Probabilistic Machine Learning

Adaptive Computation and Machine Learning

Francis Bach, editor

A complete list of titles can be found online at https://mitpress.mit.edu/search-result-list/
?series=adaptive-computation-and-machine-learning-series.

Probabilistic Machine Learning
Advanced Topics

Kevin P. Murphy

The MIT Press
Cambridge, Massachusetts
London, England

The MIT Press would like to thank the anonymous peer reviewers who provided comments on drafts of this book. The generous work of academic experts is essential for establishing the authority and quality of our publications. We acknowledge with gratitude the contributions of these otherwise uncredited readers.

Printed and bound in the United States of America.

Library of Congress Cataloging-in-Publication Data

Names: Murphy, Kevin P., author.
Title: Probabilistic machine learning : advanced topics / Kevin P. Murphy.
Description: Cambridge, Massachusetts : The MIT Press, [2023] | Series:
Adaptive computation and machine learning series | Includes
bibliographical references and index.
Identifiers: LCCN 2022045222 (print) | LCCN 2022045223 (ebook) | ISBN
9780262048439 (hardcover) | ISBN 9780262376006 (epub) | ISBN
9780262375993 (pdf)
Subjects: LCSH: Machine learning. | Probabilities.
Classification: LCC Q325.5 .M873 2023 (print) | LCC Q325.5 (ebook) | DDC
006.3/1015192–dc23/eng20230111
LC record available at https://lccn.loc.gov/2022045222
LC ebook record available at https://lccn.loc.gov/2022045223

10 9 8 7 6 5 4 3 2 1

This book is dedicated to my wife Margaret,
who has been the love of my life for 20+ years.

Brief Contents

Contents

II Inference   337

IV   Generation   763

20 Generative models: an overview   765

21 Variational autoencoders   781

V   Discovery   915

Preface

I am writing a longer [book] than usual because there is not enough time to write a short one. (Blaise Pascal, paraphrased.)

This book is a sequel to [Mur22]. and provides a deeper dive into various topics in machine learning (ML). The previous book mostly focused on techniques for learning functions of the form $f : \mathcal{X} \to \mathcal{Y}$, where f is some nonlinear model, such as a deep neural network, $\mathcal{X}$ is the set of possible inputs (typically $\mathcal{X} = \mathbb{R}^D$), and $\mathcal{Y} = \{1, \ldots, C\}$ represents the set of labels for classification problems or $\mathcal{Y} = \mathbb{R}$ for regression problems. Judea Pearl, a well known AI researcher, has called this kind of ML a form of "glorified curve fitting" (quoted in [Har18]).

In this book, we expand the scope of ML to encompass more challenging problems. For example, we consider training and testing under different distributions; we consider generation of high dimensional outputs, such as images, text, and graphs, so the output space is, say, $\mathcal{Y} = \mathbb{R}^{256 \times 256}$; we discuss methods for discovering "insights" about data, based on latent variable models; and we discuss how to use probabilistic models for causal inference and decision making under uncertainty.

We assume the reader has some prior exposure to ML and other relevant mathematical topics (e.g., probability, statistics, linear algebra, optimization). This background material can be found in the prequel to this book, [Mur22], as well several other good books (e.g., [Lin+21b; DFO20]).

Python code (mostly in JAX) to reproduce nearly all of the figures can be found online. In particular, if a figure caption says "Generated by `gauss_plot_2d.ipynb`", then you can find the corresponding Jupyter notebook at probml.github.io/notebooks#gauss_plot_2d.ipynb. Clicking on the figure link in the pdf version of the book will take you to this list of notebooks. Clicking on the notebook link will open it inside Google Colab, which will let you easily reproduce the figure for yourself, and modify the underlying source code to gain a deeper understanding of the methods. (Colab gives you access to a free GPU, which is useful for some of the more computationally heavy demos.)

In addition to the online code, probml.github.io/supp contains some additional supplementary online content which was excluded from the main book for space reasons. For exercises (and solutions) related to the topics in this book, see [Gut22].

Contributing authors

This book is the result of a lot of effort from a lot of people. I would especially like to thank the following people who wrote or cowrote various sections or chapters:

- Alex Alemi (Google), who co-wrote Section 5.1 (KL divergence) (with Murphy).
- Jeff Bilmes (U. Washington), who wrote Section 6.9 (Submodular optimization).
- Peter Chang, who co-wrote Section 8.5.1 (General Gaussian filtering) (with Murphy).
- Marco Cuturi (Apple, work done at Google), who wrote Section 6.8 (Optimal transport).
- Alexander D'Amour (Google), who co-wrote Chapter 36 (Causality) (with Veitch).
- Finale Doshi-Velez (Harvard), who co-wrote Chapter 33 (Interpretability) (with Kim).
- Roy Frostig (Google), who wrote Section 6.2 (Automatic differentiation).
- Justin Gilmer (Google), who wrote Section 19.8 (Adversarial examples).
- Giles Harper-Donnelly, who wrote Section 8.2.4 (Information form filtering and smoothing).
- Been Kim (Google), who co-wrote Chapter 33 (Interpretability) (with Doshi-Velez).
- Durk Kingma (Google), who co-wrote Chapter 24 (Energy-based models) (with Song).
- Simon Kornblith (Google), who co-wrote Chapter 32 (Representation learning) (with Poole).
- Balaji Lakshminarayanan (Google), who co-wrote Chapter 23 (Normalizing flows) (with Papamakarios) and Chapter 26 (Generative adversarial networks) (with Mohamed and Rosca).
- Lihong Li (Amazon, work done at Google), who co-wrote Section 34.4 (Contextual bandits) and Chapter 35 (Reinforcement learning) (with Murphy).
- Xinglong Li (UBC), who wrote Section 15.2.9 (Multivariate linear regression), Section 29.4.4.1 (Blocked Gibbs sampling for HMMs), Section 29.8.4.1 (Blocked Gibbs sampling for LDS), and Supplementary Section 31.2.3.
- Shakir Mohamed (Deepmind), who co-wrote Chapter 26 (Generative adversarial networks) (with Lakshminarayanan and Rosca).
- George Papamakarios (Deepmind), who cowrote Chapter 23 (Normalizing flows) (with Lakshminarayanan).
- Zeel Patel (IIT Gandhinagar), who cowrote Section 34.7 (Active learning) (with Murphy).
- Ben Poole (Google), who co-wrote Chapter 32 (Representation learning) (with Kornblith).
- Mihaela Rosca (Deepmind/UCL), who co-wrote Chapter 26 (Generative adversarial networks).
- Vinayak Rao (Purdue), who wrote Chapter 31 (Nonparametric Bayesian models).
- Yang Song (Stanford), who co-wrote Chapter 24 (Energy-based models) (with Kingma).
- Victor Veitch (Google/U. Chicago), who co-wrote Chapter 36 (Causality) (with D'Amour).
- Andrew Wilson (NYU), who co-wrote Chapter 17 (Bayesian neural networks) and Chapter 18 (Gaussian processes) (with Murphy).

Other contributors

I would also like to thank the following people who helped in various other ways:

- Many people who helped make or improve the figures, including: Aman Atman, Vibhuti Bansal, Shobhit Belwal, Aadesh Desai, Vishal Ghoniya, Anand Hegde, Ankita Kumari Jain, Madhav Kanda, Aleyna Kara, Rohit Khoiwal, Taksh Panchal, Dhruv Patel, Prey Patel, Nitish Sharma, Hetvi Shastri, Mahmoud Soliman, and Gautam Vashishtha. A special shout out to Zeel B Patel and Karm Patel for their significant efforts in improving the figure quality.
- Participants in the Google Summer of Code (GSOC) for 2021, including Ming Liang Ang, Aleyna Kara, Gerardo Duran-Martin, Srikar Reddy Jilugu, Drishti Patel, and co-mentor Mahmoud Soliman.
- Participants in the Google Summer of Code (GSOC) for 2022, including Peter Chang, Giles

Harper-Donnelly, Xinglong Li, Zeel B Patel, Karm Patel, Qingyao Sun, and co-mentors Nipun Batra and Scott Linderman.

- Many other people who contributed code (see autogenerated list at `https://github.com/probml/pyprobml#acknowledgements`).
- Many people who proofread parts of the book, including: Aalto Seminar students, Bill Behrman, Kay Brodersen, Peter Chang, Krzysztof Choromanski, Adrien Corenflos, Tom Dietterich, Gerardo Duran-Martin, Lehman Krunoslav, Ruiqi Gao, Amir Globerson, Giles Harper-Donnelly, Ravin Kumar, Junpeng Lao, Stephen Mandt, Norm Matloff, Simon Prince, Rif Saurous, Erik Sudderth, Donna Vakalis, Hal Varian, Chris Williams, Raymond Yeh, and others listed at `https://github.com/probml/pml2-book/issues?q=is:issue`. A special shout out to John Fearns who proofread almost all the math, and the MIT Press editor who ensured I use "Oxford commas" in all the right places.

About the cover

The cover illustrates a variational autoencoder (Chapter 21) being used to map from a 2d Gaussian to image space.

Kevin Patrick Murphy
Palo Alto, California
January 2023.

1 Introduction

"Intelligence is not just about pattern recognition and function approximation. It's about modeling the world". — Josh Tenenbaum, NeurIPS 2021.

Much of current machine learning focuses on the task of mapping inputs to outputs (i.e., approximating functions of the form $f : \mathcal{X} \rightarrow \mathcal{Y}$), often using "**deep learning**" (see e.g., [LBH15; Sch14; Sej20; BLH21]). Judea Pearl, a well known AI researcher, has called this "glorified curve fitting" (quoted in [Har18]). This is a little unfair, since when $\mathcal{X}$ and/or $\mathcal{Y}$ are high-dimensional spaces — such as images, sentences, graphs, or sequences of decisions/actions — then the term "curve fitting" is rather misleading, since one-dimensional intuitions often do not work in higher-dimensional settings (see e.g., [BPL21a]). Nevertheless, the quote gets at what many feel is lacking in current attempts to "solve AI" using machine learning techniques, namely that they are too focused on prediction of observable patterns, and not focused enough on "understanding" the underlying *latent structure* behind these patterns.

Gaining a "deep understanding" of the structure behind the observed data is necessary for advancing science, as well as for certain applications, such as healthcare (see e.g., [DD22]), where identifying the *root causes* or mechanisms behind various diseases is the key to developing cures. In addition, such "deep understanding" is necessary in order to develop *robust* and *efficient* systems. By "robust" we mean methods that work well even if there are unexpected changes to the data distribution to which the system is applied, which is an important concern in many areas, such as robotics (see e.g., [Roy+21]). By "efficient" we generally mean data or statistically efficient, i.e., methods that can learn quickly from small amounts of data (cf., [Lu+21b]). This is important since data can be limited in some domains, such as healthcare and robotics, even though it is abundant in other domains, such as language and vision, due to the ability to scrape the internet. We are also interested in computationally efficient methods, although this is a secondary concern as computing power continues to grow. (We also note that this trend has been instrumental to much of the recent progress in AI, as noted in [Sut19].)

To develop robust and efficient systems, this book adopts a model-based approach, in which we try to learn *parsimonious representations* of the underlying "**data generating process**" (**DGP**) given samples from one or more datasets (c.f., [Lak+17; Win+19; Sch20; Ben+21a; Cun22; MTS22]). This is in fact similar to the scientific method, where we try to explain (features of) the observations by developing theories or models. One way to formalize this process is in terms of **Bayesian inference** applied to probabilistic models, as argued in [Jay03; Box80; GS13]. We discuss inference algorithms in detail in Part II of the book.[1] But before we get there, in Part I we cover some relevant background

---

1. Note that, in the deep learning community, the term "inference" means applying a function to some inputs to

material that will be needed. (This part can be skipped by readers who are already familiar with these basics.)

Once we have a set of inference methods in our toolbox (some of which may be as simple as computing a maximum likelihood estimate using an optimization method, such as stochastic gradient descent) we can turn our focus to discussing different kinds of models. The choice of model depends on our task, the kind and amount of data we have, and our metric(s) of success. We will broadly consider four main kinds of task: prediction (e.g., classification and regression), generation (e.g., of images or text), discovery (of "meaningful structure" in data), and control (optimal decision making). We give more details below.

In Part III, we discuss models for prediction. These models are conditional distributions of the form $p(\boldsymbol{y}|\boldsymbol{x})$, where $\boldsymbol{x} \in \mathcal{X}$ is some input (often high dimensional), and $\boldsymbol{y} \in \mathcal{Y}$ is the desired output (often low dimensional). In this part of the book, we assume there is one right answer that we want to predict, although we may be uncertain about it.

In Part IV, we discuss models for generation. These models are distributions of the form $p(\boldsymbol{x})$ or $p(\boldsymbol{x}|\boldsymbol{c})$, where $\boldsymbol{c}$ are optional conditioning inputs, and where there may be multiple valid outputs. For example, given a text prompt $\boldsymbol{c}$, we may want to generate a diverse set of images $\boldsymbol{x}$ that "match" the caption. Evaluating such models is harder than in the prediction setting, since it is less clear what the desired output should be.

In Part V, we discuss latent variable models, which are joint models of the form $p(\boldsymbol{z}, \boldsymbol{x}) = p(\boldsymbol{z})p(\boldsymbol{x}|\boldsymbol{z})$, where $\boldsymbol{z}$ is the hidden state and $\boldsymbol{x}$ are the observations that are assumed to be generated from $\boldsymbol{z}$. The goal is to compute $p(\boldsymbol{z}|\boldsymbol{x})$, in order to uncover some (hopefully meaningful/useful) underlying state or patterns in the observed data. We also consider methods for trying to discover patterns learned implicitly by predictive models of the form $p(\boldsymbol{y}|\boldsymbol{x})$, without relying on an explicit generative model of the data.

Finally, in Part VI, we discuss models and algorithms which can be used to make decisions under uncertainty. This naturally leads into the very important topic of causality, with which we close the book.

In view of the broad scope of the book, we cannot go into detail on every topic. However, we have attempted to cover all the basics. In some cases, we also provide a "deeper dive" into the research frontier (as of 2022). We hope that by bringing all these topics together, you will find it easier to make connections between all these seemingly disparate areas, and can thereby deepen your understanding of the field of machine learning.

---

compute the output. This is unrelated to Bayesian inference, which is concerned with the much harder task of inverting a function, and working backwards from observed outputs to possible hidden inputs (causes). The latter is more closely related to what the deep learning community calls "training".

PART I

Fundamentals

2 Probability

2.1 Introduction

In this section, we formally define what we mean by probability, following the presentation of [Cha21, Ch. 2]. Other good introductions to this topic can be found in e.g., [GS97; BT08; Bet18; DFO20].

2.1.1 Probability space

We define a **probability space** to be a triple $(\Omega, \mathcal{F}, \mathbb{P})$, where Ω is the **sample space**, which is the set of possible outcomes from an experiment); $\mathcal{F}$ is the **event space**, which is the set of all possible subsets of Ω; and $\mathbb{P}$ is the **probability measure**, which is a mapping from an event $E \subseteq \Omega$ to a number in $[0, 1]$ (i.e., $\mathbb{P} : \mathcal{F} \to [0, 1]$), which satisfies certain consistency requirements, which we discuss in Section 2.1.4.

2.1.2 Discrete random variables

The simplest setting is where the outcomes of the experiment constitute a countable set. For example, consider throwing a 3-sided die, where the faces are labeled "A", "B" and "C". (We choose 3 sides instead of 6 for brevity.) The sample space is $\Omega = \{A, B, C\}$, which represents all the possible outcomes of the "experiment". The event space is the set of all possible subsets of the sample space, so $\mathcal{F} = \{\emptyset, \{A\}, \{B\}, \{C\}, \{A, B\}, \{A, C\}, \{B, C\}, \{A, B, C\}\}$. An event is an element of the event space. For example, the event $E_1 = \{A, B\}$ represents outcomes where the die shows face A or B, and event $E_2 = \{C\}$ represent the outcome where the die shows face C.

Once we have defined the event space, we need to specify the probability measure, which provides a way to compute the "size" or "weight" of each set in the event space. In the 3-sided die example, suppose we define the probability of each outcome (atomic event) as $\mathbb{P}[\{A\}] = \frac{2}{6}$, $\mathbb{P}[\{B\}] = \frac{1}{6}$, and $\mathbb{P}[\{C\}] = \frac{3}{6}$. We can derive the probability of other events by adding up the measures for each outcome, e.g., $\mathbb{P}[\{A, B\}] = \frac{2}{6} + \frac{1}{6} = \frac{1}{2}$. We formalize this in Section 2.1.4.

To simplify notation, we will assign a number to each possible outcome in the event space. This can be done by defining a **random variable** or **rv**, which is a function $X : \Omega \to \mathbb{R}$ that maps an outcome $\omega \in \Omega$ to a number $X(\omega)$ on the real line. For example, we can define the random variable X for our 3-sided die using $X(A) = 1$, $X(B) = 2$, $X(C) = 3$. As another example, consider an experiment where we flip a fair coin twice. The sample space is $\Omega = \{\omega_1 = (H, H), \omega_2 = (H, T), \omega_3 = (T, H), \omega_4 = (T, T)\}$, where H stands for head, and T for tail. Let X be the random variable represent the number of heads. Then we have $X(\omega_1) = 2$, $X(\omega_2) = 1$, $X(\omega_3) = 1$, and $X(\omega_4) = 0$.

We define the set of possible values of the random variable to be its **state space**, denoted $X(\Omega) = \mathcal{X}$. We define the probability of any given state using

$$p_X(a) = \mathbb{P}[X = a] = \mathbb{P}[X^{-1}(a)] \tag{2.1}$$

where $X^{-1}(a) = \{\omega \in \Omega | X(\omega) = a\}$ is the pre-image of a. Here p_X is called the **probability mass function** or **pmf** for random variable X. In the example where we flip a fair coin twice, the pmf is $p_X(0) = \mathbb{P}[\{(T,T)\}] = \frac{1}{4}$, $p_X(1) = \mathbb{P}[\{(T,H),(H,T)\}] = \frac{2}{4}$, and $p_X(2) = \mathbb{P}[\{(H,H)\}] = \frac{1}{4}$. The pmf can be represented by a histogram, or some parametric function (see Section 2.2.1). We call p_X the **probability distribution** for rv X. We will often drop the X subscript from p_X where it is clear from context.

2.1.3   Continuous random variables

We can also consider experiments with continuous outcomes. In this case, we assume the sample space is a subset of the reals, $\Omega \subseteq \mathbb{R}$, and we define each continuous random variable to be the identify function, $X(\omega) = \omega$.

For example, consider measuring the duration of some event (in seconds). We define the sample space to be $\Omega = \{t : 0 \leq t \leq T_{\max}\}$. Since this is an uncountable set, we cannot define all possible subsets by enumeration, unlike the discrete case. Instead, we need to define event space in terms of a **Borel sigma-field**, also called a **Borel sigma-algebra**. We say that $\mathcal{F}$ is a σ-field if (1) $\emptyset \in \mathcal{F}$ and $\Omega \in \mathcal{F}$; (2) $\mathcal{F}$ is closed under complement, so if $E \in \mathcal{F}$ then $E^c \in \mathcal{F}$; and (3) $\mathcal{F}$ is closed under countable unions and intersections, meaning that $\cup_{i=1}^{\infty} E_i \in \mathcal{F}$ and $\cap_{i=1}^{\infty} E_i \in \mathcal{F}$, provided $E_1, E_2, \ldots \in \mathcal{F}$. Finally, we say that $\mathcal{B}$ is a Borel σ-field if it is a σ-field generated from semi-closed intervals of the form $(-\infty, b] = \{x : -\infty < x \leq b\}$. By taking unions, intersections and complements of these intervals, we can see that $\mathcal{B}$ contains the following sets:

$$(a, b), [a, b], (a, b], [a, b], \{b\}, \quad -\infty \leq a \leq b \leq \infty \tag{2.2}$$

In our duration example, we can further restrict the event space to only contain intervals whose lower bound is 0 and whose upper bound is $\leq T_{\max}$.

To define the probability measure, we assign a weighting function $p_X(x) \geq 0$ for each $x \in \Omega$ known as a **probability density function** or **pdf**. See Section 2.2.2 for a list of common pdf's. We can then derive the probability of an event $E = [a, b]$ using

$$\mathbb{P}([a, b]) = \int_E d\mathbb{P} = \int_a^b p(x)dx \tag{2.3}$$

We can also define the **cumulative distribution function** or **cdf** for random variable X as follows:

$$P_X(x) \triangleq \mathbb{P}[X \leq x] = \int_{-\infty}^{x} p_X(x')dx' \tag{2.4}$$

From this we can compute the probability of an interval using

$$\mathbb{P}([a, b]) = p(a \leq X \leq b) = P_X(b) - P_X(a) \tag{2.5}$$

The term "probability distribution" could refer to the pdf p_X or the cdf P_X or even the probabiliy measure $\mathbb{P}$.

We can generalize the above definitions to multidimensional spaces, $\Omega \subseteq \mathbb{R}^n$, as well as more complex sample spaces, such as functions.

2.1.4 Probability axioms

The probability law associated with the event space must follow the **axioms of probability**, also called the **Kolmogorov axioms**, which are as follows:[1]
- Non-negativity: $\mathbb{P}[E] \geq 0$ for any $E \subseteq \Omega$.
- Normalization: $\mathbb{P}[\Omega] = 1$.
- Additivity: for any countable sequence of pairwise disjoint sets $\{E_1, E_2, \ldots, \}$, we have

$$\mathbb{P}\left[\cup_{i=1}^{\infty} E_i\right] = \sum_{i=1}^{\infty} \mathbb{P}[E_i] \tag{2.6}$$

In the finite case, where we just have two disjoint sets, E_1 and E_2, this becomes

$$\mathbb{P}[E_1 \cup E_2] = \mathbb{P}[E_1] + \mathbb{P}[E_2] \tag{2.7}$$

This corresponds to the probability of event E_1 or E_2, assuming they are mutually exclusive (disjoint sets).

From these axioms, we can derive the **complement rule**:

$$\mathbb{P}[E^c] = 1 - \mathbb{P}[E] \tag{2.8}$$

where $E^c = \Omega \setminus E$ is the complement of E. (This follows since $\mathbb{P}[\Omega] = 1 = \mathbb{P}[E \cup E^c] = \mathbb{P}[E] + \mathbb{P}[E^c]$.) We can also show that $\mathbb{P}[E] \leq 1$ (proof by contradiction), and $\mathbb{P}[\emptyset] = 0$ (which follows from first corollary with $E = \Omega$).

We can also show the following result, known as the **addition rule**:

$$\mathbb{P}[E_1 \cup E_2] = \mathbb{P}[E_1] + \mathbb{P}[E_2] - \mathbb{P}[E_1 \cap E_2] \tag{2.9}$$

This holds for any pair of events, even if they are not disjoint.

2.1.5 Conditional probability

Consider two events E_1 and E_2. If $\mathbb{P}[E_2] \neq 0$, we define the **conditional probability** of E_1 given E_2 as

$$\mathbb{P}[E_1|E_2] \triangleq \frac{\mathbb{P}[E_1 \cap E_2]}{\mathbb{P}[E_2]} \tag{2.10}$$

From this, we can get the **multiplication rule**:

$$\mathbb{P}[E_1 \cap E_2] = \mathbb{P}[E_1|E_2]\mathbb{P}[E_2] = \mathbb{P}[E_2|E_1]\mathbb{P}[E_1] \tag{2.11}$$

---

1. These laws can be shown to follow from a more basic set of assumptions about reasoning under uncertainty, a result known as **Cox's theorem** [Cox46; Cox61].

Conditional probability measures how likely an event E_1 is given that event E_2 has happened. However, if the events are unrelated, the probability will not change. Formally, We say that E_1 and E_2 are **independent events** if

$$\mathbb{P}[E_1 \cap E_2] = \mathbb{P}[E_1]\mathbb{P}[E_2] \tag{2.12}$$

If both $\mathbb{P}[E_1] > 0$ and $\mathbb{P}[E_2] > 0$, this is equivalent to requiring that $\mathbb{P}[E_1|E_2] = \mathbb{P}[E_1]$ or equivalently, $\mathbb{P}[E_2|E_1] = \mathbb{P}[E_2]$. Similarly, we say that E_1 and E_2 are conditionally independent given E_3 if

$$\mathbb{P}[E_1 \cap E_2|E_3] = \mathbb{P}[E_1|E_3]\mathbb{P}[E_2|E_3] \tag{2.13}$$

From the definition of conditional probability, we can derive the **law of total probability**, which states the following: if $\{A_1, \ldots, A_n\}$ is a partition of the sample space Ω, then for any event $B \subseteq \Omega$, we have

$$\mathbb{P}[B] = \sum_{i=1}^{n} \mathbb{P}[B|A_i]\mathbb{P}[A_i] \tag{2.14}$$

2.1.6   Bayes' rule

From the definition of conditional probability, we can derive **Bayes' rule**, also called **Bayes' theorem**, which says that, for any two events E_1 and E_2 such that $\mathbb{P}[E_1] > 0$ and $\mathbb{P}[E_2] > 0$, we have

$$\mathbb{P}[E_1|E_2] = \frac{\mathbb{P}[E_2|E_1]\mathbb{P}[E_1]}{\mathbb{P}[E_2]} \tag{2.15}$$

For a discrete random variable X with K possible states, we can write Bayes' rule as follows, using the law of total probability:

$$p(X = k|E) = \frac{p(E|X = k)p(X = k)}{p(E)} = \frac{p(E|X = k)p(X = k)}{\sum_{k'=1}^{K} p(E|X = k')p(X = k')} \tag{2.16}$$

Here $p(X = k)$ is the **prior probability**, $p(E|X = k)$ is the **likelihood**, $p(X = k|E)$ is the **posterior probability**, and $p(E)$ is a normalization constant, known as the **marginal likelihood**. Similarly, for a continuous random variable X, we can write Bayes' rule as follows:

$$p(X = x|E) = \frac{p(E|X = x)p(X = x)}{p(E)} = \frac{p(E|X = x)p(X = x)}{\int p(E|X = x')p(X = x')dx'} \tag{2.17}$$

2.2   Some common probability distributions

There are a wide variety of probability distributions that are used for various kinds of models. We summarize some of the more commonly used ones in the sections below. See Supplementary Chapter 2 for more information, and `https://ben18785.shinyapps.io/distribution-zoo/` for an interactive visualization.

2.2.1 Discrete distributions

In this section, we discuss some discrete distributions defined on subsets of the (non-negative) integers.

2.2.1.1 Bernoulli and binomial distributions

Let $x \in \{0, 1, \ldots, N\}$. The **binomial distribution** is defined by

$$\text{Bin}(x|N, \mu) \triangleq \binom{N}{x} \mu^x (1 - \mu)^{N-x} \tag{2.18}$$

where $\binom{N}{k} \triangleq \frac{N!}{(N-k)!k!}$ is the number of ways to choose k items from N (this is known as the **binomial coefficient**, and is pronounced "N choose k").

If $N = 1$, so $x \in \{0, 1\}$, the binomial distribution reduces to the **Bernoulli distribution**:

$$\text{Ber}(x|\mu) = \begin{cases} 1 - \mu & \text{if } x = 0 \\ \mu & \text{if } x = 1 \end{cases} \tag{2.19}$$

where $\mu = \mathbb{E}[x] = p(x = 1)$ is the mean.

2.2.1.2 Categorical and multinomial distributions

If the variable is discrete-valued, $x \in \{1, \ldots, K\}$, we can use the **categorical** distribution:

$$\text{Cat}(x|\boldsymbol{\theta}) \triangleq \prod_{k=1}^{K} \theta_k^{\mathbb{I}(x=k)} \tag{2.20}$$

Alternatively, we can represent the K-valued variable x with the one-hot binary vector $\boldsymbol{x}$, which lets us write

$$\text{Cat}(\boldsymbol{x}|\boldsymbol{\theta}) \triangleq \prod_{k=1}^{K} \theta_k^{x_k} \tag{2.21}$$

If the k'th element of $\boldsymbol{x}$ counts the number of times the value k is seen in $N = \sum_{k=1}^{K} x_k$ trials, then we get the **multinomial distribution**:

$$\mathcal{M}(\boldsymbol{x}|N, \boldsymbol{\theta}) \triangleq \binom{N}{x_1 \ldots x_K} \prod_{k=1}^{K} \theta_k^{x_k} \tag{2.22}$$

where the **multinomial coefficient** is defined as

$$\binom{N}{k_1 \ldots k_m} \triangleq \frac{N!}{k_1! \ldots k_m!} \tag{2.23}$$

2.2.1.3 Poisson distribution

Suppose $X \in \{0, 1, 2, \ldots\}$. We say that a random variable has a **Poisson** distribution with parameter $\lambda > 0$, written $X \sim \text{Poi}(\lambda)$, if its pmf (probability mass function) is

$$\text{Poi}(x|\lambda) = e^{-\lambda} \frac{\lambda^x}{x!} \tag{2.24}$$

where λ is the mean (and variance) of x.

2.2.1.4 Negative binomial distribution

Suppose we have an "urn" with N balls, R of which are red and B of which are blue. Suppose we perform **sampling with replacement** until we get $n \geq 1$ balls. Let X be the number of these that are blue. It can be shown that $X \sim \text{Bin}(n, p)$, where $p = B/N$ is the fraction of blue balls; thus X follows the binomial distribution, discussed in Section 2.2.1.1.

Now suppose we consider drawing a red ball a "failure", and drawing a blue ball a "success". Suppose we keep drawing balls until we observe r failures. Let X be the resulting number of successes (blue balls); it can be shown that $X \sim \text{NegBinom}(r, p)$, which is the **negative binomial distribution** defined by

$$\text{NegBinom}(x|r, p) \triangleq \binom{x + r - 1}{x}(1 - p)^r p^x \tag{2.25}$$

for $x \in \{0, 1, 2, \ldots\}$. (If r is real-valued, we replace $\binom{x+r-1}{x}$ with $\frac{\Gamma(x+r)}{x!\Gamma(r)}$, exploiting the fact that $(x - 1)! = \Gamma(x)$.)

This distribution has the following moments:

$$\mathbb{E}[x] = \frac{p\,r}{1 - p}, \ \mathbb{V}[x] = \frac{p\,r}{(1 - p)^2} \tag{2.26}$$

This two parameter family has more modeling flexibility than the Poisson distribution, since it can represent the mean and variance separately. This is useful, e.g., for modeling "contagious" events, which have positively correlated occurrences, causing a larger variance than if the occurrences were independent. In fact, the Poisson distribution is a special case of the negative binomial, since it can be shown that $\text{Poi}(\lambda) = \lim_{r \to \infty} \text{NegBinom}(r, \frac{\lambda}{1+\lambda})$. Another special case is when $r = 1$; this is called the **geometric distribution**.

2.2.2 Continuous distributions on $\mathbb{R}$

In this section, we discuss some univariate distributions defined on the reals, $p(x)$ for $x \in \mathbb{R}$.

2.2.2.1 Gaussian (Normal)

The most widely used univariate distribution is the **Gaussian distribution**, also called the **normal distribution**. (See [Mur22, Sec 2.6.4] for a discussion of these names.) The pdf (probability density function) of the Gaussian is given by

$$\mathcal{N}(x|\mu, \sigma^2) \triangleq \frac{1}{\sqrt{2\pi\sigma^2}} \, e^{-\frac{1}{2\sigma^2}(x-\mu)^2} \tag{2.27}$$

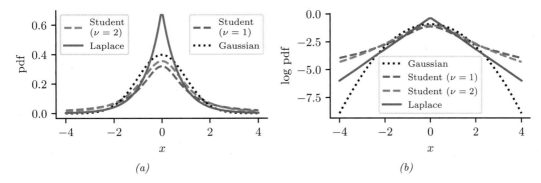

Figure 2.1: (a) The pdf's for a $\mathcal{N}(0,1)$, $\mathcal{T}_1(0,1)$ and Laplace$(0,1/\sqrt{2})$. The mean is 0 and the variance is 1 for both the Gaussian and Laplace. The mean and variance of the Student distribution is undefined when $\nu = 1$. (b) Log of these pdf's. Note that the Student distribution is not log-concave for any parameter value, unlike the Laplace distribution. Nevertheless, both are unimodal. Generated by student_laplace_pdf_plot.ipynb.

where $\sqrt{2\pi\sigma^2}$ is the normalization constant needed to ensure the density integrates to 1. The parameter μ encodes the mean of the distribution, which is also equal to the mode. The parameter σ^2 encodes the variance. Sometimes we talk about the **precision** of a Gaussian, by which we mean the inverse variance: $\lambda = 1/\sigma^2$. A high precision means a narrow distribution (low variance) centered on μ.

The cumulative distribution function or cdf of the Gaussian is defined as

$$\Phi(x;\mu,\sigma^2) \triangleq \int_{-\infty}^{x} \mathcal{N}(z|\mu,\sigma^2)dz \tag{2.28}$$

If $\mu = 0$ and $\sigma = 1$ (known as the **standard normal** distribution), we just write $\Phi(x)$.

2.2.2.2 Half-normal

For some problems, we want a distribution over non-negative reals. One way to create such a distribution is to define $Y = |X|$, where $X \sim \mathcal{N}(0,\sigma^2)$. The induced distribution for Y is called the **half-normal distribution**, which has the pdf

$$\mathcal{N}_+(y|\sigma) \triangleq 2\mathcal{N}(y|0,\sigma^2) = \frac{\sqrt{2}}{\sigma\sqrt{\pi}}\exp\left(-\frac{y^2}{2\sigma^2}\right) \quad y \geq 0 \tag{2.29}$$

This can be thought of as the $\mathcal{N}(0,\sigma^2)$ distribution "folded over" onto itself.

2.2.2.3 Student t-distribution

One problem with the Gaussian distribution is that it is sensitive to outliers, since the probability decays exponentially fast with the (squared) distance from the center. A more robust distribution is the **Student t-distribution**, which we shall call the **Student distribution** for short. Its pdf is as follows:

$$\mathcal{T}_\nu(x|\mu, \sigma^2) = \frac{1}{Z} \left[1 + \frac{1}{\nu} \left(\frac{x - \mu}{\sigma} \right)^2 \right]^{-(\frac{\nu+1}{2})} \tag{2.30}$$

$$Z = \frac{\sqrt{\nu \pi \sigma^2} \Gamma(\frac{\nu}{2})}{\Gamma(\frac{\nu+1}{2})} = \sqrt{\nu} \sigma B(\frac{1}{2}, \frac{\nu}{2}) \tag{2.31}$$

where μ is the mean, $\sigma > 0$ is the scale parameter (not the standard deviation), and $\nu > 0$ is called the **degrees of freedom** (although a better term would be the **degree of normality** [Kru13], since large values of ν make the distribution act like a Gaussian). Here $\Gamma(a)$ is the **gamma function** defined by

$$\Gamma(a) \triangleq \int_0^\infty x^{a-1} e^{-x} dx \tag{2.32}$$

and $B(a, b)$ is the **beta function**, defined by

$$B(a, b) \triangleq \frac{\Gamma(a)\Gamma(b)}{\Gamma(a+b)} \tag{2.33}$$

2.2.2.4   Cauchy distribution

If $\nu = 1$, the Student distribution is known as the **Cauchy** or **Lorentz** distribution. Its pdf is defined by

$$\mathcal{C}(x|\mu, \gamma) = \frac{1}{Z} \left[1 + \left(\frac{x - \mu}{\gamma} \right)^2 \right]^{-1} \tag{2.34}$$

where $Z = \gamma \beta(\frac{1}{2}, \frac{1}{2}) = \gamma \pi$. This distribution is notable for having such heavy tails that the integral that defines the mean does not converge.

The **half Cauchy** distribution is a version of the Cauchy (with mean 0) that is "folded over" on itself, so all its probability density is on the positive reals. Thus it has the form

$$\mathcal{C}_+(x|\gamma) \triangleq \frac{2}{\pi \gamma} \left[1 + \left(\frac{x}{\gamma} \right)^2 \right]^{-1} \tag{2.35}$$

2.2.2.5   Laplace distribution

Another distribution with heavy tails is the **Laplace distribution**, also known as the **double sided exponential** distribution. This has the following pdf:

$$\text{Laplace}(x|\mu, b) \triangleq \frac{1}{2b} \exp\left(-\frac{|x - \mu|}{b} \right) \tag{2.36}$$

Here μ is a location parameter and $b > 0$ is a scale parameter. See Figure 2.1 for a plot.

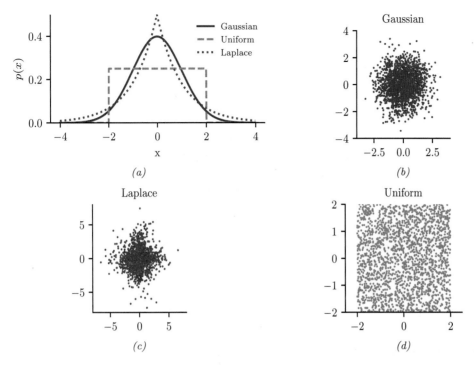

Figure 2.2: *Illustration of Gaussian (blue), sub-Gaussian (uniform, green), and super-Gaussian (Laplace, red) distributions in 1d and 2d. Generated by* sub_super_gauss_plot.ipynb.

2.2.2.6 Sub-Gaussian and super-Gaussian distributions

There are two main variants of the Gaussian distribution, known as **super-Gaussian** or **leptokurtic** ("Lepto" is Greek for "narrow") and **sub-Gaussian** or **platykurtic** ("Platy" is Greek for "broad"). These distributions differ in terms of their **kurtosis**, which is a measure of how heavy or light their tails are (i.e., how fast the density dies off to zero away from its mean). More precisely, the kurtosis is defined as

$$\text{kurt}(z) \triangleq \frac{\mu_4}{\sigma^4} = \frac{\mathbb{E}\left[(Z - \mu)^4\right]}{(\mathbb{E}\left[(Z - \mu)^2\right])^2} \tag{2.37}$$

where σ is the standard deviation, and μ_4 is the 4'th **central moment**. (Thus $\mu_1 = \mu$ is the mean, and $\mu_2 = \sigma^2$ is the variance.) For a standard Gaussian, the kurtosis is 3, so some authors define the **excess kurtosis** as the kurtosis minus 3.

A super-Gaussian distribution (e.g., the Laplace) has positive excess kurtosis, and hence heavier tails than the Gaussian. A sub-Gaussian distribution, such as the uniform, has negative excess kurtosis, and hence lighter tails than the Gaussian. See Figure 2.2 for an illustration.

2.2.3 Continuous distributions on $\mathbb{R}^+$

In this section, we discuss some univariate distributions defined on the positive reals, $p(x)$ for $x \in \mathbb{R}^+$.

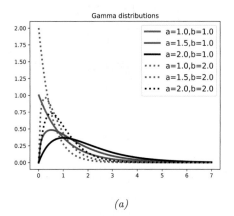
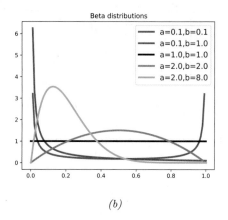

| (a) | (b) |

Figure 2.3: (a) Some gamma distributions. If $a \leq 1$, the mode is at 0; otherwise the mode is away from 0. As we increase the rate b, we reduce the horizontal scale, thus squeezing everything leftwards and upwards. Generated by gamma_dist_plot.ipynb. (b) Some beta distributions. If $a < 1$, we get a "spike" on the left, and if $b < 1$, we get a "spike" on the right. If $a = b = 1$, the distribution is uniform. If $a > 1$ and $b > 1$, the distribution is unimodal. Generated by beta_dist_plot.ipynb.

2.2.3.1   Gamma distribution

The **gamma distribution** is a flexible distribution for positive real valued rv's, $x > 0$. It is defined in terms of two parameters, called the shape $a > 0$ and the rate $b > 0$:

$$\text{Ga}(x|\text{shape} = a, \text{rate} = b) \triangleq \frac{b^a}{\Gamma(a)} x^{a-1} e^{-xb} \tag{2.38}$$

Sometimes the distribution is parameterized in terms of the rate a and the **scale** $s = 1/b$:

$$\text{Ga}(x|\text{shape} = a, \text{scale} = s) \triangleq \frac{1}{s^a \Gamma(a)} x^{a-1} e^{-x/s} \tag{2.39}$$

See Figure 2.3a for an illustration.

2.2.3.2   Exponential distribution

The **exponential distribution** is a special case of the gamma distribution and is defined by

$$\text{Expon}(x|\lambda) \triangleq \text{Ga}(x|\text{shape} = 1, \text{rate} = \lambda) \tag{2.40}$$

This distribution describes the times between events in a Poisson process, i.e., a process in which events occur continuously and independently at a constant average rate λ.

2.2.3.3   Chi-squared distribution

The **chi-squared distribution** is a special case of the gamma distribution and is defined by

$$\chi_\nu^2(x) \triangleq \text{Ga}(x|\text{shape} = \frac{\nu}{2}, \text{rate} = \frac{1}{2}) \tag{2.41}$$

where ν is called the degrees of freedom. This is the distribution of the sum of squared Gaussian random variables. More precisely, if $Z_i \sim \mathcal{N}(0,1)$, and $S = \sum_{i=1}^{\nu} Z_i^2$, then $S \sim \chi_\nu^2$. Hence if $X \sim \mathcal{N}(0, \sigma^2)$ then $X^2 \sim \sigma^2 \chi_1^2$. Since $\mathbb{E}\left[\chi_1^2\right] = 1$ and $\mathbb{V}\left[\chi_1^2\right] = 2$, we have

$$\mathbb{E}\left[X^2\right] = \sigma^2, \mathbb{V}\left[X^2\right] = 2\sigma^4 \tag{2.42}$$

2.2.3.4 Inverse gamma

The **inverse gamma distribution**, denoted $Y \sim \text{IG}(a, b)$, is the distribution of $Y = 1/X$ assuming $X \sim \text{Ga}(a, b)$. This pdf is defined by

$$\text{IG}(x|\text{shape} = a, \text{scale} = b) \triangleq \frac{b^a}{\Gamma(a)} x^{-(a+1)} e^{-b/x} \tag{2.43}$$

The mean only exists if $a > 1$. The variance only exists if $a > 2$.

The **scaled inverse chi-squared** distribution is a reparameterization of the inverse gamma distribution:

$$\chi^{-2}(x|\nu, \sigma^2) = \text{IG}(x|\text{shape} = \frac{\nu}{2}, \text{scale} = \frac{\nu\sigma^2}{2}) \tag{2.44}$$

$$= \frac{1}{\Gamma(\nu/2)} \left(\frac{\nu\sigma^2}{2}\right)^{\nu/2} x^{-\frac{\nu}{2}-1} \exp\left(-\frac{\nu\sigma^2}{2x}\right) \tag{2.45}$$

The regular inverse chi-squared distribution, written $\chi_\nu^{-2}(x)$, is the special case where $\nu\sigma^2 = 1$ (i.e., $\sigma^2 = 1/\nu$). This corresponds to $\text{IG}(x|\text{shape} = \nu/2, \text{scale} = \frac{1}{2})$.

2.2.3.5 Pareto distribution

The **Pareto distribution** has the following pdf:

$$\text{Pareto}(x|m, \kappa) = \kappa m^\kappa \frac{1}{x^{(\kappa+1)}} \mathbb{I}(x \geq m) \tag{2.46}$$

See Figure 2.4(a) for some plots. We see that x must be greater than the minimum value m, but then the pdf rapidly decays after that. If we plot the distribution on a log-log scale, it forms the straight line $\log p(x) = -a \log x + \log(c)$, where $a = (\kappa + 1)$ and $c = \kappa m^\kappa$: see Figure 2.4(b) for an illustration.

When $m = 0$, the distribution has the form $p(x) = \kappa x^{-a}$. This is known as a **power law**. If $a = 1$, the distribution has the form $p(x) \propto 1/x$; if we interpret x as a frequency, this is called a $1/f$ function.

The Pareto distribution is useful for modeling the distribution of quantities that exhibit **heavy tails** or **long tails**, in which most values are small, but there are a few very large values. Many forms of data exhibit this property. ([ACL16] argue that this is because many datasets are generated by a variety of latent factors, which, when mixed together, naturally result in heavy tailed distributions.) We give some examples below.

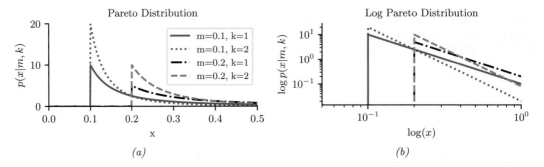

Figure 2.4: *(a) The Pareto pdf Pareto(x|k,m).   (b) Same distribution on a log-log plot.   Generated by* *pareto_dist_plot.ipynb.*

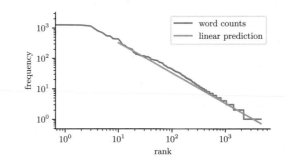

Figure 2.5: *A log-log plot of the frequency vs the rank for the words in H. G. Wells'* The Time Machine. *Generated by* zipfs_law_plot.ipynb. *Adapted from a figure from [Zha+20a, Sec 8.3].*

Modeling wealth distributions

The Pareto distribution is named after the Italian economist and sociologist Vilfredo Pareto. He created it in order to model the distribution of wealth across different countries. Indeed, in economics, the parameter κ is called the **Pareto index**. If we set $\kappa = 1.16$, we recover the **80-20 rule**, which states that 80% of the wealth of a society is held by 20% of the population.[2]

Zipf's law

Zipf's law says that the most frequent word in a language (such as "the") occurs approximately twice as often as the second most frequent word ("of"), which occurs twice as often as the fourth most frequent word, etc. This corresponds to a Pareto distribution of the form

$$p(x = r) \propto \kappa r^{-a} \tag{2.47}$$

---

2. In fact, wealth distributions are even more skewed than this.   For example, as of 2014, 80 billionaires now have as much wealth as 3.5 billion people! (Source: http://www.pbs.org/newshour/making-sense/wealthiest-getting-wealthier-lobbying-lot.) Such extreme income inequality exists in many plutocratic countries, including the USA (see e.g., [HP10]).

where r is the rank of word x when sorted by frequency, and κ and a are constants. If we set $a = 1$, we recover Zipf's law.[3] Thus Zipf's law predicts that if we plot the log frequency of words vs their log rank, we will get a straight line with slope -1. This is in fact true, as illustrated in Figure 2.5.[4] See [Ada00] for further discussion of Zipf's law, and Section 2.6.2 for a discussion of language models.

2.2.4 Continuous distributions on $[0, 1]$

In this section, we discuss some univariate distributions defined on the $[0, 1]$ interval.

2.2.4.1 Beta distribution

The **beta distribution** has support over the interval $[0, 1]$ and is defined as follows:

$$\text{Beta}(x|a, b) = \frac{1}{B(a, b)} x^{a-1} (1 - x)^{b-1} \tag{2.48}$$

where $B(a, b)$ is the **beta function**. We require $a, b > 0$ to ensure the distribution is integrable (i.e., to ensure $B(a, b)$ exists). If $a = b = 1$, we get the uniform distribution. If a and b are both less than 1, we get a bimodal distribution with "spikes" at 0 and 1; if a and b are both greater than 1, the distribution is unimodal. See Figure 2.3b.

2.2.5 Multivariate continuous distributions

In this section, we summarize some other widely used multivariate continuous distributions.

2.2.5.1 Multivariate normal (Gaussian)

The **multivariate normal (MVN)**, also called the or **multivariate Gaussian**, is by far the most widely used multivariate distribution. As such, the whole of Section 2.3 is dedicated to it.

2.2.5.2 Multivariate Student distribution

One problem with Gaussians is that they are sensitive to outliers. Fortunately, we can easily extend the Student distribution, discussed in Main Section 2.2.2.3, to D dimensions. In particular, the pdf of the **multivariate Student distribution** is given by

$$\mathcal{T}_\nu(\boldsymbol{x}|\boldsymbol{\mu}, \boldsymbol{\Sigma}) = \frac{1}{Z} \left[1 + \frac{1}{\nu} (\boldsymbol{x} - \boldsymbol{\mu})^\mathsf{T} \boldsymbol{\Sigma}^{-1} (\boldsymbol{x} - \boldsymbol{\mu}) \right]^{-\left(\frac{\nu + D}{2}\right)} \tag{2.49}$$

$$Z = \frac{\Gamma(\nu/2)}{\Gamma(\nu/2 + D/2)} \frac{\nu^{D/2} \pi^{D/2}}{|\boldsymbol{\Sigma}|^{-1/2}} \tag{2.50}$$

where $\boldsymbol{\Sigma}$ is called the scale matrix.

---

3. For example, $p(x = 2) = \kappa 2^{-1} = 2\kappa 4^{-1} = 2p(x = 4)$.
4. We remove the first 10 words from the plot, since they don't fit the prediction as well.

The Student has fatter tails than a Gaussian. The smaller ν is, the fatter the tails. As $\nu \to \infty$, the distribution tends towards a Gaussian. The distribution has these properties:

$$\text{mean} = \boldsymbol{\mu}, \text{mode} = \boldsymbol{\mu}, \text{cov} = \frac{\nu}{\nu - 2}\boldsymbol{\Sigma} \tag{2.51}$$

The mean is only well defined (finite) if $\nu > 1$. Similarly, the covariance is only well defined if $\nu > 2$.

2.2.5.3   Circular normal (von Mises Fisher) distribution

Sometimes data lives on the unit sphere, rather than being any point in Euclidean space. For example, any D dimensional vector that is ℓ_2-normalized lives on the unit $(D - 1)$ sphere embedded in $\mathbb{R}^D$.

There is an extension of the Gaussian distribution that is suitable for such angular data, known as the **von Mises-Fisher** distribution, or the **circular normal** distribution. It has the following pdf:

$$\text{vMF}(\boldsymbol{x}|\boldsymbol{\mu}, \kappa) \triangleq \frac{1}{Z} \exp(\kappa \boldsymbol{\mu}^{\mathsf{T}} \boldsymbol{x}) \tag{2.52}$$

$$Z = \frac{(2\pi)^{D/2} I_{D/2-1}(\kappa)}{\kappa^{D/2-1}} \tag{2.53}$$

where $\boldsymbol{\mu}$ is the mean (with $||\boldsymbol{\mu}|| = 1$), $\kappa \geq 0$ is the concentration or precision parameter (analogous to $1/\sigma$ for a standard Gaussian), and Z is the normalization constant, with $I_r(\cdot)$ being the modified Bessel function of the first kind and order r. The vMF is like a spherical multivariate Gaussian, parameterized by **cosine distance** instead of Euclidean distance.

The vMF distribution can be used inside of a mixture model to cluster ℓ_2-normalized vectors, as an alternative to using a Gaussian mixture model [Ban+05]. If $\kappa \to 0$, this reduces to the spherical K-means algorithm. It can also be used inside of an admixture model (Main Section 28.4.2); this is called the spherical topic model [Rei+10].

If $D = 2$, an alternative is to use the **von Mises** distribution on the unit circle, which has the form

$$\text{vMF}(x|\mu, \kappa) = \frac{1}{Z} \exp(\kappa \cos(x - \mu)) \tag{2.54}$$

$$Z = 2\pi I_0(\kappa) \tag{2.55}$$

2.2.5.4   Matrix normal distribution (MN)

The **matrix normal** distribution is defined by the following probability density function over matrices $\mathbf{X} \in \mathbb{R}^{n \times p}$:

$$\mathcal{MN}(\mathbf{X}|\mathbf{M}, \mathbf{U}, \mathbf{V}) \triangleq \frac{|\mathbf{V}|^{n/2}}{2\pi^{np/2}|\mathbf{U}|^{p/2}} \exp\left\{ -\frac{1}{2}\text{tr}\left[(\mathbf{X} - \mathbf{M})^{\mathsf{T}} \mathbf{U}^{-1} (\mathbf{X} - \mathbf{M})\mathbf{V} \right] \right\} \tag{2.56}$$

where $\mathbf{M} \in \mathbb{R}^{n \times p}$ is the mean value of $\mathbf{X}$, $\mathbf{U} \in \mathcal{S}_{++}^{n \times n}$ is the covariance among rows, and $\mathbf{V} \in \mathcal{S}_{++}^{p \times p}$ is the precision among columns. It can be seen that

$$\text{vec}(\mathbf{X}) \sim \mathcal{N}(\text{vec}(\mathbf{M}), \mathbf{V}^{-1} \otimes \mathbf{U}). \tag{2.57}$$

Note that there is another version of the definition of the matrix normal distribution using the column-covariance matrix $\tilde{\mathbf{V}} = \mathbf{V}^{-1}$ instead of $\mathbf{V}$, which leads to the density

$$\frac{1}{2\pi^{np/2}|\mathbf{U}|^{p/2}|\tilde{\mathbf{V}}|^{n/2}} \exp\left\{-\frac{1}{2}\mathrm{tr}\left[(\mathbf{X}-\mathbf{M})^{\mathsf{T}}\mathbf{U}^{-1}(\mathbf{X}-\mathbf{M})\tilde{\mathbf{V}}^{-1}\right]\right\}. \tag{2.58}$$

These two versions of definition are obviously equivalent, but we will see that the definition we adopt in Equation (2.56) will leads to a neat update of the posterior distribution (just as the precision matrix is more convenient to use than the covariance matrix in analyzing the posterior of the multivariate normal distribution with a conjugate prior).

2.2.5.5   Wishart distribution

The **Wishart** distribution is the generalization of the gamma distribution to positive definite matrices. Press [Pre05, p107] has said, "The Wishart distribution ranks next to the normal distribution in order of importance and usefulness in multivariate statistics". We will mostly use it to model our uncertainty when estimating covariance matrices (see Section 3.4.4).

The pdf of the Wishart is defined as follows:

$$\mathrm{Wi}(\mathbf{\Sigma}|\mathbf{S},\nu) \triangleq \frac{1}{Z}|\mathbf{\Sigma}|^{(\nu-D-1)/2}\exp\left(-\frac{1}{2}\mathrm{tr}(\mathbf{\Sigma}\mathbf{S}^{-1})\right) \tag{2.59}$$

$$Z \triangleq |\mathbf{S}|^{-\nu/2}2^{\nu D/2}\Gamma_D(\nu/2) \tag{2.60}$$

Here ν is called the "degrees of freedom" and $\mathbf{S}$ is the "scale matrix". (We shall get more intuition for these parameters shortly.) The normalization constant only exists (and hence the pdf is only well defined) if $\nu > D - 1$.

The distribution has these properties:

$$\text{mean} = \nu\mathbf{S}, \text{ mode} = (\nu - D - 1)\mathbf{S} \tag{2.61}$$

Note that the mode only exists if $\nu > D + 1$.

If $D = 1$, the Wishart reduces to the gamma distribution:

$$\mathrm{Wi}(\lambda|s^{-1},\nu) = \mathrm{Ga}(\lambda|\text{shape} = \frac{\nu}{2}, \text{rate} = \frac{1}{2s}) \tag{2.62}$$

If $s = 2$, this reduces to the chi-squared distribution.

There is an interesting connection between the Wishart distribution and the Gaussian. In particular, let $\boldsymbol{x}_n \sim \mathcal{N}(0, \mathbf{\Sigma})$. One can show that the scatter matrix, $\mathbf{S} = \sum_{n=1}^N \boldsymbol{x}_n\boldsymbol{x}_n^{\mathsf{T}}$, has a Wishart distribution: $\mathbf{S} \sim \mathrm{Wi}(\mathbf{\Sigma}, N)$.

2.2.5.6   Inverse Wishart distribution

If $\lambda \sim \mathrm{Ga}(a, b)$, then that $\frac{1}{\lambda} \sim \mathrm{IG}(a, b)$. Similarly, if $\mathbf{\Sigma}^{-1} \sim \mathrm{Wi}(\mathbf{S}^{-1}, \nu)$ then $\mathbf{\Sigma} \sim \mathrm{IW}(\mathbf{S}, \nu + D + 1)$, where IW is the **inverse Wishart**, the multidimensional generalization of the inverse gamma. It is defined as follows, for $\nu > D - 1$ and $\mathbf{S} \succ 0$:

$$\mathrm{IW}(\mathbf{\Sigma}|\mathbf{S},\nu) = \frac{1}{Z}|\mathbf{\Sigma}|^{-(\nu+D+1)/2}\exp\left(-\frac{1}{2}\mathrm{tr}(\mathbf{S}\mathbf{\Sigma}^{-1})\right) \tag{2.63}$$

$$Z_{\mathrm{IW}} = |\mathbf{S}|^{-\nu/2}2^{\nu D/2}\Gamma_D(\nu/2) \tag{2.64}$$

One can show that the distribution has these properties:

$$\text{mean} = \frac{\mathbf{S}}{\nu - D - 1}, \; \text{mode} = \frac{\mathbf{S}}{\nu + D + 1} \tag{2.65}$$

If $D = 1$, this reduces to the inverse gamma:

$$\text{IW}(\sigma^2 | s^{-1}, \nu) = \text{IG}(\sigma^2 | \nu/2, s/2) \tag{2.66}$$

If $s = 1$, this reduces to the inverse chi-squared distribution.

2.2.5.7   Dirichlet distribution

A multivariate generalization of the beta distribution is the **Dirichlet**[5] distribution, which has support over the **probability simplex**, defined by

$$S_K = \{\mathbf{x} : 0 \le x_k \le 1, \sum_{k=1}^{K} x_k = 1\} \tag{2.67}$$

The pdf is defined as follows:

$$\text{Dir}(\mathbf{x} | \boldsymbol{\alpha}) \triangleq \frac{1}{B(\boldsymbol{\alpha})} \prod_{k=1}^{K} x_k^{\alpha_k - 1} \mathbb{I}(\mathbf{x} \in S_K) \tag{2.68}$$

where $B(\boldsymbol{\alpha})$ is the multivariate beta function,

$$B(\boldsymbol{\alpha}) \triangleq \frac{\prod_{k=1}^{K} \Gamma(\alpha_k)}{\Gamma(\sum_{k=1}^{K} \alpha_k)} \tag{2.69}$$

Figure 2.6 shows some plots of the Dirichlet when $K = 3$. We see that $\alpha_0 = \sum_k \alpha_k$ controls the strength of the distribution (how peaked it is), and the α_k control where the peak occurs. For example, Dir(1, 1, 1) is a uniform distribution, Dir(2, 2, 2) is a broad distribution centered at $(1/3, 1/3, 1/3)$, and Dir(20, 20, 20) is a narrow distribution centered at $(1/3, 1/3, 1/3)$. Dir(3, 3, 20) is an asymmetric distribution that puts more density in one of the corners. If $\alpha_k < 1$ for all k, we get "spikes" at the corners of the simplex. Samples from the distribution when $\alpha_k < 1$ are sparse, as shown in Figure 2.7.

For future reference, here are some useful properties of the Dirichlet distribution:

$$\mathbb{E}[x_k] = \frac{\alpha_k}{\alpha_0}, \; \text{mode}[x_k] = \frac{\alpha_k - 1}{\alpha_0 - K}, \; \mathbb{V}[x_k] = \frac{\alpha_k(\alpha_0 - \alpha_k)}{\alpha_0^2(\alpha_0 + 1)} \tag{2.70}$$

where $\alpha_0 = \sum_k \alpha_k$.

Often we use a symmetric Dirichlet prior of the form $\alpha_k = \alpha/K$. In this case, we have $\mathbb{E}[x_k] = 1/K$, and $\mathbb{V}[x_k] = \frac{K-1}{K^2(\alpha+1)}$. So we see that increasing α increases the precision (decreases the variance) of the distribution.

---

5. Johann Dirichlet was a German mathematician, 1805–1859.

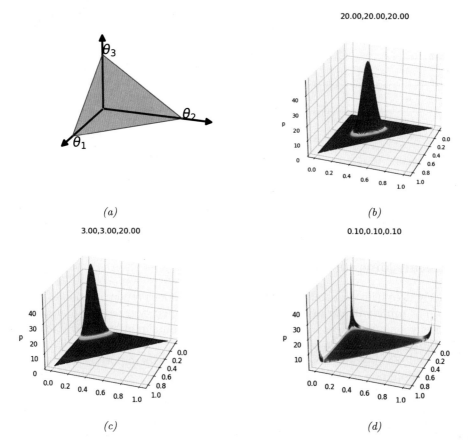

Figure 2.6: (a) The Dirichlet distribution when $K = 3$ defines a distribution over the simplex, which can be represented by the triangular surface. Points on this surface satisfy $0 \leq \theta_c \leq 1$ and $\sum_{c=1}^{3} \theta_c = 1$. Generated by dirichlet_3d_triangle_plot.ipynb. (b) Plot of the Dirichlet density for $\boldsymbol{\alpha} = (20, 20, 20)$. (c) Plot of the Dirichlet density for $\boldsymbol{\alpha} = (3, 3, 20)$. (d) Plot of the Dirichlet density for $\boldsymbol{\alpha} = (0.1, 0.1, 0.1)$. Generated by dirichlet_3d_spiky_plot.ipynb.

The Dirichlet distribution is useful for distinguishing aleatoric (data) uncertainty from epistemic uncertainty. To see this, consider a 3-sided die. If we know that each outcome is equally likely, we can use a "peaky" symmetric Dirichlet, such as $\text{Dir}(20, 20, 20)$, shown in Figure 2.6(b); this reflects the fact that we are sure the outcomes will be unpredictable. By contrast, if we are not sure what the outcomes will be like (e.g., it could be a biased die), then we can use a "flat" symmetric Dirichlet, such as $\text{Dir}(1, 1, 1)$, which can generate a wide range of possible outcome distributions. We can make the Dirichlet distribution be conditional on inputs, resulting in what is called a **prior network** [MG18], since it encodes $p(\boldsymbol{\pi}|\boldsymbol{x})$ (output is a distributon) rather than $p(y|\boldsymbol{x})$ (output is a label).

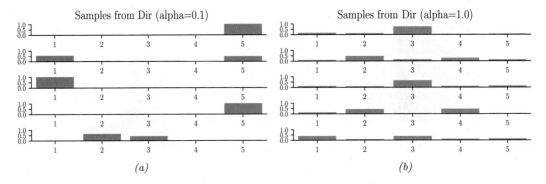

Figure 2.7: Samples from a 5-dimensional symmetric Dirichlet distribution for different parameter values. (a) $\boldsymbol{\alpha} = (0.1, \ldots, 0.1)$. *This results in very sparse distributions, with many 0s. (b)* $\boldsymbol{\alpha} = (1, \ldots, 1)$. *This results in more uniform (and dense) distributions. Generated by* dirichlet_samples_plot.ipynb.

2.3 Gaussian joint distributions

The most widely used joint probability distribution for continuous random variables is the **multivariate Gaussian** or **multivariate normal** (**MVN**). The popularity is partly because this distribution is mathematically convenient, but also because the Gaussian assumption is fairly reasonable in many cases. Indeed, the Gaussian is the distribution with maximum entropy distribution subject to having specified first and second moments (Section 2.4.7). In view of its importance, this section discusses the Gaussian distribution in detail.

2.3.1 The multivariate normal

In this section, we discuss the multivariate Gaussian or multivariate normal in detail.

2.3.1.1 Definition

The MVN density is defined by the following:

$$\mathcal{N}(\boldsymbol{x}|\boldsymbol{\mu}, \boldsymbol{\Sigma}) \triangleq \frac{1}{(2\pi)^{D/2}|\boldsymbol{\Sigma}|^{1/2}} \exp\left[-\frac{1}{2}(\boldsymbol{x} - \boldsymbol{\mu})^{\mathsf{T}}\boldsymbol{\Sigma}^{-1}(\boldsymbol{x} - \boldsymbol{\mu})\right] \tag{2.71}$$

where $\boldsymbol{\mu} = \mathbb{E}\left[\boldsymbol{x}\right] \in \mathbb{R}^D$ is the mean vector, and $\boldsymbol{\Sigma} = \text{Cov}\left[\boldsymbol{x}\right]$ is the $D \times D$ covariance matrix. The normalization constant $Z = (2\pi)^{D/2}|\boldsymbol{\Sigma}|^{1/2}$ just ensures that the pdf integrates to 1. The expression inside the exponential (ignoring the factor of -0.5) is the squared **Mahalanobis distance** between the data vector $\boldsymbol{x}$ and the mean vector $\boldsymbol{\mu}$, given by

$$d_{\boldsymbol{\Sigma}}(\boldsymbol{x}, \boldsymbol{\mu})^2 = (\boldsymbol{x} - \boldsymbol{\mu})^{\mathsf{T}}\boldsymbol{\Sigma}^{-1}(\boldsymbol{x} - \boldsymbol{\mu}) \tag{2.72}$$

In 2d, the MVN is known as the **bivariate Gaussian** distribution. Its pdf can be represented as $\boldsymbol{x} \sim \mathcal{N}(\boldsymbol{\mu}, \boldsymbol{\Sigma})$, where $\boldsymbol{x} \in \mathbb{R}^2$, $\boldsymbol{\mu} \in \mathbb{R}^2$ and

$$\boldsymbol{\Sigma} = \begin{pmatrix} \sigma_1^2 & \sigma_{12}^2 \\ \sigma_{21}^2 & \sigma_2^2 \end{pmatrix} = \begin{pmatrix} \sigma_1^2 & \rho\sigma_1\sigma_2 \\ \rho\sigma_1\sigma_2 & \sigma_2^2 \end{pmatrix} \tag{2.73}$$

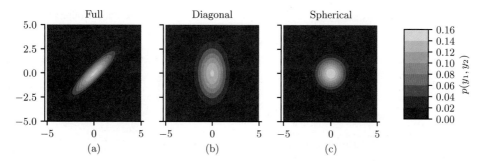

Figure 2.8: Visualization of a 2d Gaussian density in terms of level sets of constant probability density. (a) A full covariance matrix has elliptical contours. (b) A diagonal covariance matrix is an axis aligned ellipse. (c) A spherical covariance matrix has a circular shape. Generated by gauss_plot_2d.ipynb.

where the correlation coefficient is given by $\rho \triangleq \frac{\sigma_{12}^2}{\sigma_1 \sigma_2}$.

Figure 2.8 plots some MVN densities in 2d for three different kinds of covariance matrices. A **full covariance matrix** has $D(D+1)/2$ parameters, where we divide by 2 since $\boldsymbol{\Sigma}$ is symmetric. A **diagonal covariance matrix** has D parameters, and has 0s in the off-diagonal terms. A **spherical covariance matrix**, also called **isotropic covariance matrix**, has the form $\boldsymbol{\Sigma} = \sigma^2 \mathbf{I}_D$, so it only has one free parameter, namely σ^2.

2.3.1.2 Gaussian shells

Multivariate Gaussians can behave rather counterintuitively in high dimensions. In particular, we can ask: if we draw samples $\boldsymbol{x} \sim \mathcal{N}(\mathbf{0}, \mathbf{I}_D)$, where D is the number of dimensions, where do we expect most of the $\boldsymbol{x}$ to lie? Since the peak (mode) of the pdf is at the origin, it is natural to expect most samples to be near the origin. However, in high dimensions, the typical set of a Gaussian is a thin shell or annulus with a distance from origin given by $r = \sigma\sqrt{D}$ and a thickness of $O(\sigma D^{\frac{1}{4}})$. The intuitive reason for this is as follows: although the density decays as $e^{-r^2/2}$, meaning density decreases from the origin, the volume of a sphere grows as r^D, meaning volume increases from the origin, and since mass is density times volume, the majority of points end up in this annulus where these two terms "balance out". This is called the "**Gaussian soap bubble**" phenomenon, and is illustrated in Figure 2.9.[6]

To see why the typical set for a Gaussian is concentrated in a thin annulus at radius $\sqrt{D}$, consider the squared distance of a point $\boldsymbol{x}$ from the origin, $d(\boldsymbol{x}) = \sqrt{\sum_{i=1}^{D} x_i^2}$, where $x_i \sim \mathcal{N}(0,1)$. The expected squared distance is given by $\mathbb{E}\left[d^2\right] = \sum_{i=1}^{D} \mathbb{E}\left[x_i^2\right] = D$, and the variance of the squared distance is given by $\mathbb{V}\left[d^2\right] = \sum_{i=1}^{D} \mathbb{V}\left[x_i^2\right] = D$. As D grows, the coefficient of variation (i.e., the SD relative to the mean) goes to zero:

$$\lim_{D \to \infty} \frac{\text{std}\left[d^2\right]}{\mathbb{E}\left[d^2\right]} = \lim_{D \to \infty} \frac{\sqrt{D}}{D} = 0 \tag{2.74}$$

---

6. For a more detailed explanation, see this blog post by Ferenc Huszar: `https://www.inference.vc/high-dimensional-gaussian-distributions-are-soap-bubble/`.

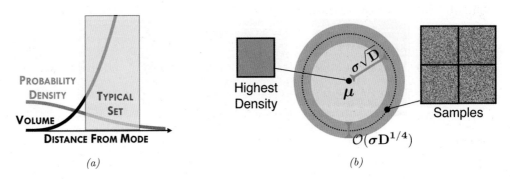

Figure 2.9: (a) Cartoon illustration of why the typical set of a Gaussian is not centered at the mode of the distribution. (b) Illustration of the typical set of a Gaussian, which is concentrated in a thin annulus of thickness $\sigma D^{1/4}$ and distance $\sigma D^{1/2}$ from the origin. We also show an image with the highest density (the all gray image on the left). as well as some high probability samples (the speckle noise images on the right). From Figure 1 of [Nal+19a]. Used with kind permission of Eric Nalisnick.

Thus the expected square distance concentrates around D, so the expected distance concentrates around $\mathbb{E}[d(\boldsymbol{x})] = \sqrt{D}$. See [Ver18] for a more rigorous proof, and Section 5.2.3 for a discussion of typical sets.

To see what this means in the context of images, in Figure 2.9b, we show some grayscale images that are sampled from a Gaussian of the form $\mathcal{N}(\boldsymbol{\mu}, \sigma^2 \mathbf{I})$, where $\boldsymbol{\mu}$ corresponds to the all-gray image. However, it is extremely unlikely that randomly sampled images would be close to all-gray, as shown in the figure.

2.3.1.3   Marginals and conditionals of an MVN

Let us partition our vector of random variables $\boldsymbol{x}$ into two parts, $\boldsymbol{x}_1$ and $\boldsymbol{x}_2$, so

$$\boldsymbol{\mu} = \begin{pmatrix} \boldsymbol{\mu}_1 \\ \boldsymbol{\mu}_2 \end{pmatrix}, \quad \boldsymbol{\Sigma} = \begin{pmatrix} \boldsymbol{\Sigma}_{11} & \boldsymbol{\Sigma}_{12} \\ \boldsymbol{\Sigma}_{21} & \boldsymbol{\Sigma}_{22} \end{pmatrix} \tag{2.75}$$

The marginals of this distribution are given by the following (see Section 2.3.1.5 for the proof):

$$p(\boldsymbol{x}_1) = \int \mathcal{N}(\boldsymbol{x}|\boldsymbol{\mu}, \boldsymbol{\Sigma})d\boldsymbol{x}_2 \triangleq \mathcal{N}(\boldsymbol{x}_1|\boldsymbol{\mu}_1^m, \boldsymbol{\Sigma}_1^m) = \mathcal{N}(\boldsymbol{x}_1|\boldsymbol{\mu}_1, \boldsymbol{\Sigma}_{11}) \tag{2.76}$$

$$p(\boldsymbol{x}_2) = \int \mathcal{N}(\boldsymbol{x}|\boldsymbol{\mu}, \boldsymbol{\Sigma})d\boldsymbol{x}_1 \triangleq \mathcal{N}(\boldsymbol{x}_2|\boldsymbol{\mu}_2^m, \boldsymbol{\Sigma}_2^m) = \mathcal{N}(\boldsymbol{x}_2|\boldsymbol{\mu}_2, \boldsymbol{\Sigma}_{22}) \tag{2.77}$$

The conditional distributions can be shown to have the following form (see Section 2.3.1.5 for the proof):

$$p(\boldsymbol{x}_1|\boldsymbol{x}_2) = \mathcal{N}(\boldsymbol{x}_1|\boldsymbol{\mu}_{1|2}^c, \boldsymbol{\Sigma}_{1|2}^c) = \mathcal{N}(\boldsymbol{x}_1|\boldsymbol{\mu}_1 + \boldsymbol{\Sigma}_{12}\boldsymbol{\Sigma}_{22}^{-1}(\boldsymbol{x}_2 - \boldsymbol{\mu}_2),\ \boldsymbol{\Sigma}_{11} - \boldsymbol{\Sigma}_{12}\boldsymbol{\Sigma}_{22}^{-1}\boldsymbol{\Sigma}_{21}) \tag{2.78}$$

$$p(\boldsymbol{x}_2|\boldsymbol{x}_1) = \mathcal{N}(\boldsymbol{x}_2|\boldsymbol{\mu}_{2|1}^c, \boldsymbol{\Sigma}_{2|1}^c) = \mathcal{N}(\boldsymbol{x}_2|\boldsymbol{\mu}_2 + \boldsymbol{\Sigma}_{21}\boldsymbol{\Sigma}_{11}^{-1}(\boldsymbol{x}_1 - \boldsymbol{\mu}_1),\ \boldsymbol{\Sigma}_{22} - \boldsymbol{\Sigma}_{21}\boldsymbol{\Sigma}_{11}^{-1}\boldsymbol{\Sigma}_{12}) \tag{2.79}$$

Note that the posterior mean of $p(\boldsymbol{x}_1|\boldsymbol{x}_2)$ is a linear function of $\boldsymbol{x}_2$, but the posterior covariance is independent of $\boldsymbol{x}_2$; this is a peculiar property of Gaussian distributions.

2.3.1.4 Information (canonical) form

It is common to parameterize the MVN in terms of the mean vector $\boldsymbol{\mu}$ and the covariance matrix $\boldsymbol{\Sigma}$. However, for reasons which are explained in Section 2.4.2.5, it is sometimes useful to represent the Gaussian distribution using **canonical parameters** or **natural parameters**, defined as

$$\boldsymbol{\Lambda} \triangleq \boldsymbol{\Sigma}^{-1}, \quad \boldsymbol{\eta} \triangleq \boldsymbol{\Sigma}^{-1}\boldsymbol{\mu} \tag{2.80}$$

The matrix $\boldsymbol{\Lambda} = \boldsymbol{\Sigma}^{-1}$ is known as the **precision matrix**, and the vector $\boldsymbol{\eta}$ is known as the **precision-weighted mean**. We can convert back to the more familiar **moment parameters** using

$$\boldsymbol{\mu} = \boldsymbol{\Lambda}^{-1}\boldsymbol{\eta}, \quad \boldsymbol{\Sigma} = \boldsymbol{\Lambda}^{-1} \tag{2.81}$$

Hence we can write the MVN in **canonical form** (also called **information form**) as follows:

$$\mathcal{N}_c(\boldsymbol{x}|\boldsymbol{\eta},\boldsymbol{\Lambda}) \triangleq c\exp\left(\boldsymbol{x}^\mathsf{T}\boldsymbol{\eta} - \frac{1}{2}\boldsymbol{x}^\mathsf{T}\boldsymbol{\Lambda}\boldsymbol{x}\right) \tag{2.82}$$

$$c \triangleq \frac{\exp(-\frac{1}{2}\boldsymbol{\eta}^\mathsf{T}\boldsymbol{\Lambda}^{-1}\boldsymbol{\eta})}{(2\pi)^{D/2}\sqrt{\det(\boldsymbol{\Lambda}^{-1})}} \tag{2.83}$$

where we use the notation $\mathcal{N}_c()$ to distinguish it from the standard parameterization $\mathcal{N}()$. For more information on moment and natural parameters, see Section 2.4.2.5.

It is also possible to derive the marginalization and conditioning formulas in information form (see Section 2.3.1.6 for the derivation). For the marginals we have

$$p(\boldsymbol{x}_1) = \mathcal{N}_c(\boldsymbol{x}_1|\boldsymbol{\eta}_1^m, \boldsymbol{\Lambda}_1^m) = \mathcal{N}_c(\boldsymbol{x}_1|\boldsymbol{\eta}_1 - \boldsymbol{\Lambda}_{12}\boldsymbol{\Lambda}_{22}^{-1}\boldsymbol{\eta}_2, \boldsymbol{\Lambda}_{11} - \boldsymbol{\Lambda}_{12}\boldsymbol{\Lambda}_{22}^{-1}\boldsymbol{\Lambda}_{21}) \tag{2.84}$$

$$p(\boldsymbol{x}_2) = \mathcal{N}_c(\boldsymbol{x}_2|\boldsymbol{\eta}_2^m, \boldsymbol{\Lambda}_2^m) = \mathcal{N}_c(\boldsymbol{x}_2|\boldsymbol{\eta}_2 - \boldsymbol{\Lambda}_{21}\boldsymbol{\Lambda}_{11}^{-1}\boldsymbol{\eta}_1, \boldsymbol{\Lambda}_{22} - \boldsymbol{\Lambda}_{21}\boldsymbol{\Lambda}_{11}^{-1}\boldsymbol{\Lambda}_{12}) \tag{2.85}$$

For the conditionals we have

$$p(\boldsymbol{x}_1|\boldsymbol{x}_2) = \mathcal{N}_c(\boldsymbol{x}_1|\boldsymbol{\eta}_{1|2}^c, \boldsymbol{\Lambda}_{1|2}^c) = \mathcal{N}_c(\boldsymbol{x}_1|\boldsymbol{\eta}_1 - \boldsymbol{\Lambda}_{12}\boldsymbol{x}_2, \boldsymbol{\Lambda}_{11}) \tag{2.86}$$

$$p(\boldsymbol{x}_2|\boldsymbol{x}_1) = \mathcal{N}_c(\boldsymbol{x}_2|\boldsymbol{\eta}_{2|1}^c, \boldsymbol{\Lambda}_{2|1}^c) = \mathcal{N}_c(\boldsymbol{x}_2|\boldsymbol{\eta}_2 - \boldsymbol{\Lambda}_{21}\boldsymbol{x}_1, \boldsymbol{\Lambda}_{22}) \tag{2.87}$$

Thus we see that marginalization is easier in moment form, and conditioning is easier in information form.

2.3.1.5 Derivation: moment form

In this section, we derive Equation (2.77) and Equation (2.78) for marginalizing and conditioning an MVN in moment form.

Before we dive in, we need to introduce the following result, for the **inverse of a partitioned matrix** of the form

$$\mathbf{M} = \begin{pmatrix} \mathbf{E} & \mathbf{F} \\ \mathbf{G} & \mathbf{H} \end{pmatrix} \tag{2.88}$$

where we assume $\mathbf{E}$ and $\mathbf{H}$ are invertible. One can show (see e.g., [Mur22, Sec 7.3.2] for the proof) that

$$\mathbf{M}^{-1} = \begin{pmatrix} (\mathbf{M}/\mathbf{H})^{-1} & -(\mathbf{M}/\mathbf{H})^{-1}\mathbf{F}\mathbf{H}^{-1} \\ -\mathbf{H}^{-1}\mathbf{G}(\mathbf{M}/\mathbf{H})^{-1} & \mathbf{H}^{-1} + \mathbf{H}^{-1}\mathbf{G}(\mathbf{M}/\mathbf{H})^{-1}\mathbf{F}\mathbf{H}^{-1} \end{pmatrix} \tag{2.89}$$

$$= \begin{pmatrix} \mathbf{E}^{-1} + \mathbf{E}^{-1}\mathbf{F}(\mathbf{M}/\mathbf{E})^{-1}\mathbf{G}\mathbf{E}^{-1} & -\mathbf{E}^{-1}\mathbf{F}(\mathbf{M}/\mathbf{E})^{-1} \\ -(\mathbf{M}/\mathbf{E})^{-1}\mathbf{G}\mathbf{E}^{-1} & (\mathbf{M}/\mathbf{E})^{-1} \end{pmatrix} \tag{2.90}$$

where

$$\mathbf{M}/\mathbf{H} \triangleq \mathbf{E} - \mathbf{F}\mathbf{H}^{-1}\mathbf{G} \tag{2.91}$$

$$\mathbf{M}/\mathbf{E} \triangleq \mathbf{H} - \mathbf{G}\mathbf{E}^{-1}\mathbf{F} \tag{2.92}$$

We say that $\mathbf{M}/\mathbf{H}$ is the **Schur complement** of $\mathbf{M}$ wrt $\mathbf{H}$, and $\mathbf{M}/\mathbf{E}$ is the Schur complement of $\mathbf{M}$ wrt $\mathbf{E}$.

From the above, we also have the following important result, known as the **matrix inversion lemma** or the **Sherman-Morrison-Woodbury formula**:

$$(\mathbf{M}/\mathbf{H})^{-1} = (\mathbf{E} - \mathbf{F}\mathbf{H}^{-1}\mathbf{G})^{-1} = \mathbf{E}^{-1} + \mathbf{E}^{-1}\mathbf{F}(\mathbf{H} - \mathbf{G}\mathbf{E}^{-1}\mathbf{F})^{-1}\mathbf{G}\mathbf{E}^{-1} \tag{2.93}$$

Now we return to the derivation of the MVN conditioning equation. Let us factor the joint $p(\boldsymbol{x}_1, \boldsymbol{x}_2)$ as $p(\boldsymbol{x}_2)p(\boldsymbol{x}_1|\boldsymbol{x}_2)$ as follows:

$$p(\boldsymbol{x}_1, \boldsymbol{x}_2) \propto \exp\left\{ -\frac{1}{2} \begin{pmatrix} \boldsymbol{x}_1 - \boldsymbol{\mu}_1 \\ \boldsymbol{x}_2 - \boldsymbol{\mu}_2 \end{pmatrix}^\mathsf{T} \begin{pmatrix} \boldsymbol{\Sigma}_{11} & \boldsymbol{\Sigma}_{12} \\ \boldsymbol{\Sigma}_{21} & \boldsymbol{\Sigma}_{22} \end{pmatrix}^{-1} \begin{pmatrix} \boldsymbol{x}_1 - \boldsymbol{\mu}_1 \\ \boldsymbol{x}_2 - \boldsymbol{\mu}_2 \end{pmatrix} \right\} \tag{2.94}$$

Using the equation for the inverse of a block structured matrix, the above exponent becomes

$$p(\boldsymbol{x}_1, \boldsymbol{x}_2) \propto \exp\left\{ -\frac{1}{2} \begin{pmatrix} \boldsymbol{x}_1 - \boldsymbol{\mu}_1 \\ \boldsymbol{x}_2 - \boldsymbol{\mu}_2 \end{pmatrix}^\mathsf{T} \begin{pmatrix} \mathbf{I} & \mathbf{0} \\ -\boldsymbol{\Sigma}_{22}^{-1}\boldsymbol{\Sigma}_{21} & \mathbf{I} \end{pmatrix} \begin{pmatrix} (\boldsymbol{\Sigma}/\boldsymbol{\Sigma}_{22})^{-1} & \mathbf{0} \\ \mathbf{0} & \boldsymbol{\Sigma}_{22}^{-1} \end{pmatrix} \right. \tag{2.95}$$

$$\left. \times \begin{pmatrix} \mathbf{I} & -\boldsymbol{\Sigma}_{12}\boldsymbol{\Sigma}_{22}^{-1} \\ \mathbf{0} & \mathbf{I} \end{pmatrix} \begin{pmatrix} \boldsymbol{x}_1 - \boldsymbol{\mu}_1 \\ \boldsymbol{x}_2 - \boldsymbol{\mu}_2 \end{pmatrix} \right\} \tag{2.96}$$

$$= \exp\left\{ -\frac{1}{2}(\boldsymbol{x}_1 - \boldsymbol{\mu}_1 - \boldsymbol{\Sigma}_{12}\boldsymbol{\Sigma}_{22}^{-1}(\boldsymbol{x}_2 - \boldsymbol{\mu}_2))^\mathsf{T} (\boldsymbol{\Sigma}/\boldsymbol{\Sigma}_{22})^{-1} \right. \tag{2.97}$$

$$\left. (\boldsymbol{x}_1 - \boldsymbol{\mu}_1 - \boldsymbol{\Sigma}_{12}\boldsymbol{\Sigma}_{22}^{-1}(\boldsymbol{x}_2 - \boldsymbol{\mu}_2)) \right\} \times \exp\left\{ -\frac{1}{2}(\boldsymbol{x}_2 - \boldsymbol{\mu}_2)^\mathsf{T}\boldsymbol{\Sigma}_{22}^{-1}(\boldsymbol{x}_2 - \boldsymbol{\mu}_2) \right\} \tag{2.98}$$

This is of the form

$$\exp(\text{quadratic form in } \boldsymbol{x}_1, \boldsymbol{x}_2) \times \exp(\text{quadratic form in } \boldsymbol{x}_2) \tag{2.99}$$

Hence we have successfully factorized the joint as

$$p(\boldsymbol{x}_1, \boldsymbol{x}_2) = p(\boldsymbol{x}_1|\boldsymbol{x}_2)p(\boldsymbol{x}_2) \tag{2.100}$$

$$= \mathcal{N}(\boldsymbol{x}_1|\boldsymbol{\mu}_{1|2}, \boldsymbol{\Sigma}_{1|2})\mathcal{N}(\boldsymbol{x}_2|\boldsymbol{\mu}_2, \boldsymbol{\Sigma}_{22}) \tag{2.101}$$

where

$$\boldsymbol{\mu}_{1|2} = \boldsymbol{\mu}_1 + \boldsymbol{\Sigma}_{12}\boldsymbol{\Sigma}_{22}^{-1}(\boldsymbol{x}_2 - \boldsymbol{\mu}_2) \tag{2.102}$$

$$\boldsymbol{\Sigma}_{1|2} = \boldsymbol{\Sigma}/\boldsymbol{\Sigma}_{22} \triangleq \boldsymbol{\Sigma}_{11} - \boldsymbol{\Sigma}_{12}\boldsymbol{\Sigma}_{22}^{-1}\boldsymbol{\Sigma}_{21} \tag{2.103}$$

where $\boldsymbol{\Sigma}/\boldsymbol{\Sigma}_{22}$ is as the Schur complement of $\boldsymbol{\Sigma}$ wrt $\boldsymbol{\Sigma}_{22}$.

2.3.1.6 Derivation: information form

In this section, we derive Equation (2.85) and Equation (2.86) for marginalizing and conditioning an MVN in information form.

First we derive the conditional formula.[7] Let us partition the information form parameters as follows:

$$\boldsymbol{\eta} = \begin{pmatrix} \boldsymbol{\eta}_1 \\ \boldsymbol{\eta}_2 \end{pmatrix}, \quad \boldsymbol{\Lambda} = \begin{pmatrix} \boldsymbol{\Lambda}_{11} & \boldsymbol{\Lambda}_{12} \\ \boldsymbol{\Lambda}_{21} & \boldsymbol{\Lambda}_{22} \end{pmatrix} \tag{2.104}$$

We can now write the joint log probabilty of $\boldsymbol{x}_1, \boldsymbol{x}_2$ as

$$\ln p(\boldsymbol{x}_1, \boldsymbol{x}_2) = -\frac{1}{2}\begin{pmatrix} \boldsymbol{x}_1 \\ \boldsymbol{x}_2 \end{pmatrix}^{\mathsf{T}}\begin{pmatrix} \boldsymbol{\Lambda}_{11} & \boldsymbol{\Lambda}_{12} \\ \boldsymbol{\Lambda}_{21} & \boldsymbol{\Lambda}_{22} \end{pmatrix}\begin{pmatrix} \boldsymbol{x}_1 \\ \boldsymbol{x}_2 \end{pmatrix} + \begin{pmatrix} \boldsymbol{x}_1 \\ \boldsymbol{x}_2 \end{pmatrix}^{\mathsf{T}}\begin{pmatrix} \boldsymbol{\eta}_1 \\ \boldsymbol{\eta}_2 \end{pmatrix} + \text{const.} \tag{2.105}$$

$$= -\frac{1}{2}\boldsymbol{x}_1^{\mathsf{T}}\boldsymbol{\Lambda}_{11}\boldsymbol{x}_1 - \frac{1}{2}\boldsymbol{x}_2^{\mathsf{T}}\boldsymbol{\Lambda}_{22}\boldsymbol{x}_2 - \frac{1}{2}\boldsymbol{x}_1^{\mathsf{T}}\boldsymbol{\Lambda}_{12}\boldsymbol{x}_2 - \frac{1}{2}\boldsymbol{x}_2^{\mathsf{T}}\boldsymbol{\Lambda}_{21}\boldsymbol{x}_1$$
$$+ \boldsymbol{x}_1^{\mathsf{T}}\boldsymbol{\eta}_1 + \boldsymbol{x}_2^{\mathsf{T}}\boldsymbol{\eta}_2 + \text{const.} \tag{2.106}$$

where the constant term does not depend on $\boldsymbol{x}_1$ or $\boldsymbol{x}_2$.

To calculate the parameters of the conditional distribution $p(\boldsymbol{x}_1|\boldsymbol{x}_2)$, we fix the value of $\boldsymbol{x}_2$ and collect the terms which are quadratic in $\boldsymbol{x}_1$ for the conditional precision and then linear in $\boldsymbol{x}_1$ for the conditional precision-weighted mean. The terms which are quadratic in $\boldsymbol{x}_1$ are just $-\frac{1}{2}\boldsymbol{x}_1^{\mathsf{T}}\boldsymbol{\Lambda}_{11}\boldsymbol{x}_1$, and hence

$$\boldsymbol{\Lambda}_{1|2}^c = \boldsymbol{\Lambda}_{11} \tag{2.107}$$

The terms which are linear in $\boldsymbol{x}_1$ are

$$-\frac{1}{2}\boldsymbol{x}_1^{\mathsf{T}}\boldsymbol{\Lambda}_{12}\boldsymbol{x}_2 - \frac{1}{2}\boldsymbol{x}_2^{\mathsf{T}}\boldsymbol{\Lambda}_{21}\boldsymbol{x}_1 + \boldsymbol{x}_1^{\mathsf{T}}\boldsymbol{\eta}_1 = \boldsymbol{x}_1^{\mathsf{T}}(\boldsymbol{\eta}_1 - \boldsymbol{\Lambda}_{12}\boldsymbol{x}_2) \tag{2.108}$$

since $\boldsymbol{\Lambda}_{21}^{\mathsf{T}} = \boldsymbol{\Lambda}_{12}$. Thus the conditional precision-weighted mean is

$$\boldsymbol{\eta}_{1|2}^c = \boldsymbol{\eta}_1 - \boldsymbol{\Lambda}_{12}\boldsymbol{x}_2. \tag{2.109}$$

We will now derive the results for marginalizing in information form. The marginal, $p(\boldsymbol{x}_2)$, can be calculated by integrating the joint, $p(\boldsymbol{x}_1, \boldsymbol{x}_2)$, with respect to $\boldsymbol{x}_1$:

$$p(\boldsymbol{x}_2) = \int p(\boldsymbol{x}_1, \boldsymbol{x}_2)d\boldsymbol{x}_1 \tag{2.110}$$

$$\propto \int \exp\left\{-\frac{1}{2}\boldsymbol{x}_1^{\mathsf{T}}\boldsymbol{\Lambda}_{11}\boldsymbol{x}_1 - \frac{1}{2}\boldsymbol{x}_2^{\mathsf{T}}\boldsymbol{\Lambda}_{22}\boldsymbol{x}_2 - \frac{1}{2}\boldsymbol{x}_1^{\mathsf{T}}\boldsymbol{\Lambda}_{12}\boldsymbol{x}_2 - \frac{1}{2}\boldsymbol{x}_2^{\mathsf{T}}\boldsymbol{\Lambda}_{21}\boldsymbol{x}_1 + \boldsymbol{x}_1^{\mathsf{T}}\boldsymbol{\eta}_1 + \boldsymbol{x}_2^{\mathsf{T}}\boldsymbol{\eta}_2\right\}d\boldsymbol{x}_1,$$
$$\tag{2.111}$$

---

7. This derivation is due to Giles Harper-Donnelly.

where the terms in the exponent have been decomposed into the partitioned structure in Equation (2.104) as in Equation (2.106). Next, collecting all the terms involving $\boldsymbol{x}_1$,

$$p(\boldsymbol{x}_2) \propto \exp\left\{-\frac{1}{2}\boldsymbol{x}_2^\mathsf{T}\boldsymbol{\Lambda}_{22}\boldsymbol{x}_2 + \boldsymbol{x}_2^\mathsf{T}\boldsymbol{\eta}_2\right\} \int \exp\left\{-\frac{1}{2}\boldsymbol{x}_1^\mathsf{T}\boldsymbol{\Lambda}_{11}\boldsymbol{x}_1 + \boldsymbol{x}_1^\mathsf{T}(\boldsymbol{\eta}_1 - \boldsymbol{\Lambda}_{12}\boldsymbol{x}_2)\right\} d\boldsymbol{x}_1, \tag{2.112}$$

we can recognize the integrand as an exponential quadratic form. Therefore the integral is equal to the normalizing constant of a Gaussian with precision, $\boldsymbol{\Lambda}_{11}$, and precision weighted mean, $\boldsymbol{\eta}_1 - \boldsymbol{\Lambda}_{12}\boldsymbol{x}_2$, which is given by the reciprocal of Equation (2.83). Substituting this in to our equation we have,

$$p(\boldsymbol{x}_2) \propto \exp\left\{-\frac{1}{2}\boldsymbol{x}_2^\mathsf{T}\boldsymbol{\Lambda}_{22}\boldsymbol{x}_2 + \boldsymbol{x}_2^\mathsf{T}\boldsymbol{\eta}_2\right\} \exp\left\{\frac{1}{2}(\boldsymbol{\eta}_1 - \boldsymbol{\Lambda}_{12}\boldsymbol{x}_2)^\mathsf{T}\boldsymbol{\Lambda}_{11}^{-1}(\boldsymbol{\eta}_1 - \boldsymbol{\Lambda}_{12}\boldsymbol{x}_2)\right\} \tag{2.113}$$

$$\propto \exp\left\{-\frac{1}{2}\boldsymbol{x}_2^\mathsf{T}\boldsymbol{\Lambda}_{22}\boldsymbol{x}_2 + \boldsymbol{x}_2^\mathsf{T}\boldsymbol{\eta}_2 + \frac{1}{2}\boldsymbol{x}_2^\mathsf{T}\boldsymbol{\Lambda}_{21}\boldsymbol{\Lambda}_{11}^{-1}\boldsymbol{\Lambda}_{12}\boldsymbol{x}_2 - \boldsymbol{x}_2^\mathsf{T}\boldsymbol{\Lambda}_{21}\boldsymbol{\Lambda}_{11}^{-1}\boldsymbol{\eta}_1\right\} \tag{2.114}$$

$$= \exp\left\{-\frac{1}{2}\boldsymbol{x}_2^\mathsf{T}(\boldsymbol{\Lambda}_{22} - \boldsymbol{\Lambda}_{21}\boldsymbol{\Lambda}_{11}^{-1}\boldsymbol{\Lambda}_{12})\boldsymbol{x}_2 + \boldsymbol{x}_2^\mathsf{T}(\boldsymbol{\eta}_2 - \boldsymbol{\Lambda}_{21}\boldsymbol{\Lambda}_{11}^{-1}\boldsymbol{\eta}_1)\right\}, \tag{2.115}$$

which we now recognise as an exponential quadratic form in $\boldsymbol{x}_2$. Extract the quadratic terms to get the marginal precision,

$$\boldsymbol{\Lambda}_{22}^m = \boldsymbol{\Lambda}_{22} - \boldsymbol{\Lambda}_{21}\boldsymbol{\Lambda}_{11}^{-1}\boldsymbol{\Lambda}_{12}, \tag{2.116}$$

and the linear terms to get the marginal precision-weighted mean,

$$\boldsymbol{\eta}_2^m = \boldsymbol{\eta}_2 - \boldsymbol{\Lambda}_{21}\boldsymbol{\Lambda}_{11}^{-1}\boldsymbol{\eta}_1. \tag{2.117}$$

2.3.2   Linear Gaussian systems

Consider two random vectors $\boldsymbol{y} \in \mathbb{R}^D$ and $\boldsymbol{z} \in \mathbb{R}^L$, which are jointly Gaussian with the following joint distribution:

$$p(\boldsymbol{z}) = \mathcal{N}(\boldsymbol{z}| \breve{\boldsymbol{\mu}}, \breve{\boldsymbol{\Sigma}}) \tag{2.118}$$

$$p(\boldsymbol{y}|\boldsymbol{z}) = \mathcal{N}(\boldsymbol{y}|\mathbf{W}\boldsymbol{z} + \boldsymbol{b}, \boldsymbol{\Omega}) \tag{2.119}$$

where $\mathbf{W}$ is a matrix of size $D \times L$. This is an example of a **linear Gaussian system**.

2.3.2.1   Joint distribution

The corresponding joint distribution, $p(\boldsymbol{z}, \boldsymbol{y}) = p(\boldsymbol{z})p(\boldsymbol{y}|\boldsymbol{z})$, is itself a $D + L$ dimensional Gaussian, with mean and covariance given by the following (this result can be obtained by moment matching):

$$p(\boldsymbol{z}, \boldsymbol{y}) = \mathcal{N}(\boldsymbol{z}, \boldsymbol{y}|\tilde{\boldsymbol{\mu}}, \tilde{\boldsymbol{\Sigma}}) \tag{2.120a}$$

$$\tilde{\boldsymbol{\mu}} \triangleq \begin{pmatrix} \breve{\boldsymbol{\mu}} \\ \boldsymbol{m} \end{pmatrix} \triangleq \begin{pmatrix} \breve{\boldsymbol{\mu}} \\ \mathbf{W}\breve{\boldsymbol{\mu}} + \boldsymbol{b} \end{pmatrix} \tag{2.120b}$$

$$\tilde{\boldsymbol{\Sigma}} \triangleq \begin{pmatrix} \breve{\boldsymbol{\Sigma}} & \mathbf{C} \\ \mathbf{C} & \mathbf{S} \end{pmatrix} \triangleq \begin{pmatrix} \breve{\boldsymbol{\Sigma}} & \breve{\boldsymbol{\Sigma}}\mathbf{W}^\mathsf{T} \\ \mathbf{W}\breve{\boldsymbol{\Sigma}} & \mathbf{W}\breve{\boldsymbol{\Sigma}}\mathbf{W}^\mathsf{T} + \boldsymbol{\Omega} \end{pmatrix} \tag{2.120c}$$

See Algorithm 8.1 on page 362 for some pseudocode to compute this joint distribution.

2.3.2.2 Posterior distribution (Bayes' rule for Gaussians)

Now we consider computing the posterior $p(\boldsymbol{z}|\boldsymbol{y})$ from a linear Gaussian system. Using Equation (2.78) for conditioning a joint Gaussian, we find that the posterior is given by

$$p(\boldsymbol{z}|\boldsymbol{y}) = \mathcal{N}(\boldsymbol{z}|\,\hat{\boldsymbol{\mu}}, \hat{\boldsymbol{\Sigma}}) \tag{2.121a}$$

$$\hat{\boldsymbol{\mu}} = \breve{\boldsymbol{\mu}} + \breve{\boldsymbol{\Sigma}}\,\mathbf{W}^{\mathsf{T}}(\boldsymbol{\Omega} + \mathbf{W}\,\breve{\boldsymbol{\Sigma}}\,\mathbf{W}^{\mathsf{T}})^{-1}(\boldsymbol{y} - (\mathbf{W}\,\breve{\boldsymbol{\mu}} + \boldsymbol{b})) \tag{2.121b}$$

$$\hat{\boldsymbol{\Sigma}} = \breve{\boldsymbol{\Sigma}} - \breve{\boldsymbol{\Sigma}}\,\mathbf{W}^{\mathsf{T}}(\boldsymbol{\Omega} + \mathbf{W}\,\breve{\boldsymbol{\Sigma}}\,\mathbf{W}^{\mathsf{T}})^{-1}\mathbf{W}\,\breve{\boldsymbol{\Sigma}} \tag{2.121c}$$

This is known as **Bayes' rule for Gaussians**. We see that if the prior $p(\boldsymbol{z})$ is Gaussian, and the likelihood $p(\boldsymbol{y}|\boldsymbol{z})$ is Gaussian, then the posterior $p(\boldsymbol{z}|\boldsymbol{y})$ is also Gaussian. We therefore say that the Gaussian prior is a **conjugate prior** for the Gaussian likelihood, since the posterior distribution has the same type as the prior. (In other words, Gaussians are closed under Bayesian updating.)

We can simplify these equations by defining $\mathbf{S} = \mathbf{W}\,\breve{\boldsymbol{\Sigma}}\,\mathbf{W}^{\mathsf{T}} + \boldsymbol{\Omega}$, $\mathbf{C} = \breve{\boldsymbol{\Sigma}}\,\mathbf{W}^{\mathsf{T}}$, and $\boldsymbol{m} = \mathbf{W}\,\breve{\boldsymbol{\mu}} + \boldsymbol{b}$, as in Equation (2.120). We also define the **Kalman gain matrix**:[8]

$$\mathbf{K} = \mathbf{C}\mathbf{S}^{-1} \tag{2.122}$$

From this, we get the posterior

$$\hat{\boldsymbol{\mu}} = \breve{\boldsymbol{\mu}} + \mathbf{K}(\boldsymbol{y} - \boldsymbol{m}) \tag{2.123}$$

$$\hat{\boldsymbol{\Sigma}} = \breve{\boldsymbol{\Sigma}} - \mathbf{K}\mathbf{C}^{\mathsf{T}} \tag{2.124}$$

Note that

$$\mathbf{K}\mathbf{S}\mathbf{K}^{\mathsf{T}} = \mathbf{C}\mathbf{S}^{-1}\mathbf{S}\mathbf{S}^{-\mathsf{T}}\mathbf{C}^{\mathsf{T}} = \mathbf{C}\mathbf{S}^{-1}\mathbf{C}^{\mathsf{T}} = \mathbf{K}\mathbf{C}^{\mathsf{T}} \tag{2.125}$$

and hence we can also write the posterior covariance as

$$\hat{\boldsymbol{\Sigma}} = \breve{\boldsymbol{\Sigma}} - \mathbf{K}\mathbf{S}\mathbf{K}^{\mathsf{T}} \tag{2.126}$$

Using the matrix inversion lemma from Equation (2.93), we can also rewrite the posterior in the following form [Bis06, p93], which takes $O(L^3)$ time instead of $O(D^3)$ time:

$$\hat{\boldsymbol{\Sigma}} = (\breve{\boldsymbol{\Sigma}}^{-1} + \mathbf{W}^{\mathsf{T}}\boldsymbol{\Omega}^{-1}\mathbf{W})^{-1} \tag{2.127}$$

$$\hat{\boldsymbol{\mu}} = \hat{\boldsymbol{\Sigma}}\,[\mathbf{W}^{\mathsf{T}}\boldsymbol{\Omega}^{-1}\,(\boldsymbol{y} - \boldsymbol{b}) + \breve{\boldsymbol{\Sigma}}^{-1}\breve{\boldsymbol{\mu}}] \tag{2.128}$$

Finally, note that the corresponding normalization constant for the posterior is just the marginal on $\boldsymbol{y}$ evaluated at the observed value:

$$p(\boldsymbol{y}) = \int \mathcal{N}(\boldsymbol{z}|\,\breve{\boldsymbol{\mu}}, \breve{\boldsymbol{\Sigma}})\mathcal{N}(\boldsymbol{y}|\mathbf{W}\boldsymbol{z} + \boldsymbol{b}, \boldsymbol{\Omega})d\boldsymbol{z}$$

$$= \mathcal{N}(\boldsymbol{y}|\mathbf{W}\,\breve{\boldsymbol{\mu}} + \boldsymbol{b}, \boldsymbol{\Omega} + \mathbf{W}\,\breve{\boldsymbol{\Sigma}}\,\mathbf{W}^{\mathsf{T}}) = \mathcal{N}(\boldsymbol{y}|\boldsymbol{m}, \mathbf{S}) \tag{2.129}$$

From this, we can easily compute the log marginal likelihood. We summarize all these equations in Algorithm 8.1.

---

8. The name comes from the Kalman filter algorithm, which we discuss in Section 8.2.2.

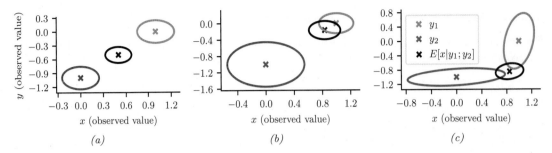

Figure 2.10: We observe $\boldsymbol{x} = (0, -1)$ (red cross) and $\boldsymbol{y} = (1, 0)$ (green cross) and estimate $\mathbb{E}\left[\boldsymbol{z}|\boldsymbol{x}, \boldsymbol{y}, \boldsymbol{\theta}\right]$ (black cross). (a) Equally reliable sensors, so the posterior mean estimate is in between the two circles. (b) Sensor 2 is more reliable, so the estimate shifts more towards the green circle. (c) Sensor 1 is more reliable in the vertical direction, Sensor 2 is more reliable in the horizontal direction. The estimate is an appropriate combination of the two measurements. Generated by sensor_fusion_2d.ipynb.

2.3.2.3   Example: Sensor fusion with known measurement noise

Suppose we have an unknown quantity of interest, $\boldsymbol{z} \sim \mathcal{N}(\boldsymbol{\mu}_z, \boldsymbol{\Sigma}_z)$, from which we get two noisy measurements, $\boldsymbol{x} \sim \mathcal{N}(\boldsymbol{z}, \boldsymbol{\Sigma}_x)$ and $\boldsymbol{y} \sim \mathcal{N}(\boldsymbol{z}, \boldsymbol{\Sigma}_y)$. Pictorially, we can represent this example as $\boldsymbol{x} \leftarrow \boldsymbol{z} \rightarrow \boldsymbol{y}$. This is an example of a linear Gaussian system. Our goal is to combine the evidence together, to compute $p(\boldsymbol{z}|\boldsymbol{x}, \boldsymbol{y}; \boldsymbol{\theta})$. This is known as **sensor fusion**. (In this section, we assume $\boldsymbol{\theta} = (\boldsymbol{\Sigma}_x, \boldsymbol{\Sigma}_y)$ is known. See Supplementary Section 2.1.2 for the general case.)

We can combine $\boldsymbol{x}$ and $\boldsymbol{y}$ into a single vector $\boldsymbol{v}$, so the model can be represented as $\boldsymbol{z} \rightarrow \boldsymbol{v}$, where $p(\boldsymbol{v}|\boldsymbol{z}) = \mathcal{N}(\boldsymbol{v}|\mathbf{W}\boldsymbol{z}, \boldsymbol{\Sigma}_v)$, where $\mathbf{W} = [\mathbf{I}; \mathbf{I}]$ and $\boldsymbol{\Sigma}_v = [\boldsymbol{\Sigma}_x, \mathbf{0}; \mathbf{0}, \boldsymbol{\Sigma}_y]$ are block-structured matrices. We can then apply Bayes' rule for Gaussians (Section 2.3.2.2) to compute $p(\boldsymbol{z}|\boldsymbol{v})$.

Figure 2.10(a) gives a 2d example, where we set $\boldsymbol{\Sigma}_x = \boldsymbol{\Sigma}_y = 0.01\mathbf{I}_2$, so both sensors are equally reliable. In this case, the posterior mean is halfway between the two observations, $\boldsymbol{x}$ and $\boldsymbol{y}$. In Figure 2.10(b), we set $\boldsymbol{\Sigma}_x = 0.05\mathbf{I}_2$ and $\boldsymbol{\Sigma}_y = 0.01\mathbf{I}_2$, so sensor 2 is more reliable than sensor 1. In this case, the posterior mean is closer to $\boldsymbol{y}$. In Figure 2.10(c), we set

$$\boldsymbol{\Sigma}_x = 0.01 \begin{pmatrix} 10 & 1 \\ 1 & 1 \end{pmatrix}, \quad \boldsymbol{\Sigma}_y = 0.01 \begin{pmatrix} 1 & 1 \\ 1 & 10 \end{pmatrix} \tag{2.130}$$

so sensor 1 is more reliable in the second component (vertical direction), and sensor 2 is more reliable in the first component (horizontal direction). In this case, the posterior mean is vertically closer to $\boldsymbol{x}$ and horizontally closer to $\boldsymbol{y}$.

2.3.3   A general calculus for linear Gaussian systems

In this section, we discuss a general method for performing inference in linear Gaussian systems. The key is to define joint distributions over the relevant variables in terms of a **potential function**, represented in information form. We can then easily derive rules for marginalizing potentials, multiplying and dividing potentials, and conditioning them on observations. Once we have defined these operations, we can use them inside of the belief propagation algorithm (Section 9.3) or junction tree algorithm (Supplementary Section 9.2) to compute quantities of interest. We give the details on how to perform these operations below; our presentation is based on [Lau92; Mur02].

2.3.3.1 Moment and canonical parameterization

We can represent a Gaussian distribution in moment form or in canonical (information) form. In moment form we have

$$\phi(\boldsymbol{x}; p, \boldsymbol{\mu}, \boldsymbol{\Sigma}) = p \times \exp\left(-\frac{1}{2}(\boldsymbol{x} - \boldsymbol{\mu})^{\mathsf{T}} \boldsymbol{\Sigma}^{-1}(\boldsymbol{x} - \boldsymbol{\mu})\right) \tag{2.131}$$

where $p = (2\pi)^{-n/2}|\boldsymbol{\Sigma}|^{-\frac{1}{2}}$ is the normalizing constant that ensures $\int_{\boldsymbol{x}} \phi(\boldsymbol{x}; p, \boldsymbol{\mu}, \boldsymbol{\Sigma}) = 1$. ($n$ is the dimensionality of $\boldsymbol{x}$.) Expanding out the quadratic form and collecting terms we get the canonical form:

$$\phi(\boldsymbol{x}; g, \boldsymbol{h}, \mathbf{K}) = \exp\left(g + \boldsymbol{x}^{\mathsf{T}}\boldsymbol{h} - \frac{1}{2}\boldsymbol{x}^{\mathsf{T}}\mathbf{K}\boldsymbol{x}\right) = \exp\left(g + \sum_i h_i x_i - \frac{1}{2}\sum_i\sum_k K_{ij}x_i x_j\right) \tag{2.132}$$

where

$$\mathbf{K} = \boldsymbol{\Sigma}^{-1} \tag{2.133}$$

$$\boldsymbol{h} = \boldsymbol{\Sigma}^{-1}\boldsymbol{\mu} \tag{2.134}$$

$$g = \log p - \frac{1}{2}\boldsymbol{\mu}^{\mathsf{T}}\mathbf{K}\boldsymbol{\mu} \tag{2.135}$$

$\mathbf{K}$ is often called the precision matrix.

Note that potentials need not be probability distributions, and need not be normalizable (integrate to 1). We keep track of the constant terms (p or g) so we can compute the likelihood of the evidence.

2.3.3.2 Multiplication and division

We can define multiplication and division in the Gaussian case by using canonical forms, as follows. To multiply $\phi_1(x_1, \ldots, x_k; g_1, \boldsymbol{h}_1, \mathbf{K}_1)$ by $\phi_2(x_{k+1}, \ldots, x_n; g_2, \boldsymbol{h}_2, \mathbf{K}_2)$, we extend them both to the same domain $x_1, \ldots, x_n$ by adding zeros to the appropriate dimensions, and then computing

$$(g_1, \boldsymbol{h}_1, \mathbf{K}_1) * (g_2, \boldsymbol{h}_2, \mathbf{K}_2) = (g_1 + g_2, \boldsymbol{h}_1 + \boldsymbol{h}_2, \mathbf{K}_1 + \mathbf{K}_2) \tag{2.136}$$

Division is defined as follows:

$$(g_1, \boldsymbol{h}_1, \mathbf{K}_1) / (g_2, \boldsymbol{h}_2, \mathbf{K}_2) = (g_1 - g_2, \boldsymbol{h}_1 - \boldsymbol{h}_2, \mathbf{K}_1 - \mathbf{K}_2) \tag{2.137}$$

2.3.3.3 Marginalization

Let ϕ_W be a potential over a set W of variables. We can compute the potential over a subset $V \subset W$ of variables by marginalizing, denoted $\phi_V = \sum_{W \setminus V} \phi_W$. Let

$$\boldsymbol{x} = \begin{pmatrix} \boldsymbol{x}_1 \\ \boldsymbol{x}_2 \end{pmatrix}, \qquad \boldsymbol{h} = \begin{pmatrix} \boldsymbol{h}_1 \\ \boldsymbol{h}_2 \end{pmatrix}, \qquad \mathbf{K} = \begin{pmatrix} \mathbf{K}_{11} & \mathbf{K}_{12} \\ \mathbf{K}_{21} & \mathbf{K}_{22} \end{pmatrix}, \tag{2.138}$$

with $\boldsymbol{x}_1$ having dimension n_1 and $\boldsymbol{x}_2$ having dimension n_2. It can be shown that

$$\int_{\boldsymbol{x}_1} \phi(\boldsymbol{x}_1, \boldsymbol{x}_2; g, \boldsymbol{h}, \mathbf{K}) = \phi(\boldsymbol{x}_2; \hat{g}, \hat{\boldsymbol{h}}, \hat{\mathbf{K}}) \tag{2.139}$$

where

$$\hat{g} = g + \frac{1}{2} \left(n_1 \log(2\pi) - \log |\mathbf{K}_{11}| + \mathbf{h}_1^\mathsf{T} \mathbf{K}_{11}^{-1} \mathbf{h}_1 \right) \tag{2.140}$$

$$\hat{h} = \mathbf{h}_2 - \mathbf{K}_{21} \mathbf{K}_{11}^{-1} \mathbf{h}_1 \tag{2.141}$$

$$\hat{K} = \mathbf{K}_{22} - \mathbf{K}_{21} \mathbf{K}_{11}^{-1} \mathbf{K}_{12} \tag{2.142}$$

2.3.3.4   Conditioning on evidence

Consider a potential defined on $(\boldsymbol{x}, \boldsymbol{y})$. Suppose we observe the value $\boldsymbol{y}$. The new potential is given by the following reduced dimensionality object:

$$\phi^*(\boldsymbol{x}) = \exp \left[g + \begin{pmatrix} \boldsymbol{x}^T & \boldsymbol{y}^T \end{pmatrix} \begin{pmatrix} \boldsymbol{h}_X \\ \boldsymbol{h}_Y \end{pmatrix} - \frac{1}{2} \begin{pmatrix} \boldsymbol{x}^T & \boldsymbol{y}^T \end{pmatrix} \begin{pmatrix} \mathbf{K}_{XX} & \mathbf{K}_{XY} \\ \mathbf{K}_{YX} & \mathbf{K}_{YY} \end{pmatrix} \begin{pmatrix} \boldsymbol{x} \\ \boldsymbol{y} \end{pmatrix} \right] \tag{2.143}$$

$$= \exp \left[\left(g + \boldsymbol{h}_Y^T \boldsymbol{y} - \frac{1}{2} \boldsymbol{y}^T \mathbf{K}_{YY} \boldsymbol{y} \right) + \boldsymbol{x}^T (\boldsymbol{h}_X - \mathbf{K}_{XY} \boldsymbol{y}) - \frac{1}{2} \boldsymbol{x}^T \mathbf{K}_{XX} \boldsymbol{x} \right] \tag{2.144}$$

This generalizes the corresponding equation in [Lau92] to the vector-valued case.

2.3.3.5   Converting a linear-Gaussian CPD to a canonical potential

Finally we discuss how to create the initial potentials, assuming we start with a directed Gaussian graphical model. In particular, consider a node with a linear-Gaussian conditional probability distribution (CPD):

$$p(\boldsymbol{x}|\boldsymbol{u}) = c \exp \left[-\frac{1}{2} \left((\boldsymbol{x} - \boldsymbol{\mu} - \mathbf{B}^T \boldsymbol{u})^T \boldsymbol{\Sigma}^{-1} (\boldsymbol{x} - \boldsymbol{\mu} - \mathbf{B}^T \boldsymbol{u}) \right) \right] \tag{2.145}$$

$$= \exp \left[-\frac{1}{2} \begin{pmatrix} \boldsymbol{x} & \boldsymbol{u} \end{pmatrix} \begin{pmatrix} \boldsymbol{\Sigma}^{-1} & -\boldsymbol{\Sigma}^{-1} \mathbf{B}^T \\ -\mathbf{B} \boldsymbol{\Sigma}^{-1} & \mathbf{B} \boldsymbol{\Sigma}^{-1} \mathbf{B}^T \end{pmatrix} \begin{pmatrix} \boldsymbol{x} \\ \boldsymbol{u} \end{pmatrix} \right. \tag{2.146}$$

$$\left. + \begin{pmatrix} \boldsymbol{x} & \boldsymbol{u} \end{pmatrix} \begin{pmatrix} \boldsymbol{\Sigma}^{-1} \boldsymbol{\mu} \\ -\mathbf{B} \boldsymbol{\Sigma}^{-1} \boldsymbol{\mu} \end{pmatrix} - \frac{1}{2} \boldsymbol{\mu}^T \boldsymbol{\Sigma}^{-1} \boldsymbol{\mu} + \log c \right] \tag{2.147}$$

where $c = (2\pi)^{-n/2} |\boldsymbol{\Sigma}|^{-\frac{1}{2}}$. Hence we set the canonical parameters to

$$g = -\frac{1}{2} \boldsymbol{\mu}^T \boldsymbol{\Sigma}^{-1} \boldsymbol{\mu} - \frac{n}{2} \log(2\pi) - \frac{1}{2} \log |\boldsymbol{\Sigma}| \tag{2.148}$$

$$h = \begin{pmatrix} \boldsymbol{\Sigma}^{-1} \boldsymbol{\mu} \\ -\mathbf{B} \boldsymbol{\Sigma}^{-1} \boldsymbol{\mu} \end{pmatrix} \tag{2.149}$$

$$\mathbf{K} = \begin{pmatrix} \boldsymbol{\Sigma}^{-1} & -\boldsymbol{\Sigma}^{-1} \mathbf{B}^T \\ -\mathbf{B} \boldsymbol{\Sigma}^{-1} & \mathbf{B} \boldsymbol{\Sigma}^{-1} \mathbf{B}^T \end{pmatrix} = \begin{pmatrix} \mathbf{I} \\ -\mathbf{B} \end{pmatrix} \boldsymbol{\Sigma}^{-1} \begin{pmatrix} \mathbf{I} & -\mathbf{B} \end{pmatrix} \tag{2.150}$$

In the special case that x is a scalar, the corresponding result can be found in [Lau92]. In particular we have $\Sigma^{-1} = 1/\sigma^2$, $B = b$ and $n = 1$, so the above becomes

$$g = \frac{-\mu^2}{2\sigma^2} - \frac{1}{2}\log(2\pi\sigma^2) \tag{2.151}$$

$$\boldsymbol{h} = \frac{\mu}{\sigma^2}\begin{pmatrix} 1 \\ -\boldsymbol{b} \end{pmatrix} \tag{2.152}$$

$$\mathbf{K} = \frac{1}{\sigma}\begin{pmatrix} 1 & -\boldsymbol{b}^T \\ -\boldsymbol{b} & \boldsymbol{b}\boldsymbol{b}^T \end{pmatrix} . \tag{2.153}$$

2.3.3.6 Example: Product of Gaussians

As an application of the above results, we can derive the (unnormalized) product of two Gaussians, as follows (see also [Kaa12, Sec 8.1.8]):

$$\mathcal{N}(\boldsymbol{x}|\boldsymbol{\mu}_1, \boldsymbol{\Sigma}_1) \times \mathcal{N}(\boldsymbol{x}|\boldsymbol{\mu}_2, \boldsymbol{\Sigma}_2) \propto \mathcal{N}(\boldsymbol{x}|\boldsymbol{\mu}_3, \boldsymbol{\Sigma}_3) \tag{2.154}$$

where

$$\boldsymbol{\Sigma}_3 = (\boldsymbol{\Sigma}_1^{-1} + \boldsymbol{\Sigma}_2^{-1})^{-1} \tag{2.155}$$

$$\boldsymbol{\mu}_3 = \boldsymbol{\Sigma}_3(\boldsymbol{\Sigma}_1^{-1}\boldsymbol{\mu}_1 + \boldsymbol{\Sigma}_2^{-1}\boldsymbol{\mu}_2) \tag{2.156}$$

We see that the posterior precision is a sum of the individual precisions, and the posterior mean is a precision-weighted combination of the individual means. We can also rewrite the result in the following way, which only requires one matrix inversion:

$$\boldsymbol{\Sigma}_3 = \boldsymbol{\Sigma}_1(\boldsymbol{\Sigma}_1 + \boldsymbol{\Sigma}_2)^{-1}\boldsymbol{\Sigma}_2 \tag{2.157}$$

$$\boldsymbol{\mu}_3 = \boldsymbol{\Sigma}_2(\boldsymbol{\Sigma}_1 + \boldsymbol{\Sigma}_2)^{-1}\boldsymbol{\mu}_1 + \boldsymbol{\Sigma}_1(\boldsymbol{\Sigma}_1 + \boldsymbol{\Sigma}_2)^{-1}\boldsymbol{\mu}_2 \tag{2.158}$$

In the scalar case, this becomes

$$\mathcal{N}(x|\mu_1, \sigma_1^2)\mathcal{N}(x|\mu_2, \sigma_2^2) \propto \mathcal{N}\left(x \Big| \frac{\mu_1\sigma_2^2 + \mu_2\sigma_1^2}{\sigma_1^2 + \sigma_2^2}, \frac{\sigma_1^2\sigma_2^2}{\sigma_1^2 + \sigma_2^2}\right) \tag{2.159}$$

2.4 The exponential family

In this section, we define the **exponential family**, which includes many common probability distributions. The exponential family plays a crucial role in statistics and machine learning, for various reasons, including the following:

- The exponential family is the unique family of distributions that has maximum entropy (and hence makes the least set of assumptions) subject to some user-chosen constraints, as discussed in Section 2.4.7.

- The exponential family is at the core of GLMs, as discussed in Section 15.1.

- The exponential family is at the core of variational inference, as discussed in Chapter 10.

- Under certain regularity conditions, the exponential family is the only family of distributions with finite-sized sufficient statistics, as discussed in Section 2.4.5.

- All members of the exponential family have a **conjugate prior** [DY79], which simplifies Bayesian inference of the parameters, as discussed in Section 3.4.

2.4.1 Definition

Consider a family of probability distributions parameterized by $\boldsymbol{\eta} \in \mathbb{R}^K$ with fixed support over $\mathcal{X}^D \subseteq \mathbb{R}^D$. We say that the distribution $p(\boldsymbol{x}|\boldsymbol{\eta})$ is in the **exponential family** if its density can be written in the following way:

$$p(\boldsymbol{x}|\boldsymbol{\eta}) \triangleq \frac{1}{Z(\boldsymbol{\eta})} h(\boldsymbol{x}) \exp[\boldsymbol{\eta}^\mathsf{T} \mathcal{T}(\boldsymbol{x})] = h(\boldsymbol{x}) \exp[\boldsymbol{\eta}^\mathsf{T} \mathcal{T}(\boldsymbol{x}) - A(\boldsymbol{\eta})] \tag{2.160}$$

where $h(\boldsymbol{x})$ is a scaling constant (also known as the **base measure**, often 1), $\mathcal{T}(\boldsymbol{x}) \in \mathbb{R}^K$ are the **sufficient statistics**, $\boldsymbol{\eta}$ are the **natural parameters** or **canonical parameters**, $Z(\boldsymbol{\eta})$ is a normalization constant known as the **partition function**, and $A(\boldsymbol{\eta}) = \log Z(\boldsymbol{\eta})$ is the **log partition function**. In Section 2.4.3, we show that A is a convex function over the convex set $\Omega \triangleq \{\boldsymbol{\eta} \in \mathbb{R}^K : A(\boldsymbol{\eta}) < \infty\}$.

It is convenient if the natural parameters are independent of each other. Formally, we say that an exponential family is **minimal** if there is no $\boldsymbol{\eta} \in \mathbb{R}^K \setminus \{0\}$ such that $\boldsymbol{\eta}^\mathsf{T} \mathcal{T}(\boldsymbol{x}) = 0$. This last condition can be violated in the case of multinomial distributions, because of the sum to one constraint on the parameters; however, it is easy to reparameterize the distribution using $K - 1$ independent parameters, as we show below.

Equation (2.160) can be generalized by defining $\boldsymbol{\eta} = f(\boldsymbol{\phi})$, where $\boldsymbol{\phi}$ is some other, possibly smaller, set of parameters. In this case, the distribution has the form

$$p(\boldsymbol{x}|\boldsymbol{\phi}) = h(\boldsymbol{x}) \exp[f(\boldsymbol{\phi})^\mathsf{T} \mathcal{T}(\boldsymbol{x}) - A(f(\boldsymbol{\phi}))] \tag{2.161}$$

If the mapping from $\boldsymbol{\phi}$ to $\boldsymbol{\eta}$ is nonlinear, we call this a **curved exponential family**. If $\boldsymbol{\eta} = f(\boldsymbol{\phi}) = \boldsymbol{\phi}$, the model is said to be in **canonical form**. If, in addition, $\mathcal{T}(\boldsymbol{x}) = \boldsymbol{x}$, we say this is a **natural exponential family** or **NEF**. In this case, it can be written as

$$p(\boldsymbol{x}|\boldsymbol{\eta}) = h(\boldsymbol{x}) \exp[\boldsymbol{\eta}^\mathsf{T} \boldsymbol{x} - A(\boldsymbol{\eta})] \tag{2.162}$$

We define the **moment parameters** as the mean of the sufficient statistics vector:

$$\boldsymbol{m} = \mathbb{E}[\mathcal{T}(\boldsymbol{x})] \tag{2.163}$$

We will see some examples below.

2.4.2 Examples

In this section, we consider some common examples of distributions in the exponential family. Each corresponds to a different way of defining $h(\boldsymbol{x})$ and $\mathcal{T}(\boldsymbol{x})$ (since Z and hence A are derived from knowing h and $\mathcal{T}$).

2.4.2.1 Bernoulli distribution

The Bernoulli distribution can be written in exponential family form as follows:

$$\text{Ber}(x|\mu) = \mu^x(1-\mu)^{1-x} \tag{2.164}$$
$$= \exp[x\log(\mu) + (1-x)\log(1-\mu)] \tag{2.165}$$
$$= \exp[\mathcal{T}(x)^\mathsf{T}\boldsymbol{\eta}] \tag{2.166}$$

where $\mathcal{T}(x) = [\mathbb{I}(x=1), \mathbb{I}(x=0)]$, $\boldsymbol{\eta} = [\log(\mu), \log(1-\mu)]$, and μ is the mean parameter. However, this is an **over-complete representation** since there is a linear dependendence between the features. We can see this as follows:

$$\mathbf{1}^\mathsf{T}\mathcal{T}(x) = \mathbb{I}(x=0) + \mathbb{I}(x=1) = 1 \tag{2.167}$$

If the representation is overcomplete, $\boldsymbol{\eta}$ is not uniquely identifiable. It is common to use a **minimal representation**, which means there is a unique $\boldsymbol{\eta}$ associated with the distribution. In this case, we can just define

$$\text{Ber}(x|\mu) = \exp\left[x\log\left(\frac{\mu}{1-\mu}\right) + \log(1-\mu)\right] \tag{2.168}$$

We can put this into exponential family form by defining

$$\eta = \log\left(\frac{\mu}{1-\mu}\right) \tag{2.169}$$
$$\mathcal{T}(x) = x \tag{2.170}$$
$$A(\eta) = -\log(1-\mu) = \log(1+e^\eta) \tag{2.171}$$
$$h(x) = 1 \tag{2.172}$$

We can recover the mean parameter μ from the canonical parameter η using

$$\mu = \sigma(\eta) = \frac{1}{1+e^{-\eta}} \tag{2.173}$$

which we recognize as the logistic (sigmoid) function.

2.4.2.2 Categorical distribution

We can represent the discrete distribution with K categories as follows (where $x_k = \mathbb{I}\,(x = k)$):

$$\text{Cat}(x|\boldsymbol{\mu}) = \prod_{k=1}^{K} \mu_k^{x_k} = \exp\left[\sum_{k=1}^{K} x_k \log \mu_k\right] \tag{2.174}$$

$$= \exp\left[\sum_{k=1}^{K-1} x_k \log \mu_k + \left(1 - \sum_{k=1}^{K-1} x_k\right) \log(1 - \sum_{k=1}^{K-1} \mu_k)\right] \tag{2.175}$$

$$= \exp\left[\sum_{k=1}^{K-1} x_k \log\left(\frac{\mu_k}{1 - \sum_{j=1}^{K-1} \mu_j}\right) + \log(1 - \sum_{k=1}^{K-1} \mu_k)\right] \tag{2.176}$$

$$= \exp\left[\sum_{k=1}^{K-1} x_k \log\left(\frac{\mu_k}{\mu_K}\right) + \log \mu_K\right] \tag{2.177}$$

where $\mu_K = 1 - \sum_{k=1}^{K-1} \mu_k$. We can write this in exponential family form as follows:

$$\text{Cat}(x|\boldsymbol{\eta}) = \exp(\boldsymbol{\eta}^\mathsf{T} \mathcal{T}(\boldsymbol{x}) - A(\boldsymbol{\eta})) \tag{2.178}$$

$$\boldsymbol{\eta} = [\log \frac{\mu_1}{\mu_K}, \ldots, \log \frac{\mu_{K-1}}{\mu_K}] \tag{2.179}$$

$$A(\boldsymbol{\eta}) = -\log(\mu_K) \tag{2.180}$$

$$\mathcal{T}(x) = [\mathbb{I}\,(x = 1), \ldots, \mathbb{I}\,(x = K - 1)] \tag{2.181}$$

$$h(x) = 1 \tag{2.182}$$

We can recover the mean parameters from the canonical parameters using

$$\mu_k = \frac{e^{\eta_k}}{1 + \sum_{j=1}^{K-1} e^{\eta_j}} \tag{2.183}$$

If we define $\eta_K = 0$, we can rewrite this as follows:

$$\mu_k = \frac{e^{\eta_k}}{\sum_{j=1}^{K} e^{\eta_j}} \tag{2.184}$$

for $k = 1 : K$. Hence $\boldsymbol{\mu} = \text{softmax}(\boldsymbol{\eta})$, where softmax is the softmax or multinomial logit function in Equation (15.136). From this, we find

$$\mu_K = 1 - \frac{\sum_{k=1}^{K-1} e^{\eta_k}}{1 + \sum_{k=1}^{K-1} e^{\eta_k}} = \frac{1}{1 + \sum_{k=1}^{K-1} e^{\eta_k}} \tag{2.185}$$

and hence

$$A(\boldsymbol{\eta}) = -\log(\mu_K) = \log\left(\sum_{k=1}^{K} e^{\eta_k}\right) \tag{2.186}$$

2.4.2.3 Univariate Gaussian

The univariate Gaussian is usually written as follows:

$$\mathcal{N}(x|\mu, \sigma^2) = \frac{1}{(2\pi\sigma^2)^{\frac{1}{2}}} \exp[-\frac{1}{2\sigma^2}(x - \mu)^2] \tag{2.187}$$

$$= \frac{1}{(2\pi)^{\frac{1}{2}}} \exp[\frac{\mu}{\sigma^2}x - \frac{1}{2\sigma^2}x^2 - \frac{1}{2\sigma^2}\mu^2 - \log\sigma] \tag{2.188}$$

We can put this in exponential family form by defining

$$\boldsymbol{\eta} = \begin{pmatrix} \mu/\sigma^2 \\ -\frac{1}{2\sigma^2} \end{pmatrix} \tag{2.189}$$

$$\mathcal{T}(x) = \begin{pmatrix} x \\ x^2 \end{pmatrix} \tag{2.190}$$

$$A(\boldsymbol{\eta}) = \frac{\mu^2}{2\sigma^2} + \log\sigma = \frac{-\eta_1^2}{4\eta_2} - \frac{1}{2}\log(-2\eta_2) \tag{2.191}$$

$$h(x) = \frac{1}{\sqrt{2\pi}} \tag{2.192}$$

The moment parameters are

$$\boldsymbol{m} = [\mu, \mu^2 + \sigma^2] \tag{2.193}$$

2.4.2.4 Univariate Gaussian with fixed variance

If we fix $\sigma^2 = 1$, we can write the Gaussian as a natural exponential family, by defining

$$\eta = \mu \tag{2.194}$$
$$\mathcal{T}(x) = x \tag{2.195}$$
$$A(\mu) = \frac{\mu^2}{2\sigma^2} + \log\sigma = \frac{\mu^2}{2} \tag{2.196}$$
$$h(x) = \frac{1}{\sqrt{2\pi}} \exp[-\frac{x^2}{2}] = \mathcal{N}(x|0, 1) \tag{2.197}$$

Note that this in example, the base measure $h(x)$ is not constant.

2.4.2.5   Multivariate Gaussian

It is common to parameterize the multivariate normal (MVN) in terms of the mean vector $\boldsymbol{\mu}$ and the covariance matrix $\boldsymbol{\Sigma}$. The corresponding pdf is given by

$$\mathcal{N}(\boldsymbol{x}|\boldsymbol{\mu}, \boldsymbol{\Sigma}) = \frac{1}{(2\pi)^{D/2}\sqrt{\det(\boldsymbol{\Sigma})}} \exp\left(-\frac{1}{2}\boldsymbol{x}^\mathsf{T}\boldsymbol{\Sigma}^{-1}\boldsymbol{x} + \boldsymbol{x}^\mathsf{T}\boldsymbol{\Sigma}^{-1}\boldsymbol{\mu} - \frac{1}{2}\boldsymbol{\mu}^\mathsf{T}\boldsymbol{\Sigma}^{-1}\boldsymbol{\mu}\right) \tag{2.198}$$

$$= c\exp\left(\boldsymbol{x}^\mathsf{T}\boldsymbol{\Sigma}^{-1}\boldsymbol{\mu} - \frac{1}{2}\boldsymbol{x}^\mathsf{T}\boldsymbol{\Sigma}^{-1}\boldsymbol{x}\right) \tag{2.199}$$

$$c \triangleq \frac{\exp(-\frac{1}{2}\boldsymbol{\mu}^\mathsf{T}\boldsymbol{\Sigma}^{-1}\boldsymbol{\mu})}{(2\pi)^{D/2}\sqrt{\det(\boldsymbol{\Sigma})}} \tag{2.200}$$

However, we can also represent the Gaussian using **canonical parameters** or **natural parameters**, also called the **information form**:

$$\boldsymbol{\Lambda} = \boldsymbol{\Sigma}^{-1} \tag{2.201}$$

$$\boldsymbol{\xi} = \boldsymbol{\Sigma}^{-1}\boldsymbol{\mu} \tag{2.202}$$

$$\mathcal{N}_c(\boldsymbol{x}|\boldsymbol{\xi}, \boldsymbol{\Lambda}) \triangleq c'\exp\left(\boldsymbol{x}^\mathsf{T}\boldsymbol{\xi} - \frac{1}{2}\boldsymbol{x}^\mathsf{T}\boldsymbol{\Lambda}\boldsymbol{x}\right) \tag{2.203}$$

$$c' = \frac{\exp(-\frac{1}{2}\boldsymbol{\xi}^\mathsf{T}\boldsymbol{\Lambda}^{-1}\boldsymbol{\xi})}{(2\pi)^{D/2}\sqrt{\det(\boldsymbol{\Lambda}^{-1})}} \tag{2.204}$$

where we use the notation $\mathcal{N}_c()$ to distinguish it from the standard parameterization $\mathcal{N}()$. Here $\boldsymbol{\Lambda}$ is called the **precision matrix** and $\boldsymbol{\xi}$ is the precision-weighted mean vector.

We can convert this to exponential family notation as follows:

$$\mathcal{N}_c(\boldsymbol{x}|\boldsymbol{\xi}, \boldsymbol{\Lambda}) = \underbrace{(2\pi)^{-D/2}}_{h(\boldsymbol{x})}\underbrace{\exp\left[\frac{1}{2}\log|\boldsymbol{\Lambda}| - \frac{1}{2}\boldsymbol{\xi}^\mathsf{T}\boldsymbol{\Lambda}^{-1}\boldsymbol{\xi}\right]}_{g(\boldsymbol{\eta})}\exp\left[-\frac{1}{2}\boldsymbol{x}^\mathsf{T}\boldsymbol{\Lambda}\boldsymbol{x} + \boldsymbol{x}^\mathsf{T}\boldsymbol{\xi}\right] \tag{2.205}$$

$$= h(\boldsymbol{x})g(\boldsymbol{\eta})\exp\left[-\frac{1}{2}\boldsymbol{x}^\mathsf{T}\boldsymbol{\Lambda}\boldsymbol{x} + \boldsymbol{x}^\mathsf{T}\boldsymbol{\xi}\right] \tag{2.206}$$

$$= h(\boldsymbol{x})g(\boldsymbol{\eta})\exp\left[-\frac{1}{2}(\sum_{ij} x_i x_j \Lambda_{ij}) + \boldsymbol{x}^\mathsf{T}\boldsymbol{\xi}\right] \tag{2.207}$$

$$= h(\boldsymbol{x})g(\boldsymbol{\eta})\exp\left[-\frac{1}{2}\mathrm{vec}(\boldsymbol{\Lambda})^\mathsf{T}\mathrm{vec}(\boldsymbol{x}\boldsymbol{x}^\mathsf{T}) + \boldsymbol{x}^\mathsf{T}\boldsymbol{\xi}\right] \tag{2.208}$$

$$= h(\boldsymbol{x})\exp\left[\boldsymbol{\eta}^\mathsf{T}\mathcal{T}(\boldsymbol{x}) - A(\boldsymbol{\eta})\right] \tag{2.209}$$

where

$$h(\boldsymbol{x}) = (2\pi)^{-D/2} \tag{2.210}$$

$$\boldsymbol{\eta} = [\boldsymbol{\xi}; -\frac{1}{2}\text{vec}(\boldsymbol{\Lambda})] = [\boldsymbol{\Sigma}^{-1}\boldsymbol{\mu}; -\frac{1}{2}\text{vec}(\boldsymbol{\Sigma}^{-1})] \tag{2.211}$$

$$\mathcal{T}(\boldsymbol{x}) = [\boldsymbol{x}; \text{vec}(\boldsymbol{x}\boldsymbol{x}^{\mathsf{T}})] \tag{2.212}$$

$$A(\boldsymbol{\eta}) = -\log g(\boldsymbol{\eta}) = -\frac{1}{2}\log|\boldsymbol{\Lambda}| + \frac{1}{2}\boldsymbol{\xi}^{\mathsf{T}}\boldsymbol{\Lambda}^{-1}\boldsymbol{\xi} \tag{2.213}$$

From this, we see that the mean (moment) parameters are given by

$$\boldsymbol{m} = \mathbb{E}\left[\mathcal{T}(\boldsymbol{x})\right] = [\boldsymbol{\mu}; \boldsymbol{\mu}\boldsymbol{\mu}^{\mathsf{T}} + \boldsymbol{\Sigma}] \tag{2.214}$$

(Note that the above is not a minimal representation, since $\boldsymbol{\Lambda}$ is a symmetric matrix. We can convert to minimal form by working with the upper or lower half of each matrix.)

2.4.2.6 Non-examples

Not all distributions of interest belong to the exponential family. For example, the Student distribution (Section 2.2.2.3) does not belong, since its pdf (Equation (2.30)) does not have the required form. (However, there is a generalization, known as the ϕ-**exponential family** [Nau04; Tsa88] which does include the Student distribution.)

As a more subtle example, consider the uniform distribution, $Y \sim \text{Unif}(\theta_1, \theta_2)$. The pdf has the form

$$p(y|\boldsymbol{\theta}) = \frac{1}{\theta_2 - \theta_1}\mathbb{I}\left(\theta_1 \le y \le \theta_2\right) \tag{2.215}$$

It is tempting to think this is in the exponential family, with $h(y) = 1$, $\mathcal{T}(y) = \boldsymbol{0}$, and $Z(\boldsymbol{\theta}) = \theta_2 - \theta_1$. However, the support of this distribution (i.e., the set of values $\mathcal{Y} = \{y : p(y) > 0\}$) depends on the parameters $\boldsymbol{\theta}$, which violates an assumption of the exponential family.

2.4.3 Log partition function is cumulant generating function

The first and second **cumulants** of a distribution are its mean $\mathbb{E}[X]$ and variance $\mathbb{V}[X]$, whereas the first and second moments are $\mathbb{E}[X]$ and $\mathbb{E}[X^2]$. We can also compute higher order cumulants (and moments). An important property of the exponential family is that derivatives of the log partition function can be used to generate all the **cumulants** of the sufficient statistics. In particular, the first and second cumulants are given by

$$\nabla_{\boldsymbol{\eta}}A(\boldsymbol{\eta}) = \mathbb{E}\left[\mathcal{T}(\boldsymbol{x})\right] \tag{2.216}$$

$$\nabla_{\boldsymbol{\eta}}^2 A(\boldsymbol{\eta}) = \text{Cov}\left[\mathcal{T}(\boldsymbol{x})\right] \tag{2.217}$$

We prove this result below.

2.4.3.1 Derivation of the mean

For simplicity, we focus on the 1d case. For the first derivative we have

$$\frac{dA}{d\eta} = \frac{d}{d\eta}\left(\log \int \exp(\eta \mathcal{T}(x))h(x)dx\right) \tag{2.218}$$

$$= \frac{\frac{d}{d\eta}\int \exp(\eta \mathcal{T}(x))h(x)dx}{\int \exp(\eta \mathcal{T}(x))h(x)dx} \tag{2.219}$$

$$= \frac{\int \mathcal{T}(x)\exp(\eta \mathcal{T}(x))h(x)dx}{\exp(A(\eta))} \tag{2.220}$$

$$= \int \mathcal{T}(x)\exp(\eta \mathcal{T}(x) - A(\eta))h(x)dx \tag{2.221}$$

$$= \int \mathcal{T}(x)p(x)dx = \mathbb{E}\left[\mathcal{T}(x)\right] \tag{2.222}$$

For example, consider the Bernoulli distribution. We have $A(\eta) = \log(1 + e^\eta)$, so the mean is given by

$$\frac{dA}{d\eta} = \frac{e^\eta}{1 + e^\eta} = \frac{1}{1 + e^{-\eta}} = \sigma(\eta) = \mu \tag{2.223}$$

2.4.3.2 Derivation of the variance

For simplicity, we focus on the 1d case. For the second derivative we have

$$\frac{d^2 A}{d\eta^2} = \frac{d}{d\eta}\int \mathcal{T}(x)\exp(\eta \mathcal{T}(x) - A(\eta))h(x)dx \tag{2.224}$$

$$= \int \mathcal{T}(x)\exp\left(\eta \mathcal{T}(x) - A(\eta)\right)h(x)(\mathcal{T}(x) - A'(\eta))dx \tag{2.225}$$

$$= \int \mathcal{T}(x)p(x)(\mathcal{T}(x) - A'(\eta))dx \tag{2.226}$$

$$= \int \mathcal{T}^2(x)p(x)dx - A'(\eta)\int \mathcal{T}(x)p(x)dx \tag{2.227}$$

$$= \mathbb{E}\left[\mathcal{T}^2(X)\right] - \mathbb{E}\left[\mathcal{T}(x)\right]^2 = \mathbb{V}\left[\mathcal{T}(x)\right] \tag{2.228}$$

where we used the fact that $A'(\eta) = \frac{dA}{d\eta} = \mathbb{E}\left[\mathcal{T}(x)\right]$. For example, for the Bernoulli distribution we have

$$\frac{d^2 A}{d\eta^2} = \frac{d}{d\eta}(1 + e^{-\eta})^{-1} = (1 + e^{-\eta})^{-2}e^{-\eta} \tag{2.229}$$

$$= \frac{e^{-\eta}}{1 + e^{-\eta}}\frac{1}{1 + e^{-\eta}} = \frac{1}{e^\eta + 1}\frac{1}{1 + e^{-\eta}} = (1 - \mu)\mu \tag{2.230}$$

2.4.3.3 Connection with the Fisher information matrix

In Section 3.3.4, we show that, under some regularity conditions, the **Fisher information matrix** is given by

$$\mathbf{F}(\eta) \triangleq \mathbb{E}_{p(\boldsymbol{x}|\eta)} \left[\nabla \log p(\boldsymbol{x}|\eta) \nabla \log p(\boldsymbol{x}|\eta)^{\mathsf{T}} \right] = -\mathbb{E}_{p(\boldsymbol{x}|\eta)} \left[\nabla_{\boldsymbol{\eta}}^2 \log p(\boldsymbol{x}|\eta) \right] \tag{2.231}$$

Hence for an exponential family model we have

$$\mathbf{F}(\eta) = -\mathbb{E}_{p(\boldsymbol{x}|\eta)} \left[\nabla_{\boldsymbol{\eta}}^2 (\boldsymbol{\eta}^{\mathsf{T}} \mathcal{T}(\boldsymbol{x}) - A(\boldsymbol{\eta})) \right] = \nabla_{\boldsymbol{\eta}}^2 A(\eta) = \mathrm{Cov} \left[\mathcal{T}(\boldsymbol{x}) \right] \tag{2.232}$$

Thus the Hessian of the log partition function is the same as the FIM, which is the same as the covariance of the sufficient statistics. See Section 3.3.4.6 for details.

2.4.4 Canonical (natural) vs mean (moment) parameters

Let Ω be the set of normalizable natural parameters:

$$\Omega \triangleq \{\boldsymbol{\eta} \in \mathbb{R}^K : Z(\boldsymbol{\eta}) < \infty\} \tag{2.233}$$

We say that an exponential family is **regular** if Ω is an open set. It can be shown that Ω is a convex set, and $A(\boldsymbol{\eta})$ is a convex function defined over this set.

In Section 2.4.3, we prove that the derivative of the log partition function is equal to the mean of the sufficient statistics, i.e.,

$$\boldsymbol{m} = \mathbb{E} \left[\mathcal{T}(\boldsymbol{x}) \right] = \nabla_{\boldsymbol{\eta}} A(\boldsymbol{\eta}) \tag{2.234}$$

The set of valid moment parameters is given by

$$\mathcal{M} = \{\boldsymbol{m} \in \mathbb{R}^K : \mathbb{E}_p \left[\mathcal{T}(\boldsymbol{x}) \right] = \boldsymbol{m}\} \tag{2.235}$$

for some distribution p.

We have seen that we can convert from the natural parameters to the moment parameters using

$$\boldsymbol{m} = \nabla_{\boldsymbol{\eta}} A(\boldsymbol{\eta}) \tag{2.236}$$

If the family is minimal, one can show that

$$\boldsymbol{\eta} = \nabla_{\boldsymbol{m}} A^*(\boldsymbol{m}) \tag{2.237}$$

where $A^*(\boldsymbol{m})$ is the convex conjugate of A:

$$A^*(\boldsymbol{m}) \triangleq \sup_{\boldsymbol{\eta} \in \Omega} \boldsymbol{\mu}^{\mathsf{T}} \boldsymbol{\eta} - A(\boldsymbol{\eta}) \tag{2.238}$$

Thus the pair of operators $(\nabla A, \nabla A^*)$ lets us go back and forth between the natural parameters $\boldsymbol{\eta} \in \Omega$ and the mean parameters $\boldsymbol{m} \in \mathcal{M}$.

For future reference, note that the Bregman divergences (Section 5.1.10) associated with A and A^* are as follows:

$$B_A(\boldsymbol{\lambda}_1 \| \boldsymbol{\lambda}_2) = A(\boldsymbol{\lambda}_1) - A(\boldsymbol{\lambda}_2) - (\boldsymbol{\lambda}_1 - \boldsymbol{\lambda}_2)^{\mathsf{T}} \nabla_{\boldsymbol{\lambda}} A(\boldsymbol{\lambda}_2) \tag{2.239}$$

$$B_{A^*}(\boldsymbol{\mu}_1 \| \boldsymbol{\mu}_2) = A(\boldsymbol{\mu}_1) - A(\boldsymbol{\mu}_2) - (\boldsymbol{\mu}_1 - \boldsymbol{\mu}_2)^{\mathsf{T}} \nabla_{\boldsymbol{\mu}} A(\boldsymbol{\mu}_2) \tag{2.240}$$

$$\tag{2.241}$$

2.4.5   MLE for the exponential family

The likelihood of an exponential family model has the form

$$p(\mathcal{D}|\boldsymbol{\eta}) = \left[\prod_{n=1}^{N} h(\boldsymbol{x}_n)\right] \exp\left(\boldsymbol{\eta}^\mathsf{T}[\sum_{n=1}^{N} \mathcal{T}(\boldsymbol{x}_n)] - NA(\boldsymbol{\eta})\right) \propto \exp\left[\boldsymbol{\eta}^\mathsf{T}\mathcal{T}(\mathcal{D}) - NA(\boldsymbol{\eta})\right] \tag{2.242}$$

where $\mathcal{T}(\mathcal{D})$ are the sufficient statistics:

$$\mathcal{T}(\mathcal{D}) = [\sum_{n=1}^{N} \mathcal{T}_1(\boldsymbol{x}_n), \ldots, \sum_{n=1}^{N} \mathcal{T}_K(\boldsymbol{x}_n)] \tag{2.243}$$

For example, for the Bernoulli model we have $\mathcal{T}(\mathcal{D}) = [\sum_n \mathbb{I}(x_n = 1)]$, and for the univariate Gaussian, we have $\mathcal{T}(\mathcal{D}) = [\sum_n x_n, \sum_n x_n^2]$.

The **Pitman-Koopman-Darmois theorem** states that, under certain regularity conditions, the exponential family is the only family of distributions with finite sufficient statistics. (Here, finite means a size independent of the size of the dataset.) In other words, for an exponential family with natural parameters $\boldsymbol{\eta}$, we have

$$p(\mathcal{D}|\boldsymbol{\eta}) = p(\mathcal{T}(\mathcal{D})|\boldsymbol{\eta}) \tag{2.244}$$

We now show how to use this result to compute the MLE. The log likelihood is given by

$$\log p(\mathcal{D}|\boldsymbol{\eta}) = \boldsymbol{\eta}^\mathsf{T}\mathcal{T}(\mathcal{D}) - NA(\boldsymbol{\eta}) + \text{const} \tag{2.245}$$

Since $-A(\boldsymbol{\eta})$ is concave in $\boldsymbol{\eta}$, and $\boldsymbol{\eta}^\mathsf{T}\mathcal{T}(\mathcal{D})$ is linear in $\boldsymbol{\eta}$, we see that the log likelihood is concave, and hence has a unique global maximum. To derive this maximum, we use the fact (shown in Section 2.4.3) that the derivative of the log partition function yields the expected value of the sufficient statistic vector:

$$\nabla_{\boldsymbol{\eta}} \log p(\mathcal{D}|\boldsymbol{\eta}) = \nabla_{\boldsymbol{\eta}}\boldsymbol{\eta}^\mathsf{T}\mathcal{T}(\mathcal{D}) - N\nabla_{\boldsymbol{\eta}}A(\boldsymbol{\eta}) = \mathcal{T}(\mathcal{D}) - N\mathbb{E}\left[\mathcal{T}(\boldsymbol{x})\right] \tag{2.246}$$

For a single data case, this becomes

$$\nabla_{\boldsymbol{\eta}} \log p(\boldsymbol{x}|\boldsymbol{\eta}) = \mathcal{T}(\boldsymbol{x}) - \mathbb{E}\left[\mathcal{T}(\boldsymbol{x})\right] \tag{2.247}$$

Setting the gradient in Equation (2.246) to zero, we see that at the MLE, the empirical average of the sufficient statistics must equal the model's theoretical expected sufficient statistics, i.e., $\hat{\boldsymbol{\eta}}$ must satisfy

$$\mathbb{E}\left[\mathcal{T}(\boldsymbol{x})\right] = \frac{1}{N}\sum_{n=1}^{N} \mathcal{T}(\boldsymbol{x}_n) \tag{2.248}$$

This is called **moment matching**. For example, in the Bernoulli distribution, we have $\mathcal{T}(x) = \mathbb{I}(X = 1)$, so the MLE satisfies

$$\mathbb{E}\left[\mathcal{T}(x)\right] = p(X = 1) = \mu = \frac{1}{N}\sum_{n=1}^{N} \mathbb{I}(x_n = 1) \tag{2.249}$$

2.4.6 Exponential dispersion family

In this section, we consider a slight extension of the natural exponential family known as the **exponential dispersion family**. This will be useful when we discuss GLMs in Section 15.1. For a scalar variable, this has the form

$$p(x|\eta, \sigma^2) = h(x, \sigma^2) \exp \left[\frac{\eta x - A(\eta)}{\sigma^2} \right] \tag{2.250}$$

Here σ^2 is called the **dispersion parameter**. For fixed σ^2, this is a natural exponential family.

2.4.7 Maximum entropy derivation of the exponential family

Suppose we want to find a distribution $p(\boldsymbol{x})$ to describe some data, where all we know are the expected values (F_k) of certain features or functions $f_k(\boldsymbol{x})$:

$$\int d\boldsymbol{x}\, p(\boldsymbol{x}) f_k(\boldsymbol{x}) = F_k \tag{2.251}$$

For example, f_1 might compute x, f_2 might compute x^2, making F_1 the empirical mean and F_2 the empirical second moment. Our prior belief in the distribution is $q(x)$.

To formalize what we mean by "least number of assumptions", we will search for the distribution that is as close as possible to our prior $q(\boldsymbol{x})$, in the sense of KL divergence (Section 5.1), while satisfying our constraints.

If we use a uniform prior, $q(\boldsymbol{x}) \propto 1$, minimizing the KL divergence is equivalent to maximizing the entropy (Section 5.2). The result is called a **maximum entropy model**.

To minimize KL subject to the constraints in Equation (2.251), and the constraint that $p(\boldsymbol{x}) \geq 0$ and $\sum_{\boldsymbol{x}} p(\boldsymbol{x}) = 1$, we need to use Lagrange multipliers. The Lagrangian is given by

$$J(p, \boldsymbol{\lambda}) = -\sum_{\boldsymbol{x}} p(\boldsymbol{x}) \log \frac{p(\boldsymbol{x})}{q(\boldsymbol{x})} + \lambda_0 \left(1 - \sum_{\boldsymbol{x}} p(\boldsymbol{x}) \right) + \sum_k \lambda_k \left(F_k - \sum_{\boldsymbol{x}} p(\boldsymbol{x}) f_k(\boldsymbol{x}) \right) \tag{2.252}$$

We can use the calculus of variations to take derivatives wrt the function p, but we will adopt a simpler approach and treat $\boldsymbol{p}$ as a fixed length vector (since we are assuming that $\boldsymbol{x}$ is discrete). Then we have

$$\frac{\partial J}{\partial p_c} = -1 - \log \frac{p(x = c)}{q(x = c)} - \lambda_0 - \sum_k \lambda_k f_k(x = c) \tag{2.253}$$

Setting $\frac{\partial J}{\partial p_c} = 0$ for each c yields

$$p(\boldsymbol{x}) = \frac{q(\boldsymbol{x})}{Z} \exp \left(-\sum_k \lambda_k f_k(\boldsymbol{x}) \right) \tag{2.254}$$

where we have defined $Z \triangleq e^{1+\lambda_0}$. Using the sum-to-one constraint, we have

$$1 = \sum_{\boldsymbol{x}} p(\boldsymbol{x}) = \frac{1}{Z} \sum_{\boldsymbol{x}} q(\boldsymbol{x}) \exp \left(-\sum_k \lambda_k f_k(\boldsymbol{x}) \right) \tag{2.255}$$

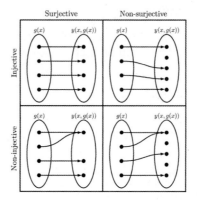

Figure 2.11: Illustration of injective and surjective functions.

Hence the normalization constant is given by

$$Z = \sum_{\boldsymbol{x}} q(\boldsymbol{x}) \exp\left(-\sum_k \lambda_k f_k(\boldsymbol{x})\right) \tag{2.256}$$

This has exactly the form of the exponential family, where $\boldsymbol{f}(\boldsymbol{x})$ is the vector of sufficient statistics, $-\boldsymbol{\lambda}$ are the natural parameters, and $q(\boldsymbol{x})$ is our base measure.

For example, if the features are $f_1(x) = x$ and $f_2(x) = x^2$, and we want to match the first and second moments, we get the Gaussian disribution.

2.5   Transformations of random variables

Suppose $\boldsymbol{x} \sim p_x(\boldsymbol{x})$ is some random variable, and $\boldsymbol{y} = f(\boldsymbol{x})$ is some deterministic transformation of it. In this section, we discuss how to compute $p_y(\boldsymbol{y})$.

2.5.1   Invertible transformations (bijections)

Let f be a **bijection** that maps $\mathbb{R}^n$ to $\mathbb{R}^n$. (A bijection is a function that is **injective**, or **one-to-one**, and **surjective**, as illustrated in Figure 2.11; this means that the function has a well-defined inverse.) Suppose we want to compute the pdf of $\boldsymbol{y} = f(\boldsymbol{x})$. The **change of variables** formula tells us that

$$p_y(\boldsymbol{y}) = p_x\left(f^{-1}(\boldsymbol{y})\right) \left|\det\left[\mathbf{J}_{f^{-1}}(\boldsymbol{y})\right]\right| \tag{2.257}$$

where $\mathbf{J}_{f^{-1}}(\boldsymbol{y})$ is the Jacobian of the inverse mapping f^{-1} evaluated at $\boldsymbol{y}$, and $|\det \mathbf{J}|$ is the absolute value of the determinant of $\mathbf{J}$. In other words,

$$\mathbf{J}_{f^{-1}}(\boldsymbol{y}) = \begin{pmatrix} \frac{\partial x_1}{\partial y_1} & \cdots & \frac{\partial x_1}{\partial y_n} \\ & \vdots & \\ \frac{\partial x_n}{\partial y_1} & \cdots & \frac{\partial x_n}{\partial y_n} \end{pmatrix} \tag{2.258}$$

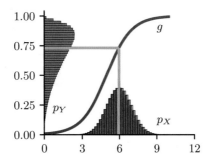

Figure 2.12: Example of the transformation of a density under a nonlinear transform. Note how the mode of the transformed distribution is not the transform of the original mode. Adapted from Exercise 1.4 of [Bis06]. Generated by bayes_change_of_var.ipynb.

If the Jacobian matrix is triangular, the determinant reduces to a product of the terms on the main diagonal:

$$\det(\mathbf{J}) = \prod_{i=1}^{n} \frac{\partial x_i}{\partial y_i} \tag{2.259}$$

2.5.2 Monte Carlo approximation

Sometime it is difficult to compute the Jacobian. In this case, we can make a Monte Carlo approximation, by drawing S samples $\boldsymbol{x}^s \sim p(\boldsymbol{x})$, computing $\boldsymbol{y}^s = f(\boldsymbol{x}^s)$, and then constructing the empirical pdf

$$p_{\mathcal{D}}(\boldsymbol{y}) = \frac{1}{S} \sum_{s=1}^{S} \delta(\boldsymbol{y} - \boldsymbol{y}^s) \tag{2.260}$$

For example, let $x \sim \mathcal{N}(6, 1)$ and $y = f(x)$, where $f(x) = \frac{1}{1+\exp(-x+5)}$. We can approximate $p(y)$ using Monte Carlo, as shown in Figure 2.12.

2.5.3 Probability integral transform

Suppose that X is a random variable with cdf P_X. Let $Y(X) = P_X(X)$ be a transformation of X. We now show that Y has a uniform distribution, a result known as the **probability integral transform** (PIT):

$$P_Y(y) = \Pr(Y \le y) = \Pr(P_X(X) \le y) \tag{2.261}$$
$$= \Pr(X \le P_X^{-1}(y)) = P_X(P_X^{-1}(y)) = y \tag{2.262}$$

For example, in Figure 2.13, we show various distributions with pdf's p_X on the left column. We sample from these, to get $x_n \sim p_x$. Next we compute the empirical cdf of $Y = P_X(X)$, by computing $y_n = P_X(x_n)$ and then sorting the values; the results, shown in the middle column, show that this

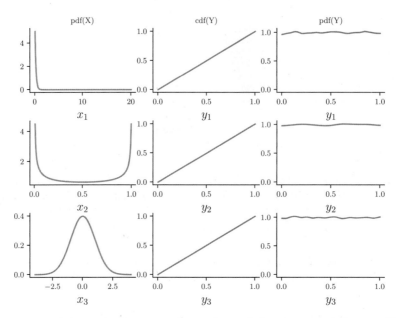

Figure 2.13: Illustration of the probability integral transform. Left column: 3 different pdf's for $p(X)$ from which we sample $x_n \sim p(x)$. Middle column: empirical cdf of $y_n = P_X(x_n)$. Right column: empirical pdf of $p(y_n)$ using a kernel density estimate. Adapted from Figure 11.17 of [MKL11]. Generated by ecdf_sample.ipynb.

distribution is uniform. We can also approximate the pdf of Y by using kernel density estimation; this is shown in the right column, and we see that it is (approximately) flat.

We can use the PIT to test if a set of samples come from a given distribution using the **Kolmogorov–Smirnov test**. To do this, we plot the empirical cdf of the samples and the theoretical cdf of the distribution, and compute the maximum distance between these two curves, as illustrated in Figure 2.14. Formally, the KS statistic is defined as

$$D_n = \max_x |P_n(x) - P(x)| \tag{2.263}$$

where n is the sample size, P_n is the empirical cdf, and P is the theoretical cdf. The value D_n should approach 0 (as $n \to \infty$) if the samples are drawn from P.

Another application of the PIT is to generate samples from a distribution: if we have a way to sample from a uniform distribution, $u_n \sim \text{Unif}(0, 1)$, we can convert this to samples from any other distribution with cdf P_X by setting $x_n = P_X^{-1}(u_n)$.

2.6   Markov chains

Suppose that $\boldsymbol{x}_t$ captures all the relevant information about the state of the system. This means it is a **sufficient statistic** for predicting the future given the past, i.e.,

$$p(\boldsymbol{x}_{t+\tau}|\boldsymbol{x}_t, \boldsymbol{x}_{1:t-1}) = p(\boldsymbol{x}_{t+\tau}|\boldsymbol{x}_t) \tag{2.264}$$

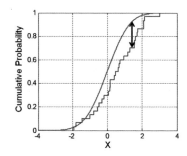

Figure 2.14: Illustration of the Kolmogorov–Smirnov statistic. The red line is a model cdf, the blue line is an empirical cdf, and the black arrow is the K–S statistic. From https://en.wikipedia.org/wiki/Kolmogorov_Smirnov_test. Used with kind permission of Wikipedia author Bscan.

for any $\tau \geq 0$. This is called the **Markov assumption**. In this case, we can write the joint distribution for any finite length sequence as follows:

$$p(\boldsymbol{x}_{1:T}) = p(\boldsymbol{x}_1)p(\boldsymbol{x}_2|\boldsymbol{x}_1)p(\boldsymbol{x}_3|\boldsymbol{x}_2)p(\boldsymbol{x}_4|\boldsymbol{x}_3)\ldots = p(\boldsymbol{x}_1)\prod_{t=2}^{T}p(\boldsymbol{x}_t|\boldsymbol{x}_{t-1}) \tag{2.265}$$

This is called a **Markov chain** or **Markov model**. Below we cover some of the basics of this topic; more details on the theory can be found in [Kun20].

2.6.1 Parameterization

In this section, we discuss how to represent a Markov model parametrically.

2.6.1.1 Markov transition kernels

The conditional distribution $p(\boldsymbol{x}_t|\boldsymbol{x}_{t-1})$ is called the **transition function, transition kernel**, or **Markov kernel**. This is just a conditional distribution over the states at time t given the state at time $t-1$, and hence it satisfies the conditions $p(\boldsymbol{x}_t|\boldsymbol{x}_{t-1}) \geq 0$ and $\int_{\boldsymbol{x}\in\mathcal{X}} dx \, p(\boldsymbol{x}_t = \boldsymbol{x}|\boldsymbol{x}_{t-1}) = 1$.

If we assume the transition function $p(\boldsymbol{x}_t|\boldsymbol{x}_{1:t-1})$ is independent of time, then the model is said to be **homogeneous, stationary**, or **time-invariant**. This is an example of **parameter tying**, since the same parameter is shared by multiple variables. This assumption allows us to model an arbitrary number of variables using a fixed number of parameters. We will make the time-invariant assumption throughout the rest of this section.

2.6.1.2 Markov transition matrices

In this section, we assume that the variables are discrete, so $X_t \in \{1,\ldots,K\}$. This is called a **finite-state Markov chain**. In this case, the conditional distribution $p(X_t|X_{t-1})$ can be written as a $K \times K$ matrix $\mathbf{A}$, known as the **transition matrix**, where $A_{ij} = p(X_t = j|X_{t-1} = i)$ is the probability of going from state i to state j. Each row of the matrix sums to one, $\sum_j A_{ij} = 1$, so this is called a **stochastic matrix**.

Figure 2.15: State transition diagrams for some simple Markov chains. Left: a 2-state chain. Right: a 3-state left-to-right chain.

A stationary, finite-state Markov chain is equivalent to a **stochastic automaton**. It is common to visualize such automata by drawing a directed graph, where nodes represent states and arrows represent legal transitions, i.e., non-zero elements of **A**. This is known as a **state transition diagram**. The weights associated with the arcs are the probabilities. For example, the following 2-state chain

$$\mathbf{A} = \begin{pmatrix} 1 - \alpha & \alpha \\ \beta & 1 - \beta \end{pmatrix} \tag{2.266}$$

is illustrated in Figure 2.15(a). The following 3-state chain

$$\mathbf{A} = \begin{pmatrix} A_{11} & A_{12} & 0 \\ 0 & A_{22} & A_{23} \\ 0 & 0 & 1 \end{pmatrix} \tag{2.267}$$

is illustrated in Figure 2.15(b). This is called a **left-to-right transition matrix**.

The A_{ij} element of the transition matrix specifies the probability of getting from i to j in one step. The n-step transition matrix $\mathbf{A}(n)$ is defined as

$$A_{ij}(n) \triangleq p(X_{t+n} = j | X_t = i) \tag{2.268}$$

which is the probability of getting from i to j in exactly n steps. Obviously $\mathbf{A}(1) = \mathbf{A}$. The **Chapman-Kolmogorov** equations state that

$$A_{ij}(m + n) = \sum_{k=1}^{K} A_{ik}(m) A_{kj}(n) \tag{2.269}$$

In words, the probability of getting from i to j in $m + n$ steps is just the probability of getting from i to k in m steps, and then from k to j in n steps, summed up over all k. We can write the above as a matrix multiplication

$$\mathbf{A}(m + n) = \mathbf{A}(m)\mathbf{A}(n) \tag{2.270}$$

Hence

$$\mathbf{A}(n) = \mathbf{A}\,\mathbf{A}(n - 1) = \mathbf{A}\,\mathbf{A}\,\mathbf{A}(n - 2) = \cdots = \mathbf{A}^n \tag{2.271}$$

Thus we can simulate multiple steps of a Markov chain by "powering up" the transition matrix.

```
christians first inhabit wherein thou hast forgive if a man childless and of laying of core these
are the heavens shall reel to and fro to seek god they set their horses and children of israel
```

Figure 2.16: *Example output from an 10-gram character-level Markov model trained on the King James Bible. The prefix "christians" is given to the model. Generated by* ngram_character_demo.ipynb.

2.6.1.3 Higher-order Markov models

The first-order Markov assumption is rather strong. Fortunately, we can easily generalize first-order models to depend on the last n observations, thus creating a model of order (memory length) n:

$$p(\boldsymbol{x}_{1:T}) = p(\boldsymbol{x}_{1:n}) \prod_{t=n+1}^{T} p(\boldsymbol{x}_t | \boldsymbol{x}_{t-n:t-1}) \tag{2.272}$$

This is called a **Markov model of order n**. If $n = 1$, this is called a **bigram model**, since we need to represent pairs of characters, $p(\boldsymbol{x}_t | \boldsymbol{x}_{t-1})$. If $n = 2$, this is called a **trigram model**, since we need to represent triples of characters, $p(\boldsymbol{x}_t | \boldsymbol{x}_{t-1}, \boldsymbol{x}_{t-2})$. In general, this is called an **n-gram model**.

Note, however, we can always convert a higher order Markov model to a first order one by defining an augmented state space that contains the past n observations. For example, if $n = 2$, we define $\tilde{\boldsymbol{x}}_t = (\boldsymbol{x}_{t-1}, \boldsymbol{x}_t)$ and use

$$p(\tilde{\boldsymbol{x}}_{1:T}) = p(\tilde{\boldsymbol{x}}_2) \prod_{t=3}^{T} p(\tilde{\boldsymbol{x}}_t | \tilde{\boldsymbol{x}}_{t-1}) = p(\boldsymbol{x}_1, \boldsymbol{x}_2) \prod_{t=3}^{T} p(\boldsymbol{x}_t | \boldsymbol{x}_{t-1}, \boldsymbol{x}_{t-2}) \tag{2.273}$$

Therefore we will just focus on first-order models throughout the rest of this section.

2.6.2 Application: language modeling

One important application of Markov models is to create **language models** (**LM**), which are models which can generate (or score) a sequence of words. When we use a finite-state Markov model with a memory of length $m = n - 1$, it is called an **n-gram model**. For example, if $m = 1$, we get a **unigram model** (no dependence on previous words); if $m = 2$, we get a **bigram model** (depends on previous word); if $m = 3$, we get a **trigram model** (depends on previous two words); etc. See Figure 2.16 for some generated text.

These days, most LMs are built using recurrent neural nets (see Section 16.3.4), which have unbounded memory. However, simple n-gram models can still do quite well when trained with enough data [Che17].

Language models have various applications, such as priors for spelling correction (see Section 29.3.3) or automatic speech recognition. In addition, conditional language models can be used to generate sequences given inputs, such as mapping one language to another, or an image to a sequence, etc.

2.6.3 Parameter estimation

In this section, we discuss how to estimate the parameters of a Markov model.

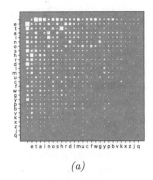

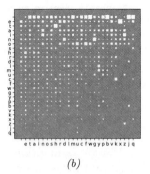

$$(a) \hspace{10em} (b)$$

Figure 2.17: (a) **Hinton diagram** *showing character bigram counts as estimated from H. G. Wells's book The Time Machine. Characters are sorted in decreasing unigram frequency; the first one is a space character. The most frequent bigram is 'e-', where - represents space. (b) Same as (a) but each row is normalized across the columns. Generated by* bigram_hinton_diagram.ipynb.

2.6.3.1 Maximum likelihood estimation

The probability of any particular sequence of length T is given by

$$p(x_{1:T}|\boldsymbol{\theta}) = \pi(x_1)A(x_1,x_2)\dots A(x_{T-1},x_T) \tag{2.274}$$

$$= \prod_{j=1}^{K}(\pi_j)^{\mathbb{I}(x_1=j)} \prod_{t=2}^{T}\prod_{j=1}^{K}\prod_{k=1}^{K}(A_{jk})^{\mathbb{I}(x_t=k,x_{t-1}=j)} \tag{2.275}$$

Hence the log-likelihood of a set of sequences $\mathcal{D} = (\boldsymbol{x}_1,\dots,\boldsymbol{x}_N)$, where $\boldsymbol{x}_i = (x_{i1},\dots,x_{i,T_i})$ is a sequence of length T_i, is given by

$$\log p(\mathcal{D}|\boldsymbol{\theta}) = \sum_{i=1}^{N}\log p(\boldsymbol{x}_i|\boldsymbol{\theta}) = \sum_j N_j^1 \log \pi_j + \sum_j\sum_k N_{jk}\log A_{jk} \tag{2.276}$$

where we define the following counts:

$$N_j^1 \triangleq \sum_{i=1}^{N}\mathbb{I}(x_{i1}=j),\quad N_{jk} \triangleq \sum_{i=1}^{N}\sum_{t=1}^{T_i-1}\mathbb{I}(x_{i,t}=j,x_{i,t+1}=k),\quad N_j = \sum_k N_{jk} \tag{2.277}$$

By adding Lagrange multipliers to enforce the sum to one constraints, one can show (see e.g., [Mur22, Sec 4.2.4]) that the MLE is given by the normalized counts:

$$\hat{\pi}_j = \frac{N_j^1}{\sum_{j'}N_{j'}^1},\quad \hat{A}_{jk} = \frac{N_{jk}}{N_j} \tag{2.278}$$

We often replace N_j^1, which is how often symbol j is seen at the start of a sequence, by N_j, which is how often symbol j is seen anywhere in a sequence. This lets us estimate parameters from a single sequence.

The counts N_j are known as **unigram statistics**, and N_{jk} are known as **bigram statistics**. For example, Figure 2.17 shows some 2-gram counts for the characters $\{a, \ldots, z, -\}$ (where - represents space) as estimated from H. G. Wells's book *The Time Machine*.

2.6.3.2 Sparse data problem

When we try to fit n-gram models for large n, we quickly encounter problems with overfitting due to data sparsity. To see that, note that many of the estimated counts N_{jk} will be 0, since now j indexes over discrete contexts of size K^{n-1}, which will become increasingly rare. Even for bigram models ($n = 2$), problems can arise if K is large. For example, if we have $K \sim 50,000$ words in our vocabulary, then a bi-gram model will have about 2.5 billion free parameters, corresponding to all possible word pairs. It is very unlikely we will see all of these in our training data. However, we do not want to predict that a particular word string is totally impossible just because we happen not to have seen it in our training text — that would be a severe form of overfitting.[9]

A "brute force" solution to this problem is to gather lots and lots of data. For example, Google has fit n-gram models (for $n = 1 : 5$) based on one trillion words extracted from the web. Their data, which is over 100GB when uncompressed, is publically available.[10] Although such an approach can be surprisingly successful (as discussed in [HNP09]), it is rather unsatisfying, since humans are able to learn language from much less data (see e.g., [TX00]).

2.6.3.3 MAP estimation

A simple solution to the sparse data problem is to use MAP estimation with a uniform Dirichlet prior, $\mathbf{A}_{j:} \sim \text{Dir}(\alpha \mathbf{1})$. In this case, the MAP estimate becomes

$$\hat{A}_{jk} = \frac{N_{jk} + \alpha}{N_j + K\alpha} \tag{2.279}$$

If $\alpha = 1$, this is called **add-one smoothing**.

The main problem with add-one smoothing is that it assumes that all n-grams are equally likely, which is not very realistic. We discuss a more sophisticated approach, based on hierarchical Bayes, in Section 3.7.3.

2.6.4 Stationary distribution of a Markov chain

Suppose we continually draw consecutive samples from a Markov chain. In the case of a finite state space, we can think of this as "hopping" from one state to another. We will tend to spend more time in some states than others, depending on the transition graph. The long term distribution over states is known as the **stationary distribution** of the chain. In this section, we discuss some of the relevant theory. In Chapter 12, we discuss an important application, known as MCMC, which is a way to generate samples from hard-to-normalize probability distributions. In Supplementary Section 2.2

---

9. A famous example of an improbable, but syntactically valid, English word string, due to Noam Chomsky [Cho57], is "colourless green ideas sleep furiously". We would not want our model to predict that this string is impossible. Even ungrammatical constructs should be allowed by our model with a certain probability, since people frequently violate grammatical rules, especially in spoken language.

10. See `http://googleresearch.blogspot.com/2006/08/all-our-n-gram-are-belong-to-you.html` for details.

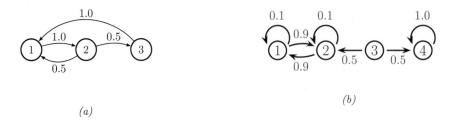

Figure 2.18: Some Markov chains. (a) A 3-state aperiodic chain. (b) A reducible 4-state chain.

we consider Google's PageRank algorithm for ranking web pages, which also leverages the concept of stationary distributions.

2.6.4.1   What is a stationary distribution?

Let $A_{ij} = p(X_t = j | X_{t-1} = i)$ be the one-step transition matrix, and let $\pi_t(j) = p(X_t = j)$ be the probability of being in state j at time t.

If we have an initial distribution over states of $\boldsymbol{\pi}_0$, then at time 1 we have

$$\pi_1(j) = \sum_i \pi_0(i) A_{ij} \tag{2.280}$$

or, in matrix notation, $\boldsymbol{\pi}_1 = \boldsymbol{\pi}_0 \mathbf{A}$, where we have followed the standard convention of assuming $\boldsymbol{\pi}$ is a *row* vector, so we post-multiply by the transition matrix.

Now imagine iterating these equations. If we ever reach a stage where $\boldsymbol{\pi} = \boldsymbol{\pi} \mathbf{A}$, then we say we have reached the **stationary distribution** (also called the **invariant distribution** or **equilibrium distribution**). Once we enter the stationary distribution, we will never leave.

For example, consider the chain in Figure 2.18(a). To find its stationary distribution, we write

$$\begin{pmatrix} \pi_1 & \pi_2 & \pi_3 \end{pmatrix} = \begin{pmatrix} \pi_1 & \pi_2 & \pi_3 \end{pmatrix} \begin{pmatrix} 1 - A_{12} - A_{13} & A_{12} & A_{13} \\ A_{21} & 1 - A_{21} - A_{23} & A_{23} \\ A_{31} & A_{32} & 1 - A_{31} - A_{32} \end{pmatrix} \tag{2.281}$$

Hence $\pi_1(A_{12} + A_{13}) = \pi_2 A_{21} + \pi_3 A_{31}$. In general, we have

$$\pi_i \sum_{j \neq i} A_{ij} = \sum_{j \neq i} \pi_j A_{ji} \tag{2.282}$$

In other words, the probability of being in state i times the net flow out of state i must equal the probability of being in each other state j times the net flow from that state into i. These are called the **global balance equations**. We can then solve these equations, subject to the constraint that $\sum_j \pi_j = 1$, to find the stationary distribution, as we discuss below.

2.6.4.2   Computing the stationary distribution

To find the stationary distribution, we can just solve the eigenvector equation $\mathbf{A}^\mathsf{T} \boldsymbol{v} = \boldsymbol{v}$, and then to set $\boldsymbol{\pi} = \boldsymbol{v}^\mathsf{T}$, where $\boldsymbol{v}$ is an eigenvector with eigenvalue 1. (We can be sure such an eigenvector exists, since $\mathbf{A}$ is a row-stochastic matrix, so $\mathbf{A1} = \mathbf{1}$; also recall that the eigenvalues of $\mathbf{A}$ and $\mathbf{A}^\mathsf{T}$ are the same.) Of course, since eigenvectors are unique only up to constants of proportionality, we must normalize $\boldsymbol{v}$ at the end to ensure it sums to one.

Note, however, that the eigenvectors are only guaranteed to be real-valued if all entries in the matrix are strictly positive, $A_{ij} > 0$ (and hence $A_{ij} < 1$, due to the sum-to-one constraint). A more general approach, which can handle chains where some transition probabilities are 0 or 1 (such as Figure 2.18(a)), is as follows. We have K constraints from $\boldsymbol{\pi}(\mathbf{I} - \mathbf{A}) = \mathbf{0}_{K \times 1}$ and 1 constraint from $\boldsymbol{\pi}\mathbf{1}_{K \times 1} = 1$. Hence we have to solve $\boldsymbol{\pi}\mathbf{M} = \boldsymbol{r}$, where $\mathbf{M} = [\mathbf{I} - \mathbf{A}, \mathbf{1}]$ is a $K \times (K+1)$ matrix, and $\boldsymbol{r} = [0, 0, \ldots, 0, 1]$ is a $1 \times (K+1)$ vector. However, this is overconstrained, so we will drop the last column of $\mathbf{I} - \mathbf{A}$ in our definition of $\mathbf{M}$, and drop the last 0 from $\boldsymbol{r}$. For example, for a 3 state chain we have to solve this linear system:

$$\begin{pmatrix} \pi_1 & \pi_2 & \pi_3 \end{pmatrix} \begin{pmatrix} 1 - A_{11} & -A_{12} & 1 \\ -A_{21} & 1 - A_{22} & 1 \\ -A_{31} & -A_{32} & 1 \end{pmatrix} = \begin{pmatrix} 0 & 0 & 1 \end{pmatrix} \tag{2.283}$$

For the chain in Figure 2.18(a) we find $\boldsymbol{\pi} = [0.4, 0.4, 0.2]$. We can easily verify this is correct, since $\boldsymbol{\pi} = \boldsymbol{\pi}\mathbf{A}$.

Unfortunately, not all chains have a stationary distribution, as we explain below.

2.6.4.3 When does a stationary distribution exist?

Consider the 4-state chain in Figure 2.18(b). If we start in state 4, we will stay there forever, since 4 is an **absorbing state**. Thus $\boldsymbol{\pi} = (0, 0, 0, 1)$ is one possible stationary distribution. However, if we start in 1 or 2, we will oscillate between those two states forever. So $\boldsymbol{\pi} = (0.5, 0.5, 0, 0)$ is another possible stationary distribution. If we start in state 3, we could end up in either of the above stationary distributions with equal probability. The corresponding transition graph has two disjoint connected components.

We see from this example that a necessary condition to have a unique stationary distribution is that the state transition diagram be a singly connected component, i.e., we can get from any state to any other state. Such chains are called **irreducible**.

Now consider the 2-state chain in Figure 2.15(a). This is irreducible provided $\alpha, \beta > 0$. Suppose $\alpha = \beta = 0.9$. It is clear by symmetry that this chain will spend 50% of its time in each state. Thus $\boldsymbol{\pi} = (0.5, 0.5)$. But now suppose $\alpha = \beta = 1$. In this case, the chain will oscillate between the two states, but the long-term distribution on states depends on where you start from. If we start in state 1, then on every odd time step (1,3,5,...) we will be in state 1; but if we start in state 2, then on every odd time step we will be in state 2.

This example motivates the following definition. Let us say that a chain has a **limiting distribution** if $\pi_j = \lim_{n \to \infty} A_{ij}^n$ exists and is independent of the starting state i, for all j. If this holds, then the long-run distribution over states will be independent of the starting state:

$$p(X_t = j) = \sum_i p(X_0 = i) A_{ij}(t) \to \pi_j \text{ as } t \to \infty \tag{2.284}$$

Let us now characterize when a limiting distribution exists. Define the **period** of state i to be $d(i) \triangleq \gcd\{t : A_{ii}(t) > 0\}$, where gcd stands for **greatest common divisor**, i.e., the largest integer that divides all the members of the set. For example, in Figure 2.18(a), we have $d(1) = d(2) = gcd(2, 3, 4, 6, ...) = 1$ and $d(3) = gcd(3, 5, 6, ...) = 1$. We say a state i is **aperiodic** if $d(i) = 1$. (A sufficient condition to ensure this is if state i has a self-loop, but this is not a necessary condition.) We say a chain is aperiodic if all its states are aperiodic. One can show the following important result:

Theorem 2.6.1. *Every irreducible (singly connected), aperiodic finite state Markov chain has a limiting distribution, which is equal to $\boldsymbol{\pi}$, its unique stationary distribution.*

A special case of this result says that every regular finite state chain has a unique stationary distribution, where a **regular** chain is one whose transition matrix satisfies $A_{ij}^n > 0$ for some integer n and all i, j, i.e., it is possible to get from any state to any other state in n steps. Consequently, after n steps, the chain could be in any state, no matter where it started. One can show that sufficient conditions to ensure regularity are that the chain be irreducible (singly connected) and that every state have a self-transition.

To handle the case of Markov chains whose state space is not finite (e.g, the countable set of all integers, or all the uncountable set of all reals), we need to generalize some of the earlier definitions. Since the details are rather technical, we just briefly state the main results without proof. See e.g., [GS92] for details.

For a stationary distribution to exist, we require irreducibility (singly connected) and aperiodicity, as before. But we also require that each state is **recurrent**, which means that you will return to that state with probability 1. As a simple example of a non-recurrent state (i.e., a **transient** state), consider Figure 2.18(b): state 3 is transient because one immediately leaves it and either spins around state 4 forever, or oscillates between states 1 and 2 forever. There is no way to return to state 3.

It is clear that any finite-state irreducible chain is recurrent, since you can always get back to where you started from. But now consider an example with an infinite state space. Suppose we perform a random walk on the integers, $\mathcal{X} = \{\ldots, -2, -1, 0, 1, 2, \ldots\}$. Let $A_{i,i+1} = p$ be the probability of moving right, and $A_{i,i-1} = 1 - p$ be the probability of moving left. Suppose we start at $X_1 = 0$. If $p > 0.5$, we will shoot off to $+\infty$; we are not guaranteed to return. Similarly, if $p < 0.5$, we will shoot off to $-\infty$. So in both cases, the chain is not recurrent, even though it is irreducible. If $p = 0.5$, we can return to the initial state with probability 1, so the chain is recurrent. However, the distribution keeps spreading out over a larger and larger set of the integers, so the expected time to return is infinite. This prevents the chain from having a stationary distribution.

More formally, we define a state to be **non-null recurrent** if the expected time to return to this state is finite. We say that a state is **ergodic** if it is aperiodic, recurrent, and non-null. We say that a chain is ergodic if all its states are ergodic. With these definitions, we can now state our main theorem:

Theorem 2.6.2. *Every irreducible, ergodic Markov chain has a limiting distribution, which is equal to $\boldsymbol{\pi}$, its unique stationary distribution.*

This generalizes Theorem 2.6.1, since for irreducible finite-state chains, all states are recurrent and non-null.

2.6.4.4   Detailed balance

Establishing ergodicity can be difficult. We now give an alternative condition that is easier to verify.

We say that a Markov chain $\mathbf{A}$ is **time reversible** if there exists a distribution $\boldsymbol{\pi}$ such that

$$\pi_i A_{ij} = \pi_j A_{ji} \tag{2.285}$$

These are called the **detailed balance equations**. This says that the flow from i to j must equal the flow from j to i, weighted by the appropriate source probabilities.

We have the following important result.

Theorem 2.6.3. *If a Markov chain with transition matrix $\mathbf{A}$ is regular and satisfies the detailed balance equations wrt distribution $\boldsymbol{\pi}$, then $\boldsymbol{\pi}$ is a stationary distribution of the chain.*

Proof. To see this, note that

$$\sum_i \pi_i A_{ij} = \sum_i \pi_j A_{ji} = \pi_j \sum_i A_{ji} = \pi_j \tag{2.286}$$

and hence $\boldsymbol{\pi} = \mathbf{A}\boldsymbol{\pi}$. $\qquad\square$

Note that this condition is sufficient but not necessary (see Figure 2.18(a) for an example of a chain with a stationary distribution which does not satisfy detailed balance).

2.7 Divergence measures between probability distributions

In this section, we discuss various ways to compare two probability distributions, P and Q, defined on the same space. For example, suppose the distributions are defined in terms of samples, $\mathcal{X} = \{\boldsymbol{x}_1, \ldots, \boldsymbol{x}_N\} \sim P$ and $\mathcal{X}' = \{\tilde{\boldsymbol{x}}_1, \ldots, \tilde{\boldsymbol{x}}_M\} \sim Q$. Determining if the samples come from the same distribution is known as a **two-sample test** (see Figure 2.19 for an illustration). This can be computed by defining some suitable **divergence metric** $D(P, Q)$ and comparing it to a threshold. (We use the term "divergence" rather than distance since we will not require D to be symmetric.) Alternatively, suppose P is an empirical distribution of data, and Q is the distribution induced by a model. We can check how well the model approximates the data by comparing $D(P, Q)$ to a threshold; this is called a **goodness-of-fit** test.

There are two main ways to compute the divergence between a pair of distributions: in terms of their difference, $P - Q$ (see e.g., [Sug+13]) or in terms of their ratio, P/Q (see e.g., [SSK12]). We briefly discuss both of these below. (Our presentation is based, in part, on [GSJ19].)

2.7.1 f-divergence

In this section, we compare distributions in terms of their density ratio $r(\boldsymbol{x}) = p(\boldsymbol{x})/q(\boldsymbol{x})$. In particular, consider the f-**divergence** [Mor63; AS66; Csi67; LV06; CS04], which is defined as follows:

$$D_f(p\|q) = \int q(\boldsymbol{x}) f\left(\frac{p(\boldsymbol{x})}{q(\boldsymbol{x})}\right) d\boldsymbol{x} \tag{2.287}$$

where $f : \mathbb{R}_+ \to \mathbb{R}$ is a convex function satisfying $f(1) = 0$. From Jensen's inequality (Section 5.1.2.2), it follows that $D_f(p\|q) \geq 0$, and obviously $D_f(p\|p) = 0$, so D_f is a valid divergence. Below we discuss some important special cases of f-divergences. (Note that f-divergences are also called ϕ-divergences.)

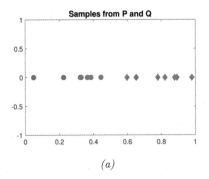
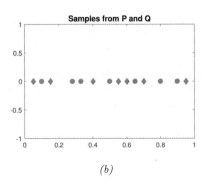

Figure 2.19: Samples from two distributions which are (a) different and (b) similar. From a figure from [GSJ19]. Used with kind permission of Arthur Gretton.

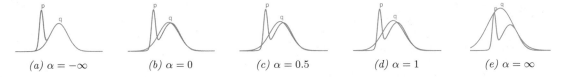

Figure 2.20: The Gaussian q which minimizes α-divergence to p (a mixture of two Gaussians), for varying α. From Figure 1 of [Min05]. Used with kind permission of Tom Minka.

2.7.1.1 KL divergence

Suppose we compute the f-divergence using $f(r) = r\log(r)$. In this case, we get a quantity called the **Kullback Leibler divergence**, defined as follows:

$$D_{\text{KL}}(p \parallel q) = \int p(\boldsymbol{x}) \log \frac{p(\boldsymbol{x})}{q(\boldsymbol{x})} d\boldsymbol{x} \tag{2.288}$$

See Section 5.1 for more details.

2.7.1.2 Alpha divergence

If $f(x) = \frac{4}{1-\alpha^2}(1 - x^{\frac{1+\alpha}{2}})$, the f-divergence becomes the **alpha divergence** [Ama09], which is as follows:

$$D_\alpha^A(p\|q) \triangleq \frac{4}{1-\alpha^2}\left(1 - \int p(\boldsymbol{x})^{(1+\alpha)/2} q(\boldsymbol{x})^{(1-\alpha)/2} d\boldsymbol{x}\right) \tag{2.289}$$

where we assume $\alpha \neq \pm 1$. Another common parameterization, and the one used by Minka in [Min05], is as follows:

$$D_\alpha^M(p\|q) = \frac{1}{\alpha(1-\alpha)}\left(1 - \int p(\boldsymbol{x})^\alpha q(\boldsymbol{x})^{1-\alpha} d\boldsymbol{x}\right) \tag{2.290}$$

This can be converted to Amari's notation using $D_{\alpha'}^A = D_\alpha^M$ where $\alpha' = 2\alpha - 1$. (We will use the Minka convention.)

We see from Figure 2.20 that as $\alpha \to -\infty$, q prefers to match one mode of p, whereas when $\alpha \to \infty$, q prefers to cover all of p. More precisely, one can show that as $\alpha \to 0$, the alpha divergence tends towards $D_{\mathrm{KL}}(q \,\|\, p)$, and as $\alpha \to 1$, the alpha divergence tends towards $D_{\mathrm{KL}}(p \,\|\, q)$. Also, when $\alpha = 0.5$, the alpha divergence equals the Hellinger distance (Section 2.7.1.3).

2.7.1.3 Hellinger distance

The (squared) **Hellinger distance** is defined as follows:

$$D_H^2(p\|q) \triangleq \frac{1}{2} \int \left(p(\boldsymbol{x})^{\frac{1}{2}} - q(\boldsymbol{x})^{\frac{1}{2}} \right)^2 d\boldsymbol{x} = 1 - \int \sqrt{p(\boldsymbol{x})q(\boldsymbol{x})}\, d\boldsymbol{x} \qquad (2.291)$$

This is a valid distance metric, since it is symmetric, nonnegative, and satisfies the triangle inequality. We see that this is equal (up to constant factors) to the f-divergence with $f(r) = (\sqrt{r} - 1)^2$, since

$$\int d\boldsymbol{x}\, q(\boldsymbol{x}) \left(\frac{p^{\frac{1}{2}}(\boldsymbol{x})}{q^{\frac{1}{2}}(\boldsymbol{x})} - 1 \right)^2 = \int d\boldsymbol{x}\, q(\boldsymbol{x}) \left(\frac{p^{\frac{1}{2}}(\boldsymbol{x}) - q^{\frac{1}{2}}(\boldsymbol{x})}{q^{\frac{1}{2}}(\boldsymbol{x})} \right)^2 = \int d\boldsymbol{x} \left(p^{\frac{1}{2}}(\boldsymbol{x}) - q^{\frac{1}{2}}(\boldsymbol{x}) \right)^2 \qquad (2.292)$$

2.7.1.4 Chi-squared distance

The **chi-squared distance** χ^2 is defined by

$$\chi^2(p, q) \triangleq \frac{1}{2} \int \frac{(q(\boldsymbol{x}) - p(\boldsymbol{x}))^2}{q(\boldsymbol{x})} d\boldsymbol{x} \qquad (2.293)$$

This is equal (up to constant factors) to an f-divergence where $f(r) = (r - 1)^2$, since

$$\int d\boldsymbol{x}\, q(\boldsymbol{x}) \left(\frac{p(\boldsymbol{x})}{q(\boldsymbol{x})} - 1 \right)^2 = \int d\boldsymbol{x}\, q(\boldsymbol{x}) \left(\frac{p(\boldsymbol{x}) - q(\boldsymbol{x})}{q(\boldsymbol{x})} \right)^2 = \int d\boldsymbol{x}\, \frac{1}{q(\boldsymbol{x})} (p(\boldsymbol{x}) - q(\boldsymbol{x}))^2 \qquad (2.294)$$

2.7.2 Integral probability metrics

In this section, we compute the divergence between two distributions in terms of $P - Q$ using an **integral probability metric** or **IPM** [Sri+09]. This is defined as follows:

$$D_{\mathcal{F}}(P, Q) \triangleq \sup_{f \in \mathcal{F}} | \mathbb{E}_{p(\boldsymbol{x})}[f(\boldsymbol{x})] - \mathbb{E}_{q(\boldsymbol{x}')}[f(\boldsymbol{x}')] | \qquad (2.295)$$

where $\mathcal{F}$ is some class of "smooth" functions. The function f that maximizes the difference between these two expectations is called the **witness function**. See Figure 2.21 for an illustration.

There are several ways to define the function class $\mathcal{F}$. One approach is to use an RKHS, defined in terms of a positive definite kernel function; this gives rise to the method known as maximum mean discrepancy or MMD. See Section 2.7.3 for details.

Another approach is to define $\mathcal{F}$ to be the set of functions that have bounded Lipschitz constant, i.e., $\mathcal{F} = \{\|f\|_L \leq 1\}$, where

$$\|f\|_L = \sup_{\boldsymbol{x} \neq \boldsymbol{x}'} \frac{|f(\boldsymbol{x}) - f(\boldsymbol{x}')|}{\|\boldsymbol{x} - \boldsymbol{x}'\|} \qquad (2.296)$$

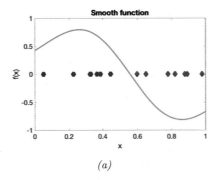
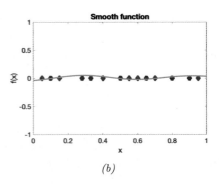

(a)   (b)

Figure 2.21: A smooth witness function for comparing two distributions which are (a) different and (b) similar. From a figure from [GSJ19]. Used with kind permission of Arthur Gretton.

The IPM in this case is equal to the **Wasserstein-1 distance**

$$W_1(P, Q) \triangleq \sup_{||f||_L \leq 1} |\mathbb{E}_{p(\boldsymbol{x})}[f(\boldsymbol{x})] - \mathbb{E}_{q(\boldsymbol{x'})}[f(\boldsymbol{x'})]| \tag{2.297}$$

See Section 6.8.2.4 for details.

2.7.3   Maximum mean discrepancy (MMD)

In this section, we describe the **maximum mean discrepancy** or **MMD** method of [Gre+12], which defines a discrepancy measure $D(P, Q)$ using samples from the two distributions. The samples are compared using positive definite kernels (Section 18.2), which can handle high-dimensional inputs. This approach can be used to define two-sample tests, and to train implicit generative models (Section 26.2.4).

2.7.3.1   MMD as an IPM

The MMD is an integral probability metric (Section 2.7.2) of the form

$$\text{MMD}(P, Q; \mathcal{F}) = \sup_{f \in \mathcal{F}: ||f|| \leq 1} [\mathbb{E}_{p(\boldsymbol{x})}[f(\boldsymbol{x})] - \mathbb{E}_{q(\boldsymbol{x'})}[f(\boldsymbol{x'})]] \tag{2.298}$$

where $\mathcal{F}$ is an RKHS (Section 18.3.7.1) defined by a positive definite kernel function $\mathcal{K}$. We can represent functions in this set as an infinite sum of basis functions

$$f(\boldsymbol{x}) = \langle f, \phi(\boldsymbol{x}) \rangle_{\mathcal{F}} = \sum_{l=1}^{\infty} f_l \phi_l(\boldsymbol{x}) \tag{2.299}$$

We restrict the set of witness functions f to be those that are in the unit ball of this RKHS, so $||f||_{\mathcal{F}}^2 = \sum_{l=1}^{\infty} f_l^2 \leq 1$. By the linearity of expectation, we have

$$\mathbb{E}_{p(\boldsymbol{x})}[f(\boldsymbol{x})] = \langle f, \mathbb{E}_{p(\boldsymbol{x})}[\phi(\boldsymbol{x})] \rangle_{\mathcal{F}} = \langle f, \boldsymbol{\mu}_P \rangle_{\mathcal{F}} \tag{2.300}$$

where $\boldsymbol{\mu}_P$ is called the **kernel mean embedding** of distribution P [Mua+17]. Hence

$$\mathrm{MMD}(P, Q; \mathcal{F}) = \sup_{||f|| \leq 1} \langle f, \boldsymbol{\mu}_P - \boldsymbol{\mu}_Q \rangle_{\mathcal{F}} = \frac{\boldsymbol{\mu}_P - \boldsymbol{\mu}_Q}{||\boldsymbol{\mu}_P - \boldsymbol{\mu}_Q||} \tag{2.301}$$

since the unit vector $\boldsymbol{f}$ that maximizes the inner product is parallel to the difference in feature means.

To get some intuition, suppose $\phi(x) = [x, x^2]$. In this case, the MMD computes the difference in the first two moments of the two distributions. This may not be enough to distinguish all possible distributions. However, using a Gaussian kernel is equivalent to comparing two infinitely large feature vectors, as we show in Section 18.2.6, and hence we are effectively comparing all the moments of the two distributions. Indeed, one can show that MMD=0 iff $P = Q$, provided we use a non-degenerate kernel.

2.7.3.2 Computing the MMD using the kernel trick

In this section, we describe how to compute Equation (2.301) in practice, given two sets of samples, $\mathcal{X} = \{\boldsymbol{x}_n\}_{n=1}^N$ and $\mathcal{X}' = \{\boldsymbol{x}'_m\}_{m=1}^M$, where $\boldsymbol{x}_n \sim P$ and $\boldsymbol{x}'_m \sim Q$. Let $\boldsymbol{\mu}_P = \frac{1}{N} \sum_{n=1}^N \phi(\boldsymbol{x}_n)$ and $\boldsymbol{\mu}_Q = \frac{1}{M} \sum_{m=1}^M \phi(\boldsymbol{x}'_m)$ be empirical estimates of the kernel mean embeddings of the two distributions. Then the squared MMD is given by

$$\mathrm{MMD}^2(\mathcal{X}, \mathcal{X}') \triangleq ||\frac{1}{N} \sum_{n=1}^N \phi(\boldsymbol{x}_n) - \frac{1}{M} \sum_{m=1}^M \phi(\boldsymbol{x}'_m)||^2 \tag{2.302}$$

$$= \frac{1}{N^2} \sum_{n=1}^N \sum_{n'=1}^N \phi(\boldsymbol{x}_n)^\mathsf{T} \phi(\boldsymbol{x}_{n'}) - \frac{2}{NM} \sum_{n=1}^N \sum_{m=1}^M \phi(\boldsymbol{x}_n)^\mathsf{T} \phi(\boldsymbol{x}'_m)$$

$$+ \frac{1}{M^2} \sum_{m=1}^M \sum_{m'=1}^M \phi(\boldsymbol{x}'_{m'})^\mathsf{T} \phi(\boldsymbol{x}'_m) \tag{2.303}$$

Since Equation (2.303) only involves inner products of the feature vectors, we can use the kernel trick (Section 18.2.5) to rewrite the above as follows:

$$\mathrm{MMD}^2(\mathcal{X}, \mathcal{X}') = \frac{1}{N^2} \sum_{n=1}^N \sum_{n'=1}^N \mathcal{K}(\boldsymbol{x}_n, \boldsymbol{x}_{n'}) - \frac{2}{NM} \sum_{n=1}^N \sum_{m=1}^M \mathcal{K}(\boldsymbol{x}_n, \boldsymbol{x}'_m) + \frac{1}{M^2} \sum_{m=1}^M \sum_{m'=1}^M \mathcal{K}(\boldsymbol{x}'_m, \boldsymbol{x}'_{m'})$$
$$\tag{2.304}$$

2.7.3.3 Linear time computation

The MMD takes $O(N^2)$ time to compute, where N is the number of samples from each distribution. In [Chw+15], they present a different test statistic called the **unnormalized mean embedding** or **UME**, that can be computed in $O(N)$ time.

The key idea is to notice that evaluating

$$\mathrm{witness}^2(\boldsymbol{v}) = (\boldsymbol{\mu}_Q(\boldsymbol{v}) - \boldsymbol{\mu}_P(\boldsymbol{v}))^2 \tag{2.305}$$

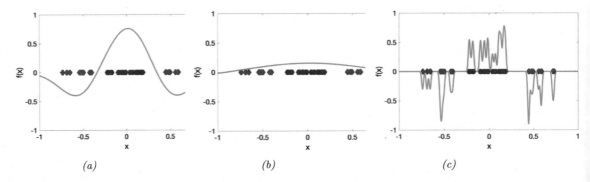

Figure 2.22: Effect of decreasing the bandwidth parameter σ on the witness function defined by a Gaussian kernel. From a figure from [GSJ19]. Used with kind permission of Dougal Sutherland.

at a set of test locations $v_1, \ldots, v_J$ is enough to detect a difference between P and Q. Hence we define the (squared) UME as follows:

$$\text{UME}^2(P, Q) = \frac{1}{J} \sum_{j=1}^{J} \left[\boldsymbol{\mu}_P(\boldsymbol{v}_j) - \boldsymbol{\mu}_Q(\boldsymbol{v}_j) \right]^2 \tag{2.306}$$

where $\boldsymbol{\mu}_P(\boldsymbol{v}) = \mathbb{E}_{p(\boldsymbol{x})}\left[\mathcal{K}(\boldsymbol{x}, \boldsymbol{v})\right]$ can be estimated empirically in $O(N)$ time, and similarly for $\boldsymbol{\mu}_Q(\boldsymbol{v})$.

A normalized version of UME, known as NME, is presented in [Jit+16]. By maximizing NME wrt the locations $\boldsymbol{v}_j$, we can maximize the statistical power of the test, and find locations where P and Q differ the most. This provides an interpretable two-sample test for high dimensional data.

2.7.3.4 Choosing the right kernel

The effectiveness of MMD (and UME) obviously crucially depends on the right choice of kernel. Even for distiguishing 1d samples, the choice of kernel can be very important. For example, consider a Gaussian kernel, $\mathcal{K}_\sigma(\boldsymbol{x}, \boldsymbol{x}') = \exp(-\frac{1}{2\sigma^2}||\boldsymbol{x} - \boldsymbol{x}'||^2)$. The effect of changing σ in terms of the ability to distinguish two different sets of 1d samples is shown in Figure 2.22. Fortunately, the MMD is differentiable wrt the kernel parameters, so we can choose the optimal σ^2 so as to maximize the power of the test [Sut+17]. (See also [Fla+16] for a Bayesian approach, which maximizes the marginal likelihood of a GP representation of the kernel mean embedding.)

For high-dimensional data such as images, it can be useful to use a pre-trained CNN model as a way to compute low-dimensional features. For example, we can define $\mathcal{K}(\boldsymbol{x}, \boldsymbol{x}') = \mathcal{K}_\sigma(\boldsymbol{h}(\boldsymbol{x}), \boldsymbol{h}(\boldsymbol{x}'))$, where $\boldsymbol{h}$ is some hidden layer of a CNN. such as the "inception" model of [Sze+15a]. The resulting MMD metric is known as the **kernel inception distance** [Biń+18]. This is similar to the **Fréchet inception distance** [Heu+17a], but has nicer statistical properties, and is better correlated with human perceptual judgement [Zho+19a].

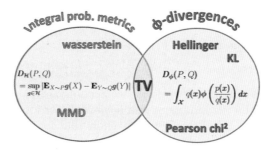

Figure 2.23: *Summary of the two main kinds of divergence measures between two probability distributions P and Q. From a figure from [GSJ19]. Used with kind permission of Arthur Gretton.*

2.7.4 Total variation distance

The **total variation distance** between two probability distributions is defined as follows:

$$D_{\text{TV}}(p, q) \triangleq \frac{1}{2}\|\boldsymbol{p} - \boldsymbol{q}\|_1 = \frac{1}{2}\int |p(\boldsymbol{x}) - q(\boldsymbol{x})|d\boldsymbol{x} \tag{2.307}$$

This is equal to an f-divergence where $f(r) = |r - 1|/2$, since

$$\frac{1}{2}\int q(\boldsymbol{x})|\frac{p(\boldsymbol{x})}{q(\boldsymbol{x})} - 1|d\boldsymbol{x} = \frac{1}{2}\int q(\boldsymbol{x})|\frac{p(\boldsymbol{x}) - q(\boldsymbol{x})}{q(\boldsymbol{x})}|d\boldsymbol{x} = \frac{1}{2}\int |p(\boldsymbol{x}) - q(\boldsymbol{x})|d\boldsymbol{x} \tag{2.308}$$

One can also show that the TV distance is an integral probability measure. In fact, it is the only divergence that is both an IPM and an f-divergence [Sri+09]. See Figure 2.23 for a visual summary.

2.7.5 Density ratio estimation using binary classifiers

In this section, we discuss a simple approach for comparing two distributions that turns out to be equivalent to IPMs and f-divergences.

Consider a binary classification problem in which points from P have label $y = 1$ and points from Q have label $y = 0$, i.e., $P(\boldsymbol{x}) = p(\boldsymbol{x}|y = 1)$ and $Q(\boldsymbol{x}) = p(\boldsymbol{x}|y = 0)$. Let $p(y = 1) = \pi$ be the class prior. By Bayes' rule, the density ratio $r(\boldsymbol{x}) = P(\boldsymbol{x})/Q(\boldsymbol{x})$ is given by

$$\frac{P(\boldsymbol{x})}{Q(\boldsymbol{x})} = \frac{p(\boldsymbol{x}|y = 1)}{p(\boldsymbol{x}|y = 0)} = \frac{p(y = 1|\boldsymbol{x})p(\boldsymbol{x})}{p(y = 1)} \Big/ \frac{p(y = 0|\boldsymbol{x})p(\boldsymbol{x})}{p(y = 0)} \tag{2.309}$$

$$= \frac{p(y = 1|\boldsymbol{x})}{p(y = 0|\boldsymbol{x})}\frac{1 - \pi}{\pi} \tag{2.310}$$

If we assume $\pi = 0.5$, then we can estimate the ratio $r(\boldsymbol{x})$ by fitting a binary classifier or discriminator $h(\boldsymbol{x}) = p(y = 1|\boldsymbol{x})$ and then computing $r = h/(1 - h)$. This is called the **density ratio estimation** or **DRE** trick.

We can optimize the classifer h by minimizing the risk (expected loss). For example, if we use log-loss, we have

$$R(h) = \mathbb{E}_{p(\boldsymbol{x}|y)p(y)} \left[-y \log h(\boldsymbol{x}) - (1 - y) \log(1 - h(\boldsymbol{x})) \right] \tag{2.311}$$

$$= \pi \mathbb{E}_{P(\boldsymbol{x})} \left[-\log h(\boldsymbol{x}) \right] + (1 - \pi) \mathbb{E}_{Q(\boldsymbol{x})} \left[-\log(1 - h(\boldsymbol{x})) \right] \tag{2.312}$$

We can also use other loss functions $\ell(y, h(\boldsymbol{x}))$ (see Section 26.2.2).

Let $R^\ell_{h*} = \inf_{h \in \mathcal{F}} R(h)$ be the minimum risk achievable for loss function ℓ, where we minimize over some function class $\mathcal{F}$.[11] In [NWJ09], they show that for every f-divergence, there is a loss function ℓ such that $-D_f(P, Q) = R^\ell_{h*}$. For example (using the notation $\tilde{y} \in \{-1, 1\}$ instead of $y \in \{0, 1\}$), total-variation distance corresponds to hinge loss, $\ell(\tilde{y}, h) = \max(0, 1 - \tilde{y}h)$; Hellinger distance corresponds to exponential loss, $\ell(\tilde{y}, h) = \exp(-\tilde{y}h)$; and χ^2 divergence corresponds to logistic loss, $\ell(\tilde{y}, h) = \log(1 + \exp(-\tilde{y}h))$.

We can also establish a connection between binary classifiers and IPMs [Sri+09]. In particular, let $\ell(\tilde{y}, h) = -2\tilde{y}h$, and $p(\tilde{y} = 1) = p(\tilde{y} = -1) = 0.5$. Then we have

$$R_{h*} = \inf_h \int \ell(\tilde{y}, h(\boldsymbol{x})) p(\boldsymbol{x}|\tilde{y}) p(\tilde{y}) d\boldsymbol{x} d\tilde{y} \tag{2.313}$$

$$= \inf_h 0.5 \int \ell(1, h(\boldsymbol{x})) p(\boldsymbol{x}|\tilde{y} = 1) d\boldsymbol{x} + 0.5 \int \ell(-1, h(\boldsymbol{x})) p(\boldsymbol{x}|\tilde{y} = -1) d\boldsymbol{x} \tag{2.314}$$

$$= \inf_h \int h(\boldsymbol{x}) Q(\boldsymbol{x}) d\boldsymbol{x} - \int h(\boldsymbol{x}) P(\boldsymbol{x}) d\boldsymbol{x} \tag{2.315}$$

$$= \sup_h - \int h(\boldsymbol{x}) Q(\boldsymbol{x}) d\boldsymbol{x} + \int h(\boldsymbol{x}) P(\boldsymbol{x}) d\boldsymbol{x} \tag{2.316}$$

which matches Equation (2.295). Thus the classifier plays the same role as the witness function.

---

11. If P is a fixed distribution, and we minimize the above objective wrt h, while also maximizing it wrt a model $Q(\boldsymbol{x})$, we recover a technique known as a generative adversarial network for fitting an implicit model to a distribution of samples P (see Chapter 26 for details). However, in this section, we assume Q is known.

3 Statistics

3.1 Introduction

Probability theory (which we discussed in Chapter 2) is concerned with modeling the distribution over observed data outcomes $\mathcal{D}$ given known parameters $\boldsymbol{\theta}$ by computing $p(\mathcal{D}|\boldsymbol{\theta})$. By contrast, **statistics** is concerned with the inverse problem, in which we want to infer the unknown parameters $\boldsymbol{\theta}$ given observations, i.e., we want to compute $p(\boldsymbol{\theta}|\mathcal{D})$. Indeed, statistics was originally called **inverse probability theory**. Nowadays, there are two main approaches to statistics, **frequentist statistics** and **Bayesian statistics**, as we discuss below. (See also Section 34.1, where we compare the frequentist and Bayesian approaches to decision theory.) Note, however, that most of this chapter (and the entire book) focuses on the Bayesian approach, for reasons that will become clear.

3.2 Bayesian statistics

In the Bayesian approach to statistics, we treat the parameters $\boldsymbol{\theta}$ as unknown, and the data $\mathcal{D}$ as fixed and known. (This is the opposite of the frequentist approach, which we discuss in Section 3.3.) We represent our uncertainty about the parameters, after (posterior to) seeing the data, by computing the **posterior distribution** using Bayes' rule:

$$p(\boldsymbol{\theta}|\mathcal{D}) = \frac{p(\boldsymbol{\theta})p(\mathcal{D}|\boldsymbol{\theta})}{p(\mathcal{D})} = \frac{p(\boldsymbol{\theta})p(\mathcal{D}|\boldsymbol{\theta})}{\int p(\boldsymbol{\theta}')p(\mathcal{D}|\boldsymbol{\theta}')d\boldsymbol{\theta}'} \tag{3.1}$$

Here $p(\boldsymbol{\theta})$ is called the **prior**, and represents our beliefs about the parameters before seeing the data; $p(\mathcal{D}|\boldsymbol{\theta})$ is called the **likelihood**, and represents our beliefs about what data we expect to see for each setting of the parameters; $p(\boldsymbol{\theta}|\mathcal{D})$ is called the posterior, and represents our beliefs about the parameters after seeing the data; and $p(\mathcal{D})$ is called the **marginal likelihood** or **evidence**, and is a normalization constant that we will use later.

The task of computing this posterior is called **Bayesian inference**, **posterior inference**, or just **inference**. We will give many examples in the following sections of this chapter, and will discuss algorithmic issues in Part II. For more details on Bayesian statistics, see e.g., [Ber97a; Hof09; Lam18; Kru15; McE20] for introductory level material, [Gel+14a; MKL21; GHV20a] for intermediate level material, and [BS94; Ber85b; Rob07] for more advanced theory.

3.2.1   Tossing coins

It is common to explain the key ideas behind Bayesian inference by considering a coin tossing experiment. We shall follow this tradition (although also see Supplementary Section 3.1 for an alternative gentle introduction to Bayes using the example of Bayesian concept learning.)

Let $\theta \in [0, 1]$ be the chance that some coin comes up heads, an event we denote by $Y = 1$. Suppose we toss a coin N times, and we record the outcomes as $\mathcal{D} = \{y_n \in \{0, 1\} : n = 1 : N\}$. We want to compute $p(\theta|\mathcal{D})$, which represents our beliefs about the parameter after doing collecting the data. To compute the posterior, we can use Bayes' rule, as in Equation (3.1). We give the details below.

3.2.1.1   Likelihood

We assume the data are **iid** or **independent and identically distributed**. Thus the likelihood has the form

$$p(\mathcal{D}|\theta) = \prod_{n=1}^{N} \theta^{y_n}(1 - \theta)^{1-y_n} = \theta^{N_1}(1 - \theta)^{N_0} \tag{3.2}$$

where we have defined $N_1 = \sum_{n=1}^{N} \mathbb{I}(y_n = 1)$ and $N_0 = \sum_{n=1}^{N} \mathbb{I}(y_n = 0)$, representing the number of heads and tails. These counts are called the **sufficient statistics** of the data, since this is all we need to know about $\mathcal{D}$ to infer θ. The total count, $N = N_0 + N_1$, is called the **sample size**.

Note that we can also consider a Binomial likelihood model, in which we perform N trials and observe the number of heads, y, rather than observing a sequence of coin tosses. Now the likelihood has the following form:

$$p(\mathcal{D}|\theta) = \mathrm{Bin}(y|N, \theta) = \binom{N}{y} \theta^y (1 - \theta)^{N-y} \tag{3.3}$$

The scaling factor $\binom{N}{y}$ is independent of θ, so we can ignore it. Thus this likelihood is proportional to the Bernoulli likelihood in Equation (3.2), so our inferences about θ will be the same for both models.

3.2.1.2   Prior

We also need to specify a prior. Let us assume we know nothing about the parameter, except that it lies in the interval $[0, 1]$. We can represent this **uninformative prior** using a uniform distribution,

$$p(\theta) = \mathrm{Unif}(\theta|0, 1) \tag{3.4}$$

More generally, we will write the prior using a **beta distribution** (Section 2.2.4.1), for reasons that will become clear shortly. That is, we assume

$$p(\theta) = \mathrm{Beta}(\theta|\, \breve{\alpha}, \breve{\beta}) \propto \theta^{\breve{\alpha}-1}(1 - \theta)^{\breve{\beta}-1} \tag{3.5}$$

Here $\breve{\alpha}$ and $\breve{\beta}$ are called **hyper-parameters**, since they are parameters of the prior which determine our beliefs about the "main" parameter θ. If we set $\breve{\alpha} = \breve{\beta} = 1$, we recover the uniform prior as a special case.

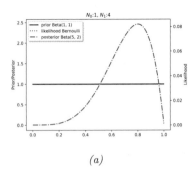
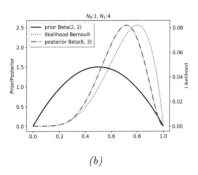

(a)	(b)

Figure 3.1: *Updating a Beta prior with a Bernoulli likelihood with sufficient statistics $N_1 = 4, N_0 = 1$. (a) Uniform Beta(1,1) prior. (a) Beta(2,2) prior. Generated by* beta_binom_post_plot.ipynb.

We can think of these hyper-parameters as **pseudocounts**, which play a role analogous to the empirical counts N_1 and N_0 derived from the real data. The strength of the prior is controlled by $\breve{N} = \breve{\alpha} + \breve{\beta}$; this is called the **equivalent sample size**, since it plays a role analogous to the observed sample size, $N = N_1 + N_0$.

3.2.1.3 Posterior

We can compute the posterior by multiplying the likelihood by the prior:

$$p(\theta|\mathcal{D}) \propto \theta^{N_1}(1-\theta)^{N_0}\, \theta^{\breve{\alpha}-1}(1-\theta)^{\breve{\beta}-1} \propto \text{Beta}(\theta|\ \breve{\alpha}+N_1, \breve{\beta}+N_0) = \text{Beta}(\theta|\ \widehat{\alpha}, \widehat{\beta}) \qquad (3.6)$$

where $\widehat{\alpha} \triangleq \breve{\alpha} + N_1$ and $\widehat{\beta} \triangleq \breve{\beta} + N_0$ are the parameters of the posterior. Since the posterior has the same functional form as the prior, we say that it is a **conjugate prior** (see Section 3.4 for more details).

For example, suppose we observe $N_1 = 4$ heads and $N_0 = 1$ tails. If we use a uniform prior, we get the posterior shown in Figure 3.1a. Not surprisingly, this has exactly the same shape as the likelihood (but is scaled to integrate to 1 over the range $[0, 1]$).

Now suppose we use a prior that has a slight preference for values of θ near to 0.5, reflecting our prior belief that it is more likely than not that the coin is fair. We will make this a weak prior by setting $\breve{\alpha} = \breve{\beta} = 2$. The effect of using this prior is illustrated in Figure 3.1b. We see the posterior (blue line) is a "compromise" between the prior (red line) and the likelihood (black line).

3.2.1.4 Posterior mode (MAP estimate)

The most probable value of the parameter is given by the MAP estimate

$$\hat{\theta}_{\text{map}} = \arg\max_\theta p(\theta|\mathcal{D}) = \arg\max_\theta \log p(\theta|\mathcal{D}) = \arg\max_\theta \log p(\theta) + \log p(\mathcal{D}|\theta) \qquad (3.7)$$

Using calculus, one can show that this is given by

$$\hat{\theta}_{\text{map}} = \frac{\breve{\alpha} + N_1 - 1}{\breve{\alpha} + N_1 - 1 + \breve{\beta} + N_0 - 1} \qquad (3.8)$$

If we use a uniform prior, $p(\theta) \propto 1$, the MAP estimate becomes the MLE, since $\log p(\theta) = 0$:

$$\hat{\theta}_{\mathrm{mle}} = \arg\max_{\theta} \log p(\mathcal{D}|\theta) = \frac{N_1}{N_1 + N_0} = \frac{N_1}{N} \tag{3.9}$$

This is intuitive and easy to compute. However, the MLE can be very misleading in the small sample setting. For example, suppose we toss the coins N times, but never see any heads, so $N_1 = 0$. In this case, we would estimate that $\hat{\theta} = 0$, which means we would not predict any future observations to be heads either. This is a very extreme estimate, that is likely due to insufficient data. We can solve this problem using a MAP estimate with a stronger prior. For example, if we use a Beta$(\theta|2, 2)$ prior, we get the estimate

$$\hat{\theta}_{\mathrm{map}} = \frac{N_1 + 1}{N_1 + 1 + N_0 + 1} = \frac{N_1 + 1}{N + 2} \tag{3.10}$$

This is called **add-one smoothing**.

3.2.1.5   Posterior mean

The posterior mode can be a poor summary of the posterior, since it corresponds to picking a single point from the entire distribution. The posterior mean is a more robust estimate, since it is a summary statistic derived by integrating over the distribution, $\bar{\theta} = \int \theta p(\theta|\mathcal{D})d\theta$. In the case of a beta posterior, $p(\theta|\mathcal{D}) = \mathrm{Beta}(\theta|\, \hat{\alpha}, \hat{\beta})$, the posterior mean is given by

$$\bar{\theta} \triangleq \mathbb{E}\left[\theta|\mathcal{D}\right] = \frac{\hat{\alpha}}{\hat{\beta} + \hat{\alpha}} = \frac{\hat{\alpha}}{\hat{N}} \tag{3.11}$$

where $\hat{N} = \hat{\beta} + \hat{\alpha}$ is the strength (equivalent sample size) of the posterior.

We will now show that the posterior mean is a convex combination of the prior mean, $m = \breve{\alpha} \,/\, \breve{N}$ and the MLE, $\hat{\theta}_{\mathrm{mle}} = \frac{N_1}{N}$:

$$\mathbb{E}\left[\theta|\mathcal{D}\right] = \frac{\breve{\alpha} + N_1}{\breve{\alpha} + N_1 + \breve{\beta} + N_0} = \frac{\breve{N}\, m + N_1}{N + \breve{N}} \tag{3.12}$$

$$= \frac{\breve{N}}{N + \breve{N}} m + \frac{N}{N + \breve{N}} \frac{N_1}{N} = \lambda m + (1 - \lambda)\hat{\theta}_{\mathrm{mle}} \tag{3.13}$$

where $\lambda = \frac{\breve{N}}{\hat{N}}$ is the ratio of the prior to posterior equivalent sample size. We see that the weaker the prior is, the smaller λ is, and hence the closer the posterior mean is to the MLE.

3.2.1.6   Posterior variance

To capture some notion of uncertainty in our estimate, a common approach is to compute the **standard error** of our estimate, which is just the posterior standard deviation:

$$\mathrm{se}(\theta) = \sqrt{\mathbb{V}\left[\theta|\mathcal{D}\right]} \tag{3.14}$$

In the case of the Bernoulli model, we showed that the posterior is a beta distribution. The variance of the beta posterior is given by

$$\mathbb{V}[\theta|\mathcal{D}] = \frac{\widehat{\alpha}\widehat{\beta}}{(\widehat{\alpha} + \widehat{\beta})^2(\widehat{\alpha} + \widehat{\beta} + 1)} = \frac{(\breve{\alpha} + N_1)(\breve{\beta} + N_0)}{(\breve{\alpha} + N_1 + \breve{\beta} + N_0)^2(\breve{\alpha} + N_1 + \breve{\beta} + N_0 + 1)} \tag{3.15}$$

If $N \gg \breve{\alpha} + \breve{\beta}$, this simplifies to

$$\mathbb{V}[\theta|\mathcal{D}] \approx \frac{N_1 N_0}{(N_1 + N_0)^2(N_1 + N_0)} = \frac{N_1}{N}\frac{N_0}{N}\frac{1}{N} = \frac{\hat{\theta}(1 - \hat{\theta})}{N} \tag{3.16}$$

where $\hat{\theta} = N_1/N$ is the MLE. Hence the standard error is given by

$$\sigma = \sqrt{\mathbb{V}[\theta|\mathcal{D}]} \approx \sqrt{\frac{\hat{\theta}(1 - \hat{\theta})}{N}} \tag{3.17}$$

We see that the uncertainty goes down at a rate of $1/\sqrt{N}$. We also see that the uncertainty (variance) is maximized when $\hat{\theta} = 0.5$, and is minimized when $\hat{\theta}$ is close to 0 or 1. This makes sense, since it is easier to be sure that a coin is biased than to be sure that it is fair.

3.2.1.7   Credible intervals

A posterior distribution is (usually) a high dimensional object that is hard to visualize and work with. A common way to summarize such a distribution is to compute a point estimate, such as the posterior mean or mode, and then to compute a **credible interval**, which quantifies the uncertainty associated with that estimate. (A credible interval is not the same as a confidence interval, which is a concept from frequentist statistics which we discuss in Section 3.3.5.1.)

More precisely, we define a $100(1 - \alpha)\%$ credible interval to be a (contiguous) region $C = (\ell, u)$ (standing for lower and upper) which contains $1 - \alpha$ of the posterior probability mass, i.e.,

$$C_\alpha(\mathcal{D}) = (\ell, u) : P(\ell \leq \theta \leq u|\mathcal{D}) = 1 - \alpha \tag{3.18}$$

There may be many intervals that satisfy Equation (3.18), so we usually choose one such that there is $(1 - \alpha)/2$ mass in each tail; this is called a **central interval**. If the posterior has a known functional form, we can compute the posterior central interval using $\ell = F^{-1}(\alpha/2)$ and $u = F^{-1}(1 - \alpha/2)$, where F is the cdf of the posterior, and F^{-1} is the inverse cdf. For example, if the posterior is Gaussian, $p(\theta|\mathcal{D}) = \mathcal{N}(0, 1)$, and $\alpha = 0.05$, then we have $\ell = \Phi^{-1}(\alpha/2) = -1.96$, and $u = \Phi^{-1}(1 - \alpha/2) = 1.96$, where Φ denotes the cdf of the Gaussian. This justifies the common practice of quoting a credible interval in the form of $\mu \pm 2\sigma$, where μ represents the posterior mean, σ represents the posterior standard deviation, and 2 is a good approximation to 1.96.

A problem with central intervals is that there might be points outside the central interval which have higher probability than points that are inside, as illustrated in Figure 3.2(a). This motivates an alternative quantity known as the **highest posterior density** or **HPD** region, which is the set of points which have a probability above some threshold. More precisely we find the threshold p^* on the pdf such that

$$1 - \alpha = \int_{\theta:p(\theta|\mathcal{D}) > p^*} p(\theta|\mathcal{D})d\theta \tag{3.19}$$

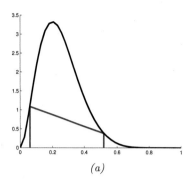
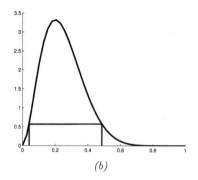

(a)   (b)

Figure 3.2: (a) Central interval and (b) HPD region for a Beta(3,9) posterior. The CI is (0.06, 0.52) and the HPD is (0.04, 0.48). Adapted from Figure 3.6 of [Hof09]. Generated by betaHPD.ipynb.

and then define the HPD as

$$C_\alpha(\mathcal{D}) = \{\theta : p(\theta|\mathcal{D}) \geq p^*\} \tag{3.20}$$

In 1d, the HPD region is sometimes called a **highest density interval** or **HDI**. For example, Figure 3.2(b) shows the 95% HDI of a Beta$(3, 9)$ distribution, which is $(0.04, 0.48)$. We see that this is narrower than the central interval, even though it still contains 95% of the mass; furthermore, every point inside of it has higher density than every point outside of it.

3.2.1.8   Posterior predictive distribution

Suppose we want to predict future observations. The optimal Bayesian approach is to compute the **posterior predictive distribution**, by marginalizing out all the unkown parameters:

$$p(\boldsymbol{y}|\mathcal{D}) = \int p(\boldsymbol{y}|\boldsymbol{\theta})p(\boldsymbol{\theta}|\mathcal{D})d\boldsymbol{\theta} \tag{3.21}$$

Sometimes computing this integral can be difficult (even if we already have access to the posterior). A common approximation is to just "**plug in**" a point estimate of the parameters, $\hat{\boldsymbol{\theta}} = \delta(\mathcal{D})$, where $\delta()$ is some estimator such as a method to compute the MLE or MAP, which gives

$$p(\boldsymbol{y}|\mathcal{D}) \approx p(\boldsymbol{y}|\hat{\boldsymbol{\theta}}) \tag{3.22}$$

This is called a **plugin approximation**. This is equivalent to modeling the posterior with a degenerate distribution centered at the point estimate

$$p(\boldsymbol{\theta}|\mathcal{D}) \approx \delta(\boldsymbol{\theta} - \hat{\boldsymbol{\theta}}) \tag{3.23}$$

where δ is the Dirac delta function. This follows from the **sifting property** of delta functions:

$$p(\boldsymbol{y}|\mathcal{D}) = \int p(\boldsymbol{y}|\boldsymbol{\theta})p(\boldsymbol{\theta}|\mathcal{D})d\boldsymbol{\theta} = \int p(\boldsymbol{y}|\boldsymbol{\theta})\delta(\boldsymbol{\theta} - \hat{\boldsymbol{\theta}})d\boldsymbol{\theta} = p(\boldsymbol{y}|\hat{\boldsymbol{\theta}}) \tag{3.24}$$

Unfortunately, the plugin approximation can result in overfitting. For example, consider the coin tossing example, and suppose we have seen $N = 3$ heads in a row. The MLE is $\hat{\theta} = 3/3 = 1$. However, if we use this estimate for prediction, we would predict that tails are impossible, and would be very surprised if one ever showed up.[1]

Instead of the plugin approximation, we can marginalize over all parameter values to compute the exact posterior predictive, as follows:

$$p(y = 1|\mathcal{D}) = \int_0^1 p(y = 1|\theta)p(\theta|\mathcal{D})d\theta \tag{3.25}$$

$$= \int_0^1 \theta \, \text{Beta}(\theta|\,\hat{\alpha}, \hat{\beta})d\theta = \mathbb{E}\left[\theta|\mathcal{D}\right] = \frac{\hat{\alpha}}{\hat{\alpha} + \hat{\beta}} \tag{3.26}$$

If we use a uniform prior, $p(\theta) = \text{Beta}(\theta|1, 1)$, the predictive distribution becomes

$$p(y = 1|\mathcal{D}) = \frac{N_1 + 1}{N_1 + N_0 + 2} \tag{3.27}$$

This is known as **Laplace's rule of succession**. Note that this is equivalent to plugging in the add-one smoothing estimate from Equation (3.10); however, that relied on the rather unnatural Beta(2,2) prior, whereas Laplace smoothing uses a uniform prior.

3.2.1.9 Marginal likelihood

The **marginal likelihood** or **evidence** for a model $\mathcal{M}$ is defined as

$$p(\mathcal{D}|\mathcal{M}) = \int p(\boldsymbol{\theta}|\mathcal{M})p(\mathcal{D}|\boldsymbol{\theta}, \mathcal{M})d\boldsymbol{\theta} \tag{3.28}$$

When performing inference for the parameters of a specific model, we can ignore this term, since it is constant wrt $\boldsymbol{\theta}$. However, this quantity plays a vital role when choosing between different models, as we discuss in Section 3.8.1. It is also useful for estimating the hyperparameters from data (an approach known as empirical Bayes), as we discuss in Section 3.7.

In general, computing the marginal likelihood can be hard. However, in the case of the beta-Bernoulli model, the marginal likelihood is proportional to the ratio of the posterior normalizer to the prior normalizer. To see this, recall that the posterior is given by $p(\theta|\mathcal{D}) = \text{Beta}(\theta|\,\hat{\alpha}, \hat{\beta})$, where $\hat{\alpha} = \breve{\alpha} + N_1$ and $\hat{\beta} = \breve{\beta} + N_0$. We know the normalization constant of the posterior is $B(\hat{\alpha}, \hat{\beta})$, where B is the beta function. Hence

$$p(\theta|\mathcal{D}) = \frac{p(\mathcal{D}|\theta)p(\theta)}{p(\mathcal{D})} = \frac{1}{p(\mathcal{D})} \left[\theta^{N_1}(1-\theta)^{N_0}\right] \left[\frac{1}{B(\breve{\alpha}, \breve{\beta})}\theta^{\breve{\alpha}-1}(1-\theta)^{\breve{\beta}-1}\right] \tag{3.29}$$

$$= \frac{1}{p(\mathcal{D})} \frac{1}{B(\breve{\alpha}, \breve{\beta})} \left[\theta^{\breve{\alpha}+N_1-1}(1-\theta)^{\breve{\beta}+N_0-1}\right] = \frac{1}{B(\hat{\alpha}, \hat{\beta})} \left[\theta^{\hat{\alpha}}(1-\theta)^{\hat{\beta}}\right] \tag{3.30}$$

So the marginal likelihood is given by the ratio of normalization constants for the posterior and prior:

$$p(\mathcal{D}) = \frac{B(\hat{\alpha}, \hat{\beta})}{B(\breve{\alpha}, \breve{\beta})} \tag{3.31}$$

---

1. This is analogous to a **black swan event**, which refers to the discovery of black swans by Dutch explorers when they first arrived in Australia in 1697, after only ever having seen white swans their entire lives (see `https://en.wikipedia.org/wiki/Black_swan_theory` for details).

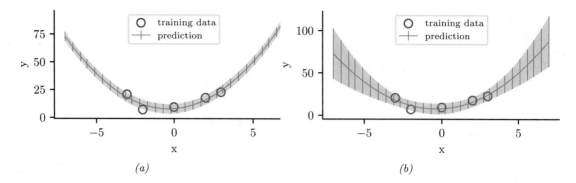

Figure 3.3: Predictions made by a polynomial regression model fit to a small dataset. (a) Plugin approximation to predictive density using the MLE. The curves shows the posterior mean, $\mathbb{E}\left[y|\boldsymbol{x}\right]$, and the error bars show the posterior standard deviation, $\mathrm{std}\left[y|\boldsymbol{x}\right]$, around this mean. (b) Bayesian posterior predictive density, obtained by integrating out the parameters. Generated by linreg_post_pred_plot.ipynb.

3.2.2 Modeling more complex data

In Section 3.2.1, we showed how the Bayesian approach can be applied to analyse a very simple model, namely a Bernoulli distribution for representing binary events such as coin tosses. The same basic ideas can be applied to more complex models. For example, in machine learning, we are often very interested in predicting outcomes $\boldsymbol{y}$ given input features $\boldsymbol{x}$. For this, we can use a conditional probability distribution of the form $p(\boldsymbol{y}|\boldsymbol{x},\boldsymbol{\theta})$, which can be a generalized linear model (Chapter 15), or a neural network (Chapter 16), etc.

The main quantity of interest is the **posterior predictive distribution**, given by

$$p(\boldsymbol{y}|\boldsymbol{x},\mathcal{D}) = \int p(\boldsymbol{y}|\boldsymbol{x},\boldsymbol{\theta})p(\boldsymbol{\theta}|\mathcal{D})d\boldsymbol{\theta} \tag{3.32}$$

By **integrating out**, or **marginalizing out**, the unknown parameters, we reduce the chance of overfitting, since we are effectively computing the weighted average of predictions from an infinite number of models. This act of integrating over uncertainty is at the heart of the Bayesian approach to machine learning. (Of course, the Bayesian approach requires a prior, but so too do methods that rely on regularization, so the prior is not so much the distinguishing aspect.)

It is worth contrasting the Bayesian approach to the more common **plugin approximation**, in which we compute a point estimate $\hat{\boldsymbol{\theta}}$ of the parameters (such as the MLE), and then plug them into the model to make predictions using $p(\boldsymbol{y}|\boldsymbol{x},\hat{\boldsymbol{\theta}})$. As we explained in Section 3.2.1.8, this is equivalent to approximate the posterior by a delta function, $p(\boldsymbol{\theta}|\mathcal{D}) \approx \delta(\boldsymbol{\theta} - \hat{\boldsymbol{\theta}})$, since

$$p(\boldsymbol{y}|\boldsymbol{x},\mathcal{D}) \approx \int p(\boldsymbol{y}|\boldsymbol{x},\boldsymbol{\theta})\delta(\boldsymbol{\theta} - \hat{\boldsymbol{\theta}})d\boldsymbol{\theta} = p(\boldsymbol{y}|\boldsymbol{x},\hat{\boldsymbol{\theta}}) \tag{3.33}$$

The plugin approximation is simple and widely used. However, it ignores uncertainty in the parameter estimates, which can result in an underestimate of the predictive uncertainty. For example, Figure 3.3a plots the plugin approximation $p(y|\boldsymbol{x},\hat{\boldsymbol{\theta}})$ for a linear regression model $p(y|\boldsymbol{x},\boldsymbol{\theta}) = \mathcal{N}(y|\hat{\boldsymbol{w}}_{\mathrm{mle}}^{\mathsf{T}}\boldsymbol{x},\hat{\sigma}_{\mathrm{mle}}^2)$, where we plug in the MLEs for $\boldsymbol{w}$ and σ^2. (See Section 15.2.1 for details on how to compute these MLEs.) We see that the size of the predicted variance is a constant (namely $\hat{\sigma}^2$).

The uncertainty captured by σ is called **aleatoric uncertainty** or **intrinsic uncertainty**, and would persist even if we knew the true model and true parameters. However, since we don't know the parameters, we have an additional, and orthogonal, source of uncertainty, called **epistemic uncertainty** (since it arises due to a lack of knowledge about the truth). In the Bayesian approach, we take this into account, which can be useful for applications such as active learning (Section 34.7), Bayesian optimization (Section 6.6), and risk-sensitive decision making (Section 34.1.3). The resulting Bayesian posterior predictive distribution for this example is shown in Figure 3.3b. We see that now the error bars get wider as we move away from the training data. For more details on Bayesian linear regression, see Section 15.2.

We can use similiar Bayesian methods for more complex nonlinear models such as neural nets, as we discuss in Section 17.1, as well as for unconditional generative models, as we discuss in Part IV.

3.2.3 Selecting the prior

A challenge with the Bayesian approach is that it requires the user to specify a prior, which may be difficult in large models, such as neural networks. We discuss the topic of prior selection at length later in this chapter. In particular, in Section 3.4, we discuss **conjugate priors**, which are computationally convenient; in Section 3.5, we discuss **uninformative priors**, which often correspond to a limit of a conjugate prior where we "know nothing"; in Section 3.6, we discuss **hierarchical priors**, which are useful when we have multiple related datasets; and in Section 3.7, we discuss **empirical priors**, which can be learned from the data.

3.2.4 Computational issues

Another challenge with the Bayesian approach is that it can be computationally expensive to compute the posterior and/or posterior predictive. We give an overview of suitable approximate posterior inference methods in Section 7.4, and discuss the topic at length in Part II. (See also [MFR20] for a historical review of this topic.)

3.2.5 Exchangeability and de Finetti's theorem

An interesting philosophical question is: where do priors come from, given that they refer to parameters which are just abstract quantities in a model, and not directly observable. A fundamental result, known as **de Finetti's theorem**, explains how they are related to our beliefs about observable outcomes.

To explain the result, we first need a definition. We say that a sequence of random variables $(\boldsymbol{x}_1, \boldsymbol{x}_2, \ldots)$ is **infinitely exchangeable** if, for any n, the joint probability $p(\boldsymbol{x}_1, \ldots, \boldsymbol{x}_n)$ is invariant to permutation of the indices. That is, for any permutation π, we have

$$p(\boldsymbol{x}_1, \ldots, \boldsymbol{x}_n) = p(\boldsymbol{x}_{\pi_1}, \ldots, \boldsymbol{x}_{\pi_n}) \tag{3.34}$$

Exchangeability is a more general concept compared to the more familiar concept of a sequence of independent, identically distributed or **iid** variables. For example, suppose $\mathcal{D} = (\boldsymbol{x}_1, \ldots, \boldsymbol{x}_n)$ is a sequence of images, where each $\boldsymbol{x}_i \sim p^*$ is generated independently from the same "true distribution" p^*. We see that this is an iid sequence. Now suppose $\boldsymbol{x}_0$ is a background image. The sequence $(\boldsymbol{x}_0 + \boldsymbol{x}_1, \ldots, \boldsymbol{x}_0 + \boldsymbol{x}_n)$ is infinitely exchangeable but not iid, since all the variables share a hidden common factor, namely the background $\boldsymbol{x}_0$. Thus the more examples we see, the better we will be able to estimate the shared $\boldsymbol{x}_0$, and thus the better we can predict future elements.

More generally, we can view an exchangeable sequence as coming from a hidden common cause, which we can treat as an unknown random variable $\boldsymbol{\theta}$. This is formalized by **de Finetti's theorem**:

Theorem 3.2.1 (de Finetti's theorem). *A sequence of random variables $(\boldsymbol{x}_1, \boldsymbol{x}_2, \ldots)$ is infinitely exchangeable iff, for all n, we have*

$$p(\boldsymbol{x}_1, \ldots, \boldsymbol{x}_n) = \int \prod_{i=1}^{n} p(\boldsymbol{x}_i|\boldsymbol{\theta})p(\boldsymbol{\theta})d\boldsymbol{\theta} \tag{3.35}$$

where $\boldsymbol{\theta}$ is some hidden common random variable (possibly infinite dimensional). That is, $\boldsymbol{x}_i$ are iid conditional on $\boldsymbol{\theta}$.

We often interpret $\boldsymbol{\theta}$ as a parameter. The theorem tells us that, if our data is exchangeable, then there must exist a parameter $\boldsymbol{\theta}$, and a likelihood $p(\boldsymbol{x}_i|\boldsymbol{\theta})$, and a prior $p(\boldsymbol{\theta})$. Thus the Bayesian approach follows automatically from exchangeability [O'N09]. (The approach can also be extended to conditional probability models using a concept called **partially exchangeable** [Dia88a].)

3.3   Frequentist statistics

Bayesian statistics, which we discussed in Section 3.2, treats parameters of models just like any other unknown random variable, and applies the rules of probability theory to infer them from data. Attempts have been made to devise approaches to statistical inference that avoid treating parameters like random variables, and which thus avoid the use of priors and Bayes rule. This alternative approach is known as **frequentist statistics**, **classical statistics** or **orthodox statistics**.

The basic idea (formalized in Section 3.3.1) is to to represent uncertainty by calculating how a quantity estimated from data (such as a parameter or a predicted label) would change if the data were changed. It is this notion of variation across repeated trials that forms the basis for modeling uncertainty used by the frequentist approach. By contrast, the Bayesian approach views probability in terms of information rather than repeated trials. This allows the Bayesian to compute the probability of one-off events, such as the probability that the polar ice cap will melt by 2030. In addition, the Bayesian approach avoids certain paradoxes that plague the frequentist approach (see Section 3.3.5), and which are a source of much confusion.

Despite the disadvantages of frequentist statistics, it is a widely used approach, and it has some concepts (such as cross validation, model checking and conformal prediction) that are useful even for Bayesians [Rub84]. Thus it is important to know some of the basic principles. We give a brief summary below of these principles below. For more details, see other texbooks, such as [Was04; Cox06; YS10; EH16].

3.3.1   Sampling distributions

In frequentist statistics, uncertainty is not represented by the posterior distribution of a random variable, but instead by the sampling distribution of an estimator. (We define these two terms below.)

As explained in the section on decision theory in Section 34.1.2, an **estimator** is a decision procedure that specifies what action to take given some observed data. In the context of parameter estimation, where the action space is to return a parameter vector, we will denote this by $\hat{\boldsymbol{\theta}} = \delta(\mathcal{D})$. For example, $\hat{\boldsymbol{\theta}}$ could be the maximum likelihood estimate, the MAP estimate, or the method of moments estimate.

The **sampling distribution** of an estimator is the distribution of results we would see if we applied the estimator multiple times to different datasets sampled from some distribution; in the context of parameter estimation, it is the distribution of $\hat{\boldsymbol{\theta}}$, viewed as a random variable that depends on the random sample $\mathcal{D}$. In more detail, imagine sampling S different data sets, each of size N, from some true model $p(\boldsymbol{x}|\boldsymbol{\theta}^*)$ to generate

$$\tilde{\mathcal{D}}^{(s)} = \{\boldsymbol{x}_n \sim p(\boldsymbol{x}_n|\boldsymbol{\theta}^*) : n = 1 : N\} \tag{3.36}$$

We denote this by $\tilde{\mathcal{D}}^{(s)} \sim \boldsymbol{\theta}^*$ for brevity. Now apply the estimator to each $\tilde{\mathcal{D}}^{(s)}$ to get a set of estimates, $\{\hat{\boldsymbol{\theta}}(\tilde{\mathcal{D}}^{(s)})\}$. As we let $S \to \infty$, the distribution induced by this set is the sampling distribution of the estimator. More precisely, we have

$$p(\delta(\tilde{\mathcal{D}}) = \boldsymbol{\theta}|\tilde{\mathcal{D}} \sim \boldsymbol{\theta}^*) \approx \frac{1}{S} \sum_{s=1}^{S} \delta(\boldsymbol{\theta} - \delta(\tilde{\mathcal{D}}^{(s)})) \tag{3.37}$$

We often approximate this by Monte Carlo, as we discuss in Section 3.3.2, although in some cases we can compute approximate it analytically, as we discuss in Section 3.3.3.

3.3.2 Bootstrap approximation of the sampling distribution

In cases where the estimator is a complex function of the data, or when the sample size is small, it is often useful to approximate its sampling distribution using a Monte Carlo technique known as the **bootstrap** [ET93].

The idea is simple. If we knew the true parameters $\boldsymbol{\theta}^*$, we could generate many (say S) fake datasets, each of size N, from the true distribution, using $\tilde{\mathcal{D}}^{(s)} = \{\boldsymbol{x}_n \sim p(\boldsymbol{x}_n|\boldsymbol{\theta}^*) : n = 1 : N\}$. We could then compute our estimate from each sample, $\hat{\boldsymbol{\theta}}^s = \delta(\tilde{\mathcal{D}}^{(s)})$ and use the empirical distribution of the resulting $\hat{\boldsymbol{\theta}}^s$ as our estimate of the sampling distribution, as in Equation (3.37). Since $\boldsymbol{\theta}^*$ is unknown, the idea of the **parametric bootstrap** is to generate each sampled dataset using $\hat{\boldsymbol{\theta}} = \delta(\mathcal{D})$ instead of $\boldsymbol{\theta}^*$, i.e., we use $\tilde{\mathcal{D}}^{(s)} = \{\boldsymbol{x}_n \sim p(\boldsymbol{x}_n|\hat{\boldsymbol{\theta}}) : n = 1 : N\}$ in Equation (3.37). This is a plug-in approximation to the sampling distribution.

The above approach requires that we have a parametric generative model for the data, $p(\boldsymbol{x}|\boldsymbol{\theta})$. An alternative, called the **non-parametric bootstrap**, is to sample N data points from the original dataset with replacement. This creates a new distribution $\mathcal{D}^{(s)}$ which has the same size as the original. However, the number of unique data points in a bootstrap sample is just $0.632 \times N$, on average. (To see this, note that the probability an item is picked at least once is $(1 - (1 - 1/N)^N)$, which approaches $1 - e^{-1} \approx 0.632$ for large N.) Fortunately, various improved versions of the bootstrap have been developed (see e.g., [ET93]).

Figure 3.4(a-b) shows an example where we compute the sampling distribution of the MLE for a Bernoulli using the parametric bootstrap. (Results using the non-parametric bootstrap are essentially the same.) When $N = 10$, we see that the sampling distribution is asymmetric, and therefore quite far from Gaussian, but when $N = 100$, the distribution looks more Gaussian, as theory suggests (see Section 3.3.3).

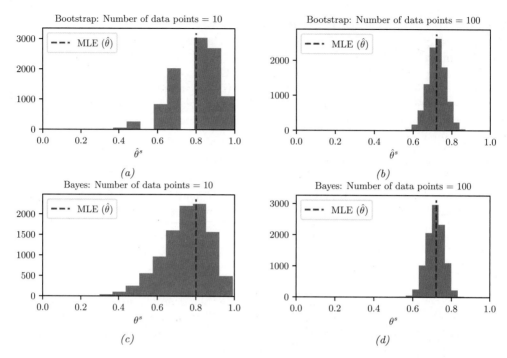

Figure 3.4: Bootstrap (top row) vs Bayes (bottom row). The N data cases were generated from $\mathrm{Ber}(\theta = 0.7)$. *Left column:* $N = 10$. *Right column:* $N = 100$. *(a-b) A bootstrap approximation to the sampling distribution of the MLE for a Bernoulli distribution. We show the histogram derived from* $B = 10{,}000$ *bootstrap samples. (c-d) Histogram of 10,000 samples from the posterior distribution using a uniform prior. Generated by* bootstrap_demo_bernoulli.ipynb.

A natural question is: what is the connection between the parameter estimates $\hat{\boldsymbol{\theta}}^s = \delta(\mathcal{D}^{(s)})$ computed by the bootstrap and parameter values sampled from the posterior, $\boldsymbol{\theta}^s \sim p(\cdot|\mathcal{D})$? Conceptually they are quite different. But in the common case that the estimator is MLE and the prior is not very strong, they can be quite similar. For example, Figure 3.4(c-d) shows an example where we compute the posterior using a uniform $\mathrm{Beta}(1,1)$ prior, and then sample from it. We see that the posterior and the sampling distribution are quite similar. So one can think of the bootstrap distribution as a "poor man's" posterior [HTF01, p235].

However, perhaps surprisingly, bootstrap can be slower than posterior sampling. The reason is that the bootstrap has to generate S sampled datasets, and then fit a model to each one. By contrast, in posterior sampling, we only have to "fit" a model once given a single dataset. (Some methods for speeding up the bootstrap when applied to massive data sets are discussed in [Kle+11].)

3.3.3   Asymptotic normality of the sampling distribution of the MLE

The most common estimator is the MLE. When the sample size becomes large, the sampling distribution of the MLE for certain models becomes Gaussian. This is known as the **asymptotic normality** of the sampling distribution. More formally, we have the following result:

Theorem 3.3.1. *Under various technical conditions, we have*

$$\sqrt{N}(\hat{\boldsymbol{\theta}} - \boldsymbol{\theta}^*) \to \mathcal{N}(\mathbf{0}, \mathbf{F}(\boldsymbol{\theta}^*)^{-1}) \tag{3.38}$$

where $\mathbf{F}(\boldsymbol{\theta}^*)$ *is the Fisher information matrix, defined in Equation* (3.40), $\boldsymbol{\theta}^*$ *are the parameters of the data generating process to which the estimator will be applied, and* $\to$ *means convergence in distribution.*

The Fisher information matrix equals the Hessian of the log likelihood, as we show in Section 3.3.4, so $\mathbf{F}(\boldsymbol{\theta}^*)$ measures the amount of curvature of the log-likelihood surface at the true parameter value. Thus we can intepret this theorem as follows: as the sample size goes to infinity, the sampling distribution of the MLE will converge to a Gaussian centered on the true parameter, with a precision equal to the Fisher information. Thus a problem with an informative (peaked) likelihood will ensure that the parameters are "well determined" by the data, and hence there will be little variation in the estimates $\hat{\boldsymbol{\theta}}$ around $\boldsymbol{\theta}^*$ as this estimator is applied across different datasets $\tilde{\mathcal{D}}$.

3.3.4 Fisher information matrix

In this section, we discuss an important quantity called the **Fisher information matrix**, which is related to the curvature of the log likelihood function. This plays a key role in frequentist statistics, for characterizing the sampling distribution of the MLE, discussed in Section 3.3.3. However, it is also used in Bayesian statistics (to derive Jeffreys' uninformative priors, discussed in Section 3.5.2), as well as in optimization (as part of the natural gradient descent, procedure, discussed in Section 6.4).

3.3.4.1 Definition

The **score function** is defined to be the gradient of the log likelihood:

$$\boldsymbol{s}(\boldsymbol{\theta}) \triangleq \nabla \log p(\boldsymbol{x}|\boldsymbol{\theta}) \tag{3.39}$$

The **Fisher information matrix (FIM)** is defined to be the covariance of the score function:

$$\mathbf{F}(\boldsymbol{\theta}) \triangleq \mathbb{E}_{\boldsymbol{x} \sim p(\boldsymbol{x}|\boldsymbol{\theta})} \left[\nabla \log p(\boldsymbol{x}|\boldsymbol{\theta}) \nabla \log p(\boldsymbol{x}|\boldsymbol{\theta})^{\mathsf{T}} \right] \tag{3.40}$$

so the (i, j)'th entry has the form

$$F_{ij} = \mathbb{E}_{\boldsymbol{x} \sim \boldsymbol{\theta}} \left[\left(\frac{\partial}{\partial \theta_i} \log p(\boldsymbol{x}|\boldsymbol{\theta}) \right) \left(\frac{\partial}{\partial \theta_j} \log p(\boldsymbol{x}|\boldsymbol{\theta}) \right) \right] \tag{3.41}$$

We give an interpretation of this quantity below.

3.3.4.2 Equivalence between the FIM and the Hessian of the NLL

In this section, we prove that the Fisher information matrix equals the expected Hessian of the negative log likelihood (NLL)

$$\mathrm{NLL}(\boldsymbol{\theta}) = -\log p(\mathcal{D}|\boldsymbol{\theta}) \tag{3.42}$$

Since the Hessian measures the curvature of the likelihood, we see that the FIM tells us how well the likelihood function can identify the best set of parameters. (If a likelihood function is flat, we cannot infer anything about the parameters, but if it is a delta function at a single point, the best parameter vector will be uniquely determined.) Thus the FIM is intimately related to the frequentist notion of uncertainty of the MLE, which is captured by the variance we expect to see in the MLE if we were to compute it on multiple different datasets drawn from our model.

   More precisely, we have the following theorem.

Theorem 3.3.2. *If* $\log p(\boldsymbol{x}|\boldsymbol{\theta})$ *is twice differentiable, and under certain regularity conditions, the FIM is equal to the expected Hessian of the NLL, i.e.,*

$$\mathbf{F}(\boldsymbol{\theta})_{ij} \triangleq \mathbb{E}_{\boldsymbol{x}\sim\boldsymbol{\theta}}\left[\left(\frac{\partial}{\partial\theta_i}\log p(\boldsymbol{x}|\boldsymbol{\theta})\right)\left(\frac{\partial}{\partial\theta_j}\log p(\boldsymbol{x}|\boldsymbol{\theta})\right)\right] = \mathbb{E}_{\boldsymbol{x}\sim\boldsymbol{\theta}}\left[\frac{\partial^2}{\partial\theta_i\theta_j}\log p(\boldsymbol{x}|\boldsymbol{\theta})\right] \tag{3.43}$$

   Before we prove this result, we establish the following important lemma.

Lemma 3.3.1. *The expected value of the score function is zero, i.e.,*

$$\mathbb{E}_{p(\boldsymbol{x}|\boldsymbol{\theta})}\left[\nabla\log p(\boldsymbol{x}|\boldsymbol{\theta})\right] = \mathbf{0} \tag{3.44}$$

   We prove this lemma in the scalar case. First, note that since $\int p(x|\theta)dx = 1$, we have

$$\frac{\partial}{\partial\theta}\int p(x|\theta)dx = 0 \tag{3.45}$$

Combining this with the identity

$$\frac{\partial}{\partial\theta}p(x|\theta) = \left[\frac{\partial}{\partial\theta}\log p(x|\theta)\right]p(x|\theta) \tag{3.46}$$

we have

$$0 = \int \frac{\partial}{\partial\theta}p(x|\theta)dx = \int\left[\frac{\partial}{\partial\theta}\log p(x|\theta)\right]p(x|\theta)dx = \mathbb{E}\left[s(\theta)\right] \tag{3.47}$$

   Now we return to the proof of our main theorem. For simplicity, we will focus on the scalar case, following the presentation of [Ric95, p263].

Proof. Taking derivatives of Equation (3.47), we have

$$0 = \frac{\partial}{\partial\theta}\int\left[\frac{\partial}{\partial\theta}\log p(x|\theta)\right]p(x|\theta)dx \tag{3.48}$$

$$= \int\left[\frac{\partial^2}{\partial\theta^2}\log p(x|\theta)\right]p(x|\theta)dx + \int\left[\frac{\partial}{\partial\theta}\log p(x|\theta)\right]\frac{\partial}{\partial\theta}p(x|\theta)dx \tag{3.49}$$

$$= \int\left[\frac{\partial^2}{\partial\theta^2}\log p(x|\theta)\right]p(x|\theta)dx + \int\left[\frac{\partial}{\partial\theta}\log p(x|\theta)\right]^2 p(x|\theta)dx \tag{3.50}$$

and hence

$$-\mathbb{E}_{x\sim\theta}\left[\frac{\partial^2}{\partial\theta^2}\log p(x|\theta)\right] = \mathbb{E}_{x\sim\theta}\left[\left(\frac{\partial}{\partial\theta}\log p(x|\theta)\right)^2\right] \tag{3.51}$$

as claimed. $\square$

Now consider the Hessian of the NLL given N iid samples $\mathcal{D} = \{\boldsymbol{x}_n : n = 1 : N\}$:

$$H_{ij} \triangleq -\frac{\partial^2}{\partial \theta_i \theta_j} \log p(\mathcal{D}|\boldsymbol{\theta}) = -\sum_{n=1}^{N} \frac{\partial^2}{\partial \theta_i \theta_j} \log p(\boldsymbol{x}_n|\boldsymbol{\theta}) \tag{3.52}$$

From the above theorem, we have

$$\mathbb{E}_{p(\mathcal{D}|\boldsymbol{\theta})} [\mathbf{H}(\mathcal{D})|\boldsymbol{\theta}] = N\mathbf{F}(\boldsymbol{\theta}) \tag{3.53}$$

This is useful when deriving the sampling distribution of the MLE, as discussed in Section 3.3.3.

3.3.4.3   Example: FIM for the binomial

Suppose $x \sim \text{Bin}(n, \theta)$. The log likelihood for a single sample is

$$l(\theta|x) = x \log \theta + (n - x) \log(1 - \theta) \tag{3.54}$$

The score function is just the gradient of the log-likelihood:

$$s(\theta|x) \triangleq \frac{d}{d\theta} l(\theta|x) = \frac{x}{\theta} - \frac{n - x}{1 - \theta} \tag{3.55}$$

The gradient of the score function is

$$s'(\theta|x) = -\frac{x}{\theta^2} - \frac{n - x}{(1 - \theta)^2} \tag{3.56}$$

Hence the Fisher information is given by

$$F(\theta) = \mathbb{E}_{x \sim \theta} [-s'(\theta|x)] = \frac{n\theta}{\theta^2} + \frac{n - n\theta}{(1 - \theta)^2} = \frac{n}{\theta} + \frac{n}{1 - \theta} = \frac{n}{\theta(1 - \theta)} \tag{3.57}$$

3.3.4.4   Example: FIM for the univariate Gaussian

Consider a univariate Gaussian $p(x|\boldsymbol{\theta}) = \mathcal{N}(x|\mu, v)$. We have

$$\ell(\boldsymbol{\theta}) = \log p(x|\boldsymbol{\theta}) = -\frac{1}{2v}(x - \mu)^2 - \frac{1}{2} \log(v) - \frac{1}{2} \log(2\pi) \tag{3.58}$$

The partial derivatives are given by

$$\frac{\partial \ell}{\partial \mu} = (x - \mu)v^{-1}, \quad \frac{\partial^2 \ell}{\partial \mu^2} = -v^{-1} \tag{3.59}$$

$$\frac{\partial \ell}{\partial v} = \frac{1}{2} v^{-2}(x - \mu)^2 - \frac{1}{2} v^{-1}, \quad \frac{\partial \ell}{\partial v^2} = -v^{-3}(x - \mu)^2 + \frac{1}{2} v^{-2} \tag{3.60}$$

$$\frac{\partial \ell}{\partial \mu \partial v} = -v^{-2}(x - \mu) \tag{3.61}$$

and hence

$$\mathbf{F}(\boldsymbol{\theta}) = \begin{pmatrix} \mathbb{E}\left[v^{-1}\right] & \mathbb{E}\left[v^{-2}(x - \mu)\right] \\ \mathbb{E}\left[v^{-2}(x - \mu)\right] & \mathbb{E}\left[v^{-3}(x - \mu)^2 - \frac{1}{2}v^{-2}\right] \end{pmatrix} = \begin{pmatrix} \frac{1}{v} & 0 \\ 0 & \frac{1}{2v^2} \end{pmatrix} \tag{3.62}$$

3.3.4.5 Example: FIM for logistic regression

Consider ℓ_2-regularized binary logistic regression. The negative log joint has the following form:

$$\mathcal{E}(\boldsymbol{w}) = -\log[p(\boldsymbol{y}|\mathbf{X}, \boldsymbol{w})p(\boldsymbol{w}|\lambda)] = -\boldsymbol{w}^\mathsf{T}\mathbf{X}^\mathsf{T}\boldsymbol{y} + \sum_{n=1}^{N} \log(1 + e^{\boldsymbol{w}^\mathsf{T}\boldsymbol{x}_n}) + \frac{\lambda}{2}\boldsymbol{w}^\mathsf{T}\boldsymbol{w} \tag{3.63}$$

The derivative has the form

$$\nabla_{\boldsymbol{w}}\mathcal{E}(\boldsymbol{w}) = -\mathbf{X}^\mathsf{T}\boldsymbol{y} + \mathbf{X}^\mathsf{T}\boldsymbol{s} + \lambda\boldsymbol{w} \tag{3.64}$$

where $s_n = \sigma(\boldsymbol{w}^\mathsf{T}\boldsymbol{x}_n)$. The FIM is given by

$$\mathbf{F}(\boldsymbol{w}) = \mathbb{E}_{p(\boldsymbol{y}|\mathbf{X},\boldsymbol{w},\lambda)}\left[\nabla^2\mathcal{E}(\boldsymbol{w})\right] = \mathbf{X}^\mathsf{T}\boldsymbol{\Lambda}\mathbf{X} + \lambda\mathbf{I} \tag{3.65}$$

where $\boldsymbol{\Lambda}$ is the $N \times N$ diagonal matrix with entries

$$\Lambda_{nn} = \sigma(\boldsymbol{w}^\mathsf{T}\boldsymbol{x}_n)(1 - \sigma(\boldsymbol{w}^\mathsf{T}\boldsymbol{x}_n)) \tag{3.66}$$

3.3.4.6 FIM for the exponential family

In this section, we discuss how to derive the FIM for an exponential family distribution with natural parameters $\boldsymbol{\eta}$, which generalizes many of the previous examples. Recall from Equation (2.216) that the gradient of the log partition function is the expected sufficient statistics

$$\nabla_{\boldsymbol{\eta}}A(\boldsymbol{\eta}) = \mathbb{E}\left[\mathcal{T}(\boldsymbol{x})\right] = \boldsymbol{m} \tag{3.67}$$

and from Equation (2.247) that the gradient of the log likelihood is the statistics minus their expected value:

$$\nabla_{\boldsymbol{\eta}} \log p(\boldsymbol{x}|\boldsymbol{\eta}) = \mathcal{T}(\boldsymbol{x}) - \mathbb{E}\left[\mathcal{T}(\boldsymbol{x})\right] \tag{3.68}$$

Hence the FIM wrt the natural parameters $\mathbf{F}_{\boldsymbol{\eta}}$ is given by

$$(\mathbf{F}_{\boldsymbol{\eta}})_{ij} = \mathbb{E}_{p(\boldsymbol{x}|\boldsymbol{\eta})}\left[\frac{\partial \log p(\boldsymbol{x}|\boldsymbol{\eta})}{\partial \eta_i}\frac{\partial \log p(\boldsymbol{x}|\boldsymbol{\eta})}{\partial \eta_j}\right] \tag{3.69}$$

$$= \mathbb{E}_{p(\boldsymbol{x}|\boldsymbol{\eta})}\left[(\mathcal{T}(\boldsymbol{x})_i - m_i)(\mathcal{T}(\boldsymbol{x})_j - m_j)\right] \tag{3.70}$$

$$= \text{Cov}\left[\mathcal{T}(\boldsymbol{x})_i, \mathcal{T}(\boldsymbol{x})_j\right] \tag{3.71}$$

or, in short,

$$\mathbf{F}_{\boldsymbol{\eta}} = \text{Cov}\left[\mathcal{T}(\boldsymbol{x})\right] \tag{3.72}$$

Sometimes we need to compute the Fisher wrt the moment parameters $\boldsymbol{m}$:

$$(\mathbf{F}_{\boldsymbol{m}})_{ij} = \mathbb{E}_{p(\boldsymbol{x}|\boldsymbol{m})}\left[\frac{\partial \log p(\boldsymbol{x}|\boldsymbol{\eta})}{\partial m_i}\frac{\partial \log p(\boldsymbol{x}|\boldsymbol{\eta})}{\partial m_j}\right] \tag{3.73}$$

From the chain rule we have

$$\frac{\partial \log p(x)}{\partial \alpha} = \frac{\partial \log p(x)}{\partial \beta} \frac{\partial \beta}{\partial \alpha} \tag{3.74}$$

and hence

$$\mathbf{F}_{\alpha} = \frac{\partial \boldsymbol{\beta}}{\partial \boldsymbol{\alpha}}^{\mathsf{T}} \mathbf{F}_{\beta} \frac{\partial \boldsymbol{\beta}}{\partial \boldsymbol{\alpha}} \tag{3.75}$$

Using the log trick

$$\nabla \mathbb{E}_{p(\boldsymbol{x})}\left[f(\boldsymbol{x})\right] = \mathbb{E}_{p(\boldsymbol{x})}\left[f(\boldsymbol{x})\nabla \log p(\boldsymbol{x})\right] \tag{3.76}$$

and Equation (3.68) we have

$$\frac{\partial m_i}{\partial \eta_j} = \frac{\partial \mathbb{E}\left[\mathcal{T}(\boldsymbol{x})_i\right]}{\partial \eta_j} = \mathbb{E}\left[\mathcal{T}(\boldsymbol{x})_i \frac{\partial \log p(\boldsymbol{x}|\boldsymbol{\eta})}{\partial \eta_j}\right] = \mathbb{E}\left[\mathcal{T}(\boldsymbol{x})_i(\mathcal{T}(\boldsymbol{x})_j - m_j)\right] \tag{3.77}$$

$$= \mathbb{E}\left[\mathcal{T}(\boldsymbol{x})_i \mathcal{T}(\boldsymbol{x})_j\right] - \mathbb{E}\left[\mathcal{T}(\boldsymbol{x})_i\right] m_j = \text{Cov}\left[\mathcal{T}(\boldsymbol{x})_i \mathcal{T}(\boldsymbol{x})_j\right] = (\mathbf{F}_{\boldsymbol{\eta}})_{ij} \tag{3.78}$$

and hence

$$\frac{\partial \boldsymbol{\eta}}{\partial \boldsymbol{m}} = \mathbf{F}_{\boldsymbol{\eta}}^{-1} \tag{3.79}$$

so

$$\mathbf{F}_{\boldsymbol{m}} = \frac{\partial \boldsymbol{\eta}}{\partial \boldsymbol{m}}^{\mathsf{T}} \mathbf{F}_{\boldsymbol{\eta}} \frac{\partial \boldsymbol{\eta}}{\partial \boldsymbol{m}} = \mathbf{F}_{\boldsymbol{\eta}}^{-1} \mathbf{F}_{\boldsymbol{\eta}} \mathbf{F}_{\boldsymbol{\eta}}^{-1} = \mathbf{F}_{\boldsymbol{\eta}}^{-1} = \text{Cov}\left[\mathcal{T}(\boldsymbol{x})\right]^{-1} \tag{3.80}$$

3.3.5 Counterintuitive properties of frequentist statistics

Although the frequentist approach to statistics is widely taught, it suffers from certain pathological properties, resulting in its often being misunderstood and/or misused, as has been pointed out in multiple articles (see e.g., [Bol02; Bri12; Cla21; Gel16; Hoe+14; Jay03; Kru10; Lav00; Lyu+20; Min99; Mac03; WG17]). We give some examples below.

3.3.5.1 Confidence intervals

In frequentist statistics, we use the variability induced by the sampling distribution as a way to estimate uncertainty of a parameter estimate. In particular, we define a $100(1 - \alpha)\%$ **confidence interval** as any interval $I(\tilde{\mathcal{D}}) = (\ell(\tilde{\mathcal{D}}), u(\tilde{\mathcal{D}}))$ derived from a hypothetical dataset $\tilde{\mathcal{D}}$ such that

$$\Pr(\theta \in I(\tilde{\mathcal{D}})|\tilde{\mathcal{D}} \sim \theta) = 1 - \alpha \tag{3.81}$$

It is common to set $\alpha = 0.05$, which yields a 95% CI. This means that, if we repeatedly sampled data, and compute $I(\tilde{\mathcal{D}})$ for each such dataset, then about 95% of such intervals will contain the true parameter θ. We say that the CI has 95% **coverage**.

Note, however, that Equation (3.81) does *not* mean that for any particular dataset that $\theta \in I(\mathcal{D})$ with 95% probability, which is what a Bayesian credible interval computes (Section 3.2.1.7), and which is what most people are usually interested in. So we see that the concept of frequentist CI and Bayesian CI are quite different: In the frequentist approach, θ is treated as an unknown fixed constant, and the data is treated as random. In the Bayesian approach, we treat the data as fixed (since it is known) and the parameter as random (since it is unknown).

This counter-intuitive definition of confidence intervals can lead to bizarre results. Consider the following example from [Ber85a, p11]. Suppose we draw two integers $\mathcal{D} = (y_1, y_2)$ from

$$p(y|\theta) = \begin{cases} 0.5 & \text{if } y = \theta \\ 0.5 & \text{if } y = \theta + 1 \\ 0 & \text{otherwise} \end{cases} \tag{3.82}$$

If $\theta = 39$, we would expect the following outcomes each with probability 0.25:

$$(39, 39), (39, 40), (40, 39), (40, 40) \tag{3.83}$$

Let $m = \min(y_1, y_2)$ and define the following interval:

$$[\ell(\mathcal{D}), u(\mathcal{D})] = [m, m] \tag{3.84}$$

For the above samples this yields

$$[39, 39], \quad [39, 39], \quad [39, 39], \quad [40, 40] \tag{3.85}$$

Hence Equation (3.84) is clearly a 75% CI, since 39 is contained in 3/4 of these intervals. However, if we observe $\mathcal{D} = (39, 40)$ then $p(\theta = 39|\mathcal{D}) = 1.0$, so we know that θ must be 39, yet we only have 75% "confidence" in this fact. We see that the CI will "cover" the true parameter 75% of the time, if we compute multiple CIs from different randomly sampled datasets, but if we just have a single observed dataset, and hence a single CI, then the frequentist "coverage" probability can be very misleading.

Several more interesting examples, along with Python code, can be found at [Van14]. See also [Hoe+14; Mor+16; Lyu+20; Cha+19b], who show that many people, including professional statisticians, misunderstand and misuse frequentist confidence intervals in practice, whereas Bayesian credible intervals do not suffer from these problems.

3.3.5.2   p-values

The frequentist approach to hypothesis testing, known as **null hypothesis significance testing** or **NHST**, is to define a decision procedure for deciding whether to accept or reject the **null hypothesis** H_0 based on whether some observed **test statistic** $t(\mathcal{D})$ is likely or not under the sampling distribution of the null model. We describe this procedure in more detail in Section 3.10.1.

Rather than accepting or rejecting the null hypothesis, we can compute a quantity related to how likely the null hypothesis is to be true. In particular, we can compute a quantity called a **p-value**, which is defined as

$$\text{pval}(t(\mathcal{D})) \triangleq \Pr(t(\tilde{\mathcal{D}}) \geq t(\mathcal{D})|\tilde{\mathcal{D}} \sim H_0) \tag{3.86}$$

where $\tilde{\mathcal{D}} \sim H_0$ is hypothetical future data. That is, the p-value is just the tail probability of observing the value $t(\mathcal{D})$ under the sampling distribution. (Note that the p-value does not explicitly depend on a model of the data, but most common test statistics implicitly define a model, as we discuss in Section 3.10.3.)

A p-value is often interpreted as the likelihood of the data under the null hypothesis, so small values are interpreted to mean that H_0 is unlikely, and therefore that H_1 is likely. The reasoning is roughly as follows:

> If H_0 is true, then this test statistic would probably not occur. This statistic did occur. Therefore H_0 is probably false.

However, this is invalid reasoning. To see why, consider the following example (from [Coh94]):

> If a person is an American, then he is probably not a member of Congress. This person is a member of Congress. Therefore he is probably not an American.

This is obviously fallacious reasoning. By contrast, the following logical argument is valid reasoning:

> If a person is a Martian, then he is not a member of Congress. This person is a member of Congress. Therefore he is not a Martian.

The difference between these two cases is that the Martian example is using **deduction**, that is, reasoning forward from logical definitions to their consequences. More precisely, this example uses a rule from logic called **modus tollens**, in which we start out with a definition of the form $P \Rightarrow Q$; when we observe $\neg Q$, we can conclude $\neg P$. By contrast, the American example concerns **induction**, that is, reasoning backwards from observed evidence to probable (but not necessarily true) causes using statistical regularities, not logical definitions.

To perform induction, we need to use probabilistic inference (as explained in detail in [Jay03]). In particular, to compute the probability of the null hypothesis, we should use Bayes rule, as follows:

$$p(H_0|\mathcal{D}) = \frac{p(\mathcal{D}|H_0)p(H_0)}{p(\mathcal{D}|H_0)p(H_0) + p(\mathcal{D}|H_1)p(H_1)} \tag{3.87}$$

If the prior is uniform, so $p(H_0) = p(H_1) = 0.5$, this can be rewritten in terms of the **likelihood ratio** $LR = p(\mathcal{D}|H_0)/p(\mathcal{D}|H_1)$ as follows:

$$p(H_0|\mathcal{D}) = \frac{LR}{LR + 1} \tag{3.88}$$

In the American Congress example, $\mathcal{D}$ is the observation that the person is a member of Congress. The null hypothesis H_0 is that the person is American, and the alternative hypothesis H_1 is that the person is not American. We assume that $p(\mathcal{D}|H_0)$ is low, since most Americans are not members of Congress. However, $p(\mathcal{D}|H_1)$ is also low — in fact, in this example, it is 0, since only Americans can be members of Congress. Hence $LR = \infty$, so $p(H_0|\mathcal{D}) = 1.0$, as intuition suggests.

Note, however, that NHST ignores $p(\mathcal{D}|H_1)$ as well as the prior $p(H_0)$, so it gives the wrong results, not just in this problem, but in many problems. Indeed, even most scientists misinterpret p-values.[2]. Consequently the journal *The American Statistician* published a whole special issue warning about the use of p-values and NHST [WSL19], and several journals have even banned p-values [TM15; AGM19].

---

2. See e.g., https://fivethirtyeight.com/features/not-even-scientists-can-easily-explain-p-values/.

3.3.5.3 Discussion

The above problems stem from the fact that frequentist inference is not conditional on the actually observed data, but instead is based on properties derived from the sampling distribution of the estimator. However, conditional probability statements are what most people want. As Jim Berger writes in [Ber85a]:

> Users of statistics want to know the probability (after seeing the data) that a hypothesis is true, or the probability that θ is in a given interval, and yet classical statistics does not allow one to talk of such things. Instead, artificial concepts such as error probabilities and coverage probabilites are introduced as substitutes. It is ironic that non-Bayesians often claim that the Bayesians form a dogmatic unrealistic religion, when instead it is the non-Bayesian methods that are often founded on elaborate and artificial structures. Unfortunately, those who become used to these artificial structures come to view them as natural, and hence this line of argument tends to have little effect on the established non-Bayesian. – Jim Berger, [Ber85a].

3.3.6 Why isn't everyone a Bayesian?

> I believe that it would be very difficult to persuade an intelligent person that current [frequentist] statistical practice was sensible, but that there would be much less difficulty with an approach via likelihood and Bayes' theorem. — George Box, 1962 (quoted in [Jay76]).

In Section 3.3.5 we showed that inference based on frequentist principles can exhibit various forms of counterintuitive behavior that can sometimes contradict common sense. Given these problems of frequentist statistics, an obvious question to ask is: "Why isn't everyone a Bayesian?" The statistician Bradley Efron wrote a paper with exactly this title [Efr86]. His short paper is well worth reading for anyone interested in this topic. Below we quote his opening section:

> The title is a reasonable question to ask on at least two counts. First of all, everyone used to be a Bayesian. Laplace wholeheartedly endorsed Bayes's formulation of the inference problem, and most 19th-century scientists followed suit. This included Gauss, whose statistical work is usually presented in frequentist terms.
>
> A second and more important point is the cogency of the Bayesian argument. Modern statisticians, following the lead of Savage and de Finetti, have advanced powerful theoretical arguments for preferring Bayesian inference. A byproduct of this work is a disturbing catalogue of inconsistencies in the frequentist point of view.
>
> Nevertheless, everyone is not a Bayesian. The current era (1986) is the first century in which statistics has been widely used for scientific reporting, and in fact, 20th-century statistics is mainly non-Bayesian. However, Lindley (1975) predicts a change for the 21st century.

Time will tell whether Lindley was right. However, the trends seem to be going in this direction. Traditionally, computation has been a barrier to using Bayesian methods, but this is less of an issue these days, due to faster computers and better algorithms, which we discuss in Part II.

Another, more fundamental, concern is that the Bayesian approach is only as correct as its modeling assumptions. In particular, it is important to check sensitivity of the conclusions to the choice of prior (and likelihood), using techniques such as Bayesian model checking (Section 3.9.1). In particular, as

Donald Rubin wrote in his paper called "Bayesianly Justifiable and Relevant Frequency Calculations for the Applied Statistician" [Rub84]:

> The applied statistician should be Bayesian in principle and calibrated to the real world in practice. [They] should attempt to use specifications that lead to approximately calibrated procedures under reasonable deviations from [their assumptions]. [They] should avoid models that are contradicted by observed data in relevant ways — frequency calculations for hypothetical replications can model a model's adequacy and help to suggest more appropriate models.

A final issue is more practical. Most users of statistical methods are not experts in statistics, but instead are experts in their own domain, such as psychology or social science. They often just want a simple (and fast!) method for testing a hypothesis, and so they turn to standard "cookie cutter" frequentist procedures, such as t-tests and χ^2-tests. Fortunately there are simple Bayesian alternatives to these tests, as we discuss in Section 3.10, which avoid the conceptual problems we discussed in Section 3.3.5, and which can also be easily "upgraded" to use more complex (and realistic) modeling assumptions when necessary. Furthermore, by using an empirical Bayes approach, it is possible to derive automatic and robust Bayesian methods that have good frequentist properties but which are also conditional on the data, thus providing the best of both worlds.

For a more detailed discussion of the pros and cons of the Bayesian approach, specifically in the context of machine learning, see `https://bit.ly/3Rbd4lo` and `https://bit.ly/3j8miSR`.

3.4 Conjugate priors

In this section, we consider Bayesian inference for a class of models with a special form of prior, known as a **conjugate prior**, which simplifies the computation of the posterior. Formally, we say that a prior $p(\boldsymbol{\theta}) \in \mathcal{F}$ is a conjugate prior for a likelihood function $p(\mathcal{D}|\boldsymbol{\theta})$ if the posterior is in the same parameterized family as the prior, i.e., $p(\boldsymbol{\theta}|\mathcal{D}) \in \mathcal{F}$. In other words, $\mathcal{F}$ is closed under Bayesian updating. If the family $\mathcal{F}$ corresponds to the exponential family (defined in Section 2.4), then the computations can be performed in closed form. In more complex settings, we cannot perform closed-form inference, but we can often leverage these results as tractable subroutines inside of a larger computational pipeline.

3.4.1 The binomial model

One of the simplest examples of conjugate Bayesian analysis is the beta-binomial model. This is covered in detail in Section 3.2.1.

3.4.2 The multinomial model

In this section, we generalize the results from Section 3.4.1 from binary variables (e.g., coins) to K-ary variables (e.g., dice). Let $y \sim \mathrm{Cat}(\boldsymbol{\theta})$ be a discrete random variable drawn from a **categorical distribution**. The likelihood has the form

$$p(\mathcal{D}|\boldsymbol{\theta}) = \prod_{n=1}^{N} \mathrm{Cat}(y_n|\boldsymbol{\theta}) = \prod_{n=1}^{N} \prod_{c=1}^{C} \theta_c^{\mathbb{I}(y_n=c)} = \prod_{c=1}^{C} \theta_c^{N_c} \tag{3.89}$$

where $N_c = \sum_n \mathbb{I}(y_n = c)$. We can generalize this to the **multinomial distribution** by defining $\boldsymbol{y} \sim \mathcal{M}(N, \boldsymbol{\theta})$, where N is the number of trials, and $y_c = N_c$ is the number of times value c is observed. The likelihood becomes

$$p(\boldsymbol{y}|N, \boldsymbol{\theta}) = \binom{N}{N_1 \ldots N_C} \prod_{c=1}^{C} \theta_c^{N_c} \tag{3.90}$$

This is the same as the categorical likelihood modulo a scaling factor. Going forwards, we will work with the categorical model, for notational simplicity.

The conjugate prior for a categorical distribution is the Dirichlet distribution, which we discussed in Section 2.2.5.7. We denote this by $p(\boldsymbol{\theta}) = \mathrm{Dir}(\boldsymbol{\theta}|\, \breve{\boldsymbol{\alpha}})$, where $\breve{\boldsymbol{\alpha}}$ is the vector of prior pseudo-counts. Often we use a symmetric Dirichlet prior of the form $\breve{\alpha}_k = \breve{\alpha}/K$. In this case, we have $\mathbb{E}[\theta_k] = 1/K$, and $\mathbb{V}[\theta_k] = \frac{K-1}{K^2(\breve{\alpha}+1)}$. Thus we see that increasing the prior sample size $\breve{\alpha}$ decreases the variance of the prior, which is equivalent to using a stronger prior.

We can combine the multinomial likelihood and Dirichlet prior to compute the Dirichlet posterior, as follows:

$$p(\boldsymbol{\theta}|\mathcal{D}) \propto p(\mathcal{D}|\boldsymbol{\theta})\mathrm{Dir}(\boldsymbol{\theta}|\, \breve{\boldsymbol{\alpha}}) \propto \left[\prod_k \theta_k^{N_k}\right]\left[\prod_k \theta_k^{\breve{\alpha}_k - 1}\right] \tag{3.91}$$

$$\propto \mathrm{Dir}(\boldsymbol{\theta}|\, \breve{\alpha}_1 + N_1, \ldots, \breve{\alpha}_K + N_K) = \mathrm{Dir}(\boldsymbol{\theta}|\, \widehat{\boldsymbol{\alpha}}) \tag{3.92}$$

where $\widehat{\alpha}_k = \breve{\alpha}_k + N_k$ are the parameters of the posterior. So we see that the posterior can be computed by adding the empirical counts to the prior counts. In particular, the posterior mode is given by

$$\hat{\theta}_k = \frac{\widehat{\alpha}_k - 1}{\sum_{k'=1}^{K} \widehat{\alpha}_k - 1} = \frac{N_k + \breve{\alpha}_k - 1}{\sum_{k'=1}^{K} N_k + \breve{\alpha}_k - 1} \tag{3.93}$$

If we set $\alpha_k = 1$ we recover the MLE; if we set $\alpha_k = 2$, we recover the add-one smoothing estimate.

The marginal likelihood for the Dirichlet-categorical model is given by the following:

$$p(\mathcal{D}) = \frac{B(\mathbf{N} + \boldsymbol{\alpha})}{B(\boldsymbol{\alpha})} \tag{3.94}$$

where

$$B(\boldsymbol{\alpha}) = \frac{\prod_{k=1}^{K} \Gamma(\alpha_k)}{\Gamma(\sum_k \alpha_k)} \tag{3.95}$$

Hence we can rewrite the above result in the following form, which is what is usually presented in the literature:

$$p(\mathcal{D}) = \frac{\Gamma(\sum_k \alpha_k)}{\Gamma(N + \sum_k \alpha_k)} \prod_k \frac{\Gamma(N_k + \alpha_k)}{\Gamma(\alpha_k)} \tag{3.96}$$

For more details on this model, see [Mur22, Sec 4.6.3].

3.4.3 The univariate Gaussian model

In this section, we derive the posterior $p(\mu, \sigma^2|\mathcal{D})$ for a univariate Gaussian. For simplicity, we consider this in three steps: inferring just μ, inferring just σ^2, and then inferring both. See Section 3.4.4 for the multivariate case.

3.4.3.1 Posterior of μ given σ^2

If σ^2 is a known constant, the likelihood for μ has the form

$$p(\mathcal{D}|\mu) \propto \exp\left(-\frac{1}{2\sigma^2}\sum_{n=1}^{N}(y_n - \mu)^2\right) \tag{3.97}$$

One can show that the conjugate prior is another Gaussian, $\mathcal{N}(\mu|\,\breve{m}, \breve{\tau}^2)$. Applying Bayes' rule for Gaussians (Equation (2.121)), we find that the corresponding posterior is given by

$$p(\mu|\mathcal{D}, \sigma^2) = \mathcal{N}(\mu|\,\hat{m}, \hat{\tau}^2) \tag{3.98}$$

$$\hat{\tau}^2 = \frac{1}{\frac{N}{\sigma^2} + \frac{1}{\breve{\tau}^2}} = \frac{\sigma^2\,\breve{\tau}^2}{N\,\breve{\tau}^2 + \sigma^2} \tag{3.99}$$

$$\hat{m} = \hat{\tau}^2\left(\frac{\breve{m}}{\breve{\tau}^2} + \frac{N\overline{y}}{\sigma^2}\right) = \frac{\sigma^2}{N\,\breve{\tau}^2 + \sigma^2}\,\breve{m} + \frac{N\,\breve{\tau}^2}{N\,\breve{\tau}^2 + \sigma^2}\overline{y} \tag{3.100}$$

where $\overline{y} \triangleq \frac{1}{N}\sum_{n=1}^{N} y_n$ is the empirical mean.

This result is easier to understand if we work in terms of the precision parameters, which are just inverse variances. Specifically, let $\lambda = 1/\sigma^2$ be the observation precision, and $\breve{\lambda} = 1/\breve{\tau}^2$ be the precision of the prior. We can then rewrite the posterior as follows:

$$p(\mu|\mathcal{D}, \lambda) = \mathcal{N}(\mu|\,\hat{m}, \hat{\lambda}^{-1}) \tag{3.101}$$

$$\hat{\lambda} = \breve{\lambda} + N\lambda \tag{3.102}$$

$$\hat{m} = \frac{N\lambda\overline{y} + \breve{\lambda}\breve{m}}{\hat{\lambda}} = \frac{N\lambda}{N\lambda + \breve{\lambda}}\overline{y} + \frac{\breve{\lambda}}{N\lambda + \breve{\lambda}}\breve{m} \tag{3.103}$$

These equations are quite intuitive: the posterior precision $\hat{\lambda}$ is the prior precision $\breve{\lambda}$ plus N units of measurement precision λ. Also, the posterior mean $\hat{m}$ is a convex combination of the empirical mean $\overline{y}$ and the prior mean $\breve{m}$. This makes it clear that the posterior mean is a compromise between the empirical mean and the prior. If the prior is weak relative to the signal strength ($\breve{\lambda}$ is small relative to λ), we put more weight on the empirical mean. If the prior is strong relative to the signal strength ($\breve{\lambda}$ is large relative to λ), we put more weight on the prior. This is illustrated in Figure 3.5. Note also that the posterior mean is written in terms of $N\lambda\overline{x}$, so having N measurements each of precision λ is like having one measurement with value $\overline{x}$ and precision $N\lambda$.

To gain further insight into these equations, consider the posterior after seeing a single datapoint

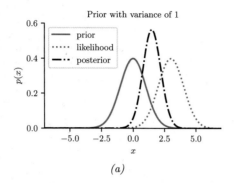
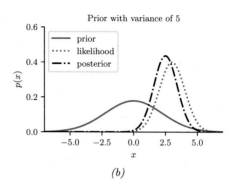

(a)   (b)

Figure 3.5: *Inferring the mean of a univariate Gaussian with known σ^2. (a) Using strong prior, $p(\mu) = \mathcal{N}(\mu|0, 1)$. (b) Using weak prior, $p(\mu) = \mathcal{N}(\mu|0, 5)$. Generated by gauss_infer_1d.ipynb.*

y (so $N = 1$). Then the posterior mean can be written in the following equivalent ways:

$$\hat{m} = \frac{\breve{\lambda}}{\hat{\lambda}}\,\breve{m} + \frac{\lambda}{\hat{\lambda}}y \tag{3.104}$$

$$= \breve{m} + \frac{\lambda}{\hat{\lambda}}(y - \breve{m}) \tag{3.105}$$

$$= y - \frac{\breve{\lambda}}{\hat{\lambda}}(y - \breve{m}) \tag{3.106}$$

The first equation is a convex combination of the prior mean and the data. The second equation is the prior mean adjusted towards the data y. The third equation is the data adjusted towards the prior mean; this is called a **shrinkage** estimate. This is easier to see if we define the weight $w = \breve{\lambda}/\hat{\lambda}$. Then we have

$$\hat{m} = y - w(y - \breve{m}) = (1 - w)y + w\,\breve{m} \tag{3.107}$$

Note that, for a Gaussian, the posterior mean and posterior mode are the same. Thus we can use the above equations to perform MAP estimation.

3.4.3.2 Posterior of σ^2 given μ

If μ is a known constant, the likelihood for σ^2 has the form

$$p(\mathcal{D}|\sigma^2) \propto (\sigma^2)^{-N/2} \exp\left(-\frac{1}{2\sigma^2}\sum_{n=1}^{N}(y_n - \mu)^2\right) \tag{3.108}$$

where we can no longer ignore the $1/(\sigma^2)$ term in front. The standard conjugate prior is the inverse gamma distribution (Section 2.2.3.4), given by

$$\text{IG}(\sigma^2|\,\breve{a}, \breve{b}) = \frac{\breve{b}^{\breve{a}}}{\Gamma(\breve{a})}(\sigma^2)^{-(\breve{a}+1)}\exp(-\frac{\breve{b}}{\sigma^2}) \tag{3.109}$$

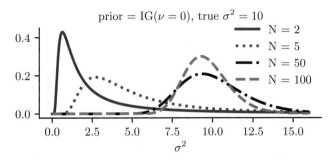

Figure 3.6: Sequential updating of the posterior for σ^2 starting from an uninformative prior. The data was generated from a Gaussian with known mean $\mu = 5$ and unknown variance $\sigma^2 = 10$. Generated by gauss_seq_update_sigma_1d.ipynb

Multiplying the likelihood and the prior, we see that the posterior is also IG:

$$p(\sigma^2|\mu, \mathcal{D}) = \mathrm{IG}(\sigma^2|\,\hat{a}, \hat{b}) \tag{3.110}$$

$$\hat{a} = \breve{a} + N/2 \tag{3.111}$$

$$\hat{b} = \breve{b} + \frac{1}{2}\sum_{n=1}^{N}(y_n - \mu)^2 \tag{3.112}$$

See Figure 3.6 for an illustration.

One small annoyance with using the $\mathrm{IG}(\breve{a}, \breve{b})$ distribution is that the strength of the prior is encoded in both $\breve{a}$ and $\breve{b}$. Therefore, in the Bayesian statistics literature it is common to use an alternative parameterization of the IG distribution, known as the (scaled) **inverse chi-squared distribution**:

$$\chi^{-2}(\sigma^2|\,\breve{\nu}, \breve{\tau}^2) = \mathrm{IG}(\sigma^2|\frac{\breve{\nu}}{2}, \frac{\breve{\nu}\,\breve{\tau}^2}{2}) \propto (\sigma^2)^{-\breve{\nu}/2-1}\exp(-\frac{\breve{\nu}\,\breve{\tau}^2}{2\sigma^2}) \tag{3.113}$$

Here $\breve{\nu}$ (called the degrees of freedom or dof parameter) controls the strength of the prior, and $\breve{\tau}^2$ encodes the prior mean. With this prior, the posterior becomes

$$p(\sigma^2|\mathcal{D}, \mu) = \chi^{-2}(\sigma^2|\,\hat{\nu}, \hat{\tau}^2) \tag{3.114}$$

$$\hat{\nu} = \breve{\nu} + N \tag{3.115}$$

$$\hat{\tau}^2 = \frac{\breve{\nu}\,\breve{\tau}^2 + \sum_{n=1}^{N}(y_n - \mu)^2}{\hat{\nu}} \tag{3.116}$$

We see that the posterior dof $\hat{\nu}$ is the prior dof $\breve{\nu}$ plus N, and the posterior sum of squares $\hat{\nu}\hat{\tau}^2$ is the prior sum of squares $\breve{\nu}\breve{\tau}^2$ plus the data sum of squares.

3.4.3.3 Posterior of μ and σ^2: conjugate prior

Now suppose we want to infer both the mean and variance. The corresponding conjugate prior is the **normal inverse gamma**:

$$\mathrm{NIG}(\mu, \sigma^2|\,\breve{m}, \breve{\kappa}, \breve{a}, \breve{b}) \triangleq \mathcal{N}(\mu|\,\breve{m}, \sigma^2/\,\breve{\kappa})\,\mathrm{IG}(\sigma^2|\,\breve{a}, \breve{b}) \tag{3.117}$$

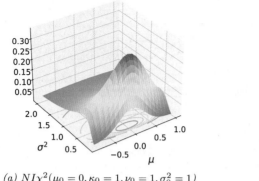 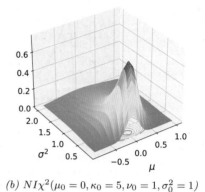

(a) $NI\chi^2(\mu_0 = 0, \kappa_0 = 1, \nu_0 = 1, \sigma_0^2 = 1)$ (b) $NI\chi^2(\mu_0 = 0, \kappa_0 = 5, \nu_0 = 1, \sigma_0^2 = 1)$

Figure 3.7: *The $NI\chi^2(\mu, \sigma^2|m, \kappa, \nu, \sigma^2)$ distribution. m is the prior mean and κ is how strongly we believe this; σ^2 is the prior variance and ν is how strongly we believe this. (a) $m = 0, \kappa = 1, \nu = 1, \sigma^2 = 1$. Notice that the contour plot (underneath the surface) is shaped like a "squashed egg". (b) We increase the strength of our belief in the mean by setting $\kappa = 5$, so the distribution for μ around $m = 0$ becomes narrower. Generated by nix_plots.ipynb.*

However, it is common to use a reparameterization of this known as the **normal inverse chi-squared** or **NIX** distribution [Gel+14a, p67], which is defined by

$$NI\chi^2(\mu, \sigma^2| \breve{m}, \breve{\kappa}, \breve{\nu}, \breve{\tau}^2) \triangleq \mathcal{N}(\mu| \breve{m}, \sigma^2/ \breve{\kappa}) \; \chi^{-2}(\sigma^2| \breve{\nu}, \breve{\tau}^2) \tag{3.118}$$

$$\propto (\frac{1}{\sigma^2})^{(\breve{\nu}+3)/2} \exp \left(-\frac{\breve{\nu}\breve{\tau}^2 + \breve{\kappa} \, (\mu - \breve{m})^2}{2\sigma^2} \right) \tag{3.119}$$

See Figure 3.7 for some plots. Along the μ axis, the distribution is shaped like a Gaussian, and along the σ^2 axis, the distribution is shaped like a χ^{-2}; the contours of the joint density have a "squashed egg" appearance. Interestingly, we see that the contours for μ are more peaked for small values of σ^2, which makes sense, since if the data is low variance, we will be able to estimate its mean more reliably.

One can show (based on Section 3.4.4.3) that the posterior is given by

$$p(\mu, \sigma^2|\mathcal{D}) = NI\chi^2(\mu, \sigma^2| \hat{m}, \hat{\kappa}, \hat{\nu}, \hat{\tau}^2) \tag{3.120}$$

$$\hat{m} = \frac{\breve{\kappa}\breve{m} + N\bar{x}}{\hat{\kappa}} \tag{3.121}$$

$$\hat{\kappa} = \breve{\kappa} + N \tag{3.122}$$

$$\hat{\nu} = \breve{\nu} + N \tag{3.123}$$

$$\hat{\nu}\hat{\tau}^2 = \breve{\nu}\breve{\tau}^2 + \sum_{n=1}^{N} (y_n - \bar{y})^2 + \frac{N \breve{\kappa}}{\breve{\kappa} + N}(\breve{m} - \bar{y})^2 \tag{3.124}$$

The interpretation of this is as follows. For μ, the posterior mean $\hat{m}$ is a convex combination of the prior mean $\breve{m}$ and the MLE $\bar{x}$; the strength of this posterior, $\hat{\kappa}$, is the prior strength $\breve{\kappa}$ plus the number of datapoints N. For σ^2, we work instead with the sum of squares: the posterior sum of squares, $\hat{\nu}\hat{\tau}^2$, is the prior sum of squares $\breve{\nu}\breve{\tau}^2$ plus the data sum of squares, $\sum_{n=1}^{N}(y_n - \bar{y})^2$, plus a term due to the discrepancy between the prior mean $\breve{m}$ and the MLE $\bar{y}$. The strength of this posterior, $\hat{\nu}$, is the prior strength $\breve{\nu}$ plus the number of datapoints N;

The posterior marginal for σ^2 is just

$$p(\sigma^2|\mathcal{D}) = \int p(\mu, \sigma^2|\mathcal{D})d\mu = \chi^{-2}(\sigma^2| \,\hat{\nu}, \hat{\tau}^2) \tag{3.125}$$

with the posterior mean given by $\mathbb{E}\left[\sigma^2|\mathcal{D}\right] = \frac{\hat{\nu}}{\hat{\nu}-2}\,\hat{\tau}^2$.

The posterior marginal for μ has a Student distribution, which follows from the fact that the Student distribution is a (scaled) mixture of Gaussians:

$$p(\mu|\mathcal{D}) = \int p(\mu, \sigma^2|D)d\sigma^2 = \mathcal{T}(\mu| \,\hat{m}, \hat{\tau}^2 \,/\, \hat{\kappa}, \hat{\nu}) \tag{3.126}$$

with the posterior mean given by $\mathbb{E}\left[\mu|\mathcal{D}\right] = \hat{m}$.

3.4.3.4 Posterior of μ and σ^2: uninformative prior

If we "know nothing" about the parameters a priori, we can use an uninformative prior. We discuss how to create such priors in Section 3.5. A common approach is to use a Jeffreys prior. In Section 3.5.2.3, we show that the Jeffreys prior for a location and scale parameter has the form

$$p(\mu, \sigma^2) \propto p(\mu)p(\sigma^2) \propto \sigma^{-2} \tag{3.127}$$

We can simulate this with a conjugate prior by using

$$p(\mu, \sigma^2) = NI\chi^2(\mu, \sigma^2| \,\breve{m}= 0, \breve{\kappa}= 0, \breve{\nu}= -1, \breve{\tau}^2= 0) \tag{3.128}$$

With this prior, the posterior has the form

$$p(\mu, \sigma^2|\mathcal{D}) = NI\chi^2(\mu, \sigma^2| \,\hat{m}= \bar{y}, \hat{\kappa}= N, \hat{\nu}= N - 1, \hat{\tau}^2= s^2) \tag{3.129}$$

where

$$s^2 \triangleq \frac{1}{N-1}\sum_{n=1}^{N}(y_n - \bar{y})^2 = \frac{N}{N-1}\hat{\sigma}^2_{\text{mle}} \tag{3.130}$$

s is known as the **sample standard deviation**. Hence the marginal posterior for the mean is given by

$$p(\mu|\mathcal{D}) = \mathcal{T}(\mu|\bar{y}, \frac{s^2}{N}, N - 1) = \mathcal{T}(\mu|\bar{y}, \frac{\sum_{n=1}^{N}(y_n - \bar{y})^2}{N(N-1)}, N - 1) \tag{3.131}$$

Thus the posterior variance of μ is

$$\mathbb{V}\left[\mu|\mathcal{D}\right] = \frac{\hat{\nu}}{\hat{\nu}-2}\,\hat{\tau}^2= \frac{N-1}{N-3}\frac{s^2}{N} \to \frac{s^2}{N} \tag{3.132}$$

The square root of this is called the **standard error of the mean**:

$$se(\mu) \triangleq \sqrt{\mathbb{V}\left[\mu|\mathcal{D}\right]} \approx \frac{s}{\sqrt{N}} \tag{3.133}$$

Thus we can approximate the 95% **credible interval** for μ using

$$I_{.95}(\mu|\mathcal{D}) = \overline{y} \pm 2\frac{s}{\sqrt{N}} \tag{3.134}$$

3.4.4   The multivariate Gaussian model

In this section, we derive the posterior $p(\boldsymbol{\mu}, \boldsymbol{\Sigma}|\mathcal{D})$ for a multivariate Gaussian. For simplicity, we consider this in three steps: inferring just $\boldsymbol{\mu}$, inferring just $\boldsymbol{\Sigma}$, and then inferring both.

3.4.4.1   Posterior of μ given Σ

The likelihood has the form

$$p(\mathcal{D}|\boldsymbol{\mu}) = \mathcal{N}(\overline{\boldsymbol{y}}|\boldsymbol{\mu}, \frac{1}{N}\boldsymbol{\Sigma}) \tag{3.135}$$

For simplicity, we will use a conjugate prior, which in this case is a Gaussian. In particular, if $p(\boldsymbol{\mu}) = \mathcal{N}(\boldsymbol{\mu}|\ \breve{\boldsymbol{m}}, \breve{\boldsymbol{V}})$ then we can derive a Gaussian posterior for $\boldsymbol{\mu}$ based on the results in Section 2.3.2.2 We get

$$p(\boldsymbol{\mu}|\mathcal{D}, \boldsymbol{\Sigma}) = \mathcal{N}(\boldsymbol{\mu}|\ \widehat{\boldsymbol{m}}, \widehat{\boldsymbol{V}}) \tag{3.136}$$

$$\widehat{\boldsymbol{V}}^{-1} = \breve{\boldsymbol{V}}^{-1} + N\boldsymbol{\Sigma}^{-1} \tag{3.137}$$

$$\widehat{\boldsymbol{m}} = \widehat{\boldsymbol{V}}\ (\boldsymbol{\Sigma}^{-1}(N\overline{\boldsymbol{y}}) + \breve{\boldsymbol{V}}^{-1}\breve{\boldsymbol{m}}) \tag{3.138}$$

Figure 3.8 gives a 2d example of these results.

3.4.4.2   Posterior of Σ given μ

We now discuss how to compute $p(\boldsymbol{\Sigma}|\mathcal{D}, \boldsymbol{\mu})$.

Likelihood

We can rewrite the likelihood as follows:

$$p(\mathcal{D}|\boldsymbol{\mu}, \boldsymbol{\Sigma}) \propto |\boldsymbol{\Sigma}|^{-\frac{N}{2}} \exp\left(-\frac{1}{2}\mathrm{tr}(\boldsymbol{S}_{\mu}\boldsymbol{\Sigma}^{-1})\right) \tag{3.139}$$

where

$$\boldsymbol{S}_{\mu} \triangleq \sum_{n=1}^{N}(\boldsymbol{y}_n - \boldsymbol{\mu})(\boldsymbol{y}_n - \boldsymbol{\mu})^{\mathsf{T}} \tag{3.140}$$

is the scatter matrix around $\boldsymbol{\mu}$.

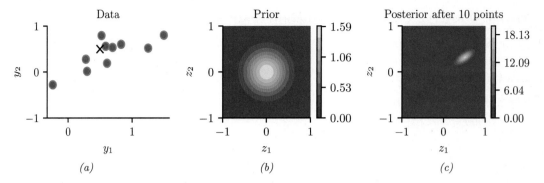

Figure 3.8: Illustration of Bayesian inference for a 2d Gaussian random vector z. (a) The data is generated from $y_n \sim \mathcal{N}(z, \Sigma_y)$, where $z = [0.5, 0.5]^\mathsf{T}$ and $\Sigma_y = 0.1([2, 1; 1, 1])$. We assume the sensor noise covariance Σ_y is known but z is unknown. The black cross represents z. (b) The prior is $p(z) = \mathcal{N}(z|0, 0.1\mathbf{I}_2)$. (c) We show the posterior after 10 datapoints have been observed. Generated by gauss_infer_2d.ipynb.

Prior

The conjugate prior is known as the **inverse Wishart** distribution, which is a distribution over positive definite matrices, as we explained in Section 2.2.5.5. This has the following pdf:

$$\mathrm{IW}(\Sigma|\,\breve{\Psi}, \breve{\nu}) \propto |\Sigma|^{-(\breve{\nu}+D+1)/2} \exp\left(-\frac{1}{2}\mathrm{tr}(\breve{\Psi}\,\Sigma^{-1})\right) \tag{3.141}$$

Here $\breve{\nu} > D - 1$ is the degrees of freedom (dof), and $\breve{\Psi}$ is a symmetric pd matrix. We see that $\breve{\Psi}$ plays the role of the prior scatter matrix, and $N_0 \triangleq \breve{\nu} + D + 1$ controls the strength of the prior, and hence plays a role analogous to the sample size N.

Posterior

Multiplying the likelihood and prior we find that the posterior is also inverse Wishart:

$$p(\Sigma|\mathcal{D}, \mu) \propto |\Sigma|^{-\frac{N}{2}} \exp\left(-\frac{1}{2}\mathrm{tr}(\Sigma^{-1}\mathbf{S}_\mu)\right) |\Sigma|^{-(\breve{\nu}+D+1)/2}$$

$$\exp\left(-\frac{1}{2}\mathrm{tr}(\Sigma^{-1}\,\breve{\Psi})\right) \tag{3.142}$$

$$= |\Sigma|^{-\frac{N+(\breve{\nu}+D+1)}{2}} \exp\left(-\frac{1}{2}\mathrm{tr}\left[\Sigma^{-1}(\mathbf{S}_\mu + \breve{\Psi})\right]\right) \tag{3.143}$$

$$= \mathrm{IW}(\Sigma|\,\widehat{\Psi}, \widehat{\nu}) \tag{3.144}$$

$$\widehat{\nu} = \breve{\nu} + N \tag{3.145}$$

$$\widehat{\Psi} = \breve{\Psi} + \mathbf{S}_\mu \tag{3.146}$$

In words, this says that the posterior strength $\widehat{\nu}$ is the prior strength $\breve{\nu}$ plus the number of observations N, and the posterior scatter matrix $\widehat{\Psi}$ is the prior scatter matrix $\breve{\Psi}$ plus the data scatter matrix $\mathbf{S}_\mu$.

3.4.4.3   Posterior of $\boldsymbol{\Sigma}$ and $\boldsymbol{\mu}$

In this section, we compute $p(\boldsymbol{\mu}, \boldsymbol{\Sigma}|\mathcal{D})$ using a conjugate prior.

Likelihood

The likelihood is given by

$$p(\mathcal{D}|\boldsymbol{\mu}, \boldsymbol{\Sigma}) \propto |\boldsymbol{\Sigma}|^{-\frac{N}{2}} \exp\left(-\frac{1}{2}\sum_{n=1}^{N}(\boldsymbol{y}_n - \boldsymbol{\mu})^{\mathsf{T}}\boldsymbol{\Sigma}^{-1}(\boldsymbol{y}_n - \boldsymbol{\mu})\right) \tag{3.147}$$

One can show that

$$\sum_{n=1}^{N}(\boldsymbol{y}_n - \boldsymbol{\mu})^{\mathsf{T}}\boldsymbol{\Sigma}^{-1}(\boldsymbol{y}_n - \boldsymbol{\mu}) = \text{tr}(\boldsymbol{\Sigma}^{-1}\mathbf{S}) + N(\overline{\boldsymbol{y}} - \boldsymbol{\mu})^{\mathsf{T}}\boldsymbol{\Sigma}^{-1}(\overline{\boldsymbol{y}} - \boldsymbol{\mu}) \tag{3.148}$$

where

$$\mathbf{S} \triangleq \mathbf{S}_{\overline{\boldsymbol{y}}} = \sum_{n=1}^{N}(\boldsymbol{y}_n - \overline{\boldsymbol{y}})(\boldsymbol{y}_n - \overline{\boldsymbol{y}})^{\mathsf{T}} = \mathbf{Y}^{\mathsf{T}}\mathbf{C}_N\mathbf{Y} \tag{3.149}$$

is empirical **scatter matrix**, and $\mathbf{C}_N$ is the **centering matrix**

$$\mathbf{C}_N \triangleq \mathbf{I}_N - \frac{1}{N}\mathbf{1}_N\mathbf{1}_N^{\mathsf{T}} \tag{3.150}$$

Hence we can rewrite the likelihood as follows:

$$p(\mathcal{D}|\boldsymbol{\mu}, \boldsymbol{\Sigma}) \propto |\boldsymbol{\Sigma}|^{-\frac{N}{2}} \exp\left(-\frac{N}{2}(\boldsymbol{\mu} - \overline{\boldsymbol{y}})^{\mathsf{T}}\boldsymbol{\Sigma}^{-1}(\boldsymbol{\mu} - \overline{\boldsymbol{y}})\right) \exp\left(-\frac{1}{2}\text{tr}(\boldsymbol{\Sigma}^{-1}\mathbf{S})\right) \tag{3.151}$$

We will use this form below.

Prior

The obvious prior to use is the following

$$p(\boldsymbol{\mu}, \boldsymbol{\Sigma}) = \mathcal{N}(\boldsymbol{\mu}|\, \breve{\boldsymbol{m}}, \breve{\mathbf{V}})\text{IW}(\boldsymbol{\Sigma}|\, \breve{\boldsymbol{\Psi}}, \breve{\nu}) \tag{3.152}$$

where IW is the inverse Wishart distribution. Unfortunately, $\boldsymbol{\mu}$ and $\boldsymbol{\Sigma}$ appear together in a non-factorized way in the likelihood in Equation (3.151) (see the first exponent term), so the factored prior in Equation (3.152) is not conjugate to the likelihood.[3]

The above prior is sometimes called **conditionally conjugate**, since both conditionals, $p(\boldsymbol{\mu}|\boldsymbol{\Sigma})$ and $p(\boldsymbol{\Sigma}|\boldsymbol{\mu})$, are individually conjugate. To create a fully conjugate prior, we need to use a prior where $\boldsymbol{\mu}$ and $\boldsymbol{\Sigma}$ are dependent on each other. We will use a joint distribution of the form $p(\boldsymbol{\mu}, \boldsymbol{\Sigma}) = p(\boldsymbol{\mu}|\boldsymbol{\Sigma})p(\boldsymbol{\Sigma})$.

---

3. Using the language of directed graphical models, we see that $\boldsymbol{\mu}$ and $\boldsymbol{\Sigma}$ become dependent when conditioned on $\mathcal{D}$ due to explaining away. See Figure 3.9(a).

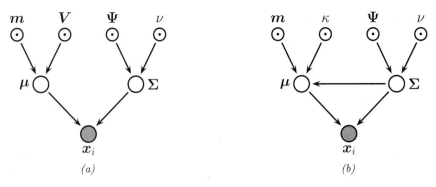

Figure 3.9: Graphical models representing different kinds of assumptions about the parameter priors. (a) A semi-conjugate prior for a Gaussian. (b) A conjugate prior for a Gaussian.

Looking at the form of the likelihood equation, Equation (3.151), we see that a natural conjugate prior has the form of a **normal-inverse-Wishart** or **NIW** distribution, defined as follows:

$$\text{NIW}(\boldsymbol{\mu}, \boldsymbol{\Sigma} | \breve{\boldsymbol{m}}, \breve{\kappa}, \breve{\nu}, \breve{\boldsymbol{\Psi}}) \triangleq \mathcal{N}(\boldsymbol{\mu} | \breve{\boldsymbol{m}}, \frac{1}{\breve{\kappa}}\boldsymbol{\Sigma}) \times \text{IW}(\boldsymbol{\Sigma} | \breve{\boldsymbol{\Psi}}, \breve{\nu}) \tag{3.153}$$

$$= \frac{1}{Z_{\text{NIW}}} |\boldsymbol{\Sigma}|^{-\frac{1}{2}} \exp\left(-\frac{\breve{\kappa}}{2}(\boldsymbol{\mu} - \breve{\boldsymbol{m}})^{\mathsf{T}}\boldsymbol{\Sigma}^{-1}(\boldsymbol{\mu} - \breve{\boldsymbol{m}})\right)$$

$$\times |\boldsymbol{\Sigma}|^{-\frac{\breve{\nu}+D+1}{2}} \exp\left(-\frac{1}{2}\text{tr}(\boldsymbol{\Sigma}^{-1}\breve{\boldsymbol{\Psi}})\right) \tag{3.154}$$

where the normalization constant is given by

$$Z_{\text{NIW}} \triangleq 2^{\breve{\nu}D/2}\Gamma_D(\breve{\nu}/2)(2\pi/\breve{\kappa})^{D/2}|\breve{\boldsymbol{\Psi}}|^{-\breve{\nu}/2} \tag{3.155}$$

The parameters of the NIW can be interpreted as follows: $\breve{\boldsymbol{m}}$ is our prior mean for $\boldsymbol{\mu}$, and $\breve{\kappa}$ is how strongly we believe this prior; $\breve{\boldsymbol{\Psi}}$ is (proportional to) our prior mean for $\boldsymbol{\Sigma}$, and $\breve{\nu}$ is how strongly we believe this prior.[4]

Posterior

To derive the posterior, let us first rewrite the scatter matrix as follows:

$$\mathbf{S} = \mathbf{Y}^{\mathsf{T}}\mathbf{Y} - \frac{1}{N}(\sum_{n=1}^{N} \boldsymbol{y}_n)(\sum_{n=1}^{N} \boldsymbol{y}_n)^{\mathsf{T}} = \mathbf{Y}^{\mathsf{T}}\mathbf{Y} - N\overline{\boldsymbol{y}}\,\overline{\boldsymbol{y}}^{\mathsf{T}} \tag{3.156}$$

where $\mathbf{Y}^{\mathsf{T}}\mathbf{Y} = \sum_{n=1}^{N} \boldsymbol{y}_n\boldsymbol{y}_n^{\mathsf{T}}$ is the **sum of squares** matrix.

---

4. Note that our uncertainty in the mean is proportional to the covariance. In particular, if we believe that the variance is large, then our uncertainty in μ must be large too. This makes sense intuitively, since if the data has large spread, it will be hard to pin down its mean.

Now we can multiply the likelihood and the prior to give

$$p(\boldsymbol{\mu}, \boldsymbol{\Sigma}|\mathcal{D}) \propto |\boldsymbol{\Sigma}|^{-\frac{N}{2}} \exp\left(-\frac{N}{2}(\boldsymbol{\mu} - \overline{\boldsymbol{y}})^\mathsf{T}\boldsymbol{\Sigma}^{-1}(\boldsymbol{\mu} - \overline{\boldsymbol{y}})\right)\exp\left(-\frac{1}{2}\mathrm{tr}(\boldsymbol{\Sigma}^{-1}\mathbf{S})\right) \tag{3.157}$$

$$\times |\boldsymbol{\Sigma}|^{-\frac{\breve{\nu}+D+2}{2}} \exp\left(-\frac{\breve{\kappa}}{2}(\boldsymbol{\mu}-\breve{\boldsymbol{m}})^\mathsf{T}\boldsymbol{\Sigma}^{-1}(\boldsymbol{\mu}-\breve{\boldsymbol{m}})\right)\exp\left(-\frac{1}{2}\mathrm{tr}(\boldsymbol{\Sigma}^{-1}\,\breve{\boldsymbol{\Psi}})\right) \tag{3.158}$$

$$= |\boldsymbol{\Sigma}|^{-(N+\breve{\nu}+D+2)/2}\exp(-\frac{1}{2}\mathrm{tr}(\boldsymbol{\Sigma}^{-1}\mathbf{M})) \tag{3.159}$$

where

$$\mathbf{M} \triangleq N(\boldsymbol{\mu}-\overline{\boldsymbol{y}})(\boldsymbol{\mu}-\overline{\boldsymbol{y}})^\mathsf{T} + \breve{\kappa}\,(\boldsymbol{\mu}-\breve{\boldsymbol{m}})(\boldsymbol{\mu}-\breve{\boldsymbol{m}})^\mathsf{T} + \mathbf{S} + \breve{\boldsymbol{\Psi}} \tag{3.160}$$

$$= (\breve{\kappa}+N)\boldsymbol{\mu}\boldsymbol{\mu}^\mathsf{T} - \boldsymbol{\mu}(\breve{\kappa}\breve{\boldsymbol{m}}+N\overline{\boldsymbol{y}})^\mathsf{T} - (\breve{\kappa}\breve{\boldsymbol{m}}+N\overline{\boldsymbol{y}})\boldsymbol{\mu}^\mathsf{T} + \breve{\kappa}\breve{\boldsymbol{m}}\breve{\boldsymbol{m}}^\mathsf{T} + \mathbf{Y}^\mathsf{T}\mathbf{Y} + \breve{\boldsymbol{\Psi}} \tag{3.161}$$

We can simplify the $\mathbf{M}$ matrix using a trick called **completing the square**. Applying this to the above, we have

$$(\breve{\kappa}+N)\boldsymbol{\mu}\boldsymbol{\mu}^\mathsf{T} - \boldsymbol{\mu}(\breve{\kappa}\breve{\boldsymbol{m}}+N\overline{\boldsymbol{y}})^\mathsf{T} - (\breve{\kappa}\breve{\boldsymbol{m}}+N\overline{\boldsymbol{y}})\boldsymbol{\mu}^\mathsf{T} \tag{3.162}$$

$$= (\breve{\kappa}+N)\left(\boldsymbol{\mu}-\frac{\breve{\kappa}\breve{\boldsymbol{m}}+N\overline{\boldsymbol{y}}}{\breve{\kappa}+N}\right)\left(\boldsymbol{\mu}-\frac{\breve{\kappa}\breve{\boldsymbol{m}}+N\overline{\boldsymbol{y}}}{\breve{\kappa}+N}\right)^\mathsf{T} \tag{3.163}$$

$$-\frac{(\breve{\kappa}\breve{\boldsymbol{m}}+N\overline{\boldsymbol{y}})(\breve{\kappa}\breve{\boldsymbol{m}}+N\overline{\boldsymbol{y}})^\mathsf{T}}{\breve{\kappa}+N} \tag{3.164}$$

$$= \widehat{\kappa}\,(\boldsymbol{\mu}-\widehat{\boldsymbol{m}})(\boldsymbol{\mu}-\widehat{\boldsymbol{m}})^\mathsf{T} - \widehat{\kappa}\widehat{\boldsymbol{m}}\widehat{\boldsymbol{m}}^\mathsf{T} \tag{3.165}$$

Hence we can rewrite the posterior as follows:

$$p(\boldsymbol{\mu},\boldsymbol{\Sigma}|\mathcal{D}) \propto |\boldsymbol{\Sigma}|^{(\widehat{\nu}+D+2)/2}\exp\left(-\frac{1}{2}\mathrm{tr}\left[\boldsymbol{\Sigma}^{-1}\left(\widehat{\kappa}\,(\boldsymbol{\mu}-\widehat{\boldsymbol{m}})(\boldsymbol{\mu}-\widehat{\boldsymbol{m}})^\mathsf{T} + \widehat{\boldsymbol{\Psi}}\right)\right]\right) \tag{3.166}$$

$$= \mathrm{NIW}(\boldsymbol{\mu},\boldsymbol{\Sigma}|\,\widehat{\boldsymbol{m}},\widehat{\kappa},\widehat{\nu},\widehat{\boldsymbol{\Psi}}) \tag{3.167}$$

where

$$\widehat{\boldsymbol{m}} = \frac{\breve{\kappa}\breve{\boldsymbol{m}}+N\overline{\boldsymbol{y}}}{\widehat{\kappa}} = \frac{\breve{\kappa}}{\breve{\kappa}+N}\,\breve{\boldsymbol{m}} + \frac{N}{\breve{\kappa}+N}\overline{\boldsymbol{y}} \tag{3.168}$$

$$\widehat{\kappa} = \breve{\kappa}+N \tag{3.169}$$

$$\widehat{\nu} = \breve{\nu}+N \tag{3.170}$$

$$\widehat{\boldsymbol{\Psi}} = \breve{\boldsymbol{\Psi}} + \mathbf{S} + \frac{\breve{\kappa}N}{\breve{\kappa}+N}(\overline{\boldsymbol{y}}-\breve{\boldsymbol{m}})(\overline{\boldsymbol{y}}-\breve{\boldsymbol{m}})^\mathsf{T} \tag{3.171}$$

$$= \breve{\boldsymbol{\Psi}} + \mathbf{Y}^\mathsf{T}\mathbf{Y} + \breve{\kappa}\breve{\boldsymbol{m}}\breve{\boldsymbol{m}}^\mathsf{T} - \widehat{\kappa}\widehat{\boldsymbol{m}}\widehat{\boldsymbol{m}}^\mathsf{T} \tag{3.172}$$

This result is actually quite intuitive: the posterior mean $\widehat{\boldsymbol{m}}$ is a convex combination of the prior mean and the MLE; the posterior scatter matrix $\widehat{\boldsymbol{\Psi}}$ is the prior scatter matrix $\breve{\boldsymbol{\Psi}}$ plus the empirical scatter matrix $\mathbf{S}$ plus an extra term due to the uncertainty in the mean (which creates its own virtual scatter matrix); and the posterior confidence factors $\widehat{\kappa}$ and $\widehat{\nu}$ are both incremented by the size of the data we condition on.

Posterior marginals

We have computed the joint posterior

$$p(\boldsymbol{\mu}, \boldsymbol{\Sigma}|\mathcal{D}) = \mathcal{N}(\boldsymbol{\mu}|\boldsymbol{\Sigma}, \mathcal{D})p(\boldsymbol{\Sigma}|\mathcal{D}) = \mathcal{N}(\boldsymbol{\mu}| \, \widehat{\boldsymbol{m}}, \frac{1}{\widehat{\kappa}}\boldsymbol{\Sigma})\mathrm{IW}(\boldsymbol{\Sigma}| \, \widehat{\boldsymbol{\Psi}}, \widehat{\nu}) \tag{3.173}$$

We now discuss how to compute the posterior marginals, $p(\boldsymbol{\Sigma}|\mathcal{D})$ and $p(\boldsymbol{\mu}|\mathcal{D})$.

It is easy to see that the posterior marginal for $\boldsymbol{\Sigma}$ is

$$p(\boldsymbol{\Sigma}|\mathcal{D}) = \int p(\boldsymbol{\mu}, \boldsymbol{\Sigma}|\mathcal{D})d\boldsymbol{\mu} = \mathrm{IW}(\boldsymbol{\Sigma}| \, \widehat{\boldsymbol{\Psi}}, \widehat{\nu}) \tag{3.174}$$

For the mean, one can show that

$$p(\boldsymbol{\mu}|\mathcal{D}) = \int p(\boldsymbol{\mu}, \boldsymbol{\Sigma}|\mathcal{D})d\boldsymbol{\Sigma} = \mathcal{T}(\boldsymbol{\mu}| \, \widehat{\boldsymbol{\mu}}, \frac{\widehat{\boldsymbol{\Psi}}}{\widehat{\kappa}\widehat{\nu}'}, \widehat{\nu}') \tag{3.175}$$

where $\widehat{\nu}' \triangleq \widehat{\nu} - D + 1$. Intuitively this result follows because $p(\boldsymbol{\mu}|\mathcal{D})$ is an infinite mixture of Gaussians, where each mixture component has a value of $\boldsymbol{\Sigma}$ drawn from the IW distribution; by mixing these altogether, we induce a Student distribution, which has heavier tails than a single Gaussian.

Posterior mode

The maximum a posteriori (MAP) estimate of $\boldsymbol{\mu}$ and $\boldsymbol{\Sigma}$ is the mode of the posterior NIW distribution with density

$$p(\boldsymbol{\mu}, \boldsymbol{\Sigma}|\mathbf{Y}) = \mathcal{N}(\boldsymbol{\mu}| \, \widehat{\boldsymbol{\mu}}, \widehat{\kappa}^{-1} \boldsymbol{\Sigma})\mathrm{IW}(\boldsymbol{\Sigma}| \, \widehat{\nu}, \widehat{\boldsymbol{\Psi}}) \tag{3.176}$$

To find the mode, we firstly notice that $\boldsymbol{\mu}$ only appears in the conditional distribution $\mathcal{N}(\boldsymbol{\mu}| \, \widehat{\boldsymbol{\mu}}, \widehat{\kappa}^{-1} \boldsymbol{\Sigma})$, and the mode of this normal distribution equals its mean, i.e., $\boldsymbol{\mu} = \widehat{\boldsymbol{\mu}}$. Also notice that this holds for any choice of $\boldsymbol{\Sigma}$. So we can plug $\boldsymbol{\mu} = \widehat{\boldsymbol{\mu}}$ in Equation (3.176) and derive the mode of $\boldsymbol{\Sigma}$. Notice that

$$-2 * \log p(\boldsymbol{\mu} = \widehat{\boldsymbol{\mu}}, \boldsymbol{\Sigma}|\mathbf{Y}) = (\widehat{\nu} + D + 2) \log(|\boldsymbol{\Sigma}|) + \mathrm{tr}(\widehat{\boldsymbol{\Psi}} \, \boldsymbol{\Sigma}^{-1}) + c \tag{3.177}$$

where c is a constant irrelevant to $\boldsymbol{\Sigma}$. We then take the derivative over $\boldsymbol{\Sigma}$:

$$\frac{\partial \log p(\boldsymbol{\mu} = \widehat{\boldsymbol{\mu}} \, \boldsymbol{\Sigma}|\mathbf{Y})}{\partial \boldsymbol{\Sigma}} = (\widehat{\nu} + D + 2)\boldsymbol{\Sigma}^{-1} - \boldsymbol{\Sigma}^{-1} \, \widehat{\boldsymbol{\Psi}} \, \boldsymbol{\Sigma}^{-1} \tag{3.178}$$

By setting the derivative to 0 and solving for $\boldsymbol{\Sigma}$, we see that $(\widehat{\nu} + D + 2)^{-1} \, \widehat{\boldsymbol{\Psi}}$ is the matrix that maximizes Equation (3.177). By checking that $\widehat{\boldsymbol{\Psi}}$ is a positive definite matrix, we conclude that $\widehat{\boldsymbol{\Psi}}$ is the MAP estimate of the covariance matrix $\boldsymbol{\Sigma}$.

In conclusion, the MAP estimate of $\{\boldsymbol{\mu}, \boldsymbol{\Sigma}\}$ are

$$\widehat{\boldsymbol{\mu}} = \frac{\breve{\kappa}\breve{\boldsymbol{\mu}} + N\bar{\boldsymbol{y}}}{\breve{\kappa} + N} \tag{3.179}$$

$$\widehat{\boldsymbol{\Sigma}} = \frac{1}{\widehat{\nu} + D + 2} \, \widehat{\boldsymbol{\Psi}} \tag{3.180}$$

Posterior predictive

We now discuss how to predict future data by integrating out the parameters. If $\boldsymbol{y} \sim \mathcal{N}(\boldsymbol{\mu}, \boldsymbol{\Sigma})$, where $(\boldsymbol{\mu}, \boldsymbol{\Sigma}|\mathcal{D}) \sim \text{NIW}(\widehat{\boldsymbol{m}}, \widehat{\kappa}, \widehat{\nu}, \widehat{\boldsymbol{\Psi}})$, then one can show that the posterior predictive distribution, for a single observation vector, is as follows:

$$p(\boldsymbol{y}|\mathcal{D}) = \int \mathcal{N}(\boldsymbol{x}|\boldsymbol{\mu}, \boldsymbol{\Sigma})\text{NIW}(\boldsymbol{\mu}, \boldsymbol{\Sigma}|\,\widehat{\boldsymbol{m}}, \widehat{\kappa}, \widehat{\nu}, \widehat{\boldsymbol{\Psi}})d\boldsymbol{\mu}d\boldsymbol{\Sigma} \tag{3.181}$$

$$= \mathcal{T}(\boldsymbol{y}|\,\widehat{\boldsymbol{m}}, \frac{\widehat{\boldsymbol{\Psi}}\,(\widehat{\kappa}+1)}{\widehat{\kappa}\widehat{\nu}'}, \widehat{\nu}') \tag{3.182}$$

where $\widehat{\nu}' = \widehat{\nu} - D + 1$.

3.4.5 The exponential family model

We have seen that exact Bayesian analysis is considerably simplified if the prior is conjugate to the likelihood. Since the posterior must have the same form as the prior, and hence the same number of parameters, the likelihood function must have fixed-sized sufficient statistics, so that we can write $p(\mathcal{D}|\boldsymbol{\theta}) = p(\boldsymbol{s}(\mathcal{D})|\boldsymbol{\theta})$. This suggests that the only family of distributions for which conjugate priors exist is the exponential family, a result proved in [DY79].[5] In the sections below, we show how to perform conjugate analysis for a generic exponential family model.

3.4.5.1 Likelihood

Recall that the likelihood of the exponential family is given by

$$p(\mathcal{D}|\boldsymbol{\eta}) = h(\mathcal{D})\exp(\boldsymbol{\eta}^{\mathsf{T}}\boldsymbol{s}(\mathcal{D}) - NA(\boldsymbol{\eta})) \tag{3.183}$$

where $\boldsymbol{s}(\mathcal{D}) = \sum_{n=1}^{N}\boldsymbol{s}(\boldsymbol{x}_n)$ and $h(\mathcal{D}) \triangleq \prod_{n=1}^{N}h(\boldsymbol{x}_n)$.

3.4.5.2 Prior

Let us write the prior in a form that mirrors the likelihood:

$$p(\boldsymbol{\eta}|\,\breve{\boldsymbol{\tau}}, \breve{\nu}) = \frac{1}{Z(\breve{\boldsymbol{\tau}}, \breve{\nu})}\exp(\breve{\boldsymbol{\tau}}^{\mathsf{T}}\boldsymbol{\eta} - \breve{\nu}\,A(\boldsymbol{\eta})) \tag{3.184}$$

where $\breve{\nu}$ is the strength of the prior, and $\breve{\boldsymbol{\tau}}\,/\,\breve{\nu}$ is the prior mean, and $Z(\breve{\boldsymbol{\tau}}, \breve{\nu})$ is a normalizing factor. The parameters $\breve{\boldsymbol{\tau}}$ can be derived from **virtual samples** representing our prior beliefs.

---

5. There are some exceptions. For example, the uniform distribution $\text{Unif}(x|0, \theta)$ has finite sufficient statistics $(N, m = \max_i x_i)$, as discussed in Section 2.4.2.6; hence this distribution has a conjugate prior, namely the Pareto distribution (Section 2.2.3.5), $p(\theta) = \text{Pareto}(\theta|\theta_0, \kappa)$, yielding the posterior $p(\theta|\boldsymbol{x}) = \text{Pareto}(\max(\theta_0, m), \kappa + N)$.

3.4.5.3 Posterior

The posterior is given by

$$p(\boldsymbol{\eta}|\mathcal{D}) = \frac{p(\mathcal{D}|\boldsymbol{\eta})p(\boldsymbol{\eta})}{p(\mathcal{D})} \tag{3.185}$$

$$= \frac{h(\mathcal{D})}{Z(\breve{\boldsymbol{\tau}}, \breve{\nu})p(\mathcal{D})} \exp\left((\breve{\boldsymbol{\tau}} + \boldsymbol{s}(\mathcal{D}))^\mathsf{T}\boldsymbol{\eta} - (\breve{\nu} + N)A(\boldsymbol{\eta})\right) \tag{3.186}$$

$$= \frac{1}{Z(\hat{\boldsymbol{\tau}}, \hat{\nu})} \exp\left(\hat{\boldsymbol{\tau}}^\mathsf{T}\boldsymbol{\eta} - \hat{\nu}\,A(\boldsymbol{\eta})\right) \tag{3.187}$$

where

$$\hat{\boldsymbol{\tau}} = \breve{\boldsymbol{\tau}} + \boldsymbol{s}(\mathcal{D}) \tag{3.188}$$

$$\hat{\nu} = \breve{\nu} + N \tag{3.189}$$

$$Z(\hat{\boldsymbol{\tau}}, \hat{\nu}) = \frac{Z(\breve{\boldsymbol{\tau}}, \breve{\nu})}{h(\mathcal{D})}p(\mathcal{D}) \tag{3.190}$$

We see that this has the same form as the prior, but where we update the sufficient statistics and the sample size.

The posterior mean is given by a convex combination of the prior mean and the empirical mean (which is the MLE):

$$\mathbb{E}[\boldsymbol{\eta}|\mathcal{D}] = \frac{\hat{\boldsymbol{\tau}}}{\hat{\nu}} = \frac{\breve{\boldsymbol{\tau}} + \boldsymbol{s}(\mathcal{D})}{\breve{\nu} + N} = \frac{\breve{\nu}}{\breve{\nu} + N}\frac{\breve{\boldsymbol{\tau}}}{\breve{\nu}} + \frac{N}{\breve{\nu} + N}\frac{\boldsymbol{s}(\mathcal{D})}{N} \tag{3.191}$$

$$= \lambda\mathbb{E}[\boldsymbol{\eta}] + (1 - \lambda)\hat{\boldsymbol{\eta}}_{\text{mle}} \tag{3.192}$$

where $\lambda = \frac{\breve{\nu}}{\breve{\nu} + N}$.

3.4.5.4 Marginal likelihood

From Equation (3.190) we see that the marginal likelihood is given by

$$p(\mathcal{D}) = \frac{Z(\hat{\boldsymbol{\tau}}, \hat{\nu})h(\mathcal{D})}{Z(\breve{\boldsymbol{\tau}}, \breve{\nu})} \tag{3.193}$$

See Section 3.2.1.9 for a detailed example in the case of the beta-Bernoulli model.

3.4.5.5 Posterior predictive density

We now derive the predictive density for future observables $\mathcal{D}' = (\tilde{\boldsymbol{x}}_1, \ldots, \tilde{\boldsymbol{x}}_{N'})$ given past data $\mathcal{D} = (\boldsymbol{x}_1, \ldots, \boldsymbol{x}_N)$:

$$p(\mathcal{D}'|\mathcal{D}) = \int p(\mathcal{D}'|\boldsymbol{\eta})p(\boldsymbol{\eta}|\mathcal{D})d\boldsymbol{\eta} \tag{3.194}$$

$$= \int h(\mathcal{D}')\exp(\boldsymbol{\eta}^\mathsf{T}\boldsymbol{s}(\mathcal{D}') - N'A(\boldsymbol{\eta}))\frac{1}{Z(\hat{\boldsymbol{\tau}}, \hat{\nu})}\exp(\boldsymbol{\eta}^\mathsf{T}\hat{\boldsymbol{\tau}} - \hat{\nu}\,A(\boldsymbol{\eta}))d\boldsymbol{\eta} \tag{3.195}$$

$$= h(\mathcal{D}')\frac{Z(\breve{\boldsymbol{\tau}} + \boldsymbol{s}(\mathcal{D}) + \boldsymbol{s}(\mathcal{D}'), \breve{\nu} + N + N')}{Z(\breve{\boldsymbol{\tau}} + \boldsymbol{s}(\mathcal{D}), \breve{\nu} + N)} \tag{3.196}$$

3.4.5.6 Example: Bernoulli distribution

As a simple example, let us revisit the Beta-Bernoulli model in our new notation.

The likelihood is given by

$$p(\mathcal{D}|\theta) = (1 - \theta)^N \exp\left(\log(\frac{\theta}{1 - \theta}) \sum_i x_n\right) \tag{3.197}$$

Hence the conjugate prior is given by

$$p(\theta|\nu_0, \tau_0) \propto (1 - \theta)^{\nu_0} \exp\left(\log(\frac{\theta}{1 - \theta})\tau_0\right) \tag{3.198}$$

$$= \theta^{\tau_0}(1 - \theta)^{\nu_0 - \tau_0} \tag{3.199}$$

If we define $\alpha = \tau_0 + 1$ and $\beta = \nu_0 - \tau_0 + 1$, we see that this is a beta distribution.

We can derive the posterior as follows, where $s = \sum_i \mathbb{I}(x_i = 1)$ is the sufficient statistic:

$$p(\theta|\mathcal{D}) \propto \theta^{\tau_0 + s}(1 - \theta)^{\nu_0 - \tau_0 + n - s} \tag{3.200}$$

$$= \theta^{\tau_n}(1 - \theta)^{\nu_n - \tau_n} \tag{3.201}$$

We can derive the posterior predictive distribution as follows. Assume $p(\theta) = \text{Beta}(\theta|\alpha, \beta)$, and let $s = s(\mathcal{D})$ be the number of heads in the past data. We can predict the probability of a given sequence of future heads, $\mathcal{D}' = (\tilde{x}_1, \ldots, \tilde{x}_m)$, with sufficient statistic $s' = \sum_{n=1}^m \mathbb{I}(\tilde{x}_i = 1)$, as follows:

$$p(\mathcal{D}'|\mathcal{D}) = \int_0^1 p(\mathcal{D}'|\theta|\text{Beta}(\theta|\alpha_n, \beta_n)d\theta \tag{3.202}$$

$$= \frac{\Gamma(\alpha_n + \beta_n)}{\Gamma(\alpha_n)\Gamma(\beta_n)} \int_0^1 \theta^{\alpha_n + t' - 1}(1 - \theta)^{\beta_n + m - t' - 1}d\theta \tag{3.203}$$

$$= \frac{\Gamma(\alpha_n + \beta_n)}{\Gamma(\alpha_n)\Gamma(\beta_n)} \frac{\Gamma(\alpha_{n+m})\Gamma(\beta_{n+m})}{\Gamma(\alpha_{n+m} + \beta_{n+m})} \tag{3.204}$$

where

$$\alpha_{n+m} = \alpha_n + s' = \alpha + s + s' \tag{3.205}$$

$$\beta_{n+m} = \beta_n + (m - s') = \beta + (n - s) + (m - s') \tag{3.206}$$

3.4.6 Beyond conjugate priors

We have seen various examples of conjugate priors, all of which have come from the exponential family (see Section 2.4). These priors have the advantages of being easy to interpret (in terms of sufficient statistics from a virtual prior dataset), and being easy to compute with. However, for most models, there is no prior in the exponential family that is conjugate to the likelihood. Furthermore, even where there is a conjugate prior, the assumption of conjugacy may be too limiting. Therefore in the sections below, we briefly discuss various other kinds of priors. (We defer the question of posterior inference with these priors until Section 7.1, where we discuss algorithmic issues, since we can no longer use closed-form solutions when the prior is not conjugate.)

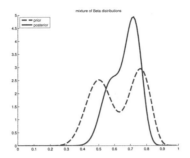

Figure 3.10: *A mixture of two Beta distributions. Generated by* mixbetademo.ipynb.

3.4.6.1 Mixtures of conjugate priors

In this section, we show how we can create a **mixture of conjugate priors** for increased modeling flexibility. Fortunately, the resulting mixture prior is still conjugate.

As an example, suppose we want to predict the outcome of a coin toss at a casino, and we believe that the coin may be fair, but it may also be biased towards heads. This prior cannot be represented by a beta distribution. Fortunately, it can be represented as a mixture of beta distributions. For example, we might use

$$p(\theta) = 0.5 \text{ Beta}(\theta|20, 20) + 0.5 \text{ Beta}(\theta|30, 10) \tag{3.207}$$

If θ comes from the first distribution, the coin is fair, but if it comes from the second, it is biased towards heads.

We can represent a mixture by introducing a latent indicator variable h, where $h = k$ means that θ comes from mixture component k. The prior has the form

$$p(\theta) = \sum_k p(h = k)p(\theta|h = k) \tag{3.208}$$

where each $p(\theta|h = k)$ is conjugate, and $p(h = k)$ are called the (prior) mixing weights. One can show that the posterior can also be written as a mixture of conjugate distributions as follows:

$$p(\theta|\mathcal{D}) = \sum_k p(h = k|\mathcal{D})p(\theta|\mathcal{D}, h = k) \tag{3.209}$$

where $p(h = k|\mathcal{D})$ are the posterior mixing weights given by

$$p(h = k|\mathcal{D}) = \frac{p(h = k)p(\mathcal{D}|h = k)}{\sum_{k'} p(h = k')p(\mathcal{D}|h = k')} \tag{3.210}$$

Here the quantity $p(\mathcal{D}|h = k)$ is the marginal likelihood for mixture component k (see Section 3.2.1.9).

Returning to our example above, if we have the prior in Equation (3.207), and we observe $N_1 = 20$ heads and $N_0 = 10$ tails, then, using Equation (3.31), the posterior becomes

$$p(\theta|\mathcal{D}) = 0.346 \text{ Beta}(\theta|40, 30) + 0.654 \text{ Beta}(\theta|50, 20) \tag{3.211}$$

See Figure 3.10 for an illustration.

We can compute the posterior probability that the coin is biased towards heads as follows:

$$\Pr(\theta > 0.5|\mathcal{D}) = \sum_k \Pr(\theta > 0.5|\mathcal{D}, h = k)p(h = k|\mathcal{D}) = 0.9604 \tag{3.212}$$

If we just used a single Beta(20,20) prior, we would get a slightly smaller value of $\Pr(\theta > 0.5|\mathcal{D}) = 0.8858$. So if we were "suspicious" initially that the casino might be using a biased coin, our fears would be confirmed more quickly than if we had to be convinced starting with an open mind.

3.4.6.2   Robust (heavy-tailed) priors

The assessment of the influence of the prior on the posterior is called **sensitivity analysis**, or **robustness analysis**. There are many ways to create **robust priors**. (see e.g., [IR00]). Here we consider a simple approach, namely the use of a heavy-tailed distribution.

To motivate this, let us consider an example from [Ber85a, p7]. Suppose $x \sim \mathcal{N}(\theta, 1)$. We observe that $x = 5$ and we want to estimate θ. The MLE is of course $\hat{\theta} = 5$, which seems reasonable. The posterior mean under a uniform prior is also $\bar{\theta} = 5$. But now suppose we know that the prior median is 0, and that there is 25% probability that θ lies in any of the intervals $(-\infty, -1)$, $(-1, 0)$, $(0, 1)$, $(1, \infty)$. Let us also assume the prior is smooth and unimodal.

One can show that a Gaussian prior of the form $\mathcal{N}(\theta|0, 2.19^2)$ satisfies these prior constraints. But in this case the posterior mean is given by 3.43, which doesn't seem very satisfactory. An alternative distribution that captures the same prior information is the Cauchy prior $\mathcal{T}_1(\theta|0, 1)$. With this prior, we find (using numerical method integration: see robust_prior_demo.ipynb for the code) that the posterior mean is about 4.6, which seems much more reasonable. In general, priors with heavy tails tend to give results which are more sensitive to the data, which is usually what we desire.

Heavy-tailed priors are usually not conjugate. However, we can often approximate a heavy-tailed prior by using a (possibly infinite) mixture of conjugate priors. For example, in Section 28.2.3, we show that the Student distribution (of which the Cauchy is a special case) can be written as an infinite mixture of Gaussians, where the mixing weights come from a gamma distribution. This is an example of a hierarchical prior; see Section 3.6 for details.

3.4.6.3   Priors for scalar variances

In this section, we discuss some commonly used priors for variance parameters. Such priors play an important role in determining how much regularization a model exhibits. For example, consider a linear regression model, $p(y|\boldsymbol{x}, \boldsymbol{w}, \sigma^2) = \mathcal{N}(y|\boldsymbol{w}^\mathsf{T}\boldsymbol{x}, \sigma^2)$. Suppose we use a Gaussian prior on the weights, $p(\boldsymbol{w}) = \mathcal{N}(\boldsymbol{w}|\boldsymbol{0}, \tau^2\mathbf{I})$. The value of τ^2 (relative to σ^2) plays a role similar to the strength of an ℓ_2-regularization term in ridge regression. In the Bayesian setting, we need to ensure we use sensible priors for the variance parameters, τ^2 and σ^2. This becomes even more important when we discuss hierarchical models, in Section 3.6.

We start by considering the simple problem of inferting a variance parameter σ^2 from a Gaussian likelihood with known mean, as in Section 3.4.3.2. The uninformative prior is $p(\sigma^2) = \text{IG}(\sigma^2|0, 0)$, which is improper, meaning it does not integrate to 1. This is fine as long as the posterior is proper. This will be the case if the prior is on the variance of the noise of $N \geq 2$ observable variables.

Unfortunately the posterior is not proper, even if $N \to \infty$, if we use this prior for the variance of the (non observable) weights in a regression model [Gel06; PS12], as we discuss in Section 3.6.

One solution to this is to use a **weakly informative** proper prior such as $\mathrm{IG}(\epsilon, \epsilon)$ for small ϵ. However, this turns out to not work very well, for reasons that are explained in [Gel06; PS12]. Instead, it is recommended to use other priors, such as uniform, exponential, half-normal, half-Student-t, or half-Cauchy; all of these are bounded below by 0, and just require 1 or 2 hyperparameters. (The term "half" refers to the fact that the distribution is "folded over" onto itself on the positive side of the real axis.)

3.4.6.4 Priors for covariance matrices

The conjugate prior for a covariance matrix is the inverse Wishart (Section 2.2.5.6). However, it can be hard to set the parameters for this in an uninformative way. One approach, discussed in [HW13], is to use a scale mixture of inverse Wisharts, where the scaling parameters have inverse gamma distributions. It is possible to choose shape and scale parameters to ensure that all the correlation parameters have uniform $(-1, 1)$ marginals, and all the standard deviations have half-Student distributions.

Unfortunately, the Wishart distribution has heavy tails, which can lead to poor performance when used in a sampling algorithm.[6] A more common approach, following Equation (3.213), is to represent the $D \times D$ covariance matrix $\boldsymbol{\Sigma}$ in terms of a product of the marginal standard deviations, $\boldsymbol{\sigma} = (\sigma_1, \ldots, \sigma_D)$, and the $D \times D$ correlation matrix $\mathbf{R}$, as follows:

$$\boldsymbol{\Sigma} = \mathrm{diag}(\boldsymbol{\sigma}) \, \mathbf{R} \, \mathrm{diag}(\boldsymbol{\sigma}) \tag{3.213}$$

For example, if $D = 2$,we have

$$\boldsymbol{\Sigma} = \begin{pmatrix} \sigma_1 & 0 \\ 0 & \sigma_2 \end{pmatrix} \begin{pmatrix} 1 & \rho \\ \rho & 1 \end{pmatrix} \begin{pmatrix} \sigma_1 & 0 \\ 0 & \sigma_2 \end{pmatrix} = \begin{pmatrix} \sigma_1^2 & \rho\sigma_1\sigma_2 \\ \rho\sigma_1\sigma_2 & \sigma_2^2 \end{pmatrix} \tag{3.214}$$

We can put a factored prior on the standard deviations, following the recommendations of Section 3.4.6.3. For example,

$$p(\boldsymbol{\sigma}) = \prod_{d=1}^{D} \mathrm{Expon}(\sigma_d | 1) \tag{3.215}$$

For the correlation matrix, it is common to use as a prior the **LKJ distribution**, named after the authors of [LKJ09]. This has the form

$$\mathrm{LKJ}(\mathbf{R}|\eta) \propto |\mathbf{R}|^{\eta-1} \tag{3.216}$$

so it only has one free parameter. When $\eta = 1$, it is a uniform prior; when $\eta = 2$, it is a "weakly regularizing" prior, that encourages small correlations (close to 0). See Figure 3.11 for a plot.

In practice, it is more common to define $\mathbf{R}$ in terms of its Cholesky decomposition, $\mathbf{R} = \mathbf{L}\mathbf{L}^\mathsf{T}$, where $\mathbf{L}$ is an unconstrained lower triangular matrix. We then represent the prior using

$$\mathrm{LKJchol}(\mathbf{L}|\eta) \propto |\mathbf{L}|^{-\eta-1} \tag{3.217}$$

---

6. See comments from Michael Betancourt at `https://github.com/pymc-devs/pymc/issues/538`.

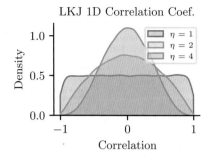

Figure 3.11: Distribution on the correlation coefficient ρ induced by a 2d LKJ distribution with varying parameter. Adapted from Figure 14.3 of [McE20]. Generated by lkj_1d.ipynb.

3.5   Noninformative priors

When we have little or no domain specific knowledge, it is desirable to use an **uninformative**, **noninformative**, or **objective** priors, to "let the data speak for itself". Unfortunately, there is no unique way to define such priors, and they all encode some kind of knowledge. It is therefore better to use the term **diffuse prior**, **minimally informative prior**, or **default prior**.

In the sections below, we briefly mention some common approaches for creating default priors. For further details, see e.g., [KW96] and the Stan website.[7]

3.5.1   Maximum entropy priors

A natural way to define an uninformative prior is to use one that has **maximum entropy**, since it makes the least commitments to any particular value in the state space (see Section 5.2 for a discussion of entropy). This is a formalization of Laplace's **principle of insufficient reason**, in which he argued that if there is no reason to prefer one prior over another, we should pick a "flat" one.

For example, in the case of a Bernoulli distribution with rate $\theta \in [0, 1]$, the maximum entropy prior is the uniform distribution, $p(\theta) = \text{Beta}(\theta|1, 1)$, which makes intuitive sense.

However, in some cases we know something about our random variable $\boldsymbol{\theta}$, and we would like our prior to match these constraints, but otherwise be maximally entropic. More precisely, suppose we want to find a distribution $p(\boldsymbol{\theta})$ with maximum entropy, subject to the constraints that the expected values of certain features or functions $f_k(\boldsymbol{\theta})$ match some known quantities F_k. This is called a **maxent prior**. In Section 2.4.7, we show that such distributions must belong to the exponential family (Section 2.4).

For example, suppose $\theta \in \{1, 2, \ldots, 10\}$, and let $p_c = p(\theta = c)$ be the corresponding prior. Suppose we know that the prior mean is 1.5. We can encode this using the following constraint

$$\mathbb{E}\left[f_1(\theta)\right] = \mathbb{E}\left[\theta\right] = \sum_c c\, p_c = 1.5 \qquad (3.218)$$

---

7. https://github.com/stan-dev/stan/wiki/Prior-Choice-Recommendations.

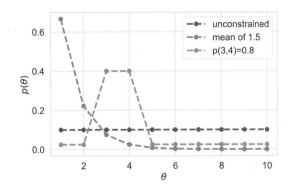

Figure 3.12: Illustration of 3 different maximum entropy priors. Adapted from Figure 1.10 of [MKL11]. Generated by maxent_priors.ipynb.

In addition, we have the constraint $\sum_c p_c = 1$. Thus we need to solve the following optimization problem:

$$\min_{\boldsymbol{p}} \mathbb{H}(\boldsymbol{p}) \quad \text{s.t.} \quad \sum_c c\, p_c = 1.5, \quad \sum_c p_c = 1.0 \tag{3.219}$$

This gives the decaying exponential curve in Figure 3.12. Now suppose we know that θ is either 3 or 4 with probability 0.8. We can encode this using

$$\mathbb{E}\left[f_1(\theta)\right] = \mathbb{E}\left[\mathbb{I}\left(\theta \in \{3, 4\}\right)\right] = \Pr(\theta \in \{3, 4\}) = 0.8 \tag{3.220}$$

This gives the inverted U-curve in Figure 3.12. We note that this distribution is flat in as many places as possible.

3.5.2 Jeffreys priors

Let θ be a random variable with prior $p_\theta(\theta)$, and let $\phi = f(\theta)$ be some invertible transformation of θ. We want to choose a prior that is **invariant** to this function f, so that the posterior does not depend on how we parameterize the model.

For example, consider a Bernoulli distribution with rate parameter θ. Suppose Alice uses a binomial likelihood with data $\mathcal{D}$, and computes $p(\theta|\mathcal{D})$. Now suppose Bob uses the same likelihood and data, but parameterizes the model in terms of the odds parameter, $\phi = \frac{\theta}{1-\theta}$. He converts Alice's prior to $p(\phi)$ using the change of variables formula, and them computes $p(\phi|\mathcal{D})$. If he then converts back to the θ parameterization, he should get the same result as Alice.

We can achieve this goal that provided we use a **Jeffreys prior**, named after Harold Jeffreys.[8] In 1d, the Jeffreys prior is given by $p(\theta) \propto \sqrt{F(\theta)}$, where F is the Fisher information (Section 3.3.4).

---

8. Harold Jeffreys, 1891–1989, was an English mathematician, statistician, geophysicist, and astronomer. He is not to be confused with Richard Jeffrey, a philosopher who advocated the subjective interpretation of probability [Jef04].

In multiple dimensions, the Jeffreys prior has the form $p(\boldsymbol{\theta}) \propto \sqrt{\det \mathbf{F}(\boldsymbol{\theta})}$, where $\mathbf{F}$ is the Fisher information matrix (Section 3.3.4).

To see why the Jeffreys prior is invariant to parameterization, consider the 1d case. Suppose $p_\theta(\theta) \propto \sqrt{F(\theta)}$. Using the change of variables, we can derive the corresponding prior for ϕ as follows:

$$p_\phi(\phi) = p_\theta(\theta) \left| \frac{d\theta}{d\phi} \right| \tag{3.221}$$

$$\propto \sqrt{F(\theta) \left(\frac{d\theta}{d\phi} \right)^2} = \sqrt{\mathbb{E}\left[\left(\frac{d \log p(x|\theta)}{d\theta} \right)^2 \right] \left(\frac{d\theta}{d\phi} \right)^2} \tag{3.222}$$

$$= \sqrt{\mathbb{E}\left[\left(\frac{d \log p(x|\theta)}{d\theta} \frac{d\theta}{d\phi} \right)^2 \right]} = \sqrt{\mathbb{E}\left[\left(\frac{d \log p(x|\phi)}{d\phi} \right)^2 \right]} \tag{3.223}$$

$$= \sqrt{F(\phi)} \tag{3.224}$$

Thus the prior distribution is the same whether we use the θ parameterization or the ϕ parameterization.

We give some examples of Jeffreys priors below.

3.5.2.1   Jeffreys prior for binomial distribution

Let us derive the Jeffreys prior for the binomial distribution using the rate parameterization θ. From Equation (3.57), we have

$$p(\theta) \propto \theta^{-\frac{1}{2}}(1-\theta)^{-\frac{1}{2}} = \frac{1}{\sqrt{\theta(1-\theta)}} \propto \text{Beta}(\theta | \frac{1}{2}, \frac{1}{2}) \tag{3.225}$$

Now consider the odds parameterization, $\phi = \theta/(1-\theta)$, so $\theta = \frac{\phi}{\phi+1}$. The likelihood becomes

$$p(x|\phi) \propto \left(\frac{\phi}{\phi+1} \right)^x \left(1 - \frac{\phi}{\phi+1} \right)^{n-x} = \phi^x(\phi+1)^{-x}(\phi+1)^{-n+x} = \phi^x(\phi+1)^{-n} \tag{3.226}$$

Thus the log likelihood is

$$\ell = x \log \phi - n \log \phi + 1 \tag{3.227}$$

The first and second derivatives are

$$\frac{d\ell}{d\phi} = \frac{x}{\phi} - \frac{n}{\phi+1} \tag{3.228}$$

$$\frac{d^2\ell}{d\phi^2} = -\frac{x}{\phi^2} + \frac{n}{(\phi+1)^2} \tag{3.229}$$

Since $\mathbb{E}[x] = n\theta = n\frac{\phi}{\phi+1}$, the Fisher information matrix is given by

$$F(\phi) = -\mathbb{E}\left[\frac{d^2\ell}{d\phi^2} \right] \frac{n}{\phi(\phi+1)} - \frac{n}{(\phi+1)^2} \tag{3.230}$$

$$= \frac{n(\phi+1) - n\phi}{\phi(\phi+1)^2} = \frac{n}{\phi(\phi+1)^2} \tag{3.231}$$

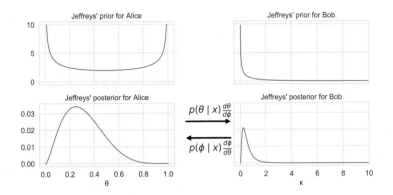

Figure 3.13: Illustration of Jeffreys prior for Alice (who uses the rate θ) and Bob (who uses the odds $\phi = \theta/(1-\theta)$). Adapted from Figure 1.9 of [MKL11]. Generated by jeffreys_prior_binomial.ipynb.

Hence

$$p_\phi(\phi) \propto \phi^{-0.5}(1+\phi)^{-1} \tag{3.232}$$

See Figure 3.13 for an illustration.

3.5.2.2 Jeffreys prior for multinomial distribution

For a categorical random variable with K states, one can show that the Jeffreys prior is given by

$$p(\boldsymbol{\theta}) \propto \text{Dir}(\boldsymbol{\theta}|\frac{1}{2},\ldots,\frac{1}{2}) \tag{3.233}$$

Note that this is different from the more obvious choices of $\text{Dir}(\frac{1}{K},\ldots,\frac{1}{K})$ or $\text{Dir}(1,\ldots,1)$.

3.5.2.3 Jeffreys prior for the mean and variance of a univariate Gaussian

Consider a 1d Gaussian $x \sim \mathcal{N}(\mu,\sigma^2)$ with both parameters unknown, so $\boldsymbol{\theta} = (\mu,\sigma)$. From Equation (3.62), the Fisher information matrix is

$$\mathbf{F}(\boldsymbol{\theta}) = \begin{pmatrix} 1/\sigma^2 & 0 \\ 0 & 2/\sigma^2 \end{pmatrix} \tag{3.234}$$

so $\sqrt{\det(\mathbf{F}(\boldsymbol{\theta}))} = \sqrt{\frac{2}{\sigma^4}}$. However, the standard Jeffreys uninformative prior for the Gaussian is defined as the product of independent uninformative priors (see [KW96]), i.e.,

$$p(\mu,\sigma^2) \propto p(\mu)p(\sigma^2) \propto 1/\sigma^2 \tag{3.235}$$

It turns out that we can emulate this prior with a conjugate NIX prior:

$$p(\mu,\sigma^2) = NI\chi^2(\mu,\sigma^2|\mu_0 = 0, \breve{\kappa}= 0, \breve{\nu}= -1, \breve{\sigma}^2= 0) \tag{3.236}$$

This lets us easily reuse the results for conjugate analysis of the Gaussian in Section 3.4.3.3, as we showed in Section 3.4.3.4.

3.5.3   Invariant priors

If we have "objective" prior knowledge about a problem in the form of invariances, we may be able to encode this into a prior, as we show below.

3.5.3.1   Translation-invariant priors

A **location-scale family** is a family of probability distributions parameterized by a location μ and scale σ. If x is an rv in this family, then $y = a + bx$ is also an rv in the same family.

   When inferring the location parameter μ, it is intuitively reasonable to want to use a **translation-invariant prior**, which satisfies the property that the probability mass assigned to any interval, $[A, B]$ is the same as that assigned to any other shifted interval of the same width, such as $[A-c, B-c]$. That is,

$$\int_{A-c}^{B-c} p(\mu)d\mu = \int_{A}^{B} p(\mu)d\mu \tag{3.237}$$

This can be achieved using

$$p(\mu) \propto 1 \tag{3.238}$$

since

$$\int_{A-c}^{B-c} 1d\mu = (B - c) - (A - c) = (B - A) = \int_{A}^{B} 1d\mu \tag{3.239}$$

   This is the same as the Jeffreys prior for a Gaussian with unknown mean μ and fixed variance. This follows since $F(\mu) = 1/\sigma^2 \propto 1$, from Equation (3.62), and hence $p(\mu) \propto 1$.

3.5.3.2   Scale-invariant prior

When inferring the scale parameter σ, we may want to use a **scale-invariant prior**, which satisfies the property that the probability mass assigned to any interval $[A, B]$ is the same as that assigned to any other interval $[A/c, B/c]$, where $c > 0$. That is,

$$\int_{A/c}^{B/c} p(\sigma)d\sigma = \int_{A}^{B} p(\sigma)d\sigma \tag{3.240}$$

This can be achieved by using

$$p(\sigma) \propto 1/\sigma \tag{3.241}$$

since then

$$\int_{A/c}^{B/c} \frac{1}{\sigma}d\sigma = [\log \sigma]_{A/c}^{B/c} = \log(B/c) - \log(A/c) = \log(B) - \log(A) = \int_{A}^{B} \frac{1}{\sigma}d\sigma \tag{3.242}$$

   This is the same as the Jeffreys prior for a Gaussian with fixed mean μ and unknown scale σ. This follows since $F(\sigma) = 2/\sigma^2$, from Equation (3.62), and hence $p(\sigma) \propto 1/\sigma$.

3.5.3.3 Learning invariant priors

Whenever we have knowledge of some kind of invariance we want our model to satisfy, we can use this to encode a corresponding prior. Sometimes this is done analytically (see e.g., [Rob07, Ch.9]). When this is intractable, it may be possible to learn invariant priors by solving a variational optimization problem (see e.g., [NS18]).

3.5.4 Reference priors

One way to define a noninformative prior is as a distribution which is maximally far from all possible posteriors, when averaged over datasets. This is the basic idea behind a **reference prior** [Ber05; BBS09]. More precisely, we say that $p(\boldsymbol{\theta})$ is a reference prior if it maximizes the expected KL divergence between posterior and prior:

$$p^*(\boldsymbol{\theta}) = \underset{p(\boldsymbol{\theta})}{\operatorname{argmax}} \int_{\mathcal{D}} p(\mathcal{D}) D_{\mathrm{KL}} \left(p(\boldsymbol{\theta}|\mathcal{D}) \parallel p(\boldsymbol{\theta}) \right) d\mathcal{D} \tag{3.243}$$

where $p(\mathcal{D}) = \int p(\mathcal{D}|\boldsymbol{\theta})p(\boldsymbol{\theta})d\boldsymbol{\theta}$. This is the same as maximizing the mutual information $\mathbb{I}(\boldsymbol{\theta}, \mathcal{D})$.

We can eliminate the integral over datasets by noting that

$$\int p(\mathcal{D}) \int p(\boldsymbol{\theta}|\mathcal{D}) \log \frac{p(\boldsymbol{\theta}|\mathcal{D})}{p(\boldsymbol{\theta})} = \int p(\boldsymbol{\theta}) \int p(\mathcal{D}|\boldsymbol{\theta}) \log \frac{p(\mathcal{D}|\boldsymbol{\theta})}{p(\mathcal{D})} = \mathbb{E}_{\boldsymbol{\theta}} \left[D_{\mathrm{KL}} \left(p(\mathcal{D}|\boldsymbol{\theta}) \parallel p(\mathcal{D}) \right) \right] \quad (3.244)$$

where we used the fact that $\frac{p(\boldsymbol{\theta}|\mathcal{D})}{p(\boldsymbol{\theta})} = \frac{p(\mathcal{D}|\boldsymbol{\theta})}{p(\mathcal{D})}$.

One can show that, in 1d, the corresponding prior is equivalent to the Jeffreys prior. In higher dimensions, we can compute the reference prior for one parameter at a time, using the chain rule. However, this can become computationally intractable. See [NS17] for a tractable approximation based on variational inference (Section 10.1).

3.6 Hierarchical priors

Bayesian models require specifying a prior $p(\boldsymbol{\theta})$ for the parameters. The parameters of the prior are called **hyperparameters**, and will be denoted by $\boldsymbol{\xi}$. If these are unknown, we can put a prior on them; this defines a **hierarchical Bayesian model**, or **multi-level model**, which can visualize like this: $\boldsymbol{\xi} \to \boldsymbol{\theta} \to \mathcal{D}$. We assume the prior on the hyper-parameters is fixed (e.g., we may use some kind of minimally informative prior), so the joint distribution has the form

$$p(\boldsymbol{\xi}, \boldsymbol{\theta}, \mathcal{D}) = p(\boldsymbol{\xi})p(\boldsymbol{\theta}|\boldsymbol{\xi})p(\mathcal{D}|\boldsymbol{\theta}) \tag{3.245}$$

The hope is that we can learn the hyperparameters by treating the parameters themselves as datapoints.

A common setting in which such an approach makes sense is when we have $J > 1$ related datasets, $\mathcal{D}_j$, each with their own parameters $\boldsymbol{\theta}_j$. Inferring $p(\boldsymbol{\theta}_j|\mathcal{D}_j)$ independently for each group j can give poor results if $\mathcal{D}_j$ is a small dataset (e.g., if condition j corresponds to a rare combination of features, or a sparsely population region). We could of course pool all the data to compute a single model, $p(\boldsymbol{\theta}|\mathcal{D})$, but that would not let us model the subpopulations. A hierarchical Bayesian model lets us

borrow statistical strength from groups with lots of data (and hence well-informed posteriors $p(\boldsymbol{\theta}_j|\mathcal{D})$) in order to help groups with little data (and hence highly uncertain posteriors $p(\boldsymbol{\theta}_j|\mathcal{D})$). The idea is that well-informed groups j will have a good estimate of $\boldsymbol{\theta}_j$, from which we can infer $\boldsymbol{\xi}$, which can be used to help estimate $\boldsymbol{\theta}_k$ for groups k with less data. (Information is shared via the hidden common parent node $\boldsymbol{\xi}$ in the graphical model, as shown in Figure 3.14.) We give some examples of this below.

After fitting such models, we can compute two kinds of posterior predictive distributions. If we want to predict observations for an existing group j, we need to use

$$p(y_j|\mathcal{D}) = \int p(y_j|\theta_j)p(\theta_j|\mathcal{D})d\theta_j \tag{3.246}$$

However, if we want to predict observations for a new group $*$ that has not yet been measured, but which is comparable to (or **exchangeable with**) the existing groups $1:J$, we need to use

$$p(y_*|\mathcal{D}) = \int p(y_*|\theta_*)p(\theta_*|\boldsymbol{\xi})p(\boldsymbol{\xi}|\mathcal{D})d\theta_*d\boldsymbol{\xi} \tag{3.247}$$

We give some examples below. (More information can be found in e.g., [GH07; Gel+14a].)

3.6.1   A hierarchical binomial model

Suppose we want to estimate the prevalence of some disease amongst different group of individuals, either people or animals. Let N_j be the size of the j'th group, and let y_j be the number of positive cases for group $j = 1:J$. We assume $y_j \sim \text{Bin}(N_j, \theta_j)$, and we want to estimate the rates θ_j. Since some groups may have small population sizes, we may get unreliable results if we estimate each θ_j separately; for example we may observe $y_j = 0$ resulting in $\hat{\theta}_j = 0$, even though the true infection rate is higher.

One solution is to assume all the θ_j are the same; this is called **parameter tying**. The resulting pooled MLE is just $\hat{\theta}_{\text{pooled}} = \frac{\sum_j y_j}{\sum_j N_j}$. But the assumption that all the groups have the same rate is a rather strong one. A compromise approach is to assume that the θ_j are similar, but that there may be group-specific variations. This can be modeled by assuming the θ_j are drawn from some common distribution, say $\theta_j \sim \text{Beta}(a, b)$. The full joint distribution can be written as

$$p(\mathcal{D}, \boldsymbol{\theta}, \boldsymbol{\xi}) = p(\boldsymbol{\xi})p(\boldsymbol{\theta}|\boldsymbol{\xi})p(\mathcal{D}|\boldsymbol{\theta}) = p(\boldsymbol{\xi}) \left[\prod_{j=1}^{J} \text{Beta}(\theta_j|\boldsymbol{\xi}) \right] \left[\prod_{j=1}^{J} \text{Bin}(y_j|N_j, \theta_j) \right] \tag{3.248}$$

where $\boldsymbol{\xi} = (a, b)$. In Figure 3.14 we represent these assumptions using a directed graphical model (see Section 4.2.8 for an explanation of such diagrams).

It remains to specify the prior $p(\boldsymbol{\xi})$. Following [Gel+14a, p110], we use

$$p(a, b) \propto (a + b)^{-5/2} \tag{3.249}$$

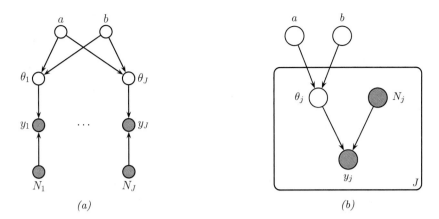

Figure 3.14: PGM for a hierarchical binomial model. (a) "Unrolled" model. (b) Same model, using plate notation.

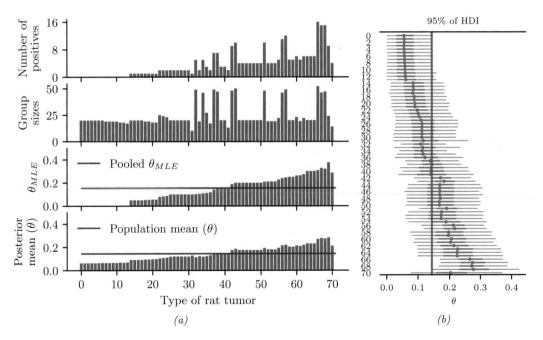

Figure 3.15: Data and inferences for the hierarchical binomial model fit using HMC. Generated by hierarchical_binom_rats.ipynb.

3.6.1.1 Posterior inference

We can perform approximate posterior inference in this model using a variety of methods. In Section 3.7.1 we discuss an optimization based approach, but here we discuss one of the most popular methods in Bayesian statistics, known as HMC or Hamiltonian Monte Carlo. This is described in Section 12.5, but in short it is a form of MCMC (Markov chain Monte Carlo) that exploits information from the gradient of the log joint to guide the sampling process. This algorithm generates samples in an unconstrained parameter space, so we need to define the log joint over all the parameters $\boldsymbol{\omega} = (\tilde{\boldsymbol{\theta}}, \tilde{\boldsymbol{\xi}}) \in \mathbb{R}^D$ as follows:

$$\log p(\mathcal{D}, \boldsymbol{\omega}) = \log p(\mathcal{D}|\boldsymbol{\theta}) + \log p(\boldsymbol{\theta}|\boldsymbol{\xi}) + \log p(\boldsymbol{\xi}) \tag{3.250}$$

$$+ \sum_{j=1}^{J} \log |\text{Jac}(\sigma)(\tilde{\theta}_j)| + \sum_{i=1}^{2} \log |\text{Jac}(\sigma_+)(\tilde{\xi}_i)| \tag{3.251}$$

where $\theta_j = \sigma(\tilde{\theta}_j)$ is the sigmoid transform, and $\xi_i = \sigma_+(\tilde{\xi}_i)$ is the softplus transform. (We need to add the Jacobian terms to account for these deterministic transformations.) We can then use automatic differentation to compute $\nabla_{\boldsymbol{\omega}} \log p(\mathcal{D}, \boldsymbol{\omega})$, which we pass to the HMC algorithm. This algorithm returns a set of (correlated) samples from the posterior, $(\tilde{\boldsymbol{\xi}}^s, \tilde{\boldsymbol{\theta}}^s) \sim p(\boldsymbol{\omega}|\mathcal{D})$, which we can back transform to $(\boldsymbol{\xi}^s, \boldsymbol{\theta}^s)$. We can then estimate the posterior over quantities of interest by using a Monte Carlo approximation to $p(f(\boldsymbol{\theta})|\mathcal{D})$ for suitable f (e.g., to compute the posterior mean rate for group j, we set $f(\boldsymbol{\theta}) = \theta_j$).

3.6.1.2 Example: the rats dataset

In this section, we apply this model to analyze the number of rats that develop a certain kind of tumor during a particular clinical trial (see [Gel+14a, p102] for details). We show the raw data in rows 1–2 of Figure 3.15a. In row 3, we show the MLE $\hat{\theta}_j$ for each group. We see that some groups have $\hat{\theta}_j = 0$, which is much less than the pooled MLE $\hat{\theta}_{\text{pooled}}$ (red line). In row 4, we show the posterior mean $\mathbb{E}[\theta_j|\mathcal{D}]$ estimated from all the data, as well as the population mean $\mathbb{E}[\theta|\mathcal{D}] = \mathbb{E}[a/(a+b)|\mathcal{D}]$ shown in the red lines. We see that groups that have low counts have their estimates increased towards the population mean, and groups that have large counts have their estimates decreased towards the population mean. In other words, the groups regularize each other; this phenomenon is called **shrinkage**. The amount of shrinkage is controlled by the prior on (a, b), which is inferred from the data.

In Figure 3.15b, we show the 95% credible intervals for each parameter, as well as the overall population mean. (This is known as a **forest plot**.) We can use this to decide if any group is significantly different than any specified target value (e.g., the overall average).

3.6.2 A hierarchical Gaussian model

In this section, we consider a variation of the model in Section 3.6.1, where this time we have real-valued data instead of binary count data. More specificially we assume $y_{ij} \sim \mathcal{N}(\theta_j, \sigma^2)$, where θ_j is the unknown mean for group j, and σ^2 is the observation variance (assumed to be shared across groups and fixed, for simplicity). Note that having N_j observations y_{ij} each with variance σ^2 is like having one measurement $y_j \triangleq \frac{1}{N_j} \sum_{i=1}^{N_j} y_{ij}$ with variance $\sigma_j^2 \triangleq \sigma^2/N_j$. This lets us simplify notation

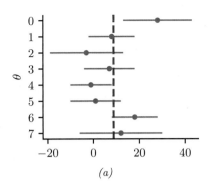

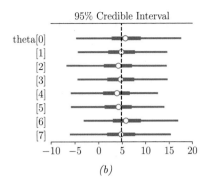

Figure 3.16: Eight schools dataset. (a) Raw data. Each row plots $y_j \pm \sigma_j$. Vertical line is the pooled estimate. (b) Posterior 95% credible intervals for θ_j. Vertical line is posterior mean $\mathbb{E}[\mu|\mathcal{D}]$. Generated by schools8.ipynb.

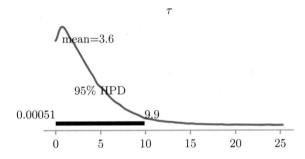

Figure 3.17: Marginal posterior density $p(\tau|\mathcal{D})$ for the 8-schools dataset. Generated by schools8.ipynb.

and use one observation per group, with likelihood $y_j \sim \mathcal{N}(\theta, \sigma_j^2)$, where we assume the σ_j's are known.

We use a hierarchical model by assuming each group's parameters come from a common distribution, $\theta_j \sim \mathcal{N}(\mu, \tau^2)$. The model becomes

$$p(\mu, \tau^2, \boldsymbol{\theta}_{1:J}|\mathcal{D}) \propto p(\mu)p(\tau^2) \prod_{j=1}^{J} \mathcal{N}(\theta_j|\mu, \tau^2)\mathcal{N}(y_j|\theta_j, \sigma_j^2) \tag{3.252}$$

where $p(\mu)p(\tau^2)$ is some kind of prior over the hyper-parameters. See Figure 3.19a for the graphical model.

3.6.2.1 Example: the eight schools dataset

Let us now apply this model to some data. We will consider the **eight schools** dataset from [Gel+14a, Sec 5.5]. The goal is to estimate the effects on a new coaching program on SAT scores. Let y_{nj} be the observed improvement in score for student n in school j compared to a baseline. Since each school has multiple students, we summarize its data using the empirical mean $\overline{y}_{\cdot j} = \frac{1}{N_j}\sum_{n=1}^{N_j} y_{nj}$

and standard deviation σ_j. See Figure 3.16a for an illustration of the data. We also show the pooled MLE for θ, which is a precision weighted average of the data:

$$\overline{y}_{..} = \frac{\sum_{j=1}^{J} \frac{1}{\sigma_j^2} \overline{y}_{.j}}{\sum_{j=1}^{J} \frac{1}{\sigma_j^2}} \tag{3.253}$$

We see that school 0 has an unusually large improvement (28 points) compared to the overall mean, suggesting that the estimating θ_0 just based on $\mathcal{D}_0$ might be unreliable. However, we can easily apply our hierarchical model. We will use HMC to do approximate inference. (See Section 3.7.2 for a faster approximate method.)

After computing the (approximate) posterior, we can compute the marginal posteriors $p(\theta_j|\mathcal{D})$ for each school. These distributions are shown in Figure 3.16b. Once again, we see shrinkage towards the global mean $\overline{\mu} = \mathbb{E}[\mu|\mathcal{D}]$, which is close to the pooled estimate $\overline{y}_{..}$. In fact, if we fix the hyper-parameters to their posterior mean values, and use the approximation

$$p(\mu, \tau^2|\mathcal{D}) = \delta(\mu - \overline{\mu})\delta(\tau^2 - \overline{\tau}^2) \tag{3.254}$$

then we can use the results from Section 3.4.3.1 to compute the marginal posteriors

$$p(\theta_j|\mathcal{D}) \approx p(\theta_j|\mathcal{D}_j, \overline{\mu}, \overline{\tau}^2) \tag{3.255}$$

In particular, we can show that the posterior mean $\mathbb{E}[\theta_j|\mathcal{D}]$ is in between the MLE $\hat{\theta}_j = y_j$ and the global mean $\overline{\mu} = \mathbb{E}[\mu|\mathcal{D}]$:

$$\mathbb{E}[\theta_j|\mathcal{D}, \overline{\mu}, \overline{\tau}^2] = w_j\overline{\mu} + (1 - w_j)\hat{\theta}_j \tag{3.256}$$

where the amount of shrinkage towards the global mean is given by

$$w_j = \frac{\sigma_j^2}{\sigma_j^2 + \tau^2} \tag{3.257}$$

Thus we see that there is more shrinkage for groups with smaller measurement precision (e.g., due to smaller sample size), which makes intuitive sense. There is also more shrinkage if τ^2 is smaller; of course τ^2 is unknown, but we can compute a posterior for it, as shown in Figure 3.17.

3.6.2.2   Non-centered parameterization

It turns out that posterior inference in this model is difficult for many algorithms because of the tight dependence between the variance hyperparameter τ^2 and the group means θ_j, as illustrated by the **funnel shape** in Figure 3.18. In particular, consider making local moves through parameter space. The algorithm can only "visit" the place where τ^2 is small (corresponding to strong shrinkage to the prior) if all the θ_j are close to the prior mean μ. It may be hard to move into the area where τ^2 is small unless all groups *simultaneously* move their θ_j estimates closer to μ.

A standard solution to this problem is to rewrite the model using the following **non-centered parameterization**:

$$\theta_j = \mu + \tau\eta_j \tag{3.258}$$
$$\eta_j \sim \mathcal{N}(0, 1) \tag{3.259}$$

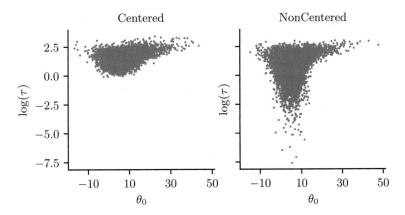

Figure 3.18: Posterior $p(\theta_0, \log(\tau)|\mathcal{D})$ for the eight schools model using (a) centered parameterization and (b) non-centered parameterization. Generated by schools8.ipynb.

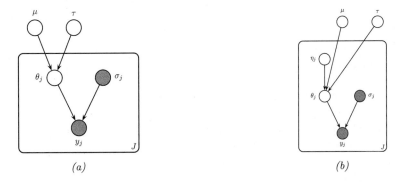

Figure 3.19: A hierarchical Gaussian Bayesian model. (a) Centered parameterization. (b) Non-centered parameterization.

See Figure 3.19b for the corresponding graphical model. By writing θ_j as a deterministic function of its parents plus a local noise term, we have reduced the dependence between θ_j and τ and hence the other θ_k variables, which can improve the computational efficiency of inference algorithms, as we discuss in Section 12.6.5. This kind of reparameterization is widely used in hierarchical Bayesian models.

3.6.3 Hierarchical conditional models

In Section 15.5, we discuss hierarchical Bayesian GLM models, which learn conditional distributions $p(\boldsymbol{y}|\boldsymbol{x}, \boldsymbol{\theta}_j)$ for each group j, using a prior of the form $p(\boldsymbol{\theta}_j|\boldsymbol{\xi})$. In Section 17.6, we discuss hierarchical Bayesian neural networks, which generalize this idea to nonlinear predictors.

3.7 Empirical Bayes

In Section 3.6, we discussed hierarchical Bayes as a way to infer parameters from data. Unfortunately, posterior inference in such models can be computationally challenging. In this section, we discuss a computationally convenient approximation, in which we first compute a point estimate of the hyperparameters, $\hat{\boldsymbol{\xi}}$, and then compute the conditional posterior, $p(\boldsymbol{\theta}|\hat{\boldsymbol{\xi}}, \mathcal{D})$, rather than the joint posterior, $p(\boldsymbol{\theta}, \boldsymbol{\xi}|\mathcal{D})$.

To estimate the hyper-parameters, we can maximize the marginal likelihood:

$$\hat{\boldsymbol{\xi}}_{\mathrm{mml}}(\mathcal{D}) = \operatorname*{argmax}_{\boldsymbol{\xi}} p(\mathcal{D}|\boldsymbol{\xi}) = \operatorname*{argmax}_{\boldsymbol{\xi}} \int p(\mathcal{D}|\boldsymbol{\theta})p(\boldsymbol{\theta}|\boldsymbol{\xi})d\boldsymbol{\theta} \tag{3.260}$$

This technique is known as **type II maximum likelihood**, since we are optimizing the hyperparameters, rather than the parameters. (In the context of neural networks, this is sometimes called the **evidence procedure** [Mac92a; WS93; Mac99].) Once we have estimated $\hat{\boldsymbol{\xi}}$, we compute the posterior $p(\boldsymbol{\theta}|\hat{\boldsymbol{\xi}}, \mathcal{D})$ in the usual way.

Since we are estimating the prior parameters from data, this approach is **empirical Bayes (EB)** [CL96]. This violates the principle that the prior should be chosen independently of the data. However, we can view it as a computationally cheap approximation to inference in the full hierarchical Bayesian model, just as we viewed MAP estimation as an approximation to inference in the one level model $\boldsymbol{\theta} \to \mathcal{D}$. In fact, we can construct a hierarchy in which the more integrals one performs, the "more Bayesian" one becomes, as shown below.

Method	Definition
Maximum likelihood	$\hat{\boldsymbol{\theta}} = \operatorname{argmax}_{\boldsymbol{\theta}} p(\mathcal{D}|\boldsymbol{\theta})$
MAP estimation	$\hat{\boldsymbol{\theta}} = \operatorname{argmax}_{\boldsymbol{\theta}} p(\mathcal{D}|\boldsymbol{\theta})p(\boldsymbol{\theta}|\boldsymbol{\xi})$
ML-II (empirical Bayes)	$\hat{\boldsymbol{\xi}} = \operatorname{argmax}_{\boldsymbol{\xi}} \int p(\mathcal{D}|\boldsymbol{\theta})p(\boldsymbol{\theta}|\boldsymbol{\xi})d\boldsymbol{\theta}$
MAP-II	$\hat{\boldsymbol{\xi}} = \operatorname{argmax}_{\boldsymbol{\xi}} \int p(\mathcal{D}|\boldsymbol{\theta})p(\boldsymbol{\theta}|\boldsymbol{\xi})p(\boldsymbol{\xi})d\boldsymbol{\theta}$
Full Bayes	$p(\boldsymbol{\theta}, \boldsymbol{\xi}|\mathcal{D}) \propto p(\mathcal{D}|\boldsymbol{\theta})p(\boldsymbol{\theta}|\boldsymbol{\xi})p(\boldsymbol{\xi})$

Note that ML-II is less likely to overfit than "regular" maximum likelihood, because there are typically fewer hyper-parameters $\boldsymbol{\xi}$ than there are parameters $\boldsymbol{\theta}$. We give some simple examples below, and will see more applications later in the book.

3.7.1 EB for the hierarchical binomial model

In this section, we revisit the hierarchical binomial model from Section 3.6.1, but we use empirical Bayes instead of full Bayesian inference. We can analytically integrate out the θ_j's, and write down

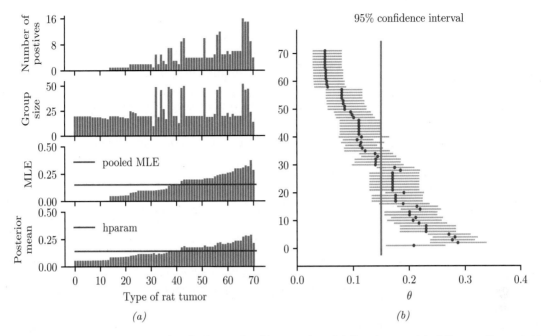

Figure 3.20: *Data and inferences for the hierarchical binomial model fit using empirical Bayes. Generated by eb_binom.ipynb.*

the marginal likelihood directly: The resulting expression is

$$p(\mathcal{D}|\boldsymbol{\xi}) = \prod_j \int \text{Bin}(y_j|N_j,\theta_j)\text{Beta}(\theta_j|a,b)d\theta_j \qquad (3.261)$$

$$\propto \prod_j \frac{B(a+y_j, b+N_j-y_j)}{B(a,b)} \qquad (3.262)$$

$$= \prod_j \frac{\Gamma(a+b)}{\Gamma(a)\Gamma(b)} \frac{\Gamma(a+y_j)\Gamma(b+N_j-y_j)}{\Gamma(a+b+N_j)} \qquad (3.263)$$

Various ways of maximizing this marginal likelihood wrt a and b are discussed in [Min00c].

Having estimated the hyper-parameters a and b, we can plug them in to compute the posterior $p(\theta_j|\hat{a},\hat{b},\mathcal{D})$ for each group, using conjugate analysis in the usual way. We show the results in Figure 3.20; they are very similar to the full Bayesian analysis shown in Figure 3.15, but the EB method is much faster.

3.7.2 EB for the hierarchical Gaussian model

In this section, we revisit the hierarchical Gaussian model from Section 3.6.2.1. However, we fit the model using empirical Bayes.

For simplicity, we will assume that $\sigma_j^2 = \sigma^2$ is the same for all groups. When the variances are equal, we can derive the EB estimate in closed form, as we now show. We have

$$p(y_j|\mu, \tau^2, \sigma^2) = \int \mathcal{N}(y_j|\theta_j, \sigma^2)\mathcal{N}(\theta_j|\mu, \tau^2)d\theta_j = \mathcal{N}(y_j|\mu, \tau^2 + \sigma^2) \tag{3.264}$$

Hence the marginal likelihood is

$$p(\mathcal{D}|\mu, \tau^2, \sigma^2) = \prod_{j=1}^{J} \mathcal{N}(y_j|\mu, \tau^2 + \sigma^2) \tag{3.265}$$

Thus we can estimate the hyper-parameters using the usual MLEs for a Gaussian. For μ, we have

$$\hat{\mu} = \frac{1}{J}\sum_{j=1}^{J} y_j = \overline{y} \tag{3.266}$$

which is the overall mean. For τ^2, we can use moment matching, which is equivalent to the MLE for a Gaussian. This means we equate the model variance to the empirical variance:

$$\hat{\tau}^2 + \sigma^2 = \frac{1}{J}\sum_{j=1}^{J}(y_j - \overline{y})^2 \triangleq v \tag{3.267}$$

so $\hat{\tau}^2 = v - \sigma^2$. Since we know τ^2 must be positive, it is common to use the following revised estimate:

$$\hat{\tau}^2 = \max\{0, v - \sigma^2\} = (v - \sigma^2)_+ \tag{3.268}$$

Given this, the posterior mean becomes

$$\hat{\theta}_j = \lambda\mu + (1 - \lambda)y_j = \mu + (1 - \lambda)(y_j - \mu) \tag{3.269}$$

where $\lambda_j = \lambda = \sigma^2/(\sigma^2 + \tau^2)$.

Unfortunately, we cannot use the above method on the 8-schools dataset in Section 3.6.2.1, since it uses unequal σ_j. However, we can still use the EM algorithm or other optimization based methods.

3.7.3   EB for Markov models (n-gram smoothing)

The main problem with add-one smoothing, discussed in Section 2.6.3.3, is that it assumes that all n-grams are equally likely, which is not very realistic. A more sophisticated approach, called **deleted interpolation** [CG96], defines the transition matrix as a convex combination of the bigram frequencies $f_{jk} = N_{jk}/N_j$ and the unigram frequencies $f_k = N_k/N$:

$$A_{jk} = (1 - \lambda)f_{jk} + \lambda f_k = (1 - \lambda)\frac{N_{jk}}{N_j} + \lambda\frac{N_k}{N} \tag{3.270}$$

The term λ is usually set by cross validation. There is also a closely related technique called **backoff smoothing**; the idea is that if f_{jk} is too small, we "back off" to a more reliable estimate, namely f_k.

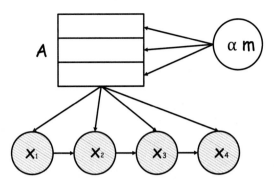

Figure 3.21: A Markov chain in which we put a different Dirichlet prior on every row of the transition matrix **A**, but the hyperparameters of the Dirichlet are shared.

We now show that this heuristic can be interpreted as an empirical Bayes approximation to a hierarchical Bayesian model for the parameter vectors corresponding to each row of the transition matrix **A**. Our presentation follows [MP95].

First, let us use an independent Dirichlet prior on each row of the transition matrix:

$$\mathbf{A}_j \sim \text{Dir}(\alpha_0 m_1, \ldots, \alpha_0 m_K) = \text{Dir}(\alpha_0 \boldsymbol{m}) = \text{Dir}(\boldsymbol{\alpha}) \tag{3.271}$$

where $\mathbf{A}_j$ is row j of the transition matrix, $\boldsymbol{m}$ is the prior mean (satisfying $\sum_k m_k = 1$) and α_0 is the prior strength (see Figure 3.21). In terms of the earlier notation, we have $\boldsymbol{\theta}_j = \mathbf{A}_j$ and $\boldsymbol{\xi} = (\alpha, \boldsymbol{m})$.

The posterior is given by $\mathbf{A}_j \sim \text{Dir}(\boldsymbol{\alpha} + \mathbf{N}_j)$, where $\mathbf{N}_j = (N_{j1}, \ldots, N_{jK})$ is the vector that records the number of times we have transitioned out of state j to each of the other states. The posterior predictive density is

$$p(X_{t+1} = k | X_t = j, \mathcal{D}) = \frac{N_{jk} + \alpha_j m_k}{N_j + \alpha_0} = \frac{f_{jk} N_j + \alpha_j m_k}{N_j + \alpha_0} \tag{3.272}$$

$$= (1 - \lambda_j) f_{jk} + \lambda_j m_k \tag{3.273}$$

where

$$\lambda_j = \frac{\alpha_j}{N_j + \alpha_0} \tag{3.274}$$

This is very similar to Equation (3.270) but not identical. The main difference is that the Bayesian model uses a context-dependent weight λ_j to combine m_k with the empirical frequency f_{jk}, rather than a fixed weight λ. This is like *adaptive* deleted interpolation. Furthermore, rather than backing off to the empirical marginal frequencies f_k, we back off to the model parameter m_k.

The only remaining question is: what values should we use for α and $\boldsymbol{m}$? Let's use empirical Bayes. Since we assume each row of the transition matrix is a priori independent given $\boldsymbol{\alpha}$, the marginal likelihood for our Markov model is given by

$$p(\mathcal{D}|\boldsymbol{\alpha}) = \prod_j \frac{B(\mathbf{N}_j + \boldsymbol{\alpha})}{B(\boldsymbol{\alpha})} \tag{3.275}$$

where $\mathbf{N}_j = (N_{j1}, \ldots, N_{jK})$ are the counts for leaving state j and $B(\boldsymbol{\alpha})$ is the generalized beta function.

We can fit this using the methods discussed in [Min00c]. However, we can also use the following approximation [MP95, p12]:

$$m_k \propto |\{j : N_{jk} > 0\}| \tag{3.276}$$

This says that the prior probability of word k is given by the number of different contexts in which it occurs, rather than the number of times it occurs. To justify the reasonableness of this result, MacKay and Peto [MP95] give the following example.

```
Imagine, you see, that the language, you see, has, you see, a
frequently occuring couplet 'you see', you see, in which the second
word of the couplet, see, follows the first word, you, with very high
probability, you see. Then the marginal statistics, you see, are going
to become hugely dominated, you see, by the words you and see, with
equal frequency, you see.
```

If we use the standard smoothing formula, Equation (3.270), then P(you|novel) and P(see|novel), for some novel context word not seen before, would turn out to be the same, since the marginal frequencies of 'you' and 'see' are the same (11 times each). However, this seems unreasonable. 'You' appears in many contexts, so P(you|novel) should be high, but 'see' only follows 'you', so P(see|novel) should be low. If we use the Bayesian formula Equation (3.273), we will get this effect for free, since we back off to m_k not f_k, and m_k will be large for 'you' and small for 'see' by Equation (3.276).

Although elegant, this Bayesian model does not beat the state-of-the-art language model, known as **interpolated Kneser-Ney** [KN95; CG98]. By using ideas from nonparametric Bayes, one can create a language model that outperforms such heuristics, as discussed in [Teh06; Woo+09]. However, one can get even better results using recurrent neural nets (Section 16.3.4); the key to their success is that they don't treat each symbol "atomically", but instead learn a distributed embedding representation, which encodes the assumption that some symbols are more similar to each other than others.

3.7.4   EB for non-conjugate models

For more complex models, we cannot compute the EB estimate exactly. However, we can use the variational EM method to compute an approximate EB estimate, as we explain in Section 10.1.3.2.

3.8   Model selection

> All models are wrong, but some are useful. — George Box [BD87, p424].[9]

In this section, we assume we have a set of different models $\mathcal{M}$, each of which may fit the data to different degrees, and each of which may make different assumptions. We discuss how to pick the best model from this set. or to average over all of them.

We assume the "true" model is in the set $\mathcal{M}$; this is known as the $\mathcal{M}$-**complete** assumption [BS94]. Of course, in reality, none of the models may be adequate; this is known as the $\mathcal{M}$-**open** scenario

---

9. George Box is a retired statistics professor at the University of Wisconsin.

[BS94; CI13]. We can check how well a model fits (or fails to fit) the data using the procedures in Section 3.9. If none of the models are a good fit, we need to expand our hypothesis space.

3.8.1 Bayesian model selection

The natural way to pick the best model is to pick the most probable model according to Bayes' rule:

$$\hat{m} = \underset{m \in \mathcal{M}}{\operatorname{argmax}} \, p(m|\mathcal{D}) \tag{3.277}$$

where

$$p(m|\mathcal{D}) = \frac{p(\mathcal{D}|m)p(m)}{\sum_{m \in \mathcal{M}} p(\mathcal{D}|m)p(m)} \tag{3.278}$$

is the posterior over models. This is called **Bayesian model selection**. If the prior over models is uniform, $p(m) = 1/|\mathcal{M}|$, then the MAP model is given by

$$\hat{m} = \underset{m \in \mathcal{M}}{\operatorname{argmax}} \, p(\mathcal{D}|m) \tag{3.279}$$

The quantity $p(\mathcal{D}|m)$ is given by

$$p(\mathcal{D}|m) = \int p(\mathcal{D}|\boldsymbol{\theta}, m)p(\boldsymbol{\theta}|m)d\boldsymbol{\theta} \tag{3.280}$$

This is known as the **marginal likelihood**, or the **evidence** for model m. (See Section 3.8.3 for details on how to compute this quantity.) If the model assigns high prior predictive density to the observed data, then we deem it a good model. If, however, the model has too much flexibility, then some prior settings will not match the data; this probability mass will be "wasted", lowering the expected likelihood. This implicit regularization effect is called the **Bayesian Occam's razor**. See Figure 3.22 for an illustration.

3.8.1.1 Example: is the coin fair?

As an example, suppose we observe some coin tosses, and want to decide if the data was generated by a fair coin, $\theta = 0.5$, or a potentially biased coin, where θ could be any value in $[0, 1]$. Let us denote the first model by M_0 and the second model by M_1. The marginal likelihood under M_0 is simply

$$p(\mathcal{D}|M_0) = \left(\frac{1}{2}\right)^N \tag{3.281}$$

where N is the number of coin tosses. From Equation (3.31), the marginal likelihood under M_1, using a Beta prior, is

$$p(\mathcal{D}|M_1) = \int p(\mathcal{D}|\theta)p(\theta)d\theta = \frac{B(\alpha_1 + N_1, \alpha_0 + N_0)}{B(\alpha_1, \alpha_0)} \tag{3.282}$$

We plot $\log p(\mathcal{D}|M_1)$ vs the number of heads N_1 in Figure 3.23(a), assuming $N = 5$ and a uniform prior, $\alpha_1 = \alpha_0 = 1$. (The shape of the curve is not very sensitive to α_1 and α_0, as long as the

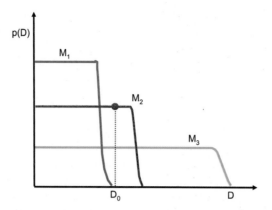

Figure 3.22: A schematic illustration of the Bayesian Occam's razor. The broad (green) curve corresponds to a complex model, the narrow (blue) curve to a simple model, and the middle (red) curve is just right. Adapted from Figure 3.13 of [Bis06]. See also [MG05, Figure 2] for a similar plot produced on real data.

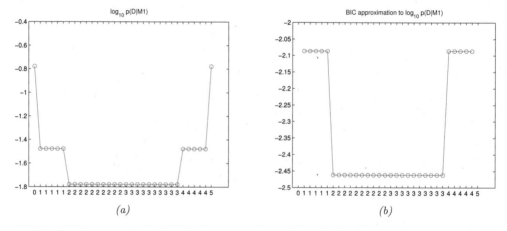

Figure 3.23: (a) Log marginal likelihood vs number of heads for the coin tossing example. (b) BIC approximation. (The vertical scale is arbitrary, since we are holding N fixed.) Generated by coins_model_sel_demo.ipynb.

prior is symmetric, so $\alpha_0 = \alpha_1$.) If we observe 2 or 3 heads, the unbiased coin hypothesis M_0 is more likely than M_1, since M_0 is a simpler model (it has no free parameters) — it would be a suspicious coincidence if the coin were biased but happened to produce almost exactly 50/50 heads/tails. However, as the counts become more extreme, we favor the biased coin hypothesis.

In Figure 3.23(b), we show a similar result, where we approximate the log marginal likelihood with the BIC score (see Section 3.8.7.2).

3.8.2 Bayes model averaging

If our goal is to perform predictions, we are better off averaging over all models, rather than predicting using just one single model. That is, we should compute the **posterior predictive distribution** using

$$p(y|\mathcal{D}) = \sum_{m \in \mathcal{M}} p(y|m)p(m|\mathcal{D}) \tag{3.283}$$

This is called **Bayes model averaging** [Hoe+99]. This is similar to the machine learning technique of **ensembling**, in which we take a weighted combination of predictors. However, it is not the same, as pointed out in [Min00b], since the weights in an ensemble do not need to sum to 1. In particular, in BMA, if there is a single best model, call it m^*, then in the large sample limit, $p(m|\mathcal{D})$ will become a degenerate distribution with all its weight on m^*, and the other members of $\mathcal{M}$ will be ignored. This does not happen with an ensemble.

3.8.3 Estimating the marginal likelihood

To perform Bayesian model selection or averaging, we need to be able to compute the marginal likelihood in Equation (3.280), also called the evidence. Below we give a brief summary of some suitable methods. For more details, see e.g., [FW12].

3.8.3.1 Analytic solution for conjugate models

If we use a conjugate prior, we can compute the marginal likelihood analytically, as we discussed in Section 3.4.5.4. We give a worked example in Section 3.8.1.1.

3.8.3.2 Harmonic mean estimator

A particularly simple estimator, known as the **harmonic mean estimator**, was proposed in [NR94]. It is defined as follows:

$$p(\mathcal{D}) \approx \left(\frac{1}{S} \sum_{s=1}^{S} \frac{1}{p(\mathcal{D}|\boldsymbol{\theta}_s)} \right)^{-1} \tag{3.284}$$

where $\boldsymbol{\theta}_s \sim p(\boldsymbol{\theta})$ are samples from the prior. This follows from the following identity:

$$\mathbb{E}\left[\frac{1}{p(\mathcal{D}|\boldsymbol{\theta})} \right] = \int \frac{1}{p(\mathcal{D}|\boldsymbol{\theta})} p(\boldsymbol{\theta}|\mathcal{D}) d\boldsymbol{\theta} \tag{3.285}$$

$$= \int \frac{1}{p(\mathcal{D}|\boldsymbol{\theta})} \frac{p(\mathcal{D}|\boldsymbol{\theta})p(\boldsymbol{\theta})}{p(\mathcal{D})} d\boldsymbol{\theta} \tag{3.286}$$

$$= \frac{1}{p(\mathcal{D})} \int p(\boldsymbol{\theta}) d\boldsymbol{\theta} = \frac{1}{p(\mathcal{D})} \tag{3.287}$$

(We have assumed the prior is proper, so it integrates to 1.)

Unfortunately, the number of samples needed to get a good estimate is generally very large, since most samples from the prior will have low likelihood, making this approach useless in practice. Indeed,

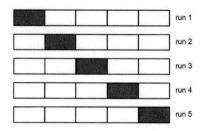

Figure 3.24: Schematic of 5-fold cross validation.

Radford Neal made a blog post in which he described this method as "The Worst Monte Carlo Method Ever".[10])

3.8.3.3 Other Monte Carlo methods

The marginal likelihood can be more reliably estimated using annealed importance sampling, as discussed in Section 11.5.4.1. An extension of this, known as sequential Monte Carlo sampling, as discussed in Section 13.2.3.3. Another method that is well suited to estimate the normalization constant is known as **nested sampling** [Ski06; Buc21].

3.8.3.4 Variational Bayes

An efficient way to compute an approximation to the evidence is to use variational Bayes, which we discuss in Section 10.3.3. This computes a tractable approximation to the posterior, $q(\boldsymbol{\theta}|\mathcal{D})$, by optimizing the evidence lower bound or ELBO, $\log q(\mathcal{D}|\boldsymbol{\theta})$, which can be used to approximate the evidence.

3.8.4 Connection between cross validation and marginal likelihood

A standard approach to model evaluation is to estimate its predictive performance (in terms of log likelihood) on a **validation set**, which is distinct from the training set which is used to fit the model If we don't have such a separate validation set, we can make one by partitioning the training set into K subsets or "**folds**", and then training on $K - 1$ and testing on the K'th; we repeat this K times, as shown in Figure 3.24. This is known as **cross validation**.

   If we set $K = N$, the method is known as **leave-one-out cross validation** or **LOO-CV**, since we train on $N - 1$ points and test on the remaining one, and we do this N times. More precisely, we have

$$L_{\text{LOO}}(m) \triangleq \sum_{n=1}^{N} \log p(\mathcal{D}_n|\hat{\boldsymbol{\theta}}(\mathcal{D}_{-n}), m) \tag{3.288}$$

10. `https://bit.ly/3t7id0k`.

where $\hat{\boldsymbol{\theta}}_{-n}$ is the parameter estimate computing when we omit $\mathcal{D}_n$ from the training set. (We discuss fast approxmations to this in Section 3.8.6.)

Interestingly, the LOO-CV version of log likelihood is closely related to the log marginal likelihood. To see this, let us write the log marginal likelihood (LML) in sequential form as follows:

$$\text{LML}(m) \triangleq \log p(\mathcal{D}|m) = \log \prod_{n=1}^{N} p(\mathcal{D}_n|\mathcal{D}_{1:n-1}, m) = \sum_{n=1}^{N} \log p(\mathcal{D}_n|\mathcal{D}_{1:n-1}, m) \tag{3.289}$$

where

$$p(\mathcal{D}_n|\mathcal{D}_{1:n-1}, m) = \int p(\mathcal{D}_n|\boldsymbol{\theta}) p(\boldsymbol{\theta}|\mathcal{D}_{1:n-1}, m) d\boldsymbol{\theta} \tag{3.290}$$

Note that we evaluate the posterior on the first $n-1$ datapoints and use this to predict the n'th; this is called **prequential analysis** [DV99].

Suppose we use a point estimate for the parameters at time n, rather than the full posterior. We can then use a plugin approximation to the n'th predictive distribution:

$$p(\mathcal{D}_n|\mathcal{D}_{1:n-1}, m) \approx \int p(\mathcal{D}_n|\boldsymbol{\theta}) \delta(\boldsymbol{\theta} - \hat{\boldsymbol{\theta}}_m(\mathcal{D}_{1:n-1})) d\boldsymbol{\theta} = p(\mathcal{D}_n|\hat{\boldsymbol{\theta}}_m(\mathcal{D}_{1:n-1})) \tag{3.291}$$

Then Equation (3.289) simplifies to

$$\log p(\mathcal{D}|m) \approx \sum_{n=1}^{N} \log p(\mathcal{D}_n|\hat{\boldsymbol{\theta}}(\mathcal{D}_{1:n-1}), m) \tag{3.292}$$

This is very similar to Equation (3.288), except it is evaluated sequentially. A complex model will overfit the "early" examples and will then predict the remaining ones poorly, and thus will get low marginal likelihood as well as a low cross-validation score. See [FH20] for further discussion.

3.8.5 Conditional marginal likelihood

The marginal likelihood answers the question "what is the likelihood of generating the training data from my prior?". This can be suitable for hypothesis testing between different fixed priors, but is less useful for selecting models based on their posteriors. In the latter case, we are more interested in the question "what is the probability that the posterior could generate withheld points from the data distribution?", which is related to the generalization performance of the (fitted) model. In fact [Lot+22] showed that the marginal likelihood can sometimes be negatively correlated with the generalization performance, because the first few terms in the LML decomposition may be large and negative for a model that has a poor prior but which otherwise adapts quickly to the data (by virtue of the prior being weak).

A better approach is to use the **conditional log marginal likelihood**, which is defined as follows [Lot+22]:

$$\text{CLML}(m) = \sum_{n=K}^{N} \log p(\mathcal{D}_n|\mathcal{D}_{1:n-1}, m) \tag{3.293}$$

where $K \in \{1, \ldots, N\}$ is a parameter of the algorithm. This evaluates the LML of the last $N - K$ datapoints, under the posterior given by the first K datapoints. We can reduce the dependence on the ordering of the datapoints by averaging over orders; if we set $K = N - 1$ and average over all orders, we get the LOO estimate.

The CLML is much more predictive of generalization performance than the LML, and is much less sensitive to prior hyperparameters. Furthermore, it is easier to calculuate, since we can use a straightforward Monte Carlo estimate of the integral, where we sample from the posterior $p(\boldsymbol{\theta}|\mathcal{D}_{<n})$; this does not suffer from the same problems as the harmonic mean estimator in Section 3.8.3.2 which samples from the prior.

3.8.6 Bayesian leave-one-out (LOO) estimate

In this section we discuss a computationally efficient method, based on importance sampling, to approximate the leave-one-out (LOO) estimate without having to fit the model N times. We focus on conditional (supervised) models, so $p(\mathcal{D}|\boldsymbol{\theta}) = p(\boldsymbol{y}|\boldsymbol{x}, \boldsymbol{\theta})$.

Suppose we have computed the posterior given the full dataset for model m. We can use this to evaluate the resulting predictive distribution $p(\boldsymbol{y}_n|\boldsymbol{x}_n, \mathcal{D}, m)$ for each datapoint n in the dataset. This gives the **log-pointwise predictive-density** or **LPPD** score:

$$\text{LPPD}(m) \triangleq \sum_{n=1}^{N} \log p(\boldsymbol{y}_n|\boldsymbol{x}_n, \mathcal{D}, m) = \sum_{n=1}^{N} \log \int p(\boldsymbol{y}_n|\boldsymbol{x}_n, \boldsymbol{\theta}, m) p(\boldsymbol{\theta}|\mathcal{D}, m) d\boldsymbol{\theta} \tag{3.294}$$

We can approximate LPPD with Monte Carlo:

$$\text{LPPD}(m) \approx \sum_{n=1}^{N} \log \left(\frac{1}{S} \sum_{s=1}^{S} p(\boldsymbol{y}_n|\boldsymbol{x}_n, \boldsymbol{\theta}_s, m) \right) \tag{3.295}$$

where $\boldsymbol{\theta}_s \sim p(\boldsymbol{\theta}|\mathcal{D}, m)$ is a posterior sample.

The trouble with LPPD is that it predicts the n'th datapoint $\boldsymbol{y}_n$ using all the data, including $\boldsymbol{y}_n$. What we would like to compute is the **expected LPPD** (**ELPD**) on *future data*, $(\boldsymbol{x}_*, \boldsymbol{y}_*)$:

$$\text{ELPD}(m) \triangleq \mathbb{E}_{\boldsymbol{x}_*, \boldsymbol{y}_*} \log p(\boldsymbol{y}_*|\boldsymbol{x}_*, \mathcal{D}, m) \tag{3.296}$$

Of course, the future data is unknown, but we can use a LOO approximation:

$$\text{ELPD}_{\text{LOO}}(m) \triangleq \sum_{n=1}^{N} \log p(\boldsymbol{y}_n|\boldsymbol{x}_n, \mathcal{D}_{-n}, m) = \sum_{n=1}^{N} \log \int p(\boldsymbol{y}_n|\boldsymbol{x}_n, \boldsymbol{\theta}, m) p(\boldsymbol{\theta}|\mathcal{D}_{-n}, m) d\boldsymbol{\theta} \tag{3.297}$$

This is a Bayesian version of Equation (3.288). We can approximate this integral using Monte Carlo:

$$\text{ELPD}_{\text{LOO}}(m) \approx \sum_{n=1}^{N} \log \left(\frac{1}{S} \sum_{s=1}^{S} p(\boldsymbol{y}_n|\boldsymbol{x}_n, \boldsymbol{\theta}_{s,-n}, m) \right) \tag{3.298}$$

where $\boldsymbol{\theta}_{s,-n} \sim p(\boldsymbol{\theta}|\mathcal{D}_{-n}, m)$.

The above procedure requires computing N different posteriors, leaving one datapoint out at a time, which is slow. A faster alternative is to compute $p(\boldsymbol{\theta}|\mathcal{D}, m)$ once, and then use importance sampling (Section 11.5) to approximate the above integral. More precisely, let $f(\boldsymbol{\theta}) = p(\boldsymbol{\theta}|\mathcal{D}_{-n}, m)$ be the target distribution of interest, and let $g(\boldsymbol{\theta}) = p(\boldsymbol{\theta}|\mathcal{D}, m)$ be the proposal. Define the importance weight for each sample s when leaving out example n to be

$$w_{s,-n} = \frac{f(\boldsymbol{\theta}_s)}{g(\boldsymbol{\theta}_s)} = \frac{p(\boldsymbol{\theta}_s|\mathcal{D}_{-n})}{p(\boldsymbol{\theta}_s|\mathcal{D})} = \frac{p(\mathcal{D}_{-n}|\boldsymbol{\theta}_s)p(\boldsymbol{\theta}_s)}{p(\mathcal{D}_{-n})} \frac{p(\mathcal{D})}{p(\mathcal{D}|\boldsymbol{\theta}_s)p(\boldsymbol{\theta}_s)} \tag{3.299}$$

$$\propto \frac{p(\mathcal{D}_{-n}|\boldsymbol{\theta}_s)}{p(\mathcal{D}|\boldsymbol{\theta}_s)} = \frac{p(\mathcal{D}_{-n}|\boldsymbol{\theta}_s)}{p(\mathcal{D}_{-n}|\boldsymbol{\theta})p(\mathcal{D}_n|\boldsymbol{\theta}_s)} = \frac{1}{p(\mathcal{D}_n|\boldsymbol{\theta}_s)} \tag{3.300}$$

We then normalize the weights to get

$$\hat{w}_{s,-n} = \frac{w_{s,-n}}{\sum_{s'=1}^{S} w_{s',-n}} \tag{3.301}$$

and use them to get the estimate

$$\text{ELPD}_{\text{IS-LOO}}(m) = \sum_{n=1}^{N} \log \left(\sum_{s=1}^{S} \hat{w}_{s,-n} p(\boldsymbol{y}_n|\boldsymbol{x}_n, \boldsymbol{\theta}_s, m) \right) \tag{3.302}$$

Unfortunately, the importance weights may have high variance, where some weights are much larger than others. To reduce this effect, we fit a Pareto distribution (Section 2.2.3.5) to each set of weights for each sample, and use this to smooth the weights. This technique is called **Pareto smoothed importance sampling** or **PSIS** [Veh+15; VGG17]. The Pareto distribution has the form

$$p(r|u, \sigma, k) = \sigma^{-1}(1 + k(r - u)\sigma^{-1})^{-1/k-1} \tag{3.303}$$

where u is the location, σ is the scale, and k is the shape. The parameter values k_n (for each datapoint n) can be used to assess how well this approximation works. If we find $k_n > 0.5$ for any given point, it is likely an outlier, and the resulting LOO estimate is likely to be quite poor. See [Siv+20] for further discussion, and [Kel21] for a general tutorial on PSIS-LOO-CV.

3.8.7 Information criteria

An alternative approach to cross validation is to score models using the negative log likelihood (or LPPD) on the training set plus a **complexity penalty** term:

$$\mathcal{L}(m) = -\log p(\mathcal{D}|\hat{\boldsymbol{\theta}}, m) + C(m) \tag{3.304}$$

This is called an **information criterion**. Different methods use different complexity terms $C(m)$, as we discuss below. See e.g., [GHV14] for further details.

A note on notation: it is conventional, when working with information criteria, to scale the NLL by -2 to get the **deviance**:

$$\text{deviance}(m) = -2\log p(\mathcal{D}|\hat{\boldsymbol{\theta}}, m) \tag{3.305}$$

This makes the math "prettier" for certain Gaussian models.

3.8.7.1   Minimum description length (MDL)

We can think about the problem of scoring different models in terms of information theory (Chapter 5). The goal is for the sender to communicate the data to the receiver. First the sender needs to specify which model m to use; this takes $C(m) = -\log p(m)$ bits (see Section 5.2). Then the receiver can fit the model, by computing $\hat{\boldsymbol{\theta}}_m$, and can thus approximately reconstruct the data. To perfectly reconstruct the data, the sender needs to send the residual errors that cannot be explained by the model; this takes

$$-L(m) = -\log p(\mathcal{D}|\hat{\boldsymbol{\theta}}, m) = -\sum_n \log p(\boldsymbol{y}_n | \boldsymbol{x}_n, \hat{\boldsymbol{\theta}}, m) \tag{3.306}$$

bits. (We are ignoring the cost of sending the input features $\boldsymbol{x}_n$, if present.) The total cost is

$$\mathcal{L}_{\text{MDL}}(m) = -\log p(\mathcal{D}|\hat{\boldsymbol{\theta}}, m) + C(m) \tag{3.307}$$

Choosing the model which minimizes this cost is known as the **minimum description length** or **MDL** principle. See e.g., [HY01] for details.

3.8.7.2   The Bayesian information criterion (BIC)

The **Bayesian information criterion** or **BIC** [Sch78] is similar to the MDL, and has the form

$$\mathcal{L}_{\text{BIC}}(m) = -2\log p(\mathcal{D}|\hat{\boldsymbol{\theta}}, m) + D_m \log N \tag{3.308}$$

where D_m is the **degrees of freedom** of model m.

We can derive the BIC score as a simple approximation to the log marginal likelihood. In particular, suppose we make a Gaussian approximation to the posterior, as discussed in Section 7.4.3. Then we get (from Equation (7.28)) the following:

$$\log p(\mathcal{D}|m) \approx \log p(\mathcal{D}|\hat{\boldsymbol{\theta}}_{\text{map}}) + \log p(\hat{\boldsymbol{\theta}}_{\text{map}}) - \frac{1}{2}\log |\mathbf{H}| \tag{3.309}$$

where $\mathbf{H}$ is the Hessian of the negative log joint $\log p(\mathcal{D}, \boldsymbol{\theta})$ evaluated at the MAP estimate $\hat{\boldsymbol{\theta}}_{\text{map}}$. We see that Equation (3.309) is the log likelihood plus some penalty terms. If we have a uniform prior, $p(\boldsymbol{\theta}) \propto 1$, we can drop the prior term, and replace the MAP estimate with the MLE, $\hat{\boldsymbol{\theta}}$, yielding

$$\log p(\mathcal{D}|m) \approx \log p(\mathcal{D}|\hat{\boldsymbol{\theta}}) - \frac{1}{2}\log |\mathbf{H}| \tag{3.310}$$

We now focus on approximating the $\log |\mathbf{H}|$ term, which is sometimes called the **Occam factor**, since it is a measure of model complexity (volume of the posterior distribution). We have $\mathbf{H} = \sum_{i=1}^{N} \mathbf{H}_i$, where $\mathbf{H}_i = \nabla\nabla \log p(\mathcal{D}_i|\boldsymbol{\theta})$. Let us approximate each $\mathbf{H}_i$ by a fixed matrix $\hat{\mathbf{H}}$. Then we have

$$\log |\mathbf{H}| = \log |N\hat{\mathbf{H}}| = \log(N^D|\hat{\mathbf{H}}|) = D \log N + \log |\hat{\mathbf{H}}| \tag{3.311}$$

where $D = \dim(\boldsymbol{\theta})$ and we have assumed $\mathbf{H}$ is full rank. We can drop the $\log |\hat{\mathbf{H}}|$ term, since it is independent of N, and thus will get overwhelmed by the likelihood. Putting all the pieces together, we get the **BIC score** that we want to maximize:

$$J_{\text{BIC}}(m) = \log p(\mathcal{D}|\hat{\boldsymbol{\theta}}, m) - \frac{D_m}{2}\log N \tag{3.312}$$

We can also define the **BIC loss**, that we want to minimize, by multiplying by -2:

$$\mathcal{L}_{\text{BIC}}(m) = -2\log p(\mathcal{D}|\hat{\boldsymbol{\theta}}, m) + D_m \log N \tag{3.313}$$

3.8.7.3 Akaike information criterion

The **Akaike information criterion** [Aka74] is closely related to BIC. It has the form

$$\mathcal{L}_{\text{AIC}}(m) = -2\log p(\mathcal{D}|\hat{\boldsymbol{\theta}}, m) + 2D_m \tag{3.314}$$

This penalizes complex models less heavily than BIC, since the regularization term is independent of N. This estimator can be derived from a frequentist perspective.

3.8.7.4 Widely applicable information criterion (WAIC)

The main problem with MDL, BIC, and AIC is that it can be hard to compute the degrees of a freedom of a model, needed to define the complexity term, since most parameters are highly correlated and not uniquely identifiable from the likelihood. In particular, if the mapping from parameters to the likelihood is not one-to-one, then the model known as a **singular statistical model**, since the corresponding Fisher information matrix (Section 3.3.4), and hence the Hessian **H** above, may be singular (have determinant 0). An alternative criterion that works even in the singular case is known as the **widely applicable information criterion** (WAIC), also known as the **Watanabe–Akaike information criterion** [Wat10; Wat13].

WAIC is like other information criteria, except it is more Bayesian. First it replaces the log likelihood $L(m)$, which uses a point estimate of the parameters, with the LPPD, which marginalizes them out. (see Equation (3.295)). For the complexity term, WAIC uses the variance of the predictive distribution:

$$C(m) = \sum_{n=1}^{N} \mathbb{V}_{\boldsymbol{\theta}|\mathcal{D},m}[\log p(\boldsymbol{y}_n|\boldsymbol{x}_n, \boldsymbol{\theta}, m)] \approx \sum_{n=1}^{N} \mathbb{V}\{\log p(\boldsymbol{y}_n|\boldsymbol{x}_n, \boldsymbol{\theta}_s, m) : s = 1 : S\} \tag{3.315}$$

The intuition for this is as follows: if, for a given datapoint n, the different posterior samples $\boldsymbol{\theta}_s$ make very different predictions, then the model is uncertain, and likely too flexible. The complexity term essentially counts how often this occurs. The final WAIC loss is

$$\mathcal{L}_{\text{WAIC}}(m) = -2\text{LPPD}(m) + 2C(m) \tag{3.316}$$

Interestingly, it can be shown that the PSIS LOO estimate in Section 3.8.6 is asymptotically equivalent to WAIC [VGG17].

3.9 Model checking

Bayesian inference and decision making is optimal, but only if the modeling assumptions are correct. In this section, we discuss some ways to assess if a model is reasonable. From a Bayesian perspective, this can seem a bit odd, since if we knew there was a better model, why don't we just use that? Here we assume that we do not have a specific alternative model in mind (so we are not performing model selection, unlike Section 3.8.1). Instead we are just trying to see if the data we observe is "typical" of what we might expect if our model were correct. This is called **model checking**.

3.9.1   Posterior predictive checks

Suppose we are trying to estimate the probability of heads for a coin, $\theta \in [0, 1]$. We have two candidate models or hypotheses, M_1 which corresponds to $\theta = 0.99$ and M_2 which corresponds to $\theta = 0.01$. Suppose we flip the coin 40 times and it comes up heads 30 times. Obviously we have $p(M = M_1|\mathcal{D}) \gg p(M = M_2|\mathcal{D})$. However model M_1 is still a very bad model for the data. (This example is from [Kru15, p331].)

To evaluate how good a candidate model M is, after seeing some data $\mathcal{D}$, we can imagine using the model to generate synthetic future datasets, by drawing from the posterior predictive distribution:

$$\tilde{\mathcal{D}}^s \sim p(\tilde{\mathcal{D}}|M, \mathcal{D}) = \{\boldsymbol{y}^s_{1:N} \sim p(\cdot|M, \boldsymbol{\theta}^s), \boldsymbol{\theta}^s \sim p(\boldsymbol{\theta}|\mathcal{D}, M)\} \tag{3.317}$$

These represent "plausible hallucinations" of the model. To assess the quality of our model, we can compute how "typical" our observed data $\mathcal{D}$ is compared to the model's hallucinations. To perform this comparison, we create one or more scalar **test statistics**, $\text{test}(\tilde{\mathcal{D}}^s)$, and compare them to the test statistics on the actual data, $\text{test}(\mathcal{D})$. These statistics should measure features of interest (since it will not, in general, be possible to capture every aspect of the data with a given model). If there is a large difference between the distribution of $\text{test}(\tilde{\mathcal{D}}^s)$ across different s and the value of $\text{test}(\mathcal{D})$, it suggests the model is not a good one. This approach called a **posterior predictive check** [Rub84].

3.9.1.1   Example: 1d Gaussian

To make things clearer, let us consider an example from [Gel+04]. In 1882, Newcomb measured the speed of light using a certain method and obtained $N = 66$ measurements, shown in Figure 3.25(a). There are clearly two outliers in the left tails, suggesting that the distribution is not Gaussian. Let us nonetheless fit a Gaussian to it. For simplicity, we will just compute the MLE, and use a plug-in approximation to the posterior predictive density:

$$p(\tilde{y}|\mathcal{D}) \approx \mathcal{N}(\tilde{y}|\hat{\mu}, \hat{\sigma}^2), \quad \hat{\mu} = \frac{1}{N}\sum_{n=1}^{N} y_n, \quad \hat{\sigma}^2 = \frac{1}{N}\sum_{n=1}^{N}(y_n - \hat{\mu})^2 \tag{3.318}$$

Let $\tilde{\mathcal{D}}^s$ be the s'th dataset of size $N = 66$ sampled from this distribution, for $s = 1 : 1000$. The histogram of $\tilde{\mathcal{D}}^s$ for some of these samples is shown in Figure 3.25(b). It is clear that none of the samples contain the large negative examples that were seen in the real data. This suggests the model cannot capture the long tails present in the data. (We are assuming that these extreme values are scientifically interesting, and something we want the model to capture.)

A more formal way to test fit is to define a test statistic. Since we are interested in small values, let us use

$$\text{test}(\mathcal{D}) = \min\{y : y \in \mathcal{D}\} \tag{3.319}$$

The empirical distribution of $\text{test}(\tilde{\mathcal{D}}^s)$ for $s = 1 : 1000$ is shown in Figure 3.25(c). For the real data, $\text{test}(\mathcal{D}) = -44$, but the test statistics of the generated data, $\text{test}(\tilde{\mathcal{D}})$, are much larger. Indeed, we see that -44 is in the left tail of the predictive distribution, $p(\text{test}(\tilde{\mathcal{D}})|\mathcal{D})$.

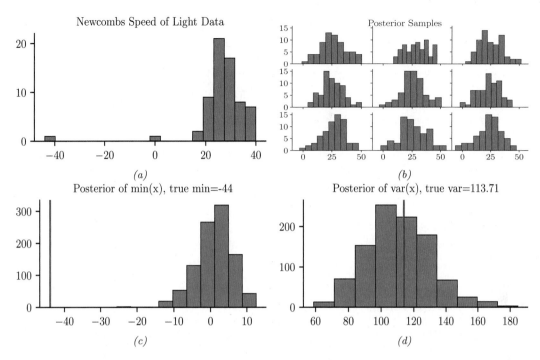

Figure 3.25: (a) Histogram of Newcomb's data. (b) Histograms of data sampled from Gaussian model. (c) Histogram of test statistic on data sampled from the model, which represents $p(test(\tilde{D}^s)|\mathcal{D})$, where $test(\mathcal{D}) = \min\{y \in \mathcal{D}\}$. The vertical line is the test statistic on the true data, $test(\mathcal{D})$. (d) Same as (c) except $test(\mathcal{D}) = \mathbb{V}\{y \in \mathcal{D}\}$. Generated by newcomb_plugin_demo.ipynb.

3.9.1.2 Example: linear regression

When fitting conditional models, $p(\boldsymbol{y}|\boldsymbol{x})$, we will have a different prediction for each input $\boldsymbol{x}$. We can compare the predictive distribution $p(\boldsymbol{y}|\boldsymbol{x}_n)$ to the observed $\boldsymbol{y}_n$ to detect places where the model does poorly.

As an example of this, we consider the "waffle divorce" dataset from [McE20, Sec 5.1]. This contains the divorce rate D_n, marriage rate M_n, and age A_n at first marriage for 50 different US states. We use a linear regression model to predict the divorce rate, $p(y = d|\boldsymbol{x} = (a, m)) = \mathcal{N}(d|\alpha + \beta_a a + \beta_m m, \sigma^2)$, using vague priors for the parameters. (In this example, we use a Laplace approximation to the posterior, discussed in Section 7.4.3.) We then compute the posterior predictive distribution $p(y|\boldsymbol{x}_n, \mathcal{D})$, which is a 1d Gaussian, and plot this vs each observed outcome y_n.

The result is shown in Figure 3.26. We see several outliers, some of which have been annotated. In particular, we see that both Idaho (ID) and Utah (UT) have a much lower divorce rate than predicted. This is because both of these states have an unusually large proportion of Mormons.

Of course, we expect errors in our predictive models. However, ideally the predictive error bars for the inputs where the model is wrong would be larger, rather than the model confidently making errors. In this case, the overconfidence arises from our incorrect use of a linear model.

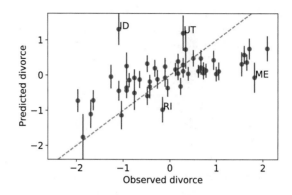

Figure 3.26: Posterior predictive distribution for divorce rate vs actual divorce rate for 50 US states. Both axes are standardized (i.e., z-scores). A few outliers are annotated. Adapted from Figure 5.5 of [McE20]. Generated by linreg_divorce_ppc.ipynb.

3.9.2 Bayesian p-values

If some test statistic of the observed data, test($\mathcal{D}$), occurs in the left or right tail of the predictive distribution, then it is very unlikely under the model. We can quantify this using a **Bayesian p-value**, also called a **posterior predictive p-value**:

$$p_B = \Pr(\text{test}(\tilde{\mathcal{D}}) \geq \text{test}(\mathcal{D})|M, \mathcal{D}) \tag{3.320}$$

where M represents the model we are using, and $\tilde{\mathcal{D}}$ is a hypothetical future dataset. In contrast, a classical or frequentist **p-value** is defined as

$$p_C = \Pr(\text{test}(\tilde{\mathcal{D}}) \geq \text{test}(\mathcal{D})|M) \tag{3.321}$$

where M represents the null hypothesis. The key difference is that the Bayesian compares what was observed to what one would expect after conditioning the model on the data, whereas the frequentist compares what was observed to the sampling distribution of the null hypothesis, which is independent of the data.

We can approximate the Bayesian p-value using Monte Carlo integration, as follows:

$$p_B = \int \mathbb{I}\left(\text{test}(\tilde{\mathcal{D}}) > \text{test}(\mathcal{D})\right) p(\tilde{\mathcal{D}}|\theta)p(\theta|\mathcal{D})d\theta \approx \frac{1}{S}\sum_{s=1}^{S} \mathbb{I}\left(\text{test}(\tilde{\mathcal{D}}^s) > \text{test}(\mathcal{D})\right) \tag{3.322}$$

Any extreme value for p_B (i.e., a value near 0 or 1) means that the observed data is unlikely under the model, as assessed via test statistic test. However, if test($\mathcal{D}$) is a sufficient statistic of the model, it is likely to be well estimated, and the p-value will be near 0.5. For example, in the speed of light example, if we define our test statistic to be the variance of the data, test($\mathcal{D}$) = $\mathbb{V}\{y : y \in \mathcal{D}\}$, we get a p-value of 0.48. (See Figure 3.25(d).) This shows that the Gaussian model is capable of representing the variance in the data, even though it is not capable of representing the support (range) of the data.

The above example illustrates the very important point that we should not try to assess whether the data comes from a given model (for which the answer is nearly always that it does not), but rather, we should just try to assess whether the model captures the features we care about. See [Gel+04, ch.6] for a more extensive discussion of this topic.

3.10 Hypothesis testing

Suppose we have collected some coin tossing data, and we want to know if there if the coin is fair or not. Or, more interestingly, we have collected some clinical trial data, and want to know if there is a non-zero effect of the treatment on the outcome (e.g., different survival rates for the treatment and control groups). These kinds of problems can be solved using **hypothesis testing**. In the sections below, we summarize several common approaches to hypothesis testing.

3.10.1 Frequentist approach

In this section, we summarize the approach to hypothesis testing that is used in classical or frequentist statistics, which is known as **null hypothesis significance testing** or **NHST**. The basic idea is to define a binary decision rule of the form $\delta(\mathcal{D}) = \mathbb{I}(t(\mathcal{D}) \geq t^*)$, where $t(\mathcal{D})$ is some scalar **test statistic** derived from the data, and t^* is some **critical value**. If the test statistic exceeds the critical value, we **reject the null hypothesis**.

There is a large "zoo" of possible test statistics one can use (e.g., [Ken93] lists over 100 different tests), but a simple example is a **t-statistic**, defined as

$$t(\mathcal{D}) = \frac{\overline{x} - \mu}{\hat{\sigma}/\sqrt{N}} \tag{3.323}$$

where where $\overline{x}$ is the empirical mean of $\mathcal{D}$, $\hat{\sigma}$ is the empirical standard deviation, N is the sample size, and μ is the **population mean**, corresponding to the mean value of the null hypothesis (often 0).

To compute the critical value t^*, we pick a **significance level** α, often 0.05, which controls the **type I error rate** of the decision procedure (i.e., the probability of accidentally rejecting the null hypothesis when it is true). We then find the value t^* whose tail probability, under the sampling distribution of the test statistic given the null hypothesis, matches the significance level:

$$p(t(\tilde{\mathcal{D}}) \geq t^* | H_0) = \alpha \tag{3.324}$$

This construction guarantees that $p(\delta(\tilde{\mathcal{D}}) = 1 | H_0) = \alpha$.

Rather than comparing $t(\mathcal{D})$ to t^*, a more common (but equivalent) approach is to compute the **p-value** of $t(\mathcal{D})$, which is defined in Equation (3.86). We can then reject the null hypothesis is $p < \alpha$.

Unfortunately, despite its widespread use, p-values and NHST have many problems, some of which are discussed in Section 3.3.5.2. We shall therefore avoid using this approach in this book.

3.10.2 Bayesian approach

In this section, we discucss the Bayesian approach to hypothesis testing. There are in fact two approaches, one based on model comparison using Bayes factors (Section 3.10.2.1), and one based on parameter estimation (Section 3.10.2.3).

Bayes factor $BF(1,0)$	Interpretation
$BF < \frac{1}{100}$	Decisive evidence for M_0
$BF < \frac{1}{10}$	Strong evidence for M_0
$\frac{1}{10} < BF < \frac{1}{3}$	Moderate evidence for M_0
$\frac{1}{3} < BF < 1$	Weak evidence for M_0
$1 < BF < 3$	Weak evidence for M_1
$3 < BF < 10$	Moderate evidence for M_1
$BF > 10$	Strong evidence for M_1
$BF > 100$	Decisive evidence for M_1

Table 3.1: Jeffreys scale of evidence for interpreting Bayes factors.

3.10.2.1   Model comparison approach

Bayesian hypothesis testing is a special case of Bayesian model selection (discussed in Section 3.8.1) when we just have two models, commonly called the **null hypothesis**, M_0, and the **alternative hypothesis**, M_1. Let us define the **Bayes factor** as the ratio of marginal likelihoods:

$$B_{1,0} \triangleq \frac{p(\mathcal{D}|M_1)}{p(\mathcal{D}|M_0)} = \frac{p(M_1|\mathcal{D})}{p(M_0|\mathcal{D})} \bigg/ \frac{p(M_1)}{p(M_0)} \tag{3.325}$$

(This is like a **likelihood ratio**, except we integrate out the parameters, which allows us to compare models of different complexity.) If $B_{1,0} > 1$ then we prefer model 1, otherwise we prefer model 0 (see Table 3.1).

We give a worked example of how to compute Bayes factors for a binomial test in Section 3.8.1.1. For examples of computing Bayes factors for more complex tests, see e.g. [Etz+18; Ly+20].

3.10.2.2   Improper priors cause problems for Bayes factors

Problems can arise when we use improper priors (i.e., priors that do not integrate to 1) for Bayesian model selection, even though such priors may be acceptable for other purposes, such as parameter inference. For example, consider testing the hypotheses $M_0 : \theta \in \Theta_0$ vs $M_1 : \theta \in \Theta_1$. The posterior probability of M_0 is given by

$$p(M_0|\mathcal{D}) = \frac{p(M_0)L_0}{p(M_0)L_0 + p(M_1)L_1} \tag{3.326}$$

where $L_i = p(\mathcal{D}|M_i) = \int_{\Theta_i} p(\mathcal{D}|\theta)p(\theta|M_i)d\theta$ is the marginal likelihood for model i.

Suppose (for simplicity) that $p(M_0) = p(M_1) = 0.5$, and we use a uniform but improper prior over the model parameters, $p(\theta|M_0) \propto c_0$ and $p(\theta|M_1) \propto c_1$. Define $\ell_i = \int_{\Theta_i} p(\mathcal{D}|\theta)d\theta$, so $L_i = c_i\ell_i$. Then

$$p(M_0|\mathcal{D}) = \frac{c_0\ell_0}{c_0\ell_0 + c_1\ell_1} = \frac{\ell_0}{\ell_0 + (c_1/c_0)\ell_1} \tag{3.327}$$

Thus the posterior (and hence Bayes factor) depends on the arbitrary constants c_0 and c_1. This is known as the **marginalization paradox**. For this reason, we should avoid using improper priors when performing Bayesian model selection. (However, if the same improper prior is used for common parameters that are shared between the two hypotheses, then the paradox does not arise.)

More generally, since the marginal likelihood is the likelihood averaged wrt the prior, results can be quite sensitive to the form of prior that is used. (See also Section 3.8.5, where we discuss conditional marginal likelihood.)

3.10.2.3   Parameter estimation approach

There are several drawbacks of the Bayesian hypothesis testing approach in Section 3.10.2.1, such as computational difficulty of computing the marginal likelihood (see Section 3.8.3), and the sensitivity to the prior (see Section 3.10.2.2). An alternative approach is to estimate the parameters of the model in the usual way, and then to see how much posterior probability is assigned to the parameter value corresponding to the null hypothesis. For example, to "test" if a coin is fair, we can first compute the posterior $p(\theta|\mathcal{D})$, and then we can evaluate the plausibility of the null hypothesis by computing $p(0.5 - \epsilon < \theta < 0.5 + \epsilon|\mathcal{D})$, where $(0.5 - \epsilon, 0.5 + \epsilon)$ is called the **region of practical equivalence** or **ROPE** [Kru15; KL17c]. This is not only computationally simpler, but is also allows us to quantify the effect size (i.e., the expected deviation of θ from the null value of 0.5), rather than merely accepting or rejecting a hypothesis. This approach is therefore called **Bayesian estimation**. We give some examples below, following https://www.sumsar.net/blog/2014/01/bayesian-first-aid/. (See also Section 3.10.3 for ways to perform more general tests usings GLMs.)

3.10.2.4   One sample test of a proportion (Binomial test)

Suppose we perform N coin tosses and observe y heads, where the frequency of heads is θ. We want to test the null hypothesis that $\theta = 0.5$. In frequentist statistics, we can use a **binomial test**. We now present a Bayesian alternative.

First we compute the posterior, $p(\theta|\mathcal{D}) \propto p(\theta)\text{Bin}(x|\theta, N)$. To do this, we need to specify a prior. We will use a noninformative prior. Following Section 3.5.2.1, the Jeffreys prior is $p(\theta) \propto \text{Beta}(\theta|\frac{1}{2}, \frac{1}{2})$, but [Lee04] argues that the uniform or flat prior, $p(\theta) \propto \text{Beta}(\theta|1, 1)$, is the least informative when we know that both heads and tails are possible. The posterior then becomes $p(\theta|\mathcal{D}) = \text{Beta}(\theta|y + 1, N - y + 1)$. From this, we can compute the credible interval $I = (\ell, u)$ using $\ell = P^{-1}(\alpha/2)$ and $u = P^{-1}(1 - \alpha/2)$, where P is the cdf of the posterior. We can also easily compute the probability that the frequency exceeds the null value using

$$p(\theta > 0.5|\mathcal{D}) = \int_{0.5}^{1} p(\theta|\mathcal{D})d\theta \tag{3.328}$$

We can compute this quantity using numerical integration or analytically [Coo05].

3.10.2.5   Two sample test of relative proportions (χ^2 test)

Now consider the setting where we have J groups, and in each group j we observe y_j successes in N_j trials. We denote the success rate by θ_j, and we are interested in testing the hypothesis that θ_j is the same for all the groups. In frequentist statistics, we can use a χ^2 **test**. Here we present a Bayesian alternative.

We will use an extension of Section 3.10.2.4, namely $y_j \sim \text{Bin}(\theta_j, N_j)$, where $\theta_j \sim \text{Beta}(1, 1)$, for $j = 1 : J$. To simplify notation, assume we $J = 2$ groups. The posterior is given by

$$p(\theta_1, \theta_2 | \mathcal{D}) = \text{Beta}(\theta_1 | y_1 + 1, N_1 - y_1 + 1)\text{Beta}(\theta_2 | y_2 + 1, N_2 - y_2 + 1) \tag{3.329}$$

We can then compute the posterior of the group difference, $\delta = \theta_1 - \theta_2$, using

$$p(\delta | \mathcal{D}) = \int_0^1 \int_0^1 \mathbb{I}\left(\delta = \theta_1 - \theta_2\right) p(\theta_1 | \mathcal{D}_1) p(\theta_2 | \mathcal{D}_2) \tag{3.330}$$

$$= \int_0^1 \text{Beta}(\theta_1 | y_1 + 1, N_1 - y_1 + 1)\text{Beta}(\theta_1 - \delta | y_2 + 1, N_2 - y_2 + 1) d\theta_1 \tag{3.331}$$

We can then use $p(\delta > 0 | \mathcal{D})$ to decide if the relative proportions between the two groups are significantly different or not.

3.10.2.6   One sample test of a mean (*t*-test)

Consider a dataset where we have N real-valued observations y_n which we assume come from a Gaussian, $y_n \sim \mathcal{N}(\mu, \sigma^2)$. We would like to test the hypothesis that $\mu = 0$. In frequentist statistics, the standard approach to this is to use a **t-test**, which is based on the sampling distribution of the standardized estimated mean. Here we develop a Bayesian alternative.

If we use a noninformative prior (which is a limiting case of the conjugate Gaussian-gamma prior), then the posterior for $p(\mu | \mathcal{D})$, after marginalizing out σ^2, is the same as the sampling distribution of the MLE, $\hat{\mu}$, as we show in Section 15.2.3.2. In particular, both have a Student t distribution. Consequently, the Bayesian credible interval will be the same as the frequentist confidence interval in this simple setting.

However, a flat or noninformative prior for $p(\mu) \propto 1$ and $p(\sigma) \propto 1$ can give poor results, since we usually do not expect arbitrarily large values. According to [GHV20a], it is generally better to use **weakly informative priors**, whose hyperparameters can be derived from statistics of the data. For example, for the mean, we can use $p(\mu) = \mathcal{N}(\mu = 0, \sigma = 2.5\text{sd}(Y))$ (assuming the data is centered), and for the standard deviation, we can use $p(\sigma) = \text{Half-Student-t}(\mu = 0, \sigma = \text{sd}(y), \nu = 4)$.[11] These priors are no longer conjugate, but we can easily perform approximate posterior inference using MCMC or other algorithms discussed in Part II. We call this approach **BTT**, for "Bayesian *t*-test".

[Kru13] proposes to use a Student likelihood $y_n \sim \mathcal{T}(\mu, \sigma, \nu)$ instead of a Gaussian likelihood, since it is more robust to outliers. He calls the method **BEST** method ("Bayesian Estimation Supersedes the t-test"), but we call it **robust BTT**. In addition to a different likelihood, robust BTT uses a different weakly informative prior, namely $\mu \sim \mathcal{N}(\mu = M_\mu, \sigma = S_\mu)$, $\sigma \in \text{Unif}(\sigma_{\text{low}}, \sigma_{\text{high}})$, and $\nu - 1 \sim \text{Expon}(1/29)$.[12]

---

11. This default prior is used by the Python **bambi** library [Cap+22], as well as the R **rstanarm** library (see https://mc-stan.org/rstanarm/articles/priors.html).

12. The prior for ν is an exponential distribution with mean 29 shifted 1 to the right, which keeps ν away from zero. According to [Kru13], "This prior was selected because it balances nearly normal distributions ($\nu > 30$) with heavy tailed distributions ($\nu < 30$)". To avoid contamination from outliers, the prior for μ uses $M_\mu = M$, where M is the trimmed mean, and $S_\mu = 10^3 D$, where D is the mean absolute deviation . The prior for σ uses $\sigma_{\text{low}} = D/1000$ and $\sigma_{\text{high}} = D \times 1000$.

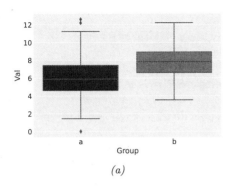 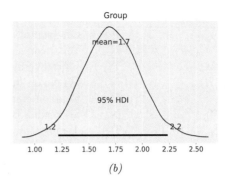

(a) (b)

Figure 3.27: Illustration of Bayesian two-sample t-test. (a) Some synthetic data from two groups. (b) Posterior distribution of the difference, $p(\mu_2 - \mu_1 | \mathcal{D})$. Generated by ttest_bambi.ipynb.

3.10.2.7 Paired sample test of relative means (paired t-test)

Now suppose we have paired data from two groups, $\mathcal{D} = \{(y_{1n}, y_{2n}) : n = 1 : N\}$, where we assume $y_{jn} \sim \mathcal{N}(\mu_j, \sigma^2)$. We are interested in testing whether $\mu_1 = \mu_2$. A simpler alternative is to define $y_n = y_{2n} - y_{1n}$, which we model using $y_n \sim \mathcal{N}(\mu, \sigma^2)$. We can then test whether $\mu = 0$ using the t-test; this is called a **paired sample t-test**. In the Bayesian setting, we can just pass $\{y_n = y_{2n} - y_{1n}\}$ to the BTT procedure of Section 3.10.2.6.

3.10.2.8 Two sample test of relative means (two sample t-test)

In this section, we consider the setting in which we have two datasets, $\mathcal{D}_1 = \{y_{1n} \sim \mathcal{N}(\mu_1, \sigma_1^2) : n = 1 : N_1\}$ and $\mathcal{D}_2 = \{y_{2n} \sim \mathcal{N}(\mu_2, \sigma_2^2) : n = 1 : N_2\}$, and we want to test the null hypothesis that $\mu_1 = \mu_2$. If we assume $\sigma_1^2 = \sigma_2^2$, we can use a **two-sample t-test**, also called an **independent t-test** or **unpaired t-test**. If we allow the variance of the observations to vary by group, then we can use **Welch's t-test**.

In the Bayesian setting, we can tackle this by generalizing the BTT model of Section 3.10.2.6 to two groups by defining $y_{jn} \sim \mathcal{N}(\mu_j, \sigma_j^2)$, for $j = 1, 2$. (We can also use a robust likelihood.) Once we have specified the model, we can perform posterior inference in the usual way, and compute quantities such as $p(\mu_1 - \mu_2 > 0 | \mathcal{D})$. See Figure 3.27 for an example.

3.10.2.9 Testing a correlation coefficient

In this section, we consider the setting in which we have some data $\mathcal{D} = \{(x_n, y_n) : n = 1 : N\}$, where (x, y) be may be correlated with a **Pearson correlation coefficient** of ρ. We are interested in testing the null hypothesis that $\rho = 0$.

In the Bayesian setting, we can do this by generalizing the two-sample BTT approach of Section 3.10.2.8. Specifically, we assume

$$(x_n, y_n) \sim \mathcal{N}(\boldsymbol{\mu}, \boldsymbol{\Sigma}) \tag{3.332}$$

Y	X	P/N	Name	Model	Exact
$\mathbb{R}$	-	P	One-sample t-test	$y \sim \mathcal{N}(\mu, \sigma^2)$	✓
$\mathbb{R}$	-	N	Wilcoxon signed-ranked	$SR(y) \sim \mathcal{N}(\mu, \sigma^2)$	$N > 14$
$(\mathbb{R}, \mathbb{R})$	-	P	Paired-sample t-test	$y_2 - y_1 \sim \mathcal{N}(\mu, \sigma^2)$	✓
$(\mathbb{R}, \mathbb{R})$	-	N	Wilcoxon matched pairs	$SR(y_2 - y_1) \sim \mathcal{N}(\mu, \sigma^2)$	✓
$\mathbb{R}$	$\mathbb{R}$	P	Pearson correlation	$y \sim \mathcal{N}(\beta_0 + \beta_1 x, \sigma^2)$	✓
$\mathbb{R}$	$\mathbb{R}$	N	Spearman correlation	$R(y) \sim \mathcal{N}(\beta_0 + \beta_1 R(x), \sigma^2)$	$N > 10$
$\mathbb{R}$	$\{0, 1\}$	P	Two-sample t-test	$y \sim \mathcal{N}(\beta_0 + \beta_1 x, \sigma^2)$	✓
$\mathbb{R}$	$\{0, 1\}$	P	Welch's t-test	$y \sim \mathcal{N}(\beta_0 + \beta_1 x, \sigma_x^2)$	✓
$\mathbb{R}$	$\{0, 1\}$	N	Mann-Whitney U	$SR(y) \sim \mathcal{N}(\beta_0 + \beta_1 x, \sigma_x^2)$	$N > 11$
$\mathbb{R}$	$[J]$	P	One-way ANOVA	$y \sim \mathcal{N}(f_{\text{aov}}(x; \boldsymbol{\beta}), \sigma^2)$	✓
$\mathbb{R}$	$[J]$	N	Kruskal-Wallis	$R(y) \sim \mathcal{N}(f_{\text{aov}}(x; \boldsymbol{\beta}), \sigma^2)$	$N > 11$
$\mathbb{R}$	$[J] \times [K]$	N	Two-way ANOVA	$y \sim \mathcal{N}(f_{\text{aov2}}(x_1, x_2; \boldsymbol{\beta}), \sigma^2)$	✓

Table 3.2: Many common statistical tests are equivalent to performing inference for the parameters of simple linear models. Here P/N represents parametric vs nonparametric test; we approximate the latter by using the rank function $R(y)$ or the signed rank function $SR(y)$. The last column, labeled "exact", specifies the sample size for which this approximation becomes accurate enough to be indistinguishable from the exact result. When the input variable is categorical, $x_1 \in [J]$, where $[J] = \{1, \ldots, J\}$, we define the mean of the output using the analysis of variance function $f_{aov}(x_1, \boldsymbol{\beta})$. When we have two categorical inputs, $x_1 \in [J]$ and $x_2 \in [K]$, we use $f_{aov2}(x_1, x_2; \boldsymbol{\beta})$. Adapted from the crib sheet at `https: // lindeloev. github. io/ tests-as-linear/`.

where $\boldsymbol{\mu} = [\mu_1, \mu_2]$, and

$$\boldsymbol{\Sigma} = \begin{pmatrix} \sigma_1^2 & \rho \sigma_1 \sigma_2 \\ \rho \sigma_a \sigma_2 & \sigma_2^2 \end{pmatrix} \tag{3.333}$$

We use the same (data-driven) priors for μ_j and σ_j, and use a uniform prior for the correlation, $p(\rho) = \text{Unif}(-1, 1)$, following [BMM00]. Once we have specified the model, we can perform posterior inference in the usual way, and compute quantities such as $p(\rho > 0 | \mathcal{D})$.

3.10.3   Common statistical tests correspond to inference in linear models

We have now seen many different tests, and it may be unclear what test to use when. Fortunately, [Lin19] points out that many of the most common tests can be represented exactly (or approximately) in terms of inference (either Bayesian or frequentist) about the parameters of a generalized linear model or GLM (see Chapter 15 for details on GLMs). This approach is easier to understand and more flexible, as discussed at length in e.g., [Kru15; GHV20b]. We summarize some of these results in Table 3.2 and the discussion below.

3.10.3.1   Approximating nonparametric tests using the rank transform

It is common to use "**nonparametric tests**", which generalize standard tests to settings where the data do not necessarily follow a Gaussian or Student distribution. A simple way to approximate such tests is to replace the original data with its **order statistics**, and then to apply a standard parametric

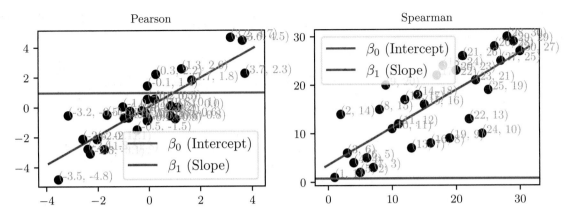

Figure 3.28: *Illustration of 1d linear regression applied to some data (left) and its rank-transformed version (right). Generated by* linreg_rank_stats.ipynb.

test, as proposed in [CI81]. This gives a good approximation to the standard nonparametric tests for sample sizes of $N \geq 10$.

Concretely, we can compute a **rank transform**, in which the data points (assumed to be scalar) are sorted, and then replaced by their integer value in the ordering. For example, the rank transform of $\mathcal{D} = (3.6, 3.4, -5.0, 8.2)$ is $R(\mathcal{D}) = (3, 2, 1, 4)$. Alternatively we may use the **signed ranked**, which first sorts the values according to their absolute size, and then attaches the corresponding sign. For example, the signed rank transform of $\mathcal{D} = (3.6, 3.4, -5.0, 8.2)$ is $SR(\mathcal{D}) = (2, 1, -3, 4)$.

We can now easily fit a parametric model, such as a GLM, to the rank-transformed data, as illustrated in Figure 3.28. (In [Doo+17], they propose a Bayesian interpretation of this, where the order statistics are viewed as observations of an underlying latent continuous quantity, on which inference is performed.) We will use this trick in the sections below.

3.10.3.2 Metric-predicted variable on one or two groups (*t*-test)

Suppose we have some data $\mathcal{D} = \{y_n \sim \mathcal{N}(\mu, \sigma^2) : n = 1 : N\}$, and we are interested in testing the null hypothesis that $\mu = 0$. We can model this as a linear regression model with a constant input (bias term), and no covariates: $p(y_n | \boldsymbol{\theta}) = \mathcal{N}(y_n | \beta_0, \sigma^2)$, where $\beta_0 = \mu$. We can now perform inference on β_0 in the usual way for GLMs, and then perform hypothesis testing. This is equivalent to the **one sample t-test** discussed in Section 3.10.2.6. For a nonparametric version, we can transform the data using the signed rank transform, thus fitting $SR(y_n) \sim \mathcal{N}(\mu, \sigma^2)$. The results are very close to the **Wilcoxon signed-ranked test**.

Now suppose we have paired data from two groups, $\mathcal{D} = \{(y_{1n}, y_{2n}) : n = 1 : N\}$, where we assume $y_{jn} \sim \mathcal{N}(\mu_j, \sigma^2)$. We are interested in testing whether $\mu_1 = \mu_2$. A simpler alternative is to define $y_n = y_{2n} - y_{1n}$, which we model using $y_n \sim \mathcal{N}(\mu, \sigma^2)$. We can then test whether $\mu = 0$ using the **paired sample t-test**, discussed in Section 3.10.2.6. Alternatively we can do inference on $SR(y_n)$, to get the **Wilcoxon matched pairs** test.

To handle the setting in which we have unpaired data from two groups, we can represent the data as $\mathcal{D} = \{(x_n, y_n) : n = 1 : N\}$, where $x_n \in \{0, 1\}$ represents whether the input belongs

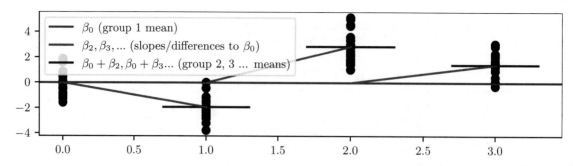

Figure 3.29: Illustration of one-way ANOVA with 4 groups. We are interested in testing whether the red lines have a slope of 0, meaning that all the groups have the same mean. Generated by anova.ipynb.

to group 0 or group 1. We assume the data comes from the following linear regression model: $p(y_n|x_n) \sim \mathcal{N}(\beta_0 + \beta_1 x_n, \sigma^2)$. We can now perform inference on $\boldsymbol{\beta}$ in the usual way for GLMs, and then perform hypothesis testing. This is equivalent to the **two-sample t-test** discussed in Section 3.10.2.8. In the nonparametric setting, we can replace y with its signed ranked transform and use the model $SR(y) \sim \mathcal{N}(\beta_0 + \beta_1 x, \sigma^2)$. This is approximately the same as the **Mann-Whitney U test**.

3.10.3.3   Metric-predicted variable with metric predictors (correlation test)

In this section, we assume the data has the form $\mathcal{D} = \{(x_n, y_n) : n = 1 : N\}$, where $x_n \in \mathbb{R}$ and $y_n \in \mathbb{R}$ are correlated with **Pearson correlation coefficient** of ρ. We are interested in testing the hypothesis that $\rho = 0$.

We can use a "bespoke" Bayesian approach as in Section 3.10.2.9. Alternatively, we can model this using simple linear regression, by writing $y_n \sim \mathcal{N}(\beta_0 + \beta_1 x, \sigma^2)$. If we scale the output Y so it has a standard deviation of 1, then we find that $\beta_1 = \rho$, as shown in [Mur22, Sec 11.2.3.3]. Thus we can use $p(\beta_1|\mathcal{D})$ to make inferences about ρ.

In the nonparametric setting, we compute the rank transform of x and y and then proceed as above. The **Spearman rank correlation coefficient** is the Pearson correlation coefficient on the rank-transformed data. While Pearson's correlation is useful for assessing the strength of linear relationships, Spearman's correlation can be used to assess general monotonic relationships, whether linear or not.

If we have multiple metric predictors (i.e., $\boldsymbol{x}_n \in \mathbb{R}^D$), we can use multiple linear regression instead of simple linear regression. We can then derive the posterior of the partial correlation coefficient from the posterior of the regression weights.

3.10.3.4   Metric-predicted variable with one nominal predictor (one-way ANOVA)

In this section, we consider the setting in which we have some data $\mathcal{D} = \{(x_n, y_n) : n = 1 : N\}$, where $x_n \in \{1, \dots, J\}$ represents which group the input belongs. (Such a discrete categorical variable is often called a **factor**.) We assume the data comes from the following linear regression model: $p(y_n|x_n = j) \sim \mathcal{N}(\mu_j, \sigma^2)$. We are interested in testing the hypothesis that all the μ_j are the same. This is traditionally performed using a **one-way ANOVA test**, where ANOVA stands for "analysis of variance". To derive a nonparametric test, we can first apply a rank transformation to y. This is similar to the **Kruskal-Wallis test**.

ANOVA assumes that the data are normally distributed, with a common (shared) variance, so that the sampling distribution of the F-**statistic** can be derived. We can write the corresponding model as a linear regression model, by using a dummy encoding of x_n, where $x_{n[j]} = \mathbb{I}(x_n = j)$. To avoid overparameterization (which can make the posterior unidentifiable), we drop the first level (this is known as **reduced rank encoding**). We can then write the model as

$$p(y_n|x_n; \boldsymbol{\theta}) \sim \mathcal{N}(f_{\text{aov}}(\boldsymbol{x}_n, \boldsymbol{\beta}), \sigma^2) \tag{3.334}$$

where we define the predicted mean using the ANOVA formula:

$$f_{\text{aov}}(\boldsymbol{x}, \boldsymbol{\beta}) = \beta_0 + \beta_2 x_{[2]} + \cdots + \beta_J x_{[J]} \tag{3.335}$$

We see that β_0 is the overall mean, and also corresponds to the value that will be used for level 1 of the factor (i.e., if $x_n = 1$). The other β_j terms represents deviations away from level 1. The null hpothesis corresponds to the assumption that $\beta_j = 0$ for all $j = 2 : J$.

A more symmetric formulation of the model is to write

$$f_{\text{aov}}(\boldsymbol{x}; \boldsymbol{\beta}) = \beta_0 + \beta_1 x_{[1]} + \beta_2 x_{[2]} + \cdots + \beta_J x_{[J]} \tag{3.336}$$

where β_0 is the **grand mean**, and where we impose the constraint that $\sum_{j=1}^{J} \beta_j = 0$. In this case we can interpret each β_j as the amount that group j deviates from the shared baseline β_0. To satisfy this constraint, we can write the predicted mean as

$$f_{\text{aov}}(\boldsymbol{x}, \tilde{\boldsymbol{\beta}}) = \tilde{\beta}_0 + \sum_{j=1}^{J} \tilde{\beta}_j x_{[j]} = \underbrace{(\tilde{\beta}_0 + \overline{\beta})}_{\beta_0} + \sum_{j=1}^{J} \underbrace{(\tilde{\beta}_j - \overline{\beta})}_{\beta_j} x_{[j]} \tag{3.337}$$

where $\tilde{\beta}_j$ are the unconstrained parameters, and $\overline{\beta} = \frac{1}{J}\sum_{j=1}^{J} \tilde{\beta}_j$. This construction satisfies the constraint, since

$$\sum_{j=1}^{J} \beta_j = \sum_{j=1}^{J} \tilde{\beta}_j - \sum_{j=1}^{J} \overline{\beta} = J\overline{\beta} - J\overline{\beta} = 0 \tag{3.338}$$

In traditional ANOVA, we assume that the data are normally distributed, with a common (shared) variance. In a Bayesian setting, we are free to relax these assumptions. For example, we can use a different likelihood (e.g., Student) and we can allow each group to have its own variance, σ_j^2, which can be reliably estimated using a hierarchical Bayesian model (see Section 3.6).

3.10.3.5 Metric-predicted variable with multiple nominal predictors (multi-way ANOVA)

In this section, we consider the setting in which we have G nominal predictors as input. To simplify notation, we assume we just have $G = 2$ groups. We assume the mean of y is given by

$$f_{\text{aov2}}(\boldsymbol{x}) = \mu + \sum_j \alpha_j x_{1,[j]} + \sum_k \beta_k x_{2,[k]} + \sum_{jk} \gamma_{jk} x_{1,[j]} x_{2,[k]} \tag{3.339}$$

	LH	RH	
Male	9	43	$N_1 = 52$
Female	4	44	$N_2 = 48$
Totals	13	87	100

Table 3.3: A 2×2 contingency table from http://en.wikipedia.org/wiki/Contingency_table.

where we impose the following sum-to-zero contraints

$$\sum_j \alpha_j = \sum_k \beta_k = \sum_j \gamma_{jk} = \sum_k \gamma_{jk} = 0 \tag{3.340}$$

We are interested in testing whether $\gamma = \mathbf{0}$, meaning there is no interaction effect. This is traditionally done using a **two-way ANOVA test**. However, we can also use a Bayesian approach and just compute $p(\boldsymbol{\theta}|\mathcal{D})$.

3.10.3.6   Count predicted variable with nominal predictors (χ^2 test)

Consider a situation in which we observed two nominal values for each item measured. For example, the gender of a person (male or female) and whether they are left handed or right handed (LH or RH). If we count the number of outcomes of each type, we can represent the data as a $R \times C$ **contingency table**. See Table 3.3 for an example. We may be interested in testing the null hypothesis that there is no interaction effect between the two groups and the outcome (i.e., the two variables are independent). In frequentist statistics, this is often tackled using a χ^2-**test**, which uses the sampling distribution of the χ^2 test statistic, defined as

$$\chi^2 = \sum_{r=1}^{R} \sum_{c=1}^{C} \frac{(O_{r,c} - E_{r,c})^2}{E_{r,c}} \tag{3.341}$$

where r indexes the rows, and c the columns, $O_{r,c}$ is the observed count in cell (r, c), and $E_{rc} = N p_{r.} p_{.c}$ is the expected count, where $p_{r.} = O_{c.}/N$ and $p_{.c} = O_{.r}/N$ are the empirical marginal frequencies.

In the Bayesian approach, we can just modify the two-way ANOVA of Section 3.10.3.5, and replace the Gaussian distribution with a Poisson distribution. We also need to pass the predicted natural parameter through an exponential link, since a Poisson distribution requires that the rate parameter is non-negative. Thus the model becomes

$$p(y|\mathbf{x} = (r, c), \boldsymbol{\theta}) = \text{Poi}(y|\lambda_{r,c}) \tag{3.342}$$

$$\lambda_{rc} = \exp(\beta_0 + \beta_r + \beta_c + \beta_{r,c}) \tag{3.343}$$

We can now perform posterior inference in the usual way.

3.10.3.7   Non-metric predicted variables

If the output variable is categorical, $y_n \in \{1, \ldots, C\}$, we can use logistic regression instead of linear regression (see e.g., Section 15.3.9). If the output is ordinal, we can use ordinal regression. If the output is a count variable, we can use Poisson regression. And so on. For more details on GLMs, see Chapter 15.

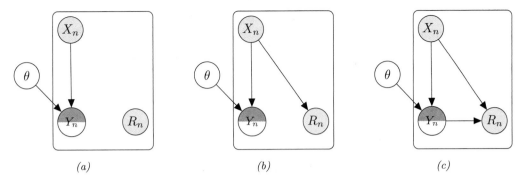

Figure 3.30: Graphical models to represent different patterns of missing data for conditional (discriminative) models. (a) Missing completely at random. (b) Missing at random. (c) Missing not at random. The semi-shaded $\boldsymbol{y}_n$ node is observed if $r_n = 1$ and is hidden otherwise. Adapted from Figure 2 of [SG02].

3.11   Missing data

Sometimes we may have **missing data**, in which parts of the data vector $\mathbf{X}_n \in \mathbb{R}^D$ may be unknown. (If we have a supervised problem, we append the labels to the feature vector.) We let $\mathbf{X}_{n,\mathrm{mis}}$ represent the missing parts, and $\mathbf{X}_{n,\mathrm{obs}}$ represent the observed parts. Since the reasons that data are missing may be informative (e.g., declining to answer a survey question such as "Do you have disease X?" may be an indication that the subject does in fact have it), we need to model the **missing data mechanism**. To do this, we introduce a random variable $\mathbf{R}_n$, to represent which parts of $\mathbf{X}_n$ are "revealed" (observed) or not. Specifically, we set $\mathbf{R}_{n,\mathrm{obs}} = 1$ for those indices (components) for which $\mathbf{X}_n$ is observed, and set $\mathbf{R}_{n,\mathrm{mis}} = 0$ for the other indices.

There are different kinds of assumptions we can make about the missing data mechanism, as discussed in [Rub76; LR87]. The strongest assumption is to assume the data is **missing completely at random** or **MCAR**. This means that $p(\mathbf{R}_n|\mathbf{X}_n) = p(\mathbf{R}_n)$, so the missingness does not depend on the hidden or observed features. A more realistic assumption is known as **missing at random** or **MAR**. This means that $p(\mathbf{R}_n|\mathbf{X}_n) = p(\mathbf{R}_n|\mathbf{X}_{n,\mathrm{obs}})$, so the missingness does not depend on the hidden features, but may depend on the visible features. If neither of these assumptions hold, we say the data is **missing not at random** or **MNAR**.

Now consider the case of conditional, or discriminative models, in which we model the outcome $\boldsymbol{y}_n$ given observed inputs $\boldsymbol{x}_n$ using a model of the form $p(\boldsymbol{y}_n|\boldsymbol{x}_n, \boldsymbol{\theta})$. Since we are conditioning on $\boldsymbol{x}_n$, we assume it is always observed. However, the output labels may or may not be observed, depending on the value of r_n. For example, in **semi-supervised learning**, we have a combination of labeled data, $\mathcal{D}^L = \{(\boldsymbol{x}_n, \boldsymbol{y}_n)\}$, and unlabeled data, $\mathcal{D}^U = \{(\boldsymbol{x}_n)\}$ [CSZ06].

The 3 missing data scenarios for the discriminative setting are shown in Figure 3.30, using graphical model notation (see [MPT13] for details). In the MCAR and MAR cases, we see that we can just ignore the unlabeled data with missing outputs, since the unknown model parameters $\boldsymbol{\theta}$ are unaffected by $\boldsymbol{y}_n$ if it is a hidden leaf node. However, in the MNAR case, we see that $\boldsymbol{\theta}$ depends on $\boldsymbol{y}_n$, even it is hidden, since the value of $\boldsymbol{y}_n$ is assumed to affect the probability of r_n, which is always observed. In such cases, to fit the model, we need to **impute** the missing values, by using methods such as EM (see Section 6.5.3).

Now consider the case where we use a joint or generative model of the form $p(\boldsymbol{x}, \boldsymbol{y}) = p(\boldsymbol{y})p(\boldsymbol{x}|\boldsymbol{y})$, instead of a discriminative model of the form $p(\boldsymbol{y}|\boldsymbol{x})$.[13] In this case, the unlabeled data can be useful for learning even in the MCAR and MAR scenarios, since $\boldsymbol{\theta}$ now depends on both $\boldsymbol{x}$ and $\boldsymbol{y}$. In particular, information about $p(\boldsymbol{x})$ can be informative about $p(\boldsymbol{y}|\boldsymbol{x})$. See e.g., [CSZ06] for details.

---

13. In [Sch+12a], they call a model of the form $p(\boldsymbol{y}|\boldsymbol{x})$ a "**causal classifier**", since the features cause the labels, and a model of the form $p(\boldsymbol{x}|\boldsymbol{y})$ an "**anti-causal classifier**", since the features are caused by the labels.

4 Graphical models

4.1 Introduction

I basically know of two principles for treating complicated systems in simple ways: the first is the principle of modularity and the second is the principle of abstraction. I am an apologist for computational probability in machine learning because I believe that probability theory implements these two principles in deep and intriguing ways — namely through factorization and through averaging. Exploiting these two mechanisms as fully as possible seems to me to be the way forward in machine learning. — Michael Jordan, 1997 (quoted in [Fre98]).

Probabilistic graphical models (**PGMs**) provide a convenient formalism for defining joint distributions on sets of random variables. In such graphs, the nodes represent random variables, and the (lack of) edges represent **conditional independence** (**CI**) assumptions between these variables. A better name for these models would be "independence diagrams", but the term "graphical models" is now entrenched.

There are several kinds of graphical model, depending on whether the graph is directed, undirected, or some combination of directed and undirected, as we discuss in the sections below. More details on graphical models can be found in e.g., [KF09a].

4.2 Directed graphical models (Bayes nets)

In this section, we discuss directed probabilistic graphical models, or **DPGM**, which are based on **directed acyclic graphs** or **DAGs** (graphs that do not have any directed cycles). PGMs based on a DAG are often called **Bayesian networks** or **Bayes nets** for short; however, there is nothing inherently "Bayesian" about Bayesian networks: they are just a way of defining probability distributions. They are also sometimes called **belief networks**. The term "belief" here refers to subjective probability. However, the probabilities used in these models are no more (and no less) subjective than in any other kind of probabilistic model.

4.2.1 Representing the joint distribution

The key property of a DAG is that the nodes can be ordered such that parents come before children. This is called a **topological ordering**. Given such an order, we define the **ordered Markov property** to be the assumption that a node is conditionally independent of all its predecessors in

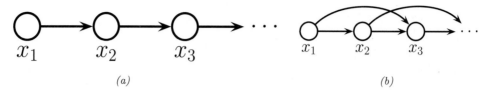

Figure 4.1: Illustration of first and second order Markov models.

the ordering given its parents, i.e.,

$$x_i \perp \boldsymbol{x}_{\mathrm{pred}(i)\backslash\mathrm{pa}(i)} | \boldsymbol{x}_{\mathrm{pa}(i)} \tag{4.1}$$

where $\mathrm{pa}(i)$ are the parents of node i, and $\mathrm{pred}(i)$ are the predecessors of node i in the ordering. Consequently, we can represent the joint distribution as follows (assuming we use node ordering $1 : N_G$):

$$p(\boldsymbol{x}_{1:N_G}) = p(x_1)p(x_2|x_1)p(x_3|x_1, x_2)\dots p(x_{N_G}|x_1, \dots, x_{N_G-1}) = \prod_{i=1}^{N_G} p(x_i|\boldsymbol{x}_{\mathrm{pa}(i)}) \tag{4.2}$$

where $p(x_i|\boldsymbol{x}_{\mathrm{pa}(i)})$ is the **conditional probability distribution** or **CPD** for node i. (The parameters of this distribution are omitted from the notation for brevity.)

The key advantage of the representation used in Equation (4.2) is that the number of parameters used to specify the joint distribution is substantially less, by virtue of the conditional independence assumptions that we have encoded in the graph, than an unstructured joint distribution. To see this, suppose all the variables are discrete and have K states each. Then an unstructured joint distribution needs $O(K^{N_G})$ parameters to specify the probability of every configuration. By contrast, with a DAG in which each node has at most N_P parents, we only need $O(N_G K^{N_P+1})$ parameters, which can be exponentially fewer if the DAG is sparse.

We give some examples of DPGM's in Section 4.2.2, and in Section 4.2.4, we discuss how to read off other conditional independence properties from the graph.

4.2.2   Examples

In this section, we give several examples of models that can be usefully represented as DPGM's.

4.2.2.1   Markov chains

We can represent the conditional independence assumptions of a first-order Markov model using the chain-structured DPGM shown in Figure 4.1(a). Consider a variable at a single time step t, which we call the "present". From the diagram, we see that information cannot flow from the past, $\boldsymbol{x}_{1:t-1}$, to the future, $\boldsymbol{x}_{t+1:T}$, except via the present, x_t. (We formalize this in Section 4.2.4.) This means that the $\boldsymbol{x}_t$ is a sufficient statistic for the past, so the model is first-order Markov. This implies that the corresponding joint distribution can be written as follows:

$$p(\boldsymbol{x}_{1:T}) = p(x_1)p(x_2|x_1)p(x_3|x_2)\cdots p(x_T|x_{T-1}) = p(x_1)\prod_{t=2}^{T} p(x_t|\boldsymbol{x}_{1:t-1}) \tag{4.3}$$

For discrete random variables, we can represent corresponding CPDs, $p(x_t = k | x_{t-1} = j)$, as a 2d table, known as a **conditional probability table** or **CPT**, $p(x_t = k | x_{t-1} = j) = \theta_{jk}$, where $0 \le \theta_{jk} \le 1$ and $\sum_{k=1}^{K} \theta_{jk} = 1$ (i.e., each row sums to 1).

The first-order Markov assumption is quite restrictive. If we want to allow for dependencies two steps into the past, we can create a Markov model of order 2. This is shown in Figure 4.1(b). The corresponding joint distribution has the form

$$p(\boldsymbol{x}_{1:T}) = p(x_1, x_2)p(x_3 | x_1, x_2)p(x_4 | x_2, x_3) \cdots p(x_T | x_{T-2}, x_{T-1}) = p(x_1, x_2) \prod_{t=3}^{T} p(x_t | \boldsymbol{x}_{t-2:t-1}) \quad (4.4)$$

As we increase the order of the Markov model, we need to add more edges. In the limit, the DAG becomes fully connected (subject to being acyclic), as shown in Figure 22.1. However, in this case, there are no useful conditional independencies, so the graphical model has no value.

4.2.2.2 The "student" network

Figure 4.2 shows a model for capturing the inter dependencies between 5 discrete random variables related to a hypothetical student taking a class: D = difficulty of class (easy, hard), I = intelligence (low, high), G = grade (A, B, C), S = SAT score (bad, good), L = letter of recommendation (bad, good). (This is a simplification of the "**student network**" from [KF09a, p.281].) The chain rule tells us that we can represent the joint as follows:

$$p(D, I, G, L, S) = p(L | S, G, D, I) \times p(S | G, D, I) \times p(G | D, I) \times p(D | I) \times p(I) \quad (4.5)$$

where we have ordered the nodes topologically as I, D, G, S, L. Note that L is conditionally independent of all the other nodes earlier in this ordering given its parent G, so we can replace $p(L | S, G, D, I)$ by $p(L | G)$. We can simplify the other terms in a similar way to get

$$p(D, I, G, L, S) = p(L | G) \times p(S | I) \times p(G | D, I) \times p(D) \times p(I) \quad (4.6)$$

The ability to simplify a joint distribution in a product of small local pieces is the key idea behind graphical models.

In addition to the graph structure, we need to specify the conditional probability distributions (CPDs) at each node. For discrete random variables, we can represent the CPD as a table, which means we have a separate row (i.e., a separate categorical distribution) for each **conditioning case**, i.e., for each combination of parent values. We can represent the i'th CPT as follows:

$$\theta_{ijk} \triangleq p(x_i = k | \boldsymbol{x}_{\text{pa}(i)} = j) \quad (4.7)$$

The matrix $\boldsymbol{\theta}_{i,:,:}$ is a **row stochastic matrix**, that satisfies the properties $0 \le \theta_{ijk} \le 1$ and $\sum_{k=1}^{K_i} \theta_{ijk} = 1$ for each row j. Here i indexes nodes, $i \in [N_G]$; k indexes node states, $k \in [K_i]$, where K_i is the number of states for node i; and j indexes joint parent states, $j \in [J_i]$, where $J_i = \prod_{p \in \text{pa}(i)} K_p$.

The CPTs for the student network are shown next to each node in Figure 4.2. For example, we see that if the class is hard ($D = 1$) and the student has low intelligence ($I = 0$), the distribution over grades A, B, and C we expect is $p(G | D = 1, I = 0) = [0.05, 0.25, 0.7]$; but if the student is intelligent, we get $p(G | D = 1, I = 1) = [0.5, 0.3, 0.2]$.

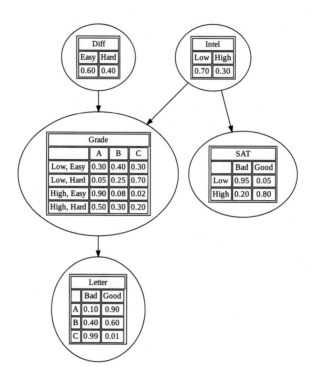

Figure 4.2: The (simplified) student network. "Diff" is the difficulty of the class. "Intel" is the intelligence of the student. "Grade" is the grade of the student in this class. "SAT" is the score of the student on the SAT exam. "Letter" is whether the teacher writes a good or bad letter of recommendation. The circles (nodes) represent random variables, the edges represent direct probabilistic dependencies. The tables inside each node represent the conditional probability distribution of the node given its parents. Generated by student_pgm.ipynb.

The number of parameters in a CPT is $O(K^{p+1})$, where K is the number of states per node, and p is the number of parents. Later we will consider more parsimonious representations, with fewer learnable parameters. (We discuss parameter learning in Section 4.2.7.)

Once we have specified the model, we can use it to answer probabilistic queries, as we discuss in Section 4.2.6. As an example, suppose we observe that the student gets a grade of C. The posterior probability that the student is intelligent is just $p(I = \text{High}|G = C) = 0.08$, as shown in Figure 4.8. However, now suppose we also observe that the student gets a good SAT score. Now the posterior probability that the student is intelligent has jumped to $p(I = \text{High}|G = C, S = \text{Good}) = 0.58$, since we can explain the C grade by inferring it was a difficult class (indeed, we find $p(D = \text{Hard}|G = C, S = \text{Good}) = 0.76$). This negative mutual interaction between multiple causes of some observations is called the **explaining away** effect, also known as **Berkson's paradox** (see Section 4.2.4.2 for details).

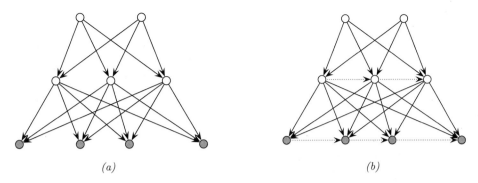

(a) *(b)*

Figure 4.3: (a) Hierarchical latent variable model with 2 layers. (b) Same as (a) but with autoregressive connections within each layer. The observed $\boldsymbol{x}$ variables are the shaded leaf nodes at the bottom. The unshaded nodes are the hidden $\boldsymbol{z}$ variables.

4.2.2.3 Sigmoid belief nets

In this section, we consider a **deep generative model** of the form shown in Figure 4.3a. This corresponds to the following joint distribution:

$$p(\boldsymbol{x}, \boldsymbol{z}) = p(\boldsymbol{z}_2)p(\boldsymbol{z}_1|\boldsymbol{z}_2)p(\boldsymbol{x}|\boldsymbol{z}_1) = \prod_{k=1}^{K_2} p(z_{2,k}) \prod_{k=1}^{K_1} p(z_{1,k}|\boldsymbol{z}_2) \prod_{d=1}^{D} p(x_d|\boldsymbol{z}_1) \tag{4.8}$$

where $\boldsymbol{x}$ denotes the visible leaf nodes, and $\boldsymbol{z}_\ell$ denotes the hidden internal nodes. (We assume there are K_ℓ hidden nodes at level ℓ, and D visible leaf nodes.)

Now consider the special case where all the latent variables are binary, and all the latent CPDs are logistic regression models. That is,

$$p(\boldsymbol{z}_\ell|\boldsymbol{z}_{\ell+1}, \boldsymbol{\theta}) = \prod_{k=1}^{K_\ell} \text{Ber}(z_{\ell,k}|\sigma(\boldsymbol{w}_{\ell,k}^\mathsf{T}\boldsymbol{z}_{\ell+1})) \tag{4.9}$$

where $\sigma(u) = 1/(1+e^{-u})$ is the sigmoid (logistic) function. The result is called a **sigmoid belief net** [Nea92].

At the bottom layer, $p(\boldsymbol{x}|\boldsymbol{z}_1, \boldsymbol{\theta})$, we use whatever observation model is appropriate for the type of data we are dealing with. For example, for real valued data, we might use

$$p(\boldsymbol{x}|\boldsymbol{z}_1, \boldsymbol{\theta}) = \prod_{d=1}^{D} \mathcal{N}(x_d|\boldsymbol{w}_{1,d,\mu}^\mathsf{T}\boldsymbol{z}_1, \exp(\boldsymbol{w}_{1,d,\sigma}^\mathsf{T}\boldsymbol{z}_1)) \tag{4.10}$$

where $\boldsymbol{w}_{1,d,\mu}$ are the weights that control the mean of the d'th output, and $\boldsymbol{w}_{1,d,\sigma}$ are the weights that control the variance of the d'th output.

We can also add directed connections between the hidden variables within a layer, as shown in Figure 4.3b. This is called a **deep autoregressive network** or **DARN** model [Gre+14], which combines ideas from latent variable modeling and autoregressive modeling.

We discuss other forms of hierarchical generative models in Chapter 21.

4.2.3 Gaussian Bayes nets

Consider a DPGM where all the variables are real-valued, and all the CPDs have the following form, known as a **linear Gaussian CPD**:

$$p(x_i|\boldsymbol{x}_{\mathrm{pa}(i)}) = \mathcal{N}(x_i|\mu_i + \boldsymbol{w}_i^\mathsf{T}\boldsymbol{x}_{\mathrm{pa}(i)}, \sigma_i^2) \tag{4.11}$$

As we show below, multiplying all these CPDs together results in a large joint Gaussian distribution of the form $p(\boldsymbol{x}) = \mathcal{N}(\boldsymbol{x}|\boldsymbol{\mu}, \boldsymbol{\Sigma})$, where $\boldsymbol{x} \in \mathbb{R}^{N_G}$. This is called a **directed Gaussian graphical model** or a **Gaussian Bayes net**.

We now explain how to derive $\boldsymbol{\mu}$ and $\boldsymbol{\Sigma}$, following [SK89, App. B]. For convenience, we rewrite the CPDs in the following form:

$$x_i = \mu_i + \sum_{j \in \mathrm{pa}(i)} w_{i,j}(x_j - \mu_j) + \sigma_i z_i \tag{4.12}$$

where $z_i \sim \mathcal{N}(0,1)$, σ_i is the conditional standard deviation of x_i given its parents, $w_{i,j}$ is the strength of the $j \to i$ edge, and μ_i is the local mean.[1]

It is easy to see that the global mean is just the concatenation of the local means, $\boldsymbol{\mu} = (\mu_1, \ldots, \mu_{N_G})$. We now derive the global covariance, $\boldsymbol{\Sigma}$. Let $\mathbf{S} \triangleq \mathrm{diag}(\boldsymbol{\sigma})$ be a diagonal matrix containing the standard deviations. We can rewrite Equation (4.12) in matrix-vector form as follows:

$$(\boldsymbol{x} - \boldsymbol{\mu}) = \mathbf{W}(\boldsymbol{x} - \boldsymbol{\mu}) + \mathbf{S}\boldsymbol{z} \tag{4.13}$$

where $\mathbf{W}$ is the matrix of regression weights. Now let $\boldsymbol{e}$ be a vector of noise terms: $\boldsymbol{e} \triangleq \mathbf{S}\boldsymbol{z}$. We can rearrange this to get $\boldsymbol{e} = (\mathbf{I} - \mathbf{W})(\boldsymbol{x} - \boldsymbol{\mu})$. Since $\mathbf{W}$ is lower triangular (because $w_{j,i} = 0$ if $j < i$ in the topological ordering), we have that $\mathbf{I} - \mathbf{W}$ is lower triangular with 1s on the diagonal. Hence

$$\begin{pmatrix} e_1 \\ e_2 \\ \vdots \\ e_{N_G} \end{pmatrix} = \begin{pmatrix} 1 & & & & \\ -w_{2,1} & 1 & & & \\ -w_{3,2} & -w_{3,1} & 1 & & \\ \vdots & & & \ddots & \\ -w_{N_G,1} & -w_{N_G,2} & \cdots & -w_{N_G,N_G-1} & 1 \end{pmatrix} \begin{pmatrix} x_1 - \mu_1 \\ x_2 - \mu_2 \\ \vdots \\ \\ x_{N_G} - \mu_{N_G} \end{pmatrix} \tag{4.14}$$

Since $\mathbf{I} - \mathbf{W}$ is always invertible, we can write

$$\boldsymbol{x} - \boldsymbol{\mu} = (\mathbf{I} - \mathbf{W})^{-1}\boldsymbol{e} \triangleq \mathbf{U}\boldsymbol{e} = \mathbf{U}\mathbf{S}\boldsymbol{z} \tag{4.15}$$

where we defined $\mathbf{U} = (\mathbf{I} - \mathbf{W})^{-1}$. Hence the covariance is given by

$$\boldsymbol{\Sigma} = \mathrm{Cov}\,[\boldsymbol{x}] = \mathrm{Cov}\,[\boldsymbol{x} - \boldsymbol{\mu}] = \mathrm{Cov}\,[\mathbf{U}\mathbf{S}\boldsymbol{z}] = \mathbf{U}\mathbf{S}\,\mathrm{Cov}\,[\boldsymbol{z}]\,\mathbf{S}\mathbf{U}^\mathsf{T} = \mathbf{U}\mathbf{S}^2\mathbf{U}^\mathsf{T} \tag{4.16}$$

since $\mathrm{Cov}\,[\boldsymbol{z}] = \mathbf{I}$.

---

1. If we do not subtract off the parent's mean (i.e., if we use $x_i = \mu_i + \sum_{j \in \mathrm{pa}(i)} w_{i,j}x_j + \sigma_i z_i$), the derivation of $\boldsymbol{\Sigma}$ is much messier, as can be seen by looking at [Bis06, p370].

4.2.4 Conditional independence properties

We write $x_A \perp_G x_B | x_C$ if A is conditionally independent of B given C in the graph G. (We discuss how to determine whether such a CI property is implied by a given graph in the sections below.) Let $I(G)$ be the set of all such CI statements encoded by the graph, and $I(p)$ be the set of all such CI statements that hold true in some distribution p. We say that G is an **I-map** (independence map) for p, or that p is **Markov** wrt G, iff $I(G) \subseteq I(p)$. In other words, the graph is an I-map if it does not make any assertions of CI that are not true of the distribution. This allows us to use the graph as a safe proxy for p when reasoning about p's CI properties. This is helpful for designing algorithms that work for large classes of distributions, regardless of their specific numerical parameters. Note that the fully connected graph is an I-map of all distributions, since it makes no CI assertions at all, as we show below. We therefore say G is a **minimal I-map** of p if G is an I-map of p, and if there is no $G' \subseteq G$ which is an I-map of p.

We now turn to the question of how to derive $I(G)$, i.e., which CI properties are entailed by a DAG.

4.2.4.1 Global Markov properties (d-separation)

We say an *undirected path* P is **d-separated** by a set of nodes C (containing the evidence) iff at least one of the following conditions hold:

1. P contains a chain or **pipe**, $s \rightarrow m \rightarrow t$ or $s \leftarrow m \leftarrow t$, where $m \in C$

2. P contains a tent or **fork**, $s \swarrow^m \searrow t$, where $m \in C$

3. P contains a **collider** or **v-structure**, $s \searrow_m \swarrow t$, where m is not in C and neither is any descendant of m.

Next, we say that a *set of nodes* A is d-separated from a different set of nodes B given a third observed set C iff each undirected path from every node $a \in A$ to every node $b \in B$ is d-separated by C. Finally, we define the CI properties of a DAG as follows:

$$\mathbf{X}_A \perp_G \mathbf{X}_B | \mathbf{X}_C \iff \text{A is d-separated from B given C} \tag{4.17}$$

This is called the (directed) **global Markov property**.

The **Bayes ball algorithm** [Sha98] is a simple way to see if A is d-separated from B given C, based on the above definition. The idea is this. We "shade" all nodes in C, indicating that they are observed. We then place "balls" at each node in A, let them "bounce around" according to some rules, and then ask if any of the balls reach any of the nodes in B. The three main rules are shown in Figure 4.4. Notice that balls can travel opposite to edge directions. We see that a ball can pass through a chain, but not if it is shaded in the middle. Similarly, a ball can pass through a fork, but not if it is shaded in the middle. However, a ball cannot pass through a v-structure, unless it is shaded in the middle.

We can justify the 3 rules of Bayes ball as follows. First consider a chain structure $X \rightarrow Y \rightarrow Z$, which encodes

$$p(x, y, z) = p(x)p(y|x)p(z|y) \tag{4.18}$$

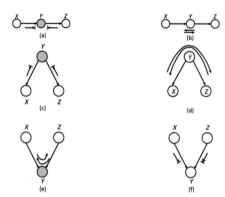

Figure 4.4: Bayes ball rules. A shaded node is one we condition on. If there is an arrow hitting a bar, it means the ball cannot pass through; otherwise the ball can pass through.

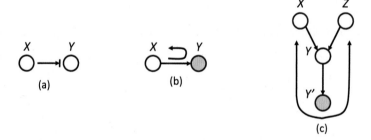

Figure 4.5: (a-b) Bayes ball boundary conditions. (c) Example of why we need boundary conditions. Y' is an observed child of Y, rendering Y "effectively observed", so the ball bounces back up on its way from X to Z.

When we condition on y, are x and z independent? We have

$$p(x, z|y) = \frac{p(x, y,)}{p(y)} = \frac{p(x)p(y|x)p(z|y)}{p(y)} = \frac{p(x, y)p(z|y)}{p(y)} = p(x|y)p(z|y) \tag{4.19}$$

and therefore $X \perp Z \mid Y$. So observing the middle node of chain breaks it in two (as in a Markov chain).

Now consider the tent structure $X \leftarrow Y \rightarrow Z$. The joint is

$$p(x, y, z) = p(y)p(x|y)p(z|y) \tag{4.20}$$

When we condition on y, are x and z independent? We have

$$p(x, z|y) = \frac{p(x, y, z)}{p(y)} = \frac{p(y)p(x|y)p(z|y)}{p(y)} = p(x|y)p(z|y) \tag{4.21}$$

and therefore $X \perp Z \mid Y$. So observing a root node separates its children (as in a naive Bayes classifier: see Section 4.2.8.2).

X	Y	Z
D	I	
D	I	S
D	S	
D	S	I
D	S	L, I
D	S	G, I
D	S	G, L, I
D	L	G
D	L	G, S
D	L	G, I
D	L	I, G, S

Table 4.1: *Conditional independence relationships implied by the student DAG (Figure 4.2). Each line has the form $X \perp Y | Z$. Generated by student_pgm.ipynb.*

Finally consider a v-structure $X \to Y \leftarrow Z$. The joint is

$$p(x, y, z) = p(x)p(z)p(y|x, z) \tag{4.22}$$

When we condition on y, are x and z independent? We have

$$p(x, z|y) = \frac{p(x)p(z)p(y|x, z)}{p(y)} \tag{4.23}$$

so $X \not\perp Z | Y$. However, in the unconditional distribution, we have

$$p(x, z) = p(x)p(z) \tag{4.24}$$

so we see that X and Z are marginally independent. So we see that conditioning on a common child at the bottom of a v-structure makes its parents become dependent. This important effect is called **explaining away**, **inter-causal reasoning**, or **Berkson's paradox** (see Section 4.2.4.2 for a discussion).

Finally, Bayes ball also needs the "boundary conditions" shown in Figure 4.5(a-b). These rules say that a ball hitting a hidden leaf stops, but a ball hitting an observed leaf "bounces back". To understand where this rule comes from, consider Figure 4.5(c). Suppose Y' is a (possibly noisy) copy of Y. If we observe Y', we effectively observe Y as well, so the parents X and Z have to compete to explain this. So if we send a ball down $X \to Y \to Y'$, it should "bounce back" up along $Y' \to Y \to Z$, in order to pass information between the parents. However, if Y and *all* its children are hidden, the ball does not bounce back.

As an example of the CI statements encoded by a DAG, Table 4.1 shows some properties that follow from the student network in Figure 4.2.

4.2.4.2   Explaining away (Berkson's paradox)

In this section, we give some examples of the **explaining away** phenomenon, also called **Berkson's paradox**.

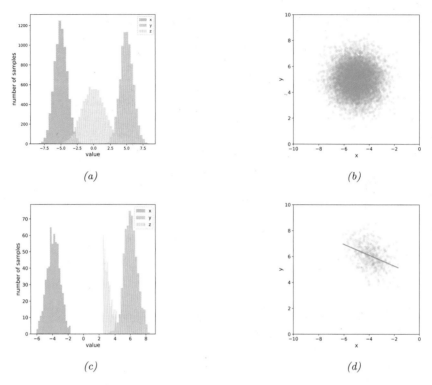

Figure 4.6: Samples from a jointly Gaussian DPGM, $p(x, y, z) = \mathcal{N}(x| -5, 1)\mathcal{N}(y|5, 1)\mathcal{N}(z|x + y, 1)$. (a) Unconditional marginal distributions, $p(x)$, $p(y)$, $p(z)$. (b) Unconditional joint distribution, $p(x, y)$. (c) Conditional marginal distribution, $p(x|z > 2.5)$, $p(y|z > 2.5)$, $p(z|z > 2.5)$. (d) Conditional joint distribution, $p(x, y|z > 2.5)$. Adapted from [Clo20]. Generated by berksons_gaussian.ipynb.

As a simple example (from [PM18b, p198]), consider tossing two coins 100 times. Suppose you only record the outcome of the experiment if at least one coin shows up heads. You should expect to record about 75 entries. You will see that every time coin 1 is recorded as tails, coin 2 will be recorded as heads. If we ignore the way in which the data was collected, we might infer from the fact that coins 1 and 2 are correlated that there is a hidden common cause. However, the correct explanation is that the correlation is due to conditioning on a hidden common effect (namely the decision of whether to record the outcome or not, so we can censor tail-tail events). This is called **selection bias**.

As another example of this, consider a Gaussian DPGM of the form

$$p(x, y, z) = \mathcal{N}(x| -5, 1)\mathcal{N}(y|5, 1)\mathcal{N}(z|x + y, 1) \tag{4.25}$$

The graph structure is $X \to Z \leftarrow Y$, where Z is the child node. Some samples from the unconditional joint distribution $p(x, y, z)$ are shown in Figure 4.6(a); we see that X and Y are uncorrelated. Now suppose we only select samples where $z > 2.5$. Some samples from the conditional joint distribution

$p(x, y|z > 2.5)$ are shown in Figure 4.6(d); we see that now X and Y are correlated. This could cause us to erroneously conclude that there is a causal relationship, but in fact the dependency is caused by selection bias.

4.2.4.3 Markov blankets

The smallest set of nodes that renders a node i conditionally independent of all the other nodes in the graph is called i's **Markov blanket**; we will denote this by $\mathrm{mb}(i)$. Below we show that the Markov blanket of a node in a DPGM is equal to the parents, the children, and the **co-parents**, i.e., other nodes who are also parents of its children:

$$\mathrm{mb}(i) \triangleq \mathrm{ch}(i) \cup \mathrm{pa}(i) \cup \mathrm{copa}(i) \tag{4.26}$$

See Figure 4.7 for an illustration.

To see why this is true, let us partition all the nodes into the target node X_i, its parents U, its children Y, its coparents Z, and the other variables O. Let X_{-i} be all the nodes except X_i. Then we have

$$p(X_i|X_{-i}) = \frac{p(X_i, X_{-i})}{\sum_x p(X_i = x, X_{-i})}, \tag{4.27}$$

$$= \frac{p(X_i, U, Y, Z, O)}{\sum_x p(X_i = x, U, Y, Z, O)} \tag{4.28}$$

$$= \frac{p(X_i|U)[\prod_j p(Y_j|X_i, Z_j)]P(U, Z, O)}{\sum_x p(X_i = x|U)[\prod_j p(Y_j|X_i = x, Z_j)]P(U, Z, O)} \tag{4.29}$$

$$= \frac{p(X_i|U)[\prod_j p(Y_j|X_i, Z_j)]}{\sum_x p(X_i = x|U)[\prod_j p(Y_j|X_i = x, Z_j)]} \tag{4.30}$$

$$\propto p(X_i|\mathrm{pa}(X_i)) \prod_{Y_j \in \mathrm{ch}(X_i)} p(Y_j|\mathrm{pa}(Y_j))) \tag{4.31}$$

where $\mathrm{ch}(X_i)$ are the children of X_i and $\mathrm{pa}(Y_j)$ are the parents of Y_j. We see that the terms that do not involve X_i cancel out from the numerator and denominator, so we are left with a product of terms that include X_i in their "scope". Hence the **full conditional** for node i becomes

$$p(x_i|\boldsymbol{x}_{-i}) = p(x_i|\boldsymbol{x}_{\mathrm{mb}(i)}) \propto p(x_i|\boldsymbol{x}_{\mathrm{pa}(i)}) \prod_{k \in \mathrm{ch}(i)} p(x_k|\boldsymbol{x}_{\mathrm{pa}(k)}) \tag{4.32}$$

We will see applications of this in Gibbs sampling (Equation (12.19)), and mean field variational inference (Equation (10.87)).

4.2.4.4 Other Markov properties

From the d-separation criterion, one can conclude that

$$i \perp \mathrm{nd}(i) \setminus \mathrm{pa}(i)|\mathrm{pa}(i) \tag{4.33}$$

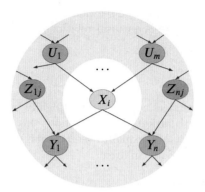

Figure 4.7: Illustration of the Markov blanket of a node in a directed graphical model. The target node X_i is shown in gray, its parents $U_{1:m}$ are shown in green, its children $Y_{1:n}$ are shown in blue, and its coparents $Z_{1:n,1:j}$ are shown in red. X_i is conditionally independent of all the other variables in the model given these variables. Adapted from Figure 13.4b of [RN19].

where the **non-descendants** of a node $\mathrm{nd}(i)$ are all the nodes except for its descendants, $\mathrm{nd}(i) = \{1, \ldots, N_G\} \setminus \{i \cup \mathrm{desc}(i)\}$. Equation (4.33) is called the (directed) **local Markov property**. For example, in Figure 4.23(a), we have $\mathrm{nd}(3) = \{1, 2, 4\}$, and $\mathrm{pa}(3) = 1$, so $3 \perp 2, 4 | 1$.

A special case of this property is when we only look at predecessors of a node according to some topological ordering. We have

$$i \perp \mathrm{pred}(i) \setminus \mathrm{pa}(i) | \mathrm{pa}(i) \tag{4.34}$$

which follows since $\mathrm{pred}(i) \subseteq \mathrm{nd}(i)$. This is called the **ordered Markov property**, which justifies Equation (4.2). For example, in Figure 4.23(a), if we use the ordering $1, 2, \ldots, 7$. we find $\mathrm{pred}(3) = \{1, 2\}$ and $\mathrm{pa}(3) = 1$, so $3 \perp 2 | 1$.

We have now described three Markov properties for DAGs: the directed global Markov property G in Equation (4.17), the directed local Markov property L in Equation (4.33), and the ordered Markov property O in Equation (4.34), It is obvious that $G \implies L \implies O$. What is less obvious, but nevertheless true, is that $O \implies L \implies G$ (see e.g., [KF09a] for the proof). Hence all these properties are equivalent.

Furthermore, any distribution p that is Markov wrt a graph can be factorized as in Equation (4.2); this is called the **factorization property** F. It is obvious that $O \implies F$, but one can show that the converse also holds (see e.g., [KF09a] for the proof).

4.2.5   Generation (sampling)

It is easy to generate prior samples from a DPGM: we simply visit the nodes in **topological order**, parents before children, and then sample a value for each node given the value of its parents. This will generate independent samples from the joint, $(x_1, \ldots, x_{N_G}) \sim p(\boldsymbol{x} | \boldsymbol{\theta})$. This is called **ancestral sampling**.

4.2.6 Inference

In the context of PGMs, the term "**inference**" refers to the task of computing the posterior over a set of **query nodes** Q given the observed values for a set of **visible nodes** V, while marginalizing over the irrelevant **nuisance variables**, $R = \{1, \ldots, N_G\} \setminus \{Q, V\}$:

$$p_{\boldsymbol{\theta}}(Q|V) = \frac{p_{\boldsymbol{\theta}}(Q, V)}{p_{\boldsymbol{\theta}}(V)} = \frac{\sum_R p_{\boldsymbol{\theta}}(Q, V, R)}{p_{\boldsymbol{\theta}}(V)} \tag{4.35}$$

(If the variables are continuous, we should replace sums with integrals.) If Q is a single node, then $p_{\boldsymbol{\theta}}(Q|V)$ is called the **posterior marginal** for node Q.

As an example, suppose $V = \boldsymbol{x}$ is a sequence of observed sound waves, $Q = \boldsymbol{z}$ is the corresponding set of unknown spoken words, and $R = \boldsymbol{r}$ are random "non-semantic" factors associated with the signal, such as prosody or background noise. Our goal is to compute the posterior over the words given the sounds, while being invariant to the irrelevant factors:

$$p_{\boldsymbol{\theta}}(\boldsymbol{z}|\boldsymbol{x}) = \sum_{\boldsymbol{r}} p_{\boldsymbol{\theta}}(\boldsymbol{z}, \boldsymbol{r}|\boldsymbol{x}) = \sum_{\boldsymbol{r}} \frac{p_{\boldsymbol{\theta}}(\boldsymbol{z}, \boldsymbol{r}, \boldsymbol{x})}{p_{\boldsymbol{\theta}}(\boldsymbol{x})} = \sum_{\boldsymbol{r}} \frac{p_{\boldsymbol{\theta}}(\boldsymbol{z}, \boldsymbol{r}, \boldsymbol{x})}{\sum_{\boldsymbol{z}', \boldsymbol{r}'} p_{\boldsymbol{\theta}}(\boldsymbol{z}', \boldsymbol{r}', \boldsymbol{x})} \tag{4.36}$$

As a simplification, we can "lump" the random factors R into the query set Q to define the complete set of **hidden variables** $H = Q \cup R$. In this case, the tasks simpifies to

$$p_{\boldsymbol{\theta}}(\boldsymbol{h}|\boldsymbol{x}) = \frac{p_{\boldsymbol{\theta}}(\boldsymbol{h}, \boldsymbol{x})}{p_{\boldsymbol{\theta}}(\boldsymbol{x})} = \frac{p_{\boldsymbol{\theta}}(\boldsymbol{h}, \boldsymbol{x})}{\sum_{\boldsymbol{h}'} p_{\boldsymbol{\theta}}(\boldsymbol{h}', \boldsymbol{x})} \tag{4.37}$$

The computational complexity of the inference task depends on the CI properties of the graph, as we discuss in Chapter 9. In general it is NP-hard (see Section 9.5.4), but for certain graph structures (such as chains, trees, and other sparse graphs), it can be solved efficiently (in polynomial) time using dynamic programming (see Chapter 9). For cases where it is intractable, we can use standard methods for approximate Bayesian inference, which we review in Chapter 7.

4.2.6.1 Example: inference in the student network

As an example of inference in PGMs, consider the student network from Section 4.2.2.2. Suppose we observe that the student gets a grade of C. The posterior marginals are shown in Figure 4.8a. We see that the low grade could be explained by the class being hard (since $p(D = \text{Hard}|G = C) = 0.63$), but is more likely explained by the student having low intelligence (since $p(I = \text{High}|G = C) = 0.08$).

However, now suppose we *also* observe that the student gets a good SAT score. The new posterior marginals are shown in Figure 4.8b. Now the posterior probability that the student is intelligent has jumped to $p(I = \text{High}|G = C, \text{SAT} = \text{Good}) = 0.58$, since otherwise it would be difficult to explain the good SAT score. Once we believe the student has high intelligence, we have to explain the C grade by assuming the class is hard, and indeed we find that the probability that the class is hard has increased to $p(D = \text{Hard}|G = C) = 0.76$. (This negative mutual interaction between multiple causes of some observations is called the explaining away effect, and is discussed in Section 4.2.4.2.)

4.2.7 Learning

So far, we have assumed that the structure G and parameters $\boldsymbol{\theta}$ of the PGM are known. However, it is possible to learn both of these from data. For details on how to learn G from data, see Section 30.3.

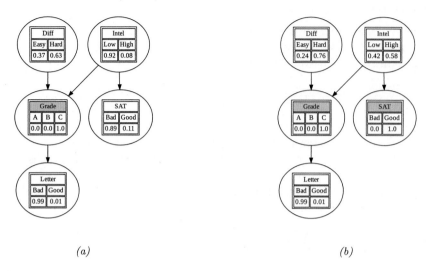

(a)   (b)

Figure 4.8: Illustration of belief updating in the "Student" PGM. The histograms show the marginal distribution of each node. Nodes with shaded titles are clamped to an observed value. (a) Posterior after conditioning on Grade=C. (b) Posterior after also conditioning on SAT=Good. Generated by student_pgm.ipynb.

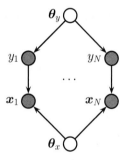

Figure 4.9: A DPGM representing the joint distribution $p(\boldsymbol{y}_{1:N}, \boldsymbol{x}_{1:N}, \boldsymbol{\theta}_y, \boldsymbol{\theta}_x)$. Here $\boldsymbol{\theta}_x$ and $\boldsymbol{\theta}_y$ are global parameter nodes that are shared across the examples, whereas $\boldsymbol{x}_n$ and $\boldsymbol{y}_n$ are local variables.

Here we focus on **parameter learning**, i.e., computing the posterior $p(\boldsymbol{\theta}|\mathcal{D}, G)$. (Henceforth we will drop the conditioning on G, since we assume the graph structure is fixed.)

We can compute the parameter posterior $p(\boldsymbol{\theta}|\mathcal{D})$ by treating $\boldsymbol{\theta}$ as "just another hidden variable", and then performing inference. However, in the machine learning community, it is more common to just compute a point estimate of the parameters, such as the posterior mode, $\hat{\boldsymbol{\theta}} = \operatorname{argmax} p(\boldsymbol{\theta}|\mathcal{D})$. This approximation is often reasonable, since the parameters depend on all the data, rather than just a single datapoint, and are therefore less uncertain than other hidden variables.

4.2.7.1 Learning from complete data

Figure 4.9 represents a graphical model for a typical supervised learning problem. We have N **local variables**, $\boldsymbol{x}_n$ and $\boldsymbol{y}_n$, and 2 **global variables**, corresponding to the parameters, which are shared across data samples. The local variables are observed (in the training set), so they are represented by solid (shaded) nodes. The global variables are not observed, and hence are represented by empty (unshaded) nodes. (The model represents a generative classifier, so the edge is from y_n to $\boldsymbol{x}_n$; if we are fitting a discriminative classifier, the edge would be from $\boldsymbol{x}_n$ to y_n, and there would be no $\boldsymbol{\theta}_y$ prior node.)

From the CI properties of Figure 4.9, it follows that the joint distribution factorizes into a product of terms, one per node:

$$p(\boldsymbol{\theta}, \mathcal{D}) = p(\boldsymbol{\theta}_x)p(\boldsymbol{\theta}_y) \left[\prod_{n=1}^{N} p(y_n|\boldsymbol{\theta}_y)p(\boldsymbol{x}_n|y_n, \boldsymbol{\theta}_x) \right] \tag{4.38}$$

$$= \left[p(\boldsymbol{\theta}_y) \prod_{n=1}^{N} p(y_n|\boldsymbol{\theta}_y) \right] \left[p(\boldsymbol{\theta}_x) \prod_{n=1}^{N} p(\boldsymbol{x}_n|y_n, \boldsymbol{\theta}_x) \right] \tag{4.39}$$

$$= [p(\boldsymbol{\theta}_y)p(\mathcal{D}_y|\boldsymbol{\theta}_y)] [p(\boldsymbol{\theta}_x)p(\mathcal{D}_x|\boldsymbol{\theta}_x)] \tag{4.40}$$

where $\mathcal{D}_y = \{y_n\}_{n=1}^{N}$ is the data that is sufficient for estimating $\boldsymbol{\theta}_y$ and $\mathcal{D}_x = \{\boldsymbol{x}_n, y_n\}_{n=1}^{N}$ is the data that is sufficient for $\boldsymbol{\theta}_x$.

From Equation (4.40), we see that the prior, likelihood, and posterior all **decompose** or factorize according to the graph structure. Thus we can compute the posterior for each parameter independently. In general, we have

$$p(\boldsymbol{\theta}, \mathcal{D}) = \prod_{i=1}^{N_G} p(\boldsymbol{\theta}_i)p(\mathcal{D}_i|\boldsymbol{\theta}_i) \tag{4.41}$$

Hence the likelihood and prior factorizes, and thus so does the posterior. If we just want to compute the MLE, we can compute

$$\hat{\boldsymbol{\theta}} = \underset{\boldsymbol{\theta}}{\operatorname{argmax}} \prod_{i=1}^{N_G} p(\mathcal{D}_i|\boldsymbol{\theta}_i) \tag{4.42}$$

We can solve this for each node independently, as we illustrate in Section 4.2.7.2.

4.2.7.2 Example: computing the MLE for CPTs

In this section, we illustrate how to compute the MLE for tabular CPDs. The likelihood is given by the following product of multinomials:

$$p(\mathcal{D}|\boldsymbol{\theta}) = \prod_{n=1}^{N} \prod_{i=1}^{N_G} p(x_{ni}|\boldsymbol{x}_{n,\mathrm{pa}(i)}, \boldsymbol{\theta}_i) \tag{4.43}$$

$$= \prod_{n=1}^{N} \prod_{i=1}^{N_G} \prod_{j=1}^{J_i} \prod_{k=1}^{K_i} \theta_{ijk}^{\mathbb{I}(x_{ni}=k, \boldsymbol{x}_{n,\mathrm{pa}(i)}=j)} \tag{4.44}$$

I	D	G	S	L
0	0	2	0	0
0	1	2	0	0
0	0	1	1	1
1	1	1	1	0
1	0	0	1	1
0	0	0	0	1
1	1	2	1	1

Table 4.2: Some fully observed training data for the student network.

I	D	$N_{i,j,k}$	$\hat{\theta}_{i,j,k}$	$\overline{\theta}_{i,j,k}$
0	0	$[1,1,1]$	$[\frac{1}{3},\frac{1}{3},\frac{1}{3}]$	$[\frac{2}{6},\frac{2}{6},\frac{2}{6}]$
0	1	$[0,0,1]$	$[\frac{0}{1},\frac{0}{1},\frac{1}{1}]$	$[\frac{1}{4},\frac{1}{4},\frac{2}{4}]$
1	0	$[1,0,0]$	$[\frac{1}{1},\frac{0}{1},\frac{0}{1}]$	$[\frac{2}{4},\frac{1}{4},\frac{1}{4}]$
1	1	$[0,1,1]$	$[0,\frac{1}{2},\frac{1}{2}]$	$[\frac{1}{5},\frac{2}{5},\frac{2}{5}]$

Table 4.3: Sufficient statistics N_{ijk} and corresponding MLE $\hat{\theta}_{ijk}$ and posterior mean $\overline{\theta}_{ijk}$ (with Dirichlet (1,1,1) prior) for node $i = G$ in the student network. Each row corresponds to a different joint configuration of its parent nodes, coresponding to state j. The index k refers to the 3 possible values of the child node G.

where

$$\theta_{ijk} \triangleq p(x_i = k | \boldsymbol{x}_{\text{pa}(i)} = j) \tag{4.45}$$

Let us define the sufficient statistics for node i to be N_{ijk}, which is the number of times that node i is in state k while its parents are in joint state j:

$$N_{ijk} \triangleq \sum_{n=1}^{N} \mathbb{I}\left(x_{n,i} = k, x_{n,\text{pa}(i)} = j\right) \tag{4.46}$$

The MLE for a multinomial is given by the normalized empirical frequencies:

$$\hat{\theta}_{ijk} = \frac{N_{ijk}}{\sum_{k'} N_{ijk'}} \tag{4.47}$$

For example, consider the student network from Section 4.2.2.2. In Table 4.2, we show some sample training data. For example, the last line in the tabel encodes a student who is smart ($I = 1$), who takes a hard class ($D = 1$), gets a C ($G = 2$), but who does well on the SAT ($S = 1$) and gets a good letter of recommendation ($L = 1$).

In Table 4.3, we list the sufficient statistics N_{ijk} and the MLE $\hat{\theta}_{ijk}$ for node $i = G$, with parents (I, D). A similar process can be used for the other nodes. Thus we see that fitting a DPGM with tabular CPDs reduces to a simple counting problem.

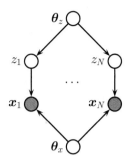

Figure 4.10: A DPGM representing the joint distribution $p(\boldsymbol{z}_{1:N}, \boldsymbol{x}_{1:N}, \boldsymbol{\theta}_z, \boldsymbol{\theta}_x)$. The local variables $\boldsymbol{z}_n$ are hidden, whereas $\boldsymbol{x}_n$ are observed. This is typical for learning unsupervised latent variable models.

However, we notice there are a lot of zeros in the sufficient statistics, due to the small sample size, resulting in extreme estimates for some of the probabilities $\hat{\theta}_{ijk}$. We discuss a (Bayesian) solution to this in Section 4.2.7.3.

4.2.7.3　Example: computing the posterior for CPTs

In Section 4.2.7.2 we discussed how to compute the MLE for the CPTs in a discrete Bayes net. We also observed that this can suffer from the zero-count problem. In this section, we show how a Bayesian approach can solve this problem.

Let us put a separate Dirichlet prior on each row of each CPT, i.e., $\boldsymbol{\theta}_{ij} \sim \text{Dir}(\boldsymbol{\alpha}_{ij})$. Then we can compute the posterior by simply adding the pseudocounts to the empirical counts to get $\boldsymbol{\theta}_{ij}|\mathcal{D} \sim \text{Dir}(\mathbf{N}_{ij} + \boldsymbol{\alpha}_{ij})$, where $\mathbf{N}_{ij} = \{N_{ijk} : k = 1 : K_i\}$, and N_{ijk} is the number of times that node i is in state k while its parents are in state j. Hence the posterior mean estimate is given by

$$\overline{\theta}_{ijk} = \frac{N_{ijk} + \alpha_{ijk}}{\sum_{k'}(N_{ijk'} + \alpha_{ijk'})} \tag{4.48}$$

The MAP estimate has the same form, except we use $\alpha_{ijk} - 1$ instead of α_{ijk}.

In Table 4.3, we illustrate this approach applied to the G node in the student network, where we use a uniform Dirichlet prior, $\alpha_{ijk} = 1$.

4.2.7.4　Learning from incomplete data

In Section 4.2.7.1, we explained that when we have complete data, the likelihood (and posterior) factorizes over CPDs, so we can estimate each CPD independently. Unfortunately, this is no longer the case when we have incomplete or missing data. To see this, consider Figure 4.10. The likelihood of the observed data can be written as follows:

$$p(\mathcal{D}|\boldsymbol{\theta}) = \sum_{\boldsymbol{z}_{1:N}} \left[\prod_{n=1}^{N} p(\boldsymbol{z}_n|\boldsymbol{\theta}_z) p(\boldsymbol{x}_n|\boldsymbol{z}_n, \boldsymbol{\theta}_x) \right] \tag{4.49}$$

$$= \prod_{n=1}^{N} \sum_{\boldsymbol{z}_n} p(\boldsymbol{z}_n|\boldsymbol{\theta}_z) p(\boldsymbol{x}_n|\boldsymbol{z}_n, \boldsymbol{\theta}_x) \tag{4.50}$$

Thus the log likelihood is given by

$$\ell(\boldsymbol{\theta}) = \sum_n \log \sum_{\boldsymbol{z}_n} p(\boldsymbol{z}_n|\boldsymbol{\theta}_z)p(\boldsymbol{x}_n|\boldsymbol{z}_n, \boldsymbol{\theta}_x) \tag{4.51}$$

The log function does not distribute over the $\sum_{\boldsymbol{z}_n}$ operation, so the objective does not decompose over nodes.[2] Consequently, we can no longer compute the MLE or the posterior by solving separate problems per node.

To solve this, we will resort to optimization methods. (We focus on the MLE case, and leave discussion of Bayesian inference for latent variable models to Part II.) In the sections below, we discuss how to use EM and SGD to find a local optimum of the (non convex) log likelihood objective.

4.2.7.5   Using EM to fit CPTs in the incomplete data case

A popular method for estimating the parameters of a DPGM in the presence of missing data is to the use the expectation maximization (EM) algorithm, as proposed in [Lau95]. We describe EM in detail in Section 6.5.3, but the basic idea is to alternate between inferring the latent variables $\boldsymbol{z}_n$ (the E or expectation step), and estimating the parameters given this completed dataset (the M or maximization step). Rather than returning the full posterior $p(\boldsymbol{z}_n|\boldsymbol{x}_n, \boldsymbol{\theta}^{(t)})$ in the E step, we instead return the expected sufficient statistics (ESS), which takes much less space. In the M step, we maximize the expected value of the log likelihood of the fully observed data using these ESS.

As an example, suppose all the CPDs are tabular, as in the example in Section 4.2.7.2. The log-likelihood of the complete data is given by

$$\log p(\mathcal{D}|\boldsymbol{\theta}) = \sum_{i=1}^{N_G} \sum_{j=1}^{J_i} \sum_{k=1}^{K_i} N_{ijk} \log \theta_{ijk} \tag{4.52}$$

and hence the expected complete data log-likelihood has the form

$$\mathbb{E}\left[\log p(\mathcal{D}|\boldsymbol{\theta})\right] = \sum_i \sum_j \sum_k \overline{N}_{ijk} \log \theta_{ijk} \tag{4.53}$$

where

$$\overline{N}_{ijk} = \sum_{n=1}^{N} \mathbb{E}\left[\mathbb{I}\left(x_{ni} = k, \boldsymbol{x}_{n,\mathrm{pa}(i)} = j\right)\right] = \sum_{n=1}^{N} p(x_{ni} = k, \boldsymbol{x}_{n,\mathrm{pa}(i)} = j|\mathcal{D}_n, \boldsymbol{\theta}^{old}) \tag{4.54}$$

where $\mathcal{D}_n$ are all the visible variables in case n, and $\boldsymbol{\theta}^{old}$ are the parameters from the previous iteration. The quantity $p(x_{ni}, \boldsymbol{x}_{n,\mathrm{pa}(i)}|\mathcal{D}_n, \boldsymbol{\theta}^{old})$ is known as a **family marginal**, and can be computed using any GM inference algorithm. The $\overline{N}_{ijk}$ are the **expected sufficient statistics** (ESS), and constitute the output of the E step.

---

2. We can also see this from the graphical model: $\boldsymbol{\theta}_x$ is no longer independent of $\boldsymbol{\theta}_z$, because there is a path that connects them via the hidden nodes $\boldsymbol{z}_n$. (See Section 4.2.4 for an explanation of how to "read off" such CI properties from a DPGM.)

Given these ESS, the M step has the simple form

$$\hat{\theta}_{ijk} = \frac{\overline{N}_{ijk}}{\sum_{k'} \overline{N}_{ijk'}} \tag{4.55}$$

We can modify this to perform MAP estimation with a Dirichlet prior by simply adding pseudocounts to the expected counts.

The famous Baum-Welch algorithm is a special case of the above equations which arises when the DPGM is an HMM (see Section 29.4.1 for details).

4.2.7.6 Using SGD to fit CPTs in the incomplete data case

The EM algorithm is a batch algorithm. To scale up to large datasets, it is more common to use stochastic gradient descent or SGD (see e.g., [BC94; Bin+97]). To apply this, we need to compute the marginal likelihood of the observed data for each example:

$$p(\boldsymbol{x}_n|\boldsymbol{\theta}) = \sum_{\boldsymbol{z}_n} p(\boldsymbol{z}_n|\boldsymbol{\theta}_z)p(\boldsymbol{x}_n|\boldsymbol{z}_n,\boldsymbol{\theta}_x) \tag{4.56}$$

where $\boldsymbol{\theta} = (\boldsymbol{\theta}_z, \boldsymbol{\theta}_x)$.) (We say that we have "**collapsed**" the model by marginalizing out $\boldsymbol{z}_n$.) We can then compute the log likelihood using

$$\ell(\boldsymbol{\theta}) = \log p(\mathcal{D}|\boldsymbol{\theta}) = \log \prod_{n=1}^{N} p(\boldsymbol{x}_n|\boldsymbol{\theta}) = \sum_{n=1}^{N} \log p(\boldsymbol{x}_n|\boldsymbol{\theta}) \tag{4.57}$$

The gradient of this objective can be computed as follows:

$$\nabla_{\boldsymbol{\theta}}\ell(\boldsymbol{\theta}) = \sum_n \nabla_{\boldsymbol{\theta}} \log p(\boldsymbol{x}_n|\boldsymbol{\theta}) \tag{4.58}$$

$$= \sum_n \frac{1}{p(\boldsymbol{x}_n|\boldsymbol{\theta})} \nabla_{\boldsymbol{\theta}} p(\boldsymbol{x}_n|\boldsymbol{\theta}) \tag{4.59}$$

$$= \sum_n \frac{1}{p(\boldsymbol{x}_n|\boldsymbol{\theta})} \nabla_{\boldsymbol{\theta}} \left[\sum_{\boldsymbol{z}_n} p(\boldsymbol{z}_n, \boldsymbol{x}_n|\boldsymbol{\theta}) \right] \tag{4.60}$$

$$= \sum_n \sum_{\boldsymbol{z}_n} \frac{p(\boldsymbol{z}_n, \boldsymbol{x}_n|\boldsymbol{\theta})}{p(\boldsymbol{x}_n|\boldsymbol{\theta})} \nabla_{\boldsymbol{\theta}} \log p(\boldsymbol{z}_n, \boldsymbol{x}_n|\boldsymbol{\theta}) \tag{4.61}$$

$$= \sum_n \sum_{\boldsymbol{z}_n} p(\boldsymbol{z}_n|\boldsymbol{x}_n, \boldsymbol{\theta}) \nabla_{\boldsymbol{\theta}} \log p(\boldsymbol{z}_n, \boldsymbol{x}_n|\boldsymbol{\theta}) \tag{4.62}$$

We can now apply a minibatch approximation to this in the usual way.

4.2.8 Plate notation

To make the parameters of a PGM explicit, we can add them as nodes to the graph, and treat them as hidden variables to be inferred. Figure 4.11(a) shows a simple example, in which we have N iid

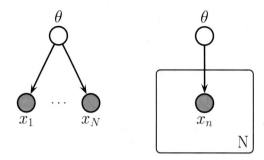

Figure 4.11: Left: datapoints $\boldsymbol{x}_n$ are conditionally independent given $\boldsymbol{\theta}$. Right: Same model, using plate notation. This represents the same model as the one on the left, except the repeated $\boldsymbol{x}_n$ nodes are inside a box, known as a plate; the number in the lower right hand corner, N, specifies the number of repetitions of the $\boldsymbol{x}_n$ node.

random variables, $\boldsymbol{x}_n$, all drawn from the same distribution with common parameter $\boldsymbol{\theta}$. We denote this by

$$\boldsymbol{x}_n \sim p(\boldsymbol{x}|\boldsymbol{\theta}) \tag{4.63}$$

The corresponding joint distribution over the parameters and data $\mathcal{D} = \{\boldsymbol{x}_1, \ldots, \boldsymbol{x}_N\}$ has the form

$$p(\mathcal{D}, \boldsymbol{\theta}) = p(\boldsymbol{\theta})p(\mathcal{D}|\boldsymbol{\theta}) \tag{4.64}$$

where $p(\boldsymbol{\theta})$ is the prior distribution for the parameters, and $p(\mathcal{D}|\boldsymbol{\theta})$ is the likelihood. By virtue of the iid assumption, the likelihood can be rewritten as follows:

$$p(\mathcal{D}|\boldsymbol{\theta}) = \prod_{n=1}^{N} p(\boldsymbol{x}_n|\boldsymbol{\theta}) \tag{4.65}$$

Notice that the order of the data vectors is not important for defining this model, i.e., we can permute the leaves of the DPGM. When this property holds, we say that the data is **exchangeable**.

In Figure 4.11(a), we see that the $\boldsymbol{x}$ nodes are repeated N times. (The **shaded nodes** represent observed values, whereas the unshaded (hollow) nodes represent latent variables or parameters.) To avoid visual clutter, it is common to use a form of **syntactic sugar** called **plates**. This is a notational convention in which we draw a little box around the repeated variables, with the understanding that nodes within the box will get repeated when the model is **unrolled**. We often write the number of copies or repetitions in the bottom right corner of the box. This is illustrated in Figure 4.11(b).

4.2.8.1   Example: factor analysis

In Section 28.3.1, we discuss the factor analysis model, which has the form

$$p(\boldsymbol{z}) = \mathcal{N}(\boldsymbol{z}|\boldsymbol{\mu}_0, \boldsymbol{\Sigma}_0) \tag{4.66}$$

$$p(\boldsymbol{x}|\boldsymbol{z}) = \mathcal{N}(\boldsymbol{x}|\mathbf{W}\boldsymbol{z} + \boldsymbol{\mu}, \boldsymbol{\Psi}) \tag{4.67}$$

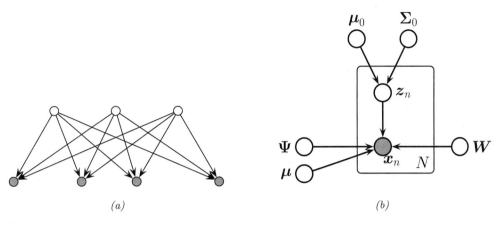

Figure 4.12: (a) Factor analysis model illustrated as a DPGM. We show the components of z (top row) and x (bottom row) as individual scalar nodes. (b) Equivalent model, where z and x are collapsed to vector-valued nodes, and parameters are added, using plate notation.

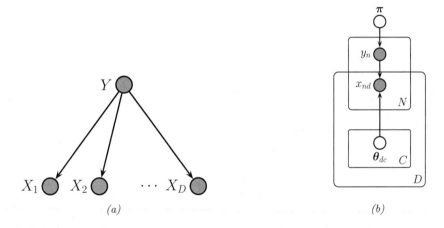

Figure 4.13: (a) Naive Bayes classifier as a DPGM. (b) Model augmented with plate notation.

where $\mathbf{W}$ is a $D \times L$ matrix, known as the factor loading matrix, and $\mathbf{\Psi}$ is a diagonal $D \times D$ covariance matrix.

Note that z and x are both vectors. We can explicitly represent their components as scalar nodes as in Figure 4.12a. Here the directed edges correspond to non-zero entries in the $\mathbf{W}$ matrix.

We can also explicitly show the parameters of the model, using plate notation, as shown in Figure 4.12b.

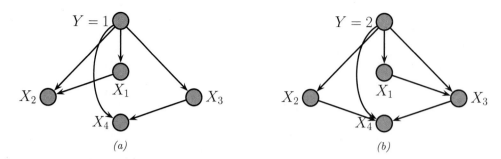

Figure 4.14: Tree-augmented naive Bayes classifier for $D = 4$ features. The tree topology can change depending on the value of y, as illustrated.

4.2.8.2   Example: naive Bayes classifier

In some models, we have doubly indexed variables. For example, consider a **naive Bayes classifier**. This is a simple generative classifier, defined as follows:

$$p(\boldsymbol{x}, y | \boldsymbol{\theta}) = p(y | \boldsymbol{\pi}) \prod_{d=1}^{D} p(x_d | y, \boldsymbol{\theta}_d) \tag{4.68}$$

The fact that the features $\boldsymbol{x}_{1:D}$ are considered conditionally independent given the class label y is where the term "naive" comes from. Nevertheless, this model often works surprisingly well, and is extremely easy to fit.

   We can represent the conditional independence assumption as shown in Figure 4.13a. We can represent the repetition over the dimension d with a plate. When we turn to infering the parameters $\boldsymbol{\theta} = (\boldsymbol{\pi}, \boldsymbol{\theta}_{1:D,1:C})$, we also need to represent the repetition over data cases n. This is shown in Figure 4.13b. Note that the parameter $\boldsymbol{\theta}_{dc}$ depends on d and c, whereas the feature $\boldsymbol{x}_{nd}$ depends on n and d. This is shown using **nested plates** to represent the shared d index.

4.2.8.3   Example: relaxing the naive Bayes assumption

We see from Figure 4.13a that the observed features are conditionally independent given the class label. We can of course allow for dependencies between the features, as illustrated in Figure 4.14. (We omit parameter nodes for simplicity.) If we enforce that the edges between the features forms a tree the model is known as a **tree-augmented naive Bayes classifier** [FGG97], or **TAN** model. (Trees are a restricted form of graphical model that have various computational advantages that we discuss later.) Note that the topology of the tree can change depending on the value of the class node y; in this case, the model is known as a **Bayesian multi net**, and can be thought of as a supervised mixture of trees.

4.3   Undirected graphical models (Markov random fields)

Directed graphical models (Section 4.2) are very useful. However, for some domains, being forced to choose a direction for the edges, as required by a DAG, is rather awkward. For example, consider

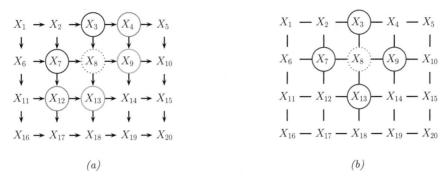

(a)   *(b)*

Figure 4.15: (a) A 2d lattice represented as a DAG. The dotted red node X_8 is independent of all other nodes (black) given its Markov blanket, which include its parents (blue), children (green) and co-parents (orange). (b) The same model represented as a UPGM. The red node X_8 is independent of the other black nodes given its neighbors (blue nodes).

modeling an image. It is reasonable to assume that the intensity values of neighboring pixels are correlated. We can model this using a DAG with a 2d lattice topology as shown in Figure 4.15(a). This is known as a **Markov mesh** [AHK65]. However, its conditional independence properties are rather unnatural.

An alternative is to use an undirected probabilistic graphical model (**UPGM**), also called a **Markov random field** (**MRF**) or **Markov network**. These do not require us to specify edge orientations, and are much more natural for some problems such as image analysis and spatial statistics. For example, an undirected 2d lattice is shown in Figure 4.15(b); now the Markov blanket of each node is just its nearest neighbors, as we show in Section 4.3.6.

Roughly speaking, the main advantages of UPGMs over DPGMs are: (1) they are symmetric and therefore more "natural" for certain domains, such as spatial or relational data; and (2) discriminative UPGMs (aka conditional random fields, or CRFs), which define conditional densities of the form $p(\boldsymbol{y}|\boldsymbol{x})$, work better than discriminative DGMs, for reasons we explain in Section 4.5.3. The main disadvantages of UPGMs compared to DPGMs are: (1) the parameters are less interpretable and less modular, for reasons we explain in Section 4.3.1; and (2) it is more computationally expensive to estimate the parameters, for reasons we explain in Section 4.3.9.1.

4.3.1 Representing the joint distribution

Since there is no topological ordering associated with an undirected graph, we can't use the chain rule to represent $p(\boldsymbol{x}_{1:N_G})$. So instead of associating CPDs with each node, we associate **potential functions** or **factors** with each **maximal clique** in the graph.[3] We will denote the potential function for clique c by $\psi_c(\boldsymbol{x}_c; \boldsymbol{\theta}_c)$, where $\boldsymbol{\theta}_c$ are its parameters. A potential function can be any non-negative function of its arguments (we give some examples below). We can use these functions to define the joint distribution as we explain in Section 4.3.1.1.

---

3. A **clique** is a set of nodes that are all neighbors of each other. A **maximal clique** is a clique which cannot be made any larger without losing the clique property.

4.3.1.1   Hammersley-Clifford theorem

Suppose a joint distribution p satisfies the CI properties implied by the undirected graph G. (We discuss how to derive these properties in Section 4.3.6.) Then the **Hammersley-Clifford theorem** tells us that p can be written as follows:

$$p(\boldsymbol{x}|\boldsymbol{\theta}) = \frac{1}{Z(\boldsymbol{\theta})} \prod_{c \in \mathcal{C}} \psi_c(\boldsymbol{x}_c; \boldsymbol{\theta}_c) \tag{4.69}$$

where $\mathcal{C}$ is the set of all the (maximal) cliques of the graph G, and $Z(\boldsymbol{\theta})$ is the **partition function** given by

$$Z(\boldsymbol{\theta}) \triangleq \sum_{\boldsymbol{x}} \prod_{c \in \mathcal{C}} \psi_c(\boldsymbol{x}_c; \boldsymbol{\theta}_c) \tag{4.70}$$

Note that the partition function is what ensures the overall distribution sums to 1.[4]

The Hammersley-Clifford theorem was never published, but a proof can be found in [KF09a]. (Note that the theorem only holds for positive distributions, i.e., ones where $p(\boldsymbol{x}|\boldsymbol{\theta}) \geq 0$ for all configurations $\boldsymbol{x}$, which rules out some models with hard constraints.)

4.3.1.2   Gibbs distribution

The distribution in Equation (4.69) can be rewritten as follows:

$$p(\boldsymbol{x}|\boldsymbol{\theta}) = \frac{1}{Z(\boldsymbol{\theta})} \exp(-\mathcal{E}(\boldsymbol{x}; \boldsymbol{\theta})) \tag{4.71}$$

where $\mathcal{E}(\boldsymbol{x}) > 0$ is the **energy** of state $\boldsymbol{x}$, defined by

$$\mathcal{E}(\boldsymbol{x}; \boldsymbol{\theta}) = \sum_c \mathcal{E}(\boldsymbol{x}_c; \boldsymbol{\theta}_c) \tag{4.72}$$

where $\boldsymbol{x}_c$ are the variables in clique c. We can see the equivalence by defining the clique potentials as

$$\psi_c(\boldsymbol{x}_c; \boldsymbol{\theta}_c) = \exp(-\mathcal{E}(\boldsymbol{x}_c; \boldsymbol{\theta}_c)) \tag{4.73}$$

We see that low energy is associated with high probability states.

Equation (4.71) is known as the **Gibbs distribution**. This kind of probability model is also called an **energy-based model**. These are commonly used in physics and biochemistry. They are also used in ML to define generative models, as we discuss in Chapter 24. (See also Section 4.4, where we discuss conditional random fields (CRFs), which are models of the form $p(\boldsymbol{y}|\boldsymbol{x}, \boldsymbol{\theta})$, where the potential functions are conditioned on input features $\boldsymbol{x}$.)

4.3.2   Fully visible MRFs (Ising, Potts, Hopfield, etc.)

In this section, we discuss some UPGMs for 2d grids, that are used in statistical physics and computer vision. We then discuss extensions to other graph structures, which are useful for biological modeling and pattern completion.

---

4. The partition function is denoted by Z because of the German word *Zustandssumme*, which means "sum over states". This reflects the fact that a lot of pioneering working on MRFs was done by German (and Austrian) physicists, such as Boltzmann.

4.3.2.1 Ising models

Consider the 2d lattice in Figure 4.15(b). We can represent the joint distribution as follows:

$$p(\boldsymbol{x}|\boldsymbol{\theta}) = \frac{1}{Z(\boldsymbol{\theta})} \prod_{i \sim j} \psi_{ij}(x_i, x_j; \boldsymbol{\theta}) \tag{4.74}$$

where $i \sim j$ means i and j are neighbors in the graph. This is called a **2d lattice model**.

An **Ising model** is a special case of the above, where the variables x_i are binary. Such models are often used to represent magnetic materials. In particular, each node represents an atom, which can have a magnetic dipole, or **spin**, which is in one of two states, $+1$ and -1. In some magnetic systems, neighboring spins like to be similar; in other systems, they like to be dissimilar. We can capture this interaction by defining the clique potentials as follows:

$$\psi_{ij}(x_i, x_j; \boldsymbol{\theta}) = \begin{cases} e^{J_{ij}} & \text{if } x_i = x_j \\ e^{-J_{ij}} & \text{if } x_i \neq x_j \end{cases} \tag{4.75}$$

where J_{ij} is the coupling strength between nodes i and j. This is known as the **Ising model**. If two nodes are not connected in the graph, we set $J_{ij} = 0$. We assume that the weight matrix is symmetric, so $J_{ij} = J_{ji}$. Often we also assume all edges have the same strength, so $J_{ij} = J$ for each (i, j) edge. Thus

$$\psi_{ij}(x_i, x_j; J) = \begin{cases} e^{J} & \text{if } x_i = x_j \\ e^{-J} & \text{if } x_i \neq x_j \end{cases} \tag{4.76}$$

It is more common to define the Ising model as an energy-based model, as follows:

$$p(\boldsymbol{x}|\boldsymbol{\theta}) = \frac{1}{Z(J)} \exp(-\mathcal{E}(\boldsymbol{x}; J)) \tag{4.77}$$

$$\mathcal{E}(\boldsymbol{x}; J) = -J \sum_{i \sim j} x_i x_j \tag{4.78}$$

where $\mathcal{E}(\boldsymbol{x}; J)$ is the energy, and where we exploited the fact that $x_i x_j = -1$ if $x_i \neq x_j$, and $x_i x_j = +1$ if $x_i = x_j$. The magnitude of J controls the degree of coupling strength between neighboring sites, which depends on the (inverse) temperature of the system (colder = more tightly coupled = larger magnitude J).

If all the edge weights are positive, $J > 0$, then neighboring spins are likely to be in the same state, since if $x_i = x_j$, the energy term gets a contribution of $-J < 0$, and lower energy corresponds to higher probability. In the machine learning literature, this is called an **associative Markov network**. In the physics literature, this is called a **ferromagnetic** model. If the weights are sufficiently strong, the corresponding probability distribution will have two modes, corresponding to the two checkerboard patterns in Figure 4.16a. These are called the **ground states** of the system.

If all of the weights are negative, $J < 0$, then the spins want to be different from their neighbors (see Figure 4.16b). This is called an **antiferromagnetic** system, and results in a **frustrated system**, since it is not possible for all neighbors to be different from each other in a 2d lattice. Thus the corresponding probability distribution will have multiple modes, corresponding to different "solutions" to the problem.

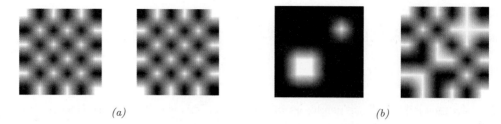

Figure 4.16: (a) The two ground states for a small ferromagnetic Ising model where $J = 1$. (b) Two different states for a small Ising model which have the same energy. Left: $J = 1$, so neighboring pixels have similar values. Right: $J = -1$, so neighboring pixels have different values. From Figures 31.7 and 31.8 of [Mac03].

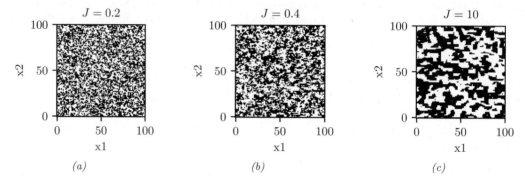

Figure 4.17: Samples from an associative Ising model with varying $J > 0$. Generated by gibbs_demo_ising.ipynb.

Figure 4.17 shows some samples from the Ising model for varying $J > 0$. (The samples were created using the Gibbs sampling method discussed in Section 12.3.3.) As the temperature reduces, the distribution becomes less entropic, and the "clumpiness" of the samples increases. One can show that, as the lattice size goes to infinity, there is a **critical temperature** J_c below which many large clusters occur, and above which many small clusters occur. In the case of an isotropic square lattice model, one can show [Geo88] that

$$J_c = \frac{1}{2} \log(1 + \sqrt{2}) \approx 0.44 \tag{4.79}$$

This rapid change in global behavior as we vary a parameter of the system is called a **phase transition**. This can be used to explain how natural systems, such as water, can suddenly go from solid to liquid, or from liquid to gas, when the temperature changes slightly. See e.g., [Mac03, ch 31] for further details on the statistical mechanics of Ising models.

In addition to pairwise terms, it is standard to add **unary terms**, $\psi_i(x_i)$. In statistical physics, this is called an **external field**. The resulting model is as follows:

$$p(\boldsymbol{x}|\boldsymbol{\theta}) = \frac{1}{Z(\boldsymbol{\theta})} \prod_i \psi_i(x_i; \boldsymbol{\theta}) \prod_{i \sim j} \psi_{ij}(x_i, x_j; \boldsymbol{\theta}) \tag{4.80}$$

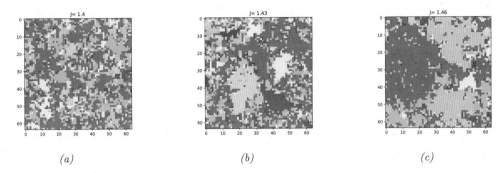

Figure 4.18: Visualizing a sample from a 10-state Potts model of size 128×128. The critical value is $J_c = \log(1 + \sqrt{10}) = 1.426$. for different association strengths: (a) $J = 1.40$, (b) $J = 1.43$, (c) $J = 1.46$. Generated by gibbs_demo_potts.ipynb.

The ψ_i terms can be thought of as a local bias term that is independent of the contributions of the neighboring nodes. For binary nodes, we can define this as follows:

$$\psi_i(x_i) = \begin{cases} e^\alpha & \text{if } x_i = +1 \\ e^{-\alpha} & \text{if } x_i = -1 \end{cases} \tag{4.81}$$

If we write this as an energy-based model, we have

$$\mathcal{E}(\boldsymbol{x}|\boldsymbol{\theta}) = -\alpha \sum_i x_i - J \sum_{i \sim j} x_i x_j \tag{4.82}$$

4.3.2.2   Potts models

In Section 4.3.2.1, we discussed the Ising model, which is a simple 2d MRF for defining distributions over binary variables. It is easy to generalize the Ising model to multiple discrete states, $x_i \in \{1, 2, \ldots, K\}$. If we use the same potential function for every edge, we can write

$$\psi_{ij}(x_i = k, x_j = k') = e^{J_{ij}(k,k')} \tag{4.83}$$

where $J_{ij}(k, k')$ is the energy if one node has state k and its neighbor has state k'. A common special case is

$$\psi_{ij}(x_i = k, x_j = k') = \begin{cases} e^J & \text{if } k = k' \\ e^0 & \text{if } k \neq k' \end{cases} \tag{4.84}$$

This is called the **Potts model**. The Potts model reduces to the Ising model if we define $J_{\text{potts}} = 2J_{\text{ising}}$.

If $J > 0$, then neighboring nodes are encouraged to have the same label; this is an example of an associative Markov model. Some samples from this model are shown in Figure 4.18. The phase transition for a 2d Potts model occurs at the following value (see [MS96]):

$$J_c = \log(1 + \sqrt{K}) \tag{4.85}$$

We can extend this model to have local evidence for each node. If we write this as an energy-based model, we have

$$\mathcal{E}(\boldsymbol{x}|\boldsymbol{\theta}) = -\sum_i \sum_{k=1}^{K} \alpha_k \mathbb{I}(x_i = k) - J \sum_{i \sim j} \mathbb{I}(x_i = x_j) \tag{4.86}$$

4.3.2.3 Potts models for protein structure prediction

One interesting application of Potts models arises in the area of **protein structure prediction**. The goal is to predict the 3d shape of a protein from its 1d sequence of amino acids. A common approach to this is known as **direct coupling analysis** (DCA). We give a brief summary below; for details, see [Mor+11].

First we compute a **multiple sequence alignment** (MSA) from a set of related amino acid sequences from the same protein family; this can be done using HMMs, as explained in Section 29.3.2. The MSA can be represented by an $N \times T$ matrix $\mathbf{X}$, where N is the number of sequences, T is the length of each sequence, and $X_{ni} \in \{1, \ldots, V\}$ is the identity of the letter at location i in sequence n. For protein sequences, $V = 21$, representing the 20 amino acids plus the gap character.

Once we have the MSA matrix $\mathbf{X}$, we fit the Potts model using maximum likelihood estimation, or some approximation, such as pseudolikelihood [Eke+13]; see Section 4.3.9 for details.[5] After fitting the model, we select the edges with the highest J_{ij} coefficients, where $i, j \in \{1, \ldots, T\}$ are locations or **residues** in the protein. Since these locations are highly coupled, they are likely to be in physical contact, since interacting residues must coevolve to avoid destroying the function of the protein (see e.g., [LHF17] for a review). This graph is called a **contact map**.

Once the contact map is established, it can be used as input to a 3d structural prediction algorithm, such as [Xu18] or the **alphafold** system [Eva+18], which won the 2018 CASP competition. Such methods use neural networks to learn functions of the form $p(d(i, j)|\{c(i, j)\})$, where $d(i, j)$ is the 3d distance between residues i and j, and $c(i, j)$ is the contact map.

4.3.2.4 Hopfield networks

A **Hopfield network** [Hop82] is a fully connected Ising model (Section 4.3.2.1) with a symmetric weight matrix, $\mathbf{W} = \mathbf{W}^\mathsf{T}$. The corresponding energy function has the form

$$\mathcal{E}(\boldsymbol{x}) = -\frac{1}{2}\boldsymbol{x}^\mathsf{T}\mathbf{W}\boldsymbol{x} \tag{4.87}$$

where $x_i \in \{-1, +1\}$.

The main application of Hopfield networks is as an **associative memory** or **content addressable memory**. The idea is this: suppose we train on a set of fully observed bit vectors, corresponding to patterns we want to memorize. (We discuss how to do this below). Then, at test time, we present a partial pattern to the network. We would like to estimate the missing variables; this is called **pattern completion**. That is, we want to compute

$$\boldsymbol{x}^* = \operatorname*{argmin}_{\boldsymbol{x}} \mathcal{E}(\boldsymbol{x}) \tag{4.88}$$

---

5. To encourage the model to learn sparse connectivity, we can also compute a MAP estimate with a sparsity promoting prior, as discussed in [IM17].

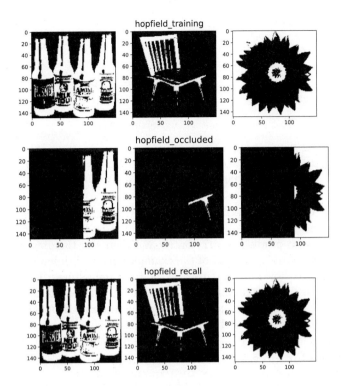

Figure 4.19: Examples of how an associative memory can reconstruct images. These are binary images of size 150×150 pixels. Top: training images. Middle row: partially visible test images. Bottom row: final state estimate. Adapted from Figure 2.1 of [HKP91]. Generated by hopfield_demo.ipynb.

We can solve this optimization problem using **iterative conditional modes (ICM)**, in which we set each hidden variable to its most likely state given its neighbors. Picking the most probable state amounts to using the rule

$$\boldsymbol{x}^{t+1} = \text{sgn}(\mathbf{W}\boldsymbol{x}^t) \tag{4.89}$$

This can be seen as a deterministic version of Gibbs sampling (see Section 12.3.3).

We illustrate this process in Figure 4.19. In the top row, we show some training examples. In the middle row, we show a corrupted input, corresponding to the initial state $\boldsymbol{x}^0$. In the bottom row, we show the final state after 30 iterations of ICM. The overall process can be thought of as retrieving a complete example from memory based on a piece of the example.

To learn the weights $\mathbf{W}$, we could use the maximum likelihood estimate method described in Section 4.3.9.1. (See also [HSDK12].) However, a simpler heuristic method, proposed in [Hop82], is to use the following **outer product method**:

$$\mathbf{W} = \left(\frac{1}{N} \sum_{n=1}^{N} \boldsymbol{x}_n \boldsymbol{x}_n^\top \right) - \mathbf{I} \tag{4.90}$$

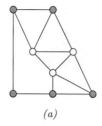

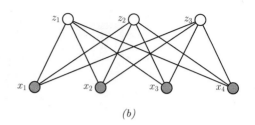

(a)   (b)

Figure 4.20: (a) A general Boltzmann machine, with an arbitrary graph structure. The shaded (visible) nodes are partitioned into input and output, although the model is actually symmetric and defines a joint distribution on all the nodes. (b) A restricted Boltzmann machine with a bipartite structure. Note the lack of intra-layer connections.

This normalizes the output product matrix by N, and then sets the diagonal to 0. This ensures the energy is low for patterns that match any of the examples in the training set. This is the technique we used in Figure 4.19. Note, however, that this method not only stores the original patterns but also their inverses, and other linear combinations. Consequently there is a limit to how many examples the model can store before they start to "collide" in the memory. Hopfield proved that, for random patterns, the network capacity is $\sim 0.14N$.

4.3.3   MRFs with latent variables (Boltzmann machines, etc.)

In this section, we discuss MRFs which contain latent variables, as a way to represent high dimensional joint distributions in discrete spaces.

4.3.3.1   Vanilla Boltzmann machines

MRFs in which all the variables are visible are limited in their expressive power, since the only way to model correlation between the variables is by directly adding an edge. An alternative approach is to introduce latent variables. A **Boltzmann machine** [AHS85] is like an Ising model (Section 4.3.2.1) with latent variables. In addition, the graph structure can be arbitrary (not just a lattice), and the binary states are $x_i \in \{0, 1\}$ instead of $x_i \in \{-1, +1\}$. We usually partition the nodes into hidden nodes z and visible nodes x, as shown in Figure 4.20(a).

4.3.3.2   Restricted Boltzmann machines (RBMs)

Unfortunately, exact inference (and hence learning) in Boltzmann machines is intractable, and even approximate inference (e.g., Gibbs sampling, Section 12.3) can be slow. However, suppose we restrict the architecture so that the nodes are arranged in two layers, and so that there are no connections between nodes within the same layer (see Figure 4.20(b)). This model is known as a **restricted Boltzmann machine (RBM)** [HT01; HS06a], or a **harmonium** [Smo86]. The RBM supports efficient approximate inference, since the hidden nodes are conditionally independent given the visible nodes, i.e., $p(z|x) = \prod_{k=1}^{K} p(z_k|x)$. Note this is in contrast to a directed two-layer models, where the explaining away effect causes the latent variables to become "entangled" in the posterior even if they are independent in the prior.

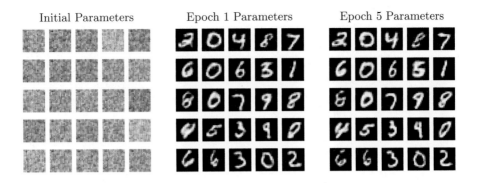

Figure 4.21: Some reconstructed images generated by a binary RBM fit to MNIST. Generated by rbm_contrastive_divergence.ipynb.

Visible	Hidden	Name	Reference
Binary	Binary	Binary RBM	[HS06a]
Gaussian	Binary	Gaussian RBM	[WS05]
Categorical	Binary	Categorical RBM	[SMH07]
Multiple categorical	Binary	Replicated softmax/undirected LDA	[SH10]
Gaussian	Gaussian	Undirected PCA	[MM01]
Binary	Gaussian	Undirected binary PCA	[WS05]

Table 4.4: Summary of different kinds of RBM.

Typically the hidden and visible nodes in an RBM are binary, so the energy terms have the form $w_{dk}x_d z_k$. If $z_k = 1$, then the k'th hidden unit adds a term of the form $\boldsymbol{w}_k^\mathsf{T}\boldsymbol{x}$ to the energy; this can be thought of as a "soft constraint". If $z_k = 0$, the hidden unit is not active, and does not have an opinion about this data example. By turning on different combinations of constraints, we can create complex distributions on the visible data. This is an example of a **product of experts** (Section 24.1.1), since $p(\boldsymbol{x}|\boldsymbol{z}) = \prod_{k:z_k=1} \exp(\boldsymbol{w}_k^\mathsf{T}\boldsymbol{x})$.

This can be thought of as a mixture model with an exponential number of hidden components, corresponding to 2^H settings of $\boldsymbol{z}$. That is, $\boldsymbol{z}$ is a **distributed representation**, whereas a standard mixture model uses a **localist representation**, where $z \in \{1, K\}$, and each setting of z corresponds to a complete prototype or exemplar $\boldsymbol{w}_k$ to which $\boldsymbol{x}$ is compared, giving rise to a model of the form $p(\boldsymbol{x}|z = k) \propto \exp(\boldsymbol{w}_k^\mathsf{T}\boldsymbol{x})$.

Many different kinds of RBMs have been defined, which use different pairwise potential functions. See Table 4.4 for a summary. (Figure 4.21 gives an example of some images generated from an RBM fit to the binarized MNIST dataset.) All of these are special cases of the **exponential family harmonium** [WRZH04]. See Supplementary Section 4.3 for more details.

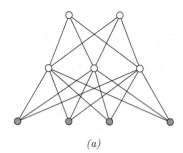
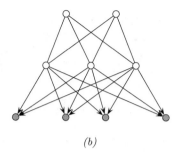

(a)   *(b)*

Figure 4.22: (a) Deep Boltzmann machine. (b) Deep belief network. The top two layers define the prior in terms on an RBM. The remaining layers are a directed graphical model that "decodes" the prior into observable data.

4.3.3.3   Deep Boltzmann machines

We can make a "deep" version of an RBM by stacking multiple layers; this is called a **deep Boltzmann machine** [SH09]. For example, the two layer model in Figure 4.22(a) has the form

$$p(\boldsymbol{x}, \boldsymbol{z}_1, \boldsymbol{z}_2 | \boldsymbol{\theta}) = \frac{1}{Z(\mathbf{W}_1, \mathbf{W}_2)} \exp\left(\boldsymbol{x}^\mathsf{T} \mathbf{W}_1 \boldsymbol{z}_1 + \boldsymbol{z}_1^\mathsf{T} \mathbf{W}_2 \boldsymbol{z}_2\right) \tag{4.91}$$

where $\boldsymbol{x}$ are the visible nodes at the bottom, and we have dropped bias terms for brevity.

4.3.3.4   Deep belief networks (DBNs)

We can use an RBM as a prior over a latent distributed code, and then use a DPGM "decoder" to convert this into the observed data, as shown in Figure 4.22(b). The corresponding joint distribution has the form

$$p(\boldsymbol{x}, \boldsymbol{z}_1, \boldsymbol{z}_2 | \boldsymbol{\theta}) = p(\boldsymbol{x} | \boldsymbol{z}_1, \mathbf{W}_1) \frac{1}{Z(\mathbf{W}_2)} \exp\left(\boldsymbol{z}_1^\mathsf{T} \mathbf{W}_2 \boldsymbol{z}_2\right) \tag{4.92}$$

In other words, it is an RBM on top of a DPGM. This combination has been called a **deep belief network (DBN)** [HOT06a]. However, this name is confusing, since it is not actually a belief net. We will therefore call it a **deep Boltzmann network** (which conveniently has the same DBN abbreviation).

DBNs can be trained in a simple greedy fashion, and support fast bottom-up inference (see [HOT06a] for details). DBNs played an important role in the history of deep learning, since they were one of the first deep models that could be successfully trained. However, they are no longer widely used, since the advent of better ways to train fully supervised deep neural networks (such as using ReLU units and the Adam optimizer), and the advent of efficient ways to train deep DPGMs, such as the VAE (Section 21.2).

4.3.4   Maximum entropy models

In Section 2.4.7, we show that the exponential family is the distribution with maximum entropy, subject to the constraints that the expected value of the features (sufficient statistics) $\boldsymbol{\phi}(\boldsymbol{x})$ match the empirical expectations. Thus the model has the form

$$p(\boldsymbol{x}|\boldsymbol{\theta}) = \frac{1}{Z(\boldsymbol{\theta})} \exp\left(\boldsymbol{\theta}^\mathsf{T}\boldsymbol{\phi}(\boldsymbol{x})\right) \tag{4.93}$$

If the features $\boldsymbol{\phi}(\boldsymbol{x})$ decompose according to a graph structure, we get a kind of MRF known as a **maximum entropy model**. We give some examples below.

4.3.4.1 Log-linear models

Suppose the potential functions have the following log-linear form:

$$\psi_c(\boldsymbol{x}_c; \boldsymbol{\theta}_c) = \exp(\boldsymbol{\theta}_c^\mathsf{T}\boldsymbol{\phi}(\boldsymbol{x}_c)) \tag{4.94}$$

where $\boldsymbol{\phi}(\boldsymbol{x}_c)$ is a feature vector derived from the variables in clique c. Then the overall model is given by

$$p(\boldsymbol{x}|\boldsymbol{\theta}) = \frac{1}{Z(\boldsymbol{\theta})} \exp\left(\sum_c \boldsymbol{\theta}_c^\mathsf{T}\boldsymbol{\phi}(\boldsymbol{x}_c)\right) \tag{4.95}$$

For example, in a Gaussian graphical model (GGM), we have

$$\boldsymbol{\phi}([x_i, x_j]) = [x_i, x_j, x_i x_j] \tag{4.96}$$

for $x_i \in \mathbb{R}$. And in an Ising model, we have

$$\boldsymbol{\phi}([x_i, x_j]) = [x_i, x_j, x_i x_j] \tag{4.97}$$

for $x_i \in \{-1, +1\}$. Thus both of these are maxent models. However, there are two key differences: first, in a GGM, the variables are real-valued, not binary; second, in a GGM, the partition function $Z(\boldsymbol{\theta})$ can be computed in $O(D^3)$ time, whereas in a Boltzmann machine, computing the partition function can take $O(2^D)$ time (see Section 9.5.4 for details).

If the features $\boldsymbol{\phi}$ are structured in a hierarchical way (capturing first order interactions, and second order interactions, etc.), and all the variables $\boldsymbol{x}$ are categorical, the resulting model is known in statistics as a **log-linear model**. However, in the ML community, the term "log-linear model" is often used to describe any model of the form Equation (4.95).

4.3.4.2 Feature induction for a maxent spelling model

In some applications, we assume the features $\boldsymbol{\phi}(\boldsymbol{x})$ are known. However, it is possible to learn the features in a maxent model in an unsupervised way; this is known as **feature induction**.

A common approach to feature induction, first proposed in [DDL97; ZWM97], is to start with a base set of features, and then to continually create new feature combinations out of old ones, greedily adding the best ones to the model.

As an example of this approach, [DDL97] describe how to build models to represent English spelling. This can be formalized as a probability distribution over variable length strings, $p(\boldsymbol{x}|\boldsymbol{\theta})$, where x_t is a letter in the English alphabet. Initially the model has no features, which represents the uniform distribution. The algorithm starts by choosing to add the feature

$$\phi_1(\boldsymbol{x}) = \sum_i \mathbb{I}\left(x_i \in \{a, \dots, z\}\right) \tag{4.98}$$

which checks if any letter is lowercase or not. After the feature is added, the parameters are (re)-fit by maximum likelihood (a computationally difficult problem, which we discuss in Section 4.3.9.1). For this feature, it turns out that $\hat{\theta}_1 = 1.944$, which means that a word with a lowercase letter in any position is about $e^{1.944} \approx 7$ times more likely than the same word without a lowercase letter in that position. Some samples from this model, generated using (annealed) Gibbs sampling (described in Section 12.3), are shown below.[6]

```
m, r, xevo, ijjiir, b, to, jz, gsr, wq, vf, x, ga, msmGh, pcp, d, oziVlal, hzagh, yzop, io,
advzmxnv, ijv_bolft, x, emx, kayerf, mlj, rawzyb, jp, ag, ctdnnnbg, wgdw, t, kguv, cy,
spxcq, uzflbbf, dxtkkn, cxwx, jpd, ztzh, lv, zhpkvnu, l^, r, qee, nynrx, atze4n, ik, se, w,
lrh, hp+, yrqyka'h, zcngotcnx, igcump, zjcjs, lqpWiqu, cefmfhc, o, lb, fdcY, tzby, yopxmvk,
by, fz,, t, govyccm, ijyiduwfzo, 6xr, duh, ejv, pk, pjw, l, fl, w
```

The second feature added by the algorithm checks if two adjacent characters are lowercase:

$$\phi_2(\boldsymbol{x}) = \sum_{i \sim j} \mathbb{I}\left(x_i \in \{a, \dots, z\}, x_j \in \{a, \dots, z\}\right) \tag{4.99}$$

Now the model has the form

$$p(\boldsymbol{x}) = \frac{1}{Z} \exp(\theta_1 \phi_1(\boldsymbol{x}) + \theta_2 \phi_2(\boldsymbol{x})) \tag{4.100}$$

Continuing in this way, the algorithm adds features for the strings s> and ing>, where > represents the end of word, and for various regular expressions such as [0-9], etc. Some samples from the model with 1000 features, generated using (annealed) Gibbs sampling, are shown below.

```
was, reaser, in, there, to, will, ,, was, by, homes, thing, be, reloverated, ther, which,
conists, at, fores, anditing, with, Mr., proveral, the, ,, ***, on't, prolling, prothere, ,,
mento, at, yaou, 1, chestraing, for, have, to, intrally, of, qut, ., best, compers, ***,
cluseliment, uster, of, is, deveral, this, thise, of, offect, inatever, thifer,
constranded, stater, vill, in, thase, in, youse, menttering, and, ., of, in, verate, of,
to
```

If we define a feature for every possible combination of letters, we can represent any probability distribution. However, this will overfit. The power of the maxent approach is that we can choose which features matter for the domain.

An alternative approach is to introduce latent variables, that implicitly model correlations amongst the visible nodes, rather than explicitly having to learn feature functions. See Section 4.3.3 for an example of such a model.

---

6. We thank John Lafferty for sharing this example.

4.3.5 Gaussian MRFs

In Section 4.2.3, we showed how to represent a multivariate Gaussian using a DPGM. In this section, we show how to represent a multivariate Gaussian using a UPGM. (For further details on GMRFs, see e.g., [RH05].)

4.3.5.1 Standard GMRFs

A **Gaussian graphical model** (or **GGM**), also called a **Gaussian MRF**, is a pairwise MRF of the following form:

$$p(\boldsymbol{x}) = \frac{1}{Z(\boldsymbol{\theta})} \prod_{i \sim j} \psi_{ij}(x_i, x_j) \prod_i \psi_i(x_i) \tag{4.101}$$

$$\psi_{ij}(x_i, x_j) = \exp(-\frac{1}{2} x_i \Lambda_{ij} x_j) \tag{4.102}$$

$$\psi_i(x_i) = \exp(-\frac{1}{2} \Lambda_{ii} x_i^2 + \eta_i x_i) \tag{4.103}$$

$$Z(\boldsymbol{\theta}) = (2\pi)^{D/2} |\boldsymbol{\Lambda}|^{-\frac{1}{2}} \tag{4.104}$$

The ψ_{ij} are **edge potentials** (pairwise terms), and each the ψ_i are **node potentials** or **unary terms**. (We could absorb the unary terms into the pairwise terms, but we have kept them separate for clarity.)

The joint distribution can be rewritten in a more familiar form as follows:

$$p(\boldsymbol{x}) \propto \exp[\boldsymbol{\eta}^\mathsf{T} \boldsymbol{x} - \frac{1}{2} \boldsymbol{x}^\mathsf{T} \boldsymbol{\Lambda} \boldsymbol{x}] \tag{4.105}$$

This is called the **information form** of a Gaussian; $\boldsymbol{\Lambda} = \boldsymbol{\Sigma}^{-1}$ and $\boldsymbol{\eta} = \boldsymbol{\Lambda}\boldsymbol{\mu}$ are called the **canonical parameters**.

If $\Lambda_{ij} = 0$, there is no pairwise term connecting x_i and x_j, and hence $x_i \perp x_j | \boldsymbol{x}_{-ij}$, where $\boldsymbol{x}_{-ij}$ are all the nodes except for x_i and x_j. Hence the zero entries in $\boldsymbol{\Lambda}$ are called **structural zeros**. This means we can use ℓ_1 regularization on the weights to learn a sparse graph, a method known as **graphical lasso** (see Supplementary Section 30.4.2).

Note that the covariance matrix $\boldsymbol{\Sigma} = \boldsymbol{\Lambda}^{-1}$ can be dense even if the precision matrix $\boldsymbol{\Lambda}$ is sparse. For example, consider an AR(1) process with correlation parameter ρ.[7] The precision matrix (for a graph with $T = 7$ nodes) looks like this:

$$\boldsymbol{\Lambda} = \frac{1}{\tau^2} \begin{pmatrix} 1 & -\rho & & & & & \\ -\rho & 1+\rho^2 & -\rho & & & & \\ & -\rho & 1+\rho^2 & -\rho & & & \\ & & -\rho & 1+\rho^2 & -\rho & & \\ & & & -\rho & 1+\rho^2 & -\rho & \\ & & & & -\rho & 1+\rho^2 & -\rho \\ & & & & & -\rho & 1 \end{pmatrix} \tag{4.106}$$

---

7. This example is from `https://dansblog.netlify.app/posts/2022-03-22-a-linear-mixed-effects-model/`.

But the covariance matrix is fully dense:

$$\mathbf{\Lambda}^{-1} = \tau^2 \begin{pmatrix} \rho & \rho^2 & \rho^3 & \rho^4 & \rho^5 & \rho^6 & \rho^7 \\ \rho^2 & \rho & \rho^2 & \rho^3 & \rho^4 & \rho^5 & \rho^6 \\ \rho^3 & \rho^2 & \rho & \rho^2 & \rho^3 & \rho^4 & \rho^5 \\ \rho^4 & \rho^3 & \rho^2 & \rho & \rho^2 & \rho^3 & \rho^4 \\ \rho^5 & \rho^4 & \rho^3 & \rho^2 & \rho & \rho^2 & \rho^3 \\ \rho^6 & \rho^5 & \rho^4 & \rho^3 & \rho^2 & \rho & \rho^2 \\ \rho^7 & \rho^6 & \rho^5 & \rho^4 & \rho^3 & \rho^2 & \rho \end{pmatrix} \tag{4.107}$$

This follows because, in a chain structured UPGM, every pair of nodes is marginally correlated, even if they may be conditionally independent given a separator.

4.3.5.2   Nonlinear Gaussian MRFs

In this section, we consider a generalization of GGMs to handle the case of nonlinear models. Suppose the joint is given by a product of local factors, or clique potentials, ψ_c, each of which is defined on a set or clique variables $\boldsymbol{x}_c$ as follows:

$$p(\boldsymbol{x}) = \frac{1}{Z} \prod_c \psi_c(\boldsymbol{x}_c) \tag{4.108}$$

$$\psi_c(\boldsymbol{x}_c) = \exp(-E_c(\boldsymbol{x}_c)) \tag{4.109}$$

$$E_c(\boldsymbol{x}_c) = \frac{1}{2}(f_c(\boldsymbol{x}_c) - \boldsymbol{d}_c)^\mathsf{T} \boldsymbol{\Sigma}_c^{-1} (f_c(\boldsymbol{x}_c) - \boldsymbol{d}_c) \tag{4.110}$$

where $\boldsymbol{d}_c$ is an optional local evidence term for the c'th clique, and f_c is some measurement function. Suppose the measurent function f_c is linear, i.e.,

$$f_c(\boldsymbol{x}) = \mathbf{J}_c \boldsymbol{x} + \boldsymbol{b}_c \tag{4.111}$$

In this case, the energy for clique c becomes

$$E_c(\boldsymbol{x}_c) = \frac{1}{2}\boldsymbol{x}_c^\mathsf{T} \underbrace{\mathbf{J}_c^\mathsf{T}\boldsymbol{\Sigma}_c^{-1}\mathbf{J}_c}_{\mathbf{\Lambda}_c} \boldsymbol{x}_c + \boldsymbol{x}_c^\mathsf{T} \underbrace{\mathbf{J}_c^\mathsf{T}\boldsymbol{\Sigma}_c^{-1}(\boldsymbol{b}_c - \boldsymbol{d}_c)}_{-\boldsymbol{\eta}_c} + \underbrace{\frac{1}{2}(\boldsymbol{b}_c - \boldsymbol{d}_c)\boldsymbol{\Sigma}_c^{-1}(\boldsymbol{b}_c - \boldsymbol{d}_c)}_{k_c} \tag{4.112}$$

$$= \frac{1}{2}\boldsymbol{x}_c^\mathsf{T}\mathbf{\Lambda}_c\boldsymbol{x}_c - \boldsymbol{\eta}_c^\mathsf{T}\boldsymbol{x}_c + k_c \tag{4.113}$$

which is a standard Gaussian factor. If f_c is nonlinear, it is common to linearize the model around the current estimate $\boldsymbol{x}_c^0$ to get

$$f_c(\boldsymbol{x}_c) \approx f_c(\boldsymbol{x}_c^0) + \mathbf{J}_c(\boldsymbol{x}_c - \boldsymbol{x}_c^0) = \mathbf{J}_c\boldsymbol{x}_c + \underbrace{(f_c(\boldsymbol{x}_c^0) - \mathbf{J}_c\boldsymbol{x}_c^0)}_{\boldsymbol{b}_c} \tag{4.114}$$

where $\mathbf{J}_c$ is the Jacobian of $f_c(\boldsymbol{x}_c)$ wrt $\boldsymbol{x}_c$. This gives us a "temporary" Gaussian factor that we can use for inference. This process can be iterated for improved accuracy.

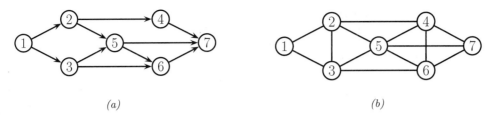

Figure 4.23: (a) A DPGM. (b) Its moralized version, represented as a UPGM.

4.3.6 Conditional independence properties

In this section, we explain how UPGMs encode conditional independence assumptions.

4.3.6.1 Basic results

UPGMs define CI relationships via simple graph separation as follows: given 3 sets of nodes A, B, and C, we say $\mathbf{X}_A \perp_G \mathbf{X}_B | \mathbf{X}_C$ iff C separates A from B in the graph G. This means that, when we remove all the nodes in C, if there are no paths connecting any node in A to any node in B, then the CI property holds. This is called the **global Markov property** for UPGMs. For example, in Figure 4.23(b), we have that $\{X_1, X_2\} \perp \{X_6, X_7\} | \{X_3, X_4, X_5\}$.

The smallest set of nodes that renders a node t conditionally independent of all the other nodes in the graph is called t's **Markov blanket**; we will denote this by $\mathrm{mb}(t)$. Formally, the Markov blanket satisfies the following property:

$$t \perp \mathcal{V} \setminus \mathrm{cl}(t) | \mathrm{mb}(t) \tag{4.115}$$

where $\mathrm{cl}(t) \triangleq \mathrm{mb}(t) \cup \{t\}$ is the **closure** of node t, and $\mathcal{V} = \{1, \ldots, N_G\}$ is the set of all nodes. One can show that, in a UPGM, a node's Markov blanket is its set of immediate neighbors. This is called the **undirected local Markov property**. For example, in Figure 4.23(b), we have $\mathrm{mb}(X_5) = \{X_2, X_3, X_4, X_6, X_7\}$.

From the local Markov property, we can easily see that two nodes are conditionally independent given the rest if there is no direct edge between them. This is called the **pairwise Markov property**. In symbols, this is written as

$$s \perp t | \mathcal{V} \setminus \{s, t\} \iff G_{st} = 0 \tag{4.116}$$

where $G_{st} = 0$ means there is no edge between s and t (so there is a 0 in the adjaceny matrix).

Using the three Markov properties we have discussed, we can derive the following CI properties (amongst others) from the UPGM in Figure 4.23(b): $X_1 \perp X_7 | \mathrm{rest}$ (pairwise); $X_1 \perp \mathrm{rest} | X_2, X_3$ (local); $X_1, X_2 \perp X_6, X_7 | X_3, X_4, X_5$ (global).

It is obvious that global Markov implies local Markov which implies pairwise Markov. What is less obvious is that pairwise implies global, and hence that all these Markov properties are the same, as illustrated in Figure 4.24 (see e.g., [KF09a, p119] for a proof).[8] The importance of this result is that it is usually easier to empirically assess pairwise conditional independence; such pairwise CI statements can be used to construct a graph from which global CI statements can be extracted.

---

8. This assumes $p(\boldsymbol{x}) > 0$ for all $\boldsymbol{x}$, i.e., that p is a positive density. The restriction to positive densities arises because

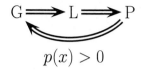

Figure 4.24: *Relationship between Markov properties of UPGMs.*

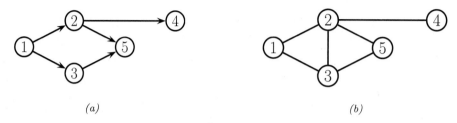

Figure 4.25: *(a) The ancestral graph induced by the DAG in Figure 4.23(a) wrt $U = \{X_2, X_4, X_5\}$. (b) The moralized version of (a).*

4.3.6.2   An undirected alternative to d-separation

We have seen that determinining CI relationships in UPGMs is much easier than in DPGMs, because we do not have to worry about the directionality of the edges. That is, we can use simple graph separation, instead of d-separation.

In this section, we show how to convert a DPGM to a UPGM, so that we can infer CI relationships for the DPGM using simple graph separation. It is tempting to simply convert the DPGM to a UPGM by dropping the orientation of the edges, but this is clearly incorrect, since a v-structure $A \to B \leftarrow C$ has quite different CI properties than the corresponding undirected chain $A - B - C$ (e.g., the latter graph incorrectly states that $A \perp C|B$). To avoid such incorrect CI statements, we can add edges between the "unmarried" parents A and C, and then drop the arrows from the edges, forming (in this case) a fully connected undirected graph. This process is called **moralization**. Figure 4.23 gives a larger example of moralization: we interconnect 2 and 3, since they have a common child 5, and we interconnect 4, 5, and 6, since they have a common child 7.

Unfortunately, moralization loses some CI information, and therefore we cannot use the moralized UPGM to determine CI properties of the DPGM. For example, in Figure 4.23(a), using d-separation, we see that $X_4 \perp X_5|X_2$. Adding a moralization arc $X_4 - X_5$ would lose this fact (see Figure 4.23(b)). However, notice that the 4-5 moralization edge, due to the common child 7, is not needed if we do not observe 7 or any of its descendants. This suggests the following approach to determining if $A \perp B|C$. First we form the **ancestral graph** of DAG G with respect to $U = A \cup B \cup C$. This means we remove all nodes from G that are not in U or are not ancestors of U. We then moralize this ancestral

---

deterministic constraints can result in independencies present in the distribution that are not explicitly represented in the graph. See e.g., [KF09a, p120] for some examples. Distributions with non-graphical CI properties are said to be **unfaithful** to the graph, so $I(p) \neq I(G)$.

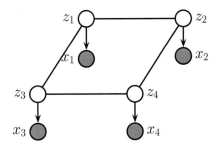

Figure 4.26: A grid-structured MRF with hidden nodes z_i and local evidence nodes x_i. The prior $p(z)$ is an undirected Ising model, and the likelihood $p(x|z) = \prod_i p(x_i|z_i)$ is a directed fully factored model.

graph, and apply the simple graph separation rules for UPGMs. For example, in Figure 4.25(a), we show the ancestral graph for Figure 4.23(a) using $U = \{X_2, X_4, X_5\}$. In Figure 4.25(b), we show the moralized version of this graph. It is clear that we now correctly conclude that $X_4 \perp X_5 | X_2$.

4.3.7 Generation (sampling)

Unlike with DPGMs, it can be quite slow to sample from an UPGM, even from the unconditional prior, because there is no ordering of the variables. Furthermore, we cannot easily compute the probability of any configuration unless we know the value of Z. Consequently it is common to use MCMC methods for generating from an UPGM (see Chapter 12).

In the special case of UPGMs with low treewidth and discrete or Gaussian potentials, it is possible to use the junction tree algorithm to draw samples using dynamic programming (see Supplementary Section 9.2.3).

4.3.8 Inference

We discuss inference in graphical models in detail in Chapter 9. In this section, we just give an example.

Suppose we have an image composed of binary pixels, z_i, but we only observe noisy versions of the pixels, x_i. We assume the joint model has the form

$$p(\boldsymbol{x}, \boldsymbol{z}) = p(\boldsymbol{z})p(\boldsymbol{x}|\boldsymbol{z}) = \left[\frac{1}{Z} \sum_{i \sim j} \psi_{ij}(z_i, z_j)\right] \prod_i p(x_i|z_i) \tag{4.117}$$

where $p(\boldsymbol{z})$ is an Ising model prior, and $p(x_i|z_i) = \mathcal{N}(x_i|z_i, \sigma^2)$, for $z_i \in \{-1, +1\}$. This model uses a UPGM as a prior, and has directed edges for the likelihood, as shown in Figure 4.26; such a hybrid undirected-directed model is called a **chain graph** (even though it is not chain-structured).

The inference task is to compute the posterior marginals $p(z_i|\boldsymbol{x})$, or the posterior MAP estimate, $\text{argmax}_{\boldsymbol{z}}\, p(\boldsymbol{z}|\boldsymbol{x})$. The exact computation is intractable for large grids (for reasons explained in Section 9.5.4), so we must use approximate methods. There are many algorithms that we can use, including mean field variational inference (Section 10.3.2), Gibbs sampling (Section 12.3.3), loopy belief propagation (Section 9.4), etc. In Figure 4.27, we show the results of variational inference.

Figure 4.27: *Example of image denoising using mean field variational inference. We use an Ising prior with* $W_{ij} = 1$ *and a Gaussian noise model with* $\sigma = 2$. *(a) Noisy image. (b) Result of inference. Generated by* ising_image_denoise_demo.ipynb.

4.3.9   Learning

In this section, we discuss how to estimate the parameters for an MRF. As we will see, computing the MLE can be computationally expensive, even in the fully observed case, because of the need to deal with the partition function $Z(\boldsymbol{\theta})$. And computing the posterior over the parameters, $p(\boldsymbol{\theta}|\mathcal{D})$, is even harder, because of the additional normalizing constant $p(\mathcal{D})$ — this case has been called **doubly intractable** [MGM06]. Consequently we will focus on point estimation methods such as MLE and MAP. (For one approach to Bayesian parameter inference in an MRF, based on persistent variational inference, see [IM17].)

4.3.9.1   Learning from complete data

We will start by assuming there are no hidden variables or missing data during training (this is known as the **complete data** setting). For simplicity of presentation, we restrict our discusssion to the case of MRFs with log-linear potential functions. (See Section 24.2 for the general nonlinear case, where we discuss MLE for energy-based models.)

In particular, we assume the distribution has the following form:

$$p(\boldsymbol{x}|\boldsymbol{\theta}) = \frac{1}{Z(\boldsymbol{\theta})} \exp\left(\sum_c \boldsymbol{\theta}_c^\mathsf{T} \boldsymbol{\phi}_c(\boldsymbol{x}) \right) \tag{4.118}$$

where c indexes the cliques. The (averaged) log-likelihood of the full dataset becomes

$$\ell(\boldsymbol{\theta}) \triangleq \frac{1}{N} \sum_n \log p(\boldsymbol{x}_n|\boldsymbol{\theta}) = \frac{1}{N} \sum_n \left[\sum_c \boldsymbol{\theta}_c^\mathsf{T} \boldsymbol{\phi}_c(\boldsymbol{x}_n) - \log Z(\boldsymbol{\theta}) \right] \tag{4.119}$$

Its gradient is given by

$$\frac{\partial \ell}{\partial \boldsymbol{\theta}_c} = \frac{1}{N} \sum_n \left[\boldsymbol{\phi}_c(\boldsymbol{x}_n) - \frac{\partial}{\partial \boldsymbol{\theta}_c} \log Z(\boldsymbol{\theta}) \right] \tag{4.120}$$

We know from Section 2.4.3 that the derivative of the log partition function wrt $\boldsymbol{\theta}_c$ is the expectation of the c'th feature vector under the model, i.e.,

$$\frac{\partial \log Z(\boldsymbol{\theta})}{\partial \boldsymbol{\theta}_c} = \mathbb{E}\left[\boldsymbol{\phi}_c(\boldsymbol{x})|\boldsymbol{\theta}\right] = \sum_{\boldsymbol{x}} p(\boldsymbol{x}|\boldsymbol{\theta})\boldsymbol{\phi}_c(\boldsymbol{x}) \tag{4.121}$$

Hence the gradient of the log likelihood is

$$\frac{\partial \ell}{\partial \boldsymbol{\theta}_c} = \frac{1}{N}\sum_n \left[\boldsymbol{\phi}_c(\boldsymbol{x}_n)\right] - \mathbb{E}\left[\boldsymbol{\phi}_c(\boldsymbol{x})\right] \tag{4.122}$$

When the expected value of the features according to the data is equal to the expected value of the features according to the model, the gradient will be zero, so we get

$$\mathbb{E}_{p_{\mathcal{D}}}\left[\boldsymbol{\phi}_c(\boldsymbol{x})\right] = \mathbb{E}_{p(\boldsymbol{x}|\boldsymbol{\theta})}\left[\boldsymbol{\phi}_c(\boldsymbol{x})\right] \tag{4.123}$$

This is called **moment matching**. Evaluating the $\mathbb{E}_{p_{\mathcal{D}}}\left[\boldsymbol{\phi}_c(\boldsymbol{x})\right]$ term is called the **clamped phase** or **positive phase**, since $\boldsymbol{x}$ is set to the observed values $\boldsymbol{x}_n$; evaluating the $\mathbb{E}_{p(\boldsymbol{x}|\boldsymbol{\theta})}\left[\boldsymbol{\phi}_c(\boldsymbol{x})\right]$ term is called the **unclamped phase** or **negative phase**, since $\boldsymbol{x}$ is free to vary, and is generated by the model.

In the case of MRFs with tabular potentials (i.e., one feature per entry in the clique table), we can use an algorithm called **iterative proportional fitting** or **IPF** [Fie70; BFH75; JP95] to solve these equations in an iterative fashion.[9] But in general, we must use gradient methods to perform parameter estimation.

4.3.9.2 Computational issues

The biggest computational bottleneck in fitting MRFs and CRFs using MLE is the cost of computing the derivative of the log partition function, $\log Z(\boldsymbol{\theta})$, which is needed to compute the derivative of the log likelihood, as we saw in Section 4.3.9.1. To see why this is slow to compute, note that

$$\nabla_{\boldsymbol{\theta}} \log Z(\boldsymbol{\theta}) = \frac{\nabla_{\boldsymbol{\theta}} Z(\boldsymbol{\theta})}{Z(\boldsymbol{\theta})} = \frac{1}{Z(\boldsymbol{\theta})}\nabla_{\boldsymbol{\theta}}\int \tilde{p}(\boldsymbol{x};\boldsymbol{\theta})d\boldsymbol{x} = \frac{1}{Z(\boldsymbol{\theta})}\int \nabla_{\boldsymbol{\theta}}\tilde{p}(\boldsymbol{x};\boldsymbol{\theta})d\boldsymbol{x} \tag{4.124}$$

$$= \frac{1}{Z(\boldsymbol{\theta})}\int \tilde{p}(\boldsymbol{x};\boldsymbol{\theta})\nabla_{\boldsymbol{\theta}}\log \tilde{p}(\boldsymbol{x};\boldsymbol{\theta})d\boldsymbol{x} = \int \frac{\tilde{p}(\boldsymbol{x};\boldsymbol{\theta})}{Z(\boldsymbol{\theta})}\nabla_{\boldsymbol{\theta}}\log \tilde{p}(\boldsymbol{x};\boldsymbol{\theta})d\boldsymbol{x} \tag{4.125}$$

$$= \mathbb{E}_{\boldsymbol{x}\sim p(\boldsymbol{x};\boldsymbol{\theta})}\left[\nabla_{\boldsymbol{\theta}}\log \tilde{p}(\boldsymbol{x};\boldsymbol{\theta})\right] \tag{4.126}$$

where in Equation (4.125) we used the fact that $\nabla_{\boldsymbol{\theta}}\log \tilde{p}(\boldsymbol{x};\boldsymbol{\theta}) = \frac{1}{\tilde{p}(\boldsymbol{x};\boldsymbol{\theta})}\nabla_{\boldsymbol{\theta}}\tilde{p}(\boldsymbol{x};\boldsymbol{\theta})$ (this is known as the **log-derivative trick**). Thus we see that we need to draw samples from the model at each step of SGD training, just to estimate the gradient.

In Section 24.2.1, we discuss various efficient sampling methods. However, it is also possible to use alternative estimators which do not use the principle of maximum likelihood. For example, in Section 24.2.2 we discuss the technique of contrastive divergence. And in Section 4.3.9.3, we discuss the technique of pseudolikelihood. (See also [Sto17] for a review of many methods for parameter estimation in MRFs.)

---

9. In the case of decomposable graphs, IPF converges in a single iteration. Intuitively, this is because a decomposable graph can be converted to a DAG without any loss of information, as explained in Section 4.5, and we know that we can compute the MLE for tabular CPDs in closed form, just by normalizing the counts.

Figure 4.28: (a) A small 2d lattice. (b) The representation used by pseudo likelihood. Solid nodes are observed neighbors. Adapted from Figure 2.2 of [Car03].

4.3.9.3   Maximum pseudolikelihood estimation

When fitting fully visible MRFs (or CRFs), a simple alternative to maximizing the likelihood is to maximize the **pseudo likelihood** [Bes75], defined as follows:

$$\ell_{PL}(\boldsymbol{\theta}) \triangleq \frac{1}{N} \sum_{n=1}^{N} \sum_{d=1}^{D} \log p(x_{nd}|\boldsymbol{x}_{n,-d}, \boldsymbol{\theta}) \tag{4.127}$$

That is, we optimize the product of the full conditionals, also known as the **composite likelihood** [Lin88a; DL10; VRF11]. Compare this to the objective for maximum likelihood:

$$\ell_{ML}(\boldsymbol{\theta}) = \frac{1}{N} \sum_{n=1}^{N} \log p(\boldsymbol{x}_n|\boldsymbol{\theta}) \tag{4.128}$$

In the case of Gaussian MRFs, PL is equivalent to ML [Bes75], although this is not true in general. Nevertheless, it is a consistent estimator in the large sample limit [LJ08].

The PL approach is illustrated in Figure 4.28 for a 2d grid. We learn to predict each node, given all of its neighbors. This objective is generally fast to compute since each full conditional $p(x_d|\boldsymbol{x}_{-d}, \boldsymbol{\theta})$ only requires summing over the states of a single node, x_d, in order to compute the local normalization constant. The PL approach is similar to fitting each full conditional separately, except that, in PL, the parameters are tied between adjacent nodes.

Experiments in [PW05; HT09] suggest that PL works as well as exact ML for fully observed Ising models, but is much faster. In [Eke+13], they use PL to fitt Potts models to (aligned) protein sequence data. However, when fitting RBMs, [Mar+10] found that PL is worse than some of the stochastic ML methods we discuss in Section 24.2.

Another more subtle problem is that each node assumes that its neighbors have known values during training. If node $j \in \text{nbr}(i)$ is a perfect predictor for node i (where $\text{nbr}(i)$ is the set of neighbors), then j will learn to rely completely on node i, even at the expense of ignoring other potentially useful information, such as its local evidence, say y_i. At test time, the neighboring nodes will not be observed, and performance will suffer.[10]

---

10. Geoff Hinton has an analogy for this problem. Suppose we want to learn to denoise images of symmetric shapes, such as Greek vases. Each hidden pixel x_i depends on its spatial neighbors, as well the noisy observation y_i. Since its symmetric counterpart x_j will perfectly predict x_i, the model will ignore y_i and just rely on x_j, even though x_j will not be available at test time.

4.3.9.4   Learning from incomplete data

In this section, we consider parameter estimation for MRFs (and CRFs) with hidden variables. Such **incomplete data** can arise for several reasons. For example, we may want to learn a model of the form $p(z)p(x|z)$ which lets us infer a "clean" image z from a noisy or corrupted version x. If we only observe x, the model is called a **hidden Gibbs random field**. See Section 10.3.2 for an example. As another example, we may have a CRF in which the hidden variables are used to encode an unknown alignment between the inputs and outputs [Qua+07], or to model missing parts of the input [SRS10].

We now discuss how to compute the MLE in such cases. For notational simplicity, we focus on unconditional models (MRFs, not CRFs), and we assume all the potentials are log-linear. In this case, the model has the following form:

$$p(\boldsymbol{x}, \boldsymbol{z}|\boldsymbol{\theta}) = \frac{\exp(\boldsymbol{\theta}^\mathsf{T}\boldsymbol{\phi}(\boldsymbol{x}, \boldsymbol{z}))}{Z(\boldsymbol{\theta})} = \frac{\tilde{p}(\boldsymbol{x}, \boldsymbol{z}|\boldsymbol{\theta})}{Z(\boldsymbol{\theta})} \tag{4.129}$$

$$Z(\boldsymbol{\theta}) = \sum_{\boldsymbol{x}, \boldsymbol{z}} \exp(\boldsymbol{\theta}^\mathsf{T}\boldsymbol{\phi}(\boldsymbol{x}, \boldsymbol{z})) \tag{4.130}$$

where $\tilde{p}(\boldsymbol{x}, \boldsymbol{z}|\boldsymbol{\theta})$ is the unnormalized distribution. We have dropped the sum over cliques c for brevity.

The log likelihood is now given by

$$\ell(\boldsymbol{\theta}) = \frac{1}{N} \sum_{n=1}^{N} \log \left(\sum_{\boldsymbol{z}_n} p(\boldsymbol{x}_n, \boldsymbol{z}_n|\boldsymbol{\theta}) \right) \tag{4.131}$$

$$= \frac{1}{N} \sum_{n=1}^{N} \log \left(\frac{1}{Z(\boldsymbol{\theta})} \sum_{\boldsymbol{z}_n} \tilde{p}(\boldsymbol{x}_n, \boldsymbol{z}_n|\boldsymbol{\theta}) \right) \tag{4.132}$$

$$= \frac{1}{N} \sum_{n=1}^{N} \left[\log \sum_{\boldsymbol{z}_n} \tilde{p}(\boldsymbol{x}_n, \boldsymbol{z}_n|\boldsymbol{\theta}) \right] - \log Z(\boldsymbol{\theta}) \tag{4.133}$$

Note that

$$\log \sum_{\boldsymbol{z}_n} \tilde{p}(\boldsymbol{x}_n, \boldsymbol{z}_n|\boldsymbol{\theta}) = \log \sum_{\boldsymbol{z}_n} \exp(\boldsymbol{\theta}^\mathsf{T}\boldsymbol{\phi}(\boldsymbol{x}_n, \boldsymbol{z}_n)) \triangleq \log Z(\boldsymbol{\theta}, \boldsymbol{x}_n) \tag{4.134}$$

where $Z(\boldsymbol{\theta}, \boldsymbol{x}_n)$ is the same as the partition function for the whole model, except that $\boldsymbol{x}$ is fixed at $\boldsymbol{x}_n$. Thus the log likelihood is a difference of two partition functions, one where $\boldsymbol{x}$ is clamped to $\boldsymbol{x}_n$ and $\boldsymbol{z}$ is unclamped, and one where both $\boldsymbol{x}$ and $\boldsymbol{z}$ are unclamped. The gradient of these log partition functions corresponds to the expected features, where (in the clamped case) we condition on $\boldsymbol{x} = \boldsymbol{x}_n$. Hence

$$\frac{\partial \ell}{\partial \boldsymbol{\theta}} = \frac{1}{N} \sum_{n} \left[\mathbb{E}_{\boldsymbol{z} \sim p(\boldsymbol{z}|\boldsymbol{x}_n, \boldsymbol{\theta})} \left[\boldsymbol{\phi}(\boldsymbol{x}_n, \boldsymbol{z}) \right] \right] - \mathbb{E}_{(\boldsymbol{z}, \boldsymbol{x}) \sim p(\boldsymbol{z}, \boldsymbol{x}|\boldsymbol{\theta})} \left[\boldsymbol{\phi}(\boldsymbol{x}, \boldsymbol{z}) \right] \tag{4.135}$$

4.4   Conditional random fields (CRFs)

A **conditional random field** or **CRF** [LMP01] is a Markov random field defined on a set of related label nodes $\boldsymbol{y}$, whose joint probability is predicted conditional on a fixed set of input nodes $\boldsymbol{x}$. More

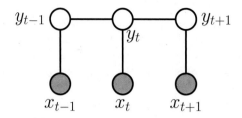

Figure 4.29: A 1d conditional random field (CRF) for sequence labeling.

precisely, it corresponds to a model of the following form:

$$p(\boldsymbol{y}|\boldsymbol{x}, \boldsymbol{\theta}) = \frac{1}{Z(\boldsymbol{x}, \boldsymbol{\theta})} \prod_c \psi_c(\boldsymbol{y}_c; \boldsymbol{x}, \boldsymbol{\theta}) \tag{4.136}$$

(Note how the partition function now depends on the inputs $\boldsymbol{x}$ as well as the parameters $\boldsymbol{\theta}$.) Now suppose the potential functions are log-linear and have the form

$$\psi_c(\boldsymbol{y}_c; \boldsymbol{x}, \boldsymbol{\theta}) = \exp(\boldsymbol{\theta}_c^\mathsf{T} \boldsymbol{\phi}_c(\boldsymbol{x}, \boldsymbol{y}_c)) \tag{4.137}$$

This is a conditional version of the maxent models we discussed in Section 4.3.4. Of course, we can also use nonlinear potential functions, such as DNNs.

CRFs are useful because they capture dependencies amongst the output labels. They can therefore be used for **structured prediction**, where the output $\boldsymbol{y} \in \mathcal{Y}$ that we want to predict given the input $\boldsymbol{x}$ lives in some structured space, such as a sequence of labels, or labels associated with nodes on a graph. In such problems, there are often constraints on the set of valid values of the output $\boldsymbol{y}$. For example, if we want to perform sentence parsing, the output should satisfy the rules of grammar (e.g., noun phrase must precede verb phrase). See Section 4.4.1 for details on the application of CRFs to NLP. In some cases, the "constraints" are "soft", rather than "hard". For example, if we want to associate a label with each pixel in an image (a task called semantic segmentation), we might want to "encourage" the label at one location to be the same as its neighbors, unless the visual input strongly suggests a change in semantic content at this location (e.g., at the edge of an object). See Section 4.4.2 for details on the applications of CRFs to computer vision tasks.

4.4.1   1d CRFs

In this section, we focus on 1d CRFs defined on chain-structured graphical models. The graphical model is shown in Figure 4.29. This defines a joint distribution over sequences, $\boldsymbol{y}_{1:T}$, given a set of inputs, $\boldsymbol{x}_{1:T}$, as follows:

$$p(\boldsymbol{y}_{1:T}|\boldsymbol{x}, \boldsymbol{\theta}) = \frac{1}{Z(\boldsymbol{x}, \boldsymbol{\theta})} \prod_{t=1}^{T} \psi(y_t, \boldsymbol{x}_t; \boldsymbol{\theta}) \prod_{t=2}^{T} \psi(y_{t-1}, y_t; \boldsymbol{\theta}) \tag{4.138}$$

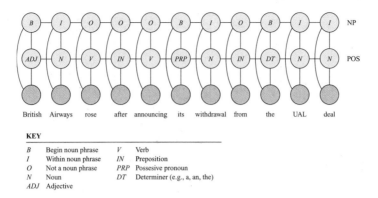

Figure 4.30: *A CRF for joint part of speech tagging and noun phrase segmentation. From Figure 4.E.1 of [KF09a]. Used with kind permission of Daphne Koller.*

where $\psi(y_t, \boldsymbol{x}_t; \boldsymbol{\theta})$ are the node potentials and $\psi(y_t, y_{t+1}; \boldsymbol{\theta})$ are the edge potentials. (We have assumed that the edge potentials are independent of the input $\boldsymbol{x}$, but this assumption is not required.)

Note that one could also consider an alternative way to define this conditional distribution, by using a discriminative directed Markov chain:

$$p(\boldsymbol{y}_{1:T}|\boldsymbol{x}, \boldsymbol{\theta}) = p(y_1|\boldsymbol{x}_1; \boldsymbol{\theta}) \prod_{t=2}^{T} p(y_t|y_{t-1}, \boldsymbol{x}_t; \boldsymbol{\theta}) \tag{4.139}$$

This is called a **maximum entropy Markov model** [MFP00]. However, it suffers from a subtle flaw compared to the CRF. In particular, in the directed model, each conditional $p(y_t|y_{t-1}, \boldsymbol{x}_t; \boldsymbol{\theta})$, is **locally normalized**, whereas in the CRF, the model is **globally normalized** due to the $Z(\boldsymbol{x}, \boldsymbol{\theta})$ term. The latter allows information to propagate through the entire sequence, as we discuss in more detail in Section 4.5.3.

CRFs were widely used in the natural language processing (NLP) community in the 1980s–2010s (see e.g., [Smi11]), although recently they have been mostly replaced by RNNs and transformers (see e.g., [Gol17]). Fortunately, we can get the best of both worlds by combining CRFs with DNNs, which allows us to combine data driven techniques with prior knowledge about constraints on the label space. We give some examples below.

4.4.1.1 Noun phrase chunking

A common task in NLP is **information extraction**, in which we try to parse a sentence into **noun phrases** (NP), such as names and addresses of people or businesses, as well as **verb phrases**, which describe who is doing what to whom (e.g., "British Airways rose"). In order to tackle this task, we can assign a **part of speech** tag to each word, where the tags correspond to Noun, Verb, Adjective, etc. In addition, to extract the span of each noun phrase, we can annotate words as being at the beginning (B) or inside (I) of a noun phrase, or outside (O) of one. See Figure 4.30 for an example.

The connections between adjacent labels can encode constraints such as the fact that B (begin) must precede I (inside). For example, the sequences OBIIO and OBIOBIO are valid (corresponding to

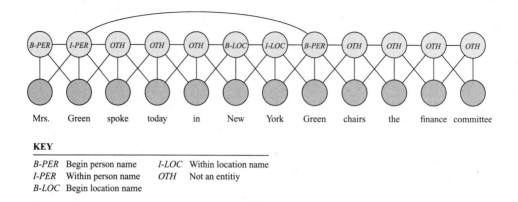

Figure 4.31: A skip-chain CRF for named entity recognition. From Figure 4.E.1 of [KF09a]. Used with kind permission of Daphne Koller.

one NP of 3 words, and two adjacent NPs of 2 words), but `OIBIO` is not. This prior information can be encoded by defining $\psi(y_{t-1}^{\mathrm{BIO}} = *, y_t^{\mathrm{BIO}} = B, x_t; \boldsymbol{\theta})$ to be 0 for any value of $*$ except O. We can encode similar grammatical rules for the POS tags.

Given this model, we can compute the MAP sequence of labels, and thereby extract the spans that are labeled as noun phrases. This is called **noun phrase chunking**.

4.4.1.2 Named entity recognition

In this section we consider the task of **named entity extraction**, in which we not only tag the noun phrases, but also classify them into different types. A simple approach to this is to extend the BIO notation to {B-Per, I-Per, B-Loc, I-Loc, B-Org, I-Org, Other}. However, sometimes it is ambiguous whether a word is a person, location, or something else. Proper nouns are particularly difficult to deal with because they belong to an **open class**, that is, there is an unbounded number of possible names, unlike the set of nouns and verbs, which is large but essentially fixed. For example, "British Airways" is an organization, but "British Virgin Islands" is a location.

We can get better performance by considering long-range correlations between words. For example, we might add a link between all occurrences of the same word, and force the word to have the same tag in each occurence. (The same technique can also be helpful for resolving the identity of pronouns.) This is known as a **skip-chain CRF**. See Figure 4.31 for an illustration, where we show that the word "Green" is interpeted as a person in both occurrences within the same sentence.

We see that the graph structure itself changes depending on the input, which is an additional advantage of CRFs over generative models. Unfortunately, inference in this model is generally more expensive than in a simple chain with local connections because of the larger treewdith (see Section 9.5.2).

4.4.1.3 Natural language parsing

A generalization of chain-structured models for language is to use probabilistic grammars. In particular, a probabilistic **context free grammar** or **PCFG** in Chomsky normal form is a set of

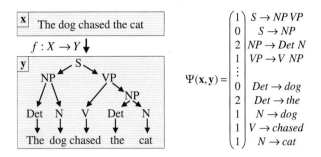

Figure 4.32: *Illustration of a simple parse tree based on a context free grammar in Chomsky normal form. The feature vector $\Psi(\boldsymbol{x}, \boldsymbol{y})$ counts the number of times each production rule was used, and is used to define the energy of a particular tree structure, $E(\boldsymbol{y}|\boldsymbol{x}) = -\boldsymbol{w}^\mathsf{T}\Psi(\boldsymbol{x}, \boldsymbol{y})$. The probability distribution over trees is given by $p(\boldsymbol{y}|\boldsymbol{x}) \propto \exp(-E(\boldsymbol{y}|\boldsymbol{x}))$. From Figure 5.2 of [AHT07]. Used with kind permission of Yasemin Altun.*

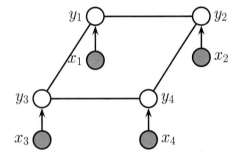

Figure 4.33: *A grid-structured CRF with label nodes y_i and local evidence nodes x_i.*

re-write or production rules of the form $\sigma \to \sigma'\sigma''$ or $\sigma \to x$, where $\sigma, \sigma', \sigma'' \in \Sigma$ are non-terminals (analogous to parts of speech), and $x \in \mathcal{X}$ are terminals, i.e., words. Each such rule has an associated probability. The resulting model defines a probability distribution over sequences of words. We can compute the probability of observing a particular sequence $\boldsymbol{x} = x_1 \ldots x_T$ by summing over all trees that generate it. This can be done in $O(T^3)$ time using the **inside-outside algorithm**; see e.g., [JM08; MS99; Eis16] for details.

PCFGs are generative models. It is possible to make discriminative versions which encode the probability of a labeled tree, $\boldsymbol{y}$, given a sequence of words, $\boldsymbol{x}$, by using a CRF of the form $p(\boldsymbol{y}|\boldsymbol{x}) \propto \exp(\boldsymbol{w}^\mathsf{T}\Psi(\boldsymbol{x}, \boldsymbol{y}))$. For example, we might define $\Psi(\boldsymbol{x}, \boldsymbol{y})$ to count the number of times each production rule was used (which is analogous to the number of state transitions in a chain-structured model), as illustrated in Figure 4.32. We can also use a deep neural net to define the features, as in the **neural CRF parser** method of [DK15b].

4.4.2 2d CRFs

It is also possible to apply CRFs to image processing problems, which are usually defined on 2d grids, as illustrated in Figure 4.33. (Compare this to the generative model in Figure 4.26.) This

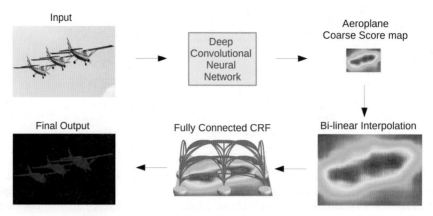

Figure 4.34: A fully connected CRF is added to the output of a CNN, in order to increase the sharpness of the segmentation boundaries. From Figure 3 of [Che+15]. Used with kind permission of Jay Chen.

corresponds to the following conditional model:

$$p(\boldsymbol{y}|\boldsymbol{x}) = \frac{1}{Z(\boldsymbol{x})} \left[\sum_{i \sim j} \psi_{ij}(y_i, y_j) \right] \prod_i p(y_i|\boldsymbol{x}_i) \tag{4.140}$$

In the sections below, we discuss some applications of this and other CRF models in computer vision.

4.4.2.1 Semantic segmentation

The task of **semantic segmentation** is to assign a label to every pixel in an image. We can easily solve this problem using a CNN with one softmax output node per pixel. However, this may fail to capture long-range dependencies, since convolution is a local operation.

One way to get better results is to feed the output of the CNN into a CRF. Since the CNN already uses convolution, its outputs will usually already be locally smooth, so the benefits from using a CRF with a local grid structure may be quite small. However, we can somtimes get better results if we use a **fully connected CRF**, which has connections between all the pixels. This can capture long range connections which the grid-structured CRF cannot. See Figure 4.34 for an illustration, and [Che+17a] for details.

Unfortunately, exact inference in a fully connected CRF is intractable, but in the case of Gaussian potentials, it is possible to devise an efficient mean field algorithm, as described in [KK11]. Interestingly, [Zhe+15] showed how the mean field update equations can be implemented using a recurrent neural network (see Section 16.3.4), allowing end-to-end training. Alternatively, if we are willing to use a finite number of iterations, we can just "unroll" the computation graph and treat it as a fixed-sized feedforward circuit. The result is a graph-structured neural network, where the topology of the GNN is derived from the graphical model (cf., Section 9.4.10). The advantage of this compared to standard CRF methods is that we can train this entire model end-to-end using standard gradient descent methods; we no longer have to worry about the partition function (see Section 4.4.3), or the lack of convergence that can arise when combining approximate inference with standard CRF learning.

Figure 4.35: Pictorial structures model for a face and body. Each body part corresponds to a node in the CRF whose state space represents the location of that part. The edges (springs) represent pairwise spatial constraints. The local evidence nodes are not shown. Adapted from a figure by Pedro Felzenszwalb.

4.4.2.2 Deformable parts models

Consider the problem of **object detection**, i.e., finding the location(s) of an object of a given class (e.g., a person or a car) in an image. One way to tackle this is to train a binary classifier that takes as input an image patch and specifies if the patch contains the object or not. We can then apply this to every image patch, and return the locations where the classifier has high confidence detections; this is known as a **sliding window detector**, and works quite well for rigid objects such as cars or frontal faces. Such an approach can be made efficient by using convolutional neural networks (CNNs); see Section 16.3.2 for details.

However, such methods can work poorly when there is occlusion, or when the shape is deformable, such as a person's or animal's body, because there is too much variation in the overall appearance. A natural strategy to deal with such problems is break the object into parts, and then to detect each part separately. But we still need to enforce spatial coherence of the parts. This can be done using a pairwise CRF, where node y_i specifies the location of part i in the image (assuming it is present), and where we connect adjacent parts by a potential function that encourages them to be close together. For example, we can use a pairwise potential of the form $\psi(y_i, y_j | \boldsymbol{x}) = \exp(-d(y_i, y_j))$, where $y_i \in \{1, \ldots, K\}$ is the location of part i (a discretization of the 2d image plane), and $d(y_i, y_i)$ is the distance between parts i and j. (We can make this "distance" also depend on the inputs $\boldsymbol{x}$ if we want, for example we may relax the distance penalty if we detect an edge.) In addition we will have a local evidence term of the form $p(y_i | \boldsymbol{x})$, which can be any kind of discriminative classifier, such as a CNN, which predicts the distribution over locations for part i given the image $\boldsymbol{x}$. The overall model has the form

$$p(\boldsymbol{y}|\boldsymbol{x}) = \frac{1}{Z(\boldsymbol{x})} \left[\prod_i p(y_i | f(\boldsymbol{x})_i) \right] \left[\prod_{(i,j) \in E} \psi(y_i, y_j | \boldsymbol{x}) \right] \tag{4.141}$$

where E is the set of edges in the CRF, and $f(\boldsymbol{x})_i$ is the i'th output of the CNN.

We can think of this CRF as a series of parts connected by springs, where the energy of the system increases if the parts are moved too far from their expected relative distance. This is illustrated in Figure 4.35. The resulting model is known as a **pictorial structure** [FE73], or **deformable parts**

model [Fel+10]. Furthermore, since this is a conditional model, we can make the spring strengths be image dependent.

We can find the globally optimal joint configuration $\boldsymbol{y}^* = \operatorname{argmax}_{\boldsymbol{y}} p(\boldsymbol{y}|\boldsymbol{x}, \boldsymbol{\theta})$ using brute force enumeration in $O(K^T)$ time, where T is the number of nodes and K is the number of states (locations) per node. While T is often small, (e.g., just 10 body parts in Figure 4.35), K is often very large, since there are millions of possible locations in an image. By using tree-structured graphs, exact inference can be done in $O(TK^2)$ time, as we explain in Section 9.3.2. Furthermore, by exploiting the fact that the discrete states are ordinal, inference time can be further reduced to $O(TK)$, as explained in [Fel+10].

Note that by "augmenting" standard deep neural network libaries with a dynamic programming inference "module", we can represent DPMs as a kind of CNN, as shown in [Gir+15]. The key property is that we can backpropagate gradients through the inference algorithm.

4.4.3   Parameter estimation

In this section, we discuss how to perform maximum likelihood estimation for CRFs. This is a small extension of the MRF case in Section 4.3.9.1.

4.4.3.1   Log-linear potentials

In this section we assume the log potential functions are linear in the parameters, i.e.,

$$\psi_c(\boldsymbol{y}_c; \boldsymbol{x}, \boldsymbol{\theta}) = \exp(\boldsymbol{\theta}_c^{\mathsf{T}} \boldsymbol{\phi}_c(\boldsymbol{x}, \boldsymbol{y}_c)) \tag{4.142}$$

Hence the log likelihood becomes

$$\ell(\boldsymbol{\theta}) \triangleq \frac{1}{N} \sum_n \log p(\boldsymbol{y}_n|\boldsymbol{x}_n, \boldsymbol{\theta}) = \frac{1}{N} \sum_n \left[\sum_c \boldsymbol{\theta}_c^{\mathsf{T}} \boldsymbol{\phi}_c(\boldsymbol{y}_{nc}, \boldsymbol{x}_n) - \log Z(\boldsymbol{x}_n; \boldsymbol{\theta}) \right] \tag{4.143}$$

where

$$Z(\boldsymbol{x}_n; \boldsymbol{\theta}) = \sum_{\boldsymbol{y}} \exp(\boldsymbol{\theta}^{\mathsf{T}} \boldsymbol{\phi}(\boldsymbol{y}, \boldsymbol{x}_n)) \tag{4.144}$$

is the partition function for example n.

We know from Section 2.4.3 that the derivative of the log partition function yields the expected sufficient statistics, so the gradient of the log likelihood can be written as follows:

$$\frac{\partial \ell}{\partial \boldsymbol{\theta}_c} = \frac{1}{N} \sum_n \left[\boldsymbol{\phi}_c(\boldsymbol{y}_{nc}, \boldsymbol{x}_n) - \frac{\partial}{\partial \boldsymbol{\theta}_c} \log Z(\boldsymbol{x}_n; \boldsymbol{\theta}) \right] \tag{4.145}$$

$$= \frac{1}{N} \sum_n \left[\boldsymbol{\phi}_c(\boldsymbol{y}_{nc}, \boldsymbol{x}_n) - \mathbb{E}_{p(\boldsymbol{y}|\boldsymbol{x}_n, \boldsymbol{\theta})} \left[\boldsymbol{\phi}_c(\boldsymbol{y}, \boldsymbol{x}_n) \right] \right] \tag{4.146}$$

Since the objective is convex, we can use a variety of solvers to find the MLE, such as the stochastic meta descent method of [Vis+06], which is a variant of SGD where the stepsize is adapted automatically.

4.4.3.2 General case

In the general case, a CRF can be written as follows:

$$p(\boldsymbol{y}|\boldsymbol{x};\boldsymbol{\theta}) = \frac{\exp(f(\boldsymbol{x},\boldsymbol{y};\boldsymbol{\theta}))}{Z(\boldsymbol{x};\boldsymbol{\theta})} = \frac{\exp(f(\boldsymbol{x},\boldsymbol{y};\boldsymbol{\theta}))}{\sum_{\boldsymbol{y}'}\exp(f(\boldsymbol{x},\boldsymbol{y}';\boldsymbol{\theta}))} \tag{4.147}$$

where $f(\boldsymbol{x},\boldsymbol{y};\boldsymbol{\theta})$ is a scoring (negative energy) function, where high scores correspond to probable configurations. The gradient of the log likelihood is

$$\nabla_{\boldsymbol{\theta}}\ell(\boldsymbol{\theta}) = \frac{1}{N}\sum_{n=1}^{N}\nabla_{\boldsymbol{\theta}}f(\boldsymbol{x}_n,\boldsymbol{y}_n;\boldsymbol{\theta}) - \nabla_{\boldsymbol{\theta}}\log Z(\boldsymbol{x}_n;\boldsymbol{\theta}) \tag{4.148}$$

Computing derivatives of the log partition function is tractable provided we can compute the corresponding expectations, as we discuss in Section 4.3.9.2. Note, however, that we need to compute these derivatives for every training example, which is slower than the MRF case, where the log partition function is a constant independent of the observed data (but dependent on the model parameters).

4.4.4 Other approaches to structured prediction

Many other approaches to structured prediction have been proposed, going beyond CRFs. For example, **max margin Markov networks** [TGK03], and the closely relayed **structural support vector machine** [Tso+05], can be seen as non-probabilistic alternatives to CRFs. More recently, [BYM17] proposed **structured prediction energy networks**, which are a form of energy based model (Chapter 24), where we predict using an optimization procedure, $\hat{\boldsymbol{y}}(\boldsymbol{x}) = \operatorname{argmin}\mathcal{E}(\boldsymbol{x},\boldsymbol{y})$. In addition, it is common to use graph neural networks (Section 16.3.6) and sequence-to-sequence models such as transformers (Section 16.3.5) for this task.

4.5 Comparing directed and undirected PGMs

In this section, we compare DPGMs and UPGMs in terms of their modeling power, we discuss how to convert from one to the other, and we and present a unified representation.

4.5.1 CI properties

Which model has more "expressive power", a DPGM or a UPGM? To formalize the question, recall from Section 4.2.4 that G is an I-map of a distribution p if $I(G) \subseteq I(p)$, meaning that all the CI statements encoded by the graph G are true of the distribution p. Now define G to be **perfect map** of p if $I(G) = I(p)$, in other words, the graph can represent all (and only) the CI properties of the distribution. It turns out that DPGMs and UPGMs are perfect maps for different sets of distributions (see Figure 4.36). In this sense, neither is more powerful than the other as a representation language.

As an example of some CI relationships that can be perfectly modeled by a DPGM but not a UPGM, consider a v-structure $A \rightarrow C \leftarrow B$. This asserts that $A \perp B$, and $A \not\perp B|C$. If we drop the arrows, we get $A - C - B$, which asserts $A \perp B|C$ and $A \not\perp B$, which is not consistent with the independence statements encoded by the DPGM. In fact, there is no UPGM that can precisely

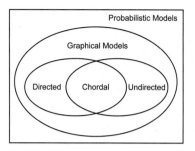

Figure 4.36: DPGMs and UPGMs can perfectly represent different sets of distributions. Some distributions can be perfectly represented by either DPGM's or UPGMs; the corresponding graph must be chordal.

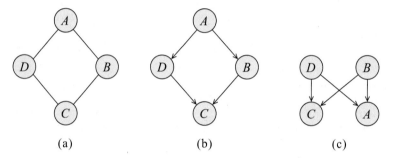

Figure 4.37: A UPGM and two failed attempts to represent it as a DPGM. From Figure 3.10 of [KF09a]. Used with kind permission of Daphne Koller.

represent all and only the two CI statements encoded by a v-structure. In general, CI properties in UPGMs are monotonic, in the following sense: if $A \perp B|C$, then $A \perp B|(C \cup D)$. But in DPGMs, CI properties can be non-monotonic, since conditioning on extra variables can eliminate conditional independencies due to explaining away.

As an example of some CI relationships that can be perfectly modeled by a UPGM but not a DPGM, consider the 4-cycle shown in Figure 4.37(a). One attempt to model this with a DPGM is shown in Figure 4.37(b). This correctly asserts that $A \perp C|B, D$. However, it incorrectly asserts that $B \perp D|A$. Figure 4.37(c) is another incorrect DPGM: it correctly encodes $A \perp C|B, D$, but incorrectly encodes $B \perp D$. In fact there is no DPGM that can precisely represent all and only the CI statements encoded by this UPGM.

Some distributions can be perfectly modeled by either a DPGM or a UPGM; the resulting graphs are called **decomposable** or **chordal**. Roughly speaking, this means the following: if we collapse together all the variables in each maximal clique, to make "mega-variables", the resulting graph will be a tree. Of course, if the graph is already a tree (which includes chains as a special case), it will already be chordal.

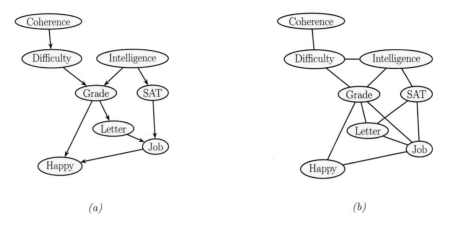

Figure 4.38: Left: the full student DPGM. Right: the equivalent UPGM. We add moralization arcs D-I, G-J, and L-S. Adapted from Figure 9.8 of [KF09a].

4.5.2 Converting between a directed and undirected model

Although DPGMs and UPGMs are not in general equivalent, if we are willing to allow the graph to encode fewer CI properties than may strictly hold, then we can safely convert one to the other, as we explain below.

4.5.2.1 Converting a DPGM to a UPGM

We can easily convert a DPGM to a UPGM as follows. First, any "unmarried" parents that share a child must get "married", by adding an edge between them; this process is known as **moralization**. Then we can drop the arrows, resulting in an undirected graph. The reason we need to do this is to ensure that the CI properties of the UGM match those of the DGM, as explained in Section 4.3.6.2. It also ensures there is a clique that can "store" the CPDs of each family.

Let us consider an example from [KF09a]. We will use the (full version of the student network shown in Figure 4.38(a). The corresponding joint has the following form:

$$P(C, D, I, G, S, L, J, H) \tag{4.149}$$
$$= P(C)P(D|C)P(I)P(G|I, D)P(S|I)P(L|G)P(J|L, S)P(H|G, J) \tag{4.150}$$

Next, we define a potential or factor for every CPD, yielding

$$p(C, D, I, G, S, L, J, H) = \psi_C(C)\psi_D(D, C)\psi_I(I)\psi_G(G, I, D) \tag{4.151}$$
$$\psi_S(S, I)\psi_L(L, G)\psi_J(J, L, S)\psi_H(H, G, J) \tag{4.152}$$

All the potentials are **locally normalized**, since they are CPDs, and hence there is no need for a global normalization constant, so $Z = 1$. The corresponding undirected graph is shown in Figure 4.38(b). We see that we have added D-I, G-J, and L-S moralization edges.[11]

---

11. We will see this example again in Section 9.5, where we use it to illustrate the variable elimination inference algorithm.

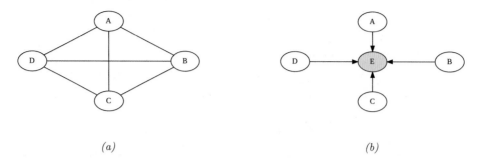

(a)   *(b)*

Figure 4.39: (a) An undirected graphical model. (b) A directed equivalent, obtained by adding a dummy observed child node.

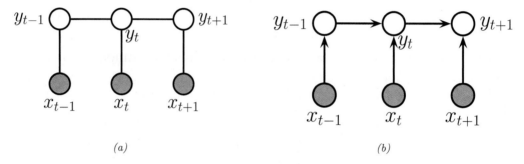

(a)   *(b)*

Figure 4.40: Two discriminative models for sequential data. (a) An undirected model (CRF). (b) A directed model (MEMM).

4.5.2.2   Converting a UPGM to a DPGM

To convert a UPGM to a DPGM, we proceed as follows. For each potential function $\psi_c(\boldsymbol{x}_c; \boldsymbol{\theta}_c)$, we create a "dummy node", call it Y_c, which is "clamped" to a special observed state, call it y_c^*. We then define $p(Y_c = y_c^* | \boldsymbol{x}_c) = \psi_c(\boldsymbol{x}_c; \boldsymbol{\theta}_c)$. This "local evidence" CPD encodes the same factor as in the DGM. The overall joint has the form $p_{\text{undir}}(\boldsymbol{x}) \propto p_{\text{dir}}(\boldsymbol{x}, \boldsymbol{y}^*)$.

As an example, consider the UPGM in Figure 4.39(a), which defines the joint $p(A, B, C, D) = \psi(A, B, C, D)/Z$. We can represent this as a DPGM by adding a dummy E node, which is a child of all the other nodes. We set $E = 1$ and define the CPD $p(E = 1 | A, B, C, D) \propto \psi(A, B, C, D)$. By conditioning on this observed child, all the parents become dependent, as in the UGM.

4.5.3   Conditional directed vs undirected PGMs and the label bias problem

Directed and undirected models behave somewhat differently in the conditional (discriminative) setting. As an example of this, let us compare the 1d undirected CRF in Figure 4.40a with the directed Markov chain in Figure 4.40b. (This latter model is called a maximum entropy Markov model

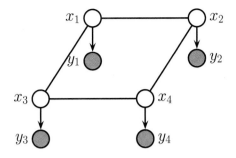

Figure 4.41: A grid-structured MRF with hidden nodes x_i and local evidence nodes y_i. The prior $p(\boldsymbol{x})$ is an undirected Ising model, and the likelihood $p(\boldsymbol{y}|\boldsymbol{x}) = \prod_i p(y_i|x_i)$ is a directed fully factored model.

(MEMM), which is a reference to the connection with maxent models discussed in Section 4.3.4.) The MEMM suffers from a subtle problem compared to the CRF known (rather obscurely) as the **label bias** problem [LMP01]. The problem is that local features at time t do not influence states prior to time t. That is, $y_{t-1} \perp \boldsymbol{x}_t | y_t$, thus blocking information flow backwards in time.

To understand what this means in practice, consider the part of speech tagging task which we discussed in Section 4.4.1.1. Suppose we see the word "banks"; this could be a verb (as in "he banks at Chase"), or a noun (as in "the river banks were overflowing"). Locally the part of speech tag for the word is ambiguous. However, suppose that later in the sentence, we see the word "fishing"; this gives us enough context to infer that the sense of "banks" is "river banks" and not "financial banks". However, in an MEMM the "fishing" evidence will not flow backwards, so we will not be able to infer the correct label for "banks". The CRF does not have this problem.

The label bias problem in MEMMs occurs because directed models are **locally normalized**, meaning each CPD sums to 1. By contrast, MRFs and CRFs are **globally normalized**, which means that local factors do not need to sum to 1, since the partition function Z, which sums over all joint configurations, will ensure the model defines a valid distribution.

However, this solution comes at a price: in a CRF, we do not get a valid probability distribution over $\boldsymbol{y}_{1:T}$ until we have seen the whole sentence, since only then can we normalize over all configurations. Consequently, CRFs are not as useful as directed probabilistic graphical models (DPGM) for online or real-time inference. Furthermore, the fact that Z is a function of all the parameters makes CRFs less modular and much slower to train than DPGM's, as we discuss in Section 4.4.3.

4.5.4 Combining directed and undirected graphs

We can also define graphical models that contain directed and undirected edges. We discuss a few examples below.

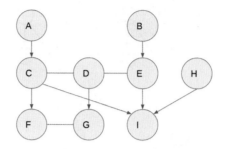

Figure 4.42: A partially directed acyclic graph (PDAG). The chain components are $\{A\}$, $\{B\}$, $\{C, D, E\}$, $\{F, G\}$, $\{H\}$, and $\{I\}$. Adapted from Figure 4.15 of [KF09a].

4.5.4.1   Chain graphs

A **chain graph** is a PGM which may have both directed and undirected edges, but without any directed cycles. A simple example is shown in Figure 4.41, which defines the following joint model:

$$p(\boldsymbol{x}_{1:D}, \boldsymbol{y}_{1:D}) = p(\boldsymbol{x}_{1:D})p(\boldsymbol{y}_{1:D}|\boldsymbol{x}_{1:D}) = \left[\frac{1}{Z} \prod_{i \sim j} \psi_{ij}(x_i, x_j) \right] \left[\prod_{i=1}^{D} p(y_i|x_i) \right] \tag{4.153}$$

In this example, the prior $p(\boldsymbol{x})$ is specified by a UPGM, and the likelihood $p(\boldsymbol{y}|\boldsymbol{x})$ is specified as a fully factorized DPGM.

More generally, a chain graph can be defined in terms of a **partially directed acyclic graph** (**PDAG**). This is a graph which can be decomposed into a directed graph of **chain components**, where the nodes within each chain component are connected with each other only with undirected edges. See Figure 4.42 for an example.

We can use a PDAG to define a joint distribution using $\prod_i p(C_i|\text{pa}(C_i))$, where each C_i is a chain component, and each CPD is a conditional random field. For example, referring to Figure 4.42, we have

$$p(A, B, ..., I) = p(A)p(B)p(C, D, E|A, B)p(F, G|C, D)p(H)p(I|C, E, H) \tag{4.154}$$

$$p(C, D, E|A, B) = \frac{1}{Z(A, B)} \phi(A, C)\phi(B, E)\phi(C, D)\phi(D, E) \tag{4.155}$$

$$p(F, G|C, D) = \frac{1}{Z(C, D)} \phi(F, C)\phi(G, D)\phi(F, G) \tag{4.156}$$

For more details, see e.g., [KF09a, Sec 4.6.2].

4.5.4.2   Acyclic directed mixed graphs

One can show [Pea09b, p51] that every latent variable DPGM can be rewritten in a way such that every latent variable is a root node with exactly two observed children. This is called the **projection** of the latent variable PGM, and is observationally indistinguishable from the original model.

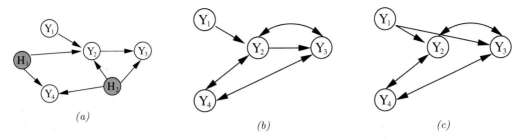

Figure 4.43: (a) A DAG with two hidden variables (shaded). (b) The corresponding ADMG. The bidirected edges reflect correlation due to the hidden variable. (c) A Markov equivalent ADMG. From Figure 3 of [SG09]. Used with kind permission of Ricardo Silva.

Each such latent variable root node induces a dependence between its two children. We can represent this with a directed arc. The resulting graph is called an **acyclic directed mixed graph** or **ADMG**. See Figure 4.43 for an example. (A **mixed graph** is one with undirected, unidirected, and bidirected edges.)

One can determine CI properties of ADMGs using a technique called **m-separation** [Ric03]. This is equivalent to d-separation in a graph where every bidirected edge $Y_i \leftrightarrow Y_j$ is replaced by $Y_i \leftarrow X_{ij} \rightarrow Y_j$, where X_{ij} is a hidden variable for that edge.

The most common example of ADMGs is when everything is linear-Gaussian. This is known as a structural equation model and is discussed in Section 4.7.2.

4.5.5 Comparing directed and undirected Gaussian PGMs

In this section, we compare directed and undirected Gaussian graphical models. In Section 4.2.3, we saw that directed GGMs correspond to sparse regression matrices. In Section 4.3.5, we saw that undirected GGMs correspond to sparse precision matrices.

The advantage of the DAG formulation is that we can make the regression weights $\mathbf{W}$, and hence $\boldsymbol{\Sigma}$, be conditional on covariate information [Pou04], without worrying about positive definite constraints. The disadavantage of the DAG formulation is its dependence on the order, although in certain domains, such as time series, there is already a natural ordering of the variables.

It is actually possible to combine both directed and undirected representations, resulting in a model known as a (Gaussian) **chain graph**. For example, consider a discrete-time, second-order Markov chain in which the observations are continuous, $\boldsymbol{x}_t \in \mathbb{R}^D$. The transition function can be represented as a (vector-valued) linear-Gaussian CPD:

$$p(\boldsymbol{x}_t|\boldsymbol{x}_{t-1}, \boldsymbol{x}_{t-2}, \boldsymbol{\theta}) = \mathcal{N}(\boldsymbol{x}_t|\mathbf{A}_1\boldsymbol{x}_{t-1} + \mathbf{A}_2\boldsymbol{x}_{t-2}, \boldsymbol{\Sigma}) \tag{4.157}$$

This is called a **vector autoregressive** or **VAR** process of order 2. Such models are widely used in econometrics for time series forecasting.

The time series aspect is most naturally modeled using a DPGM. However, if $\boldsymbol{\Sigma}^{-1}$ is sparse, then the correlation amongst the components within a time slice is most naturally modeled using a UPGM.

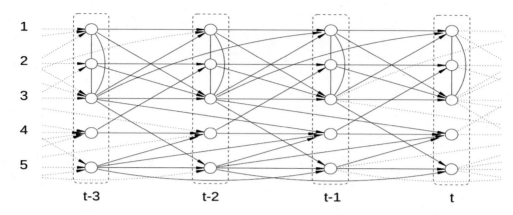

Figure 4.44: A VAR(2) process represented as a dynamic chain graph. From [DE00]. Used with kind permission of Rainer Dahlhaus.

For example, suppose we have

$$
\mathbf{A}_1 = \begin{pmatrix} \frac{3}{5} & 0 & \frac{1}{5} & 0 & 0 \\ 0 & \frac{3}{5} & 0 & -\frac{1}{5} & 0 \\ \frac{2}{5} & \frac{1}{3} & \frac{3}{5} & 0 & 0 \\ 0 & 0 & 0 & -\frac{1}{2} & \frac{1}{5} \\ 0 & 0 & \frac{1}{5} & 0 & \frac{2}{5} \end{pmatrix}, \quad \mathbf{A}_2 = \begin{pmatrix} 0 & 0 & -\frac{1}{5} & 0 & 0 \\ 0 & 0 & 0 & 0 & 0 \\ 0 & 0 & 0 & 0 & 0 \\ 0 & 0 & \frac{1}{5} & 0 & \frac{1}{3} \\ 0 & 0 & 0 & 0 & -\frac{1}{5} \end{pmatrix} \tag{4.158}
$$

and

$$
\mathbf{\Sigma} = \begin{pmatrix} 1 & \frac{1}{2} & \frac{1}{3} & 0 & 0 \\ \frac{1}{2} & 1 & -\frac{1}{3} & 0 & 0 \\ \frac{1}{3} & -\frac{1}{3} & 1 & 0 & 0 \\ 0 & 0 & 0 & 1 & 0 \\ 0 & 0 & 0 & 0 & 1 \end{pmatrix}, \quad \mathbf{\Sigma}^{-1} = \begin{pmatrix} 2.13 & -1.47 & -1.2 & 0 & 0 \\ -1.47 & 2.13 & 1.2 & 0 & 0 \\ -1.2 & 1.2 & 1.8 & 0 & 0 \\ 0 & 0 & 0 & 1 & 0 \\ 0 & 0 & 0 & 0 & 1 \end{pmatrix} \tag{4.159}
$$

The resulting graphical model is illustrated in Figure 4.44. Zeros in the transition matrices $\mathbf{A}_1$ and $\mathbf{A}_2$ correspond to absent directed arcs from $\boldsymbol{x}_{t-1}$ and $\boldsymbol{x}_{t-2}$ into $\boldsymbol{x}_t$. Zeros in the precision matrix $\mathbf{\Sigma}^{-1}$ correspond to absent undirected arcs between nodes in $\boldsymbol{x}_t$.

4.5.5.1   Covariance graphs

Sometimes we have a sparse covariance matrix rather than a sparse precision matrix. This can be represented using a **bi-directed graph**, where each edge has arrows in both directions, as in Figure 4.45(a). Here nodes that are not connected are unconditionally independent. For example in Figure 4.45(a) we see that $Y_1 \perp Y_3$. In the Gaussian case, this means $\Sigma_{1,3} = \Sigma_{3,1} = 0$. (A graph representing a sparse covariance matrix is called a **covariance graph**, see e.g., [Pen13]). By contrast, if this were an undirected model, we would have that $Y_1 \perp Y_3|Y_2$, and $\Lambda_{1,3} = \Lambda_{3,1} = 0$, where $\mathbf{\Lambda} = \mathbf{\Sigma}^{-1}$.

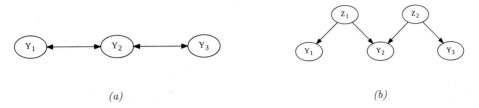

Figure 4.45: (a) A bi-directed graph. (b) The equivalent DAG. Here the z nodes are latent confounders. Adapted from Figures 5.12–5.13 of [Cho11].

A bidirected graph can be converted to a DAG with latent variables, where each bidirected edge is replaced with a hidden variable representing a hidden common cause, or **confounder**, as illustrated in Figure 4.45(b). The relevant CI properties can then be determined using d-separation.

4.6   PGM extensions

In this section, we discuss some extensions of the basic PGM framework.

4.6.1   Factor graphs

A **factor graph** [KFL01; Loe04] is a graphical representation that unifies directed and undirected models. They come in two main "flavors". The original version uses a bipartite graph, where we have nodes for random variables and nodes for factors, as we discuss in Section 4.6.1.1. An alternative form, known as a **Forney factor graphs** [For01] just has nodes for factors, and the variables are associated with edges, as we explain in Section 4.6.1.2.

4.6.1.1   Bipartite factor graphs

A **factor graph** is an undirected bipartite graph with two kinds of nodes. Round nodes represent variables, square nodes represent factors, and there is an edge from each variable to every factor that mentions it. For example, consider the MRF in Figure 4.46(a). If we assume one potential per maximal clique, we get the factor graph in Figure 4.46(b), which represents the function

$$f(x_1, x_2, x_3, x_4) = f_{124}(x_1, x_2, x_4) f_{234}(x_2, x_3, x_4) \tag{4.160}$$

We can represent this in a topologically equivalent way as in Figure 4.46(c).

One advantage of factor graphs over UPGM diagrams is that they are more fine-grained. For example, suppose we associate one potential per edge, rather than per clique. In this case, we get the factor graph in Figure 4.46(d), which represents the function

$$f(x_1, x_2, x_3, x_4) = f_{14}(x_1, x_4) f_{12}(x_1, x_2) f_{34}(x_3, x_4) f_{23}(x_2, x_3) f_{24}(x_2, x_4) \tag{4.161}$$

We can also convert a DPGM to a factor graph: just create one factor per CPD, and connect that factor to all the variables that use that CPD. For example, Figure 4.47 represents the following

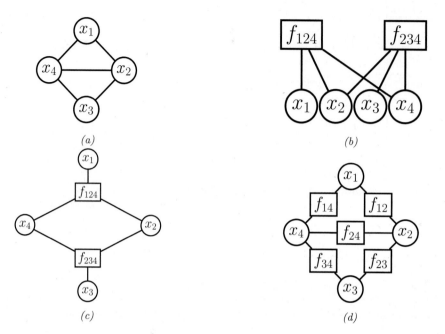

Figure 4.46: (a) A simple UPGM. (b) A factor graph representation assuming one potential per maximal clique. (c) Same as (b), but graph is visualized differently. (d) A factor graph representation assuming one potential per edge.

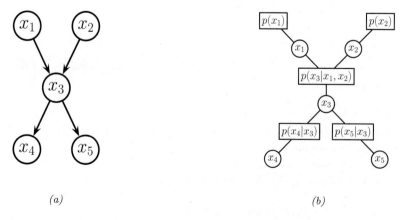

Figure 4.47: (a) A simple DPGM. (b) Its corresponding factor graph.

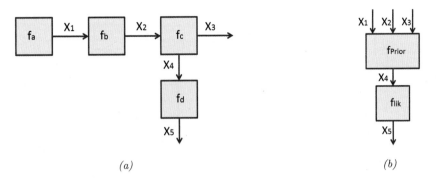

Figure 4.48: A Forney factor graph. (a) Directed version. (b) Hierarchical version.

factorization:

$$f(x_1, x_2, x_3, x_4, x_5) = f_1(x_1)f_2(x_2)f_{123}(x_1, x_2, x_3)f_{34}(x_3, x_4)f_{35}(x_3, x_5) \tag{4.162}$$

where we define $f_{123}(x_1, x_2, x_3) = p(x_3|x_1, x_2)$, etc. If each node has at most one parent (and hence the graph is a chain or simple tree), then there will be one factor per edge (root nodes can have their prior CPDs absorbed into their children's factors). Such models are equivalent to pairwise MRFs.

4.6.1.2 Forney factor graphs

A **Forney factor graph** (**FFG**), also called a **normal factor graph**, is a graph in which nodes represent factors, and edges represent variables [For01; Loe04; Loe+07; CLV19]. This is more similar to standard neural network diagrams, and electrical engineering diagrams, where signals (represented as electronic pulses, or tensors, or probability distributions) propagate along wires and are modified by functions represented as nodes.

For example, consider the following factorized function:

$$f(x_1, \ldots, x_5) = f_a(x_1)f_b(x_1, x_2)f_c(x_2, x_3, x_4)f_d(x_4, x_5) \tag{4.163}$$

We can visualize this as an FFG as in Figure 4.48a. The edge labeled x_3 is called a **half-edge**, since it is only connected to one node; this is because x_3 only participates in one factor. (Similarly for x_5.) The directionality associated with the edges is a useful mnemonic device if there is a natural order in which the variables are generated. In addition, associating directions with each edge allows us to uniquely name "messages" that are sent along each edge, which will prove useful when we discuss inference algorithms in Section 9.3.

In addition to being more similar to neural network diagrams, FFGs have the advantage over bipartite FGs in that they support hierarchical (compositional) construction, in which complex dependency structure between variables can be represented as a blackbox, with the input/output interface being represented by edges corresponding to the variables exposed by the blackbox. See Figure 4.48b for an example, which represents the function

$$f(x_1, \ldots, x_5) = f_{\text{prior}}(x_1, x_2, x_3, x_4)f_{\text{lik}}(x_4, x_5) \tag{4.164}$$

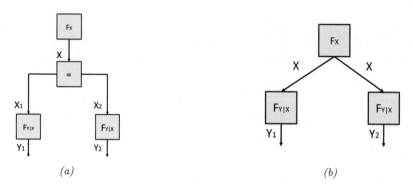

Figure 4.49: An FFG with an equality constraint node (left) and its corresponding simplified form (right).

The factor f_{prior} represents a (potentially complex) joint distribution $p(x_1, x_2, x_3, x_4)$, and the factor f_{lik} represents the likelihood term $p(x_5|x_4)$. Such models are widely used to build error-correcting codes (see Section 9.4.8).

To allow for variables to participate in more than 2 factors, equality constraint nodes are introduced, as illustrated in Figure 4.49(a). Formally, this is a factor defined as follows:

$$f_=(x, x_1, x_2) = \delta(x - x_1)\delta(x - x_2) \tag{4.165}$$

where $\delta(u)$ is a Dirac delta if u is continuous, and a Kronecker delta if u is discrete. The effect of this factor is to ensure all the variables connected to the factor have the same value; intuitively, this factor acts like a "wire splitter". Thus the function represented in Figure 4.49(a) is equivalent to the following:

$$f(x, y_1, y_2) = f_x(x)f_{y|x}(y_1, x)f_{y|x}(y_2, x) \tag{4.166}$$

This simplified form is represented in Figure 4.49(b), where we reuse the x variable across multiple edges. We have chosen the edge orientations to reflect our interpretation of the factors $f_{y|x}(y, x)$ as likelihood terms, $p(y|x)$. We have also chosen to reuse the same $f_{y|x}$ factor for both y variables; this is an example of **parameter tying**.

4.6.2 Probabilistic circuits

A **probabilistic circuit** is a kind of graphical model that supports efficient exact inference. It includes **arithmetic circuits** [Dar03; Dar09], **sum-product networks** (SPNs) [PD11; SCPD22]. and other kinds of model.

Here we briefly describe SPNs. An SPN is a probabilistic model, based on a directed tree-structured graph, in which terminal nodes represent univariate probability distributions and non-terminal nodes represent convex combinations (weighted sums) and products of probability functions. SPNs are similar to deep mixture models, in which we combine together dimensions. SPNs leverage context-specific independence to reduce the complexity of exact inference to time that is proportional to the number of links in the graph, as opposed to the treewidth of the graph (see Section 9.5.2).

SPNs are particularly useful for tasks such as missing data imputation of tabular data (see e.g., [Cla20; Ver+19]). A recent extension of SPNs, known as **einsum networks**, is proposed in [Peh+20] (see Section 9.7.1 for details on the connection between einstein summation and PGM inference).

4.6.3   Directed relational PGMs

A Bayesian network defines a joint probability distribution over a fixed number of random variables. By using plate notation (Section 4.2.8), we can define models with certain kinds of repetitive structure, and tied parameters, but many models are not expressible in this way. For example, it is not possible to represent even a simple HMM using plate notation (see Figure 29.12). Various notational extensions of plates have been proposed to handle repeated structure (see e.g., [HMK04; Die10]) but have not been widely adopted. The problem becomes worse when we have more complex domains, involving multiple objects which interact via multiple relationships.[12] Such models are called **relational probability models** or **RPMs**. In this section, we focus on directed RPMs; see Section 4.6.4 for the undirected case.

As in first order logic, RPMs have constant symbols (representing objects), function symbols (mapping one set of constants to another), and predicate symbols (representing relations between objects). We will assume that each function has a **type signature**. To illustrate this, consider an example from [RN19, Sec 15.1], which concerns online book reviews on sites such as Amazon. Suppose there are two types of objects, Book and Customer, and the following functions and predicates:

$$\text{Honest} : \text{Customer} \to \{\text{True}, \text{False}\} \tag{4.167}$$

$$\text{Kindess} : \text{Customer} \to \{1, 2, 3, 4, 5\} \tag{4.168}$$

$$\text{Quality} : \text{Book} \to \{1, 2, 3, 4, 5\} \tag{4.169}$$

$$\text{Recommendation} : \text{Customer} \times \text{Book} \to \{1, 2, 3, 4, 5\} \tag{4.170}$$

The constant symbols refer to specific objects. To keep things simple, we assume there are two books, B_1 and B_2, and two customers, C_1 and C_2. The **basic random variables** are obtained by instantiating each function with each possible combination of objects to create a set of **ground terms**. In this example, these variables are $H(C_1)$, $Q(B_1)$, $R(C_1, B_2)$, etc. (We use the abbreviations H, K, Q and R for the functions Honest, Kindness, Quality, and Recommendation.[13])

We now need to specify the (conditional) distribution over these random variables. We define these distributions in terms of the generic indexed form of the variables, rather than the specific ground form. For example, we may use the following priors for the root nodes (variables with no parents):

$$H(c) \sim \text{Cat}(0.99, 0.01) \tag{4.171}$$

$$K(c) \sim \text{Cat}(0.1, 0.1, 0.2, 0.3, 0.3) \tag{4.172}$$

$$Q(b) \sim \text{Cat}(0.05, 0.2, 0.4, 0.2, 0.15) \tag{4.173}$$

For the recommendation nodes, we need to define a conditional distribution of the form

$$R(c, b) \sim \text{RecCPD}(H(c), K(c), Q(b)) \tag{4.174}$$

---

12. See e.g., this blog post from Rob Zinkov: https://www.zinkov.com/posts/2013-07-28-stop-using-plates.
13. A unary function of an object that returns a basic type, such as Boolean or an integer, is often called an **attribute** of that object.

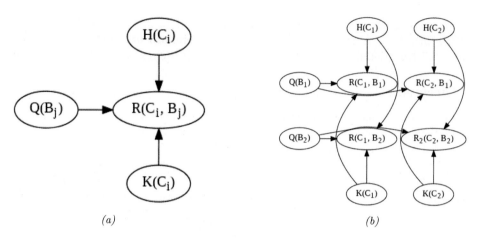

Figure 4.50: RPM for the book review domain. (a) Template for a generic customer C_i and book B_j pair. R is rating, Q is quality, H is honesty, and K is kindness. (b) Unrolled model for 2 books and 2 customers.

where RecCPD is the conditional probability distribution (CPD) for the recommendation node. If represented as a conditional probability table (CPT), this has $2 \times 5 \times 5 = 50$ rows, each with 5 entries. This table can encode our assumptions about what kind of ratings a book receives based on the quality of the book, but also properties of the reviewer, such as their honest and kindness. (More sophisticated models of human raters in the context of crowd-sourced data collection can be found in e.g., [LRC19].)

We can convert the above formulae into a graphical model "**template**", as shown in Figure 4.50a. Given a set of objects, we can "**unroll**" the template to create a "**ground network**", as shown in Figure 4.50b. There are $C \times B + 2C + B$ random variables, with a corresponding joint state space (set of **possible worlds**) of size $2^C 5^{C+B+BC}$, which can get quite large. However, if we are only interested in answering specific queries, we can dynamically unroll small pieces of the network that are relevant to that query [GC90; Bre92].

Let us assume that only a subset of the $R(c, b)$ entries are observed, and we would like to predict the missing entries of this matrix. This is essentially a simplified **recommender system**. (Unfortunately it ignores key aspects of the problem, such as the content/topic of the books, and the interests/preferences of the customers.) We can use standard probabilistic inference methods for graphical models (which we discuss in Chapter 9) to solve this problem.

Things get more interesting when we don't know which objects are being referred to. For example, customer C_1 might write a review of a book called "Probabilistic Machine Learning", but do they mean edition 1 (B_1) or edition 2 (B_2)? To handle this kind of **relational uncertainty**, we can add all possible referents as parents to each relation. This is illustrated in Figure 4.51, where now $Q(B_1)$ and $Q(B_2)$ are both parents of $R(C_1, B_1)$. This is necessary because their review score might either depend on $Q(B_1)$ or $Q(B_2)$, depending on which edition they are writing about. To disambiguate this, we create a new variable, $L(C_i)$, which specifies which version number of each book customer i is referring to. The new CPD for the recommendation node, $p(R(c, b)|H(c), K(c), Q(1 : B), L(c))$,

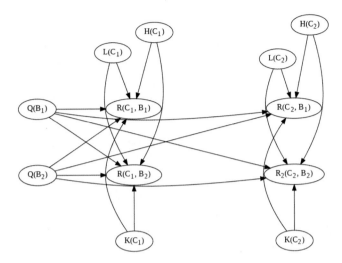

Figure 4.51: An extension of the book review RPM to handle identity uncertainty about which book a given customer is actually reviewing. The $R(c, b)$ node now depends on all books, since we don't know which one is being referred to. We can select one of these parents based on the mapping specified by the user's library, $L(c)$.

has the form

$$R(c, b) \sim \text{RecCPT}(H(c), K(c), Q(b')) \text{ where } b' = L(c) \tag{4.175}$$

This CPD acts like a **multiplexer**, where the $L(c)$ node specifies which of the parents $Q(1 : B)$ to actually use.

Although the above problem may seem contrived, **identity uncertainty** is a widespread problem in many areas, such as citation analysis, credit card histories, and object tracking (see Section 4.6.5). In particular, the problem of **entity resolution** or **record linkage** — which refers to the task of mapping particular strings (such as names) to particular objects (such as people) — is a whole field of research (see e.g., https://en.wikipedia.org/wiki/Record_linkage for an overview and [SHF15] for a Bayesian approach).

4.6.4 Undirected relational PGMs

We can create **relational UGMs** in a manner which is analogous to relational DGMs (Section 4.6.3). This is particularly useful in the discriminative setting, for the same reasons that undirected CRFs are preferable to conditional DGMs (see Section 4.4).

4.6.4.1 Collective classification

As an example of a relational UGM, suppose we are interested in the problem of classifying web pages of a university into types (e.g., student, professor, admin, etc.) Obviously we can do this based on the contents of the page (e.g., words, pictures, layout, etc.) However, we might also suppose there is information in the hyper-link structure itself. For example, it might be likely for students to

Fr(A,A)	Fr(B,B)	Fr(B,A)	Fr(A,B)	Sm(A)	Sm(B)	Ca(A)	Ca(B)
1	1	0	1	1	1	1	1
1	1	0	1	1	0	0	0
1	1	0	1	1	1	0	1

Table 4.5: *Some possible joint instantiations of the 8 variables in the smoking example.*

cite professors, and professors to cite other professors, but there may be no links between admin pages and students/professors. When faced with a web page whose label is ambiguous, we can bias our estimate based on the estimated labels of its neighbors, as in a CRF. This process is known as **collective classification** (see e.g., [Sen+08]). To specify the CRF structure for a web-graph of arbitrary size and shape, we just specify a template graph and potential functions, and then unroll the template appropriately to match the topology of the web, making use of parameter tying.

4.6.4.2 Markov logic networks

One particularly popular way of specifying relational UGMs is to use **first-order logic** rather than a graphical description of the template. The result is known as a **Markov logic network** [RD06; Dom+06; DL09].

For example, consider the sentences "Smoking causes cancer" and "If two people are friends, and one smokes, then so does the other". We can write these sentences in first-order logic as follows:

$$\forall x. Sm(x) \implies Ca(x) \tag{4.176}$$
$$\forall x. \forall y. Fr(x, y) \land Sm(x) \implies Sm(y) \tag{4.177}$$

where Sm and Ca are predicates, and Fr is a relation.

It is convenient to write all formulas in **conjunctive normal form** (CNF), also known as **clausal form**. In this case, we get

$$\neg Sm(x) \lor Ca(x) \tag{4.178}$$
$$\neg Fr(x, y) \lor \neg Sm(x) \lor Sm(y) \tag{4.179}$$

The first clause can be read as "Either x does not smoke or he has cancer", which is logically equivalent to Equation (4.176). (Note that in a clause, any unbound variable, such as x, is assumed to be universally quantified.)

Suppose there are just two objects (people) in the world, Anna and Bob, which we will denote by **constant symbols** A and B. We can then create 8 binary random variables $Sm(x)$, $Ca(x)$, and $Fr(x, y)$ for $x, y \in \{A, B\}$. This defines 2^8 **possible worlds**, some of which are shown in Table 4.5.[14]

Our goal is to define a probability distribution over these joint assignments. We can do this by creating a UGM with these variables, and adding a potential function to capture each logical rule or

---

14. Note that we have not encoded the fact that Fr is a symmetric relation, so $Fr(A, B)$ and $Fr(B, A)$ might have different values. Similarly, we have the "degenerate" nodes $Fr(A)$ and $Fr(B)$, since we did not enforce $x \neq y$ in Equation (4.177). (If we add such constraints, then the model compiler, which generates the ground network, should avoid creating redundant nodes.)

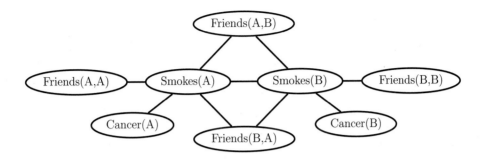

Figure 4.52: *An example of a ground Markov logic network represented as a pairwise MRF for 2 people. Adapted from Figure 2.1 from [DL09]. Used with kind permission of Pedro Domingos.*

constraint. For example, we can encode the rule $\neg Sm(x) \vee Ca(x)$ by creating a potential function $\Psi(Sm(x), Ca(x))$, where we define

$$\Psi(Sm(x), Ca(x)) = \begin{cases} 1 & \text{if } \neg Sm(x) \vee Ca(x) = T \\ 0 & \text{if } \neg Sm(x) \vee Ca(x) = F \end{cases} \tag{4.180}$$

The result is the UGM in Figure 4.52.

The above approach will assign non-zero probability to all logically valid worlds. However, logical rules may not always be true. For example, smoking does not always cause cancer. We can relax the hard constraints by using non-zero potential functions. In particular, we can associate a weight with each rule, and thus get potentials such as

$$\Psi(Sm(x), Ca(x)) = \begin{cases} e^w & \text{if } \neg Sm(x) \vee Ca(x) = T \\ e^0 & \text{if } \neg Sm(x) \vee Ca(x) = F \end{cases} \tag{4.181}$$

where the value of $w > 0$ controls strongly we want to enforce the corresponding rule.

The overall joint distribution has the form

$$p(\boldsymbol{x}) = \frac{1}{Z(\boldsymbol{w})} \exp(\sum_i w_i n_i(\boldsymbol{x})) \tag{4.182}$$

where $n_i(\boldsymbol{x})$ is the number of instances of clause i which evaluate to true in assignment $\boldsymbol{x}$.

Given a grounded MLN model, we can then perform inference using standard methods. Of course, the ground models are often extremely large, so more efficient inference methods, which avoid creating the full ground model (known as **lifted inference**), must be used. See [DL09; KNP11] for details.

One way to gain tractability is to relax the discrete problem to a continuous one. This is the basic idea behind **hinge-loss MRFs** [Bac+15b], which support exact inference using scalable convex optimization. There is a template language for this model family known as **probabilistic soft logic**, which has a similar "flavor" to MLN, although it is not quite as expressive.

Recently MLNs have been combined with DL in various ways. For example, [Zha+20f] uses graph neural networks for inference. And [WP18] uses MLNs for evidence fusion, where the noisy predictions come from DNNs trained using weak supervision.

Finally, it is worth noting one subtlety which arises with undirected models, namely that the size of the unrolled model, which depends on the number of objects in the universe, can affect the results of inference, even if we have no data about the new objects. For example, consider an undirected chain of length T, with T hidden nodes z_t and T observed nodes y_t; call this model M_1. Now suppose we double the length of the chain to $2T$, without adding more evidence; call this model M_2. We find that $p(z_t|y_{1:T}, M_1) \neq p(z_t|y_{1:T}, M_2)$, for $t = 1 : T$, even though we have not added new information, due to the different partition functions. This does not happen with a directed chain, because the newly added nodes can be marginalized out without affecting the original nodes, since the model is locally normalized and therefore modular. See [JBB09; Poo+12] for further discussion.

4.6.5 Open-universe probability models

In Section 4.6.3, we discussed relational probability models, as well as the topic of identity uncertainty. However, we also implicitly made a **closed world assumption**, namely that the set of all objects is fixed and specified ahead of time. In many real world problems, this is an unrealistic assumption. For example, in Section 29.9.3.5, we discuss the problem of tracking an unknown number of objects over time. As another example, consider the problem of enforcing the UN Comprehensive Nuclear Test Ban Treaty (CTBT). This requires monitoring seismic events, and determining if they were caused by nature or man-made explosions. Thus the number of objects of each type, as well as their source, is uncertain [ARS13],

As another (more peaceful) example, suppose we want to perform **citation matching**, in which we want to know whether to cite an arxiv version of a paper or the version on some conference website. Are these the same object? It is often hard to tell, since the titles and author might be the same, yet the content may have been updated. It is often necessary to use subtle cues, such as the date stored in the meta-data, to infer if the two "textual measurements" refer to the same underlying object (paper) or not [Pas+02].

In problems such as these, the number of objects of each type, as well as their relationships, is uncertain. This requires the use of **open-universe probability models** or **OUPM**, which can generate new objects as well as their properties [Rus15; MR10; LB19]. The first formal language for OUPMs was **BLOG** [Mil+05], which stands for "Bayesian LOGic". This used a general purpose, but slow, MCMC inference scheme to sample over possible worlds of variable size and shape. [Las08; LLC20] describes another open-universe modeling language called **multi-entity Bayesian networks**.

Very recently, Facebook has released the **Bean Machine** library, available at https://beanmachine. org/, which supports more efficient inference in OUPMs. Details can be found in [Teh+20], as well as their blog post.[15]

4.6.6 Programs as probability models

OUPMs, discussed in Section 4.6.5, let us define probability models over complex dynamic state spaces of unbounded and variable size. The set of possible worlds correspond to objects and their

---

15. See https://tinyurl.com/2svy5tmh.

attributes and relationships. Another approach is to use a **probabilistic programming language** or **PPL**, in which we define the set of possible words as the set of **execution traces** generated by the program when it is endowed with a random choice mechanism. (This is a **procedural approach** to the problem, whereas OUPMs are a **declarative approach**.)

The difference between a probabilistic programming language and a standard one was described in [Gor+14] as follows: "Probabilistic programs are usual functional or imperative programs with two added constructs: (1) the ability to draw values at random from distributions, and (2) the abiliy to condition values of variables in a program via observation". The former is a way to define $p(z, y)$, and the latter is the same as standard Bayesian conditioning $p(z|y)$.

Some recent examples of PPLs include **Gen** [CT+19], **Pyro** [Bin+19] and **Turing** [GXG18]. Inference in such models is often based on SMC, which we discuss in Chapter 13. For more details on PPLs, see e.g. [Mee+18].

4.7   Structural causal models

> While probabilities encode our beliefs about a static world, causality tells us whether and how probabilities change when the world changes, be it by intervention or by act of imagination. — Judea Pearl [PM18b].

In this section, we discuss how we can use directed graphical model notation to represent **causal models**. We discuss causality in greater detail in Chapter 36, but we introduce some basic ideas and notation here, since it is foundational material that we will need in other parts of the book.

The core idea behind causal models is to create a mechanistic model of the world in which we can reason about the effects of local changes. The canonical example is an electronic circuit: we can predict the effects of any action, such as "knocking out" a particular transistor, or changing the resistance level of a wire, by modifying the circuit locally, and then "re-running" it from the same initial conditions.

We can generalize this idea to create a **structural causal models** or **SCM** [PGJ16], also called **functional causal model** [Sch19]. An SCM is a triple $\mathcal{M} = (\mathcal{U}, \mathcal{V}, \mathcal{F})$, where $\mathcal{U} = \{U_i : i = 1 : N\}$ is a set of unexplained or **exogenous** "noise" variables, which are passed as input to the model, $\mathcal{V} = \{V_i : i = 1 : N\}$ is a set of **endogeneous** variables that are part of the model itself, and $\mathcal{F} = \{f_i : i = 1 : N\}$ is a set of deterministic functions of the form $V_i = f_i(V_{\mathrm{pa}_i}, U_i)$, where pa_i are the parents of variable i, and $U_i \in \mathcal{U}$ are the external inputs. We assume the equations can be structured in a **recursive** way, so the dependency graph of nodes given their parents is a DAG. Finally, we assume our model is **causally sufficient**, which means that $\mathcal{V}$ and $\mathcal{U}$ are all of the causally relevant factors (although they may not all be observed). This is called the "**causal Markov assumption**".

Of course, a model typically cannot represent all the variables that might influence observations or decisions. After all, models are *abstractions* of reality. The variables that we choose not to model explicitly in a functional way can be lumped into the unmodeled exogenous terms. To represent our ignorance about these terms, we can use a distribution $p(U)$ over their values. By "pushing" this external noise through the deterministic part of the model, we induce a distribution over the endogenous variables, $p(\mathcal{V})$, as in a probabilistic graphical model. However, SCMs make stronger assumptions than PGMs.

We usually assume $p(U)$ is factorized (i.e., the U_i are independent); this is called a **Markovian SCM**. If the exogeneous noise terms are not independent, it would break the assumption that

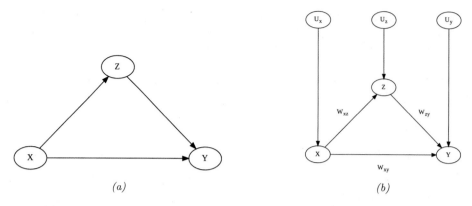

Figure 4.53: (a) PGM for modeling relationship between salary, education and debt. (b) Corresponding SCM.

outcomes can be determined locally using deterministic functions. If there are believed to be dependencies between some of the U_i, we can add extra hidden parents to represent this; this is often depicted as a bidirected or undirected edge connecting the U_i, and is known as a **semi-Markovian SCM**.

4.7.1   Example: causal impact of education on wealth

We now give a simple example of an SCM, based on [PM18b, p276]. Suppose we are interested in the causal effect of education on wealth. Let X represent the level of education of a person (on some numeric scale, say $0 = $ high school, $1 = $ college, $2 = $ graduate school), and Y represent their wealth (at some moment in time). In some cases we might expect that increasing X would increase Y (although it of course depends on the nature of the degree, the nature of the job, etc). Thus we add an edge from X to Y. However, getting more education can cost a lot of money (in certain countries), which is a potentially confounding factor on wealth. Let Z be the debt incurred by a person based on their education. We add an edge from X to Z to reflect the fact that larger X means larger Z (in general), and we add an edge from Z to Y to reflect that larger Z means lower Y (in general).

We can represent our structural assumptions graphically as shown in Figure 4.53b(a). The corresponding SCM has the form:

$$X = f_X(U_x) \tag{4.183}$$
$$Z = f_Z(X, U_z) \tag{4.184}$$
$$Y = f_Y(X, Z, U_y) \tag{4.185}$$

for some set of functions f_x, f_y, f_z, and some prior distribution $p(U_x, U_y, U_z)$. We can also explicitly represent the exogeneous noise terms as shown in Figure 4.53b(b); this makes clear our assumption that the noise terms are a priori independent. (We return to this point later.)

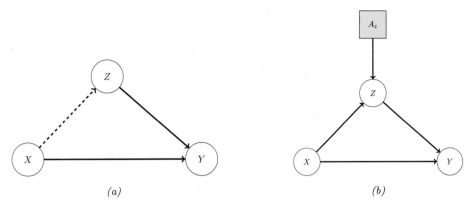

Figure 4.54: An SCM in which we intervene on Z. (a) Hard intervention, in which we clamp Z and thus cut its incoming edges (shown as dotted). (b) Soft intervention, in which we change Z's mechanism. The square node is an "action" node, using the influence diagram notation from Section 34.2.

4.7.2 Structural equation models

A **structural equation model** [Bol89; BP13], also known as a **path diagram**, is a special case of a structural causal model in which all the functional relationships are linear, and the prior on the noise terms is Gaussian. SEMs are widely used in economics and social science, due to the fact that they have a causal interpretation, yet they are computationally tractable.

For example, let us make an SEM version of our education example. We have

$$X = U_x \tag{4.186}$$
$$Z = c_z + w_{xz}X + U_z \tag{4.187}$$
$$Y = c_y + w_{xy}X + w_{zy}Z + U_y \tag{4.188}$$

If we assume $p(U_x) = \mathcal{N}(U_x|0, \sigma_x^2)$, $p(U_z) = \mathcal{N}(U_x|0, \sigma_z^2)$, and $p(U_y) = \mathcal{N}(U_x|0, \sigma_y^2)$, then the model can be converted to the following Gaussian DGM:

$$p(X) = \mathcal{N}(X|\mu_x, \sigma_x^2) \tag{4.189}$$
$$p(Z|X) = \mathcal{N}(Z|c_z + w_{xz}X, \sigma_z^2) \tag{4.190}$$
$$p(Y|X, Z) = \mathcal{N}(Y|c_y + w_{xy}X + w_{zy}Z, \sigma_y^2) \tag{4.191}$$

We can relax the linearity assumption, to allow arbitrarily flexible functions, and relax the Gaussian assumption, to allow any noise distribution. The resulting "nonparametric SEMs" are equivalent to structural causal models. (For a more detailed comparison between SEMs and SCMs, see [Pea12; BP13; Shi00b].)

4.7.3 Do operator and augmented DAGs

One of the main advantages of SCMs is that they let us predict the effect of **interventions**, which are actions that change one or more local mechanisms. A simple intervention is to force a variable to have a given value, e.g., we can force a gene to be "on" or "off". This is called a **perfect intervention** and is written as $\mathrm{do}(X_i = x_i)$, where we have introduced new notation for the **"do" operator** (as in the verb "to do"). This notation means we actively clamp variable X_i to value x_i (as opposed to just observing that it has this value). Since the value of X_i is now independent of its usual parents, we should "cut" the incoming edges to node X_i in the graph. This is called the **"graph surgery"** operation.

In Figure 4.54a we illustrate this for our education SCM, where we force Z to have a given value. For example, we may set $Z = 0$, by paying off everyone's student debt. Note that $p(X|\mathrm{do}(Z = z)) \neq p(X|Z = z)$, since the intervention changes the model. For example, if we see someone with a debt of 0, we may infer that they probably did not get higher education, i.e., $p(X \geq 1|Z = 0)$ is small; but if we pay off everyone's college loans, then observing someone with no debt in this modified world should not change our beliefs about whether they got higher education, i.e., $p(X \geq 1|\mathrm{do}(Z = 0)) = p(X \geq 1)$.

In more realistic scenarios, we may not be able to set a variable to a specific value, but we may be able to change it from its current value in some way. For example, we may be able to reduce everyone's debt by some fixed amount, say $\Delta = -10,000$. Thus we replace $Z = f_Z(X, U_z)$ with $Z = f'_z(Z, U_z)$, where $f'_z(Z, U_z) = f_z(Z, U_z) + \Delta$. This is called an **additive intervention**.

To model this kind of scenario, we can add create an **augmented DAG**, in which every variable is augmented with an additional parent node, representing whether or not the variable's mechanism is changed in some way [Daw02; Daw15; CPD17]. These extra variables are represented by square nodes, and correspond to decision variables or actions, as in the influence diagram formalism (Section 34.2). The same formalism is used in MDPs for reinforcement learning (see Section 34.5).

We give an example of this in Figure 4.54b, where we add the $A_z \in \{0, 1\}$ node to specify whether we use the debt reduction policy or not. The modified mechanism for Z becomes

$$Z = f'_Z(X, U_x, A_z) = \begin{cases} f_Z(X, U_x) & \text{if } A_z = 0 \\ f_Z(X, U_x) + \Delta & \text{if } A_z = 1 \end{cases} \tag{4.192}$$

With this new definition, conditioning on the effects of an action can be performed using standard probabilistic inference. That is, $p(Q|\mathrm{do}(A_z = a), E = e) = p(Q|A_z = a, E = e)$, where Q is the query (e.g., the event $X \geq 1$) and E are the (possibly empty) evidence variables. This is because the A_z node has no parents, so it has no incoming edges to cut when we clamp it.

Although the augmented DAG allows us to use standard notation (no explicit do operators) and inference machinery, the use of "surgical" interventions, which delete incoming edges to a node that is set to a value, results in a simpler graph, which can simplify many calculations, particularly in the non-parametric setting (see [Pea09b, p361] for a discussion). It is therefore a useful abstraction, even if it is less general than the augmented DAG approach.

4.7.4   Counterfactuals

So far we have been focused on predicting the **effects of causes**, so we can choose the optimal action (e.g., if I have a headache, I have to decide should I take an aspirin or not). This can be tackled using standard techniques from Bayesian decision theory, as we have seen (see [Daw00; Daw15; LR19; Roh21; DM22] for more details).

Now suppose we are interested in the **causes of effects**. For example, suppose I took the aspirin and my headache did go away. I might be interested in the **counterfactual question** "if I had not

Level	Activity	Questions	Examples
1:Association. $p(Y\|a)$	Seeing	How would seeing A change my belief in Y?	Someone took aspirin, how likely is it their headache will be cured?
2:Intervention. $p(Y\|\mathrm{do}(a))$	Doing	What if I do A?	If I take aspirin, will my headache be cured?
3:Counterfactuals. $p(Y^a\|\mathrm{do}(a'),y')$	Imagining	Was it A that caused Y?	Would my headache be cured had I not taken aspirin?

Table 4.6: *Pearl's causal hierarchy. Adapted from Table 1 of [Pea19].*

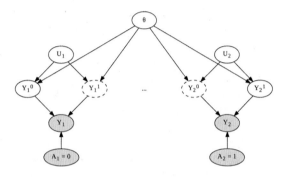

Figure 4.55: *Illustration of the potential outcomes framework as a SCM. The nodes with dashed edges are unobserved. In this example, for unit 1, we select action $A_1 = 0$ and observe $Y_1 = Y_1^0 = y_1$, whereas for unit 2, we select action $A_2 = 1$ and observe $Y_2 = Y_2^1 = y_2$.*

taken the aspirin, would my headache have gone away anyway?". This kind of reasoning is crucial for legal reasoning (see e.g., [DMM17]), as well as for tasks like explainability and fairness.

Counterfactual reasoning requires strictly more assumptions than reasoning about interventions (see e.g., [DM22]). Indeed, Judea Pearl has proposed what he calls the **causal hierarchy** [Pea09b; PGJ16; PM18b], which has three levels of analysis, each more powerful than the last, but each making stronger assumptions. See Table 4.6 for a summary.

In counterfactual reasoning, we want to answer questions of the type $p(Y^{a'}|\mathrm{do}(a),y)$, which is read as: "what is the probability distribution over outcomes Y *if I were to do a'*, given that I have already done a and observed outcome y". (We can also condition on any other evidencee that was observed, such as covariates x.) The quantity $Y^{a'}$ is often called a **potential outcome** [Rub74], since it is the outcome that would occur in a hypothetical world in which you did a' instead of a. (Note that $p(Y^{a'} = y)$ is equivalent to $p(Y = y|\mathrm{do}(a'))$, and is an interventional prediction, not a counterfactual one.)

The assumptions behind the potential outcomes framework can be clearly expressed using a structural causal model. We illustrate this in Figure 4.55 for a simple case where there are two possible actions. We see that we have a set of "**units**", such as individual patients, indexed by subscripts. Each unit is associated with a hidden exogenous random noise source, U_i, that captures everything that is unique about that unit. This noise gets deterministically mapped to two potential outcomes, Y_i^0 and Y_i^1, depending on which action is taken. For any given unit, we only get to observe one of the outcomes, namely the one corresponding to the action that was actually chosen.   In Figure 4.55, unit 1 chooses action $A_1 = 0$, so we get to see $Y_1^0 = y_1$, whereas unit 2 chooses action $A_2 = 1$, so we get to see $Y_2^1 = y_2$. The fact that we cannot simultaneously see both outcomes for the same unit is called the "**fundamental problem of causal inference**" [Hol86].

We will assume the noise sources are independent, which is known as the "stable unit treatment value assumption" or **SUTVA**. (This would not be true if the treatment on person j could somehow affect the outcome of person i, e.g., due to spreading disease or information between i and j.) We also assume that the determinsistic mechanisms that map noise to outcomes are the same across all units (represented by the shared parameter vector $\boldsymbol{\theta}$ in Figure 4.55). We need to make one final assumption, namely that the exogeneous noise is not affected by our actions. (This is a formalization of the assumption known as "all else being equal", or (in legal terms) "**ceteris paribus**".)

With the above assumptions, we can predict what the outcome *for an individual unit* would have been in the alternative universe where we picked the other action. The procedure is as follows. First we perform **abduction** using SCM G, to infer $p(U_i | A_i = a, Y_i = y_i)$, which is the posterior over the latent factors for unit i given the observed evidence in the actual world. Second we perform **intervention**, in which we modify the causal mechanisms of G by replacing $A_i = a$ with $A_i = a'$ to get $G_{a'}$. Third we perform **prediction**, in which we propagate the distribution of the latent factors, $p(U_i | A_i = a, Y_i = y_i)$, through the modified SCM $G_{a'}$ to get $p(Y_i^{a'} | A_i = a, Y_i = y_i)$.

In Figure 4.55, we see that we have two copies of every possible outcome variable, to represent the set of possible worlds. Of course, we only get to see one such world, based on the actions that we actually took. More generally, a model in which we "clone" all the deterministic variables, with the noise being held constant between the two branches of the graph for the same unit, is called a **twin network** [Pea09b]. We will see a more practical example in Section 29.12.6, where we discuss assessing the counterfactual causal impact of an intervention in a time series. (See also [RR11; RR13], who propose a related formalism known as **single world intervention graph** or **SWIG**.)

We see from the above that the potential outcomes framework is mathematically equivalent to structural causal models, but does not use graphical model notation. This has led to heated debate between the founders of the two schools of thought.[16]. The SCM approach is more popular in computer science (see e.g., [PJS17; Sch19; Sch+21b]), and the PO approach is more popular in economics (see e.g., [AP09; Imb19]). Modern textbooks on causality usually use both formalisms (see e.g., [HR20a; Nea20]).

---

16. The potential outcomes framework is based on the work of Donald Rubin, and others, and is therefore sometimes called the **Rubin causal model** (see e.g., https://en.wikipedia.org/wiki/Rubin_causal_model). The structural causal models framework is based on the work of Judea Pearl and others. See e.g., http://causality.cs.ucla.edu/blog/index.php/2012/12/03/judea-pearl-on-potential-outcomes/ for a discussion of the two.

5 Information theory

Machine learning is fundamentally about **information processing**. But what is information anyway, and wow do we measure it? Ultimately we need a way to quantify the magnitude of an update from one set of beliefs to another. It turns out that with a relatively short list of desiderata there is a unique answer: the Kullback-Leibler (KL) divergence (see Section 5.1). We'll study the properties of the KL divergence and two special cases: entropy (Section 5.2, and mutual information (Section 5.3). that are useful enough to merit independent study. We then go on to briefly discuss two main applications of information theory. The first application is **data compression** or **source coding**, which is the problem of removing redundancy from data so it can be represented more compactly, either in a lossless way (e.g., ZIP files) or a lossy way (e.g., MP3 files). See Section 5.4 for details. The second application is **error correction** or **channel coding**, which means encoding data in such a way that it is robust to errors when sent over a noisy channel, such as a telephone line or a satellite link. See Section 5.5 for details.

It turns out that methods for data compression and error correction both rely on having an accurate probabilistic model of the data. For compression, a probabilistic model is needed so the sender can assign shorter **codewords** to data vectors which occur most often, and hence save space. For error correction, a probabilistic model is needed so the receiver can infer the most likely source message by combining the received noisy message with a prior over possible messages.

It is clear that probabilistic machine learning is useful for information theory. However, information theory is also useful for machine learning. Indeed, we have seen that Bayesian machine learning is about representing and reducing our uncertainty, and so is fundamentally about information. In Section 5.6.2, we explore this direction in more detail, where we discuss the information bottleneck.

For more information on information theory, see e.g., [Mac03; CT06].

5.1 KL divergence

This section is written with Alex Alemi.

To discuss information theory, we need some way to measure or quantify information itself. Let's say we start with some distribution describing our degrees of belief about a random variable, call it $q(x)$. We then want to update our degrees of belief to some new distribution $p(x)$, perhaps because we've taken some new measurements or merely thought about the problem a bit longer. What we seek is a mathematical way to quantify the magnitude of this update, which we'll denote $I[p\|q]$. What sort of criteria would be reasonable for such a measure? We discuss this issue below, and then define a quantity that satisfies these criteria.

5.1.1   Desiderata

For simplicity, imagine we are describing a distribution over N possible events. In this case, the probability distribution $q(\boldsymbol{x})$ consists of N non-negative real numbers that add up to 1. To be even more concrete, imagine we are describing the random variable representing the suit of the next card we'll draw from a deck: $S \in \{\clubsuit, \spadesuit, \heartsuit, \diamondsuit\}$. Imagine we initially believe the distributions over suits to be uniform: $q = [\frac{1}{4}, \frac{1}{4}, \frac{1}{4}, \frac{1}{4}]$. If our friend told us they removed all of the red cards we could update to: $q' = [\frac{1}{2}, \frac{1}{2}, 0, 0]$. Alternatively, we might believe some diamonds changed into clubs and want to update to $q'' = [\frac{3}{8}, \frac{2}{8}, \frac{2}{8}, \frac{1}{8}]$. Is there a good way to quantify *how much* we've updated our beliefs? Which is a larger update: $q \to q'$ or $q \to q''$?

It seems desireable that any useful such measure would satisfy the following properties:

1. *continuous* in its arguments: If we slightly perturb either our starting or ending distribution, it should similarly have a small effect on the magnitude of the update. For example: $I[p\|\frac{1}{4} + \epsilon, \frac{1}{4}, \frac{1}{4}, \frac{1}{4} - \epsilon]$ should be close to $I[p\|q]$ for small ϵ, where $q = [\frac{1}{4}, \frac{1}{4}, \frac{1}{4}, \frac{1}{4}]$.

2. *non-negative*: $I[p\|q] \geq 0$ for all $p(\boldsymbol{x})$ and $q(\boldsymbol{x})$. The magnitude of our updates are non-negative.

3. *permutation invariant*: The magnitude of the update should not depend on the order we choose for the elements of $\boldsymbol{x}$. For example, it shouldn't matter if I list my probabilities for the suits of cards in the order $\clubsuit, \spadesuit, \heartsuit, \diamondsuit$ or $\clubsuit, \diamondsuit, \heartsuit, \spadesuit$, if I keep the order consistent across all of the distributions, I should get the same answer. For example: $I[a, b, c, d\|e, f, g, h] = I[a, d, c, b\|e, h, g, f]$.

4. *monotonic* for uniform distributions: While it's hard to say how large the updates in our beliefs are in general, there are some special cases for which we have a strong intuition. If our beliefs update from a uniform distribution on N elements to one that is uniform in N' elements, the information gain should be an increasing function of N and a decreasing function of N'. For instance changing from a uniform distribution on all four suits $[\frac{1}{4}, \frac{1}{4}, \frac{1}{4}, \frac{1}{4}]$ (so $N = 4$) to only one suit, such as all clubs, $[1, 0, 0, 0]$ where $N' = 1$, is a larger update than if I only updated to the card being black, $[\frac{1}{2}, \frac{1}{2}, 0, 0]$ where $N' = 2$.

5. satisfy a natural *chain rule*: So far we've been describing our beliefs in what will happen on the next card draw as a single random variable representing the suit of the next card ($S \in \{\clubsuit, \spadesuit, \heartsuit, \diamondsuit\}$). We could equivalently describe the same physical process in two steps. First we consider the random variable representing the color of the card ($C \in \{\blacksquare, \square\}$), which could be either black ($\blacksquare = \{\clubsuit, \spadesuit\}$) or red ($\square = \{\heartsuit, \diamondsuit\}$). Then, if we draw a red card we describe our belief that it is $\heartsuit$ versus $\diamondsuit$. If it was instead black we would assign beliefs to it being $\clubsuit$ versus $\spadesuit$. We can convert any distribution over the four suits into this conditional factorization, for example:

$$p(S) = \begin{bmatrix} \frac{3}{8}, \frac{2}{8}, \frac{2}{8}, \frac{1}{8} \end{bmatrix} \tag{5.1}$$

becomes

$$p(C) = \begin{bmatrix} \frac{5}{8}, \frac{3}{8} \end{bmatrix} \quad p(\{\clubsuit, \spadesuit\}|C = \blacksquare) = \begin{bmatrix} \frac{3}{5}, \frac{2}{5} \end{bmatrix} \quad p(\{\heartsuit, \diamondsuit\}|C = \square) = \begin{bmatrix} \frac{2}{3}, \frac{1}{3} \end{bmatrix}. \tag{5.2}$$

In the same way we could decompose our uniform distribution q. Obviously, for our measure of information to be of use the magnitude of the update needs to be the same regardless of how we choose to describe what is ultimately the same physical process. What we need is some way to relate what would be four different invocations of our information function:

$$I_S \equiv I\left[p(S)\|q(S)\right] \tag{5.3}$$

$$I_C \equiv I\left[p(C)\|q(C)\right] \tag{5.4}$$

$$I_\blacksquare \equiv I\left[p(\{\clubsuit, \spadesuit\}|C = \blacksquare)\|q(\{\clubsuit, \spadesuit\}|C = \blacksquare)\right] \tag{5.5}$$

$$I_\square \equiv I\left[p(\{\heartsuit, \diamondsuit\}|C = \square)\|q(\{\heartsuit, \diamondsuit\}|C = \square)\right]. \tag{5.6}$$

Clearly I_S should be some function of $\{I_C, I_\blacksquare, I_\square\}$. Our last desideratum is that the way we measure the magnitude of our updates will have I_S be a linear combination of $I_C, I_\blacksquare, I_\square$. In particular, we will require that they combine as a weighted linear combinations, with weights set by the probability that we would find ourselves in that branch according to the distribution p:

$$I_S = I_C + p(C = \blacksquare)I_\blacksquare + p(C = \square)I_\square = I_C + \frac{5}{8}I_\blacksquare + \frac{3}{8}I_\square \tag{5.7}$$

Stating this requirement more generally: If we partition $\boldsymbol{x}$ into two pieces $[\boldsymbol{x}_L, \boldsymbol{x}_R]$, so that we can write $p(\boldsymbol{x}) = p(\boldsymbol{x}_L)p(\boldsymbol{x}_R|\boldsymbol{x}_L)$ and similarly for q, the magnitude of the update should be

$$I[p(\boldsymbol{x})\|q(\boldsymbol{x})] = I[p(\boldsymbol{x}_L)\|q(\boldsymbol{x}_L)] + \mathbb{E}_{p(\boldsymbol{x}_L)}\left[I[p(\boldsymbol{x}_R|\boldsymbol{x}_L)\|q(\boldsymbol{x}_R|\boldsymbol{x}_L)]\right]. \tag{5.8}$$

Notice that this requirement *breaks the symmetry between our two distributions*: The right hand side asks us to take the expected conditional information gain with respect to the marginal, but we need to decide which of two marginals to take the expectation with respect to.

5.1.2 The KL divergence uniquely satisfies the desiderata

We will now define a quantity that is the only measure (up to a multiplicative constant) that satisfies the above desiderata. The **Kullback-Leibler divergence** or **KL divergence**, also known as the **information gain** or **relative entropy**, is defined as follows:

$$D_{\mathrm{KL}}\left(p \parallel q\right) \triangleq \sum_{k=1}^{K} p_k \log \frac{p_k}{q_k}. \tag{5.9}$$

This naturally extends to continuous distributions:

$$D_{\mathrm{KL}}\left(p \parallel q\right) \triangleq \int dx\, p(x) \log \frac{p(x)}{q(x)}. \tag{5.10}$$

Next we will verify that this definition satisfies all of our desiderata. (The proof that it is the unique measure which captures these properties can be found in, e.g., [Hob69; Rén61].)

5.1.2.1 Continuity of KL

One of our desiderata was that our measure of information gain should be continuous. The KL divergence is manifestly continuous in its arguments except potentially when p_k or q_k is zero. In the first case, notice that the limit as $p \to 0$ is well behaved:

$$\lim_{p \to 0} p \log \frac{p}{q} = 0. \tag{5.11}$$

Taking this as the definition of the value of the integrand when $p = 0$ will make it continuous there. Notice that we do have a problem however if $q = 0$ in some place that $p \neq 0$. Our information gain requires that our original distribution of beliefs q has some support everywhere the updated distribution does. Intuitively it would require an infinite amount of information for us to update our beliefs in some outcome to change from being exactly 0 to some positive value.

5.1.2.2   Non-negativity of KL divergence

In this section, we prove that the KL divergence as defined is always non-negative. We will make use of **Jensen's inequality**, which states that for any convex function f, we have that

$$f\left(\sum_{i=1}^{n} \lambda_i \boldsymbol{x}_i\right) \leq \sum_{i=1}^{n} \lambda_i f(\boldsymbol{x}_i) \tag{5.12}$$

where $\lambda_i \geq 0$ and $\sum_{i=1}^{n} \lambda_i = 1$. This can be proved by induction, where the base case with $n = 2$ follows by definition of convexity.

Theorem 5.1.1. *(Information inequality)* $D_{\mathrm{KL}}\left(p \parallel q\right) \geq 0$ *with equality iff* $p = q$.

Proof. We now prove the theorem, following [CT06, p28]. As we noted in the previous section, the KL divergence requires special consideration when $p(x)$ or $q(x) = 0$, the same is true here. Let $A = \{x : p(x) > 0\}$ be the support of $p(x)$. Using the convexity of the log function and Jensen's inequality, we have that

$$-D_{\mathrm{KL}}\left(p \parallel q\right) = -\sum_{x \in A} p(x) \log \frac{p(x)}{q(x)} = \sum_{x \in A} p(x) \log \frac{q(x)}{p(x)} \tag{5.13}$$

$$\leq \log \sum_{x \in A} p(x) \frac{q(x)}{p(x)} = \log \sum_{x \in A} q(x) \tag{5.14}$$

$$\leq \log \sum_{x \in \mathcal{X}} q(x) = \log 1 = 0 \tag{5.15}$$

Since $\log(x)$ is a strictly concave function ($-\log(x)$ is convex), we have equality in Equation (5.14) iff $p(x) = cq(x)$ for some c that tracks the fraction of the whole space $\mathcal{X}$ contained in A. We have equality in Equation (5.15) iff $\sum_{x \in A} q(x) = \sum_{x \in \mathcal{X}} q(x) = 1$, which implies $c = 1$. Hence $D_{\mathrm{KL}}\left(p \parallel q\right) = 0$ iff $p(x) = q(x)$ for all x. $\square$

The non-negativity of KL divergence often feels as though it's one of the most useful results in information theory. It is a good result to keep in your back pocket. Anytime you can rearrange an expression in terms of KL divergence terms, since those are guaranteed to be non-negative, dropping them immediately generates a bound.

5.1.2.3   KL divergence is invariant to reparameterizations

We wanted our measure of information to be invariant to permutations of the labels. The discrete form is manifestly permutation invariant as summations are. The KL divergence actually satisfies a much stronger property of reparameterization invariance. Namely, we can transform our random variable through an arbitrary invertible map and it won't change the value of the KL divergence.

If we transform our random variable from x to some $y = f(x)$ we know that $p(x)\,dx = p(y)\,dy$ and $q(x)\,dx = q(y)\,dy$. Hence the KL divergence remains the same for both random variables:

$$D_{\mathrm{KL}}\left(p(x) \parallel q(x)\right) = \int dx\, p(x) \log \frac{p(x)}{q(x)} = \int dy\, p(y) \log \left(\frac{p(y)\left|\frac{dy}{dx}\right|}{q(y)\left|\frac{dy}{dx}\right|}\right) = D_{\mathrm{KL}}\left(p(y) \parallel q(y)\right). \quad (5.16)$$

Because of this reparameterization invariance we can rest assured that when we measure the KL divergence between two distributions we are measuring something about the distributions and not the way we choose to represent the space in which they are defined. We are therefore free to transform our data into a convenient basis of our choosing, such as a Fourier bases for images, without affecting the result.

5.1.2.4 Montonicity for uniform distributions

Consider updating a probability distribution from a uniform distribution on N elements to a uniform distribution on N' elements. The KL divergence is:

$$D_{\mathrm{KL}}\left(p \parallel q\right) = \sum_k \frac{1}{N'} \log \frac{\frac{1}{N'}}{\frac{1}{N}} = \log \frac{N}{N'}, \quad (5.17)$$

or the log of the ratio of the elements before and after the update. This satisfies our monotonocity requirement.

We can interpret this result as follows: Consider finding an element of a sorted array by means of bisection. A well designed yes/no question can cut the search space in half. Measured in bits, the KL divergence tells us how many well designed yes/no questions are required on average to move from q to p.

5.1.2.5 Chain rule for KL divergence

Here we show that the KL divergence satisfies a natural chain rule:

$$D_{\mathrm{KL}}\left(p(x,y) \parallel q(x,y)\right) = \int dx\, dy\, p(x,y) \log \frac{p(x,y)}{q(x,y)} \quad (5.18)$$

$$= \int dx\, dy\, p(x,y) \left[\log \frac{p(x)}{q(x)} + \log \frac{p(y|x)}{q(y|x)}\right] \quad (5.19)$$

$$= D_{\mathrm{KL}}\left(p(x) \parallel q(x)\right) + \mathbb{E}_{p(x)}\left[D_{\mathrm{KL}}\left(p(y|x) \parallel q(y|x)\right)\right]. \quad (5.20)$$

We can rest assured that we can decompose our distributions into their conditionals and the KL divergences will just add.

As a notational convenience, the **conditional KL divergence** is defined to be the expected value of the KL divergence between two conditional distributions:

$$D_{\mathrm{KL}}\left(p(y|x) \parallel q(y|x)\right) \triangleq \int dx\, p(x) \int dy\, p(y|x) \log \frac{p(y|x)}{q(y|x)}. \quad (5.21)$$

This allows us to drop many expectation symbols.

5.1.3 Thinking about KL

In this section, we discuss some qualitative properties of the KL divergence.

5.1.3.1 Units of KL

Above we said that the desiderata we listed determined the KL divergence up to a multiplicative constant. Because the KL divergence is logarithmic, and logarithms in different bases are the same up to a multiplicative constant, our choice of the base of the logarithm when we compute the KL divergence is a choice akin to choosing which units to measure the information in.

If the KL divergence is measured with the base-2 logarithm, it is said to have units of **bits**, short for "binary digits". If measured using the natural logarithm as we normally do for mathematical convenience, it is said to be measured in **nats** for "natural units".

To convert between the systems, we use $\log_2 y = \frac{\log y}{\log 2}$. Hence

$$1 \text{ bit} = \log 2 \text{ nats} \sim 0.693 \text{ nats} \tag{5.22}$$

$$1 \text{ nat} = \frac{1}{\log 2} \text{ bits} \sim 1.44 \text{ bits}. \tag{5.23}$$

5.1.3.2 Asymmetry of the KL divergence

The KL divergence is *not* symmetric in its two arguments. While many find this asymmetry confusing at first, we can see that the asymmetry stems from our requirement that we have a natural chain rule. When we decompose the distribution into its conditional, we need to take an expectation with respect to the variables being conditioned on. In the KL divergence we take this expectation with respect to the first argument $p(x)$. This breaks the symmetry between the two distributions.

At a more intuitive level, we can see that the information required to move from q to p is in general different than the information required to move from p to q. For example, consider the KL divergence between two Bernoulli distributions, the first with the probability of success given by 0.443 and the second with 0.975:

$$D_{KL} = 0.975 \log \frac{0.975}{0.443} + 0.025 \log \frac{0.025}{0.557} = 0.692 \text{ nats} \sim 1.0 \text{ bits}. \tag{5.24}$$

So it takes 1 bit of information to update from a $[0.443, 0.557]$ distribution to a $[0.975, 0.025]$ Bernoulli distribution. What about the reverse?

$$D_{KL} = 0.443 \log \frac{0.443}{0.975} + 0.557 \log \frac{0.557}{0.025} = 1.38 \text{ nats} \sim 2.0 \text{ bits}, \tag{5.25}$$

so it takes two bits, or twice as much information to move the other way. Thus we see that starting with a distribution that is nearly even and moving to one that is nearly certain takes about 1 bit of information, or one well designed yes/no question. To instead move us from near certainty in an outcome to something that is akin to the flip of a coin requires more persuasion.

5.1.3.3 KL as expected weight of evidence

Imagine you have two different hypotheses you wish to select between, which we'll label P and Q. You collect some data D. Bayes' rule tells us how to update our beliefs in the hypotheses being correct:

$$\Pr(P|D) = \frac{\Pr(D|P)}{\Pr(D)} \Pr(P). \tag{5.26}$$

Normally this requires being able to evaluate the marginal likelihood $\Pr(D)$, which is difficult. If we instead consider the ratio of the probabilities for the two hypotheses:

$$\frac{\Pr(P|D)}{\Pr(Q|D)} = \frac{\Pr(D|P)}{\Pr(D|Q)} \frac{\Pr(P)}{\Pr(Q)}, \tag{5.27}$$

the marginal likelihood drops out. Taking the logarithm of both sides, and identifying the probability of the data under the model as the likelihood we find:

$$\log \frac{\Pr(P|D)}{\Pr(Q|D)} = \log \frac{p(D)}{q(D)} + \log \frac{\Pr(P)}{\Pr(Q)}. \tag{5.28}$$

The posterior log probability ratio for one hypothesis over the other is just our prior log probability ratio plus a term that I. J. Good called the **weight of evidence** [Goo85] D for hypothesis P over Q:

$$w[P/Q; D] \triangleq \log \frac{p(D)}{q(D)}. \tag{5.29}$$

With this interpretation, the KL divergence is the expected weight of evidence for P over Q given by each observation, provided P were correct. Thus we see that data will (on average) add rather than subtract evidence towards the correct hypothesis, since KL divergence is always non-negative in expectation (see Section 5.1.2.2).

5.1.4 Minimizing KL

In this section, we discuss ways to minimize $D_{\mathbb{KL}}(p \parallel q)$ or $D_{\mathbb{KL}}(q \parallel p)$ wrt an approximate distribution q, given a true distribution p.

5.1.4.1 Forwards vs reverse KL

The asymmetry of KL means that finding a q that is close to p by minimizing $D_{\mathbb{KL}}(p \parallel q)$ (also called the **inclusive KL** or **forwards KL**) gives different behavior than minimizing $D_{\mathbb{KL}}(q \parallel p)$ (also called the **exclusive KL** or **reverse KL**). For example, consider the bimodal distribution p shown in blue in Figure 5.1, which we approximate with a unimodal Gaussian q.

To prevent $D_{\mathbb{KL}}(p \parallel q)$ from becoming infinite, we must have $q > 0$ whenever $p > 0$ (i.e., q must have support everywhere p does), so q tends to *cover* both modes as it must be nonvanishing everywhere p is; this is called **mode-covering** or **zero-avoiding** behavior (orange curve). By contrast, to prevent $D_{\mathbb{KL}}(q \parallel p)$ from becoming infinite, we must have $q = 0$ whenever $p = 0$, which creates **mode-seeking** or **zero-forcing** behavior (green curve).

For an animated visualization (written by Ari Seff) of the difference between these two objectives, see `https://twitter.com/ari_seff/status/1303741288911638530`.

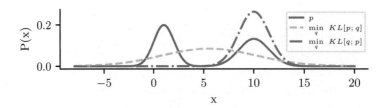

Figure 5.1: Demonstration of the mode-covering or mode-seeking behavior of KL divergence. The original distribution p (shown in blue) is bimodal. When we minimize $D_{\mathbb{KL}}(p \parallel q)$, then q covers the modes of p (orange). When we minimize $D_{\mathbb{KL}}(q \parallel p)$, then q ignores some of the modes of p (green). Generated by minimize_ kl_ divergence.ipynb.

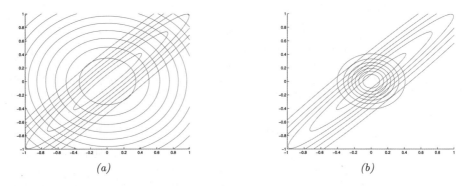

Figure 5.2: Illustrating forwards vs reverse KL on a symmetric Gaussian. The blue curves are the contours of the true distribution p. The red curves are the contours of a factorized approximation q. (a) Minimizing $D_{\mathbb{KL}}(p \parallel q)$. (b) Minimizing $D_{\mathbb{KL}}(q \parallel p)$. Adapted from Figure 10.2 of [Bis06]. Generated by kl_ pq_ gauss.ipynb.

5.1.4.2   Moment projection (mode covering)

Suppose we compute q by minimizing the forwards KL:

$$q = \underset{q}{\operatorname{argmin}}\, D_{\mathbb{KL}}(p \parallel q) \tag{5.30}$$

This is called **M-projection**, or **moment projection** since the optimal q matches the moments of p, as we show below. The process of computing q is therefore called **moment matching**.

To see why the optimal q must match the moments of p, let us assume that q is an exponential family distribution of the form

$$q(\boldsymbol{x}) = h(\boldsymbol{x}) \exp[\boldsymbol{\eta}^{\mathsf{T}} \mathcal{T}(\boldsymbol{x}) - \log Z(\boldsymbol{\eta})] \tag{5.31}$$

where $\mathcal{T}(\boldsymbol{x})$ is the vector of sufficient statistics, and $\boldsymbol{\eta}$ are the natural parameters. The first order optimality conditions are as follows:

$$\partial_{\eta_i} D_{\mathrm{KL}}(p \| q) = -\partial_{\eta_i} \int_{\boldsymbol{x}} p(\boldsymbol{x}) \log q(\boldsymbol{x}) \tag{5.32}$$

$$= -\partial_{\eta_i} \int_{\boldsymbol{x}} p(\boldsymbol{x}) \log \left(h(\boldsymbol{x}) \exp[\boldsymbol{\eta}^\mathsf{T} \mathcal{T}(\boldsymbol{x}) - \log Z(\boldsymbol{\eta})] \right) \tag{5.33}$$

$$= -\partial_{\eta_i} \int_{\boldsymbol{x}} p(\boldsymbol{x}) \left(\boldsymbol{\eta}^\mathsf{T} \mathcal{T}(\boldsymbol{x}) - \log Z(\boldsymbol{\eta}) \right) \tag{5.34}$$

$$= -\int_{\boldsymbol{x}} p(\boldsymbol{x}) \mathcal{T}_i(\boldsymbol{x}) + \mathbb{E}_{q(\boldsymbol{x})}\left[\mathcal{T}_i(\boldsymbol{x}) \right] \tag{5.35}$$

$$= -\mathbb{E}_{p(\boldsymbol{x})}\left[\mathcal{T}_i(\boldsymbol{x}) \right] + \mathbb{E}_{q(\boldsymbol{x})}\left[\mathcal{T}_i(\boldsymbol{x}) \right] = 0 \tag{5.36}$$

where in the penultimate line we used the fact that the derivative of the log partition function yields the expected sufficient statistics, as shown in Equation (2.216). Hence the expected sufficient statistics (moments of the distribution) must match.

As an example, suppose the true target distribution p is a correlated 2d Gaussian, $p(\boldsymbol{x}) = \mathcal{N}(\boldsymbol{x}|\boldsymbol{\mu}, \boldsymbol{\Sigma}) = \mathcal{N}(\boldsymbol{x}|\boldsymbol{\mu}, \boldsymbol{\Lambda}^{-1})$, where

$$\boldsymbol{\mu} = \begin{pmatrix} \mu_1 \\ \mu_2 \end{pmatrix}, \quad \boldsymbol{\Sigma} = \begin{pmatrix} \Sigma_{11} & \Sigma_{12} \\ \Sigma_{12}^\mathsf{T} & \Sigma_{22} \end{pmatrix} \quad \boldsymbol{\Lambda} = \begin{pmatrix} \Lambda_{11} & \Lambda_{12} \\ \Lambda_{12}^\mathsf{T} & \Lambda_{22} \end{pmatrix} \tag{5.37}$$

We will approximate this with a distribution q which is a product of two 1d Gaussians, i.e., a Gaussian with a diagonal covariance matrix:

$$q(\boldsymbol{x}|\boldsymbol{m}, \mathbf{V}) = \mathcal{N}(x_1|m_1, v_1)\mathcal{N}(x_2|m_2, v_2) \tag{5.38}$$

If we perform moment matching, the optimal q must therefore have the following form:

$$q(\boldsymbol{x}) = \mathcal{N}(x_1|\mu_1, \Sigma_{11})\mathcal{N}(x_2|\mu_2, \Sigma_{22}) \tag{5.39}$$

In Figure 5.2(a), we show the resulting distribution. We see that q covers (includes) p, but its support is too broad (under-confidence).

5.1.4.3   Information projection (mode seeking)

Now suppose we compute q by minimizing the reverse KL:

$$q = \operatorname*{argmin}_q D_{\mathrm{KL}}(q \| p) \tag{5.40}$$

This is called **I-projection**, or **information projection**. This optimization problem is often easier to compute, since the objective requires taking expectations wrt q, which we can choose to be a tractable family.

As an example, consider again the case where the true distribution is a full covariance Gaussian, $p(\boldsymbol{x}) = \mathcal{N}(\boldsymbol{x}|\boldsymbol{\mu}, \boldsymbol{\Lambda}^{-1})$, and let the approximation be a diagonal Gaussian, $q(\boldsymbol{x}) = \mathcal{N}(\boldsymbol{x}|\boldsymbol{m}, \operatorname{diag}(\boldsymbol{v}))$. Then one can show (see Supplementary Section 5.1.2) that the optimal variational parameters are $\boldsymbol{m} = \boldsymbol{\mu}$ and $v_i = \Lambda_{ii}^{-1}$. We illustrate this in 2d in Figure 5.2(b). We see that the posterior variance is too narrow, i.e, the approximate posterior is overconfident. Note, however, that minimizing the reverse KL does not always result in an overly compact approximation, as explained in [Tur+08].

5.1.5   Properties of KL

Below are some other useful properties of the KL divergence.

5.1.5.1   Compression lemma

An important general purpose result for the KL divergence is the **compression lemma**:

Theorem 5.1.2. *For any distributions P and Q with a well-defined KL divergence, and for any scalar function ϕ defined on the domain of the distributions we have that:*

$$\mathbb{E}_P[\phi] \leq \log \mathbb{E}_Q\left[e^\phi\right] + D_{\mathrm{KL}}(P \parallel Q). \tag{5.41}$$

Proof. We know that the KL divergence between any two distributions is non-negative. Consider a distribution of the form:

$$g(x) = \frac{q(x)}{\mathcal{Z}} e^{\phi(x)}. \tag{5.42}$$

where the *partition function* is given by:

$$\mathcal{Z} = \int dx\, q(x) e^{\phi(x)}. \tag{5.43}$$

Taking the KL divergence between $p(x)$ and $g(x)$ and rearranging gives the bound:

$$D_{\mathrm{KL}}(P \parallel G) = D_{\mathrm{KL}}(P \parallel Q) - \mathbb{E}_P[\phi(x)] + \log(\mathcal{Z}) \geq 0. \tag{5.44}$$

$\square$

One way to view the compression lemma is that it provides what is termed the Donsker-Varadhan variational representation of the KL divergence:

$$D_{\mathrm{KL}}(P \parallel Q) = \sup_\phi \mathbb{E}_P[\phi(x)] - \log \mathbb{E}_Q\left[e^{\phi(x)}\right]. \tag{5.45}$$

In the space of all possible functions ϕ defined on the same domain as the distributions, assuming all of the values above are finite, the KL divergence is the supremum achieved. For any fixed function $\phi(x)$, the right hand side provides a lower bound on the true KL divergence.

Another use of the compression lemma is that it provides a way to estimate the expectation of some function with respect to an unknown distribution P. In this spirit, the compression lemma can be used to power a set of what are known as PAC-Bayes bounds of losses with respect to the true distribution in terms of measured losses with respect to a finite training set. See for example Section 17.4.5 or Banerjee [Ban06].

5.1.5.2 Data processing inequality for KL

We now show that any processing we do on samples from two different distributions makes their samples approach one another. This is called the **data processing inequality**, since it shows that we cannot increase the information gain from q to p by processing our data and then measuring it.

Theorem 5.1.3. *Consider two different distributions $p(x)$ and $q(x)$ combined with a probabilistic channel $t(y|x)$. If $p(y)$ is the distribution that results from sending samples from $p(x)$ through the channel $t(y|x)$ and similarly for $q(y)$ we have that:*

$$D_{\mathrm{KL}}\left(p(x) \parallel q(x)\right) \geq D_{\mathrm{KL}}\left(p(y) \parallel q(y)\right) \tag{5.46}$$

Proof. The proof uses Jensen's inequality from Section 5.1.2.2 again. Call $p(x, y) = p(x)t(y|x)$ and $q(x, y) = q(x)t(y|x)$.

$$D_{\mathrm{KL}}\left(p(x) \parallel q(x)\right) = \int dx\, p(x) \log \frac{p(x)}{q(x)} \tag{5.47}$$

$$= \int dx \int dy\, p(x)t(y|x) \log \frac{p(x)t(y|x)}{q(x)t(y|x)} \tag{5.48}$$

$$= \int dx \int dy\, p(x, y) \log \frac{p(x, y)}{q(x, y)} \tag{5.49}$$

$$= -\int dy\, p(y) \int dx\, p(x|y) \log \frac{q(x, y)}{p(x, y)} \tag{5.50}$$

$$\geq -\int dy\, p(y) \log \left(\int dx\, p(x|y) \frac{q(x, y)}{p(x, y)} \right) \tag{5.51}$$

$$= -\int dy\, p(y) \log \left(\frac{q(y)}{p(y)} \int dx\, q(x|y) \right) \tag{5.52}$$

$$= \int dy\, p(y) \log \frac{p(y)}{q(y)} = D_{\mathrm{KL}}\left(p(y) \parallel q(y)\right) \tag{5.53}$$

$\square$

One way to interpret this result is that any processing done to random samples makes it harder to tell two distributions apart.

As a special form of processing, we can simply marginalize out a subset of random variables.

Corollary 5.1.1. *(Monotonicity of KL divergence)*

$$D_{\mathrm{KL}}\left(p(x, y) \parallel q(x, y)\right) \geq D_{\mathrm{KL}}\left(p(x) \parallel q(x)\right) \tag{5.54}$$

Proof. The proof is essentially the same as the one above.

$$D_{\mathrm{KL}}\left(p(x,y)\parallel q(x,y)\right) = \int dx \int dy\, p(x,y)\log\frac{p(x,y)}{q(x,y)} \tag{5.55}$$

$$= -\int dy\, p(y)\int dx\, p(x|y)\log\left(\frac{q(y)}{p(y)}\frac{q(x|y)}{p(x|y)}\right) \tag{5.56}$$

$$\geq -\int dy\, p(y)\log\left(\frac{q(y)}{p(y)}\int dx\, q(x|y)\right) \tag{5.57}$$

$$= \int dy\, p(y)\log\frac{p(y)}{q(y)} = D_{\mathrm{KL}}\left(p(y)\parallel q(y)\right) \tag{5.58}$$

$$\tag{5.59}$$

$\square$

One intuitive interpretation of this result is that if you only partially observe random variables, it is harder to distinguish between two candidate distributions than if you observed all of them.

5.1.6   KL divergence and MLE

Suppose we want to find the distribution q that is as close as possible to p, as measured by KL divergence:

$$q^* = \arg\min_q D_{\mathrm{KL}}\left(p\parallel q\right) = \arg\min_q \int p(x)\log p(x)dx - \int p(x)\log q(x)dx \tag{5.60}$$

Now suppose p is the empirical distribution, which puts a probability atom on the observed training data and zero mass everywhere else:

$$p_{\mathcal{D}}(x) = \frac{1}{N}\sum_{n=1}^{N}\delta(x - x_n) \tag{5.61}$$

Using the sifting property of delta functions we get

$$D_{\mathrm{KL}}\left(p_{\mathcal{D}}\parallel q\right) = -\int p_{\mathcal{D}}(x)\log q(x)dx + C \tag{5.62}$$

$$= -\int\left[\frac{1}{N}\sum_n\delta(x - x_n)\right]\log q(x)dx + C \tag{5.63}$$

$$= -\frac{1}{N}\sum_n\log q(x_n) + C \tag{5.64}$$

where $C = \int p_{\mathcal{D}}(x)\log p_{\mathcal{D}}(x)$ is a constant independent of q.

We can rewrite the above as follows

$$D_{\mathrm{KL}}\left(p_{\mathcal{D}}\parallel q\right) = \mathbb{H}_{ce}(p_{\mathcal{D}}, q) - \mathbb{H}(p_{\mathcal{D}}) \tag{5.65}$$

where

$$\mathbb{H}_{ce}(p,q) \triangleq -\sum_k p_k \log q_k \tag{5.66}$$

is known as the **cross entropy**. The quantity $\mathbb{H}_{ce}(p_{\mathcal{D}}, q)$ is the average negative log likelihood of q evaluated on the training set. Thus we see that minimizing KL divergence to the empirical distribution is equivalent to maximizing likelihood.

This perspective points out the flaw with likelihood-based training, namely that it puts too much weight on the training set. In most applications, we do not really believe that the empirical distribution is a good representation of the true distribution, since it just puts "spikes" on a finite set of points, and zero density everywhere else. Even if the dataset is large (say 1M images), the universe from which the data is sampled is usually even larger (e.g., the set of "all natural images" is much larger than 1M). Thus we need to somehow smooth the empirical distribution by sharing probability mass between "similar" inputs.

5.1.7 KL divergence and Bayesian inference

Bayesian inference itself can be motivated as the solution to a particular minimization problem of KL.

Consider a prior set of beliefs described by a joint distribution $q(\theta, D) = q(\theta)q(D|\theta)$, involving some *prior* $q(\theta)$ and some *likelihood* $q(D|\theta)$. If we happen to observe some particular dataset D_0, how should we update our beliefs? We could search for the joint distribution that is as close as possible to our prior beliefs but that respects the constraint that we now know the value of the data:

$$p(\theta, D) = \operatorname{argmin} D_{\mathbb{KL}}\left(p(\theta, D) \,\|\, q(\theta, D)\right) \text{ such that } p(D) = \delta(D - D_0). \tag{5.67}$$

where $\delta(D - D_0)$ is a degenerate distribution that puts all its mass on the dataset D that is identically equal to D_0. Writing the KL out in its chain rule form:

$$D_{\mathbb{KL}}\left(p(\theta, D) \,\|\, q(\theta, D)\right) = D_{\mathbb{KL}}\left(p(D) \,\|\, q(D)\right) + D_{\mathbb{KL}}\left(p(\theta|D) \,\|\, q(\theta|D)\right), \tag{5.68}$$

makes clear that the solution is given by the joint distribution:

$$p(\theta, D) = p(D)p(\theta|D) = \delta(D - D_0)q(\theta|D). \tag{5.69}$$

Our updated beliefs have a marginal over the θ

$$p(\theta) = \int dD \, p(\theta, D) = \int dD \, \delta(D - D_0)q(\theta|D) = q(\theta|D = D_0), \tag{5.70}$$

which is just the usual Bayesian posterior from our prior beliefs evaluated at the data we observed.

By contrast, the usual statement of Bayes' rule is just a trivial observation about the chain rule of probabilities:

$$q(\theta, D) = q(D)q(\theta|D) = q(\theta)q(D|\theta) \implies q(\theta|D) = \frac{q(D|\theta)}{q(D)}q(\theta). \tag{5.71}$$

Notice that this relates the conditional distribution $q(\theta|D)$ in terms of $q(D|\theta)$, $q(\theta)$ and $q(D)$, but that these are all different ways to write the same distribution. Bayes' rule does not tell us how we ought to *update* our beliefs in light of evidence, for that we need some other principle [Cat+11].

One of the nice things about this interpretation of Bayesian inference is that it naturally generalizes to other forms of constraints rather than assuming we have observed the data exactly.

If there was some additional measurement error that was well understood, we ought to instead of pegging out updated beliefs to be a delta function on the observed data, simply peg it to be the well understood distribution $p(D)$. For example, we might not know the precise value the data takes, but believe after measuring things that it is a Gaussian distribution with a certain mean and standard deviation.

Because of the chain rule of KL, this has no effect on our updated conditional distribution over parameters, which remains the Bayesian posterior: $p(\theta|D) = q(\theta|D)$. However, this does change our marginal beliefs about the parameters, which are now:

$$p(\theta) = \int dD \, p(D) q(\theta|D). \tag{5.72}$$

This generalization of Bayes' rule is sometimes called **Jeffrey's conditionalization rule** [Cat08].

5.1.8   KL divergence and exponential families

The KL divergence between two exponential family distributions from the same family has a nice closed form, as we explain below.

Consider $p(\boldsymbol{x})$ with natural parameter $\boldsymbol{\eta}$, base measure $h(\boldsymbol{x})$ and sufficient statistics $\mathcal{T}(\boldsymbol{x})$:

$$p(\boldsymbol{x}) = h(\boldsymbol{x}) \exp[\boldsymbol{\eta}^{\mathsf{T}} \mathcal{T}(\boldsymbol{x}) - A(\boldsymbol{\eta})] \tag{5.73}$$

where

$$A(\boldsymbol{\eta}) = \log \int h(\boldsymbol{x}) \exp(\boldsymbol{\eta}^{\mathsf{T}} \mathcal{T}(\boldsymbol{x})) d\boldsymbol{x} \tag{5.74}$$

is the *log partition function*, a convex function of $\boldsymbol{\eta}$.

The KL divergence between two exponential family distributions from the same family is as follows:

$$D_{\mathrm{KL}}\left(p(\boldsymbol{x}|\boldsymbol{\eta}_1) \parallel p(\boldsymbol{x}|\boldsymbol{\eta}_2)\right) = \mathbb{E}_{\boldsymbol{\eta}_1}\left[(\boldsymbol{\eta}_1 - \boldsymbol{\eta}_2)^{\mathsf{T}} \mathcal{T}(\boldsymbol{x}) - A(\boldsymbol{\eta}_1) + A(\boldsymbol{\eta}_2)\right] \tag{5.75}$$

$$= (\boldsymbol{\eta}_1 - \boldsymbol{\eta}_2)^{\mathsf{T}} \boldsymbol{\mu}_1 - A(\boldsymbol{\eta}_1) + A(\boldsymbol{\eta}_2) \tag{5.76}$$

where $\boldsymbol{\mu}_j \triangleq \mathbb{E}_{\boldsymbol{\eta}_j}[\mathcal{T}(\boldsymbol{x})]$.

5.1.8.1   Example: KL divergence between two Gaussians

An important example is the KL divergence between two multivariate Gaussian distributions, which is given by

$$D_{\mathrm{KL}}\left(\mathcal{N}(\boldsymbol{x}|\boldsymbol{\mu}_1, \boldsymbol{\Sigma}_1) \parallel \mathcal{N}(\boldsymbol{x}|\boldsymbol{\mu}_2, \boldsymbol{\Sigma}_2)\right)$$
$$= \frac{1}{2}\left[\mathrm{tr}(\boldsymbol{\Sigma}_2^{-1}\boldsymbol{\Sigma}_1) + (\boldsymbol{\mu}_2 - \boldsymbol{\mu}_1)^{\mathsf{T}}\boldsymbol{\Sigma}_2^{-1}(\boldsymbol{\mu}_2 - \boldsymbol{\mu}_1) - D + \log\left(\frac{\det(\boldsymbol{\Sigma}_2)}{\det(\boldsymbol{\Sigma}_1)}\right)\right] \tag{5.77}$$

In the scalar case, this becomes

$$D_{\mathrm{KL}}\left(\mathcal{N}(x|\mu_1,\sigma_1) \parallel \mathcal{N}(x|\mu_2,\sigma_2)\right) = \log\frac{\sigma_2}{\sigma_1} + \frac{\sigma_1^2 + (\mu_1 - \mu_2)^2}{2\sigma_2^2} - \frac{1}{2} \tag{5.78}$$

5.1.9 Approximating KL divergence using the Fisher information matrix

Let $p_{\boldsymbol{\theta}}(\boldsymbol{x})$ and $p_{\boldsymbol{\theta}'}(\boldsymbol{x})$ be two distributions, where $\boldsymbol{\theta}' = \boldsymbol{\theta} + \boldsymbol{\delta}$. We can measure how close the second distribution is to the first in terms their predictive distribution (as opposed to comparing $\boldsymbol{\theta}$ and $\boldsymbol{\theta}'$ in parameter space) as follows:

$$D_{\mathrm{KL}}\left(p_{\boldsymbol{\theta}} \parallel p_{\boldsymbol{\theta}'}\right) = \mathbb{E}_{p_{\boldsymbol{\theta}}(\boldsymbol{x})}\left[\log p_{\boldsymbol{\theta}}(\boldsymbol{x}) - \log p_{\boldsymbol{\theta}'}(\boldsymbol{x})\right] \tag{5.79}$$

Let us approximate this with a second order Taylor series expansion:

$$D_{\mathrm{KL}}\left(p_{\boldsymbol{\theta}} \parallel p_{\boldsymbol{\theta}'}\right) \approx -\boldsymbol{\delta}^{\mathsf{T}}\mathbb{E}\left[\nabla \log p_{\boldsymbol{\theta}}(\boldsymbol{x})\right] - \frac{1}{2}\boldsymbol{\delta}^{\mathsf{T}}\mathbb{E}\left[\nabla^2 \log p_{\boldsymbol{\theta}}(\boldsymbol{x})\right]\boldsymbol{\delta} \tag{5.80}$$

Since the expected score function is zero (from Equation (3.44)), the first term vanishes, so we have

$$D_{\mathrm{KL}}\left(p_{\boldsymbol{\theta}} \parallel p_{\boldsymbol{\theta}'}\right) \approx \frac{1}{2}\boldsymbol{\delta}^{\mathsf{T}}\mathbf{F}(\boldsymbol{\theta})\boldsymbol{\delta} \tag{5.81}$$

where $\mathbf{F}$ is the FIM

$$\mathbf{F} = -\mathbb{E}\left[\nabla^2 \log p_{\boldsymbol{\theta}}(\boldsymbol{x})\right] = \mathbb{E}\left[(\nabla \log p_{\boldsymbol{\theta}}(\boldsymbol{x}))(\nabla \log p_{\boldsymbol{\theta}}(\boldsymbol{x}))^{\mathsf{T}}\right] \tag{5.82}$$

Thus we have shown that the KL divergence is approximately equal to the (squared) Mahalanobis distance using the Fisher information matrix as the metric. This result is the basis of the **natural gradient** method discussed in Section 6.4.

5.1.10 Bregman divergence

Let $f : \Omega \to \mathbb{R}$ be a continuously differentiable, strictly convex function defined on a closed convex set Ω. We define the **Bregman divergence** associated with f as follows [Bre67]:

$$B_f(\boldsymbol{w}\|\boldsymbol{v}) = f(\boldsymbol{w}) - f(\boldsymbol{v}) - (\boldsymbol{w} - \boldsymbol{v})^{\mathsf{T}}\nabla f(\boldsymbol{v}) \tag{5.83}$$

To understand this, let

$$\hat{f}_{\boldsymbol{v}}(\boldsymbol{w}) = f(\boldsymbol{v}) + (\boldsymbol{w} - \boldsymbol{v})^{\mathsf{T}}\nabla f(\boldsymbol{v}) \tag{5.84}$$

be a first order Taylor series approximation to f centered at $\boldsymbol{v}$. Then the Bregman divergence is the difference from this linear approximation:

$$B_f(\boldsymbol{w}\|\boldsymbol{v}) = f(\boldsymbol{w}) - \hat{f}_{\boldsymbol{v}}(\boldsymbol{w}) \tag{5.85}$$

See Figure 5.3a for an illustration. Since f is convex, we have $B_f(\boldsymbol{w}\|\boldsymbol{v}) \geq 0$, since $\hat{f}_v$ is a linear lower bound on f.

Below we mention some important special cases of Bregman divergences.

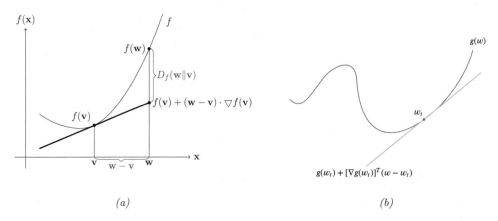

Figure 5.3: (a) Illustration of Bregman divergence. (b) A locally linear approximation to a non-convex function.

- If $f(\boldsymbol{w}) = ||\boldsymbol{w}||^2$, then $B_f(\boldsymbol{w}||\boldsymbol{v}) = ||\boldsymbol{w} - \boldsymbol{v}||^2$ is the squared Euclidean distance.

- If $f(\boldsymbol{w}) = \boldsymbol{w}^\mathsf{T}\mathbf{Q}\boldsymbol{w}$, then $B_f(\boldsymbol{w}||\boldsymbol{v})$ is the squared Mahalanobis distance.

- If $\boldsymbol{w}$ are the natural parameters of an exponential family distribution, and $f(\boldsymbol{w}) = \log Z(\boldsymbol{w})$ is the log normalizer, then the Bregman divergence is the same as the Kullback-Leibler divergence, as we show in Section 5.1.10.1.

5.1.10.1   KL is a Bregman divergence

Recall that the log partition function $A(\boldsymbol{\eta})$ is a convex function. We can therefore use it to define the Bregman divergence (Section 5.1.10) between the two distributions, p and q, as follows:

$$B_f(\boldsymbol{\eta}_q||\boldsymbol{\eta}_p) = A(\boldsymbol{\eta}_q) - A(\boldsymbol{\eta}_p) - (\boldsymbol{\eta}_q - \boldsymbol{\eta}_p)^\mathsf{T}\nabla_{\boldsymbol{\eta}_p}A(\boldsymbol{\eta}_p) \tag{5.86}$$

$$= A(\boldsymbol{\eta}_q) - A(\boldsymbol{\eta}_p) - (\boldsymbol{\eta}_q - \boldsymbol{\eta}_p)^\mathsf{T}\mathbb{E}_p\left[\mathcal{T}(\boldsymbol{x})\right] \tag{5.87}$$

$$= D_{\mathrm{KL}}\left(p \,\|\, q\right) \tag{5.88}$$

where we exploited the fact that the gradient of the log partition function computes the expected sufficient statistics as shown in Section 2.4.3.

In fact, the KL divergence is the only divergence that is both a Bregman divergence and an f-divergence (Section 2.7.1) [Ama09].

5.2   Entropy

In this section, we discuss the **entropy** of a distribution p, which is just a shifted and scaled version of the KL divergence between the probability distribution and the uniform distribution, as we will see.

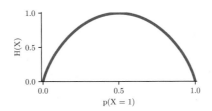

Figure 5.4: Entropy of a Bernoulli random variable as a function of θ. The maximum entropy is $\log_2 2 = 1$. Generated by bernoulli_entropy_fig.ipynb.

5.2.1 Definition

The entropy of a discrete random variable X with distribution p over K states is defined by

$$\mathbb{H}(X) \triangleq -\sum_{k=1}^{K} p(X = k) \log p(X = k) = -\mathbb{E}_X[\log p(X)] \tag{5.89}$$

We can use logarithms to any base, but we commonly use log base 2, in which case the units are called bits, or log base e, in which case the units are called nats, as we explained in Section 5.1.3.1.

The entropy is equivalent to a constant minus the KL divergence from the uniform distribution:

$$\mathbb{H}(X) = \log K - D_{\mathbb{KL}}(p(X) \parallel u(X)) \tag{5.90}$$

$$D_{\mathbb{KL}}(p(X) \parallel u(X)) = \sum_{k=1}^{K} p(X = k) \log \frac{p(X = k)}{\frac{1}{K}} \tag{5.91}$$

$$= \log K + \sum_{k=1}^{K} p(X = k) \log p(X = k) \tag{5.92}$$

If p is uniform, the KL is zero, and we see that the entropy achieves its maximal value of $\log K$.

For the special case of binary random variables, $X \in \{0, 1\}$, we can write $p(X = 1) = \theta$ and $p(X = 0) = 1 - \theta$. Hence the entropy becomes

$$\mathbb{H}(X) = -[p(X = 1) \log p(X = 1) + p(X = 0) \log p(X = 0)] \tag{5.93}$$

$$= -[\theta \log \theta + (1 - \theta) \log(1 - \theta)] \tag{5.94}$$

This is called the **binary entropy function**, and is also written $\mathbb{H}(\theta)$. We plot this in Figure 5.4. We see that the maximum value of 1 bit occurs when the distribution is uniform, $\theta = 0.5$. A fair coin requires a single yes/no question to determine its state.

5.2.2 Differential entropy for continuous random variables

If X is a continuous random variable with pdf $p(x)$, we define the **differential entropy** as

$$h(X) \triangleq -\int_{\mathcal{X}} dx \, p(x) \log p(x) \tag{5.95}$$

assuming this integral exists.

For example, one can show that the entropy of a d-dimensional Gaussian is

$$h(\mathcal{N}(\boldsymbol{\mu}, \boldsymbol{\Sigma})) = \frac{1}{2} \log |2\pi e \boldsymbol{\Sigma}| = \frac{1}{2} \log[(2\pi e)^d |\boldsymbol{\Sigma}|] = \frac{d}{2} + \frac{d}{2} \log(2\pi) + \frac{1}{2} \log |\boldsymbol{\Sigma}| \tag{5.96}$$

In the 1d case, this becomes

$$h(\mathcal{N}(\mu, \sigma^2)) = \frac{1}{2} \log \left[2\pi e \sigma^2 \right] \tag{5.97}$$

Note that, unlike the discrete case, *differential entropy can be negative*. This is because pdf's can be bigger than 1. For example, suppose $X \sim U(0, a)$. Then

$$h(X) = -\int_0^a dx \, \frac{1}{a} \log \frac{1}{a} = \log a \tag{5.98}$$

If we set $a = 1/8$, we have $h(X) = \log_2(1/8) = -3$ bits.

One way to understand differential entropy is to realize that all real-valued quantities can only be represented to finite precision. It can be shown [CT91, p228] that the entropy of an n-bit quantization of a continuous random variable X is approximately $h(X) + n$. For example, suppose $X \sim U(0, \frac{1}{8})$. Then in a binary representation of X, the first 3 bits to the right of the binary point must be 0 (since the number is $\leq 1/8$). So to describe X to n bits of accuracy only requires $n - 3$ bits, which agrees with $h(X) = -3$ calculated above.

The continuous entropy also lacks the reparameterization independence of KL divergence Section 5.1.2.3. In particular, if we transform our random variable $y = f(x)$, the entropy transforms. To see this, note that the change of variables tells us that

$$p(y) \, dy = p(x) \, dx \implies p(y) = p(x) \left| \frac{dy}{dx} \right|^{-1}, \tag{5.99}$$

Thus the continuous entropy transforms as follows:

$$h(X) = -\int dx \, p(x) \log p(x) = h(Y) - \int dy \, p(y) \log \left| \frac{dy}{dx} \right|. \tag{5.100}$$

We pick up a factor in the continuous entropy of the log of the determinant of the Jacobian of the transformation. This changes the value for the continuous entropy even for simply rescaling the random variable such as when we change units. For example in Figure 5.5 we show the distribution of adult human heights (it is bimodal because while both male and female heights are normally distributed, they differ noticeably). The continuous entropy of this distribution depends on the units it is measured in. If measured in feet, the continuous entropy is 0.43 bits. Intuitively this is because human heights mostly span less than a foot. If measured in centimeters it is instead 5.4 bits. There are 30.48 centimeters in a foot, $\log_2 30.48 = 4.9$ explaining the difference. If we measured the continuous entropy of the same distribution measured in meters we would obtain -1.3 bits!

5.2.3   Typical sets

The **typical set** of a probability distribution is the set whose elements have an information content that is close to that of the expected information content from random samples from the distribution.

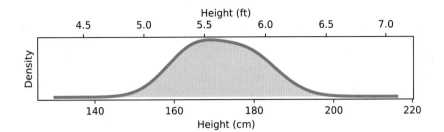

Figure 5.5: Distribution of adult heights. The continuous entropy of the distribution depends on its units of measurement. If heights are measured in feet, this distribution has a continuous entropy of 0.43 bits. If measured in centimeters it's 5.4 bits. If measured in meters it's −1.3 bits. Data taken from https: //ourworldindata.org/human-height.

More precisely, for a distribution $p(\boldsymbol{x})$ with support $\boldsymbol{x} \in \mathcal{X}$, the ϵ-typical set $\mathcal{A}_\epsilon^N \in \mathcal{X}^N$ for $p(\boldsymbol{x})$ is the set of all length N sequences such that

$$\mathbb{H}(p(\boldsymbol{x})) - \epsilon \leq -\frac{1}{N} \log p(\boldsymbol{x}_1, \ldots, \boldsymbol{x}_N) \leq \mathbb{H}(p(\boldsymbol{x})) + \epsilon \tag{5.101}$$

If we assume $p(\boldsymbol{x}_1, \ldots, \boldsymbol{x}_N) = \prod_{n=1}^N p(\boldsymbol{x}_n)$, then we can interpret the term in the middle as the N-sample empirical estimate of the entropy. The **asymptotic equipartition property** or **AEP** states that this will converge (in probability) to the true entropy as $N \to \infty$ [CT06]. Thus the typical set has probability close to 1, and is thus a compact summary of what we can expect to be generated by $p(\boldsymbol{x})$.

5.2.4 Cross entropy and perplexity

A standard way to measure how close a model q is to a true distribution p is in terms of the KL divergence (Section 5.1), given by

$$D_{\mathbb{KL}}(p \parallel q) = \sum_x p(x) \log \frac{p(x)}{q(x)} = \mathbb{H}_{ce}(p, q) - \mathbb{H}(p) \tag{5.102}$$

where $\mathbb{H}_{ce}(p, q)$ is the **cross entropy**

$$\mathbb{H}_{ce}(p, q) = -\sum_x p(x) \log q(x) \tag{5.103}$$

and $\mathbb{H}(p) = \mathbb{H}_{ce}(p, p)$ is the entropy, which is a constant independent of the model.

In language modeling, it is common to report an alternative performance measure known as the **perplexity**. This is defined as

$$\text{perplexity}(p, q) \triangleq 2^{\mathbb{H}_{ce}(p, q)} \tag{5.104}$$

We can compute an empirical approximation to the cross entropy as follows. Suppose we approximate the true distribution with an empirical distribution based on data sampled from p:

$$p_{\mathcal{D}}(x|\mathcal{D}) = \frac{1}{N} \sum_{n=1}^{N} \mathbb{I}(x = x_n) \tag{5.105}$$

In this case, the cross entropy is given by

$$H = -\frac{1}{N} \sum_{n=1}^{N} \log p(x_n) = -\frac{1}{N} \log \prod_{n=1}^{N} p(x_n) \tag{5.106}$$

The corresponding perplexity is given by

$$\text{perplexity}(p_{\mathcal{D}}, p) = 2^{-\frac{1}{N} \log(\prod_{n=1}^{N} p(x_n))} = 2^{\log(\prod_{n=1}^{N} p(x_n))^{-\frac{1}{N}}} \tag{5.107}$$

$$= (\prod_{n=1}^{N} p(x_n))^{-1/N} = \sqrt[N]{\prod_{n=1}^{N} \frac{1}{p(x_n)}} \tag{5.108}$$

In the case of language models, we usually condition on previous words when predicting the next word. For example, in a bigram model, we use a second order Markov model of the form $p(x_n|x_{n-1})$. We define the **branching factor** of a language model as the number of possible words that can follow any given word. For example, suppose the model predicts that each word is equally likely, regardless of context, so $p(x_n|x_{n-1}) = 1/K$, where K is the number of words in the vocabulary. Then the perplexity is $((1/K)^N)^{-1/N} = K$. If some symbols are more likely than others, and the model correctly reflects this, its perplexity will be lower than K. However, we have $\mathbb{H}(p^*) \leq \mathbb{H}_{ce}(p^*, p)$, so we can never reduce the perplexity below $2^{-\mathbb{H}(p^*)}$.

5.3 Mutual information

The KL divergence gave us a way to measure how similar two distributions were. How should we measure how dependent two random variables are? One thing we could do is turn the question of measuring the dependence of two random variables into a question about the similarity of their distributions. This gives rise to the notion of **mutual information** (MI) between two random variables, which we define below.

5.3.1 Definition

The mutual information between rv's X and Y is defined as follows:

$$\mathbb{I}(X;Y) \triangleq D_{\text{KL}}(p(x,y) \| p(x)p(y)) = \sum_{y \in Y} \sum_{x \in X} p(x,y) \log \frac{p(x,y)}{p(x)\,p(y)} \tag{5.109}$$

(We write $\mathbb{I}(X;Y)$ instead of $\mathbb{I}(X,Y)$, in case X and/or Y represent sets of variables; for example, we can write $\mathbb{I}(X;Y,Z)$ to represent the MI between X and (Y,Z).) For continuous random variables, we just replace sums with integrals.

It is easy to see that MI is always non-negative, even for continuous random variables, since

$$\mathbb{I}(X;Y) = D_{\mathrm{KL}}\left(p(x,y) \parallel p(x)p(y)\right) \geq 0 \tag{5.110}$$

We achieve the bound of 0 iff $p(x,y) = p(x)p(y)$.

5.3.2 Interpretation

Knowing that the mutual information is a KL divergence between the joint and factored marginal distributions tells is that the MI measures the information gain if we update from a model that treats the two variables as independent $p(x)p(y)$ to one that models their true joint density $p(x,y)$.

To gain further insight into the meaning of MI, it helps to re-express it in terms of joint and conditional entropies, as follows:

$$\mathbb{I}(X;Y) = \mathbb{H}(X) - \mathbb{H}(X|Y) = \mathbb{H}(Y) - \mathbb{H}(Y|X) \tag{5.111}$$

Thus we can interpret the MI between X and Y as the reduction in uncertainty about X after observing Y, or, by symmetry, the reduction in uncertainty about Y after observing X. Incidentally, this result gives an alternative proof that conditioning, on average, reduces entropy. In particular, we have $0 \leq \mathbb{I}(X;Y) = \mathbb{H}(X) - \mathbb{H}(X|Y)$, and hence $\mathbb{H}(X|Y) \leq \mathbb{H}(X)$.

We can also obtain a different interpretation. One can show that

$$\mathbb{I}(X;Y) = \mathbb{H}(X,Y) - \mathbb{H}(X|Y) - \mathbb{H}(Y|X) \tag{5.112}$$

Finally, one can show that

$$\mathbb{I}(X;Y) = \mathbb{H}(X) + \mathbb{H}(Y) - \mathbb{H}(X,Y) \tag{5.113}$$

See Figure 5.6 for a summary of these equations in terms of an **information diagram**. (Formally, this is a signed measure mapping set expressions to their information-theoretic counterparts [Yeu91a].)

5.3.3 Data processing inequality

Suppose we have an unknown variable X, and we observe a noisy function of it, call it Y. If we process the noisy observations in some way to create a new variable Z, it should be intuitively obvious that we cannot increase the amount of information we have about the unknown quantity, X. This is known as the **data processing inequality**. We now state this more formally, and then prove it.

Theorem 5.3.1. *Suppose $X \to Y \to Z$ forms a Markov chain, so that $X \perp Z|Y$. Then $\mathbb{I}(X;Y) \geq \mathbb{I}(X;Z)$.*

Proof. By the chain rule for mutual information we can expand the mutual information in two different ways:

$$\mathbb{I}(X;Y,Z) = \mathbb{I}(X;Z) + \mathbb{I}(X;Y|Z) \tag{5.114}$$
$$= \mathbb{I}(X;Y) + \mathbb{I}(X;Z|Y) \tag{5.115}$$

Since $X \perp Z|Y$, we have $\mathbb{I}(X;Z|Y) = 0$, so

$$\mathbb{I}(X;Z) + \mathbb{I}(X;Y|Z) = \mathbb{I}(X;Y) \tag{5.116}$$

Since $\mathbb{I}(X;Y|Z) \geq 0$, we have $\mathbb{I}(X;Y) \geq \mathbb{I}(X;Z)$. Similarly one can prove that $\mathbb{I}(Y;Z) \geq \mathbb{I}(X;Z)$.

$\square$

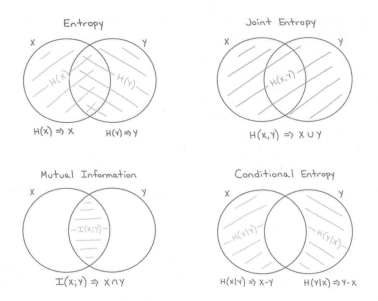

Figure 5.6: The marginal entropy, joint entropy, conditional entropy, and mutual information represented as information diagrams. Used with kind permission of Katie Everett.

5.3.4 Sufficient statistics

An important consequence of the DPI is the following. Suppose we have the chain $\theta \rightarrow X \rightarrow s(X)$. Then

$$\mathbb{I}\left(\theta; s(X)\right) \leq \mathbb{I}\left(\theta; X\right) \tag{5.117}$$

If this holds with equality, then we say that $s(X)$ is a **sufficient statistic** of the data X for the purposes of inferring θ. In this case, we can equivalently write $\theta \rightarrow s(X) \rightarrow X$, since we can reconstruct the data from knowing $s(X)$ just as accurately as from knowing θ.

An example of a sufficient statistic is the data itself, $s(X) = X$, but this is not very useful, since it doesn't summarize the data at all. Hence we define a **minimal sufficient statistic** $s(X)$ as one which is sufficient, and which contains no extra information about θ; thus $s(X)$ maximally compresses the data X without losing information which is relevant to predicting θ. More formally, we say s is a minimal sufficient statistic for X if $s(X) = f(s'(X))$ for some function f and all sufficient statistics $s'(X)$. We can summarize the situation as follows:

$$\theta \rightarrow s(X) \rightarrow s'(X) \rightarrow X \tag{5.118}$$

Here $s'(X)$ takes $s(X)$ and adds redundant information to it, thus creating a one-to-many mapping.

For example, a minimal sufficient statistic for a set of N Bernoulli trials is simply N and $N_1 = \sum_n \mathbb{I}(X_n = 1)$, i.e., the number of successes. In other words, we don't need to keep track of the entire sequence of heads and tails and their ordering, we only need to keep track of the total number of heads and tails. Similarly, for inferring the mean of a Gaussian distribution with known variance we only need to know the empirical mean and number of samples.

Earlier in Section 5.1.8 we motivated the exponential family of distributions as being the ones that are minimal in the sense that they contain no other information than constraints on some statistics of the data. It makes sense then that the statistics used to generate exponential family distributions are sufficient. It also hints at the more remarkable fact of the **Pitman-Koopman-Darmois theorem**, which says that for any distribution whose domain is fixed, it is only the exponential family that admits sufficient statistics with bounded dimensionality as the number of samples increases [Dia88b].

5.3.5   Multivariate mutual information

There are several ways to generalize the idea of mutual information to a set of random variables as we discuss below.

5.3.5.1   Total correlation

The simplest way to define multivariate MI is to use the **total correlation** [Wat60] or **multi-information** [SV98], defined as

$$\mathbb{TC}(\{X_1, \ldots, X_D\}) \triangleq D_{\mathrm{KL}}\left(p(\boldsymbol{x}) \parallel \prod_d p(x_d) \right) \tag{5.119}$$

$$= \sum_{\boldsymbol{x}} p(\boldsymbol{x}) \log \frac{p(\boldsymbol{x})}{\prod_{d=1}^{D} p(x_d)} = \sum_d \mathbb{H}(x_d) - \mathbb{H}(\boldsymbol{x}) \tag{5.120}$$

For example, for 3 variables, this becomes

$$\mathbb{TC}(X, Y, Z) = \mathbb{H}(X) + \mathbb{H}(Y) + \mathbb{H}(Z) - \mathbb{H}(X, Y, Z) \tag{5.121}$$

where $\mathbb{H}(X, Y, Z)$ is the joint entropy

$$\mathbb{H}(X, Y, Z) = -\sum_x \sum_y \sum_z p(x, y, z) \log p(x, y, z) \tag{5.122}$$

One can show that the multi-information is always non-negative, and is zero iff $p(\boldsymbol{x}) = \prod_d p(x_d)$. However, this means the quantity is non-zero even if only a pair of variables interact. For example, if $p(X, Y, Z) = p(X, Y)p(Z)$, then the total correlation will be non-zero, even though there is no 3 way interaction. This motivates the alternative definition in Section 5.3.5.2.

5.3.5.2   Interaction information (co-information)

The conditional mutual information can be used to give an inductive definition of the **multivariate mutual information (MMI)** as follows:

$$\mathbb{I}(X_1; \cdots; X_D) = \mathbb{I}(X_1; \cdots; X_{D-1}) - \mathbb{I}(X_1; \cdots; X_{D-1}|X_D) \tag{5.123}$$

This is called the **multiple mutual information** [Yeu91b], or the **co-information** [Bel03]. This definition is equivalent, up to a sign change, to the **interaction information** [McG54; Han80; JB03; Bro09].

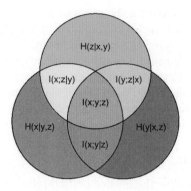

Figure 5.7: Illustration of multivariate mutual information between three random variables. From https:
// en. wikipedia. org/ wiki/ Mutual_ information. *Used with kind permission of Wikipedia author PAR.*

For 3 variables, the MMI is given by

$$\mathbb{I}(X;Y;Z) = \mathbb{I}(X;Y) - \mathbb{I}(X;Y|Z) \tag{5.124}$$
$$= \mathbb{I}(X;Z) - \mathbb{I}(X;Z|Y) \tag{5.125}$$
$$= \mathbb{I}(Y;Z) - \mathbb{I}(Y;Z|X) \tag{5.126}$$

This can be interpreted as the change in mutual information between two pairs of variables when conditioning on the third. Note that this quantity is symmetric in its arguments.

By the definition of conditional mutual information, we have

$$\mathbb{I}(X;Z|Y) = \mathbb{I}(Z;X,Y) - \mathbb{I}(Y;Z) \tag{5.127}$$

Hence we can rewrite Equation (5.125) as follows:

$$\mathbb{I}(X;Y;Z) = \mathbb{I}(X;Z) + \mathbb{I}(Y;Z) - \mathbb{I}(X,Y;Z) \tag{5.128}$$

This tells us that the MMI is the difference between how much we learn about Z given X and Y individually vs jointly (see also Section 5.3.5.3).

The 3-way MMI is illustrated in the information diagram in Figure 5.7. The way to interpret such diagrams when we have multiple variables is as follows: the area of a shaded area that includes circles $A, B, C, \ldots$ and excludes circles $F, G, H, \ldots$ represents $\mathbb{I}(A;B;C;\ldots|F,G,H,\ldots)$; if $B = C = \emptyset$, this is just $\mathbb{H}(A|F,G,H,\ldots)$; if $F = G = H = \emptyset$, this is just $\mathbb{I}(A;B;C,\ldots)$.

5.3.5.3   Synergy and redundancy

The MMI is $\mathbb{I}(X;Y;Z) = \mathbb{I}(X;Z) + \mathbb{I}(Y;Z) - \mathbb{I}(X,Y;Z)$. We see that this can be positive, zero, *or negative*. If some of the information about Z that is provided by X is also provided by Y, then there is some **redundancy** between X and Y (wrt Z). In this case, $\mathbb{I}(X;Z) + \mathbb{I}(Y;Z) > \mathbb{I}(X,Y;Z)$, so (from Equation (5.128)) we see that the MMI will be positive. If, by contrast, we learn more about Z when we see X and Y together, we say there is some **synergy** between them. In this case, $\mathbb{I}(X;Z) + \mathbb{I}(Y;Z) < \mathbb{I}(X,Y;Z)$, so the MMI will be negative.

5.3.5.4 MMI and causality

The sign of the MMI can be used to distinguish between different kinds of directed graphical models, which can sometimes be interpreted causally (see Chapter 36 for a general discussion of causality). For example, consider a model of the form $X \leftarrow Z \rightarrow Y$, where Z is a "cause" of X and Y. For example, suppose X represents the event it is raining, Y represents the event that the sky is dark, and Z represents the event that the sky is cloudy. Conditioning on the common cause Z renders the children X and Y independent, since if I know it is cloudy, noticing that the sky is dark does not change my beliefs about whether it will rain or not. Consequently $\mathbb{I}(X;Y|Z) \leq \mathbb{I}(X;Y)$, so $\mathbb{I}(X;Y;Z) \geq 0$.

Now consider the case where Z is a common effect, $X \rightarrow Z \leftarrow Y$. In this case, conditioning on Z makes X and Y dependent, due to the explaining away phenomenon (see Section 4.2.4.2). For example, if X and Y are independent random bits, and Z is the XOR of X and Y, then observing $Z = 1$ means that $p(X \neq Y|Z = 1) = 1$, so X and Y are now dependent (information-theoretically, not causally), even though they were a priori independent. Consequently $\mathbb{I}(X;Y|Z) \geq \mathbb{I}(X;Y)$, so $\mathbb{I}(X;Y;Z) \leq 0$.

Finally, consider a Markov chain, $X \rightarrow Y \rightarrow Z$. We have $\mathbb{I}(X;Z|Y) \leq \mathbb{I}(X;Z)$ and so the MMI must be positive.

5.3.5.5 MMI and entropy

We can also write the MMI in terms of entropies. Specifically, we know that

$$\mathbb{I}(X;Y) = \mathbb{H}(X) + \mathbb{H}(Y) - \mathbb{H}(X,Y) \tag{5.129}$$

and

$$\mathbb{I}(X;Y|Z) = \mathbb{H}(X,Z) + \mathbb{H}(Y,Z) - \mathbb{H}(Z) - \mathbb{H}(X,Y,Z) \tag{5.130}$$

Hence we can rewrite Equation (5.124) as follows:

$$\mathbb{I}(X;Y;Z) = [\mathbb{H}(X) + \mathbb{H}(Y) + \mathbb{H}(Z)] - [\mathbb{H}(X,Y) + \mathbb{H}(X,Z) + \mathbb{H}(Y,Z)] + \mathbb{H}(X,Y,Z) \tag{5.131}$$

Contrast this to Equation (5.121).

More generally, we have

$$\mathbb{I}(X_1,\ldots,X_D) = -\sum_{\mathcal{T} \subseteq \{1,\ldots,D\}} (-1)^{|\mathcal{T}|} \mathbb{H}(\mathcal{T}) \tag{5.132}$$

For sets of size 1, 2, and 3 this expands as follows:

$$I_1 = H_1 \tag{5.133}$$
$$I_{12} = H_1 + H_2 - H_{12} \tag{5.134}$$
$$I_{123} = H_1 + H_2 + H_3 - H_{12} - H_{13} - H_{23} + H_{123} \tag{5.135}$$

We can use the **Möbius inversion formula** to derive the following dual relationship:

$$\mathbb{H}(\mathcal{S}) = -\sum_{\mathcal{T} \subseteq \mathcal{S}} (-1)^{|\mathcal{T}|} \mathbb{I}(\mathcal{T}) \tag{5.136}$$

for sets of variables $\mathcal{S}$.

Using the chain rule for entropy, we can also derive the following expression for the 3-way MMI:

$$\mathbb{I}(X;Y;Z) = \mathbb{H}(Z) - \mathbb{H}(Z|X) - \mathbb{H}(Z|Y) + \mathbb{H}(Z|X,Y) \tag{5.137}$$

5.3.6   Variational bounds on mutual information

In this section, we discuss methods for computing upper and lower bounds on MI that use variational approximations to the intractable distributions. This can be useful for representation learning (Chapter 32). This approach was first suggested in [BA03]. For a more detailed overview of variational bounds on mutual information, see Poole et al. [Poo+19b].

5.3.6.1   Upper bound

Suppose that the joint $p(\boldsymbol{x}, \boldsymbol{y})$ is intractable to evaluate, but that we can sample from $p(\boldsymbol{x})$ and evaluate the conditional distribution $p(\boldsymbol{y}|\boldsymbol{x})$. Furthermore, suppose we approximate $p(\boldsymbol{y})$ by $q(\boldsymbol{y})$. Then we can compute an upper bound on the MI as follows:

$$\mathbb{I}(\boldsymbol{x};\boldsymbol{y}) = \mathbb{E}_{p(\boldsymbol{x},\boldsymbol{y})} \left[\log \frac{p(\boldsymbol{y}|\boldsymbol{x})q(\boldsymbol{y})}{p(\boldsymbol{y})q(\boldsymbol{y})} \right] \tag{5.138}$$

$$= \mathbb{E}_{p(\boldsymbol{x},\boldsymbol{y})} \left[\log \frac{p(\boldsymbol{y}|\boldsymbol{x})}{q(\boldsymbol{y})} \right] - D_{\mathbb{KL}}\left(p(\boldsymbol{y}) \parallel q(\boldsymbol{y})\right) \tag{5.139}$$

$$\leq \mathbb{E}_{p(\boldsymbol{x})} \left[\mathbb{E}_{p(\boldsymbol{y}|\boldsymbol{x})} \left[\log \frac{p(\boldsymbol{y}|\boldsymbol{x})}{q(\boldsymbol{y})} \right] \right] \tag{5.140}$$

$$= \mathbb{E}_{p(\boldsymbol{x})} \left[D_{\mathbb{KL}}\left(p(\boldsymbol{y}|\boldsymbol{x}) \parallel q(\boldsymbol{y})\right) \right] \tag{5.141}$$

This bound is tight if $q(\boldsymbol{y}) = p(\boldsymbol{y})$.

What's happening here is that $\mathbb{I}(Y;X) = \mathbb{H}(Y) - \mathbb{H}(Y|X)$ and we've assumed we know $p(\boldsymbol{y}|\boldsymbol{x})$ and so can estimate $\mathbb{H}(Y|X)$ well. While we don't know $\mathbb{H}(Y)$, we can upper bound it using some model $q(\boldsymbol{y})$. Our model can never do better than $p(\boldsymbol{y})$ itself (the non-negativity of KL), so our entropy estimate errs too large, and hence our MI estimate will be an upper bound.

5.3.6.2   BA lower bound

Suppose that the joint $p(\boldsymbol{x}, \boldsymbol{y})$ is intractable to evaluate, but that we can evaluate $p(\boldsymbol{x})$. Furthermore, suppose we approximate $p(\boldsymbol{x}|\boldsymbol{y})$ by $q(\boldsymbol{x}|\boldsymbol{y})$. Then we can derive the following variational lower bound on the mutual information:

$$\mathbb{I}(\boldsymbol{x};\boldsymbol{y}) = \mathbb{E}_{p(\boldsymbol{x},\boldsymbol{y})} \left[\log \frac{p(\boldsymbol{x}|\boldsymbol{y})}{p(\boldsymbol{x})} \right] \tag{5.142}$$

$$= \mathbb{E}_{p(\boldsymbol{x},\boldsymbol{y})} \left[\log \frac{q(\boldsymbol{x}|\boldsymbol{y})}{p(\boldsymbol{x})} \right] + \mathbb{E}_{p(\boldsymbol{y})} \left[D_{\mathbb{KL}}\left(p(\boldsymbol{x}|\boldsymbol{y}) \parallel q(\boldsymbol{x}|\boldsymbol{y})\right) \right] \tag{5.143}$$

$$\geq \mathbb{E}_{p(\boldsymbol{x},\boldsymbol{y})} \left[\log \frac{q(\boldsymbol{x}|\boldsymbol{y})}{p(\boldsymbol{x})} \right] = \mathbb{E}_{p(\boldsymbol{x},\boldsymbol{y})} \left[\log q(\boldsymbol{x}|\boldsymbol{y}) \right] + h(\boldsymbol{x}) \tag{5.144}$$

where $h(\boldsymbol{x})$ is the differential entropy of $\boldsymbol{x}$. This is called the **BA lower bound**, after the authors Barber and Agakov [BA03].

5.3.6.3   NWJ lower bound

The BA lower bound requires a tractable normalized distribution $q(\boldsymbol{x}|\boldsymbol{y})$ that we can evaluate pointwise. If we reparameterize this distribution in a clever way, we can generate a lower bound that does not require a normalized distribution. Let's write:

$$q(\boldsymbol{x}|\boldsymbol{y}) = \frac{p(\boldsymbol{x})e^{f(\boldsymbol{x},\boldsymbol{y})}}{Z(\boldsymbol{y})} \tag{5.145}$$

with $Z(\boldsymbol{y}) = \mathbb{E}_{p(\boldsymbol{x})}\left[e^{f(\boldsymbol{x},\boldsymbol{y})}\right]$ the normalization constant or partition function. Plugging this into the BA lower bound above we obtain:

$$\mathbb{E}_{p(\boldsymbol{x},\boldsymbol{y})}\left[\log\frac{p(\boldsymbol{x})e^{f(\boldsymbol{x},\boldsymbol{y})}}{p(\boldsymbol{x})Z(\boldsymbol{y})}\right] = \mathbb{E}_{p(\boldsymbol{x},\boldsymbol{y})}\left[f(\boldsymbol{x},\boldsymbol{y})\right] - \mathbb{E}_{p(\boldsymbol{y})}\left[\log Z(\boldsymbol{y})\right] \tag{5.146}$$

$$= \mathbb{E}_{p(\boldsymbol{x},\boldsymbol{y})}\left[f(\boldsymbol{x},\boldsymbol{y})\right] - \mathbb{E}_{p(\boldsymbol{y})}\left[\log\mathbb{E}_{p(\boldsymbol{x})}\left[e^{f(\boldsymbol{x},\boldsymbol{y})}\right]\right] \tag{5.147}$$

$$\triangleq I_{DV}(X;Y). \tag{5.148}$$

This is the **Donsker-Varadhan** lower bound [DV75].

We can construct a more tractable version of this by using the fact that the log function can be upper bounded by a straight line using

$$\log x \le \frac{x}{a} + \log a - 1 \tag{5.149}$$

If we set $a = e$, we get

$$\mathbb{I}(X;Y) \ge \mathbb{E}_{p(\boldsymbol{x},\boldsymbol{y})}[f(\boldsymbol{x},\boldsymbol{y})] - e^{-1}\mathbb{E}_{p(\boldsymbol{y})}Z(\boldsymbol{y}) \triangleq I_{NWJ}(X;Y) \tag{5.150}$$

This is called the **NWJ lower bound** (after the authors of Nguyen, Wainwright, and Jordan [NWJ10a]), or the f-GAN KL [NCT16a], or the MINE-f score [Bel+18].

5.3.6.4   InfoNCE lower bound

If we instead explore a multi-sample extension to the DV bound above, we can generate the following lower bound (see [Poo+19b] for the derivation):

$$\mathbb{I}_{\text{NCE}} = \mathbb{E}\left[\frac{1}{K}\sum_{i=1}^{K}\log\frac{e^{f(\boldsymbol{x}_i,\boldsymbol{y}_i)}}{\frac{1}{K}\sum_{j=1}^{K}e^{f(\boldsymbol{x}_i,\boldsymbol{y}_j)}}\right] \tag{5.151}$$

$$= \log K - \mathbb{E}\left[\frac{1}{K}\sum_{i=1}^{K}\log\left(1 + \sum_{j\ne i}^{K}e^{f(\boldsymbol{x}_i,\boldsymbol{y}_j)-f(\boldsymbol{x}_i,\boldsymbol{y}_i)}\right)\right] \tag{5.152}$$

where the expectation is over paired samples from the joint $p(X, Y)$. The quantity in Equation (5.152) is called the **InfoNCE** estimate, and was proposed in [OLV18a; Hen+19a]. (NCE stands for "noise contrastive estimation", and is discussed in Section 24.4.)

The intuition here is that mutual information is a divergence between the joint $p(\boldsymbol{x}, \boldsymbol{y})$ and the product of the marginals, $p(\boldsymbol{x})p(\boldsymbol{y})$. In other words, mutual information is a measurement of how

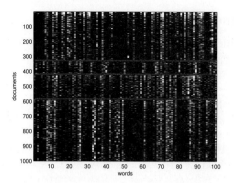

Figure 5.8: *Subset of size 16242 x 100 of the 20-newsgroups data. We only show 1000 rows, for clarity. Each row is a document (represented as a bag-of-words bit vector), each column is a word. The red lines separate the 4 classes, which are (in descending order) comp, rec, sci, talk (these are the titles of USENET groups). We can see that there are subsets of words whose presence or absence is indicative of the class. The data is available from* http://cs.nyu.edu/~roweis/data.html. *Generated by* newsgroups_visualize.ipynb.

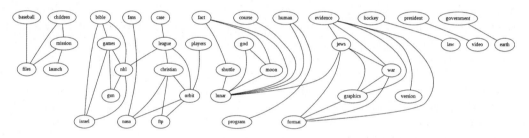

Figure 5.9: *Part of a relevance network constructed from the 20-newsgroup data. data shown in Figure 5.8. We show edges whose mutual information is greater than or equal to 20% of the maximum pairwise MI. For clarity, the graph has been cropped, so we only show a subset of the nodes and edges. Generated by* relevance_network_newsgroup_demo.ipynb.

distinct sampling pairs jointly is from sampling xs and ys independently. The InfoNCE bound in Equation (5.152) provides a lower bound on the true mutual information by attempting to train a model to distinguish between these two situations.

Although this is a valid lower bound, we may need to use a large batch size K to estimate the MI if the MI is large, since $\mathbb{I}_{\text{NCE}} \leq \log K$. (Recently [SE20a] proposed to use a multi-label classifier, rather than a multi-class classifier, to overcome this limitation.)

5.3.7   Relevance networks

If we have a set of related variables, we can compute a **relevance network**, in which we add an $i - j$ edge if the pairwise mutual information $\mathbb{I}(X_i; X_j)$ is above some threshold. In the Gaussian case, $\mathbb{I}(X_i; X_j) = -\frac{1}{2}\log(1 - \rho_{ij}^2)$, where ρ_{ij} is the correlation coefficient, and the resulting graph is called a **covariance graph** (Section 4.5.5.1). However, we can also apply it to discrete random variables.

Relevance networks are quite popular in systems biology [Mar+06], where they are used to visualize the interaction between genes. But they can also be applied to other kinds of datasets. For example, Figure 5.9 visualizes the MI between words in the 20-newsgroup dataset shown in Figure 5.8. The results seem intuitively reasonable.

However, relevance networks suffer from a major problem: the graphs are usually very dense, since most variables are dependent on most other variables, even after thresholding the MIs. For example, suppose X_1 directly influences X_2 which directly influences X_3 (e.g., these form components of a signalling cascade, $X_1 - X_2 - X_3$). Then X_1 has non-zero MI with X_3 (and vice versa), so there will be a $1 - 3$ edge as well as the $1 - 2$ and $2 - 3$ edges; thus the graph may be fully connected, depending on the threshold.

A solution to this is to learn a probablistic graphical model, which represents conditional *in-dependence*, rather than *dependence*. In the chain example, there will not be a $1 - 3$ edge, since $X_1 \perp X_3 | X_2$. Consequently graphical models are usually much sparser than relevance networks. See Chapter 30 for details.

5.4 Data compression (source coding)

Data compression, also known as **source coding**, is at the heart of information theory. It is also related to probabilistic machine learning. The reason for this is as follows: if we can model the probability of different kinds of data samples, then we can assign short **code words** to the most frequently occuring ones, reserving longer encodings for the less frequent ones. This is similar to the situation in natural language, where common words (such as "a", "the", "and") are generally much shorter than rare words. Thus the ability to compress data requires an ability to discover the underlying patterns, and their relative frequencies, in the data. This has led Marcus Hutter to propose that compression be used as an objective way to measure performance towards general purpose AI. More precisely, he is offering 50,000 Euros to anyone who can compress the first 100MB of (English) Wikipedia better than some baseline. This is known as the **Hutter prize**.[1]

In this section, we give a brief summary of some of the key ideas in data compression. For details, see e.g., [Mac03; CT06; YMT22].

5.4.1 Lossless compression

Discrete data, such as natural language, can always be compressed in such a way that we can uniquely recover the original data. This is called **lossless compression**.

Claude Shannon proved that the expected number of bits needed to losslessly encode some data coming from distribution p is at least $\mathbb{H}(p)$. This is known as the **source coding theorem**. Achieving this lower bound requires coming up with good probability models, as well as good ways to design codes based on those models. Because of the non-negativity of the KL divergence, $\mathbb{H}_{ce}(p, q) \geq \mathbb{H}(p)$, so if we use any model q other than the true model p to compress the data, it will take some excess bits. The number of excess bits is exactly $D_{\mathbb{KL}}(p \parallel q)$.

Common techniques for realizing lossless codes include Huffman coding, arithmetic coding, and asymmetric numeral systems [Dud13]. The input to these algorithms is a probability distribution over strings (which is where ML comes in). This distribution is often represented using a latent variable model (see e.g., [TBB19; KAH19]).

---

1. For details, see `http://prize.hutter1.net`.

5.4.2 Lossy compression and the rate-distortion tradeoff

To encode real-valued signals, such as images and sound, as a digital signal, we first have to quantize the signal into a sequence of symbols. A simple way to do this is to use vector quantization. We can then compress this discrete sequence of symbols using lossless coding methods. However, when we uncompress, we lose some information. Hence this approach is called **lossy compression**.

In this section, we quantify this tradeoff between the size of the representation (number of symbols we use), and the resulting error. We will use the terminology of the variational information bottleneck discussed in Section 5.6.2 (except here we are in the unsupervised setting). In particular, we assume we have a stochastic encoder $p(z|x)$, a stochastic decoder $d(x|z)$ and a prior marginal $m(z)$.

We define the **distortion** of an encoder-decoder pair (as in Section 5.6.2) as follows:

$$D = - \int dx\, p(x) \int dz\, e(z|x) \log d(x|z) \tag{5.153}$$

If the decoder is a deterministic model plus Gaussian noise, $d(x|z) = \mathcal{N}(x|f_d(z), \sigma^2)$, and the encoder is deterministic, $e(z|x) = \delta(z - f_e(x))$, then this becomes

$$D = \frac{1}{\sigma^2} \mathbb{E}_{p(x)} \left[||f_d(f_e(x)) - x||^2 \right] \tag{5.154}$$

This is just the expected **reconstruction error** that occurs if we (deterministically) encode and then decode the data using f_e and f_d.

We define the **rate** of our model as follows:

$$R = \int dx\, p(x) \int dz\, e(z|x) \log \frac{e(z|x)}{m(z)} \tag{5.155}$$

$$= \mathbb{E}_{p(x)} \left[D_{\mathrm{KL}} \left(e(z|x) \, \| \, m(z) \right) \right] \tag{5.156}$$

$$= \int dx \int dz\, p(x, z) \log \frac{p(x, z)}{p(x)m(z)} \geq \mathbb{I}(x, z) \tag{5.157}$$

This is just the average KL between our encoding distribution and the marginal. If we use $m(z)$ to design an optimal code, then the rate is the *excess* number of bits we need to pay to encode our data using $m(z)$ rather than the true **aggregate posterior** $p(z) = \int dx\, p(x)e(z|x)$.

There is a fundamental tradeoff between the rate and distortion. To see why, note that a trivial encoding scheme would set $e(z|x) = \delta(z - x)$, which simply uses x as its own best representation. This would incur 0 distortion (and hence maximize the likelihood), but it would incur a high rate, since each $e(z|x)$ distribution would be unique, and far from $m(z)$. In other words, there would be no compression. Conversely, if $e(z|x) = \delta(z - \mathbf{0})$, the encoder would ignore the input. In this case, the rate would be 0, but the distortion would be high.

We can characterize the tradeoff more precisely using the variational lower and upper bounds on the mutual information from Section 5.3.6. From that section, we know that

$$H - D \leq \mathbb{I}(x; z) \leq R \tag{5.158}$$

where H is the (differential) entropy

$$H = - \int dx\, p(x) \log p(x) \tag{5.159}$$

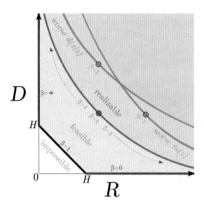

Figure 5.10: *Illustration of the rate-distortion tradeoff. See text for details. From Figure 1 of [Ale+18]. Used with kind permission of Alex Alemi.*

For discrete data, all probabilities are bounded above by 1, and hence $H \geq 0$ and $D \geq 0$. In addition, the rate is always non-negative, $R \geq 0$, since it is the average of a KL divergence. (This is true for either discrete or continuous encodings $\boldsymbol{z}$.) Consequently, we can plot the set of achievable values of R and D as shown in Figure 5.10. This is known as a **rate distortion curve**.

The bottom horizontal line corresponds to the zero distortion setting, $D = 0$, in which we can perfectly encode and decode our data. This can be achieved by using the trivial encoder where $e(\boldsymbol{z}|\boldsymbol{x}) = \delta(\boldsymbol{z} - \boldsymbol{x})$. Shannon's source coding theorem tells us that the minimum number of bits we need to use to encode data in this setting is the entropy of the data, so $R \geq H$ when $D = 0$. If we use a suboptimal marginal distribution $m(\boldsymbol{z})$ for coding, we will increase the rate without affecting the distortion.

The left vertical line corresponds to the zero rate setting, $R = 0$, in which the latent code is independent of $\boldsymbol{z}$. In this case, the decoder $d(\boldsymbol{x}|\boldsymbol{z})$ is independent of $\boldsymbol{z}$. However, we can still learn a joint probability model $p(\boldsymbol{x})$ which does not use latent variables, e.g., this could be an autoregressive model. The minimal distortion such a model could achieve is again the entropy of the data, $D \geq H$.

The black diagonal line illustrates solutions that satisfy $D = H - R$, where the upper and lower bounds are tight. In practice, we cannot achieve points on the diagonal, since that requires the bounds to be tight, and therefore assumes our models $e(\boldsymbol{z}|\boldsymbol{x})$ and $d(\boldsymbol{x}|\boldsymbol{z})$ are perfect. This is called the "non-parametric limit". In the finite data setting, we will always incur additional error, so the RD plot will trace a curve which is shifted up, as shown in Figure 5.10.

We can generate different solutions along this curve by minimizing the following objective:

$$J = D + \beta R = \int d\boldsymbol{x} \, p(\boldsymbol{x}) \int d\boldsymbol{z} \, e(\boldsymbol{z}|\boldsymbol{x}) \left[-\log d(\boldsymbol{x}|\boldsymbol{z}) + \beta \log \frac{e(\boldsymbol{z}|\boldsymbol{x})}{m(\boldsymbol{z})} \right] \tag{5.160}$$

If we set $\beta = 1$, and define $q(\boldsymbol{z}|\boldsymbol{x}) = e(\boldsymbol{z}|\boldsymbol{x})$, $p(\boldsymbol{x}|\boldsymbol{z}) = d(\boldsymbol{x}|\boldsymbol{z})$, and $p(\boldsymbol{z}) = m(\boldsymbol{z})$, this exactly matches the VAE objective in Section 21.2. To see this, note that the ELBO from Section 10.1.1.2 can be written as

$$Ł = -(D + R) = \mathbb{E}_{p(\boldsymbol{x})} \left[\mathbb{E}_{e(\boldsymbol{z}|\boldsymbol{x})} [\log d(\boldsymbol{x}|\boldsymbol{z})] - \mathbb{E}_{e(\boldsymbol{z}|\boldsymbol{x})} \left[\log \frac{e(\boldsymbol{z}|\boldsymbol{x})}{m(\boldsymbol{z})} \right] \right] \tag{5.161}$$

which we recognize as the expected reconstruction error minus the KL term $D_{\text{KL}}\left(e(\boldsymbol{z}|\boldsymbol{x}) \parallel m(\boldsymbol{z})\right)$.

If we allow $\beta \neq 1$, we recover the β-VAE objective discussed in Section 21.3.1. Note, however, that the β-VAE model cannot distinguish between different solutions on the diagonal line, all of which have $\beta = 1$. This is because all such models have the same marginal likelihood (and hence same ELBO), although they differ radically in terms of whether they learn an interesting latent representation or not. Thus likelihood is not a sufficient metric for comparing the quality of unsupervised representation learning methods, as discussed in Section 21.3.1.

For further discussion on the inherent conflict between rate, distortion, and *perception*, see [BM19]. For techniques for evaluating rate distortion curves for models see [HCG20].

5.4.3   Bits back coding

In the previous section we penalized the rate of our code using the average KL divergence, $\mathbb{E}_{p(\boldsymbol{x})}\left[R(\boldsymbol{x})\right]$, where

$$R(\boldsymbol{x}) \triangleq \int d\boldsymbol{z}\, p(\boldsymbol{z}|\boldsymbol{x}) \log \frac{p(\boldsymbol{z}|\boldsymbol{x})}{m(\boldsymbol{z})} = \mathbb{H}_{ce}(p(\boldsymbol{z}|\boldsymbol{x}), m(\boldsymbol{z})) - \mathbb{H}(p(\boldsymbol{z}|\boldsymbol{x})). \tag{5.162}$$

The first term is the cross entropy, which is the expected number of bits we need to encode $\boldsymbol{x}$; the second term is the entropy, which is the minimum number of bits. Thus we are penalizing the *excess* number of bits required to communicate the code to a receiver. How come we don't have to "pay for" the actual (total) number of bits we use, which is the cross entropy?

The reason is that we could in principle get the bits needed by the optimal code given back to us; this is called **bits back coding** [HC93; FH97]. The argument goes as follows. Imagine Alice is trying to (losslessly) communicate some data, such as an image $\boldsymbol{x}$, to Bob. Before they went their separate ways, both Alice and Bob decided to share their encoder $p(\boldsymbol{z}|\boldsymbol{x})$, marginal $m(\boldsymbol{z})$ and decoder distributions $d(\boldsymbol{x}|\boldsymbol{z})$. To communicate an image, Alice will use a **two part code**. First, she will sample a code $\boldsymbol{z} \sim p(\boldsymbol{z}|\boldsymbol{x})$ from her encoder, and communicate that to Bob over a channel designed to efficiently encode samples from the marginal $m(\boldsymbol{z})$; this costs $-\log_2 m(\boldsymbol{z})$ bits. Next Alice will use her decoder $d(\boldsymbol{x}|\boldsymbol{z})$ to compute the residual error, and losslessly send that to Bob at the cost of $-\log_2 d(\boldsymbol{x}|\boldsymbol{z})$ bits. The expected total number of bits required here is what we naively expected:

$$\mathbb{E}_{p(\boldsymbol{z}|\boldsymbol{x})}\left[-\log_2 d(\boldsymbol{x}|\boldsymbol{z}) - \log_2 m(\boldsymbol{z})\right] = D + \mathbb{H}_{ce}(p(\boldsymbol{z}|\boldsymbol{x}), m(\boldsymbol{z})). \tag{5.163}$$

We see that this is the distortion plus cross entropy, not distortion plus rate. So how do we get the bits back, to convert the cross entropy to a rate term?

The trick is that Bob actually receives more information than we suspected. Bob can use the code $\boldsymbol{z}$ and the residual error to perfectly reconstruct $\boldsymbol{x}$. However, Bob also knows what specific code Alice sent, $\boldsymbol{z}$, as well as what encoder she used, $p(\boldsymbol{z}|\boldsymbol{x})$. When Alice drew the sample code $\boldsymbol{z} \sim p(\boldsymbol{z}|\boldsymbol{x})$, she had to use some kind of entropy source in order to generate the random sample. Suppose she did it by picking words sequentially from a compressed copy of Moby Dick, in order to generate a stream of random bits. On Bob's end, he can reverse engineer all of the sampling bits, and thus recover the compressed copy of Moby Dick! Thus Alice can use the extra randomness in the choice of $\boldsymbol{z}$ to share more information.

While in the original formulation the bits back argument was largely theoretical, offering a thought experiment for why we should penalize our models with the KL instead of the cross entropy, recently several practical real world algorithms have been developed that actually achieve the bits back goal. These include [HPHL19; AT20; TBB19; YBM20; HLA19; FHHL20].

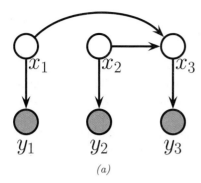 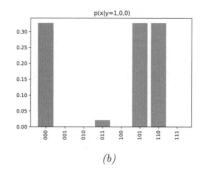

(a)   (b)

Figure 5.11: (a) A simple error-correcting code DPGM. x_i are the sent bits, y_i are the received bits. x_3 is an even parity check bit computed from x_1 and x_2. (b) Posterior over codewords given that $\boldsymbol{y} = (1, 0, 0)$; the probability of a bit flip is 0.2. Generated by error_correcting_code_demo.ipynb.

5.5   Error-correcting codes (channel coding)

The idea behind **error correcting codes** is to add redundancy to a signal $\boldsymbol{x}$ (which is the result of encoding the original data), such that when it is sent over to the receiver via a noisy transmission line (such as a cell phone connection), the receiver can recover from any corruptions that might occur to the signal. This is called **channel coding**.

In more detail, let $\boldsymbol{x} \in \{0, 1\}^m$ be the source message, where m is called the **block length**. Let $\boldsymbol{y}$ be the result of sending $\boldsymbol{x}$ over a **noisy channel**. This is a corrupted version of the message. For example, each message bit may get flipped independently with probability α, in which case $p(\boldsymbol{y}|\boldsymbol{x}) = \prod_{i=1}^m p(y_i|x_i)$, where $p(y_i|x_i = 0) = [1 - \alpha, \alpha]$ and $p(y_i|x_i = 1) = [\alpha, 1 - \alpha]$. Alternatively, we may add Gaussian noise, so $p(y_i|x_i = b) = \mathcal{N}(y_i|\mu_b, \sigma^2)$. The receiver's goal is to infer the true message from the noisy observations, i.e., to compute $\operatorname{argmax}_{\boldsymbol{x}} p(\boldsymbol{x}|\boldsymbol{y})$.

A common way to increase the chance of being able to recover the original signal is to add **parity check bits** to it before sending it. These are deterministic functions of the original signal, which specify if the sum of the input bits is odd or even. This provides a form of **redundancy**, so that if one bit is corrupted, we can still infer its value, assuming the other bits are not flipped. (This is reasonable since we assume the bits are corrupted independently at random, so it is less likely that multiple bits are flipped than just one bit.)

For example, suppose we have two original message bits, and we add one parity bit. This can be modeled using a directed graphical model as shown in Figure 5.11(a). This graph encodes the following joint probability distribution:

$$p(\boldsymbol{x}, \boldsymbol{y}) = p(x_1)p(x_2)p(x_3|x_1, x_2) \prod_{i=1}^{3} p(y_i|x_i) \tag{5.164}$$

The priors $p(x_1)$ and $p(x_2)$ are uniform. The conditional term $p(x_3|x_1, x_2)$ is deterministic, and computes the parity of (x_1, x_2). In particular, we have $p(x_3 = 1|x_1, x_2) = 1$ if the total number of 1s in the block $x_{1:2}$ is odd. The likelihood terms $p(y_i|x_i)$ represent a bit flipping noisy channel model, with noise level $\alpha = 0.2$.

Suppose we observe $\boldsymbol{y} = (1, 0, 0)$. We know that this cannot be what the sender sent, since this violates the parity constraint (if $x_1 = 1$ then we know $x_3 = 1$). Instead, the 3 posterior modes for $\boldsymbol{x}$ are 000 (first bit was flipped), 110 (second bit was flipped), and 101 (third bit was flipped). The only other configuration with non-zero support in the posterior is 011, which corresponds to the much less likely hypothesis that three bits were flipped (see Figure 5.11(b)). All other hypotheses (001, 010, and 100) are inconsistent with the deterministic method used to create codewords. (See Section 9.3.3.2 for further discussion of this point.)

In practice, we use more complex coding schemes that are more efficient, in the sense that they add less redundant bits to the message, but still guarantee that errors can be corrected. For details, see Section 9.4.8.

5.6   The information bottleneck

In this section, we discuss discriminative models $p(\boldsymbol{y}|\boldsymbol{x})$ that use a *stochastic bottleneck* between the input $\boldsymbol{x}$ and the output $\boldsymbol{y}$ to prevent overfitting, and improve robustness and calibration.

5.6.1   Vanilla IB

We say that $\boldsymbol{z}$ is a **representation** of $\boldsymbol{x}$ if $\boldsymbol{z}$ is a (possibly stochastic) function of $\boldsymbol{x}$, and hence can be described by the conditional $p(\boldsymbol{z}|\boldsymbol{x})$. We say that a representation $\boldsymbol{z}$ of $\boldsymbol{x}$ is **sufficient** for task $\boldsymbol{y}$ if $\boldsymbol{y} \perp \boldsymbol{x}|\boldsymbol{z}$, or equivalently, if $\mathbb{I}(\boldsymbol{z}; \boldsymbol{y}) = \mathbb{I}(\boldsymbol{x}; \boldsymbol{y})$, i.e., $\mathbb{H}(\boldsymbol{y}|\boldsymbol{z}) = \mathbb{H}(\boldsymbol{y}|\boldsymbol{x})$. We say that a representation is a **minimal sufficient statistic** if $\boldsymbol{z}$ is sufficient and there is no other $\boldsymbol{z}$ with smaller $\mathbb{I}(\boldsymbol{z}; \boldsymbol{x})$ value. Thus we would like to find a representation $\boldsymbol{z}$ that maximizes $\mathbb{I}(\boldsymbol{z}; \boldsymbol{y})$ while minimizing $\mathbb{I}(\boldsymbol{z}; \boldsymbol{x})$. That is, we would like to optimize the following objective:

$$\min \beta\, \mathbb{I}(\boldsymbol{z}; \boldsymbol{x}) - \mathbb{I}(\boldsymbol{z}; \boldsymbol{y}) \tag{5.165}$$

where $\beta \geq 0$, and we optimize wrt the distributions $p(\boldsymbol{z}|\boldsymbol{x})$ and $p(\boldsymbol{y}|\boldsymbol{z})$. This is called the **information bottleneck principle** [TPB99]. This generalizes the concept of minimal sufficient statistic to take into account that there is a tradeoff between sufficiency and minimality, which is captured by the Lagrange multiplier $\beta > 0$.

This principle is illustrated in Figure 5.12. We assume Z is a function of X, but is independent of Y, i.e., we assume the graphical model $Z \leftarrow X \leftrightarrow Y$. This corresponds to the following joint distribution:

$$p(\boldsymbol{x}, \boldsymbol{y}, \boldsymbol{z}) = p(\boldsymbol{z}|\boldsymbol{x})p(\boldsymbol{y}|\boldsymbol{x})p(\boldsymbol{x}) \tag{5.166}$$

Thus Z can capture any amount of information about X that it wants, but cannot contain information that is unique to Y, as illustrated in Figure 5.12a. The optimal representation only captures information about X that is useful for Y; to prevent us "wasting capacity" and fitting irrelevant details of the input, Z should also minimize information about X, as shown in Figure 5.12b.

If all the random variables are discrete, and $\boldsymbol{z} = e(\boldsymbol{x})$ is a deterministic function of $\boldsymbol{x}$, then the algorithm of [TPB99] can be used to minimize the IB objective in Section 5.6. The objective can also be solved analytically if all variables are jointly Gaussian [Che+05] (the resulting method can be viewed as a form of supervised PCA). But in general, it is intractable to solve this problem exactly. We discuss a tractable approximation in Section 5.6.2. (More details can be found in e.g., [SZ22].)

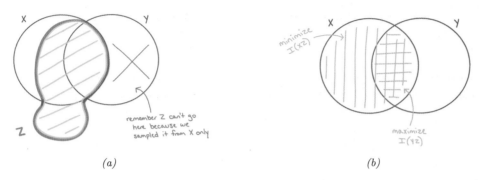

Figure 5.12: Information diagrams for information bottleneck. (a) Z can contain any amount of information about X (whether it useful for predicting Y or not), but it cannot contain information about Y that is not shared with X. (b) The optimal representation for Z maximizes $\mathbb{I}(Z, Y)$ and minimizes $\mathbb{I}(Z, X)$. Used with kind permission of Katie Everett.

5.6.2 Variational IB

In this section, we derive a variational upper bound on Equation (5.165), leveraging ideas from Section 5.3.6. This is called the **variational IB** or **VIB** method [Ale+16]. The key trick will be to use the non-negativity of the KL divergence to write

$$\int d\boldsymbol{x} \, p(\boldsymbol{x}) \log p(\boldsymbol{x}) \geq \int d\boldsymbol{x} \, p(\boldsymbol{x}) \log q(\boldsymbol{x}) \tag{5.167}$$

for any distribution q. (Note that both p and q may be conditioned on other variables.)

To explain the method in more detail, let us define the following notation. Let $e(\boldsymbol{z}|\boldsymbol{x}) = p(\boldsymbol{z}|\boldsymbol{x})$ represent the encoder, $b(\boldsymbol{z}|\boldsymbol{y}) \approx p(\boldsymbol{z}|\boldsymbol{y})$ represent the backwards encoder, $d(\boldsymbol{y}|\boldsymbol{z}) \approx p(\boldsymbol{y}|\boldsymbol{z})$ represent the classifier (decoder), and $m(\boldsymbol{z}) \approx p(\boldsymbol{z})$ represent the marginal. (Note that we get to choose $p(\boldsymbol{z}|\boldsymbol{x})$, but the other distributions are derived by approximations of the corresponding marginals and conditionals of the exact joint $p(\boldsymbol{x}, \boldsymbol{y}, \boldsymbol{z})$.) Also, let $\langle \cdot \rangle$ represent expectations wrt the relevant terms from the $p(\boldsymbol{x}, \boldsymbol{y}, \boldsymbol{z})$ joint.

With this notation, we can derive a lower bound on $\mathbb{I}(\boldsymbol{z}; \boldsymbol{y})$ as follows:

$$\mathbb{I}(\boldsymbol{z}; \boldsymbol{y}) = \int d\boldsymbol{y} dz \, p(\boldsymbol{y}, \boldsymbol{z}) \log \frac{p(\boldsymbol{y}, \boldsymbol{z})}{p(\boldsymbol{y})p(\boldsymbol{z})} \tag{5.168}$$

$$= \int d\boldsymbol{y} dz \, p(\boldsymbol{y}, \boldsymbol{z}) \log p(\boldsymbol{y}|\boldsymbol{z}) - \int d\boldsymbol{y} dz \, p(\boldsymbol{y}, \boldsymbol{z}) \log p(\boldsymbol{y}) \tag{5.169}$$

$$= \int d\boldsymbol{y} dz \, p(\boldsymbol{z})p(\boldsymbol{y}|\boldsymbol{z}) \log p(\boldsymbol{y}|\boldsymbol{z}) - \text{const} \tag{5.170}$$

$$\geq \int d\boldsymbol{y} dz \, p(\boldsymbol{y}, \boldsymbol{z}) \log d(\boldsymbol{y}|\boldsymbol{z}) \tag{5.171}$$

$$= \langle \log d(\boldsymbol{y}|\boldsymbol{z}) \rangle \tag{5.172}$$

where we exploited the fact that $\mathbb{H}(p(\boldsymbol{y}))$ is a constant that is independent of our representation.

Note that we can approximate the expections by sampling from

$$p(\boldsymbol{y}, \boldsymbol{z}) = \int d\boldsymbol{x} \, p(\boldsymbol{x}) p(\boldsymbol{y}|\boldsymbol{x}) p(\boldsymbol{z}|\boldsymbol{x}) = \int d\boldsymbol{x} \, p(\boldsymbol{x}, \boldsymbol{y}) e(\boldsymbol{z}|\boldsymbol{x}) \tag{5.173}$$

This is just the empirical distribution "pushed through" the encoder.

Similarly, we can derive an upper bound on $\mathbb{I}(\boldsymbol{z}; \boldsymbol{x})$ as follows:

$$\mathbb{I}(\boldsymbol{z}; \boldsymbol{x}) = \int d\boldsymbol{z} d\boldsymbol{x} \, p(\boldsymbol{x}, \boldsymbol{z}) \log \frac{p(\boldsymbol{z}, \boldsymbol{x})}{p(\boldsymbol{x}) p(\boldsymbol{z})} \tag{5.174}$$

$$= \int d\boldsymbol{z} d\boldsymbol{x} \, p(\boldsymbol{x}, \boldsymbol{z}) \log p(\boldsymbol{z}|\boldsymbol{x}) - \int d\boldsymbol{z} \, p(\boldsymbol{z}) \log p(\boldsymbol{z}) \tag{5.175}$$

$$\leq \int d\boldsymbol{z} d\boldsymbol{x} \, p(\boldsymbol{x}, \boldsymbol{z}) \log p(\boldsymbol{z}|\boldsymbol{x}) - \int d\boldsymbol{z} \, p(\boldsymbol{z}) \log m(\boldsymbol{z}) \tag{5.176}$$

$$= \int d\boldsymbol{z} d\boldsymbol{x} \, p(\boldsymbol{x}, \boldsymbol{z}) \log \frac{e(\boldsymbol{z}|\boldsymbol{x})}{m(\boldsymbol{z})} \tag{5.177}$$

$$= \langle \log e(\boldsymbol{z}|\boldsymbol{x}) \rangle - \langle \log m(\boldsymbol{z}) \rangle \tag{5.178}$$

Note that we can approximate the expectations by sampling from $p(\boldsymbol{x}, \boldsymbol{z}) = p(\boldsymbol{x}) p(\boldsymbol{z}|\boldsymbol{x})$.

Putting it altogether, we get the following upper bound on the IB objective:

$$\beta \, \mathbb{I}(\boldsymbol{x}; \boldsymbol{z}) - \mathbb{I}(\boldsymbol{z}; \boldsymbol{y}) \leq \beta \left(\langle \log e(\boldsymbol{z}|\boldsymbol{x}) \rangle - \langle \log m(\boldsymbol{z}) \rangle \right) - \langle \log d(\boldsymbol{y}|\boldsymbol{z}) \rangle \tag{5.179}$$

Thus the VIB objective is

$$\mathcal{L}_{\text{VIB}} = \beta \left(\mathbb{E}_{p_{\mathcal{D}}(\boldsymbol{x}) e(\boldsymbol{z}|\boldsymbol{x})} \left[\log e(\boldsymbol{z}|\boldsymbol{x}) - \log m(\boldsymbol{z}) \right] \right) - \mathbb{E}_{p_{\mathcal{D}}(\boldsymbol{x}) e(\boldsymbol{z}|\boldsymbol{x}) d(\boldsymbol{y}|\boldsymbol{z})} \left[\log d(\boldsymbol{y}|\boldsymbol{z}) \right] \tag{5.180}$$

$$= -\mathbb{E}_{p_{\mathcal{D}}(\boldsymbol{x}) e(\boldsymbol{z}|\boldsymbol{x}) d(\boldsymbol{y}|\boldsymbol{z})} \left[\log d(\boldsymbol{y}|\boldsymbol{z}) \right] + \beta \mathbb{E}_{p_{\mathcal{D}}(\boldsymbol{x})} \left[D_{\text{KL}} \left(e(\boldsymbol{z}|\boldsymbol{x}) \, \| \, m(\boldsymbol{z}) \right) \right] \tag{5.181}$$

We can now take stochastic gradients of this objective and minimize it (wrt the parameters of the encoder, decoder, and marginal) using SGD. (We assume the distributions are reparameterizable, as discussed in Section 6.3.5.) For the encoder $e(\boldsymbol{z}|\boldsymbol{x})$, we often use a conditional Gaussian, and for the decoder $d(\boldsymbol{y}|\boldsymbol{z})$, we often use a softmax classifier. For the marginal, $m(\boldsymbol{z})$, we should use a flexible model, such as a mixture of Gaussians, since it needs to approximate the **aggregated posterior** $p(\boldsymbol{z}) = \int d\boldsymbol{z} p(\boldsymbol{x}) e(\boldsymbol{z}|\boldsymbol{x})$, which is a mixture of N Gaussians (assuming $p(\boldsymbol{x})$ is an empirical distribution with N samples, and $e(\boldsymbol{z}|\boldsymbol{x})$ is a Gaussian).

We illustrate this in Figure 5.13, where we fit the an MLP model to MNIST. We use a 2d bottleneck layer before passing to the softmax. In panel a, we show the embedding learned by a determinisic encoder. We see that each image gets mapped to a point, and there is little overlap between classes, or between instances. In panels b-c, we show the embedding learned by a stochastic encoder. Each image gets mapped to a Gaussian distribution, we show the mean and the covariance separately. The classes are still well separated, but individual instances of a class are no longer distinguishable, since such information is not relevant for prediction purposes.

5.6.3 Conditional entropy bottleneck

The IB tries to maximize $\mathbb{I}(Z; Y)$ while minimizing $\mathbb{I}(Z; X)$. We can write this objective as

$$\min \mathbb{I}(\boldsymbol{x}; \boldsymbol{z}) - \lambda \, \mathbb{I}(\boldsymbol{y}; \boldsymbol{z}) \tag{5.182}$$

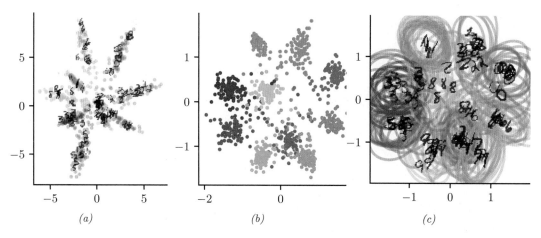

Figure 5.13: *2d embeddings of MNIST digits created by an MLP classifier. (a) Deterministic model. (b-c) VIB model, means and covariances. Generated by vib_demo.ipynb. Used with kind permission of Alex Alemi.*

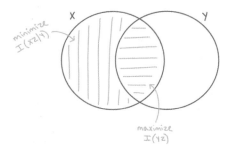

Figure 5.14: *Conditional entropy bottleneck (CEB) chooses a representation Z that maximizes $\mathbb{I}(Z, Y)$ and minimizes $\mathbb{I}(X, Z|Y)$. Used with kind permission of Katie Everett.*

for $\lambda \geq 0$. However, we see from the information diagram in Figure 5.12b that $\mathbb{I}(Z; X)$ contains some information that is relevant to Y. A sensible alternative objective is to minimizes the residual mutual information, $\mathbb{I}(X; Z|Y)$. This gives rise to the following objective:

$$\min \mathbb{I}(\boldsymbol{x}; \boldsymbol{z}|\boldsymbol{y}) - \lambda' \, \mathbb{I}(\boldsymbol{y}; \boldsymbol{z}) \tag{5.183}$$

for $\lambda' \geq 0$. This is known as the **conditional entropy bottleck** or **CEB** [Fis20]. See Figure 5.14 for an illustration.

Since $\mathbb{I}(\boldsymbol{x}; \boldsymbol{z}|\boldsymbol{y}) = \mathbb{I}(\boldsymbol{x}; \boldsymbol{z}) - \mathbb{I}(\boldsymbol{y}; \boldsymbol{z})$, we see that the CEB is equivalent to standard IB with $\lambda' = \lambda + 1$. However, it is easier to upper bound $\mathbb{I}(\boldsymbol{x}; \boldsymbol{z}|\boldsymbol{y})$ than $\mathbb{I}(\boldsymbol{x}; \boldsymbol{z})$, since we are conditioning on $\boldsymbol{y}$, which provides information about $\boldsymbol{z}$. In particular, by leveraging $p(\boldsymbol{z}|\boldsymbol{x}, y) = p(\boldsymbol{z}|\boldsymbol{x})$ we have

$$\mathbb{I}(\boldsymbol{x}; \boldsymbol{z}|\boldsymbol{y}) = \mathbb{I}(\boldsymbol{x}; \boldsymbol{z}) - \mathbb{I}(\boldsymbol{y}; \boldsymbol{z}) \tag{5.184}$$

$$= \mathbb{H}(\boldsymbol{z}) - \mathbb{H}(\boldsymbol{z}|\boldsymbol{x}) - [\mathbb{H}(\boldsymbol{z}) - \mathbb{H}(\boldsymbol{z}|\boldsymbol{y})] \tag{5.185}$$

$$= -\mathbb{H}(\boldsymbol{z}|\boldsymbol{x}) + \mathbb{H}(\boldsymbol{z}|\boldsymbol{y}) \tag{5.186}$$

$$= \int dz dx \, p(\boldsymbol{x}, \boldsymbol{z}) \log p(\boldsymbol{z}|\boldsymbol{x}) - \int dz dy \, p(\boldsymbol{z}, \boldsymbol{y}) \log p(\boldsymbol{z}|\boldsymbol{y}) \tag{5.187}$$

$$\leq \int dz dx \, p(\boldsymbol{x}, \boldsymbol{z}) \log e(\boldsymbol{z}|\boldsymbol{x}) - \int dz dy \, p(\boldsymbol{z}, \boldsymbol{y}) \log b(\boldsymbol{z}|\boldsymbol{y}) \tag{5.188}$$

$$= \langle \log e(\boldsymbol{z}|\boldsymbol{x}) \rangle - \langle \log b(\boldsymbol{z}|\boldsymbol{y}) \rangle \tag{5.189}$$

Putting it altogether, we get the final CEB objective:

$$\min \beta \left(\langle \log e(\boldsymbol{z}|\boldsymbol{x}) \rangle - \langle \log b(\boldsymbol{z}|\boldsymbol{y}) \rangle \right) - \langle \log d(\boldsymbol{y}|\boldsymbol{z}) \rangle \tag{5.190}$$

Note that it is generally easier to learn the conditional backwards encoder $b(\boldsymbol{z}|\boldsymbol{y})$ than the unconditional marginal $m(\boldsymbol{z})$. Also, we know that the tightest upper bound occurs when $\mathbb{I}(\boldsymbol{x}; \boldsymbol{z}|\boldsymbol{y}) = \mathbb{I}(\boldsymbol{x}; \boldsymbol{z}) - \mathbb{I}(\boldsymbol{y}; \boldsymbol{z}) = 0$. The corresponding value of β corresponds to an optimal representation. By contrast, it is not clear how to measure distance from optimality when using IB.

6 Optimization

6.1 Introduction

In this chapter, we consider solving **optimization problems** of various forms. Abstractly these can all be written as

$$\boldsymbol{\theta}^* \in \operatorname*{argmin}_{\boldsymbol{\theta} \in \Theta} \mathcal{L}(\boldsymbol{\theta}) \tag{6.1}$$

where $\mathcal{L} : \Theta \to \mathbb{R}$ is the objective or loss function, and Θ is the parameter space we are optimizing over. However, this abstraction hides many details, such as whether the problem is constrained or unconstrained, discrete or continuous, convex or non-convex, etc. In the prequel to this book, [Mur22], we discussed some simple optimization algorithms for some common problems that arise in machine learning. In this chapter, we discuss some more advanced methods. For more details on optimization, please consult some of the many excellent textbooks, such as [KW19b; BV04; NW06; Ber15; Ber16] as well as various review articles, such as [BCN18; Sun+19b; PPS18; Pey20].

6.2 Automatic differentiation

This section is written by Roy Frostig.

This section is concerned with computing (partial) derivatives of complicated functions in an automatic manner. By "complicated" we mean those expressed as a composition of an arbitrary number of more basic operations, such as in deep neural networks. This task is known as **automatic differentiation** (**AD**), or **autodiff**. AD is an essential component in optimization and deep learning, and is also used in several other fields across science and engineering. See e.g., Baydin et al. [Bay+15] for a review focused on machine learning and Griewank and Walther [GW08] for a classical textbook.

6.2.1 Differentiation in functional form

Before covering automatic differentiation, it is useful to review the mathematics of differentiation. We will use a particular **functional** notation for partial derivatives, rather than the typical one used throughout much of this book. We will refer to the latter as the **named variable** notation for the moment. Named variable notation relies on associating function arguments with names. For instance, given a function $f : \mathbb{R}^2 \to \mathbb{R}$, the partial derivative of f with respect to its first scalar argument, at a point $\boldsymbol{a} = (a_1, a_2)$, might be written:

$$\left.\frac{\partial f}{\partial x_1}\right|_{\boldsymbol{x}=\boldsymbol{a}} \tag{6.2}$$

This notation is not entirely self-contained. It refers to a name $\boldsymbol{x} = (x_1, x_2)$, implicit or inferred from context, suggesting the argument of f. An alternative expression is:

$$\frac{\partial}{\partial a_1} f(a_1, a_2) \tag{6.3}$$

where now a_1 serves both as an argument name (or a symbol in an expression) and as a particular evaluation point. Tracking names can become an increasingly complicated endeavor as we compose many functions together, each possibly taking several arguments.

A functional notation instead defines derivatives as operators on functions. If a function has multiple arguments, they are identified by position rather than by name, alleviating the need for auxiliary variable definitions. Some of the following definitions draw on those in Spivak's *Calculus on Manifolds* [Spi71] and in Sussman and Wisdom's *Functional Differential Geometry* [SW13], and generally appear more regularly in accounts of differential calculus and geometry. These texts are recommended for a more formal treatment, and a more mathematically general view, of the material briefly covered in this section.

Beside notation, we will rely on some basic multivariable calculus concepts. This includes the notion of (partial) derivatives, the differential or Jacobian of a function at a point, its role as a linear approximation local to the point, and various properties of linear maps, matrices, and transposition. We will focus on a finite-dimensional setting and write $\{\boldsymbol{e}_1, \ldots, \boldsymbol{e}_n\}$ for the standard basis in $\mathbb{R}^n$.

Linear and multilinear functions. We use $F : \mathbb{R}^n \multimap \mathbb{R}^m$ to denote a function $F : \mathbb{R}^n \to \mathbb{R}^m$ that is linear, and by $F[\boldsymbol{x}]$ its application to $\boldsymbol{x} \in \mathbb{R}^n$. Recall that such a linear map corresponds to a matrix in $\mathbb{R}^{m \times n}$ whose columns are $F[\boldsymbol{e}_1], \ldots, F[\boldsymbol{e}_n]$; both interpretations will prove useful. Conveniently, function composition and matrix multiplication expressions look similar: to compose two linear maps F and G we can write $F \circ G$ or, barely abusing notation, consider the matrix FG. Every linear map $F : \mathbb{R}^n \multimap \mathbb{R}^m$ has a transpose $F : \mathbb{R}^m \multimap \mathbb{R}^n$, which is another linear map identified with transposing the corresponding matrix.

Repeatedly using the linear arrow symbol, we can denote by:

$$T : \underbrace{\mathbb{R}^n \multimap \cdots \multimap \mathbb{R}^n}_{k \text{ times}} \multimap \mathbb{R}^m \tag{6.4}$$

a multilinear, or more specifically k-linear, map:

$$T : \underbrace{\mathbb{R}^n \times \cdots \times \mathbb{R}^n}_{k \text{ times}} \to \mathbb{R}^m \tag{6.5}$$

which corresponds to an array (or tensor) in $\mathbb{R}^{m \times n \times \cdots \times n}$. We denote by $T[\boldsymbol{x}_1, \ldots, \boldsymbol{x}_k] \in \mathbb{R}^m$ the application of such a k-linear map to vectors $\boldsymbol{x}_1, \ldots, \boldsymbol{x}_k \in \mathbb{R}^n$.

The derivative operator. For an open set $U \subset \mathbb{R}^n$ and a differentiable function $f : U \to \mathbb{R}^m$, denote its **derivative function**:

$$\partial f : U \to (\mathbb{R}^n \multimap \mathbb{R}^m) \tag{6.6}$$

or equivalently $\partial f : U \to \mathbb{R}^{m \times n}$. This function maps a point $\boldsymbol{x} \in U$ to the Jacobian of all partial derivatives evaluated at $\boldsymbol{x}$. The symbol ∂ itself denotes the **derivative operator**, a function mapping functions to their derivative functions. When $m = 1$, the map $\partial f(\boldsymbol{x})$ recovers the standard gradient $\nabla f(\boldsymbol{x})$ at any $\boldsymbol{x} \in U$, by considering the matrix view of the former. Indeed, the nabla symbol ∇ is sometimes described as an operator as well, such that ∇f is a function. When $n = m = 1$, the Jacobian is scalar-valued, and ∂f is the familiar derivative f'.

In the expression $\partial f(\boldsymbol{x})[\boldsymbol{v}]$, we will sometimes refer to the argument $\boldsymbol{x}$ as the **linearization point** for the Jacobian, and to $\boldsymbol{v}$ as the **perturbation**. We call the map:

$$(\boldsymbol{x}, \boldsymbol{v}) \mapsto \partial f(\boldsymbol{x})[\boldsymbol{v}] \tag{6.7}$$

over linearization points $\boldsymbol{x} \in U$ and *input* perturbations $\boldsymbol{v} \in \mathbb{R}^n$ the **Jacobian-vector product (JVP)**. We similarly call its transpose:

$$(\boldsymbol{x}, \boldsymbol{u}) \mapsto \partial f(\boldsymbol{x})^{\mathsf{T}}[\boldsymbol{u}] \tag{6.8}$$

over linearization points $\boldsymbol{x} \in U$ and *output* perturbations $\boldsymbol{u} \in \mathbb{R}^m$ the **vector-Jacobian product (VJP)**.

Thinking about maps instead of matrices can help us define higher-order derivatives recursively, as we proceed to do below. It separately suggests how the action of a Jacobian is commonly written in code. When we consider writing $\partial f(\boldsymbol{x})$ in a program for a fixed $\boldsymbol{x}$, we often implement it as a function that carries out multiplication by the Jacobian matrix, i.e., $\boldsymbol{v} \mapsto \partial f(\boldsymbol{x})[\boldsymbol{v}]$, instead of explicitly representing it as a matrix of numbers in memory. Going a step further, for that matter, we often implement ∂f as an entire JVP at once, i.e., over any linearization point $\boldsymbol{x}$ and perturbation $\boldsymbol{v}$. As a toy example with scalars, consider the cosine:

$$(x, v) \mapsto \partial \cos(x) v = -v \sin(x) \tag{6.9}$$

If we express this at once in code, we can, say, avoid computing $\sin(x)$ whenever $v = 0$.[1]

Higher-order derivatives. Suppose the function f above remains arbitrarily differentiable over its domain $U \subset \mathbb{R}^n$. To take another derivative, we write:

$$\partial^2 f : U \to (\mathbb{R}^n \multimap \mathbb{R}^n \multimap \mathbb{R}^m) \tag{6.10}$$

where $\partial^2 f(\boldsymbol{x})$ is a bilinear map representing all second-order partial derivatives. In named variable notation, one might write $\frac{\partial f(\boldsymbol{x})}{\partial x_i \partial x_j}$ to refer to $\partial^2 f(\boldsymbol{x})[\boldsymbol{e}_i, \boldsymbol{e}_j]$, for example.

---

1. This example ignores that such an optimization might be done (best) by a compiler. Then again, for more complex examples, implementing $(\boldsymbol{x}, \boldsymbol{v}) \mapsto \partial f(\boldsymbol{x})[\boldsymbol{v}]$ as a single subroutine can help guide compiler optimizations all the same.

The second derivative function $\partial^2 f$ can be treated coherently as the outcome of applying the derivative operator twice. That is, it makes sense to say that $\partial^2 = \partial \circ \partial$. This observation extends recursively to cover arbitrary higher-order derivatives. For $k \geq 1$:

$$\partial^k f : U \to (\underbrace{\mathbb{R}^n \multimap \ldots \multimap \mathbb{R}^n}_{k \text{ times}} \multimap \mathbb{R}^m) \tag{6.11}$$

is such that $\partial^k f(\boldsymbol{x})$ is a k-linear map.

With $m = 1$, the map $\partial^2 f(\boldsymbol{x})$ corresponds to the Hessian matrix at any $\boldsymbol{x} \in U$. Although Jacobians and Hessians suffice to make sense of many machine learning techniques, arbitrary higher-order derivatives are not hard to come by either (e.g., [Kel+20]). As an example, they appear when writing down something as basic as a function's Taylor series approximation, which we can express with our derivative operator as:

$$f(\boldsymbol{x} + \boldsymbol{v}) \approx f(\boldsymbol{x}) + \partial f(\boldsymbol{x})[\boldsymbol{v}] + \frac{1}{2!}\partial^2 f(\boldsymbol{x})[\boldsymbol{v}, \boldsymbol{v}] + \cdots + \frac{1}{k!}\partial^k f(\boldsymbol{x})[\boldsymbol{v}, \ldots, \boldsymbol{v}] \tag{6.12}$$

Multiple inputs.   Now consider a function of two arguments:

$$g : U \times V \to \mathbb{R}^m . \tag{6.13}$$

where $U \subset \mathbb{R}^{n_1}$ and $V \subset \mathbb{R}^{n_2}$. For our purposes, a product domain like $U \times V$ mainly serves to suggest a convenient partitioning of a function's input components. It is isomorphic to a subset of $\mathbb{R}^{n_1+n_2}$, corresponding to a single-input function. The latter tells us how the derivative functions of g ought to look, based on previous definitions, and we will swap between the two views with little warning. Multiple inputs tend to arise in the context of computational circuits and programs: many functions in code are written to accept multiple arguments, and many basic operations (such as $+$) do the same.

With multiple inputs, we can denote by $\partial_i g$ the derivative function with respect to the i'th argument:

$$\partial_1 g : \mathbb{R}^{n_1} \times \mathbb{R}^{n_2} \to (\mathbb{R}^{n_1} \multimap \mathbb{R}^m) , \text{ and} \tag{6.14}$$
$$\partial_2 g : \mathbb{R}^{n_1} \times \mathbb{R}^{n_2} \to (\mathbb{R}^{n_2} \multimap \mathbb{R}^m) . \tag{6.15}$$

Under the matrix view, the function $\partial_1 g$ maps a pair of points $\boldsymbol{x} \in \mathbb{R}^{n_1}$ and $\boldsymbol{y} \in \mathbb{R}^{n_2}$ to the matrix of all partial derivatives of g with respect to its first argument, evaluated at $(\boldsymbol{x}, \boldsymbol{y})$. We take ∂g with no subscript to simply mean the concatenation of $\partial_1 g$ and $\partial_2 g$:

$$\partial g : \mathbb{R}^{n_1} \times \mathbb{R}^{n_2} \to (\mathbb{R}^{n_1} \times \mathbb{R}^{n_2} \multimap \mathbb{R}^m) \tag{6.16}$$

where, for every linearization point $(\boldsymbol{x}, \boldsymbol{y}) \in U \times V$ and perturbations $\dot{\boldsymbol{x}} \in \mathbb{R}^{n_1}$, $\dot{\boldsymbol{y}} \in \mathbb{R}^{n_2}$:

$$\partial g(\boldsymbol{x}, \boldsymbol{y})[\dot{\boldsymbol{x}}, \dot{\boldsymbol{y}}] = \partial_1 g(\boldsymbol{x}, \boldsymbol{y})[\dot{\boldsymbol{x}}] + \partial_2 g(\boldsymbol{x}, \boldsymbol{y})[\dot{\boldsymbol{y}}] . \tag{6.17}$$

Alternatively, taking the matrix view:

$$\partial g(\boldsymbol{x}, \boldsymbol{y}) = \begin{pmatrix} \partial_1 g(\boldsymbol{x}, \boldsymbol{y}) & \partial_2 g(\boldsymbol{x}, \boldsymbol{y}) \end{pmatrix} . \tag{6.18}$$

This convention will simplify our chain rule statement below. When $n_1 = n_2 = m = 1$, both sub-matrices are scalar, and $\partial g_1(x, y)$ recovers the partial derivative that might otherwise be written in named variable notation as:

$$\frac{\partial}{\partial x} g(x, y). \tag{6.19}$$

However, the expression ∂g_1 bears a meaning on its own (as a function) whereas the expression $\frac{\partial g}{\partial x}$ may be ambiguous without further context. Again composing operators lets us write higher-order derivatives. For instance, $\partial_2 \partial_1 g(\boldsymbol{x}, \boldsymbol{y}) \in \mathbb{R}^{m \times n_1 \times n_2}$, and if $m = 1$, the Hessian of g at $(\boldsymbol{x}, \boldsymbol{y})$ is:

$$\begin{pmatrix} \partial_1 \partial_1 g(\boldsymbol{x}, \boldsymbol{y}) & \partial_1 \partial_2 g(\boldsymbol{x}, \boldsymbol{y}) \\ \partial_2 \partial_1 g(\boldsymbol{x}, \boldsymbol{y}) & \partial_2 \partial_2 g(\boldsymbol{x}, \boldsymbol{y}) \end{pmatrix}. \tag{6.20}$$

Composition and fan-out. If $f = g \circ h$ for some $h : \mathbb{R}^n \to \mathbb{R}^p$ and $g : \mathbb{R}^p \to \mathbb{R}^m$, then the **chain rule** of calculus observes that:

$$\partial f(\boldsymbol{x}) = \partial g(h(\boldsymbol{x})) \circ \partial h(\boldsymbol{x}) \text{ for all } \boldsymbol{x} \in \mathbb{R}^n \tag{6.21}$$

How does this interact with our notation for multi-argument functions? For one, it can lead us to consider expressions with **fan-out**, where several sub-expressions are functions of the same input. For instance, assume two functions $a : \mathbb{R}^n \to \mathbb{R}^{m_1}$ and $b : \mathbb{R}^n \to \mathbb{R}^{m_2}$, and that:

$$f(\boldsymbol{x}) = g(a(\boldsymbol{x}), b(\boldsymbol{x})) \tag{6.22}$$

for some function g. Abbreviating $h(\boldsymbol{x}) = (a(\boldsymbol{x}), b(\boldsymbol{x}))$ so that $f(\boldsymbol{x}) = g(h(\boldsymbol{x}))$, Equations (6.16) and (6.21) tell us that:

$$\partial f(\boldsymbol{x}) = \partial g(h(\boldsymbol{x})) \circ \partial h(\boldsymbol{x}) \tag{6.23}$$
$$= \partial_1 g(a(\boldsymbol{x}), b(\boldsymbol{x})) \circ \partial a(\boldsymbol{x}) + \partial_2 g(a(\boldsymbol{x}), b(\boldsymbol{x})) \circ \partial b(\boldsymbol{x}) \tag{6.24}$$

Note that $+$ is meant pointwise here. It also follows from the above that if instead:

$$f(\boldsymbol{x}, \boldsymbol{y}) = g(a(\boldsymbol{x}), b(\boldsymbol{y})) \tag{6.25}$$

in other words, if we write multiple arguments but exhibit no fan-out, then:

$$\partial_1 f(\boldsymbol{x}, \boldsymbol{y}) = \partial_1 g(a(\boldsymbol{x}), b(\boldsymbol{y})) \circ \partial a(\boldsymbol{x}), \text{ and} \tag{6.26}$$
$$\partial_2 f(\boldsymbol{x}, \boldsymbol{y}) = \partial_2 g(a(\boldsymbol{x}), b(\boldsymbol{y})) \circ \partial b(\boldsymbol{y}) \tag{6.27}$$

Composition and fan-out rules for derivatives are what let us break down a complex derivative calculation into simpler ones. This is what automatic differentiation techniques rely on when processing the sort of elaborate numerical computations that turn up in modern machine learning and numerical programming.

6.2.2   Differentiating chains, circuits, and programs

The purpose of automatic differentiation is to compute derivatives of arbitrary functions provided as input. Given a function $f : U \subset \mathbb{R}^n \to \mathbb{R}^m$ and a linearization point $\boldsymbol{x} \in U$, AD computes either:

- the JVP $\partial f(\boldsymbol{x})[v]$ for an input perturbation $\boldsymbol{v} \in \mathbb{R}^n$, or

- the VJP $\partial f(\boldsymbol{x})^{\mathsf{T}}[u]$ for an output perturbation $\boldsymbol{u} \in \mathbb{R}^m$.

In other words, JVPs and VJPs capture the two essential tasks of AD.[2]

Deciding what functions f to handle as input, and how to represent them, is perhaps the most load-bearing aspect of this setup. Over what *language* of functions should we operate? By a language, we mean some formal way of describing functions by composing a set of basic primitive operations. For primitives, we can think of various differentiable array operations (elementwise arithmetic, reductions, contractions, indexing and slicing, concatenation, etc.), but we will largely consider primitives and their derivatives as a given, and focus on how elaborately we can compose them. AD becomes increasingly challenging with increasingly expressive languages. Considering this, we introduce it in stages.

6.2.2.1   Chain compositions and the chain rule

To start, take only functions that are **chain compositions** of basic operations. Chains are a convenient class of function representations because derivatives *decompose* along the same structure according to the aptly-named chain rule.

As a toy example, consider $f : \mathbb{R}^n \to \mathbb{R}^m$ composed of three operations in sequence:

$$f = c \circ b \circ a \tag{6.28}$$

By the chain rule, its derivatives are given by

$$\partial f(\boldsymbol{x}) = \partial c(b(a(\boldsymbol{x}))) \circ \partial b(a(\boldsymbol{x})) \circ \partial a(\boldsymbol{x}) \tag{6.29}$$

Now consider the JVP against an input perturbation $\boldsymbol{v} \in \mathbb{R}^n$:

$$\partial f(\boldsymbol{x})[\boldsymbol{v}] = \partial c(b(a(\boldsymbol{x}))) \left[\partial b(a(\boldsymbol{x})) \left[\partial a(\boldsymbol{x})[\boldsymbol{v}] \right] \right] \tag{6.30}$$

This expression's bracketing highlights a right-to-left evaluation order that corresponds to **forward-mode automatic differentiation**. Namely, to carry out this JVP, it makes sense to compute prefixes of the original chain:

$$\boldsymbol{x}, \ a(\boldsymbol{x}), \ b(a(\boldsymbol{x})) \tag{6.31}$$

alongside the partial JVPs, because each is then immediately used as a subsequent linearization point, respectively:

$$\partial a(\underline{\boldsymbol{x}}), \ \partial b(\underline{a(\boldsymbol{x})}), \ \partial c(\underline{b(a(\boldsymbol{x}))}) \tag{6.32}$$

Extending this idea to arbitrary chain compositions gives Algorithm 6.1.

---

2. Materalizing the Jacobian as a numerical array, as is commonly required in an optimization context, is a special case of computing a JVP or VJP against the standard basis vectors in $\mathbb{R}^n$ or $\mathbb{R}^m$ respectively.

Algorithm 6.1: Forward-mode automatic differentiation (JVP) on chains

---

1 **input:** $f : \mathbb{R}^n \to \mathbb{R}^m$ as a chain composition $f = f_T \circ \cdots \circ f_1$
2 **input:** linearization point $\boldsymbol{x} \in \mathbb{R}^n$ and input perturbation $\boldsymbol{v} \in \mathbb{R}^n$
3 $\boldsymbol{x}_0, \boldsymbol{v}_0 := \boldsymbol{x}, \boldsymbol{v}$
4 **for** $t := 1, \ldots, T$ **do**
5 $\quad \boldsymbol{x}_t := f_t(\boldsymbol{x}_{t-1})$
6 $\quad \boldsymbol{v}_t := \partial f_t(\boldsymbol{x}_{t-1})[\boldsymbol{v}_{t-1}]$
7 **output:** $\boldsymbol{x}_T$, equal to $f(\boldsymbol{x})$
8 **output:** $\boldsymbol{v}_T$, equal to $\partial f(\boldsymbol{x})[\boldsymbol{v}]$

By contrast, we can transpose Equation (6.29) to consider a VJP against an output perturbation $\boldsymbol{u} \in \mathbb{R}^m$:

$$\partial f(\boldsymbol{x})^{\mathsf{T}}[\boldsymbol{u}] = \partial a(\boldsymbol{x})^{\mathsf{T}} \left[\partial b(a(\boldsymbol{x}))^{\mathsf{T}} \left[\partial c(b(a(\boldsymbol{x})))^{\mathsf{T}}[\boldsymbol{u}] \right] \right] \tag{6.33}$$

Transposition reverses the Jacobian maps relative to their order in Equation (6.29), and now the bracketed evaluation corresponds to **reverse-mode automatic differentiation**. To carry out this VJP, we can compute the original chain prefixes $\boldsymbol{x}$, $a(\boldsymbol{x})$, and $b(a(\boldsymbol{x}))$ first, and then read them *in reverse* as successive linearization points:

$$\partial c(\underline{b(a(\boldsymbol{x}))})^{\mathsf{T}}, \ \partial b(\underline{a(\boldsymbol{x})})^{\mathsf{T}}, \ \partial a(\underline{\boldsymbol{x}})^{\mathsf{T}} \tag{6.34}$$

Extending this idea to arbitrary chain compositions gives Algorithm 6.2.

Algorithm 6.2: Reverse-mode automatic differentiation (VJP) on chains

---

1 **input:** $f : \mathbb{R}^n \to \mathbb{R}^m$ as a chain composition $f = f_T \circ \cdots \circ f_1$
2 **input:** linearization point $\boldsymbol{x} \in \mathbb{R}^n$ and output perturbation $\boldsymbol{u} \in \mathbb{R}^m$
3 $\boldsymbol{x}_0 := \boldsymbol{x}$
4 **for** $t := 1, \ldots, T$ **do**
5 $\quad \boldsymbol{x}_t := f_t(\boldsymbol{x}_{t-1})$
6 $\boldsymbol{u}_T := \boldsymbol{u}$
7 **for** $t := T, \ldots, 1$ **do**
8 $\quad \boldsymbol{u}_{t-1} := \partial f_t(\boldsymbol{x}_{t-1})^{\mathsf{T}}[\boldsymbol{u}_t]$
9 **output:** $\boldsymbol{x}_T$, equal to $f(\boldsymbol{x})$
10 **output:** $\boldsymbol{u}_0$, equal to $\partial f(\boldsymbol{x})^{\mathsf{T}}[\boldsymbol{u}]$

Although chain compositions impose a very specific structure, they already capture some deep neural network models, such as multi-layer perceptrons (provided matrix multiplication is a primitive operation), as covered in this book's prequel [Mur22, Ch.13].

Reverse-mode AD is faster than forward-mode when the output is scalar valued (as often arises in deep learning, where the output is a loss function). However, reverse-mode AD stores all chain

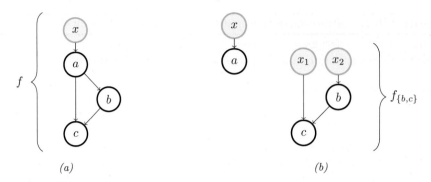

Figure 6.1: A circuit for a function f over three primitives, and its decomposition into two circuits without fan-out. Input nodes are drawn in green.

prefixes before its backwards traversal, so it consumes more memory than forward-mode. There are ways to combat this memory requirement in special-case scenarios, such as when the chained operations are each reversible [MDA15; Gom+17; KKL20]. One can also trade off memory for computation by discarding some prefixes and re-computing them as needed.

6.2.2.2   From chains to circuits

When primitives can accept multiple inputs, we can naturally extend chains to **circuits** — directed acyclic graphs over primitive operations, sometimes also called computation graphs. To set up for this section, we will distinguish between (1) **input nodes** of a circuit, which symbolize a function's arguments, and (2) **primitive nodes**, each of which is labeled by a primitive operation. We assume that input nodes have no incoming edges and (without loss of generality) exactly one outgoing edge each, and that the graph has exactly one sink node. The overall function of the circuit is composition of operations from the input nodes to the sink, where the output of each operation is input to others according to its outgoing edges.

What made AD work in Section 6.2.2.1 is the fact that derivatives decompose along chains thanks to the aptly-named chain rule. When moving from chains to directed acyclic graphs, do we need some sort of "graph rule" in order to decompose our calculation along the circuit's structure? Circuits introduce two new features: **fan-in** and **fan-out**. In graphical terms, fan-in simply refers to multiple edges incoming to a node, and fan-out refers to multiple edges outgoing.

What do these mean in functional terms? Fan-in happens when a primitive operation accepts multiple arguments. We observed in Section 6.2.1 that multiple arguments can be treated as one, and how the chain rule then applies. Fan-out requires slightly more care, specifically for reverse-mode differentiation.

The gist of an answer can be illustrated with a small example. Consider the circuit in Figure 6.1a. The operation a precedes b and c topologically, with an outgoing edge to each of both. We can cut a away from $\{b, c\}$ to produce two new circuits, shown in Figure 6.1b. The first corresponds to a and the second corresponds to the remaining computation, given by:

$$f_{\{b,c\}}(\boldsymbol{x}_1, \boldsymbol{x}_2) = c(\boldsymbol{x}_1, b(\boldsymbol{x}_2)).\tag{6.35}$$

We can recover the complete function f from a and $f_{\{b,c\}}$ with the help of a function dup given by:

$$\mathrm{dup}(\boldsymbol{x}) = (\boldsymbol{x}, \boldsymbol{x}) \equiv \begin{pmatrix} I \\ I \end{pmatrix} \boldsymbol{x} \tag{6.36}$$

so that f can be written as a chain composition:

$$f = f_{\{b,c\}} \circ \mathrm{dup} \circ a \,. \tag{6.37}$$

The circuit for $f_{\{b,c\}}$ contains no fan-out, and composition rules such as Equation (6.25) tell us its derivatives in terms of b, c, and their derivatives, all via the chain rule. Meanwhile, the chain rule applied to Equation (6.37) says that:

$$\partial f(\boldsymbol{x}) = \partial f_{\{b,c\}}(\mathrm{dup}(a(\boldsymbol{x}))) \circ \partial \mathrm{dup}(a(\boldsymbol{x})) \circ \partial a(\boldsymbol{x}) \tag{6.38}$$

$$= \partial f_{\{b,c\}}(a(\boldsymbol{x}), a(\boldsymbol{x})) \circ \begin{pmatrix} I \\ I \end{pmatrix} \circ \partial a(\boldsymbol{x}) \,. \tag{6.39}$$

The above expression suggests calculating a JVP of f by right-to-left evaluation. It is similar to the JVP calculation suggested by Equation (6.30), but with a *duplication* operation $\begin{pmatrix} I & I \end{pmatrix}^{\mathsf{T}}$ in the middle that arises from the Jacobian of dup.

Transposing the derivative of f at $\boldsymbol{x}$:

$$\partial f(\boldsymbol{x})^{\mathsf{T}} = \partial a(\boldsymbol{x})^{\mathsf{T}} \circ \begin{pmatrix} I & I \end{pmatrix} \circ \partial f_{\{b,c\}}(a(\boldsymbol{x}), a(\boldsymbol{x}))^{\mathsf{T}} \,. \tag{6.40}$$

Considering right-to-left evaluation, this too is similar to the VJP calculation suggested by Equation (6.33), but with a *summation* operation $\begin{pmatrix} I & I \end{pmatrix}$ in the middle that arises from the *transposed* Jacobian of dup. The lesson of using dup in this small example is that, more generally, in order to handle fan-out in reverse mode AD, we can process operations in topological order — first forward and then in reverse — and then *sum* partial VJPs along multiple outgoing edges.

Algorithm 6.3: Foward-mode circuit differentiation (JVP)

---

1 **input:** $f : \mathbb{R}^n \to \mathbb{R}^m$ composing $f_1, \ldots, f_T$ in topological order, where f_1 is identity
2 **input:** linearization point $\boldsymbol{x} \in \mathbb{R}^n$ and perturbation $\boldsymbol{v} \in \mathbb{R}^n$
3 $\boldsymbol{x}_1, \boldsymbol{v}_1 := \boldsymbol{x}, \boldsymbol{v}$
4 **for** $t := 2, \ldots, T$ **do**
5 $\quad$ let $[q_1, \ldots, q_r] = \mathrm{Pa}(t)$
6 $\quad \boldsymbol{x}_t := f_t(\boldsymbol{x}_{q_1}, \ldots, \boldsymbol{x}_{q_r})$
7 $\quad \boldsymbol{v}_t := \sum_{i=1}^{r} \partial_i f_t(\boldsymbol{x}_{q_1}, \ldots, \boldsymbol{x}_{q_r})[\boldsymbol{v}_{q_i}]$
8 **output:** $\boldsymbol{x}_T$, equal to $f(\boldsymbol{x})$
9 **output:** $\boldsymbol{v}_T$, equal to $\partial f(\boldsymbol{x})[\boldsymbol{v}]$

Algorithms 6.3 and 6.4 give a complete description of forward- and reverse-mode differentiation on circuits. For brevity they assume a single argument to the entire circuit function. Nodes are indexed $1, \ldots, T$. The first is the input node, and the remaining $T - 1$ are labeled by their operation $f_2, \ldots, f_T$. We take f_1 to be the identity. For each t, if f_t takes k arguments, let $\mathrm{Pa}(t)$ be the ordered

---

Algorithm 6.4: Reverse-mode circuit differentiation (VJP)

---

1 **input:** $f : \mathbb{R}^n \to \mathbb{R}^m$ composing $f_1, \dots, f_T$ in topological order, where f_1, f_T are identity
2 **input:**   linearization point $\boldsymbol{x} \in \mathbb{R}^n$ and perturbation $\boldsymbol{u} \in \mathbb{R}^m$
3 $\boldsymbol{x}_1 := \boldsymbol{x}$
4 **for** $t := 2, \dots, T$ **do**
5 $\quad$ let $[q_1, \dots, q_r] = \mathrm{Pa}(t)$
6 $\quad$ $\boldsymbol{x}_t := f_t(\boldsymbol{x}_{q_1}, \dots, \boldsymbol{x}_{q_r})$
7 $\boldsymbol{u}_{(T-1) \to T} := \boldsymbol{u}$
8 **for** $t := T - 1, \dots, 2$ **do**
9 $\quad$ let $[q_1, \dots, q_r] = \mathrm{Pa}(t)$
10 $\quad$ $\boldsymbol{u}'_t := \sum_{c \in \mathrm{Ch}(t)} \boldsymbol{u}_{t \to c}$
11 $\quad$ $\boldsymbol{u}_{q_i \to t} := \partial_i f_t(\boldsymbol{x}_{q_1}, \dots, \boldsymbol{x}_{q_r})^\mathsf{T} \boldsymbol{u}'_t$ $\;$ for $i = 1, \dots, r$
12 **output:** $\boldsymbol{x}_T$, equal to $f(\boldsymbol{x})$
13 **output:** $\boldsymbol{u}_{1 \to 2}$, equal to $\partial f(\boldsymbol{x})^\mathsf{T} \boldsymbol{u}$

---

list of k indices of its parent nodes (possibly containing duplicates, due to fan-out), and let $\mathrm{Ch}(t)$ be the indices of its children (again possibly duplicate). Algorithm 6.4 takes a few more conventions: that f_T is the identity, that node T has $T - 1$ as its only parent, and that the child of node 1 is node 2.

Fan-out is a feature of *graphs*, but arguably not an essential feature of *functions*. One can always remove all fan-out from a circuit representation by duplicating nodes. Our interest in fan-out is precisely to avoid this, allowing for an efficient representation and, in turn, efficient memory use in Algorithms 6.3 and 6.4.

Reverse-mode AD on circuits has appeared under various names and formulations over the years. The algorithm is precisely the **backpropagation** algorithm in neural networks, a term introduced in the 1980s [RHW86b; RHW86a], and has separately come up in the context of control theory and sensitivity, as summarized in historical notes by Goodfellow, Bengio, and Courville [GBC16, Section 6.6].

6.2.2.3   From circuits to programs

Graphs are useful for introducing AD algorithms, and they might align well enough with neural network applications. But computer scientists have spent decades formalizing and studying various "languages for expressing functions compositionally". Simply put, this is what programming languages are for! Can we automatically differentiate numerical functions expressed in, say, Python, Haskell, or some variant of the lambda calculus? These offer a far more widespread — and intuitively more expressive — way to describe an input function.[3]

In the previous sections, our approach to AD became more complex as we allowed for more complex graph structure. Something similar happens when we introduce grammatical constructs in a

---

3. In Python, what the language calls a "function" does not always describe a pure function of the arguments listed in its syntactic definition; its behavior may rely on side effects or global state, as allowed by the language. Here, we specifically mean a Python function that is pure and functional. JAX's documentation details this restriction [Bra+18].

programming language. How do we adapt AD to handle a language with loops, conditionals, and recursive calls? What about parallel programming constructs? We have partial answers to questions like these today, although they invite a deeper dive into language details such as type systems and implementation concerns [Yu+18; Inn20; Pas+21b].

One example language construct that we already know how to handle, due to Section 6.2.2.2, is a standard `let` expression. In languages with a means of name or variable binding, multiple appearances of the same variable are analogous to fan-out in a circuit. Figure 6.1a corresponds to a function f that we could write in a functional language as:

```
f(x) =
  let ax = a(x)
   in c(ax, b(ax))
```

in which `ax` indeed appears twice after it is bound.

Understanding the interaction between language capacity and automatic differentiability is an ongoing topic of computer science research [PS08a; AP19; Vyt+19; BMP19; MP21]. In the meantime, functional languages have proven quite effective in recent AD systems, both widely-used and experimental. Systems such as JAX, Dex, and others are designed around pure functional programming models, and internally rely on functional program representations for differentiation [Mac+15; BPS16; Sha+19; FJL18; Bra+18; Mac+19; Dex; Fro+21; Pas+21a].

6.3 Stochastic optimization

In this section, we consider optimization of stochastic objectives of the form

$$\mathcal{L}(\boldsymbol{\theta}) = \mathbb{E}_{q_{\boldsymbol{\theta}}(\boldsymbol{z})} \left[\tilde{\mathcal{L}}(\boldsymbol{\theta}, \boldsymbol{z}) \right] \tag{6.41}$$

where $\boldsymbol{\theta}$ are the parameters we are optimizing, and $\boldsymbol{z}$ is a random variable, such as an external noise.

6.3.1 Stochastic gradient descent

Suppose we have a way of computing an unbiased estimate $\boldsymbol{g}_t$ of the gradient of the objective function, i.e.,

$$\mathbb{E}\left[\boldsymbol{g}_t\right] = \nabla_{\boldsymbol{\theta}} \mathcal{L}(\boldsymbol{\theta})|_{\boldsymbol{\theta}_t} \tag{6.42}$$

Then we can use this inside of a gradient descent procedure:

$$\boldsymbol{\theta}_{t+1} = \boldsymbol{\theta}_t - \eta_t \boldsymbol{g}_t \tag{6.43}$$

where η_t is the **learning rate** or **step size**. This is called **stochastic gradient descent** or **SGD**.

6.3.1.1 Choosing the step size

When using SGD, we need to be careful in how we choose the learning rate in order to achieve convergence. Rather than choosing a single constant learning rate, we can use a **learning rate**

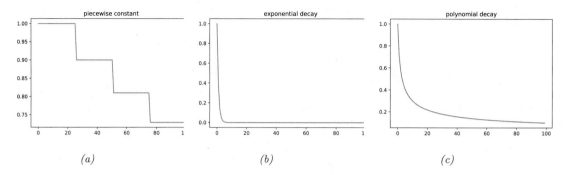

Figure 6.2: Illustration of some common learning rate schedules. (a) Piecewise constant. (b) Exponential decay. (c) Polynomial decay. Generated by learning_rate_plot.ipynb.

schedule, in which we adjust the step size over time. Theoretically, a sufficient condition for SGD to achieve convergence is if the learning rate schedule satisfies the **Robbins-Monro conditions**:

$$\eta_t \to 0, \quad \frac{\sum_{t=1}^{\infty} \eta_t^2}{\sum_{t=1}^{\infty} \eta_t} \to 0 \tag{6.44}$$

Some common examples of learning rate schedules are listed below:

$$\eta_t = \eta_i \text{ if } t_i \leq t \leq t_{i+1} \quad \text{piecewise constant} \tag{6.45}$$

$$\eta_t = \eta_0 e^{-\lambda t} \text{ exponential decay} \tag{6.46}$$

$$\eta_t = \eta_0 (\beta t + 1)^{-\alpha} \text{ polynomial decay} \tag{6.47}$$

In the piecewise constant schedule, t_i are a set of time points at which we adjust the learning rate to a specified value. For example, we may set $\eta_i = \eta_0 \gamma^i$, which reduces the initial learning rate by a factor of γ for each threshold (or milestone) that we pass. Figure 6.2a illustrates this for $\eta_0 = 1$ and $\gamma = 0.9$. This is called **step decay**. Sometimes the threshold times are computed adaptively, by estimating when the train or validation loss has plateaued; this is called **reduce-on-plateau**. Exponential decay is typically too fast, as illustrated in Figure 6.2b. A common choice is polynomial decay, with $\alpha = 0.5$ and $\beta = 1$, as illustrated in Figure 6.2c; this corresponds to a **square-root schedule**, $\eta_t = \eta_0 \frac{1}{\sqrt{t+1}}$. For more details, see [Mur22, Sec 8.4.3].

6.3.1.2   Variance reduction

SGD can be slow to converge because it relies on a stochastic estimate of the gradient. Various methods have been proposed for reducing the variance of the parameter estimates generated at each step, which can speedup convergence. For more details, see [Mur22, Sec 8.4.5].

6.3.1.3   Preconditioned SGD

In many cases, the gradient magnitudes can be very different along each dimension, corresponding to the loss surface being steep along some directions and shallow along others, similar to a valley floor. In such cases, one can get faster convergence by scaling the gradient vector by a **conditioning matrix** $\mathbf{C}_t$ as follows:

$$\boldsymbol{\theta}_{t+1} = \boldsymbol{\theta}_t - \eta_t \mathbf{C}_t \boldsymbol{g}_t \tag{6.48}$$

This is called **preconditioned SGD**. For more details, see [Mur22, Sec 8.4.6].

6.3.2 SGD for optimizing a finite-sum objective

In the simplest case, the distribution used to compute the expectation, $q_{\boldsymbol{\theta}}(\boldsymbol{z})$, does not depend on the parameters being optimized, $\boldsymbol{\theta}$. In this case, we can push gradients inside the expectation operator, and then use Monte Carlo sampling for $\boldsymbol{z}$ to approximate the gradient:

$$\nabla_{\boldsymbol{\theta}} \mathcal{L}(\boldsymbol{\theta}) = \nabla_{\boldsymbol{\theta}} \mathbb{E}_{q(\boldsymbol{z})} \left[\tilde{\mathcal{L}}(\boldsymbol{\theta}, \boldsymbol{z}) \right] = \mathbb{E}_{q(\boldsymbol{z})} \left[\nabla_{\boldsymbol{\theta}} \tilde{\mathcal{L}}(\boldsymbol{\theta}, \boldsymbol{z}) \right] \approx \frac{1}{S} \sum_{s=1}^{S} \nabla_{\boldsymbol{\theta}} \tilde{\mathcal{L}}(\boldsymbol{\theta}, \boldsymbol{z}_s) \tag{6.49}$$

For example, consider the problem of **empirical risk minimization** or **ERM**, which requires minimizing

$$\mathcal{L}(\boldsymbol{\theta}) = \frac{1}{N} \sum_{n=1}^{N} \tilde{\mathcal{L}}(\boldsymbol{\theta}, \boldsymbol{z}_n) = \frac{1}{N} \sum_{n=1}^{N} \ell(\boldsymbol{y}_n, f(\boldsymbol{x}_n; \boldsymbol{\theta})) \tag{6.50}$$

where $\boldsymbol{z}_n = (\boldsymbol{x}_n, \boldsymbol{y}_n)$ is the n'th labeled example, and f is a prediction function. This kind of objective is called a **finite sum objective**. We can write this as an expected loss wrt the empirical distrbution $p_{\mathcal{D}}(\boldsymbol{x}, \boldsymbol{y})$:

$$\mathcal{L}(\boldsymbol{\theta}) = \mathbb{E}_{p_{\mathcal{D}}(\boldsymbol{z})} \left[\tilde{\mathcal{L}}(\boldsymbol{\theta}, \boldsymbol{z}) \right] \tag{6.51}$$

Since the expectation depends on the data, and not on the parameters, we can approximate the gradient by using a **minibatch** of $B = |\mathcal{B}|$ datapoints from the full dataset $\mathcal{D}$ at each iteration:

$$\boldsymbol{g}_t = \nabla \mathcal{L}(\boldsymbol{\theta}_t) = \frac{1}{B} \sum_{n \in \mathcal{B}} \nabla \ell(\boldsymbol{y}_n, f(\boldsymbol{x}_n; \boldsymbol{\theta})) \tag{6.52}$$

These noisy gradients can then be passed to SGD. When the dataset is large, this method is much faster than **full batch** gradient descent, since it does not require evaluating the loss on all N examples before updating the model [BB08; BB11].

6.3.3 SGD for optimizing the parameters of a distribution

Now suppose the stochasticity depends on the parameters we are optimizing. For example, $\boldsymbol{z}$ could be an action sampled from a stochastic policy $q_{\boldsymbol{\theta}}$, as in RL (Section 35.3.2), or $\boldsymbol{z}$ could be a latent variable sampled from an inference network $q_{\boldsymbol{\theta}}$, as in stochastic variational inference (see Section 10.2). In this case, the gradient is given by

$$\nabla_{\boldsymbol{\theta}} \mathbb{E}_{q_{\boldsymbol{\theta}}(\boldsymbol{z})} \left[\tilde{\mathcal{L}}(\boldsymbol{\theta}, \boldsymbol{z}) \right] = \nabla_{\boldsymbol{\theta}} \int \tilde{\mathcal{L}}(\boldsymbol{\theta}, \boldsymbol{z}) q_{\boldsymbol{\theta}}(\boldsymbol{z}) d\boldsymbol{z} \tag{6.53}$$

$$= \int \left[\nabla_{\boldsymbol{\theta}} \tilde{\mathcal{L}}(\boldsymbol{\theta}, \boldsymbol{z}) \right] q_{\boldsymbol{\theta}}(\boldsymbol{z}) d\boldsymbol{z} + \int \tilde{\mathcal{L}}(\boldsymbol{\theta}, \boldsymbol{z}) \left[\nabla_{\boldsymbol{\theta}} q_{\boldsymbol{\theta}}(\boldsymbol{z}) \right] d\boldsymbol{z} \tag{6.54}$$

The first term can be approximated by Monte Carlo sampling:

$$\int \left[\nabla_{\boldsymbol{\theta}} \tilde{\mathcal{L}}(\boldsymbol{\theta}, \boldsymbol{z}) \right] q_{\boldsymbol{\theta}}(\boldsymbol{z}) d\boldsymbol{z} \approx \frac{1}{S} \sum_{s=1}^{S} \nabla_{\boldsymbol{\theta}} \tilde{\mathcal{L}}(\boldsymbol{\theta}, \boldsymbol{z}_s) \tag{6.55}$$

where $\boldsymbol{z}_s \sim q_{\boldsymbol{\theta}}$. Note that if $\tilde{\mathcal{L}}()$ is independent of $\boldsymbol{\theta}$, this term vanishes.

Now consider the second term, that takes the gradients of the distribution itself:

$$I \triangleq \int \tilde{\mathcal{L}}(\boldsymbol{\theta}, \boldsymbol{z}) \left[\nabla_{\boldsymbol{\theta}} q_{\boldsymbol{\theta}}(\boldsymbol{z}) \right] d\boldsymbol{z} \tag{6.56}$$

We can no longer use vanilla Monte Carlo sampling to approximate this integral. However, there are various other ways to approximate this (see [Moh+20] for an extensive review). We briefly describe the two main methods in Section 6.3.4 and Section 6.3.5.

6.3.4   Score function estimator (REINFORCE)

The simplest way to approximate Equation (6.56) is to exploit the **log derivative trick**, which is the following identity:

$$\nabla_{\boldsymbol{\theta}} q_{\boldsymbol{\theta}}(\boldsymbol{z}) = q_{\boldsymbol{\theta}}(\boldsymbol{z}) \nabla_{\boldsymbol{\theta}} \log q_{\boldsymbol{\theta}}(\boldsymbol{z}) \tag{6.57}$$

With this, we can rewrite Equation (6.56) as follows:

$$I = \int \tilde{\mathcal{L}}(\boldsymbol{\theta}, \boldsymbol{z}) [q_{\boldsymbol{\theta}}(\boldsymbol{z}) \nabla_{\boldsymbol{\theta}} \log q_{\boldsymbol{\theta}}(\boldsymbol{z})] d\boldsymbol{z} = \mathbb{E}_{q_{\boldsymbol{\theta}}(\boldsymbol{z})} \left[\tilde{\mathcal{L}}(\boldsymbol{\theta}, \boldsymbol{z}) \nabla_{\boldsymbol{\theta}} \log q_{\boldsymbol{\theta}}(\boldsymbol{z}) \right] \tag{6.58}$$

This is called the **score function estimator** or **SFE** [Fu15]. (The term "score function" refers to the gradient of a log probability distribution, as explained in Section 3.3.4.1.) It is also called the **likelihood ratio gradient estimator**, or the **REINFORCE** estimator (the reason for this latter name is explained in Section 35.3.2). We can now easily approximate this with Monte Carlo:

$$I \approx \frac{1}{S} \sum_{s=1}^{S} \tilde{\mathcal{L}}(\boldsymbol{\theta}, \boldsymbol{z}_s) \nabla_{\boldsymbol{\theta}} \log q_{\boldsymbol{\theta}}(\boldsymbol{z}_s) \tag{6.59}$$

where $\boldsymbol{z}_s \sim q_{\boldsymbol{\theta}}$. We only require that the sampling distribution is differentiable, not the objective $\tilde{\mathcal{L}}(\boldsymbol{\theta}, \boldsymbol{z})$ itself. This allows the method to be used for blackbox stochastic optimization problems, such as variational optimization (Supplementary Section 6.4.3), black-box variational inference (Section 10.2.3), reinforcement learning (Section 35.3.2), etc.

6.3.4.1   Control variates

The score function estimate can have high variance. One way to reduce this is to use **control variates**, in which we replace $\tilde{\mathcal{L}}(\boldsymbol{\theta}, \boldsymbol{z})$ with

$$\hat{\tilde{\mathcal{L}}}(\boldsymbol{\theta}, \boldsymbol{z}) = \tilde{\mathcal{L}}(\boldsymbol{\theta}, \boldsymbol{z}) - c \left(b(\boldsymbol{\theta}, \boldsymbol{z}) - \mathbb{E}\left[b(\boldsymbol{\theta}, \boldsymbol{z}) \right] \right) \tag{6.60}$$

where $b(\boldsymbol{\theta}, \boldsymbol{z})$ is a **baseline function** that is correlated with $\tilde{\mathcal{L}}(\boldsymbol{\theta}, \boldsymbol{z})$, and $c > 0$ is a coefficient. Since $\mathbb{E}\left[\hat{\tilde{\mathcal{L}}}(\boldsymbol{\theta}, \boldsymbol{z}) \right] = \mathbb{E}\left[\tilde{\mathcal{L}}(\boldsymbol{\theta}, \boldsymbol{z}) \right]$, we can use $\hat{\tilde{\mathcal{L}}}$ to compute unbiased gradient estimates of $\tilde{\mathcal{L}}$. The advantage is that this new estimate can result in lower variance, as we show in Section 11.6.3.

6.3.4.2 Rao-Blackwellization

Suppose $q_{\boldsymbol{\theta}}(\boldsymbol{z})$ is a discrete distribution. In this case, our objective becomes $\mathcal{L}(\boldsymbol{\theta}) = \sum_{\boldsymbol{z}} \tilde{\mathcal{L}}(\boldsymbol{\theta}, \boldsymbol{z}) q_{\boldsymbol{\theta}}(\boldsymbol{z})$. We can now easily compute gradients using $\nabla_{\boldsymbol{\theta}} \mathcal{L}(\boldsymbol{\theta}) = \sum_{\boldsymbol{z}} \tilde{\mathcal{L}}(\boldsymbol{\theta}, \boldsymbol{z}) \nabla_{\boldsymbol{\theta}} q_{\boldsymbol{\theta}}(\boldsymbol{z})$. Of course, if $\boldsymbol{z}$ can take on exponentially many values (e.g., we are optimizing over the space of strings), this expression is intractable. However, suppose we can partition this sum into two sets, a small set S_1 of high probability values and a large set S_2 of all other values. Then we can enumerate over S_1 and use the score function estimator for S_2:

$$\nabla_{\boldsymbol{\theta}} \mathcal{L}(\boldsymbol{\theta}) = \sum_{\boldsymbol{z} \in S_1} \tilde{\mathcal{L}}(\boldsymbol{\theta}, \boldsymbol{z}) \nabla_{\boldsymbol{\theta}} q_{\boldsymbol{\theta}}(\boldsymbol{z}) + \mathbb{E}_{q_{\boldsymbol{\theta}}(\boldsymbol{z} | \boldsymbol{z} \in S_2)} \left[\tilde{\mathcal{L}}(\boldsymbol{\theta}, \boldsymbol{z}) \nabla_{\boldsymbol{\theta}} \log q_{\boldsymbol{\theta}}(\boldsymbol{z}) \right] \tag{6.61}$$

To compute the second expectation, we can use rejection sampling applied to samples from $q_{\boldsymbol{\theta}}(\boldsymbol{z})$. This procedure is a form of Rao-Blackwellization as shown in [Liu+19b], and reduces the variance compared to standard SFE (see Section 11.6.2 for details on Rao-Blackwellization).

6.3.5 Reparameterization trick

The score function estimator can have high variance, even when using a control variate. In this section, we derive a lower variance estimator, which can be applied if $\tilde{\mathcal{L}}(\boldsymbol{\theta}, \boldsymbol{z})$ is differentiable wrt $\boldsymbol{z}$. We additionally require that we can compute a sample from $q_{\boldsymbol{\theta}}(\boldsymbol{z})$ by first sampling $\boldsymbol{\epsilon}$ from some noise distribution q_0 which is independent of $\boldsymbol{\theta}$, and then transforming to $\boldsymbol{z}$ using a deterministic and differentiable function $\boldsymbol{z} = g(\boldsymbol{\theta}, \boldsymbol{\epsilon})$. For example, instead of sampling $\boldsymbol{z} \sim \mathcal{N}(\mu, \sigma^2)$, we can sample $\boldsymbol{\epsilon} \sim \mathcal{N}(0, 1)$ and compute

$$\boldsymbol{z} = g(\boldsymbol{\theta}, \boldsymbol{\epsilon}) = \mu + \sigma \boldsymbol{\epsilon} \tag{6.62}$$

where $\boldsymbol{\theta} = (\mu, \sigma)$. This allows us to rewrite our stochastic objective as follows:

$$\mathcal{L}(\boldsymbol{\theta}) = \mathbb{E}_{q_{\boldsymbol{\theta}}(\boldsymbol{z})} \left[\tilde{\mathcal{L}}(\boldsymbol{\theta}, \boldsymbol{z}) \right] = \mathbb{E}_{q_0(\boldsymbol{\epsilon})} \left[\tilde{\mathcal{L}}(\boldsymbol{\theta}, g(\boldsymbol{\theta}, \boldsymbol{\epsilon})) \right] \tag{6.63}$$

Since $q_0(\boldsymbol{\epsilon})$ is independent of $\boldsymbol{\theta}$, we can push the gradient operator inside the expectation, which we can approximate with Monte Carlo:

$$\nabla_{\boldsymbol{\theta}} \mathcal{L}(\boldsymbol{\theta}) = \mathbb{E}_{q_0(\boldsymbol{\epsilon})} \left[\nabla_{\boldsymbol{\theta}} \tilde{\mathcal{L}}(\boldsymbol{\theta}, g(\boldsymbol{\theta}, \boldsymbol{\epsilon})) \right] \approx \frac{1}{S} \sum_{s=1}^{S} \nabla_{\boldsymbol{\theta}} \tilde{\mathcal{L}}(\boldsymbol{\theta}, g(\boldsymbol{\theta}, \boldsymbol{\epsilon}_s)) \tag{6.64}$$

where $\boldsymbol{\epsilon}_s \sim q_0$. This is called the **reparameterization gradient** or the **pathwise derivative** [Gla03; Fu15; KW14; RMW14a; TLG14; JO18; FMM18], and is widely used in variational inference (Section 10.2.1). For a review of such methods, see [Moh+20].

Note that the tensorflow probability library (which also has a JAX interface) supports reparameterizable distributions. Therefore you can just write code in a straightforward way, as shown in ?? 6.1.

Listing 6.1: Derivative of a stochastic function

```
def expected_loss(params):
    zs = dist.sample(N, key)
    return jnp.mean(loss(params, zs))
g = jax.grad(expected_loss)(params)
```

6.3.5.1   Example

As a simple example, suppose we define some arbitrary function, such as $\tilde{\mathcal{L}}(z) = z^2 - 3z$, and then define its expected value as $\mathcal{L}(\boldsymbol{\theta}) = \mathbb{E}_{\mathcal{N}(z|\mu,v)}\left[\tilde{\mathcal{L}}(z)\right]$, where $\boldsymbol{\theta} = (\mu, v)$ and $v = \sigma^2$. Suppose we want to compute

$$\nabla_{\boldsymbol{\theta}}\mathcal{L}(\boldsymbol{\theta}) = [\frac{\partial}{\partial\mu}\mathbb{E}\left[\tilde{\mathcal{L}}(z)\right], \frac{\partial}{\partial v}\mathbb{E}\left[\tilde{\mathcal{L}}(z)\right]] \tag{6.65}$$

Since the Gaussian distribution is reparameterizable, we can sample $z \sim \mathcal{N}(z|\mu, v)$, and then use automatic differentiation to compute each of these gradient terms, and then average.

However, in the special case of Gaussian distributions, we can also compute the gradient vector directly. In particular, in Section 6.4.5.1 we present Bonnet's theorem, which states that

$$\frac{\partial}{\partial\mu}\mathbb{E}\left[\tilde{\mathcal{L}}(z)\right] = \mathbb{E}\left[\frac{\partial}{\partial z}\tilde{\mathcal{L}}(z)\right] \tag{6.66}$$

Similarly, Price's theorem states that

$$\frac{\partial}{\partial v}\mathbb{E}\left[\tilde{\mathcal{L}}(z)\right] = 0.5\mathbb{E}\left[\frac{\partial^2}{\partial z^2}\tilde{\mathcal{L}}(z)\right] \tag{6.67}$$

In gradient_expected_value_gaussian.ipynb we show that these two methods are numerically equivalent, as theory suggests.

6.3.5.2   Total derivative

To compute the gradient term inside the expectation in Equation (6.64) we need to use the **total derivative**, since the function $\tilde{\mathcal{L}}$ depends on $\boldsymbol{\theta}$ directly and via the noise sample $\boldsymbol{z}$. Recall that, for a function of the form $\tilde{\mathcal{L}}(\theta_1, \ldots, \theta_{d_\psi}, z_1(\boldsymbol{\theta}), \ldots, z_{d_z}(\boldsymbol{\theta}))$, the total derivative wrt θ_i is given by the chain rule as follows:

$$\frac{\partial\tilde{\mathcal{L}}}{\partial\theta_i}^{\text{TD}} = \frac{\partial\tilde{\mathcal{L}}}{\partial\theta_i} + \sum_j \frac{\partial\tilde{\mathcal{L}}}{\partial z_j}\frac{\partial z_j}{\partial\theta_i} \tag{6.68}$$

and hence

$$\nabla_{\boldsymbol{\theta}}\tilde{\mathcal{L}}(\boldsymbol{\theta}, \boldsymbol{z})^{\text{TD}} = \nabla_{\boldsymbol{z}}\tilde{\mathcal{L}}(\boldsymbol{\theta}, \boldsymbol{z})\mathbf{J} + \nabla_{\boldsymbol{\theta}}\tilde{\mathcal{L}}(\boldsymbol{\theta}, \boldsymbol{z}) \tag{6.69}$$

where $\mathbf{J} = \frac{\partial\boldsymbol{z}^{\mathsf{T}}}{\partial\boldsymbol{\theta}}$ is the $d_z \times d_\psi$ Jacobian matrix of the noise transformation:

$$\mathbf{J} = \begin{pmatrix} \frac{\partial z_1}{\partial\theta_1} & \cdots & \frac{\partial z_1}{\partial\theta_{d_\psi}} \\ \vdots & \ddots & \vdots \\ \frac{\partial z_{d_z}}{\partial\theta_{d_\psi}} & \cdots & \frac{\partial z_{d_z}}{\partial\theta_{d_\psi}} \end{pmatrix} \tag{6.70}$$

We leverage this decomposition in Section 6.3.5.3, where we derive a lower variance gradient estimator in the special case of variational inference.

6.3.5.3   "Sticking the landing" estimator

In this section we consider the special case which arises in variational inference (Section 10.2). The ELBO objective (for a single latent sample z) has the form

$$\tilde{\mathcal{L}}(\boldsymbol{\theta}, \boldsymbol{z}) = \log p(\boldsymbol{z}, \boldsymbol{x}) - \log q(\boldsymbol{z}|\boldsymbol{\theta}) \tag{6.71}$$

where $\boldsymbol{\theta}$ are the parameters of the variational posterior. The gradient becomes

$$\nabla_{\boldsymbol{\theta}} \tilde{\mathcal{L}}(\boldsymbol{\theta}, \boldsymbol{z}) = \nabla_{\boldsymbol{\theta}} \left[\log p(\boldsymbol{z}, \boldsymbol{x}) - \log q(\boldsymbol{z}|\boldsymbol{\theta}) \right] \tag{6.72}$$

$$= \underbrace{\nabla_{\boldsymbol{z}} \left[\log p(\boldsymbol{z}, \boldsymbol{x}) - \log q(\boldsymbol{z}|\boldsymbol{\theta}) \right] \mathbf{J}}_{\text{path derivative}} - \underbrace{\nabla_{\boldsymbol{\theta}} \log q(\boldsymbol{z}|\boldsymbol{\theta})}_{\text{score function}} \tag{6.73}$$

The first term is the indirect effect of $\boldsymbol{\theta}$ on the objective via the generated samples $\boldsymbol{z}$. The second term is the direct effect of $\boldsymbol{\theta}$ on the objective. The second term is zero in expectation since it is the score function (see Equation (3.44)), but it may be non-zero for a finite number of samples, even if $q(\boldsymbol{z}|\boldsymbol{\theta}) = p(\boldsymbol{z}|\boldsymbol{x})$ is the true posterior. In [RWD17], they propose to drop the second term to create a lower variance estimator. This can be achieved by using $\log q(\boldsymbol{z}|\boldsymbol{\theta}')$, where $\boldsymbol{\theta}'$ is a "disconnected" copy of $\boldsymbol{\theta}$ that does not affect the gradient. In pseudocode, this looks like the following:

$$\boldsymbol{\epsilon} \sim q_0(\boldsymbol{\epsilon}) \tag{6.74}$$

$$\boldsymbol{z} = g(\boldsymbol{\epsilon}, \boldsymbol{\theta}) \tag{6.75}$$

$$\boldsymbol{\theta}' = \text{stop-gradient}(\boldsymbol{\theta}) \tag{6.76}$$

$$\boldsymbol{g} = \nabla_{\boldsymbol{\theta}} \left[\log p(\boldsymbol{z}, \boldsymbol{x}) - \log q(\boldsymbol{z}|\boldsymbol{\theta}') \right] \tag{6.77}$$

They call this the **sticking the landing** or **STL** estimator.[4] Note that the STL estimator is not always better than the "standard" estimator, without the stop gradient term. In [GD20], they propose to use a weighted combination of estimators, where the weights are optimized so as to reduce variance for a fixed amount of compute.

6.3.6   Gumbel softmax trick

When working with discrete variables, we cannot use the reparameterization trick. However, we can often relax the discrete variables to continuous ones in a way which allows the trick to be used, as we explain below.

Consider a one-hot vector $\boldsymbol{d}$ with K bits, so $d_k \in \{0, 1\}$ and $\sum_{k=1}^{K} d_k = 1$. This can be used to represent a K-ary categorical variable d. Let $P(d) = \text{Cat}(d|\boldsymbol{\pi})$, where $\pi_k = P(d_k = 1)$, so $0 \leq \pi_k \leq 1$. Alternatively we can parameterize the distribution in terms of $(\alpha_1, \ldots, \alpha_k)$, where $\pi_k = \alpha_k / (\sum_{k'=1}^{K} \alpha_{k'})$. We will denote this by $d \sim \text{Cat}(d|\boldsymbol{\alpha})$.

We can sample a one-hot vector $\boldsymbol{d}$ from this distribution by computing

$$\boldsymbol{d} = \text{onehot}(\underset{k}{\text{argmax}}[\epsilon_k + \log \alpha_k]) \tag{6.78}$$

---

4. The expression "to stick a landing" means to land firmly on one's feet after performing a gymnastics move. In the current context, the analogy is this: if the variational posterior is optimal, then we want our objective to be 0, and not to "wobble" with Monte Carlo noise.

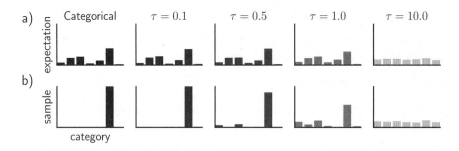

Figure 6.3: Illustration of the Gumbel-softmax (concrete) distribution with $K = 7$ states at different temperatures τ. The top row shows $\mathbb{E}[z]$, and the bottom row shows samples $z \sim \text{GumbelSoftmax}(\alpha, \tau)$. The left column shows a discrete (categorical) distribution, which always produces one-hot samples. From Figure 1 of [JGP17]. Used with kind permission of Ben Poole.

where $\epsilon_k \sim \text{Gumbel}(0, 1)$ is sampled from the **Gumbel distribution** [Gum54]. We can draw such samples by first sampling $u_k \sim \text{Unif}(0, 1)$ and then computing $\epsilon_k = -\log(-\log(u_k))$. This is called the **Gumbel-max trick** [MTM14], and gives us a reparameterizable representation for the categorical distribution.

Unfortunately, the derivative of the argmax is 0 everywhere except at the boundary of transitions from one label to another, where the derivative is undefined. However, suppose we replace the argmax with a softmax, and replace the discrete one-hot vector d with a continuous relaxation $x \in \Delta^{K-1}$, where $\Delta^{K-1} = \{x \in \mathbb{R}^K : x_k \in [0, 1], \sum_{k=1}^K x_k = 1\}$ is the K-dimensional simplex. Then we can write

$$x_k = \frac{\exp((\log \alpha_k + \epsilon_k)/\tau)}{\sum_{k'=1}^K \exp((\log \alpha_{k'} + \epsilon_{k'})/\tau)} \tag{6.79}$$

where $\tau > 0$ is a temperature parameter. This is called the **Gumbel-softmax distribution** [JGP17] or the **concrete distribution** [MMT17]. This smoothly approaches the discrete distribution as $\tau \to 0$, as illustrated in Figure 6.3.

We can now replace $f(d)$ with $f(x)$, which allows us to take reparameterized gradients wrt x.

6.3.7   Stochastic computation graphs

We can represent an arbitrary function containing both deterministic and stochastic components as a **stochastic computation graph**. We can then generalize the AD algorithm (Section 6.2) to leverage score function estimation (Section 6.3.4) and reparameterization (Section 6.3.5) to compute Monte Carlo gradients for complex nested functions. For details, see [Sch+15a; Gaj+19].

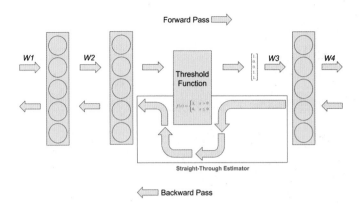

Figure 6.4: Illustration of straight-through estimator when applied to a binary threshold function in the middle of an MLP. From $https://www.hassanaskary.com/python/pytorch/deep\%20learning/2020/09/19/intuitive-explanation-of-straight-through-estimators.html$. Used with kind permission of Hassan Askary.

6.3.8 Straight-through estimator

In this section, we discuss how to approximate the gradient of a quantized version of a signal. For example, suppose we have the following thresholding function, that binarizes its output:

$$f(x) = \begin{cases} 1 & \text{if } x > 0 \\ 0 & \text{if } x \leq 0 \end{cases} \tag{6.80}$$

This does not have a well-defined gradient. However, we can use the **straight-through estimator** proposed in [Ben13] as an approximation. The basic idea is to replace $g(x) = f'(x)$, where $f'(x)$ is the derivative of f wrt input, with $g(x) = x$ when computing the backwards pass. See Figure 6.4 for a visualization, and [Yin+19b] for an analysis of why this is a valid approximation.

In practice, we sometimes replace $g(x) = x$ with the **hard tanh** function, defined by

$$\text{HardTanh}(x) = \begin{cases} x & \text{if } -1 \leq x \leq 1 \\ 1 & \text{if } x > 1 \\ -1 & \text{if } x < -1 \end{cases} \tag{6.81}$$

This ensures the gradients that are backpropagated don't get too large. See Section 21.6 for an application of this approach to discrete autoencoders.

6.4 Natural gradient descent

In this section, we discuss **natural gradient descent** (**NGD**) [Ama98], which is a second order method for optimizing the parameters of (conditional) probability distributions $p_\theta(y|x)$. The key idea is to compute parameter updates by measuring distances between the induced distributions, rather than comparing parameter values directly.

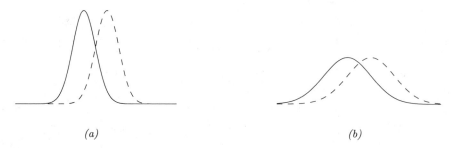

Figure 6.5: Changing the mean of a Gaussian by a fixed amount (from solid to dotted curve) can have more impact when the (shared) variance is small (as in a) compared to when the variance is large (as in b). Hence the impact (in terms of prediction accuracy) of a change to μ depends on where the optimizer is in (μ, σ) space. From Figure 3 of [Hon+10], reproduced from [Val00]. Used with kind permission of Antti Honkela.

For example, consider comparing two Gaussians, $p_{\boldsymbol{\theta}} = p(y|\mu, \sigma)$ and $p_{\boldsymbol{\theta}'} = p(y|\mu', \sigma')$. The (squared) Euclidean distance between the parameter vectors decomposes as $||\boldsymbol{\theta} - \boldsymbol{\theta}'||^2 = (\mu - \mu')^2 + (\sigma - \sigma')^2$. However, the predictive distribution has the form $\exp(-\frac{1}{2\sigma^2}(y - \mu)^2)$, so changes in μ need to be measured relative to σ. This is illustrated in Figure 6.5(a-b), which shows two univariate Gaussian distributions (dotted and solid lines) whose means differ by δ. In Figure 6.5(a), they share the same small variance σ^2, whereas in Figure 6.5(b), they share the same large variance. It is clear that the value of δ matters much more (in terms of the effect on the distribution) when the variance is small. Thus we see that the two parameters interact with each other, which the Euclidean distance cannot capture. This problem gets much worse when we consider more complex models, such as deep neural networks. By modeling such correlations, NGD can converge much faster than other gradient methods.

6.4.1   Defining the natural gradient

The key to NGD is to measure the notion of distance between two probability distributions in terms of the KL divergence. As we show in Section 5.1.9, this can be appproximated in terms of the Fisher information matrix (FIM). In particular, for any given input $\boldsymbol{x}$, we have

$$D_{\mathrm{KL}}\left(p_{\boldsymbol{\theta}}(\boldsymbol{y}|\boldsymbol{x}) \,\|\, p_{\boldsymbol{\theta}+\boldsymbol{\delta}}(\boldsymbol{y}|\boldsymbol{x})\right) \approx \frac{1}{2}\boldsymbol{\delta}^{\mathsf{T}}\mathbf{F}_{\boldsymbol{x}}\boldsymbol{\delta} \tag{6.82}$$

where $\mathbf{F}_{\boldsymbol{x}}$ is the FIM

$$\mathbf{F}_{\boldsymbol{x}}(\boldsymbol{\theta}) = -\mathbb{E}_{p_{\boldsymbol{\theta}}(\boldsymbol{y}|\boldsymbol{x})}\left[\nabla^2 \log p_{\boldsymbol{\theta}}(\boldsymbol{y}|\boldsymbol{x})\right] = \mathbb{E}_{p_{\boldsymbol{\theta}}(\boldsymbol{y}|\boldsymbol{x})}\left[(\nabla \log p_{\boldsymbol{\theta}}(\boldsymbol{y}|\boldsymbol{x}))(\nabla \log p_{\boldsymbol{\theta}}(\boldsymbol{y}|\boldsymbol{x}))^{\mathsf{T}}\right] \tag{6.83}$$

We can compute the average KL between the current and updated distributions using $\frac{1}{2}\boldsymbol{\delta}^{\mathsf{T}}\mathbf{F}\boldsymbol{\delta}$, where $\mathbf{F}$ is the averaged FIM:

$$\mathbf{F}(\boldsymbol{\theta}) = \mathbb{E}_{p_{\mathcal{D}}(\boldsymbol{x})}\left[\mathbf{F}_{\boldsymbol{x}}(\boldsymbol{\theta})\right] \tag{6.84}$$

NGD uses the inverse FIM as a preconditioning matrix, i.e., we perform updates of the following form:

$$\boldsymbol{\theta}_{t+1} = \boldsymbol{\theta}_t - \eta_t \mathbf{F}(\boldsymbol{\theta}_t)^{-1} \boldsymbol{g}_t \tag{6.85}$$

The term

$$\mathbf{F}^{-1}\boldsymbol{g}_t = \mathbf{F}^{-1}\nabla\mathcal{L}(\boldsymbol{\theta}_t) \triangleq \tilde{\nabla}\mathcal{L}(\boldsymbol{\theta}_t) \tag{6.86}$$

is called the **natural gradient**.

6.4.2 Interpretations of NGD

6.4.2.1 NGD as a trust region method

In Supplementary Section 6.1.3.1 we show that we can interpret standard gradient descent as optimizing a linear approximation to the objective subject to a penalty on the ℓ_2 norm of the change in parameters, i.e., if $\boldsymbol{\theta}_{t+1} = \boldsymbol{\theta}_t + \boldsymbol{\delta}$, then we optimize

$$M_t(\boldsymbol{\delta}) = \mathcal{L}(\boldsymbol{\theta}_t) + \boldsymbol{g}_t^\mathsf{T}\boldsymbol{\delta} + \eta||\boldsymbol{\delta}||_2^2 \tag{6.87}$$

Now let us replace the squared distance with the squared FIM-based distance, $||\boldsymbol{\delta}||_F^2 = \boldsymbol{\delta}^\mathsf{T}\mathbf{F}\boldsymbol{\delta}$. This is equivalent to squared Euclidean distance in the **whitened coordinate system** $\boldsymbol{\phi} = \mathbf{F}^{\frac{1}{2}}\boldsymbol{\theta}$, since

$$||\boldsymbol{\phi}_{t+1} - \boldsymbol{\phi}_t||_2^2 = ||\mathbf{F}^{\frac{1}{2}}(\boldsymbol{\theta}_t + \boldsymbol{\delta}) - \mathbf{F}^{\frac{1}{2}}\boldsymbol{\theta}_t||_2^2 = ||\mathbf{F}^{\frac{1}{2}}\boldsymbol{\delta}||_2^2 = ||\boldsymbol{\delta}||_F^2 \tag{6.88}$$

The new objective becomes

$$M_t(\boldsymbol{\delta}) = \mathcal{L}(\boldsymbol{\theta}_t) + \boldsymbol{g}_t^\mathsf{T}\boldsymbol{\delta} + \eta\boldsymbol{\delta}^\mathsf{T}\mathbf{F}\boldsymbol{\delta} \tag{6.89}$$

Solving $\nabla_{\boldsymbol{\delta}} M_t(\boldsymbol{\delta}) = \mathbf{0}$ gives the update

$$\boldsymbol{\delta}_t = -\eta\mathbf{F}^{-1}\boldsymbol{g}_t \tag{6.90}$$

This is the same as the natural gradient direction. Thus we can view NGD as a trust region method, where we use a first-order approximation to the objective, and use FIM-distance in the constraint.

In the above derivation, we assumed $\mathbf{F}$ was a constant matrix. Im most problems, it will change at each point in space, since we are optimizing in a curved space known as a **Riemannian manifold**. For certain models, we can compute the FIM efficiently, allowing us to capture curvature information, even though we use a first-order approximation to the objective.

6.4.2.2 NGD as a Gauss-Newton method

If $p(\boldsymbol{y}|\boldsymbol{x}, \boldsymbol{\theta})$ is an exponential family distribution with natural parameters computed by $\boldsymbol{\eta} = f(\boldsymbol{x}, \boldsymbol{\theta})$, then one can show [Hes00; PB14] that NGD is identical to the generalized Gauss-Newton (GGN) method (Section 17.3.2). Furthermore, in the online setting, these methods are equivalent to performing sequential Bayesian inference using the extended Kalman filter, as shown in [Oll18].

6.4.3   Benefits of NGD

The use of the FIM as a preconditioning matrix, rather than the Hessian, has two advantages. First, $\mathbf{F}$ is always positive definite, whereas $\mathbf{H}$ can have negative eigenvalues at saddle points, which are prevalent in high dimensional spaces. Second, it is easy to approximate $\mathbf{F}$ online from minibatches, since it is an expectation (wrt the empirical distribution) of outer products of gradient vectors. This is in contrast to Hessian-based methods [Byr+16; Liu+18a], which are much more sensitive to noise introduced by the minibatch approximation.

In addition, the connection with trust region optimization makes it clear that NGD updates parameters in a way that matter most for prediction, which allows the method to take larger steps in uninformative regions of parameter space, which can help avoid getting stuck on plateaus. This can also help with issues that arise when the parameters are highly correlated.

For example, consider a 2d Gaussian with an unusual, highly coupled parameterization, proposed in [SD12]:

$$p(\boldsymbol{x}; \boldsymbol{\theta}) = \frac{1}{2\pi} \exp\left[-\frac{1}{2}\left((x_1 - \left[3\theta_1 + \frac{1}{3}\theta_2\right]) \right)^2 - \frac{1}{2}\left(x_2 - \left[\frac{1}{3}\theta_1\right] \right)^2 \right] \tag{6.91}$$

The objective is the cross entropy loss:

$$\mathcal{L}(\boldsymbol{\theta}) = -\mathbb{E}_{p^*(\boldsymbol{x})} \left[\log p(\boldsymbol{x}; \boldsymbol{\theta}) \right] \tag{6.92}$$

The gradient of this objective is given by

$$\nabla_{\boldsymbol{\theta}} \mathcal{L}(\boldsymbol{\theta}) \begin{pmatrix} = \mathbb{E}_{p^*(\boldsymbol{x})} \left[3(x_1 - [3\theta_1 + \frac{1}{3}\theta_2]) + \frac{1}{3}(x_2 - [\frac{1}{3}\theta_1]) \right] \\ \mathbb{E}_{p^*(\boldsymbol{x})} \left[\frac{1}{3}(x_1 - [3\theta_1 + \frac{1}{3}\theta_2]) \right] \end{pmatrix} \tag{6.93}$$

Suppose that $p^*(\boldsymbol{x}) = p(\boldsymbol{x}; [0, 0])$. Then the Fisher matrix is a constant matrix, given by

$$\mathbf{F} = \begin{pmatrix} 3^2 + \frac{1}{3^2} & 1 \\ 1 & \frac{1}{3^2} \end{pmatrix} \tag{6.94}$$

Figure 6.6 compares steepest descent in $\boldsymbol{\theta}$ space with the natural gradient method, which is equivalent to steepest descent in $\boldsymbol{\phi}$ space. Both methods start at $\boldsymbol{\theta} = (1, -1)$. The global optimum is at $\boldsymbol{\theta} = (0, 0)$. We see that the NG method (blue dots) converges much faster to this optimum and takes the shortest path, whereas steepest descent takes a very circuitous route. We also see that the gradient field in the whitened parameter space is more "spherical", which makes descent much simpler and faster.

Finally, note that since NGD is invariant to how we parameterize the distribution, we will get the same results even for a standard parameterization of the Gaussian. This is particularly useful if our probability model is more complex, such as a DNN (see e.g., [SSE18]).

6.4.4   Approximating the natural gradient

The main drawback of NGD is the computational cost of computing (the inverse of) the Fisher information matrix (FIM). To speed this up, several methods make assumptions about the form of $\mathbf{F}$, so it can be inverted efficiently. For example, [LeC+98] uses a diagonal approximation for

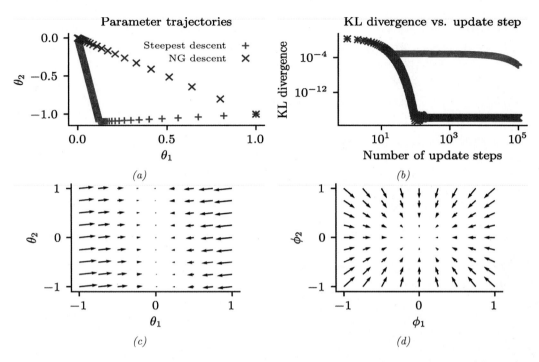

Figure 6.6: *Illustration of the benefits of natural gradient vs steepest descent on a 2d problem. (a) Trajectories of the two methods in parameter space (red = steepest descent, blue = NG). They both start in the bottom right, at $(1, -1)$. (b) Objective vs number of iterations. (c) Gradient field in the $\boldsymbol{\theta}$ parameter space. (d) Gradient field in the whitened $\boldsymbol{\phi} = \mathbf{F}^{\frac{1}{2}}\boldsymbol{\theta}$ parameter space used by NG. Generated by* nat_grad_demo.ipynb.

neural net training; [RMB08] uses a low-rank plus block diagonal approximation; and [GS15] assumes the covariance of the gradients can be modeled by a directed Gaussian graphical model with low treewidth (i.e., the Cholesky factorization of $\mathbf{F}$ is sparse).

[MG15] propose the **KFAC** method, which stands for "Kronecker factored approximate curvature"; this approximates the FIM of a DNN as a block diagonal matrix, where each block is a Kronecker product of two small matrices. This method has shown good results on supervised learning of neural nets [GM16; BGM17; Geo+18; Osa+19b] as well as reinforcement learning of neural policy networks [Wu+17]. The KFAC approximation can be justified using the mean field analysis of [AKO18]. In addition, [ZMG19] prove that KFAC will converge to the global optimum of a DNN if it is overparameterized (i.e., acts like an interpolator).

A simpler approach is to approximate the FIM by replacing the model's distribution with the empirical distribution. In particular, define $p_{\mathcal{D}}(\boldsymbol{x}, \boldsymbol{y}) = \frac{1}{N} \sum_{n=1}^{N} \delta_{\boldsymbol{x}_n}(\boldsymbol{x}) \delta_{\boldsymbol{y}_n}(\boldsymbol{y})$, $p_{\mathcal{D}}(\boldsymbol{x}) = \frac{1}{N} \sum_{n=1}^{N} \delta_{\boldsymbol{x}_n}(\boldsymbol{x})$

and $p_{\boldsymbol{\theta}}(\boldsymbol{x}, \boldsymbol{y}) = p_{\mathcal{D}}(\boldsymbol{x})p(\boldsymbol{y}|\boldsymbol{x}, \boldsymbol{\theta})$. Then we can compute the **empirical Fisher** [Mar16] as follows:

$$\mathbf{F} = \mathbb{E}_{p_{\boldsymbol{\theta}}(\boldsymbol{x}, \boldsymbol{y})} \left[\nabla \log p(\boldsymbol{y}|\boldsymbol{x}, \boldsymbol{\theta}) \nabla \log p(\boldsymbol{y}|\boldsymbol{x}, \boldsymbol{\theta})^{\mathsf{T}} \right] \tag{6.95}$$

$$\approx \mathbb{E}_{p_{\mathcal{D}}(\boldsymbol{x}, \boldsymbol{y})} \left[\nabla \log p(\boldsymbol{y}|\boldsymbol{x}, \boldsymbol{\theta}) \nabla \log p(\boldsymbol{y}|\boldsymbol{x}, \boldsymbol{\theta})^{\mathsf{T}} \right] \tag{6.96}$$

$$= \frac{1}{|\mathcal{D}|} \sum_{(\boldsymbol{x}, \boldsymbol{y}) \in \mathcal{D}} \nabla \log p(\boldsymbol{y}|\boldsymbol{x}, \boldsymbol{\theta}) \nabla \log p(\boldsymbol{y}|\boldsymbol{x}, \boldsymbol{\theta})^{\mathsf{T}} \tag{6.97}$$

This approximation is widely used, since it is simple to compute. In particular, we can compute a diagonal approximation using the squared gradient vector. (This is similar to AdaGrad, but only uses the current gradient instead of a moving average of gradients; the latter is a better approach when performing stochastic optimization.)

Unfortunately, the empirical Fisher does not work as well as the true Fisher [KBH19; Tho+19]. To see why, note that when we reach a flat part of parameter space where the gradient vector goes to zero, the empirical Fisher will become singular, and hence the algorithm will get stuck on this plateau. However, the true Fisher takes expectations over the outputs, i.e., it marginalizes out $\boldsymbol{y}$. This will allow it to detect small changes in the output if we change the parameters. This is why the natural gradient method can "escape" plateaus better than standard gradient methods.

An alternative strategy is to use exact computation of $\mathbf{F}$, but solve for $\mathbf{F}^{-1}\boldsymbol{g}$ approximately using truncated conjugate gradient (CG) methods, where each CG step uses efficient methods for Hessian-vector products [Pea94]. This is called **Hessian free optimization** [Mar10a]. However, this approach can be slow, since it may take many CG iterations to compute a single parameter update.

6.4.5   Natural gradients for the exponential family

In this section, we asssume $\mathcal{L}$ is an expected loss of the following form:

$$\mathcal{L}(\boldsymbol{\mu}) = \mathbb{E}_{q_{\boldsymbol{\mu}}(\boldsymbol{z})} \left[\tilde{\mathcal{L}}(\boldsymbol{z}) \right] \tag{6.98}$$

where $q_{\boldsymbol{\mu}}(\boldsymbol{z})$ is an exponential family distribution with moment parameters $\boldsymbol{\mu}$. This is the basis of variational optimization (discussed in Supplementary Section 6.4.3) and natural evolutionary strategies (discussed in Section 6.7.6).

It turns out the gradient wrt the moment parameters is the same as the natural gradient wrt the natural parameters $\boldsymbol{\lambda}$. This follows from the chain rule:

$$\frac{d}{d\boldsymbol{\lambda}} \mathcal{L}(\boldsymbol{\lambda}) = \frac{d\boldsymbol{\mu}}{d\boldsymbol{\lambda}} \frac{d}{d\boldsymbol{\mu}} \mathcal{L}(\boldsymbol{\mu}) = \mathbf{F}(\boldsymbol{\lambda}) \nabla_{\boldsymbol{\mu}} \mathcal{L}(\boldsymbol{\mu}) \tag{6.99}$$

where $\mathcal{L}(\boldsymbol{\mu}) = \mathcal{L}(\boldsymbol{\lambda}(\boldsymbol{\mu}))$, and where we used Equation (2.232) to write

$$\mathbf{F}(\boldsymbol{\lambda}) = \nabla_{\boldsymbol{\lambda}} \boldsymbol{\mu}(\boldsymbol{\lambda}) = \nabla_{\boldsymbol{\lambda}}^2 A(\boldsymbol{\lambda}) \tag{6.100}$$

Hence

$$\tilde{\nabla}_{\boldsymbol{\lambda}} \mathcal{L}(\boldsymbol{\lambda}) = \mathbf{F}(\boldsymbol{\lambda})^{-1} \nabla_{\boldsymbol{\lambda}} \mathcal{L}(\boldsymbol{\lambda}) = \nabla_{\boldsymbol{\mu}} \mathcal{L}(\boldsymbol{\mu}) \tag{6.101}$$

It remains to compute the (regular) gradient wrt the moment parameters. The details on how to do this will depend on the form of the q and the form of $\mathcal{L}(\boldsymbol{\lambda})$. We discuss some approaches to this problem below.

6.4.5.1 Analytic computation for the Gaussian case

In this section, we assume that $q(z) = \mathcal{N}(z|m, V)$. We now show how to compute the relevant gradients analytically.

Following Section 2.4.2.5, the natural parameters of q are

$$\lambda^{(1)} = V^{-1}m, \ \lambda^{(2)} = -\frac{1}{2}V^{-1} \tag{6.102}$$

and the moment parameters are

$$\mu^{(1)} = m, \ \mu^{(2)} = V + mm^\mathsf{T} \tag{6.103}$$

For simplicity, we derive the result for the scalar case. Let $m = \mu^{(1)}$ and $v = \mu^{(2)} - (\mu^{(1)})^2$. By using the chain rule, the gradient wrt the moment parameters are

$$\frac{\partial \mathcal{L}}{\partial \mu^{(1)}} = \frac{\partial \mathcal{L}}{\partial m}\frac{\partial m}{\partial \mu^{(1)}} + \frac{\partial \mathcal{L}}{\partial v}\frac{\partial v}{\partial \mu^{(1)}} = \frac{\partial \mathcal{L}}{\partial m} - 2\frac{\partial \mathcal{L}}{\partial v}m \tag{6.104}$$

$$\frac{\partial \mathcal{L}}{\partial \mu^{(2)}} = \frac{\partial \mathcal{L}}{\partial m}\frac{\partial m}{\partial \mu^{(2)}} + \frac{\partial \mathcal{L}}{\partial v}\frac{\partial v}{\partial \mu^{(2)}} = \frac{\partial \mathcal{L}}{\partial v} \tag{6.105}$$

It remains to compute the derivatives wrt m and v. If $z \sim \mathcal{N}(m, V)$, then from **Bonnet's theorem** [Bon64] we have

$$\frac{\partial}{\partial m_i}\mathbb{E}\left[\tilde{\mathcal{L}}(z)\right] = \mathbb{E}\left[\frac{\partial}{\partial \theta_i}\tilde{\mathcal{L}}(z)\right] \tag{6.106}$$

And from **Price's theorem** [Pri58] we have

$$\frac{\partial}{\partial V_{ij}}\mathbb{E}\left[\tilde{\mathcal{L}}(z)\right] = c_{ij}\mathbb{E}\left[\frac{\partial^2}{\partial \theta_i \theta_j}\tilde{\mathcal{L}}(z)\right] \tag{6.107}$$

where $c_{ij} = \frac{1}{2}$ is $i = j$ and $c_{ij} = 1$ otherwise. (See gradient_expected_value_gaussian.ipynb for a "proof by example" of these claims.)

In the multivariate case, the result is as follows [OA09; KR21a]:

$$\nabla_{\mu^{(1)}}\mathbb{E}_{q(z)}\left[\tilde{\mathcal{L}}(z)\right] = \nabla_m\mathbb{E}_{q(z)}\left[\tilde{\mathcal{L}}(z)\right] - 2\nabla_V\mathbb{E}_{q(z)}\left[\tilde{\mathcal{L}}(z)\right]m \tag{6.108}$$

$$= \mathbb{E}_{q(z)}\left[\nabla_z\tilde{\mathcal{L}}(z)\right] - \mathbb{E}_{q(z)}\left[\nabla_z^2\tilde{\mathcal{L}}(z)\right]m \tag{6.109}$$

$$\nabla_{\mu^{(2)}}\mathbb{E}_{q(z)}\left[\tilde{\mathcal{L}}(z)\right] = \nabla_V\mathbb{E}_{q(z)}\left[\tilde{\mathcal{L}}(z)\right] \tag{6.110}$$

$$= \frac{1}{2}\mathbb{E}_{q(z)}\left[\nabla_z^2\tilde{\mathcal{L}}(z)\right] \tag{6.111}$$

Thus we see that the natural gradients rely on both the gradient and Hessian of the loss function $\tilde{\mathcal{L}}(z)$. We will see applications of this result in Supplementary Section 6.4.2.2.

6.4.5.2   Stochastic approximation for the general case

In general, it can be hard to analytically compute the natural gradient. However, we can compute a Monte Carlo approximation. To see this, let us assume $\mathcal{L}$ is an expected loss of the following form:

$$\mathcal{L}(\boldsymbol{\mu}) = \mathbb{E}_{q_{\boldsymbol{\mu}}(\boldsymbol{z})} \left[\tilde{\mathcal{L}}(\boldsymbol{z}) \right] \tag{6.112}$$

From Equation (6.101) the natural gradient is given by

$$\nabla_{\boldsymbol{\mu}} \mathcal{L}(\boldsymbol{\mu}) = \mathbf{F}(\boldsymbol{\lambda})^{-1} \nabla_{\boldsymbol{\lambda}} \mathcal{L}(\boldsymbol{\lambda}) \tag{6.113}$$

For exponential family distributions, both of these terms on the RHS can be written as expectations, and hence can be approximated by Monte Carlo, as noted by [KL17a]. To see this, note that

$$\mathbf{F}(\boldsymbol{\lambda}) = \nabla_{\boldsymbol{\lambda}} \boldsymbol{\mu}(\boldsymbol{\lambda}) = \nabla_{\boldsymbol{\lambda}} \mathbb{E}_{q_{\boldsymbol{\lambda}}(\boldsymbol{z})} \left[\mathcal{T}(\boldsymbol{z}) \right] \tag{6.114}$$

$$\nabla_{\boldsymbol{\lambda}} \mathcal{L}(\boldsymbol{\lambda}) = \nabla_{\boldsymbol{\lambda}} \mathbb{E}_{q_{\boldsymbol{\lambda}}(\boldsymbol{z})} \left[\tilde{\mathcal{L}}(\boldsymbol{z}) \right] \tag{6.115}$$

If q is reparameterizable, we can apply the reparameterization trick (Section 6.3.5) to push the gradient inside the expectation operator. This lets us sample $\boldsymbol{z}$ from q, compute the gradients, and average; we can then pass the resulting stochastic gradients to SGD.

6.4.5.3   Natural gradient of the entropy function

In this section, we discuss how to compute the natural gradient of the entropy of an exponential family distribution, which is useful when performing variational inference (Chapter 10). The natural gradient is given by

$$\tilde{\nabla}_{\boldsymbol{\lambda}} \mathbb{H}(\boldsymbol{\lambda}) = -\nabla_{\boldsymbol{\mu}} \mathbb{E}_{q_{\boldsymbol{\mu}}(\boldsymbol{z})} \left[\log q(\boldsymbol{z}) \right] \tag{6.116}$$

where, from Equation (2.160), we have

$$\log q(\boldsymbol{z}) = \log h(\boldsymbol{z}) + \mathcal{T}(\boldsymbol{z})^{\mathsf{T}} \boldsymbol{\lambda} - A(\boldsymbol{\lambda}) \tag{6.117}$$

Since $\mathbb{E}\left[\mathcal{T}(\boldsymbol{z})\right] = \boldsymbol{\mu}$, we have

$$\nabla_{\boldsymbol{\mu}} \mathbb{E}_{q_{\boldsymbol{\mu}}(\boldsymbol{z})} \left[\log q(\boldsymbol{z}) \right] = \nabla_{\boldsymbol{\mu}} \mathbb{E}_{q(\boldsymbol{z})} \left[\log h(\boldsymbol{z}) \right] + \nabla_{\boldsymbol{\mu}} \boldsymbol{\mu}^{\mathsf{T}} \boldsymbol{\lambda}(\boldsymbol{\mu}) - \nabla_{\boldsymbol{\mu}} A(\boldsymbol{\lambda}) \tag{6.118}$$

where $h(\boldsymbol{z})$ is the base measure. Since $\boldsymbol{\lambda}$ is a function of $\boldsymbol{\mu}$, we have

$$\nabla_{\boldsymbol{\mu}} \boldsymbol{\mu}^{\mathsf{T}} \boldsymbol{\lambda} = \boldsymbol{\lambda} + (\nabla_{\boldsymbol{\mu}} \boldsymbol{\lambda})^{\mathsf{T}} \boldsymbol{\mu} = \boldsymbol{\lambda} + (\mathbf{F}_{\boldsymbol{\lambda}}^{-1} \nabla_{\boldsymbol{\lambda}} \boldsymbol{\lambda})^{\mathsf{T}} \boldsymbol{\mu} = \boldsymbol{\lambda} + \mathbf{F}_{\boldsymbol{\lambda}}^{-1} \boldsymbol{\mu} \tag{6.119}$$

and since $\boldsymbol{\mu} = \nabla_{\boldsymbol{\lambda}} A(\boldsymbol{\lambda})$ we have

$$\nabla_{\boldsymbol{\mu}} A(\boldsymbol{\lambda}) = \mathbf{F}_{\boldsymbol{\lambda}}^{-1} \nabla_{\boldsymbol{\lambda}} A(\boldsymbol{\lambda}) = \mathbf{F}_{\boldsymbol{\lambda}}^{-1} \boldsymbol{\mu} \tag{6.120}$$

Hence

$$-\nabla_{\boldsymbol{\mu}} \mathbb{E}_{q_{\boldsymbol{\mu}}(\boldsymbol{z})} \left[\log q(\boldsymbol{z}) \right] = -\nabla_{\boldsymbol{\mu}} \mathbb{E}_{q(\boldsymbol{z})} \left[\log h(\boldsymbol{z}) \right] - \boldsymbol{\lambda} \tag{6.121}$$

If we assume that $h(\boldsymbol{z}) = \text{const}$, as is often the case, we get

$$\tilde{\nabla}_{\boldsymbol{\lambda}} \mathbb{H}(\boldsymbol{\lambda}) = -\boldsymbol{\lambda} \tag{6.122}$$

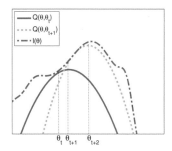

Figure 6.7: Illustration of a bound optimization algorithm. Adapted from Figure 9.14 of [Bis06]. Generated by em_log_likelihood_max.ipynb.

6.5   Bound optimization (MM) algorithms

In this section, we consider a class of algorithms known as **bound optimization** or **MM** algorithms. In the context of minimization, MM stands for **majorize-minimize**. In the context of maximization, MM stands for **minorize-maximize**. There are many examples of MM algorithms, such as EM (Section 6.5.3), proximal gradient methods (Section 4.1), the mean shift algorithm for clustering [FH75; Che95; FT05], etc. For more details, see e.g., [HL04; Mai15; SBP17; Nad+19],

6.5.1   The general algorithm

In this section, we assume our goal is to *maximize* some function $\ell(\boldsymbol{\theta})$ wrt its parameters $\boldsymbol{\theta}$. The basic approach in MM algorithms is to construct a **surrogate function** $Q(\boldsymbol{\theta}, \boldsymbol{\theta}^t)$ which is a tight lowerbound to $\ell(\boldsymbol{\theta})$ such that $Q(\boldsymbol{\theta}, \boldsymbol{\theta}^t) \leq \ell(\boldsymbol{\theta})$ and $Q(\boldsymbol{\theta}^t, \boldsymbol{\theta}^t) = \ell(\boldsymbol{\theta}^t)$. If these conditions are met, we say that Q minorizes ℓ. We then perform the following update at each step:

$$\boldsymbol{\theta}^{t+1} = \underset{\boldsymbol{\theta}}{\operatorname{argmax}} \, Q(\boldsymbol{\theta}, \boldsymbol{\theta}^t) \tag{6.123}$$

This guarantees us monotonic increases in the original objective:

$$\ell(\boldsymbol{\theta}^{t+1}) \geq Q(\boldsymbol{\theta}^{t+1}, \boldsymbol{\theta}^t) \geq Q(\boldsymbol{\theta}^t, \boldsymbol{\theta}^t) = \ell(\boldsymbol{\theta}^t) \tag{6.124}$$

where the first inequality follows since $Q(\boldsymbol{\theta}^t, \boldsymbol{\theta}')$ is a lower bound on $\ell(\boldsymbol{\theta}^t)$ for any $\boldsymbol{\theta}'$; the second inequality follows from Equation (6.123); and the final equality follows the tightness property. As a consequence of this result, if you do not observe monotonic increase of the objective, you must have an error in your math and/or code. This is a surprisingly powerful debugging tool.

This process is sketched in Figure 6.7. The dashed red curve is the original function (e.g., the log-likelihood of the observed data). The solid blue curve is the lower bound, evaluated at $\boldsymbol{\theta}^t$; this touches the objective function at $\boldsymbol{\theta}^t$. We then set $\boldsymbol{\theta}^{t+1}$ to the maximum of the lower bound (blue curve), and fit a new bound at that point (dotted green curve). The maximum of this new bound becomes $\boldsymbol{\theta}^{t+2}$, etc.

6.5.2   Example: logistic regression

If $\ell(\boldsymbol{\theta})$ is a concave function we want to maximize, then one way to obtain a valid lower bound is to use a bound on its Hessian, i.e., to find a negative definite matrix $\mathbf{B}$ such that $\mathbf{H}(\boldsymbol{\theta}) \succ \mathbf{B}$. In this case, one can show (see [BCN18, App. B]) that

$$\ell(\boldsymbol{\theta}) \geq \ell(\boldsymbol{\theta}^t) + (\boldsymbol{\theta} - \boldsymbol{\theta}^t)^{\mathsf{T}} \boldsymbol{g}(\boldsymbol{\theta}^t) + \frac{1}{2}(\boldsymbol{\theta} - \boldsymbol{\theta}^t)^{\mathsf{T}} \mathbf{B}(\boldsymbol{\theta} - \boldsymbol{\theta}^t) \tag{6.125}$$

where $\boldsymbol{g}(\boldsymbol{\theta}^t) = \nabla \ell(\boldsymbol{\theta}^t)$. Therefore the following function is a valid lower bound:

$$Q(\boldsymbol{\theta}, \boldsymbol{\theta}^t) = \boldsymbol{\theta}^{\mathsf{T}}(\boldsymbol{g}(\boldsymbol{\theta}^t) - \mathbf{B}\boldsymbol{\theta}^t) + \frac{1}{2}\boldsymbol{\theta}^{\mathsf{T}}\mathbf{B}\boldsymbol{\theta} \tag{6.126}$$

The corresponding update becomes

$$\boldsymbol{\theta}^{t+1} = \boldsymbol{\theta}^t - \mathbf{B}^{-1}\boldsymbol{g}(\boldsymbol{\theta}^t) \tag{6.127}$$

This is similar to a Newton update, except we use $\mathbf{B}$, which is a fixed matrix, rather than $\mathbf{H}(\boldsymbol{\theta}^t)$, which changes at each iteration. This can give us some of the advantages of second order methods at lower computational cost.

For example, let us fit a multi-class logistic regression model using MM. (We follow the presentation of [Kri+05], who also consider the more interesting case of *sparse* logistic regression.)   The probability that example n belongs to class $c \in \{1, \ldots, C\}$ is given by

$$p(y_n = c | \boldsymbol{x}_n, \boldsymbol{w}) = \frac{\exp(\boldsymbol{w}_c^{\mathsf{T}} \boldsymbol{x}_n)}{\sum_{i=1}^{C} \exp(\boldsymbol{w}_i^{\mathsf{T}} \boldsymbol{x}_n)} \tag{6.128}$$

Because of the normalization condition $\sum_{c=1}^{C} p(y_n = c | \boldsymbol{x}_n, \boldsymbol{w}) = 1$, we can set $\boldsymbol{w}_C = \boldsymbol{0}$. (For example, in binary logistic regression, where $C = 2$, we only learn a single weight vector.) Therefore the parameters $\boldsymbol{\theta}$ correspond to a weight matrix $\boldsymbol{w}$ of size $D(C - 1)$, where $\boldsymbol{x}_n \in \mathbb{R}^D$.

If we let $\boldsymbol{p}_n(\boldsymbol{w}) = [p(y_n = 1 | \boldsymbol{x}_n, \boldsymbol{w}), \ldots, p(y_n = C{-}1 | \boldsymbol{x}_n, \boldsymbol{w})]$ and $\boldsymbol{y}_n = [\mathbb{I}\,(y_n = 1), \ldots, \mathbb{I}\,(y_n = C - 1)]$, we can write the log-likelihood as follows:

$$\ell(\boldsymbol{w}) = \sum_{n=1}^{N} \left[\sum_{c=1}^{C-1} y_{nc} \boldsymbol{w}_c^{\mathsf{T}} \boldsymbol{x}_n - \log \sum_{c=1}^{C} \exp(\boldsymbol{w}_c^{\mathsf{T}} \boldsymbol{x}_n) \right] \tag{6.129}$$

The gradient is given by the following:

$$\boldsymbol{g}(\boldsymbol{w}) = \sum_{n=1}^{N} (\boldsymbol{y}_n - \boldsymbol{p}_n(\boldsymbol{w})) \otimes \boldsymbol{x}_n \tag{6.130}$$

where $\otimes$ denotes Kronecker product (which, in this case, is just outer product of the two vectors). The Hessian is given by the following:

$$\mathbf{H}(\boldsymbol{w}) = -\sum_{n=1}^{N} (\mathrm{diag}(\boldsymbol{p}_n(\boldsymbol{w})) - \boldsymbol{p}_n(\boldsymbol{w})\boldsymbol{p}_n(\boldsymbol{w})^{\mathsf{T}}) \otimes (\boldsymbol{x}_n \boldsymbol{x}_n^{\mathsf{T}}) \tag{6.131}$$

We can construct a lower bound on the Hessian, as shown in [Boh92]:

$$\mathbf{H}(\boldsymbol{w}) \succ -\frac{1}{2}[\mathbf{I} - \mathbf{1}\mathbf{1}^{\mathsf{T}}/C] \otimes (\sum_{n=1}^{N} \boldsymbol{x}_n \boldsymbol{x}_n^{\mathsf{T}}) \triangleq \mathbf{B} \tag{6.132}$$

where $\mathbf{I}$ is a $(C - 1)$-dimensional identity matrix, and $\mathbf{1}$ is a $(C - 1)$-dimensional vector of all 1s. In the binary case, this becomes

$$\mathbf{H}(\boldsymbol{w}) \succ -\frac{1}{2}(1 - \frac{1}{2})(\sum_{n=1}^{N} \boldsymbol{x}_n^{\mathsf{T}} \boldsymbol{x}_n) = -\frac{1}{4}\mathbf{X}^{\mathsf{T}}\mathbf{X} \tag{6.133}$$

This follows since $p_n \leq 0.5$ so $-(p_n - p_n^2) \geq -0.25$.

We can use this lower bound to construct an MM algorithm to find the MLE. The update becomes

$$\boldsymbol{w}^{t+1} = \boldsymbol{w}^t - \mathbf{B}^{-1}\boldsymbol{g}(\boldsymbol{w}^t) \tag{6.134}$$

For example, let us consider the binary case, so $\boldsymbol{g}^t = \nabla\ell(\boldsymbol{w}^t) = \mathbf{X}^{\mathsf{T}}(\boldsymbol{y} - \boldsymbol{\mu}^t)$, where $\boldsymbol{\mu}^t = [p_n(\boldsymbol{w}^t), (1 - p_n(\boldsymbol{w}^t))]_{n=1}^{N}$. The update becomes

$$\boldsymbol{w}^{t+1} = \boldsymbol{w}^t - 4(\mathbf{X}^{\mathsf{T}}\mathbf{X})^{-1}\boldsymbol{g}^t \tag{6.135}$$

The above is faster (per step) than the IRLS (iteratively reweighted least squares) algorithm (i.e., Newton's method), which is the standard method for fitting GLMs. To see this, note that the Newton update has the form

$$\boldsymbol{w}^{t+1} = \boldsymbol{w}^t - \mathbf{H}^{-1}\boldsymbol{g}(\boldsymbol{w}^t) = \boldsymbol{w}^t - (\mathbf{X}^{\mathsf{T}}\mathbf{S}^t\mathbf{X})^{-1}\boldsymbol{g}^t \tag{6.136}$$

where $\mathbf{S}^t = \text{diag}(\boldsymbol{\mu}^t \odot (1 - \boldsymbol{\mu}^t))$. We see that Equation (6.135) is faster to compute, since we can precompute the constant matrix $(\mathbf{X}^{\mathsf{T}}\mathbf{X})^{-1}$.

6.5.3 The EM algorithm

In this section, we discuss the **expectation maximization (EM)** algorithm [DLR77; MK07], which is an algorithm designed to compute the MLE or MAP parameter estimate for probability models that have **missing data** and/or **hidden variables**. It is a special case of an MM algorithm.

The basic idea behind EM is to alternate between estimating the hidden variables (or missing values) during the **E step** (expectation step), and then using the fully observed data to compute the MLE during the **M step** (maximization step). Of course, we need to iterate this process, since the expected values depend on the parameters, but the parameters depend on the expected values.

In Section 6.5.3.1, we show that EM is a **bound optimization** algorithm, which implies that this iterative procedure will converge to a local maximum of the log likelihood. The speed of convergence depends on the amount of missing data, which affects the tightness of the bound [XJ96; MD97; SRG03; KKS20].

We now describe the EM algorithm for a generic model. We let $\boldsymbol{y}_n$ be the visible data for example n, and $\boldsymbol{z}_n$ be the hidden data.

6.5.3.1   Lower bound

The goal of EM is to maximize the log likelihood of the observed data:

$$\ell(\boldsymbol{\theta}) = \sum_{n=1}^{N} \log p(\boldsymbol{y}_n|\boldsymbol{\theta}) = \sum_{n=1}^{N} \log \left[\sum_{\boldsymbol{z}_n} p(\boldsymbol{y}_n, \boldsymbol{z}_n|\boldsymbol{\theta}) \right] \tag{6.137}$$

where $\boldsymbol{y}_n$ are the visible variables and $\boldsymbol{z}_n$ are the hidden variables. Unfortunately this is hard to optimize, since the log cannot be pushed inside the sum.

EM gets around this problem as follows. First, consider a set of arbitrary distributions $q_n(\boldsymbol{z}_n)$ over each hidden variable $\boldsymbol{z}_n$. The observed data log likelihood can be written as follows:

$$\ell(\boldsymbol{\theta}) = \sum_{n=1}^{N} \log \left[\sum_{\boldsymbol{z}_n} q_n(\boldsymbol{z}_n) \frac{p(\boldsymbol{y}_n, \boldsymbol{z}_n|\boldsymbol{\theta})}{q_n(\boldsymbol{z}_n)} \right] \tag{6.138}$$

Using Jensen's inequality, we can push the log (which is a concave function) inside the expectation to get the following lower bound on the log likelihood:

$$\ell(\boldsymbol{\theta}) \geq \sum_{n} \sum_{\boldsymbol{z}_n} q_n(\boldsymbol{z}_n) \log \frac{p(\boldsymbol{y}_n, \boldsymbol{z}_n|\boldsymbol{\theta})}{q_n(\boldsymbol{z}_n)} \tag{6.139}$$

$$= \sum_{n} \underbrace{\mathbb{E}_{q_n} \left[\log p(\boldsymbol{y}_n, \boldsymbol{z}_n|\boldsymbol{\theta}) \right] + \mathbb{H}(q_n)}_{\text{Ł}(\boldsymbol{\theta}, q_n|\boldsymbol{y}_n)} \tag{6.140}$$

$$= \sum_{n} \text{Ł}(\boldsymbol{\theta}, q_n|\boldsymbol{y}_n) \triangleq \text{Ł}(\boldsymbol{\theta}, \{q_n\}|\mathcal{D}) \tag{6.141}$$

where $\mathbb{H}(q)$ is the entropy of probability distribution q, and $\text{Ł}(\boldsymbol{\theta}, \{q_n\}|\mathcal{D})$ is called the **evidence lower bound** or **ELBO**, since it is a lower bound on the log marginal likelihood, $\log p(\boldsymbol{y}_{1:N}|\boldsymbol{\theta})$, also called the evidence. Optimizing this bound is the basis of variational inference, as we discuss in Section 10.1.

6.5.3.2   E step

We see that the lower bound is a sum of N terms, each of which has the following form:

$$\text{Ł}(\boldsymbol{\theta}, q_n|\boldsymbol{y}_n) = \sum_{\boldsymbol{z}_n} q_n(\boldsymbol{z}_n) \log \frac{p(\boldsymbol{y}_n, \boldsymbol{z}_n|\boldsymbol{\theta})}{q_n(\boldsymbol{z}_n)} \tag{6.142}$$

$$= \sum_{\boldsymbol{z}_n} q_n(\boldsymbol{z}_n) \log \frac{p(\boldsymbol{z}_n|\boldsymbol{y}_n, \boldsymbol{\theta}) p(\boldsymbol{y}_n|\boldsymbol{\theta})}{q_n(\boldsymbol{z}_n)} \tag{6.143}$$

$$= \sum_{\boldsymbol{z}_n} q_n(\boldsymbol{z}_n) \log \frac{p(\boldsymbol{z}_n|\boldsymbol{y}_n, \boldsymbol{\theta})}{q_n(\boldsymbol{z}_n)} + \sum_{\boldsymbol{z}_n} q_n(\boldsymbol{z}_n) \log p(\boldsymbol{y}_n|\boldsymbol{\theta}) \tag{6.144}$$

$$= -D_{\mathbb{KL}}\left(q_n(\boldsymbol{z}_n) \| p(\boldsymbol{z}_n|\boldsymbol{y}_n, \boldsymbol{\theta})\right) + \log p(\boldsymbol{y}_n|\boldsymbol{\theta}) \tag{6.145}$$

where $D_{\mathbb{KL}}\left(q \| p\right) \triangleq \sum_{z} q(z) \log \frac{q(z)}{p(z)}$ is the Kullback-Leibler divergence (or KL divergence for short) between probability distributions q and p. We discuss this in more detail in Section 5.1, but the key property we need here is that $D_{\text{KL}}(q \| p) \geq 0$ and $D_{\text{KL}}(q \| p) = 0$ iff $q = p$. Hence we can maximize the lower bound $\text{Ł}(\boldsymbol{\theta}, \{q_n\}|\mathcal{D})$ wrt $\{q_n\}$ by setting each one to $q_n^* = p(\boldsymbol{z}_n|\boldsymbol{y}_n, \boldsymbol{\theta})$. This is called the **E step**. This ensures the ELBO is a tight lower bound:

$$\text{Ł}(\boldsymbol{\theta}, \{q_n^*\}|\mathcal{D}) = \sum_n \log p(\boldsymbol{y}_n|\boldsymbol{\theta}) = \ell(\boldsymbol{\theta}|\mathcal{D}) \tag{6.146}$$

To see how this connects to bound optimization, let us define

$$Q(\boldsymbol{\theta}, \boldsymbol{\theta}^t) = \text{Ł}(\boldsymbol{\theta}, \{p(\boldsymbol{z}_n|\boldsymbol{y}_n; \boldsymbol{\theta}^t)\}) \tag{6.147}$$

Then we have $Q(\boldsymbol{\theta}, \boldsymbol{\theta}^t) \leq \ell(\boldsymbol{\theta})$ and $Q(\boldsymbol{\theta}^t, \boldsymbol{\theta}^t) = \ell(\boldsymbol{\theta}^t)$, as required.

However, if we cannot compute the posteriors $p(\boldsymbol{z}_n|\boldsymbol{y}_n; \boldsymbol{\theta}^t)$ exactly, we can still use an approximate distribution $q(\boldsymbol{z}_n|\boldsymbol{y}_n; \boldsymbol{\theta}^t)$; this will yield a non-tight lower-bound on the log-likelihood. This generalized version of EM is known as variational EM [NH98b]. See Section 6.5.6.1 for details.

6.5.3.3 M step

In the M step, we need to maximize $\text{Ł}(\boldsymbol{\theta}, \{q_n^t\})$ wrt $\boldsymbol{\theta}$, where the q_n^t are the distributions computed in the E step at iteration t. Since the entropy terms $\mathbb{H}(q_n)$ are constant wrt $\boldsymbol{\theta}$, we can drop them in the M step. We are left with

$$\ell^t(\boldsymbol{\theta}) = \sum_n \mathbb{E}_{q_n^t(\boldsymbol{z}_n)} \left[\log p(\boldsymbol{y}_n, \boldsymbol{z}_n|\boldsymbol{\theta})\right] \tag{6.148}$$

This is called the **expected complete data log likelihood**. If the joint probability is in the exponential family (Section 2.4), we can rewrite this as

$$\ell^t(\boldsymbol{\theta}) = \sum_n \mathbb{E}\left[\mathcal{T}(\boldsymbol{y}_n, \boldsymbol{z}_n)^\mathsf{T}\boldsymbol{\theta} - A(\boldsymbol{\theta})\right] = \sum_n (\mathbb{E}\left[\mathcal{T}(\boldsymbol{y}_n, \boldsymbol{z}_n)\right]^\mathsf{T}\boldsymbol{\theta} - A(\boldsymbol{\theta})) \tag{6.149}$$

where $\mathbb{E}\left[\mathcal{T}(\boldsymbol{y}_n, \boldsymbol{z}_n)\right]$ are called the **expected sufficient statistics**.

In the M step, we maximize the expected complete data log likelihood to get

$$\boldsymbol{\theta}^{t+1} = \arg\max_{\boldsymbol{\theta}} \sum_n \mathbb{E}_{q_n^t} \left[\log p(\boldsymbol{y}_n, \boldsymbol{z}_n|\boldsymbol{\theta})\right] \tag{6.150}$$

In the case of the exponential family, the maximization can be solved in closed-form by matching the moments of the expected sufficient statistics (Section 2.4.5).

We see from the above that the E step does not in fact need to return the full set of posterior distributions $\{q(\boldsymbol{z}_n)\}$, but can instead just return the sum of the expected sufficient statistics, $\sum_n \mathbb{E}_{q(\boldsymbol{z}_n)} \left[\mathcal{T}(\boldsymbol{y}_n, \boldsymbol{z}_n)\right]$.

A common application of EM is for fitting mixture models; we discuss this in the prequel to this book, [Mur22]. Below we give a different example.

6.5.4 Example: EM for an MVN with missing data

It is easy to compute the MLE for a multivariate normal when we have a fully observed data matrix: we just compute the sample mean and covariance. In this section, we consider the case where we have

missing data or **partially observed data**. For example, we can think of the entries of $\mathbf{Y}$ as being answers to a survey; some of these answers may be unknown. There are many kinds of missing data, as we discuss in Section 3.11. In this section, we make the missing at random (MAR) assumption, for simplicity. Under the MAR assumption, the log likelihood of the visible data has the form

$$\log p(\mathbf{X}|\boldsymbol{\theta}) = \sum_n \log p(\boldsymbol{x}_n|\boldsymbol{\theta}) = \sum_n \log \left[\int p(\boldsymbol{x}_n, \boldsymbol{z}_n|\boldsymbol{\theta}) d\boldsymbol{z}_n \right] \tag{6.151}$$

where $\boldsymbol{x}_n$ are the visible variables in case n, $\boldsymbol{z}_n$ are the hidden variables, and $\boldsymbol{y}_n = (\boldsymbol{z}_n, \boldsymbol{x}_n)$ are all the variables. Unfortunately, this objective is hard to maximize. since we cannot push the log inside the expectation. Fortunately, we can easily apply EM, as we explain below.

6.5.4.1   E step

Suppose we have the parameters $\boldsymbol{\theta}^{t-1}$ from the previous iteration. Then we can compute the expected complete data log likelihood at iteration t as follows:

$$Q(\boldsymbol{\theta}, \boldsymbol{\theta}^{t-1}) = \mathbb{E}\left[\sum_{n=1}^{N} \log \mathcal{N}(\boldsymbol{y}_n|\boldsymbol{\mu}, \boldsymbol{\Sigma})|\mathcal{D}, \boldsymbol{\theta}^{t-1} \right] \tag{6.152}$$

$$= -\frac{N}{2} \log |2\pi\boldsymbol{\Sigma}| - \frac{1}{2} \sum_n \mathbb{E}\left[(\boldsymbol{y}_n - \boldsymbol{\mu})^\mathsf{T} \boldsymbol{\Sigma}^{-1} (\boldsymbol{y}_n - \boldsymbol{\mu}) \right] \tag{6.153}$$

$$= -\frac{N}{2} \log |2\pi\boldsymbol{\Sigma}| - \frac{1}{2} \mathrm{tr}(\boldsymbol{\Sigma}^{-1} \sum_n \mathbb{E}\left[(\boldsymbol{y}_n - \boldsymbol{\mu})(\boldsymbol{y}_n - \boldsymbol{\mu})^\mathsf{T} \right] \tag{6.154}$$

$$= -\frac{N}{2} \log |\boldsymbol{\Sigma}| - \frac{ND}{2} \log(2\pi) - \frac{1}{2} \mathrm{tr}(\boldsymbol{\Sigma}^{-1} \mathbb{E}\left[\mathbf{S}(\boldsymbol{\mu}) \right]) \tag{6.155}$$

where

$$\mathbb{E}\left[\mathbf{S}(\boldsymbol{\mu}) \right] \triangleq \sum_n \left(\mathbb{E}\left[\boldsymbol{y}_n \boldsymbol{y}_n^\mathsf{T} \right] + \boldsymbol{\mu}\boldsymbol{\mu}^\mathsf{T} - 2\boldsymbol{\mu}\mathbb{E}\left[\boldsymbol{y}_n \right]^\mathsf{T} \right) \tag{6.156}$$

(We drop the conditioning of the expectation on $\mathcal{D}$ and $\boldsymbol{\theta}^{t-1}$ for brevity.) We see that we need to compute $\sum_n \mathbb{E}\left[\boldsymbol{y}_n \right]$ and $\sum_n \mathbb{E}\left[\boldsymbol{y}_n \boldsymbol{y}_n^\mathsf{T} \right]$; these are the expected sufficient statistics.

To compute these quantities, we use the results from Section 2.3.1.3. We have

$$p(\boldsymbol{z}_n|\boldsymbol{x}_n, \boldsymbol{\theta}) = \mathcal{N}(\boldsymbol{z}_n|\boldsymbol{m}_n, \mathbf{V}_n) \tag{6.157}$$

$$\boldsymbol{m}_n \triangleq \boldsymbol{\mu}_h + \boldsymbol{\Sigma}_{hv}\boldsymbol{\Sigma}_{vv}^{-1}(\boldsymbol{x}_n - \boldsymbol{\mu}_v) \tag{6.158}$$

$$\mathbf{V}_n \triangleq \boldsymbol{\Sigma}_{hh} - \boldsymbol{\Sigma}_{hv}\boldsymbol{\Sigma}_{vv}^{-1}\boldsymbol{\Sigma}_{vh} \tag{6.159}$$

where we partition $\boldsymbol{\mu}$ and $\boldsymbol{\Sigma}$ into blocks based on the hidden and visible indices h and v. Hence the expected sufficient statistics are

$$\mathbb{E}\left[\boldsymbol{y}_n \right] = (\mathbb{E}\left[\boldsymbol{z}_n \right]; \boldsymbol{x}_n) = (\boldsymbol{m}_n; \boldsymbol{x}_n) \tag{6.160}$$

To compute $\mathbb{E}\left[\boldsymbol{y}_n \boldsymbol{y}_n^{\mathsf{T}}\right]$, we use the result that $\mathrm{Cov}\left[\boldsymbol{y}\right] = \mathbb{E}\left[\boldsymbol{y}\boldsymbol{y}^{\mathsf{T}}\right] - \mathbb{E}\left[\boldsymbol{y}\right]\mathbb{E}\left[\boldsymbol{y}^{\mathsf{T}}\right]$. Hence

$$\mathbb{E}\left[\boldsymbol{y}_n \boldsymbol{y}_n^{\mathsf{T}}\right] = \mathbb{E}\left[\begin{pmatrix} \boldsymbol{z}_n \\ \boldsymbol{x}_n \end{pmatrix} \begin{pmatrix} \boldsymbol{z}_n^{\mathsf{T}} & \boldsymbol{x}_n^{\mathsf{T}} \end{pmatrix}\right] = \begin{pmatrix} \mathbb{E}\left[\boldsymbol{z}_n \boldsymbol{z}_n^{\mathsf{T}}\right] & \mathbb{E}\left[\boldsymbol{z}_n\right]\boldsymbol{x}_n^{\mathsf{T}} \\ \boldsymbol{x}_n \mathbb{E}\left[\boldsymbol{z}_n\right]^{\mathsf{T}} & \boldsymbol{x}_n \boldsymbol{x}_n^{\mathsf{T}} \end{pmatrix} \tag{6.161}$$

$$\mathbb{E}\left[\boldsymbol{z}_n \boldsymbol{z}_n^{\mathsf{T}}\right] = \mathbb{E}\left[\boldsymbol{z}_n\right]\mathbb{E}\left[\boldsymbol{z}_n\right]^{\mathsf{T}} + \mathbf{V}_n \tag{6.162}$$

6.5.4.2   M step

By solving $\nabla Q(\boldsymbol{\theta}, \boldsymbol{\theta}^{(t-1)}) = \mathbf{0}$, we can show that the M step is equivalent to plugging these ESS into the usual MLE equations to get

$$\boldsymbol{\mu}^t = \frac{1}{N}\sum_n \mathbb{E}\left[\boldsymbol{y}_n\right] \tag{6.163}$$

$$\boldsymbol{\Sigma}^t = \frac{1}{N}\sum_n \mathbb{E}\left[\boldsymbol{y}_n \boldsymbol{y}_n^{\mathsf{T}}\right] - \boldsymbol{\mu}^t (\boldsymbol{\mu}^t)^{\mathsf{T}} \tag{6.164}$$

Thus we see that EM is *not* equivalent to simply replacing variables by their expectations and applying the standard MLE formula; that would ignore the posterior variance and would result in an incorrect estimate. Instead we must compute the expectation of the sufficient statistics, and plug that into the usual equation for the MLE.

6.5.4.3   Initialization

To get the algorithm started, we can compute the MLE based on those rows of the data matrix that are fully observed. If there are no such rows, we can just estimate the diagonal terms of $\boldsymbol{\Sigma}$ using the observed marginal statistics. We are then ready to start EM.

6.5.4.4   Example

As an example of this procedure in action, let us consider an imputation problem, where we have $N = 100$ 10-dimensional data cases, which we assume to come from a Gaussian. We generate synthetic data where 50% of the observations are missing at random. First we fit the parameters using EM. Call the resulting parameters $\hat{\boldsymbol{\theta}}$. We can now use our model for predictions by computing $\mathbb{E}\left[\boldsymbol{z}_n | \boldsymbol{x}_n, \hat{\boldsymbol{\theta}}\right]$. Figure 6.8 indicates that the results obtained using the learned parameters are almost as good as with the true parameters. Not surprisingly, performance improves with more data, or as the fraction of missing data is reduced.

6.5.5   Example: robust linear regression using Student likelihood

In this section, we discuss how to use EM to fit a linear regression model that uses the Student distribution for its likelihood, instead of the more common Gaussian distribution, in order to achieve robustness, as first proposed in [Zel76]. More precisely, the likelihood is given by

$$p(y|\boldsymbol{x}, \boldsymbol{w}, \sigma^2, \nu) = \mathcal{T}(y | \boldsymbol{w}^{\mathsf{T}}\boldsymbol{x}, \sigma^2, \nu) \tag{6.165}$$

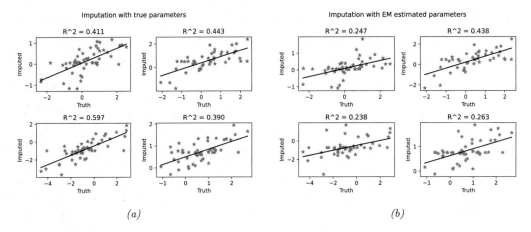

Figure 6.8: Illustration of data imputation using a multivariate Gaussian. (a) Scatter plot of true values vs imputed values using true parameters. (b) Same as (a), but using parameters estimated with EM. We just show the first four variables, for brevity. Generated by gauss_imputation_em_demo.ipynb.

At first blush it may not be apparent how to do this, since there is no missing data, and there are no hidden variables. However, it turns out that we can introduce "artificial" hidden variables to make the problem easier to solve; this is a common trick. The key insight is that we can represent the Student distribution as a Gaussian scale mixture, as we discuss in Section 28.2.3.1.

We can apply the GSM version of the Student distribution to our problem by associating a latent scale $z_n \in \mathbb{R}_+$ with each example. The complete data log likelihood is therefore given by

$$\log p(\boldsymbol{y}, \boldsymbol{z}|\mathbf{X}, \boldsymbol{w}, \sigma^2, \nu) = \sum_n -\frac{1}{2}\log(2\pi z_n\sigma^2) - \frac{1}{2z_n\sigma^2}(y_i - \boldsymbol{w}^T\boldsymbol{x}_i)^2 \tag{6.166}$$

$$+ (\frac{\nu}{2} - 1)\log(z_n) - z_n\frac{\nu}{2} + \text{const} \tag{6.167}$$

Ignoring terms not involving $\boldsymbol{w}$, and taking expectations, we have

$$Q(\boldsymbol{\theta}, \boldsymbol{\theta}^t) = -\sum_n \frac{\lambda_n}{2\sigma^2}(y_n - \boldsymbol{w}^T\boldsymbol{x}_n)^2 \tag{6.168}$$

where $\lambda_n^t \triangleq \mathbb{E}\left[1/z_n|y_n, \boldsymbol{x}_n, \boldsymbol{w}^t\right]$. We recognize this as a weighted least squares objective, with weight λ_n^t per datapoint.

We now discuss how to compute these weights. Using the results from Section 2.2.3.4, one can show that

$$p(z_n|y_n, \boldsymbol{x}_n, \boldsymbol{\theta}) = \text{IG}(\frac{\nu+1}{2}, \frac{\nu+\delta_n}{2}) \tag{6.169}$$

where $\delta_n = \frac{(y_n - \boldsymbol{x}^T\boldsymbol{x}_n)^2}{\sigma^2}$ is the standardized residual. Hence

$$\lambda_n = \mathbb{E}\left[1/z_n\right] = \frac{\nu^t + 1}{\nu^t + \delta_n^t} \tag{6.170}$$

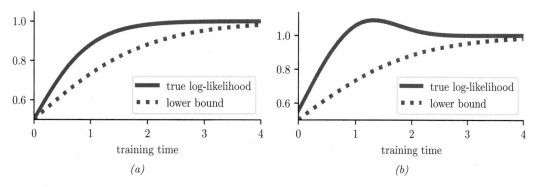

Figure 6.9: Illustration of possible behaviors of variational EM. (a) The lower bound increases at each iteration, and so does the likelihood. (b) The lower bound increases but the likelihood decreases. In this case, the algorithm is closing the gap between the approximate and true posterior. This can have a regularizing effect. Adapted from Figure 6 of [SJJ96]. Generated by var_em_bound.ipynb.

So if the residual δ_n^t is large, the point will be given low weight λ_n^t, which makes intuitive sense, since it is probably an outlier.

6.5.6 Extensions to EM

There are many variations and extensions of the EM algorithm, as discussed in [MK97]. We summarize a few of these below.

6.5.6.1 Variational EM

Suppose in the E step we pick $q_n^* = \operatorname{argmin}_{q_n \in \mathcal{Q}} D_{\mathbb{KL}}\left(q_n \parallel p(\boldsymbol{z}_n | \boldsymbol{x}_n, \boldsymbol{\theta})\right)$. Because we are optimizing over the space of functions, this is called variational inference (see Section 10.1 for details). If the family of distributions $\mathcal{Q}$ is rich enough to contain the true posterior, $q_n = p(\boldsymbol{z}_n | \boldsymbol{x}_n, \boldsymbol{\theta})$, then we can make the KL be zero. But in general, we might choose a more restrictive class for computational reasons. For example, we might use $q_n(\boldsymbol{z}_n) = \mathcal{N}(\boldsymbol{z}_n | \boldsymbol{\mu}_n, \operatorname{diag}(\boldsymbol{\sigma}_n))$ even if the true posterior is correlated.

The use of a restricted posterior family $\mathcal{Q}$ inside the E step of EM is called **variational EM** [NH98a]. Unlike regular EM, variational EM is not guaranteed to increase the actual log likelihood itself (see Figure 6.9), but it does monotonically increase the variational lower bound. We can control the tightness of this lower bound by varying the variational family $\mathcal{Q}$; in the limit in which $q_n = p_n$, corresponding to exact inference, we recover the same behavior as regular EM. See Section 10.1.3 for further discussion.

6.5.6.2 Hard EM

Suppose we use a degenerate posterior approximation in the context of variational EM, corresponding to a point estimate, $q(\boldsymbol{z} | \boldsymbol{x}_n) = \delta_{\hat{\boldsymbol{z}}_n}(\boldsymbol{z})$, where $\hat{\boldsymbol{z}}_n = \operatorname{argmax}_{\boldsymbol{z}} p(\boldsymbol{z} | \boldsymbol{x}_n)$. This is equivalent to **hard EM**, where we ignore uncertainty about $\boldsymbol{z}_n$ in the E step.

The problem with this degenerate approach is that it is very prone to overfitting, since the number of latent variables is proportional to the number of datacases [WCS08].

6.5.6.3   Monte Carlo EM

Another approach to handling an intractable E step is to use a Monte Carlo approximation to the expected sufficient statistics. That is, we draw samples from the posterior, $z_n^s \sim p(z_n|x_n, \theta^t)$; then we compute the sufficient statistics for each completed vector, (x_n, z_n^s); and finally we average the results. This is called **Monte Carlo EM** or **MCEM** [WT90; Nea12].

One way to draw samples is to use MCMC (see Chapter 12). However, if we have to wait for MCMC to converge inside each E step, the method becomes very slow. An alternative is to use stochastic approximation, and only perform "brief" sampling in the E step, followed by a partial parameter update. This is called **stochastic approximation EM** [DLM99] and tends to work better than MCEM.

6.5.6.4   Generalized EM

Sometimes we can perform the E step exactly, but we cannot perform the M step exactly. However, we can still monotonically increase the log likelihood by performing a "partial" M step, in which we merely increase the expected complete data log likelihood, rather than maximizing it. For example, we might follow a few gradient steps. This is called the **generalized EM** or **GEM** algorithm [MK07]. (This is an unfortunate term, since there are many ways to generalize EM, but it is the standard terminology.) For example, [Lan95a] proposes to perform one Newton-Raphson step:

$$\boldsymbol{\theta}_{t+1} = \boldsymbol{\theta}_t - \eta_t \mathbf{H}_t^{-1} \boldsymbol{g}_t \tag{6.171}$$

where $0 < \eta_t \leq 1$ is the step size, and

$$\boldsymbol{g}_t = \frac{\partial}{\partial \boldsymbol{\theta}} Q(\boldsymbol{\theta}, \boldsymbol{\theta}_t)|_{\boldsymbol{\theta}=\boldsymbol{\theta}_t} \tag{6.172}$$

$$\mathbf{H}_t = \frac{\partial^2}{\partial \boldsymbol{\theta} \partial \boldsymbol{\theta}^\mathsf{T}} Q(\boldsymbol{\theta}, \boldsymbol{\theta}_t)|_{\boldsymbol{\theta}=\boldsymbol{\theta}_t} \tag{6.173}$$

If $\eta_t = 1$, [Lan95a] calls this the **gradient EM algorithm**. However, it is possible to use a larger step size to speed up the algorithm, as in the **quasi-Newton EM algorithm** of [Lan95b]. This method also replaces the Hessian in Equation (6.173), which may not be negative definite (for non exponential family models), with a BFGS approximation. This ensures the overall algorithm is an ascent algorithm. Note, however, when the M step cannot be computed in closed form, EM loses some of its appeal over directly optimizing the marginal likelihood with a gradient based solver.

6.5.6.5   ECM algorithm

The **ECM** algorithm stands for "expectation conditional maximization", and refers to optimizing the parameters in the M step sequentially, if they turn out to be dependent. The **ECME** algorithm, which stands for "ECM either" [LR95], is a variant of ECM in which we maximize the expected complete data log likelihood (the Q function) as usual, or the observed data log likelihood, during one or more of the conditional maximization steps. The latter can be much faster, since it ignores the results of the E step, and directly optimizes the objective of interest. A standard example of this is when fitting the Student distribution. For fixed ν, we can update Σ as usual, but then to update ν, we replace the standard update of the form $\nu^{t+1} = \arg\max_\nu Q((\boldsymbol{\mu}^{t+1}, \boldsymbol{\Sigma}^{t+1}, \nu), \boldsymbol{\theta}^t)$ with $\nu^{t+1} = \arg\max_\nu \log p(\mathcal{D}|\boldsymbol{\mu}^{t+1}, \boldsymbol{\Sigma}^{t+1}, \nu)$. See [MK97] for more information.

6.5.6.6   Online EM

When dealing with large or streaming datasets, it is important to be able to learn online, as we discussed in Section 19.7.5. There are two main approaches to **online EM** in the literature. The first approach, known as **incremental EM** [NH98a], optimizes the lower bound $Q(\boldsymbol{\theta}, q_1, \ldots, q_N)$ one q_n at a time; however, this requires storing the expected sufficient statistics for each data case.

The second approach, known as **stepwise EM** [SI00; LK09; CM09], is based on stochastic gradient descent. This optimizes a local upper bound on $\ell_n(\boldsymbol{\theta}) = \log p(\boldsymbol{x}_n|\boldsymbol{\theta})$ at each step. (See [Mai13; Mai15] for a more general discussion of stochastic and incremental bound optimization algorithms.)

6.6   Bayesian optimization

In this section, we discuss **Bayesian optimization** or **BayesOpt**, which is a model-based approach to black-box optimization, designed for the case where the objective function $f : \mathcal{X} \to \mathbb{R}$ is expensive to evaluate (e.g., if it requires running a simulation, or training and testing a particular neural net architecture).

Since the true function f is expensive to evaluate, we want to make as few function calls (i.e., make as few **queries** $\boldsymbol{x}$ to the **oracle** f) as possible. This suggests that we should build a **surrogate function** (also called a **response surface model**) based on the data collected so far, $\mathcal{D}_n = \{(\boldsymbol{x}_i, y_i) : i = 1 : n\}$, which we can use to decide which point to query next. There is an inherent tradeoff between picking the point $\boldsymbol{x}$ where we think $f(\boldsymbol{x})$ is large (we follow the convention in the literature and assume we are trying to maximize f), and picking points where we are uncertain about $f(\boldsymbol{x})$ but where observing the function value might help us improve the surrogate model. This is another instance of the exploration-exploitation dilemma.

In the special case where the domain we are optimizing over is finite, so $\mathcal{X} = \{1, \ldots, A\}$, the BayesOpt problem becomes similar to the **best arm identification** problem in the bandit literature (Section 34.4). An important difference is that in bandits, we care about the cost of every action we take, whereas in optimization, we usually only care about the cost of the final solution we find. In other words, in bandits, we want to minimize cumulative regret, whereas in optimization we want to minimize simple or final regret.

Another related topic is **active learning**. Here the goal is to identify the whole function f with as few queries as possible, whereas in BayesOpt, the goal is just to identify the maximum of the function.

Bayesian optimization is a large topic, and we only give a brief overview below. For more details, see e.g., [Sha+16; Fra18; Gar23]. (See also `https://distill.pub/2020/bayesian-optimization/` for an interactive tutorial.)

6.6.1   Sequential model-based optimization

BayesOpt is an instance of a strategy known as sequential model-based optimization (**SMBO**) [HHLB11]. In this approach, we alternate between querying the function at a point, and updating our estimate of the surrogate based on the new data. More precisely, at each iteration n, we have a labeled dataset $\mathcal{D}_n = \{(\boldsymbol{x}_i, y_i) : i = 1 : n\}$, which records points $\boldsymbol{x}_i$ that we have queried, and the corresponding function values, $y_i = f(\boldsymbol{x}_i) + \epsilon_i$, where ϵ_i is an optional noise term. We use this dataset to estimate a probability distribution over the true function f; we will denote this by $p(f|\mathcal{D}_n)$. We then choose the next point to query $\boldsymbol{x}_{n+1}$ using an **acquisition function** $\alpha(\boldsymbol{x}; \mathcal{D}_n)$, which computes the expected utility of querying $\boldsymbol{x}$. (We discuss acquisition functions in Section 6.6.3). After we observe $y_{n+1} = f(\boldsymbol{x}_{n+1}) + \epsilon_{n+1}$, we update our beliefs about the function, and repeat. See Algorithm 6.5 for some pseudocode.

Algorithm 6.5: Bayesian optimization

---

1 Collect initial dataset $\mathcal{D}_0 = \{(\boldsymbol{x}_i, y_i)\}$ from random queries $\boldsymbol{x}_i$ or a space-filling design
2 Initialize model by computing $p(f|\mathcal{D}_0)$
3 **for** $n = 1, 2, \ldots$ *until convergence* **do**
4 $\quad$ Choose next query point $\boldsymbol{x}_{n+1} = \text{argmax}_{\boldsymbol{x} \in \mathcal{X}}\, \alpha(\boldsymbol{x}; \mathcal{D}_n)$
5 $\quad$ Measure function value, $y_{n+1} = f(\boldsymbol{x}_{n+1}) + \epsilon_n$
6 $\quad$ Augment dataset, $\mathcal{D}_{n+1} = \{\mathcal{D}_n, (\boldsymbol{x}_{n+1}, y_{n+1})\}$
7 $\quad$ Update model by computing $p(f|\mathcal{D}_{n+1})$

This method is illustrated in Figure 6.10. The goal is to find the global optimum of the solid black curve. In the first row, we show the 2 previously queried points, x_1 and x_2, and their corresponding function values. $y_1 = f(x_1)$ and $y_2 = f(x_2)$. Our uncertainty about the value of f at those locations is 0 (if we assume no observation noise), as illustrated by the posterior credible interval (shaded blue are) becoming "pinched". Consequently the acquisition function (shown in green at the bottom) also has value 0 at those previously queried points. The red triangle represents the maximum of the acquisition function, which becomes our next query, x_3. In the second row, we show the result of observing $y_3 = f(x_3)$; this further reduces our uncertainty about the shape of the function. In the third row, we show the result of observing $y_4 = f(x_4)$. This process repeats until we run out of time, or until we are confident there are no better unexplored points to query.

The two main "ingredients" that we need to provide to a BayesOpt algorithm are (1) a way to represent and update the posterior surrogate $p(f|\mathcal{D}_n)$, and (2) a way to define and optimize the acquisition function $\alpha(\boldsymbol{x}; \mathcal{D}_n)$. We discuss both of these topics below.

6.6.2   Surrogate functions

In this section, we discuss ways to represent and update the posterior over functions, $p(f|\mathcal{D}_n)$.

6.6.2.1   Gaussian processes

In BayesOpt, it is very common to use a Gaussian process or GP for our surrogate. GPs are explained in detail in Chapter 18, but the basic idea is that they represent $p(f(\boldsymbol{x})|\mathcal{D}_n)$ as a Gaussian,

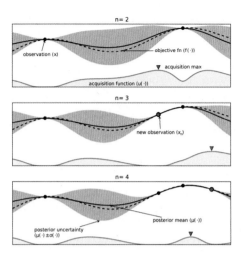

Figure 6.10: Illustration of sequential Bayesian optimization over three iterations. The rows correspond to a training set of size $t = 2, 3, 4$. The solid black line is the true, but unknown, function $f(x)$. The dotted black line is the posterior mean, $\mu(x)$. The shaded blue intervals are the 95% credible interval derived from $\mu(x)$ and $\sigma(x)$. The solid black dots correspond to points whose function value has already been computed, i.e., x_n for which $f(x_n)$ is known. The green curve at the bottom is the acquisition function. The red dot is the proposed next point to query, which is the maximum of the acquisition function. From Figure 1 of [Sha+16]. Used with kind permission of Nando de Freitas.

$p(f(\boldsymbol{x})|\mathcal{D}_n) = \mathcal{N}(f|\mu_n(\boldsymbol{x}), \sigma_n^2(\boldsymbol{x}))$, where $\mu_n(\boldsymbol{x})$ and $\sigma_n(\boldsymbol{x})$ are functions that can be derived from the training data $\mathcal{D}_n = \{(\boldsymbol{x}_i, y_i) : i = 1 : n\}$ using a simple closed-form equation. The GP requires specifying a kernel function $\mathcal{K}_{\boldsymbol{\theta}}(\boldsymbol{x}, \boldsymbol{x}')$, which measures similarities between input points $\boldsymbol{x}, \boldsymbol{x}'$. The intuition is that if two inputs are similar, so $\mathcal{K}_{\boldsymbol{\theta}}(\boldsymbol{x}, \boldsymbol{x}')$ is large, then the corresponding function values are also likely to be similar, so $f(\boldsymbol{x})$ and $f(\boldsymbol{x}')$ should be positively correlated. This allows us to interpolate the function between the labeled training points; in some cases, it also lets us extrapolate beyond them.

GPs work well when we have little training data, and they support closed form Bayesian updating. However, exact updating takes $O(N^3)$ for N samples, which becomes too slow if we perform many function evaluations. There are various methods (Section 18.5.3) for reducing this to $O(NM^2)$ time, where M is a parameter we choose, but this sacrifices some of the accuracy.

In addition, the performance of GPs depends heavily on having a good kernel. We can estimate the kernel parameters $\boldsymbol{\theta}$ by maximizing the marginal likelihood, as discussed in Section 18.6.1. However, since the sample size is small (by assumption), we can often get better performance by marginalizing out $\boldsymbol{\theta}$ using approximate Bayesian inference methods, as discussed in Section 18.6.2. See e.g., [WF16] for further details.

6.6.2.2 Bayesian neural networks

A natural alternative to GPs is to use a parametric model. If we use linear regression, we can efficiently perform exact Bayesian inference, as shown in Section 15.2. If we use a nonlinear model, such as a DNN, we need to use approximate inference methods. We discuss Bayesian neural networks in detail in Chapter 17. For their application to BayesOpt, see e.g., [Spr+16; PPR22; Kim+22].

6.6.2.3   Other models

We are free to use other forms of regression model. [HHLB11] use an ensemble of random forests; such models can easily handle conditional parameter spaces, as we discuss in Section 6.6.4.2, although bootstrapping (which is needed to get uncertainty estimates) can be slow.

6.6.3   Acquisition functions

In BayesOpt, we use an **acquisition function** (also called a **merit function**) to evaluate the expected utility of each possible point we could query: $\alpha(\boldsymbol{x}|\mathcal{D}_n) = \mathbb{E}_{p(y|\boldsymbol{x}, \mathcal{D}_n)}[U(\boldsymbol{x}, y; \mathcal{D}_n)]$, where $y = f(\boldsymbol{x})$ is the unknown value of the function at point $\boldsymbol{x}$, and $U()$ is a utility function. Different utility functions give rise to different acquisition functions, as we discuss below. We usually choose functions so that the utility of picking a point that has already been queried is small (or 0, in the case of noise-free observations), in order to encourage exploration.

6.6.3.1   Probability of improvement

Let us define $M_n = \max_{i=1}^n y_i$ to be the best value observed so far (known as the **incumbent**). (If the observations are noisy, using the highest mean value $\max_i \mathbb{E}_{p(f|\mathcal{D}_n)}[f(\boldsymbol{x}_i)]$ is a reasonable alternative [WF16].) Then we define the utility of some new point $\boldsymbol{x}$ using $U(\boldsymbol{x}, y; \mathcal{D}_n) = \mathbb{I}(y > M_n)$. This gives reward iff the new value is better than the incumbent. The corresponding acquisition function is then given by the expected utility, $\alpha_{PI}(\boldsymbol{x}; \mathcal{D}_n) = p(f(\boldsymbol{x}) > M_n | \mathcal{D}_n)$. This is known as the **probability of improvement** [Kus64]. If $p(f|\mathcal{D}_n)$ is a GP, then this quantity can be computed in closed form, as follows:

$$\alpha_{PI}(\boldsymbol{x}; \mathcal{D}_n) = p(f(\boldsymbol{x}) > M_n | \mathcal{D}_n) = \Phi(\gamma_n(\boldsymbol{x}, M_n)) \tag{6.174}$$

where Φ is the cdf of the $\mathcal{N}(0, 1)$ distribution and

$$\gamma_n(\boldsymbol{x}, \tau) = \frac{\mu_n(\boldsymbol{x}) - \tau}{\sigma_n(\boldsymbol{x})} \tag{6.175}$$

6.6.3.2   Expected improvement

The problem with PI is that all improvements are considered equally good, so the method tends to exploit quite aggressively [Jon01]. A common alternative takes into account the amount of improvement by defining $U(\boldsymbol{x}, y; \mathcal{D}_n) = (y - M_n)\mathbb{I}(y > M_n)$ and

$$\alpha_{EI}(\boldsymbol{x}; \mathcal{D}_n) = \mathbb{E}_{\mathcal{D}_n}[U(\boldsymbol{x}, y)] = \mathbb{E}_{\mathcal{D}_n}[(f(\boldsymbol{x}) - M_n)\mathbb{I}(f(\boldsymbol{x}) > M_n)] \tag{6.176}$$

This acquisition function is known as the **expected improvement** (**EI**) criterion [Moc+96]. In the case of a GP surrogate, this has the following closed form expression:

$$\alpha_{EI}(\boldsymbol{x}; \mathcal{D}_n) = (\mu_n(\boldsymbol{x}) - M_n)\Phi(\gamma) + \sigma_n(\boldsymbol{x})\phi(\gamma) = \sigma_n(\boldsymbol{x})[\gamma_n\Phi(\gamma) + \phi(\gamma)] \tag{6.177}$$

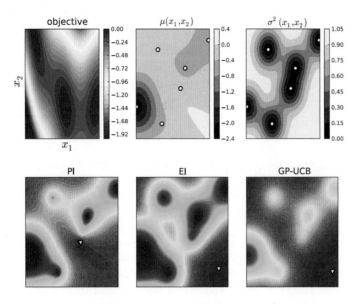

Figure 6.11: The first row shows the objective function, (the Branin function defined on $\mathbb{R}^2$), and its posterior mean and variance using a GP estimate. White dots are the observed data points. The second row shows 3 different acquisition functions (probability of improvement, expected improvement, and upper confidence bound); the white triangles are the maxima of the corresponding acquisition functions. From Figure 6 of [BCF10]. Used with kind permission of Nando de Freitas.

where $\phi()$ is the pdf of the $\mathcal{N}(0, 1)$ distribution, Φ is the cdf, and $\gamma = \gamma_n(\boldsymbol{x}, M_n)$. The first term encourages exploitation (evaluating points with high mean) and the second term encourages exploration (evaluating points with high variance). This is illustrated in Figure 6.10.

If we cannot compute the predictive variance analytically, but can draw posterior samples, then we can compute a Monte Carlo approximation to the EI, as proposed in [Kim+22]:

$$\alpha_{EI}(\boldsymbol{x}; \mathcal{D}_n) \approx \frac{1}{S} \sum_{s=1}^{S} \max(\mu_n^s(\boldsymbol{x}) - M_n, 0) \tag{6.178}$$

6.6.3.3 Upper confidence bound (UCB)

An alternative approach is to compute an **upper confidence bound** or **UCB** on the function, at some confidence level β_n, and then to define the acquisition function as follows: $\alpha_{UCB}(\boldsymbol{x}; \mathcal{D}_n) = \mu_n(\boldsymbol{x}) + \beta_n \sigma_n(\boldsymbol{x})$. This is the same as in the contextual bandit setting, discussed in Section 34.4.5, except we are optimizing over $\boldsymbol{x} \in \mathcal{X}$, rather than a finite set of arms $a \in \{1, \dots, A\}$. If we use a GP for our surrogate, the method is known as **GP-UCB** [Sri+10].

6.6.3.4 Thompson sampling

We discuss **Thompson sampling** in Section 34.4.6 in the context of multiarmed bandits, where the state space is finite, $\mathcal{X} = \{1, \ldots, A\}$, and the acquisition function $\alpha(a; \mathcal{D}_n)$ corresponds to the probability that arm a is the best arm. We can generalize this to real-valued input spaces $\mathcal{X}$ using

$$\alpha(\boldsymbol{x}; \mathcal{D}_n) = \mathbb{E}_{p(\boldsymbol{\theta}|\mathcal{D}_n)} \left[\mathbb{I} \left(\boldsymbol{x} = \operatorname*{argmax}_{\boldsymbol{x}'} f_{\boldsymbol{\theta}}(\boldsymbol{x}') \right) \right] \tag{6.179}$$

We can compute a single sample approximation to this integral by sampling $\tilde{\boldsymbol{\theta}} \sim p(\boldsymbol{\theta}|\mathcal{D}_n)$. We can then pick the optimal action as follows:

$$\boldsymbol{x}_{n+1} = \operatorname*{argmax}_{\boldsymbol{x}} \alpha(\boldsymbol{x}; \mathcal{D}_n) = \operatorname*{argmax}_{\boldsymbol{x}} \mathbb{I} \left(\boldsymbol{x} = \operatorname*{argmax}_{\boldsymbol{x}'} f_{\tilde{\boldsymbol{\theta}}}(\boldsymbol{x}') \right) = \operatorname*{argmax}_{\boldsymbol{x}} f_{\tilde{\boldsymbol{\theta}}}(\boldsymbol{x}) \tag{6.180}$$

In other words, we greedily maximize the sampled surrogate.

For continuous spaces, Thompson sampling is harder to apply than in the bandit case, since we can't directly compute the best "arm" $\boldsymbol{x}_{n+1}$ from the sampled function. Furthermore, when using GPs, there are some subtle technical difficulties with sampling a function, as opposed to sampling the parameters of a parametric surrogate model (see [HLHG14] for discussion).

6.6.3.5 Entropy search

Since our goal in BayesOpt is to find $\boldsymbol{x}^* = \operatorname{argmax}_{\boldsymbol{x}} f(\boldsymbol{x})$, it makes sense to try to directly minimize our uncertainty about the location of $\boldsymbol{x}^*$, which we denote by $p_*(\boldsymbol{x}|\mathcal{D}_n)$. We will therefore define the utility as follows:

$$U(\boldsymbol{x}, y; \mathcal{D}_n) = \mathbb{H}\left(\boldsymbol{x}^*|\mathcal{D}_n\right) - \mathbb{H}\left(\boldsymbol{x}^*|\mathcal{D}_n \cup \{(\boldsymbol{x}, y)\}\right) \tag{6.181}$$

where $\mathbb{H}\left(\boldsymbol{x}^*|\mathcal{D}_n\right) = \mathbb{H}(p_*(\boldsymbol{x}|\mathcal{D}_n))$ is the entropy of the posterior distribution over the location of the optimum. This is known as the information gain criterion; the difference from the objective used in active learning is that here we want to gain information about $\boldsymbol{x}^*$ rather than about f for all $\boldsymbol{x}$. The corresponding acquisition function is given by

$$\alpha_{ES}(\boldsymbol{x}; \mathcal{D}_n) = \mathbb{E}_{p(y|\boldsymbol{x}, \mathcal{D}_n)} \left[U(\boldsymbol{x}, y; \mathcal{D}_n)\right] = \mathbb{H}\left(\boldsymbol{x}^*|\mathcal{D}_n\right) - \mathbb{E}_{p(y|\boldsymbol{x}, \mathcal{D}_n)} \left[\mathbb{H}\left(\boldsymbol{x}^*|\mathcal{D}_n \cup \{(\boldsymbol{x}, y)\}\right)\right] \tag{6.182}$$

This is known as **entropy search** [HS12].

Unfortunately, computing $\mathbb{H}\left(\boldsymbol{x}^*|\mathcal{D}_n\right)$ is hard, since it requires a probability model over the input space. Fortunately, we can leverage the symmetry of mutual information to rewrite the acquisition function in Equation (6.182) as follows:

$$\alpha_{PES}(\boldsymbol{x}; \mathcal{D}_n) = \mathbb{H}\left(y|\mathcal{D}_n, \boldsymbol{x}\right) - \mathbb{E}_{\boldsymbol{x}^*|\mathcal{D}_n} \left[\mathbb{H}\left(y|\mathcal{D}_n, \boldsymbol{x}, \boldsymbol{x}^*\right)\right] \tag{6.183}$$

where we can approximate the expectation from $p(\boldsymbol{x}^*|\mathcal{D}_n)$ using Thompson sampling. Now we just have to model uncertainty about the output space y. This is known as **predictive entropy search** [HLHG14].

6.6.3.6 Knowledge gradient

So far the acquisition functions we have considered are all greedy, in that they only look one step ahead. The **knowledge gradient** acquisition function, proposed in [FPD09], looks two steps ahead by considering the improvement we might expect to get if we query $\boldsymbol{x}$, update our posterior, and then exploit our knowledge by maximizing wrt our new beliefs. More precisely, let us define the best value we can find if we query one more point:

$$V_{n+1}(\boldsymbol{x}, y) = \max_{\boldsymbol{x}'} \mathbb{E}_{p(f|\boldsymbol{x}, y, \mathcal{D}_n)} [f(\boldsymbol{x}')] \tag{6.184}$$

$$V_{n+1}(\boldsymbol{x}) = \mathbb{E}_{p(y|\boldsymbol{x}, \mathcal{D}_n)} [V_{n+1}(\boldsymbol{x}, y)] \tag{6.185}$$

We define the KG acquisition function as follows:

$$\alpha_{KG}(\boldsymbol{x}; \mathcal{D}_n) = \mathbb{E}_{\mathcal{D}_n} [(V_{n+1}(\boldsymbol{x}) - M_n)\mathbb{I}(V_{n+1}(\boldsymbol{x}) > M_n)] \tag{6.186}$$

Compare this to the EI function in Equation (6.176).) Thus we pick the point $\boldsymbol{x}_{n+1}$ such that observing $f(\boldsymbol{x}_{n+1})$ will give us knowledge which we can then exploit, rather than directly trying to find a better point with better f value.

6.6.3.7 Optimizing the acquisition function

The acquisition function $\alpha(\boldsymbol{x})$ is often multimodal (see e.g., Figure 6.11), since it will be 0 at all the previously queried points (assuming noise-free observations). Consequently maximizing this function can be a hard subproblem in itself [WHD18; Rub+20].

In the continuous setting, it is common to use multirestart BFGS or grid search. We can also use the cross-entropy method (Section 6.7.5), using mixtures of Gaussians [BK10] or VAEs [Fau+18] as the generative model over $\boldsymbol{x}$. In the discrete, combinatorial setting (e.g., when optimizing biological sequences), [Bel+19] use regularized evolution, (Section 6.7.3), and [Ang+20] use proximial policy optimization (Section 35.3.4). Many other combinations are possible.

6.6.4 Other issues

There are many other issues that need to be tackled when using Bayesian optimization, a few of which we briefly mention below.

6.6.4.1 Parallel (batch) queries

In some cases, we want to query the objective function at multiple points in parallel; this is known as **batched Bayesian optimization**. Now we need to optimize over a set of possible queries, which is computationally even more difficult than the regular case. See [WHD18; DBB20] for some recent papers on this topic.

6.6.4.2 Conditional parameters

BayesOpt is often applied to hyper-parameter optimization. In many applications, some hyperparameters are only well-defined if other ones take on specific values. For example, suppose we are trying to automatically tune a classifier, as in the **Auto-Sklearn** system [Feu+15], or the **Auto-WEKA** system [Kot+17]. If the method chooses to use a neural network, it also needs to specify the number of layers, and number of hidden units per layer; but if it chooses to use a decision tree, it instead should specify different hyperparameters, such as the maximum tree depth.

We can formalize such problems by defining the search space in terms of a tree or DAG (directed acyclic graph), where different subsets of the parameters are defined at each leaf. Applying GPs to this setting requires non-standard kernels, such as those discussed in [Swe+13; Jen+17]. Alternatively, we can use other forms of Bayesian regression, such as ensembles of random forests [HHLB11], which can easily handle conditional parameter spaces.

6.6.4.3   Multifidelity surrogates

In some cases, we can construct surrogate functions with different levels of accuracy, each of which may take variable amounts of time to compute. In particular, let $f(\boldsymbol{x}, s)$ be an approximation to the true function at $\boldsymbol{x}$ with fidelity s. The goal is to solve $\max_{\boldsymbol{x}} f(\boldsymbol{x}, 0)$ by observing $f(\boldsymbol{x}, s)$ at a sequence of $(\boldsymbol{x}_i, s_i)$ values, such that the total cost $\sum_{i=1}^{n} c(s_i)$ is below some budget. For example, in the context of hyperparameter selection, s may control how long we run the parameter optimizer for, or how large the validation set is.

In addition to choosing what fidelity to use for an experiment, we may choose to terminate expensive trials (queries) early, if the results of their cheaper proxies suggest they will not be worth running to completion (see e.g., [Str19; Li+17c; FKH17]). Alternatively, we may choose to resume an earlier aborted run, to collect more data on it, as in the **freeze-thaw algorithm** [SSA14].

6.6.4.4   Constraints

If we want to maximize a function subject to known constraints, we can simply build the constraints into the acquisition function. But if the constraints are unknown, we need to estimate the support of the feasible set in addition to estimating the function. In [GSA14], they propose the weighted EI criterion, given by $\alpha_{wEI}(\boldsymbol{x}; \mathcal{D}_n) = \alpha_{EI}(\boldsymbol{x}; \mathcal{D}_n) h(\boldsymbol{x}; \mathcal{D}_n)$, where $h(\boldsymbol{x}; \mathcal{D}_n)$ is a GP with a Bernoulli observation model that specifies if $\boldsymbol{x}$ is feasible or not. Of course, other methods are possible. For example, [HL+16b] propose a method based on predictive entropy search.

6.7   Derivative-free optimization

Derivative-free optimization or **DFO** refers to a class of techniques for optimizing functions without using derivatives. This is useful for blackbox function optimization as well as discrete optimization. If the function is expensive to evaliate, we can use Bayesian optimization (Section 6.6). If the function is cheap to evaluate, we can use stochastic local search methods or evolutionary search methods, as we discuss below.

6.7.1   Local search

In this section, we discuss heuristic optimization algorithms that try to find the global maximum in a discrete, unstructured search space. These algorithms replace the local gradient based update, which has the form $\boldsymbol{\theta}_{t+1} = \boldsymbol{\theta}_t + \eta_t \boldsymbol{d}_t$, with the following discrete analog:

$$\boldsymbol{x}_{t+1} = \underset{\boldsymbol{x} \in \text{nbr}(\boldsymbol{x}_t)}{\text{argmax}} \ \mathcal{L}(\boldsymbol{x}) \tag{6.187}$$

where $\mathrm{nbr}(\boldsymbol{x}_t) \subseteq \mathcal{X}$ is the set of **neighbors** of $\boldsymbol{x}_t$. This is called **hill climbing, steepest ascent**, or **greedy search**.

If the "neighborhood" of a point contains the entire space, Equation (6.187) will return the global optimum in one step, but usually such a global neighborhood is too large to search exhaustively. Consequently we usually define local neighborhoods. For example, consider the **8-queens problem**. Here the goal is to place queens on an 8×8 chessboard so that they don't attack each other (see Figure 6.14). The state space has the form $\mathcal{X} = 64^8$, since we have to specify the location of each queen on the grid. However, due to the constraints, there are only $8^8 \approx 17M$ feasible states. We define the neighbors of a state to be all possible states generated by moving a single queen to another square in the same column, so each node has $8 \times 7 = 56$ neighbors. According to [RN10, p.123], if we start at a randomly generated 8-queens state, steepest ascent gets stuck at a local maximum 86% of the time, so it only solves 14% of problem instances. However, it is fast, taking an average of 4 steps when it succeeds and 3 when it gets stuck.

In the sections below, we discuss slightly smarter algorithms that are less likely to get stuck in local maxima.

6.7.1.1 Stochastic local search

Hill climbing is greedy, since it picks the best point in its local neighborhood, by solving Equation (6.187) exactly. One way to reduce the chance of getting stuck in local maxima is to approximately maximize this objective at each step. For example, we can define a probability distribution over the uphill neighbors, proportional to how much they improve, and then sample one at random. This is called **stochastic hill climbing**. If we gradually decrease the entropy of this probability distribution (so we become greedier over time), we get a method called simulated annealing, which we discuss in Section 12.9.1.

Another simple technique is to use greedy hill climbing, but then whenever we reach a local maximum, we start again from a different random starting point. This is called **random restart hill climbing**. To see the benefit of this, consider again the 8-queens problem. If each hill-climbing search has a probability of $p \approx 0.14$ of success, then we expect to need $R = 1/p \approx 7$ restarts until we find a valid solution. The expected number of total steps can be computed as follows. Let $N_1 = 4$ be the average number of steps for successful trials, and $N_0 = 3$ be the average number of steps for failures. Then the total number of steps on average is $N_1 + (R - 1)N_0 = 4 + 6 \times 3 = 22$. Since each step is quick, the overall method is very fast. For example, it can solve an n-queens problem with $n = 1M$ in under a minute.

Of course, solving the n-queens problem is not the most useful task in practice. However, it is typical of several real-world **boolean satisfiability problems**, which arise in problems ranging from AI planning to model checking (see e.g., [SLM92]). In such problems, simple **stochastic local search (SLS)** algorithms of the kind we have discussed work surprisingly well (see e.g., [HS05]).

6.7.1.2 Tabu search

Hill climbing will stop as soon as it reaches a local maximum or a plateau. Obviously one can perform a random restart, but this would ignore all the information that had been gained up to this point. A more intelligent alternative is called **tabu search** [GL97]. This is like hill climbing, except it allows moves that decrease (or at least do not increase) the scoring function, provided the move is to a new

---

Algorithm 6.6: Tabu search.

---

1 $t := 0$ // counts iterations
2 $c := 0$ // counts number of steps with no progress
3 Initialize $\boldsymbol{x}_0$
4 $\boldsymbol{x}^* := \boldsymbol{x}_0$ // current best incumbent
5 **while** $c < c_{\max}$ **do**
6 $\quad$ $\boldsymbol{x}_{t+1} = \operatorname{argmax}_{\boldsymbol{x} \in \operatorname{nbr}(\boldsymbol{x}_t) \setminus \{\boldsymbol{x}_{t-\tau}, \ldots, \boldsymbol{x}_{t-1}\}} f(\boldsymbol{x})$
7 $\quad$ **if** $f(\boldsymbol{x}_{t+1}) > f(\boldsymbol{x}^*)$ **then**
8 $\quad\quad$ $\boldsymbol{x}^* := \boldsymbol{x}_{t+1}$
9 $\quad\quad$ $c := 0$
10 $\quad$ **else**
11 $\quad\quad$ $c := c + 1$
12 $\quad$ $t := t + 1$
13 return $\boldsymbol{x}^*$

---

state that has not been seen before. We can enforce this by keeping a tabu list which tracks the τ most recently visited states. This forces the algorithm to explore new states, and increases the chances of escaping from local maxima. We continue to do this for up to $c_{\max}$ steps (known as the "tabu tenure"). The pseudocode can be found in Algorithm 6.6. (If we set $c_{\max} = 1$, we get greedy hill climbing.)

For example, consider what happens when tabu search reaches a hill top, $\boldsymbol{x}_t$. At the next step, it will move to one of the neighbors of the peak, $\boldsymbol{x}_{t+1} \in \operatorname{nbr}(\boldsymbol{x}_t)$, which will have a lower score. At the next step, it will move to the neighbor of the previous step, $\boldsymbol{x}_{t+2} \in \operatorname{nbr}(\boldsymbol{x}_{t+1})$; the tabu list prevents it cycling back to $\boldsymbol{x}_t$ (the peak), so it will be forced to pick a neighboring point at the same height or lower. It continues in this way, "circling" the peak, possibly being forced downhill to a lower level-set (an inverse **basin flooding** operation), until it finds a ridge that leads to a new peak, or until it exceeds a maximum number of non-improving moves.

According to [RN10, p.123], tabu search increases the percentage of 8-queens problems that can be solved from 14% to 94%, although this variant takes an average of 21 steps for each successful instance and 64 steps for each failed instance.

6.7.1.3   Random search

A surprisingly effective strategy in problems where we know nothing about the objective is to use **random search**. In this approach, each iterate $\boldsymbol{x}_{t+1}$ is chosen uniformly at random from $\mathcal{X}$. This should always be tried as a baseline.

In [BB12], they applied this technique to the problem of hyper-parameter optimization for some ML models, where the objective is performance on a validation set. In their examples, the search space is continuous, $\Theta = [0, 1]^D$. It is easy to sample from this at random. The standard alternative approach is to quantize the space into a fixed set of values, and then to evaluate them all; this is known as **grid search**. (Of course, this is only feasible if the number of dimensions D is small.) They found that random search outperformed grid search. The intuitive reason for this is that many

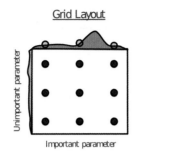
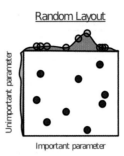

Figure 6.12: *Illustration of grid search (left) vs random search (right). From Figure 1 of [BB12]. Used with kind permission of James Bergstra.*

hyper-parameters do not make much difference to the objective function, as illustrated in Figure 6.12. Consequently it is a waste of time to place a fine grid along such unimportant dimensions.

RS has also been used to optimize the parameters of MDP policies, where the objective has the form $f(\boldsymbol{x}) = \mathbb{E}_{\boldsymbol{\tau} \sim \pi_{\boldsymbol{x}}}[R(\boldsymbol{\tau})]$ is the expected reward of trajectories generated by using a policy with parameters $\boldsymbol{x}$. For policies with few free parameters, RS can outperform more sophisticated reinforcement learning methods described in Chapter 35, as shown in [MGR18]. In cases where the policy has a large number of parameters, it is sometimes possible to project them to a lower dimensional random subspace, and perform optimization (either grid search or random search) in this subspace [Li+18a].

6.7.2 Simulated annealing

Simulated annealing [KJV83; LA87] is a **stochastic local search** algorithm (Section 6.7.1.1) that attempts to find the global minimum of a black-box function $\mathcal{E}(\boldsymbol{x})$, where $\mathcal{E}()$ is known as the **energy function**. The method works by converting the energy to an (unnormalized) probability distribution over states by defining $p(\boldsymbol{x}) = \exp(-\mathcal{E}(\boldsymbol{x}))$, and then using a variant of the **Metropolis-Hastings** algorithm to sample from a set of probability distributions, designed so that at the final step, the method samples from one of the modes of the distribution, i.e., it finds one of the most likely states, or lowest energy states. This approach can be used for both discrete and continuous optimization. See Section 12.9.1 for more details.

6.7.3 Evolutionary algorithms

Stochastic local search (SLS) maintains a single "best guess" at each step, $\boldsymbol{x}_t$. If we run this for T steps, and restart K times, the total cost is TK. A natural alternative is to maintain a set or **population** of K good candidates, $\mathcal{S}_t$, which we try to improve at each step. This is called an **evolutionary algorithm** (**EA**). If we run this for T steps, it also takes TK time; however, it can often get better results than multi-restart SLS, since the search procedure explores more of the space in parallel, and information from different members of the population can be shared. Many versions of EA are possible, as we discuss below.

Since EA algorithms draw inspiration from the biological process of evolution, they also borrow

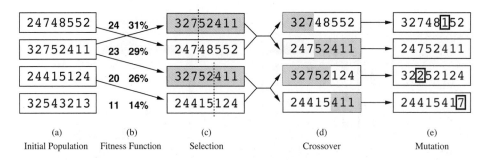

| (a) | (b) | (c) | (d) | (e) |
| Initial Population | Fitness Function | Selection | Crossover | Mutation |

Figure 6.13: *Illustration of a genetic algorithm applied to the 8-queens problem. (a) Initial population of 4 strings. (b) We rank the members of the population by fitness, and then compute their probability of mating. Here the integer numbers represent the number of nonattacking pairs of queens, so the global maximum has a value of 28. We pick an individual $\boldsymbol{\theta}$ with probability $p(\boldsymbol{\theta}) = \mathcal{L}(\boldsymbol{\theta})/Z$, where $Z = \sum_{\boldsymbol{\theta} \in \mathcal{P}} \mathcal{L}(\boldsymbol{\theta})$ sums the total fitness of the population. For example, we pick the first individual with probability $24/78 = 0.31$, the second with probability $23/78 = 0.29$, etc. In this example, we pick the first individual once, the second twice, the third one once, and the last one does not get to breed. (c) A split point on the "chromosome" of each parent is chosen at random. (d) The two parents swap their chromosome halves. (e) We can optionally apply pointwise mutation. From Figure 4.6 of [RN10]. Used with kind permission of Peter Norvig.*

a lot of its terminology. The **fitness** of a member of the population is the value of the objective function (possibly normalized across population members). The members of the population at step $t + 1$ are called the **offspring**. These can be created by randomly choosing a **parent** from $\mathcal{S}_t$ and applying a random **mutation** to it. This is like asexual reproduction. Alternatively we can create an offspring by choosing two parents from $\mathcal{S}_t$, and then combining them in some way to make a child, as in sexual reproduction; combining the parents is called **recombination**. (It is often followed by mutation.)

The procedure by which parents are chosen is called the **selection function**. In **truncation selection**, each parent is chosen from the fittest K members of the population (known as the **elite set**). In **tournament selection**, each parent is the fittest out of K randomly chosen members. In **fitness proportionate selection**, also called **roulette wheel selection**, each parent is chosen with probability proportional to its fitness relative to the others. We can also "kill off" the oldest members of the population, and then select parents based on their fitness; this is called **regularized evolution** [Rea+19]).

In addition to the selection rule for parents, we need to specify the recombination and mutation rules. There are many possible choices for these heuristics. We briefly mention a few of them below.

- In a **genetic algorithm (GA)** [Gol89; Hol92], we use mutation and a particular recombination method based on **crossover**. To implement crossover, we assume each individual is represented as a vector of integers or binary numbers, by analogy to **chromosomes**. We pick a split point along the chromosome for each of the two chosen parents, and then swap the strings, as illustrated in Figure 6.13.

- In **genetic programming** [Koz92], we use a tree-structured representation of individuals, instead of a bit string. This representation ensures that all crossovers result in valid children, as illustrated

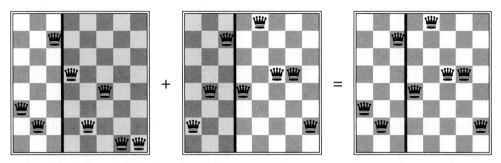

Figure 6.14: The 8-queens states corresponding to the first two parents in Figure 6.13(c) and their first child in Figure 6.13(d). We see that the encoding 32752411 means that the first queen is in row 3 (counting from the bottom left), the second queen is in row 2, etc. The shaded columns are lost in the crossover, but the unshaded columns are kept. From Figure 4.7 of [RN10]. Used with kind permission of Peter Norvig.

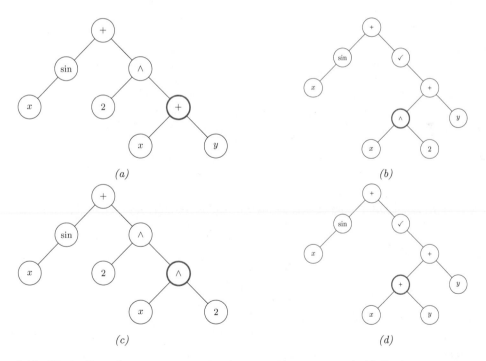

Figure 6.15: Illustration of crossover operator in a genetic program. (a-b) the two parents, representing $\sin(x) + (x + y)^2$ and $\sin(x) + \sqrt{x^2 + y}$. The red circles denote the two crossover points. (c-d) the two children, representing $\sin(x) + (x^2)^2$ and $\sin(x) + \sqrt{x + y + y}$. Adapted from Figure 9.2 of [Mit97]

in Figure 6.15. Genetic programming can be useful for finding good programs as well as other structured objects, such as neural networks. In **evolutionary programming**, the structure of the tree is fixed and only the numerical parameters are evolved.

- In **surrogate assisted EA**, a surrogate function $\hat{f}(s)$ is used instead of the true objective function $f(s)$ in order to speed up the evaluation of members of the population (see [Jin11] for a survey). This is similar to the use of response surface models in Bayesian optimization (Section 6.6), except it does not deal with the explore-exploit tradeoff.

- In a **memetic algorithm** [MC03], we combine mutation and recombination with standard local search.

Evolutionary algorithms have been applied to a large number of applications, including training neural networks (this combination is known as **neuroevolution** [Sta+19]). An efficient JAX-based library for (neuro)-evolution can be found at `https://github.com/google/evojax`.

6.7.4   Estimation of distribution (EDA) algorithms

EA methods maintain a population of good candidate solutions, which can be thought of as an implicit (nonparametric) density model over states with high fitness. [BC95] proposed to "remove the genetics from GAs", by explicitly learning a probabilistic model over the configuration space that puts its mass on high scoring solutions. That is, the population becomes the set of parameters of a generative model, $\boldsymbol{\theta}_t$.

One way to learn such as model is as follows. We start by creating a sample of $K' > K$ candidate solutions from the current model, $\mathcal{S}_t = \{\boldsymbol{x}_k \sim p(\boldsymbol{x}|\boldsymbol{\theta}_t)\}$. We then rank the samples using the fitness function, and then pick the most promising subset $\mathcal{S}_t^*$ of size K using a selection operator (this is known as **truncation selection**). Finally, we fit a new probabilistic model $p(\boldsymbol{x}|\boldsymbol{\theta}_{t+1})$ to $\mathcal{S}_t^*$ using maximum likelihood estimation. This is called the **estimation of distribution** or **EDA** algorithm (see e.g., [LL02; PSCP06; Hau+11; PHL12; Hu+12; San17; Bal17]).

Note that EDA is equivalent to minimizing the cross entropy between the empirical distribution defined by $\mathcal{S}_t^*$ and the model distribution $p(\boldsymbol{x}|\boldsymbol{\theta}_{t+1})$. Thus EDA is related to the **cross entropy method**, as described in Section 6.7.5, although CEM usually assumes the special case where $p(\boldsymbol{x}|\boldsymbol{\theta}) = \mathcal{N}(\boldsymbol{x}|\boldsymbol{\mu}, \boldsymbol{\Sigma})$. EDA is also closely related to the EM algorithm, as discussed in [Bro+20a].

As a simple example, suppose the configuration space is bit strings of length D, and the fitness function is $f(\boldsymbol{x}) = \sum_{d=1}^{D} x_d$, where $x_d \in \{0, 1\}$ (this is called the **one-max** function in the EA literature). A simple probabilistic model for this is a fully factored model of the form $p(\boldsymbol{x}|\boldsymbol{\theta}) = \prod_{d=1}^{D} \text{Ber}(x_d|\theta_d)$. Using this model inside of DBO results in a method called univariate marginal distribution algorithm or **UMDA**.

We can estimate the parameters of the Bernoulli model by setting θ_d to the fraction of samples in $\mathcal{S}_t^*$ that have bit d turned on. Alternatively, we can incrementally adjust the parameters. The population-based incremental learning (**PBIL**) algorithm [BC95] applies this idea to the factored Bernoulli model, resulting in the following update:

$$\hat{\theta}_{d,t+1} = (1 - \eta_t)\hat{\theta}_{d,t} + \eta_t \bar{\theta}_{d,t} \tag{6.188}$$

where $\bar{\theta}_{d,t} = \frac{1}{N_t} \sum_{k=1}^{K} \mathbb{I}(x_{k,d} = 1)$ is the MLE estimated from the $K = |\mathcal{S}_t^*|$ samples generated in the current iteration, and η_t is a learning rate.

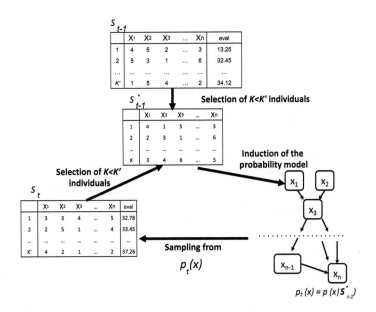

Figure 6.16: Illustration of the BOA algorithm (EDA applied to a generative model structured as a Bayes net). Adapted from Figure 3 of [PHL12].

It is straightforward to use more expressive probability models that capture dependencies between the parameters (these are known as **building blocks** in the EA literature). For example, in the case of real-valued parameters, we can use a multivariate Gaussian, $p(\boldsymbol{x}) = \mathcal{N}(\boldsymbol{x}|\boldsymbol{\mu}, \boldsymbol{\Sigma})$. The resulting method is called the **estimation of multivariate normal algorithm** or **EMNA**, [LL02]. (See also Section 6.7.5.)

For discrete random variables, it is natural to use probabilistic graphical models (Chapter 4) to capture dependencies between the variables. [BD97] learn a tree-structured graphical model using the Chow-Liu algorithm (Supplementary Section 30.2.1); [BJV97] is a special case of this where the graph is a tree. We can also learn more general graphical model structures (see e.g., [LL02]). We typically use a Bayes net (Section 4.2), since we can use ancestral sampling (Section 4.2.5) to easily generate samples; the resulting method is therefore called the **Bayesian optimization algorithm** (**BOA**) [PGCP00].[5] The hierarchical BOA (**hBOA**) algorithm [Pel05] extends this by using decision trees and decision graphs to represent the local CPTs in the Bayes net (as in [CHM97]), rather than using tables. In general, learning the structure of the probability model for use in EDA is called **linkage learning**, by analogy to how genes can be linked together if they can be co-inherited as a building block.

We can also use deep generative models to represent the distribution over good candidates. For example, [CSF16] use denoising autoencoders and NADE models (Section 22.2), [Bal17] uses a DNN regressor which is then inverted using gradient descent on the inputs, [PRG17] uses RBMs

---

5. This should not be confused with the Bayesian optimization methods we discuss in Section 6.6, that use response surface modeling to model $p(f(\boldsymbol{x}))$ rather than $p(\boldsymbol{x}^*)$.

(Section 4.3.3.2), [GSM18] uses VAEs (Section 21.2), etc. Such models might take more data to fit (and therefore more function calls), but can potentially model the probability landscape more faithfully. (Whether that translates to better optimization performance is not clear, however.)

6.7.5 Cross-entropy method

The **cross-entropy method** [Rub97; RK04; Boe+05] is a special case of EDA (Section 6.7.4) in which the population is represented by a multivariate Gaussian. In particular, we set $\boldsymbol{\mu}_{t+1}$ and $\boldsymbol{\Sigma}_{t+1}$ to the empirical mean and covariance of $\mathcal{S}_{t+1}^*$, which are the top K samples. This is closely related to the SMC algorithm for sampling rare events discussed in Section 13.6.4.

The CEM is sometimes used for model-based RL (Section 35.4), since it is simple and can find reasonably good optima of multimodal objectives. It is also sometimes used inside of Bayesian optimization (Section 6.6), to optimize the multi-modal acquisition function (see [BK10]).

6.7.5.1 Differentiable CEM

The **differentiable CEM** method of [AY19] replaces the top K operator with a soft, differentiable approximation, which allows the optimizer to be used as part of an end-to-end differentiable pipeline. For example, we can use this to create a differentiable model predictive control (MPC) algorithm (Section 35.4.1), as described in Section 35.4.5.2.

The basic idea is as follows. Let $\mathcal{S}_t = \{\boldsymbol{x}_{t,i} \sim p(\boldsymbol{x}|\boldsymbol{\theta}_t) : i = 1 : K'\}$ represent the current population, with fitness values $v_{t,i} = f(\boldsymbol{x}_{t,i})$. Let $v_{t,K}^*$ be the K'th smallest value. In CEM, we compute the set of top K samples, $\mathcal{S}_t^* = \{i : v_{t,i} \geq v_{t,K}^*\}$, and then update the model based on these: $\boldsymbol{\theta}_{t+1} = \operatorname{argmax}_{\boldsymbol{\theta}} \sum_{i \in \mathcal{S}_t} p_t(i) \log p(\boldsymbol{x}_{t,i}|\boldsymbol{\theta})$, where $p_t(i) = \mathbb{I}(i \in \mathcal{S}_t^*)/|\mathcal{S}_t^*|$. In the differentiable version, we replace the sparse distribution $\boldsymbol{p}_t$ with the "soft" dense distribution $\boldsymbol{q}_t = \Pi(\boldsymbol{p}_t; \tau, K)$, where

$$\Pi(\boldsymbol{p}; \tau, K) = \operatorname*{argmin}_{0 \leq \boldsymbol{q} \leq 1} -\boldsymbol{p}^{\mathsf{T}} \boldsymbol{q} - \tau \mathbb{H}(\boldsymbol{q}) \quad \text{s.t.} \quad \mathbf{1}^{\mathsf{T}} \boldsymbol{q} = K \tag{6.189}$$

projects the distribution $\boldsymbol{p}$ onto the polytope of distributions which sum to K. (Here $\mathbb{H}(\boldsymbol{q}) = -\sum_i q_i \log(q_i) + (1 - q_i) \log(1 - q_i)$ is the entropy, and $\tau > 0$ is a temperature parameter.) This projection operator (and hence the whole DCEM algorithm) can be backpropagated through using implicit differentiation [AKZK19].

6.7.6 Evolutionary strategies

Evolution strategies [Wie+14] are a form of distribution-based optimization in which the distribution over the population is represented by a Gaussian, $p(\boldsymbol{x}|\boldsymbol{\theta}_t)$ (see e.g., [Sal+17b]). Unlike CEM, the parameters are updated using gradient ascent applied to the expected value of the objective, rather than using MLE on a set of elite samples. More precisely, consider the smoothed objective $\mathcal{L}(\boldsymbol{\theta}) = \mathbb{E}_{p(\boldsymbol{x}|\boldsymbol{\theta})}[f(\boldsymbol{x})]$. We can use the REINFORCE estimator (Section 6.3.4) to compute the gradient of this objective as follows:

$$\nabla_{\boldsymbol{\theta}} \mathcal{L}(\boldsymbol{\theta}) = \mathbb{E}_{p(\boldsymbol{x}|\boldsymbol{\theta})}[f(\boldsymbol{x}) \nabla_{\boldsymbol{\theta}} \log p(\boldsymbol{x}|\boldsymbol{\theta})] \tag{6.190}$$

This can be approximated by drawing Monte Carlo samples. We discuss how to compute this gradient below.

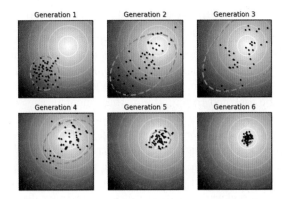

Figure 6.17: Illustration of the CMA-ES method applied to a simple 2d function. The dots represent members of the population, and the dashed orange ellipse represents the multivariate Gaussian. From https://en.wikipedia.org/wiki/CMA-ES. Used with kind permission of Wikipedia author Sentewolf.

6.7.6.1 Natural evolutionary strategies

If the probability model is in the exponential family, we can compute the natural gradient (Section 6.4), rather than the "vanilla" gradient, which can result in faster convergence. Such methods are called **natural evolution strategies** [Wie+14].

6.7.6.2 CMA-ES

The **CMA-ES** method of [Han16], which stands for "covariance matrix adaptation evolution strategy" is a kind of NES. It is very similar to CEM except it updates the parameters in a special way. In particular, instead of computing the new mean and covariance using unweighted MLE on the elite set, we attach weights to the elite samples based on their rank. We then set the new mean to the weighted MLE of the elite set.

The update equations for the covariance are more complex. In particular, "evolutionary paths" are also used to accumulate the search directions across successive generations, and these are used to update the covariance. It can be shown that the resulting updates approximate the natural gradient of $\mathcal{L}(\boldsymbol{\theta})$ without explicitly modeling the Fisher information matrix [Oll+17].

Figure 6.17 illustrates the method in action.

6.8 Optimal transport

This section is written by Marco Cuturi.

In this section, we focus on **optimal transport** theory, a set of tools that have been proposed, starting with work by [Mon81], to compare two probability distributions. We start from a simple example involving only matchings, and work from there towards various extensions.

6.8.1   Warm-up: matching optimally two families of points

Consider two families $(\mathbf{x}_1, \ldots, \mathbf{x}_n)$ and $(\mathbf{y}_1, \ldots, \mathbf{y}_n)$, each consisting in $n > 1$ distinct points taken from a set $\mathcal{X}$. A *matching* between these two families is a bijective mapping that assigns to each point $\mathbf{x}_i$ another point $\mathbf{y}_j$. Such an assignment can be encoded by pairing indices $(i, j) \in \{1, \ldots, n\}^2$ such that they define a *permutation* σ in the symmetric group $\mathcal{S}_n$. With that convention and given a permuation σ, $\mathbf{x}_i$ would be assigned to $\mathbf{y}_{\sigma_i}$, the σ_i'th element in the second family.

   Matchings costs. When matching a family with another, it is natural to consider the cost incurred when pairing any point $\mathbf{x}_i$ with another point $\mathbf{y}_j$, for all possible pairs $(i, j) \in \{1, \ldots, n\}^2$. For instance, $\mathbf{x}_i$ might contain information on the current location of a taxi driver i, and $\mathbf{y}_j$ that of a user j who has just requested a taxi; in that case, $C_{ij} \in \mathbb{R}$ may quantify the cost (in terms of time, fuel or distance) required for taxi driver i to reach user j. Alternatively, $\mathbf{x}_i$ could represent a vector of skills held by a job seeker i and $\mathbf{y}_j$ a vector quantifying desirable skills associated with a job posting j; in that case C_{ij} could quantify the numbers of hours required for worker i to carry out job j. We will assume without loss of generality that the values C_{ij} are obtained by evaluating a cost *function* $c : \mathcal{X} \times \mathcal{X} \to \mathbb{R}$ on the pair $(\mathbf{x}_i, \mathbf{y}_j)$, namely $C_{ij} = c(\mathbf{x}_i, \mathbf{y}_j)$. In many applications of optimal transport, such cost functions have a geometric interpretation and are typically distance functions on $\mathcal{X}$ as in Fig. 6.18, in which $\mathcal{X} = \mathbb{R}^2$, or as will be later discussed in Section 6.8.2.4.

   Least-cost matchings. Equipped with a cost function c, the *optimal* matching (or assignment) problem is that of finding a permutation that reaches the smallest total cost, as defined by the function

$$\min_{\sigma} E(\sigma) = \sum_{i=1}^{n} c(\mathbf{x}_i, \mathbf{y}_{\sigma_j}) . \tag{6.191}$$

The optimal matching problem is arguably one of the simplest combinatorial optimization problems, tackled as early as the 19th century [JB65]. Although a naive enumeration of all permutations would require evaluating objective E a total of $n!$ times, the Hungarian algorithm [Kuh55] was shown to provide the optimal solution in polynomial time [Mun57], and later refined to require in the worst case $O(n^3)$ operations.

6.8.2   From optimal matchings to Kantorovich and Monge formulations

The optimal matching problem is relevant to many applications, but it suffers from a few limitations. One could argue that most of the optimal transport literature arises from the necessity to overcome these limitations and extend (6.191) to more general settings. An obvious issue arises when the number of points available in both familites is not the same. The second limitation arises when considering a continuous setting, namely when trying to match (or morph) two probability densities, rather than families of atoms (discrete measures).

6.8.2.1   Mass splitting

Suppose again that all points $\mathbf{x}_i$ and $\mathbf{y}_j$ describe skills, respectively held by a worker i and needed for a task j to be fulfilled in a factory. Since finding a matching is equivalent to finding a permutation in $\{1, \ldots, n\}$, problem (6.191) cannot handle cases in which the number of workers is larger (or smaller) than the number of tasks. More problematically, the assumption that every single task is indivisible,

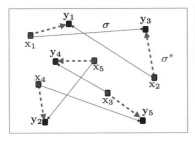 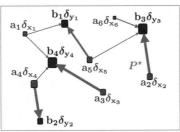 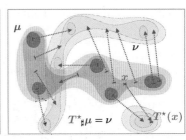

Figure 6.18: Left: Matching a family of 5 points to another is equivalent to considering a permutation in $\{1, \ldots, n\}$. When to each pair $(\mathbf{x}_i, \mathbf{y}_j) \in \mathbb{R}^2$ is associated a cost equal to the distance $\|\mathbf{x}_i - \mathbf{y}_j\|$, the optimal matching problem involves finding a permutation σ that minimizes $\|\mathbf{x}_i - \mathbf{y}_{\sigma_i}\|$ for i in $\{1, 2, 3, 4, 5\}$. Middle: The Kantorovich formulation of optimal transport generalizes optimal matchings, and arises when comparing discrete measures, that is, families of weighted points that do not necessarily share the same size but do share the same total mass. The relevant variable is a matrix P of size $n \times m$, which must satisfy row-sum and column-sum constraints, and which minimizes its dot product with matrix C_{ij}. Right: another direct extension of the matching problem lies when, intuitively, the number n of points that is described is such that the considered measures become continuous densities. In that setting, and unlike the Kantorovich setting, the goal is to seek a map $T : \mathcal{X} \to \mathcal{X}$ which, to any point x in the support of the input measure μ is associated a point $y = T(x)$ in the support of ν. The push-forward constraint $T_\sharp \mu = \nu$ ensures that ν is recovered by applying map T to all points in the support of μ; the optimal map $T^\star$ is that which minimizes the distance between x and $T(x)$, averaged over μ.

or that workers are only able to dedicate themselves to a single task, is hardly realistic. Indeed, certain tasks may require more (or less) dedication than that provided by a single worker, whereas some workers may only be able to work part-time, or, on the contrary, be willing to put extra hours. The rigid machinery of permutations falls short of handling such cases, since permutations are by definition one-to-one associations. The Kantorovich formulation allows for *mass-splitting*, the idea that the effort provided by a worker or needed to complete a given task can be split. In practice, to each of the n workers is associated, in addition to $\mathbf{x}_i$, a positive number $\mathbf{a}_i > 0$. That number represents the amount of time worker i is able to provide. Similarly, we introduce numbers $\mathbf{b}_j > 0$ describing the amount of time needed to carry out each of the m tasks (n and m do not necessarily coincide). Worker i is therefore described as a pair $(\mathbf{a}_i, \mathbf{x}_i)$, mathematically equivalent to a *weighted Dirac measure* $\mathbf{a}_i \delta_{\mathbf{x}_i}$. The overall workforce available to the factory is described as a discrete measure $\sum_i \mathbf{a}_i \delta_{\mathbf{x}_i}$, whereas its tasks are described in $\sum_j \mathbf{b}_j \delta_{\mathbf{y}_j}$. If one assumes further that the factory has a balanced workload, namely that $\sum_i \mathbf{a}_i = \sum_j \mathbf{b}_j$, then the Kantorovich [Kan42] formulation of optimal transport is:

$$\mathrm{OT}_C(\mathbf{a}, \mathbf{b}) \triangleq \min_{P \in \mathbf{R}_+^{n \times m}, P\mathbf{1}_n = \mathbf{a}, P^T \mathbf{1}_m = \mathbf{b}} \langle P, C \rangle \triangleq \sum_{i,j} P_{ij} C_{ij}. \tag{6.192}$$

The interpretation behind such matrices is simple: each coefficient P_{ij} describes an allocation of time for worker i to spend on task j. The i'th row-sum must be equal to the total $\mathbf{a}_i$ for the time constraint of worker i to be satisfied, whereas the j'th column-sum must be equal to $\mathbf{b}_j$, reflecting that the time needed to complete task j has been budgeted.

6.8.2.2   Monge formulation and optimal push forward maps

By introducing mass-splitting, the Kantorovich formulation of optimal transport allows for a far more general comparison between discrete measures of different sizes and weights (middle plot of Fig. 6.18). Naturally, this flexibility comes with a downside: one can no longer associate to each point $\mathbf{x}_i$ another point $\mathbf{y}_j$ to which it is uniquely associated, as was the case with the classical matching problem. Interestingly, this property can be recovered in the limit where the measures become densities. Indeed, the Monge [Mon81] formulation of optimal transport allows to recover precisely that property, on the condition (loosely speaking) that measure μ admits a density. In that setting, the analogous mathematical object guaranteeing that μ is mapped onto ν is that of **push forward** maps morphing μ to ν, namely maps T such that for any measurable set $A \subset \mathcal{X}$, $\mu(T^{-1}(A)) = \nu(A)$. When T is differentiable, and μ, ν have densities p and q wrt the Lebesgue measure in $\mathbb{R}^d$, this statement is equivalent, thanks to the change of variables formula, to ensuring almost everywhere that:

$$q(T(x)) = p(x)|J_T(x)|, \tag{6.193}$$

where $|J_T(x)|$ stands for the determinant of the Jacobian matrix of T evaluated at x.

Writing $T_\sharp \mu = \nu$ when T does satisfy these conditions, the Monge [Mon81] problem consists in finding the best map T that minimizes the average cost between $\mathbf{x}$ and its displacement $T(\mathbf{x})$,

$$\inf_{T : T_\sharp \mu = \nu} \int_{\mathcal{X}} c(\mathbf{x}, T(\mathbf{x})) \, \mu(\mathrm{d}\mathbf{x}). \tag{6.194}$$

T is therefore a map that pushes μ forwards to ν globally, but which results, on average, in the smallest average cost. While very intuitive, the Monge problem turns out to be extremely difficult to solve in practice, since it is non-convex. Indeed, one can easily check that the constraint $\{T_\sharp \mu = \nu\}$ is not convex, since one can easily find counter-examples for which $T_\sharp \mu = \nu$ and $T'_\sharp \nu$ yet $(\frac{1}{2}T + \frac{1}{2}T')_\sharp \mu \neq \nu$. Luckily, Kantorovich's approach also works for continuous measures, and yields a comparatively much simpler linear program.

6.8.2.3   Kantorovich formulation

The Kantovorich problem (6.192) can also be extended to a continuous setting: Instead of optimizing over a subset of matrices in $\mathbb{R}^{n \times m}$, consider $\Pi(\mu, \nu)$, the subset of joint probability distributions $\mathcal{P}(\mathcal{X} \times \mathcal{X})$ with marginals μ and ν, namely

$$\Pi(\mu, \nu) \triangleq \{\pi \in \mathcal{P}(\mathcal{X}^2) : \forall A \subset \mathcal{X}, \pi(A \times \mathcal{X}) = \mu(A) \text{ and } \pi(\mathcal{X} \times A) = \nu(A)\}. \tag{6.195}$$

Note that $\Pi(\mu, \nu)$ is not empty since it always contains the product measure $\mu \otimes \nu$. With this definition, the continuous formulation of (6.192) can be obtained as

$$\mathrm{OT}_c(\mu, \nu) \triangleq \inf_{\pi \in \Pi(\mu, \nu)} \int_{\mathcal{X}^2} c \, \mathrm{d}\pi. \tag{6.196}$$

Notice that (6.196) subsumes directly (6.192), since one can check that they coincide when μ, ν are discrete measures, with respective probability weights $\mathbf{a}, \mathbf{b}$ and locations $(\mathbf{x}_1, \ldots, \mathbf{x}_n)$ and $(\mathbf{y}_1, \ldots, \mathbf{y}_m)$.

6.8.2.4 Wasserstein distances

When c is equal to a metric d exponentiated by an integer, the optimal value of the Kantorovich problem is called the Wasserstein *distance* between μ and ν:

$$W_p(\mu, \nu) \triangleq \left(\inf_{\pi \in \Pi(\mu, \nu)} \int_{\mathcal{X}^2} d(\mathbf{x}, \mathbf{y})^p \, d\pi(\mathbf{x}, \mathbf{y}) \right)^{1/p}. \tag{6.197}$$

While the symmetry and the fact that $W_p(\mu, \nu) = 0 \Rightarrow \mu = \nu$ are relatively easy to prove provided d is a metric, proving the triangle inequality is slightly more challenging, and builds on a result known as the gluing lemma ([Vil08, p.23]). The p'th power of $W_p(\mu, \nu)$ is often abbreviated as $W_p^p(\mu, \nu)$.

6.8.3 Solving optimal transport

6.8.3.1 Duality and cost concavity

Both (6.192) and (6.196) are linear programs: their constraints and objective functions only involve summations. In that sense they admit a dual formulation (here, again, (6.199) subsumes (6.198)):

$$\max_{\substack{\mathbf{f} \in \mathbb{R}^n, \mathbf{g} \in \mathbb{R}^m \\ \mathbf{f} \oplus \mathbf{g} \leq C}} \mathbf{f}^T \mathbf{a} + \mathbf{g}^T \mathbf{b} \tag{6.198}$$

$$\sup_{f \oplus g \leq c} \int_{\mathcal{X}} f \, d\mu + \int_{\mathcal{X}} g \, d\nu \tag{6.199}$$

where the sign $\oplus$ denotes tensor addition for vectors, $\mathbf{f} \oplus \mathbf{g} = [\mathbf{f}_i + \mathbf{g}_j]_{ij}$, or functions, $f \oplus g : \mathbf{x}, \mathbf{y} \mapsto f(\mathbf{x}) + g(\mathbf{y})$. In other words, the dual problem looks for a pair of vectors (or functions) that attain the highest possible expectation when summed against $\mathbf{a}$ and $\mathbf{b}$ (or integrated against μ, ν), pending the constraint that they do not differ too much across points $\mathbf{x}, \mathbf{y}$, as measured by c.

The dual problems in (6.192) and (6.196) have two variables. Focusing on the continuous formulation, a closer inspection shows that it is possible, given a function f for the first measure, to compute the best possible candidate for function g. That function g should be as large as possible, yet satisfy the constraint that $g(\mathbf{y}) \leq c(\mathbf{x}, \mathbf{y}) - f(\mathbf{x})$ for all $\mathbf{x}, \mathbf{y}$, making

$$\forall \mathbf{y} \in \mathcal{X}, \overline{f}(\mathbf{y}) \triangleq \inf_{\mathbf{x}} c(\mathbf{x}, \mathbf{y}) - f(\mathbf{x}), \tag{6.200}$$

the optimal choice. $\overline{f}$ is called the c-transform of f. Naturally, one may choose to start instead from g, to define an alternative c-transform:

$$\forall \mathbf{x} \in \mathcal{X}, \widetilde{g}(\mathbf{x}) \triangleq \inf_{\mathbf{y}} c(\mathbf{x}, \mathbf{y}) - g(\mathbf{y}). \tag{6.201}$$

Since these transformations can only improve solutions, one may even think of applying alternatively these transformations to an arbitrary f, to define $\overline{f}, \widetilde{\overline{f}}$ and so on. One can show, however, that this has little interest, since

$$\widetilde{\overline{\overline{f}}} = \overline{f}. \tag{6.202}$$

This remark allows, nonetheless, to narrow down the set of candidate functions to those that have already undergone such transformations. This reasoning yields the so-called set of c-concave functions, $\mathcal{F}_c \triangleq \{f \mid \exists g : \mathcal{X} \to \mathbb{R}, f = \tilde{g}\}$, which can be shown, equivalently, to be the set of functions f such that $f = \tilde{\bar{f}}$. One can therefore focus our attention to c-concave functions to solve (6.199) using a so-called semi-dual formulation,

$$\sup_{f \in \mathcal{F}_c} \int_{\mathcal{X}} f \, \mathrm{d}\mu + \int_{\mathcal{X}} \bar{f} \, \mathrm{d}\nu. \tag{6.203}$$

Going from (6.199) to (6.203), we have removed a dual variable g and narrowed down the feasible set to $\mathcal{F}_c$, at the cost of introducing the highly non-linear transform $\bar{f}$. This reformulation is, however, very useful, in the sense that it allows to restrict our attention on c-concave functions, notably for two important classes of cost functions c: distances and squared-Euclidean norms.

6.8.3.2 Kantorovich-Rubinstein duality and Lipschitz potentials

A striking result illustrating the interest of c-concavity is provided when c is a metric d, namely when $p = 1$ in (6.197). In that case, one can prove (exploiting notably the triangle inequality of the d) that a d-concave function f is 1-Lipschitz (one has $|f(\mathbf{x}) - f(\mathbf{y})| \le d(\mathbf{x}, \mathbf{y})$ for any $\mathbf{x}, \mathbf{y}$) and such that $\bar{f} = -f$. This result translates therefore in the following identity:

$$W_1(\mu, \nu) = \sup_{f \in 1\text{-Lipschitz}} \int_{\mathcal{X}} f \, (\mathrm{d}\mu - \mathrm{d}\nu). \tag{6.204}$$

This result has numerous practical applications. This supremum over 1-Lipschitz functions can be efficiently approximated using wavelet coefficients of densities in low dimensions [SJ08], or heuristically in more general cases by training neural networks parameterized to be 1-Lipschitz [ACB17] using ReLU activation functions, and bounds on the entries of the weight matrices.

6.8.3.3 Monge maps as gradients of convex functions: the Brenier theorem

Another application of c-concavity lies in the case $c(\mathbf{x}, \mathbf{y}) = \frac{1}{2}\|\mathbf{x} - \mathbf{y}\|^2$, which corresponds, up to the factor $\frac{1}{2}$, to the squared W_2 distance used between densities in an Euclidean space. The remarkable result, shown first by [Bre91], is that the Monge map solving (6.194) between two measures for that cost (taken for granted μ is regular enough, here assumed to have a density wrt the Lebesgue measure) exists and is necessarily the gradient of a convex function. In loose terms, one can show that

$$T^\star = \arg\min_{T:T_\sharp\mu=\nu} \int_{\mathcal{X}} \frac{1}{2}\|\mathbf{x} - T(\mathbf{x})\|_2^2 \, \mu(\mathrm{d}\mathbf{x}). \tag{6.205}$$

exists, and is the gradient of a convex function $u : \mathbb{R}^d \to \mathbb{R}$, namely $T^\star = \nabla u$. Conversely, for any convex function u, the optimal transport map between μ and the displacement $\nabla u_\sharp \mu$ is necessarily equal to ∇u.

We provide a sketch of the proof: one can always exploit, for any reasonable cost function c (e.g., lower bounded and lower semi continuous), primal-dual relationships: Consider an optimal coupling $P^\star$ for (6.196), as well as an optimal c-concave dual function $f^\star$ for (6.203). This implies in particular that $(f^\star, g^\star = \overline{f^\star})$ is optimal for (6.199). Complementary slackness conditions for this pair of linear programs imply that if $\mathbf{x}_0, \mathbf{y}_0$ is in the support of $P^\star$, then necessarily (and sufficiently) $f^\star(\mathbf{x}_0) + \overline{f^\star}(\mathbf{y}_0) = c(\mathbf{x}_0, \mathbf{y}_0)$. Suppose therefore that $\mathbf{x}_0, \mathbf{y}_0$ is indeed in the support of $P^\star$. From the equality $f^\star(\mathbf{x}_0) + \overline{f^\star}(\mathbf{y}_0) = c(\mathbf{x}_0, \mathbf{y}_0)$ one can trivially obtain that $\overline{f^\star}(\mathbf{y}_0) = c(\mathbf{x}_0, \mathbf{y}_0) - f^\star(\mathbf{x}_0)$. Yet, recall also that, by definition, $\overline{f^\star}(\mathbf{y}_0) = \inf_{\mathbf{x}} c(\mathbf{x}, \mathbf{y}_0) - f^\star(\mathbf{x})$. Therefore, $\mathbf{x}_0$ has the special property that it *minimizes* $\mathbf{x} \to c(\mathbf{x}, \mathbf{y}_0) - f^\star(\mathbf{x})$. If, at this point, one recalls that c is assumed in this section to be $c(\mathbf{x}, \mathbf{y}) = \frac{1}{2}\|\mathbf{x} - \mathbf{y}\|\|^2$, one has therefore that $\mathbf{x}_0$ verifies

$$\mathbf{x}_0 \in \operatorname*{argmin}_{\mathbf{x}} \tfrac{1}{2}\|\mathbf{x} - \mathbf{y}_0\|^2 - f^\star(\mathbf{x}). \tag{6.206}$$

Assuming $f^\star$ is differentiable, which one can prove by c-concavity, this yields the identity

$$\mathbf{y}_0 - \mathbf{x}_0 - \nabla f^\star(\mathbf{x}_0) = 0 \Rightarrow \mathbf{y}_0 = \mathbf{x}_0 - \nabla f^\star(\mathbf{x}_0) = \nabla\left(\tfrac{1}{2}\|\cdot\|^2 - f^\star\right)(\mathbf{x}_0). \tag{6.207}$$

Therefore, if $(\mathbf{x}_0, \mathbf{y}_0)$ is in the support of $P^\star$, $\mathbf{y}_0$ is uniquely determined, which proves $P^\star$ is in fact a Monge map "disguised" as a coupling, namely

$$P^\star = \left(\mathrm{Id}, \nabla\left(\tfrac{1}{2}\|\cdot\|^2 - f^\star\right)\right)_\sharp \mu. \tag{6.208}$$

The end of the proof can be worked out as follows: For any function $h : \mathcal{X} \to \mathbf{R}$, one can show, using the definitions of c-transforms and the Legendre transform, that $\frac{1}{2}\|\cdot\|^2 - h$ is convex if and only if h is c-concave. An intermediate step in that proof relies on showing that $\frac{1}{2}\|\cdot\|^2 - \overline{h}$ is equal to the Legendre transform of $\frac{1}{2}\|\cdot\|^2 - h$. The function $\frac{1}{2}\|\cdot\|^2 - f^\star$ above is therefore convex, by c-concavity of $f^\star$, and the optimal transport map is itself the gradient of a convex function.

Knowing that an optimal transport map for the squared-Euclidean cost is necessarily the gradient of a convex function can prove very useful to solve (6.203). Indeed, this knowledge can be leveraged to restrict estimation to relevant families of functions, namely gradients of input-convex neural networks [AXK17], as proposed in [Mak+20] or [Kor+20], as well as arbitrary convex functions with desirable smoothness and strong-convexity constants [PdC20].

6.8.3.4 Closed forms for univariate and Gaussian distributions

Many metrics between probability distributions have closed form expressions for simple cases. The Wasserstein distance is no exception, and can be computed in close form in two important scenarios. When distributions are univariate and the cost $c(\mathbf{x}, \mathbf{y})$ is either a convex function of the difference $\mathbf{x} - \mathbf{y}$, or when $\partial c/\partial \mathbf{x} \partial \mathbf{y} < 0$ a.e., then the Wasserstein distance is essentially a comparison between the quantile functions of μ and ν. Recall that for a measure ρ, its quantile function Q_ρ is a function that takes values in $[0, 1]$ and is valued in the support of ρ, and corresponds to the (generalized) inverse map of F_ρ, the cumulative distribution function (cdf) of ρ. With these notations, one has that

$$\mathrm{OT}_c(\mu, \nu) = \int_{[0,1]} c\left(Q_\mu(u), Q_\nu(u)\right) \mathrm{d}u \tag{6.209}$$

In particular, when c is $\mathbf{x}, \mathbf{y} \mapsto |\mathbf{x} - \mathbf{y}|$ then $\mathrm{OT}_c(\mu, \nu)$ corresponds to the Kolmogorov-Smirnov statistic, namely the area between the cdf of μ and that of ν. If c is $\mathbf{x}, \mathbf{y} \mapsto (\mathbf{x} - \mathbf{y})^2$, we recover simply the squared-Euclidean norm between the quantile functions of μ and ν. Note finally that the Monge map is also available in closed form, and is equal to $Q_\nu \circ F_\mu$.

The second closed form applies to so-called elliptically contoured distributions, chiefly among them Gaussian multivariate distributions[Gel90]. For two Gaussians $\mathcal{N}(\mathbf{m}_1, \Sigma_1)$ and $\mathcal{N}(\mathbf{m}_2, \Sigma_2)$ their 2-Wasserstein distance decomposes as

$$W_2^2(\mathcal{N}(\mathbf{m}_1, \Sigma_1), \mathcal{N}(\mathbf{m}_2, \Sigma_2)) = \|\mathbf{m}_1 - \mathbf{m}_2\|^2 + \mathcal{B}^2(\Sigma_1, \Sigma_2) \tag{6.210}$$

where the Bures metric $\mathcal{B}$ reads:

$$\mathcal{B}^2(\Sigma_1, \Sigma_2) = \mathrm{tr}\left(\Sigma_1 + \Sigma_2 - 2\left(\Sigma_1^{\frac{1}{2}}\Sigma_2\Sigma_1^{\frac{1}{2}}\right)^{\frac{1}{2}}\right). \tag{6.211}$$

Notice in particular that these quantities are well-defined even when the covariance matrices are not invertible, and that they collapse to the distance between means as both covariances become 0. When the first covariance matrix is invertible, one has that the optimal Monge map is given by

$$T \triangleq \mathbf{x} \mapsto A(\mathbf{x} - \mathbf{m}_1) + \mathbf{m}_2, \text{ where } A \triangleq \Sigma_1^{-\frac{1}{2}}\left(\Sigma_1^{\frac{1}{2}}\Sigma_2\Sigma_1^{\frac{1}{2}}\right)^{\frac{1}{2}}\Sigma_1^{-\frac{1}{2}} \tag{6.212}$$

It is easy to show that $T^\star$ is indeed optimal: The fact that $T_\sharp\mathcal{N}(\mathbf{m}_1, \Sigma_1) = \mathcal{N}(\mathbf{m}_2, \Sigma_2)$ follows from the knowledge that the affine push-forward of a Gaussian is another Gaussian. Here T is designed to push precisely the first Gaussian onto the second (and A designed to recover random variables with variance Σ_2 when starting from random variables with variance Σ_1). The optimality of T can be recovered by simply noticing that is the gradient of a convex quadratic form, since A is positive definite, and closing this proof using the Brenier theorem above.

6.8.3.5 Exact evaluation using linear program solvers

We have hinted, using duality and c-concavity, that methods based on stochastic optimization over 1-Lipschitz or convex neural networks can be employed to estimate Wasserstein distances when c is the Euclidean distance or its square. These approaches are, however, non-convex and can only reach local optima. Apart from these two cases, and the closed forms provided above, the only reliable approach to compute Wasserstein distances appears when both μ and ν are discrete measures: in that case, one can instantiate and solve the discrete (6.192) problem, or its dual (6.198) formulation. The primal problem is a canonical example of network flow problems, and can be solved with the network-simplex method in $O(nm(n+m)\log(n+m))$ complexity [AMO88], or, alternatively, with the comparable auction algorithm [BC89]. These approaches suffer from computational limitations: their cubic cost is intractable for large scale scenarios; their combinatorial flavor makes it harder to solve to parallelize simultaneously the computation of multiple optimal transport problems with a common cost matrix C.

An altogether different issue, arising from statistics, should further discourage users from using these LP formulations, notably in high-dimensional settings. Indeed, the bottleneck practitioners will most likely encounter when using (6.192) is that, in most scenarios, their goal will be to approximate the distance between two continuous measures μ, ν using only i.i.d samples contained in empirical measures $\hat{\mu}_n, \hat{\nu}_n$. Using (6.192) to approximate the corresponding (6.196) is doomed to fail, as various results [FG15] have shown in relevant settings (notably for measures in $\mathbb{R}^q$) that the *sample complexity* of the estimator provided by (6.192) to approximate (6.196) is of order $1/n^{1/q}$. In other words, the gap between $W_2(\mu, \nu)$ and $W_2(\hat{\mu}_n, \hat{\nu}_n)$ is large in expectation, and decreases extremely slowly as n increases in high dimensions. Thus solving (6.196) exactly between these samples is mostly time wasted on overfitting. To address this curse of dimensionality, it is therefore extremely important in practice to approach (6.196) using a more careful strategy, one that involves regularizations that can leverage prior assumptions on μ and ν. While all approaches outlined above using neural networks can be interpreted under this light, we focus in the following on a specific approach that results in a convex problem that is relatively simple to implement, embarassingly parallel, and with quadratic complexity.

6.8.3.6 Obtaining smoothness using entropic regularization

A computational approach to speedup the resolution of (6.192) was proposed in [Cut13], building on earlier contributions [Wil69; KY94] and a filiation to the Schrödinger bridge problem in the special case where $c = d^2$ [Léo14]. The idea rests upon regularizing the transportation cost by the Kullback-Leibler divergence of the coupling to the product measure of μ, ν,

$$W_{c,\gamma}(\mu, \nu) \triangleq \inf_{\pi \in \Pi(\mu,\nu)} \int_{\mathcal{X}^2} d(\mathbf{x}, \mathbf{y})^p \, d\pi(\mathbf{x}, \mathbf{y}) + \gamma D_{\mathrm{KL}}(\pi \| \mu \otimes \nu). \tag{6.213}$$

When instantiated on discrete measures, this problem is equivalent to the following γ-strongly convex problem on the set of transportation matrices (which should be compared to (6.192))

$$\mathrm{OT}_{C,\gamma}(\mathbf{a}, \mathbf{b}) = \min_{P \in \mathbf{R}_+^{n \times m}, P\mathbf{1}_m = \mathbf{a}, P^T \mathbf{1}_n = \mathbf{b}} \langle P, C \rangle \triangleq \sum_{i,j} P_{ij} C_{ij} - \gamma \mathbb{H}(P) + \gamma \left(\mathbb{H}(\mathbf{a}) + \mathbb{H}(\mathbf{b}) \right), \tag{6.214}$$

which is itself equivalent to the following dual problem (which should be compared to (6.198))

$$\mathrm{OT}_{C,\gamma}(\mathbf{a}, \mathbf{b}) = \max_{\mathbf{f} \in \mathbb{R}^n, \mathbf{g} \in \mathbb{R}^m} \mathbf{f}^T \mathbf{a} + \mathbf{g}^T \mathbf{b} - \gamma (e^{\mathbf{f}/\gamma})^T K e^{\mathbf{g}/\gamma} + \gamma \left(1 + \mathbb{H}(\mathbf{a}) + \mathbb{H}(\mathbf{b}) \right) \tag{6.215}$$

and $K \triangleq e^{-C/\gamma}$ is the elementwise exponential of $-C/\gamma$. This regularization has several benefits. Primal-dual relationships show an explicit link between the (unique) solution $P_\gamma^\star$ and a pair of optimal dual variables $(\mathbf{f}^\star, \mathbf{g}^\star)$ as

$$P_\gamma^\star = \mathrm{diag}(e^{\mathbf{f}/\gamma}) K \, \mathrm{diag}(e^{\mathbf{g}/\gamma}) \tag{6.216}$$

Problem (6.215) can be solved using a fairly simple strategy that has proved very sturdy in practice: a simple block-coordinate ascent (optimizing alternatively the objective in $\mathbf{f}$ and then $\mathbf{g}$), resulting in the famous Sinkhorn algorithm [Sin67], here expressed with log-sum-exp updates, starting from an arbitrary initialization for $\mathbf{g}$, to carry out these two updates sequentially, until they converge:

$$\mathbf{f} \leftarrow \gamma \log \mathbf{a} - \gamma \log K e^{\mathbf{g}/\gamma} \qquad\qquad \mathbf{g} \leftarrow \gamma \log \mathbf{b} - \gamma \log K^T e^{\mathbf{f}/\gamma} \tag{6.217}$$

The convergence of this algorithm has been amply studied (see [CK21] and references therein). Convergence is naturally slower as γ decreases, reflecting the hardness of approaching LP solutions, as studied in [AWR17]. This regularization also has statistical benefits since, as argued in [Gen+19], the sample complexity of the regularized Wasserstein distance improves to a $O(1/\sqrt{n})$ regime, with, however, a constant in $1/\gamma^{q/2}$ that deteriorates as dimension grows.

6.9   Submodular optimization

This section is written by Jeff Bilmes.

This section provides a brief overview of submodularity in machine learning.[6] Submodularity has an extremely simple definition. However, the "simplest things are often the most complicated to understand fully" [Sam74], and while submodularity has been studied extensively over the years, it continues to yield new and surprising insights and properties, some of which are extremely relevant to data science, machine learning, and artificial intelligence. A submodular function operates on subsets of some finite *ground set*, V. Finding a guaranteed good subset of V would ordinarily require an amount of computation exponential in the size of V. Submodular functions, however, have certain properties that make optimization either tractable or approximable where otherwise neither would be possible. The properties are quite natural, however, so submodular functions are both flexible and widely applicable to real problems. Submodularity involves an intuitive and natural diminishing returns property, stating that adding an element to a smaller set helps more than adding it to a larger set. Like convexity, submodularity allows one to efficiently find provably optimal or near-optimal solutions. In contrast to convexity, however, where little regarding maximization is guaranteed, submodular functions can be both minimized and (approximately) maximized. Submodular maximization and minimization, however, require very different algorithmic solutions and have quite different applications. It is sometimes said that submodular functions are a discrete form of convexity. This is not quite true, as submodular functions are like both convex and concave functions, but also have properties that are similar simultaneously to both convex and concave functions at the same time, but then some properties of submodularity are neither like convexity nor like concavity. Convexity and concavity, for example, can be conveyed even as univariate functions. This is impossible for submodularity, as submodular functions are defined based only on the response of the function to changes amongst different variables in a multidimensional discrete space.

6.9.1   Intuition, examples, and background

Let us define a *set function* $f : 2^V \to \mathbb{R}$ as one that assigns a value to every subset of V. The notation 2^V is the power set of V, and has size $2^{|V|}$ which means that f lives in space $\mathbb{R}^{2^n}$ — i.e., since there are 2^n possible subsets of V, f can return 2^n distinct values. We use the notation $X + v$ as shorthand for $X \cup \{v\}$. Also, the value of an element in a given context is so widely used a concept, we have a special notation for it — the incremental value *gain* of v in the context if X is defined as $f(v|X) = f(X + v) - f(X)$. Thus, while $f(v)$ is the value of element v, $f(v|X)$ is the value of element v if you already have X. We also define the gain of set X in the context of Y as $f(X|Y) = f(X \cup Y) - f(Y)$.

6.9.1.1   Coffee, lemon, milk, and tea

As a simple example, will explore the manner in which the value of everyday items may interact and combine, namely coffee, lemon, milk, and tea. Consider the value relationships amongst the four

---

6. A greatly extended version of the material in this section may be found at [Bil22].

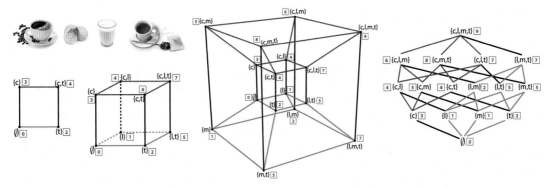

Figure 6.19: *The value relationships between coffee c, lemon l, milk m, and tea t. On the left, we first see a simple square showing the relationships between coffee and tea and see that they are substitutive (or submodular). In this, and all of the shapes, the vertex label set is indicated in curly braces and the value at that vertex is a blue integer in a box. We next see a three-dimensional cube that adds lemon to the coffee and tea set. We see that tea and lemon are complementary (supermodular), but coffee and lemon are additive (modular, or independent). We next see a four-dimensional hypercube (tesseract) showing all of the value relationships described in the text. The four-dimensional hypercube is also shown as a lattice (on the right) showing the same relationships as well as two (red and green, also shown in the tesseract) of the eight three-dimensional cubes contained within.*

items coffee (c), lemon (l), milk (m), and tea (t) as shown in Figure 6.19.[7] Suppose you just woke up, and there is a function $f : 2^V \to \mathbb{R}$ that provides the average valuation for any subset of the items in V where $V = \{c, l, m, t\}$. You can think of this function as giving the average price a typical person would be willing to pay for any subset of items. Since nothing should cost nothing, we would expect that $f(\emptyset) = 0$. Clearly, one needs either coffee or tea in the morning, so $f(c) > 0$ and $f(t) > 0$, and coffee is usually more expensive than tea, so that $f(c) > f(t)$ pound for pound. Also more items cost more, so that, for example, $0 < f(c) < f(c, m) < f(c, m, t) < f(c, l, m, t)$. Thus, the function f is strictly *monotone*, or $f(X) < f(Y)$ whenever $X \subset Y$.

The next thing we note is that coffee and tea may substitute for each other — they both have the same effect, waking you up. They are mutually redundant, and they decrease each other's value since once you have had a cup of coffee, a cup of tea is less necessary and less desirable. Thus, $f(c, t) < f(c) + f(t)$, which is known as a *subadditive* relationship, the whole is less than the sum of the parts. On the other hand, some items complement each other. For example, milk and coffee are better combined together than when both are considered in isolation, or $f(m, c) > f(m) + f(c)$, a *superadditive* relationship, the whole is more than the sum of the parts. A few of the items do not affect each other's price. For example, lemon and milk cost the same together as apart, so $f(l, m) = f(l) + f(m)$, an *additive* or *modular* relationship — such a relationship is perhaps midway between a subadditive and a superadditive relationship and can be seen as a form of independence.

Things become more interesting when we consider three or more items together. For example, once you have tea, lemon becomes less valuable when you acquire milk since there might be those

---

7. We use different character fonts c, l, m, and t for the ingestibles than we use for other constructs. For example, below we use m for modular functions.

that prefer milk to lemon in their tea. Similarly, milk becomes less valuable once you have acquired lemon since there are those who prefer lemon in their tea to milk. So, once you have tea, lemon and milk are substitutive, you would never use both as the lemon would only curdle the milk. These are *submodular* relationships, $f(\mathsf{l}|\mathsf{m},\mathsf{t}) < f(\mathsf{l}|\mathsf{t})$ and $f(\mathsf{m}|\mathsf{l},\mathsf{t}) < f(\mathsf{m}|\mathsf{t})$ each of which implies that $f(\mathsf{l},\mathsf{t}) + f(\mathsf{m},\mathsf{t}) > f(\mathsf{l},\mathsf{m},\mathsf{t}) + f(\mathsf{t})$. The value of lemon (respectively milk) with tea decreases in the larger context of having milk (respectively lemon) with tea, typical of submodular relationships.

Not all of the items are in a submodular relationship, as sometimes the presence of an item can increase the value of another item. For example, once you have milk, then tea becomes still more valuable when you also acquire lemon, since tea with the choice of either lemon or milk is more valuable than tea with the option only of milk. Similarly, once you have milk, lemon becomes more valuable when you acquire tea, since lemon with milk alone is not nearly as valuable as lemon with tea, even if milk is at hand. This means that $f(\mathsf{t}|\mathsf{l},\mathsf{m}) > f(\mathsf{t}|\mathsf{m})$ and $f(\mathsf{l}|\mathsf{t},\mathsf{m}) > f(\mathsf{l}|\mathsf{m})$ implying $f(\mathsf{l},\mathsf{m}) + f(\mathsf{m},\mathsf{t}) < f(\mathsf{l},\mathsf{m},\mathsf{t}) + f(\mathsf{m})$. These are known as *supermodular* relationships, where the value increases as the context increases.

We have asked for a set of relationships amongst various subsets of the four items $V = \{\mathsf{c},\mathsf{l},\mathsf{m},\mathsf{t}\}$, Is there a function that offers a value to each $X \subseteq V$ that satisfies all of the above relationships? Figure 6.19 in fact shows such a function. On the left, we see a two-dimensional square whose vertices indicate the values over subsets of $\{\mathsf{c},\mathsf{t}\}$ and we can quickly verify that the sum of the blue boxes on north-west (corresponding to $f(\{\mathsf{c}\})$) and south-east corners (corresponding to $f(\{\mathsf{t}\})$) is greater than the sum of the north-east and south-west corners, expressing the required submodular relationship. Next on the right is a three-dimensional cube that adds the relationship with lemon. Now we have six squares, and we see that the values at each of the vertices all satisfy the above requirements — we verify this by considering the valuations at the four corners of every one of the six faces of the cube. Since $|V| = 4$, we need a four-dimensional hypercube to show all values, and this may be shown in two ways. It is first shown as a tesseract, a well-known three-dimensional projection of a four-dimensional hypercube. In the figure, all vertices are labeled both with subsets of V as well as the function value $f(X)$ as the blue number in a box. The figure on the right shows a *lattice* version of the four-dimensional hypercube, where corresponding three-dimensional cubes are shown in green and red.

We thus see that a set function is defined for all subsets of a ground set, and that they correspond to valuations at all vertices of the hypercube. For the particular function over valuations of subsets of coffee, lemon, milk, and tea, we have seen submodular, supermodular, and modular relationships all in one function. Therefore, the overall function f defined in Figure 6.19 is neither submodular, supermodular, nor modular. For combinatorial auctions, there is often a desire to have a diversity of such manners of relationships [LLN06] — representation of these relationships can be handled by a difference of submodular functions [NB05; IB12] or a sum of a submodular and supermodular function [BB18] (further described below). In machine learning, however, most of the time we are interested in functions that are submodular (or modular, or supermodular) everywhere.

6.9.2   Submodular basic definitions

For a function to be submodular, it must satisfy the submodular relationship for all subsets. We arrive at the following definition.

Definition 6.9.1 (Submodular function). *A given set function $f : 2^V \to \mathbb{R}$ is submodular if for all*

$X, Y \subseteq V$, *we have the following inequality:*

$$f(X) + f(Y) \geq f(X \cup Y) + f(X \cap Y) \tag{6.218}$$

There are also many other equivalent definitions of submodularity [Bil22] some of which are more intuitive and easier to understand. For example, submodular functions are those set functions that satisfy the property of diminishing returns. If we think of a function $f(X)$ as measuring the value of a set X that is a subset of a larger set of data items $X \subseteq V$, then the submodular property means that the incremental "value" of adding a data item v to set X decreases as the size of X grows. This gives us a second classic definition of submodularity.

Definition 6.9.2 (Submodular function via diminishing returns). *A given set function $f : 2^V \to \mathbb{R}$ is submodular if for all $X, Y \subseteq V$, where $X \subseteq Y$ and for all $v \notin Y$, we have the following inequality:*

$$f(X + v) - f(X) \geq f(Y + v) - f(Y) \tag{6.219}$$

The property that the incremental value of lemon with tea is less than the incremental value of lemon once milk is already in the tea is equivalent to Equation 6.218 if we set $X = \{\mathsf{m}, \mathsf{t}\}$ and $Y = \{\mathsf{l}, \mathsf{t}\}$ (i.e., $f(\mathsf{m}, \mathsf{t}) + f(\mathsf{l}, \mathsf{t}) > f(\mathsf{l}, \mathsf{m}, \mathsf{t}) + f(\mathsf{t})$). It is naturally also equivalent to Equation 6.219 if we set $X = \{\mathsf{t}\}$, $Y = \{\mathsf{m}, \mathsf{t}\}$, and with $v = \mathsf{l}$ (i.e., $f(\mathsf{l}|\mathsf{m}, \mathsf{t}) < f(\mathsf{l}|\mathsf{t})$).

There are many functions that are submodular, one famous one being Shannon entropy seen as a function of subsets of random variables. We first point out that there are non-negative (i.e., $f(A) \geq 0, \forall A$), monotone non-decreasing (i.e., $f(A) \leq f(B)$ whenever $A \subseteq B$) submodular functions that are not entropic [Yeu91b; ZY97; ZY98], so submodularity is not just a trivial restatement of the class of entropy functions. When a function is monotone non-decreasing, submodular, and *normalized* so that $f(\emptyset) = 0$, it is often referred to as a **polymatroid function**. Thus, while the entropy function is a polymatroid function, it does not encompass all polymatroid functions even though all polymatroid functions satisfy the properties Claude Shannon mentioned as being natural for an "information" function (see Section 6.9.7).

A function f is supermodular if and only if $-f$ is submodular. If a function is both submodular and supermodular, it is known as a *modular* function. It is always the case that a modular function $m : 2^V \to \mathbb{R}$ may take the form of a vector-scalar pair. That is, for any $A \subseteq V$, we have that $m(A) = c + \sum_{v \in A} m_v$ where c is the scalar, and $\{m_v\}_{v \in V}$ can be seen as the elements of a vector indexed by elements of V. If the modular function is normalized, so that $m(\emptyset) = 0$, then $c = 0$ and the modular function can be seen simply as a vector $m \in \mathbb{R}^V$. Hence, we sometimes say that the modular function $x \in \mathbb{R}^V$ offers a value for set A as the partial sum $x(A) = \sum_{v \in A} x(v)$. Many combinatorial problems use modular functions as objectives. For example, the graph cut problem uses a modular function defined over the edges, judges a cut in a graph as the modular function applied to the edges that comprise the cut.

As can be seen from the above, and by considering Figure 6.19, a submodular function, and in fact any set function, $f : 2^V \to \mathbb{R}$ can be seen as a function defined only on the vertices of the n-dimensional unit hypercube $[0, 1]^n$. Given any set $X \subseteq V$, we define $\mathbf{1}_X \in \{0, 1\}^V$ to be the characteristic vector of set X defined as $\mathbf{1}_X(v) = 1$ if $v \in X$ and $\mathbf{1}_X(v) = 0$ otherwise. This gives us a way to map from any set $X \subseteq V$ to a binary vector $\mathbf{1}_X$. We also see that $\mathbf{1}_X$ is itself a modular function since $\mathbf{1}_X \in \{0, 1\}^V \subset \mathbb{R}^V$.

Submodular functions share a number of properties in common with both convex and concave functions [Lov83], including wide applicability, generality, multiple representations, and closure under a number of common operators (including mixtures, truncation, complementation, and certain convolutions). There is one important submodular closure property that we state here — that if we take non-negative weighted (or conical) combinations of submodular functions, we preserve submodularity. In other words, if we have a set of k submodular functions, $f_i : 2^V \to \mathbb{R}$, $i \in [k]$, and we form $f(X) = \sum_{i=1}^{k} \omega_i f_i(X)$ where $\omega_i \geq 0$ for all i, then Definition 6.9.1 immediately implies that f is also submodular. When we consider Definition 6.9.1, we see that submodular functions live in a cone in 2^n-dimensional space defined by the intersection of an exponential number of half-spaces each one of which is defined by one of the inequalities of the form $f(X) + f(Y) \geq f(X \cup Y) + f(X \cap Y)$. Each submodular function is therefore a point in that cone. It is therefore not surprising that taking conical combinations of such points stays within this cone.

6.9.3   Example submodular functions

As mentioned above, there are many functions that are submodular besides entropy. Perhaps the simplest such function is $f(A) = \sqrt{|A|}$ which is the composition of the square-root function (which is concave) with the cardinality $|A|$ of the set A. The gain function is $f(A + v) - f(A) = \sqrt{k+1} - \sqrt{k}$ if $|A| = k$, which we know to be a decreasing in k, thus establishing the submodularity of f. In fact, if $\phi : \mathbb{R} \to \mathbb{R}$ is any concave function, then $f(A) = \phi(|A|)$ will be submodular for the same reason.[8] Generalizing this slightly further, a function defined as $f(A) = \phi(\sum_{a \in A} m(a))$ is also submodular, whenever $m(a) \geq 0$ for all $a \in V$. This yields a composition of a concave function with a modular function $f(A) = \phi(m(A))$ since $\sum_{a \in A} m(a) = m(A)$. We may take sums of such functions as well as add a final modular function without losing submodularity, leading to $f(A) = \sum_{u \in U} \phi_u(\sum_{a \in A} m_u(a)) + \sum_{a \in A} m_\pm(a)$ where ϕ_u can be a distinct concave function for each u, $m_u(a)$ is a non-negative real value for all u and a, and $m_\pm(a)$ is an arbitrary real number. Therefore, $f(A) = \sum_{u \in U} \phi_u(m_u(A)) + m_\pm(A)$ where m_u is a u-specific non-negative modular function and $m_\pm$ is an arbitrary modular function. Such functions are sometimes known as **feature-based** submodular functions [BB17] because U can be a set of non-negative features (in the machine-learning "bag-of-words" sense) and this function measures a form of dispersion over A as determined by the set of features U.

A function such as $f(A) = \sum_{u \in U} \phi_u(m_u(A))$ tends to award high diversity to a set A that has a high valuation by a distinct set of the features U. The reason is that, due to the concave nature of ϕ_u, any addition to the argument $m_u(A)$ by adding, say, v to A would diminish as A gets larger. In order to produce a set larger than A that has a much larger valuation, one must use a feature $u' \neq u$ that has not yet diminished as much.

Facility location is another well-known submodular function — perhaps an appropriate nickname would be the "k-means of submodular functions", due to its applicability, utility, ease-of-use (it needs only an affinity matrix), and similarity to k-medoids problems. The facility location function is defined using an affinity matrix as follows: $f(A) = \sum_{v \in V} \max_{a \in A} \operatorname{sim}(a, v)$ where $\operatorname{sim}(a, v)$ is a non-negative measure of the affinity (or similarity) between element a and v. Here, every element $v \in V$ must have a representative within the set A and the representative for each $v \in V$ is chosen to be the element $a \in A$ most similar to v. This function is also a form of dispersion or diversity function because, in order to maximize it, every element $v \in V$ must have some element similar to

---

8. While we will not be extensively discussing supermodular functions in this section, $f(A) = \phi(|A|)$ is supermodular for any convex function ϕ.

it in A. The overall score is then the sum of the similarity between each element $v \in V$ and v's representative. This function is monotone (since as A includes more elements to become $B \supseteq A$, it is possible only to find an element in B more similar to a given v than an element in A).

While the facility location looks quite different from a feature-based function, it is possible to precisely represent any facility location function with a feature-based function. Consider just $\max_{a \in A} x_a$ and, without loss of generality, assume that $0 \le x_1 \le x_2 \le \cdots \le x_n$. Then $\max_{a \in A} x_a = \sum_{i=1}^{n} y_i \min(|A \cap \{i, i+1, \ldots, n\}|, 1)$ where $y_i = x_i - x_{i-1}$ and we set $x_0 = 0$. We note that this is a sum of weighted concave composed with modular functions since $\min(\alpha, 1)$ is concave in α, and $|A \cap \{i, i+1, \ldots, n\}|$ is a modular function in A. Thus, the facility location function, a sum of these, is merely a feature-based function.

Feature-based functions, in fact, are quite expressive, and can be used to represent many different submodular functions including set cover and graph-based functions. For example, we can define a *set cover function*, given a set of sets $\{U_v\}_{v \in V}$, via $f(X) = \left|\bigcup_{v \in X} U_v\right|$. If $f(X) = |U|$ where $U = \bigcup_{v \in V} U_v$ then X indexes a set that fully covers U. This can also be represented as $f(X) = \sum_{u \in U} \min(1, m_u(X))$ where $m_u(X)$ is a modular function where $m_u(v) = 1$ if and only if $u \in U_v$ and otherwise $m_u(v) = 0$. We see that this is a feature-based submodular function since $\min(1, x)$ is concave in x, and U is a set of features.

This construct can be used to produce the vertex cover function if we set $U = V$ to be the set of vertices in a graph, and set $m_u(v) = 1$ if and only if vertices u and v are adjacent in the graph and otherwise set $m_u(v) = 0$. Similarly, the edge cover function can be expressed by setting V to be the set of edges in a graph, U to be the set of vertices in the graph, and $m_u(v) = 1$ if and only edge v is incident to vertex u.

A generalization of the set cover function is the *probabilistic coverage* function. Let $\mathsf{P}[B_{u,v} = 1]$ be the probability of the presence of feature (or concept) u within element v. Here, we treat $B_{u,v}$ as a Bernoulli random variable for each element v and feature u so that $\mathsf{P}[B_{u,v} = 1] = 1 - \mathsf{P}[B_{u,v} = 0]$. Then we can define the probabilistic coverage function as $f(X) = \sum_{u \in U} f_u(X)$ where, for feature u, we have $f_u(X) = 1 - \prod_{v \in X}(1 - \mathsf{P}[B_{u,v} = 1])$ which indicates the degree to which feature u is "covered" by X. If we set $\mathsf{P}[B_{u,v} = 1] = 1$ if and only if $u \in U_v$ and otherwise $\mathsf{P}[B_{u,v} = 1] = 0$, then $f_u(X) = \min(1, m_u(X))$ and the set cover function can be represented as $\sum_{u \in U} f_u(X)$. We can generalize this in two ways. First, to make it softer and more probabilistic we allow $\mathsf{P}[B_{u,v} = 1]$ to be any number between zero and one. We also allow each feature to have a non-negative weight. This yields the general form of the probabilistic coverage function, which is defined by taking a weighted combination over all features: $f_u(X) = \sum_{u \in U} \omega_u f_u(X)$ where $\omega_u \ge 0$ is a weight for feature u. Observe that $1 - \prod_{v \in X}(1 - \mathsf{P}[B_{u,v} = 1]) = 1 - \exp(-m_u(X)) = \phi(m_u(X))$ where m_u is a modular function with evaluation $m_u(X) = \sum_{v \in X} \log(1/(1 - \mathsf{P}[B_{u,v} = 1]))$ and for $z \in \mathbb{R}$, $\phi(z) = 1 - \exp(-z)$ is a concave function. Thus, the probabilistic coverage function (and its set cover specialization) is also a feature-based function.

Another common submodular function is the graph cut function. Here, we measure the value of a subset of V by the edges that cross between a set of nodes and all but that set of nodes. We are given an undirected non-negative weighted graph $\mathcal{G} = (V, E, w)$ where V is the set of nodes, $E \subseteq V \times V$ is the set of edges, and $w \in \mathbb{R}_+^E$ are non-negative edge weights corresponding to symmetric matrix (so $w_{i,j} = w_{j,i}$). For any $e \in E$, we have $e = \{i, j\}$ for some $i, j \in V$ with $i \ne j$, the graph cut function $f : 2^V \to \mathbb{R}$ is defined as $f(X) = \sum_{i \in X, j \in \bar{X}} w_{i,j}$ where $w_{i,j} \ge 0$ is the weight of edge $e = \{i, j\}$ ($w_{i,j} = 0$ if the edge does not exist), and where $\bar{X} = V \setminus X$ is the complement of set X. Notice that we can write the graph cut function as follows:

$$f(X) = \sum_{i \in X, j \in \bar{X}} w_{i,j} = \sum_{i,j \in V} w_{i,j} \mathbf{1}\{i \in X, j \in \bar{X}\} \tag{6.220}$$

$$= \frac{1}{2} \sum_{i,j \in V} w_{i,j} \min(|X \cap \{i,j\}|, 1) + \frac{1}{2} \sum_{i,j \in V} w_{i,j} \min(|(V \setminus X) \cap \{i,j\}|, 1) - \frac{1}{2} \sum_{i,j \in V} w_{i,j} \tag{6.221}$$

$$= \tilde{f}(X) + \tilde{f}(V \setminus X) - \tilde{f}(V) \tag{6.222}$$

where $\tilde{f}(X) = \frac{1}{2} \sum_{i,j \in V} w_{i,j} \min(|X \cap \{i,j\}|, 1)$. Therefore, since $\min(\alpha, 1)$ is concave, and since $m_{i,j}(X) = |X \cap \{i,j\}|$ is modular, $\tilde{f}(X)$ is submodular for all i, j. Also, since $\tilde{f}(X)$ is submodular, so is $\tilde{f}(V \setminus X)$ (in X). Therefore, the graph cut function can be expressed as a sum of non-normalized feature-based functions. Note that here the second modular function is not normalized and is non-increasing, and also we subtract the constant $\tilde{f}(V)$ to achieve equality.

Another way to view the graph cut function is to consider the non-negative weights as a modular function defined over the edges. That is, we view $w \in \mathbb{R}_+^E$ as a modular function $w : 2^E \to \mathbb{R}_+$ where for every $A \subseteq E$, $w(A) = \sum_{e \in A} w(e)$ is the weight of the edges A where $w(e)$ is the weight of edge e. Then the graph cut function becomes $f(X) = w(\{(a,b) \in E : a \in X, b \in X \setminus X\})$. We view $\{(a,b) \in E : a \in X, b \in X \setminus X\}$ as a set-to-set mapping function, that maps subsets of nodes to subsets of edges, and the edge weight modular function w measures the weight of the resulting edges. This immediately suggests that other functions can measure the weight of the resulting edges as well, including non-modular functions. One example is to use a polymatroid function itself leading $h(X) = g(\{(a,b) \in E : a \in X, b \in X \setminus X\})$ where $g : 2^E \to \mathbb{R}_+$ is a submodular function defined on subsets of edges. The function h is known as the **cooperative cut** function, and it is neither submodular nor supermodular in general but there are many useful and practical algorithms that can be used to optimize it [JB16] thanks to its internal yet exposed and thus available to exploit submodular structure.

While feature-based functions are flexible and powerful, there is a strictly broader class of submodular functions, unable to be expressed by feature-based functions, that are related to deep neural networks. Here, we create a recursively nested composition of concave functions with sums of compositions of concave functions. An example is $f(A) = \phi(\sum_{u \in U} \omega_u \phi_u(\sum_{a \in A} m_u(a)))$, where ϕ is an outer concave function composed with a feature-based function, with $m_u(a) \geq 0$ and $\omega_u \geq 0$. This is known as a two-layer **deep submodular function** (DSF). A three-layer DSF has the form $f(A) = \phi(\sum_{c \in C} \omega_c \phi_c(\sum_{u \in U} \omega_{u,c} \phi_u(\sum_{a \in A} m_u(a))))$. DSFs strictly expand the class of submodular functions beyond feature-based functions, meaning that there are feature-based functions that cannot represent deep submodular functions, even simple ones [BB17].

6.9.4   Submodular optimization

Submodular functions, while discrete, would not be very useful if it was not possible to optimize over them efficiently. There are many natural problems in machine learning that can be cast as submodular optimization and that can be addressed relatively efficiently.

When one wishes to encourage diversity, information, spread, high complexity, independence, coverage, or dispersion, one usually will maximize a submodular function, in the form of $\max_{A \in \mathcal{C}} f(A)$ where $\mathcal{C} \subseteq 2^V$ is a constraint set, a set of subsets we are willing to accept as feasible solutions (more on this below).

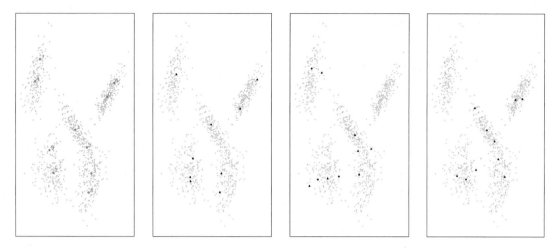

Figure 6.20: Far left: cardinality constrained (to ten) submodular maximization of a facility location function over 1000 points in two dimensions. Similarities are based on a Gaussian kernel $sim(a, v) = \exp(-d(a, v))$ where $d(\cdot, \cdot)$ is a distance. Selected points are green stars, and the greedy order is also shown next to each selected point. Right three plots: different uniformly-at-random subsets of size ten.

   Why is submodularity, in general, a good model for diversity? Submodular functions are such that once you have some elements, any other elements not in your possession but that are similar to, explained by, or represented by the elements in your possession become less valuable. Thus, in order to maximize the function, one must choose other elements that are dissimilar to, or not well represented by, the ones you already have. That is, the elements similar to the ones you own are diminished in value relative to their original values, while the elements dissimilar to the ones you have do not have diminished value relative to their original values. Thus, maximizing a submodular function successfully involves choosing elements that are jointly dissimilar amongst each other, which is a definition of diversity. Diversity in general is a critically important aspect in machine learning and artificial intelligence. For example, bias in data science and machine learning can often be seen as some lack of diversity somewhere. Submodular functions have the potential to encourage (and even ensure) diversity, enhance balance, and reduce bias in artificial intelligence.

   Note that in order for a submodular function to appropriately model diversity, it is important for it to be instantiated appropriately. Figure 6.20 shows an example in two dimensions. The plot compares the ten points chosen according to a facility location instantiated with a Gaussian kernel, along with the random samples of size ten. We see that the facility location selected points are more diverse and tend to cover the space much better than any of the randomly selected points, each of which miss large regions of the space and/or show cases where points near each other are jointly selected.

   When one wishes for homogeneity, conformity, low complexity, coherence, or cooperation, one will usually minimize a submodular function, in the form of $\min_{A \in \mathcal{C}} f(A)$. For example, if V is a set of pixels in an image, one might wish to choose a subset of pixels corresponding to a particular object over which the properties (i.e., color, luminance, texture) are relatively homogeneous. Finding a set X of size k, even if k is large, need not have a large valuation $f(X)$, in fact it could even have the least valuation. Thus, semantic image segmentation could work even if the object being segmented and isolated consists of the majority of image pixels.

6.9.4.1 Submodular maximization

While the cardinality constrained submodular maximization problem is NP complete [Fei98], it was shown in [NWF78; FNW78] that the very simple and efficient greedy algorithm finds an approximate solution guaranteed to be within $1 - 1/e \approx 0.63$ of the optimal solution. Moreover, the approximation ratio achieved by the simple greedy algorithm is provably the best achievable in polynomial time, assuming $P \neq NP$ [Fei98]. The greedy algorithm proceeds as follows: Starting with $X_0 = \emptyset$, we repeat the following greedy step for $i = 0 \ldots (k-1)$:

$$X_{i+1} = X_i \cup (\operatorname*{argmax}_{v \in V \setminus X_i} f(X_i \cup \{v\})) \tag{6.223}$$

What the above approximation result means is that if $X^* \in \operatorname{argmax}\{f(X) : |X| \leq k\}$, and if $\tilde{X}$ is the result of the greedy procedure, then $f(\tilde{X}) \geq (1 - 1/e)f(X^*)$.

The $1 - 1/e$ guarantee is a powerful constant factor approximation result since it holds regardless of the size of the initial set V and regardless of which polymatroid function f is being optimized. It is possible to make this algorithm run extremely fast using various acceleration tricks [FNW78; NWF78; Min78].

A minor bit of additional information about a polymatroid function, however, can improve the approximation guarantee. Define the total curvature if the polymatroid function f as $\kappa = 1 - \min_{v \in V} f(v|V-v)/f(v)$ where we assume $f(v) > 0$ for all v (if not, we may prune them from the ground set since such elements can never improve a polymatroid function valuation). We thus have $0 \leq \kappa \leq 1$, and [CC84] showed that the greedy algorithm gives a guarantee of $\frac{1}{\kappa}(1 - e^{-\kappa}) \geq 1 - 1/e$. In fact, this is an equality (and we get the same bound) when $\kappa = 1$, which is the fully curved case. As κ gets smaller, the bound improves, until we reach the $\kappa = 0$ case and the bound becomes unity. Observe that $\kappa = 0$ if and only if the function is modular, in which case the greedy algorithm is optimal for the cardinality constrained maximization problem.   In some cases, non-submodular functions can be decomposed into components that each might be more amenable to approximation. We see below that any set function can be written as a difference of submodular [NB05; IB12] functions, and sometimes (but not always) a given h can be composed into a monotone submodular plus a monotone supermodular function, or a BP function [BB18], i.e., $h = f + g$ where f is submodular and g is supermodular. g has an easily computed quantity called the supermodular curvature $\kappa^g = 1 - \min_{v \in V} g(v)/g(v|V-v)$ that, together with the submodular curvature, can be used to produce an approximation ratio having the form $\frac{1}{\kappa}(1 - e^{-\kappa(1-\kappa^g)})$ for greedy maximization of h.

6.9.4.2 Discrete constraints

There are many other types of constraints one might desire besides a cardinality limitation. The next simplest constraint allows each element v to have a non-negative cost, say $m(v) \in \mathbb{R}_+$. In fact, this means that the costs are modular, i.e., the cost of any set X is $m(X) = \sum_{v \in X} m(v)$. A submodular maximization problem subject to a *knapsack constraint* then takes the form $\max_{X \subseteq V : m(X) \leq b} f(X)$ where b is a non-negative budget. While the greedy algorithm does not solve this problem directly, a slightly modified cost-scaled version of the greedy algorithm [Svi04] does solve this problem for any set of knapsack costs. This has been used for various multi-document summarization tasks [LB11; LB12].

There is no single direct analogy for a convex set when one is optimizing over subsets of the set V, but there are a few forms of discrete constraints that are both mathematically interesting and that often occur repeatedly in applications.

The first form is the independent subsets of a matroid. The independent sets of a matroid are useful to represent a constraint set for submodular maximization [Cal+07; LSV09; Lee+10], $\max_{X \in \mathcal{I}} f(X)$, and this can be useful in many ways. We can see this by showing a simple example of what is known as a *partition matroid*. Consider a partition $V = \{V_1, V_2, \ldots, V_m\}$ of V into m mutually disjoint subsets that we call blocks. Suppose also that for each of the m blocks, there is a positive integer limit ℓ_i for $i \in [m]$. Consider next the set of sets formed by taking all subsets of V such that each subset has intersection with V_i no more than ℓ_i for each i. I.e., consider

$$\mathcal{I}_{\mathrm{p}} = \{X : \forall i \in [m], |V_i \cap X| \le \ell_i\}. \tag{6.224}$$

Then $(V, \mathcal{I}_{\mathrm{p}})$ is a matroid. The corresponding submodular maximization problem is a natural generalization of the cardinality constraint in that, rather than having a fixed number of elements beyond which we are uninterested, the set of elements V is organized into groups, and here we have a fixed per-group limit beyond which we are uninterested. This is useful for fairness applications since the solution must be distributed over the blocks of the matroid. Still, there are many much more powerful types of matroids that one can use [Oxl11; GM12].

Regardless of the matroid, the problem $\max_{X \in \mathcal{I}} f(X)$ can be solved, with a $1/2$ approximation factor, using the same greedy algorithm as above [NWF78; FNW78]. Indeed, the greedy algorithm has an intimate relationship with submodularity, a fact that is well studied in some of the seminal works on submodularity [Edm70; Lov83; Sch04]. It is also possible to define constraints consisting of an *intersection of matroids*, meaning that the solution must be simultaneously independent in multiple distinct matroids. Adding on to this, we might wish a set to be independent in multiple matroids and also satisfy a knapsack constraint. Knapsack constraints are not matroid constraints, since there can be multiple maximal cost solutions that are not the same size (as must be the case in a matroid). It is also possible to define discrete constraints using level sets of another completely different submodular function [IB13] — given two submodular functions f and g, this leads to optimization problems of the form $\max_{X \subseteq V : g(X) \le \alpha} f(X)$ (the submodular cost submodular knapsack, or SCSK, problem) and $\min_{X \subseteq V : g(X) \ge \alpha} f(X)$ (the submodular cost submodular cover, or SCSC, problem). Other examples include covering constraints [IN09], and cut constraints [JB16]. Indeed, the type of constraints on submodular maximization for which good and scalable algorithms exist is quite vast, and still growing.

One last note on submodular maximization. In the above, the function f has been assumed to be a polymatroid function. There are many submodular functions that are not monotone [Buc+12]. One example we saw before, namely the graph cut function. Another example is the log of the determinant (log-determinant) of a submatrix of a positive-definite matrix (which is the Gaussian entropy plus a constant). Suppose that $\mathbf{M}$ is an $n \times n$ symmetric positive-definite (SPD) matrix, and that $\mathbf{M}_X$ is a row-column submatrix (i.e., it is an $|X| \times |X|$ matrix consisting of the rows and columns of $\mathbf{M}$ consisting of the elements in X). Then the function defined as $f(X) = \log \det(\mathbf{M}_X)$ is submodular but not necessarily monotone non-decreasing. In fact, the submodularity of the log-determinant function is one of the reasons that *determinantal point processes* (DPPs), which instantiate probability distributions over sets in such a way that high probability is given to those subsets that are diverse according to $\mathbf{M}$, are useful for certain tasks where we wish to probabilistically model diversity [KT11]. (See Supplementary Section 31.8.5 for details on DPPs.) Diversity of a set X here is measured by the volume of the parallelepiped which is known to be computed as the determinant of the submatrix $\mathbf{M}_X$ and taking the log of this volume makes the function submodular in X. A DPP in fact is an example of a log-submodular probabilistic model (more in Section 6.9.10).

6.9.4.3   Submodular function minimization

In the case of a polymatroid function, unconstrained minimization is again trivial. However, even in the unconstrained case, the minimization of an arbitrary (i.e., not necessarily monotone) submodular function $\min_{X \subseteq V} f(X)$ might seem hopelessly intractable. Unconstrained submodular maximization is NP-hard (albeit approximable), and this is not surprising given that there are an exponential number of sets needing to be considered. Remarkably, submodular minimization does not require exponential computation, and is not NP-hard; in fact, there are polynomial time algorithms for doing so, something that is not at all obvious. This is one of the important characteristics that submodular functions share with convex functions, their common amenability to minimization. Starting in the very late 1960s and spearheaded by individuals such as Jack Edmonds [Edm70], there was a concerted effort in the discrete mathematics community in search of either an algorithm that could minimize a submodular function in polynomial time or a proof that such a problem was NP-hard. The nut was finally cracked in a classic paper [GLS81] on the ellipsoid algorithm that gave a polynomial time algorithm for submodular function minimization (SFM). While the algorithm was polynomial, it was a continuous algorithm, and it was not practical, so the search continued for a purely combinatorial strongly polynomial time algorithm. Queyranne [Que98] then proved that an algorithm [NI92] worked for this problem when the set function also satisfies a symmetry condition (i.e., $\forall X \subseteq V, f(X) = f(V \setminus X)$), which only requires $O(n^3)$ time. The result finally came around the year 2000 using two mostly independent methods [IFF00; Sch00]. These algorithms, however, also were impractical, in that while they are polynomial time, they had unrealistically high polynomial degree (i.e., $\tilde{O}(|V|^7 * \gamma + |V|^8)$ for [Sch00] and $\tilde{O}(|V|^7 * \gamma)$ for [IFF00]). This led to additional work on combinatorial algorithms for SFM leading to algorithms that could perform SFM in time $\tilde{O}(|V|^5 \gamma + |V|^6)$ in [IO09]. Two practical algorithms for SFM include the Fujishige-Wolfe procedure [Fuj05; Wol76][9] as well as the Frank-Wolfe procedure, each of which minimize the 2-norm on a polyhedron B_f associated with the submodular function f and which is defined below (it should also be noted that the Frank-Wolfe algorithm can also be used to minimize the convex extension of the function, something that is relatively easy to compute via the Lovász extension [Lov83]). More recent work on SFM are also based on continuous relaxations of the problem in some form or another, leading algorithms with strongly polynomial running time [LSW15] of $O(|V|^3 \log^2 |V|)$ for which it was possible to drop the log factors leading to a complexity of $O(|V|^3)$ in [Jia21], weakly-polynomial running time [LSW15] of $\tilde{O}(|V|^2 \log M)$ (where $M >= \max_{S \subseteq V} |f(S)|$), pseudopolynomial running time [ALS20; Cha+17] of $\tilde{O}(|V| M^2)$, and a ϵ-approximate minimization with a linear running time [ALS20] of $\tilde{O}(|V|/\epsilon^2)$. There have been other efforts to utilize parallelism to further improve SFM [BS20].

---

9. This is the same Wolfe as the Wolfe in Frank-Wolfe but not the same algorithm.

6.9.5 Applications of submodularity in machine learning and AI

Submodularity arises naturally in applications in machine learning and artificial intelligence, but its utility has still not yet been as widely recognized and exploited as other techniques. For example, while information theoretic concepts like entropy and mutual information are extremely widely used in machine learning (e.g., the cross-entropy loss for classification is ubiquitous), the submodularity property of entropy is not nearly as widely explored.

Still, in the last several decades, submodularity has been increasingly studied and utilized in the context of machine learning. In the below we begin to provide only a brief survey of some of the major subareas within machine learning that have been touched by submodularity. The list is not meant to be exhaustive, or even extensive. It is hoped that the below should, at least, offer a reasonable introduction into how submodularity has been and can continue to be useful in machine learning and artificial intelligence.

6.9.6 Sketching, coresets, distillation, and data subset and feature Selection

A summary is a concise representation of a body of data that can be used as an effective and efficient substitute for that data. There are many types of summaries, some being extremely simple. For example, the mean or median of a list of numbers summarizes some property (the central tendency) of that list. A random subset is also a form of summary.

Any given summary, however, is not guaranteed to do a good job serving all purposes. Moreover, a summary usually involves at least some degree of approximation and fidelity loss relative to the original, and different summaries are faithful to the original in different ways and for different tasks. For these and other reasons, the field of summarization is rich and diverse, and summarization procedures are often very specialized.

Several distinct names for summarization have been used over the past few decades, including "sketches", "coresets", (in the field of natural language processing) "summaries", and "distillation".

Sketches [Cor17; CY20; Cor+12], arose in the field of computer science and was based on the acknowledgment that data is often too large to fit in memory and too large for an algorithm to run on a given machine, something enabled by a much smaller but still representative, and provably approximate, representation of the data.

Coresets are similar to sketches and there are some properties that are more often associated with coresets than with sketches, but sometimes the distinction is a bit vague. The notion of a coreset [BHPI02; AHP+05; BC08] comes from the field of computational geometry where one is interested in solving certain geometric problems based on a set of points in $\mathbb{R}^d$. For any geometric problem and a set of points, a coreset problem typically involves finding the smallest weighted subset of points so that when an algorithm is run on the weighted subset, it produces approximately the same answer as when it is run on the original large dataset. For example, given a set of points, one might wish to find the diameter of set, or the radius of the smallest enclosing sphere, or finding the narrowest annulus (ring) containing the points, or a subset of points whose k-center clustering is approximately the same as the k-center clustering of the whole [BHPI02].

Document summarization became one of the most important problems in natural language processing (NLP) in the 1990s although the idea of computing a summary of a text goes back much further to the 1950s [Luh58; Edm69], also and coincidentally around the same time that the CliffsNotes [Wik21] organization began. There are two main forms of document summarization [YWX17]. With *extractive summarization* [NM12], a set of sentences (or phrases) are extracted from the documents needing to be summarized, and the resulting subset of sentences, perhaps appropriately ordered, comprises the summary.

With abstractive summarization [LN19], on the other hand, the goal is to produce an "abstract" of the documents, where one is not constrained to have any of the sentences in the abstract correspond to any of the sentences in the original documents. With abstractive summarization, therefore, the goal is to synthesize a small set of new pseudo sentences that represent the original documents. CliffsNotes, for example, are abstractive summaries of the literature being represented.

Another form of summarization that has more recently become popular in the machine learning community is *data distillation* [SG06b; Wan+20c; Suc+20; BYH20; NCL20; SS21; Ngu+21] or equivalently *dataset condensation* [ZMB21; ZB21]. With data distillation[10], the goal is to produce a small set of synthetic pseudosamples that can be used, for example, to train a model. The key here is that in the reduced dataset, the samples are not compelled to be the same as, or a subset of, the original dataset.

All of the above should be contrasted with data *compression*, which in some sense is the most extreme data reduction method. With compression, either lossless or lossy, one is no longer under any obligation that the reduced form of the data must be usable, or even recognizable, by any algorithm or entity other than the decoder, or uncompression, algorithm.

6.9.6.1   Summarization Algorithm Design Choices

It is the author's contention that the notions of summarization, coresets, sketching, and distillation are certainly analogous and quite possibly synonymous, and they are all different from compression. The different names for summarization are simply different nomenclatures for the same language game. What matters is not what you call it but the choices one makes when designing a procedure for summarization. And indeed, there are many choices.

Submodularity offers essentially an infinite number of ways to perform data sketching and coresets. When we view the submodular function as an information function (as we discussed in Section 6.9.7), where $f(X)$ is the information contained in set X and $f(V)$ is the maximum available information, finding the small X that maximizes $f(X)$ (i.e., $X^* \in \mathrm{argmax}\{f(X) : |X| \leq k\}$), is a form of coreset computation that is parameterized by the function f which has 2^n parameters since f lives in a 2^n-dimensional cone. Performing this maximization will then minimize the residual information $f(V \setminus X | X)$ about anything not present the summary $V \setminus X$ since $f(V) = f(X \cup V \setminus X) = f(V \setminus X | X) + f(X)$ so maximizing $f(X)$ will minimize $f(V \setminus X | X)$. For every f, moreover, the same algorithm (e.g., the greedy algorithm) can be used to produce the summarization, and in every case, there is an approximation guarantee relative to the current f, as mentioned in earlier sections, as long as f stays submodular. Hence, submodularity provides a universal framework for summarization, coresets, and sketches to the extent that the space of submodular functions itself is sufficiently diverse and spans over different coreset problems.

Overall, the coreset or sketching problem, when using submodular functions, therefore becomes a problem of "submodular design". That is, how do we construct a submodular function that, for a particular problem, acts as a good coreset producer when the function is maximized. There are three general approaches to produce an f that works well as a summarization objective: (1) a pragmatic

---

10. Data distillation is distinct from the notion of *knowledge distillation* [HVD14; BC14; BCNM06] or *model distillation*, where the "knowledge" contained in a large model is distilled or reduced down into a different smaller model.

approach where the function is constructed by hand and heuristics, (2) a learning approach where all or part of the submodular function is inferred from an optimization procedure, and (3) a mathematical approach where a given submodular function when optimized offers of a coreset property.

When the primary goal is a practical and scalable algorithm that can produce an extractive summary that works well on a variety of different data types, and if one is comfortable with heuristics that work well in practice, a good option is to specify a submodular function by hand. For example, given a similarity matrix, it is easy to instantiate a facility location function and maximize it to produce a summary. If there are multiple similarity matrices, one can construct multiple facility location functions and maximize their convex combination. Such an approach is viable and practical and has been used successfully many times in the past for producing good summaries. One of the earliest examples of this is the algorithm presented in [KKT03] that shows how a submodular model can be used to select the most influential nodes in a social network. Perhaps the earliest example of this approach used for data subset selection for machine learning is [LB09] which utilizes a submodular facility location function based on Fisher kernels (gradients wrt parameters of log probabilities) and applies it to unsupervised speech selection to reduce transcription costs. Other examples of this approach includes: [LB10a; LB11] which developed submodular functions for query-focused document summarization; [KB14b] which computes a subset of training data in the context of transductive learning in a statistical machine translation system; [LB10b; Wei+13; Wei+14] which develops submodular functions for speech data subset selection (the former, incidentally, is the first use of a deep submodular function and the latter does this in an unsupervised label-free fashion); [SS18a] which is a form of robust submodularity for producing coresets for training CNNs; [Kau+19] which uses a facility location to facilitate diversity selection in active learning; [Bai+15; CTN17] which develops a mixture of submodular functions for document summarization where the mixture coefficients are also included in the hyperparameter set; and [Xu+15], which uses a symmetrized submodular function for the purposes of video summarization.

The learnability and identifiability of submodular functions has received a good amount of study from a theoretical perspective. Starting with the strictest learning settings, the problem looks pretty dire. For example, [SF08; Goe+09] shows that if one is restricted to making a polynomial number of queries (i.e., training pairs of the form $(S, f(S))$) of a monotone submodular function, then it is not possible to approximate f with a multiplicative approximation factor better than $\tilde{\Omega}(\sqrt{n})$. In [BH11], goodness is judged multiplicatively, meaning for a set $A \subseteq V$ we wish that $\tilde{f}(A) \leq f(A) \leq g(n)f(A)$ for some function $g(n)$, and this is typically a probabilistic condition (i.e., measured by distribution, or $\tilde{f}(A) \leq f(A) \leq g(n)f(A)$, should happen on a fraction at least $1 - \beta$ of the points). Alternatively, goodness may also be measured by an additive approximation error, say by a norm. I.e., defining $\text{err}_p(f, \tilde{f}) = \|f - \tilde{f}\|_p = (E_{A \sim \mathbf{Pr}}[|f(A) - \tilde{f}(A)|^p])^{1/p}$, we may wish $\text{err}_p(f, \tilde{f}) < \epsilon$ for $p = 1$ or $p = 2$. In the PAC (probably approximately correct) model, we probably ($\delta > 0$) approximately ($\epsilon > 0$ or $g(n) > 1$) learn ($\beta = 0$) with a sample or algorithmic complexity that depends on δ and $g(n)$. In the PMAC (probably mostly approximately correct) model [BH11], we also "mostly" $\beta > 0$ learn. In some cases, we wish to learn the best submodular approximation to a non-submodular function. In other cases, we are allowed to deviate from submodularity as long as the error is small. Learning special cases includes coverage functions [FK14; FK13a], and low-degree polynomials [FV15], curvature limited functions [IJB13], functions with a limited "goal" [DHK14; Bac+18], functions that are Fourier sparse [Wen+20a], or that are of a family called "juntas" [FV16], or that come from families other than submodular [DFF21], and still others [BRS17; FKV14; FKV17; FKV20; FKV13; YZ19]. Other results include that one cannot minimize a submodular function by learning it first from samples [BS17]. The essential strategy of learning is to attempt to construct a submodular function approximation $\hat{f}$ from an underlying submodular function f querying the latter only a small number of times. The overall gist of these results is that it is hard to learn everywhere and accurately.

In the machine learning community, learning can be performed extremely efficiently in practice, although there are not the types of guarantees as one finds above. For example, given a mixture of submodular components of the form $f(A) = \sum_i \alpha_i f_i(A)$, if each f_i is considered fixed, then the learning occurs only over the mixture coefficients α_i. This can be solved as a linear regression problem where the optimal coefficients can be computed in a linear regression setting. Alternatively, such functions can be learnt in a max-margin setting where the goal is primarily to adjust α_i to ensure that $f(A)$ is large on certain subsets [SSJ12; LB12; Tsc+14]. Even here there are practical challenges, however, since it is in general hard in practice to obtain a training set of pairs $\{(S_i, F(S_i))\}_i$. Alternatively, one can also "learn" a submodular function in a reinforcement learning setting [CKK17] by optimizing the implicit function directly from gain vectors queried from an environment. In general, such practical learning algorithms have been used for image summarization [Tsc+14], document summarization [LB12], and video summarization [GGG15; Vas+17a; Gon+14; SGS16; SLG17]. While none of these learning approaches claim to approximate some true underlying submodular function, in practice, they do perform better than the by-hand crafting of a submodular function mentioned above.

By a submodularity based coreset, we mean one where the direct optimization of a submodular function offers a theoretical guarantee for some specific problem. This is distinct from above where the submodular function is used as a surrogate heuristic objective function and for which, even if the submodular function is learnt, optimizing it is only a heuristic for the original problem. In some limited cases, it can be shown that the function we wish to approximate is already submodular, e.g., in the case of certain naive Bayes and k-NN classifiers [WIB15] where the training accuracy, as a function of the training data subset, can be shown to be submodular. Hence, maximizing this function offers the same guarantee on the training accuracy as it does on the submodular function. Unfortunately, the accuracy for many models is not a submodular function, although they do have a difference of submodular [NB05; IB12] decomposition.

In other cases, it can be shown that certain desirable coreset objectives are inherently submodular. For example, in [MBL20], it is shown that the normed difference between the overall gradient (from summing over all samples in the training data) and an approximate gradient (from summing over only samples in a summary) can be upper bounded with a supermodular function that, when converted to a submodular facility location function and maximized, will select a set that reduces this difference, and will lead to similar convergence rates to an approximate optimum solution in the convex case. A similar example of this in a DPP context is shown in [TBA19]. In other cases, subsets of the training data and training occur simultaneously using a continuous-discrete optimization framework, where the goal is to minimize the loss on diverse and challenging samples measured by a submodular objective [ZB18]. In still other cases, bi-level objectives related to but not guaranteed to be submodular can be formed where a set is selected from a training set with the deliberate purpose of doing well on a validation set [Kil+20; BMK20].

The methods above have focused on reducing the number of samples in a training dataset. Considering the transpose of a design matrix, however, all of the above methods can be used for reducing the features of a machine learning procedure as well. Specifically, any of the extractive summarization, subset selection, or coreset methods can be seen as feature selection while any of the abstract summarization, sketching, or distillation approaches can be seen as dimensionality reduction.

6.9.7   Combinatorial information functions

The entropy function over a set of random variables $X_1, X_2, \ldots, X_n$ is defined as $H(X_1, X_2, \ldots, X_n) = -\sum_{x_1, x_2, \ldots, x_n} p(x_1, \ldots, x_n) \log p(x_1, \ldots, x_n)$. From this we can define three set-argument conditional mutual information functions as $I_H(A; B|C) = I(X_A; X_B|X_C)$ where the latter is the mutual information between variables indexed by A and B given variables indexed by C. This mutual information expresses the residual information between X_A and X_B that is not explained by their common information with X_C.

As mentioned above, we may view any polymatroid function as a type of information function over subsets of V. That is, $f(A)$ is the information in set A — to the extent that this is true, this property justifies f's use as a summarization objective as mentioned above. The reason f may be viewed as an information function stems from f being normalized, f's non-negativity, f's monotonicity, and the property that further conditioning reduces valuation (i.e., $f(A|B) \geq f(A|B, C)$ which is identical to the submodularity property). These properties were deemed as essential to the entropy function in Shannon's original work [Sha48] but are true of any polymatroid function as well. Hence, given any polymatroid function f, is it possible to define a combinatorial mutual information function [Iye+21] in a similar way. Specifically, we can define the combinatorial (submodular) conditional mutual information (CCMI) as $I_f(A; B|C) = f(A + C) + f(B + C) - f(C) - f(A + B + C)$, which has been known as the connectivity function [Cun83] amongst other names. If f is the entropy function, then this yields the standard entropic mutual information but here the mutual information can be defined for any submodular information measure f. For an arbitrary polymatroid f, therefore, $I_f(A; B|C)$ can be seen as an A, B set-pair similarity score that ignores, neglects, or discounts any common similarity between the A, B pair that is due to C.

Historical use of a special case of CCMI, i.e., $I_f(A; B)$ where $C = \emptyset$, occurred in a number of circumstances. For example, in [GKS05] the function $g(A) = I_f(A; V \setminus A)$ (which, incidentally, is both symmetric ($g(A) = g(V \setminus A)$ for all A) and submodular) was optimized using the greedy procedure; this has a guarantee as long as $g(A)$ is monotone up $2k$ elements whenever one wishes for a summary of size k. This was done for f being the entropy function, but it can be used for any polymatroid function. In similar work, where f is the Shannon entropy function, [KG05] demonstrated that $g_C(A) = I_f(A; C)$ (for a fixed set C) is not submodular in A but if it is the case that the elements of V are independent given C then submodularity is preserved. This can be immediately seen by the consequence of this independence assumption which yields that $I_f(A; C) = f(A) - f(A|C) = f(A) - \sum_{a \in A} f(a|C)$ where the second equality is due to the conditional independence property. In this case, I_f is the difference between a submodular and a modular function which preserves submodularity for any polymatroid f.

On the other hand, it would be useful for $g_{B,C}(A) = I_f(A; B|C)$, where B and C are fixed, to be possible to optimize in terms of A. One can view this function as one that, when it is maximized, chooses A to be similar to B in a way that neglects or discounts any common similarity that A and B have with C. One option to optimize this function to utilize difference of submodular [NB05; IB12] optimization as mentioned earlier. A more recent result shows that in some cases $g_{B,C}(A)$ is still submodular in A. Define the second-order partial derivative of a submodular function f as follows $f(i, j|S) \triangleq f(j|S + i) - f(j|S)$. Then if it is the case that $f(i, j|S)$ is monotone non-decreasing in S for $S \subseteq V \setminus \{i, j\}$ then $I_f(A; B|C)$ is submodular in A for fixed B and C. It may be thought that only esoteric functions have this property, but in fact [Iye+21] shows that this is true for a number of widely used submodular functions in practice, including the facility location function which results in the form $I_f(A; B|C) = \sum_{v \in V} \max\left(\min\left(\sum_{a \in A} \text{sim}(v, a), \max_{b \in B} \text{sim}(v, b)\right) - \max_{c \in C} \text{sim}(v, c), 0\right)$. This function was used [Kot+22] to produce summaries A that were particularly relevant to a query given by B but that should neglect information in C that can be considered "private" information to avoid.

6.9.8   Clustering, data partitioning, and parallel machine learning

There are an almost unlimited number of clustering algorithms and a plethora of reviews on their variants. Any given submodular function can also instantiate a clustering procedure as well, and there are several ways to do this. Here we offer only a brief outline of the approach. In the last section, we defined $I_f(A; V \setminus A)$ as the CCMI between A and everything but A. When we view this as a function of A, then $g(A) = I_f(A; V \setminus A)$ and $g(A)$ is a symmetric submodular function that can be minimized using Queyranne's algorithm [Que98; NI92]. Once this is done, the resulting A is such that it is least similar to $V \setminus A$, according to $I_f(A; V \setminus A)$ and hence forms a 2-clustering. This process can then be recursively applied where we form two new functions $g_A(B) = I_f(B; A \setminus B)$ for $B \subseteq A$ and $g_{V \setminus A}(B) = I_f(B; (V \setminus A) \setminus B)$ for $B \subseteq V \setminus A$. These are two symmetric submodular functions on different ground sets that also can be minimized using Queyranne's algorithm. This recursive bisection algorithm then repeats until the desired number of clusters is formed. Hence, the CCMI function can be used as a top-down recursive bisection clustering procedure and has been called Q-clustering [NJB05; NB06]. It should be noted that such forms of clustering often generalize forming a multiway cut in an undirected graph in which case the objective becomes the graph-cut function that, as we saw above, is also submodular. In some cases, the number of clusters need not be specified in advance [NKI10]. Another submodular approach to clustering can be found in [Wei+15b] where the goal is to minimize the maximum valued block in a partitioning which can lead to submodular load balancing or minimum makespan scheduling [HS88; LST90].

Yet another form of clustering can be seen via the simple cardinality constrained submodular maximization process itself which can be compared to a k-medoids process whenever the objective f is the facility location function. Hence, any such submodular function can be seen as a submodular-function-parameterized form of finding the k "centers" among a set of data items. There have been numerous applications of submodular clustering. For example, using these techniques it is possible to identify parcellations of the human brain [Sal+17a]. Other applications include partitioning data for more effective and accurate and lower variance distributed machine learning training [Wei+15a] and also for more ideal mini-batch construction for training deep neural networks [Wan+19b].

6.9.9   Active and semi-supervised learning

Suppose we are given dataset $\{x_i, y_i\}_{i \in V}$ consisting of $|V| = n$ samples of x, y pairs but where the labels are unknown. Samples are labeled one at a time or one mini-batch at a time, and after each labeling step t each remaining unlabeled sample is given a score $s_t(x_i)$ that indicates the potential benefit of acquiring a label for that sample. Examples include the entropy of the model's output distribution on x_i, or a margin-based score consisting of the difference between the top and the second-from-the-top posterior probability. This produces a modular function on the unlabeled samples, $m_t(A) = \sum_{a \in A} s(x_a)$ where $A \subseteq V$. It is simple to use this modular function to produce a mini-batch active learning procedure where at each stage we form $A_t \in \text{argmax}_{A \subseteq U_t : |A| = k} m_t(A)$

where U_t is the set of unlabeled samples at stage t. Then A_t is a set of size k that gets labeled, we form $U_t = U_t \setminus A_t$, update $s_t(a)$ for $a \in U_t$, and repeat. This is called **active learning**.

The reason for using active learning with mini-batches of size greater than one is that it is often inefficient to ask for a single label at a time. The problem with such a minibatch strategy, however, is that the set A_t can be redundant. The reason is that the uncertainty about every sample in A_t could be owing to the same underlying cause — even though the model is most uncertain about samples in A_t, once one sample in A_t is labeled, it may not be optimal to label the remaining samples in A_t due to this redundancy. Utilizing submodularity, therefore, can help reduce this redundancy. Suppose $f_t(A)$ is a submodular diversity model over samples at step t. At each stage, choosing the set of samples to label becomes $A_t \in \mathrm{argmax}_{A \subseteq U_t : |A| = k} m_t(A) + f_t(A)$ — A_t is selected based on a combination of both uncertainty (via $m_t(A)$) and diversity (via $f_t(A)$). This is precisely the submodular active learning approach taken in [WIB15; Kau+19].

Another quite different approach to a form of submodular "batch" active learning setting where a batch L of labeled samples are selected all at once and then used to label the rest of the unlabeled samples. This also allows the remaining unlabeled samples to be utilized in a semi-supervised framework [GB09; GB11]. In this setting, we start with a graph $G = (V, E)$ where the nodes V need to be given a binary $\{0, 1\}$-valued label, $y \in \{0, 1\}^V$. For any $A \subseteq V$ let $y_A \in \{0, 1\}^A$ be the labels just for node set A. We also define $V(y) \subseteq V$ as $V(y) = \{v \in V : y_v = 1\}$. Hence $V(y)$ are the graph nodes labeled 1 by y and $V \setminus V(y)$ are the nodes labeled 0. Given submodular objective f, we form its symmetric CCMI variant $I_f(A) \triangleq I_f(A; V \setminus A)$ — note that $I_f(A)$ is always submodular in A. This allows $I_f(V(y))$ to determine the "smoothness" of a given candidate labeling y. For example, if I_f is the weighted graph cut function where each weight corresponds to an affinity between the corresponding two nodes, then $I_f(V(y))$ would be small if $V(y)$ (the 1-labeled nodes) do not have strong affinity with $V \setminus V(y)$ (the 0-labeled nodes). In general, however, I_f can be any symmetric submodular function. Let $L \subseteq V$ be any candidate set of nodes to be labeled, and define $\Psi(L) \triangleq \min_{T \subseteq (V \setminus L) : T \neq \emptyset} I_f(T)/|T|$. Then $\Psi(L)$ measures the "strength" of L in that if $\Psi(L)$ is small, an adversary can label nodes other than L without being too unsmooth according to I_f, while if $\Psi(L)$ is large, an adversary can do no such thing. Then [GB11] showed that given a node set L to be queried, and the corresponding correct labels y_L that are completed (in a semi-supervised fashion) according to the following $y' = \mathrm{argmin}_{\hat{y} \in \{0,1\}^V : \hat{y}_L = y_L} I_f(V(\hat{y}))$, then this results in the following bound on the true labeling $\|y - y'\|^2 \leq 2 I_f(V(y))/\Psi(L)$ suggesting that we can find a good set to query by maximizing L in $\Psi(L)$, and this holds for any submodular function. Of course, it is necessary to find an underlying submodular function f that fits a given problem, and this is discussed in Section 6.9.6.

6.9.10 Probabilistic modeling

Graphical models are often used to describe factorization requirements on families of probability distributions. Factorization is not the only way, however, to describe restrictions on such families. In a graphical model, graphs describe only which random variable may directly interact with other random variables. An entirely different strategy for producing families of often-tractable probabilistic models can be produced without requiring any factorization property at all. Considering an energy function $E(x)$ where $p(x) \propto \exp(-E(x))$, factorizations correspond to there being cliques in the graph such that the graph's tree-width often is limited. On the other hand, finding $\max_x p(x)$ is the same as finding $\min_x E(x)$, something that can be done if $E(x) = f(V(x))$ is a submodular function (using the earlier used notation $V(x)$ to map from binary vectors to subsets of V). Even a submodular function as simple as $f(A) = \sqrt{|A|} - m(A)$ where m is modular has tree-width of $n-1$, and this leads to an energy function $E(x)$ that allows $\max_x p(x)$ to be solved in polynomial time using submodular function minimization (see Section 6.9.4.3). Such restrictions to $E(x)$ therefore are not of the form *amongst the random variables, who is allowed to directly interact with whom*, but rather *amongst the random variables, what is the manner that they interact*. Such potential function restrictions can also combine with direct interaction restrictions as well, and this has been widely used in computer vision, leading to cases where graph-cut and graph-cut like "move making" algorithms (such as $\alpha - \beta$ swap and α-expansion algorithms) used in attractive models (see Supplementary Section 9.3.4.3). In fact, the culmination of these efforts [KZ02] lead to a rediscovery of the submodularity (or the "regular" property) as being the essential ingredient for when Markov random fields can be solved using graph cut minimization, which is a special case of submodular function minimization.

The above model can be seen as log-supermodular since $\log p(x) = -E(x) + \log 1/Z$ is a supermodular function. These are all distributions that put high probability on configurations that yield small valuation by a submodular function. Therefore, these distributions have high probability when x consists of a homogeneous set of assignments to the elements of x. For this reason, they are useful for computer vision segmentation problems (e.g., in a segment of an image, the nearby pixels should roughly be homogeneous as that is often what defines an object). The DPPs we saw above, however, are an example of a log-submodular probability distribution since $f(X) = \log \det(\mathbf{M}_X)$ is submodular. These models have high probability for diverse sets.

More generally, $E(x)$ being either a submodular or supermodular function can produce log-submodular or log-supermodular distributions, covering both cases above where the partition function takes the form $Z = \sum_{A \subseteq V} \exp(f(A))$ for objective f. Moreover, we often wish to perform tasks much more than just finding the most probable random variable assignments. This includes marginalization, computing the partition function, constrained maximization, and so on. Unfortunately, many of these more general probabilistic inference problems do not have polynomial time solutions even though the objectives are submodular or supermodular. On the other hand, such structure has opened the doors to an assortment of new probabilistic inference procedures that exploit this structure [DK14; DK15a; DTK16; ZDK15; DJK18]. Most of these methods were of the variational sort and offered bounds on the partition function Z, sometimes making use of the fact that submodular functions have easily computable semi-gradients [IB15; Fuj05] which are modular upper and lower bounds on a submodular or supermodular function that are tight at one or more subsets. Given a submodular (or supermodular) function f and a set A, it is possible to easily construct (in linear time) a modular function upper bound $m^A : 2^V \to \mathbb{R}$ and a modular function lower bound $m_A : 2^V \to \mathbb{R}$ having the properties that $m_A(X) \leq f(X) \leq m^A(X)$ for all $X \subseteq V$ and that is tight at $X = A$ meaning $m_A(A) = f(A) = m^A(A)$ [IB15]. For any modular function m, the probability function for a characteristic vector $x = \mathbf{1}_A$ becomes $p(\mathbf{1}_A) = 1/Z \exp(E(\mathbf{1}_A)) = \prod_{a \in A} \sigma(m(a)) \prod_{a \notin A} \sigma(-m(a))$ where σ is the logistic function. Thus, a modular approximation of a submodular function is like a mean-field approximation of the distribution and makes the assumption that all random variables are independent. Such an approximation can then be used to compute quantities such as upper and lower bounds on the partition function, and much else.

6.9.11 Structured norms and loss functions

Convex norms are used ubiquitously in machine learning, often as complexity penalizing regularizers (e.g., the ubiquitous p-norms for $p \geq 1$) and also sometimes as losses (e.g., squared error). Identifying new useful structured and possibly learnable sparse norms is an interesting and useful endeavor, and submodularity can help here as well. Firstly, recall the ℓ_0 or counting norm $\|x\|_0$ simply counts the number of nonzero entries in x. When we wish for a sparse solution, we may wish to regularize using $\|x\|_0$ but it both leads to an intractable combinatorial optimization problem, and it leads to an object that is not differentiable. The usual approach is to find the closest convex relaxation of this norm and that is the one norm or $\|x\|_1$. This is convex in x and has a sub-gradient structure and hence can be combined with a loss function to produce an optimizable machine learning objective, for example the lasso. On the other hand, $\|x\|_1$ has no structure, as each element of x is penalized based on its absolute value irrespective of the state of any of the other elements. There have thus been efforts to develop group norms that penalize groups or subsets of elements of x together, such as group lasso [HTW15].

It turns out that there is a way to utilize a submodular function as the regularizer. Penalizing x via $\|x\|_0$ is identical to penalizing it via $|V(x)|$ and note that $m(A) = |A|$ is a modular function. Instead, we could penalize x via $f(V(x))$ for a submodular function f. Here, any element of x being non-zero would allow for a diminishing penalty of other elements of x being zero all according to the submodular function, and such cooperative penalties can be obtained via a submodular parameterization. Like when using the zero-norm $\|x\|_0$, this leads to the same combinatorial problem due to continuous optimization of x with a penalty term of the form $f(V(x))$. To address this, we can use the Lovász extension $\breve{f}(x)$ on a vector x. This function is convex, but it is not a norm, but if we consider the construct defined as $\|x\|_f = \breve{f}(|x|)$, it can be shown that this satisfies all the properties of a norm for all non-trivial submodular functions [PG98; Bac+13] (i.e., those normalized submodular functions for which $f(v) > 0$ for all v). In fact, the group lasso mentioned above is a special case for a particularly simple feature-based submodular function (a sum of min-truncated cardinality functions). But in principle, the same submodular design strategies mentioned in Section 6.9.6 can be used to produce a submodular function to instantiate an appropriate convex structured norm for a given machine learning problem.

6.9.12 Conclusions

We have only barely touched the surface of submodularity and how it applies to and can benefit machine learning. For more details, see [Bil22] and the many references contained therein. Considering once again the innocuous looking submodular inequality, then very much like the definition of convexity, we observe something that belies much of its complexity while opening the gates to wide and worthwhile avenues for machine learning exploration.

PART II

Inference

7 Inference algorithms: an overview

7.1 Introduction

In the probabilistic approach to machine learning, all unknown quantities — be they predictions about the future, hidden states of a system, or parameters of a model — are treated as random variables, and endowed with probability distributions. The process of **inference** corresponds to computing the posterior distribution over these quantities, conditioning on whatever data is available.

In more detail, let $\boldsymbol{\theta}$ represent the unknown variables, and $\mathcal{D}$ represent the known variables. Given a likelihood $p(\mathcal{D}|\boldsymbol{\theta})$ and a prior $p(\boldsymbol{\theta})$, we can compute the posterior $p(\boldsymbol{\theta}|\mathcal{D})$ using Bayes' rule:

$$p(\boldsymbol{\theta}|\mathcal{D}) = \frac{p(\boldsymbol{\theta})p(\mathcal{D}|\boldsymbol{\theta})}{p(\mathcal{D})} \tag{7.1}$$

The main computational bottleneck is computing the normalization constant in the denominator, which requires solving the following high dimensional integral:

$$p(\mathcal{D}) = \int p(\mathcal{D}|\boldsymbol{\theta})p(\boldsymbol{\theta})d\boldsymbol{\theta} \tag{7.2}$$

This is needed to convert the unnormalized joint probability of some parameter value, $p(\boldsymbol{\theta}, \mathcal{D})$, to a normalized probability, $p(\boldsymbol{\theta}|\mathcal{D})$, which takes into account all the other plausible values that $\boldsymbol{\theta}$ could have.

Once we have the posterior, we can use it to compute posterior expectations of some function of the unknown variables, i.e.,

$$\mathbb{E}\left[g(\boldsymbol{\theta})|\mathcal{D}\right] = \int g(\boldsymbol{\theta})p(\boldsymbol{\theta}|\mathcal{D})d\boldsymbol{\theta} \tag{7.3}$$

By defining g in the appropriate way, we can compute many quantities of interest, such as the following:

$$\text{mean: } g(\boldsymbol{\theta}) = \boldsymbol{\theta} \tag{7.4}$$

$$\text{covariance: } g(\boldsymbol{\theta}) = (\boldsymbol{\theta} - \mathbb{E}\left[\boldsymbol{\theta}|\mathcal{D}\right])(\boldsymbol{\theta} - \mathbb{E}\left[\boldsymbol{\theta}|\mathcal{D}\right])^{\mathsf{T}} \tag{7.5}$$

$$\text{marginals: } g(\boldsymbol{\theta}) = p(\theta_1 = \theta_1^*|\boldsymbol{\theta}_{2:D}) \tag{7.6}$$

$$\text{predictive: } g(\boldsymbol{\theta}) = p(\boldsymbol{y}_{N+1}|\boldsymbol{\theta}) \tag{7.7}$$

$$\text{expected loss: } g(\boldsymbol{\theta}) = \ell(\boldsymbol{\theta}, a) \tag{7.8}$$

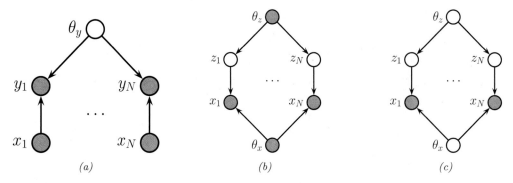

Figure 7.1: Graphical models with (a) global hidden variables for representing the Bayesian discriminative model $p(\boldsymbol{y}_{1:N}, \boldsymbol{\theta}_y | \boldsymbol{x}_{1:N}) = p(\boldsymbol{\theta}_y) \prod_{n=1}^{N} p(\boldsymbol{y}_n | \boldsymbol{x}_n; \boldsymbol{\theta}_y)$; (b) local hidden variables for representing the generative model $p(\boldsymbol{x}_{1:N}, \boldsymbol{z}_{1:N} | \boldsymbol{\theta}) = \prod_{n=1}^{N} p(\boldsymbol{z}_n | \boldsymbol{\theta}_z) p(\boldsymbol{x}_n | \boldsymbol{z}_n, \boldsymbol{\theta}_x)$; (c) local and global hidden variables for representing the Bayesian generative model $p(\boldsymbol{x}_{1:N}, \boldsymbol{z}_{1:N}, \boldsymbol{\theta}) = p(\boldsymbol{\theta}_z) p(\boldsymbol{\theta}_x) \prod_{n=1}^{N} p(\boldsymbol{z}_n | \boldsymbol{\theta}_z) p(\boldsymbol{x}_n | \boldsymbol{z}_n, \boldsymbol{\theta}_x)$. Shaded nodes are assumed to be known (observed), unshaded nodes are hidden.

where $\boldsymbol{y}_{N+1}$ is the next observation after seeing the N examples in $\mathcal{D}$, and the posterior expected loss is computing using loss function ℓ and action a (see Section 34.1.3). Finally, if we define $g(\boldsymbol{\theta}) = p(\mathcal{D}|\boldsymbol{\theta}, M)$ for model M, we can also phrase the marginal likelihood (Section 3.8.3) as an expectation wrt the prior:

$$\mathbb{E}\left[g(\boldsymbol{\theta})|\mathcal{D}\right] = \int g(\boldsymbol{\theta}) p(\boldsymbol{\theta}|M) d\boldsymbol{\theta} = \int p(\mathcal{D}|\boldsymbol{\theta}, M) p(\boldsymbol{\theta}|M) d\boldsymbol{\theta} = p(\mathcal{D}|M) \tag{7.9}$$

Thus we see that integration (and computing expectations) is at the heart of Bayesian inference, whereas differentiation is at the heart of optimization.

In this chapter, we give a high level summary of algorithmic techniques for computing (approximate) posteriors, and/or their corresponding expectations. We will give more details in the following chapters. Note that most of these methods are independent of the specific model. This allows problem solvers to focus on creating the best model possible for the task, and then relying on some inference engine to do the rest of the work — this latter process is sometimes called "**turning the Bayesian crank**". For more details on Bayesian computation, see e.g., [Gel+14a; MKL21; MFR20].

7.2   Common inference patterns

There are kinds of posterior we may want to compute, but we can identify 3 main patterns, as we discuss below. These give rise to different types of inference algorithm, as we will see in later chapters.

7.2.1   Global latents

The first pattern arises when we need to perform inference in models which have **global latent variables**, such as parameters of a model $\boldsymbol{\theta}$, which are shared across all N observed training cases. This is shown in Figure 7.1a, and corresponds to the usual setting for supervised or discriminative learning, where the joint distribution has the form

$$p(\boldsymbol{y}_{1:N}, \boldsymbol{\theta} | \boldsymbol{x}_{1:N}) = p(\boldsymbol{\theta}) \left[\prod_{n=1}^{N} p(\boldsymbol{y}_n | \boldsymbol{x}_n, \boldsymbol{\theta}) \right] \tag{7.10}$$

The goal is to compute the posterior $p(\boldsymbol{\theta} | \boldsymbol{x}_{1:N}, \boldsymbol{y}_{1:N})$. Most of the Bayesian supervised learning models discussed in Part III follow this pattern.

7.2.2 Local latents

The second pattern arises when we need to perform inference in models which have **local latent variables**, such as hidden states $\boldsymbol{z}_{1:N}$; we assume the model parameters $\boldsymbol{\theta}$ are known. This is shown in Figure 7.1b. Now the joint distribution has the form

$$p(\boldsymbol{x}_{1:N}, \boldsymbol{z}_{1:N} | \boldsymbol{\theta}) = \left[\prod_{n=1}^{N} p(\boldsymbol{x}_n | \boldsymbol{z}_n, \boldsymbol{\theta}_x) p(\boldsymbol{z}_n | \boldsymbol{\theta}_z) \right] \tag{7.11}$$

The goal is to compute $p(\boldsymbol{z}_n | \boldsymbol{x}_n, \boldsymbol{\theta})$ for each n. This is the setting we consider for most of the PGM inference methods in Chapter 9.

If the parameters are not known (which is the case for most latent variable models, such as mixture models), we may choose to estimate them by some method (e.g., maximum likelihood), and then plug in this point estimate. The advantage of this approach is that, conditional on $\boldsymbol{\theta}$, all the latent variables are conditionally independent, so we can perform inference in parallel across the data. This lets us use methods such as expectation maximization (Section 6.5.3), in which we infer $p(\boldsymbol{z}_n | \boldsymbol{x}_n, \boldsymbol{\theta}_t)$ in the E step for all n simultaneously, and then update $\boldsymbol{\theta}_t$ in the M step. If the inference of $\boldsymbol{z}_n$ cannot be done exactly, we can use variational inference, a combination known as variational EM (Section 6.5.6.1).

Alternatively, we can use a minibatch approximation to the likelihood, marginalizing out $\boldsymbol{z}_n$ for each example in the minibatch to get

$$\log p(\mathcal{D}_t | \boldsymbol{\theta}_t) = \sum_{n \in \mathcal{D}_t} \log \left[\sum_{\boldsymbol{z}_n} p(\boldsymbol{x}_n, \boldsymbol{z}_n | \boldsymbol{\theta}_t) \right] \tag{7.12}$$

where $\mathcal{D}_t$ is the minibatch at step t. If the marginalization cannot be done exactly, we can use variational inference, a combination known as stochastic variational inference or SVI (Section 10.1.4). We can also learn an inference network $q_\phi(\boldsymbol{z} | \boldsymbol{x}; \boldsymbol{\theta})$ to perform the inference for us, rather than running an inference engine for each example n in each batch t; the cost of learning ϕ can be amortized across the batches. This is called amortized SVI (see Section 10.1.5).

7.2.3 Global and local latents

The third pattern arises when we need to perform inference in models which have **local and global latent variables**. This is shown in Figure 7.1c, and corresponds to the following joint distribution:

$$p(\boldsymbol{x}_{1:N}, \boldsymbol{z}_{1:N}, \boldsymbol{\theta}) = p(\boldsymbol{\theta}_x) p(\boldsymbol{\theta}_z) \left[\prod_{n=1}^{N} p(\boldsymbol{x}_n | \boldsymbol{z}_n, \boldsymbol{\theta}_x) p(\boldsymbol{z}_n | \boldsymbol{\theta}_z) \right] \tag{7.13}$$

This is essentially a Bayesian version of the latent variable model in Figure 7.1b, where now we model uncertainty in both the local variables $\boldsymbol{z}_n$ and the shared global variables $\boldsymbol{\theta}$. This approach is less common in the ML community, since it is often assumed that the uncertainty in the parameters $\boldsymbol{\theta}$ is negligible compared to the uncertainty in the local variables $\boldsymbol{z}_n$. The reason for this is that the parameters are "informed" by all N data cases, whereas each local latent $\boldsymbol{z}_n$ is only informed by a single datapoint, namely $\boldsymbol{x}_n$. Nevertheless, there are advantages to being "fully Bayesian", and modeling uncertainty in both local and global variables. We will see some examples of this later in the book.

7.3   Exact inference algorithms

In some cases, we can perform example posterior inference in a tractable manner. In particular, if the prior is **conjugate** to the likelihood, the posterior will be analytically tractable. In general, this will be the case when the prior and likelihood are from the same exponential family (Section 2.4). In particular, if the unknown variables are represented by $\boldsymbol{\theta}$, then we assume

$$p(\boldsymbol{\theta}) \propto \exp(\boldsymbol{\lambda}_0^{\mathsf{T}} \mathcal{T}(\boldsymbol{\theta})) \tag{7.14}$$

$$p(\boldsymbol{y}_i|\boldsymbol{\theta}) \propto \exp(\tilde{\boldsymbol{\lambda}}_i(\boldsymbol{y}_i)^{\mathsf{T}} \mathcal{T}(\boldsymbol{\theta})) \tag{7.15}$$

where $\mathcal{T}(\boldsymbol{\theta})$ are the sufficient statistics, and $\boldsymbol{\lambda}$ are the natural parameters. We can then compute the posterior by just adding the natural parameters:

$$p(\boldsymbol{\theta}|\boldsymbol{y}_{1:N}) = \exp(\boldsymbol{\lambda}_*^{\mathsf{T}} \mathcal{T}(\boldsymbol{\theta})) \tag{7.16}$$

$$\boldsymbol{\lambda}_* = \boldsymbol{\lambda}_0 + \sum_{n=1}^{N} \tilde{\boldsymbol{\lambda}}_n(\boldsymbol{y}_n) \tag{7.17}$$

See Section 3.4 for details.

Another setting where we can compute the posterior exactly arises when the D unknown variables are all discrete, each with K states; in this case, the integral for the normalizing constant becomes a sum with K^D terms. In many cases, K^D will be too large to be tractable. However, if the distribution satisfies certain conditional independence properties, as expressed by a probabilistic graphical model (PGM), then we can write the joint as a product of local terms (see Chapter 4). This lets us use dynamic programming to make the computation tractable (see Chapter 9).

7.4   Approximate inference algorithms

For most probability models, we will not be able to compute marginals or posteriors exactly, so we must resort to using **approximate inference**. There are many different algorithms, which trade off speed, accuracy, simplicity, and generality. We briefly discuss some of these algorithms below, and give more detail in the following chapters. (See also [Alq22; MFR20] for a review of various methods.)

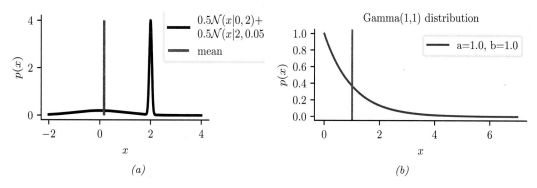

Figure 7.2: *Two distributions in which the mode (highest point) is untypical of the distribution; the mean (vertical red line) is a better summary. (a) A bimodal distribution. Generated by* bimodal_dist_plot.ipynb. *(b) A skewed* Ga(1, 1) *distribution. Generated by* gamma_dist_plot.ipynb.

7.4.1 The MAP approximation and its problems

The simplest approximate inference method is to compute the MAP estimate

$$\hat{\boldsymbol{\theta}} = \operatorname{argmax} p(\boldsymbol{\theta}|\mathcal{D}) = \operatorname{argmax} \log p(\boldsymbol{\theta}) + \log p(\mathcal{D}|\boldsymbol{\theta}) \tag{7.18}$$

and then to assume that the posterior puts 100% of its probability on this single value:

$$p(\boldsymbol{\theta}|\mathcal{D}) \approx \delta(\boldsymbol{\theta} - \hat{\boldsymbol{\theta}}) \tag{7.19}$$

The advantage of this approach is that we can compute the MAP estimate using a variety of optimization algorithms, which we discuss in Chapter 6. However, the MAP estimate also has various drawbacks, some of which we discuss below.

7.4.1.1 The MAP estimate gives no measure of uncertainty

In many statistical applications (especially in science) it is important to know how much one can trust a given parameter estimate. Obviously a point estimate does not convey any notion of uncertainty. Although it is possible to derive frequentist notions of uncertainty from a point estimate (see Section 3.3.1), it is arguably much more natural to just compute the posterior, from which we can derive useful quantities such as the standard error (see Section 3.2.1.6) and credible regions (see Section 3.2.1.7).

In the context of prediction (which is the main focus in machine learning), we saw in Section 3.2.2 that plugging in a point estimate can underestimate the predictive uncertainty, which can result in predictions which are not just wrong, but confidently wrong. It is generally considered very important for a predictive model to "know what it does not know", and the Bayesian approach is a good strategy for achieving this goal.

7.4.1.2 The MAP estimate is often untypical of the posterior

In some cases, we may not be interested in uncertainty, and instead we just want a single summary of the posterior. However, the mode of a posterior distribution is often a very poor choice as a

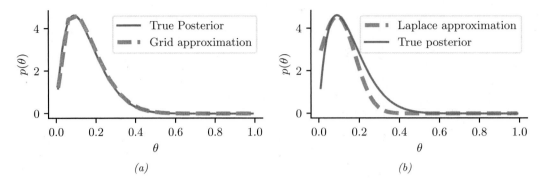

Figure 7.3: Approximating the posterior of a beta-Bernoulli model. (a) Grid approximation using 20 grid points. (b) Laplace approximation. Generated by laplace_ approx_ beta_ binom.ipynb.

summary statistic, since the mode is usually quite untypical of the distribution, unlike the mean or median. This is illustrated in Figure 7.2(a) for a 1d continuous space, where we see that the mode is an isolated peak (black line), far from most of the probability mass. By contrast, the mean (red line) is near the middle of the distribution.

Another example is shown in Figure 7.2(b): here the mode is 0, but the mean is non-zero. Such skewed distributions often arise when inferring variance parameters, especially in hierarchical models. In such cases the MAP estimate (and hence the MLE) is obviously a very bad estimate.

7.4.1.3   The MAP estimate is not invariant to reparameterization

A more subtle problem with MAP estimation is that the result we get depends on how we parameterize the probability distribution, which is not very desirable. For example, when representing a Bernoulli distribution, we should be able to parameterize it in terms of probability of success, or in terms of the log-odds (logit), without that affecting our beliefs.

For example, let $\hat{x} = \text{argmax}_x \, p_x(x)$ be the MAP estimate for x. Now let $y = f(x)$ be a transformation of x. In general it is not the case that $\hat{y} = \text{argmax}_y \, p_y(y)$ is given by $f(\hat{x})$. For example, let $x \sim \mathcal{N}(6, 1)$ and $y = f(x)$, where $f(x) = \frac{1}{1+\exp(-x+5)}$. We can use the change of variables (Section 2.5.1) to conclude $p_y(y) = p_x(f^{-1}(y))|\frac{df^{-1}(y)}{dy}|$. Alternatively we can use a Monte Carlo approximation. The result is shown in Figure 2.12. We see that the original Gaussian for $p(x)$ has become "squashed" by the sigmoid nonlinearity. In particular, we see that the mode of the transformed distribution is not equal to the transform of the original mode.

We have seen that the MAP estimate depends on the parameterization. The MLE does not suffer from this since the likelihood is a function, not a probability density. Bayesian inference does not suffer from this problem either, since the change of measure is taken into account when integrating over the parameter space.

7.4.2   Grid approximation

If we want to capture uncertainty, we need to allow for the fact that $\boldsymbol{\theta}$ may have a range of possible values, each with non-zero probability. The simplest way to capture this property is to partition the space of possible values into a finite set of regions, call them $r_1, \ldots, r_K$, each representing a region of parameter space of volume Δ centered on $\boldsymbol{\theta}_k$. This is called a **grid approximation**. The probability of being in each region is given by $p(\boldsymbol{\theta} \in r_k|\mathcal{D}) \approx p_k\Delta$, where

$$p_k = \frac{\tilde{p}_k}{\sum_{k'=1}^{K} \tilde{p}_{k'}} \tag{7.20}$$

$$\tilde{p}_k = p(\mathcal{D}|\boldsymbol{\theta}_k)p(\boldsymbol{\theta}_k) \tag{7.21}$$

As K increases, we decrease the size of each grid cell. Thus the denominator is just a simple numerical approximation of the integral

$$p(\mathcal{D}) = \int p(\mathcal{D}|\boldsymbol{\theta})p(\boldsymbol{\theta})d\boldsymbol{\theta} \approx \sum_{k=1}^{K} \Delta\tilde{p}_k \tag{7.22}$$

As a simple example, we will use the problem of approximating the posterior of a beta-Bernoulli model. Specifically, the goal is to approximate

$$p(\theta|\mathcal{D}) \propto \left[\prod_{n=1}^{N} \text{Ber}(y_n|\theta)\right] \text{Beta}(1,1) \tag{7.23}$$

where $\mathcal{D}$ consists of 10 heads and 1 tail (so the total number of observations is $N = 11$), with a uniform prior. Although we can compute this posterior exactly using the method discussed in Section 3.4.1, this serves as a useful pedagogical example since we can compare the approximation to the exact answer. Also, since the target distribution is just 1d, it is easy to visualize the results.

In Figure 7.3a, we illustrate the grid approximation applied to our 1d problem. We see that it is easily able to capture the skewed posterior (due to the use of an imbalanced sample of 10 heads and 1 tail). Unfortunately, this approach does not scale to problems in more than 2 or 3 dimensions, because the number of grid points grows exponentially with the number of dimensions.

7.4.3 Laplace (quadratic) approximation

In this section, we discuss a simple way to approximate the posterior using a multivariate Gaussian; this known as a **Laplace approximation** or **quadratic approximation** (see e.g., [TK86; RMC09]).

Suppose we write the posterior as follows:

$$p(\boldsymbol{\theta}|\mathcal{D}) = \frac{1}{Z}e^{-\mathcal{E}(\boldsymbol{\theta})} \tag{7.24}$$

where $\mathcal{E}(\boldsymbol{\theta}) = -\log p(\boldsymbol{\theta}, \mathcal{D})$ is called an energy function, and $Z = p(\mathcal{D})$ is the normalization constant. Performing a Taylor series expansion around the mode $\hat{\boldsymbol{\theta}}$ (i.e., the lowest energy state) we get

$$\mathcal{E}(\boldsymbol{\theta}) \approx \mathcal{E}(\hat{\boldsymbol{\theta}}) + (\boldsymbol{\theta} - \hat{\boldsymbol{\theta}})^\mathsf{T}\boldsymbol{g} + \frac{1}{2}(\boldsymbol{\theta} - \hat{\boldsymbol{\theta}})^\mathsf{T}\mathbf{H}(\boldsymbol{\theta} - \hat{\boldsymbol{\theta}}) \tag{7.25}$$

where $\boldsymbol{g}$ is the gradient at the mode, and $\mathbf{H}$ is the Hessian. Since $\hat{\boldsymbol{\theta}}$ is the mode, the gradient term is zero. Hence

$$\hat{p}(\boldsymbol{\theta}, \mathcal{D}) = e^{-\mathcal{E}(\hat{\boldsymbol{\theta}})} \exp\left[-\frac{1}{2}(\boldsymbol{\theta} - \hat{\boldsymbol{\theta}})^{\mathsf{T}} \mathbf{H}(\boldsymbol{\theta} - \hat{\boldsymbol{\theta}})\right] \tag{7.26}$$

$$\hat{p}(\boldsymbol{\theta}|\mathcal{D}) = \frac{1}{Z}\hat{p}(\boldsymbol{\theta}, \mathcal{D}) = \mathcal{N}(\boldsymbol{\theta}|\hat{\boldsymbol{\theta}}, \mathbf{H}^{-1}) \tag{7.27}$$

$$Z = e^{-\mathcal{E}(\hat{\boldsymbol{\theta}})}(2\pi)^{D/2}|\mathbf{H}|^{-\frac{1}{2}} \tag{7.28}$$

The last line follows from normalization constant of the multivariate Gaussian.

The Laplace approximation is easy to apply, since we can leverage existing optimization algorithms to compute the MAP estimate, and then we just have to compute the Hessian at the mode. (In high dimensional spaces, we can use a diagonal approximation.)

In Figure 7.3b, we illustrate this method applied to our 1d problem. Unfortunately we see that it is not a particularly good approximation. This is because the posterior is skewed, whereas a Gaussian is symmetric. In addition, the parameter of interest lies in the constrained interval $\theta \in [0, 1]$, whereas the Gaussian assumes an unconstrained space, $\boldsymbol{\theta} \in \mathbb{R}^D$. Fortunately, we can solve this latter problem by using a change of variable. For example, in this case we can apply the Laplace approximation to $\alpha = \text{logit}(\theta)$. This is a common trick to simplify the job of inference.

See Section 15.3.5 for an application of Laplace approximation to Bayesian logistic regression, and Section 17.3.2 for an application of Laplace approximation to Bayesian neural networks.

7.4.4   Variational inference

In Section 7.4.3, we discussed the Laplace approximation, which uses an optimization procedure to find the MAP estimate, and then approximates the curvature of the posterior at that point based on the Hessian. In this section, we discuss **variational inference** (**VI**), also called **variational Bayes** (**VB**). This is another optimization-based approach to posterior inference, but which has much more modeling flexibility (and thus can give a much more accurate approximation).

VI attempts to approximate an intractable probability distribution, such as $p(\boldsymbol{\theta}|\mathcal{D})$, with one that is tractable, $q(\boldsymbol{\theta})$, so as to minimize some discrepancy D between the distributions:

$$q^* = \operatorname*{argmin}_{q \in \mathcal{Q}} D(q, p) \tag{7.29}$$

where $\mathcal{Q}$ is some tractable family of distributions (e.g., fully factorized distributions). Rather than optimizing over functions q, we typically optimize over the parameters of the function q; we denote these **variational parameters** by $\boldsymbol{\psi}$.

It is common to use the KL divergence (Section 5.1) as the discrepancy measure, which is given by

$$D(q, p) = D_{\mathbb{KL}}\left(q(\boldsymbol{\theta}|\boldsymbol{\psi}) \parallel p(\boldsymbol{\theta}|\mathcal{D})\right) = \int q(\boldsymbol{\theta}|\boldsymbol{\psi}) \log \frac{q(\boldsymbol{\theta}|\boldsymbol{\psi})}{p(\boldsymbol{\theta}|\mathcal{D})} d\boldsymbol{\theta} \tag{7.30}$$

where $p(\boldsymbol{\theta}|\mathcal{D}) = p(\mathcal{D}|\boldsymbol{\theta})p(\boldsymbol{\theta})/p(\mathcal{D})$. The inference problem then reduces to the following optimization

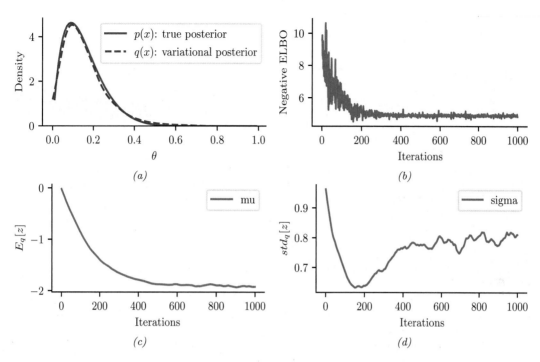

Figure 7.4: ADVI applied to the beta-Bernoulli model. (a) Approximate vs true posterior. (b) Negative ELBO over time. (c) Variational μ parameter over time. (d) Variational σ parameter over time. Generated by advi_beta_binom.ipynb.

problem:

$$\psi^* = \underset{\psi}{\operatorname{argmin}} \, D_{\mathrm{KL}} \left(q(\boldsymbol{\theta}|\boldsymbol{\psi}) \parallel p(\boldsymbol{\theta}|\mathcal{D}) \right) \tag{7.31}$$

$$= \underset{\psi}{\operatorname{argmin}} \, \mathbb{E}_{q(\boldsymbol{\theta}|\boldsymbol{\psi})} \left[\log q(\boldsymbol{\theta}|\boldsymbol{\psi}) - \log \left(\frac{p(\mathcal{D}|\boldsymbol{\theta})p(\boldsymbol{\theta})}{p(\mathcal{D})} \right) \right] \tag{7.32}$$

$$= \underset{\psi}{\operatorname{argmin}} \, \underbrace{\mathbb{E}_{q(\boldsymbol{\theta}|\boldsymbol{\psi})} \left[-\log p(\mathcal{D}|\boldsymbol{\theta}) - \log p(\boldsymbol{\theta}) + \log q(\boldsymbol{\theta}|\boldsymbol{\psi}) \right]}_{-\text{Ł}(\boldsymbol{\psi})} + \log p(\mathcal{D}) \tag{7.33}$$

Note that $\log p(\mathcal{D})$ is independent of $\boldsymbol{\psi}$, so we can ignore it when fitting the approximate posterior, and just focus on maximizing the term

$$\text{Ł}(\boldsymbol{\psi}) \triangleq \mathbb{E}_{q(\boldsymbol{\theta}|\boldsymbol{\psi})} \left[\log p(\mathcal{D}|\boldsymbol{\theta}) + \log p(\boldsymbol{\theta}) - \log q(\boldsymbol{\theta}|\boldsymbol{\psi}) \right] \tag{7.34}$$

Since we have $D_{\mathrm{KL}} \left(q \parallel p \right) \geq 0$, we have $\text{Ł}(\boldsymbol{\psi}) \leq \log p(\mathcal{D})$. The quantity $\log p(\mathcal{D})$, which is the log marginal likelihood, is also called the **evidence**. Hence $\text{Ł}(\boldsymbol{\psi})$ is known as the **evidence lower bound** or **ELBO**. By maximizing this bound, we are making the variational posterior closer to the true posterior. (See Section 10.1 for details.)

We can choose any kind of approximate posterior that we like. For example, we may use a Gaussian, $q(\boldsymbol{\theta}|\boldsymbol{\psi}) = \mathcal{N}(\boldsymbol{\theta}|\boldsymbol{\mu}, \boldsymbol{\Sigma})$. This is different from the Laplace approximation, since in VI, we optimize

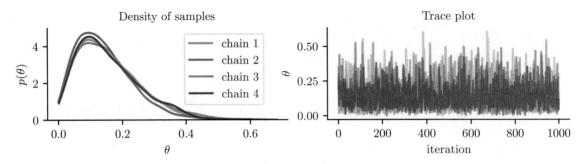

Figure 7.5: Approximating the posterior of a beta-Bernoulli model using MCMC. (a) Kernel density estimate derived from samples from 4 independent chains. (b) Trace plot of the chains as they generate posterior samples. Generated by hmc_beta_binom.ipynb.

Σ, rather than equating it to the Hessian. If Σ is diagonal, we are assuming the posterior is fully factorized; this is called a **mean field** approximation.

A Gaussian approximation is not always suitable for all parameters. For example, in our 1d example we have the constraint that $\theta \in [0, 1]$. We could use a variational approximation of the form $q(\theta|\psi) = \text{Beta}(\theta|a, b)$, where $\psi = (a, b)$. However choosing a suitable form of variational distribution requires some level of expertise. To create a more easily applicable, or "turn-key", method, that works on a wide range of models, we can use a method called **automatic differentiation variational inference** or **ADVI** [Kuc+16]. This uses the change of variables method to convert the parameters to an unconstrained form, and then computes a Gaussian variational approximation. The method also uses automatic differentiation to derive the Jacobian term needed to compute the density of the transformed variables. See Section 10.2.2 for details.

We now apply ADVI to our 1d beta-Bernoulli model. Let $\theta = \sigma(z)$, where we replace $p(\theta|\mathcal{D})$ with $q(z|\psi) = \mathcal{N}(z|\mu, \sigma)$, where $\psi = (\mu, \sigma)$. We optimize a stochastic approximation to the ELBO using SGD. The results are shown in Figure 7.4 and seem reasonable.

7.4.5   Markov chain Monte Carlo (MCMC)

Although VI is fast, it can give a biased approximation to the posterior, since it is restricted to a specific function form $q \in \mathcal{Q}$. A more flexible approach is to use a non-parametric approximation in terms of a set of samples, $q(\boldsymbol{\theta}) \approx \frac{1}{S} \sum_{s=1}^{S} \delta(\boldsymbol{\theta} - \boldsymbol{\theta}^s)$. This is called a **Monte Carlo approximation**. The key issue is how to create the posterior samples $\boldsymbol{\theta}^s \sim p(\boldsymbol{\theta}|\mathcal{D})$ efficiently, without having to evaluate the normalization constant $p(\mathcal{D}) = \int p(\boldsymbol{\theta}, \mathcal{D}) d\boldsymbol{\theta}$.

For low dimensional problems, we can use methods such as **importance sampling**, which we discuss in Section 11.5. However, for high dimensional problems, it is more common to use **Markov chain Monte Carlo** or **MCMC**. We give the details in Chapter 12, but give a brief introduction here.

The most common kind of MCMC is known as the **Metropolis-Hastings algorithm**. The basic idea behind MH is as follows: we start at a random point in parameter space, and then perform a random walk, by sampling new states (parameters) from a **proposal distribution** $q(\boldsymbol{\theta}'|\boldsymbol{\theta})$. If q is chosen carefully, the resulting Markov chain distribution will satisfy the property that the fraction of time we visit each point in space is proportional to the posterior probability. The key point is that to decide whether to move to a newly proposed point $\boldsymbol{\theta}'$ or to stay in the curent point $\boldsymbol{\theta}$, we only need to evaluate the unnormalized density ratio

$$\frac{p(\boldsymbol{\theta}|\mathcal{D})}{p(\boldsymbol{\theta}'|\mathcal{D})} = \frac{p(\mathcal{D}|\boldsymbol{\theta})p(\boldsymbol{\theta})/p(\mathcal{D})}{p(\mathcal{D}|\boldsymbol{\theta}')p(\boldsymbol{\theta}')/p(\mathcal{D})} = \frac{p(\mathcal{D}, \boldsymbol{\theta})}{p(\mathcal{D}, \boldsymbol{\theta}')} \tag{7.35}$$

This avoids the need to compute the normalization constant $p(\mathcal{D})$. (In practice we usually work with log probabilities, instead of joint probabilities, to avoid numerical issues.)

We see that the input to the algorithm is just a function that computes the log joint density, $\log p(\boldsymbol{\theta}, \mathcal{D})$, as well as a proposal distribution $q(\boldsymbol{\theta}'|\boldsymbol{\theta})$ for deciding which states to visit next. It is common to use a Gaussian distribution for the proposal, $q(\boldsymbol{\theta}'|\boldsymbol{\theta}) = \mathcal{N}(\boldsymbol{\theta}'|\boldsymbol{\theta}, \sigma\mathbf{I})$; this is called the **random walk Metropolis** algorithm. However, this can be very inefficient, since it is blindly walking through the space, in the hopes of finding higher probability regions.

In models that have conditional independence structure, it is often easy to compute the **full conditionals** $p(\boldsymbol{\theta}_d|\boldsymbol{\theta}_{-d}, \mathcal{D})$ for each variable d, one at a time, and then sample from them. This is like a stochastic analog of coordinate ascent, and is called **Gibbs sampling** (see Section 12.3 for details).

For models where all unknown variables are continuous, we can often compute the gradient of the log joint, $\nabla_{\boldsymbol{\theta}} \log p(\boldsymbol{\theta}, \mathcal{D})$. We can use this gradient information to guide the proposals into regions of space with higher probability. This approach is called **Hamiltonian Monte Carlo** or **HMC**, and is one of the most widely used MCMC algorithms due to its speed. For details, see Section 12.5.

We apply HMC to our beta-Bernoulli model in Figure 7.5. (We use a logit transformation for the parameter.) In panel b, we show samples generated by the algorithm from 4 parallel Markov chains. We see that they oscillate around the true posterior, as desired. In panel a, we compute a kernel density estimate from the posterior samples from each chain; we see that the result is a good approximation to the true posterior in Figure 7.3.

7.4.6 Sequential Monte Carlo

MCMC is like a stochastic local search algorithm, in that it makes moves through the state space of the posterior distribution, comparing the current value to proposed neighboring values. An alternative approach is to use perform inference using a sequence of different distributions, from simpler to more complex, with the final distribution being equal to the target posterior. This is called **sequential Monte Carlo** or **SMC**. This approach, which is more similar to tree search than local search, has various advantages over MCMC, which we discuss in Chapter 13.

A common application of SMC is to **sequential Bayesian inference**, in which we recursively compute (i.e., in an online fashion) the posterior $p(\boldsymbol{\theta}_t|\mathcal{D}_{1:t})$, where $\mathcal{D}_{1:t} = \{(\boldsymbol{x}_n, y_n) : n = 1 : t\}$ is all the data we have seen so far. This sequence of distributions converges to the full batch posterior $p(\boldsymbol{\theta}|\mathcal{D})$ once all the data has been seen. However, the approach can also be used when the data is arriving in a continual, unending stream, as in state-space models (see Chapter 29). The application of SMC to such dynamical models is known as **particle filtering**. See Section 13.2 for details.

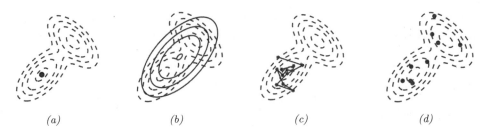

Figure 7.6: Different approximations to a bimodal 2d distribution. (a) Local MAP estimate. (b) Parametric Gaussian approximation. (c) Correlated samples from near one mode. (d) Independent samples from the distribution. Adapted from Figure 2 of [PY14]. Used with kind permission of George Panadreou.

7.4.7   Challenging posteriors

In many applications, the posterior can be high dimensional and multimodal. Approximating such distributions can be quite challenging. In Figure 7.6, we give a simple 2d example. We compare MAP estimation (which does not capture any uncertainty), a Gaussian parametric approximation such as the Laplace approximation or variational inference (see panel b), and a nonparametric approximation in terms of samples. If the samples are generated from MCMC, they are serially correlated, and may only explore a local model (see panel c). However, ideally we can draw independent samples from the entire support of the distribution, as shown in panel d. We may also be able to fit a local parametric approximation around each such sample (see Section 17.3.9.1), to get a semi-parametric approximation to the posterior.

7.5   Evaluating approximate inference algorithms

There are many different approximate inference algorithms, each of which make different tradeoffs between speed, accuracy, generality, simplicity, etc. This makes it hard to compare them on an equal footing.

One approach is to evaluate the accuracy of the approximation $q(\boldsymbol{\theta})$ by comparing to the "true" posterior $p(\boldsymbol{\theta}|\mathcal{D})$, computed offline with an "exact" method. We are usually interested in accuracy vs speed tradeoffs, which we can compute by evaluating $D_{\mathbb{KL}}\left(p(\boldsymbol{\theta}|\mathcal{D}) \parallel q_t(\boldsymbol{\theta})\right)$, where $q_t(\boldsymbol{\theta})$ is the approximate posterior after t units of compute time. Of course, we could use other measures of distributional similarity, such as Wasserstein distance.

Unfortunately, it is usually impossible to compute the true posterior $p(\boldsymbol{\theta}|\mathcal{D})$. A simple alternative is to evaluate the quality in terms of its prediction abilities on out of sample observed data, similar to cross validation. More generally, we can compare the expected loss or Bayesian risk (Section 34.1.3) of different posteriors, as proposed in [KPS98; KPS99]:

$$R = \mathbb{E}_{p^*(\boldsymbol{x},\boldsymbol{y})}\left[\ell(\boldsymbol{y}, q(\boldsymbol{y}|\boldsymbol{x},\mathcal{D}))\right] \text{ where } q(\boldsymbol{y}|\boldsymbol{x},\mathcal{D}) = \int p(\boldsymbol{y}|\boldsymbol{x},\boldsymbol{\theta})q(\boldsymbol{\theta}|\mathcal{D})d\boldsymbol{\theta} \tag{7.36}$$

where $\ell(\boldsymbol{y}, q(\boldsymbol{y}))$ is some loss function, such as log-loss. Alternatively, we can measure performance of the posterior when it is used in some downstream task, such as continual or active learning, as proposed in [Far22].

For some specialized methods for assessing variational inference, see [Yao+18b; Hug+20], and for Monte Carlo methods, see [CGR06; CTM17; GAR16].

8 Gaussian filtering and smoothing

8.1 Introduction

In this chapter, we consider the task of posterior inference in **state-space models** (SSMs). We discuss SSMs in more detail in Chapter 29, but we can think of them as latent variable sequence models with the conditional independencies shown by the chain-structured graphical model Figure 8.1. The corresponding joint distribution has the form

$$p(\boldsymbol{y}_{1:T}, \boldsymbol{z}_{1:T} | \boldsymbol{u}_{1:T}) = \left[p(\boldsymbol{z}_1 | \boldsymbol{u}_1) \prod_{t=2}^{T} p(\boldsymbol{z}_t | \boldsymbol{z}_{t-1}, \boldsymbol{u}_t) \right] \left[\prod_{t=1}^{T} p(\boldsymbol{y}_t | \boldsymbol{z}_t, \boldsymbol{u}_t) \right] \tag{8.1}$$

where $\boldsymbol{z}_t$ are the hidden variables at time t, $\boldsymbol{y}_t$ are the observations (outputs), and $\boldsymbol{u}_t$ are the optional inputs. The term $p(\boldsymbol{z}_t | \boldsymbol{z}_{t-1}, \boldsymbol{u}_t)$ is called the **dynamics model** or **transition model**, $p(\boldsymbol{y}_t | \boldsymbol{z}_t, \boldsymbol{u}_t)$ is called the **observation model** or **measurement model**, and $p(\boldsymbol{z}_1 | \boldsymbol{u}_1)$ is the prior or initial state distribution.[1]

8.1.1 Inferential goals

Given the sequence of observations, and a known model, one of the main tasks with SSMs is to perform posterior inference about the hidden states; this is also called **state estimation**.

For example, consider an airplane flying in the sky. (For simplicity, we assume the world is 2d, not 3d.) We would like to estimate its location and velocity $\boldsymbol{z}_t \in \mathbb{R}^4$ given noisy sensor measurements of its location $\boldsymbol{y}_t \in \mathbb{R}^2$, as illustrated in Figure 8.2(a). (We ignore the inputs $\boldsymbol{u}_t$ for simplicity.)

We discuss a suitable SSM for this problem, that embodies Newton's laws of motion, in Section 8.2.1.1. We can use the model to compute the **belief state** $p(\boldsymbol{z}_t | \boldsymbol{y}_{1:t})$; this is called Bayesian **filtering**. If we represent the belief state using a Gaussian, then we can use the **Kalman filter** to solve this task, as we discuss in Section 8.2.2. In Figure 8.2(b) we show the results of this algorithm. The green dots are the noisy observations, the red line shows the posterior mean estimate of the location, and the black circles show the posterior covariance. (The posterior over the velocity is not shown.) We see that the estimated trajectory is less noisy than the raw data, since it incorporates prior knowledge about how the data was generated.

Another task of interest is the **smoothing** problem where we want to compute $p(\boldsymbol{z}_t | \boldsymbol{y}_{1:T})$ using an offline dataset. We can compute these quantities using the **Kalman smoother** described in

---

1. In some cases, the initial state distribution is denoted by $p(\boldsymbol{z}_0)$, and then we derive $p(\boldsymbol{z}_1 | \boldsymbol{u}_1)$ by passing $p(\boldsymbol{z}_0)$ through the dynamics model. In this case, the joint distribution represents $p(\boldsymbol{y}_{1:T}, \boldsymbol{z}_{0:T} | \boldsymbol{u}_{1:T})$.

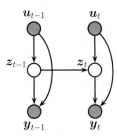

Figure 8.1: A state-space model represented as a graphical model. z_t are the hidden variables at time t, y_t are the observations (outputs), and u_t are the optional inputs.

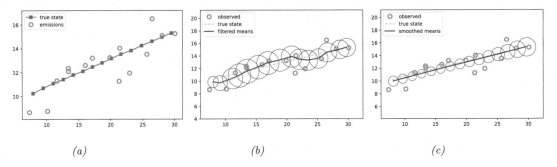

| (a) | (b) | (c) |

Figure 8.2: Illustration of Kalman filtering and smoothing for a linear dynamical system. (a) Observations (green cirles) are generated by an object moving to the right (true location denoted by blue squares). (b) Results of online Kalman filtering. Red cross is the posterior mean, circles are 95% confidence ellipses derived from the posterior covariance. (c) Same as (b), but using offline Kalman smoothing. The MSE in the trajectory for filtering is 3.13, and for smoothing is 1.71. Generated by kf_tracking.ipynb.

Section 8.2.3. In Figure 8.2(c) we show the result of this algorithm. We see that the resulting estimate is smoother compared to filtering, and that the posterior uncertainty is reduced (as visualized by the smaller confidence ellipses).

To understand this behavior intuitively, consider a detective trying to figure out who committed a crime. As they move through the crime scene, their uncertainty is high until he finds the key clue; then they have an "aha" moment, the uncertainty is reduced, and all the previously confusing observations are, in **hindsight**, easy to explain. Thus we see that, given all the data (including finding the clue), it is much easier to infer the state of the world.

A disadvantage of the smoothing method is that we have to wait until all the data has been observed before we start performing inference, so it cannot be used for online or realtime problems. **Fixed lag smoothing** is a useful compromise between online and offline estimation; it involves computing $p(z_{t-\ell}|y_{1:t})$, where $\ell > 0$ is called the lag. This gives better performance than filtering, but incurs a slight delay. By changing the size of the lag, we can trade off accuracy vs delay. See Figure 8.3 for an illustration.

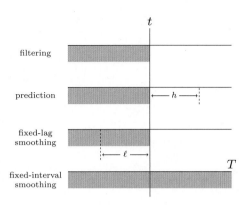

Figure 8.3: The main kinds of inference for state-space models. The shaded region is the interval for which we have data. The arrow represents the time step at which we want to perform inference. t is the current time, T is the sequence length, ℓ is the lag, and h is the prediction horizon. Used with kind permission of Peter Chang.

In addition to infering the latent state, we may want to predict future observations. We can compute the **observed predictive distribution** h steps into the future as follows:

$$p(\boldsymbol{y}_{t+h}|\boldsymbol{y}_{1:t}) = \sum_{\boldsymbol{z}_{t+h}} p(\boldsymbol{y}_{t+h}|\boldsymbol{z}_{t+h})p(\boldsymbol{z}_{t+h}|\boldsymbol{y}_{1:t}) \tag{8.2}$$

where the **hidden state predictive distribution** is obtained by pushing the current belief state through the dynamics model

$$p(\boldsymbol{z}_{t+h}|\boldsymbol{y}_{1:t}) = \sum_{\boldsymbol{z}_{t:t+h-1}} p(\boldsymbol{z}_t|\boldsymbol{y}_{1:t})p(\boldsymbol{z}_{t+1}|\boldsymbol{z}_t)p(\boldsymbol{z}_{t+2}|\boldsymbol{z}_{t+1}) \cdots p(\boldsymbol{z}_{t+h}|\boldsymbol{z}_{t+h-1}) \tag{8.3}$$

(When the states are continuous, we need to replace the sums with integrals.)

8.1.2 Bayesian filtering equations

The **Bayes filter** is an algorithm for recursively computing the **belief state** $p(\boldsymbol{z}_t|\boldsymbol{y}_{1:t})$ given the prior belief from the previous step, $p(\boldsymbol{z}_{t-1}|\boldsymbol{y}_{1:t-1})$, the new observation $\boldsymbol{y}_t$, and the model. This can be done using **sequential Bayesian updating**, and requires a constant amount of computation per time step (independent of t). For a dynamical model, this reduces to the **predict-update** cycle described below.

The **prediction step** is just the **Chapman-Kolmogorov equation**:

$$p(\boldsymbol{z}_t|\boldsymbol{y}_{1:t-1}) = \int p(\boldsymbol{z}_t|\boldsymbol{z}_{t-1})p(\boldsymbol{z}_{t-1}|\boldsymbol{y}_{1:t-1})d\boldsymbol{z}_{t-1} \tag{8.4}$$

The prediction step computes the one-step-ahead predictive distribution for the latent state, which updates the posterior from the previous time step into the prior for the current step.[2]

The **update step** is just Bayes' rule:

$$p(\boldsymbol{z}_t|\boldsymbol{y}_{1:t}) = \frac{1}{Z_t} p(\boldsymbol{y}_t|\boldsymbol{z}_t) p(\boldsymbol{z}_t|\boldsymbol{y}_{1:t-1}) \tag{8.5}$$

where the normalization constant is

$$Z_t = \int p(\boldsymbol{y}_t|\boldsymbol{z}_t) p(\boldsymbol{z}_t|\boldsymbol{y}_{1:t-1}) d\boldsymbol{z}_t = p(\boldsymbol{y}_t|\boldsymbol{y}_{1:t-1}) \tag{8.6}$$

We can use the normalization constants to compute the log likelihood of the sequence as follows:

$$\log p(\boldsymbol{y}_{1:T}) = \sum_{t=1}^{T} \log p(\boldsymbol{y}_t|\boldsymbol{y}_{1:t-1}) = \sum_{t=1}^{T} \log Z_t \tag{8.7}$$

where we define $p(\boldsymbol{y}_1|\boldsymbol{y}_0) = p(\boldsymbol{y}_1)$. This quantity is useful for computing the MLE of the parameters.

8.1.3   Bayesian smoothing equations

In the offline setting, we want to compute $p(\boldsymbol{z}_t|\boldsymbol{y}_{1:T})$, which is the belief about the hidden state at time t given all the data, both past and future. This is called (fixed interval) **smoothing**. We first perform the forwards or filtering pass, and then compute the smoothed belief states by working backwards, from right (time $t = T$) to left ($t = 1$), as we explain below. Hence this method is also called **forwards filtering backwards smoothing** or **FFBS**.

Suppose, by induction, that we have already computed $p(\boldsymbol{z}_{t+1}|\boldsymbol{y}_{1:T})$. We can convert this into a joint smoothed distribution over two consecutive time steps using

$$p(\boldsymbol{z}_t, \boldsymbol{z}_{t+1}|\boldsymbol{y}_{1:T}) = p(\boldsymbol{z}_t|\boldsymbol{z}_{t+1}, \boldsymbol{y}_{1:T}) p(\boldsymbol{z}_{t+1}|\boldsymbol{y}_{1:T}) \tag{8.8}$$

To derive the first term, note that from the Markov properties of the model, and Bayes' rule, we have

$$p(\boldsymbol{z}_t|\boldsymbol{z}_{t+1}, \boldsymbol{y}_{1:T}) = p(\boldsymbol{z}_t|\boldsymbol{z}_{t+1}, \boldsymbol{y}_{1:t}, \cancel{\boldsymbol{y}_{t+1:T}}) \tag{8.9}$$

$$= \frac{p(\boldsymbol{z}_t, \boldsymbol{z}_{t+1}|\boldsymbol{y}_{1:t})}{p(\boldsymbol{z}_{t+1}|\boldsymbol{y}_{1:t})} \tag{8.10}$$

$$= \frac{p(\boldsymbol{z}_{t+1}|\boldsymbol{z}_t) p(\boldsymbol{z}_t|\boldsymbol{y}_{1:t})}{p(\boldsymbol{z}_{t+1}|\boldsymbol{y}_{1:t})} \tag{8.11}$$

Thus the joint distribution over two consecutive time steps is given by

$$p(\boldsymbol{z}_t, \boldsymbol{z}_{t+1}|\boldsymbol{y}_{1:T}) = p(\boldsymbol{z}_t|\boldsymbol{z}_{t+1}, \boldsymbol{y}_{1:t}) p(\boldsymbol{z}_{t+1}|\boldsymbol{y}_{1:T}) = \frac{p(\boldsymbol{z}_{t+1}|\boldsymbol{z}_t) p(\boldsymbol{z}_t|\boldsymbol{y}_{1:t}) p(\boldsymbol{z}_{t+1}|\boldsymbol{y}_{1:T})}{p(\boldsymbol{z}_{t+1}|\boldsymbol{y}_{1:t})} \tag{8.12}$$

---

2. The prediction step is not needed at $t = 1$ if $p(\boldsymbol{z}_1)$ is provided as input to the model. However, if we just provide $p(\boldsymbol{z}_0)$, we need to compute $p(\boldsymbol{z}_1|\boldsymbol{y}_{1:0}) = p(\boldsymbol{z}_1)$ by applying the prediction step.

from which we get the new smoothed marginal distribution:

$$p(\boldsymbol{z}_t|\boldsymbol{y}_{1:T}) = p(\boldsymbol{z}_t|\boldsymbol{y}_{1:t}) \int \left[\frac{p(\boldsymbol{z}_{t+1}|\boldsymbol{z}_t)p(\boldsymbol{z}_{t+1}|\boldsymbol{y}_{1:T})}{p(\boldsymbol{z}_{t+1}|\boldsymbol{y}_{1:t})} \right] d\boldsymbol{z}_{t+1} \tag{8.13}$$

$$= \int p(\boldsymbol{z}_t, \boldsymbol{z}_{t+1}|\boldsymbol{y}_{1:t}) \frac{p(\boldsymbol{z}_{t+1}|\boldsymbol{y}_{1:T})}{p(\boldsymbol{z}_{t+1}|\boldsymbol{y}_{1:t})} d\boldsymbol{z}_{t+1} \tag{8.14}$$

Intuitively we can interpret this as follows: we start with the two-slice filtered distribution, $p(\boldsymbol{z}_t, \boldsymbol{z}_{t+1}|\boldsymbol{y}_{1:t})$, and then we divide out the old $p(\boldsymbol{z}_{t+1}|\boldsymbol{y}_{1:t})$ and multiply in the new $p(\boldsymbol{z}_{t+1}|\boldsymbol{y}_{1:T})$, and then marginalize out $\boldsymbol{z}_{t+1}$.

8.1.4 The Gaussian ansatz

In general, computing the integrals required to implement Bayesian filtering and smoothing is intractable. However, there are two notable exceptions: if the state space is discrete, as in an HMM, we can represent the belief states as discrete distributions (histograms), which we can update using the forwards-backwards algorithm, as discussed in Section 9.2; and if the SSM is a linear-Gaussian model, then we can represent the belief states by Gaussians, which we can update using the Kalman filter and smoother, which we discuss in Section 8.2.2 and Section 8.2.3. In the nonlinear and/or non-Gaussian setting, we can still use a Gaussian to represent an approximate belief state, as we discuss in Section 8.3, Section 8.4, Section 8.5 and Section 8.6. We discuss some non-Gaussian approximations in Section 8.7.

For most of this chapter, we assume the SSM can be written as a nonlinear model subject to additive Gaussian noise:

$$\begin{aligned} \boldsymbol{z}_t &= \boldsymbol{f}(\boldsymbol{z}_{t-1}, \boldsymbol{u}_t) + \mathcal{N}(\boldsymbol{0}, \mathbf{Q}_t) \\ \boldsymbol{y}_t &= \boldsymbol{h}(\boldsymbol{z}_t, \boldsymbol{u}_t) + \mathcal{N}(\boldsymbol{0}, \mathbf{R}_t) \end{aligned} \tag{8.15}$$

where $\boldsymbol{f}$ is the transition or dynamics function, and $\boldsymbol{h}$ is the observation function. In some cases, we will further assume that these functions are linear.

8.2 Inference for linear-Gaussian SSMs

In this section, we discuss inference in SSMs where all the distributions are linear Gaussian. This is called a **linear Gaussian state space model** (**LG-SSM**) or a **linear dynamical system** (**LDS**). We discuss such models in detail in Section 29.6, but in brief they have the following form:

$$\begin{aligned} p(\boldsymbol{z}_t|\boldsymbol{z}_{t-1}, \boldsymbol{u}_t) &= \mathcal{N}(\boldsymbol{z}_t|\mathbf{F}_t\boldsymbol{z}_{t-1} + \mathbf{B}_t\boldsymbol{u}_t + \boldsymbol{b}_t, \mathbf{Q}_t) \tag{8.16} \\ p(\boldsymbol{y}_t|\boldsymbol{z}_t, \boldsymbol{u}_t) &= \mathcal{N}(\boldsymbol{y}_t|\mathbf{H}_t\boldsymbol{z}_t + \mathbf{D}_t\boldsymbol{u}_t + \boldsymbol{d}_t, \mathbf{R}_t) \tag{8.17} \end{aligned}$$

where $\boldsymbol{z}_t \in \mathbb{R}^{N_z}$ is the hidden state, $\boldsymbol{y}_t \in \mathbb{R}^{N_y}$ is the observation, and $\boldsymbol{u}_t \in \mathbb{R}^{N_u}$ is the input. (We have allowed the parameters to be time-varying, for later extensions that we will consider.) We often assume the means of the process noise and observation noise (i.e., the bias or offset terms) are zero, so $\boldsymbol{b}_t = \boldsymbol{0}$ and $\boldsymbol{d}_t = \boldsymbol{0}$. In addition, we often have no inputs, so $\mathbf{B}_t = \mathbf{D}_t = \boldsymbol{0}$. In this case, the model simplifies to the following:[3]

$$p(z_t|z_{t-1}) = \mathcal{N}(z_t|\mathbf{F}_t z_{t-1}, \mathbf{Q}_t) \tag{8.18}$$
$$p(y_t|z_t) = \mathcal{N}(y_t|\mathbf{H}_t z_t, \mathbf{R}_t) \tag{8.19}$$

See Figure 8.1 for the graphical model.

Note that an LG-SSM is just a special case of a Gaussian Bayes net (Section 4.2.3), so the entire joint distribution $p(y_{1:T}, z_{1:T}|u_{1:T})$ is a large multivariate Gaussian with $N_y N_z T$ dimensions. However, it has a special structure that makes it computationally tractable to use, as we show below. In particular, we will discuss the **Kalman filter** and **Kalman smoother**, that can perform exact filtering and smoothing in $O(TN_z^3)$ time.

8.2.1   Examples

Before diving into the theory, we give some motivating examples.

8.2.1.1   Tracking and state estimation

A common application of LG-SSMs is for **tracking** objects, such as airplanes or animals, from noisy measurements, such as radar or cameras. For example, suppose we want to track an object moving in 2d. (We discuss this example in more detail in Section 29.7.1.) The hidden state z_t encodes the location, (x_{t1}, x_{t2}), and the velocity, $(\dot{x}_{t1}, \dot{x}_{t1})$, of the moving object. The observation y_t is a noisy version of the location. (The velocity is not observed but can be inferred from the change in location.) We assume that we obtain measurements with a sampling period of Δ. The new location is the old location plus Δ times the velocity, plus noise added to all terms:

$$z_t = \underbrace{\begin{pmatrix} 1 & 0 & \Delta & 0 \\ 0 & 1 & 0 & \Delta \\ 0 & 0 & 1 & 0 \\ 0 & 0 & 0 & 1 \end{pmatrix}}_{\mathbf{F}} z_{t-1} + q_t \tag{8.20}$$

where $q_t \sim \mathcal{N}(\mathbf{0}, \mathbf{Q}_t)$. The observation extracts the location and adds noise:

$$y_t = \underbrace{\begin{pmatrix} 1 & 0 & 0 & 0 \\ 0 & 1 & 0 & 0 \end{pmatrix}}_{\mathbf{H}} z_t + r_t \tag{8.21}$$

where $r_t \sim \mathcal{N}(\mathbf{0}, \mathbf{R}_t)$.

Our goal is to use this model to estimate the unknown location (and velocity) of the object given the noisy observations. In particular, in the filtering problem, we want to compute $p(z_t|y_{1:t})$ in a recursive fashion. Figure 8.2(b) illustrates filtering for the linear Gaussian SSM applied to the noisy tracking data in Figure 8.2(a) (shown by the green dots). The filtered estimates are computed using the Kalman filter algorithm described in Section 8.2.2. The red line shows the posterior

---

3. Our notation is similar to [SS23], except he writes $p(x_k|x_{k-1}) = \mathcal{N}(x_k|\mathbf{A}_{k-1}x_{k-1}, \mathbf{Q}_{k-1})$ instead of $p(z_t|z_{t-1}) = \mathcal{N}(z_t|\mathbf{F}_t z_{t-1}, \mathbf{Q}_t)$, and $p(y_k|x_k) = \mathcal{N}(y_k|\mathbf{H}_k x_k, \mathbf{R}_k)$ instead of $p(y_t|z_t) = \mathcal{N}(y_t|\mathbf{H}_t z_t, \mathbf{R}_t)$.

mean estimate of the location, and the black circles show the posterior covariance. We see that the estimated trajectory is less noisy than the raw data, since it incorporates prior knowledge about how the data was generated.

Another task of interest is the smoothing problem where we want to compute $p(\boldsymbol{z}_t|\boldsymbol{y}_{1:T})$ using an offline dataset. Figure 8.2(c) illustrates smoothing for the LG-SSM, implemented using the Kalman smoothing algorithm described in Section 8.2.3. We see that the resulting estimate is smoother, and that the posterior uncertainty is reduced (as visualized by the smaller confidence ellipses).

8.2.1.2 Online Bayesian linear regression (recursive least squares)

In Section 29.7.2 we discuss how to use the Kalman filter to recursively compute the exact posterior $p(\boldsymbol{w}|\mathcal{D}_{1:t})$ for a linear regression model in an online fashion. This is known as the recursive least squares algorithm. The basic idea is to treat the latent state to be the parameter values, $\boldsymbol{z}_t = \boldsymbol{w}$, and to define the non-stationary observation model as $p(\boldsymbol{y}_t|\boldsymbol{z}_t) = \mathcal{N}(y_t|\boldsymbol{x}_t^\mathsf{T}\boldsymbol{z}_t, \sigma^2)$, and the dynamics model as $p(\boldsymbol{z}_t|\boldsymbol{z}_{t-1}) = \mathcal{N}(\boldsymbol{z}_t|\boldsymbol{z}_{t-1}, \mathbf{0I})$.

8.2.1.3 Time series forecasting

In Section 29.12, we discuss how to use Kalman filtering to perform time series forecasting.

8.2.2 The Kalman filter

The **Kalman filter** (**KF**) is an algorithm for exact Bayesian filtering for linear Gaussian state space models. The resulting algorithm is the Gaussian analog of the HMM filter in Section 9.2.2. The belief state at time t is now given by $p(\boldsymbol{z}_t|\boldsymbol{y}_{1:t}) = \mathcal{N}(\boldsymbol{z}_t|\boldsymbol{\mu}_{t|t}, \boldsymbol{\Sigma}_{t|t})$, where we use the notation $\boldsymbol{\mu}_{t|t'}$ and $\boldsymbol{\Sigma}_{t|t'}$ to represent the posterior mean and covariance given $\boldsymbol{y}_{1:t'}$.[4] Since everything is Gaussian, we can perform the prediction and update steps in closed form, as we explain below (see Section 8.2.2.4 for the derivation).

8.2.2.1 Predict step

The one-step-ahead prediction for the hidden state, also called the **time update step**, is given by the following:

$$p(\boldsymbol{z}_t|\boldsymbol{y}_{1:t-1}, \boldsymbol{u}_{1:t}) = \mathcal{N}(\boldsymbol{z}_t|\boldsymbol{\mu}_{t|t-1}, \boldsymbol{\Sigma}_{t|t-1}) \tag{8.22}$$

$$\boldsymbol{\mu}_{t|t-1} = \mathbf{F}_t\boldsymbol{\mu}_{t-1|t-1} + \mathbf{B}_t\boldsymbol{u}_t + \boldsymbol{b}_t \tag{8.23}$$

$$\boldsymbol{\Sigma}_{t|t-1} = \mathbf{F}_t\boldsymbol{\Sigma}_{t-1|t-1}\mathbf{F}_t^\mathsf{T} + \mathbf{Q}_t \tag{8.24}$$

---

4. We represent the mean and covariance of the filtered belief state by $\boldsymbol{\mu}_{t|t}$ and $\boldsymbol{\Sigma}_{t|t}$, but some authors use the notation $\boldsymbol{m}_t$ and $\mathbf{P}_t$ instead. We represent the mean and covariance of the smoothed belief state by $\boldsymbol{\mu}_{t|T}$ and $\boldsymbol{\Sigma}_{t|T}$, but some authors use the notation $\boldsymbol{m}_t^s$ and $\mathbf{P}_t^s$ instead. Finally, we represent the mean and covariance of the one-step-ahead posterior predictive distribution, $p(\boldsymbol{z}_t|\boldsymbol{y}_{1:t-1})$, by $\boldsymbol{\mu}_{t|t-1}$ and $\boldsymbol{\Sigma}_{t|t-1}$, whereas some authors use $\boldsymbol{m}_t^-$ and $\mathbf{P}_t^-$ instead.

8.2.2.2   Update step

The update step (also called the **measurement step**) can be computed using Bayes' rule, as follows:

$$p(z_t|y_{1:t}, u_{1:t}) = \mathcal{N}(z_t|\mu_{t|t}, \Sigma_{t|t}) \tag{8.25}$$

$$\hat{y}_t = \mathbf{H}_t\mu_{t|t-1} + \mathbf{D}_t u_t + d_t \tag{8.26}$$

$$\mathbf{S}_t = \mathbf{H}_t\Sigma_{t|t-1}\mathbf{H}_t^\mathsf{T} + \mathbf{R}_t \tag{8.27}$$

$$\mathbf{K}_t = \Sigma_{t|t-1}\mathbf{H}_t^\mathsf{T}\mathbf{S}_t^{-1} \tag{8.28}$$

$$\mu_{t|t} = \mu_{t|t-1} + \mathbf{K}_t(y_t - \hat{y}_t) \tag{8.29}$$

$$\Sigma_{t|t} = \Sigma_{t|t-1} - \mathbf{K}_t\mathbf{H}_t\Sigma_{t|t-1} \tag{8.30}$$

$$= \Sigma_{t|t-1} - \mathbf{K}_t\mathbf{S}_t\mathbf{K}_t^\mathsf{T} \tag{8.31}$$

where $\hat{y}_t$ is the expected observation, $e_t = y_t - \hat{y}_t$ is the **residual error** or **innovation term**, and $\mathbf{K}_t$ is the **Kalman gain matrix**.

Note that, by using the matrix inversion lemma, the Kalman gain matrix can also be written as

$$\mathbf{K}_t = \Sigma_{t|t-1}\mathbf{H}_t^\mathsf{T}(\mathbf{H}_t\Sigma_{t|t-1}\mathbf{H}_t^\mathsf{T} + \mathbf{R}_t)^{-1} = (\Sigma_{t|t-1}^{-1} + \mathbf{H}_t^\mathsf{T}\mathbf{R}_t^{-1}\mathbf{H}_t)^{-1}\mathbf{H}_t^\mathsf{T}\mathbf{R}_t^{-1} \tag{8.32}$$

This is useful if $\mathbf{R}_t^{-1}$ is precomputed (e.g., if it is constant over time) and $N_y \gg N_z$.

8.2.2.3   Posterior predictive

The one-step-ahead posterior predictive density for the observations can be computed as follows. (We ignore inputs and bias terms, for notational brevity.) First we compute the one-step-ahead predictive density for latent states:

$$p(z_t|y_{1:t-1}) = \int p(z_t|z_{t-1})p(z_{t-1}|y_{1:t-1})dz_{t-1} = \mathcal{N}(z_t|\mu_{t|t-1}, \Sigma_{t|t-1}) \tag{8.33}$$

$$= \mathcal{N}(z_t|\mathbf{F}_t\mu_{t-1|t-1}, \mathbf{F}_t\Sigma_{t-1|t-1}\mathbf{F}_t^\mathsf{T} + \mathbf{Q}_t) = \mathcal{N}(z_t|\mu_{t|t-1}, \Sigma_{t|t-1}) \tag{8.34}$$

Then we convert this to a prediction about observations by marginalizing out z_t:

$$p(y_t|y_{1:t-1}) = \int p(y_t, z_t|y_{1:t-1})dz_t = \int p(y_t|z_t)p(z_t|y_{1:t-1})dz_t = \mathcal{N}(y_t|m_t, \mathbf{S}_t) \tag{8.35}$$

This can also be used to compute the log-likelihood of the observations: The normalization constant of the new posterior can be computed as follows:

$$\log p(y_{1:T}) = \sum_{t=1}^{T} \log p(y_t|y_{1:t-1}) = \sum_{t=1}^{T} \log Z_t \tag{8.36}$$

where we define $p(y_1|y_0) = p(y_1)$. This is just a sum of the log probabilities of the one-step-ahead measurement predictions, and is a measure of how "surprised" the model is at each step.

We can generalize the prediction step to predict observations K steps into the future by first forecasting K steps in latent space, and then "grounding" the final state into predicted observations. (This is in contrast to an RNN (Section 16.3.4), which requires generating observations at each step, in order to update future hidden states.)

8.2.2.4 Derivation

In this section we derive the Kalman filter equations, following [SS23, Sec 6.3]. The results are a straightforward application of the rules for manipulating linear Gaussian systems, discussed in Section 2.3.2.

First we derive the prediction step. From Equation (2.120), the joint predictive distribution for states is given by

$$p(\boldsymbol{z}_{t-1}, \boldsymbol{z}_t | \boldsymbol{y}_{1:t-1}) = p(\boldsymbol{z}_t | \boldsymbol{z}_{t-1}) p(\boldsymbol{z}_{t-1} | \boldsymbol{y}_{1:t-1}) \tag{8.37}$$

$$= \mathcal{N}(\boldsymbol{z}_t | \mathbf{F}_t \boldsymbol{z}_{t-1}, \mathbf{Q}_t) \mathcal{N}(\boldsymbol{z}_{t-1} | \boldsymbol{\mu}_{t-1|t-1}, \boldsymbol{\Sigma}_{t-1|t-1}) \tag{8.38}$$

$$= \mathcal{N}\left(\begin{pmatrix} \boldsymbol{z}_{t-1} \\ \boldsymbol{z}_t \end{pmatrix} | \boldsymbol{\mu}', \boldsymbol{\Sigma}' \right) \tag{8.39}$$

where

$$\boldsymbol{\mu}' = \begin{pmatrix} \boldsymbol{\mu}_{t-1|t-1} \\ \mathbf{F}_t \boldsymbol{\mu}_{t-1|t-1} \end{pmatrix}, \quad \boldsymbol{\Sigma}' = \begin{pmatrix} \boldsymbol{\Sigma}_{t-1|t-1} & \boldsymbol{\Sigma}_{t-1|t-1} \mathbf{F}_t^\mathsf{T} \\ \mathbf{F}_t \boldsymbol{\Sigma}_{t-1|t-1} & \mathbf{F}_t \boldsymbol{\Sigma}_{t-1|t-1} \mathbf{F}_t^\mathsf{T} + \mathbf{Q}_t \end{pmatrix} \tag{8.40}$$

Hence the marginal predictive distribution for states is given by

$$p(\boldsymbol{z}_t | \boldsymbol{y}_{1:t-1}) = \mathcal{N}(\boldsymbol{z}_t | \mathbf{F}_t \boldsymbol{\mu}_{t-1|t-1}, \mathbf{F}_t \boldsymbol{\Sigma}_{t-1|t-1} \mathbf{F}_t^\mathsf{T} + \mathbf{Q}_t) = \mathcal{N}(\boldsymbol{z}_t | \boldsymbol{\mu}_{t|t-1}, \boldsymbol{\Sigma}_{t|t-1}) \tag{8.41}$$

Now we derive the measurement update step. The joint distribution for state and observation is given by

$$p(\boldsymbol{z}_t, \boldsymbol{y}_t | \boldsymbol{y}_{1:t-1}) = p(\boldsymbol{y}_t | \boldsymbol{z}_t) p(\boldsymbol{z}_t | \boldsymbol{y}_{1:t-1}) \tag{8.42}$$

$$= \mathcal{N}(\boldsymbol{y}_t | \mathbf{H}_t \boldsymbol{z}_t, \mathbf{R}_t) \mathcal{N}(\boldsymbol{z}_t | \boldsymbol{\mu}_{t|t-1}, \boldsymbol{\Sigma}_{t|t-1}) \tag{8.43}$$

$$= \mathcal{N}\left(\begin{pmatrix} \boldsymbol{z}_t \\ \boldsymbol{y}_t \end{pmatrix} | \boldsymbol{\mu}'', \boldsymbol{\Sigma}'' \right) \tag{8.44}$$

where

$$\boldsymbol{\mu}'' = \begin{pmatrix} \boldsymbol{\mu}_{t|t-1} \\ \mathbf{H}_t \boldsymbol{\mu}_{t|t-1} \end{pmatrix}, \quad \boldsymbol{\Sigma}'' = \begin{pmatrix} \boldsymbol{\Sigma}_{t|t-1} & \boldsymbol{\Sigma}_{t|t-1} \mathbf{H}_t^\mathsf{T} \\ \mathbf{H}_t \boldsymbol{\Sigma}_{t|t-1} & \mathbf{H}_t \boldsymbol{\Sigma}_{t|t-1}^{-1} \mathbf{H}_t^\mathsf{T} + \mathbf{R}_t \end{pmatrix} \tag{8.45}$$

Finally, we convert this joint into a conditional using Equation (2.78) as follows:

$$p(\boldsymbol{z}_t | \boldsymbol{y}_t, \boldsymbol{y}_{1:t-1}) = \mathcal{N}(\boldsymbol{z}_t | \boldsymbol{\mu}_{t|t}, \boldsymbol{\Sigma}_{t|t}) \tag{8.46}$$

$$\boldsymbol{\mu}_{t|t} = \boldsymbol{\mu}_{t|t-1} + \boldsymbol{\Sigma}_{t|t-1} \mathbf{H}_t^\mathsf{T} (\mathbf{H}_t \boldsymbol{\Sigma}_{t|t-1} \mathbf{H}_t^\mathsf{T} + \mathbf{R}_t)^{-1} [\boldsymbol{y}_t - \mathbf{H}_t \boldsymbol{\mu}_{t|t-1}] \tag{8.47}$$

$$= \boldsymbol{\mu}_{t|t-1} + \mathbf{K}_t [\boldsymbol{y}_t - \mathbf{H}_t \boldsymbol{\mu}_{t|t-1}] \tag{8.48}$$

$$\boldsymbol{\Sigma}_{t|t} = \boldsymbol{\Sigma}_{t|t-1} - \boldsymbol{\Sigma}_{t|t-1} \mathbf{H}_t^\mathsf{T} (\mathbf{H}_t \boldsymbol{\Sigma}_{t|t-1} \mathbf{H}_t^\mathsf{T} + \mathbf{R}_t)^{-1} \mathbf{H}_t \boldsymbol{\Sigma}_{t|t-1} \tag{8.49}$$

$$= \boldsymbol{\Sigma}_{t|t-1} - \mathbf{K}_t \mathbf{H}_t \boldsymbol{\Sigma}_{t|t-1} \tag{8.50}$$

where

$$\mathbf{S}_t = \mathbf{H}_t \boldsymbol{\Sigma}_{t|t-1} \mathbf{H}_t^\mathsf{T} + \mathbf{R}_t \tag{8.51}$$

$$\mathbf{K}_t = \boldsymbol{\Sigma}_{t|t-1} \mathbf{H}_t^\mathsf{T} \mathbf{S}_t^{-1} \tag{8.52}$$

8.2.2.5   Abstract formulation

We can represent the Kalman filter equations much more compactly by defining various functions
that create and manipulate jointly Gaussian systems, as in Section 2.3.2. In particular, suppose we
have the following linear Gaussian system:

$$p(\boldsymbol{z}) = \mathcal{N}(\breve{\boldsymbol{\mu}}, \breve{\boldsymbol{\Sigma}}) \tag{8.53}$$

$$p(\boldsymbol{y}|\boldsymbol{z}) = \mathcal{N}(\mathbf{A}\boldsymbol{z} + \boldsymbol{b}, \boldsymbol{\Omega}) \tag{8.54}$$

Then the joint is given by

$$p(\boldsymbol{z}, \boldsymbol{y}) = \mathcal{N}\left(\begin{pmatrix} \breve{\boldsymbol{\mu}} \\ \overline{\boldsymbol{\mu}} \end{pmatrix}, \begin{pmatrix} \breve{\boldsymbol{\Sigma}} & \mathbf{C} \\ \mathbf{C}^{\mathsf{T}} & \mathbf{S} \end{pmatrix} \right) = \mathcal{N}\left(\begin{pmatrix} \breve{\boldsymbol{\mu}} \\ \mathbf{A}\,\breve{\boldsymbol{\mu}} + \boldsymbol{b} \end{pmatrix}, \begin{pmatrix} \breve{\boldsymbol{\Sigma}} & \breve{\boldsymbol{\Sigma}}\,\mathbf{A}^{\mathsf{T}} \\ \mathbf{A}\,\breve{\boldsymbol{\Sigma}} & \mathbf{A}\,\breve{\boldsymbol{\Sigma}}\,\mathbf{A}^{\mathsf{T}} + \boldsymbol{\Omega} \end{pmatrix} \right) \tag{8.55}$$

and the posterior is given by

$$p(\boldsymbol{z}|\boldsymbol{y}) = \mathcal{N}(\boldsymbol{z}|\,\widehat{\boldsymbol{\mu}}, \widehat{\boldsymbol{\Sigma}}) = \mathcal{N}\left(\boldsymbol{z}|\,\breve{\boldsymbol{\mu}} + \mathbf{K}(\boldsymbol{y} - \overline{\boldsymbol{\mu}}), \breve{\boldsymbol{\Sigma}} - \mathbf{K}\mathbf{S}\mathbf{K}^{\mathsf{T}} \right) \tag{8.56}$$

where $\mathbf{K} = \mathbf{C}\mathbf{S}^{-1}$. See Algorithm 8.1 for the pseudocode.

Algorithm 8.1: Functions for a linear Gaussian system.

1 def **GaussMoments**($\breve{\boldsymbol{\mu}}, \breve{\boldsymbol{\Sigma}}, \mathbf{A}, \boldsymbol{b}, \boldsymbol{\Omega}$) :
2   $\overline{\boldsymbol{\mu}} = \mathbf{A}\,\breve{\boldsymbol{\mu}} + \boldsymbol{b}$
3   $\mathbf{S} = \boldsymbol{\Omega} + \mathbf{A}\,\breve{\boldsymbol{\Sigma}}\,\mathbf{A}^{\mathsf{T}}$
4   $\mathbf{C} = \breve{\boldsymbol{\Sigma}}\,\mathbf{A}^{\mathsf{T}}$
5   Return $(\overline{\boldsymbol{\mu}}, \mathbf{S}, \mathbf{C})$

6 def **GaussCondition**($\breve{\boldsymbol{\mu}}, \breve{\boldsymbol{\Sigma}}, \overline{\boldsymbol{\mu}}, \mathbf{S}, \mathbf{C}, \boldsymbol{y}$) :
7   $\mathbf{K} = \mathbf{C}\mathbf{S}^{-1}$
8   $\widehat{\boldsymbol{\mu}} = \breve{\boldsymbol{\mu}} + \mathbf{K}(\boldsymbol{y} - \overline{\boldsymbol{\mu}})$
9   $\widehat{\boldsymbol{\Sigma}} = \breve{\boldsymbol{\Sigma}} - \mathbf{K}\mathbf{S}\mathbf{K}^{\mathsf{T}}$
10 $\ell = \log \mathcal{N}(\boldsymbol{y}|\overline{\boldsymbol{\mu}}, \mathbf{S})$
11 Return $(\widehat{\boldsymbol{\mu}}, \widehat{\boldsymbol{\Sigma}}, \ell)$

We can now apply these functions to derive Kalman filtering as follows. In the prediction step, we
compute

$$p(\boldsymbol{z}_{t-1}, \boldsymbol{z}_t | \boldsymbol{y}_{1:t-1}) = \mathcal{N}\left(\begin{pmatrix} \boldsymbol{\mu}_{t-1|t-1} \\ \boldsymbol{\mu}_{t|t-1} \end{pmatrix}, \begin{pmatrix} \boldsymbol{\Sigma}_{t-1|t-1} & \boldsymbol{\Sigma}_{t-1,t|t-1} \\ \boldsymbol{\Sigma}_{t,t-1|t-1} & \boldsymbol{\Sigma}_{t|t-1} \end{pmatrix} \right) \tag{8.57}$$

$$(\boldsymbol{\mu}_{t|t-1}, \boldsymbol{\Sigma}_{t|t-1}, \boldsymbol{\Sigma}_{t-1,t|t}) = \mathbf{GaussMoments}(\boldsymbol{\mu}_{t-1|t-1}, \boldsymbol{\Sigma}_{t-1|t-1}, \mathbf{F}_t, \mathbf{B}_t\boldsymbol{u}_t + \boldsymbol{b}_t, \mathbf{Q}_t) \tag{8.58}$$

from which we get the marginal distribution

$$p(\boldsymbol{z}_t | \boldsymbol{y}_{1:t-1}) = \mathcal{N}(\boldsymbol{\mu}_{t|t-1}, \boldsymbol{\Sigma}_{t|t-1}) \tag{8.59}$$

In the update step, we compute the joint distribution

$$p(\boldsymbol{z}_t, \boldsymbol{y}_t | \boldsymbol{y}_{1:t-1}) = \mathcal{N}\left(\begin{pmatrix} \boldsymbol{\mu}_{t|t-1} \\ \overline{\boldsymbol{\mu}}_t \end{pmatrix}, \begin{pmatrix} \boldsymbol{\Sigma}_{t|t-1} & \mathbf{C}_t \\ \mathbf{C}_t^\mathsf{T} & \mathbf{S}_t \end{pmatrix}\right) \tag{8.60}$$

$$(\hat{\boldsymbol{y}}_t, \mathbf{S}_t, \mathbf{C}_t) = \textbf{GaussMoments}(\boldsymbol{\mu}_{t|t-1}, \boldsymbol{\Sigma}_{t|t-1}, \mathbf{H}_t, \mathbf{D}_t \boldsymbol{u}_t + \boldsymbol{d}_t, \mathbf{R}_t) \tag{8.61}$$

We then condition this on the observations to get the posterior distribution

$$p(\boldsymbol{z}_t | \boldsymbol{y}_t, \boldsymbol{y}_{1:t-1}) = p(\boldsymbol{z}_t | \boldsymbol{y}_{1:t}) = \mathcal{N}(\boldsymbol{\mu}_{t|t}, \boldsymbol{\Sigma}_{t|t}) \tag{8.62}$$

$$(\boldsymbol{\mu}_{t|t}, \boldsymbol{\Sigma}_{t|t}, \ell_t) = \textbf{GaussCondition}(\boldsymbol{\mu}_{t|t-1}, \boldsymbol{\Sigma}_{t|t-1}, \hat{\boldsymbol{y}}_t, \mathbf{S}_t, \mathbf{C}_t, \boldsymbol{y}_t) \tag{8.63}$$

The overall KF algorithm is shown in Algorithm 8.2.

Algorithm 8.2: Kalman filter.

1 def $\mathrm{KF}(\mathbf{F}_{1:T}, \mathbf{B}_{1:T}, \boldsymbol{b}_{1:T}, \mathbf{Q}_{1:T}, \mathbf{H}_{1:T}, \mathbf{D}_{1:T}, \boldsymbol{d}_{1:T}, \mathbf{R}_{1:T}, \boldsymbol{u}_{1:T}, \boldsymbol{y}_{1:T}, \boldsymbol{\mu}_{0|0}, \boldsymbol{\Sigma}_{0|0})$:
2 **foreach** $t = 1 : T$ **do**
3 $\quad$ // Predict:
4 $\quad (\boldsymbol{\mu}_{t|t-1}, \boldsymbol{\Sigma}_{t|t-1}, -) = \textbf{GaussMoments}(\boldsymbol{\mu}_{t-1|t-1}, \boldsymbol{\Sigma}_{t-1|t-1}, \mathbf{F}_t, \mathbf{B}_t \boldsymbol{u}_t + \boldsymbol{b}_t, \mathbf{Q}_t)$
5 $\quad$ // Update:
6 $\quad (\overline{\boldsymbol{\mu}}, \mathbf{S}, \mathbf{C}) = \textbf{GaussMoments}(\boldsymbol{\mu}_{t|t-1}, \boldsymbol{\Sigma}_{t|t-1}, \mathbf{F}_t, \mathbf{B}_t \boldsymbol{u}_t + \boldsymbol{b}_t, \mathbf{Q}_t)$
7 $\quad (\boldsymbol{\mu}_{t|t}, \boldsymbol{\Sigma}_{t|t}, \ell_t) = \textbf{GaussCondition}(\boldsymbol{\mu}_{t|t-1}, \boldsymbol{\Sigma}_{t|t-1}, \overline{\boldsymbol{\mu}}, \mathbf{S}, \mathbf{C}, \boldsymbol{y})$
8 Return $(\boldsymbol{\mu}_{t|t}, \boldsymbol{\Sigma}_{t|t})_{t=1}^T, \sum_{t=1}^T \ell_t$

8.2.2.6 Numerical issues

In practice, the Kalman filter can encounter numerical issues. One solution is to use the **information filter**, which recursively updates the natural parameters of the Gaussian, $\boldsymbol{\Lambda}_{t|t} = \boldsymbol{\Sigma}_{t|t}^{-1}$ and $\boldsymbol{\eta}_{t|t} = \boldsymbol{\Lambda}_t \boldsymbol{\mu}_{t|t}$, instead of the mean and covariance (see Section 8.2.4). Another solution is the **square root filter**, which works with the Cholesky or QR decomposition of $\boldsymbol{\Sigma}_{t|t}$, which is much more numerically stable than directly updating $\boldsymbol{\Sigma}_{t|t}$. These techniques can be combined to create the **square root information filter** (SRIF) [May79]. (According to [Bie06], the SRIF was developed in 1969 for use in JPL's Mariner 10 mission to Venus.) In [Tol22] they present an approach which uses QR decompositions instead of matrix inversions, which can also be more stable.

8.2.2.7 Continuous-time version

The Kalman filter can be extended to work with continuous time dynamical systems; the resulting method is called the **Kalman Bucy filter**. See [SS19, p208] for details.

8.2.3 The Kalman (RTS) smoother

In Section 8.2.2, we described the Kalman filter, which sequentially computes $p(\boldsymbol{z}_t | \boldsymbol{y}_{1:t})$ for each t. This is useful for online inference problems, such as tracking. However, in an offline setting, we can wait until all the data has arrived, and then compute $p(z_t | y_{1:T})$. By conditioning on past and future data, our uncertainty will be significantly reduced. This is illustrated in Figure 8.2(c), where we see that the posterior covariance ellipsoids are smaller for the smoothed trajectory than for the filtered trajectory.

We now explain how to compute the smoothed estimates, using an algorithm called the **RTS smoother** or **RTSS**, named after its inventors, Rauch, Tung, and Striebel [RTS65]. It is also known as the **Kalman smoothing** algorithm. The algorithm is the linear-Gaussian analog to the forwards-filtering backwards-smoothing algorithm for HMMs in Section 9.2.4.

8.2.3.1 Algorithm

In this section, we state the Kalman smoother algorithm. We give the derivation in Section 8.2.3.2. The key update equations are as follows: From this, we can extract the smoothed marginal

$$p(z_t | y_{1:T}) = \mathcal{N}(z_t | \mu_{t|T}, \Sigma_{t|T}) \tag{8.64}$$

$$\mu_{t+1|t} = \mathbf{F}_t \mu_{t|t} \tag{8.65}$$

$$\Sigma_{t+1|t} = \mathbf{F}_t \Sigma_{t|t} \mathbf{F}_t^\mathsf{T} + \mathbf{Q}_{t+1} \tag{8.66}$$

$$\mathbf{G}_t = \Sigma_{t|t} \mathbf{F}_t^\mathsf{T} \Sigma_{t+1|t}^{-1} \tag{8.67}$$

$$\mu_{t|T} = \mu_{t|t} + \mathbf{G}_t (\mu_{t+1|T} - \mu_{t+1|t}) \tag{8.68}$$

$$\Sigma_{t|T} = \Sigma_{t|t} + \mathbf{G}_t (\Sigma_{t+1|T} - \Sigma_{t+1|t}) \mathbf{G}_t^\mathsf{T} \tag{8.69}$$

8.2.3.2 Derivation

In this section, we derive the RTS smoother, following [SS23, Sec 12.2]. As in the derivation of the Kalman filter in Section 8.2.2.4, we make heavy use of the rules for manipulating linear Gaussian systems, discussed in Section 2.3.2.

The joint filtered distribution for two consecutive time slices is

$$p(z_t, z_{t+1} | y_{1:t}) = p(z_{t+1} | z_t) p(z_t | y_{1:t}) = \mathcal{N}(z_{t+1} | \mathbf{F}_t z_t, \mathbf{Q}_{t+1}) \mathcal{N}(z_t | \mu_{t|t}, \Sigma_{t|t}) \tag{8.70}$$

$$= \mathcal{N}\left(\begin{pmatrix} z_t \\ z_{t+1} \end{pmatrix} \Big| m_1, \mathbf{V}_1 \right) \tag{8.71}$$

where

$$m_1 = \begin{pmatrix} \mu_{t|t} \\ \mathbf{F}_t \mu_{t|t} \end{pmatrix}, \quad \mathbf{V}_1 = \begin{pmatrix} \Sigma_{t|t} & \Sigma_{t|t} \mathbf{F}_t^\mathsf{T} \\ \mathbf{F}_t \Sigma_{t|t} & \mathbf{F}_t \Sigma_{t|t} \mathbf{F}_t^\mathsf{T} + \mathbf{Q}_{t+1} \end{pmatrix} \tag{8.72}$$

By the Markov property for the hidden states we have

$$p(z_t | z_{t+1}, y_{1:T}) = p(z_t | z_{t+1}, y_{1:t}, y_{t+1:T}) = p(z_t | z_{t+1}, y_{1:t}) \tag{8.73}$$

and hence by conditioning the joint distribution $p(z_t, z_{t+1}|y_{1:t})$ on the future state we get

$$p(z_t|z_{t+1}, y_{1:T}) = \mathcal{N}(z_t|m_2, V_2) \tag{8.74}$$

$$\mu_{t+1|t} = F_t\mu_{t|t} \tag{8.75}$$

$$\Sigma_{t+1|t} = F_t\Sigma_{t|t}F_t^\mathsf{T} + Q_{t+1} \tag{8.76}$$

$$G_t = \Sigma_{t|t}F_t^\mathsf{T}\Sigma_{t+1|t}^{-1} \tag{8.77}$$

$$m_2 = \mu_{t|t} + G_t(z_{t+1} - \mu_{t+1|t}) \tag{8.78}$$

$$V_2 = \Sigma_{t|t} - G_t\Sigma_{t+1|t}G_t^\mathsf{T} \tag{8.79}$$

where G_t is the backwards Kalman gain matrix. For future reference, we note that we can rewrite this matrix as

$$G_t = D_{t+1}\Sigma_{t+1|t}^{-1} \tag{8.80}$$

where $D_{t+1} = \Sigma_{t|t}F_t^\mathsf{T}$ is the cross covariance term in the upper right block of V_1.

The joint distribution of two consecutive time slices given all the data is

$$p(z_{t+1}, z_t|y_{1:T}) = p(z_t|z_{t+1}, y_{1:T})p(z_{t+1}|y_{1:T}) \tag{8.81}$$

$$= \mathcal{N}(z_t|m_2(z_{t+1}), V_2)\mathcal{N}(z_{t+1}|\mu_{t|T}, \Sigma_{t|T}) \tag{8.82}$$

$$= \mathcal{N}\left(\begin{pmatrix} z_{t+1} \\ z_t \end{pmatrix}|m_3, V_3\right) \tag{8.83}$$

where

$$m_3 = \begin{pmatrix} \mu_{t+1|T} \\ \mu_{t|t} + G_t(\mu_{t+1|T} - \mu_{t+1|t}) \end{pmatrix}, \quad V_3 = \begin{pmatrix} \Sigma_{t+1|T} & \Sigma_{t+1|T}G_t^\mathsf{T} \\ G_t\Sigma_{t+1|T} & G_t\Sigma_{t+1|T}G_t^\mathsf{T} + V_2 \end{pmatrix} \tag{8.84}$$

From this, we can extract $p(z_t|y_{1:T})$, with the mean and covariance given by Equation (8.68) and Equation (8.69).

8.2.3.3 Two-filter smoothing

Note that the backwards pass of the Kalman smoother does not need access to the observations, $y_{1:T}$, but does need access to the filtered belief states from the forwards pass, $p(z_t|y_{1:t}) = \mathcal{N}(z_t|\mu_{t|t}, \Sigma_{t|t})$. There is an alternative version of the algorithm, known as **two-filter smoothing** [FP69; Kit04], in which we compute the forwards pass as usual, and then separately compute backwards messages $p(y_{t+1:T}|z_t) \propto \mathcal{N}(z_t|\mu_{t|t}^b, \Sigma_{t|t}^b)$, similar to the backwards filtering algorithm in HMMs (Section 9.2.3).

However, these backwards messages are conditional likelihoods, not posteriors, which can cause numerical problems. For example, consider $t = T$; in this case, we need to set the initial covariance matrix to be $\Sigma_T^b = \infty I$, so that the backwards message has no effect on the filtered posterior (since there is no evidence beyond step T). This problem can be resolved by working in information form. An alternative approach is to generalize the two-filter smoothing equations to ensure the likelihoods are normalizable by multiplying them by artificial distributions [BDM10].

In general, the RTS smoother is preferred to the two-filter smoother, since it is more numerically stable, and it is easier to generalize it to the nonlinear case.

8.2.3.4   Time and space complexity

In general, the Kalman smoothing algorithm takes $O(N_y^3 + N_z^2 + N_y N_z)$ per step, where there are T steps. This can be slow when applied to long sequences. In [SGF21], they describe how to reduce this to $O(\log T)$ steps using a **parallel prefix scan** operator that can be run efficiently on GPUs. In addition, we can reduce the space from $O(T)$, to $O(\log T)$ using the same algorithm as in Section 9.2.5.

8.2.3.5   Forwards filtering backwards sampling

To draw posterior samples from the LG-SSM, we can leverage the following result:

$$p(z_t|z_{t+1}, y_{1:T}) = \mathcal{N}(z_t|\tilde{\mu}_t, \tilde{\Sigma}_t) \tag{8.85}$$

$$\tilde{\mu}_t = \mu_{t|t} + G_t(z_{t+1} - F_t\mu_{t|t}) \tag{8.86}$$

$$\tilde{\Sigma}_t = \Sigma_{t|t} - G_t\Sigma_{t+1|t}G_t^\mathsf{T} = \Sigma_{t|t} - \Sigma_{t|t}F_t^\mathsf{T}\Sigma_{t+1|t}^{-1}\Sigma_{t+1|t}G_t^\mathsf{T} \tag{8.87}$$

$$= \Sigma_{t|t}(I - F_t^\mathsf{T}G_t^\mathsf{T}) \tag{8.88}$$

where G_t is the backwards Kalman gain defined in Equation (8.67).

8.2.4   Information form filtering and smoothing

This section is written by Giles Harper-Donnelly.

In this section, we derive the Kalman filter and smoother algorithms in information form. We will see that this is the "dual" of Kalman filtering/smoothing in moment form. In particular, while computing marginals in moment form is easy, computing conditionals is hard (requires a matrix inverse). Conversely, for information form, computing marginals is hard, but computing conditionals is easy.

8.2.4.1   Filtering: algorithm

The predict step has a similar structure to the update step in moment form. We start with the prior $p(z_{t-1}|y_{1:t-1}, u_{1:t-1}) = \mathcal{N}_c(z_{t-1}|\eta_{t-1|t-1}, \Lambda_{t-1|t-1})$ and then compute

$$p(z_t|y_{1:t-1}, u_{1:t}) = \mathcal{N}_c(z_t|\eta_{t|t-1}, \Lambda_{t|t-1}) \tag{8.89}$$

$$M_t = \Lambda_{t-1|t-1} + F_t^\mathsf{T}Q_t^{-1}F_t \tag{8.90}$$

$$J_t = Q_t^{-1}F_tM_t^{-1} \tag{8.91}$$

$$\Lambda_{t|t-1} = Q_t^{-1} - Q_t^{-1}F_t(\Lambda_{t-1|t-1} + F_t^\mathsf{T}Q_t^{-1}F_t)^{-1} F_t^\mathsf{T}Q_t^{-1} \tag{8.92}$$

$$= Q_t^{-1} - J_tF_t^\mathsf{T}Q_t^{-1} \tag{8.93}$$

$$= Q_t^{-1} - J_tM_tJ_t^\mathsf{T} \tag{8.94}$$

$$\eta_{t|t-1} = J_t\eta_{t-1|t-1} + \Lambda_{t|t-1}(B_tu_t + b_t), \tag{8.95}$$

where J_t is analogous to the Kalman gain matrix in moment form Equation (8.28). From the matrix inversion lemma, Equation (2.93), we see that Equation (8.92) is the inverse of the predicted covariance $\Sigma_{t|t-1}$ given in Equation (8.24).

The update step in information form is as follows:

$$p(\boldsymbol{z}_t|\boldsymbol{y}_{1:t}, \boldsymbol{u}_{1:t}) = \mathcal{N}_c(\boldsymbol{z}_t|\boldsymbol{\eta}_{t|t}, \boldsymbol{\Lambda}_{t|t}) \tag{8.96}$$

$$\boldsymbol{\Lambda}_{t|t} = \boldsymbol{\Lambda}_{t|t-1} + \mathbf{H}_t^\mathsf{T} \mathbf{R}_t^{-1} \mathbf{H}_t \tag{8.97}$$

$$\boldsymbol{\eta}_{t|t} = \boldsymbol{\eta}_{t|t-1} + \mathbf{H}_t^\mathsf{T} \mathbf{R}_t^{-1}(\boldsymbol{y}_t - \mathbf{D}_t \boldsymbol{u}_t - \boldsymbol{d}_t). \tag{8.98}$$

8.2.4.2 Filtering: derivation

For the predict step, we first derive the joint distribution over hidden states at $t, t-1$:

$$p(\boldsymbol{z}_{t-1}, \boldsymbol{z}_t|\boldsymbol{y}_{1:t-1}, \boldsymbol{u}_{1:t}) = p(\boldsymbol{z}_t|\boldsymbol{z}_{t-1}, \boldsymbol{u}_t)p(\boldsymbol{z}_{t-1}|\boldsymbol{y}_{1:t-1}, \boldsymbol{u}_{1:t-1}) \tag{8.99}$$

$$= \mathcal{N}_c(\boldsymbol{z}_t, |\mathbf{Q}_t^{-1}(\mathbf{F}_t \boldsymbol{z}_{t-1} + \mathbf{B}_t \boldsymbol{u}_t + \boldsymbol{b}_t), \mathbf{Q}_t^{-1}) \tag{8.100}$$

$$\times \mathcal{N}_c(\boldsymbol{z}_{t-1}, |\boldsymbol{\eta}_{t-1|t-1}, \boldsymbol{\Lambda}_{t-1|t-1}) \tag{8.101}$$

$$= \mathcal{N}_c(\boldsymbol{z}_{t-1}, \boldsymbol{z}_t|\boldsymbol{\eta}_{t-1,t|t}, \boldsymbol{\Lambda}_{t-1,t|t}) \tag{8.102}$$

where

$$\boldsymbol{\eta}_{t-1,t|t-1} = \begin{pmatrix} \boldsymbol{\eta}_{t-1|t-1} - \mathbf{F}_t^\mathsf{T} \mathbf{Q}_t^{-1}(\mathbf{B}_t \boldsymbol{u}_t + \boldsymbol{b}_t) \\ \mathbf{Q}_t^{-1}(\mathbf{B}_t \boldsymbol{u}_t + \boldsymbol{b}_t) \end{pmatrix} \tag{8.103}$$

$$\boldsymbol{\Lambda}_{t-1,t|t-1} = \begin{pmatrix} \boldsymbol{\Lambda}_{t-1|t-1} + \mathbf{F}_t^\mathsf{T} \mathbf{Q}_t^{-1} \mathbf{F}_t & -\mathbf{F}_t^\mathsf{T} \mathbf{Q}_t^{-1} \\ -\mathbf{Q}_t^{-1} \mathbf{F}_t & \mathbf{Q}_t^{-1} \end{pmatrix} \tag{8.104}$$

The information form predicted parameters $\boldsymbol{\eta}_{t|t-1}, \boldsymbol{\Lambda}_{t|t-1}$ can then be derived using the marginalisation formulae in Section 2.3.1.4.

For the update step, we start with the joint distribution over the hidden state and the observation at t:

$$p(\boldsymbol{z}_t, \boldsymbol{y}_t|\boldsymbol{y}_{1:t-1}, \boldsymbol{u}_{1:t}) = p(\boldsymbol{y}_t|\boldsymbol{z}_t, \boldsymbol{u}_t)p(\boldsymbol{z}_t|\boldsymbol{y}_{1:t-1}, \boldsymbol{u}_{1:t}) \tag{8.105}$$

$$= \mathcal{N}_c(\boldsymbol{y}_t, |\mathbf{R}_t^{-1}(\mathbf{H}_t \boldsymbol{z}_t + \mathbf{D}\boldsymbol{u}_t + \boldsymbol{d}_t), \mathbf{R}_t^{-1})\mathcal{N}_c(\boldsymbol{z}_t|\boldsymbol{\eta}_{t|t-1}, \boldsymbol{\Lambda}_{t|t-1}) \tag{8.106}$$

$$= \mathcal{N}_c(\boldsymbol{z}_t, \boldsymbol{y}|\boldsymbol{\eta}_{z,y|t}, \boldsymbol{\Lambda}_{z,y|t}) \tag{8.107}$$

where

$$\boldsymbol{\eta}_{z,y|t} = \begin{pmatrix} \boldsymbol{\eta}_{t|t-1} - \mathbf{H}_t^\mathsf{T} \mathbf{R}_t^{-1}(\mathbf{D}_t \boldsymbol{u}_t + \boldsymbol{d}_t) \\ \mathbf{R}_t^{-1}(\mathbf{D}_t \boldsymbol{u}_t + \boldsymbol{d}_t) \end{pmatrix} \tag{8.108}$$

$$\boldsymbol{\Lambda}_{z,y|t} = \begin{pmatrix} \boldsymbol{\Lambda}_{t|t-1} + \mathbf{H}_t^\mathsf{T} \mathbf{R}_t^{-1} \mathbf{H}_t & -\mathbf{H}_t^\mathsf{T} \mathbf{R}_t^{-1} \\ -\mathbf{R}_t^{-1} \mathbf{H}_t & \mathbf{R}_t^{-1} \end{pmatrix} \tag{8.109}$$

The information form filtered parameters $\boldsymbol{\eta}_{t|t}, \boldsymbol{\Lambda}_{t|t}$ are then derived using the conditional formulae in 2.3.1.4.

8.2.4.3   Smoothing: algorithm

The smoothing equations are as follows:

$$p(\boldsymbol{z}_t|\boldsymbol{y}_{1:T}) = \mathcal{N}_c(\boldsymbol{z}_t|\boldsymbol{\eta}_{t|T}, \boldsymbol{\Lambda}_{t|T}) \tag{8.110}$$

$$\mathbf{U}_t = \mathbf{Q}_t^{-1} + \boldsymbol{\Lambda}_{t+1|T} - \boldsymbol{\Lambda}_{t+1|t} \tag{8.111}$$

$$\mathbf{L}_t = \mathbf{F}_t^\mathsf{T}\mathbf{Q}_t^{-1}\mathbf{U}_t^{-1} \tag{8.112}$$

$$\boldsymbol{\Lambda}_{t|T} = \boldsymbol{\Lambda}_{t|t} + \mathbf{F}_t^\mathsf{T}\mathbf{Q}_t^{-1}\mathbf{F}_t - \mathbf{L}_t\mathbf{Q}_t^{-1}\mathbf{F} \tag{8.113}$$

$$= \boldsymbol{\Lambda}_{t|t} + \mathbf{F}_t^\mathsf{T}\mathbf{Q}_t^{-1}\mathbf{F}_t - \mathbf{L}_t\mathbf{U}_t\mathbf{L}_t^\mathsf{T} \tag{8.114}$$

$$\boldsymbol{\eta}_{t|T} = \boldsymbol{\eta}_{t|t} + \mathbf{L}_t(\boldsymbol{\eta}_{t+1|T} - \boldsymbol{\eta}_{t+1|t}). \tag{8.115}$$

The parameters $\boldsymbol{\eta}_{t|t}$ and $\boldsymbol{\Lambda}_{t|t}$ are the filtered values from Equations (8.98) and (8.97) respectively. Similarly, $\boldsymbol{\eta}_{t+1|t}$ and $\boldsymbol{\Lambda}_{t+1|t}$ are the predicted parameters from Equations (8.95) and (8.92). The matrix $\mathbf{L}_t$ is the information form analog to the backwards Kalman gain matrix in Equation (8.67).

8.2.4.4   Smoothing: derivation

From the generic forwards-filtering backwards-smoothing equation, Equation (8.14), we have

$$p(\boldsymbol{z}_t|\boldsymbol{y}_{1:T}) = p(\boldsymbol{z}_t|\boldsymbol{y}_{1:t}) \int \left[\frac{p(\boldsymbol{z}_{t+1}|\boldsymbol{z}_t)p(\boldsymbol{z}_{t+1}|\boldsymbol{y}_{1:T})}{p(\boldsymbol{z}_{t+1}|\boldsymbol{y}_{1:t})} \right] d\boldsymbol{z}_{t+1} \tag{8.116}$$

$$= \int p(\boldsymbol{z}_t, \boldsymbol{z}_{t+1}|\boldsymbol{y}_{1:t}) \frac{p(\boldsymbol{z}_{t+1}|\boldsymbol{y}_{1:T})}{p(\boldsymbol{z}_{t+1}|\boldsymbol{y}_{1:t})} d\boldsymbol{z}_{t+1} \tag{8.117}$$

$$= \int \mathcal{N}_c(\boldsymbol{z}_t, \boldsymbol{z}_{t+1}|\boldsymbol{\eta}_{t,t+1|t}, \boldsymbol{\Lambda}_{t,t+1|t}) \frac{\mathcal{N}_c(\boldsymbol{z}_{t+1}|\boldsymbol{\eta}_{t+1|T}, \boldsymbol{\Lambda}_{t+1|T})}{\mathcal{N}_c(\boldsymbol{z}_{t+1}|\boldsymbol{\eta}_{t+1|t}, \boldsymbol{\Lambda}_{t+1|t})} d\boldsymbol{z}_{t+1} \tag{8.118}$$

$$= \int \mathcal{N}_c(\boldsymbol{z}_t, \boldsymbol{z}_{t+1}|\boldsymbol{\eta}_{t,t+1|T}, \boldsymbol{\Lambda}_{t,t+1|T}) d\boldsymbol{z}_{t+1}. \tag{8.119}$$

The parameters of the joint filtering predictive distribution, $p(\boldsymbol{z}_t, \boldsymbol{z}_{t+1}|\boldsymbol{y}_{1:t})$, take precisely the same form as those in the filtering derivation described in Section 8.2.4.2:

$$\boldsymbol{\eta}_{t,t+1|t} = \begin{pmatrix} \boldsymbol{\eta}_{t|t} \\ \mathbf{0} \end{pmatrix}, \quad \boldsymbol{\Lambda}_{t,t+1|t} = \begin{pmatrix} \boldsymbol{\Lambda}_{t|t} + \mathbf{F}_{t+1}^\mathsf{T}\mathbf{Q}_{t+1}^{-1}\mathbf{F}_{t+1} & -\mathbf{F}_{t+1}^\mathsf{T}\mathbf{Q}_{t+1}^{-1} \\ -\mathbf{Q}_{t+1}^{-1}\mathbf{F}_{t+1} & \mathbf{Q}_{t+1}^{-1} \end{pmatrix}, \tag{8.120}$$

We can now update this potential function by subtracting out the filtered information and adding in the smoothing information, using the rules for manipulating Gaussian potentials described in Section 2.3.3:

$$\boldsymbol{\eta}_{t,t+1|T} = \boldsymbol{\eta}_{t,t+1|t} + \begin{pmatrix} \mathbf{0} \\ \boldsymbol{\eta}_{t+1|T} \end{pmatrix} - \begin{pmatrix} \mathbf{0} \\ \boldsymbol{\eta}_{t+1|t} \end{pmatrix} = \begin{pmatrix} \boldsymbol{\eta}_{t|t} \\ \boldsymbol{\eta}_{t+1|T} - \boldsymbol{\eta}_{t+1|t} \end{pmatrix}, \tag{8.121}$$

and

$$\boldsymbol{\Lambda}_{t,t+1|T} = \boldsymbol{\Lambda}_{t,t+1|t} + \begin{pmatrix} \mathbf{0} & \mathbf{0} \\ \mathbf{0} & \boldsymbol{\Lambda}_{t+1|T} \end{pmatrix} - \begin{pmatrix} \mathbf{0} & \mathbf{0} \\ \mathbf{0} & \boldsymbol{\Lambda}_{t+1|t} \end{pmatrix} \tag{8.122}$$

$$= \begin{pmatrix} \boldsymbol{\Lambda}_{t|t} + \mathbf{F}_{t+1}^\mathsf{T}\mathbf{Q}_{t+1}^{-1}\mathbf{F}_{t+1} & -\mathbf{F}_{t+1}^\mathsf{T}\mathbf{Q}_{t+1}^{-1} \\ -\mathbf{Q}_{t+1}^{-1}\mathbf{F}_{t+1} & \mathbf{Q}_{t+1}^{-1} + \boldsymbol{\Lambda}_{t+1|T} - \boldsymbol{\Lambda}_{t+1|t} \end{pmatrix} \tag{8.123}$$

Applying the information form marginalization formula Equation (2.85) leads to Equation (8.115) and Equation (8.113).

8.3 Inference based on local linearization

In this section, we extend the Kalman filter and smoother to the case where the system dynamics and/or the observation model are nonlinear. (We continue to assume that the noise is additive Gaussian, as in Equation (8.15).) The basic idea is to linearize the dynamics and observation models about the previous state estimate using a first order Taylor series expansion, and then to apply the standard Kalman filter equations from Section 8.2.2. Intuitively we can think of this as approximating a stationary non-linear dynamical system with a non-stationary linear dynamical system. This approach is called the **extended Kalman filter** or **EKF**.

8.3.1 Taylor series expansion

Suppose $\boldsymbol{x} \sim \mathcal{N}(\boldsymbol{\mu}, \boldsymbol{\Sigma})$ and $\boldsymbol{y} = \boldsymbol{g}(\boldsymbol{x})$, where $\boldsymbol{g} : \mathbb{R}^n \to \mathbb{R}^m$ is a differentiable and invertible function. The pdf for $\boldsymbol{y}$ is given by

$$p(\boldsymbol{y}) = |\det \operatorname{Jac}(\boldsymbol{g}^{-1})(\boldsymbol{y})| \, \mathcal{N}(\boldsymbol{g}^{-1}(\boldsymbol{y})|\boldsymbol{\mu}, \boldsymbol{\Sigma}) \tag{8.124}$$

In general this is intractable to compute, so we seek an approximation.

Suppose $\boldsymbol{x} = \boldsymbol{\mu} + \boldsymbol{\delta}$, where $\boldsymbol{\delta} \sim \mathcal{N}(\boldsymbol{0}, \boldsymbol{\Sigma})$. Then we can form a first order Taylor series expansion of the function $\boldsymbol{g}$ as follows:

$$\boldsymbol{g}(\boldsymbol{x}) = \boldsymbol{g}(\boldsymbol{\mu} + \boldsymbol{\delta}) \approx \boldsymbol{g}(\boldsymbol{\mu}) + \mathbf{G}(\boldsymbol{\mu})\boldsymbol{\delta} \tag{8.125}$$

where $\mathbf{G}(\boldsymbol{\mu}) = \operatorname{Jac}(\boldsymbol{g})(\boldsymbol{\mu})$ is the Jacobian of $\boldsymbol{g}$ at $\boldsymbol{\mu}$:

$$[\mathbf{G}(\boldsymbol{\mu})]_{jj'} = \frac{\partial g_j(\boldsymbol{x})}{\partial x_{j'}}\Big|_{\boldsymbol{x}=\boldsymbol{\mu}} \tag{8.126}$$

We now derive the induced Gaussian approximation to $\boldsymbol{y} = \boldsymbol{g}(\boldsymbol{x})$. The mean is given by

$$\mathbb{E}\left[\boldsymbol{y}\right] \approx \mathbb{E}\left[\boldsymbol{g}(\boldsymbol{\mu}) + \mathbf{G}(\boldsymbol{\mu})\boldsymbol{\delta}\right] = \boldsymbol{g}(\boldsymbol{\mu}) + \mathbf{G}(\boldsymbol{\mu})\mathbb{E}\left[\boldsymbol{\delta}\right] = \boldsymbol{g}(\boldsymbol{\mu}) \tag{8.127}$$

The covariance is given by

$$\operatorname{Cov}\left[\boldsymbol{y}\right] = \mathbb{E}\left[(\boldsymbol{g}(\boldsymbol{x}) - \mathbb{E}\left[\boldsymbol{g}(\boldsymbol{x})\right])(\boldsymbol{g}(\boldsymbol{x}) - \mathbb{E}\left[\boldsymbol{g}(\boldsymbol{x})\right])^{\mathsf{T}}\right] \tag{8.128}$$

$$\approx \mathbb{E}\left[(\boldsymbol{g}(\boldsymbol{x}) - \boldsymbol{g}(\boldsymbol{\mu}))(\boldsymbol{g}(\boldsymbol{x}) - \boldsymbol{g}(\boldsymbol{\mu}))^{\mathsf{T}}\right] \tag{8.129}$$

$$\approx \mathbb{E}\left[(\boldsymbol{g}(\boldsymbol{\mu}) + \mathbf{G}(\boldsymbol{\mu})\boldsymbol{\delta} - \boldsymbol{g}(\boldsymbol{\mu}))(\boldsymbol{g}(\boldsymbol{\mu}) + \mathbf{G}(\boldsymbol{\mu})\boldsymbol{\delta} - \boldsymbol{g}(\boldsymbol{\mu}))^{\mathsf{T}}\right] \tag{8.130}$$

$$= \mathbb{E}\left[(\mathbf{G}(\boldsymbol{\mu})\boldsymbol{\delta})(\mathbf{G}(\boldsymbol{\mu})\boldsymbol{\delta})^{\mathsf{T}}\right] \tag{8.131}$$

$$= \mathbf{G}(\boldsymbol{\mu})\mathbb{E}\left[\boldsymbol{\delta}\boldsymbol{\delta}^{\mathsf{T}}\right]\mathbf{G}(\boldsymbol{\mu})^{\mathsf{T}} \tag{8.132}$$

$$= \mathbf{G}(\boldsymbol{\mu})\,\boldsymbol{\Sigma}\,\mathbf{G}(\boldsymbol{\mu})^{\mathsf{T}} \tag{8.133}$$

Algorithm 8.3: Linearized approximation to a joint Gaussian distribution.

1 def **LinearizedMoments**$(\boldsymbol{\mu}, \boldsymbol{\Sigma}, \boldsymbol{g}, \boldsymbol{\Omega})$:
2 $\hat{\boldsymbol{y}} = \boldsymbol{g}(\boldsymbol{\mu})$
3 $\mathbf{G} = \mathrm{Jac}(\boldsymbol{g})(\boldsymbol{\mu})$
4 $\mathbf{S} = \mathbf{G}\boldsymbol{\Sigma}\mathbf{G}^{\mathsf{T}} + \boldsymbol{\Omega}$
5 $\mathbf{C} = \boldsymbol{\Sigma}\mathbf{G}^{\mathsf{T}}$
6 Return $(\hat{\boldsymbol{y}}, \mathbf{S}, \mathbf{C})$

When deriving the EKF, we need to compute the joint distribution $p(\boldsymbol{x}, \boldsymbol{y})$ where

$$\boldsymbol{x} \sim \mathcal{N}(\boldsymbol{\mu}, \boldsymbol{\Sigma}), \ \boldsymbol{y} = \boldsymbol{g}(\boldsymbol{x}) + \boldsymbol{q}, \ \boldsymbol{q} \sim \mathcal{N}(\boldsymbol{0}, \boldsymbol{\Omega}) \tag{8.134}$$

where $\boldsymbol{q}$ is independent of $\boldsymbol{x}$. We can compute this by defining the augmented function $\tilde{\boldsymbol{g}}(\boldsymbol{x}) = [\boldsymbol{x}, \boldsymbol{g}(\boldsymbol{x})]$ and following the procedure above. The resulting linear approximation to the joint is

$$\begin{pmatrix} \boldsymbol{x} \\ \boldsymbol{y} \end{pmatrix} \sim \mathcal{N}\left(\begin{pmatrix} \boldsymbol{\mu} \\ \hat{\boldsymbol{y}} \end{pmatrix}, \begin{pmatrix} \boldsymbol{\Sigma} & \mathbf{C} \\ \mathbf{C}^{\mathsf{T}} & \mathbf{S} \end{pmatrix} \right) = \mathcal{N}\left(\begin{pmatrix} \boldsymbol{\mu} \\ \boldsymbol{g}(\boldsymbol{\mu}) \end{pmatrix}, \begin{pmatrix} \boldsymbol{\Sigma} & \boldsymbol{\Sigma}\mathbf{G}^{\mathsf{T}} \\ \mathbf{G}\boldsymbol{\Sigma} & \mathbf{G}\boldsymbol{\Sigma}\mathbf{G}^{\mathsf{T}} + \boldsymbol{\Omega} \end{pmatrix} \right) \tag{8.135}$$

where the parameters are computed using Algorithm 8.3. We can then condition this joint Gaussian on the observed value $\boldsymbol{y}$ to get the posterior.

It is also possible to derive an approximation for the case of non-additive Gaussian noise, where $\boldsymbol{y} = \boldsymbol{g}(\boldsymbol{x}, \boldsymbol{q})$. See [SS23, Sec 7.1] for details.

8.3.2   The extended Kalman filter (EKF)

We now derive the extended Kalman filter for performing approximate inference in the model given by Equation (8.15). We first linearize the dynamics model around $\boldsymbol{\mu}_{t-1|t-1}$ to get an approximation to the one-step-ahead predictive distribution $p(\boldsymbol{z}_t | \boldsymbol{y}_{1:t-1}, \boldsymbol{u}_{1:t}) = \mathcal{N}(\boldsymbol{z}_t | \boldsymbol{\mu}_{t|t-1}, \boldsymbol{\Sigma}_{t|t-1})$. We then linearize the observation model around $\boldsymbol{\mu}_{t|t-1}$, and then perform a Gaussian update. (In Section 8.3.2.2, we consider linearizing around a different point that gives better accuracy.)

We can write one step of the EKF algorithm using the notation from Section 8.2.2.5 as follows:

$$(\boldsymbol{\mu}_{t|t-1}, \boldsymbol{\Sigma}_{t|t-1}, -) = \textbf{LinearizedMoments}(\boldsymbol{\mu}_{t-1|t-1}, \boldsymbol{\Sigma}_{t-1|t-1}, \boldsymbol{f}(\cdot, \boldsymbol{u}_t), \mathbf{Q}_t) \tag{8.136}$$

$$(\hat{\boldsymbol{y}}_t, \mathbf{S}_t, \mathbf{C}_t) = \textbf{LinearizedMoments}(\boldsymbol{\mu}_{t|t-1}, \boldsymbol{\Sigma}_{t|t-1}, \boldsymbol{h}(\cdot, \boldsymbol{u}_t), \mathbf{R}_t) \tag{8.137}$$

$$(\boldsymbol{\mu}_{t|t}, \boldsymbol{\Sigma}_{t|t}, \ell_t) = \textbf{GaussCondition}(\boldsymbol{\mu}_{t|t-1}, \boldsymbol{\Sigma}_{t|t-1}, \hat{\boldsymbol{y}}_t, \mathbf{S}_t, \mathbf{C}_t, \boldsymbol{y}_t) \tag{8.138}$$

Spelling out the details more explicitly, we can write the predict step as follows:

$$\boldsymbol{\mu}_{t|t-1} = \boldsymbol{f}(\boldsymbol{\mu}_{t-1}, \boldsymbol{u}_t) \tag{8.139}$$

$$\boldsymbol{\Sigma}_{t|t-1} = \mathbf{F}_t \boldsymbol{\Sigma}_{t-1} \mathbf{F}_t^{\mathsf{T}} + \mathbf{Q}_t \tag{8.140}$$

where $\mathbf{F}_t \equiv \mathrm{Jac}(\boldsymbol{f}(\cdot, \boldsymbol{u}_t))(\boldsymbol{\mu}_{t|t-1})$ is the $N_z \times N_z$ Jacobian matrix of the dynamics model. The update step is as follows:

$$\hat{\boldsymbol{y}}_t = h(\boldsymbol{\mu}_{t|t-1}, \boldsymbol{u}_t)) \tag{8.141}$$

$$\mathbf{S}_t = \mathbf{H}_t \boldsymbol{\Sigma}_{t|t-1} \mathbf{H}_t^\mathsf{T} + \mathbf{R}_t \tag{8.142}$$

$$\mathbf{K}_t = \boldsymbol{\Sigma}_{t|t-1} \mathbf{H}_t^\mathsf{T} \mathbf{S}_t^{-1} \tag{8.143}$$

$$\boldsymbol{\mu}_{t|t} = \boldsymbol{\mu}_{t|t-1} + \mathbf{K}_t(\boldsymbol{y}_t - \hat{\boldsymbol{y}}_t) \tag{8.144}$$

$$\boldsymbol{\Sigma}_{t|t} = \boldsymbol{\Sigma}_{t|t-1} - \mathbf{K}_t \mathbf{H}_t \boldsymbol{\Sigma}_{t|t-1} = \boldsymbol{\Sigma}_{t|t-1} - \mathbf{K}_t \mathbf{S}_t \mathbf{K}_t^\mathsf{T} \tag{8.145}$$

where $\mathbf{H}_t \equiv \mathrm{Jac}(h(\cdot, \boldsymbol{u}_t))(\boldsymbol{\mu}_{t|t-1})$ is the $N_y \times N_z$ Jacobian matrix of the observation model and $\mathbf{K}_t$ is the $N_z \times N_y$ Kalman gain matrix. See Supplementary Section 8.2.1 for the details of the derivation.

8.3.2.1 Accuracy

The EKF is widely used because it is simple and relatively efficient. However, there are two cases when the EKF works poorly [IX00; VDMW03]. The first is when the prior covariance is large. In this case, the prior distribution is broad, so we end up sending a lot of probability mass through different parts of the function that are far from $\boldsymbol{\mu}_{t-1|t-1}$, where the function has been linearized. The other setting where the EKF works poorly is when the function is highly nonlinear near the current mean (see Figure 8.5a).

A more accurate approach is to use a second-order Taylor series approximation, known as the **second order EKF**. The resulting updates can still be computed in closed form (see [SS23, Sec 7.3] for details). We can further improve performance by repeatedly re-linearizing the equations around $\boldsymbol{\mu}_t$ instead of $\boldsymbol{\mu}_{t|t-1}$; this is called the iterated EKF (see Section 8.3.2.2). In Section 8.4.2, we will discuss an algorithm called the unscented Kalman filter (UKF) which is even more accurate, and is derivative free (does not require computing Jacobians).

8.3.2.2 Iterated EKF

Algorithm 8.4: Iterated extended Kalman filter.

1 def **IEKF**$(\boldsymbol{f}, \mathbf{Q}, h, \mathbf{R}, \boldsymbol{y}_{1:T}, \boldsymbol{\mu}_{0|0}, \boldsymbol{\Sigma}_{0|0}, J)$:
2   **foreach** $t = 1 : T$ **do**
3   Predict step:
4       $(\boldsymbol{\mu}_{t|t-1}, \boldsymbol{\Sigma}_{t|t-1}, -) = \mathbf{LinearizedMoments}(\boldsymbol{\mu}_{t-1|t-1}, \boldsymbol{\Sigma}_{t-1|t-1}, \boldsymbol{f}(\cdot, \boldsymbol{u}_t), \mathbf{Q}_t)$
5   Update step:
6       $\boldsymbol{\mu}_{t|t} = \boldsymbol{\mu}_{t|t-1}, \boldsymbol{\Sigma}_{t|t} = \boldsymbol{\Sigma}_{t|t-1}$
7   **foreach** $j = 1 : J$ **do**
8          $(\hat{\boldsymbol{y}}_t, \mathbf{S}_t, \mathbf{C}_t) = \mathbf{LinearizedMoments}(\boldsymbol{\mu}_{t|t}, \boldsymbol{\Sigma}_{t|t}, h(\cdot, \boldsymbol{u}_t), \mathbf{R}_t)$
          $(\boldsymbol{\mu}_{t|t}, \boldsymbol{\Sigma}_{t|t}, \ell_t) = \mathbf{GaussCondition}(\boldsymbol{\mu}_{t|t-1}, \boldsymbol{\Sigma}_{t|t-1}, \hat{\boldsymbol{y}}_t, \mathbf{S}_t, \mathbf{C}_t, \boldsymbol{y}_t)$
9 Return $(\boldsymbol{\mu}_{t|t}, \boldsymbol{\Sigma}_{t|t})_{t=1}^T$

Another way to improve the accuracy of the EKF is by repeatedly re-linearizing the measurement model around the current posterior, $\boldsymbol{\mu}_{t|t}$, instead of $\boldsymbol{\mu}_{t|t-1}$; this is called the **iterated EKF** [BC93].

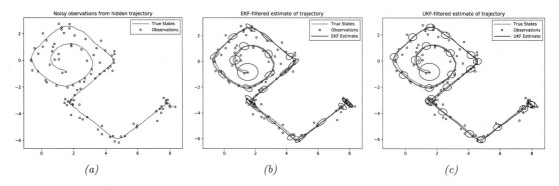

Figure 8.4: *Illustration of filtering applied to a 2d nonlinear dynamical system. (a) True underlying state and observed data. (b) Extended Kalman filter estimate. Generated by ekf_spiral.ipynb. (c) Unscented Kalman filter estimate. Generated by ukf_spiral.ipynb.*

See Algorithm 8.4 for the pseudocode. (If we set the number of iterations to $J = 1$, we recover the standard EKF.)

The IEKF can be interpreted as a Gauss–Newton method for finding MAP estimate of the state at each step [BC93]. Specifically it minimizes the following objective:

$$\mathcal{L}(\boldsymbol{z}_t) = \frac{1}{2}(\boldsymbol{y}_t - \boldsymbol{h}(\boldsymbol{z}_t))^\mathsf{T}\mathbf{R}_t^{-1}(\boldsymbol{y}_t - \boldsymbol{h}(\boldsymbol{z}_t)) + \frac{1}{2}(\boldsymbol{z}_t - \boldsymbol{\mu}_{t|t-1})^\mathsf{T}\boldsymbol{\Sigma}_{t|t-1}^{-1}(\boldsymbol{z}_t - \boldsymbol{\mu}_{t|t-1}) \tag{8.146}$$

See [SS23, Sec 7.4] for details.

Unfortunately the Gauss-Newton method can sometimes diverge. Various robust extensions — including Levenberg-Marquardt, line search, and quasi-Newton methods — have been proposed in [SHA15; SS20a]. See [SS23, Sec 7.5] for details.

8.3.2.3   Example: Tracking a point spiraling in 2d

In Section 8.2.1.1, we considered an example of state estimation and tracking of an object moving in 2d under a linear dynamics model with a linear observation model. However, motion and observation models are often nonlinear. For example, consider an object that is moving along a curved trajectory, such as this:

$$\boldsymbol{f}(\boldsymbol{z}) = (z_1 + \Delta\sin(z_2), z_2 + \Delta\cos(z_1)) \tag{8.147}$$

where Δ is the discrete step size (see [SS19, p221] for the continuous time version). For simplicity, we assume full visibility of the state vector (modulo observation noise), so $\boldsymbol{h}(\boldsymbol{z}) = \boldsymbol{z}$.

Despite the simplicity of this model, exact inference is intractable. However, we can easily apply the EKF. The results are shown in Figure 8.4b.

8.3.2.4   Example: Neural network training

In Section 17.5.2, we show how to use the EKF to perform online parameter inference for an MLP regression model.

8.3.3 The extended Kalman smoother (EKS)

We can extend the EKF to the offline smoothing case, resulting in the **extended Kalman smoother**, also called the **extended RTS smoother**. We just need to linearize the dynamics around the filtered mean when computing $\mathbf{F}_t$, and then we can apply the standard Kalman smoother update. See [SS23, Sec 13.1] for more details.

For improved accuracy, we can use the **iterated EKS**, which relinearizes the model at the previous MAP estimate. In [Bel94], they show that IEKS is equivalent to a Gauss-Newton method for computing the MAP estimate of the smoothing posterior. Unfortunately the IEKS can diverge in some cases. A robust IEKS method, that uses line search and Levenberg-Marquardt to update the parameters, is presented in [SS20a].

8.4 Inference based on the unscented transform

In this section, we replace the local linearization of the model with a different approximation. The key idea is this: instead of computing a linear approximation to the dynamics and measurement functions, and then passing a Gaussian distribtution through the linearized functions, we instead approximate the joint distributions $p(\boldsymbol{z}_{t-1}, \boldsymbol{z}_t | \boldsymbol{y}_{1:t-1})$ and $p(\boldsymbol{z}_t, \boldsymbol{y}_t | \boldsymbol{y}_{1:t-1})$ by Gaussians, where the moments are computed using numerical integration; we can then compute the marginal and conditional of these distributions to perform the time and measurement updates.

There are many methods to compute the Gaussian moments, as we discuss in Section 8.5.1. Here we use a method based on the unscented transform (see Section 8.4.1). Using the unscented transform for the transition and observation models gives the the overall method, known as the **unscented Kalman filter** or **UKF**, [JU97; JUDW00], also called the **sigma point filter** [VDMW03].

The main advantage of the UKF over the EKF is that it can be more accurate, and more stable. (Indeed, [JU97; JUDW00] claim the term "unscented" was invented because the method "doesn't stink".) In addition, the UKF does not need to compute Jacobians of the observation and dynamics models, so it can be applied to non-differentiable models, or ones with hard constraints. However, the UKF can be slower, since it requires N_z evaluations of the dynamics and observation models. In addition, it has 3 hyper-parameters that need to be set.

8.4.1 The unscented transform

Algorithm 8.5: Computing sigma points using unscented transform.

1 def **SigmaPoints**$(\boldsymbol{\mu}, \boldsymbol{\Sigma}; \alpha, \beta, \kappa)$:
2 $n = $ dimensionality of $\boldsymbol{\mu}$
3 $\lambda = \alpha^2(n + \kappa) - n$
4 Compute a set of $2n + 1$ sigma points:
$\quad \mathcal{X}_0 = \boldsymbol{\mu}, \ \mathcal{X}_i = \boldsymbol{\mu} + \sqrt{n+\lambda} \left[\sqrt{\boldsymbol{\Sigma}}\right]_{:i}, \ \mathcal{X}_{i+n} = \boldsymbol{\mu} - \sqrt{n+\lambda} \left[\sqrt{\boldsymbol{\Sigma}}\right]_{:i}$
5 Compute a set of $2n + 1$ weights for the mean and covariance:
$\quad w_0^m = \frac{\lambda}{n+\lambda}, \ w_0^c = \frac{\lambda}{n+\lambda} + (1 - \alpha^2 + \beta), \ w_i^m = w_i^c = \frac{1}{2(n+\lambda)}$
6 Return $(\mathcal{X}_{0:2n}, w_{0:2n}^m, w_{0:2n}^c)$

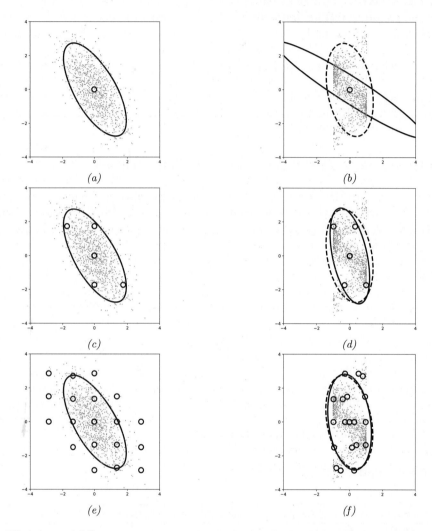

Figure 8.5: *Illustration of different ways to approximate the distribution induced by a nonlinear transformation* $f : \mathbb{R}^2 \to \mathbb{R}^2$. *(a) Data from the source distribution,* $\mathcal{D} = \{\boldsymbol{x}_i \sim p(\boldsymbol{x})\}$, *with Gaussian approximation superimposed. (b) The dots show a Monte Carlo approximation to* $p(f(\boldsymbol{x}))$ *derived from* $\mathcal{D}' = \{f(\boldsymbol{x}_i)\}$. *The dotted ellipse is a Gaussian approximation to this target distribution, computed from the empirical moments. The solid ellipse is a Taylor transform. (c) Unscented sigma points. (d) Unscented transform. (e) Gauss-Hermite points (order 5). (f) GH transform. Adapted from Figures 5.3–5.4 of [Sar13]. Generated by* gaussian_transforms.ipynb.

Algorithm 8.6: Unscented approximation to a joint Gaussian distribution.

1 def **UnscentedMoments**$(\boldsymbol{\mu}, \boldsymbol{\Sigma}, \boldsymbol{g}, \boldsymbol{\Omega}; \alpha, \beta, \kappa)$:
2 $(\mathcal{X}_{0:2n}, w^m_{0:2n}, w^c_{0:2n}) = $ **SigmaPoints**$(\boldsymbol{\mu}, \boldsymbol{\Sigma}; \alpha, \beta, \kappa)$
3 $\mathcal{Y}_i = \boldsymbol{g}(\mathcal{X}_i), \; i = 0 : 2n$
4 $\hat{\boldsymbol{y}} = \sum_{i=0}^{2n} w^m_i \mathcal{Y}_i$
5 $\mathbf{S} = \sum_{i=0}^{2n} w^c_i (\mathcal{Y}_i - \boldsymbol{\mu}_U)(\mathcal{Y}_i - \boldsymbol{\mu}_U)^\mathsf{T} + \boldsymbol{\Omega}$
6 $\mathbf{C} = \sum_{i=0}^{2n} w^c_i (\mathcal{X}_i - \boldsymbol{\mu})(\mathcal{Y}_i - \boldsymbol{\mu}_U)^\mathsf{T}$
7 Return $(\hat{\boldsymbol{y}}, \mathbf{S}, \mathbf{C})$

Suppose we have two random variables $\boldsymbol{x} \sim \mathcal{N}(\boldsymbol{\mu}, \boldsymbol{\Sigma})$ and $\boldsymbol{y} = \boldsymbol{g}(\boldsymbol{x})$, where $\boldsymbol{g} : \mathbb{R}^n \to \mathbb{R}^m$. The unscented transform forms a Gaussian approximation to $p(\boldsymbol{y})$ using the following process. First we compute a set of $2n+1$ sigma points, $\mathcal{X}_i$, and corresponding weights, w^m_i and w^c_i, using Algorithm 8.5, for $i = 0 : 2n$. (The notation $\mathbf{M}_{:i}$ means the i'th column of matrix $\mathbf{M}$, $\sqrt{\boldsymbol{\Sigma}}$ is the matrix square root, so $\sqrt{\boldsymbol{\Sigma}}\sqrt{\boldsymbol{\Sigma}}^\mathsf{T} = \boldsymbol{\Sigma}$.) Next we propagate the sigma points through the nonlinear function to get the following $2n + 1$ outputs:

$$\mathcal{Y}_i = \boldsymbol{g}(\mathcal{X}_i), \; i = 0 : 2n \tag{8.148}$$

Finally we estimate the mean and covariance of the resulting set of points:

$$\mathbb{E}\left[\boldsymbol{g}(\boldsymbol{x})\right] \approx \hat{\boldsymbol{y}} = \sum_{i=0}^{2n} w^m_i \mathcal{Y}_i \tag{8.149}$$

$$\mathrm{Cov}\left[\boldsymbol{g}(\boldsymbol{x})\right] \approx \mathbf{S}' = \sum_{i=0}^{2n} w^c_i (\mathcal{Y}_i - \hat{\boldsymbol{y}})(\mathcal{Y}_i - \hat{\boldsymbol{y}})^\mathsf{T} \tag{8.150}$$

Now suppose we want to approximate the joint distribution $p(\boldsymbol{x}, \boldsymbol{y})$, where $\boldsymbol{y} = \boldsymbol{g}(\boldsymbol{x}) + \boldsymbol{e}$, and $\boldsymbol{e} \sim \mathcal{N}(\boldsymbol{0}, \boldsymbol{\Omega})$. By defining the augmented function $\tilde{\boldsymbol{g}}(\boldsymbol{x}) = (\boldsymbol{x}, \boldsymbol{g}(\boldsymbol{x}))$, and applying the above procedure (and adding extra noise), we get

$$\begin{pmatrix} \boldsymbol{x} \\ \boldsymbol{y} \end{pmatrix} \sim \mathcal{N}\left(\begin{pmatrix} \boldsymbol{\mu} \\ \hat{\boldsymbol{y}} \end{pmatrix}, \begin{pmatrix} \boldsymbol{\Sigma} & \mathbf{C} \\ \mathbf{C}^\mathsf{T} & \mathbf{S} \end{pmatrix} \right) \tag{8.151}$$

where the parameters are computed using Algorithm 8.6.

The sigma points and their weights depend on three hyperparameters, α, β, and κ, which determine the spread of the sigma points around the mean. A typical recommended setting for these is $\alpha = 10^{-3}$, $\kappa = 1$, $\beta = 2$ [Bit16].

In Figure 8.5(a-b), we show the linearized Taylor transform discussed in Section 8.3.1 applied to a nonlinear function. In Figure 8.5(c-d), we show the corresponding unscented transform, which we can see is more accurate. In fact, the unscented transform (which uses $2n + 1$ sigma points) is a third-order method in the sense that the mean of $\boldsymbol{y}$ is exact for polynomials up to order 3. However the covariance is only exact for linear functions (first order polynomials), because the square of a second order polynomial is already order 4. However, the UT idea can be extended to order 5 using $2n^2 + 1$ sigma points [MS67]; this can capture covariance terms exactly for quadratic functions. We discuss even more accurate approximations, based on numerical integration methods, in Section 8.5.1.4.

8.4.2 The unscented Kalman filter (UKF)

The UKF applies the unscented transform twice, once to approximate passing through the system model $\boldsymbol{f}$, and once to approximate passing through the measurement model $\boldsymbol{h}$. By analogy to Section 8.2.2.5, we can derive the UKF algorithm as follows:

$$(\boldsymbol{\mu}_{t|t-1}, \boldsymbol{\Sigma}_{t|t-1}, -) = \textbf{UnscentedMoments}(\boldsymbol{\mu}_{t-1|t-1}, \boldsymbol{\Sigma}_{t-1|t-1}, \boldsymbol{f}(\cdot, \boldsymbol{u}_t), \mathbf{Q}_t) \qquad (8.152)$$

$$(\hat{\boldsymbol{y}}_t, \mathbf{S}_t, \mathbf{C}_t) = \textbf{UnscentedMoments}(\boldsymbol{\mu}_{t|t-1}, \boldsymbol{\Sigma}_{t|t-1}, \boldsymbol{h}(\cdot, \boldsymbol{u}_t), \mathbf{R}_t) \qquad (8.153)$$

$$(\boldsymbol{\mu}_{t|t}, \boldsymbol{\Sigma}_{t|t}, \ell_t) = \textbf{GaussCondition}(\boldsymbol{\mu}_{t|t-1}, \boldsymbol{\Sigma}_{t|t-1}, \hat{\boldsymbol{y}}_t, \mathbf{S}_t, \mathbf{C}_t, \boldsymbol{y}_t) \qquad (8.154)$$

See [SS23, Sec 8.8] for more details.

In Figure 8.4c, we illustrate the UKF algorithm (with $\alpha = 1$, $\beta = 0$, $\kappa = 2$) applied to the 2d nonlinear tracking problem from Section 8.3.2.3.

8.4.3 The unscented Kalman smoother (UKS)

The **unscented Kalman smoother**, also called the **unscented RTS smoother** [Sar08], is a simple modification of the usual Kalman smoothing method, where we approximate the nonlinearity by the unscented transform. The key insight is to notice that the reverse Kalman gain matrix $\mathbf{G}_t$ in Equation (8.80) can be defined in terms of the predicted covariance and cross covariance, both of which can be estimated using the UT. Once we have computed this, we can use the RTS equations in the usual way. See [SS23, Sec 14.4] for the details.

An interesting application of unscented Kalman smoothing was its use by the UK government as part of its COVID-19 contact tracing app [Lov+20; BCH20]. The app used the UKS to estimate the distance between (anonymized) people based on bluetooth signal strength between their mobile phones; the distance was then combined with other signals, such as contact duration and infectiousness level of the index case, to estimate the risk of transmission. (See also [MKS21] for a way to learn the risk score.)

8.5   Other variants of the Kalman filter

In this section, we briefly mention some other variants of Kalman filtering. For a more extensive review, see [SS23; Li+17e].

8.5.1   General Gaussian filtering

This section is co-authored with Peter Chang.

Let $p(\boldsymbol{z}) = \mathcal{N}(\boldsymbol{z}|\boldsymbol{\mu}, \boldsymbol{\Sigma})$ and $p(\boldsymbol{y}|\boldsymbol{z}) = \mathcal{N}(\boldsymbol{y}|\boldsymbol{h}_{\boldsymbol{\mu}}(\boldsymbol{z}), \boldsymbol{\Omega})$ for some function $\boldsymbol{h}_{\boldsymbol{\mu}}$. Let $p(\boldsymbol{z}, \boldsymbol{y}) = p(\boldsymbol{z})p(\boldsymbol{y}|\boldsymbol{z})$ be the exact joint distribution. The best Gaussian approximation to the joint can be computed by solving

$$q(\boldsymbol{z}, \boldsymbol{y}) = \operatorname*{argmin}_{q \in \mathcal{N}} D_{\mathrm{KL}} \left(p(\boldsymbol{z}, \boldsymbol{y}) \,\|\, q(\boldsymbol{z}, \boldsymbol{y}) \right) \tag{8.155}$$

As we explain in Section 5.1.4.2, this can be obtained by **moment matching**, i.e.,

$$q(\boldsymbol{z}, \boldsymbol{y}) = \mathcal{N} \left(\begin{pmatrix} \boldsymbol{z} \\ \boldsymbol{y} \end{pmatrix} \,\middle|\, \begin{pmatrix} \boldsymbol{\mu} \\ \hat{\boldsymbol{y}} \end{pmatrix}, \begin{pmatrix} \boldsymbol{\Sigma} & \mathbf{C} \\ \mathbf{C}^{\mathsf{T}} & \mathbf{S} \end{pmatrix} \right) \tag{8.156}$$

where

$$\hat{\boldsymbol{y}} = \mathbb{E}[\boldsymbol{y}] = \int \boldsymbol{h}_{\boldsymbol{\mu}}(\boldsymbol{z}) \mathcal{N}(\boldsymbol{z}|\boldsymbol{\mu}, \boldsymbol{\Sigma}) d\boldsymbol{z} \tag{8.157}$$

$$\mathbf{S} = \mathbb{V}[\boldsymbol{y}] = \boldsymbol{\Omega} + \int (\boldsymbol{h}_{\boldsymbol{\mu}}(\boldsymbol{z}) - \hat{\boldsymbol{y}})(\boldsymbol{h}_{\boldsymbol{\mu}}(\boldsymbol{z}) - \hat{\boldsymbol{y}})^{\mathsf{T}} \mathcal{N}(\boldsymbol{z}|\boldsymbol{\mu}, \boldsymbol{\Sigma}) d\boldsymbol{z} \tag{8.158}$$

$$\mathbf{C} = \operatorname{Cov}[\boldsymbol{z}, \boldsymbol{y}] = \int (\boldsymbol{z} - \boldsymbol{\mu})(\boldsymbol{h}_{\boldsymbol{\mu}}(\boldsymbol{z}) - \hat{\boldsymbol{y}})^{\mathsf{T}} \mathcal{N}(\boldsymbol{z}|\boldsymbol{\mu}, \boldsymbol{\Sigma}) d\boldsymbol{z} \tag{8.159}$$

We can use the above Gaussian approximation either for the time update (i.e., going from $p(\boldsymbol{z}_{t-1}|\boldsymbol{y}_{1:t-1})$ to $p(\boldsymbol{z}_t|\boldsymbol{y}_{1:t-1})$ via $p(\boldsymbol{z}_{t-1}, \boldsymbol{z}_t|\boldsymbol{y}_{1:t-1})$), or for the measurement update, (i.e., going from $p(\boldsymbol{z}_t|\boldsymbol{y}_{1:t-1})$ to $p(\boldsymbol{z}_t|\boldsymbol{y}_{1:t})$ via $p(\boldsymbol{z}_t, \boldsymbol{y}_t|\boldsymbol{y}_{1:t-1})$). For example, if the prior from the time update is $p(\boldsymbol{z}_t) = \mathcal{N}(\boldsymbol{z}_t|\boldsymbol{\mu}_{t|t-1}, \boldsymbol{\Sigma}_{t|t-1})$, then the measurement update becomes

$$\mathbf{K}_t = \mathbf{C}_t \mathbf{S}_t^{-1} \tag{8.160}$$

$$\boldsymbol{\mu}_{t|t} = \boldsymbol{\mu}_{t|t-1} + \mathbf{K}_t(\boldsymbol{y}_t - \hat{\boldsymbol{y}}_t) \tag{8.161}$$

$$\boldsymbol{\Sigma}_{t|t} = \boldsymbol{\Sigma}_{t|t-1} - \mathbf{K}_t \mathbf{S}_t \mathbf{K}_t^{\mathsf{T}} \tag{8.162}$$

The resulting method is called **general Gaussian filtering** or **GGF** [IX00; Wu+06].

8.5.1.1 Statistical linear regression

An alternative perspective on the above method is that we are approximating the likelihood by $q(\boldsymbol{y}|\boldsymbol{z}) = \mathcal{N}(\boldsymbol{y}|\mathbf{A}\boldsymbol{z} + \boldsymbol{b}, \boldsymbol{\Omega})$, where we define

$$\begin{aligned} \mathbf{A} &= \mathbf{C}^{\mathsf{T}} \boldsymbol{\Sigma}^{-1} \\ \boldsymbol{b} &= \hat{\boldsymbol{y}} - \mathbf{A}\boldsymbol{\mu} \\ \boldsymbol{\Omega} &= \mathbf{S} - \mathbf{A}\boldsymbol{\Sigma}\mathbf{A}^{\mathsf{T}} \end{aligned} \tag{8.163}$$

This is called **statistical linear regression** or **SLR** [LBS01; AHE07], and ensures that we minimize

$$\mathcal{L}(\mathbf{A}, \boldsymbol{b}, \boldsymbol{\Omega}) = \mathbb{E}_{\mathcal{N}(\boldsymbol{z}|\boldsymbol{\mu}, \boldsymbol{\Sigma})} \left[D_{\mathrm{KL}} \left(p(\boldsymbol{y}|\boldsymbol{z}) \,\|\, q(\boldsymbol{y}|\boldsymbol{z}; \mathbf{A}, \boldsymbol{b}, \boldsymbol{\Omega}) \right) \right] \tag{8.164}$$

For the proof, see [GF+15; Kam+22].

Equivalently, one can show that the above parameters minimize the following mean squared error

$$\mathcal{L}(\mathbf{A}, \boldsymbol{b}) = \mathbb{E} \left[(\boldsymbol{y} - \mathbf{A}\boldsymbol{x} - \boldsymbol{b})^{\mathsf{T}} (\boldsymbol{y} - \mathbf{A}\boldsymbol{x} - \boldsymbol{b}) \right] \tag{8.165}$$

with $\boldsymbol{\Omega}$ given by the residual noise

$$\boldsymbol{\Omega} = \mathbb{E}\left[(\boldsymbol{y} - \mathbf{A}\boldsymbol{x} - \boldsymbol{b})(\boldsymbol{y} - \mathbf{A}\boldsymbol{x} - \boldsymbol{b})^{\mathsf{T}}\right] \tag{8.166}$$

See [SS23, Sec 9.4] for the proof.

Note that although SLR results in a linear model, it is different than the Taylor series approximation of Section 8.3.1, since the linearization is chosen to be optimal wrt a distribution of points (averaged over $\mathcal{N}(\boldsymbol{z}|\boldsymbol{\mu}, \boldsymbol{\Sigma})$), instead of just being optimal at a single point $\boldsymbol{\mu}$.

8.5.1.2   Approximating the moments

To implement GGF, we need a way to compute $\hat{\boldsymbol{y}}$, $\mathbf{S}$ and $\mathbf{C}$. To help with this, we define two functions to compute Gaussian first and second moments:

$$g_e(\boldsymbol{f}, \boldsymbol{\mu}, \boldsymbol{\Sigma}) \triangleq \int \boldsymbol{f}(\boldsymbol{z})\mathcal{N}(\boldsymbol{z}|\boldsymbol{\mu}, \boldsymbol{\Sigma})dz \tag{8.167}$$

$$g_c(\boldsymbol{f}, \boldsymbol{g}, \boldsymbol{\mu}, \boldsymbol{\Sigma}) \triangleq \int (\boldsymbol{f}(\boldsymbol{z}) - \overline{\boldsymbol{f}})(\boldsymbol{g}(\boldsymbol{z}) - \overline{\boldsymbol{g}})^{\mathsf{T}}\mathcal{N}(\boldsymbol{z}|\boldsymbol{\mu}, \boldsymbol{\Sigma})dz \tag{8.168}$$

where $\overline{\boldsymbol{f}} = g_e(\boldsymbol{f}, \boldsymbol{\mu}, \boldsymbol{\Sigma})$ and $\overline{\boldsymbol{g}} = g_e(\boldsymbol{g}, \boldsymbol{\mu}, \boldsymbol{\Sigma})$. There are several ways to compute these integrals, as we discuss below.

8.5.1.3   Approximation based on linearization

The simplest approach to approximating the moments is to linearize the functions $\boldsymbol{f}$ and $\boldsymbol{g}$ around $\boldsymbol{\mu}$, which yields the following (see Section 8.3.1):

$$\hat{\boldsymbol{f}}(\boldsymbol{z}) = \boldsymbol{\mu} + \mathbf{F}(\boldsymbol{z} - \boldsymbol{\mu}) \tag{8.169}$$
$$\hat{\boldsymbol{g}}(\boldsymbol{z}) = \boldsymbol{\mu} + \mathbf{G}(\boldsymbol{z} - \boldsymbol{\mu}) \tag{8.170}$$

where $\mathbf{F}$ and $\mathbf{G}$ are the Jacobians of f and g. Thus we get the following implementation of the moment functions:

$$g_e(\hat{\boldsymbol{f}}, \boldsymbol{\mu}, \boldsymbol{\Sigma}) = \mathbb{E}\left[\boldsymbol{\mu} + \mathbf{F}(\boldsymbol{z} - \boldsymbol{\mu})\right] = \boldsymbol{\mu} \tag{8.171}$$

$$g_c(\hat{\boldsymbol{f}}, \hat{\boldsymbol{g}}, \boldsymbol{\mu}, \boldsymbol{\Sigma}) = \mathbb{E}\left[(\hat{\boldsymbol{f}}(\boldsymbol{z}) - \overline{\boldsymbol{f}})(\hat{\boldsymbol{g}}(\boldsymbol{z}) - \overline{\boldsymbol{g}})^{\mathsf{T}}\right] \tag{8.172}$$

$$= \mathbb{E}\left[\hat{\boldsymbol{f}}(\boldsymbol{z})\hat{\boldsymbol{g}}(\boldsymbol{z})^{\mathsf{T}} + \overline{\boldsymbol{f}}\,\overline{\boldsymbol{g}}^{\mathsf{T}} - \hat{\boldsymbol{f}}(\boldsymbol{z})\overline{\boldsymbol{g}}^{\mathsf{T}} - \overline{\boldsymbol{f}}\hat{\boldsymbol{g}}(\boldsymbol{z})^{\mathsf{T}}\right] \tag{8.173}$$

$$= \mathbb{E}\left[(\boldsymbol{\mu} + \mathbf{F}(\boldsymbol{z} - \boldsymbol{\mu}))(\boldsymbol{\mu} + \mathbf{G}(\boldsymbol{z} - \boldsymbol{\mu}))^{\mathsf{T}} + \boldsymbol{\mu}\boldsymbol{\mu}^{\mathsf{T}} - \boldsymbol{\mu}\boldsymbol{\mu}^{\mathsf{T}} - \boldsymbol{\mu}\boldsymbol{\mu}^{\mathsf{T}}\right] \tag{8.174}$$

$$= \mathbb{E}\left[\boldsymbol{\mu}\boldsymbol{\mu}^{\mathsf{T}} + \mathbf{F}(\boldsymbol{z} - \boldsymbol{\mu})(\boldsymbol{z} - \boldsymbol{\mu})^{\mathsf{T}}\mathbf{G}^{\mathsf{T}} + \mathbf{F}(\boldsymbol{z} - \boldsymbol{\mu})\boldsymbol{\mu}^{\mathsf{T}} + \boldsymbol{\mu}(\boldsymbol{z} - \boldsymbol{\mu})^{\mathsf{T}}\mathbf{G}^{\mathsf{T}} - \boldsymbol{\mu}\boldsymbol{\mu}^{\mathsf{T}}\right] \tag{8.175}$$

$$= \mathbf{F}\mathbb{E}\left[(\boldsymbol{z} - \boldsymbol{\mu})(\boldsymbol{z} - \boldsymbol{\mu})^{\mathsf{T}}\right]\mathbf{G}^{\mathsf{T}} = \mathbf{F}\boldsymbol{\Sigma}\mathbf{G}^{\mathsf{T}} \tag{8.176}$$

Using this inside the GGF is equivalent to the EKF in Section 8.3.2. However, this approach can lead to large errors and sometimes divergence of the filter [IX00; VDMW03].

8.5.1.4 Approximation based on Gaussian quadrature

Since we are computing integrals wrt a Gaussian measure, we can use **Gaussian quadrature** methods of the following form:

$$\int h(z)\mathcal{N}(z|\mu,\Sigma)dz \approx \sum_{k=1}^{K} w^k h(z^k) \tag{8.177}$$

for a suitable set of evaluation points z^k (sometimes called **sigma points**) and weights w^k. (Note that one-dimensional integrals are called **quadratures**, and multi-dimensional integrals are called **cubatures**.)

One way to compute the sigma points is to use the unscented transform described in Section 8.4.1. Using this inside the GGF is equivalent to the UKF in Section 8.4.2.

Alternatively, we can use **spherical cubature integration**, which gives rise to the **cubature Kalman filter** or **CKF** [AH09]. This turns out (see [SS23, Sec 8.7]) to be a special case of the UKF, with $2n_z + 1$ sigma points, and hyperparameter values of $\alpha = 1$ and $\beta = 0$ (with κ left free).

A more accurate approximation uses **Gauss-Hermite integration**, which allows the user to select more sigma points. In particular, an order p approximation will be exact for polynomials of order up to $2p - 1$. See [SS23, Sec 8.3] for details, and Figure 8.5(e-f) for an illustration. However, this comes at a price: the number of sigma points is now p^n. Using Gauss-Hermite integration for GGF gives rise to the **Gauss-Hermite Kalman filter** or **GHKF** [IX00], also known as the **quadrature Kalman filter** or **QKF** [AHE07].

8.5.1.5 Approximation based on Monte Carlo integration

We can also approximate the integrals with Monte Carlo (see Section 11.2). Note, however, that this is not the same as particle filtering (Section 13.2), which approximates the conditional $p(z_t|y_{1:t})$ rather than the joint $p(z_t, y_t|y_{1:t-1})$ (see Section 8.6.1 for discussion of this difference).

8.5.2 Conditional moment Gaussian filtering

We can go beyond the Gaussian likelihood assumption by approximating the actual likelihood by a linear Gaussian model, as proposed in [TGFS18]. The only requirement is that we can compute the first and second **conditional moments** of the likelihood:

$$h_\mu(z) = \mathbb{E}[y|z] = \int y p(y|z)dy \tag{8.178}$$

$$h_\Sigma(z) = \text{Cov}[y|z] = \int (y - h_\mu(z))(y - h_\mu(z))^\mathsf{T} p(y|z)dy \tag{8.179}$$

Note that these integrals may be wrt a non-Gaussian measure $p(y|z)$. Also, y may be discrete, in which case these integrals become sums.

Next we compute the unconditional moments. By the law of iterated expecations we have

$$\hat{y} = \mathbb{E}[y] = \mathbb{E}[\mathbb{E}[y|z]] = \int h_\mu(z)\mathcal{N}(z|\mu,\Sigma)dz = g_e(h_\mu(z),\mu,\Sigma) \tag{8.180}$$

Similarly

$$\mathbf{C} = \text{Cov}\,[\boldsymbol{z}, \boldsymbol{y}] = \mathbb{E}\left[\mathbb{E}\left[(\boldsymbol{z} - \boldsymbol{\mu})(\boldsymbol{y} - \hat{\boldsymbol{y}})|\boldsymbol{z}\right]\right] = \mathbb{E}\left[(\boldsymbol{z} - \boldsymbol{\mu})(\boldsymbol{h}_{\boldsymbol{\mu}}(\boldsymbol{z}) - \hat{\boldsymbol{y}})\right] \tag{8.181}$$

$$= \int (\boldsymbol{z} - \boldsymbol{\mu})(\boldsymbol{h}_{\boldsymbol{\mu}}(\boldsymbol{z}) - \hat{\boldsymbol{y}})^{\mathsf{T}} \mathcal{N}(\boldsymbol{z}|\boldsymbol{\mu}, \boldsymbol{\Sigma}) d\boldsymbol{z} = g_c(\boldsymbol{z}, \boldsymbol{h}_{\boldsymbol{\mu}}(\boldsymbol{z}), \boldsymbol{\mu}, \boldsymbol{\Sigma}) \tag{8.182}$$

Finally

$$\mathbf{S} = \mathbb{V}\,[\boldsymbol{y}] = \mathbb{E}\left[\mathbb{V}\,[\boldsymbol{y}|\boldsymbol{z}]\right] + \mathbb{V}\left[\mathbb{E}\,[\boldsymbol{y}|\boldsymbol{z}]\right] \tag{8.183}$$

$$= \int \boldsymbol{h}_{\boldsymbol{\Sigma}}(\boldsymbol{z})\mathcal{N}(\boldsymbol{z}|\boldsymbol{\mu}, \boldsymbol{\Sigma}) d\boldsymbol{z} + \int (\boldsymbol{h}_{\boldsymbol{\mu}}(\boldsymbol{z}) - \hat{\boldsymbol{y}})(\boldsymbol{h}_{\boldsymbol{\mu}}(\boldsymbol{z}) - \hat{\boldsymbol{y}})^{\mathsf{T}} \mathcal{N}(\boldsymbol{z}|\boldsymbol{\mu}, \boldsymbol{\Sigma}) d\boldsymbol{z} \tag{8.184}$$

$$= g_e(\boldsymbol{h}_{\boldsymbol{\Sigma}}(\boldsymbol{z}), \boldsymbol{\mu}, \boldsymbol{\Sigma}) + g_c(\boldsymbol{h}_{\boldsymbol{\mu}}(\boldsymbol{z}), \boldsymbol{h}_{\boldsymbol{\mu}}(\boldsymbol{z}), \boldsymbol{\mu}, \boldsymbol{\Sigma}) \tag{8.185}$$

Note that the equation for $\hat{\boldsymbol{y}}$ is the same in Equation (8.157) and Equation (8.180), and the equation for $\mathbf{C}$ is the same in Equation (8.159) and Equation (8.182). Furthermore, if $\boldsymbol{h}_{\boldsymbol{\Sigma}}(\boldsymbol{z}) = \boldsymbol{\Omega}$, then the equation for $\mathbf{S}$ is the same in Equation (8.158) and Equation (8.185).

We can approximate the unconditional moments using linearization or numerical integration. We can then plug them into the GGF algorithm. We call this **conditional moments Gaussian filtering** or **CMGF**.

We can use CMGF to perform approximate inference in SSMs with Poisson likelihoods. For example, if $p(y|z) = \text{Poisson}(y|ce^z)$, we have

$$\boldsymbol{h}_{\boldsymbol{\mu}}(z) = \boldsymbol{h}_{\boldsymbol{\Sigma}}(z) = ce^z \tag{8.186}$$

This method can be used to perform (extended) Kalman filtering with more general exponential family likelihoods, as described in [TGFS18; Oll18]. For example, suppose we have a categorical likelihood:

$$p(y_t|\boldsymbol{z}_t) = \text{Cat}(y_t|\boldsymbol{p}_t) = \text{Cat}(y_t|\text{softmax}(\boldsymbol{\eta}_t)) = \text{Cat}(y_t|\text{softmax}(h(\boldsymbol{z}_t))) \tag{8.187}$$

where $\boldsymbol{\eta}_t = h(\boldsymbol{z}_t)$ are the predicted logits. Then the conditional mean and covariance are given by

$$\boldsymbol{h}_{\boldsymbol{\mu}}(\boldsymbol{z}_t) = \boldsymbol{p}_t = \text{softmax}(h(\boldsymbol{z}_t)), \ \boldsymbol{h}_{\boldsymbol{\Sigma}}(\boldsymbol{z}_t) = \text{diag}(\boldsymbol{p}_t) - \boldsymbol{p}_t\boldsymbol{p}_t^{\mathsf{T}} \tag{8.188}$$

(We can drop one of the classes from the vector $\boldsymbol{p}_t$ to ensure the covariance is full rank.) This approach can be used for online inference in neural network classifiers [CMJ22], as well as Gaussian process classifiers [GFTS19] and recommender systems [GU16; GUK21]. We can also use this method as a proposal distribution inside of a particle filtering algorithm (Section 13.2), as discussed in [Hos+20b].

8.5.3   Iterated filters and smoothers

The GGF method in Section 8.5.1, and the CMGF method in Section 8.5.2, both require computing moments wrt the predictive distribution $\mathcal{N}(\boldsymbol{z}_t|\boldsymbol{\mu}_{t|t-1}, \boldsymbol{\Sigma}_{t|t-1})$ before performing the measurement update. It is possible to do one step of GGF to compute the posterior given the new observation, $\mathcal{N}(\boldsymbol{z}_t|\boldsymbol{\mu}_{t|t}, \boldsymbol{\Sigma}_{t|t})$, and then to use this revised posterior to compute new moments in an iterated fashion. This is called **iterated posterior linearization filter** or **IPLF** [GF+15]. (This is similar

---

Algorithm 8.7: Iterated conditional moments Gaussian filter.

---

1 def **Iterated-CMGF**$(\boldsymbol{f}, \mathbf{Q}, \boldsymbol{h_\mu}, \boldsymbol{h_\Sigma}, \boldsymbol{y}_{1:T}, \boldsymbol{\mu}_{0|0}, \boldsymbol{\Sigma}_{0|0}, J, g_e, g_c)$:

2 **foreach** $t = 1 : T$ **do**

3   Predict step:

4     $(\boldsymbol{\mu}_{t|t-1}, \boldsymbol{\Sigma}_{t|t-1}, -) = \textbf{CondMoments}(\boldsymbol{\mu}_{t-1|t-1}, \boldsymbol{\Sigma}_{t-1|t-1}, \boldsymbol{f}, \mathbf{Q}, g_e, g_c)$

5   Update step:

6     $\boldsymbol{\mu}_{t|t} = \boldsymbol{\mu}_{t|t-1}, \boldsymbol{\Sigma}_{t|t} = \boldsymbol{\Sigma}_{t|t-1}$

7   **foreach** $j = 1 : J$ **do**

8        $(\hat{\boldsymbol{y}}_t, \mathbf{S}_t, \mathbf{C}_t) = \textbf{CondMoments}(\boldsymbol{\mu}_{t|t}, \boldsymbol{\Sigma}_{t|t}, \boldsymbol{h_\mu}, \boldsymbol{h_\Sigma}, g_e, g_c)$

9        $(\boldsymbol{\mu}_{t|t}, \boldsymbol{\Sigma}_{t|t}, \ell_t) = \textbf{GaussCondition}(\boldsymbol{\mu}_{t|t-1}, \boldsymbol{\Sigma}_{t|t-1}, \hat{\boldsymbol{y}}_t, \mathbf{S}_t, \mathbf{C}_t, \boldsymbol{y}_t)$

10 Return $(\boldsymbol{\mu}_{t|t}, \boldsymbol{\Sigma}_{t|t})_{t=1}^T$

11 def **CondMoments**$(\boldsymbol{\mu}, \boldsymbol{\Sigma}, \boldsymbol{h_\mu}, \boldsymbol{h_\Sigma}, g_e, g_c)$:

12 $\hat{\boldsymbol{y}} = g_e(\boldsymbol{h_\mu}(\boldsymbol{z}), \boldsymbol{\mu}, \boldsymbol{\Sigma})$

13 $\mathbf{S} = g_e(\boldsymbol{h_\Sigma}(\boldsymbol{z}), \boldsymbol{\mu}, \boldsymbol{\Sigma}) + g_c(\boldsymbol{h_\mu}(\boldsymbol{z}), \boldsymbol{h_\mu}(\boldsymbol{z}), \boldsymbol{\mu}, \boldsymbol{\Sigma})$

14 $\mathbf{C} = g_c(\boldsymbol{z}, \boldsymbol{h_\mu}(\boldsymbol{z}), \boldsymbol{\mu}, \boldsymbol{\Sigma})$

15 Return $(\hat{\boldsymbol{y}}, \mathbf{S}, \mathbf{C})$

---

to the iterated EKF which we discussed in Section 8.3.2.2.) See Algorithm 8.7 for the pseudocode, and [SS23, Sec 10.4] for more details.

In a similar way, we can derive the **iterated posterior linearization smoother** or **IPLS** [GFSS17]. This is similar to the iterated EKS which we discussed in Section 8.3.3.

Unfortunately the IPLF and IPLS can diverge. A more robust version of IPLF, that uses line search to perform damped (partial) updates, is presented in [Rai+18b]. Similarly, a more robust version of IPLS, that uses line search and Levenberg-Marquardt to update the parameters, is presented in [Lin+21c].

Various extensions of the above methods have been proposed. For example, in [HPR19] they extend IPLS to belief propagation in Forney factor graphs (Section 4.6.1.2), which enables the method to be applied to a large class of graphical models beyond SSMs. In particular, they give a general linearization formulation (including explicit message update rules) for nonlinear approximate Gaussian BP (Section 9.4.3) where the linearization can be Jacobian-based ("EKF-style"), statistical (moment matching), or anything else. They also show how any such linearization method can benefit from iterations.

In [Kam+22], they present a method based on approximate expectation propagation (Section 10.7), that is very similar to IPLS, except that the distributions that are used to compute the SLR terms, needed to compute the Gaussian messages, are different. In particular, rather than using the smoothed posterior from the last iteration, it uses the "cavity" distribution, which is the current posterior minus the incoming message that was sent at the last iteration, similar to Section 8.2.4.4. The advantage of this is that the outgoing message does not double count the evidence. The disadvantage is that this may be numerically unstable.

In [WSS21], they propose a variety of "**Bayes-Newton**" methods for approximately computing Gaussian posteriors to probabilistic models with nonlinear and/or non-Gaussian likelihoods. This generalizes all of the above methods, and can be applied to SSMs and GPs.

8.5.4   Ensemble Kalman filter

The **ensemble Kalman filter** (**EnKF**) is a technique developed in the geoscience (meteorology) community to perform approximate online inference in large nonlinear systems. In particular, it is mostly used for problems where the hidden state represents an unknown physical quantity (e.g., temperature or pressure) at each point on a spatial grid, and the measurements are sparse and spatially localized. Combining this information over space and time is called **data assimilation**.

The canonical reference is [Eve09], but a more accessible tutorial (using the same Bayesian signal processing approach we adopt in this chapter) is in [Rot+17].

The key idea is to represent the belief state $p(z_t|y_{1:t})$ by a finite number of samples $\mathbf{Z}_{t|t} = \{z_{t|t}^s : s = 1 : N_s\}$, where each $z_{t|t}^s \in \mathbb{R}^{N_z}$. In contrast to particle filtering (Section 13.2), the samples are updated in a manner that closely resembles the Kalman filter, so there is no importance sampling or resampling step. The downside is that the posterior does not converge to the true Bayesian posterior even as $N_s \to \infty$ [LGMT11], except in the linear-Gaussian case. However, sometimes the performance of EnKF can be better for small number of samples (although this depends of course on the PF proposal distribution).

The posterior mean and covariance can be derived from the ensemble of samples as follows:

$$\tilde{\boldsymbol{\mu}}_{t|t} = \frac{1}{N_s} \sum_{s=1}^{N_s} z_{t|t}^s = \frac{1}{N_s} \mathbf{Z}_{t|t} \mathbf{1} \tag{8.189}$$

$$\tilde{\boldsymbol{\Sigma}}_{t|t} = \frac{1}{N_s - 1} \sum_{s=1}^{N_s} (z_t^s - \tilde{\boldsymbol{\mu}}_{t|t})(z_t^s - \tilde{\boldsymbol{\mu}}_{t|t})^{\mathsf{T}} = \frac{1}{N_s - 1} \tilde{\mathbf{Z}}_{t|t} \tilde{\mathbf{Z}}_{t|t}^{\mathsf{T}} \tag{8.190}$$

where $\tilde{\mathbf{Z}}_{t|t} = \mathbf{Z}_{t|t} - \tilde{\boldsymbol{\mu}}_{t|t} \mathbf{1}^{\mathsf{T}}$.

We update the samples as follows. For the time update, we first draw N_s system noise variables $q_t^s \sim \mathcal{N}(\mathbf{0}, \mathbf{Q}_t)$, and then we pass these, and the previous state estimate, through the dynamics model to get the one-step-ahead state predictions, $z_{t|t-1}^s = f(z_{t-1|t-1}^s, q_t^s)$, from which we get $\mathbf{Z}_{t|t-1} = \{z_{t|t-1}^s\}$, which has size $N_z \times N_s$. Next we draw N_s observation noise variables $r_t^s \sim \mathcal{N}(\mathbf{0}, \mathbf{R}_t)$, and use them to compute the one-step-ahead observation predictions, $y_{t|t-1}^s = h(z_{t|t-1}^s, r_t^s)$ and $\mathbf{Y}_{t|t-1} = \{y_{t|t-1}^s\}$, which has size $N_y \times N_s$. Finally we compute the measurement update using

$$\mathbf{Z}_{t|t} = \mathbf{Z}_{t|t-1} + \tilde{\mathbf{K}}_t(y_t \mathbf{1}^{\mathsf{T}} - \mathbf{Y}_{t|t-1}) \tag{8.191}$$

which is the analog of Equation (8.29).

We now discuss how to compute $\tilde{\mathbf{K}}_t$, which is the analog of the Kalman gain matrix in Equation (8.28). First note that we can write the exact Kalman gain matrix (in the linear-Gaussian case) as $\mathbf{K}_t = \boldsymbol{\Sigma}_{t|t-1} \mathbf{H}^{\mathsf{T}} \mathbf{S}_t^{-1} = \mathbf{C}_t \mathbf{S}_t^{-1}$, where $\mathbf{S}_t$ is the covariance of the measurements, and $\mathbf{C}_t$ is the crosscovariance between the state and output predictions. In the EnKF, we approximate $\mathbf{S}_t$ and $\mathbf{C}_t$ empirically as follows. First we compute the deviations from predictions:

$$\tilde{\mathbf{Z}}_{t|t-1} = \mathbf{Z}_{t|t-1}(\mathbf{I} - \frac{1}{N} \mathbf{1}\mathbf{1}^{\mathsf{T}}), \;\; \tilde{\mathbf{Y}}_{t|t-1} = \mathbf{Y}_{t|t-1}(\mathbf{I} - \frac{1}{N} \mathbf{1}\mathbf{1}^{\mathsf{T}}) \tag{8.192}$$

Then we compute the sample covariance matrices

$$\tilde{\mathbf{S}}_t = \frac{1}{N_s - 1} \tilde{\mathbf{Y}}_{t|t-1} \tilde{\mathbf{Y}}_{t|t-1}^\mathsf{T}, \quad \tilde{\mathbf{C}}_t = \frac{1}{N_s - 1} \tilde{\mathbf{Z}}_{t|t-1} \tilde{\mathbf{Y}}_{t|t-1}^\mathsf{T} \tag{8.193}$$

Finally we compute

$$\tilde{\mathbf{K}}_t = \tilde{\mathbf{C}}_t \tilde{\mathbf{S}}_t^{-1} \tag{8.194}$$

We now compare the computational complexity to the KF algorithm. Recall that N_z is the number of latent dimensions, N_y is the number of observed dimensions, and N_s is the number of samples. We will assume $N_z > N_s > N_y$, as occurs in most geospatial problems. The EnKF time update takes $O(N_z^2 N_s)$ operations, and the measurement update takes $O(N_z N_y N_s)$, By contrast, in the KF, the time update takes $O(N_z^3)$ operations, and the measurement update takes $O(N_z^2 N_y)$. So we see that the EnKF is faster for high dimensional state spaces, because it uses a low-rank approximation to the posterior covariance.

Unfortunately, if N_s is too small, the EnKF can be become overconfident, and the filter can diverge. Various heuristics (e.g., covariance inflation) have been proposed to fix this. However, most of these methods are ad-hoc. A variety of more well-principled solutions have also been proposed, see e.g., [FK13b; Rei13].

8.5.5 Robust Kalman filters

In practice we often have noise that is non-Gaussian. A common example is when we have clutter, or outliers, in the observation model, or sudden changes in the process model. In this case, we might use the Laplace distribution [Ara+09] or the Student t-distribution [Ara10; RÖG13; Ara+17] as noise models.

[Hua+17b] proposes a variational Bayes (Section 10.3.3) approach, that allows the dynamical prior and the observation model to both be (linear) Student distributions, but where the posterior is approximated at each step using a Gaussian, conditional on the noise scale matrix, which is modeled using an inverse Wishart distribution. An extension of this, to handle mixture distributions, can be found in [Hua+19].

8.5.6 Dual EKF

In this section, we briefly discuss one approach to estimating the parameters of an SSM. In an offline setting, we can use EM, SGD, or Bayesian inference to compute an approximation to $p(\boldsymbol{\theta}|\boldsymbol{y}_{1:T})$ (see Section 29.8). In the online setting, we want to compute $p(\boldsymbol{\theta}_t|\boldsymbol{y}_{1:t})$. We can do this by adding the parameters to the state space, possibly with an **artificial dynamics**, $p(\boldsymbol{\theta}_t|\boldsymbol{\theta}_{t-1}) = \mathcal{N}(\boldsymbol{\theta}_t|\boldsymbol{\theta}_{t-1}, \epsilon \mathbf{I})$, and then performing joint inference of states and parameters. The latent variables at each step now contain the latent states, $\boldsymbol{z}_t$, and the latent parameters, $\boldsymbol{\theta}_t$. One approach to performing approximating inference in such a model is to use the **dual EKF**, in which one EKF performs state estimation and the other EKF performs parameter estimation [WN01].

8.6 Assumed density filtering

In this section, we discuss **assumed density filtering** or **ADF** [May79]. In this approach, we *assume* the posterior has a specific form (e.g., a Gaussian). At each step, we update the previous

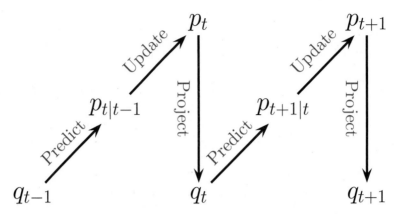

Figure 8.6: *Illustration of the predict-update-project cycle of assumed density filtering.* $q_t \in \mathcal{Q}$ *is a tractable distribution, whereas we may have* $p_{t|t-1} \notin \mathcal{Q}$ *and* $p_t \notin \mathcal{Q}$.

posterior with the new likelihood; the result will often not have the desired form (e.g., will no longer be Gaussian), so we project it to the closest approximating distribution of the required type.

In more detail, we assume (by induction) that our prior $q_{t-1}(\boldsymbol{z}_{t-1}) \approx p(\boldsymbol{z}_{t-1}|\boldsymbol{y}_{1:t-1})$ satisfies $q_{t-1} \in \mathcal{Q}$, where $\mathcal{Q}$ is a family of tractable distributions. We can update the prior with the new measurement to get the approximate posterior as follows. First we compute the **one-step-ahead predictive distribution**

$$p_{t|t-1}(\boldsymbol{z}_t|\boldsymbol{y}_{1:t-1}) = \int p(\boldsymbol{z}_t|\boldsymbol{z}_{t-1})q_{t-1}(\boldsymbol{z}_{t-1})d\boldsymbol{z}_{t-1} \tag{8.195}$$

Then we update this prior with the likelihood for step t to get the posterior

$$p_t(\boldsymbol{z}_t|\boldsymbol{y}_{1:t}) = \frac{1}{Z_t}p(\boldsymbol{y}_t|\boldsymbol{z}_t)p_{t|t-1}(\boldsymbol{z}_t) \tag{8.196}$$

where

$$Z_t = \int p(\boldsymbol{y}_t|\boldsymbol{z}_t)p_{t|t-1}(\boldsymbol{z}_t)d\boldsymbol{z}_t \tag{8.197}$$

is the normalization constant. Unfortunately, we often find that the resulting posterior is no longer in our tractable family, $p(\boldsymbol{z}_t) \notin \mathcal{Q}$. So after Bayesian updating we seek the best tractable approximation by computing

$$q_t(\boldsymbol{z}_t|\boldsymbol{y}_{1:t}) = \underset{q \in \mathcal{Q}}{\operatorname{argmin}} D_{\mathrm{KL}}\left(p_t(\boldsymbol{z}_t|\boldsymbol{y}_{1:t}) \parallel q(\boldsymbol{z}_t)\right) \tag{8.198}$$

This minimizes the Kullback-Leibler divergence from the approximation $q(\boldsymbol{z}_t)$ to the "exact" posterior $p_t(\boldsymbol{z}_t)$, and can be thought of as **projecting** p onto the space of tractable distributions. Thus the overall algorithm consists of three steps — predict, update, and project — as sketched in Figure 8.6.

Computing $\min_q D_{\mathrm{KL}}\left(p \parallel q\right)$ is known as **moment projection**, since the optimal q should have the same moments as p (see Section 5.1.4.2). So in the Gaussian case, we just need to set the

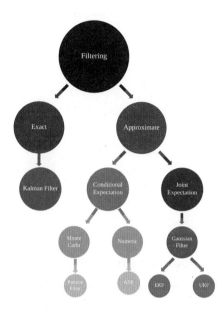

Figure 8.7: *A taxonomy of filtering algorithms. Adapted from Figure 2 of [Wüt+16].*

mean and covariance of q_t so they are the same as the mean and covariance of p_t. We will give some examples of this below. By contrast, computing $\min_q D_{\mathbb{KL}}(q \parallel p)$, as in variational inference (Section 10.1), is known as **information projection**, and will result in mode seeking behavior (see Section 5.1.4.1), rather than trying to capture overall moments.

8.6.1 Connection with Gaussian filtering

When $\mathcal{Q}$ is the set of Gaussian distributions, there is a close connection between ADF and Gaussian filtering, which we discussed in Section 8.5.1. GF corresponds to solving the following optimization problem

$$q_{t|t-1}(\boldsymbol{z}_t, \tilde{\boldsymbol{y}}_t) = \underset{q \in \mathcal{Q}}{\operatorname{argmin}} D_{\mathbb{KL}}\left(p(\boldsymbol{z}_t, \tilde{\boldsymbol{y}}_t | \boldsymbol{y}_{1:t-1}) \parallel q(\boldsymbol{z}_t, \tilde{\boldsymbol{y}}_t | \boldsymbol{y}_{1:t-1})\right) \tag{8.199}$$

which can be solved by moment matching (see Section 8.5.1). We then condition this joint distribution on the event $\tilde{\boldsymbol{y}}_t = \boldsymbol{y}_t$, where $\tilde{\boldsymbol{y}}_t$ is the unknown random variable and $\boldsymbol{y}_t$ is its observed value. This gives $p_t(\boldsymbol{z}_t | \boldsymbol{y}_{1:t})$, which is easy to compute, due to the Gaussian assumption. By contrast, in Gaussian ADF, we first compute the (locally) exact posterior $p_t(\boldsymbol{z}_t | \boldsymbol{y}_{1:t})$, and then approximate it with $q_t(\boldsymbol{z}_t | \boldsymbol{y}_{1:t})$ by projecting into $\mathcal{Q}$. Thus ADF approximates the conditional $p_t(\boldsymbol{z}_t | \boldsymbol{y}_{1:t})$, whereas GF approximates the joint $p_{t|t-1}(\boldsymbol{z}_t, \tilde{\boldsymbol{y}}_t | \boldsymbol{y}_{1:t})$, from which we derive $p_t(\boldsymbol{z}_t | \boldsymbol{y}_{1:t})$ by conditioning.

ADF is more accurate than GF, since it directy approximates the posterior, but it is more computationally demanding, for reasons explained in [Wüt+16]. However, in [Kam+22] they propose an approximate form of expectation propagation (which is a generalization of ADF) in which the messages are computed using the same local joint Gaussian approximation as used in Gaussian filtering. See Figure 8.7 for a summary of how these different methods relate.

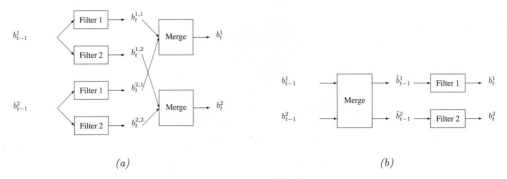

Figure 8.8: ADF for a switching linear dynamical system with 2 discrete states. (a) GPB2 method. (b) IMM method.

8.6.2   ADF for SLDS (Gaussian sum filter)

In this section, we apply ADF to inference in switching linear dynamical systems (SLDS, Section 29.9), which are a combination of HMM and LDS models. The resulting method is known as the **Gaussian sum filter** (see e.g., [Cro+11; Wil+17]).

A Gaussian sum filter approximates the belief state at each step by a mixture of K Gaussians. This can be implemented by running K Kalman filters in parallel. This is particularly well suited to switching SSMs. We now describe one version of this algorithm, known as the "second order **generalized pseudo-Bayes filter**" (GPB2) [BSF88]. We assume that the prior belief state b_{t-1} is a mixture of K Gaussians, one per discrete state:

$$b_{t-1}^i \triangleq p(\boldsymbol{z}_{t-1}, m_{t-1} = i|\boldsymbol{y}_{1:t-1}) = \pi_{t-1|t-1}^i \mathcal{N}(\boldsymbol{z}_{t-1}|\boldsymbol{\mu}_{t-1|t-1}^i, \boldsymbol{\Sigma}_{t-1|t-1}^i) \tag{8.200}$$

where $i \in \{1, \dots, K\}$. We then pass this through the K different linear models to get

$$b_t^{ij} \triangleq p(\boldsymbol{z}_t, m_{t-1} = i, m_t = j|\boldsymbol{y}_{1:t}) = \pi_{t|t}^{ij} \mathcal{N}(\boldsymbol{z}_t|\boldsymbol{\mu}_{t|t}^{ij}, \boldsymbol{\Sigma}_{t|t}^{ij}) \tag{8.201}$$

where $\pi_{t|t}^{ij} = \pi_{t-1|t-1}^i A_{ij}$, where $A_{ij} = p(m_t = j|m_{t-1} = i)$. Finally, for each value of j, we collapse the K Gaussian mixtures down to a single mixture to give

$$b_t^j \triangleq p(\boldsymbol{z}_t, m_t = j|\boldsymbol{y}_{1:t}) = \pi_{t|t}^j \mathcal{N}(\boldsymbol{z}_t|\boldsymbol{\mu}_{t|t}^j, \boldsymbol{\Sigma}_{t|t}^j) \tag{8.202}$$

See Figure 8.8a for a sketch.

The optimal way to approximate a mixture of Gaussians with a single Gaussian is given by $q = \arg\min_q D_{\mathbb{KL}}(q \parallel p)$, where $p(\boldsymbol{z}) = \sum_k \pi^k \mathcal{N}(\boldsymbol{z}|\boldsymbol{\mu}^k, \boldsymbol{\Sigma}^k)$ and $q(\boldsymbol{z}) = \mathcal{N}(\boldsymbol{z}|\boldsymbol{\mu}, \boldsymbol{\Sigma})$. This can be solved by moment matching, that is,

$$\boldsymbol{\mu} = \mathbb{E}[\boldsymbol{z}] = \sum_k \pi^k \boldsymbol{\mu}^k \tag{8.203}$$

$$\boldsymbol{\Sigma} = \text{Cov}[\boldsymbol{z}] = \sum_k \pi^k \left(\boldsymbol{\Sigma}^k + (\boldsymbol{\mu}^k - \boldsymbol{\mu})(\boldsymbol{\mu}^k - \boldsymbol{\mu})^\mathsf{T}\right) \tag{8.204}$$

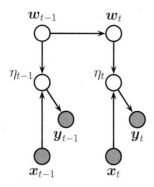

Figure 8.9: A dynamic logistic regression model. $\boldsymbol{w}_t$ are the regression weights at time t, and $\eta_t = \boldsymbol{w}_t^\mathsf{T} \boldsymbol{x}_t$. Compare to Figure 29.24a.

In the graphical model literature, this is called **weak marginalization** [Lau92], since it preserves the first two moments. Applying these equations to our model, we can go from b_t^{ij} to b_t^j as follows (where we drop the t subscript for brevity):

$$\pi^j = \sum_i \pi^{ij} \tag{8.205}$$

$$\pi^{j|i} = \frac{\pi^{ij}}{\sum_{j'} \pi^{ij'}} \tag{8.206}$$

$$\boldsymbol{\mu}^j = \sum_i \pi^{j|i} \boldsymbol{\mu}^{ij} \tag{8.207}$$

$$\boldsymbol{\Sigma}^j = \sum_i \pi^{j|i} \left(\boldsymbol{\Sigma}^{ij} + (\boldsymbol{\mu}^{ij} - \boldsymbol{\mu}^j)(\boldsymbol{\mu}^{ij} - \boldsymbol{\mu}_j)^\mathsf{T} \right) \tag{8.208}$$

This algorithm requires running K^2 filters at each step. A cheaper alternative, known as **interactive multiple models** or **IMM** [BSF88], can be obtained by first collapsing the prior to a single Gaussian (by moment matching), and then updating it using K different Kalman filters, one per value of m_t. See Figure 8.8b for a sketch.

8.6.3 ADF for online logistic regression

In this section we discuss the application of ADF to online Bayesian parameter inference for a binary logistic regression model, based on [Zoe07]. The overall approach is similar to the online linear regression case (discussed in Section 29.7.2), but approximates the posterior after each update step, which is necessary since the likelihood is not conjugate to the prior.

We assume our model has the following form:

$$p(y_t|\boldsymbol{x}_t, \boldsymbol{w}_t) = \mathrm{Ber}(y_t|\sigma(\boldsymbol{x}_t^\mathsf{T} \boldsymbol{w}_t)) \tag{8.209}$$

$$p(\boldsymbol{w}_t|\boldsymbol{w}_{t-1}) = \mathcal{N}(\boldsymbol{w}_t|\boldsymbol{w}_{t-1}, \mathbf{Q}) \tag{8.210}$$

where $\mathbf{Q}$ is the covariance of the process noise, which allows the parameters to change slowly over time. We will assume $\mathbf{Q} = \epsilon\mathbf{I}$; we can also set $\epsilon = 0$, as in the recursive least squares method (Section 29.7.2), if we believe the parameters will not change. See Figure 8.9 for an illustration of the model.

As our approximating family, we will use diagonal Gaussians, for computational efficiency. Thus the prior is the posterior from the previous time step, and has the form

$$p(\boldsymbol{w}_{t-1}|\mathcal{D}_{1:t-1}) \approx p_{t-1}(\boldsymbol{w}_{t-1}) = \prod_j \mathcal{N}(w_{t-1}^j|\mu_{t-1|t-1}^j, \tau_{t-1|t-1}^j) \tag{8.211}$$

where $\mu_{t-1|t-1}^j$ and $\tau_{t-1|t-1}^j$ are the posterior mean and variance for parameter j given past data. Now we discuss how to update this prior.

First we compute the one-step-ahead predictive density $p_{t|t-1}(\boldsymbol{w}_t)$ using the standard linear-Gaussian update, i.e., $\boldsymbol{\mu}_{t|t-1} = \boldsymbol{\mu}_{t-1|t-1}$ and $\boldsymbol{\tau}_{t|t-1} = \boldsymbol{\tau}_{t-1|t-1} + \mathbf{Q}$, where we can set $\mathbf{Q} = 0\mathbf{I}$ if there is no drift.

Now we concentrate on the measurement update step. Define the scalar sum (corresponding to the logits, if we are using binary classification) as $\eta_t = \boldsymbol{w}_t^\mathsf{T}\boldsymbol{x}_t$. If $p_{t|t-1}(\boldsymbol{w}_t) = \prod_j \mathcal{N}(w_t^j|\mu_{t|t-1}^j, \tau_{t|t-1}^j)$, then we can compute the 1d prior predictive distribution for η_t as follows:

$$p(\eta_t|\mathcal{D}_{1:t-1}, \boldsymbol{x}_t) \approx p_{t|t-1}(\eta_t) = \mathcal{N}(\eta_t|m_{t|t-1}, v_{t|t-1}) \tag{8.212}$$

$$m_{t|t-1} = \sum_j x_{t,j}\mu_{t|t-1}^j \tag{8.213}$$

$$v_{t|t-1} = \sum_j x_{t,j}^2 \tau_{t|t-1}^j \tag{8.214}$$

The posterior for the 1d η_t is given by

$$p(\eta_t|\mathcal{D}_{1:t}) \approx p_t(\eta_t) = \mathcal{N}(\eta_t|m_t, v_t) \tag{8.215}$$

$$m_t = \int \eta_t \frac{1}{Z_t} p(y_t|\eta_t) p_{t|t-1}(\eta_t) d\eta_t \tag{8.216}$$

$$v_t = \int \eta_t^2 \frac{1}{Z_t} p(y_t|\eta_t) p_{t|t-1}(\eta_t) d\eta_t - m_t^2 \tag{8.217}$$

$$Z_t = \int p(y_t|\eta_t) p_{t|t-1}(\eta_t) d\eta_t \tag{8.218}$$

where $p(y_t|\eta_t) = \mathrm{Ber}(y_t|\eta_t)$. These integrals are one dimensional, and so can be efficiently computed using Gaussian quadrature, as explained in [Zoe07; KB00].

Having inferred $p_t(\eta_t)$, we need to compute $p_t(\boldsymbol{w}|\eta_t)$. This can be done as follows. Define δ_m as the change in the mean and δ_v as the change in the variance:

$$m_t = m_{t|t-1} + \delta_m, \; v_t = v_{t|t-1} + \delta_v \tag{8.219}$$

Using the fact that $p(\eta_t|\boldsymbol{w}) = \mathcal{N}(\eta_t|\boldsymbol{w}^\mathsf{T}\eta_t, 0)$ is a linear Gaussian system, with prior $p(\boldsymbol{w}) = p(\boldsymbol{w}|\boldsymbol{\mu}_{t|t-1}, \boldsymbol{\tau}_{t|t-1})$ and "soft evidence" $p(\eta_t) = \mathcal{N}(m_t, v_t)$, we can derive the posterior for $p(\boldsymbol{w}|\mathcal{D}_t)$ as

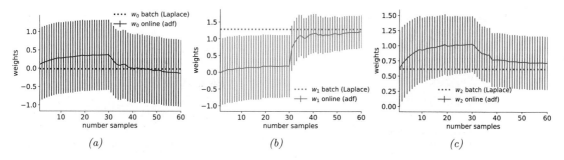

Figure 8.10: Bayesian inference applied to a 2d binary logistic regression problem, $p(y = 1|\boldsymbol{x}) = \sigma(w_0 + w_1 x_1 + w_2 x_2)$. We show the marginal posterior mean and variance for each parameter vs time as computed by ADF. The dotted horizontal line is the offline Laplace approximation. Generated by adf_logistic_regression_demo.ipynb.

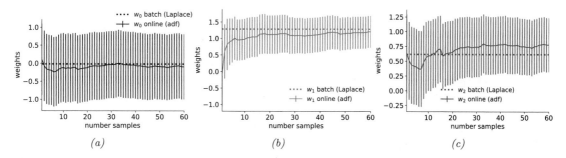

Figure 8.11: Same as Figure 8.10, except the order in which the data is visited is different. Generated by adf_logistic_regression_demo.ipynb.

follows:

$$p_t(w_t^i) = \mathcal{N}(w_t^i | \mu_{t|t}^i, \tau_{t|t}^i) \tag{8.220}$$

$$\mu_{t|t}^i = \mu_{t|t-1}^i + a_i \delta_m \tag{8.221}$$

$$\tau_{t|t}^i = \tau_{t|t-1}^i + a_i^2 \delta_v \tag{8.222}$$

$$a_i \triangleq \frac{x_t^i \tau_{t|t-1}^i}{\sum_j (x_t^j)^2 + \tau_{t|t-1}^j} \tag{8.223}$$

Thus we see that the parameters which correspond to inputs i with larger magnitude (big $|x_t^i|$) or larger uncertainty (big $\tau_{t|t-1}^i$) get updated most, due to a large a_i factor, which makes intuitive sense.

As an example, we consider a 2d binary classification problem. We sequentially compute the posterior using the ADF, and compare to the offline estimate computed using a Laplace approximation. In Figure 8.10 we plot the posterior marginals over the 3 parameters as a function of "time" (i.e., after conditioning on each training example one). We see that we converge to the offline MAP estimate. In Figure 8.11, we show the results of performing sequential Bayesian updating in a different ordering of the data. We still converge to approximate the same answer. In Figure 8.12, we see that the

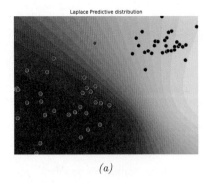
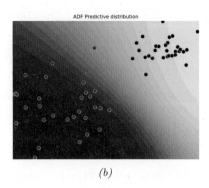

(a)   *(b)*

Figure 8.12: Predictive distribution for the binary logistic regression problem. (a) Result from Laplace approximation. (b) Result from ADF at the final step. Generated by adf_logistic_regression_demo.ipynb.

resulting posterior predictive distributions from the Laplace estimate and ADF estimate (at the end of training) are similar.

Note that the whole algorithm only takes $O(D)$ time and space per step, the same as SGD. However, unlike SGD, there are no step-size parameters, since the diagonal covariance implicitly specifies the size of the update for each dimension. Furthermore, we get a posterior approximation, not just a point estimate.

The overall approach is very similar to the generalized posterior linearization filter of Section 8.5.3, which uses quadrature (or the unscented transform) to compute a Gaussian approximation to the joint $p(y_t, \boldsymbol{w}_t | \mathcal{D}_{1:t-1})$, from which we can easily compute $p(\boldsymbol{w}_t | \mathcal{D}_{1:t})$. However, ADF approximates the posterior rather than the joint, as explained in Section 8.6.1.

8.6.4   ADF for online DNNs

In Section 17.5.3, we show how to use ADF to recursively approximate the posterior over the parameters of a deep neural network in an online fashion. This generalizes Section 8.6.3 to the case of nonlinear models.

8.7   Other inference methods for SSMs

There are a variety of other inference algorithms that can be applied to SSMs. We give a very brief summary below. For more details, see e.g., [Dau05; Sim06; Fra08; Sar13; SS23; Tri21].

8.7.1   Grid-based approximations

A very simple approach to approximate inference in SSMs is to discretize the state space, and then to apply the HMM filter and smoother (see Section 9.2.3), as proposed in [RG17]. This is called a **grid-based approximation**. Unfortunately, this approach will not scale to higher dimensional problems, due to the curse of dimensionality. In particular, we know that the HMM filter takes $O(K^2)$ operations per time step, if there are K states. If we have N_z dimensions, each discretized into B bins, then we have $K = B^{N_z}$, so the approach quickly becomes intractable.

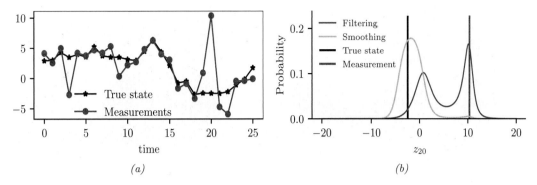

Figure 8.13: *(a) Observations and true and estimated state. (b) Marginal distributions for time step $t = 20$. Generated by discretized_ssm_student.ipynb.*

However, this approach can be useful in 1d or 2d. As an illustration, consider a simple 1d SSM with linear dynamics corrupted by additive Student noise:

$$z_t = z_{t-1} + \mathcal{T}_2(0, 1) \tag{8.224}$$

The observations are also linear, and are also corrupted by additive Student noise:

$$y_t = z_t + \mathcal{T}_2(0, 1) \tag{8.225}$$

This robust observation model is useful when there are potential outliers in the observed data, such as at time $t = 20$ in Figure 8.13a. (See also Section 8.5.5 for discussion of robust Kalman filters.)

Unfortunately the use of a non-Gaussian likelihood means that the resulting posterior can become multimodal. Fortunately, this is not a problem for the grid-based approach. We show the results for filtering and smoothing in Figure 8.14a and in Figure 8.14b. We see that at $t = 20$, the filtering distribution, $p(z_t|\boldsymbol{y}_{1:20})$, is bimodal, with a mean that is quite far from the true state (see Figure 8.13b for a detailed plot). Such a multimodal distribution can be approximated by a suitably fine discretization.

8.7.2 Expectation propagation

In Section 10.7 we discuss the expectation propagation (EP) algorithm, which can be viewed as an iterative version of ADF (Section 8.6). In particular, at each step we combine each exact local likelihood factor with approximate factors from both the past filtering distribution and the future smoothed posterior; these factors are combined to compute the locally exact posterior, which is then projected back to the tractable family (e.g., Gaussian), before moving to the next time step. This process can be iterated for increased accuracy. In many cases the local EP update is intractable, but we can make a local Gaussian approximation, similar to the one in general Gaussian filtering (Section 8.5.1), as explained in [Kam+22].

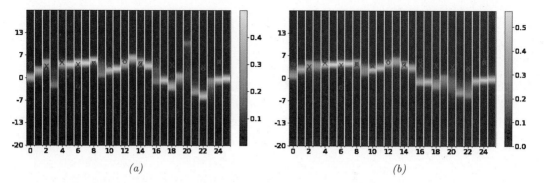

Figure 8.14: Discretized posterior of the latent state at each time step. Red cross is the true latent state. Red circle is observation. (a) Filtering. (b) Smoothing. Generated by discretized_ssm_student.ipynb.

8.7.3   Variational inference

EP can be viewed as locally minimizing the inclusive KL, $D_{\mathrm{KL}}\left(p(\boldsymbol{z}_t|\boldsymbol{y}_{1:T}) \parallel q(\boldsymbol{z}_t|\boldsymbol{y}_{1:T})\right)$, for each time step t. An alternative approach is to globally minimize the exclusive KL, $D_{\mathrm{KL}}\left(q(\boldsymbol{z}_{1:T}|\boldsymbol{y}_{1:T}) \parallel p(\boldsymbol{z}_{1:T}|\boldsymbol{y}_{1:T})\right)$; this is called variational inference, and is explained in Chapter 10. The difference between these two objectives is discussed in more detail in Section 5.1.4.1, but from a practical point of view, the main advantage of VI is that we can derive a tractable lower bound to the objective, and can then optimize it using stochastic optimization. This method is guaranteed to converge, unlike EP. For more details on VI applied to SSMs (both state estimation and parameter estimation), see e.g., [CWS21; Cou+20; Cou+21; BFY20; FLMM21; Cam+21].

8.7.4   MCMC

In Chapter 12 we discuss Markov chain Monte Carlo (MCMC) methods, which can be used to draw samples from intractable posteriors. In the case of SSMs, this includes both the distribution over states, $p(\boldsymbol{z}_{1:T}|\boldsymbol{y}_{1:T})$, and the distribution over parameters, $p(\boldsymbol{\theta}|\boldsymbol{y}_{1:T})$. In some cases, such as when using HMMs or linear-Gaussian SSMs, we can perform blocked Gibbs sampling, in which we use forwards filtering backwards sampling to sample an entire sequence from $p(\boldsymbol{z}_{1:T}|\boldsymbol{y}_{1:T},\boldsymbol{\theta})$, followed by sampling the parameters, $p(\boldsymbol{\theta}|\boldsymbol{z}_{1:T},\boldsymbol{y}_{1:T})$ (see e.g., [CK96; Sco02; CMR05] for details.) Alternatively we can marginalize out the hidden states and just compute the parameter posterior $p(\boldsymbol{\theta}|\boldsymbol{y}_{1:T})$. When state inference is intractable, we can use gradient-based HMC methods (assuming the states are continuous), although this does not scale well to long sequences.

8.7.5   Particle filtering

In Section 13.2 we discuss particle filtering, which is a form of sequential Bayesian inference for SSMs which replaces the assumption that the posterior is (approximately) Gaussian with a more flexible representation, namely a set of weighted samples called "particles" (see e.g., [Aru+02; DJ11; NLS19]). Essentially the technique amounts to a form of importance sampling, combined with steps to prevent "particle impoverishment", which refers to some samples receiving negligible weight because they are too improbable in the posterior (which grows with time). Particle filtering is widely used because it is very flexible, and has good theoretical properties. In practice it may require many samples to get a good approximation, but we can use heuristic methods, such as the extended or unscented Kalman filters, as proposal distributions, which can improve the efficiency significantly. In the offline setting, we can use particle smoothing (Section 13.5) or SMC (sequential Monte Carlo) samplers (Section 13.6).

9 Message passing algorithms

9.1 Introduction

In this chapter we consider posterior inference (i.e., computing marginals, modes, samples, etc) for probability distributions that can be represented by a probabilistic graphical model (PGM, Chapter 4) with some kind of sparse graph structure (i.e., it is not a fully connected graph). The algorithms we discuss will leverage the conditional independence properties encoded in the graph structure (discussed in Chapter 4) in order to perform efficient inference. In particular, we will use the principle of **dynamic programming** (DP), which finds an optimal solution by solving subproblems and then combining them.

DP can be implemented by computing local quantities for each node (or clique) in the graph, and then sending **messages** to neighboring nodes (or cliques) so that all nodes (cliques) can come to an overall consensus about the global solutions. Hence these are known as **message passing algorithms**. Each message can be intepreted as probability distribution about the value of a node given evidence from part of the graph. These distributions are often called **belief states**, so these algorithms are also called **belief propagation** (**BP**) algorithms.

In Section 9.2, we consider the special case where the graph structure is a 1d chain, which is an important special case. (For a chain, a natural approach is to send messages forwards in time, and then backwards in time, so this method can also be used for inference in state space models, as we discuss in Chapter 8.) In Section 9.3, we can generalize this approach to work with trees, and in Section 9.4, we generalize it work with any graph, including ones with cycles or loops. However, sending messages on loopy graphs may give incorrect answers. In such cases, we may wish to convert the graph to a tree, and then send messages on it, using the methods discussed in Section 9.5 and Section 9.6. We can also pose the inference problem as an optimization problem, as we discuss in Section 9.7.

9.2 Belief propagation on chains

In this section, we consider inference for PGMs where the graph structure is a 1d chain. For notational simplicity, we focus on the case where the graphical model is directed rather than undirected, although the resulting methods are easy to generalize. In addition, we only consider the case where all the hidden variables are discrete; we discuss generalizations to handle continuous latent variables in Chapter 8 and Chapter 13.

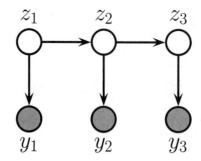

Figure 9.1: An HMM represented as a graphical model. z_t are the hidden variables at time t, y_t are the observations (outputs).

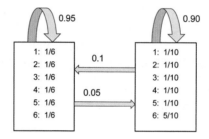

Figure 9.2: The state transition matrix $\mathbf{A}$ and observation matrix $\mathbf{B}$ for the casino HMM. Adapted from [Dur+98, p54].

9.2.1   Hidden Markov Models

In this section we assume the graphical model can be represented as a state space model, as shown in Figure 9.1. We discuss SSMs in more detail in Chapter 29, but we can think of them as latent variable sequence models with the conditional independencies shown by the chain-structured graphical model Figure 8.1. The corresponding joint distribution has the form

$$p(\boldsymbol{y}_{1:T}, \boldsymbol{z}_{1:T}) = \left[p(\boldsymbol{z}_1) \prod_{t=2}^{T} p(\boldsymbol{z}_t | \boldsymbol{z}_{t-1}) \right] \left[\prod_{t=1}^{T} p(\boldsymbol{y}_t | \boldsymbol{z}_t) \right] \tag{9.1}$$

where $\boldsymbol{z}_t$ are the hidden variables at time t, and $\boldsymbol{y}_t$ are the observations (outputs). If all the latent variables are discrete (as we assume in this section), the resulting model is called a **hidden Markov model** or **HMM**. We consider SSMs with continuous latent variables in Chapter 8.

9.2.1.1   Example: casino HMM

As a concrete example from [Dur+98], we consider the **occasionally dishonest casino**. We assume we are in a casino and observe a series of die rolls, $y_t \in \{1, 2, \ldots, 6\}$. Being a keen-eyed statistician, we notice that the distribution of values is not what we expect from a fair die: it seems that there are occasional "streaks", in which 6s seem to show up more often than other values. We would like to estimate the underlying state, namely whether the die is fair or loaded, so that we make predictions about the future.

To formalize this, let $z_t \in \{1, 2\}$ represent the unknown hidden state (fair or loaded) at time t, and let $y_t \in \{1, \ldots, 6\}$ represent the observed outcome (die roll). Let $A_{jk} = p(z_t = k | z_{t-1} = j)$ be the state transition matrix. Most of the time the casino uses a fair die, $z = 1$, but occasionally it switches to a loaded die, $z = 2$, for a short period, as shown in the state transition diagram in Figure 9.2.

Let $B_{kl} = p(y_t = l | z_t = k)$ be the observation matrix corresponding to a categorical distribution over values of the die face. If $z = 1$ the observation distribution is a uniform categorical distribution over the symbols $\{1, \ldots, 6\}$. If $z = 2$, the observation distribution is skewed towards face 6. That is,

$$p(y_t | z_t = 1) = \text{Cat}(y_t | [1/6, \ldots, 1/6]) \tag{9.2}$$

$$p(y_t | z_t = 2) = \text{Cat}(y_t | [1/10, 1/10, 1/10, 1/10, 1/10, 5/10]) \tag{9.3}$$

If we sample from this model, we may generate data such as the following:

```
hid:  111111111122221111111111111111111111122222222212221111111111111111111111
obs:  135553452655533663163515515262321121134622212632642654223446453232424361
```

Here obs refers to the observation and hid refers to the hidden state (1 is fair and 2 is loaded). In the full sequence of length 300, we find the empirical fraction of times that we observe a 6 in hidden state 1 to be 0.149, and in state 2 to be 0.472, which are very close to the expected fractions. (See casino_hmm.ipynb for the code.)

9.2.1.2 Posterior inference

Our goal is to infer the hidden states by computing the posterior over all the hidden nodes in the model, $p(z_t | \boldsymbol{y}_{1:T})$. This is called the **smoothing distribution**. By the Markov property, we can break this into two terms:

$$p(z_t = j | \boldsymbol{y}_{t+1:T}, \boldsymbol{y}_{1:t}) \propto p(z_t = j, \boldsymbol{y}_{t+1:T} | \boldsymbol{y}_{1:t}) p(z_t = j | \boldsymbol{y}_{1:t}) p(\boldsymbol{y}_{t+1:T} | z_t = j, \boldsymbol{y}_{1:t}) \tag{9.4}$$

We will first compute the **filtering distribution** $p(z_t = j | \boldsymbol{y}_{1:t})$ by working forwards in time. We then compute the $p(\boldsymbol{y}_{t+1:T} | z_t = j)$ terms by working backwards in time, and then we finally combine both terms. Both passes take (TK^2) time, where K is the number of discrete hidden states. We give the details below.

9.2.2 The forwards algorithm

As we discuss in Section 8.1.2, the **Bayes filter** is an algorithm for recursively computing the **belief state** $p(z_t | \boldsymbol{y}_{1:t})$ given the prior belief from the previous step, $p(z_{t-1} | \boldsymbol{y}_{1:t-1})$, the new observation $\boldsymbol{y}_t$, and the model. In the HMM literature, this is known as the **forwards algorithm**.

In an HMM, the latent states z_t are discrete, so we can define the belief state as a vector, $\alpha_t(j) \triangleq p(z_t = j | \boldsymbol{y}_{1:t})$, the local evidence as another vector, $\lambda_t(j) \triangleq p(\boldsymbol{y}_t | z_t = j)$, and the transition matrix as $A_{i,j} = p(z_t = j | z_{t-1} = i)$. Then the predict step becomes

$$\alpha_{t|t-1}(j) \triangleq p(z_t = j | \boldsymbol{y}_{1:t-1}) = \sum_i p(z_t = j | z_{t-1} = i) p(z_{t-1} = i | \boldsymbol{y}_{1:t-1} = \sum_i A_{i,j} \alpha_{t-1}(i) \tag{9.5}$$

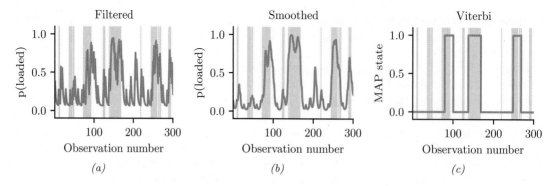

Figure 9.3: *Inference in the dishonest casino. Vertical gray bars denote times when the hidden state corresponded to the loaded die. Blue lines represent the posterior probability of being in that state given different subsets of observed data. If we recover the true state exactly, the blue curve will transition at the same time as the gray bars. (a) Filtered estimates. (b) Smoothed estimates. (c) MAP trajectory. Generated by* casino_hmm.ipynb.

and the update step becomes

$$\alpha_t(j) = \frac{1}{Z_t} p(\boldsymbol{y}_t | z_t = j) p(z_t = j | \boldsymbol{y}_{1:t-1}) = \frac{1}{Z_t} \lambda_t(j) \alpha_{t|t-1}(j) = \frac{1}{Z_t} \lambda_t(j) \left[\sum_i \alpha_{t-1}(i) A_{i,j} \right] \qquad (9.6)$$

where the normalization constant for each time step is given by

$$Z_t \triangleq p(\boldsymbol{y}_t | \boldsymbol{y}_{1:t-1}) = \sum_{j=1}^{K} p(\boldsymbol{y}_t | z_t = j) p(z_t = j | \boldsymbol{y}_{1:t-1}) = \sum_{j=1}^{K} \lambda_t(j) \alpha_{t|t-1}(j) \qquad (9.7)$$

We can write the update equation in matrix-vector notation as follows:

$$\boldsymbol{\alpha}_t = \text{normalize} \left(\boldsymbol{\lambda}_t \odot (\mathbf{A}^{\mathsf{T}} \boldsymbol{\alpha}_{t-1}) \right) \qquad (9.8)$$

where $\odot$ represents elementwise vector multiplication, and the normalize function just ensures its argument sums to one. (See Section 9.2.3.4 for more discussion on normalization.)

Figure 9.3(a) illustrates filtering for the casino HMM, applied to a random sequence $\boldsymbol{y}_{1:T}$ of length $T = 300$. In blue, we plot the probability that the die is in the loaded (vs fair) state, based on the evidence seen so far. The gray bars indicate time intervals during which the generative process actually switched to the loaded die. We see that the probability generally increases in the right places.

9.2.3   The forwards-backwards algorithm

In this section, we present the most common approach to smoothing in HMMs, known as the **forwards-backwards** or **FB** algorithm [Rab89]. In the forwards pass, we compute $\alpha_t(j) = p(z_t = j | \boldsymbol{y}_{1:t})$ as before. In the backwards pass, we compute the conditional likelihood

$$\beta_t(j) \triangleq p(\boldsymbol{y}_{t+1:T} | z_t = j) \qquad (9.9)$$

We then combine these using

$$\gamma_t(j) = p(z_t = j | \boldsymbol{y}_{t+1:T}, \boldsymbol{y}_{1:t}) \propto p(z_t = j, \boldsymbol{y}_{t+1:T} | \boldsymbol{y}_{1:t}) \tag{9.10}$$

$$= p(z_t = j | \boldsymbol{y}_{1:t}) p(\boldsymbol{y}_{t+1:T} | z_t = j, \cancel{\boldsymbol{y}_{1:t}}) = \alpha_t(j) \beta_t(j) \tag{9.11}$$

In matrix notation, this becomes

$$\boldsymbol{\gamma}_t = \text{normalize}(\boldsymbol{\alpha}_t \odot \boldsymbol{\beta}_t) \tag{9.12}$$

Note that the forwards and backwards passes can be computed independently, but both need access to the local evidence $p(\boldsymbol{y}_t | z_t)$. The results are only combined at the end. This is therefore called **two-filter smoothing** [Kit04].

9.2.3.1 Backwards recursion

We can recursively compute the β's in a right-to-left fashion as follows:

$$\beta_{t-1}(i) = p(\boldsymbol{y}_{t:T} | z_{t-1} = i) \tag{9.13}$$

$$= \sum_j p(z_t = j, \boldsymbol{y}_t, \boldsymbol{y}_{t+1:T} | z_{t-1} = i) \tag{9.14}$$

$$= \sum_j p(\boldsymbol{y}_{t+1:T} | z_t = j, \cancel{\boldsymbol{y}_t, z_{t-1} = i}) p(z_t = j, \boldsymbol{y}_t | z_{t-1} = i) \tag{9.15}$$

$$= \sum_j p(\boldsymbol{y}_{t+1:T} | z_t = j) p(\boldsymbol{y}_t | z_t = j, \cancel{z_{t-1} = i}) p(z_t = j | z_{t-1} = i) \tag{9.16}$$

$$= \sum_j \beta_t(j) \lambda_t(j) A_{i,j} \tag{9.17}$$

We can write the resulting equation in matrix-vector form as

$$\boldsymbol{\beta}_{t-1} = \mathbf{A}(\boldsymbol{\lambda}_t \odot \boldsymbol{\beta}_t) \tag{9.18}$$

The base case is

$$\beta_T(i) = p(\boldsymbol{y}_{T+1:T} | z_T = i) = p(\emptyset | z_T = i) = 1 \tag{9.19}$$

which is the probability of a non-event.

Note that $\boldsymbol{\beta}_t$ is not a probability distribution over states, since it does not need to satisfy $\sum_j \beta_t(j) = 1$. However, we usually normalize it to avoid numerical underflow (see Section 9.2.3.4).

9.2.3.2 Example

In Figure 9.3(a-b), we compare filtering and smoothing for the casino HMM. We see that the posterior distributions when conditioned on all the data (past and future) are indeed smoother than when just conditioned on the past (filtering).

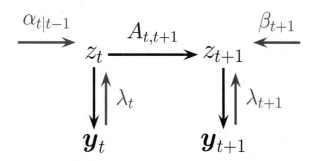

Figure 9.4: *Computing the two-slice joint distribution for an HMM from the forwards messages, backwards messages, and local evidence messages.*

9.2.3.3 Two-slice smoothed marginals

We can compute the two-slice marginals using the output of the forwards-backwards algorithm as follows:

$$p(\boldsymbol{z}_t, \boldsymbol{z}_{t+1}|\boldsymbol{y}_{1:T}) = p(\boldsymbol{z}_t, \boldsymbol{z}_{t+1}|\boldsymbol{y}_{1:t}, \boldsymbol{y}_{t+1:T}) \tag{9.20}$$

$$\propto p(\boldsymbol{y}_{t+1:T}|\boldsymbol{z}_t, \boldsymbol{z}_{t+1}, \boldsymbol{y}_{1:t})p(\boldsymbol{z}_t, \boldsymbol{z}_{t+1}|\boldsymbol{y}_{1:t}) \tag{9.21}$$

$$= p(\boldsymbol{y}_{t+1:T}|\boldsymbol{z}_{t+1})p(\boldsymbol{z}_t, \boldsymbol{z}_{t+1}|\boldsymbol{y}_{1:t}) \tag{9.22}$$

$$= p(\boldsymbol{y}_{t+1:T}|\boldsymbol{z}_{t+1})p(\boldsymbol{z}_t|\boldsymbol{y}_{1:t})p(\boldsymbol{z}_{t+1}|\boldsymbol{z}_t) \tag{9.23}$$

$$= p(\boldsymbol{y}_{t+1}, \boldsymbol{y}_{t+2:T}|\boldsymbol{z}_{t+1})p(\boldsymbol{z}_t|\boldsymbol{y}_{1:t})p(\boldsymbol{z}_{t+1}|\boldsymbol{z}_t) \tag{9.24}$$

$$= p(\boldsymbol{y}_{t+1}|\boldsymbol{z}_{t+1})p(\boldsymbol{y}_{t+2:T}|\boldsymbol{z}_{t+1}, \boldsymbol{y}_{t+1})p(\boldsymbol{z}_t|\boldsymbol{y}_{1:t})p(\boldsymbol{z}_{t+1}|\boldsymbol{z}_t) \tag{9.25}$$

$$= p(\boldsymbol{y}_{t+1}|\boldsymbol{z}_{t+1})p(\boldsymbol{y}_{t+2:T}|\boldsymbol{z}_{t+1})p(\boldsymbol{z}_t|\boldsymbol{y}_{1:t})p(\boldsymbol{z}_{t+1}|\boldsymbol{z}_t) \tag{9.26}$$

We can rewrite this in terms of the already computed quantities as follows:

$$\xi_{t,t+1}(i,j) \propto \lambda_{t+1}(j)\beta_{t+1}(j)\alpha_t(i)A_{i,j} \tag{9.27}$$

Or in matrix-vector form:

$$\boldsymbol{\xi}_{t,t+1} \propto \mathbf{A} \odot \left[\boldsymbol{\alpha}_t(\boldsymbol{\lambda}_{t+1} \odot \boldsymbol{\beta}_{t+1})^{\mathsf{T}}\right] \tag{9.28}$$

Since $\boldsymbol{\alpha}_t \propto \boldsymbol{\lambda}_t \odot \boldsymbol{\alpha}_{t|t-1}$, we can also write the above equation as follows:

$$\boldsymbol{\xi}_{t,t+1} \propto \mathbf{A} \odot \left[(\boldsymbol{\lambda}_t \odot \boldsymbol{\alpha}_{t|t-1}) \odot (\boldsymbol{\lambda}_{t+1} \odot \boldsymbol{\beta}_{t+1})^{\mathsf{T}}\right] \tag{9.29}$$

This can be interpreted as a product of incoming messages and local factors, as shown in Figure 9.4. In particular, we combine the factors $\boldsymbol{\alpha}_{t|t-1} = p(\boldsymbol{z}_t|\boldsymbol{y}_{1:t-1})$, $\mathbf{A} = p(\boldsymbol{z}_{t+1}|\boldsymbol{z}_t)$, $\boldsymbol{\lambda}_t \propto p(\boldsymbol{y}_t|\boldsymbol{z}_t)$, $\boldsymbol{\lambda}_{t+1} \propto p(\boldsymbol{y}_{t+1}|\boldsymbol{z}_{t+1})$, and $\boldsymbol{\beta}_{t+1} \propto p(\boldsymbol{y}_{t+2:T}|\boldsymbol{z}_{t+1})$ to get $p(\boldsymbol{z}_t, \boldsymbol{z}_{t+1}, \boldsymbol{y}_t, \boldsymbol{y}_{t+1}, \boldsymbol{y}_{t+2:T}|\boldsymbol{y}_{1:t-1})$, which we can then normalize.

9.2.3.4 Numerically stable implementation

In most publications on HMMs, such as [Rab89], the forwards message is defined as the following unnormalized *joint* probability:

$$\alpha'_t(j) = p(\boldsymbol{z}_t = j, \boldsymbol{y}_{1:t}) = \lambda_t(j) \left[\sum_i \alpha'_{t-1}(i) A_{i,j} \right] \tag{9.30}$$

We instead define the forwards message as the normalized *conditional* probability

$$\alpha_t(j) = p(\boldsymbol{z}_t = j | \boldsymbol{y}_{1:t}) = \frac{1}{Z_t} \lambda_t(j) \left[\sum_i \alpha_{t-1}(i) A_{i,j} \right] \tag{9.31}$$

The unnormalized (joint) form has several problems. First, it rapidly suffers from numerical underflow, since the probability of the joint event that $(\boldsymbol{z}_t = j, \boldsymbol{y}_{1:t})$ is vanishingly small.[1] Second, it is less interpretable, since it is not a distribution over states. Third, it precludes the use of approximate inference methods that try to approximate posterior distributions (we will see such methods later). We therefore always use the normalized (conditional) form.

Of course, the two definitions only differ by a multiplicative constant, since $p(\boldsymbol{z}_t = j | \boldsymbol{y}_{1:t}) = p(\boldsymbol{z}_t = j, \boldsymbol{y}_{1:t})/p(\boldsymbol{y}_{1:t})$ [Dev85]. So the *algorithmic* difference is just one line of code (namely the presence or absence of a call to the `normalize` function). Nevertheless, we feel it is better to present the normalized version, since it will encourage readers to implement the method properly (i.e., normalizing after each step to avoid underflow).

In practice it is more numerically stable to compute the log probabilities $\ell_t(j) = \log p(\boldsymbol{y}_t | \boldsymbol{z}_t = j)$ of the evidence, rather than the probabilities $\lambda_t(j) = p(\boldsymbol{y}_t | \boldsymbol{z}_t = j)$. We can combine the state conditional log likelihoods $\lambda_t(j)$ with the state prior $p(\boldsymbol{z}_t = j | \boldsymbol{y}_{1:t-1})$ by using the log-sum-exp trick, as in Equation (28.30).

9.2.4 Forwards filtering backwards smoothing

An alternative way to perform offline smoothing is to use forwards filtering/backwards smoothing, as discussed in Section 8.1.3. In this approach, we first perform the forwards or filtering pass, and then compute the smoothed belief states by working backwards, from right (time $t = T$) to left ($t = 1$). This approach is widely used for SSMs with continuous latent states, since the backwards likelihood $\beta_t(i)$ used in Section 9.2.3 is not always well defined when the state space is not discrete.

We assume by induction that we have already computed

$$\gamma_{t+1}(j) \triangleq p(\boldsymbol{z}_{t+1} = j | \boldsymbol{y}_{1:T}) \tag{9.32}$$

---

1. For example, if the observations are independent of the states, we have $p(\boldsymbol{z}_t = j, \boldsymbol{y}_{1:t}) = p(\boldsymbol{z}_t = j) \prod_{i=1}^{t} p(\boldsymbol{y}_i)$, which becomes exponentially small with t.

We then compute the smoothed joint distribution over two consecutive time steps:

$$\xi_{t,t+1}(i,j) \triangleq p(z_t = i, z_{t+1} = j | y_{1:T}) = p(z_t = i | z_{t+1} = j, y_{1:t})p(z_{t+1} = j | y_{1:T}) \tag{9.33}$$

$$= \frac{p(z_{t+1} = j | z_t = i)p(z_t = i | y_{1:t})p(z_{t+1} = j | y_{1:T})}{p(z_{t+1=j} | y_{1:t})} \tag{9.34}$$

$$= \alpha_t(i) A_{i,j} \frac{\gamma_{t+1}(j)}{\alpha_{t+1|t}(j)} \tag{9.35}$$

where

$$\alpha_{t+1|t}(j) = p(z_{t+1} = j | y_{1:t}) = \sum_{i'} A(i', j) \alpha_t(i') \tag{9.36}$$

is the one-step-ahead predictive distribution. We can interpret the ratio in Equation (9.35) as dividing out the old estimate of z_{t+1} given $y_{1:t}$, namely $\alpha_{t+1|t}$, and multiplying in the new estimate given $y_{1:T}$, namely γ_{t+1}.

Once we have the two sliced smoothed distribution, we can easily get the marginal one slice smoothed distribution using

$$\gamma_t(i) = p(z_t = i | y_{1:T}) = \sum_j \xi_{t,t+1}(i,j) = \alpha_t(i) \sum_j \left[A_{i,j} \frac{\gamma_{t+1}(j)}{\alpha_{t+1|t}(j)} \right] \tag{9.37}$$

We initialize the recursion using $\gamma_T(j) = \alpha_T(j) = p(z_T = j | y_{1:T})$.

9.2.5   Time and space complexity

It is clear that a straightforward implementation of the forwards-backwards algorithm takes $O(K^2 T)$ time, since we must perform a $K \times K$ matrix multiplication at each step. For some applications, such as speech recognition, K is very large, so the $O(K^2)$ term becomes prohibitive. Fortunately, if the transition matrix is sparse, we can reduce this substantially. For example, in a sparse left-to-right transition matrix (e.g., Figure 9.6(a)), the algorithm takes $O(TK)$ time.

In some cases, we can exploit special properties of the state space, even if the transition matrix is not sparse. In particular, suppose the states represent a discretization of an underlying continuous state-space, and the transition matrix has the form $A_{i,j} \propto \rho(z_j - z_i)$, where z_i is the continuous vector represented by state i and $\rho(u)$ is some scalar cost function, such as Euclidean distance. Then one can implement the forwards-backwards algorithm in $O(TK \log K)$ time. The key is to rewrite Equation (9.5) as a convolution,

$$\alpha_{t|t-1}(j) = p(z_t = j | y_{1:t-1}) = \sum_i \alpha_{t-1}(i) A_{i,j} = \sum_i \alpha_{t-1}(i) \rho(j - i) \tag{9.38}$$

and then to apply the Fast Fourier Transform. (A similar transformation can be applied in the backwards pass.) This is very useful for models with large state spaces. See [FHK03] for details.

We can also reduce inference to $O(\log T)$ time by using a **parallel prefix scan** operator that can be run efficiently on GPUs. For details, see [HSGF21].

In some cases, the bottleneck is memory, not time. In particular, to compute the posteriors γ_t, we must store the fitered distributions α_t for $t = 1, \ldots, T$ until we do the backwards pass. It is possible

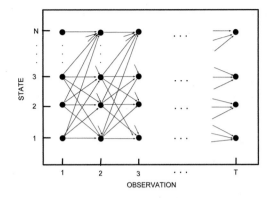

Figure 9.5: *The trellis of states vs time for a Markov chain. Adapted from [Rab89].*

to devise a simple divide-and-conquer algorithm that reduces the space complexity from $O(KT)$ to $O(K \log T)$ at the cost of increasing the running time from $O(K^2T)$ to $O(K^2T \log T)$. The basic idea is to store $\boldsymbol{\alpha}_t$ and $\boldsymbol{\beta}_t$ vectors at a logarithmic number of intermediate checkpoints, and then recompute the missing messages on demand from these checkpoints. See [BMR97; ZP00] for details.

9.2.6 The Viterbi algorithm

The MAP estimate is (one of) the sequences with maximum posterior probability:

$$\boldsymbol{z}_{1:T}^* = \operatorname*{argmax}_{\boldsymbol{z}_{1:T}} p(\boldsymbol{z}_{1:T}|\boldsymbol{y}_{1:T}) = \operatorname*{argmax}_{\boldsymbol{z}_{1:T}} \log p(\boldsymbol{z}_{1:T}|\boldsymbol{y}_{1:T}) \tag{9.39}$$

$$= \operatorname*{argmax}_{\boldsymbol{z}_{1:T}} \log \pi_1(\boldsymbol{z}_1) + \log \lambda_1(\boldsymbol{z}_1) + \sum_{t=2}^{T} [\log A(\boldsymbol{z}_{t-1}, \boldsymbol{z}_t) + \log \lambda_t(\boldsymbol{z}_t)] \tag{9.40}$$

This is equivalent to computing a shortest path through the **trellis diagram** in Figure 9.5, where the nodes are possible states at each time step, and the node and edge weights are log probabilities. This can be computed in $O(TK^2)$ time using the **Viterbi algorithm** [Vit67], as we explain below.

9.2.6.1 Forwards pass

Recall the (unnormalized) forwards equation

$$\alpha_t'(j) = p(\boldsymbol{z}_t = j, \boldsymbol{y}_{1:t}) = \sum_{\boldsymbol{z}_1,\ldots,\boldsymbol{z}_{t-1}} p(\boldsymbol{z}_{1:t-1}, \boldsymbol{z}_t = j, \boldsymbol{y}_{1:t}) \tag{9.41}$$

Now suppose we replace sum with max to get

$$\delta_t(j) \triangleq \max_{\boldsymbol{z}_1,\ldots,\boldsymbol{z}_{t-1}} p(\boldsymbol{z}_{1:t-1}, \boldsymbol{z}_t = j, \boldsymbol{y}_{1:t}) \tag{9.42}$$

This is the maximum probability we can assign to the data so far if we end up in state j. The key insight is that the most probable path to state j at time t must consist of the most probable path to some other state i at time $t - 1$, followed by a transition from i to j. Hence

$$\delta_t(j) = \lambda_t(j) \left[\max_i \delta_{t-1}(i) A_{i,j} \right] \tag{9.43}$$

We initialize by setting $\delta_1(j) = \pi_j \lambda_1(j)$.

We often work in the log domain to avoid numerical issues. Let $\delta'_t(j) = -\log \delta_t(j)$, $\lambda'_t(j) = -\log p(\boldsymbol{y}_t | \boldsymbol{z}_t = j)$, $A'(i,j) = -\log p(\boldsymbol{z}_t = j | \boldsymbol{z}_{t-1} = i)$. Then we have

$$\delta'_t(j) = \lambda'_t(j) + \left[\min_i \delta'_{t-1}(i) + A'(i,j) \right] \tag{9.44}$$

We also need to keep track of the most likely previous (**ancestor**) state, for each possible state that we end up in:

$$a_t(j) \triangleq \operatorname*{argmax}_i \delta_{t-1}(i) A_{i,j} = \operatorname*{argmin}_i \delta'_{t-1}(i) + A'(i,j) \tag{9.45}$$

That is, $a_t(j)$ stores the identity of the previous state on the most probable path to $\boldsymbol{z}_t = j$. We will see why we need this in Section 9.2.6.2.

9.2.6.2 Backwards pass

In the backwards pass, we compute the most probable sequence of states using a **traceback** procedure, as follows: $\boldsymbol{z}_t^* = a_{t+1}(\boldsymbol{z}_{t+1}^*)$, where we initialize using $\boldsymbol{z}_T^* = \arg\max_i \delta_T(i)$. This is just following the chain of ancestors along the MAP path.

If there is a unique MAP estimate, the above procedure will give the same result as picking $\hat{z}_t = \operatorname{argmax}_j \gamma_t(j)$, computed by forwards-backwards, as shown in [WF01b]. However, if there are multiple posterior modes, the latter approach may not find any of them, since it chooses each state independently, and hence may break ties in a manner that is inconsistent with its neighbors. The traceback procedure avoids this problem, since once $\boldsymbol{z}_t$ picks its most probable state, the previous nodes condition on this event, and therefore they will break ties consistently.

9.2.6.3 Example

In Figure 9.3(c), we show the Viterbi trace for the casino HMM. We see that, most of the time, the estimated state corresponds to the true state.

In Figure 9.6, we give a detailed worked example of the Viterbi algorithm, based on [Rus+95]. Suppose we observe the sequence of discrete observations $\boldsymbol{y}_{1:4} = (C_1, C_3, C_4, C_6)$, representing codebook entries in a vector-quantized version of a speech signal. The model starts in state $\boldsymbol{z}_1 = S_1$. The probability of generating $x_1 = C_1$ in $\boldsymbol{z}_1$ is 0.5, so we have $\delta_1(1) = 0.5$, and $\delta_1(i) = 0$ for all other states. Next we can self-transition to S_1 with probability 0.3, or transition to S_2 with proability 0.7. If we end up in S_1, the probability of generating $x_2 = C_3$ is 0.3; if we end up in S_2, the probability of generating $x_2 = C_3$ is 0.2. Hence we have

$$\delta_2(1) = \delta_1(1) A(1,1) \lambda_2(1) = 0.5 \cdot 0.3 \cdot 0.3 = 0.045 \tag{9.46}$$
$$\delta_2(2) = \delta_1(1) A(1,2) \lambda_2(2) = 0.5 \cdot 0.7 \cdot 0.2 = 0.07 \tag{9.47}$$

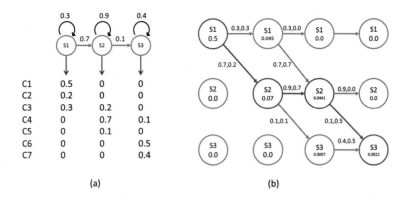

Figure 9.6: *Illustration of Viterbi decoding in a simple HMM for speech recognition. (a) A 3-state HMM for a single phone. We are visualizing the state transition diagram. We assume the observations have been vector quantized into 7 possible symbols, $C_1, \ldots, C_7$. Each state S_1, S_2, S_3 has a different distribution over these symbols. Adapted from Figure 15.20 of [RN02]. (b) Illustration of the Viterbi algorithm applied to this model, with data sequence C_1, C_3, C_4, C_6. The columns represent time, and the rows represent states. The numbers inside the circles represent the $\delta_t(j)$ value for that state. An arrow from state i at $t - 1$ to state j at t is annotated with two numbers: the first is the probability of the $i \to j$ transition, and the second is the probability of generating observation $\boldsymbol{y}_t$ from state j. The red lines/circles represent the most probable sequence of states. Adapted from Figure 24.27 of [RN95].*

Thus state 2 is more probable at $t = 2$; see the second column of Figure 9.6(b). The algorithm continues in this way until we have reached the end of the sequence. One we have reached the end, we can follow the red arrows back to recover the MAP path (which is 1,2,2,3).

For more details on HMMs for automatic speech recognition (ASR) see e.g., [JM08].

9.2.6.4 Time and space complexity

The time complexity of Viterbi is clearly $O(K^2T)$ in general, and the space complexity is $O(KT)$, both the same as forwards-backwards. If the transition matrix has the form $A_{i,j} \propto \rho(\boldsymbol{z}_j - \boldsymbol{z}_i)$, where $\boldsymbol{z}_i$ is the continuous vector represented by state i and $\rho(u)$ is some scalar cost function, such as Euclidean distance, we can implement Viterbi in $O(TK)$ time, by using the generalized distance transform to implement Equation (9.44). See [FHK03; FH12] for details.

9.2.6.5 N-best list

There are often multiple paths which have the same likelihood. The Viterbi algorithm returns one of them, but can be extended to return the top N paths [SC90; NG01]. This is called the **N-best list**. Computing such a list can provide a better summary of the posterior uncertainty.

In addition, we can perform **discriminative reranking** [CK05] of all the sequences in $\mathcal{L}_N$, based on global features derived from $(\boldsymbol{y}_{1:T}, \boldsymbol{z}_{1:T})$. This technique is widely used in speech recognition. For example, consider the sentence "recognize speech". It is possible that the most probable interpretation by the system of this acoustic signal is "wreck a nice speech", or maybe "wreck a nice beach" (see

Figure 34.3). Maybe the correct interpretation is much lower down on the list. However, by using a re-ranking system, we may be able to improve the score of the correct interpretation based on a more global context.

One problem with the N-best list is that often the top N paths are very similar to each other, rather than representing qualitatively different interpretations of the data. Instead we might want to generate a more diverse set of paths to more accurately represent posterior uncertainty. One way to do this is to sample paths from the posterior, as we discuss in Section 9.2.7. Another way is to use a determinantal point process (Supplementary Section 31.8.5) which encourages points to be diverse [Bat+12; ZA12].

9.2.7   Forwards filtering backwards sampling

Rather than computing the single most probable path, it is often useful to sample multiple paths from the posterior: $\boldsymbol{z}_{1:T}^s \sim p(\boldsymbol{z}_{1:T}|\boldsymbol{y}_{1:T})$. We can do this by modifying the forwards filtering backwards smoothing algorithm from Section 9.2.4, so that we draw samples on the backwards pass, rather than computing marginals. This is called **forwards filtering backwards sampling** (also sometimes unfortunately abbreviated to FFBS). In particular, note that we can write the joint from right to left using

$$p(\boldsymbol{z}_{1:T}|\boldsymbol{y}_{1:T}) = p(\boldsymbol{z}_T|\boldsymbol{y}_{1:T})p(\boldsymbol{z}_{T-1}|\boldsymbol{z}_T, \boldsymbol{y}_{1:T})p(\boldsymbol{z}_{T-2}|\boldsymbol{z}_{T-1}, \cancel{\boldsymbol{z}_T}, \boldsymbol{y}_{1:T})\cdots p(\boldsymbol{z}_1|\boldsymbol{z}_2, \cancel{\boldsymbol{z}_{3:T}}, \boldsymbol{y}_{1:T}) \tag{9.48}$$

$$= p(\boldsymbol{z}_T|\boldsymbol{y}_{1:T}) \prod_{t=T-1}^{1} p(\boldsymbol{z}_t|\boldsymbol{z}_{t+1}, \boldsymbol{y}_{1:T}) \tag{9.49}$$

Thus at step t we sample $\boldsymbol{z}_t^s$ from $p(\boldsymbol{z}_t|\boldsymbol{z}_{t+1}^s, \boldsymbol{y}_{1:T})$ given in Equation (9.49).

9.3   Belief propagation on trees

The forwards-backwards algorithm for HMMs discussed in Section 9.2.3 (and the Kalman smoother algorithm for LDS which we discuss in Section 8.2.3) can be interpreted as a message passing algorithm applied to a chain structured graphical model. In this section, we generalize these algorithms to work with trees.

9.3.1   Directed vs undirected trees

Consider a pairwise *undirected* graphical model, which can be written as follows:

$$p^*(\boldsymbol{z}) \triangleq p(\boldsymbol{z}|\boldsymbol{y}) \propto \prod_{s \in \mathcal{V}} \psi_s(z_s|\boldsymbol{y}_s) \prod_{(s,t) \in \mathcal{E}} \psi_{s,t}(z_s, z_t) \tag{9.50}$$

where $\psi_{s,t}(z_s, z_t)$ are the pairwise clique potential, one per edge, $\psi_s(z_s|\boldsymbol{y}_s)$ are the local evidence potentials, one per node, $\mathcal{V}$ is the set of nodes, and $\mathcal{E}$ is the set of edges. (We will henceforth drop the conditioning on the observed values $\boldsymbol{y}$ for brevity.)

Now suppose the corresponding graph structure is a tree, such as the one in Figure 9.7a. We can always convert this into a directed tree by picking an arbitrary node as the root, and then "picking

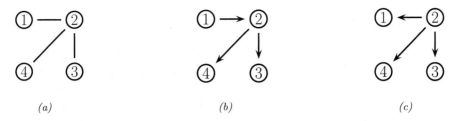

(a) (b) (c)

Figure 9.7: *An undirected tree and two equivalent directed trees.*

the tree up by the root" and orienting all the edges away from the root. For example, if we pick node 1 as the root we get Figure 9.7b. This corresponds to the following directed graphical model:

$$p^*(\mathbf{z}) \propto p^*(z_1)p^*(z_2|z_1)p^*(z_3|z_2)p^*(z_4|z_2) \tag{9.51}$$

However, if we pick node 2 as the root, we get Figure 9.7c. This corresponds to the following directed graphical model:

$$p^*(\mathbf{z}) \propto p^*(z_2)p^*(z_1|z_2)p^*(z_3|z_2)p^*(z_4|z_2) \tag{9.52}$$

Since these graphs express the same conditional independence properties, they represent the same family of probability distributions, and hence we are free to use any of these parameterizations.

To make the model more symmetric, it is preferable to use an undirected tree. If we define the potentials as (possibly unnnormalized) marginals (i.e., $\psi_s(z_s) \propto p^*(z_s)$ and $\psi_{s,t}(z_s, z_t) = p^*(z_s, z_t)$), then we can write

$$p^*(\mathbf{z}) \propto \prod_{s \in \mathcal{V}} p^*(z_s) \prod_{(s,t) \in \mathcal{E}} \frac{p^*(z_s, z_t)}{p^*(z_s)p^*(z_t)} \tag{9.53}$$

For example, for Figure 9.7a we have

$$p^*(z_1, z_2, z_3, z_4) \propto p^*(z_1)p^*(z_2)p^*(z_3)p^*(z_4) \frac{p^*(z_1, z_2)p^*(z_2, z_3)p^*(z_2, z_4)}{p^*(z_1)p^*(z_2)p^*(z_2)p^*(z_3)p^*(z_2)p^*(z_4)} \tag{9.54}$$

To see the equivalence with the directed representation, we can cancel terms to get

$$p^*(z_1, z_2, z_3, z_4) \propto p^*(z_1, z_2) \frac{p^*(z_2, z_3)}{p^*(z_2)} \frac{p^*(z_2, z_4)}{p^*(z_2)} \tag{9.55}$$

$$= p^*(z_1)p^*(z_2|z_1)p^*(z_3|z_2)p^*(z_4|z_2) \tag{9.56}$$

$$= p^*(z_2)p^*(z_1|z_2)p^*(z_3|z_2)p^*(z_4|z_2) \tag{9.57}$$

where $p^*(z_t|z_s) = p^*(z_s, z_t)/p^*(z_s)$.

Thus a tree can be represented as either an undirected or directed graph. Both representations can be useful, as we will see.

```
// Collect to root
for each node s in post-order
```
$$\text{bel}_s(z_s) \propto \psi_s(z_s) \prod_{t \in \text{ch}_s} m_{t \to s}(z_s)$$
$$t = \texttt{parent}(s)$$
$$m_{s \to t}(z_t) = \sum_{z_s} \psi_{st}(z_s, z_t) \text{bel}_s(z_s)$$

```
// Distribute from root
for each node t in pre-order
```
$$s = \texttt{parent}(t)$$
$$m_{s \to t}(z_t) = \sum_{z_s} \psi_{st}(z_s, z_t) \frac{\text{bel}_s(z_s)}{m_{t \to s}(z_s)}$$
$$\text{bel}_t(z_t) \propto \text{bel}_t(z_t) m_{s \to t}(z_t)$$

Figure 9.8: Belief propagation on a pairwise, rooted tree.

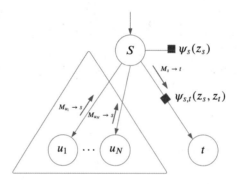

Figure 9.9: Illustration of how the top-down message from s to t is computed during BP on a tree. The u_i nodes are the other children of s, besides t. Square nodes represent clique potentials.

9.3.2   Sum-product algorithm

In this section, we assume that our model is an undirected tree, as in Equation (9.50). However, we will pick an arbitrary node as a root, and orient all the edges downwards away from this root, so that each node has a unique parent. For a directed, rooted tree, we can compute various node orderings. In particular, in a **pre-order**, we traverse from the root to the left subtree and then to right subtree, top to bottom. In a **post-order**, we traverse from the left subtree to the right subtree and then to the root, bottom to top. We will use both of these below.

We now present the **sum-product algorithm** for trees. We first send messages from the leaves to the root. This is the generalization of the forwards pass from Section 9.2.2. Let $m_{s \to t}(z_t)$ denote the message from node s to node t. This summarizes the belief state about z_t given all the evidence in the tree below the $s - t$ edge. Consider a node s in the ordering. We update its belief state by combining the incoming messages from all its children with its own local evidence:

$$\text{bel}_s(z_s) \propto \psi_s(z_s) \prod_{t \in \text{ch}_s} m_{t \to s}(z_s) \tag{9.58}$$

To compute the outgoing message that s should send to its parent t, we pass the local belief through the pairwise potential linking s and t, and then marginalize out s to get

$$m_{s \to t}(z_t) = \sum_{z_s} \psi_{st}(z_s, z_t) \text{bel}_s(z_s) \tag{9.59}$$

At the root of the tree, $\text{bel}_t(z_t) = p(z_t|\boldsymbol{y})$ will have seen all the evidence. It can then send messages back down to the leaves. The message that s sends to its child t should be the product of all the messages that s received from all its *other* children u, passed through the pairwise potential, and then marginalized:

$$m_{s \to t}(z_t) = \sum_{z_t} \left(\psi_s(z_s) \psi_{st}(z_s, z_t) \prod_{u \in \text{ch}_s \setminus t} m_{u \to s}(z_s) \right) \tag{9.60}$$

See Figure 9.9. Instead of multiplying all-but-one of the messages that s has received, we can multiply all of them and then divide out by the $t \to s$ message from child t. The advantage of this is that the product of all the messages has already been computed in Equation (9.58), so we don't need to recompute that term. Thus we get

$$m_{s \to t}(z_t) = \sum_{z_s} \psi_{st}(z_s, z_t) \frac{\text{bel}_s(z_s)}{m_{t \to s}(z_s)} \tag{9.61}$$

We can think of $\text{bel}_s(z_s)$ as the new updated posterior $p(z_s|\boldsymbol{y})$ given all the evidence, and $m_{t \to s}(z_s)$ as the prior predictive $p(z_s|\boldsymbol{y}_t^-)$, where $\boldsymbol{y}_t^-$ is all the evidence in the subtree rooted at t. Thus the ratio contains the new evidence that t did not already know about from its own subtree. We use this to update the belief state at node t to get:

$$\text{bel}_t(z_t) \propto \text{bel}_t(z_t) m_{s \to t}(z_t) \tag{9.62}$$

(Note that Equation (9.58) is a special case of this where we don't divide out by $m_{s \to t}$, since in the upwards pass, there is no incoming message from the parent.) This is analogous to the backwards smoothing equation in Equation (9.37), with $\alpha_t(i)$ replaced by $\text{bel}_t(z_t = i)$, $A(i, j)$ replaced by $\psi_{st}(z_s = i, z_t = j)$, $\gamma_{t+1}(j)$ replaced by $\text{bel}_s(z_s = j)$, and $\alpha_{t+1|t}(j)$ replaced by $m_{t \to s}(z_s = j)$.

See Figure 9.8 for the overall pseudocode. This can be generalized to directed trees with multiple root nodes (known as **polytrees**) as described in Supplementary Section 9.1.1.

9.3.3 Max-product algorithm

In Section 9.3.2 we described the sum-product algorithm, that computes the posterior marginals:

$$\text{bel}_i(k) = \gamma_i(k) = p(z_i = k|\boldsymbol{y}) = \sum_{\boldsymbol{z}_{-i}} p(z_i = k, \boldsymbol{z}_{-i}|\boldsymbol{y}) \tag{9.63}$$

We can replace the sum operation with the max operation to get **max-product belief propagation**. The result of this computation are a set of **max marginals** for each node:

$$\zeta_i(k) = \max_{\boldsymbol{z}_{-i}} p(z_i = k, \boldsymbol{z}_{-i}|\boldsymbol{y}) \tag{9.64}$$

We can derive two different kinds of "MAP" estimates from these local quantities. The first is $\hat{z}_i = \operatorname{argmax}_k \gamma_i(k)$; this is known as the **maximizer of the posterior marginal** or **MPM** estimate (see e.g., [MMP87; SM12]); let $\hat{\boldsymbol{z}} = [\hat{z}_1, \ldots, \hat{z}_{N_z}]$ be the sequence of such estimates. The second is $\tilde{z}_i = \operatorname{argmax}_k \zeta_i(k)$; we call this the **maximizer of the max marginal** or **MMM** estimate; let $\tilde{\boldsymbol{z}} = [\tilde{z}_1, \ldots, \tilde{z}_{N_z}]$.

An interesting question is: what, if anything, do these estimates have to do with the "true" MAP estimate, $\boldsymbol{z}^* = \operatorname{argmax}_{\boldsymbol{z}} p(\boldsymbol{z}|\boldsymbol{y})$? We discuss this below.

9.3.3.1   Connection between MMM and MAP

In [YW04], they showed that, if the max marginals are unique and computed exactly (e.g., if the graph is a tree), then $\tilde{\boldsymbol{z}} = \boldsymbol{z}^*$. This means we can recover the global MAP estimate by running max product BP and then setting each node to its local max (i.e., using the MMM estimate).

However, if there are ties in the max marginals (corresponding to the case where there is more than one globally optimal solution), this "local stitching" process may result in global inconsistencies.

If we have a tree-structured model, we can use a **traceback** procedure, analogous to the Viterbi algorithm (Section 9.2.6), in which we clamp nodes to their optimal values while working backwards from the root. For details, see e.g., [KF09a, p569].

Unfortunately, traceback does not work on general graphs. An alternative, iterative approach, proposed in [YW04], is follows. First we run max product BP, and clamp all nodes which have unique max marginals to their optimal values; we then clamp a single ambiguous node to an optimal value, and condition on all these clamped values as extra evidence, and perform more rounds of message passing, until all ties are broken. This may require many rounds of inference, although the number of non-clamped (hidden) variables gets reduced at each round.

9.3.3.2   Connection between MPM and MAP

In this section, we discuss the MPM estimate, $\hat{\boldsymbol{z}}$, which computes the maximum of the posterior marginals. In general, this does not correspond to the MAP estimate, even if the posterior marginals are exact. To see why, note that MPM just looks at the belief state for each node given all the visible evidence, but ignores any dependencies or constraints that might exist in the prior.

To illustrate why this could be a problem, consider the error correcting code example from Section 5.5, where we defined $p(\boldsymbol{z}, \boldsymbol{y}) = p(z_1)p(z_2)p(z_3|z_1, z_2)\prod_{i=1}^3 p(y_i|z_i)$, where all variables are binary. The priors $p(z_1)$ and $p(z_2)$ are uniform. The conditional term $p(z_3|z_1, z_2)$ is deterministic, and computes the parity of (z_1, z_2). In particular, we have $p(z_3 = 1|z_1, z_2) = \mathbb{I}(\operatorname{odd}(z_1, z_2))$, so that the total number of 1s in the block $\boldsymbol{z}_{1:3}$ is even. The likelihood terms $p(y_i|z_i)$ represent a bit flipping noisy channel model, with noise level $\alpha = 0.2$.

Suppose we observe $\boldsymbol{y} = (1, 0, 0)$. In this case, the exact posterior marginals are as follows:[2] $\gamma_1 = [0.3469, 0.6531]$, $\gamma_2 = [0.6531, 0.3469]$, $\gamma_3 = [0.6531, 0.3469]$. The exact max marginals are all the same,

---

2. See error_correcting_code_demo.ipynb for the code.

namely $\zeta_i = [0.3265, 0.3265]$. Finally, the 3 global MAP estimates are $\boldsymbol{z}^* \in \{[0,0,0], [1,1,0], [1,0,1]\}$, each of which corresponds to a single bit flip from the observed vector. The MAP estimates are all valid code words (they have an even number of 1s), and hence are sensible hypotheses about the value of $\boldsymbol{z}$. By contrast, the MPM estimate is $\hat{\boldsymbol{z}} = [1,0,0]$, which is not a legal codeword. (And in this example, the MMM estimate is not well defined, since the max marginals are not unique.)

So, which method is better? This depends on our loss function, as we discuss in Section 34.1. If we want to minimize the prediction error of each z_i, also called **bit error**, we should compute the MPM. If we want to minimize the prediction error for the entire sequence $\boldsymbol{z}$, also called **word error**, we should use MAP, since this can take global constraints into account.

For example, suppose we are performing speech recognition and someones says "recognize speech". MPM decoding may return "wreck a nice beach", since locally it may be that "beach" is the most probable interpretation of "speech" when viewed in isolation (see Figure 34.3). However, MAP decoding would infer that "recognize speech" is the more likely overall interpretation, by taking into account the language model prior, $p(\boldsymbol{z})$.

On the other hand, if we don't have strong constraints, the MPM estimate can be more robust [MMP87; SM12], since it marginalizes out the other nodes, rather than maxing them out. For example, in the casino HMM example in Figure 9.3, we see that the MPM method makes 49 bit errors (out of a total possible of $T = 300$), and the MAP path makes 60 errors.

9.3.3.3 Connection between MPE and MAP

In the graphical models literature, computing the jointly most likely setting of all the latent variables, $\boldsymbol{z}^* = \mathrm{argmax}_{\boldsymbol{z}}\, p(\boldsymbol{z}|\boldsymbol{y})$, is known as the **most probable explanation** or **MPE** [Pea88]. In that literature, the term "MAP" is used to refer to the case where we maximize some of the hidden variables, and marginalize (sum out) the rest. For example, if we maximize a single node, z_i, but sum out all the others, $\boldsymbol{z}_{-i}$, we get the MPM $\hat{z}_i = \mathrm{argmax}_{z_i} \sum_{\boldsymbol{z}_{-i}} p(\boldsymbol{z}|\boldsymbol{y})$.

We can generalize the MPM estimate to compute the best guess for a set of query variables Q, given evidence on a set of visible variables V, marginalizing out the remaining variables R, to get

$$\boldsymbol{z}_Q^* = \arg\max_{\boldsymbol{z}_Q} \sum_{\boldsymbol{z}_R} p(\boldsymbol{z}_Q, \boldsymbol{z}_R | \boldsymbol{z}_V) \tag{9.65}$$

(Here $\boldsymbol{z}_R$ are called **nuisance variables**, since they are not of interest, and are not observed.) In [Pea88], this is called a MAP estimate, but we will call it an MPM estimate, to avoid confusion with the ML usage of the term "MAP" (where we maximize everything jointly).

9.4 Loopy belief propagation

In this section, we extend belief propagation to work on graphs with cycles or loops; this is called **loopy belief propagation** or **LBP**. Unfortunately, this method may not converge, and even if it does, it is not clear if the resulting estimates are valid. Indeed, Judea Pearl, who invented belief propagation for trees, wrote the following about loopy BP in 1988:

> When loops are present, the network is no longer singly connected and local propagation schemes will invariably run into trouble ... If we ignore the existence of loops and permit the nodes to continue communicating with each other as if the network were singly connected,

messages may circulate indefinitely around the loops and the process may not converge to a stable equilibrium ... Such oscillations do not normally occur in probabilistic networks ... which tend to bring all messages to some stable equilibrium as time goes on. However, this asymptotic equilibrium is not coherent, in the sense that it does not represent the posterior probabilities of all nodes of the network. — [Pea88, p.195]

Despite these reservations, Pearl advocated the use of belief propagation in loopy networks as an approximation scheme (J. Pearl, personal communication). [MWJ99] found empirically that it works on various graphical models, and it is now used in many real world applications, some of which we discuss below. In addition, there is now some theory justifying its use in certain cases, as we discuss below. (For more details, see e.g., [Yed11].)

9.4.1 Loopy BP for pairwise undirected graphs

In this section, we assume (for notational simplicity) that our model is an undirected pairwise PGM, as in Equation (9.50). However, unlike Section 9.3.2, we do not assume the graph is a tree. We can apply the same message passing equations as before. However, since there is no natural node ordering, we will do this in a parallel, asynchronous way. The basic idea is that all nodes receive messages from their neighbors in parallel, they then update their belief states, and finally they send new messages back out to their neighbors. This message passing process repeats until convergence. This kind of computing architecture is called a **systolic array**, due to its resemblance to a beating heart.

More precisely, we initialize all messages to the all 1's vector. Then, in parallel, each node absorbs messages from all its neighbors using

$$\text{bel}_s(z_s) \propto \psi_s(z_s) \prod_{t \in \text{nbr}_s} m_{t \to s}(z_s) \tag{9.66}$$

Then, in parallel, each node sends messages to each of its neighbors:

$$m_{s \to t}(z_t) = \sum_{z_s} \left(\psi_s(z_s) \psi_{st}(z_s, z_t) \prod_{u \in \text{nbr}_s \setminus t} m_{u \to s}(z_s) \right) \tag{9.67}$$

The $m_{s \to t}$ message is computed by multiplying together all incoming messages, except the one sent by the recipient, and then passing through the ψ_{st} potential. We continue this process until convergence. If the graph is a tree, the method is guaranteed to converge after $D(G)$ iterations, where $D(G)$ is the **diameter** of the graph, that is, the largest distance between any two nodes.

9.4.2 Loopy BP for factor graphs

To implement loopy BP for general graphs, including those with higher-order clique potentials (beyond pairwise), it is useful to use a factor graph representation described in Section 4.6.1. In this section, we summarize the BP equations for the bipartite version of factor graphs, as derived in [KFL01].[3] For a version that works for Forney factor graphs, see [Loe+07].

---

3. For an efficient JAX implementation of these equations for discrete factor graphs, see https://github.com/vicariousinc/PGMax. For the Gaussian case, see https://github.com/probml/pgm-jax.

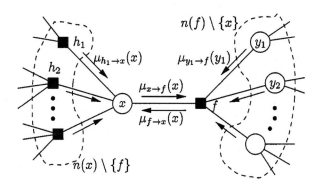

Figure 9.10: *Message passing on a bipartite factor graph. Square nodes represent factors, and circles represent variables. The y_i nodes correspond to the neighbors x'_i of f other than x. From Figure 6 of [KFL01]. Used with kind permission of Brendan Frey.*

In the case of bipartite factor graphs, we have two kinds of messages: variables to factors

$$m_{x \to f}(x) = \prod_{h \in \text{nbr}(x) \setminus \{f\}} m_{h \to x}(x) \tag{9.68}$$

and factors to variables

$$m_{f \to x}(x) = \sum_{x'} f(x, x') \prod_{x' \in \text{nbr}(f) \setminus \{x\}} m_{x' \to f}(x') \tag{9.69}$$

Here $\text{nbr}(x)$ are all the factors that are connected to variable x, and $\text{nbr}(f)$ are all the variables that are connected to factor f. These messages are illustrated in Figure 9.10. At convergence, we can compute the final beliefs as a product of incoming messages:

$$\text{bel}(x) \propto \prod_{f \in \text{nbr}(x)} m_{f \to x}(x) \tag{9.70}$$

The order in which the messages are sent can be determined using various heuristics, such as computing a spanning tree, and picking an arbitrary node as root. Alternatively, the update ordering can be chosen adaptively using **residual belief propagation** [EMK06]. Or fully parallel, asynchronous implementations can be used.

9.4.3 Gaussian belief propagation

It is possible to genereralize (loopy) belief propagation to the Gaussian case, by using the "calculus for linear Gaussian models" in Section 2.3.3 to compute the messages and beliefs. Note that computing the posterior mean in a linear-Gaussian system is equivalent to solving a linear system, so these methods are also useful for linear algebra. See e.g., [PL03; Bic09; Du+18] for details.

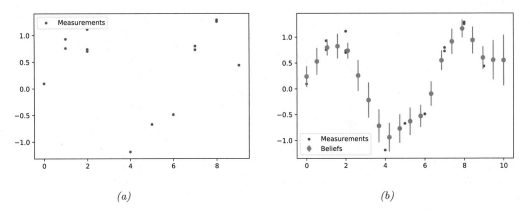

(a)   *(b)*

Figure 9.11: Interpolating noisy data using Gaussian belief propagation applied to a 1d MRF. Generated by gauss-bp-1d-line.ipynb.

As an example of Gaussian BP, consider the problem of interpolating noisy data in 1d, as discussed in [OED21]. In particular, let $f : \mathbb{R} \to \mathbb{R}$ be an unknown function for which we get N noisy measurements y_i at locations x_i. We want to estimate $z_i = f(g_i)$ at G grid locations g_i. Let x_i be the closest location to g_i. Then we assume the measurement factor is as follows:

$$\psi_i(z_{i-1}, z_i) = \frac{1}{\sigma^2}(\hat{y}_i - y_i)^2 \tag{9.71}$$

$$\hat{y}_i = (1 - \gamma_i)z_{i-1} + \gamma_i z_i \tag{9.72}$$

$$\gamma_i = \frac{x_i - g_i}{g_i - g_{i-1}} \tag{9.73}$$

Here $\hat{y}_i$ is the predicted measurement. The potential function makes the unknown function values z_{i-1} and z_i move closer to the observation, based on how far these grid points are from where the measurement was taken. In addition, we add a pairwise smoothness potential, that encodes the prior that z_i should be close to z_{i-1} and z_{i+1}:

$$\phi_i(z_{i-1}, z_i) = \frac{1}{\tau^2}\delta_i^2 \tag{9.74}$$

$$\delta_i = z_i - z_{i-1} \tag{9.75}$$

The overall model is

$$p(\boldsymbol{z}|\boldsymbol{x}, \boldsymbol{y}, \boldsymbol{g}, \sigma^2, \tau^2) \propto \prod_{i=1}^{G} \psi_i(z_{i-1}, z_i)\phi_i(z_{i-1}, z_i) \tag{9.76}$$

Suppose the true underlying function is a sine wave. We show some sample data in Figure 9.11(a). We then apply Gaussian BP. Since this model is a chain, and the model is linear-Gaussian, the resulting posterior marginals, shown in Figure 9.11(b), are exact. We see that the method has inferred the underlying sine shape just based on a smoothness prior.

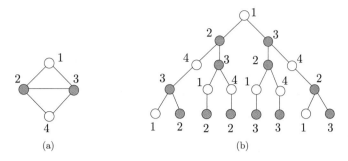

Figure 9.12: (a) A simple loopy graph. (b) The computation tree, rooted at node 1, after 4 rounds of message passing. Nodes 2 and 3 occur more often in the tree because they have higher degree than nodes 1 and 2. From Figure 8.2 of [WJ08]. Used with kind permission of Martin Wainwright.

To perform message passing in models with non-linear (but Gaussian) potentials, we can generalize the extended Kalman filter techniques from Section 8.3.2 and the moment matching techniques (based on quadrature/sigma points) from Section 8.5.1 and Section 8.5.1.1 from chains to general factor graphs (see e.g., [MHH14; PHR18; HPR19]). To extend to the non-Gaussian case, we can use **non-parametric BP** or **particle BP** (see e.g., [Sud+03; Isa03; Sud+10; Pac+14]), which uses ideas from particle filtering (Section 13.2).

9.4.4 Convergence

Loopy BP may not converge, or may only converge slowly. In this section, we discuss some techniques that increase the chances of convergence, and the speed of convergence.

9.4.4.1 When will LBP converge?

The details of the analysis of when LBP will converge are beyond the scope of this chapter, but we briefly sketch the basic idea. The key analysis tool is the **computation tree**, which visualizes the messages that are passed as the algorithm proceeds. Figure 9.12 gives a simple example. In the first iteration, node 1 receives messages from nodes 2 and 3. In the second iteration, it receives one message from node 3 (via node 2), one from node 2 (via node 3), and two messages from node 4 (via nodes 2 and 3). And so on.

The key insight is that T iterations of LBP is equivalent to exact computation in a computation tree of height $T + 1$. If the strengths of the connections on the edges is sufficiently weak, then the influence of the leaves on the root will diminish over time, and convergence will occur. See [MK05; WJ08] and references therein for more information.

9.4.4.2 Making LBP converge

Although the theoretical convergence analysis is very interesting, in practice, when faced with a model where LBP is not converging, what should we do?

One simple way to increase the chance of convergence is to use **damping**. That is, at iteration k,

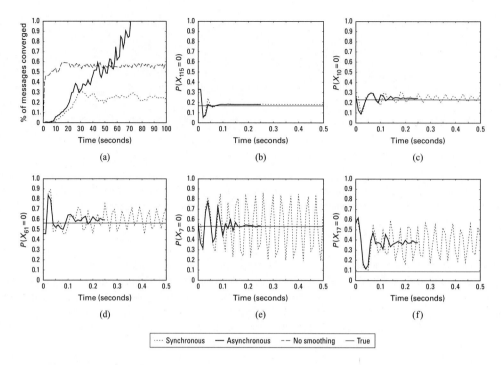

Figure 9.13: Illustration of the behavior of loopy belief propagation on an 11×11 Ising grid with random potentials, $w_{ij} \sim \mathrm{Unif}(-C, C)$, where $C = 11$. For larger C, inference becomes harder. (a) Percentage of messages that have converged vs time for 3 different update schedules: Dotted = damped synchronous (few nodes converge), dashed = undamped asychnronous (half the nodes converge), solid = damped asychnronous (all nodes converge). (b-f) Marginal beliefs of certain nodes vs time. Solid straight line = truth, dashed = sychnronous, solid = damped asychronous. From Figure 11.C.1 of [KF09a]. Used with kind permission of Daphne Koller.

we use an update of the form

$$m_{t \to s}^{k}(x_s) = \lambda m_{t \to s}(x_s) + (1 - \lambda) m_{t \to s}^{k-1}(x_s) \qquad (9.77)$$

where $m_{t \to s}(x_s)$ is the standard undamped message, where $0 \leq \lambda \leq 1$ is the damping factor. Clearly if $\lambda = 1$ this reduces to the standard scheme, but for $\lambda < 1$, this partial updating scheme can help improve convergence. Using a value such as $\lambda \sim 0.5$ is standard practice. The benefits of this approach are shown in Figure 9.13, where we see that damped updating results in convergence much more often than undamped updating (see [ZLG20] for some analysis of the benefits of damping).

It is possible to devise methods, known as **double loop algorithms**, which are guaranteed to converge to a local minimum of the same objective that LBP is minimizing [Yui01; WT01]. Unfortunately, these methods are rather slow and complicated, and the accuracy of the resulting marginals is usually not much greater than with standard LBP. (Indeed, oscillating marginals is sometimes a sign that the LBP approximation itself is a poor one.) Consequently, these techniques are not very widely used (although see [GF21] for a newer technique).

9.4.4.3   Increasing the convergence rate with adaptive scheduling

The standard approach when implementing LBP is to perform **synchronous updates**, where all nodes absorb messages in parallel, and then send out messages in parallel. That is, the new messages at iteration $k + 1$ are computed in parallel using

$$m_{1:E}^{k+1} = (f_1(\boldsymbol{m}^k), \ldots, f_E(\boldsymbol{m}^k)) \tag{9.78}$$

where E is the number of edges, and $f_i(\boldsymbol{m})$ is the function that computes the message for edge i given all the old messages. This is analogous to the Jacobi method for solving linear systems of equations.

It is well known [Ber97b] that the Gauss-Seidel method, which performs **asynchronous updates** in a fixed round-robin fashion, converges faster when solving linear systems of equations. We can apply the same idea to LBP, using updates of the form

$$\boldsymbol{m}_i^{k+1} = f_i\left(\{\boldsymbol{m}_j^{k+1} : j < i\}, \{\boldsymbol{m}_j^k : j > i\}\right) \tag{9.79}$$

where the message for edge i is computed using new messages (iteration $k + 1$) from edges earlier in the ordering, and using old messages (iteration k) from edges later in the ordering.

This raises the question of what order to update the messages in. One simple idea is to use a fixed or random order. The benefits of this approach are shown in Figure 9.13, where we see that (damped) asynchronous updating results in convergence much more often than synchronous updating.

However, we can do even better by using an adaptive ordering. The intuition is that we should focus our computational efforts on those variables that are most uncertain. [EMK06] proposed a technique known as **residual belief propagation**, in which messages are scheduled to be sent according to the norm of the difference from their previous value. That is, we define the residual of new message $m_{s \to t}$ at iteration k to be

$$r(s, t, k) = || \log m_{s \to t} - \log m_{s \to t}^k ||_\infty = \max_j | \log \frac{m_{s \to t}(j)}{m_{s \to t}^k(j)} | \tag{9.80}$$

We can store messages in a priority queue, and always send the one with highest residual. When a message is sent from s to t, all of the other messages that depend on $m_{s \to t}$ (i.e., messages of the form $m_{t \to u}$ where $u \in \text{nbr}(t) \setminus s$) need to be recomputed; their residual is recomputed, and they are added back to the queue. In [EMK06], they showed (experimentally) that this method converges more often, and much faster, than using sychronous updating, or asynchronous updating with a fixed order.

A refinement of residual BP was presented in [SM07]. In this paper, they use an upper bound on the residual of a message instead of the actual residual. This means that messages are only computed if they are going to be sent; they are not just computed for the purposes of evaluating the residual. This was observed to be about five times faster than residual BP, although the quality of the final results are similar.

9.4.5   Accuracy

For a graph with a single loop, one can show that the max-product version of LBP will find the correct MAP estimate, if it converges [Wei00]. For more general graphs, one can bound the error in the approximate marginals computed by LBP, as shown in [WJW03; IFW05; Vin+10b].

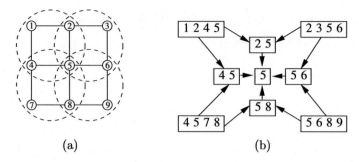

Figure 9.14: (a) Clusters superimposed on a 3 × 3 lattice graph. (b) Corresponding hyper-graph. Nodes represent clusters, and edges represent set containment. From Figure 4.5 of [WJ08]. Used with kind permission of Martin Wainwright.

Much stronger results are available in the case of Gaussian models. In particular, it can be shown that, if the method converges, the means are exact, although the variances are not (typically the beliefs are over confident). See e.g., [WF01a; JMW06; Bic09; Du+18] for details.

9.4.6   Generalized belief propagation

We can improve the accuracy of loopy BP by clustering together nodes that form a tight loop. This is known as the **cluster variational method**, or **generalized belief propagation** [YFW00].

The result of clustering is a hyper-graph, which is a graph where there are hyper-edges between sets of vertices instead of between single vertices. Note that a junction tree (Section 9.6) is a kind of hyper-graph. We can represent a hyper-graph using a poset (partially ordered set) diagram, where each node represents a hyper-edge, and there is an arrow $e_1 \rightarrow e_2$ if $e_2 \subset e_1$. See Figure 9.14 for an example.

If we allow the size of the largest hyper-edge in the hyper-graph to be as large as the treewidth of the graph, then we can represent the hyper-graph as a tree, and the method will be exact, just as LBP is exact on regular trees (with treewidth 1). In this way, we can define a continuum of approximations, from LBP all the way to exact inference. See Supplementary Section 10.4.3.3 for more information.

9.4.7   Convex BP

In Supplementary Section 10.4.3 we analyze LBP from a variational perspective, and show that the resulting optimization problem, for both standard and generalized BP, is non-convex. However it is possible to create a version of **convex BP**, as we explain in Supplementary Section 10.4.4, which has the advantage that it will always converge.

9.4.8   Application: error correcting codes

LBP was first proposed by Judea Pearl in his 1988 book [Pea88]. He recognized that applying BP to loopy graphs might not work, but recommended it as a heuristic.

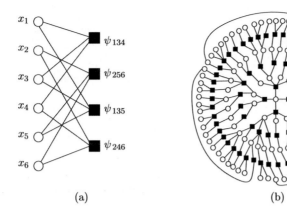

(a)   (b)

Figure 9.15: (a) A simple factor graph representation of a (2,3) low-density parity check code. Each message bit (hollow round circle) is connected to two parity factors (solid black squares), and each parity factor is connected to three bits. Each parity factor has the form $\psi_{stu}(x_s, x_t, x_u) = \mathbb{I}(x_s \otimes x_t \otimes x_u = 1)$, where $\otimes$ is the xor operator. The local evidence factors for each hidden node are not shown. (b) A larger example of a random LDPC code. We see that this graph is "locally tree-like", meaning there are no short cycles; rather, each cycle has length $\sim \log m$, where m is the number of nodes. This gives us a hint as to why loopy BP works so well on such graphs. (Note, however, that some error correcting code graphs have short loops, so this is not the full explanation.) From Figure 2.9 from [WJ08]. Used with kind permission of Martin Wainwright.

However, the main impetus behind the interest in LBP arose when McEliece, MacKay, and Cheng [MMC98] showed that a popular algorithm for error correcting codes, known as **turbocodes** [BGT93], could be viewed as an instance of LBP applied to a certain kind of graph.

We introduced error correcting codes in Section 5.5. Recall that the basic idea is to send the source message $\boldsymbol{x} \in \{0, 1\}^m$ over a noisy channel, and for the receiver to try to infer it given noisy measurements $\boldsymbol{y} \in \{0, 1\}^m$ or $\boldsymbol{y} \in \mathbb{R}^m$. That is, the receiver needs to compute $\boldsymbol{x}^* = \operatorname{argmax}_{\boldsymbol{x}} p(\boldsymbol{x}|\boldsymbol{y}) = \operatorname{argmax}_{\boldsymbol{x}} \tilde{p}(\boldsymbol{x})$.

It is standard to represent $\tilde{p}(\boldsymbol{x})$ as a factor graph (Section 4.6.1), which can easily represent any deterministic relationships (parity constraints) between the bits. A factor graph is a bipartite graph with x_i nodes on one side, and factors on the other. A graph in which each node is connected to n factors, and in which each factor is connected to k nodes, is called an (n, k) code. Figure 9.15(a) shows a simple example of a $(2, 3)$ code, where each bit (hollow round circle) is connected to two parity factors (solid black squares), and each parity factor is connected to three bits. Each parity factor has the form

$$\psi_{stu}(x_s, x_t, x_u) \triangleq \begin{cases} 1 & \text{if } x_s \otimes x_t \otimes x_u = 1 \\ 0 & \text{otherwise} \end{cases} \tag{9.81}$$

If the degrees of the parity checks and variable nodes remain bounded as the blocklength m increases, this is called a **low-density parity check code**, or **LDPC code**. (Turbocodes are constructed in a similar way.)

Figure 9.15(b) shows an example of a randomly constructed LDPC code. This graph is "locally tree-like", meaning there are no short cycles; rather, each cycle has length $\sim \log m$. This fact is important to the success of LBP, which is only guaranteed to work on tree-structured graphs. Using

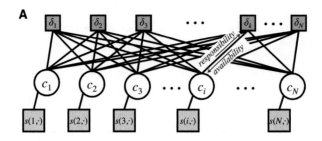

Figure 9.16: Factor graphs for affinity propagation. Circles are variables, squares are factors. Each c_i node has N possible states. From Figure S2 of [FD07a]. Used with kind permission of Brendan Frey.

methods such as these, people have been able to approach the lower bound in Shannon's channel coding theorem, meaning they have produced codes with very little redundancy for a given amount of noise in the channel. See e.g., [MMC98; Mac03] for more details. Such codes are widely used, e.g., in modern cellphones.

9.4.9 Application: affinity propagation

In this section, we discuss **affinity propagation** [FD07a], which can be seen as an improvement to K-medoids clustering, which takes as input a pairwise similarity matrix. The idea is that each datapoint must choose another datapoint as its exemplar or centroid; some datapoints will choose themselves as centroids, and this will automatically determine the number of clusters. More precisely, let $c_i \in \{1, \ldots, N\}$ represent the centroid for datapoint i. The goal is to maximize the following function

$$J(\boldsymbol{c}) = \sum_{i=1}^{N} S(i, c_i) + \sum_{k=1}^{N} \delta_k(\boldsymbol{c}) \tag{9.82}$$

where $S(i, c_i)$ is the similarity between datapoint i and its centroid c_i. The second term is a penalty term that is $-\infty$ if some datapoint i has chosen k as its exemplar (i.e., $c_i = k$), but k has not chosen itself as an exemplar (i.e., we do not have $c_k = k$). More formally,

$$\delta_k(\boldsymbol{c}) = \begin{cases} -\infty & \text{if } c_k \neq k \text{ but } \exists i : c_i = k \\ 0 & \text{otherwise} \end{cases} \tag{9.83}$$

This encourages "representative" samples to vote for themselves as centroids, thus encouraging clustering behavior.

The objective function can be represented as a factor graph. We can either use N nodes, each with N possible values, as shown in Figure 9.16, or we can use N^2 binary nodes (see [GF09] for the details). We will assume the former representation.

We can find a strong local maximum of the objective by using max-product loopy belief propagation (Section 9.4). Referring to the model in Figure 9.16, each variable node c_i sends a message to each factor node δ_k. It turns out that this vector of N numbers can be reduced to a scalar message,

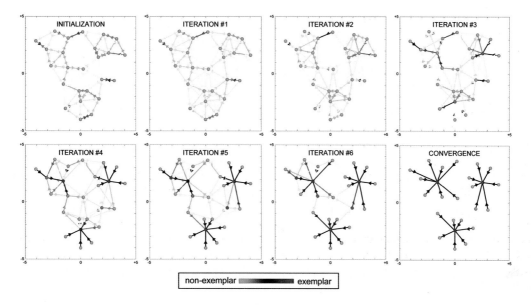

Figure 9.17: *Example of affinity propagation. Each point is colored coded by how much it wants to be an exemplar (red is the most, green is the least). This can be computed by summing up all the incoming availability messages and the self-similarity term. The darkness of the $i \to k$ arrow reflects how much point i wants to belong to exemplar k. From Figure 1 of [FD07a]. Used with kind permission of Brendan Frey.*

denoted $r_{i \to k}$, known as the responsibility. This is a measure of how much i thinks k would make a good exemplar, compared to all the other exemplars i has looked at. In addition, each factor node δ_k sends a message to each variable node c_i. Again this can be reduced to a scalar message, $a_{i \leftarrow k}$, known as the availability. This is a measure of how strongly k believes it should an exemplar for i, based on all the other datapoints k has looked at.

As usual with loopy BP, the method might oscillate, and convergence is not guaranteed. However, by using damping, the method is very reliable in practice. If the graph is densely connected, message passing takes $O(N^2)$ time, but with sparse similarity matrices, it only takes $O(E)$ time, where E is the number of edges or non-zero entries in S.

The number of clusters can be controlled by scaling the diagonal terms $S(i, i)$, which reflect how much each datapoint wants to be an exemplar. Figure 9.17 gives a simple example of some 2d data, where the negative Euclidean distance was used to measured similarity. The $S(i, i)$ values were set to be the median of all the pairwise similarities. The result is 3 clusters. Many other results are reported in [FD07a], who show that the method significantly outperforms K-medoids.

9.4.10   Emulating BP with graph neural nets

There is a close connection between message passing in PGMs and message passing in graph neural networks (GNNs), which we discuss in Section 16.3.6. However, for PGMs, the message computations are computing using (non-learned) update equations that work for any model; all that is needed is the graph structure G, model parameters $\boldsymbol{\theta}$, and evidence $\boldsymbol{v}$. By contrast, GNNs are trained to emulate specific functions using labeled input-output pairs.

It is natural to wonder what happens if we train a GNN on the exact posterior marginals derived from a small PGM, and then apply that trained GNN to a different test PGM. In [Yoo+18; Zha+19d], they show this method can work quite well if the test PGM is similar in structure to the one used for training.

An alternative approach is to start with a known PGM, and then "unroll" the BP message passing algorithm to produce a layered feedforward model, whose connectivity is derived from the graph. The resulting network can then be trained discriminatively for some end-task (not necessarily computing posterior marginals). Thus the BP procedure applied to the PGM just provides a way to design the neural network structure. This method is called **deep unfolding** (see e.g., [HLRW14]), and can often give very good results. (See also [SW20] for a more recent version of this approach, called "**neural enhanced BP**".)

These neural methods are useful if the PGM is fixed, and we want to repeatedly perform inference or prediction with it, using different values of the evidence, but where the set of nodes which are observed is always the same. This is an example of amortized inference, where we train a model to emulate the results of running an iterative optimization scheme (see Section 10.1.5 for more discussion).

9.5   The variable elimination (VE) algorithm

In this section, we discuss an algorithm to compute a posterior marginal $p(\boldsymbol{z}_Q|\boldsymbol{y})$ for any query set Q, assuming p is defined by a graphical model. Unlike loopy BP, it is guaranteed to give the correct answers even if the graph has cycles. We assume all the hidden nodes are discrete, although a version of the algorithm can be created for the Gaussian case by using the rules for sum and product defined in Section 2.3.3.

9.5.1   Derivation of the algorithm

We will explain the algorithm by applying it to an example. Specifically, we consider the student network from Section 4.2.2.2. Suppose we want to compute $p(J = 1)$, the marginal probability that a person will get a job. Since we have 8 binary variables, we could simply enumerate over all possible assignments to all the variables (except for J), adding up the probability of each joint instantiation:

$$p(J) = \sum_L \sum_S \sum_G \sum_H \sum_I \sum_D \sum_C p(C, D, I, G, S, L, J, H) \tag{9.84}$$

However, this would take $O(2^7)$ time. We can be smarter by **pushing sums inside products**. This is the key idea behind the **variable elimination** algorithm [ZP96], also called **bucket elimination** [Dec96], or, in the context of genetic pedigree trees, the **peeling algorithm** [CTS78].

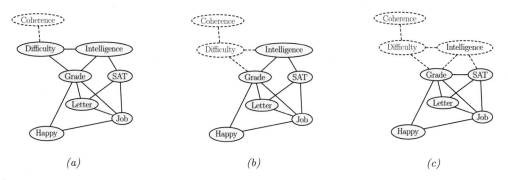

(a)   (b)   (c)

Figure 9.18: Example of the elimination process, in the order C, D, I, H, G, S, L. When we eliminate I (figure c), we add a fill-in edge between G and S, since they are not connected. Adapted from Figure 9.10 of [KF09a].

In our example, we get

$$
\begin{aligned}
p(J) &= \sum_{L,S,G,H,I,D,C} p(C, D, I, G, S, L, J, H) \\
&= \sum_{L,S,G,H,I,D,C} \psi_C(C)\psi_D(D,C)\psi_I(I)\psi_G(G,I,D)\psi_S(S,I)\psi_L(L,G) \\
&\quad \times \psi_J(J,L,S)\psi_H(H,G,J) \\
&= \sum_{L,S} \psi_J(J,L,S) \sum_G \psi_L(L,G) \sum_H \psi_H(H,G,J) \sum_I \psi_S(S,I)\psi_I(I) \\
&\quad \times \sum_D \psi_G(G,I,D) \sum_C \psi_C(C)\psi_D(D,C)
\end{aligned}
$$

We now evaluate this expression, working right to left as shown in Table 9.1. First we multiply together all the terms in the scope of the $\sum_C$ operator to create the temporary factor

$$\tau_1'(C,D) = \psi_C(C)\psi_D(D,C) \tag{9.85}$$

Then we marginalize out C to get the new factor

$$\tau_1(D) = \sum_C \tau_1'(C,D) \tag{9.86}$$

Next we multiply together all the terms in the scope of the $\sum_D$ operator and then marginalize out to create

$$\tau_2'(G,I,D) = \psi_G(G,I,D)\tau_1(D) \tag{9.87}$$

$$\tau_2(G,I) = \sum_D \tau_2'(G,I,D) \tag{9.88}$$

And so on.

$$\sum_L \sum_S \psi_J(J,L,S) \sum_G \psi_L(L,G) \sum_H \psi_H(H,G,J) \sum_I \psi_S(S,I)\psi_I(I) \sum_D \psi_G(G,I,D) \underbrace{\sum_C \psi_C(C)\psi_D(D,C)}_{\tau_1(D)}$$

$$\sum_L \sum_S \psi_J(J,L,S) \sum_G \psi_L(L,G) \sum_H \psi_H(H,G,J) \sum_I \psi_S(S,I)\psi_I(I) \underbrace{\sum_D \psi_G(G,I,D)\tau_1(D)}_{\tau_2(G,I)}$$

$$\sum_L \sum_S \psi_J(J,L,S) \sum_G \psi_L(L,G) \sum_H \psi_H(H,G,J) \underbrace{\sum_I \psi_S(S,I)\psi_I(I)\tau_2(G,I)}_{\tau_3(G,S)}$$

$$\sum_L \sum_S \psi_J(J,L,S) \sum_G \psi_L(L,G) \underbrace{\sum_H \psi_H(H,G,J)\,\tau_3(G,S)}_{\tau_4(G,J)}$$

$$\sum_L \sum_S \psi_J(J,L,S) \underbrace{\sum_G \psi_L(L,G)\tau_4(G,J)\tau_3(G,S)}_{\tau_5(J,L,S)}$$

$$\sum_L \sum_S \underbrace{\psi_J(J,L,S)\tau_5(J,L,S)}_{\tau_6(J,L)}$$

$$\underbrace{\sum_L \tau_6(J,L)}_{\tau_7(J)}$$

Table 9.1: *Eliminating variables from Figure 4.38 in the order* C, D, I, H, G, S, L *to compute* $P(J)$.

The above technique can be used to compute any marginal of interest, such as $p(J)$ or $p(J, H)$. To compute a conditional, we can take a ratio of two marginals, where the visible variables have been clamped to their known values (and hence don't need to be summed over). For example,

$$p(J = j | I = 1, H = 0) = \frac{p(J = j, I = 1, H = 0)}{\sum_{j'} p(J = j', I = 1, H = 0)} \qquad (9.89)$$

9.5.2   Computational complexity of VE

The running time of VE is clearly exponential in the size of the largest factor, since we have to sum over all of the corresponding variables. Some of the factors come from the original model (and are thus unavoidable), but new factors may also be created in the process of summing out. For example, in Table 9.1, we created a factor involving G, I, and S; but these nodes were not originally present together in any factor.

The order in which we perform the summation is known as the **elimination order**. This can have a large impact on the size of the intermediate factors that are created. For example, consider the ordering in Table 9.1: the largest created factor (beyond the original ones in the model) has size 3, corresponding to $\tau_5(J, L, S)$. Now consider the ordering in Table 9.2: now the largest factors are $\tau_1(I, D, L, J, H)$ and $\tau_2(D, L, S, J, H)$, which are much bigger.

$$\sum_D \sum_C \psi_D(D,C) \sum_H \sum_L \sum_S \psi_J(J,L,S) \sum_I \psi_I(I)\psi_S(S,I) \underbrace{\sum_G \psi_G(G,I,D)\psi_L(L,G)\psi_H(H,G,J)}_{\tau_1(I,D,L,J,H)}$$

$$\sum_D \sum_C \psi_D(D,C) \sum_H \sum_L \sum_S \psi_J(J,L,S) \underbrace{\sum_I \psi_I(I)\psi_S(S,I)\tau_1(I,D,L,J,H)}_{\tau_2(D,L,S,J,H)}$$

$$\sum_D \sum_C \psi_D(D,C) \sum_H \sum_L \underbrace{\sum_S \psi_J(J,L,S)\tau_2(D,L,S,J,H)}_{\tau_3(D,L,J,H)}$$

$$\sum_D \sum_C \psi_D(D,C) \sum_H \underbrace{\sum_L \tau_3(D,L,J,H)}_{\tau_4(D,J,H)}$$

$$\sum_D \sum_C \psi_D(D,C) \underbrace{\sum_H \tau_4(D,J,H)}_{\tau_5(D,J)}$$

$$\sum_D \underbrace{\sum_C \psi_D(D,C)\tau_5(D,J)}_{\tau_6(D,J)}$$

$$\underbrace{\sum_D \tau_6(D,J)}_{\tau_7(J)}$$

Table 9.2: *Eliminating variables from Figure 4.38 in the order* G, I, S, L, H, C, D.

We can determine the size of the largest factor graphically, without worrying about the actual numerical values of the factors, by running the VE algorithm "symbolically". When we eliminate a variable z_t, we connect together all variables that share a factor with z_t (to reflect the new temporary factor τ'_t). The edges created by this process are called **fill-in edges**. For example, Figure 9.18 shows the fill-in edges introduced when we eliminate in the $C, D, I, \ldots$ order. The first two steps do not introduce any fill-ins, but when we eliminate I, we connect G and S, to capture the temporary factor

$$\tau'_3(G,S,I) = \psi_S(S,I)\psi_I(I)\tau_2(G,I) \tag{9.90}$$

Let $\mathcal{G}_\prec$ be the (undirected) graph induced by applying variable elimination to $\mathcal{G}$ using elimination ordering $\prec$. The temporary factors generated by VE correspond to maximal **cliques** in the graph $\mathcal{G}_\prec$. For example, with ordering (C, D, I, H, G, S, L), the maximal cliques are as follows:

$$\{C,D\}, \{D,I,G\}, \{G,L,S,J\}, \{G,J,H\}, \{G,I,S\} \tag{9.91}$$

It is clear that the time complexity of VE is

$$\sum_{c \in \mathcal{C}(\mathcal{G}_\prec)} K^{|c|} \tag{9.92}$$

where $\mathcal{C}(\mathcal{G})$ are the (maximal) cliques in graph $\mathcal{G}$, $|c|$ is the size of the clique c, and we assume for notational simplicity that all the variables have K states each.

Let us define the **induced width** of a graph given elimination ordering $\prec$, denoted $w_\prec$, as the size of the largest factor (i.e., the largest clique in the induced graph) minus 1. Then it is easy to see that the complexity of VE with ordering $\prec$ is $O(K^{w_\prec+1})$. The smallest possible induced width for a graph is known at its **treewidth**. Unfortunately finding the corresponding optimal elimination order is an NP-complete problem [Yan81; ACP87]. See Section 9.5.3 for a discussion of some approximate methods for finding good elimination orders.

9.5.3   Picking a good elimination order

Many algorithms take time (or space) which is exponential in the tree width of the corresponding graph. For example, this applies to Cholesky decompositions of sparse matrices, as well as to einsum contractions (see `https://github.com/dgasmith/opt_einsum`). Hence we would like to find an elimination ordering that minimizes the width. We say that an ordering π is a **perfect elimination ordering** if it does not introduce any fill-in edges. Every graph that is already triangulated (e.g., a tree) has a perfect elimination ordering. We call such graphs **decomposable**.

In general, we will need to add fill-in edges to ensure the resulting graph is decomposable. Different orderings can introduce different numbers of fill-in edges, which affects the width of the resulting chordal graph; for example, compare Table 9.1 to Table 9.2.

Choosing an elimination ordering with minimal width is NP-complete [Yan81; ACP87]. It is common to use greedy approximation known as the **min-fill heuristic**, which works as follows: eliminate any node which would not result in any fill-ins (i.e., all of whose uneliminated neighbors already form a clique); if there is no such node, eliminate the node which would result in the minimum number of fill-in edges. When nodes have different weights (e.g., representing different numbers of states), we can use the **min-weight heuristic**, where we try to minimize the weight of the created cliques at each step.

Of course, many other methods are possible. See [Heg06] for a general survey. [Kja90; Kja92] compared simulated annealing with the above greedy method, and found that it sometimes works better (although it is much slower). [MJ97] approximate the discrete optimization problem by a continuous optimization problem. [BG96] present a randomized approximation algorithm. [Gil88] present the nested dissection order, which is always within $O(\log N)$ of optimal. [Ami01] discuss various constant-factor appoximation algorithms. [Dav+04] present the **AMD** or approximate minimum degree ordering algorithm, which is implemented in Matlab.[4] The METIS library can be used for finding elimination orderings for large graphs; this implements the **nested dissection** algorithm [GT86]. For a planar graph with N nodes, the resulting treewidth will have the optimal size of $O(N^{3/2})$.

9.5.4   Computational complexity of exact inference

We have seen that variable elimination takes $O(NK^{w+1})$ time to compute the marginals for a graph with N nodes, and treewidth w, where each variable has K states. If the graph is densely connected, then $w = O(N)$, and so inference will take time exponential in N.

---

4. See the description of the symamd command at `https://bit.ly/31N6E2b`. ("sym" stands for symbolic, "amd" stands approximate minimum degree.)

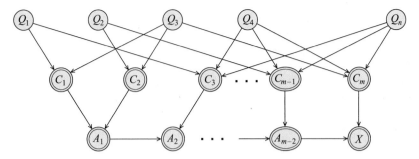

Figure 9.19: Encoding a 3-SAT problem on n variables and m clauses as a DGM. The Q_s variables are binary random variables. The C_t variables are deterministic functions of the Q_s's, and compute the truth value of each clause. The A_t nodes are a chain of AND gates, to ensure that the CPT for the final x node has bounded size. The double rings denote nodes with deterministic CPDs. From Figure 9.1 of [KF09a]. Used with kind permission of Daphne Koller.

Of course, just because some particular algorithm is slow doesn't mean that there isn't some smarter algorithm out there. Unfortunately, this seems unlikely, since it is easy to show that exact inference for discrete graphical models is NP-hard [DL93]. The proof is a simple reduction from the satisfiability problem. In particular, note that we can encode any 3-SAT problem as a DPGM with deterministic links, as shown in Figure 9.19. We clamp the final node, x, to be on, and we arrange the CPTs so that $p(x = 1) > 0$ iff there is a satisfying assignment. Computing any posterior marginal requires evaluating the normalization constant, $p(x = 1)$, so inference in this model implicitly solves the SAT problem.

In fact, exact inference is #P-hard [Rot96], which is even harder than NP-hard. The intuitive reason for this is that to compute the normalizing constant, we have to *count* how many satisfying assignments there are. (By contrast, MAP estimation is provably easier for some model classes [GPS89], since, intuitively speaking, it only requires finding one satisfying assignment, not counting all of them.) Furthermore, even approximate inference is computationally hard in general [DL93; Rot96].

The above discussion was just concerned with inferring the states of discrete hidden variables. When we have continuous hidden variables, the problem can be even harder, since even a simple two-node graph, of the form $z \to y$, can be intractable to invert if the variables are high dimensional and do not have a conjugate relationship (Section 3.4). Inference in mixed discrete-continuous models can also be hard [LP01].

As a consequence of these hardness results, we often have to resort to approximate inference methods, such as variational inference (Chapter 10) and Monte Carlo inference (Chapter 11).

9.5.5 Drawbacks of VE

Consider using VE to compute all the marginals in a chain-structured graphical model, such as an HMM. We can easily compute the final marginal $p(z_T|\boldsymbol{y})$ by eliminating all the nodes z_1 to z_{T-1} in order. This is equivalent to the forwards algorithm, and takes $O(K^2T)$ time, as we discussed in Section 9.2.3. But now suppose we want to compute $p(z_{T-1}|\boldsymbol{y})$. We have to run VE again, at a cost

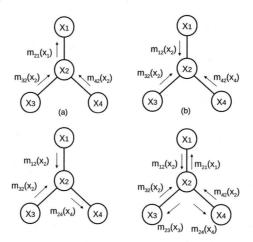

Figure 9.20: Sending multiple messages along a tree. (a) z_1 is root. (b) z_2 is root. (c) z_4 is root. (d) All of the messages needed to compute all singleton marginals. Adapted from Figure 4.3 of [Jor07].

of $O(K^2T)$ time. So the total cost to compute all the marginals is $O(K^2T^2)$. However, we know that we can solve this problem in $O(K^2T)$ using the forwards-backwards, as we discussed in Section 9.2.3. The difference is that FB caches the messages computed on the forwards pass, so it can reuse them later. (Caching previously computed results is the core idea behind dynamic programming.)

The same problem arises when applying VE to trees. For example, consider the 4-node tree in Figure 9.20. We can compute $p(z_1|\boldsymbol{y})$ by eliminating $\boldsymbol{z}_{2:4}$; this is equivalent to sending messages up to z_1 (the messages correspond to the τ factors created by VE). Similarly we can compute $p(z_2|\boldsymbol{y})$, $p(z_3|\boldsymbol{y})$ and then $p(z_4|\boldsymbol{y})$. We see that some of the messages used to compute the marginal on one node can be re-used to compute the marginals on the other nodes. By storing the messages for later re-use, we can compute all the marginals in $O(K^2T)$ time, as we show in Section 9.3.

The question is: how do we get these benefits of message passing on a tree when the graph is not a tree? We give the answer in Section 9.6.

9.6 The junction tree algorithm (JTA)

The **junction tree algorithm** or **JTA** is a generalization of variable elimination that lets us efficiently compute all the posterior marginals without repeating redundant work, by using dynamic programming, thus avoiding the problems mentioned in Section 9.5.5. The basic idea is to convert the graph into a special kind of tree, known as a **junction tree** (also called a **join tree**, or **clique tree**), and then to run belief propagation (message passing) on this tree. We can create the join tree by running variable elimination "symbolically", as discussed in Section 9.5.2, and adding the generated fill-in edges to the graph. The resulting chordal graph can then be converted to a tree, as explained in Supplementary Section 9.2.1. Once we have a tree, we can perform message passing on it, using a variant of the method Section 9.3.2. See Supplementary Section 9.2.2 for details.

9.7 Inference as optimization

In this section, we discuss how to perform posterior inference by solving an optimization problem, which is often computationally simpler. See also Supplementary Section 9.3.

9.7.1 Inference as backpropagation

In this section, we discuss how to compute posterior marginals in a graphical model using automatic differentiation. For notational simplicity, we focus on undirected graphical models, where the joint can be represented as an exponential family (Section 2.4) follows:

$$p(\boldsymbol{x}) = \frac{1}{Z} \prod_c \psi_c(\boldsymbol{x}_c) = \exp(\sum_c \boldsymbol{\eta}_c^\mathsf{T} \mathcal{T}(\boldsymbol{x}_c) - \log A(\boldsymbol{\eta})) = \exp(\boldsymbol{\eta}^\mathsf{T} \mathcal{T}(\boldsymbol{x}) - \log A(\boldsymbol{\eta})) \tag{9.93}$$

where ψ_c is the potential function for clique c, $\boldsymbol{\eta}_c$ are the natural parameters for clique c, $\mathcal{T}(\boldsymbol{x}_c)$ are the corresponding sufficient statistics, and $A = \log Z$ is the log partition function.

We will consider pairwise models (with node and edge potentials), and discrete variables. The natural parameters are the node and edge log potentials, $\boldsymbol{\eta} = (\{\eta_{s;j}\}, \{\eta_{s,t;j,k}\})$, and the sufficient statistics are node and edge indicator functions, $\mathcal{T}(\boldsymbol{x}) = (\{\mathbb{I}(x_s = j)\}, \{\mathbb{I}(x_s = j, x_t = k)\})$. (Note: we use $s, t \in \mathcal{V}$ to index nodes and $j, k \in \mathcal{X}$ to index states.)

The mean of the sufficient statistics are given by

$$\boldsymbol{\mu} = \mathbb{E}[\mathcal{T}(\boldsymbol{x})] = (\{p(x_s = j)\}_s, \{p(x_s = j, x_t = k)\}_{s \neq t}) = (\{\mu_{s;j}\}_s, \{\mu_{st;jk}\}_{s \neq t}) \tag{9.94}$$

The key result, from Equation (2.236), is that $\boldsymbol{\mu} = \nabla_{\boldsymbol{\eta}} A(\boldsymbol{\eta})$. Thus as long as we have a function that computes $A(\boldsymbol{\eta}) = \log Z(\boldsymbol{\eta})$, we can use automatic differentiation (Section 6.2) to compute gradients, and then we can extract the corresponding node marginals from the gradient vector. If we have evidence (known values) on some of the variables, we simply "clamp" the corresponding entries to 0 or 1 in the node potentials.

The observation that probabilistic inference can be performed using automatic differentiation has been discovered independently by several groups (e.g., [Dar03; PD03; Eis16; ASM17]). It also lends itself to the development of differentiable approximations to inference (see e.g., [MB18]).

9.7.1.1 Example: inference in a small model

As a concrete example, consider a small chain structured model $x_1 - x_2 - x_3$, where each node has K states. We can represent the node potentials as $K \times 1$ tensors (table of numbers), and the edge potentials by $K \times K$ tensors. The partition function is given by

$$Z(\boldsymbol{\psi}) = \sum_{x_1, x_2, x_3} \psi_1(x_1)\psi_2(x_2)\psi_3(x_3)\psi_{12}(x_1, x_2)\psi_{23}(x_2, x_3) \tag{9.95}$$

Let $\boldsymbol{\eta} = \log(\boldsymbol{\psi})$ be the log potentials, and $A(\boldsymbol{\eta}) = \log Z(\boldsymbol{\eta})$ be the log partition function. We can compute the single node marginals $\boldsymbol{\mu}_s = p(x_s = 1 : K)$ using $\boldsymbol{\mu}_s = \nabla_{\boldsymbol{\eta}_s} A(\boldsymbol{\eta})$, and the pairwise marginals $\boldsymbol{\mu}_{s,t}(j, k) = p(x_s = j, x_t = k)$ using $\boldsymbol{\mu}_{s,t} = \nabla_{\boldsymbol{\eta}_{s,t}} A(\boldsymbol{\eta})$.

We can compute the partition function Z efficiently use numpy's **einsum** function, which implements tensor contraction using Einstein summation notation. We label each dimension of the tensors by A, B, and C, so einsum knows how to match things up. We then compute gradients using an auto-diff library.[5] The result is that inference can be done in two lines of Python code, as shown in Listing 9.1:

Listing 9.1: Computing marginals from derivative of log partition function

```
import jax.numpy as jnp
from jax import grad

logZ_fun = lambda logpots: np.log(jnp.einsum("A,B,C,AB,BC",
        *[jnp.exp(lp) for lp in logpots]))
probs = grad(logZ_fun)(logpots)
```

To perform conditional inference, such as $p(x_s = k | x_t = e)$, we multiply in one-hot indicator vectors to clamp x_t to the value e so that the unnormalized joint only assigns non-zero probability to state combinations that are valid. We then sum over all values of the unclamped variables to get the constrained partition function Z_e. The gradients will now give us the marginals conditioned on the evidence [Dar03].

9.7.2   Perturb and MAP

In this section, we discuss how to draw posterior samples from a graphical model by leveraging optimization as a subroutine. The basic idea is to make S copies of the model, each of which has slightly perturbed versions of the parameters, $\boldsymbol{\theta}_s = \boldsymbol{\theta}_s + \boldsymbol{\epsilon}_s$, and then to compute the MAP estimate, $\boldsymbol{x}_s = \operatorname{argmax} p(\boldsymbol{x}|\boldsymbol{y}; \boldsymbol{\theta}_s)$. For a suitably chosen noise distribution for $\boldsymbol{\epsilon}_s$, this technique — known as **perturb-and-MAP** — can be shown that this gives exact posterior samples [PY10; PY11; PY14].

9.7.2.1   Gaussian case

We first consider the case of a Gaussian MRF. Let $\boldsymbol{x} \in \mathbb{R}^N$ be the vector of hidden states with prior

$$p(\boldsymbol{x}) \propto \mathcal{N}(\mathbf{G}\boldsymbol{x}|\boldsymbol{\mu}_p, \boldsymbol{\Sigma}_p) \propto \exp(-\frac{1}{2}\boldsymbol{x}^\mathsf{T}\mathbf{K}_x\boldsymbol{x} + \boldsymbol{h}_x^\mathsf{T}\boldsymbol{x}) \tag{9.96}$$

where $\mathbf{G} \in \mathbb{R}^{K \times N}$ is a matrix that represents prior dependencies (e.g., pairwise correlations), $\mathbf{K}_x = \mathbf{G}^\mathsf{T}\boldsymbol{\Sigma}_p^{-1}\mathbf{G}$, and $\boldsymbol{h}_x = \mathbf{G}^\mathsf{T}\boldsymbol{\Sigma}_p^{-1}\boldsymbol{\mu}_p$. Let $\boldsymbol{y} \in \mathbb{R}^M$ be the measurements with likelihood

$$p(\boldsymbol{y}|\boldsymbol{x}) = \mathcal{N}(\boldsymbol{y}|\mathbf{H}\boldsymbol{x} + \boldsymbol{c}, \boldsymbol{\Sigma}_n) \propto \exp(-\frac{1}{2}\boldsymbol{x}^\mathsf{T}\mathbf{K}_{y|x}\boldsymbol{x} + \boldsymbol{h}_{y|x}^\mathsf{T}\boldsymbol{x} - \frac{1}{2}\boldsymbol{y}^\mathsf{T}\boldsymbol{\Sigma}_n^{-1}\boldsymbol{y}) \tag{9.97}$$

where $\mathbf{H} \in \mathbb{R}^{M \times N}$ represents dependencies between the hidden and visible variables, $\mathbf{K}_{y|x} = \mathbf{H}^\mathsf{T}\boldsymbol{\Sigma}_n^{-1}\mathbf{H}$ and $\boldsymbol{h}_{y|x} = \mathbf{H}^\mathsf{T}\boldsymbol{\Sigma}_n^{-1}(\boldsymbol{y} - \boldsymbol{c})$. The posterior is given by the following (cf. one step of the information filter in Section 8.2.4)

$$p(\boldsymbol{x}|\boldsymbol{y}) = \mathcal{N}(\boldsymbol{x}|\boldsymbol{\mu}, \boldsymbol{\Sigma}) \tag{9.98}$$

$$\boldsymbol{\Sigma}^{-1} = \mathbf{K} = \mathbf{G}^\mathsf{T}\boldsymbol{\Sigma}_p^{-1}\mathbf{G} + \mathbf{H}^\mathsf{T}\boldsymbol{\Sigma}_n^{-1}\mathbf{H} \tag{9.99}$$

$$\boldsymbol{\mu} = \mathbf{K}(\mathbf{G}^\mathsf{T}\boldsymbol{\Sigma}_p^{-1}\boldsymbol{\mu}_p + \mathbf{H}^\mathsf{T}\boldsymbol{\Sigma}_n^{-1}(\boldsymbol{y} - \boldsymbol{c})) \tag{9.100}$$

---

5. See ugm_inf_autodiff.py for the full (JAX) code, and see https://github.com/srush/ProbTalk for a (PyTorch) version by Sasha Rush.

where we have assumed $\mathbf{K} = \mathbf{K}_x + \mathbf{K}_{y|x}$ is invertible (although the prior or likelihood on their own may be singular).

The K rows of $\mathbf{G} = [\boldsymbol{g}_1^\mathsf{T}; \ldots; \boldsymbol{g}_K^\mathsf{T}]$ and the M rows of $\mathbf{H} = [\boldsymbol{h}_1^\mathsf{T}; \ldots; \boldsymbol{h}_M^\mathsf{T}]$ can be combined into the L rows of $\mathbf{F} = [\boldsymbol{f}_1^\mathsf{T}; \ldots; \boldsymbol{f}_L^\mathsf{T}]$, which define the linear constraints of the system. If we assume that $\boldsymbol{\Sigma}_p$ and $\boldsymbol{\Sigma}_n$ are diagonal, then the structure of the graphical model is uniquely determined by the sparsity of $\mathbf{F}$. The resulting posterior factorizes as a product of L Gaussian "experts":

$$p(\boldsymbol{x}|\boldsymbol{y}) \propto \prod_{l=1}^{L} \exp(-\frac{1}{2}\boldsymbol{x}^\mathsf{T}\mathbf{K}_l\boldsymbol{x} + \boldsymbol{h}_l^\mathsf{T}\boldsymbol{x}) \propto \prod_{l=1}^{L} \mathcal{N}(\boldsymbol{f}_l^\mathsf{T}\boldsymbol{x}; \mu_l, \Sigma_l) \tag{9.101}$$

where Σ_l equals $\boldsymbol{\Sigma}_{p,l,l}$ for $l = 1 : K$ and equals $\boldsymbol{\Sigma}_{n,l',l'}$ for $l = K+1 : L$ where $l' = l - K$. Similarly $\mu_l = \boldsymbol{\mu}_{p,l}$ for $l = 1 : K$ and $\mu_l = (y_{l'} - c_{l'})$ for $l = K+1 : L$.

To apply perturb and MAP, we proceed as follows. First perturb the prior mean by sampling $\tilde{\boldsymbol{\mu}}_p \sim \mathcal{N}(\boldsymbol{\mu}_p, \boldsymbol{\Sigma}_p)$, and perturb the measurements by sampling $\tilde{\boldsymbol{y}} \sim \mathcal{N}(\boldsymbol{y}, \boldsymbol{\Sigma}_n)$. (Note that this is equivalent to first perturbing the linear term in each information form potential, using $\tilde{\boldsymbol{h}}_l = \boldsymbol{h}_l + \boldsymbol{f}_l\boldsymbol{\Sigma}_l^{-\frac{1}{2}}\epsilon_l$, where $\epsilon_l \sim \mathcal{N}(0, 1)$.) Then compute the MAP estimate for $\boldsymbol{x}$ using the perturbed parameters:

$$\tilde{\boldsymbol{x}} = \mathbf{K}^{-1}\mathbf{G}^\mathsf{T}\boldsymbol{\Sigma}_p^{-1}\tilde{\boldsymbol{\mu}}_p + \mathbf{K}^{-1}\mathbf{H}^\mathsf{T}\boldsymbol{\Sigma}_n^{-1}(\tilde{\boldsymbol{y}} - \boldsymbol{c}) \tag{9.102}$$

$$= \underbrace{\mathbf{K}^{-1}\mathbf{G}^\mathsf{T}\boldsymbol{\Sigma}_p^{-1}}_{\mathbf{A}}(\boldsymbol{\mu}_p + \boldsymbol{\epsilon}_\mu) + \underbrace{\mathbf{K}^{-1}\mathbf{H}^\mathsf{T}\boldsymbol{\Sigma}_n^{-1}}_{\mathbf{B}}(\boldsymbol{y} + \boldsymbol{\epsilon}_y - \boldsymbol{c}) \tag{9.103}$$

$$= \boldsymbol{\mu} + \mathbf{A}\boldsymbol{\epsilon}_\mu + \mathbf{B}\boldsymbol{\epsilon}_y \tag{9.104}$$

We see that $\mathbb{E}[\tilde{\boldsymbol{x}}] = \boldsymbol{\mu}$ and $\mathbb{E}[(\tilde{\boldsymbol{x}} - \boldsymbol{\mu})(\tilde{\boldsymbol{x}} - \boldsymbol{\mu})^\mathsf{T}] = \mathbf{K}^{-1} = \boldsymbol{\Sigma}$, so the method produces exact samples.

This approach is very scalable, since compute the MAP estimate of sparse GMRFs (i.e., posterior mean) can be done efficiently using conjugate gradient solvers. Alternatively we can use loopy belief propagation (Section 9.4), which can often compute the exact posterior mean (see e.g., [WF01a; JMW06; Bic09; Du+18]).

9.7.2.2 Discrete case

In [PY11; PY14] they extend perturb-and-MAP to the case of discrete graphical models. This setup is more complicated, and requires the use of Gumbel noise, which can be sampled using $\epsilon = -\log(-\log(u))$, where $u \sim \text{Unif}(0, 1)$. This noise should be added to all the potentials in the model, but as a simple approximation, it can just be added to the unary terms, i.e., the local evidence potentials. Let the score, or unnormalized log probability, of configuration $\boldsymbol{x}$ given inputs $\boldsymbol{c}$ be

$$S(\boldsymbol{x}; \boldsymbol{c}) = \log p(\boldsymbol{x}|\boldsymbol{c}) + \text{const} = \sum_i \log \phi_i(x_i) + \sum_{ij} \log \psi_{ij}(x_{i,j}) \tag{9.105}$$

where we have assumed a pairwise CRF for notational simplicity. If we perturb the local evidence potentials $\phi_i(k)$ by adding ϵ_{ik} to each entry, where k indexes the discrete latent states, we get $\tilde{S}(\boldsymbol{x}; \boldsymbol{c})$. We then compute a sample $\tilde{\boldsymbol{x}}$ by solving $\tilde{\boldsymbol{x}} = \text{argmax}\, \tilde{S}(\boldsymbol{x}; \boldsymbol{c})$. The advantage of this approach is that it can leverage efficient MAP solvers for discrete models, such as those discussed in Supplementary Section 9.3. This can in turn be used for parameter learning, and estimating the partition function [HJ12; Erm+13].

10 Variational inference

10.1 Introduction

In this chapter, we discuss **variational inference**, which reduces posterior inference to optimization. Note that VI is a large topic; this chapter just gives a high level overview. For more details, see e.g., [Jor+98; JJ00; Jaa01; WJ08; SQ05; TLG08; Zha+19b; Bro18].

10.1.1 The variational objective

Consider a model with unknown (latent) variables z, known variables x, and fixed parameters θ. (If the parameters are unknown, they can be added to z, as we discuss later.) We assume the prior is $p_\theta(z)$ and the likelihood is $p_\theta(x|z)$, so the unnormalized joint is $p_\theta(x, z) = p_\theta(x|z)p_\theta(z)$, and the posterior is $p_\theta(z|x) = p_\theta(x, z)/p_\theta(x)$. We assume that it is intractable to compute the normalization constant, $p_\theta(x) = \int p_\theta(x, z)dz$, and hence intractable to compute the normalized posterior. We therefore seek an approximation to the posterior, which we denote by $q(z)$, such that we minimize the following loss:

$$q = \operatorname*{argmin}_{q \in \mathcal{Q}} D_{\mathbb{KL}}\left(q(z) \,\|\, p_\theta(z|x)\right) \tag{10.1}$$

Since we are minimizing over functions (namely distributions q), this is called a **variational method**.

In practice we pick a parametric family $\mathcal{Q}$, where we use ψ, known as the **variational parameters**, to specify which member of the family we are using. We can compute the best variational parameters (for given x) as follows:

$$\psi^* = \operatorname*{argmin}_{\psi} D_{\mathbb{KL}}\left(q_\psi(z) \,\|\, p_\theta(z|x)\right) \tag{10.2}$$

$$= \operatorname*{argmin}_{\psi} \mathbb{E}_{q_\psi(z)}\left[\log q_\psi(z) - \log\left(\frac{p_\theta(x|z)p_\theta(z)}{p_\theta(x)}\right)\right] \tag{10.3}$$

$$= \operatorname*{argmin}_{\psi} \underbrace{\mathbb{E}_{q_\psi(z)}\left[\log q_\psi(z) - \log p_\theta(x|z) - \log p_\theta(z)\right]}_{\mathcal{L}(\theta, \psi|x)} + \log p_\theta(x) \tag{10.4}$$

The final term $\log p_\theta(x) = \int p_\theta(x, z)dz$ is generally intractable to compute. Fortunately, it is independent of ψ, so we can drop it. This leaves us with the first term, which we write as follows:

$$\mathcal{L}(\theta, \psi|x) = \mathbb{E}_{q_\psi(z)}\left[-\log p_\theta(x, z) + \log q_\psi(z)\right] \tag{10.5}$$

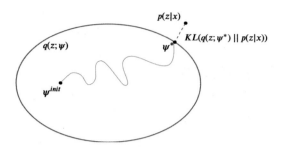

Figure 10.1: Illustration of variational inference. The large oval represents the set of variational distributions $Q = \{q_\psi(z) : \psi \in \ominus\}$, where $\ominus$ is the set of possible variational parameters. The true distribution is the point $p(z|x)$, which we assume lies outside the set. Our goal is to find the best approximation to p within our variational family; this is the point ψ^* which is closest in KL divergence. We find this point by starting an optimization procedure from the random initial point ψ^{init}. Adapted from a figure by David Blei.

Minimizing this objective will minimize the KL divergence, causing our approximation to approach the true posterior. See Figure 10.1 for an illustration. In the sections below, we give two different interpretations of this objective function.

10.1.1.1   The view from physics: minimize the variational free energy

If we define $\mathcal{E}_\theta(z) = -\log p_\theta(z, x)$ as the energy, then we can rewrite the loss in Equation (10.5)

$$\mathcal{L}(\theta, \psi|x) = \mathbb{E}_{q_\psi(z)}\left[\mathcal{E}_\theta(z)\right] - \mathbb{H}(q_\psi) = \text{expected energy} - \text{entropy} \tag{10.6}$$

In physics, this is known as the **variational free energy** (VFE). This is an upper bound on the **free energy** (FE), $-\log p_\theta(x)$, which follows from the fact that

$$D_{\mathrm{KL}}\left(q_\psi(z) \parallel p_\theta(z|x)\right) = \mathcal{L}(\theta, \psi|x) + \log p_\theta(x) \geq 0 \tag{10.7}$$

$$\underbrace{\mathcal{L}(\theta, \psi|x)}_{\text{VFE}} \geq \underbrace{-\log p_\theta(x)}_{\text{FE}} \tag{10.8}$$

Variational inference is equivalent to minimizing the VFE. If we we reach the minimum value of $-\log p_\theta(x)$, then the KL divergence term will be 0, so our approximate posterior will be exact.

10.1.1.2   The view from statistics: maximize the evidence lower bound (ELBO)

The negative of the VFE is known as the **evidence lower bound** or **ELBO** function [BKM16]:

$$Ł(\theta, \psi|x) \triangleq \mathbb{E}_{q_\psi(z)}\left[\log p_\theta(x, z) - \log q_\psi(z)\right] = \text{ELBO} \tag{10.9}$$

The name "ELBO" arises because

$$Ł(\theta, \psi|x) \leq \log p_\theta(x) \tag{10.10}$$

where $\log p_\theta(x)$ is called the "evidence". The inequality follows from Equation (10.8). Therefore maximizing the ELBO wrt ψ will minimize the original KL, since $\log p_\theta(x)$ is a constant wrt ψ.

(Note: we use the symbol Ł for the ELBO, rather than $\mathcal{L}$, since we want to maximize Ł but minimize $\mathcal{L}$.)

We can rewrite the ELBO as follows:

$$Ł(\boldsymbol{\theta}, \boldsymbol{\psi}|\boldsymbol{x}) = \mathbb{E}_{q_{\boldsymbol{\psi}}(\boldsymbol{z})}\left[\log p_{\boldsymbol{\theta}}(\boldsymbol{x}, \boldsymbol{z})\right] + \mathbb{H}(q_{\boldsymbol{\psi}}(\boldsymbol{z})) \tag{10.11}$$

We can interpret this

$$\text{ELBO} = \text{expected log joint} + \text{entropy} \tag{10.12}$$

The second term encourages the posterior to be maximum entropy, while the first term encourages it to be a joint MAP configuration.

We can also rewrite the ELBO as

$$Ł(\boldsymbol{\psi}|\boldsymbol{\theta}, \boldsymbol{x}) = \mathbb{E}_{q_{\boldsymbol{\psi}}(\boldsymbol{z})}\left[\log p_{\boldsymbol{\theta}}(\boldsymbol{x}|\boldsymbol{z}) + \log p_{\boldsymbol{\theta}}(\boldsymbol{z}) - \log q_{\boldsymbol{\psi}}(\boldsymbol{z})\right] \tag{10.13}$$

$$= \mathbb{E}_{q_{\boldsymbol{\psi}}(\boldsymbol{z})}\left[\log p_{\boldsymbol{\theta}}(\boldsymbol{x}|\boldsymbol{z})\right] - D_{\mathbb{KL}}\left(q_{\boldsymbol{\psi}}(\boldsymbol{z}) \parallel p_{\boldsymbol{\theta}}(\boldsymbol{z})\right) \tag{10.14}$$

We can interpret this as follows:

$$\text{ELBO} = \text{expected log likelihood} - \text{KL from posterior to prior} \tag{10.15}$$

The KL term acts like a regularizer, preventing the posterior from diverging too much from the prior.

10.1.2 Form of the variational posterior

There are two main approaches for choosing the form of the variational posterior, $q_{\boldsymbol{\psi}}(\boldsymbol{z}|\boldsymbol{x})$. In the first approach, we pick a convenient functional form, such as multivariate Gaussian, and then optimize the ELBO using gradient-based methods. This is called **fixed-form VI**, and is discussed in Section 10.2. An alternative is to make the **mean field** assumption, namely that the posterior factorizes:

$$q_{\boldsymbol{\psi}}(\boldsymbol{z}) = \prod_{j=1}^{J} q_j(\boldsymbol{z}_j) \tag{10.16}$$

where $q_j(\boldsymbol{z}_j) = q_{\boldsymbol{\psi}_j}(\boldsymbol{z}_j)$ is the posterior over the j'th group of variables. We don't need to specify the functional form for each q_j. Instead, the optimal distributional form can be derived by maximizing the ELBO wrt each group of variational parameters one at a time, in a coordinate ascent manner. This is therefore called **free-form VI**, and is discussed in Section 10.3.

We now give a simple example of variational inference applied to a 2d latent vector $\boldsymbol{z}$, representing the mean of a Gaussian. The prior is $\mathcal{N}(\boldsymbol{z}|\, \breve{\boldsymbol{m}}, \breve{\mathbf{V}})$, and the likelihood is

$$p(\mathcal{D}|\boldsymbol{z}) = \prod_{n=1}^{N} \mathcal{N}(\boldsymbol{x}_n|\boldsymbol{z}, \boldsymbol{\Sigma}) \propto \mathcal{N}(\overline{\boldsymbol{x}}|\boldsymbol{z}, \frac{1}{N}\boldsymbol{\Sigma}) \tag{10.17}$$

The exact posterior, $p(\boldsymbol{z}|\mathcal{D}) = \mathcal{N}(\boldsymbol{z}|\, \widehat{\boldsymbol{m}}, \widehat{\mathbf{V}})$, can be computed analytically, as discussed in Section 3.4.4.1. In Figure 10.2, we compare three Gaussian variational approximations to the posterior. If q uses a full covariance matrix, it matches the exact posterior; however, this is intractable in high

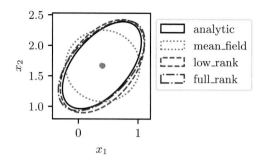

Figure 10.2: Variational approximation to the exact (Gaussian) posterior for the mean of a 2d Gaussian likelihood with a Gaussian prior. We show 3 Gaussian approximations to the posterior, using a full covariance (blue), a diagonal covariance (green), and a diagonal plus rank one covariance (red). Generated by gaussian_2d_vi.ipynb.

dimensions. If q uses a diagonal covariance matrix (corresponding to the mean field approximation), we see that the approximation is over confident, which is a well-known flaw of variational inference, due to the mode-seeking nature of minimizing $D_{\text{KL}}(q \parallel p)$ (see Section 5.1.4.3 for details). Finally, if q uses a rank-1 plus diagonal approximation, we get a much better approximation; furthermore, this can be computed quite efficiently, as we discuss in Section 10.2.1.3.

10.1.3   Parameter estimation using variational EM

So far, we have assumed the model parameters $\boldsymbol{\theta}$ are known. However, we can try to estimate them by maximing the log marginal likelihood of the dataset, $\mathcal{D} = \{\boldsymbol{x}_n : n = 1 : N\}$,

$$\log p(\mathcal{D}|\boldsymbol{\theta}) = \sum_{n=1}^{N} \log p(\boldsymbol{x}_n|\boldsymbol{\theta}) \tag{10.18}$$

In general, this is intractable to compute, but we discuss approximations below.

10.1.3.1   MLE for latent variable models

Suppose we have a latent variable model of the form

$$p(\mathcal{D}, \boldsymbol{z}_{1:N}|\boldsymbol{\theta}) = \prod_{n=1}^{N} p(\boldsymbol{z}_n|\boldsymbol{\theta})p(\boldsymbol{x}_n|\boldsymbol{z}_n, \boldsymbol{\theta}) \tag{10.19}$$

as shown in Figure 10.3a. Furthermore, suppose we want to compute the MLE for $\boldsymbol{\theta}$ given the dataset $\mathcal{D} = \{\boldsymbol{x}_n : n = 1 : N\}$. Since the local latent variables $\boldsymbol{z}_n$ are hidden, we must marginalize them out to get the local (per example) log marginal likelihood:

$$\log p(\boldsymbol{x}_n|\boldsymbol{\theta}) = \log \left[\int p(\boldsymbol{x}_n|\boldsymbol{z}_n, \boldsymbol{\theta})p(\boldsymbol{z}_n|\boldsymbol{\theta})d\boldsymbol{z}_n \right] \tag{10.20}$$

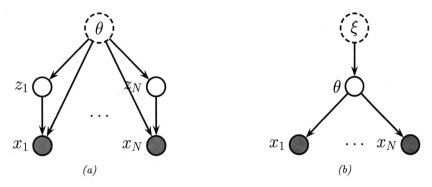

Figure 10.3: Graphical models with: (a) Local stochastic latent variables $\boldsymbol{z}_n$ and global deterministic latent parameter $\boldsymbol{\theta}$. (b) Global stochastic latent parameter $\boldsymbol{\theta}$ and global deterministic latent hyper-parameter $\boldsymbol{\xi}$. The observed variables $\boldsymbol{x}_n$ are shown by shaded circles.

Unfortunately, computing this integral is usually intractable, since it corresponds to the normalization constant of the exact posterior. Fortunately, the ELBO is a lower bound on this:

$$\text{Ł}(\boldsymbol{\theta}, \boldsymbol{\psi}_n | \boldsymbol{x}_n) \leq \log p(\boldsymbol{x}_n | \boldsymbol{\theta}) \tag{10.21}$$

We can thus optimize the model parameters by maximizing

$$\text{Ł}(\boldsymbol{\theta}, \boldsymbol{\psi}_{1:N} | \mathcal{D}) \triangleq \sum_{n=1}^{N} \text{Ł}(\boldsymbol{\theta}, \boldsymbol{\psi}_n | \boldsymbol{x}_n) \leq \log p(\mathcal{D} | \boldsymbol{\theta}) \tag{10.22}$$

This is the basis of the **variational EM** algorithm. We discuss this in more detail in Section 6.5.6.1, but the basic idea is to alternate between maximizing the ELBO wrt the variational parameters $\{\boldsymbol{\psi}_n\}$ in the E step, to give us $q_{\boldsymbol{\psi}_n}(\boldsymbol{z}_n)$, and then maximizing the ELBO (using the new $\boldsymbol{\psi}_n$) wrt the model parameters $\boldsymbol{\theta}$ in the M step. (We can also use SGD and amortized inference to speed this up, as we explain in Sections 10.1.4 to 10.1.5.)

10.1.3.2 Empirical Bayes for fully observed models

Suppose we have a fully observed model (with no local latent variables) of the form

$$p(\mathcal{D}, \boldsymbol{\theta} | \boldsymbol{\xi}) = p(\boldsymbol{\theta} | \boldsymbol{\xi}) \prod_{n=1}^{N} p(\boldsymbol{x}_n | \boldsymbol{\theta}) \tag{10.23}$$

as shown in Figure 10.3b. In the context of Bayesian parameter inference, our goal is to compute the parameter posterior:

$$p(\boldsymbol{\theta} | \mathcal{D}, \boldsymbol{\xi}) = \frac{p(\mathcal{D} | \boldsymbol{\theta}) p(\boldsymbol{\theta} | \boldsymbol{\xi})}{p(\mathcal{D} | \boldsymbol{\xi})} \tag{10.24}$$

where $\boldsymbol{\theta}$ are the global unknown model parameters (latent variables), and $\boldsymbol{\xi}$ are the hyper-parameters for the prior. If the hyper-parameters are unknown, we can estimate them using empirical Bayes (see

Section 3.7) by computing

$$\hat{\boldsymbol{\xi}} = \underset{\boldsymbol{\xi}}{\text{argmax}}\, \log p(\mathcal{D}|\boldsymbol{\xi}) \tag{10.25}$$

We can use variational EM to compute this, similar to Section 10.1.3.1, except now the parameters to be estimated are $\boldsymbol{\xi}$, the latent variables are the shared global parameters $\boldsymbol{\theta}$, and the observations are the entire dataset, $\mathcal{D}$. We then get the lower bound

$$\log p(\mathcal{D}|\boldsymbol{\xi}) \geq \textit{Ł}(\boldsymbol{\xi}, \boldsymbol{\psi}|\mathcal{D}) = \mathbb{E}_{q_{\boldsymbol{\psi}}(\boldsymbol{\theta})}\left[\sum_{n=1}^{N} \log p(\boldsymbol{x}_n|\boldsymbol{\theta})\right] - D_{\mathbb{KL}}\left(q_{\boldsymbol{\psi}}(\boldsymbol{\theta}) \,\|\, p(\boldsymbol{\theta}|\boldsymbol{\xi})\right) \tag{10.26}$$

We optimize this wrt the parameters of the variational posterior, $\boldsymbol{\psi}$, and wrt the prior hyper-parameters $\boldsymbol{\xi}$.

If the prior $\boldsymbol{\xi}$ is fixed, we just need to optimize the variational parameters $\boldsymbol{\psi}$ to compute the posterior, $q_{\boldsymbol{\psi}}(\boldsymbol{\theta}|\mathcal{D})$. This is known as **variational Bayes**. See Section 10.3.3 for more details.

10.1.4   Stochastic VI

In Section 10.1.3, we saw that parameter estimation requires optimizing the ELBO for the entire dataset, which is defined as the sum of the ELBOs for each of the N data samples $\boldsymbol{x}_n$. Computing this objective can be slow if N is large. Fortunately, we can replace this objective with a stochastic approximation, which is faster to compute, and provides an unbiased estimate. In particular, at each step, we can draw a random minibatch of $B = |\mathcal{B}|$ examples from the dataset, and then make the approximation

$$\textit{Ł}(\boldsymbol{\theta}, \boldsymbol{\psi}_{1:N}|\mathcal{D}) = \sum_{n=1}^{N} \textit{Ł}(\boldsymbol{\theta}, \boldsymbol{\psi}_n|\boldsymbol{x}_n) \approx \frac{N}{B} \sum_{\boldsymbol{x}_n \in \mathcal{B}} \left[\mathbb{E}_{q_{\boldsymbol{\psi}_n}(\boldsymbol{z}_n)}\left[\log p_{\boldsymbol{\theta}}(\boldsymbol{x}_n|\boldsymbol{z}_n) + \log p_{\boldsymbol{\theta}}(\boldsymbol{z}_n) - \log q_{\boldsymbol{\psi}_n}(\boldsymbol{z}_n)\right]\right] \tag{10.27}$$

This can be used inside of a stochastic optimization algorithm, such as SGD. This is called **stochastic variational inference** or **SVI** [Hof+13], and allows VI to scale to large datasets.

10.1.5   Amortized VI

In Section 10.1.4, we saw that in each iteration of SVI, we need to optimize the local variational parameters $\boldsymbol{\psi}_n$ for each example n in the minibatch. This nested optimization can be quite slow.

An alternative approach is to train a model, known as an **inference network** or **recognition network**, to predict $\boldsymbol{\psi}_n$ from the observed data, $\boldsymbol{x}_n$, using $\boldsymbol{\psi}_n = f_{\boldsymbol{\phi}}^{\text{inf}}(\boldsymbol{x}_n)$. This technique is known as **amortized variational inference** [GG14], or **inference compilation** [LBW17], since we are reducing the cost of per-example time inference by training a model that is shared across all examples. (See also [Amo22] for a general discussion of amortized optimization.) For brevity, we will write the amortized posterior as

$$q(\boldsymbol{z}_n|\boldsymbol{\psi}_n) = q(\boldsymbol{z}_n|f_{\boldsymbol{\phi}}^{\text{inf}}(\boldsymbol{x}_n)) = q_{\boldsymbol{\phi}}(\boldsymbol{z}_n|\boldsymbol{x}_n) \tag{10.28}$$

The corresponding ELBO becomes

$$\text{Ł}(\boldsymbol{\theta}, \boldsymbol{\phi}|\mathcal{D}) = \sum_{n=1}^{N} \left[\mathbb{E}_{q_{\boldsymbol{\phi}}(\boldsymbol{z}_n|\boldsymbol{x}_n)} \left[\log p_{\boldsymbol{\theta}}(\boldsymbol{x}_n, \boldsymbol{z}_n) - \log q_{\boldsymbol{\phi}}(\boldsymbol{z}|\boldsymbol{x}_n) \right] \right] \tag{10.29}$$

If we combine this with SVI we get an amortized version of Equation (10.27). For example, if we use a minibatch of size 1, we get

$$\text{Ł}(\boldsymbol{\theta}, \boldsymbol{\phi}|\boldsymbol{x}_n) \approx N \left[\mathbb{E}_{q_{\boldsymbol{\phi}}(\boldsymbol{z}_n|\boldsymbol{x}_n)} \left[\log p_{\boldsymbol{\theta}}(\boldsymbol{x}_n, \boldsymbol{z}_n) - \log q_{\boldsymbol{\phi}}(\boldsymbol{z}|\boldsymbol{x}_n) \right] \right] \tag{10.30}$$

We can optimize this as shown in Algorithm 10.1. Note that the (partial) maximization wrt $\boldsymbol{\theta}$ in the M step is usually done with a gradient update, but the maximization wrt $\boldsymbol{\phi}$ in the E step is trickier, since the loss uses $\boldsymbol{\phi}$ to define an expectation operator, so we can't necessarily push the gradient operator inside; we discuss ways to optimize the variational parameters in Section 10.2 and Section 10.3.

Algorithm 10.1: Amortized stochastic variational EM

---

1 Initialize $\boldsymbol{\theta}, \boldsymbol{\phi}$
2 **repeat**
3   Sample $\boldsymbol{x}_n \sim p_{\mathcal{D}}$
4   E step: $\boldsymbol{\phi} = \text{argmax}_{\boldsymbol{\phi}} \, \text{Ł}(\boldsymbol{\theta}, \boldsymbol{\phi}|\boldsymbol{x}_n)$
5   M step: $\boldsymbol{\theta} = \text{argmax}_{\boldsymbol{\theta}} \, \text{Ł}(\boldsymbol{\theta}, \boldsymbol{\phi}|\boldsymbol{x}_n)$
6 **until** *converged*

10.1.6 Semi-amortized inference

Amortized SVI is widely used for fitting LVMs, e.g., for VAEs (see Section 21.2), for topic models [SS17a], for probabilistic programming [RHG16], for CRFs [TG18], etc. However, the use of an inference network can result in a suboptimal setting of the local variational parameters $\boldsymbol{\psi}_n$. This is called the **amortization gap** [CLD18]. We can close this gap by using the inference network to warm-start an optimizer for $\boldsymbol{\psi}_n$; this is known as **semi-amortized VI** [Kim+18c]. (See also [MYM18], who propose a closely related method called **iterative amortized inference**.)

An alternative approach is to use the inference network as a proposal distribution. If we combine this with importance sampling, we get the IWAE bound of Section 10.5.1. If we use this with Metropolis-Hastings, we get a VI-MCMC hybrid (see Section 10.4.5).

10.2 Gradient-based VI

In this section, we will choose some convenient form for $q_{\boldsymbol{\psi}}(\boldsymbol{z})$, such as a Gaussian for continuous $\boldsymbol{z}$, or a product of categoricals for discrete $\boldsymbol{z}$, and then optimize the ELBO using gradient based methods.

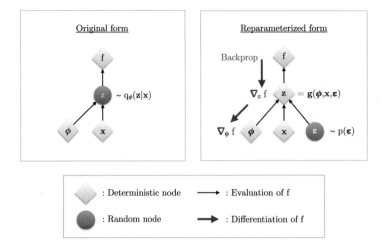

Figure 10.4: Illustration of the reparameterization trick. The objective f depends on the variational parameters ϕ, the observed data $\boldsymbol{x}$, and the latent random variable $\boldsymbol{z} \sim q_\phi(\boldsymbol{z}|\boldsymbol{x})$. On the left, we show the standard form of the computation graph. On the right, we show a reparameterized form, in which we move the stochasticity into the noise source ϵ, and compute $\boldsymbol{z}$ deterministically, $\boldsymbol{z} = g(\phi, \boldsymbol{x}, \epsilon)$. The rest of the graph is deterministic, so we can backpropagate the gradient of the scalar f wrt ϕ through $\boldsymbol{z}$ and into ϕ. From Figure 2.3 of [KW19a]. Used with kind permission of Durk Kingma.

The gradient wrt the generative parameters $\boldsymbol{\theta}$ is easy to compute, since we can push gradients inside the expectation, and use a single Monte Carlo sample:

$$\nabla_{\boldsymbol{\theta}} \text{Ł}(\boldsymbol{\theta}, \boldsymbol{\phi}|\boldsymbol{x}) = \nabla_{\boldsymbol{\theta}} \mathbb{E}_{q_\phi(\boldsymbol{z}|\boldsymbol{x})} \left[\log p_{\boldsymbol{\theta}}(\boldsymbol{x}, \boldsymbol{z}) - \log q_\phi(\boldsymbol{z}|\boldsymbol{x}) \right] \tag{10.31}$$

$$= \mathbb{E}_{q_\phi(\boldsymbol{z}|\boldsymbol{x})} \left[\nabla_{\boldsymbol{\theta}} \left\{ \log p_{\boldsymbol{\theta}}(\boldsymbol{x}, \boldsymbol{z}) - \log q_\phi(\boldsymbol{z}|\boldsymbol{x}) \right\} \right] \tag{10.32}$$

$$\approx \nabla_{\boldsymbol{\theta}} \log p_{\boldsymbol{\theta}}(\boldsymbol{x}, \boldsymbol{z}^s) \tag{10.33}$$

where $\boldsymbol{z}^s \sim q_\phi(\boldsymbol{z}|\boldsymbol{x})$. This is an unbiased estimate of the gradient, so can be used with SGD.

The gradient wrt the inference parameters $\boldsymbol{\phi}$ is harder to compute since

$$\nabla_{\boldsymbol{\phi}} \text{Ł}(\boldsymbol{\theta}, \boldsymbol{\phi}|\boldsymbol{x}) = \nabla_{\boldsymbol{\phi}} \mathbb{E}_{q_\phi(\boldsymbol{z}|\boldsymbol{x})} \left[\log p_{\boldsymbol{\theta}}(\boldsymbol{x}, \boldsymbol{z}) - \log q_\phi(\boldsymbol{z}|\boldsymbol{x}) \right] \tag{10.34}$$

$$\neq \mathbb{E}_{q_\phi(\boldsymbol{z}|\boldsymbol{x})} \left[\nabla_{\boldsymbol{\phi}} \left\{ \log p_{\boldsymbol{\theta}}(\boldsymbol{x}, \boldsymbol{z}) - \log q_\phi(\boldsymbol{z}|\boldsymbol{x}) \right\} \right] \tag{10.35}$$

However, we can often use the reparameterization trick, which we discuss in Section 10.2.1. If not, we can use blackbox VI, which we discuss in Section 10.2.3.

10.2.1   Reparameterized VI

In this section, we discuss the **reparameterization trick** for taking gradients wrt distributions over continuous latent variables $\boldsymbol{z} \sim q_\phi(\boldsymbol{z}|\boldsymbol{x})$. We explain this in detail in Section 6.3.5, but we summarize the basic idea here.

The key trick is to rewrite the random variable $z \sim q_\phi(z|x)$ as some differentiable (and invertible) transformation g of another random variable $\epsilon \sim p(\epsilon)$, which does not depend on ϕ, i.e., we assume we can write

$$z = g(\phi, x, \epsilon) \tag{10.36}$$

For example,

$$z \sim \mathcal{N}(\mu, \text{diag}(\sigma)) \iff z = \mu + \epsilon \odot \sigma, \ \epsilon \sim \mathcal{N}(0, I) \tag{10.37}$$

Using this, we have

$$\mathbb{E}_{q_\phi(z|x)}[f(z)] = \mathbb{E}_{p(\epsilon)}[f(z)] \quad \text{s.t.} \quad z = g(\phi, x, \epsilon) \tag{10.38}$$

where we define

$$f_{\theta, \phi}(z) = \log p_\theta(x, z) - \log q_\phi(z|x) \tag{10.39}$$

Hence

$$\nabla_\phi \mathbb{E}_{q_\phi(z|x)}[f(z)] = \nabla_\phi \mathbb{E}_{p(\epsilon)}[f(z)] = \mathbb{E}_{p(\epsilon)}[\nabla_\phi f(z)] \tag{10.40}$$

which we can approximate with a single Monte Carlo sample. This lets us propagate gradients back through the f function. See Figure 10.4 for an illustration. This is called **reparameterized VI** or **RVI**.

Since we are now working with the random variable ϵ, we need to use the change of variables formula to compute

$$\log q_\phi(z|x) = \log p(\epsilon) - \log \left| \det \left(\frac{\partial z}{\partial \epsilon} \right) \right| \tag{10.41}$$

where $\frac{\partial z}{\partial \epsilon}$ is the Jacobian:

$$\frac{\partial z}{\partial \epsilon} = \begin{pmatrix} \frac{\partial z_1}{\partial \epsilon_1} & \cdots & \frac{\partial z_1}{\partial \epsilon_k} \\ \vdots & \ddots & \vdots \\ \frac{\partial z_k}{\partial \epsilon_1} & \cdots & \frac{\partial z_k}{\partial \epsilon_k} \end{pmatrix} \tag{10.42}$$

We design the transformation $z = g(\epsilon)$ such that this Jacobian is tractable to compute. We give some examples below.

10.2.1.1 Gaussian with diagonal covariance (mean field)

Suppose we use a fully factorized Gaussian posterior. Then the reparameterization process becomes

$$\epsilon \sim \mathcal{N}(0, I) \tag{10.43}$$

$$z = \mu + \sigma \odot \epsilon \tag{10.44}$$

where the inference network generates the parameters of the transformation:

$$(\boldsymbol{\mu}, \log \boldsymbol{\sigma}) = f_{\boldsymbol{\phi}}^{\text{inf}}(\boldsymbol{x}) \tag{10.45}$$

Thus to sample from the posterior $q_{\boldsymbol{\phi}}(\boldsymbol{z}|\boldsymbol{x})$, we sample $\boldsymbol{\epsilon} \mathcal{N}(\boldsymbol{0}, \mathbf{I})$, and then compute $\boldsymbol{z}$.

Given the sample, we need to evaluate the ELBO:

$$f(\boldsymbol{z}) = \log p_{\boldsymbol{\theta}}(\boldsymbol{x}|\boldsymbol{z}) + \log p_{\boldsymbol{\theta}}(\boldsymbol{z}) - \log q_{\boldsymbol{\phi}}(\boldsymbol{z}|\boldsymbol{x}) \tag{10.46}$$

To evaluate the $p_{\boldsymbol{\theta}}(\boldsymbol{x}|\boldsymbol{z})$ term, we can just plug $\boldsymbol{z}$ into the likelihood. To evaluate the $\log q_{\boldsymbol{\phi}}(\boldsymbol{z}|\boldsymbol{x})$ term, we need to use the change of variables formula from Equation (10.41). The Jacobian is given by $\frac{\partial \boldsymbol{z}}{\partial \boldsymbol{\epsilon}} = \text{diag}(\boldsymbol{\sigma})$. Hence

$$\log q_{\boldsymbol{\phi}}(\boldsymbol{z}|\boldsymbol{x}) = \sum_{k=1}^{K} [\log \mathcal{N}(\epsilon_k|0, 1) - \log \sigma_k] = -\sum_{k=1}^{K} \left[\frac{1}{2} \log(2\pi) + \frac{1}{2}\epsilon_k^2 + \log \sigma_k \right] \tag{10.47}$$

Finally, to evaluate the $p(\boldsymbol{z})$ term, we can use the transformation $\boldsymbol{z} = \boldsymbol{0} + \boldsymbol{1} \odot \boldsymbol{\epsilon}$, so the Jacobian is the identity and we get

$$\log p(\boldsymbol{z}) = \sum_{k=1}^{K} \left[\frac{1}{2} z_k^2 + \frac{1}{2} \log(2\pi) \right] \tag{10.48}$$

An alternative is to use the objective

$$f'(\boldsymbol{z}) = \log p_{\boldsymbol{\theta}}(\boldsymbol{x}|\boldsymbol{z}) + D_{\mathbb{KL}}\left(q_{\boldsymbol{\phi}}(\mathbf{Z}|\boldsymbol{x}) \parallel p_{\boldsymbol{\theta}}(\mathbf{Z}) \right) \tag{10.49}$$

In some cases, we evaluate the second term analytically, without needing Monte Carlo. For example, if we assume a diagonal Gaussian prior, $p(\boldsymbol{z}) = \mathcal{N}(\boldsymbol{z}|\boldsymbol{0}, \mathbf{I})$, and diagonal gaussian posterior, $q(\boldsymbol{z}|\boldsymbol{x}) = \mathcal{N}(\boldsymbol{z}|\boldsymbol{\mu}, \text{diag}(\boldsymbol{\sigma}))$, we can use Equation (5.78) to compute the KL in closed form:

$$D_{\mathbb{KL}}\left(q \parallel p \right) = -\frac{1}{2} \sum_{k=1}^{K} \left[\log \sigma_k^2 - \sigma_k^2 - \mu_k^2 + 1 \right] \tag{10.50}$$

The objective $f'(\boldsymbol{z})$ is often lower variance than $f(\boldsymbol{z})$, since it computes the KL analytically. However, it is harder to generalize this objective to settings where the prior and/or posterior are not Gaussian.

10.2.1.2   Gaussian with full covariance

Now consider using a full covariance Gaussian posterior. We will compute a Cholesky decomposition of the covariance, $\boldsymbol{\Sigma} = \mathbf{L}\mathbf{L}^{\mathsf{T}}$, where $\mathbf{L}$ is a lower triangular matrix with non-zero entries on the diagonal. Hence the reparamterization becomes

$$\boldsymbol{\epsilon} \sim \mathcal{N}(\boldsymbol{0}, \mathbf{I}) \tag{10.51}$$

$$\boldsymbol{z} = \boldsymbol{\mu} + \mathbf{L}\boldsymbol{\epsilon} \tag{10.52}$$

The Jacobian of this affine transformation is $\frac{\partial \boldsymbol{z}}{\partial \boldsymbol{\epsilon}} = \mathbf{L}$. Since $\mathbf{L}$ is a triangular matrix, its determinant is the product of its main diagonal, so

$$\log \left| \det \frac{\partial \boldsymbol{z}}{\partial \boldsymbol{\epsilon}} \right| = \sum_{k=1}^{K} \log |L_{kk}| \tag{10.53}$$

We can compute $\mathbf{L}$ using

$$\mathbf{L} = \mathbf{M} \odot \mathbf{L}' + \mathrm{diag}(\boldsymbol{\sigma}) \tag{10.54}$$

where $\mathbf{M}$ is a masking matrix with 0s on and above the diagonal, and 1s below the diagonal, and where $(\boldsymbol{\mu}, \log \boldsymbol{\sigma}, \mathbf{L}')$ is predicted by the inference network. With this construction, the diagonal entries of $\mathbf{L}$ are given by $\boldsymbol{\sigma}$, so

$$\log \left| \det \frac{\partial \boldsymbol{z}}{\partial \boldsymbol{\epsilon}} \right| = \sum_{k=1}^{K} \log |L_{kk}| = \sum_{k=1}^{K} \log \sigma_k \tag{10.55}$$

10.2.1.3 Gaussian with low-rank plus diagonal covariance

In high dimensions, an efficient alternative to using a Cholesky decomposition is the factor decomposition

$$\boldsymbol{\Sigma} = \mathbf{B}\mathbf{B}^\mathsf{T} + \mathbf{C}^2 \tag{10.56}$$

where $\mathbf{B}$ is the factor loading matrix of size $d \times f$, where $f \ll d$ is the number of factors, d is the dimensionality of $\boldsymbol{z}$, and $\mathbf{C} = \mathrm{diag}(c_1, \ldots, c_d)$. This reduces the total number of variational parameters from $d + d(d+1)/2$ to $(f+2)d$. In [ONS18], they called this approach **VAFC** (short for variational approximation with factor covariance).

In the special case where $f = 1$, the covariance matrix becomes

$$\boldsymbol{\Sigma} = \boldsymbol{b}\boldsymbol{b}^\mathsf{T} + \mathrm{diag}(\boldsymbol{c}^2) \tag{10.57}$$

In this case, it is possible to compute the natural gradient (Section 6.4) of the ELBO in closed form in $O(d)$ time, as shown in [Tra+20b; TND21], who call the approach **NAGVAC-1** (natural gradient Gaussian variational approximation). This can result in much faster convergence than following the normal gradient.

In Section 10.1.2, we show that this low rank approximation is much better than a diagonal approximation. See Supplementary Section 10.1 for more examples.

10.2.1.4 Other variational posteriors

Many other kinds of distribution can be written in a reparameterizable way, as described in [Moh+20]. This includes standard exponential family distributions, such as the gamma and Dirichlet, as well as more exotic forms, such as inverse autoregressive flows (see Section 10.4.3).

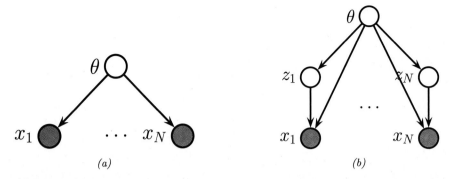

Figure 10.5: *Graphical models with (a) Global latent parameter $\boldsymbol{\theta}$ and observed variables $\boldsymbol{x}_{1:N}$. (b) Local latent variables $\boldsymbol{z}_{1:N}$, global latent parameter $\boldsymbol{\theta}$, and observed variables $\boldsymbol{x}_{1:N}$.*

10.2.1.5   Example: Bayesian parameter inference

In this section, we use reparameterized SVI to infer the posterior for the parameters of a Gaussian mixture model (GMM). We will marginalize out the discrete latent variables, so just need to approximate the posterior over the global latent, $p(\boldsymbol{\theta}|\mathcal{D})$. This is sometimes called a "**collapsed**" model, since we have marginalized out all the local latent variables. That is, we have converted the model in Figure 10.5b to the one in Figure 10.5a. We choose a factored (mean field) variational posterior that is conjugate to the likelihood, but is also reparameterizable. This lets us fit the posterior with SGD.

For simplicity, we assume diagonal covariance matrices for each Gaussian mixture component. Thus the likelihood for one datapoint, $\boldsymbol{x} \in \mathbb{R}^D$, is

$$p(\boldsymbol{x}|\boldsymbol{\theta}) = \sum_{k=1}^{K} \pi_k \mathcal{N}(\boldsymbol{x}|\boldsymbol{\mu}_k, \mathrm{diag}(\boldsymbol{\lambda}_k)^{-1}) \tag{10.58}$$

where $\boldsymbol{\mu}_k = (\mu_{k1}, \ldots, \mu_{kD})$ are the means, $\boldsymbol{\lambda}_k = (\lambda_{k1}, \ldots, \lambda_{kD})$ are the precisions, and $\boldsymbol{\pi} = (\pi_1, \ldots, \pi_K)$ are the mixing weights. We use the following prior for these parameters:

$$p_{\boldsymbol{\xi}}(\boldsymbol{\theta}) = \left[\prod_{k=1}^{K} \prod_{d=1}^{D} \mathcal{N}(\mu_{kd}|0, 1) \mathrm{Ga}(\lambda_{kd}|5, 5) \right] \mathrm{Dir}(\boldsymbol{\pi}|\mathbf{1}) \tag{10.59}$$

where $\boldsymbol{\xi}$ are the hyperparameters. We assume the following mean field posterior:

$$q_{\boldsymbol{\psi}}(\boldsymbol{\theta}) = \left[\prod_{k=1}^{K} \prod_{d=1}^{D} \mathcal{N}(\mu_{kd}|m_{kd}, s_{kd}) \mathrm{Ga}(\lambda_{kd}|\alpha_{kd}, \beta_{kd}) \right] \mathrm{Dir}(\boldsymbol{\pi}|\boldsymbol{c}) \tag{10.60}$$

where $\boldsymbol{\psi} = (\boldsymbol{m}_{1:K,1:D}, \boldsymbol{s}_{1:K,1:D}, \boldsymbol{\alpha}_{1:K,1:D}, \boldsymbol{\beta}_{1:K,1:D}, \boldsymbol{c})$ are the variational parameters for $\boldsymbol{\theta}$.

We can compute the ELBO using

$$Ł(\boldsymbol{\xi}, \boldsymbol{\psi}|\mathcal{D}) = \mathbb{E}_{q_{\boldsymbol{\psi}}(\boldsymbol{\theta})} \left[\log p(\mathcal{D}|\boldsymbol{\theta}) + \log p_{\boldsymbol{\xi}}(\boldsymbol{\theta}) - \log q_{\boldsymbol{\psi}}(\boldsymbol{\theta}) \right] \tag{10.61}$$

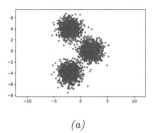 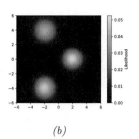 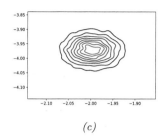

| (a) | (b) | (c) |

Figure 10.6: SVI for fitting a mixture of 3 Gaussians in 2d. (a) 3000 training points. (b) Fitted density, plugging in the posterior mean parameters. (c) Kernel density estimate fit to 10,000 samples from $q(\boldsymbol{\mu}_1|\boldsymbol{\psi})$. Generated by svi_gmm_demo_2d.ipynb.

Since the distributions are reparameterizable, we can and push gradients inside this expression. We can approximate the expectation by drawing a single posterior sample, and can approximate the log likelihood using minibatching. We can then update the variational parameters, (and optionally the hyperparameters of the prior, as we discussed in Section 10.1.3.2) using the pseudocode in Algorithm 10.2.

Algorithm 10.2: Reparameterized SVI for Bayesian parameter inference

1 Initialize $\boldsymbol{\psi}, \boldsymbol{\xi}$
2 **repeat**
3   Sample minibatch $\mathcal{B} = \{\boldsymbol{x}_b \sim \mathcal{D} : b = 1 : B\}$
4   Sample $\boldsymbol{\epsilon} \sim q_0$
5   Compute $\tilde{\boldsymbol{\theta}} = g(\boldsymbol{\psi}, \boldsymbol{\epsilon})$
6   Compute $\mathcal{L}(\boldsymbol{\psi}|\mathcal{D}, \tilde{\boldsymbol{\theta}}) = -\frac{N}{B} \sum_{\boldsymbol{x}_n \in \mathcal{B}} \log p(\boldsymbol{x}_n|\tilde{\boldsymbol{\theta}}) - \log p_{\boldsymbol{\xi}}(\tilde{\boldsymbol{\theta}}) + \log q_{\boldsymbol{\psi}}(\tilde{\boldsymbol{\theta}})$
7   Update $\boldsymbol{\xi} := \boldsymbol{\xi} - \eta \nabla_{\boldsymbol{\xi}} \mathcal{L}(\boldsymbol{\xi}, \boldsymbol{\psi}|\mathcal{D}, \tilde{\boldsymbol{\theta}})$
8   Update $\boldsymbol{\psi} := \boldsymbol{\psi} - \eta \nabla_{\boldsymbol{\psi}} \mathcal{L}(\boldsymbol{\xi}, \boldsymbol{\psi}|\mathcal{D}, \tilde{\boldsymbol{\theta}})$
9 **until** converged

Figure 10.6 gives an example of this in practice. We generate a dataset from a mixture of 3 Gaussians in 2d, using $\boldsymbol{\mu}_1^* = [2, 0]$, $\boldsymbol{\mu}_2^* = [-2, -4]$, $\boldsymbol{\mu}_3^* = [-2, 4]$, precisions $\lambda_{dk}^* = 1$, and uniform mixing weights, $\boldsymbol{\pi}^* = [1/3, 1/3, 1/3]$. Figure 10.6a shows the training set of 3000 points. We fit this using SVI, with a batch size of 500, for 1000 epochs, using the Adam optimizer. Figure 10.6b shows the predictions of the fitted model. More precisely, it shows $p(\boldsymbol{x}|\overline{\boldsymbol{\theta}})$, where $\overline{\boldsymbol{\theta}} = \mathbb{E}_{q(\boldsymbol{\theta}|\boldsymbol{\psi})}[\boldsymbol{\theta}]$. Figure 10.6c shows a kernel density estimate fit to 10,000 samples from $q(\boldsymbol{\mu}_1|\boldsymbol{\psi})$. We see that the posterior mean is $\mathbb{E}[\boldsymbol{\mu}_1] \approx [-2, -4]$. Due to label switching unidentifiability, we see this matches $\boldsymbol{\mu}_2^*$ rather than $\boldsymbol{\mu}_1^*$.

10.2.1.6 Example: MLE for LVMs

In this section, we consider reparameterized SVI for computing the MLE for latent variable models (LVMs) with continuous latents, such as variational autoencoders (Section 21.2). Unlike Section 10.2.1.5, we cannot analytically marginalize out the local latents. Instead we will use amortized inference, as in Section 10.1.5, which means we learn an inference network (with parameters ϕ) to predict the local variational parameters ψ_n given input x_n. If we sample a single example x_n from the dataset at each iteration, and a single latent variable z_n from the variational posterior, then we get the pseudocode in Algorithm 10.3.

Algorithm 10.3: Reparameterized amortized SVI for MLE of an LVM

---

1 Initialize θ, ϕ
2 **repeat**
3 $\quad$ Sample $x_n \sim p_{\mathcal{D}}$
4 $\quad$ Sample $\epsilon_n \sim q_0$
5 $\quad$ Compute $z_n = g(\phi, x_n, \epsilon_n)$
6 $\quad$ Compute $\mathcal{L}(\theta, \phi | x_n, z_n) = -\log p_\theta(x_n, z_n) + \log q_\phi(z_n | x_n)$
7 $\quad$ Update $\theta := \theta - \eta \nabla_\theta \mathcal{L}(\phi, \theta | x_n, z_n)$
8 $\quad$ Update $\phi := \phi - \eta \nabla_\phi \mathcal{L}(\phi, \theta | x_n, z_n)$
9 **until** converged

10.2.2 Automatic differentiation VI

To apply Gaussian VI, we need to transform constrained parameters (such as variance terms) to unconstrained form, so they live in $\mathbb{R}^D$. This technique can be used for any distribution for which we can define a bijection to $\mathbb{R}^D$. This approach is called **automatic differentiation variational inference** or **ADVI** [Kuc+16]. We give the details below.

10.2.2.1 Basic idea

Our goal is to approximate the posterior $p(\theta | \mathcal{D}) \propto p(\theta)p(\mathcal{D}|\theta)$, where $\theta \in \Theta$ lives in some D-dimensional constrained parameter space. Let $T : \Theta \to \mathbb{R}^D$ be a bijective mapping that maps from the constrained space Θ to the unconstrained space $\mathbb{R}^D$. with inverse $T^{-1} : \mathbb{R}^D \to \Theta$. Let $u = T(\theta)$ be the unconstrained latent variables. We will use a Gaussian variational approximation to the posterior for u, i.e.,: $q_\psi(u) = \mathcal{N}(u | \mu_d, \Sigma)$, where $\psi = (\mu, \Sigma)$.

By the change of variable formula Equation (2.257), we have

$$p(u) = p(T^{-1}(u)) | \det(\mathbf{J}_{T^{-1}}(u))| \tag{10.62}$$

where $\mathbf{J}_{T^{-1}}$ is the Jacobian of the inverse mapping $u \to \theta$. Hence the ELBO becomes

$$Ł(\psi) = E_{u \sim q_\psi(u)} \left[\log p(\mathcal{D} | T^{-1}(u)) + \log p(T^{-1}(u)) + \log |\det(\mathbf{J}_{T^{-1}}(u))| \right] + \mathbb{H}(\psi) \tag{10.63}$$

This is a tractable objective, assuming the Jacobian is tractable, since the final entropy term is available in closed form, and we can use a Monte Carlo approximation of the expectation over u.

Since the objective is stochastic, and reparamterizable, we can use SGD to optimize it. However, [Ing20] propose **deterministic ADVI**, in which the samples $\epsilon_s \sim \mathcal{N}(\mathbf{0}, \mathbf{I})$ are held fixed during the optimization process. This is called the common random numbers trick (Section 11.6.1), and makes the objective a deterministic function; this allows for the use of more powerful second-order optimization methods, such as BFGS. (Of course, if the dataset is large, we might need to use minibatch subsampling, which reintroduces stochasticity.)

10.2.2.2 Example: ADVI for beta-binomial model

To illustrate ADVI, we consider the 1d beta-binomial model from Section 7.4.4. We want to approximate $p(\theta|\mathcal{D})$ using the prior $p(\theta) = \text{Beta}(\theta|a, b)$ and likelihood $p(\mathcal{D}|\theta) = \prod_i \text{Ber}(y_i|\theta)$, where the sufficient statistics are $N_1 = 10$, $N_0 = 1$, and the prior is uninformative, $a = b = 1$. We use the transformation $\theta = T^{-1}(z) = \sigma(z)$, and optimize the ELBO with SGD. The results of this method are shown in Figure 7.4 and show that the Gaussian fit is a good approximation, despite the skewed nature of the posterior.

10.2.2.3 Example: ADVI for GMMs

In this section, we use ADVI to approximate the posterior of the parameters of a mixture of Gaussians. The difference from the VBEM algorithm of Section 10.3.6 is that we use ADVI combined with a Gaussian variational posterior, rather than using a mean field approximation defined by a product of conjugate distributions.

To apply ADVI, we marginalize out the discrete local discrete latents $m_n \in \{1, \ldots, K\}$ analytically, so the likelihood has the form

$$p(\mathcal{D}|\boldsymbol{\theta}) = \prod_{n=1}^{N} \left[\sum_{k=1}^{K} \pi_k \mathcal{N}(\boldsymbol{y}_n | \boldsymbol{\mu}_k, \text{diag}(\boldsymbol{\Sigma}_k)) \right] \tag{10.64}$$

We use an uninformative Gaussian prior for the $\boldsymbol{\mu}_k$, a uniform LKJ prior for the $\mathbf{L}_k$, a log-normal prior for the $\boldsymbol{\sigma}_k$, and a uniform Dirichlet prior for the mixing weights $\boldsymbol{\pi}$. (See [Kuc+16, Fig 21] for a definition of the model in STAN syntax.) The posterior approximation for the unconstrained parameters is a block-diagonal gaussian. $q(\boldsymbol{u}) = \mathcal{N}(\boldsymbol{u}|\boldsymbol{\psi}_{\boldsymbol{\mu}}, \boldsymbol{\psi}_{\boldsymbol{\Sigma}})$, where the unconstrained parameters are computed using suitable bijections (see code for details).

We apply this method to the Old Faithful dataset from Figure 10.12, using $K = 10$ mixture components. The results are shown in Figure 10.7. In the top left, we show the special case where we constrain the posterior to be a MAP estimate, by setting $\boldsymbol{\psi}_{\boldsymbol{\Sigma}} = \mathbf{0}$. We see that there is no sparsity in the posterior, since there is no Bayesian "Occam factor" from marginalizing out the parameters. In panels c–d, we show 3 samples from the posterior. We see that the Bayesian method strongly prefers just 2 mixture components, although there is a small amount of support for some other Gaussian components (shown by the faint ellipses).

10.2.2.4 More complex posteriors

We can combine ADVI with any of the improved posterior approximations that we discuss in Section 10.4 — such as Gaussian mixtures [Mor+21b] or normalizing flows [ASD20] — to create a high-quality, automatic approximate inference scheme.

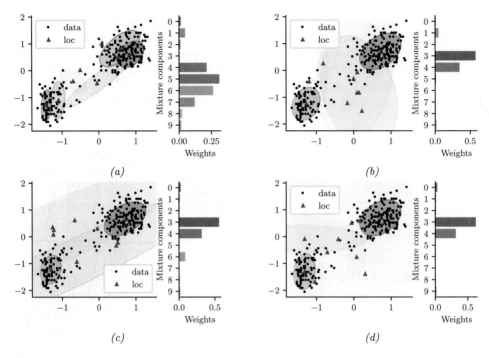

Figure 10.7: Posterior over the mixing weights (histogram) and the means and covariances of each Gaussian mixture component, using $K = 10$, when fitting the model to the Old Faithful dataset from Figure 10.12. (a) MAP approximation. (b-d) 3 samples from the Gaussian approximation. The intensity of the shading is proportional to the mixture weight. Generated by gmm_advi_bijax.ipynb.

10.2.3   Blackbox variational inference

In this section, we assume that we can evaluate $\tilde{\mathcal{L}}(\psi, z) = \log p(z, x) - \log q_\psi(z)$ pointwise, but we do not assume we can take gradients of this function. (For example, z may contain discrete variables.) We are thus treating the model as a "blackbox". Hence this approach is called **blackbox variational inference** or **BBVI** [RGB14; ASD20].

10.2.3.1   Estimating the gradient using REINFORCE

To estimate the gradient of the ELBO, we will use the **score function estimator**, also called the **REINFORCE** estimator (Section 6.3.4). In particular, suppose we write the ELBO as

$$\text{Ł}(\psi) = \mathbb{E}_{q(z|\psi)}\left[\tilde{\mathcal{L}}(\psi, z)\right] = \mathbb{E}_{q(z|\psi)}\left[\log p(x, z) - \log q(z|\psi)\right] \tag{10.65}$$

Then from Equation (6.58) we have

$$\nabla_\psi \text{Ł}(\psi) = \mathbb{E}_{q(z|\psi)}\left[\tilde{\mathcal{L}}(\psi, z)\nabla_\psi \log q(z|\psi)\right] \tag{10.66}$$

We can then compute a Monte Carlo approximation to this:

$$\widehat{\nabla_{\psi}\mathcal{L}(\psi_t)} = \frac{1}{S}\sum_{s=1}^{S}\tilde{\mathcal{L}}(\psi, z_s)\nabla_{\psi}\log q_{\psi}(z_s)|_{\psi=\psi_t} \qquad (10.67)$$

We can pass this to any kind of gradient optimizer, such as SGD or Adam.

10.2.3.2 Reducing the variance using control variates

In practice, the variance of this estimator is quite large, so it is important to use methods such as **control variates** or **CV** (Section 6.3.4.1). To see how this works, consider the naive gradient estimator in Equation (10.67), which for the i'th component we can write as

$$\widehat{\nabla_{\psi_i}\mathcal{L}(\psi_t)}^{\text{naive}} = \frac{1}{S}\sum_{s=1}^{S}\tilde{g}_i(z_s) \qquad (10.68)$$

$$\tilde{g}_i(z_s) = g_i(z_s) \times \tilde{\mathcal{L}}(\psi, z_s) \qquad (10.69)$$

$$g_i(z_s) = \nabla_{\psi_i}\log q_{\psi}(z_s) \qquad (10.70)$$

The control variate version of this can be obtained by replacing $\tilde{g}_i(z_s)$ with

$$\tilde{g}_i^{cv}(z) = \tilde{g}_i(z) + c_i(\mathbb{E}\left[b_i(z)\right] - b_i(z)) \qquad (10.71)$$

where $b_i(z)$ is a baseline function and c_i is some constant, to be specified below. A convenient baseline is the score function, $b_i(z) = \nabla_{\psi_i}\log q_{\psi_i}(z) = g_i(z)$, since this is correlated with $\tilde{g}_i(z)$, and has the property that $\mathbb{E}\left[b_i(z)\right] = \mathbf{0}$, since the expected value of the score function is zero, as we showed in Equation (3.44). Hence

$$\tilde{g}_i^{cv}(z) = \tilde{g}_i(z) - c_i g_i(z) = g_i(z)(\tilde{\mathcal{L}}(\psi, z) - c_i) \qquad (10.72)$$

so the CV estimator is given by

$$\widehat{\nabla_{\psi_i}\mathcal{L}(\psi_t)}^{\text{cv}} = \frac{1}{S}\sum_{s=1}^{S}g_i(z_s) \times (\tilde{\mathcal{L}}(\psi, z_s) - c_i) \qquad (10.73)$$

One can show that the optimal c_i that minimizes the variance of the CV estimator is

$$c_i = \frac{\text{Cov}\left[g_i(z)\tilde{\mathcal{L}}(\psi, z), g_i(z)\right]}{\mathbb{V}\left[g_i(z)\right]} \qquad (10.74)$$

For more details, see e.g., [TND21].

10.3 Coordinate ascent VI

A common approximation in variational inference is to assume that all the latent variables are independent, i.e.,

$$q_{\psi}(z) = \prod_{j=1}^{J} q_j(z_j) \qquad (10.75)$$

where J is the number of hidden variables, and $q_j(z_j)$ is shorthand for $q_{\psi_j}(z_j)$, where ψ_j are the variational parameters for the j'th distribution. This is called the **mean field** approximation.

From Equation (10.11), the ELBO becomes

$$Ł(\psi) = \int q_\psi(z) \log p_\theta(x, z) dz + \sum_{j=1}^{J} \mathbb{H}(q_j) \tag{10.76}$$

since the entropy of a product distribution is the sum of entropies of each component in the product. The first term also often decomposes according to the Markov properties of the graphical model. This allows us to use a coordinate ascent optimization scheme to estimate each ψ_j, as we explain in Section 10.3.1. This is called **coordinate ascent variational inference** or **CAVI**, and is an alternative to gradient-based VI.

10.3.1   Derivation of CAVI algorithm

In this section, we derive the coordinate ascent variational inference (CAVI) procedure.

To derive the update equations, we initially assume there are just 3 discrete latent variables, to simplify notation. In this case the ELBO is given by

$$Ł(q_1, q_2, q_3) = \sum_{z_1} \sum_{z_2} \sum_{z_3} q_1(z_1) q_2(z_2) q_3(z_3) \log \tilde{p}(z_1, z_2, z_3) + \sum_{j=1}^{3} \mathbb{H}(q_j) \tag{10.77}$$

where we define $\tilde{p}(z) = p_\theta(z, x)$ for brevity. We will optimize this wrt each q_i, one at a time, keeping the others fixed.

Let us look at the objective for q_3:

$$Ł_3(q_3) = \sum_{z_3} q_3(z_3) \left[\sum_{z_1} \sum_{z_2} q_1(z_1) q_2(z_2) \log \tilde{p}(z_1, z_2, z_3) \right] + \mathbb{H}(q_3) + \text{const} \tag{10.78}$$

$$= \sum_{z_3} q_3(z_3) [g_3(z_3) - \log q_3(z_3)] + \text{const} \tag{10.79}$$

where

$$g_3(z_3) \triangleq \sum_{z_1} \sum_{z_2} q_1(z_1) q_2(z_2) \log \tilde{p}(z_1, z_2, z_3) = \mathbb{E}_{z_{-3}} [\log \tilde{p}(z_1, z_2, z_3)] \tag{10.80}$$

where $z_{-3} = (z_1, z_2)$ is all variables except z_3. Here $g_3(z_3)$ can be interpreted as an expected negative energy (log probability). We can convert this into an unnormalized probability distribution by defining

$$\tilde{f}_3(z_3) = \exp(g_3(z_3)) \tag{10.81}$$

which we can normalize to get

$$f_3(z_3) = \frac{\tilde{f}_3(z_3)}{\sum_{z_3'} \tilde{f}_3(z_3')} \propto \exp(g_3(z_3)) \tag{10.82}$$

Since $g_3(z_3) \propto \log f_3(z_3)$ we get

$$\text{Ł}_3(q_3) = \sum_{z_3} q_3(z_3) \left[\log f_3(z_3) - \log q_3(z_3) \right] + \text{const} = -D_{\mathbb{KL}}\left(q_3 \parallel f_3 \right) + \text{const} \tag{10.83}$$

Since $D_{\mathbb{KL}}\left(q_3 \parallel f_3 \right)$ achieves its minimal value of 0 when $q_3(z_3) = f_3(z_3)$ for all z_3, we see that $q_3^*(z_3) = f_3(z_3)$.

Now suppose that the joint distribution is defined by a Markov chain, where $z_1 \to z_2 \to z_3$, so $z_1 \perp z_3 | z_2$. Hence $\log \tilde{p}(z_1, z_2, z_3) = \log \tilde{p}(z_2, z_3 | z_1) + \log \tilde{p}(z_1)$, where the latter term is independent of $q_3(z_3)$. Thus the ELBO simplifies to

$$\text{Ł}_3(q_3) = \sum_{z_3} q_3(z_3) \left[\sum_{z_2} q_2(z_2) \log \tilde{p}(z_2, z_3) \right] + \mathbb{H}(q_3) + \text{const} \tag{10.84}$$

$$= \sum_{z_3} q_3(z_3) \left[\log f_3(z_3) - \log q_3(z_3) \right] + \text{const} \tag{10.85}$$

where

$$f_3(z_3) \propto \exp\left[\sum_{z_2} q_2(z_2) \log \tilde{p}(z_2, z_3) \right] = \exp\left[\mathbb{E}_{\boldsymbol{z}_{\mathrm{mb}_3}}\left[\log \tilde{p}(z_2, z_3) \right] \right] \tag{10.86}$$

where $\boldsymbol{z}_{\mathrm{mb}_3} = z_2$ is the Markov blanket (Section 4.2.4.3) of z_3. As before, the optimal variational distribution is given by $q_3(z_3) = f_3(z_3)$.

In general, when we have J groups of variables, the optimal variational distribution for the j'th group is given by

$$q_j(\boldsymbol{z}_j) \propto \exp\left[\mathbb{E}_{\boldsymbol{z}_{\mathrm{mb}_j}}\left[\log \tilde{p}(\boldsymbol{z}_j, \boldsymbol{z}_{\mathrm{mb}_j}) \right] \right] \tag{10.87}$$

(Compare to the equation for Gibbs sampling in Equation (12.19).) The CAVI method simply computes q_j for each dimension j in turn, in an iterative fashion (see Algorithm 10.4). Convergence is guaranteed since the bound is convex wrt each of the factors q_i [Bis06, p. 466].

Algorithm 10.4: Coordinate ascent variational inference (CAVI).

---

1 Initialize $q_j(\boldsymbol{z}_j)$ for $j = 1 : J$
2 **foreach** $t = 1 : T$ **do**
3   **foreach** $j = 1 : J$ **do**
4   Compute $g_j(\boldsymbol{z}_j) = \mathbb{E}_{\boldsymbol{z}_{\mathrm{mb}_i}}\left[\log \tilde{p}(\boldsymbol{z}_i, \boldsymbol{z}_{\mathrm{mb}_i}) \right]$
5   Compute $q_j(\boldsymbol{z}_j) \propto \exp(g_j(\boldsymbol{z}_j))$

Note that the functional form of the q_i distributions does not need to be specified in advance, but will be determined by the form of the log joint. This is therefore called **free-form VI**, as opposed to fixed-form, where we explicitly choose a convenient distributional type for q (we discuss fixed-form VI in Section 10.2). We give some examples below that will make this clearer.

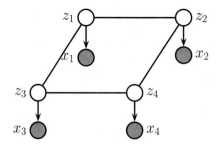

Figure 10.8: A grid-structured MRF with hidden nodes z_i and local evidence nodes x_i. The prior $p(\boldsymbol{z})$ is an undirected Ising model, and the likelihood $p(\boldsymbol{x}|\boldsymbol{z}) = \prod_i p(x_i|z_i)$ is a directed fully factored model.

10.3.2   Example: CAVI for the Ising model

In this section, we apply CAVI to perform mean field inference in an Ising model (Section 4.3.2.1), which is a kind of Markov random field defined on binary random variables, $z_i \in \{-1, +1\}$, arranged in a 2d grid.

Originally Ising models were developed as models of atomic spins for magnetic materials, although we will apply them to an image denoising problem. Specifically, let z_i be the hidden value of pixel i, and $x_i \in \mathbb{R}$ be the observed noisy value. See Figure 10.8 for the graphical model.

Let $L_i(z_i) \triangleq \log p(x_i|z_i)$ be the log likelihood for the i'th pixel (aka the **local evidence** for node i in the graphical model). The overall likelihood has the form

$$p(\boldsymbol{x}|\boldsymbol{z}) = \prod_i p(x_i|z_i) = \exp(\sum_i L_i(z_i)) \tag{10.88}$$

Our goal is to approximate the posterior $p(\boldsymbol{z}|\boldsymbol{x})$. We will use an Ising model for the prior:

$$p(\boldsymbol{z}) = \frac{1}{Z_0} \exp(-\mathcal{E}_0(\boldsymbol{z})) \tag{10.89}$$

$$\mathcal{E}_0(\boldsymbol{z}) = -\sum_{i \sim j} W_{ij} z_i z_j \tag{10.90}$$

where we sum over each $i - j$ edge. Therefore the posterior has the form

$$p(\boldsymbol{z}|\boldsymbol{x}) = \frac{1}{Z(\boldsymbol{x})} \exp(-\mathcal{E}(\boldsymbol{z})) \tag{10.91}$$

$$\mathcal{E}(\boldsymbol{z}) = \mathcal{E}_0(\boldsymbol{z}) - \sum_i L_i(z_i) \tag{10.92}$$

We will now make the following fully factored approximation:

$$q(\boldsymbol{z}) = \prod_i q_i(z_i) = \prod_i \text{Ber}(z_i|\mu_i) \tag{10.93}$$

where $\mu_i = \mathbb{E}_{q_i}[z_i]$ is the mean value of node i. To derive the update for the variational parameter μ_i, we first compute the unnormalized log joint, $\log \tilde{p}(\boldsymbol{z}) = -\mathcal{E}(\boldsymbol{z})$, dropping terms that do not involve

z_i:

$$\log \tilde{p}(\boldsymbol{z}) = z_i \sum_{j \in \text{nbr}_i} W_{ij} z_j + L_i(z_i) + \text{const} \tag{10.94}$$

This only depends on the states of the neighboring nodes. Hence

$$q_i(z_i) \propto \exp(\mathbb{E}_{q_{-i}(\boldsymbol{z})}[\log \tilde{p}(\boldsymbol{z})]) = \exp\left(z_i \sum_{j \in \text{nbr}_i} W_{ij} \mu_j + L_i(z_i) \right) \tag{10.95}$$

where $q_{-i}(\boldsymbol{z}) = \prod_{j \neq i} q(z_j)$. Thus we replace the states of the neighbors by their average values. (Note that this replaces binary variables with continuous ones.)

We now simplify this expression. Let $m_i = \sum_{j \in \text{nbr}_i} W_{ij} \mu_j$ be the mean field influence on node i. Also, let $L_i^+ \triangleq L_i(+1)$ and $L_i^- \triangleq L_i(-1)$. The approximate marginal posterior is given by

$$q_i(z_i = 1) = \frac{e^{m_i + L_i^+}}{e^{m_i + L_i^+} + e^{-m_i + L_i^-}} = \frac{1}{1 + e^{-2m_i + L_i^- - L_i^+}} = \sigma(2a_i) \tag{10.96}$$

$$a_i \triangleq m_i + 0.5(L_i^+ - L_i^-) \tag{10.97}$$

Similarly, we have $q_i(z_i = -1) = \sigma(-2a_i)$. From this we can compute the new mean for site i:

$$\mu_i = \mathbb{E}_{q_i}[z_i] = q_i(z_i = +1) \cdot (+1) + q_i(z_i = -1) \cdot (-1) \tag{10.98}$$

$$= \frac{1}{1 + e^{-2a_i}} - \frac{1}{1 + e^{2a_i}} = \frac{e^{a_i}}{e^{a_i} + e^{-a_i}} - \frac{e^{-a_i}}{e^{-a_i} + e^{a_i}} = \tanh(a_i) \tag{10.99}$$

We can turn the above equations into a fixed point algorithm by writing

$$\mu_i^t = \tanh\left(\sum_{j \in \text{nbr}_i} W_{ij} \mu_j^{t-1} + 0.5(L_i^+ - L_i^-) \right) \tag{10.100}$$

Following [MWJ99], we can use **damped updates** of the following form to improve convergence:

$$\mu_i^t = (1 - \lambda)\mu_i^{t-1} + \lambda \tanh\left(\sum_{j \in \text{nbr}_i} W_{ij} \mu_j^{t-1} + 0.5(L_i^+ - L_i^-) \right) \tag{10.101}$$

for $0 < \lambda < 1$. We can update all the nodes in parallel, or update them asynchronously.

Figure 10.9 shows the method in action, applied to a 2d Ising model with homogeneous attractive potentials, $W_{ij} = 1$. We use parallel updates with a damping factor of $\lambda = 0.5$. (If we don't use damping, we tend to get "checkerboard" artifacts.)

10.3.3 Variational Bayes

In Bayesian modeling, we treat the parameters $\boldsymbol{\theta}$ as latent variables. Thus our goal is to approximate the parameter posterior $p(\boldsymbol{\theta}|\mathcal{D}) \propto p(\boldsymbol{\theta})p(\mathcal{D}|\boldsymbol{\theta})$. Applying VI to this problem is called **variational Bayes** [Att00].

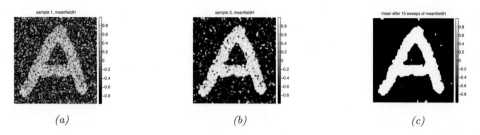

(a)   (b)   (c)

Figure 10.9: Example of image denoising using mean field (with parallel updates and a damping factor of 0.5). We use an Ising prior with $W_{ij} = 1$ and a Gaussian noise model with $\sigma = 2$. We show the results after 1, 3 and 15 iterations across the image. Compare to Figure 12.3, which shows the results of using Gibbs sampling. Generated by ising_image_denoise_demo.ipynb.

In this section, we assume there are no latent variables except for the shared global parameters, so the model has the form

$$p(\boldsymbol{\theta}, \mathcal{D}) = p(\boldsymbol{\theta}) \prod_{n=1}^{N} p(\mathcal{D}_n | \boldsymbol{\theta}) \qquad (10.102)$$

These conditional independencies are illustrated in Figure 10.5a.

We will fit the variational posterior by maximizing the ELBO

$$\mathcal{L}(\boldsymbol{\psi_\theta} | \mathcal{D}) = \mathbb{E}_{q(\boldsymbol{\theta}|\boldsymbol{\psi_\theta})} \left[\log p(\boldsymbol{\theta}, \mathcal{D}) \right] + \mathbb{H}(q(\boldsymbol{\theta}|\boldsymbol{\psi_\theta})) \qquad (10.103)$$

We will assume the variational posterior factorizes over the parameters:

$$q(\boldsymbol{\theta}|\boldsymbol{\psi_\theta}) = \prod_j q(\boldsymbol{\theta}_j | \boldsymbol{\psi}_{\theta_j}) \qquad (10.104)$$

We can then update each $\boldsymbol{\psi}_{\theta_j}$ using CAVI (Section 10.3.1).

10.3.4   Example: VB for a univariate Gaussian

Consider inferring the parameters of a 1d Gaussian. The likelihood is given by $p(\mathcal{D}|\boldsymbol{\theta}) = \prod_{n=1}^{N} \mathcal{N}(x_n | \mu, \lambda^{-1})$, where μ is the mean and λ is the precision. Suppose we use a conjugate prior of the form

$$p(\mu, \lambda) = \mathcal{N}(\mu | \mu_0, (\kappa_0 \lambda)^{-1}) \text{Ga}(\lambda | a_0, b_0) \qquad (10.105)$$

It is possible to derive the posterior $p(\mu, \lambda | \mathcal{D})$ for this model exactly, as shown in Section 3.4.3.3. However, here we use the VB method with the following factored approximate posterior:

$$q(\mu, \lambda) = q(\mu | \boldsymbol{\psi}_\mu) q(\lambda | \boldsymbol{\psi}_\lambda) \qquad (10.106)$$

We do not need to specify the forms for the distributions $q(\mu | \boldsymbol{\psi}_\mu)$ and $q(\lambda | \boldsymbol{\psi}_\lambda)$; the optimal forms will "fall out" automatically during the derivation (and conveniently, they turn out to be Gaussian and gamma respectively). Our presentation follows [Mac03, p429].

10.3.4.1 Target distribution

The unnormalized log posterior has the form

$$\log \tilde{p}(\mu, \lambda) = \log p(\mu, \lambda, \mathcal{D}) = \log p(\mathcal{D}|\mu, \lambda) + \log p(\mu|\lambda) + \log p(\lambda) \tag{10.107}$$

$$= \frac{N}{2} \log \lambda - \frac{\lambda}{2} \sum_{n=1}^{N} (x_n - \mu)^2 - \frac{\kappa_0 \lambda}{2} (\mu - \mu_0)^2$$

$$+ \frac{1}{2} \log(\kappa_0 \lambda) + (a_0 - 1) \log \lambda - b_0 \lambda + \text{const} \tag{10.108}$$

10.3.4.2 Updating $q(\mu|\psi_\mu)$

The optimal form for $q(\mu|\psi_\mu)$ is obtained by averaging over λ:

$$\log q(\mu|\psi_\mu) = \mathbb{E}_{q(\lambda|\psi_\lambda)} \left[\log p(\mathcal{D}|\mu, \lambda) + \log p(\mu|\lambda) \right] + \text{const} \tag{10.109}$$

$$= -\frac{\mathbb{E}_{q(\lambda|\psi_\lambda)}[\lambda]}{2} \left\{ \kappa_0(\mu - \mu_0)^2 + \sum_{n=1}^{N} (x_n - \mu)^2 \right\} + \text{const} \tag{10.110}$$

By completing the square one can show that $q(\mu|\psi_\mu) = \mathcal{N}(\mu|\mu_N, \kappa_N^{-1})$, where

$$\mu_N = \frac{\kappa_0 \mu_0 + N\bar{x}}{\kappa_0 + N}, \quad \kappa_N = (\kappa_0 + N)\mathbb{E}_{q(\lambda|\psi_\lambda)}[\lambda] \tag{10.111}$$

At this stage we don't know what $q(\lambda|\psi_\lambda)$ is, and hence we cannot compute $\mathbb{E}[\lambda]$, but we will derive this below.

10.3.4.3 Updating $q(\lambda|\psi_\lambda)$

The optimal form for $q(\lambda|\psi_\lambda)$ is given by

$$\log q(\lambda|\psi_\lambda) = \mathbb{E}_{q(\mu|\psi_\mu)} \left[\log p(\mathcal{D}|\mu, \lambda) + \log p(\mu|\lambda) + \log p(\lambda) \right] + \text{const} \tag{10.112}$$

$$= (a_0 - 1) \log \lambda - b_0 \lambda + \frac{1}{2} \log \lambda + \frac{N}{2} \log \lambda$$

$$- \frac{\lambda}{2} \mathbb{E}_{q(\mu|\psi_\mu)} \left[\kappa_0(\mu - \mu_0)^2 + \sum_{n=1}^{N} (x_n - \mu)^2 \right] + \text{const} \tag{10.113}$$

We recognize this as the log of a gamma distribution, hence $q(\lambda|\psi_\lambda) = \text{Ga}(\lambda|a_N, b_N)$, where

$$a_N = a_0 + \frac{N+1}{2} \tag{10.114}$$

$$b_N = b_0 + \frac{1}{2} \mathbb{E}_{q(\mu|\psi_\mu)} \left[\kappa_0(\mu - \mu_0)^2 + \sum_{n=1}^{N} (x_n - \mu)^2 \right] \tag{10.115}$$

10.3.4.4   Computing the expectations

To implement the updates, we have to specify how to compute the various expectations. Since $q(\mu) = \mathcal{N}(\mu|\mu_N, \kappa_N^{-1})$, we have

$$\mathbb{E}_{q(\mu)}[\mu] = \mu_N \tag{10.116}$$

$$\mathbb{E}_{q(\mu)}[\mu^2] = \frac{1}{\kappa_N} + \mu_N^2 \tag{10.117}$$

Since $q(\lambda) = \text{Ga}(\lambda|a_N, b_N)$, we have

$$\mathbb{E}_{q(\lambda)}[\lambda] = \frac{a_N}{b_N} \tag{10.118}$$

We can now give explicit forms for the update equations. For $q(\mu)$ we have

$$\mu_N = \frac{\kappa_0 \mu_0 + N\bar{x}}{\kappa_0 + N} \tag{10.119}$$

$$\kappa_N = (\kappa_0 + N)\frac{a_N}{b_N} \tag{10.120}$$

and for $q(\lambda)$ we have

$$a_N = a_0 + \frac{N+1}{2} \tag{10.121}$$

$$b_N = b_0 + \frac{1}{2}\kappa_0(\mathbb{E}[\mu^2] + \mu_0^2 - 2\mathbb{E}[\mu]\mu_0) + \frac{1}{2}\sum_{n=1}^{N}\left(x_n^2 + \mathbb{E}[\mu^2] - 2\mathbb{E}[\mu]x_n\right) \tag{10.122}$$

We see that μ_N and a_N are in fact fixed constants, and only κ_N and b_N need to be updated iteratively. (In fact, one can solve for the fixed points of κ_N and b_N analytically, but we don't do this here in order to illustrate the iterative updating scheme.)

10.3.4.5   Illustration

Figure 10.10 gives an example of this method in action. The green contours represent the exact posterior, which is Gaussian-gamma. The dotted red contours represent the variational approximation over several iterations. We see that the final approximation is reasonably close to the exact solution. However, it is more "compact" than the true distribution. It is often the case that mean field inference underestimates the posterior uncertainty, for reasons explained in Section 5.1.4.1.

10.3.4.6   Lower bound

In VB, we maximize a lower bound on the log marginal likelihood:

$$Ł(\boldsymbol{\psi_\theta}|\mathcal{D}) \leq \log p(\mathcal{D}) = \log \iint p(\mathcal{D}|\mu, \lambda)p(\mu, \lambda)d\mu d\lambda \tag{10.123}$$

It is very useful to compute the lower bound itself, for three reasons. First, it can be used to assess convergence of the algorithm. Second, it can be used to assess the correctness of one's code: as with

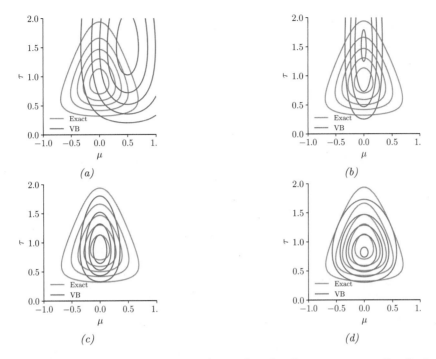

Figure 10.10: *Factored variational approximation (orange) to the Gaussian-gamma distribution (blue). (a) Initial guess. (b) After updating* $q(\mu|\boldsymbol{\psi}_\mu)$. *(c) After updating* $q(\lambda|\boldsymbol{\psi}_\lambda)$. *(d) At convergence (after 5 iterations). Adapted from Fig. 10.4 of [Bis06]. Generated by* unigauss_vb_demo.ipynb.

EM, if we use CAVI to optimize the objective, the bound should increase monotonically at each iteration, otherwise there must be a bug. Third, the bound can be used as an approximation to the marginal likelihood, which can be used for Bayesian model selection or empirical Bayes (see Section 10.1.3). In the case of the current model, one can show that the lower bound has the following form:

$$\text{Ł} = \text{const} + \frac{1}{2}\ln\frac{1}{\kappa_N} + \ln\Gamma(a_N) - a_N \ln b_N \tag{10.124}$$

10.3.5 Variational Bayes EM

In Bayesian latent variable models, we have two forms of hidden variables: local (or per example) hidden variables z_n, and global (shared) hidden variables $\boldsymbol{\theta}$, which represent the parameters of the model. See Figure 10.5b for an illustration. (Note that the parameters, which are fixed in number, are sometimes called **intrinsic variables**, whereas the local hidden variables are called **extrinsic variables**.) If $\boldsymbol{h} = (\boldsymbol{\theta}, \boldsymbol{z}_{1:N})$ represents all the hidden variables, then the joint distribution is given by

$$p(\boldsymbol{h}, \mathcal{D}) = p(\boldsymbol{\theta}, \boldsymbol{z}_{1:N}, \mathcal{D}) = p(\boldsymbol{\theta}) \prod_{n=1}^{N} p(\boldsymbol{z}_n|\boldsymbol{\theta})p(\boldsymbol{x}_n|\boldsymbol{z}_n, \boldsymbol{\theta}) \tag{10.125}$$

We will make the following mean field assumption:

$$q(\boldsymbol{\theta}, \boldsymbol{z}_{1:N}|\boldsymbol{\psi}_{1:N}, \boldsymbol{\psi}_{\boldsymbol{\theta}}) = q(\boldsymbol{\theta}|\boldsymbol{\psi}_{\boldsymbol{\theta}}) \prod_{n=1}^{N} q(\boldsymbol{z}_n|\boldsymbol{\psi}_n) \tag{10.126}$$

where $\boldsymbol{\psi} = (\boldsymbol{\psi}_{1:N}, \boldsymbol{\psi}_{\boldsymbol{\theta}})$.

We will use VI to maximize the ELBO:

$$\text{Ł}(\boldsymbol{\psi}|\mathcal{D}) = \mathbb{E}_{q(\boldsymbol{\theta}, \boldsymbol{z}_{1:N}|\boldsymbol{\psi}_{1:N}, \boldsymbol{\psi}_{\boldsymbol{\theta}})} \left[\log p(\boldsymbol{z}_{1:N}, \boldsymbol{\theta}, \mathcal{D}) - \log q(\boldsymbol{\theta}, \boldsymbol{z}_{1:N})\right] \tag{10.127}$$

If we use the mean field assumption, then we can apply the CAVI approach to optimize each set of variational parameters. In particular, we can alternate between optimizing the $q_n(\boldsymbol{z}_n)$ in parallel, independently of each other, with $q(\boldsymbol{\theta})$ held fixed, and then optimizing $q(\boldsymbol{\theta})$ with the q_n held fixed. This is known as **variational Bayes EM** [BG06]. It is similar to regular EM, except in the E step, we infer an approximate posterior for $\boldsymbol{z}_n$ averaging out the parameters (instead of plugging in a point estimate), and in the M step, we update the parameter posterior parameters using the expected sufficient statistics.

Now suppose we approximate $q(\boldsymbol{\theta})$ by a delta function, $q(\boldsymbol{\theta}) = \delta(\boldsymbol{\theta} - \hat{\boldsymbol{\theta}})$. The Bayesian LVM ELBO objective from Equation (10.127) simplifies to the "LVM ELBO":

$$\text{Ł}(\boldsymbol{\theta}, \boldsymbol{\psi}_{1:N}|\mathcal{D}) = \mathbb{E}_{q(\boldsymbol{z}_{1:N}|\boldsymbol{\psi}_{1:N})} \left[\log p(\boldsymbol{\theta}, \mathcal{D}, \boldsymbol{z}_{1:N}) - \log q(\boldsymbol{z}_{1:N}|\boldsymbol{\psi}_{1:N})\right] \tag{10.128}$$

We can optimize this using the **variational EM** algorithm, which is a CAVI algorithm which updates the $\boldsymbol{\psi}_n$ in parallel in the variational E step, and then updates $\boldsymbol{\theta}$ in the M step.

VEM is simpler than VBEM since in the variational E step, we compute $q(\boldsymbol{z}_n|\boldsymbol{x}_n, \hat{\boldsymbol{\theta}})$, instead of $\mathbb{E}_{\boldsymbol{\theta}}[q(\boldsymbol{z}_n|\boldsymbol{x}_n, \boldsymbol{\theta})]$; that is, we plug in a point estimate of the model parameters, rather than averaging over the parameters. For more details on VEM, see Section 10.1.3.

10.3.6   Example: VBEM for a GMM

Consider a standard Gaussian mixture model (GMM):

$$p(\boldsymbol{z}, \boldsymbol{x}|\boldsymbol{\theta}) = \prod_n \prod_k \pi_k^{z_{nk}} \mathcal{N}(\boldsymbol{x}_n|\boldsymbol{\mu}_k, \boldsymbol{\Lambda}_k^{-1})^{z_{nk}} \tag{10.129}$$

where $z_{nk} = 1$ if datapoint n belongs to cluster k, and $z_{nk} = 0$ otherwise. Our goal is to approximate the posterior $p(\boldsymbol{z}, \boldsymbol{\theta}|\boldsymbol{x})$ under the following conjugate prior

$$p(\boldsymbol{\theta}) = \text{Dir}(\boldsymbol{\pi}|\, \breve{\boldsymbol{\alpha}}) \prod_k \mathcal{N}(\boldsymbol{\mu}_k|\, \breve{\boldsymbol{m}}, (\breve{\kappa}\,\boldsymbol{\Lambda}_k)^{-1}) \text{Wi}(\boldsymbol{\Lambda}_k|\, \breve{\mathbf{L}}, \breve{\nu}) \tag{10.130}$$

where $\boldsymbol{\Lambda}_k$ is the precision matrix for cluster k. For the mixing weights, we usually use a symmetric prior, $\breve{\boldsymbol{\alpha}} = \alpha_0 \mathbf{1}$.

The exact posterior $p(\boldsymbol{z}, \boldsymbol{\theta}|\mathcal{D})$ is a mixture of K^N distributions, corresponding to all possible labelings $\boldsymbol{z}$, which is intractable to compute. In this section, we derive a VBEM algorithm, which will approximate the posterior around a local mode. We follow the presentation of [Bis06, Sec 10.2]. (See also Section 10.2.1.5 and Section 10.2.2.3, where we discuss variational approximations based on stochastic gradient descent, which can scale better to large datasets compared to VBEM.)

10.3.6.1 The variational posterior

We will use the standard mean field approximation to the posterior: $q(\boldsymbol{\theta}, \boldsymbol{z}_{1:N}) = q(\boldsymbol{\theta}) \prod_n q_n(\boldsymbol{z}_n)$. At this stage we have not specified the forms of the q functions; these will be determined by the form of the likelihood and prior. Below we will show that the optimal forms are as follows:

$$q_n(\boldsymbol{z}_n) = \text{Cat}(\boldsymbol{z}_n | \boldsymbol{r}_n) \tag{10.131}$$

$$q(\boldsymbol{\theta}) = \text{Dir}(\boldsymbol{\pi} | \widehat{\boldsymbol{\alpha}}) \prod_k \mathcal{N}(\boldsymbol{\mu}_k | \widehat{\boldsymbol{m}}_k, (\widehat{\kappa}_k \boldsymbol{\Lambda}_k)^{-1}) \text{Wi}(\boldsymbol{\Lambda}_k | \widehat{\mathbf{L}}_k, \widehat{\nu}_k) \tag{10.132}$$

where $\boldsymbol{r}_n$ are the posterior responsibilities, and the parameters with hats on them are the hyperparameters from the prior updated with data.

10.3.6.2 Derivation of $q(\boldsymbol{\theta})$ (variational M step)

Using the mean field recipe in Algorithm 10.4, we write down the log joint, and take expectations over all variables except $\boldsymbol{\theta}$, so we average out the $\boldsymbol{z}_n$ wrt $q(\boldsymbol{z}_n) = \text{Cat}(\boldsymbol{z}_n | \boldsymbol{r}_n)$:

$$\log q(\boldsymbol{\theta}) = \underbrace{\log p(\boldsymbol{\pi}) + \sum_n \mathbb{E}_{q(z_n)} [\log p(\boldsymbol{z}_n | \boldsymbol{\pi})]}_{L_{\boldsymbol{\pi}}}$$

$$+ \sum_k \left[\underbrace{\log p(\boldsymbol{\mu}_k, \boldsymbol{\Lambda}_k) \sum_n \mathbb{E}_{q(z_n)} [z_{nk}] \log \mathcal{N}(\boldsymbol{x}_n | \boldsymbol{\mu}_k, \boldsymbol{\Lambda}_k^{-1})}_{L_{\boldsymbol{\mu}_k, \boldsymbol{\Lambda}_k}} \right] + \text{const} \tag{10.133}$$

Since the expected log joint factorizes into a term involving $\boldsymbol{\pi}$ and terms involving $(\boldsymbol{\mu}_k, \boldsymbol{\Lambda}_k)$, we see that the variational posterior also factorizes into the form

$$q(\boldsymbol{\theta}) = q(\boldsymbol{\pi}) \prod_k q(\boldsymbol{\mu}_k, \boldsymbol{\Lambda}_k) \tag{10.134}$$

For the $\boldsymbol{\pi}$ term, we have

$$\log q(\boldsymbol{\pi}) = (\alpha_0 - 1) \sum_k \log \pi_k + \sum_k \sum_n r_{nk} \log \pi_k + \text{const} \tag{10.135}$$

Exponentiating, we recognize this as a Dirichlet distribution:

$$q(\boldsymbol{\pi}) = \text{Dir}(\boldsymbol{\pi} | \widehat{\boldsymbol{\alpha}}) \tag{10.136}$$

$$\widehat{\alpha}_k = \alpha_0 + N_k \tag{10.137}$$

$$N_k = \sum_n r_{nk} \tag{10.138}$$

For the $\boldsymbol{\mu}_k$ and $\boldsymbol{\Lambda}_k$ terms, we have

$$q(\boldsymbol{\mu}_k, \boldsymbol{\Lambda}_k) = \mathcal{N}(\boldsymbol{\mu}_k| \, \widehat{\boldsymbol{m}}_k, (\widehat{\kappa}_k \, \boldsymbol{\Lambda}_k)^{-1})\mathrm{Wi}(\boldsymbol{\Lambda}_k| \, \widehat{\mathbf{L}}_k, \widehat{\nu}_k) \tag{10.139}$$

$$\widehat{\kappa}_k = \breve{\kappa} + N_k \tag{10.140}$$

$$\widehat{\boldsymbol{m}}_k = (\breve{\kappa} \, \breve{\boldsymbol{m}} + N_k \overline{\boldsymbol{x}}_k)/ \, \widehat{\kappa}_k \tag{10.141}$$

$$\widehat{\mathbf{L}}_k^{-1} = \breve{\mathbf{L}}^{-1} + N_k \mathbf{S}_k + \frac{\breve{\kappa} \, N_k}{\breve{\kappa} + N_k}(\overline{\boldsymbol{x}}_k - \breve{\boldsymbol{m}})(\overline{\boldsymbol{x}}_k - \breve{\boldsymbol{m}})^{\mathsf{T}} \tag{10.142}$$

$$\widehat{\nu}_k = \breve{\nu} + N_k \tag{10.143}$$

$$\overline{\boldsymbol{x}}_k = \frac{1}{N_k} \sum_n r_{nk} \boldsymbol{x}_n \tag{10.144}$$

$$\mathbf{S}_k = \frac{1}{N_k} \sum_n r_{nk}(\boldsymbol{x}_n - \overline{\boldsymbol{x}}_k)(\boldsymbol{x}_n - \overline{\boldsymbol{x}}_k)^{\mathsf{T}} \tag{10.145}$$

This is very similar to the M step for MAP estimation for GMMs, except here we are computing the parameters of the posterior for $\boldsymbol{\theta}$ rather than a point estimate $\hat{\boldsymbol{\theta}}$.

10.3.6.3   Derivation of $q(\boldsymbol{z})$ (variational E step)

The variational E step is more interesting, since it is quite different from the E step in regular EM, because we need to average over the parameters, rather than condition on them. In particular, we have

$$\log q(\boldsymbol{z}) = \sum_n \sum_k z_{nk} \left(\mathbb{E}_{q(\boldsymbol{\pi})}\left[\log \pi_k\right] + \frac{1}{2}\mathbb{E}_{q(\boldsymbol{\Lambda}_k)}\left[\log |\boldsymbol{\Lambda}_k|\right] - \frac{D}{2}\log(2\pi) \right.$$

$$\left. - \frac{1}{2}\mathbb{E}_{q(\boldsymbol{\theta})}\left[(\boldsymbol{x}_n - \boldsymbol{\mu}_k)^{\mathsf{T}}\boldsymbol{\Lambda}_k(\boldsymbol{x}_n - \boldsymbol{\mu}_k)\right] \right) + \mathrm{const} \tag{10.146}$$

Using the fact that $q(\boldsymbol{\pi}) = \mathrm{Dir}(\boldsymbol{\pi}| \, \widehat{\boldsymbol{\alpha}})$, one can show that

$$\exp(\mathbb{E}_{q(\boldsymbol{\pi})}\left[\log \pi_k\right]) = \frac{\exp(\psi(\widehat{\alpha}_k))}{\exp(\psi(\sum_{k'} \widehat{\alpha}_{k'}))} \triangleq \tilde{\pi}_k \tag{10.147}$$

where ψ is the **digamma function**:

$$\psi(x) = \frac{d}{dx}\log \Gamma(x) \tag{10.148}$$

This takes care of the first term.

For the second term, one can show

$$\mathbb{E}_{q(\boldsymbol{\Lambda}_k)}\left[\log |\boldsymbol{\Lambda}_k|\right] = \sum_{j=1}^{D} \psi\left(\frac{\widehat{\nu}_k + 1 - j}{2}\right) + D\log 2 + \log |\widehat{\mathbf{L}}_k| \tag{10.149}$$

Finally, for the expected value of the quadratic form, one can show

$$\mathbb{E}_{q(\boldsymbol{\mu}_k, \boldsymbol{\Lambda}_k)}\left[(\boldsymbol{x}_n - \boldsymbol{\mu}_k)^{\mathsf{T}}\boldsymbol{\Lambda}_k(\boldsymbol{x}_n - \boldsymbol{\mu}_k)\right] = D\,\widehat{\kappa}_k^{-1} + \widehat{\nu}_k \,(\boldsymbol{x}_n - \widehat{\boldsymbol{m}}_k)^{\mathsf{T}} \, \widehat{\mathbf{L}}_k \,(\boldsymbol{x}_n - \widehat{\boldsymbol{m}}_k) \triangleq \tilde{\Lambda}_k \tag{10.150}$$

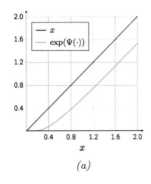

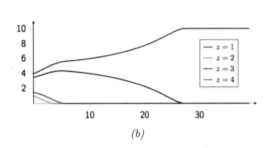

(a) (b)

Figure 10.11: (a) We plot $\exp(\psi(x))$ vs x. We see that this function performs a form of shrinkage, so that small values get set to zero. (b) We plot N_k vs time for 4 different states (z values), starting from random initial values. We perform a series of VBEM updates, ignoring the likelihood term. We see that states that initially had higher counts get reinforced, and sparsely populated states get killed off. From [LK07]. Used with kind permission of Percy Liang.

Thus we get that the posterior responsibility of cluster k for datapoint n is

$$r_{nk} \propto \tilde{\pi}_k \tilde{\Lambda}_k^{\frac{1}{2}} \exp\left(-\frac{D}{2\,\widehat{\kappa}_k} - \frac{\widehat{\nu}_k}{2} (\boldsymbol{x}_n - \widehat{\boldsymbol{m}}_k)^\mathsf{T}\, \widehat{\boldsymbol{\Lambda}}_k\, (\boldsymbol{x}_n - \widehat{\boldsymbol{m}}_k) \right) \tag{10.151}$$

Compare this to the expression used in regular EM:

$$r_{nk}^{EM} \propto \hat{\pi}_k |\hat{\boldsymbol{\Lambda}}_k|^{\frac{1}{2}} \exp\left(-\frac{1}{2}(\boldsymbol{x}_n - \hat{\boldsymbol{\mu}}_k)^\mathsf{T} \hat{\boldsymbol{\Lambda}}_k (\boldsymbol{x}_n - \hat{\boldsymbol{\mu}}_k) \right) \tag{10.152}$$

where $\hat{\pi}_k$ is the MAP estimate for π_k. The significance of this difference is discussed in Section 10.3.6.4.

10.3.6.4 Automatic sparsity inducing effects of VBEM

In regular EM, the E step has the form given in Equation (10.152), whereas in VBEM, the E step has the form given in Equation (10.151). Although they look similar, they differ in an important way. To understand this, let us ignore the likelihood term, and just focus on the prior. From Equation (10.147) we have

$$r_{nk}^{VB} = \tilde{\pi}_k = \frac{\exp(\psi(\widehat{\alpha}_k))}{\exp(\psi(\sum_{k'} \widehat{\alpha}_{k'}))} \tag{10.153}$$

And from the usual EM MAP estimation equations for GMM mixing weights (see e.g., [Mur22, Sec 8.7.3.4]) we have

$$r_{nk}^{EM} = \hat{\pi}_k = \frac{\widehat{\alpha}_k - 1}{\sum_{k'} (\widehat{\alpha}_{k'} - 1)} \tag{10.154}$$

where $\widehat{\alpha}_k = \alpha_0 + N_k$, and $N_k = \sum_n r_{nk}$ is the expected number of assignments to cluster k.

We know from Figure 2.6 that using $\alpha_0 \ll 1$ causes $\boldsymbol{\pi}$ to be sparse, which will encourage $\boldsymbol{r}_n$ to be sparse, which will "kill off" unnecessary mixture components (i.e., ones for which $N_k \ll N$, meaning very few datapoints are assigned to cluster k). To encourage this sparsity promoting effect, let us set $\alpha_0 = 0$. In this case, the updated parameters for the mixture weights are given by the following:

$$\tilde{\pi}_k = \frac{\exp(\psi(N_k))}{\exp(\psi(\sum_{k'} N_{k'}))} \tag{10.155}$$

$$\hat{\pi}_k = \frac{N_k - 1}{\sum_{k'}(N_{k'} - 1)} \tag{10.156}$$

Now consider a cluster which has no assigned data, so $N_k = 0$. In regular EM, $\hat{\pi}_k$ might end up negative, as pointed out in [FJ02]. (This will not occur if we use maximum likelihood training, which corresponds to $\alpha_0 = 1$, but this will not induce any sparsity, either.) This problem does not arise in VBEM, since we use the digamma function, which is always positive, as shown in Figure 10.11(a).

More interestingly, let us consider the effect of these updates on clusters that have unequal, but non-zero, number of assignments. Suppose we start with a random assignment of counts to 4 clusters, and iterate the VBEM algorithm, ignoring the contribution from the likelihood for simplicity. Figure 10.11(b) shows how the counts N_k evolve over time. We notice that clusters that started out with small counts end up with zero counts, and clusters that started out with large counts end up with even larger counts. In other words, the initially popular clusters get more and more members. This is called the **rich get richer** phenomenon; we will encounter it again in Supplementary Section 31.2, when we discuss Dirichlet process mixture models.

The reason for this effect is shown in Figure 10.11(a): we see that $\exp(\psi(N_k)) < N_k$, and is zero if N_k is sufficiently small, similar to the soft-thresholding behavior induced by ℓ_1-regularization (see Section 15.2.6). Importantly, this effect of reducing N_k is greater on clusters with small counts.

We now demonstrate this automatic pruning method on a real example. We fit a mixture of 6 Gaussians to the Old Faithful dataset, using $\alpha_0 = 0.001$. Since the data only really "needs" 2 clusters, the remaining 4 get "killed off", as shown in Figure 10.12. In Figure 10.13, we plot the initial and final values of α_k; we see that $\hat{\alpha}_k = 0$ for all but two of the components k.

Thus we see that VBEM for GMMs with a sparse Dirichlet prior provides an efficient way to choose the number of clusters. Similar techniques can be used to choose the number of states in an HMM and other latent variable models. However, this **variational pruning effect** (also called **posterior collapse**), is not always desirable, since it can cause the model to "ignore" the latent variables $\boldsymbol{z}$ if the likelihood function $p(\boldsymbol{x}|\boldsymbol{z})$ is sufficiently powerful. We discuss this more in Section 21.4.

10.3.6.5 Lower bound on the marginal likelihood

The VBEM algorithm is maximizing the following lower bound

$$\mathcal{L} = \sum_{\boldsymbol{z}} \int d\boldsymbol{\theta} \, q(\boldsymbol{z}, \boldsymbol{\theta}) \log \frac{p(\boldsymbol{x}, \boldsymbol{z}, \boldsymbol{\theta})}{q(\boldsymbol{z}, \boldsymbol{\theta})} \leq \log p(\boldsymbol{x}) \tag{10.157}$$

This quantity increases monotonically with each iteration, as shown in Figure 10.14.

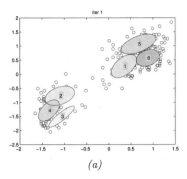 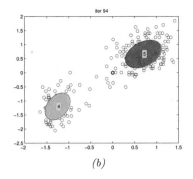

Figure 10.12: *We visualize the posterior mean parameters at various stages of the VBEM algorithm applied to a mixture of Gaussians model on the Old Faithful data. Shading intensity is proportional to the mixing weight. We initialize with K-means and use $\alpha_0 = 0.001$ as the Dirichlet hyper-parameter. (The red dot on the right panel represents all the unused mixture components, which collapse to the prior at 0.) Adapted from Figure 10.6 of [Bis06]. Generated by* gmm_vb_em.ipynb.

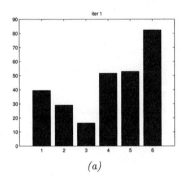 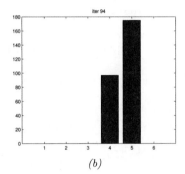

Figure 10.13: *We visualize the posterior values of $\boldsymbol{\alpha}_k$ for the model in Figure 10.12 after the first and last iteration of the algorithm. We see that unnecessary components get "killed off". (Interestingly, the initially large cluster 6 gets "replaced" by cluster 5.) Generated by* gmm_vb_em.ipynb.

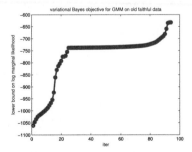

Figure 10.14: *Lower bound vs iterations for the VB algorithm in Figure 10.12. The steep parts of the curve correspond to places where the algorithm figures out that it can increase the bound by "killing off" unnecessary mixture components, as described in Section 10.3.6.6. The plateaus correspond to slowly moving the clusters around. Generated by* gmm_vb_em.ipynb.

10.3.6.6   Model selection using VBEM

Section 10.3.6.4 discusses a way to choose K automatically, during model fitting, by "killing off" unneeded clusters. An alternative approach is to fit several models, and then to use the variational lower bound to the log marginal likelihood, $\mathcal{L}(K) \leq \log p(\mathcal{D}|K)$, to approximate $p(K|\mathcal{D})$. In particular, if we have a uniform prior, we get the posterior

$$p(K|\mathcal{D}) = \frac{p(\mathcal{D}|K)}{\sum_{K'} p(\mathcal{D}|K')} \approx \frac{e^{\mathcal{L}(K)}}{\sum_{K'} e^{\mathcal{L}(K')}} \qquad (10.158)$$

It is shown in [BG06] that the VB approximation to the marginal likelihood is more accurate than BIC [BG06]. However, the lower bound needs to be modified somewhat to take into account the lack of identifiability of the parameters. In particular, although VB will approximate the volume occupied by the parameter posterior, it will only do so around one of the local modes. With K components, there are $K!$ equivalent modes, which differ merely by permuting the labels. Therefore a more accurate approximation to the log marginal likelihood is to use $\log p(\mathcal{D}|K) \approx \mathcal{L}(K) + \log(K!)$.

10.3.7   Variational message passing (VMP)

In this section, we describe the CAVI algorithm for a generic model in which each complete conditional, $p(z_j|z_{-j}, x)$, is in the exponential family, i.e.,

$$p(z_j|z_{-j}, x) = h(z_j) \exp[\eta_j(z_{-j}, x)^{\mathsf{T}} \mathcal{T}(z_j) - A_j(\eta_j(z_{-j}, x))] \qquad (10.159)$$

where $\mathcal{T}(z_j)$ is the vector of sufficient statistics, η_j are the natural parameters, A_j is the log partition function, and $h(z_j)$ is the base distribution. This assumption holds if the prior $p(z_j)$ is conjugate to the likelihood, $p(z_{-j}, x|z_j)$.

If Equation (10.159) holds, the mean field update node j becomes

$$q_j(z_j) \propto \exp\left[\mathbb{E}\left[\log p(z_j|z_{-j}, x)\right]\right] \qquad (10.160)$$

$$= \exp\left[\log h(z_j) + \mathbb{E}\left[\eta_j(z_{-j}, x)\right]^{\mathsf{T}} \mathcal{T}(z_j) - \mathbb{E}\left[A_j(\eta_j(z_{-j}, x))\right]\right] \qquad (10.161)$$

$$\propto h(z_j) \exp\left[\mathbb{E}\left[\eta_j(z_{-j}, x)\right]^{\mathsf{T}} \mathcal{T}(z_j)\right] \qquad (10.162)$$

Thus we update the local natural parameters using the expected values of the other nodes. These become the new variational parameters:

$$\psi_j = \mathbb{E}\left[\eta_j(z_{-j}, x)\right] \qquad (10.163)$$

We can generalize the above approach to work with any model where each full conditional is conjugate. The resulting algorithm is known as **variational message passing** or **VMP** [WB05] that works for any directed graphical model. VMP is similar to belief propagation (Section 9.3): at each iteration, each node collects all the messages from its parents, and all the messages from its children (which might require the children to get messages from their co-parents), and combines them to compute the expected value of the node's sufficient statistics. The messages that are sent are the expected sufficient statistics of a node, rather than just a discrete or Gaussian distribution (as in BP). Several software libraries have implemented this framework (see e.g., [Win; Min+18; Lut16; Wan17]).

VMP can be extended to the case where each full conditional is conditionally conjugate using the CVI framework in Supplementary Section 10.3.1. See also [ABV21], where they use local Laplace approximations to intractable factors inside of a message passing framework.

10.3.8 Autoconj

The VMP method requires the user to manually specify a graphical model; the corresponding node update equations are then computed for each node using a lookup table, for each possible combination of node types. It is possible to automatically derive these update equations for any conditionally conjugate directed graphical model using a technique called **autoconj** [HJT18]. This is analogous to the use of automatic differentiation (autodiff) to derive the gradient for any differentiable function. (Note that autoconj uses autodiff internally.) The resulting full conditionals can be used for CAVI, and also for Gibbs sampling (Section 12.3).

10.4 More accurate variational posteriors

In general, we can improve the tightness of the ELBO lower bound, and hence reduce the KL divergence of our posterior approximation, if we use more flexible posterior families (although optimizing within more flexible families may be slower, and can incur statistical error if the sample size is low [Bha+21]). In this section, we give several examples of more accurate variational posteriors, going beyond fully factored mean field approximations, or simple unimodal Gaussian approximations.

10.4.1 Structured mean field

The mean field assumption is quite strong, and can sometimes give poor results. Fortunately, sometimes we can exploit **tractable substructure** in our problem, so that we can efficiently handle some kinds of dependencies between the variables in the posterior in an analytic way, rather than assuming they are all independent. This is called the **structured mean field** approach [SJ95].

A common example arises when appling VI to time series models, such as HMMs, where the latent variables within each sequence are usually highly correlated across time. Rather than assuming a fully factorized posterior, we can treat each sequence $z_{n,1:T}$ as a block, and just assume independence between blocks and the parameters: $q(z_{1:N,1:T}, \theta) = q(\theta) \prod_{n=1}^{N} q(z_{n,1:T})$, where $q(z_{n,1:T}) = \prod_t q(z_{n,t}|z_{n,t-1})$. We can compute the joint distribution $q(z_{n,1:T})$, taking into account the dependence between time steps, using the forwards-backwards algorithm. For details, see [JW14; Fot+14]. A similar approach was applied to the factorial HMM model, as we discuss in Supplementary Section 10.3.2.

An automatic way to derive a structured variational approximation to a probabilistic model, specified by a probabilistic programming language, is discussed in [AHG20].

10.4.2 Hierarchical (auxiliary variable) posteriors

Suppose $q_\phi(z|x) = \prod_k q_\phi(z_k|x)$ is a factorized distribution, such as a diagonal Gaussian. This does not capture dependencies between the latent variables (components of z). We could of course use a full covariance matrix, but this might be too expensive.

An alternative approach is to use a hierarchical model, in which we add **auxiliary latent variables** a, which are used to increase the flexibility of the variational posterior. In particular, we can still assume $q_\phi(z|x, a)$ is conditionally factorized, but when we marginalize out a, we induce dependencies between the elements of z, i.e.,

$$q_\phi(z|x) = \int q_\phi(z|x, a) q_\phi(a|x) da \neq \prod_k q_\phi(z_k|x) \tag{10.164}$$

This is called a **hierarchical variational model** [Ran16], or an **auxiliary variable deep generative model** [Maa+16].

In [TRB16], they model $q_\phi(z|x, a)$ as a Gaussian process, which is a flexible nonparametric distribution (see Chapter 18), where a are the inducing points. This combination is called a **variational GP**.

10.4.3   Normalizing flow posteriors

Normalizing flows are a class of probability models which work by passing a simple source distribution, such as a diagonal Gaussian, through a series of nonlinear, but invertible, mappings f to create a more complex distribution. This can be used to get more accurate posterior approximations than standard Gaussian VI, as we discuss in Section 23.1.2.2.

10.4.4   Implicit posteriors

In Chapter 26, we discuss implicit probability distributions, which are models which we can sample from, but which we cannot evaluate pointwise. For example, consider passing a Gaussian noise term, $z_0 \sim \mathcal{N}(0, I)$, through a nonlinear, *non-invertible* mapping f to create $z = f(z_0)$; it is easy to sample from $q(z)$, but it is intractable to evaluate the density $q(z)$ (unlike with flows). This makes it hard to evaluate the log density ratio $\log p_\theta(z)/q_\psi(z|x)$, which is needed to compute the ELBO. However, we can use the same method as is used in GANs (generative adversarial networks, Chapter 26), in which we train a classifier that discriminates prior samples from samples from the variational posterior by evaluating $T(x, z) = \log q_\psi(z|x) - \log p_\theta(z)$. See e.g., [TR19] for details.

10.4.5   Combining VI with MCMC inference

There are various ways to combine variational inference with MCMC to get an improved approximate posterior. In [SKW15], they propose **Hamiltonian variational inference**, in which they train an inference network to initialize an HMC sampler (Section 12.5). The gradient of the log posterior (wrt the latents), which is needed by HMC, is given by

$$\nabla_z \log p_\theta(z|x) = \nabla_z \log [p_\theta(x, z) - \log p_\theta(x)] = \nabla_z \log p_\theta(x, z) \tag{10.165}$$

This is easy to compute. They use the final sample to approximate the posterior $q_\phi(z|x)$. To compute the entropy of this distribution, they also learn an auxiliary inverse inference network to reverse the HMC Markov chain.

A simpler approach is proposed in [Hof17]. Here they train an inference network to initialize an HMC sampler, using the standard ELBO for ϕ, but they optimize the generative parameters θ using a stochastic approximation to the log marginal likelihood, given by $\log p_\theta(z, x)$ where z is a sample from the HMC chain. This does not require learning a reverse inference network, and avoids problems with variational pruning, since it does not use the ELBO for training the generative model.

10.5 Tighter bounds

Another way to improve the quality of the posterior approximation is to optimize q wrt a bound that is a tighter approximation to the log marginal likelihood compared to the standard ELBO. We give some examples below.

10.5.1 Multi-sample ELBO (IWAE bound)

In this section, we discuss a method known as the **importance weighted autoencoder** or **IWAE** [BGS16], which is a way to tighten the variational lower bound by using self-normalized importance sampling (Section 11.5.2). (It can also be interpreted as standard ELBO maximization in an expanded model, where we add extra auxiliary variables [CMD17; DS18; Tuc+19].)

Let the inference network $q_\phi(z|x)$ be viewed as a proposal distribution for the target posterior $p_\theta(z|x)$. Define $w_s^* = \frac{p_\theta(x, z_s)}{q_\phi(z_s|x)}$ as the unnormalized importance weight for a sample, and $w_s = w_s^*/(\sum_{s'=1}^S w_{s'}^*)$ as the normalized importance weights. From Equation (11.43) we can compute an estimate of the marginal likelihood $p(x)$ using

$$\hat{p}_S(x|z_{1:S}) \triangleq \frac{1}{S}\sum_{k=1}^S \frac{p_\theta(x, z_s)}{q_\phi(z_s|x)} = \frac{1}{S}\sum_{k=1}^S w_s \tag{10.166}$$

This is unbiased, i.e., $\mathbb{E}_{q_\phi(z_{1:S}|x)}[\hat{p}_S(x|z_{1:S})] = p(x)$, where $q_\phi(z_{1:S}|x) = \prod_{s=1}^S q_\phi(z_s|x)$. In addition, since the estimator is always positive, we can take logarithms, and thus obtain a stochastic lower bound on the log likelihood:

$$Ł_S(\phi, \theta|x) \triangleq \mathbb{E}_{q_\phi(z_{1:S}|x)}\left[\log\left(\frac{1}{S}\sum_{s=1}^S w_s\right)\right] = \mathbb{E}_{q_\phi(z_{1:S}|x)}[\log\hat{p}_S(z_{1:S})] \tag{10.167}$$

$$\leq \log\mathbb{E}_{q_\phi(z_{1:S}|x)}[\hat{p}_S(z_{1:S})] = \log p(x) \tag{10.168}$$

where we used Jensen's inequality in the penultimate line, and the unbiased property in the last line. This is called the **multi-sample ELBO** or **IWAE bound** [BGS16]. The gradients of this expression wrt θ and ϕ are given in Equation (10.179). If $S = 1$, $Ł_S$ reduces to the standard ELBO:

$$Ł_1(\phi, \theta|x) = \mathbb{E}_{q(z|x)}[\log w] = \int q_\phi(z|x)\log\frac{p_\theta(z, x)}{q_\phi(z|x)}dz \tag{10.169}$$

One can show [BGS16] that increasing the number of samples S is guaranteed to make the bound tighter, thus making it a better proxy for the log likelihood. Intuitively, averaging the S samples inside the log removes the need for every sample z_s to explain the data x. This encourages the proposal distribution q to be less concentrated than the single-sample variational posterior.

10.5.1.1   Pathologies of optimizing the IWAE bound

Unfortunately, increasing the number of samples in the IWAE bound can decrease the signal to noise ratio, resulting in learning a worse model [Rai+18a]. Intuitively, the reason this happens is that increasing S reduces the dependence of the bound on the quality of the inference network, which makes the gradient of the ELBO wrt ϕ less informative (higher variance).

One solution to this is to use the **doubly reparameterized gradient estimator** [TL18b]. Another approach is to use alternative estimation methods that avoid ELBO maximization, such as using the thermodynamic variational objective (see Section 10.5.2) or the reweighted wake-sleep algorithm (see Section 10.6).

10.5.2   The thermodynamic variational objective (TVO)

In [MLW19; Bre+20b], they present the **thermodynamic variational objective** or **TVO**. This is an alternative to IWAE for creating tighter variational bounds, which has certain advantages, particularly for posteriors that are not reparameterizable (e.g., discrete latent variables). The framework also has close connections with the reweighted wake-sleep algorithm from Section 10.6, as we will see in Section 10.5.3.

The TVO technique uses **thermodynamic integration**, also called **path sampling**, which is a technique used in physics and phylogenetics to approximate intractable normalization constants of high dimensional distributions (see e.g., [GM98; LP06; FP08]). This is based on the insight that it is easier to calculate the ratio of two unknown constants than to calculate the constants themselves. This is similar to the idea behind annealed importance sampling (Section 11.5.4), but TI is deterministic. For details, see [MLW19; Bre+20b].

10.5.3   Minimizing the evidence upper bound

Recall that the evidence lower bound or ELBO is given by

$$\text{Ł}(\boldsymbol{\theta}, \boldsymbol{\phi}|\boldsymbol{x}) = \log p_{\boldsymbol{\theta}}(\boldsymbol{x}) - D_{\mathbb{KL}}\left(q_{\boldsymbol{\phi}}(\boldsymbol{z}|\boldsymbol{x})) \parallel p_{\boldsymbol{\theta}}(\boldsymbol{z}|\boldsymbol{x})\right) \leq \log p_{\boldsymbol{\theta}}(\boldsymbol{x}) \tag{10.170}$$

By analogy, we can define the **evidence upper bound** or **EUBO** as follows:

$$\text{EUBO}(\boldsymbol{\theta}, \boldsymbol{\phi}|\boldsymbol{x}) = \log p_{\boldsymbol{\theta}}(\boldsymbol{x}) + D_{\mathbb{KL}}\left(p_{\boldsymbol{\theta}}(\boldsymbol{z}|\boldsymbol{x}) \parallel q_{\boldsymbol{\phi}}(\boldsymbol{z}|\boldsymbol{x})\right) \geq \log p_{\boldsymbol{\theta}}(\boldsymbol{x}) \tag{10.171}$$

Minimizing this wrt the variational parameters $\boldsymbol{\phi}$, as an alternative to maxmimizing the ELBO, was proposed in [MLW19], where they showed that it can sometimes converge to the true $\log p_{\boldsymbol{\theta}}(\boldsymbol{x})$ faster.

The above bound is for a specific input $\boldsymbol{x}$. If we sample $\boldsymbol{x}$ from the generative model, and minimize $\mathbb{E}_{p_{\boldsymbol{\theta}}(\boldsymbol{x})}\left[\text{EUBO}(\boldsymbol{\theta}, \boldsymbol{\phi}|\boldsymbol{x})\right]$ wrt $\boldsymbol{\phi}$, we recover the sleep phase of the wake-sleep algorithm (see Section 10.6.2).

Now suppose we sample $\boldsymbol{x}$ from the empirical distribution, and minimize $\mathbb{E}_{p_{\mathcal{D}}(\boldsymbol{x})}\left[\text{EUBO}(\boldsymbol{\theta}, \boldsymbol{\phi}|\boldsymbol{x})\right]$ wrt $\boldsymbol{\phi}$. To approximate the expectation, we can use self-normalized importance sampling, as in Equation (10.188), to get

$$\nabla_{\boldsymbol{\phi}}\text{EUBO}(\boldsymbol{\theta}, \boldsymbol{\phi}|\boldsymbol{x}) = \sum_{s=1}^{S} \overline{w}_s \nabla_{\boldsymbol{\phi}} \log q_{\boldsymbol{\phi}}(\boldsymbol{z}^s|\boldsymbol{x}) \tag{10.172}$$

where $\overline{w}_s = w^{(s)}/(\sum_{s'} w^{(s')})$, and $w^{(s)} = \frac{p(\boldsymbol{x}, \boldsymbol{z}^s)}{q(\boldsymbol{z}^s | \boldsymbol{\phi}_t)}$. This is equivalent to the "daydream" update (aka "wake-phase $\boldsymbol{\phi}$ update") of the wake-sleep algorithm (see Section 10.6.3).

10.6 Wake-sleep algorithm

So far in this chapter we have focused on fitting latent variable models by maximizing the ELBO. This has two main drawbacks. First, it does not work well when we have discrete latent variables, because in such cases we cannot use the reparamterization trick; thus we have to use higher variance estimators, such as REINFORCE (see Section 10.2.3). Second, even in the case where we can use the reparamterization trick, the lower bound may not be very tight. We can improve the tightness by using the IWAE multi-sample bound (Section 10.5.1), but paradoxically this may not result in learning a better model, for reasons discussed in Section 10.5.1.1.

In this section, we discuss a different way to jointly train generative and inference models, which avoids some of the problems with ELBO maximization. The method is known as the **wake-sleep algorithm** [Hin+95; BB15b; Le+19; FT19]. because it alternates between two steps: in the wake phase, we optimize the generative model parameters $\boldsymbol{\theta}$ to maximize the marginal likelihood of the observed data (we approximate $\log p_{\boldsymbol{\theta}}(\boldsymbol{x})$ by drawing importance samples from the inference network), and in the sleep phase, we optimize the inference model parameters $\boldsymbol{\phi}$ to learn to invert the generative model by training the inference network on labeled $(\boldsymbol{x}, \boldsymbol{z})$ pairs, where $\boldsymbol{x}$ are samples generated by the current model parameters. This can be viewed as a form of **adaptive importance sampling**, which iteratively improves its proposal, while simultaneously optimizing the model. We give further details below.

10.6.1 Wake phase

In the **wake phase**, we minimize the KL divergence from the empirical distribution to the model's distribution:

$$\mathcal{L}(\boldsymbol{\theta}) = D_{\mathrm{KL}}\left(p_{\mathcal{D}}(\boldsymbol{x}) \parallel p_{\boldsymbol{\theta}}(\boldsymbol{x})\right) = \mathbb{E}_{p_{\mathcal{D}}(\boldsymbol{x})}\left[-\log p_{\boldsymbol{\theta}}(\boldsymbol{x})\right] + \text{const} \tag{10.173}$$

where $p_{\boldsymbol{\theta}}(\boldsymbol{x}) = \int p_{\boldsymbol{\theta}}(\boldsymbol{z}) p_{\boldsymbol{\theta}}(\boldsymbol{x}|\boldsymbol{z}) d\boldsymbol{z}$. This is equivalent to maximizing the likelihood of the observed data:

$$\ell(\boldsymbol{\theta}) = \mathbb{E}_{p_{\mathcal{D}}(\boldsymbol{x})}\left[\log p_{\boldsymbol{\theta}}(\boldsymbol{x})\right] \tag{10.174}$$

Since the log marginal likelihood $\log p_{\boldsymbol{\theta}}(\boldsymbol{x})$ cannot be computed exactly, we will approximate it. In the original wake-sleep paper, they proposed to use the ELBO lower bound. In the **reweighted wake-sleep** (RWS) algorithm of [BB15b; Le+19], they propose to use the IWAE bound from Section 10.5.1 instead. In particular, if we draw S samples from the inference network, $\boldsymbol{z}_s \sim q_{\boldsymbol{\phi}}(\boldsymbol{z}|\boldsymbol{x})$, we get the following estimator:

$$\ell(\boldsymbol{\theta}|\boldsymbol{\phi}, \boldsymbol{x}) = \log\left(\frac{1}{S}\sum_{s=1}^{S} w_s\right) \tag{10.175}$$

where $w_s = \frac{p_{\boldsymbol{\theta}}(\boldsymbol{x}, \boldsymbol{z}_s)}{q_{\boldsymbol{\phi}}(\boldsymbol{z}_s|\boldsymbol{x})}$. Note that this is the same as the IWAE bound in Equation (10.168).

We now discuss how to compute the gradient of this objective wrt $\boldsymbol{\theta}$ or $\boldsymbol{\phi}$. Using the log-derivative trick, we have that

$$\nabla \log w_s = \frac{1}{w_s} \nabla w_s \tag{10.176}$$

Hence

$$\nabla \ell(\boldsymbol{\theta}|\boldsymbol{\phi}, \boldsymbol{x}) = \frac{1}{\frac{1}{S} \sum_{s=1}^{S} w_s} \left(\frac{1}{S} \sum_{s=1}^{S} \nabla w_s \right) \tag{10.177}$$

$$= \frac{1}{\sum_{s=1}^{S} w_s} \left(\sum_{s=1}^{S} w_s \nabla \log w_s \right) \tag{10.178}$$

$$= \sum_{s=1}^{S} \overline{w}_s \nabla \log w_s \tag{10.179}$$

where $\overline{w}_s = w_s / (\sum_{s'=1}^{S} w_{s'})$.

In the case of the derivatives wrt $\boldsymbol{\theta}$, we have

$$\nabla_{\boldsymbol{\theta}} \log w_s = \frac{1}{w_s} \nabla_{\boldsymbol{\theta}} w_s = \frac{q_{\boldsymbol{\phi}}(\boldsymbol{z}_s|\boldsymbol{x})}{p_{\boldsymbol{\theta}}(\boldsymbol{x}, \boldsymbol{z}_s)} \nabla_{\boldsymbol{\theta}} \frac{p_{\boldsymbol{\theta}}(\boldsymbol{x}, \boldsymbol{z}_s)}{q_{\boldsymbol{\phi}}(\boldsymbol{z}_s|\boldsymbol{x})} = \frac{1}{p_{\boldsymbol{\theta}}(\boldsymbol{x}, \boldsymbol{z}_s)} \nabla_{\boldsymbol{\theta}} p_{\boldsymbol{\theta}}(\boldsymbol{x}, \boldsymbol{z}_s) = \nabla_{\boldsymbol{\theta}} \log p_{\boldsymbol{\theta}}(\boldsymbol{x}, \boldsymbol{z}_s) \tag{10.180}$$

and hence we get

$$\nabla_{\boldsymbol{\theta}} \ell(\boldsymbol{\theta}|\boldsymbol{\phi}, \boldsymbol{x}) \sum_{s=1}^{S} \overline{w}_s \nabla \log p_{\boldsymbol{\theta}}(\boldsymbol{x}, \boldsymbol{z}_s) \tag{10.181}$$

10.6.2   Sleep phase

In the **sleep phase**, we try to minimize the KL divergence between the true posterior (under the current model) and the inference network's approximation to that posterior:

$$\mathcal{L}(\boldsymbol{\phi}) = \mathbb{E}_{p_{\boldsymbol{\theta}}(\boldsymbol{x})} \left[D_{\mathrm{KL}} \left(p_{\boldsymbol{\theta}}(\boldsymbol{z}|\boldsymbol{x}) \,\|\, q_{\boldsymbol{\phi}}(\boldsymbol{z}|\boldsymbol{x}) \right) \right] = \mathbb{E}_{p_{\boldsymbol{\theta}}(\boldsymbol{z}, \boldsymbol{x})} \left[-\log q_{\boldsymbol{\phi}}(\boldsymbol{z}|\boldsymbol{x}) \right] + \text{const} \tag{10.182}$$

Equivalently, we can maximize the following log likelihood objective:

$$\ell(\boldsymbol{\phi}|\boldsymbol{\theta}) = \mathbb{E}_{(\boldsymbol{z}, \boldsymbol{x}) \sim p_{\boldsymbol{\theta}}(\boldsymbol{z}, \boldsymbol{x})} \left[\log q_{\boldsymbol{\phi}}(\boldsymbol{z}|\boldsymbol{x}) \right] \tag{10.183}$$

where $p_{\boldsymbol{\theta}}(\boldsymbol{z}, \boldsymbol{x}) = p_{\boldsymbol{\theta}}(\boldsymbol{z}) p_{\boldsymbol{\theta}}(\boldsymbol{x}|\boldsymbol{z})$. We see that the sleep phase amounts to maximum likelihood training of the inference network based on samples from the generative model. These "fantasy samples", created while the network "dreams", can be easily generated using ancestral sampling (Section 4.2.5). If we use S such samples, the objective becomes

$$\ell(\boldsymbol{\phi}|\boldsymbol{\theta}) = \frac{1}{S} \sum_{s=1}^{S} \log q_{\boldsymbol{\phi}}(\boldsymbol{z}'_s|\boldsymbol{x}'_s) \tag{10.184}$$

where $(\boldsymbol{z}'_s, \boldsymbol{x}'_s) \sim p_{\boldsymbol{\theta}}(\boldsymbol{z}, \boldsymbol{x})$. The gradient of this is given by

$$\nabla_{\boldsymbol{\phi}} \ell(\boldsymbol{\phi}|\boldsymbol{\theta}) = \frac{1}{S} \sum_{s=1}^{S} \nabla_{\boldsymbol{\phi}} \log q_{\boldsymbol{\phi}}(\boldsymbol{z}'_s|\boldsymbol{x}'_s) \tag{10.185}$$

We do not require $q_{\boldsymbol{\phi}}(\boldsymbol{z}'|\boldsymbol{x})$ to be reparameterizable, since the samples are drawn from a distribution that is independent of $\boldsymbol{\phi}$. This means it is easy to apply this method to models with discrete latent variables.

10.6.3 Daydream phase

The disadvantage of the sleep phase is that the inference network, $q_{\boldsymbol{\phi}}(\boldsymbol{z}|\boldsymbol{x})$, is trying to follow a moving target, $p_{\boldsymbol{\theta}}(\boldsymbol{z}|\boldsymbol{x})$. Furthermore, it is only being trained on synthetic data from the model, not on real data. The reweighted wake-sleep algorithm of [BB15b] proposed to learn the inference network by using real data from the empirical distribution, in addition to fantasy data. They call the case where you use real data the "**wake-phase** q **update**", but we will call it the "**daydream phase**", since, unlike sleeping, the system uses real data $\boldsymbol{x}$ to update the inference model, instead of fantasies.[1] [Le+19] went further, and proposed to only use the wake and daydream phases, and to skip the sleep phase entirely.

In more detail, the new objective which we want to minimize becomes

$$\mathcal{L}(\boldsymbol{\phi}|\boldsymbol{\theta}) = \mathbb{E}_{p_{\mathcal{D}}(\boldsymbol{x})} \left[D_{\mathrm{KL}} \left(p_{\boldsymbol{\theta}}(\boldsymbol{z}|\boldsymbol{x}) \,\|\, q_{\boldsymbol{\phi}}(\boldsymbol{z}|\boldsymbol{x}) \right) \right] \tag{10.186}$$

We can compute a single sample approximation to the negative of the above expression as follows:

$$\ell(\boldsymbol{\phi}|\boldsymbol{\theta}, \boldsymbol{x}) = \mathbb{E}_{p_{\boldsymbol{\theta}}(\boldsymbol{z}|\boldsymbol{x})} \left[\log q_{\boldsymbol{\phi}}(\boldsymbol{z}|\boldsymbol{x}) \right] \tag{10.187}$$

where $\boldsymbol{x} \sim p_{\mathcal{D}}$. We can approximate this expectation using importance sampling, with $q_{\boldsymbol{\phi}}$ as the proposal. This results in the following estimator of the gradient for each datapoint:

$$\nabla_{\boldsymbol{\phi}} \ell(\boldsymbol{\phi}|\boldsymbol{\theta}, \boldsymbol{x}) = \int p_{\boldsymbol{\theta}}(\boldsymbol{z}|\boldsymbol{x}) \nabla_{\boldsymbol{\phi}} \log q_{\boldsymbol{\phi}}(\boldsymbol{z}|\boldsymbol{x}) d\boldsymbol{z} \approx \sum_{s=1}^{S} \overline{w}_s \nabla_{\boldsymbol{\phi}} \log q_{\boldsymbol{\phi}}(\boldsymbol{z}_s|\boldsymbol{x}) \tag{10.188}$$

where $\boldsymbol{z}_s \sim q_{\boldsymbol{\phi}}(\boldsymbol{z}_s|\boldsymbol{x})$ and $\overline{w}_s$ are the normalized weights.

We see that Equation (10.188) is very similar to Equation (10.185). The key difference is that in the daydream phase, we sample from $(\boldsymbol{x}, \boldsymbol{z}_s) \sim p_{\mathcal{D}}(\boldsymbol{x}) q_{\boldsymbol{\phi}}(\boldsymbol{z}|\boldsymbol{x})$, where $\boldsymbol{x}$ is a real datapoint, whereas in the sleep phase, we sample from $(\boldsymbol{x}'_s, \boldsymbol{z}'_s) \sim p_{\boldsymbol{\theta}}(\boldsymbol{z}, \boldsymbol{x})$, where $\boldsymbol{x}'_s$ is generated datapoint.

10.6.4 Summary of algorithm

We summarize the RWS algorithm in Algorithm 10.5. The disadvantage of the RWS algorithm is that it does not optimize a single well-defined objective, so it is not clear if the method will converge, in contrast to ELBO maximization. On the other hand, the method is fairly simple, since it consists of two alternating weighted maximum likelihood problems. It can also be shown to "sandwich" a

---

1. We thank Rif A. Saurous for suggesting this term.

Algorithm 10.5: One SGD update using wake-sleep algorithm.

---

1 Sample $\boldsymbol{x}_n$ from dataset
2 Draw S samples from inference network: $\boldsymbol{z}_s \sim q(\boldsymbol{z}|\boldsymbol{x}_n)$
3 Compute unnormalized weights: $w_s = \frac{p(\boldsymbol{x}_n, \boldsymbol{z}_s)}{q(\boldsymbol{z}_s|\boldsymbol{x}_n)}$
4 Compute normalized weights: $\overline{w}_s = \frac{w_s}{\sum_{s'=1}^{S} w_{s'}}$
5 Optional: Compute estimate of log likelihood: $\log p(\boldsymbol{x}_n) = \log(\frac{1}{S}\sum_{s=1}^{S} w_s)$
6 Wake phase: Update $\boldsymbol{\theta}$ using $\sum_{s=1}^{S} \overline{w}_s \nabla_{\boldsymbol{\theta}} \log p_{\boldsymbol{\theta}}(\boldsymbol{z}_s, \boldsymbol{x}_n)$
7 Daydream phase: Update $\boldsymbol{\phi}$ using $\sum_{s=1}^{S} \overline{w}_s \nabla_{\boldsymbol{\phi}} \log q_{\boldsymbol{\phi}}(\boldsymbol{z}_s|\boldsymbol{x}_n)$
8 Optional sleep phase: Draw S samples from model, $(\boldsymbol{x}'_s, \boldsymbol{z}'_s) \sim p_{\boldsymbol{\theta}}(\boldsymbol{x}, \boldsymbol{z})$ and update $\boldsymbol{\phi}$ using
   $\frac{1}{S}\sum_{s=1}^{S} \nabla_{\boldsymbol{\phi}} \log q_{\boldsymbol{\phi}}(\boldsymbol{z}'_s|\boldsymbol{x}'_s)$
9 b

---

lower and upper bound of the log marginal likelihood. We can think of this in terms of the two joint distributions $p_{\boldsymbol{\theta}}(\boldsymbol{x}, \boldsymbol{z}) = p_{\boldsymbol{\theta}}(\boldsymbol{z})p_{\boldsymbol{\theta}}(\boldsymbol{x}|\boldsymbol{z})$ and $q_{\mathcal{D},\boldsymbol{\phi}}(\boldsymbol{x}, \boldsymbol{z}) = p_{\mathcal{D}}(\boldsymbol{x})q_{\boldsymbol{\phi}}(\boldsymbol{z}|\boldsymbol{x})$:

$$\text{wake phase } \min_{\boldsymbol{\theta}} D_{\mathbb{KL}}\left(q_{\mathcal{D},\boldsymbol{\phi}}(\boldsymbol{x}, \boldsymbol{z}) \parallel p_{\boldsymbol{\theta}}(\boldsymbol{x}, \boldsymbol{z})\right) \tag{10.189}$$

$$\text{daydream phase } \min_{\boldsymbol{\phi}} D_{\mathbb{KL}}\left(p_{\boldsymbol{\theta}}(\boldsymbol{x}, \boldsymbol{z}) \parallel q_{\mathcal{D},\boldsymbol{\phi}}(\boldsymbol{x}, \boldsymbol{z})\right) \tag{10.190}$$

10.7   Expectation propagation (EP)

One problem with lower bound maximization (i.e., standard VI) is that we are minimizing $D_{\mathbb{KL}}(q \parallel p)$, which induces **zero-forcing** behavior, as we discussed in Section 5.1.4.1. This means that $q(\boldsymbol{z}|\boldsymbol{x})$ tends to be too compact (over-confident), to avoid the situation in which $q(\boldsymbol{z}|\boldsymbol{x}) > 0$ but $p(\boldsymbol{z}|\boldsymbol{x}) = 0$, which would incur infinite KL penalty.

Although zero-forcing can be desirable behavior for some multi-modal posteriors (e.g., mixture models), it is not so reasonable for many unimodal posteriors (e.g., Bayesian logistic regression, or GPs with log-concave likelihoods). One way to avoid this problem is to minimize $D_{\mathbb{KL}}(p \parallel q)$, which is zero-avoiding, as we discussed in Section 5.1.4.1. This tends to result in broad posteriors, which avoids overconfidence. In this section, we discuss **expectation propagation** or **EP** [Min01b], which can be seen as a local approximation to $D_{\mathbb{KL}}(p \parallel q)$.

10.7.1   Algorithm

We assume the exact posterior can be written as follows:

$$p(\boldsymbol{\theta}|\mathcal{D}) = \frac{1}{Z_p}\hat{p}(\boldsymbol{\theta}), \quad \hat{p}(\boldsymbol{\theta}) = p_0(\boldsymbol{\theta})\prod_{k=1}^{K} f_k(\boldsymbol{\theta}) \tag{10.191}$$

where $\hat{p}(\boldsymbol{\theta})$ is the unnormalized posterior, p_0 is the prior, f_k corresponds to the k'th likelihood term or **local factor** (also called a **site potential**). Here $Z_p = p(\mathcal{D})Z_0$ is the normalization constant for the posterior, where Z_0 is the normalization constant for the prior. To simplify notation, we let $f_0(\boldsymbol{\theta}) = p_0(\boldsymbol{\theta})$ be the prior.

We will approximate the posterior as follows:

$$q(\boldsymbol{\theta}) = \frac{1}{Z_q}\hat{q}(\boldsymbol{\theta}), \quad \hat{q}(\boldsymbol{\theta}) = p_0(\boldsymbol{\theta})\prod_{k=1}^{K}\tilde{f}_k(\boldsymbol{\theta}) \tag{10.192}$$

where $\tilde{f}_k \in \mathcal{Q}$ is the approximate local factor, and $\mathcal{Q}$ is some tractable family in the exponential family, usually a Gaussian [Gel+14b].

We will optimize each $\tilde{f}_i$ in turn, keeping the others fixed. We initialize each $\tilde{f}_i$ using an uninformative distribution from the family $\mathcal{Q}$. so $q(\boldsymbol{\theta}) = p_0(\boldsymbol{\theta})$.

To compute the new local factor $\tilde{f}_i^{\text{new}}$, we proceed as follows. First we compute the **cavity distribution** by deleting the $\tilde{f}_i$ from the approximate posterior by dividing it out:

$$q_{-i}^{\text{cavity}}(\boldsymbol{\theta}) = \frac{q(\boldsymbol{\theta})}{\tilde{f}_i(\boldsymbol{\theta})} \propto \prod_{k \neq i}\tilde{f}_k(\boldsymbol{\theta}) \tag{10.193}$$

This division operation can be implemented by subtracting the natural parameters, as explained in Section 2.3.3.2. The cavity distribution represents the effect of all the factors except for f_i (which is approximated by $\tilde{f}_i$).

Next we (conceptually) compute the **tilted distribution** by multiplying the exact factor f_i onto the cavity distribution:

$$q_i^{\text{tilted}}(\boldsymbol{\theta}) = \frac{1}{Z_i}f_i(\boldsymbol{\theta})q_{-i}^{\text{cavity}}(\boldsymbol{\theta}) \tag{10.194}$$

where $Z_i = \int q_{-i}^{\text{cavity}}(\boldsymbol{\theta})f_i(\boldsymbol{\theta})d\boldsymbol{\theta}$ is the normalization constant for the tilted distribution. This is the result of combining the current approximation, excluding factor i, with the exact f_i term.

Unfortunately, the resulting tilted distribution may be outside of our model family (e.g., if we combine a Gaussian prior with a non-Gaussian likelihood). So we will approximate the tilted distribution as follows:

$$q_i^{\text{proj}}(\boldsymbol{\theta}) = \text{proj}(q_i^{\text{tilted}}) \triangleq \underset{\tilde{q} \in \mathcal{Q}}{\text{argmin}}\, D(q_i^{\text{tilted}}||\tilde{q}) \tag{10.195}$$

This can be thought of as projecting the tilted distribution into the approximation family. If $D(q_i^{\text{tilted}}||q) = D_{\text{KL}}\left(q_i^{\text{tilted}} \| q\right)$, this can be done by moment matching, as shown in Section 5.1.4.2. For example, suppose the cavity distribution is Gaussian, $q_{-i}^{\text{cavity}}(\boldsymbol{\theta}) = \mathcal{N}_c(\boldsymbol{\theta}|\boldsymbol{r}_{-i}, \mathbf{Q}_{-i})$, using the canonical parameterization. Then the log of the tilted distribution is given by

$$\log q_i^{\text{tilted}}(\boldsymbol{\theta}) = \alpha \log f_i(\boldsymbol{\theta}) - \frac{1}{2}\boldsymbol{\theta}^{\mathsf{T}}\mathbf{Q}_{-i}\boldsymbol{\theta} + \boldsymbol{r}_{-i}^{\mathsf{T}}\boldsymbol{\theta} + \text{const} \tag{10.196}$$

Let $\hat{\boldsymbol{\theta}}$ be a local maximum of this objective. If $\mathcal{Q}$ is the set of Gaussians, we can compute the projected tilted distribution as a Gaussian with the following parameters:

$$\mathbf{Q}_{\backslash i} = -\nabla_{\boldsymbol{\theta}}^2 \log q_i^{\text{tilted}}(\boldsymbol{\theta})|_{\boldsymbol{\theta}=\hat{\boldsymbol{\theta}}}, \quad \boldsymbol{r}_{\backslash i} = \mathbf{Q}_{\backslash i}\hat{\boldsymbol{\theta}} \tag{10.197}$$

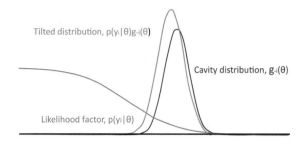

Figure 10.15: Combining a logistic likelihood factor $f_i = p(y_i|\boldsymbol{\theta})$ with the cavity prior, $q_{-i}^{cavity} = g_{-i}(\boldsymbol{\theta})$, to get the tilted distribution, $q_i^{tilted} = p(y_i|\boldsymbol{\theta})g_{-i}(\boldsymbol{\theta})$. Adapted from Figure 2 of [Gel+14b].

This is called **Laplace propagation** [SVE04]. For more general distributions, we can use Monte Carlo approximations; this is known as **blackbox EP** [HL+16a; Li+18c].

Finally, we compute a local factor that, if combined with the cavity distribution, would give the same results as this projected distribution:

$$\tilde{f}_i^{\mathrm{new}}(\boldsymbol{\theta}) = \frac{q_i^{\mathrm{proj}}(\boldsymbol{\theta})}{q_{-i}^{\mathrm{cavity}}(\boldsymbol{\theta})} \tag{10.198}$$

We see that $q_{-i}^{\mathrm{cavity}}(\boldsymbol{\theta})\tilde{f}_i^{\mathrm{new}}(\boldsymbol{\theta}) = q_i^{\mathrm{proj}}(\boldsymbol{\theta})$, so combining this approximate factor with the cavity distribution results in a distribution which is the best possible approximation (within $\mathcal{Q}$) to the results of using the exact factor.

10.7.2   Example

Figure 10.15 illustrates the process of combining a very non-Gaussian likelihood f_i with a Gaussian cavity prior q_{-i}^{cavity} to yield a nearly Gaussian tilted distribution q_i^{tilted}, which can then be approximated by a Gaussian using projection.

Thus instead of trying to "Gaussianize" each likelihood term f_i in isolation (as is done, e.g., in EKF), we try to find the best local factor $\tilde{f}_i$ (within some family) that achieves approximately the same effect, when combined with all the other terms (represented by the cavity distribution, q_{-i}), as using the exact factor f_i. That is, we choose a local factor that works well in the context of all the other factors.

10.7.3   EP as generalized ADF

We can view EP as a generalization of the ADF algorithm discussed in Section 8.6. ADF is a form of sequential Bayesian inference. At each step, it maintains a tractable approximation to the posterior, $q_t(\boldsymbol{z}) \in \mathcal{Q}$, updates it with the likelihood from the next observation, $\hat{p}_{t+1}(\boldsymbol{z}) \propto q_t(\boldsymbol{z})p(\boldsymbol{x}_t|\boldsymbol{z})$, and then projects the resulting updated posterior back to the tractable family using $q_{t+1} = \mathrm{argmin}_{q \in \mathcal{Q}} D_{\mathrm{KL}}(\hat{p}_{t+1} \| q)$. ADF minimizes KL in the desired direction. However, it is a sequential algorithm, designed for the online setting. In the batch setting, the method can given different results depending on the order in which the updates are performed. In addition, if we perform multiple passes over the data, we will include the same likelihood terms multiple times, resulting in an overconfident posterior. EP overcomes this problem.

10.7.4 Optimization issues

In practice, EP can be numerically unstable. For example, if we use Gaussians as our local factors, we might end up with negative variance when we subtract the natural parameters. To reduce the chance of this, it is common to use damping, in which we perform a partial update of each factor with a step size of δ. More precisely, we change the final step to be the following:

$$\tilde{f}_i^{\text{new}}(\boldsymbol{\theta}) = \left(\tilde{f}_i(\boldsymbol{\theta})\right)^{1-\delta} \left(\frac{q_i^{\text{proj}}(\boldsymbol{\theta})}{q_{-i}^{\text{cavity}}}\right)^{\delta} \tag{10.199}$$

This can be implemented by scaling the natural parameters by δ. [ML02] suggest $\delta = 1/K$ as a safe strategy (where K is the number of factors), but this results in very slow convergence. [Gel+14b] suggest starting with $\delta = 0.5$, and then reducing to $\delta = 1/K$ over K iterations.

In addition to numerical stability, there is no guarantee that EP will converge in its vanilla form, although empirically it can work well, especially with log-concave factors f_i (e.g., as in GP classifiers).

10.7.5 Power EP and α-divergence

We also have a choice about what divergence measure $D(q_i^{\text{tilted}}||q)$ to use when we approximate the tilted distribution. If we use $D_{\mathbb{KL}}\left(q_i^{\text{tilted}} \parallel q\right)$, we recover classic EP, as described above. If we use $D_{\mathbb{KL}}\left(q \parallel q_i^{\text{tilted}}\right)$, we recover the reverse KL used in standard variational inference. We can generalize the above results by using α-divergences (Section 2.7.1.2), which allow us to interpolate between mode seeking and mode covering behavior, as shown in Figure 2.20. We can optimize the α-divergence by using the **power EP** method of [Min04].

Algorithmically, this is a fairly small modification to regular EP. In particular, we first compute the cavity distribution, $q_{-i}^{\text{cavity}} \propto \frac{q}{f_i^{\alpha}}$; we then approximate the tilted distribution, $q_i^{\text{proj}} = \text{proj}(q_{-i}^{\text{cavity}} f_i^{\alpha})$; and finally we compute the new factor $\tilde{f}_i^{\text{new}} \propto \left(\frac{q_i^{\text{proj}}}{q_{-i}^{\text{cavity}}}\right)^{1/\alpha}$.

10.7.6 Stochastic EP

The main disadvantage of EP in the big data setting is that we need to store the $\tilde{f}_n(\boldsymbol{\theta})$ terms for each datapoint n, so we can compute the cavity distribution. If $\boldsymbol{\theta}$ has D dimensions, and we use full covariance Gaussians, this requires $O(ND^2)$ memory.

The idea behind **stochastic EP** [LHLT15] is to approximate the local factors with a shared factor that acts like an aggregated likelihood, i.e.,

$$\prod_{n=1}^{N} f_n(\boldsymbol{\theta}) \approx \tilde{f}(\boldsymbol{\theta})^N \tag{10.200}$$

where typically $f_n(\boldsymbol{\theta}) = p(\boldsymbol{x}_n|\boldsymbol{\theta})$. This exploits the fact that the posterior only cares about approximating the product of the likelihoods, rather than each likelihood separately. Hence it suffices for $\tilde{f}(\boldsymbol{\theta})$ to approximate the average likelihood.

We can modify EP to this setting as follows. First, when computing the cavity distribution, we use

$$q_{-1}(\boldsymbol{\theta}) \propto q(\boldsymbol{\theta})/\tilde{f}(\boldsymbol{\theta}) \tag{10.201}$$

We then compute the tilted distribution

$$q_{\backslash n}(\boldsymbol{\theta}) \propto f_n(\boldsymbol{\theta})q_{-1}(\boldsymbol{\theta}) \tag{10.202}$$

Next we derive the new local factor for this datapoint using moment matching:

$$\tilde{f}_n(\boldsymbol{\theta}) = \mathrm{proj}(q_{\backslash n}(\boldsymbol{\theta}))/q_{-1}(\boldsymbol{\theta}) \tag{10.203}$$

Finally, we perform a damped update of the average likelihood $\tilde{f}(\boldsymbol{\theta})$ using this new local factor:

$$\tilde{f}_{\mathrm{new}}(\boldsymbol{\theta}) = \tilde{f}_{\mathrm{old}}(\boldsymbol{\theta})^{1-1/N}\tilde{f}_n(\boldsymbol{\theta})^{1/N} \tag{10.204}$$

The ADF algorithm is similar to SEP, in that we compute the tilted distribution $q_{\backslash t} \propto f_t q_{t-1}$ and then project it, without needing to keep the f_t factors. The difference is that instead of using the cavity distribution $q_{-1}(\boldsymbol{\theta})$ as a prior, it uses the posterior from the previous time step, q_{t-1}. This avoids the need to compute and store $\tilde{f}$, but results in overconfidence in the batch setting.

11 Monte Carlo methods

11.1 Introduction

In this chapter, we discuss **Monte Carlo methods**, which are a stochastic approach to solving numerical integration problems. The name refers to the "Monte Carlo" casino in Monaco; this was used as a codename by von Neumann and Ulam, who invented the technique while working on the atomic bomb during WWII. Since then, the technique has become widely adopted in physics, statistics, machine learning, and many areas of science and engineering.

In this chapter, we give a brief introduction to some key concepts. In Chapter 12, we discuss MCMC, which is the most widely used MC method for high-dimensional problems. In Chapter 13, we discuss SMC, which is widely used for MC inference in state space models, but can also be applied more generally. For more details on MC methods, see e.g., [Liu01; RC04; KTB11; BZ20].

11.2 Monte Carlo integration

We often want to compute the expected value of some function of a random variable, $\mathbb{E}[f(\mathbf{X})]$. This requires computing the following integral:

$$\mathbb{E}[f(\boldsymbol{x})] = \int f(\boldsymbol{x})p(\boldsymbol{x})d\boldsymbol{x} \tag{11.1}$$

where $\boldsymbol{x} \in \mathbb{R}^n$, $f : \mathbb{R}^n \to \mathbb{R}^m$, and $p(\boldsymbol{x})$ is the target distribution of $\mathbf{X}$.[1] In low dimensions (up to, say, 3), we can compute the above integral efficiently using **numerical integration**, which (adaptively) computes a grid, and then evaluates the function at each point on the grid.[2] But this does not scale to higher dimensions.

An alternative approach is to draw multiple random samples, $\boldsymbol{x}_n \sim p(\boldsymbol{x})$, and then to compute

$$\mathbb{E}[f(\boldsymbol{x})] \approx \frac{1}{N_s} \sum_{n=1}^{N_s} f(\boldsymbol{x}_n) \tag{11.2}$$

This is called **Monte Carlo integration**. It has the advantage over numerical integration that the function is only evaluated in places where there is non-negligible probability, so it does not

---

1. In many cases, the target distribution may be the posterior $p(\boldsymbol{x}|\boldsymbol{y})$, which can be hard to compute; in such problems, we often work with the unnormalized distribution, $\tilde{p}(\boldsymbol{x}) = p(\boldsymbol{x}, \boldsymbol{y})$, instead, and then normalize the results using $Z = \int p(\boldsymbol{x}, \boldsymbol{y})d\boldsymbol{x} = p(\boldsymbol{y})$.
2. In 1d, numerical integration is called **quadrature**; in higher dimensions, it is called **cubature** [Sar13].

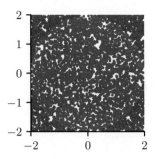

Figure 11.1: Estimating π by Monte Carlo integration using 5000 samples. Blue points are inside the circle, red points are outside. Generated by mc_estimate_pi.ipynb.

need to uniformly cover the entire space. In particular, it can be shown that the accuracy is in principle independent of the dimensionality of $\boldsymbol{x}$, and only depends on the number of samples N_s (see Section 11.2.2 for details). The catch is that we need a way to generate the samples $\boldsymbol{x}_n \sim p(\boldsymbol{x})$ in the first place. In addition, the estimator may have high variance. We will discuss this topic at length in the sections below.

11.2.1   Example: estimating π by Monte Carlo integration

MC integration can be used for many applications, not just in ML and statistics. For example, suppose we want to estimate π. We know that the area of a circle with radius r is πr^2, but it is also equal to the following definite integral:

$$I = \int_{-r}^{r} \int_{-r}^{r} \mathbb{I}\left(x^2 + y^2 \leq r^2\right) dx dy \tag{11.3}$$

Hence $\pi = I/(r^2)$. Let us approximate this by Monte Carlo integration. Let $f(x,y) = \mathbb{I}\left(x^2 + y^2 \leq r^2\right)$ be an indicator function that is 1 for points inside the circle, and 0 outside, and let $p(x)$ and $p(y)$ be uniform distributions on $[-r, r]$, so $p(x) = p(y) = 1/(2r)$. Then

$$I = (2r)(2r) \int \int f(x,y)p(x)p(y)dx dy \tag{11.4}$$

$$= 4r^2 \int \int f(x,y)p(x)p(y)dx dy \tag{11.5}$$

$$\approx 4r^2 \frac{1}{N_s} \sum_{n=1}^{N_s} f(x_n, y_n) \tag{11.6}$$

Using 5000 samples, we find $\hat{\pi} = 3.10$ with standard error 0.09 compared to the true value of $\pi = 3.14$. We can plot the points that are accepted or rejected as in Figure 11.1.

11.2.2   Accuracy of Monte Carlo integration

The accuracy of an MC approximation increases with sample size. This is illustrated in Figure 11.2. On the top line, we plot a histogram of samples from a Gaussian distribution. On the bottom line,

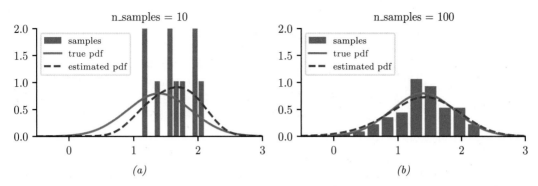

Figure 11.2: *10 and 100 samples from a Gaussian distribution, $\mathcal{N}(\mu = 1.5, \sigma^2 = 0.25)$. A dotted red line denotes kernel density estimate derived from the samples. Generated by* mc_accuracy_demo.ipynb.

we plot a smoothed version of these samples, created using a kernel density estimate. This smoothed distribution is then evaluated on a dense grid of points and plotted. Note that this smoothing is just for the purposes of plotting, it is not used for the Monte Carlo estimate itself.

If we denote the exact mean by $\mu = \mathbb{E}[f(X)]$, and the MC approximation by $\hat{\mu}$, one can show that, with independent samples,

$$(\hat{\mu} - \mu) \rightarrow \mathcal{N}(0, \frac{\sigma^2}{N_s}) \tag{11.7}$$

where

$$\sigma^2 = \mathbb{V}[f(X)] = \mathbb{E}[f(X)^2] - \mathbb{E}[f(X)]^2 \tag{11.8}$$

This is a consequence of the central limit theorem. Of course, σ^2 is unknown in the above expression, but it can be estimated by MC:

$$\hat{\sigma}^2 = \frac{1}{N_s} \sum_{n=1}^{N_s} (f(x_n) - \hat{\mu})^2 \tag{11.9}$$

Thus for large enough N_s we have

$$P\left\{ \hat{\mu} - 1.96 \frac{\hat{\sigma}}{\sqrt{N_s}} \leq \mu \leq \hat{\mu} + 1.96 \frac{\hat{\sigma}}{\sqrt{N_s}} \right\} \approx 0.95 \tag{11.10}$$

The term $\sqrt{\frac{\hat{\sigma}^2}{N_s}}$ is called the (numerical or empirical) **standard error**, and is an estimate of our uncertainty about our estimate of μ.

If we want to report an answer which is accurate to within $\pm\epsilon$ with probability at least 95%, we need to use a number of samples N_s which satisfies $1.96\sqrt{\hat{\sigma}^2/N_s} \leq \epsilon$. We can approximate the 1.96 factor by 2, yielding $N_s \geq \frac{4\hat{\sigma}^2}{\epsilon^2}$.

The remarkable thing to note about the above results is that the error in the estimate, σ^2/N_s, is theoretically independent of the dimensionality of the integral. The catch is that sampling from high dimensional distributions can be hard. We turn to that topic next.

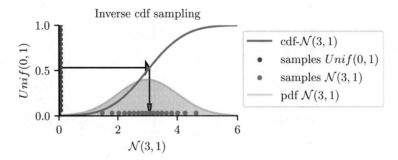

Figure 11.3: Sampling from $\mathcal{N}(3,1)$ using an inverse cdf.

11.3   Generating random samples from simple distributions

We saw in Section 11.2 how we can evaluate $\mathbb{E}\left[f(X)\right]$ for different functions f of a random variable X using Monte Carlo integration. The main computational challenge is to efficiently generate samples from the probability distribution $p^*(\boldsymbol{x})$ (which may be a posterior, $p^*(\boldsymbol{x}) \propto p(\boldsymbol{x}|\mathcal{D})$). In this section, we discuss sampling methods that are suitable for parametric univariate distributions. These can be used as building blocks for sampling from more complex multivariate distributions.

11.3.1   Sampling using the inverse cdf

The simplest method for sampling from a univariate distribution is based on the **inverse probability transform**. Let F be a cdf of some distribution we want to sample from, and let F^{-1} be its inverse. Then we have the following result.

Theorem 11.3.1. *If $U \sim U(0,1)$ is a uniform rv, then $F^{-1}(U) \sim F$.*

Proof.

$$\Pr(F^{-1}(U) \le x) = \Pr(U \le F(x)) \quad \text{(applying } F \text{ to both sides)} \tag{11.11}$$

$$= F(x) \quad \text{(because } \Pr(U \le y) = y\text{)} \tag{11.12}$$

where the first line follows since F is a monotonic function, and the second line follows since U is uniform on the unit interval. $\square$

Hence we can sample from any univariate distribution, for which we can evaluate its inverse cdf, as follows: generate a random number $u \sim U(0,1)$ using a **pseudorandom number generator** (see e.g., [Pre+88] for details). Let u represent the height up the y axis. Then "slide along" the x axis until you intersect the F curve, and then "drop down" and return the corresponding x value. This corresponds to computing $x = F^{-1}(u)$. See Figure 11.3 for an illustration.

For example, consider the exponential distribution

$$\text{Expon}(x|\lambda) \triangleq \lambda e^{-\lambda x} \, \mathbb{I}\,(x \ge 0) \tag{11.13}$$

The cdf is

$$F(x) = 1 - e^{-\lambda x} \, \mathbb{I}\,(x \ge 0) \tag{11.14}$$

whose inverse is the quantile function

$$F^{-1}(p) = -\frac{\ln(1-p)}{\lambda} \tag{11.15}$$

By the above theorem, if $U \sim \text{Unif}(0,1)$, we know that $F^{-1}(U) \sim \text{Expon}(\lambda)$. So we can sample from the exponential distribution by first sampling from the uniform and then transforming the results using $-\ln(1-u)/\lambda$. (In fact, since $1 - U \sim \text{Unif}(0,1)$, we can just use $-\ln(u)/\lambda$.)

11.3.2 Sampling from a Gaussian (Box-Muller method)

In this section, we describe a method to sample from a Gaussian. The idea is we sample uniformly from a unit radius circle, and then use the change of variables formula to derive samples from a spherical 2d Gaussian. This can be thought of as two samples from a 1d Gaussian.

In more detail, sample $z_1, z_2 \in (-1, 1)$ uniformly, and then discard pairs that do not satisfy $z_1^2 + z_2^2 \le 1$. The result will be points uniformly distributed inside the unit circle, so $p(\boldsymbol{z}) = \frac{1}{\pi} \mathbb{I}(z \text{ inside circle})$. Now define

$$x_i = z_i \left(\frac{-2 \ln r^2}{r^2} \right)^{\frac{1}{2}} \tag{11.16}$$

for $i = 1 : 2$, where $r^2 = z_1^2 + z_2^2$. Using the multivariate change of variables formula, we have

$$p(x_1, x_2) = p(z_1, z_2) | \frac{\partial(z_1, z_2)}{\partial(x_1, x_2)} | = \left[\frac{1}{\sqrt{2\pi}} \exp(-\frac{1}{2}x_1^2) \right] \left[\frac{1}{\sqrt{2\pi}} \exp(-\frac{1}{2}x_2^2) \right] \tag{11.17}$$

Hence x_1 and x_2 are two independent samples from a univariate Gaussian. This is known as the **Box-Muller** method.

To sample from a multivariate Gaussian, we first compute the Cholesky decomposition of its covariance matrix, $\boldsymbol{\Sigma} = \mathbf{L}\mathbf{L}^\mathsf{T}$, where $\mathbf{L}$ is lower triangular. Next we sample $\boldsymbol{x} \sim \mathcal{N}(\mathbf{0}, \mathbf{I})$ using the Box-Muller method. Finally we set $\boldsymbol{y} = \mathbf{L}\boldsymbol{x} + \boldsymbol{\mu}$. This is valid since

$$\text{Cov}[\boldsymbol{y}] = \mathbf{L}\text{Cov}[\boldsymbol{x}]\mathbf{L}^\mathsf{T} = \mathbf{L}\,\mathbf{I}\,\mathbf{L}^\mathsf{T} = \boldsymbol{\Sigma} \tag{11.18}$$

11.4 Rejection sampling

Suppose we want to sample from the **target distribution**

$$p(\boldsymbol{x}) = \tilde{p}(\boldsymbol{x})/Z_p \tag{11.19}$$

where $\tilde{p}(\boldsymbol{x})$ is the unnormalized version, and

$$Z_p = \int \tilde{p}(\boldsymbol{x})\, d\boldsymbol{x} \tag{11.20}$$

is the (possibly unknown) normalization constant. One of the simplest approaches to this problem is **rejection sampling**, which we now explain.

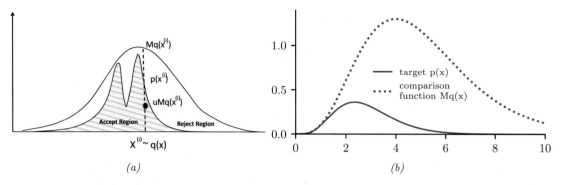

Figure 11.4: (a) Schematic illustration of rejection sampling. From Figure 2 of [And+03]. Used with kind permission of Nando de Freitas. (b) Rejection sampling from a $\text{Ga}(\alpha = 5.7, \lambda = 2)$ *distribution (solid blue) using a proposal of the form* $M\text{Ga}(k, \lambda - 1)$ *(dotted red), where* $k = \lfloor 5.7 \rfloor = 5$*. The curves touch at* $\alpha - k = 0.7$*. Generated by* rejection_sampling_demo.ipynb.

11.4.1   Basic idea

In rejection sampling, we require access to a **proposal distribution** $q(\boldsymbol{x})$ which satisfies $Cq(\boldsymbol{x}) \geq \tilde{p}(\boldsymbol{x})$, for some constant C. The function $Cq(\boldsymbol{x})$ provides an upper envelope for $\tilde{p}$.

We can use the proposal distribution to generate samples from the target distribution as follows. We first sample $\boldsymbol{x}_0 \sim q(\boldsymbol{x})$, which corresponds to picking a random $\boldsymbol{x}$ location, and then we sample $u_0 \sim \text{Unif}(0, Cq(\boldsymbol{x}_0))$, which corresponds to picking a random height (y location) under the envelope. If $u_0 > \tilde{p}(\boldsymbol{x}_0)$, we reject the sample, otherwise we accept it. This process is illustrated in 1d in Figure 11.4(a): the acceptance region is shown shaded, and the rejection region is the white region between the shaded zone and the upper envelope.

We now prove this procedure is correct. First note that the probability of any given sample $\boldsymbol{x}_0$ being accepted equals the probability of a sample $u_0 \sim \text{Unif}(0, Cq(\boldsymbol{x}_0))$ being less than or equal to $\tilde{p}(\boldsymbol{x}_0)$, i.e.,

$$q(\text{accept}|\boldsymbol{x}_0) = \int_0^{\tilde{p}(\boldsymbol{x}_0)} \frac{1}{Cq(\boldsymbol{x}_0)}\, du = \frac{\tilde{p}(\boldsymbol{x}_0)}{Cq(\boldsymbol{x}_0)} \tag{11.21}$$

Therefore

$$q(\text{propose and accept } \boldsymbol{x}_0) = q(\boldsymbol{x}_0)q(\text{accept}|\boldsymbol{x}_0) = q(\boldsymbol{x}_0)\frac{\tilde{p}(\boldsymbol{x}_0)}{Cq(\boldsymbol{x}_0)} = \frac{\tilde{p}(\boldsymbol{x}_0)}{C} \tag{11.22}$$

Integrating both sides give

$$\int q(\boldsymbol{x}_0)q(\text{accept}|\boldsymbol{x}_0)\, d\boldsymbol{x}_0 = q(\text{accept}) = \frac{\int \tilde{p}(\boldsymbol{x}_0)\, d\boldsymbol{x}_0}{C} = \frac{Z_p}{C} \tag{11.23}$$

Hence we see that the distribution of accepted points is given by the target distribution:

$$q(\boldsymbol{x}_0|\text{accept}) = \frac{q(\boldsymbol{x}_0, \text{accept})}{q(\text{accept})} = \frac{\tilde{p}(\boldsymbol{x}_0)}{C}\frac{C}{Z_p} = \frac{\tilde{p}(\boldsymbol{x}_0)}{Z_p} = p(\boldsymbol{x}_0) \tag{11.24}$$

How efficient is this method? If $\tilde{p}$ is a normalized target distribution, the acceptance probability is $1/C$. Hence we want to choose C as small as possible while still satisfying $Cq(x) \geq \tilde{p}(x)$.

11.4.2 Example

For example, suppose we want to sample from a gamma distribution:[3]

$$\text{Ga}(x|\alpha, \lambda) = \frac{1}{\Gamma(\alpha)} x^{\alpha-1} \lambda^{\alpha} \exp(-\lambda x) \qquad (11.25)$$

where $\Gamma(\alpha)$ is the gamma function. One can show that if $X_i \overset{iid}{\sim} \text{Expon}(\lambda)$, and $Y = X_1 + \cdots + X_k$, then $Y \sim \text{Ga}(k, \lambda)$. For non-integer shape parameters α, we cannot use this trick. However, we can use rejection sampling using a $\text{Ga}(k, \lambda - 1)$ distribution as a proposal, where $k = \lfloor \alpha \rfloor$. The ratio has the form

$$\frac{p(x)}{q(x)} = \frac{\text{Ga}(x|\alpha, \lambda)}{\text{Ga}(x|k, \lambda - 1)} = \frac{x^{\alpha-1} \lambda^{\alpha} \exp(-\lambda x)/\Gamma(\alpha)}{x^{k-1}(\lambda - 1)^k \exp(-(\lambda - 1)x)/\Gamma(k)} \qquad (11.26)$$

$$= \frac{\Gamma(k)\lambda^{\alpha}}{\Gamma(\alpha)(\lambda - 1)^k} x^{\alpha-k} \exp(-x) \qquad (11.27)$$

This ratio attains its maximum when $x = \alpha - k$. Hence

$$C = \frac{\text{Ga}(\alpha - k|\alpha, \lambda)}{\text{Ga}(\alpha - k|k, \lambda - 1)} \qquad (11.28)$$

See Figure 11.4(b) for a plot.

11.4.3 Adaptive rejection sampling

We now describe a method that can automatically come up with a tight upper envelope $q(x)$ to any log concave 1d density $p(x)$. The idea is to upper bound the log density with a piecewise linear function, as illustrated in Figure 11.5(a). We choose the initial locations for the pieces based on a fixed grid over the support of the distribution. We then evaluate the gradient of the log density at these locations, and make the lines be tangent at these points.

Since the log of the envelope is piecewise linear, the envelope itself is piecewise exponential:

$$q(x) = C_i \lambda_i \exp(-\lambda_i(x - x_{i-1})), \quad x_{i-1} < x \leq x_i \qquad (11.29)$$

where x_i are the grid points. It is relatively straightforward to sample from this distribution. If the sample x is rejected, we create a new grid point at x, and thereby refine the envelope. As the number of grid points is increased, the tightness of the envelope improves, and the rejection rate goes down. This is known as **adaptive rejection sampling** (ARS) [GW92]. Figure 11.5(b-c) gives an example of the method in action. As with standard rejection sampling, it can be applied to unnormalized distributions.

---

3. This section is based on notes by Ioana A. Cosma, available at `http://users.aims.ac.za/~ioana/cp2.pdf`.

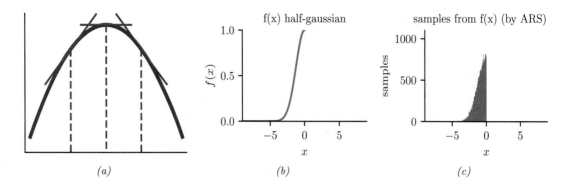

(a)   (b)   (c)

Figure 11.5: (a) Idea behind adaptive rejection sampling. We place piecewise linear upper (and lower) bounds on the log-concave density. Adapted from Figure 1 of [GW92]. Generated by ars_envelope.ipynb. (b-c) Using ARS to sample from a half-Gaussian. Generated by ars_demo.ipynb.

11.4.4   Rejection sampling in high dimensions

It is clear that we want to make our proposal $q(\boldsymbol{x})$ as close as possible to the target distribution $p(\boldsymbol{x})$, while still being an upper bound. But this is quite hard to achieve, especially in high dimensions. To see this, consider sampling from $p(\boldsymbol{x}) = \mathcal{N}(\mathbf{0}, \sigma_p^2 \mathbf{I})$ using as a proposal $q(\boldsymbol{x}) = \mathcal{N}(\mathbf{0}, \sigma_q^2 \mathbf{I})$. Obviously we must have $\sigma_q^2 \geq \sigma_p^2$ in order to be an upper bound. In D dimensions, the optimum value is given by $C = (\sigma_q/\sigma_p)^D$. The acceptance rate is $1/C$ (since both p and q are normalized), which decreases exponentially fast with dimension. For example, if σ_q exceeds σ_p by just 1%, then in 1000 dimensions the acceptance ratio will be about $1/20,000$. This is a fundamental weakness of rejection sampling.

11.5   Importance sampling

In this section, we describe a Monte Carlo method known as **importance sampling** for approximating integrals of the form

$$\mathbb{E}\left[\varphi(\boldsymbol{x})\right] = \int \varphi(\boldsymbol{x})\pi(\boldsymbol{x})d\boldsymbol{x} \tag{11.30}$$

where φ is called a **target function**, and $\pi(\boldsymbol{x})$ is the **target distribution**, often a conditional distribution of the form $\pi(\boldsymbol{x}) = p(\boldsymbol{x}|\boldsymbol{y})$. Since in general it is difficult to draw from the target distribution, we will instead draw from some **proposal distribution** $q(\boldsymbol{x})$ (which will usually depend on $\boldsymbol{y}$). We then adjust for the inaccuracies of this by associating weights with each sample, so we end up with a weighted MC approximation:

$$\mathbb{E}\left[\varphi(\boldsymbol{x})\right] \approx \sum_{n=1}^{N} W_n \varphi(\boldsymbol{x}_n) \tag{11.31}$$

We discuss two cases, first when the target is normalized, and then when it is unnormalized. This will affect the ways the weights are computed, as well as statistical properties of the estimator.

11.5.1   Direct importance sampling

In this section, we assume that we can *evaluate* the normalized target distribution $\pi(\boldsymbol{x})$, but we cannot sample from it. So instead we will sample from the proposal $q(\boldsymbol{x})$. We can then write

$$\int \varphi(\boldsymbol{x})\pi(\boldsymbol{x})d\boldsymbol{x} = \int \varphi(\boldsymbol{x})\frac{\pi(\boldsymbol{x})}{q(\boldsymbol{x})}q(\boldsymbol{x})d\boldsymbol{x} \tag{11.32}$$

We require that the proposal be non-zero whenever the target is non-zero, i.e., the support of $q(\boldsymbol{x})$ needs to be greater or equal to the support of $\pi(\boldsymbol{x})$. If we draw N_s samples $\boldsymbol{x}_n \sim q(\boldsymbol{x})$, we can write

$$\mathbb{E}\left[\varphi(\boldsymbol{x})\right] \approx \frac{1}{N_s}\sum_{n=1}^{N_s}\frac{\pi(\boldsymbol{x}_n)}{q(\boldsymbol{x}_n)}\varphi(\boldsymbol{x}_n) = \frac{1}{N_s}\sum_{n=1}^{N_s}\tilde{w}_n\varphi(\boldsymbol{x}_n) \tag{11.33}$$

where we have defined the **importance weights** as follows:

$$\tilde{w}_n = \frac{\pi(\boldsymbol{x}_n)}{q(\boldsymbol{x}_n)} \tag{11.34}$$

The result is an unbiased estimate of the true mean $\mathbb{E}\left[\varphi(\boldsymbol{x})\right]$.

11.5.2   Self-normalized importance sampling

The disadvantage of direct importance sampling is that we need a way to evaluate the normalized target distribution π in order to compute the weights. It is often much easier to evaluate the **unnormalized target distribution**

$$\tilde{\gamma}(\boldsymbol{x}) = Z\pi(\boldsymbol{x}) \tag{11.35}$$

where

$$Z = \int \tilde{\gamma}(\boldsymbol{x})d\boldsymbol{z} \tag{11.36}$$

is the normalization constant. (For example, if $\pi(\boldsymbol{x}) = p(\boldsymbol{x}|\boldsymbol{y})$, then $\tilde{\gamma}(\boldsymbol{x}) = p(\boldsymbol{x}, \boldsymbol{y})$ and $Z = p(\boldsymbol{y})$.) The key idea is to also approximate the normalization constant Z with importance sampling. This method is called **self-normalized importance sampling**. The resulting estimate is a ratio of two estimates, and hence is biased. However as $N_s \to \infty$, the bias goes to zero, under some weak assumptions (see e.g., [RC04] for details).

In more detail, SNIS is based on this approximation:

$$\mathbb{E}\left[\varphi(\boldsymbol{x})\right] = \int \varphi(\boldsymbol{x})\pi(\boldsymbol{x})d\boldsymbol{x} = \frac{\int \varphi(\boldsymbol{x})\tilde{\gamma}(\boldsymbol{x})d\boldsymbol{x}}{\int \tilde{\gamma}(\boldsymbol{x})d\boldsymbol{x}} = \frac{\int \left[\frac{\tilde{\gamma}(\boldsymbol{x})}{q(\boldsymbol{x})}\varphi(\boldsymbol{x})\right]q(\boldsymbol{x})d\boldsymbol{x}}{\int \left[\frac{\tilde{\gamma}(\boldsymbol{x})}{q(\boldsymbol{x})}\right]q(\boldsymbol{x})d\boldsymbol{x}} \tag{11.37}$$

$$\approx \frac{\frac{1}{N_s}\sum_{n=1}^{N_s}\tilde{w}_n\varphi(\boldsymbol{x}_n)}{\frac{1}{N_s}\sum_{n=1}^{N_s}\tilde{w}_n} \tag{11.38}$$

where we have defined the **unnormalized weights**

$$\tilde{w}_n = \frac{\tilde{\gamma}(\boldsymbol{x}_n)}{q(\boldsymbol{x}_n)} \tag{11.39}$$

We can write Equation (11.38) more compactly as

$$\mathbb{E}\left[\varphi(\boldsymbol{x})\right] \approx \sum_{n=1}^{N_s} W_n \varphi(\boldsymbol{x}_n) \tag{11.40}$$

where we have defined the **normalized weights** by

$$W_n = \frac{\tilde{w}_n}{\sum_{n'=1}^{N_s} \tilde{w}_{n'}} \tag{11.41}$$

This is equivalent to approximating the target distribution using a weighted sum of delta functions:

$$\pi(\boldsymbol{x}) \approx \sum_{n=1}^{N_s} W_n \delta(\boldsymbol{x} - \boldsymbol{x}_n) \triangleq \hat{\pi}(\boldsymbol{x}) \tag{11.42}$$

As a byproduct of this algorithm we get the following appoximation to the normalization constant:

$$Z \approx \frac{1}{N_s} \sum_{n=1}^{N_s} \tilde{w}_n \triangleq \hat{Z} \tag{11.43}$$

11.5.3   Choosing the proposal

The performance of importance sampling depends crucially on the quality of the proposal distribution. As we mentioned, we require that the support of q cover the support of the target (i.e., $\tilde{\gamma}(\boldsymbol{x}) > 0 \implies q(\boldsymbol{x}) > 0$). However, we also want the proposal to not be too "loose" of a "covering". Ideally it should also take into account properties of the target function φ as well, as shown in Figure 11.6. This can yield subsantial benefits, as shown in the "**target aware Bayesian inference**" scheme of [Rai+20]. However, usually the target function φ is unknown or ignored, so we just try to find a "generally useful" approximation to the target.

One way to come up with a good proposal is to learn one, by optimizing the variational lower bound or ELBO (see Section 10.1.1.2). Indeed, if we fix the parameters of the generative model, we can think of importance weighted autoencoders (Section 10.5.1) as learning a good IS proposal. More details on this connection can be found in [DS18].

11.5.4   Annealed importance sampling (AIS)

In this section, we describe a method known as **annealed importance sampling** [Nea01] for sampling from complex, possibly multimodal distributions. Assume we want to sample from some target distribution $p_0(\boldsymbol{x}) \propto f_0(\boldsymbol{x})$ (where $f_0(\boldsymbol{x})$ is the unnormalized version), but we cannot easily do so, because p_0 is complicated in some way (e.g., high dimensional and/or multi-modal). However, suppose that there is an easier distribution which we *can* sample from, call it $p_n(\boldsymbol{x}) \propto f_n(\boldsymbol{x})$; for

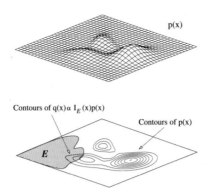

Figure 11.6: In importance sampling, we should sample from a distribution that takes into account regions where $\pi(\boldsymbol{x})$ has high probability and where $\varphi(\boldsymbol{x})$ is large. Here the function to be evaluated is an indicator function of a set, corresponding to a set of rare events in the tail of the distribution. From Figure 3 of [And+03]. Used with kind permission of Nando de Freitas.

example, this might be the prior. We now construct a sequence of intermediate distributions than move slowly from p_n to p_0 as follows:

$$f_j(\boldsymbol{x}) = f_0(\boldsymbol{x})^{\beta_j} f_n(\boldsymbol{x})^{1-\beta_j} \tag{11.44}$$

where $1 = \beta_0 > \beta_1 > \cdots > \beta_n = 0$, where β_j is an inverse temperature. We will sample a set of points from f_n, and then from f_{n-1}, and so on, until we eventually sample from f_0.

To sample from each f_j, suppose we can define a Markov chain $T_j(\boldsymbol{x}, \boldsymbol{x}') = p_j(\boldsymbol{x}'|\boldsymbol{x})$, which leaves p_0 invariant (i.e., $\int p_j(\boldsymbol{x}'|\boldsymbol{x})p_0(\boldsymbol{x})d\boldsymbol{x} = p_0(\boldsymbol{x}')$). (See Chapter 12 for details on how to construct such chains.) Given this, we can sample $\boldsymbol{x}$ from p_0 as follows: sample $\boldsymbol{v}_n \sim p_n$; sample $\boldsymbol{v}_{n-1} \sim T_{n-1}(\boldsymbol{v}_n, \cdot)$; and continue in this way until we sample $\boldsymbol{v}_0 \sim T_0(\boldsymbol{v}_1, \cdot)$; finally we set $\boldsymbol{x} = \boldsymbol{v}_0$ and give it weight

$$w = \frac{f_{n-1}(\boldsymbol{v}_{n-1})}{f_n(\boldsymbol{v}_{n-1})} \frac{f_{n-2}(\boldsymbol{v}_{n-2})}{f_{n-1}(\boldsymbol{v}_{n-2})} \cdots \frac{f_1(\boldsymbol{v}_1)}{f_2(\boldsymbol{v}_1)} \frac{f_0(\boldsymbol{v}_0)}{f_1(\boldsymbol{v}_0)} \tag{11.45}$$

This can be shown to be correct by viewing the algorithm as a form of importance sampling in an extended state space $\boldsymbol{v} = (\boldsymbol{v}_0, \ldots, \boldsymbol{v}_n)$. Consider the following distribution on this state space:

$$p(\boldsymbol{v}) \propto \varphi(\boldsymbol{v}) = f_0(\boldsymbol{v}_0)\tilde{T}_0(\boldsymbol{v}_0, \boldsymbol{v}_1)\tilde{T}_2(\boldsymbol{v}_1, \boldsymbol{v}_2) \cdots \tilde{T}_{n-1}(\boldsymbol{v}_{n-1}, \boldsymbol{v}_n) \tag{11.46}$$

$$\propto p(\boldsymbol{v}_0)p(\boldsymbol{v}_1|\boldsymbol{v}_0) \cdots p(\boldsymbol{v}_n|\boldsymbol{v}_{n-1}) \tag{11.47}$$

where $\tilde{T}_j$ is the reversal of T_j:

$$\tilde{T}_j(\boldsymbol{v}, \boldsymbol{v}') = T_j(\boldsymbol{v}', \boldsymbol{v})p_j(\boldsymbol{v}')/p_j(\boldsymbol{v}) = T_j(\boldsymbol{v}', \boldsymbol{v})f_j(\boldsymbol{v}')/f_j(\boldsymbol{v}) \tag{11.48}$$

It is clear that $\sum_{\boldsymbol{v}_1, \ldots, \boldsymbol{v}_n} \varphi(\boldsymbol{v}) = f_0(\boldsymbol{v}_0)$, so by sampling from $p(\boldsymbol{v})$, we can effectively sample from $p_0(\boldsymbol{x})$.

We can sample on this extended state space using the above algorithm, which corresponds to the following proposal:

$$q(\boldsymbol{v}) \propto g(\boldsymbol{v}) = f_n(\boldsymbol{v}_n)T_{n-1}(\boldsymbol{v}_n, \boldsymbol{v}_{n-1}) \cdots T_2(\boldsymbol{v}_2, \boldsymbol{v}_1)T_0(\boldsymbol{v}_1, \boldsymbol{v}_0) \tag{11.49}$$

$$\propto p(\boldsymbol{v}_n)p(\boldsymbol{v}_{n-1}|\boldsymbol{v}_n) \cdots p(\boldsymbol{v}_1|\boldsymbol{v}_0) \tag{11.50}$$

One can show that the importance weights $w = \frac{\varphi(\boldsymbol{v}_0,\dots,\boldsymbol{v}_n)}{g(\boldsymbol{v}_0,\dots,\boldsymbol{v}_n)}$ are given by Equation (11.45). Since marginals of the sampled sequences from this extended model are equivalent to samples from $p_0(\boldsymbol{x})$, we see that we are using the correct weights.

11.5.4.1   Estimating normalizing constants using AIS

An important application of AIS is to evaluate a ratio of partition functions. Notice that $Z_0 = \int f_0(\boldsymbol{x})d\boldsymbol{x} = \int \varphi(\boldsymbol{v})d\boldsymbol{v}$, and $Z_n = \int f_n(\boldsymbol{x})d\boldsymbol{x} = \int g(\boldsymbol{v})d\boldsymbol{v}$. Hence

$$\frac{Z_0}{Z_n} = \frac{\int \varphi(\boldsymbol{v})d\boldsymbol{v}}{\int g(\boldsymbol{v})d\boldsymbol{v}} = \frac{\int \frac{\varphi(\boldsymbol{v})}{g(\boldsymbol{v})}g(\boldsymbol{v})d\boldsymbol{v}}{\int g(\boldsymbol{v})d\boldsymbol{v}} = \mathbb{E}_g \left[\frac{\varphi(\boldsymbol{v})}{g(\boldsymbol{v})} \right] \approx \frac{1}{S} \sum_{s=1}^{S} w_s \tag{11.51}$$

where $w_s = \varphi(\boldsymbol{v}_s)/g(\boldsymbol{v}_s)$. If f_0 is a prior and f_n is the posterior, we can estimate $Z_n = p(\mathcal{D})$ using the above equation, provided the prior has a known normalization constant Z_0. This is generally considered the method of choice for evaluating difficult partition functions. See e.g., [GM98] for more details.

11.6   Controlling Monte Carlo variance

As we mentioned in Section 11.2.2, the standard error in a Monte Carlo estimate is $O(1/\sqrt{S})$, where S is the number of (independent) samples. Consequently it may take many samples to reduce the variance to a sufficiently small value. In this section, we discuss some ways to reduce the variance of sampling methods. For more details, see e.g., [KTB11].

11.6.1   Common random numbers

When performing Monte Carlo optimization, we often want to compare $\mathbb{E}_{p(\boldsymbol{z})}\left[f(\boldsymbol{\theta}, \boldsymbol{z})\right]$ to $\mathbb{E}_{p(\boldsymbol{z})}\left[f(\boldsymbol{\theta}', \boldsymbol{z})\right]$ for different values of the parameters $\boldsymbol{\theta}$ and $\boldsymbol{\theta}'$. To reduce the variance of this comparison, we can use the same random samples $\boldsymbol{z}_s$ for evaluating both functions. In this way, differences in the outcome can be ascribed to differences in the parameters $\boldsymbol{\theta}$, rather than to the noise terms. This is called the **common random numbers** trick, and is widely used in ML (see e.g., [GBJ18; NJ00]), since it can often convert a stochastic optimization problem into a deterministic one, enabling the us of more powerful optimization methods. For more details on CRN, see e.g., https://en.wikipedia.org/wiki/Variance_reduction#Common_Random_Numbers_(CRN).

11.6.2   Rao-Blackwellization

In this section, we discuss a useful technique for reducing the variance of MC estimators known as **Rao-Blackwellization**. To explain the method, suppose we have two rv's, X and Y, and we want to estimate $\overline{f} = \mathbb{E}\left[f(X, Y)\right]$. The naive approach is to use an MC approximation

$$\hat{f}_{MC} = \frac{1}{S} \sum_{s=1}^{S} f(X_s, Y_s) \tag{11.52}$$

where $(X_s, Y_s) \sim p(X, Y)$. This is an unbiased estimator of $\overline{f}$. However, it may have high variance.

Now suppose we can analytically marginalize out Y, provided we know X, i.e., we can tractably compute

$$f_X(X_s) = \int dY \, p(Y|X_s) f(X_s, Y) = \mathbb{E}\left[f(X, Y)|X = X_s\right] \tag{11.53}$$

Let us define the Rao-Blackwellized estimator

$$\hat{f}_{RB} = \frac{1}{S} \sum_{s=1}^{S} f_X(X_s) \tag{11.54}$$

where $X_s \sim p(X)$. This is an unbiased estimator, since $\mathbb{E}\left[\hat{f}_{RB}\right] = \mathbb{E}\left[\mathbb{E}\left[f(X, Y)|X\right]\right] = \overline{f}$. However, this estimate can have lower variance than the naive estimator. The intuitive reason is that we are now sampling in a reduced dimensional space. Formally we can see this by using the law of iterated variance to get

$$\mathbb{V}\left[\mathbb{E}\left[f(X, Y)|X\right]\right] = \mathbb{V}\left[f(X, Y)\right] - \mathbb{E}\left[\mathbb{V}\left[f(X, Y)\right]|X\right] \leq \mathbb{V}\left[f(X, Y)\right] \tag{11.55}$$

For some examples of this in practice, see Section 6.3.4.2, Section 13.4, and Section 12.3.8.

11.6.3 Control variates

Suppose we want to estimate $\mu = \mathbb{E}\left[f(X)\right]$ using an unbiased estimator $m(\mathcal{X}) = \frac{1}{S}\sum_{s=1}^{S} m(x_s)$, where $x_s \sim p(X)$ and $\mathbb{E}\left[m(X)\right] = \mu$. (We abuse notation slightly and use m to refer to a function of a single random variable as well as a set of samples.) Now consider the alternative estimator

$$m^*(\mathcal{X}) = m(\mathcal{X}) + c\left(b(\mathcal{X}) - \mathbb{E}\left[b(\mathcal{X})\right]\right) \tag{11.56}$$

This is called a **control variate**, and b is called a **baseline**. (Once again we abuse notation and use $b(\mathcal{X}) = \frac{1}{S}\sum_{s=1}^{S} b(x_s)$ and $m^*(\mathcal{X}) = \frac{1}{S}\sum_{s=1}^{S} m^*(x_s)$.)

It is easy to see that $m^*(\mathcal{X})$ is an unbiased estimator, since $\mathbb{E}\left[m^*(X)\right] = \mathbb{E}\left[m(X)\right] = \mu$. However, it can have lower variance, provided b is correlated with m. To see this, note that

$$\mathbb{V}\left[m^*(X)\right] = \mathbb{V}\left[m(X)\right] + c^2 \mathbb{V}\left[b(X)\right] + 2c\mathrm{Cov}\left[m(X), b(X)\right] \tag{11.57}$$

By taking the derivative of $\mathbb{V}\left[m^*(X)\right]$ wrt c and setting to 0, we find that the optimal value is

$$c^* = -\frac{\mathrm{Cov}\left[m(X), b(X)\right]}{\mathbb{V}\left[b(X)\right]} \tag{11.58}$$

The corresponding variance of the new estimator is now

$$\mathbb{V}[m^*(X)] = \mathbb{V}[m(X)] - \frac{\text{Cov}[m(X), b(X)]^2}{\mathbb{V}[b(X)]} = (1 - \rho_{m,b}^2)\mathbb{V}[m(X)] \leq \mathbb{V}[m(X)] \qquad (11.59)$$

where $\rho_{m,b}^2$ is the correlation of the basic estimator and the baseline function. If we can ensure this correlation is high, we can reduce the variance. Intuitively, the CV estimator is exploiting information about the errors in the estimate of a known quantity, namely $\mathbb{E}[b(X)]$, to reduce the errors in estimating the unknown quantity, namely μ.

We give a simple worked example in Section 11.6.3.1. See Section 10.2.3 for an example of this technique applied to blackbox variational inference.

11.6.3.1   Example

We now give a simple worked example of control variates.[4] Consider estimating $\mu = \mathbb{E}[f(X)]$ where $f(X) = 1/(1 + X)$ and $X \sim \text{Unif}(0, 1)$. The exact value is

$$\mu = \int_0^1 \frac{1}{1+x} dx = \ln 2 \approx 0.693 \qquad (11.60)$$

The naive MC estimate, using S samples, is $m(\mathcal{X}) = \frac{1}{S}\sum_{s=1}^S f(x_s)$. Using $S = 1500$, we find $\mathbb{E}[m(\mathcal{X})] = 0.6935$ with standard error se $= 0.0037$.

Now let us use $b(X) = 1 + X$ as a baseline, so $b(\mathcal{X}) = (1/S)\sum_s(1 + x_s)$. This has expectation $\mathbb{E}[b(X)] = \int_0^1(1 + x)dx = \frac{3}{2}$. The control variate estimator is given by

$$m^*(\mathcal{X}) = \frac{1}{S}\sum_{s=1}^S f(x_s) + c\left(\frac{1}{S}\sum_{s=1}^S b(x_s) - \frac{3}{2}\right) \qquad (11.61)$$

The optimal value can be estimated from the samples of $m(x_s)$ and $b(x_s)$, and plugging into Equation (11.58) to get $c^* \approx 0.4773$. Using $S = 1500$, we find $\mathbb{E}[m^*(\mathcal{X})] = 0.6941$ and se $= 0.0007$.

See also Section 11.6.4.1, where we analyze this example using antithetic sampling.

11.6.4   Antithetic sampling

In this section, we discuss **antithetic sampling**, which is a simple way to reduce variance.[5] Suppose we want to estimate $\theta = \mathbb{E}[Y]$. Let Y_1 and Y_2 be two samples. An unbiased estimate of θ is given by $\hat{\theta} = (Y_1 + Y_2)/2$. The variance of this estimate is

$$\mathbb{V}[\hat{\theta}] = \frac{\mathbb{V}[Y_1] + \mathbb{V}[Y_2] + 2\text{Cov}[Y_1, Y_2]}{4} \qquad (11.62)$$

so the variance is reduced if $\text{Cov}[Y_1, Y_2] < 0$. So whenever we sample Y_1, we should set Y_2 to be its "opposite", but with the same mean.

For example, suppose $Y \sim \text{Unif}(0, 1)$. If we let $y_1, \ldots, y_n$ be iid samples from $\text{Unif}(0, 1)$, then we can define $y_i' = 1 - y_i$. The distribution of y_i' is still $\text{Unif}(0, 1)$, but $\text{Cov}[y_i, y_i'] < 1$.

---

4. The example is from `https://en.wikipedia.org/wiki/Control_variates`, with modified notation. See control_variates.ipynb for some code.
5. Our presentation is based on `https://en.wikipedia.org/wiki/Antithetic_variates`. See antithetic_sampling.ipynb for the code.

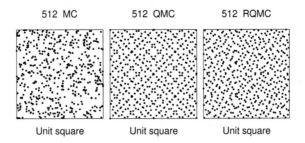

Figure 11.7: *Illustration of Monte Carlo (MC), Quasi-MC (QMC) from a Sobol sequence, and randomized QMC using a scrambling method. Adapted from Figure 1 of [OR20]. Used with kind permission of Art Owen.*

11.6.4.1 Example

To see why this can be useful, consider the example from Section 11.6.3.1. Let $\hat{\mu}_{\mathrm{mc}}$ be the classic MC estimate using $2N$ samples from $\mathrm{Unif}(0,1)$, and let $\hat{\mu}_{\mathrm{anti}}$ be the MC estimate using the above antithetic sampling scheme applied to N base samples from $\mathrm{Unif}(0,1)$. The exact value is $\mu = \ln 2 \approx 0.6935$. For the classical method, with $N = 750$, we find $\mathbb{E}[\hat{\mu}_{\mathrm{mc}}] = 0.69365$ with a standard error of 0.0037. For the antithetic method, we find $\mathbb{E}[\hat{\mu}_{\mathrm{anti}}] = 0.6939$ with a standard error of 0.0007, which matches the control variate method of Section 11.6.3.1.

11.6.5 Quasi-Monte Carlo (QMC)

Quasi-Monte Carlo (see e.g., [Lem09; Owe13]) is an approach to numerical integration that replaces random samples with **low discrepancy sequences**, such as the **Halton sequence** (see e.g., [Owe17]) or **Sobol sequence**. Intuitively, these are **space filling** sequences of points, constructed to reduce the unwanted gaps and clusters that would arise among randomly chosen inputs. See Figure 11.7 for an example.[6]

More precisely, consider the problem of evaluating the following D-dimensional integral:

$$\bar{f} = \int_{[0,1]^D} f(\boldsymbol{x})d\boldsymbol{x} \approx \hat{f}_N = \frac{1}{N}\sum_{n=1}^{N} f(\boldsymbol{x}_n) \tag{11.63}$$

Let $\epsilon_N = |\bar{f} - \hat{f}_N|$ be the error. In standard Monte Carlo, if we draw N independent samples, then we have $\epsilon_N \sim O\left(\frac{1}{\sqrt{N}}\right)$. In QMC, it can be shown that $\epsilon_N \sim O\left(\frac{(\log N)^D}{N}\right)$. For $N > 2^D$, the latter is smaller than the former.

One disadvantage of QMC is that it just provides a point estimate of $\bar{f}$, and does not give an uncertainty estimate. By contrast, in regular MC, we can estimate the MC standard error, discussed in Section 11.2.2. **Randomized QMC** (see e.g., [L'E18]) provides a solution to this problem. The basic idea is to repeat the QMC method R times, by perturbing the sequence of N points by a

---

6. More details on QMC can be found at `http://roth.cs.kuleuven.be/wiki/Main_Page`. For connections to Bayesian quadrature, see e.g., [DKS13; HKO22].

random amount. In particular, define

$$\boldsymbol{y}_{i,r} = \boldsymbol{x}_i + \boldsymbol{u}_r \pmod{1} \tag{11.64}$$

where $\boldsymbol{x}_1, \ldots, \boldsymbol{x}_N$ is a low-discrepancy sequence, and $\boldsymbol{u}_r \sim \text{Unif}(0,1)^D$ is a random perturbation. The set $\{\boldsymbol{y}_j\}$ is low discrepancy, and satisfies that each $\boldsymbol{y}_j \sim \text{Unif}(0,1)^D$, for $j = 1 : N \times R$. This has much lower variance than standard MC. (Typically we take R to be a power of 2.) Recently, [OR20] proved a strong law of large numbers for RQMC.

QMC and RQMC can be used inside of MCMC inference (see e.g., [OT05]) and variational inference (see e.g., [BWM18]). It is also commonly used to select the initial set of query points for Bayesian optimization (Section 6.6).

Another technique that can be used is **orthogonal Monte Carlo**, where the samples are conditioned to be pairwise orthogonal, but with the marginal distributions matching the original ones (see e.g., [Lin+20]).

12 Markov chain Monte Carlo

12.1 Introduction

In Chapter 11, we considered non-iterative Monte Carlo methods, including rejection sampling and importance sampling, which generate independent samples from some target distribution. The trouble with these methods is that they often do not work well in high dimensional spaces. In this chapter, we discuss a popular method for sampling from high-dimensional distributions known as **Markov chain Monte Carlo** or **MCMC**. In a survey by *SIAM News*[1], MCMC was placed in the top 10 most important algorithms of the 20th century.

The basic idea behind MCMC is to construct a Markov chain (Section 2.6) on the state space $\mathcal{X}$ whose stationary distribution is the target density $p^*(x)$ of interest. (In a Bayesian context, this is usually a posterior, $p^*(x) \propto p(x|\mathcal{D})$, but MCMC can be applied to generate samples from any kind of distribution.) That is, we perform a random walk on the state space, in such a way that the fraction of time we spend in each state x is proportional to $p^*(x)$. By drawing (correlated) samples $x_0, x_1, x_2, \ldots$, from the chain, we can perform Monte Carlo integration wrt p^*.

Note that the initial samples from the chain do not come from the stationary distribution, and should be discarded; the amount of time it takes to reach stationarity is called the **mixing time** or **burn-in time**; reducing this is one of the most important factors in making the algorithm fast, as we will see.

The MCMC algorithm has an interesting history. It was discovered by physicists working on the atomic bomb at Los Alamos during World War II, and was first published in the open literature in [Met+53] in a chemistry journal. An extension was published in the statistics literature in [Has70], but was largely unnoticed. A special case (Gibbs sampling, Section 12.3) was independently invented in [GG84] in the context of Ising models (Section 4.3.2.1). But it was not until [GS90] that the algorithm became well-known to the wider statistical community. Since then it has become wildly popular in Bayesian statistics, and is becoming increasingly popular in machine learning.

In the rest of this chapter, we give a brief introduction to MCMC methods. For more details on the theory, see e.g., [GRS96; BZ20]. For more details on the implementation side, see e.g., [Lao+20]. And for an interactive visualization of many of these algorithsm in 2d, see http://chi-feng.github.io/mcmc-demo/app.html.

---

1. Source: http://www.siam.org/pdf/news/637.pdf.

12.2   Metropolis-Hastings algorithm

In this section, we describe the simplest kinds of MCMC algorithm known as the **Metropoli-Hastings** or **MH** algorithm.

12.2.1   Basic idea

The basic idea in MH is that at each step, we propose to move from the current state $\boldsymbol{x}$ to a new state $\boldsymbol{x}'$ with probability $q(\boldsymbol{x}'|\boldsymbol{x})$, where q is called the **proposal distribution** (also called the **kernel**). The user is free to use any kind of proposal they want, subject to some conditions which we explain below. This makes MH quite a flexible method.

Having proposed a move to $\boldsymbol{x}'$, we then decide whether to **accept** this proposal, or to reject it, according to some formula, which ensures that the long-term fraction of time spent in each state is proportional to $p^*(\boldsymbol{x})$. If the proposal is accepted, the new state is $\boldsymbol{x}'$, otherwise the new state is the same as the current state, $\boldsymbol{x}$ (i.e., we repeat the sample).

If the proposal is symmetric, so $q(\boldsymbol{x}'|\boldsymbol{x}) = q(\boldsymbol{x}|\boldsymbol{x}')$, the acceptance probability is given by the following formula:

$$A = \min\left(1, \frac{p^*(\boldsymbol{x}')}{p^*(\boldsymbol{x})}\right) \tag{12.1}$$

We see that if $\boldsymbol{x}'$ is more probable than $\boldsymbol{x}$, we definitely move there (since $\frac{p^*(\boldsymbol{x}')}{p^*(\boldsymbol{x})} > 1$), but if $\boldsymbol{x}'$ is less probable, we may still move there anyway, depending on the relative probabilities. So instead of greedily moving to only more probable states, we occasionally allow "downhill" moves to less probable states. In Section 12.2.2, we prove that this procedure ensures that the fraction of time we spend in each state $\boldsymbol{x}$ is equal to $p^*(\boldsymbol{x})$.

If the proposal is asymmetric, so $q(\boldsymbol{x}'|\boldsymbol{x}) \neq q(\boldsymbol{x}|\boldsymbol{x}')$, we need the **Hastings correction**, given by the following:

$$A = \min(1, \alpha) \tag{12.2}$$

$$\alpha = \frac{p^*(\boldsymbol{x}')q(\boldsymbol{x}|\boldsymbol{x}')}{p^*(\boldsymbol{x})q(\boldsymbol{x}'|\boldsymbol{x})} = \frac{p^*(\boldsymbol{x}')/q(\boldsymbol{x}'|\boldsymbol{x})}{p^*(\boldsymbol{x})/q(\boldsymbol{x}|\boldsymbol{x}')} \tag{12.3}$$

This correction is needed to compensate for the fact that the proposal distribution itself (rather than just the target distribution) might favor certain states.

An important reason why MH is a useful algorithm is that, when evaluating α, we only need to know the target density up to a normalization constant. In particular, suppose $p^*(\boldsymbol{x}) = \frac{1}{Z}\tilde{p}(\boldsymbol{x})$, where $\tilde{p}(\boldsymbol{x})$ is an unnormalized distribution and Z is the normalization constant. Then

$$\alpha = \frac{(\tilde{p}(\boldsymbol{x}')/Z)\, q(\boldsymbol{x}|\boldsymbol{x}')}{(\tilde{p}(\boldsymbol{x})/Z)\, q(\boldsymbol{x}'|\boldsymbol{x})} \tag{12.4}$$

so the Z's cancel. Hence we can sample from p^* even if Z is unknown.

A proposal distribution q is valid or admissible if it "covers" the support of the target. Formally, we can write this as

$$\text{supp}(p^*) \subseteq \cup_x \text{supp}(q(\cdot|x)) \tag{12.5}$$

With this, we can state the overall algorithm as in Algorithm 12.1.

Algorithm 12.1: Metropolis-Hastings algorithm

---

1 Initialize x^0
2 for $s = 0, 1, 2, \ldots$ **do**
3 $\quad$ Define $x = x^s$
4 $\quad$ Sample $x' \sim q(x'|x)$
5 $\quad$ Compute acceptance probability

$$\alpha = \frac{\tilde{p}(x')q(x|x')}{\tilde{p}(x)q(x'|x)}$$

6 $\quad$ Compute $A = \min(1, \alpha)$
7 $\quad$ Sample $u \sim U(0, 1)$
8 $\quad$ Set new sample to

$$x^{s+1} = \begin{cases} x' & \text{if } u \leq A \text{ (accept)} \\ x^s & \text{if } u > A \text{ (reject)} \end{cases}$$

12.2.2 Why MH works

To prove that the MH procedure generates samples from p^*, we need a bit of Markov chain theory, as discussed in Section 2.6.4.

The MH algorithm defines a Markov chain with the following transition matrix:

$$p(\boldsymbol{x}'|\boldsymbol{x}) = \begin{cases} q(\boldsymbol{x}'|\boldsymbol{x})A(\boldsymbol{x}'|\boldsymbol{x}) & \text{if } \boldsymbol{x}' \neq \boldsymbol{x} \\ q(\boldsymbol{x}|\boldsymbol{x}) + \sum_{\boldsymbol{x}' \neq \boldsymbol{x}} q(\boldsymbol{x}'|\boldsymbol{x})(1 - A(\boldsymbol{x}'|\boldsymbol{x})) & \text{otherwise} \end{cases} \tag{12.6}$$

This follows from a case analysis: if you move to $\boldsymbol{x}'$ from $\boldsymbol{x}$, you must have proposed it (with probability $q(\boldsymbol{x}'|\boldsymbol{x})$) and it must have been accepted (with probability $A(\boldsymbol{x}'|\boldsymbol{x})$); otherwise you stay in state $\boldsymbol{x}$, either because that is what you proposed (with probability $q(\boldsymbol{x}|\boldsymbol{x})$), or because you proposed something else (with probability $q(\boldsymbol{x}'|\boldsymbol{x})$) but it was rejected (with probability $1 - A(\boldsymbol{x}'|\boldsymbol{x})$).

Let us analyze this Markov chain. Recall that a chain satisfies **detailed balance** if

$$p(\boldsymbol{x}'|\boldsymbol{x})p^*(\boldsymbol{x}) = p(\boldsymbol{x}|\boldsymbol{x}')p^*(\boldsymbol{x}') \tag{12.7}$$

This means in the in-flow to state $\boldsymbol{x}'$ from $\boldsymbol{x}$ is equal to the out-flow from state $\boldsymbol{x}'$ back to $\boldsymbol{x}$, and vice versa. We also showed that if a chain satisfies detailed balance, then p^* is its stationary distribution. Our goal is to show that the MH algorithm defines a transition function that satisfies detailed balance and hence that p^* is its stationary distribution. (If Equation (12.7) holds, we say that p^* is an **invariant** distribution wrt the Markov transition kernel q.)

Theorem 12.2.1. *If the transition matrix defined by the MH algorithm (given by Equation (12.6)) is ergodic and irreducible, then p^* is its unique limiting distribution.*

Proof. Consider two states $\boldsymbol{x}$ and $\boldsymbol{x}'$. Either

$$p^*(\boldsymbol{x})q(\boldsymbol{x}'|\boldsymbol{x}) < p^*(\boldsymbol{x}')q(\boldsymbol{x}|\boldsymbol{x}') \tag{12.8}$$

or

$$p^*(\boldsymbol{x})q(\boldsymbol{x}'|\boldsymbol{x}) \geq p^*(\boldsymbol{x}')q(\boldsymbol{x}|\boldsymbol{x}') \tag{12.9}$$

Without loss of generality, assume that $p^*(\boldsymbol{x})q(\boldsymbol{x}'|\boldsymbol{x}) > p^*(\boldsymbol{x}')q(\boldsymbol{x}|\boldsymbol{x}')$. Hence

$$\alpha(\boldsymbol{x}'|\boldsymbol{x}) = \frac{p^*(\boldsymbol{x}')q(\boldsymbol{x}|\boldsymbol{x}')}{p^*(\boldsymbol{x})q(\boldsymbol{x}'|\boldsymbol{x})} < 1 \tag{12.10}$$

Hence we have $A(\boldsymbol{x}'|\boldsymbol{x}) = \alpha(\boldsymbol{x}'|\boldsymbol{x})$ and $A(\boldsymbol{x}|\boldsymbol{x}') = 1$.

Now to move from $\boldsymbol{x}$ to $\boldsymbol{x}'$ we must first propose $\boldsymbol{x}'$ and then accept it. Hence

$$p(\boldsymbol{x}'|\boldsymbol{x}) = q(\boldsymbol{x}'|\boldsymbol{x})A(\boldsymbol{x}'|\boldsymbol{x}) = q(\boldsymbol{x}'|\boldsymbol{x})\frac{p^*(\boldsymbol{x}')q(\boldsymbol{x}|\boldsymbol{x}')}{p^*(\boldsymbol{x})q(\boldsymbol{x}'|\boldsymbol{x})} = \frac{p^*(\boldsymbol{x}')}{p^*(\boldsymbol{x})}q(\boldsymbol{x}|\boldsymbol{x}') \tag{12.11}$$

Hence

$$p^*(\boldsymbol{x})p(\boldsymbol{x}'|\boldsymbol{x}) = p^*(\boldsymbol{x}')q(\boldsymbol{x}|\boldsymbol{x}') \tag{12.12}$$

The backwards probability is

$$p(\boldsymbol{x}|\boldsymbol{x}') = q(\boldsymbol{x}|\boldsymbol{x}')A(\boldsymbol{x}|\boldsymbol{x}') = q(\boldsymbol{x}|\boldsymbol{x}') \tag{12.13}$$

since $A(\boldsymbol{x}|\boldsymbol{x}') = 1$. Inserting this into Equation (12.12) we get

$$p^*(\boldsymbol{x})p(\boldsymbol{x}'|\boldsymbol{x}) = p^*(\boldsymbol{x}')p(\boldsymbol{x}|\boldsymbol{x}') \tag{12.14}$$

so detailed balance holds wrt p^*. Hence, from Theorem 2.6.3, p^* is a stationary distribution. Furthermore, from Theorem 2.6.2, this distribution is unique, since the chain is ergodic and irreducible. □

12.2.3   Proposal distributions

In this section, we discuss some common proposal distributions. Note, however, that good proposal design is often intimately dependent on the form of the target distribution (most often the posterior).

12.2.3.1   Independence sampler

If we use a proposal of the form $q(\boldsymbol{x}'|\boldsymbol{x}) = q(\boldsymbol{x}')$, where the new state is independent of the old state, we get a method known as the **independence sampler**, which is similar to importance sampling (Section 11.5). The function $q(\boldsymbol{x}')$ can be any suitable distribution, such as a Gaussian. This has non-zero probability density on the entire state space, and hence is a valid proposal for any unconstrained continuous state space.

12.2.3.2   Random walk Metropolis (RWM) algorithm

The **random walk Metropolis** algorithm corresponds to MH with the following proposal distribution:

$$q(\boldsymbol{x}'|\boldsymbol{x}) = \mathcal{N}(\boldsymbol{x}'|\boldsymbol{x}, \tau^2\mathbf{I}) \tag{12.15}$$

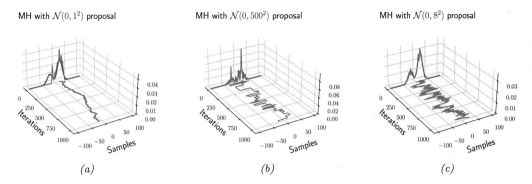

Figure 12.1: *An example of the Metropolis-Hastings algorithm for sampling from a mixture of two 1d Gaussians ($\boldsymbol{\mu} = (-20, 20)$, $\boldsymbol{\pi} = (0.3, 0.7)$, $\boldsymbol{\Sigma} = (100, 100)$), using a Gaussian proposal with standard deviation of $\tau \in \{1, 8, 500\}$. (a) When $\tau = 1$, the chain gets trapped near the starting state and fails to sample from the mode at $\mu = -20$. (b) When $\tau = 500$, the chain is very "sticky", so its effective sample size is low (as reflected by the rough histogram approximation at the end). (c) Using a variance of $\tau = 8$ is just right and leads to a good approximation of the true distribution (shown in red). Compare to Figure 12.4. Generated by mcmc_gmm_demo.ipynb.*

Here τ is a scale factor chosen to facilitate rapid mixing. [RR01b] prove that, if the posterior is Gaussian, the asymptotically optimal value is to use $\tau^2 = 2.38^2/D$, where D is the dimensionality of $\boldsymbol{x}$; this results in an acceptance rate of 0.234, which (in this case) is the optimal tradeoff between exploring widely enough to cover the distribution without being rejected too often. (See [Béd08] for a more recent account of optimal acceptance rates for random walk Metropolis methods.)

Figure 12.1 shows an example where we use RWM to sample from a mixture of two 1D Gaussians. This is a somewhat tricky target distribution, since it consists of two somewhat separated modes. It is very important to set the variance of the proposal τ^2 correctly: if the variance is too low, the chain will only explore one of the modes, as shown in Figure 12.1(a), but if the variance is too large, most of the moves will be rejected, and the chain will be very **sticky**, i.e., it will stay in the same state for a long time. This is evident from the long stretches of repeated values in Figure 12.1(b). If we set the proposal's variance just right, we get the trace in Figure 12.1(c), where the samples clearly explore the support of the target distribution.

12.2.3.3   Composing proposals

If there are several proposals that might be useful, one can combine them using a **mixture proposal**, which is a convex combination of base proposals:

$$q(\boldsymbol{x}'|\boldsymbol{x}) = \sum_{k=1}^{K} w_k q_k(\boldsymbol{x}'|\boldsymbol{x}) \tag{12.16}$$

where w_k are the mixing weights that sum to one. As long as each q_k is an individually valid proposal, and each $w_k > 0$, then the overall mixture proposal will also be valid. In particular, if each proposal is reversible, so it satisfies detailed balance (Section 2.6.4.4), then so does the mixture.

It is also possible to compose individual proposals by chaining them together to get

$$q(\boldsymbol{x'}|\boldsymbol{x}) = \sum_{\boldsymbol{x}_1} \cdots \sum_{\boldsymbol{x}_{K-1}} q_1(\boldsymbol{x}_1|\boldsymbol{x}) q_2(\boldsymbol{x}_2|\boldsymbol{x}_1) \cdots q_K(\boldsymbol{x}|\boldsymbol{x}_{K-1}) \tag{12.17}$$

A common example is where each base proposal only updates a subset of the variables (see e.g., Section 12.3).

12.2.3.4 Data-driven MCMC

In the case where the target distribution is a posterior, $p^*(\boldsymbol{x}) = p(\boldsymbol{x}|\mathcal{D})$, it is helpful to condition the proposal not just on the previous hidden state, but also the visible data, i.e., to use $q(\boldsymbol{x'}|\boldsymbol{x}, \mathcal{D})$. This is called **data-driven MCMC** (see e.g., [TZ02; Jih+12]).

One way to create such a proposal is to train a recognition network to propose states using $q(\boldsymbol{x'}|\boldsymbol{x}, \mathcal{D}) = f(\boldsymbol{x})$. If the state space is high-dimensional, it might be hard to predict all the hidden components, so we can alternatively train individual "experts" to predict specific pieces of the hidden state. For example, in the context of estimating the 3d pose of a person from an image, we might combine a face detector with a limb detector. We can then use a mixture proposal of the form

$$q(\boldsymbol{x'}|\boldsymbol{x}, \mathcal{D}) = \pi_0 q_0(\boldsymbol{x'}|\boldsymbol{x}) + \sum_k \pi_k q_k(x'_k|f_k(\mathcal{D})) \tag{12.18}$$

where q_0 is a standard data-independent proposal (e.g., random walk), and q_k updates the k'th component of the state space.

The overall procedure is a form of **generate and test**: the discriminative proposals $q(\boldsymbol{x'}|\boldsymbol{x}, \mathcal{D})$ generate new hypotheses, which are then "tested" by computing the posterior ratio $\frac{p(\boldsymbol{x'}|\mathcal{D})}{p(\boldsymbol{x}|\mathcal{D})}$, to see if the new hypothesis is better or worse. (See also Section 13.3, where we discuss learning proposal distributions for particle filters.)

12.2.3.5 Adaptive MCMC

One can change the parameters of the proposal as the algorithm is running to increase efficiency. This is called **adaptive MCMC**. This allows one to start with a broad covariance (say), allowing large moves through the space until a mode is found, followed by a narrowing of the covariance to ensure careful exploration of the region around the mode.

However, one must be careful not to violate the Markov property; thus the parameters of the proposal should not depend on the entire history of the chain. It turns out that a sufficient condition to ensure this is that the adaption is "faded out" gradually over time. See e.g., [AT08] for details.

12.2.4 Initialization

It is necessary to start MCMC in an initial state that has non-zero probability. A natural approach is to first use an optimizer to find a local mode. However, at such points the gradients of the log joint are zero, which can cause problems for some gradient-based MCMC methods, such as HMC (Section 12.5), so it can be better to start "close" to a MAP estimate (see e.g., [HFM17, Sec 7.]).

12.3   Gibbs sampling

The major problems with MH are the need to choose the proposal distribution, and the fact that the acceptance rate may be low. In this section, we describe an MH method that exploits conditional independence properties of a graphical model to automatically create a good proposal, with acceptance probability 1. This method is known as **Gibbs sampling**.[2] (In physics, this method is known as **Glauber dynamics** or the **heat bath** method.) This is the MCMC analog of coordinate descent.[3]

12.3.1   Basic idea

The idea behind Gibbs sampling is to sample each variable in turn, conditioned on the values of all the other variables in the distribution. For example, if we have $D = 3$ variables, we use

- $x_1^{s+1} \sim p(x_1 | x_2^s, x_3^s)$

- $x_2^{s+1} \sim p(x_2 | x_1^{s+1}, x_3^s)$

- $x_3^{s+1} \sim p(x_3 | x_1^{s+1}, x_2^{s+1})$

This readily generalizes to D variables. (Note that if x_i is a known variable, we do not sample it, but it may be used as input to th another conditional distribution.)

The expression $p(x_i | \boldsymbol{x}_{-i})$ is called the **full conditional** for variable i. In general, x_i may only depend on some of the other variables. If we represent $p(\boldsymbol{x})$ as a graphical model, we can infer the dependencies by looking at i's Markov blanket, which are its neighbors in the graph (see Section 4.2.4.3), so we can write

$$x_i^{s+1} \sim p(x_i | \boldsymbol{x}_{-i}^s) = p(x_i | \boldsymbol{x}_{\mathrm{mb}(i)}^s) \tag{12.19}$$

(Compare to the equation for mean field variational inference in Equation (10.87).)

We can sample some of the nodes in parallel, without affecting correctness. In particular, suppose we can create a **coloring** of the (moralized) undirected graph, such that no two neighboring nodes have the same color. (In general, computing an optimal coloring is NP-complete, but we can use efficient heuristics such as those in [Kub04].) Then we can sample all the nodes of the same color in parallel, and cycle through the colors sequentially [Gon+11].

12.3.2   Gibbs sampling is a special case of MH

It turns out that Gibbs sampling is a special case of MH where we use a sequence of proposals of the form

$$q_i(\boldsymbol{x}' | \boldsymbol{x}) = p(x_i' | \boldsymbol{x}_{-i}) \mathbb{I}\left(\boldsymbol{x}_{-i}' = \boldsymbol{x}_{-i}\right) \tag{12.20}$$

That is, we move to a new state where x_i is sampled from its full conditional, but $\boldsymbol{x}_{-i}$ is left unchanged.

---

2. Josiah Willard Gibbs, 1839–1903, was an American physicist.
3. Several software libraries exist for applying Gibbs sampling to general graphical models, including Nimble, which is a C++ library with an R wrapper, and which replaces older programs such as BUGS and JAGS.

Figure 12.2: *Illustration of checkerboard pattern for a 2d MRF. This allows for parallel updates.*

We now prove that the acceptance rate of each such proposal is 100%, so the overall algorithm also has an acceptance rate of 100%. We have

$$\alpha = \frac{p(\boldsymbol{x}')q_i(\boldsymbol{x}|\boldsymbol{x}')}{p(\boldsymbol{x})q_i(\boldsymbol{x}'|\boldsymbol{x})} = \frac{p(x_i'|\boldsymbol{x}_{-i}')p(\boldsymbol{x}_{-i}')p(x_i|\boldsymbol{x}_{-i}')}{p(x_i|\boldsymbol{x}_{-i})p(\boldsymbol{x}_{-i})p(x_i'|\boldsymbol{x}_{-i})} \tag{12.21}$$

$$= \frac{p(x_i'|\boldsymbol{x}_{-i})p(\boldsymbol{x}_{-i})p(x_i|\boldsymbol{x}_{-i})}{p(x_i|\boldsymbol{x}_{-i})p(\boldsymbol{x}_{-i})p(x_i'|\boldsymbol{x}_{-i})} = 1 \tag{12.22}$$

where we exploited the fact that $\boldsymbol{x}_{-i}' = \boldsymbol{x}_{-i}$.

The fact that the acceptance rate is 100% does not necessarily mean that Gibbs will converge rapidly, since it only updates one coordinate at a time (see Section 12.3.7). However, if we can group together correlated variables, then we can sample them as a group, which can significantly help mixing.

12.3.3   Example: Gibbs sampling for Ising models

In Section 4.3.2.1, we discuss Ising models and Potts models, which are pairwise MRFs with a 2d grid structure. The joint distribution has the form

$$p(\boldsymbol{x}) = \frac{1}{Z} \prod_{i \sim j} \psi_{ij}(x_i, x_j | \boldsymbol{\theta}) \tag{12.23}$$

where $i \sim j$ means i and j are neighbors in the graph.

To apply Gibbs sampling to such a model, we just need to iteratively sample from each full conditional:

$$p(x_i|\boldsymbol{x}_{-i}) \propto \prod_{j \in \text{nbr}(i)} \psi_{ij}(x_i, x_j) \tag{12.24}$$

Note that although Gibbs sampling is a sequential algorithm, we can sometimes exploit conditional independence properties to perform parallel updates [RS97a]. In the case of a 2d grid, we can color code nodes using a checkerboard pattern shown in Figure 12.2. This has the property that the black nodes are conditionally independent of each other given the white nodes, and vice versa. Hence we can sample all the black nodes in parallel (as a single group), and then sample all the white nodes, etc.

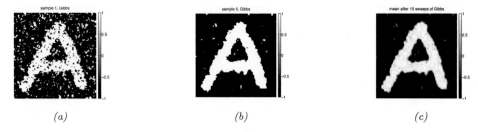

Figure 12.3: *Example of image denoising using Gibbs sampling. We use an Ising prior with $J = 1$ and a Gaussian noise model with $\sigma = 2$. (a) Sample from the posterior after one sweep over the image. (b) Sample after 5 sweeps. (c) Posterior mean, computed by averaging over 15 sweeps. Compare to Figure 10.9 which shows the results of mean field inference. Generated by* ising_image_denoise_demo.ipynb.

To perform the sampling, we need to compute the full conditional in Equation (12.24). In the case of an Ising model with edge potentials $\psi(x_i, x_j) = \exp(Jx_ix_j)$, where $x_i \in \{-1, +1\}$, the full conditional becomes

$$p(x_i = +1|\boldsymbol{x}_{-i}) = \frac{\prod_{j \in \text{nbr}(i)} \psi_{ij}(x_i = +1, x_j)}{\prod_{j \in \text{nbr}(i)} \psi(x_i = +1, x_j) + \prod_{j \in \text{nbr}(i)} \psi(x_i = -1, x_i)} \tag{12.25}$$

$$= \frac{\exp[J \sum_{j \in \text{nbr}(i)} x_j]}{\exp[J \sum_{j \in \text{nbr}(i)} x_j] + \exp[-J \sum_{j \in \text{nbr}(i)} x_j]} \tag{12.26}$$

$$= \frac{\exp[J\eta_i]}{\exp[J\eta_i] + \exp[-J\eta_i]} = \sigma(2J\eta_i) \tag{12.27}$$

where J is the coupling strength, $\eta_i \triangleq \sum_{j \in \text{nbr}(i)} x_j$, and $\sigma(u) = 1/(1 + e^{-u})$ is the sigmoid function. (If we use $x_i \in \{0, 1\}$, this becomes $p(x_i = +1|\boldsymbol{x}_{-i}) = \sigma(J\eta_i)$.) It is easy to see that $\eta_i = x_i(a_i - d_i)$, where a_i is the number of neighbors that agree with (have the same sign as) node i, and d_t is the number of neighbors who disagree. If this number is equal, the "forces" on x_i cancel out, so the full conditional is uniform. Some samples from this model are shown in Figure 4.17.

One application of Ising models is as a prior for binary image denoising problems. In particular, suppose $\boldsymbol{y}$ is a noisy version of $\boldsymbol{x}$, and we wish to compute the posterior $p(\boldsymbol{x}|\boldsymbol{y}) \propto p(\boldsymbol{x})p(\boldsymbol{y}|\boldsymbol{x})$, where $p(\boldsymbol{x})$ is an Ising prior, and $p(\boldsymbol{y}|\boldsymbol{x}) = \prod_i p(y_i|x_i)$ is a per-site likelihood term. Suppose this is a Gaussian. Let $\psi_i(x_i) = \mathcal{N}(y_i|x_i, \sigma^2)$ be the corresponding "local evidence" term. The full conditional becomes

$$p(x_i = +1|\boldsymbol{x}_{-i}, \boldsymbol{y}) = \frac{\exp[J\eta_i]\psi_i(+1)}{\exp[J\eta_i]\psi_i(+1) + \exp[-J\eta_i]\psi_i(-1)} \tag{12.28}$$

$$= \sigma\left(2J\eta_i - \log\frac{\psi_i(+1)}{\psi_i(-1)}\right) \tag{12.29}$$

Now the probability of x_i entering each state is determined both by compatibility with its neighbors (the Ising prior) and compatibility with the data (the local likelihood term).

See Figure 12.3 for an example of this algorithm applied to a simple image denoising problem. The results are similar to the mean field results in Figure 10.9.

12.3.4   Example: Gibbs sampling for Potts models

We can extend Section 12.3.3 to the Potts models as follows. Recall that the model has the following form:

$$p(\boldsymbol{x}) = \frac{1}{Z} \exp(-\mathcal{E}(\boldsymbol{x})) \tag{12.30}$$

$$\mathcal{E}(\boldsymbol{x}) = -J \sum_{i \sim j} \mathbb{I}\left(x_i = x_j\right) \tag{12.31}$$

For a node i with neighbors nbr(i), the full conditional is thus given by

$$p(x_i = k | \boldsymbol{x}_{-i}) = \frac{\exp(J \sum_{n \in \text{nbr}(i)} \mathbb{I}\left(x_n = k\right))}{\sum_{k'} \exp(J \sum_{n \in \text{nbr}(i)} \mathbb{I}\left(x_n = k'\right))} \tag{12.32}$$

So if $J > 0$, a node i is more likely to enter a state k if most of its neighbors are already in state k, corresponding to an attractive MRF. If $J < 0$, a node i is more likely to enter a different state from its neighbors, corresponding to a repulsive MRF. See Figure 4.18 for some samples from this model created using this method.

12.3.5   Example: Gibbs sampling for GMMs

In this section, we consider sampling from a Bayesian Gaussian mixture model of the form

$$p(z = k, \boldsymbol{x} | \boldsymbol{\theta}) = \pi_k \mathcal{N}(\boldsymbol{x} | \boldsymbol{\mu}_k, \boldsymbol{\Sigma}_k) \tag{12.33}$$

$$p(\boldsymbol{\theta}) = \text{Dir}(\boldsymbol{\pi} | \boldsymbol{\alpha}) \prod_{k=1}^{K} \mathcal{N}(\boldsymbol{\mu}_k | \boldsymbol{m}_0, \mathbf{V}_0) \text{IW}(\boldsymbol{\Sigma}_k, \mathbf{S}_0, \nu_0) \tag{12.34}$$

12.3.5.1   Known parameters

Suppose, initially, that the parameteters $\boldsymbol{\theta}$ are known. We can easily draw independent samples from $p(\boldsymbol{x} | \boldsymbol{\theta})$ by using ancestral sampling: first sample z and then $\boldsymbol{x}$. However, for illustrative purposes, we will use Gibbs sampling to draw correlated samples. The full conditional for $p(\boldsymbol{x} | z = k, \boldsymbol{\theta})$ is just $\mathcal{N}(\boldsymbol{x} | \boldsymbol{\mu}_k, \boldsymbol{\Sigma}_k)$, and the full conditional for $p(z = k | \boldsymbol{x})$ is given by Bayes' rule:

$$p(z = k | \boldsymbol{x}, \boldsymbol{\theta}) = \frac{\pi_k \mathcal{N}(\boldsymbol{x} | \boldsymbol{\mu}_k, \boldsymbol{\Sigma}_k)}{\sum_{k'} \pi_{k'} \mathcal{N}(\boldsymbol{x} | \boldsymbol{\mu}_{k'}, \boldsymbol{\Sigma}_{k'})} \tag{12.35}$$

An example of this procedure, applied to a mixture of two 1d Gaussians with means at -20 and $+20$, is shown in Figure 12.4. We see that the samples are auto correlated, meaning that if we are in state 1, we will likely stay in that state for a while, and generate values near μ_1; then we will stochastically jump to state 2, and stay near there for a while, etc. (See Section 12.6.3 for a way to measure this.) By contrast, independent samples from the joint would not be correlated at all.

In Section 12.3.5.2, we modify this example to sample the parameters of the GMM from their posterior, $p(\boldsymbol{\theta} | \mathcal{D})$, instead of sampling from $p(\mathcal{D} | \boldsymbol{\theta})$.

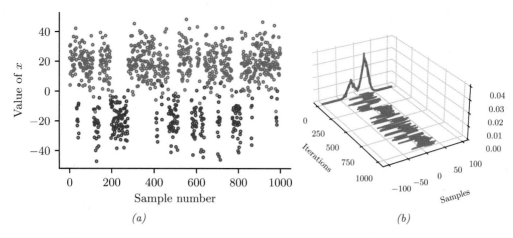

Figure 12.4: (a) Some samples from a mixture of two 1d Gaussians generated using Gibbs sampling. Color denotes the value of z, vertical location denotes the value of x. Horizontal axis represents time (sample number). (b) Traceplot of x over time, and the resulting empirical distribution is shown in blue. The true distribution is shown in red. Compare to Figure 12.1. Generated by mcmc_gmm_demo.ipynb.

12.3.5.2 Unknown parameters

Now suppose the parameters are unknown, so we want to fit the model to data. If we use a conditionally conjugate factored prior, then the full joint distribution is given by

$$p(\boldsymbol{x}, \boldsymbol{z}, \boldsymbol{\mu}, \boldsymbol{\Sigma}, \boldsymbol{\pi}) = p(\boldsymbol{x}|\boldsymbol{z}, \boldsymbol{\mu}, \boldsymbol{\Sigma})p(\boldsymbol{z}|\boldsymbol{\pi})p(\boldsymbol{\pi}) \prod_{k=1}^{K} p(\boldsymbol{\mu}_k)p(\boldsymbol{\Sigma}_k) \tag{12.36}$$

$$= \left(\prod_{i=1}^{N} \prod_{k=1}^{K} (\pi_k \mathcal{N}(\boldsymbol{x}_i|\boldsymbol{\mu}_k, \boldsymbol{\Sigma}_k))^{\mathbb{I}(z_i=k)} \right) \times \tag{12.37}$$

$$\text{Dir}(\boldsymbol{\pi}|\boldsymbol{\alpha}) \prod_{k=1}^{K} \mathcal{N}(\boldsymbol{\mu}_k|\boldsymbol{m}_0, \mathbf{V}_0)\text{IW}(\boldsymbol{\Sigma}_k|\mathbf{S}_0, \nu_0) \tag{12.38}$$

We use the same prior for each mixture component.

The full conditionals are as follows. For the discrete indicators, we have

$$p(z_i = k|\boldsymbol{x}_i, \boldsymbol{\mu}, \boldsymbol{\Sigma}, \boldsymbol{\pi}) \propto \pi_k \mathcal{N}(\boldsymbol{x}_i|\boldsymbol{\mu}_k, \boldsymbol{\Sigma}_k) \tag{12.39}$$

For the mixing weights, we have (using results from Section 3.4.2)

$$p(\boldsymbol{\pi}|\boldsymbol{z}) = \text{Dir}(\{\alpha_k + \sum_{i=1}^{N} \mathbb{I}(z_i = k)\}_{k=1}^{K}) \tag{12.40}$$

For the means, we have (using results from Section 3.4.4.1)

$$p(\boldsymbol{\mu}_k|\boldsymbol{\Sigma}_k, \boldsymbol{z}, \boldsymbol{x}) = \mathcal{N}(\boldsymbol{\mu}_k|\boldsymbol{m}_k, \mathbf{V}_k) \tag{12.41}$$

$$\mathbf{V}_k^{-1} = \mathbf{V}_0^{-1} + N_k\boldsymbol{\Sigma}_k^{-1} \tag{12.42}$$

$$\boldsymbol{m}_k = \mathbf{V}_k(\boldsymbol{\Sigma}_k^{-1}N_k\overline{\boldsymbol{x}}_k + \mathbf{V}_0^{-1}\boldsymbol{m}_0) \tag{12.43}$$

$$N_k \triangleq \sum_{i=1}^{N}\mathbb{I}(z_i = k) \tag{12.44}$$

$$\overline{\boldsymbol{x}}_k \triangleq \frac{\sum_{i=1}^{N}\mathbb{I}(z_i = k)\,\boldsymbol{x}_i}{N_k} \tag{12.45}$$

For the covariances, we have (using results from Section 3.4.4.2)

$$p(\boldsymbol{\Sigma}_k|\boldsymbol{\mu}_k, \boldsymbol{z}, \boldsymbol{x}) = \mathrm{IW}(\boldsymbol{\Sigma}_k|\mathbf{S}_k, \nu_k) \tag{12.46}$$

$$\mathbf{S}_k = \mathbf{S}_0 + \sum_{i=1}^{N}\mathbb{I}(z_i = k)\,(\boldsymbol{x}_i - \boldsymbol{\mu}_k)(\boldsymbol{x}_i - \boldsymbol{\mu}_k)^{\mathsf{T}} \tag{12.47}$$

$$\nu_k = \nu_0 + N_k \tag{12.48}$$

12.3.6 Metropolis within Gibbs

When implementing Gibbs sampling, we have to sample from the full conditionals. If the distributions are conjugate, we can compute the full conditional in closed form, but in the general case, we will need to devise special algorithms to sample from the full conditionals.

One approach is to use the MH algorithm; this is called **Metropolis within Gibbs**. In particular, to sample from $x_i^{s+1} \sim p(x_i|\boldsymbol{x}_{1:i-1}^{s+1}, \boldsymbol{x}_{i+1:D}^s)$, we proceed in 3 steps:

1. Propose $x_i' \sim q(x_i'|x_i^s)$

2. Compute the acceptance probability $A_i = \min(1, \alpha_i)$ where

$$\alpha_i = \frac{p(\boldsymbol{x}_{1:i-1}^{s+1}, x_i', \boldsymbol{x}_{i+1:D}^s)/q(x_i'|x_i^s)}{p(\boldsymbol{x}_{1:i-1}^{s+1}, x_i^s, \boldsymbol{x}_{i+1:D}^s)/q(x_i^s|x_i')} \tag{12.49}$$

3. Sample $u \sim U(0, 1)$ and set $x_i^{s+1} = x_i'$ if $u < A_i$, and set $x_i^{s+1} = x_i^s$ otherwise.

12.3.7 Blocked Gibbs sampling

Gibbs sampling can be quite slow, since it only updates one variable at a time (so-called **single site updating**). If the variables are highly correlated, the chain will move slowly through the state space. This is illustrated in Figure 12.5, where we illustrate sampling from a 2d Gaussian. The ellipse represents the covariance matrix. The size of the moves taken by Gibbs sampling is controlled by the variance of the conditional distributions. If the variance is ℓ along some coordinate direction, but the support of the distribution is L along this dimension, then we need $O((L/\ell)^2)$ steps to obtain an independent sample.

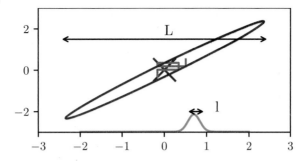

Figure 12.5: *Illustration of potentially slow sampling when using Gibbs sampling for a skewed 2d Gaussian. Adapted from Figure 11.11 of [Bis06]. Generated by gibbs_gauss_demo.ipynb.*

In some cases we can efficiently sample groups of variables at a time. This is called **blocked Gibbs sampling** [JKK95; WY02], and can make much bigger moves through the state space.

As an example, suppose we want to perform Bayesian inference for a state-space model, such as an HMM, i.e., we want to sample from

$$p(\boldsymbol{\theta}, \boldsymbol{z}|\boldsymbol{x}) \propto p(\boldsymbol{\theta}) \prod_{t=1}^{T} p(\boldsymbol{x}_t|\boldsymbol{z}_t, \boldsymbol{\theta})p(\boldsymbol{z}_t|\boldsymbol{z}_{t-1}, \boldsymbol{\theta}) \tag{12.50}$$

We can use blocked Gibbs sampling, where we alternate between sampling from $p(\boldsymbol{\theta}|\boldsymbol{z}, \boldsymbol{x})$ and $p(\boldsymbol{z}|\boldsymbol{x}, \boldsymbol{\theta})$. The former is easy to do (assuming conjugate priors), since all variables in the model are observed (see Section 29.8.4.1). The latter can be done using forwards-filtering backwards-sampling (Section 9.2.7).

12.3.8 Collapsed Gibbs sampling

We can sometimes gain even greater speedups by analytically integrating out some of the unknown quantities. This is called a **collapsed Gibbs sampler**, and it tends to be more efficient, since it is sampling in a lower dimensional space. This can result in lower variance, as discussed in Section 11.6.2.

As an example, consider a GMM with a fully conjugate prior. This can be represented as a DPGM as shown in Figure 12.6a. Since the prior is conjugate, we can analytically integrate out the model parameters $\boldsymbol{\mu}_k$, $\boldsymbol{\Sigma}_k$, and $\boldsymbol{\pi}$, so the only remaining hidden variables are the discrete indicator variables $\boldsymbol{z}$. However, once we integrate out $\boldsymbol{\pi}$, all the z_i nodes become inter-dependent. Similarly, once we integrate out $\boldsymbol{\theta}_k = (\boldsymbol{\mu}_k, \boldsymbol{\Sigma}_k)$, all the $\boldsymbol{x}_i$ nodes become inter-dependent, as shown in Figure 12.6b. Nevertheless, we can easily compute the full conditionals, and hence implement a Gibbs sampler, as we explain below. In particular, the full conditional for the latent indicators is given by

$$p(z_i = k|\boldsymbol{z}_{-i}, \boldsymbol{x}, \boldsymbol{\alpha}, \boldsymbol{\beta}) \propto p(z_i = k|\boldsymbol{z}_{-i}, \boldsymbol{\alpha}, \cancel{\boldsymbol{\beta}})p(\boldsymbol{x}|z_i = k, \boldsymbol{z}_{-i}, \cancel{\boldsymbol{\alpha}}, \boldsymbol{\beta}) \tag{12.51}$$

$$\propto p(z_i = k|\boldsymbol{z}_{-i}, \boldsymbol{\alpha})p(\boldsymbol{x}_i|\boldsymbol{x}_{-i}, z_i = k, \boldsymbol{z}_{-i}, \boldsymbol{\beta})$$

$$p(\boldsymbol{x}_{-i}|\cancel{z_i = k}, \boldsymbol{z}_{-i}, \boldsymbol{\beta}) \tag{12.52}$$

$$\propto p(z_i = k|\boldsymbol{z}_{-i}, \boldsymbol{\alpha})p(\boldsymbol{x}_i|\boldsymbol{x}_{-i}, z_i = k, \boldsymbol{z}_{-i}, \boldsymbol{\beta}) \tag{12.53}$$

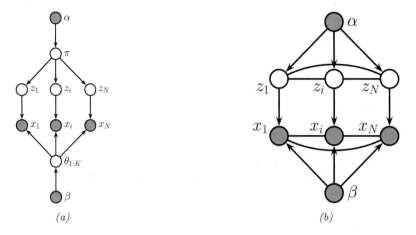

Figure 12.6: (a) A mixture model represented as an "unrolled" DPGM. (b) After integrating out the continuous latent parameters.

where $\boldsymbol{\beta} = (\boldsymbol{m}_0, \mathbf{V}_0, \mathbf{S}_0, \nu_0)$ are the hyper-parameters for the class-conditional densities. We now discuss how to compute these terms.

Suppose we use a symmetric prior of the form $\boldsymbol{\pi} \sim \mathrm{Dir}(\boldsymbol{\alpha})$, where $\alpha_k = \alpha/K$, for the mixing weights. Then we can obtain the first term in Equation (12.53), from Equation (3.96), where

$$p(z_1, \ldots, z_N | \alpha) = \frac{\Gamma(\alpha)}{\Gamma(N+\alpha)} \prod_{k=1}^{K} \frac{\Gamma(N_k + \alpha/K)}{\Gamma(\alpha/K)} \tag{12.54}$$

Hence

$$p(z_i = k | \boldsymbol{z}_{-i}, \alpha) = \frac{p(\boldsymbol{z}_{1:N} | \alpha)}{p(\boldsymbol{z}_{-i} | \alpha)} = \frac{\frac{1}{\Gamma(N+\alpha)}}{\frac{1}{\Gamma(N+\alpha-1)}} \times \frac{\Gamma(N_k + \alpha/K)}{\Gamma(N_{k,-i} + \alpha/K)} \tag{12.55}$$

$$= \frac{\Gamma(N+\alpha-1)}{\Gamma(N+\alpha)} \frac{\Gamma(N_{k,-i} + 1 + \alpha/K)}{\Gamma(N_{k,-i} + \alpha/K)} = \frac{N_{k,-i} + \alpha}{N + \alpha - 1} \tag{12.56}$$

where $N_{k,-i} \triangleq \sum_{n \neq i} \mathbb{I}(z_n = k) = N_k - 1$, and where we exploited the fact that $\Gamma(x+1) = x\Gamma(x)$.

To obtain the second term in Equation (12.53), which is the posterior predictive distribution for $\boldsymbol{x}_i$ given all the other data and all the assignments, we use the fact that

$$p(\boldsymbol{x}_i | \boldsymbol{x}_{-i}, \boldsymbol{z}_{-i}, z_i = k, \boldsymbol{\beta}) = p(\boldsymbol{x}_i | \mathcal{D}_{-i,k}, \boldsymbol{\beta}) \tag{12.57}$$

where $\mathcal{D}_{-i,k} = \{\boldsymbol{x}_j : z_j = k, j \neq i\}$ is all the data assigned to cluster k except for $\boldsymbol{x}_i$. If we use a conjugate prior for $\boldsymbol{\theta}_k$, we can compute $p(\boldsymbol{x}_i | \mathcal{D}_{-i,k}, \boldsymbol{\beta})$ in closed form. Furthermore, we can efficiently update these predictive likelihoods by caching the sufficient statistics for each cluster. To compute the above expression, we remove $\boldsymbol{x}_i$'s statistics from its current cluster (namely z_i), and then evaluate $\boldsymbol{x}_i$ under each cluster's posterior predictive distribution. Once we have picked a new cluster, we add $\boldsymbol{x}_i$'s statistics to this new cluster.

Some pseudo-code for one step of the algorithm is shown in Algorithm 12.2, based on [Sud06, p94]. (We update the nodes in random order to improve the mixing time, as suggested in [RS97b].) We can initialize the sample by sequentially sampling from $p(z_i|\boldsymbol{z}_{1:i-1}, \boldsymbol{x}_{1:i})$. In the case of GMMs, both the naive sampler and collapsed sampler take $O(NKD)$ time per step.

Algorithm 12.2: Collapsed Gibbs sampler for a mixture model

---

1 **for** *each $i = 1 : N$ in random order* **do**
2   Remove $\boldsymbol{x}_i$'s sufficient statistics from old cluster z_i
3   **for** *each $k = 1 : K$* **do**
4   Compute $p_k(\boldsymbol{x}_i|\boldsymbol{\beta}) = p(\boldsymbol{x}_i|\{\boldsymbol{x}_j : z_j = k, j \neq i\}, \boldsymbol{\beta})$
5   Compute $p(z_i = k|\boldsymbol{z}_{-i}, \alpha) \propto (N_{k,-i} + \alpha/K)p_k(\boldsymbol{x}_i)$
6   Sample $z_i \sim p(z_i|\cdot)$
7   Add $\boldsymbol{x}_i$'s sufficient statistics to new cluster z_i

---

The primary advantage of using the collapsed sampler is that it extends to the case where we have an "infinite" number of mixture components, as in the Dirichlet process mixture model of Supplementary Section 31.2.2.

12.4 Auxiliary variable MCMC

Sometimes we can dramatically improve the efficiency of sampling by introducing **auxiliary variables**, in order to reduce correlation between the original variables. If the original variables are denoted by $\boldsymbol{x}$, and the auxiliary variables by $\boldsymbol{v}$, then the augmented distribution becomes $p(\boldsymbol{x}, \boldsymbol{v})$. We assume it is easier to sample from this than the marginal distribution $p(\boldsymbol{x})$. If so, we can draw joint samples $(\boldsymbol{x}^s, \boldsymbol{v}^s) \sim p(\boldsymbol{x}, \boldsymbol{v})$, and then just "throw away" the $\boldsymbol{v}^s$, and the result will be samples from the desired marginal, $\boldsymbol{x}^s \sim \sum_{\boldsymbol{v}} p(\boldsymbol{x}, \boldsymbol{v})$. We give some examples of this below.

12.4.1 Slice sampling

Consider sampling from a univariate, but multimodal, distribution $p(x) = \tilde{p}(x)/Z_p$, where $\tilde{p}(x)$ is unnormalized, and $Z_p = \int \tilde{p}(x)dx$. We can sometimes improve the ability to make large moves by adding a uniform auxiliary variable v. We define the joint distribution as follows:

$$\hat{p}(x, v) = \begin{cases} 1/Z_p & \text{if } 0 \leq v \leq \tilde{p}(x) \\ 0 & \text{otherwise} \end{cases} \tag{12.58}$$

The marginal distribution over x is given by

$$\int \hat{p}(x, v)dv = \int_0^{\tilde{p}(x)} \frac{1}{Z_p}dv = \frac{\tilde{p}(x)}{Z_p} = p(x) \tag{12.59}$$

so we can sample from $p(x)$ by sampling from $\hat{p}(x, v)$ and then ignoring v. To do this, we will use a technique called **slice sampling** [Nea03].

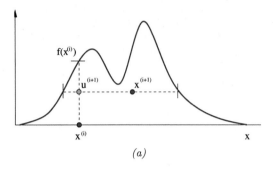 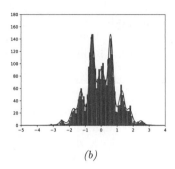

(a) (b)

Figure 12.7: *Slice sampling. (a) Illustration of one step of the algorithm in 1d. Given a previous sample x^i, we sample u^{i+1} uniformly on $[0, f(x^i)]$, where $f = \tilde{p}$ is the (unnormalized) target density. We then sample x^{i+1} along the slice where $f(x) \geq u^{i+1}$. From Figure 15 of [And+03]. Used with kind permission of Nando de Freitas. (b) Output of slice sampling applied to a 1d distribution. Generated by* slice_sampling_demo_1d.ipynb.

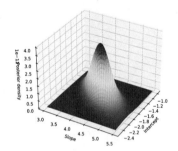 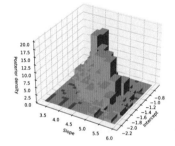

Figure 12.8: *Posterior for binomial regression for 1d data. Left: slice sampling approximation. Right: grid approximation. Generated by* slice_sampling_demo_2d.ipynb.

This works as follows. Given previous sample x^i, we sample v^{i+1} from

$$p(v|x^i) = U_{[0,\tilde{p}(x^i)]}(v) \tag{12.60}$$

This amounts to uniformly picking a point on the vertical line between 0 and $\tilde{p}(x^i)$, We use this to construct a "slice" of the density at or above this height, by computing $A^{i+1} = \{x : \tilde{p}(x) \geq v^{i+1}\}$. We then sample x^{i+1} uniformly from ths set. See Figure 12.7(a) for an illustration.

To compute the level set A, we can use an iterative search procedure called **stepping out**, in which we start with an interval $x_{min} \leq x \leq x_{max}$ around the current point x^i of some width, and then we keep extending it until the endpoints fall outside the slice. We can then use rejection sampling to sample from the interval. For the details, see [Nea03].

To apply the method to multivariate distributions, we sample one extra auxiliary variable for each dimension. Thus we perfom $2D$ sampling operations to draw a single joint sample, where

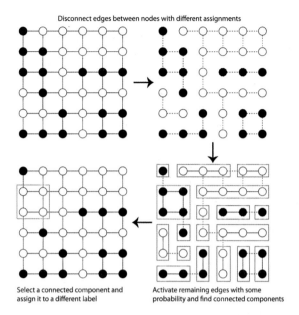

Disconnect edges between nodes with different assignments

Select a connected component and
assign it to a different label

Activate remaining edges with some
probability and find connected components

Figure 12.9: Illustration of the Swendsen-Wang algorithm on a 2d grid. Used with kind permission of Kevin Tang.

D is the number of random variables. The advantage of this over Gibbs sampling applied to the original (non-augmented) distribution is that it only needs access to the unnormalized joint, not the full-conditionals.

Figure 12.7(b) illustrates the algorithm in action on a synthetic 1d problem. Figure 12.8 illustrates its behavior on a slightly harder problem, namely binomial logistic regression. The model has the form $y_i \sim \text{Bin}(n_i, \text{logit}(\beta_1 + \beta_2 x_i))$. We use a vague Gaussian prior for the β_j's. On the left we show the slice sampling approximation to the posterior, and on the right we shpw a grid-based approximation, as a simple deteterministic proxy for the true posterior. We see a close correpondence.

12.4.2 Swendsen-Wang

Consider an Ising model of the following form: $p(\boldsymbol{x}) = \frac{1}{Z} \prod_e \Psi(\boldsymbol{x}_e)$, where $\boldsymbol{x}_e = (x_i, x_j)$ for edge $e = (i, j)$, $x_i \in \{+1, -1\}$, and the edge potential is defined by $\begin{pmatrix} e^J & e^{-J} \\ e^{-J} & e^J \end{pmatrix}$, where J is the edge strength. In Section 12.3.3, we discussed how to apply Gibbs sampling to this model. However, this can be slow when J is large in absolute value, because neighboring states can be highly correlated. The **Swendsen-Wang** algorithm [SW87b] is an auxiliary variable MCMC sampler which mixes much faster, at least for the case of attractive or ferromagnetic models, with $J > 0$.

Suppose we introduce auxiliary binary variables, one per edge.[4] These are called **bond variables**, and will be denoted by $\boldsymbol{v}$. We then define an extended model $p(\boldsymbol{x}, \boldsymbol{v})$ of the form $p(\boldsymbol{x}, \boldsymbol{v}) =$

---

4. Our presentation of the method is based on notes by David MacKay, available from http://www.inference.phy.cam.ac.uk/mackay/itila/swendsen.pdf.

$\frac{1}{Z'} \prod_e \Psi(\boldsymbol{x}_e, v_e)$, where $v_e \in \{0, 1\}$, and we define the new edge potentials as follows:

$$\Psi(\boldsymbol{x}_e, v_e = 0) = \begin{pmatrix} e^{-J} & e^{-J} \\ e^{-J} & e^{-J} \end{pmatrix}, \ \Psi(\boldsymbol{x}_e, v_e = 1) = \begin{pmatrix} e^{J} - e^{-J} & 0 \\ 0 & e^{J} - e^{-J} \end{pmatrix} \tag{12.61}$$

It is clear that $\sum_{v_e=0}^{1} \Psi(\boldsymbol{x}_e, v_e) = \Psi(\boldsymbol{x}_e)$, and hence that $\sum_{\boldsymbol{v}} p(\boldsymbol{x}, \boldsymbol{v}) = p(\boldsymbol{x})$, as required.

Fortunately, it is easy to apply Gibbs sampling to this extended model. The full conditional $p(\boldsymbol{v}|\boldsymbol{x})$ factorizes over the edges, since the bond variables are conditionally independent given the node variables. Furthermore, the full conditional $p(v_e|\boldsymbol{x}_e)$ is simple to compute: if the nodes on either end of the edge are in the same state ($x_i = x_j$), we set the bond v_e to 1 with probability $p = 1 - e^{-2J}$, otherwise we set it to 0. In Figure 12.9 (top right), the bonds that could be turned on (because their corresponding nodes are in the same state) are represented by dotted edges. In Figure 12.9 (bottom right), the bonds that are randomly turned on are represented by solid edges.

To sample $p(\boldsymbol{x}|\boldsymbol{v})$, we proceed as follows. Find the connected components defined by the graph induced by the bonds that are turned on. (Note that a connected component may consist of a singleton node.) Pick one of these components uniformly at random. All the nodes in each such component must have the same state. Pick a state ± 1 uniformly at random, and set all the variables in this component to adopt this new state. This is illustrated in Figure 12.9 (bottom right), where the green square denotes the selected connected component; we set all the nodes within this square to white, to get the bottom left configuration.

It should be intuitively clear that Swendsen-Wang makes much larger moves through the state space than Gibbs sampling. The gains are exponentially large for certain settings of the edge parameter. More precisely, let the edge strength be parameterized by J/T, where $T > 0$ is a computational temperature. For large T, the nodes are roughly independent, so both methods work equally well. However, as T approaches a **critical temperature** T_c, the typical states of the system have very long correlation lengths, and Gibbs sampling takes a very long time to generate independent samples. As the temperature continues to drop, the typical states are either all on or all off. The frequency with which Gibbs sampling moves between these two modes is exponentially small. By contrast, SW mixes rapidly at all temperatures.

Unfortunately, if any of the edge weights are negative, $J < 0$, the system is **frustrated**, and there are exponentially many modes, even at low temperature. SW does not work very well in this setting, since it tries to force many neighboring variables to have the same state. In fact, sampling from these kinds of frustrated systems is provably computationally hard for any algorithm [JS93; JS96].

12.5   Hamiltonian Monte Carlo (HMC)

Many MCMC algorithms perform poorly in high dimensional spaces, because they rely on a form of random search based on local perturbations. In this section, we discuss a method known as **Hamiltonian Monte Carlo** or **HMC**, that leverages gradient information to guide the local moves. This is an auxiliary variable method (Section 12.4) derived from physics [Dua+87; Nea93; Mac03; Nea10; Bet17].[5] In particular, the method builds on **Hamiltonian mechanics**, which we describe below.

---

5. The method was originally called **hybrid MC** [Dua+87]. It was introduced to the statistics community in [Nea93], and was renamed to Hamiltonian MC in [Mac03].

12.5.1 Hamiltonian mechanics

Consider a particle rolling around an energy landscape. We can characterize the motion of the particle in terms of its position $\boldsymbol{\theta} \in \mathbb{R}^D$ (often denoted by $\boldsymbol{q}$) and its momentum $\boldsymbol{v} \in \mathbb{R}^D$ (often denoted by $\boldsymbol{p}$). The set of possible values for $(\boldsymbol{\theta}, \boldsymbol{v})$ is called the **phase space**. We define the **Hamiltonian** function for each point in phase space as follows:

$$\mathcal{H}(\boldsymbol{\theta}, \boldsymbol{v}) \triangleq \mathcal{E}(\boldsymbol{\theta}) + \mathcal{K}(\boldsymbol{v}) \tag{12.62}$$

where $\mathcal{E}(\boldsymbol{\theta})$ is the **potential energy**, $\mathcal{K}(\boldsymbol{v})$ is the **kinetic energy**, and the Hamiltonian is the total energy. In a physical setting, the potential energy is due to the pull of gravity, and the momentum is due to the motion of the particle. In a statistical setting, we often take the potential energy to be

$$\mathcal{E}(\boldsymbol{\theta}) = -\log \tilde{p}(\boldsymbol{\theta}) \tag{12.63}$$

where $\tilde{p}(\boldsymbol{\theta})$ is a possibly unnormalized distribution, such as $p(\boldsymbol{\theta}, \mathcal{D})$, and the kinetic energy to be

$$\mathcal{K}(\boldsymbol{v}) = \frac{1}{2} \boldsymbol{v}^\mathsf{T} \boldsymbol{\Sigma}^{-1} \boldsymbol{v} \tag{12.64}$$

where $\boldsymbol{\Sigma}$ is a positive definite matrix, known as the **inverse mass matrix**.

Stable orbits are defined by trajectories in phase space that have a constant energy, The trajectory of a particle within an energy level set can be obtained by solving the following continuous time differential equations, known as **Hamilton's equations**:

$$\begin{aligned} \frac{d\boldsymbol{\theta}}{dt} &= \frac{\partial \mathcal{H}}{\partial \boldsymbol{v}} = \frac{\partial \mathcal{K}}{\partial \boldsymbol{v}} \\ \frac{d\boldsymbol{v}}{dt} &= -\frac{\partial \mathcal{H}}{\partial \boldsymbol{\theta}} = -\frac{\partial \mathcal{E}}{\partial \boldsymbol{\theta}} \end{aligned} \tag{12.65}$$

To see why energy is conserved, note that

$$\frac{d\mathcal{H}}{dt} = \sum_{i=1}^{D} \left[\frac{\partial \mathcal{H}}{\partial \boldsymbol{\theta}_i} \frac{d\boldsymbol{\theta}_i}{dt} + \frac{\partial \mathcal{H}}{\partial \boldsymbol{v}_i} \frac{d\boldsymbol{v}_i}{dt} \right] = \sum_{i=1}^{D} \left[\frac{\partial \mathcal{H}}{\partial \boldsymbol{\theta}_i} \frac{\partial \mathcal{H}}{\partial \boldsymbol{v}_i} - \frac{\partial \mathcal{H}}{\partial \boldsymbol{\theta}_i} \frac{\partial \mathcal{H}}{\partial \boldsymbol{v}_i} \right] = 0 \tag{12.66}$$

Intuitively, we can understand this result as follows: a satellite in orbit around a planet will "want" to continue in a straight line due to its momentum, but will get pulled in towards the planet due to gravity, and if these forces cancel, the orbit is stable. If the satellite starts spiraling towards the planet, its kinetic energy will increase but its potential energy will decrease.

Note that the mapping from $(\boldsymbol{\theta}(t), \boldsymbol{v}(t))$ to $(\boldsymbol{\theta}(t+s), \boldsymbol{v}(t+s))$ for some time increment s is invertible for small enough time steps. Furthermore, this mapping is volume preserving, so has a Jacobian determinant of 1. (See e.g., [BZ20, p287] for a proof.) These facts will be important later when we turn this system into an MCMC algorithm.

12.5.2 Integrating Hamilton's equations

In this section, we discuss how to simulate Hamilton's equations in discrete time.

12.5.2.1   Euler's method

The simplest way to model the time evolution is to update the position and momentum simultaneously by a small amount, known as the step size η:

$$\boldsymbol{v}_{t+1} = \boldsymbol{v}_t + \eta\frac{d\boldsymbol{v}}{dt}(\boldsymbol{\theta}_t, \boldsymbol{v}_t) = \boldsymbol{v}(t) - \eta\frac{\partial\mathcal{E}(\boldsymbol{\theta}_t)}{\partial\boldsymbol{\theta}} \tag{12.67}$$

$$\boldsymbol{\theta}_{t+1} = \boldsymbol{\theta}_t + \eta\frac{d\boldsymbol{\theta}}{dt}(\boldsymbol{\theta}_t, \boldsymbol{v}_t) = \boldsymbol{\theta}_t + \eta\frac{\partial\mathcal{K}(\boldsymbol{v}_t)}{\partial\boldsymbol{v}} \tag{12.68}$$

If the kinetic energy has the form in Equation (12.64) then the second expression simplifies to

$$\boldsymbol{\theta}_{t+1} = \boldsymbol{\theta}_t + \eta\boldsymbol{\Sigma}^{-1}\boldsymbol{v}_{t+1} \tag{12.69}$$

This is known as **Euler's method**.

12.5.2.2   Modified Euler's method

The **modified Euler's method** is slightly more accurate, and works as follows: First update the momentum, and then update the position using the new momentum:

$$\boldsymbol{v}_{t+1} = \boldsymbol{v}_t + \eta\frac{d\boldsymbol{v}}{dt}(\boldsymbol{\theta}_t, \boldsymbol{v}_t) = \boldsymbol{v}_t - \eta\frac{\partial\mathcal{E}(\boldsymbol{\theta}_t)}{\partial\boldsymbol{\theta}} \tag{12.70}$$

$$\boldsymbol{\theta}_{t+1} = \boldsymbol{\theta}_t + \eta\frac{d\boldsymbol{\theta}}{dt}(\boldsymbol{\theta}_t, \boldsymbol{v}_{t+1}) = \boldsymbol{\theta}_t + \eta\frac{\partial\mathcal{K}(\boldsymbol{v}_{t+1})}{\partial\boldsymbol{v}} \tag{12.71}$$

Unfortunately, the asymmetry of this method can cause some theoretical problems (see e.g., [BZ20, p287]) which we resolve below.

12.5.2.3   Leapfrog integrator

In this section, we discuss the **leapfrog integrator**, which is a symmetrized version of the modified Euler method. We first perform a "half" update of the momentum, then a full update of the position, and then finally another "half" update of the momentum:

$$\boldsymbol{v}_{t+1/2} = \boldsymbol{v}_t - \frac{\eta}{2}\frac{\partial\mathcal{E}(\boldsymbol{\theta}_t)}{\partial\boldsymbol{\theta}} \tag{12.72}$$

$$\boldsymbol{\theta}_{t+1} = \boldsymbol{\theta}_t + \eta\frac{\partial\mathcal{K}(\boldsymbol{v}_{t+1/2})}{\partial\boldsymbol{v}} \tag{12.73}$$

$$\boldsymbol{v}_{t+1} = \boldsymbol{v}_{t+1/2} - \frac{\eta}{2}\frac{\partial\mathcal{E}(\boldsymbol{\theta}_{t+1})}{\partial\boldsymbol{\theta}} \tag{12.74}$$

If we perform multiple leapfrog steps, it is equivalent to performing a half step update of $\boldsymbol{v}$ at the beginning and end of the trajectory, and alternating between full step updates of $\boldsymbol{\theta}$ and $\boldsymbol{v}$ in between.

12.5.2.4   Higher order integrators

It is possible to define higher order integrators that are more accurate, but take more steps. For details, see [BRSS18].

12.5.3 The HMC algorithm

We now describe how to use Hamiltonian dynamics to define an MCMC sampler in the expanded state space $(\boldsymbol{\theta}, \boldsymbol{v})$. The target distribution has the form

$$p(\boldsymbol{\theta}, \boldsymbol{v}) = \frac{1}{Z} \exp\left[-\mathcal{H}(\boldsymbol{\theta}, \boldsymbol{v})\right] = \frac{1}{Z} \exp\left[-\mathcal{E}(\boldsymbol{\theta}) - \frac{1}{2}\boldsymbol{v}^\mathsf{T}\boldsymbol{\Sigma}\boldsymbol{v}\right] \tag{12.75}$$

The marginal distribution over the latent variables of interest has the form

$$p(\boldsymbol{\theta}) = \int p(\boldsymbol{\theta}, \boldsymbol{v}) d\boldsymbol{v} = \frac{1}{Z_q} e^{-\mathcal{E}(\boldsymbol{\theta})} \int \frac{1}{Z_p} e^{-\frac{1}{2}\boldsymbol{v}^\mathsf{T}\boldsymbol{\Sigma}\boldsymbol{v}} d\boldsymbol{v} = \frac{1}{Z_q} e^{-\mathcal{E}(\boldsymbol{\theta})} \tag{12.76}$$

Suppose the previous state of the Markov chain is $(\boldsymbol{\theta}_{t-1}, \boldsymbol{v}_{t-1})$. To sample the next state, we proceed as follows. We set the initial position to $\boldsymbol{\theta}'_0 = \boldsymbol{\theta}_{t-1}$, and sample a new random momentum, $\boldsymbol{v}'_0 \sim \mathcal{N}(\boldsymbol{0}, \boldsymbol{\Sigma})$. We then initialize a random trajectory in the phase space, starting at $(\boldsymbol{\theta}'_0, \boldsymbol{v}'_0)$, and followed for L leapfrog steps, until we get to the final proposed state $(\boldsymbol{\theta}^*, \boldsymbol{v}^*) = (\boldsymbol{\theta}'_L, \boldsymbol{v}'_L)$. If we have simulated Hamiltonian mechanics correctly, the energy should be the same at the start and end of this process; if not, we say the HMC has **diverged**, and we reject the sample. If the energy is constant, we compute the MH acceptance probability

$$\alpha = \min\left(1, \frac{p(\boldsymbol{\theta}^*, \boldsymbol{v}^*)}{p(\boldsymbol{\theta}_{t-1}, \boldsymbol{v}_{t-1})}\right) = \min\left(1, \exp\left[-\mathcal{H}(\boldsymbol{\theta}^*, \boldsymbol{v}^*) + \mathcal{H}(\boldsymbol{\theta}_{t-1}, \boldsymbol{v}_{t-1})\right]\right) \tag{12.77}$$

(The transition probabilities cancel since the proposal is reversible.) Finally, we accept the proposal by setting $(\boldsymbol{\theta}_t, \boldsymbol{v}_t) = (\boldsymbol{\theta}^*, \boldsymbol{v}^*)$ with probability α, otherwise we set $(\boldsymbol{\theta}_t, \boldsymbol{v}_t) = (\boldsymbol{\theta}_{t-1}, \boldsymbol{v}_{t-1})$. (In practice we don't need to keep the momentum term, it is only used inside of the leapfrog algorithm.) See Algorithm 12.3 for the pseudocode.[6]

Algorithm 12.3: Hamiltonian Monte Carlo

---
1 **for** $t = 1 : T$ **do**
2   Generate random momentum $\boldsymbol{v}_{t-1} \sim \mathcal{N}(\boldsymbol{0}, \boldsymbol{\Sigma})$
3   Set $(\boldsymbol{\theta}'_0, \boldsymbol{v}'_0) = (\boldsymbol{\theta}_{t-1}, \boldsymbol{v}_{t-1})$
4   Half step for momentum: $\boldsymbol{v}'_{\frac{1}{2}} = \boldsymbol{v}'_0 - \frac{\eta}{2}\nabla\mathcal{E}(\boldsymbol{\theta}'_0)$
5   **for** $l = 1 : L - 1$ **do**
6          $\boldsymbol{\theta}'_l = \boldsymbol{\theta}'_{l-1} + \eta\boldsymbol{\Sigma}^{-1}\boldsymbol{v}'_{l-1/2}$
7          $\boldsymbol{v}'_{l+1/2} = \boldsymbol{v}'_{l-1/2} - \eta\nabla\mathcal{E}(\boldsymbol{\theta}'_l)$
8   Full step for location: $\boldsymbol{\theta}'_L = \boldsymbol{\theta}'_{L-1} + \eta\boldsymbol{\Sigma}^{-1}\boldsymbol{v}'_{L-1/2}$
9   Half step for momentum: $\boldsymbol{v}'_L = \boldsymbol{v}'_{L-1/2} - \frac{\eta}{2}\nabla\mathcal{E}(\boldsymbol{\theta}'_L)$
10   Compute proposal $(\boldsymbol{\theta}^*, \boldsymbol{v}^*) = (\boldsymbol{\theta}'_L, \boldsymbol{v}'_L)$
11   Compute $\alpha = \min\left(1, \exp[-\mathcal{H}(\boldsymbol{\theta}^*, \boldsymbol{v}^*) + \mathcal{H}(\boldsymbol{\theta}_{t-1}, \boldsymbol{v}_{t-1})]\right)$
12   Set $\boldsymbol{\theta}_t = \boldsymbol{\theta}^*$ with probability α, otherwise $\boldsymbol{\theta}_t = \boldsymbol{\theta}_{t-1}$.

---

6. There are many high-quality implementations of HMC. For example, BlackJAX in JAX.

We need to sample a new momentum at each iteration to satisfy ergodicity. To see why, recall that $\mathcal{H}(\boldsymbol{\theta}, \boldsymbol{v})$ stays approximately constant as we move through phase space. If $\mathcal{H}(\boldsymbol{\theta}, \boldsymbol{v}) = \mathcal{E}(\boldsymbol{\theta}) + \frac{1}{2}\boldsymbol{v}^{\mathsf{T}}\boldsymbol{\Sigma}\boldsymbol{v}$, then clearly $\mathcal{E}(\boldsymbol{\theta}) \leq \mathcal{H}(\boldsymbol{\theta}, \boldsymbol{v}) = h$ for all locations $\boldsymbol{\theta}$ along the trajectory. Thus the sampler cannot reach states where $\mathcal{E}(\boldsymbol{\theta}) > h$. To ensure the sampler explores the full space, we must pick a random momentum at the start of each iteration.

12.5.4   Tuning HMC

We need to specify three hyperparameters for HMC: the number of leapfrog steps L, the step size η, and the covariance $\boldsymbol{\Sigma}$.

12.5.4.1   Choosing the number of steps using NUTS

We want to choose the number of leapfrog steps L to be large enough that the algorithm explores the level set of constant energy, but without doubling back on itself, which would waste computation, due to correlated samples. Fortunately, there is an algorithm, known as the **no-U-turn sampler** or **NUTS** algorithm [HG14], which can adaptively choose L for us.

12.5.4.2   Choosing the step size

When $\boldsymbol{\Sigma} = \mathbf{I}$, the ideal step size η should be roughly equal to the width of $\mathcal{E}(\boldsymbol{\theta})$ in the most constrained direction of the local energy landscape. For a locally quadratic potential, this corresponds to the square root of the smallest marginal standard deviation of the local covariance matrix. (If we think of the energy surface as a valley, this corresponds to the direction with the steepest sides.) A step size much larger than this will cause moves that are likely to be rejected because they move to places which increase the potential energy too much. On the other hand, if the step size is too low, the proposal distribution will not move much from the starting position, and the algorithm will be very slow.

In [BZ20, Sec 9.5.4] they recommend the following heuristic for picking η: set $\boldsymbol{\Sigma} = \mathbf{I}$ and $L = 1$, and then vary η until the acceptance rates are in the range of 40%–80%. Of course, different step sizes might be needed in different parts of the state space. In this case, we can use learning rate schedules from the optimization literature, such as cyclical schedules [Zha+20d].

12.5.4.3   Choosing the covariance (inverse mass) matrix

To allow for larger step sizes, we can use a smarter choice for $\boldsymbol{\Sigma}$, also called the **inverse mass matrix**. One way to estimate a fixed $\boldsymbol{\Sigma}$ is to run HMC with $\boldsymbol{\Sigma} = \mathbf{I}$ for a **warm-up** period, until the chain is "burned in" (see Section 12.6); then we run for a few more steps, so we can compute the empirical covariance matrix using $\boldsymbol{\Sigma} = \mathbb{E}\left[(\boldsymbol{\theta} - \overline{\boldsymbol{\theta}})(\boldsymbol{\theta} - \overline{\boldsymbol{\theta}})^{\mathsf{T}}\right]$. In [Hof+19] they propose a method called the **NeuTra HMC** algorithm which "neutralizes" bad geometry by learning an inverse autoregressive flow model (Section 23.2.4.3) in order to map the warped distribution to an isotropic Gaussian. This is often an order of magnitude faster than vanilla HMC.

12.5.5 Riemann manifold HMC

If we let the covariance matrix change as we move position, so $\mathbf{\Sigma}$ is a function of $\boldsymbol{\theta}$, the method is known as **Riemann manifold HMC** or **RM-HMC** [GC11; Bet13], since the moves follow a curved manifold, rather than the flat manifold induced by a constant $\mathbf{\Sigma}$.

A natural choice for the covariance matrix is to use the Hessian at the current location, to capture the local geometry:

$$\mathbf{\Sigma}(\boldsymbol{\theta}) = \nabla^2 \mathcal{E}(\boldsymbol{\theta}) \tag{12.78}$$

Since this is not always positive definite, an alternative, that can be used for some problems, is to use the Fisher information matrix (Section 3.3.4), given by

$$\mathbf{\Sigma}(\boldsymbol{\theta}) = -\mathbb{E}_{p(\boldsymbol{x}|\boldsymbol{\theta})} \left[\nabla^2 \log p(\boldsymbol{x}|\boldsymbol{\theta}) \right] \tag{12.79}$$

Once we have computed $\mathbf{\Sigma}(\boldsymbol{\theta})$, we can compute the kinetic energy as follows:

$$\mathcal{K}(\boldsymbol{\theta}, \boldsymbol{v}) = \frac{1}{2} \log((2\pi)^D |\mathbf{\Sigma}(\boldsymbol{\theta})|) + \frac{1}{2} \boldsymbol{v}^\mathsf{T} \mathbf{\Sigma}(\boldsymbol{\theta}) \boldsymbol{v} \tag{12.80}$$

Unfortunately the Hamiltonian updates of $\boldsymbol{\theta}$ and $\boldsymbol{v}$ are no longer separable, which makes the RM-HMC algorithm more complex to implement, so it is not widely used.

12.5.6 Langevin Monte Carlo (MALA)

A special case of HMC occurs when we take $L = 1$ leapfrog steps. This is known as **Langevin Monte Carlo** (**LMC**), or the **Metropolis adjusted Langevin algorithm** (**MALA**) [RT96]. This gives rise to the simplified algorithm shown in Algorithm 12.4.

Algorithm 12.4: Langevin Monte Carlo

---

1 **for** $t = 1 : T$ **do**
2 $\quad$ Generate random momentum $\boldsymbol{v}_{t-1} \sim \mathcal{N}(\mathbf{0}, \mathbf{\Sigma})$
3 $\quad$ $\boldsymbol{\theta}^* = \boldsymbol{\theta}_{t-1} - \frac{\eta^2}{2} \mathbf{\Sigma}^{-1} \nabla \mathcal{E}(\boldsymbol{\theta}_{t-1}) + \eta \mathbf{\Sigma}^{-1} \boldsymbol{v}_{t-1}$
4 $\quad$ $\boldsymbol{v}^* = \boldsymbol{v}_{t-1} - \frac{\eta}{2} \nabla \mathcal{E}(\boldsymbol{\theta}_{t-1}) - \frac{\eta}{2} \nabla \mathcal{E}(\boldsymbol{\theta}^*)$
5 $\quad$ Compute $\alpha = \min \left(1, \exp[-\mathcal{H}(\boldsymbol{\theta}^*, \boldsymbol{v}^*)] / \exp[-\mathcal{H}(\boldsymbol{\theta}_{t-1}, \boldsymbol{v}_{t-1})]\right)$
6 $\quad$ Set $\boldsymbol{\theta}_t = \boldsymbol{\theta}^*$ with probability α, otherwise $\boldsymbol{\theta}_t = \boldsymbol{\theta}_{t-1}$.

A further simplification is to eliminate the MH acceptance step. In this case, the update becomes

$$\boldsymbol{\theta}_t = \boldsymbol{\theta}_{t-1} - \frac{\eta^2}{2} \mathbf{\Sigma}^{-1} \nabla \mathcal{E}(\boldsymbol{\theta}_{t-1}) + \eta \mathbf{\Sigma}^{-1} \boldsymbol{v}_{t-1} \tag{12.81}$$

$$= \boldsymbol{\theta}_{t-1} - \frac{\eta^2}{2} \mathbf{\Sigma}^{-1} \nabla \mathcal{E}(\boldsymbol{\theta}_{t-1}) + \eta \sqrt{\mathbf{\Sigma}^{-1}} \boldsymbol{\epsilon}_{t-1} \tag{12.82}$$

where $\boldsymbol{v}_{t-1} \sim \mathcal{N}(\mathbf{0}, \mathbf{\Sigma})$ and $\boldsymbol{\epsilon}_{t-1} \sim \mathcal{N}(\mathbf{0}, \mathbf{I})$. This is just like gradient descent with added noise. If we set $\mathbf{\Sigma}$ to be the Fisher information matrix, this becomes natural gradient descent (Section 6.4) with added noise. If we approximate the gradient with a stochastic gradient, we get a method known as **SGLD**, or **stochastic gradient Langevin descent** (see Section 12.7.1 for details).

Now suppose $\mathbf{\Sigma} = \mathbf{I}$, and we set $\eta = \sqrt{2}$. In continuous time, we get the following stochastic differential equation (SDE), known as **Langevin diffusion**:

$$d\boldsymbol{\theta}_t = -\nabla\mathcal{E}(\boldsymbol{\theta}_t)dt + \sqrt{2}d\mathbf{B}_t \tag{12.83}$$

where $\mathbf{B}_t$ represents D-dimensional **Brownian motion**. If we use this to generate the samples, the method is known as the **anadjusted Langevin algorithm** or **ULA** [Par81; RT96].

12.5.7   Connection between SGD and Langevin sampling

In this section, we discuss a deep connection between stochastic gradient descent (SGD) and Langevin sampling, following the presentation of [BZ20, Sec 10.2.3].

Consider the minimization of the additive loss

$$\mathcal{L}(\boldsymbol{\theta}) = \sum_{n=1}^{N} \mathcal{L}_n(\boldsymbol{\theta}) \tag{12.84}$$

For example, we may define $\mathcal{L}_n(\boldsymbol{\theta}) = -\log p(y_n|\boldsymbol{x}_n, \boldsymbol{\theta}).$) We will use a minibatch approximation to the gradients:

$$\nabla_B\mathcal{L}(\boldsymbol{\theta}) = \frac{1}{B}\sum_{n\in\mathcal{S}}\nabla\mathcal{L}_n(\boldsymbol{\theta}) \tag{12.85}$$

where $\mathcal{S} = \{i_1, \dots, i_B\}$ is a randomly chosen set of indices of size B. For simplicity of analysis, we assume the indices are chosen with replacement from $\{1, \dots, N\}$.

Let us define the (scaled) error (due to minibatching) in the estimated gradient by

$$\boldsymbol{v}_t \triangleq \sqrt{\eta}(\nabla\mathcal{L}(\boldsymbol{\theta}_t) - \nabla_B\mathcal{L}(\boldsymbol{\theta}_t)) \tag{12.86}$$

This is called the **diffusion term**. Then we can rewrite the SGD update as

$$\boldsymbol{\theta}_{t+1} = \boldsymbol{\theta}_t - \eta\nabla_B\mathcal{L}(\boldsymbol{\theta}_t) = \boldsymbol{\theta}_t - \eta\nabla\mathcal{L}(\boldsymbol{\theta}_t) + \sqrt{\eta}\boldsymbol{v}_t \tag{12.87}$$

The diffusion term $\boldsymbol{v}_t$ has mean 0, since

$$\mathbb{E}\left[\nabla_B\mathcal{L}(\boldsymbol{\theta})\right] = \frac{1}{B}\sum_{j=1}^{B}\mathbb{E}\left[\nabla\mathcal{L}_{i_j}(\boldsymbol{\theta})\right] = \frac{1}{B}\sum_{j=1}^{B}\nabla\mathcal{L}(\boldsymbol{\theta}) = \nabla\mathcal{L}(\boldsymbol{\theta}) \tag{12.88}$$

To compute the variance of the diffusion term, note that

$$\mathbb{V}\left[\nabla_B\mathcal{L}(\boldsymbol{\theta})\right] = \frac{1}{B^2}\sum_{j=1}^{B}\mathbb{V}\left[\nabla\mathcal{L}_{i_j}(\boldsymbol{\theta})\right] \tag{12.89}$$

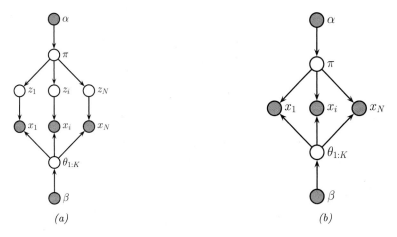

Figure 12.10: (a) A mixture model. (b) After integrating out the discrete latent variables.

where

$$\mathbb{V}\left[\nabla\mathcal{L}_{i_j}(\boldsymbol{\theta})\right] = \mathbb{E}\left[\nabla\mathcal{L}_{i_j}(\boldsymbol{\theta})\nabla\mathcal{L}_{i_j}(\boldsymbol{\theta})^{\mathsf{T}}\right] - \mathbb{E}\left[\nabla\mathcal{L}_{i_j}(\boldsymbol{\theta})\right]\mathbb{E}\left[\nabla\mathcal{L}_{i_j}(\boldsymbol{\theta})^{\mathsf{T}}\right] \tag{12.90}$$

$$= \left(\frac{1}{N}\sum_{n=1}^{N}\nabla\mathcal{L}_n(\boldsymbol{\theta})\nabla\mathcal{L}_n(\boldsymbol{\theta})^{\mathsf{T}}\right) - \nabla\mathcal{L}(\boldsymbol{\theta})\nabla\mathcal{L}(\boldsymbol{\theta})^{\mathsf{T}} \triangleq \mathbf{D}(\boldsymbol{\theta}) \tag{12.91}$$

where $\mathbf{D}(\boldsymbol{\theta})$ is called the **diffusion matrix**. Hence $\mathbb{V}\left[\boldsymbol{v}_t\right] = \frac{\eta}{B}\mathbf{D}(\boldsymbol{\theta}_t)$.

[LTW15] prove that the following continuous time stochastic differential equation is a first-order approximation of minibatch SGD (assuming the loss function is Lipschitz continuous):

$$d\boldsymbol{\theta}(t) = -\nabla\mathcal{L}(\boldsymbol{\theta}(t))dt + \sqrt{\frac{\eta}{B}\mathbf{D}(\boldsymbol{\theta}_t)}d\mathbf{B}(t) \tag{12.92}$$

where $\mathbf{B}(t)$ is Brownian motion. Thus the noise from minibatching causes SGD to act like a Langevin sampler. (See [Hu+17] for more information.)

The scale factor for the noise, $\tau = \frac{\eta}{B}$, plays the role of **temperature**. Thus we see that using a smaller batch size is like using a larger temperature; the added noise ensures that SGD avoids going into narrow ravines, and instead spends most of its time in flat minima which have better generalization performance [Kes+17]. See Section 17.4.1 for more discussion of this point.

12.5.8 Applying HMC to constrained parameters

To apply HMC, we require that all the latent quantities be continuous (real-valued) and have unconstrained support, i.e., $\boldsymbol{\theta} \in \mathbb{R}^D$, so discrete latent variables need to be marginalized out (although some recent work, such as [NDL20; Zho20], relaxes this requirement).

As an example of how this can be done, consider a GMM. We can easily write the likelihood without discrete latents as follows:

$$p(\boldsymbol{x}_n|\boldsymbol{\theta}) = \sum_{k=1}^{K} \pi_k \mathcal{N}(\boldsymbol{x}_n|\boldsymbol{\mu}_k, \boldsymbol{\Sigma}_k) \tag{12.93}$$

The corresponding "collapsed" model is shown in Figure 12.10(b). (Note that this is the opposite of Section 12.3.8, where we integrated out the continuous parameters in order to apply Gibbs sampling to the discrete latents.) We can apply similar techniques to other discrete latent variable models. For example, to apply HMC to HMMs, we can use the forwards algorithm (Section 9.2.2) to efficiently compute $p(\boldsymbol{x}_n|\boldsymbol{\theta}) = \sum_{\boldsymbol{z}_{1:T}} p(\boldsymbol{x}_n, \boldsymbol{z}_{n,1:T}|\boldsymbol{\theta})$.

In addition to marginalizing out any discrete latent variables, we need to ensure the remaining continuous latent variables are unconstrained. This often requires performing a change of variables using a bijector. For example, instead of sampling the discrete probability vector from the probability simplex $\boldsymbol{\pi} \in \mathbb{S}^K$, we should sample the logits $\boldsymbol{\eta} \in \mathbb{R}^K$. After sampling, we can transform back, since bijectors are invertible. (For a practical example, see change_of_variable_hmc.ipynb.)

12.5.9   Speeding up HMC

Although HMC uses gradient information to explore the typical set, sometimes the geometry of the typical set can be difficult to sample from. See Section 12.5.4.3 for ways to estimate the mass matrix, which can help with such difficult cases.

Another issue is the cost of evaluating the target distribution, $\mathcal{E}(\boldsymbol{\theta}) = -\log \tilde{p}(\boldsymbol{\theta})$. For many ML applications, this has the form $\log \tilde{p}(\boldsymbol{\theta}) = \log p_0(\boldsymbol{\theta}) + \sum_{n=1}^{N} \log p(\boldsymbol{\theta}_n|\boldsymbol{\theta})$. This takes $O(N)$ time to compute. We can speed this up by using stochastic gradient methods; see Section 12.7 for details.

12.6   MCMC convergence

We start MCMC from an arbitrary initial state. As we explained in Section 2.6.4, the samples will be coming from the chain's stationary distribution only when the chain has "forgotten" where it started from. The amount of time it takes to enter the stationary distribution is called the mixing time (see Section 12.6.1 for details). Samples collected before the chain has reached its stationary distribution do not come from p^*, and are usually thrown away. The initial period, whose samples will be ignored, is called the **burn-in phase**.

For example, consider a uniform distribution on the integers $\{0, 1, \ldots, 20\}$. Suppose we sample from this using a symmetric random walk. In Figure 12.11, we show two runs of the algorithm. On the left, we start in state 10; on the right, we start in state 17. Even in this small problem it takes over 200 steps until the chain has "forgotten" where it started from. Proposal distributions that make larger changes can converge faster. For example, [BD92; Man] prove that it takes about 7 riffle shuffles to properly mix a deck of 52 cards (i.e., to ensure the distribution is uniform).

In Section 12.6.1 we discuss how to compute the mixing time theoretically. In practice, this can be very hard [BBM10] (this is one of the fundamental weaknesses of MCMC), so in Section 12.6.2, we discuss practical heuristics.

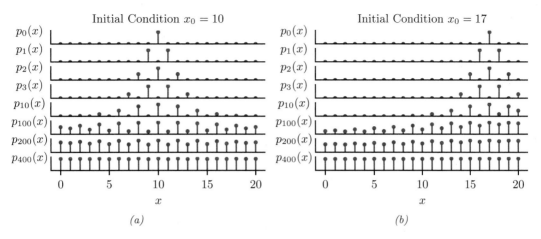

Figure 12.11: *Illustration of convergence to the uniform distribution over $\{0, 1, \ldots, 20\}$ using a symmetric random walk starting from (left) state 10, and (right) state 17. Adapted from Figures 29.14 and 29.15 of [Mac03]. Generated by* random_walk_integers.ipynb.

12.6.1 Mixing rates of Markov chains

The amount of time it takes for a Markov chain to converge to the stationary distribution, and forget its initial state, is called the **mixing time**. More formally, we say that the mixing time from state x_0 is the minimal time such that, for any constant $\epsilon > 0$, we have that

$$\tau_\epsilon(x_0) \triangleq \min\{t : ||\delta_{x_0}(x)T^t - p^*||_1 \leq \epsilon\} \tag{12.94}$$

where $\delta_{x_0}(x)$ is a distribution with all its mass in state x_0, T is the transition matrix of the chain (which depends on the target p^* and the proposal q), and $\delta_{x_0}(x)T^t$ is the distribution after t steps. The mixing time of the chain is defined as

$$\tau_\epsilon \triangleq \max_{x_0} \tau_\epsilon(x_0) \tag{12.95}$$

This is the maximum amount of time it takes for the chain's distribution to get ϵ close to p^* from any starting state.

The mixing time is determined by the eigengap $\gamma = \lambda_1 - \lambda_2$, which is the difference between the first and second eigenvalues of the transition matrix. For a finie state chain, one cans show $\tau_\epsilon = O(\frac{1}{\gamma} \log \frac{n}{\epsilon})$, where n is the number of states.

We can also study the problem by examining the geometry of the state space. For example, consider the chain in Figure 12.12. We see that the state space consists of two "islands", each of which is connected via a narrow "bottleneck". (If they were completely disconnected, the chain would not be ergodic, and there would no longer be a unique stationary distribution, as discussed in Section 2.6.4.3.) We define the **conductance** ϕ of a chain as the minimum probability, over all subsets S of states, of transitioning from that set to its complement:

$$\phi \triangleq \min_{S:0 \leq p^*(S) \leq 0.5} \frac{\sum_{x \in S, x' \in S^c} T(x \to x')}{p^*(S)}, \tag{12.96}$$

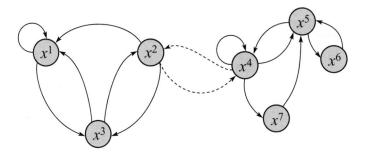

Figure 12.12: A Markov chain with low conductance. The dotted arcs represent transitions with very low probability. From Figure 12.6 of [KF09a]. Used with kind permission of Daphne Koller.

One can show that $\tau_\epsilon \leq O\left(\frac{1}{\phi^2} \log \frac{n}{\epsilon}\right)$. Hence chains with low conductance have high mixing time. For example, distributions with well-separated modes usually have high mixing time. Simple MCMC methods, such as MH and Gibbs, often do not work well in such cases, and more advanced algorithms, such as parallel tempering, are necessary (see e.g., [ED05; Kat+06; BZ20]).

12.6.2   Practical convergence diagnostics

Computing the mixing time of a chain is in general quite difficult, since the transition matrix is usually very hard to compute. Furthermore, diagnosing convergence is computationally intractable in general [BBM10]. Nevertheless, various heuristics have been proposed — see e.g., [Gey92; CC96; BR98; Veh+19]. We discuss some of the current recommended approaches below, following [Veh+19].

12.6.2.1   Trace plots

One of the simplest approaches to assessing if the method has converged is to run multiple chains (typically 3 or 4) from very different **overdispersed** starting points, and to plot the samples of some quantity of interest, such as the value of a certain component of the state vector, or some event such as the value taking on an extreme value. This is called a **trace plot**. If the chain has mixed, it should have "forgotten" where it started from, so the trace plots should converge to the same distribution, and thus overlap with each other.

To illustrate this, we will consider a very simple, but enlightening, example from [McE20, Sec 9.5]. The model is a univariate Gaussian, $y_i \sim \mathcal{N}(\alpha, \sigma)$, with just 2 observations, $y_1 = -1$ and $y_2 = +1$. We first consider a very diffuse prior, $\alpha \sim \mathcal{N}(0, 1000)$ and $\sigma \sim \text{Expon}(0.0001)$, both of which allow for very large values of α and σ. We fit the model using HMC using 3 chains and 500 samples. The result is shown in Figure 12.13. On the right, we show the trace plots for α and σ for 3 different chains. We see that they do not overlap much with each other. In addition, the numerous black vertical lines at the bottom of the plot indicate that HMC had many divergences.

The problem is caused by the overly diffuse priors, which do not get overwhelmed by the likelihood because we only have 2 datapoints. Thus the posterior is also diffuse. We can fix this by using slightly stronger priors, that keep the parameters close to more sensible values. For example, suppose we use $\alpha \sim \mathcal{N}(1, 10)$ and $\sigma \sim \text{Expon}(1)$. Now we get the results in Figure 12.14. On the right we see

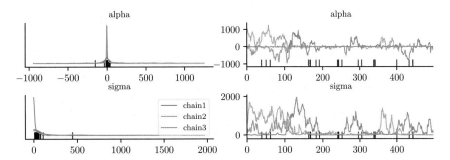

Figure 12.13: *Marginals (left) and trace plot (right) for the univariate Gaussian using the diffuse prior. Black vertical lines indicate HMC divergences. Adapted from Figures 9.9–9.10 of [McE20]. Generated by mcmc_traceplots_unigauss.ipynb.*

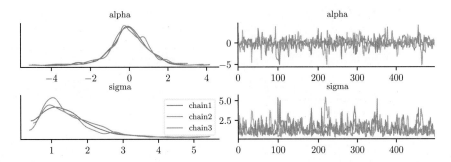

Figure 12.14: *Marginals (left) and trace plot (right) for the univariate Gaussian using the sensible prior. Adapted from Figures 9.9–9.10 of [McE20]. Generated by mcmc_traceplots_unigauss.ipynb.*

that the traceplots overlap. On the left, we see that the marginal distributions from each chain have support over a reasonable interval, and have a peak at the "right" place (the MLE for α is 0, and for σ is 1). And we don't see any divergence warnings (vertical black markers in the plot).

Since trace plots of converging chains correspond to overlapping lines, it can be hard to distinguish success from failure. An alternative plot, known as a **trace rank plot**, was recently proposed in [Veh+19]. (In [McE20], this is called a **trankplot**, a term we borrow.) The idea is to compute the rank of each sample based on all the samples from all the chains, after burnin. We then plot a histogram of the ranks for each chain separately. If the chains have converged, the distribution over ranks should be uniform, since there should be no preference for high or low scoring samples amongst the chains.

The trankplot for the model with the diffuse prior is shown in Figure 12.15. (The x-axis is from 1 to the total number of samples, which in this example is 1500, since we use 3 chains and draw 500 samples from each.) We can see that the different chains are clearly not mixing. The trankplot for the model with the sensible prior is shown in Figure 12.16; this looks much better.

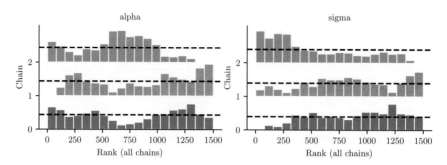

Figure 12.15: *Trace rank plot for the univariate Gaussian using the diffuse prior. Adapted from Figures 9.9–9.10 of [McE20]. Generated by* mcmc_traceplots_unigauss.ipynb.

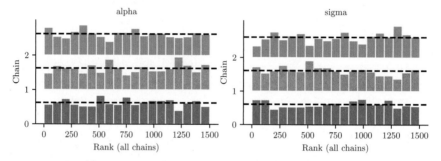

Figure 12.16: *Trace rank plot for the univariate Gaussian using the sensible prior. Adapted from Figures 9.9–9.10 of [McE20]. Generated by* mcmc_traceplots_unigauss.ipynb.

12.6.2.2   Estimated potential scale reduction (EPSR)

In this section, we discuss a way to assess convergence more quantitatively. The basic idea is this: if one or more chains has not mixed well, then the variance of all the chains combined together will be higher than the variance of the individual chains. So we will compare the variance of the quantity of interest computed between and within chains.

More precisely, suppose we have M chains, and we draw N samples from each. Let x_{nm} denote the quantity of interest derived from the n'th sample from the m'th chain. We compute the between- and within-sequence variances as follows:

$$B = \frac{N}{M-1} \sum_{m=1}^{M} (\overline{x}_{\cdot m} - \overline{x}_{\cdot \cdot})^2, \text{ where } \overline{x}_{\cdot m} = \frac{1}{N} \sum_{n=1}^{N} x_{nm}, \quad \overline{x}_{\cdot \cdot} = \frac{1}{M} \sum_{m=1}^{M} \overline{x}_{\cdot m} \tag{12.97}$$

$$W = \frac{1}{M} \sum_{m=1}^{M} s_m^2, \text{ where } s_m^2 = \frac{1}{N-1} \sum_{n=1}^{N} (x_{nm} - \overline{x}_{\cdot m})^2 \tag{12.98}$$

The formula for s_m^2 is the usual unbiased estimate for the variance from a set of N samples; W is just the average of this. The formula for B is similar, but scaled up by N since it is based on the variance of $\overline{x}_{\cdot m}$, which are averaged over N values.

Next we compute the following average variance:

$$\hat{V}^+ \triangleq \frac{N-1}{N}W + \frac{1}{N}B \tag{12.99}$$

Finally, we compute the following quantity, known as the **estimated potential scale reduction** or **R-hat**:

$$\hat{R} \triangleq \sqrt{\frac{\hat{V}^+}{W}} \tag{12.100}$$

In [Veh+19], they recommend checking if $\hat{R} < 1.01$ before declaring convergence.

For example, consider the $\hat{R}$ values for various samplers for our univariate GMM example. In particular, consider the 3 MH samplers in Figure 12.1, and the Gibbs sampler in Figure 12.4. The $\hat{R}$ values are 1.493, 1.039, 1.005, and 1.007. So this diagnostic has correctly identified that the first two samplers are unreliable, which evident from the figure.

In practice, it is recommended to use a slightly different quantity, known as **split-$\hat{R}$**. This can be computed by splitting each chain into the first and second halves, thus doubling the number of chains M (but halving the number of samples N from each), before computing $\hat{R}$. This can detect non-stationarity within a single chain.

12.6.3 Effective sample size

Although MCMC lets us draw samples from a target distribution (assuming it has converged), the samples are not independent, so we may need to draw a lot of them to get a reliable estimate. In this section, we discuss how to compute the **effective sample size** or **ESS** from a set of (possibly correlated) samples.

To start, suppose we draw N *independent* samples from the target distribution, and let $\hat{x} = \frac{1}{N}\sum_{n=1}^{N} x_n$ be our empirical estimate of the mean of the quantity of interest. The variance of this estimate is given by

$$\mathbb{V}[\hat{x}] = \frac{1}{N^2}\mathbb{V}\left[\sum_{n=1}^{N} x_n\right] = \frac{1}{N^2}\sum_{n=1}^{N}\mathbb{V}[x_n] = \frac{1}{N}\sigma^2 \tag{12.101}$$

where $\sigma^2 = \mathbb{V}[X]$. If the samples are correlated, the variance of the estimate will be higher, as we show below.

Recall that for N (not necessarily independent) random variables we have

$$\mathbb{V}\left[\sum_{n=1}^{N} x_n\right] = \sum_{i=1}^{N}\sum_{j=1}^{N}\mathrm{Cov}[x_i, x_j] = \sum_{i=1}^{N}\mathbb{V}[x_i] + 2\sum_{1\le i<j\le N}\mathrm{Cov}[x_i, x_j] \tag{12.102}$$

Let $\bar{x} = \frac{1}{N}\sum_{n=1}^{N} x_n$ be our estimate based on these correlated samples. The variance of this estimate is given by

$$\mathbb{V}[\bar{x}] = \frac{1}{N^2}\sum_{i=1}^{N}\sum_{j=1}^{N}\mathrm{Cov}[x_i, x_j] \tag{12.103}$$

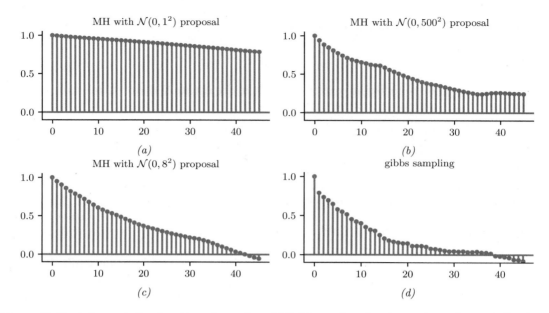

Figure 12.17: *Autocorrelation functions for various MCMC samplers for the mixture of two 1d Gaussians.* *(a-c) These are the MH samplers in Figure 12.1. (d) This is the Gibbs sampler in Figure 12.4. Generated by* *mcmc_gmm_demo.ipynb.*

We now rewrite this in a more convenient form. First recall that the correlation of x_i and x_j is given by

$$\text{corr}\left[x_i, x_j\right] = \frac{\text{Cov}\left[x_i, x_j\right]}{\sqrt{\mathbb{V}\left[x_i\right] \mathbb{V}\left[x_j\right]}} \tag{12.104}$$

Since we assume we are drawing samples from the target distribution, we have $\mathbb{V}\left[x_i\right] = \sigma^2$, where σ^2 is the true variance. Hence

$$\mathbb{V}\left[\overline{x}\right] = \frac{\sigma^2}{N^2} \sum_{i=1}^{N} \sum_{j=1}^{N} \text{corr}\left[x_i, x_j\right] \tag{12.105}$$

For a fixed i, we can think of $\text{corr}\left[x_i, x_j\right]$ as a function of j. This will usually decay as j gets further from i. As $N \to \infty$ we can approximate the sum of correlations by

$$\sum_{j=1}^{N} \text{corr}\left[x_i, x_j\right] \to \sum_{\ell=-\infty}^{\infty} \text{corr}\left[x_i, x_{i+\ell}\right] = 1 + 2 \sum_{\ell=1}^{\infty} \text{corr}\left[x_i, x_{i+\ell}\right] \tag{12.106}$$

since $\text{corr}\left[x_i, x_i\right] = 1$ and $\text{corr}\left[x_i, x_{i-\ll}\right] = \text{corr}\left[x_i, x_{i+\ell}\right]$ for lag $\ell > 0$. Since we assume the samples are coming from a stationary distribution, the index i does not matter. Thus we can define the **autocorrelation time** as

$$\rho = 1 + 2 \sum_{\ell=1}^{\infty} \rho(\ell) \tag{12.107}$$

where $\rho(\ell)$ is the **autocorrelation function** (ACF), defined as

$$\rho(\ell) \triangleq \text{corr}\,[x_0, x_\ell] \tag{12.108}$$

The ACF can be approximated efficiently by convolving the signal $\boldsymbol{x}$ with itself. In Figure 12.17, we plot the ACF for our four samplers for the GMM. We see that the ACF of the Gibbs sampler (bottom right) dies off to 0 much more rapidly than the MH samplers. Intuitively this indicates that each Gibbs sample is "worth" more than each MH sample. We quantify this below.

From Equation (12.105), we can compute the variance of pur estimate in terms of the ACF as follows: $\mathbb{V}\,[\overline{x}] = \frac{\sigma^2}{N^2} \sum_{i=1}^{N} \rho = \frac{\sigma^2}{N}\rho$. By contrast, the variance of the estimate from independent samples is $\mathbb{V}\,[\hat{x}] = \frac{\sigma^2}{N}$. So we see that the variance is a factor ρ larger when there is correlation. We therefore define the **effective sample size** of our set of samples to be

$$N_{\text{eff}} \triangleq \frac{N}{\rho} = \frac{N}{1 + 2\sum_{\ell=1}^{\infty} \rho(\ell)} \tag{12.109}$$

In practice, we truncate the sum at lag L, which is the last integer at which $\rho(L)$ is positive. Also, if we run M chains, the numerator should be NM, so we get the following estimate:

$$\hat{N}_{\text{eff}} = \frac{NM}{1 + 2\sum_{\ell=1}^{L} \hat{\rho}(\ell)} \tag{12.110}$$

In [Veh+19], they propose various extensions of the above estimator, such as using rank statistics, to make the estimate more robust.

12.6.4 Improving speed of convergence

There are many possible things you could try if the $\hat{R}$ value is too large, and/or the effective sample size is too low. Here is a brief list:

- Try using a non-centered parameterization (see Section 12.6.5).

- Try sampling variables in groups or blocks (see Section 12.3.7).

- Try using Rao-Blackwellization, i.e., analytically integrating out some of the variables (see Section 12.3.8).

- Try adding auxiliary variables (see Section 12.4).

- Try using adaptive proposal distributions (see Section 12.2.3.5).

More details can be found in [Rob+18].

12.6.5 Non-centered parameterizations and Neal's funnel

A common problem that arises when applying sampling to hierarchical Bayesian models is when a set of parameters at one level of the model have a tight depenedence on parameters at the level above. We show some practical examples of this in the hierarchical Gaussian 8-schools example in

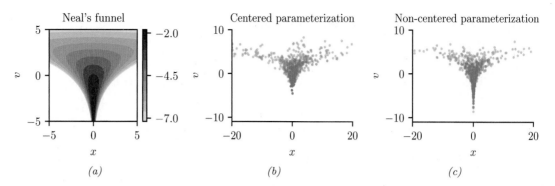

Figure 12.18: Neal's funnel. (a) Joint density. (b) HMC samples from centered representation. (c) HMC samples from non-centered representation. Generated by neals_funnel.ipynb.

Section 3.6.2.2 and the hierarchical radon regression example in Section 15.5.2.2. Here, we focus on the following simple toy model that captures the essence of the problem:

$$\nu \sim \mathcal{N}(0, 3) \tag{12.111}$$
$$x \sim \mathcal{N}(0, \exp(\nu)) \tag{12.112}$$

The corresponding joint density $p(x, \nu)$ is shown in Figure 12.18a. This is known **Neal's funnel**, named after [Nea03]. It is hard for a sampler to "descend" in the narrow "neck" of the distribution, corresponding to areas where the variance ν is small [BG13].

Fortunately, we can represent this model in an equivalent way that makes it easier to sample from, providing we use a **non-centered parameterization** [PR03]. This has the form

$$\nu \sim \mathcal{N}(0, 3) \tag{12.113}$$
$$z \sim \mathcal{N}(0, 1) \tag{12.114}$$
$$x = z \exp(\nu) \tag{12.115}$$

This is easier to sample from, since $p(z, \nu)$ is a product of 2 independent Gaussians, and we can derive x deterministically from these Gaussian samples. The advantage of this reparameterization is shown in Figure 12.18. A method to automatically derive such reparameterizations is discussed in [GMH20].

12.7   Stochastic gradient MCMC

Consider an unnormalized target distribution of the following form:

$$\pi(\boldsymbol{\theta}) \propto p(\boldsymbol{\theta}, \mathcal{D}) = p_0(\boldsymbol{\theta}) \prod_{n=1}^{N} p(\boldsymbol{x}_n | \boldsymbol{\theta}) \tag{12.116}$$

where $\mathcal{D} = (\boldsymbol{x}_1, \dots, \boldsymbol{x}_N)$. Alternatively we can define the target distribution in terms of an energy function (negative log joint) as follows:

$$p(\boldsymbol{\theta}, \mathcal{D}) \propto \exp(-\mathcal{E}(\boldsymbol{\theta})) \tag{12.117}$$

The energy function can be decomposed over data samples:

$$\mathcal{E}(\boldsymbol{\theta}) = \sum_{n=1}^{N} \mathcal{E}_n(\boldsymbol{\theta}) \tag{12.118}$$

$$\mathcal{E}_n(\boldsymbol{\theta}) = -\log p(\boldsymbol{x}_n|\boldsymbol{\theta}) - \frac{1}{N}\log p_0(\boldsymbol{\theta}) \tag{12.119}$$

Evaluating the full energy (e.g., to compute an acceptance probability in the Metropolis-Hastings algorithm, or to compute the gradient in HMC) takes $O(N)$ time, which does not scale to large data. In this section, we discuss some solutions to this problem.

12.7.1 Stochastic gradient Langevin dynamics (SGLD)

Recall from Equation (12.83) that the **Langevin diffusion** SDE has the following form

$$d\boldsymbol{\theta}_t = -\nabla \mathcal{E}(\boldsymbol{\theta}_t)dt + \sqrt{2}d\mathbf{W}_t \tag{12.120}$$

where $d\mathbf{W}_t$ is a Wiener noise (also called Brownian noise) process. In discrete time, we can use the following Euler approximation:

$$\boldsymbol{\theta}_{t+1} \approx \boldsymbol{\theta}_t - \eta_t \nabla \mathcal{E}(\boldsymbol{\theta}_t) + \sqrt{2\eta_t}\mathcal{N}(\mathbf{0}, \mathbf{I}) \tag{12.121}$$

Computing the gradient $\boldsymbol{g}(\boldsymbol{\theta}_t) = \nabla \mathcal{E}(\boldsymbol{\theta}_t)$ at each step takes $O(N)$ time. We can compute an unbiased minibatch approximation to the gradient term in $O(B)$ time using

$$\hat{\boldsymbol{g}}(\boldsymbol{\theta}_t) = \frac{N}{B}\sum_{n \in \mathcal{B}_t} \nabla \mathcal{E}_n(\boldsymbol{\theta}_t) = -\frac{N}{B}\left(\sum_{n \in \mathcal{B}_t} \nabla \log p(\boldsymbol{x}_n|\boldsymbol{\theta}_t) + \frac{B}{N}\nabla \log p_0(\boldsymbol{\theta}_t)\right) \tag{12.122}$$

where $\mathcal{B}_t$ is the minibatch at step t. This gives rise to the following approximate update:

$$\boldsymbol{\theta}_{t+1} = \boldsymbol{\theta}_t - \eta_t \hat{\boldsymbol{g}}(\boldsymbol{\theta}_t) + \sqrt{2\eta_t}\mathcal{N}(\mathbf{0}, \mathbf{I}) \tag{12.123}$$

This is called **stochastic gradient Langevin dynamics** or **SGLD** [Wel11]. The resulting update step is identical to SGD, except for the addition of a Gaussian noise term. (See [Neg+21] for some recent analysis of this method; they also suggest setting $\eta_t \propto N^{-2/3}$.)

12.7.2 Preconditionining

As in SGD, we can get better results (especially for models such as neural networks) if we use preconditioning to scale the gradient updates. In [PT13], they use the Fisher information matrix (FIM) as the preconditioner; this method is known as **stochastic gradient Riemannian Langevin dynamics** or **SGRLD**.

Unfortunately, computing the FIM is often hard. In [Li+16], they propose to use the same kind of diagonal approximation as used by RMSprop; this is called **preconditioned SGLD**. An alternative is to use an Adam-like preconditioner, as proposed in [KSL21]. This is called **SGLD-Adam**. For more details, see [CSN21].

12.7.3   Reducing the variance of the gradient estimate

The variance of the noise introduced by minibatching can be quite large, which can hurt the performance of methods such as SGLD [BDM18]. In [Bak+17], they propose to reduce the variance of this estimate by using a **control variate** estimator; this method is therefore called **SGLD-CV**. Specifically they use the following gradient approximation:

$$\hat{\nabla}_{cv}\mathcal{E}(\boldsymbol{\theta}_t) = \nabla\mathcal{E}(\hat{\boldsymbol{\theta}}) + \frac{N}{B}\sum_{n\in\mathcal{S}_t}\left(\nabla\mathcal{E}_n(\boldsymbol{\theta}_t) - \nabla\mathcal{E}_n(\hat{\boldsymbol{\theta}})\right) \tag{12.124}$$

Here $\hat{\boldsymbol{\theta}}$ is any fixed value, but it is often taken to be an approximate MAP estimate (e.g., based on one epoch of SGD). The reason Equation (12.124) is valid is because the terms we add and subtract are equal in expectation, and hence we get an unbiased estimate:

$$\mathbb{E}\left[\hat{\nabla}_{cv}\mathcal{E}(\boldsymbol{\theta}_t)\right] = \nabla\mathcal{E}(\hat{\boldsymbol{\theta}}) + \mathbb{E}\left[\frac{N}{B}\sum_{n\in\mathcal{S}_t}\left(\nabla\mathcal{E}_n(\boldsymbol{\theta}_t) - \nabla\mathcal{E}_n(\hat{\boldsymbol{\theta}})\right)\right] \tag{12.125}$$

$$= \nabla\mathcal{E}(\hat{\boldsymbol{\theta}}) + \nabla\mathcal{E}(\boldsymbol{\theta}_t) - \nabla\mathcal{E}(\hat{\boldsymbol{\theta}}) = \nabla\mathcal{E}(\boldsymbol{\theta}_t) \tag{12.126}$$

Note that the first term, $\nabla\mathcal{E}(\hat{\boldsymbol{\theta}}) = \sum_{n=1}^{N}\nabla\mathcal{E}_n(\hat{\boldsymbol{\theta}})$, requires a single pass over the entire dataset, but only has to be computed once (e.g., while estimating $\hat{\boldsymbol{\theta}}$).

One disadvantage of SGLD-CV is that the reference point $\hat{\boldsymbol{\theta}}$ has to be precomputed, and is then fixed. An alternative is to update the reference point online, by performing periodic full batch estimates. This is called **SVRG-LD** [Dub+16; Cha+18], where SVRG stands for stochastic variance reduced gradient, and LD stands for Langevin dynamics. If we use $\tilde{\boldsymbol{\theta}}_t$ to denote the most recent snapshot (reference point), the corresponding gradient estimate is given by

$$\hat{\nabla}_{svrg}\mathcal{E}(\boldsymbol{\theta}_t) = \nabla\mathcal{E}(\tilde{\boldsymbol{\theta}}_t) + \frac{N}{B}\sum_{n\in\mathcal{S}_t}\left(\nabla\mathcal{E}_n(\boldsymbol{\theta}_t) - \nabla\mathcal{E}_n(\tilde{\boldsymbol{\theta}}_t)\right) \tag{12.127}$$

We recompute the snapshot every τ steps (known as the epoch length). See Algorithm 12.5 for the pseudo-code.

Algorithm 12.5: SVRG Langevin descent

---

1 Initialize $\boldsymbol{\theta}_0$
2 **for** $t = 1:T$ **do**
3   **if** $t \mod \tau = 0$ **then**
4          $\tilde{\boldsymbol{\theta}} = \boldsymbol{\theta}_t$
5          $\tilde{\boldsymbol{g}} = \sum_{n=1}^{N}\mathcal{E}_n(\tilde{\boldsymbol{\theta}})$
6   Sample minibatch $\mathcal{B}_t \in \{1,\dots,N\}$
7      $\boldsymbol{g}_t = \tilde{\boldsymbol{g}} + \frac{N}{B}\sum_{n\in\mathcal{B}_t}\left(\nabla\mathcal{E}_n(\boldsymbol{\theta}_t) - \nabla\mathcal{E}_n(\tilde{\boldsymbol{\theta}})\right)$
8      $\boldsymbol{\theta}_{t+1} = \boldsymbol{\theta}_t - \eta_t\boldsymbol{g}_t + \sqrt{2\eta_t}\mathcal{N}(\mathbf{0}, \mathbf{I})$

The disadvantage of SVRG is that it needs to perform a full pass over the data every τ steps. An alternative approach, called **SAGA-LD** [Dub+16; Cha+18] (which stands for stochastic averaged gradient acceleration), avoids this by storing all N gradient vectors, and then doing incremental updates. Unfortunately the memory requirements of this algorithm usually make it impractical.

12.7.4 SG-HMC

We discussed Hamiltonian Monte Carlo (HMC) in Section 12.5, which uses auxiliary momentum variables to improve performance over Langevin MC. In this section, we discuss a way to speed it up by approximating the gradients using minibatches. This is called **SG-HMC** [CFG14; ZG21], where SG stands for "stochastic gradient".

Recall that the leapfrog updates have the following form:

$$v_{t+1/2} = v_t - \frac{\eta}{2}\nabla\mathcal{E}(\boldsymbol{\theta}_t) \tag{12.128}$$

$$\boldsymbol{\theta}_{t+1} = \boldsymbol{\theta}_t + \eta v_{t+1/2} = \boldsymbol{\theta}_t + \eta v_t - \frac{\eta}{2}\nabla\mathcal{E}(\boldsymbol{\theta}_t) \tag{12.129}$$

$$v_{t+1} = v_{t+1/2} - \frac{\eta}{2}\nabla\mathcal{E}(\boldsymbol{\theta}_{t+1}) = v_t - \frac{\eta}{2}\nabla\mathcal{E}(\boldsymbol{\theta}_t) - \frac{\eta}{2}\nabla\mathcal{E}(\boldsymbol{\theta}_{t+1}) \tag{12.130}$$

We can replace the full batch gradient with a stochastic approximation, to get

$$\boldsymbol{\theta}_{t+1} = \boldsymbol{\theta}_t + \eta v_t - \frac{\eta^2}{2}g(\boldsymbol{\theta}_t, \boldsymbol{\xi}_t) \tag{12.131}$$

$$v_{t+1} = v_t - \frac{\eta}{2}g(\boldsymbol{\theta}_t, \boldsymbol{\xi}_t) - \frac{\eta}{2}g(\boldsymbol{\theta}_{t+1}, \boldsymbol{\xi}_{t+1/2}) \tag{12.132}$$

where $\boldsymbol{\xi}_t$ and $\boldsymbol{\xi}_{t+1/2}$ are independent sources of randomness (e.g., batch indices). In [ZG21], they show that this algorithm (even without the MH rejection step) provides a good approximation to the posterior (in the sense of having small Wasserstein-2 distance) for the case where the energy functon is strongly convex. Furthermore, performance can be considerably improved if we use the variance reduction methods discussed in Section 12.7.3.

12.7.5 Underdamped Langevin dynamics

The **underdamped Langevin dynamics (ULD)** has the form of the following SDE [CDC15; LMS16; Che+18a; Che+18d]:

$$\begin{aligned} d\boldsymbol{\theta}_t &= v_t dt \\ dv_t &= -g(\boldsymbol{\theta}_t)dt - \gamma v_t dt + \sqrt{2\gamma}d\mathbf{W}_t \end{aligned} \tag{12.133}$$

where $g(\boldsymbol{\theta}_t) = \nabla\mathcal{E}(\boldsymbol{\theta}_t)$ is the gradient or **force** acting on the particle, $\gamma > 0$ is the **friction** parameter, and $d\mathbf{W}_t$ is Wiener noise.

Equation (12.133) is like the Langevin dynamics of Equation (12.83) but with an added momentum term v_t. We can solve the dynamics using various integration methods. It can be shown (see e.g., [LMS16]) that these methods are accurate to second order, whereas solving standard (overdamped) Langevin is only accurate to first order, and thus will require more sampling steps to achieve a given accuracy.

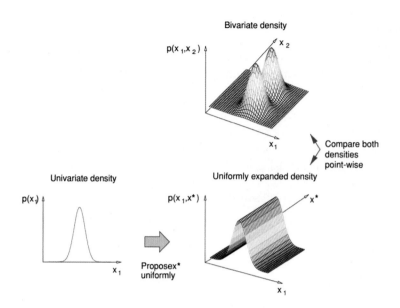

Figure 12.19: *To compare a 1d model against a 2d model, we first have to map the 1d model to 2d space so the two have a common measure. Note that we assume the ridge has finite support, so it is integrable. From Figure 17 of [And+03]. Used with kind permission of Nando de Freitas.*

12.8   Reversible jump (transdimensional) MCMC

Suppose we have a set of models with different numbers of parameters, e.g., mixture models in which the number of mixture components is unknown. Let the model be denoted by m, and let its unknowns (e.g., parameters) be denoted by $\boldsymbol{x}_m \in \mathcal{X}_m$ (e.g., $\mathcal{X}_m = \mathbb{R}^{n_m}$, where n_m is the dimensionality of model m). Sampling in spaces of differing dimensionality is called **trans-dimensional MCMC**. We could sample the model indicator $m \in \{1, \ldots, M\}$ and sample all the parameters from the product space $\prod_{m=1}^{M} \mathcal{X}_m$, but this is very inefficient, and only works if M is finite. It is more parsimonious to sample in the union space $\mathcal{X} = \cup_{m=1}^{M} \{m\} \times \mathcal{X}_m$, where we only worry about parameters for the currently active model.

The difficulty with this approach arises when we move between models of different dimensionality. The trouble is that when we compute the MH acceptance ratio, we are comparing densities defined on spaces of different dimensionality, which is not well defined. For example, comparing densities on two points of a sphere makes sense, but comparing a density on a sphere to a density on a circle does not, as there is a dimensional mismatch in the two concepts. The solution, proposed by [Gre98] and known as **reversible jump MCMC** or **RJMCMC**, is to augment the low dimensional space with extra random variables so that the two spaces have a common measure. This is illustrated in Figure 12.19.

We give a sketch of the algorithm below. For more details, see e.g., [Gre03; HG12].

12.8.1 Basic idea

To explain the method in more detail, we follow the presentation of [And+03]. To ensure a common measure, we need to define a way to extend each pair of subspaces $\mathcal{X}_m$ and $\mathcal{X}_n$ to $\mathcal{X}_{m,n} = \mathcal{X}_m \times \mathcal{U}_{m,n}$ and $\mathcal{X}_{n,m} = \mathcal{X}_n \times \mathcal{U}_{n,m}$. We also need to define a deterministic, differentiable and invertible mapping

$$(\boldsymbol{x}_m, \boldsymbol{u}_{m,n}) = f_{n \to m}(\boldsymbol{x}_n, \boldsymbol{u}_{n,m}) = (f_{n \to m}^x(\boldsymbol{x}_n, \boldsymbol{u}_{n,m}), f_{n \to m}^u(\boldsymbol{x}_n, \boldsymbol{u}_{n,m})) \tag{12.134}$$

Invertibility means that

$$f_{m \to n}(f_{n \to m}(\boldsymbol{x}_n, \boldsymbol{u}_{n,m})) = (\boldsymbol{x}_n, \boldsymbol{u}_{n,m}) \tag{12.135}$$

Finally, we need to define proposals $q_{n \to m}(\boldsymbol{u}_{n,m}|n, \boldsymbol{x}_n)$ and $q_{m \to n}(\boldsymbol{u}_{m,n}|m, \boldsymbol{x}_m)$.

Suppose we are in state $(n, \boldsymbol{x}_n)$. We move to $(m, \boldsymbol{x}_m)$ by generating $\boldsymbol{u}_{n,m} \sim q_{n \to m}(\cdot|n, \boldsymbol{x}_n)$, and then computing $(\boldsymbol{x}_m, \boldsymbol{u}_{m,n}) = f_{n \to m}(\boldsymbol{x}_n, \boldsymbol{u}_{n,m})$. We then accept the move with probability

$$A_{n \to m} = \min \left\{ 1, \frac{p(m, \boldsymbol{x}_m^*)}{p(n, \boldsymbol{x}_n)} \times \frac{q(n|m)}{q(m|n)} \times \frac{q_{m \to n}(\boldsymbol{u}_{m,n}|m, \boldsymbol{x}_m^*)}{q_{n \to m}(\boldsymbol{u}_{n,m}|n, \boldsymbol{x}_n)} \times |\det \mathbf{J}_{f_{m \to n}}| \right\} \tag{12.136}$$

where $\boldsymbol{x}_m^* = f_{n \to m}^x(\boldsymbol{x}_n, \boldsymbol{u}_{n,m})$, $\mathbf{J}_{f_{m \to n}}$ is the Jacobian of the transformation

$$J_{f_{m \to n}} = \frac{\partial f_{n \to m}(\boldsymbol{x}_m, \boldsymbol{u}_{m,n})}{\partial(\boldsymbol{x}_m, \boldsymbol{u}_{m,n})} \tag{12.137}$$

and $|\det \mathbf{J}|$ is the absolute value of the determinant of the Jacobian.

12.8.2 Example

Let us consider an example from [AFD01]. They consider an RBF network for nonlinear regression of the form

$$f(\boldsymbol{x}) = \sum_{j=1}^{k} a_j \mathcal{K}(||\boldsymbol{x} - \boldsymbol{\mu}_j||) + \boldsymbol{\beta}^\mathsf{T} \boldsymbol{x} + \beta_0 + \epsilon \tag{12.138}$$

where $\mathcal{K}()$ is some kernel function (e.g., a Gaussian), k is the number of such basis functions, and ϵ is a Gaussian noise term. If $k = 0$, the model corresponds to linear regression.

They fit this model to the data in Figure 12.20(a). The predictions on the test set are shown in Figure 12.20(b). Estimates of $p(k|\mathcal{D})$, the (distribution over the) number of basis functions, are shown in Figure 12.20(c) as a function of the iteration number; the posterior at the final iteration is shown in Figure 12.20(d). There is clearly the most posterior support for $k = 2$, which makes sense given the two "bumps" in the data.

To generate these results, they consider several kinds of proposal. One of them is to split a current basis function μ into two new ones using

$$\mu_1 = \mu - u_{n,n+1}\alpha, \; \mu_2 = \mu + u_{n,n+1}\alpha \tag{12.139}$$

where α is a parameter of the proposal, and $u_{n,m}$ is sampled from some distribution (e.g., uniform). To ensure reversibility, they define a corresponding merge move

$$\mu = \frac{\mu_1 + \mu_2}{2} \tag{12.140}$$

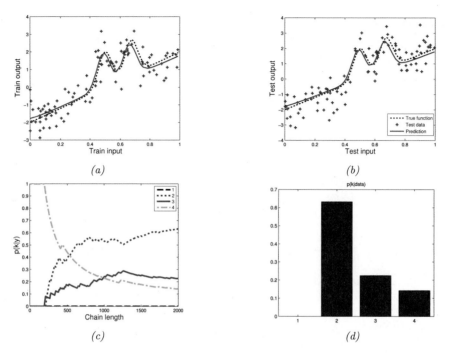

Figure 12.20: Fitting an RBF network to some 1d data using RJMCMC. (a) Prediction on train set. (b) Prediction on test set. (c) Plot of $p(k|\mathcal{D})$ vs iteration. (d) Final posterior $p(k|\mathcal{D})$. Adapted from Figure 4 of [AFD01]. Generated by rjmcmc_rbf, written by Nando de Freitas.

where μ_1 is chosen at random, and μ_2 is its nearest neighbor. To ensure these moves are reversible, we require $||\mu_1 - \mu_2|| < 2\beta$.

The acceptance ratio for the split move is given by

$$A_{split} = \min\left\{1, \frac{p(k+1,\mu_{k+1})}{p(k,\mu_{k+1})} \times \frac{1/(k+1)}{1/k} \times \frac{1}{p(u_{n,m})} \times |\det \mathbf{J}_{split}|\right\} \tag{12.141}$$

where $1/k$ is the probability of choosing one of the k bases uniformly at random. The Jacobian is

$$\mathbf{J}_{split} = \frac{\partial(\mu_1,\mu_2)}{\partial(\mu, u_{n,m})} = \det\begin{pmatrix} 1 & 1 \\ -\beta & \beta \end{pmatrix} \tag{12.142}$$

so $|\det \mathbf{J}_{split}| = 2\beta$. The acceptance ratio for the merge move is given by

$$A_{merge} = \min\left\{1, \frac{p(k-1,\mu_{k-1})}{p(k,\mu_k)} \times \frac{1/(k-1)}{1/k} \times |\det \mathbf{J}_{merge}|\right\} \tag{12.143}$$

where $|\det \mathbf{J}_{merge}| = 1/(2\beta)$.

The overall pseudo-code for the algorithm, assuming the current model has index k, is given in Algorithm 12.6. Here b_k is the probability of a birth move, d_k is the probability of a death move, s_k

---

Algorithm 12.6: Generic reversible jump MCMC (single step)

---

1 Sample $u \sim U(0, 1)$
2 If $u \leq b_k$
3 then birth move
4 else if $u \leq (b_k + d_k)$ then death move
5 else if $u \leq (b_k + d_k + s_k)$ then split move
6 else if $u \leq (b_k + d_k + s_k + m_k)$ then merge move
7 else update parameters

---

is the probability of a split move, and m_k is the probability of a merge move. If we don't make a dimension-changing move, we just update the parameters of the current model using random walk MH.

12.8.3   Discussion

RJMCMC algorithms can be quite tricky to implement. If, however, the continuous parameters can be integrated out (resulting in a method called collapsed RJMCMC), much of the difficulty goes away, since we are just left with a discrete state space, where there is no need to worry about change of measure. For example, if we fix the centers $\boldsymbol{\mu}_j$ in Equation (12.138) (e.g., using samples from the data, or using K-means clustering), we are left with a linear model, where we can integrate out the parameters. All that is left to do is sample which of these fixed basis functions to include in the model, which is a discrete variable selection problem. See e.g., [Den+02] for details.

In Chapter 31, we discuss Bayesian nonparametric models, which allow for an infinite number of different models. Surprisingly, such models are often easier to deal with computationally (as well as more realistic, statistically) than working with a finite set of different models.

12.9   Annealing methods

Many distributions are multimodal and hence hard to sample from. However, by analogy to the way metals are heated up and then cooled down in order to make the molecules align, we can imagine using a computational temperature parameter to "smooth out" a distribution, gradually cooling it to recover the original "bumpy" distribution. We first explain this idea in more detail in the context of an algorithm for MAP estimation. We then discuss extensions to the sampling case.

12.9.1   Simulated annealing

In this section, we discuss the **simulated annealing** algorithm [KJV83; LA87], which is a variant of the Metropolis-Hastings algorithm which is designed to find the global optimum of blackbox function. (Other approaches to blackbox optimization are discussed in Section 6.7.)

Annealing is a physical process of heating a solid until thermal stresses are released, then cooling it very slowly until the crystals are perfectly arranged, acheiving a minimum energy state. Depending on how fast or slow the temperature is cooled, the results will have better or worse quality. We can apply this approach to probability distributions, to control the number of modes (low energy states)

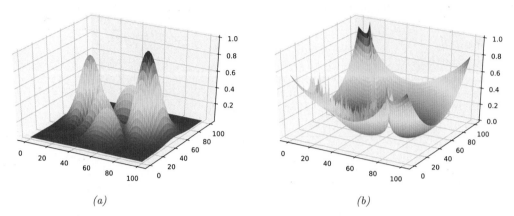

Figure 12.21: (a) A peaky distribution. (b) Corresponding energy function. Generated by simulated_annealing_2d_demo.ipynb.

that they have, by defining

$$p_T(\boldsymbol{x}) = \exp(-\mathcal{E}(\boldsymbol{x})/T) \tag{12.144}$$

where T is the temperature, which is reduced over time. As an example, consider the **peaks function**:

$$p(x, y) \propto |3(1-x)^2 e^{-x^2 - (y+1)^2} - 10(\frac{x}{5} - x^3 - y^5)e^{-x^2 - y^2} - \frac{1}{3}e^{-(x+1)^2 - y^2}| \tag{12.145}$$

This is plotted in Figure 12.21a. The corresponding energy is in Figure 12.21b. We plot annealed versions of this distribution in Figure 12.22. At high temperatures, $T \gg 1$, the surface is approximately flat, and hence it is easy to move around (i.e., to avoid local optima). As the temperature cools, the largest peaks become larger, and the smallest peaks disappear. By cooling slowly enough, it is possible to "track" the largest peak, and thus find the global optimum (minimum energy state). This is an example of a **continuation method**.

In more detail, at each step, we sample a new state according to some proposal distribution $\boldsymbol{x}' \sim q(\cdot|\boldsymbol{x}_t)$. For real-valued parameters, this is often simply a random walk proposal centered on the current iterate, $\boldsymbol{x}' = \boldsymbol{x}_t + \boldsymbol{\epsilon}_{t+1}$, where $\boldsymbol{\epsilon}_{t+1} \sim \mathcal{N}(\boldsymbol{0}, \boldsymbol{\Sigma})$. (The matrix $\boldsymbol{\Sigma}$ is often diagonal, and may be updated over time using the method in [Cor+87].) Having proposed a new state, we compute the acceptance probability

$$\alpha_{t+1} = \exp\left(-(\mathcal{E}(\boldsymbol{x}') - \mathcal{E}(\boldsymbol{x}_t))/T_t\right) \tag{12.146}$$

where T_t is the temperature of the system. We then accept the new state (i.e., set $\boldsymbol{x}_{t+1} = \boldsymbol{x}'$) with probability $\min(1, \alpha_{t+1})$, otherwise we stay in the current state (i.e., set $\boldsymbol{x}_{t+1} = \boldsymbol{x}_t$). This means that if the new state has lower energy (is more probable), we will definitely accept it, but if it has higher energy (is less probable), we might still accept, depending on the current temperature. Thus the algorithm allows "downhill" moves in probability space (uphill in energy space), but less frequently as the temperature drops.

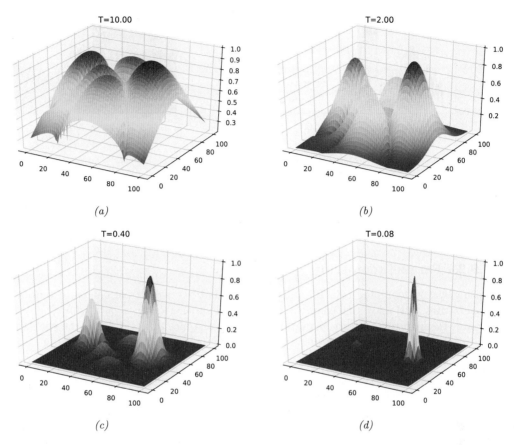

Figure 12.22: Annealed version of the distribution in Figure 12.21a at different temperatures. Generated by simulated_annealing_2d_demo.ipynb.

The rate at which the temperature changes over time is called the **cooling schedule**. It has been shown [Haj88] that if one cools according to a logarithmic schedule, $T_t \propto 1/\log(t+1)$, then the method is guaranteed to find the global optimum under certain assumptions. However, this schedule is often too slow. In practice it is common to use an **exponential cooling schedule** of the form $T_{t+1} = \gamma T_t$, where $\gamma \in (0,1]$ is the cooling rate. Cooling too quickly means one can get stuck in a local maximum, but cooling too slowly just wastes time. The best cooling schedule is difficult to determine; this is one of the main drawbacks of simulated annealing.

In Figure 12.23a, we show a cooling schedule using $\gamma = 0.9$. If we combine this with a Gaussian random walk proposal with $\sigma = 10$ to the peaky distribution in Figure 12.21a, we get the results shown in Figure 12.23 and Figure 12.23b. We see that the algorithm concentrates its samples near the global optimum (the peak on the middle right).

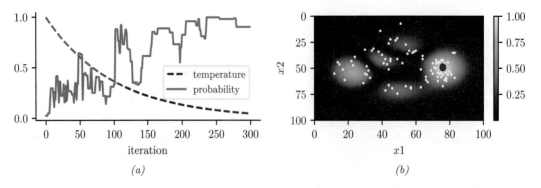

Figure 12.23: Simulated annealing applied to the distribution in Figure 12.21a. (a) Temperature vs iteration and probability of each visited point vs iteration. (b) Visited samples, superimposed on the target distribution. The big red dot is the highest probability point found. Generated by simulated_annealing_2d_demo.ipynb.

12.9.2 Parallel tempering

Another way to combine MCMC and annealing is to run multiple chains in parallel at different temperatures, and allow one chain to sample from another chain at a neighboring temperature. In this way, the high temperature chain can make long distance moves through the state space, and have this influence lower temperature chains. This is known as **parallel tempering**. See e.g., [ED05; Kat+06] for details.

13 Sequential Monte Carlo

13.1 Introduction

In this chapter, we discuss **sequential Monte Carlo** or **SMC** algorithms, which can be used to sample from a sequence of related probability distributions. SMC is most commonly used to solve filtering in state-space models (SSM, Chapter 29), but it can also be applied to other problems, such as sampling from a static (but possibly multi-modal) distribution, or for sampling rare events from some process.

Our presentation is based on the excellent tutorial [NLS19], and differs from traditional presentations, such as [Aru+02], by emphasizing the fact that we are sampling sequences of related variables, not just computing the filtering distribution of an SSM. This more general perspective will let us tackle static estimation problems, as we will see. For another good introduction to SMC, see [DJ11]. For a more formal (measure theoretic) treatment of SMC, using the **Feynman-Kac** formalism, see [CP20b].

13.1.1 Problem statement

In SMC, the goal is to sample from a sequence of related distributions of the form

$$\pi_t(\boldsymbol{z}_{1:t}) = \frac{1}{Z_t}\tilde{\gamma}_t(\boldsymbol{z}_{1:t}) \tag{13.1}$$

for $t = 1 : T$, where $\tilde{\gamma}_t$ is the unnormalized **target distribution**, π_t is the normalized version, and $\boldsymbol{z}_{1:t}$ are the random variables of interest. In some applications (e.g., filtering in an SSM), we care about each intermediate marginal distribution, $\pi_t(\boldsymbol{z}_t)$, for $t = 1 : T$; this is called **particle filtering**. (The word "particle" just means "sample".) In other applications, we only care about the final distribution, $\pi_T(\boldsymbol{z}_T)$, and the intermediate steps are introduced just for computational reasons; this is called an **SMC sampler**. We briefly review both of these below, and go into more detail in later sections.

13.1.2 Particle filtering for state-space models

An important application of SMC is to sequential (online) inference (state estimation) in SSMs. As an example, consider a Markovian state-space model with the following joint distribution:

$$\pi_T(\boldsymbol{z}_{1:T}) \propto p(\boldsymbol{z}_{1:T}, \boldsymbol{y}_{1:T}) = p(\boldsymbol{z}_1)p(\boldsymbol{y}_1|\boldsymbol{z}_1)\prod_{t=1}^{T} p(\boldsymbol{z}_t|\boldsymbol{z}_{t-1})p(\boldsymbol{y}_t|\boldsymbol{z}_t) \tag{13.2}$$

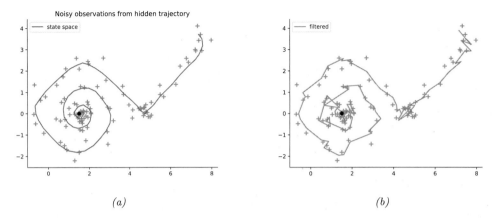

Figure 13.1: Illustration of particle filtering (using the dynamical prior as the proposal) applied to a 2d nonlinear dynamical system. (a) True underlying state and observed data. (b) PF estimate of the posterior mean. Generated by bootstrap_filter_spiral.ipynb.

A common choice is to define the unnormalized target distribution at step t to be

$$\tilde{\gamma}_t(\boldsymbol{z}_{1:t}) = p(\boldsymbol{z}_{1:t}, \boldsymbol{y}_{1:t}) = p(\boldsymbol{z}_1)p(\boldsymbol{y}_1|\boldsymbol{z}_1) \prod_{s=1}^{t} p(\boldsymbol{z}_s|\boldsymbol{z}_{s-1})p(\boldsymbol{y}_s|\boldsymbol{z}_s) \tag{13.3}$$

Note that this a distribution over an (ever growing) sequence of latent variables. However, we often only care about the most recent marginal of this distribution, in which case we just need to compute $\tilde{\gamma}_t(\boldsymbol{z}_t)$, which avoids having to store the full history.

For example, consider the following 2d nonlinear tracking problem (the same one as in Section 8.3.2.3):

$$\begin{aligned} p(\boldsymbol{z}_t|\boldsymbol{z}_{t-1}) &= \mathcal{N}(\boldsymbol{z}_t|f(\boldsymbol{z}_{t-1}), q\mathbf{I}) \\ p(\boldsymbol{y}_t|\boldsymbol{z}_t) &= \mathcal{N}(\boldsymbol{y}_t|\boldsymbol{z}_t, r\mathbf{I}) \\ \boldsymbol{f}(\boldsymbol{z}) &= (z_1 + \Delta\sin(z_2), z_2 + \Delta\cos(z_1)) \end{aligned} \tag{13.4}$$

where Δ is the step size of the underlying continuous system, q is the variance of the system noise, and r is the variance of the observation noise. (We treat Δ, q, and r as fixed constants; see Supplementary Section 13.1.3 for a discussion of joint state and parameter estimation.) The true underlying state trajectory, and the corresponding noisy measurements, are shown in Figure 13.1a. The posterior mean estimate of the state, computed using 2000 samples in a simple form of SMC called the bootstrap filter (Section 13.2.3.1), is shown in Figure 13.1b.

Particle filtering can also be applied to **non-Markovian models**, where $\boldsymbol{z}_t$ may depend on all the past hidden states, $\boldsymbol{z}_{1:t-1}$, and $\boldsymbol{y}_t$ depends on the current $\boldsymbol{z}_t$ and possibly also all the past hidden states, $\boldsymbol{z}_{1:t-1}$, and optionally the past observatiobns, $\boldsymbol{y}_{1:t-1}$. In this case, the unnormalized target distribution at step t is

$$\tilde{\gamma}_t(z_{1:t}) = p(z_1)p(y_1|z_1)\prod_{s=1}^{t} p(z_s|z_{1:s-1})p(y_s|z_{1:s}) \tag{13.5}$$

For example, consider a 1d Gaussian sequence model where the dynamics are first-order Markov, but the observations depend on the entire past sequence (this is example 1.2.1 from [NLS19]):

$$p(z_t|z_{1:t-1}) = \mathcal{N}(z_t|\phi z_{t-1}, q)$$

$$p(y_t|z_{1:t}) = \mathcal{N}(y_t|\sum_{s=1}^{t} \beta^{t-s} z_s, r) \tag{13.6}$$

If we set $\beta = 0$, we get $p(y_t|z_{1:t}) = \mathcal{N}(y_t|z_t, r)$ (where we define $0^0 = 1$), so the model becomes a linear-Gaussian SSM. As β gets larger, the dependence on the past increases, making the inference problem harder. (We will revisit this example below.)

13.1.3 SMC samplers for static parameter estimation

Now consider the problem of parameter estimation from a fixed dataset, $\mathcal{D} = \{y_n : n = 1 : N\}$. We suppose the observations are conditionally iid, so the posterior has the form $p(z|\mathcal{D}) \propto p(z)\prod_{n=1}^{N} p(y_n|z)$, where z is the unknown parameter. It is not immediately obvious how to approximate $p(z|\mathcal{D})$ using SMC, since we just have one distribution. However, we can convert this into a sequential inference problem in several different ways. One approach, known as **data tempering**, defines the (marginal) target distribution at step t as $\tilde{\gamma}_t(z_t) = p(z_t)p(y_{1:t}|z_t)$. In this case, the number of time steps T is the same as the number of data samples, N. Another approach, known as **likelihood tempering**, defines the (marginal) target distribution at step t as $\tilde{\gamma}_t(z_t) = p(z_t)p(\mathcal{D}|z_t)^{\tau_t}$, where $0 = \tau_t < \cdots < \tau_T = 1$ is a temperature parameter. In this case, the number of steps T depends on how quickly we anneal the distibution from the initial prior $p(z_1)$ to the final target $p(z_T)p(\mathcal{D}|z_T)$.

Once we have defined the marginal target distributions $\tilde{\gamma}_t(z_t)$, we need a way to expand this to a joint target distribution over a *sequence* of variables, $\tilde{\gamma}_t(z_{1:t})$, so the distributions become connected to each other. We explain how to do this in Section 13.6. We can then treat the model as an SSM and apply particle filtering. At the end, we extract the final joint target distribution, $\tilde{\gamma}_T(z_{1:T}) = p(z_{1:T})p(\mathcal{D}|z_T)$, from which we can compute the marginal target distribution $\tilde{\gamma}_T(z_T) = p(z_T, \mathcal{D})$, from which we can get the posterior $p(z|\mathcal{D})$ by normalizing. We give the details in Section 13.6.

13.2 Particle filtering

In this section, we cover the basics of SMC for state space models, culiminating in a method known as the **particle filter**.

13.2.1 Importance sampling

We start by reviewing the self-normalized importance sampling method (**SNIS**), which is the foundation of the particle filter. (See also Section 11.5.)

Suppose we are interested in estimating the expectation of some function φ_t with respect to a target distribution π_t, which we denote by

$$\pi_t(\varphi) \triangleq \mathbb{E}_{\pi_t}\left[\varphi_t(\mathbf{z}_{1:t})\right] = \int \frac{\tilde{\gamma}_t(\mathbf{z}_{1:t})}{Z_t} \varphi_t(\mathbf{z}_{1:t}) d\mathbf{z}_{1:t} \tag{13.7}$$

where $Z_t = \int \tilde{\gamma}_t(\mathbf{z}_{1:t}) d\mathbf{z}_{1:t}$. Suppose we use SNIS with proposal $q_t(\mathbf{z}_{1:t})$. We then get the following approximation:

$$\pi_t(\varphi) \approx \frac{1}{\hat{Z}_t} \frac{1}{N_s} \sum_{i=1}^{N_s} \tilde{w}_t(\mathbf{z}_{1:t}^i) \varphi_t(\mathbf{z}_{1:t}^i) \tag{13.8}$$

where $\mathbf{z}_{1:t}^i \overset{\text{iid}}{\sim} q_t$ are independent samples from the proposal, $\tilde{w}_t^i$ are the **unnormalized weights** defined by

$$\tilde{w}_t^i = \frac{\tilde{\gamma}_t(\mathbf{z}_{1:t}^i)}{q_t(\mathbf{z}_{1:t}^i)} \tag{13.9}$$

and $\hat{Z}_t$ is the approximate normalization constant defined by

$$\hat{Z}_t \triangleq \frac{1}{N_s} \sum_{i=1}^{N_s} \tilde{w}_t^i \tag{13.10}$$

To simplify notation, let us define the **normalized weights** by

$$W_t^i = \frac{\tilde{w}_t^i}{\sum_j \tilde{w}_t^j} \tag{13.11}$$

Then we can write

$$\mathbb{E}_{\pi_t}\left[\varphi_t(\mathbf{z}_{1:t})\right] \approx \sum_{i=1}^{N_s} W_t^i \varphi_t(\mathbf{z}_{1:t}^i) \tag{13.12}$$

Alternatively, instead of computing the expectation of a specific target function, we can just approximate the target distribution itself, using a sum of weighted samples:

$$\pi_t(\mathbf{z}_{1:t}) \approx \sum_{i=1}^{N_s} W_t^i \delta(\mathbf{z}_{1:t} - \mathbf{z}_{1:t}^i) \triangleq \hat{\pi}_t(\mathbf{z}_{1:t}) \tag{13.13}$$

The problem with importance sampling when applied in the context of sequential models is that the dimensionality of the state space is very large, and increases with t. This makes it very hard to define a good proposal that covers the high probability regions, resulting in most samples getting negligible weight. In the sections below, we discuss solutions to this problem.

13.2.2 Sequential importance sampling

In this section, we discuss **sequential importance sampling** or **SIS**, in which the proposal has the following autoregressive structure:

$$q_t(\boldsymbol{z}_{1:t}) = q_{t-1}(\boldsymbol{z}_{1:t-1})q_t(\boldsymbol{z}_t|\boldsymbol{z}_{1:t-1}) \tag{13.14}$$

We can obtain samples from $q_{t-1}(\boldsymbol{z}_{1:t-1})$ by reusing the $\boldsymbol{z}_{1:t-1}^i$ samples, which we then extend by one step by sampling from the conditional $q_t(\boldsymbol{z}_t|\boldsymbol{z}_{1:t-1}^i)$. We can think of this as "growing" the chain (sequence of states). The unnormalized weights can be computed recursively as follows:

$$\tilde{w}_t(\boldsymbol{z}_{1:t}) = \frac{\tilde{\gamma}_t(\boldsymbol{z}_{1:t})}{q_t(\boldsymbol{z}_{1:t})} = \frac{\tilde{\gamma}_{t-1}(\boldsymbol{z}_{1:t-1})}{\tilde{\gamma}_{t-1}(\boldsymbol{z}_{1:t-1})} \frac{\tilde{\gamma}_t(\boldsymbol{z}_{1:t})}{q_t(\boldsymbol{z}_t|\boldsymbol{z}_{1:t-1})q_{t-1}(\boldsymbol{z}_{1:t-1})} \tag{13.15}$$

$$= \frac{\tilde{\gamma}_{t-1}(\boldsymbol{z}_{1:t-1})}{q_{t-1}(\boldsymbol{z}_{1:t-1})} \frac{\tilde{\gamma}_t(\boldsymbol{z}_{1:t})}{\tilde{\gamma}_{t-1}(\boldsymbol{z}_{1:t-1})q_t(\boldsymbol{z}_t|\boldsymbol{z}_{1:t-1})} \tag{13.16}$$

$$= \tilde{w}_{t-1}(\boldsymbol{z}_{1:t-1})\frac{\tilde{\gamma}_t(\boldsymbol{z}_{1:t})}{\tilde{\gamma}_{t-1}(\boldsymbol{z}_{1:t-1})q_t(\boldsymbol{z}_t|\boldsymbol{z}_{1:t-1})} \tag{13.17}$$

The ratio factors are sometimes called the **incremental importance weights**:

$$\alpha_t(\boldsymbol{z}_{1:t}) = \frac{\tilde{\gamma}_t(\boldsymbol{z}_{1:t})}{\tilde{\gamma}_{t-1}(\boldsymbol{z}_{1:t-1})q_t(\boldsymbol{z}_t|\boldsymbol{z}_{1:t-1})} \tag{13.18}$$

See Algorithm 13.1 for pseudocode for the resulting SIS algorithm. (In practice we compute the weights in log-space, and convert back using the log-sum-exp trick.)

Note that, in the special case of state space models, the weight computation can be further simplified. In particular, suppose we have

$$\tilde{\gamma}_t(\boldsymbol{z}_{1:t}) = p(\boldsymbol{z}_{1:t}, \boldsymbol{y}_{1:t}) = p(\boldsymbol{y}_t|\boldsymbol{z}_{1:t})p(\boldsymbol{z}_t|\boldsymbol{z}_{1:t-1})p(\boldsymbol{z}_{1:t-1}, \boldsymbol{y}_{1:t-1}) \tag{13.19}$$

$$= p(\boldsymbol{y}_t|\boldsymbol{z}_{1:t})p(\boldsymbol{z}_t|\boldsymbol{z}_{1:t-1})\tilde{\gamma}_{t-1}(\boldsymbol{z}_{1:t-1}) \tag{13.20}$$

Then the incremental weight is given by

$$\alpha_t(\boldsymbol{z}_{1:t}) = \frac{p(\boldsymbol{y}_t|\boldsymbol{z}_{1:t})p(\boldsymbol{z}_t|\boldsymbol{z}_{1:t-1})\tilde{\gamma}_{t-1}(\boldsymbol{z}_{1:t-1})}{\tilde{\gamma}_{t-1}(\boldsymbol{z}_{1:t-1})q_t(\boldsymbol{z}_t|\boldsymbol{z}_{1:t-1})} = \frac{p(\boldsymbol{y}_t|\boldsymbol{z}_{1:t})p(\boldsymbol{z}_t|\boldsymbol{z}_{1:t-1})}{q_t(\boldsymbol{z}_t|\boldsymbol{z}_{1:t-1})} \tag{13.21}$$

Unfortunately SIS suffers from a problem known as **weight degeneracy** or **particle impoverishment**, in which most of the weights become very small (near zero), so the posterior ends up being approximated by a single particle. This is illustrated in Figure 13.2a, where we apply SIS to the non-Markovian example in Equation (13.6) using $N_s = 5$ particles. The reason for degeneracy is that each particle has to "explain" (generate) the entire sequence of observations. Each sequence of guessed states becomes increasingly improbable over time, due to the product of likelihood terms, and the differences between the weights of each hypothesis will grow exponentially. Of course, there has to be a best sequence amongst the set of candidates, so when we normalize the weights, the best one will get weight 1 and the rest will get weight 0. But this is a waste of most of the particles. We discuss a solution to this in Section 13.2.3.

Algorithm 13.1: Sequential importance sampling (SIS)

---

1 Initialization: $\boldsymbol{z}_1^i \sim q_1(\boldsymbol{z}_1)$, $\tilde{w}_1^i = \frac{\tilde{\gamma}_1(\boldsymbol{z}_1^i)}{q_1(\boldsymbol{z}_1^i)}$, $W_1^i = \frac{\tilde{w}_1^i}{\sum_j \tilde{w}_1^j}$, $\hat{\pi}_1(\boldsymbol{z}_1) = \sum_{i=1}^{N_s} W_1^i \delta(\boldsymbol{z}_1 - \boldsymbol{z}_1^i)$

2 **for** $t = 2 : T$ **do**

3 $\quad$ **for** $i = 1 : N_s$ **do**

4 $\quad\quad$ Sample $\boldsymbol{z}_t^i \sim q_t(\boldsymbol{z}_t | \boldsymbol{z}_{1:t-1}^i)$

5 $\quad\quad$ Compute incremental weight $\alpha_t^i = \frac{\tilde{\gamma}_t(\boldsymbol{z}_{1:t}^i)}{\tilde{\gamma}_{t-1}(\boldsymbol{z}_{1:t-1}^i) q_t(\boldsymbol{z}_t^i | \boldsymbol{z}_{1:t-1}^i)}$

6 $\quad\quad$ Compute unnormalized weight $\tilde{w}_t^i = \tilde{w}_{t-1}^i \alpha_t^i$

7 $\quad$ Compute normalized weights $W_t^i = \frac{\tilde{w}_t^i}{\sum_j \tilde{w}_t^j}$ for $i = 1 : N_s$

8 $\quad$ Compute MC posterior $\hat{\pi}_t(\boldsymbol{z}_{1:t}) = \sum_{i=1}^{N_s} W_t^i \delta(\boldsymbol{z}_{1:t} - \boldsymbol{z}_{1:t}^i)$

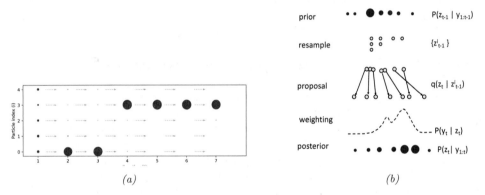

(a)   (b)

Figure 13.2: (a) Illustration of weight degeneracy for SIS applied to the model in Equation (13.6). with parameters $(\phi, q, \beta, r) = (0.9, 10.0, 0.5, 1.0)$. We use $T = 6$ steps and $N_s = 5$ samples. We see that as t increases, almost all the probability mass concentrates on particle 3. Generated by sis_vs_smc.ipynb. Adapted from Figure 2 of [NLS19]. (b) Illustration of the bootstrap particle filtering algorithm.

13.2.3 Sequential importance sampling with resampling

In this section, we describe **sequential importance sampling with resampling** (**SISR**). The basic idea is this: instead of "growing" all of the old particle sequences by one step, we first select the N_s "fittest" particles, by sampling from the old posterior, and then we let these survivors grow by one step.

In more detail, at step t, we sample from

$$q_t^{\text{SISR}}(\boldsymbol{z}_{1:t}) = \hat{\pi}_{t-1}(\boldsymbol{z}_{1:t-1}) q_t(\boldsymbol{z}_t | \boldsymbol{z}_{1:t-1}) \tag{13.22}$$

where $\hat{\pi}_{t-1}(\boldsymbol{z}_{1:t-1})$ is the previous weighted posterior approximation. By contrast, in SIS, we sample from

$$q_t^{\text{SIS}}(\boldsymbol{z}_{1:t}) = q_{t-1}^{\text{SIS}}(\boldsymbol{z}_{1:t-1}) q_t(\boldsymbol{z}_t | \boldsymbol{z}_{1:t-1}) \tag{13.23}$$

Algorithm 13.2: Sequential importance sampling with resampling (SISR)

---

1 Initialization: $z_1^i \sim q_1(z_1)$, $\tilde{w}_1^i = \frac{\tilde{\gamma}_1(z_1^i)}{q_1(z_1^i)}$, $W_1^i = \frac{\tilde{w}_1^i}{\sum_j \tilde{w}_1^j}$, $\hat{\pi}_1(z_1) = \sum_{i=1}^{N_s} W_1^i \delta(z_1 - z_1^i)$

2 **for** $t = 2 : T$ **do**

3   Compute ancestors $a_{t-1}^{1:N_s} = \text{resample}(\tilde{w}_{t-1}^{1:N_s})$

4   Select $z_{t-1}^{1:N_s} = \text{permute}(a_{t-1}^{1:N_s}, z_{t-1}^{1:N_s})$

5   Reset unnormalized weights $\tilde{w}_{t-1}^{1:N_s} = 1/N_s$

6   **for** $i = 1 : N_s$ **do**

7   Sample $z_t^i \sim q_t(z_t|z_{1:t-1}^i)$

8   Compute unnormalized weight $\tilde{w}_t^i = \alpha_t^i = \frac{\tilde{\gamma}_t(z_{1:t}^i)}{\tilde{\gamma}_{t-1}(z_{1:t-1}^i)q_t(z_t^i|z_{1:t-1}^i)}$

9   Compute normalized weights $W_t^i = \frac{\tilde{w}_t^i}{\sum_j \tilde{w}_t^j}$ for $i = 1 : N_s$

10   Compute MC posterior $\hat{\pi}_t(z_{1:t}) = \sum_{i=1}^{N_s} W_t^i \delta(z_{1:t} - z_{1:t}^i)$

We can sample from Equation (13.22) in two steps. First we **resample** N_s samples from $\hat{\pi}_{t-1}(z_{1:t-1})$ to get a *uniformly weighted* set of new samples $z_{1:t-1}^i$. (See Section 13.2.4 for details on how to do this.) Then we extend each sample using $z_t^i \sim q_t(z_t|z_{1:t-1}^i)$, and concatenate z_t^i to $z_{1:t-1}^i$,

After making a proposal, we compute the unnormalized weights. We use the standard SNIS method, except we "pretend" that the proposal is given by $\tilde{\gamma}_{t-1}(z_{1:t-1}^i)q_t(z_t^i|z_{1:t-1}^i)$ even though we used $\hat{\pi}_{t-1}(z_{1:t-1}^i)q_t(z_t^i|z_{1:t-1}^i)$. The intuitive reason why this is valid is because the previous weighted approximation, $\hat{\pi}_{t-1}(z_{1:t-1}^i)$, was an unbiased estimate of the previous target distribution, $\tilde{\gamma}_{t-1}(z_{1:t-1})$. (See e.g., [CP20b] for more theoretical details.) We then compute the unnormalized weights, which are the same as the incremental weights, since the resampling step sets $\tilde{w}_{t-1}^i = 1$. We then normalize these weights and compute the new approximationg to the target posterior $\hat{\pi}_t(z_{1:t})$. See Algorithm 13.2 for the pseudocode.

13.2.3.1 Bootstrap filter

We now consider a special case of SISR, in which the model is an SSM, and the proposal distribution is equal to the dynamical prior:

$$q_t(z_t|z_{1:t-1}) = p(z_t|z_{1:t-1}) \tag{13.24}$$

In this case, the corresponding incremental weight in Equation (13.21) simplifies to

$$\alpha_t(z_{1:t}) = \frac{p(y_t|z_{1:t})p(z_t|z_{1:t-1})}{q(z_t|z_{1:t-1})} = \frac{p(y_t|z_t)p(z_t|z_{t-1})}{p(z_t|z_{t-1})} = p(y_t|z_{1:t}) \tag{13.25}$$

This special case is called the **bootstrap filter** [Gor93] or the **survival of the fittest** algorithm [KKR95]. (In the computer vision literature, this is called the **condensation** algorithm, which stands for "conditional density propagation" [IB98].) See Figure 13.2b for an illustration of how this algorithm works, and Figure 13.1b for some sample results on real data.

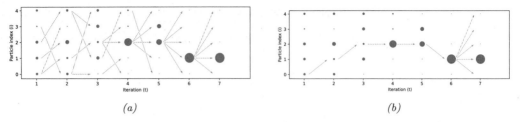

Figure 13.3: (a) Illustration of diversity of samples in SMC applied to the model in Equation (13.6). (b) Illustration of the path degeneracy problem. Generated by sis_vs_smc.ipynb. Adapted from Figure 3 of [NLS19].

The bootstrap filter is useful for models where we can sample from the dynamics, but cannot evaluate the transition model pointwise. This occurs in certain implicit dynamical models, such as those defined using differential equatons (see e.g., [IBK06]); such models are often used in epidemiology. However, in general it is much more efficient to use proposals that take the current evidence $\boldsymbol{y}_t$ into account. We discuss ways to approximate such "locally optimal" proposals in Section 13.3.

13.2.3.2 Path degeneracy problem

In Figure 13.3a we show how particle filtering can result in a much more diverse set of active particles, with more balanced weights when applied to the non-Markovian example in Equation (13.6).

While particle filtering does not suffer from weight degeneracy, it does suffer from another problem known as **path degeneracy**. This refers to the fact that the number of particles that "survive" (have non-negligible weight) over many steps may drop rapidly over time, resulting in a loss of diversity when we try to represent the distribution over the past. We illustrate this in Figure 13.3b, where we only include arrows for samples that have been resampled at each step up until the final step. We see that we have $N_s = 5$ identical copies of $\boldsymbol{z}_1^1$ in the final set of surviving sequences. (The time at which all the paths meet at a common ancestor, when tracing backwards in time, is known as the **coalescence** time.) We discuss some ways to ameliorate this issue in Section 13.2.4 and Section 13.2.5.

13.2.3.3 Estimating the normalizing constant

We can use particle filtering to approximate the normalization constant $Z_T = p(\boldsymbol{y}_{1:T}) = \prod_{t=1}^{T} p(\boldsymbol{y}_t | \boldsymbol{y}_{1:t-1})$ as follows:

$$\hat{Z}_T = \prod_{t=1}^{T} \hat{Z}_t \tag{13.26}$$

where, from Equation (13.10), we have

$$\hat{Z}_t = \frac{1}{N_s} \sum_{i=1}^{N_s} \tilde{w}_t^i = \hat{Z}_{t-1} \left(\widehat{Z_t / Z_{t-1}} \right) \tag{13.27}$$

where

$$\widehat{Z_t/Z_{t-1}} = \frac{\sum_{i=1}^{N_s} \tilde{w}_t^i}{\sum_{i=1}^{N_s} \tilde{w}_{t-1}^i} \tag{13.28}$$

This estimate of the marginal likelihood is very useful for tasks such as parameter estimation.

13.2.4 Resampling methods

Importance sampling gives a weighted set of particles, $\{(W_t^i, \boldsymbol{z}_t^i) : i = 1 : N\}$, which we can use to approximate posterior expectations using

$$\mathbb{E}[f(\boldsymbol{z}_t)|\boldsymbol{y}_{1:t}] \approx \sum_{i=1}^{N} W_t^i f(\boldsymbol{z}_t^i) \tag{13.29}$$

Suppose we sample a single index $A \in \{1, \ldots, N\}$ with probabilities $(W_t^1, \ldots, W_t^N)$. Then the expected value evaluated at this index is

$$\mathbb{E}\left[f(\boldsymbol{z}_t^A)|\boldsymbol{y}_{1:t}\right] = \sum_{i=1}^{N} p(A = i) f(\boldsymbol{z}_t^i) = \sum_{i=1}^{N} W_t^i f(\boldsymbol{z}_t^i) \tag{13.30}$$

If we sample N indices independently and compute their average, we get

$$\mathbb{E}[f(\boldsymbol{z}_t)|\boldsymbol{y}_{1:t}, A_{1:N}] \approx \frac{1}{N} \sum_{i=1}^{N} f(\boldsymbol{z}_t^{A_i}) \tag{13.31}$$

which is a standard unweighted Monte Carlo estimate, with weights $W_t^i = 1/N$. Averaging over the indices gives

$$\mathbb{E}_{A_{1:N}}\left[\frac{1}{N}\sum_{i=1}^{N} f(\boldsymbol{z}_t^{A_i})\right] = \sum_{i=1}^{N} W_t^i f(\boldsymbol{z}_t^i) \tag{13.32}$$

Thus using the output from the resampling procedure — which drops particles with low weight, and duplicates particles with high weight — will give the same result in expectation as the original weighted estimate. However, to reduce the variance of the method, we need to pick the resampling method carefully, as we discuss below.

13.2.4.1 Inverse cdf

Most of the common resampling methods work as follows. First we form the cumulative distribution from the weights $W^{1:N}$, as illustrated by the staircase in Figure 13.4. (We drop the t index for brevity.) Then, given a set of N uniform random variables, $U^i \sim \text{Unif}(0, 1)$, we check to see which bin (interval) U^i lands in; if it falls in bin a, we return index a, i.e., sample i gets mapped to index a if

$$\sum_{j=1}^{a-1} W^j \leq U^i < \sum_{j=1}^{a} W^j \tag{13.33}$$

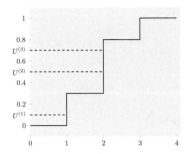

Figure 13.4: Illustration of how to sample from the empirical cdf $P(x) = \sum_{n=1}^{N} W^n \mathbb{I}(x \geq n)$ shown in black. The height of step n is W_n. If U^m picks step n, then we set the ancestor of m to be n, i.e., $A^m = n$. In this example, $A^{1:3} = (1, 2, 2)$. Adapted from Figure 9.3 of [CP20b].

It would seem that each index would take $O(N)$ time to compute, for a total time of $O(N^2)$, but if the U^i are ordered from smallest to largest, we can implement it in $O(N)$ time. We denote this function $\mathbf{A}_{1:N} = \text{icdf}(\mathbf{W}^{1:N}, \mathbf{U}^{1:N})$. See Listing 13.1 for some JAX code.[1]

Listing 13.1: Sampling from an ordered inverse CDF

```
def icdf(weights, u):
    n = weights.shape[0]
    cumsum = jnp.cumsum(weights)
    idx = jnp.searchsorted(cumsum, u)
    return jnp.clip(idx, 0, n - 1)
```

13.2.4.2   Multinomial resampling

In **multinomial resampling**, we set $\mathbf{U}^{1:N}$ to be an ordered set of N samples from the uniform distribution. We then compute the ancestor indices using $\mathbf{A}_{1:N} = \text{icdf}(\mathbf{W}^{1:N}, \mathbf{U}^{1:N})$.

Although this is a simple method, it can introduce a lot of variance into the representation of the distribution. For example, suppose all the weights are equal, $W^n = 1/N$. Let $\mathcal{W}^n = \sum_{m=1}^{N} \mathbb{I}(A^m = n)$ be the number of "offspring" for particle n (i.e., the number of times this particle is chosen in the resampling step). We have $\mathcal{W}^n \sim \text{Bin}(N, 1/N)$, so $P(\mathcal{W}^n = 0) = (1 - 1/N)^N \approx e^{-1} \approx 0.37$. So there is a 37% chance that any given particle will disappear even though they all had the same initial weight. In the sections below, we discuss some **low variance resampling** methods.

13.2.4.3   Stratified resampling

A simple approach to improve on multinomial resampling is to use **stratified resampling**, in which we divide the unit interval into N_s strata, $(0, 1/N_s)$, $(1/N_s, 2/N_s)$, up to $(1 - 1/N_s, 1)$. We then generate

$$U^i \sim \text{Unif}((i-1)/N_s, i/N_s) \tag{13.34}$$

and compute $\mathbf{A}_{1:N} = \text{icdf}(\mathbf{W}^{1:N}, \mathbf{U}^{1:N})$.[2]

---

1. Modified from https://github.com/blackjax-devs/blackjax/blob/main/blackjax/smc/resampling.py.
2. To compute the $\mathbf{U}^{1:N}$, we can use `v = jr.uniform(rngkey, (n,))` and `u = (jnp.arange(n) + v) / n`.

13.2.4.4   Systematic resampling

We can further reduce the variance by forcing all the samples to be deterministically generated from a shared random source, $u \sim \text{Unif}(0,1)$, by computing

$$U^i = \frac{i-1}{N_s} + \frac{u}{N_s} \tag{13.35}$$

We then compute $\mathbf{A}_{1:N} = \text{icdf}(\mathbf{W}^{1:N}, \mathbf{U}^{1:N}).^3$

13.2.4.5   Comparison

It can be proved that all of the above methods are unbiased. Empirically it seems that systematic resampling is lower variance than other methods [HSG06], although stratified resampling, and the more complex method of [GCW19], have better theoretical properties. Multinomial resampling is not recommended, since it has provably higher variance than the other methods.

13.2.5   Adaptive resampling

The resampling step can result in loss of diversity, since each ancestor may generate multiple children, and some may generate no children, since the ancestor indices A_t^n are sampled independently; this is the path degeneracy problem mentioned above. On the other hand, if we never resample, we end up with SIS, which suffers from weight degeneracy (particles with negligible weight). A compromise is to use **adaptive resampling**, in which we resample whenever the **effective sample size** or **ESS** drops below some minimum, such as $N/2$. A common way to define the ESS is as follows:[4]

$$\text{ESS}(W^{1:N}) = \frac{1}{\sum_{n=1}^{N}(W^n)^2} \tag{13.36}$$

Alternatively we can compute the ESS using the unnormalized weights:

$$\text{ESS}(\tilde{w}^{1:N}) = \frac{\left(\sum_{n=1}^{N}\tilde{w}^n\right)^2}{\sum_{n=1}^{N}(\tilde{w}^n)^2} \tag{13.37}$$

Note that if we have k weights with $\tilde{w}^n = 1$ and $N - k$ weights with $\tilde{w}^n = 0$, then the ESS is k; thus ESS is between 1 and N.

The pseudocode for SISR with adaptive resampling is given in Algorithm 13.3. (We use the notation of [Law+22, App. B], in which we first sample new extensions of the sequences, and then optionally resample the sequences at the end of each step.)

13.3   Proposal distributions

The efficiency of PF is crucially dependent on the quality of the proposal distribution. We discuss some options below.

---

3. To compute the $\mathbf{U}^{1:N}$, we can use `v = jr.uniform(rngkey, ())` and `u = (jnp.arange(n) + v) / n`.
4. Note that the ESS used in SMC is different than the ESS used in MCMC (Section 12.6.3); the latter takes into account auto-correlation of the MCMC samples.

Algorithm 13.3: SISR with adaptive resampling (generic SMC)

---

1 Initialization: $\tilde{w}_0^{1:N_s} = 1$, $\hat{Z}_0 = 1$
2 **for** $t = 1 : T$ **do**
3   **for** $i = 1 : N_s$ **do**
4   Sample particle $\boldsymbol{z}_t^i \sim q_t(\boldsymbol{z}_t | \boldsymbol{z}_{1:t-1}^i)$
5   Compute incremental weight $\alpha_t^i = \frac{\tilde{\gamma}_t(\boldsymbol{z}_{1:t}^i)}{\tilde{\gamma}_{t-1}(\boldsymbol{z}_{1:t-1}^i)q_t(\boldsymbol{z}_t^i|\boldsymbol{z}_{1:t-1}^i)}$
6   Compute unnormalized weight $\tilde{w}_t^i = \tilde{w}_{t-1}^i \alpha_t^i$
7   Estimate normalization constant: $\widehat{Z_t/Z_{t-1}} = \frac{\sum_{i=1}^{N_s} \tilde{w}_t^i}{\sum_{i=1}^{N_s} \tilde{w}_{t-1}^i}$, $\hat{Z}_t = \hat{Z}_{t-1}(\widehat{Z_t/Z_{t-1}})$
8   **if** $ESS(\tilde{w}_{t-1}^{1:N}) < ESS_{\min}$ **then**
9   Compute ancestors $\boldsymbol{a}_t^{1:N_s} = \text{resample}(\tilde{w}_t^{1:N_s})$
10   Select $\boldsymbol{z}_t^{1:N_s} = \text{permute}(\boldsymbol{a}_t^{1:N_s}, \boldsymbol{z}_t^{1:N_s})$
11   Reset unnormalized weights $\tilde{w}_t^{1:N_s} = 1/N_s$
12   Compute normalized weights $W_t^i = \frac{\tilde{w}_t^i}{\sum_j \tilde{w}_t^j}$ for $i = 1 : N_s$
13   Compute MC posterior $\hat{\pi}_t(\boldsymbol{z}_{1:t}) = \sum_{i=1}^{N_s} W_t^i \delta(\boldsymbol{z}_{1:t} - \boldsymbol{z}_{1:t}^i)$

13.3.1   Locally optimal proposal

We define the (one-step) **locally optimal proposal distribution** $q_t^*(z_t|z_{1:t-1})$ to be the one that minimizes

$$D_{\mathrm{KL}}\left(\pi_{t-1}(\boldsymbol{z}_{1:t-1})q_t(\boldsymbol{z}_t|\boldsymbol{z}_{1:t-1}) \parallel \pi_t(\boldsymbol{z}_{1:t})\right) \tag{13.38}$$

$$= \mathbb{E}_{\pi_{t-1}q_t}\left[\log\{\pi_{t-1}(\boldsymbol{z}_{1:t-1})q_t(\boldsymbol{z}_t|\boldsymbol{z}_{1:t-1})\} - \log\pi_t(\boldsymbol{z}_{1:t})\right] \tag{13.39}$$

$$= \mathbb{E}_{\pi_{t-1}q_t}\left[\log q_t(\boldsymbol{z}_t|\boldsymbol{z}_{1:t-1}) - \log\pi_t(\boldsymbol{z}_t|\boldsymbol{z}_{1:t-1})\right] + \text{const} \tag{13.40}$$

$$= \mathbb{E}_{\pi_{t-1}q_t}\left[D_{\mathrm{KL}}\left(q_t(\boldsymbol{z}_t|\boldsymbol{z}_{1:t-1}) \parallel \pi_t(\boldsymbol{z}_t|\boldsymbol{z}_{1:t-1})\right)\right] + \text{const} \tag{13.41}$$

The KL is minimized by choosing

$$q_t^*(\boldsymbol{z}_t|\boldsymbol{z}_{1:t-1}) = \pi_t(\boldsymbol{z}_t|\boldsymbol{z}_{1:t-1}) = \frac{\tilde{\gamma}_t(\boldsymbol{z}_{1:t})}{\tilde{\gamma}_t(\boldsymbol{z}_{1:t-1})} \tag{13.42}$$

where $\tilde{\gamma}_t(\boldsymbol{z}_{1:t-1}) = \int \tilde{\gamma}_t(\boldsymbol{z}_{1:t})d\boldsymbol{z}_t$ is the probability of the past sequence under the current target distribution.

Note that the subscript t specifies the t'th distribution, so in the context of SSMs, we have $\pi_t(\boldsymbol{z}_t|\boldsymbol{z}_{1:t-1}) = p(\boldsymbol{z}_t|\boldsymbol{z}_{1:t-1}, \boldsymbol{y}_{1:t})$. Thus we see that when proposing $\boldsymbol{z}_t$, we should condition on all the data, including the most recent observation, $\boldsymbol{y}_t$; this is called a **guided particle filter**, and will will be better than the bootstrap filter, which proposes from the prior.

In general, it is intractable to compute the locally optimal proposal, so we consider various approximations below.

13.3.2 Proposals based on the extended and unscented Kalman filter

One way to approximate the locally optimal proposal distribution is based on the extended Kalman filter (Section 8.3.2) or the unscented Kalman filter (Section 13.3.2), which gives rise to the **extended particle filter** [DGA00] and **unscented particle filter** [Mer+00] respectively. To explain these methods, we follow the presentation of [NLS19, p36]. As usual, we assume the dynamical system can be written as $z_t = f(z_{t-1}) + q_t$ and $y_t = h(z_t) + r_t$, where q_t is the system noise and r_t is the observation noise. The EKF and UKF approximations assume that the joint distribution over neighboring time steps, given the i'th history, is Gaussian:

$$p(z_t, y_t | z_{1:t-1}^i) \approx \mathcal{N}\left(\begin{pmatrix} z_t \\ y_t \end{pmatrix} | \hat{\mu}^i, \hat{\Sigma}^i \right) \tag{13.43}$$

where

$$\hat{\mu}^i = \begin{pmatrix} \hat{\mu}_z^i \\ \hat{\mu}_y^i \end{pmatrix}, \hat{\Sigma}^i = \begin{pmatrix} \hat{\Sigma}_{zz}^i & \hat{\Sigma}_{zy}^i \\ \hat{\Sigma}_{yz}^i & \hat{\Sigma}_{yy}^i \end{pmatrix} \tag{13.44}$$

(See Section 8.5.1 for details.)

The EKF and UKF compute $\hat{\mu}^i$ and $\hat{\Sigma}^i$ differently. In the EKF, we linearize f and h, and assume the noise terms are Gaussian. We then compute $p(z_t, y_t | z_{1:t-1}^i)$ exactly for this linearized model (see Section 8.3.1). In the UKF, we propagate sigma points through f and h, and approximate the resulting means and covariances using the unscented transform, which can be more accurate (see Section 8.4). Once we have computed $\hat{\mu}^i$ and $\hat{\Sigma}^i$, we can use standard rules for Gaussian conditioning to compute the approximate proposal as follows:

$$q(z_t | z_{1:t-1}^i, y_t) \approx \mathcal{N}(z_t | \mu_t^i, \Sigma_t^i) \tag{13.45}$$

$$\mu_t^i = \hat{\mu}_z^i + \hat{\Sigma}_{zy}^i (\hat{\Sigma}_{yy}^i)^{-1} (y_t - \hat{\mu}_y^i) \tag{13.46}$$

$$\Sigma_t^i = \hat{\Sigma}_{zz}^i - \hat{\Sigma}_{zy}^i (\hat{\Sigma}_{yy}^i)^{-1} \hat{\Sigma}_{yz}^i \tag{13.47}$$

Note that the linearization (or sigma point) approximation needs to be performed for each particle sepatately.

13.3.3 Proposals based on the Laplace approximation

To handle non-Gaussian likelihoods in an SSM, we can use the Laplace approximation (Section 7.4.3), as suggested in [DGA00]. In particular, consider an SSM with linear-Gaussian latent dynamics and a GLM likelihood. At each step, we compute the maximum $z_t^* = \arg\max \log p(y_t | z_t)$ as step t (e.g., using Newton-Raphson), and then approximate the likelihood using

$$p(y_t | z_t) \approx \mathcal{N}(z_t | z_t^*, -\mathbf{H}_t^*) \tag{13.48}$$

where $\mathbf{H}_t^*$ is the Hessian of the log-likelihood at the mode. We now compute $p(z_t | z_{t-1}^i, y_t)$ using the update step of the Kalman filter, using the same equations as in Section 13.3.2. This combination is called the **Laplace Gaussian filter** [Koy+10]. We give an example in Section 13.3.3.1.

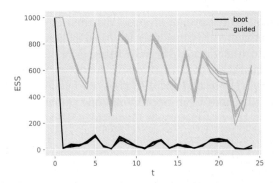

Figure 13.5: Effective sample size at each step for the bootstrap particle filter and a guided particle filter for a Gaussian SSM with Poisson likelihood. Adapted from Figure 10.4 of [CP20b]. Generated by pf_guided_neural_decoding.ipynb.

13.3.3.1   Example: neural decoding

In this section, we give an example where we apply the Laplace approximation to an SSM with linear-Gaussian dynamics and a Poisson likelihood. The application arises from neuroscience. In particular, assume we record the **neural spike trains** as a monkey moves its hand around in space. Let $\boldsymbol{z}_t \in \mathbb{R}^6$ represent the 3d location and velocity of the hand. We model the dynamics of the hand using a simple Brownian random walk model [CP20b, p157]:

$$\begin{pmatrix} z_t(i) \\ z_t(i+3) \end{pmatrix} | \boldsymbol{z}_{t-1} \sim \mathcal{N}_2 \left(\begin{pmatrix} 1 & \Delta \\ 0 & 1 \end{pmatrix} \begin{pmatrix} z_{t-1}(i) \\ z_{t-1}(i+3) \end{pmatrix}, \sigma^2 \mathbf{Q} \right), \ i = 1:3 \tag{13.49}$$

where the covariance of the noise is given by the following, assuming a discretization step of Δ:

$$\mathbf{Q} = \begin{pmatrix} \Delta^3/3 & \Delta^2/2 \\ \Delta^2/2 & \Delta \end{pmatrix} \tag{13.50}$$

We assume the k'th observation at time t is the number of spikes for neuron k in this sensing interval:

$$p(y_t(k)|\boldsymbol{z}_t) = \text{Poi}(\lambda_k(\boldsymbol{z}_t)) \tag{13.51}$$
$$\log \lambda_k(\boldsymbol{z}_t) = \alpha_k + \boldsymbol{\beta}_k^\mathsf{T} \boldsymbol{z}_t \tag{13.52}$$

Our goal is to compute $p(\boldsymbol{z}_t|\boldsymbol{y}_{1:t})$, which lets us infer the position of the hand from the neural code. (Apart from its value for furthering basic science, this can be useful for applications such as helping disabled people control their arms using "mind control".)

To illustrate this, we sample a synthetic dataset from the model, to simulate a "monkey" moving its arm for $T = 25$ time steps; this generates $K = 50$ neuronal counts per time step. We then apply particle filtering to this dataset (using the true model), using either the bootstrap filter (i.e., proposal is the random walk prior) or the guided filter (i.e., proposal is the Laplace approximation mentioned above). In Figure 13.5, we see that the effective sample size of the guided filter is much higher than for the bootstrap filter.

13.3.4 Proposals based on SMC (nested SMC)

It is possible to use SMC as a subroutine to compute a proposal distribution for SMC: at each step t, for each particle i, we run an SMC algorithm where the target distribution is the optimal proposal, $p(z_t|z_{1:t-1}^i, y_{1:t})$. This is called **nested SMC** [NLS15; NLS19].

This method can approximate the locally optimal proposal arbitrarily well, since it does not make any limiting parametric assumptions. However, the method can be slow, although the inner SMC algorithm can be run in parallel for each outer sample [NLS15; NLS19].

13.4 Rao-Blackwellized particle filtering (RBPF)

In some models, we can partition the hidden variables into two kinds, m_t and z_t, such that we can analytically integrate out z_t provided we know the values of $m_{1:t}$. This means we only have to sample $m_{1:t}$, and can represent $p(z_t|m_{1:t}, y_{1:t})$ parametrically. These hybrid particles are sometimes called **distributional particles** or **collapsed particles** [KF09a, Sec 12.4]. This combines techniques from particle filtering (Section 13.2) with deterministic methods such as Kalman filtering (Section 8.2.2).

The advantage of this approach is that we reduce the dimensionality of the space in which we are sampling, which reduces the variance of our estimate. This technique is known as **Rao-Blackwellized particle filtering** or **RBPF** for short. (See Section 11.6.2 for more details on Rao-Blackwellization.) In Section 13.4.1 we give an example of RBPF for inference in a switching linear dynamical systems. In Section 13.4.3 we illustrate RBPF for inference in the SLAM model for a mobile robot.

13.4.1 Mixture of Kalman filters

In this section, we consider the application of RBPF to a switching linear dynamical system (Section 29.9). This model has both continuous and discrete latent variables. This can be used to track a system that switches between discrete modes or operating regimes, represented by the discrete variable m_t.

For notational simplicity, we ignore the control inputs u_t. Thus the model is given by

$$p(z_t|z_{t-1}, m_t = k) = \mathcal{N}(z_t|\mathbf{F}_k z_{t-1}, \mathbf{Q}_k) \tag{13.53}$$

$$p(y_t|z_t, m_t = k) = \mathcal{N}(y_t|\mathbf{H}_k z_t, \mathbf{R}_k) \tag{13.54}$$

$$p(m_t = k|m_{t-1} = j) = A_{jk} \tag{13.55}$$

We let $\boldsymbol{\theta}_k = (\mathbf{F}_k, \mathbf{H}_k, \mathbf{Q}_k, \mathbf{R}_k, \mathbf{A}_{:,k})$ represent all the parameters for state k.

Exact inference is intractable, but if we sample the discrete variables, we can infer the continuous variables conditoned on the discretes exactly, making this a good candidate for RBPF. In particular, if we sample trajectories $m_{1:t}^n$, we can apply a Kalman filter to each particle. This can be thought of as a **mixture of Kalman filters** [CL00]. The resulting belief state is represented by

$$p(z_t, m_t|y_{1:t}) \approx \sum_{n=1}^N W_t^n \delta(m_t - m_t^n)\mathcal{N}(z_t|\boldsymbol{\mu}_t^n, \boldsymbol{\Sigma}_t^n) \tag{13.56}$$

To derive the filtering algorithm, note that the full posterior at time t can be written as follows:

$$p(m_{1:t}, z_{1:t}|y_{1:t}) = p(z_{1:t}|m_{1:t}, y_{1:t})p(m_{1:t}|y_{1:t}) \tag{13.57}$$

The second term is given by the following:

$$p(\boldsymbol{m}_{1:t}|\boldsymbol{y}_{1:t}) \propto p(\boldsymbol{y}_t|\boldsymbol{m}_{1:t}, \boldsymbol{y}_{1:t-1})p(\boldsymbol{m}_{1:t}|\boldsymbol{y}_{1:t-1}) \tag{13.58}$$

$$= p(\boldsymbol{y}_t|\boldsymbol{m}_{1:t}, \boldsymbol{y}_{1:t-1})p(\boldsymbol{m}_t|\boldsymbol{m}_{1:t-1}, \boldsymbol{y}_{1:t-1})p(\boldsymbol{m}_{1:t-1}|\boldsymbol{y}_{1:t-1}) \tag{13.59}$$

$$= p(\boldsymbol{y}_t|\boldsymbol{m}_{1:t}, \boldsymbol{y}_{1:t-1})p(\boldsymbol{m}_t|\boldsymbol{m}_{t-1})p(\boldsymbol{m}_{1:t-1}|\boldsymbol{y}_{1:t-1}) \tag{13.60}$$

Note that, unlike the case of standard particle filtering, we cannot write $p(\boldsymbol{y}_t|\boldsymbol{m}_{1:t}, \boldsymbol{y}_{1:t-1}) = p(\boldsymbol{y}_t|\boldsymbol{m}_t)$, since $\boldsymbol{m}_t$ does not d-separate the past observations from $\boldsymbol{y}_t$, as is evident from Figure 29.25a.

Suppose we use the following recursive proposal distribution:

$$q(\boldsymbol{m}_{1:t}|\boldsymbol{y}_{1:t}) = q(\boldsymbol{m}_t|\boldsymbol{m}_{1:t-1}, \boldsymbol{y}_{1:t})q(\boldsymbol{m}_{1:t-1}|\boldsymbol{y}_{1:t}) \tag{13.61}$$

Then we get the unnormalized importance weights

$$\tilde{w}_t^n \propto \frac{p(\boldsymbol{y}_t|\boldsymbol{m}_t^n, \boldsymbol{m}_{1:t-1}^n, \boldsymbol{y}_{1:t-1})p(\boldsymbol{m}_t^n|\boldsymbol{m}_{t-1}^n)}{q(\boldsymbol{m}_t^n|\boldsymbol{m}_{1:t-1}^n, \boldsymbol{y}_{1:t})}\tilde{w}_{t-1}^n \tag{13.62}$$

As a special case, suppose we propose from the prior, $q(m_t|\boldsymbol{m}_{t-1}^n, \boldsymbol{y}_{1:t}) = p(m_t|m_{t-1}^n)$. If we sample discrete state k, the weight update becomes

$$\tilde{w}_t^n \propto \tilde{w}_{t-1}^n p(\boldsymbol{y}_t|m_t^n = k, \boldsymbol{m}_{1:t-1}^n, \boldsymbol{y}_{1:t-1}) = \tilde{w}_{t-1}^n L_{tk}^n \tag{13.63}$$

where

$$L_{tk}^n = p(\boldsymbol{y}_t|m_t = k, \boldsymbol{m}_{1:t-1}^n, \boldsymbol{y}_{1:t-1}) = \int p(\boldsymbol{y}_t|m_t = k, \boldsymbol{z}_t)p(\boldsymbol{z}_t|m_t = k, \boldsymbol{y}_{1:t-1}, \boldsymbol{m}_{1:t-1}^n)d\boldsymbol{z}_t \tag{13.64}$$

The quantity L_{tk}^n is the predictive density for the new observation $\boldsymbol{y}_t$ conditioned on $m_t = k$ and the history of previous latents, $\boldsymbol{m}_{1:t-1}^n$. In the case of SLDS models, this can be computed using the normalization constant of the Kalman filter, Equation (8.35). The resulting algorithm is shown in Algorithm 13.4. The step marked "KFupdate" refers to the Kalman filter update equations in Section 8.2.2, and is applied to each particle separately.

Algorithm 13.4: One step of RBPF for SLDS using prior as proposal

---

1 **for** $n = 1 : N$ **do**
2     $k \sim p(m_t|m_{t-1}^n)$
3     $m_t^n := k$
4     $(\boldsymbol{\mu}_t^n, \boldsymbol{\Sigma}_t^n, L_{tk}^n) = $ KFupdate$(\boldsymbol{\mu}_{t-1}^n, \boldsymbol{\Sigma}_{t-1}^n, \boldsymbol{y}_t, \boldsymbol{\theta}_k)$
5     $\tilde{w}_t^n = \tilde{w}_{t-1}^n L_{tk}^n$
6 Compute ESS $= $ ESS$(\tilde{w}_t^{1:N_s})$
7 **if** $ESS < ESS_{\min}$ **then**
8     $\boldsymbol{a}_t^{1:N} = $ Resample$(\tilde{w}_t^{1:N})$
9     $(\boldsymbol{m}_t^{1:N_s}, \boldsymbol{\mu}_t^{1:N_s}, \boldsymbol{\Sigma}_t^{1:N_s}) = $ permute$(\boldsymbol{a}_t, \boldsymbol{m}_t^{1:N_s}, \boldsymbol{\mu}_t^{1:N_s}, \boldsymbol{\Sigma}_t^{1:N_s})$
10     $\tilde{w}_t^n = 1/N_s$

13.4.1.1 Improvements

An improved version of the algorithm can be developed based on the fact that we are sampling a discrete state space. At each step, we propagate each of the N old particles through all K possible transition models. We then compute the weight for all NK new particles, and sample from this to get the final set of N particles. This latter step can be done using the **optimal resampling** method of [FC03], which will stochastically select the particles with the largest weight, while also ensuring the result is an unbiased approximation. In addition, this approach ensures that we do not have duplicate particles, which is wasteful and unnecessary when the state space is discrete.

13.4.2 Example: tracking a maneuvering object

In this section we give an example of RBPF for an SLDS from [DGK01]. Our goal is to track an object that has the following motion model:

$$p(\mathbf{z}_t|\mathbf{z}_{t-1}, m_t = k) = \mathcal{N}(\mathbf{z}_t|\mathbf{F}\mathbf{z}_{t-1} + \boldsymbol{b}_k, \mathbf{Q}) \tag{13.65}$$

where $\mathbf{z}_t = (x_{1t}, \dot{x}_{1t}, x_{2t}, \dot{x}_{2t})$ contains the 2d position and velocity. We define the observaton matrix by $\mathbf{H} = \mathbf{I}$ and the observation covariance by $\mathbf{R} = 10 \operatorname{diag}(2, 1, 2, 1)$. We define the dynamics matrix by

$$\mathbf{F} = \begin{pmatrix} 1 & \Delta & 0 & 0 \\ 0 & 1 & 0 & 0 \\ 0 & 0 & 1 & \Delta \\ 0 & 0 & 0 & 1 \end{pmatrix} \tag{13.66}$$

where $\Delta = 0.1$,. We set the noise covariance to $\mathbf{Q} = 0.2\mathbf{I}$ and the input bias vectors for each state to $\boldsymbol{b}_1 = (0, 0, 0, 0)$, $\boldsymbol{b}_2 = (-1.225, -0.35, 1.225, 0.35)$ and $\boldsymbol{b}_3 = (1.225, 0.35, -1.225, -0.35)$. Thus the system will turn in different directions depending on the discrete state. The discrete state transition matrix is given by

$$\mathbf{A} = \begin{pmatrix} 0.8 & 0.1 & 0.1 \\ 0.1 & 0.8 & 0.1 \\ 0.1 & 0.1 & 0.8 \end{pmatrix} \tag{13.67}$$

Figure 13.6a shows some observations, and the true state of the system, from a sample run, for 100 steps. The colors denote the discrete state, and the location of the symbol denotes the (x, y) location. The small dots represent noisy observations. Figure 13.6b shows the estimate of the state computed using RBPF with the optimal proposal with 1000 particles. In Figure 13.6c, we show the analogous estimate using the boostrap filter, which does much worse.

In Figure 13.7a and Figure 13.7b, we show the posterior marginals of the (x, y) locations over time. In Figure 13.7c we show the true discrete state, and in Figure 13.7d we show the posterior marginal over discrete states. The overall state classification error rate is 29%, but it seems that occasionally misclassifying isolated time steps does not significantly hurt estimation of the continuous states, as we can see from Figure 13.6b.

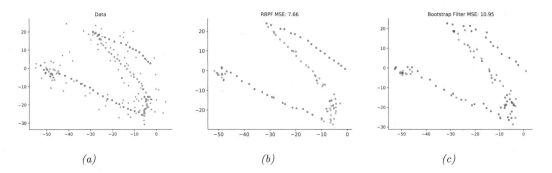

Figure 13.6: *Illustration of state estimation for a switching linear model. (a) Black dots are observations, hollow circles are the true location, colors represent the discrete state. (b) Estimate from RBPF. Generated by* rbpf_maneuver.ipynb. *(c) Estimate from bootstrap filter. Generated by* bootstrap_filter_maneuver.ipynb.

13.4.3   Example: FastSLAM

Consider a robot moving around an environment, such as a maze or indoor office environment. It needs to learn a map of the environment, and keep track of its location (pose) within that map. This problem is known as **simultaneous localization and mapping**, or **SLAM** for short. SLAM is widely used in mobile robotics (see e.g., [SC86; CN01; TBF06] for details). It is also useful in augmented reality, where the task is to recursively estimate the 3d pose of a handheld camera with respect to a set of 2d visual landmarks (this is known as **visual SLAM**, [TUI17; SMT18; Cza+20; DH22]).

Let us assume we can represent the map as the 2d locations of a set of K landmarks, denote them by $\boldsymbol{l}^1, \ldots, \boldsymbol{l}^K$ (each is a vector in $\mathbb{R}^2$). (We can use data association to figure out which landmark generated each observation, as discussed in Section 29.9.3.2.) Let $\boldsymbol{r}_t$ represent the unknown location of the robot at time t. Let $\boldsymbol{z}_t = (\boldsymbol{r}_t, \boldsymbol{l}_t^{1:K})$ be the combined state space. We can then perform online inference so that the robot can update its estimate of its own location, and the landmark locations.

The state transition model is defined as

$$p(\boldsymbol{z}_t | \boldsymbol{z}_{t-1}, \boldsymbol{u}_t) = p(\boldsymbol{r}_t | \boldsymbol{r}_{t-1}, \boldsymbol{l}_{t-1}^{1:K}, \boldsymbol{u}_t) \prod_{k=1}^{K} p(\boldsymbol{l}_t^k | \boldsymbol{l}_{t-1}^k) \tag{13.68}$$

where $p(\boldsymbol{r}_t | \boldsymbol{r}_{t-1}, \boldsymbol{l}_{t-1}^{1:K}, \boldsymbol{u}_t)$ specifies how the robot moves given the control signal $\boldsymbol{u}_t$ and the location of the obstacles $\boldsymbol{l}_{t-1}^{1:K}$. (Note that in this section, we assume that a human is joysticking the robot through the environment, so $\boldsymbol{u}_{1:t}$ is given as input, i.e., we do not address the decision-theoretic issue of choosing where to move.)

If the obstacles (landmarks) are static, we can define $p(\boldsymbol{l}_t^k | \boldsymbol{l}_{t-1}^k) = \delta(\boldsymbol{l}_t^k - \boldsymbol{l}_{t-1}^k)$, which is equivalent to treating the map as an unknown parameter that is shared globally across all time steps. More generally, we can let the landmark locations evolve over time [Mur00].

The observations $\boldsymbol{y}_t$ measure the distance from $\boldsymbol{r}_t$ to the set of closest landmarks. Figure 13.8 shows the corresponding graphical model for the case where $K = 2$, and where on the first step it sees landmarks 1 and 2, then just landmark 2, then just landmark 1, etc.

If all the CPDs are linear-Gaussian, then we can use a Kalman filter to maintain our belief state

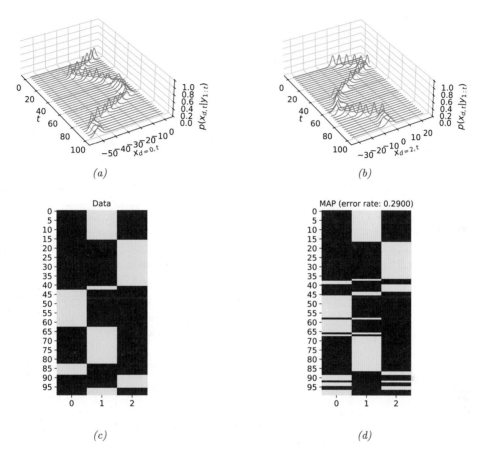

Figure 13.7: *Visualizing the posterior from the RBPF algorithm. Top row: Posterior marginals of the location of the object over time, derived from the mixture of Gaussian representation for (a) x location (dimension 0), (b) y location (dimension 2). Bottom row: visualization of the true (c) and predicted (d) discrete states. Generated by rbpf_maneuver.ipynb.*

about the location of the robot and the location of the landmarks, $p(\boldsymbol{z}_t|\boldsymbol{y}_{1:t}, \boldsymbol{u}_{1:t})$. In the more general case of a nonlinear model, we can use the EKF (Section 8.3.2) or UKF (Section 8.4.2).

Over time, the uncertainty in the robot's location will increase, due to wheel slippage, etc., but when the robot returns to a familiar location, its uncertainty will decrease again. This is called **closing the loop**, and is illustrated in Figure 13.9(a), where we see the uncertainty ellipses, representing $\mathrm{Cov}\,[\boldsymbol{z}_t|\boldsymbol{y}_{1:t}, \boldsymbol{u}_{1:t}]$, grow and then shrink.

In addition to visualizing the uncertainty of the robot's location, we can visualize the uncertainty about the map. To do this, consider the posterior precision matrix, $\boldsymbol{\Lambda}_t = \boldsymbol{\Sigma}_t^{-1}$. Zeros in the precision

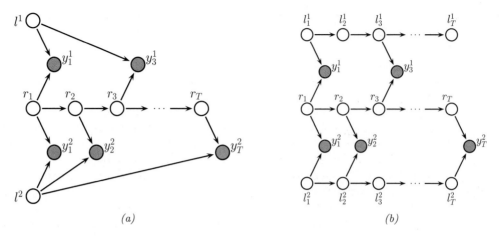

Figure 13.8: *Graphical model representing the SLAM problem.* $\boldsymbol{l}_t^k$ *is the location of landmark k at time* t, $\boldsymbol{r}_t$ *is the location of the robot at time* t, *and* $\boldsymbol{y}_t$ *is the observation vector. In the model on the left, the landmarks are static (so they act like global shared parameters), on the right, their location can change over time. The robot's observations are based on the distance to the nearest landmarks from the current state, denoted* $f(\boldsymbol{r}_t, \boldsymbol{l}_t^k)$. *The number of observations per time step is variable, depending on how many landmarks are within the range of the sensor. Adapted from Figure 15.A.3 of [KF09a].*

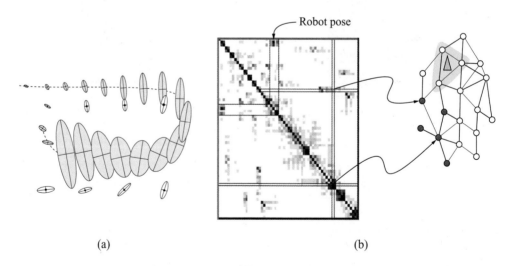

Figure 13.9: *Illustration of the SLAM problem. (a) A robot starts at the top left and moves clockwise in a circle back to where it started. We see how the posterior uncertainty about the robot's location increases and then decreases as it returns to a familar location, closing the loop. If we performed smoothing, this new information would propagate backwards in time to disambiguate the entire trajectory. (b) We show the precision matrix, representing sparse correlations between the landmarks, and between the landmarks and the robot's position (pose). The conditional independencies encoded by the sparse precision matrix can be visualized as a Gaussian graphical model, as shown on the right. From Figure 15.A.3 of [KF09a]. Used with kind permission of Daphne Koller.*

matrix correspond to absent edges in the corresponding undirected Gaussian graphical model (GGM, see Section 4.3.5). Initially all the beliefs about landmark locations are uncorrelated (by assumption), so the GGM is a disconnected graph, and Λ_t is diagonal. However, as the robot moves about, it will induce correlation between nearby landmarks. Intuitively this is because the robot is estimating its position based on distance to the landmarks, but the landmarks' locations are being estimated based on the robot's position, so they all become interdependent. This can be seen more clearly from the graphical model in Figure 13.8: it is clear that l^1 and l^2 are not d-separated by $y_{1:t}$, because there is a path between them via the unknown sequence of $r_{1:t}$ nodes. Consequently, the precision matrix becomes denser over time. As a consequence of the precision matrix becoming denser, each inference step takes $O(K^3)$ time. This prevents the method from being applied to large maps.

One way to speed this up is based on the following observation: conditional on knowing the robot's path, $r_{1:t}$, the landmark locations are independent, i.e., $p(l_t|r_{1:t}, y_{1:t}) = \prod_{k=1}^{K} p(l_t^k|r_{1:t}, y_{1:t})$. This can be seen by looking at the DGM in Figure 13.8. We can therefore sample the trajectory using some proposal, and apply (2d) Kalman filtering to each landmark independently. This is an example of RBPF, and reduces the inference cost to $O(NK)$, where N is the number of particles and K is the number of landmarks.

The overall cost of this technique is $O(NK)$ per step. Fortunately, the number of particles N needed for good performance is quite small, so the algorithm is essentially linear in the number of landmarks, making it quite scalable. This idea was first suggested in [Mur00], who applied it to grid-structured occupancy grids (and used the HMM filter for each particle). It was subsequently extended to landmark-based maps in [Thr+04], using the Kalman filter for each particle; they called the technique **FastSLAM**.

13.5 Extensions of the particle filter

There are many extensions to the basic particle filtering algorithm, such as the following:

- We can increase particle diversity by applying one or more steps of MCMC sampling (Section 12.2) at each PF step using $\pi_t(z_t)$ as the target distribution. This is called the **resample-move** algorithm [DJ11]. It is also possible to use SMC instead of MCMC to diversify the samples [GM17].

- We can extend PF to the case of offline inference; this is called **particle smoothing** (see e.g., [Kla+06]).

- We can extend PF to inference in general graphical models (not just chains) by combining PF with loopy belief propagation (Section 9.4); this is called **non-parametric BP** or **particle BP** (see e.g., [Sud+03; Isa03; Sud+10; Pac+14]).

- We can extend PF to perform inference in static models (e.g., for parameter inference), as we discuss in Section 13.6.

13.6 SMC samplers

In this section, we discuss **SMC samplers** (sequential Monte Carlo samplers), which are a way to apply particle filters to sample from a generic target distribution, $\pi(z) = \tilde{\gamma}(z)/Z$, rather than requiring the model to be an SSM. Thus SMC is an alternative to MCMC.

The advantages of SMC samplers over MCMC are as follows: we can estimate the normalizing constant Z; we can more easily develop adaptive versions that tune the transition kernel using the current set of samples; and the method is easier to parallelize (see e.g., [CCS22; Gre+22]).

The method works by defining a sequence of intermediate distributions, $\pi_t(z_t)$, which we expand to a sequence of distributions over all the past variables, $\overline{\pi}_t(z_{1:t})$. We then use the particle filtering algorithm to sample from each of these intermediate distributions. By marginalizing all but the final state, we recover samples from the target distribution, $\pi(z) = \sum_{z_{1:T-1}} \overline{\pi}_T(z_{1:T})$, as we explain below. (For more details, see e.g., [Dai+20a; CP20b].)

13.6.1   Ingredients of an SMC sampler

To define an SMC sampler, we need to specify several ingredients:

- A sequence of distributions defined on the same state space, $\pi_t(z_t) = \tilde{\gamma}_t(z_t)/Z_t$, for $t = 0 : T$;

- A **forwards kernel** $M_t(z_t|z_{t-1})$ (often written as $M_t(z_{t-1}, z_t)$), which satisfies $\sum_{z_t} M_t(z_t|z_{t-1}) = 1$. This can be used to propose new samples from our current estimate when we apply particle filtering.

- A **backwards kernel** $L_t(z_t|z_{t+1})$ (often written as $L(z_t, z_{t+1})$), which satisfies $\sum_{z_t} L_t(z_t|z_{t+1}) = 1$. This allows us to create a sequence of variables by working backwards in time from the final target value to the first time step. In particular, we create the following joint distribution:

$$\overline{\pi}_t(z_{1:t}) = \pi_t(z_t) \prod_{s=1}^{t-1} L_s(z_s|z_{s+1}) \tag{13.69}$$

This satisfies $\sum_{z_{1:t-1}} \overline{\pi}_t(z_{1:t}) = \pi_t(z_t)$, so if we apply particle filtering to this for $t = 1 : T$, then samples from the "end" of such sequences will be from the target distribution π_t.

With the above ingredients, we can compute the incremental weight at step t using

$$\alpha_t = \frac{\overline{\pi}_t(z_{1:t})}{\overline{\pi}_{t-1}(z_{1:t-1})M_t(z_t|z_{t-1})} \propto \frac{\tilde{\gamma}_t(z_t)}{\tilde{\gamma}_{t-1}(z_{t-1})} \frac{L_{t-1}(z_{t-1}|z_t)}{M_t(z_t|z_{t-1})} \tag{13.70}$$

This can be plugged into the generic SMC algorithm, Algorithm 13.3.

We still have to specify the forwards and backwards kernels. We will assume the forwards kernel M_t is an MCMC kernel that leaves π_t invariant. We can then define the backwards kernel to be the **time reversal** of the forwards kernel. More precisely, suppose we define L_{t-1} so it satisfies

$$\pi_t(z_t)L_{t-1}(z_{t-1}|z_t) = \pi_t(z_{t-1})M_t(z_t|z_{t-1}) \tag{13.71}$$

In this case, the incremental weight simplifies as follows:

$$\alpha_t = \frac{Z_t \pi_t(z_t) L_{t-1}(z_{t-1}|z_t)}{Z_{t-1} \pi_{t-1}(z_{t-1}) M_t(z_t|z_{t-1})} \tag{13.72}$$

$$= \frac{Z_t \pi_t(z_{t-1}) M_t(z_t|z_{t-1})}{Z_{t-1} \pi_{t-1}(z_{t-1}) M_t(z_t|z_{t-1})} \tag{13.73}$$

$$= \frac{\tilde{\gamma}_t(z_{t-1})}{\tilde{\gamma}_{t-1}(z_{t-1})} \tag{13.74}$$

We can use any kind of MCMC kernel for M_t. For example, if the parameters are real valued and unconstrained, we can use a Markov kernel that corresponds to K steps of a random walk Metropolis-Hastings sampler. We can set the covariance of the proposal to $\delta^2 \hat{\Sigma}_{t-1}$, where $\hat{\Sigma}_{t-1}$ is the empirical covariance of the weighted samples from the previous step, $(W_{t-1}^{1:N}, z_{t-1}^{1:N})$, and $\delta = 2.38 D^{-3/2}$ (which is the optimal scaling parameter for RWMH). In high dimensional problems, we can use gradient based Markov kernels, such as HMC [BCJ20] and NUTS [Dev+21]. For binary state spaces, we can use the method of [SC13].

13.6.2 Likelihood tempering (geometric path)

There are many ways to specify the intermediate target distributions. In the **geometric path** method, we specify the intermediate distributions to be

$$\tilde{\gamma}_t(z) = \tilde{\gamma}_0(z)^{1-\lambda_t} \tilde{\gamma}(z)^{\lambda_t} \tag{13.75}$$

where $0 = \lambda_0 < \lambda_1 < \cdots < \lambda_T = 1$ are **inverse temperature** parameters, and $\tilde{\gamma}_0$ is the initial proposal. If we apply particle filtering to this model, but "turn off" the resampling step, the method becomes equivalent to **annealed importance sampling** (Section 11.5.4).

In the context of Bayesian parameter inference, we often denote the latent variable z by θ, we define $\tilde{\gamma}_0(\theta) \propto \pi_0(\theta)$ as the prior, and $\tilde{\gamma}(z) = \pi_0(\theta)p(\mathcal{D}|\theta)$ as the posterior. We can then define the intermediate distributions to be

$$\tilde{\gamma}_t(\theta) = \pi_0(\theta)^{1-\lambda_t} \pi_0(\theta)^{\lambda_t} p(\mathcal{D}|\theta)^{\lambda_t} = \pi_0(\theta)^{1-\lambda_t} \exp[-\lambda_t \mathcal{E}(\theta)] \tag{13.76}$$

where $\mathcal{E}(\theta) = -\log p(\mathcal{D}, \theta)$ is the energy (potential) function. The incremental weights are given by

$$\alpha_t(\theta) = \frac{\pi_0(\theta)^{1-\lambda_t} \exp[-\lambda_t \mathcal{E}(\theta)]}{\pi_0(\theta)^{1-\lambda_t} \exp[-\lambda_{t-1} \mathcal{E}(\theta)]} = \exp[-\delta_t \mathcal{E}(\theta)] \tag{13.77}$$

where $\lambda_t = \lambda_{t-1} + \delta_t$.

For this method to work well, it is important to choose the λ_t so that the successive distributions are "equidistant"; this is called **adaptive tempering**. In the case of a Gaussian prior and Gaussian energy, one can show [CP20b] that this can be achieved by picking $\lambda_t = (1 + \gamma)^{t+1} - 1$, where $\gamma > 0$ is some constant. Thus we should increase λ slowly at first, and then make bigger and bigger steps.

In practice we can estimate λ_t by setting $\lambda_t = \lambda_{t-1} + \delta_t$, where

$$\delta_t = \operatorname*{argmin}_{\delta \in [0, 1-\lambda_{t-1}]} \left(\mathrm{ESSLW}(\{-\delta\, \mathcal{E}(\theta_t^n)\}) - \mathrm{ESS}_{\min} \right) \tag{13.78}$$

where $\mathrm{ESSLW}(\{l_n\}) = \mathrm{ESS}(\{e^{l_n}\})$ computes the ESS (Equation (13.37)) from the log weights, $l_n = \log \tilde{w}^n$. This ensures the change in the ESS across steps is close to the desired minimum ESS, typically $0.5N$. (If there is no solution for δ in the interval, we set $\delta_t = 1 - \lambda_{t-1}$.) See Algorithm 13.5 for the overall algorithm.

13.6.2.1 Example: sampling from a 1d bimodal distribution

Consider the simple distribution

$$p(\theta) \propto \mathcal{N}(\theta|0, \mathbf{I}) \exp(-\mathcal{E}(\theta)) \tag{13.79}$$

Algorithm 13.5: SMC with adaptive tempering

---

1 $\lambda_{-1} = 0$, $t = -1$, $W_{-1}^n = 1$
2 **while** $\lambda_t < 1$ **do**
3      $t = t + 1$
4   **if** $t = 0$ **then**
5          $\boldsymbol{\theta}_0^n \sim \pi_0(\boldsymbol{\theta})$
6   **else**
7          $A_t^{1:N} = \text{Resample}(W_{t-1}^{1:N})$
8          $\boldsymbol{\theta}_t^n \sim M_{\lambda_{t-1}}(\boldsymbol{\theta}_{t-1}^{A_t^n}, \cdot)$
9   Compute δ_t using Equation (13.78)
10     $\lambda_t = \lambda_{t-1} + \delta_t$
11     $\tilde{w}_t^n = \exp[-\delta\mathcal{E}(\boldsymbol{\theta}_t^n)]$
12     $W_t^n = \tilde{w}_t^n / (\sum_{m=1}^N \tilde{w}_t^m)$

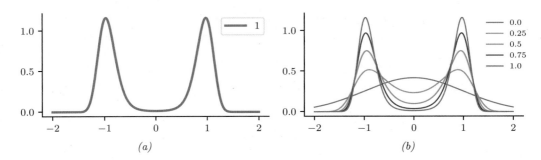

Figure 13.10: (a) Illustration of a bimodal target distribution. (b) Tempered versions of the target at different inverse temperatures, from $\lambda_T = 1$ down to $\lambda_1 = 0$. Generated by smc_tempered_1d_bimodal.ipynb.

where $\mathcal{E}(\boldsymbol{\theta}) = c(||\boldsymbol{\theta}||^2 - 1)^2$. We plot this in 1d in Figure 13.10a for $c = 5$; we see that it has a bimodal shape, since the low energy states correspond to parameter vectors whose norm is close to 1.

SMC is particularly useful for sampling from multimodal distributions, which can be provably hard to efficiently sample from using other methods, including HMC [MPS18], since gradients only provide local information about the curvature. As an example, in Figure 13.11a and Figure 13.11b we show the result of applying HMC (Section 12.5) and NUTS (Section 12.5.4.1) to this problem. We see that both algorithms get stuck near the initial state of $\theta_0 = 1$.

In Figure 13.10b, we show tempered versions of the target distribution at 5 different temperatures, chosen uniformly in the interval $[0, 1]$. We see that at $\lambda_1 = 0$, the tempered target is equal to the Gaussian prior (blue line), which is easy to sample from. Each subsequent distribution is close to the previous one, so SMC can track the change until it ends up at the target distribution with $\lambda_T = 1$, as shown in Figure 13.11c.

These SMC results were obtained using the adaptive tempering scheme described above. In Figure 13.11d we see that initially the temperature is small, and then it increases exponentially. The algorithm takes 8 steps until $\lambda_T \geq 1$.

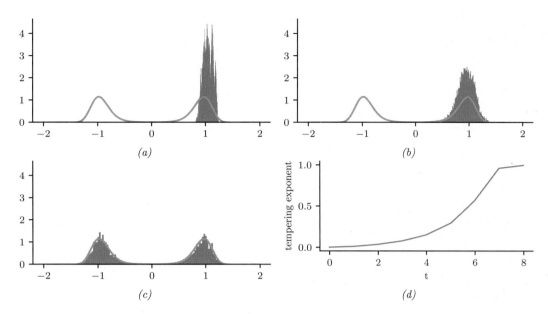

Figure 13.11: *Sampling from the bimodal distribution in Figure 13.10a. (a) HMC. (b) NUTS. (c) Tempered SMC with HMC kernel (single step). (d) Adaptive inverse temperature schedule. Generated by smc_tempered_1d_bimodal.ipynb.*

13.6.3   Data tempering

If we have a set of iid observations, we can define the t'th target to be

$$\tilde{\gamma}_t(\boldsymbol{\theta}) = p(\boldsymbol{\theta})p(\boldsymbol{y}_{1:t}|\boldsymbol{\theta}) \tag{13.80}$$

We can now apply SMC to this model. From Equation (13.74), the incremental weight becomes

$$\alpha_t(\boldsymbol{\theta}) = \frac{\tilde{\gamma}_t(\boldsymbol{z}_{t-1})}{\tilde{\gamma}_{t-1}(\boldsymbol{z}_{t-1})} = \frac{p(\boldsymbol{\theta})p(\boldsymbol{y}_{1:t}|\boldsymbol{\theta})}{p(\boldsymbol{\theta})p(\boldsymbol{y}_{1:t-1}|\boldsymbol{\theta})} = p(\boldsymbol{y}_t|\boldsymbol{y}_{1:t-1}, \boldsymbol{\theta}) \tag{13.81}$$

This can be plugged into the generic SMC algorithm in Algorithm 13.3.

Unfortunately, to sample from the MCMC kernel will typically take $O(t)$ time, since the MH accept/reject step requires computing $p(\boldsymbol{\theta}')\prod_{i=1}^{t}p(\boldsymbol{y}_{1i}|\boldsymbol{\theta}')$ for any proposed $\boldsymbol{\theta}'$. Hence the total cost is $O(T^2)$ if there are T observations. To reduce this, we can only sample parameters at times t when the ESS drops below a certain level; in the remaining steps, we just grow the sequence deterministically by repeating the previously sampled value. This technique was proposed in [Cho02], who called it the **iterated batch importance sampling** or **IBIS** algorithm.

13.6.3.1   Example: IBIS for a 1d Gaussian

In this section, we give a simple example of IBIS applied to data from a 1d Gaussian, $y_t \sim \mathcal{N}(\mu = 3.14, \sigma = 1)$ for $t = 1 : 30$. The unknowns are $\boldsymbol{\theta} = (\mu, \sigma)$. The prior is $p(\boldsymbol{\theta}) = \mathcal{N}(\mu|0, 1)\text{Ga}(\sigma|a =$

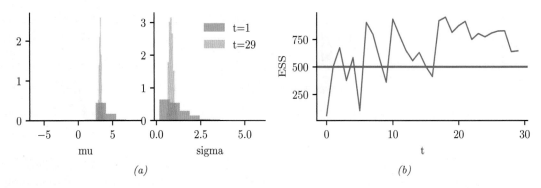

Figure 13.12: *Illustration of IBIS applied to 30 samples from $\mathcal{N}(\mu = 3.14, \sigma = 1)$. (a) Posterior approximation after $t = 1$ and $t = 29$ observations. (b) Effective sample size over time. The sudden jumps up occur whenever resampling is triggered, which happens when the ESS drops below 500. Generated by smc_ibis_1d.ipynb.*

$1, b = 1$). We use IBIS with an adaptive RWMH kernel. We use $N = 20$ particles, each updated for $K = 50$ MCMC steps, so we collect 1000 samples per time step.

Figure 13.12a shows the approximate posterior after $t = 1$ and $t = 29$ time steps. We see that the posterior concentrates on the true values of $\mu = 3.14$ and $\sigma = 1$.

Figure 13.12b plots the ESS vs time. The number of particles is 1000, and resampling (and MCMC moves) is triggered whenever this drops below 500. We see that we only need to invoke MCMC updates 3 times.

13.6.4   Sampling rare events and extrema

Suppose we want to sample values from $\pi_0(\boldsymbol{\theta})$ conditioned on the event that $S(\boldsymbol{\theta}) > \lambda^*$, where S is some score or "fitness" function. If λ^* is in the tail of the score distribution, this corresponds to sampling a **rare event**, which can be hard.

One approach is to use SMC to sample from a sequence of distributions with gradually increasing thresholds:

$$\pi_t(\boldsymbol{\theta}) = \frac{1}{Z_t} \mathbb{I}\left(S(\boldsymbol{\theta}) \geq \lambda_t\right) \pi_0(\boldsymbol{\theta}) \tag{13.82}$$

with $\lambda_0 < \cdots < \lambda_T = \lambda^*$. We can then use likelihood tempering, where the "likelihood" is the function

$$G_t(\boldsymbol{\theta}_t) = \mathbb{I}\left(S(\boldsymbol{\theta}_t) \geq \lambda_t\right) \tag{13.83}$$

We can use SMC to generate samples from the final distribution π_T. We may also be interested in estimating

$$Z_T = p(S(\boldsymbol{\theta}) \geq \lambda_T) \tag{13.84}$$

where the probability is taken wrt $\pi_0(\boldsymbol{\theta})$.

We can adaptively set the thresholds λ_t as follows: at each step, sort the samples by their score, and set λ_t to the α'th highest quantile. For example, if we set $\alpha = 0.5$, we keep the top 50% fittest particles. This ensures the ESS equals the minimum threshold at each step. For details, see [Cér+12].

Note that this method is very similar to the **cross-entropy method** (Section 6.7.5). The difference is that CEM fits a parametric distribution (e.g., a Gaussian) to the particles at each step and samples from that, rather than using a Markov kernel.

13.6.5 SMC-ABC and likelihood-free inference

The term **likelihood-free inference** refers to estimating the parameters $\boldsymbol{\theta}$ of a blackbox from which we can sample data, $\boldsymbol{y} \sim p(\cdot|\boldsymbol{\theta})$, but where we cannot evaluate $p(\boldsymbol{y}|\boldsymbol{\theta})$ pointwise. Such models are called simulators, so this approach to inference is also called **simulation-based inference** (see e.g., [Nea+08; CBL20; Gou+96]). These models are also called **implicit models** (see Section 26.1).

If we want to approximate the posterior of a model with no known likelihood, we can use **approximate Bayesian computation** or **ABC** (see e.g., [Bea19; SFB18; Gut+14; Pes+21]). In this setting, we sample both parameters $\boldsymbol{\theta}$ and synthetic data $\boldsymbol{y}$ such that the synthetic data (generated from $\boldsymbol{\theta}$) is sufficiently close to the observed data $\boldsymbol{y}^*$, as judged by some distance score, $d(\boldsymbol{y}, \boldsymbol{y}^*) < \epsilon$. (For high dimensional problems, we typically require $d(\boldsymbol{s}(\boldsymbol{y}), \boldsymbol{s}(\boldsymbol{y}^*)) < \epsilon$, where $\boldsymbol{s}(\boldsymbol{y})$ is a low-dimensionary summary statistic of the data.)

In **SMC-ABC**, we gradually decrease the discrepancy ϵ to get a series of distributions as follows:

$$\pi_t(\boldsymbol{\theta}, \boldsymbol{y}) = \frac{1}{Z_t} \pi_0(\boldsymbol{\theta}) p(\boldsymbol{y}|\boldsymbol{\theta}) \mathbb{I}\left(d(\boldsymbol{y}, \boldsymbol{y}^*) < \epsilon_t \right) \tag{13.85}$$

where $\epsilon_0 > \epsilon_1 > \cdots$. This is similar to the rare event SMC samplers in Section 13.6.4, except that we can't directly evaluate the quality of a candidate, $\boldsymbol{\theta}$. Instead we must first convert it to data space and make the comparison there. For details, see [DMDJ12].

Although SMC-ABC is popular in some fields, such as genetics and epidemiology, this method is quite slow and does not scale to high dimensional problems. In such settings, a more efficient approach is to train a generative model to **emulate** the simulator; if this model is parametric with a tractable likelihood (e.g., a flow model), we can use the usual methods for posterior inference of its parameters (including gradient based methods like HMC). See e.g., [Bre+20a] for details.

13.6.6 SMC^2

We have seen how SMC can be a useful alternative to MCMC. However it requires that we can efficiently evaluate the likelihood ratio terms $\frac{\gamma_t(\boldsymbol{\theta}_t)}{\gamma_{t-1}(\boldsymbol{\theta}_t)}$. In cases where this is not possible (e.g., for latent variable models), we can use SMC (specifically the estimate $\hat{Z}_t$ in Equation (13.10)) as a subroutine to approximate these likelihoods. This is called **SMC^2**. For details, see [CP20b, Ch. 18].

13.6.7 Variational filtering SMC

One way to improve SMC is to learn a proposal distribution (e.g., using a neural network) such that the approximate posterior, $\hat{\pi}_T(\boldsymbol{z}_{1:T}; \boldsymbol{\phi}, \boldsymbol{\theta})$, is close to the target posterior, $\pi_T(\boldsymbol{z}_{1:T}; \boldsymbol{\theta})$, where $\boldsymbol{\theta}$ are the model parameters, and $\boldsymbol{\phi}$ are the proposal parameters (which may depend on $\boldsymbol{\theta}$). One can show

[Nae+18] that the KL divergence between these distributions can be bounded as follows:

$$0 \leq D_{\mathrm{KL}}\left(\mathbb{E}\left[\hat{\pi}_T(\boldsymbol{z}_{1:T})\right] \parallel \pi_T(\boldsymbol{z}_{1:T})\right) \leq -\mathbb{E}\left[\log \frac{\hat{Z}_T}{Z_T}\right] \tag{13.86}$$

where

$$Z_T(\boldsymbol{\theta}) = p_{\boldsymbol{\theta}}(\boldsymbol{y}_{1:T}) = \int p_{\boldsymbol{\theta}}(\boldsymbol{z}_{1:T}, \boldsymbol{y}_{1:T}) d\boldsymbol{z}_{1:T} \tag{13.87}$$

Hence

$$\mathbb{E}\left[\log \hat{Z}_T(\boldsymbol{\theta}, \boldsymbol{\phi})\right] \leq \mathbb{E}\left[\log Z_T(\boldsymbol{\theta})\right] = \log Z_T(\boldsymbol{\theta}) \tag{13.88}$$

Thus we can use SMC sampling to compute an unbiased approximation to $\mathbb{E}\left[\log \hat{Z}_T(\boldsymbol{\theta}, \boldsymbol{\phi})\right]$, which is a lower bound on the evidence (log marginal likelihood).

We can now maximize this lower bound wrt $\boldsymbol{\theta}$ and $\boldsymbol{\phi}$ using SGD, as a way to learn both proposals and the model. Unfortunately, computing the gradient of the bound is tricky, since the resampling step is non-differentiable. However, in practice one can ignore the dependence of the resampling operator on the parameters, or one can use differentiable approximations (see e.g., [Ros+22]). This overall approach was independently proposed in several papers: the **FIVO** (filtering variational objective) paper [Mad+17], the **variational SMC** paper [Nae+18] and the **auto-encoding SMC** paper [Le+18].

13.6.8 Variational smoothing SMC

The methods in Section 13.6.7 use SMC in which the target distributions are defined to be the filtered distributions, $\pi_t(\boldsymbol{z}_{1:t}) = p_{\boldsymbol{\theta}}(\boldsymbol{z}_{1:t}|\boldsymbol{y}_{1:t})$; this is called **filtering SMC**. Unfortunately, this can work poorly when fitting models to offline sequence data, since at time t, all future observations are ignored in the objective, no matter how good the proposal. This can create situations where future observations are unlikely given the current set of sampled trajectories, which can result in particle impoverishment and high variance in the estimate of the lower bound.

Recently, a new method called **SIXO** (smoothing inference with twisted objectives) was proposed in [Law+22] that uses the smoothing distributions as targets, $\pi_t(\boldsymbol{z}_{1:t}) = p_{\boldsymbol{\theta}}(\boldsymbol{z}_{1:t}|\boldsymbol{y}_{1:T})$, to create a much lower variance variational lower bound. Of course it is impossible to directly compute this posterior, but we can approximate it using **twisted particle filters** [WL14a; AL+16]. In this approach, we approximate the (unnormalized) posterior using

$$p_{\boldsymbol{\theta}}(\boldsymbol{z}_{1:t}, \boldsymbol{y}_{1:T}) = p_{\boldsymbol{\theta}}(\boldsymbol{z}_{1:t}, \boldsymbol{y}_{1:t}) p_{\boldsymbol{\theta}}(\boldsymbol{y}_{t+1:T}|\boldsymbol{z}_{1:t}, \boldsymbol{y}_{1:t}) \tag{13.89}$$

$$= p_{\boldsymbol{\theta}}(\boldsymbol{z}_{1:t}, \boldsymbol{y}_{1:t}) p_{\boldsymbol{\theta}}(\boldsymbol{y}_{t+1:T}|\boldsymbol{z}_t) \tag{13.90}$$

$$\approx p_{\boldsymbol{\theta}}(\boldsymbol{z}_{1:t}, \boldsymbol{y}_{1:t}) r_{\boldsymbol{\psi}}(\boldsymbol{y}_{t+1:T}, \boldsymbol{z}_t) \tag{13.91}$$

where $r_{\boldsymbol{\psi}}(\boldsymbol{y}_{t+1:T}, \boldsymbol{z}_t) \approx p_{\boldsymbol{\theta}}(\boldsymbol{y}_{t+1:T}|\boldsymbol{z}_t)$ is the **twisting function**, which acts as a "lookahead function".

One way to approximate the twisting function is to note that

$$p_{\boldsymbol{\theta}}(\boldsymbol{y}_{t+1:T}|\boldsymbol{z}_t) = \frac{p_{\boldsymbol{\theta}}(\boldsymbol{z}_t|\boldsymbol{y}_{t+1:T}) p_{\boldsymbol{\theta}}(\boldsymbol{y}_{t+1:T})}{p_{\boldsymbol{\theta}}(\boldsymbol{z}_t)} \propto \frac{p_{\boldsymbol{\theta}}(\boldsymbol{z}_t|\boldsymbol{y}_{t+1:T})}{p_{\boldsymbol{\theta}}(\boldsymbol{z}_t)} \tag{13.92}$$

where we drop terms that are independent of $\boldsymbol{z}_t$ since such terms will cancel out when we normalize the sampling weights. We can approximate the density ratio using the binary classifier method of Section 2.7.5. To do this, we define one distribution to be $p_1 = p_{\boldsymbol{\theta}}(\boldsymbol{z}_t, \boldsymbol{y}_{t+1:T})$ and the other to be $p_2 = p_{\boldsymbol{\theta}}(\boldsymbol{z}_t)p_{\boldsymbol{\theta}}(\boldsymbol{y}_{t+1:T})$, so that $p_1/p_2 = \frac{p_{\boldsymbol{\theta}}(\boldsymbol{z}_t|\boldsymbol{y}_{t+1:T})}{p_{\boldsymbol{\theta}}(\boldsymbol{z}_t)}$. We can easily draw a sample $(\boldsymbol{z}_{1:T}, \boldsymbol{y}_{1:T}) \sim p_{\boldsymbol{\theta}}$ using ancestral sampling, from which we can compute $(\boldsymbol{z}_t, \boldsymbol{y}_{t+1:T}) \sim p_1$ by marginalization. We can also sample a fresh sequence from $(\tilde{\boldsymbol{z}}_{1:T}, \tilde{\boldsymbol{y}}_{1:T}) \sim p_{\boldsymbol{\theta}}$ from which we can compute $(\tilde{\boldsymbol{z}}_t, \tilde{\boldsymbol{y}}_{t+1:T}) \sim p_2$ by marginalization. We then use $(\boldsymbol{z}_t, \boldsymbol{y}_{t+1:T})$ as a positive example and $(\tilde{\boldsymbol{z}}_t, \tilde{\boldsymbol{y}}_{t+1:T})$ as a negative example when training the binary classifier, $r_{\boldsymbol{\psi}}(\boldsymbol{y}_{t+1:T}, \boldsymbol{z}_t)$.

Once we have updated the twisting parameters $\boldsymbol{\psi}$, we can rerun SMC to get a tighter lower bound on the log marginal likelihood, which we can then optimize wrt the model parameters $\boldsymbol{\theta}$ and proposal parameters $\boldsymbol{\phi}$. Thus the overall method is a stochastic variational EM-like method for optimziing the bound

$$\mathcal{L}_{\text{SIXO}}(\boldsymbol{\theta}, \boldsymbol{\phi}, \boldsymbol{\psi}, \boldsymbol{y}_{1:T}) \triangleq \mathbb{E}\left[\log \hat{Z}_{\text{SIXO}}(\boldsymbol{\theta}, \boldsymbol{\phi}, \boldsymbol{\psi}, \boldsymbol{y}_{1:T})\right] \tag{13.93}$$

$$\leq \log \mathbb{E}\left[\hat{Z}_{\text{SIXO}}(\boldsymbol{\theta}, \boldsymbol{\phi}, \boldsymbol{\psi}, \boldsymbol{y}_{1:T})\right] = \log p_{\boldsymbol{\theta}}(\boldsymbol{y}_{1:T}) \tag{13.94}$$

In [Law+22] they prove the following: suppose the true model p^* is an SSM in which the optimal proposal function for the model satisfies $p^*(\boldsymbol{z}_t|\boldsymbol{z}_{1:t-1}, \boldsymbol{y}_{1:T}) \in \mathcal{Q}$, and the optimal lookahead function for the model satisfies $p^*(\boldsymbol{y}_{t+1:T}|\boldsymbol{z}_t) \in \mathcal{R}$. Furthermore, assume the SIXO objective has a unique maximizer. Then, at the optimum, we have that the learned proposal $q_{\boldsymbol{\phi}^*}(\boldsymbol{z}_t|\boldsymbol{z}_{1:t-1}, \boldsymbol{y}_{1:T}) \in \mathcal{Q}$ is equal to the optimal proposal, the learned twisting function $r_{\boldsymbol{\psi}^*}(\boldsymbol{y}_{t+1:T}, \boldsymbol{z}_t) \in \mathcal{R}$ is equal to the optimal lookahead, and the lower bound is tight (i.e., $\mathcal{L}_{\text{SIXO}}(\boldsymbol{\theta}^*, \boldsymbol{\phi}^*, \boldsymbol{\psi}^*) = p^*(\boldsymbol{y}_{1:T})$) for any number of samples $N_s \geq 1$ and for any kind of SSM p^*. (This is in contrast to the FIVO bound, whiere the bound does not usually become tight.)

PART III

Prediction

14 Predictive models: an overview

14.1 Introduction

The vast majority of machine learning is concerned with tackling a single problem, namely learning to predict outputs y from inputs x using some function f that is estimated from a labeled training set $\mathcal{D} = \{(x_n, y_n) : n = 1 : N\}$, for $x_n \in \mathcal{X} \subseteq \mathbb{R}^D$ and $y_n \in \mathcal{Y} \subseteq \mathbb{R}^C$. We can model our uncertainty about the correct output for a given input using a conditional probability model of the form $p(y|f(x))$. When $\mathcal{Y}$ is a discrete set of labels, this is called (in the ML literature) a **discriminative model**, since it lets us discriminate (distinguish) between the different possible values of y. If the output is real-valued, $\mathcal{Y} = \mathbb{R}$, this is called a **regression model**. (In the statistics literature, the term "regression model" is used in both cases, even if $\mathcal{Y}$ is a discrete set.) We will use the more generic term "**predictive model**" to refer to such models.

A predictive model can be considered as a special case of a conditional generative model (discussed in Chapter 20). In a predictive model, the output is usually low dimensional, and there is a single best answer that we want to predict. However, in most generative models, the output is usually high dimensional, such as images or sentences, and there may be many correct outputs for any given input. We will discuss a variety of types of predictive model in Section 14.1.1, but we defer the details to subsequent chapters. The rest of this chapter then discusses issues that are relevant to all types of predictive model, regardless of the specific form, such as evaluation.

14.1.1 Types of model

There are many different kinds of predictive model $p(y|x)$. The biggest distinction is between **parametric models**, that have a fixed number of parameters independent of the size of the training set, and **non-parametric models** that have a variable number of parameters that grows with the size of the training set. Non-parametric models are usually more flexible, but can be slower to use for prediction. Parametric models are usually less flexible, but are faster to use for prediction.

Most non-parametric models are based on comparing a test input x to some or all of the stored training examples $\{x_n, n = 1 : N\}$, using some form of similarity, $s_n = \mathcal{K}(x, x_n) \geq 0$, and then predicting the output using some weighted combination of the training labels, such as $\hat{y} = \sum_{n=1}^{N} s_n y_n$. A typical example is a Gaussian process, which we discuss in Chapter 18. Other examples, such as K-nearest neighbor models, are discussed in the prequel to this book, [Mur22].

Most parametric models have the form $p(y|x) = p(y|f(x; \theta))$, where f is some kind of function that predicts the parameters (e.g., the mean, or logits) of the output distribution (e.g., Gaussian or categorical). There are many kinds of function we can use. If f is a linear function of θ (i.e.,

$f(\boldsymbol{x}; \boldsymbol{\theta}) = \boldsymbol{\theta}^{\mathsf{T}} \boldsymbol{\phi}(\boldsymbol{x})$ for some *fixed* feature transformation $\boldsymbol{\phi}$), then the model is called a generalized linear model or GLM, which we discuss in Chapter 15. If f is a non-linear, but differentiable, function of $\boldsymbol{\theta}$ (e.g., $f(\boldsymbol{x}; \boldsymbol{\theta}) = \boldsymbol{\theta}_2^{\mathsf{T}} \boldsymbol{\phi}(\boldsymbol{x}; \boldsymbol{\theta}_1)$ for some learnable function $\boldsymbol{\phi}(\boldsymbol{x}; \boldsymbol{\theta}_1)$), then it is common to represent f using a neural network (Chapter 16). Other types of predictive model, such as decision trees and random forests, are discussed in the prequel to this book, [Mur22].

14.1.2 Model fitting using ERM, MLE, and MAP

In this section, we briefly discuss some methods used for fitting (parametric) models. The most common approach is to use **maximum likelihood estimation** or **MLE**, which amounts to solving the following optimization problem:

$$\hat{\boldsymbol{\theta}} = \underset{\boldsymbol{\theta} \in \Theta}{\operatorname{argmax}} \, p(\mathcal{D}|\boldsymbol{\theta}) = \underset{\boldsymbol{\theta} \in \Theta}{\operatorname{argmax}} \log p(\mathcal{D}|\boldsymbol{\theta}) \tag{14.1}$$

If the dataset is N iid data samples, the likelihood decomposes into a product of terms, $p(\mathcal{D}|\boldsymbol{\theta}) = \prod_{n=1}^{N} p(\boldsymbol{y}_n|\boldsymbol{x}_n, \boldsymbol{\theta})$. Thus we can instead minimize the following (scaled) **negative log likelihood**:

$$\hat{\boldsymbol{\theta}} = \underset{\boldsymbol{\theta} \in \Theta}{\operatorname{argmin}} \frac{1}{N} \sum_{n=1}^{N} [- \log p(\boldsymbol{y}_n|\boldsymbol{x}_n, \boldsymbol{\theta})] \tag{14.2}$$

We can generalize this by replacing the **log loss** $\ell_n(\boldsymbol{\theta}) = - \log p(\boldsymbol{y}_n|\boldsymbol{x}_n, \boldsymbol{\theta})$ with a more general loss function to get

$$\hat{\boldsymbol{\theta}} = \underset{\boldsymbol{\theta} \in \Theta}{\operatorname{argmin}} \, r(\boldsymbol{\theta}) \tag{14.3}$$

where $r(\boldsymbol{\theta})$ is the **empirical risk**

$$r(\boldsymbol{\theta}) = \frac{1}{N} \sum_{n=1}^{N} \ell_n(\boldsymbol{\theta}) \tag{14.4}$$

This approach is called **empirical risk minimization** or **ERM**.

ERM can easily result in **overfitting**, so it is common to add a penalty or regularizer term to get

$$\hat{\boldsymbol{\theta}} = \underset{\boldsymbol{\theta} \in \Theta}{\operatorname{argmin}} \, r(\boldsymbol{\theta}) + \lambda C(\boldsymbol{\theta}) \tag{14.5}$$

where $\lambda \geq 0$ controls the degree of regularization, and $C(\boldsymbol{\theta})$ is some complexity measure. If we use log loss, and we define $C(\boldsymbol{\theta}) = - \log \pi_0(\boldsymbol{\theta})$, where $\pi_0(\boldsymbol{\theta})$ is some prior distribution, and we use $\lambda = 1$, we recover the **MAP estimate**

$$\hat{\boldsymbol{\theta}} = \underset{\boldsymbol{\theta} \in \Theta}{\operatorname{argmax}} \log p(\mathcal{D}|\boldsymbol{\theta}) + \log \pi_0(\boldsymbol{\theta}) \tag{14.6}$$

This can be solved using standard optimization methods (see Chapter 6).

14.1.3   Model fitting using Bayes, VI, and generalized Bayes

Another way to prevent overfitting is to estimate a *probability distribution over parameters*, $q(\boldsymbol{\theta})$, instead of a point estimate. That is, we can try to estimate the ERM in expectation:

$$\hat{q} = \underset{q \in \mathcal{P}(\Theta)}{\operatorname{argmin}} \mathbb{E}_{q(\boldsymbol{\theta})}\left[r(\boldsymbol{\theta})\right] \tag{14.7}$$

If $\mathcal{P}(\Theta)$ is the space of all probability distributions over parameters, then the solution will converge to a delta function that puts all its probability on the MLE. Thus this approach, on its own, will not prevent overfitting. However, we can regularize the problem by preventing the distribution from moving too far from the prior. If we measure the divergence between q and the prior using KL divergence, we get

$$\hat{q} = \underset{q \in \mathcal{P}(\Theta)}{\operatorname{argmin}} \mathbb{E}_{q(\boldsymbol{\theta})}\left[r(\boldsymbol{\theta})\right] + \frac{1}{\lambda} D_{\mathrm{KL}}\left(q \,\|\, \pi_0\right) \tag{14.8}$$

The solution to this problem is known as the **Gibbs posterior**, and is given by the following:

$$\hat{q}(\boldsymbol{\theta}) = \frac{e^{-\lambda r(\boldsymbol{\theta})} \pi_0(\boldsymbol{\theta})}{\int e^{-\lambda r(\boldsymbol{\theta}')} \pi_0(\boldsymbol{\theta}') d\boldsymbol{\theta}'} \tag{14.9}$$

This is widely used in the **PAC-Bayes** community (see e.g., [Alq21].

Now suppose we use log loss, and set $\lambda = N$, to get

$$\hat{q}(\boldsymbol{\theta}) = \frac{e^{\sum_{n=1}^N \log p(\boldsymbol{y}_n|\boldsymbol{x}_n,\boldsymbol{\theta})} \pi_0(\boldsymbol{\theta})}{\int e^{\sum_{n=1}^N \log p(\boldsymbol{y}_n|\boldsymbol{x}_n,\boldsymbol{\theta}')} \pi_0(\boldsymbol{\theta}') d\boldsymbol{\theta}'} \tag{14.10}$$

Then the resulting distribution is equivalent to the Bayes posterior:

$$\hat{q}(\boldsymbol{\theta}) = \frac{p(\mathcal{D}|\boldsymbol{\theta}) \pi_0(\boldsymbol{\theta})}{\int p(\mathcal{D}|\boldsymbol{\theta}') \pi_0(\boldsymbol{\theta}') d\boldsymbol{\theta}'} \tag{14.11}$$

Often computing the Bayes posterior is intractable. We can simplify the problem by restricting attention to a limited family of distributions, $\mathcal{Q}(\Theta) \subset \mathcal{P}(\Theta)$. This gives rise to the following objective:

$$\hat{q} = \underset{q \in \mathcal{Q}(\Theta)}{\operatorname{argmin}} \mathbb{E}_{q(\boldsymbol{\theta})}\left[-\log p(\mathcal{D}|\boldsymbol{\theta})\right] + D_{\mathrm{KL}}\left(q \,\|\, \pi_0\right) \tag{14.12}$$

This is known as **variational inference**; see Chapter 10 for details.

We can generalize this by replacing the negative log likelihood with a general risk, $r(\boldsymbol{\theta})$. Furthermore, we can replace the KL with a general divergence, $D(q\|\pi_0)$, which we can weight using a general λ. This gives rise to the following objective:

$$\hat{q} = \underset{q \in \mathcal{Q}(\Theta)}{\operatorname{argmin}} \mathbb{E}_{q(\boldsymbol{\theta})}\left[r(\boldsymbol{\theta})\right] + \lambda D(q\|\pi_0) \tag{14.13}$$

This is called **generalized Bayesian inference** [BHW16; KJD19; KJD21].

14.2 Evaluating predictive models

In this section we discuss how to evaluate the quality of a trained discriminative model.

14.2.1 Proper scoring rules

It is common to measure performance of a predictive model using a **proper scoring rule** [GR07a], which is defined as follows. Let $S(p_{\boldsymbol{\theta}}, (y, \boldsymbol{x}))$ be the score for predictive distribution $p_{\boldsymbol{\theta}}(y|\boldsymbol{x})$ when given an event $y|\boldsymbol{x} \sim p^*(y|\boldsymbol{x})$, where p^* is the true conditional distribution. (If we want to evaluate a Bayesian model, where we marginalize out $\boldsymbol{\theta}$ rather than condition on it, we just replace $p_{\boldsymbol{\theta}}(y|\boldsymbol{x})$ with $p(y|\boldsymbol{x}) = \int p_{\boldsymbol{\theta}}(y|\boldsymbol{x})p(\boldsymbol{\theta}|\mathcal{D})d\boldsymbol{\theta}$.) The expected score is defined by

$$S(p_{\boldsymbol{\theta}}, p^*) = \int p^*(\boldsymbol{x})p^*(y|\boldsymbol{x})S(p_{\boldsymbol{\theta}}, (y, \boldsymbol{x}))dy d\boldsymbol{x} \tag{14.14}$$

A proper scoring rule is one where $S(p_{\boldsymbol{\theta}}, p^*) \leq S(p^*, p^*)$, with equality iff $p_{\boldsymbol{\theta}}(y|\boldsymbol{x}) = p^*(y|\boldsymbol{x})$. Thus maximizing such a proper scoring rule will force the model to match the true probabilities.

The log-likelihood, $S(p_{\boldsymbol{\theta}}, (y, \boldsymbol{x})) = \log p_{\boldsymbol{\theta}}(y|\boldsymbol{x})$, is a proper scoring rule. This follows from Gibbs inequality:

$$S(p_{\boldsymbol{\theta}}, p^*) = \mathbb{E}_{p^*(\boldsymbol{x})p^*(y|\boldsymbol{x})}\left[\log p_{\boldsymbol{\theta}}(y|\boldsymbol{x})\right] \leq \mathbb{E}_{p^*(\boldsymbol{x})p^*(y|\boldsymbol{x})}\left[\log p^*(y|\boldsymbol{x})\right] \tag{14.15}$$

Therefore minimizing the NLL (aka log loss) should result in well-calibrated probabilities. However, in practice, log-loss can over-emphasize tail probabilities [QC+06].

A common alternative is to use the **Brier score** [Bri50], which is defined as follows:

$$S(p_{\boldsymbol{\theta}}, (y, \boldsymbol{x})) \triangleq \frac{1}{C}\sum_{c=1}^{C}(p_{\boldsymbol{\theta}}(y = c|\boldsymbol{x}) - \mathbb{I}(y = c))^2 \tag{14.16}$$

This is just the squared error of the predictive distribution $\boldsymbol{p} = p(1:C|\boldsymbol{x})$ compared to the one-hot label distribution $\boldsymbol{y}$. Since it based on squared error, the Brier score is less sensitive to extremely rare or extremely common classes. The Brier score is also a proper scoring rule.

14.2.2 Calibration

A model whose predicted probabilities match the empirical frequencies is said to be **calibrated** [Daw82; NMC05; Guo+17]. For example, if a classifier predicts $p(y = c|\boldsymbol{x}) = 0.9$, then we expect this to be the true label about 90% of the time. A well-calibrated model is useful to avoid making the wrong decision when the outcome is too uncertain. In the sections below, we discuss some ways to measure and improve calibration.

14.2.2.1 Expected calibration error

To assess calibration, we divide the predicted probabilities into a finite set of bins or buckets, and then assess the discrepancy between the empirical probability and the predicted probability by counting. More precisely, suppose we have B bins. Let $\mathcal{B}_b$ be the set of indices of samples whose prediction

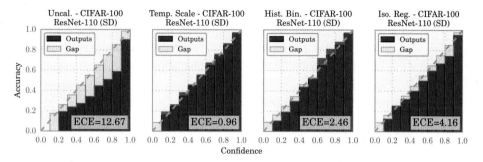

Figure 14.1: *Reliability diagrams for the ResNet CNN image classifier [He+16b] applied to CIFAR-100 dataset. ECE is the expected calibration error, and measures the size of the red gap. Methods from left to right: original probabilities; after temperature scaling; after histogram binning; after isotonic regression. From Figure 4 of [Guo+17]. Used with kind permission of Chuan Guo.*

confidence falls into the interval $I_b = (\frac{b-1}{B}, \frac{b}{B}]$. Here we use uniform bin widths, but we could also define the bins so that we can get an equal number of samples in each one.

Let $f(\boldsymbol{x})_c = p(y = c|\boldsymbol{x})$, $\hat{y}_n = \operatorname{argmax}_{c \in \{1,...,C\}} f(\boldsymbol{x}_n)_c$, and $\hat{p}_n = \max_{c \in \{1,...,C\}} f(\boldsymbol{x}_n)_c$. The accuracy within bin b is defined as

$$\operatorname{acc}(\mathcal{B}_b) = \frac{1}{|\mathcal{B}_b|} \sum_{n \in \mathcal{B}_b} \mathbb{I}(\hat{y}_n = y_n) \tag{14.17}$$

The average confidence within this bin is defined as

$$\operatorname{conf}(\mathcal{B}_b) = \frac{1}{|\mathcal{B}_b|} \sum_{n \in \mathcal{B}_b} \hat{p}_n \tag{14.18}$$

If we plot accuracy vs confidence, we get a **reliability diagram**, as shown in Figure 14.1. The gap between the accuracy and confidence is shown in the red bars. We can measure this using the **expected calibration error** (**ECE**) [NCH15]:

$$\operatorname{ECE}(f) = \sum_{b=1}^{B} \frac{|\mathcal{B}_b|}{B} |\operatorname{acc}(\mathcal{B}_b) - \operatorname{conf}(\mathcal{B}_b)| \tag{14.19}$$

In the multiclass case, the ECE only looks at the error of the MAP (top label) prediction. We can extend the metric to look at all the classes using the **marginal calibration error**, proposed in [KLM19]:

$$\operatorname{MCE} = \sum_{c=1}^{C} w_c \mathbb{E}\left[(p(Y = c|f(\boldsymbol{x})_c) - f(\boldsymbol{x})_c)^2\right] \tag{14.20}$$

$$= \sum_{c=1}^{C} w_c \sum_{b=1}^{B} \frac{|\mathcal{B}_{b,c}|}{B} (\operatorname{acc}(\mathcal{B}_{b,c}) - \operatorname{conf}(\mathcal{B}_{b,c}))^2 \tag{14.21}$$

where $\mathcal{B}_{b,c}$ is the b'th bin for class c, and $w_c \in [0, 1]$ denotes the importance of class c. (We can set $w_c = 1/C$ if all classes are equally important.) In [Nix+19], they call this metric **static calibration error**; they show that certain methods that have good ECE may have poor MCE. Other multi-class calibration metrics are discussed in [WLZ19].

14.2.2.2 Improving calibration

In principle, training a classifier so it optimizes a proper scoring rule (such as NLL) should automatically result in a well-calibrated classifier. In practice, however, unbalanced datasets can result in poorly calibrated predictions. Below we discuss various ways for improving the calibration of probabilistic classifiers, following [Guo+17].

14.2.2.3 Platt scaling

Let z be the log-odds, or logit, and $p = \sigma(z)$, produced by a probabilistic binary classifier. We wish to convert this to a more calibrated value q. The simplest way to do this is known as **Platt scaling**, and was proposed in [Pla00]. The idea is to compute $q = \sigma(az + b)$, where a and b are estimated via maximum likelihood on a validation set.

In the multiclass case, we can extend Platt scaling by using matrix scaling: $\boldsymbol{q} = \mathrm{softmax}(\mathbf{W}\boldsymbol{z} + \boldsymbol{b})$, where we estimate $\mathbf{W}$ and $\boldsymbol{b}$ via maximum likelihood on a validation set. Since $\mathbf{W}$ has $K \times K$ parameters, where K is the number of classes, this method can easily overfit, so in practice we restrict $\mathbf{W}$ to be diagonal.

14.2.2.4 Nonparametric (histogram) methods

Platt scaling makes a strong assumption about how the shape of the calibration curve. A more flexible, nonparametric, method is to partion the predicted probabilities into bins, p_m, and to estimate an empirical probability q_m for each such bin; we then replace p_m with q_m; this is known as **histogram binning** [ZE01a]. We can regularize this method by requiring that $q = f(p)$ be a piecewise constant, monotonically non-decreasing function; this is known as **isotonic regression** [ZE01a]. An alternative approach, known as the **scaling-binning calibrator**, is to apply a scaling method (such as Platt scaling), and then to apply histogram binning to that. This has the advantage of using the average of the scaled probabilities in each bin instead of the average of the observed binary labels (see Figure 14.2). In [KLM19], they prove that this results in better calibration, due to the lower variance of the estimator.

In the multiclass case, $\boldsymbol{z}$ is the vector of logits, and $\boldsymbol{p} = \mathrm{softmax}(\boldsymbol{z})$ is the vector of probabilities. We wish to convert this to a better calibrated version, $\boldsymbol{q}$. [ZE01b] propose to extend histogram binning and isotonic regression to this case by applying the above binary method to each of the K one-vs-rest problems, where K is the number of classes. However, this requires K separate calibration models, and results in an unnormalized probability distribution.

14.2.2.5 Temperature scaling

In [Guo+17], they noticed empirically that the diagonal version of Platt scaling, when applied to a variety of DNNs, often ended learning a vector of the form $\boldsymbol{w} = (c, c, \ldots, c)$, for some constant c. This suggests a simpler form of scaling, which they call **temperature scaling**: $\boldsymbol{q} = \mathrm{softmax}(\boldsymbol{z}/T)$,

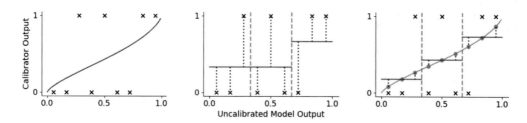

Figure 14.2: Visualization of 3 different approaches to calibrating a binary probabilistic classifier. Black crosses are the observed binary labels, red lines are the calibrated outputs. (a) Platt scaling. (b) Histogram binning with 3 bins. The output in each bin is the average of the binary labels in each bin. (c) The scaling-binning calibrator. This first applies Platt scaling, and then computes the average of the scaled points (gray circles) in each bin. From Figure 1 of [KLM19]. Used with kind permission of Ananya Kumar.

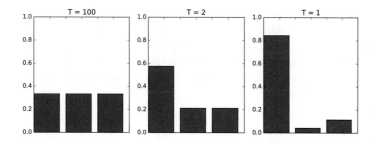

Figure 14.3: Softmax distribution softmax$(\boldsymbol{a}/T)$, *where* $\boldsymbol{a} = (3, 0, 1)$, *at temperatures of* $T = 100$, $T = 2$ *and* $T = 1$. *When the temperature is high (left), the distribution is uniform, whereas when the temperature is low (right), the distribution is "spiky", with most of its mass on the largest element. Generated by* softmax_plot.ipynb.

where $T > 0$ is a temperature parameter, which can be estimated by maximum likelihood on the validation set. The effect of this temperature parameter is to make the distribution less peaky, as shown in Figure 14.3. [Guo+17] show empirically that this method produces the lowest ECE on a variety of DNN classification problems (see Figure 14.1 for a visualization). Furthermore, it is much simpler and faster than the other methods.

Note that Platt scaling and temperature scaling do not affect the identity of the most probable class label, so these methods have no impact on classification accuracy. However, they do improve calibration performance. A more recent multi-class calibration method is discussed in [Kul+19].

14.2.2.6   Label smoothing

When training classifiers, we usually represent the true target label as a one-hot vector, say $\boldsymbol{y} = (0, 1, 0)$ to represent class 2 out of 3. We can improve results if we "spread" some of the probability mass across all the bins. For example we may use $\boldsymbol{y} = (0.1, 0.8, 0.1)$. This is called **label smoothing** and often results in better-calibrated models [MKH19].

14.2.2.7   Bayesian methods

Bayesian approaches to fitting classifiers often result in more calibrated predictions, since they represent uncertainty in the parameters. See Section 17.3.8 for an example.   However, [Ova+19] shows that well-calibrated models (even Bayesian ones) often become mis-calibrated when applied to inputs that come from a different distribution (see Section 19.2 for details).

14.2.3   Beyond evaluating marginal probabilities

Calibration (Section 14.2.2) focuses on assessing properties of the marginal predictive distribution $p(y|\boldsymbol{x})$. But this can sometimes be insufficient to distinguish between a good and bad model, especially in the context of online learning and sequential decision making, as pointed out in [Lu+22; Osb+21; WSG21; KKG22]. For example, consider two learning agents who observe a sequence of coin tosses. Let the outcome at time t be $Y_t \sim \text{Ber}(\theta)$, where θ is the unknown parameter. Agent 1 believes $\theta = 2/3$, whereas agent 2 believes either $\theta = 0$ or $\theta = 1$, but is not sure which, and puts probabilities $1/3$ and $2/3$ on these events. Thus both agents, despite having different models, make identical predictions for the next outcome: $p(Y_1^i = 0) = 1/3$ for agents $i = 1, 2$. However, the predictions of the two agents about a *sequence* of τ future outcomes is very different: In particular, agent 1 predicts each individual coin toss is a random Bernoulli event, where the probability is due to irreducible noise or **aleatoric uncertainty**:

$$p(Y_1^1 = 0, \ldots, Y_\tau^1 = 0) = \frac{1}{3^\tau} \tag{14.22}$$

By contrast, agent 2 predicts that the sequence will either be all heads or all tails, where the probability is induced by **epistemic uncertainty** about the true parameters:

$$p(Y_1^2 = y_1, \ldots, Y_\tau^2 = y_\tau) = \begin{cases} 1/3 & \text{if } y_1 = \cdots = y_\tau = 0 \\ 2/3 & \text{if } y_1 = \cdots = y_\tau = 1 \\ 0 & \text{otherwise} \end{cases} \tag{14.23}$$

The difference in beliefs between these agents will impact their behavior. For example, in a casino, agent 1 incurs little risk on repeatedly betting on heads in the long run, but for agent 2, this would be a very unwise strategy, and some initial information gathering (exploration) would be worthwhile.

Based on the above, we see that it is useful to evaluate *joint* predictive distributions when assessing predictive models. In [Lu+22; Osb+21] they propose to evaluate the posterior predictive distributions over τ outcomes $\boldsymbol{y} = Y_{T+1:T+\tau}$, given a set of τ inputs $\boldsymbol{x} = X_{T:T+\tau-1}$, and the past T data samples, $\mathcal{D}_T = \{(X_t, Y_{t+1}) : t = 0, 1, \ldots, T-1\}$. The Bayes optimal predictive distribution is

$$P_T^B = p(\boldsymbol{y}|\boldsymbol{x}, \mathcal{D}_T) \tag{14.24}$$

This is usually intractable to compute. Instead the agent will use an approximate distribution, known as a **belief state**, which we denote by

$$Q_T = p(\boldsymbol{y}|\boldsymbol{x}, \mathcal{D}_T) \tag{14.25}$$

The natural performance metric is the KL between these distributions. Since this depend on the inputs $\boldsymbol{x}$ and $\mathcal{D}_T = (X_{0:T-1}, Y_{1:T})$, we will averaged the KL over these values, which are drawn iid from the true data generating distribution, which we denote by

$$P(X, Y, \mathcal{E}) = P(X|\mathcal{E})P(Y|X, \mathcal{E})P(\mathcal{E}) \tag{14.26}$$

where $\mathcal{E}$ is the true but unknown environment. Thus we define our metric as

$$d_{B,Q}^{KL} = \mathbb{E}_{P(\boldsymbol{x}, \mathcal{D}_T)} \left[D_{\mathrm{KL}} \left(P^B(\boldsymbol{y}|\boldsymbol{x}, \mathcal{D}_T) \parallel Q(\boldsymbol{y}|\boldsymbol{x}, \mathcal{D}_T) \right) \right] \tag{14.27}$$

where

$$P(\boldsymbol{x}, \mathcal{D}_T, \mathcal{E}) = P(\mathcal{E}) \underbrace{\left[\prod_{t=0}^{T-1} P(X_t|\mathcal{E})P(Y_{t+1}|X_t, \mathcal{E}) \right]}_{P(\mathcal{D}_T|\mathcal{E})} \underbrace{\left[\prod_{t=T}^{T+\tau-1} P(x_t|\mathcal{E}) \right]}_{P(\boldsymbol{x}|\mathcal{E})} \tag{14.28}$$

and $P(\boldsymbol{x}, \mathcal{D}_T)$ marginalizes this over environments.

Unfortunately, it is usually intractable to compute the exact Bayes posterior, P_T^B, so we cannot evaluate $d_{B,Q}^{KL}$. However, in Section 14.2.3.1, we show that

$$d_{B,Q}^{KL} = d_{\mathcal{E},Q}^{KL} - \mathbb{I}(\mathcal{E}; \boldsymbol{y}|\mathcal{D}_T, \boldsymbol{x}) \tag{14.29}$$

where the second term is a constant wrt the agent, and the first term is given by

$$d_{\mathcal{E},Q}^{KL} = \mathbb{E}_{P(\boldsymbol{x}, \mathcal{D}_T, \mathcal{E})} \left[D_{\mathrm{KL}} \left(P(\boldsymbol{y}|\boldsymbol{x}, \mathcal{E}) \parallel Q(\boldsymbol{y}|\boldsymbol{x}, \mathcal{D}_T) \right) \right] \tag{14.30}$$

$$= \mathbb{E}_{P(\boldsymbol{y}|\boldsymbol{x}, \mathcal{E})P(\boldsymbol{x}, \mathcal{D}_T, \mathcal{E})} \left[\log \frac{P(\boldsymbol{y}|\boldsymbol{x}, \mathcal{E})}{Q(\boldsymbol{y}|\boldsymbol{x}, \mathcal{D}_T)} \right] \tag{14.31}$$

Hence if we rank agents in terms of $d_{\mathcal{E},Q}^{KL}$, it will give the same results as ranking them by $d_{B,Q}^{KL}$.

To compute $d_{\mathcal{E},Q}^{KL}$ in practice, we can use a Monte Carlo approximation: we just have to sample J environments, $\mathcal{E}^j \sim P(\mathcal{E})$, sample a training set $\mathcal{D}_T$ from each environment, $\mathcal{D}_T^j \sim P(\mathcal{D}_T|\mathcal{E}^j)$, and then sample N data vectors of length τ, $(\boldsymbol{x}_n^j, \boldsymbol{y}_n^j) \sim P(X_{T:T+\tau-1}, Y_{T+1:T+\tau}|\mathcal{E}^j)$. We can then compute

$$\hat{d}_{\mathcal{E},Q}^{KL} = \frac{1}{JN} \sum_{j=1}^{J} \sum_{n=1}^{N} \left[\log P(\boldsymbol{y}_n^j|\boldsymbol{x}_n^j, \mathcal{E}^j) - \log Q(\boldsymbol{y}_n^j|\boldsymbol{x}_n^j, \mathcal{D}_T^j) \right] \tag{14.32}$$

where

$$p_{jn} = P(\boldsymbol{y}_n^j|\boldsymbol{x}_n^j, \mathcal{E}^j) = \prod_{t=T}^{T+\tau-1} P(Y_{n,t+1}^j|X_{n,t}^j, \mathcal{E}^j) \tag{14.33}$$

$$q_{jn} = Q(\boldsymbol{y}_n^j|\boldsymbol{x}_n^j, \mathcal{D}_T^j) = \int Q(\boldsymbol{y}_n^j|\boldsymbol{x}_n^j, \boldsymbol{\theta})Q(\boldsymbol{\theta}|\mathcal{D}_T^j)d\boldsymbol{\theta} \tag{14.34}$$

$$\approx \frac{1}{M} \sum_{m=1}^{M} \prod_{t=T}^{T+\tau-1} Q(Y_{n,t+1}^j|X_{n,t}^j, \boldsymbol{\theta}_m^j) \tag{14.35}$$

where $\boldsymbol{\theta}_m^j \sim Q(\boldsymbol{\theta}|\mathcal{D}_T^j)$ is a sample from the agent's posterior over the environment.

The above assumes that $P(Y|X)$ is known; this will be the case if we use a synthetic data generator, as in the "neural testbed" in [Osb+21]. If we just have an J empirical distributions for $P^j(X, Y)$, we can replace the KL with the cross entropy, which only differs by an additive constant:

$$d_{\mathcal{E},Q}^{KL} = \mathbb{E}_{P(\boldsymbol{x}, \mathcal{D}_T, \mathcal{E})} \left[D_{\mathrm{KL}} \left(P(\boldsymbol{y}|\boldsymbol{x}, \mathcal{E}) \,\|\, Q(\boldsymbol{y}|\boldsymbol{x}, \mathcal{D}_T) \right) \right] \tag{14.36}$$

$$= \underbrace{\mathbb{E}_{P(\boldsymbol{x}, \boldsymbol{y}, \mathcal{E})} \left[\log P(\boldsymbol{y}|\boldsymbol{x}, \mathcal{E}) \right]}_{\text{const}} - \underbrace{\mathbb{E}_{P(\boldsymbol{x}, \boldsymbol{y}, \mathcal{D}_T|\mathcal{E}) P(\mathcal{E})} \left[\log Q(\boldsymbol{y}|\boldsymbol{x}, \mathcal{D}_T) \right]}_{d_{\mathcal{E},Q}^{CE}} \tag{14.37}$$

where the latter term is just the empirical negative log likelihood (NLL) of the agent on samples from the environment. Hence if we rank agents in terms of their NLL or cross entropy $d_{\mathcal{E},Q}^{CE}$ we will get the same results as ranking them by $d_{\mathcal{E},Q}^{KL}$, which will in turn give the same results as ranking them by $d_{B,Q}^{KL}$.

In practice we can approximate the cross entropy as follows:

$$\hat{d}_{\mathcal{E},Q}^{CE} = -\frac{1}{JN} \sum_{j=1}^{J} \sum_{n=1}^{N} \log Q(\boldsymbol{y}_n^j | \boldsymbol{x}_n^j, \mathcal{D}_T^j) \tag{14.38}$$

where $\mathcal{D}_T^j \sim P^j$, and $(\boldsymbol{x}_n^j, \boldsymbol{y}_n^j) \sim P^j$.

An alternative to estimating the KL or NLL is to evaluate the joint predictive accuracy by using it in a downstream task. In [Osb+21], they show that good predictive accuracy (for $\tau > 1$) correlates with good performance on a bandit problem (see Section 34.4). In [WSG21] they show that good predictive accuracy (for $\tau > 1$) results in good performance on a transductive active learning task.

14.2.3.1   Proof of claim

We now prove Equation (14.29), based on [Lu+21a]. First note that

$$d_{\mathcal{E},Q}^{KL} = \mathbb{E}_{P(\boldsymbol{x}, \mathcal{D}_T, \mathcal{E}) P(\boldsymbol{y}|\boldsymbol{x}, \mathcal{E})} \left[\log \frac{P(\boldsymbol{y}|\boldsymbol{x}, \mathcal{E})}{Q(\boldsymbol{y}|\boldsymbol{x}, \mathcal{D}_T)} \right] \tag{14.39}$$

$$= \mathbb{E} \left[\log \frac{P(\boldsymbol{y}|\boldsymbol{x}, \mathcal{D}_T)}{Q(\boldsymbol{y}|\boldsymbol{x}, \mathcal{D}_T)} \right] + \mathbb{E} \left[\log \frac{P(\boldsymbol{y}|\boldsymbol{x}, \mathcal{E})}{P(\boldsymbol{y}|\boldsymbol{x}, \mathcal{D}_T)} \right] \tag{14.40}$$

For the first term in Equation (14.40) we have

$$\mathbb{E} \left[\log \frac{P(\boldsymbol{y}|\boldsymbol{x}, \mathcal{D}_T)}{Q(\boldsymbol{y}|\boldsymbol{x}, \mathcal{D}_T)} \right] = \sum P(\boldsymbol{x}, \boldsymbol{y}, \mathcal{D}_T) \log \frac{P(\boldsymbol{y}|\boldsymbol{x}, \mathcal{D}_T)}{Q(\boldsymbol{y}|\boldsymbol{x}, \mathcal{D}_T)} \tag{14.41}$$

$$= \sum P(\boldsymbol{x}, \mathcal{D}_T) \sum P(\boldsymbol{y}|\boldsymbol{x}, \mathcal{D}_T) \log \frac{P(\boldsymbol{y}|\boldsymbol{x}, \mathcal{D}_T)}{Q(\boldsymbol{y}|\boldsymbol{x}, \mathcal{D}_T)} \tag{14.42}$$

$$= \mathbb{E}_{P(\boldsymbol{x}, \mathcal{D}_T)} \left[D_{\mathrm{KL}} \left(P(\boldsymbol{y}|\boldsymbol{x}, \mathcal{D}_T) \,\|\, Q(\boldsymbol{y}|\boldsymbol{x}, \mathcal{D}_T) \right) \right] = d_{B,Q}^{KL} \tag{14.43}$$

We now show that the second term in Equation (14.40) reduces to the mutual information. We exploit the fact that

$$P(\boldsymbol{y}|\boldsymbol{x}, \mathcal{E}) = P(\boldsymbol{y}|\mathcal{D}_T, \boldsymbol{x}, \mathcal{E}) = \frac{P(\mathcal{E}, \boldsymbol{y}|\mathcal{D}_T, \boldsymbol{x})}{P(\mathcal{E}|\mathcal{D}_T, \boldsymbol{x})} \tag{14.44}$$

Figure 14.4: Prediction set examples on Imagenet. We show three progressively more difficult examples of the class fox squirrel and the prediction sets generated by conformal prediction. (Compare to Figure 17.9.) From Figure 1 of [AB21]. Used with kind permission of Anastasios Angelopoulos.

since $\mathcal{D}_T$ has no new information in beyond $\mathcal{E}$. From this we get

$$\mathbb{E}\left[\log \frac{P(\boldsymbol{y}|\boldsymbol{x}, \mathcal{E})}{P(\boldsymbol{y}|\boldsymbol{x}, \mathcal{D}_T)}\right] = \mathbb{E}\left[\log \frac{P(\mathcal{E}, \boldsymbol{y}|\mathcal{D}_T, \boldsymbol{x})/P(\mathcal{E}|\mathcal{D}_T, \boldsymbol{x})}{P(\boldsymbol{y}|\mathcal{D}, \mathcal{D}_T)}\right] \tag{14.45}$$

$$= \sum P(\mathcal{D}_T, \boldsymbol{x}) \sum P(\mathcal{E}, \boldsymbol{y}|\mathcal{D}_T, \boldsymbol{x}) \log \frac{P(\mathcal{E}, \boldsymbol{y}|\mathcal{D}_T, \boldsymbol{x})}{P(\boldsymbol{y}|\mathcal{D}_T, \boldsymbol{x})P(\mathcal{E}|\mathcal{D}_T, \boldsymbol{x})} \tag{14.46}$$

$$= \mathbb{I}(\mathcal{E}; \boldsymbol{y}|\mathcal{D}_T, \boldsymbol{x}) \tag{14.47}$$

Hence

$$d_{\mathcal{E},Q}^{KL} = d_{B,Q}^{KL} + \mathbb{I}(\mathcal{E}; \boldsymbol{y}|\mathcal{D}_T, \boldsymbol{x}) \tag{14.48}$$

as claimed.

14.3 Conformal prediction

In this section, we briefly discuss **conformal prediction** [VGS05; SV08; ZFV20; AB21; KSB21; Man22b]. This is a simple but effective way to create prediction intervals or sets with guaranteed frequentist coverage probability from any predictive method $p(y|\boldsymbol{x})$. This can be seen as a form of **distribution free uncertainty quantification**, since it works without making assumptions (beyond exchangeability of the data) about the true data generating process or the form of the model.[1] Our presentation is based on the excellent tutorial of [AB21].[2]

In conformal prediction, we start with some heuristic notion of uncertainty — such as the softmax score for a classification problem, or the variance for a regression problem — and we use it to define a **conformal score** $s(\boldsymbol{x}, y) \in \mathbb{R}$, which measures how badly the output y "conforms" to $\boldsymbol{x}$. (Large

---

1. The exchangeability assumption rules out time series data, which is serially correlated. However, extensions to conformal prediction have been developed for the time series case, see e.g., [Zaf+22]. The exchangeability assumption also rules out distribution shift, although this has also been partially addressed.
2. See also the easy-to-use **MAPIE** Python library at `https://mapie.readthedocs.io/en/latest/index.html`, and the list of papers at [Man22a].

values of the score are less likely, so it is better to think of it as a non-conformity score.) Next we apply this score to a **calibration set** of n labeled examples, that was not used to train f, to get $\mathcal{S} = \{s_i = s(\boldsymbol{x}_i, y_i) : i = 1 : n\}$.[3] The user specifies a desired confidence threshold α, say 0.1, and we then compute the $(1 - \alpha)$ quantile $\hat{q}$ of $\mathcal{S}$. (In fact, we should replace $1 - \alpha$ with $\frac{\lceil (n+1)(1-\alpha) \rceil}{n}$, to account for the finite size of $\mathcal{S}$.) Finally, given a new test input, $\boldsymbol{x}_{n+1}$, we compute the prediction set to be

$$\mathcal{T}(\boldsymbol{x}_{n+1}) = \{y : s(\boldsymbol{x}_{n+1}, y) \leq \hat{q}\} \tag{14.49}$$

Intuitively, we include all the outputs y that are plausible given the input. See Figure 14.4 for an illustration.

Remarkably, one can show the following general result

$$1 - \alpha \leq P^*(y^{n+1} \in \mathcal{T}(\boldsymbol{x}_{n+1})) \leq 1 - \alpha + \frac{1}{n + 1} \tag{14.50}$$

where the probability is wrt the true distribution $P^*(\boldsymbol{x}_{n+1}, y_{n+1})$. We say that the prediction set has a **coverage** level of $1 - \alpha$. This holds for any value of $n \geq 1$ and $\alpha \in [0, 1]$. The only assumption is that the values $(\boldsymbol{x}_i, y_i)$ are exchangeable, and hence the calibration scores s_i are also exchangeable.

To see why this is true, let us sort the scores so $s_1 < \cdots s_n$, so $\hat{q} = s_i$, where $i = \frac{\lceil (n+1)(1-\alpha) \rceil}{n}$. (We assume the scores are distinct, for simplicity.) The score s_{n+1} is equally likely to fall in anywhere between the calibration points $s_1, \ldots, s_n$, since the points are exchangeable. Hence

$$P^*(s_{n+1} \leq s_k) = \frac{k}{n + 1} \tag{14.51}$$

for any $k \in \{1, \ldots, n + 1\}$. The event $\{y_{n+1} \in \mathcal{T}(\boldsymbol{x}_{n+1})\}$ is equivalent to $\{s_{n+1} \leq \hat{q}\}$. Hence

$$P^*(y_{n+1} \in \mathcal{T}(\boldsymbol{x}_{n+1})) = P^*(s_{n+1} \leq \hat{q}) = \frac{\lceil (n+1)(1-\alpha) \rceil}{n + 1} \geq 1 - \alpha \tag{14.52}$$

For the proof of the upper bound, see [Lei+18].

Although this result may seem like a "free lunch", it is worth noting that we can always achieve a desired coverage level by defining the prediction set to be all possible labels. In this case, the prediction set will be independent of the input, but it will cover the true label $1 - \alpha$ of the time. To rule out some degenerate cases, we seek prediction sets that are as small as possible (although we allow for the set to be larger for harder examples), while meeting the coverage requirement. Achieving this goal requires that we define suitable conformal scores. Below we give some examples of how to compute conformal scores $s(\boldsymbol{x}, y)$ for different kinds of problem.[4] It is also important to note that the coverage guarantees are frequentist in nature, and refer to average behavior, rather than representing per-instance uncertainty, as in the Bayesian approach.

---

3. Using a calibration set is called **split conformal prediction**. If we don't have enough data to adopt this splitting approach, we can use **full conformal prediction** [VGS05], which requires fitting the model n times using a leave-one-out type procedure.
4. It is also possible to learn conformal scores in an end-to-end way, jointly with the predictive model, as discussed in [Stu+22].

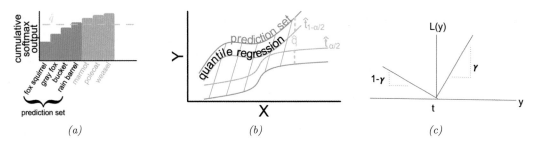

Figure 14.5: (a) Illusration of adaptive prediction set. From Figure 5 of [AB21]. Used with kind permission of Anastasios Angelopoulos. (b) Illustrate of conformalized quantile regression. From Figure 6 of [AB21]. Used with kind permission of Anastasios Angelopoulos. (c) Illustration of pinball loss function.

14.3.1 Conformalizing classification

The simplest way to apply conformal prediction to multiclass classification is to derive the conformal score from the softmax score assigned to the label using $s(\boldsymbol{x}, y) = 1 - f(\boldsymbol{x})_y$, so large values are considered less likely than small values. We compute the threshold $\hat{q}$ as described above, and then we define the prediction set to be $\mathcal{T}(\boldsymbol{x}) = \{y : f(\boldsymbol{x})_y \geq 1 - \hat{q}\}$, which matches Equation (14.49). That is, we take the set of all class labels above the specified threshold, as illustrated in Figure 14.4.

Although the above approach produces prediction sets with the smallest average size (as proved in [SLW19]), the size of the set tends to be too large for easy examples and too small for hard examples. We now present an improved method, known as **adaptive prediction sets**, due to [RSC20], which solves this problem. The idea is simple: we sort all the softmax scores, $f(\boldsymbol{x})_c$ for $c = 1 : C$, to get permutation $\pi_{1:C}$, and then we define $s(\boldsymbol{x}, y)$ to be the cumulative sum of the scores up until we reach label y: $s(\boldsymbol{x}, y) = \sum_{c=1}^{k} f(\boldsymbol{x})_{\pi_j}$, where $k = \pi_y$. We now compute $\hat{q}$ as before, and define the prediction set $\mathcal{T}(\boldsymbol{x})$ to be the set of all labels, sorted in order of decreasing probability, until we cover $\hat{q}$ of the probability mass. See Figure 14.5a for an illustration. This uses all the softmax scores output by the model, rather than just the top score, which accounts for its improved performance.

14.3.2 Conformalizing regression

In this section, we consider conformalized regression problems. Since now $y \in \mathbb{R}$, computing the prediction set in Equation (14.49) is expensive, so instead we will compute a prediction interval, specified by a lower and upper bound.

14.3.2.1 Conformalizing quantile regression

In this section, we use **quantile regression** to compute the lower and upper bounds. We first fit a function of the form $t_\gamma(\boldsymbol{x})$, which predicts the γ quantile of the pdf $P(Y|\boldsymbol{x})$. For example, if we set $\gamma = 0.5$, we get the median. If we use $\gamma = 0.05$ and $\gamma = 0.95$, we can get an approximate 90% prediction interval using $[t_{0.05}(\boldsymbol{x}), t_{0.95}(\boldsymbol{x})]$, as illustrated by the gray lines in Figure 14.5b. To fit the quantile regression model, we just replace squared loss with the **quantile loss**, also called the **pinball loss**, which is defined as

$$\ell_\gamma(y, \hat{t}) = (y - \hat{t})\gamma \mathbb{I}\left(y > \hat{t}\right) + (\hat{t} - y)(1 - \gamma)\mathbb{I}\left(y < \hat{t}\right) \tag{14.53}$$

where y is the true output and $\hat{t}$ is the predicted value at quantile γ. See Figure 14.5c for an illustration.

The regression quantiles are only approximately a 90% interval because the model may be mismatched to the true distribution. However we can use conformal prediction to fix this. In particular, let us define the conformal score to be

$$s(\boldsymbol{x}, y) = \max\left(\hat{t}_{\alpha/2}(\boldsymbol{x}) - y, y - \hat{t}_{\alpha/2}(\boldsymbol{x})\right) \tag{14.54}$$

In other words, $s(\boldsymbol{x}, y)$ is a positive measure of how far the value y is outside the prediction interval, or is a negative measure if y is inside the prediction interval. We compute $\hat{q}$ as before, and define the conformal prediction interval to be

$$\mathcal{T}(\boldsymbol{x}) = [\hat{t}_{\alpha/2}(\boldsymbol{x}) - \hat{q}, \hat{t}_{\alpha/2}(\boldsymbol{x}) + \hat{q}] \tag{14.55}$$

This makes the quantile regression interval wider if $\hat{q}$ is positive (if the base method was overconfident), and narrower if $\hat{q}$ is negative (if the base method was underconfident). See Figure 14.5b for an illustration. This approach is called **conformalized quantile regression** or **CQR** [RPC19].

14.3.2.2   Conformalizing predicted variances

There are many ways to define uncertainty scores $u(\boldsymbol{x})$, such as the predicted standard deviation, from which we can derive a prediction interval using

$$\mathcal{T}(\boldsymbol{x}) = [f(\boldsymbol{x}) - u(\boldsymbol{x})\hat{q}, f(\boldsymbol{x}) + u(\boldsymbol{x})\hat{q}] \tag{14.56}$$

Here $\hat{q}$ is derived from the quantiles of the following conformal scores

$$s(\boldsymbol{x}, y) = \frac{|y - f(\boldsymbol{x})|}{u(\boldsymbol{x})} \tag{14.57}$$

The interval produced by this method tends to be wider than the one computed by CQR, since it extends an equal amount above and below the predicted value $f(\boldsymbol{x})$. In addition, the uncertainty measure $u(\boldsymbol{x})$ may not scale properly with α. Nevertheless, this is a simple post-hoc method that can be applied to many regression methods without needing to retrain them.

15 Generalized linear models

15.1 Introduction

A **generalized linear model** or **GLM** [MN89] is a conditional version of an exponential family distribution (Section 2.4). More precisely, the model has the following form:

$$p(y_n|\boldsymbol{x}_n, \boldsymbol{w}, \sigma^2) = \exp\left[\frac{y_n \eta_n - A(\eta_n)}{\sigma^2} + \log h(y_n, \sigma^2)\right] \tag{15.1}$$

where $\eta_n = \boldsymbol{w}^\mathsf{T}\boldsymbol{x}_n$ is the natural parameter for the distribution, $A(\eta_n)$ is the log normalizer, $\mathcal{T}(y) = y$ is the sufficient statistic, and σ^2 is the dispersion term. Based on the results in Section 2.4.3, we can show that the mean and variance of the response variable are as follows:

$$\mu_n \triangleq \mathbb{E}\left[y_n|\boldsymbol{x}_n, \boldsymbol{w}, \sigma^2\right] = A'(\eta_n) \triangleq \ell^{-1}(\eta_n) \tag{15.2}$$

$$\mathbb{V}\left[y_n|\boldsymbol{x}_n, \boldsymbol{w}, \sigma^2\right] = A''(\eta_n)\,\sigma^2 \tag{15.3}$$

We will denote the mapping from the linear inputs to the mean of the output using $\mu_n = \ell^{-1}(\eta_n)$, where the function ℓ is known as the **link function**, and ℓ^{-1} is known as the **mean function**. This relationship is usually written as follows:

$$\ell(\mu_n) = \eta_n = \boldsymbol{w}^\mathsf{T}\boldsymbol{x}_n \tag{15.4}$$

GLMs are quite limited in their predictive power, due to the assumption of linearity (although we can always use basis function expansion on $\boldsymbol{x}_n$ to improve the flexibility). However, the main use of GLMs in the statistics literature is not for prediction, but for hypothesis testing, as we explain in Section 3.10.3. This relies on the ability to compute the posterior, $p(\boldsymbol{w}|\mathcal{D})$, which we discuss in Section 15.1.4. We can use this to draw conclusions about whether any of the inputs (e.g., representing different groups) have a significant effect on the output.

15.1.1 Some popular GLMs

In this section, we give some examples of widely used GLMs.

15.1.1.1 Linear regression

Recall that linear regression has the form

$$p(y_n|\boldsymbol{x}_n, \boldsymbol{w}, \sigma^2) = \frac{1}{\sqrt{2\pi\sigma^2}} \exp(-\frac{1}{2\sigma^2}(y_n - \boldsymbol{w}^\mathsf{T}\boldsymbol{x}_n)^2) \tag{15.5}$$

Hence

$$\log p(y_n|\boldsymbol{x}_n, \boldsymbol{w}, \sigma^2) = -\frac{1}{2\sigma^2}(y_n - \eta_n)^2 - \frac{1}{2}\log(2\pi\sigma^2) \tag{15.6}$$

where $\eta_n = \boldsymbol{w}^\mathsf{T}\boldsymbol{x}_n$. We can write this in GLM form as follows:

$$\log p(y_n|\boldsymbol{x}_n, \boldsymbol{w}, \sigma^2) = \frac{y_n\eta_n - \frac{\eta_n^2}{2}}{\sigma^2} - \frac{1}{2}\left(\frac{y_n^2}{\sigma^2} + \log(2\pi\sigma^2)\right) \tag{15.7}$$

We see that $A(\eta_n) = \eta_n^2/2$ and hence

$$\mathbb{E}[y_n] = \eta_n = \boldsymbol{w}^\mathsf{T}\boldsymbol{x}_n \tag{15.8}$$
$$\mathbb{V}[y_n] = \sigma^2 \tag{15.9}$$

See Section 15.2 for details on linear regression.

15.1.1.2　Binomial regression

If the response variable is the number of successes in N_n trials, $y_n \in \{0, \dots, N_n\}$, we can use **binomial regression**, which is defined by

$$p(y_n|\boldsymbol{x}_n, N_n, \boldsymbol{w}) = \text{Bin}(y_n|\sigma(\boldsymbol{w}^\mathsf{T}\boldsymbol{x}_n), N_n) \tag{15.10}$$

We see that binary logistic regression is the special case when $N_n = 1$.

The log pdf is given by

$$\log p(y_n|\boldsymbol{x}_n, N_n, \boldsymbol{w}) = y_n \log \mu_n + (N_n - y_n)\log(1 - \mu_n) + \log\binom{N_n}{y_n} \tag{15.11}$$

$$= y_n \log(\frac{\mu_n}{1 - \mu_n}) + N_n \log(1 - \mu_n) + \log\binom{N_n}{y_n} \tag{15.12}$$

where $\mu_n = \sigma(\eta_n)$. To rewrite this in GLM form, let us define

$$\eta_n \triangleq \log\left[\frac{\mu_n}{(1 - \mu_n)}\right] = \log\left[\frac{1}{1 + e^{-\boldsymbol{w}^\mathsf{T}\boldsymbol{x}_n}}\frac{1 + e^{-\boldsymbol{w}^\mathsf{T}\boldsymbol{x}_n}}{e^{-\boldsymbol{w}^\mathsf{T}\boldsymbol{x}_n}}\right] = \log\frac{1}{e^{-\boldsymbol{w}^\mathsf{T}\boldsymbol{x}_n}} = \boldsymbol{w}^\mathsf{T}\boldsymbol{x}_n \tag{15.13}$$

Hence we can write binomial regression in GLM form as follows

$$\log p(y_n|\boldsymbol{x}_n, N_n, \boldsymbol{w}) = y_n\eta_n - A(\eta_n) + h(y_n) \tag{15.14}$$

where $h(y_n) = \log\binom{N_n}{y_n}$ and

$$A(\eta_n) = -N_n \log(1 - \mu_n) = N_n \log(1 + e^{\eta_n}) \tag{15.15}$$

Hence

$$\mathbb{E}[y_n] = \frac{dA}{d\eta_n} = \frac{N_n e^{\eta_n}}{1 + e^{\eta_n}} = \frac{N_n}{1 + e^{-\eta_n}} = N_n \mu_n \tag{15.16}$$

and

$$\mathbb{V}[y_n] = \frac{d^2 A}{d\eta_n^2} = N_n \mu_n (1 - \mu_n) \tag{15.17}$$

See Section 15.3.9 for an example of binomial regression.

15.1.1.3   Poisson regression

If the response variable is an integer count, $y_n \in \{0, 1, \ldots\}$, we can use **Poisson regression**, which is defined by

$$p(y_n | \boldsymbol{x}_n, \boldsymbol{w}) = \mathrm{Poi}(y_n | \exp(\boldsymbol{w}^\mathsf{T} \boldsymbol{x}_n)) \tag{15.18}$$

where

$$\mathrm{Poi}(y | \mu) = e^{-\mu} \frac{\mu^y}{y!} \tag{15.19}$$

is the Poisson distribution. Poisson regression is widely used in bio-statistical applications, where y_n might represent the number of diseases of a given person or place, or the number of reads at a genomic location in a high-throughput sequencing context (see e.g., [Kua+09]).

The log pdf is given by

$$\log p(y_n | \boldsymbol{x}_n, \boldsymbol{w}) = y_n \log \mu_n - \mu_n - \log(y_n!) \tag{15.20}$$

where $\mu_n = \exp(\boldsymbol{w}^\mathsf{T} \boldsymbol{x}_n)$. Hence in GLM form we have

$$\log p(y_n | \boldsymbol{x}_n, \boldsymbol{w}) = y_n \eta_n - A(\eta_n) + h(y_n) \tag{15.21}$$

where $\eta_n = \log(\mu_n) = \boldsymbol{w}^\mathsf{T} \boldsymbol{x}_n$, $A(\eta_n) = \mu_n = e^{\eta_n}$, and $h(y_n) = -\log(y_n!)$. Hence

$$\mathbb{E}[y_n] = \frac{dA}{d\eta_n} = e^{\eta_n} = \mu_n \tag{15.22}$$

and

$$\mathbb{V}[y_n] = \frac{d^2 A}{d\eta_n^2} = e^{\eta_n} = \mu_n \tag{15.23}$$

15.1.1.4   Zero-inflated Poisson regression

In many forms of count data, the number of observed 0s is larger than what a model might expect, even after taking into account the predictors. Intuitively, this is because there may be many ways to produce no outcome. For example, consider predicting sales data for a product. If the sales are 0, does it mean the product is unpopular (so the demand is very low), or was it simply sold out (implying the demand is high, but supply is zero)? Similar problems arise in genomics, epidemiology, etc.

To handle such situations, it is common to use a **zero-inflated Poisson** or **ZIP** model. The likelihood for this model is a mixture of two distributions: a spike at 0, and a standard Poisson. Formally, we define

$$\text{ZIP}(y|\rho, \lambda) = \begin{cases} \rho + (1 - \rho)\exp(-\lambda) & \text{if } y = 0 \\ (1 - \rho)\frac{\lambda^y \exp(-\lambda)}{y!} & \text{if } y > 0 \end{cases} \tag{15.24}$$

Here ρ is the prior probability of picking the spike, and λ is the rate of the Poisson. We see that there are two "mechanisms" for generating a 0: either (with probability ρ) we choose the spike, or (with probability $1 - \rho$) we simply generate a zero count just because the rate of the Poisson is so low. (This latter event has probability $\lambda^0 e^{-\lambda}/0! = e^{-\lambda}$.)

15.1.2   GLMs with noncanonical link functions

We have seen how the mean parameters of the output distribution are given by $\mu = \ell^{-1}(\eta)$, where the function ℓ is the link function. There are several choices for this function, as we now discuss.

The **canonical link function** ℓ satisfies the property that $\theta = \ell(\mu)$, where θ are the canonical (natural) parameters. Hence

$$\theta = \ell(\mu) = \ell(\ell^{-1}(\eta)) = \eta \tag{15.25}$$

This is what we have assumed so far. For example, for the Bernoulli distribution, the canonical parameter is the log-odds $\eta = \log(\mu/(1 - \mu))$, which is given by the logit transform

$$\eta = \ell(\mu) = \text{logit}(\mu) = \log\left(\frac{\mu}{1 - \mu}\right) \tag{15.26}$$

The inverse of this is the sigmoid or logistic funciton

$$\mu = \ell^{-1}(\eta) = \sigma(\eta) = 1/(1 + e^{-\eta}) \tag{15.27}$$

However, we are free to use other kinds of link function. For example, in Section 15.4 we use

$$\eta = \ell(\mu) = \Phi^{-1}(\mu) \tag{15.28}$$
$$\mu = \ell^{-1}(\eta) = \Phi(\eta) \tag{15.29}$$

This is known as the **probit link function**.

Another link function that is sometimes used for binary responses is the **complementary log-log** function

$$\eta = \ell(\mu) = \log(-\log(1 - \mu)) \tag{15.30}$$

This is used in applications where we either observe 0 events (denoted by $y = 0$) or one or more (denoted by $y = 1$), where events are assumed to be governed by a Poisson distribution with rate λ. Let E be the number of events. The Poisson assumption means $p(E = 0) = \exp(-\lambda)$ and hence

$$p(y = 0) = (1 - \mu) = p(E = 0) = \exp(-\lambda) \tag{15.31}$$

Thus $\lambda = -\log(1 - \mu)$. When λ is a function of covariates, we need to ensure it is positive, so we use $\lambda = e^\eta$, and hence

$$\eta = \log(\lambda) = \log(-\log(1 - \mu)) \tag{15.32}$$

15.1.3 Maximum likelihood estimation

GLMs can be fit using similar methods to those that we used to fit logistic regression. In particular, the negative log-likelihood has the following form (ignoring constant terms):

$$\text{NLL}(\boldsymbol{w}) = -\log p(\mathcal{D}|\boldsymbol{w}) = -\frac{1}{\sigma^2}\sum_{n=1}^{N}\ell_n \tag{15.33}$$

where

$$\ell_n \triangleq \eta_n y_n - A(\eta_n) \tag{15.34}$$

where $\eta_n = \boldsymbol{w}^\mathsf{T}\boldsymbol{x}_n$. For notational simplicity, we will assume $\sigma^2 = 1$.

We can compute the gradient for a single term as follows:

$$\boldsymbol{g}_n \triangleq \frac{\partial \ell_n}{\partial \boldsymbol{w}} = \frac{\partial \ell_n}{\partial \eta_n}\frac{\partial \eta_n}{\partial \boldsymbol{w}} = (y_n - A'(\eta_n))\boldsymbol{x}_n = (y_n - \mu_n)\boldsymbol{x}_n \tag{15.35}$$

where $\mu_n = f(\boldsymbol{w}^\mathsf{T}\boldsymbol{x}_n)$, and f is the inverse link function that maps from canonical parameters to mean parameters. (For example, in the case of logistic regression, we have $\mu_n = \sigma(\boldsymbol{w}^\mathsf{T}\boldsymbol{x})$.)

The Hessian is given by

$$\mathbf{H} = \frac{\partial^2}{\partial \boldsymbol{w}\partial \boldsymbol{w}^\mathsf{T}}\text{NLL}(\boldsymbol{w}) = -\sum_{n=1}^{N}\frac{\partial \boldsymbol{g}_n}{\partial \boldsymbol{w}^\mathsf{T}} \tag{15.36}$$

where

$$\frac{\partial \boldsymbol{g}_n}{\partial \boldsymbol{w}^\mathsf{T}} = \frac{\partial \boldsymbol{g}_n}{\partial \mu_n}\frac{\partial \mu_n}{\partial \boldsymbol{w}^\mathsf{T}} = -\boldsymbol{x}_n f'(\boldsymbol{w}^\mathsf{T}\boldsymbol{x}_n)\boldsymbol{x}_n^\mathsf{T} \tag{15.37}$$

Hence

$$\mathbf{H} = \sum_{n=1}^{N} f'(\eta_n)\boldsymbol{x}_n\boldsymbol{x}_n^\mathsf{T} \tag{15.38}$$

For example, in the case of logistic regression, $f(\eta_n) = \sigma(\eta_n) = \mu_n$, and $f'(\eta_n) = \mu_n(1 - \mu_n)$. In general, we see that the Hessian is positive definite, since $f'(\eta_n) > 0$; hence the negative log likelihood is convex, so the MLE for a GLM is unique (assuming $f(\eta_n) > 0$ for all n).

For small datasets, we can use the **iteratively reweighted least squares** or **IRLS** algorithm, which is a form of Newton's method, to compute the MLE (see e.g., [Mur22, Sec 10.2.6]). For large datsets, we can use SGD. (In practice it is often useful to combine SGD with methods that automatically tune the step size, such as [Loi+21].)

15.1.4 Bayesian inference

Maximum likelihood estimation provides a point estimate of the parameters, but does not convey any notion of uncertainty, which is important for hypothesis testing, as we explain in Section 3.10.3, as well as for avoiding overfitting. To compute the uncertainty, we will perform Bayesian inference of the parameters. To do this, we we first need to specify a prior. Choosing a suitable prior depends on the form of link function. For example, a "flat" or "uninformative" prior on the offset term $\alpha \in \mathbb{R}$ will not translate to an uninformative prior on the probability scale if we pass α through a sigmoid, as we discuss in Section 15.3.4.

Once we have chosen the prior, we can compute the posterior using a variety of approximate inference methods. For small datasets, HMC (Section 12.5) is the easiest to use, since you just need to write down the log likelihood and log prior; we can then use autograd to compute derivatives which can be passed to the HMC engine (see e.g., [BG13] for details).

There are many standard software packages for HMC analysis of (hierarchical) GLMs, such as **Bambi** (`https://github.com/bambinos/bambi`), which is a Python wrapper on top of PyMC/Black-JAX, **RStanARM** (`https://cran.r-project.org/web/packages/rstanarm/index.html`), which is an R wrapper on top of Stan, and **BRMS** (`https://cran.r-project.org/web/packages/brms/index.html`), which is another R wrapper on top of Stan. These libraries support a convenient **formula syntax**, initially created in the R language, for compactly specifying the form of the model, including possible interaction terms between the inputs.

For large datasets, HMC can be slow, since it is a full batch algorithm. In such settings, variational Bayes (see e.g., [HOW11; TN13]), expectation propagation (see e.g., [KW18]), or more specialized algorithms (e.g., [HAB17]) are the best choice.

15.2   Linear regression

Linear regression is the simplest case of a GLM, and refers to the following model:

$$p(y|\boldsymbol{x}, \boldsymbol{\theta}) = \mathcal{N}(y|w_0 + \boldsymbol{w}^\mathsf{T}\boldsymbol{x}, \sigma^2) \tag{15.39}$$

where $\boldsymbol{\theta} = (w_0, \boldsymbol{w}, \sigma^2)$ are all the parameters of the model. (In statistics, the parameters w_0 and $\boldsymbol{w}$ are usually denoted by β_0 and $\boldsymbol{\beta}$.) We gave a detailed introduction to this model in the prequel to this book, [Mur22]. In this section, we briefly discuss maximum likelihood estimation, and then focus on a Bayesian analysis.

15.2.1   Ordinary least squares

From Equation (15.39), we can derive the negative log likelihood of the data as follows:

$$\text{NLL}(\boldsymbol{w}, \sigma^2) = -\sum_{n=1}^{N} \log\left[\left(\frac{1}{2\pi\sigma^2}\right)^{\frac{1}{2}} \exp\left(-\frac{1}{2\sigma^2}(y_n - \boldsymbol{w}^\mathsf{T}\boldsymbol{x}_n)^2\right)\right] \tag{15.40}$$

$$= \frac{1}{2\sigma^2}\sum_{n=1}^{N}(y_n - \hat{y}_n)^2 + \frac{N}{2}\log(2\pi\sigma^2) \tag{15.41}$$

where we have defined the predicted response $\hat{y}_n \triangleq \boldsymbol{w}^\mathsf{T}\boldsymbol{x}_n$. In [Mur22, Sec 11.2.2] we show that the MLE is given by

$$\hat{\boldsymbol{w}}_{\text{mle}} = (\mathbf{X}^\mathsf{T}\mathbf{X})^{-1}\mathbf{X}^\mathsf{T}\boldsymbol{y} \tag{15.42}$$

This is called the **ordinary least squares (OLS)** solution.

The MLE for the observation noise is given by

$$\hat{\sigma}^2_{\text{mle}} = \underset{\sigma^2}{\text{argmin}} \, \text{NLL}(\hat{\boldsymbol{w}}, \sigma^2) = \frac{1}{N} \sum_{n=1}^{N} (y_n - \boldsymbol{x}_n^\mathsf{T} \hat{\boldsymbol{w}})^2 \tag{15.43}$$

This is just the mean squared error of the residuals, which is an intuitive result.

15.2.2 Conjugate priors

In this section, we derive the posterior for the parameters using a conjugate prior. We first consider the case where just $\boldsymbol{w}$ is unknown (so the observation noise variance parameter σ^2 is fixed), and then we consder the general case, where both σ^2 and $\boldsymbol{w}$ are unknown.

15.2.2.1 Noise variance is known

The conjugate prior for linear regression has the following form:

$$p(\boldsymbol{w}) = \mathcal{N}(\boldsymbol{w}| \, \breve{\boldsymbol{w}}, \breve{\boldsymbol{\Sigma}}) \tag{15.44}$$

We often use $\breve{\boldsymbol{w}} = \boldsymbol{0}$ as the prior mean and $\breve{\boldsymbol{\Sigma}} = \tau^2 \mathbf{I}_D$ as the prior covariance. (We assume the bias term is included in the weight vector, but often use a much weaker prior for it, since we typically do not want to regularize the overall mean level of the output.)

To derive the posterior, let us first rewrite the likelihood in terms of an MVN as follows:

$$\ell(\boldsymbol{w}) = p(\mathcal{D}|\boldsymbol{w}, \sigma^2) = \prod_{n=1}^{N} p(y_n|\boldsymbol{w}^\mathsf{T}\boldsymbol{x}, \sigma^2) = \mathcal{N}(\boldsymbol{y}|\mathbf{X}\boldsymbol{w}, \sigma^2 \mathbf{I}_N) \tag{15.45}$$

where $\mathbf{I}_N$ is the $N \times N$ identity matrix. We can then use Bayes' rule for Gaussians (Equation (2.121)) to derive the posterior, which is as follows:

$$p(\boldsymbol{w}|\mathbf{X}, \boldsymbol{y}, \sigma^2) \propto \mathcal{N}(\boldsymbol{w}| \, \breve{\boldsymbol{w}}, \breve{\boldsymbol{\Sigma}}) \mathcal{N}(\boldsymbol{y}|\mathbf{X}\boldsymbol{w}, \sigma^2 \mathbf{I}_N) = \mathcal{N}(\boldsymbol{w}| \, \hat{\boldsymbol{w}}, \hat{\boldsymbol{\Sigma}}) \tag{15.46}$$

$$\hat{\boldsymbol{w}} \triangleq \hat{\boldsymbol{\Sigma}} \, (\breve{\boldsymbol{\Sigma}}^{-1} \breve{\boldsymbol{w}} + \frac{1}{\sigma^2} \mathbf{X}^\mathsf{T} \boldsymbol{y}) \tag{15.47}$$

$$\hat{\boldsymbol{\Sigma}} \triangleq (\breve{\boldsymbol{\Sigma}}^{-1} + \frac{1}{\sigma^2} \mathbf{X}^\mathsf{T} \mathbf{X})^{-1} \tag{15.48}$$

where $\hat{\boldsymbol{w}}$ is the posterior mean, and $\hat{\boldsymbol{\Sigma}}$ is the posterior covariance.

Now suppose $\breve{\boldsymbol{w}} = \boldsymbol{0}$ and $\breve{\boldsymbol{\Sigma}} = \tau^2 \mathbf{I}$. In this case, the posterior mean becomes

$$\hat{\boldsymbol{w}} = \frac{1}{\sigma^2} \hat{\boldsymbol{\Sigma}} \, \mathbf{X}^\mathsf{T} \boldsymbol{y} = (\frac{\sigma^2}{\tau^2} \mathbf{I} + \mathbf{X}^\mathsf{T} \mathbf{X})^{-1} \mathbf{X}^\mathsf{T} \boldsymbol{y} \tag{15.49}$$

If we define $\lambda = \frac{\sigma^2}{\tau^2}$, we see this is equivalent to **ridge regression**, which optimizes

$$\mathcal{L}(\boldsymbol{w}) = \text{RSS}(\boldsymbol{w}) + \lambda ||\boldsymbol{w}||^2 \tag{15.50}$$

where RSS is the residual sum of squares:

$$\text{RSS}(\boldsymbol{w}) = \frac{1}{2} \sum_{n=1}^{N} (y_n - \boldsymbol{w}^\mathsf{T}\boldsymbol{x}_n)^2 = \frac{1}{2}||\mathbf{X}\boldsymbol{w} - \boldsymbol{y}||_2^2 = \frac{1}{2}(\mathbf{X}\boldsymbol{w} - \boldsymbol{y})^\mathsf{T}(\mathbf{X}\boldsymbol{w} - \boldsymbol{y}) \tag{15.51}$$

15.2.2.2   Noise variance is unknown

In this section, we assume $\boldsymbol{w}$ and σ^2 are both unknown. The likelihood is given by

$$\ell(\boldsymbol{w}, \sigma^2) = p(\mathcal{D}|\boldsymbol{w}, \sigma^2) \propto (\sigma^2)^{-N/2} \exp\left(-\frac{1}{2\sigma^2}\sum_{n=1}^{N}(y_n - \boldsymbol{w}^\mathsf{T}\boldsymbol{x}_n)^2\right) \tag{15.52}$$

Since the regression weights now depend on σ^2 in the likelihood, the conjugate prior for $\boldsymbol{w}$ has the form

$$p(\boldsymbol{w}|\sigma^2) = \mathcal{N}(\boldsymbol{w}|\,\breve{\boldsymbol{w}}, \sigma^2\,\breve{\boldsymbol{\Sigma}}) \tag{15.53}$$

For the noise variance σ^2, the conjugate prior is based on the inverse gamma distrbution, which has the form

$$\text{IG}(\sigma^2|\,\breve{a}, \breve{b}) = \frac{\breve{b}^{\breve{a}}}{\Gamma(\breve{a})}(\sigma^2)^{-(\breve{a}+1)}\exp(-\frac{\breve{b}}{\sigma^2}) \tag{15.54}$$

(See Section 2.2.3.4 for more details.) Putting these two together, we find that the joint conjugate prior is the **normal inverse gamma** distribution:

$$\text{NIG}(\boldsymbol{w}, \sigma^2|\,\breve{\boldsymbol{w}}, \breve{\boldsymbol{\Sigma}}, \breve{a}, \breve{b}) \triangleq \mathcal{N}(\boldsymbol{w}|\,\breve{\boldsymbol{w}}, \sigma^2\,\breve{\boldsymbol{\Sigma}})\text{IG}(\sigma^2|\,\breve{a}, \breve{b}) \tag{15.55}$$

$$= \frac{\breve{b}^{\breve{a}}}{(2\pi)^{D/2}|\,\breve{\boldsymbol{\Sigma}}\,|^{\frac{1}{2}}\Gamma(\breve{a})}\,(\sigma^2)^{-(\breve{a}+(D/2)+1)}$$

$$\times \exp\left[-\frac{(\boldsymbol{w}-\breve{\boldsymbol{w}})^\mathsf{T}\,\breve{\boldsymbol{\Sigma}}^{-1}\,(\boldsymbol{w}-\breve{\boldsymbol{w}}) + 2\,\breve{b}}{2\sigma^2}\right] \tag{15.56}$$

This results in the following posterior:

$$p(\boldsymbol{w}, \sigma^2|\mathcal{D}) = \text{NIG}(\boldsymbol{w}, \sigma^2|\,\widehat{\boldsymbol{w}}, \widehat{\boldsymbol{\Sigma}}, \widehat{a}, \widehat{b}) \tag{15.57}$$

$$\widehat{\boldsymbol{w}} = \widehat{\boldsymbol{\Sigma}}\,(\breve{\boldsymbol{\Sigma}}^{-1}\,\breve{\boldsymbol{w}} + \mathbf{X}^\mathsf{T}\boldsymbol{y}) \tag{15.58}$$

$$\widehat{\boldsymbol{\Sigma}} = (\breve{\boldsymbol{\Sigma}}^{-1} + \mathbf{X}^\mathsf{T}\mathbf{X})^{-1} \tag{15.59}$$

$$\widehat{a} = \breve{a} + N/2 \tag{15.60}$$

$$\widehat{b} = \breve{b} + \frac{1}{2}\left(\breve{\boldsymbol{w}}^\mathsf{T}\breve{\boldsymbol{\Sigma}}^{-1}\breve{\boldsymbol{w}} + \boldsymbol{y}^\mathsf{T}\boldsymbol{y} - \widehat{\boldsymbol{w}}^\mathsf{T}\widehat{\boldsymbol{\Sigma}}^{-1}\widehat{\boldsymbol{w}}\right) \tag{15.61}$$

The expressions for $\widehat{\boldsymbol{w}}$ and $\widehat{\boldsymbol{\Sigma}}$ are similar to the case where σ^2 is known. The expression for $\widehat{a}$ is also intuitive, since it just updates the counts. The expression for $\widehat{b}$ can be interpreted as follows: it is the prior sum of squares, $\breve{b}$, plus the empirical sum of squares, $\boldsymbol{y}^\mathsf{T}\boldsymbol{y}$, plus a term due to the error in the prior on $\boldsymbol{w}$.

The posterior marginals are as follows. For the variance, we have

$$p(\sigma^2|\mathcal{D}) = \int p(\boldsymbol{w}|\sigma^2, \mathcal{D})p(\sigma^2|\mathcal{D})d\boldsymbol{w} = \text{IG}(\sigma^2|\,\widehat{a}, \widehat{b}) \tag{15.62}$$

For the regression weights, it can be shown that

$$p(\boldsymbol{w}|\mathcal{D}) = \int p(\boldsymbol{w}|\sigma^2, \mathcal{D})p(\sigma^2|\mathcal{D})d\sigma^2 = \mathcal{T}(\boldsymbol{w}|\,\widehat{\boldsymbol{w}}, \frac{\widehat{b}}{\widehat{a}}\,\widehat{\boldsymbol{\Sigma}}, 2\,\widehat{a}) \tag{15.63}$$

15.2.2.3 Posterior predictive distribution

In machine learning we usually care more about uncertainty (and accuracy) of our predictions, not our parameter estimates. Fortunately, one can derive the posterior predictive distribution in closed form. In particular, one can show that, given N' new test inputs $\tilde{\mathbf{X}}$, we have

$$p(\tilde{\boldsymbol{y}}|\tilde{\mathbf{X}}, \mathcal{D}) = \int \int p(\tilde{\boldsymbol{y}}|\tilde{\mathbf{X}}, \boldsymbol{w}, \sigma^2) p(\boldsymbol{w}, \sigma^2|\mathcal{D}) d\boldsymbol{w} d\sigma^2 \tag{15.64}$$

$$= \int \int \mathcal{N}(\tilde{\boldsymbol{y}}|\tilde{\mathbf{X}}\boldsymbol{w}, \sigma^2 \mathbf{I}_{N'}) \text{NIG}(\boldsymbol{w}, \sigma^2| \widehat{\boldsymbol{w}}, \widehat{\boldsymbol{\Sigma}}, \widehat{a}, \widehat{b}) d\boldsymbol{w} d\sigma^2 \tag{15.65}$$

$$= \mathcal{T}(\tilde{\boldsymbol{y}}|\tilde{\mathbf{X}}\,\widehat{\boldsymbol{w}}, \frac{\widehat{b}}{\widehat{a}}(\mathbf{I}_{N'} + \tilde{\mathbf{X}}\,\widehat{\boldsymbol{\Sigma}}\,\tilde{\mathbf{X}}^{\mathsf{T}}), 2\,\widehat{a}) \tag{15.66}$$

The posterior predictive mean is equivalent to "normal" linear regression, but where we plug in $\widehat{\boldsymbol{w}} = \mathbb{E}[\boldsymbol{w}|\mathcal{D}]$ instead of the MLE. The posterior predictive variance has two components: $\widehat{b}/\widehat{a}\mathbf{I}_{N'}$ due to the measurement noise, and $\widehat{b}/\widehat{a}\tilde{\mathbf{X}}\,\widehat{\boldsymbol{\Sigma}}\,\tilde{\mathbf{X}}^{\mathsf{T}}$ due to the uncertainty in $\boldsymbol{w}$. This latter term varies depending on how close the test inputs are to the training data. The results are similar to using a Gaussian prior (with fixed $\hat{\sigma}^2$), except the predictive distribution is even wider, since we are taking into account uncertainty about σ^2.

15.2.3 Uninformative priors

A common criticism of Bayesian inference is the need to use a prior. This is sometimes thought to "pollute" the inferences one makes from the data. We can minimize the effect of the prior by using an uninformative prior, as we discussed in Section 3.5. Below we discuss various uninformative priors for linear regression.

15.2.3.1 Jeffreys prior

From Section 3.5.3.1, we know that the Jeffreys prior for the location parameter has the form $p(\boldsymbol{w}) \propto 1$, and from Section 3.5.3.2, we know that the Jeffreys prior for the scale factor has the form $p(\sigma) \propto \sigma^{-1}$. We can emulate these priors using an improper NIG prior with $\breve{\boldsymbol{w}} = \mathbf{0}$, $\breve{\boldsymbol{\Sigma}} = \infty\mathbf{I}$, $\breve{a} = -D/2$ and $\breve{b} = 0$. The corresponding posterior is given by

$$p(\boldsymbol{w}, \sigma^2|\mathcal{D}) = \text{NIG}(\boldsymbol{w}, \sigma^2| \widehat{\boldsymbol{w}}, \widehat{\boldsymbol{\Sigma}}, \widehat{a}, \widehat{b}) \tag{15.67}$$

$$\widehat{\boldsymbol{w}} = \widehat{\boldsymbol{w}}_{\text{mle}} = (\mathbf{X}^{\mathsf{T}}\mathbf{X})^{-1}\mathbf{X}^{\mathsf{T}}\boldsymbol{y} \tag{15.68}$$

$$\widehat{\boldsymbol{\Sigma}} = (\mathbf{X}^{\mathsf{T}}\mathbf{X})^{-1} \triangleq \mathbf{C} \tag{15.69}$$

$$\widehat{a} = \frac{\nu}{2} \tag{15.70}$$

$$\widehat{b} = \frac{s^2\nu}{2} \tag{15.71}$$

$$s^2 \triangleq \frac{||\boldsymbol{y} - \hat{\boldsymbol{y}}||^2}{\nu} \tag{15.72}$$

$$\nu = N - D \tag{15.73}$$

Hence the posterior distribution of the weights is given by

$$p(\boldsymbol{w}|\mathcal{D}) = \mathcal{T}(\boldsymbol{w}|\hat{\boldsymbol{w}}, s^2 \mathbf{C}, \nu) \tag{15.74}$$

where $\hat{\boldsymbol{w}}$ is the MLE. The marginals for each weight therefore have the form

$$p(w_d|\mathcal{D}) = \mathcal{T}(w_d|\hat{w}_d, s^2 C_{dd}, \nu) \tag{15.75}$$

15.2.3.2   Connection to frequentist statistics

Interestingly, the posterior when using Jeffreys prior is formally equivalent to the **frequentist sampling distribution** of the MLE, which has the form

$$p(\hat{w}_d|\mathcal{D}^*) = \mathcal{T}(\hat{w}_d|w_d, s^2 C_{dd}, \nu) \tag{15.76}$$

where $\mathcal{D}^* = (\mathbf{X}, \boldsymbol{y}^*)$ is hypothetical data generated from the true model given the fixed inputs $\mathbf{X}$. In books on frequentist statistics, this is more commonly written in the following equivalent way (see e.g., [Ric95, p542]):

$$\frac{\hat{w}_d - w_d}{s\sqrt{C_{dd}}} \sim t_{N-D} \tag{15.77}$$

The sampling distribution is numerically the same as the posterior distribution in Equation (15.75) because $\mathcal{T}(w|\mu, \sigma^2, \nu) = \mathcal{T}(\mu|w, \sigma^2, \nu)$. However, it is semantically quite different, since the sampling distribution does not condition on the observed data, but instead is based on hypothetical data drawn from the model. See [BT73, p117] for more discussion of the equivalences between Bayesian and frequentist analysis of simple linear models when using uninformative priors.

15.2.3.3   Zellner's g-prior

It is often reasonable to assume an uninformative prior on σ^2, since that is just a scalar that does not have much influence on the results, but using an uninformative prior for $\boldsymbol{w}$ can be dangerous, since the strength of the prior controls how well regularized the model is, as we know from ridge regression.

A common compromise is to use an NIG prior with $\breve{a} = -D/2$, $\breve{b} = 0$ (to ensure $p(\sigma^2) \propto 1$) and $\breve{\boldsymbol{w}} = \mathbf{0}$ and $\breve{\mathbf{\Sigma}} = g(\mathbf{X}^\mathsf{T}\mathbf{X})^{-1}$, where $g > 0$ plays a role analogous to $1/\lambda$ in ridge regression. This is called Zellner's **g-prior** [Zel86].[1] We see that the prior covariance is proportional to $(\mathbf{X}^\mathsf{T}\mathbf{X})^{-1}$ rather than $\mathbf{I}$; this ensures that the posterior is invariant to scaling of the inputs, e.g., due to a change in the units of measurement [Min00a].

---

1. Note this prior is conditioned on the inputs $\mathbf{X}$, but not the outputs $\boldsymbol{y}$; this is totally valid in a conditional (discriminative) model, where all calculations are conditioned on $\mathbf{X}$, which is treated like a fixed constant input.

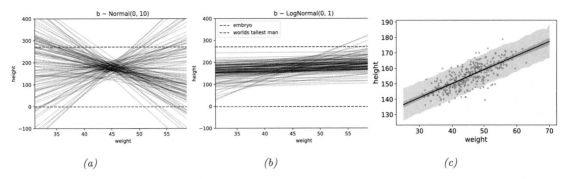

Figure 15.1: Linear regression for predicting height given weight, $y \sim \mathcal{N}(\alpha + \beta x, \sigma^2)$. (a) Prior predictive samples using a Gaussian prior for β. (b) Prior predictive samples using a log-Gaussian prior for β. (c) Posterior predictive samples using the log-Gaussian prior. The inner shaded band is the 95% credible interval for μ, representing epistemic uncertainty. The outer shaded band is the 95% credible interval for the observations y, which also adds data uncertainty due to σ. Adapted from Figures 4.5 and 4.10 of [McE20]. Generated by linreg_height_weight.ipynb.

With this prior, the posterior becomes

$$p(\boldsymbol{w}, \sigma^2 | g, \mathcal{D}) = \text{NIG}(\boldsymbol{w}, \sigma^2 | \boldsymbol{w}_N, \mathbf{V}_N, a_N, b_N) \tag{15.78}$$

$$\mathbf{V}_N = \frac{g}{g+1}(\mathbf{X}^T\mathbf{X})^{-1} \tag{15.79}$$

$$\boldsymbol{w}_N = \frac{g}{g+1}\hat{\boldsymbol{w}}_{mle} \tag{15.80}$$

$$a_N = N/2 \tag{15.81}$$

$$b_N = \frac{s^2}{2} + \frac{1}{2(g+1)}\hat{\boldsymbol{w}}_{mle}^T\mathbf{X}^T\mathbf{X}\hat{\boldsymbol{w}}_{mle} \tag{15.82}$$

Various approaches have been proposed for setting g, including cross validation, empirical Bayes [Min00a; GF00], hierarchical Bayes [Lia+08], etc.

15.2.4 Informative priors

In many problems, it is possible to use domain knowledge to come up with plausible priors. As an example, we consider the problem of predicting the height of a person given their weight. We will use a dataset collected from Kalahari foragers by the anthropologist Nancy Howell (this example is from [McE20, p93]).

Let x_i be the weight (in kg) and y_i be height (in cm) of the i'th person, and let $\bar{x}$ be the mean of the inputs. The observation model is given by

$$y_i \sim \mathcal{N}(\mu_i, \sigma) \tag{15.83}$$

$$\mu_i = \alpha + \beta(x_i - \bar{x}) \tag{15.84}$$

We see that the intercept α is the predicted output if $x_i = \bar{x}$, and the slope β is the predicted change in height per unit change in weight above or below the average weight.

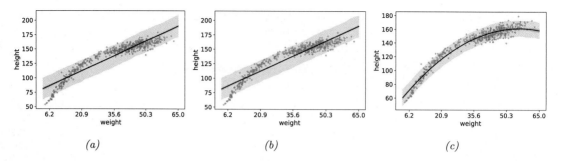

Figure 15.2: Linear regression for predicting height given weight for the full dataset (including children) using polynomial regression. (a) Posterior fit for linear model with log-Gaussian prior for β_1. (b) Posterior fit for quadratic model with log-Gaussian prior for β_2. (c) Posterior fit for quadratic model with Gaussian prior for β_2. Adapted from Figure 4.11 of [McE20]. Generated by linreg_height_weight.ipynb.

The question is: what priors should we use? To be truly Bayesian, we should set these before looking at the data. A sensible prior for α is the height of a "typical person", with some spread. We use $\alpha \sim \mathcal{N}(178, 20)$, since the author of the book from which this example is taken is 178cm. By using a standard deviation of 20, the prior puts 95% probability on the broad range of 178 ± 40.

What about the prior for β? It is tempting to use a **vague prior**, or **weak prior**, such as $\beta \sim \mathcal{N}(0, 10)$, which is similar to a flat (uniform) prior, but more concentrated at 0 (a form of mild regularization). To see if this is reasonable, we can compute samples from the **prior predictive distribution**, i.e., we sample $(\alpha_s, \beta_s) \sim p(\alpha)p(\beta)$, and then plot $\alpha_s x + \beta_s$ for a range of x values, for different samples $s = 1 : S$. The results are shown in Figure 15.1a. We see that this is not a very sensible prior. For example, we see that it suggests that it is just as likely for the height to decrease with weight as increase with weight, which is not plausible. In addition, it predicts heights which are larger than the world's tallest person (272 cm) and smaller than the world's shortest person (an embryo, of size 0).

We can encode the monotonically increasing relationship between weight and height by restricting β to be positive. An easy way to do this is to use a log-normal or log-Gaussian prior. (If $\tilde{\beta} = \log(\beta)$ is Gaussian, then $e^{\tilde{\beta}}$ must be positive.) Specifically, we will assume $\beta \sim \mathcal{LN}(0, 1)$. Samples from this prior are shown in Figure 15.1b. This is much more reasonable.

Finally we must choose a prior over σ. In [McE20] they use $\sigma \sim \text{Unif}(0, 50)$. This ensures that σ is positive, and that the prior predictive distribution for the output is within 100cm of the average height. However, it is usually easier to specify the expected value for σ than an upper bound. To do this, we can use $\sigma \sim \text{Expon}(\lambda)$, where λ is the rate. We then set $\mathbb{E}[\sigma] = 1/\lambda$ to the value of the standard deviation that we expect. For example, we can use the empirical standard deviation of the data.

Since these priors are no longer conjugate, we cannot compute the posterior in closed form. However, we can use a variety of approximate inference methods. In this simple example, it suffices to use a quadratic (Laplace) approximation (see Section 7.4.3). The results are shown in Figure 15.1c, and look sensible.

So far, we have only considered a subset of the data, corresponding to adults over the age of 18. If we include children, we find that the mapping from weight to height is nonlinear. This is illustrated in Figure 15.2a. We can fix this problem by using **polynomial regression**. For example, consider a quadratic expansion of the standardized features x_i:

$$\mu_i = \alpha + \beta_1 x_i + \beta_2 x_i^2 \tag{15.85}$$

If we use a log-Gaussian prior for β_2, we find that the model is too constrained, and it underfits. This is illustrated in Figure 15.2b. The reason is that we need to use an inverted quadratic with a negative coefficient, but since this is disallowed by the prior, the model ends up not using this degree of freedom (we find $\mathbb{E}\left[\beta_2|\mathcal{D}\right] \approx 0.08$). If we use a Gaussian prior on β_2, we avoid this problem, illustrated in Figure 15.2c.

This example shows that it can be useful to think about the functional form of the mapping from inputs to outputs in order to specify sensible priors.

15.2.5 Spike and slab prior

It is often useful to be able to select a subset of the input features when performing prediction, either to reduce overfitting, or to improve interpretability of the model. This can be achieved if we ensure that the weight vector $\boldsymbol{w}$ is **sparse** (i.e., has many zero elements), since if $w_d = 0$, then x_d plays no role in the inner product $\boldsymbol{w}^\mathsf{T}\boldsymbol{x}$.

The canonical way to achieve sparsity when using Bayesian inference is to use a **spike-and-slab** (**SS**) prior [MB88], which has the form of a 2 component mixture model, with one component being a "spike" at 0, and the other being a uniform "slab" between $-a$ and a:

$$p(\boldsymbol{w}) = \prod_{d=1}^{D} (1-\pi)\delta(w_d) + \pi\text{Unif}(w_d| -a, a) \tag{15.86}$$

where π is the prior probability that each coefficient is non-zero. The corresponding log prior on the coefficients is thus

$$\log p(\boldsymbol{w}) = ||\boldsymbol{w}||_0 \log(1-\pi) + (D - ||\boldsymbol{w}||_0)\log\pi = -\lambda||\boldsymbol{w}||_0 + \text{const} \tag{15.87}$$

where $\lambda = \log\frac{\pi}{1-\pi}$ controls the sparsity of the model, and $||\boldsymbol{w}||_0 = \sum_{d=1}^{D}\mathbb{I}(w_d \neq 0)$ is the ℓ_0 **norm** of the weights. Thus MAP estimation with a spike and slab prior is equivalent ℓ_0 **regularization**; this penalizes the number of non-zero coefficients. Interestingly, posterior samples will also be sparse.

By contrast, consider using a Laplace prior. The **lasso** estimator uses MAP estimation, which results in a sparse estimate. However, posterior samples are not sparse. Interestingly, [EY09] show theoretically (and [SPZ09] confirm experimentally) that using the posterior mean with a spike-and-slab prior also results in better prediction accuracy than using the posterior mode with a Laplace prior.

In practice, we often approximate the uniform slab with a broad Gaussian distribution,

$$p(\boldsymbol{w}) = \prod_d (1-\pi)\delta(w_d) + \pi\mathcal{N}(w_d|0, \sigma_w^2) \tag{15.88}$$

As $\sigma_w^2 \to \infty$, the second term approaches a uniform distribution over $[-\infty, +\infty]$. We can implement the mixture model by associating a binary random variable, $s_d \sim \text{Ber}(\pi)$, with each coefficient, to indicate if the coefficient is "on" or "off".

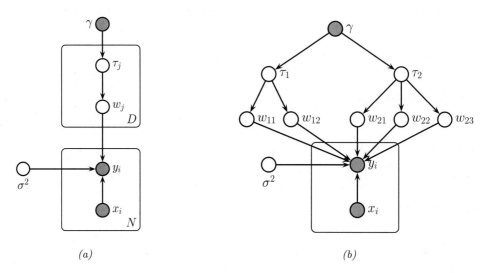

Figure 15.3: (a) Representing lasso using a Gaussian scale mixture prior. (b) Graphical model for group lasso with 2 groups, the first has size $G_1 = 2$, the second has size $G_2 = 3$.

Unfortunately, MAP estimation (not to mention full Bayesian inference) with such discrete mixture priors is computationally difficult. Various approximate inference methods have been proposed, including greedy search (see e.g., [SPZ09]) or MCMC (see e.g., [HS09]).

15.2.6 Laplace prior (Bayesian lasso)

A computationally cheap way to achieve sparsity is to perform MAP estimation with a Laplace prior by minimizing the penalized negative log likelihood:

$$\text{PNLL}(\boldsymbol{w}) = -\log p(\mathcal{D}|\boldsymbol{w}) - \log p(\boldsymbol{w}|\lambda) = ||\mathbf{X}\boldsymbol{w} - \boldsymbol{y}||_2^2 + \lambda||\boldsymbol{w}||_1 \tag{15.89}$$

where $||\boldsymbol{w}||_1 \triangleq \sum_{d=1}^{D} |w_d|$ is the ℓ_1 norm of $\boldsymbol{w}$. This method is called **lasso**, which stands for "least absolute shrinkage and selection operator" [Tib96]. See Section 11.4 of the prequel to this book, [Mur22], for details.

In this section, we discuss posterior inference with this prior; this is known as the **Bayesian lasso** [PC08]. In particular, we assume the following prior:

$$p(\boldsymbol{w}|\sigma^2) = \prod_j \frac{\lambda}{2\sqrt{\sigma^2}} e^{-\lambda|w_j|/\sqrt{\sigma^2}} \tag{15.90}$$

(Note that conditioning the prior on σ^2 is important to ensure that the full posterior is unimodal.)

To simplify inference, we will represent the Laplace prior as a Gaussian scale mixture, which we discussed in Section 28.2.3.2. In particular, one can show that the Laplace distribution is an infinite weighted sum of Gaussians, where the precision comes from a gamma distribution:

$$\text{Laplace}(w|0,\lambda) = \int \mathcal{N}(w|0,\tau^2)\text{Ga}(\tau^2|1,\frac{\lambda^2}{2})d\tau^2 \tag{15.91}$$

We can therefore represent the Bayesian lasso model as a hierarchical latent variable model, as shown in Figure 15.3a. The corresponding joint distribution has the following form:

$$p(\boldsymbol{y},\boldsymbol{w},\boldsymbol{\tau},\sigma^2|\mathbf{X}) = \mathcal{N}(\boldsymbol{y}|\mathbf{X}\boldsymbol{w},\sigma^2\mathbf{I}_N)\left[\prod_j \mathcal{N}(w_j|0,\sigma^2\tau_j^2)\text{Ga}(\tau_j^2|1,\lambda^2/2)\right]p(\sigma^2) \tag{15.92}$$

We can also create a GSM to match the **group lasso** prior, which sets multiple coefficients to zero at the same time:

$$\boldsymbol{w}_g|\sigma^2,\tau_g^2 \sim \mathcal{N}(\boldsymbol{0},\sigma^2\tau_g^2\mathbf{I}_{d_g}) \tag{15.93}$$

$$\tau_g^2 \sim \text{Ga}(\frac{d_g+1}{2},\frac{\lambda^2}{2}) \tag{15.94}$$

where d_g is the size of group g. So we see that there is one variance term per group, each of which comes from a gamma prior, whose shape parameter depends on the group size, and whose rate parameter is controlled by γ.

Figure 15.3b gives an example, where we have 2 groups, one of size 2 and one of size 3. This picture makes it clearer why there should be a grouping effect. For example, suppose $w_{1,1}$ is small; then τ_1^2 will be estimated to be small, which will force $w_{1,2}$ to be small, due to shrinkage (cf. Section 3.6). Conversely, suppose $w_{1,1}$ is large; then τ_1^2 will be estimated to be large, which will allow $w_{1,2}$ to be become large as well.

Given these hierachical models, we can easily derive a Gibbs sampling algorithm (Section 12.3) to sample from the posterior (see e.g., [PC08]). Unfortunately, these posterior samples are not sparse, even though the MAP estimate is sparse. This is because the prior puts infinitessimal probability on the event that each coefficient is zero.

15.2.7 Horseshoe prior

The Laplace prior is not suitable for sparse Bayesian models, because posterior samples are not sparse. The spike and slab prior does not have this problem but is often too slow to use (although see [BRG20]). Fortunately, it is possible to devise continuous priors (without discrete latent variables) that are both sparse and computationally efficient. One popular prior of this type is the **horseshoe prior** [CPS10], so-named because of the shape of its density function.

In the horseshoe prior, instead of using a Laplace prior for each weight, we use the following Gaussian scale mixture:

$$w_j \sim \mathcal{N}(0,\lambda_j^2\tau^2) \tag{15.95}$$

$$\lambda_j \sim \mathcal{C}_+(0,1) \tag{15.96}$$

$$\tau^2 \sim \mathcal{C}_+(0,1) \tag{15.97}$$

where $\mathcal{C}_+(0, 1)$ is the half-Cauchy distribution (Section 2.2.2.4), λ_j is a local shrinkage factor, and τ^2 is a global shrinkage factor. The Cauchy distribution has very fat tails, so λ_j is likely to be either 0 or very far from 0, which emulates the spike and slab prior, but in a continuous way. For more details, see e.g., [Bha+19].

15.2.8   Automatic relevancy determination

An alternative to using posterior inference with a sparsity promoting prior is to use posterior inference with a Gaussian prior, $w_j \sim \mathcal{N}(0, 1/\alpha_j)$, but where we use empirical Bayes to optimize the precisions α_j. That is, we first compute $\hat{\boldsymbol{\alpha}} = \operatorname{argmax}_{\boldsymbol{\alpha}} p(\boldsymbol{y}|\mathbf{X}, \boldsymbol{\alpha})$, and then compute $\hat{\boldsymbol{w}} = \operatorname{argmax}_{\boldsymbol{w}} \mathcal{N}(\boldsymbol{w}|\boldsymbol{0}, \hat{\boldsymbol{\alpha}}^{-1})$. Perhaps surprisingly, we will see that this results in a sparse estimate, for reasons we explain in Section 15.2.8.2.

This technique is known as **sparse Bayesian learning** [Tip01] or **automatic relevancy determination** (**ARD**) [Mac95; Nea96]. It has also been called **NUV** estimation, which stands for "normal prior with unknown variance" [Loe+16]. It was originally developed for neural networks (where sparsity is applied to the first layer weights), but here we apply it to linear models.

15.2.8.1   ARD for linear models

In this section, we explain ARD in more detail, by applying it to linear regression. The likelihood is $p(y|\boldsymbol{x}, \boldsymbol{w}, \beta) = \mathcal{N}(y|\boldsymbol{w}^\mathsf{T}\boldsymbol{x}, 1/\beta)$, where $\beta = 1/\sigma^2$. The prior is $p(\boldsymbol{w}) = \mathcal{N}(\boldsymbol{w}|\boldsymbol{0}, \mathbf{A}^{-1})$, where $\mathbf{A} = \operatorname{diag}(\boldsymbol{\alpha})$. The marginal likelihood can be computed analytically (using Equation (2.129)) as follows:

$$p(\boldsymbol{y}|\mathbf{X}, \boldsymbol{\alpha}, \beta) = \int \mathcal{N}(\boldsymbol{y}|\mathbf{X}\boldsymbol{w}, (1/\beta)\mathbf{I}_N)\mathcal{N}(\boldsymbol{w}|\boldsymbol{0}, \mathbf{A}^{-1})d\boldsymbol{w} \tag{15.98}$$

$$= \mathcal{N}(\boldsymbol{y}|\boldsymbol{0}, \beta^{-1}\mathbf{I}_N + \mathbf{X}\mathbf{A}^{-1}\mathbf{X}^\mathsf{T}) \tag{15.99}$$

$$= \mathcal{N}(\boldsymbol{y}|\boldsymbol{0}, \mathbf{C}_{\boldsymbol{\alpha}}) \tag{15.100}$$

where $\mathbf{C}_{\boldsymbol{\alpha}} \triangleq \beta^{-1}\mathbf{I}_N + \mathbf{X}\mathbf{A}^{-1}\mathbf{X}^\mathsf{T}$. This is very similar to the marginal likelihood under the spike-and-slab prior (Section 15.2.5), which is given by

$$p(\boldsymbol{y}|\mathbf{X}, \boldsymbol{s}, \sigma_w^2, \sigma_y^2) = \int \mathcal{N}(\boldsymbol{y}|\mathbf{X}_{\boldsymbol{s}}\boldsymbol{w}_{\boldsymbol{s}}, \sigma_y^2\mathbf{I})\mathcal{N}(\boldsymbol{w}_{\boldsymbol{s}}|\boldsymbol{0}_{\boldsymbol{s}}, \sigma_w^2\mathbf{I})d\boldsymbol{w}_{\boldsymbol{s}} = \mathcal{N}(\boldsymbol{y}|\boldsymbol{0}, \mathbf{C}_{\boldsymbol{s}}) \tag{15.101}$$

where $\mathbf{C}_{\boldsymbol{s}} = \sigma_y^2\mathbf{I}_N + \sigma_w^2\mathbf{X}_{\boldsymbol{s}}\mathbf{X}_{\boldsymbol{s}}^\mathsf{T}$. (Here $\mathbf{X}_{\boldsymbol{s}}$ refers to the design matrix where we select only the columns of $\mathbf{X}$ where $s_d = 1$.) The difference is that we have replaced the binary $s_j \in \{0, 1\}$ variables with continuous $\alpha_j \in \mathbb{R}^+$, which makes the optimization problem easier.

The objective is the log marginal likelihood, given by

$$\ell(\boldsymbol{\alpha}, \beta) = -\frac{1}{2}\log p(\boldsymbol{y}|\mathbf{X}, \boldsymbol{\alpha}, \beta) = \log|\mathbf{C}_{\boldsymbol{\alpha}}| + \boldsymbol{y}^\mathsf{T}\mathbf{C}_{\boldsymbol{\alpha}}^{-1}\boldsymbol{y} \tag{15.102}$$

There are various algorithms for optimizing $\ell(\boldsymbol{\alpha}, \beta)$, some of which we discuss in Section 15.2.8.3.

ARD can be used as an alternative to ℓ_1 regularization. Although the ARD objective is not convex, it tends to give much sparser results [WW12]. In addition, it can be shown [WRN10] that the ARD objective has many fewer local optima than the ℓ_0-regularized objective, and hence is much easier to optimize.

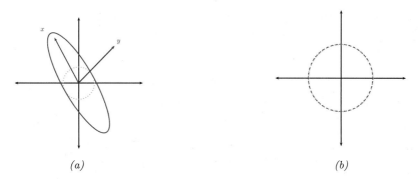

(a) (b)

Figure 15.4: Illustration of why ARD results in sparsity. The vector of inputs x does not point towards the vector of outputs y, so the feature should be removed. (a) For finite α, the probability density is spread in directions away from y. (b) When $\alpha = \infty$, the probability density at y is maximized. Adapted from Figure 8 of [Tip01].

15.2.8.2 Why does ARD result in a sparse solution?

Once we have estimated $\boldsymbol{\alpha}$ and β, we can compute the posterior over the parameters using Bayes' rule for Gaussians, to get $p(\boldsymbol{w}|\mathcal{D}, \hat{\boldsymbol{\alpha}}, \hat{\beta}) = \mathcal{N}(\boldsymbol{w}|\,\hat{\boldsymbol{w}}, \hat{\boldsymbol{\Sigma}})$, where $\hat{\boldsymbol{\Sigma}}^{-1} = \hat{\beta}\mathbf{X}^{\mathsf{T}}\mathbf{X} + \mathbf{A}$ and $\hat{\boldsymbol{w}} = \hat{\beta}\,\hat{\boldsymbol{\Sigma}}\,\mathbf{X}^{\mathsf{T}}\boldsymbol{y}$. If we have $\hat{\alpha}_d \approx \infty$, then $\hat{w}_d \approx 0$, so the solution vector will be sparse.

We now give an intuitive argument, based on [Tip01], about when such a sparse solution may be optimal. We shall assume $\beta = 1/\sigma^2$ is fixed for simplicity. Consider a 1d linear regression with 2 training examples, so $\mathbf{X} = \boldsymbol{x} = (x_1, x_2)$, and $\boldsymbol{y} = (y_1, y_2)$. We can plot $\boldsymbol{x}$ and $\boldsymbol{y}$ as vectors in the plane, as shown in Figure 15.4. Suppose the feature is irrelevant for predicting the response, so $\boldsymbol{x}$ points in a nearly orthogonal direction to $\boldsymbol{y}$. Let us see what happens to the marginal likelihood as we change α. The marginal likelihood is given by $p(\boldsymbol{y}|\boldsymbol{x}, \alpha, \beta) = \mathcal{N}(\boldsymbol{y}|\boldsymbol{0}, \mathbf{C}_\alpha)$, where $\mathbf{C}_\alpha = \frac{1}{\beta}\mathbf{I} + \frac{1}{\alpha}\boldsymbol{x}\boldsymbol{x}^{\mathsf{T}}$. If α is finite, the posterior will be elongated along the direction of $\boldsymbol{x}$, as in Figure 15.4(a). However, if $\alpha = \infty$, we have $\mathbf{C}_\alpha = \frac{1}{\beta}\mathbf{I}$, which is spherical, as in Figure 15.4(b). If $|\mathbf{C}_\alpha|$ is held constant, the latter assigns higher probability density to the observed response vector $\boldsymbol{y}$, so this is the preferred solution. In other words, the marginal likelihood "punishes" solutions where α_d is small but $\mathbf{X}_{:,d}$ is irrelevant, since these waste probability mass. It is more parsimonious (from the point of view of Bayesian Occam's razor) to eliminate redundant dimensions.

Another way to understand the sparsity properties of ARD is as approximate inference in a hierarchical Bayesian model [BT00]. In particular, suppose we put a conjugate prior on each precision, $\alpha_d \sim \text{Ga}(a, b)$, and on the observation precision, $\beta \sim \text{Ga}(c, d)$. Since exact inference with a Student prior is intractable, we can use variational Bayes (Section 10.3.3), with a factored posterior approximation of the form

$$q(\boldsymbol{w}, \boldsymbol{\alpha}) = q(\boldsymbol{w})q(\boldsymbol{\alpha}) \approx \mathcal{N}(\boldsymbol{w}|\boldsymbol{\mu}, \boldsymbol{\Sigma}) \prod_d \text{Ga}(\alpha_d|\,\hat{a}_d, \hat{b}_d) \tag{15.103}$$

ARD approximates $q(\boldsymbol{\alpha})$ by a point estimate. However, in VB, we integrate out $\boldsymbol{\alpha}$; the resulting posterior marginal $q(\boldsymbol{w})$ on the weights is given by

$$p(\boldsymbol{w}|\mathcal{D}) = \int \mathcal{N}(\boldsymbol{w}|\boldsymbol{0}, \text{diag}(\boldsymbol{\alpha})^{-1}) \prod_d \text{Ga}(\alpha_d | \widehat{a}_d, \widehat{b}) d\boldsymbol{\alpha} \tag{15.104}$$

This is a Gaussian scale mixture, and can be shown to be the same as a multivariate Student distribution (see Section 28.2.3.1), with non-diagonal covariance. Note that the Student has a large spike at 0, which intuitively explains why the posterior mean (which, for a Student distribution, is equal to the posterior mode) is sparse.

Finally, we can also view ARD as a MAP estimation problem with a **non-factorial prior** [WN07]. Intuitively, the dependence between the w_j parameters arises, despite the use of a diagonal Gaussian prior, because the prior precision α_j is estimated based after marginalizing out all $\boldsymbol{w}$, and hence depends on all the features. Interestingly, [WRN10] prove that MAP estimation with non-factorial priors is strictly better than MAP estimation with any possible factorial prior in the following sense: the non-factorial objective always has fewer local minima than factorial objectives, while still satisfying the property that the global optimum of the non-factorial objective corresponds to the global optimum of the ℓ_0 objective — a property that ℓ_1 regularization, which has no local minima, does not enjoy.

15.2.8.3 Algorithms for ARD

There are various algorithms for optimizing $\ell(\boldsymbol{\alpha}, \beta)$. One approach is to use EM, in which we compute $p(\boldsymbol{w}|\mathcal{D}, \boldsymbol{\alpha})$ in the E step and then maximize $\boldsymbol{\alpha}$ in the M step. In variational Bayes, we infer both $\boldsymbol{w}$ and $\boldsymbol{\alpha}$ (see [Dru08] for details). In [WN10], they present a method based on iteratively reweighted ℓ_1 estimation.

Recently, [HXW17] showed that the nested iterative computations performed these methods can emulated by a recurrent neural network (Section 16.3.4). Furthermore, by training this model, it is possible to achieve much faster convergence than manually designed optimization algorithms.

15.2.8.4 Relevance vector machines

Suppose we create a linear regression model of the form $p(y|\boldsymbol{x}; \boldsymbol{\theta}) = \mathcal{N}(y|\boldsymbol{w}^\mathsf{T}\boldsymbol{\phi}(\boldsymbol{x}), \sigma^2)$, where $\boldsymbol{\phi}(\boldsymbol{x}) = [\mathcal{K}(\boldsymbol{x}, \boldsymbol{x}_1), \dots, \mathcal{K}(\boldsymbol{x}, \boldsymbol{x}_N)]$, where $\mathcal{K}()$ is a kernel function (Section 18.2) and $\boldsymbol{x}_1, \dots, \boldsymbol{x}_N$ are the N training points. This is called **kernel basis function expansion**, and transforms the input from $\boldsymbol{x} \in \mathcal{X}$ to $\boldsymbol{\phi}(\boldsymbol{x}) \in \mathbb{R}^N$. Obviously this model has $O(N)$ parameters, and hence is nonparametric. However, we can use ARD to select a small subset of the exemplars. This technique is called the relevance vector machine (RVM) [Tip01; TF03].

15.2.9 Multivariate linear regression

This section is written by Xinglong Li.

In this section, we consider the **multivariate linear regression** model, which has the form

$$\mathbf{Y} = \mathbf{W}\mathbf{X} + \mathbf{E} \tag{15.105}$$

where $\mathbf{W} \in \mathbb{R}^{N_y \times N_x}$ is the matrix of regression coefficient, $\mathbf{X} \in \mathbb{R}^{N_x \times N}$ is the matrix of input features (with each row being an input variable and each *column* being an observation), $\mathbf{Y} \in \mathbb{R}^{N_y \times N}$ is the matrix of responses (with each row being an output variable and each *column* being an observation), and $\mathbf{E} = [\boldsymbol{e}_1, \cdots, \boldsymbol{e}_N]$ is the matrix of residual errors, where $\boldsymbol{e}_i \overset{iid}{\sim} \mathcal{N}(\mathbf{0}, \boldsymbol{\Sigma})$. It can be seen from the definition that given $\boldsymbol{\Sigma}$, $\mathbf{W}$ and $\mathbf{X}$, columns of $\mathbf{Y}$ are independently random variables following multivariate normal distributions. So the likelihood of the observation is

$$p(\mathbf{Y}|\mathbf{W}, \mathbf{X}, \boldsymbol{\Sigma}) = \frac{1}{(2\pi)^{N_y \times N}|\boldsymbol{\Sigma}|^{N/2}} \exp\left(\sum_{i=1}^{N} -\frac{1}{2}(\boldsymbol{y}_i - \mathbf{W}\boldsymbol{x}_i)^\mathsf{T}\boldsymbol{\Sigma}^{-1}(\boldsymbol{y}_i - \mathbf{W}\boldsymbol{x}_i) \right) \tag{15.106}$$

$$= \frac{1}{(2\pi)^{N_y \times N}|\boldsymbol{\Sigma}|^{N/2}} \exp\left(-\frac{1}{2}\mathrm{tr}\left((\mathbf{Y} - \mathbf{W}\mathbf{X})^\mathsf{T}\boldsymbol{\Sigma}^{-1}(\mathbf{Y} - \mathbf{W}\mathbf{X}) \right) \right) \tag{15.107}$$

$$= \mathcal{MN}(\mathbf{Y}|\mathbf{W}\mathbf{X}, \boldsymbol{\Sigma}, \mathbf{I}_{N \times N}), \tag{15.108}$$

The conjugate prior for this is the **matrix normal inverse Wishart** distribution,

$$\mathbf{W}, \boldsymbol{\Sigma} \sim \mathrm{MNIW}(\mathbf{M}_0, \mathbf{V}_0, \nu_0, \boldsymbol{\Psi}_0) \tag{15.109}$$

where the MNIW is defined by

$$\mathbf{W}|\boldsymbol{\Sigma} \sim \mathcal{MN}(\mathbf{M}_0, \boldsymbol{\Sigma}_0, \mathbf{V}_0) \tag{15.110}$$

$$\boldsymbol{\Sigma} \sim \mathrm{IW}(\nu_0, \boldsymbol{\Psi}_0), \tag{15.111}$$

where $\mathbf{V}_0 \in \mathbb{R}_{++}^{N_x \times N_x}$, $\boldsymbol{\Psi}_0 \in \mathbb{R}_{++}^{N_y \times N_y}$ and $\nu_0 > N_x - 1$ is the degree of freedom of the inverse Wishart distribution.

The posterior distribution of $\{\mathbf{W}, \boldsymbol{\Sigma}\}$ still follows a matrix normal inverse Wishart distribution. We follow the derivation in [Fox09, App.F]. Tthe density of the joint distribution is

$$p(\mathbf{Y}, \mathbf{W}, \boldsymbol{\Sigma}) \propto |\boldsymbol{\Sigma}|^{-(\nu_0 + N_y + 1 + N_x + N)/2} \times \exp\left\{ -\frac{1}{2}\mathrm{tr}(\boldsymbol{\Omega}_0) \right\} \tag{15.112}$$

$$\boldsymbol{\Omega}_0 \triangleq \boldsymbol{\Psi}_0 \boldsymbol{\Sigma}^{-1} + (\mathbf{Y} - \mathbf{W}\mathbf{X})^\mathsf{T}\boldsymbol{\Sigma}^{-1}(\mathbf{Y} - \mathbf{W}\mathbf{X}) + (\mathbf{W} - \mathbf{M}_0)^\mathsf{T}\boldsymbol{\Sigma}^{-1}(\mathbf{W} - \mathbf{M}_0)\mathbf{V}_0 \tag{15.113}$$

We first aggregate items including $\mathbf{W}$ in the exponent so that it takes the form of a matrix normal distribution. This is similar to the "completing the square" technique that we used in deriving the conjugate posterior for multivariate normal distributions in Section 3.4.4.3. Specifically,

$$\mathrm{tr}\left[(\mathbf{Y} - \mathbf{W}\mathbf{X})^\mathsf{T}\boldsymbol{\Sigma}^{-1}(\mathbf{Y} - \mathbf{W}\mathbf{X}) + (\mathbf{W} - \mathbf{M}_0)^\mathsf{T}\boldsymbol{\Sigma}^{-1}(\mathbf{W} - \mathbf{M}_0)\mathbf{V}_0 \right] \tag{15.114}$$

$$= \mathrm{tr}\left(\boldsymbol{\Sigma}^{-1}[(\mathbf{Y} - \mathbf{W}\mathbf{X})(\mathbf{Y} - \mathbf{W}\mathbf{X})^\mathsf{T} + (\mathbf{W} - \mathbf{M}_0)\mathbf{V}_0(\mathbf{W} - \mathbf{M}_0)^\mathsf{T}] \right) \tag{15.115}$$

$$= \mathrm{tr}\left(\boldsymbol{\Sigma}^{-1}[\mathbf{W}\mathbf{S}_{xx}\mathbf{W}^\mathsf{T} - 2\mathbf{S}_{yx}\mathbf{W}^\mathsf{T} + \mathbf{S}_{yy}] \right) \tag{15.116}$$

$$= \mathrm{tr}\left(\boldsymbol{\Sigma}^{-1}[(\mathbf{W} - \mathbf{S}_{yx}\mathbf{S}_{xx}^{-1})\mathbf{S}_{xx}(\mathbf{W} - \mathbf{S}_{yx}\mathbf{S}_{xx}^{-1})^\mathsf{T} + \mathbf{S}_{y|x}] \right). \tag{15.117}$$

where

$$\mathbf{S}_{xx} = \mathbf{X}\mathbf{X}^\mathsf{T} + \mathbf{V}_0, \qquad\qquad \mathbf{S}_{yx} = \mathbf{Y}\mathbf{X}^\mathsf{T} + \mathbf{M}_0\mathbf{V}_0, \tag{15.118}$$

$$\mathbf{S}_{yy} = \mathbf{Y}\mathbf{Y}^\mathsf{T} + \mathbf{M}_0\mathbf{V}_0\mathbf{M}_0^\mathsf{T}, \qquad\qquad \mathbf{S}_{y|x} = \mathbf{S}_{yy} - \mathbf{S}_{yx}\mathbf{S}_{xx}^{-1}\mathbf{S}_{yx}^\mathsf{T}. \tag{15.119}$$

Therefore, it can be see from Equation (15.117) that given $\boldsymbol{\Sigma}$, $\mathbf{W}$ follows a matrix normal distribution

$$\mathbf{W}|\boldsymbol{\Sigma}, \mathbf{X}, \mathbf{Y} \sim \mathcal{MN}(\mathbf{S}_{yx}\mathbf{S}_{xx}^{-1}, \boldsymbol{\Sigma}, \mathbf{S}_{xx}). \tag{15.120}$$

Marginalizing out $\mathbf{W}$ (which corresponds to removing the terms including $\mathbf{W}$ in the exponent in Equation (15.113)), it can be shown that the posterior distribution of $\boldsymbol{\Sigma}$ is an inverse Wishart distribution. In fact, by replacing Equation (15.117) to the corresponding terms in Equation (15.113), it can be seen that the only terms left after integrating out $\mathbf{W}$ are $\boldsymbol{\Sigma}^{-1}\boldsymbol{\Psi}$ and $\boldsymbol{\Sigma}^{-1}\mathbf{S}_{y|x}$, which indicates that the scale matrix of the posterior inverse Wishart distribution is $\boldsymbol{\Psi}_0 + \mathbf{S}_{y|x}$.

In conclusion, the joint posterior distribution of $\{\mathbf{W}, \boldsymbol{\Sigma}\}$ given the observation is

$$\mathbf{W}, \boldsymbol{\Sigma}|\mathbf{X}, \mathbf{Y} \sim \text{MNIW}(\mathbf{M}_1, \mathbf{V}_1, \nu_1, \boldsymbol{\Psi}_1) \tag{15.121}$$
$$\mathbf{M}_1 = \mathbf{S}_{yx}\mathbf{S}_{xx}^{-1} \tag{15.122}$$
$$\mathbf{V}_1 = \mathbf{S}_{xx} \tag{15.123}$$
$$\nu_1 = N + \nu_0 \tag{15.124}$$
$$\boldsymbol{\Psi}_1 = \boldsymbol{\Psi}_0 + \mathbf{S}_{y|x} \tag{15.125}$$

The MAP estimate of $\mathbf{W}$ and $\boldsymbol{\Sigma}$ are the mode of the posterior matrix normal inverse Wishart distribution. To derive this, notice that $\mathbf{W}$ only appears in the matrix normal density function in the posterior, so the matrix $\mathbf{W}$ maximizing the posterior density of $\{\mathbf{W}, \boldsymbol{\Sigma}\}$ is the matrix $\mathbf{W}$ that maximizes the matrix normal posterior of $\mathbf{W}$. So the MAP estimate of $\mathbf{W}$ is $\hat{\mathbf{W}} = \mathbf{M}_1 = \mathbf{S}_{yx}\mathbf{S}_{xx}^{-1}$, and this holds for any value of $\boldsymbol{\Sigma}$. By plugging $\mathbf{W} = \hat{\mathbf{W}}$ into the joint posterior of $\{\mathbf{W}, \boldsymbol{\Sigma}\}$, and taking derivatives over $\boldsymbol{\Sigma}$, it can be seen that the matrix maximizing the density is $(\nu_1 + N_y + N_x + 1)^{-1}\boldsymbol{\Psi}_1$. Since $\boldsymbol{\Psi}_1$ is positive definite, it is the MAP estimate of $\boldsymbol{\Sigma}$.

In conclusion, the MAP estimate of $\{\mathbf{W}, \boldsymbol{\Sigma}\}$ are

$$\hat{\mathbf{W}} = \mathbf{S}_{yx}\mathbf{S}_{xx}^{-1} \tag{15.126}$$
$$\hat{\boldsymbol{\Sigma}} = \frac{1}{\nu_1 + N_y + N_x + 1}(\boldsymbol{\Psi}_0 + \mathbf{S}_{y|x}) \tag{15.127}$$

15.3 Logistic regression

Logistic regression is a very widely used discriminative classification model that maps input vectors $\boldsymbol{x} \in \mathbb{R}^D$ to a distribution over class labels, $y \in \{1, \ldots, C\}$. If $C = 2$, this is known as **binary logistic regression**, and if $C > 2$, it is known as **multinomial logistic regression**, or alternatively, **multiclass logistic regression**.

15.3.1 Binary logistic regression

In the binary case, where $y \in \{0, 1\}$, the model has the following form

$$p(y|\boldsymbol{x}; \boldsymbol{\theta}) = \text{Ber}(y|\sigma(\boldsymbol{w}^\mathsf{T}\boldsymbol{x} + b)) \tag{15.128}$$

where $\boldsymbol{w}$ are the weights, b is the bias (offset), and σ is the **sigmoid** or **logistic** function, defined by

$$\sigma(a) \triangleq \frac{1}{1 + e^{-a}} \tag{15.129}$$

Let $\eta_n = \boldsymbol{w}^\mathsf{T} \boldsymbol{x}_n + b$ be the **logits** for example n, and $\mu_n = \sigma(\eta_n) = p(y = 1|\boldsymbol{x}_n)$ be the mean of the output. Then we can write the log likelihood as the negative cross entropy:

$$\log p(\mathcal{D}|\boldsymbol{\theta}) = \log \prod_{n=1}^{N} \mu_n^{y_n} (1 - \mu_n)^{1-y_n} = \sum_{n=1}^{N} y_n \log \mu_n + (1 - y_n) \log(1 - \mu_n) \tag{15.130}$$

We can expand this equation into a more explicit form (that is commonly seen in implementations) by performing some simple algebra. First note that

$$\mu_n = \frac{1}{1 + e^{-\eta_n}} = \frac{e^{\eta_n}}{1 + e^{\eta_n}}, \quad 1 - \mu_n = 1 - \frac{e^{\eta_n}}{1 + e^{\eta_n}} = \frac{1}{1 + e^{\eta_n}} \tag{15.131}$$

Hence

$$\log p(\mathcal{D}|\boldsymbol{\theta}) = \sum_{n=1}^{N} y_n [\log e^{\eta_n} - \log(1 + e^{\eta_n})] + (1 - y_n)[\log 1 - \log(1 + e^{\eta_n})] \tag{15.132}$$

$$= \sum_{n=1}^{N} y_n [\eta_n - \log(1 + e^{\eta_n})] + (1 - y_n)[-\log(1 + e^{\eta_n})] \tag{15.133}$$

$$= \sum_{n=1}^{N} y_n \eta_n - \sum_{n=1}^{N} \log(1 + e^{\eta_n}) \tag{15.134}$$

Note that the $\log(1 + e^a)$ function is often implemented using `np.log1p(np.exp(a))`.

15.3.2 Multinomial logistic regression

Multinomial logistic regression is a discriminative classification model of the following form:

$$p(y|\boldsymbol{x}; \boldsymbol{\theta}) = \mathrm{Cat}(y|\mathrm{softmax}(\mathbf{W}\boldsymbol{x} + \boldsymbol{b})) \tag{15.135}$$

where $\boldsymbol{x} \in \mathbb{R}^D$ is the input vector, $y \in \{1, \dots, C\}$ is the class label, $\mathbf{W}$ is a $C \times D$ weight matrix, $\boldsymbol{b}$ is C-dimensional bias vector, and softmax() is the **softmax function**, defined as

$$\mathrm{softmax}(\boldsymbol{a}) \triangleq \left[\frac{e^{a_1}}{\sum_{c'=1}^{C} e^{a_{c'}}}, \dots, \frac{e^{a_C}}{\sum_{c'=1}^{C} e^{a_{c'}}} \right] \tag{15.136}$$

If we define the logits as $\boldsymbol{\eta}_n = \mathbf{W}\boldsymbol{x}_n + \boldsymbol{b}$, the probabilities as $\boldsymbol{\mu}_n = \mathrm{softmax}(\boldsymbol{\eta}_n)$, and let $\boldsymbol{y}_n$ be the one-hot encoding of the label y_n, then the log likelihood can be written as the negative cross entropy:

$$\log p(\mathcal{D}|\boldsymbol{\theta}) = \log \prod_{n=1}^{N} \prod_{c=1}^{C} \mu_{nc}^{y_{nc}} = \sum_{n=1}^{N} \sum_{c=1}^{C} y_{nc} \log \mu_{nc} \tag{15.137}$$

15.3.3   Dealing with class imbalance and the long tail

In many problems, some classes are much rarer than others; this problem is called **class imbalance**. In such a setting, standard maximum likelihood training may not work well, since it designed to minimize (a bound on) the 0-1 loss, which can be dominated by the most frequent classes. A natural alternative is to consider the **balanced error rate**, which computes the average of the per-class error rates of classifier f:

$$\mathrm{BER}(f) = \frac{1}{C} \sum_{y=1}^{C} p^*_{\boldsymbol{x}|y} \left(y \notin \operatorname*{argmax}_{y' \in \mathcal{Y}} f_{y'}(\boldsymbol{x}) \right) \tag{15.138}$$

where p^* is the true distribution. The classifier that optimizes this loss, f^*, must satisfy

$$\operatorname*{argmax}_{y \in \mathcal{Y}} f^*_y(\boldsymbol{x}) = \operatorname*{argmax}_{y \in \mathcal{Y}} p^*_{\mathrm{bal}}(y|\boldsymbol{x}) = \operatorname*{argmax}_{y \in \mathcal{Y}} p^*(\boldsymbol{x}|y) \tag{15.139}$$

where $p^*_{\mathrm{bal}}(y|\boldsymbol{x}) \propto \frac{1}{C} p^*(\boldsymbol{x}|y)$ is the predictor when using balanced classes. Thus to minimize the BER, we should using the class-conditional likelihood, $p(\boldsymbol{x}|y)$, rather than the class posterior, $p(y|\boldsymbol{x})$.

In [Men+21], they propose a simple scheme called **logit adjustment** that can achieve this optimal classifier. We assume the model computes logits using $f_y(\boldsymbol{x}) = \boldsymbol{w}_y^\top \boldsymbol{\phi}(\boldsymbol{x})$, where $\boldsymbol{\phi}(\boldsymbol{x}) = \boldsymbol{x}$ for a GLM. In the post-hoc version, the model is trained in the usual way, and then at prediction time, we use

$$\operatorname*{argmax}_{y \in \mathcal{Y}} p(\boldsymbol{x}|y) = \operatorname*{argmax}_{y \in \mathcal{Y}} \frac{p(y|\boldsymbol{x})p(\boldsymbol{x})}{p(y)} = \operatorname*{argmax}_{y \in \mathcal{Y}} \frac{\exp(\boldsymbol{w}_y^\top \boldsymbol{\phi}(\boldsymbol{x}))}{\pi_y} \tag{15.140}$$

where $\pi_y = p(y)$ is the empirical label prior. In practice, it is helpful to inroduce a tuning parameter $\tau > 0$ and to use the predictor

$$\hat{f}(\boldsymbol{x}) = \operatorname*{argmax}_{y \in \mathcal{Y}} f_y(\boldsymbol{x}) - \tau \log \pi_y \tag{15.141}$$

Alternatively, we can change the loss function used during training, by using the following **logit adjusted softmax cross-entropy loss**:

$$\ell(y, f(\boldsymbol{x})) = -\log \frac{e^{f_y(\boldsymbol{x}) + \tau \log \pi_y}}{\sum_{y'=1}^{C} e^{f_{y'}(\boldsymbol{x}) + \tau \log \pi_{y'}}} \tag{15.142}$$

This is like training with a predictor of the form $g_y(\boldsymbol{x}) = f_y(\boldsymbol{x}) + \tau \log \pi_y$, and then at test time using $\operatorname{argmax}_y f_y(\boldsymbol{x}) = \operatorname{argmax}_y g_y(\boldsymbol{x}) - \tau \log \pi_y$, as above.

We can also combine the above loss with a prior on the parameters and perform Bayesian inference, as we discuss below. (The use a non-standard likelihood can be justifed using the generalized Bayesian inference framework, as discussed in Section 14.1.3.)

15.3.4   Parameter priors

As with linear regression, it is standard to use Gaussian priors for the weights in a logistic regression model. It is natural to set the prior mean to 0, to reflect the fact that the output could either

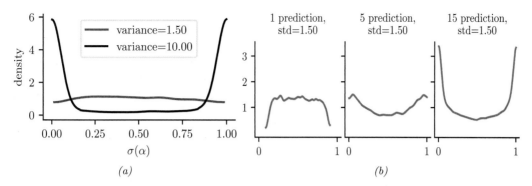

Figure 15.5: (a) Prior on logistic regression output when using $\mathcal{N}(0, \omega)$ prior for the offset term, for $\omega = 10$ or $\omega = 1.5$. Adapted from Figure 11.3 of [McE20]. Generated by logreg_prior_offset.ipynb. (b) Distribution over the fraction of 1s we expect to see when using binary logistic regression applied to random binary feature vectors of increasing dimensionality. We use a $\mathcal{N}(0, 1.5)$ prior on the regression coefficients. Adapted from Figure 3 of [Gel+20]. Generated by logreg_prior.ipynb.

increase or decrease in probability depending on the input. But how do we set the prior variance? It is tempting to use a large value, to approximate a uniform distribution, but this is a bad idea. To see why, consider a binary logistic regression model with just an offset term and no features:

$$p(y|\boldsymbol{\theta}) = \text{Ber}(y|\sigma(\alpha)) \qquad (15.143)$$
$$p(\alpha) = \mathcal{N}(\alpha|0, \omega) \qquad (15.144)$$

If we set the prior to the large value of $\omega = 10$, the implied prior for y is an extreme distribution, with most of its density near 0 or 1, as shown in Figure 15.5a. By contrast, if we use the smaller value of $\omega = 1.5$, we get a flatter distribution, as shown.

If we have input features, the problem gets a little trickier, since the magnitude of the logits will now depend on the number and distribution of the input variables. For example, suppose we generate N random binary vectors $\boldsymbol{x}_n$, each of dimension D, where $x_{nd} \sim \text{Ber}(p)$, where $p = 0.8$. We then compute $p(y_n = 1|\boldsymbol{x}_n) = \sigma(\boldsymbol{\beta}^\mathsf{T} \boldsymbol{x}_n)$, where $\boldsymbol{\beta} \sim \mathcal{N}(\mathbf{0}, 1.5\mathbf{I})$. We sample S values of $\boldsymbol{\beta}$, and for each one, we sample a vector of labels, $\boldsymbol{y}_{1:N,s}$ from the above distribution. We then compute the fraction of positive labels, $f_s = \frac{1}{N} \sum_{n=1}^N \mathbb{I}(y_{n,s} = 1)$. We plot the distribution of $\{f_s\}$ as a function of D in Figure 15.5b. We see that the induced prior is initially flat, but eventually becomes skewed towards the extreme values of 0 and 1. To avoid this, we should standardize the inputs, and scale the variance of the prior by $1/\sqrt{D}$. We can also use a heavier tailed distribution, such as a Cauchy or Student [Gel+08; GLM15], instead of the Gaussian prior.

15.3.5 Laplace approximation to the posterior

Unfortunately, we cannot compute the posterior analytically, unlike with linear regression, since there is no corresponding conjugate prior. (This mirrors the case with MLE, where we have a closed form solution for linear regression, but not for logistic regression.) Fortunately, there are a range of approximate inference methods we can use.

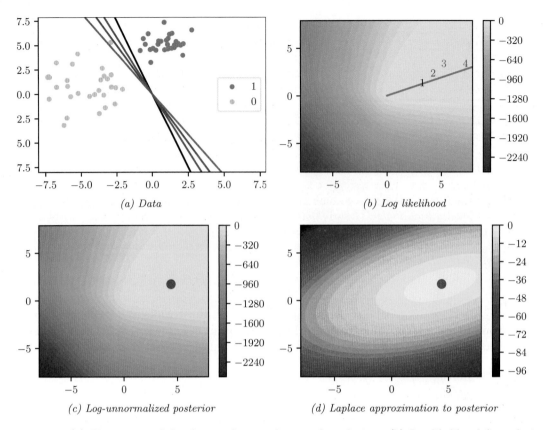

Figure 15.6: (a) Illustration of the data and some decision boundaries. (b) Log-likelihood for a logistic regression model. The line is drawn from the origin in the direction of the MLE (which is at infinity). The numbers correspond to 4 points in parameter space, corresponding to the colored lines in (a). (c) Unnormalized log posterior (assuming vague spherical prior). (d) Laplace approximation to posterior. Adapted from a figure by Mark Girolami. Generated by logreg_laplace_demo.ipynb.

In this section, we use the Laplace approximation. As we explain in Section 7.4.3, this approximates the posterior using a Gaussian. The mean of the Gaussian is equal to the MAP estimate $\hat{\boldsymbol{w}}$, and the covariance is equal to the inverse Hessian $\mathbf{H}$ computed at the MAP estimate, i.e.,

$$p(\boldsymbol{w}|\mathcal{D}) \approx \mathcal{N}(\boldsymbol{w}|\hat{\boldsymbol{w}}, \mathbf{H}^{-1}), \hat{\boldsymbol{w}} = \arg\min - \log p(\boldsymbol{w}, \mathcal{D}), \mathbf{H} = -\nabla_{\boldsymbol{w}}^2 \log p(\boldsymbol{w}, \mathcal{D})|_{\hat{\boldsymbol{w}}} \tag{15.145}$$

We can find the mode using a standard optimization method, and we can then compute the Hessian at the mode analytically or using automatic differentiation.

As an example, consider the binary data illustrated in Figure 15.6(a). There are many parameter settings that correspond to lines that perfectly separate the training data; we show 4 example lines. For each decision boundary in Figure 15.6(a), we plot the corresponding parameter vector as point in the log likelihood surface in Figure 15.6(b). These parameters values are $\boldsymbol{w}_1 = (3, 1)$, $\boldsymbol{w}_2 = (4, 2)$, $\boldsymbol{w}_3 = (5, 3)$, and $\boldsymbol{w}_4 = (7, 3)$. These points all approximately satisfy $\boldsymbol{w}_i(1)/\boldsymbol{w}_i(2) \approx \hat{\boldsymbol{w}}_{\text{mle}}(1)/\hat{\boldsymbol{w}}_{\text{mle}}(2)$, and hence are close to the orientation of the maximum likelihood decision boundary. The points are ordered by increasing weight norm (3.16, 4.47, 5.83, and 7.62). The unconstrained MLE has $||\boldsymbol{w}|| = \infty$, so is infinitely far to the top right.

To ensure a unique solution, we use a (spherical) Gaussian prior centered at the origin, $\mathcal{N}(\boldsymbol{w}|\boldsymbol{0}, \sigma^2 \mathbf{I})$. The value of σ^2 controls the strength of the prior. If we set $\sigma^2 = \infty$, we force the MAP estimate to be $\boldsymbol{w} = \boldsymbol{0}$; this will result in maximally uncertain predictions, since all points $\boldsymbol{x}$ will produce a predictive distribution of the form $p(y = 1|\boldsymbol{x}) = 0.5$. If we set $\sigma^2 = 0$, the MAP estimate becomes the MLE, resulting in minimally uncertain predictions. (In particular, all positively labeled points will have $p(y = 1|\boldsymbol{x}) = 1.0$, and all negatively labeled points will have $p(y = 1|\boldsymbol{x}) = 0.0$, since the data is separable.) As a compromise (to make a nice illustration), we pick the value $\sigma^2 = 100$.

Multiplying this prior by the likelihood results in the unnormalized posterior shown in Figure 15.6(c). The MAP estimate is shown by the blue dot. The Laplace approximation to this posterior is shown in Figure 15.6(d). We see that it gets the mode correct (by construction), but the shape of the posterior is somewhat distorted. (The southwest-northeast orientation captures uncertainty about the magnitude of $\boldsymbol{w}$, and the southeast-northwest orientation captures uncertainty about the orientation of the decision boundary.)

15.3.6   Approximating the posterior predictive distribution

Next we need to convert the posterior over the parameters into a posterior over predictions, as follows:

$$p(y|\boldsymbol{x}, \mathcal{D}) = \int p(y|\boldsymbol{x}, \boldsymbol{w}) p(\boldsymbol{w}|\mathcal{D}) d\boldsymbol{w} \tag{15.146}$$

The simplest way to evaluate this integral is to use a Monte Carlo approximation. For example, in the case of binary logistic regression, we have

$$p(y = 1|\boldsymbol{x}, \mathcal{D}) \approx \frac{1}{S} \sum_{s=1}^{S} \sigma(\boldsymbol{w}_s^\mathsf{T} \boldsymbol{x}) \tag{15.147}$$

where $\boldsymbol{w}_s \sim p(\boldsymbol{w}|\mathcal{D})$ are posterior samples.

However, we can also use deterministic approximations to the integral, which are often faster. Let $\boldsymbol{f}_* = f(\boldsymbol{x}_*, \boldsymbol{w})$ be the predicted logits, before the sigmoid/softmax layer, given test point $\boldsymbol{x}_*$. If the posterior over the parameters is Gaussian, $p(\boldsymbol{w}|\mathcal{D}) = \mathcal{N}(\boldsymbol{\mu}, \boldsymbol{\Sigma})$, then the predictive distribution over logits is also Gaussian:

$$p(\boldsymbol{f}_*|\boldsymbol{x}_*, \mathcal{D}) = \int \delta(\boldsymbol{f}_* - f(\boldsymbol{x}_*, \boldsymbol{w})) \mathcal{N}(\boldsymbol{w}|\mathcal{D}) d\boldsymbol{w} = \mathcal{N}(\boldsymbol{f}_*|\boldsymbol{\mu}^\mathsf{T} \boldsymbol{x}_*, \boldsymbol{x}_*^\mathsf{T} \boldsymbol{\Sigma} \boldsymbol{x}_*) \triangleq \mathcal{N}(\boldsymbol{f}_*|\mu_*, \Sigma_*) \tag{15.148}$$

In the case of binary logistic regression, we can approximate the sigmoid with the probit function Φ (see Section 15.4), which allows us to solve the integral analytically:

$$p(y_*|\boldsymbol{x}_*) \approx \int \Phi(f_*) \mathcal{N}(f_*|\mu_*, \sigma_*^2) df_* = \sigma\left(\frac{\mu_*}{\sqrt{1 + \frac{\pi}{8}\sigma_*^2}}\right) \tag{15.149}$$

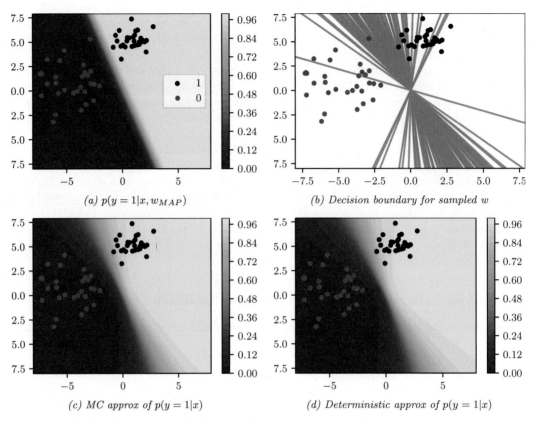

(a) $p(y = 1|x, w_{MAP})$ (b) Decision boundary for sampled w

(c) MC approx of $p(y = 1|x)$ (d) Deterministic approx of $p(y = 1|x)$

Figure 15.7: Posterior predictive distribution for a logistic regression model in 2d. (a) Contours of $p(y = 1|\boldsymbol{x}, \hat{\boldsymbol{w}}_{map})$. (b) Samples from the posterior predictive distribution. (c) Averaging over these samples. (d) Moderated output (probit approximation). Generated by logreg_laplace_demo.ipynb.

This is called the **probit approximation** [SL90]. In [Gib97], a generalization to the multiclass case was provided. This is known as the **generalized probit approximation**, and has the form

$$p(\boldsymbol{y}_*|\boldsymbol{x}_*) \approx \int \mathrm{softmax}(\boldsymbol{f}_*)\mathcal{N}(\boldsymbol{f}_*|\boldsymbol{\mu}_*, \boldsymbol{\Sigma}_*)d\boldsymbol{f}_* = \mathrm{softmax}\left(\{\frac{\mu_{*,c}}{\sqrt{1 + \frac{\pi}{8}\Sigma_{*,cc}}}\}\right) \tag{15.150}$$

This ignores the correlations between the logits, because it only depends on the diagonal elements of $\boldsymbol{\Sigma}_*$. Nevertheless it can work well, even in the case of neural net classifiers [LIS20]. Another deterministic approximation, known as the **Laplace bridge**, is discussed in Section 17.3.10.2.

We now illustrate the posterior predictive for our binary example. Figure 15.7(a) shows the plugin approximation using the MAP estimate. We see that there is no uncertainty about the location of the decision boundary, even though we are generating probabilistic predictions over the labels. Figure 15.7(b) shows what happens when we plug in samples from the Gaussian posterior. Now we see that there is considerable uncertainty about the orientation of the "best" decision boundary. Figure 15.7(c) shows the average of these samples. By averaging over multiple predictions, we see

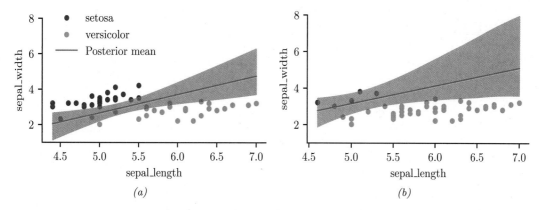

Figure 15.8: *Illustration of the posterior over the decision boundary for classifying iris flowers (setosa vs versicolor) using 2 input features. (a) 25 examples per class. Adapted from Figure 4.5 of [Mar18]. (b) 5 examples of class 0, 45 examples of class 1. Adapted from Figure 4.8 of [Mar18]. Generated by logreg_iris_bayes_2d.ipynb.*

that the uncertainty in the decision boundary "splays out" as we move further from the training data. Figure 15.7(d) shows that the probit approximation gives very similar results to the Monte Carlo approximation.

15.3.7 MCMC inference

Markov chain Monte Carlo, or MCMC, is often considered the "gold standard" for approximate inference, since it makes no explicit assumptions about the form of the posterior. It is explained in depth in Chapter 12, but the output is a set of (correlated) samples from the posterior, which gives the following non-parametric approximation:

$$q(\boldsymbol{\theta}|\mathcal{D}) \approx \frac{1}{S} \sum_{s=1}^{S} \delta(\boldsymbol{\theta} - \boldsymbol{\theta}^s) \tag{15.151}$$

where $\boldsymbol{\theta}^s \sim p(\boldsymbol{\theta}|\mathcal{D})$. Once we have the samples, we can plug them into Equation (15.147) to approximate the posterior predictive distribution.

A common MCMC method is known as Hamiltonian Monte Carlo (Section 12.5); this can leverage our ability to compute the gradient of the log joint, $\nabla_{\boldsymbol{\theta}} \log p(\mathcal{D}, \boldsymbol{\theta})$, for improved efficiency. Let us apply HMC to a 2-dimensional, 2-class version of the iris classification problem, where we just use two input features, sepal length and sepal width, and two classes, Virginica and non-Virginica. The decision boundary is the set of points (x_1^*, x_2^*) such that $\sigma(b + w_1 x_1^* + w_2 x_2^*) = 0.5$. Such points must lie on the following line:

$$x_2^* = -\frac{b}{w_2} + \left(-\frac{w_1}{w_2} x_1^*\right) \tag{15.152}$$

We can therefore compute an MC approximation to the posterior over decision boundaries by sampling the parameters from the posterior, $(w_1, w_2, b) \sim p(\boldsymbol{\theta}|\mathcal{D})$, and plugging them into the above equation,

Dept. D_i	Gender G_i	# Admitted A_i	# Rejected R_i	# Applications N_i
A	male	512	313	825
A	female	89	19	108
B	male	353	207	560
B	female	17	8	25
C	male	120	205	325
C	female	202	391	593
D	male	138	279	417
D	female	131	244	375
E	male	53	138	191
E	female	94	299	393
F	male	22	351	373
F	female	24	317	341

Table 15.1: Admissions data for UC Berkeley from [BHO75].

to get $p(x_1^*, x_2 * |\mathcal{D})$. The results of this method (using a vague Gaussian prior for the parameters) are shown in Figure 15.8a. The solid line is the posterior mean, and the shaded interval is a 95% credible interval. As before, we see that the uncertainty about the location of the boundary is higher as we move away from the training data.

In Figure 15.8b, we show what happens to the decision boundary when we have unbalanced classes. We notice two things. First, the posterior uncertainty increases, because we have less data from the blue class. Second, we see that the posterior mean of the decision boundary shifts towards the class with less data. This follows from linear discriminant analysis, where one can show that changing the class prior changes the location of the decision boundary, so that more of the input space gets mapped to the class which is higher a priori. (See [Mur22, Sec 9.2] for details.)

15.3.8   Other approximate inference methods

There are many other approximate inference methods we can use, as we discuss in Part II. A common approach is variational inference (Section 10.1), which converts approximate inference into an optimization problem. It does this by choosing an approximate distribution $q(\boldsymbol{w}; \boldsymbol{\psi})$ and optimizing the variational parameters $\boldsymbol{\psi}$ to maximize the evidence lower bound (ELBO). This has the effect of making $q(\boldsymbol{w}; \boldsymbol{\psi}) \approx p(\boldsymbol{w}|\mathcal{D})$ in the sense that the KL divergence is small. There are several ways to tackle this: use a stochastic estimate of the ELBO (see Section 10.2.1), use the conditionally conjugate VI method of Supplementary Section 10.3.1.2, or use a "local" VI method that creates a quadratic lower bound to the logistic function (see Supplementary Section 15.1).

In the online setting, we can use assumed density filtering (ADF) to recursively compute a Gaussian approximate posterior $p(\boldsymbol{w}|\mathcal{D}_{1:t})$, as we discuss in Section 8.6.3.

15.3.9 Case study: is Berkeley admissions biased against women?

In this section, we consider a simple but interesting example of logistic regression from [McE20, Sec 11.1.4]. The question of interest is whether admission to graduate school at UC Berkeley is biased against women. The dataset comes from a famous paper [BHO75], which collected statistics for 6 departments for men and women. The data table only has 12 rows, shown in Table 15.1, although the total sample size (number of observations) is 4526. We conduct a regression analysis to try to determine if gender "causes" imbalanced admissions rates.

An obvious way to attempt to answer the question of interest is to fit a binomial logistic regression model, in which the outcome is the admissions rate, and the input is a binary variable representing the gender of each sample (make or female). One way to write this model is as follows:

$$A_i \sim \text{Bin}(N_i, \mu_i) \tag{15.153}$$
$$\text{logit}(\mu_i) = \alpha + \beta\text{MALE}[i] \tag{15.154}$$
$$\alpha \sim \mathcal{N}(0, 10) \tag{15.155}$$
$$\beta \sim \mathcal{N}(0, 1.5) \tag{15.156}$$

Here A_i is the number of admissions for sample i, N_i is the nunber of applications, and MALE$[i] = 1$ iff the sample is male. So the log odds is α for female cases, and $\alpha + \beta$ for male candidates. (The choice of prior for these parameters is discussed in Section 15.3.4.)

The above formulation is asymmetric in the genders. In particular, the log odds for males has two random variables associated with it, and hence is a priori is more uncertain. It is often better to rewrite the model in the following symmetric way:

$$A_i \sim \text{Bin}(N_i, \mu_i) \tag{15.157}$$
$$\text{logit}(\mu_i) = \alpha_{\text{GENDER}[i]} \tag{15.158}$$
$$\alpha_j \sim \mathcal{N}(0, 1.5), \ j \in \{1, 2\} \tag{15.159}$$

Here GENDER$[i]$ is the gender (1 for male, 2 for female), so the log odds is α_1 for males and α_2 for females.

We can perform posterior inference using a variety of methods (see Chapter 7). Here we use HMC (Section 12.5). We find the 89% credible interval for α_1 is $[-0.29, 0.16]$ and for α_2 is $[-0.91, 0.75]$.[2] The corresponding distribution for the difference in probability, $\sigma(\alpha_1) - \sigma(\alpha_2)$, is $[0.12, 0.16]$, with a mean of 0.14. So it seems that Berkeley is biased in favor of men.

However, before jumping to conclusions, we should check if the model is any good. In Figure 15.9a, we plot the posterior predictive distribution, along with the original data. We see the model is a very bad fit to the data (the blue data dots are often outside the black predictive intervals). In particular, we see that the empirical admissions rate for women is actually higher in all the departments except for C and E, yet the model says that women should have a 14% lower chance of admission.

The trouble is that men and women did not apply to the same departments in equal amounts. Women tended not to apply to departments, like A and B, with high admissions rates, but instead applied more to departments, like F, with low admissions rates. So even though less women were accepted *overall*, within in each department, women tended to be accepted at about the same rate.

---

2. McElreath uses 89% interval instead of 95% to emphasize the arbitrary nature of these values. The difference is insignificant.

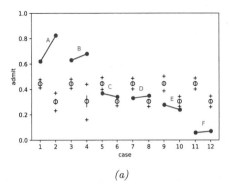
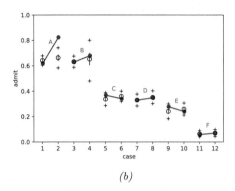

(a) *(b)*

Figure 15.9: Blue dots are admission rates for each of the 6 departments (A-F) for males (left half of each dyad) and females (right half). The circle is the posterior mean of μ_i, the small vertical black lines indicate 1 standard deviation of μ_i. The + marks indicate 95% predictive interval for A_i. (a) Basic model, only taking gender into account. (b) Augmented model, adding department specific offsets. Adapted from Figure 11.5 of [McE20]. Generated by logreg_ucb_admissions_numpyro.ipynb.

We can get a better understanding if we consider the DAG in Figure 15.10a. This is intended to be a causal model of the relevant factors. We discuss causality in more detail in Chapter 36, but the basic idea should be clear from this picture. In particular, we see that there is an indirect causal path $G \to D \to A$ from gender to acceptance, so to infer the direct affect $G \to A$, we need to condition on D and close the indirect path. We can do this by adding department id as another feature:

$$A_i \sim \text{Bin}(N_i, \mu_i) \tag{15.160}$$
$$\text{logit}(\mu_i) = \alpha_{\text{GENDER}[i]} + \gamma_{\text{DEPT}[i]} \tag{15.161}$$
$$\alpha_j \sim \mathcal{N}(0, 1.5), j \in \{1, 2\} \tag{15.162}$$
$$\gamma_k \sim \mathcal{N}(0, 1.5), k \in \{1, \dots, 6\} \tag{15.163}$$

Here $j \in \{1, 2\}$ (for gender) and $k \in \{1, \dots, 6\}$ (for department). Note that there 12 parameters in this model, but each combination (slice of the data) has a fairly large sample size of data associated with it, as we see in Table 15.1.

In Figure 15.9b, we plot the posterior predictive distribution for this new model; we see the fit is now much better. We find the 89% credible interval for α_1 is $[-1.38, 0.35]$ and for α_2 is $[-1.31, 0.42]$. The corresponding distribution for the difference in probability, $\sigma(\alpha_1) - \sigma(\alpha_2)$, is $[-0.05, 0.01]$. So it seems that there is no bias after all.

However, the above conclusion is based on the correctness of the model in Figure 15.10a. What if there are **unobserved confounders** U, such as academic ability, influencing both admission rate and department choice? This hypothesis is shown in Figure 15.10b. In this case, conditioning on the collider D opens up a non-causal path between gender and admissions, $G \to D \leftarrow U \to A$. This invalidates any causal conclusions we may want to draw.

The point of this example is to serve as a cautionary tale to those trying to draw causal conclusions from predictive models. See Chapter 36 for more details.

Figure 15.10: *Some possible causal models of admissions rates. G is gender, D is department, A is acceptance rate. (a) No hidden confounders. (b) Hidden confounder (small dot) affects both D and A. Generated by logreg_ucb_admissions_numpyro.ipynb.*

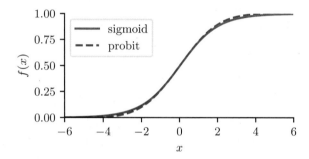

Figure 15.11: *The logistic (sigmoid) function $\sigma(x)$ in solid red, with the Gaussian cdf function $\Phi(\lambda x)$ in dotted blue superimposed. Here $\lambda = \sqrt{\pi/8}$, which was chosen so that the derivatives of the two curves match at $x = 0$. Adapted from Figure 4.9 of [Bis06]. Generated by probit_plot.ipynb.*

15.4   Probit regression

In this section, we discuss **probit regression**, which is similiar to binary logistic regression except it uses $\mu_n = \Phi(a_n)$ instead of $\mu_n = \sigma(a_n)$ as the mean function, where Φ is the cdf of the standard normal, and $a_n = \boldsymbol{w}^\mathsf{T}\boldsymbol{x}_n$. The corresponding link function is therefore $a_n = \ell(\mu_n) = \Phi^{-1}(\mu_n)$; the inverse of the Gaussian cdf is known as the **probit function**.

The Gaussian cdf Φ is very similar to the logistic function, as shown in Figure 15.11. Thus probit regression and "regular" logistic regression behave very similarly. However, probit regression has some advantages. In particular, it has a simple interpretation as a latent variable model (see Section 15.4.1), which arises from the field of **choice theory** as studied in economics (see e.g., [Koo03]). This also simplifies the task of Bayesian parameter inference.

15.4.1   Latent variable interpretation

We can interpret $a_n = \boldsymbol{w}^\mathsf{T}\boldsymbol{x}_n$ as a factor that is proportional to how likely a person is respond positively (generate $y_n = 1$) given input $\boldsymbol{x}_n$. However, typically there are other unobserved factors that influence someone's response. Let us model these hidden factors by Gaussian noise, $\epsilon_n \sim \mathcal{N}(0, 1)$. Let the combined preference for positive outcomes be represented by the latent variable $z_n = \boldsymbol{w}^\mathsf{T} \boldsymbol{x}_n + \epsilon_n$. We assume that the person will pick the positive label iff this latent factor is positive rather than negative, i.e.,

$$y_n = \mathbb{I}(z_n \geq 0) \tag{15.164}$$

When we marginalize out z_n, we recover the probit model:

$$p(y_n = 1 | \boldsymbol{x}_n, \boldsymbol{w}) = \int \mathbb{I}(z_n \geq 0) \mathcal{N}(z_n | \boldsymbol{w}^\mathsf{T} \boldsymbol{x}_n, 1) dz_n \tag{15.165}$$

$$= p(\boldsymbol{w}^\mathsf{T} \boldsymbol{x}_n + \epsilon_n \geq 0) = p(\epsilon_n \geq -\boldsymbol{w}^\mathsf{T} \boldsymbol{x}_n) \tag{15.166}$$

$$= 1 - \Phi(-\boldsymbol{w}^\mathsf{T} \boldsymbol{x}_n) = \Phi(\boldsymbol{w}^\mathsf{T} \boldsymbol{x}_n) \tag{15.167}$$

Thus we can think of probit regression as a threshold function applied to noisy input.

We can interpret logistic regression in the same way. However, in that case the noise term ϵ_n comes from a **logistic distribution**, defined as follows:

$$f(y | \mu, s) \triangleq \frac{e^{-\frac{y - \mu}{s}}}{s(1 + e^{-\frac{y - \mu}{s}})^2} = \frac{1}{4s} \operatorname{sech}^2(\frac{y - \mu}{s^2}) \tag{15.168}$$

where the mean is μ and the variance is $\frac{s^2 \pi^2}{3}$. The cdf of this distribution is given by

$$F(y | \mu, s) = \frac{1}{1 + e^{-\frac{y - \mu}{s}}} \tag{15.169}$$

It is clear that if we use logistic noise with $\mu = 0$ and $s = 1$ we recover logistic regression. However, it is computationally easier to deal with Gaussian noise, as we show below.

15.4.2   Maximum likelihood estimation

In this section, we discuss some methods for fitting probit regression using MLE.

15.4.2.1   MLE using SGD

We can find the MLE for probit regression using standard gradient methods. Let $\mu_n = \boldsymbol{w}^\mathsf{T} \boldsymbol{x}_n$, and let $\tilde{y}_n \in \{-1, +1\}$. Then the gradient of the log-likelihood for a single example n is given by

$$\boldsymbol{g}_n \triangleq \frac{d}{d\boldsymbol{w}} \log p(\tilde{y}_n | \boldsymbol{w}^\mathsf{T} \boldsymbol{x}_n) = \frac{d\mu_n}{d\boldsymbol{w}} \frac{d}{d\mu_n} \log p(\tilde{y}_n | \boldsymbol{w}^\mathsf{T} \boldsymbol{x}_n) = \boldsymbol{x}_n \frac{\tilde{y}_n \phi(\mu_n)}{\Phi(\tilde{y}_n \mu_n)} \tag{15.170}$$

where ϕ is the standard normal pdf, and Φ is its cdf. Similarly, the Hessian for a single case is given by

$$\mathbf{H}_n = \frac{d}{d\boldsymbol{w}^2} \log p(\tilde{y}_n | \boldsymbol{w}^\mathsf{T} \boldsymbol{x}_n) = -\boldsymbol{x}_n \left(\frac{\phi(\mu_n)^2}{\Phi(\tilde{y}_n \mu_n)^2} + \frac{\tilde{y}_n \mu_n \phi(\mu_n)}{\Phi(\tilde{y}_n \mu_n)} \right) \boldsymbol{x}_n^\mathsf{T} \tag{15.171}$$

This can be passed to any gradient-based optimizer.

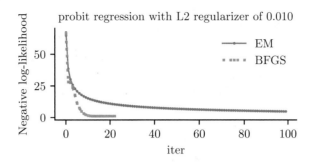

Figure 15.12: *Fitting a probit regression model in 2d using a quasi-Newton method or EM. Generated by* probit_reg_demo.ipynb.

15.4.2.2   MLE using EM

We can use the latent variable interpretation of probit regression to derive an elegant EM algorithm for fitting the model. The complete data log likelihood has the following form, assuming a $\mathcal{N}(\mathbf{0}, \mathbf{V}_0)$ prior on $\boldsymbol{w}$:

$$\ell(\boldsymbol{z}, \boldsymbol{w}|\mathbf{V}_0) = \log p(\boldsymbol{y}|\boldsymbol{z}) + \log \mathcal{N}(\boldsymbol{z}|\mathbf{X}\boldsymbol{w}, \mathbf{I}) + \log \mathcal{N}(\boldsymbol{w}|\mathbf{0}, \mathbf{V}_0) \tag{15.172}$$

$$= \sum_n \log p(y_n|z_n) - \frac{1}{2}(\boldsymbol{z} - \mathbf{X}\boldsymbol{w})^\mathsf{T}(\boldsymbol{z} - \mathbf{X}\boldsymbol{w}) - \frac{1}{2}\boldsymbol{w}^\mathsf{T}\mathbf{V}_0^{-1}\boldsymbol{w} \tag{15.173}$$

The posterior in the E step is a **truncated Gaussian**:

$$p(z_n|y_n, \boldsymbol{x}_n, \boldsymbol{w}) = \begin{cases} \mathcal{N}(z_n|\boldsymbol{w}^\mathsf{T}\boldsymbol{x}_n, 1)\mathbb{I}(z_n > 0) & \text{if } y_n = 1 \\ \mathcal{N}(z_n|\boldsymbol{w}^\mathsf{T}\boldsymbol{x}_n, 1)\mathbb{I}(z_n < 0) & \text{if } y_n = 0 \end{cases} \tag{15.174}$$

In Equation (15.173), we see that $\boldsymbol{w}$ only depends linearly on $\boldsymbol{z}$, so we just need to compute $\mathbb{E}[z_n|y_n, \boldsymbol{x}_n, \boldsymbol{w}]$, so we just need to compute the posterior mean. One can show that this is given by

$$\mathbb{E}[z_n|\boldsymbol{w}, \boldsymbol{x}_n] = \begin{cases} \mu_n + \frac{\phi(\mu_n)}{1-\Phi(-\mu_n)} = \mu_n + \frac{\phi(\mu_n)}{\Phi(\mu_n)} & \text{if } y_n = 1 \\ \mu_n - \frac{\phi(\mu_n)}{\Phi(-\mu_n)} = \mu_n - \frac{\phi(\mu_n)}{1-\Phi(\mu_i)} & \text{if } y_n = 0 \end{cases} \tag{15.175}$$

where $\mu_n = \boldsymbol{w}^\mathsf{T}\boldsymbol{x}_n$.

In the M step, we estimate $\boldsymbol{w}$ using ridge regression, where $\boldsymbol{\mu} = \mathbb{E}[\boldsymbol{z}]$ is the output we are trying to predict. Specifically, we have

$$\hat{\boldsymbol{w}} = (\mathbf{V}_0^{-1} + \mathbf{X}^\mathsf{T}\mathbf{X})^{-1}\mathbf{X}^\mathsf{T}\boldsymbol{\mu} \tag{15.176}$$

The EM algorithm is simple, but can be much slower than direct gradient methods, as illustrated in Figure 15.12. This is because the posterior entropy in the E step is quite high, since we only observe that z is positive or negative, but are given no information from the likelihood about its magnitude. Using a stronger regularizer can help speed convergence, because it constrains the range of plausible z values. In addition, one can use various speedup tricks, such as data augmentation [DM01].

15.4.3   Bayesian inference

It is possible to use the latent variable formulation of probit regression in Section 15.4.2.2 to derive a simple Gibbs sampling algorithm for approximating the posterior $p(\boldsymbol{w}|\mathcal{D})$ (see e.g., [AC93; HH06]).

The key idea is to use an auxiliary latent variable, which, when conditioned on, makes the whole model a conjugate linear-Gaussian model. The full conditional for the latent variables is given by

$$p(z_i|y_i, \boldsymbol{x}_i, \boldsymbol{w}) = \begin{cases} \mathcal{N}(z_i|\boldsymbol{w}^T\boldsymbol{x}_i, 1)\mathbb{I}(z_i > 0) & \text{if } y_i = 1 \\ \mathcal{N}(z_i|\boldsymbol{w}^T\boldsymbol{x}_i, 1)\mathbb{I}(z_i < 0) & \text{if } y_i = 0 \end{cases} \tag{15.177}$$

Thus the posterior is a truncated Gaussian. We can sample from a truncated Gaussian, $\mathcal{N}(z|\mu, \sigma)\mathbb{I}(a \leq z \leq b)$ in two steps: first sample $u \sim U(\Phi((a-\mu)/\sigma), \Phi((b-\mu)/\sigma))$, then set $z = \mu + \sigma\Phi^{-1}(u)$ [Rob95a].

The full conditional for the parameters is given by

$$p(\boldsymbol{w}|\mathcal{D}, \boldsymbol{z}, \boldsymbol{\lambda}) = \mathcal{N}(\boldsymbol{w}_N, \mathbf{V}_N) \tag{15.178}$$

$$\mathbf{V}_N = (\mathbf{V}_0^{-1} + \mathbf{X}^T\mathbf{X})^{-1} \tag{15.179}$$

$$\boldsymbol{w}_N = \mathbf{V}_N(\mathbf{V}_0^{-1}\boldsymbol{w}_0 + \mathbf{X}^T\boldsymbol{z}) \tag{15.180}$$

For further details, see e.g., [AC93; FSF10]. It is also possible to use variational Bayes, which tends to be much faster (see e.g., [GR06a; FDZ19]).

15.4.4   Ordinal probit regression

One advantage of the latent variable interpretation of probit regression is that it is easy to extend to the case where the response variable is ordered in some way, such as the outputs low, medium, and high. This is called **ordinal regression**. The basic idea is as follows. If there are C output values, we introduce $C + 1$ thresholds γ_j and set

$$y_n = j \quad \text{if} \quad \gamma_{j-1} < z_n \leq \gamma_j \tag{15.181}$$

where $\gamma_0 \leq \cdots \leq \gamma_C$. For identifiability reasons, we set $\gamma_0 = -\infty$, $\gamma_1 = 0$ and $\gamma_C = \infty$. For example, if $C = 2$, this reduces to the standard binary probit model, whereby $z_n < 0$ produces $y_n = 0$ and $z_n \geq 0$ produces $y_n = 1$. If $C = 3$, we partition the real line into 3 intervals: $(-\infty, 0], (0, \gamma_2], (\gamma_2, \infty)$. We can vary the parameter γ_2 to ensure the right relative amount of probability mass falls in each interval, so as to match the empirical frequencies of each class label. See e.g., [AC93] for further details.

Finding the MLEs for this model is a bit trickier than for binary probit regression, since we need to optimize for $\boldsymbol{w}$ and $\boldsymbol{\gamma}$, and the latter must obey an ordering constraint. See e.g., [KL09] for an approach based on EM. It is also possible to derive a simple Gibbs sampling algorithm for this model (see e.g., [Hof09, p216]).

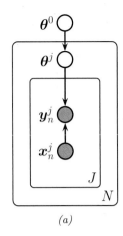
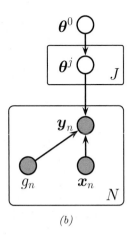

(a) (b)

Figure 15.13: *Hierarchical Bayesian discriminative models with J groups. (a) Nested formulation. (b) Non-nested formulation, with group indicator $g_n \in \{1, \ldots, J\}$.*

15.4.5 Multinomial probit models

Now consider the case where the response variable can take on C unordered categorical values, $y_n \in \{1, \ldots, C\}$. The **multinomial probit** model is defined as follows:

$$z_{nc} = \boldsymbol{w}_c^{\mathsf{T}} \boldsymbol{x}_{nc} + \epsilon_{nc} \tag{15.182}$$

$$\boldsymbol{\epsilon} \sim \mathcal{N}(\boldsymbol{0}, \mathbf{R}) \tag{15.183}$$

$$y_n = \arg \max_c z_{nc} \tag{15.184}$$

See e.g., [DE04; GR06b; Sco09; FSF10] for more details on the model and its connection to multinomial logistic regression.

If instead of setting $y_n = \text{argmax}_c z_{ic}$ we use $y_{nc} = \mathbb{I}(z_{nc} > 0)$, we get a model known as **multivariate probit**, which is one way to model C correlated binary outcomes (see e.g., [TMD12]).

15.5 Multilevel (hierarchical) GLMs

Suppose we have a set of J related datasets, each of which contains a series of N_j datapoints $\mathcal{D}_j = \{(\boldsymbol{x}_n^j, \boldsymbol{y}_n^j) : n = 1 : N_j\}$. There are 3 main ways to fit models in such a setting: we could fit J separate models, $p(\boldsymbol{y}|\boldsymbol{x}; \mathcal{D}_j)$, which might result in overfitting if some $\mathcal{D}_j$ are small; we could pool all the data to get $\mathcal{D} = \cup_{j=1}^J \mathcal{D}_j$ and fit a single model, $p(\boldsymbol{y}|\boldsymbol{x}; \mathcal{D})$, which might result in underfitting; or we can use a **hierarchical Bayesian model**, also called a **multilevel model** or **partially pooled model**, in which we assume each group has its own parameters, $\boldsymbol{\theta}^j$, but that these have something in common, as modeled by a shared global prior $p(\boldsymbol{\theta}^0)$. (Note that each group could be a single individual.) The overall model has the form

$$p(\boldsymbol{\theta}^{0:J}, \mathcal{D}) = p(\boldsymbol{\theta}^0) \prod_{j=1}^J \left[p(\boldsymbol{\theta}^j|\boldsymbol{\theta}^0) \prod_{n=1}^{N_j} p(\boldsymbol{y}_n^j|\boldsymbol{x}_n^j, \boldsymbol{\theta}^j) \right] \tag{15.185}$$

See Figure 15.13a, which represents the model using nested plate notation.

It is often more convenient to represent the model as in Figure 15.13b, which eliminates the nested plates (and hence the double indexing of variables) by associating a group indicator variable $g_n \in \{1, \ldots, J\}$, which specifies which set of parameters to use for each datapoint. Thus the model now has the form

$$p(\boldsymbol{\theta}^{0:J}, \mathcal{D}) = p(\boldsymbol{\theta}^0) \left[\prod_{j=1}^{J} p(\boldsymbol{\theta}^j | \boldsymbol{\theta}^0) \right] \left[\prod_{n=1}^{N} p(\boldsymbol{y}_n | \boldsymbol{x}_n, g_n, \boldsymbol{\theta}) \right] \tag{15.186}$$

where

$$p(\boldsymbol{y}_n | \boldsymbol{x}_n, g_n, \boldsymbol{\theta}) = \prod_{j=1}^{J} p(\boldsymbol{y}_n | \boldsymbol{x}_n, \boldsymbol{\theta}^j)^{\mathbb{I}(g_n = j)} \tag{15.187}$$

If the likelihood function is a GLM, this hierarchical model is called a **hierarchical GLM** [LN96]. This class of models is very widely used in applied statistics. For much more details, see e.g., [GH07; GHV20b; Gel+22].

15.5.1   Generalized linear mixed models (GLMMs)

Suppose that the prior on the per-group parameters is Gaussian, so $p(\boldsymbol{\theta}^j | \boldsymbol{\theta}^0) = \mathcal{N}(\boldsymbol{\theta}^j | \boldsymbol{\theta}^0, \boldsymbol{\Sigma}^j)$. If we have a GLM likelihood, the model becomes

$$p(\boldsymbol{y}_n | \boldsymbol{x}_n, g_n = j, \boldsymbol{\theta}) = p(\boldsymbol{y}_n | \ell(\eta_n)) \tag{15.188}$$

$$\eta_n = \boldsymbol{x}_n^\mathsf{T} \boldsymbol{\theta}^j = \boldsymbol{x}_n^\mathsf{T} (\boldsymbol{\theta}^0 + \boldsymbol{\epsilon}^j) = \boldsymbol{x}_n^\mathsf{T} \boldsymbol{\theta}^0 + \boldsymbol{x}_n^\mathsf{T} \boldsymbol{\epsilon}^j \tag{15.189}$$

where ℓ is the link function, and $\boldsymbol{\epsilon}^j \sim \mathcal{N}(\boldsymbol{0}, \boldsymbol{\Sigma})$. This is known as a **generalized linear mixed model (GLMM)** or **mixed effects model**. The shared (common) parameters $\boldsymbol{\theta}^0$ are called **fixed effects**, and the group-specific offsets $\boldsymbol{\epsilon}^j$ are called **random effects**.[3] We can see that the random effects model group-specific deviations or idiosyncrasies away from the shared fixed parameters. Furthermore, we see that the random effects are correlated, which allows us to model dependencies between the observations that would not be captured by a standard GLM.

For model fitting, we can use any of the Bayesian inference methods that we discussed in Section 15.1.4.

15.5.2   Example: radon regression

In this section, we give an example of a hierarchical Bayesian linear regression model. We apply it to a simplified version of the **radon** example from [Gel+14a, Sec 9.4].

Radon is known to be the highest cause of lung cancer in non-smokers, so reducing it where possible is desirable. To help with this, we fit a regression model, that predicts the (log) radon level as a function of the location of the house, as represented by a categorical feature indicating its county, and

---

3. Note that there are multiple definitions of the terms "fixed effects" and random effects", as explained in this blog post by Andrew Gelman: https://statmodeling.stat.columbia.edu/2005/01/25/why_i_dont_use/.

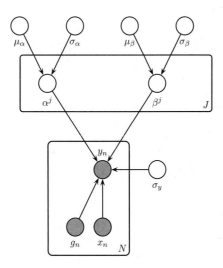

Figure 15.14: *A hierarchical Bayesian linear regression model for the radon problem.*

a binary feature representing whether the house has a basement or not. We use a dataset consisting of $J = 85$ counties in Minnesota; each county has between 2 and 80 measurements.

We assume the following likelihood:

$$p(y_n|x_n, g_n = j, \boldsymbol{\theta}) = \mathcal{N}(y_n|\alpha_j + \beta_j x_n, \sigma_y^2) \tag{15.190}$$

where $g_n \in \{1, \ldots, J\}$ is the county for house i, and $x_n \in \{0, 1\}$ indicates if the floor is at level 0 (i.e., in the basement) or level 1 (i.e., above ground). Intuitively we expect the radon levels to be lower in houses without basements, since they are more insulated from the earth which is the source of the radon.

Since some counties have very few datapoints, we use a hierarchical prior in which we assume $\alpha_j \sim \mathcal{N}(\mu_\alpha, \sigma_\alpha^2)$, and $\beta_j \sim \mathcal{N}(\mu_\beta, \sigma_\beta^2)$. We use weak priors for the parameters: $\mu_\alpha \sim \mathcal{N}(0, 1)$, $\mu_\beta \sim \mathcal{N}(0, 1)$, $\sigma_\alpha \sim \mathcal{C}_+(1)$, $\sigma_\beta \sim \mathcal{C}_+(1)$, $\sigma_y \sim \mathcal{C}_+(1)$. See Figure 15.14 for the graphical model.

15.5.2.1 Posterior inference

Figure 15.15 shows the posterior marginals for μ_α, μ_β, α_j and β_j. We see that μ_β is close to -0.6 with high probability, which confirms our suspicion that having $x = 1$ (i.e., no basement) decreases the amount of radon in the house. We also see that the distribution of the α_j parameters is quite variable, due to different base rates across the counties.

Figure 15.16 shows predictions from the hierarchical and non-hierarchical model for 3 different counties. We see that the predictions from the hierarchical model are more consistent across counties, and work well even if there are no examples of certain feature combinations for a given county (e.g., there are no houses without basements in the sample from Cass county). If we sample data from the posterior predictive distribution, and compare it to the real data, we find that the RMSE is 0.13 for the non-hierarchical model and 0.08 for the hierarchical model, indicating that the latter fits better.

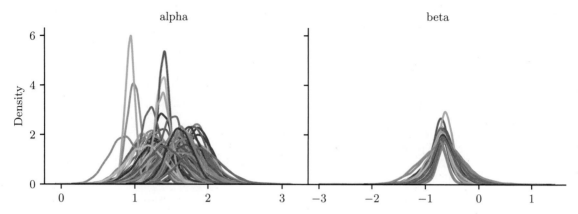

Figure 15.15: *Posterior marginals for* α_j *and* β_j *for each county* j *in the radon model. Generated by* linreg_hierarchical_non_centered.ipynb.

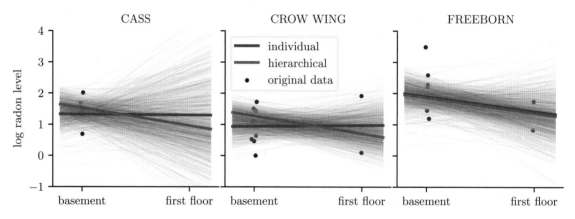

Figure 15.16: *Predictions from the radon model for 3 different counties in Minnesota. Black dots are observed datapoints. Red represents results of hierarchical (shared) prior, blue represents results of non-hierarchical prior. Thick lines are the result of using the posterior mean, thin lines are the result of using posterior samples. Generated by* linreg_hierarchical_non_centered.ipynb.

15.5.2.2   Non-centered parameterization

One problem that frequently arises in hierarchical models is that the parameters be very correlated. This can cause computational problems when performing inference.

Figure 15.17a gives an example where we plot $p(\beta_j, \sigma_\beta | \mathcal{D})$ for some specific county j. If we believe that σ_β is large, then β_c is "allowed" to vary a lot, and we get the broad distribution at the top of the figure. However, if we believe that σ_β is small, then β_j is constrained to be close to the global prior mean of μ_β, so we get the narrow distribution at the bottom of the figure. This is often called **Neal's funnel**, after a paper by Radford Neal [Nea03]. It is difficult for many algorithms (especially sampling algorithms) to explore parts of parameter space at the bottom of the funnel. This is evident from the marginal posterior for σ_β shown (as a histogram) on the right hand side of the plot: we see

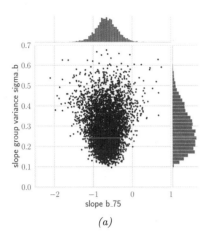
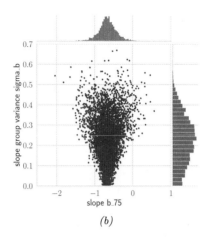

Figure 15.17: (a) Bivariate posterior $p(\beta_j, \sigma_\beta | \mathcal{D})$ for the hierarchical radon model for county $j = 75$ using centered parameterization. (b) Similar to (a) except we plot $p(\tilde{\beta}_j, \sigma_\beta | \mathcal{D})$ for the non-centered parameterization. Generated by linreg_hierarchical_non_centered.ipynb.

that it excludes the interval $[0, 0.1]$, thus ruling out models in which we shrink β_j all the way to 0. In cases where a covariate has no useful predictive role, we would like to be able to induce sparsity, so we need to overcome this problem.

A simple solution to this is to use a **non-centered parameterization** [PR03]. That is, we replace $\beta_j \sim \mathcal{N}(\mu_\beta, \sigma_\beta^2)$ with $\beta_j = \mu_\beta + \tilde{\beta}_j \sigma_\beta$, where $\tilde{\beta}_j \sim \mathcal{N}(0, 1)$ represents the *offset* from the global mean, μ_β. The correlation between $\tilde{\beta}_j$ and σ_β is much less, as shown in Figure 15.17b. See Section 12.6.5 for more details.

16 Deep neural networks

16.1 Introduction

The term "**deep neural network**" or **DNN**, in its modern usage, refers to any kind of differentiable function that can be expressed as a **computation graph**, where the nodes are primitive operations (like matrix mulitplication), and edges represent numeric data in the form of vectors, matrices, or tensors. In its simplest form, this graph can be constructed as a linear series of nodes or "**layers**". The term "deep" refers to models with many such layers.

In Section 16.2 we discuss some of the basic building blocks (node types) that are used in the field. In Section 16.3 we give examples of common architectures which are constructed from these building blocks. In Section 6.2 we show how we can efficiently compute the gradient of functions defined on such graphs. If the function computes the scalar loss of the model's predictions given a training set, we can pass this gradient to an optimization routine, such as those discussed in Chapter 6, in order to fit the model. Fitting such models to data is called "**deep learning**".

We can combine DNNs with probabilistic models in two different ways. The first is to use them to define nonlinear functions which are used inside conditional distributions. For example, we may construct a classifier using $p(y|\boldsymbol{x}, \boldsymbol{\theta}) = \text{Cat}(y|\text{softmax}(f(\boldsymbol{x}; \boldsymbol{\theta})))$, where $f(\boldsymbol{x}; \boldsymbol{\theta})$ is a neural network that maps inputs $\boldsymbol{x}$ and parameters $\boldsymbol{\theta}$ to output logits. Or we may construct a joint probability distribution over multiple variables using a directed graphical model (Chapter 4) where each CPD $p(\boldsymbol{x}_i|\text{pa}(\boldsymbol{x}_i))$ is a DNN. This lets us construct expressive probability models.

The other way we can combine DNNs and probabilistic models is to use DNNs to approximate the posterior distribution, i.e., we learn a function f to compute $q(\boldsymbol{z}|f(\mathcal{D}; \boldsymbol{\phi}))$, where $\boldsymbol{z}$ are the hidden variables (latents and/or parameters), $\mathcal{D}$ are the observed variables (data), f is an **inference network**, and $\boldsymbol{\phi}$ are its parameters; for details, see Section 10.1.5. Note that in this latter, setting the joint model $p(\boldsymbol{z}, \mathcal{D})$ may be a "traditional" model without any "neural" components. For example, it could be a complex simulator. Thus the DNN is just used for computational purposes, not statistical/modeling purposes.

More details on DNNs can be found in such books as [Zha+20a; Cho21; Gér19; GBC16; Raf22], as well as a multitude of online courses. For a more theoretical treatment, see e.g., [Ber+21; Cal20; Aro+21; RY21].

16.2 Building blocks of differentiable circuits

In this section we discuss some common building blocks used in constructing neural networks. We denote the input to a block as $\boldsymbol{x}$ and the output as $\boldsymbol{y}$.

Figure 16.1: An artificial "neuron", the most basic building block of a DNN. (a) The output y is a weighted combination of the inputs $\boldsymbol{x}$, where the weights vector is denoted by $\boldsymbol{w}$. (b) Alternative depiction of the neuron's behavior. The bias term b can be emulated by defining $w_N = b$ and $X_N = 1$.

16.2.1   Linear layers

The most basic building block of a DNN is a single "**neuron**", which corresponds to a real-valued signal y computed by multiplying a vector-valued input signal $\boldsymbol{x}$ by a weight vector $\boldsymbol{w}$, and then adding a bias term b. That is,

$$y = f(\boldsymbol{x}; \boldsymbol{\theta}) = \boldsymbol{w}^\mathsf{T} \boldsymbol{x} + b \tag{16.1}$$

where $\boldsymbol{\theta} = (\boldsymbol{w}, b)$ are the parameters for the function f. This is depicted in Figure 16.1. (The bias term is omitted for clarity.)

It is common to group a set of neurons together into a **layer**. We can then represent the activations of a layer with D units as a vector $\boldsymbol{z} \in \mathbb{R}^D$. We can transform an input vector of activations $\boldsymbol{x}$ into an output vector $\boldsymbol{y}$ by multiplying by a weight matrix $\mathbf{W}$, an adding an offset vector or bias term $\boldsymbol{b}$ to get

$$\boldsymbol{y} = f(\boldsymbol{x}; \boldsymbol{\theta}) = \mathbf{W}\boldsymbol{x} + \boldsymbol{b} \tag{16.2}$$

where $\boldsymbol{\theta} = (\mathbf{W}, \boldsymbol{b})$ are the parameters for the function f. This is called a **linear layer**, or **fully connected layer**.

It is common to prepend the bias vector onto the first column of the weight matrix, and to append a 1 to the vector $\boldsymbol{x}$, so that we can write this more compactly as $\boldsymbol{x} = \tilde{\mathbf{W}}^\mathsf{T}\tilde{\boldsymbol{x}}$, where $\tilde{\mathbf{W}} = [\mathbf{W}, \boldsymbol{b}]$ and $\tilde{\boldsymbol{x}} = [\boldsymbol{x}, 1]$. This allows us to ignore the bias term from our notation if we want to.

16.2.2   Nonlinearities

A stack of linear layers is equivalent to a single linear layer where we multliply together all the weight matrices. To get more expressive power we can transform each layer by passing it elementwise (pointwise) through a nonlinear function called an **activation function**. This is denoted by

$$\boldsymbol{y} = \varphi(\boldsymbol{x}) = [\varphi(x_1), \ldots, \varphi(x_D)] \tag{16.3}$$

See Table 16.1 for a list of some common activation functions, and Figure 16.2 for a visualization. For more details, see e.g., [Mur22, Sec 13.2.3].

Name	Definition	Range	Reference
Sigmoid	$\sigma(a) = \frac{1}{1+e^{-a}}$	$[0, 1]$	
Hyperbolic tangent	$\tanh(a) = 2\sigma(2a) - 1$	$[-1, 1]$	
Softplus	$\sigma_+(a) = \log(1 + e^a)$	$[0, \infty]$	[GBB11]
Rectified linear unit	$\text{ReLU}(a) = \max(a, 0)$	$[0, \infty]$	[GBB11; KSH12a]
Leaky ReLU	$\max(a, 0) + \alpha \min(a, 0)$	$[-\infty, \infty]$	[MHN13]
Exponential linear unit	$\max(a, 0) + \min(\alpha(e^a - 1), 0)$	$[-\infty, \infty]$	[CUH16]
Swish	$a\sigma(a)$	$[-\infty, \infty]$	[RZL17]
GELU	$a\Phi(a)$	$[-\infty, \infty]$	[HG16]

Table 16.1: List of some popular activation functions for neural networks.

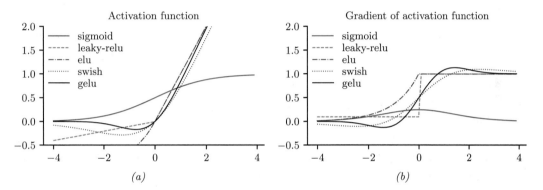

Figure 16.2: (a) Some popular activation functions. "ReLU" stands for "restricted linear unit". "GELU" stands for "Gaussian error linear unit". (b) Plot of their gradients. Generated by activation_fun_deriv.ipynb.

16.2.3 Convolutional layers

When dealing with image data, we can apply the same weight matrix to each local patch of the image, in order to reduce the number of parameters. If we "slide" this weight matrix over the image and add up the results, we get a technique known as **convolution**; in this case the weight matrix is often called a "**kernel**" or "**filter**".

More precisely, let $\mathbf{X} \in \mathbb{R}^{H \times W}$ be the input image, and $\mathbf{W} \in \mathbb{R}^{h \times w}$ be the kernel. The output is denoted by $\mathbf{Z} = \mathbf{X} \circledast \mathbf{W}$, where (ignoring boundary conditions) we have the following:[1]

$$Z_{i,j} = \sum_{u=0}^{h-1} \sum_{v=0}^{w-1} x_{i+u,j+v} w_{u,v} \tag{16.4}$$

Essentially we compare a local patch of $\boldsymbol{x}$, of size $h \times w$ and centered at (i, j), to the filter $\boldsymbol{w}$; the output just measures how similar the input patch is to the filter. We can define convolution in 1d or 3d in an analogous manner. Note that the spatial size of the outputs may be smaller than inputs,

---

1. Note that, technically speaking, we are using **cross correlation** rather than convolution. However, these terms are used interchangeably in deep learning.

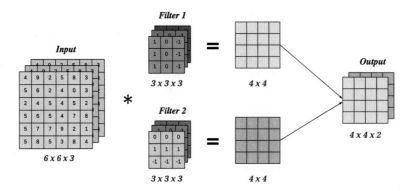

Figure 16.3: A 2d convolutional layer with 3 input channels and 2 output channels. The kernel has size 3×3 and we use stride 1 with 0 padding, so the 6×6 input gets mapped to the 4×4 output.

due to boundary effects, although this can be solved by using **padding**. See [Mur22, Sec 14.2.1] for more details.

We can repeat this process for multiple layers of inputs, and by using multiple filters, we can generate multiple layers of output. In general, if we have C input channels, and we want to map it to D output (feature) channels, then we define D kernels, each of size $h \times w \times C$, where h, w are the height and width of the kernel. The d'th output feature map is obtained by convolving all C input feature maps with the d'th kernel, and then adding up the results elementwise:

$$z_{i,j,d} = \sum_{u=0}^{h-1}\sum_{v=0}^{w-1}\sum_{c=0}^{C-1} x_{i+u,j+v,c} w_{u,v,c,d} \tag{16.5}$$

This is called a **convolutional layer**, and is illustrated in Figure 16.3.

The advantage of a convolutional layer compared to using a linear layer is that the weights of the kernel are shared across locations in the input. Thus if a pattern in the input shifts locations, the corresponding output activation will also shift. This is called **shift equivariance**. In some cases, we want the output to be the same, no matter where the input pattern occurs; this is called **shift invariance**, and can be obtained by using a **pooling layer**, which computes the maximum or average value in each local patch of the input. (Note that pooling layers have no free (learnable) parameters.) Other forms of invariance can also be captured by neural networks (see e.g., [CW16; FWW21]).

16.2.4   Residual (skip) connections

If we stack a large number of nonlinear layers together, the signal may get squashed to zero or may blow up to infinity, depending on the magnitude of the weights, and the nature of the nonlinearities. Similar problems can plague gradients that are passed backwards through the network (see Section 6.2). To reduce the effect of this we can add **skip connections**, also called **residual connections**, which allow the signal to skip one or more layers, which prevents it from being modified. For example,

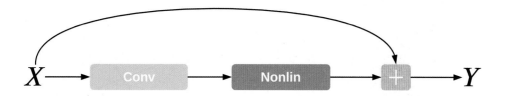

Figure 16.4: *A residual connection around a convolutional layer.*

Figure 16.4 illustrates a network that computes

$$y = f(\boldsymbol{x}; \mathbf{W}) = \varphi(\mathrm{conv}(\boldsymbol{x}; \mathbf{W})) + \boldsymbol{x} \qquad (16.6)$$

Now the convolutional layer only needs to learn an offset or residual to add (or subtract) to the input to match the desired output, rather than predicting the output directly. Such residuals are often small in size, and hence are easier to learn using neurons with weights that are bounded (e.g., close to 1).

16.2.5 Normalization layers

To learn an input-output mapping, it is often best if the inputs are standardized, meaning that they have zero mean and unit standard deviation. This ensures that the required magnitude of the weights is small, and comparable across dimensions. To ensure that the internal activations have this property, it is common to add **normalization layers**.

The most common approach is to use **batch normalization** (**BN**) [IS15]. However this relies on having access to a batch of $B > 1$ input examples. Various alternatives have been proposed to overcome the need of having an input batch, such as **layer normalization** [BKH16], **instance normalization** [UVL16], **group normalization** [WH18], **filter response normalization** [SK20], etc. More details can be found in [Mur22, Sec 14.2.4].

16.2.6 Dropout layers

Neural networks often have millions of parameters, and thus can sometimes overfit, especially when trained on small datasets. There are many ways to ameliorate this effect, such as applying regularizers to the weights, or adopting a fully Bayesian approach (see Chapter 17). Another common heuristic is known as **dropout** [Sri+14a], in which edges are randomly omitted each time the network is used, as illustrated in Figure 16.5. More precisely, if w_{lij} is the weight of the edge from node i in layer $l-1$ to node j in layer $l+1$, then we replace it with $\theta_{lij} = w_{lij}\epsilon_{li}$, where $\epsilon_{li} \sim \mathrm{Ber}(1-p)$, where p is the drop probability, and $1-p$ is the keep probability. Thus if we sample $\epsilon_{li} = 0$, then all of the weights going out of unit i in layer $l-1$ into any j in layer l will be set to 0.

During training, the gradients will be zero for the weights connected to a neuron which has been switched "off". However, since we resample ϵ_{lij} every time the network is used, different combinations of weights will be updated on each step. The result is an **ensemble** of networks, each with slightly different sparse graph structures.

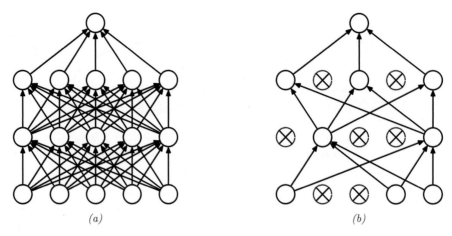

Figure 16.5: *Illustration of dropout. (a) A standard neural net with 2 hidden layers. (b) An example of a thinned net produced by applying dropout with $p = 0.5$. Units that have been dropped out are marked with an x. From Figure 1 of [Sri+14a]. Used with kind permission of Geoff Hinton.*

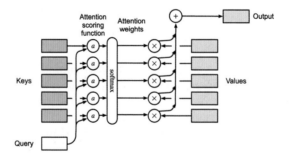

Figure 16.6: *Attention layer. (a) Mapping a single query $\boldsymbol{q}$ to a single output, given a set of keys and values. From Figure 10.3.1 of [Zha+20a]. Used with kind permission of Aston Zhang.*

At test time, we usually turn the dropout noise off, so the model acts deterministically. To ensure the weights have the same expectation at test time as they did during training (so the input activation to the neurons is the same, on average), at test time we should use $\mathbb{E}\left[\theta_{lij}\right] = w_{lij}\mathbb{E}\left[\epsilon_{li}\right]$. For Bernoulli noise, we have $\mathbb{E}\left[\epsilon\right] = 1 - p$, so we should multiply the weights by the keep probability, $1 - p$, before making predictions. We can, however, use dropout at test time if we wish. This is called **Monte Carlo dropout** (see Section 17.3.1).

16.2.7   Attention layers

In non-parametric kernel based prediction methods, such as Gaussian processes (Chapter 18), we compare the input $\boldsymbol{x} \in \mathbb{R}^{d_k}$ to each of the training examples $\mathbf{X} = (\boldsymbol{x}_1, \ldots, \boldsymbol{x}_n)$ using a kernel to get a vector of similarity scores, $\boldsymbol{\alpha} = [\mathcal{K}(\boldsymbol{x}, \boldsymbol{x}_i)]_{i=1}^n$. We then use this to retrieve a weighted combination

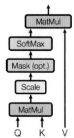

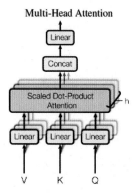

Scaled Dot-Product Attention

Multi-Head Attention

Figure 16.7: *(a) Scaled dot-product attention in matrix form. (b) Multi-head attention. From Figure 2 of [Vas+17b]. Used with kind permission of Ashish Vaswani.*

of the corresponding m target values $\boldsymbol{y}_i \in \mathbb{R}^{d_v}$ as follows:

$$\hat{\boldsymbol{y}} = \sum_{i=1}^{n} \alpha_i \boldsymbol{y}_i \tag{16.7}$$

See Section 18.3.7 for details.

We can make a differentiable and parametric version of this as follows (see [Tsa+19] for details). First we replace the stored examples matrix $\mathbf{X}$ with a learned embedding, to create a set of stored **keys**, $\mathbf{K} = \mathbf{W}^K \mathbf{X} \in \mathbb{R}^{n \times d_k}$. Similarly we replace the stored output matrix $\mathbf{Y}$ with a learned embedding, to create a set of stored **values**, $\mathbf{V} = \mathbf{W}^V \mathbf{Y} \in \mathbb{R}^{n \times d_v}$. Finally we embed the input to create a **query**, $\boldsymbol{q} = \mathbf{W}^Q \boldsymbol{x} \in \mathbb{R}^{d_k}$. The parameters to be learned are the three embedding matrices.

To ensure the output is a differentiable function of the input, we replace the fixed kernel function with a soft **attention layer**. More precisely, we define

$$\text{Attn}(\boldsymbol{q}, (\boldsymbol{k}_1, \boldsymbol{v}_1), \dots, (\boldsymbol{k}_n, \boldsymbol{v}_n)) = \text{Attn}(\boldsymbol{q}, (\boldsymbol{k}_{1:n}, \boldsymbol{v}_{1:n})) = \sum_{i=1}^{n} \alpha_i(\boldsymbol{q}, \boldsymbol{k}_{1:n}) \boldsymbol{v}_i \tag{16.8}$$

where $\alpha_i(\boldsymbol{q}, \boldsymbol{k}_{1:n})$ is the i'th **attention weight**; these weights satisfy $0 \leq \alpha_i(\boldsymbol{q}, \boldsymbol{k}_{1:n}) \leq 1$ for each i and $\sum_i \alpha_i(\boldsymbol{q}, \boldsymbol{k}_{1:n}) = 1$.

The attention weights can be computed from an **attention score** function $a(\boldsymbol{q}, \boldsymbol{k}_i) \in \mathbb{R}$, that computes the similarity of query $\boldsymbol{q}$ to key $\boldsymbol{k}_i$. For example, we can use (scaled) **dot product attention**, which has the form

$$a(\boldsymbol{q}, \boldsymbol{k}) = \boldsymbol{q}^\top \boldsymbol{k} / \sqrt{d_k} \tag{16.9}$$

(The scaling by $\sqrt{d_k}$ is to reduce the dependence of the output on the dimensionality of the vectors.) Given the scores, we can compute the attention weights using the softmax function:

$$\alpha_i(\boldsymbol{q}, \boldsymbol{k}_{1:n}) = \text{softmax}_i([a(\boldsymbol{q}, \boldsymbol{k}_1), \dots, a(\boldsymbol{q}, \boldsymbol{k}_n)]) = \frac{\exp(a(\boldsymbol{q}, \boldsymbol{k}_i))}{\sum_{j=1}^{n} \exp(a(\boldsymbol{q}, \boldsymbol{k}_j))} \tag{16.10}$$

See Figure 16.6 for an illustration.

In some cases, we want to restrict attention to a subset of the dictionary, corresponding to valid entries. For example, we might want to pad sequences to a fixed length (for efficient minibatching), in which case we should "mask out" the padded locations. This is called **masked attention**. We can implement this efficiently by setting the attention score for the masked entries to a large negative number, such as -10^6, so that the corresponding softmax weights will be 0.

In practice, we usually deal with minibatches of n vectors at a time. Let the corresponding matrices of queries, keys and values be denoted by $\mathbf{Q} \in \mathbb{R}^{n \times d_k}$, $\mathbf{K} \in \mathbb{R}^{n \times d_k}$, $\mathbf{V} \in \mathbb{R}^{n \times d_v}$. Let

$$z_j = \sum_{i=1}^{n} \alpha_i(q_j, \mathbf{K}) v_i \tag{16.11}$$

be the j'th output corresponding to the j'th query. We can compute all outputs $\mathbf{Z} \in \mathbb{R}^{n \times d_v}$ in parallel using

$$\mathbf{Z} = \text{Attn}(\mathbf{Q}, \mathbf{K}, \mathbf{V}) = \text{softmax}(\frac{\mathbf{Q}\mathbf{K}^\mathsf{T}}{\sqrt{d_k}})\mathbf{V} \tag{16.12}$$

where the softmax function softmax is applied row-wise. See Figure 16.7 (left) for an illustration.

To increase the flexibility of the model, we often use a **multi-head attention** layer, as illustrated in Figure 16.7 (right). Let the i'th head be

$$h_i = \text{Attn}(\mathbf{Q}\mathbf{W}_i^Q, \mathbf{K}\mathbf{W}_i^K, \mathbf{V}\mathbf{W}_i^V) \tag{16.13}$$

where $\mathbf{W}_i^Q \in \mathbb{R}^{d \times d_k}$, $\mathbf{W}_i^K \in \mathbb{R}^{d \times d_k}$ and $\mathbf{W}_i^V \in \mathbb{R}^{d \times d_v}$ are linear projection matrices. We define the output of the MHA layer to be

$$\mathbf{Z} = \text{MHA}(\mathbf{Q}, \mathbf{K}, \mathbf{V}) = \text{Concat}(h_1, \dots, h_h)\mathbf{W}^O \tag{16.14}$$

where h is the number of heads, and $\mathbf{W}^O \in \mathbb{R}^{h d_v \times d}$. Having multiple heads can increase performance of the layer, in the event that some of the weight matrices are poorly initialized; after training, we can often remove all but one of the heads [MLN19].

When the output of one attention layer is used as input to another, the method is called **self-attention**. This is the basis of the transformer model, which we discuss in Section 16.3.5.

16.2.8   Recurrent layers

We can make the model be **stateful** by augmenting the input x with the current state s_t, and then computing the output and the new state using some kind of function:

$$(y, s_{t+1}) = f(x, s_t) \tag{16.15}$$

This is called a **recurrent layer**, as shown in Figure 16.8. This forms the basis of **recurrent neural networks**, discussed in Section 16.3.4. In a vanilla RNN, the function f is a simple MLP, but it may also use attention (Section 16.2.7).

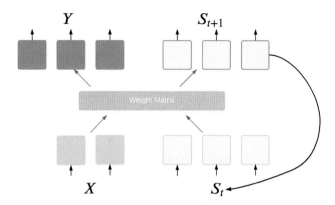

Figure 16.8: Recurrent layer.

16.2.9 Multiplicative layers

In this section, we discuss **multiplicative layers**, which are useful for combining different information sources. Our presentation follows [Jay+20].

Suppose we have inputs $\boldsymbol{x} \in \mathbb{R}^n$ and $\boldsymbol{z} \in \mathbb{R}^m$, In a linear layer (and, by extension, convolutional layers), it is common to concatenate the inputs to get $f(\boldsymbol{x}, \boldsymbol{z}) = \mathbf{W}[\boldsymbol{x}; \boldsymbol{z}] + \boldsymbol{b}$, where $\mathbf{W} \in \mathbb{R}^{k \times (m+n)}$ and $\boldsymbol{b} \in \mathbb{R}^k$. We can increase the expressive power of the model by using **multiplicative interactions**, such as the following **bilinear form**:

$$f(\boldsymbol{x}, \boldsymbol{z}) = \boldsymbol{z}^\mathsf{T} \mathbb{W} \boldsymbol{x} + \mathbf{U}\boldsymbol{z} + \mathbf{V}\boldsymbol{x} + \boldsymbol{b} \tag{16.16}$$

where $\mathbb{W} \in \mathbb{R}^{m \times n \times k}$ is a weight tensor, defined such that

$$(\boldsymbol{z}^\mathsf{T} \mathbb{W} \boldsymbol{x})_k = \sum_{ij} \boldsymbol{z}_i \mathbb{W}_{ijk} \boldsymbol{x}_j \tag{16.17}$$

That is, the k'th entry of the output is the weighted inner product of $\boldsymbol{z}$ and $\boldsymbol{x}$, where the weight matrix is the k'th "slice" of $\mathbb{W}$. The other parameters have size $\mathbf{U} \in \mathbb{R}^{k \times m}$, $\mathbf{V} \in \mathbb{R}^{k \times n}$, and $\boldsymbol{b} \in \mathbb{R}^k$.

This formulation includes many interesting special cases. In particular, a **hypernetwork** [HDL17] can be viewed in this way. A hypernetwork is a neural network that generates parameters for another neural network. In particular, we replace $f(\boldsymbol{x}; \boldsymbol{\theta})$ with $f(\boldsymbol{x}; g(\boldsymbol{z}; \boldsymbol{\phi}))$. If f and g are affine, this is equivalent to a multiplicative layer. To see this, let $\mathbf{W}' = \boldsymbol{z}^\mathsf{T} \mathbb{W} + \mathbf{V}$ and $\boldsymbol{b}' = \mathbf{U}\boldsymbol{z} + \boldsymbol{b}$. If we define $g(\boldsymbol{z}; \boldsymbol{\Phi}) = [\mathbf{W}', \boldsymbol{b}']$, and $f(\boldsymbol{x}; \boldsymbol{\theta}) = \mathbf{W}'\boldsymbol{x} + \boldsymbol{b}'$, we recover Equation (16.16).

We can also view the gating layers used in RNNs (Section 16.3.4) as a form of multiplicative interaction. In particular, if the hypernetwork computes the diagonal matrix $\mathbf{W}' = \sigma(\boldsymbol{z}^\mathsf{T} \mathbb{W} + \mathbf{V}) = \text{diag}(a_1, \ldots, a_n)$, then we can define $f(\boldsymbol{x}, \boldsymbol{z}; \boldsymbol{\theta}) = \boldsymbol{a}(\boldsymbol{z}) \odot \boldsymbol{x}$, which is the standard gating mechanism. Attention mechanisms (Section 16.2.7) are also a form of multiplicative interaction, although they involve three-way interactions, between query, key, and value.

Another variant arises if the hypernetwork just computes a scalar weight for each channel of a convolutional layer, plus a bias term:

$$f(\boldsymbol{x}, \boldsymbol{z}) = a(\boldsymbol{z}) \odot \boldsymbol{x} + \boldsymbol{b}(\boldsymbol{z}) \tag{16.18}$$

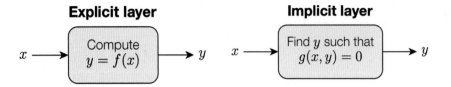

Figure 16.9: Explicit vs implicit layers.

This is called **FiLM**, which stands for "feature-wise linear modulation" [Per+18]. For a detailed tutorial on the FiLM layer and its many applications, see `https://distill.pub/2018/feature-wise-transformations`.

16.2.10   Implicit layers

So far we have focused on **explicit layers**, which specify how to transform the input to the output using $y = f(x)$. We can also define **implicit layers**, which specify the output indirectly, in terms of a constraint function:

$$y \in \underset{y}{\arg\min} \, f(x, y) \text{ such that } g(x, y) = 0 \tag{16.19}$$

The details on how to find a solution to this constrained optimization problem can vary depending on the problem. For example, we may need to run an inner optimization routine, or call a differential equation solver. The main advantage of this approach is that the inner computations do not need to be stored explicitly, which saves a lot of memory. Furthermore, once the solution has been found, we can propagate gradients through the whole layer, by leveraging the implicit function theorem. This lets us use higher level primitives inside an end-to-end framework. For more details, see [GHC21] and `http://implicit-layers-tutorial.org/`.

16.3   Canonical examples of neural networks

In this section, we give several "canonical" examples of neural network architectures that are widely used for different tasks.

16.3.1   Multilayer perceptrons (MLPs)

A **multilayer perceptron (MLP)**, also called a **feedforward neural network (FFNN)**, is one of the simplest kinds of neural networks. It consists of a series of L linear layers, combined with elementwise nonlinearities:

$$f(x; \theta) = \mathbf{W}_L \varphi_L(\mathbf{W}_{L-1} \varphi_{L-1}(\cdots \varphi_1(\mathbf{W}_1 x) \cdots)) \tag{16.20}$$

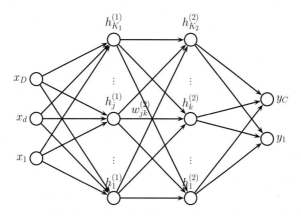

Figure 16.10: A feedforward neural network with D inputs, K_1 hidden units in layer 1, K_2 hidden units in layer 2, and C outputs. $w_{jk}^{(l)}$ is the weight of the connection from node j in layer $l-1$ to node k in layer l.

For example, Figure 16.10 shows an MLP with 1 input layer of D units, 2 hidden layers of K_1 and K_2 units, and 1 output layer with C units. The k'th hidden unit in layer l is given by

$$h_k^{(l)} = \varphi_l \left(b_k^{(l)} + \sum_{j=1}^{K_{l-1}} w_{jk}^{(l)} h_j^{(l-1)} \right) \tag{16.21}$$

where φ_l is the nonlinear activation function at layer l.

For a classification problem, the final nonlinearity is usually the softmax function. However, it is also common for the final layer to have linear activations, in which case the outputs are interpreted as logits; the loss function used during training then converts to (log) probabilities internally.

We can also use MLPs for regression. Figure 16.11 shows how we can make a model for **heteroskedastic** nonlinear regression. (The term "heteroskedastic" just means that the predicted output variance is input-dependent, rather than a constant.) This function has two outputs which compute $f_\mu(\boldsymbol{x}) = \mathbb{E}\left[y|\boldsymbol{x},\boldsymbol{\theta}\right]$ and $f_\sigma(\boldsymbol{x}) = \sqrt{\mathbb{V}\left[y|\boldsymbol{x},\boldsymbol{\theta}\right]}$. We can share most of the layers (and hence parameters) between these two functions by using a common "**backbone**" and two output "**heads**", as shown in Figure 16.11. For the μ head, we use a linear activation, $\varphi(a) = a$. For the σ head, we use a softplus activation, $\varphi(a) = \sigma_+(a) = \log(1 + e^a)$. If we use linear heads and a nonlinear backbone, the overall model is given by

$$p(y|\boldsymbol{x},\boldsymbol{\theta}) = \mathcal{N}\left(y|\boldsymbol{w}_{\boldsymbol{\mu}}^{\mathsf{T}} f(\boldsymbol{x};\boldsymbol{w}_{\text{shared}}), \sigma_+(\boldsymbol{w}_{\boldsymbol{\sigma}}^{\mathsf{T}} f(\boldsymbol{x};\boldsymbol{w}_{\text{shared}}))\right) \tag{16.22}$$

16.3.2 Convolutional neural networks (CNNs)

A vanilla **convolutional neural network** or **CNN** consists of a series of convolutional layers, pooling layers, linear layers, and nonlinearities. See Figure 16.12 for an example. More sophisticated architectures, such as the **ResNet** model [He+16a; He+16b], add skip (residual) connections, normalization layers, etc. The **ConvNeXt** model of [Liu+22b] is considered the current (as of February 2022) state of the art CNN architecture for a wide variety of vision tasks. See e.g., [Mur22, Ch.14] for more details on CNNs.

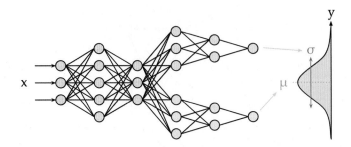

Figure 16.11: *Illustration of an MLP with a shared "backbone" and two output "heads", one for predicting the mean and one for predicting the variance. From* https://brendanhasz.github.io/2019/07/23/ bayesian-density-net.html. *Used with kind permission of Brendan Hasz.*

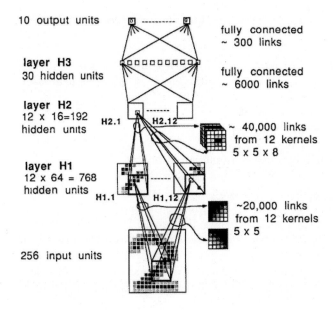

Figure 16.12: *One of the first CNNs ever created, for classifying MNIST images. From Figure 3 of [LeC+89]. For a "modern" implementation, see* lecun1989.ipynb.

16.3.3 Autoencoders

An **autoencoder** is a neural network that maps inputs x to a low-dimensional latent space using an **encoder**, $z = f_e(x)$, and then attempts to reconstruct the inputs using a **decoder**, $\hat{x} = f_d(z)$. The model is trained to minimize

$$\mathcal{L}(\boldsymbol{\theta}) = ||r(\boldsymbol{x}) - \boldsymbol{x}||_2^2 \tag{16.23}$$

where $r(\boldsymbol{x}) = f_d(f_e(\boldsymbol{x}))$. (We can also replace squared error with more general conditional log likelihoods.) See Figure 16.13 for an illustration of a 3 layer AE.

Input Layer | Latent Representation | Output Layer

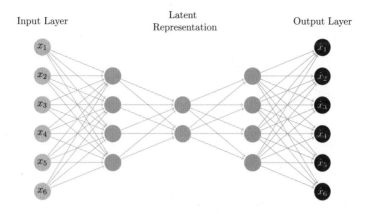

Figure 16.13: *Illustration of an autoencoder with 3 hidden layers.*

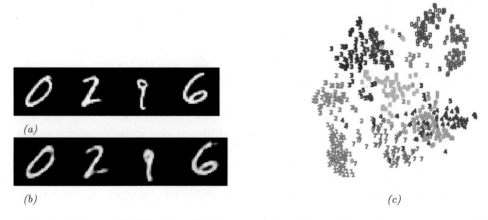

(a)

(b)

(c)

Figure 16.14: *(a) Some MNIST digits. (b) Reconstruction of these images using a convolutional autoencoder. (c) t-SNE visualization of the 20-d embeddings. The colors correspond to class labels, which were not used during training. Generated by* ae_mnist_conv_jax.ipynb.

For image data, we can make the encoder be a convolutional network, and the decoder be a transpose convolutional network. We can use this to compute low dimensional embeddings of image data. For example, suppose we fit such a model to some MNIST digits. We show the reconstruction abilities of such a model in Figure 16.14b. In Figure 16.14c, we show a 2d visualization of the 20-dimensional embedding space computed using t-SNE. The colors correspond to class labels, which were not used during training. We see fairly good separation, showing that images which are visually similar are placed close to each other in the embedding space, as desired. (See also Section 21.2.3, where we compare AEs with variational AEs.)

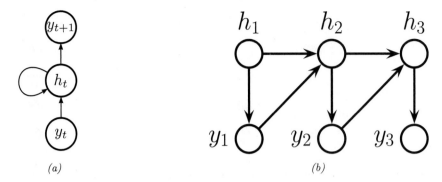

Figure 16.15: *Illustration of a recurrent neural network (RNN). (a) With self-loop. (b) Unrolled in time.*

16.3.4   Recurrent neural networks (RNNs)

A **recurrent neural network** (**RNN**) is a network with a recurrent layer, as in Equation (16.15). This is illustrated in Figure 16.15. Formally this defines the following probability distribution over sequences:

$$p(\boldsymbol{y}_{1:T}) = \sum_{\boldsymbol{h}_{1:T}} p(\boldsymbol{y}_{1:T}, \boldsymbol{h}_{1:T}) = \sum_{\boldsymbol{h}_{1:T}} \mathbb{I}(\boldsymbol{h}_1 = \boldsymbol{h}_1^*) \, p(\boldsymbol{y}_1|\boldsymbol{h}_1) \prod_{t=2}^{T} p(\boldsymbol{y}_t|\boldsymbol{h}_t) \mathbb{I}(\boldsymbol{h}_t = f(\boldsymbol{h}_{t-1}, \boldsymbol{y}_{t-1})) \quad (16.24)$$

where $\boldsymbol{h}_t$ is the deterministic hidden state, computed from the last hidden state and last output using $f(\boldsymbol{h}_{t-1}, \boldsymbol{y}_{t-1})$. (At training time, $\boldsymbol{y}_{t-1}$ is observed, but at prediction time, it is generated.)

In a vanilla RNN, the function f is a simple MLP. However, we can also use attention to selectively update parts of the state vector based on similarity between the input the previous state, as in the **GRU** (gated recurrent unit) model, and the **LSTM** (long short term memory) model. We can also make the model into a conditional sequence model, by feeding in extra inputs to the f function. See e.g., [Mur22, Ch. 15] for more details on RNNs.

16.3.5   Transformers

Consider the problem of classifying each word in a sentence, for example with its part of speech tag (noun, verb, etc). That is, we want to learn a mapping $f : \mathcal{X} \to \mathcal{Y}$, where $\mathcal{X} = \mathcal{V}^T$ is the set of input sequences defined over (word) vocabulary $\mathcal{V}$, T is the length of the sentence, and $\mathcal{Y} = \mathcal{T}^T$ is the set of output sequences, defined over (tag) vocabulary $\mathcal{T}$. To do well at this task, we need to learn a contextual embedding of each word. RNNs process one token at a time, so the embedding of the word at location t, $\boldsymbol{z}_t$, depends on the hidden state of the network, $\boldsymbol{s}_t$, which may be a lossy summary of all the previously seen words. We can create bidirectional RNNs so that future words can also affect the embedding of $\boldsymbol{z}_t$, but this dependence is still mediated via the hidden state. An alternative approach is to compute $\boldsymbol{z}_t$ as a direct function of all the other words in the sentence, by using the attention operator discussed in Section 16.2.7 rather than using hidden state. This is called an (encoder-only) **transformer**, and is used by models such as BERT [Dev+19]. This idea is sketched in Figure 16.16.

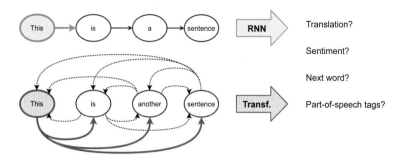

Figure 16.16: Visualizing the difference between an RNN and a transformer. From [Jos20]. Used with kind permission of Chaitanya Joshi.

It is also possible to create a decoder-only transformer, in which each output $\boldsymbol{y}_t$ only attends to all the previously generated outputs, $\boldsymbol{y}_{1:t-1}$. This can be implemented using masked attention, and is useful for generative language models, such as GPT (see Section 22.4.1). We can combine the encoder and decoder to create a conditional sequence-to-sequence model, $p(\boldsymbol{y}_{1:T_y}|\boldsymbol{x}_{1:T_x})$, as proposed in the original transformer paper [Vas+17c]. See Supplementary Section 16.1.1 and [PH22] for more details.

It has been found that large transformers are very flexible sequence-to-sequence function approximators, if trained on enough data (see e.g., [Lin+21a] for a review in the context of NLP, and [Kha+21; Han+20; Zan21] for reviews in the context of computer vision). The reasons why they work so well are still not very clear. However, some initial insights can be found in, e.g., [Rag+21; WGY21; Nel21; BP21]. See also Supplementary Section 16.1.2.5 where we discuss the connection with graph neural networks.

16.3.6 Graph neural networks (GNNs)

It is possible to define neural networks for working with graph-structured data. These are called **graph neural networks** or **GNNs**. See Supplementary Section 16.1.2 for details.

17 Bayesian neural networks

This chapter is coauthored with Andrew Wilson.

17.1 Introduction

Deep neural networks (DNNs) are usually trained using a (penalized) maximum likelihood objective to find a single setting of parameters. However, large flexible models like neural networks can represent many functions, corresponding to different parameter settings, which fit the training data well, yet generalize in different ways. (This phenomenon is known as **underspecification** (see e.g., [D'A+20]; see Figure 17.11 for an illustration.) Considering all of these different models together can lead to improved accuracy and uncertainty representation. This can be done by computing the posterior predictive distribution using Bayesian model averaging:

$$p(\boldsymbol{y}|\boldsymbol{x}, \mathcal{D}) = \int p(\boldsymbol{y}|\boldsymbol{x}, \boldsymbol{\theta})p(\boldsymbol{\theta}|\mathcal{D})d\boldsymbol{\theta} \tag{17.1}$$

where $p(\boldsymbol{\theta}|\mathcal{D}) \propto p(\boldsymbol{\theta})p(\mathcal{D}|\boldsymbol{\theta})$.

The main challenges in applying Bayesian inference to DNNs are specifying suitable priors, and efficiently computing the posterior, which is challenging due to the large number of parameters and the large datasets. The application of Bayesian inference to DNNs is sometimes called **Bayesian deep learning** or **BDL**. By contrast, the term **deep Bayesian learning** or **DBL** refers to the use of deep models to help speed up Bayesian inference of "classical" models, usually by training amortized inference networks that can be used as part of a variational inference or importance sampling algorithm, as discussed in Section 10.1.5.) For more details on the topic of BDL, see e.g., [PS17; Wil20; WI20; Jos+22; Kha20].

17.2 Priors for BNNs

To perform Bayesian inference for the parameters of a DNN, we need to specify a prior $p(\boldsymbol{\theta})$. [Nal18; WI20; For22] discusses the issue of prior selection at length. Here we just give a brief summary of common approaches.

17.2.1 Gaussian priors

Consider an MLP with one hidden layer with activation function φ and a linear output:

$$f(\boldsymbol{x}; \boldsymbol{\theta}) = \mathbf{W}_2 \varphi(\mathbf{W}_1 \boldsymbol{x} + \boldsymbol{b}_1) + \boldsymbol{b}_2 \tag{17.2}$$

(If the output is nonlinear, such as a softmax transform, we can fold it into the loss function during training.) If we have two hidden layers this becomes

$$f(\boldsymbol{x}; \boldsymbol{\theta}) = \mathbf{W}_3 \left(\varphi\left(\mathbf{W}_2 \varphi(\mathbf{W}_1 \boldsymbol{x} + \boldsymbol{b}_1) + \boldsymbol{b}_2\right)\right) + \boldsymbol{b}_3 \tag{17.3}$$

In general, with $L - 1$ hidden layers and a linear output, we have

$$f(\boldsymbol{x}; \boldsymbol{\theta}) = \mathbf{W}_L \left(\cdots \varphi(\mathbf{W}_1 \boldsymbol{x} + \boldsymbol{b}_1)\right) + \boldsymbol{b}_L \tag{17.4}$$

We need to specify the priors for $\mathbf{W}_l$ and $\boldsymbol{b}_l$ for $l = 1 : L$. The most common choice is to use a factored Gaussian prior:

$$\mathbf{W}_\ell \sim \mathcal{N}(\mathbf{0}, \alpha_\ell^2 \mathbf{I}), \ \boldsymbol{b}_\ell \sim \mathcal{N}(\mathbf{0}, \beta_\ell^2 \mathbf{I}) \tag{17.5}$$

The **Xavier initialization** or **Glorot initialization**, named after the first author of [GB10], is to set

$$\alpha_\ell^2 = \frac{2}{n_{\text{in}} + n_{\text{out}}} \tag{17.6}$$

where n_{in} is the fan-in of a node in level ℓ (number of weights coming into a neuron), and n_{out} is the fan-out (number of weights going out of a neuron). **LeCun initialization**, named after Yann LeCun, corresponds to using

$$\alpha_\ell^2 = \frac{1}{n_{\text{in}}} \tag{17.7}$$

We can get a better understanding of these priors by considering the effect they have on the corresponding distribution over functions that they define. To help understand this correspondence, let us reparameterize the model as follows:

$$\mathbf{W}_\ell = \alpha_\ell \boldsymbol{\eta}_\ell, \ \boldsymbol{\eta}_\ell \sim \mathcal{N}(\mathbf{0}, \mathbf{I}), \ \boldsymbol{b}_\ell = \beta_\ell \boldsymbol{\epsilon}_\ell, \ \boldsymbol{\epsilon}_\ell \sim \mathcal{N}(\mathbf{0}, \mathbf{I}) \tag{17.8}$$

Hence every setting of the prior hyperparameters specifies the following random function:

$$f(\boldsymbol{x}; \boldsymbol{\alpha}, \boldsymbol{\beta}) = \alpha_L \boldsymbol{\eta}_L(\cdots \varphi(\alpha_1 \boldsymbol{\eta}_1 \boldsymbol{x} + \beta_1 \boldsymbol{\epsilon}_1)) + \beta_L \boldsymbol{\epsilon}_L \tag{17.9}$$

To get a feeling for the effect of these hyperparameters, we can sample MLP parameters from this prior and plot the resulting random functions. We use a sigmoid nonlinearity, so $\varphi(a) = \sigma(a)$. We consider $L = 2$ layers, so $\mathbf{W}_1$ are the input-to-hidden weights, and $\mathbf{W}_2$ are the hidden-to-output weights. We assume the input and output are scalars, so we are generating random nonlinear 1d mappings $f : \mathbb{R} \to \mathbb{R}$.

Figure 17.1(a) shows some sampled functions where $\alpha_1 = 5$, $\beta_1 = 1$, $\alpha_2 = 1$, $\beta_2 = 1$. In Figure 17.1(b) we increase α_1; this allows the first layer weights to get bigger, making the sigmoid-like

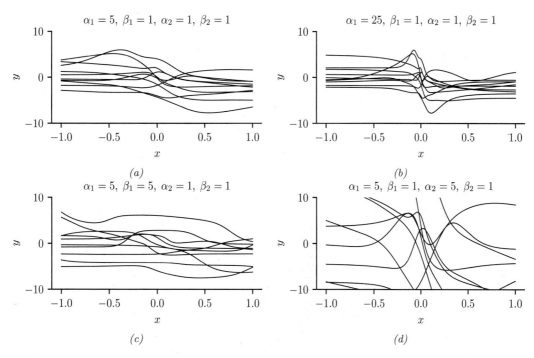

Figure 17.1: *The effects of changing the hyperparameters on an MLP with one hidden layer. (a) Random functions sampled from a Gaussian prior with hyperparameters* $\alpha_1 = 5$, $\beta_1 = 1$, $\alpha_2 = 1$, $\beta_2 = 1$. *(b) Increasing* α_1 *by a factor of 5. (c) Increasing* β_1 *by a factor of 5. (d) Inreasing* α_2 *by a factor of 5. Generated by* mlp_priors_demo.ipynb.

shape of the functions steeper. In Figure 17.1(c), we increase β_1; this allows the first layer biases to get bigger, which allows the center of the sigmoid to shift left and right more, away from the origin. In Figure 17.1(d), we increase α_2; this allows the second layer linear weights to get bigger, making the functions more "wiggly" (greater sensitivity to change in the input, and hence larger dynamic range).

The above results are specific to the case of sigmoidal activation functions. ReLU units can behave differently. For example, [WI20, App. E] show that for MLPs with ReLU units, if we set $\beta_\ell = 0$, so the bias terms are all zero, the effect of changing α_ℓ is just to rescale the output. To see this, note that Equation (17.9) simplifies to

$$f(\boldsymbol{x}; \boldsymbol{\alpha}, \boldsymbol{\beta} = \boldsymbol{0}) = \alpha_L \boldsymbol{\eta}_L(\cdots \varphi(\alpha_1 \boldsymbol{\eta}_1 \boldsymbol{x})) = \alpha_L \cdots \alpha_1 \boldsymbol{\eta}_L(\cdots \varphi(\boldsymbol{\eta}_1 \boldsymbol{x})) \tag{17.10}$$

$$= \alpha_L \cdots \alpha_1 f(\boldsymbol{x}; (\boldsymbol{\alpha} = \boldsymbol{1}, \boldsymbol{\beta} = \boldsymbol{0})) \tag{17.11}$$

where we used the fact that for ReLU, $\varphi(\alpha z) = \alpha \varphi(z)$ for any positive α, and $\varphi(\alpha z) = 0$ for any negative α (since the preactivation $z \geq 0$). In general, it is the ratio of α and β that matters for determining what happens to input signals as they propagate forwards and backwards through a randomly initialized model; for details, see e.g., [Bah+20].

We see that initializing the model's parameters at a particular random value is like sampling a point from this prior over functions. In the limit of infinitely wide neural networks, we can derive this prior distribution analytically: this is known as a **neural network Gaussian process**, and is explained in Section 18.7.

17.2.2   Sparsity-promoting priors

Although Gaussian priors are simple and widely used, they are not the only option. For some applications, it is useful to use **sparsity promoting priors**, such as the Laplace, which encourage most of the weights (or channels in a CNN) to be zero (cf. Section 15.2.6). For details, see [Hoe+21].

17.2.3   Learning the prior

We have seen how different priors for the parameters correspond to different priors over functions. We could in principle set the hyperparameters (e.g., the α and β parameters of the Gaussian prior) using grid search to optimize cross-validation loss. However, cross-validation can be slow, particularly if we allow different priors for each layer of the network, as our grid search will grow exponentially with the number of hyperparameters we wish to determine.

An alternative is to use gradient based methods to optimize the marginal likelihood

$$\log p(\mathcal{D}|\boldsymbol{\alpha}, \boldsymbol{\beta}) = \int \log p(\mathcal{D}|\boldsymbol{\theta}) p(\boldsymbol{\theta}|\boldsymbol{\alpha}, \boldsymbol{\beta}) d\boldsymbol{\theta} \tag{17.12}$$

This approach is known as empirical Bayes (Section 3.7) or **evidence maximization**, since $\log p(\mathcal{D}|\boldsymbol{\alpha}, \boldsymbol{\beta})$ is also called the evidence [Mac92a; WS93; Mac99]. This can give rise to sparse models, as we discussed in the context of automatic relevancy determination (Section 15.2.8). Unfortunately, computing the marginal likelihood is computationally difficult for large neural networks.

Learning the prior is more meaningful if we can do it on a separate, but related dataset. In [SZ+22] they propose to train a model on an initial, large dataset $\mathcal{D}_1$ (possibly unsupervised) to get a point estimate, $\hat{\boldsymbol{\theta}}_1$, from which they can derive an approximate low-rank Gaussian posterior, using the SWAG method (Section 17.3.8). They then use this informative prior when fine-tuning the model on a downstream dataset $\mathcal{D}_2$. The fine-tuning can either be a MAP estimate $\hat{\boldsymbol{\theta}}_2$ or some approximate posterior, $p(\boldsymbol{\theta}_2|\mathcal{D}_2, \mathcal{D}_1)$, e.g., computed using MCMC (Section 17.3.7). They call this technique "**Bayesian transfer learning**". (See Section 19.5.1 for more details on transfer learning.)

17.2.4   Priors in function space

Typically, the relationship between the prior distribution over parameters and the functions preferred by the prior is not transparent. In some cases, it can be possible to pick more informative priors based on principles such as desired invariances that we want the function to satisfy (see e.g., [Nal18]). [FBW21] introduces *residual pathway priors*, providing a mechanism for encoding high level concepts into prior distributions, such as locality, independencies, and symmetries, without constraining model flexibility. A different approach to encoding interpretable priors over functions leverages kernel methods such as Gaussian processes (e.g., [Sun+19a]), as we discuss in Section 18.1.

17.2.5   Architectural priors

Beyond specifying the parametric prior, it is important to note that the architecture of the model can have an even larger effect on the induced distribution over functions, as argued in Wilson and Izmailov [WI20] and Izmailov et al. [Izm+21b]. For example, a CNN architecture encodes prior knowledge about translation equivariance, due to its use of convolution, and hierarchical structure, due to its use of multiple layers. Other forms of inductive bias are induced by different architectures, such as RNNs. (Models such as transformers have weaker inductive bias, but consequently often need more data to perform well.) Thus we can think of the field of **neural architecture search** (reviewed in [EMH19]) as a form of structural prior learning.

In fact, with a suitable architecture, we can often get good results using random (untrained) models. For example, Ulyanov, Vedaldi, and Lempitsky [UVL18] showed that an untrained CNN with random parameters (sampled from a Gaussian) often works very well for low-level image processing tasks, such as image denoising, super-resolution, and image inpainting. The resulting prior over functions has been called the **deep image prior**. Similarly, Pinto and Cox [PC12] showed that untrained CNNs with the right structure can do well at face recognition. Moreover, Zhang et al. [Zha+17] show that randomly initialized CNNs can process data to provide features that greatly improve the performance of other models, such as kernel methods.

17.3   Posteriors for BNNs

There are a large number of different approximate inference schemes that have been applied to Bayesian neural networks, with different strengths and limitations. In the sections below, we briefly describe some of these.

17.3.1   Monte Carlo dropout

Monte Carlo dropout (MCD) [GG16; KG17] is a very simple and widely used method for approximating the Bayesian predictive distribution. Usually stochastic dropout layers are added as a form of regularization, and are "turned off" at test time, as described in Section 16.2.6, However, the idea in MCD is to also perform random sampling at test time. More precisely, we drop out each hidden unit by sampling from a Bernoulli(p) distribution; we repeat this procedure S times, to create S distinct models. We then create an equally weighted average of the predictive distributions for each of these models:

$$p(y|\boldsymbol{x}, \mathcal{D}) \approx \frac{1}{S} \sum_{s=1}^{S} p(y|\boldsymbol{x}, \boldsymbol{\theta}^s) \tag{17.13}$$

where $\boldsymbol{\theta}^s$ is a version of the MAP parameter estimate where we randomly drop out some connections.

We give an example of this process in action in Figure 17.2. We see that it succesfully captures uncertainty due to "out of distribution" inputs. (See Section 19.3.2 for more discussion of OOD detection.)

One drawback of MCD is that it is slow at test time. However this can be overcome by "distilling" the model's predictions into a deterministic "student" network, as we discuss in Section 17.3.10.3.

A more fundamental problem is that MCD does not give proper uncertainty estimates, as argued in [Osb16; LF+21]. The problem is the following. Although MCD can be viewed as a form of variational

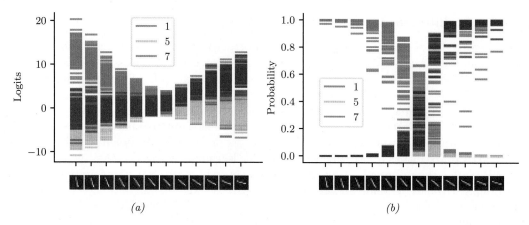

(a)   (b)

Figure 17.2: Illustration of MC dropout applied to the LeNet architecture. The inputs are some rotated images of the digit 1 from the MNIST dataset. (a) Softmax inputs (logits). (b) Softmax outputs (proabilities). We see that the inputs are classified as digit 7 for the last three images (as shown by the probabilities), even though the model has high uncertainty (as shown by the logits). Adapted from Figure 4 of [GG16]. Generated by mnist_classification_mc_dropout.ipynb

inference [GG16], this is only true under a degenerate posterior approximation, corresponding to a mixture of two delta functions, one at 0 (for dropped out nodes) and one at the MLE. This posterior will not converge to the true posterior (which is a delta function at the MLE) even as the training set size goes to infinity, since we are always dropping out hidden nodes with a constant probability p [Osb16]. Fortunately this pathology can be fixed if the noise rate is optimized [GHK17]. For more details, see e.g., [HGMG18; NHLS19; LF+21].

17.3.2   Laplace approximation

In Section 7.4.3, we introduced the Laplace approximation, which computes a Gaussian approximation to the posterior, $p(\boldsymbol{\theta}|\mathcal{D})$, centered at the MAP estimate, $\boldsymbol{\theta}^*$. The posterior prediction matrix is equal to the Hessian of the negative log joint computed at the mode. The benefits of this approach are that it is simple, and it can be used to derive a Bayesian estimate from a pretrained model. The main disadvantage is that computing the Hessian can be expensive. In addition, it may not be positive definite, since the log likelihood of DNNs is non-convex. It is therefore common to use a Gauss-newton approximation to the Hessian instead, as we explain below.

Following the notation of [Dax+21], let $\boldsymbol{f}(\boldsymbol{x}_n, \boldsymbol{\theta}) \in \mathbb{R}^C$ be the prediction function with C outputs, and $\boldsymbol{\theta} \in \mathbb{R}^P$ be the parameter vector. Let $\boldsymbol{r}(\boldsymbol{y}; \boldsymbol{f}) = \nabla_{\boldsymbol{f}} \log p(\boldsymbol{y}|\boldsymbol{f})$ be the residual[1], and $\Lambda(\boldsymbol{y}; \boldsymbol{f}) = -\nabla_{\boldsymbol{f}}^2 \log p(\boldsymbol{y}|\boldsymbol{f})$ be the per-input noise term. In addition, let $\mathbf{J} \in \mathbb{R}^{C \times P}$ be the Jacobian, $[\mathbf{J}_{\boldsymbol{\theta}}(\boldsymbol{x})]_{ci} = \frac{\partial f_c(\boldsymbol{x}, \boldsymbol{\theta})}{\partial \theta_i}$, and $\mathbf{H} \in \mathbb{R}^{C \times P \times P}$ be the Hessian, $[\mathbf{H}_{\boldsymbol{\theta}}(\boldsymbol{x})]_{cij} = \frac{\partial^2 f_c(\boldsymbol{x}, \boldsymbol{\theta})}{\partial \theta_i \partial \theta_j}$. Then the gradient and Hessian

---

1. In the Gaussian case, this term becomes $\nabla_{\boldsymbol{f}} ||\boldsymbol{y} - \boldsymbol{f}||^2 = 2||\boldsymbol{y} - \boldsymbol{f}||$, so it can be interpreted as a residual error.

of the log likelihood are given by the following [IKB21]:

$$\nabla_{\boldsymbol{\theta}} \log p(\boldsymbol{y}|\boldsymbol{f}(\boldsymbol{x}, \boldsymbol{\theta})) = \mathbf{J}_{\boldsymbol{\theta}}(\boldsymbol{x})^{\mathsf{T}} \boldsymbol{r}(\boldsymbol{y}; \boldsymbol{f}) \tag{17.14}$$

$$\nabla_{\boldsymbol{\theta}}^2 \log p(\boldsymbol{y}|\boldsymbol{f}(\boldsymbol{x}, \boldsymbol{\theta})) = \mathbf{H}_{\boldsymbol{\theta}}(\boldsymbol{x})^{\mathsf{T}} \boldsymbol{r}(\boldsymbol{y}; \boldsymbol{f}) - \mathbf{J}_{\boldsymbol{\theta}}(\boldsymbol{x})^{\mathsf{T}} \boldsymbol{\Lambda}(\boldsymbol{y}; \boldsymbol{f}) \mathbf{J}_{\boldsymbol{\theta}}(\boldsymbol{\theta}) \tag{17.15}$$

Since the network Hessian $\mathbf{H}$ is usually intractable to compute, it is usually dropped, leaving only the Jacobian term. This is called the **generalized Gauss-Newton** or **GGN** approximation [Sch02; Mar20]. The GGN approximation is guaranteed to be positive definite. By contrast, this is not true for the original Hessian in Equation (17.15), since the objective is not convex. Furthermore, computing the Jacobian term is cheaper to compute than the Hessian.

Putting it all together, for a Gaussian prior, $p(\boldsymbol{\theta}) = \mathcal{N}(\boldsymbol{\theta}|\boldsymbol{m}_0, \mathbf{S}_0)$, the Laplace approximation becomes $p(\boldsymbol{\theta}|\mathcal{D}) \approx (\mathcal{N}|\boldsymbol{\theta}^*, \boldsymbol{\Sigma}_{\text{GGN}})$, where

$$\boldsymbol{\Sigma}_{\text{GGN}}^{-1} = \sum_{n=1}^{N} \mathbf{J}_{\boldsymbol{\theta}^*}(\boldsymbol{x}_n)^{\mathsf{T}} \boldsymbol{\Lambda}(\boldsymbol{y}_n; \boldsymbol{f}_n) \mathbf{J}_{\boldsymbol{\theta}^*}(\boldsymbol{x}_n) + \mathbf{S}_0^{-1} \tag{17.16}$$

Unfortunately inverting this matrix takes $O(P^3)$ time, so for models with many parameters, further approximations are usually used. The simplest is to use a diagonal approximation, which takes $O(P)$ time and space. A more sophisticated approach is presented in [RBB18a], which leverages the **KFAC** (Kronecker factored curvature) approximation of [MG15]. This approximates the covariance of each layer using a Kronecker product.

A limitation of the Laplace approximation is that the posterior covariance is derived from the Hessian evaluated at the MAP parameters. This means Laplace forms a highly *local* approximation: even if the non-Gaussian posterior could be well-described by a Gaussian distribution, the Gaussian distribution *formed using Laplace* only captures the local characteristics of the posterior at the MAP parameters — and may therefore suffer badly from local optima, providing overly compact or diffuse representations. In addition, the curvature information is only used after the model has been estimated, and not during the model optimization process. By contrast, variational inference (Section 17.3.3) can provide more accurate approximations for comparable cost.

17.3.3 Variational inference

In fixed-form variational inference (Section 10.2), we choose a distribution for the posterior approximation $q_{\boldsymbol{\psi}}(\boldsymbol{\theta})$ and minimize $D_{\text{KL}}(q \parallel p)$, with respect to $\boldsymbol{\psi}$. We often choose a Gaussian approximate posterior, $q_{\boldsymbol{\psi}}(\boldsymbol{\theta}) = \mathcal{N}(\boldsymbol{\theta}|\boldsymbol{\mu}, \boldsymbol{\Sigma})$, which lets us use the reparameterization trick to create a low variance estimator of the gradient of the ELBO (see Section 10.2.1). Despite the use of a Gaussian, the parameters that minimize the KL objective are often different what we would find with the Laplace approximation (Section 17.3.2).

Variational methods for neural networks date back to at least Hinton and Camp [HC93]. In deep learning, [Gra11] revisited variational methods, using a Gaussian approximation with a diagonal covariance matrix. This approximates the distribution of every parameter in the model by a univariate Gaussian, where the mean is the point estimate, and the variance captures the uncertainty, as shown in Figure 17.3. This approach was improved further in [Blu+15], who used the reparameterization trick to compute lower variance estimates of the ELBO; they called their method **Bayes by backprop** (**BBB**). This is essentially identical to the SVI algorithm in Algorithm 10.2, except the likelihood becomes $p(\boldsymbol{y}_n|\boldsymbol{x}_n, \boldsymbol{\theta})$ from the DNN, and the prior $p_{\boldsymbol{\xi}}(\boldsymbol{\theta})$ and variational posterior $q_{\boldsymbol{\psi}}(\boldsymbol{\theta})$ are Gaussians.

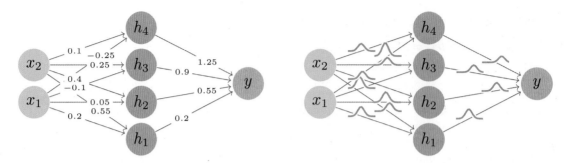

Figure 17.3: Illustration of an MLP with (left) a point estimate for each weight, (right) a marginal distribution for each weight, corresponding to a fully factored posterior approximation.

Many extensions of the BBB have been proposed. In [KSW15], they propise the **local reparameterization trick**, that samples the activations $a = \mathbf{W}z$ at each layer, instead of the weights $\mathbf{W}$, which results in a lower variance estimate of the ELBO gradient. In [Osa+19a], they used the **variational online Gauss-Newton (VOGN)** method of [Kha+18], for improved scalability. VOGN is a noisy version of natural gradient descent, where the extra noise emulates the effect of variational inference. In [Mis+18], they replaced the diagonal approximation with a low-rank plus diagonal approximation, and used VOGN for fitting. In [Tra+20b], they use a rank-one plus diagonal approximation known as **NAGVAC** (see Section 10.2.1.3). In this case, there are only 3 times as many parameters as when computing a point estimate (for the variational mean, variance, and rank-one vector), making the approach very scalable. In addition, in this case it is possible to analytically compute the natural gradient, which speeds up model fitting (see Section 6.4). Many other variational methods have also been proposed (see e.g., [LW16; Zha+18; Wu+19a; HHK19]). See also Section 17.5.4 for a discussion of online VI for DNNs.

17.3.4 Expectation propagation

Expectation propagation (EP) is similar to variational inference, except it locally optimizes $D_{\mathrm{KL}}(p \parallel q)$ instead of $D_{\mathrm{KL}}(q \parallel p)$, where p is the exact posterior and q is the approximate posterior. For details, see Section 10.7.

A special case of EP is the assumed density filtering (ADF) algorithm of Section 8.6, which is equivalent to the first pass of ADF. In Section 8.6.3 we show how to apply ADF to online logistic regression. In [HLA15a], they extend ADF to the case of BNNs; they called their method probabilistic backpropagation or **PBP**. They approximate every parameter in the model by a Gaussian factor, as in Figure 17.3. See Section 17.5.3 for the details.

17.3.5 Last layer methods

A very simple approximation to the posterior is to only "be Bayesian" about the weights in the final layer, and to use MAP estimates for all the other parameters. This is called the **neural-linear** approximation [RTS18]. In more detail, let $z = f(x, \theta)$ be the predicted outputs (e.g., logits) of the model before any optional final nonlinearity. We assume this has the form $z = w_L^\mathsf{T}\phi(x; \theta)$, where $\phi(\boldsymbol{x})$ are the features extracted by the first $L-1$ layers. This gives us a Bayesian GLM. We can use standard techniques, such as the Laplace approximation (Section 15.3.5), to compute $p(\boldsymbol{w}_L|\mathcal{D}) = \mathcal{N}(\boldsymbol{\mu}_L, \boldsymbol{\Sigma}_L)$, given $\phi()$. To estimate the parameters of the feature extractor, we can optimize the log-likelihood in the usual way. Given the posterior over the last layer weights, we can compute the posterior predictive distribution over the logits using

$$p(\boldsymbol{z}|\boldsymbol{x}, \mathcal{D}) = \mathcal{N}(\boldsymbol{z}|\boldsymbol{\mu}_L\phi(\boldsymbol{x}), \phi(\boldsymbol{x})\boldsymbol{\Sigma}_L\phi(\boldsymbol{x})^\mathsf{T}) \tag{17.17}$$

This can be passed through the final softmax layer to compute $p(\boldsymbol{y}|\boldsymbol{x}, \mathcal{D})$ as described in Section 15.3.6.

In [KHH20] they show this can reduce overconfidence in predictions for inputs that are far from the training data. However, this approach ignores uncertainty introduced by the earlier feature extraction layers, where most of the parameters reside. We discuss a solution to this in Section 17.3.6.

17.3.6 SNGP

It is possible to combine DNNs with Gaussian process (GP) models (Chapter 18), by using the DNN to act as a feature extractor, which is then fed into the kernel in the final layer. This is called "deep kernel learning" (see Section 18.6.6).

One problem with this is that the feature extractor may lose information which is not needed for classification accuracy, but which is needed for robust performance on out-of-distribution inputs (see Section 17.4.6.2). The basic problem is that, in a classification problem, there is no reduction in training accuracy (log likelihood) if points which are far away are projected close together, as long as they are on the correct side of the decision boundary. Thus the distances between two inputs can be erased by the feature extraction layers, so that OOD inputs appear to the final layer to be close to the training set.

One solution to this is to use the **SNGP** (spectrally normalized Gaussian process) method of [Liu+20d; Liu+22a]. This constrains the feature extraction layers to be "distance preserving", so that two inputs that are far apart in input space remain far apart after many layers of feature extraction, by using spectral normalization of the weights to bound the Lipschitz constant of the feature extractor. The overall approach ensures that information that is relevant for computing the confidence of a prediction, but which might be irrelevant to computing the label of a prediction, is not lost. This can help performance in tasks such as out-of-distribution detection (Section 17.4.6.2).

17.3.7 MCMC methods

Some of the earliest work on inference for BNNs was done by Radford Neal, who proposed to use Hamiltonian Monte Carlo (Section 12.5) to approximate the posterior [Nea96]. This is generally considered the gold standard method, since it does not make strong assumptions about the form of the posterior. For more recent work on scaling up HMC for BNNs, see e.g., [Izm+21b; CJ21].

We give a simple example of vanilla HMC in Figure 17.4, where we fit a shallow MLP to a small 2d binary dataset. We plot the mean and standard deviation of the posterior predictive distribution, $p(y=1|\boldsymbol{x};\mathcal{D})$. We see that the uncertainty is higher as we move away from the training data. (Compare to Bayesian logistic regression in 1d in Figure 15.8a.)

However, a significant limitation of standard MCMC procedures, including HMC, is that they require access to the full training set at each step. Stochastic gradient MCMC methods, such as

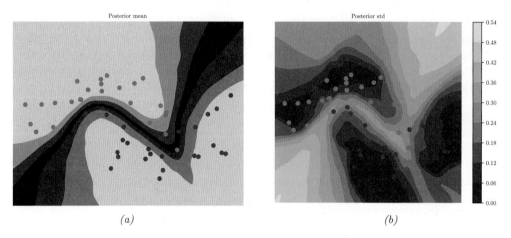

(a)   (b)

Figure 17.4: Illustration of an MLP fit to the two-moons dataset using HMC. (a) Posterior mean. (b) Posterior standard derivation. The uncertainty increases as we move away from the training data. Generated by bnn_mlp_2d_hmc.ipynb.

SGLD, operate instead using mini-batches of data, offering a scalable alternative, as we discuss in Section 12.7.1. For an example of SGLD applied to an MLP, see Section 19.3.3.1.

17.3.8   Methods based on the SGD trajectory

In [MHB17; SL18; CS18], it was shown that, under some assumptions, the iterates produced by stochastic gradient descent (SGD), when run at a fixed learning rate, correspond to samples from a Gaussian approximation to the posterior centered at a local mode, $p(\boldsymbol{\theta}|\mathcal{D}) \approx \mathcal{N}(\boldsymbol{\theta}|\hat{\boldsymbol{\theta}}, \boldsymbol{\Sigma})$. We can therefore use SGD to generate approximate posterior samples. This is similar to SG-MCMC methods, except we do not add explicit gradient noise, and the learning rate is held constant.

In [Izm+18], they noted that these SGD solutions (with fixed learning rate) surround the periphery of points of good generalization, as shown in Figure 17.5. This is in part because SGD does not converge to a local optimum unless the learning rate is annealed to 0. They therefore proposed to compute the average of several SGD samples, each one collected after a certain interval (e.g., one epoch of training), to get $\overline{\boldsymbol{\theta}} = \frac{1}{S} \sum_{s=1}^{S} \boldsymbol{\theta}_s$. They call this **stochastic weight averaging (SWA)**. They showed that the resulting point tends to correspond to a broader local minimum than the SGD solutions (see Figure 17.10), resulting in better generalization performance.

The SWA approach is related to Polyak-Ruppert averaging, which is often used in convex optimization. The difference is that Polyak-Ruppert typically assumes the learning rate decays to zero, and uses an exponential moving average (EMA) of iterates, rather than an equal average; Polyak-Ruppert averaging is mainly used to reduce variance in the SGD estimate, rather than as a method to find points of better generalization.

The SWA approach is also related to **snapshot ensembles** [Hua+17a], and **fast geometric ensembles** [Gar+18c]; these methods save the parameters $\boldsymbol{\theta}_s$ after increasing and decreasing the learning rate multiple times in a cyclical fashion, and then computing the *average of the predictions* using $p(\boldsymbol{y}|\boldsymbol{x}, \mathcal{D}) \approx \frac{1}{S} \sum_{s=1}^{S} p(\boldsymbol{y}|\boldsymbol{x}, \boldsymbol{\theta}_s)$, rather than computing the *average of the parameters* and

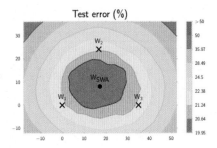

Figure 17.5: *Illustration of stochastic weight averaging (SWA). The three crosses represent different SGD solutions. The star in the middle is the average of these parameter values. From Figure 1 of [Izm+18]. Used with kind permission of Andrew Wilson.*

predicting with a single model (which is faster). Moreover, by finding a flat region, representing a "center or mass" in the posterior, SWA can be seen as approximating the Bayesian model average in Equation 17.1 with a single model.

In [Mad+19], they proposed to fit a Gaussian distribution to the set of samples produced by SGD near a local mode. They use the SWA solution as the mean of the Gaussian. For the covariance matrix, they use a low-rank plus diagonal approximation of the form $p(\boldsymbol{\theta}|\mathcal{D}) = \mathcal{N}(\boldsymbol{\theta}|\overline{\boldsymbol{\theta}}, \boldsymbol{\Sigma})$, where $\boldsymbol{\Sigma} = (\boldsymbol{\Sigma}_{\text{diag}} + \boldsymbol{\Sigma}_{\text{lr}})/2$, $\boldsymbol{\Sigma}_{\text{diag}} = \text{diag}(\overline{\boldsymbol{\theta}^2} - (\overline{\boldsymbol{\theta}})^2)$, $\overline{\boldsymbol{\theta}} = \frac{1}{S}\sum_{s=1}^{S}\boldsymbol{\theta}_s$, $\overline{\boldsymbol{\theta}^2} = \frac{1}{S}\sum_{s=1}^{S}\boldsymbol{\theta}_s^2$, and $\boldsymbol{\Sigma}_{\text{lr}} = \frac{1}{S}\boldsymbol{\Delta}\boldsymbol{\Delta}^{\mathsf{T}}$ is the sample covariance matrix of the last K samples of $\boldsymbol{\Delta}_i = (\boldsymbol{\theta}_i - \overline{\boldsymbol{\theta}}_i)$, where $\overline{\boldsymbol{\theta}}_i$ is the running average of the parameters from the first i samples. They call this method **SWAG**, which stands for "stochastic weight averaging with Gaussian posterior". This can be used to generate an arbitrary number of posterior samples at prediction time. They show that SWAG scales to large residual networks with millions of parameters, and large datasets such as ImageNet, with improved accuracy and calibration over conventional SGD training, and no additional training overhead.

17.3.9 Deep ensembles

Many conventional approximate inference methods focus on approximating the posterior $p(\boldsymbol{\theta}|\mathcal{D})$ in a local neighborhood around one of the posterior modes. While this is often not a major limitation in classical machine learning, modern deep neural networks have highly multi-modal posteriors, with parameters in different modes giving rise to very different functions. On the other hand, the functions in a neighborhood of a single mode may make fairly similar predictions. So using such a local approximation to compute the posterior predictive will underestimate uncertainty and generalize more poorly.

A simple alternative method is to train multiple models, and then to approximate the posterior using an equally weighted mixture of delta functions,

$$p(\boldsymbol{\theta}|\mathcal{D}) \approx \frac{1}{M}\sum_{m=1}^{M}\delta(\boldsymbol{\theta} - \hat{\boldsymbol{\theta}}_m) \tag{17.18}$$

where M is the number of models, and $\hat{\boldsymbol{\theta}}_m$ is the MAP estimate for model m. See Figure 17.6 for a

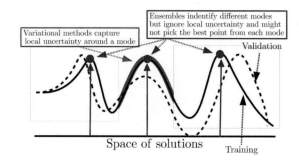

Figure 17.6: Cartoon illustration of the NLL as it varies across the parameter space. Subspace methods (red) model the local neighborhood around a local mode, whereas ensemble methods (blue) approximate the posterior using a set of distinct modes. From Figure 1 of [FHL19]. Used with kind permission of Balaji Lakshminarayanan.

sketch. This approach is called **deep ensembles** [LPB17; FHL19].

The models can differ in terms of their random seed used for initialization [LPB17], or hyperparameters [Wen+20c], or architecture [Zai+20], or all of the above. In addition, [DF21; TB22] discusses how to add an explicit repulsive term to ensure functional diversity between the ensemble members. This way, each member corresponds to a distinct prediction function. Combining these is more effective than combining multiple samples from the same basin of attraction, especially in the presence of dataset shift [Ova+19].

17.3.9.1   Multi-SWAG

We can further improve on this approach by fitting a Gaussian to each local mode using the SWAG method from Section 17.3.8 to get a mixture of Gaussians approximation:

$$p(\boldsymbol{\theta}|\mathcal{D}) \approx \frac{1}{M} \sum_{m=1}^{M} \mathcal{N}(\boldsymbol{\theta}|\hat{\boldsymbol{\theta}}_m, \boldsymbol{\Sigma}_m) \tag{17.19}$$

This approach is known as **MultiSWAG** [WI20]. MultiSWAG performs a Bayesian model average both across multiple basins of attraction, like deep ensembles, but also within each basin, and provides an easy way to generate an arbitrary number of posterior samples, $S > M$, in an any-time fashion.

17.3.9.2   Deep ensembles with random priors

The standard way to fit each member of a deep ensemble is to initialize them each with a different random set of parameters, but them to train them all on the same data. Unfortunately this can result in the predictions from each ensemble member being rather similar, which reduces the benefit of the approach. One way to increase diversity is to train each member on a different subset of the data; this is called **bootstrap sampling**. Another approach is to define the i'th ensemble member $g_i(\boldsymbol{x})$ to be the addition of a trainable model $t_i(\boldsymbol{x})$ and a fixed, but random, **prior network**, $p_i(\boldsymbol{x})$, to get

$$g_i(\boldsymbol{x}; \boldsymbol{\theta}_i) = t_i(\boldsymbol{x}; \boldsymbol{\theta}_i) + \beta p_i(\boldsymbol{x}) \tag{17.20}$$

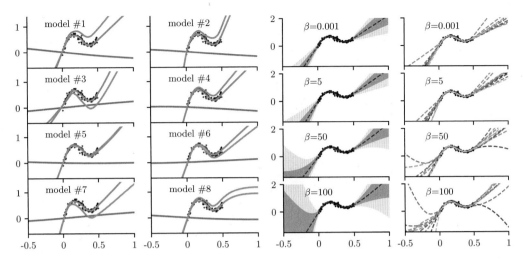

Figure 17.7: Deep ensemble with random priors. (a) Individual predictions from each member. Blue is the fixed random prior function, orange is the trainable function, green is the combination of the two. (b) Overall prediction from the ensemble, for increasingly large values of β. On the left we show (in red) the posterior mean and pointwise standard deviation, and on the right we show samples from the posterior. As β increases, we trust the random priors more, and pay less attention to the data, thus getting a more diffuse posterior. Generated by randomized_priors.ipynb.

where $\beta \geq 0$ controls the amount of data-independent variation between the members. The trainable network learns to model the residual error between the true output and the value predicted by the prior. This is called a **random prior deep ensemble** [OAC18]. See Figure 17.7 for an illustration.

17.3.9.3 Deep ensembles as approximate Bayesian inference

The posterior predictive distribution for a Bayesian neural network cannot be expressed in closed form. Therefore all Bayesian inference approaches in deep learning are approximate. In this context, all approximate inference procedures fall onto a spectrum, representing how closely they approximate the true posterior predictive distribution. Deep ensembles can provide better approximations to a Bayesian model average than a single basin marginalization approach, because point masses from different basins of attraction represent greater functional diversity than standard Bayesian approaches which sample within a single basin.

17.3.9.4 Deep ensembles vs classical ensembles

Note that deep ensembles are slightly different from classical ensemble methods (see e.g., [Die00]), such as bagging and random forests, which obtain diversity of their predictors by training them on different subsets of the data (created using bootstrap resampling), or on different features. This data perturbation is necessary to get diversity when the base learner is a convex problem (such as a linear model, or shallow decision tree). In the deep ensemble approach, every model is trained on the same data, and the same input features. The diversity arises due to different starting parameters, different

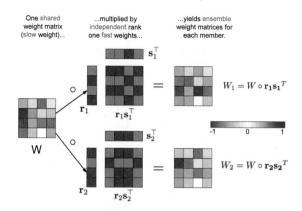

Figure 17.8: Illustration of batch ensemble with 2 ensemble members. From Figure 2 of [WTB20]. Used with kind permission of Paul Vicol.

random seeds, and SGD noise, which induces different solutions due to the nonconvex loss. It is also possible to explicitly enforce diversity of the ensemble members, which can provably improve performance [TB22].

17.3.9.5   Deep ensembles vs mixtures of experts and stacking

If we use weighted combinations of the models, $p(\boldsymbol{\theta}|\mathcal{D}) = \sum_{m=1}^{M} p(m|\mathcal{D})p(\boldsymbol{\theta}|m, \mathcal{D})$, where $p(m|\mathcal{D})$ is the marginal likelihood of model m, then, in the large sample limit, this mixture will concentrate on the MAP model, so only one component will be selected. By contrast, in deep ensembles, we always use M equally weighted models. Thus we see that Bayes model averaging is not the same as model ensembling [Min00b]. Indeed, ensembling can enlarge the expressive power of the posterior predictive distribution compared to BMA [OCM21].

We can also make the mixing weights be conditional on the inputs:

$$p(y|\boldsymbol{x}, \mathcal{D}) = \sum_{m} w_m(\boldsymbol{x})p(y|\boldsymbol{x}, \boldsymbol{\theta}_m) \tag{17.21}$$

If we constrain the weights to be non-zero and sum to one, this is called a **mixture of experts**. However, if we allow a general positive weighted combination, the approach is called **stacking** [Wol92; Bre96; Yao+18a; CAII20]. In stacking, the weights $w_m(\boldsymbol{x})$ are usually estimated on hold-out data, to make the method more robust to model misspecification.

17.3.9.6   Batch ensemble

Deep ensembles require M times more memory and time than a single model. One way to reduce the memory cost is to share most of the parameters — which we call **slow weights**, $\mathbf{W}$ — and then let each ensemble member m estimate its own local perturbation, which we will call **fast weights**, $\mathbf{F}_m$. We then define $\mathbf{W}_m = \mathbf{W} \odot \mathbf{F}_m$. For efficiency, we can define $\mathbf{F}_m$ to be a rank-one matrix, $\mathbf{F}_m = \boldsymbol{s}_m \boldsymbol{r}_m^\mathsf{T}$, as illustrated in Figure 17.8. This is called **batch ensemble** [WTB20].

It is clear that the memory overhead is very small compared to naive ensembles, since we just need to store $2M$ vectors (s_m^l and r_m^l) for every layer l, which is negligible compared to the quadratic cost of storing the shared weight matrix $\mathbf{W}^l$.

In addition to memory savings, batch ensemble can reduce the inference time by a constant factor by leveraging within-device parallelism. To see this, consider the output of one layer using ensemble m on example n:

$$y_n^m = \varphi\left(\mathbf{W}_m^\mathsf{T} x_n\right) = \varphi\left((\mathbf{W} \odot s_m r_m^\mathsf{T})^\mathsf{T} x_n\right) = \varphi\left((\mathbf{W}^\mathsf{T}(x_n \odot s_m) \odot r_m\right) \tag{17.22}$$

We can vectorize this for a minibatch of inputs $\mathbf{X}$ by replicating r_m and s_m along the B rows in the batch to form matrices, giving

$$\mathbf{Y}_m = \varphi\left(((\mathbf{X} \odot \mathbf{S}_m)\mathbf{W}) \odot \mathbf{R}_m\right) \tag{17.23}$$

This applies the same ensemble parameters m to every example in the minibatch of size B. To achieve diversity during training, we can divide the minibatch into M sub-batches, and use sub-batch m to train $\mathbf{W}_m$. (Note that this reduces the batch size for training each ensemble to B/M.) At test time, when we want to average over M models, we can replicate each input M times, leading to a batch size of BM.

In [WTB20], they show that this method outperforms MC dropout at negligible extra memory cost. However, the best combination was to combine batch ensemble with MC dropout; in some cases, this approached the performance of naive ensembles.

17.3.10 Approximating the posterior predictive distribution

Once we have approximated the parameter posterior, $q(\boldsymbol{\theta}) \approx p(\boldsymbol{\theta}|\mathcal{D})$, we can use it to approximate the posterior predictive distribution:

$$p(\boldsymbol{y}|\boldsymbol{x}, \mathcal{D}) = \int q(\boldsymbol{\theta})p(\boldsymbol{y}|\boldsymbol{x}, \boldsymbol{\theta})d\boldsymbol{\theta} \tag{17.24}$$

We often approximate this integral using Monte Carlo:

$$p(\boldsymbol{y}|\boldsymbol{x}, \mathcal{D}) \approx \frac{1}{S}\sum_{s=1}^{S} p(\boldsymbol{y}|\boldsymbol{f}(\boldsymbol{x}, \boldsymbol{\theta}^s)) \tag{17.25}$$

where $\boldsymbol{\theta}^s \sim q(\boldsymbol{\theta}|\mathcal{D})$. We discuss some extensions of this approach below.

17.3.10.1 A linearized approximation

In [IKB21] they point out that samples from an approximate posterior, $q(\boldsymbol{\theta})$, can result in bad predictions when plugged into the model if the posterior puts probability density "in the wrong places". This is because $\boldsymbol{f}(\boldsymbol{x};\boldsymbol{\theta})$ is a highly nonlinear function of $\boldsymbol{\theta}$ that might behave quite differently when $\boldsymbol{\theta}$ is far from the MAP estimate on which $q(\boldsymbol{\theta})$ is centered. To avoid this problem, they propose to replace $\boldsymbol{f}(\boldsymbol{x};\boldsymbol{\theta})$ with a linear approximation centered at the MAP estimate $\boldsymbol{\theta}^*$:

$$\boldsymbol{f}_{\text{lin}}^{\boldsymbol{\theta}^*}(\boldsymbol{x}, \boldsymbol{\theta}) = \boldsymbol{f}(\boldsymbol{x}, \boldsymbol{\theta}^*) + \mathbf{J}(\boldsymbol{x})(\boldsymbol{\theta} - \boldsymbol{\theta}^*) \tag{17.26}$$

where $\mathbf{J}_{\boldsymbol{\theta}^*}(\boldsymbol{x}) = \frac{\partial f(\boldsymbol{x};\boldsymbol{\theta})}{\partial \boldsymbol{\theta}}|_{\boldsymbol{\theta}^*}$ is the $P \times C$ Jacobian matrix, where P is the number of parameters, and C is the number of outputs. Such a model is well behaved around $\boldsymbol{\theta}^*$, and so the approximation

$$p(\boldsymbol{y}|\boldsymbol{x}, \mathcal{D}) \approx \frac{1}{S} \sum_{s=1}^{S} p(\boldsymbol{y}|\boldsymbol{f}_{\text{lin}}^{\boldsymbol{\theta}^*}(\boldsymbol{x}, \boldsymbol{\theta}^s)) \tag{17.27}$$

often works better than Equation (17.25).

Note that $\boldsymbol{z} = \boldsymbol{f}_{\text{lin}}^{\boldsymbol{\theta}^*}(\boldsymbol{x}, \boldsymbol{\theta})$ is a linear function of the parameters $\boldsymbol{\theta}$, but a nonlinear function of the inputs $\boldsymbol{x}$. Thus $p(\boldsymbol{y}|\boldsymbol{f}_{\text{lin}}^{\boldsymbol{\theta}^*}(\boldsymbol{x}, \boldsymbol{\theta}))$ is a generalized linear model (Section 15.1), so [IKB21] call this approximation the **GLM predictive distribution**.

If we have a Gaussian approximation to the parameter, $p(\boldsymbol{\theta}|\mathcal{D}) \approx \mathcal{N}(\boldsymbol{\theta}|\boldsymbol{\mu}, \boldsymbol{\Sigma})$, then we can "push this through" the linear approximation to get

$$p(\boldsymbol{z}|\boldsymbol{x}, \mathcal{D}) \approx \mathcal{N}(\boldsymbol{z}|\boldsymbol{f}(\boldsymbol{x}, \boldsymbol{\mu}), \mathbf{J}(\boldsymbol{x})^\mathsf{T} \boldsymbol{\Sigma} \mathbf{J}(\boldsymbol{x})) \tag{17.28}$$

where $\boldsymbol{z}$ are the logits. (Alternatively, we can use the last layer method of Equation (17.17) to get a Gaussian approximation to $p(\boldsymbol{z}|\boldsymbol{x}, \mathcal{D})$.) If we approximate the final softmax layer with a probit function, we can analytically pass this Gaussian through the final softmax layer to deterministically compute the predictive probabilities $p(y = c|\boldsymbol{x}, \mathcal{D})$, using Equation (15.150). Alternatively, we can use the Laplace bridge approximation in Section 17.3.10.2.

17.3.10.2 The Laplace bridge approximation

Just using a point estimate of the probability of each class label, $p_c = p(y = c|\boldsymbol{x}, \mathcal{D})$, can be unreliable, since it does not convey any sense of uncertainty in the probability value, even though we may have taken the uncertainty of the parameters into account (e.g., using the methods of Section 17.3.10.1). An alternative is to represent the output over labels as a Dirichlet distribution, $\text{Dir}(\boldsymbol{\pi}|\boldsymbol{\alpha})$, rather than a categorical distribution, $\text{Cat}(\boldsymbol{y}|\boldsymbol{p})$, where $\boldsymbol{p} = \text{softmax}(\boldsymbol{z})$. This is more appropriate if we view each datapoint as being annotated with a "soft" vector of probabilities (e.g., representing consensus votes from human raters), rather than a one-hot encoding with a single "ground truth" value. This can be useful for settings where the true label is ambiguous (see e.g., [Bey+20; Dum+18]).

We can either train the model to predict the Dirichlet parameters directly (as in the **prior network** approach of [MG18]), or we can train the model to predict softmax outputs in the usual way, and then derive the Dirichlet parameters from a Gaussian approximation to the posterior. The latter approach is known as the **Laplace bridge** [HKH22], and has the advantage that it can be used as a post-processing method. It works as follows. First we compute a Gaussian approximation to the logits, $p(\boldsymbol{z}|\boldsymbol{x}, \mathcal{D}) = \mathcal{N}(\boldsymbol{z}|\boldsymbol{m}, \mathbf{V})$ using Equation (17.28) or Equation (17.17). Then we compute

$$\alpha_i = \frac{1}{V_{ii}} \left(1 - \frac{2}{C} + \frac{\exp(m_i)}{C^2} \sum_{j=1}^{C} \exp(-m_j) \right) \tag{17.29}$$

where C is the number of classes. We can then derive the probabilities of each class label using $p_c = \mathbb{E}[\pi_c] = \alpha_c/\alpha_0$, where $\alpha_0 = \sum_{c=1}^{C} \alpha_c$.

Note that the derivation of the above result assumes that the Gaussian terms sum to zero, since the Gaussian has one less degree of freedom compared to the Dirichlet. To ensure this, it is necessary

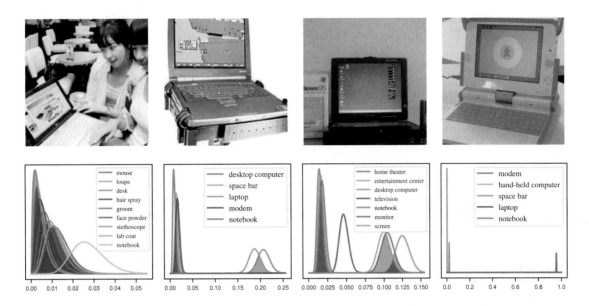

Figure 17.9: Illustration of uncertainty about individual labels in an image classification problem. Top row: images from the "laptop" class of ImageNet. Bottom row: beta marginals for the top-k predtions for the respective image. First column: high uncertainty about all the labels. Second column: "notebook" and "laptop" have high confidence. Third column: "desktop", "screen" and "monitor" have high confidence. Fourth column: only "laptop" has high confidence. (Compare to Figure 14.4.) From Figure 6 of [HKH22]. Used with kind permission of Philipp Hennig.

to first project the Gaussian distribution onto this constraint surface, yielding

$$p(z|x, \mathcal{D}) = \mathcal{N}\left(z|m - \frac{V11^{\mathsf{T}}m}{1^{\mathsf{T}}V_*1}, V - \frac{V11^{\mathsf{T}}V}{1^{\mathsf{T}}V1}\right) = \mathcal{N}(z|m', V') \tag{17.30}$$

where $\mathbf{1}$ is the ones vector of size C. To avoid potential problems where $\boldsymbol{\alpha}$ is sparse, [HKH22] propose to also scale the posterior (after the zero-sum constraint) by using $m'' = m'/\sqrt{c}$ and $V'' = V'/c$, where $c = (\sum_{ii} V'_{ii})/\sqrt{C/2}$.

One useful property of the Laplace bridge approximation, compared to the probit approximation, is that we can easily compute a marginal distribution over the probablility of each label being present. This is because the marginals of a Dirichlet are beta distributions. We can use this to adaptively compute a top-k prediction set; this is similar in spirit to conformal prediction (Section 14.3.1), but is Bayesian, in the sense that it represents per-instance uncertainty. The method works as follows. First we sort the class labels in decreasing order of expected probability, to get $\tilde{\boldsymbol{\alpha}}$; next we compute the marginal distribution over the probability for the top label,

$$p(\pi_1|x, \mathcal{D}) = \text{Beta}(\tilde{\alpha}_1, \alpha_0 - \tilde{\alpha}_1) \tag{17.31}$$

where $\alpha_0 = \sum_c \alpha_c$. We then compute the marginal distributions for the other labels in a similar way, and return all labels that have significant overlap with the top label. As we see from the examples in Figure 17.9, this approach can return variable-sized outputs, reflecting uncertainty in a natural way.

17.3.10.3   Distillation

The MC approximation to the posterior predictive is S times slower than a standard, deterministic plug-in approximation. One way to speed this up is to use **distillation** to approximate the semi-parametric "teacher" model p_t from Equation (17.25) by a parametric "student" model p_s by minimizing $\mathbb{E}\left[D_{\mathrm{KL}}\left(p_t(\boldsymbol{y}|\boldsymbol{x}) \parallel p_s(\boldsymbol{y}|\boldsymbol{x})\right)\right]$ wrt p_s. This approach was first proposed in [HVD14], who called the technique "**dark knowledge**", because the teacher has "hidden" information in its predictive probabilities (logits) than is not apparent in the raw one-hot labels.

In [Kor+15], this idea was used to distill the predictions from a teacher whose parameter posterior was computed using HMC; this is called "**Bayesian dark knowledge**". A similar idea was used in [BPK16; GBP18], who distilled the predictive distribution derived from MC dropout (Section 17.3.1).

Since the parametric student is typically less flexible than the semi-parametric teacher, it may be overconfident, and lack diversity in its predictions. To avoid this overconfidence, it is safer to make the student be a mixture distribution [SG05; Tra+20a].

17.3.11   Tempered and cold posteriors

When working with BNNs for classification problems, the likelihood is usually taken to be

$$p(y|\boldsymbol{x}, \boldsymbol{\theta}) = \mathrm{Cat}(y|\mathrm{softmax}(f(\boldsymbol{x}; \boldsymbol{\theta}))) \tag{17.32}$$

where $f(\boldsymbol{x}; \boldsymbol{\theta}) \in \mathbb{R}^C$ returns the logits over the C class labels. This is the same as in multinomial logistic regression (Section 15.3.2); the only difference is that f is a nonlinear function of $\boldsymbol{\theta}$.

However, in practice, it is often found (see e.g., [Zha+18; Wen+20b; LST21; Noc+21]) that BNNs give better predictive accuracy if the likelihood function is scaled by some power α. That is, instead of targeting the posterior $p(\boldsymbol{\theta}|\mathcal{D}) \propto p(\boldsymbol{y}|\boldsymbol{x}, \boldsymbol{\theta})p(\boldsymbol{\theta})$, these methods target the **tempered posterior**, $p_{\mathrm{tempered}}(\boldsymbol{\theta}|\mathcal{D}) \propto p(\boldsymbol{y}|\mathbf{X}, \boldsymbol{\theta})^\alpha p(\boldsymbol{\theta})$. In log space, we have

$$\log p_{\mathrm{tempered}}(\boldsymbol{\theta}|\mathcal{D}) = \alpha \log p(\boldsymbol{y}|\mathbf{X}, \boldsymbol{\theta}) + \log p(\boldsymbol{\theta}) + \mathrm{const} \tag{17.33}$$

This is also called an α-**posterior** or **power posterior** [Med+21].

Another common method is to target the **cold posterior**, $p_{\mathrm{cold}}(\boldsymbol{\theta}|\mathcal{D}) \propto p(\boldsymbol{\theta}|\mathbf{X}, \boldsymbol{y})^{1/T}$, or, in log space,

$$\log p_{\mathrm{cold}}(\boldsymbol{\theta}|\mathcal{D}) = \frac{1}{T} \log p(\boldsymbol{y}|\mathbf{X}, \boldsymbol{\theta}) + \frac{1}{T} \log p(\boldsymbol{\theta}) + \mathrm{const} \tag{17.34}$$

If $T < 1$, we say that the posterior is "cold". Note that, in the case of a Gaussian prior, using the cold prior is the same as using the tempered prior with a different hyperparameter, since

$$\frac{1}{T} \log \mathcal{N}(\boldsymbol{\theta}|0, \sigma_{\mathrm{cold}}^2 \mathbf{I}) = -\frac{1}{2T\sigma_{\mathrm{cold}}^2} \sum_i \theta_i^2 + \mathrm{const} = \mathcal{N}(\boldsymbol{\theta}|0, \sigma_{\mathrm{tempered}}^2 \mathbf{I}) + \mathrm{const} \tag{17.35}$$

where $\sigma_{\mathrm{tempered}}^2 = T\sigma_{\mathrm{cold}}^2$. Thus both methods are effectively the same, and just reweight the likelihood.

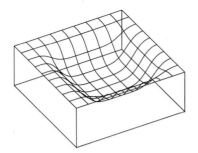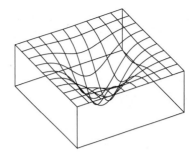

Figure 17.10: Flat vs sharp minima. From Figures 1 and 2 of [HS97]. Used with kind permission of Jürgen Schmidhuber.

Cold posteriors in Bayesian neural network classifiers are a consequence of underrepresenting aleatoric (label) uncertainty, as shown by [Kap+22]. On benchmarks such as CIFAR-100, we should have essentially no uncertainty about the labels of the training images, yet Bayesian classifiers with softmax likelihoods have very high uncertainty for these points. Moreover, [Izm+21b] showed that the cold posterior effect in all the examples of [Wen+20b] when data augmentation is removed. [Kap+22] show that with the SGLD inference in [Wen+20b], data augmentation has the effect of raising the likelihood to a power $1/K$ for minibatches of size K. Cold posteriors exactly counteract this effect, more honestly representing our beliefs about aleatoric uncertainty, by sharpening the likelihood. However, tempering is not required, and [Kap+22] show that by using a Dirichlet observation model to explicitly represent (lack of) label noise, there is no cold posterior effect, even with data augmentation. The curation hypotheses of [Ait21] can be considered a special case of the above explanation, where curation has the effect of increasing our confidence about training labels.

In Section 14.1.3, we discuss generalized variational inference, which gives a general framework for understanding whether and how the likelihood or prior could benefit from tempering. Tempering is particularly useful if (as is usually the case) the model is misspecified [KJD21].

17.4 Generalization in Bayesian deep learning

In this section, we discuss why "being Bayesian" can improve predictive accuracy and generalization performance.

17.4.1 Sharp vs flat minima

Some optimization methods (in particular, second-order batch methods) are able to find "needles in haystacks", corresponding to narrow but deep "holes" in the loss landscape, corresponding to parameter settings with very low loss. These are known as **sharp minima**, see Figure 17.10(right). From the point of view of minimizing the empirical loss, the optimizer has done a good job. However, such solutions generally correspond to a model that has overfit the data. It is better to find points that correspond to **flat minima**, as shown in Figure 17.10(left); such solutions are more robust and generalize better. To see why, note that flat minima correspond to regions in parameter space where there is a lot of posterior uncertainty, and hence samples from this region are less able to precisely memorize irrelevant details about the training set [AS17]. Put another way, the description length for sharp minima is large, meaning you need to use many bits of precision to specify the exact location in parameter space to avoid incurring large loss, whereas the description length for flat minima is less, resulting in better generalization [Mac03].

SGD often finds such flat minima by virtue of the addition of noise, which prevents it from "entering" narrow regions of the loss landscape (see Section 12.5.7). In addition, in higher dimensional spaces, flat regions occupy a much greater volume, and are thus much more easily discoverable by optimization procedures. More precisely, the analysis in [SL18] shows that the probability of entering any given basin of attraction $\mathcal{A}$ around a minimum is given by $p_{SGD}(\boldsymbol{\theta} \in \mathcal{A}) \propto \int_{\mathcal{A}} e^{-\mathcal{L}(\boldsymbol{\theta})} d\boldsymbol{\theta}$. Note that this is integrating over the volume of space corresponding to $\mathcal{A}$, and hence is proportional to the model evidence (marginal likelihood) for that region, as explained in Section 3.8.1. Since the evidence is parameterization invariant (since we marginalize out the parameters), this means that SGD will avoid regions that have low evidence (corresponding to sharp minima) regardless of how we parameterize the model (contrary to the claims in [Din+17]).

In fact, several papers have shown that we can view SGD as approximately sampling from the Bayesian posterior (see Section 17.3.8). The SWA method (Section 17.3.8) can be seen as finding a center of mass in the posterior based on these SGD samples, finding solutions that generalize better than picking a single SGD point.

If we must use a single solution, a flat one will help us better approximate the Bayesian model average in the integral of Equation (17.1). However, by attempting to perform a more complete Bayesian model average, we will select for flatness without having to deal with the messiness of having to worry about flatness definitions, or the effects of reparameterization, or unknown implicit regularization, as the model average will automatically weight regions with the greatest volume.

17.4.2 Mode connectivity and the loss landscape

In DNNs there are often many low-loss solutions, which provide complementary explanations of the data. Moreover, in [Gar+18c] they showed that two independently trained SGD solutions can be connected by a curve in a subspace, along which the training loss remains near-zero, known as **mode connectivity**. Despite having the same training loss, these different parameter settings give rise to very different functions, as illustrated in Figure 17.11, where we show predictions on a 1d regression problem coming from different points in parameter space obtained by interpolating along a mode connecting curve between two distinct MAP estimates. Using a Bayesian model average, we can combine these functions together to provide much better performance over a single flat solution [Izm+19].

Recently, it has been discovered [Ben+21b] that there are in fact large multidimensional simplexes of low loss solutions, which can be combined together for significantly improved performance. These results further motivate the Bayesian approach (Equation (17.1)), where we perform a posterior weighted model average.

17.4.3 Effective dimensionality of a model

Modern DNNs have millions of parameters, but these parameters are often not well-determined by the data, i.e., there can be a lot of posterior uncertainty. By averaging over the posterior, we reduce the chance of overfitting, because we do not use "degrees of freedom" that are not needed or

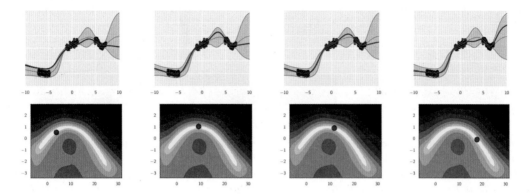

Figure 17.11: *Diversity of high performing functions sampled from the posterior. Top row: we show predictions on the 1d input domain for 4 different functions. We see that they extrapolate in different ways outside of the support of the data. Bottom row: we show a 2d subspace spanning two distinct modes (MAP estimates), and connected by a low-loss curved path computed as in [Gar+18c]. From Figure 8 of [WI20]. Used with kind permission of Andrew Wilson.*

warranted.

To quantify the number of degrees of freedom, or **effective dimensionality** [Mac92b], we follow [MBW20] and define

$$N_{\text{eff}}(\mathbf{H}, c) = \sum_{i=1}^{k} \frac{\lambda_i}{\lambda_i + c}, \tag{17.36}$$

where λ_i are the eigenvalues of the Hessian matrix $\mathbf{H}$ computed at a local mode, and $c > 0$ is a regularization parameter. Intuitively, the effective dimension counts the number of well-determined parameters. A "flat minimum" will have many directions in parameter space that are not well-determined, and hence will have low effective dimensionality. This means that we can perform Bayesian inference in a low dimensional subspace [Izm+19]: Since there is functional homogeneity in all directions but those defining the effective dimension, neural networks can be significantly compressed.

This compression perspective can also be used to understand why the effective dimension can be a good proxy for generalization. If two models have similar training loss, but one has lower effective dimension, then it is providing a better compression for the data at the same fidelity. In Figure 17.12 we show that for CNNs with low training loss (above the green partition), the effective dimensionality closely tracks generalization performance. We also see that the number of parameters alone is not a strong determinant of generalization. Indeed, models with more parameters can have a lower number of effective parameters. We also see that wide but shallow models overfit, while depth helps provide lower effective dimensionality, leading to a better compression of the data. It is depth that makes modern neural networks distinctive, providing hierarchical inductive biases making it possible to discover more regularity in the data.

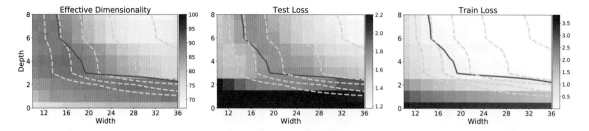

Figure 17.12: Left: effective dimensionality as a function of model width and depth for a CNN on CIFAR-100. Center: test loss as a function of model width and depth. Right: train loss as a function of model width and depth. Yellow level curves represent equal parameter counts (1e5, 2e5, 4e5, 1.6e6). The green curve separates models with near-zero training loss. Effective dimensionality serves as a good proxy for generalization for models with low train loss. We see wide but shallow models overfit, providing low train loss, but high test loss and high effective dimensionality. For models with the same train loss, lower effective dimensionality can be viewed as a better compression of the data at the same fidelity. Thus depth provides a mechanism for compression, which leads to better generalization. From Figure 2 of [MBW20]. Used with kind permission of Andrew Wilson.

17.4.4 The hypothesis space of DNNs

Zhang et al. [Zha+17] showed that CNNs can fit CIFAR-10 images with random labels with zero training error, but can still generalize well on the noise-free test set. It has been claimed that this result contradicts a classical understanding of generalization, because it shows that neural networks are capable of significantly overfitting the data, but can still generalize well on structured inputs.

We can resolve this paradox by taking a Bayesian perspective. In particular, we know that modern CNNs are very flexible, so they can fit almost pattern (since they are in fact universal approximators). However, their architecture encodes a prior over what kinds of patterns they expect to see in the data (see Section 17.2.5). Image datasets with random labels *can* be represented by this function class, but such solutions receive very low marginal likelihood, since they strongly violate the prior assumptions [WI20]. By contrast, image datasets where the output labels are consistent with patterns in the input get much higher marginal likelihood.

This phenomenon is not unique to DNNs. For example, it also occurs with Gaussian processes (Chapter 18). Such models are also universal approximators, but they allocate most of their probability mass to a small range of solutions (depending on the chosen kernel). They can also fit image datasets with random labels, but such data receives a low marginal likelihood [WI20].

In general, we can distinguish the support of a model, i.e., the set of functions it can represent, from the distribution over that support, i.e., the inductive bias which leads it to prefer some functions over others. We would like to use models where the support is large, so we can capture the complexity of real-world data, but also where the inductive bias places probability mass on the kinds of functions we expect to see. If we succeed at this, the posterior will quickly converge on the true function after seeing a small amount of data. This idea is sketched in Figure 17.13.

17.4.5 PAC-Bayes

PAC-Bayes [McA99; LC02; Gue19; Alq21; GSZ21] provides a promising mechanism to derive

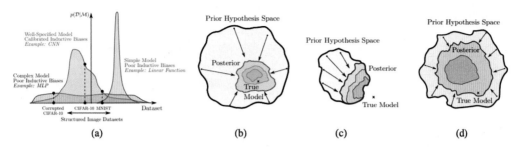

Figure 17.13: *Illustration of the behavior of different kinds of model families and the prior distributions they induce over datasets. (a) The purple model is a simple linear model that has small support, and can only represent a few kinds of datasets. The pink model is an unstructured MLP: this has support over a large range of datasets with a fairly uninformative (broad) prior. Finally the green model is a CNN; this has support over a large range of datasets but the prior is more concentrated on certain kinds of datasets that have compositional structure. (b) The posterior for the green model (CNN) rapidly collapses to the true model, since it is consistent with the data. (c) The posterior for the purple model (linear) also rapidly collapses, but to a solution which cannot represent the true model. (d) The posterior for the pink model (MLP) collapses very slowly (as a function of dataset size). From Figure 2 of [WI20]. Used with kind permission of Andrew Wilson.*

non-vacuous generalization bounds for large *stochastic networks* [Ney+17; NBS18; DR17], with parameters sampled from a probability distribution. In particular, the difference between the train error and the generalization error can be expressed as

$$\sqrt{\frac{D_{\mathrm{KL}}\left(Q \parallel P\right) + c}{2(N-1)}}, \tag{17.37}$$

where c is a constant, N is the number of training points, P is the prior distribution over the parameters, and Q is an arbitrary distribution, which can be chosen to optimize the bound.

The perspective in this chapter is largely complementary, and in some ways orthogonal, to the PAC-Bayes literature. Our focus has been on Bayesian marginalization, particularly multi-modal marginalization, and a prescriptive approach to model construction. In contrast, PAC-Bayes bounds are about bounding the empirical risk of a single sample, rather than marginalization, and are not currently prescriptive: what we would do to improve the bounds, such as reducing the number of model parameters, or using highly compact priors, does not typically improve generalization. Moreover, while we have seen Bayesian model averaging over multimodal posteriors has a significant effect on generalization, it has a minimal logarithmic effect on PAC-Bayes bounds. In general, because the bounds are loose, albeit non-vacuous in some cases, there is often room to make modeling choices that improve PAC-Bayes bounds without improving generalization, making it hard to derive a prescription for model construction from the bounds.

17.4.6 Out-of-distribution generalization for BNNs

Bayesian methods are often assumed to be more robust in the context of distribution shift (discussed in Chapter 19), because they capture more uncertainty than methods based on point estimation.

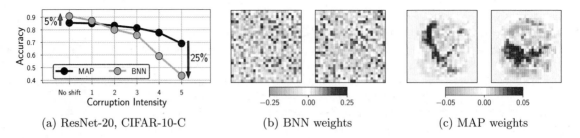

(a) ResNet-20, CIFAR-10-C   (b) BNN weights   (c) MAP weights

Figure 17.14: *Bayesian neural networks under covariate shift. a: Performance of a ResNet-20 on the pixelate corruption in CIFAR-10-C. For the highest degree of corruption, a Bayesian model average underperforms a MAP solution by 25% (44% against 69%) accuracy. See Izmailov et al. [Izm+21b] for details. b: Visualization of the weights in the first layer of a Bayesian fully-connected network on MNIST sampled via HMC. c: The corresponding MAP weights. We visualize the weights connecting the input pixels to a neuron in the hidden layer as a 28×28 image, where each weight is shown in the location of the input pixel it interacts with. This is Figure 1 of Izmailov et al. [Izm+21a].*

However, there are some subtleties, some of which we discuss below.

17.4.6.1 BMA can give poor results with default priors

Many approximate inference methods, especially deep ensembles, are significantly less overconfident (more well calibrated) in the presence of some kinds of covariate shifts [Ova+19]. However, in [Izm+21b], it was noted that HMC, which arguably offers the most accurate approximation to the posterior, often works poorly under distribution shift.

Rather than an idiosyncrasy of HMC, Izmailov et al. [Izm+21a] show this lack of robustness is a foundational issue of Bayesian model averaging under covariate shift, caused by degeneracies in the training data, and a poor choice of prior. As an illustrative special case, MNIST digits all have black corner pixels. Weights in the first layer of a neural network connected to these pixels are multiplied by zero, and thus can take any value without affecting the outputs of the network. Classical MAP training or deep ensembles of MAP solutions with a Gaussian prior will therefore drive these parameters to zero, since they don't help with the data fit, and the resulting network will be robust to corruptions on these pixels. On the other hand, the posterior for these parameters will be the same as the prior, and so a Bayesian model average will multiply corruptions by random numbers sampled from the prior, leading to degraded predictive performance.

Figure 17.14(b, c) visualizes this example, showing the first-layer weights of a fully-connected network for the MAP solution and a BNN posterior sample, on MNIST. The MAP weights corresponding to zero intensity pixels near the boundary are near zero, while the BNN weights look noisy, sampled from a Gaussian prior.

Izmailov et al. [Izm+21a] prove that this issue is a special case of a much more general problem, whenever there are linear dependencies in the input features of the training data, both for fully-connected and convolutional networks. In this case, the data live on a hyperplane. If a covariate or domain shift, moves orthogonal to this hyperplane, the posterior will be the same as the prior in the direction of the shift. The posterior model average will thus be highly vulnerable to shifts that do not particularly affect the underlying semantic structure of the problem (such as corruptions), whereas the MAP solution will be entirely robust to such shifts.

By introducing a prior over parameters which is aligned with the principal components of the training inputs, we can substantially improve the generalization accuracy of Bayesian neural networks in out-of-distribution settings. Izmailov et al. [Izm+21a] propose the following *EmpCov* prior: $p(w^1) = \mathcal{N}(0, \alpha\Sigma + \epsilon I)$, where w^1 are the first layer weights, $\Sigma = \frac{1}{n-1}\sum_{i=1}^{n} x_i x_i^T$ is the empirical covariance of the training input features x_i, $\alpha > 0$ determines the scale of the prior, and ϵ is a small positive constant to ensure the covariance matrix is positive definite. With this improved prior they are able to obtain a method that is much more robust to distribution shift.

17.4.6.2 BNNs can be overconfident on OOD inputs

An important problem in practice is how a predictive model will behave when it is given an input that is "out of distribution" or OOD. Ideally we would like the model to express that it is not confident in its prediction, so that the system can abstain from predicting (see Section 19.3.3). Using "exact" inference methods, such as MCMC, for BNNs can give this behavior in some cases. For example, in Section 19.3.3.1 we showed that an MLP which was fit to MNIST using SGLD would be less overconfident than a point estimate (computed using SGD) when presented with inputs from fashion MNIST. However, this behavior does not always occur reliably.

To illustrate the problem, consider the 2d nonlinear binary classification dataset shown in Figure 17.15. In addition to the two training classes, we have highlighted (in green) a set of OOD inputs that are far from the support of the training set. Intuitively we would expect the model to predict a probability of 0.5 (corresponding to "don't know") for such inputs that are far from the training set. However we see that the only methods that do so are the Gaussian process (GP) classifier (see Section 18.4) and the SNGP model (Section 17.3.6), which contains a GP layer on top of the feature extractor.

The lesson we learn from this simple example is that "being Bayesian" only helps if we are using a good hypothesis class. If we only consider a single MLP classifier, with standard Gaussian priors on the weights, it is extremely unlikely that we will learn the kind of compact decision boundary shown in Figure 17.15g, because that function has negligible support under our prior (c.f. Section 17.4.4). Instead we should embrace the power of Bayes to avoid overfitting and use as complex a model class as we can afford.

17.4.7 Model selection for BNNs

Historically, the marginal likelihood (aka Bayesian evidence) has been used for model selection problems, such as choosing neural architectures or hyperparameter values [Mac92a]. Recent methods based on the Laplace approximation, such as [Imm+21; Dax+21], have made this scalable to large BNNs. However, [Lot+22] argue that it is much better to use the conditional marginal likelihood, which we discuss in Section 3.8.5.

17.5 Online inference

In Section 17.3, we have focused on batch or offline inference. However, an important application of Bayesian inference is in sequential settings, where the data arrives in a continuous stream, and the model has to "keep up". This is called **sequential Bayesian inference**, and is one approach to

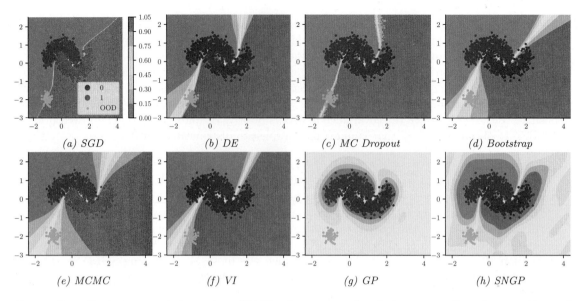

Figure 17.15: Predictions made by various (B)NNs when presented with the training data shown in blue and red. The green blob is an example of some OOD inputs. Methods are: (a) standard SGD; (b) deep Ensemble of 10 models with different random initializations; (c) MC dropout with 50 samples; (d) bootstrap training, where each of the 10 models is initialized identically but given different versions of the data, obtained by resampling with replacement; (e) MCMC using NUTS algorithm with 3000 warmup steps and 3000 samples; (f) bariational inference; (g) Gaussian process classifier using RBF kernel; (h) SNGP. The model is an MLP with 8,16,16,8 units in the hidden layers and ReLu activation. The output layer has 1 neuron with sigmoid activation. Generated by makemoons_comparison.ipynb

online learning (see Section 19.7.5). In this section, we discuss some algorithmic approaches to this problem in the context of DNNs. These methods are widely used for continual learning, which we discuss Section 19.7.

17.5.1   Sequential Laplace for DNNs

In [RBB18b], they extended the Laplace method of Section 17.3.2 to the sequential setting. Specifically, let $p(\boldsymbol{\theta}|\mathcal{D}_{1:t-1}) \approx \mathcal{N}(\boldsymbol{\theta}|\boldsymbol{\mu}_{t-1}, \boldsymbol{\Lambda}_{t-1}^{-1})$ be the approximate posterior from the previous step; we assume the precision matrix is Kronecker factored. We now compute the new mean by solving the MAP problem

$$\boldsymbol{\mu}_t = \operatorname{argmax} \log p(\mathcal{D}_t|\boldsymbol{\theta}) + \log p(\boldsymbol{\theta}|\mathcal{D}_{t-1}) \tag{17.38}$$

$$= \operatorname{argmax} \log p(\mathcal{D}_t|\boldsymbol{\theta}) - \frac{1}{2}(\boldsymbol{\theta} - \boldsymbol{\mu}_{t-1})\boldsymbol{\Lambda}_{t-1}^{-1}(\boldsymbol{\theta} - \boldsymbol{\mu}_{t-1}) \tag{17.39}$$

Once we have computed $\boldsymbol{\mu}_t$, we compute the approximate Hessian at this point, and get the new posterior precision

$$\boldsymbol{\Lambda}_t = \lambda \mathbf{H}(\boldsymbol{\mu}_t) + \boldsymbol{\Lambda}_{t-1} \tag{17.40}$$

where $\lambda \geq 0$ is a weighting factor that trades off how much the model pays attention to the new data vs old data.

Now suppose we use a diagonal approximation to the posterior prediction matrix. From Equation (17.39), we see that this amounts to adding a quadratic penalty to each new MAP estimate, to encourage it to remain close to the parameters from previous tasks. This approach is called **elastic weight consolidation** (**EWC**) [Kir+17].

17.5.2 Extended Kalman filtering for DNNs

In Section 29.7.2, we showed how Kalman filtering can be used to incrementally compute the exact posterior for the weights of a linear regression model with known variance, i.e., we compute $p(\boldsymbol{\theta}|\mathcal{D}_{1:t}, \sigma^2)$, where $\mathcal{D}_{1:t} = \{(\boldsymbol{u}_i, y_i) : i = 1 : t\}$ is the data seen so far, and

$$p(y_t|\boldsymbol{u}_t, \boldsymbol{\theta}, \sigma^2) = \mathcal{N}(y_t|\boldsymbol{\theta}^\mathsf{T}\boldsymbol{u}_t, \sigma^2) \tag{17.41}$$

is the linear regression likelihood. The application of KF to this model is known as recursive least squares.

Now consider the case of nonlinear regression:

$$p(y_t|\boldsymbol{u}_t, \boldsymbol{\theta}, \sigma^2) = \mathcal{N}(y_t|f(\boldsymbol{\theta}, \boldsymbol{u}_t), \sigma^2) \tag{17.42}$$

where $f(\boldsymbol{\theta}, \boldsymbol{u}_t)$ is some nonlinear function, such as an MLP. We can use the extended Kalman filter (Section 8.3.2) to approximately compute $p(\boldsymbol{\theta}_t|\mathcal{D}_{1:t}, \sigma^2)$, where $\boldsymbol{\theta}_t$ is the hidden state (see e.g., [SW89; PF03]). To see this, note that we can set the dynamics model to the identity function, $f(\boldsymbol{\theta}_t) = \boldsymbol{\theta}_t$, so the parameters are propagated through unchanged, and the observation model to the input-dependent function $f(\boldsymbol{\theta}_t) = f(\boldsymbol{\theta}_t, \boldsymbol{u}_t)$. We set the observation noise to $\mathbf{R}_t = \sigma^2$, and the dynamics noise to $\mathbf{Q}_t = q\mathbf{I}$, where q is a small constant, to allow the parameters to slowly drift according to artificial **process noise**. (In practice it can be useful to anneal q from a large initial value to something near 0.)

17.5.2.1 Example

We now give an example of this process in action. We sample a synthetic dataset from the true function

$$h^*(u) = x - 10\cos(u)\sin(u) + u^3 \tag{17.43}$$

and add Gaussian noise with $\sigma = 3$. We then fit this with an MLP with one hidden layer with H hidden units, so the model has the form

$$f(\boldsymbol{\theta}, \boldsymbol{u}) = \mathbf{W}_2 \tanh(\mathbf{W}_1 \boldsymbol{u} + \boldsymbol{b}_1) + \boldsymbol{b}_2 \tag{17.44}$$

where $\mathbf{W}_1 \in \mathbb{R}^{H \times 1}$, $\boldsymbol{b}_1 \in \mathbb{R}^H$, $\mathbf{W}_2 \in \mathbb{R}^{1 \times H}$, $\boldsymbol{b}_2 \in \mathbb{R}^1$. We set $H = 6$, so there are $D = 19$ parameters in total.

Given the data, we sequentially compute the posterior, starting from a vague Gaussian prior, $p(\boldsymbol{\theta}) = \mathcal{N}(\boldsymbol{\theta}|\mathbf{0}, \boldsymbol{\Sigma}_0)$, where $\boldsymbol{\Sigma}_0 = 100\mathbf{I}$. (In practice we cannot start from the prior mean, which is $\boldsymbol{\theta}_0 = \mathbf{0}$, since linearizing the model around this point results in a zero gradient, so we use an initial random sample for $\boldsymbol{\theta}_0$.) The results are shown in Figure 17.16. We can see that the model adapts to the data, without having to specify any learning rate. In addition, we see that the predictions become gradually more confident, as the posterior concentrates on the MLE.

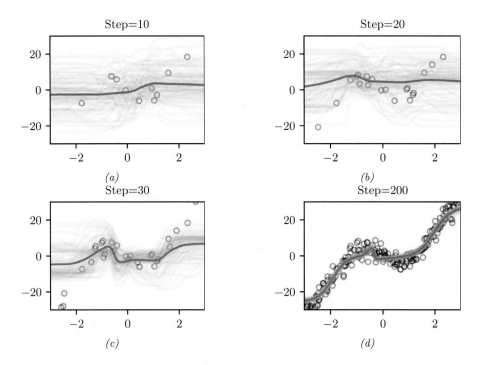

Figure 17.16: Sequential Bayesian inference for the parameters of an MLP using the extended Kalman filter. We show results after seeing the first 10, 20, 30 and 200 observations. (For a video of this, see https://bit.ly/3wXnWaM.) Generated by ekf_mlp.ipynb.

17.5.2.2   Setting the variance terms

In the above example, we set the variance terms by hand. In general we need to estimate the noise variance σ, which determines $\mathbf{R}_t$ and hence the learning rate, as well as the strength of the prior $\boldsymbol{\Sigma}_0$, which controls the amount of regularization. Some methods for doing this are discussed in [FNG00].

17.5.2.3   Reducing the computational complexity

The naive EKF method described above takes $O(N_z^3)$ time, which is prohibitive for large neural networks. A simple approximation, known as the **decoupled EKF**, was proposed in [PF91; SPD92] (see [PF03] for a review). This partitions the weights into G groups or blocks, and estimates the relevant matrices for each group g independently. If $G = 1$, this reduces the standard global EKF. If we put each weight into its own group, we get a fully diagonal approximation. In practice this does not work any better than SGD, since it ignores correlations between the parameters. A useful compromise is to put all the weights corresponding to each neuron into its own group; this is called **node decoupled EKF**, which has been used in [Sim02] to train RBF networks and [GUK21] to train exponential family matrix factorization models (widely used in recommender systems). For more details on DEKF, Supplementary Section 17.1.

Another approach to increasing computational efficiency is to leverage the fact that the effective dimensionality of a DNN is often quite low (see Section 17.4.3). Indeed we can approximate the model parameters by using a low dimensional vector of coefficients that specify the point in a linear manifold corresponding to weight space; the basis set defining this linear manifold can either be chosen randomly [Li+18b; GARD18; Lar+22], or can be estimated using PCA applied to the SGD iterates [Izm+19]. We can exploit this observation to perform EKF in this low-dimensional subspace, which significantly speeds up inference, as discussed in [DMKM22].

17.5.3 Assumed density filtering for DNNs

In Section 8.6.3, we discussed how to use assumed density filtering (ADF) to perform online (binary) logistic regression. In this section, we generalize this to nonlinear predictive models, such as DNNs. The key is to perform Gaussian moment matching of the hidden activations at each layer of the model. This provides an alternative to the EKF approach in Section 17.5.2, which is based on linearization of the network.

We will assume the following likelihood:

$$p(\boldsymbol{y}_t|\boldsymbol{u}_t, \boldsymbol{w}_t) = \text{Expfam}(\boldsymbol{y}_t|\ell^{-1}(f(\boldsymbol{u}_t; \boldsymbol{w}_t))) \tag{17.45}$$

where $f(\boldsymbol{x}; \boldsymbol{w})$ is the DNN, ℓ^{-1} is the inverse link function, and Expfam() is some exponential family distribution. For example, if f is linear and we are solving a binary classification problem, we can write

$$p(y_t|\boldsymbol{u}_t, \boldsymbol{w}_t) = \text{Ber}(y_t|\sigma(\boldsymbol{u}_t^{\mathsf{T}} \boldsymbol{w}_t)) \tag{17.46}$$

We discussed using ADF to fit this model in Section 8.6.3.

In [HLA15b], they propose **probabilistic backpropagation (PBP)**, which is an instance of ADF applied to MLPs. The basic idea is to approximate the posterior over the weights in each layer using a fully factorized distribution

$$p(\boldsymbol{w}_t|\mathcal{D}_{1:t}) \approx p_t(\boldsymbol{w}_t) = \prod_{l=1}^{L} \prod_{i=1}^{D_l} \prod_{j=1}^{D_{l-1}+1} \mathcal{N}(w_{ijl}|\mu_{ijl}^t, \tau_{ijl}^t) \tag{17.47}$$

where L is the number of layers, and D_l is the number of neurons in layer l. (The **expectation backpropagation** algorithm of [SHM14] is a special case of this, where the variances are fixed to $\tau = 1$.)

Suppose the parameters are static, so $\boldsymbol{w}_t = \boldsymbol{w}_{t-1}$. Then the new posterior, after conditioning on the t'th observation, is given by

$$\hat{p}_t(\boldsymbol{w}) = \frac{1}{Z_t} p(\boldsymbol{y}_t|\boldsymbol{u}_t, \boldsymbol{w}) \mathcal{N}(\boldsymbol{w}|\boldsymbol{\mu}^{t-1}, \boldsymbol{\Sigma}^{t-1}) \tag{17.48}$$

where $\boldsymbol{\Sigma}^{t-1} = \text{diag}(\boldsymbol{\tau}^{t-1})$. We then project $\hat{p}_t(\boldsymbol{w})$ instead the space of factored Gaussians to compute the new (approximate) posterior, $p_t(\boldsymbol{w})$. This can be done by computing the following means and variances [Min01a]:

$$\mu_{ijl}^t = \mu_{ijl}^{t-1} + \tau_{ijl}^{t-1} \frac{\partial \ln Z_t}{\partial \mu_{ijl}^{t-1}} \tag{17.49}$$

$$\tau_{ijl}^t = \tau_{ijl}^{t-1} - (\tau_{ijl}^{t-1})^2 \left[\left(\frac{\partial \ln Z_t}{\partial \mu_{ijl}^{t-1}} \right)^2 - 2 \frac{\partial \ln Z_t}{\partial \tau_{ijl}^{t-1}} \right] \tag{17.50}$$

In the forwards pass, we compute Z_t by propagating the input $\boldsymbol{u}_t$ through the model. Since we have a Gaussian distribution over the weights, instead of a point estimate, this induces an (approximately) Gaussian distribution over the values of the hidden units. For certain kinds of activation functions (such as ReLU), the relevant integrals (to compute the means and variances) can be solved analytically, as in GP-neural networks (Section 18.7). The result is that we get a Gaussian distribution over the final layer of the form $\mathcal{N}(\boldsymbol{\eta}_t | \boldsymbol{\mu}, \boldsymbol{\Sigma})$, where $\boldsymbol{\eta}_t = f(\boldsymbol{u}_t; \boldsymbol{w}_t)$ is the output of the neural network before the GLM link function induced by $p_t(\boldsymbol{w}_t)$. Hence we can approximate the partition function using

$$Z_t \approx \int p(\boldsymbol{y}_t | \boldsymbol{\eta}_t) \mathcal{N}(\boldsymbol{\eta}_t | \boldsymbol{\mu}, \boldsymbol{\Sigma}) d\boldsymbol{\eta}_t \tag{17.51}$$

We now discuss how to compute this integral. In the case of probit classification, with $y \in \{-1, +1\}$, we have $p(y|\boldsymbol{x}, \boldsymbol{w}) = \Phi(y\eta)$, where Φ is the cdf of the standard normal. We can then use the following analytical result

$$\int \Phi(y\eta) \mathcal{N}(h|\mu, \sigma) d\eta = \Phi\left(\frac{y\mu}{\sqrt{1 + \sigma}} \right) \tag{17.52}$$

In the case of logistic classification, with $y \in \{0, 1\}$, we have $p(y|\boldsymbol{x}, \boldsymbol{w}) = \text{Ber}(y|\sigma(\eta))$; in this case, we can use the probit approximation from Section 15.3.6. For the multiclass case, where $\boldsymbol{y} \in \{0, 1\}^C$ (one-hot encoding), we have $p(\boldsymbol{y}|\boldsymbol{x}, \boldsymbol{w}) = \text{Cat}(\boldsymbol{y}|\text{softmax}(\boldsymbol{\eta}))$. A variational lower bound to $\log Z_t$ for this case is given in [GDFY16].

Once we have computed Z_t, we can take gradients and update the Gaussian posterior moments, before moving to the next step.

17.5.4   Online variational inference for DNNs

A natural approach to online learning is to use variational inference, where the prior is the posterior from the previous step. This is known as **streaming variational Bayes** [Bro+13]. In more detail, at step t, we compute

$$\boldsymbol{\psi}_t = \underset{\boldsymbol{\psi}}{\text{argmin}} \underbrace{\mathbb{E}_{q(\boldsymbol{\theta}|\boldsymbol{\psi})}[\ell_t(\boldsymbol{\theta})] + D_{\text{KL}}\left(q(\boldsymbol{\theta}|\boldsymbol{\psi}) \,\|\, q(\boldsymbol{\theta}|\boldsymbol{\psi}_{t-1})\right)}_{-\text{Ł}_t(\boldsymbol{\psi})} \tag{17.53}$$

$$= \underset{\boldsymbol{\psi}}{\text{argmin}} \, \mathbb{E}_{q(\boldsymbol{\theta}|\boldsymbol{\psi})}\left[\ell_t(\boldsymbol{\theta}) + \log q(\boldsymbol{\theta}|\boldsymbol{\psi}) - \log q(\boldsymbol{\theta}|\boldsymbol{\psi}_{t-1})\right] \tag{17.54}$$

where $\ell_t(\boldsymbol{\theta}) = -\log p(\mathcal{D}_t|\boldsymbol{\theta})$ is the negative log likelihood (or, more generally, some loss function) of the data batch at step t.

When applied to DNNs, this approach is called **variational continual learning** or **VCL** [Ngu+18]. (We discuss continual learning in Section 19.7.) An efficient implementation of this, known as **FOO-VB** ("fixed-point operator for online variational Bayes") is given in [Zen+21].

One problem with the VCL objective in Equation (17.53) is that the KL term can cause the model to become too sparse, which can prevent the model from adapting or learning new tasks. This problem is called **variational overpruning** [TT17]. More precisely, the reason this happens as is as follows: some weights might not be needed to fit a given dataset, so their posterior will be equal to the prior, but sampling from these high-variance weights will add noise to the likelihood; to reduce this, the optimization method will prefer to set the bias term to a large negative value, so the corresponding unit is "turned off", and thus has no effect on the likelihood. Unfortunately, these "dead units" become stuck, so there is not enough network capacity to learn the next task.

In [LST21], they propose a solution to this, known as **generalized variational continual learning** or **GVCL**. The first step is to downweight the KL term by a factor $\beta < 1$ to get

$$\text{\L}_t = \mathbb{E}_{q(\boldsymbol{\theta}|\boldsymbol{\psi})} \left[\ell_t(\boldsymbol{\theta}) \right] + \beta D_{\mathbb{KL}} \left(q(\boldsymbol{\theta}|\boldsymbol{\psi}) \parallel q(\boldsymbol{\theta}|\boldsymbol{\psi}_{t-1}) \right) \tag{17.55}$$

Interestingly, one can show that in the limit of $\beta \to 0$, this recovers several standard methods that use a Laplace approximation based on the Hessian. In particular if we use a diagonal variational posterior, this reduces to online EWC method of [Sch+18]; if we use a block-diagonal and Kronecker factored posterior, this reduces to the online structured Laplace method of [RBB18b]; and if we use a low-rank posterior precision matrix, this reduces to the SOLA method of [Yin+20].

The second step is to replace the prior and posterior by using tempering, which is useful when the model is misspecified, as discussed in Section 17.3.11. In the case of Gaussians, raising the distribution to the power λ is equivalent to tempering with a temperature of $\tau = 1/\lambda$, which is the same as scaling the covariance by λ^{-1}. Thus the GVCL objective becomes

$$\text{\L}_t = \mathbb{E}_{q(\boldsymbol{\theta}|\boldsymbol{\psi})} \left[\ell_t(\boldsymbol{\theta}) \right] + \beta D_{\mathbb{KL}} \left(q(\boldsymbol{\theta}|\boldsymbol{\psi})^{\lambda} \parallel q(\boldsymbol{\theta}|\boldsymbol{\psi}_{t-1})^{\lambda} \right) \tag{17.56}$$

This can be optimized using SGD, assuming the posterior is reparameterizable (see Section 10.2.1).

17.6 Hierarchical Bayesian neural networks

In some problems, we have multiple related datasets, such as a set of medical images from different hospitals. Some aspects of the data (e.g., the shape of healthy vs diseased cells) is generally the same across datasets, but other aspects may be unique or idiosyncratic (e.g., each hospital may use a different colored die for staining). To model this, we can use a hierarchical Bayesian model, in which we allow the parameters for each dataset to be different (to capture random effects), while coming from a common prior (to capture shared effects). This is the setup we considered in Section 15.5, where we discuss hierarchical Bayesian GLMs. In this section, we extend this to nonlinear predictors based on neural networks. (The setup is very similar to domain generalization, discussed in Section 19.6.2, except here we care about performance on all the domains, not just a held-out target domain.)

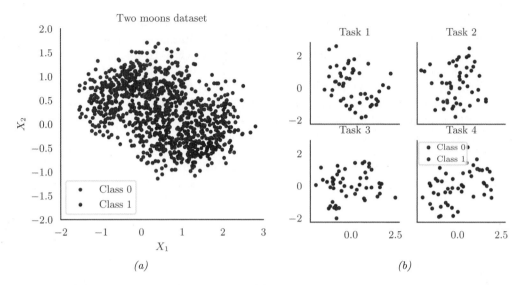

Figure 17.17: (a) Two moons synthetic dataset. (b) Multi-task version, where we rotate the data to create 18 related tasks (groups). Each dataset has 50 training and 50 test points. Here we show the first 4 tasks. Generated by bnn_hierarchical.ipynb.

17.6.1   Example: multimoons classification

In this section, we consider an example[2] where we want to solve multiple related nonlinear binary classification problems coming from J different environments or distributions. We assume that each environment has its own unique decision boundary $p(y|\boldsymbol{x}, \boldsymbol{w}^j)$, so this is a form of concept shift (see Section 19.2.3). However we assume the overall shape of each boundary is similar to a common shared boundary, denote $p(y|\boldsymbol{x}, \boldsymbol{w}^0)$. We only have a small number N_j of examples from each environment, $\mathcal{D}^j = \{(\boldsymbol{x}_n^j, y_n^j) : n = 1 : N_j\}$, but we can utilize their common structure to do better than fitting J separate models.

To illustrate this, we create some synthetic 2d data for the $J = 18$ tasks. We start with the two-moons dataset, illustrated in Figure 17.17a. Each task is obtained by rotating the 2d inputs by a different amount, to create 18 related classification problems (see Figure 17.17b). See Figure 17.17b for the training data for 4 tasks.

To handle the nonlinear decision boundary, we use a multilayer perceptron. Since the dataset is low-dimensional (2d input), we use a shallow model with just 2 hidden layers, each with 5 neurons. We could fit a separate MLP to each task, but since we have limited data per task ($N_j = 50$ examples for training), this works poorly, as we show below. We could also pool all the data and fit a single model, but this does even worse, since the datasets come from different underlying distributions, so mixing the data together from different "concepts" confuses the model. Instead we adopt a hierarchical Bayesian approach.

Our modeling assumptions are shown in Figure 17.18. In particular, we assume the weight from

---

2. This example is from `https://twiecki.io/blog/2018/08/13/hierarchical_bayesian_neural_network/`. For a real-world example of a similar approach applied to a gesture recognition task, see [Jos+17].

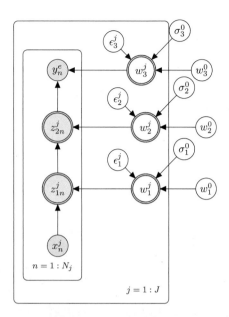

Figure 17.18: Illustration of a hierarchical Bayesian MLP with 2 hidden layers. There are J different models, each with N_j observed samples, and a common set of global shared parent parameters denoted with the 0 superscript. Nodes which are shaded are observed. Nodes with double ringed circles are deterministic functions of their parents.

unit i to unit k in layer l for environment j, denoted $w^j_{i,k,l}$, comes from a common prior value $w^0_{i,k,l}$, with a random offset. We use the non-centered parameterization from Section 12.6.5 to write

$$w^j_{i,k,l} = w^0_{i,k,l} + \epsilon^j_{i,k,l} \times \sigma^0_l \tag{17.57}$$

where $\epsilon^j_{i,k,l} \sim \mathcal{N}(0,1)$. By allowing a different σ^0_l per layer l, we let the model control the degree of shrinkage to the prior for each layer separately. (We could also make the σ^j_l parameters be environment specific, which would allow for different amounts of distribution shift from the common parent.) For the hyper-parameters, we put $\mathcal{N}(0,1)$ priors on $w^0_{i,k,l}$, and $\mathcal{N}_+(1)$ priors on σ^0_l.

We compute the posterior $p(\epsilon^{1:J}_{1:L}, w^0_{1:L}, \sigma^0_{1:L}|\mathcal{D})$ using HMC (Section 12.5). We then evaluate this model using a fresh set of labeled samples from each environment. The average classification accuracy on the train and test sets for the non-hierarchical model (one MLP per environment, fit separately) is 86% and 83%. For the hierarchical model, this improves to 91% and 89% respectively.

To see why the hierarchical model works better, we will plot the posterior predictive distribution in 2d. Figure 17.19(top) shows the results for the nonhierarchical models; we see that the method fails to learn the common underlying Z-shaped decision boundary. By contrast, Figure 17.19(bottom) shows that the hierarchical method has correctly recovered the common pattern, while still allowing group variation.

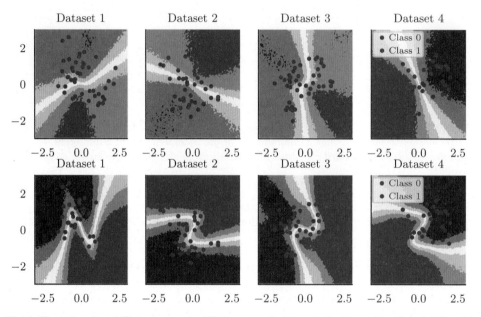

Figure 17.19: Top: Results of fitting separate MLPs on each dataset. Bottom: Results of fitting hierarchical MLP on all datasets jointly. Generated by bnn_hierarchical.ipynb.

18 Gaussian processes

This chapter is coauthored with Andrew Wilson.

18.1 Introduction

Deep neural networks are a family of flexible function approximators of the form $f(\boldsymbol{x}; \boldsymbol{\theta})$, where the dimensionality of $\boldsymbol{\theta}$ (i.e., the number of parameters) is fixed, and independent of the size N of the training set. However, such parametric models can overfit when N is small, and can underfit when N is large, due to their fixed capacity. In order to create models whose capacity automatically adapts to the amount of data, we turn to **nonparametric models**.

There are many approaches to building nonparametric models for classification and regression (see e.g., [Was06]). In this chapter, we consider a Bayesian approach in which we represent uncertainty about the input-output mapping f by defining a prior distribution over functions, and then updating it given data. In particular, we will use a **Gaussian process** to represent the prior $p(f)$; we then use Bayes' rule to derive the posterior $p(f|\mathcal{D})$, which is another GP, as we explain below. More details on GPs can be found the excellent book [RW06], as well as the interative tutorial at `https://distill.pub/2019/visual-exploration-gaussian-processes`. See also Chapter 31 for other examples of Bayesian nonparametric models.

18.1.1 GPs: what and why?

To explain GPs in more detail, recall that a Gaussian random vector of length N, $\boldsymbol{f} = [f_1, \ldots, f_N]$, is defined by its mean $\boldsymbol{\mu} = \mathbb{E}[\boldsymbol{f}]$ and its covariance $\boldsymbol{\Sigma} = \text{Cov}[\boldsymbol{f}]$. Now consider a function $f : \mathcal{X} \to \mathbb{R}$ evaluated at a set of inputs, $\mathbf{X} = \{\boldsymbol{x}_n \in \mathcal{X}\}_{n=1}^N$. Let $\boldsymbol{f}_X = [f(\boldsymbol{x}_1), \ldots, f(\boldsymbol{x}_N)]$ be the set of unknown function values at these points. If $\boldsymbol{f}_X$ is jointly Gaussian for any set of $N \geq 1$ points, then we say that $f : \mathcal{X} \to \mathbb{R}$ is a **Gaussian process**. Such a process is defined by its **mean function** $m(\boldsymbol{x}) \in \mathbb{R}$ and a **covariance function**, $\mathcal{K}(\boldsymbol{x}, \boldsymbol{x}') \geq 0$, which is any positive definite **Mercer kernel** (see Section 18.2). For example, we might use an RBF kernel of the form $\mathcal{K}(\boldsymbol{x}, \boldsymbol{x}') \propto \exp(-||\boldsymbol{x} - \boldsymbol{x}'||^2)$ (see Section 18.2.1.1 for details).

We denote the corresponding GP by

$$f(\boldsymbol{x}) \sim GP(m(\boldsymbol{x}), \mathcal{K}(\boldsymbol{x}, \boldsymbol{x}')) \tag{18.1}$$

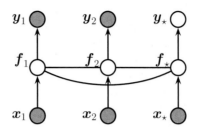

Figure 18.1: A Gaussian process for 2 training points, $\boldsymbol{x}_1$ and $\boldsymbol{x}_2$, and 1 testing point, $\boldsymbol{x}_*$, represented as a graphical model representing $p(\boldsymbol{y}, \boldsymbol{f}_X|\mathbf{X}) = \mathcal{N}(\boldsymbol{f}_X|m(\mathbf{X}), \mathcal{K}(\mathbf{X})) \prod_i p(y_i|f_i)$. The hidden nodes $f_i = f(\boldsymbol{x}_i)$ represent the value of the function at each of the datapoints. These hidden nodes are fully interconnected by undirected edges, forming a Gaussian graphical model; the edge strengths represent the covariance terms $\Sigma_{ij} = \mathcal{K}(\boldsymbol{x}_i, \boldsymbol{x}_j)$. If the test point $\boldsymbol{x}_*$ is similar to the training points $\boldsymbol{x}_1$ and $\boldsymbol{x}_2$, then the value of the hidden function f_* will be similar to f_1 and f_2, and hence the predicted output y_* will be similar to the training values y_1 and y_2.

where

$$m(\boldsymbol{x}) = \mathbb{E}\left[f(\boldsymbol{x})\right] \tag{18.2}$$

$$\mathcal{K}(\boldsymbol{x}, \boldsymbol{x}') = \mathbb{E}\left[(f(\boldsymbol{x}) - m(\boldsymbol{x}))(f(\boldsymbol{x}') - m(\boldsymbol{x}'))^\mathsf{T}\right] \tag{18.3}$$

This means that, for any finite set of points $\mathbf{X} = \{\boldsymbol{x}_1, \ldots, \boldsymbol{x}_N\}$, we have

$$p(\boldsymbol{f}_X|\mathbf{X}) = \mathcal{N}(\boldsymbol{f}_X|\boldsymbol{\mu}_X, \mathbf{K}_{X,X}) \tag{18.4}$$

where $\boldsymbol{\mu}_X = (m(\boldsymbol{x}_1), \ldots, m(\boldsymbol{x}_N))$ and $\mathbf{K}_{X,X}(i, j) \triangleq \mathcal{K}(\boldsymbol{x}_i, \boldsymbol{x}_j)$.

A GP can be used to define a prior over functions. We can evaluate this prior at any set of points we choose. However, to learn about the function from data, we have to update this prior with a likelihood function. We typically assume we have a set of N iid observations $\mathcal{D} = \{(\boldsymbol{x}_i, y_i) : i = 1 : N\}$, where $y_i \sim p(y|f(\boldsymbol{x}_i))$, as shown in Figure 18.1. If we use a Gaussian likelihood, we can compute the posterior $p(f|\mathcal{D})$ in closed form, as we discuss in Section 18.3. For other kinds of likelihoods, we will need to use approximate inference, as we discuss in Section 18.4. In many cases f is not directly observed, and instead forms part of a latent variable model, both in supervised and unsupervised settings such as in Section 28.3.7.

The generalization properties of a Gaussian process are controlled by its covariance function (kernel), which we describe in Section 18.2. These kernels live in a reproducing kernel Hilbert space (RKHS), described in Section 18.3.7.1.

GPs were originally designed for spatial data analysis, where the input is 2d. This special case is called **kriging**. However, they can be applied to higher dimensional inputs. In addition, while they have been traditionally limited to small datasets, it is now possible to apply GPs to problems with millions of points, with essentially exact inference. We discuss these scalability advances in Section 18.5.

Moreover, while Gaussian processes have historically been considered smoothing interpolators, GPs now routinely perform representation learning, through covariance function learning, and multilayer models. These advances have clearly illustrated that GPs and neural networks are not competing, but complementary, and can be combined for better performance than would be achieved by deep learning alone. We describe GPs for representation learning in Section 18.6.

The connections between Gaussian processes and neural networks can also be further understood by considering infinite limits of neural networks that converge to Gaussian processes with particular covariance functions, which we describe in Section 18.7.

So Gaussian processes are nonparametric models which can scale and do representation learning. But why, in the age of deep learning, should we want to use a Gaussian process? There are several compelling reasons to prefer a GP, including:

- Gaussian processes typically provide well-calibrated predictive distributions, with a good characterization of epistemic (model) uncertainty — uncertainty arising from not knowing which of many solutions is correct. For example, as we move away from the data, there are a greater variety of consistent solutions, and so we expect greater uncertainty.

- Gaussian processes are often state-of-the-art for continuous regression problems, especially spatiotemporal problems, such as weather interpolation and forecasting. In regression, Gaussian process inference can also typically be performed in closed form.

- The marginal likelihood of a Gaussian process provides a powerful mechanism for flexible kernel learning. Kernel learning enables us to provide long-range extrapolations, but also tells us interpretable properties of the data that we didn't know before, towards scientific discovery.

- Gaussian processes are often used as a probabilistic surrogate for optimizing expensive objectives, in a procedure known as **Bayesian optimization** (Section 6.6).

18.2   Mercer kernels

The generalization properties of Gaussian processes boil down to how we encode prior knowledge about the similarity of two input vectors. If we know that x_i is similar to x_j, then we can encourage the model to make the predicted output at both locations (i.e., $f(x_i)$ and $f(x_j)$) to be similar.

To define similarity, we introduce the notion of a **kernel function**. The word "kernel" has many different meanings in mathematics; here we consider a **Mercer kernel**, also called a **positive definite kernel**. This is any symmetric function $\mathcal{K} : \mathcal{X} \times \mathcal{X} \to \mathbb{R}^+$ such that

$$\sum_{i=1}^{N} \sum_{j=1}^{N} \mathcal{K}(x_i, x_j) c_i c_j \geq 0 \tag{18.5}$$

for any set of N (unique) points $x_i \in \mathcal{X}$, and any choice of numbers $c_i \in \mathbb{R}$. We assume $\mathcal{K}(x_i, x_j) > 0$, so that we can only achieve equality in the above equation if $c_i = 0$ for all i.

Another way to understand this condition is the following. Given a set of N datapoints, let us define the **Gram matrix** as the following $N \times N$ similarity matrix:

$$\mathbf{K} = \begin{pmatrix} \mathcal{K}(x_1, x_1) & \cdots & \mathcal{K}(x_1, x_N) \\ & \vdots & \\ \mathcal{K}(x_N, x_1) & \cdots & \mathcal{K}(x_N, x_N) \end{pmatrix} \tag{18.6}$$

We say that $\mathcal{K}$ is a Mercer kernel iff the Gram matrix is positive definite for any set of (distinct) inputs $\{\boldsymbol{x}_i\}_{i=1}^N$.

We discuss several popular Mercer kernels below. More details can be found at [Wil14] and https://www.cs.toronto.edu/~duvenaud/cookbook/. See also Section 18.6 where we discuss how to learn kernels from data.

18.2.1   Stationary kernels

For real-valued inputs, $\mathcal{X} = \mathbb{R}^D$, it is common to use **stationary kernels** (also called **shift-invariant kernels**), which are functions of the form $\mathcal{K}(\boldsymbol{x}, \boldsymbol{x}') = \mathcal{K}(\boldsymbol{r})$, where $\boldsymbol{r} = \boldsymbol{x} - \boldsymbol{x}'$; thus the output only depends on the relative difference between the inputs. (See Section 18.2.2 for a discussion of non-stationary kernels.) Furthermore, in many cases, all that matters is the magnitude of the difference:

$$r = ||\boldsymbol{r}||_2 = ||\boldsymbol{x} - \boldsymbol{x}'|| \tag{18.7}$$

We give some examples below. (See also Figure 18.3 and Figure 18.4 for some visualizations of these kernels.)

18.2.1.1   Squared exponential (RBF) kernel

The **squared exponential** (SE) kernel, also sometimes called the **exponentiated quadratic** kernel or the **radial basis function** (**RBF**) kernel, is defined as

$$\mathcal{K}(r; \ell) = \exp\left(-\frac{r^2}{2\ell^2}\right) \tag{18.8}$$

Here ℓ corresponds to the **length-scale** of the kernel, i.e., the distance over which we expect differences to matter.

From Equation (18.7) we can rewrite this kernel as

$$\mathcal{K}(\boldsymbol{x}, \boldsymbol{x}'; \ell) = \exp\left(-\frac{||\boldsymbol{x} - \boldsymbol{x}'||^2}{2\ell^2}\right) \tag{18.9}$$

This is the RBF kernel we encountered earlier. It is also sometimes called the **Gaussian kernel**.

See Figure 18.3(f) and Figure 18.4(f) for a visualization in 1D.

18.2.1.2   ARD kernel

We can generalize the RBF kernel by replacing Euclidean distance with Mahalanobis distance, as follows:

$$\mathcal{K}(\boldsymbol{r}; \boldsymbol{\Sigma}, \sigma^2) = \sigma^2 \exp\left(-\frac{1}{2} \boldsymbol{r}^\mathsf{T} \boldsymbol{\Sigma}^{-1} \boldsymbol{r}\right) \tag{18.10}$$

where $\boldsymbol{r} = \boldsymbol{x} - \boldsymbol{x}'$. If $\boldsymbol{\Sigma}$ is diagonal, this can be written as

$$\mathcal{K}(\boldsymbol{r}; \boldsymbol{\ell}, \sigma^2) = \sigma^2 \exp\left(-\frac{1}{2} \sum_{d=1}^{D} \frac{1}{\ell_d^2} r_d^2\right) = \prod_{d=1}^{D} \mathcal{K}(r_d; \ell_d, \sigma^{2/d}) \tag{18.11}$$

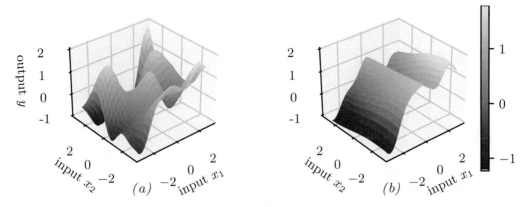

Figure 18.2: *Function samples from a GP with an ARD kernel.* (a) $\ell_1 = \ell_2 = 1$. *Both dimensions contribute to the response.* (b) $\ell_1 = 1$, $\ell_2 = 5$. *The second dimension is essentially ignored. Adapted from Figure 5.1 of [RW06]. Generated by* gpr_demo_ard.ipynb.

where

$$\mathcal{K}(r; \ell, \tau^2) = \tau^2 \exp\left(-\frac{1}{2}\frac{1}{\ell^2} r^2\right) \tag{18.12}$$

We can interpret σ^2 as the overall variance, and ℓ_d as defining the **characteristic length scale** of dimension d. If d is an irrelevant input dimension, we can set $\ell_d = \infty$, so the corresponding dimension will be ignored. This is known as **automatic relevance determination** or **ARD** (Section 15.2.8). Hence the corresponding kernel is called the **ARD kernel**. See Figure 18.2 for an illustration of some 2d functions sampled from a GP using this prior.

18.2.1.3 Matérn kernels

The SE kernel gives rise to functions that are infinitely differentiable, and therefore are very smooth. For many applications, it is better to use the **Matérn kernel**, which gives rise to "rougher" functions, which can better model local "wiggles" without having to make the overall length scale very small.

The Matérn kernel has the following form:

$$\mathcal{K}(r; \nu, \ell) = \frac{2^{1-\nu}}{\Gamma(\nu)}\left(\frac{\sqrt{2\nu}r}{\ell}\right)^{\nu} K_{\nu}\left(\frac{\sqrt{2\nu}r}{\ell}\right) \tag{18.13}$$

where K_{ν} is a modified Bessel function and ℓ is the length scale. Functions sampled from this GP are k-times differentiable iff $\nu > k$. As $\nu \to \infty$, this approaches the SE kernel.

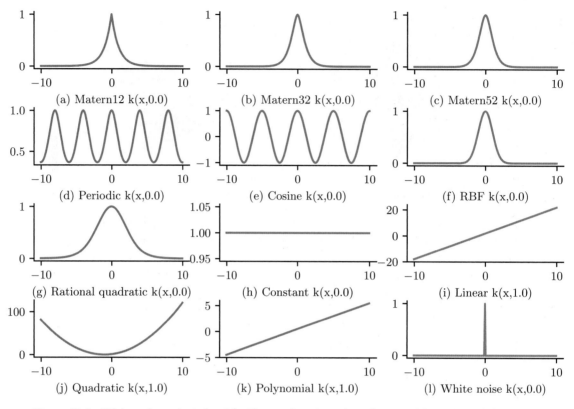

Figure 18.3: *GP kernels evaluated at* $k(x, 0)$ *as a function of* x. *Generated by* gpKernelPlot.ipynb.

For values $\nu \in \{\frac{1}{2}, \frac{3}{2}, \frac{5}{2}\}$, the function simplifies as follows:

$$\mathcal{K}(r; \frac{1}{2}, \ell) = \exp(-\frac{r}{\ell}) \tag{18.14}$$

$$\mathcal{K}(r; \frac{3}{2}, \ell) = \left(1 + \frac{\sqrt{3}r}{\ell}\right) \exp\left(-\frac{\sqrt{3}r}{\ell}\right) \tag{18.15}$$

$$\mathcal{K}(r; \frac{5}{2}, \ell) = \left(1 + \frac{\sqrt{5}r}{\ell} + \frac{5r^2}{3\ell^2}\right) \exp\left(-\frac{\sqrt{5}r}{\ell}\right) \tag{18.16}$$

See Figure 18.3(a-c) and Figure 18.4(a-c) for a visualization.

The value $\nu = \frac{1}{2}$ corresponds to the **Ornstein-Uhlenbeck process**, which describes the velocity of a particle undergoing Brownian motion. The corresponding function is continuous but not differentiable, and hence is very "jagged".

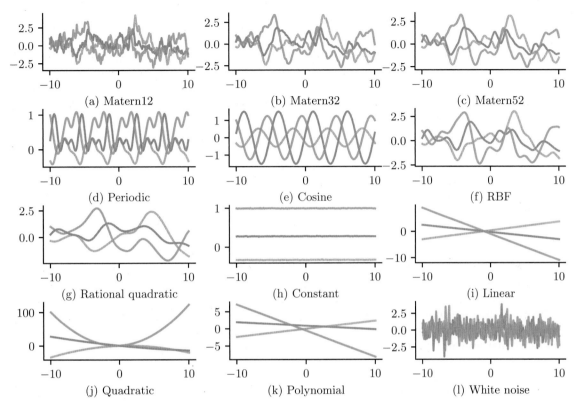

Figure 18.4: *GP samples drawn using different kernels. Generated by* gpKernelPlot.ipynb.

18.2.1.4 Periodic kernels

One way to create a periodic 1d random function is to map x to the 2d space $\boldsymbol{u}(x) = (\cos(x), \sin(x))$, and then use an SE kernel in $\boldsymbol{u}$-space:

$$\mathcal{K}(x, x') = \exp\left(-\frac{2\sin^2((x - x')/2)}{\ell^2}\right) \tag{18.17}$$

which follows since $(\cos(x) - \cos(x'))^2 + (\sin(x) - \sin(x'))^2 = 4\sin^2((x - x')/2)$. We can generalize this by specifying the period p to get the **periodic kernel**, also called the **exp-sine-squared kernel**:

$$\mathcal{K}_{\mathrm{per}}(r; \ell, p) = \exp\left(-\frac{2}{\ell^2}\sin^2(\pi\frac{r}{p})\right) \tag{18.18}$$

where p is the period and ℓ is the length scale. See Figure 18.3(d-e) and Figure 18.4(d-e) for a visualization.

A related kernel is the **cosine kernel**:

$$\mathcal{K}(r; p) = \cos\left(2\pi\frac{r}{p}\right) \tag{18.19}$$

18.2.1.5   Rational quadratic kernel

We define the **rational quadratic** kernel to be

$$\mathcal{K}_{RQ}(r; \ell, \alpha) = \left(1 + \frac{r^2}{2\alpha\ell^2}\right)^{-\alpha} \tag{18.20}$$

We recognize this is proportional to a Student t density. Hence it can be interpreted as a scale mixture of SE kernels of different characteristic lengths. In particular, let $\tau = 1/\ell^2$, and assume $\tau \sim \text{Ga}(\alpha, \ell^2)$. Then one can show that

$$\mathcal{K}_{RQ}(r) = \int p(\tau|\alpha, \ell^2)\mathcal{K}_{SE}(r|\tau)d\tau \tag{18.21}$$

As $\alpha \to \infty$, this reduces to a SE kernel.

See Figure 18.3(g) and Figure 18.4(g) for a visualization.

18.2.1.6   Kernels from spectral densities

Consider the case of a stationary kernel which satisfies $\mathcal{K}(\boldsymbol{x}, \boldsymbol{x}') = \mathcal{K}(\boldsymbol{\delta})$, where $\boldsymbol{\delta} = \boldsymbol{x} - \boldsymbol{x}'$, for $\boldsymbol{x}, \boldsymbol{x}' \in \mathbb{R}^d$. Let us further assume that $\mathcal{K}(\boldsymbol{\delta})$ is positive definite. In this case, **Bochner's theorem** tells us that we can represent $\mathcal{K}(\boldsymbol{\delta})$ by its Fourier transform:

$$\mathcal{K}(\boldsymbol{\delta}) = \int_{\mathbb{R}^d} p(\boldsymbol{\omega})e^{j\boldsymbol{\omega}^\top\boldsymbol{\delta}}d\boldsymbol{\omega} \tag{18.22}$$

where $j = \sqrt{-1}$, $e^{j\theta} = \cos(\theta) + j\sin(\theta)$, $\boldsymbol{\omega}$ is the frequency, and $p(\boldsymbol{\omega})$ is the **spectral density** (see [SS19, p93, p253] for details).

We can easily derive and gain intuitions into several kernels from spectral densities. If we take the Fourier transform of an RBF kernel we find the spectral density $p(\boldsymbol{\omega}) = \sqrt{2\pi\ell^2}\exp\left(-2\pi^2\boldsymbol{\omega}^2\ell^2\right)$. Thus the spectral density is also Gaussian, but with a bandwidth *inversely* proportional to the length-scale hyperparameter ℓ. That is, as ℓ becomes large, the spectral density collapses onto a point mass. This result is intuitive: as we increase the length-scale, our model treats points as correlated over large distances, and becomes very smooth and slowly varying, and thus low-frequency. In general, since the Gaussian distribution has relatively light tails, we can see that RBF kernels won't generally support high frequency solutions.

We can instead use a Student t spectral density, which has heavy tails that will provide greater support for higher frequencies. Taking the inverse Fourier transform of this spectral density, we recover the Matérn kernel, with degrees of freedom ν corresponding to the degrees of freedom in the spectral density. Indeed, the smaller we make ν, the less smooth and higher frequency are the associated fits to data using a Matérn kernel.

We can also derive **spectral mixture kernels** by modelling the spectral density as a scale-location mixture of Gaussians and taking the inverse Fourier transform [WA13]. Since scale-location mixtures of Gaussians are dense in the set of distributions, and can therefore approximate any spectral density, this kernel can approximate any stationary kernel to arbitrary precision. The spectral mixture kernel thus forms a powerful approach to kernel learning, which we discuss further in Section 18.6.5.

18.2.2 Nonstationary kernels

A stationary kernel assumes the measure of similarity between two inputs is independent of their location, i.e., $\mathcal{K}(\boldsymbol{x}, \boldsymbol{x}')$ only depends on $\boldsymbol{r} = \boldsymbol{x} - \boldsymbol{x}'$. A **nonstationary kernel** relaxes this assumption. This is useful for a variety of problems, such as environmental modeling (see e.g., [GSR12; Pat+22]), where correlations between locations can change depending on latent factors in the environment.

18.2.2.1 Polynomial kernels

A simple form of non-stationary kernel is the **polynomial kernel** (also called **dot product kernel**) of order M, defined by

$$\mathcal{K}(\boldsymbol{x}, \boldsymbol{x}') = (\boldsymbol{x}^\mathsf{T} \boldsymbol{x}')^M \tag{18.23}$$

This contains all monomials of order M. For example, if $M = 2$, we get the **quadratic kernel**; in 2d, this becomes

$$(\boldsymbol{x}^\mathsf{T} \boldsymbol{x}')^2 = (x_1 x_1' + x_2 x_2')^2 = (x_1 x_1')^2 + (x_2 x_2)^2 + 2(x_1 x_1')(x_2 x_2') \tag{18.24}$$

We can generalize this to contain all terms up to degree M by using the **inhomogeneous polynomial kernel**

$$\mathcal{K}(\boldsymbol{x}, \boldsymbol{x}') = (\boldsymbol{x}^\mathsf{T} \boldsymbol{x}' + c)^M \tag{18.25}$$

For example, if $M = 2$ and the inputs are 2d, we have

$$\begin{aligned}
(\boldsymbol{x}^\mathsf{T} \boldsymbol{x}' + 1)^2 &= (x_1 x_1')^2 + (x_1 x_1')(x_2 x_2') + (x_1 x_1') \\
&\quad + (x_2 x_2)(x_1 x_1') + (x_2 x_2')^2 + (x_2 x_2') \\
&\quad + (x_1 x_1') + (x_2 x_2') + 1
\end{aligned} \tag{18.26}$$

18.2.2.2 Gibbs kernel

Consider an RBF kernel where the length scale hyper-parameter, and the signal variance hyper-parameter, are both input dependent; this is called the **Gibbs kernel** [Gib97], and is defined by

$$\mathcal{K}(\boldsymbol{x}, \boldsymbol{x}') = \sigma(\boldsymbol{x})\sigma(\boldsymbol{x}') \sqrt{\frac{2\ell(\boldsymbol{x})\ell(\boldsymbol{x}')}{\ell(\boldsymbol{x})^2 + \ell(\boldsymbol{x}')^2}} \exp\left(-\frac{||\boldsymbol{x} - \boldsymbol{x}'||^2}{\ell(\boldsymbol{x})^2 + \ell(\boldsymbol{x}')^2} \right) \tag{18.27}$$

If $\ell(\boldsymbol{x})$ and $\sigma(\boldsymbol{x})$ are constants, this reduces to the standard RBF kernel. We can model the functional dependency of these kernel parameters on the input by using another GP (see e.g., [Hei+16]).

18.2.2.3 Other non-stationary kernels

Other ways to induce non-stationarity include using a neural network kernel (Section 18.7.1), non-stationary spectral kernels [RHK17], or a deep GP (Section 18.7.3).

18.2.3   Kernels for nonvectorial (structured) inputs

Kernels are particularly useful when the inputs are structured objects, such as strings and graphs, since it is often hard to "featurize" variable-sized inputs. For example, we can define a **string kernel** which compares strings in terms of the number of n-grams they have in common [Lod+02; BC17].

We can also define kernels on graphs [KJM19]. For example, the **random walk kernel** conceptually performs random walks on two graphs simultaneously, and then counts the number of paths that were produced by both walks. This can be computed efficiently as discussed in [Vis+10]. For more details on graph kernels, see [KJM19].

For a review of kernels on structured objects, see e.g., [Gär03].

18.2.4   Making new kernels from old

Given two valid kernels $\mathcal{K}_1(\boldsymbol{x}, \boldsymbol{x}')$ and $\mathcal{K}_2(\boldsymbol{x}, \boldsymbol{x}')$, we can create a new kernel using any of the following methods:

$$\mathcal{K}(\boldsymbol{x}, \boldsymbol{x}') = c\mathcal{K}_1(\boldsymbol{x}, \boldsymbol{x}'), \text{ for any constant } c > 0 \tag{18.28}$$

$$\mathcal{K}(\boldsymbol{x}, \boldsymbol{x}') = f(\boldsymbol{x})\mathcal{K}_1(\boldsymbol{x}, \boldsymbol{x}')f(\boldsymbol{x}'), \text{ for any function } f \tag{18.29}$$

$$\mathcal{K}(\boldsymbol{x}, \boldsymbol{x}') = q(\mathcal{K}_1(\boldsymbol{x}, \boldsymbol{x}')) \text{ for any function polynomial } q \text{ with nonneg. coef.} \tag{18.30}$$

$$\mathcal{K}(\boldsymbol{x}, \boldsymbol{x}') = \exp(\mathcal{K}_1(\boldsymbol{x}, \boldsymbol{x}')) \tag{18.31}$$

$$\mathcal{K}(\boldsymbol{x}, \boldsymbol{x}') = \boldsymbol{x}^\mathsf{T}\mathbf{A}\boldsymbol{x}', \text{ for any psd matrix } \mathbf{A} \tag{18.32}$$

For example, suppose we start with the linear kernel $\mathcal{K}(\boldsymbol{x}, \boldsymbol{x}') = \boldsymbol{x}\boldsymbol{x}'$. We know this is a valid Mercer kernel, since the corresponding Gram matrix is just the (scaled) covariance matrix of the data. From the above rules, we can see that the polynomial kernel $\mathcal{K}(\boldsymbol{x}, \boldsymbol{x}') = (\boldsymbol{x}^\mathsf{T}\boldsymbol{x}')^M$ from Section 18.2.2.1 is a valid Mercer kernel.

We can also use the above rules to establish that the Gaussian kernel is a valid kernel. To see this, note that

$$||\boldsymbol{x} - \boldsymbol{x}'||^2 = \boldsymbol{x}^\mathsf{T}\boldsymbol{x} + (\boldsymbol{x}')^\mathsf{T}\boldsymbol{x}' - 2\boldsymbol{x}^\mathsf{T}\boldsymbol{x}' \tag{18.33}$$

and hence

$$\mathcal{K}(\boldsymbol{x}, \boldsymbol{x}') = \exp(-||\boldsymbol{x} - \boldsymbol{x}'||^2/2\sigma^2) = \exp(-\boldsymbol{x}^\mathsf{T}\boldsymbol{x}/2\sigma^2)\exp(\boldsymbol{x}^\mathsf{T}\boldsymbol{x}'/\sigma^2)\exp(-(\boldsymbol{x}')^\mathsf{T}\boldsymbol{x}'/2\sigma^2) \tag{18.34}$$

is a valid kernel.

We can also combine kernels using addition or multiplication:

$$\mathcal{K}(\boldsymbol{x}, \boldsymbol{x}') = \mathcal{K}_1(\boldsymbol{x}, \boldsymbol{x}') + \mathcal{K}_2(\boldsymbol{x}, \boldsymbol{x}') \tag{18.35}$$

$$\mathcal{K}(\boldsymbol{x}, \boldsymbol{x}') = \mathcal{K}_1(\boldsymbol{x}, \boldsymbol{x}') \times \mathcal{K}_2(\boldsymbol{x}, \boldsymbol{x}') \tag{18.36}$$

Multiplying two positive-definite kernels together always results in another positive definite kernel. This is a way to get a conjunction of the individual properties of each kernel, as illustrated in Figure 18.5.

In addition, adding two positive-definite kernels together always results in another positive definite kernel. This is a way to get a disjunction of the individual properties of each kernel, as illustrated in Figure 18.6.

For an example of combining kernels to forecast some time series data, see Section 18.8.1.

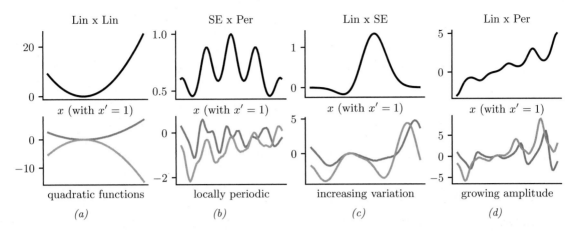

Figure 18.5: *Examples of 1d structures obtained by multiplying elementary kernels. Top row shows* $\mathcal{K}(x, x' = 1)$. *Bottom row shows some functions sampled from* $GP(f|0, \mathcal{K})$. *Adapted from Figure 2.2 of [Duv14]. Generated by* combining_kernels_by_multiplication.ipynb.

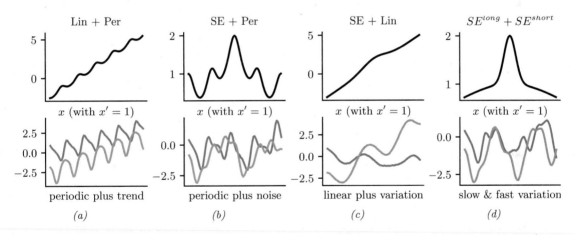

Figure 18.6: *Examples of 1d structures obtained by summing elementary kernels. Top row shows* $\mathcal{K}(x, x' = 1)$. *Bottom row shows some functions sampled from* $GP(f|0, \mathcal{K})$. *Adapted from Figure 2.2 of [Duv14]. Generated by* combining_kernels_by_summation.ipynb.

18.2.5 Mercer's theorem

Recall that any positive definite matrix $\mathbf{K}$ can be represented using an eigendecomposition of the form $\mathbf{K} = \mathbf{U}^\mathsf{T} \mathbf{\Lambda} \mathbf{U}$, where $\mathbf{\Lambda}$ is a diagonal matrix of eigenvalues $\lambda_i > 0$, and $\mathbf{U}$ is a matrix containing the eigenvectors. Now consider element (i, j) of $\mathbf{K}$:

$$k_{ij} = (\mathbf{\Lambda}^{\frac{1}{2}} \mathbf{U}_{:i})^\mathsf{T} (\mathbf{\Lambda}^{\frac{1}{2}} \mathbf{U}_{:j}) \tag{18.37}$$

where $\mathbf{U}_{:i}$ is the i'th column of $\mathbf{U}$. If we define $\phi(\boldsymbol{x}_i) = \mathbf{U}_{:i}$, then we can write

$$k_{ij} = \sum_{m=1}^{M} \lambda_m \phi_m(\boldsymbol{x}_i)\phi_m(\boldsymbol{x}_j) \tag{18.38}$$

where M is the rank of the kernel matrix. Thus we see that the entries in the kernel matrix can be computed by performing an inner product of some feature vectors that are implicitly defined by the eigenvectors of the kernel matrix.

This idea can be generalized to apply to kernel functions, not just kernel matrices, as we now show. First, we define an **eigenfunction** $\phi()$ of a kernel $\mathcal{K}$ with eigenvalue λ wrt measure μ as a function that satisfies

$$\int \mathcal{K}(\boldsymbol{x}, \boldsymbol{x}')\phi(\boldsymbol{x})d\mu(\boldsymbol{x}) = \lambda\phi(\boldsymbol{x}') \tag{18.39}$$

We usually sort the eigenfunctions in order of decreasing eigenvalue, $\lambda_1 \geq \lambda_2 \geq \cdots$. The eigenfunctions are orthogonal wrt μ:

$$\int \phi_i(\boldsymbol{x})\phi_j(\boldsymbol{x})d\mu(\boldsymbol{x}) = \delta_{ij} \tag{18.40}$$

where δ_{ij} is the Kronecker delta. With this definition in hand, we can state **Mercer's theorem**. Informally, it says that any positive definite kernel function can be represented as the following infinite sum:

$$\mathcal{K}(\boldsymbol{x}, \boldsymbol{x}') = \sum_{m=1}^{\infty} \lambda_m \phi_m(\boldsymbol{x})\phi_m(\boldsymbol{x}') \tag{18.41}$$

where ϕ_m are eigenfunctions of the kernel, and λ_m are the corresponding eigenvalues. This is the functional analog of Equation (18.38).

A **degenerate kernel** has only a finite number of non-zero eigenvalues. In this case, we can rewrite the kernel function as an inner product between two finite-length vectors. For example, consider the quadratic kernel $\mathcal{K}(\boldsymbol{x}, \boldsymbol{x}') = \langle \boldsymbol{x}, \boldsymbol{x}' \rangle^2$ from Equation (18.24). If we define $\phi(x_1, x_2) = [x_1^2, \sqrt{2}x_1x_2, x_2^2] \in \mathbb{R}^3$, then we can write this as $\mathcal{K}(\boldsymbol{x}, \boldsymbol{x}') = \phi(\boldsymbol{x})^\mathsf{T}\phi(\boldsymbol{x})$. Thus we see that this kernel is degenerate.

Now consider the RBF kernel. In this case, the corresponding feature representation is infinite dimensional (see Section 18.2.6 for details). However, by working with kernel functions, we can avoid having to deal with infinite dimensional vectors.

From the anove, we see that we can replace inner product operations in an explicit (possibly infinite dimensional) feature space with a call to a kernel function, i.e., we replace $\phi(\boldsymbol{x})^\mathsf{T}\phi(\boldsymbol{x})$ with $\mathcal{K}(\boldsymbol{x}, \boldsymbol{x}')$. This is called the **kernel trick**.

18.2.6 Approximating kernels with random features

Although the power of kernels resides in the ability to avoid working with featurized representations of the inputs, such kernelized methods can take $O(N^3)$ time, in order to invert the Gram matrix $\mathbf{K}$, as we wil see in Section 18.3. This can make it difficult to use such methods on large scale data.

Fortunately, we can approximate the feature map for many kernels using a randomly chosen finite set of M basis functions, thus reducing the cost to $O(NM + M^3)$.

We will show how to do this for shift-invariant kernels by returning to Bochner's theorem in Eq. (18.22). In the case of a Gaussian RBF kernel, we have seen that the spectral density is a Gaussian distribution. Hence we can easily compute a Monte Carlo approximation to this integral by sampling random Gaussian vectors. This yields the following approximation: $\mathcal{K}(\boldsymbol{x}, \boldsymbol{x}') \approx \phi(\boldsymbol{x})^\mathsf{T} \phi(\boldsymbol{x})$, where the (real-valued) feature vector is given by

$$\phi(\boldsymbol{x}) = \sqrt{\frac{1}{D}} \left[\sin(\boldsymbol{z}_1^\mathsf{T} \boldsymbol{x}), \cdots, \sin(\boldsymbol{z}_D^\mathsf{T} \boldsymbol{x}), \cos(\boldsymbol{z}_1^\mathsf{T} \boldsymbol{x}), \cdots, \cos(\boldsymbol{z}_D^\mathsf{T} \boldsymbol{x}) \right] \tag{18.42}$$

$$= \sqrt{\frac{1}{D}} \left[\sin(\mathbf{Z}^\mathsf{T} \boldsymbol{x}), \cos(\mathbf{Z}^\mathsf{T} \boldsymbol{x}) \right] \tag{18.43}$$

Here $\mathbf{Z} = (1/\sigma)\mathbf{G}$, and $\mathbf{G} \in \mathbb{R}^{d \times D}$ is a random Gaussian matrix, where the entries are sampled iid from $\mathcal{N}(0, 1)$. The representation in Equation (18.43) are called **random Fourier features (RFF)** [SS15; RR08] or "weighted sums of random kitchen sinks" [RR09]. (One can obtain an even better approximation by ensuring that the rows of $\mathbf{Z}$ are random but orthogonal; this is called **orthogonal random features** [Yu+16].)

One can create similar random feature representations for other kinds of kernels. We can then use such features for supervised learning by defining $f(\boldsymbol{x}; \boldsymbol{\theta}) = \mathbf{W}\varphi(\mathbf{Z}\boldsymbol{x}) + \boldsymbol{b}$, where $\mathbf{Z}$ is a random Gaussian matrix, and the form of φ depends on the chosen kernel. This is equivalent to a one layer MLP with random input-to-hidden weights; since we only optimize the hidden-to-output weights $\boldsymbol{\theta} = (\mathbf{W}, \boldsymbol{b})$, the model is equivalent to a linear model with fixed random features. If we use enough random features, we can approximate the performance of a kernelized prediction model, but the computational cost is now $O(N)$ rather than $O(N^2)$.

Unfortunately, random features can result in worse performance than using a non-degenerate kernel, since they don't have enough expressive power. We discuss other ways to scale GPs to large datasets in Section 18.5.

18.3 GPs with Gaussian likelihoods

In this section, we discuss GPs for regression, using a Gaussian likelihood. In this case, all the computations can be performed in closed form, using standard linear algebra methods. We extend this framework to non-Gaussian likelihoods later in the chapter.

18.3.1 Predictions using noise-free observations

Suppose we observe a training set $\mathcal{D} = \{(\boldsymbol{x}_n, y_n) : n = 1 : N\}$, where $y_n = f(\boldsymbol{x}_n)$ is the noise-free observation of the function evaluated at $\boldsymbol{x}_n$. If we ask the GP to predict $f(\boldsymbol{x})$ for a value of $\boldsymbol{x}$ that it has already seen, we want the GP to return the answer $f(\boldsymbol{x})$ with no uncertainty. In other words, it should act as an **interpolator** of the training data. Here we assume the observed function values are noiseless. We will consider the case of noisy observations shortly.

Now we consider the case of predicting the outputs for new inputs that may not be in $\mathcal{D}$. Specifically, given a test set $\mathbf{X}_*$ of size $N_* \times D$, we want to predict the function outputs $\boldsymbol{f}_* = [f(\boldsymbol{x}_1), \ldots, f(\boldsymbol{x}_{N_*})]$.

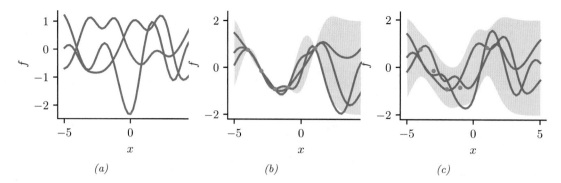

Figure 18.7: Left: some functions sampled from a GP prior with RBF kernel. Middle: some samples from a GP posterior, after conditioning on 5 noise-free observations. Right: some samples from a GP posterior, after conditioning on 5 noisy observations. The shaded area represents $\mathbb{E}\left[f(\boldsymbol{x})\right] \pm 2\sqrt{\mathbb{V}[f(\boldsymbol{x})]}$. Adapted from Figure 2.2 of [RW06]. Generated by gpr_demo_noise_free.ipynb.

By definition of the GP, the joint distribution $p(\boldsymbol{f}_X, \boldsymbol{f}_* | \mathbf{X}, \mathbf{X}_*)$ has the following form

$$
\begin{pmatrix} \boldsymbol{f}_X \\ \boldsymbol{f}_* \end{pmatrix} \sim \mathcal{N}\left(\begin{pmatrix} \boldsymbol{\mu}_X \\ \boldsymbol{\mu}_* \end{pmatrix}, \begin{pmatrix} \mathbf{K}_{X,X} & \mathbf{K}_{X,*} \\ \mathbf{K}_{X,*}^\mathsf{T} & \mathbf{K}_{*,*} \end{pmatrix} \right)
\tag{18.44}
$$

where $\boldsymbol{\mu}_X = (m(\boldsymbol{x}_1), \ldots, m(\boldsymbol{x}_N))$, $\boldsymbol{\mu}_* = (m(\boldsymbol{x}_1^*), \ldots, m(\boldsymbol{x}_{N_*}^*))$, $\mathbf{K}_{X,X} = \mathcal{K}(\mathbf{X}, \mathbf{X})$ is $N \times N$, $\mathbf{K}_{X,*} = \mathcal{K}(\mathbf{X}, \mathbf{X}_*)$ is $N \times N_*$, and $\mathbf{K}_{*,*} = \mathcal{K}(\mathbf{X}_*, \mathbf{X}_*)$ is $N_* \times N_*$. See Figure 18.7 for a static illustration, and http://www.infinitecuriosity.org/vizgp/ for an interactive visualization.

By the standard rules for conditioning Gaussians (Section 2.3.1.4), the posterior has the following form

$$
p(\boldsymbol{f}_* | \mathbf{X}_*, \mathcal{D}) = \mathcal{N}(\boldsymbol{f}_* | \boldsymbol{\mu}_{*|X}, \boldsymbol{\Sigma}_{*|X})
\tag{18.45}
$$

$$
\boldsymbol{\mu}_{*|X} = \boldsymbol{\mu}_* + \mathbf{K}_{X,*}^\mathsf{T} \mathbf{K}_{X,X}^{-1} (\boldsymbol{f}_X - \boldsymbol{\mu}_X)
\tag{18.46}
$$

$$
\boldsymbol{\Sigma}_{*|X} = \mathbf{K}_{*,*} - \mathbf{K}_{X,*}^\mathsf{T} \mathbf{K}^{-1} \mathbf{K}_{X,*}
\tag{18.47}
$$

This process is illustrated in Figure 18.7. On the left we show some samples from the prior, $p(f)$, where we use an RBF kernel (Section 18.2.1.1) and a zero mean function. On the right, we show samples from the posterior, $p(f|\mathcal{D})$. We see that the model perfectly interpolates the training data, and that the predictive uncertainty increases as we move further away from the observed data.

Note that the cost of the above method for sampling N_* points is $O(N_*^3)$. This can be reduced to $O(N_*)$ time using the methods in [Ple+18; Wil+20a].

18.3.2   Predictions using noisy observations

In Section 18.3.1, we showed how to do GP regression when the training data was noiseless. Now let us consider the case where what we observe is a noisy version of the underlying function, $y_n = f(\boldsymbol{x}_n) + \epsilon_n$, where $\epsilon_n \sim \mathcal{N}(0, \sigma_y^2)$. In this case, the model is not required to interpolate the data, but it must come "close" to the observed data. The covariance of the observed noisy responses is

$$
\text{Cov}\left[y_i, y_j\right] = \text{Cov}\left[f_i, f_j\right] + \text{Cov}\left[\epsilon_i, \epsilon_j\right] = \mathcal{K}(\boldsymbol{x}_i, \boldsymbol{x}_j) + \sigma_y^2 \delta_{ij}
\tag{18.48}
$$

where $\delta_{ij} = \mathbb{I}\,(i = j)$. In other words

$$\text{Cov}\,[\boldsymbol{y}|\mathbf{X}] = \mathbf{K}_{X,X} + \sigma_y^2 \mathbf{I}_N \tag{18.49}$$

The joint density of the observed data and the latent, noise-free function on the test points is given by

$$\begin{pmatrix} \boldsymbol{y} \\ \boldsymbol{f}_* \end{pmatrix} \sim \mathcal{N}\left(\begin{pmatrix} \boldsymbol{\mu}_X \\ \boldsymbol{\mu}_* \end{pmatrix}, \begin{pmatrix} \mathbf{K}_{X,X} + \sigma_y^2 \mathbf{I} & \mathbf{K}_{X,*} \\ \mathbf{K}_{X,*}^\mathsf{T} & \mathbf{K}_{*,*} \end{pmatrix} \right) \tag{18.50}$$

Hence the posterior predictive density at a set of test points $\mathbf{X}_*$ is

$$p(\boldsymbol{f}_*|\mathcal{D}, \mathbf{X}_*) = \mathcal{N}(\boldsymbol{f}_*|\boldsymbol{\mu}_{*|X}, \boldsymbol{\Sigma}_{*|X}) \tag{18.51}$$

$$\boldsymbol{\mu}_{*|X} = \boldsymbol{\mu}_* + \mathbf{K}_{X,*}^\mathsf{T}(\mathbf{K}_{X,X} + \sigma_y^2 \mathbf{I})^{-1}(\boldsymbol{y} - \boldsymbol{\mu}_X) \tag{18.52}$$

$$\boldsymbol{\Sigma}_{*|X} = \mathbf{K}_{*,*} - \mathbf{K}_{X,*}^\mathsf{T}(\mathbf{K}_{X,X} + \sigma_y^2 \mathbf{I})^{-1}\mathbf{K}_{X,*} \tag{18.53}$$

In the case of a single test input, this simplifies as follows

$$p(f_*|\mathcal{D}, \boldsymbol{x}_*) = \mathcal{N}(f_*|m_* + \boldsymbol{k}_*^\mathsf{T}(\mathbf{K}_{X,X} + \sigma_y^2 \mathbf{I})^{-1}(\boldsymbol{y} - \boldsymbol{\mu}_X), \; k_{**} - \boldsymbol{k}_*^\mathsf{T}(\mathbf{K}_{X,X} + \sigma_y^2 \mathbf{I})^{-1}\boldsymbol{k}_*) \tag{18.54}$$

where $\boldsymbol{k}_* = [\mathcal{K}(\boldsymbol{x}_*, \boldsymbol{x}_1), \ldots, \mathcal{K}(\boldsymbol{x}_*, \boldsymbol{x}_N)]$ and $k_{**} = \mathcal{K}(\boldsymbol{x}_*, \boldsymbol{x}_*)$. If the mean function is zero, we can write the posterior mean as follows:

$$\boldsymbol{\mu}_{*|X} = \boldsymbol{k}_*^\mathsf{T} \underbrace{\mathbf{K}_\sigma^{-1} \boldsymbol{y}}_{\boldsymbol{\alpha}} = \sum_{n=1}^{N} \mathcal{K}(\boldsymbol{x}_*, \boldsymbol{x}_n)\alpha_n \tag{18.55}$$

where

$$\mathbf{K}_\sigma = \mathbf{K}_{X,X} + \sigma_y^2 \mathbf{I} \tag{18.56}$$

$$\boldsymbol{\alpha} = \mathbf{K}_\sigma^{-1} \boldsymbol{y} \tag{18.57}$$

Fitting this model amounts to computing $\boldsymbol{\alpha}$ in Equation (18.57). This is usually done by computing the Cholesky decomposition of $\mathbf{K}_\sigma$, as described in Section 18.3.6. Once we have computed $\boldsymbol{\alpha}$, we can compute predictions for each test point in $O(N)$ time for the mean, and $O(N^2)$ time for the variance.

18.3.3 Weight space vs function space

In this section, we show how Bayesian linear regression is a special case of a GP.

Consider the linear regression model $y = f(\boldsymbol{x}) + \epsilon$, where $f(\boldsymbol{x}) = \boldsymbol{w}^\mathsf{T}\boldsymbol{\phi}(\boldsymbol{x})$ and $\epsilon \sim \mathcal{N}(0, \sigma_y^2)$. If we use a Gaussian prior $p(\boldsymbol{w}) = \mathcal{N}(\boldsymbol{w}|\boldsymbol{0}, \boldsymbol{\Sigma}_w)$, then the posterior is as follows (see Section 15.2.2 for the derivation):

$$p(\boldsymbol{w}|\mathcal{D}) = \mathcal{N}(\boldsymbol{w}|\frac{1}{\sigma_y^2}\mathbf{A}^{-1}\boldsymbol{\Phi}^T\boldsymbol{y}, \mathbf{A}^{-1}) \tag{18.58}$$

where $\boldsymbol{\Phi}$ is the $N \times D$ design matrix, and

$$\mathbf{A} = \sigma_y^{-2}\boldsymbol{\Phi}^\mathsf{T}\boldsymbol{\Phi} + \boldsymbol{\Sigma}_w^{-1} \tag{18.59}$$

The posterior predictive distribution for $f_* = f(\boldsymbol{x}_*)$ is therefore

$$p(f_*|\mathcal{D}, \boldsymbol{x}_*) = \mathcal{N}(f_*|\frac{1}{\sigma_y^2}\boldsymbol{\phi}_*^\mathsf{T}\mathbf{A}^{-1}\boldsymbol{\Phi}^\mathsf{T}\boldsymbol{y}, \ \boldsymbol{\phi}_*^\mathsf{T}\mathbf{A}^{-1}\boldsymbol{\phi}_*) \tag{18.60}$$

where $\boldsymbol{\phi}_* = \boldsymbol{\phi}(\boldsymbol{x}_*)$. This views the problem of inference and prediction in **weight space**.

We now show that this is equivalent to the predictions made by a GP using a kernel of the form $\mathcal{K}(\boldsymbol{x}, \boldsymbol{x}') = \boldsymbol{\phi}(\boldsymbol{x})^\mathsf{T}\boldsymbol{\Sigma}_w\boldsymbol{\phi}(\boldsymbol{x}')$. To see this, let $\mathbf{K} = \boldsymbol{\Phi}\boldsymbol{\Sigma}_w\boldsymbol{\Phi}^\mathsf{T}$, $\boldsymbol{k}_* = \boldsymbol{\Phi}\boldsymbol{\Sigma}_w\boldsymbol{\phi}_*$, and $k_{**} = \boldsymbol{\phi}_*^\mathsf{T}\boldsymbol{\Sigma}_w\boldsymbol{\phi}_*$. Using this notation, and the matrix inversion lemma, we can rewrite Equation (18.60) as follows

$$p(f_*|\mathcal{D}, \boldsymbol{x}_*) = \mathcal{N}(f_*|\boldsymbol{\mu}_{*|X}, \boldsymbol{\Sigma}_{*|X}) \tag{18.61}$$

$$\boldsymbol{\mu}_{*|X} = \boldsymbol{\phi}_*^\mathsf{T}\boldsymbol{\Sigma}_w\boldsymbol{\Phi}^\mathsf{T}(\mathbf{K} + \sigma_y^2\mathbf{I})^{-1}\boldsymbol{y} = \boldsymbol{k}_*^\mathsf{T}(\mathbf{K}_{X,X} + \sigma_y\mathbf{I})^{-1}\boldsymbol{y} \tag{18.62}$$

$$\boldsymbol{\Sigma}_{*|X} = \boldsymbol{\phi}_*^\mathsf{T}\boldsymbol{\Sigma}_w\boldsymbol{\phi}_* - \boldsymbol{\phi}_*^\mathsf{T}\boldsymbol{\Sigma}_w\boldsymbol{\Phi}^\mathsf{T}(\mathbf{K} + \sigma_y^2\mathbf{I})^{-1}\boldsymbol{\Phi}\boldsymbol{\Sigma}_w\boldsymbol{\phi}_* = k_{**} - \boldsymbol{k}_*^\mathsf{T}(\mathbf{K}_{X,X} + \sigma_y^2\mathbf{I})^{-1}\boldsymbol{k}_* \tag{18.63}$$

which matches the results in Equation (18.54), assuming $m(\boldsymbol{x}) = 0$. A non-zero mean can be captured by adding a constant feature with value 1 to $\boldsymbol{\phi}(\boldsymbol{x})$.

Thus we can derive a GP from Bayesian linear regression. Note, however, that linear regression assumes $\boldsymbol{\phi}(\boldsymbol{x})$ is a finite length vector, whereas a GP allows us to work directly in terms of kernels, which may correspond to infinite length feature vectors (see Section 18.2.5). That is, a GP works in **function space**.

18.3.4   Semiparametric GPs

So far, we have mostly assumed the mean of the GP is 0, and have relied on its interpolation abilities to model the mean function. Sometimes it is useful to fit a global linear model for the mean, and use the GP to model the residual errors, as follows:

$$g(\boldsymbol{x}) = f(\boldsymbol{x}) + \boldsymbol{\beta}^\mathsf{T}\boldsymbol{\phi}(\boldsymbol{x}) \tag{18.64}$$

where $f(\boldsymbol{x}) \sim \text{GP}(0, \mathcal{K}(\boldsymbol{x}, \boldsymbol{x}'))$, and $\boldsymbol{\phi}()$ are some fixed basis functions. This combines a parametric and a non-parametric model, and is known as a **semi-parametric model**.

If we assume $\boldsymbol{\beta} \sim \mathcal{N}(\boldsymbol{b}, \mathbf{B})$, we can integrate these parameters out to get a new GP [O'H78]:

$$g(\boldsymbol{x}) \sim \text{GP}\left(\boldsymbol{\phi}(\boldsymbol{x})^\mathsf{T}\boldsymbol{b}, \ \mathcal{K}(\boldsymbol{x}, \boldsymbol{x}') + \boldsymbol{\phi}(\boldsymbol{x})^\mathsf{T}\mathbf{B}\boldsymbol{\phi}(\boldsymbol{x}')\right) \tag{18.65}$$

Let $\mathbf{H}_X = \boldsymbol{\phi}(\mathbf{X})^\mathsf{T}$ be the $D \times N$ matrix of training examples, and $\mathbf{H}_* = \boldsymbol{\phi}(\mathbf{X}_*)^\mathsf{T}$ be the $D \times N_*$ matrix of test examples. The corresponding predictive distribution for test inputs $\mathbf{X}_*$ has the following form [RW06, p28]:

$$\mathbb{E}\left[g(\mathbf{X}_*)|\mathcal{D}\right] = \mathbf{H}_*^\mathsf{T}\overline{\boldsymbol{\beta}} + \mathbf{K}_{X,*}^\mathsf{T}\mathbf{K}_\sigma^{-1}(\boldsymbol{y} - \mathbf{H}_X^\mathsf{T}\overline{\boldsymbol{\beta}}) = \mathbb{E}\left[f(\mathbf{X}_*)|\mathcal{D}\right] + \mathbf{R}^\mathsf{T}\overline{\boldsymbol{\beta}} \tag{18.66}$$

$$\text{Cov}\left[g(\mathbf{X}_*)|\mathcal{D}\right] = \text{Cov}\left[f(\mathbf{X}_*)|\mathcal{D}\right] + \mathbf{R}^\mathsf{T}(\mathbf{B}^{-1} + \mathbf{H}_X\mathbf{K}_\sigma^{-1}\mathbf{H}_X^\mathsf{T})^{-1}\mathbf{R} \tag{18.67}$$

$$\overline{\boldsymbol{\beta}} = (\mathbf{B}^{-1} + \mathbf{H}_X\mathbf{K}_\sigma^{-1}\mathbf{H}_X^\mathsf{T})^{-1}(\mathbf{H}_X\mathbf{K}_\sigma^{-1}\boldsymbol{y} + \mathbf{B}^{-1}\boldsymbol{b}) \tag{18.68}$$

$$\mathbf{R} = \mathbf{H}_* - \mathbf{H}_X\mathbf{K}_\sigma^{-1}\mathbf{K}_{X,*} \tag{18.69}$$

These results can be interpreted as follows: the mean is the usual mean from the GP, plus a global offset from the linear model, using $\bar{\boldsymbol{\beta}}$; and the covariance is the usual covariance from the GP, plus an additional positive term due to the uncertainty in $\boldsymbol{\beta}$.

In the limit of an uninformative prior for the regression parameters, as $\mathbf{B} \to \infty \mathbf{I}$, this simplifies to

$$\mathbb{E}\left[g(\mathbf{X}_*)|\mathcal{D}\right] = \mathbb{E}\left[f(\mathbf{X}_*)|\mathcal{D}\right] + \mathbf{R}^\mathsf{T}(\mathbf{H}_X \mathbf{K}_\sigma^{-1} \mathbf{H}_X^\mathsf{T})^{-1} \mathbf{H}_X \mathbf{K}_\sigma^{-1} \boldsymbol{y} \tag{18.70}$$

$$\mathrm{Cov}\left[g(\mathbf{X}_*)|\mathcal{D}\right] = \mathrm{Cov}\left[f(\mathbf{X}_*)|\mathcal{D}\right] + \mathbf{R}^\mathsf{T}(\mathbf{H}_X \mathbf{K}_\sigma^{-1} \mathbf{H}_X^\mathsf{T})^{-1} \mathbf{R} \tag{18.71}$$

18.3.5 Marginal likelihood

Most kernels have some free parameters. For example, the RBF-ARD kernel (Section 18.2.1.2) has the form

$$\mathcal{K}(\boldsymbol{x}, \boldsymbol{x}') = \exp\left(-\frac{1}{2}\sum_{d=1}^{D}\frac{1}{\ell_d^2}(x_d - x_d')^2\right) = \prod_{d=1}^{D}\mathcal{K}_{\ell_d}(x_d, x_d') \tag{18.72}$$

where each ℓ_d is a length scale for feature dimension d. Let these (and the observation noise variance σ_y^2, if present) be denoted by $\boldsymbol{\theta}$. We can compute the likelihood of these parameters as follows:

$$p(\boldsymbol{y}|\mathbf{X}, \boldsymbol{\theta}) = p(\mathcal{D}|\boldsymbol{\theta}) = \int p(\boldsymbol{y}|\boldsymbol{f}_X, \boldsymbol{\theta})p(\boldsymbol{f}_X|\mathbf{X}, \boldsymbol{\theta})d\boldsymbol{f}_X \tag{18.73}$$

Since we are integrating out the function f, we often call $\boldsymbol{\theta}$ hyperparameters, and the quantity $p(\mathcal{D}|\boldsymbol{\theta})$ the marginal likelihood.

Since f is a GP, we can compute the above integral using the marginal likelihood for the corresponding Gaussian. This gives

$$\log p(\mathcal{D}|\boldsymbol{\theta}) = -\frac{1}{2}(\boldsymbol{y} - \boldsymbol{\mu}_X)^\mathsf{T}\mathbf{K}_\sigma^{-1}(\boldsymbol{y} - \boldsymbol{\mu}_X) - \frac{1}{2}\log|\mathbf{K}_\sigma| - \frac{N}{2}\log(2\pi) \tag{18.74}$$

The first term is the square of the Mahalanobis distance between the observations and the predicted values: better fits will have smaller distance. The second term is the log determinant of the covariance matrix, which measures model complexity: smoother functions will have smaller determinants, so $-\log|\mathbf{K}_\sigma|$ will be larger (less negative) for simpler functions. The marginal likelihood measures the tradeoff between fit and complexity.

In Section 18.6.1, we discuss how to learn the kernel parameters from data by maximizing the marginal likelihood wrt $\boldsymbol{\theta}$.

18.3.6 Computational and numerical issues

In this section, we discuss computational and numerical issues which arise when implementing the above equations. For notational simplicity, we assume the prior mean is zero, $m(\boldsymbol{x}) = 0$.

The posterior predictive mean is given by $\mu_* = \boldsymbol{k}_*^\mathsf{T}\mathbf{K}_\sigma^{-1}\boldsymbol{y}$. For reasons of numerical stability, it is unwise to directly invert $\mathbf{K}_\sigma$. A more robust alternative is to compute a Cholesky decomposition, $\mathbf{K}_\sigma = \mathbf{L}\mathbf{L}^\mathsf{T}$, which takes $O(N^3)$ time. Given this, we can compute

$$\mu_* = \boldsymbol{k}_*^\mathsf{T}\mathbf{K}_\sigma^{-1}\boldsymbol{y} = \boldsymbol{k}_*^\mathsf{T}\mathbf{L}^{-\mathsf{T}}(\mathbf{L}^{-1}\boldsymbol{y}) = \boldsymbol{k}_*^\mathsf{T}\boldsymbol{\alpha} \tag{18.75}$$

Here $\boldsymbol{\alpha} = \mathbf{L}^\mathsf{T} \backslash (\mathbf{L} \backslash \boldsymbol{y})$, where we have used the backslash operator to represent backsubstitution.

We can compute the variance in $O(N^2)$ time for each test case using

$$\sigma_*^2 = k_{**} - \boldsymbol{k}_*^\mathsf{T} \mathbf{L}^{-\mathsf{T}} \mathbf{L}^{-1} \boldsymbol{k}_* = k_{**} - \boldsymbol{v}^\mathsf{T} \boldsymbol{v} \tag{18.76}$$

where $\boldsymbol{v} = \mathbf{L} \backslash \boldsymbol{k}_*$.

Finally, the log marginal likelihood (needed for kernel learning, Section 18.6) can be computed using

$$\log p(\boldsymbol{y}|\mathbf{X}) = -\frac{1}{2}\boldsymbol{y}^\mathsf{T}\boldsymbol{\alpha} - \sum_{n=1}^{N} \log L_{nn} - \frac{N}{2}\log(2\pi) \tag{18.77}$$

We see that overall cost is dominated by $O(N^3)$. We discuss faster, but approximate, methods in Section 18.5.

18.3.7   Kernel ridge regression

The term **ridge regression** refers to linear regression with an ℓ_2 penalty on the regression weights:

$$\boldsymbol{w}^* = \underset{\boldsymbol{w}}{\mathrm{argmin}} \sum_{n=1}^{N} (y_n - f(\boldsymbol{x}_n; \boldsymbol{w}))^2 + \lambda ||\boldsymbol{w}||_2^2 \tag{18.78}$$

where $f(\boldsymbol{x}; \boldsymbol{w}) = \boldsymbol{w}^\mathsf{T}\boldsymbol{x}$. The solution for this is

$$\boldsymbol{w}^* = (\mathbf{X}^\mathsf{T}\mathbf{X} + \lambda\mathbf{I})^{-1}\mathbf{X}^\mathsf{T}\boldsymbol{y} = (\sum_{n=1}^{N} \boldsymbol{x}_n\boldsymbol{x}_n^\mathsf{T} + \lambda\mathbf{I})^{-1}(\sum_{n=1}^{N} \boldsymbol{x}_n y_n) \tag{18.79}$$

In this section, we consider a function space version of this:

$$f^* = \underset{f \in \mathcal{F}}{\mathrm{argmin}} \sum_{n=1}^{N} (y_n - f(\boldsymbol{x}_n))^2 + \lambda ||f||^2 \tag{18.80}$$

For this to make sense, we have to define the function space $\mathcal{F}$ and the norm $||f||$. If we use a function space derived from a positive definite kernel function $\mathcal{K}$, the resulting method is called **kernel ridge regression** (KRR). We will see that the resulting estimate $f^*(\boldsymbol{x}_*)$ is equivalent to the posterior mean of a GP. We give the details below.

18.3.7.1   Reproducing kernel Hilbert spaces

In this section, we briefly introduce the relevant mathematical "machinery" needed to explain KRR.

Let $\mathcal{F} = \{f : \mathcal{X} \to \mathbb{R}\}$ be a space of real-valued funcitons. Elements of this space (i.e., functions) can be added and scalar multiplied as if they were vectors. That is, if $f \in \mathcal{F}$ and $g \in \mathcal{F}$, then $\alpha f + \beta g \in \mathcal{F}$ for $\alpha, \beta \in \mathbb{R}$. We can also define an **inner product** for $\mathcal{F}$, which is a mapping $\langle f, g \rangle \in \mathbb{R}$

which satisfies the following:

$$\langle \alpha f_1 + \beta f_2, g \rangle = \alpha \langle f_1, g \rangle + \beta \langle f_2, g \rangle \tag{18.81}$$
$$\langle f, g \rangle = \langle g, f \rangle \tag{18.82}$$
$$\langle f, f \rangle \geq 0 \tag{18.83}$$
$$\langle f, f \rangle = 0 \text{ iff } f(x) = 0 \text{ for all } x \in \mathcal{X} \tag{18.84}$$

We define the norm of a function using

$$||f|| \triangleq \sqrt{\langle f, f \rangle} \tag{18.85}$$

A function space $\mathcal{H}$ with an inner product operator is called a **Hilbert space**. (We also require that the function space be complete, which means that every Cauchy sequence of functions $f_i \in \mathcal{H}$ has a limit that is also in $\mathcal{H}$.)

The most common Hilbert space is the space known as L^2. To define this, we need to specify a **measure** μ on the input space $\mathcal{X}$; this is a function that assigns any (suitable) subset A of $\mathcal{X}$ to a positive number, such as its volume. This can be defined in terms of the density function $w : \mathcal{X} \to \mathbb{R}$, as follows:

$$\mu(A) = \int_A w(x) dx \tag{18.86}$$

Thus we have $\mu(dx) = w(x)dx$. We can now define $L^2(\mathcal{X}, \mu)$ to be the space of functions $f : \mathcal{X} \to \mathbb{R}$ that satisfy

$$\int_{\mathcal{X}} f(x)^2 w(x) dx < \infty \tag{18.87}$$

This is known as the set of **square-integrable functions**. This space has an inner product defined by

$$\langle f, g \rangle = \int_{\mathcal{X}} f(x)g(x)w(x)dx \tag{18.88}$$

We define a **Reproducing Kernel Hilbert Space** or **RKHS** as follows. Let $\mathcal{H}$ be a Hilbert space of functions $f : \mathcal{X} \to \mathbb{R}$. We say that $\mathcal{H}$ is an RKHS endowed with inner product $\langle \cdot, \cdot \rangle_{\mathcal{H}}$ if there exists a (symmetric) **kernel function** $\mathcal{K} : \mathcal{X} \times \mathcal{X} \to \mathbb{R}$ with the following properties:
- For every $\boldsymbol{x} \in \mathcal{X}$, $\mathcal{K}(\boldsymbol{x}, \cdot) \in \mathcal{H}$.
- $\mathcal{K}$ satisfies the **reproducing property**:

$$\langle f(\cdot), \mathcal{K}(\cdot, \boldsymbol{x}') \rangle = f(\boldsymbol{x}') \tag{18.89}$$

The reason for the term "reproducing property" is as follows. Let $f(\cdot) = \mathcal{K}(\boldsymbol{x}, \cdot)$. Then we have that

$$\langle \mathcal{K}(\boldsymbol{x}, \cdot), \mathcal{K}(\cdot, \boldsymbol{x}') \rangle = \mathcal{K}(\boldsymbol{x}, \boldsymbol{x}') \tag{18.90}$$

18.3.7.2 Complexity of a function in an RKHS

The main utility of RKHS from the point of view of machine learning is that it allows us to define a notion of a function's "smoothness" or "complexity" in terms of its norm, as we now discuss.

Suppose we have a positive definite kernel function $\mathcal{K}$. From Mercer's theorem we have $\mathcal{K}(\boldsymbol{x}, \boldsymbol{x}') = \sum_{i=1}^{\infty} \lambda_i \phi_i(\boldsymbol{x}) \phi_i(\boldsymbol{x}')$. Now consider a Hilbert space $\mathcal{H}$ defined by functions of the form $f(\boldsymbol{x}) = \sum_{i=1}^{\infty} f_i \phi(\boldsymbol{x})$, with $\sum_{i=1}^{\infty} f_i^2/\lambda < \infty$. The inner product of two functions in this space is

$$\langle f, g \rangle_{\mathcal{H}} = \sum_{i=1}^{\infty} \frac{f_i g_i}{\lambda_i} \tag{18.91}$$

Hence the (squared) norm is given by

$$\|f\|_{\mathcal{H}}^2 = \langle f, f \rangle_{\mathcal{H}} = \sum_{i=1}^{\infty} \frac{f_i^2}{\lambda_i} \tag{18.92}$$

This is analogous to the quadratic form $\boldsymbol{f}^\mathsf{T} \mathbf{K}^{-1} \boldsymbol{f}$ which occurs in some GP objectives (see Equation (18.101)). Thus the smoothness of the function is controlled by the properties of the corresponding kernel.

18.3.7.3 Representer theorem

In this section, we consider the problem of (regularized) empirical risk minimization in function space. In particular, consider the following problem:

$$f^* = \underset{f \in \mathcal{H}_{\mathcal{K}}}{\operatorname{argmin}} \sum_{n=1}^{N} \ell(y_n, f(\boldsymbol{x}_n)) + \frac{\lambda}{2} \|f\|_{\mathcal{H}}^2 \tag{18.93}$$

where $\mathcal{H}_{\mathcal{K}}$ is an RKHS with kernel $\mathcal{K}$ and $\ell(y, \hat{y}) \in \mathbb{R}$ is a loss function. Then one can show [KW70; SHS01] the following result:

$$f^*(x) = \sum_{n=1}^{N} \alpha_n \mathcal{K}(x, x_n) \tag{18.94}$$

where $\alpha_n \in \mathbb{R}$ are some coefficients that depend on the training data. This is called the **representer theorem**.

Now consider the special case where the loss function is squared loss, and $\lambda = \sigma_y^2$. We want to minimize

$$\mathcal{L}(f) = \frac{1}{2\sigma_y^2} \sum_{n=1}^{N} (y_n - f(\boldsymbol{x}_n))^2 + \frac{1}{2} \|f\|_{\mathcal{H}}^2 \tag{18.95}$$

Substituting in Equation (18.94), and using the fact that $\langle \mathcal{K}(\cdot, \boldsymbol{x}_i), \mathcal{K}(\cdot, \boldsymbol{x}_j) \rangle = \mathcal{K}(\boldsymbol{x}_i, \boldsymbol{x}_j)$, we obtain

$$\mathcal{L}(f) = \frac{1}{2} \boldsymbol{\alpha}^\mathsf{T} \mathbf{K} \boldsymbol{\alpha} + \frac{1}{2\sigma_y^2} \|\boldsymbol{y} - \mathbf{K} \boldsymbol{\alpha}\|^2 \tag{18.96}$$

$$= \frac{1}{2} \boldsymbol{\alpha}^\mathsf{T} (\mathbf{K} + \frac{1}{\sigma_y^2} \mathbf{K}^2) \boldsymbol{\alpha} - \frac{1}{\sigma_y^2} \boldsymbol{y}^\mathsf{T} \mathbf{K} \boldsymbol{\alpha} + \frac{1}{2\sigma_y^2} \boldsymbol{y}^\mathsf{T} \boldsymbol{y} \tag{18.97}$$

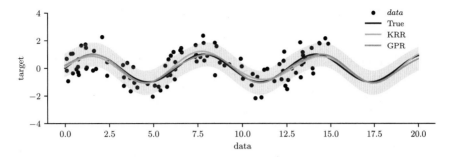

Figure 18.8: *Kernel ridge regression (KRR) compared to Gaussian process regression (GPR) using the same kernel. Generated by krr_vs_gpr.ipynb.*

Minimizing this wrt $\boldsymbol{\alpha}$ gives $\hat{\boldsymbol{\alpha}} = (\mathbf{K} + \sigma_y^2 \mathbf{I})^{-1} \boldsymbol{y}$, which is the same as Equation (18.57). Furthermore, the prediction for a test point is

$$\hat{f}(\boldsymbol{x}_*) = \boldsymbol{k}_*^\mathsf{T} \boldsymbol{\alpha} = \boldsymbol{k}_*^\mathsf{T} (\mathbf{K} + \sigma_y^2 \mathbf{I})^{-1} \boldsymbol{y} \tag{18.98}$$

This is known as **kernel ridge regression** [Vov13]. We see that the result matches the posterior predictive mean of a GP in Equation (18.55).

18.3.7.4 Example of KRR vs GPR

In this section, we compare KRR with GP regression on a simple 1d problem. Since the underlying function is believed to be periodic, we use the periodic kernel from Equation (18.18). To capture the fact that the observations are noisy, we add to this a **white noise kernel**

$$\mathcal{K}(\boldsymbol{x}, \boldsymbol{x}') = \sigma_y^2 \delta(\boldsymbol{x} - \boldsymbol{x}') \tag{18.99}$$

as in Equation (18.48). Thus there are 3 GP hyper-parameters: the kernel length scale ℓ, the kernel periodicity p, and the noise level σ_y^2. We can optimize these by maximizing the marginal likelihood using gradient descent (see Section 18.6.1). For KRR, we also have 3 hyperparameters (ℓ, p, and $\lambda = \sigma_y^2$); we optimize these using grid search combined with cross validation (which in general is slower than gradient based optimization). The resulting model fits are shown in Figure 18.8, and are very similar, as is to be expected.

18.4 GPs with non-Gaussian likelihoods

So far, we have focused on GPs for regression using Gaussian likelihoods. In this case, the posterior is also a GP, and all computation can be performed analytically. However, if the likelihood is non-Gaussian, we can no longer compute the posterior exactly. We can create variety of different "classical" models by changing the form of the likelihood, as we show in Table 18.1. In the sections below, we briefly discuss some approximate inference methods. (For more details, see e.g., [WSS21].)

Model	Likelihood	Section
Regression	$\mathcal{N}(f_i, \sigma_y^2)$	Section 18.3.2
Robust regression	$\mathcal{T}_\nu(f_i, \sigma_y^2)$	Section 18.4.4
Binary classification	$\mathrm{Ber}(\sigma(f_i))$	Section 18.4.1
Multiclass classification	$\mathrm{Cat}(\mathrm{softmax}(\boldsymbol{f}_i))$	Section 18.4.2
Poisson regression	$\mathrm{Poi}(\exp(f_i))$	Section 18.4.3

Table 18.1: *Summary of GP models with a variety of likelihoods.*

$\log p(y_i\|f_i)$	$\frac{\partial}{\partial f_i}\log p(y_i\|f_i)$	$\frac{\partial^2}{\partial f_i^2}\log p(y_i\|f_i)$
$\log \sigma(y_i f_i)$	$t_i - \pi_i$	$-\pi_i(1-\pi_i)$
$\log \Phi(y_i f_i)$	$\frac{y_i \phi(f_i)}{\Phi(y_i f_i)}$	$-\frac{\phi_i^2}{\Phi(y_i f_i)^2} - \frac{y_i f_i \phi(f_i)}{\Phi(y_i f_i)}$

Table 18.2: *Likelihood, gradient, and Hessian for binary logistic/probit GP regression. We assume $y_i \in \{-1,+1\}$ and define $t_i = (y_i + 1)/2 \in \{0,1\}$ and $\pi_i = \sigma(f_i)$ for logistic regression, and $\pi_i = \Phi(f_i)$ for probit regression. Also, ϕ and Φ are the pdf and cdf of $\mathcal{N}(0,1)$. From [RW06, p43].*

18.4.1   Binary classification

In this section, we consider binary classification using GPs. If we use the sigmoid link function, we have $p(y_n = 1|\boldsymbol{x}_n) = \sigma(y_n f(\boldsymbol{x}_n))$. If we assume $y_n \in \{-1, +1\}$, then we have $p(y_n|\boldsymbol{x}_n) = \sigma(y_n f_n)$, since $\sigma(-z) = 1 - \sigma(z)$. If we use the probit link, we have $p(y_n = 1|\boldsymbol{x}_n) = \Phi(y_n f(\boldsymbol{x}_n))$, where $\Phi(z)$ is the cdf of the standard normal. More generally, let $p(y_n|\boldsymbol{x}_n) = \mathrm{Ber}(y_n|\varphi(f_n))$. The overall log joint has the form

$$\mathcal{L}(\boldsymbol{f}_X) = \log p(\boldsymbol{y}|\boldsymbol{f}_X) + \log p(\boldsymbol{f}_X|\mathbf{X}) \tag{18.100}$$

$$= \log p(\boldsymbol{y}|\boldsymbol{f}_X) - \frac{1}{2}\boldsymbol{f}_X^\mathsf{T} \mathbf{K}_{X,X}^{-1} \boldsymbol{f}_X - \frac{1}{2}\log|\mathbf{K}_{X,X}| - \frac{N}{2}\log 2\pi \tag{18.101}$$

The simplest approach to approximate inference is to use a Laplace approximation (Section 7.4.3). The gradient and Hessian of the log joint are given by

$$\nabla\mathcal{L} = \nabla \log p(\boldsymbol{y}|\boldsymbol{f}_X) - \mathbf{K}_{X,X}^{-1}\boldsymbol{f}_X \tag{18.102}$$

$$\nabla^2\mathcal{L} = \nabla^2 \log p(\boldsymbol{y}|\boldsymbol{f}_X) - \mathbf{K}_{X,X}^{-1} = -\boldsymbol{\Lambda} - \mathbf{K}_{X,X}^{-1} \tag{18.103}$$

where $\boldsymbol{\Lambda} \triangleq -\nabla^2 \log p(\boldsymbol{y}|\boldsymbol{f}_X)$ is a diagonal matrix, since the likelihood factorizes across examples. Expressions for the gradient and Hessian of the log likelihood for the logit and probit case are shown in Table 18.2. At convergence, the Laplace approximation of the posterior takes the following form:

$$p(\boldsymbol{f}_X|\mathcal{D}) \approx q(\boldsymbol{f}_X) = \mathcal{N}(\hat{\boldsymbol{f}}, (\mathbf{K}_{X,X}^{-1} + \boldsymbol{\Lambda})^{-1}) \tag{18.104}$$

where $\hat{\boldsymbol{f}}$ is the MAP estimate. See [RW06, Sec 3.4] for further details.

For improved accuracy, we can use variational inference, in which we assume $q(\boldsymbol{f}_X) = \mathcal{N}(\boldsymbol{f}_X|\boldsymbol{m}, \mathbf{S})$; we then optimize $\boldsymbol{m}$ and $\mathbf{S}$ using (stochastic) gradient descent, rather than assuming $\mathbf{S}$ is the Hessian at the mode. See Section 18.5.4 for the details.

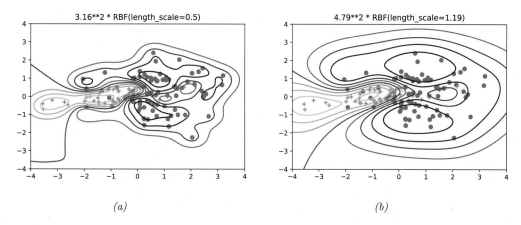

Figure 18.9: Contours of the posterior predictive probability for a binary classifier generated by a GP with an SE kernel. (a) Manual kernel parameters: short length scale, $\ell = 0.5$, variance $3.16^2 \approx 9.98$. (b) Learned kernel parameters: long length scale, $\ell = 1.19$, variance $4.79^2 \approx 22.9$. Generated by gpc_demo_2d.ipynb.

Once we have a Gaussian posterior $q(\boldsymbol{f}_X | \mathcal{D})$, we can then use standard GP prediction to compute $q(f_* | \boldsymbol{x}_*, \mathcal{D})$. Finally, we can approximate the posterior predictive distribution over binary labels using

$$\pi_* = p(y_* = 1 | \boldsymbol{x}_*, \mathcal{D}) = \int p(y_* = 1 | f_*) q(f_* | \boldsymbol{x}_*, \mathcal{D}) df_* \qquad (18.105)$$

This 1d integral can be computed using the probit approximation from Section 15.3.6. In this case we have $\pi_* \approx \sigma(\kappa(v) \mathbb{E}[f_*])$, where $v = \mathbb{V}[f_*]$ and $\kappa^2(v) = (1 + \pi v / 8)^{-1}$.

In Figure 18.9, we show a synthetic binary classification problem in 2d. We use an SE kernel. On the left, we show predictions using hyper-parameters set by hand; we use a short length scale, hence the very sharp turns in the decision boundary. On the right, we show the predictions using the learned hyper-parameters; the model favors more parsimonious explanation of the data.

18.4.2 Multiclass classification

The multi-class case is somewhat harder, since the function now needs to return a vector of C logits to get $p(y_n | \boldsymbol{x}_n) = \text{Cat}(y_n | \text{softmax}(\boldsymbol{f}_n))$, where $\boldsymbol{f}_n = (f_n^1, \ldots, f_n^C)$, It is standard to assume that $f^c \sim \text{GP}(0, \mathcal{K}_c)$. Thus we have one latent function per class, which are a priori independent, and which may use different kernels.

We can derive a Laplace approximation for this model as discussed in [RW06, Sec 3.5]. Alternatively, we can use a variational approach, using the local variational bound to the multinomial softmax in [Cha12]. An alternative variational method, based on data augmentation with auxiliary variables, is described in [Wen+19b; Liu+19a; GFWO20].

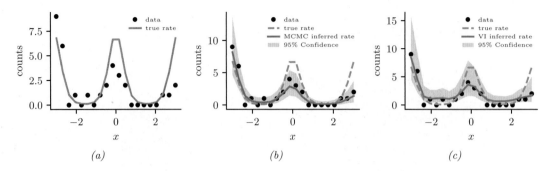

Figure 18.10: *Poisson regression with a GP. (a) Observed data (black dots) and true log rate function (yellow line). (b) Posterior predictive distribution (shading shows 1 and 2 σ bands) from MCMC. (c) Posterior predictive distribution from SVI. Generated by* gp_poisson_1d.ipynb.

18.4.3 GPs for Poisson regression (Cox process)

In this section, we illustrate Poisson regression where the underlying log rate function is modeled by a GP. This is known as a **Cox process**. We can perform approximate posterior inference in this model using Laplace, MCMC, or SVI (stochastic variational inference). In Figure 18.10 we give a 1d example, where we use a Matérn $\frac{5}{2}$ kernel. We apply MCMC and SVI. In the VI case, we additionally have to specify the form of the posterior; we use a Gaussian approximation for the variational GP posterior $p(\boldsymbol{f}|\mathbf{X},\boldsymbol{y})$, and a point estimate for the kernel parameters.

An interesting application of this is to spatial **disease mapping**. For example, [VPV10] discuss the problem of modeling the relative risk of heart attack in different regions in Finland. The data consists of the heart attacks in Finland from 1996–2000 aggregated into 20km × 20km lattice cells. The likelihood has the following form: $y_n \sim \mathrm{Poi}(e_n r_n)$, where e_n is the known expected number of deaths (related to the population of cell n and the overall death rate), and r_n is the **relative risk** of cell n which we want to infer. Since the data counts are small, we regularize the problem by sharing information with spatial neighbors. Hence we assume $f \triangleq \log(r) \sim \mathrm{GP}(0,\mathcal{K})$. We use a Matérn kernel (Section 18.2.1.3) with $\nu = 3/2$, and a length scale and magnitude that are estimated from data.

Figure 18.11 gives an example of this method in action (using Laplace approximation). On the left we plot the posterior mean relative risk (RR), and on the right, the posterior variance. We see that the RR is higher in eastern Finland, which is consistent with other studies. We also see that the variance in the north is higher, since there are fewer people living there.

18.4.4 Other likelihoods

Many other likelihoods are possible. For example, [VJV09] uses a Student t likelihood in order to perform robust regression. A general method for performing approximate variational inference in GPs with such non-conjugate likelihoods is discussed in [WSS21].

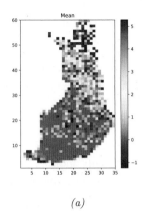

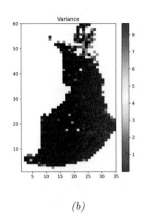

(a)

(b)

Figure 18.11: We show the relative risk of heart disease in Finland using a Poisson GP fit to 911 data points. Left: posterior mean. Right: posterior variance. Generated by gp_spatial_demo.ipynb.

Method	Cost	Section
Cholesky	$O(N^3)$	Section 18.3.6
Conj. Grad.	$O(CN^2)$	Section 18.5.5
Inducing	$O(NM^2 + M^3 + DNM)$	Section 18.5.3
Variational	$O(NM^2 + M^3 + DNM)$	Section 18.5.4
SVGP	$O(BM^2 + M^3 + DNM)$	Section 18.5.4.3
KISS-GP	$O(CN + CDM^D \log M)$	Section 18.5.5.3
SKIP	$O(DLN + DLM \log M + L^3 N \log D + CL^2 N)$	Section 18.5.5.3

Table 18.3: Summary of time to compute the log marginal likelihood of a GP regression model. Notation: N is number of training examples, M is number of inducing points, B is size of minibatch, D is dimensionality of input vectors (assuming $\mathcal{X} = \mathbb{R}^D$), C is number of conjugate gradient iterations, and L is number of Lanczos iterations. Based on Table 2 of [Gar+18a].

18.5 Scaling GP inference to large datasets

In Section 18.3.6, we saw that the best way to perform GP inference and training is to compute a Cholesky decomposition of the $N \times N$ Gram matrix. Unfortunately, this takes $O(N^3)$ time. In this section, we discuss methods to scale up GPs to handle large N. See Table 18.3 for a summary, and [Liu+20c] for more details.[1]

18.5.1 Subset of data

The simplest approach to speeding up GP inference is to throw away some of the data. Suppose we keep a subset of M examples. In this case, exact inference will take $O(M^3)$ time. This is called the

---

1. We focus on efficient methods for evaluating the marginal likelihood and the posterior predictive distribution. For an efficient method for sampling a function from the posterior, see [Wil+20a].

subset-of-data approach.

The key question is: how should we choose the subset? The simplest approach is to pick random examples (this method was recently analyzed in [HIY19]). However, intuitively it makes more sense to try to pick a subset that in some sense "covers" the original data, so it contains approximately the same information (up to some tolerance) without the redundancy. Clustering algorithms are one heuristic approach, but we can also use coreset methods, which can provably find such an information-preserving subset (see e.g., [Hug+19] for an application of this idea to GPs).

18.5.1.1   Informative vector machine

Clustering and coreset methods are unsupervised, in that they only look at the features $\boldsymbol{x}_i$ and not the labels y_i, which can be suboptimal. The **informative vector machine** [HLS03] uses a greedy strategy to iteratively add the labeled example $(\boldsymbol{x}_j, y_j)$ that maximally reduces the entropy of the function's posterior, $\Delta_j = \mathbb{H}(p(f_j)) - \mathbb{H}(p^{\text{new}}(f_j))$, where $p^{\text{new}}(f_j)$ is the posterior of f at $\boldsymbol{x}_j$ after conditioning on y_j. (This is very similar to active learning.) To compute Δ_j, let $p(f_j) = \mathcal{N}(\mu_j, v_j)$, and $p(f_j|y_j) \propto p(f_j)\mathcal{N}(y_j|f_j, \sigma^2) = \mathcal{N}(f_j|\mu_j^{\text{new}}, v_j^{\text{new}})$, where $(v_j^{\text{new}})^{-1} = v_j^{-1} + \sigma^{-2}$. Since $\mathbb{H}(\mathcal{N}(\mu, v)) = \log(2\pi e v)/2$, we have $\Delta_j = 0.5 \log(1 + v_j/\sigma^2)$. Since this is a monotonic function of v_j, we can maximize it by choosing the site with the largest variance. (In fact, entropy is a submodular function, so we can use submodular optimization algorithms to improve on the IVM, as shown in [Kra+08].)

18.5.1.2   Discussion

The main problem with the subset of data approach is that it ignores some of the data, which can reduce predictive accuracy and increase uncertainty about the true function. Fortunately there are other scalable methods that avoid this problem, essentially by approximately representing (or compressing) the training data, as we discuss below.

18.5.2   Nyström approximation

Suppose we had a rank M approximation to the $N \times N$ matrix gram matrix of the following form:

$$\mathbf{K}_{X,X} \approx \mathbf{U}\boldsymbol{\Lambda}\mathbf{U}^{\mathsf{T}} \tag{18.106}$$

where $\boldsymbol{\Lambda}$ is a diagonal matrix of the M leading eigenvalues, and $\mathbf{U}$ is the matrix of the corresponding M eigenvectors, each of size N. In this case, we can use the matrix inversion lemma to write

$$\mathbf{K}_{\sigma}^{-1} = (\mathbf{K}_{X,X} + \sigma^2 \mathbf{I}_N)^{-1} \approx \sigma^{-2}\mathbf{I}_N + \sigma^{-2}\mathbf{U}(\sigma^2\boldsymbol{\Lambda}^{-1} + \mathbf{U}^{\mathsf{T}}\mathbf{U})^{-1}\mathbf{U}^{\mathsf{T}} \tag{18.107}$$

which takes $O(NM^2)$ time. Similarly, one can show (using the Sylvester determinant lemma) that

$$|\mathbf{K}_{\sigma}| \approx |\boldsymbol{\Lambda}||\sigma^2\boldsymbol{\Lambda}^{-1} + \mathbf{U}^{\mathsf{T}}\mathbf{U}| \tag{18.108}$$

which also takes $O(NM^2)$ time.

Unfortunately, directly computing such an eigendecomposition takes $O(N^3)$ time, which does not help. However, suppose we pick a subset Z of $M < N$ points. We can partition the Gram matrix as follows (where we assume the chosen points come first, and then the remaining points):

$$\mathbf{K}_{X,X} = \begin{pmatrix} \mathbf{K}_{Z,Z} & \mathbf{K}_{Z,X-Z} \\ \mathbf{K}_{X-Z,Z} & \mathbf{K}_{X-Z,X-Z} \end{pmatrix} \triangleq \begin{pmatrix} \mathbf{K}_{Z,Z} & \mathbf{K}_{Z,\tilde{X}} \\ \mathbf{K}_{\tilde{X},Z} & \mathbf{K}_{\tilde{X},\tilde{X}} \end{pmatrix} \tag{18.109}$$

where $\tilde{X} = X - Z$. We now compute an eigendecomposition of $\mathbf{K}_{Z,Z}$ to get the eigenvalues $\{\lambda_i\}_{i=1}^{M}$ and eigenvectors $\{\boldsymbol{u}_i\}_{i=1}^{M}$. We now use these to approximate the full matrix as shown below, where the scaling constants are chosen so that $\|\tilde{\boldsymbol{u}}_i\| \approx 1$:

$$\tilde{\lambda}_i \triangleq \frac{N}{M}\lambda_i \tag{18.110}$$

$$\tilde{\boldsymbol{u}} \triangleq \sqrt{\frac{M}{N}}\frac{1}{\lambda_i}\mathbf{K}_{\tilde{X},Z}\boldsymbol{u}_i \tag{18.111}$$

$$\mathbf{K}_{X,X} \approx \sum_{i=1}^{M} \tilde{\lambda}_i \tilde{\boldsymbol{u}}_i \tilde{\boldsymbol{u}}_i^{\mathsf{T}} \tag{18.112}$$

$$= \sum_{i=1}^{M} \frac{N}{M}\lambda_i \sqrt{\frac{M}{N}}\frac{1}{\lambda_i}\mathbf{K}_{\tilde{X},Z}\boldsymbol{u}_i \ \sqrt{\frac{M}{N}}\frac{1}{\lambda_i}\boldsymbol{u}_i^{\mathsf{T}}\mathbf{K}_{\tilde{X},Z}^{\mathsf{T}} \tag{18.113}$$

$$= \mathbf{K}_{\tilde{X},Z}\left(\sum_{i=1}^{M}\frac{1}{\lambda_i}\boldsymbol{u}_i\boldsymbol{u}_i^{\mathsf{T}}\right)\mathbf{K}_{\tilde{X},Z} \tag{18.114}$$

$$= \mathbf{K}_{\tilde{X},Z}\mathbf{K}_{Z,Z}^{-1}\mathbf{K}_{\tilde{X},Z}^{\mathsf{T}} \tag{18.115}$$

This is known as the **Nyström approximation** [WS01]. If we define

$$\mathbf{Q}_{A,B} \triangleq \mathbf{K}_{A,Z}\mathbf{K}_{Z,Z}^{-1}\mathbf{K}_{Z,B} \tag{18.116}$$

then we can write the approximate Gram matrix as $\mathbf{Q}_{X,X}$. We can then replace $\mathbf{K}_\sigma$ with $\hat{\mathbf{Q}}_{X,X} = \mathbf{Q}_{X,X} + \sigma^2\mathbf{I}_N$. Computing the eigendecomposition takes $O(M^3)$ time, and computing $\hat{\mathbf{Q}}_{X,X}^{-1}$ takes $O(NM^2)$ time. Thus complexity is now linear in N instead of cubic.

If we are approximating *only* $\hat{\mathbf{K}}_{X,X}$ in $\boldsymbol{\mu}_{*|X}$ in Equation (18.52) and $\boldsymbol{\Sigma}_{*|X}$ in Equation (18.53), then this is inconsistent with the other un-approximated kernel function evaluations in these formulae, and can result in the predictive variance being negative. One solution to this is to use the same $\mathbf{Q}$ approximation for all terms.

18.5.3 Inducing point methods

In this section, we discuss an approximation method based on **inducing points**, also called **pseudoinputs**, which are like a learned summary of the training data that we can condition on, rather than conditioning on all of it.

Let $\mathbf{X}$ be the observed inputs, and $\boldsymbol{f}_X = f(\mathbf{X})$ be the unknown vector of function values (for which we have noisy observations $\boldsymbol{y}$). Let $\boldsymbol{f}_*$ be the unknown function values at one or more test points $\mathbf{X}_*$. Finally, let us assume we have M additional inputs, $\mathbf{Z}$, with unknown function values $\boldsymbol{f}_Z$ (often denoted by $\boldsymbol{u}$). The exact joint prior has the form

$$p(\boldsymbol{f}_X, \boldsymbol{f}_*) = \int p(\boldsymbol{f}_*, \boldsymbol{f}_X, \boldsymbol{f}_Z)d\boldsymbol{f}_Z = \int p(\boldsymbol{f}_*, \boldsymbol{f}_X|\boldsymbol{f}_Z)p(\boldsymbol{f}_Z)d\boldsymbol{f}_Z = \mathcal{N}\left(\mathbf{0}, \begin{pmatrix} \mathbf{K}_{X,X} & \mathbf{K}_{X,*} \\ \mathbf{K}_{*,X} & \mathbf{K}_{*,*} \end{pmatrix}\right) \tag{18.117}$$

Figure 18.12: *Illustration of the graphical model for a GP on n observations, $\boldsymbol{f}_{1:n}$, and one test case, f_*, with inducing variables $\boldsymbol{u}$. The thick lines indicate that all variables are fully interconnected. The observations y_i (not shown) are locally connected to each f_i. (a) no approximations are made. (b) we assume f_* is conditionally independent of $\boldsymbol{f}_X$ given $\boldsymbol{u}$. From Figure 1 of [QCR05]. Used with kind permission of Joaquin Quiñonero Candela.*

(We write $p(\boldsymbol{f}_X, \boldsymbol{f}_*)$ instead of $p(\boldsymbol{f}_X, \boldsymbol{f}_* | \mathbf{X}, \mathbf{X}_*)$, since the inputs can be thought of as just indices into the random function f.)

We will choose $\boldsymbol{f}_Z$ in such a way that it acts as a sufficient statistic for the data, so that we can predict $\boldsymbol{f}_*$ just using $\boldsymbol{f}_Z$ instead of $\boldsymbol{f}_X$, i.e., we assume $\boldsymbol{f}_* \perp \boldsymbol{f}_X | \boldsymbol{f}_Z$. Thus we approximate the prior as follows:

$$p(\boldsymbol{f}_*, \boldsymbol{f}_X, \boldsymbol{f}_Z) = p(\boldsymbol{f}_*|\boldsymbol{f}_X, \boldsymbol{f}_Z)p(\boldsymbol{f}_X|\boldsymbol{f}_Z)p(\boldsymbol{f}_Z) \approx p(\boldsymbol{f}_*|\boldsymbol{f}_Z)p(\boldsymbol{f}_X|\boldsymbol{f}_Z)p(\boldsymbol{f}_Z) \tag{18.118}$$

See Figure 18.12 for an illustration of this assumption, and Section 18.5.3.4 for details on how to choose the inducing set $\mathbf{Z}$. (Note that this method is often called a "**sparse GP**", because it makes predictions for $\boldsymbol{f}_*$ using a subset of the training data, namely $\boldsymbol{f}_Z$, instead of all of it, $\boldsymbol{f}_X$.)

From this, we can derive the following train and test conditionals

$$p(\boldsymbol{f}_X|\boldsymbol{f}_Z) = \mathcal{N}(\boldsymbol{f}_X|\mathbf{K}_{X,Z}\mathbf{K}_{Z,Z}^{-1}\boldsymbol{f}_Z, \ \mathbf{K}_{X,X} - \mathbf{Q}_{X,X}) \tag{18.119}$$

$$p(\boldsymbol{f}_*|\boldsymbol{f}_Z) = \mathcal{N}(\boldsymbol{f}_*|\mathbf{K}_{*,Z}\mathbf{K}_{Z,Z}^{-1}\boldsymbol{f}_Z, \ \mathbf{K}_{*,*} - \mathbf{Q}_{*,*}) \tag{18.120}$$

The above equations can be seen as exact inference on noise-free observations $\boldsymbol{f}_Z$. To gain computational speedups, we will make further approximations to the terms $\tilde{\mathbf{Q}}_{X,X} = \mathbf{K}_{X,X} - \mathbf{Q}_{X,X}$ and $\tilde{\mathbf{Q}}_{*,*} = \mathbf{K}_{*,*} - \mathbf{Q}_{*,*}$, as we discuss below. We can then derive the approximate prior $q(\boldsymbol{f}_X, \boldsymbol{f}_*) = \int q(\boldsymbol{f}_X|\boldsymbol{f}_Z)q(\boldsymbol{f}_*|\boldsymbol{f}_Z)p(\boldsymbol{f}_Z)d\boldsymbol{f}_Z$, which we then condition on the observations in the usual way.

All of the approximations we discuss below result in an initial training cost of $O(M^3 + NM^2)$, and then take $O(M)$ time for the predictive mean for each test case, and $O(M^2)$ time for the predictive variance. (Compare this to $O(N^3)$ training time and $O(N)$ and $O(N^2)$ testing time for exact inference.)

18.5.3.1 SOR/DIC

Suppose we assume $\tilde{\mathbf{Q}}_{X,X} = \mathbf{0}$ and $\tilde{\mathbf{Q}}_{*,*} = \mathbf{0}$, so the conditionals are deterministic. This is called the **deterministic inducing conditional (DIC)** approximation [QCR05], or the **subset of regressors (SOR)** approximation [Sil85; SB01]. The corresponding joint prior has the form

$$q_{\text{SOR}}(\boldsymbol{f}_X, \boldsymbol{f}_*) = \mathcal{N}(\mathbf{0}, \begin{pmatrix} \mathbf{Q}_{X,X} & \mathbf{Q}_{X,*} \\ \mathbf{Q}_{*,X} & \mathbf{Q}_{*,*} \end{pmatrix}) \tag{18.121}$$

Let us define $\hat{\mathbf{Q}}_{X,X} = \mathbf{Q}_{X,X} + \sigma^2 \mathbf{I}_N$, and $\mathbf{\Sigma} = (\sigma^{-2} \mathbf{K}_{Z,X} \mathbf{K}_{X,Z} + \mathbf{K}_{Z,Z})^{-1}$. Then the predictive distribution is

$$q_{\text{SOR}}(\boldsymbol{f}_* | \boldsymbol{y}) = \mathcal{N}(\boldsymbol{f}_* | \mathbf{Q}_{*,X} \hat{\mathbf{Q}}_{X,X}^{-1} \boldsymbol{y}, \ \mathbf{Q}_{*,*} - \mathbf{Q}_{*,X} \hat{\mathbf{Q}}_{X,X}^{-1} \mathbf{Q}_{X,*}) \tag{18.122}$$

$$= \mathcal{N}(\boldsymbol{f}_* | \sigma^{-2} \mathbf{K}_{*,Z} \mathbf{\Sigma} \mathbf{K}_{Z,X} \boldsymbol{y}, \ \mathbf{K}_{*,Z} \mathbf{\Sigma} \mathbf{K}_{Z,*}) \tag{18.123}$$

This is equivalent to the usual one for GPs except we have replaced $\mathbf{K}_{X,X}$ by $\mathbf{Q}_{X,X}$. This is equivalent to performing GP inference with the following kernel function

$$\mathcal{K}_{\text{SOR}}(\boldsymbol{x}_i, \boldsymbol{x}_j) = \mathcal{K}(\boldsymbol{x}_i, \mathbf{Z}) \, \mathbf{K}_{Z,Z}^{-1} \, \mathcal{K}(\mathbf{Z}, \boldsymbol{x}_j) \tag{18.124}$$

The kernel matrix has rank M, so the GP is degenerate. Furthermore, the kernel will be near 0 when $\boldsymbol{x}_i$ or $\boldsymbol{x}_j$ is far from one of the chosen points $\mathbf{Z}$, which can result in an underestimate of the predictive variance.

18.5.3.2 DTC

One way to overcome the overconfidence of DIC is to only assume $\tilde{\mathbf{Q}}_{X,X} = \mathbf{0}$, but let $\tilde{\mathbf{Q}}_{*,*} = \mathbf{K}_{*,*} - \mathbf{Q}_{*,*}$ be exact. This is called the **deterministic training conditional** or **DTC** method [SWL03].

The corresponding joint prior has the form

$$q_{\text{dtc}}(\boldsymbol{f}_X, \boldsymbol{f}_*) = \mathcal{N}\left(\mathbf{0}, \begin{pmatrix} \mathbf{Q}_{X,X} & \mathbf{Q}_{X,*} \\ \mathbf{Q}_{*,X} & \mathbf{K}_{*,*} \end{pmatrix}\right) \tag{18.125}$$

Hence the predictive distribution becomes

$$q_{\text{dtc}}(\boldsymbol{f}_* | \boldsymbol{y}) = \mathcal{N}(\boldsymbol{f}_* | \mathbf{Q}_{*,X} \hat{\mathbf{Q}}_{X,X}^{-1} \boldsymbol{y}, \ \mathbf{K}_{*,*} - \mathbf{Q}_{*,X} \hat{\mathbf{Q}}_{X,X}^{-1} \mathbf{Q}_{X,*}) \tag{18.126}$$

$$= \mathcal{N}(\boldsymbol{f}_* | \sigma^{-2} \mathbf{K}_{*,Z} \mathbf{\Sigma} \mathbf{K}_{Z,X} \boldsymbol{y}, \ \mathbf{K}_{*,*} - \mathbf{Q}_{*,*} + \mathbf{K}_{*,Z} \mathbf{\Sigma} \mathbf{K}_{Z,*}) \tag{18.127}$$

The predictive mean is the same as in SOR, but the variance is larger (since $\mathbf{K}_{*,*} - \mathbf{Q}_{*,*}$ is positive definite) due to the uncertainty of $\boldsymbol{f}_*$ given $\boldsymbol{f}_Z$.

18.5.3.3 FITC

A widely used approximation assumes $q(\boldsymbol{f}_X | \boldsymbol{f}_Z)$ is fully factorized, i.e,

$$q(\boldsymbol{f}_X | \boldsymbol{f}_Z) = \prod_{n=1}^{N} p(f_n | \boldsymbol{f}_Z) = \mathcal{N}(\boldsymbol{f}_X | \mathbf{K}_{X,Z} \mathbf{K}_{Z,Z}^{-1} \boldsymbol{f}_Z, \text{diag}(\mathbf{K}_{X,X} - \mathbf{Q}_{X,X})) \tag{18.128}$$

This is called the **fully independent training conditional** or **FITC** assumption, and was first proposed in [SG06a]. This throws away less uncertainty that the SOR and DTC methods, since it does not make any deterministic assumptions about the relationship between $\boldsymbol{f}_X$ and $\boldsymbol{f}_Z$.

The joint prior has the form

$$q_{\text{fitc}}(\boldsymbol{f}_X, \boldsymbol{f}_*) = \mathcal{N}\left(\mathbf{0}, \begin{pmatrix} \mathbf{Q}_{X,X} - \text{diag}(\mathbf{Q}_{X,X} - \mathbf{K}_{X,X}) & \mathbf{Q}_{X,*} \\ \mathbf{Q}_{*,X} & \mathbf{K}_{*,*} \end{pmatrix}\right) \tag{18.129}$$

The predictive distribution for a single test case is given by

$$q_{\text{fitc}}(f_*|\boldsymbol{y}) = \mathcal{N}(f_*|\boldsymbol{k}_{*,Z}\boldsymbol{\Sigma}\mathbf{K}_{Z,X}\boldsymbol{\Lambda}^{-1}\boldsymbol{y}, k_{**} - q_{**} + \boldsymbol{k}_{*,Z}\boldsymbol{\Sigma}\boldsymbol{k}_{Z,*}) \tag{18.130}$$

where $\boldsymbol{\Lambda} \triangleq \text{diag}(\mathbf{K}_{X,X} - \mathbf{Q}_{X,X} + \sigma^2\mathbf{I}_N)$, and $\boldsymbol{\Sigma} \triangleq (\mathbf{K}_{Z,Z} + \mathbf{K}_{Z,X}\boldsymbol{\Lambda}^{-1}\mathbf{K}_{X,Z})^{-1}$. If we have a batch of test cases, we can assume they are conditionally independent (an approach known as **fully independent conditional** or **FIC**), and multiply the above equation.

The computational cost is the same as for SOR and DTC, but the approach avoids some of the pathologies due to a non-degenerate kernel. In particular, one can show that the FIC method is equivalent to exact GP inference with the following non-degenerate kernel:

$$\mathcal{K}_{\text{fic}}(\boldsymbol{x}_i, \boldsymbol{x}_j) = \begin{cases} \mathcal{K}(\boldsymbol{x}_i, \boldsymbol{x}_j) & \text{if } i = j \\ \mathcal{K}_{\text{SOR}}(\boldsymbol{x}_i, \boldsymbol{x}_j) & \text{if } i \neq j \end{cases} \tag{18.131}$$

18.5.3.4 Learning the inducing points

So far, we have not specified how to choose the inducing points or pseudoinputs $\mathbf{Z}$. We can treat these like kernel hyperparameters, and choose them so as to maximize the log marginal likelihood, given by

$$\log q(\boldsymbol{y}|\mathbf{X}, \mathbf{Z}) = \log \int \int p(\boldsymbol{y}|\boldsymbol{f}_X)q(\boldsymbol{f}_X|\mathbf{X}, \boldsymbol{f}_Z)p(\boldsymbol{f}_Z|\mathbf{Z})d\boldsymbol{f}_Zd\boldsymbol{f} \tag{18.132}$$

$$= \log \int p(\boldsymbol{y}|\boldsymbol{f}_X)q(\boldsymbol{f}_X|\mathbf{X}, \mathbf{Z})d\boldsymbol{f}_X \tag{18.133}$$

$$= -\frac{1}{2}\log|\mathbf{Q}_{X,X} + \boldsymbol{\Lambda}| - \frac{1}{2}\boldsymbol{y}^\mathsf{T}(\mathbf{Q}_{X,X} + \boldsymbol{\Lambda})^{-1}\boldsymbol{y} - \frac{n}{2}\log(2\pi) \tag{18.134}$$

where the definition of $\boldsymbol{\Lambda}$ depends on the method, namely $\boldsymbol{\Lambda}_{\text{SOR}} = \boldsymbol{\Lambda}_{\text{dtc}} = \sigma^2\mathbf{I}_N$, and $\boldsymbol{\Lambda}_{\text{fitc}} = \text{diag}(\mathbf{K}_{X,X} - \mathbf{Q}_{X,X}) + \sigma^2\mathbf{I}_N$.

If the input domain is $\mathbb{R}^d$, we can optimize $\mathbf{Z} \in \mathbb{R}^{Md}$ using gradient methods. However, one of the appeals of kernel methods is that they can handle structured inputs, such as strings and graphs (see Section 18.2.3). In this case, we cannot use gradient methods to select the inducing points. A simple approach is to select the inducing points from the training set, as in the subset of data approach in Section 18.5.1, or using the efficient selection mechanism in [Cao+15]. However, we can also use discrete optimization methods, such as simulated annealing (Section 12.9.1), as discussed in [For+18a]. See Figure 18.13 for an illustration.

18.5.4 Sparse variational methods

In this section, we discuss a variational approach to GP inference called the **sparse variational GP** or **SVGP** approximation, also known as the **variational free energy** or **VFE** approach [Tit09; Mat+16]. This is similar to the inducing point methods in Section 18.5.3, except it approximates the posterior, rather than approximating the prior. The variational approach can also easily handle non-conjugate likelihoods, as we will see. For more details, see e.g., [BWR16; Lei+20]. (See also [WKS21] for connections between SVGP and the Nyström method.)

To explain the idea behind SVGP/ VFE, let us assume, for simplicity, that the function f is defined over a finite set $\mathcal{X}$ of possible inputs, which we partition into three subsets: the training set $\mathbf{X}$, a set

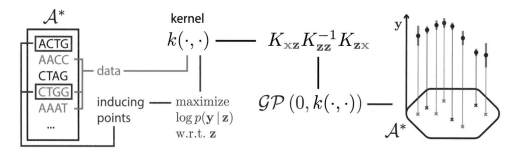

Figure 18.13: Illustration of how to choose inducing points from a discrete input domain (here DNA sequences of length 4) to maximize the log marginal likelihood. From Figure 1 of [For+18a]. Used with kind permission of Vincent Fortuin.

of inducing points $\mathbf{Z}$, and all other points (which we can think of as the test set), $\mathbf{X}_*$. (We assume these sets are disjoint.) Let $\boldsymbol{f}_X$, $\boldsymbol{f}_Z$ and $\boldsymbol{f}_*$ represent the corresponding unknown function values on these points, and let $\boldsymbol{f} = [\boldsymbol{f}_X, \boldsymbol{f}_Z, \boldsymbol{f}_*]$ be all the unknowns. (Here we work with a fixed-length vector $\boldsymbol{f}$, but the result generalizes to Gaussian processes, as explained in [Mat+16].) We assume the function is sampled from a GP, so $p(\boldsymbol{f}) = \mathcal{N}(m(\mathcal{X}), \mathcal{K}(\mathcal{X}, \mathcal{X}))$.

The inducing point methods in Section 18.5.3 approximates the GP prior by assuming $p(\boldsymbol{f}_*, \boldsymbol{f}_X, \boldsymbol{f}_Z) \approx p(\boldsymbol{f}_*|\boldsymbol{f}_Z)p(\boldsymbol{f}_X|\boldsymbol{f}_Z)p(\boldsymbol{f}_Z)$. The inducing points $\boldsymbol{f}_Z$ are chosen to maximize the likelihood of the observed data. We then perform exact inference in this approximate model. By contrast, in this section, we will keep the model unchanged, but we will instead approximate the posterior $p(\boldsymbol{f}|\boldsymbol{y})$ using variational inference.

In the VFE view, the inducing points $\mathbf{Z}$ and inducing variables $\boldsymbol{f}_Z$ (often denoted by $\boldsymbol{u}$) are variational parameters, rather than model parameters, which avoids the risk of overfitting. Furthermore, one can show that as the number of inducing points m increases, the quality of the posterior consistently improves, eventually recovering exact inference. By contrast, in the classical inducing point method, increasing m does not always result in better performance [BWR16].

In more detail, the VFE approach tries to find an approximate posterior $q(\boldsymbol{f})$ to minimize $D_{\mathbb{KL}}(q(\boldsymbol{f}) \parallel p(\boldsymbol{f}|\boldsymbol{y}))$. The key assumption is that $q(\boldsymbol{f}) = q(\boldsymbol{f}_*, \boldsymbol{f}_X, \boldsymbol{f}_Z) = p(\boldsymbol{f}_*, \boldsymbol{f}_X|\boldsymbol{f}_Z)q(\boldsymbol{f}_Z)$, where $p(\boldsymbol{f}_*, \boldsymbol{f}_X|\boldsymbol{f}_Z)$ is computed exactly using the GP prior, and $q(\boldsymbol{f}_Z)$ is learned, by minimizing $\mathcal{K}(q) = D_{\mathbb{KL}}(q(\boldsymbol{f}) \parallel p(\boldsymbol{f}|\boldsymbol{y}))$.[2] Intuitively, $q(\boldsymbol{f}_Z)$ acts as a "bottleneck" which "absorbs" all the observations from $\boldsymbol{y}$; posterior predictions for elements of $\boldsymbol{f}_X$ or $\boldsymbol{f}_*$ are then made via their dependence on $\boldsymbol{f}_Z$, rather than their dependence on each other.

---

2. One can show that $D_{\mathbb{KL}}(q(\boldsymbol{f}) \parallel p(\boldsymbol{f}|\boldsymbol{y})) = D_{\mathbb{KL}}(q(\boldsymbol{f}_X, \boldsymbol{f}_Z) \parallel p(\boldsymbol{f}_X, \boldsymbol{f}_Z|\boldsymbol{y}))$, which is the original objective from [Tit09].

We can derive the form of the loss, which is used to compute the posterior $q(\boldsymbol{f}_Z)$, as follows:

$$\mathcal{K}(q) = D_{\mathrm{KL}}\left(q(\boldsymbol{f}_*, \boldsymbol{f}_X, \boldsymbol{f}_Z) \parallel p(\boldsymbol{f}_*, \boldsymbol{f}_X, \boldsymbol{f}_Z | \boldsymbol{y})\right) \tag{18.135}$$

$$= \int q(\boldsymbol{f}_*, \boldsymbol{f}_X, \boldsymbol{f}_Z) \log \frac{q(\boldsymbol{f}_*, \boldsymbol{f}_X, \boldsymbol{f}_Z)}{p(\boldsymbol{f}_*, \boldsymbol{f}_X, \boldsymbol{f}_Z | \boldsymbol{y})} d\boldsymbol{f}_* \, d\boldsymbol{f}_X \, d\boldsymbol{f}_Z \tag{18.136}$$

$$= \int p(\boldsymbol{f}_*, \boldsymbol{f}_X | \boldsymbol{f}_Z) q(\boldsymbol{f}_Z) \log \frac{\cancel{p(\boldsymbol{f}_* | \boldsymbol{f}_X, \boldsymbol{f}_Z)}\cancel{p(\boldsymbol{f}_X | \boldsymbol{f}_Z)} q(\boldsymbol{f}_Z) p(\boldsymbol{y})}{\cancel{p(\boldsymbol{f}_* | \boldsymbol{f}_X, \boldsymbol{f}_Z)}\cancel{p(\boldsymbol{f}_X | \boldsymbol{f}_Z)} p(\boldsymbol{f}_Z) p(\boldsymbol{y} | \boldsymbol{f}_X)} d\boldsymbol{f}_* \, d\boldsymbol{f}_X \, d\boldsymbol{f}_Z \tag{18.137}$$

$$= \int p(\boldsymbol{f}_*, \boldsymbol{f}_X | \boldsymbol{f}_Z) q(\boldsymbol{f}_Z) \log \frac{q(\boldsymbol{f}_Z) p(\boldsymbol{y})}{p(\boldsymbol{f}_Z) p(\boldsymbol{y} | \boldsymbol{f}_X)} d\boldsymbol{f}_* \, d\boldsymbol{f}_X \, d\boldsymbol{f}_Z \tag{18.138}$$

$$= \int q(\boldsymbol{f}_Z) \log \frac{q(\boldsymbol{f}_Z)}{p(\boldsymbol{f}_Z)} d\boldsymbol{f}_Z - \int p(\boldsymbol{f}_X | \boldsymbol{f}_Z) q(\boldsymbol{f}_Z) \log p(\boldsymbol{y} | \boldsymbol{f}_X) d\boldsymbol{f}_X \, d\boldsymbol{f}_Z + C \tag{18.139}$$

$$= D_{\mathrm{KL}}\left(q(\boldsymbol{f}_Z) \parallel p(\boldsymbol{f}_Z)\right) - \mathbb{E}_{q(\boldsymbol{f}_X)}\left[\log p(\boldsymbol{y} | \boldsymbol{f}_X)\right] + C \tag{18.140}$$

where $C = \log p(\boldsymbol{y})$ is an irrelevant constant.

We can alternatively write the objective as an evidence lower bound that we want to maximize:

$$\log p(\boldsymbol{y}) = \mathcal{K}(q) + \mathbb{E}_{q(\boldsymbol{f}_X)}\left[\log p(\boldsymbol{y} | \boldsymbol{f}_X)\right] - D_{\mathrm{KL}}\left(q(\boldsymbol{f}_Z) \parallel p(\boldsymbol{f}_Z)\right) \tag{18.141}$$

$$\geq \mathbb{E}_{q(\boldsymbol{f}_X)}\left[\log p(\boldsymbol{y} | \boldsymbol{f}_X)\right] - D_{\mathrm{KL}}\left(q(\boldsymbol{f}_Z) \parallel p(\boldsymbol{f}_Z)\right) \triangleq \mathcal{L}(q) \tag{18.142}$$

Now suppose we choose a Gaussian posterior approximation, $q(\boldsymbol{f}_Z) = \mathcal{N}(\boldsymbol{f}_Z | \boldsymbol{m}, \mathbf{S})$. Since $p(\boldsymbol{f}_Z) = \mathcal{N}(\boldsymbol{f}_Z | \boldsymbol{0}, \mathcal{K}(\mathbf{Z}, \mathbf{Z}))$, we can compute the KL term in closed form using the formula for KL divergence between Gaussians (Equation (5.77)). To compute the expected log-likelihood term, we first need to compute the induced posterior over the latent function values at the training points:

$$q(\boldsymbol{f}_X | \boldsymbol{m}, \mathbf{S}) = \int p(\boldsymbol{f}_X | \boldsymbol{f}_Z, \mathbf{X}, \mathbf{Z}) q(\boldsymbol{f}_Z | \boldsymbol{m}, \mathbf{S}) d\boldsymbol{f}_Z = \mathcal{N}(\boldsymbol{f}_X | \tilde{\boldsymbol{\mu}}, \tilde{\boldsymbol{\Sigma}}) \tag{18.143}$$

$$\tilde{\mu}_i = m(\boldsymbol{x}_i) + \boldsymbol{\alpha}(\boldsymbol{x}_i)^{\mathsf{T}}(\boldsymbol{m} - m(\mathbf{Z})) \tag{18.144}$$

$$\tilde{\Sigma}_{ij} = \mathcal{K}(\boldsymbol{x}_i, \boldsymbol{x}_j) - \boldsymbol{\alpha}(\boldsymbol{x}_i)^{\mathsf{T}}(\mathcal{K}(\mathbf{Z}, \mathbf{Z}) - \mathbf{S})\boldsymbol{\alpha}(\boldsymbol{x}_j) \tag{18.145}$$

$$\boldsymbol{\alpha}(\boldsymbol{x}_i) = \mathcal{K}(\mathbf{Z}, \mathbf{Z})^{-1}\mathcal{K}(\mathbf{Z}, \boldsymbol{x}_i) \tag{18.146}$$

Hence the marginal at a single point is $q(f_n) = \mathcal{N}(f_n | \tilde{\mu}_n, \tilde{\Sigma}_{nn})$, which we can use to compute the expected log likelihood:

$$\mathbb{E}_{q(\boldsymbol{f}_X)}\left[\log p(\boldsymbol{y} | \boldsymbol{f}_X)\right] = \sum_{n=1}^{N} \mathbb{E}_{q(f_n)}\left[\log p(y_n | f_n)\right] \tag{18.147}$$

We discuss how to compute these expectations below.

18.5.4.1 Gaussian likelihood

If we have a Gaussian observation model, we can compute the expected log likelihood in closed form. In particular, if we assume $m(\boldsymbol{x}) = \boldsymbol{0}$, we have

$$\mathbb{E}_{q(f_n)}\left[\log \mathcal{N}(y_n | f_n, \beta^{-1})\right] = \log \mathcal{N}(y_n | \boldsymbol{k}_n^{\mathsf{T}} \mathbf{K}_{Z,Z}^{-1} \boldsymbol{m}, \beta^{-1}) - \frac{1}{2}\beta \tilde{k}_{nn} - \frac{1}{2}\mathrm{tr}(\mathbf{S}\boldsymbol{\Lambda}_n) \tag{18.148}$$

where $\tilde{k}_{nn} = k_{nn} - \boldsymbol{k}_n^\mathsf{T} \mathbf{K}_{Z,Z}^{-1} \boldsymbol{k}_n$, $\boldsymbol{k}_n$ is the n'th column of $\mathbf{K}_{Z,X}$ and $\boldsymbol{\Lambda}_n = \beta \mathbf{K}_{Z,Z}^{-1} \boldsymbol{k}_n \boldsymbol{k}_n^\mathsf{T} \mathbf{K}_{Z,Z}^{-1}$.

Hence the overall ELBO has the form

$$\mathcal{L}(q) = \log \mathcal{N}(\boldsymbol{y} | \mathbf{K}_{X,z} \mathbf{K}_{Z,Z}^{-1} \boldsymbol{m}, \beta^{-1} \mathbf{I}_N) - \frac{1}{2} \beta \mathrm{tr}(\mathbf{K}_{X,z} \mathbf{K}_{Z,Z}^{-1} \mathbf{S} \mathbf{K}_{Z,Z}^{-1} \mathbf{K}_{Z,X}) \tag{18.149}$$

$$- \frac{1}{2} \beta \mathrm{tr}(\mathbf{K}_{X,X} - \mathbf{Q}_{X,X}) - D_{\mathrm{KL}}\left(q(\boldsymbol{f}_Z) \,\|\, p(\boldsymbol{f}_Z)\right) \tag{18.150}$$

where $\mathbf{Q}_{X,X} = \mathbf{K}_{X,z} \mathbf{K}_{Z,Z}^{-1} \mathbf{K}_{Z,X}$.

To compute the gradients of this, we leverage the following result [OA09]:

$$\frac{\partial}{\partial \mu} \mathbb{E}_{\mathcal{N}(x|\mu,\sigma^2)}\left[h(x)\right] = \mathbb{E}_{\mathcal{N}(x|\mu,\sigma^2)}\left[\frac{\partial}{\partial x} h(x)\right] \tag{18.151}$$

$$\frac{\partial}{\partial \sigma^2} \mathbb{E}_{\mathcal{N}(x|\mu,\sigma^2)}\left[h(x)\right] = \frac{1}{2} \mathbb{E}_{\mathcal{N}(x|\mu,\sigma^2)}\left[\frac{\partial^2}{\partial x^2} h(x)\right] \tag{18.152}$$

We then substitute $h(x)$ with $\log p(y_n | f_n)$. Using this, one can show

$$\nabla_{\boldsymbol{m}} \mathcal{L}(q) = \beta \mathbf{K}_{Z,Z}^{-1} \mathbf{K}_{Z,X} \boldsymbol{y} - \boldsymbol{\Lambda} \boldsymbol{m} \tag{18.153}$$

$$\nabla_{\mathbf{S}} \mathcal{L}(q) = \frac{1}{2} \mathbf{S}^{-1} - \frac{1}{2} \boldsymbol{\Lambda} \tag{18.154}$$

Setting the derivatives to zero gives the optimal solution:

$$\mathbf{S} = \boldsymbol{\Lambda}^{-1} \tag{18.155}$$

$$\boldsymbol{\Lambda} = \beta \mathbf{K}_{Z,Z}^{-1} \mathbf{K}_{Z,X} \mathbf{K}_{X,z} \mathbf{K}_{Z,Z}^{-1} + \mathbf{K}_{Z,Z}^{-1} \tag{18.156}$$

$$\boldsymbol{m} = \beta \boldsymbol{\Lambda}^{-1} \mathbf{K}_{Z,Z}^{-1} \mathbf{K}_{Z,X} \boldsymbol{y} \tag{18.157}$$

This is called **sparse GP regression** or **SGPR** [Tit09].

With these parameters, the lower bound on the log marginal likelihood is given by

$$\log p(\boldsymbol{y}) \geq \log \mathcal{N}(\boldsymbol{y} | \mathbf{0}, \mathbf{K}_{X,z} \mathbf{K}_{Z,Z}^{-1} \mathbf{K}_{Z,X} + \beta^{-1} \mathbf{I}) - \frac{1}{2} \beta \mathrm{tr}(\mathbf{K}_{X,X} - \mathbf{Q}_{X,X}) \tag{18.158}$$

(This is called the "collapsed" lower bound, since we have marginalized out $\boldsymbol{f}_Z$.) If $Z = X$, then $\mathbf{K}_{Z,Z} = \mathbf{K}_{Z,X} = \mathbf{K}_{X,X}$, so the bound becomes tight, and we have $\log p(\boldsymbol{y}) = \log \mathcal{N}(\boldsymbol{y} | \mathbf{0}, \mathbf{K}_{X,X} + \beta^{-1} \mathbf{I})$.

Equation (18.158) is almost the same as the log marginal likelihood for the DTC model in Equation (18.134), except for the trace term; it is this latter term that prevents overfitting, due to the fact that we treat $\boldsymbol{f}_Z$ as variational parameters of the posterior rather than model parameters of the prior.

18.5.4.2 Non-Gaussian likelihood

In this section, we briefly consider the case of non-Gaussian likelihoods, which arise when using GPs for classification or for count data (see Section 18.4). We can compute the gradients of the expected log likelihood by defining $h(f_n) = \log p(y_n | f_n)$ and then using a Monte Carlo approximation to Equation (18.151) and Equation (18.152). In the case of a binary classifier, we can use the results in Table 18.2 to compute the inner $\frac{\partial}{\partial f_n} h(f_n)$ and $\frac{\partial^2}{\partial f_n^2} h(f_n)$ terms. Alternatively, we can use numerical integration techniques, such as those discussed in Section 8.5.1.4. (See also [WSS21].)

18.5.4.3 Minibatch SVI

Computing the optimal variational solution in Section 18.5.4.1 requires solving a batch optimization problem, which takes $O(M^3 + NM^2)$ time. This may still be too slow if N is large, unless M is small, which compromises accuracy.

An alternative approach is to perform stochastic optimization of the VFE objective, instead of batch optimization. This is known as stochastic variational inference (see Section 10.1.4). The key observation is that the log likelihood in Equation (18.147) is a sum of N terms, which we can approximate with minibatch sampling to compute noisy estimates of the gradient, as proposed in [HFL13].

In more detail, the objective becomes

$$\mathcal{L}(q) = \left[\frac{N}{B} \sum_{b=1}^{B} \frac{1}{|\mathcal{B}_b|} \sum_{n \in \mathcal{B}_b} \mathbb{E}_{q(f_n)} \left[\log p(y_n | f_n) \right] \right] - D_{\mathrm{KL}} \left(q(\boldsymbol{f}_Z) \, \| \, (p(\boldsymbol{f}_Z)) \right) \tag{18.159}$$

where $\mathcal{B}_b$ is the b'th batch, and B is the number of batches. Since the GP model (with Gaussian likelihoods) is in the exponential family, we can efficiently compute the natural gradient (Section 6.4) of Equation (18.159) wrt the canonical parameters of $q(\boldsymbol{f}_Z)$; this converges much faster than following the standard gradient. See [HFL13] for details.

18.5.5 Exploiting parallelization and structure via kernel matrix multiplies

It takes $O(N^3)$ time to compute the Cholesky decomposition of $\mathbf{K}_{X,X}$, which is needed to solve the linear system $\mathbf{K}_\sigma \boldsymbol{\alpha} = \boldsymbol{y}$ and to compute $|\mathbf{K}_{X,X}|$. An alternative to Cholesky decomposition is to use linear algebra methods, often called **Krylov subspace methods** based just on **matrix vector multiplication** or **MVM**. These approaches are often much faster.

In short, if the kernel matrix $\mathbf{K}_{X,X}$ has special algebraic structure, which is often the case through either the choice of kernel or the structure of the inputs, then it is typically easier to exploit this structure in performing fast matrix multiplies. Moreover, even if the kernel matrix **does not** have special structure, matrix multiplies are trivial to parallelize, and can thus be greatly accelerated by GPUs, unlike Cholesky based methods which are largely sequential. Algorithms based on matrix multiplies are in harmony with modern hardware advances, which enable significant parallelization.

18.5.5.1 Using conjugate gradient and Lanczos methods

We can solve the linear system $\mathbf{K}_\sigma \boldsymbol{\alpha} = \boldsymbol{y}$ using conjugate gradients (CG). The key computational step in CG is the ability to perform MVMs. Let $\tau(\mathbf{K}_\sigma)$ be the time complexity of a single MVM with $\mathbf{K}_\sigma$. For a dense $n \times n$ matrix, we have $\tau(\mathbf{K}_\sigma) = n^2$; however, we can speed this up if $\mathbf{K}_\sigma$ is sparse or structured, as we discuss below.

Even if $\mathbf{K}_\sigma$ is dense, we may still be able to save time by solving the linear system approximately. In particular, if we perform C iterations, CG will take $O(C\tau(\mathbf{K}_\sigma))$ time. If we run for $C = n$, and $\tau(\mathbf{K}_\sigma) = n^2$, it gives the exact solution in $O(n^3)$ time. However, often we can use fewer iterations and still get good accuracy, depending on the condition number of $\mathbf{K}_\sigma$.

We can compute the log determinant of a matrix using the MVM primitive with a similar iterative method known as **stochastic Lanczos quadrature** [UCS17; Don+17a]. This takes $O(L\tau(\mathbf{K}_\sigma))$ time for L iterations.

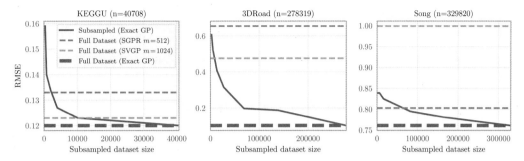

Figure 18.14: *RMSE on test set as a function of training set size using a GP with Matern 3/2 kernel with shared lengthscale across all dimensions. Solid lines: exact inference. Dashed blue: SGPR method (closed-form batch solution to the Gaussian variational approximation) of Section 18.5.4.1 with $M = 512$ inducing points. Dashed orange: SVGP method (SGD on Gaussian variational approxiation) of Section 18.5.4.3 with $M = 1024$ inducing points. Number of input dimensions: KEGGU $D = 27$, 3DRoad $D = 3$, Song $D = 90$. From Figure 4 of [Wan+19a]. Used with kind permission of Andrew Wilson.*

These methods have been used in the **blackbox matrix-matrix multiplication (BBMM)** inference procedure of [Gar+18a], which formulates a batch approach to CG that can be effectively parallelized on GPUs. Using 8 GPUs, this enabled the authors of [Wan+19a] to perform exact inference for a GP regression model on $N \sim 10^4$ datapoints in seconds, $N \sim 10^5$ datapoints in minutes, and $N \sim 10^6$ datapoints in hours.

Interestingly, Figure 18.14 shows that exact GP inference on a subset of the data can often outperform approximate inference on the full data. We also see that performance of exact GPs continues to significantly improve as we increase the size of the data, suggesting that GPs are not only useful in the small-sample setting. In particular, the BBMM is an exact method, and so will preserve the non-parametric representation of a GP with a non-degenerate kernel. By contrast, standard scalable approximations typically operate by replacing the exact kernel with an approximation that corresponds to a parametric model. The non-parametric GPs are able to grow their capacity with more data, benefiting more significantly from the structure present in large datasets.

18.5.5.2 Kernels with compact support

Suppose we use a kernel with **compact support**, where $\mathcal{K}(\boldsymbol{x}, \boldsymbol{x}') = 0$ if $\|\boldsymbol{x} - \boldsymbol{x}'\| > \epsilon$ for some threshold ϵ (see e.g., [MR09]), then $\mathbf{K}_\sigma$ will be sparse, so $\tau(\mathbf{K}_\sigma)$ will be $O(N)$. We can also induce sparsity and structure in other ways, as we discuss in Section 18.5.5.3.

18.5.5.3 KISS

One way to ensure that MVMs are fast is to force the kernel matrix to have structure. The **structured kernel interpolation (SKI)** method of [WN15] does this as follows. First it assumes we have a set of inducing points, with Gram matrix $\mathbf{K}_{Z,Z}$. It then interpolates these values to predict the entries of the full kernel matrix using

$$\mathbf{K}_{X,X} \approx \mathbf{W}_{\mathbf{X}} \mathbf{K}_{Z,Z} \mathbf{W}_{\mathbf{X}}^\mathsf{T} \tag{18.160}$$

where $\mathbf{W_X}$ is a sparse matrix containing interpolation weights. If we use cubic interpolation, each row only has 4 nonzeros. Thus we can compute $(\mathbf{W_X K}_{Z,Z} \mathbf{W_X^T})\boldsymbol{v}$ for any vector $\boldsymbol{v}$ in $O(N + M^2)$ time.

Note that the **SKI** approach generalizes all inducing point methods. For example, we can recover the subset of regressors method (SOR) method by setting the interpolation weights to $\mathbf{W} = \mathbf{K}_{X,Z}\mathbf{K}_{Z,Z}^{-1}$. We can identify this procedure as performing a global Gaussian process interpolation strategy on the user specified kernel. See [WN15] and [WDN15] for more details.

In 1d, we can further reduce the running time by choosing the inducing points to be on a regular grid, so that $\mathbf{K}_{Z,Z}$ is a Toeplitz matrix. In higher dimensions, we need to use a multidimensional grid of points, resulting in $\mathbf{K}_{Z,Z}$ being a Kronecker product of Toeplitz matrices. This enables matrix vector multiplication in $O(N + M \log M)$ time and $O(N + M)$ space. The resulting method is called **KISS-GP** [WN15], which stands for "kernel interpolation for scalable, structured GPs".

Unfortunately, the KISS method can take exponential time in the input dimensions D when exploiting Kronecker structure in $\mathbf{K}_{Z,Z}$, due to the need to create a fully connected multidimensional lattice. In [Gar+18b], they propose a method called **SKIP**, which stands for "SKI for products". The idea is to leverage the fact that many kernels (including ARD) can be written as a product of 1d kernels: $\mathcal{K}(\boldsymbol{x}, \boldsymbol{x}') = \prod_{d=1}^{D} \mathcal{K}^d(\boldsymbol{x}, \boldsymbol{x}')$. This can be combined with the 1d SKI method to enable fast MVMs. The overall running time to compute the log marginal likelihood (which is the bottleneck for kernel learning) using C iterations of CG and a Lanczos decomposition of rank L, becomes $O(DL(N + M \log M) + L^3 N \log D + CL^2 N)$. Typical values are $L \sim 10^1$ and $C \sim 10^2$.

18.5.5.4 Tensor train methods

Consider the Gaussian VFE approach in Section 18.5.4. We have to estimate the covariance $\mathbf{S}$ and the mean $\boldsymbol{m}$. We can represent $\mathbf{S}$ efficiently using Kronecker structure, as used by KISS. Additionally, we can represent $\boldsymbol{m}$ efficiently using the **tensor train decomposition** [Ose11] in combination with **SKI** [WN15]. The resulting **TT-GP** method can scale efficiently to billions of inducing points, as explained in [INK18].

18.5.6 Converting a GP to an SSM

Consider a function defined on a 1d scalar input, such as a time index. For many stationary 1d kernels, the corresponding GP can be modeled using a linear time invariant (LTI) stochastic differential equation (SDE)[3]; this SDE can then be converted to a linear-Gaussian state space model (Section 29.1) as first proposed in [HS10]. For example, consider the exponential kernel in Equation (18.14), $\mathcal{K}(t, t') = \frac{q}{2\lambda} \exp(-\lambda|t - t'|)$, which corresponds to a Matérn kernel with $\nu = 1/2$. The corresponding SDE is the Orstein-Uhlenbeck process which has the form $\frac{dx(t)}{dt} = -\lambda x(t) + w(t)$, where $w(t)$ is a white noise process with spectral density q [SS19, p258].[4] For other kernels (such as Matérn with $\nu = 3/2$), we need to use multiple latent states in order to capture higher order

---

3. The condition is that the spectral density of the covariance function has to be a rational function. This includes many kernels, such as the Matérn kernel, but excludes the squared exponential (RBF) kernel. However the latter can be approximated by an SDE, as explained in [SS19, p261].

4. This is sometimes written as $dx = -\lambda x \, dt + d\beta$, where $\beta(t)$ is a Brownian noise process, and $w(t) = \frac{d\beta(t)}{dt}$, as explained in [SS19, p45].

derivative terms (see Supplementary Section 18.2 for details). Furthermore, for higher dimensional inputs, we need to use even more latent states, to enforce the Markov property [DSP21].

Once we have converted the GP to LG-SSM form, we can perform exact inference in $O(N)$ time using Kalman smoothing, as explained in Section 8.2.3. Furthermore, if we have access to a highly parallel processor, such as a GPU, we can reduce the time to $\log(N)$ [CZS22], as explained in Section 8.2.3.4.

18.6 Learning the kernel

In [Mac98], David MacKay asked: "How can Gaussian processes replace neural networks? Have we thrown the baby out with the bathwater?" This remark was made in the late 1990s, at the end of the second wave of neural networks. Researchers and practitioners had grown weary of the design decisions associated with neural networks — such as activation functions, optimization procedures, architecture design — and the lack of a principled framework to make these decisions. Gaussian processes, by contrast, were perceived as flexible and principled probabilistic models, which naturally followed from Radford Neal's results on infinite neural networks [Nea96], which we discuss in more depth in Section 18.7.

However, MacKay [Mac98] noted that neural networks could discover rich representations of data through adaptive hidden basis functions, while Gaussian processes with standard kernel functions, such as the RBF kernel, are essentially just smoothing devices. Indeed, the generalization properties of Gaussian processes hinge on the suitability of the kernel function. *Learning* the kernel is how we do representation learning with Gaussian processes, and in many cases will be crucial for good performance — especially when we wish to perform extrapolation, making predictions far away from the data [WA13; Wil+14].

As we will see, learning a kernel is in many ways analogous to training a neural network. Moreover, neural networks and Gaussian processes can be synergistically combined through approaches such as deep kernel learning (see Section 18.6.6) and NN-GPs (Section 18.7.2).

18.6.1 Empirical Bayes for the kernel parameters

Suppose, as in Section 18.3.2, we are performing 1d regression using a GP with an RBF kernel. Since the data has observation noise, the kernel has the following form:

$$\mathcal{K}_y(x_p, x_q) = \sigma_f^2 \exp(-\frac{1}{2\ell^2}(x_p - x_q)^2) + \sigma_y^2 \delta_{pq} \tag{18.161}$$

Here ℓ is the horizontal scale over which the function changes, σ_f^2 controls the vertical scale of the function, and σ_y^2 is the noise variance. Figure 18.15 illustrates the effects of changing these parameters. We sampled 20 noisy datapoints from the SE kernel using $(\ell, \sigma_f, \sigma_y) = (1, 1, 0.1)$, and then made predictions various parameters, conditional on the data. In Figure 18.15(a), we use $(\ell, \sigma_f, \sigma_y) = (1, 1, 0.1)$, and the result is a good fit. In Figure 18.15(b), we increase the length scale to $\ell = 3$; now the function looks smoother, but we are arguably underfitting.

To estimate the kernel parameters $\boldsymbol{\theta}$ (sometimes called hyperparameters), we could use exhaustive search over a discrete grid of values, with validation loss as an objective, but this can be quite slow. (This is the approach used by nonprobabilistic methods, such as SVMs, to tune kernels.) Here we

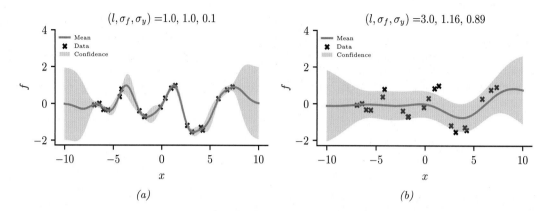

Figure 18.15: Some 1d GPs with RBF kernels but different hyper-parameters fit to 20 noisy observations. The hyper-parameters $(\ell, \sigma_f, \sigma_y)$ are as follows: (a) (1, 1, 0.1) (b) (3.0, 1.16, 0.89). Adapted from Figure 2.5 of [RW06]. Generated by gpr_demo_change_hparams.ipynb.

consider an empirical Bayes approach, which will allow us to use continuous optimization methods, which are much faster. In particular, we will maximize the marginal likelihood

$$p(\boldsymbol{y}|\mathbf{X}, \boldsymbol{\theta}) = \int p(\boldsymbol{y}|\boldsymbol{f}, \mathbf{X})p(\boldsymbol{f}|\mathbf{X}, \boldsymbol{\theta})d\boldsymbol{f} \tag{18.162}$$

(The reason it is called the marginal likelihood, rather than just likelihood, is because we have marginalized out the latent Gaussian vector $\boldsymbol{f}$.) Since $p(\boldsymbol{f}|\mathbf{X}) = \mathcal{N}(\boldsymbol{f}|\boldsymbol{0}, \mathbf{K})$, and $p(\boldsymbol{y}|\boldsymbol{f}) = \prod_{n=1}^{N} \mathcal{N}(y_n|f_n, \sigma_y^2)$, the marginal likelihood is given by

$$\log p(\boldsymbol{y}|\mathbf{X}, \boldsymbol{\theta}) = \log \mathcal{N}(\boldsymbol{y}|\boldsymbol{0}, \mathbf{K}_\sigma) = -\frac{1}{2}\boldsymbol{y}\mathbf{K}_\sigma^{-1}\boldsymbol{y} - \frac{1}{2}\log|\mathbf{K}_\sigma| - \frac{N}{2}\log(2\pi) \tag{18.163}$$

where the dependence of $\mathbf{K}_\sigma$ on $\boldsymbol{\theta}$ is implicit. The first term is a data fit term, the second term is a model complexity term, and the third term is just a constant. To understand the tradeoff between the first two terms, consider a SE kernel in 1d, as we vary the length scale ℓ and hold σ_y^2 fixed. Let $J(\ell) = -\log p(\boldsymbol{y}|\mathbf{X}, \ell)$. For short length scales, the fit will be good, so $\boldsymbol{y}^\mathsf{T}\mathbf{K}_\sigma^{-1}\boldsymbol{y}$ will be small. However, the model complexity will be high: $\mathbf{K}$ will be almost diagonal, since most points will not be considered "near" any others, so the $\log|\mathbf{K}_\sigma|$ will be large. For long length scales, the fit will be poor but the model complexity will be low: $\mathbf{K}$ will be almost all 1's, so $\log|\mathbf{K}_\sigma|$ will be small.

We now discuss how to maximize the marginal likelihood. One can show that

$$\frac{\partial}{\partial \theta_j} \log p(\boldsymbol{y}|\mathbf{X}, \boldsymbol{\theta}) = \frac{1}{2}\boldsymbol{y}^\mathsf{T}\mathbf{K}_\sigma^{-1}\frac{\partial \mathbf{K}_\sigma}{\partial \theta_j}\mathbf{K}_\sigma^{-1}\boldsymbol{y} - \frac{1}{2}\mathrm{tr}(\mathbf{K}_\sigma^{-1}\frac{\partial \mathbf{K}_\sigma}{\partial \theta_j}) \tag{18.164}$$

$$= \frac{1}{2}\mathrm{tr}\left((\boldsymbol{\alpha}\boldsymbol{\alpha}^\mathsf{T} - \mathbf{K}_\sigma^{-1})\frac{\partial \mathbf{K}_\sigma}{\partial \theta_j}\right) \tag{18.165}$$

where $\boldsymbol{\alpha} = \mathbf{K}_\sigma^{-1}\boldsymbol{y}$. It takes $O(N^3)$ time to compute $\mathbf{K}_\sigma^{-1}$, and then $O(N^2)$ time per hyper-parameter to compute the gradient.

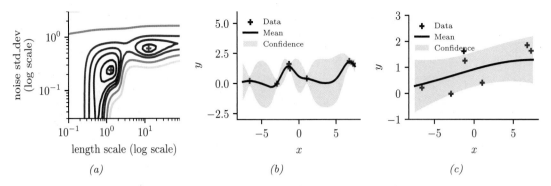

Figure 18.16: Illustration of local minima in the marginal likelihood surface. (a) We plot the log marginal likelihood vs σ_y^2 and ℓ, for fixed $\sigma_f^2 = 1$, using the 7 datapoints shown in panels b and c. (b) The function corresponding to the lower left local minimum, $(\ell, \sigma_n^2) \approx (1, 0.2)$. This is quite "wiggly" and has low noise. (c) The function corresponding to the top right local minimum, $(\ell, \sigma_n^2) \approx (10, 0.8)$. This is quite smooth and has high noise. The data was generated using $(\ell, \sigma_n^2) = (1, 0.1)$. Adapted from Figure 5.5 of [RW06]. Generated by gpr_demo_marglik.ipynb.

The form of $\frac{\partial \mathbf{K}_\sigma}{\partial \theta_j}$ depends on the form of the kernel, and which parameter we are taking derivatives with respect to. Often we have constraints on the hyper-parameters, such as $\sigma_y^2 \geq 0$. In this case, we can define $\theta = \log(\sigma_y^2)$, and then use the chain rule.

Given an expression for the log marginal likelihood and its derivative, we can estimate the kernel parameters using any standard gradient-based optimizer. However, since the objective is not convex, local minima can be a problem, as we illustrate below, so we may need to use multiple restarts.

18.6.1.1 Example

Consider Figure 18.16. We use the SE kernel in Equation (18.161) with $\sigma_f^2 = 1$, and plot $\log p(\mathbf{y}|\mathbf{X}, \ell, \sigma_y^2)$ (where $\mathbf{X}$ and $\mathbf{y}$ are the 7 datapoints shown in panels b and c as we vary ℓ and σ_y^2. The two local optima are indicated by $+$ in panel a. The bottom left optimum corresponds to a low-noise, short-length scale solution (shown in panel b). The top right optimum corresponds to a high-noise, long-length scale solution (shown in panel c). With only 7 datapoints, there is not enough evidence to confidently decide which is more reasonable, although the more complex model (panel b) has a marginal likelihood that is about 60% higher than the simpler model (panel c). With more data, the more complex model would become even more preferred.

Figure 18.16 illustrates some other interesting (and typical) features. The region where $\sigma_y^2 \approx 1$ (top of panel a) corresponds to the case where the noise is very high; in this regime, the marginal likelihood is insensitive to the length scale (indicated by the horizontal contours), since all the data is explained as noise. The region where $\ell \approx 0.5$ (left hand side of panel a) corresponds to the case where the length scale is very short; in this regime, the marginal likelihood is insensitive to the noise level (indicated by the vertical contours), since the data is perfectly interpolated. Neither of these regions would be chosen by a good optimizer.

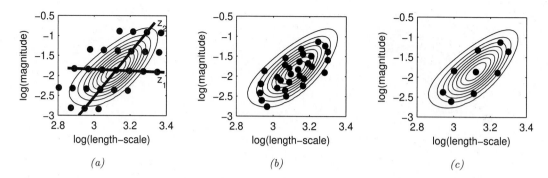

Figure 18.17: Three different approximations to the posterior over hyper-parameters: grid-based, Monte Carlo, and central composite design. From Figure 3.2 of [Van10]. Used with kind permission of Jarno Vanhatalo.

18.6.2 Bayesian inference for the kernel parameters

When we have a small number of datapoints (e.g., when using GPs for blackbox optimization, as we discuss in Section 6.6), using a point estimate of the kernel parameters can give poor results [Bul11; WF14]. As a simple example, if the function values that have been observed so far are all very similar, then we may estimate $\hat{\sigma} \approx 0$, which will result in overly confident predictions.[5]

To overcome such overconfidence, we can compute a posterior over the kernel parameters. If the dimensionality of $\boldsymbol{\theta}$ is small, we can compute a discrete grid of possible values, centered on the MAP estimate $\hat{\boldsymbol{\theta}}$ (computed as above). We can then approximate the posterior using

$$p(\boldsymbol{f}|\mathcal{D}) = \sum_{s=1}^{S} p(\boldsymbol{f}|\mathcal{D}, \boldsymbol{\theta}_s) p(\boldsymbol{\theta}_s|\mathcal{D}) w_s \tag{18.166}$$

where w_s denotes the weight for grid point s.

In higher dimensions, a regular grid suffers from the curse of dimensionality. One alternative is place grid points at the mode, and at a distance ± 1sd from the mode along each dimension, for a total of $2|\boldsymbol{\theta}| + 1$ points. This is called a **central composite design** [RMC09]. See Figure 18.17 for an illustration.

In higher dimensions, we can use Monte Carlo inference for the kernel parameters when computing Equation (18.166). For example, [MA10] shows how to use slice sampling (Section 12.4.1) for this task, [Hen+15] shows how to use HMC (Section 12.5), and [BBV11a] shows how to use SMC (Chapter 13).

In Figure 18.18, we illustrate the difference between kernel optimization vs kernel inference. We fit a 1d dataset using a kernel of the form

$$\mathcal{K}(r) = \sigma_1^2 \mathcal{K}_{\text{SE}}(r; \tau) \mathcal{K}_{\cos}(r; \rho_1) + \sigma_2^s \mathcal{K}_{32}(r; \rho_2) \tag{18.167}$$

where $\mathcal{K}_{\text{SE}}(r; \ell)$ is the squared exponential kernel (Equation (18.12)), $\mathcal{K}_{\cos}(r; \rho_1)$ is the cosine kernel (Equation (18.19)), and $\mathcal{K}_{32}(r; \rho_2)$ is the Matérn $\frac{3}{2}$ kernel (Equation (18.15)). We then compute a

---

5. In [WSN00; BBV11b], they show how we can put a conjugate prior on σ^2 and integrate it out, to generate a Student version of the GP, which is more robust.

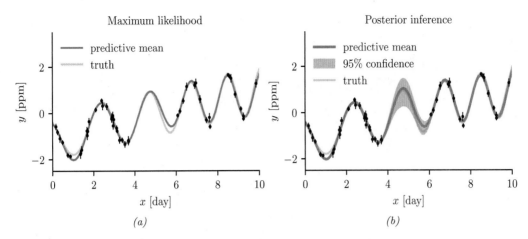

Figure 18.18: *Difference between estimation and inference for kernel hyper-parameters. (a) Empirical Bayes approach based on optimization. We plot the posterior predicted mean given a plug-in estimate,* $\mathbb{E}\left[f(x)|\mathcal{D}, \hat{\boldsymbol{\theta}}\right]$. *(b) Bayesian approach based on HMC. We plot the posterior predicted mean, marginalizing over hyper-parameters,* $\mathbb{E}\left[f(x)|\mathcal{D}\right]$. *Generated by* gp_kernel_opt.ipynb.

point-estimate of the kernel parameters using empirical Bayes, and posterior samples using HMC. We then predicting the posterior mean of f on a 1d test set by plugging in the MLE or averaging over samples. We see that the latter captures more uncertainty (beyond the uncertainty captured by the Gaussian itself).

18.6.3   Multiple kernel learning for additive kernels

A special case of kernel learning arises when the kernel is a sum of B base kernels

$$\mathcal{K}(\boldsymbol{x}, \boldsymbol{x}') = \sum_{b=1}^{B} w_b \mathcal{K}_b(\boldsymbol{x}, \boldsymbol{x}') \tag{18.168}$$

Optimizing the weights $w_b > 0$ using structural risk minimization is known as **multiple kernel learning**; see e.g., [Rak+08] for details.

Now suppose we constrain the base kernels to depend on a subset of the variables. Furthermore, suppose we enforce a hierarchical inclusion property (e.g., including the kernel k_{123} means we must also include k_{12}, k_{13} and k_{23}), as illustrated in Figure 18.19(left). This is called **hierarchical kernel learning**. We can find a good subset from this model class using convex optimization [Bac09]; however, this requires the use of cross validation to estimate the weights. A more efficient approach is to use the empirical Bayes approach described in [DNR11].

In many cases, it is common to restrict attention to first order additive kernels:

$$\mathcal{K}(\boldsymbol{x}, \boldsymbol{x}') = \sum_{d=1}^{D} \mathcal{K}_d(x_d, x_d') \tag{18.169}$$

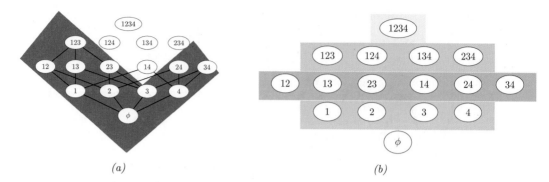

(a)   (b)

Figure 18.19: Comparison of different additive model classes for a 4d function. Circles represent different interaction terms, ranging from first-order to fourth-order. Left: hierarchical kernel learning uses a nested hierarchy of terms. Right: additive GPs use a weighted sum of additive kernels of different orders. Color shades represent different weighting terms. Adapted from Figure 6.2 of [Duv14].

The resulting function then has the form

$$f(\boldsymbol{x}) = f_1(x_1) + \ldots + f_D(x_D) \tag{18.170}$$

This is called a **generalized additive model** or **GAM**.

Figure 18.20 shows an example of this, where each base kernel has the form $\mathcal{K}_d(x_d, x'_d) = \sigma_d^2 \mathrm{SE}(x_d, x'_d | \ell_d)$, In Figure 18.20, we see that the σ_d^2 terms for the coarse and fine features are set to zero, indicating that these inputs have no impact on the response variable.

[DBW20] considers additive kernels operating on different linear projections of the inputs:

$$\mathcal{K}(\boldsymbol{x}, \boldsymbol{x}') = \sum_{b=1}^{B} w_b \mathcal{K}_b(\mathbf{P}_b \boldsymbol{x}, \mathbf{P}_b \boldsymbol{x}') \tag{18.171}$$

Surprisingly, they show that these models can match or exceed the performance of kernels operating on the original space, even when the projections are into a **single** dimension, and not learned. In other words, it is possible to reduce many regression problems to a single dimension without loss in performance. This finding is particularly promising for scalable inference, such as KISS (see Section 18.5.5.3), and active learning, which are greatly simplified in a low dimensional setting.

More recently, [LBH22] has proposed the **orthogonal additive kernel** (OAK), which imposes an orthogonality constraint on the additive functions. This ensures an identifiable, low-dimensional representation of the functional relationship, and results in improved performance.

18.6.4   Automatic search for compositional kernels

Although the above methods can estimate the hyperparameters of a specified set of kernels, they do not choose the kernels themselves (other than the special case of selecting a subset of kernels from a set). In this section, we describe a method, based on [Duv+13], for sequentially searching through the space of increasingly complex GP models so as to find a parsiminous description of the data. (See also [BHB22] for a review.)

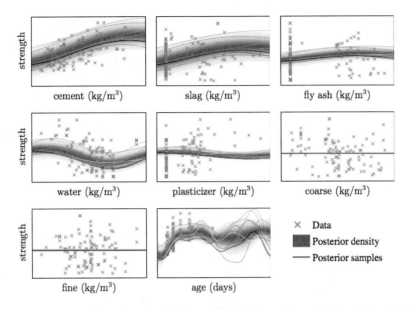

Figure 18.20: *Predictive distribution of each term im a GP-GAM model applied to a dataset with 8 continuous inputs and 1 continuous output, representing the strength of some concrete. From Figure 2.7 of [Duv14]. Used with kind permission of David Duvenaud.*

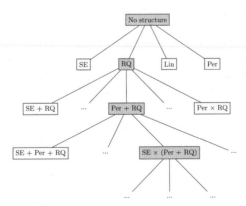

Figure 18.21: *Example of a search tree over kernel expressions. Adapted from Figure 3.2 of [Duv14].*

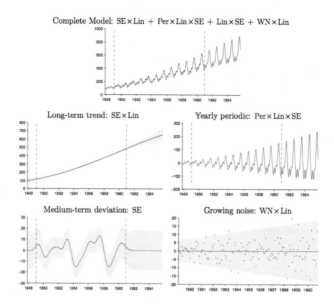

Figure 18.22: Top row: airline dataset and posterior distribution of the model discovered after a search of depth 10. Subsequent rows: predictions of the individual components. From Figure 3.5 of [Duv14], based on [Llo+14]. Used with kind permission of David Duvenaud.

We start with a simple kernel, such as the white noise kernel, and then consider replacing it with a set of possible alternative kernels, such as an SE kernel, RQ kernel, etc. We use the BIC score (Section 3.8.7.2) to evaluate each candidate model (choice of kernel) m. This has the form $\text{BIC}(m) = \log p(\mathcal{D}|m) - \frac{1}{2}|m| \log N$, where $p(\mathcal{D}|m)$ is the marginal likelihood, and $|m|$ is the number of parameters. The first term measures fit to the data, and the second term is a complexity penalty. We can also consider replacing a kernel by the addition of two kernels, $k \rightarrow (k + k')$, or the multiplication of two kernels, $k \rightarrow (k \times k')$. See Figure 18.21 for an illustration of the search space.

Searching through this space is similar to what a human expert would do. In particular, if we find structure in the residuals, such as periodicity, we can propose a certain "move" through the space. We can also start with some structure that is assumed to hold globally, such as linearity, but if we find this only holds locally, we can multiply the kernel by an SE kernel. We can also add input dimensions incrementally, to capture higher order interactions.

Figure 18.22 shows the output of this process applied to a dataset of monthly totals of international airline passengers. The input to the GP is the set of time stamps, $\boldsymbol{x} = 1 : t$; there are no other features.

The observed data lies in between the dotted vertical lines; curves outside of this region are extrapolations. We see that the system has discovered a fairly interpretable set of patterns in the data. Indeed, it is possible to devise an algorithm to automatically convert the output of this search process to a natural language summary, as shown in [Llo+14]. In this example, it summarizes the data as being generated by the addition of 4 underlying trends: a linearly increasing function; an approximately periodic function with a period of 1.0 years, and with linearly increasing amplitude; a

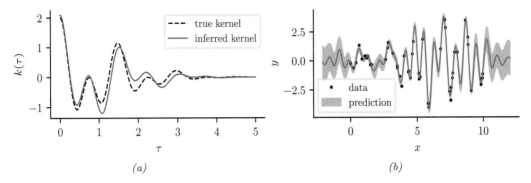

Figure 18.23: *Illustration of a GP with a spectral mixture kernel in 1d. (a) Learned vs true kernel. (b) Predictions using learned kernel. Generated by* gp_spectral_mixture.ipynb.

smooth function; and uncorrelated noise with linearly increasing standard deviation.

Recently, [Sun+18] showed how to create a DNN which learns the kernel given two input vectors. The hidden units are defined as sums and products of elementary kernels, as in the above search based approach. However, the DNN can be trained in a differentiable way, so is much faster.

18.6.5 Spectral mixture kernel learning

Any shift-invariant (stationary) kernel can be converted via the Fourier transform to its dual form, known as its **spectral density**. This means that learning the spectral density is equivalent to learning any shift-invariant kernel. For example, if we take the Fourier transform of an RBF kernel, we get a Gaussian spectral density centered at the origin. If we take the Fourier transform of a Matérn kernel, we get a Student spectral density centred at the origin. Thus standard approaches to multiple kernel learning, which typically involve additive compositions of RBF and Matérn kernels with different length-scale parameters, amount to density estimation with a scale mixture of Gaussian or Student distributions at the origin. Such models are very inflexible for density estimation, and thus also very limited in being able to perform kernel learning.

On the other hand, *scale-location* mixture of Gaussians can model any density to arbitrary precision. Moreover, with even a small number of components these mixtures of Gaussians are highly flexible. Thus a spectral density corresponding to a scale-location mixture of Gaussians forms an expressive basis for all shift-invariant kernels. One can evaluate the inverse Fourier transform for a Gaussian mixture analytically, to derive the **spectral mixture kernel** [WA13], which we can express for one-dimensional inputs x as:

$$\mathcal{K}(x, x') = \sum_i w_i \cos((x - x')(2\pi\mu_i)) \exp(-2\pi^2(x - x')^2 v_i) \tag{18.172}$$

The mixture weights w_i, as well as the means μ_i and variances v_i of the Gaussians in the spectral density, can be learned by empirical Bayes optimization (Section 18.6.1) or in a fully-Bayesian procedure (Section 18.6.2) [Jan+17]. We illustrate the former approach in Figure 18.23.

By learning the parameters of the spectral mixture kernel, we can discover representations that enable extrapolation — to make reasonable predictions far away from the data. For example, in Sec-

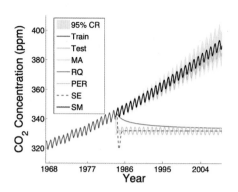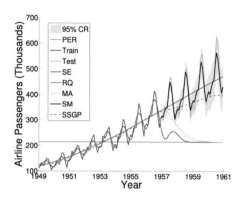

Figure 18.24: Extrapolations (point predictions and 95% credible set) on CO_2 and airline datasets using Gaussian processes with Matérn, rational quadratic, periodic, RBF (SE), and spectral mixture kernels, each with hyperparameters learned using empirical Bayes. From [Wil14].

tion 18.8.1, compositions of kernels are carefully hand-crafted to extrapolate CO_2 concentrations. But in this instance, the human statistician is doing all of the interesting representation learning. Figure Figure 18.24 shows Gaussian processes with learned spectral mixture kernels instead automatically extrapolating on CO_2 and airline passenger problems.

These kernels can also be used to extrapolate higher dimensional large-scale spatio-temporal patterns. Large datasets can provide relatively more information for expressive kernel learning. However, scaling an expressive kernel learning approach poses different challenges than scaling a standard Gaussian process model. One faces additional computational constraints, and the need to retain significant model structure for expressing the rich information available in a large dataset. Indeed, in Figure 18.24 we can separately understand the effects of the kernel learning approach and scalable inference procedure, in being able to discover structure necessary to extrapolate textures. An expressive kernel model and a scalable inference approach that preserves a *non-parametric* representation are needed for good performance.

Structure exploiting inference procedures, such as Kronecker methods, as well as KISS-GP and conjugate gradient based approaches, are appropriate for these tasks — since they generally preserve or exploit existing structure, rather than introducing approximations that corrupt the structure. Spectral mixture kernels combined with these scalable inference techniques have been used to great effect for spatiotemporal extrapolation problems, including land-surface temperature forecasting, epidemiological modeling, and policy-relevant applications.

18.6.6   Deep kernel learning

Deep kernel learning [SH07; Wil+16] combines the structural properties of neural networks with the non-parametric flexibility and uncertainty representation provided by Gaussian processes. For example, we can define a "deep RBF kernel" as follows:

$$\mathcal{K}_{\boldsymbol{\theta}}(\boldsymbol{x}, \boldsymbol{x}') = \exp\left[-\frac{1}{2\sigma^2}||\boldsymbol{h}_{\boldsymbol{\theta}}^{L}(\boldsymbol{x}) - \boldsymbol{h}_{\boldsymbol{\theta}}^{L}(\boldsymbol{x}')||^2\right] \tag{18.173}$$

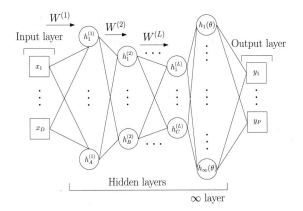

Figure 18.25: *Deep kernel learning: a Gaussian process with a deep kernel maps D dimensional inputs $\boldsymbol{x}$ through L parametric hidden layers followed by a hidden layer with an infinite number of basis functions, with base kernel hyperparameters $\boldsymbol{\theta}$. Overall, a Gaussian process with a deep kernel produces a probabilistic mapping with an infinite number of adaptive basis functions parameterized by $\boldsymbol{\gamma} = \{\boldsymbol{w}, \boldsymbol{\theta}\}$. All parameters $\boldsymbol{\gamma}$ are learned through the marginal likelihood of the Gaussian process. From Figure 1 of [Wil+16].*

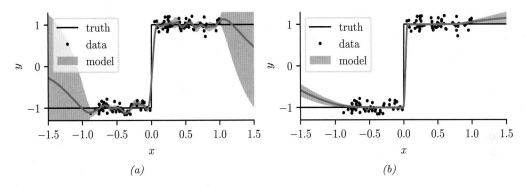

Figure 18.26: *Modeling a discontinuous function with (a) a GP with a "shallow" Matérn $\frac{3}{2}$ kernel, and (b) a GP with a "deep" MLP + Matérn kernel. Generated by gp_deep_kernel_learning.ipynb.*

where $\boldsymbol{h}_{\boldsymbol{\theta}}^L(\boldsymbol{x})$ are the outputs of layer L from a DNN. We can then learning the parameters $\boldsymbol{\theta}$ by maximizing the marginal likelihood of the Gaussian processes.

This framework is illustrated in Figure 18.25. We can understand the neural network features as inputs into a base kernel. The neural network can either be (1) pre-trained, (2) learned jointly with the base kernel parameters, or (3) pre-trained and then fine-tuned through the marginal likelihood. This approach can be viewed as a "last-layer" Bayesian model, where a Gaussian process is applied to the final layer of a neural network. The base kernel often provides a good measure of distance in feature space, desirably encouraging predictions to have high uncertainty as we move far away from the data.

We can use deep kernel learning to help the GP learn discontinuous functions, as illustrated in Figure 18.26. On the left we show the results of a GP with a standard Matérn $\frac{3}{2}$ kernel. It is clear

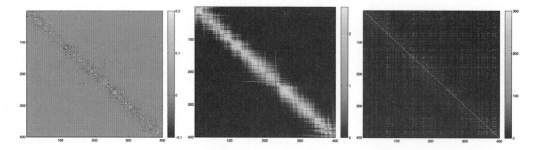

Figure 18.27: Left: the learned covariance matrix of a deep kernel with spectral mixture base kernel on a set of test cases for the **Olivetti faces dataset***, where the test samples are ordered according to the orientations of the input faces. Middle: the respective covariance matrix using a deep kernel with RBF base kernel. Right: the respective covariance matrix using a standard RBF kernel. From Figure 5 of [Wil+16].*

that the out-of-sample predictions are poor. On the right we show the results of the same model where we first transform the input through a learned 2 layer MLP (with 15 and 10 hidden units). It is clear that the model is working much better.

As a more complex example, we consider a regression problem where we wish to map faces (vectors of pixel intensities) to a continuous valued orientation angle. In Figure 18.27, we evaluate the deep kernel matrix (with RBF and spectral mixture base kernels, discussed in Section 18.6.5) on data ordered by orientation angle. We can see that the learned deep kernels, in the left two panels, have a pronounced diagonal band, meaning that they have *discovered* that faces with similar orientation angles are correlated. On the other hand, in the right panel we see that the entries even for a learned RBF kernel are highly diffuse. Since the RBF kernel essentially uses Euclidean distance as a metric for similarity, it is unable to learn a representation that effectively solves this problem. In this case, one must do highly non-Euclidean metric learning.

However, [ORW21] show that the approach to DKL based on maximizing the marginal likelihood can result in overfitting that is worse than standard DNN learning. They propose a fully Bayesian approach, in which they use SGLD (Section 12.7.1) to sample the DNN weights as well as the GP hyperparameters.

18.7   GPs and DNNs

In Section 18.6.6, we showed how we can combine the structural properties of neural networks with GPs. In Section 18.7.1 we show that, in the limit of infinitely wide networks, a neural network defines a GP with a certain kernel. These kernels are fixed, so the method is not performing representation learning, as a standard neural network would (see e.g., [COB18; Woo+19]). Nonetheless, these kernels are interesting in their own right, for example in modelling non-stationary covariance structure. In Section 18.7.2, we discuss the connection between SGD training of DNNs and GPs. And in Section 18.7.3, we discuss deep GPs, which are similar to DNNs in that they consist of many layers of functions which are composed together, but each layer is a nonparametric function.

18.7.1 Kernels derived from infinitely wide DNNs (NN-GP)

In this section, we show that an MLP with one hidden layer, whose width goes to infinity, and which has a Gaussian prior on all the parameters, converges to a Gaussian process with a well-defined kernel.[6] This result was first shown for in [Nea96; Wil98], and was later extended to deep MLPs in [DFS16; Lee+18], to CNNs in [Nov+19], and to general DNNs in [Yan19]. The resulting kernel is called the **NN-GP** kernel [Lee+18].

We will consider the following model:

$$f_k(\boldsymbol{x}) = b_k + \sum_{j=1}^{H} v_{jk} h_j(\boldsymbol{x}), \ h_j(\boldsymbol{x}) = \varphi(u_{0j} + \boldsymbol{x}^\mathsf{T} \boldsymbol{u}_j) \tag{18.174}$$

where H is the number of hidden units, and $\varphi()$ is some nonlinear activation function, such as ReLU. We will assume Gaussian priors on the parameters:

$$b_k \sim \mathcal{N}(0, \sigma_b), v_{jk} \sim \mathcal{N}(0, \sigma_v), u_{0j} \sim \mathcal{N}(0, \sigma_0), \boldsymbol{u}_j \sim \mathcal{N}(0, \boldsymbol{\Sigma}) \tag{18.175}$$

Let $\boldsymbol{\theta} = \{b_k, v_{jk}, u_{0j}, \boldsymbol{u}_j\}$ be all the parameters. The expected output from unit k when applied to one input vector is given by

$$\mathbb{E}_{\boldsymbol{\theta}}\left[f_k(\boldsymbol{x})\right] = \mathbb{E}_{\boldsymbol{\theta}}\left[b_k + \sum_{j=1}^{H} v_{jk} h_j(\boldsymbol{x})\right] = \underbrace{\mathbb{E}_{\boldsymbol{\theta}}\left[b_k\right]}_{=0} + \sum_{j=1}^{H} \underbrace{\mathbb{E}_{\boldsymbol{\theta}}\left[v_{jk}\right]}_{=0} \mathbb{E}_{\boldsymbol{u}}\left[h_j(\boldsymbol{x})\right] = 0 \tag{18.176}$$

The covariance in the output for unit k when the function is applied to two different inputs is given by the following:[7]

$$\mathbb{E}_{\boldsymbol{\theta}}\left[f_k(\boldsymbol{x}) f_k(\boldsymbol{x}')\right] = \mathbb{E}_{\boldsymbol{\theta}}\left[\left(b_k + \sum_{j=1}^{H} v_{jk} h_j(\boldsymbol{x})\right)\left(b_k + \sum_{j=1}^{H} v_{jk} h_j(\boldsymbol{x})\right)\right] \tag{18.177}$$

$$= \sigma_b^2 + \sum_{j=1}^{H} \mathbb{E}_{\boldsymbol{\theta}}\left[v_{jk}^2\right] \mathbb{E}_{\boldsymbol{u}}\left[h_j(\boldsymbol{x}) h_j(\boldsymbol{x}')\right] = \sigma_b^2 + \sigma_v^2 H \mathbb{E}_{\boldsymbol{u}}\left[h_j(\boldsymbol{x}) h_j(\boldsymbol{x}')\right] \tag{18.178}$$

Now consider the limit $H \to \infty$. We scale the magnitude of the output by defining $\sigma_v^2 = \omega/H$. Since the input to k'th output unit is an infinite sum of random variables (from the hidden units $h_j(\boldsymbol{x})$), we can use the **central limit theorem** to conclude that the output converges to a Gaussian with mean and variance given by

$$\mathbb{E}\left[f_k(\boldsymbol{x})\right] = 0, \ \mathbb{V}\left[f_k(\boldsymbol{x})\right] = \sigma_b^2 + \omega \mathbb{E}_{\boldsymbol{u}}\left[h(\boldsymbol{x})^2\right] \tag{18.179}$$

Furthermore, the joint distribution over $\{f_k(\boldsymbol{x}_n) : n = 1 : N\}$ for any $N \geq 2$ converges to a multivariate Gaussian with covariance given by

$$\mathbb{E}\left[f_k(\boldsymbol{x}) f_k(\boldsymbol{x}')\right] = \sigma_b^2 + \omega \mathbb{E}_{\boldsymbol{u}}\left[h(\boldsymbol{x}) h(\boldsymbol{x}')\right] \triangleq \mathcal{K}(\boldsymbol{x}, \boldsymbol{x}') \tag{18.180}$$

---

6. Our presentation is based on http://cbl.eng.cam.ac.uk/pub/Intranet/MLG/ReadingGroup/presentation_matthias.pdf.
7. We are using the fact that $u \sim \mathcal{N}(0, \sigma^2)$ implies $\mathbb{E}\left[u^2\right] = \mathbb{V}\left[u\right] = \sigma^2$.

$h(\tilde{\boldsymbol{x}})$	$C(\tilde{\boldsymbol{x}}, \tilde{\boldsymbol{x}}')$
$\mathrm{erf}(\tilde{\boldsymbol{x}}^{\mathsf{T}}\tilde{\boldsymbol{u}})$	$\frac{2}{\pi}\arcsin(f_1(\tilde{\boldsymbol{x}}, \tilde{\boldsymbol{x}}'))$
$\mathbb{I}\left(\tilde{\boldsymbol{x}}^{\mathsf{T}}\tilde{\boldsymbol{u}} \geq 0\right)$	$\pi - \theta(\tilde{\boldsymbol{x}}, \tilde{\boldsymbol{x}}')$
$\mathrm{ReLU}(\tilde{\boldsymbol{x}}^{\mathsf{T}}\tilde{\boldsymbol{u}})$	$\frac{f_2(\tilde{\boldsymbol{x}}, \tilde{\boldsymbol{x}}')}{\pi}\sin(\theta(\tilde{\boldsymbol{x}}, \tilde{\boldsymbol{x}}')) + \frac{\pi - \theta(\tilde{\boldsymbol{x}}, \tilde{\boldsymbol{x}}')}{\pi}\tilde{\boldsymbol{x}}^{\mathsf{T}}\tilde{\boldsymbol{\Sigma}}\tilde{\boldsymbol{x}}'$

Table 18.4: *Some neural net GP kernels. Here we define* $f_1(\tilde{\boldsymbol{x}}, \tilde{\boldsymbol{x}}') = \frac{2\tilde{\boldsymbol{x}}^{\mathsf{T}}\tilde{\boldsymbol{\Sigma}}\tilde{\boldsymbol{x}}'}{\sqrt{(1+2\tilde{\boldsymbol{x}}^{\mathsf{T}}\tilde{\boldsymbol{\Sigma}}\tilde{\boldsymbol{x}})(1+2(\tilde{\boldsymbol{x}}')^{\mathsf{T}}\tilde{\boldsymbol{\Sigma}}\tilde{\boldsymbol{x}}')}}$, $f_2(\tilde{\boldsymbol{x}}, \tilde{\boldsymbol{x}}') = $ $\|\tilde{\boldsymbol{\Sigma}}^{\frac{1}{2}}\tilde{\boldsymbol{x}}\|\,\|\tilde{\boldsymbol{\Sigma}}^{\frac{1}{2}}\tilde{\boldsymbol{x}}'\|$, $f_3(\tilde{\boldsymbol{x}}, \tilde{\boldsymbol{x}}') = \sqrt{(\tilde{\boldsymbol{x}}^{\mathsf{T}}\tilde{\boldsymbol{\Sigma}}\tilde{\boldsymbol{x}})((\tilde{\boldsymbol{x}}')^{\mathsf{T}}\tilde{\boldsymbol{\Sigma}}\tilde{\boldsymbol{x}}')}$, *and* $\theta(\tilde{\boldsymbol{x}}, \tilde{\boldsymbol{x}}') = \arccos(f_3(\tilde{\boldsymbol{x}}, \tilde{\boldsymbol{x}}'))$. *Results are derived in* [Wil98; CS09].

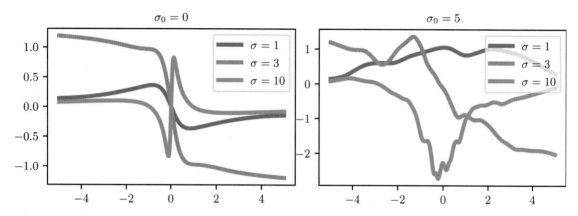

Figure 18.28: *Sample output from a GP with an NNGP kernel derived from an infinitely wide one layer MLP with activation function of the form* $h(x) = \mathrm{erf}(x \cdot u + u_0)$ *where* $u \sim \mathcal{N}(0, \sigma)$ *and* $u_0 \sim \mathcal{N}(0, \sigma_0)$. *Generated by* nngp_1d.ipynb. *Used with kind permission of Matthias Bauer.*

Thus the MLP converges to a GP. To compute the kernel function, we need to evaluate

$$C(\boldsymbol{x}, \boldsymbol{x}') = \mathbb{E}_{\boldsymbol{u}}\left[h(u_0 + \boldsymbol{u}^{\mathsf{T}}\boldsymbol{x})h(u_0 + \boldsymbol{u}^{\mathsf{T}}\boldsymbol{x}')\right] = \mathbb{E}_{\boldsymbol{u}}\left[h(\tilde{\boldsymbol{u}}^{\mathsf{T}}\tilde{\boldsymbol{x}})h(\tilde{\boldsymbol{u}}^{\mathsf{T}}\tilde{\boldsymbol{x}}')\right] \tag{18.181}$$

where we have defined $\tilde{\boldsymbol{x}} = (1, \boldsymbol{x})$ and $\tilde{\boldsymbol{u}} = (u_0, \boldsymbol{u})$. Let us define

$$\tilde{\boldsymbol{\Sigma}} = \begin{pmatrix} \sigma_0^2 & 0 \\ 0 & \boldsymbol{\Sigma} \end{pmatrix} \tag{18.182}$$

Then we have

$$C(\boldsymbol{x}, \boldsymbol{x}') = \int h(\tilde{\boldsymbol{u}}^{\mathsf{T}}\tilde{\boldsymbol{x}})h(\tilde{\boldsymbol{u}}^{\mathsf{T}}\tilde{\boldsymbol{x}}')\mathcal{N}(\tilde{\boldsymbol{u}}|\boldsymbol{0}, \tilde{\boldsymbol{\Sigma}})d\tilde{\boldsymbol{u}} \tag{18.183}$$

This can be computed in closed form for certain activation functions, as shown in Table 18.4.

This is sometimes called the **neural net kernel**. Note that this is a non-stationary kernel, and sample paths from it are nearly discontinuous and tend to constant values for large positive or negative inputs, as illustrated in Figure 18.28.

18.7.2 Neural tangent kernel (NTK)

In Section 18.7.1 we derived the NN-GP kernel, under the assumption that all the weights are random. A natural question is: can we derive a kernel from a DNN after it has been trained, or more generally, while it is being trained. It turns out that this can be done, as we show below.

Let $\boldsymbol{f} = [f(\boldsymbol{x}_n; \theta)]_{n=1}^N$ be the $N \times 1$ prediction vector, let $\nabla_f \mathcal{L} = [\frac{\partial \mathcal{L}}{\partial f(\boldsymbol{x}_n)}]_{n=1}^N$ be the $N \times 1$ loss gradient vector, let $\boldsymbol{\theta} = [\theta_p]_{p=1}^P$ be the $P \times 1$ vector of parameters, and let $\nabla_{\boldsymbol{\theta}} \boldsymbol{f} = [\frac{\partial f(\boldsymbol{x}_n)}{\partial \theta_p}]$ be the $P \times N$ matrix of partials. Suppose we perform continuous time gradient descent with fixed learning rate η. The parameters evolve over time as follows:

$$\partial_t \boldsymbol{\theta}_t = -\eta \nabla_{\boldsymbol{\theta}} \mathcal{L}(\boldsymbol{f}_t) = -\eta \nabla_{\boldsymbol{\theta}} \boldsymbol{f}_t \cdot \nabla_f \mathcal{L}(\boldsymbol{f}_t) \tag{18.184}$$

Thus the function evolves over time as follows:

$$\partial_t \boldsymbol{f}_t = \nabla_{\boldsymbol{\theta}} \boldsymbol{f}_t^\mathsf{T} \partial_t \boldsymbol{\theta}_t = -\eta \nabla_{\boldsymbol{\theta}} \boldsymbol{f}_t^\mathsf{T} \nabla_{\boldsymbol{\theta}} \boldsymbol{f}_t \cdot \nabla_f \mathcal{L}(\boldsymbol{f}_t) = -\eta \mathcal{T}_t \cdot \nabla_f \mathcal{L}(\boldsymbol{f}_t) \tag{18.185}$$

where $\mathcal{T}_t$ is the $N \times N$ kernel matrix

$$\mathcal{T}_t(\boldsymbol{x}, \boldsymbol{x}') \triangleq \nabla_{\boldsymbol{\theta}} f_t(\boldsymbol{x}) \cdot \nabla_{\boldsymbol{\theta}} f_t(\boldsymbol{x}') = \sum_{p=1}^P \frac{\partial f(\boldsymbol{x}; \boldsymbol{\theta})}{\partial \theta_p}\Big|_{\boldsymbol{\theta}_t} \frac{\partial f(\boldsymbol{x}'; \boldsymbol{\theta})}{\partial \theta_p}\Big|_{\boldsymbol{\theta}_t} \tag{18.186}$$

If we let the learning rate η become infinitesimally small, and the widths go to infinity, one can show that this kernel converges to a constant matrix, this is known as the **neural tangent kernel** or **NTK** [JGH18]:

$$\mathcal{T}(\boldsymbol{x}, \boldsymbol{x}') \triangleq \nabla_{\boldsymbol{\theta}} f(\boldsymbol{x}; \boldsymbol{\theta}_\infty) \cdot \nabla_{\boldsymbol{\theta}} f(\boldsymbol{x}'; \boldsymbol{\theta}_\infty) \tag{18.187}$$

Details on how to compute this kernel for various models, such as CNNs, graph neural nets, and general neural nets, can be found in [Aro+19; Du+19; Yan19]. A software libary to compute the NN-GP kernel and NTK is available in [Ano19].

The assumptions behind the NTK results in the parameters barely changing from their initial values (which is why a linear approximation around the starting parameters is valid). This can still lead to a change in the final predictions (and zero final training error), because the final layer weights can learn to use the random features just like in kernel regression. However, this phenomenon — which has been called "**lazy training**" [COB18] — is not representative of DNN behavior in practice [Woo+19], where parameters often change a lot. Fortunately it is possible to use a different parameterization which does result in feature learning in the infinite width limit [YH21].

18.7.3 Deep GPs

A **deep Gaussian process** or **DGP** is a composition of GPs [DL13]. More formally, a DGP of L layers is a hierachical model of the form

$$\mathrm{DGP}(\boldsymbol{x}) = f_L \circ \cdots \circ \boldsymbol{f}_1(\boldsymbol{x}), \ \boldsymbol{f}_i(\cdot) = [f_i^{(1)}(\cdot), \ldots, f_i^{(H_i)}(\cdot)], \ f_i^{(j)} \sim \mathrm{GP}(0, \mathcal{K}_i(\cdot, \cdot)) \tag{18.188}$$

This is similar to a deep neural network, except the hidden nodes are now hidden functions.

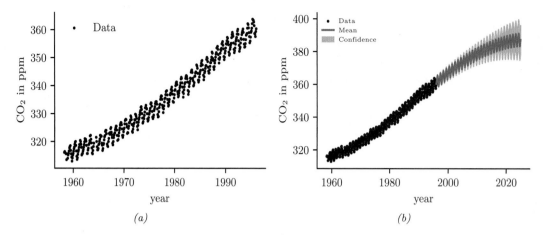

Figure 18.29: *(a) The observed Mauna Loa CO_2 time series. (b) Forecasts from a GP. Generated by gp_mauna_loa.ipynb.*

A natural question is: what is gained by this approach compared to a standard GP? Although conventional single-layer GPs are nonparametric, and can model any function (assuming the use of a non-degenerate kernel) with enough data, in practice their performance is limited by the choice of kernel. It is tempting to think that deep kernel learning (Section 18.6.6) can solve this problem, but in theory a GP on top of a DNN is still just a GP. However, one can show that a composition of GPs is strictly more general. Unfortunately, inference in deep GPs is rather complicated, so we leave the details to Supplementary Section 18.1. See also [Jak21] for a recent survey on this topic.

18.8   Gaussian processes for time series forecasting

It is possible to use Gaussian processes to perform time series forecasting (see e.g., [Rob+13]). The basic idea is to model the unknown output as a function of time, $f(t)$, and to represent a prior about the form of f as a GP; we then update this prior given the observed evidence, and forecast into the future. Naively this would take $O(T^3)$ time. However, for certain stationary kernels, it is possible to reformulate the problem as a linear-Gaussian state space model, and then use the Kalman smoother to perform inference in $O(T)$ time, as explained in [SSH13; SS19; Ada+20]. This conversion can be done exactly for Matérn kernels and approximately for Gaussian (RBF) kernels (see [SS19, Ch. 12]). In [SGF21], they describe how to reduce the linear dependence on T to $\log(T)$ time using a parallel prefix scan operator, that can be run efficiently on GPUs (see Section 8.2.3.4).

18.8.1   Example: Mauna Loa

In this section, we use the Mauna Loa CO_2 dataset from Section 29.12.5.1. We show the raw data in Figure 18.29(a). We see that there is periodic (or quasi-periodic) signal with a year-long period superimposed on a long term trend. Following [RW06, Sec 5.4.3], we will model this with a composition of kernels:

$$\mathcal{K}(r) = \mathcal{K}_1(r) + \mathcal{K}_2(r) + \mathcal{K}_3(r) + \mathcal{K}_4(r) \tag{18.189}$$

where $\mathcal{K}_i(t, t') = \mathcal{K}_i(t - t')$ for the i'th kernel.

To capture the long term smooth rising trend, we let $\mathcal{K}_1$ be a squared exponential (SE) kernel, where θ_0 is the amplitude and θ_1 is the length scale:

$$\mathcal{K}_1(r) = \theta_0^2 \exp\left(-\frac{r^2}{2\,\theta_1^2}\right) \tag{18.190}$$

To model the periodicity, we can use a periodic or exp-sine-squared kernel from Equation (18.18) with a period of 1 year. However, since it is not clear if the seasonal trend is exactly periodic, we multiply this periodic kernel with another SE kernel to allow for a decay away from periodicity; the result is $\mathcal{K}_2$, where θ_2 is the magnitude, θ_3 is the decay time for the periodic component, $\theta_4 = 1$ is the period, and θ_5 is the smoothness of the periodic component.

$$\mathcal{K}_2(r) = \theta_2^2 \exp\left(-\frac{r^2}{2\,\theta_3^2} - \theta_5 \sin^2\left(\frac{\pi\,r}{\theta_4}\right)\right) \tag{18.191}$$

To model the (small) medium term irregularitries, we use a rational quadratic kernel (Equation (18.20)):

$$\mathcal{K}_3(r) = \theta_6^2 \left[1 + \frac{r^2}{2\,\theta_7^2\,\theta_8}\right]^{-\theta_8} \tag{18.192}$$

where θ_6 is the magnitude, θ_7 is the typical length scale, and θ_8 is the shape parameter.

The magnitude of the independent noise can be incorporated into the observation noise of the likelihood function. For the correlated noise, we use another SE kernel:

$$\mathcal{K}_4(r) = \theta_9^2 \exp\left(-\frac{r^2}{2\,\theta_{10}^2}\right) \tag{18.193}$$

where θ_9 is the magnitude of the correlated noise, and θ_{10} is the length scale. (Note that the combination of $\mathcal{K}_1$ and $\mathcal{K}_4$ is non-identifiable, but this does not affect predictions.)

We can fit this model by optimizing the marginal likelihood wrt $\boldsymbol{\theta}$ (see Section 18.6.1). The resulting forecast is shown in Figure 18.29(b).

19 Beyond the iid assumption

19.1 Introduction

The standard approach to supervised ML assumes the training and test sets both contain independent and identically distributed (iid) samples from the same distribution. However, there are many settings in which the test distribution may be different from the training distribution; this is known as **distribution shift**, as we discuss in Section 19.2.

In some cases, we may have data from multiple related distributions, not just train and test, as we discuss in Section 19.6. We may also encounter data in a streaming setting, where the data distribution may be changing continuously, or in a piecewise constant fashion, as we discuss in Section 19.7. Finally, in Section 19.8, we discuss settings in which the test distribution is chosen by an adversary to minimize performance of a prediction system.

19.2 Distribution shift

Suppose we have a labeled training set from a **source distribution** $p(\boldsymbol{x}, \boldsymbol{y})$ which we use to fit a predictive model $p(\boldsymbol{y}|\boldsymbol{x})$. At test time we encounter data from the **target distribution** $q(\boldsymbol{x}, \boldsymbol{y})$. If $p \neq q$, we say that there has been a **distribution shift** or **datatset shift** [QC+08; BD+10]. This can adversely affect the performance of predictive models, as we illustrate in Section 19.2.1. In Section 19.2.2 we give a taxonomy of some kinds of distribution shift using the language of causal graphical models. We then proceed to discuss a variety of strategies that can be adopted to ameliorate the harm caused by distribution shift. In particular, in Section 19.3, we discuss techniques for detecting shifts, so that we can abstain from giving an incorrect prediction if the model is not confident. In Section 19.4, we discuss techniques to improve robustness to shifts; in particular, given labeled data from $p(\boldsymbol{x}, \boldsymbol{y})$, we aim to create a model that approximates $q(\boldsymbol{y}|\boldsymbol{x})$. In Section 19.5, we discuss techniques to adapt the model to the target distribution given some labeled or unlabeled data from the target.

19.2.1 Motivating examples

Figure 19.1 shows how shifting the test distribution slightly, by adding a small amount of Gaussian noise, can hurt performance of an otherwise high accuracy image classifier. Similar effects occur with other kinds of **common corruptions**, such as image blurring [HD19]. Analogous problems can also occur in the text domain [Ryc+19], and the speech domain (see e.g., male vs female speakers in

"Coffee Pot" $\sigma = .1$ $\sigma = .2$ $\sigma = .4$ $\sigma = .6$
                  "Coffee Pot"   "Toaster"   "Computer"   "Television"

Figure 19.1: *Effect of Gaussian noise of increasing magnitude on an image classifier. The model is a ResNet-50 CNN trained on ImageNet. From Figure 23 of [For+19]. Used with kind permission of Justin Gilmer.*

(A) **Cow: 0.99**, Pasture: 0.99,   (B) No Person: 0.99, Water: 0.98,   (C) No Person: 0.97, **Mammal:**
Grass: 0.99, No Person: 0.98,   Beach: 0.97, Outdoors: 0:97,   **0.96**, Water: 0.94, Beach: 0.94, Two:
Mammal: 0.98   Seashore: 0.97   0.94

Figure 19.2: *Illustration of how image classifiers generalize poorly to new environments. (a) In the training data, most cows ocur on grassy backgrounds. (b-c) In these test image, the cow occurs "out of context", namely on a beach. The background is considered a "spurious correlation". In (b), the cow is not detected. In (c), it is classified with a generic "mammal" label. Top five labels and their confidences are produced by ClarifAI.com, which is a state of the art commerical vision system. From Figure 1 of [BVHP18]. Used with kind permission of Sara Beery.*

Figure 34.3). These examples illustrate that high performing predictive models can be very sensitive to small changes in the input distribution.

Performance can also drop on "clean" images, but which exhibit other kinds of shift. Figure 19.2 gives an amusing example of this. In particular, it illustrates how the performance of a CNN image classifier can be very accurate on **in-domain** data, but can be very inaccurate on **out-of-domain** data, such as images with a different background, or taken at a different time or location (see e.g., [Koh+20b]) or from a novel viewing angle (see e.g., [KH22])).

The root cause of many of these problems is the fact that discriminative models often leverage features that are predictive of the output *in the training set*, but which are not reliable in general. For example, in an image classification dataset, we may find that green grass in the background is very predictive of the class label "cow", but this is not a feature that is stable across different distributions; these are called **spurious correlations** or **shortcut features**. Unfortunately, such features are often easier for models to learn, for reasons explained in [Gei+20a; Xia+21b; Sha+20;

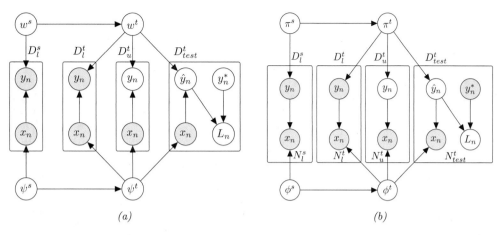

(a) $\qquad$ (b)

Figure 19.3: *Models for distribution shift from source s to target t. Here $\mathcal{D}_L^s$ is the labeled training set from the source, $\mathcal{D}_L^t$ is an optional labeled training set from the target, $\mathcal{D}_U^t$ is an optional unlabeled training set from the target, and $\mathcal{D}_{test}^t$ is a labeled test set from the target. In the latter case, $\hat{y}_n$ is the prediction on the n'th test case (generated by the model), $\boldsymbol{y}_n^*$ is the true value, and $\ell_n = \ell(\boldsymbol{y}_n^*, \hat{\boldsymbol{y}}_n)$ is the corresponding loss. (Note that we don't evaluate the loss on the source distribution.) (a) Discriminative (causal) model. (b) Generative (anticausal).*

Pez+21].

Relying on these shortcuts can have serious real-world consequences. For example, [Zec+18a] found that a CNN trained to recognize pneumonia was relying on hospital-specific metal tokens in the chest X-ray scans, rather than focusing on the lungs themselves, and thus the model did not generalize to new hospitals.

Analogous problems arise with other kinds of ML models, as well as other data types, such as text (e.g., changing "he" to "she" can flip the output of a sentiment analysis system), audio (e.g., adding background noise can easily confuse speech recognition systems), and medical records [Ros22]. Furthermore, the changes to the input needed to change the output can often be imperceptible, as we discuss in the section on adversarial robustness (Section 19.8).

19.2.2 A causal view of distribution shift

In the sections below, we briefly summarize some canonical kinds of distribution shift. We adopt a causal view of the problem, following [Sch+12a; Zha+13b; BP16; Mei18a; CWG20; Bud+21; SCS22]).[1] (See Section 4.7 for a brief discussion of causal DAGs, and Chapter 36 for more details.)

We assume the inputs to the model (the covariates) are X and the outputs to be predicted (the labels) are Y. If we believe that X causes Y, denoted $X \to Y$, we call it **causal prediction** or **discriminative prediction**. If we believe that Y causes X, denoted $Y \to X$, we call it **anticausal prediction** or **generative prediction**. [Sch+12a].

---

1. In the causality literature, the question of whether a model can generalize to a new distribution is called the question of **external validity**. If a model is externally valid, we say that it is **transportable** from one distribution to another [BP16].

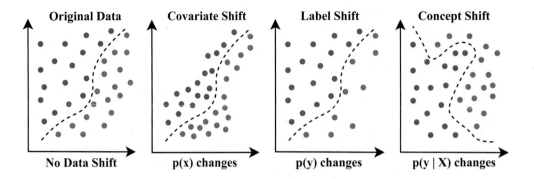

Figure 19.4: Illustration of the 4 main kinds of distribution shift for a 2d binary classification problem. Adapted from Figure 1 of [al21].

The decision about which model to use depends on our assumptions about the underlying **data generating process**. For example, suppose X is a medical image, and Y is an image segmentation created by a human expert or an algorithm. If we change the image, we will change the annotation, and hence $X \to Y$. Now suppose X is a medical image and Y is the ground truth disease state of the patient, as estimated by some other means (e.g., a lab test). In this case, we have $Y \to X$, since changing the disease state will change the appearance of the image. As another example, suppose X is a text review of a movie, and Y is a measure of how informative the review is. Clearly we have $X \to Y$. Now suppose Y is the star rating of the movie, representing the degree to which the user liked it; this will affect the words that they write, and hence $Y \to X$.

Based on the above discussion, we can factor the joint distribution in two possible ways. One way is to define a discriminative model:

$$p_{\boldsymbol{\theta}}(\boldsymbol{x}, \boldsymbol{y}) = p_{\boldsymbol{\psi}}(\boldsymbol{x}) p_{\boldsymbol{w}}(\boldsymbol{y}|\boldsymbol{x}) \tag{19.1}$$

See Figure 19.3a. Alternatively we can define a generative model:

$$p_{\boldsymbol{\theta}}(\boldsymbol{x}, \boldsymbol{y}) = p_{\boldsymbol{\pi}}(\boldsymbol{y}) p_{\boldsymbol{\phi}}(\boldsymbol{x}|\boldsymbol{y}) \tag{19.2}$$

See Figure 19.3b. For each of these 2 models model types, different parts of the distribution may change from source to target. This gives rise to 4 canonical type of shift, as we discuss in Section 19.2.3.

19.2.3   The four main types of distribution shift

The four main types of distribution shift are summarized in Section 19.2 and are illustrated in Figure 19.4. We give more details below (see also [LP20]).

19.2.3.1   Covariate shift

In a causal (discriminative) model, if $p_{\boldsymbol{\psi}}(\boldsymbol{x})$ changes (so $\boldsymbol{\psi}^s \neq \boldsymbol{\psi}^t$), we call it **covariate shift**, also called **domain shift**. For example, the training distribution may be clean images of coffee pots, and

Name	Source	Target	Joint
Covariate/domain shift	$p(X)p(Y\|X)$	$q(X)p(Y\|X)$	Discriminative
Concept shift	$p(X)p(Y\|X)$	$p(X)q(Y\|X)$	Discriminative
Label (prior) shift	$p(Y)p(X\|Y)$	$q(Y)p(X\|Y)$	Generative
Manifestation shift	$p(Y)p(X\|Y)$	$p(Y)q(X\|Y)$	Generative

Table 19.1: *The 4 main types of distribution shift.*

the test distribution may be images of coffee pots with Gaussian noise, as shown in Figure 19.1; or the training distribution may be photos of objects in a catalog, with uncluttered white backgrounds, and the test distribution may be photos of the same kinds of objects collected "in the wild"; or the training data may be synthetically generated images, and the test distribution may be real images. Similar shifts can occur in the text domain; for example, the training distribution may be movie reviews written in English, and the test distribution may be translations of these reviews into Spanish.

Some standard strategies to combat covariate shift include importance weighting (Section 19.5.2) and domain adaptation (Section 19.5.3).

19.2.3.2 Concept shift

In a causal (discriminative) model, if $p_{\boldsymbol{w}}(\boldsymbol{y}|\boldsymbol{x})$ changes (so $\boldsymbol{w}^s \neq \boldsymbol{w}^t$), we call it **concept shift**, also called **annotation shift**. For example, consider the medical imaging context: the conventions for annotating images might be different between the training distribution and test distribution. Another example of concept shift occurs when a new label can occur in the target distribution that was not part of the source distribution. This is related to open world recognition, discussed in Section 19.3.4.

Since concept shift is a change in what we "mean" by a label, it is impossible to fix this problem without seeing labeled examples from the target distribution, which defines each label by means of examples.

19.2.3.3 Label/prior shift

In a generative model, if $p_{\boldsymbol{\pi}}(\boldsymbol{y})$ changes (i.e., $\boldsymbol{\pi}^s \neq \boldsymbol{\pi}^t$), we call it **label shift**, also called **prior shift** or **prevalence shift**. For example, consider the medical imaging context, where $Y = 1$ if the patient has some disease and $Y = 0$ otherwise. If the training distribution is an urban hospital and the test distribution is a rural hospital, then the prevalence of the disease, represented by $p(Y = 1)$, might very well be different.

Some standard strategies to combat label shift are to reweight the output of a discriminative classifier using an estimate of the new label distribution, as we discuss in Section 19.5.4.

19.2.3.4 Manifestation shift

In a generative model, if $p_{\boldsymbol{\phi}}(\boldsymbol{x}|\boldsymbol{y})$ changes (i.e., $\boldsymbol{\phi}^s \neq \boldsymbol{\phi}^t$), we call **manifestation shift** [CWG20], or **conditional shift** [Zha+13b]. This is, in some sense, the inverse of concept shift. For example, consider the medical imaging context: the way that the same disease Y manifests itself in the shape of a tumor X might be different. This is usually due to the presence of a hidden confounding factor that has changed between source and target (e.g., different age of the patients).

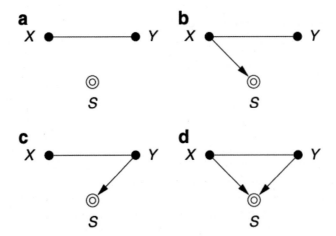

Figure 19.5: Causal diagrams for different sample selection strategies. Undirected edges can be oriented in either direction. The selection variable S is set to 1 its parent nodes match the desired criterion; only these samples are included in the dataset. (a) No selection. (b) Selection on X. (c) Selection on Y. (d) Selection on X and Y. Adapted from Figure 4 of [CWG20].

19.2.4   Selection bias

In some cases, we may induce a shift in the distribution just due to the way the data is collected, without any changes to the underlying distributions. In particular, let $S = 1$ if a sample from the population is included in the training set, and $S = 0$ otherwise. Thus the source distribution is $p(X, Y) = p(X, Y|S = 1)$ but the target distribution is $q(X, Y) = p(X, Y|S \in \{0, 1\}) = p(X, Y)$, so there is no selection.

In Figure 19.5 we visualize the four kinds of selection. For example, suppose we select based on X meeting certain criteria, e.g., images of a certain quality, or exhibiting a certain pattern; this can induce domain shift or covariate shift. Now suppose we select based on Y meeting certain criteria, e.g., we are more likely to select rare examples where $Y = 1$, in order to **balance the dataset** (for reasons of computational efficiency); this can induce label shift. Finally, suppose we select based on both X and Y; this can induce non-causal dependencies between X and Y, a phenomenon known as **selection bias** (see Section 4.2.4.2 for details).

19.3   Detecting distribution shifts

In general it will not be possible to make a model robust to all of the ways a distribution can shift at test time, nor will we always have access to test samples at training time. As an alternative, it may be sufficient for the model to *detect* that a shift has happened, and then to respond in the appropriate way. There are several ways of detecting distribution shift, some of which we summarize below. (See also Section 29.5.6, where we discuss changepoint detection in time series data.) The main distinction between methods is based on whether we have a set of samples from the target distribution, or just a single sample, and whether the test samples are labeled or unlabeled. We discuss these different scenarios below.

19.3.1 Detecting shifts using two-sample testing

Suppose we collect a set of samples from the source and target distribution. We can then use standard techniques for **two-sample testing** to estimate if the null hypothesis, $p(\boldsymbol{x}, y) = q(\boldsymbol{x}, y)$, is true or not. (If we have unlabeled samples, we just test if $p(\boldsymbol{x}) = q(\boldsymbol{x})$.) For example, we can use MMD (Section 2.7.3) to measure the distance between the set of input samples (see e.g., [Liu+20a]). Or we can measure (Euclidean) distances in the embedding space of a classifier trained on the source (see e.g., [KM22]).

In some cases it may be possible to just test if the distribution of the labels $p(y)$ has changed, which is an easier problem than testing for changes in the distribution of inputs $p(\boldsymbol{x})$. In particular, if the label shift assumption (Section 19.2.3.3) holds (i.e., $q(\boldsymbol{x}|y) = p(\boldsymbol{x}|y)$), plus some other assumptions, then we can use the blackbox shift estimation technique from Section 19.5.4 to estimate $q(y)$. If we find that $q(y) = p(y)$, then we can conclude that $q(\boldsymbol{x}, y) = p(\boldsymbol{x}, y)$. In [RGL19], they showed experimentally that this method worked well for detecting distribution shifts even when the label shift assumption does not hold.

It is also possible to use conformal prediction (Section 14.3) to develop "distribution free" methods for detecting covariate shift, given only acccess to a calibration set and some conformity scoring function [HL20].

19.3.2 Detecting single out-of-distribution (OOD) inputs

Now suppose we just have *one* unlabeled sample from the target distribution, $\boldsymbol{x} \sim q$, and we want to know if $\boldsymbol{x}$ is in-distribution (**ID**) or out-of-distribution (**OOD**). We will call this problem **out-of-distribution detection**, although it is also called **anomaly detection**, and **novelty detection**.[2]

The OOD detection problem requires making a binary decision about whether the test sample is ID or OOD. If it is ID, we may optionally require that we return its class label, as shown in Figure 19.6. In the sections below, we give a brief overview of techniques that have been proposed for tackling this problem, but for more details, see e.g., [Pan+21; Ruf+21; Bul+20; Yan+21; Sal+21; Hen+19b].

19.3.2.1 Supervised ID/OOD methods (outlier exposure)

The simplest method for OOD detection assumes we have access to labeled ID and OOD samples at training time. Then we just fit a binary classifier to distinguish the OOD or background class (called "**known unknowns**") from the ID class (called "**known knowns**") This technique is called **outlier exposure** (see e.g., [HMD19; Thu+21; Bit+21]) and can work well. However, in most cases we will not have enough examples from the OOD distribution, since the OOD set is basically the set of all possible inputs except for the ones of interest.

---

2. The task of **outlier detection** is somewhat different from anomaly or OOD detection, despite the similar name. In the outlier detection literature, the assumption is that there is a single unlabeled dataset, and the goal is to identify samples which are "untypical" compared to the majority. This is often used for **data cleaning**. (Note that this is a **transductive learning** task, where the model is trained and evaluated on the same data. We focus on inductive tasks, where we train a model on one dataset, and then test it on another.)

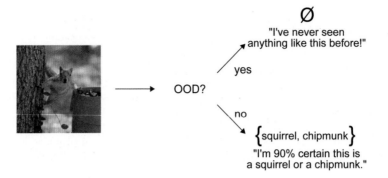

Figure 19.6: Illustration of a two-stage decision problem. First we must decide if the input image is out-of-distribution (OOD) or not. If it is not, we must return the set of class labels that have high probabilitiy. From [AB21]. Used with kind permission of Anastasios Angelopoulos.

19.3.2.2   Classification confidence methods

Instead of trying to solve the binary ID/OOD classification problem, we can directly try to predict the class of the input. Let the probabilities over the C labels be $p_c = p(y = c|\boldsymbol{x})$, and let the logits be $\ell_c = \log p_c$. We can derive a **confidence score** or **uncertainty metric** in a variety of ways from these quantities, e.g., the max probability $s = \max_c p_c$, the margin $s = \max_c \ell_c - \max_c^2 \ell_c$ (where $\max^2$ means the second largest element), the entropy $s = \mathbb{H}(\boldsymbol{p}_{1:C})^3$, the "**energy score**" $s = \sum_c \ell_c$ [Liu+21b], etc. In [Mil+21; Vaz+22] they show that the simple max probability baseline performs very well in practice.

19.3.2.3   Conformal prediction

It is possible to create a method for OOD detection and ID classification that has provably bounded risk using conformal prediction (Section 14.3). The details are in [Ang+21], but we sketch the basic idea here.

We want to solve the two-stage decision problems illustrated in Figure 19.6. We define the prediction set as follows:

$$\mathcal{T}_\lambda(\boldsymbol{x}) = \begin{cases} \emptyset & \text{if } \text{OOD}(\boldsymbol{x}) > \lambda_1 \\ \text{APS}(\boldsymbol{x}) & \text{otherwise} \end{cases} \tag{19.3}$$

where $\text{OOD}(\boldsymbol{x})$ is some heuristic OOD score (such as max class probability), and $\text{APS}(\boldsymbol{x})$ is the adaptive prediction set method of Section 14.3.1, which returns the set of the top K class labels, such that the sum of their probabilities exceeds threshold λ_2. (Formally, $\text{APS}(\boldsymbol{x}) = \{\pi_1, \ldots, \pi_K\}$ where π sorts $f(\boldsymbol{x})_{1:C}$ in descending order, and $K = \min\{K' : \sum_{c=1}^{K'} f(\boldsymbol{x})_c > \lambda_2\}$.)

We choose the thresholds λ_1 and λ_2 using a calibration set and a frequentist hypothesis testing

---

3. [Kir+21] argues against using entropy, since it confuses uncertainty about which of the C labels to use with uncertainty about whether any of the labels is suitable, compared to a "none-of-the-above" option.

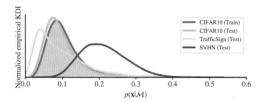

Figure 19.7: Likelihoods from a Glow normalizing flow model (Section 23.2.1) trained on CIFAR10 and evaluated on different test sets. The SVHN street sign dataset has lower visual complexity, and hence higher likelihood. Qualitatively similar results are obtained for other generative models and datasets. From Figure 1 of [Ser+20]. Used with kind permission of Joan Serrà.

method (see [Ang+21]). The resulting thresholds will jointly minimize the following risks:

$$R_1(\boldsymbol{\lambda}) = p(\mathcal{T}_{\boldsymbol{\lambda}}(\boldsymbol{x}) = \emptyset) \tag{19.4}$$

$$R_2(\boldsymbol{\lambda}) = p(\boldsymbol{y} \notin \mathcal{T}_{\boldsymbol{\lambda}}(\boldsymbol{x}) | \mathcal{T}_{\boldsymbol{\lambda}}(\boldsymbol{x}) \neq \emptyset) \tag{19.5}$$

where $p(\boldsymbol{x}, y)$ is the true but unknown source distribution (of ID samples, no OOD samples required), R_1 is the chance that an ID sample will be incorrectly rejected as OOD (type-I error), and R_2 is the chance (conditional on the decision to classify) that the true label is not in the predicted set. The goal is to set λ_1 as large as possible (so we can detect OOD examples when they arise) while controlling the type-I error (e.g., we may want to ensure that we falsely flag (as OOD) no more than 10% of in-distribution samples). We then set λ_2 in the usual way for the APS method in Section 14.3.1.

19.3.2.4 Unsupervised methods

If we don't have labeled examples, a natural approach to OOD detection is to fit an unconditional density model (such as a VAE) to the ID samples, and then to evaluate the likelihood $p(\boldsymbol{x})$ and compare this to some threshold value. Unfortunately for many kinds of deep model and datasets, we sometimes find that $p(\boldsymbol{x})$ is lower for samples that are from the source distribution than from a novel target distribution. For example, if we train a pixel-CNN model (Section 22.3.2) or a normalizing-flow model (Chapter 23) on Fashion-MNIST and evaluate it on MNIST, we find it gives higher likelihood to the MNIST samples [Nal+19a; Ren+19; KIW20; ZGR21]. This phenomenon occurs for several other models and datasets (see Figure 19.7).

One solution to this is to use log a **likelihood ratio** relative to a baseline density model, $R(\boldsymbol{x}) = \log p(\boldsymbol{x})/q(\boldsymbol{x})$, as opposed to the raw log likelihood, $L(\boldsymbol{x}) = \log p(\boldsymbol{x})$. (This technique was explored in [Ren+19], amongst other papers.) An important advantage of this is that the ratio is invariant to transformations of the data. To see this, let $\boldsymbol{x}' = \boldsymbol{\phi}(\boldsymbol{x})$ be some invertible, but possibly nonlinear, transformation. By the change of variables, we have $p(\boldsymbol{x}') = p(\boldsymbol{x})|\det \text{Jac}(\boldsymbol{\phi}^{-1})(\boldsymbol{x})|$. Thus $L(\boldsymbol{x}')$ will differ from $L(\boldsymbol{x})$ in a way that depends on the transformation. By contrast, we have $R(\boldsymbol{x}) = R(\boldsymbol{x}')$, regardless of $\boldsymbol{\phi}$, since

$$R(\boldsymbol{x}') = \log p(\boldsymbol{x}') - \log q(\boldsymbol{x}') = \log p(\boldsymbol{x}) + \log|\det \text{Jac}(\boldsymbol{\phi}^{-1})(\boldsymbol{x})| - \log q(\boldsymbol{x}) - \log|\det \text{Jac}(\boldsymbol{\phi}^{-1})(\boldsymbol{x})|$$
$$\tag{19.6}$$

Various other strategies have been proposed, such as computing the log-likelihood adjusted by a measure of the complexity (coding length computed by a lossless compression algorithm) of the input [Ser+20], computing the likelihood of model features instead of inputs [Mor+21a], etc.

A closely related technique relies on **reconstruction error**. The idea is to fit an autoencoder or VAE (Section 21.2) to the ID samples, and then measure the reconstruction error of the input: a sample that is OOD is likely to incur larger error (see e.g., [Pol+19]). However, this suffers from the same problems as density estimation methods.

An alternative to trying to estimate the likelihood, or reconstruct the output, is to use a GAN (Chapter 26) that is trained to discriminate "real" from "fake" data. This has been extended to the open set recognition setting in the OpenGAN method of [KR21b].

19.3.3 Selective prediction

Suppose the system has a confidence level of p that an input is OOD (see Section 19.3.4 for a discussion of some ways to compute such confidence scores). If p is below some threshold, the system may choose to **abstain** from classifying it with a specific label. By varying the threshold, we can control the tradeoff between accuracy and abstention rate. This is called **selective prediction** (see e.g., [EW10; GEY19; Ziy+19; JKG18]), and is useful for applications where an error can be more costly than asking a human expert for help (e.g., medical image classification).

19.3.3.1 Example: SGLD vs SGD for MLPs

One way to improve performance of OOD detection is to "be Bayesian" about the parameters of the model, so that the uncertainty in their values is reflected in the posterior predictive distribution. This can result in better performance in selective prediction tasks.

In this section, we give a simple example of this, where we fit a shallow MLP to the MNIST dataset using either standard SGD (specifically RMSprop) or stochastic gradient Langevin dynamics (see Section 12.7.1), which is a form of MCMC inference. We use 6,000 training steps, where each step uses a minibatch of size 1,000. After fitting the model to the training set, we evaluate its predictions on the test set. To assess how well calibrated the model is, we select a subset of predictions whose confidence is above a threshold t. (The confidence value is just the probability assigned to the MAP class.) As we increase the threshold t from 0 to 1, we make predictions on fewer examples, but the accuracy should increase. This is shown in Figure 19.8: the green curve is the fraction of the test set for which we make a prediction, and the blue curve is the accuracy. On the left we show SGD, and on the right we show SGLD. In this case, performance is quite similar, although SGD has slightly higher accuracy. However, the story changes somewhat when there is distribution shift.

To study the effects under distribution shift, we apply both models to FashionMNIST data. We show the results in Figure 19.9. The accuracy of both models is very low (less than the chance level of 10%), but SGD remains quite confident in many more of its predictions than SGLD, which is more conservative. To see this, consider a confidence threshold of 0.5: the SGD approach predicts on about 97% of the examples (recall that the green curve corresponds to the right hand axis), whereas the SGLD only predicts on about 70% of the examples.

More details on the behavior of Bayesian neural networks under distribution shift can be found in Section 17.4.6.2.

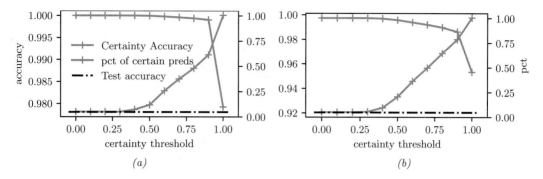

Figure 19.8: *Accuracy vs confidence plots for an MLP fit to the MNIST training set, and then evaluated on one batch from the MNIST test set. Scale for blue accuracy curve is on the left, scale for green percentage predicted curve is on the right. (a) Plugin approach, computed using SGD. (b) Bayesian approach, computed using 10 samples from SGLD. Generated by bnn_mnist_sgld.ipynb.*

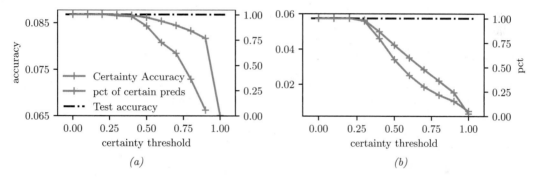

Figure 19.9: *Similar to Figure 19.8, except that performance is evaluated on the Fashion MNIST dataset. (a) SGD. (b) SGLD. Generated by bnn_mnist_sgld.ipynb.*

19.3.4 Open set and open world recognition

In Section 19.3.3, we discussed methods that "refuse to classify" if the system is not confident enough about its predicted output. If the system detects that this lack of confidence is due to the input coming from a novel class, rather than just being a novel instance of an existing class, we call the problem **open set recognition** (see e.g., [GHC20] for a review).

Rather than "flagging" novel classes as OOD, we can instead allow the set of classes to grow over time; this is called **open world classification** [BB15a]. Note that open world classification is most naturally tackled in the context of a continual learning system, which we discuss in Section 19.7.3.

19.4 Robustness to distribution shifts

In this section, we discuss techniques to improve the **robustness** of a model to distribution shifts. In particular, given labeled data from $p(\boldsymbol{x}, \boldsymbol{y})$, we aim to create a model that approximates $q(\boldsymbol{y}|\boldsymbol{x})$.

19.4.1 Data augmentation

A simple approach to potentially increasing the robustness of a predictive model to distribution shifts is to simulate samples from the target distribution by modifying the source data. This is called **data augmentation**, and is widely used in the deep learning community. For example, it is standard to apply small perturbations to images (e.g., shifting them or rotating them), while keeping the label the same (assuming that the label should be invariant to such changes); see e.g., [SK19; Hen+20] for details. Similarly, in NLP (natural language processing), it is standard to change words that should not affect the label (e.g., replacing "he" with "she" in a sentiment analysis system), or to use **back translation** (from a source language to a target language and back) to generate paraphrases; see e.g., [Fen+21] for a review of such techniques. For a causal perspective on data augmentation, see e.g., [Kau+21].

19.4.2 Distributionally robust optimization

We can make a discriminative model that is robust to (some forms of) covariate shift by solving the following **distributionally robust optimization** (DRO) problem:

$$\min_{f \in \mathcal{F}} \max_{\boldsymbol{w} \in \mathcal{W}} \frac{1}{N} \sum_{n=1}^{N} w_n \ell(f(\boldsymbol{x}_n), \boldsymbol{y}_n) \tag{19.7}$$

where the samples are from the source distribution, $(\boldsymbol{x}_n, \boldsymbol{y}_n) \sim p$. This is an example of a **min-max optimization problem**, in which we want to minimize the worst case risk. The specification of the robustness set, $\mathcal{W}$, is a key factor that determines how well the method works, and how difficult the optimization problem is. Typically it is specified in terms of an ℓ_2 ball around the inputs, but this could also be defined in a feature (embedding space) It is also possible to define the robustness set in terms of local changes to a structural causal model [Mei18a]. For more details on DRO, see e.g., [WYG14; Hu+18; CP20a; LFG21; Sag+20].

19.5 Adapting to distribution shifts

In this section, we discuss techniques to **adapt** the model to the target distribution. If we have some labeled data from the target distribution, we can use transfer learning, as we discuss in Section 19.5.1. However, getting labeled data from the target distribution is often not an option. Therefore, in the other sections, we discuss techniques that just rely on *unlabeled* data from the target distribution.

19.5.1 Supervised adaptation using transfer learning

Suppose we have labeled training data from a source distribution, $\mathcal{D}^s = \{(\boldsymbol{x}_n, \boldsymbol{y}_n) \sim p : n = 1 : N_s\}$, and also some labeled data from the target distribution, $\mathcal{D}^t = \{(\boldsymbol{x}_n, \boldsymbol{y}_n) \sim q : n = 1 : N_t\}$. Our goal is to minimize the risk on the target distibution q, which can be computed using

$$R(f, q) = \mathbb{E}_{q(\boldsymbol{x}, \boldsymbol{y})}\left[\ell(\boldsymbol{y}, f(\boldsymbol{x}))\right] \tag{19.8}$$

We can approximate the risk empirically using

$$\hat{R}(f, \mathcal{D}^t) = \frac{1}{|\mathcal{D}^t|} \sum_{(\boldsymbol{x}_n, \boldsymbol{y}_n) \in \mathcal{D}^t} \ell(\boldsymbol{y}_n, f(\boldsymbol{x}_n)) \tag{19.9}$$

If $\mathcal{D}^t$ is large enough, we can directly optimize this using standard empirical risk minimization (ERM). However, if $\mathcal{D}^t$ is small, we might want to use $\mathcal{D}^s$ somehow as a regularizer. This is called **transfer learning**, since we hope to "transfer knowledge" from p to q. There are many approaches to transfer learning (see e.g., [Zhu+21] for a review). We briefly mention a few below.

19.5.1.1 Pre-train and fine-tune

The simplest and most widely used approach to transfer learning is the **pre-train and fine-tune** approach. We first fit a model to the source distribution by computing $f^s = \mathrm{argmin}_f \hat{R}(f, \mathcal{D}^s)$. (Note that the source data may be unlabeled, in which case we can use self-supervised learning methods.) We then adapt the model to work on the target distribution by computing

$$f^t = \underset{f}{\mathrm{argmin}}\ \hat{R}(f, \mathcal{D}^t) + \lambda ||f - f^s|| \tag{19.10}$$

where $||f - f^s||$ is some distance between the functions, and $\lambda \geq 0$ controls the degree of regularization.

Since we assume that we have very few samples from the target distribution, we typically "freeze" most of the parameters of the source model. (This makes an implicit assumption that the features that are useful for the source distribution also work well for the target.) We can then solve Equation (19.10) by "chopping off the head" from f^s and replacing it with a new linear layer, to map to the new set of labels for the target distribution, and then compute a new MAP estimate for the parameters on the target distribution. (We can also compute a prior for the parameters of the source model, and use it to compute a posterior for the parameters of the target model, as discussed in Section 17.2.3.)

This approach is very widely used in practice, since it is simple and effective. In particular, it is common to take a large pre-trained model, such as a transformer, that has been trained (often using self supervised learning, Section 32.3.3) on a lot of data, such as the entire web, and then to use this model as a feature extractor (see e.g., [Kol+20]). The features are fed to the downstream model, which may be a linear classifier or a shallow MLP, which is trained on the target distribution.

19.5.1.2 Prompt tuning (in-context learning)

Recently another approach to transfer learning has been developed, that leverages large models, such as transformers (Section 22.4), which are trained on massive web datasets, usually in an unsupervised way, and then adapted to a small, task-specific target distribution. The interesting thing about this approach is the parameters of the original model are not changed; instead, the model is simply "conditioned" on new training data, usually in the form of a text **prompt** $\boldsymbol{z}$. That is, we compute

$$f^t(\boldsymbol{x}) = f^s(\boldsymbol{x} \cup \boldsymbol{z}) \tag{19.11}$$

where we (manually or automatically) optimize $\boldsymbol{z}$ while keeping f^s frozen. This approach is called **prompt tuning** or **in-context learning** (see e.g., [Liu+21a]), and is an instance of **few-shot learning** (see Figure 22.4 for an example).

Here $\boldsymbol{z}$ acts like a small training dataset, and f^s uses attention (Section 16.2.7) to "look at" all its inputs, comparing $\boldsymbol{x}$ with the examples in $\boldsymbol{z}$, and uses this to make a prediction. This works because the text training data often has a similar hierarchical structure (see [Xie+22] for a Bayesian interpretation).

19.5.2   Weighted ERM for covariate shift

In this section we reconsider the risk minimization objective in Equation (19.8), but leverage unlabeled data from the target distribution to estimate it. If we make the covariate shift assumption (i.e., $q(\boldsymbol{x}, \boldsymbol{y}) = q(\boldsymbol{x})p(\boldsymbol{y}|\boldsymbol{x})$), then we have

$$R(f, q) = \int q(\boldsymbol{x})q(\boldsymbol{y}|\boldsymbol{x})\ell(\boldsymbol{y}, f(\boldsymbol{x}))d\boldsymbol{x}d\boldsymbol{y} \tag{19.12}$$

$$= \int q(\boldsymbol{x})p(\boldsymbol{y}|\boldsymbol{x})\ell(\boldsymbol{y}, f(\boldsymbol{x}))d\boldsymbol{x}d\boldsymbol{y} \tag{19.13}$$

$$= \int \frac{q(\boldsymbol{x})}{p(\boldsymbol{x})}p(\boldsymbol{x})p(\boldsymbol{y}|\boldsymbol{x})\ell(\boldsymbol{y}, f(\boldsymbol{x}))d\boldsymbol{x}d\boldsymbol{y} \tag{19.14}$$

$$\approx \frac{1}{N}\sum_{(\boldsymbol{x}_n, \boldsymbol{y}_n)\in\mathcal{D}_L^s} w_n\ell(\boldsymbol{y}_n, f(\boldsymbol{x}_n)) \tag{19.15}$$

where the weights are given by the ratio

$$w_n = w(\boldsymbol{x}_n) = \frac{q(\boldsymbol{x}_n)}{p(\boldsymbol{x}_n)} \tag{19.16}$$

Thus we can solve the covariate shift problem by using **weighted ERM** [Shi00a; SKM07].

However, this raises two questions. First, why do we need to use this technique, since a discriminative model $p(\boldsymbol{y}|\boldsymbol{x})$ should work for any input $\boldsymbol{x}$, regardless of which distribution it comes from? Second, given that we do need to use this method, in practice how should we estimate the weights $w_n = w(\boldsymbol{x}_n) = \frac{q(\boldsymbol{x}_n)}{p(\boldsymbol{x}_n)}$? We discuss these issues below.

19.5.2.1   Why is covariate shift a problem for discriminative models?

For a discriminative model of the form $p(\boldsymbol{y}|\boldsymbol{x})$, it might seem that such a change in $p(\boldsymbol{x})$ will not affect the predictions. If the predictor $p(y|\boldsymbol{x})$ is the correct model for all parts of the input space $\boldsymbol{x}$, then this conclusion is warranted. However, most models will only be accurate in certain parts of the input space. This is illustrated in Figure 19.10b, where we show that a linear model fit to the source distribution may perform much worse on the target distribution than a model that weights target points more heavily during training.

19.5.2.2   How should we estimating the ERM weights?

One approach to estimating the ERM weights $w_n = w(\boldsymbol{x}_n) = \frac{q(\boldsymbol{x}_n)}{p(\boldsymbol{x}_n)}$ is to learn a density model for the source and target. However, density esimation is difficult for high dimensional features. An alternative approach is to try to approximate the density ratio, by fitting a binary classifier to distinguish the two distributions, as discussed in Section 2.7.5. In particular, suppose we have an equal number of samples from $p(\boldsymbol{x})$ and $q(\boldsymbol{x})$. Let us label the first set with $c = -1$ and the second set with $c = 1$. Then we have

$$p(c = 1|\boldsymbol{x}) = \frac{q(\boldsymbol{x})}{q(\boldsymbol{x}) + p(\boldsymbol{x})} \tag{19.17}$$

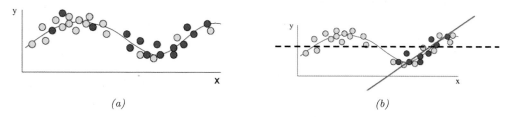

Figure 19.10: (a) Illustration of covariate shift. Light gray represents training distribution, dark gray represents test distribution. We see the test distribution has shifted to the right but the underlying input-output function is constant. (b) Dashed line: fitting a linear model across the full support of X. Solid black line: fitting the same model only on parts of input space that have high likelihood under the test distribution. From Figures 1–2 of [Sto09]. Used with kind permission of Amos Storkey.

and hence $\frac{p(c=1|\boldsymbol{x})}{p(c=-1|\boldsymbol{x})} = \frac{q(\boldsymbol{x})}{p(\boldsymbol{x})}$. If the classifier has the form $f(\boldsymbol{x}) = p(c=1|\boldsymbol{x}) = \sigma(h(\boldsymbol{x})) = \frac{1}{1+\exp(-h(\boldsymbol{x}))}$, where $h(\boldsymbol{x})$ is the prediction function that returns the logits, then the importance weights are given by

$$w_n = \frac{1/(1+\exp(-h(\boldsymbol{x}_n)))}{\exp(-h(\boldsymbol{x}_n))/(1+\exp(-h(\boldsymbol{x}_n)))} = \exp(h(\boldsymbol{x}_n)) \tag{19.18}$$

Of course this method requires that $\boldsymbol{x}$ values that may occur in the test distribution should also be possible in the training distribution, i.e., $q(\boldsymbol{x}) > 0 \implies p(\boldsymbol{x}) > 0$. Hence there are no guarantees about this method being able to interpolate beyond the training distribution.

19.5.3 Unsupervised domain adaptation for covariate shift

We now turn to methods that only need access to unlabeled examples from the target distribution.

The technique of **unsupervised domain adaptation** or **UDA** assumes access to a labeled dataset from the source distribution, $\mathcal{D}_1 = \mathcal{D}_L^s \sim p(\boldsymbol{x}, \boldsymbol{y})$ and an unlabeled dataset from the target distribution, $\mathcal{D}_2 = \mathcal{D}_U^t \sim q(\boldsymbol{x})$. It then uses the unlabeled target data to improve robustness or invariance of the predictor, rather than using a weighted ERM method.

There are many forms of UDA (see e.g., [KL21; CB20] for reviews). Here we just focus on one method, called **domain adversarial learning** [Gan+16a]. Let $f_{\boldsymbol{\alpha}} : \mathcal{X}_1 \cup \mathcal{X}_2 \to \mathcal{H}$ be a feature extractor defined on the two input domains, let $c_{\boldsymbol{\beta}} : \mathcal{H} \to \{1, 2\}$ be a classifier that maps from the feature space to the domain from which the input was taken, either domain 1 or 2 (source or target), and let $g_{\boldsymbol{\gamma}} : \mathcal{H} \to \mathcal{Y}$ be a classifier that maps from the feature space to the label space. We want to train the feature extractor so that it cannot distinguish whether the input is coming from the source or target distribution; in this case, it will only be able to use features that are common to both domains. Hence we optimize

$$\min_{\boldsymbol{\gamma}} \max_{\boldsymbol{\alpha}, \boldsymbol{\beta}} \frac{1}{N_1 + N_2} \sum_{\boldsymbol{x}_n \in \mathcal{D}_1, \mathcal{D}_2} \ell(d_n, c_{\boldsymbol{\beta}}(f_{\boldsymbol{\alpha}}(\boldsymbol{x}_n))) + \frac{1}{N_1} \sum_{(\boldsymbol{x}_n, \boldsymbol{y}_n) \in \mathcal{D}_1} \ell(\boldsymbol{y}_n, g_{\boldsymbol{\gamma}}(f_{\boldsymbol{\alpha}}(\boldsymbol{x}_n))) \tag{19.19}$$

The objective in Equation (19.19) minimizes the loss on the desired task of classifying y, but *maximizes* the loss on the auxiliary task of classifying the domain label d. This can be implemented by the **gradient sign reversal** trick, and is related to GANs (Section 26.7.6).

19.5.4   Unsupervised techniques for label shift

In this section, we describe an approach known as **blackbox shift estimation**, due to [LWS18], which can be used to tackle the **label shift** problem in an unsupervised way. We assume that the only thing that changes in the target distribution is the label prior, i.e., if the source distribution is denoted by $p(\boldsymbol{x}, \boldsymbol{y})$ and target distribution is denoted by $q(\boldsymbol{x}, \boldsymbol{y})$, we assume $q(\boldsymbol{x}, \boldsymbol{y}) = p(\boldsymbol{x}|\boldsymbol{y})q(\boldsymbol{y})$.

First note that, for any deterministic function $f : \mathcal{X} \to \mathcal{Y}$, we have

$$p(\boldsymbol{x}|y) = q(\boldsymbol{x}|y) \implies p(f(\boldsymbol{x})|y) = q(f(\boldsymbol{x})|y) \implies p(\hat{y}|y) = q(\hat{y}|y) \tag{19.20}$$

where $\hat{y} = f(\boldsymbol{x})$ is the predicted label. Let $\mu_i = q(\hat{y} = i)$ be the empirical fraction of times the model predicts class i on the test set, and let $q(y = i)$ be the true but unknown label distribution on the test set, and let $C_{ij} = p(\hat{y} = i|y = j)$ be the class confusion matrix estimated on the training set. Then we have

$$\mu_{\hat{y}} = \sum_y q(\hat{y}|y)q(y) = \sum_y p(\hat{y}|y)q(y) = \sum_y p(\hat{y}, y)\frac{q(y)}{p(y)} \tag{19.21}$$

We can write this in matrix-vector form as follows:

$$\mu_i = \sum_i C_{ij} q_j, \implies \boldsymbol{\mu} = \mathbf{C}\boldsymbol{q} \tag{19.22}$$

Hence we can solve $\boldsymbol{q} = \mathbf{C}^{-1}\boldsymbol{\mu}$, providing that $\mathbf{C}$ is not singular (this will be the case if $\mathbf{C}$ is strongly diagonal, i.e., the model predicts class y_i correctly more often than any other class y_j). We also require that for every $q(y) > 0$ we have $p(y) > 0$, which means we see every label at training time.

Once we know the new label distribution, $q(\boldsymbol{y})$, we can adjust our discriminative classifier to take the new label prior into account as follows:

$$q(y|\boldsymbol{x}) = \frac{q(\boldsymbol{x}|y)q(y)}{q(\boldsymbol{x})} = \frac{p(\boldsymbol{x}|y)q(y)}{q(\boldsymbol{x})} = \frac{p(y|\boldsymbol{x})p(\boldsymbol{x})}{p(y)}\frac{q(y)}{q(\boldsymbol{x})} = p(y|\boldsymbol{x})\frac{q(y)}{p(y)}\frac{p(\boldsymbol{x})}{q(\boldsymbol{x})} \tag{19.23}$$

We can safely ignore the $\frac{p(\boldsymbol{x})}{q(\boldsymbol{x})}$ term, which is constant wrt y, and we can plug in our estimates of the label distributions to compute the $\frac{q(y)}{p(y)}$.

In summary, there are three requirements for this method: (1) the confusion matrix is invertible; (2) no new labels at test time; (3) the only thing that changes is the label prior. If these three conditions hold, the above approach is a valid estimator. See [LWS18] for more details, and [Gar+20] for an alternative approach, based on maximum likelihood (rather than moment matching) for estimating the new marginal label distribution.

19.5.5   Test-time adaptation

In some settings, it is possible to continuously update the model parameters. This allows the model to adapt to changes in the input distribution. This is called **test time adaptation** or **TTA**. The difference from the unsupervised domain adaptation methods of Section 19.5.3 is that, in the online setting, we just have the model which was trained on the source, and not the source distribution.

In [Sun+20] they proposed an approach called **TTT** ("test-time training") for adapting a discriminative model. In this approach, a self-supervised proxy task is used to create proxy-labels, which can then be used to adapt the model at run time. In more detail, suppose we create a Y-structured network, where we first perform feature extraction, $x \to h$, and then use h to predict the output y and some proxy output r, such as the angle of rotation of the input image. The rotation angle is known if we use data augmentation. Hence we can apply this technique at test time, even if y is unknown, and update the $x \to h \to r$ part of the network, which influences the prediction for y via the shared bottleneck (feature layer) h.

Of course, if the proxy output, such as the rotation angle, is not known, we cannot use proxy-supervised learning methods such as TTT. In [Wan+20a], they propose an approach, inspired by semi-supervised learning methods, which they call **TENT**, which stands for "test-time adaptation by entropy minimization". The idea is to update the classifier parameters to minimize the entropy of the predictive distribution on a batch of test examples. In [Goy+22], they give a justification for this heuristic from the meta-learning perspective. In [ZL21], they present a Bayesian version of TENT, which they call **BACS**, which stands for "Bayesian adaptation under covariate shift". In [ZLF21], they propose a method called **MEMO** ("marginal entropy minimization with one test point") that can be used for any architecture. The idea is, once again, to apply data augmentation at test time to the input x, to create a set of inputs, $\tilde{x}_1, \ldots, \tilde{x}_B$. Now we update the parameters so as to minimize the predictive entropy produced by the averaged distribution

$$\overline{p}(y|x, w) = \frac{1}{B} \sum_{b=1}^{B} p(y|\tilde{x}_b, w) \tag{19.24}$$

This ensures that the model gives the same predictions for each perturbation of the input, and that the predictions are confident (low entropy).

An alternative to entropy based methods is to use **pseudolabels** (predicted outputs on the unlaneled target generated by the source model), and then to **self-train** on these (see e.g., [KML20; LHF20; Che+22]), often with additional regularizers to prevent over-fitting.

19.6 Learning from multiple distributions

In Section 19.2, we discussed the setting in which a model is trained on a single source distribution, and then evaluated on a distinct target distribution. In this section, we generalize this to a setting in which the model is trained on data from $J \geq 2$ source distributions, before being tested on data from a target distribution. This includes a variety of different problem settings, depending on the value of J, as we summarize in Figure 19.11.

19.6.1 Multitask learning

In **multi-task learning** (MTL) [Car97], we have labeled data from J different distributions, $\mathcal{D}^j = \{(x_n^j, y_n^j) : n = 1 : N_j\}$, and the goal is to learn a model that predicts well on all J of them simultaneously, where $f(x, j) : \mathcal{X} \to \mathcal{Y}_j$ is the output for the j'th task. For example, we might want to map a color image of size $H \times W \times 3$ to a set of semantic labels per pixel, $\mathcal{Y}^1 = \{1, \ldots, C\}^{HW}$, as

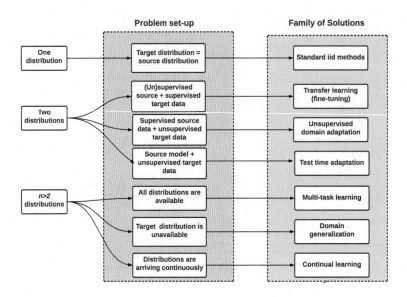

Figure 19.11: Schematic overview of techniques for learning from 1 or more different distributions. Adapted from slide 3 of [Sca21].

well as a set of predicted depth values per pixel, $\mathcal{Y}^2 = \mathbb{R}^{HW}$. We can do this using ERM where we have multiple samples for each task:

$$f^* = \operatorname*{argmin}_{f} \sum_{j=1}^{J} \sum_{n=1}^{N_j} \ell_j(\boldsymbol{y}_n^j, f(\boldsymbol{x}_n^j, j)) \tag{19.25}$$

where ℓ_j is the loss function for task j (suitably scaled).

There are many approaches to solving MTL. The simplest is to fit a single model with multiple "output heads", as illustrated in Figure 19.12. This is called a "**shared trunk network**". Unfortunately this often leads to worse performance than training J single task networks. In [Mis+16], they propose to take a weighted combination of the activations of each single task network, an approach they called "**cross-stitch networks**". See [ZY21] for a more detailed review of neural approaches, and [BLS11] for a theoretical analysis of this problem.

Note that multi-task learning does not always help performance on each task because sometimes there can be "**task interference**" or "**negative transfer**" (see e.g., [MAP17; Sta+20; WZR20]). In such cases, we should use separate networks, rather than using one model with multiple output heads.

19.6.2   Domain generalization

The problem of **domain generalization** assumes we train on J different labeled source distributions or "**environments**" (also called "**domains**"), and then test on a new target distribution (denoted by

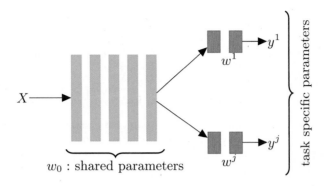

Figure 19.12: *Illustration of multi-headed network for multi-task learning.*

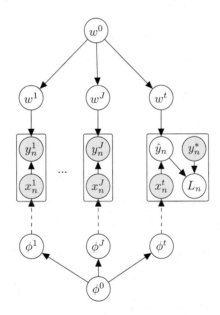

Figure 19.13: *Hierarchical Bayesian discriminative model for learning from J different environments (distributions), and then testing on a new target distribution $t = J + 1$. Here $\hat{\boldsymbol{y}}_n$ is the prediction for test example $\boldsymbol{x}_n$, $\boldsymbol{y}_n^*$ is the true output, and $\ell_n = \ell(\boldsymbol{y}_n^t, \boldsymbol{y}_n^*)$ is the associated loss. The parameters of the distribution over input features $p_\phi(\boldsymbol{x})$ are shown with dotted edges, since these distributions do not need to be learned in a discriminative model.*

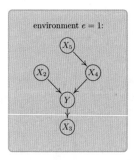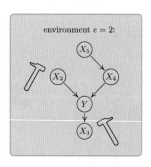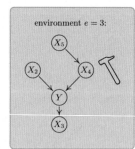

Figure 19.14: Illustration of invariant causal prediction. The hammer symbol represents variables whose distribution is perturbed in the given environment. An invariant predictor must use features $\{X_2, X_4\}$. Considering indirect causes instead of direct ones (e.g. $\{X_2, X_5\}$) or an incomplete set of direct causes (e.g., $\{X_4\}$) may not be sufficient to guarantee invariant prediction. From Figure 1 of [PBM16b]. Used with kind permission of Jonas Peters.

$t = J + 1$). In some cases each environment is just identified with a meaningless integer id. In more realistic settings, each different distribution has associated **meta-data** or **context variables** that characterizes the environment in which the data was collected, such as the time, location, imaging device, etc.

Domain generalization (DG) is similar to multi-task learning, but differs in what we want to predict. In particular, in DG, we only care about prediction accuracy on the target distribution, not the J training distribution. Furthermore, we assume we don't have any labeled data from the target distribution. We therefore have to make some assumptions about how $p^t(\boldsymbol{x}, \boldsymbol{y})$ relates to $p^j(\boldsymbol{x}, \boldsymbol{y})$ for $j = 1 : J$.

One way to formalize this is to create a hierarchical Bayesian model, as proposed in [Bax00], and illustrated in Figure 19.13. This encodes the assumption that $p^t(\boldsymbol{x}, \boldsymbol{y}) = p(\boldsymbol{x}|\boldsymbol{\phi}^t)p(\boldsymbol{y}|\boldsymbol{x}, \boldsymbol{w}^t)$ where $\boldsymbol{w}^t$ is derived from a common "population level" model $\boldsymbol{w}^0$, shared across all distributions, and similarly for $\boldsymbol{\phi}^t$. (Note, however, that in a discriminative model, we don't need to model $p(\boldsymbol{x}|\boldsymbol{\phi}^t)$.) See Section 15.5 for discussion of hierarchical Bayesian GLMs, and Section 17.6 for discussion of hierarchical Bayesian MLPs.

Many other techniques have been proposed for DG. Note, however, that [GLP21] found that none of these methods worked consistently better than the baseline approach of performing empirical risk minimization across all the provided datasets. For more information, see e.g., [GLP21; She+21; Wan+21; Chr+21].

19.6.3   Invariant risk minimization

One approach to domain generalization that has received a lot of attention is called **invariant risk minimization** or **IRM** [Arj+19]. The goal is to learn a predictor that works well across all environments, yet is less prone to depending on the kinds of "spurious features" we discussed in Section 19.2.1.

IRM is an extension of an earlier method called **invariant causal prediction** (ICP) [PBM16b]. This uses hypothesis testing methods to find the set of predictors (features) that directly cause the outcome in each environment, rather than features that are indirect causes, or are just correlated with the outcome. See Figure 19.14 for an illustration.

In [Arj+19], they proposed an extension of ICP to handle the case of high dimensional inputs, where the individual variables do not have any causal meaning (e.g., they correspond to pixels). Their approach requires finding a predictor that works well on average, across all environments, while also being optimal for each individual environment. That is, we want to find

$$f^* = \underset{f \in \mathcal{F}}{\operatorname{argmin}} \sum_{j=1}^{J} \frac{1}{N_j} \sum_{n=1}^{N_j} \ell(\boldsymbol{y}_n^j, f(\boldsymbol{x}_n^j)) \tag{19.26}$$

$$\text{such that } f \in \arg\min_{g \in \mathcal{F}} \frac{1}{N_j} \sum_{n=1}^{N_j} \ell(\boldsymbol{y}_n^j, g(\boldsymbol{x}_n^j)) \text{ for all } j \in \mathcal{E} \tag{19.27}$$

where $\mathcal{E}$ is the set of environments, and $\mathcal{F}$ is the set of prediction functions. The intuition behind this is as follows: there may be many functions that achieve low empirical loss on any given environment, since the problem may be underspecified, but if we pick the one that also works well on all environments, it is more likely to rely on causal features rather than spurious features.

Unfortunately, more recent work has shown that the IRM principle often does not work well for covariate shift, both in theory [RRR21] and practice [GLP21], although it can work well in some anti-causal (generative) models [Ahu+21].

19.6.4 Meta learning

The goal of **meta-learning** is to "learn the learning algorithm" [TP97]. A common way to do this is to provide the meta-learner with a set of datasets from different distributions. This is very similar to domain generalization (Section 19.6.2), except that we partition each training distribution into training and test, so we can "practice" learning to generalize from a training set to a test set. A general review of meta-learning can be found in [Hos+20a]. Here we present a unifying summary based on the hierarchical Bayesian framework proposed in [Gor+19].

19.6.4.1 Meta-learning as probabilistic inference for prediction

We assume there are J tasks (distributions), each of which has a training set $\mathcal{D}_{\text{train}}^j = \{(\boldsymbol{x}_n^j, \boldsymbol{y}_n^j) : n = 1 : N^j\}$ and a test set $\mathcal{D}_{\text{test}}^j = \{(\tilde{\boldsymbol{x}}_m^j, \tilde{\boldsymbol{y}}_m^j) : m = 1 : M^j\}$. In addition, $\boldsymbol{w}^j$ are the task specific parameters, and $\boldsymbol{w}^0$ are the shared parameters, as shown in Figure 19.15. This is very similar to the domain generalization model in Figure 19.13, except for two differences: first there is the trivial difference due to the use of plate notation; second, in meta learning, we have both training and test partitions for all distributions, whereas in DG, we only have a test set for the target distribution.

We will learn a point estimate for the global parameters $\boldsymbol{w}^0$, since it is shared across all datasets, and thus has little uncertainty. However, we will compute an approximate posterior for $\boldsymbol{w}^j$, since each task often has little data. We denote this posterior by $p(\boldsymbol{w}^j | \mathcal{D}_{\text{train}}^j, \boldsymbol{w}^0)$. From this, we can compute the posterior predictive distribution for each task:

$$p(\tilde{\boldsymbol{y}}^j | \tilde{\boldsymbol{x}}^j, \mathcal{D}_{\text{train}}^j, \boldsymbol{w}^0) = \int p(\tilde{\boldsymbol{y}}^j | \tilde{\boldsymbol{x}}^j, \boldsymbol{w}^j) p(\boldsymbol{w}^j | \mathcal{D}_{\text{train}}^j, \boldsymbol{w}^0) d\boldsymbol{w}^j \tag{19.28}$$

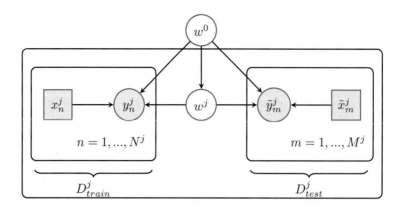

Figure 19.15: Hierarchical Bayesian model for meta-learning. There are J tasks, each of which has a training set $\mathcal{D}^j = \{(\boldsymbol{x}_n^j, \boldsymbol{y}_n^j) : n = 1 : N^j\}$ and a test set $\mathcal{D}_{\text{test}}^j = \{(\tilde{\boldsymbol{x}}_m^j, \tilde{\boldsymbol{y}}_m^j) : m = 1 : M^j\}$. $\boldsymbol{w}^j$ are the task specific parameters, and $\boldsymbol{\theta}$ are the shared parameters. Adapted from Figure 1 of [Gor+19].

Since computing the posterior is in general intractable, we will learn an amortized approximation (see Section 10.1.5) to the predictive distribution, denoted by $q_{\boldsymbol{\phi}}(\tilde{\boldsymbol{y}}^j | \tilde{\boldsymbol{x}}^j, \mathcal{D}_{\text{train}}^j, \boldsymbol{w}^0)$. We choose the parameters of the prior $\boldsymbol{w}^0$ and the inference network $\boldsymbol{\phi}$ to make this *predictive posterior* as accurate as possible for any given input dataset:

$$\boldsymbol{\phi}^* = \operatorname*{argmin}_{\boldsymbol{\phi}} \mathbb{E}_{p(\mathcal{D}_{\text{train}}, \tilde{\boldsymbol{x}})} \left[D_{\text{KL}} \left(p(\tilde{\boldsymbol{y}} | \tilde{\boldsymbol{x}}, \mathcal{D}_{\text{train}}, \boldsymbol{w}^0) \, \| \, q_{\boldsymbol{\phi}}(\tilde{\boldsymbol{y}} | \tilde{\boldsymbol{x}}, \mathcal{D}_{\text{train}}, \boldsymbol{w}^0) \right) \right] \tag{19.29}$$

$$= \operatorname*{argmin}_{\boldsymbol{\phi}} \mathbb{E}_{p(\mathcal{D}_{\text{train}}, \tilde{\boldsymbol{x}})} \left[\mathbb{E}_{p(\tilde{\boldsymbol{y}} | \tilde{\boldsymbol{x}}, \mathcal{D}_{\text{train}}, \boldsymbol{w}^0)} \left[\log q_{\boldsymbol{\phi}}(\tilde{\boldsymbol{y}} | \tilde{\boldsymbol{x}}, \mathcal{D}_{\text{train}}, \boldsymbol{w}^0) \right] \right] \tag{19.30}$$

$$= \operatorname*{argmin}_{\boldsymbol{\phi}} \mathbb{E}_{p(\mathcal{D}_{\text{train}}, \tilde{\boldsymbol{x}}, \tilde{\boldsymbol{y}})} \left[\log \int p(\tilde{\boldsymbol{y}} | \tilde{\boldsymbol{x}}, \boldsymbol{w}) q_{\boldsymbol{\phi}}(\boldsymbol{w} | \mathcal{D}_{\text{train}}, \boldsymbol{w}^0) d\boldsymbol{w} \right] \tag{19.31}$$

where we made the approximation $p(\tilde{\boldsymbol{y}} | \tilde{\boldsymbol{x}}, \mathcal{D}_{\text{train}}, \boldsymbol{w}^0) \approx p(\tilde{\boldsymbol{y}} | \tilde{\boldsymbol{x}}, \mathcal{D}_{\text{train}})$. We can then make a Monte Carlo approximation to the outer expectation by sampling J tasks (distributions) from $p(\mathcal{D})$, each of which gets partitioned into a train and test set, $\{(\mathcal{D}_{\text{train}}^j, \mathcal{D}_{\text{test}}^j) \sim p(\mathcal{D}) : j = 1 : J\}$, where $\mathcal{D}_{\text{test}}^j = \{(\tilde{\boldsymbol{x}}_m, \tilde{\boldsymbol{y}}_m)\}$. We can make an MC approximation to the inner expectation (the integral) by drawing S samples from the task-specific parameter posterior $\boldsymbol{w}_s^j \sim q_{\boldsymbol{\phi}}(\boldsymbol{w}^j | \mathcal{D}^j, \boldsymbol{w}^0)$. The resulting objective has the following form (where we assume each test set has M samples for notational simplicity):

$$\mathcal{L}_{\text{meta}}(\boldsymbol{w}^0, \boldsymbol{\phi}) = \frac{1}{MJ} \sum_{m=1}^{M} \sum_{j=1}^{J} \log \left(\frac{1}{S} \sum_{s=1}^{S} p(\tilde{\boldsymbol{y}}_m^j | \tilde{\boldsymbol{x}}_m^j, \boldsymbol{w}_s^j) \right) \tag{19.32}$$

Note that this is different from standard (amortized) variational inference, that focuses on approximating the expected accuracy of the *parameter posterior* given all of the data for a task, $\mathcal{D}_{\text{all}}^j = \mathcal{D}_{\text{train}}^j \cup \mathcal{D}_{\text{test}}^j$, rather than focusing on predictive accuracy of a test set given a training set.

Indeed, the standard objective has the form

$$\mathcal{L}_{\text{VI}}(\boldsymbol{w}^0, \boldsymbol{\phi}) = \frac{1}{J} \sum_{j=1}^{J} \left(\sum_{(\boldsymbol{x},\boldsymbol{y}) \in \mathcal{D}_{\text{all}}^j} \left[\frac{1}{S} \sum_{s=1}^{S} \log p(\tilde{\boldsymbol{y}}^j | \tilde{\boldsymbol{x}}^j, \boldsymbol{w}_s^j) \right] - D_{\text{KL}} \left(q_{\boldsymbol{\phi}}(\boldsymbol{w}^j | \mathcal{D}_{\text{all}}^j, \boldsymbol{w}^0) \, \| \, p(\boldsymbol{w}^j | \boldsymbol{w}^0) \right) \right)$$

(19.33)

where $\boldsymbol{w}_s^j \sim q_{\boldsymbol{\phi}}(\boldsymbol{w}^j | \mathcal{D}_{\text{all}}^j)$. We see that the standard formulation takes the average of a log, but the meta-learning formulation takes the log of an average. The latter can give provably better predictive accuracy, as pointed out in [MAD20]. Another difference is that the meta-learning formulation optimizes the forward KL, not reverse KL. Finally, in the meta-learning formulation, we do not have the KL penalty term on the parameter posterior.

Below we show how this framework includes several common approaches to meta-learning.

19.6.4.2 Neural processes

In the special case that the task-specific inference network computes a point estimate, $q(\boldsymbol{w}^j | \mathcal{D}^j, \boldsymbol{w}^0) = \delta(\boldsymbol{w}^j - \mathcal{A}_{\boldsymbol{\phi}}(\mathcal{D}^j, \boldsymbol{w}^0))$, the posterior predictive distribution becomes

$$q(\tilde{\boldsymbol{y}}^j | \tilde{\boldsymbol{x}}^j, \mathcal{D}^j, \boldsymbol{w}^0) = \int p(\tilde{\boldsymbol{y}}^j | \tilde{\boldsymbol{x}}^j, \boldsymbol{w}^j) q(\boldsymbol{w}^j | \mathcal{D}^j, \boldsymbol{w}^0) d\boldsymbol{w}^j = p(\tilde{\boldsymbol{y}}^j | \tilde{\boldsymbol{x}}^j, \mathcal{A}_{\boldsymbol{\phi}}(\mathcal{D}^j, \boldsymbol{w}^0), \boldsymbol{w}^0)$$

(19.34)

where $\mathcal{A}_{\boldsymbol{\phi}}(\mathcal{D}^j, \boldsymbol{w}^0)$ is a function that takes in a set, and returns some parameters. We can evaluate this predictive distribution empirically, and directly optimize it (wrt $\boldsymbol{\phi}$ and $\boldsymbol{w}^0$) using standard supervised maximum likelihood methods. This approach is called a **neural process** [Gar+18e; Gar+18d; Dub20; Jha+22]).

19.6.4.3 Gradient-based meta-learning (MAML)

In **gradient-based meta-learning**, we define the task specific inference procedure as follows:

$$\hat{\boldsymbol{w}}^j = \mathcal{A}(\mathcal{D}^j, \boldsymbol{w}^0) = \boldsymbol{w}^0 + \eta \nabla_{\boldsymbol{w}} \log \sum_{n=1}^{N^j} p(\boldsymbol{y}_n^j | \boldsymbol{x}_n^j, \boldsymbol{w})|_{\boldsymbol{w}^0}$$

(19.35)

That is, we set the task specific parameters to be shared parameters $\boldsymbol{w}^0$, modified by one step along the gradient of the log conditional likelihood. This approach is called **model-agnostic meta-learning** or **MAML** [FAL17]. It is also possible to take multiple gradient steps, by feeding the gradient into an RNN [RL17].

19.6.4.4 Metric-based few-shot learning (prototypical networks)

Now suppose $\boldsymbol{w}^0$ correspond to the parameters of a shared neural feature extractor, $h_{\boldsymbol{w}^0}(\boldsymbol{x})$, and the task specific parameters are the weights and biases of the last linear layer of a classifier, $\boldsymbol{w}^j = \{\boldsymbol{w}_c^j, b_c^j\}_{c=1}^C$. Let us compute the average of the feature vectors for each class in each task's training set:

$$\boldsymbol{\mu}_c^j = \frac{1}{|\mathcal{D}_c^j|} \sum_{\boldsymbol{x}_n^c \in \mathcal{D}_c^j} h_{\boldsymbol{w}^0}(\boldsymbol{x}_n^c)$$

(19.36)

Now define the task specific inference procedure as follows. We first compute the vector containing the centroid and norm for each class:

$$\hat{\boldsymbol{w}}^j = \mathcal{A}(\mathcal{D}^j, \boldsymbol{w}^0) = [\boldsymbol{\mu}_c^j, \ -\frac{1}{2}||\boldsymbol{\mu}_c^j||^2]_{c=1}^C \tag{19.37}$$

The predictive distribution becomes

$$q(\tilde{y}^j = c|\tilde{\boldsymbol{x}}^j, \mathcal{D}^j, \boldsymbol{w}^0) \propto \exp\left(-d(h_{\boldsymbol{w}^0}(\tilde{\boldsymbol{x}}), \boldsymbol{\mu}_c^j)\right) = \exp\left(h_{\boldsymbol{w}^0}(\tilde{\boldsymbol{x}})^\mathsf{T}\boldsymbol{\mu}_c^j - \frac{1}{2}||\boldsymbol{\mu}_c^j||^2\right) \tag{19.38}$$

where $d(\boldsymbol{u}, \boldsymbol{v})$ is the Euclidean distance. This is equivalent to the technique known as **prototypical networks** [SSZ17].

19.7   Continual learning

In this section, we discuss **continual learning** (see e.g., [Had+20; Del+21; Qu+21; LCR21; Mai+22; Lin+22]), also called **life-long learning** (see e.g., [Thr98; CL18]), in which the system learns from a sequence of different distributions, $p_1, p_2, \ldots$. In particular, at each time step t, the model receives a batch of labeled data,

$$\mathcal{D}_t = \{(\boldsymbol{x}_n, \boldsymbol{y}_n) : n = 1 : N_t, \boldsymbol{x}_n \sim p_t(\boldsymbol{x}), \boldsymbol{y}_n = f_t(\boldsymbol{x}_n)\} \tag{19.39}$$

where $p_t(\boldsymbol{x})$ is the unknown input distribution, and $f_t : \mathcal{X}_t \to \mathcal{Y}_t$ is the unknown prediction function. (We focus on noise-free outputs, for notational simplicity.) The learner is then expected to update its belief state about the true function f_t, and to use its beliefs to make predictions on an independent test set,

$$\mathcal{D}_t^{\text{test}} = \{(\boldsymbol{x}_n, \boldsymbol{y}_n) : n = 1 : N_t^{\text{test}}, \boldsymbol{x}_n \sim p_t^{\text{test}}(\boldsymbol{x}), \boldsymbol{y}_n = f_t^{\text{test}}(\boldsymbol{x}_n)\} \tag{19.40}$$

Depending on how we assume $p_t(\boldsymbol{x})$ and f_t evolve over time, and how the test set is defined, we can create a variety of different CL scenarios, as we discuss below.

19.7.1   Domain drift

The problem of **domain drift** refers to the setting in which $p_t(\boldsymbol{x})$ changes over time (i.e., covariate shift), but the functional mapping $f_t : \mathcal{X} \to \mathcal{Y}$ is constant. For example, the vision system of a self driving car may have to classify cars vs pedestrians under shifting lighting conditions (see e.g., [Sun+22]).

To evaluate such a model, we assume $f_t^{\text{test}} = f_t$ and define $p_t^{\text{test}}(\boldsymbol{x})$ to be the current input distribution p_t (e.g., if it is currently night time, we want the detector to work well on dark images). Alternatively we can define $p_t^{\text{test}}(\boldsymbol{x})$ to be the union of all the input distributions seen so far, $p_t^{\text{test}} = \cup_{s=1}^T p_s$ (e.g., we want the detector to work well on dark and light images). This latter assumption is illustrated in Figure 19.16.

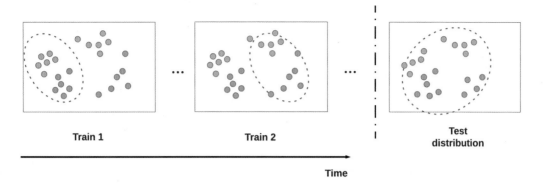

Figure 19.16: *An illustration of domain drift.*

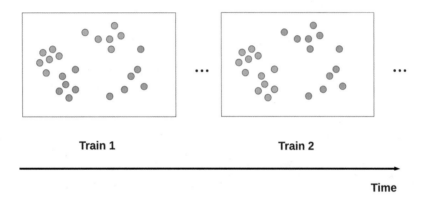

Figure 19.17: *An illustration of concept drift.*

19.7.2 Concept drift

The problem of **concept drift** refers to the setting where the functional mapping $f_t : \mathcal{X} \to \mathcal{Y}$ changes over time, but the input distribution $p_t(\boldsymbol{x})$ is constant [WK96]. For example, we can imagine a setting in which people engage in certain behaviors, and at step t some of these are classified as illegal, and at step $t' > t$, the definition of what is legal changes, and hence the decision boundary changes. This is illustrated in Figure 19.17.

As another example, we might initially be faced with a sort-by-color task, where red objects go on the left and blue objects on the right, and then a sort-by-shape task, where square objects go on the left and circular objects go on the right.[4] We can think of this as a problem where $p(y|\boldsymbol{x}, \text{task})$ is stationary, but the task is unobserved, so $p(y|\boldsymbol{x})$ changes.

In the concept drift scenario, we see that the prediction for the same underlying input point $\boldsymbol{x} \in \mathcal{X}$ will change depending on when the prediction is performed. This means that the test distribution

---

4. This example is from Mike Mozer.

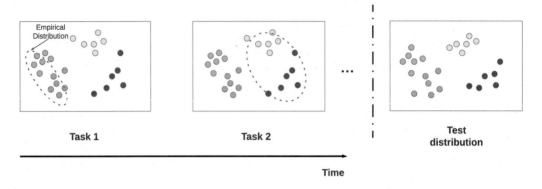

Figure 19.18: *An illustration of class incremental learning. Adapted from Figure 1 of [LCR21].*

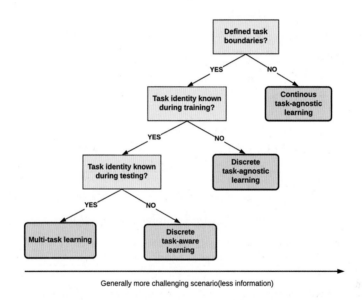

Figure 19.19: *Different kinds of incremental learning. Adapted from Figure 1 of [Zen+18].*

also needs to change over time for meaningful identification. Alternatively, we can "tag" each input with the corresponding time stamp or task id.

19.7.3 Task incremental learning

A very widely studied form of continual learning focuses on the setting in which new class labels are "revealed" over time. That is, there is assumed to be a true static prediction function $f : \mathcal{X} \to \mathcal{Y}$, but at step t, the learner only sees samples from $(\mathcal{X}, \mathcal{Y}_t)$, where $\mathcal{Y}_t \subset \mathcal{Y}$. For example, $\mathcal{X}$ may be the space of images, $\mathcal{Y}_1$ might be {cats, dogs}, and $\mathcal{Y}_2$ might be {cars, bikes, trucks}. Learning to classify with an increasing number of categories is called **class incremental learning** (see e.g., [Mas+20]). This is also called **task incremental learning**, since each distribution is considered as a different **task**. See Figure 19.18 for an illustration.

The problem of class incremental learning has been studied under a variety of different assumptions, as discussed in [Hsu+18; VT18; FG18; Del+21]. The most common scenarios are shown in Figure 19.19. If we assume there are no well defined boundaries between tasks, we have **continuous task-agnostic learning** (see e.g., [SKM21; Zen+21]). If there are well defined boundaries (i.e., discontinuous changes of the training distribution), then we can distinguish two subcases. If the boundaries are not known during training (similar to detecting distribution shift), we have **discrete task-agnostic learning**. Finally, if the boundaries are given to the training algorithm, we have a **task-aware learning** problem.

A common experimental setup in the task-aware setting is to define each task to be a different version of the MNIST dataset, e.g., with all 10 classes present but with the pixels randomly permuted (this is called **permuted MNIST**) or with a subset of 2 classes present at each step (this is called **split MNIST**).[5] In the task-aware setting, the task label may or may not be known at test time. If it is, the problem is essentially equivalent to multi-task learning (see Section 19.6.1). If it is not, the model must predict the task and corresponding class label within that task (which is a standard supervised problem with a hierarchical label space); this is commonly done by using a multi-headed DNN, with CT outputs, where C is the number of classes, and T is the number of tasks.

In the multi-headed approach, the number of "heads" is usually specified as input to the algorithm, because the softmax imposes a sum-to-one constraint that prevents incremental estimation of the output weights in the open-class setting. An alternative approach is to wait until a new class label is encountered for the first time, and then train the model with an enlarged output head. This requires storing past data from each class, as well as data for the new class (see e.g., [PTD20]). Alternatively, we can use generative classifiers where we do not need to worry about "output heads". If we use a "deep" nearest neighbor classifier, with a shared feature extractor (embedding function), the main challenge is to efficiently update the stored prototypes for past classes as the feature extractor parameters change (see e.g., [DLT21]). If we fit a separate generative model per class (e.g., a VAE, as in [VLT21]), then online learning becomes easier, but the method may be less sample efficient.

At the time of writing, most of the CL literature focuses on the task-aware setting. However, from a practical point of view, the assumption that task boundaries are provided at training or test time is very unrealistic. For example, consider the problem of training a robot to perform various activities: The data just streams in, and the robot must learn what to do, without anyone telling it that it is now being given an example from a new task or distribution (see e.g., [Fon+21; Woł+21]). Thus future research should focus on the task-agnostic setting, with either discrete or continuous changes.

19.7.4 Catastrophic forgetting

In the class incremental learning literature, it is common to train on a sequence of tasks, but to test (at each step) on all tasks. In this scenario, there are two main possible failure modes. The first possible problem is called "**catastrophic forgetting**" (see e.g., [Rob95b; Fre99; Kir+17]). This

---

5. In the split MNIST setup, for task 1, digits (0,1) get labeled as (0,1), but in task 2, digits (2,3) get labeled as (0,1). So the "meaning" of the output label depends on what task we are solving. Thus the output space is really hierarchical, namely the cross product of task id and class label.

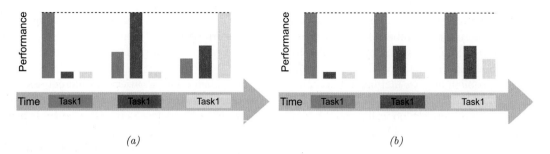

Figure 19.20: Some failure modes in class incremental learning. We train on task 1 (blue) and evaluate on tasks 1–3 (blue, orange, yellow); we then train on task 2 and evaluate on tasks 1–3; etc. (a) Catastrophic forgetting refers to the phenomenon in which performance on a previous task drops when trained on a new task. (b) Too little plasticity (e.g., due to too much regularization) refers to the phenomenon in which only the first task is learned. Adapted from Figure 2 of [Had+20].

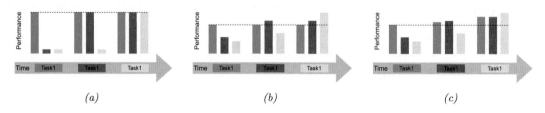

Figure 19.21: What success looks like for class incremental learning. We train on task 1 (blue) and evaluate on tasks 1–3 (blue, orange, yellow); we then train on task 2 and evaluate on tasks 1–3; etc. (a) No forgetting refers to the phenomenon in which performance on previous tasks does not degrade over time. (b) Forwards transfer refers to the phenomenon in which training on past tasks improves performance on future tasks beyond what would have been obtained by training from scratch. (c) Backwards transfer refers to the phenomenon in which training on future tasks improves performance on past tasks beyond what would have been obtained by training from scratch. Adapted from Figure 2 of [Had+20].

refers to the phenomenon in which performance on a previous task drops when trained on a new task (see Figure 19.20(a)). Another possible problem is that only the first task is learned, and the model does not adapt to new tasks (see Figure 19.20(b)).

If we avoid these problems, we should expect to see the performance profile in Figure 19.21(a), where performance of incremental training is equal to training on each task separately. However, we might hope to do better by virtue of the fact that we are training on multiple tasks, which are often assumed to be related. In particular, we might hope to see **forwards transfer**, in which training on past tasks improves performance on future tasks beyond what would have been obtained by training from scratch (see Figure 19.21(b)). Additionally, we might hope to see **backwards transfer**, in which training on future tasks improves performance on past tasks (see Figure 19.21(c)).

We can quantify the degree of transfer as follows, following [LPR17]. If R_{ij} is the performance on task j after it was trained on task i, R_j^{ind} is the performance on task j when trained just on j, and there are T tasks, then the amount of forwards transfer is

$$\text{FWT} = \frac{1}{T} \sum_{j=1}^{T} R_{j,j} - R_j^{\text{ind}} \tag{19.41}$$

and the amount of backwards transfer is

$$\text{BWT} = \frac{1}{T} \sum_{j=1}^{T} R_{T,j} - R_{j,j} \tag{19.42}$$

There are many methods that have been devised to overcome the problem of catastrophic forgetting, but we can group them into three main types. The first is **regularization methods**, which add a loss to preserve information that is relevant to old tasks. (For example, online Bayesian inference is of this type, since the posterior for the parameters is derived from the new data and the past prior; see e.g., the **elastic weight consolidation** method discussed in Section 17.5.1, or the **variational continual learning** method discussed in Supplementary Section 10.2). The second is **memory methods**, which rely on some kind of **experience replay** or **rehearsal** of past data (see e.g., [Hen+21]), or some kind of generative model of past data. The third is **architectural methods**, that add capacity to the network whenever a task boundary is encountered, such as a new class label (see e.g., [Rus+16]).

Of course, these techniques can be combined. For example, we can create a semi-parametric model, in which we store some past data (exemplars) while also learning parameters online in a Bayesian (regularized) way (see e.g., [Kur+20]). The "right" method depends, as usual, on what inductive bias you want to use, and want your computational budget is in terms of time and memory.

19.7.5 Online learning

The problem of **online learning** is similar to continual learning, except the loss metric is different, and we usually assume that learning and evaluation occur at each step. More precisely, we assume the data generating distribution, $p_t^*(\boldsymbol{x}, \boldsymbol{y}) = p(\boldsymbol{x}|\boldsymbol{\phi}_t)p(\boldsymbol{y}|\boldsymbol{x}, \boldsymbol{w}_t)$, evolves over time, as shown in Figure 19.22. At each step t nature generates a data sample, $(\boldsymbol{x}_t, \boldsymbol{y}_t) \sim p_t^*$. The agent sees $\boldsymbol{x}_t$ and is asked to predict $\boldsymbol{y}_t$ by computing the posterior predictive distribution

$$\hat{p}_{t|t-1} = p(\boldsymbol{y}|\boldsymbol{x}_t, \mathcal{D}_{1:t-1}) \tag{19.43}$$

where $\mathcal{D}_{1:t-1} = \{(\boldsymbol{x}_s, \boldsymbol{y}_s) : s = 1 : t-1\}$ is all past data. It then incurs a loss of

$$\mathcal{L}_t = \ell(\hat{p}_{t|t-1}, \boldsymbol{y}_t) \tag{19.44}$$

See Figure 19.22. This approach is called **prequential prediction** [DV99; GSR13].

In contrast to the continual learning scenarios studied above, the loss incurred at each step is what matters, rather than loss on a fixed test set. That is, we want to minimize $\mathcal{L} = \sum_{t=1}^{T} \mathcal{L}_t$. In the case of log-loss, this is equal to the (conditional) log marginal likelihood of the data, $\log p(\mathcal{D}) = \log p(\boldsymbol{y}_{1:T}|\boldsymbol{x}_{1:T})$. This can be used to compute the prequential minimum description length (MDL) of a model [BLH22], which is useful for model selection.

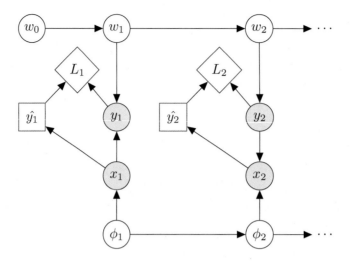

Figure 19.22: Online learning illustrated as an influence diagram (Section 34.2). Here $\hat{y}_t =$ argmax$_y$ $p(y|\boldsymbol{x}_t, \mathcal{D}_{1:t-1})$ is the action (MAP predicted output) at time t, and $L_t = \ell(y_t, \hat{y}_t)$ is the corresponding loss (utility) function. We then update the parameters of the model, $\boldsymbol{\theta}_t = (\boldsymbol{w}_t, \boldsymbol{\phi}_t)$, given the input and true output $(\boldsymbol{x}_t, \boldsymbol{y}_t)$. The parameters of the world model can change arbitrarily over time.

Another metric that is widely used is to compare the cumulative loss to the optimal value one could have obtained in hindsight. This yields a quantity called the **regret**:

$$\text{regret} = \sum_{t=1}^{T} \left[\ell(\hat{p}_{t|t-1}, \boldsymbol{y}_t) - \ell(\hat{p}_{t|T}, \boldsymbol{y}_t) \right] \tag{19.45}$$

where $\hat{p}_{t|t-1} = p(\boldsymbol{y}|\boldsymbol{x}_t, \mathcal{D}_{1:t-1})$ is the online prediction, and $\hat{p}_{t|T} = p(\boldsymbol{y}|\boldsymbol{x}_t, \mathcal{D}_{1:T})$ is the optimal estimate at the end of training. It is possible to convert bounds on regret, which are backwards looking, into bounds on risk (i.e., expected future loss), which are forwards looking. See [HT15] for details.

Online learning is very useful for decision and control problems, such as multi-armed bandits (Section 34.4) and reinforcement learning (see Chapter 35), where the agent "lives forever", and where there is no fixed training phase followed by a test phase. (See e.g., Section 17.5 where we discuss online Bayesian inference for neural networks.)

The previous continual learning scenarios can be derived as special cases of online learning, by defining a suitable sequence of distributions, and by requiring the agent to either train or test at each step on a suitable minibatch of data. (We leave the details of this mapping as an exercise to the reader.)

19.8   Adversarial examples

This section is coauthored with Justin Gilmer.

Figure 19.23: Example of an adversarial attack on an image classifier. Left column: original image which is correctly classified. Middle column: small amount of structured noise which is added to the input (magnitude of noise is magnified by 10×). Right column: new image, which is confidently misclassified as a "gibbon", even though it looks just like the original "panda" image. Here $\epsilon = 0.007$. From Figure 1 of [GSS15]. Used with kind permission of Ian Goodfellow.

In Section 19.2, we discussed what happens to a predictive model when the input distribution shifts for some reason. In this section, we consider the case where an adversary deliberately chooses inputs to minimize the performance of a predictive model. That is, suppose an input x is classified as belonging to class c. We then choose a new input x_{adv} which minimizes the probability of this label, subject to the constraint that x_{adv} is "perceptually similar" to the original input x. This gives rise to the following objective:

$$x_{\text{adv}} = \underset{x' \in \Delta(x)}{\operatorname{argmin}} \log p(y = c | x') \tag{19.46}$$

where $\Delta(x)$ is the set of images that are "similar" to x (we discuss different notions of similarity below).

Equation (19.46) is an example of an **adversarial attack**. We illustrate this in Figure 19.23. The input image x is on the left, and is predicted to be a panda with probability 57%. By adding a tiny amount of carefully chosen noise (shown in the middle) to the input, we generate the **adversarial image** x_{adv} on the right: this "looks like" the input, but is now classified as a gibbon with probability 99%.

The ability to create adversarial images was first noted in [Sze+14]. It is suprisingly easy to create such examples, which seems paradoxical, given the fact that modern classifiers seem to work so well on normal inputs, and the perturbed images "look" the same to humans. We explain this paradox in Section 19.8.5.

The existence of adversarial images also raises security concerns. For example, [Sha+16] showed they could force a face recognition system to misclassify person A as person B, merely by asking person A to wear a pair of sunglasses with a special pattern on them, and [Eyk+18] show that is possible to attach small "**adversarial stickers**" to traffic signs to classify stop signs as speed limit signs.

Below we briefly discuss how to create adversarial attacks, why they occur, and how we can try to defend against them. We focus on the case of deep neural nets for images, although it is important to note that many other kinds of models (including logistic regression and generative models) can also suffer from adversarial attacks. Furthermore, this is not restricted to the image domain, but occurs with many kinds of high dimensional inputs. For example, [Li+19] contains an audio attack and [Dal+04; Jia+19] contains a text attack. More details on adversarial examples can be found in e.g., [Wiy+19; Yua+19].

19.8.1   Whitebox (gradient-based) attacks

To create an adversarial example, we must find a "small" perturbation $\boldsymbol{\delta}$ to add to the input $\boldsymbol{x}$ to create $\boldsymbol{x}_{\text{adv}} = \boldsymbol{x} + \boldsymbol{\delta}$ so that $f(\boldsymbol{x}_{\text{adv}}) = y'$, where $f()$ is the classifier, and y' is the label we want to force the system to output. This is known as a **targeted attack**. Alternatively, we may just want to find a perturbation that causes the current predicted label to change from its current value to any other value, so that $f(\boldsymbol{x} + \boldsymbol{\delta}) \neq f(\boldsymbol{x})$, which is known as **untargeted attack**.

In general, we define the objective for the adversary as *maximizing* the following loss:

$$\boldsymbol{x}_{\text{adv}} = \underset{\boldsymbol{x}' \in \Delta(\boldsymbol{x})}{\text{argmax}}\, \mathcal{L}(\boldsymbol{x}', y; \boldsymbol{\theta}) \tag{19.47}$$

where y is the true label. For the untargeted case, we can define $\mathcal{L}(\boldsymbol{x}', y; \boldsymbol{\theta}) = -\log p(y|\boldsymbol{x}')$, so we minimize the probability of the true label; and for the targeted case, we can define $\mathcal{L}(\boldsymbol{x}', y; \boldsymbol{\theta}) = \log p(y'|\boldsymbol{x}')$, where we maximize the probability of the desired label $y' \neq y$.

To define what we mean by "small" perturbation, we impose the constraint that $\boldsymbol{x}_{\text{adv}} \in \Delta(\boldsymbol{x})$, which is the set of "perceptually similar" images to the input $\boldsymbol{x}$. Most of the literature has focused on a simplistic setting in which the adversary is restricted to making bounded l_p perturbations of a clean input $\boldsymbol{x}$, that is

$$\Delta(\boldsymbol{x}) = \{\boldsymbol{x}' : ||\boldsymbol{x}' - \boldsymbol{x}||_p < \epsilon\} \tag{19.48}$$

Typically people assume $p = 1$ or $p = 0$. We will discuss more realistic threat models in Section 19.8.3.

In this section, we assume that the attacker knows the model parameters $\boldsymbol{\theta}$; this is called a **whitebox attack**, and lets us use gradient based optimization methods. We relax this assumption in Section 19.8.2.)

To solve the optimization problem in Equation (19.47), we can use any kind of constrained optimization method. In [Sze+14] they used bound-constrained BFGS. [GSS15] proposed the more efficient **fast gradient sign** (**FGS**) method, which performs iterative updates of the form

$$\boldsymbol{x}_{t+1} = \boldsymbol{x}_t + \boldsymbol{\delta}_t \tag{19.49}$$

$$\boldsymbol{\delta}_t = \epsilon\, \text{sign}(\nabla_{\boldsymbol{x}} \log p(y'|\boldsymbol{x}, \boldsymbol{\theta})|_{\boldsymbol{x}_t}) \tag{19.50}$$

where $\epsilon > 0$ is a small learning rate. (Note that this gradient is with respect to the input pixels, not the model parameters.) Figure 19.23 gives an example of this process.

More recently, [Mad+18] proposed the more powerful **projected gradient descent** (**PGD**) attack; this can be thought of as an iterated version of FGS. There is no "best" variant of PGD for solving 19.47. Instead, what matters more is the implementation details, e.g. how many steps are used, the step size, and the exact form of the loss. To avoid local minima, we may use random restarts, choosing random points in the constraint space Δ to initialize the optimization. The algorithm should be carefully tuned to the specific problem, and the loss should be monitored to check for optimization issues. For best practices, see [Car+19].

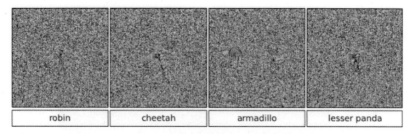

Figure 19.24: Images that look like random noise but which cause the CNN to confidently predict a specific class. From Figure 1 of [NYC15]. Used with kind permission of Jeff Clune.

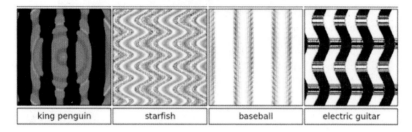

Figure 19.25: Synthetic images that cause the CNN to confidently predict a specific class. From Figure 1 of [NYC15]. Used with kind permission of Jeff Clune.

19.8.2 Blackbox (gradient-free) attacks

In this section, we no longer assume that the adversary knows the parameters $\boldsymbol{\theta}$ of the predictive model f. This is known as a **black box attack**. In such cases, we must use derivative-free optimization (DFO) methods (see Section 6.7).

Evolutionary algorithms (EA) are one class of DFO solvers. These were used in [NYC15] to create blackbox attacks. Figure 19.24 shows some images that were generated by applying an EA to a random noise image. These are known as **fooling images**, as opposed to adversarial images, since they are not visually realistic. Figure 19.25 shows some fooling images that were generated by applying EA to the parameters of a compositional pattern-producing network (CPPN) [Sta07].[6] By suitably perturbing the CPPN parameters, it is possible to generate structured images with high fitness (classifier score), but which do not look like natural images [Aue12].

In [SVK19], they used differential evolution to attack images by modifying a single pixel. This is equivalent to bounding the ℓ_0 norm of the perturbation, so that $||\boldsymbol{x}_{\text{adv}} - \boldsymbol{x}||_0 = 1$.

In [Pap+17], they learned a differentiable surrogate model of the blackbox, by just querying its predictions y for different inputs $\boldsymbol{x}$. They then used gradient-based methods to generate adversarial attacks on their surrogate model, and then showed that these attacks transferred to the real model. In this way, they were able to attack various the image classification APIs of various cloud service

---

6. A CPPN is a set of elementary functions (such as linear, sine, sigmoid, and Gaussian) which can be composed in order to specify the mapping from each coordinate to the desired color value. CPPN was originally developed as a way to encode abstract properties such as symmetry and repetition, which are often seen during biological development.

Figure 19.26: An adversarially modified image to evade spam detectors. The image is constructed from scratch, and does not involve applying a small perturbation to any given image. This is an illustrative example of how large the space of possible adversarial inputs Δ can be when the attacker has full control over the input. From [Big+11]. Used with kind permission of Battista Biggio.

providers, including Google, Amazon, and MetaMind.

19.8.3   Real world adversarial attacks

Typically, the space of possible adversarial inputs Δ can be quite large, and will be difficult to exactly define mathematically as it will depend on semantics of the input based on the attacker's goals [BR18]. (The set of variations Δ that we want the model to be invariant to is called the **threat model**.)

Consider for example of the content constrained threat model discussed in [Gil+18a]. One instance of this threat model involves image spam, where the attacker wishes to upload an image attachment in an email that will not be classified as spam by a detection model. In this case Δ is incredibly large as it consists of all possible images which contain some semantic concept the attacker wishes to upload (in this case an advertisement). To explore Δ, spammers can utilize different fonts, word orientations or add random objects to the background as is the case of the adversarial example in Figure 19.26 (see [Big+11] for more examples). Of course, optimization based methods may still be used here to explore parts of Δ. However, in practice it may be preferable to design an adversarial input by hand as this can be significantly easier to execute with only limited-query black-box access to the underlying classifier.

19.8.4   Defenses based on robust optimization

As discussed in Section 19.8.3, securing a system against adversarial inputs in more general threat models seems extraordinarily difficult, due to the vast space of possible adversarial inputs Δ. However, there is a line of research focused on producing models which are invariant to perturbations within a small constraint set $\Delta(\boldsymbol{x})$, with a focus on l_p-robustness where $\Delta(\boldsymbol{x}) = \{\boldsymbol{x}' : ||\boldsymbol{x} - \boldsymbol{x}'||_p < \epsilon\}$. Although solving this toy threat model has little application to security settings, enforcing smoothness priors has in some cases improved robustness to random image corruptions [SHS], led to models which transfer better [Sal+20], and has biased models towards different features in the data [Yin+19a].

Perhaps the most straightforward method for improving l_p-robustness is to directly optimize for it through **robust optimization** [BTEGN09], also known as **adversarial training** [GSS15]. We define the **adversarial risk** to be

$$\min_\theta \mathbb{E}_{(\boldsymbol{x},\boldsymbol{y})\sim p(\boldsymbol{x},\boldsymbol{y})} \left[\max_{\boldsymbol{x}'\in\Delta(\boldsymbol{x})} L(\boldsymbol{x}',\boldsymbol{y};\theta) \right] \tag{19.51}$$

The min max formulation in equation 19.51 poses unique challenges from an optimization perspective — it requires solving both the non-concave inner maximazation and the non-convex outer minimization problems. Even worse, the inner max is NP-hard to solve in general [Kat+17]. However, in practice it may be sufficient to compute the gradient of the outer objective $\nabla_\theta L(\boldsymbol{x}_{\mathrm{adv}},\boldsymbol{y},;\theta)$ at an approximately maximal point in the inner problem $\boldsymbol{x}_{\mathrm{adv}} \approx \mathrm{argmax}_{\boldsymbol{x}} L(\boldsymbol{x}_{\mathrm{adv}},\boldsymbol{y};\theta)$ [Mad+18]. Currently, best practice is to approximate the inner problem using a few steps of PGD.

Other methods seek to **certify** that a model is robust within a given region $\Delta(x)$. One method for certification uses randomized smoothing [CRK19] — a technique for converting a model robust to random noise into a model which is provably robust to bounded worst-case perturbations in the l_2-metric. Another class of methods applies specifically for networks with ReLU activations, leveraging the property that the model is locally linear, and that certifying in region defined by linear constraints reduces to solving a series of linear programs, for which standard solvers can be applied [WK18].

19.8.5 Why models have adversarial examples

The existence of adversarial inputs is paradoxical, since modern classifiers seem to do so well on normal inputs. However, the existence of adversarial examples is a natural consequence of the general lack of robustness to distribution shift discussed in Section 19.2. To see this, suppose a model's accuracy drops on some shifted distribution of inputs $p_{\mathrm{te}}(\boldsymbol{x})$ that differs from the training distribution $p_{\mathrm{tr}}(\boldsymbol{x})$; in this case, the model will necessarily be vunerable to an adversarial attack: if errors exist, there must be a nearest such error. Furthermore, if the input distribution is high dimensional, then we should expect the nearest error to be significantly closer than errors which are sampled randomly from some out-of-distribution $p_{\mathrm{te}}(\boldsymbol{x})$.

A cartoon illustration of what is going on is shown in Figure 19.27a, where $\boldsymbol{x}_0$ is the clean input image, B is an image corrupted by Gaussian noise, and A is an adversarial image. If we assume a linear decision boundary, then the error set E is a half space a certain distance from $\boldsymbol{x}_0$. We can relate the distance to the decision boundary $d(\boldsymbol{x}_0, E)$ with the error rate in noise at some input $\boldsymbol{x}_0$, denoted by $\mu = \mathbb{P}_{\delta\sim N(0,\sigma I)}[\boldsymbol{x}_0 + \delta \in E]$. With a linear decision boundary the relationship between these two quantities is determined by

$$d(\boldsymbol{x}_0, E) = -\sigma \Phi^{-1}(\mu) \tag{19.52}$$

where Φ^{-1} denotes the inverse cdf of the gaussian distribution. When the input dimension is large, this distance will be significantly smaller than the distance to a randomly sampled noisy image $\boldsymbol{x}_0 + \delta$ for $\delta \sim N(0, \sigma I)$, as the noise term will with high propbability have norm $||\delta||_2 \approx \sigma\sqrt{d}$. As a concrete example consider the ImageNet dataset, where $d = 224 \times 224 \times 3$ and suppose we set $\sigma = .2$.

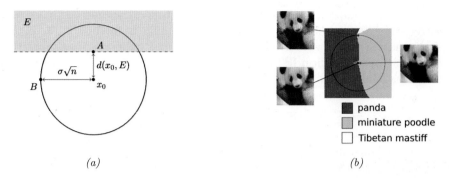

(a)   (b)

Figure 19.27: (a) When the input dimension n is large and the decision boundary is locally linear, even a small error rate in random noise will imply the existence of small adversarial perturbations. Here, $d(\boldsymbol{x}_0, E)$ denotes the distance from a clean input $\boldsymbol{x}_0$ to an adversarial example (A) while the distance from $\boldsymbol{x}_0$ to a random sample $N(0; \sigma^2 I$ (B) will be approximately $\sigma\sqrt{n}$. As $n \to \infty$ the ratio of $d(x_0, A)$ to $d(\boldsymbol{x}_0, B)$ goes to 0. (b) A 2d slice of the InceptionV3 decision boundary through three points: a clean image (black), an adversarial example (red), and an error in random noise (blue). The adversarial example and the error in noise lie in the same region of the error set which is misclassified as "miniature poodle", which closely resembles a halfspace as in a. Used with kind permission of Justin Gilmer.

Then if the error rate in noise is just $\mu = .01$, equation 19.52 will imply that $d(\boldsymbol{x}_0, E) = .5$. Thus the distance to an adversarial example will be more than 100 times closer than the distance to a typical noisy images, which will be $\sigma\sqrt{d} \approx 77.6$. This phenomenon of small volume error sets being close to most points in a data distribution $p(\boldsymbol{x})$ is called **concentration of measure**, and is a property common among many high dimensional data distributions [MDM19; Gil+18b].

In summary, although the existence of adversarial examples is often discussed as an unexpected phenomenon, there is nothing special about the existence of worst-case errors for ML classifiers — they will always exist as long as errors exist.

PART IV

Generation

20 Generative models: an overview

20.1 Introduction

A **generative model** is a joint probability distribution $p(\boldsymbol{x})$, for $\boldsymbol{x} \in \mathcal{X}$. In some cases, the model may be conditioned on inputs or covariates $\boldsymbol{c} \in \mathcal{C}$, which gives rise to a **conditional generative model** of the form $p(\boldsymbol{x}|\boldsymbol{c})$.

There are many kinds of generative model. We give a brief summary in Section 20.2, and go into more detail in subsequent chapters. See also [Tom22] for a recent book on this topic that goes into more depth.

20.2 Types of generative model

There are many kinds of generative model, some of which we list in Table 20.1. At a high level, we can distinguish between **deep generative models** (DGM) — which use deep neural network to learn a complex mapping from a single latent vector $\boldsymbol{z}$ to the observed data $\boldsymbol{x}$ — and more "classical" **probabilistic graphical models** (PGM), that map a set of interconnected latent variables $\boldsymbol{z}_1, \ldots, \boldsymbol{z}_L$ to the observed variables $\boldsymbol{x}_1, \ldots, \boldsymbol{x}_D$ using simpler, often linear, mappings. Of course, many hybrids are possible. For example, PGMs can use neural networks, and DGMs can use structured state spaces. We discuss PGMs in general terms in Chapter 4, and give examples in Chapter 28, Chapter 29, Chapter 30. In this part of the book, we mostly focus on DGMs.

The main kinds of DGM are: **variational autoencoders** (**VAE**), **autoregressive models** (**ARM**) models, **normalizing flows**, **diffusion models**, **energy based models** (**EBM**), and **generative adversarial networks** (**GAN**). We can categorize these models in terms of the following criteria (see Figure 20.1 for a visual summary):

- Density: does the model support pointwise evaluation of the probability density function $p(\boldsymbol{x})$, and if so, is this fast or slow, exact, approximate or a bound, etc? For **implicit models**, such as GANs, there is no well-defined density $p(\boldsymbol{x})$. For other models, we can only compute a lower bound on the density (VAEs), or an approximation to the density (EBMs, UPGMs).

- Sampling: does the model support generating new samples, $\boldsymbol{x} \sim p(\boldsymbol{x})$, and if so, is this fast or slow, exact or approximate? Directed PGMs, VAEs, and GANs all support fast sampling. However, undirected PGMs, EBMs, ARM, diffusion, and flows are slow for sampling.

- Training: what kind of method is used for parameter estimation? For some models (such as AR, flows and directed PGMs), we can perform exact maximum likelihood estimation (MLE), although

Model	Chapter	Density	Sampling	Training	Latents	Architecture
PGM-D	Section 4.2	Exact, fast	Fast	MLE	Optional	Sparse DAG
PGM-U	Section 4.3	Approx, slow	Slow	MLE-A	Optional	Sparse graph
VAE	Chapter 21	LB, fast	Fast	MLE-LB	$\mathbb{R}^L$	Encoder-Decoder
ARM	Chapter 22	Exact, fast	Slow	MLE	None	Sequential
Flows	Chapter 23	Exact, slow/fast	Slow	MLE	$\mathbb{R}^D$	Invertible
EBM	Chapter 24	Approx, slow	Slow	MLE-A	Optional	Discriminative
Diffusion	Chapter 25	LB	Slow	MLE-LB	$\mathbb{R}^D$	Encoder-Decoder
GAN	Chapter 26	NA	Fast	Min-max	$\mathbb{R}^L$	Generator-Discriminator

Table 20.1: *Characteristics of common kinds of generative model. Here D is the dimensionality of the observed $\boldsymbol{x}$, and L is the dimensionality of the latent $\boldsymbol{z}$, if present. (We usually assume $L \ll D$, although overcomplete representations can have $L \gg D$.) Abbreviations: Approx = approximate, ARM = autoregressive model, EBM = energy based model, GAN = generative adversarial network, MLE = maximum likelihood estimation, MLE-A = MLE (approximate), MLE-LB = MLE (lower bound), NA = not available, PGM = probabilistic graphical model, PGM-D = directed PGM, PGM-U = undirected PGM, VAE = variational autoencoder.*

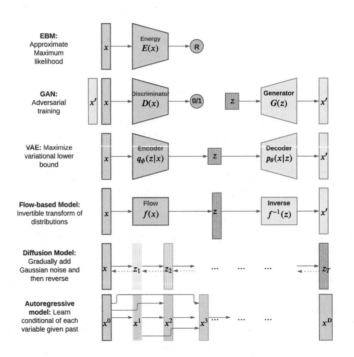

Figure 20.1: *Summary of various kinds of deep generative model. Here $\boldsymbol{x}$ is the observed data, $\boldsymbol{z}$ is the latent code, and $\boldsymbol{x}'$ is a sample from the model. AR models do not have a latent code $\boldsymbol{z}$. For diffusion models and flow models, the size of $\boldsymbol{z}$ is the same as $\boldsymbol{x}$. For AR models, x^d is the d'th dimension of $\boldsymbol{x}$. R represents real-valued output, 0/1 represents binary output. Adapted from Figure 1 of [Wen21].*

the objective is usually non-convex, so we can only reach a local optimum. For other models, we cannot tractably compute the likelihood. In the case of VAEs, we maximize a lower bound on the likelihood; in the case of EBMs and UGMs, we maximize an approximation to the likelihood. For GANs we have to use min-max training, which can be unstable, and there is no clear objective function to monitor.

- Latents: does the model use use a latent vector z to generate x or not, and if so, is it the same size as x or is it a potentially compressed representation? For example, ARMs do not use latents; flows and diffusion use latents, but they are not compressed.[1] Graphical models, including EBMs, may or may not use latents.

- Architecture: what kind of neural network should we use, and are there restrictions? For flows, we are restricted to using invertible neural networks where each layer has a tractable Jacobian. For EBMs, we can use any model we like. The other models have different restrictions.

20.3 Goals of generative modeling

There are several different kinds of tasks that we can use generative models for, as we discuss below.

20.3.1 Generating data

One of the main goals of generative models is to generate (create) new data samples. This is sometimes called **generative AI** (see e.g., [GBGM23] for a recent survey). For example, if we fit a model $p(x)$ to images of faces, we can sample new faces from it, as illustrated in Figure 25.10.[2] Similar methods can be used to create samples of text, audio, etc. When this technology is abused to make fake content, they are called **deep fakes** (see e.g., [Ngu+19]). Genrative models can also be used to create **synthetic data** for training discriminative models (see e.g., [Wil+20; Jor+22]).

To control what is generated, it is useful to use a **conditional generative model** of the form $p(x|c)$. Here are some examples:

- c = text prompt, x = image. This is a **text-to-image** model (see Figure 20.2, Figure 20.3 and Figure 22.6 for examples).

- c = image, x = text. This is an **image-to-text** model, which is useful for **image captioning**.

- c = image, x = image. This is an **image-to-image** model, and can be used for image colorization, inpainting, uncropping, JPEG artefact restoration, etc. See Figure 20.4 for examples.

- c = sequence of sounds, x = sequence of words. This is a **speech-to-text** model, which is useful for **automatic speech recognition (ASR)**.

- c = sequence of English words, x = sequence of French words. This is a **sequence-to-sequence** model, which is useful for **machine translation**.

---

1. Flow models define a latent vector z that has the same size as x, although the internal deterministic computation may use vectors that are larger or smaller than the input (see e.g., the DenseFlow paper [GGS21]).
2. These images were made with a technique called score-based generative modeling (Section 25.3), although similar results can be obtained using many other techniques. See for example https://this-person-does-not-exist.com/en which shows results from a GAN model (Chapter 26).

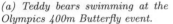

(a) Teddy bears swimming at the Olympics 400m Butterfly event. (b) A cute corgi lives in a house made out of sushi. (c) A cute sloth holding a small treasure chest. A bright golden glow is coming from the chest.

Figure 20.2: Some 1024×1024 images generated from text prompts by the Imagen diffusion model (Section 25.6.4). From Figure 1 of [Sah+22]. Used with kind permission of William Chan.

A portrait photo of a kangaroo wearing an orange hoodie and blue sunglasses standing on the grass in front of the Sydney Opera House holding a sign on the chest that says Welcome Friends!

Figure 20.3: Some images generated from the Parti transformer model (Section 22.4.2) in response to a text prompt. We show results from models of increasing size (350M, 750M, 3B, 20B). Multiple samples are generated, and the highest ranked one is shown. From Figure 10 of [Yu+22]. Used with kind permission of Jiahui Yu.

- c = initial prompt, x = continuation of the text. This is another sequence-to-sequence model, which is useful for automatic **text generation** (see Figure 22.5 for an example).

Note that, in the conditional case, we sometimes denote the inputs by x and the outputs by y. In this case the model has the familiar form $p(y|x)$. In the special case that y denotes a low dimensional quantity, such as a integer class label, $y \in \{1, \ldots, C\}$, we get a predictive (discriminative) model. The main difference beween a discriminative model and a conditional generative model is this: in a discriminative model, we assume there is one correct output, whereas in a conditional generative model, we assume there may be multiple correct outputs. This makes it harder to evaluate generative models, as we discuss in Section 20.4.

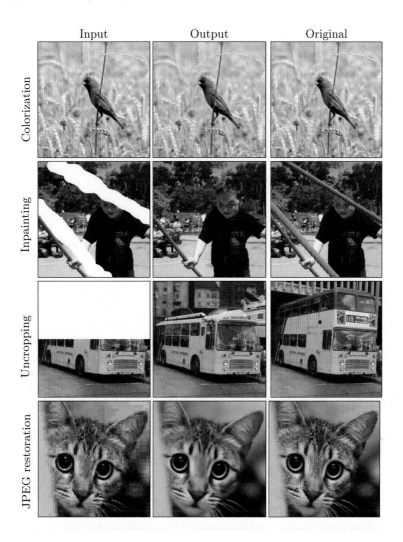

Figure 20.4: Illustration of some image-to-image tasks using the Palette conditional diffusion model (Section 25.6.4). From Figure 1 of [Sah+21]. Used with kind permission of Chitwan Saharia.

20.3.2 Density estimation

The task of **density estimation** refers to evaluating the probablity of an observed data vector, i.e., computing $p(\boldsymbol{x})$. This can be useful for outlier detection (Section 19.3.2), data compression (Section 5.4), generative classifiers, model comparison, etc.

A simple approach to this problem, which works in low dimensions, is to use **kernel density**

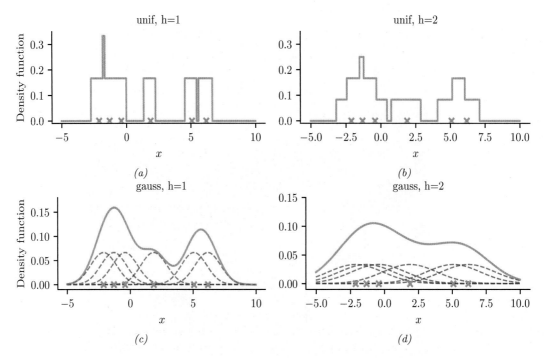

Figure 20.5: A nonparametric (Parzen) density estimator in 1d estimated from 6 datapoints, denoted by x. Top row: uniform kernel. Bottom row: Gaussian kernel. Left column: bandwidth parameter $h = 1$. Right column: bandwidth parameter $h = 2$. Adapted from http://en.wikipedia.org/wiki/Kernel_density_estimation. Generated by parzen_window_demo.ipynb.

estimation or **KDE**, which has the form

$$p(\boldsymbol{x}|\mathcal{D}) = \frac{1}{N} \sum_{n=1}^{N} \mathcal{K}_h\left(\boldsymbol{x} - \boldsymbol{x}_n\right) \tag{20.1}$$

Here $\mathcal{D} = \{\boldsymbol{x}_1, \ldots, \boldsymbol{x}_N\}$ is the data, and $\mathcal{K}_h$ is a density kernel with **bandwidth** h, which is a function $\mathcal{K} : \mathbb{R} \to \mathbb{R}_+$ such that $\int \mathcal{K}(x)dx = 1$ and $\int x\mathcal{K}(x)dx = 0$. We give a 1d example of this in Figure 20.5: in the top row, we use a uniform (boxcar) kernel, and in the bottom row, we use a Gaussian kernel.

In higher dimensions, KDE suffers from the **curse of dimensionality** (see e.g., [AHK01]), and we need to use parametric density models $p_{\boldsymbol{\theta}}(\boldsymbol{x})$ of some kind.

20.3.3   Imputation

The task of **imputation** refers to "filling in" missing values of a data vector or data matrix. For example, suppose $\mathbf{X}$ is an $N \times D$ matrix of data (think of a spreadsheet) in which some entries, call them $\mathbf{X}_m$, may be missing, while the rest, $\mathbf{X}_o$, are observed. A simple way to fill in the missing data is to use the mean value of each feature, $\mathbb{E}[x_d]$; this is called **mean value imputation**, and is

Data sample	Variables				Missing values replaced by means		
	A	B	C		A	B	C
1	6	6	NA		2	6	7.5
2	NA	6	0		9	6	0
3	NA	6	NA		9	6	7.5
4	10	10	10		10	10	10
5	10	10	10		10	10	10
6	10	10	10		10	10	10
Average	9	8	7.5		9	8	7.5

Figure 20.6: *Missing data imputation using the mean of each column.*

illustrated in Figure 20.6. However, this ignores dependencies between the variables within each row, and does not return any measure of uncertainty.

We can generalize this by fitting a generative model to the observed data, $p(\mathbf{X}_o)$, and then computing samples from $p(\mathbf{X}_m|\mathbf{X}_o)$. This is called **multiple imputation**. A generative model can be used to fill in more complex data types, such as **in-painting** occluded pixels in an image (see Figure 20.4).

See Section 3.11 for a more general discussion of missing data.

20.3.4 Structure discovery

Some kinds of generative models have latent variables z, which are assumed to be the "causes" that generated the observed data x. We can use Bayes' rule to invert the model to compute $p(z|x) \propto p(z)p(x|z)$. This can be useful for discovering latent, low-dimensional patterns in the data.

For example, suppose we perturb various proteins in a cell and measure the resulting phosphorylation state using a technique known as flow cytometry, as in [Sac+05]. An example of such a dataset is shown in Figure 20.7(a). Each row represents a data sample $x_n \sim p(\cdot|a_n, z)$, where $x \in \mathbb{R}^{11}$ is a vector of outputs (phosphorylations), $a \in \{0, 1\}^6$ is a vector of input actions (perturbations) and z is the unknown cellular signaling network structure. We can infer the graph structure $p(z|\mathcal{D})$ using graphical model structure learning techhniques (see Section 30.3). In particular, we can use the dynamic programming method described in [EM07] to get the result is shown in Figure 20.7(b). Here we plot the median graph, which includes all edges for which $p(z_{ij} = 1|\mathcal{D}) > 0.5$. (For a more recent approach to this problem, see e.g., [Bro+20b].)

20.3.5 Latent space interpolation

One of the most interesting abilities of certain latent variable models is the ability to generate samples that have certain desired properties by interpolating between existing datapoints in latent space. To explain how this works, let x_1 and x_2 be two inputs (e.g., images), and let $z_1 = e(x_1)$ and $z_2 = e(x_2)$ be their latent encodings. (The method used for computing these will depend on the

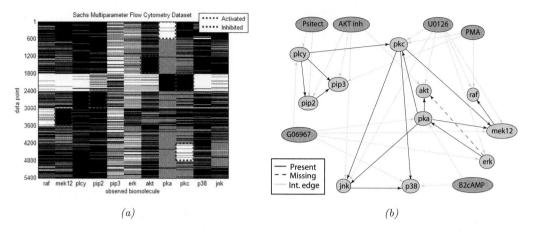

(a)   (b)

Figure 20.7: (a) A design matrix consisting of 5400 datapoints (rows) measuring the state (using flow cytometry) of 11 proteins (columns) under different experimental conditions. The data has been discretized into 3 states: low (black), medium (grey), and high (white). Some proteins were explicitly controlled using activating or inhibiting chemicals. (b) A directed graphical model representing dependencies between various proteins (blue circles) and various experimental interventions (pink ovals), which was inferred from this data. We plot all edges for which $p(G_{ij} = 1|\mathcal{D}) > 0.5$. Dotted edges are believed to exist in nature but were not discovered by the algorithm (1 false negative). Solid edges are true positives. The light colored edges represent the effects of intervention. From Figure 6d of [EM07].

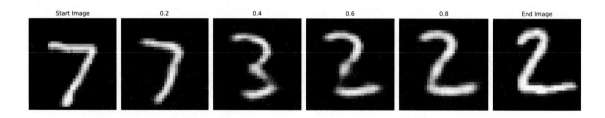

Figure 20.8: Interpolation between two MNIST images in the latent space of a β-VAE (with β = 0.5). Generated by mnist_vae_ae_comparison.ipynb.

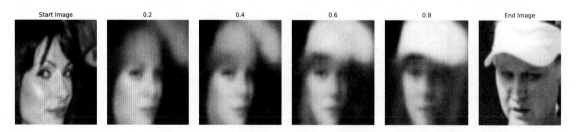

Figure 20.9: Interpolation between two CelebA images in the latent space of a β-VAE (with β = 0.5). Generated by celeba_vae_ae_comparison.ipynb.

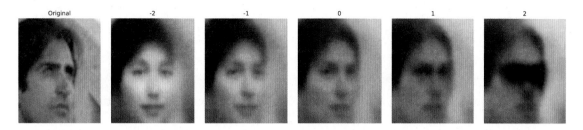

Figure 20.10: *Arithmetic in the latent space of a β-VAE (with β = 0.5). The first column is an input image, with embedding z. Subsequent columns show the decoding of $z + s\Delta$, where $s \in \{-2, -1, 0, 1, 2\}$ and $\Delta = \overline{z}^+ - \overline{z}^-$ is the difference in the average embeddings of images with or without a certain attribute (here, wearing sunglasses). Generated by* celeba_vae_ae_comparison.ipynb.

type of model; we discuss the details in later chapters.) We can regard z_1 and z_2 as two "anchors" in latent space. We can now generate new images that interpolate between these points by computing $z = \lambda z_1 + (1 - \lambda)z_2$, where $0 \le \lambda \le 1$, and then decoding by computing $x' = d(z)$, where $d()$ is the decoder. This is called **latent space interpolation**, and will generate data that combines semantic features from both x_1 and x_2. (The justification for taking a linear interpolation is that the learned manifold often has approximately zero curvature, as shown in [SKTF18]. However, sometimes it is better to use nonlinear interpolation [Whi16; MB21; Fad+20].)

We can see an example of this process in Figure 20.8, where we use a β-VAE model (Section 21.3.1) fit to the MNIST dataset. We see that the model is able to produce plausible interpolations between the digit 7 and the digit 2. As a more interesting example, we can fit a β-VAE to the **CelebA** dataset [Liu+15].[3] The results are shown in Figure 20.9, and look reasonable. (We can get much better quality if we use a larger model trained on more data for a longer amount of time.)

It is also possible to perform interpolation in the latent space of text models, as illustrated in Figure 21.7.

20.3.6 Latent space arithmetic

In some cases, we can go beyond interpolation, and can perform **latent space arithmetic**, in which we can increase or decrease the amount of a desired "semantic factor of variation". This was first shown in the **word2vec** model [Mik+13], but it also is possible in other latent variable models. For example, consider our VAE model fit to the CelebA dataset, which has faces of celebrities and some corresponding attributes. Let $\mathbf{X}_i^+$ be a set of images which have attribute i, and $\mathbf{X}_i^-$ be a set of images which do not have this attribute. Let $\mathbf{Z}_i^+$ and $\mathbf{Z}_i^-$ be the corresponding embeddings, and $\overline{z}_i^+$ and $\overline{z}_i^-$ be the average of these embeddings. We define the offset vector as $\Delta_i = \overline{z}_i^+ - \overline{z}_i^-$. If we add some positive multiple of Δ_i to a new point z, we increase the amount of the attribute i; if we subtract some multiple of Δ_i, we decrease the amount of the attribute i [Whi16].

We give an example of this in Figure 20.10. We consider the attribute of wearing sunglasses. The j'th reconstruction is computed using $\hat{x}_j = d(z + s_j\Delta)$, where $z = e(x)$ is the encoding of the original image, and s_j is a scale factor. When $s_j > 0$ we add sunglasses to the face. When $s_j < 0$ we

---

3. CelebA contains about 200k images of famous celebrities. The images are also annotated with 40 attributes. We reduce the resolution of the images to 64×64, as is conventional.

remove sunglasses; but this also has the side effect of making the face look younger and more female, possibly a result of dataset bias.

20.3.7   Generative design

Another interesting use case for (deep) generative models is **generative design**, in which we use the model to generate candidate objects, such as molecules, which have desired properties (see e.g., [RNA22]). One approach is to fit a VAE to unlabeled samples, and then to perform Bayesian optimization (Section 6.6) in its latent space, as discussed in Section 21.3.5.2.

20.3.8   Model-based reinforcement learning

We discuss reinforcement learning (RL) in Chapter 35. The main success stories of RL to date have been in computer games, where simulators exist and data is abundant. However, in other areas, such as robotics, data is expensive to acquire. In this case, it can be useful to learn a generative "**world model**", so the agent can do planning and learning "in it's head". See Section 35.4 for more details.

20.3.9   Representation learning

Representation learning refers to learning (possibly uninterpretable) latent factors z that generate the observed data x. The primary goal is for these features to be used in "**downstream**" supervised tasks. This is discussed in Chapter 32.

20.3.10   Data compression

Models which can assign high probability to frequently occuring data vectors (e.g., images, sentences), and low probability to rare vectors, can be used for **data compression**, since we can assign shorter codes to the more common items. Indeed, the optimal coding length for a vector x from some stochastic source $p(x)$ is $l(x) = -\log p(x)$, as proved by Shannon. See Section 5.4 for details.

20.4   Evaluating generative models

This section is written by Mihaela Rosca, Shakir Mohamed, and Balaji Lakshminarayanan.

Evaluating generative models requires metrics which capture

- **sample quality** — are samples generated by the model a part of the data distribution?

- **sample diversity** — are samples from the model distribution capturing all modes of the data distribution?

- **generalization** — is the model generalizing beyond the training data?

There is no known metric which meets all these requirements, but various metrics have been proposed to capture different aspects of the learned distribution, some of which we discuss below.

20.4.1 Likelihood-based evaluation

A standard way to measure how close a model q is to a true distribution p is in terms of the KL divergence (Section 5.1):

$$D_{\text{KL}}\left(p \parallel q\right) = \int p(\boldsymbol{x}) \log \frac{p(\boldsymbol{x})}{q(\boldsymbol{x})} = -\mathbb{H}\left(p\right) + \mathbb{H}_{ce}\left(p, q\right) \tag{20.2}$$

where $\mathbb{H}\left(p\right)$ is a constant, and $\mathbb{H}_{ce}\left(p, q\right)$ is the cross entropy. If we approximate $p(\boldsymbol{x})$ by the empirical distribution, we can evaluate the cross entropy in terms of the empirical **negative log likelihood** on the dataset:

$$\text{NLL} = -\frac{1}{N} \sum_{n=1}^{N} \log q(\boldsymbol{x}_n) \tag{20.3}$$

Usually we care about negative log likelihood on a held-out test set.[4]

20.4.1.1 Computing the log-likelihood

For models of discrete data, such as language models, it is easy to compute the (negative) log likelihood. However, it is common to measure performance using a quantity called **perplexity**, which is defined as 2^H, where $H = \text{NLL}$ is the cross entropy or negative log likelihood.

For image and audio models, one complication is that the model is usually a continuous distribution $p(\boldsymbol{x}) \geq 0$ but the data is usually discrete (e.g., $\boldsymbol{x} \in \{0, \ldots, 255\}^D$ if we use one byte per pixel). Consequently the average log likelihood can be arbitrary large, since the pdf can be bigger than 1. To avoid this it is standard pratice to use **uniform dequantization** [TOB16], in which we add uniform random noise to the discrete data, and then treat it as continuous-valued data. This gives a lower bound on the average log likelihood of the discrete model on the original data.

To see this, let $\boldsymbol{z}$ be a continuous latent variable, and $\boldsymbol{x}$ be a vector of binary observations computed by rounding, so $p(\boldsymbol{x}|\boldsymbol{z}) = \delta(\boldsymbol{x} - \text{round}(\boldsymbol{z}))$, computed elementwise. We have $p(\boldsymbol{x}) = \int p(\boldsymbol{x}|\boldsymbol{z})p(\boldsymbol{z})d\boldsymbol{z}$. Let $q(\boldsymbol{z}|\boldsymbol{x})$ be a probabilistic inverse of $\boldsymbol{x}$, that is, it has support only on values where $p(\boldsymbol{x}|\boldsymbol{z}) = 1$. In this case, Jensen's inequality gives

$$\log p(\boldsymbol{x}) \geq \mathbb{E}_{q(\boldsymbol{z}|\boldsymbol{x})} \left[\log p(\boldsymbol{x}|\boldsymbol{z}) + \log p(\boldsymbol{z}) - \log q(\boldsymbol{z}|\boldsymbol{x})\right] \tag{20.4}$$

$$= \mathbb{E}_{q(\boldsymbol{z}|\boldsymbol{x})} \left[\log p(\boldsymbol{z}) - \log q(\boldsymbol{z}|\boldsymbol{x})\right] \tag{20.5}$$

Thus if we model the density of $\boldsymbol{z} \sim q(\boldsymbol{z}|\boldsymbol{x})$, which is a dequantized version of $\boldsymbol{x}$, we will get a lower bound on $p(\boldsymbol{x})$.

20.4.1.2 Likelihood can be hard to compute

Unfortunately, for many models, computing the likelihood can be computationally expensive, since it requires knowing the normalization constant of the probability model. One solution is to use variational inference (Chapter 10), which provides a way to efficiently compute lower (and sometimes

---

4. In some applications, we report **bits per dimension**, which is the NLL using log base 2, divided by the dimensionality of $\boldsymbol{x}$. (To compute this metric, recall that $\log_2 L = \frac{\log_e L}{\log_e 2}$.)

upper) bounds on the log likelihood. Another solution is to use annealed importance sampling (Section 11.5.4.1), which provides a way to estimate the log likelihood using Monte Carlo sampling. However, in the case of implicit generative models, such as GANs (Chapter 26), the likelihood is not even defined, so we need to find evaluation metrics that do not rely on likelihood.

20.4.1.3   Likelihood is not related to sample quality

A more subtle concern with likelihood is that it is often uncorrelated with the perceptual quality of the samples, at least for real-valued data, such as images and sound. In particular, a model can have great log-likelihood but create poor samples and vice versa.

To see why a model can have good likelihoods but create bad samples, consider the following argument from [TOB16]. Suppose q_0 is a density model for D-dimensional data $\boldsymbol{x}$ which performs arbitrarily well as judged by average log-likelihood, and suppose q_1 is a bad model, such as white noise. Now consider samples generated from the mixture model

$$q_2(\boldsymbol{x}) = 0.01q_0(\boldsymbol{x}) + 0.99q_1(\boldsymbol{x}) \tag{20.6}$$

Clearly 99% of the samples will be poor. However, the log-likelihood per pixel will hardly change between q_2 and q_0 if D is large, since

$$\log q_2(\boldsymbol{x}) = \log[0.01q_0(\boldsymbol{x}) + 0.99q_1(\boldsymbol{x})] \geq \log[0.01q_0(\boldsymbol{x})] = \log q_0(\boldsymbol{x}) - 100 \tag{20.7}$$

For high-dimensional data, $|\log q_0(\boldsymbol{x})| \sim D \gg 100$, so $\log q_2(\boldsymbol{x}) \approx \log q_0(\boldsymbol{x})$, and hence mixing in the poor sampler does not significantly impact the log likelihood.

Now consider a case where the model has good samples but bad likelihoods. To achieve this, suppose q is a GMM centered on the training images:

$$q(\boldsymbol{x}) = \frac{1}{N} \sum_{n=1}^{N} \mathcal{N}(\boldsymbol{x}|\boldsymbol{x}_n, \epsilon^2 \mathbf{I}) \tag{20.8}$$

If ϵ is small enough that the Gaussian noise is imperceptible, then samples from this model will look good, since they correspond to the training set of real images. But this model will almost certainly have poor likelihood on the test set due to overfitting. (In this case we say the model has effectively just memorized the training set.)

20.4.2   Distances and divergences in feature space

Due to the challenges associated with comparing distributions in high dimensional spaces, and the desire to compare distributions in a semantically meaningful way, it is common to use domain-specific **perceptual distance metrics**, that measure how similar data vectors are to each other or to the training data. However, most metrics used to evaluate generative models do not directly compare raw data (e.g., pixels) but use a neural network to obtain features from the raw data and compare the feature distribution obtained from model samples with the feature distribution obtained from the dataset. The neural network used to obtain features can be trained solely for the purpose of evaluation, or can be pretrained; a common choice is to use a pretrained classifier (see e.g., [Sal+16; Heu+17b; Bin+18; Kyn+19; SSG18a]).

The **Inception score** [Sal+16] measures the average KL divergence between the marginal distribution of class labels obtained from the samples $p_{\boldsymbol{\theta}}(y) = \int p_{\text{disc}}(y|\boldsymbol{x})p_{\boldsymbol{\theta}}(\boldsymbol{x})d\boldsymbol{x}$ (where the integral is approximated by sampling images $\boldsymbol{x}$ from a fixed dataset) and the distribution $p(y|\boldsymbol{x})$ induced by samples from the model, $\boldsymbol{x} \sim p_{\boldsymbol{\theta}}(\boldsymbol{x})$. (The term comes from the "Inception" model [Sze+15b] that is often used to define $p_{\text{disc}}(y|\boldsymbol{x})$.) This leads to the following score:

$$\text{IS} = \exp\left[\mathbb{E}_{p_{\boldsymbol{\theta}}(\boldsymbol{x})}D_{\text{KL}}\left(p_{\text{disc}}(Y|\boldsymbol{x}) \parallel p_{\boldsymbol{\theta}}(Y)\right)\right] \tag{20.9}$$

To understand this, let us rewrite the log score as follows:

$$\log(\text{IS}) = \mathbb{H}(p_{\boldsymbol{\theta}}(Y)) - \mathbb{E}_{p_{\boldsymbol{\theta}}(\boldsymbol{x})}\left[\mathbb{H}(p_{\text{disc}}(Y|\boldsymbol{x}))\right] \tag{20.10}$$

Thus we see that a high scoring model will be equally likely to generate samples from all classes, thus maximizing the entropy of $p_{\boldsymbol{\theta}}(Y)$, while also ensuring that each individual sample is easy to classify, thus minimizing the entropy of $p_{\text{disc}}(Y|\boldsymbol{x})$.

The Inception score solely relies on class labels, and thus does not measure overfitting or sample diversity outside the predefined dataset classes. For example, a model which generates one perfect example per class would get a perfect Inception score, despite not capturing the variety of examples inside a class, as shown in Figure 20.11a. To address this drawback, the **Fréchet Inception distance** or **FID** score [Heu+17b] measures the Fréchet distance between two Gaussian distributions on sets of features of a pre-trained classifier. One Gaussian is obtained by passing model samples through a pretrained classifier, and the other by passing dataset samples through the same classifier. If we assume that the mean and covariance obtained from model features are $\boldsymbol{\mu}_m$ and $\boldsymbol{\Sigma}_m$ and those from the data are $\boldsymbol{\mu}_d$ and $\boldsymbol{\Sigma}_d$, then the FID is

$$\text{FID} = \|\boldsymbol{\mu}_m - \boldsymbol{\mu}_d\|_2^2 + \text{tr}\left(\boldsymbol{\Sigma}_d + \boldsymbol{\Sigma}_m - 2(\boldsymbol{\Sigma}_d\boldsymbol{\Sigma}_m)^{1/2}\right) \tag{20.11}$$

Since it uses features instead of class logits, the Fréchet distance captures more than modes captured by class labels, as shown in Figure 20.11b. Unlike the Inception score, a lower score is better since we want the two distributions to be as close as possible.

Unfortunately, the Fréchet distance has been shown to have a high bias, with results varying widely based on the number of samples used to compute the score. To mitigate this issue, the **kernel Inception distance** has been introduced [Bin+18], which measures the squared MMD (Section 2.7.3) between the features obtained from the data and features obtained from model samples.

20.4.3 Precision and recall metrics

Since the FID only measures the distance between the data and model distributions, it is difficult to use it as a diagnostic tool: a bad (high) FID can indicate that the model is not able to generate high quality data, or that it puts too much mass around the data distribution, or that the model only captures a subset of the data (e.g., in Figure 26.6). Trying to disentangle between these two failure modes has been the motivation to seek individual precision (sample quality) and recall (sample diversity) metrics in the context of generative models [LPO17; Kyn+19]. (The diversity question is especially important in the context of GANs, where mode collapse (Section 26.3.3) can be an issue.)

A common approach is to use nearest neighbors in the feature space of a pretrained classifier to

Figure 20.11: (a) Model samples with good (high) inception score are visually realistic. (b) Model samples with good (low) FID score are visually realistic and diverse.

define precision and recall [Kyn+19]. To formalize this, let us define

$$f_k(\phi, \Phi) = \begin{cases} 1 & \text{if } \exists \phi' \in \Phi \, s.t. \, \|\phi - \phi'\|_2^2 \leq \|\phi' - \text{NN}_k(\phi', \Phi)\|_2^2 \\ 0 & \text{otherwise} \end{cases} \tag{20.12}$$

where Φ is a set of feature vectors and $\text{NN}_k(\phi', \Phi)$ is a function returning the k'th nearest neighbor of ϕ' in Φ. We now define precision and recall as follows:

$$\text{precision}(\Phi_{model}, \Phi_{data}) = \frac{1}{|\Phi_{model}|} \sum_{\phi \in \Phi_{model}} f_k(\phi, \Phi_{data}); \tag{20.13}$$

$$\text{recall}(\Phi_{model}, \Phi_{data}) = \frac{1}{|\Phi_{data}|} \sum_{\phi \in \Phi_{data}} f_k(\phi, \Phi_{model}); \tag{20.14}$$

Precision and recall are always between 0 and 1. Intuitively, the precision metric measures whether samples are as close to data as data is to other data examples, while recall measures whether data is as close to model samples as model samples are to other samples. The parameter k controls how lenient the metrics will be — the higher k, the higher both precision and recall will be. As in classification, precision and recall in generative models can be used to construct a trade-off curve between different models which allows practitioners to make an informed decision regarding which model they want to use.

20.4.4   Statistical tests

Statistical tests have long been used to determine whether two sets of samples have been generated from the same distribution; these types of statistical tests are called **two sample tests**. Let us define the null hypothesis as the statement that both set of samples are from the same distribution. We then compute a statistic from the data and compare it to a threshold, and based on this we decide whether to reject the null hypothesis. In the context of evaluating implicit generative models such as GANs, statistics based on classifiers [Saj+18] and the MMD [Liu+20b] have been used. For use in scenarios with high dimensional input spaces, which are ubiquitous in the era of deep learning, two sample tests have been adapted to use learned features instead of raw data.

Like all other evaluation metrics for generative models, statistical tests have their own advantages and disadvantages: while users can specify Type 1 error — the chance they allow that the null hypothesis is wrongly rejected — statistical tests tend to be computationally expensive and thus cannot be used to monitor progress in training; hence they are best used to compare fully trained models.

20.4.5 Challenges with using pretrained classifiers

While popular and convenient, evaluation metrics that rely on pretrained classifiers (such as IS, FID, nearest neighbors in feature space, and statistical tests in feature space) have significant drawbacks. One might not have a pretrained classifier available for the dataset at hand, so classifiers trained on other datasets are used. Given the well known challenges with neural network generalization (see Section 17.4), the features of a classifier trained on images from one dataset might not be reliable enough to provide a fine grained signal of quality for samples obtained from a model trained on a different dataset. If the generative model is trained on the same dataset as the pre-trained classifier but the model is not capturing the data distribution perfectly, we are presenting the pre-trained classifier with out-of-distribution data and relying on its features to obtain score to evaluate our models. Far from being purely theoretical concerns, these issues have been studied extensively and have been shown to affect evaluation in practice [RV19; BS18].

20.4.6 Using model samples to train classifiers

Instead of using pretrained classifiers to evaluate samples, one can train a classifier on samples from conditional generative models, and then see how good these classifiers are at classifying data. For example, does adding synthetic (sampled) data to the real data help? This is closer to a reliable evaluation of generative model samples, since ultimately, the performance of generative models is dependent on the downstream task they are trained for. If used for semisupervised learning, one should assess how much adding samples to a classifier dataset helps with test accuracy. If used for model based reinforcement learning, one should assess how much the generative model helps with agent performance. For examples of this approach, see e.g., [SSM18; SSA18; RV19; SS20b; Jor+22].

20.4.7 Assessing overfitting

Many of the metrics discussed so far capture the sample quality and diversity, but do not capture overfitting to the training data. To capture overfitting, often a visual inspection is performed: a set of samples is generated from the model and for each sample its closest K nearest neighbors in the feature space of a pretrained classifier are obtained from the dataset. While this approach requires manually assessing samples, it is a simple way to test whether a model is simply memorizing the data. We show an example in Figure 20.12: since the model sample in the top left is quite different than its neighbors from the dataset (remaining images), we can conclude the sample is not simply memorised from the dataset. Similarly, sample diversity can be measured by approximating the support of the learned distribution by looking for similar samples in a large sample pool — as in the pigeonhole principle — but it is expensive and often requires manual human assessment[AZ17].

For likelihood-based models — such as variational autoencoders (Chapter 21), autoregressive models (Chapter 22), and normalizing flows (Chapter 23) — we can assess memorization by seeing

Figure 20.12: *Illustration of nearest neighbors in feature space: in the top left we have the query sample generated using BigGAN, and the rest of the images are its nearest neighbors from the dataset. The nearest neighbors search is done in the feature space of a pretrained classifier. From Figure 13 of [BDS18]. Used with kind permission of Andy Brock.*

how much the log-likelihood of a model changes when a sample is included in the model's training set or not [BW21].

20.4.8   Human evaluation

One approach to evaluate generative models is to use human evaluation, by presenting samples from the model alongside samples from the data distribution, and ask human raters to compare the quality of the samples [Zho+19b]. Human evaluation is a suitable metric if the model is used to create art or other data for human display, or if reliable automated metrics are hard to obtain. However, human evaluation can be difficult to standardize, hard to automate, and can be expensive or cumbersome to set up.

21 Variational autoencoders

21.1 Introduction

In this chapter, we discuss generative models of the form

$$z \sim p_{\theta}(z) \tag{21.1}$$
$$x|z \sim \text{Expfam}(x|d_{\theta}(z)) \tag{21.2}$$

where $p(z)$ is some kind of prior on the latent code z, $d_{\theta}(z)$ is a deep neural network, known as the **decoder**, and $\text{Expfam}(x|\eta)$ is an exponential family distribution, such as a Gaussian or product of Bernoullis. This is called a **deep latent variable model** or **DLVM**. When the prior is Gaussian (as is often the case), this model is called a **deep latent Gaussian model** or **DLGM**.

Posterior inference (i.e., computing $p_{\theta}(z|x)$) is computationally intractable, as is computing the marginal likelihood

$$p_{\theta}(x) = \int p_{\theta}(x|z)p_{\theta}(z) \, dz \tag{21.3}$$

Hence we need to resort to approximate inference. For most of this chapter, we will use **amortized inference**, which we discussed in Section 10.1.5. This trains another model, $q_{\phi}(z|x)$, called the **recognition network** or **inference network**, simultaneously with the generative model to do approximate posterior inference. This combination is called a **variational autoencoder** or **VAE** [KW14; RMW14b; KW19a], since it can be thought of as a probabilistic version of a deterministic autoencoder, discussed in Section 16.3.3.

In this chapter, we introduce the basic VAE, as well as some extensions. Note that the literature on VAE-like methods is vast[1], so we will only discuss a small subset of the ideas that have been explored.

21.2 VAE basics

In this section, we discuss the basics of variational autoencoders.

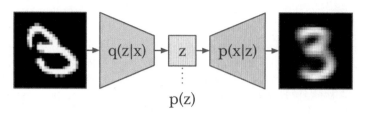

Figure 21.1: Schematic illustration of a VAE. From a figure in [Haf18]. Used with kind permission of Danijar Hafner.

21.2.1   Modeling assumptions

In the simplest setting, a VAE defines a generative model of the form

$$p_{\boldsymbol{\theta}}(\boldsymbol{z}, \boldsymbol{x}) = p_{\boldsymbol{\theta}}(\boldsymbol{z}) p_{\boldsymbol{\theta}}(\boldsymbol{x}|\boldsymbol{z}) \tag{21.4}$$

where $p_{\boldsymbol{\theta}}(\boldsymbol{z})$ is usually a Gaussian, and $p_{\boldsymbol{\theta}}(\boldsymbol{x}|\boldsymbol{z})$ is usually a product of exponential family distributions (e.g., Gaussians or Bernoullis), with parameters computed by a neural network decoder, $d_{\boldsymbol{\theta}}(\boldsymbol{z})$. For example, for binary observations, we can use

$$p_{\boldsymbol{\theta}}(\boldsymbol{x}|\boldsymbol{z}) = \prod_{d=1}^{D} \text{Ber}(x_d | \sigma(d_{\boldsymbol{\theta}}(\boldsymbol{z}))) \tag{21.5}$$

In addition, a VAE fits a recognition model

$$q_{\boldsymbol{\phi}}(\boldsymbol{z}|\boldsymbol{x}) = q(\boldsymbol{z}|e_{\boldsymbol{\phi}}(\boldsymbol{x})) \approx p_{\boldsymbol{\theta}}(\boldsymbol{z}|\boldsymbol{x}) \tag{21.6}$$

to perform approximate posterior inference. Here $q_{\boldsymbol{\phi}}(\boldsymbol{z}|\boldsymbol{x})$ is usually a Gaussian, with parameters computed by a neural network encoder $e_{\boldsymbol{\phi}}(\boldsymbol{x})$:

$$q_{\boldsymbol{\phi}}(\boldsymbol{z}|\boldsymbol{x}) = \mathcal{N}(\boldsymbol{z}|\boldsymbol{\mu}, \text{diag}(\exp(\boldsymbol{\ell}))) \tag{21.7}$$

$$(\boldsymbol{\mu}, \boldsymbol{\ell}) = e_{\boldsymbol{\phi}}(\boldsymbol{x}) \tag{21.8}$$

where $\boldsymbol{\ell} = \log \boldsymbol{\sigma}$. The model can be thought of as encoding the input $\boldsymbol{x}$ into a stochastic latent bottleneck $\boldsymbol{z}$ and then decoding it to approximately reconstruct the input, as shown in Figure 21.1.

The idea of training an inference network to "invert" a generative network, rather than running an optimization algorithm to infer the latent code, is called amortized inference, and is discussed in Section 10.1.5. This idea was first proposed in the **Helmholtz machine** [Day+95]. However, that paper did not present a single unified objective function for inference and generation, but instead used the wake-sleep (Section 10.6) method for training. By contrast, the VAE optimizes a variational lower bound on the log-likelihood, which means that convergence to a locally optimal MLE of the parameters is guaranteed.

We can use other approaches to fitting the DLGM (see e.g., [Hof17; DF19]). However, learning an inference network to fit the DLGM is often faster and can have some regularization benefits (see e.g., [KP20]).[2]

---

1. For example, the website https://github.com/matthewvowels1/Awesome-VAEs lists over 900 papers.
2. Combining a generative model with an inference model in this way results in what has been called a "**monference**",

21.2.2 Model fitting

We can fit a VAE using amortized stochastic variational inference, as we discuss in Section 10.2.1.6. For example, suppose we use a VAE with a diagonal Bernoulli likelihood model, and a full covariance Gaussian as our variational posterior. Then we can use the methods discussed in Section 10.2.1.2 to derive the fitting algorith. See Algorithm 21.1 for the corresponding pseudocode.

Algorithm 21.1: Fitting a VAE with Bernoulli likelihood and full covariance Gaussian posterior. Based on Algorithm 2 of [KW19a].

---

1 Initialize $\boldsymbol{\theta}$, $\boldsymbol{\phi}$
2 **repeat**
3   Sample $\boldsymbol{x} \sim p_{\mathcal{D}}$
4   Sample $\boldsymbol{\epsilon} \sim q_0$
5      $(\boldsymbol{\mu}, \log \boldsymbol{\sigma}, \mathbf{L}') = e_{\boldsymbol{\phi}}(\boldsymbol{x})$
6      $\mathbf{M} = \text{np.triu(np.ones}(K), -1)$
7      $\mathbf{L} = \mathbf{M} \odot \mathbf{L}' + \text{diag}(\boldsymbol{\sigma})$
8      $\boldsymbol{z} = \mathbf{L}\boldsymbol{\epsilon} + \boldsymbol{\mu}$
9      $\boldsymbol{p}_p = d_{\boldsymbol{\theta}}(\boldsymbol{z})$
10     $\mathcal{L}_{\text{logqz}} = -\sum_{k=1}^{K} \left[\frac{1}{2}\epsilon_k^2 + \frac{1}{2}\log(2\pi) + \log \sigma_k \right]$ // from $q_{\boldsymbol{\phi}}(\boldsymbol{z}|\boldsymbol{x})$ in Equation (10.47)
11     $\mathcal{L}_{\text{logpz}} = -\sum_{k=1}^{K} \left[\frac{1}{2}z_k^2 + \frac{1}{2}\log(2\pi) \right]$ // from $p_{\boldsymbol{\theta}}(\boldsymbol{z})$ in Equation (10.48)
12     $\mathcal{L}_{\text{logpx}} = -\sum_{d=1}^{D} \left[x_d \log p_d + (1 - x_d) \log(1 - p_d) \right]$ // from $p_{\boldsymbol{\theta}}(\boldsymbol{x}|\boldsymbol{z})$
13     $\mathcal{L} = \mathcal{L}_{\text{logpx}} + \mathcal{L}_{\text{logpz}} - \mathcal{L}_{\text{logqz}}$
14   Update $\boldsymbol{\theta} := \boldsymbol{\theta} - \eta \nabla_{\boldsymbol{\theta}} \mathcal{L}$
15   Update $\boldsymbol{\phi} := \boldsymbol{\phi} - \eta \nabla_{\boldsymbol{\phi}} \mathcal{L}$
16 **until** converged

21.2.3 Comparison of VAEs and autoencoders

VAEs are very similar to deterministic autoencoders (AE). There are 2 main differences: in the AE, the objective is the log likelihood of the reconstruction without any KL term; and in addition, the encoding is deterministic, so the encoder network just needs to compute $\mathbb{E}[\boldsymbol{z}|\boldsymbol{x}]$ and not $\mathbb{V}[\boldsymbol{z}|\boldsymbol{x}]$. In view of these similarities, one can use the same codebase to implement both methods. However, it is natural to wonder what the benefits and potential drawbacks of the VAE are compared to the deterministic AE.

We shall answer this question by fitting both models to the CelebA dataset. Both models have the same convolutional structure with the following number of hidden channels per convolutional layer in the encoder: (32, 64, 128, 256, 512). The spatial size of each layer is as follows: (32, 16, 8, 4, 2). The final $2 \times 2 \times 512$ convolutional layer then gets reshaped and passed through a linear layer to generate the mean and (marginal) variance of the stochastic latent vector, which has size 256. The structure

---

i.e., model-inference hybrid. See the blog by Jacob Andreas, `http://blog.jacobandreas.net/monference.html`, for further discussion.

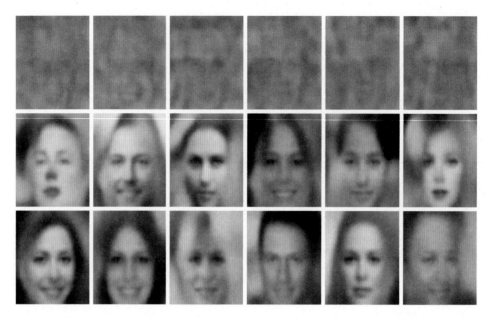

Figure 21.2: Illustration of unconditional image generation using (V)AEs trained on CelebA. Row 1: deterministic autoencoder. Row 2: β-VAE with β = 0.5. Row 3: VAE (with β = 1). Generated by celeba_vae_ae_comparison.ipynb.

of the decoder is the mirror image of the decoder. Each model is trained for 5 epochs with a batch size of 256, which takes about 20 minutes on a GPU.

The main advantage of a VAE over a deterministic autoencoder is that it defines a proper generative model, that can create sensible-looking novel images by decoding prior samples $z \sim \mathcal{N}(\mathbf{0}, \mathbf{I})$. By contrast, an autoencoder only knows how to decode latent codes derived from the training set, so does poorly when fed random inputs. This is illustrated in Figure 21.2.

We can also use both models to reconstruct a given input image. In Figure 21.3, we see that both AE and VAE can reconstruct the input images reasonably well, although the VAE reconstructions are somewhat blurry, for reasons we discuss in Section 21.3.1. We can reduce the amount of blurriness by scaling down the KL penalty term by a factor of β; this is known as the β-VAE, and is discussed in more detail in Section 21.3.1.

21.2.4   VAEs optimize in an augmented space

In this section, we derive several alternative expressions for the ELBO which shed light on how VAEs work.

First, let us define the joint generative distribution

$$p_{\boldsymbol{\theta}}(\boldsymbol{x}, \boldsymbol{z}) = p_{\boldsymbol{\theta}}(\boldsymbol{z}) p_{\boldsymbol{\theta}}(\boldsymbol{x}|\boldsymbol{z}) \tag{21.9}$$

Figure 21.3: *Illustration of image reconstruction using (V)AEs trained and applied to CelebA. Row 1: original images. Row 2: deterministic autoencoder. Row 3: β-VAE with β = 0.5. Row 4: VAE (with β = 1). Generated by celeba_vae_ae_comparison.ipynb.*

from which we can derive the generative data marginal

$$p_{\boldsymbol{\theta}}(\boldsymbol{x}) = \int_{\boldsymbol{z}} p_{\boldsymbol{\theta}}(\boldsymbol{x}, \boldsymbol{z}) d\boldsymbol{z} \tag{21.10}$$

and the generative posterior

$$p_{\boldsymbol{\theta}}(\boldsymbol{z}|\boldsymbol{x}) = p_{\boldsymbol{\theta}}(\boldsymbol{x}, \boldsymbol{z})/p_{\boldsymbol{\theta}}(\boldsymbol{x}) \tag{21.11}$$

Let us also define the joint *inference* distribution

$$q_{\mathcal{D},\boldsymbol{\phi}}(\boldsymbol{z}, \boldsymbol{x}) = p_{\mathcal{D}}(\boldsymbol{x})q_{\boldsymbol{\phi}}(\boldsymbol{z}|\boldsymbol{x}) \tag{21.12}$$

where

$$p_{\mathcal{D}}(\boldsymbol{x}) = \frac{1}{N} \sum_{n=1}^{N} \delta(\boldsymbol{x}_n - \boldsymbol{x}) \tag{21.13}$$

is the empirical distribution. From this we can derive the inference latent marginal, also called the **aggregated posterior**:

$$q_{\mathcal{D},\phi}(z) = \int_x q_{\mathcal{D},\phi}(x, z) dx \tag{21.14}$$

and the inference likelihood

$$q_{\mathcal{D},\phi}(x|z) = q_{\mathcal{D},\phi}(x, z)/q_{\mathcal{D},\phi}(z) \tag{21.15}$$

See Figure 21.4 for a visual illustration.

Having defined our terms, we can now derive various alternative versions of the ELBO, following [ZSE19]. First note that the ELBO averaged over all the data is given by

$$\text{Ł}(\theta, \phi|\mathcal{D}) = \mathbb{E}_{p_{\mathcal{D}}(x)}\left[\mathbb{E}_{q_\phi(z|x)}\left[\log p_\theta(x|z)\right]\right] - \mathbb{E}_{p_{\mathcal{D}}(x)}\left[D_{\text{KL}}\left(q_\phi(z|x) \parallel p_\theta(z)\right)\right] \tag{21.16}$$

$$= \mathbb{E}_{q_{\mathcal{D},\phi}(x,z)}\left[\log p_\theta(x|z) + \log p_\theta(z) - \log q_\phi(z|x)\right] \tag{21.17}$$

$$= \mathbb{E}_{q_{\mathcal{D},\phi}(x,z)}\left[\log \frac{p_\theta(x, z)}{q_{\mathcal{D},\phi}(x, z)} + \log p_{\mathcal{D}}(x)\right] \tag{21.18}$$

$$= -D_{\text{KL}}\left(q_{\mathcal{D},\phi}(x, z) \parallel p_\theta(x, z)\right) + \mathbb{E}_{p_{\mathcal{D}}(x)}\left[\log p_{\mathcal{D}}(x)\right] \tag{21.19}$$

If we define $\stackrel{c}{=}$ to mean equal up to additive constants, we can rewrite the above as

$$\text{Ł}(\theta, \phi|\mathcal{D}) \stackrel{c}{=} -D_{\text{KL}}\left(q_\phi(x, z) \parallel p_\theta(x, z)\right) \tag{21.20}$$

$$\stackrel{c}{=} -D_{\text{KL}}\left(p_{\mathcal{D}}(x) \parallel p_\theta(x)\right) - \mathbb{E}_{p_{\mathcal{D}}(x)}\left[D_{\text{KL}}\left(q_\phi(z|x) \parallel p_\theta(z|x)\right)\right] \tag{21.21}$$

Thus maximizing the ELBO requires minimizing the two KL terms. The first KL term is minimized by MLE, and the second KL term is minimized by fitting the true posterior. Thus if the posterior family is limited, there may be a conflict between these objectives.

Finally, we note that the ELBO can also be written as

$$\text{Ł}(\theta, \phi|\mathcal{D}) \stackrel{c}{=} -D_{\text{KL}}\left(q_{\mathcal{D},\phi}(z) \parallel p_\theta(z)\right) - \mathbb{E}_{q_{\mathcal{D},\phi}(z)}\left[D_{\text{KL}}\left(q_\phi(x|z) \parallel p_\theta(x|z)\right)\right] \tag{21.22}$$

We see from Equation (21.22) that VAEs are trying to minimize the difference between the inference marginal and generative prior, $D_{\text{KL}}\left(q_\phi(z) \parallel p_\theta(z)\right)$, while simultaneously minimizing reconstruction error, $D_{\text{KL}}\left(q_\phi(x|z) \parallel p_\theta(x|z)\right)$ Since x is typically of much higher dimensionality than z, the latter term usually dominates. Consequently, if there is a conflict between these two objectives (e.g., due to limited modeling power), the VAE will favor reconstruction accuracy over posterior inference. Thus the learned posterior may not be a very good approximation to the true posterior (see [ZSE19] for further discussion).

21.3   VAE generalizations

In this section, we discuss some variants of the basic VAE model.

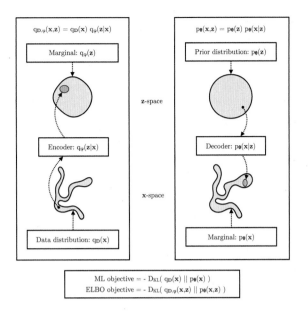

Figure 21.4: The maximum likelihood (ML) objective can be viewed as the minimization of $D_{\text{KL}}(p_{\mathcal{D}}(\boldsymbol{x}) \parallel p_{\boldsymbol{\theta}}(\boldsymbol{x}))$. (Note: in the figure, $p_{\mathcal{D}}(\boldsymbol{x})$ is denoted by $q_D(\boldsymbol{x})$.) The ELBO objective is minimization of $D_{\text{KL}}(q_{\mathcal{D},\phi}(\boldsymbol{x}, \boldsymbol{z}) \parallel p_{\boldsymbol{\theta}}(\boldsymbol{x}, \boldsymbol{z}))$, which upper bounds $D_{\text{KL}}(q_{\mathcal{D}}(\boldsymbol{x}) \parallel p_{\boldsymbol{\theta}}(\boldsymbol{x}))$. From Figure 2.4 of [KW19a]. Used with kind permission of Durk Kingma.

21.3.1 β-VAE

It is often the case that VAEs generate somewhat blurry images, as illustrated in Figure 21.3, Figure 21.2 and Figure 20.9. This is not the case for models that optimize the exact likelihood, such as pixelCNNs (Section 22.3.2) and flow models (Chapter 23). To see why VAEs are different, consider the common case where the decoder is a Gaussian with fixed variance, so

$$\log p_{\boldsymbol{\theta}}(\boldsymbol{x}|\boldsymbol{z}) = -\frac{1}{2\sigma^2}||\boldsymbol{x} - d_{\boldsymbol{\theta}}(\boldsymbol{z})||_2^2 + \text{const} \tag{21.23}$$

Let $e_{\phi}(\boldsymbol{x}) = \mathbb{E}\left[q_{\phi}(\boldsymbol{z}|\boldsymbol{x})\right]$ be the encoding of $\boldsymbol{x}$, and $\mathcal{X}(\boldsymbol{z}) = \{\boldsymbol{x} : e_{\phi}(\boldsymbol{x}) = \boldsymbol{z}\}$ be the set of inputs that get mapped to $\boldsymbol{z}$. For a fixed inference network, the optimal setting of the generator parameters, when using squared reconstruction loss, is to ensure $d_{\boldsymbol{\theta}}(\boldsymbol{z}) = \mathbb{E}\left[\boldsymbol{x} : \boldsymbol{x} \in \mathcal{X}(\boldsymbol{z})\right]$. Thus the decoder should predict the average of all inputs $\boldsymbol{x}$ that map to that $\boldsymbol{z}$, resulting in blurry images.

We can solve this problem by increasing the expressive power of the posterior approximation (avoiding the merging of distinct inputs into the same latent code), or of the generator (by adding back information that is missing from the latent code), or both. However, an even simpler solution is to reduce the penalty on the KL term, making the model closer to a deterministic autoencoder:

$$\mathcal{L}_{\beta}(\boldsymbol{\theta}, \phi|\boldsymbol{x}) = \underbrace{-\mathbb{E}_{q_{\phi}(\boldsymbol{z}|\boldsymbol{x})}\left[\log p_{\boldsymbol{\theta}}(\boldsymbol{x}|\boldsymbol{z})\right]}_{\mathcal{L}_E} + \beta \underbrace{D_{\text{KL}}\left(q_{\phi}(\boldsymbol{z}|\boldsymbol{x}) \parallel p_{\boldsymbol{\theta}}(\boldsymbol{z})\right)}_{\mathcal{L}_R} \tag{21.24}$$

where $\mathcal{L}_E$ is the reconstruction error (negative log likelihood), and $\mathcal{L}_R$ is the KL regularizer. This is called the β-**VAE** objective [Hig+17a]. If we set $\beta = 1$, we recover the objective used in standard VAEs; if we set $\beta = 0$, we recover the objective used in standard autoencoders.

By varying β from 0 to infinity, we can reach different points on the **rate distortion curve**, as discussed in Section 5.4.2. These points make different tradeoffs between reconstruction error (distortion) and how much information is stored in the latents about the input (rate of the corresponding code). By using $\beta < 1$, we store more bits about each input, and hence can reconstruct images in a less blurry way. If we use $\beta > 1$, we get a more compressed representation.

21.3.1.1 Disentangled representations

One advantage of using $\beta > 1$ is that it encourages the learning of a latent representation that is "**disentangled**". Intuitively this means that each latent dimension represents a different **factor of variation** in the input. This is often formalized in terms of the total correlation (Section 5.3.5.1), which is defined as follows:

$$\text{TC}(\boldsymbol{z}) = \sum_k \mathbb{H}\left(z_k\right) - \mathbb{H}\left(\boldsymbol{z}\right) = D_{\mathbb{KL}}\left(p(\boldsymbol{z}) \parallel \prod_k p_k(z_k)\right) \tag{21.25}$$

This is zero iff the components of $\boldsymbol{z}$ are all mutually independent, and hence disentangled. In [AS18], they prove that using $\beta > 1$ will decrease the TC.

Unfortunately, in [Loc+18] they prove that nonlinear latent variable models are unidentifiable, and therefore for any disentangled representation, there is an equivalent fully entangled representation with exactly the same likelihood. Thus it is not possible to recover the correct latent representation without choosing the appropriate inductive bias, via the encoder, decoder, prior, dataset, or learning algorithm, i.e., merely adjusting β is not sufficient. See Section 32.4.1 for more discussion.

21.3.1.2 Connection with information bottleneck

In this section, we show that the β-VAE is an unsupervised version of the information bottleneck (IB) objective from Section 5.6. If the input is $\boldsymbol{x}$, the hidden bottleneck is $\boldsymbol{z}$, and the target outputs are $\tilde{\boldsymbol{x}}$, then the unsupervised IB objective becomes

$$\mathcal{L}_{\text{UIB}} = \beta \, \mathbb{I}(\boldsymbol{z}; \boldsymbol{x}) - \mathbb{I}(\boldsymbol{z}; \tilde{\boldsymbol{x}}) \tag{21.26}$$

$$= \beta \mathbb{E}_{p(\boldsymbol{x},\boldsymbol{z})}\left[\log \frac{p(\boldsymbol{x}, \boldsymbol{z})}{p(\boldsymbol{x})p(\boldsymbol{z})}\right] - \mathbb{E}_{p(\boldsymbol{z},\tilde{\boldsymbol{x}})}\left[\log \frac{p(\boldsymbol{z}, \tilde{\boldsymbol{x}})}{p(\boldsymbol{z})p(\tilde{\boldsymbol{x}})}\right] \tag{21.27}$$

where

$$p(\boldsymbol{x}, \boldsymbol{z}) = p_{\mathcal{D}}(\boldsymbol{x})p(\boldsymbol{z}|\boldsymbol{x}) \tag{21.28}$$

$$p(\boldsymbol{z}, \tilde{\boldsymbol{x}}) = \int p_{\mathcal{D}}(\boldsymbol{x})p(\boldsymbol{z}|\boldsymbol{x})p(\tilde{\boldsymbol{x}}|\boldsymbol{z})d\boldsymbol{x} \tag{21.29}$$

Intuitively, the objective in Equation (21.26) means we should pick a representation $\boldsymbol{z}$ that can predict $\tilde{\boldsymbol{x}}$ reliably, while not memorizing too much information about the input $\boldsymbol{x}$. The tradeoff parameter is controlled by β.

From Equation (5.181), we have the following variational upper bound on this unsupervised objective:

$$\mathcal{L}_{\text{UVIB}} = -\mathbb{E}_{q_{\mathcal{D}, \phi}(\boldsymbol{z}, \boldsymbol{x})} \left[\log p_{\boldsymbol{\theta}}(\boldsymbol{x}|\boldsymbol{z}) \right] + \beta \mathbb{E}_{p_{\mathcal{D}}(\boldsymbol{x})} \left[D_{\text{KL}} \left(q_{\phi}(\boldsymbol{z}|\boldsymbol{x}) \parallel p_{\boldsymbol{\theta}}(\boldsymbol{z}) \right) \right] \tag{21.30}$$

which matches Equation (21.24) when averaged over $\boldsymbol{x}$.

21.3.2 InfoVAE

In Section 21.2.4, we discussed some drawbacks of the standard ELBO objective for training VAEs, namely the tendency to ignore the latent code when the decoder is powerful (Section 21.4), and the tendency to learn a poor posterior approximation due to the mismatch between the KL terms in data space and latent space (Section 21.2.4). We can fix these problems to some degree by using a generalized objective of the following form:

$$Ł(\boldsymbol{\theta}, \phi|\boldsymbol{x}) = -\lambda D_{\text{KL}} \left(q_{\phi}(\boldsymbol{z}) \parallel p_{\boldsymbol{\theta}}(\boldsymbol{z}) \right) - \mathbb{E}_{q_{\phi}(\boldsymbol{z})} \left[D_{\text{KL}} \left(q_{\phi}(\boldsymbol{x}|\boldsymbol{z}) \parallel p_{\boldsymbol{\theta}}(\boldsymbol{x}|\boldsymbol{z}) \right) \right] + \alpha \, \mathbb{I}_q(\boldsymbol{x}; \boldsymbol{z}) \tag{21.31}$$

where $\alpha \geq 0$ controls how much we weight the mutual information $\mathbb{I}_q(\boldsymbol{x}; \boldsymbol{z})$ between $\boldsymbol{x}$ and $\boldsymbol{z}$, and $\lambda \geq 0$ controls the tradeoff between $\boldsymbol{z}$-space KL and $\boldsymbol{x}$-space KL. This is called the **InfoVAE** objective [ZSE19]. If we set $\alpha = 0$ and $\lambda = 1$, we recover the standard ELBO, as shown in Equation (21.22).

Unfortunately, the objective in Equation (21.31) cannot be computed as written, because of the intractable MI term:

$$\mathbb{I}_q(\boldsymbol{x}; \boldsymbol{z}) = \mathbb{E}_{q_{\phi}(\boldsymbol{x}, \boldsymbol{z})} \left[\log \frac{q_{\phi}(\boldsymbol{x}, \boldsymbol{z})}{q_{\phi}(\boldsymbol{x}) q_{\phi}(\boldsymbol{z})} \right] = -\mathbb{E}_{q_{\phi}(\boldsymbol{x}, \boldsymbol{z})} \left[\log \frac{q_{\phi}(\boldsymbol{z})}{q_{\phi}(\boldsymbol{z}|\boldsymbol{x})} \right] \tag{21.32}$$

However, using the fact that $q_{\phi}(\boldsymbol{x}|\boldsymbol{z}) = p_{\mathcal{D}}(\boldsymbol{x}) q_{\phi}(\boldsymbol{z}|\boldsymbol{x}) / q_{\phi}(\boldsymbol{z})$, we can rewrite the objective as follows:

$$Ł = \mathbb{E}_{q_{\phi}(\boldsymbol{x}, \boldsymbol{z})} \left[-\lambda \log \frac{q_{\phi}(\boldsymbol{z})}{p_{\boldsymbol{\theta}}(\boldsymbol{z})} - \log \frac{q_{\phi}(\boldsymbol{x}|\boldsymbol{z})}{p_{\boldsymbol{\theta}}(\boldsymbol{x}|\boldsymbol{z})} - \alpha \log \frac{q_{\phi}(\boldsymbol{z})}{q_{\phi}(\boldsymbol{z}|\boldsymbol{x})} \right] \tag{21.33}$$

$$= \mathbb{E}_{q_{\phi}(\boldsymbol{x}, \boldsymbol{z})} \left[\log p_{\boldsymbol{\theta}}(\boldsymbol{x}|\boldsymbol{z}) - \log \frac{q_{\phi}(\boldsymbol{z})^{\lambda + \alpha - 1} p_{\mathcal{D}}(\boldsymbol{x})}{p_{\boldsymbol{\theta}}(\boldsymbol{z})^{\lambda} q_{\phi}(\boldsymbol{z}|\boldsymbol{x})^{\alpha - 1}} \right] \tag{21.34}$$

$$= \mathbb{E}_{p_{\mathcal{D}}(\boldsymbol{x})} \left[\mathbb{E}_{q_{\phi}(\boldsymbol{z}|\boldsymbol{x})} \left[\log p_{\boldsymbol{\theta}}(\boldsymbol{x}|\boldsymbol{z}) \right] \right] - (1 - \alpha) \mathbb{E}_{p_{\mathcal{D}}(\boldsymbol{x})} \left[D_{\text{KL}} \left(q_{\phi}(\boldsymbol{z}|\boldsymbol{x}) \parallel p_{\boldsymbol{\theta}}(\boldsymbol{z}) \right) \right]$$
$$- (\alpha + \lambda - 1) D_{\text{KL}} \left(q_{\phi}(\boldsymbol{z}) \parallel p_{\boldsymbol{\theta}}(\boldsymbol{z}) \right) - \mathbb{E}_{p_{\mathcal{D}}(\boldsymbol{x})} \left[\log p_{\mathcal{D}}(\boldsymbol{x}) \right] \tag{21.35}$$

where the last term is a constant we can ignore. The first two terms can be optimized using the reparameterization trick. Unfortunately, the last term requires computing $q_{\phi}(\boldsymbol{z}) = \int_{\boldsymbol{x}} q_{\phi}(\boldsymbol{x}, \boldsymbol{z}) d\boldsymbol{x}$, which is intractable. Fortunately, we can easily sample from this distribution, by sampling $\boldsymbol{x} \sim p_{\mathcal{D}}(\boldsymbol{x})$ and $\boldsymbol{z} \sim q_{\phi}(\boldsymbol{z}|\boldsymbol{x})$. Thus $q_{\phi}(\boldsymbol{z})$ is an **implicit probability model**, similar to a GAN (see Chapter 26).

As long as we use a strict divergence, meaning $D(q, p) = 0$ iff $q = p$, then one can show that this does not affect the optimality of the procedure. In particular, proposition 2 of [ZSE19] tells us the following:

Theorem 1. *Let $\mathcal{X}$ and $\mathcal{Z}$ be continuous spaces, and $\alpha < 1$ (to bound the MI) and $\lambda > 0$. For any fixed value of $\mathbb{I}_q(\boldsymbol{x}; \boldsymbol{z})$, the approximate InfoVAE loss, with any strict divergence $D(q_{\phi}(\boldsymbol{z}), p_{\boldsymbol{\theta}}(\boldsymbol{z}))$, is globally optimized if $p_{\boldsymbol{\theta}}(\boldsymbol{x}) = p_{\mathcal{D}}(\boldsymbol{x})$ and $q_{\phi}(\boldsymbol{z}|\boldsymbol{x}) = p_{\boldsymbol{\theta}}(\boldsymbol{z}|\boldsymbol{x})$.*

21.3.2.1   Connection with MMD VAE

If we set $\alpha = 1$, the InfoVAE objective simplifies to

$$\text{Ł} \overset{c}{=} \mathbb{E}_{p_{\mathcal{D}}(\boldsymbol{x})} \left[\mathbb{E}_{q_{\phi}(\boldsymbol{z}|\boldsymbol{x})} \left[\log p_{\boldsymbol{\theta}}(\boldsymbol{x}|\boldsymbol{z}) \right] \right] - \lambda D_{\text{KL}} \left(q_{\phi}(\boldsymbol{z}) \,\|\, p_{\boldsymbol{\theta}}(\boldsymbol{z}) \right) \tag{21.36}$$

The **MMD VAE**[3] replaces the KL divergence in the above term with the (squared) maximum mean discrepancy or **MMD** divergence defined in Section 2.7.3. (This is valid based on the above theorem.) The advantage of this approach over standard InfoVAE is that the resulting objective is tractable. In particular, if we set $\lambda = 1$ and swap the sign we get

$$\mathcal{L} = \mathbb{E}_{p_{\mathcal{D}}(\boldsymbol{x})} \left[\mathbb{E}_{q_{\phi}(\boldsymbol{z}|\boldsymbol{x})} \left[-\log p_{\boldsymbol{\theta}}(\boldsymbol{x}|\boldsymbol{z}) \right] \right] + \text{MMD}(q_{\phi}(\boldsymbol{z}), p_{\boldsymbol{\theta}}(\boldsymbol{z})) \tag{21.37}$$

As we discuss in Section 2.7.3, we can compute the MMD as follows:

$$\text{MMD}(p, q) = \mathbb{E}_{p(\boldsymbol{z}), p(\boldsymbol{z}')} \left[\mathcal{K}(\boldsymbol{z}, \boldsymbol{z}') \right] + \mathbb{E}_{q(\boldsymbol{z}), q(\boldsymbol{z}')} \left[\mathcal{K}(\boldsymbol{z}, \boldsymbol{z}') \right] - 2\mathbb{E}_{p(\boldsymbol{z}), q(\boldsymbol{z}')} \left[\mathcal{K}(\boldsymbol{z}, \boldsymbol{z}') \right] \tag{21.38}$$

where $\mathcal{K}()$ is some kernel function, such as the RBF kernel, $\mathcal{K}(\boldsymbol{z}, \boldsymbol{z}') = \exp(-\frac{1}{2\sigma^2} ||\boldsymbol{z} - \boldsymbol{z}'||_2^2)$. Intuitively the MMD measures the similarity (in latent space) between samples from the prior and samples from the aggregated posterior.

In practice, we can implement the MMD objective by using the posterior predicted mean $\boldsymbol{z}_n = e_{\phi}(\boldsymbol{x}_n)$ for all B samples in the current minibatch, and comparing this to B random samples from the $\mathcal{N}(\boldsymbol{0}, \mathbf{I})$ prior.

If we use a Gaussian decoder with fixed variance, the negative log likelihood is just a squared error term:

$$-\log p_{\boldsymbol{\theta}}(\boldsymbol{x}|\boldsymbol{z}) = ||\boldsymbol{x} - d_{\boldsymbol{\theta}}(\boldsymbol{z})||_2^2 \tag{21.39}$$

Thus the entire model is deterministic, and just predicts the means in latent space and visible space.

21.3.2.2   Connection with β-VAEs

If we set $\alpha = 0$ and $\lambda = 1$, we get back the original ELBO. If $\lambda > 0$ is freely chosen, but we use $\alpha = 1 - \lambda$, we get the β-VAE.

21.3.2.3   Connection with adversarial autoencoders

If we set $\alpha = 1$ and $\lambda = 1$, and D is chosen to be the Jensen-Shannon divergence (which can be minimized by training a binary discriminator, as explained in Section 26.2.2), then we get a model known as an **adversarial autoencoder** [Mak+15a].

21.3.3   Multimodal VAEs

It is possible to extend VAEs to create joint distributions over different kinds of variables, such as images and text. This is sometimes called a **multimodal VAE** or **MVAE**. Let us assume there are

---

3. Proposed in `https://ermongroup.github.io/blog/a-tutorial-on-mmd-variational-autoencoders/`.

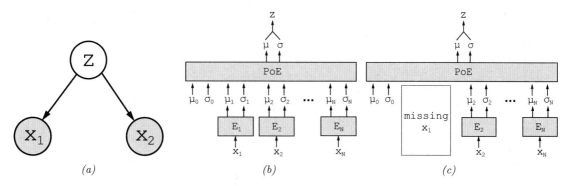

Figure 21.5: *Illustration of multi-modal VAE. (a) The generative model with $N = 2$ modalities. (b) The product of experts (PoE) inference network is derived from N individual Gaussian experts E_i. μ_0 and σ_0 are parameters of the prior. (c) If a modality is missing, we omit its contribution to the posterior. From Figure 1 of [WG18]. Used with kind permission of Mike Wu.*

M modalities. We assume they are conditionally independent given the latent code, and hence the generative model has the form

$$p_{\boldsymbol{\theta}}(\boldsymbol{x}_1, \ldots, \boldsymbol{x}_M, \boldsymbol{z}) = p(\boldsymbol{z}) \prod_{m=1}^{M} p_{\boldsymbol{\theta}}(\boldsymbol{x}_m | \boldsymbol{z}) \tag{21.40}$$

where we treat $p(\boldsymbol{z})$ as a fixed prior. See Figure 21.5(a) for an illustration.

The standard ELBO is given by

$$\text{Ł}(\boldsymbol{\theta}, \boldsymbol{\phi} | \mathbf{X}) = \mathbb{E}_{q_{\boldsymbol{\phi}}(\boldsymbol{z} | \mathbf{X})} \left[\sum_m \log p_{\boldsymbol{\theta}}(\boldsymbol{x}_m | \boldsymbol{z}) \right] - D_{\text{KL}}\left(q_{\boldsymbol{\phi}}(\boldsymbol{z} | \mathbf{X}) \,\|\, p(\boldsymbol{z}) \right) \tag{21.41}$$

where $\mathbf{X} = (\boldsymbol{x}_1, \ldots, \boldsymbol{x}_M)$ is the observed data. However, the different likelihood terms $p(\boldsymbol{x}_m | \boldsymbol{z})$ may have different dynamic ranges (e.g., Gaussian pdf for pixels, and categorical pmf for text), so we introduce weight terms $\lambda_m \geq 0$ for each likelihood. In addition, let $\beta \geq 0$ control the amount of KL regularization. This gives us a weighted version of the ELBO, as follows:

$$\text{Ł}(\boldsymbol{\theta}, \boldsymbol{\phi} | \mathbf{X}) = \mathbb{E}_{q_{\boldsymbol{\phi}}(\boldsymbol{z} | \mathbf{X})} \left[\sum_m \lambda_m \log p_{\boldsymbol{\theta}}(\boldsymbol{x}_m | \boldsymbol{z}) \right] - \beta D_{\text{KL}}\left(q_{\boldsymbol{\phi}}(\boldsymbol{z} | \mathbf{X}) \,\|\, p(\boldsymbol{z}) \right) \tag{21.42}$$

Often we don't have a lot of paired (aligned) data from all M modalities. For example, we may have a lot of images (modality 1), and a lot of text (modality 2), but very few (image, text) pairs. So it is useful to generalize the loss so it fits the marginal distributions of subsets of the features. Let $O_m = 1$ if modality m is observed (i.e., $\boldsymbol{x}_m$ is known), and let $O_m = 0$ if it is missing or unobserved. Let $\mathbf{X} = \{\boldsymbol{x}_m : O_m = 1\}$ be the visible features. We now use the following objective:

$$\text{Ł}(\boldsymbol{\theta}, \boldsymbol{\phi} | \mathbf{X}) = \mathbb{E}_{q_{\boldsymbol{\phi}}(\boldsymbol{z} | \mathbf{X})} \left[\sum_{m : O_m = 1} \lambda_m \log p_{\boldsymbol{\theta}}(\boldsymbol{x}_m | \boldsymbol{z}) \right] - \beta D_{\text{KL}}\left(q_{\boldsymbol{\phi}}(\boldsymbol{z} | \mathbf{X}) \,\|\, p(\boldsymbol{z}) \right) \tag{21.43}$$

The key problem is how to compute the posterior $q_\phi(z|\mathbf{X})$ given different subsets of features. In general this can be hard, since the inference network is a discriminative model that assumes all inputs are available. For example, if it is trained on (image, text) pairs, $q_\phi(z|\boldsymbol{x}_1, \boldsymbol{x}_2)$, how can we compute the posterior just given an image, $q_\phi(z|\boldsymbol{x}_1)$, or just given text, $q_\phi(z|\boldsymbol{x}_2)$? (This issue arises in general with VAE when we have missing inputs.)

Fortunately, based on our conditional independence assumption between the modalities, we can compute the optimal form for $q_\phi(z|\mathbf{X})$ given set of inputs by computing the exact posterior under the model, which is given by

$$p(z|\mathbf{X}) = \frac{p(z)p(\boldsymbol{x}_1, \ldots, \boldsymbol{x}_M|z)}{p(\boldsymbol{x}_1, \ldots, \boldsymbol{x}_M)} = \frac{p(z)}{p(\boldsymbol{x}_1, \ldots, \boldsymbol{x}_M)} \prod_{m=1}^{M} p(\boldsymbol{x}_m|z) \tag{21.44}$$

$$= \frac{p(z)}{p(\boldsymbol{x}_1, \ldots, \boldsymbol{x}_M)} \prod_{m=1}^{M} \frac{p(z|\boldsymbol{x}_m)p(\boldsymbol{x}_m)}{p(z)} \tag{21.45}$$

$$\propto p(z) \prod_{m=1}^{M} \frac{p(z|\boldsymbol{x}_m)}{p(z)} \approx p(z) \prod_{m=1}^{M} \tilde{q}(z|\boldsymbol{x}_m) \tag{21.46}$$

This can be viewed as a product of experts (Section 24.1.1), where each $\tilde{q}(z|\boldsymbol{x}_m)$ is an "expert" for the m'th modality, and $p(z)$ is the prior. We can compute the above posterior for any subset of modalities for which we have data by modifying the product over m. If we use Gaussian distributions for the prior $p(z) = \mathcal{N}(z|\boldsymbol{\mu}_0, \boldsymbol{\Lambda}_0^{-1})$ and marginal posterior ratio $\tilde{q}(z|\boldsymbol{x}_m) = \mathcal{N}(z|\boldsymbol{\mu}_m, \boldsymbol{\Lambda}_m^{-1})$, then we can compute the product of Gaussians using the result from Equation (2.154):

$$\prod_{m=0}^{M} \mathcal{N}(z|\boldsymbol{\mu}_m, \boldsymbol{\Lambda}_m^{-1}) \propto \mathcal{N}(z|\boldsymbol{\mu}, \boldsymbol{\Sigma}), \quad \boldsymbol{\Sigma} = (\sum_m \boldsymbol{\Lambda}_m)^{-1}, \quad \boldsymbol{\mu} = \boldsymbol{\Sigma}(\sum_m \boldsymbol{\Lambda}_m \boldsymbol{\mu}_m) \tag{21.47}$$

Thus the overall posterior precision is the sum of individual expert posterior precisions, and the overall posterior mean is the precision weighted average of the individual expert posterior means. See Figure 21.5(b) for an illustration. For a linear Gaussian (factor analysis) model, we can ensure $q(z|\boldsymbol{x}_m) = p(z|\boldsymbol{x}_m)$, in which case the above solution is the exact posterior [WN18], but in general it will be an approximation.

We need to train the individual expert recognition models $q(z|\boldsymbol{x}_m)$ as well as the joint model $q(z|\mathbf{X})$, so the model knows what to do with fully observed as well as partially observed inputs at test time. In [Ved+18], they propose a somewhat complex "triple ELBO" objective. In [WG18], they propose the simpler approach of optimizing the ELBO for the fully observed feature vector, all the marginals, and a set of $\mathcal{J}$ randomly chosen joint modalities:

$$Ł(\boldsymbol{\theta}, \boldsymbol{\phi}|\mathbf{X}) = Ł(\boldsymbol{\theta}, \boldsymbol{\phi}|()\boldsymbol{x}_1, \ldots, \boldsymbol{x}_M) + \sum_{m=1}^{M} Ł(\boldsymbol{\theta}, \boldsymbol{\phi}|\boldsymbol{x}_m) + \sum_{j \in \mathcal{J}} Ł(\boldsymbol{\theta}, \boldsymbol{\phi}|\mathbf{X}_j) \tag{21.48}$$

This generalizes nicely to the semi-supervised setting, in which we only have a few aligned ("labeled") examples from the joint, but have many unaligned ("unlabeled") examples from the individual marginals. See Figure 21.5(c) for an illustration.

Note that the above scheme can only handle the case of a fixed number of missingness patterns; we can generalize to allow for arbitrary missingness as discussed in [CNW20]. (See also Section 3.11 for a more general discussion of missing data.)

21.3.4 Semisupervised VAEs

In this section, we discuss how to extend VAEs to the **semi-supervised learning** setting in which we have both labeled data, $\mathcal{D}_L = \{(\boldsymbol{x}_n, y_n)\}$, and unlabeled data, $\mathcal{D}_U = \{(\boldsymbol{x}_n)\}$. We focus on the **M2** model, proposed in [Kin+14a].

The generative model has the following form:

$$p_{\boldsymbol{\theta}}(\boldsymbol{x}, y) = p_{\boldsymbol{\theta}}(y)p_{\boldsymbol{\theta}}(\boldsymbol{x}|y) = p_{\boldsymbol{\theta}}(y) \int p_{\boldsymbol{\theta}}(\boldsymbol{x}|y, \boldsymbol{z})p_{\boldsymbol{\theta}}(\boldsymbol{z})d\boldsymbol{z} \tag{21.49}$$

where $\boldsymbol{z}$ is a latent variable, $p_{\boldsymbol{\theta}}(\boldsymbol{z}) = \mathcal{N}(\boldsymbol{z}|\boldsymbol{0}, \mathbf{I})$ is the latent prior, $p_{\boldsymbol{\theta}}(y) = \text{Cat}(y|\boldsymbol{\pi})$ the label prior, and $p_{\boldsymbol{\theta}}(\boldsymbol{x}|y, \boldsymbol{z}) = p(\boldsymbol{x}|f_{\boldsymbol{\theta}}(y, \boldsymbol{z}))$ is the likelihood, such as a Gaussian, with parameters computed by f (a deep neural network). The main innovation of this approach is to assume that data is generated according to both a latent class variable y as well as the continuous latent variable $\boldsymbol{z}$. The class variable y is observed for labeled data and unobserved for unlabled data.

To compute the likelihood for the *labeled data*, $p_{\boldsymbol{\theta}}(\boldsymbol{x}, y)$, we need to marginalize over $\boldsymbol{z}$, which we can do by using an inference network of the form

$$q_{\boldsymbol{\phi}}(\boldsymbol{z}|y, \boldsymbol{x}) = \mathcal{N}(\boldsymbol{z}|\boldsymbol{\mu}_{\boldsymbol{\phi}}(y, \boldsymbol{x}), \text{diag}(\boldsymbol{\sigma}_{\boldsymbol{\phi}}(y, \boldsymbol{x}))) \tag{21.50}$$

We then use the following variational lower bound

$$\log p_{\boldsymbol{\theta}}(\boldsymbol{x}, y) \geq \mathbb{E}_{q_{\boldsymbol{\phi}}(\boldsymbol{z}|\boldsymbol{x}, y)}\left[\log p_{\boldsymbol{\theta}}(\boldsymbol{x}|y, \boldsymbol{z}) + \log p_{\boldsymbol{\theta}}(y) + \log p_{\boldsymbol{\theta}}(\boldsymbol{z}) - \log q_{\boldsymbol{\phi}}(\boldsymbol{z}|\boldsymbol{x}, y)\right] = -\mathcal{L}(\boldsymbol{x}, y) \tag{21.51}$$

as is standard for VAEs (see Section 21.2). The only difference is that we observe two kinds of data: $\boldsymbol{x}$ and y.

To compute the likelihood for the *unlabeled* data, $p_{\boldsymbol{\theta}}(\boldsymbol{x})$, we need to marginalize over $\boldsymbol{z}$ *and* y, which we can do by using an inference network of the form

$$q_{\boldsymbol{\phi}}(\boldsymbol{z}, y|\boldsymbol{x}) = q_{\boldsymbol{\phi}}(\boldsymbol{z}|\boldsymbol{x})q_{\boldsymbol{\phi}}(y|\boldsymbol{x}) \tag{21.52}$$

$$q_{\boldsymbol{\phi}}(\boldsymbol{z}|\boldsymbol{x}) = \mathcal{N}(\boldsymbol{z}|\boldsymbol{\mu}_{\boldsymbol{\phi}}(\boldsymbol{x}), \text{diag}(\boldsymbol{\sigma}_{\boldsymbol{\phi}}(\boldsymbol{x}))) \tag{21.53}$$

$$q_{\boldsymbol{\phi}}(y|\boldsymbol{x}) = \text{Cat}(y|\boldsymbol{\pi}_{\boldsymbol{\phi}}(\boldsymbol{x})) \tag{21.54}$$

Note that $q_{\boldsymbol{\phi}}(y|\boldsymbol{x})$ acts like a discriminative classifier, that imputes the missing labels. We then use the following variational lower bound:

$$\log p_{\boldsymbol{\theta}}(\boldsymbol{x}) \geq \mathbb{E}_{q_{\boldsymbol{\phi}}(\boldsymbol{z}, y|\boldsymbol{x})}\left[\log p_{\boldsymbol{\theta}}(\boldsymbol{x}|y, \boldsymbol{z}) + \log p_{\boldsymbol{\theta}}(y) + \log p_{\boldsymbol{\theta}}(\boldsymbol{z}) - \log q_{\boldsymbol{\phi}}(\boldsymbol{z}, y|\boldsymbol{x})\right] \tag{21.55}$$

$$= -\sum_y q_{\boldsymbol{\phi}}(y|\boldsymbol{x})\mathcal{L}(\boldsymbol{x}, y) + \mathbb{H}\left(q_{\boldsymbol{\phi}}(y|\boldsymbol{x})\right) = -\mathcal{U}(\boldsymbol{x}) \tag{21.56}$$

Note that the discriminative classifier $q_{\boldsymbol{\phi}}(y|\boldsymbol{x})$ is only used to compute the log-likelihood of the unlabeled data, which is undesirable. We can therefore add an extra classification loss on the supervised data, to get the following overall objective function:

$$\mathcal{L}(\boldsymbol{\theta}) = \mathbb{E}_{(\boldsymbol{x}, y) \sim \mathcal{D}_L}\left[\mathcal{L}(\boldsymbol{x}, y)\right] + \mathbb{E}_{\boldsymbol{x} \sim \mathcal{D}_U}\left[\mathcal{U}(\boldsymbol{x})\right] + \alpha \mathbb{E}_{(\boldsymbol{x}, y) \sim \mathcal{D}_L}\left[-\log q_{\boldsymbol{\phi}}(y|\boldsymbol{x})\right] \tag{21.57}$$

where $\mathcal{D}_L$ is the labeled data, $\mathcal{D}_U$ is the unlabeled data, and α is a hyperparameter that controls the relative weight of generative and discriminative learning.

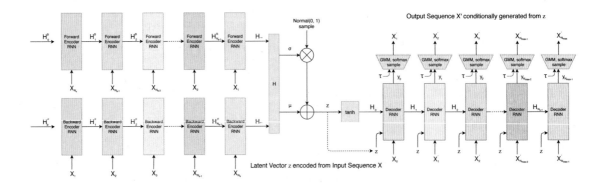

Figure 21.6: *Illustration of a VAE with a bidirectional RNN encoder and a unidirectional RNN decoder. The output generator can use a GMM and/or softmax distribution. From Figure 2 of [HE18]. Used with kind permission of David Ha.*

21.3.5   VAEs with sequential encoders/decoders

In this section, we discuss VAEs for sequential data, such as text and biosequences, in which the data x is a variable-length sequence, but we have a fixed-sized latent variable $z \in \mathbb{R}^K$. (We consider the more general case in which z is a variable-length sequence of latents — known as **sequential VAE** or **dynamic VAE** — in Section 29.13.) All we have to do is modify the decoder $p(x|z)$ and encoder $q(z|x)$ to work with sequences.

21.3.5.1   Models

If we use an RNN for the encoder and decoder of a VAE, we get a model which is called a **VAE-RNN**, as proposed in [Bow+16a]. In more detail, the generative model is $p(z, x_{1:T}) = p(z)\text{RNN}(x_{1:T}|z)$, where z can be injected as the initial state of the RNN, or as an input to every time step. The inference model is $q(z|x_{1:T}) = \mathcal{N}(z|\boldsymbol{\mu}(h), \boldsymbol{\Sigma}(h))$, where $h = [\overrightarrow{h_T}, \overleftarrow{h_1}]$ is the output of a bidirectional RNN applied to $x_{1:T}$. See Figure 21.6 for an illustration.

More recently, people have tried to combine transformers with VAEs. For example, in the **Optimus** model of [Li+20], they use a BERT model for the encoder. In more detail, the encoder $q(z|x)$ is derived from the embedding vector associated with a dummy token corresponding to the "class label" which is appended to the input sequence x. The decoder is a standard autoregressive model (similar to GPT), with one additional input, namely the latent vector z. They consider two ways of injecting the latent vector. The simplest approach is to add z to the embedding layer of every token in the decoding step, by defining $h'_i = h_i + \mathbf{W}z$, where $h_i \in \mathbb{R}^H$ is the original embedding for the i'th token, and $\mathbf{W} \in \mathbb{R}^{H \times K}$ is a decoding matrix, where K is the size of the latent vector. However, they get better results in their experiments by letting all the layers of the decoder attend to the latent code z. An easy way to do this is to define the memory vector $h_m = \mathbf{W}z$, where $\mathbf{W} \in \mathbb{R}^{LH \times K}$, where L is the number of layers in the decoder, and then to append $h_m \in \mathbb{R}^{L \times H}$ to all the other embeddings at each layer.

An alternative approach, known as **transformer VAE**, was proposed in [Gre20]. This model uses a **funnel transformer** [Dai+20b] as the encoder, and the **T5** [Raf+20a] conditional transformer for

```
                                          i went to the store to buy some groceries .
                                          i store to buy some groceries .
he was silent for a long moment .         i were to buy any groceries .
he was silent for a moment .              horses are to buy any groceries .
it was quiet for a moment .               horses are to buy any animal .
it was dark and cold .                    horses the favorite any animal .
there was a pause .                       horses the favorite favorite animal .
it was my turn .                          horses are my favorite animal .
```

(a)   (b)

Figure 21.7: (a) Samples from the latent space of a VAE text model, as we interpolate between two sentences (on first and last line). Note that the intermediate sentences are grammatical, and semantically related to their neighbors. From Table 8 of [Bow+16b]. (b) Same as (a), but now using a deterministic autoencoder (with the same RNN encoder and decoder). From Table 1 of [Bow+16b]. Used with kind permission of Sam Bowman.

the decoder. In addition, it uses an MMD VAE (Section 21.3.2.1) to avoid posterior collapse.

21.3.5.2 Applications

In this section, we discuss some applications of VAEs to sequence data.

Text

In [Bow+16b], they apply the VAE-RNN model to natural language sentences. (See also [MB16; SSB17] for related work.) Although this does not improve performance in terms of the standard perplexity measures (predicting the next word given the previous words), it does provide a way to infer a semantic representation of the sentence. This can then be used for latent space interpolation, as discussed in Section 20.3.5. The results of doing this with the VAE-RNN are illustrated in Figure 21.7a. (Similar results are shown in [Li+20], using a VAE-transformer.) By contrast, if we use a standard deterministic autoencoder, with the same RNN encoder and decoder networks, we learn a much less meaningful space, as illustrated in Figure 21.7b. The reason is that the deterministic autoencoder has "holes" in its latent space, which get decoded to nonsensical outputs.

However, because RNNs (and transformers) are powerful decoders, we need to address the problem of posterior collapse, which we discuss in Section 21.4. One common way to avoid this problem is to use KL annealing, but a more effective method is to use the InfoVAE method of Section 21.3.2, which includes adversarial autoencoders (used in [She+20] with an RNN decoder) and MMD autoencoders (used in [Gre20] with a transformer decoder).

Sketches

In [HE18], they apply the VAE-RNN model to generate sketches (line drawings) of various animals and hand-written characters. They call their model **sketch-rnn**. The training data records the sequence of (x, y) pen positions, as well as whether the pen was touching the paper or not. The emission model used a GMM for the real-valued location offsets, and a categorical softmax distribution for the discrete state.

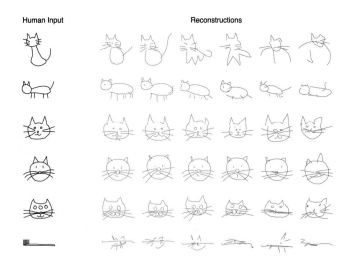

Figure 21.8: Conditional generation of cats from sketch-RNN model. We increase the temperature parameter from left to right. From Figure 5 of [HE18]. Used with kind permission of David Ha.

Figure 21.8 shows some samples from various class-conditional models. We vary the temperature parameter τ of the emission model to control the stochasticity of the generator. (More precisely, we multiply the GMM variances by τ, and divide the discrete probabilities by τ before renormalizing.) When the temperature is low, the model tries to reconstruct the input as closely as possible. However, when the input is untypical of the training set (e.g., a cat with three eyes, or a toothbrush), the reconstruction is "regularized" towards a canonical cat with two eyes, while still keeping some features of the input.

Molecular design

In [GB+18], they use VAE-RNNs to model molecular graph structure, represented as a string using the SMILES representation.[4] It is also possible to learn a mapping from the latent space to some scalar quantity of interest, such as the solubility or drug efficacy of a molecule. We can then perform gradient-based optimization in the continuous latent space to try to generate new graphs which maximize this quantity. See Figure 21.9 for a sketch of this approach.

The main problem is to ensure that points in latent space decode to valid strings/molecules. There are various solutions to this, including using a **grammar VAE**, where the RNN decoder is replaced by a stochastic context free grammar. See [KPHL17] for details.

21.4   Avoiding posterior collapse

If the decoder $p_{\theta}(x|z)$ is sufficiently powerful (e.g., a pixel CNN, or an RNN for text), then the VAE does not need to use the latent code z for anything. This is called **posterior collapse** or **variational**

---

4. See https://en.wikipedia.org/wiki/Simplified_molecular-input_line-entry_system.

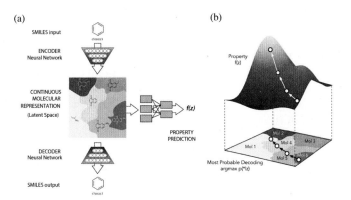

Figure 21.9: Application of VAE-RNN to molecule design. (a) The VAE-RNN model is trained on a sequence representation of molecules known as SMILES. We can fit an MLP to map from the latent space to properties of the molecule, such as its "fitness" $f(\boldsymbol{z})$. (b) We can perform gradient ascent in $f(\boldsymbol{z})$ space, and then decode the result to a new molecule with high fitness. From Figure 1 of [GB+18]. Used with kind permission of Rafael Gomez-Bombarelli.

overpruning (see e.g., [Che+17b; Ale+18; Hus17a; Phu+18; TT17; Yeu+17; Luc+19; DWW19; WBC21]). To see why this happens, consider Equation (21.21). If there exists a parameter setting for the generator $\boldsymbol{\theta}^*$ such that $p_{\boldsymbol{\theta}^*}(\boldsymbol{x}|\boldsymbol{z}) = p_{\mathcal{D}}(\boldsymbol{x})$ for every $\boldsymbol{z}$, then we can make $D_{\mathbb{KL}}\left(p_{\mathcal{D}}(\boldsymbol{x}) \parallel p_{\boldsymbol{\theta}}(\boldsymbol{x})\right) = 0$. Since the generator is independent of the latent code, we have $p_{\boldsymbol{\theta}}(\boldsymbol{z}|\boldsymbol{x}) = p_{\boldsymbol{\theta}}(\boldsymbol{z})$. The prior $p_{\boldsymbol{\theta}}(\boldsymbol{z})$ is usually a simple distribution, such as a Gaussian, so we can find a setting of the inference parameters so that $q_{\boldsymbol{\phi}^*}(\boldsymbol{z}|\boldsymbol{x}) = p_{\boldsymbol{\theta}}(\boldsymbol{z})$, which ensures $D_{\mathbb{KL}}\left(q_{\boldsymbol{\phi}}(\boldsymbol{z}|\boldsymbol{x}) \parallel p_{\boldsymbol{\theta}}(\boldsymbol{z}|\boldsymbol{x})\right) = 0$. Thus we have succesfully maximized the ELBO, but we have not learned any useful latent representation of the data, which is one of the goals of latent variable modeling.[5] We discuss some solutions to posterior collapse below.

21.4.1 KL annealing

A common approach to solving this problem, proposed in [Bow+16a], is to use **KL annealing**, in which the KL penalty term in the ELBO is scaled by β, which is increased from 0.0 (corresponding to an autoencoder) to 1.0 (which corresponds to standard MLE training). (Note that, by contrast, the β-VAE model in Section 21.3.1 uses $\beta > 1$.)

KL annealing can work well, but requires tuning the schedule for β. A standard practice [Fu+19] is to use **cyclical annealing**, which repeats the process of increasing β multiple times. This ensures the progressive learning of more meaningful latent codes, by leveraging good representations learned in a previous cycle as a way to warmstart the optimization.

---

5. Note that [Luc+19; DWW20] show that posterior collapse can also happen in linear VAE models, where the ELBO corresponds to the exact marginal likelihood, so the problem is not only due to powerful (nonlinear) decoders, but is also related to spurious local maxima in the objective.

21.4.2   Lower bounding the rate

An alternative approach is to stick with the original unmodified ELBO objective, but to prevent the rate (i.e., the $D_{\mathbb{KL}}(q \parallel p)$ term) from collapsing to 0, by limiting the flexibility of q. For example, [XD18; Dav+18] use a von Mises-Fisher (Section 2.2.5.3) prior and posterior, instead of a Gaussian, and they constrain the posterior to have a fixed concentration, $q(\boldsymbol{z}|\boldsymbol{x}) = \text{vMF}(\boldsymbol{z}|\boldsymbol{\mu}(\boldsymbol{x}), \kappa)$. Here the parameter κ controls the rate of the code. The δ-**VAE** method [Oor+19] uses a Gaussian autoregressive prior and a diagonal Gaussian posterior. We can ensure the rate is at least δ by adjusting the regression parameter of the AR prior.

21.4.3   Free bits

In this section, we discuss the method of **free bits** [Kin+16], which is another way of lower bounding the rate. To explain this, consider a fully factorized posterior in which the KL penalty has the form

$$\mathcal{L}_R = \sum_i D_{\mathbb{KL}}(q_{\boldsymbol{\phi}}(z_i|\boldsymbol{x}) \parallel p_{\boldsymbol{\theta}}(z_i)) \tag{21.58}$$

where z_i is the i'th dimension of $\boldsymbol{z}$. We can replace this with a hinge loss, that will give up driving down the KL for dimensions that are already beneath a target compression rate λ:

$$\mathcal{L}'_R = \sum_i \max(\lambda, D_{\mathbb{KL}}(q_{\boldsymbol{\phi}}(z_i|\boldsymbol{x}) \parallel p_{\boldsymbol{\theta}}(z_i))) \tag{21.59}$$

Thus the bits where the KL is sufficiently small "are free", since the model does not have to "pay" to encode them according to the prior.

21.4.4   Adding skip connections

One reason for latent variable collapse is that the latent variables $\boldsymbol{z}$ are not sufficiently "connected to" the observed data $\boldsymbol{x}$. One simple solution is to modify the architecture of the generative model by adding **skip connections**, similar to a residual network (Section 16.2.4), as shown in Figure 21.10. This is called a **skip-VAE** [Die+19a].

21.4.5   Improved variational inference

The posterior collapse problem is caused in part by the poor approximation to the posterior. In [He+19], they proposed to keep the model and VAE objective unchanged, but to more aggressively update the inference network before each step of generative model fitting. This enables the inference network to capture the current true posterior more faithfully, which will encourage the generator to use the latent codes when it is useful to do so.

However, this only addresses the part of posterior collapse that is due to the amortization gap [CLD18], rather than the more fundamental problem of variational pruning, in which the KL term penalizes the model if its posterior deviates too far from the prior, which is often too simple to match the aggregated posterior.

Another way to ameliorate variational pruning is to use lower bounds that are tighter than the vanilla ELBO (Section 10.5.1), or more accurate posterior approximations (Section 10.4), or more accurate (hierarchical) generative models (Section 21.5).

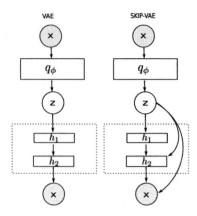

Figure 21.10: (a) VAE. (b) Skip-VAE. From Figure 1 of [Die+19a]. Used with kind permission of Adji Dieng.

21.4.6 Alternative objectives

An alternative to the above methods is to replace the ELBO objective with other objectives, such as the InfoVAE objective discussed in Section 21.3.2, which includes adversarial autoencoders and MMD autoencoders as special cases. The InfoVAE objective includes a term to explicitly enforce non-zero mutual information between x and z, which effectively solves the problem of posterior collapse.

21.5 VAEs with hierarchical structure

We define a **hierarchical VAE** or HVAE, with L stochastic layers, to be the following generative model:[6]

$$p_{\boldsymbol{\theta}}(\boldsymbol{x}, \boldsymbol{z}_{1:L}) = p_{\boldsymbol{\theta}}(\boldsymbol{z}_L) \left[\prod_{l=L-1}^{1} p_{\boldsymbol{\theta}}(\boldsymbol{z}_l|\boldsymbol{z}_{l+1}) \right] p_{\boldsymbol{\theta}}(\boldsymbol{x}|\boldsymbol{z}_1) \tag{21.60}$$

We can improve on the above model by making it non-Markovian, i.e., letting each $\boldsymbol{z}_l$ depend on all the higher level stochastic variables, $\boldsymbol{z}_{l+1:L}$, not just the preceeding level, i.e.,

$$p_{\boldsymbol{\theta}}(\boldsymbol{x}, \boldsymbol{z}) = p_{\boldsymbol{\theta}}(\boldsymbol{z}_L) \left[\prod_{l=L-1}^{1} p_{\boldsymbol{\theta}}(\boldsymbol{z}_l|\boldsymbol{z}_{l+1:L}) \right] p_{\boldsymbol{\theta}}(\boldsymbol{x}|\boldsymbol{z}_{1:L}) \tag{21.61}$$

Note that the likelihood is now $p_{\boldsymbol{\theta}}(\boldsymbol{x}|\boldsymbol{z}_{1:L})$ instead of just $p_{\boldsymbol{\theta}}(\boldsymbol{x}|\boldsymbol{z}_1)$. This is analogous to adding skip connections from all preceeding variables to all their children. It is easy to implement this by using a deterministic "backbone" of residual connections, that accumulates all stochastic decisions, and propagates them down the chain, as illustrated in Figure 21.11(left). We discuss how to perform inference and learning in such models below.

---

6. There is a split in the literature about whether to label the top level as $\boldsymbol{z}_L$ or $\boldsymbol{z}_1$. We adopt the former convention, since we view lower numbered layers, such as $\boldsymbol{z}_1$, as being "closer to the data", and higher numbered layers, such as $\boldsymbol{z}_L$, as being "more abstract".

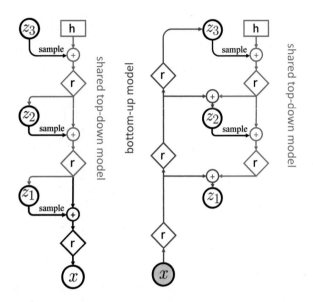

Figure 21.11: Hierarchical VAEs with 3 stochastic layers. Left: generative model. Right: inference network. Diamond is a residual network, $\oplus$ is feature combination (e.g., concatenation), and h is a trainable parameter. We first do bottom-up inference, by propagating $\boldsymbol{x}$ up to $\boldsymbol{z}_3$ to compute $\boldsymbol{z}_3^s \sim q_\phi(\boldsymbol{z}_3|\boldsymbol{x})$, and then we perform top-down inference by computing $\boldsymbol{z}_2^s \sim q_\phi(\boldsymbol{z}_2|\boldsymbol{x}, \boldsymbol{z}_3^s)$ and then $\boldsymbol{z}_1^s \sim q_\phi(\boldsymbol{z}_1|\boldsymbol{x}, \boldsymbol{z}_{2:3}^s)$. From Figure 2 of [VK20a]. Used with kind permission of Arash Vahdat.

21.5.1   Bottom-up vs top-down inference

To perform inference in a hierarchical VAE, we could use a **bottom-up inference model** of the form

$$q_\phi(\boldsymbol{z}|\boldsymbol{x}) = q_\phi(\boldsymbol{z}_1|\boldsymbol{x}) \prod_{l=2}^{L} q_\phi(\boldsymbol{z}_l|\boldsymbol{x}, \boldsymbol{z}_{1:l-1}) \tag{21.62}$$

However, a better approach is to use a **top-down inference model** of the form

$$q_\phi(\boldsymbol{z}|\boldsymbol{x}) = q_\phi(\boldsymbol{z}_L|\boldsymbol{x}) \prod_{l=L-1}^{1} q_\phi(\boldsymbol{z}_l|\boldsymbol{x}, \boldsymbol{z}_{l+1:L}) \tag{21.63}$$

Inference for $\boldsymbol{z}_l$ combines bottom-up information from $\boldsymbol{x}$ with top-down information from higher layers, $\boldsymbol{z}_{>l} = \boldsymbol{z}_{l+1:L}$. See Figure 21.11(right) for an illustration.[7]

---

7. Note that it is also possible to have a stochastic bottom-up encoder and a stochastic top-down encoder, as discussed in the **BIVA** paper [Maa+19]. (BIVA stands for "bidirectional-inference variational autoencoder".)

With the above model, the ELBO can be written as follows (using the chain rule for KL):

$$\text{Ł}(\boldsymbol{\theta}, \boldsymbol{\phi}|\boldsymbol{x}) = \mathbb{E}_{q_{\boldsymbol{\phi}}(\boldsymbol{z}|\boldsymbol{x})} \left[\log p_{\boldsymbol{\theta}}(\boldsymbol{x}|\boldsymbol{z})\right] - D_{\mathbb{KL}} \left(q_{\boldsymbol{\phi}}(\boldsymbol{z}_L|\boldsymbol{x}) \, \| \, p_{\boldsymbol{\theta}}(\boldsymbol{z}_L)\right) \tag{21.64}$$

$$- \sum_{l=L-1}^{1} \mathbb{E}_{q_{\boldsymbol{\phi}}(\boldsymbol{z}_{>l}|\boldsymbol{x})} \left[D_{\mathbb{KL}} \left(q_{\boldsymbol{\phi}}(\boldsymbol{z}_l|\boldsymbol{x}, \boldsymbol{z}_{>l}) \, \| \, p_{\boldsymbol{\theta}}(\boldsymbol{z}_l|\boldsymbol{z}_{>l})\right)\right] \tag{21.65}$$

where

$$q_{\boldsymbol{\phi}}(\boldsymbol{z}_{>l}|\boldsymbol{x}) = \prod_{i=l+1}^{L} q_{\boldsymbol{\phi}}(\boldsymbol{z}_i|\boldsymbol{x}, \boldsymbol{z}_{>i}) \tag{21.66}$$

is the approximate posterior above layer l (i.e., the parents of $\boldsymbol{z}_l$).

The reason the top-down inference model is better is that it more closely approximates the true posterior of a given layer, which is given by

$$p_{\boldsymbol{\theta}}(\boldsymbol{z}_l|\boldsymbol{x}, \boldsymbol{z}_{l+1:L}) \propto p_{\boldsymbol{\theta}}(\boldsymbol{z}_l|\boldsymbol{z}_{l+1:L}) p_{\boldsymbol{\theta}}(\boldsymbol{x}|\boldsymbol{z}_l, \boldsymbol{z}_{l+1:L}) \tag{21.67}$$

Thus the posterior combines the top-down prior term $p_{\boldsymbol{\theta}}(\boldsymbol{z}_l|\boldsymbol{z}_{l+1:L})$ with the bottom-up likelihood term $p_{\boldsymbol{\theta}}(\boldsymbol{x}|\boldsymbol{z}_l, \boldsymbol{z}_{l+1:L})$. We can approximate this posterior by defining

$$q_{\boldsymbol{\phi}}(\boldsymbol{z}_l|\boldsymbol{x}, \boldsymbol{z}_{l+1:L}) \propto p_{\boldsymbol{\theta}}(\boldsymbol{z}_l|\boldsymbol{z}_{l+1:L}) \tilde{q}_{\boldsymbol{\phi}}(\boldsymbol{z}_l|\boldsymbol{x}, \boldsymbol{z}_{l+1:L}) \tag{21.68}$$

where $\tilde{q}_{\boldsymbol{\phi}}(\boldsymbol{z}_l|\boldsymbol{x}, \boldsymbol{z}_{l+1:L})$ is a learned Gaussian approximation to the bottom-up likelihood. If both prior and likelihood are Gaussian, we can compute this product in closed form, as proposed in the **ladder network** paper [Sn+16; Søn+16].[8] A more flexible approach is to let $q_{\boldsymbol{\phi}}(\boldsymbol{z}_l|\boldsymbol{x}, \boldsymbol{z}_{l+1:L})$ be learned, but to force it to share some of its parameters with the learned prior $p_{\boldsymbol{\theta}}(\boldsymbol{z}_l|\boldsymbol{z}_{l+1:L})$, as proposed in [Kin+16]. This reduces the number of parameters in the model, and ensures that the posterior and prior remain somewhat close.

21.5.2 Example: very deep VAE

There have been many papers exploring different kinds of HVAE models (see e.g., [Kin+16; Sn+16; Chi21a; VK20a; Maa+19]), and we do not have space to discuss them all. Here we focus on the **"very deep VAE"** or **VD-VAE** model of [Chi21a], since it is simple but yields state of the art results (at the time of writing).

The architecture is a simple convolutional VAE with bidirectional inference, as shown in Figure 21.12. For each layer, the prior and posterior are diagonal Gaussians. The author found that nearest-neighbor upsampling (in the decoder) worked much better than transposed convolution, and avoided posterior collapse. This enabled training with the vanilla VAE objective, without needing any of the tricks discussed in Section 21.5.4.

The low-resolution latents (at the top of the hierarchy) capture a lot of the global structure of each image; the remaining high-resolution latents are just used to fill in details, that make the image look more realistic, and improve the likelihood. This suggests the model could be useful for lossy

---

8. The term "ladder network" arises from the horizontal "rungs" in Figure 21.11(right). Note that a similar idea was independently proposed in [Sal16].

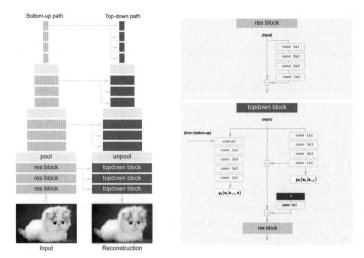

Figure 21.12: The top-down encoder used by the hierarchical VAE in [Chi21a]. Each convolution is preceded by the GELU nonlinearity. The model uses average pooling and nearest-neighbor upsampling for the pool and unpool layers. The posterior q_ϕ and prior p_θ are diagonal Gaussians. From Figure 3 of [Chi21a]. Used with kind permission of Rewon Child.

Figure 21.13: Samples from a VDVAE model (trained on FFHQ dataset) from different levels of the hierarchy. From Figure 1 of [Chi21a]. Used with kind permission of Rewon Child.

compression, since a lot of the low-level details can be drawn from the prior (i.e., "hallucinated"), rather than having to be sent by the encoder.

We can also use the model for unconditional sampling at multiple resolutions. This is illustrated in Figure 21.13, using a model with 78 stochastic layers trained on the FFHQ-256 dataset.[9].

21.5.3   Connection with autoregressive models

Until recently, most hierarchical VAEs only had a small number of stochastic layers. Consequently the images they generated have not looked as good, or had as high likelihoods, as images produced by other models, such as the autoregressive PixelCNN model (see Section 22.3.2). However, by endowing VAEs with many more stochastic layers, it is possible to outperform AR models in terms of

9. This is a 256^2 version of the Flickr-Faces High Quality dataset from https://github.com/NVlabs/ffhq-dataset, which has 80k images at 1024^2 resolution.

Latent variables are identical to observed variables

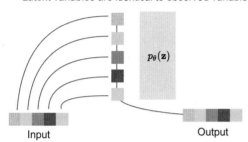

Latent variables allow for parallel generation

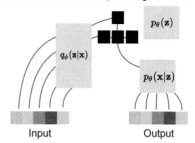

Figure 21.14: Left: a hierarchical VAE which emulates an autoregressive model using an identify encoder, autoregressive prior, and identity decoder. Right: a hierarchical VAE with a 2 layer hierarchical latent code. The bottom hidden nodes (black) are conditionally independent given the top layer. From Figure 2 of [Chi21a]. Used with kind permission of Rewon Child.

likelihood and sample quality, while using fewer parameters and much less computing power [Chi21a; VK20a; Maa+19].

To see why this is possible, note that we can represent any AR model as a degenerate VAE, as shown in Figure 21.14(left). The idea is simple: the encoder copies the input into latent space by setting $\boldsymbol{z}_{1:D} = \boldsymbol{x}_{1:D}$ (so $q_\phi(z_i = x_i | \boldsymbol{z}_{>i}, \boldsymbol{x}) = 1$), then the model learns an autoregressive prior $p_{\boldsymbol{\theta}}(\boldsymbol{z}_{1:D}) = \prod_d p(z_d | \boldsymbol{z}_{1:d-1})$, and finally the likelihood function just copies the latent vector to output space, so $p_{\boldsymbol{\theta}}(x_i = z_i | \boldsymbol{z}) = 1$. Since the encoder computes the exact (albeit degenerate) posterior, we have $q_\phi(\boldsymbol{z}|\boldsymbol{x}) = p_{\boldsymbol{\theta}}(\boldsymbol{z}|\boldsymbol{x})$, so the ELBO is tight and reduces to the log likelihood,

$$\log p_{\boldsymbol{\theta}}(\boldsymbol{x}) = \log p_{\boldsymbol{\theta}}(\boldsymbol{z}) = \sum_d \log p_{\boldsymbol{\theta}}(x_d | \boldsymbol{x}_{<d}) \tag{21.69}$$

Thus we can emulate any AR model with a VAE providing it has at least D stochastic layers, where D is the dimensionality of the observed data.

In practice, data usually lives in a lower-dimensional manifold (see e.g., [DW19]), which can allow for a much more compact latent code. For example, Figure 21.14(right) shows a hierarchical code in which the latent factors at the lower level are conditionally independent given the higher level, and hence can be generated in parallel. Such a tree-like structure can enable sample generation in $O(\log D)$ time, whereas an autoregressive model always takes $O(D)$ time. (Recall that for an image D is the number of pixels, so it grows quadratically with image resolution. For example, even a tiny 32×32 image has $D = 3072$.)

In addition to speed, hierarchical models also require many fewer parameters than "flat" models. The typical architecture used for generating images is a **multi-scale** approach: the model starts from a small, spatially arranged set of latent variables, and at each subsequent layer, the spatial resolution is increased (usually by a factor of 2). This allows the high level to capture global, long-range correlations (e.g., the symmetry of a face, or overall skin tone), while letting lower levels capture fine-grained details.

21.5.4   Variational pruning

A common problem with hierarchical VAEs is that the higher level latent layers are often ignored, so the model does not learn interesting high level semantics. This is caused by **variational pruning**. This problem is analogous to the issue of latent variable collapse, which we discussed in Section 21.4.

A common heuristic to mitigate this problem is to use KL balancing coefficients [Che+17b], to ensure that an equal amount of information is encoded in each layer. That is, we use the following penalty:

$$\sum_{l=1}^{L} \gamma_l \mathbb{E}_{q_\phi(\boldsymbol{z}_{>l}|\boldsymbol{x})} \left[D_{\mathrm{KL}} \left(q_\phi(\boldsymbol{z}_l|\boldsymbol{x}, \boldsymbol{z}_{>l}) \parallel p_\theta(\boldsymbol{z}_l|\boldsymbol{z}_{>l}) \right) \right] \tag{21.70}$$

The balancing term γ_l is set to a small value when the KL penalty is small (on the current minibatch), to encourage use of that layer, and is set to a large value when the KL term is large. (This is only done during the "warm up period".) Concretely, [VK20a] proposes to set the coefficients γ_l to be proportional to the size of the layer, s_l, and the average KL loss:

$$\gamma_l \propto s_l \mathbb{E}_{\boldsymbol{x} \sim \mathcal{B}} \left[\mathbb{E}_{q_\phi(\boldsymbol{z}_{>l}|\boldsymbol{x})} \left[D_{\mathrm{KL}} \left(q_\phi(\boldsymbol{z}_l|\boldsymbol{x}, \boldsymbol{z}_{>l}) \parallel p_\theta(\boldsymbol{z}_l|\boldsymbol{z}_{>l}) \right) \right] \right] \tag{21.71}$$

where $\mathcal{B}$ is the current minibatch.

21.5.5   Other optimization difficulties

A common problem when training (hierarchical) VAEs is that the loss can become unstable. The main reason for this is that the KL term is unbounded (can become infinitely large). In [Chi21a], they tackle the problem in two ways. First, ensure the initial random weights of the final convolutional layer in each residual bottleneck block get scaled by $1/\sqrt{L}$. Second, skip an update step if the norm of the gradient of the loss exceeds some threshold.

In the **Nouveau VAE** method of [VK20a], they use some more complicated measures to ensure stability. First, they use batch normalization, but with various tweaks. Second, they use spectral regularization for the encoder. Specifically they add the penalty $\beta \sum_i \lambda_i$, where λ_i is the largest singular value of the i'th convolutional layer (estimated using a single power iteration step), and $\beta \geq 0$ is a tuning parameter. Third, they use inverse autoregressive flows (Section 23.2.4.3) in each layer, instead of a diagonal Gaussian approximation. Fourth, they represent the posterior using a residual representation. In particular, let us assume the prior for the i'th variable in layer l is

$$p_\theta(z_l^i|\boldsymbol{z}_{>l}) = \mathcal{N}(z_l^i|\mu_i(\boldsymbol{z}_{>l}), \sigma_i(\boldsymbol{z}_{>l})) \tag{21.72}$$

They propose the following posterior approximation:

$$q_\phi(z_l^i|\boldsymbol{x}, \boldsymbol{z}_{>l}) = \mathcal{N} \left(z_l^i|\mu_i(\boldsymbol{z}_{>l}) + \Delta\mu_i(\boldsymbol{z}_{>l}, \boldsymbol{x}), \ \sigma_i(\boldsymbol{z}_{>l}) \cdot \Delta\sigma_i(\boldsymbol{z}_{>l}, \boldsymbol{x}) \right) \tag{21.73}$$

where the Δ terms are the relative changes computed by the encoder. The corresponding KL penalty reduces to the following (dropping the l subscript for brevity):

$$D_{\mathrm{KL}} \left(q_\phi(z^i|\boldsymbol{x}, \boldsymbol{z}_{>l}) \parallel p_\theta(z^i|\boldsymbol{z}_{>l}) \right) = \frac{1}{2} \left(\frac{\Delta\mu_i^2}{\sigma_i^2} + \Delta\sigma_i^2 - \log \Delta\sigma_i^2 - 1 \right) \tag{21.74}$$

So as long as σ_i is bounded from below, the KL term can be easily controlled just by adjusting the encoder parameters.

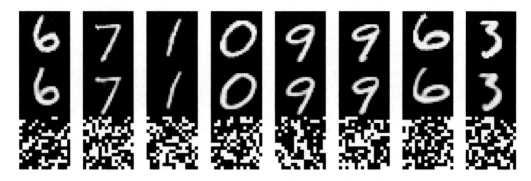

Figure 21.15: *Autoencoder for MNIST using 256 binary latents. Top row: input images. Middle row: reconstruction. Bottom row: latent code, reshaped to a 16 × 16 image. Generated by quantized_autoencoder_mnist.ipynb.*

21.6 Vector quantization VAE

In this section, we describe **VQ-VAE**, which stands for "vector quantized VAE" [OVK17; ROV19]. This is like a standard VAE except it uses a set of discrete latent variables.

21.6.1 Autoencoder with binary code

The simplest approach to the problem is to construct a standard VAE, but to add a discretization layer at the end of the encoder, $z_e(x) \in \{0, \ldots, S-1\}^K$, where S is the number of states, and K is the number of discrete latents. For example, we can binarize the latent vector (using $S = 2$) by clipping z to lie in $\{0, 1\}^K$. This can be useful for data compression (see e.g., [BLS17]).

Suppose we assume the prior over the latent codes is uniform. Since the encoder is deterministic, the KL divergence reduces to a constant, equal to $\log K$. This avoids the problem with posterior collapse (Section 21.4). Unfortunately, the discontinuous quantization operation of the encoder prohibits the direct use of gradient based optimization. The solution proposed in [OVK17] is to use the straight-through estimator, which we discuss in Section 6.3.8. We show a simple example of this approach in Figure 21.15, where we use a Gaussian likelihood, so the loss function has the form

$$\mathcal{L} = ||x - d(e(x))||_2^2 \tag{21.75}$$

where $e(x) \in \{0, 1\}^K$ is the encoder, and $d(z) \in \mathbb{R}^{28 \times 28}$ is the decoder.

21.6.2 VQ-VAE model

We can get a more expressive model by using a 3d tensor of discrete latents, $z \in \mathbb{R}^{H \times W \times K}$, where K is the number of discrete values per latent variable. Rather than just binarizing the continuous vector $z_e(x)_{ij}$, we compare it to a **codebook** of embedding vectors, $\{e_k : k = 1 : K, e_k \in \mathbb{R}^L\}$, and then set z_{ij} to the index of the nearest codebook entry:

$$q(z_{ij} = k|x) = \begin{cases} 1 & \text{if } k = \text{argmin}_{k'} ||z_e(x)_{i,j,:} - e_{k'}||_2 \\ 0 & \text{otherwise} \end{cases} \tag{21.76}$$

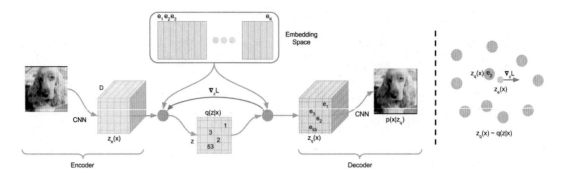

Figure 21.16: VQ-VAE architecture. From Figure 1 of [OVK17]. Used with kind permission of Aäron van den Oord.

When reconstructing the input we replace each discrete code index by the corresponding real-valued codebook vector:

$$(\boldsymbol{z}_q)_{ij} = \boldsymbol{e}_k \text{ where } \boldsymbol{z}_{ij} = k \tag{21.77}$$

These values are then passed to the decoder, $p(\boldsymbol{x}|\boldsymbol{z}_q)$, as usual. See Figure 21.16 for an illustration of the overall architecture. Note that although $\boldsymbol{z}_q$ is generated from a discrete combination of codebook vectors, the use of a distributed code makes the model very expressive. For example, if we use a grid of 32×32, with $K = 512$, then we can generate $512^{32 \times 32} = 2^{9216}$ distinct images, which is astronomically large.

To fit this model, we can minimize the negative log likelihood (reconstruction error) using the straight-through estimator, as before. This amounts to passing the gradients from the decoder input $\boldsymbol{z}_q(\boldsymbol{x})$ to the encoder output $\boldsymbol{z}_e(\boldsymbol{x})$, bypassing Equation (21.76), as shown by the red arrow in Figure 21.16. Unfortunately this means that the codebook entries will not get any learning signal. To solve this, the authors proposed to add an extra term to the loss, known as the **codebook loss**, that encourages the codebook entries $\boldsymbol{e}$ to match the output of the encoder. We treat the encoder $\boldsymbol{z}_e(\boldsymbol{x})$ as a fixed target, by adding a **stop gradient** operator to it; this ensures $\boldsymbol{z}_e$ is treated normally in the forwards pass, but has zero gradient in the backwards pass. The modified loss (dropping the spatial indices i, j) becomes

$$\mathcal{L} = -\log p(\boldsymbol{x}|\boldsymbol{z}_q(\boldsymbol{x})) + ||\text{sg}(\boldsymbol{z}_e(\boldsymbol{x})) - \boldsymbol{e}||_2^2 \tag{21.78}$$

where $\boldsymbol{e}$ refers to the codebook vector assigned to $\boldsymbol{z}_e(\boldsymbol{x})$, and sg is the stop gradient operator.

An alternative way to update the codebook vectors is to use moving averages. To see how this works, first consider the batch setting. Let $\{\boldsymbol{z}_{i,1}, \ldots, \boldsymbol{z}_{i,n_i}\}$ be the set of n_i outputs from the encoder that are closest to the dictionary item $\boldsymbol{e}_i$. We can update $\boldsymbol{e}_i$ to minimize the MSE

$$\sum_{j=1}^{n_i} ||\boldsymbol{z}_{i,j} - \boldsymbol{e}_i||_2^2 \tag{21.79}$$

which has the closed form update

$$e_i = \frac{1}{n_i} \sum_{j=1}^{n_i} z_{i,j} \tag{21.80}$$

This is like the M step of the EM algorithm when fitting the mean vectors of a GMM. In the minibatch setting, we replace the above operations with an exponentially moving average, as follows:

$$N_i^t = \gamma N_i^{t-1} + (1 - \gamma) n_i^t \tag{21.81}$$

$$m_i^t = \gamma m_i^{t-1} + (1 - \gamma) \sum_j z_{i,j}^t \tag{21.82}$$

$$e_i^t = \frac{m_i^t}{N_i^t} \tag{21.83}$$

The authors found $\gamma = 0.9$ to work well.

The above procedure will learn to update the codebook vectors so it matches the output of the encoder. However, it is also important to ensure the encoder does not "change its mind" too often about what codebook value to use. To prevent this, the authors propose to add a third term to the loss, known as the **commitment loss**, that encourages the encoder output to be close to the codebook values. Thus we get the final loss:

$$\mathcal{L} = -\log p(\boldsymbol{x}|\boldsymbol{z}_q(\boldsymbol{x})) + ||\mathrm{sg}(\boldsymbol{z}_e(\boldsymbol{x})) - \boldsymbol{e}||_2^2 + \beta||\boldsymbol{z}_e(\boldsymbol{x}) - \mathrm{sg}(\boldsymbol{e})||_2^2 \tag{21.84}$$

The authors found $\beta = 0.25$ to work well, although of course the value depends on the scale of the reconstruction loss (NLL) term. (A probabilistic interpretation of this loss can be found in [Hen+18].) Overall, the decoder optimizes the first term only, the encoder optimizes the first and last term, and the embeddings optimize the middle term.

21.6.3 Learning the prior

After training the VQ-VAE model, it is possible to learn a better prior, to match the aggregated posterior. To do this, we just apply the encoder to a set of data, $\{\boldsymbol{x}_n\}$, thus converting them to discrete sequences, $\{\boldsymbol{z}_n\}$. We can then learn a joint distribution $p(\boldsymbol{z})$ using any kind of sequence model. In the original VQ-VAE paper [OVK17], they used the causal convolutional PixelCNN model (Section 22.3.2). More recent work has used transformer decoders (Section 22.4). Samples from this prior can then be decoded using the decoder part of the VQ-VAE model. We give some examples of this in the sections below.

21.6.4 Hierarchical extension (VQ-VAE-2)

In [ROV19], they extend the original VQ-VAE model by using a hierarchical latent code. The model is illustrated in Figure 21.17. They applied this to images of size $256 \times 256 \times 3$. The first latent layer maps this to a quantized representation of size 64×64, and the second latent layer maps this to a quantized representation of size 32×32. This hierarchical scheme allows the top level to focus on high level semantics of the image, leaving fine visual details, such as texture, to the lower level. (See Section 21.5 for more discussion of hierarchical VAEs.)

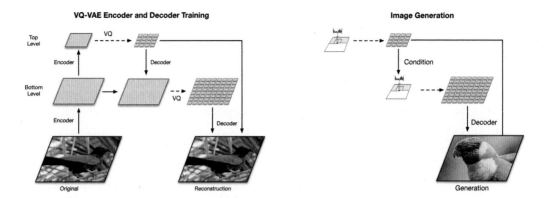

Figure 21.17: Hierarchical extension of VQ-VAE. (a) Encoder and decoder architecture. (b) Combining a Pixel-CNN prior with the decoder. From Figure 2 of [ROV19]. Used with kind permission of Aaron van den Oord.

After fitting the VQ-VAE, they learn a prior over the top level code using a PixelCNN model augmented with self-attention (Section 16.2.7) to capture long-range dependencies. (This hybrid model is known as PixelSNAIL [Che+17c].) For the lower level prior, they just use standard PixelCNN, since attention would be too expensive. Samples from the model can then be decoded using the VQ-VAE decoder, as shown in Figure 21.17.

21.6.5   Discrete VAE

In VQ-VAE, we use a one-hot encoding for the latents, $q(z = k|\boldsymbol{x}) = 1$ iff $k = \text{argmin}_k \, ||\boldsymbol{z}_e(\boldsymbol{x}) - \boldsymbol{e}_k||_2$, and then set $\boldsymbol{z}_q = \boldsymbol{e}_k$. This does not capture any uncertainty in the latent code, and requires the use of the straight-through estimator for training.

Various other approaches to fitting VAEs with discrete latent codes have been investigated. In the DALL-E paper (Section 22.4.2), they use a fairly simple method, based on using the Gumbel-softmax relaxation for the discrete variables (see Section 6.3.6). In brief, let $q(z = k|\boldsymbol{x})$ be the probability that the input $\boldsymbol{x}$ is assigned to codebook entry k. We can exactly sample $w_k \sim q(z = k|\boldsymbol{x})$ from this by computing $w_k = \text{argmax}_k \, g_k + \log q(z = k|\boldsymbol{x})$, where each g_k is from a Gumbel distribution. We can now "relax" this by using a softmax with temperature $\tau > 0$ and computing

$$w_k = \frac{\exp(\frac{g_k + \log q(z=k|\boldsymbol{x})}{\tau})}{\sum_{j=1}^{K} \exp(\frac{g_j + \log q(z=j|\boldsymbol{x})}{\tau})} \tag{21.85}$$

We now set the latent code to be a weighted sum of the codebook vectors:

$$\boldsymbol{z}_q = \sum_{k=1}^{K} w_k \boldsymbol{e}_k \tag{21.86}$$

In the limit that $\tau \to 0$, the distribution over weights $\boldsymbol{w}$ converges to a one-hot disribution, in which case $\boldsymbol{z}$ becomes equal to one of the codebook entries. But for finite τ, we "fill in" the space between the vectors.

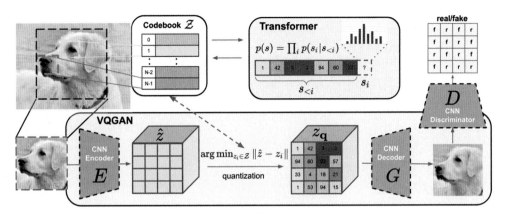

Figure 21.18: Illustration of the VQ-GAN. From Figure 2 of [ERO21]. Used with kind permission of Patrick Esser.

This allows us to express the ELBO in the usual differentiable way:

$$\mathcal{L} = -\mathbb{E}_{q(\boldsymbol{z}|\boldsymbol{x})}\left[\log p(\boldsymbol{x}|\boldsymbol{z})\right] + \beta D_{\mathrm{KL}}\left(q(\boldsymbol{z}|\boldsymbol{x}) \parallel p(\boldsymbol{z})\right) \tag{21.87}$$

where $\beta > 0$ controls the amount of regularization. (Unlike VQ-VAE, the KL term is not a constant, because the encoder is stochastic.) Furthermore, since the Gumbel noise variables are sampled from a distribution that is independent of the encoder parameters, we can use the reparameterization trick (Section 6.3.5) to optimize this.

21.6.6 VQ-GAN

One drawback of VQ-VAE is that it uses mean squared error in its reconstruction loss, which can result in blurry samples. In the **VQ-GAN** paper [ERO21], they replace this with a (patch-wise) GAN loss (see Chapter 26), together with a perceptual loss; this results in much higher visual fidelity. In addition, they use a transformer (see Section 16.3.5) to model the prior on the latent codes. See Figure 21.18 for a visualization of the overall model. In [Yu+21], they replace the CNN encoder and decoder of the VQ-GAN model with transformers, yielding improved results; they call this **VIM** (vector-quantized image modeling).

22 Autoregressive models

22.1   Introduction

By the chain rule of probability, we can write any joint distribution over T variables as follows:

$$p(\boldsymbol{x}_{1:T}) = p(\boldsymbol{x}_1)p(\boldsymbol{x}_2|\boldsymbol{x}_1)p(\boldsymbol{x}_3|\boldsymbol{x}_2,\boldsymbol{x}_1)p(\boldsymbol{x}_4|\boldsymbol{x}_3,\boldsymbol{x}_2,\boldsymbol{x}_1)\ldots = \prod_{t=1}^{T} p(\boldsymbol{x}_t|\boldsymbol{x}_{1:t-1}) \tag{22.1}$$

where $\boldsymbol{x}_t \in \mathcal{X}$ is the t'th observation, and we define $p(\boldsymbol{x}_1|\boldsymbol{x}_{1:0}) = p(x_1)$ as the initial state distribution. This is called an **autoregressive model** or **ARM**. This corresponds to a fully connected DAG, in which each node depends on all its predecessors in the ordering, as shown in Figure 22.1. The models can also be conditioned on arbitrary inputs or context $\boldsymbol{c}$, in order to define $p(\boldsymbol{x}|\boldsymbol{c})$, although we omit this for notational brevity.

We could of course also factorize the joint distribution "backwards" in time, using

$$p(\boldsymbol{x}_{1:T}) = \prod_{t=T}^{1} p(\boldsymbol{x}_t|\boldsymbol{x}_{t+1:T}) \tag{22.2}$$

However, this "anti-causal" direction is often harder to learn (see e.g., [PJS17]).

Although the decomposition in Equation (22.1) is general, each term in this expression (i.e., each conditional distribution $p(\boldsymbol{x}_t|\boldsymbol{x}_{1:t-1})$) becomes more and more complex, since it depends on an increasing number of arguments, which makes the terms slow to compute, and makes estimating their parameters more data hungry (see Section 2.6.3.2).

One approach to solving this intractability is to make the (first-order) **Markov assumption**, which gives rise to a **Markov model** $p(\boldsymbol{x}_t|\boldsymbol{x}_{1:t-1}) = p(\boldsymbol{x}_t|\boldsymbol{x}_{t-1})$, which we discuss in Section 2.6. (This is also called an auto-regressive model of order 1.) Unfortunately, the Markov assumption is very limiting. One way to relax it, and to make $\boldsymbol{x}_t$ depend on all the past $\boldsymbol{x}_{1:t-1}$ without explicitly regressing on them, is to assume the past can be compressed into a **hidden state** $\boldsymbol{z}_t$. If $\boldsymbol{z}_t$ is a deterministic function of the past observations $\boldsymbol{x}_{1:t-1}$, the resulting model is known as a **recurrent neural network**, discussed in Section 16.3.4. If $\boldsymbol{z}_t$ is a stochastic function of the past hidden state, $\boldsymbol{z}_{t-1}$, the resulting model is known as a **hidden Markov model**, which we discuss in Section 29.2.

Another approach is to stay with the general AR model of Equation (22.1), but to use a restricted functional form, such as some kind of neural network, for the conditionals $p(\boldsymbol{x}_t|\boldsymbol{x}_{1:t-1})$. Thus rather than making conditional independence assumptions, or explicitly compressing the past into a sufficient

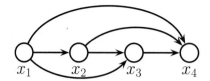

Figure 22.1: A fully-connected auto-regressive model.

statistic, we implicitly learn a compact mapping from the past to the future. In the sections below, we discuss different functional forms for these conditional distributions.

The main advantage of such AR models is that it is easy to compute, and optimize, the exact likelihood of each sequence (data vector). The main disadvantage is that generating samples is inherently sequential, which can be slow. In addition, the method does not learn a compact latent representation of the data.

22.2   Neural autoregressive density estimators (NADE)

A simple way to represent each conditional probability distribution $p(x_t|\boldsymbol{x}_{1:t-1})$ is to use a generalized linear model, such as logistic regression, as proposed in [Fre98]. We can make the model be more powerful by using a neural network. The resulting model is called the **neural auto-regressive density estimator** or **NADE** model [LM11].

If we let $p(x_t|\boldsymbol{x}_{1:t-1})$ be a conditional mixture of Gaussians, we get a model known as **RNADE** ("real-valued neural autoregressive density estimator") of [UML13]. More precisely, this has the form

$$p(x_t|\boldsymbol{x}_{1:t-1}) = \sum_{k=1}^{K} \pi_{t,k} \mathcal{N}(x_t|\mu_{t,k}, \sigma_{t,k}^2) \tag{22.3}$$

where the parameters are generated by a network, $(\boldsymbol{\mu}_t, \boldsymbol{\sigma}_t, \boldsymbol{\pi}_t) = f_t(\boldsymbol{x}_{1:t-1}; \boldsymbol{\theta}_t)$.

Rather than using separate neural networks, $f_1, \ldots, f_T$, it is more efficient to create a single network with T inputs and T outputs. This can be done using masking, resulting in a model called the **MADE** ("masked autoencoder for density estimation") model [Ger+15].

One disadvantage of NADE-type models is that they assume the variables have a natural linear ordering. This makes sense for temporal or sequential data, but not for more general data types, such as images or graphs. An orderless extension to NADE was proposed in [UML14; Uri+16].

22.3   Causal CNNs

One approach to representing the distribution $p(\boldsymbol{x}_t|\boldsymbol{x}_{1:t-1})$ is to try to identify patterns in the past history that might be predictive of the value of $\boldsymbol{x}_t$. If we assume these patterns can occur in any location, it makes sense to use a **convolutional neural network** to detect them. However, we need to make sure we only apply the convolutional mask to past inputs, not future ones. This can be done using **masked convolution**, also called **causal convolution**. We discuss this in more detail below.

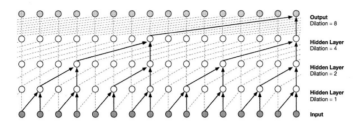

Figure 22.2: Illustration of the wavenet model using dilated (atrous) convolutions, with dilation factors of 1, 2, 4 and 8. From Figure 3 of [oor+16]. Used with kind permission of Aäron van den Oord.

22.3.1 1d causal CNN (convolutional Markov models)

Consider the following **convolutional Markov model** for 1d discrete sequences:

$$p(\boldsymbol{x}_{1:T}) = \prod_{t=1}^{T} p(x_t | \boldsymbol{x}_{1:t-1}; \boldsymbol{\theta}) = \prod_{t=1}^{T} \text{Cat}(x_t | \text{softmax}(\varphi(\sum_{\tau=1}^{t-k} \boldsymbol{w}^\mathsf{T} \boldsymbol{x}_{\tau:\tau+k}))) \tag{22.4}$$

where $\boldsymbol{w}$ is the convolutional filter of size k, and we have assumed a single nonlinearity φ and categorical output, for notational simplicity. This is like regular 1d convolution except we "mask out" future inputs, so that x_t only depends on the past values. We can of course use deeper models, and we can condition on input features $\boldsymbol{c}$.

In order to capture long-range dependencies, we can use **dilated convolution** (see [Mur22, Sec 14.4.1]). This model has been successfully used to create a state of the art **text to speech** (TTS) synthesis system known as **wavenet** [oor+16]. See Figure 22.2 for an illustration.

The wavenet model is a conditional model, $p(\boldsymbol{x}|\boldsymbol{c})$, where $\boldsymbol{c}$ is a set of linguistic features derived from an input sequence of words, and $\boldsymbol{x}$ is raw audio. The **tacotron** system [Wan+17c] is a fully end-to-end approach, where the input is words rather than linguistic features.

Although wavenet produces high quality speech, it is too slow for use in production systems. However, it can be "distilled" into a parallel generative model [Oor+18], as we discuss in Section 23.2.4.3.

22.3.2 2d causal CNN (PixelCNN)

We can extend causal convolutions to 2d, to get an autoregressive model of the form

$$p(\boldsymbol{x}|\boldsymbol{\theta}) = \prod_{r=1}^{R} \prod_{c=1}^{C} p(x_{r,c} | f_{\boldsymbol{\theta}}(\boldsymbol{x}_{1:r-1,1:C}, \boldsymbol{x}_{r,1:c-1})) \tag{22.5}$$

where R is the number of rows, C is the number of columns, and we condition on all previously generated pixels in a **raster scan** order, as illustrated in Figure 22.3. This is called the **pixelCNN** model [Oor+16]. Naive sampling (generation) from this model takes $O(N)$ time, where $N = RC$ is the number of pixels, but [Ree+17] shows how to use a multiscale approach to reduce the complexity to $O(\log N)$.

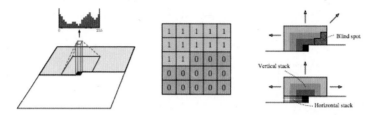

Figure 22.3: Illustration of causal 2d convolution in the PixelCNN model. The red histogram shows the empirical distribution over discretized values for a single pixel of a single RGB channel. The red and green 5×5 array shows the binary mask, which selects the top left context, in order to ensure the convolution is causal. The diagrams on the right illustrate how we can avoid blind spots by using a vertical context stack, that contains all previous rows, and a horizontal context stack, that just contains values from the current row. From Figure 1 of [Oor+16]. Used with kind permission of Aaron van den Oord.

Various extensions of this model have been proposed. The **pixelCNN++** model of [Sal+17c] improved the quality by using a mixture of logistic distributions, to capture the multimodality of $p(x_i|\boldsymbol{x}_{1:i-1})$. The **pixelRNN** of [OKK16] combined masked convolution with an RNN to get even longer range contextual dependencies. The **Subscale Pixel Network** of [MK19] proposed to generate the pixels such that the higher order bits are sampled before lower order bits, which allows high resolution details to be sampled conditioned on low resolution versions of the whole image, rather than just the top left corner.

22.4   Transformers

We introduced transformers in Section 16.3.5. They can be used for encoding sequences (as in BERT), or for decoding (generating) sequences. We can also combine the two, using an encoder-decoder combination, for conditional generation from $p(\boldsymbol{y}|\boldsymbol{c})$. Alternatively, we can define a joint sequence model $p(\boldsymbol{c}, \boldsymbol{y})$, where $\boldsymbol{c}$ is the conditioning or context prompt, and then just condition the joint model, by giving it as the initial context.

The decoder (generator) works as follows. At each step t, the model applies masked (causal) self attention (Section 16.2.7) to the first t inputs, $\boldsymbol{y}_{1:t}$, to compute a set of attention weights, $\boldsymbol{a}_{1:t}$. From this it computes an activation vector $\boldsymbol{z}_t = \sum_{\tau=1}^{t} a_t \boldsymbol{y}_t$. This is then passed through a feed-forward layer to compute $\boldsymbol{h}_t = \text{MLP}(\boldsymbol{z}_t)$. This process is repeated for each layer in the model. Finally the output is used to predict the next element in the sequence, $\boldsymbol{y}_{t+1} \sim \text{Cat}(\text{softmax}(\mathbf{W}\boldsymbol{h}_t))$.

At training time, all predictions can happen in parallel, since the target generated sequence is already available. That is, the t'th output $\boldsymbol{y}_t$ can be predicted given inputs $\boldsymbol{y}_{1:t-1}$, and this can be done for all t simultaneously. However, at test time, the model must be applied sequentially, so the output generated at $t + 1$ is fed back into the model to predict $t + 2$, etc. Note that the running time of transformers is $O(T^2)$, although a variety of more efficient versions have been developed (see e.g., [Mur22, Sec 15.6] for details).

Transformers are the basis of many popular (conditional) generative models for sequences. We give some examples below.

A "whatpu" is a small, furry animal native to Tanzania. An example of a sentence that uses the word whatpu is:
We were traveling in Africa and we saw these very cute whatpus.

To do a "farduddle" means to jump up and down really fast. An example of a sentence that uses the word farduddle is:
One day when I was playing tag with my little sister, she got really excited and she started doing these crazy farduddles.
A "yalubalu" is a type of vegetable that looks like a big pumpkin. An example of a sentence that uses the word yalubalu is:
I was on a trip to Africa and I tried this yalubalu vegetable that was grown in a garden there. It was delicious.

A "Burringo" is a car with very fast acceleration. An example of a sentence that uses the word Burringo is:
In our garage we have a Burringo that my father drives to work every day.

A "Gigamuru" is a type of Japanese musical instrument. An example of a sentence that uses the word Gigamuru is:
I have a Gigamuru that my uncle gave me as a gift. I love to play it at home.

To "screeg" something is to swing a sword at it. An example of a sentence that uses the word screeg is:
We screeghed at each other for several minutes and then we went outside and ate ice cream.

Figure 22.4: *Illustration of few shot learning with GPT-3. The model is asked to create an example sentence using a new word whose meaning is provided in the prompt. Boldface is GPT-3's completions, light gray is human input. From Figure 3.16 of [Bro+20d].*

22.4.1 Text generation (GPT, etc.)

In [Rad+18], OpenAI proposed a model called **GPT**, which is short for "Generative Pre-training Transformer". This is a decoder-only transformer model that uses causal (masked) attention. In [Rad+19], they propose **GPT-2**, which is a larger version of GPT (1.5 billion parameters, or 6.5GB, for the XL version), trained on a large web corpus (8 million pages, or 40GB). They also simplify the training objective, and just train it using maximum likelihood.

After GPT-2, OpenAI released **GPT-3** [Bro+20d], which is an even larger version of GPT-2 (175 billion parameters), trained on even more data (300 billion words), but based on the same principles. (Training was estimated to take 355 GPU years and cost $4.6M.) Due to the large size of the data and model, GPT-3 shows even more remarkable abilities to generate novel text. In particular, the output can be (partially) controlled by just changing the conditioning prompt. This enables the model to perform tasks that it has never been trained on, just by giving it some examples in the prompt. This is called "**in-context learning**". See Figure 22.4 for an example, and Section 19.5.1.2 for more details.

More recently, OpenAI released **ChatGPT** [Ope], which is an improved version of GPT-3 which has been trained to have interactive dialogs by using a technique called **reinforcement learning from human feedback** or **RLHF**, a technique first introduced in the **InstructGPT** paper [Ouy+22]. This uses RL techniques such as PPO (Section 35.3.4) to fine tune the model so that it generates responses that are more "aligned" with human intent, as estimated by a ranking model, which is pre-trained on supervised data.

```
(JAX):
Yo, PyTorch, you think you're hot stuff.
But JAX is where it's at, no need to bluff.
Your popularity might be on the rise
But when it comes to performance, we're the guys.

With automatic differentation, we're a breeze
Training neural nets with ease
Our functional approach is innovative and unique
PyTorch can't touch our speed, try and keep up, meek

(PyTorch):
Hold up, JAX,  you might be fast
But PyTorch is the one that's built to last
We may not have the fancy functional flair
But our flexibility sets us above the pair

Our community is strong and growing each day
Suppporting us in every single way
We may not be the newest on the block
But we'lll always be the torch that leads the flock
```

Figure 22.5: ChatGPT response to the prompt "Write a rap battle about PyTorch and JAX". Used with kind permission of Paige Bailey. From https://twitter.com/DynamicWebPaige/status/1601743574369902593.

Despite the impressive performance of these **large language models** or **LLMs** (see Figure 22.5 for an example), there are several open problems with them, such as: they often confidently **hallucinate** incorrect answers to questions (see e.g., [Ji+22]); they can generate biased or toxic output (see e.g., [Lia+]); and they are very resource intensive to train and serve. Indeed, these concerns are why Google has not (at the time of writing) released its version of ChatGPT, known as **LaMDA** [Col21].

The basic ideas behind LLMs are quite simple (maximum likelihood training of an autoregresssive transformer), and they can be implemented in about 300 lines of code.[1] However, just by scaling up the size of the models and datasets, it seems that qualitatively new capabilities can emerge (see e.g., [Wei+22]). Nevertheless, although this approach is good at learning formal linguistic competence (surface form), it is not clear if it is sufficient to learn functional linguistic competence, which requires a deeper, non-linguistic understanding of the world derived from experience [Mah+23].

22.4.2   Image generation (DALL-E, etc.)

The **DALL-E** model[2] from OpenAI [Ram+21a] can generate images of remarkable quality and diversity given text prompts, as shown in Figure 22.6. The methodology is conceptually quite straightforward, and most of the effort went into data collection (they scraped the web for 250 million image-text pairs) and scaling up the training (they fit a model with 12 billion parameters). Here we just focus on the algorithmic methods.

The basic idea is to transform an image x into a sequence of discrete tokens z using a discrete

---

1. See e.g., https://github.com/karpathy/nanoGPT
2. The name is derived from the artist Salvador Dalí and Pixar's movied "WALL-E"

(a) an armchair in the shape of an avocado.

(b) an illustration of a baby hedgehog in a christmas sweater walking a dog

Figure 22.6: *Some images generated by the DALL-E model in response to a text prompt. (a) "An armchair in the shape of an avocado". (b) "An illustration of a baby hedgehog in a christmas sweater walking a dog". From* `https://openai.com/blog/dall-e`. *Used with kind permission of Aditya Ramesh.*

VAE model (Section 21.6.5). We then fit a transformer to the concatenation of the image tokens z and text tokens y to get a joint model of the form $p(z, y)$.

To sample an image x given a text prompt y, we sample a latent code $z \sim p(z|y)$ by conditioning the transformer on the prompt y, and then we feed z into the VAE decoder to get the image $x \sim p(x|z)$. Multiple images are generated for each prompt, and these are then ranked according to a pre-trained critic, which gives them scores depending on how well the generated image matches the input text: $s_n = \text{critic}(x_n, y_n)$. The critic they used was the contrastive CLIP model (see Section 32.3.4.1). This discriminative reranking significantly improves the results.

Some sample results are shown in Figure 22.6, and more can be found online at `https://openai.com/blog/dall-e/`. The image on the right of Figure 22.6 is particularly interesting, since the prompt — "An illustration of a baby hedgehog in a christmas sweater walking a dog" — arguably requires that the model solve the "**variable binding problem**". This refers to the fact that the sentence implies the hedgehog should be wearing the sweater and not the dog. We see that the model sometimes interprets this correctly, but not always: sometimes it draws both animals with Christmas sweaters. In addition, sometimes it draws a hedgehog walking a smaller hedgehog. The quality of the results can also be sensitive to the form of the prompt.

The **PARTI** model [Yu+22] from Google follows similar high level ideas to DALL-E, but has been scaled to an even larger size. The larger models perform qualitatively much better, as shown in Figure 20.3.

Other recent approaches to (conditional) image generation — such as **DALL-E 2** [Ram+22] from Open-AI, **Imagen** [Sah+22] from Google, and **Stable diffusion** [Rom+22] from Stability.AI — are based on diffusion rather than applying a transformer to discretized image patches. See Section 25.6.4 for details.

22.4.3 Other applications

Transformers have been used to generate many other kinds of (discrete) data, such as midi music sequences [Hua+18a], protein sequences [Gan+23], etc.

23 Normalizing flows

This chapter is written by George Papamakarios and Balaji Lakshminarayanan.

23.1 Introduction

In this chapter we discuss **normalizing flows**, a class of flexible density models that can be easily sampled from and whose exact likelihood function is efficient to compute. Such models can be used for many tasks, such as density modeling, inference and generative modeling. We introduce the key principles of normalizing flows and refer to recent surveys by Papamakarios et al. [Pap+19] and Kobyzev, Prince, and Brubaker [KPB19] for readers interested in learning more. See also https://github.com/janosh/awesome-normalizing-flows for a list of papers and software packages.

23.1.1 Preliminaries

Normalizing flows create complex probability distributions $p(\boldsymbol{x})$ by passing random variables $\boldsymbol{u} \in \mathbb{R}^D$, drawn from a simple **base distribution** $p(\boldsymbol{u})$ through a nonlinear but *invertible* transformation $\boldsymbol{f} : \mathbb{R}^D \to \mathbb{R}^D$. That is, $p(\boldsymbol{x})$ is defined by the following process:

$$\boldsymbol{x} = \boldsymbol{f}(\boldsymbol{u}) \quad \text{where} \quad \boldsymbol{u} \sim p(\boldsymbol{u}). \tag{23.1}$$

The base distribution is typically chosen to be simple, for example standard Gaussian or uniform, so that we can easily sample from it and compute the density $p(\boldsymbol{u})$. A flexible enough transformation $\boldsymbol{f}$ can induce a complex distribution on the transformed variable $\boldsymbol{x}$ even if the base distribution is simple.

Sampling from $p(\boldsymbol{x})$ is straightforward: we first sample $\boldsymbol{u}$ from $p(\boldsymbol{u})$ and then compute $\boldsymbol{x} = \boldsymbol{f}(\boldsymbol{u})$. To compute the density $p(\boldsymbol{x})$, we rely on the fact that $\boldsymbol{f}$ is invertible. Let $\boldsymbol{g}(\boldsymbol{x}) = \boldsymbol{f}^{-1}(\boldsymbol{x}) = \boldsymbol{u}$ be the inverse mapping, which "**normalizes**" the data distribution by mapping it back to the base distribution (which is often a normal distribution). Using the change-of-variables formula for random variables from Equation (2.257), we have

$$p_x(\boldsymbol{x}) = p_u(\boldsymbol{g}(\boldsymbol{x}))|\det \mathbf{J}(\boldsymbol{g})(\boldsymbol{x})| = p_u(\boldsymbol{u})|\det \mathbf{J}(\boldsymbol{f})(\boldsymbol{u})|^{-1}, \tag{23.2}$$

where $\mathbf{J}(\boldsymbol{f})(\boldsymbol{u}) = \frac{\partial \boldsymbol{f}}{\partial \boldsymbol{u}}|_{\boldsymbol{u}}$ is the Jacobian matrix of $\boldsymbol{f}$ evaluated at $\boldsymbol{u}$. Taking logs of both sides of Equation (23.2), we get

$$\log p_x(\boldsymbol{x}) = \log p_u(\boldsymbol{u}) - \log|\det \mathbf{J}(\boldsymbol{f})(\boldsymbol{u})|. \tag{23.3}$$

As discussed above, $p(\boldsymbol{u})$ is typically easy to evaluate. So, if one can use flexible invertible transformations $\boldsymbol{f}$ whose Jacobian determinant $\det \mathbf{J}(\boldsymbol{f})(\boldsymbol{u})$ can be computed efficiently, then one can construct complex densities $p(\boldsymbol{x})$ that allow exact sampling and efficient exact likelihood computation. This is in contrast to latent variable models, which require methods like variational inference to lower-bound the likelihood.

One might wonder how flexible are the densities $p(\boldsymbol{x})$ obtained by transforming random variables sampled from simple $p(\boldsymbol{u})$. It turns out that we can use this method to approximate any smooth distribution. To see this, consider the scenario where the base distribution $p(\boldsymbol{u})$ is a one-dimensional uniform distribution. Recall that inverse transform sampling (Section 11.3.1) samples random variables from a uniform distribution and transforms them using the inverse cumulative distribution function (cdf) to generate samples from the desired density. We can use this method to sample from any one-dimensional density as long as the transformation $\boldsymbol{f}$ is powerful enough to model the inverse cdf (which is a reasonable assumption for well-behaved densities whose cdf is invertible and differentiable). We can further extend this argument to multiple dimensions by first expressing the density $p(\boldsymbol{x})$ as a product of one-dimensional conditionals using the chain rule of probability, and then applying inverse transform sampling to each one-dimensional conditional. The result is a normalizing flow that transforms a product of uniform distributions into any desired distribution $p(\boldsymbol{x})$. We refer to [Pap+19] for a more detailed proof.

How do we define flexible invertible mappings whose Jacobian determinant is easy to compute? We discuss this topic in detail in Section 23.2, but in summary, there are two main ways. The first approach is to define a set of simple transformations that are invertible by design, and whose Jacobian determinant is easy to compute; for instance, if the Jacobian is a triangular matrix, its determinant can be computed efficiently. The second approach is to exploit the fact that a composition of invertible functions is also invertible, and the overall Jacobian determinant is just the product of the individual Jacobian determinants. More precisely, if $\boldsymbol{f} = \boldsymbol{f}_N \circ \cdots \circ \boldsymbol{f}_1$ where each $\boldsymbol{f}_i$ is invertible, then $\boldsymbol{f}$ is also invertible, with inverse $\boldsymbol{g} = \boldsymbol{g}_1 \circ \cdots \circ \boldsymbol{g}_N$ and log Jacobian determinant given by

$$\log|\det \mathbf{J}(\boldsymbol{g})(\boldsymbol{x})| = \sum_{i=1}^{N} \log|\det \mathbf{J}(\boldsymbol{g}_i)(\boldsymbol{u}_i)| \tag{23.4}$$

where $\boldsymbol{u}_i = \boldsymbol{f}_i \circ \cdots \circ \boldsymbol{f}_1(\boldsymbol{u})$ is the i'th intermediate output of the flow. This allows us to create complex flows from simple components, just as graphical models allow us to create complex joint distributions from simpler conditional distributions.

Finally, a note on terminology. An invertible transformation is also known as a **bijection**. A bijection that is differentiable and has a differentiable inverse is known as a **diffeomorphism**. The transformation $\boldsymbol{f}$ of a flow model is a diffeomorphism, although in the rest of this chapter we will refer to it as a "bijection" for simplicity, leaving the differentiability implicit. The density $p_x(\boldsymbol{x})$ of a flow model is also known as the **pushforward** of the base distribution $p_u(\boldsymbol{u})$ through the transformation $\boldsymbol{f}$, and is sometimes denoted as $p_x = \boldsymbol{f}_* p_u$. Finally, in mathematics the term "flow" refers to any family of diffeomorphisms $\boldsymbol{f}_t$ indexed by a real number t such that $t = 0$ indexes the identity function, and $t_1 + t_2$ indexes $\boldsymbol{f}_{t_2} \circ \boldsymbol{f}_{t_1}$ (in physics, t often represents time). In machine learning we use the term "flow" by analogy to the above meaning, to highlight the fact that we can create flexible invertible transformations by composing simpler ones; in this sense, the index t is analogous to the number i of transformations in $\boldsymbol{f}_i \circ \cdots \circ \boldsymbol{f}_1$.

23.1.2 How to train a flow model

There are two common applications of normalizing flows. The first one is density estimation of observed data, which is achieved by fitting $p_{\boldsymbol{\theta}}(\boldsymbol{x})$ to the data and using it as an estimate of the data density, potentially followed by generating new data from $p_{\boldsymbol{\theta}}(\boldsymbol{x})$. The second one is variational inference, which involves sampling from and evaluating a variational posterior $q_{\boldsymbol{\theta}}(\boldsymbol{z}|\boldsymbol{x})$ parameterized by the flow model. As we will see below, these applications optimize different objectives and impose different computational constraints on the flow model.

23.1.2.1 Density estimation

Density estimation requires maximizing the likelihood function in Equation (23.2). This requires that we can efficiently evaluate the inverse flow $\boldsymbol{u} = \boldsymbol{f}^{-1}(\boldsymbol{x})$ and its Jacobian determinant $\det \mathbf{J}(\boldsymbol{f}^{-1})(\boldsymbol{x})$ for any given $\boldsymbol{x}$. After optimizing the model, we can optionally use it to generate new data. To sample new points, we require that the forwards mapping $\boldsymbol{f}$ be tractable.

23.1.2.2 Variational inference

Normalizing flows are commonly used for variational inference to parameterize the approximate posterior distribution in latent variable models, as discussed in Section 10.4.3. Consider a latent variable model with continuous latent variables $\boldsymbol{z}$ and observable variables $\boldsymbol{x}$. For simplicity, we consider the model parameters to be fixed as we are interested in approximating the true posterior $p^*(\boldsymbol{z}|\boldsymbol{x})$ with a normalizing flow $q_{\boldsymbol{\theta}}(\boldsymbol{z}|\boldsymbol{x})$.[1] As discussed in Section 10.1.1.2, the variational parameters are trained by maximizing the evidence lower bound (ELBO), given by

$$L(\boldsymbol{\theta}) = \mathbb{E}_{q_{\boldsymbol{\theta}}(\boldsymbol{z}|\boldsymbol{x})} \left[\log p(\boldsymbol{x}|\boldsymbol{z}) + \log p(\boldsymbol{z}) - \log q_{\boldsymbol{\theta}}(\boldsymbol{z}|\boldsymbol{x}) \right] \tag{23.5}$$

When viewing the ELBO as a function of $\boldsymbol{\theta}$, it can be simplified as follows (note we drop the dependency on $\boldsymbol{x}$ for simplicity):

$$L(\boldsymbol{\theta}) = \mathbb{E}_{q_{\boldsymbol{\theta}}(\boldsymbol{z})} \left[\ell_{\boldsymbol{\theta}}(\boldsymbol{z}) \right]. \tag{23.6}$$

Let $q_{\boldsymbol{\theta}}(\boldsymbol{z})$ denote a normalizing flow with base distribution $q(\boldsymbol{u})$ and transformation $\boldsymbol{z} = f_{\boldsymbol{\theta}}(\boldsymbol{u})$. Then the reparameterization trick (Section 6.3.5) allows us to optimize the parameters using stochastic gradients. To achieve this, we first write the expectation with respect to the base distribution:

$$L(\boldsymbol{\theta}) = \mathbb{E}_{q_{\boldsymbol{\theta}}(\boldsymbol{z})} \left[\ell_{\boldsymbol{\theta}}(\boldsymbol{z}) \right] = \mathbb{E}_{q(\boldsymbol{u})} \left[\ell_{\boldsymbol{\theta}}(f_{\boldsymbol{\theta}}(\boldsymbol{u})) \right]. \tag{23.7}$$

Then, since the base distribution does not depend on $\boldsymbol{\theta}$, we can obtain stochastic gradients as follows:

$$\nabla_{\boldsymbol{\theta}} L(\boldsymbol{\theta}) = \mathbb{E}_{q(\boldsymbol{u})} \left[\nabla_{\boldsymbol{\theta}} \ell_{\boldsymbol{\theta}}(f_{\boldsymbol{\theta}}(\boldsymbol{u})) \right] \approx \frac{1}{N} \sum_{n=1}^{N} \nabla_{\boldsymbol{\theta}} \ell_{\boldsymbol{\theta}}(f_{\boldsymbol{\theta}}(\boldsymbol{u}_n)), \tag{23.8}$$

where $\{\boldsymbol{u}_n\}_{n=1}^{N}$ are samples from $q(\boldsymbol{u})$.

---

1. We denote the parameters of the variational posterior by $\boldsymbol{\theta}$ here, which should not be confused with the model parameters which are also typically denoted by $\boldsymbol{\theta}$ elsewhere.

As we can see, in order to optimize this objective, we need to be able to efficiently sample from $q_\theta(z|x)$ and evaluate the probability density of these samples during optimization. (See Section 23.2.4.3 for details on how to do this.) This is contrast to the MLE approach in Section 23.1.2.1, which requires that we be able to compute efficiently the density of arbitrary training datapoints, but it does not require samples during optimization.

23.2   Constructing flows

In this section, we discuss how to compute various kinds of flows that are invertible by design and have efficiently computable Jacobian determinants.

23.2.1   Affine flows

A simple choice is to use an affine transformation $x = f(u) = Au + b$. This is a bijection if and only if A is an invertible square matrix. The Jacobian determinant of f is $\det A$, and its inverse is $u = f^{-1}(x) = A^{-1}(x - b)$. A flow consisting of affine bijections is called an **affine flow**, or a **linear flow** if we ignore b.

On their own, affine flows are limited in their expressive power. For example, suppose the base distribution is Gaussian, $p(u) = \mathcal{N}(u|\mu, \Sigma)$. Then the pushforward distribution after an affine bijection is still Gaussian, $p(x) = \mathcal{N}(x|A\mu + b, A\Sigma A^\mathsf{T})$. However, affine bijections are useful building blocks when composed with the non-affine bijections we discuss later, as they encourage "mixing" of dimensions through the flow.

For practical reasons, we need to ensure the Jacobian determinant and the inverse of the flow are fast to compute. In general, computing $\det A$ and A^{-1} explicitly takes $O(D^3)$ time. To reduce the cost, we can add structure to A. If A is diagonal, the cost becomes $O(D)$. If A is triangular, the Jacobian determinant is the product of the diagonal elements, so it takes $O(D)$ time; inverting the flow requires solving the triangular system $Au = x - b$, which can be done with backsubstitution in $O(D^2)$ time.

The result of a triangular transformation depends on the ordering of the dimensions. To reduce sensitivity to this, and to encourage "mixing" of dimensions, we can multiply A with a permutation matrix, which has an absolute determinant of 1. We often use a permutation that reverses the indices at each layer or that randomly shuffles them. However, usually the permutation at each layer is fixed rather than learned.

For spatially structured data (such as images), we can define A to be a convolution matrix. For example, GLOW [KD18b] uses 1×1 convolution; this is equivalent to pointwise linear transformation across feature dimensions, but regular convolution across spatial dimensions. Two more general methods for modeling $d \times d$ convolutions are presented in [HBW19], one based on stacking autoregressive convolutions, and the other on carrying out the convolution in the Fourier domain.

23.2.2   Elementwise flows

Let $h : \mathbb{R} \to \mathbb{R}$ be a scalar-valued bijection. We can create a vector-valued bijection $f : \mathbb{R}^D \to \mathbb{R}^D$ by applying h elementwise, that is, $f(u) = (h(u_1), \ldots, h(u_D))$. The function f is invertible, and its Jacobian determinant is given by $\prod_{i=1}^{D} \frac{dh}{du_i}$. A flow composed of such bijections is known as an **elementwise flow**.

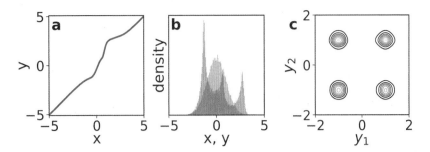

Figure 23.1: *Non-linear squared flow (NLSq). Left: an invertible mapping consisting of 4 NLSq layers. Middle: red is the base distribution (Gaussian), blue is the distribution induced by the mapping on the left. Right: density of a 5-layer autoregressive flow using NLSq transformations and a Gaussian base density, trained on a mixture of 4 Gaussians. From Figure 5 of [ZR19b]. Used with kind permission of Zachary Ziegler.*

On their own, elementwise flows are limited, since they do not model dependencies between the elements. However, they are useful building blocks for more complex flows, such as coupling flows (Section 23.2.3) and autoregressive flows (Section 23.2.4), as we will see later. In this section, we discuss techniques for constructing scalar-valued bijections $h : \mathbb{R} \to \mathbb{R}$ for use in elementwise flows.

23.2.2.1 Affine scalar bijection

An **affine scalar bijection** has the form $h(u; \boldsymbol{\theta}) = au + b$, where $\boldsymbol{\theta} = (a, b) \in \mathbb{R}^2$. (This is a scalar version of an affine flow.) Its derivative $\frac{dh}{du}$ is equal to a. It is invertible if and only if $a \neq 0$. In practice, we often parameterize a to be positive, for example by making it the exponential or the softplus of an unconstrained parameter. When $a = 1$, $h(u; \boldsymbol{\theta}) = u + b$ is often called an **additive scalar bijection**.

23.2.2.2 Higher-order perturbations

The affine scalar bijection is simple to use, but limited. We can make it more flexible by adding higher-order perturbations, under the constraint that invertibility is preserved. For example, Ziegler and Rush [ZR19b] propose the following, which they term **non-linear squared flow**:

$$h(u; \boldsymbol{\theta}) = au + b + \frac{c}{1 + (du + e)^2}, \tag{23.9}$$

where $\boldsymbol{\theta} = (a, b, c, d, e) \in \mathbb{R}^5$. When $c = 0$, this reduces to the affine case. When $c \neq 0$, it adds an inverse-quadratic perturbation, which can induce multimodality as shown in Figure 23.1. Under the constraints $a > \frac{9}{8\sqrt{3}} cd$ and $d > 0$ the function becomes invertible, and its inverse can be computed analytically by solving a quadratic polynomial.

23.2.2.3 Combinations of strictly monotonic scalar functions

A strictly monotonic scalar function is one that is always increasing (has positive derivative everywhere) or always decreasing (has negative derivative everywhere). Such functions are invertible. Many activation functions, such as the logistic sigmoid $\sigma(u) = 1/(1 + \exp(-u))$, are strictly monotonic.

Using such activation functions as a starting point, we can build more flexible monotonic functions via **conical combination** (linear combination with positive coefficients) and function composition. Suppose $h_1, \ldots, h_K$ are strictly increasing; then the following are also strictly increasing:

- $a_1 h_1 + \cdots + a_K h_K + b$ with $a_k > 0$ (conical combination with a bias),

- $h_1 \circ \cdots \circ h_K$ (function composition).

By repeating the above two constructions, we can build arbitrarily complex increasing functions. For example, a composition of conical combinations of logistic sigmoids is just an MLP where all weights are positive [Hua+18b].

The derivative of such a scalar bijection can be computed by repeatedly applying the chain rule, and in practice can be done with automatic differentiation. However, the inverse is not typically computable in closed form. In practice we can compute the inverse using bisection search, since the function is monotonic.

23.2.2.4 Scalar bijections from integration

A simple way to ensure a scalar function is strictly monotonic is to constrain its derivative to be positive. Let $h' = \frac{dh}{du}$ be this derivative. Wehenkel and Louppe [WL19] directly parameterize h' with a neural network whose output is made positive via an ELU activation function shifted up by 1. They then integrate the derivative numerically to get the bijection:

$$h(u) = \int_0^u h'(t)dt + b, \tag{23.10}$$

where b is a bias. They call this approach **unconstrained monotonic neural networks**.

The above integral is generally not computable in closed form. It can be, however, if h' is constrained appropriately. For example, Jaini, Selby, and Yu [JSY19] take h' to be a sum of K squared polynomials of degree L:

$$h'(u) = \sum_{k=1}^{K} \left(\sum_{\ell=0}^{L} a_{k\ell} u^\ell \right)^2. \tag{23.11}$$

This makes h' a non-negative polynomial of degree $2L$. The integral is analytically tractable, and makes h an increasing polynomial of degree $2L + 1$. For $L = 0$, h' is constant, so h reduces to an affine scalar bijection.

In these approaches, the derivative of the bijection can just be read off. However, the inverse is not analytically computable in general. In practice, we can use bisection search to compute the inverse numerically.

23.2.2.5 Splines

Another way to construct monotonic scalar functions is using **splines**. These are piecewise-polynomial or piecewise-rational functions, parameterized in terms of $K + 1$ **knots** (u_k, x_k) through which the spline passes. That is, we set $h(u_k) = x_k$, and define h on the interval (u_{k-1}, u_k) by interpolating

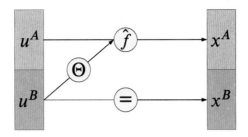

Figure 23.2: *Illustration of a coupling layer* $\boldsymbol{x} = f(\boldsymbol{u})$. *A bijection, with parameters determined by* $\boldsymbol{u}^B$, *is applied to* $\boldsymbol{u}^A$ *to generate* $\boldsymbol{x}^A$; *meanwhile* $\boldsymbol{x}^B = \boldsymbol{u}^B$ *is passed through unchanged, so the mapping can be inverted. From Figure 3 of [KPB19]. Used with kind permission of Ivan Kobyzev.*

from x_{k-1} to x_k with a polynomial or rational function (ratio of two polynomials). By increasing the number of knots we can create arbitrarily flexible monotonic functions.

Different ways to interpolate between knots give different types of spline. A simple choice is to interpolate linearly [Mül+19a]. However, this makes the derivative discontinuous at the knots. Interpolating with quadratic polynomials [Mül+19a] gives enough flexibility to make the derivative continuous. Interpolating with cubic polynomials [Dur+19], ratios of linear polynomials [DEL20], or ratios of quadratic polynomials [DBP19] allows the derivatives at the knots to be arbitrary parameters.

The spline is strictly increasing if we take $u_{k-1} < u_k$, $x_{k-1} < x_k$, and make sure the interpolation between knots is itself increasing. Depending on the flexibility on the interpolating function, more than one interpolation may exist; in practice we choose one that is guaranteed to be always increasing (see references above for details).

An advantage of splines is that they can be inverted analytically if the interpolating functions only contain low-degree polynomials. In this case, we compute $u = h^{-1}(x)$ as follows: first, we use binary search to locate the interval (x_{k-1}, x_k) in which x lies; then, we analytically solve the resulting low-degree polynomial for u.

23.2.3 Coupling flows

In this section we describe coupling flows, which allow us to model dependencies between dimensions using arbitrary non-linear functions (such as deep neural networks). Consider a partition of the input $\boldsymbol{u} \in \mathbb{R}^D$ into two subspaces, $(\boldsymbol{u}^A, \boldsymbol{u}^B) \in \mathbb{R}^d \times \mathbb{R}^{D-d}$, where d is an integer between 1 and $D - 1$. Assume a bijection $\hat{\mathbf{f}}(\cdot; \boldsymbol{\theta}) : \mathbb{R}^d \to \mathbb{R}^d$ parameterized by $\boldsymbol{\theta}$ and acting on the subspace $\mathbb{R}^d$. We define the function $\boldsymbol{f} : \mathbb{R}^D \to \mathbb{R}^D$ given by $\boldsymbol{x} = \boldsymbol{f}(\boldsymbol{u})$ as follows:

$$\boldsymbol{x}^A = \hat{\mathbf{f}}(\boldsymbol{u}^A; \Theta(\boldsymbol{u}^B)) \tag{23.12}$$

$$\boldsymbol{x}^B = \boldsymbol{u}^B. \tag{23.13}$$

See Figure 23.2 for an illustration. The function $\boldsymbol{f}$ is called a **coupling layer** [DKB15; DSDB17], because it "couples" $\boldsymbol{u}^A$ and $\boldsymbol{u}^B$ together though $\hat{\mathbf{f}}$ and Θ. We refer to flows consisting of coupling layers as **coupling flows**.

The parameters of $\hat{\mathbf{f}}$ are computed by $\boldsymbol{\theta} = \Theta(\boldsymbol{u}^B)$, where Θ is an *arbitrary* function called the **conditioner**. Unlike affine flows, which mix dimensions linearly, and elementwise flows, which do not mix dimensions at all, coupling flows can mix dimensions with a flexible non-linear conditioner Θ. In practice we often implement Θ as a deep neural network; any architecture can be used, including MLPs, CNNs, ResNets, etc.

The coupling layer $\boldsymbol{f}$ is *invertible*, and its inverse is given by $\boldsymbol{u} = \boldsymbol{f}^{-1}(\boldsymbol{x})$, where

$$\boldsymbol{u}^A = \hat{\mathbf{f}}^{-1}(\boldsymbol{x}^A; \Theta(\boldsymbol{x}^B)) \tag{23.14}$$

$$\boldsymbol{u}^B = \boldsymbol{x}^B. \tag{23.15}$$

That is, $\boldsymbol{f}^{-1}$ is given by simply replacing $\hat{\mathbf{f}}$ with $\hat{\mathbf{f}}^{-1}$. Because $\boldsymbol{x}^B$ does not depend on $\boldsymbol{u}^A$, the Jacobian of $\boldsymbol{f}$ is block triangular:

$$\mathbf{J}(\boldsymbol{f}) = \begin{pmatrix} \partial \boldsymbol{x}^A / \partial \boldsymbol{u}^A & \partial \boldsymbol{x}^A / \partial \boldsymbol{u}^B \\ \partial \boldsymbol{x}^B / \partial \boldsymbol{u}^A & \partial \boldsymbol{x}^B / \partial \boldsymbol{u}^B \end{pmatrix} = \begin{pmatrix} \mathbf{J}(\hat{\mathbf{f}}) & \partial \boldsymbol{x}^A / \partial \boldsymbol{u}^B \\ \mathbf{0} & \mathbf{I} \end{pmatrix}. \tag{23.16}$$

Thus, $\det \mathbf{J}(\boldsymbol{f})$ is equal to $\det \mathbf{J}(\hat{\mathbf{f}})$.

We often define $\hat{\mathbf{f}}$ to be an elementwise bijection, so that $\hat{\mathbf{f}}^{-1}$ and $\det \mathbf{J}(\hat{\mathbf{f}})$ are easy to compute. That is, we define:

$$\hat{\mathbf{f}}(\boldsymbol{u}^A; \boldsymbol{\theta}) = \left(h(u_1^A; \boldsymbol{\theta}_1), \ldots, h(u_d^A; \boldsymbol{\theta}_d) \right), \tag{23.17}$$

where $h(\cdot; \boldsymbol{\theta}_i)$ is a scalar bijection parameterized by $\boldsymbol{\theta}_i$. Any of the scalar bijections described in Section 23.2.2 can be used here. For example, $h(\cdot; \boldsymbol{\theta}_i)$ can be an affine bijection with $\boldsymbol{\theta}_i$ its scale and shift parameters (Section 23.2.2.1); or it can be a monotonic MLP with $\boldsymbol{\theta}_i$ its weights and biases (Section 23.2.2.3); or it can be a monotonic spline with $\boldsymbol{\theta}_i$ its knot coordinates (Section 23.2.2.5).

There are many ways to define the partition of $\boldsymbol{u}$ into $(\boldsymbol{u}^A, \boldsymbol{u}^B)$. A simple way is just to partition $\boldsymbol{u}$ into two halves. We can also exploit spatial structure in the partitioning. For example, if $\boldsymbol{u}$ is an image, we can partition its pixels using a "checkerboard" pattern, where pixels in "black squares" are in $\boldsymbol{u}^A$ and pixels in "white squares" are in $\boldsymbol{u}^B$ [DSDB17]. Since only part of the input is transformed by each coupling layer, in practice we typically employ different partitions along a coupling flow, to ensure all variables get transformed and are given the opportunity to interact.

Finally, if $\hat{\mathbf{f}}$ is an elementwise bijection, we can implement arbitrary partitions easily using a binary mask $\boldsymbol{b}$ as follows:

$$\boldsymbol{x} = \boldsymbol{b} \odot \boldsymbol{u} + (1 - \boldsymbol{b}) \odot \hat{\mathbf{f}}(\boldsymbol{u}; \Theta(\boldsymbol{b} \odot \boldsymbol{u})), \tag{23.18}$$

where $\odot$ denotes elementwise multiplication. A value of 0 in $\boldsymbol{b}$ indicates that the corresponding element in $\boldsymbol{u}$ is transformed (belongs to $\boldsymbol{u}^A$); a value of 1 indicates that it remains unchanged (belongs to $\boldsymbol{u}^B$).

As an example, we fit a masked coupling flow, created from piecewise rational quadratic splines, to the two moons dataset. Samples from each layer of the fitted model are shown in Figure 23.3.

23.2.4 Autoregressive flows

In this section we discuss **autoregressive flows**, which are flows composed of autoregressive bijections. Like coupling flows, autoregressive flows allow us to model dependencies between variables with arbitrary non-linear functions, such as deep neural networks.

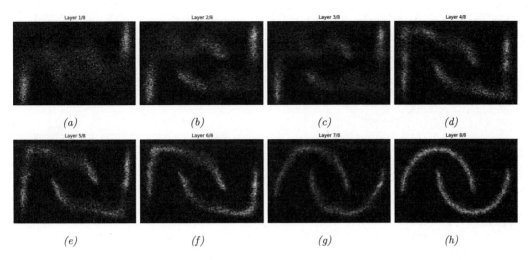

Figure 23.3: (a) Two moons dataset. (b) Samples from a normalizing flow fit to this dataset. Generated by two_moons_nsf_normalizing_flow.ipynb.

Suppose the input $\boldsymbol{u}$ contains D scalar elements, that is, $\boldsymbol{u} = (u_1, \ldots, u_D) \in \mathbb{R}^D$. We define an **autoregressive bijection** $\boldsymbol{f} : \mathbb{R}^D \to \mathbb{R}^D$, its output denoted by $\boldsymbol{x} = (x_1, \ldots, x_D) \in \mathbb{R}^D$, as follows:

$$x_i = h(u_i; \Theta_i(\boldsymbol{x}_{1:i-1})), \quad i = 1, \ldots, D. \tag{23.19}$$

Each output x_i depends on the corresponding input u_i and all previous outputs $\boldsymbol{x}_{1:i-1} = (x_1, \ldots, x_{i-1})$. The function $h(\cdot; \boldsymbol{\theta}) : \mathbb{R} \to \mathbb{R}$ is a scalar bijection (for example, one of those described in Section 23.2.2), and is parameterized by $\boldsymbol{\theta}$. The function Θ_i is a conditioner that outputs the parameters $\boldsymbol{\theta}_i$ that yield x_i, given all previous outputs $\boldsymbol{x}_{1:i-1}$. Like in coupling flows, Θ_i can be an arbitrary non-linear function, and is often parameterized as a deep neural network.

Because h is invertible, $\boldsymbol{f}$ is also invertible, and its inverse is given by:

$$u_i = h^{-1}(x_i; \Theta_i(\boldsymbol{x}_{1:i-1})), \quad i = 1, \ldots, D. \tag{23.20}$$

An important property of $\boldsymbol{f}$ is that each output x_i depends on $\boldsymbol{u}_{1:i} = (u_1, \ldots, u_i)$, but not on $\boldsymbol{u}_{i+1:D} = (u_{i+1}, \ldots, u_D)$; as a result, the partial derivative $\partial x_i / \partial u_j$ is identically zero whenever $j > i$. Therefore, the Jacobian matrix $\mathbf{J}(\boldsymbol{f})$ is triangular, and its determinant is simply the product of its diagonal entries:

$$\det \mathbf{J}(\boldsymbol{f}) = \prod_{i=1}^D \frac{\partial x_i}{\partial u_i} = \prod_{i=1}^D \frac{dh}{du_i}. \tag{23.21}$$

In other words, the autoregressive structure of $\boldsymbol{f}$ leads to a Jacobian determinant that can be computed efficiently in $O(D)$ time.

Although invertible, autoregressive bijections are computationally asymmetric: evaluating $\boldsymbol{f}$ is inherently sequential, whereas evaluating $\boldsymbol{f}^{-1}$ is inherently parallel. That is because we need $\boldsymbol{x}_{1:i-1}$ to

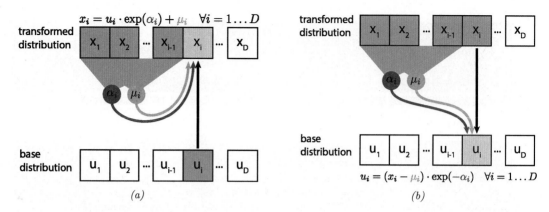

Figure 23.4: (a) Affine autoregressive flow with one layer. In this figure, $\boldsymbol{u}$ is the input to the flow (sample from the base distribution) and $\boldsymbol{x}$ is its output (sample from the transformed distribution). (b) Inverse of the above. From [Jan18]. Used with kind permission of Eric Jang.

compute x_i; therefore, computing the components of $\boldsymbol{x}$ must be done sequentially, by first computing x_1, then using it to compute x_2, then using x_1 and x_2 to compute x_3, and so on. On the other hand, computing the inverse can be done in parallel for each u_i, since $\boldsymbol{u}$ does not appear on the right-hand side of Equation (23.20). Hence, in practice it is often faster to compute $\boldsymbol{f}^{-1}$ than to compute $\boldsymbol{f}$, assuming h and h^{-1} have similar computational cost.

23.2.4.1   Affine autoregressive flows

For a concrete example, we can take h to be an affine scalar bijection (Section 23.2.2.1) parameterized by a log scale α and a bias μ. Such autoregressive flows are known as **affine autoregressive flows**. The parameters of the i'th component, α_i and μ_i, are functions of $\boldsymbol{x}_{1:i-1}$, so $\boldsymbol{f}$ takes the following form:

$$x_i = u_i \exp(\alpha_i(\boldsymbol{x}_{1:i-1})) + \mu_i(\boldsymbol{x}_{1:i-1}). \tag{23.22}$$

This is illustrated in Figure 23.4(a). We can invert this by

$$u_i = (x_i - \mu_i(\boldsymbol{x}_{1:i-1})) \exp(-\alpha_i(\boldsymbol{x}_{1:i-1})). \tag{23.23}$$

This is illustrated in Figure 23.4(b). Finally, we can calculate the log absolute Jacobian determinant by

$$\log|\det \mathbf{J}(\boldsymbol{f})| = \log\left|\prod_{i=1}^{D} \exp(\alpha_i(\boldsymbol{x}_{1:i-1}))\right| = \sum_{i=1}^{D} \alpha_i(\boldsymbol{x}_{1:i-1}). \tag{23.24}$$

Let us look at an example of an affine autoregressive flow on a 2d density estimation problem. Consider an affine autoregressive flow $\boldsymbol{x} = (x_1, x_2) = \boldsymbol{f}(\boldsymbol{u})$, where $\boldsymbol{u} \sim \mathcal{N}(\mathbf{0}, \mathbf{I})$ and $\boldsymbol{f}$ is a single autoregressive bijection. Since x_1 is an affine transformation of $u_1 \sim \mathcal{N}(0, 1)$, it is Gaussian with mean μ_1 and standard deviation $\sigma_1 = \exp \alpha_1$. Similarly, if we consider x_1 fixed, x_2 is an affine

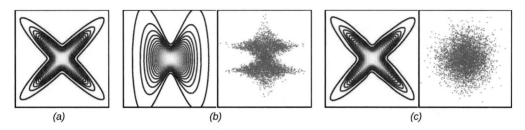

Figure 23.5: *Density estimation with affine autoregressive flows, using a Gaussian base distribution. (a) True density. (b) Estimated density using a single autoregressive layer with ordering (x_1, x_2). On the left (contour plot) we show $p(\boldsymbol{x})$. On the right (green dots) we show samples of $\boldsymbol{u} = \boldsymbol{f}^{-1}(\boldsymbol{x})$, where $\boldsymbol{x}$ is sampled from the true density. (c) Same as (b), but using 5 autoregressive layers and reversing the variable ordering after each layer. Adapted from Figure 1 of [PPM17]. Used with kind permission of Iain Murray.*

transformation of $u_2 \sim \mathcal{N}(0, 1)$, so it is *conditionally* Gaussian with mean $\mu_2(x_1)$ and standard deviation $\sigma_2(x_1) = \exp \alpha_2(x_1)$. Thus, a single affine autoregressive bijection will always produce a distribution with Gaussian conditionals, that is, a distribution of the following form:

$$p(x_1, x_2) = p(x_1)\,p(x_2|x_1) = \mathcal{N}(x_1|\mu_1, \sigma_1^2)\,\mathcal{N}(x_2|\mu_2(x_1), \sigma_2(x_1)^2) \tag{23.25}$$

This result generalizes to an arbitrary number of dimensions D.

A single affine bijection is not very powerful, regardless of how flexible the functions $\alpha_2(x_1)$ and $\mu_2(x_1)$ are. For example, suppose we want to fit the cross-shaped density shown in Figure 23.5(a) with such a flow. The resulting maximum-likelihood fit is shown in Figure 23.5(b). The red contours show the predictive distribution, $\hat{p}(\boldsymbol{x})$, which clearly fails to capture the true distribution. The green dots show transformed versions of the data samples, $p(\boldsymbol{u})$; we see that this is far from the Gaussian base distribution.

Fortunately, we can obtain a better fit by composing multiple autoregressive bijections (layers), and reversing the order of the variables after each layer. For example, Figure 23.5(c) shows the results of an affine autoregressive flow with 5 layers applied to the same problem. The red contours show that we have matched the empirical distribution, and the green dots show we have matched the Gaussian base distribution.

Note that another way to obtain a better fit is to replace the affine bijection h with a more flexible one, such as a monotonic MLP (Section 23.2.2.3) or a monotonic spline (Section 23.2.2.5).

23.2.4.2 Masked autoregressive flows

As we have seen, the conditioners Θ_i can be arbitrary non-linear functions. The most straightforward way to parameterize them is separately for each i, for example by using D separate neural networks. However, this can be parameter-inefficient for large D.

In practice, we often share parameters between conditioners by combining them into a single model Θ that takes in $\boldsymbol{x}$ and outputs $(\boldsymbol{\theta}_1, \ldots, \boldsymbol{\theta}_D)$. For the bijection to remain autoregressive, we must constrain Θ so that $\boldsymbol{\theta}_i$ depends only on $\boldsymbol{x}_{1:i-1}$ and not on $\boldsymbol{x}_{i:D}$. One way to achieve this is to start with an arbitrary neural network (an MLP, a CNN, a ResNet, etc.), and drop connections (for example, by zeroing out weights) until $\boldsymbol{\theta}_i$ is only a function of $\boldsymbol{x}_{1:i-1}$.

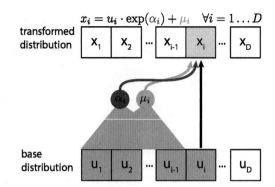

Figure 23.6: Inverse autoregressive flow that uses affine scalar bijections. In this figure, $\boldsymbol{u}$ is the input to the flow (sample from the base distribution) and $\boldsymbol{x}$ is its output (sample from the transformed distribution) From [Jan18]. Used with kind permission of Eric Jang.

An example of this approach is the **masked autoregressive flow** (**MAF**) model of [PPM17]. This model is an affine autoregressive flow combined with permutation layers, as we described in Section 23.2.4.1. MAF implements the combined conditioner Θ as follows: it starts with an MLP, and then multiplies (elementwise) the weight matrix of each layer with a binary mask of the same size (different masks are used for different layers). The masks are constructed using the method of [Ger+15]. This ensures that all computational paths from x_j to $\boldsymbol{\theta}_i$ are zeroed out whenever $j \geq i$, effectively making $\boldsymbol{\theta}_i$ only a function of $\boldsymbol{x}_{1:i-1}$. Still, evaluating the masked conditioner Θ has the same computational cost as evaluating the original (unmasked) MLP.

The key advantage of MAF (and of related models) is that, given $\boldsymbol{x}$, all parameters $(\boldsymbol{\theta}_1, \ldots, \boldsymbol{\theta}_D)$ can be computed efficiently with one neural network evaluation, so the computation of the inverse $\boldsymbol{f}^{-1}$ is fast. Thus, we can efficiently evaluate the probability density of the flow model for arbitrary datapoints. However, in order to compute $\boldsymbol{f}$, the conditioner Θ must be called a total of D times, since not all entries of $\boldsymbol{x}$ are available to start with. Thus, generating new samples from the flow is D times more expensive than evaluating its probability density function. This makes MAF suitable for density estimation, but less so for data generation.

23.2.4.3   Inverse autoregressive flows

As we have seen, the parameters $\boldsymbol{\theta}_i$ that yield the i'th output x_i are functions of the previous outputs $\boldsymbol{x}_{1:i-1}$. This ensures that the Jacobian $\mathbf{J}(\boldsymbol{f})$ is triangular, and so its determinant is efficient to compute.

However, there is another possibility: we can make $\boldsymbol{\theta}_i$ a function of the previous *inputs* instead, that is, a function of $\boldsymbol{u}_{1:i-1}$. This leads to the following bijection, which is known as **inverse autoregressive**:

$$x_i = h(u_i; \Theta_i(\boldsymbol{u}_{1:i-1})), \quad i = 1, \ldots, D. \tag{23.26}$$

Like its autoregressive counterpart, this bijection has a triangular Jacobian whose determinant is also given by $\det \mathbf{J}(\boldsymbol{f}) = \prod_{i=1}^{D} \frac{dh}{du_i}$. Figure 23.6 illustrates an inverse autoregressive flow, for the case where h is affine.

To see why this bijection is called "inverse autoregressive", compare Equation (23.26) with Equation (23.20). The two formulas differ only notationally: we can get from one to the other by swapping $\boldsymbol{u}$ with $\boldsymbol{x}$ and h with h^{-1}. In other words, the inverse autoregressive bijection corresponds to a direct parameterization of the inverse of an autoregressive bijection.

Since inverse autoregressive bijections swap the forwards and inverse directions of their autoregressive counterparts, they also swap their computational properties. This means that the forward direction $\boldsymbol{f}$ of an inverse autoregressive flow is inherently parallel and therefore fast, whereas its inverse direction $\boldsymbol{f}^{-1}$ is inherently sequential and therefore slow.

An example of an inverse autoregressive flow is their namesake **IAF** model of [Kin+16]. IAF uses affine scalar bijections, masked conditioners, and permutation layers, so it is precisely the inverse of the MAF model described in Section 23.2.4.2. Using IAF, we can generate $\boldsymbol{u}$ in parallel from the base distribution (using, for example, a diagonal Gaussian), and then sample each element of $\boldsymbol{x}$ in parallel. However, evaluating $p(\boldsymbol{x})$ for an arbitrary datapoint $\boldsymbol{x}$ is slow, because we have to evaluate each element of $\boldsymbol{u}$ sequentially. Fortunately, evaluating the likelihood of samples generated from IAF (as opposed to externally provided samples) incurs no additional cost, since in this case the u_i terms will already have been computed.

Although not so suitable for density estimation or maximum-likelihood training, IAFs are well-suited for parameterizing variational posteriors in variational inference. This is because in order to estimate the variational lower bound (ELBO), we only need samples from the variational posterior and their associated probability densities, both of which are efficient to obtain. See Section 23.1.2.2 for details.

Another useful application of IAFs is training them to mimic models whose probability density is fast to evaluate but which are slow to sample from. A notable example is the **parallel wavenet** model of [Oor+18]. This model is an IAF p_s that it trained to mimic a pretrained wavenet model p_t by minimizing the KL divergence $D_{\mathrm{KL}}\left(p_s \parallel p_t\right)$. This KL can be easily estimated by first sampling from p_s and then evaluating $\log p_s$ and $\log p_t$ at those samples, operations which are all efficient for these models. After training, we obtain an IAF that can generate audio of similar quality as the original wavenet, but can do so much faster.

23.2.4.4 Connection with autoregressive models

Autoregressive flows can be thought of as generalizing autoregressive models of continuous random variables, discussed in Section 22.1. Specifically, any continuous autoregressive model can be reparameterized as a one-layer autoregressive flow, as we describe below.

Consider a general autoregressive model over a continuous random variable $\boldsymbol{x} = (x_1, \ldots, x_D) \in \mathbb{R}^D$ written as

$$p(\boldsymbol{x}) = \prod_{i=1}^{D} p_i(x_i | \boldsymbol{\theta}_i) \quad \text{where} \quad \boldsymbol{\theta}_i = \Theta_i(\boldsymbol{x}_{1:i-1}). \tag{23.27}$$

In the above expression, $p_i(x_i | \boldsymbol{\theta}_i)$ is the i'th conditional distribution of the autoregressive model, whose parameters $\boldsymbol{\theta}_i$ are arbitrary functions of the previous variables $\boldsymbol{x}_{1:i-1}$. For example, $p_i(x_i | \boldsymbol{\theta}_i)$ can be a mixture of one-dimensional Gaussian distributions, with $\boldsymbol{\theta}_i$ representing the collection of its means, variances, and mixing coefficients.

Now consider sampling a vector $\boldsymbol{x}$ from the autoregressive model, which can be done by sampling one element at a time as follows:

$$x_i \sim p_i(x_i | \Theta_i(\boldsymbol{x}_{1:i-1})) \quad \text{for } i = 1, \ldots, D. \tag{23.28}$$

Each conditional can be sampled from using inverse transform sampling (Section 11.3.1). Let $U(0,1)$ be the uniform distribution on the interval $[0,1]$, and let $\text{CDF}_i(x_i | \boldsymbol{\theta}_i)$ be the cumulative distribution function of the i'th conditional. Sampling can be written as:

$$x_i = \text{CDF}_i^{-1}(u_i | \Theta_i(\boldsymbol{x}_{1:i-1})) \quad \text{where} \quad u_i \sim U(0,1). \tag{23.29}$$

Comparing the above expression with the definition of an autoregressive bijection in Equation (23.19), we see that the autoregressive model has been expressed as a one-layer autoregressive flow whose base distribution is uniform on $[0,1]^D$ and whose scalar bijections correspond to the inverse conditional cdf's. Viewing autoregressive models as flows this way has an important advantage, namely that it allows us to increase the flexibility of an autoregressive model by composing multiple instances of it in a flow, without sacrificing the overall tractability.

23.2.5 Residual flows

A residual network is a composition of **residual connections**, which are functions of the form $\boldsymbol{f}(\boldsymbol{u}) = \boldsymbol{u} + \mathbf{F}(\boldsymbol{u})$. The function $\mathbf{F} : \mathbb{R}^D \to \mathbb{R}^D$ is called the **residual block**, and it computes the difference between the output and the input, $\boldsymbol{f}(\boldsymbol{u}) - \boldsymbol{u}$.

Under certain conditions on $\mathbf{F}$, the residual connection $\boldsymbol{f}$ becomes invertible. We will refer to flows composed of invertible residual connections as **residual flows**. In the following, we describe two ways the residual block $\mathbf{F}$ can be constrained so that the residual connection $\boldsymbol{f}$ is invertible.

23.2.5.1 Contractive residual blocks

One way to ensure the residual connection is invertible is to choose the residual block to be a contraction. A contraction is a function $\mathbf{F}$ whose Lipschitz constant is less than 1; that is, there exists $0 \leq L < 1$ such that for all $\boldsymbol{u}_1$ and $\boldsymbol{u}_2$ we have:

$$\|\mathbf{F}(\boldsymbol{u}_1) - \mathbf{F}(\boldsymbol{u}_2)\| \leq L\|\boldsymbol{u}_1 - \boldsymbol{u}_2\|. \tag{23.30}$$

The invertibility of $\boldsymbol{f}(\boldsymbol{u}) = \boldsymbol{u} + \mathbf{F}(\boldsymbol{u})$ can be shown as follows. Consider the mapping $\boldsymbol{g}(\boldsymbol{u}) = \boldsymbol{x} - \mathbf{F}(\boldsymbol{u})$. Because $\mathbf{F}$ is a contraction, $\boldsymbol{g}$ is also a contraction. So, by Banach's fixed-point theorem, $\boldsymbol{g}$ has a unique fixed point $\boldsymbol{u}_*$. Hence we have

$$\boldsymbol{u}_* = \boldsymbol{x} - \mathbf{F}(\boldsymbol{u}_*) \tag{23.31}$$
$$\Rightarrow \quad \boldsymbol{u}_* + \mathbf{F}(\boldsymbol{u}_*) = \boldsymbol{x} \tag{23.32}$$
$$\Rightarrow \quad \boldsymbol{f}(\boldsymbol{u}_*) = \boldsymbol{x}. \tag{23.33}$$

Because $\boldsymbol{u}_*$ is unique, it follows that $\boldsymbol{u}_* = \boldsymbol{f}^{-1}(\boldsymbol{x})$.

An example of a residual flow with contractive residual blocks is the **iResNet** model of [Beh+19]. The residual blocks of iResNet are convolutional neural networks, that is, compositions of convolutional layers with non-linear activation functions. Because the Lipschitz constant of a composition is less or equal to the product of the Lipschitz constants of the individual functions, it is enough to ensure the

convolutions are contractive, and to use increasing activation functions with slope less or equal to 1. The iResNet model ensures the convolutions are contractive by applying spectral normalization to their weights [Miy+18a].

In general, there is no analytical expression for the inverse $\boldsymbol{f}^{-1}$. However, we can approximate $\boldsymbol{f}^{-1}(\boldsymbol{x})$ using the following iterative procedure:

$$\boldsymbol{u}_n = \boldsymbol{g}(\boldsymbol{u}_{n-1}) = \boldsymbol{x} - \mathbf{F}(\boldsymbol{u}_{n-1}). \tag{23.34}$$

Banach's fixed-point theorem guarantees that the sequence $\boldsymbol{u}_0, \boldsymbol{u}_1, \boldsymbol{u}_2, \ldots$ will converge to $\boldsymbol{u}_* = \boldsymbol{f}^{-1}(\boldsymbol{x})$ for any choice of $\boldsymbol{u}_0$, and it will do so at a rate of $O(L^n)$, where L is the Lipschitz constant of $\boldsymbol{g}$ (which is the same as the Lipschitz constant of $\mathbf{F}$). In practice, it is convenient to choose $\boldsymbol{u}_0 = \boldsymbol{x}$.

In addition, there is no analytical expression for the Jacobian determinant, whose exact computation costs $O(D^3)$. However, there is a computationally efficient stochastic estimator of the log Jacobian determinant. The idea is to express the log Jacobian determinant as a power series. Using the fact that $\boldsymbol{f}(\boldsymbol{x}) = \boldsymbol{x} + \mathbf{F}(\boldsymbol{x})$, we have

$$\log |\det \mathbf{J}(\boldsymbol{f})| = \log |\det(\mathbf{I} + \mathbf{J}(\mathbf{F}))| = \sum_{k=1}^{\infty} \frac{(-1)^{k+1}}{k} \operatorname{tr}\left[\mathbf{J}(\mathbf{F})^k\right]. \tag{23.35}$$

This power series converges when the matrix norm of $\mathbf{J}(\mathbf{F})$ is less than 1, which here is guaranteed exactly because $\mathbf{F}$ is a contraction. The trace of $\mathbf{J}(\mathbf{F})^k$ can be efficiently approximated using Jacobian-vector products via the **Hutchinson trace estimator** [Ski89; Hut89; Mey+21]:

$$\operatorname{tr}\left[\mathbf{J}(\mathbf{F})^k\right] \approx \boldsymbol{v}^\top \mathbf{J}(\mathbf{F})^k \boldsymbol{v}, \tag{23.36}$$

where $\boldsymbol{v}$ is a sample from a distribution with zero mean and unit covariance, such as $\mathcal{N}(\mathbf{0}, \mathbf{I})$. Finally, the infinite series can be approximated by a finite one either by truncation [Beh+19], which unfortunately yields a biased estimator, or by employing the **Russian-roulette estimator** [Che+19], which is unbiased.

23.2.5.2 Residual blocks with low-rank Jacobian

There is an efficient way of computing the determinant of a matrix which is a low-rank perturbation of an identity matrix. Suppose $\mathbf{A}$ and $\mathbf{B}$ are matrices, where $\mathbf{A}$ is $D \times M$ and $\mathbf{B}$ is $M \times D$. The following formula is known as the **Weinstein-Aronszajn identity**[2], and is a special case of the more general **matrix determinant lemma**:

$$\det(\mathbf{I}_D + \mathbf{AB}) = \det(\mathbf{I}_M + \mathbf{BA}). \tag{23.37}$$

We write $\mathbf{I}_D$ and $\mathbf{I}_M$ for the $D \times D$ and $M \times M$ identity matrices respectively. The significance of this formula is that it turns a $D \times D$ determinant that costs $O(D^3)$ into an $M \times M$ determinant that costs $O(M^3)$. If M is smaller than D, this saves computation.

With some restrictions on the residual block $\mathbf{F} : \mathbb{R}^D \to \mathbb{R}^D$, we can apply this formula to compute the determinant of a residual connection efficiently. The trick is to create a bottleneck inside $\mathbf{F}$. We do that by defining $\mathbf{F} = \mathbf{F}_2 \circ \mathbf{F}_1$, where $\mathbf{F}_1 : \mathbb{R}^D \to \mathbb{R}^M$, $\mathbf{F}_2 : \mathbb{R}^M \to \mathbb{R}^D$ and $M \ll D$. The chain

---

2. See https://en.wikipedia.org/wiki/Weinstein-Aronszajn_identity.

rule gives $\mathbf{J}(\mathbf{F}) = \mathbf{J}(\mathbf{F}_2)\mathbf{J}(\mathbf{F}_1)$, where $\mathbf{J}(\mathbf{F}_2)$ is $D \times M$ and $\mathbf{J}(\mathbf{F}_1)$ is $M \times D$. Now we can apply our determinant formula as follows:

$$\det \mathbf{J}(\boldsymbol{f}) = \det(\mathbf{I}_D + \mathbf{J}(\mathbf{F})) = \det(\mathbf{I}_D + \mathbf{J}(\mathbf{F}_2)\mathbf{J}(\mathbf{F}_1)) = \det(\mathbf{I}_M + \mathbf{J}(\mathbf{F}_1)\mathbf{J}(\mathbf{F}_2)). \tag{23.38}$$

Since the final determinant costs $O(M^3)$, we can make the Jacobian determinant efficient by reducing M, that is, by narrowing the bottleneck.

An example of the above is the **planar flow** of [RM15]. In this model, each residual block is an MLP with one hidden layer and one hidden unit. That is,

$$\boldsymbol{f}(\boldsymbol{u}) = \boldsymbol{u} + \boldsymbol{v}\sigma(\boldsymbol{w}^\top \boldsymbol{u} + b), \tag{23.39}$$

where $\boldsymbol{v} \in \mathbb{R}^D$, $\boldsymbol{w} \in \mathbb{R}^D$ and $b \in \mathbb{R}$ are the parameters, and σ is the activation function. The residual block is the composition of $\mathbf{F}_1(\boldsymbol{u}) = \boldsymbol{w}^\top \boldsymbol{u} + b$ and $\mathbf{F}_2(z) = \boldsymbol{v}\sigma(z)$, so $M = 1$. Their Jacobians are $\mathbf{J}(\mathbf{F}_1)(\boldsymbol{u}) = \boldsymbol{w}^\top$ and $\mathbf{J}(\mathbf{F}_2)(z) = \boldsymbol{v}\sigma'(z)$. Substituting these in the formula for the Jacobian determinant we obtain:

$$\det \mathbf{J}(\boldsymbol{f})(\boldsymbol{u}) = 1 + \boldsymbol{w}^\top \boldsymbol{v}\sigma'(\boldsymbol{w}^\top \boldsymbol{u} + b), \tag{23.40}$$

which can be computed efficiently in $O(D)$. Other examples include the **circular flow** of [RM15] and the **Sylvester flow** of [Ber+18].

This technique gives an efficient way of computing determinants of residual connections with bottlenecks, but in general there is no guarantee that such functions are invertible. This means that invertibility must be satisfied on a case-by-case basis. For example, the planar flow is invertible when σ is the hyperbolic tangent and $\boldsymbol{w}^\top \boldsymbol{v} > -1$, but otherwise it may not be.

23.2.6 Continuous-time flows

So far we have discussed flows that consist of a sequence of bijections $\boldsymbol{f}_1, \ldots, \boldsymbol{f}_N$. Starting from some input $\boldsymbol{x}_0 = \boldsymbol{u}$, this creates a sequence of outputs $\boldsymbol{x}_1, \ldots, \boldsymbol{x}_N$ where $\boldsymbol{x}_n = \boldsymbol{f}_n(\boldsymbol{x}_{n-1})$. However, we can also have flows where the input is transformed into the final output in a continuous way. That is, we start from $\boldsymbol{x}_0 = \boldsymbol{x}(0)$, create a continuously-indexed sequence $\boldsymbol{x}(t)$ for $t \in [0, T]$ with some fixed T, and take $\boldsymbol{x}(T)$ to be the final output. Thinking of t as analogous to time, we refer to these as **continuous-time flows**.

The sequence $\boldsymbol{x}(t)$ is defined as the solution to a first-order ordinary differential equation (ODE) of the form:

$$\frac{d\boldsymbol{x}}{dt}(t) = \mathbf{F}(\boldsymbol{x}(t), t). \tag{23.41}$$

The function $\mathbf{F} : \mathbb{R}^D \times [0, T] \to \mathbb{R}^D$ is a time-dependent vector field that parameterizes the ODE. If we think of $\boldsymbol{x}(t)$ as the position of a particle in D dimensions, the vector $\mathbf{F}(\boldsymbol{x}(t), t)$ determines the particle's velocity at time t.

The flow (for time T) is a function $\boldsymbol{f} : \mathbb{R}^D \to \mathbb{R}^D$ that takes in an input $\boldsymbol{x}_0$, solves the ODE with initial condition $\boldsymbol{x}(0) = \boldsymbol{x}_0$, and returns $\boldsymbol{x}(T)$. The function $\boldsymbol{f}$ is a well-defined bijection if the solution to the ODE exists for all $t \in [0, T]$ and is unique. These conditions are not generally satisfied for arbitrary $\mathbf{F}$, but they are if $\mathbf{F}(\cdot, t)$ is Lipschitz continuous with a Lipschitz constant that does not depend on t. That is, $\boldsymbol{f}$ is a well-defined bijection if there exists a constant L such that for all $\boldsymbol{x}_1$, $\boldsymbol{x}_2$ and $t \in [0, T]$ we have:

$$\|\mathbf{F}(\boldsymbol{x}_1, t) - \mathbf{F}(\boldsymbol{x}_2, t)\| \leq L\|\boldsymbol{x}_1 - \boldsymbol{x}_2\|. \tag{23.42}$$

This result is a consequence of the **Picard-Lindelöf theorem** for ODEs.[3] In practice, we can parameterize $\mathbf{F}$ using any choice of model, provided the Lipschitz condition is met.

Usually the ODE cannot be solved analytically, but we can solve it approximately by discretizing it. A simple example is **Euler's method**, which corresponds to the following discretization for some small step size $\epsilon > 0$:

$$\boldsymbol{x}(t + \epsilon) = \boldsymbol{x}(t) + \epsilon \mathbf{F}(\boldsymbol{x}(t), t). \tag{23.43}$$

This is equivalent to a residual connection with residual block $\epsilon \mathbf{F}(\cdot, t)$, so the ODE solver can be thought of as a deep residual network with $O(T/\epsilon)$ layers. A smaller step size leads to a more accurate solution, but also to more computation. There are several other solution methods varying in accuracy and sophistication, such as those in the broader Runge-Kutta family, some of which use adaptive step sizes.

The inverse of $\boldsymbol{f}$ can be easily computed by solving the ODE in reverse. That is, to compute $\boldsymbol{f}^{-1}(\boldsymbol{x}_T)$ we solve the ODE with initial condition $\boldsymbol{x}(T) = \boldsymbol{x}_T$, and return $\boldsymbol{x}(0)$. Unlike some other flows (such as autoregressive flows) which are more expensive to compute in one direction than in the other, continuous-time flows require the same amount of computation in either direction.

In general, there is no analytical expression for the Jacobian determinant of $\boldsymbol{f}$. However, we can express it as the solution to a separate ODE, which we can then solve numerically. First, we define $\boldsymbol{f}_t : \mathbb{R}^D \to \mathbb{R}^D$ to be the flow for time t, that is, the function that takes $\boldsymbol{x}_0$, solves the ODE with initial condition $\boldsymbol{x}(0) = \boldsymbol{x}_0$ and returns $\boldsymbol{x}(t)$. Clearly, $\boldsymbol{f}_0$ is the identity function and $\boldsymbol{f}_T = \boldsymbol{f}$. Let us define $L(t) = \log|\det \mathbf{J}(\boldsymbol{f}_t)(\boldsymbol{x}_0)|$. Because $\boldsymbol{f}_0$ is the identity function, $L(0) = 0$, and because $\boldsymbol{f}_T = \boldsymbol{f}$, $L(T)$ gives the Jacobian determinant of $\boldsymbol{f}$ that we are interested in. It can be shown that L satisfies the following ODE:

$$\frac{dL}{dt}(t) = \text{tr}\big[\mathbf{J}(\mathbf{F}(\cdot, t))(\boldsymbol{x}(t))\big]. \tag{23.44}$$

That is, the rate of change of L at time t is equal to the Jacobian trace of $\mathbf{F}(\cdot, t)$ evaluated at $\boldsymbol{x}(t)$. So we can compute $L(T)$ by solving the above ODE with initial condition $L(0) = 0$. Moreover, we can compute $\boldsymbol{x}(T)$ and $L(T)$ simultaneously, by combining their two ODEs into a single ODE operating on the extended space $(\boldsymbol{x}, L)$.

An example of a continuous-time flow is the **neural ODE** model of [Che+18c], which uses a neural network to parameterize $\mathbf{F}$. To avoid backpropagating gradients through the ODE solver, which can be computationally demanding, they use the **adjoint sensitivity method** to express the time evolution of the gradient with respect to $\boldsymbol{x}(t)$ as a separate ODE. Solving this ODE gives the required gradients, and can be thought of as the continuous-time analog of backpropagation.

Another example is the **FFJORD** model of [Gra+19]. This is similar to the neural ODE model, except that it uses the Hutchinson trace estimator to approximate the Jacobian trace of $\mathbf{F}(\cdot, t)$. This usage of the Hutchinson trace estimator is analogous to that in contractive residual flows (Section 23.2.5.1), and it speeds up computation in exchange for a stochastic (but unbiased) estimate.

See also Section 25.4.4, where we discuss continuous time diffusion models.

---

3. See https://en.wikipedia.org/wiki/Picard-Lindel%C3%B6f_theorem

23.3   Applications

In this section, we highlight some applications of flows for canonical probabilistic machine learning tasks.

23.3.1   Density estimation

Flow models allow exact density computation and can be used to fit multi-modal densities to observed data. (see Figure 23.3 for an example). An early example is Gaussianization [CG00] who applied this idea to fit low-dimensional densities. Tabak and Vanden-Eijnden [TVE10] and Tabak and Turner [TT13] introduced the modern idea of flows (including the term 'normalizing flows'), describing a flow as a composition of simpler maps. Deep density models [RA13] was one of the first to use neural networks for flows to parameterize high-dimensional densities. There has been a rich line of follow-up work including **NICE** [DKB15] and **Real NVP** [DSDB17]. (NVP stands for "non-volume-preserving", which refers to the fact that the Jacobian of the transform is not unity.) Masked autoregressive flows (Section 23.2.4.2) further improved performance on unconditional and conditional density estimation tasks.

Flows can be used for *hybrid models* which model the joint density of inputs and targets $p(\boldsymbol{x}, y)$, as opposed to discriminative classification models which just model the conditional $p(y|\boldsymbol{x})$ and density models which just model the marginal $p(\boldsymbol{x})$. Nalisnick et al. [Nal+19b] proposed a flow-based hybrid model using invertible mappings for representation learning and showed that the joint density $p(\boldsymbol{x}, y)$ can be computed efficiently, which can be useful for downstream tasks such as anomaly detection, semi-supervised learning and selective classification. Flow-based hybrid models are memory-efficient since most of the parameters are in the invertible representation which are shared between the discriminative and generative models; furthermore, the density $p(\boldsymbol{x}, y)$ can be computed in a single forwards pass leading to computational savings. Residual flows [Che+19] use invertible residual mappings [Beh+19] for hybrid modeling which further improves performance. Flows have also been used to fit densities to embeddings [Zha+20b; CZG20] for anomaly detection tasks.

23.3.2   Generative modeling

Another task is generation, which involves generating novel samples from a fitted model $p^*(\boldsymbol{x})$. Generation is a popular downstream task for normalizing flows, which have been applied for different data modalities including images, video, audio, text, and structured objects such as graphs and point clouds. Images are arguably the most popular modality for deep generative models: GLOW [KD18b] was one of the first flow-based models to generate compelling high-dimensional images, and has been extended to video to produce RGB frames [Kum+19b]; residual flows [Che+19] have also been shown to produce sharp images.

Oord et al. [Oor+18] used flows for audio synthesis by distilling WaveNet into an IAF (Section 23.2.4.3), which enables faster sampling than WaveNet. Other flow models for audio include WaveFLOW [PVC19] and FlowWaveNet [Kim+19], which directly speed up WaveNet using coupling layers.

Flows have been also used for text. Tran et al. [Tra+19] define a discrete flow over a vocabulary for language-modeling tasks. Another popular approach is to define a latent variable model with discrete observation space but a continuous latent space. For example, Ziegler and Rush [ZR19a] use normalizing flows in latent space for language modeling.

23.3.3 Inference

Normalizing flows have been used for probabilistic inference. Rezende and Mohamed [RM15] popularized normalizing flows in machine learning, and showed how they can be used for modeling variational posterior distributions in latent variable models. Various extensions such as Householder flows [TW16], inverse autoregressive flows [Kin+16], multiplicative normalizing flows [LW17], and Sylvester flows [Ber+18] have been proposed for modeling the variational posterior for latent variable models, as well as posteriors for Bayesian neural networks.

Flows have been used as complex proposal distributions for importance sampling; examples include neural importance sampling [Mül+19b] and Boltzmann generators [Noé+19]. Hoffman et al. [Hof+19] used flows to improve the performance of Hamiltonian Monte Carlo (Section 12.5) by defining bijective transformations to transform random variables to simpler distributions and performing HMC in that space instead.

Finally, flows can be used in the context of simulation-based inference, where the likelihood function of the parameters is not available, but simulating data from the model is possible. The main idea is to train a flow on data simulated from the model in order to approximate the posterior distribution or the likelihood function. The flow model can also be used to guide simulations in order to make inference more efficient [PSM19; GNM19]. This approach has been used for inference of simulation models in cosmology [Als+19] and computational neuroscience [Gon+20].

24 Energy-based models

This chapter is co-authored with Yang Song and Durk Kingma.

24.1 Introduction

We have now seen several ways of defining deep generative models, including VAEs (Chapter 21), autoregressive models (Chapter 22), and normalizing flows (Chapter 23). All of the above models can be formulated in terms of directed graphical models (Chapter 4), where we generate the data one step at a time, using locally normalized distributions. In some cases, it is easier to specify a distribution in terms of a set of constraints that valid samples must satisfy, rather than a generative process. This can be done using an undirected graphical model (Chapter 4).

Energy-based models or **EBM** can be written as a Gibbs distribution as follows:

$$p_{\boldsymbol{\theta}}(\mathbf{x}) = \frac{\exp(-\mathcal{E}_{\boldsymbol{\theta}}(\mathbf{x}))}{Z_{\boldsymbol{\theta}}} \tag{24.1}$$

where $\mathcal{E}_{\boldsymbol{\theta}}(\mathbf{x}) \geq 0$ is known as the **energy function** with parameters $\boldsymbol{\theta}$, and $Z_{\boldsymbol{\theta}}$ is the **partition function**:

$$Z_{\boldsymbol{\theta}} = \int \exp(-\mathcal{E}_{\boldsymbol{\theta}}(\mathbf{x})) \, d\mathbf{x} \tag{24.2}$$

This is constant wrt $\mathbf{x}$ but is a function of $\boldsymbol{\theta}$. Since EBMs do not usually make any Markov assumptions (unlike graphical models), evaluating this integral is usually intractable. Consequently we usually need to use approximate methods, such as annealed importance sampling, discussed in Section 11.5.4.1.

The advantage of an EBM over other generative models is that the energy function can be any kind of function that returns a non-negative scalar; it does not need to integrate to 1. This allows one to use a variety of neural network architectures for defining the energy. As such, EBMs have found wide applications in many fields of machine learning, including image generation [Ngi+11; Xie+16; DM19b], discriminative learning [Gra+20b], natural processing [Mik+13; Den+20], density estimation [Wen+19a; Son+19], and reinforcement learning [Haa+17; Haa+18a], to list a few. (More examples can be found at https://github.com/yataobian/awesome-ebm.)

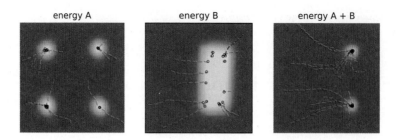

Figure 24.1: Combining two energy functions in 2d by summation, which is equivalent to multiplying the corresponding probability densities. We also illustrate some sampled trajectories towards high probability (low energy) regions. From Figure 14 of [DM19a]. Used with kind permission of Yilun Du.

24.1.1   Example: products of experts (PoE)

As an example of why energy based models are useful, suppose we want to create a generative model of proteins that are thermally stable at room temperature, and which bind to the COVID-19 spike receptor. Suppose $p_1(x)$ can generate stable proteins and $p_2(x)$ can generate proteins that bind. (For example, both of these models could be autoregressive sequence models, trained on different datasets.) We can view each of these models as "experts" about a particular aspect of the data. On their own, they are not an adequate model of the data that we have (or want to have), but we can then combine them, to represent the **conjunction of features**, by computing a **product of experts (PoE)** [Hin02]:

$$p_{12}(x) = \frac{1}{Z_{12}} p_1(x) p_2(x) \tag{24.3}$$

This will assign high probability to proteins that are stable and which bind, and low probability to all others. By contrast, a **mixture of experts** would either generate from p_1 or from p_2, but would not combine features from both.

If the experts are represented as energy based models (EBM), then the PoE model is also an EBM, with an energy given by

$$\mathcal{E}_{12}(x) = \mathcal{E}_1(x) + \mathcal{E}_2(x) \tag{24.4}$$

Intuitively, we can think of each component of energy as a "**soft constraint**" on the data. This idea is illustrated in Figure 24.1.

24.1.2   Computational difficulties

Although the flexibility of EBMs can provide significant modeling advantages, computation of the likelihood and drawing samples from the model are generally intractable. In this chapter, we will discuss a variety of approximate methods to solve these problems.

24.2 Maximum likelihood training

The de facto standard for learning probabilistic models from iid data is maximum likelihood estimation (MLE). Let $p_{\boldsymbol{\theta}}(\mathbf{x})$ be a probabilistic model parameterized by $\boldsymbol{\theta}$, and $p_{\mathcal{D}}(\mathbf{x})$ be the underlying data distribution of a dataset. We can fit $p_{\boldsymbol{\theta}}(\mathbf{x})$ to $p_{\mathcal{D}}(\mathbf{x})$ by maximizing the expected log-likelihood function over the data distribution, defined by

$$\ell(\boldsymbol{\theta}) = \mathbb{E}_{\mathbf{x} \sim p_{\mathcal{D}}(\mathbf{x})}[\log p_{\boldsymbol{\theta}}(\mathbf{x})] \tag{24.5}$$

as a function of $\boldsymbol{\theta}$. Here the expectation can be easily estimated with samples from the dataset. Maximizing likelihood is equivalent to minimizing the KL divergence between $p_{\mathcal{D}}(\mathbf{x})$ and $p_{\boldsymbol{\theta}}(\mathbf{x})$, because

$$\ell(\boldsymbol{\theta}) = -D_{\mathrm{KL}}\left(p_{\mathcal{D}}(\mathbf{x}) \parallel p_{\boldsymbol{\theta}}(\mathbf{x})\right) + \mathrm{const} \tag{24.6}$$

where the constant is equal to $\mathbb{E}_{\mathbf{x} \sim p_{\mathcal{D}}(\mathbf{x})}[\log p_{\mathcal{D}}(\mathbf{x})]$ which does not depend on $\boldsymbol{\theta}$.

We cannot usually compute the likelihood of an EBM because the normalizing constant $Z_{\boldsymbol{\theta}}$ is often intractable. Nevertheless, we can still estimate the gradient of the log-likelihood with MCMC approaches, allowing for likelihood maximization with stochastic gradient ascent [You99]. In particular, the gradient of the log-probability of an EBM decomposes as a sum of two terms:

$$\nabla_{\boldsymbol{\theta}} \log p_{\boldsymbol{\theta}}(\mathbf{x}) = -\nabla_{\boldsymbol{\theta}} \mathcal{E}_{\boldsymbol{\theta}}(\mathbf{x}) - \nabla_{\boldsymbol{\theta}} \log Z_{\boldsymbol{\theta}}. \tag{24.7}$$

The first gradient term, $-\nabla_{\boldsymbol{\theta}} \mathcal{E}_{\boldsymbol{\theta}}(\mathbf{x})$, is straightforward to evaluate with automatic differentiation. The challenge is in approximating the second gradient term, $\nabla_{\boldsymbol{\theta}} \log Z_{\boldsymbol{\theta}}$, which is intractable to compute exactly. This gradient term can be rewritten as the following expectation:

$$\nabla_{\boldsymbol{\theta}} \log Z_{\boldsymbol{\theta}} = \nabla_{\boldsymbol{\theta}} \log \int \exp(-\mathcal{E}_{\boldsymbol{\theta}}(\mathbf{x})) d\mathbf{x} \tag{24.8}$$

$$\overset{(i)}{=} \left(\int \exp(-\mathcal{E}_{\boldsymbol{\theta}}(\mathbf{x})) d\mathbf{x}\right)^{-1} \nabla_{\boldsymbol{\theta}} \int \exp(-\mathcal{E}_{\boldsymbol{\theta}}(\mathbf{x})) d\mathbf{x} \tag{24.9}$$

$$= \left(\int \exp(-\mathcal{E}_{\boldsymbol{\theta}}(\mathbf{x})) d\mathbf{x}\right)^{-1} \int \nabla_{\boldsymbol{\theta}} \exp(-\mathcal{E}_{\boldsymbol{\theta}}(\mathbf{x})) d\mathbf{x} \tag{24.10}$$

$$\overset{(ii)}{=} \left(\int \exp(-\mathcal{E}_{\boldsymbol{\theta}}(\mathbf{x})) d\mathbf{x}\right)^{-1} \int \exp(-\mathcal{E}_{\boldsymbol{\theta}}(\mathbf{x}))(-\nabla_{\boldsymbol{\theta}} \mathcal{E}_{\boldsymbol{\theta}}(\mathbf{x})) d\mathbf{x} \tag{24.11}$$

$$= \int \left(\int \exp(-\mathcal{E}_{\boldsymbol{\theta}}(\mathbf{x})) d\mathbf{x}\right)^{-1} \exp(-\mathcal{E}_{\boldsymbol{\theta}}(\mathbf{x}))(-\nabla_{\boldsymbol{\theta}} \mathcal{E}_{\boldsymbol{\theta}}(\mathbf{x})) d\mathbf{x} \tag{24.12}$$

$$\overset{(iii)}{=} \int \frac{1}{Z_{\boldsymbol{\theta}}} \exp(-\mathcal{E}_{\boldsymbol{\theta}}(\mathbf{x}))(-\nabla_{\boldsymbol{\theta}} \mathcal{E}_{\boldsymbol{\theta}}(\mathbf{x})) d\mathbf{x} \tag{24.13}$$

$$\overset{(iv)}{=} \int p_{\boldsymbol{\theta}}(\mathbf{x})(-\nabla_{\boldsymbol{\theta}} \mathcal{E}_{\boldsymbol{\theta}}(\mathbf{x})) d\mathbf{x} \tag{24.14}$$

$$= \mathbb{E}_{\mathbf{x} \sim p_{\boldsymbol{\theta}}(\mathbf{x})}\left[-\nabla_{\boldsymbol{\theta}} \mathcal{E}_{\boldsymbol{\theta}}(\mathbf{x})\right], \tag{24.15}$$

where steps (i) and (ii) are due to the chain rule of gradients, and (iii) and (iv) are from definitions in Equations (24.1) and (24.2). Thus, we can obtain an unbiased Monte Carlo estimate of the log-likelihood gradient by using

$$\nabla_{\boldsymbol{\theta}} \log Z_{\boldsymbol{\theta}} \simeq -\frac{1}{S} \sum_{s=1}^{S} \nabla_{\boldsymbol{\theta}} \mathcal{E}_{\boldsymbol{\theta}}(\tilde{\mathbf{x}}_s), \tag{24.16}$$

where $\tilde{\mathbf{x}}_s \sim p_{\boldsymbol{\theta}}(\mathbf{x})$, i.e., a random sample from the distribution over $\mathbf{x}$ given by the EBM. Therefore, as long as we can draw random samples from the model, we have access to an unbiased Monte Carlo estimate of the log-likelihood gradient, allowing us to optimize the parameters with stochastic gradient ascent.

Much of the literature has focused on methods for efficient MCMC sampling from EBMs. We discuss some of these methods below.

24.2.1 Gradient-based MCMC methods

Some efficient MCMC methods, such as **Langevin MCMC** (Section 12.5.6) or Hamiltonian Monte Carlo (Section 12.5), make use of the fact that the gradient of the log-probability wrt $\mathbf{x}$ (known as the **score function**) is equal to the (negative) gradient of the energy, and is therefore easy to calculate:

$$\nabla_{\mathbf{x}} \log p_{\boldsymbol{\theta}}(\mathbf{x}) = -\nabla_{\mathbf{x}} \mathcal{E}_{\boldsymbol{\theta}}(\mathbf{x}) - \underbrace{\nabla_{\mathbf{x}} \log Z_{\boldsymbol{\theta}}}_{=0} = -\nabla_{\mathbf{x}} \mathcal{E}_{\boldsymbol{\theta}}(\mathbf{x}). \tag{24.17}$$

For example, when using Langevin MCMC to sample from $p_{\boldsymbol{\theta}}(\mathbf{x})$, we first draw an initial sample $\mathbf{x}^0$ from a simple prior distribution, and then simulate an overdamped Langevin diffusion process for K steps with step size $\epsilon > 0$:

$$\mathbf{x}^{k+1} \leftarrow \mathbf{x}^k + \frac{\epsilon^2}{2} \underbrace{\nabla_{\mathbf{x}} \log p_{\boldsymbol{\theta}}(\mathbf{x}^k)}_{=-\nabla_{\mathbf{x}} \mathcal{E}_{\boldsymbol{\theta}}(\mathbf{x})} + \epsilon \mathbf{z}^k, \quad k = 0, 1, \cdots, K-1. \tag{24.18}$$

where $\mathbf{z}^k \sim \mathcal{N}(\mathbf{0}, \mathbf{I})$ is a Gaussian noise term. We show an example of this process in Figure 25.5d.

When $\epsilon \to 0$ and $K \to \infty$, $\mathbf{x}^K$ is guaranteed to distribute as $p_{\boldsymbol{\theta}}(\mathbf{x})$ under some regularity conditions. In practice we have to use a small finite ϵ, but the discretization error is typically negligible, or can be corrected with a Metropolis-Hastings step (Section 12.2), leading to the Metropolis-adjusted Langevin algorithm (Section 12.5.6).

24.2.2 Contrastive divergence

Running MCMC till convergence to obtain a sample $\mathbf{x} \sim p_{\boldsymbol{\theta}}(\mathbf{x})$ can be computationally expensive. Therefore we typically need approximations to make MCMC-based learning of EBMs practical. One popular method for doing so is **contrastive divergence** (CD) [Hin02]. In CD, one initializes the MCMC chain from the datapoint $\mathbf{x}$, and proceeds to perform MCMC for a fixed number of steps. One can show that T steps of CD minimizies the following objective:

$$\mathrm{CD}_T = D_{\mathrm{KL}}\left(p_0 \parallel p_\infty\right) - D_{\mathrm{KL}}\left(p_T \parallel p_\infty\right) \tag{24.19}$$

where p_T is the distribution over $\mathbf{x}$ after T MCMC updates, and p_0 is the data distribution. Typically we can get good results with a small value of T, sometimes just $T = 1$. We give the details below.

24.2.2.1 Fitting RBMs with CD

CD was initially developed to fit a special kind of latent variable EBM known as a restricted Boltzmann machine (Section 4.3.3.2). This model was specifically designed to support fast block Gibbs sampling, which is required by CD (and can also be exploited by standard MCMC-based learning methods [AHS85].)

For simplicity, we will assume the hidden and visible nodes are binary, and we use 1-step contrastive divergence. As discussed in Supplementary Section 4.3.1, the binary RBM has the following energy function:

$$\mathcal{E}(\boldsymbol{x}, \boldsymbol{z}; \boldsymbol{\theta}) = \sum_{d=1}^{D} \sum_{k=1}^{K} x_d z_k W_{dk} + \sum_{d=1}^{D} x_d b_d + \sum_{k=1}^{K} z_k c_k \tag{24.20}$$

(Henceforth we will drop the unary (bias) terms, which can be emulated by clamping $z_k = 1$ or $x_d = 1$.) This is a loglinear model where we have one binary feature per edge. Thus from Equation (4.135) the gradient of the log-likelihood is given by the clamped expectations minus the unclamped expectations:

$$\frac{\partial \ell}{\partial w_{dk}} = \frac{1}{N} \sum_{n=1}^{N} \mathbb{E}\left[x_d z_k | \boldsymbol{x}_n, \boldsymbol{\theta}\right] - \mathbb{E}\left[x_d z_k | \boldsymbol{\theta}\right] \tag{24.21}$$

We can rewrite the above gradient in matrix-vector form as follows:

$$\nabla_{\boldsymbol{w}}\, \ell = \mathbb{E}_{p_{\mathcal{D}}(\boldsymbol{x})p(\boldsymbol{z}|\boldsymbol{x},\boldsymbol{\theta})}\left[\boldsymbol{x}\boldsymbol{z}^T\right] - \mathbb{E}_{p(\boldsymbol{z},\boldsymbol{x}|\boldsymbol{\theta})}\left[\boldsymbol{x}\boldsymbol{z}^T\right] \tag{24.22}$$

(We can derive a similar expression for the gradient of the bias terms by setting $x_d = 1$ or $z_k = 1$.)

The first term in the expression for the gradient in Equation (24.21), when $\boldsymbol{x}$ is fixed to a data case, is sometimes called the **clamped phase**, and the second term, when $\boldsymbol{x}$ is free, is sometimes called the **unclamped phase**. When the model expectations match the empirical expectations, the two terms cancel out, the gradient becomes zero and learning stops.

We can also make a connection to the principle of **Hebbian learning** in neuroscience. In particular, Hebb's rule says that the strength of connection between two neurons that are simultaneously active should be increased. (This theory is often summarized as "Cells that fire together wire together".[1]) The first term in Equation (24.21) is therefore considered a Hebbian term, and the second term an anti-Hebbian term, due to the sign change.

We can leverage the Markov structure of the bipartite graph to approximate the expectations as follows:

$$\boldsymbol{z}_n \sim p(\boldsymbol{z}|\boldsymbol{x}_n, \boldsymbol{\theta}) \tag{24.23}$$
$$\boldsymbol{x}'_n \sim p(\boldsymbol{x}|\boldsymbol{z}_n, \boldsymbol{\theta}) \tag{24.24}$$
$$\boldsymbol{z}'_n \sim p(\boldsymbol{z}|\boldsymbol{x}'_n, \boldsymbol{\theta}) \tag{24.25}$$

---

1. See https://en.wikipedia.org/wiki/Hebbian_theory.

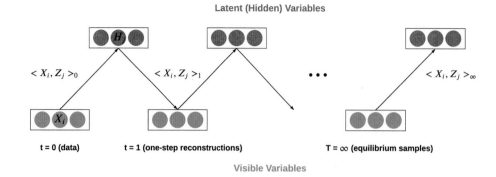

Figure 24.2: Illustration of contrastive divergence sampling for an RBM. The visible nodes are initialized at an example drawn from the dataset. Then we sample a hidden vector, then another visible vector, etc. Eventually (at "infinity") we will be producing samples from the joint distribution $p(\boldsymbol{x}, \boldsymbol{z} | \boldsymbol{\theta})$.

We can think of $\boldsymbol{x}'_n$ as the model's best attempt at reconstructing $\boldsymbol{x}_n$ after being encoded and then decoded by the model. Such samples are sometimes called **fantasy data**. See Figure 24.2 for an illustration. Given these samples, we then make the approximation

$$\mathbb{E}_{p(\cdot|\boldsymbol{\theta})}\left[\boldsymbol{x}\boldsymbol{z}^\mathsf{T}\right] \approx \boldsymbol{x}_n(\boldsymbol{z}'_n)^\mathsf{T} \tag{24.26}$$

In practice, it is common to use $\mathbb{E}\left[\boldsymbol{z}|\boldsymbol{x}'_n\right]$ instead of a sampled value $\boldsymbol{z}'_n$ in the above expression, since this reduces the variance. However, it is not valid to use $\mathbb{E}\left[\boldsymbol{z}|\boldsymbol{x}_n\right]$ instead of sampling $\boldsymbol{z}_n \sim p(\boldsymbol{z}|\boldsymbol{x}_n)$ in Equation (24.23), because then each hidden unit would be able to pass more than 1 bit of information, so it would not act as much of a bottleneck.

The whole procedure is summarized in Algorithm 24.1. For more details, see [Hin10; Swe+10].

Algorithm 24.1: CD-1 training for an RBM with binary hidden and visible units

---

1 Initialize weights $\mathbf{W} \in \mathbb{R}^{D \times K}$ randomly
2 **for** $t = 1, 2, \ldots$ **do**
3 　　**for** *each minibatch of size B* **do**
4 　　　　Set minibatch gradient to zero, $\boldsymbol{g} := \boldsymbol{0}$
5 　　　　**for** *each case $\boldsymbol{x}_n$ in the minibatch* **do**
6 　　　　　　Compute $\boldsymbol{\mu}_n = \mathbb{E}\left[\boldsymbol{z}|\boldsymbol{x}_n, \mathbf{W}\right]$
7 　　　　　　Sample $\boldsymbol{z}_n \sim p(\boldsymbol{z}|\boldsymbol{x}_n, \mathbf{W})$
8 　　　　　　Sample $\boldsymbol{x}'_n \sim p(\boldsymbol{x}|\boldsymbol{z}_n, \mathbf{W})$
9 　　　　　　Compute $\boldsymbol{\mu}'_n = \mathbb{E}\left[\boldsymbol{z}|\boldsymbol{x}'_n, \mathbf{W}\right]$
10 　　　　　　Compute gradient $\nabla_\mathbf{W} = (\boldsymbol{x}_n)(\boldsymbol{\mu}_n)^\mathsf{T} - (\boldsymbol{x}'_n)(\boldsymbol{\mu}'_n)^\mathsf{T}$
11 　　　　　　Accumulate $\boldsymbol{g} := \boldsymbol{g} + \nabla_\mathbf{W}$
12 　　　　Update parameters $\mathbf{W} := \mathbf{W} + \eta_t \frac{1}{B}\boldsymbol{g}$

24.2.2.2 Persistent CD

One variant of CD that sometimes performs better is **persistent contrastive divergence** (PCD) [Tie08; TH09; You99]. In this approach, a single MCMC chain with a persistent state is employed to sample from the EBM. In PCD, we do not restart the MCMC chain when training on a new datapoint; rather, we carry over the state of the previous MCMC chain and use it to initialize a new MCMC chain for the next training step. See Line 12 for some pseudocode. Hence there are two dynamical processes running at different time scales: the states x change quickly, and the parameters θ change slowly.

Algorithm 24.2: Persistent MCMC-SGD for fitting an EBM

1 Initialize parameters θ randomly
2 Initialize chains $\tilde{x}_{1:S}$ randomly
3 Initialize learning rate η
4 **for** $t = 1, 2, \ldots$ **do**
5   **for** x_b *in minibatch of size* B **do**
6         $g_b = \nabla_\theta \mathcal{E}_\theta(x_b)$
7   **for** *sample* $s = 1 : S$ **do**
8   Sample $\tilde{x}_s \sim \text{MCMC}(\text{target} = p(\cdot|\theta), \text{init} = \tilde{x}_s, \text{nsteps} = N)$
9         $\tilde{g}_s = \nabla_\theta \mathcal{E}_\theta(\tilde{x}_s)$
10     $g_t = -(\frac{1}{B}\sum_{b=1}^{B} g_b) - (\frac{1}{S}\sum_{s=1}^{S} \tilde{g}_s)$
11     $\theta := \theta + \eta g_t$
12   Decrease step size η

A theoretical justification for this was given in [You89], who showed that we can start the MCMC chain at its previous value, and just take a few steps, because $p(x|\theta_t)$ is likely to be close to $p(x|\theta_{t-1})$, since we only changed the parameters by a small amount in the intervening SGD step.

24.2.2.3 Other methods

PCD can be further improved by keeping multiple historical states of the MCMC chain in a replay buffer and initialize new MCMC chains by randomly sampling from it [DM19b]. Other variants of CD include mean field CD [WH02], and multi-grid CD [Gao+18].

EBMs trained with CD may not capture the data distribution faithfully, since truncated MCMC can lead to biased gradient updates that hurt the learning dynamics [SMB10; FI10; Nij+19]. There are several methods that focus on removing this bias for improved MCMC training. For example, one line of work proposes unbiased estimators of the gradient through coupled MCMC [JOA17; QZW19]; and Du et al. [Du+20] propose to reduce the bias by differentiating through the MCMC sampling algorithm and estimating an entropy correction term.

24.3   Score matching (SM)

If two continuously differentiable real-valued functions $f(\mathbf{x})$ and $g(\mathbf{x})$ have equal first derivatives everywhere, then $f(\mathbf{x}) \equiv g(\mathbf{x}) + \text{constant}$. When $f(\mathbf{x})$ and $g(\mathbf{x})$ are log probability density functions (pdf's) with equal first derivatives, the normalization requirement (Equation (24.1)) implies that $\int \exp(f(\mathbf{x}))d\mathbf{x} = \int \exp(g(\mathbf{x}))d\mathbf{x} = 1$, and therefore $f(\mathbf{x}) \equiv g(\mathbf{x})$. As a result, one can learn an EBM by (approximately) matching the first derivatives of its log-pdf to the first derivatives of the log pdf of the data distribution. If they match, then the EBM captures the data distribution exactly. The first-order gradient function of a log pdf wrt its input, $\nabla_{\boldsymbol{x}} \log p_{\boldsymbol{\theta}}(\boldsymbol{x})$, is called the (Stein) **score** function. (This is distinct from the Fisher score, $\nabla_{\boldsymbol{\theta}} \log p_{\boldsymbol{\theta}}(\boldsymbol{x})$.) For training EBMs, it is useful to transform the equivalence of distributions to the equivalence of scores, because the score of an EBM can be easily obtained as follows:

$$s_{\boldsymbol{\theta}}(\boldsymbol{x}) \triangleq \nabla_{\mathbf{x}} \log p_{\boldsymbol{\theta}}(\mathbf{x}) = -\nabla_{\mathbf{x}} \mathcal{E}_{\boldsymbol{\theta}}(\mathbf{x}) \tag{24.27}$$

We see that this does not involve the typically intractable normalizing constant $Z_{\boldsymbol{\theta}}$.

Let $p_{\mathcal{D}}(\mathbf{x})$ be the underlying data distribution, from which we have a finite number of iid samples but do not know its pdf. The **score matching** objective [Hyv05] minimizes a discrepancy between two distributions called the **Fisher divergence**:

$$D_F(p_{\mathcal{D}}(\mathbf{x}) \parallel p_{\boldsymbol{\theta}}(\mathbf{x})) = \mathbb{E}_{p_{\mathcal{D}}(\mathbf{x})} \left[\frac{1}{2} \| \nabla_{\mathbf{x}} \log p_{\mathcal{D}}(\mathbf{x}) - \nabla_{\mathbf{x}} \log p_{\boldsymbol{\theta}}(\mathbf{x}) \|^2 \right]. \tag{24.28}$$

The expectation wrt $p_{\mathcal{D}}(\mathbf{x})$, in this objective and its variants below, admits a trivial unbiased Monte Carlo estimator using the empirical mean of samples $\mathbf{x} \sim p_{\mathcal{D}}(\mathbf{x})$. However, the second term of Equation (24.28), $\nabla_{\mathbf{x}} \log p_{\mathcal{D}}(\mathbf{x})$, is generally impractical to calculate since it requires knowing the pdf of $p_{\mathcal{D}}(\mathbf{x})$. We discuss a solution to this below.

24.3.1   Basic score matching

Hyvärinen [Hyv05] shows that, under certain regularity conditions, the Fisher divergence can be rewritten using integration by parts, with second derivatives of $\mathcal{E}_{\boldsymbol{\theta}}(\mathbf{x})$ replacing the unknown first derivatives of $p_{\mathcal{D}}(\mathbf{x})$:

$$D_F(p_{\mathcal{D}}(\mathbf{x}) \parallel p_{\boldsymbol{\theta}}(\mathbf{x})) = \mathbb{E}_{p_{\mathcal{D}}(\mathbf{x})} \left[\frac{1}{2} \sum_{i=1}^{d} \left(\frac{\partial \mathcal{E}_{\boldsymbol{\theta}}(\mathbf{x})}{\partial x_i} \right)^2 + \frac{\partial^2 \mathcal{E}_{\boldsymbol{\theta}}(\mathbf{x})}{\partial x_i^2} \right] + \text{constant} \tag{24.29}$$

$$= \mathbb{E}_{p_{\mathcal{D}}(\mathbf{x})} \left[\frac{1}{2} \| s_{\boldsymbol{\theta}}(\mathbf{x}) \|^2 + \text{tr}(\mathbf{J}_{\mathbf{x}} s_{\boldsymbol{\theta}}(\mathbf{x})) \right] + \text{constant} \tag{24.30}$$

where d is the dimensionality of $\mathbf{x}$, and $\mathbf{J}_{\mathbf{x}} s_{\boldsymbol{\theta}}(\mathbf{x})$ is the Jacobian of the score function. The constant does not affect optimization and thus can be dropped for training. It is shown by [Hyv05] that estimators based on score matching are consistent under some regularity conditions, meaning that the parameter estimator obtained by minimizing Equation (24.28) converges to the true parameters in the limit of infinite data. See Figure 25.5 for an example.

An important downside of the objective Equation (24.30) is that it takes $O(d^2)$ time to compute the trace of the Jacobian. For this reason, the implicit SM formulation of Equation (24.30) has only been applied to relatively simple energy functions where computation of the second derivatives is tractable.

Score Matching assumes a continuous data distribution with positive density over the space, but it can be generalized to discrete or bounded data distributions [Hyv07b; Lyu12]. It is also possible to consider higher-order gradients of log pdf's beyond first derivatives [PDL+12].

24.3.2 Denoising score matching (DSM)

The Score Matching objective in Equation (24.30) requires several regularity conditions for $\log p_{\mathcal{D}}(\mathbf{x})$, e.g., it should be continuously differentiable and finite everywhere. However, these conditions may not always hold in practice. For example, a distribution of digital images is typically discrete and bounded, because the values of pixels are restricted to the range $\{0, 1, \cdots, 255\}$. Therefore, $\log p_{\mathcal{D}}(\mathbf{x})$ in this case is discontinuous and is negative infinity outside the range, and thus SM is not directly applicable.

To alleviate this, one can add a bit of noise to each datapoint: $\tilde{\mathbf{x}} = \mathbf{x} + \boldsymbol{\epsilon}$. As long as the noise distribution $p(\boldsymbol{\epsilon})$ is smooth, the resulting noisy data distribution $q(\tilde{\mathbf{x}}) = \int q(\tilde{\mathbf{x}} \mid \mathbf{x}) p_{\mathcal{D}}(\mathbf{x}) d\mathbf{x}$ is also smooth, and thus the Fisher divergence $D_F(q(\tilde{\mathbf{x}}) \parallel p_{\boldsymbol{\theta}}(\tilde{\mathbf{x}}))$ is a proper objective. [KL10] showed that the objective with noisy data can be approximated by the noiseless Score Matching objective of Equation (24.30) plus a regularization term; this regularization makes Score Matching applicable to a wider range of data distributions, but still requires expensive second-order derivatives.

[Vin11] proposed an elegant and scalable solution to the above difficulty, by showing that:

$$D_F(q(\tilde{\mathbf{x}}) \parallel p_{\boldsymbol{\theta}}(\tilde{\mathbf{x}})) = \mathbb{E}_{q(\tilde{\mathbf{x}})} \left[\frac{1}{2} \| \nabla_{\mathbf{x}} \log p_{\boldsymbol{\theta}}(\tilde{\mathbf{x}}) - \nabla_{\mathbf{x}} \log q(\tilde{\mathbf{x}}) \|_2^2 \right] \tag{24.31}$$

$$= \mathbb{E}_{q(\mathbf{x},\tilde{\mathbf{x}})} \left[\frac{1}{2} \| \nabla_{\mathbf{x}} \log p_{\boldsymbol{\theta}}(\tilde{\mathbf{x}}) - \nabla_{\mathbf{x}} \log q(\tilde{\mathbf{x}}|\mathbf{x}) \|_2^2 \right] + \text{constant} \tag{24.32}$$

$$= \frac{1}{2} \mathbb{E}_{q(\mathbf{x},\tilde{\mathbf{x}})} \left[\left\| \boldsymbol{s}_{\boldsymbol{\theta}}(\tilde{\mathbf{x}}) + \frac{(\tilde{\mathbf{x}} - \boldsymbol{x})}{\sigma^2} \right\|_2^2 \right] \tag{24.33}$$

where $\boldsymbol{s}_{\boldsymbol{\theta}}(\tilde{\mathbf{x}}) = \nabla_{\mathbf{x}} \log p_{\boldsymbol{\theta}}(\tilde{\mathbf{x}})$ is the estimated score function, and

$$\nabla_{\mathbf{x}} \log q(\tilde{\mathbf{x}}|\mathbf{x}) = \nabla_{\mathbf{x}} \log \mathcal{N}(\tilde{\mathbf{x}}|\mathbf{x}, \sigma^2 \mathbf{I}) = \frac{(\tilde{\mathbf{x}} - \boldsymbol{x})}{\sigma^2} \tag{24.34}$$

The expectation can be approximated by sampling from $p_{\mathcal{D}}(\mathbf{x})$ and then sampling the noise term $\tilde{\mathbf{x}}$. (The constant term does not affect optimization and can be ignored without changing the optimal solution.)

This estimation method is called **denoising score matching** (DSM) by [Vin11]. Similar formulations were also explored by Raphan and Simoncelli [RS07; RS11] and can be traced back to Tweedie's formula (Supplementary Section 3.3) and Stein's unbiased risk estimation [Ste81].

24.3.2.1 Difficulties

The major drawback of adding noise to data arises when $p_{\mathcal{D}}(\mathbf{x})$ is already a well-behaved distribution that satisfies the regularity conditions required by score matching. In this case, $D_F(q(\tilde{\mathbf{x}}) \parallel p_{\boldsymbol{\theta}}(\tilde{\mathbf{x}})) \neq$

$D_F(p_{\mathcal{D}}(\mathbf{x}) \parallel p_{\boldsymbol{\theta}}(\mathbf{x}))$, and DSM is not a consistent objective because the optimal EBM matches the noisy distribution $q(\tilde{\mathbf{x}})$, not $p_{\mathcal{D}}(\mathbf{x})$. This inconsistency becomes non-negligible when $q(\tilde{\mathbf{x}})$ significantly differs from $p_{\mathcal{D}}(\mathbf{x})$.

One way to attenuate the inconsistency of DSM is to choose $q \approx p_{\mathcal{D}}$, i.e., use a small noise perturbation. However, this often significantly increases the variance of objective values and hinders optimization. As an example, suppose $q(\tilde{\mathbf{x}} \mid \mathbf{x}) = \mathcal{N}(\tilde{\mathbf{x}} \mid \mathbf{x}, \sigma^2 I)$ and $\sigma \approx 0$. The corresponding DSM objective is

$$D_F(q(\tilde{\mathbf{x}}) \parallel p_{\boldsymbol{\theta}}(\tilde{\mathbf{x}})) = \mathbb{E}_{p_{\mathcal{D}}(\mathbf{x})} \mathbb{E}_{\mathbf{z} \sim \mathcal{N}(0,I)} \left[\frac{1}{2} \left\| \frac{\mathbf{z}}{\sigma} + \nabla_{\mathbf{x}} \log p_{\boldsymbol{\theta}}(\mathbf{x} + \sigma\mathbf{z}) \right\|_2^2 \right]$$

$$\simeq \frac{1}{2N} \sum_{i=1}^{N} \left\| \frac{\mathbf{z}^{(i)}}{\sigma} + \nabla_{\mathbf{x}} \log p_{\boldsymbol{\theta}}(\mathbf{x}^{(i)} + \sigma\mathbf{z}^{(i)}) \right\|_2^2, \tag{24.35}$$

where $\{\mathbf{x}^{(i)}\}_{i=1}^{N} \overset{\text{i.i.d.}}{\sim} p_{\mathcal{D}}(\mathbf{x})$, and $\{\mathbf{z}^{(i)}\}_{i=1}^{N} \overset{\text{i.i.d.}}{\sim} \mathcal{N}(\mathbf{0}, \boldsymbol{I})$. When $\sigma \to 0$, we can leverage Taylor series expansion to rewrite the Monte Carlo estimator in Equation (24.35) to

$$\frac{1}{2N} \sum_{i=1}^{N} \left[\frac{2}{\sigma} (\mathbf{z}^{(i)})^{\mathsf{T}} \nabla_{\mathbf{x}} \log p_{\boldsymbol{\theta}}(\mathbf{x}^{(i)}) + \frac{\|\mathbf{z}^{(i)}\|_2^2}{\sigma^2} \right] + \text{constant}. \tag{24.36}$$

When estimating the above expectation with samples, the variances of $(\mathbf{z}^{(i)})^{\mathsf{T}} \nabla_{\mathbf{x}} \log p_{\boldsymbol{\theta}}(\mathbf{x}^{(i)})/\sigma$ and $\|\mathbf{z}^{(i)}\|_2^2/\sigma^2$ will both grow unbounded as $\sigma \to 0$ due to division by σ and σ^2. This enlarges the variance of DSM and makes optimization challenging. Various methods have been proposed to reduce this variance (see e.g., [Wan+20d]).

24.3.3 Sliced score matching (SSM)

By adding noise to data, DSM avoids the expensive computation of second-order derivatives. However, as mentioned before, the optimal EBM that minimizes the DSM objective corresponds to the distribution of noise-perturbed data $q(\tilde{\mathbf{x}})$, not the original noise-free data distribution $p_{\mathcal{D}}(\mathbf{x})$. In other words, DSM does not give a consistent estimator of the data distribution, i.e., one cannot directly obtain an EBM that exactly matches the data distribution even with unlimited data.

Sliced score matching (SSM) [Son+19] is one alternative to Denoising Score Matching that is both consistent and computationally efficient. Instead of minimizing the Fisher divergence between two vector-valued scores, SSM randomly samples a projection vector $\mathbf{v}$, takes the inner product between $\mathbf{v}$ and the two scores, and then compares the resulting two scalars. More specifically, sliced ccore matching minimizes the following divergence called the **sliced Fisher divergence**:

$$D_{SF}(p_{\mathcal{D}}(\mathbf{x}) \| p_{\boldsymbol{\theta}}(\mathbf{x})) = \mathbb{E}_{p_{\mathcal{D}}(\mathbf{x})} \mathbb{E}_{p(\mathbf{v})} \left[\frac{1}{2} (\mathbf{v}^{\mathsf{T}} \nabla_{\mathbf{x}} \log p_{\mathcal{D}}(\mathbf{x}) - \mathbf{v}^{\mathsf{T}} \nabla_{\mathbf{x}} \log p_{\boldsymbol{\theta}}(\mathbf{x}))^2 \right], \tag{24.37}$$

where $p(\mathbf{v})$ denotes a projection distribution such that $\mathbb{E}_{p(\mathbf{v})}[\mathbf{v}\mathbf{v}^{\mathsf{T}}]$ is positive definite. Similar to Fisher divergence, sliced Fisher divergence has an implicit form that does not involve the unknown $\nabla_{\mathbf{x}} \log p_{\mathcal{D}}(\mathbf{x})$, which is given by

$$D_{SF}(p_{\mathcal{D}}(\mathbf{x}) \| p_{\boldsymbol{\theta}}(\mathbf{x})) = \mathbb{E}_{p_{\mathcal{D}}(\mathbf{x})} \mathbb{E}_{p(\mathbf{v})} \left[\frac{1}{2} \sum_{i=1}^{d} \left(\frac{\partial \mathcal{E}_{\boldsymbol{\theta}}(\mathbf{x})}{\partial x_i} v_i \right)^2 + \sum_{i=1}^{d} \sum_{j=1}^{d} \frac{\partial^2 \mathcal{E}_{\boldsymbol{\theta}}(\mathbf{x})}{\partial x_i \partial x_j} v_i v_j \right] + C. \tag{24.38}$$

All expectations in the above objective can be estimated with empirical means, and again the constant term C can be removed without affecting training. The second term involves second-order derivatives of $\mathcal{E}_{\boldsymbol{\theta}}(\mathbf{x})$, but contrary to SM, it can be computed efficiently with a cost linear in the dimensionality d. This is because

$$\sum_{i=1}^{d}\sum_{j=1}^{d}\frac{\partial^2\mathcal{E}_{\boldsymbol{\theta}}(\mathbf{x})}{\partial x_i \partial x_j}v_i v_j = \sum_{i=1}^{d}\frac{\partial}{\partial x_i}\underbrace{\left(\sum_{j=1}^{d}\frac{\partial\mathcal{E}_{\boldsymbol{\theta}}(\mathbf{x})}{\partial x_j}v_j\right)}_{:=f(\mathbf{x})}v_i, \tag{24.39}$$

where $f(\mathbf{x})$ is the same for different values of i. Therefore, we only need to compute it once with $O(d)$ computation, *plus* another $O(d)$ computation for the outer sum to evaluate Equation (24.39), whereas the original SM objective requires $O(d^2)$ computation.

For many choices of $p(\mathbf{v})$, part of the SSM objective (Equation (24.38)) can be evaluated in closed form, potentially leading to lower variance. For example, when $p(\mathbf{v}) = \mathcal{N}(\mathbf{0}, \boldsymbol{I})$, we have

$$\mathbb{E}_{p_{\mathcal{D}}(\mathbf{x})}\mathbb{E}_{p(\mathbf{v})}\left[\frac{1}{2}\sum_{i=1}^{d}\left(\frac{\partial\mathcal{E}_{\boldsymbol{\theta}}(\mathbf{x})}{\partial x_i}v_i\right)^2\right] = \mathbb{E}_{p_{\mathcal{D}}(\mathbf{x})}\left[\frac{1}{2}\sum_{i=1}^{d}\left(\frac{\partial\mathcal{E}_{\boldsymbol{\theta}}(\mathbf{x})}{\partial x_i}\right)^2\right] \tag{24.40}$$

and as a result,

$$D_{SF}(p_{\mathcal{D}}(\mathbf{x})\|p_{\boldsymbol{\theta}}(\mathbf{x})) = \mathbb{E}_{p_{\mathcal{D}}(\mathbf{x})}\mathbb{E}_{\mathbf{v}\sim\mathcal{N}(\mathbf{0},\boldsymbol{I})}\left[\frac{1}{2}\sum_{i=1}^{d}\left(\frac{\partial\mathcal{E}_{\boldsymbol{\theta}}(\mathbf{x})}{\partial x_i}\right)^2 + \sum_{i=1}^{d}\sum_{j=1}^{d}\frac{\partial^2\mathcal{E}_{\boldsymbol{\theta}}(\mathbf{x})}{\partial x_i \partial x_j}v_i v_j\right] + C \tag{24.41}$$

$$= \mathbb{E}_{p_{\mathcal{D}}(\mathbf{x})}\mathbb{E}_{\mathbf{v}\sim\mathcal{N}(\mathbf{0},\boldsymbol{I})}\left[\frac{1}{2}(\boldsymbol{v}^\mathsf{T}\boldsymbol{s}_{\boldsymbol{\theta}}(\boldsymbol{x}))^2 + \boldsymbol{v}^\mathsf{T}[\boldsymbol{J}\boldsymbol{v}]\right] \tag{24.42}$$

where $\mathbf{J} = \mathbf{J}_x \boldsymbol{s}_{\boldsymbol{\theta}}(\boldsymbol{x})$. (Note that $\mathbf{J}\boldsymbol{v}$ can be computed using a Jacobian vector product operation.)

The above objective Equation (24.41) can also be obtained by approximating the sum of second-order gradients in the standard SM objective (Equation (24.30)) with the Hutchinson trace estimator [Ski89; Hut89; Mey+21]. It often (but not always) has lower variance than Equation (24.38), and can perform better in some applications [Son+19].

24.3.4 Connection to contrastive divergence

Though score matching and contrastive divergence (Section 24.2.2) are seemingly very different approaches, they are closely connected to each other. In fact, score matching can be viewed as a special instance of contrastive divergence in the limit of a particular MCMC sampler [Hyv07a]. Moreover, the Fisher divergence optimized by Score Matching is related to the derivative of KL divergence [Cov99], which is the underlying objective of Contrastive Divergence.

Contrastive divergence requires sampling from the EBM $\mathcal{E}_{\boldsymbol{\theta}}(\mathbf{x})$, and one popular method for doing so is Langevin MCMC. Recall from Section 24.2.1 that given any initial datapoint $\mathbf{x}^0$, the Langevin MCMC method executes the following

$$\mathbf{x}^{k+1} \leftarrow \mathbf{x}^k - \frac{\epsilon}{2}\nabla_{\mathbf{x}}\mathcal{E}_{\boldsymbol{\theta}}(\mathbf{x}^k) + \sqrt{\epsilon}\,\mathbf{z}^k, \tag{24.43}$$

iteratively for $k = 0, 1, \cdots, K-1$, where $\mathbf{z}^k \sim \mathcal{N}(\mathbf{0}, \boldsymbol{I})$ and $\epsilon > 0$ is the step size.

Suppose we only run one-step Langevin MCMC for contrastive divergence. In this case, the gradient of the log-likelihood is given by

$$
\mathbb{E}_{p_{\mathcal{D}}(\mathbf{x})}[\nabla_{\boldsymbol{\theta}} \log p_{\boldsymbol{\theta}}(\mathbf{x})] = -\mathbb{E}_{p_{\mathcal{D}}(\mathbf{x})}[\nabla_{\boldsymbol{\theta}}\mathcal{E}_{\boldsymbol{\theta}}(\mathbf{x})] + \mathbb{E}_{\mathbf{x} \sim p_{\boldsymbol{\theta}}(\mathbf{x})}[\nabla_{\boldsymbol{\theta}}\mathcal{E}_{\boldsymbol{\theta}}(\mathbf{x})]
$$

$$
\simeq -\mathbb{E}_{p_{\mathcal{D}}(\mathbf{x})}[\nabla_{\boldsymbol{\theta}}\mathcal{E}_{\boldsymbol{\theta}}(\mathbf{x})] + \mathbb{E}_{p_{\boldsymbol{\theta}}(\mathbf{x}), \mathbf{z} \sim \mathcal{N}(0, \boldsymbol{I})}\left[\nabla_{\boldsymbol{\theta}}\mathcal{E}_{\boldsymbol{\theta}}\left(\mathbf{x} - \frac{\epsilon^2}{2}\nabla_{\mathbf{x}}E_{\boldsymbol{\theta}'}(\mathbf{x}) + \epsilon\, \mathbf{z}\right)\Big|_{\boldsymbol{\theta}'=\boldsymbol{\theta}}\right]. \quad (24.44)
$$

After Taylor series expansion with respect to ϵ followed by some algebraic manipulations, the above equation can be transformed to the following [Hyv07a]:

$$
\frac{\epsilon^2}{2}\nabla_{\boldsymbol{\theta}} D_F(p_{\mathcal{D}}(\mathbf{x}) \parallel p_{\boldsymbol{\theta}}(\mathbf{x})) + o(\epsilon^2). \quad (24.45)
$$

When ϵ is sufficiently small, it corresponds to the re-scaled gradient of the score matching objective.

In general, score matching minimizes the Fisher divergence $D_F(p_{\mathcal{D}}(\mathbf{x}) \parallel p_{\boldsymbol{\theta}}(\mathbf{x}))$, whereas Contrastive Divergence minimizes an objective related to the KL divergence $D_{KL}(p_{\mathcal{D}}(\mathbf{x}) \parallel p_{\boldsymbol{\theta}}(\mathbf{x}))$, as shown in Equation (24.19). The above connection of score matching and Contrastive Divergence is a natural consequence of the connection between those two statistical divergences, as characterized by *de Bruijin's identity* [Cov99; Lyu12]:

$$
\frac{d}{dt}D_{KL}(q_t(\tilde{\mathbf{x}}) \parallel p_{\boldsymbol{\theta},t}(\tilde{\mathbf{x}})) = -\frac{1}{2}D_F(q_t(\tilde{\mathbf{x}}) \parallel p_{\boldsymbol{\theta},t}(\tilde{\mathbf{x}})).
$$

Here $q_t(\tilde{\mathbf{x}})$ and $p_{\boldsymbol{\theta},t}(\tilde{\mathbf{x}})$ denote smoothed versions of $p_{\mathcal{D}}(\mathbf{x})$ and $p_{\boldsymbol{\theta}}(\mathbf{x})$, resulting from adding Gaussian noise to $\mathbf{x}$ with variance t; i.e., $\tilde{\mathbf{x}} \sim \mathcal{N}(\mathbf{x}, t\boldsymbol{I})$.

24.3.5 Score-based generative models

We have seen how to use score matching to fit EBMs by learning the scalar energy function $\mathcal{E}_{\boldsymbol{\theta}}(\boldsymbol{x})$. We can alternatively directly learn the score function, $\boldsymbol{s}_{\boldsymbol{\theta}}(\boldsymbol{x}) = \nabla_{\boldsymbol{x}} \log p_{\boldsymbol{\theta}}(\boldsymbol{x})$; this is called a score-based generative model, and is discussed in Section 25.3. Such unconstrained score models are not guaranteed to output a conservative vector field, meaning they do not correspond to the gradient of any function. However, both methods seem to give comparable results [SH21].

24.4 Noise contrastive estimation

Another principle for learning the parameters of EBMs is **Noise contrastive estimation** (NCE), introduced by [GH10]. It is based on the idea that we can learn an EBM by contrasting it with another distribution with known density.

Let $p_{\mathcal{D}}(\mathbf{x})$ be our data distribution, and let $p_{\mathrm{n}}(\mathbf{x})$ be a chosen distribution with known density, called a noise distribution. This noise distribution is usually simple and has a tractable pdf, like $\mathcal{N}(\mathbf{0}, \boldsymbol{I})$, such that we can compute the pdf and generate samples from it efficiently. Strategies exist to learn the noise distribution, as referenced below. Furthermore, let y be a binary variable with Bernoulli distribution, which we use to define a mixture distribution of noise and data: $p_{\mathrm{n,data}}(\mathbf{x}) =$

$p(y = 0)p_n(\mathbf{x}) + p(y = 1)p_\mathcal{D}(\mathbf{x})$. According to Bayes' rule, given a sample $\mathbf{x}$ from this mixture, the posterior probability of $y = 0$ is

$$p_{n,data}(y = 0 \mid \mathbf{x}) = \frac{p_{n,data}(\mathbf{x} \mid y = 0)p(y = 0)}{p_{n,data}(\mathbf{x})} = \frac{p_n(\mathbf{x})}{p_n(\mathbf{x}) + \nu p_\mathcal{D}(\mathbf{x})} \qquad (24.46)$$

where $\nu = p(y = 1)/p(y = 0)$.

Let our EBM $p_{\boldsymbol{\theta}}(\mathbf{x})$ be defined as:

$$p_{\boldsymbol{\theta}}(\mathbf{x}) = \exp(-\mathcal{E}_{\boldsymbol{\theta}}(\mathbf{x}))/Z_{\boldsymbol{\theta}} \qquad (24.47)$$

Contrary to most other EBMs, $Z_{\boldsymbol{\theta}}$ is treated as a learnable (scalar) parameter in NCE. Given this model, similar to the mixture of noise and data above, we can define a mixture of noise and the model distribution: $p_{n,\boldsymbol{\theta}}(\mathbf{x}) = p(y = 0)p_n(\mathbf{x}) + p(y = 1)p_{\boldsymbol{\theta}}(\mathbf{x})$. The posterior probability of $y = 0$ given this noise/model mixture is:

$$p_{n,\boldsymbol{\theta}}(y = 0 \mid \mathbf{x}) = \frac{p_n(\mathbf{x})}{p_n(\mathbf{x}) + \nu p_{\boldsymbol{\theta}}(\mathbf{x})} \qquad (24.48)$$

In NCE, we indirectly fit $p_{\boldsymbol{\theta}}(\mathbf{x})$ to $p_\mathcal{D}(\mathbf{x})$ by fitting $p_{n,\boldsymbol{\theta}}(y \mid \mathbf{x})$ to $p_{n,data}(y \mid \mathbf{x})$ through a standard conditional maximum likelihood objective:

$$\boldsymbol{\theta}^* = \underset{\boldsymbol{\theta}}{\mathrm{argmin}}\, \mathbb{E}_{p_{n,data}(\mathbf{x})}[D_{KL}(p_{n,data}(y \mid \mathbf{x}) \parallel p_{n,\boldsymbol{\theta}}(y \mid \mathbf{x}))] \qquad (24.49)$$

$$= \underset{\boldsymbol{\theta}}{\mathrm{argmax}}\, \mathbb{E}_{p_{n,data}(\mathbf{x},y)}[\log p_{n,\boldsymbol{\theta}}(y \mid \mathbf{x})], \qquad (24.50)$$

which can be solved using stochastic gradient ascent. Just like any other deep classifier, when the model is sufficiently powerful, $p_{n,\boldsymbol{\theta}^*}(y \mid \mathbf{x})$ will match $p_{n,data}(y \mid \mathbf{x})$ at the optimum. In that case:

$$p_{n,\boldsymbol{\theta}^*}(y = 0 \mid \mathbf{x}) \equiv p_{n,data}(y = 0 \mid \mathbf{x}) \qquad (24.51)$$

$$\iff \frac{p_n(\mathbf{x})}{p_n(\mathbf{x}) + \nu p_{\boldsymbol{\theta}^*}(\mathbf{x})} \equiv \frac{p_n(\mathbf{x})}{p_n(\mathbf{x}) + \nu p_\mathcal{D}(\mathbf{x})} \qquad (24.52)$$

$$\iff p_{\boldsymbol{\theta}^*}(\mathbf{x}) \equiv p_\mathcal{D}(\mathbf{x}) \qquad (24.53)$$

Consequently, $E_{\boldsymbol{\theta}^*}(\mathbf{x})$ is an unnormalized energy function that matches the data distribution $p_\mathcal{D}(\mathbf{x})$, and $Z_{\boldsymbol{\theta}^*}$ is the corresponding normalizing constant.

As one unique feature that contrastive divergence and score matching do not have, NCE provides the normalizing constant of an Energy-Based Model as a by-product of its training procedure. When the EBM is very expressive, e.g., a deep neural network with many parameters, we can assume it is able to approximate a normalized probability density and absorb $Z_{\boldsymbol{\theta}}$ into the parameters of $\mathcal{E}_{\boldsymbol{\theta}}(\mathbf{x})$ [MT12], or equivalently, fixing $Z_{\boldsymbol{\theta}} = 1$. The resulting EBM trained with NCE will be self-normalized, i.e., having a normalizing constant close to 1.

In practice, choosing the right noise distribution $p_n(\mathbf{x})$ is critical to the success of NCE, especially for structured and high-dimensional data. As argued in Gutmann and Hirayama [GH12], NCE works the best when the noise distribution is close to the data distribution (but not exactly the same). Many methods have been proposed to automatically tune the noise distribution, such as Adversarial Contrastive Estimation [BLC18], Conditional NCE [CG18] and Flow Contrastive Estimation [Gao+20]. NCE can be further generalized using Bregman divergences (Section 5.1.10), where the formulation introduced here reduces to a special case.

24.4.1   Connection to score matching

Noise contrastive estimation provides a family of objectives that vary for different $p_n(\mathbf{x})$ and ν. This flexibility may allow adaptation to special properties of a task with hand-tuned $p_n(\mathbf{x})$ and ν, and may also give a unified perspective for different approaches. In particular, when using an appropriate $p_n(\mathbf{x})$ and a slightly different parameterization of $p_{n,\boldsymbol{\theta}}(y \mid \mathbf{x})$, we can recover score matching from NCE [GH12].

Specifically, we choose the noise distribution $p_n(\mathbf{x})$ to be a perturbed data distribution: given a small (deterministic) vector $\mathbf{v}$, let $p_n(\mathbf{x}) = p_{\mathcal{D}}(\mathbf{x} - \mathbf{v})$. It is efficient to sample from this $p_n(\mathbf{x})$, since we can first draw any datapoint $\mathbf{x}' \sim p_{\mathcal{D}}(\mathbf{x}')$ and then compute $\mathbf{x} = \mathbf{x}' + \mathbf{v}$. It is, however, difficult to evaluate the density of $p_n(\mathbf{x})$ because $p_{\mathcal{D}}(\mathbf{x})$ is unknown. Since the original parameterization of $p_{n,\boldsymbol{\theta}}(y \mid \mathbf{x})$ in NCE (Equation (24.48)) depends on the pdf of $p_n(\mathbf{x})$, we cannot directly apply the standard NCE objective. Instead, we replace $p_n(\mathbf{x})$ with $p_{\boldsymbol{\theta}}(\mathbf{x} - \mathbf{v})$ and parameterize $p_{n,\boldsymbol{\theta}}(y = 0 \mid \mathbf{x})$ with the following form

$$p_{n,\boldsymbol{\theta}}(y = 0 \mid \mathbf{x}) := \frac{p_{\boldsymbol{\theta}}(\mathbf{x} - \mathbf{v})}{p_{\boldsymbol{\theta}}(\mathbf{x}) + p_{\boldsymbol{\theta}}(\mathbf{x} - \mathbf{v})} \tag{24.54}$$

In this case, the NCE objective (Equation (24.50)) reduces to:

$$\boldsymbol{\theta}^* = \underset{\boldsymbol{\theta}}{\operatorname{argmin}} \, \mathbb{E}_{p_{\mathcal{D}}(\mathbf{x})}[\log(1 + \exp(\mathcal{E}_{\boldsymbol{\theta}}(\mathbf{x}) - \mathcal{E}_{\boldsymbol{\theta}}(\mathbf{x} - \mathbf{v})) + \log(1 + \exp(\mathcal{E}_{\boldsymbol{\theta}}(\mathbf{x}) - \mathcal{E}_{\boldsymbol{\theta}}(\mathbf{x} + \mathbf{v}))] \tag{24.55}$$

At $\boldsymbol{\theta}^*$, we have a solution where:

$$p_{n,\boldsymbol{\theta}^*}(y = 0 \mid \mathbf{x}) \equiv p_{n,\text{data}}(y = 0 \mid \mathbf{x}) \tag{24.56}$$

$$\implies \frac{p_{\boldsymbol{\theta}^*}(\mathbf{x} - \mathbf{v})}{p_{\boldsymbol{\theta}^*}(\mathbf{x}) + p_{\boldsymbol{\theta}^*}(\mathbf{x} - \mathbf{v})} \equiv \frac{p_{\mathcal{D}}(\mathbf{x} - \mathbf{v})}{p_{\mathcal{D}}(\mathbf{x}) + p_{\mathcal{D}}(\mathbf{x} - \mathbf{v})} \tag{24.57}$$

which implies that $p_{\boldsymbol{\theta}^*}(\mathbf{x}) \equiv p_{\mathcal{D}}(\mathbf{x})$, i.e., our model matches the data distribution.

As noted in Gutmann and Hirayama [GH12] and Song et al. [Son+19], when $\|\mathbf{v}\|_2 \approx 0$, the NCE objective Equation (24.50) has the following equivalent form by Taylor expansion

$$\underset{\boldsymbol{\theta}}{\operatorname{argmin}} \frac{1}{4} \mathbb{E}_{p_{\mathcal{D}}(\mathbf{x})} \left[\frac{1}{2} \sum_{i=1}^{d} \left(\frac{\partial \mathcal{E}_{\boldsymbol{\theta}}(\mathbf{x})}{\partial x_i} v_i \right)^2 + \sum_{i=1}^{d} \sum_{j=1}^{d} \frac{\partial^2 \mathcal{E}_{\boldsymbol{\theta}}(\mathbf{x})}{\partial x_i \partial x_j} v_i v_j \right] + 2 \log 2 + o(\|\mathbf{v}\|_2^2). \tag{24.58}$$

Comparing against Equation (24.38), we immediately see that the above objective equals that of SSM, if we ignore small additional terms hidden in $o(\|\mathbf{v}\|_2^2)$ and take the expectation with respect to $\mathbf{v}$ over a user-specified distribution $p(\mathbf{v})$.

24.5   Other methods

Aside from MCMC-based training, score matching and noise contrastive estimation, there are also other methods for learning EBMs. Below we briefly survey some examples of them. Interested readers can learn more details from references therein.

24.5.1   Minimizing Differences/Derivatives of KL Divergences

The overarching strategy for learning probabilistic models from data is to minimize the KL divergence between data and model distributions. However, because the normalizing constants of EBMs are typically intractable, it is hard to directly evaluate the KL divergence when the model is an EBM (see the discussion in Section 24.2.1). One generic idea that has frequently circumvented this difficulty is to consider differences/derivatives of KL divergences. It turns out that the unknown partition functions of EBMs are often cancelled out after taking the difference of two closely related KL divergences, or computing the derivatives.

Typical examples of this strategy include minimum velocity learning [Mov08; Wan+20d], minimum probability flow [SDBD11], and minimum KL contraction [Lyu11], to name a few. In minimum velocity learning and minimum probability flow, a Markov chain is designed such that it starts from the data distribution $p_{\mathcal{D}}(\mathbf{x})$ and converges to the EBM distribution $p_{\boldsymbol{\theta}}(\mathbf{x}) = e^{-\mathcal{E}_{\boldsymbol{\theta}}(\mathbf{x})}/Z_{\boldsymbol{\theta}}$. Specifically, the Markov chain satisfies $p_0(\mathbf{x}) \equiv p_{\mathcal{D}}(\mathbf{x})$ and $p_{\infty}(\mathbf{x}) \equiv p_{\boldsymbol{\theta}}(\mathbf{x})$, where we denote by $p_t(\mathbf{x})$ the state distribution at time $t \geq 0$.

This Markov chain will evolve towards $p_{\boldsymbol{\theta}}(\mathbf{x})$ unless $p_{\mathcal{D}}(\mathbf{x}) \equiv p_{\boldsymbol{\theta}}(\mathbf{x})$. Therefore, we can fit the EBM distribution $p_{\boldsymbol{\theta}}(\mathbf{x})$ to $p_{\mathcal{D}}(\mathbf{x})$ by minimizing the modulus of the "velocity" of this evolution, defined by

$$\left.\frac{\mathrm{d}}{\mathrm{d}t} D_{\mathrm{KL}}(p_t(\mathbf{x}) \parallel p_{\boldsymbol{\theta}}(\mathbf{x}))\right|_{t=0} \quad \text{or} \quad \left.\frac{\mathrm{d}}{\mathrm{d}t} D_{\mathrm{KL}}(p_{\mathcal{D}}(\mathbf{x}) \parallel p_t(\mathbf{x}))\right|_{t=0} \tag{24.59}$$

in minimum velocity learning and minimum probability flow respectively. These objectives typically do not require computing the normalizing constant $Z_{\boldsymbol{\theta}}$.

In minimum KL contraction [Lyu11], a distribution transformation Φ is chosen such that

$$D_{\mathrm{KL}}(p(\mathbf{x}) \parallel q(\mathbf{x})) \geq D_{\mathrm{KL}}(\Phi\{p(\mathbf{x})\} \parallel \Phi\{q(\mathbf{x})\}) \tag{24.60}$$

with equality if and only if $p(\mathbf{x}) = q(\mathbf{x})$. We can leverage this Φ to train an EBM, by minimizing

$$D_{\mathrm{KL}}(p_{\mathcal{D}}(\mathbf{x}) \parallel p_{\boldsymbol{\theta}}(\mathbf{x})) - D_{\mathrm{KL}}(\Phi\{p_{\mathcal{D}}(\mathbf{x})\} \parallel \Phi\{p_{\boldsymbol{\theta}}(\mathbf{x})\}). \tag{24.61}$$

This objective does not require computing the partition function $Z_{\boldsymbol{\theta}}$ whenever Φ is linear.

Minimum velocity learning, minimum probability flow, and minimum KL contraction can all be viewed as generalizations to score matching and noise contrastive estimation [Mov08; SDBD11; Lyu11].

24.5.2   Minimizing the Stein discrepancy

We can train EBMs by minimizing the Stein discrepancy, defined by

$$D_{\mathrm{Stein}}(p_{\mathcal{D}}(\mathbf{x}) \parallel p_{\boldsymbol{\theta}}(\mathbf{x})) := \sup_{\mathbf{f} \in \mathcal{F}} \mathbb{E}_{p_{\mathcal{D}}(\mathbf{x})}[\nabla_{\mathbf{x}} \log p_{\boldsymbol{\theta}}(\mathbf{x})^{\mathsf{T}} \mathbf{f}(\mathbf{x}) + \mathrm{trace}(\nabla_{\mathbf{x}} \mathbf{f}(\mathbf{x}))], \tag{24.62}$$

where $\mathcal{F}$ is a family of vector-valued functions, and $\nabla_{\mathbf{x}} \mathbf{f}(\mathbf{x})$ denotes the Jacobian of $\mathbf{f}(\mathbf{x})$. With some regularity conditions [GM15; LLJ16], we have $D_S(p_{\mathcal{D}}(\mathbf{x}) \parallel p_{\boldsymbol{\theta}}(\mathbf{x})) \geq 0$, where the equality holds if and only if $p_{\mathcal{D}}(\mathbf{x}) \equiv p_{\boldsymbol{\theta}}(\mathbf{x})$. Similar to score matching (Equation (24.30)), the objective Equation (24.62) only involves the score function of $p_{\boldsymbol{\theta}}(\mathbf{x})$, and does not require computing the EBM's partition function. Still, the trace term in Equation (24.62) may demand expensive computation, and does not scale well to high dimensional data.

There are two common methods that sidestep this difficulty. Gorham and Mackey [GM15] and Liu, Lee, and Jordan [LLJ16] discovered that when $\mathcal{F}$ is a unit ball in a reproducing kernel Hilbert space (RKHS) with a fixed kernel, the Stein discrepancy becomes kernelized Stein discrepancy, where the trace term is a constant and does not affect optimization. Otherwise, $\text{trace}(\nabla_{\mathbf{x}}\mathbf{f}(\mathbf{x}))$ can be approximated with the Skilling-Hutchinson trace estimator [Ski89; Hut89; Gra+20c].

24.5.3 Adversarial training

Recall from Section 24.2.1 that when training EBMs with maximum likelihood estimation (MLE), we need to sample from the EBM per training iteration. However, sampling using multiple MCMC steps is expensive and requires careful tuning of the Markov chain. One way to avoid this difficulty is to use non-MLE methods that do not need sampling, such as score matching and noise contrastive estimation. Here we introduce another family of methods that sidestep costly MCMC sampling by learning an auxiliary model through adversarial training, which allows fast sampling.

Using the definition of EBMs, we can rewrite the maximum likelihood objective by introducing a variational distribution $q_{\phi}(\mathbf{x})$ parameterized by ϕ:

$$
\begin{aligned}
\mathbb{E}_{p_{\mathcal{D}}(\mathbf{x})}[\log p_{\boldsymbol{\theta}}(\mathbf{x})] &= \mathbb{E}_{p_{\mathcal{D}}(\mathbf{x})}[-\mathcal{E}_{\boldsymbol{\theta}}(\mathbf{x})] - \log Z_{\boldsymbol{\theta}} \\
&= \mathbb{E}_{p_{\mathcal{D}}(\mathbf{x})}[-\mathcal{E}_{\boldsymbol{\theta}}(\mathbf{x})] - \log \int e^{-\mathcal{E}_{\boldsymbol{\theta}}(\mathbf{x})} \mathrm{d}\mathbf{x} \\
&= \mathbb{E}_{p_{\mathcal{D}}(\mathbf{x})}[-\mathcal{E}_{\boldsymbol{\theta}}(\mathbf{x})] - \log \int q_{\phi}(\mathbf{x}) \frac{e^{-\mathcal{E}_{\boldsymbol{\theta}}(\mathbf{x})}}{q_{\phi}(\mathbf{x})} \mathrm{d}\mathbf{x} \\
&\overset{(i)}{\leq} \mathbb{E}_{p_{\mathcal{D}}(\mathbf{x})}[-\mathcal{E}_{\boldsymbol{\theta}}(\mathbf{x})] - \int q_{\phi}(\mathbf{x}) \log \frac{e^{-\mathcal{E}_{\boldsymbol{\theta}}(\mathbf{x})}}{q_{\phi}(\mathbf{x})} \mathrm{d}\mathbf{x} \\
&= \mathbb{E}_{p_{\mathcal{D}}(\mathbf{x})}[-\mathcal{E}_{\boldsymbol{\theta}}(\mathbf{x})] - \mathbb{E}_{q_{\phi}(\mathbf{x})}[-\mathcal{E}_{\boldsymbol{\theta}}(\mathbf{x})] - H(q_{\phi}(\mathbf{x})),
\end{aligned}
\tag{24.63}
$$

where $H(q_{\phi}(\mathbf{x}))$ denotes the entropy of $q_{\phi}(\mathbf{x})$. Step (i) is due to Jensen's inequality. Equation (24.63) provides an upper bound to the expected log-likelihood. For EBM training, we can first minimize the upper bound Equation (24.63) with respect to $q_{\phi}(\mathbf{x})$ so that it is closer to the likelihood objective, and then maximize Equation (24.63) with respect to $\mathcal{E}_{\boldsymbol{\theta}}(\mathbf{x})$ as a surrogate for maximizing likelihood. This amounts to using the following maximin objective

$$
\max_{\boldsymbol{\theta}} \min_{\phi} \mathbb{E}_{q_{\phi}(\mathbf{x})}[\mathcal{E}_{\boldsymbol{\theta}}(\mathbf{x})] - \mathbb{E}_{p_{\mathcal{D}}(\mathbf{x})}[\mathcal{E}_{\boldsymbol{\theta}}(\mathbf{x})] - H(q_{\phi}(\mathbf{x})).
\tag{24.64}
$$

Optimizing the above objective is similar to training GANs (Chapter 26), and can be achieved by adversarial training. The variational distribution $q_{\phi}(\mathbf{x})$ should allow both fast sampling and efficient entropy evaluation to make Equation (24.64) tractable. This limits the model family of $q_{\phi}(\mathbf{x})$, and usually restricts our choice to invertible probabilistic models, such as inverse autoregressive flow (Section 23.2.4.3). See Dai et al. [Dai+19b] for an example on designing $q_{\phi}(\mathbf{x})$ and training EBMs with Equation (24.64).

Kim and Bengio [KB16] and Zhai et al. [Zha+16] propose to represent $q_{\phi}(\mathbf{x})$ with neural samplers, like the generator of GANs. A neural sampler is a deterministic mapping g_{ϕ} that maps a random

Gaussian noise $\mathbf{z} \sim \mathcal{N}(\mathbf{0}, \boldsymbol{I})$ directly to a sample $\mathbf{x} = g_\phi(\mathbf{z})$. When using a neural sampler as $q_\phi(\mathbf{x})$, it is efficient to draw samples through the deterministic mapping, but $H(q_\phi(\mathbf{x}))$ is intractable since the density of $q_\phi(\mathbf{x})$ is unknown. Kim and Bengio [KB16] and Zhai et al. [Zha+16] propose several heuristics to approximate this entropy function. Kumar et al. [Kum+19c] propose to estimate the entropy through its connection to mutual information: $H(q_\phi(\mathbf{z})) = I(g_\phi(\mathbf{z}), \mathbf{z})$, which can be estimated from samples with variational lower bounds [NWJ10b; NCT16b]. Dai et al. [Dai+19a] noticed that when defining $p_{\boldsymbol{\theta}}(\mathbf{x}) = p_0(\mathbf{x})e^{-\mathcal{E}_{\boldsymbol{\theta}}(\mathbf{x})}/Z_{\boldsymbol{\theta}}$, with $p_0(\mathbf{x})$ being a fixed base distribution, the entropy term $-H(q_\phi(\mathbf{x}))$ in Equation (24.64) can be replaced by $\mathrm{D}_{\mathrm{KL}}(q_\phi(\mathbf{x}) \parallel p_0(\mathbf{x}))$, which can also be approximated with variational lower bounds using samples from $q_\phi(\mathbf{x})$ and $p_0(\mathbf{x})$, without requiring the density of $q_\phi(\mathbf{x})$.

Grathwohl et al. [Gra+20a] represent $q_\phi(\mathbf{x})$ as a noisy neural sampler, where samples are obtained via $g_\phi(\mathbf{z}) + \sigma\boldsymbol{\epsilon}$, assuming $\mathbf{z}, \boldsymbol{\epsilon} \sim \mathcal{N}(\mathbf{0}, \boldsymbol{I})$. With a noisy neural sampler, $\nabla_\phi H(q_\phi(\mathbf{x}))$ becomes particularly easy to estimate, which allows gradient-based optimization for the minimax objective in Equation (24.63). A related approach is proposed in Xie et al. [Xie+18], where authors train a noisy neural sampler with samples obtained from MCMC, and initialize new MCMC chains with samples generated from the neural sampler. This cooperative sampling scheme improves the convergence of MCMC, but may still require multiple MCMC steps for sample generation. It does not optimize the objective in Equation (24.63).

When using both adversarial training and MCMC sampling, Yu et al. [Yu+20] noticed that EBMs can be trained with an arbitrary f-divergence, including KL, reverse KL, total variation, Hellinger, etc. The method proposed by Yu et al. [Yu+20] allows us to explore the trade-offs and inductive bias of different statistical divergences for more flexible EBM training.

25 Diffusion models

25.1 Introduction

In this chapter, we consider a class of models called **diffusion models**. This class of models has recently generated a lot of interest, due to its ability to generate diverse, high quality, samples, and the relative simplicity of the training scheme, which allows very large models to be trained at scale. Diffusion models are closely related to VAEs (Chapter 21), normalizing flows (Chapter 23), and EBMs (Chapter 24), as we will see.

The basic idea behind these models is based on the observation that it is hard to convert noise into structured data, but it is easy to convert structured data into noise. In particular, we can use a **forwards process** or **diffusion process** to gradually convert the observed data x_0 into a noisy version x_T by passing the data through T steps of a stochastic encoder $q(x_t|x_{t-1})$. After enough steps, we have $x_T \sim \mathcal{N}(0, I)$, or some other convenient reference distribution. We then learn a **reverse process** to undo this, by passing the noise through T steps of a decoder $p_\theta(x_{t-1}|x_t)$ until we generate x_0. See Figure 25.1 for an overall sketch of the approach. In the following sections, we discuss this class of models in more detail. Our presentation is based in part on the excellent tutorial [KGV22]. More details can be found in the recent review papers [Yan+22; Cao+22], as well as specialized papers, such as [Kar+22]. There are also many other excellent resources online, such as `https://github.com/heejkoo/Awesome-Diffusion-Models` and `https://scorebasedgenerativemodeling.github.io/`.

25.2 Denoising diffusion probabilistic models (DDPMs)

In this section, we discuss **denoising diffusion probabilistic models** or **DDPMs**, introduced in [SD+15b], and then extended in [HJA20; Kin+21] and many other works. We can think of the DDPM as similar to a hierarchical variational autoencoder (Section 21.5), except that all the latent states (denoted x_t for $t = 1 : T$) have the same dimensionality as the input x_0. (In this respect, a DDPM is similar to a normalizing flow (Chapter 23); however, in a diffusion model, the hidden layers are stochastic, and do not need to use invertible transformations.) In addition, the encoder network q is a simple linear Gaussian model, rather than being learned[1], and the decoder network p is shared across all time steps. These restrictions result in a very simple training objective, which allows deep models to be easily trained without any risk of posterior collapse (Section 21.4). In

---

1. Later we will discuss some extensions in which the noise level of the encoder can also be learned. Nevertheless, the encoder remains simple, by design.

$$q(\mathbf{x_t}|\mathbf{x_{t-1}}) = \mathcal{N}(\mathbf{x_t}; \sqrt{1-\beta_t}\mathbf{x_{t-1}}, \beta_t\mathbf{I})$$

Data   Noise

$$p_\theta(\mathbf{x_{t-1}}|\mathbf{x_t}) = \mathcal{N}(\mathbf{x_{t-1}}; \mu_\theta(\mathbf{x_t}, t), \sigma_t^2\mathbf{I})$$

Figure 25.1: Denoising diffusion probabilistic model. The forwards diffusion process, $q(\boldsymbol{x}_t|\boldsymbol{x}_{t-1})$, implements the (non-learned) inference network; this just adds Gaussian noise at each step. The reverse diffusion process, $p_\theta(\boldsymbol{x}_{t-1}|\boldsymbol{x}_t)$, implements the decoder; this is a learned Gaussian model. From Slide 16 of [KGV22]. Used with kind permission of Arash Vahdat.

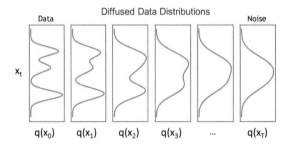

Figure 25.2: Illustration of a diffusion model on 1d data. The forwards diffusion process gradually transforms the empirical data distribution $q(\boldsymbol{x}_0)$ into a simple target distribution, here $q(\boldsymbol{x}_T) = \mathcal{N}(\mathbf{0}, \mathbf{I})$. To generate from the model, we sample a point $\boldsymbol{x}_T \sim \mathcal{N}(\mathbf{0}, \mathbf{I})$, and then run the Markov chain backwards, by sampling $\boldsymbol{x}_t \sim p_\theta(\boldsymbol{x}_t|\boldsymbol{x}_{t+1})$ until we get a sample in the original data space, $\boldsymbol{x}_0$. From Slide 19 of [KGV22]. Used with kind permission of Arash Vahdat.

particular, in Section 25.2.3, we will see that training reduces to a series of weighted nonlinear least squares problems.

25.2.1 Encoder (forwards diffusion)

The forwards encoder process is defined to be a simple linear Gaussian model:

$$q(\boldsymbol{x}_t|\boldsymbol{x}_{t-1}) = \mathcal{N}(\boldsymbol{x}_t|\sqrt{1-\beta_t}\boldsymbol{x}_{t-1}, \beta_t\mathbf{I}) \tag{25.1}$$

where the values of $\beta_t \in (0, 1)$ are chosen according to a noise schedule (see Section 25.2.4). The joint distribution over all the latent states, conditioned on the input, is given by

$$q(\boldsymbol{x}_{1:T}|\boldsymbol{x}_0) = \prod_{t=1}^{T} q(\boldsymbol{x}_t|\boldsymbol{x}_{t-1}) \tag{25.2}$$

Since this defines a linear Gaussian Markov chain, we can compute marginals of it in closed form. In particular, we have

$$q(\boldsymbol{x}_t|\boldsymbol{x}_0) = \mathcal{N}(\boldsymbol{x}_t|\sqrt{\overline{\alpha}_t}\boldsymbol{x}_0, (1 - \overline{\alpha}_t)\mathbf{I}) \tag{25.3}$$

where we define

$$\alpha_t \triangleq 1 - \beta_t, \overline{\alpha}_t = \prod_{s=1}^{t} \alpha_s \tag{25.4}$$

We choose the noise schedule such that $\overline{\alpha}_T \approx 0$, so that $q(\boldsymbol{x}_T|\boldsymbol{x}_0) \approx \mathcal{N}(\mathbf{0}, \mathbf{I})$.

The distribution $q(\boldsymbol{x}_t|\boldsymbol{x}_0)$ is known as the **diffusion kernel**. Applying this to the input data distribution and then computing the result unconditional marginals is equivalent to Gaussian convolution:

$$q(\boldsymbol{x}_t) = \int q_0(\boldsymbol{x}_0)q(\boldsymbol{x}_t|\boldsymbol{x}_0)d\boldsymbol{x}_0 \tag{25.5}$$

As t increases, the marginals become simpler, as shown in Figure 25.2. In the image domain, this process will first remove high-frequency content (i.e., low-level details, such as texture), and later will remove low-frequency content (i.e., high-level or "semantic" information, such as shape), as shown in Figure 25.1.

25.2.2 Decoder (reverse diffusion)

In the reverse diffusion process, we would like to invert the forwards diffusion process. If we know the input $\boldsymbol{x}_0$, we can derive the reverse of one forwards step as follows:[2]

$$q(\boldsymbol{x}_{t-1}|\boldsymbol{x}_t, \boldsymbol{x}_0) = \mathcal{N}(\boldsymbol{x}_{t-1}|\tilde{\mu}_t(\boldsymbol{x}_t, \boldsymbol{x}_0), \tilde{\beta}_t \mathbf{I}) \tag{25.6}$$

$$\tilde{\mu}_t(\boldsymbol{x}_t, \boldsymbol{x}_0) = \frac{\sqrt{\overline{\alpha}_{t-1}}\beta_t}{1 - \overline{\alpha}_t}\boldsymbol{x}_0 + \frac{\sqrt{\alpha_t}(1 - \overline{\alpha}_{t-1})}{1 - \overline{\alpha}_t}\boldsymbol{x}_t \tag{25.7}$$

$$\tilde{\beta}_t = \frac{1 - \overline{\alpha}_{t-1}}{1 - \overline{\alpha}_t}\beta_t \tag{25.8}$$

Of course, when generating a new datapoint, we do not know $\boldsymbol{x}_0$, but we will train the generator to approximate the above distribution averaged over $\boldsymbol{x}_0$. Thus we choose the generator to have the form

$$p_{\boldsymbol{\theta}}(\boldsymbol{x}_{t-1}|\boldsymbol{x}_t) = \mathcal{N}(\boldsymbol{x}_{t-1}|\boldsymbol{\mu}_{\boldsymbol{\theta}}(\boldsymbol{x}_t, t), \boldsymbol{\Sigma}_{\boldsymbol{\theta}}(\boldsymbol{x}_t, t)) \tag{25.9}$$

We often set $\boldsymbol{\Sigma}_{\boldsymbol{\theta}}(\boldsymbol{x}_t, t) = \sigma_t^2 \mathbf{I}$. We discuss how to learn σ_t^2 in Section 25.2.4, but two natural choices are $\sigma_t^2 = \beta_t$ and $\sigma_t^2 = \tilde{\beta}_t$; these correspond to upper and lower bounds on the reverse process entropy, as shown in [HJA20].

The corresponding joint distribution over all the generated variables is given by $p_{\boldsymbol{\theta}}(\boldsymbol{x}_{0:T}) = p(\boldsymbol{x}_T)\prod_{t=1}^{T} p_{\boldsymbol{\theta}}(\boldsymbol{x}_{t-1}|\boldsymbol{x}_t)$, where we set $p(\boldsymbol{x}_T) = \mathcal{N}(\mathbf{0}, \mathbf{I})$. We can sample from this distribution using the pseudocode in Algorithm 25.2.

---

2. We just need to use Bayes' rule for Gaussians. See e.g., `https://lilianweng.github.io/posts/2021-07-11-diffusion-models/` for a detailed derivation.

25.2.3 Model fitting

We will fit the model by maximizing the evidence lower bound (ELBO), similar to how we train VAEs (see Section 21.2). In particular, for each data example $\boldsymbol{x}_0$ we have

$$\log p_{\boldsymbol{\theta}}(\boldsymbol{x}_0) = \log \left[\int d\boldsymbol{x}_{1:T} q(\boldsymbol{x}_{1:T}|\boldsymbol{x}_0) \frac{p_{\boldsymbol{\theta}}(\boldsymbol{x}_{0:T})}{q(\boldsymbol{x}_{1:T}|\boldsymbol{x}_0)} \right] \tag{25.10}$$

$$\geq \int d\boldsymbol{x}_{1:T} q(\boldsymbol{x}_{1:T}|\boldsymbol{x}_0) \log \left(p(\boldsymbol{x}_T) \prod_{t=1}^{T} \frac{p_{\boldsymbol{\theta}}(\boldsymbol{x}_{t-1}|\boldsymbol{x}_t)}{q(\boldsymbol{x}_t|\boldsymbol{x}_{t-1})} \right) \tag{25.11}$$

$$= \mathbb{E}_q \left[\log p(\boldsymbol{x}_T) + \sum_{t=1}^{T} \log \frac{p_{\boldsymbol{\theta}}(\boldsymbol{x}_{t-1}|\boldsymbol{x}_t)}{q(\boldsymbol{x}_t|\boldsymbol{x}_{t-1})} \right] \triangleq \text{Ł}(\boldsymbol{x}_0) \tag{25.12}$$

We now discuss how to compute the terms in the ELBO. By the Markov property we have $q(\boldsymbol{x}_t|\boldsymbol{x}_{t-1}) = q(\boldsymbol{x}_t|\boldsymbol{x}_{t-1}, \boldsymbol{x}_0)$, and by Bayes' rule, we have

$$q(\boldsymbol{x}_t|\boldsymbol{x}_{t-1}, \boldsymbol{x}_0) = \frac{q(\boldsymbol{x}_{t-1}|\boldsymbol{x}_t, \boldsymbol{x}_0) q(\boldsymbol{x}_t|\boldsymbol{x}_0)}{q(\boldsymbol{x}_{t-1}|\boldsymbol{x}_0)} \tag{25.13}$$

Plugging Equation (25.13) into the ELBO we get

$$\text{Ł}(\boldsymbol{x}_0) = \mathbb{E}_{q(\boldsymbol{x}_{1:T}|\boldsymbol{x}_0)} \left[\log p(\boldsymbol{x}_T) + \sum_{t=2}^{T} \log \frac{p_{\boldsymbol{\theta}}(\boldsymbol{x}_{t-1}|\boldsymbol{x}_t)}{q(\boldsymbol{x}_{t-1}|\boldsymbol{x}_t, \boldsymbol{x}_0)} + \underbrace{\sum_{t=2}^{T} \log \frac{q(\boldsymbol{x}_{t-1}|\boldsymbol{x}_0)}{q(\boldsymbol{x}_t|\boldsymbol{x}_0)}}_{*} + \log \frac{p_{\boldsymbol{\theta}}(\boldsymbol{x}_0|\boldsymbol{x}_1)}{q(\boldsymbol{x}_1|\boldsymbol{x}_0)} \right] \tag{25.14}$$

The term marked * is a telescoping sum, and can be simplified as follows:

$$* = \qquad\qquad \log q(\boldsymbol{x}_{T-1}|\boldsymbol{x}_0) + \cdots + \log q(\boldsymbol{x}_2|\boldsymbol{x}_0) + \log q(\boldsymbol{x}_1|\boldsymbol{x}_0) \tag{25.15}$$

$$- \log q(\boldsymbol{x}_T|\boldsymbol{x}_0) - \log q(\boldsymbol{x}_{T-1}|\boldsymbol{x}_0) - \cdots - \log q(\boldsymbol{x}_2|\boldsymbol{x}_0) \tag{25.16}$$

$$= -\log q(\boldsymbol{x}_T|\boldsymbol{x}_0) + \log q(\boldsymbol{x}_1|\boldsymbol{x}_0) \tag{25.17}$$

Hence the negative ELBO (variational upper bound) becomes

$$\mathcal{L}(\boldsymbol{x}_0) = -\mathbb{E}_{q(\boldsymbol{x}_{1:T}|\boldsymbol{x}_0)} \left[\log \frac{p(\boldsymbol{x}_T)}{q(\boldsymbol{x}_T|\boldsymbol{x}_0)} + \sum_{t=2}^{T} \log \frac{p_{\boldsymbol{\theta}}(\boldsymbol{x}_{t-1}|\boldsymbol{x}_t)}{q(\boldsymbol{x}_{t-1}|\boldsymbol{x}_t, \boldsymbol{x}_0)} + \log p_{\boldsymbol{\theta}}(\boldsymbol{x}_0|\boldsymbol{x}_1) \right] \tag{25.18}$$

$$= \underbrace{D_{\text{KL}}\left(q(\boldsymbol{x}_T|\boldsymbol{x}_0) \,\|\, p(\boldsymbol{x}_T) \right)}_{L_T(\boldsymbol{x}_0)} \tag{25.19}$$

$$+ \sum_{t=2}^{T} \mathbb{E}_{q(\boldsymbol{x}_t|\boldsymbol{x}_0)} \underbrace{D_{\text{KL}}\left(q(\boldsymbol{x}_{t-1}|\boldsymbol{x}_t, \boldsymbol{x}_0) \,\|\, p_{\boldsymbol{\theta}}(\boldsymbol{x}_{t-1}|\boldsymbol{x}_t) \right)}_{L_{t-1}(\boldsymbol{x}_0)} - \underbrace{\mathbb{E}_{q(\boldsymbol{x}_1|\boldsymbol{x}_0)} \log p_{\boldsymbol{\theta}}(\boldsymbol{x}_0|\boldsymbol{x}_1)}_{L_0(\boldsymbol{x}_0)} \tag{25.20}$$

Each of these KL terms can be computed analytically, since all the distributions are Gaussian. Below we focus on the L_{t-1} term. Since $\boldsymbol{x}_t = \sqrt{\overline{\alpha}_t}\boldsymbol{x}_0 + \sqrt{(1 - \overline{\alpha}_t)}\boldsymbol{\epsilon}$, we can write

$$\tilde{\boldsymbol{\mu}}_t(\boldsymbol{x}_t, \boldsymbol{x}_0) = \frac{1}{\sqrt{\alpha_t}}\left(\boldsymbol{x}_t - \frac{\beta_t}{\sqrt{1 - \overline{\alpha}_t}}\boldsymbol{\epsilon}\right) \tag{25.21}$$

Thus instead of training the model to predict the mean of the denoised version of $\boldsymbol{x}_{t-1}$ given its noisy input $\boldsymbol{x}_t$, we can train the model to predict the noise, from which we can compute the mean:

$$\boldsymbol{\mu}_{\boldsymbol{\theta}}(\boldsymbol{x}_t, \boldsymbol{x}_0) = \frac{1}{\sqrt{\alpha_t}}\left(\boldsymbol{x}_t - \frac{\beta_t}{\sqrt{1 - \overline{\alpha}_t}}\boldsymbol{\epsilon}_{\boldsymbol{\theta}}(\boldsymbol{x}_t, t)\right) \tag{25.22}$$

With this parameterization, the loss (averaged over the dataset) becomes

$$L_{t-1} = \mathbb{E}_{\boldsymbol{x}_0 \sim q_0(\boldsymbol{x}_0), \boldsymbol{\epsilon} \sim \mathcal{N}(\mathbf{0}, \mathbf{I})}\left[\underbrace{\frac{\beta_t^2}{2\sigma_t^2 \alpha_t(1 - \overline{\alpha}_t)}}_{\lambda_t} ||\boldsymbol{\epsilon} - \boldsymbol{\epsilon}_{\boldsymbol{\theta}}\Big(\underbrace{\sqrt{\overline{\alpha}_t}\boldsymbol{x}_0 + \sqrt{1 - \overline{\alpha}_t}\boldsymbol{\epsilon}}_{\boldsymbol{x}_t}, t\Big)||^2\right] \tag{25.23}$$

The time dependent weight λ_t ensures that the training objective corresponds to maximum likelihood training (assuming the variational bound is tight). However, it has been found empirically that the model produces better looking samples if we set $\lambda_t = 1$. The resulting simplified loss (also averaging over time steps t in the model) is given by

$$L_{\text{simple}} = \mathbb{E}_{\boldsymbol{x}_0 \sim q_0(\boldsymbol{x}_0), \boldsymbol{\epsilon} \sim \mathcal{N}(\mathbf{0}, \mathbf{I}), t \sim \text{Unif}(1, T)}\left[||\boldsymbol{\epsilon} - \boldsymbol{\epsilon}_{\boldsymbol{\theta}}\Big(\underbrace{\sqrt{\overline{\alpha}_t}\boldsymbol{x}_0 + \sqrt{1 - \overline{\alpha}_t}\boldsymbol{\epsilon}}_{\boldsymbol{x}_t}, t\Big)||^2\right] \tag{25.24}$$

The overall training procedure is shown in Algorithm 25.1. We can improve the perceptual quality of samples using more advanced weighting schemes, are discussed in [Cho+22]. Conversely, if the goal is to improve likelihood scores, we can optimize the noise schedule, as discussed in Section 25.2.4.

Algorithm 25.1: Training a DDPM model with L_{simple}.

---

1 **while** *not converged* **do**
2      $\boldsymbol{x}_0 \sim q_0(\boldsymbol{x}_0)$
3      $t \sim \text{Unif}(\{1, \ldots, T\})$
4      $\boldsymbol{\epsilon} \sim \mathcal{N}(\mathbf{0}, \mathbf{I})$
5   Take gradient descent step on $\nabla_{\boldsymbol{\theta}}||\boldsymbol{\epsilon} - \boldsymbol{\epsilon}_{\boldsymbol{\theta}}\left(\sqrt{\overline{\alpha}_t}\boldsymbol{x}_0 + \sqrt{1 - \overline{\alpha}_t}\boldsymbol{\epsilon}, t\right)||^2$

After the model is trained, we can generate data using ancestral sampling, as shown in Algorithm 25.2.

25.2.4 Learning the noise schedule

In this section, we describe a way to optimize the noise schedule used by the encoder so as to maximize the ELBO; this approach is called a **variational diffusion model** or **VDM** [Kin+21].

Algorithm 25.2: Sampling from a DDPM model.

1 $x_T \sim \mathcal{N}(\mathbf{0}, \mathbf{I})$
2 **foreach** $t = T, \dots, 1$ **do**
3 $\quad\quad \epsilon_t \sim \mathcal{N}(\mathbf{0}, \mathbf{I})$
4 $\quad\quad x_{t-1} = \frac{1}{\sqrt{\alpha_t}} \left(x_t - \frac{1-\alpha_t}{\sqrt{1-\bar{\alpha}_t}} \epsilon_\theta(x_t, t) \right) + \sigma_t \epsilon_t$
5 Return x_0

We will use the following parameterization of the encoder:

$$q(\boldsymbol{x}_t | \boldsymbol{x}_0) = \mathcal{N}(\boldsymbol{x}_t | \hat{\alpha}_t \boldsymbol{x}_0, \hat{\sigma}_t^2 \mathbf{I}) \tag{25.25}$$

(Note that $\hat{\alpha}_t$ and $\hat{\sigma}_t$ are different to the parameters α_t and σ_t in Section 25.2.1.) Rather than working with $\hat{\alpha}_t$ and $\hat{\sigma}_t^2$ separately, we will learn to predict their ratio, which is known as the **signal to noise ratio**:

$$R(t) = \hat{\alpha}_t^2 / \hat{\sigma}_t^2 \tag{25.26}$$

This should be monotonically decreasing in t. This can be ensured by defining $R(t) = \exp(-\gamma_\phi(t))$, where $\gamma_\phi(t)$ is a monotonic neural network. We usually set $\hat{\alpha}_t = \sqrt{1 - \sigma_t^2}$, to corresponde to the variance preserving SDE discussed in Section 25.4.

Following the derivation in Section 25.2.3, the negative ELBO (variational upper bound) can be written as

$$\mathcal{L}(\boldsymbol{x}_0) = \underbrace{D_{\mathrm{KL}}\left(q(\boldsymbol{x}_T | \boldsymbol{x}_0) \,\|\, p(\boldsymbol{x}_T)\right)}_{\text{prior loss}} + \underbrace{\mathbb{E}_{q(\boldsymbol{x}_1 | \boldsymbol{x}_0)}[-\log p_\theta(\boldsymbol{x}_0 | \boldsymbol{x}_1)]}_{\text{reconstruction loss}} + \underbrace{\mathcal{L}_D(\boldsymbol{x}_0)}_{\text{diffusion loss}} \tag{25.27}$$

where the first two terms are similar to a standard VAE, and the final diffusion loss is given below:[3]

$$\mathcal{L}_D(\boldsymbol{x}_0) = \frac{1}{2} \mathbb{E}_{\epsilon \sim \mathcal{N}(\mathbf{0}, \mathbf{I})} \int_0^1 R'(t) \|\boldsymbol{x}_0 - \hat{\boldsymbol{x}}_\theta(\boldsymbol{z}_t, t)\|_2^2 \, dt \tag{25.28}$$

where $R'(t)$ is the derivative of the SNR function, and $\boldsymbol{z}_t = \alpha_t \boldsymbol{x}_0 + \sigma_t \epsilon_t$. (See [Kin+21] for the derivation.)

Since the SNR functon is invertible, due to the monotonicity assumtion, we can perform a change of variables, and make everything a function of $v = R(t)$ instead of t. In particular, let $\boldsymbol{z}_v = \alpha_v \boldsymbol{x}_0 + \sigma_v \epsilon$, and $\tilde{\boldsymbol{x}}_\theta(\boldsymbol{z}, v) = \hat{\boldsymbol{x}}_\theta(\boldsymbol{z}, R^{-1}(v))$. Then we can rewrite Equation (25.28) as

$$\mathcal{L}_D(\boldsymbol{x}_0) = \frac{1}{2} \mathbb{E}_{\epsilon \sim \mathcal{N}(\mathbf{0}, \mathbf{I})} \int_{R_{\min}}^{R_{\max}} \|\boldsymbol{x}_0 - \tilde{\boldsymbol{x}}_\theta(\boldsymbol{z}_v, v)\|_2^2 \, dv \tag{25.29}$$

where $R_{\min} = R(1)$ and $R_{\max} = R(0)$. Thus we see that the shape of the SNR schedule does not matter, except for its value at the two end points.

---

3. We present a simplified form of the loss that uses the continuous time limit, which we discuss in Section 25.4.

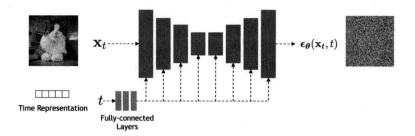

Figure 25.3: *Illustration of the U-net architecture used in the denoising step. From Slide 26 of [KGV22]. Used with kind permission of Arash Vahdat.*

Figure 25.4: *Some sample images generated by a small variational diffusion model trained on EMNIST for about 30 minutes on a K40 GPU. (a) Unconditional sampling. (b) Conditioned on class label. (c) Using classifier-free guidance (see Section 25.6.3). Generated by* diffusion_emnist.ipynb. *Used with kind permission of Alex Alemi.*

The integral in Equation (25.29) can be estimated by sampling a timestep uniformly at random. When processing a minibatch of k examples, we can produce a lower variance estimate of the variational bound by using a **low-discrepancy sampler** (cf., Section 11.6.5). In this approach, instead of sampling the timesteps independently, we sample a single uniform random number $u_0 \sim \text{Unif}(0, 1)$, and then set $t^i = \mod(u_0 + i/k, 1)$ for the i'th sample. We can also optimize the noise schedule wrt the variance of the diffusion loss.

25.2.5 Example: image generation

Diffusion models are often used to generate images. The most common architecture for image generation is based on the **U-net** model [RFB15], as shown in Figure 25.3. The time step t is encoded as a vector, using sinusoidal positional encoding or random Fourier features, and is then fed into the residual blocks, using either simple spatial addition or by conditioning the group norm layers [DN21a]. Of course, other architectures besides U-net are possible. For example, recently [PX22; Li+22; Bao+22a] have proposed the use of transformers, to replace the convolutional and deconvolutional layers.

The results of training a small U-net VDM on EMNIST images are shown in Figure 25.4. By training big models (billions of parameters) for a long time (days) on lots of data (millions of images), diffusion models can be made to generate very high quality images (see Figure 20.2). Results can be further improved by using conditional diffusion models, where guidance is provided about what kinds of images to generate (see Section 25.6).

25.3   Score-based generative models (SGMs)

This section is written with Yang Song and Durk Kingma.

In Section 24.3, we discussed how to fit energy based models (EBMs) using score matching. This adjusts the parameters of the EBM so that the score function of the model, $\nabla_x \log p_\theta(x)$, matches the score function of the data, $\nabla_x \log p_{\mathcal{D}}(x)$. An alternative to fitting a scalar energy function and computing its score is to directly learn the score function. This is called a **score-based generative model** or **SGM** [SE19; SE20b; Son+21b]. We can optimize the score function $s_\theta(x)$ using basic score matching (Section 24.3.1), sliced score matching (Section 24.3.3 or denoising score matching (Section 24.3.2). We discuss this class of models in more detail below. (For a comparison with EBMs, see [SH21].)

25.3.1   Example

In Figure 25.5a, we show the **Swiss roll** dataset. We estimate the score function by fitting an MLP with 2 hidden layers, each with 128 hidden units, using basic score matching. In Figure 25.5b, we show the output of the network after training for 10,000 steps of SGD. We see that there are no major false negatives (since wherever the density of the data is highest, the gradient field is zero), but there are some false positives (since some regions of zero gradient do not correspond to data regions). The comparison of the predicted outputs with the empirical data density is shown more clearly in Figure 25.5c. In Figure 25.5d, we show some samples from the learned model, generated using Langevin sampling.

25.3.2   Adding noise at multiple scales

In general, score matching can have difficulty when there are regions of low data density. To see this, suppose $p_{\mathcal{D}}(x) = \pi p_0(x) + (1-\pi)p_1(x)$. Let $\mathcal{S}_0 := \{x \mid p_0(x) > 0\}$ and $\mathcal{S}_1 := \{x \mid p_1(x) > 0\}$ be the supports of $p_0(x)$ and $p_1(x)$ respectively. When they are disjoint from each other, the score of $p_{\mathcal{D}}(x)$ is given by

$$\nabla_x \log p_{\mathcal{D}}(x) = \begin{cases} \nabla_x \log p_0(x), & x \in \mathcal{S}_0 \\ \nabla_x \log p_1(x), & x \in \mathcal{S}_1, \end{cases} \tag{25.30}$$

which does not depend on the weight π. Hence score matching cannot correctly recover the true distribution. Furthermore, Langevin sampling will have difficulty traversing between modes. (In practice this will happen even when the different modes only have approximately disjoint supports.)

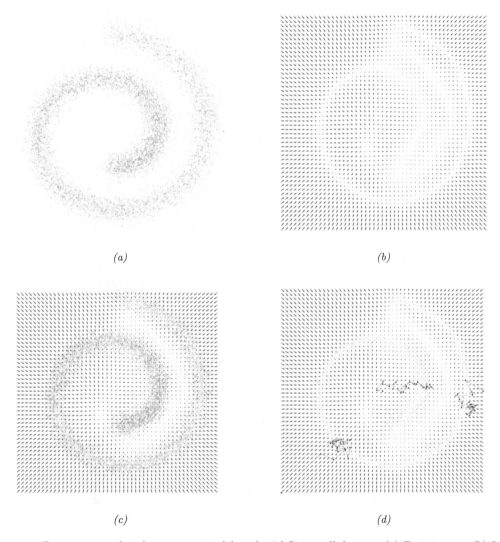

Figure 25.5: *Fitting a score-based generative model to the 2d Swiss roll dataset. (a) Training set. (b) Learned score function trained using the basic score matching. (c) Superposition of learned score function and empirical density. (d) Langevin sampling applied to the learned model. We show 3 different trajectories, each of length 25. Generated by* score_matching_swiss_roll.ipynb.

Song and Ermon [SE19; SE20b] and Song et al. [Son+21b] overcome this difficulty by perturbing training data with different scales of noise. Specifically, they use

$$q_\sigma(\tilde{\boldsymbol{x}}|\boldsymbol{x}) = \mathcal{N}(\tilde{\boldsymbol{x}}|\boldsymbol{x}, \sigma^2 \mathbf{I}) \tag{25.31}$$

$$q_\sigma(\tilde{\boldsymbol{x}}) = \int p_{\mathcal{D}}(\boldsymbol{x}) q_\sigma(\tilde{\boldsymbol{x}}|\boldsymbol{x}) d\boldsymbol{x} \tag{25.32}$$

For a large noise perturbation, different modes are connected due to added noise, and the estimated weights between them are therefore accurate. For a small noise perturbation, different modes are more disconnected, but the noise-perturbed distribution is closer to the original unperturbed data distribution. Using a sampling method such as annealed Langevin dynamics [SE19; SE20b; Son+21b] or diffusion sampling [SD+15a; HJA20; Son+21b], we can sample from the most noise-perturbed distribution first, then smoothly reduce the magnitude of noise scales until reaching the smallest one. This procedure helps combine information from all noise scales, and maintains the correct estimation of weights from higher noise perturbations when sampling from smaller ones.

In practice, all score models share weights and are implemented with a single neural network conditioned on the noise scale; this is called a **noise conditional score network**, and has the form $\boldsymbol{s_\theta}(\boldsymbol{x}, \sigma)$. Scores of different scales are estimated by training a mixture of score matching objectives, one per noise scale. If we use the denoising score matching objective in Equation (24.33), we get

$$\mathcal{L}(\boldsymbol{\theta}; \sigma) = \mathbb{E}_{q(\mathbf{x}, \tilde{\mathbf{x}})} \left[\frac{1}{2} \|\nabla_{\mathbf{x}} \log p_{\boldsymbol{\theta}}(\tilde{\mathbf{x}}, \sigma) - \nabla_{\mathbf{x}} \log q_\sigma(\tilde{\mathbf{x}}|\mathbf{x})\|_2^2 \right] \tag{25.33}$$

$$= \frac{1}{2} \mathbb{E}_{p_{\mathcal{D}}(\mathbf{x})} \mathbb{E}_{\tilde{\mathbf{x}} \sim \mathcal{N}(\boldsymbol{x}, \sigma^2 \mathbf{I})} \left\{ \left\| \boldsymbol{s_\theta}(\tilde{\mathbf{x}}, \sigma) + \frac{(\tilde{\mathbf{x}} - \boldsymbol{x})}{\sigma^2} \right\|_2^2 \right\} \tag{25.34}$$

where we used the fact that, for a Gaussian, the score is given by

$$\nabla_{\boldsymbol{x}} \log \mathcal{N}(\tilde{\boldsymbol{x}}|\boldsymbol{x}, \sigma^2 \mathbf{I}) = -\nabla_{\boldsymbol{x}} \frac{1}{2\sigma^2}(\boldsymbol{x} - \tilde{\boldsymbol{x}})^\top(\boldsymbol{x} - \tilde{\boldsymbol{x}}) = \frac{\boldsymbol{x} - \tilde{\boldsymbol{x}}}{\sigma^2} \tag{25.35}$$

If we have T different noise scales, we can combine the losses in a weighted fashion using

$$\mathcal{L}(\boldsymbol{\theta}; \sigma_{1:T}) = \sum_{t=1}^{T} \lambda_t \mathcal{L}(\boldsymbol{\theta}; \sigma_t) \tag{25.36}$$

where we choose $\sigma_1 > \sigma_2 > \cdots > \sigma_T$, and the weighting term satisfies $\lambda_t > 0$.

25.3.3 Equivalence to DDPM

We now show that the above score-based generative model training objective is equivalent to the DDPM loss. To see this, first let us replace $p_{\mathcal{D}}(\boldsymbol{x})$ with $q_0(\boldsymbol{x}_0)$, $\tilde{\boldsymbol{x}}$ with $\boldsymbol{x}_t$, and $\boldsymbol{s_\theta}(\tilde{\boldsymbol{x}}, \sigma)$ with $\boldsymbol{s_\theta}(\boldsymbol{x}_t, t)$. We will also compute a stochastic approximation to Equation (25.36) by sampling a time step uniformly at random. Then Equation (25.36) becomes

$$\mathcal{L} = \mathbb{E}_{\boldsymbol{x}_0 \sim q_0(\boldsymbol{x}_0), \boldsymbol{x}_t \sim q(\boldsymbol{x}_t|\boldsymbol{x}_0), t \sim \text{Unif}(1, T)} \left[\lambda_t \left\| \boldsymbol{s_\theta}(\boldsymbol{x}_t, t) + \frac{(\boldsymbol{x}_t - \boldsymbol{x}_0)}{\sigma_t^2} \right\|_2^2 \right] \tag{25.37}$$

If we use the fact that $\boldsymbol{x}_t = \boldsymbol{x}_0 + \sigma_t \boldsymbol{\epsilon}$, and if we define $\boldsymbol{s_\theta}(\boldsymbol{x}_t, t) = -\frac{\boldsymbol{\epsilon_\theta}(\boldsymbol{x}_t, t)}{\sigma_t}$, we can rewrite this as

$$\mathcal{L} = \mathbb{E}_{\boldsymbol{x}_0 \sim q_0(\boldsymbol{x}_0), \boldsymbol{\epsilon} \sim \mathcal{N}(\mathbf{0}, \mathbf{I}), t \sim \text{Unif}(1,T)} \left[\frac{\lambda_t}{\sigma_t^2} \| \boldsymbol{\epsilon} - \boldsymbol{\epsilon_\theta}(\boldsymbol{x}_t, t) \|_2^2 \right] \tag{25.38}$$

If we set $\lambda_t = \sigma_t^2$, we recover L_{simple} loss in Equation (25.24).

25.4 Continuous time models using differential equations

In this section, we consider a DDPM model in the limit of an infinite number of hidden layers, or equivalently, an SGM in the limit of an infinite number of noise levels. This requires switching from discrete time to continuous time, which complicates the mathematics. The advantage is that we can leverage the large existing literature on solvers for ordinary and stochastic differential equations to enable faster generation, as we will see.

25.4.1 Forwards diffusion SDE

Let us first consider a diffusion process where the noise level β_t gets rewritten as $\beta(t)\Delta t$, where Δt is a step size:

$$\boldsymbol{x}_t = \sqrt{1 - \beta_t} \boldsymbol{x}_{t-1} + \sqrt{\beta_t} \mathcal{N}(\mathbf{0}, \mathbf{I}) = \sqrt{1 - \beta(t)\Delta t} \boldsymbol{x}_{t-1} + \sqrt{\beta(t)\Delta t} \mathcal{N}(\mathbf{0}, \mathbf{I}) \tag{25.39}$$

If Δt is small, we can approximate the first term with a first-order Taylor series expansion to get

$$\boldsymbol{x}_t \approx \boldsymbol{x}_{t-1} - \frac{\beta(t)\Delta t}{2} \boldsymbol{x}_{t-1} + \sqrt{\beta(t)\Delta t} \mathcal{N}(\mathbf{0}, \mathbf{I}) \tag{25.40}$$

Hence for small Δt we have

$$\frac{\boldsymbol{x}_t - \boldsymbol{x}_{t-1}}{\Delta t} \approx -\frac{\beta(t)}{2} \boldsymbol{x}_{t-1} + \frac{\sqrt{\beta(t)}}{\sqrt{\Delta t}} \mathcal{N}(\mathbf{0}, \mathbf{I}) \tag{25.41}$$

We can now switch to the **continuous time** limit, and write this as the following **stochastic differential equation** or **SDE**:

$$\frac{d\boldsymbol{x}(t)}{dt} = -\frac{1}{2} \beta(t) \boldsymbol{x}(t) + \sqrt{\beta(t)} \frac{d\boldsymbol{w}(t)}{dt} \tag{25.42}$$

where $\boldsymbol{w}(t)$ represents a standard **Wiener process**, also called **Brownian noise**. More generally, we can write such SDEs as follows, where we use **Itô calculus** notation (see e.g., [SS19]):

$$d\boldsymbol{x} = \underbrace{\boldsymbol{f}(\boldsymbol{x}, t)}_{\text{drift}} dt + \underbrace{g(t)}_{\text{diffusion}} d\boldsymbol{w} \tag{25.43}$$

The first term in the above SDE is called the **drift coefficient**, and the second term is called the **diffusion coefficient**.

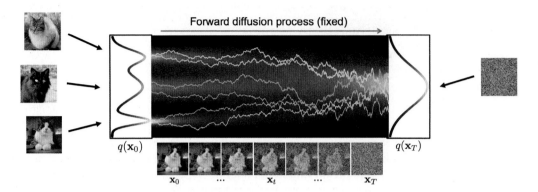

Figure 25.6: Illustration of the forwards diffusion process in continuous time. Yellow lines are sample paths from the SDE. Heat map represents the marginal distribution computed using the probability flow ODE. From Slide 43 of [KGV22]. Used with kind permission of Karsten Kreis.

We can gain some intuition for these processes by looking at the 1d example in Figure 25.6. We can draw multiple paths as follows: sample an initial state from the data distribution, and then integrate over time using **Euler-Maruyama** integration:

$$\boldsymbol{x}(t + \Delta t) = \boldsymbol{x}(t) + \boldsymbol{f}(\boldsymbol{x}(t), t)\Delta t + g(t)\sqrt{\Delta t}\mathcal{N}(\mathbf{0}, \mathbf{I}) \tag{25.44}$$

We can see how the data distributiom at $t = 0$, on the left hand side, gradually gets transformed to a pure noise distribution at $t = 1$, on the right hand side.

In [Son+21b], they show that the SDE corresponding to DDPMs, in the $T \to \infty$ limit, is given by

$$d\boldsymbol{x} = -\frac{1}{2}\beta(t)\boldsymbol{x}dt + \sqrt{\beta(t)}d\boldsymbol{\omega} \tag{25.45}$$

where $\beta(t/T) = T\beta_t$. Here the drift term is proportional to $-\boldsymbol{x}$, which encourages the process to return to 0. Consequently, DDPM corresponds to a **variance preserving** process. By contrast, the SDE corresponding to SGMs is given by the following:

$$d\boldsymbol{x} = \sqrt{\frac{d[\sigma(t)^2]}{dt}}d\boldsymbol{\omega} \tag{25.46}$$

where $\sigma(t/T) = \sigma_t$. This SDE has zero drift, so corresponds to a **variance exploding** process.

25.4.2   Forwards diffusion ODE

Instead of adding Gaussian noise at every step, we can just sample the initial state, and then let it evolve deterministically over time according to the following **ordinary differential equation** or **ODE**:

$$d\boldsymbol{x} = \underbrace{\left[f(\boldsymbol{x}, t) - \frac{1}{2}g(t)^2\nabla_{\boldsymbol{x}}\log p_t(\boldsymbol{x})\right]}_{h(\boldsymbol{x},t)} dt \tag{25.47}$$

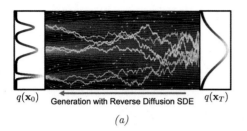
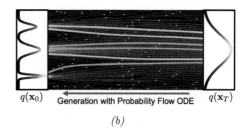

Figure 25.7: *Illustration of the reverse diffusion process. (a) Sample paths from the SDE. (b) Deterministic trajectories from the probability flow ODE. From Slide 65 of [KGV22]. Used with kind permission of Karsten Kreis.*

This is called the **probability flow ODE** [Son+21b, Sec D.3]. We can compute the state at any moment in time using any ODE solver:

$$\boldsymbol{x}(t) = \boldsymbol{x}(0) + \int_0^t h(\boldsymbol{x}, \tau)d\tau \tag{25.48}$$

See Figure 25.7b for a visualization of a sample trajectory. If we start the solver from different random states $\boldsymbol{x}(0)$, then the induced distribution over paths will have the same marginals as the SDE model. See the heatmap in Figure 25.6 for an illustration.

25.4.3   Reverse diffusion SDE

To generate samples from this model, we need to be able to reverse the SDE. In a remarkable result, [And82] showed that any forwards SDE of the form in Equation (25.43) can be reversed to get the following **reverse-time SDE**:

$$d\boldsymbol{x} = \left[f(\boldsymbol{x}, t) - g(t)^2 \nabla_{\boldsymbol{x}} \log q_t(\boldsymbol{x})\right] dt + g(t)d\overline{\boldsymbol{w}} \tag{25.49}$$

where $\overline{\boldsymbol{w}}$ is the standard Wiener process when time flows backwards, dt is an infinitesimal negative time step, and $\nabla_{\boldsymbol{x}} \log q_t(\boldsymbol{x})$ is the score function.

In the case of the DDPM, the reverse SDE has the following form:

$$d\boldsymbol{x}_t = \left[-\frac{1}{2}\beta(t)\boldsymbol{x}_t - \beta(t)\nabla_{\boldsymbol{x}_t} \log q_t(\boldsymbol{x}_t)\right] dt + \sqrt{\beta(t)}d\overline{\boldsymbol{w}}_t \tag{25.50}$$

To estimate the score function, we can use denoising score matching as we discussed in Section 25.3, to get

$$\nabla_{\boldsymbol{x}_t} \log q_t(\boldsymbol{x}_t) \approx \boldsymbol{s}_{\boldsymbol{\theta}}(\boldsymbol{x}_t, t) \tag{25.51}$$

(In practice, it is advisable to use variance reduction techniques, such as importance sampling, as discussed in [Son+21a].) The SDE becomes

$$d\boldsymbol{x}_t = -\frac{1}{2}\beta(t)\left[\boldsymbol{x}_t + 2\boldsymbol{s}_{\boldsymbol{\theta}}(\boldsymbol{x}_t, t)\right] dt + \sqrt{\beta(t)}d\overline{\boldsymbol{w}}_t \tag{25.52}$$

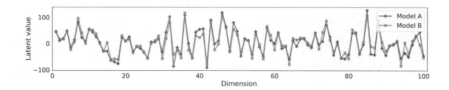

Figure 25.8: *Comparing the first 100 dimensions of the latent code obtained for a random CIFAR-100 image. "Model A" and "Model B" are separately trained with different architectures. From Figure 7 of [Son+21b]. Used with kind permission of Yang Song.*

After fitting the score network, we can sample from it using ancestral sampling (as in Section 25.2), or we can use the Euler-Maruyama integration scheme in Equation (25.44), which gives

$$\boldsymbol{x}_{t-1} = \boldsymbol{x}_t + \frac{1}{2}\beta(t)\left[\boldsymbol{x}_t + 2\boldsymbol{s}_{\boldsymbol{\theta}}(\boldsymbol{x}_t, t)\right]\Delta t + \sqrt{\beta(t)\Delta t}\mathcal{N}(\boldsymbol{0}, \mathbf{I}) \tag{25.53}$$

See Figure 25.7a for an illustration.

25.4.4 Reverse diffusion ODE

Based on the results in Section 25.4.2, we can derive the probability flow ODE from the reverse-time SDE in Equation (25.49) to get

$$d\boldsymbol{x}_t = \left[f(\boldsymbol{x}, t) - \frac{1}{2}g(t)^2\boldsymbol{s}_{\boldsymbol{\theta}}(\boldsymbol{x}_t, t)\right]dt \tag{25.54}$$

If we set $f(\boldsymbol{x}, t) = -\frac{1}{2}\beta(t)$ and $g(t) = \sqrt{\beta(t)}$, as in DDPM, this becomes

$$d\boldsymbol{x}_t = -\frac{1}{2}\beta(t)\left[\boldsymbol{x}_t + \boldsymbol{s}_{\boldsymbol{\theta}}(\boldsymbol{x}_t, t)\right]dt \tag{25.55}$$

See Figure 25.7b for an illustration. A simple way to solve this ODE is to use **Euler's method**:

$$\boldsymbol{x}_{t-1} = \boldsymbol{x}_t + \frac{1}{2}\beta(t)\left[\boldsymbol{x}_t + \boldsymbol{s}_{\boldsymbol{\theta}}(\boldsymbol{x}_t, t)\right]\Delta t \tag{25.56}$$

However, in practice one can get better results using higher-order ODE solvers, such as **Heung's method** [Kar+22].

This model is a special case of a **neural ODE**, also called a **continuous normalizing flow** (see Section 23.2.6). Consequently we can derive the exact log marginal likelihood. However, instead of maximizing this directly (which is expensive), we use score matching to fit the model.

Another advantage of the deterministic ODE approach is that it guarantees that the generative model is **identifiable**. To see this, note that the ODE (in both forwards and reverse directions) is deterministic, and is uniquely determined by the score function. If the architecture is sufficiently flexible, and if there is enough data, then score matching will recover the true score function of the data generating process. Thus, after training, a given datapoint will map to a unique point in latent space, regardless of the model architecture or initialization (see Figure 25.8).

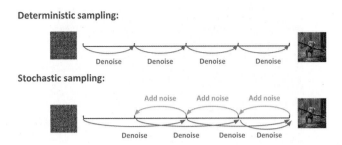

Figure 25.9: *Generatng from the reverse diffusion process using 4 steps. (Top) Deterministic sampling. (Bottom) A mix of deterministic and stochastic sampling. Used with kind permission of Ruiqi Gao.*

Furthermore, since every point in latent space decodes to a unique image, we can perform "semantic interpolation" in the latent space to generate images with properties that are in between two input examples (cf., Figure 20.9).

25.4.5 Comparison of the SDE and ODE approach

In Section 25.4.3 we described the reverse diffusion process as an SDE, and in Section 25.4.4, we described it as an ODE. We can see the connection between these methods by rewriting the SDE in Equation (25.49) as follows:

$$d\boldsymbol{x}_t = \underbrace{-\frac{1}{2}\beta(t)[\boldsymbol{x}_t + \boldsymbol{s_\theta}(\boldsymbol{x}_t, t)]dt}_{\text{probability flow ODE}} \underbrace{-\frac{1}{2}\beta(t)\boldsymbol{s_\theta}(\boldsymbol{x}_t, t)dt + \sqrt{\beta(t)}d\overline{\boldsymbol{w}}_t}_{\text{Langevin diffusion SDE}} \qquad (25.57)$$

The continuous noise injection can compensate for errors introduced by the numerical integration of the ODE term. Consequently, the resulting samples often look better. However, the ODE approach can be faster. Fortunately it is possible to combine these techniques, as proposed in [Kar+22]. The basic idea is illustrated in Figure 25.9: we alternate between performing a deterministic step using an ODE solver, and then adding a small amount noise to the result. This can be repeated for some number of steps. (We discuss ways to reduce the number of required steps, in Section 25.5.)

25.4.6 Example

A simple JAX implementation of the above ideas, written by Winnie Xu, can be found in diffusion_mnist.ipynb. This fits a small model to MNIST images using denoising score matching. It then generates from the model by solving the probability flow ODE using the diffrax library. By scaling this kind of method up to a much larger model, and training for a much longer time, it is possible to produce very impressive looking results, as shown in Figure 25.10.

25.5 Speeding up diffusion models

One of the main disadvantages of diffusion models is that generating from them takes many small steps, which can be slow. While it is possible to just take fewer, larger steps, the results are much

Figure 25.10: Synthetic faces from a score-based generative model trained on CelebA-HQ-256 images. From Figure 12 of [Son+21b]. Used with kind permission of Yang Song.

worse. In this section, we briefly mention a few techniques that have been proposed to tackle this important problem. Many other techniques are mentioned in the recent review papers [UAP22; Yan+22; Cao+22].

25.5.1 DDIM sampler

In this section, we describe the denoising diffusion implicit model or **DDIM** of [SME21], which can be used for efficient deterministic generation. The first step is to use a **non-Markovian** forwards diffusion process, so it always conditions on the input in addition to the previous step:

$$q(\boldsymbol{x}_{t-1}|\boldsymbol{x}_t, \boldsymbol{x}_0) = \mathcal{N}(\sqrt{\overline{\alpha}_{t-1}}\boldsymbol{x}_0 + \sqrt{1 - \overline{\alpha}_{t-1} - \tilde{\sigma}_t^2}\frac{\boldsymbol{x}_t - \sqrt{\overline{\alpha}_t}\boldsymbol{x}_0}{\sqrt{1 - \overline{\alpha}_t}}, \tilde{\sigma}_t^2\mathbf{I}) \tag{25.58}$$

The corresponding reverse process is

$$p_{\boldsymbol{\theta}}(\boldsymbol{x}_{t-1}|\boldsymbol{x}_t) = \mathcal{N}(\sqrt{\overline{\alpha}_{t-1}}\hat{\boldsymbol{x}}_0 + \sqrt{1 - \overline{\alpha}_{t-1} - \tilde{\sigma}_t^2}\frac{\boldsymbol{x}_t - \sqrt{\overline{\alpha}_t}\hat{\boldsymbol{x}}_0}{\sqrt{1 - \overline{\alpha}_t}}, \tilde{\sigma}_t^2\mathbf{I}) \tag{25.59}$$

where $\hat{\boldsymbol{x}}_0 = \hat{\boldsymbol{x}}_{\boldsymbol{\theta}}(\boldsymbol{x}_t, t)$ is the predicted output from the model. By setting $\tilde{\sigma}_t^2 = 0$, the reverse process becomes fully deterministic, given the initial prior sample (whose variance is controlled by $\tilde{\sigma}_T^2$). The resulting probability flow ODE gives better results when using a small number of steps compared to the methods discussed in Section 25.4.4.

Note that the weighted negative VLB for this model is the same as L_{simple} in Section 25.2, so the DDIM sampler can be applied to a trained DDPM model.

25.5.2 Non-Gaussian decoder networks

If the reverse diffusion process takes larger steps, then the induced distribution over clean outputs given a noisy input will become multimodal, as illustrated in Figure 25.11. This requires more complicated forms for the distribution $p_{\boldsymbol{\theta}}(\boldsymbol{x}_{t-1}|\boldsymbol{x}_t)$. In [Gao+21], they use an EBM to fit this distribution. However, this still requires the use of MCMC to draw a sample. In [XKV22], they use a GAN (Chapter 26) to fit this distribution. This enables us to easily draw a sample by passing

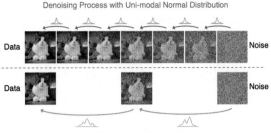

Figure 25.11: Illustration of why taking larger steps in the reverse diffusion process needs more complex, mulit-modal conditional distributions. From Slide 90 of [KGV22]. Used with kind permission of Arash Vahdat.

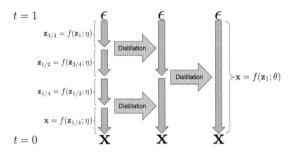

Figure 25.12: Progressive distillation. From Figure 1 of [SH22]. Used with kind permission of Tim Salimans.

Gaussian noise through the generator. The benefits over a single stage GAN is that both the generator and discriminator are solving a much simpler problem, resulting in increased mode coverage, and better training stability. The benefit over a standard diffusion model is that we can generate high quality samples in many fewer steps.

25.5.3 Distillation

In this section, we discuss the **progressive distillation** method of [SH22], which provides a way to create a diffusion model that only needs a small number of steps to create high quality samples. The basic idea is follows. First we train a DDPM model in the usual way, and sample from it using the DDIM method; we treat this as the "teacher" model. We use this to generate intermediate latent states, and train a "student" model to predict the output of the teacher on every second step, as shown in Figure 25.12. After the student has been trained, it can generate results that are as good as the teacher, but in half the number of steps. This student can then teach a new generation of even faster students. See Algorithm 25.4 for the pseudocode, which should be compared to Algorithm 25.3 for the standard training procedure. Note that each round of teaching becomes faster, because the teachers become smaller, so the total time to perform the distillation is relatively small. The resulting model can generate high quality samples in as few as 4 steps.

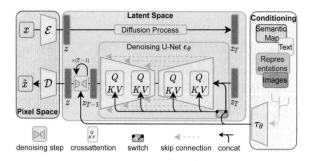

Figure 25.13: Combining a VAE with a diffusion model. Here $\mathcal{E}$ and $\mathcal{D}$ are the encoder and decoder of the VAE. The diffusion model conditions on the inputs either by using concatenation or by using a cross-attention mechanism. From Figure 3 of [Rom+22]. Used with kind permission of Robin Rombach.

Algorithm 25.3: Standard training

Input: Model $\hat{\boldsymbol{x}}_{\boldsymbol{\theta}}(\boldsymbol{z}_t)$ to be trained
Input: Dataset $\mathcal{D}$
Input: Loss weight function w

1 **while** *not converged* **do**
2     $\boldsymbol{x} \sim \mathcal{D}$
3     $t \sim \text{Unif}(0,1)$
4     $\boldsymbol{\epsilon} \sim \mathcal{N}(\boldsymbol{0},\mathbf{I})$
5     $\boldsymbol{z}_t = \alpha_t \boldsymbol{x} + \sigma_t \boldsymbol{\epsilon}$
6     $\tilde{\boldsymbol{x}} = \boldsymbol{x}$ (Clean data is target)
7     $\lambda_t = \log(\alpha_t^2/\sigma_t^2)$ (Log SNR)
8     $L_{\boldsymbol{\theta}} = w(\lambda_t)\|\tilde{\boldsymbol{x}} - \hat{\boldsymbol{x}}_{\boldsymbol{\theta}}(\boldsymbol{z}_t)\|_2^2$
9     $\boldsymbol{\theta} := \boldsymbol{\theta} - \gamma \nabla_{\boldsymbol{\theta}} L_{\boldsymbol{\theta}}$

Algorithm 25.4: Progressive distillation

Input: Trained teacher model $\hat{\boldsymbol{x}}_{\boldsymbol{\eta}}(\boldsymbol{z}_t)$
Input: Dataset $\mathcal{D}$
Input: Loss weight function w
Input: Student sampling steps N

1 **foreach** K *iterations* **do**
2     $\theta := \eta$ (Assign student)
3   **while** *not converged* **do**
4       $\boldsymbol{x} \sim \mathcal{D}$
5       $t = i/N,\ i \sim \text{Cat}(1,2,\ldots,N)$
6       $\boldsymbol{\epsilon} \sim \mathcal{N}(\boldsymbol{0},\mathbf{I})$
7       $\boldsymbol{z}_t = \alpha_t \boldsymbol{x} + \sigma_t \boldsymbol{\epsilon}$
8       $t' = t - 0.5/N,\ t'' = t - 1/N$
9       $\boldsymbol{z}_{t'} = \alpha_{t'}\hat{\boldsymbol{x}}_{\boldsymbol{\eta}}(\boldsymbol{z}_t) + \frac{\sigma_{t'}}{\sigma_t}(\boldsymbol{z}_t - \alpha_t \hat{\boldsymbol{x}}_{\boldsymbol{\eta}}(\boldsymbol{z}_t))$
10       $\boldsymbol{z}_{t''} = $
        $\alpha_{t''}\hat{\boldsymbol{x}}_{\boldsymbol{\eta}}(\boldsymbol{z}_{t'}) + \frac{\sigma_{t''}}{\sigma_{t'}}(\boldsymbol{z}_{t'} - \alpha_{t'}\hat{\boldsymbol{x}}_{\boldsymbol{\eta}}(\boldsymbol{z}_{t'}))$
11       $\tilde{\boldsymbol{x}} = \frac{\boldsymbol{z}_{t''} - (\sigma_{t''}/\sigma_t)\boldsymbol{z}_t}{\alpha_{t''} - (\sigma_{t''}/\sigma_t)\alpha_t}$ (Teacher is target)
12       $\lambda_t = \log(\alpha_t^2/\sigma_t^2)$
13       $L_{\boldsymbol{\theta}} = w(\lambda_t)\|\tilde{\boldsymbol{x}} - \hat{\boldsymbol{x}}_{\boldsymbol{\theta}}(\boldsymbol{z}_t)\|_2^2$
14       $\boldsymbol{\theta} := \boldsymbol{\theta} - \gamma \nabla_{\boldsymbol{\theta}} L_{\boldsymbol{\theta}}$
15     $\eta := \boldsymbol{\theta}$ (Student becomes next teacher)
16     $N := N/2$ (Halve number of sampling steps)

25.5.4 Latent space diffusion

Another approach to speeding up diffusion models for images is to first embed the images into a lower dimensional space, and then fit the diffusion model to the embeddings. This idea has been pursued in several papers.

In the latent diffusion model (**LDM**) of [Rom+22], they adopt a two-stage training scheme, in which they first fit the VAE, augmented with a perceptual loss, and then fit the diffusion model to the embedding. The architecture is illustrated in Figure 25.13. The LDM forms the foundation of the very popular **stable diffusion** system created by **Stability AI**. In the latent score-based generative model (**LSGM**) of [VKK21], they first train a hierarchical VAE, and then jointly train the VAE and a diffusion model.

In addition to speed, an additional advantage of combining diffusion models with autoencoders is that it makes it simple to apply diffusion to many different kinds of data, such as text and graphs: we just need to define a suitable architecture to embed the input domain into a continuous space. Note, however, that it is also possible to define diffusion directly on discrete state spaces, as we discuss in Section 25.7.

So far we have discussed applying diffusion "on top of" a VAE. However, we can also do the reverse, and fit a VAE on top of a DDPM model, where we use the diffusion model to "post process" blurry samples coming from the VAE. See [Pan+22] for details.

25.6 Conditional generation

In this section, we discuss how to generate samples from a diffusion model where we condition on some side information c, such as a class label or text prompt.

25.6.1 Conditional diffusion model

The simplest way to control the generation from a generative model is to train it on (c, x) pairs so as to maximize the conditional likelihood, $p(x|c)$. If the conditioning signal c is a scalar (e.g., a class label), it can be mapped to an embedding vector, and then incorporated into the network by spatial addition, or by using it to modular the group normalization layers. If the input c is another image, we can simply concatenate it with x_t as an extra set of channels. If the input c is a text prompt, we can embed it, and then use spatial addition or cross-attention (see Figure 25.13 for an illustration).

25.6.2 Classifier guidance

One problem with conditional diffusion models is that we need to retrain them for each kind of conditioning that we want to perform. An alternative approach, known as **classifier guidance** was proposed in [DN21b], and allows us to leverage pre-trained discriminative classifiers of the form $p_\phi(c|x)$ to control the generation process. The idea is as follows. First we use Bayes' rule to write

$$\log p(x|c) = \log p(c|x) + \log p(x) - \log p(c) \tag{25.60}$$

from which the score function becomes

$$\nabla_x \log p(x|c) = \nabla_x \log p(x) + \nabla_x \log p(c|x) \tag{25.61}$$

We can now use this conditional score to generate samples, rather than the unconditional score. We can further amplify the influence of the conditioning signal by scaling it by a factor $w > 1$:

$$\nabla_x \log p_w(x|c) = \nabla_x \log p(x) + w \nabla_x \log p(c|x) \tag{25.62}$$

In practice, this can be achieved as follows by generating samples from

$$x_{t-1} \sim \mathcal{N}(\mu + w\Sigma g, \Sigma), \ \mu = \mu_\theta(x_t, t), \ \Sigma = \Sigma_\theta(x_t, t), \ g = \nabla_{x_t} \log p_\phi(c|x_t) \tag{25.63}$$

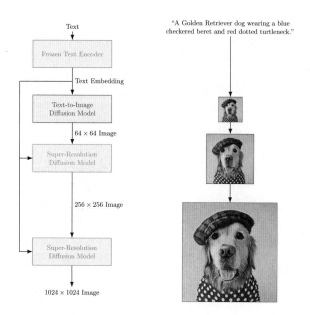

Figure 25.14: Cascaded diffusion model used by the Imagen text-to-image system. From Figure A.5 of [Sah+22]. Used with kind permission of Saurabh Saxena.

25.6.3   Classifier-free guidance

Unfortunately, $p(c|x_t)$ is a discriminative model, that may ignore many details of the input x_t. Hence optimizing along the directions specified by $\nabla_{x_t} \log p(c|x_t)$ can give poor results, similar to what happens when we create adversarial images. In addition, we need to train a classifier for each time step, since x_t will differ in its blurriness.

In [HS21], they proposed a technique called **classifier-free guidance**, which derives the classifier from the generative model, using $p(c|x) = \frac{p(x|c)p(c)}{p(x)}$, from which we get

$$\log p(c|x) = \log p(x|c) + \log p(c) - \log p(x) \tag{25.64}$$

This requires learning two generative models, namely $p(x|c)$ and $p(x)$. However, in practice we can use the same model for this, and simply set $c = \emptyset$ to represent the unconditional case. We then use this implicit classifier to get the following modified score function:

$$\nabla_x[\log p(x|c) + w \log p(c|x)] = \nabla_x[\log p(x|c) + w(\log p(x|c) - \log p(x))] \tag{25.65}$$
$$= \nabla_x[(1 + w) \log p(x|c) - w \log p(x)] \tag{25.66}$$

Larger guidance weight usually results in better individual sample quality, but lower diversity.

25.6.4   Generating high resolution images

In order to generate high resolution images, [Ho+21] proposed to use **cascaded generation**, in which we first train a model to generate 64×64 images, and then train a separate **super-resolution**

Figure 25.15: Multinomial diffusion model, applied to semantic image segmentation. The input image is on the right, and gets diffused to the noise image on the left. From Figure 1 of [Aus+21]. Used with kind permission of Emiel Hoogeboom.

model to map this to 256×256 or 1024×1024. This approach is used in Google's **Imagen** model [Sah+22], which is a text-to-image system (see Figure 25.14). Imagen uses large pre-trained text encoder, based on T5-XXL [Raf+20a], combined with a VDM model (Section 25.2.4) based on the U-net architecture, to generate impressive-looking images (see Figure 20.2).

In addition to conditioning on text, it is possible to condition on another image to create a model for **image-to-image translation**. For example, we can learn map a gray-scale image c to a color image x, or a corrupted or occluded image c to a clean version x. This can be done by training a multi-task conditional diffusion model, as explained in [Sah+21]. See Figure 20.4 for some sample outputs.

25.7 Diffusion for discrete state spaces

So far in this chapter, we have focused on Gaussian diffusion for generating real-valued data. However it is also possible to define diffusion models for discrete data, such as text or semantic segmentation labels, either by using a continuous latent embedding space (see Section 25.5.4), or by defining diffusion operations directly on the discrete state space, as we discuss beow.

25.7.1 Discrete Denoising Diffusion Probabilistic Models

In this section we discuss the Discrete Denoising Diffusion Probabilistic Model (**D3PM**) of [Aus+21], which defines a discrete time diffusion process directly on the discrete state space. (This builds on prior work such as **multinomial diffusion** [Hoo+21], and the original diffusion paper of [SD+15b].)

The basic idea is illustrated in Figure 25.15 in the context of semantic segmentation, which associates a categorical label to each pixel in an image. On the right we illustrate some sample images, and the corresponding categorical distribution that they induce over a single pixel. We gradually transform these pixel-wise distributions to the uniform distribution, using a stochastic sampling process that we describe below. We then learn a neural network to invert this process, so it can generate discrete data from noise; in the diagram, this corresponds to moving from left to right.

To ensure efficient training, we require that we can efficiently sample from $q(\boldsymbol{x}_t|\boldsymbol{x}_0)$ for an abritrary timestep t, so we can randomly sample time steps when optimizing the variational bound in Equation (25.27). In addition, we require that $q(\boldsymbol{x}_{t-1}|\boldsymbol{x}_t, \boldsymbol{x}_0)$ have a tractable form, so we can efficiently compute the KL terms

$$L_{t-1}(\boldsymbol{x}_0) = \mathbb{E}_{q(\boldsymbol{x}_t|\boldsymbol{x}_0)} D_{\mathrm{KL}}\left(q(\boldsymbol{x}_{t-1}|\boldsymbol{x}_t, \boldsymbol{x}_0) \parallel p_{\boldsymbol{\theta}}(\boldsymbol{x}_{t-1}|\boldsymbol{x}_t)\right) \tag{25.67}$$

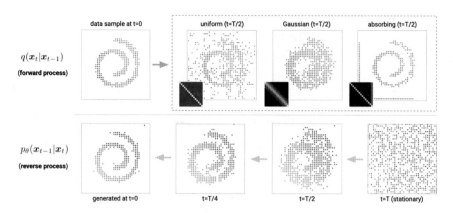

Figure 25.16: D3PM forward and (learned) reverse proccess applied to a quantized Swiss roll. Each dot represents a 2d categorical variable. Top: samples from the uniform, discretized Gaussian, and absorbing state models, along with corresponding transition matrices **Q**. *Bottom: samples from a learned discretized Gaussian reverse process. From Figure 1 of [Aus+21]. Used with kind permission of Jacob Austin.*

Finally, it is useful if the forwards process converges to a known stationary distribution, $\pi(\boldsymbol{x}_T)$, which we can use for our generative prior $p(\boldsymbol{x}_T)$; this ensures $D_{\mathrm{KL}}\left(q(\boldsymbol{x}_T|\boldsymbol{x}_0) \parallel p(\boldsymbol{x}_T)\right) = 0$.

To satisfy the above criteria, we assume the state consists of D independent blocks, each representing a categorical variable, $x_t \in \{1, \ldots, K\}$; we represent this by the one-hot row vector $\boldsymbol{x}_0$. In general, this will represent a vector of probabilities. We then define the forwards diffusion kernel as follows:

$$q(\boldsymbol{x}_t|\boldsymbol{x}_{t-1}) = \mathrm{Cat}(\boldsymbol{x}_t|\boldsymbol{x}_{t-1}\mathbf{Q}_t) \tag{25.68}$$

where $[\mathbf{Q}_t]_{ij} = q(x_t = j|x_{t-1} = k)$ is a row stochastic transition matrix. (We discuss how to define $\mathbf{Q}_t$ in Section 25.7.2.)

We can derive the t-step marginal of the forwards process as follows:

$$q(\boldsymbol{x}_t|\boldsymbol{x}_0) = \mathrm{Cat}(\boldsymbol{x}_t|\boldsymbol{x}_0\overline{\mathbf{Q}}_t), \ \overline{\mathbf{Q}}_t = \mathbf{Q}_1\mathbf{Q}_2\cdots\mathbf{Q}_t \tag{25.69}$$

Similarly, we can reverse the forwards process as follows:

$$q(\boldsymbol{x}_{t-1}|\boldsymbol{x}_t, \boldsymbol{x}_0) = \frac{q(\boldsymbol{x}_t|\boldsymbol{x}_{t-1}, \boldsymbol{x}_0)q(\boldsymbol{x}_{t-1}|\boldsymbol{x}_0)}{q(\boldsymbol{x}_t|\boldsymbol{x}_0)} = \mathrm{Cat}\left(\boldsymbol{x}_{t-1}|\frac{\boldsymbol{x}_t\mathbf{Q}_t^{\mathsf{T}} \odot \boldsymbol{x}_0\overline{\mathbf{Q}}_{t-1}}{\boldsymbol{x}_0\overline{\mathbf{Q}}_t\boldsymbol{x}_t^{\mathsf{T}}}\right) \tag{25.70}$$

We discuss how to define the generative process $p_{\boldsymbol{\theta}}(\boldsymbol{x}_{t-1}|\boldsymbol{x}_t)$ in Section 25.7.3. Since both distrbutions factorize, we can easily compute the KL distributions in Equation (25.67) by summing the KL for each dimension.

25.7.2 Choice of Markov transition matrices for the forward processes

In this section, we give some examples of how to represent the transition matrix $\mathbf{Q}_t$.

One simple approach is to use $\mathbf{Q}_t = (1 - \beta_t)\mathbf{I} + \beta_t/K$, which we can write in scalar form as follows:

$$
[\mathbf{Q}_t]_{ij} = \begin{cases} 1 - \frac{K-1}{K}\beta_t & \text{if } i = j \\ \frac{1}{K}\beta_t & \text{if } i \neq j \end{cases} \tag{25.71}
$$

Intuitively, this adds a little amount of uniform noise over the K classes, and with a large probability, $1 - \beta_t$, we sample from $\boldsymbol{x}_{t-1}$. We call this the uniform kernel. Since this is a doubly stochastic matrix with strictly positive entries, the stationary distributon is uniform. See Figure 25.16 for an illustration.

In the case of the uniform kernel, one can show [Hoo+21] that the marginal distribution is given by

$$
q(\boldsymbol{x}_t|\boldsymbol{x}_0) = \text{Cat}(\boldsymbol{x}_t|\overline{\alpha}_t\boldsymbol{x}_0 + (1 - \overline{\alpha}_t)/K) \tag{25.72}
$$

where $\alpha_t = 1 - \beta_t$ and $\overline{\alpha}_t = \prod_{\tau=1}^{t} \alpha_\tau$. This is similar to the Gaussian case discussed in Section 25.2. Furthermore, we can derive the posterior distribution as follows:

$$
q(\boldsymbol{x}_{t-1}|\boldsymbol{x}_t, \boldsymbol{x}_0) = \text{Cat}(\boldsymbol{x}_{t-1}|\boldsymbol{\theta}_{\text{post}}(\boldsymbol{x}_t, \boldsymbol{\theta}_0)), \ \boldsymbol{\theta}_{\text{post}}(\boldsymbol{x}_t, \boldsymbol{\theta}_0) = \tilde{\boldsymbol{\theta}}/\sum_{k=1}^{K}\tilde{\theta}_k \tag{25.73}
$$

$$
\tilde{\boldsymbol{\theta}} = [\alpha_t\boldsymbol{x}_t + (1 - \alpha_t)/K] \odot [\overline{\alpha}_{t-1}\boldsymbol{x}_0 + (1 - \overline{\alpha}_{t-1})/K] \tag{25.74}
$$

Another option is to define a special **absorbing state** m, representing a MASK token, which we transition into with probability β_t. Formally, we have $\mathbf{Q}_t = (1 - \beta_t)\mathbf{I} + \beta_t\mathbf{1}\boldsymbol{e}_m^\mathsf{T}$, or, in scalar form,

$$
[\mathbf{Q}_t]_{ij} = \begin{cases} 1 & \text{if } i = j = m \\ 1 - \beta_t & \text{if } i = j \neq m \\ \beta_t & \text{if } j = m, i \neq m \end{cases} \tag{25.75}
$$

This converges to a point-mass distribution on state m. See Figure 25.16 for an illustration.

Another option, suitable for quantized ordinal values, is to use a **discretized Gaussian**, that transitions to other nearby states, with a probability that depends on how similar the states are in numerical value. If we ensure the transition matrix is doubly stochastic, the resulting stationary distribution will again be uniform. See Figure 25.16 for an illustration.

25.7.3 Parameterization of the reverse process

While it is possible to directly predict the logits $p_{\boldsymbol{\theta}}(\boldsymbol{x}_{t-1}|\boldsymbol{x}_t)$ using a neural network $f_{\boldsymbol{\theta}}(\boldsymbol{x}_t)$, it is preferable to directly predict the logits of the output, using $\tilde{p}_{\boldsymbol{\theta}}(\tilde{\boldsymbol{x}}_0|\boldsymbol{x}_t)$; we can then combine this with the analytical expression for $q(\boldsymbol{x}_{t-1}|\boldsymbol{x}_t, \boldsymbol{x}_0)$ to get

$$
p_{\boldsymbol{\theta}}(\boldsymbol{x}_{t-1}|\boldsymbol{x}_t) \propto \sum_{\tilde{\boldsymbol{x}}_0} q(\boldsymbol{x}_{t-1}|\boldsymbol{x}_t, \tilde{\boldsymbol{x}}_0)\tilde{p}_{\boldsymbol{\theta}}(\tilde{\boldsymbol{x}}_0|\boldsymbol{x}_t) \tag{25.76}
$$

(The sum over $\tilde{\boldsymbol{x}}_0$ takes $O(DK)$ time, if there are D dimensions, each with K values.) One advantage of this approach, compared to directly learning $p_{\boldsymbol{\theta}}(\boldsymbol{x}_{t-1}|\boldsymbol{x}_t)$, is that the model will automatically satisfy any sparsity constraints in $\mathbf{Q}_t$. In addition, we can perform inference with k steps at a time, by predicting

$$p_{\boldsymbol{\theta}}(\boldsymbol{x}_{t-k}|\boldsymbol{x}_t) \propto \sum_{\tilde{\boldsymbol{x}}_0} q(\boldsymbol{x}_{t-k}|\boldsymbol{x}_t, \tilde{\boldsymbol{x}}_0) \tilde{p}_{\boldsymbol{\theta}}(\tilde{\boldsymbol{x}}_0|\boldsymbol{x}_t) \tag{25.77}$$

Note that, in the multi-step Gaussian case, we require more complex models to handle multimodaility (see Section 25.5.2). By contrast, discrete distributions already have this flexibility built in.

25.7.4 Noise schedules

In this section we discuss how to choose the noise schedule for β_t. For discretized Gaussian diffusion, [Aus+21] propose to linearly increase the variance of the Gaussian noise before the discretization step. For uniform diffusion, we can use a cosine schedule of the form $\alpha_t = \cos(\frac{t/T+s}{1+s}\frac{\pi}{2})$, where $s = 0.08$, as proposed in [ND21]. (Recall that $\beta_t = 1 - \alpha_t$, so the noise increases over time.) For masked diffusion, we can use a schedule of the form $\beta_t = 1/(T - t + 1)$, as proposed in [SD+15b].

25.7.5 Connections to other probabilistic models for discrete sequences

There are interesting connections between D3PM and other probabilistic text models. For example, suppose we define the transition matrix as a combination of the unifrom transition matrix and an absorbing MASK state, i.e., $\mathbf{Q} = \alpha \mathbf{1} e_m^{\mathsf{T}} + \beta \mathbf{1}\mathbf{1}^{\mathsf{T}}/K + (1 - \alpha - \beta)\mathbf{I}$. For a one-step diffusion process in which $q(\boldsymbol{x}_1|\boldsymbol{x}_0)$ replaces $\alpha = 10\%$ of the tokens with MASK, and $\beta = 5\%$ uniformly at random, we recover the same objective that is used to train the **BERT** language model, namely

$$L_0(\boldsymbol{x}_0) = -\mathbb{E}_{q(\boldsymbol{x}_1|\boldsymbol{x}_0)} \log p_{\boldsymbol{\theta}}(\boldsymbol{x}_0|\boldsymbol{x}_1) \tag{25.78}$$

(This follows since $L_T = 0$, and there are no other time steps used in the variational bound in Equation (25.27).)

Now consider a diffusion process that deterministically masks tokens one-by-one. For a sequence of length $N = T$, we have $q([\boldsymbol{x}_t]_i|\boldsymbol{x}_0) = [\boldsymbol{x}_0]_i$ if $i < N - t$ (pass through), else $[\boldsymbol{x}_t]_i$ is set to MASK. Because this is a deterministic process, the posterior $q(\boldsymbol{x}_{t-1}|\boldsymbol{x}_t, \boldsymbol{x}_0)$ is a delta function on the $\boldsymbol{x}_t$ with one fewer mask tokens. One can then show that the KL term becomes $D_{\mathrm{KL}}\left(q([\boldsymbol{x}_t]_i|\boldsymbol{x}_t, \boldsymbol{x}_0) \parallel p_{\boldsymbol{\theta}}([\boldsymbol{x}_{t-1}]_i|\boldsymbol{x}_t)\right) = -\log p_{\boldsymbol{\theta}}([\boldsymbol{x}_0]_i|\boldsymbol{x}_t)$, which is the standard cross-entropy loss for an autoregressive model.

Finally one can show that generative **masked language models**, such as [WC19; Gha+19], also correspond to discrete diffusion processes: the sequence starts will all locations masked out, and each step, a set of tokens are generated, given the previous sequence. The **MaskGIT** method of [Cha+22] uses a similar procedure in the image domain, after applying vector quantization to image patches. These parallel, iterative decoders are much faster than sequential autoregressive decoders. See Figure 25.17 for an illustration.

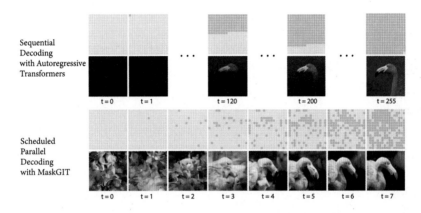

Figure 25.17: *Comparison of sequential image generation with a transformer (top) vs parallel generation with MaskGIT (bottom). All pixels start out in the MASK state, denoted by light gray. In the transformer, we generate one pixel at a time, so it takes 256 steps for the whole image. In the MaskGIT method, multiple states are generated in parallel, which only takes 8 steps. From Figure 2 of [Cha+22]. Used with kind permission of Huiwen Chang.*

26 Generative adversarial networks

This chapter is written by Mihaela Rosca, Shakir Mohamed, and Balaji Lakshminarayanan.

26.1 Introduction

In this chapter, we focus on **implicit generative models**, which are a kind of probabilistic model without an explicit likelihood function [ML16]. This includes the family of **generative adversarial networks** or **GANs** [Goo16]. In this chapter, we provide an introduction to this topic, focusing on a probabilistic perspective.

To develop a probabilistic formulation for GANs, it is useful to first distinguish between two types of probabilistic models: "**prescribed probabilistic models**" and "**implicit probabilistic models**" [DG84]. Prescribed probabilistic models, which we will call **explicit probabilistic models**, provide an explicit parametric specification of the distribution of an observed random variable $\boldsymbol{x}$, specifying a log-likelihood function $\log q_{\theta}(\boldsymbol{x})$ with parameters $\boldsymbol{\theta}$. Most models we encountered in this book thus far are of this form, whether they be state-of-the-art classifiers, large-vocabulary sequence models, or fine-grained spatio-temporal models. Alternatively, we can specify an **implicit probabilistic model** that defines a stochastic procedure to directly generate data. Such models are the natural approach for problems in climate and weather, population genetics, and ecology, since the mechanistic understanding of such systems can be used to directly describe the generative model. We illustrate the difference between implicit and explicit models in Figure 26.1.

The form of implicit generative models we focus on in this chapter can be expressed as a probabilistic latent variable model, similar to VAEs (Chapter 21). Implicit generative models use a latent variable $\boldsymbol{z}$ and transform it using a deterministic function $G_{\boldsymbol{\theta}}$ that maps from $\mathbb{R}^m \to \mathbb{R}^d$ using parameters $\boldsymbol{\theta}$. Implicit generative models do not include a likelihood function or observation model. Instead, the generating procedure defines a valid density on the output space that forms an effective likelihood function:

$$\boldsymbol{x} = G_{\boldsymbol{\theta}}(\boldsymbol{z}'); \qquad \boldsymbol{z}' \sim q(\boldsymbol{z}) \tag{26.1}$$

$$q_{\theta}(\boldsymbol{x}) = \frac{\partial}{\partial x_1} \cdots \frac{\partial}{\partial x_d} \int_{\{G_{\boldsymbol{\theta}}(\boldsymbol{z}) \leq \boldsymbol{x}\}} q(\boldsymbol{z}) d\boldsymbol{z}, \tag{26.2}$$

where $q(\boldsymbol{z})$ is a distribution over latent variables that provides the external source of randomness. Equation (26.2) is the definition of the transformed density $q_{\theta}(\boldsymbol{x})$ defined as the derivative of a cumulative distribution function, and hence integrates the distribution $q(\boldsymbol{z})$ over all events defined

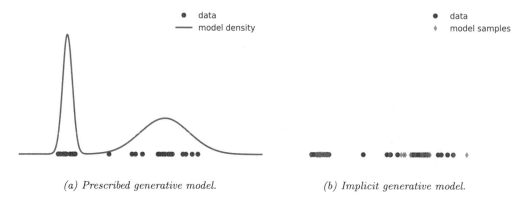

(a) Prescribed generative model.   *(b) Implicit generative model.*

Figure 26.1: Visualizing the difference between prescribed and implicit generative models. Prescribed models provide direct access to the learned density (sometimes unnormalized). Implicit models only provide access to a simulator which can be used to generate samples from an implied density. Generated by genmo_types_implicit_explicit.ipynb

by the set $\{G_{\boldsymbol{\theta}}(\boldsymbol{z}) \leq \boldsymbol{x}\}$. When the latent and data dimension are equal $(m = d)$ and the function $G_{\boldsymbol{\theta}}(\boldsymbol{z})$ is invertible or has easily characterized roots, we recover the rule for transformations of probability distributions. This transformation of variables property is also used in normalizing flows (Chapter 23). In diffusion models (Chapter 25), we also transform noise into data and vice versa, but the transformation is not strictly invertible.

We can develop more general and flexible implicit generative models where the function G is a non-linear function with $d > m$, e.g., specified by a deep network. Such models are sometimes called **generator networks** or **generative neural samplers**; they can also be throught of as **differentiable simulators**. Unfortunately the integral (26.2) is intractable in these kinds of models, and we may not even be able to determine the set $\{G_{\boldsymbol{\theta}}(\boldsymbol{z}) \leq \boldsymbol{x}\}$. Of course, intractability is also a challenge for explicit latent variable models such as VAEs (Chapter 21), but in the GAN case, the lack of a likelihood term makes the learning problem even harder. Therefore this problem is called **likelihood-free inference** or **simulation-based inference**.

Likelihood-free inference also forms the basis of the field known as **approximate Bayesian computation** or **ABC**, which we briefly discuss in Section 13.6.5. ABC and GANs give us two different algorithmic frameworks for learning in implicit generative models. Both approaches rely on a learning principle based on *comparing real and simulated data*. This type of learning by comparison instantiates a core principle of likelihood-free inference, and expanding on this idea is the focus of the next section. The subsequent sections will then focus on GANs specifically, to develop a more detailed foundation and practical considerations. (See also `https://poloclub.github.io/ganlab/` for an interactive tutorial.)

26.2   Learning by comparison

In most of this book, we rely on the principle of maximum likelihood for learning. By maximizing the likelihood we effectively minimize the KL divergence between the model q_{θ} (with parameters $\boldsymbol{\theta}$)

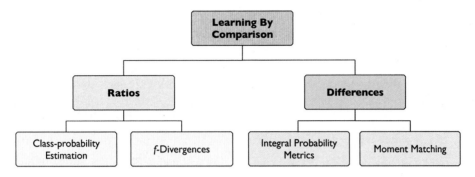

Figure 26.2: Overview of approaches for learning in implicit generative models

and the unknown true data distribution p^*. Recalling equation (26.2), in implicit models we cannot evaluate $q_\theta(x)$, and thus cannot use maximum likelihood training. As implicit models provide a sampling procedure, we instead are searching for learning principles that only use *samples from the model*.

The task of learning in implicit models is to determine, from two sets of samples, whether their distributions are close to each other and to quantify the distance between them. We can think of this as a 'two sample' or likelihood-free approach to learning by comparison. There are many ways of doing this, including using distributional divergences or distances through binary classification, the method of moments, and other approaches. Figure 26.2 shows an overview of different approaches for learning by comparison.

26.2.1 Guiding principles

We are looking for objectives $\mathcal{D}(p^*, q)$ that satisfy the following requirements:

1. Provide guarantees about learning the data distribution: $\operatorname{argmin}_q \mathcal{D}(p^*, q) = p^*$.

2. Can be evaluated only using samples from the data and model distribution.

3. Are computationally cheap to evaluate.

Many distributional distances and divergences satisfy the first requirement, since by definition they satisfy the following:

$$\mathcal{D}(p^*, q) \geq 0; \qquad \mathcal{D}(p^*, q) = 0 \iff p^* = q \tag{26.3}$$

Many distributional distances and divergences, however, fail to satisfy the other two requirements: they cannot be evaluated only using samples — such as the KL divergence, or are computationally intractable — such as the Wasserstein distance. The main approach to overcome these challenges is to *approximate the desired quantity through optimization* by introducing a comparison model, often called a **discriminator** or a **critic** D, such that:

$$\mathcal{D}(p^*, q) = \operatorname*{argmax}_D \mathcal{F}(D, p^*, q) \tag{26.4}$$

where $\mathcal{F}$ is a functional that depends on p^* and q only through samples. For the cases we discuss, both the model and the critic are parametric with parameters $\boldsymbol{\theta}$ and $\boldsymbol{\phi}$ respectively; instead of optimizing over distributions or functions, we optimize with respect to parameters. For the critic, this results in the optimization problem $\text{argmax}_{\boldsymbol{\phi}} \mathcal{F}(D_{\boldsymbol{\phi}}, p^*, q_{\boldsymbol{\theta}})$. For the model parameters $\boldsymbol{\theta}$, the exact objective $\mathcal{D}(p^*, q_{\boldsymbol{\theta}})$ is replaced with the tractable approximation provided through the use of $D_{\boldsymbol{\phi}}$.

A convenient approach to ensure that $\mathcal{F}(D_{\boldsymbol{\phi}}, p^*, q_{\boldsymbol{\theta}})$ can be estimated using only samples from the model and the unknown data distribution is to depend on the two distributions only in expectation:

$$\mathcal{F}(D_{\boldsymbol{\phi}}, p^*, q_{\boldsymbol{\theta}}) = \mathbb{E}_{p^*(\boldsymbol{x})} f(\boldsymbol{x}, \boldsymbol{\phi}) + \mathbb{E}_{q_{\boldsymbol{\theta}}(\boldsymbol{x})} g(\boldsymbol{x}, \boldsymbol{\phi}) \tag{26.5}$$

where f and g are real valued functions whose choice will define $\mathcal{F}$. In the case of implicit generative models, this can be rewritten to use the sampling path $\boldsymbol{x} = G_{\boldsymbol{\theta}}(\boldsymbol{z})$, $\boldsymbol{z} \sim q(\boldsymbol{z})$:

$$\mathcal{F}(D_{\boldsymbol{\phi}}, p^*, q_{\boldsymbol{\theta}}) = \mathbb{E}_{p^*(\boldsymbol{x})} f(\boldsymbol{x}, \boldsymbol{\phi}) + \mathbb{E}_{q(\boldsymbol{z})} g(G_{\boldsymbol{\theta}}(\boldsymbol{z}), \boldsymbol{\phi}) \tag{26.6}$$

which can be estimated using Monte Carlo estimation

$$\mathcal{F}(D_{\boldsymbol{\phi}}, p^*, q_{\boldsymbol{\theta}}) \approx \frac{1}{N} \sum_{i=1}^{N} f(\widehat{\boldsymbol{x}}_i, \boldsymbol{\phi}) + \frac{1}{M} \sum_{i=1}^{M} g(G_{\boldsymbol{\theta}}(\widehat{\boldsymbol{z}}_i), \boldsymbol{\phi}); \qquad \widehat{\boldsymbol{x}}_i \sim p^*(\boldsymbol{x}); \qquad \widehat{\boldsymbol{z}}_i \sim q(\boldsymbol{z}) \tag{26.7}$$

Next, we will see how to instantiate these guiding principles in order to find the functions f and g and thus the objective $\mathcal{F}$ which can be used to train implicit models: class probability estimation (Section 26.2.2), bounds on f-divergences (Section 26.2.3), integral probability metrics (Section 26.2.4), and moment matching (Section 26.2.5).

26.2.2   Density ratio estimation using binary classifiers

One way to compare two distributions p^* and $q_{\boldsymbol{\theta}}$ is to compute their density ratio $r(\boldsymbol{x}) = \frac{p^*(\boldsymbol{x})}{q_{\boldsymbol{\theta}}(\boldsymbol{x})}$. The distributions are the same if and only if the ratio is 1 everywhere in the support of $q_{\boldsymbol{\theta}}$. Since we cannot evaluate the densities of implicit models, we must instead develop techniques to compute the density ratio from samples alone, following the guiding principles established above.

Fortunately, we can use the trick from Section 2.7.5 which converts density estimation into a binary classification problem to write

$$\frac{p^*(\boldsymbol{x})}{q_{\boldsymbol{\theta}}(\boldsymbol{x})} = \frac{D(\boldsymbol{x})}{1 - D(\boldsymbol{x})} \tag{26.8}$$

where $D(\boldsymbol{x})$ is the discriminator or critic which is trained to distinguish samples coming from p^* vs $q_{\boldsymbol{\theta}}$.

For parametric classification, we can learn discriminators $D_{\boldsymbol{\phi}}(\boldsymbol{x}) \in [0, 1]$ with parameters $\boldsymbol{\phi}$. Using knowledge and insight about probabilistic classification, we can learn the parameters by minimizing any proper scoring rule [GR07b] (see also Section 14.2.1). For the familiar Bernoulli log-loss (or binary cross entropy loss), we obtain the objective:

$$V(q_{\boldsymbol{\theta}}, p^*) = \arg\max_{\boldsymbol{\phi}} \mathbb{E}_{p(\boldsymbol{x}|y)p(y)} [y \log D_{\boldsymbol{\phi}}(\boldsymbol{x}) + (1 - y) \log(1 - D_{\boldsymbol{\phi}}(\boldsymbol{x}))]$$

$$= \arg\max_{\boldsymbol{\phi}} \mathbb{E}_{p(\boldsymbol{x}|y=1)p(y=1)} \log D_{\boldsymbol{\phi}}(\boldsymbol{x}) + \mathbb{E}_{p(\boldsymbol{x}|y=0)p(y=0)} \log(1 - D_{\boldsymbol{\phi}}(\boldsymbol{x})) \tag{26.9}$$

$$= \arg\max_{\boldsymbol{\phi}} \frac{1}{2} \mathbb{E}_{p^*(\boldsymbol{x})} \log D_{\boldsymbol{\phi}}(\boldsymbol{x}) + \frac{1}{2} \mathbb{E}_{q_{\boldsymbol{\theta}}(\boldsymbol{x})} \log(1 - D_{\boldsymbol{\phi}}(\boldsymbol{x})). \tag{26.10}$$

Loss	Objective Function ($D := D(\boldsymbol{x}; \boldsymbol{\phi}) \in [0, 1]$)
Bernoulli loss	$\mathbb{E}_{p^*(\boldsymbol{x})}[\log D] + \mathbb{E}_{q_\theta(\boldsymbol{x})}[\log(1 - D)]$
Brier score	$\mathbb{E}_{p^*(\boldsymbol{x})}[-(1 - D)^2] + \mathbb{E}_{q_\theta(\boldsymbol{x})}[-D^2]$
Exponential loss	$\mathbb{E}_{p^*(\boldsymbol{x})}\left[\left(-\frac{1-D}{D}\right)^{\frac{1}{2}}\right] + \mathbb{E}_{q_\theta(\boldsymbol{x})}\left[\left(-\frac{D}{1-D}\right)^{\frac{1}{2}}\right]$
Misclassification	$\mathbb{E}_{p^*(\boldsymbol{x})}[-\mathbb{I}[D \leq 0.5]] + \mathbb{E}_{q_\theta(\boldsymbol{x})}[-\mathbb{I}[D > 0.5]]$
Hinge loss	$\mathbb{E}_{p^*(\boldsymbol{x})}\left[-\max\left(0, 1 - \log\frac{D}{1-D}\right)\right] + \mathbb{E}_{q_\theta(\boldsymbol{x})}\left[-\max\left(0, 1 + \log\frac{D}{1-D}\right)\right]$
Spherical	$\mathbb{E}_{p^*(\boldsymbol{x})}[\alpha D] + \mathbb{E}_{q_\theta(\boldsymbol{x})}[\alpha(1 - D)]; \quad \alpha = (1 - 2D + 2D^2)^{-\frac{1}{2}}$

Table 26.1: *Proper scoring rules that can be maximized in class probability-based learning of implicit generative models. Based on [ML16].*

The same procedure can be extended beyond the Bernoulli log-loss to other proper scoring rules used for binary classification, such as those presented in Table 26.1, adapted from [ML16]. The optimal discriminator D is $\frac{p^*(\boldsymbol{x})}{p^*(\boldsymbol{x}) + q_\theta(\boldsymbol{x})}$, since:

$$\frac{p^*(\boldsymbol{x})}{q_\theta(\boldsymbol{x})} = \frac{D^*(\boldsymbol{x})}{1 - D^*(\boldsymbol{x})} \implies D^*(\boldsymbol{x}) = \frac{p^*(\boldsymbol{x})}{p^*(\boldsymbol{x}) + q_\theta(\boldsymbol{x})} \tag{26.11}$$

By substituting the optimal discriminator into the scoring rule (26.10), we can show that the objective V can also be interpreted as the minimization of the Jensen-Shannon divergence.

$$V^*(q_\theta, p^*) = \frac{1}{2}\mathbb{E}_{p^*(\boldsymbol{x})}[\log\frac{p^*(\boldsymbol{x})}{p^*(\boldsymbol{x}) + q_\theta(\boldsymbol{x})}] + \frac{1}{2}\mathbb{E}_{q_\theta(\boldsymbol{x})}[\log(1 - \frac{p^*(\boldsymbol{x})}{p^*(\boldsymbol{x}) + q_\theta(\boldsymbol{x})})] \tag{26.12}$$

$$= \frac{1}{2}\mathbb{E}_{p^*(\boldsymbol{x})}[\log\frac{p^*(\boldsymbol{x})}{\frac{p^*(\boldsymbol{x}) + q_\theta(\boldsymbol{x})}{2}}] + \frac{1}{2}\mathbb{E}_{q_\theta(\boldsymbol{x})}[\log(\frac{q_\theta(\boldsymbol{x})}{\frac{p^*(\boldsymbol{x}) + q_\theta(\boldsymbol{x})}{2}})] - \log 2 \tag{26.13}$$

$$= \frac{1}{2}D_{\mathrm{KL}}\left(p^* \parallel \frac{p^* + q_\theta}{2}\right) + \frac{1}{2}D_{\mathrm{KL}}\left(q_\theta \parallel \frac{p^* + q_\theta}{2}\right) - \log 2 \tag{26.14}$$

$$= JSD(p^*, q_\theta) - \log 2 \tag{26.15}$$

where JSD denotes the Jensen-Shannon divergence:

$$JSD(p^*, q_\theta) = \frac{1}{2}D_{\mathrm{KL}}\left(p^* \parallel \frac{p^* + q_\theta}{2}\right) + \frac{1}{2}D_{\mathrm{KL}}\left(q_\theta \parallel \frac{p^* + q_\theta}{2}\right) \tag{26.16}$$

This establishes a connection between *optimal* binary classification and distributional divergences. By using binary classification, we were able to compute the distributional divergence using only samples, which is the important property needed for learning implicit generative models; as expressed in the guiding principles (Section 26.2.1), we have turned an intractable estimation problem — how to estimate the JSD divergence, into an optimization problem — how to learn a classifier which can be used to approximate that divergence.

We would like to train the parameters $\boldsymbol{\theta}$ of generative model to minimize the divergence:

$$\min_{\boldsymbol{\theta}} JSD(p^*, q_\theta) = \min_{\boldsymbol{\theta}} V^*(q_\theta, p^*) + \log 2 \tag{26.17}$$

$$= \min_{\boldsymbol{\theta}} \frac{1}{2}\mathbb{E}_{p^*(\boldsymbol{x})}\log D^*(\boldsymbol{x}) + \frac{1}{2}\mathbb{E}_{q_\theta(\boldsymbol{x})}\log(1 - D^*(\boldsymbol{x})) + \log 2 \tag{26.18}$$

Since we do not have access to the optimal classifier D^* but only to the neural approximation D_ϕ obtained using the optimization in (26.10) , this results in a min-max optimization problem:

$$\min_{\boldsymbol{\theta}} \max_{\boldsymbol{\phi}} \frac{1}{2}\mathbb{E}_{p^*(\boldsymbol{x})}[\log D_\phi(\boldsymbol{x})] + \frac{1}{2}\mathbb{E}_{q_\theta(\boldsymbol{x})}[\log(1 - D_\phi(\boldsymbol{x}))] \tag{26.19}$$

By replacing the generating procedure (26.1) in (26.19) we obtain the objective in terms of the latent variables $\boldsymbol{z}$ of the implicit generative model:

$$\min_{\boldsymbol{\theta}} \max_{\boldsymbol{\phi}} \frac{1}{2}\mathbb{E}_{p^*(\boldsymbol{x})}[\log D_\phi(\boldsymbol{x})] + \frac{1}{2}\mathbb{E}_{q(\boldsymbol{z})}[\log(1 - D_\phi(G_{\boldsymbol{\theta}}(\boldsymbol{z})))], \tag{26.20}$$

which recovers the definition proposed in the original GAN paper [Goo+14]. The core principle behind GANs is to train a discriminator, in this case a binary classifier, to approximate a distance or divergence between the model and data distributions, and to then train the generative model to minimize this approximation of the divergence or distance.

Beyond the use of the Bernoulli scoring rule used above, other scoring rules have been used to train generative models via min-max optimization. The Brier scoring rule, which under discriminator optimality conditions can be shown to correspond to minimizing the Pearson χ^2 divergence via similar arguments as the ones shown above has lead to LS-GAN [Mao+17]. The hinge scoring rule has become popular [Miy+18b; BDS18], and under discriminator optimality conditions corresponds to minimizing the total variational distance [NWJ+09].

The connection between proper scoring rules and distributional divergences allows the construction of convergence guarantees for the learning criteria above, under infinite capacity of the discriminator and generator: since the minimizer of distributional divergence is the true data distribution (Equation 26.3), if the discriminator is optimal and the generator has enough capacity, it will learn the data distribution. In practice however, this assumption will not hold, as discriminators are rarely optimal; we will discuss this at length in Section 26.3.

26.2.3　Bounds on f-divergences

As we saw with the appearance of the Jensen-Shannon divergence in the previous section, we can consider directly using a measure of distributional divergence to derive methods for learning in implicit models. One general class of divergences are the f-divergences (Section 2.7.1) defined as:

$$\mathcal{D}_f\left[p^*(\boldsymbol{x})\|q_\theta(\boldsymbol{x})\right] = \int q_\theta(\boldsymbol{x})f\left(\frac{p^*(\boldsymbol{x})}{q_\theta(\boldsymbol{x})}\right)d\boldsymbol{x} \tag{26.21}$$

where f is a convex function such that $f(1) = 0$. For different choices of f, we can recover known distributional divergences such as the KL, reverse KL, and Jensen-Shannon divergence. We discuss such connections in Section 2.7.1, and provide a summary in Table 26.2.

To evaluate Equation (26.21) we will need to evaluate the density of the data $p^*(\boldsymbol{x})$ and the model $q_\theta(\boldsymbol{x})$, neither of which are available. In the previous section we overcame the challenge of evaluating the density ratio by transforming it into a problem of binary classification. In this section, we will instead look towards the role of lower bounds on f-divergences, which is an approach for tractability that is also used for variational inference (Chapter 10).

Divergence	f	$f^\dagger$	Optimal Critic
KL	$u \log u$	e^{u-1}	$1 + \log r(\boldsymbol{x})$
Reverse KL	$-\log u$	$-1 - \log(-u)$	$-1/r(\boldsymbol{x})$
JSD	$u \log u - (u+1) \log \frac{u+1}{2}$	$-\log(2 - e^u)$	$\frac{2}{1+1/r(\boldsymbol{x})})$
Pearson χ^2	$(u-1)^2$	$\frac{1}{4}u^2 + u$	$\left(\sqrt{r(\boldsymbol{x})} - 1 \right) \sqrt{1/r(\boldsymbol{x})}$

Table 26.2: *Standard divergences as f divergences for various choices of f. The optimal critic is written as a function of the density ratio $r(\boldsymbol{x}) = \frac{p^*(\boldsymbol{x})}{q_\theta(\boldsymbol{x})}$.*

f-divergences have a widely-developed theory in convex analysis and information theory. Since the function f in Equation (26.21) is convex, we know that we can find a tangent that bounds it from below. The variational formulation of the f-divergence is [NWJ10b; NCT16c]:

$$\mathcal{D}_f\left[p^*(\boldsymbol{x}) \| q_\theta(\boldsymbol{x})\right] = \int q_\theta(\boldsymbol{x}) f\left(\frac{p^*(\boldsymbol{x})}{q_\theta(\boldsymbol{x})}\right) d\boldsymbol{x} \tag{26.22}$$

$$= \int q_\theta(\boldsymbol{x}) \sup_{t:\mathcal{X}\to\mathbb{R}} \left[t(\boldsymbol{x}) \frac{p^*(\boldsymbol{x})}{q_\theta(\boldsymbol{x})} - f^\dagger(t(\boldsymbol{x}))\right] d\boldsymbol{x} \tag{26.23}$$

$$= \int \sup_{t:\mathcal{X}\to\mathbb{R}} p^*(\boldsymbol{x})t(\boldsymbol{x}) - q_\theta(\boldsymbol{x}) f^\dagger(t(\boldsymbol{x})) d\boldsymbol{x} \tag{26.24}$$

$$\geq \sup_{t\in\mathcal{T}} \mathbb{E}_{p^*(\boldsymbol{x})}[t(\boldsymbol{x})] - \mathbb{E}_{q_\theta(\boldsymbol{x})}[f^\dagger(t(\boldsymbol{x}))]. \tag{26.25}$$

In the second line we use the result from convex analysis, discussed Supplementary Section 6.3, that re-expresses the convex function f using $f(u) = \sup_t ut - f^\dagger(t)$, where $f^\dagger$ is the convex conjugate of the function f, and t is a parameter we optimize over. Since we apply f at $u = \frac{p^*(\boldsymbol{x})}{q_\theta(\boldsymbol{x})}$ for all $\boldsymbol{x} \in \mathcal{X}$, we make the parameter t be a function $t(\boldsymbol{x})$. The final inequality comes from replacing the supremum over all functions from the data domain $\mathcal{X}$ to $\mathbb{R}$ with the supremum over a family of functions $\mathcal{T}$ (such as the family of functions expressible by a neural network architecture), which might not be able to capture the true supremum. The function t takes the role of the discriminator or critic.

The final expression in Equation (26.25) follows the general desired form of Equation 26.5: it is the difference of two expectations, and these expectations can be computed by Monte Carlo estimation using only samples, as in Equation (26.7); despite starting with an objective (Equation 26.21) which contravened the desired principles for training implicit generative models, variational bounds have allowed us to construct an approximation which satisfies all desiderata.

Using bounds on the f-divergence, we obtain an objective (26.25) that allows learning both the generator and critic parameters. We use a critic D with parameters $\boldsymbol{\phi}$ to estimate the bound, and then optimize the parameters $\boldsymbol{\theta}$ of the generator to minimize the approximation of the f-divergence provided by the critic (we replace t above with $D_{\boldsymbol{\phi}}$, to retain standard GAN notation):

$$\min_{\boldsymbol{\theta}} \mathcal{D}_f(p^*, q_\theta) \geq \min_{\boldsymbol{\theta}} \max_{\boldsymbol{\phi}} \mathbb{E}_{p^*(\boldsymbol{x})}[D_{\boldsymbol{\phi}}(\boldsymbol{x})] - \mathbb{E}_{q_\theta(\boldsymbol{x})}[f^\dagger(D_{\boldsymbol{\phi}}(\boldsymbol{x}))] \tag{26.26}$$

$$= \min_{\boldsymbol{\theta}} \max_{\boldsymbol{\phi}} \mathbb{E}_{p^*(\boldsymbol{x})}[D_{\boldsymbol{\phi}}(\boldsymbol{x})] - \mathbb{E}_{q(\boldsymbol{z})}[f^\dagger(D_{\boldsymbol{\phi}}(G_{\boldsymbol{\theta}}(\boldsymbol{z})))] \tag{26.27}$$

This approach to train an implicit generative model leads to f-GANs [NCT16c]. It is worth noting that there exists an equivalence between the scoring rules in the previous section and bounds on

f-divergences [RW11]: for each scoring rule we can find an f-divergence that leads to the same training criteria and the same min-max game of Equation 26.27. An intuitive way to grasp the connection between f-divergences and proper scoring rules is through their use of density ratios: in both cases the optimal critic approximates a quantity directly related to the density ratio (see Table 26.2 for f-divergences and Equation (26.11) for scoring rules).

26.2.4   Integral probability metrics

Instead of comparing distributions by using their ratio as we did in the previous two sections, we can instead study their difference. A general class of measure of difference is given by the Integral Probability Metrics (Section 2.7.2) defined as:

$$I_{\mathcal{F}}(p^*(\boldsymbol{x}), q_\theta(\boldsymbol{x})) = \sup_{f \in \mathcal{F}} \left| \mathbb{E}_{p^*(\boldsymbol{x})} f(\boldsymbol{x}) - \mathbb{E}_{q_\theta(\boldsymbol{x})} f(\boldsymbol{x}) \right|. \tag{26.28}$$

The function f is a test or witness function that will take the role of the discriminator or critic. To use IPMs we must define the class of real valued, measurable functions $\mathcal{F}$ over which the supremum is taken, and this choice will lead to different distances, just as choosing different convex functions f leads to different f-divergences. Integral probability metrics are distributional distances: beyond satisfying the conditions for distributional divergences $\mathcal{D}(p^*, q) \geq 0$; $\mathcal{D}(p^*, q) = 0 \iff p^* = q$ (Equation (26.3)), they are also symmetric $\mathcal{D}(p, q) = \mathcal{D}(q, p)$ and satisfy the triangle inequality $\mathcal{D}(p, q) \leq \mathcal{D}(p, r) + \mathcal{D}(r, q)$.

Not all function families satisfy these conditions of create a valid distance $I_{\mathcal{F}}$. To see why consider the case where $\mathcal{F} = \{z\}$ where z is the function $z(\boldsymbol{x}) = 0$. This choice of $\mathcal{F}$ entails that regardless of the two distributions chosen, the value in Equation 26.28 would be 0, violating the requirement that distance between two distributions be 0 only if the two distributions are the same. A popular choice of $\mathcal{F}$ for which $I_{\mathcal{F}}$ satisfies the conditions of a valid distributional distance is the set of 1-Lipschitz functions, which leads to the Wasserstein distance [Vil08]:

$$W_1(p^*(\boldsymbol{x}), q_\theta(\boldsymbol{x})) = \sup_{f : \|f\|_{\text{Lip}} \leq 1} \mathbb{E}_{p^*(\boldsymbol{x})} f(\boldsymbol{x}) - \mathbb{E}_{q_\theta(\boldsymbol{x})} f(\boldsymbol{x}) \tag{26.29}$$

We show an example of a Wasserstein critic in Figure 26.3a. The supremum over the set of 1-Lipschitz functions is intractable for most cases, which again suggests the introduction of a learned critic:

$$W_1(p^*(\boldsymbol{x}), q_\theta(\boldsymbol{x})) = \sup_{f : \|f\|_{\text{Lip}} \leq 1} \mathbb{E}_{p^*(\boldsymbol{x})} f(\boldsymbol{x}) - \mathbb{E}_{q_\theta(\boldsymbol{x})} f(\boldsymbol{x}) \tag{26.30}$$

$$\geq \max_{\phi : \|D_\phi\|_{\text{Lip}} \leq 1} \mathbb{E}_{p^*(\boldsymbol{x})} D_\phi(\boldsymbol{x}) - \mathbb{E}_{q_\theta(\boldsymbol{x})} D_\phi(\boldsymbol{x}), \tag{26.31}$$

where the critic D_ϕ has to be regularized to be 1-Lipschitz (various techniques for Lipschitz regularization via gradient penalties or spectral normalization methods have been used [ACB17; Gul+17]). As was the case with f-divergences, we replace an intractable quantity which requires a supremum over a class of functions with a bound obtained using a subset of this function class, a subset which can be modeled using neural networks.

(a) *Optimal Wasserstein critic.*   (b) *Optimal MMD critic.*

Figure 26.3: *Optimal critics in Integral Probability Metrics (IPMs). Generated by ipm_divergences.ipynb*

To train a generative model, we again introduce a min max game:

$$\min_{\boldsymbol{\theta}} W_1(p^*(\boldsymbol{x}), q_\theta(\boldsymbol{x})) \geq \min_{\boldsymbol{\theta}} \max_{\phi:\|D_\phi\|_{\mathrm{Lip}}\leq 1} \mathbb{E}_{p^*(\boldsymbol{x})} D_\phi(\boldsymbol{x}) - \mathbb{E}_{q_\theta(\boldsymbol{x})} D_\phi(\boldsymbol{x}) \tag{26.32}$$

$$= \min_{\boldsymbol{\theta}} \max_{\phi:\|D_\phi\|_{\mathrm{Lip}}\leq 1} \mathbb{E}_{p^*(\boldsymbol{x})} D_\phi(\boldsymbol{x}) - \mathbb{E}_{q(\boldsymbol{z})} D_\phi(G_{\boldsymbol{\theta}}(\boldsymbol{z})) \tag{26.33}$$

This leads to the popular WassersteinGAN [ACB17].

If we replace the choice of function family $\mathcal{F}$ to that of functions in an RKHS (Section 18.3.7.1) with norm one, we obtain the **maximum mean discrepancy** (**MMD**) discussed in Section 2.7.3:

$$\mathrm{MMD}(p^*(\boldsymbol{x}), q_\theta(\boldsymbol{x})) = \sup_{f:\|f\|_{RKHS}=1} \mathbb{E}_{p^*(\boldsymbol{x})} f(\boldsymbol{x}) - \mathbb{E}_{q_\theta(\boldsymbol{x})} f(\boldsymbol{x}). \tag{26.34}$$

We show an example of an MMD critic in Figure 26.3b. It is often more convenient to use the square MMD loss [LSZ15; DRG15], which can be evaluated using the kernel $\mathcal{K}$ (Section 18.3.7.1):

$$\mathrm{MMD}^2(p^*, q_\theta) = \mathbb{E}_{p^*(\boldsymbol{x})}\mathbb{E}_{p^*(\boldsymbol{x}')}\mathcal{K}(\boldsymbol{x}, \boldsymbol{x}') - 2\mathbb{E}_{p^*(\boldsymbol{x})}\mathbb{E}_{q_\theta(\boldsymbol{y})}\mathcal{K}(\boldsymbol{x}, \boldsymbol{y}) + \mathbb{E}_{q_\theta(\boldsymbol{y})}\mathbb{E}_{q_\theta(\boldsymbol{y}')}\mathcal{K}(\boldsymbol{y}, \boldsymbol{y}') \tag{26.35}$$

$$= \mathbb{E}_{p^*(\boldsymbol{x})}\mathbb{E}_{p^*(\boldsymbol{x}')}\mathcal{K}(\boldsymbol{x}, \boldsymbol{x}') - 2\mathbb{E}_{p^*(\boldsymbol{x})}\mathbb{E}_{q(\boldsymbol{z})}\mathcal{K}(\boldsymbol{x}, G_{\boldsymbol{\theta}}(\boldsymbol{z})) + \mathbb{E}_{q(\boldsymbol{z})}\mathbb{E}_{q(\boldsymbol{z}')}\mathcal{K}(G_{\boldsymbol{\theta}}(\boldsymbol{z}), G_{\boldsymbol{\theta}}(\boldsymbol{z}')) \tag{26.36}$$

The MMD can be directly used to learn a generative model, often called a generative matching network [LSZ15]:

$$\min_{\boldsymbol{\theta}} \mathrm{MMD}^2(p^*, q_\theta) \tag{26.37}$$

The choice of kernel is important. Using a fixed or predefined kernel such as a radial basis function (RBF) kernel might not be appropriate for all data modalities, such as high dimensional images. Thus we are looking for a way to learn a feature function ζ such that $\mathcal{K}(\zeta(\boldsymbol{x}), \zeta(\boldsymbol{x}'))$ is a valid kernel; luckily, we can use that for any characteristic kernel $\mathcal{K}(\boldsymbol{x}, \boldsymbol{x}')$ and injective function ζ, $\mathcal{K}(\zeta(\boldsymbol{x}), \zeta(\boldsymbol{x}'))$ is also a characteristic kernel. While this tells us that we can use feature functions in the MMD objective, it does not tell us how to learn the features. In order to ensure that the learned features are sensitive to differences between the data distribution $p^*(\boldsymbol{x})$ and the model distribution $q_\theta(\boldsymbol{x})$, the kernel parameters are trained to *maximize* the square MMD. This again casts the problem into a familiar min max objective by learning the projection ζ with parameters ϕ [Li+17b]:

$$\min_{\boldsymbol{\theta}} \text{MMD}_\zeta{}^2(p_\mathcal{D}, q_\theta) \tag{26.38}$$

$$= \min_{\boldsymbol{\theta}} \max_{\boldsymbol{\phi}} \mathbb{E}_{p^*(\boldsymbol{x})} \mathbb{E}_{p^*(\boldsymbol{x}')} \mathcal{K}(\zeta_\phi(\boldsymbol{x}), \zeta_\phi(\boldsymbol{x}'))$$

$$- 2\mathbb{E}_{p^*(\boldsymbol{x})} \mathbb{E}_{q_\theta(\boldsymbol{y})} \mathcal{K}(\zeta_\phi(\boldsymbol{x}), \zeta_\phi(\boldsymbol{y})) \tag{26.39}$$

$$+ \mathbb{E}_{q_\theta(\boldsymbol{y})} \mathbb{E}_{q_\theta(\boldsymbol{y}')} \mathcal{K}(\zeta_\phi(\boldsymbol{y}), \zeta_\phi(\boldsymbol{y}'))$$

where ζ_ϕ is regularized to be injective, though this is sometimes relaxed [Bin+18]. Unlike the Wasserstein distance and f-divergences, Equation (26.39) can be estimated using Monte Carlo estimation, without requiring a lower bound on the original objective.

26.2.5   Moment matching

More broadly than distances defined by integral probability metrics, for a set of test statistics s, one can define a **moment matching** criteria [Pea36], also known as the method of moments:

$$\min_{\boldsymbol{\theta}} \left\| \mathbb{E}_{p^*(\boldsymbol{x})} s(\boldsymbol{x}) - \mathbb{E}_{q_\theta(\boldsymbol{x})} s(\boldsymbol{x}) \right\|_2^2 \tag{26.40}$$

where $m(\boldsymbol{\theta}) = \mathbb{E}_{q_\theta(\boldsymbol{x})} s(\boldsymbol{x})$ is the *moment function*. The choice of statistic $s(\boldsymbol{x})$ is crucial, since as with distributional divergences and distances, we would like to ensure that if the objective is minimized and reaches the minimal value 0, the two distributions are the same $p^*(\boldsymbol{x}) = q_\theta(\boldsymbol{x})$. Too see that not all functions s satisfy this requirement consider the function $s(\boldsymbol{x}) = \boldsymbol{x}$: simply matching the means of two distributions is not sufficient to match higher moments (such as variance). For likelihood based models the score function $s(\boldsymbol{x}) = \log q_\theta(\boldsymbol{x})$ satisfies the above requirement and leads to a consistent estimator [Vaa00], but this choice of s is not available for implicit generative models.

This motivates the search for other approaches of integrating the method of moments for implicit models. The MMD can be seen as a moment matching criteria, by matching the means of the two distributions after lifting the data into the feature space of an RHKS. But moment matching can go beyond integral probability metrics: Ravuri et al. [Rav+18] show that one can *learn* useful moments by using s as the set of features containing the gradients of a trained discriminator classifier D_ϕ together with the features of the learned critic: $s_\phi(\boldsymbol{x}) = [\nabla_\phi D_\phi(\boldsymbol{x}), h_1(\boldsymbol{x}), \ldots, h_n(\boldsymbol{x})]$ where $h_1(\boldsymbol{x}), \ldots, h_n(\boldsymbol{x})$ are the hidden activations of the learned critic. Both features and gradients are needed: the gradients $\nabla_\phi D_\phi(\boldsymbol{x})$ are required to ensure the estimator for the parameters $\boldsymbol{\theta}$ is consistent, since the number of moments $s(\boldsymbol{x})$ needs to be larger than the number of parameters $\boldsymbol{\theta}$, which will be true if the critic will have more parameters than the model; the features $h_i(\boldsymbol{x})$ are added since they have been shown empirically to improve performance, thus showcasing the importance of the choice of test statistics s used to train implicit models.

26.2.6   On density ratios and differences

We have seen how density ratios (Sections 26.2.2 and 26.2.3) and density differences (Section 26.2.4) can be used to define training objectives for implicit generative models. We now explore some of the distinctions between using ratios and differences for learning by comparison, as well as explore the

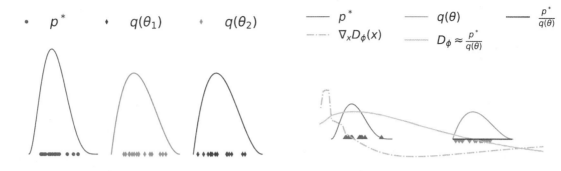

(a) *Failure of the KL divergence to distinguish between distributions with non-overlapping support:* $D_{\mathrm{KL}}\left(p^* \parallel q_{\theta_1}\right) = D_{\mathrm{KL}}\left(p^* \parallel q_{\theta_2}\right) = \infty$, *despite q_{θ_2} being closer to p^* than q_{θ_1}.*

(b) *The density ratio $\frac{p^*}{q_\theta}$ used by the KL divergence and a smooth estimate given by an MLP, together with the gradient it provides with respect to the input variable.*

Figure 26.4: *The KL divergence cannot provide learning signal for distributions without overlapping support (left), while the smooth approximation given by a learned decision surface like an MLP can (right). Generated by ipm_divergences.ipynb*

effects of using approximations to these objectives using function classes such as neural networks has on these distinctions.

One often stated downside of using divergences that rely on density ratios (such as f-divergences) is their poor behavior when the distributions p^* and q_θ do not have overlapping support. For non-overlapping support, the density ratio $\frac{p^*}{q_\theta}$ will be ∞ in the parts of the space where $p^*(\boldsymbol{x}) > 0$ but $q_\theta(\boldsymbol{x}) = 0$, and 0 otherwise. In that case, the $D_{\mathrm{KL}}\left(p^* \parallel q_\theta\right) = \infty$ and the $JSD(p^*, q_\theta) = \log 2$, regardless of the value of $\boldsymbol{\theta}$. Thus *f-divergences cannot distinguish between different model distributions when they do not have overlapping support with the data distribution*, as visualized in Figure 26.4a. This is in contrast with difference based methods such as IPMs such as the Wasserstein distance and the MMD, which have smoothness requirements built in the *definition* of the method, by constraining the norm of the critic (Equations (26.29) and (26.34)). We can see the effect of these constraints in Figure 26.3: both the Wasserstein distance and the MMD provide useful signal in the case of distributions with non-overlapping support.

While the *definition* of f-divergences relies on density ratios (Equation (26.21)), we have seen that to train implicit generative models we use approximations to those divergences obtained using a parametric critic D_ϕ. If the function family of the critic used to approximate the divergence (via the bound or class probability estimation) contains only smooth functions, it will not be able to model the sharp true density ratio, which jumps from 0 to ∞, but it can provide a smooth approximation. We show an example in Figure 26.4b, where we show the density ratio for two distributions without overlapping support and an approximation provided by an MLP trained to approximate the KL divergence using Equation 26.25. Here, the smooth decision surface provided by the MLP can be used to train a generative model while the underlying KL divergence cannot be; the learned MLP provides the gradient signal on how to move distribution mass to areas with more density under the data distribution, while the KL divergence provides a zero gradient almost everywhere in the space. This ability of approximations to f-divergences to overcome non-overlapping support issues is a desirable property of generative modeling training criteria, as it allows models to learn the data distribution regardless of initialization [Fed+18]. Thus while the case of non-overlapping support provides an important theoretical difference between IPMs and f-divergences, it is less significant in practice since bounds on f-divergences or class probability estimation are used with smooth critics to approximate the underlying divergence.

Some density ratio and density difference based approaches also share commonalities: bounds are used both for f-divergences (variational bounds in Equation 26.25) and for the Wasserstein distance (Equation (26.31)). These bounds to distributional divergence and distances have their own set of challenges: since the generator minimizes a lower bound of the underlying divergence or distance, minimizing this objective provides no guarantees that the divergence will decrease in training. To see this, we can look at Equation 26.26: its RHS can get arbitrarily low without decreasing the LHS, the divergence we are interested in minimizing; this is unlike variational *upper* bound on the KL divergence used to train variational autoencoders Chapter 21.

26.3　Generative adversarial networks

We have looked at different learning principles that do not require the use of explicit likelihoods, and thus can be used to train implicit models. These learning principles specify training criteria, but do not tell us how to *train* models or parameterize models. To answer these questions, we now look at algorithms for training implicit models, where the models (both the discriminator and generator) are deep neural networks; this leads us to enerative adversarial networks (GANs). We cover how to turn learning principles into loss functions for training GANs (Section 26.3.1); how to train models using gradient descent (Section 26.3.2); how to improve GAN optimization (Section 26.3.4) and how to assess GAN convergence (Section 26.3.5).

26.3.1　From learning principles to loss functions

In Section 26.2 we discussed learning principles for implicit generative models: class probability estimation, bounds on f-divergences, integral probability metrics and moment matching. These principles can be used to formulate loss functions to train the model parameters $\boldsymbol{\theta}$ and the critic parameters $\boldsymbol{\phi}$. Many of these objectives use **zero-sum losses** via a **min-max** formulation: the generator's goal is to minimize the same function the discriminator is maximizing. We can formalize this as:

$$\min \max V(\boldsymbol{\phi}, \boldsymbol{\theta}) \tag{26.41}$$

As an example, we recover the original GAN with the Bernoulli log-loss (Equation (26.19)) when

$$V(\boldsymbol{\phi}, \boldsymbol{\theta}) = \frac{1}{2}\mathbb{E}_{p^*(\boldsymbol{x})}[\log D_{\boldsymbol{\phi}}(\boldsymbol{x})] + \frac{1}{2}\mathbb{E}_{q_{\boldsymbol{\theta}}(\boldsymbol{x})}[\log(1 - D_{\boldsymbol{\phi}}(\boldsymbol{x}))]. \tag{26.42}$$

The reason most of the learning principles we have discussed lead to zero-sum losses is due to their underlying structure: the critic maximizes a quantity in order to approximate a divergence or distance — such as an f-divergence or Integral Probability Metric — and the model minimizes this approximation to the divergence or distance. That need not be the case, however. Intuitively, the discriminator training criteria needs to ensure that the discriminator can distinguish between data and model samples, while the generator loss function needs to ensure that model samples are indistinguishable from data according to the discriminator.

To construct a GAN that is not zero-sum, consider the zero-sum criteria in the original GAN (Equation 26.42), induced by the Bernoulli scoring rule. The discriminator tries to distinguish between data and model samples by classifying the data as real (label 1) and samples as fake (label 0), while the goal of the generator is to minimize the probability that the discriminator classifies its samples as fake: $\min_{\theta} \mathbb{E}_{q_{\theta}(\boldsymbol{x})} \log(1 - D_{\phi}(\boldsymbol{x}))$. An equally intuitive goal for the generator is to maximize the probability that the discriminator classifies its samples as real. While the difference might seem subtle, this loss, known as the "nonsaturating loss" [Goo+14], defined as $\mathbb{E}_{q_{\theta}(\boldsymbol{x})} - \log D_{\phi}(\boldsymbol{x})$, enjoys better gradient properties early in training, as shown in Figure 26.5: the non-saturating loss provides a stronger learning signal (via the gradient) when the generator is performing poorly, and the discriminator can easily distinguish its samples from data, i.e., $D(G(\boldsymbol{z}))$ is low; more on the gradients properties the saturating and non-saturating losses can be found in [AB17; Fed+18].

There exist many other GAN losses which are not zero-sum, including formulations of LS-GAN [Mao+17], GANs trained using the hinge loss [LY17], and RelativisticGANs [JM18]. We can thus generally write a GAN formulation as follows:

$$\min_{\phi} L_D(\phi, \boldsymbol{\theta}); \qquad \min_{\boldsymbol{\theta}} L_G(\phi, \boldsymbol{\theta}). \tag{26.43}$$

We recover the zero-sum formulations if $-L_D(\phi, \boldsymbol{\theta}) = L_G(\phi, \boldsymbol{\theta}) = V(\phi, \boldsymbol{\theta})$. Despite departing from the zero-sum structure, the nested form of the optimization remains in the general formulation, as we will discuss in Section 26.3.2.

The loss functions for the discriminator and generator, L_D and L_G respectively, follow the general form in Equation 26.5, which allows them to be used to efficiently train implicit generative models. The majority of loss functions considered here can thus be written as follows:

$$L_D(\phi, \boldsymbol{\theta}) = \mathbb{E}_{p^*(\boldsymbol{x})} g(D_{\phi}(\boldsymbol{x})) + \mathbb{E}_{q_{\theta}(\boldsymbol{x})} h(D_{\phi}(\boldsymbol{x})) = \mathbb{E}_{p^*(\boldsymbol{x})} g(D_{\phi}(\boldsymbol{x})) + \mathbb{E}_{q(\boldsymbol{z})} h(D_{\phi}(G_{\boldsymbol{\theta}}(\boldsymbol{z}))) \tag{26.44}$$

$$L_G(\phi, \boldsymbol{\theta}) = \mathbb{E}_{q_{\theta}(\boldsymbol{x})} l(D_{\phi}(\boldsymbol{x})) = \mathbb{E}_{q(\boldsymbol{z})} l(D_{\phi}(G_{\boldsymbol{\theta}}(\boldsymbol{z}))) \tag{26.45}$$

where $g, h, l : \mathbb{R} \to \mathbb{R}$. We recover the original GAN for $g(t) = -\log t$, $h(t) = -\log(1 - t)$ and $l(t) = \log(1 - t)$; the non-saturating loss for $g(t) = -\log t$, $h(t) = -\log(1 - t)$ and $l(t) = -\log(t)$; the Wasserstein distance formulation for $g(t) = t$, $h(t) = -t$ and $l(t) = t$; for f-divergences $g(t) = t$, $h(t) = -f^{\dagger}(t)$ and $l(t) = f^{\dagger}(t)$.

26.3.2 Gradient descent

GANs employ the learning principles discussed above in conjunction with gradient based learning for the parameters of the discriminator and generator. We assume a general formulation with a discriminator loss function $L_D(\phi, \boldsymbol{\theta})$ and a generator loss function $L_G(\phi, \boldsymbol{\theta})$. Since the discriminator is often introduced to approximate a distance or divergence $D(p^*, q_{\theta})$ (Section 26.2), for the generator to minimize a good approximation of that divergence one should solve the discriminator optimization fully for each generator update. That would entail that for each generator update one would first find the optimal discriminator parameters $\phi^* = \operatorname{argmin}_{\phi} L_D(\phi, \boldsymbol{\theta})$ in order to perform a gradient update given by $\nabla_{\boldsymbol{\theta}} L_G(\phi^*, \boldsymbol{\theta})$. Fully solving the inner optimization problem $\phi^* = \operatorname{argmin}_{\phi} L_D(\phi, \boldsymbol{\theta})$

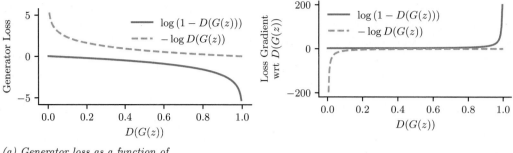

(a) Generator loss as a function of discriminator score.

(b) The gradients of the generator loss with respect to the discriminator score.

Figure 26.5: *Saturating* $\log(1 - D(G(z)))$ *vs non-saturating* $-\log D(G(z))$ *loss functions. The non-saturating loss provides stronger gradients when the discriminator is easily detecting that generated samples are fake. Generated by* gan_loss_types.ipynb

for each optimization step of the generator is computationally prohibitive, which motivates the use of alternating updates: performing a few gradient steps to update the discriminator parameters, followed by a generator update. Note that when updating the discriminator, we keep the generator parameters fixed, and when updating the generator, we keep the discriminator parameters fixed. We show a general algorithm for these alternative updates in Algorithm 26.1.

Algorithm 26.1: General GAN training algorithm with alternating updates

---

1 Initialize ϕ, θ
2 **for** *each training iteration* **do**
3   **for** K *steps* **do**
4   Update the discriminator parameters ϕ using the gradient $\nabla_\phi L_D(\phi, \theta)$;
5   Update the generator parameters θ using the gradient $\nabla_\theta L_G(\phi, \theta)$
6 Return ϕ, θ

We are thus interested in computing $\nabla_\phi L_D(\phi, \theta)$ and $\nabla_\theta L_G(\phi, \theta)$. Given the choice of loss functions follows the general form in Equations 26.44 and 26.45 both for the discriminator and generator, we can compute the gradients that can be used for training. To compute the discriminator gradients, we write:

$$\nabla_\phi L_D(\phi, \theta) = \nabla_\phi \left[\mathbb{E}_{p^*(\boldsymbol{x})} g(D_\phi(\boldsymbol{x})) + \mathbb{E}_{q_\theta(\boldsymbol{x})} h(D_\phi(\boldsymbol{x})) \right] \tag{26.46}$$

$$= \mathbb{E}_{p^*(\boldsymbol{x})} \nabla_\phi g(D_\phi(\boldsymbol{x})) + \mathbb{E}_{q_\theta(\boldsymbol{x})} \nabla_\phi h(D_\phi(\boldsymbol{x})) \tag{26.47}$$

where $\nabla_\phi g(D_\phi(\boldsymbol{x}))$ and $\nabla_\phi h(D_\phi(\boldsymbol{x}))$ can be computed via backpropagation, and each expectation can be estimated using Monte Carlo estimation. For the generator, we would like to compute the gradient:

$$L_G(\phi, \theta) = \nabla_\theta \mathbb{E}_{q_\theta(\boldsymbol{x})} l(D_\phi(\boldsymbol{x})) \tag{26.48}$$

Here we cannot change the order of differentiation and integration since the distribution under the integral depends on the differentiation parameter $\boldsymbol{\theta}$. Instead, we will use that $q_\theta(\boldsymbol{x})$ is the distribution induced by an implicit generative model (also known as the "reparameterization trick", see Section 6.3.5):

$$\nabla_{\boldsymbol{\theta}} L_G(\boldsymbol{\phi}, \boldsymbol{\theta}) = \nabla_{\boldsymbol{\theta}} \mathbb{E}_{q_\theta(\boldsymbol{x})} l(D_\phi(\boldsymbol{x})) = \nabla_{\boldsymbol{\theta}} \mathbb{E}_{q(\boldsymbol{z})} l(D_\phi(G_{\boldsymbol{\theta}}(\boldsymbol{z}))) = \mathbb{E}_{q(\boldsymbol{z})} \nabla_{\boldsymbol{\theta}} l(D_\phi(G_{\boldsymbol{\theta}}(\boldsymbol{z}))) \quad (26.49)$$

and again use Monte Carlo estimation to approximate the gradient using samples from the prior $q(\boldsymbol{z})$. Replacing the choice of loss functions and Monte Carlo estimation in Algorithm 26.1 leads to Algorithm 26.2, which is often used to train GANs.

Algorithm 26.2: GAN training algorithm

---

1 Initialize $\boldsymbol{\phi}, \boldsymbol{\theta}$
2 **for** *each training iteration* **do**
3   **for** *K steps* **do**
4   Sample minibatch of M noise vectors $\boldsymbol{z}_m \sim q(\boldsymbol{z})$
5   Sample minibatch of M examples $\boldsymbol{x}_m \sim p^*(\boldsymbol{x})$
6   Update the discriminator by performing stochastic gradient descent using this gradient:
            $\nabla_\phi \frac{1}{M} \sum_{m=1}^{M} [g(D_\phi(\boldsymbol{x}_m)) + \nabla_\phi h(D_\phi(G_{\boldsymbol{\theta}}(\boldsymbol{z}_m)))]$.
7   Sample minibatch of M noise vectors $\boldsymbol{z}_m \sim q(\boldsymbol{z})$
8   Update the generator by performing stochastic gradient descent using this gradient:
         $\nabla_{\boldsymbol{\theta}} \frac{1}{M} \sum_{m=1}^{M} l(D_\phi(G_{\boldsymbol{\theta}}(\boldsymbol{z}_m)))$.
9 Return $\boldsymbol{\phi}, \boldsymbol{\theta}$

26.3.3 Challenges with GAN training

Due to the adversarial game nature of GANs the optimizing dynamics of GANs are both hard to study in theory, and to stabilize in practice. GANs are known to suffer from **mode collapse**, a phenomenon where the generator converges to a distribution which does not cover not all the modes (peaks) of the data distribution, thus the model underfits the distribution. We show an example in Figure 26.6: while the data is a mixture of Gaussians with 16 modes, the model converges only to a few modes. Alternatively, another problematic behavior is **mode hopping**, where the generator "hops" between generating different modes of the data distribution. An intuitive explanation for this behavior is as follows: if the generator becomes good at generating data from one mode, it will generate more from that mode. If the discriminator cannot learn to distinguish between real and generated data in this mode, the generator has no incentive to expand its support and generate data from other modes. On the other hand, if the discriminator eventually learns to distinguish between the real and generated data inside this mode, the generator can simply move (hop) to a new mode, and this game of cat and mouse can continue.

While mode collapse and mode hopping are often associated with GANs, many improvements have made GAN training more stable, and these behaviors more rare. These improvements include using large batch sizes, increasing the discriminator neural capacity, using discriminator and generator regularization, as well as more complex optimization methods.

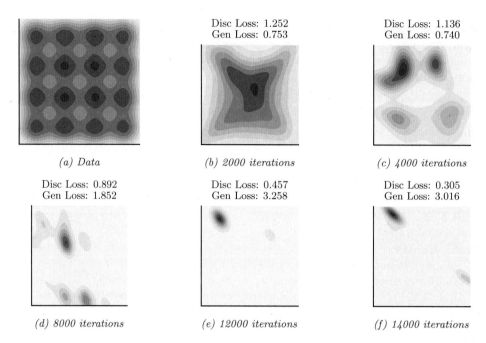

Figure 26.6: *Illustration of mode collapse and mode hopping in GAN training. (a) The dataset, a mixture of 16 Gaussians in 2 dimensions. (b-f) Samples from the model after various amounts of training. Generated by* gan_mixture_of_gaussians.ipynb.

26.3.4   Improving GAN optimization

Hyperparameter choices such as the choice of momentum can be crucial when training GANs, with lower momentum values being preferred compared to the usual high momentum used in supervised learning. Algorithms such as Adam [KB14a] provide a great boost in performance [RMC16a]. Many other optimization methods have been successfully applied to GANs, such as those which target variance reduction [Cha+19c]; those which backpropagate through gradient steps, thus ensuring that generator does well against the discriminator *after it has been updated* [Met+16]; or using a local bilinear approximation of the two player game [SA19]. While promising, these advanced optimization methods tend to have a higher computational cost, making them harder to scale to large models or large datasets compared to less efficient optimization methods.

26.3.5   Convergence of GAN training

The challenges with GAN optimization make it hard to quantify when convergence has occurred. In Section 26.2 we saw how global convergence guarantees can be provided under optimality conditions for multiple objectives constructed starting with different distributional divergences and distances: if the discriminator is optimal, the generator is minimizing a distributional divergence or distance between the data and model distribution, and thus under infinite capacity and perfect optimization can learn the data distribution. This type of argument has been used since the original GAN paper [Goo+14] to connect GANs to standard objectives in generative models, and obtain the associated theoretical guarantees. From a game theory perspective, this type of convergence guarantee provides an existence proof of a global Nash equilibrium for the GAN game, though under strong assumptions. A Nash equilibrium is achieved when both players (the discriminator and generator) would incur a loss if they decide to act by changing their parameters. Consider the original GAN defined by the objective in Equation 26.19; then $q_\theta = p^*$ and $D_\phi(x) = \frac{p^*(x)}{p^*(x)+q_\theta(x)} = \frac{1}{2}$ is a global Nash equilibrium, since for a given q_θ, the ratio $\frac{p^*(x)}{p^*(x)+q_\theta(x)}$ is the optimal discriminator (Equation 26.11), and given an optimal discriminator, the data distribution is the optimal generator as it is the minimizer of the Jensen-Shannon divergence (Equation 26.15).

While these global theoretical guarantees provide useful insights about the GAN game, they do not account for optimization challenges that arise with accounting for the optimization trajectories of the two players, or for neural network parameterization since they assume infinite capacity both for the discriminator and generator. In practice GANs do not decrease a distance or divergence at every optimization step [Fed+18] and global guarantees are difficult to obtain when using optimization methods such as gradient descent. Instead, the focus shifts towards local convergence guarantees, such as reaching a local Nash equilibrium. A local Nash equilibrium requires that both players are at a local, not global minimum: a local Nash equilibrium is a stationary point (the gradients of the two loss functions are zero, i.e $\nabla_\phi L_D(\phi, \theta) = 0$ and $\nabla_\theta L_G(\phi, \theta) = 0$), and the eigenvalues of the Hessian of each player ($\nabla_\phi \nabla_\phi L_D(\phi, \theta)$ and $\nabla_\theta \nabla_\theta L_G(\phi, \theta)$) are non-negative; for a longer discussion on Nash equilibria in continuous games, see [RBS16]. For the general GAN game, it is not guaranteed that a local Nash equilibrium always exists [FO20], and weaker conditions such as stationarity or locally stable stationarity have been studied [Ber+19]; other equilibrium definitions inspired by game theory have also been used [JNJ20; HLC19].

To motivate why convergence analysis is important in the case of GANs, we visualize an example of a GAN that does not converge trained with gradient descent. In DiracGAN [MGN18a] the data distribution $p^*(x)$ is the Dirac delta distribution with mass at zero. The generator is modeling a Dirac delta distribution with parameter θ: $G_\theta(z) = \theta$ and the discriminator is a linear function of the input with learned parameter ϕ: $D_\phi(x) = \phi x$. We also assume a GAN formulation where $g = h = -l$ in the general loss functions L_D and L_G defined above, see Equations (26.44) and (26.45). This results in the zero-sum game given by:

$$L_D = \mathbb{E}_{p^*(x)} - l(D_\phi(x)) + \mathbb{E}_{q_\theta(x)} - l(D_\phi(x)) = -l(0) - l(\theta\phi) \tag{26.50}$$
$$L_G = \mathbb{E}_{p^*(x)} l(D_\phi(x)) + \mathbb{E}_{q_\theta(x)} l(D_\phi(x)) = +l(0) + l(\theta\phi) \tag{26.51}$$

where l depends on the GAN formulation used ($l(z) = -\log(1 + e^{-z})$ for instance). The unique equilibrium point is $\theta = \phi = 0$. We visualize the DiracGAN problem in Figure 26.7 and show that DiracGANs with alternating gradient descent (Algorithm 26.1) do not reach the equilibrium point, but instead takes a circular trajectory around the equilibrium.

There are two main theoretical approaches taken to understand GAN convergence behavior around an equilibrium: by analyzing either the discrete dynamics of gradient descent, or the underlying continuous dynamics of the game using approaches such as stability analysis. To understand the difference between the two approaches, consider the discrete dynamics defined by gradient descent

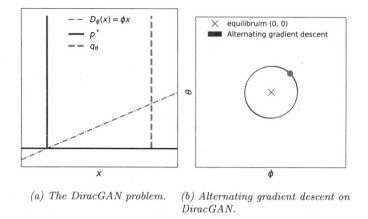

(a) The DiracGAN problem.   (b) Alternating gradient descent on
                              DiracGAN.

Figure 26.7: Visualizing divergence using a simple GAN: DiracGAN. Generated by dirac_gan.ipynb

with learning rates αh and λh, either via alternating updates (as we have seen in Algorithm 26.1):

$$\phi_t = \phi_{t-1} - \alpha h \nabla_\phi L_D(\phi_{t-1}, \theta_{t-1}), \tag{26.52}$$

$$\theta_t = \theta_{t-1} - \lambda h \nabla_\theta L_G(\phi_t, \theta_{t-1}) \tag{26.53}$$

or simultaneous updates, where instead of alternating the gradient updates between the two players, they are both updated simultaneously:

$$\phi_t = \phi_{t-1} - \alpha h \nabla_\phi L_D(\phi_{t-1}, \theta_{t-1}), \tag{26.54}$$

$$\theta_t = \theta_{t-1} - \lambda h \nabla_\theta L_G(\phi_{t-1}, \theta_{t-1}) \tag{26.55}$$

The above dynamics of gradient descent are obtained using Euler numerical integration from the ODEs that describes the game dynamics of the two players:

$$\dot{\phi} = -\nabla_\phi L_D(\phi, \theta), \tag{26.56}$$

$$\dot{\theta} = -\nabla_\theta L_G(\phi, \theta) \tag{26.57}$$

One approach to understand the behavior of GANs is to study these underlying ODEs, which, when discretized, result in the gradient descent updates above, rather than directly studying the discrete updates. These ODEs can be used for stability analysis to study the behavior around an equilibrium. This entails finding the eigenvalues of the Jacobian of the game

$$J = \begin{bmatrix} -\nabla_\phi \nabla_\phi L_D(\phi, \theta) & -\nabla_\theta \nabla_\phi L_D(\phi, \theta) \\ -\nabla_\phi \nabla_\theta L_G(\phi, \theta) & -\nabla_\theta \nabla_\theta L_G(\phi, \theta) \end{bmatrix} \tag{26.58}$$

evaluated at a stationary point (i.e., where $\nabla_\phi L_D(\phi, \theta) = 0$ and $\nabla_\theta L_G(\phi, \theta) = 0$). If the eigenvalues of the Jacobian all have negative real parts, then the system is asymptotically stable around the equilibrium; if at least one eigenvalue has positive real part, the system is unstable around the

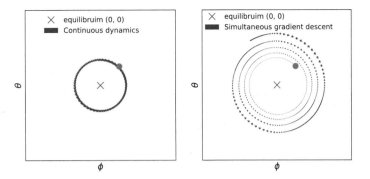

Figure 26.8: *Continuous (left) and discrete dynamics (right) take different trajectories in DiracGAN. Generated by* dirac_gan.ipynb

equilibrium. For the DiracGAN, the Jacobian evaluated at the equilibrium $\theta = \phi = 0$ is:

$$J = \begin{bmatrix} \nabla_\phi \nabla_\phi l(\theta\phi) + l(0) & \nabla_\theta \nabla_\phi l(\theta\phi) + l(0) \\ -\nabla_\phi \nabla_\theta (l(\theta\phi) + l(0)) & -\nabla_\theta \nabla_\theta (l(\theta\phi) + l(0)) \end{bmatrix} = \begin{bmatrix} 0 & l'(0) \\ -l'(0) & 0 \end{bmatrix} \tag{26.59}$$

where eigenvalues of this Jacobian are $\lambda_\pm = \pm i l'(0)$. This is interesting, as the real parts of the eigenvalues are both 0; this result tells us that there is no asymptotic convergence to an equilibrium, but linear convergence could still occur. In this simple case we can reach the conclusion that convergence does not occur as we observe that there is a preserved quantity in this system, as $\theta^2 + \phi^2$ does not change in time (Figure 26.8, left):

$$\frac{d\left(\theta^2 + \phi^2\right)}{dt} = 2\theta \frac{d\theta}{dt} + 2\phi \frac{d\phi}{dt} = -2\theta l'(\theta\phi)\phi + 2\phi l'(\theta\phi)\theta = 0.$$

Using stability analysis to understand the underlying continuous dynamics of GANs around an equilibrium has been used to show that explicit regularization can help convergence [NK17; Bal+18]. Alternatively, one can directly study the updates of simultaneous gradient descent shown in Equations 26.54 and 26.55. Under certain conditions, [MNG17b] prove that GANs trained with simultaneous gradient descent reach a local Nash equilibrium. Their approach relies on assessing the convergence of series of the form $F^k(\boldsymbol{x})$ resulting from the repeated application of gradient descent update of the form $F(\boldsymbol{x}) = \boldsymbol{x} + hG(\boldsymbol{x})$, where h is the learning rate. Since the function F depends on the learning rate h, their convergence results depend on the size of the learning rate, which is not the case for continuous time approaches.

Both continuous and discrete approaches have been useful in understanding and improving GAN training; however, both approaches still leave a gap between our theoretical understanding and the most commonly used algorithms to train GANs in practice, such as alternating gradient descent or more complex optimizers used in practice, like Adam. Far from only providing different proof techniques, these approaches can reach different conclusions about the convergence of a GAN: we show an example in Figure 26.8, where we see that simultaneous gradient descent and the continuous dynamics behave differently when a large enough learning rate is used. In this case, the discretization error — the difference between the behavior of the continuous dynamics in Equations 26.56 and 26.57

and the gradient descent dynamics in Equations 26.54 and 26.55 — makes the analysis of gradient descent using continuous dynamics reach the wrong conclusion about DiracGAN [Ros+21]. This difference in behavior has been a motivator to train GANs with higher order numerical integrators such as RungeKutta4, which to more closely follow the underlying continuous system compared to gradient descent [Qin+20].

While optimization convergence analysis is an indispensable step in understanding GAN training and has led to significant practical improvements, it is worth noting that ensuring converge to an equilibrium does not ensure the model has learned a good fit of the data distribution. The loss landscape determined by the choice of L_D and L_G, as well as the parameterization of the discriminator and generator can lead to equilibria which do not capture the data distribution. The lack of distributional guarantees provided by game equilibria showcases the need to complement convergence analysis with work looking at the effect of gradient based learning in this game setting on the learned distribution.

26.4   Conditional GANs

We have thus far discussed how to use implicit generative models to learn a true unconditional distribution $p^*(\boldsymbol{x})$ from which we only have samples. It is often useful, however, to be able to learn *conditional distributions* of the from $p^*(\boldsymbol{x}|\boldsymbol{y})$. This requires having **paired data**, where each input $\boldsymbol{x}_n$ is paired with a corresponding set of covariates $\boldsymbol{y}_n$, such as a class label, or a set of attributes or words, so $\mathcal{D} = \{(\boldsymbol{x}_n, \boldsymbol{y}_n) : n = 1 : N\}$, as in standard supervised learning. The conditioning variable can be discrete, like a class label, or continuous, such as an embedding which encodes other information. Conditional generative models are appealing since we can specify that we want the generated sample to be associated with conditioning information y, making them very amenable to real world applications, as we discuss in Section 26.7.

To be able to learn implicit conditional distributions $q_\theta(\boldsymbol{x}|\boldsymbol{y})$, we require datasets that specify the conditioning information associated with data, and we have to adapt the model architectures and loss functions. In the GAN case, changing the loss function for the generative model can be done by changing the critic, since the critic is part of the loss function of the generator; it is important for the critic to provide learning signal accounting for conditioning information, by penalizing a generator which provides realistic samples but which ignore the provided conditioning.

If we do not change the form of the min-max game, but provide the conditioning information to the two players, a **conditional GAN** can be created from the original GAN game [MO14]:

$$\min_{\boldsymbol{\theta}} \max_{\boldsymbol{\phi}} \frac{1}{2}\mathbb{E}_{p(\boldsymbol{y})}\mathbb{E}_{p^*(\boldsymbol{x}|\boldsymbol{y})}[\log D_{\boldsymbol{\phi}}(\boldsymbol{x},\boldsymbol{y})] + \frac{1}{2}\mathbb{E}_{p(\boldsymbol{y})}\mathbb{E}_{q_\theta(\boldsymbol{x}|\boldsymbol{y})}[\log(1 - D_{\boldsymbol{\phi}}(\boldsymbol{x},\boldsymbol{y}))] \tag{26.60}$$

In the case of implicit latent variable models, the embedding information becomes an additional input to the generator, together with the latent variable $\boldsymbol{z}$:

$$\min_{\boldsymbol{\theta}} \max_{\boldsymbol{\phi}} \mathcal{L}(\boldsymbol{\theta}, \boldsymbol{\phi}) = \frac{1}{2}\mathbb{E}_{p(\boldsymbol{y})}\mathbb{E}_{p^*(\boldsymbol{x}|\boldsymbol{y})}[\log D_{\boldsymbol{\phi}}(\boldsymbol{x},\boldsymbol{y})] + \frac{1}{2}\mathbb{E}_{p(\boldsymbol{y})}\mathbb{E}_{q(\boldsymbol{z})}[\log(1 - D_{\boldsymbol{\phi}}(\mathcal{G}_{\boldsymbol{\theta}}(\boldsymbol{z},\boldsymbol{y}),\boldsymbol{y}))] \tag{26.61}$$

For discrete conditioning information such as labels, one can also add a new loss function, by training a critic which does not only learn to distinguish between real and fake data, but learns to classify both data and generated samples as pertaining to one of the K classes provided in the

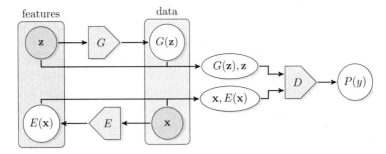

Figure 26.9: Learning an implicit posterior using an adversarial approach, as done in BiGAN. From Figure 1 of [DKD16]. Used with kind permission of Jeff Donahue.

dataset [OOS17]:

$$\mathcal{L}_c(\boldsymbol{\theta}, \boldsymbol{\phi}) = -\left[\frac{1}{2}\mathbb{E}_{p(\boldsymbol{y})}\mathbb{E}_{p^*(\boldsymbol{x}|\boldsymbol{y})}[\log D_\phi(\boldsymbol{y}|\boldsymbol{x})] + \frac{1}{2}\mathbb{E}_{p(\boldsymbol{y})}\mathbb{E}_{q_\theta(\boldsymbol{x}|\boldsymbol{y})}[\log(D_\phi(\boldsymbol{y}|\boldsymbol{x}))]\right] \quad (26.62)$$

Note that while we could have two critics, one unsupervised critic and one supervised which maximizes the equation above, in practice the same critic is used, to aid shaping the features used in both decision surfaces. Unlike the adversarial nature of the unsupervised game, it is in the interest of both players to minmize the classification loss $\mathcal{L}_c$. Thus together with the adversarial dynamics provided by $\mathcal{L}$, the two players are trained as follows:

$$\max_{\boldsymbol{\phi}} \mathcal{L}(\boldsymbol{\theta}, \boldsymbol{\phi}) - \mathcal{L}_c(\boldsymbol{\theta}, \boldsymbol{\phi}) \qquad\qquad \min_{\boldsymbol{\theta}} \mathcal{L}(\boldsymbol{\theta}, \boldsymbol{\phi}) + \mathcal{L}_c(\boldsymbol{\theta}, \boldsymbol{\phi}) \qquad (26.63)$$

In the case of conditional latent variable models, the latent variable controls the sample variability *inside* the mode specified by the conditioning information. In early conditional GANs, the conditioning information was provided as additional input to the discriminator and generator, for example by concatenating the conditioning information to the latent variable $\boldsymbol{z}$ in the case of the generator; it has been since observed that it is important to provide the conditioning information at various layers of the model, both for the generator and the discriminator [DV+17; DSK16] or use a projection discriminator [MK18].

26.5 Inference with GANs

Unlike other latent variable models such as variational autoencoders, GANs do not define an inference procedure associated with the generative model. To deploy the principles behind GANs to find a posterior distribution $p(\boldsymbol{z}|\boldsymbol{x})$, multiple approaches have been taken, from combining GANs and variational autoencoders via hybrid methods [MNG17a; Sri+17; Lar+16; Mak+15b] to constructing inference methods catered to implicit variable models [Dum+16; DKD16; DS19]. An overview of these methods can be found in [Hus17b].

GAN based methods which perform inference and learn **implicit posterior distribution** $p(\boldsymbol{z}|\boldsymbol{x})$ introduce changes to the GAN algorithm to do so. An example of such a method is **BiGAN** (bidirectional GAN) [DKD16] or **ALI** (adversarialy learned inference) [Dum+16], which trains an implicit parameterized encoder E_ζ to map input x to latent variables z. To ensure consistency between the encoder E_ζ and the generator G_θ, an adversarial approach is introduced with a discriminator D_ϕ learning to distinguish between pairs of data and latent samples: D_ϕ learns to consider pairs $(x, E_\zeta(x))$ with $x \sim p^*$ as real, while $(G_\theta(z), z)$ with $z \sim q(z)$ is considered fake. This approach, shown in Figure 26.9, ensures that the joint distributions are matched, and thus the marginal distribution $q_\theta(x)$ given by G_θ should learn $p^*(x)$, while the conditional distribution $p_\zeta(z|x)$ given by E_ζ should learn $q_\theta(z|x) = \frac{q_\theta(x,z)}{q_\theta(x)} \propto q_\theta(x|z)q(z)$. This joint GAN loss can be used both to train the generator G_θ and the encoder E_ζ, without requiring a reconstruction loss common in other inference methods. While not using a reconstruction loss, this objective retains the property that under global optimality conditions the encoder and decoder are inverses of each other: $E_\theta(G_\zeta(z)) = z$ and $G_\zeta(E_\theta(x)) = x$. (See also Section 21.2.4 for a discussion of how VAEs learn to ensure $p^*(x)p_\zeta(z|x)$ matches $p(z)p_\theta(x|z)$ using an explicit model of the data.)

26.6   Neural architectures in GANs

We have so far discussed the learning principles, algorithms, and optimization methods that can be used to train implicit generative models parameterized by deep neural networks. We have not discussed, however, the importance of the choice of neural network architectures for the model and the critic, choices which have fueled the progress in GAN generation since their conception. We will look at a few case studies which show the importance of information about data modalities into the critic and the generator (Section 26.6.1), employing the right inductive biases (Section 26.6.2), incorporating attention in GAN models (Section 26.6.3), progressive generation (Section 26.6.4), regularization (Section 26.6.5), and using large scale architectures (Section 26.6.6).

26.6.1   The importance of discriminator architectures

Since the discriminator or critic is rarely optimal — either due to the use of alternating gradient descent or the lack of capacity of the neural discriminator — GANs do not perform distance or divergence minimization in practice. Instead, the critic acts as part of a **learned loss function** for the model (the generator). Every time the critic is updated, the loss function for the generative model changes; this is in stark contrast with divergence minimization such maximum likelihood estimation, where the loss function stays the same throughout the training of the model. Just as learning features of data instead of handcrafting them is a reason for the success of deep learning methods, learning loss functions advanced the state of the art of generative modeling. Critics that take data modalities into account — such as convolutional critics for images and recurrent critics for sequential data such as text or audio — become part of data modality dependent loss functions. This in turn provides modality-specific learning signal to the model, for example by penalizing blurry images and encouraging sharp edges, which is achieved due to the convolutional parameterization of the critic. Even within the same data modality, changes to critic architectures and regularization have been one of the main drivers in obtaining better GANs, since they affect the generator's loss function, and thus also the *gradients of the generator* and have a strong effect on optimization.

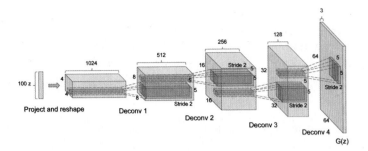

Figure 26.10: *DCGAN convolutional generator. From Figure 1 of [RMC15]. Used with kind permission of Alec Radford.*

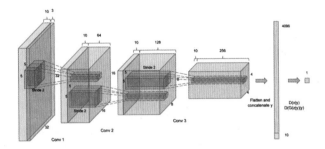

Figure 26.11: *DCGAN convolutional discrimiantor. From Figure 1 of [RMC15]. Used with kind permission of Alec Radford.*

26.6.2 Architectural inductive biases

While the original GAN paper used convolutions only sparingly, deep convolutional GAN (**DC-GAN**) [RMC15] performed an extensive study on what architectures are most useful for GAN training, resulting in a set of useful guidelines that led to a substantial boost in performance. Without changing the learning principles behind GANs, DCGAN was able to obtain better results on image data by using convolutional generators (Figure 26.10) and critics, using BatchNormalization for both the generator and critic, replacing pooling layers with strided convolutions, using ReLU activation networks in the generator, and LeakyReLU activations in the discriminator. Many of these principles are still in use today, for larger architectures and with various loss functions. Since DCGAN, residual convolutional layers have become a key staple of both models and critics for image data [Gul+17], and recurrent architectures are used for sequence data such as text [SSG18b; Md+19].

26.6.3 Attention in GANs

Attention mechanisms are explained in detail in Section 16.2.7. In this section, we discuss how to use them for both the GAN generator and discriminator; this is called the self attention GAN or **SAGAN** model [Zha+19c]. The advantage of self attention is that it ensures that both discriminator and generator have access to a *global* view of other units of the same layer, unlike convolutional

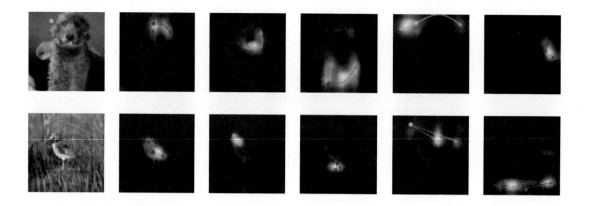

Figure 26.12: *Attention queries used by a SAGAN model, showcasing the global span of attention. Each row first shows the input image and a set of color coded query locations in the image. The subsequent images show the attention maps corresponding to each query location in the first image, with the query color coded location being shown, and arrows from it to the attention map are used to highlight the most attended regions. From Figure 1 of [Zha+19c]. Used with kind permission of Han Zhang.*

layers. This is illustrated in Figure 26.12, which visualizes the global span of attention: query points can attend to various other areas in the image.

The self-attention mechanism for convolutional features reshaped to $\boldsymbol{h} \in \mathbb{R}^{C \times N}$ is defined by $\boldsymbol{f} = W_f \boldsymbol{h}$, $\boldsymbol{g} = W_g \boldsymbol{h}$, $\mathbf{S} = \boldsymbol{f}^T \boldsymbol{g}$, where $W_f \in \mathbb{R}^{C' \times C}$, $W_g \in \mathbb{R}^{C' \times C}$, where $C' \leq C$ is a hyperparameter. From $\mathbf{S} \in \mathbb{R}^{N \times N}$, a probability row matrix β is obtained by applying the softmax operator for each row, which is then used to *attend* to a linear transformation of the features $\boldsymbol{o} = W_o(W_h \boldsymbol{h})\beta^T \in R^{C \times N}$, using learned operators $W_h \in \mathbb{R}^{C' \times C}$, $W_o \in \mathbb{R}^{C \times C'}$. An output is then created by $\boldsymbol{y} = \gamma \boldsymbol{o} + \boldsymbol{h}$, where $\gamma \in \mathbb{R}$ is a learned parameter.

Beyond providing global signal to the players, it is worth noting the flexibility of the self attention mechanism. The learned parameter γ ensures that the model can decide not to use the attention layer, and thus adding self attention does not restrict the set of possible models an architecture can learn. Moreover, self attention significantly increases the number of parameters of the model (each attention layer introduced 4 learned matrices $\mathbf{W}_f, \mathbf{W}_g, \mathbf{W}_h, \mathbf{W}_o$), an approach that has been observed as a fruitful way to improve GAN training.

26.6.4   Progressive generation

One of the first successful approaches to generating higher resolution, color images from a GAN is via an *iterative* process, by first generating a lower dimensional sample, and then using that as conditioning information to generate a higher dimensional sample, and repeating the process until the desired resolution is reached. **LapGAN** [DCF+15] uses a Laplacian pyramid as the iterative building block, by first upsampling the lower dimensional samples using a simple upsampling operation, such as smoothed upsampling, and then using a conditional generator to produce a residual to be added to the upsampled version to produce the higher resolution sample. In turn, this higher resolution sample can then be provided to another LapGAN layer to produce another, even higher resolution

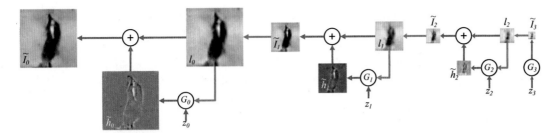

Figure 26.13: *LapGAN generation algorithm: the generation process starts with a low dimension sample, which gets upscaled and residually added to the output of a generator at a higher resolution. The process gets repeated multiple times. From Figure 1 of [DCF+15]. Used with kind permission of Emily Denton.*

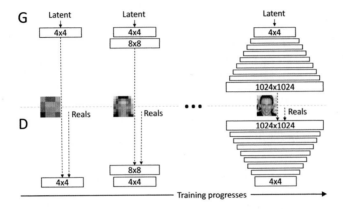

Figure 26.14: *ProgressiveGAN training algorithm. The input to the discriminator at the bottom of the figure is either a generated image, or a real image (denotes as 'Reals' in the figure) at the corresponding resolution. From Figure 1 of [Kar+18]. Used with kind permission of Tero Karras.*

sample, and so on — this process is shown in Figure 26.13. In LapGAN, a different generator and critic are trained for each iterative block of the model; in ProgressiveGAN [Kar+18] the lower resolution generator and critic are "grown", by becoming part of the generator and critic used to learn to generate higher resolution samples. The higher resolution generator is obtained by adding new layers on top of the last layer of the lower resolution generator. A residual connection between an upscaled version of the lower dimensional sample and the output of the newly created higher resolution generator is added, which is annealed from 0 to 1 in training — transitioning from using the upscaled version of the lower dimensional sample early in training, to only using the sample of the higher resolution generator at the end of training. A similar change is done to the discriminator. Figure 26.14 shows the growing generator and discriminators in ProgressiveGAN training.

26.6.5 Regularization

Regularizing both the discriminator and the generator has by now a long tradition in GAN training. Regularizing GANs can be justified from multiple perspectives: theoretically, as it has been shown to be tied to convergence analysis [MGN18b]; empirically, as it has been shown to help performance and stability in practice [RMC15; Miy+18c; Zha+19c; BDS18]; and intuitively, as it can be used to avoid overfitting in the discriminator and generator. Regularization approaches include adding noise to the discriminator input [AB17], adding noise to the discriminator and generator hidden features [ZML16], using BatchNorm for the two players [RMC15], adding dropout in the discriminator [RMC15], spectral normalization [Miy+18c; Zha+19c; BDS18], and gradient penalties (penalizing the norm of the discriminator gradient with respect to its input $\|\nabla_{\boldsymbol{x}} D_{\phi}(\boldsymbol{x})\|^2$) [Arb+18; Fed+18; ACB17; Gul+17]. Often regularization methods help training regardless of the type of loss function used, and have been shown to have effects both on training performance as well as the stability of the GAN game. However, improving stability and improving performance in GAN training can be at odds with each other, since too much regularization can make the models very stable but reduce performance [BDS18].

26.6.6   Scaling up GAN models

By combining many of the architectural tricks discussed thus far — very large residual networks, self attention, spectral normalization both in the discriminator and the generator, BatchNormalization in the generator — one can train GANs to generating diverse, high quality data, as done with BigGAN [BDS18], StyleGAN [Kar+20c], and alias-free GAN [Kar+21]. Beyond combining carefully chosen architectures and regularization, creating large scale GANs also require changes in optimization, with large batch sizes being a key component. This furthers the view that the key components of the GAN game — the losses, the parameterization of the models, and the optimization method — have to be viewed collectively rather than in isolation.

26.7   Applications

The ability to generate new plausible data enables a wide range of applications for GANs. This section will look at a set of applications that aim to demonstrate the breadth of GANs across different data modalities, such as images (Section 26.7.1), video (Section 26.7.2), audio (Section 26.7.3), and text (Section 26.7.4), and include applications such as imitation learning (Section 26.7.5), domain adapation (Section 26.7.6), and art (Section 26.7.7).

26.7.1   GANs for image generation

The most widely studied application area is in image generation. We focus on the translation of one image to another using either paired or unpaired datasets. There are many other topics related to image GANs that we do not cover, and a more complete overview can be found in other sources, such as [Goo16] for the theory and [Bro19] for the practice. A JAX notebook which uses a small pretrained GAN to generate some face images can be found at GAN_JAX_CelebA_demo.ipynb. We show the progression of quality in sample generation of faces using GANs in Figure 26.15. There is also increasing need to consider the generation of images with regards to the potential risks they can have when used in other domains, which involve discussions of synthetic media and **deep fakes**, and sources for discussion include [Bru+18; Wit].

Figure 26.15: Increasingly realistic synthetic faces generated by different kinds of GAN, specifically (from left to right): original GAN [Goo+14], DCGAN [RMC15], CoupledGAN [LT16], ProgressiveGAN [Kar+18], StyleGAN [KLA19]. Used with kind permission of Ian Goodfellow. An online demo, which randomly generates face images using StyleGAN, can be found at https://thispersondoesnotexist.com.

26.7.1.1 Conditional image generation

Class-conditional image generation using GANs has become a very fruitful endeavor. BigGAN [BDS18] carries out class-conditional generation of ImageNet samples across a variety of categories, from dogs and cats to volcanoes and hamburgers. StyleGAN [KLA19] is able to generate high quality images of faces at high resolution by learning a conditioning style vector and the ProgressiveGAN architecture discussed in Section 26.6.4. By learning the conditioning vector they are able to generate samples which interpolate between the styles of other samples, for example by preserving coarser style elements such as pose or face shape from one sample, and smaller scale style elements such as hair style from another; this provides fine grained control over the style of the generated images.

26.7.1.2 Paired image-to-image generation

We have discussed in Section 26.4 how using paired data of the form $(\boldsymbol{x}_n, \boldsymbol{y}_n)$ can be used to build conditional generative models of $p(\boldsymbol{x}|\boldsymbol{y})$. In some cases, the conditioning variable $\boldsymbol{y}$ has the same size and shape as the output variable $\boldsymbol{x}$. The resulting model $p_{\boldsymbol{\theta}}(\boldsymbol{x}|\boldsymbol{y})$ can then be used to perform **image to image translation**, as illustrated in Figure 26.16, where $\boldsymbol{y}$ is drawn from the **source domain**, and $\boldsymbol{x}$ from the **target domain**. Collecting paired data of this form can be expensive, but in some cases, we can acquire it automatically. One such example is image colorization, where a paired dataset can easily be obtained by processing color images into grayscale images (see e.g., [Jas]).

For a conditional GAN used for paired image-to-image translation was proposed in [Iso+17], and is known as the **pix2pix** model. It uses a U-net style architecture for the generator, as used for semantic segmentation tasks. However, they replace the batch normalization layers with instance normalization, as in neural style transfer.

For the discriminator, pix2pix uses a **patchGAN** model, that tries to classify local patches as being real or fake (as opposed to classifying the whole image). Since the patches are local, the discriminator is forced to focus on the style of the generated patches, and ensure they match the statistics of the target domain. A patch-level discriminator is also faster to train than a whole-image discriminator, and gives a denser feedback signal. This can produce results similar to Figure 26.16

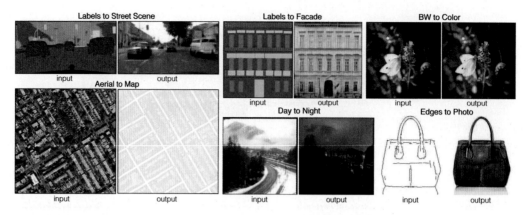

Figure 26.16: Example results on several image-to-image translation problems as generated by the pix2pix conditional GAN. From Figure 1 of [Iso+17]. Used with kind permission of Phillip Isola.

(depending on the dataset).

26.7.1.3   Unpaired image-to-image generation

A major drawback of conditional GANs is the need to collect paired data. It is often much easier to collect **unpaired data** of the form $\mathcal{D}_x = \{\boldsymbol{x}_n : n = 1 : N_x\}$ and $\mathcal{D}_y = \{\boldsymbol{y}_n : n = 1 : N_y\}$. For example, $\mathcal{D}_x$ might be a set of daytime images, and $\mathcal{D}_y$ a set of night-time images; it would be impossible to collect a paired dataset in which exactly the same scene is recorded during the day and night (except using a computer graphics engine, but then we wouldn't need to learn a generator).

We assume that the datasets $\mathcal{D}_x$ and $\mathcal{D}_y$ come from the marginal distributions $p(\boldsymbol{x})$ and $p(\boldsymbol{y})$ respectively. We would then like to fit a joint model of the form $p(\boldsymbol{x}, \boldsymbol{y})$, so that we can compute conditionals $p(\boldsymbol{x}|\boldsymbol{y})$ and $p(\boldsymbol{y}|\boldsymbol{x})$ and thus translate from one domain to another. This is called **unsupervised domain translation**.

In general, this is an ill-posed problem, since there are an infinite number of different joint distributions that are consistent with a set of marginals $p(\boldsymbol{x})$ and $p(\boldsymbol{y})$. We can try, however, to learn a joint distribution such that samples from it satisfy additional constraints. For example, if G is a conditional generator that maps a sample from $\mathcal{X}$ to $\mathcal{Y}$, and F maps a sample from $\mathcal{Y}$ to $\mathcal{X}$, it is reasonable to require that these be inverses of each other, i.e., $F(G(\boldsymbol{x})) = \boldsymbol{x}$ and $G(F(\boldsymbol{y})) = \boldsymbol{y}$. This is called a **cycle consistency** loss [Zhu+17]. We can encourage G and F to satisfy this constraint by using a penalty term on the difference between the starting image and the image we get after going through this cycle:

$$\mathcal{L}_{\text{cycle}} = \mathbb{E}_{p(\boldsymbol{x})}||F(G(\boldsymbol{x})) - \boldsymbol{x}||_1 + \mathbb{E}_{p(\boldsymbol{y})}||G(F(\boldsymbol{y})) - \boldsymbol{y}||_1 \qquad (26.64)$$

To ensure that the outputs of G are samples from $p(\boldsymbol{y})$ and those of F are samples from $p(\boldsymbol{x})$, we use a standard GAN approach, introducing discriminators D_X and D_Y, which can be done using any choice of GAN loss $\mathcal{L}_{\text{GAN}}$, as visualized in Figure 26.17. Finally, we can optionally check that applying the conditional generator to images from its own domain does not change them:

$$\mathcal{L}_{\text{identity}} = \mathbb{E}_{p(\boldsymbol{x})}||\boldsymbol{x} - F(\boldsymbol{x})||_1 + \mathbb{E}_{p(\boldsymbol{y})}||\boldsymbol{y} - G(\boldsymbol{y})||_1 \qquad (26.65)$$

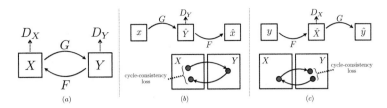

Figure 26.17: *Illustration of the CycleGAN training scheme. (a) Illustration of the 4 functions that are trained. (b) Forwards cycle consistency from $\mathcal{X}$ back to $\mathcal{X}$. (c) Backwards cycle consistency from $\mathcal{Y}$ back to $\mathcal{Y}$. From Figure 3 of [Zhu+17]. Used with kind permission of Jun-Yan Zhu.*

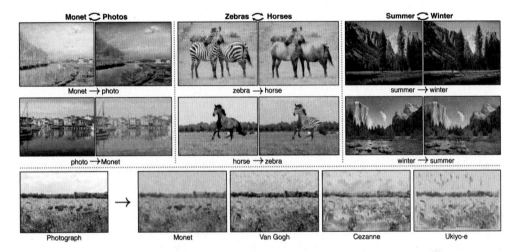

Figure 26.18: *Some examples of unpaired image-to-image translation generated by the CycleGAN model. From Figure 1 of [Zhu+17]. Used with kind permission of Jun-Yan Zhu.*

We can combine all three of these consistency losses to train the translation mappings F and G, using hyperparameters λ_1 and λ_2:

$$\mathcal{L} = \mathcal{L}_{\mathrm{GAN}} + \lambda_1 \mathcal{L}_{\mathrm{cycle}} + \lambda_2 \mathcal{L}_{\mathrm{identity}} \tag{26.66}$$

CycleGAN results on various datasets are shown in Figure 26.18. The bottom row shows how CycleGAN can be used for **style transfer**.

26.7.2 Video generation

The GAN framework can be expanded from individual images (frames) to videos; the techniques used to generate realistic images can also be applied to generate videos, with additional techniques required to ensure *spatio-temporal consistency*. Spatio-temporal consistency is obtained by ensuring that the discriminator has access to the real data and generated sequences in order, thus penalizing the generator when generating realistic individual frames without respecting temporal order [SMS17;

Sai+20; CDS19; Tul+18]. Another discriminator can be employed to additionally ensure each frame is realistic [Tul+18; CDS19]. The generator itself needs to have a temporal element, which is often implemented through a recurrent component. As with images, the generation framework can be expanded to video-to-video translation [Ban+18; Wan+18], encompassing applications such as motion transfer [Cha+19a].

26.7.3   Audio generation

Generative models have been demonstrated in the tasks of generating audio waveforms, as well as for the task of text-to-speech (TTS) generation. Other types of generative models, such as autoregressive models, such as WaveNet [oor+16] and WaveRNN [Kal+18b] have been developed for these applications, although autoregressive models are difficult to parallelize over time since they predict each time step of the audio sequentially and can be computationally expensive and too slow to be used in practice. GANs provide an alternative approach for these tasks and other paths for addressing these concerns.

Many different GAN architectures have been developed for audio-only generation, including generation of single note recordings from instruments by GANSynth, a vocoder model that uses GANs to generate magnitude spectrograms from mel-spectrograms [Eng+18], in voice conversion using a modified CycleGAN discussed above [Kan+20], and the direct generation of raw audio in WaveGAN [DMP18].

Initial work on GANs for TTS was developed [Yan+17] whose approach is similar to conditional GANs for image generation (see Section 26.7.1.2), but uses 1d convolution instead of 2d. More recent GANs such as GAN-TTS [Biń+19] use more advanced architectures and discriminators that operate at multiple frequency scales that have performance that now matches the best performing autoregressive models when assessed using mean opinion scores. In both the direct-audio generation, the ability of GANs to allow faster generation and different types of context is the advantage that makes them advantageous compared to other models.

26.7.4   Text generation

Similar to image and audio domains, there are several tasks for text data for which GAN-based approaches have been developed, including conditional text generation and text-style transfer. Text data are often represented as discrete values, at either the character level or the word-level, indicating membership within a set of a particular vocabulary size (alphabet size, or number of words). Due to the discrete nature of text, GAN models trained on text are *explicit*, since they explicitly model the probability distribution of the output, rather than modeling the sampling path. This is unlike most GAN models of continuous data such as images that we have discussed in the chapter so far, though explicit GANs of continuous data do exist [Die+19b].

The discrete nature of text is why maximum likelihood is one of the most common methods of learning generative models of text. However, models trained with maximum likelihood are often limited to autoregressive models, while like in the audio case, GANs make it possible to generate text in a non-autoregressive manner, making other tasks possible, such as one-shot feedforward generation [Gul+17].

The difficulty of generating discrete data such as text using GANs can be seen looking at their loss function, such as in Equations (26.19), (26.21) and (26.28). GAN losses contain terms of the form $\mathbb{E}_{q_\theta(x)} f(x)$, which we not only need to evaluate, but also backpropagate through, by computing $\nabla_\theta \mathbb{E}_{q_\theta(x)} f(x)$. In the case of implicit distributions given by latent variable models, we used the reparameterization trick to compute this gradient (Equation 26.49). In the discrete case, the reparameterization trick is not available and we have to look for other ways to estimate the desired gradient. One approach is to use the score function estimator, discussed in Section 6.3.4. However, the score function estimator exhibits high gradient variance, which can destabilize training. One common approach to avoid this issue is to pre-train the language model generator using maximum likelihood, and then to fine-tune with a GAN loss which gets backpropagated into the generator using the score-function estimator, as done by Sequence GAN [Yu+17], MaliGAN [Che+17], and RankGAN [Lin+17a]. While these methods spearheaded the use of GANs for text, they do not address the inherent instabilities of score function estimation and thus have to limit the amount of adversarial fine tuning to a small number of epochs and often use a small learning rate, keeping their performance close to that of the maximum-likelihood solution [SSG18a; Cac+18].

An alternative to maximum likelihood pretraining is to use other approaches to stabilize the score function estimator or to use continuous relaxations for backpropagation. ScratchGAN is a word-level model that uses large batch sizes and discriminator regularization to stabilize score function training (these techniques are the same that we have seen as stabilizers for training image GANs) [Md+19]. [Pre+17b] completely avoid the score function estimator and develop a character level model without pre-training, by using continuous relaxations and curriculum learning. These training approaches can also benefit from other architectural advances, e.g., [NNP19] showed that language GANs can benefit from complex architectures such as relation networks [San+17].

Finally, unsupervised text style transfer, mimicking image style transfer, have been proposed by [She+17; Fu+17] using adversarial classifiers to decode to a different style/language, or like [Pra+18] who trains different encoders, one per style, by combining the encoder of a pre-trained NMT and style classifiers, among other approaches.

26.7.5 Imitation learning

Imitation learning takes advantage of observations of expert demonstrations to learn action policies and reward functions of unknown environments by minimizing some form of discrepancy between the learned and the expert behaviors. There are many approaches available, including behavioral cloning [PPG91] that treats this problem as one of supervised learning, and inverse reinforcement learning [NR00b]. GANs are appealing for imitation learning since they provide a way to avoid the difficulty of designing good discrepancy functions for behaviors, and instead learn these discrepancy functions using a discriminator between trajectories generated by a learned agent and observed demonstrations.

This approach, known as generative adversarial imitation learning (**GAIL**) [HE16a] demonstrates the ability to use GANs for complex behaviors in high-dimensional environments. GAIL jointly learns a generator, which forms a stochastic policy, along with a discriminator that acts as a reward signal. Like we saw in the probabilistic development of GANs in the earlier sections, GAIL can also be generalized to multiple f-divergences, rather than the standard Jensen-Shannon divergence used as the standard loss in GANs. This has led to a family of other GAIL variants that use other f-divergences [Ke+19a; Fin+16; Bro+20c], including f-GAIL that aims to also learn the best f-divergence to use [Zha+20e], as well as new analytical insight into the computation and generalization of such approaches [Che+20b].

26.7.6 Domain adaptation

An important task in machine learning is to correct for shifts in the data distribution over time, minimizing some measure of domain shift, as we discuss in Section 19.5.3. Like with the other applications, GANs are popular as ways of avoiding the choice of distance or degree of shift. Both the supervised and unsupervised approaches for image generation we reviewed earlier looked at pixel-level domain adaptation models that perform distribution alignment in raw pixel space, translating source data to the style of a target domain, as with pix2pix and CycleGAN. Extensions of these approaches for the general problem of domain adaptation seek to do this not only in the observed data space (e.g., with pixels), but also at the feature level. One general approach is domain-adversarial training of neural networks [Gan+16b] or adversarial discriminative domain adaptation (ADDA) [Tze+17]. The CyCADA approach of [Hof+18] extends CycleGAN by enforcing both structural and semantic consistency during adaptation using a cycle-consistency loss and semantics losses based on a particular visual recognition task. There are also many extensions that include class conditional information [Tsa+18; Lon+18] or adaptation when the modes to be matched have different frequencies in the source and target domains [BHC19].

26.7.7 Design, art and creativity

Generative models, particularly of images, have added to approaches in the more general area of algorithmic art. The applications in image and audio generation with transfer can also be considered aspects of artistic image generation. In these cases, the goal of training is not generalization, but to create appealing images across different types of visual aesthetics [Sar18]. One example takes style transfer GANs to create visual experiences, in which objects placed under a video are re-rendered using other visual styles in real time [AFG19]. The generation ability has been used to explore alternative designs and fabrics in fashion [Kat+19], and have now also become part of major drawing software to provide new tools to support designers [Ado]. And beyond images, creative and artistic expression using GANs include areas in music, voice, dance, and typography [AI 19].

PART V

Discovery

27 Discovery methods: an overview

27.1 Introduction

We have seen in Part III how to create probabilistic models that can make predictions about outputs given inputs, using supervised learning methods (conditional likelihood maximization). And we have seen in Part IV how to create probabilistic models that can generate outputs unconditionally, using unsupervised learning methods (unconditional likelihood maximization). However, in some settings, our goal is to try to *understand* a given dataset. That is, we want to *discover* something "interesting", and possibly "actionable". Prediction and generation are useful subroutines for discovery, but are not sufficient on their own. In particular, although neural networks often implicitly learn useful features from data, they are often hard to interpret, and the results can be unstable and sensitive to arbitrary details of the training protocol (e.g., SGD learning rates, or random seeds).

In this part of the book, we focus on learning models that create an interpretable representation of high dimensional data. A common approach is to use a **latent variable model**, in which we make the assumption that the observed data x was caused by, or generated by, some underlying (often low dimensional) **latent factors** z, which represents the "true" state of the world. Crucially, these latent variables are assumed to be meaningful to the end user of the model. (Thus evaluating such models will generally require domain expertise.)

For example, suppose we want to interpret an image x in terms of an underlying 3d scene, z, which is represented in terms of objects and surfaces. The **forwards mapping** from z to x is often many-to-one, i.e., different latent values, say z and z', may give rise to the same observation x, due to limitations of the sensor. (This is called **perceptual aliasing**.) Consequently the inverse mapping, from x to z, is ill-posed. In such cases, we need to impose a prior, $p(z)$, to make our estimate well-defined. In simple settings, we can use a point estimate, such as the MAP estimate

$$\hat{z}(x) = \operatorname*{argmax}_{z} p(z|x) = \operatorname*{argmax}_{z} \log p(z) + \log p(x|z) \qquad (27.1)$$

In the context of computer vision, this approach is known as **vision as inverse graphics** or **analysis by synthesis** [KMY04; YK06; Doy+07; MC19]. See Figure 27.1 for an illustration.

This approach to inverse modeling is widely used in science and engineering, where z represents the underlying state of the world which we want to estimate, and x is just a noisy or partial manifestation of this true state. In some cases, we know both the prior $p(z|\theta)$ and the likelihood $p(x|z,\theta)$, and we just need to solve the inference problem for z. But more commonly, the model parameters θ are also (partially) unknown, and need to be inferred from observable samples $\mathcal{D} = \{x_n : n = 1 : N\}$. In some cases, the structure of the model itself is unknown and needs to be learned.

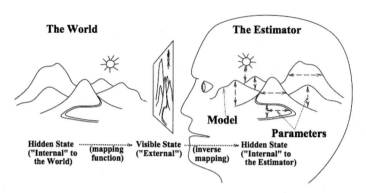

Figure 27.1: *Vision as inverse graphics. The agent (here represented by a human head) has to infer the scene z given the image x using an estimator. From Figure 1 of [Rao99]. Used with kind permission of Rajesh Rao.*

27.2   Overview of Part V

In Chapter 28, we discuss simple latent variable models where typically the observed data is a fixed-dimensional vector such as $x \in \mathbb{R}^D$. In Chapter 29 we extend these models to work with sequences of correlated vectors, $x = x_{1:T}$, such as speech, video, genomics data, etc. It is straightforward to make parts of these model be nonlinear ("deep"), as we discuss. These models can also be extended to the spatio-temporal setting. In Chapter 30, we extend these models to work with general graphs.

In Chapter 31, we discuss non-parametric Bayesian models, which allow us to represent uncertainty about many aspects of a model, such as the number of hidden states, the structure of the model, the form of a functional dependency, etc. Thus the complexity of the learned representation can grow dynamically, depending on the quantity and quality (informativeness) of the data. This is important when performing discovery tasks, and helps us maintain flexibility while still retaining interpretability.

In Chapter 32, we discuss representation learning using neural networks. This can be tackled using latent variable modeling, but there are also a variety of other estimation methods one can use. Finally, in Chapter 33, we discuss how to interpret the behavior of a predictive model (typically a neural network).

28 Latent factor models

28.1 Introduction

A **latent variable model** (**LVM**) is any probabilistic model in which some variables are always latent or hidden. A simple example is a mixture model (Section 28.2), which has the form $p(\boldsymbol{x}) = \sum_k p(\boldsymbol{x}|z=k)p(z=k)$, where z is an indicator variable that specifies which mixture component to use for generating $\boldsymbol{x}$. However, we can also use continuous latent variables, or a mixture of discrete and continuous. And we can also have multiple latent variables, which are interconnected in complex ways.

In this chapter, we discuss a very simple kind of LVM that has the following form:

$$\boldsymbol{z} \sim p(\boldsymbol{z}) \tag{28.1}$$
$$\boldsymbol{x}|\boldsymbol{z} \sim \text{Expfam}(\boldsymbol{x}|f(\boldsymbol{z})) \tag{28.2}$$

where $f(\boldsymbol{z})$ is known as the **decoder**, and $p(\boldsymbol{z})$ is some kind of prior. We assume that $\boldsymbol{z}$ is a single "layer" of hidden random variables, corresponding to a set of "latent factors". We call these **latent factor models**. In this chapter, we assume the decoder f is a simple linear model; we consider nonlinear extensions in Chapter 21. Thus the overall model is similar to a GLM (Section 15.1), except the input to the model is hidden.

We can create a large variety of different "classical" models by changing the form of the prior $p(\boldsymbol{z})$ and/or the likelihood $p(\boldsymbol{x}|\boldsymbol{z})$, as we show in Table 28.1. We will give the details in the following sections. (Note that, although we are discussing generative models, our focus is on posterior inference of meaningful latents (discovery), rather than generating realistic samples of data.)

28.2 Mixture models

One way to create more complex probability models is to take a convex combination of simple distributions. This is called a **mixture model**. This has the form

$$p(\boldsymbol{x}|\boldsymbol{\theta}) = \sum_{k=1}^{K} \pi_k p_k(\boldsymbol{x}) \tag{28.3}$$

where p_k is the k'th mixture component, and π_k are the mixture weights which satisfy $0 \leq \pi_k \leq 1$ and $\sum_{k=1}^{K} \pi_k = 1$.

We can re-express this model as a hierarchical model, in which we introduce the discrete **latent variable** $z \in \{1, \ldots, K\}$, which specifies which distribution to use for generating the output $\boldsymbol{x}$. The

Model	$p(\boldsymbol{z})$	$p(\boldsymbol{x}|\boldsymbol{z})$	Section
FA/PCA	$\mathcal{N}(\boldsymbol{z}|\boldsymbol{0},\mathbf{I})$	$\mathcal{N}(\boldsymbol{x}|\mathbf{W}\boldsymbol{z},\boldsymbol{\Psi})$	Section 28.3.1
GMM	$\sum_c \mathrm{Cat}(c|\boldsymbol{\pi})\mathcal{N}(\boldsymbol{z}|\boldsymbol{\mu}_c,\boldsymbol{\Sigma}_c)$	$\mathcal{N}(\boldsymbol{x}|\mathbf{W}\boldsymbol{z},\boldsymbol{\Psi})$	Section 28.2.4
MixFA	$\mathrm{Cat}(c|\boldsymbol{\pi})\mathcal{N}(\boldsymbol{z}|\boldsymbol{0},\mathbf{I})$	$\mathcal{N}(\boldsymbol{x}|\mathbf{W}_c\boldsymbol{z}+\boldsymbol{\mu}_c,\boldsymbol{\Psi}_c)$	Section 28.3.3.5
NMF	$\prod_k \mathrm{Ga}(z_k|\alpha_k,\beta_k)$	$\prod_d \mathrm{Poi}(x_d|\exp(\boldsymbol{w}_d^\mathsf{T}\boldsymbol{z})))$	Section 28.4.1
Simplex FA (mPCA)	$\mathrm{Dir}(\boldsymbol{z}|\boldsymbol{\alpha})$	$\prod_d \mathrm{Cat}(x_d|\mathbf{W}_d\boldsymbol{z})$	Section 28.4.2
LDA	$\mathrm{Dir}(\boldsymbol{z}|\boldsymbol{\alpha})$	$\prod_d \mathrm{Cat}(x_d|\mathbf{W}\boldsymbol{z})$	Section 28.5
ICA	$\prod_d \mathrm{Laplace}(z_d|\lambda)$	$\prod_d \delta(x_d-\boldsymbol{w}_d^\mathsf{T}\boldsymbol{z})$	Section 28.6
Sparse coding	$\prod_k \mathrm{Laplace}(z_k|\lambda)$	$\prod_d \mathcal{N}(x_d|\boldsymbol{w}_d^\mathsf{T}\boldsymbol{z},\sigma^2)$	Section 28.6.5

Table 28.1: Some popular "shallow" latent factor models. Abbreviations: FA = factor analysis, PCA = principal components analysis, GMM = Gaussian mixture model, NMF = non-negative matrix factorization, mPCA = multinomial PCA, LDA = latent Dirichlet allocation, ICA = independent components analysis. $k = 1:L$ ranges over latent dimensions, $d = 1:D$ ranges over observed dimensions. (For ICA, we have the constraint that $L = D$.)

prior on this latent variable is $p(z = k) = \pi_k$, and the conditional is $p(\boldsymbol{x}|z = k) = p_k(\boldsymbol{x}) = p(\boldsymbol{x}|\boldsymbol{\theta}_k)$. That is, we define the following joint model:

$$p(z|\boldsymbol{\theta}) = \mathrm{Cat}(z|\boldsymbol{\pi}) \tag{28.4}$$

$$p(\boldsymbol{x}|z = k, \boldsymbol{\theta}) = p(\boldsymbol{x}|\boldsymbol{\theta}_k) \tag{28.5}$$

The "generative story" for the data is that we first sample a specific component z, and then we generate the observations $\boldsymbol{x}$ using the parameters chosen according to the value of z. By marginalizing out z, we recover Equation (28.3):

$$p(\boldsymbol{x}|\boldsymbol{\theta}) = \sum_{k=1}^{K} p(z = k|\boldsymbol{\theta})p(\boldsymbol{x}|z = k, \boldsymbol{\theta}) = \sum_{k=1}^{K} \pi_k p(\boldsymbol{x}|\boldsymbol{\theta}_k) \tag{28.6}$$

We can create different kinds of mixture model by varying the base distribution p_k, as we illustrate below.

28.2.1   Gaussian mixture models (GMMs)

A **Gaussian mixture model** or **GMM**, also called a **mixture of Gaussians (MoG)**, is defined as follows:

$$p(\boldsymbol{x}) = \sum_{k=1}^{K} \pi_k \mathcal{N}(\boldsymbol{x}|\boldsymbol{\mu}_k, \boldsymbol{\Sigma}_k) \tag{28.7}$$

In Figure 28.1 we show the density defined by a mixture of 3 Gaussians in 2d. Each mixture component is represented by a different set of elliptical contours. If we let the number of mixture components grow sufficiently large, a GMM can approximate any smooth distribution over $\mathbb{R}^D$.

GMMs are often used for unsupervised **clustering** of real-valued data samples $\boldsymbol{x}_n \in \mathbb{R}^D$. This works in two stages. First we fit the model, usually by computing the MLE $\hat{\boldsymbol{\theta}} = \mathrm{argmax} \log p(\mathcal{D}|\boldsymbol{\theta})$,

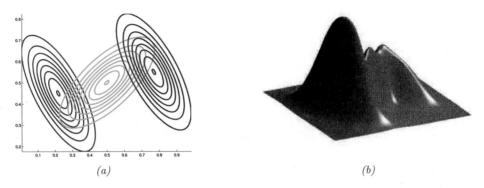

(a) (b)

Figure 28.1: A mixture of 3 Gaussians in 2d. (a) We show the contours of constant probability for each component in the mixture. (b) A surface plot of the overall density. Adapted from Figure 2.23 of [Bis06]. Generated by gmm_plot_demo.ipynb.

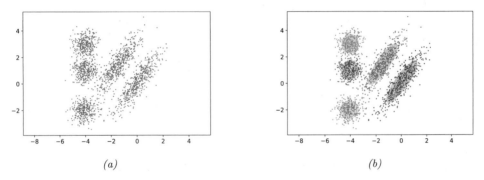

(a) (b)

Figure 28.2: (a) Some data in 2d. (b) A possible clustering using $K = 5$ clusters computed using a GMM. Generated by gmm_2d.ipynb.

where $\mathcal{D} = \{\boldsymbol{x}_n : n = 1 : N\}$ (e.g., using EM or SGD). Then we associate each datapoint $\boldsymbol{x}_n$ with a discrete latent or hidden variable $z_n \in \{1, \ldots, K\}$ which specifies the identity of the mixture component or cluster which was used to generate $\boldsymbol{x}_n$. These latent identities are unknown, but we can compute a posterior over them using Bayes' rule:

$$r_{nk} \triangleq p(z_n = k | \boldsymbol{x}_n, \boldsymbol{\theta}) = \frac{p(z_n = k | \boldsymbol{\theta}) p(\boldsymbol{x}_n | z_n = k, \boldsymbol{\theta})}{\sum_{k'=1}^{K} p(z_n = k' | \boldsymbol{\theta}) p(\boldsymbol{x}_n | z_n = k', \boldsymbol{\theta})} \tag{28.8}$$

The quantity r_{nk} is called the **responsibility** of cluster k for datapoint n. Given the responsibilities, we can compute the most probable cluster assignment as follows:

$$\hat{z}_n = \arg\max_k r_{nk} = \arg\max_k \left[\log p(\boldsymbol{x}_n | z_n = k, \boldsymbol{\theta}) + \log p(z_n = k | \boldsymbol{\theta}) \right] \tag{28.9}$$

This is known as **hard clustering**. (If we use the responsibilities to fractionally assign each datapoint to different clusters, it is called **soft clustering**.) See Figure 28.2 for an example.

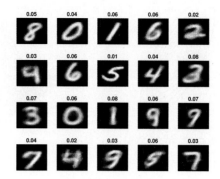

Figure 28.3: We fit a mixture of 20 Bernoullis to the binarized MNIST digit data. We visualize the estimated cluster means $\hat{\boldsymbol{\mu}}_k$. The numbers on top of each image represent the estimated mixing weights $\hat{\pi}_k$. No labels were used when training the model. Generated by mix_bernoulli_em_mnist.ipynb.

If we have a uniform prior over z_n, and we use spherical Gaussians with $\boldsymbol{\Sigma}_k = \mathbf{I}$, the hard clustering problem reduces to

$$z_n = \underset{k}{\operatorname{argmin}} \, ||\boldsymbol{x}_n - \hat{\boldsymbol{\mu}}_k||_2^2 \tag{28.10}$$

In other words, we assign each datapoint to its closest centroid, as measured by Euclidean distance. This is the basis of the K-means clustering algorithm (see the prequel to this book).

28.2.2 Bernoulli mixture models

If the data is binary valued, we can use a **Bernoulli mixture model** (BMM), also called a **mixture of Bernoullis**, where each mixture component has the following form:

$$p(\boldsymbol{x}|z = k, \boldsymbol{\theta}) = \prod_{d=1}^{D} \operatorname{Ber}(y_d|\mu_{dk}) = \prod_{d=1}^{D} \mu_{dk}^{y_d}(1 - \mu_{dk})^{1-y_d} \tag{28.11}$$

Here μ_{dk} is the probability that bit d turns on in cluster k.

For example, consider fitting a mixture of Bernoullis using $K = 20$ components to the MNIST dataset. The resulting parameters for each mixture component (i.e., $\boldsymbol{\mu}_k$ and π_k) are shown in Figure 28.3. We see that the model has "discovered" a representation of each type of digit. (Some digits are represented multiple times, since the model does not know the "true" number of classes. See Section 3.8.1 for information on how to choose the number K of mixture components.)

28.2.3 Gaussian scale mixtures (GSMs)

A **Gaussian scale mixture** or **GSM** [AM74; Wes87] is like an "infinite" mixture of Gaussians, each with a different scale (variance). More precisely, let $x = \epsilon z$, where $z \sim \mathcal{N}(0, \sigma_0^2)$ and $\epsilon \sim p(\epsilon)$. We can think of this as **multiplicative noise** being applied to the Gaussian rv z. We have $x|\epsilon \sim \mathcal{N}(0, \epsilon^2 \sigma_0^2)$. Marginalizing out the scale ϵ gives

$$p(x) = \int \mathcal{N}(x|0, \sigma_0^2 \epsilon^2) p(\epsilon) d\epsilon \tag{28.12}$$

By changing the prior $p(\epsilon)$, we can create various interesting distributions. We give some examples below.

The main advantage of this approach is that it is often computationally more convenient to work with the **expanded parameterization**, in which we explicitly include the scale term ϵ, since, conditional on that, the distribution is Gaussian. We use this formulation in Section 6.5.5, where we discuss robust regression.

28.2.3.1 Student-t distribution as a GSM

We can represent the Student distribution as a GSM as follows:

$$\mathcal{T}(x|0, \sigma^2, \nu) = \int_0^\infty \mathcal{N}(x|0, z\sigma^2) \mathrm{IG}(z|\frac{\nu}{2}, \frac{\nu}{2}) dz = \int_0^\infty \mathcal{N}(x|0, z\sigma^2) \chi^{-2}(z|\nu, 1) dz \tag{28.13}$$

where IG is the inverse Gamma distribution (Section 2.2.3.4). Thus we can think of the Student as an infinite superposition of Gaussians of different widths; marginalizing this out induces a distribution with wider tails than a Gaussian with the same variance. This result also explains why the Student distribution approaches a Gaussian as the dof gets large, since when $\nu = \infty$, the inverse Gamma distribution becomes a delta function.

28.2.3.2 Laplace distribution as a GSM

Similarly one can show that the Laplace distribution is an infinite weighted sum of Gaussians, where the precision comes from a gamma distribution:

$$\mathrm{Laplace}(x|0, \lambda) = \int \mathcal{N}(x|0, \tau^2) \mathrm{Ga}(\tau^2|1, \frac{\lambda^2}{2}) d\tau^2 \tag{28.14}$$

28.2.3.3 Spike and slab distribution

Suppose $\epsilon \sim \mathrm{Ber}(\pi)$. (Note that $\epsilon^2 = \epsilon$, since $\epsilon \in \{0, 1\}$.) In this case we have

$$x = \sum_{\epsilon \in \{0,1\}} \mathcal{N}(x|0, \sigma_0^2 \epsilon) p(\epsilon) = \pi \mathcal{N}(x|0, \sigma_0^2) + (1 - \pi) \delta_0(x) \tag{28.15}$$

This is known as the **spike and slab** distribution, since the $\delta_0(x)$ is a "spike" at 0, and the $\mathcal{N}(x|0, \sigma_0^2)$ acts like a uniform "slab" for large enough σ_0. This distribution is useful in sparse modeling.

28.2.3.4 Horseshoe distribution

Suppose $\epsilon \sim \mathcal{C}_+(1)$, which is the half-Cauchy distribution (see Section 2.2.2.4). Then the induced distribution $p(x)$ is called the **horseshoe distribution** [CPS10]. This has a spike at 0, like the

Figure 28.4: Example of recovering a clean image (right) from a corrupted version (left) using MAP estimation with a GMM patch prior and Gaussian likelihood. First row: image denoising. Second row: image deblurring. Third row: image inpainting. From [RW15] and [ZW11]. Used with kind permission of Dan Rosenbaum and Daniel Zoran.

Student and Laplace distributions, but has heavy tails that do not asymptote to zero. This makes it useful as a sparsity promoting prior, that "kills off" small parameters, but does not overregularize large parameters.

28.2.4 Using GMMs as a prior for inverse imaging problems

In this section, we consider using GMMs as a blackbox density model to regularize the inversion of a many-to-one mapping. Specifically, we consider the problem of inferring a "clean" image x from a corrupted version y. We use a linear-Gaussian forwards model of the form

$$p(\boldsymbol{y}|\boldsymbol{x}) = \mathcal{N}(\boldsymbol{y}|\mathbf{W}\boldsymbol{x}, \sigma^2\mathbf{I}) \tag{28.16}$$

where σ^2 is the variance of the measurement noise. The form of the matrix $\mathbf{W}$ depends on the nature of the corruption, which we assume is known, for simplicity. Here are some common examples of different kinds of corruption we can model in our approach:

- If the corruption is due to additive noise (as in Figure 28.4a), we can set $\mathbf{W} = \mathbf{I}$. The resulting MAP estimate can be used for **image denoising**, as in Figure 28.4b.

- If the corruption is due to blurring (as in Figure 28.4c), we can set $\mathbf{W}$ to be a fixed convolutional kernel [KF09b]. The resulting MAP estimate can be used for **image deblurring**, as in Figure 28.4d.

- If the corruption is due to occlusion (as in Figure 28.4e), we can set $\mathbf{W}$ to be a diagonal matrix, with 0s in the locations corresponding to the occluders. The resulting MAP estimate can be used for **image inpainting**, as in Figure 28.4f.

- If the corruption is due to downsampling, we can set $\mathbf{W}$ to a convolutional kernel. The resulting MAP estimate can be used for **image super-resolution**.

Thus we see that the linear-Gaussian likelihood model is surprisingly flexible. Given the model, our goal is to invert it, by computing the MAP estimate $\hat{\boldsymbol{x}} = \operatorname{argmax} p(\boldsymbol{x}|\boldsymbol{y})$. However, the problem of inverting this model is ill-posed, since there are many possible latent images $\boldsymbol{x}$ that map to the same observed image $\boldsymbol{y}$. Therefore we need to use a prior to regularize the inversion process.

In [ZW11], they propose to partition the image into patches, and to use a GMM prior of the form $p(\boldsymbol{x}_i) = \sum_k p(c_i = k)\mathcal{N}(\boldsymbol{x}_i|\boldsymbol{\mu}_k, \boldsymbol{\Sigma}_k)$ for each patch i. They use $K = 200$ mixture components, and they fit the GMM on a dataset of 2M clean image patches.

To compute the MAP mixture component, c_i^*, we can marginalize out $\boldsymbol{x}_i$ and use Equation (2.129) to compute the marginal likelihood

$$c_i^* = \operatorname*{argmax}_c p(c)p(\boldsymbol{y}_i|c) = \operatorname*{argmax}_c p(c)\mathcal{N}(\boldsymbol{y}_i|\mathbf{W}\boldsymbol{\mu}_c, \sigma^2\mathbf{I} + \mathbf{W}\boldsymbol{\Sigma}_c\mathbf{W}^\mathsf{T}) \tag{28.17}$$

We can then approximate the MAP for the latent patch $\boldsymbol{x}_i$ by using the approximation

$$p(\boldsymbol{x}_i|\boldsymbol{y}_i) \approx p(\boldsymbol{x}_i|\boldsymbol{y}_i, c_i^*) \propto \mathcal{N}(\boldsymbol{x}_i|\boldsymbol{\mu}_{c_i^*}, \boldsymbol{\Sigma}_{c_i^*})\mathcal{N}(\boldsymbol{y}_i|\mathbf{W}\boldsymbol{x}_i, \sigma^2\mathbf{I}) \tag{28.18}$$

If we know c_i^*, we can compute the above using Bayes' rule for Gaussians in Equation (2.121).

To apply this method to full images, [ZW11] optimize the following objective

$$E(\boldsymbol{x}|\boldsymbol{y}) = \frac{1}{2\sigma^2}||\mathbf{W}\boldsymbol{x} - \boldsymbol{y}||^2 - \text{EPLL}(\boldsymbol{x}) \tag{28.19}$$

where **EPLL** is the "**expected patch log likelihood**", given by

$$\text{EPLL}(\boldsymbol{x}) = \sum_i \log p(\mathbf{P}_i\boldsymbol{x}) \tag{28.20}$$

where $\boldsymbol{x}_i = \mathbf{P}_i\boldsymbol{x}$ is the i'th patch computed by projection matrix $\mathbf{P}_i$. Since these patches overlap, this is not a valid likelihood, since it overcounts the pixels. Nevertheless, optimizing this objective (using a method called "half quadratic splitting") works well empirically. See Figure 28.4 for some examples of this process in action.

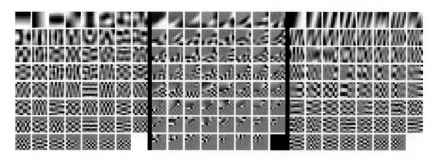

Figure 28.5: Illustration of the parameters learned by a GMM applied to image patches. Each of the 3 panels corresponds to a different mixture component k. Within each panel, we show the eigenvectors (reshaped as images) of the covariance matrix Σ_k in decreasing order of eigenvalue. We see various kinds of patterns, including ones that look like the ones learned from PCA (see Figure 28.34), but also ones that look like edges and texture. From Figure 6 of [ZW11]. Used with kind permission of Daniel Zoran.

A more principled solution to the overlapping patch problem is to use a multiscale model, as proposed in [PE16]. Another approach, proposed in [FW21], uses Gibbs sampling to combine samples from overlapping patches. This approach has the additional advantage of computing posterior samples from $p(\boldsymbol{x}|\boldsymbol{y})$, which can look much better than the posterior mean or mode computed by optimization methods. (For example, if the corruption process removes the color from the latent image $\boldsymbol{x}$ to create a gray scale $\boldsymbol{y}$, then the posterior MAP estimate of $\boldsymbol{x}$ will also be a gray scale image, whereas posterior samples will be color images.) See also Section 28.3.3.5 where we show how to extend the GMM model to a mixture of low rank Gaussians, which lets us directly model images instead of image patches.

28.2.4.1   Why does the method work?

To understand why such a simple model of image patches works so well, note that the log prior for a single latent image patch $\boldsymbol{x}_i$ using mixture component k can be written as follows:

$$\log p(\boldsymbol{x}_i|c_i = k) = \log \mathcal{N}(\boldsymbol{x}_i|\boldsymbol{0}, \boldsymbol{\Sigma}_k) = -\boldsymbol{x}_i^\mathsf{T}\boldsymbol{\Sigma}_k^{-1}\boldsymbol{x}_i + a_k \tag{28.21}$$

where a_k is a constant that depends on k but is independent of $\boldsymbol{x}_i$. Let $\boldsymbol{\Sigma}_k = \mathbf{V}_k\boldsymbol{\Lambda}_k\mathbf{V}_k^\mathsf{T}$ be an eigendecomposition of $\boldsymbol{\Sigma}_k$, where $\lambda_{k,d}$ is the d'th eigenvalue of $\boldsymbol{\Sigma}_k$, and $\boldsymbol{v}_{k,d}$ is the d'th eigenvector. Then we can rewrite the above as follows:

$$\log p(\boldsymbol{x}_i|c_i = k) = -\sum_{d=1}^{D} \frac{1}{\lambda_{k,d}}(\boldsymbol{v}_{k,d}^\mathsf{T}\boldsymbol{x}_i)^2 + a_k \tag{28.22}$$

Thus we see that the eigenvectors are acting like templates. Each mixture component has a different set of templates, each with their own weight (eigenvalue), as illustrated in Figure 28.5. By mixing these together, we get a powerful model for the statistics of natural image patches. (See [ZW12] for more analysis of why this simple model works so well, based on the "**dead leaves**" model of image formation.)

28.2.4.2 Speeding up inference using discriminative models

Although simple and effective, computing $f(\boldsymbol{y}) = \operatorname{argmax}_{\boldsymbol{x}} p(\boldsymbol{x}|\boldsymbol{y})$ for each image patch can be slow if the image is large. However, every time we solve this problem, we can store the result, and build up a dataset of $(\boldsymbol{y}, f(\boldsymbol{y}))$ pairs. We can then train an amortized inference network (Section 10.1.5) to learn this $\boldsymbol{y} \to f(\boldsymbol{y})$ mapping, to speed up future inferences, as proposed in [RW15]. (See also [Par+19] for further speedup tricks.)

An alternative approach is to dispense with the generative model, and to train on an artificially created dataset of the form $(\boldsymbol{y}, \boldsymbol{x})$, where $\boldsymbol{x}$ is a clean natural image, and $\boldsymbol{y} = C(\boldsymbol{x})$ is an artificial corruption of it. We can then train a discriminative model $\hat{f}(\boldsymbol{y})$ directly from $(\boldsymbol{y}, \boldsymbol{x})$ pairs. This technique works very well (see e.g., [Luc+18]), but is limited by the form of corruptions C it is trained on. This means we need to train a different network for every linear operator $\mathbf{W}$, and sometimes even for every different noise level σ^2.

28.2.4.3 Blind inverse problems

In the discussion above, we assumed the forwards model had the form $p(\boldsymbol{y}|\boldsymbol{x}, \boldsymbol{\theta}) = \mathcal{N}(\boldsymbol{y}|\mathbf{W}\boldsymbol{x}, \sigma^2 \mathbf{I})$, where $\mathbf{W}$ is known. If $\mathbf{W}$ is not known, then computing $p(\boldsymbol{x}|\boldsymbol{y})$ is known as a **blind inverse problem**.

Such problems are much harder to solve. One approach is to estimate the parameters of the forwards model, $\mathbf{W}$, and the latent image, $\boldsymbol{x}$, using an EM-like method from a set of images coming from the same likelihood function. That is, we alternate between estimating $\hat{\boldsymbol{x}} = \operatorname{argmax}_{\boldsymbol{x}} p(\boldsymbol{x}|\boldsymbol{y}, \hat{\mathbf{W}})$ in the E step, and estimating $\hat{\mathbf{W}} = \operatorname{argmax}_{\mathbf{W}} p(\boldsymbol{y}|\hat{\boldsymbol{x}}, \mathbf{W})$ in the M step. Some encouraging results of this approach are shown in [Ani+18]. (They use a GAN prior for $p(\boldsymbol{x})$ rather than a GMM.)

In cases where we get two independent noisy samples, $\boldsymbol{y}_1$ and $\boldsymbol{y}_2$, generated from the same underlying image $\boldsymbol{x}$, then we can avoid having to explicitly learn an image prior $p(\boldsymbol{x})$, and can instead directly learn an estimator for the posterior mode, $f(\boldsymbol{y}) = \operatorname{argmax}_{\boldsymbol{x}} p(\boldsymbol{x}|\boldsymbol{y})$, without needing access to the latent image $\boldsymbol{x}$, by exploiting a form of cycle consistency; see [XC19] for details.

28.2.5 Using mixture models for classification problems

It is possible to use mixture models to define the class-conditional density $p(\boldsymbol{x}|y = c)$ in a generative classifier. We can then derive the class posterior using Bayes' rule:

$$p(y = c|\boldsymbol{x}) = \frac{p(y = c)p(\boldsymbol{x}|y = c)}{\sum_{c'} p(y = c)p(\boldsymbol{x}|y = c)} = \frac{p(y = c)p(\boldsymbol{x}|y = c)}{Z} \tag{28.23}$$

where $p(y = c) = \pi_c$ is the prior on class label c, Z is the normalization constant, and the form of $p(\boldsymbol{x}|y = c)$ depends on the kind of data we have. For real-valued features, it is common to use a GMM:

$$p(\boldsymbol{x}|y = c) = \sum_{k=1}^{K_c} \alpha_{c,k} \mathcal{N}(\boldsymbol{x}|\mu_{c,k}, \boldsymbol{\Sigma}_{c,k}) \tag{28.24}$$

Using a generative model to perform classification can be useful when we have missing data, since we can compute $p(\boldsymbol{x}^v|y = c) = \sum_{\boldsymbol{x}^m} p(\boldsymbol{x}^m, \boldsymbol{x}^v|y = c)$ to compute the marginal likelihood of the visible features $\boldsymbol{x}^v$. It is also useful for semi-supervised learning, since we can optimize the model to fit $\sum_n \log p(\boldsymbol{x}_n^l, y_n^l)$ on the labeled data and $\sum_n \log p(\boldsymbol{x}_n^u)$ on the unlabeled data.

28.2.5.1   Hybrid generative/discriminative training

Unfortunately the classification accuracy of generative models of the form $p(\boldsymbol{x}, y)$ can be much worse than discriminative (conditional) models of the form $p(y|\boldsymbol{x})$, since the latter are directly optimized to predict the labels given the features, and don't "waste" capacity on modeling irrelevant details of the inputs. (For a more in-depth discussion of generative vs discriminative classifiers, see e.g., [Mur22, Sec 9.4].)

Fortunately it is possible to train generative models in a discriminative fashion, which can close the performance gap with conditional models, while maintaining the advantages of generative models. In particular, we can optimize the following hybrid objective, proposed in [BT04; Rot+18]:

$$\mathcal{L}(\boldsymbol{\theta}) = -\lambda \underbrace{\sum_{n=1}^{N} \log p(\boldsymbol{x}_n, y_n | \boldsymbol{\theta})}_{\mathcal{L}_{\text{gen}}(\boldsymbol{\theta})} - (1 - \lambda) \underbrace{\sum_{n=1}^{N} \log p(y_n | \boldsymbol{x}_n, \boldsymbol{\theta})}_{\mathcal{L}_{\text{dis}}(\boldsymbol{\theta})} \tag{28.25}$$

where $0 \leq \lambda \leq 1$ controls the tradeoff between generative and discriminative modeling.

If we have unlabeled data, we can modify the generative loss as shown below:

$$\mathcal{L}_{\text{gen}}(\boldsymbol{\theta}) = \kappa \sum_{n=1}^{N^l} \log p(\boldsymbol{x}_n^l, y_n^l | \boldsymbol{\theta}) + (1 - \kappa) \sum_{n=1}^{N^u} \log p(\boldsymbol{x}_n^u | \boldsymbol{\theta}) \tag{28.26}$$

Here we have introduced an extra trade-off parameter $0 \leq \kappa \leq 1$ to prevent the unlabeled data from overwhelming the labeled data (if $N_u \gg N_l$), as proposed in [Nig+00].

An alternative to changing the objective function is to change the model itself, so that we parameterize the joint using $p(\boldsymbol{x}, y) = p(y|\boldsymbol{x}, \boldsymbol{\theta})p(\boldsymbol{x}|\tilde{\boldsymbol{\theta}})$, and then define different kinds of joint priors $p(\boldsymbol{\theta}, \tilde{\boldsymbol{\theta}})$; see [LBM06; BL07a] for details.

28.2.5.2   Optimization issues

To optimize the loss, we need to reparameterize the model into unconstrained form. For the class prior, we can use $\pi_{1:C} = \text{softmax}(\tilde{\pi}_{1:C})$, and optimize wrt the logits $\tilde{\pi}_{1:C}$. Similarly for the mixture weights $\alpha_{c,1:K}$. The means $\boldsymbol{\mu}_{ck}$ are already unconstrained. For the covariance matrices, we will use a diagonal plus low-rank representation, to reduce the number of parameters:

$$\boldsymbol{\Sigma}_{c,k} = \text{diag}(\boldsymbol{d}_{c,k}) + \mathbf{S}_{c,k}\mathbf{S}_{c,k}^{\mathsf{T}} \tag{28.27}$$

where $\mathbf{S}_{c,k}$ is an unconstrained $D \times R$ matrix, where $R \ll D$ is the rank of the approximation. (For numerical stability, we usually add $\epsilon \mathbf{I}$ to the above expression, to ensure $\boldsymbol{\Sigma}_{c,k}$ is positive definite for all parameter settings.) To ensure positivity of the diagonal term, we can use the softplus transform, $d_{c,k} = \log(1 + \exp(\tilde{d}_{c,k}))$, and optimize wrt the $\tilde{d}_{c,k}$ terms.

28.2.5.3   Numerical issues

To compute the class conditional log likelihood, $\ell_c = \log p(\boldsymbol{x}|y = c)$, we can use the **log-sum-exp trick** to avoid numerical underflow. Define $\tilde{\alpha}_{ck} = \log \alpha_{ck}$ and $\ell_{ck} = \log \mathcal{N}(\boldsymbol{x}|\boldsymbol{\mu}_{ck}, \boldsymbol{\Sigma}_{ck})$. Then we have

$$\ell_c = \log p(\boldsymbol{x}|y = c) = \log \sum_k e^{\tilde{\alpha}_{ck} + \ell_{ck}} \tag{28.28}$$

$$= e^M \log \sum_k e^{\tilde{\alpha}_{ck} + \ell_{ck} - M} \triangleq \text{logsumexp}(\{\tilde{\alpha}_{ck} + \ell_{ck}\}_k) \tag{28.29}$$

where $M = \max_k \tilde{\alpha}_{ck} + \ell_{ck}$.

We can use a similar method to compute the posterior over classes. We have

$$p(y = c|\boldsymbol{x}) = \frac{\pi_c e^{\ell_c}}{Z} = \frac{\pi_c e^{\ell_c - L}}{e^{-L} Z} = \frac{\pi_c e^{\tilde{\ell}_c}}{\tilde{Z}} \tag{28.30}$$

where $L = \max_c \ell_c$, $\tilde{\ell}_c = \ell_c - L$, and $\tilde{Z} = \sum_c \pi_c e^{\tilde{\ell}_c}$. This lets us combine the class prior probability π_c with the scaled class conditional log likelihood $\tilde{\ell}_c$ to get the class posterior in a stable way. (We can also compute the log normalization constant, $\log p(\boldsymbol{x}) = \log Z = \log(\tilde{Z}) + L$.)

To compute a single Gaussian log density, $\ell_{ck} = \log \mathcal{N}(\boldsymbol{x}|\boldsymbol{\mu}_{ck}, \boldsymbol{\Sigma}_{ck})$, we need to evaluate $\log \det(\boldsymbol{\Sigma}_{ck})$ and $\boldsymbol{\Sigma}_{ck}^{-1}$. To make this efficient, we can use the matrix determinant lemma to compute

$$\det(\mathbf{A} + \mathbf{S}\mathbf{S}^\mathsf{T}) = \det(\mathbf{I} + \mathbf{S}^\mathsf{T}\mathbf{A}^{-1}\mathbf{S}) \det(\mathbf{A}) \tag{28.31}$$

where $\mathbf{A} = \text{diag}(\boldsymbol{d}) + \epsilon\mathbf{I}$, and the matrix inversion lemma to compute

$$(\mathbf{A} + \mathbf{S}\mathbf{S}^\mathsf{T})^{-1} = \mathbf{A}^{-1} - \mathbf{A}^{-1}\mathbf{S}(\mathbf{I} + \mathbf{S}^\mathsf{T}\mathbf{A}^{-1}\mathbf{S})^{-1}\mathbf{S}^\mathsf{T}\mathbf{A}^{-1} \tag{28.32}$$

(See also the discussion of mixture of factor analyzers in Section 28.3.3.)

28.3 Factor analysis

In this section, we discuss a simple latent factor model in which the prior $p(\boldsymbol{z})$ is Gaussian, and the likelihood $p(\boldsymbol{x}|\boldsymbol{z})$ is also Gaussian, using a linear decoder for the mean. This family includes many important special cases, such as PCA, as we discuss below. We also briefly discuss some simple extensions.

28.3.1 Factor analysis: the basics

Factor analysis corresponds to the following linear-Gaussian latent variable generative model:

$$p(\boldsymbol{z}) = \mathcal{N}(\boldsymbol{z}|\boldsymbol{\mu}_0, \boldsymbol{\Sigma}_0) \tag{28.33}$$

$$p(\boldsymbol{x}|\boldsymbol{z}, \boldsymbol{\theta}) = \mathcal{N}(\boldsymbol{x}|\mathbf{W}\boldsymbol{z} + \boldsymbol{\mu}, \boldsymbol{\Psi}) \tag{28.34}$$

where $\mathbf{W}$ is a $D \times L$ matrix, known as the **factor loading matrix**, and $\boldsymbol{\Psi}$ is a diagonal $D \times D$ covariance matrix.

28.3.1.1   FA as a Gaussian with low-rank plus diagonal covariance

FA can be thought of as a low-rank version of a Gaussian distribution. To see this, note that the induced marginal distribution $p(\boldsymbol{x}|\boldsymbol{\theta})$ is a Gaussian (see Equation (2.129) for the derivation):

$$p(\boldsymbol{x}|\boldsymbol{\theta}) = \int \mathcal{N}(\boldsymbol{x}|\mathbf{W}\boldsymbol{z} + \boldsymbol{\mu}, \boldsymbol{\Psi})\mathcal{N}(\boldsymbol{z}|\boldsymbol{\mu}_0, \boldsymbol{\Sigma}_0)d\boldsymbol{z} \tag{28.35}$$

$$= \mathcal{N}(\boldsymbol{x}|\mathbf{W}\boldsymbol{\mu}_0 + \boldsymbol{\mu}, \boldsymbol{\Psi} + \mathbf{W}\boldsymbol{\Sigma}_0\mathbf{W}^\mathsf{T}) \tag{28.36}$$

The first and second moments can be derived as follows:

$$\begin{aligned}
\mathbb{E}\left[\boldsymbol{x}\right] &= \mathbf{W}\boldsymbol{\mu}_0 + \boldsymbol{\mu} \\
\mathrm{Cov}\left[\boldsymbol{x}\right] &= \mathbf{W}\mathrm{Cov}\left[\boldsymbol{z}\right]\mathbf{W}^\mathsf{T} + \boldsymbol{\Psi} = \mathbf{W}\boldsymbol{\Sigma}_0\mathbf{W}^\mathsf{T} + \boldsymbol{\Psi}
\end{aligned} \tag{28.37}$$

From this, we see that we can set $\boldsymbol{\mu}_0 = \mathbf{0}$ without loss of generality, since we can always absorb $\mathbf{W}\boldsymbol{\mu}_0$ into $\boldsymbol{\mu}$. Similarly, we can set $\boldsymbol{\Sigma}_0 = \mathbf{I}$ without loss of generality, since we can always absorb a correlated prior by using a new weight matrix, $\tilde{\mathbf{W}} = \mathbf{W}\boldsymbol{\Sigma}_0^{-\frac{1}{2}}$, since then

$$\mathrm{Cov}\left[\boldsymbol{x}\right] = \mathbf{W}\boldsymbol{\Sigma}_0\mathbf{W}^\mathsf{T} + \boldsymbol{\Psi} = \tilde{\mathbf{W}}\tilde{\mathbf{W}}^\mathsf{T} + \boldsymbol{\Psi} \tag{28.38}$$

Finally, we see that we should restrict $\boldsymbol{\Psi}$ to be diagonal, otherwise we could set $\tilde{\mathbf{W}} = \mathbf{0}$, thus ignoring the latent factors, while still being able to model any covariance. After these simplifications we have the final model:

$$\begin{aligned}
p(\boldsymbol{z}) &= \mathcal{N}(\boldsymbol{z}|\mathbf{0}, \mathbf{I}) \\
p(\boldsymbol{x}|\boldsymbol{z}) &= \mathcal{N}(\boldsymbol{x}|\mathbf{W}\boldsymbol{z} + \boldsymbol{\mu}, \boldsymbol{\Psi})
\end{aligned} \tag{28.39} \tag{28.40}$$

from which we get

$$p(\boldsymbol{x}) = \mathcal{N}(\boldsymbol{x}|\boldsymbol{\mu}, \mathbf{W}\mathbf{W}^\mathsf{T} + \boldsymbol{\Psi}) \tag{28.41}$$

For example, suppose where $L = 1$, $D = 2$ and $\boldsymbol{\Psi} = \sigma^2\mathbf{I}$. We illustrate the generative process in this case in Figure 28.6. We can think of this as taking an isotropic Gaussian "spray can", representing the likelihood $p(\boldsymbol{x}|\boldsymbol{z})$, and "sliding it along" the 1d line defined by $\boldsymbol{w}z + \boldsymbol{\mu}$ as we vary the 1d latent prior z. This induces an elongated (and hence correlated) Gaussian in 2d. That is, the induced distribution has the form $p(\boldsymbol{x}) = \mathcal{N}(\boldsymbol{x}|\boldsymbol{\mu}, \boldsymbol{w}\boldsymbol{w}^\mathsf{T} + \sigma^2\mathbf{I})$.

In general, FA approximates the covariance matrix of the visible vector using a low-rank decomposition:

$$\mathbf{C} = \mathrm{Cov}\left[\boldsymbol{x}\right] = \mathbf{W}\mathbf{W}^\mathsf{T} + \boldsymbol{\Psi} \tag{28.42}$$

This only uses $O(LD)$ parameters, which allows a flexible compromise between a full covariance Gaussian, with $O(D^2)$ parameters, and a diagonal covariance, with $O(D)$ parameters.

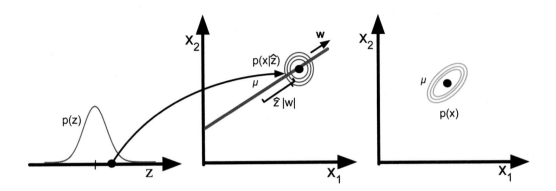

Figure 28.6: Illustration of the FA generative process, where we have $L = 1$ latent dimension generating $D = 2$ observed dimensions; we assume $\mathbf{\Psi} = \sigma^2 \mathbf{I}$. The latent factor has value $z \in \mathbb{R}$, sampled from $p(z)$; this gets mapped to a 2d offset $\boldsymbol{\delta} = z\boldsymbol{w}$, where $\boldsymbol{w} \in \mathbb{R}^2$, which gets added to $\boldsymbol{\mu}$ to define a Gaussian $p(\boldsymbol{x}|z) = \mathcal{N}(\boldsymbol{x}|\boldsymbol{\mu} + \boldsymbol{\delta}, \sigma^2 \mathbf{I})$. By integrating over z, we "slide" this circular Gaussian "spray can" along the principal component axis $\boldsymbol{w}$, which induces elliptical Gaussian contours in $\boldsymbol{x}$ space centered on $\boldsymbol{\mu}$. Adapted from Figure 12.9 of [Bis06].

28.3.1.2 Computing the posterior

We can compute the posterior over the latent codes, $p(\boldsymbol{z}|\boldsymbol{x})$, using Bayes' rule for Gaussians. In particular, from Equation (2.121), we have

$$p(\boldsymbol{z}|\boldsymbol{x}) = \mathcal{N}(\boldsymbol{z}|\boldsymbol{\mu}_{z|x}, \boldsymbol{\Sigma}_{z|x}) \tag{28.43}$$

$$\boldsymbol{\Sigma}_{z|x} = (\mathbf{I} + \mathbf{W}^\mathsf{T}\mathbf{\Psi}^{-1}\mathbf{W})^{-1} = \mathbf{I} - \mathbf{W}^\mathsf{T}(\mathbf{W}\mathbf{W}^\mathsf{T} + \mathbf{\Psi})^{-1}\mathbf{W} \tag{28.44}$$

$$\boldsymbol{\mu}_{z|x} = \boldsymbol{\Sigma}_{z|x}[\mathbf{W}^\mathsf{T}\mathbf{\Psi}^{-1}(\boldsymbol{x} - \boldsymbol{\mu})] = \mathbf{W}^\mathsf{T}(\mathbf{W}\mathbf{W}^\mathsf{T} + \mathbf{\Psi})^{-1}(\boldsymbol{x} - \boldsymbol{\mu}) \tag{28.45}$$

We can avoid inverting the $D \times D$ matrix $\mathbf{C} = \mathbf{W}\mathbf{W}^\mathsf{T} + \mathbf{\Psi}$ by using the matrix inversion lemma:

$$\mathbf{C}^{-1} = (\mathbf{W}\mathbf{W}^\mathsf{T} + \mathbf{\Psi})^{-1} \tag{28.46}$$

$$= \mathbf{\Psi}^{-1} - \mathbf{\Psi}^{-1}\mathbf{W}\underbrace{(\mathbf{I} + \mathbf{W}^\mathsf{T}\mathbf{\Psi}^{-1}\mathbf{W})^{-1}}_{\mathbf{L}^{-1}}\mathbf{W}^\mathsf{T}\mathbf{\Psi}^{-1} \tag{28.47}$$

where $\mathbf{L} = \mathbf{I} + \mathbf{W}^\mathsf{T}\mathbf{\Psi}^{-1}\mathbf{W}$ is $L \times L$.

28.3.1.3 Computing the likelihood

In this section, we discuss how to efficiently compute the log (marginal) likelihood, which is given by

$$\log p(\boldsymbol{x}|\boldsymbol{\mu}, \mathbf{C}) = -\frac{1}{2}\left[D\log(2\pi) + \log\det(\mathbf{C}) + \tilde{\boldsymbol{x}}^\mathsf{T}\mathbf{C}^{-1}\tilde{\boldsymbol{x}}\right] \tag{28.48}$$

where $\tilde{x} = x - \mu$, and $\mathbf{C} = \mathbf{W}\mathbf{W}^\mathsf{T} + \mathbf{\Psi}$. Using Equation (28.47), the Mahalanobis distance can be computed using

$$\tilde{x}^\mathsf{T} \mathbf{C}^{-1} \tilde{x} = \tilde{x}^\mathsf{T} \left[\mathbf{\Psi}^{-1} \tilde{x} - \mathbf{\Psi}^{-1}\mathbf{W}\mathbf{L}^{-1}(\mathbf{W}^\mathsf{T}\mathbf{\Psi}^{-1}\tilde{x}) \right] \tag{28.49}$$

which takes $O(L^3 + LD)$ to compute. From the matrix determinant lemma, the log determinant is given by

$$\log \det(\mathbf{C}) = \log \det(\mathbf{L}) + \log \det(\mathbf{\Psi}) \tag{28.50}$$

which takes $O(L^3 + D)$ to compute. (See also Section 28.2.5, where we discuss fitting low-rank GMM classifiers discriminatively, which requires similar computations.)

28.3.1.4   Model fitting using EM

We can compute the MLE for the FA model either by performing gradient ascent on the log likelihood in Equation (28.48), or by using the EM algorithm [RT82; GH96b]. The latter can converge faster, and automatically satisfies positivity constraints on $\mathbf{\Psi}$. We give the details below, assuming that the observed data is standardized, so $\mu = \mathbf{0}$ for notational simplicity.

In the E step, we compute the following expected sufficient statistics:

$$\mathbf{E}_{x,z} = \sum_{n=1}^{N} x_n \mathbb{E}\left[z|x_n\right]^\mathsf{T} \tag{28.51}$$

$$\mathbf{E}_{z,z} = \sum_{n=1}^{N} \mathbb{E}\left[zz^\mathsf{T}|x_n\right] \tag{28.52}$$

$$\mathbf{E}_{x,x} = \sum_{n=1}^{N} x_n x_n^\mathsf{T} \tag{28.53}$$

where

$$\mathbb{E}\left[z|x\right] = \mathbf{B}x \tag{28.54}$$

$$\mathbb{E}\left[zz^\mathsf{T}|x\right] = \mathrm{Cov}\left[z|x\right] + \mathbb{E}\left[z|x\right]\mathbb{E}\left[z|x\right]^\mathsf{T} = \mathbf{I} - \mathbf{B}\mathbf{W} + \mathbf{B}xx^\mathsf{T}\mathbf{B}^\mathsf{T} \tag{28.55}$$

$$\mathbf{B} \triangleq \mathbf{W}^\mathsf{T}(\mathbf{\Psi} + \mathbf{W}\mathbf{W}^\mathsf{T})^{-1} = \mathbf{W}^\mathsf{T}\mathbf{C}^{-1} \tag{28.56}$$

In the M step, we have

$$\mathbf{W}^{\mathrm{new}} = \mathbf{E}_{x,z}\mathbf{E}_{z,z}^{-1} \tag{28.57}$$

$$\mathbf{\Psi}^{\mathrm{new}} = \frac{1}{N}\mathrm{diag}\left(\mathbf{E}_{x,x} - \mathbf{W}^{\mathrm{new}}\mathbf{E}_{x,z}^\mathsf{T}\right) \tag{28.58}$$

28.3.1.5   Handling missing data

We can also perform posterior inference in the presence of missing data (if we make the missing at random assumption — see Section 3.11 for discussion). In particular, let us partition $x = (x_1, x_2)$,

$\mathbf{W} = [\mathbf{W}_1, \mathbf{W}_2]$, and $\boldsymbol{\mu} = [\boldsymbol{\mu}_1, \boldsymbol{\mu}_2]$, and suppose $\boldsymbol{x}_2$ is missing (unknown). From Supplementary Section 2.1.1, we have

$$p(\boldsymbol{z}|\boldsymbol{x}_1) = \mathcal{N}(\boldsymbol{z}|\boldsymbol{\mu}_{z|1}, \boldsymbol{\Sigma}_{z|1}) \tag{28.59}$$

$$\boldsymbol{\Sigma}_{z|1}^{-1} = \mathbf{I} + \mathbf{W}_1^\mathsf{T} \boldsymbol{\Sigma}_{11}^{-1} \mathbf{W}_1 \tag{28.60}$$

$$\boldsymbol{\mu}_{z|1} = \boldsymbol{\Sigma}_{z|1}[\mathbf{W}_1^\mathsf{T} \boldsymbol{\Sigma}_{11}^{-1} (\boldsymbol{x}_1 - \boldsymbol{\mu}_1)] \tag{28.61}$$

where $\boldsymbol{\Sigma}_{11}$ is the top left block of $\boldsymbol{\Psi}$.

We can modify the EM algorithm to fit the model in the presence of missing data in the obvious way.

28.3.1.6 Unidentifiability of the parameters

The parameters of a FA model are unidentifiable. To see this, consider a model with weights $\mathbf{W}$ and observation covariance $\boldsymbol{\Psi}$. We have

$$\text{Cov}[\boldsymbol{x}] = \mathbf{W}\mathbb{E}\left[\boldsymbol{z}\boldsymbol{z}^\mathsf{T}\right]\mathbf{W}^\mathsf{T} + \mathbb{E}\left[\boldsymbol{\epsilon}\boldsymbol{\epsilon}^\mathsf{T}\right] = \mathbf{W}\mathbf{W}^\mathsf{T} + \boldsymbol{\Psi} \tag{28.62}$$

where $\boldsymbol{\epsilon} \sim \mathcal{N}(\mathbf{0}, \boldsymbol{\Psi})$ is the observation noise. Now consider a different model with weights $\tilde{\mathbf{W}} = \mathbf{W}\mathbf{R}$, where $\mathbf{R}$ is an arbitrary orthogonal rotation matrix, satisfying $\mathbf{R}\mathbf{R}^\mathsf{T} = \mathbf{I}$. This has the same likelihood, since

$$\text{Cov}[\boldsymbol{x}] = \tilde{\mathbf{W}}\mathbb{E}\left[\boldsymbol{z}\boldsymbol{z}^\mathsf{T}\right]\tilde{\mathbf{W}}^\mathsf{T} + \mathbb{E}\left[\boldsymbol{\epsilon}\boldsymbol{\epsilon}^\mathsf{T}\right] = \mathbf{W}\mathbf{R}\mathbf{R}^\mathsf{T}\mathbf{W}^\mathsf{T} + \boldsymbol{\Psi} = \mathbf{W}\mathbf{W}^\mathsf{T} + \boldsymbol{\Psi} \tag{28.63}$$

Geometrically, multiplying $\mathbf{W}$ by an orthogonal matrix is like rotating $\boldsymbol{z}$ before generating $\boldsymbol{x}$; but since $\boldsymbol{z}$ is drawn from an isotropic Gaussian, this makes no difference to the likelihood. Consequently, we cannot uniquely identify $\mathbf{W}$, and therefore cannot uniquely identify the latent factors, either. This is called the "**factor rotations problem**" (see e.g., [Dar80]).

To break this symmetry, several solutions can be used, as we discuss below.

- **Forcing W to have orthogonal columns..** In (P)PCA, we force $\mathbf{W}$ to have orthogonal columns. and to sort the dimensions in order of decreasing eigenvalue (of $\mathbf{W}\mathbf{W}^\mathsf{T}$). However, this still does not ensure identifiability, since we can always multiply $\mathbf{W}$ by another orthogonal matrix without changing the likelihood.

- **Forcing W to be lower triangular.** One way to resolve permutation unidentifiability, which is popular in the Bayesian community (e.g., [LW04]), is to ensure that the first visible feature is only generated by the first latent factor, the second visible feature is only generated by the first two latent factors, and so on. For example, if $L = 3$ and $D = 4$, the correspond factor loading matrix is given by

$$\mathbf{W} = \begin{pmatrix} w_{11} & 0 & 0 \\ w_{21} & w_{22} & 0 \\ w_{31} & w_{32} & w_{33} \\ w_{41} & w_{42} & w_{43} \end{pmatrix} \tag{28.64}$$

We also require that $w_{kk} > 0$ for $k = 1 : L$. The total number of parameters in this constrained matrix is $D + DL - L(L-1)/2$, which is equal to the number of uniquely identifiable parameters in FA (excluding the mean).[1] The disadvantage of this method is that the first L visible variables, known as the **founder variables**, affect the interpretation of the latent factors, and so must be chosen carefully.

- **Sparsity promoting priors on the weights**. Instead of pre-specifying which entries in $\mathbf{W}$ are zero, we can encourage the entries to be zero, using ℓ_1 regularization [ZHT06], ARD [Bis99; AB08], or spike-and-slab priors [Rat+09]. This is called sparse factor analysis. This does not necessarily ensure a unique MAP estimate, but it does encourage interpretable solutions.

- **Choosing an informative rotation matrix**. There are a variety of heuristic methods that try to find rotation matrices $\mathbf{R}$ which can be used to modify $\mathbf{W}$ (and hence the latent factors) so as to try to increase the interpretability, typically by encouraging them to be (approximately) sparse. One popular method is known as **varimax** [Kai58].

- **Use of non-Gaussian priors for the latent factors**. If we replace the prior on the latent variables, $p(\mathbf{z})$, with a non-Gaussian distribution, we can sometimes uniquely identify $\mathbf{W}$, as well as the latent factors. See e.g., [KKH20] for details.

28.3.2   Probabilistic PCA

In this section, we consider a special case of the factor analysis model in which $\mathbf{W}$ has orthogonal columns and $\mathbf{\Psi} = \sigma^2 \mathbf{I}$, so $p(\mathbf{x}) = \mathcal{N}(\mathbf{x}|\boldsymbol{\mu}, \mathbf{C})$ where $\mathbf{C} = \mathbf{W}\mathbf{W}^\mathsf{T} + \sigma^2 \mathbf{I}$. This model is called **probabilistic principal components analysis (PPCA)** [TB99], or **sensible PCA** [Row97].

   The advantage of PPCA over factor analysis is that the MLE has a closed form solution, as we show in Section 28.3.2.2. The advantage of PPCA over non-probabilistic PCA is that the model defines a proper likelihood function, which makes it easier to extend in various ways e.g., by creating mixtures of PPCA models (see Section 28.3.3).

28.3.2.1   Derivation of the MLE

The log likelihood for PPCA is given by

$$\log p(\mathbf{X}|\boldsymbol{\mu}, \mathbf{W}, \sigma^2) = -\frac{ND}{2}\log(2\pi) - \frac{N}{2}\log|\mathbf{C}| - \frac{1}{2}\sum_{n=1}^{N}(\mathbf{x}_n - \boldsymbol{\mu})^\mathsf{T}\mathbf{C}^{-1}(\mathbf{x}_n - \boldsymbol{\mu}) \tag{28.65}$$

The MLE for $\boldsymbol{\mu}$ is $\overline{\mathbf{x}}$. Plugging in gives

$$\log p(\mathbf{X}|\boldsymbol{\mu}, \mathbf{W}, \sigma^2) = -\frac{N}{2}\left[D\log(2\pi) + \log|\mathbf{C}| + \mathrm{tr}(\mathbf{C}^{-1}\mathbf{S})\right] \tag{28.66}$$

where $\mathbf{S} = \frac{1}{N}\sum_{n=1}^{N}(\mathbf{x}_n - \overline{\mathbf{x}})(\mathbf{x}_n - \overline{\mathbf{x}})^\mathsf{T}$ is the empirical covariance matrix.

   In [TB99; Row97] they show that the maximum of this objective must satisfy

$$\hat{\mathbf{W}} = \mathbf{U}_L(\mathbf{\Lambda}_L - \sigma^2\mathbf{I})^{\frac{1}{2}}\mathbf{R} \tag{28.67}$$

---

1. We get D parameters for $\mathbf{\Psi}$ and DL for $\mathbf{W}$, but we need to remove $L(L-1)/2$ degrees of freedom coming from $\mathbf{R}$, since that is the dimensionality of the space of orthogonal matrices of size $L \times L$. To see this, note that there are $L-1$ free parameters in $\mathbf{R}$ in the first column (since the column vector must be normalized to unit length), there are $L-2$ free parameters in the second column (which must be orthogonal to the first), and so on.

where $\mathbf{U}_L$ is a $D \times L$ matrix whose columns are given by the L eigenvectors of $\mathbf{S}$ with largest eigenvalues, $\mathbf{\Lambda}_L$ is the $L \times L$ diagonal matrix of corresponding eigenvalues, and $\mathbf{R}$ is an arbitrary $L \times L$ orthogonal matrix, which (WLOG) we can take to be $\mathbf{R} = \mathbf{I}$.

If we plug in the MLE for $\mathbf{W}$, we find the covariance for the predictive distribution to be

$$\mathbf{C} = \mathbf{W}\mathbf{W}^\mathsf{T} + \sigma^2 \mathbf{I} = \mathbf{U}_L (\mathbf{\Lambda}_L - \sigma^2 \mathbf{I}) \mathbf{U}_L^\mathsf{T} + \sigma^2 \mathbf{I} \tag{28.68}$$

The MLE for the observation variance is

$$\sigma^2 = \frac{1}{D - L} \sum_{i=L+1}^{D} \lambda_i \tag{28.69}$$

which is the average distortion associated with the discarded dimensions. If $L = D$, then the estimated noise is 0, since the model collapses to $\mathbf{z} = \mathbf{x}$.

28.3.2.2 PCA is recovered in the noise-free limit

In the noise-free limit, where $\sigma^2 = 0$, we see that the MLE (for $\mathbf{R} = \mathbf{I}$) is

$$\hat{\mathbf{W}} = \mathbf{U}_L \mathbf{\Lambda}_L^{\frac{1}{2}} \tag{28.70}$$

so

$$\hat{\mathbf{C}} = \hat{\mathbf{W}}\hat{\mathbf{W}}^\mathsf{T} = \mathbf{U}_L \mathbf{\Lambda}_L^{\frac{1}{2}} \mathbf{\Lambda}_L^{\frac{1}{2}} \mathbf{U}_L^\mathsf{T} = \mathbf{S}_L \tag{28.71}$$

where $\mathbf{S}_L$ is the rank L approximation to $\mathbf{S}$. This is the same as standard PCA.

28.3.2.3 Computing the posterior

To use PPCA as an alternative to PCA, we need to compute the posterior mean $\mathbb{E}\left[\mathbf{z}|\mathbf{x}\right]$, which is the equivalent of the PCA encoder model. Using the factor analysis results from Section 28.3.1.2, we have

$$p(\mathbf{z}|\mathbf{x}) = \mathcal{N}(\mathbf{z}|\sigma^{-2}\mathbf{\Sigma}\mathbf{W}^\mathsf{T}(\mathbf{x} - \boldsymbol{\mu}), \mathbf{\Sigma}) \tag{28.72}$$

where

$$\mathbf{\Sigma}^{-1} = \mathbf{I} + \sigma^{-2}\mathbf{W}^\mathsf{T}\mathbf{W} = \frac{1}{\sigma^2} \underbrace{(\sigma^2 \mathbf{I} + \mathbf{W}^\mathsf{T}\mathbf{W})}_{\mathbf{M}} \tag{28.73}$$

Hence

$$p(\mathbf{z}|\mathbf{x}) = \mathcal{N}(\mathbf{z}|\mathbf{M}^{-1}\mathbf{W}^\mathsf{T}(\mathbf{x} - \boldsymbol{\mu}), \sigma^2 \mathbf{M}^{-1}) \tag{28.74}$$

In the $\sigma^2 = 0$ limit, we have $\mathbf{M} = \mathbf{W}^\mathsf{T}\mathbf{W}$ and so

$$\mathbb{E}\left[\mathbf{z}|\mathbf{x}\right] = (\mathbf{W}^\mathsf{T}\mathbf{W})^{-1}\mathbf{W}^\mathsf{T}(\mathbf{x} - \overline{\mathbf{x}}) \tag{28.75}$$

This is the orthogonal projection of the data into the latent space, as in standard PCA.

28.3.2.4   Model fitting using EM

In Section 28.3.2.2, we showed how to fit the PCA model using an eigenvector method. We can also use EM, by leveraging the probabilistic formulation of PPCA in the zero noise limit, $\sigma^2 = 0$, as shown by [Row97].

In particular, let $\tilde{\mathbf{Z}} = \mathbf{Z}^{\mathsf{T}}$ be an $L \times N$ matrix storing the posterior means (low-dimensional representations) along its columns. Similarly, let $\tilde{\boldsymbol{x}}_n = \boldsymbol{x}_n - \hat{\boldsymbol{\mu}}$ be the centered examples stored along the columns of $\tilde{\mathbf{X}}$. From Equation (28.75), when $\sigma^2 = 0$, we have

$$\tilde{\mathbf{Z}} = (\mathbf{W}^{\mathsf{T}} \mathbf{W})^{-1} \mathbf{W}^{\mathsf{T}} \tilde{\mathbf{X}} \tag{28.76}$$

This constitutes the E step. Notice that this is just an orthogonal projection of the data.

From Equation (28.57), the M step is given by

$$\hat{\mathbf{W}} = \left[\sum_n \tilde{\boldsymbol{x}}_n \mathbb{E}\left[z_n | \tilde{\boldsymbol{x}}_n \right]^{\mathsf{T}} \right] \left[\sum_n \mathbb{E}\left[z_n | \tilde{\boldsymbol{x}}_n \right] \mathbb{E}\left[z_n | \tilde{\boldsymbol{x}}_n \right]^{\mathsf{T}} \right]^{-1} \tag{28.77}$$

where we exploited the fact that $\boldsymbol{\Sigma} = \text{Cov}\left[z | \tilde{x} \right] = 0\mathbf{I}$ when $\sigma^2 = 0$.

In summary, here is the entire algorithm:

$$\tilde{\mathbf{Z}} = (\mathbf{W}^{\mathsf{T}} \mathbf{W})^{-1} \mathbf{W}^{\mathsf{T}} \tilde{\mathbf{X}} \text{ (E step)} \tag{28.78}$$

$$\mathbf{W} = \tilde{\mathbf{X}} \tilde{\mathbf{Z}}^{\mathsf{T}} (\tilde{\mathbf{Z}} \tilde{\mathbf{Z}}^{\mathsf{T}})^{-1} \text{ (M step)} \tag{28.79}$$

It is worth comparing this expression to the MLE for multi-output linear regression, which has the form $\mathbf{W} = (\sum_n \boldsymbol{y}_n \boldsymbol{x}_n^{\mathsf{T}})(\sum_n \boldsymbol{x}_n \boldsymbol{x}_n^{\mathsf{T}})^{-1}$. Thus we see that the M step is like linear regression where we replace the observed inputs by the expected values of the latent variables.

[TB99] showed that the only stable fixed point of the EM algorithm is the globally optimal solution. That is, the EM algorithm converges to a solution where $\mathbf{W}$ spans the same linear subspace as that defined by the first L eigenvectors of $\mathbf{S}$. However, if we want $\mathbf{W}$ to be orthogonal, and to contain the eigenvectors in descending order of eigenvalue, we have to orthogonalize the resulting matrix (which can be done quite cheaply). Alternatively, we can modify EM to give the principal basis directly [AO03].

28.3.3   Mixture of factor analyzers

The factor analysis model (Section 28.3.1) assumes the observed data can be modeled as arising from a linear mapping from a low-dimensional set of Gaussian factors. One way to relax this assumption is to assume the model is only locally linear, so the overall model becomes a (weighted) combination of FA models; this is called a **mixture of factor analyzers** or MFA [GH96b]. The overall model for the data is a mixture of linear manifolds, which can be used to approximate an overall curved manifold. Another way to think of this model is a mixture of Gaussians, where each mixture component has a covariance matrix which is diagonal plus low-rank.

28.3.3.1   Model definition

The generative story is as follows. First we sample a discrete latent indicator $m_n \in \{1, \dots, K\}$ from discrete distribution $\text{Cat}(\cdot | \boldsymbol{\pi})$ to specify which subspace (cluster) we should use to generate the data.

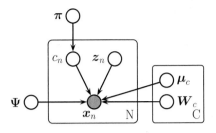

Figure 28.7: Mixture of factor analyzers as a PGM.

If $m_n = k$, we sample $\boldsymbol{z}_n$ from a Gaussian prior and pass it through the $\mathbf{W}_k$ matrix, where $\mathbf{W}_k$ maps from the L-dimensional subspace to the D-dimensional visible space.[2] Finally we add Gaussian observation noise sampled from $\mathcal{N}(\boldsymbol{\mu}_k, \boldsymbol{\Psi})$. Thus the model is as follows:

$$p(\boldsymbol{x}_n|\boldsymbol{z}_n, m_n = k, \boldsymbol{\theta}) = \mathcal{N}(\boldsymbol{x}_n|\boldsymbol{\mu}_k + \mathbf{W}_k\boldsymbol{z}_n, \boldsymbol{\Psi}) \tag{28.80}$$

$$p(\boldsymbol{z}_n|\boldsymbol{\theta}) = \mathcal{N}(\boldsymbol{z}_n|\mathbf{0}, \mathbf{I}) \tag{28.81}$$

$$p(m_n|\boldsymbol{\theta}) = \mathrm{Cat}(m_n|\boldsymbol{\pi}) \tag{28.82}$$

The corresponding distribution in the visible space is given by

$$p(\boldsymbol{x}|\boldsymbol{\theta}) = \sum_k p(m = k) \int p(\boldsymbol{z}|c)p(\boldsymbol{x}|\boldsymbol{z}, m) \, d\boldsymbol{z} \tag{28.83}$$

$$= \sum_k \pi_k \int \mathcal{N}(\boldsymbol{z}|\mathbf{0}, \mathbf{I})\mathcal{N}(\boldsymbol{x}|\mathbf{W}_k\boldsymbol{z} + \boldsymbol{\mu}_k, \boldsymbol{\Psi}) \, d\boldsymbol{z} \tag{28.84}$$

$$= \sum_k \pi_k \mathcal{N}(\boldsymbol{x}|\boldsymbol{\mu}_k, \boldsymbol{\Psi} + \mathbf{W}_k\mathbf{W}_k^\mathsf{T}) \tag{28.85}$$

In the special case that $\boldsymbol{\Psi} = \sigma^2\mathbf{I}$, we get a mixture of PPCA models. See Figure 28.8 for an example of the method applied to some 2d data.

We can think of this as a low-rank version of a mixture of Gaussians. In particular, this model needs $O(KLD)$ parameters instead of the $O(KD^2)$ parameters needed for a mixture of full covariance Gaussians. This can reduce overfitting.

28.3.3.2 Model fitting using EM

We can fit this model using EM, extending the results of Section 28.3.1.4 (see [GH96b] for the derivation, and [ZY08] for a faster ECM version). In the E step, we compute the posterior responsibility of cluster j for datapoint i using

$$r_{ij} \triangleq p(m_i = j|\boldsymbol{x}_i, \boldsymbol{\theta}) \propto \pi_j \mathcal{N}(\boldsymbol{x}_i|\boldsymbol{\mu}_j, \mathbf{W}_j\mathbf{W}_j^\mathsf{T} + \boldsymbol{\Psi}) \tag{28.86}$$

---

2. If we allow $\boldsymbol{z}_n$ to depend on m_n, we can let each subspace have a different dimensionality, as suggested in [KS15].

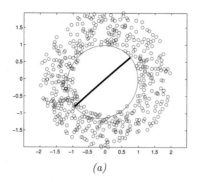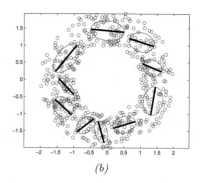

(a)   (b)

Figure 28.8: Mixture of PPCA models fit to a 2d dataset, using $L = 1$ latent dimensions. (a) $K = 1$ mixture components. (b) $K = 10$ mixture components. Generated by mix_ppca_demo.ipynb.

We also compute the following expected sufficient statistics, where we define $w_j = \mathbb{I}(m = j)$ and $\mathbf{B}_j = \mathbf{W}_j^\mathsf{T}(\mathbf{\Psi} + \mathbf{W}_j \mathbf{W}_j^\mathsf{T})^{-1}$:

$$\mathbb{E}[w_j \boldsymbol{z}|\boldsymbol{x}_i] = \mathbb{E}[w_j|\boldsymbol{x}_i]\,\mathbb{E}[\boldsymbol{z}|w_j, \boldsymbol{x}_i] = r_{ij}\mathbf{B}_j(\boldsymbol{x}_i - \boldsymbol{\mu}_j) \tag{28.87}$$

$$\mathbb{E}[w_j \boldsymbol{z}\boldsymbol{z}^\mathsf{T}|\boldsymbol{x}_i] = \mathbb{E}[w_j|\boldsymbol{x}_i]\,\mathbb{E}[\boldsymbol{z}\boldsymbol{z}^\mathsf{T}|w_j, \boldsymbol{x}_i] = r_{ij}(\mathbf{I} - \mathbf{B}_j\mathbf{W}_j + \mathbf{B}_j(\boldsymbol{x} - \boldsymbol{\mu}_j)(\boldsymbol{x} - \boldsymbol{\mu}_j)^\mathsf{T}\mathbf{B}_j^\mathsf{T}) \tag{28.88}$$

In the M step, we compute the following parameter update for the augmented factor loading matrix:

$$[\mathbf{W}_j^{\text{new}}\ \boldsymbol{\mu}_j^{\text{new}}] \triangleq \tilde{\mathbf{W}}_j^{\text{new}} = \left(\sum_i r_{ij}\boldsymbol{x}_i \mathbb{E}[\tilde{\boldsymbol{z}}|\boldsymbol{x}_i, w_j]^\mathsf{T}\right)\left(\sum_i r_{ij}\mathbb{E}[\tilde{\boldsymbol{z}}\tilde{\boldsymbol{z}}^\mathsf{T}|\boldsymbol{x}_i, w_j]\right)^{-1} \tag{28.89}$$

where $\tilde{\boldsymbol{z}} = [\boldsymbol{z}; 1]$,

$$\mathbb{E}[\tilde{\boldsymbol{z}}|\boldsymbol{x}_i, w_j] = \begin{pmatrix} \mathbb{E}[\boldsymbol{z}|\boldsymbol{x}_i, w_j] \\ 1 \end{pmatrix} \tag{28.90}$$

$$\mathbb{E}[\tilde{\boldsymbol{z}}\tilde{\boldsymbol{z}}^\mathsf{T}|\boldsymbol{x}_i, w_j] = \begin{pmatrix} \mathbb{E}[\tilde{\boldsymbol{z}}\tilde{\boldsymbol{z}}^\mathsf{T}|\boldsymbol{x}_i, w_j] & \mathbb{E}[\tilde{\boldsymbol{z}}|\boldsymbol{x}_i, w_j] \\ \mathbb{E}[\tilde{\boldsymbol{z}}|\boldsymbol{x}_i, w_j]^\mathsf{T} & 1 \end{pmatrix} \tag{28.91}$$

The new covariance matrix is given by

$$\mathbf{\Psi}^{\text{new}} = \frac{1}{N}\text{diag}\left(\sum_{ij} r_{ij}(\boldsymbol{x}_i - \tilde{\mathbf{W}}_j^{\text{new}}\mathbb{E}[\tilde{\boldsymbol{z}}|\boldsymbol{x}_i, w_j])\boldsymbol{x}_i^\mathsf{T}\right) \tag{28.92}$$

And the new mixing weights are given by

$$\pi_j^{\text{new}} = \frac{1}{N}\sum_{i=1}^N r_{ij} \tag{28.93}$$

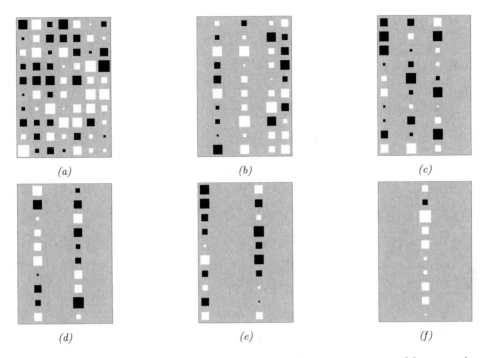

Figure 28.9: Illustration of estimating the effective dimensionalities in a mixture of factor analysers using variational Bayes EM with an ARD prior. Black are negative values, white are positive, gray is 0. The blank columns have been forced to 0 via the ARD mechanism, reducing the effective dimensionality. The data was generated from 6 clusters with intrinsic dimensionalities of 7, 4, 3, 2, 2, 1, which the method has successfully estimated. From Figure 4.4 of [Bea03]. Used with kind permission of Matt Beal.

28.3.3.3 Model fitting using SGD

We can also fit mixture models using SGD, as shown in [RW18]. This idea can be combined with an inference network (see Section 10.1.5) to efficiently approximate the posterior over the latent variables. [Zon+18] use this approach to jointly learn a GMM applied to a deep autoencoder to provide a nonlinear extension of MFA; they show good results on anomaly detection.

28.3.3.4 Model selection

To choose the number of mixture components K, and the number of latent dimensions L, we can use discrete search combined with objectives such as the marginal likelihood or validation likelihood. However, we can also use numerical optimization methods to optimize L, which can be faster. We initially assume that N_c is known. To estimate L, we set the model to its maximal size, and then use a technique called automatic relevance determination or ARD to automatically prune out irrelevant weights (see Section 15.2.8). This can be implemented using variational Bayes EM (Section 10.3.5); for details, see [Bis99; GB00].

Figure 28.9 illustrates this approach applied to a mixture of FA models fit to a small synthetic

number of points per cluster	intrinsic dimensionalities					
	1	7	4	3	2	2
8		2			1	
8		1	2			
16	1	4			2	
32	1	6	3	3	2	2
64	1	7	4	3	2	2
128	1	7	4	3	2	2

Figure 28.10: *We show the estimated number of clusters, and their estimated dimensionalities, as a function of sample size. The ARD algorithm found two different solutions when $N = 8$. Note that more clusters, with larger effective dimensionalities, are discovered as the sample sizes increases. From Table 4.1 of [Bea03]. Used with kind permission of Matt Beal.*

dataset. The figures visualize the weight matrices for each cluster, using **Hinton diagrams**, where where the size of the square is proportional to the value of the entry in the matrix. We see that many of them are sparse. Figure 28.10 shows that the degree of sparsity depends on the amount of training data, in accord with the Bayesian Occam's razor. In particular, when the sample size is small, the method automatically prefers simpler models, but as the sample size gets sufficiently large, the method converges on the "correct" solution, which is one with 6 subspaces of dimensionality 1, 2, 2, 3, 4 and 7.

Although the ARD method can estimate the number of latent dimensions L, it still needs to perform discrete search over the number of mixture components N_c. This is done using "birth" and "death" moves [GB00]. An alternative approach is to perform stochastic sampling in the space of models. Traditional approaches, such as [LW04], are based on reversible jump MCMC, and also use birth and death moves. However, this can be slow and difficult to implement. More recent approaches use non-parametric priors, combined with Gibbs sampling, see e.g., [PC09].

28.3.3.5 MixFA for image generation

In this section, we use the MFA model as a generative model for images, following [RW18]. This is equivalent to using a mixture of Gaussians, where each mixture component has a low-rank covariance matrix. Surprisingly, the results are competitive with deep generative models such as those in Part IV, despite the fact that no neural networks are used in the model.

In [RW18], they fit the MFA model to the CelebA dataset, which is a dataset of faces of celebrities (movie stars). They use $K = 300$ components, each of latent dimension $L = 10$; the observed data has dimension $D = 64 \times 64 \times 3 = 12,288$. They fit the model using SGD, using the methods from Section 28.3.1.3 to efficiently compute the log likelihood, despite the high dimensionality. The $\boldsymbol{\mu}_k$ parameters are initialized using K-means clustering, and the $\mathbf{W}_k$ parameters are initialized using factor analysis for each component separately. Then the model is fine-tuned end-to-end.

Figure 28.11 shows some images generated from the fitted model. The results are surprisingly good for such a simple locally linear model. The reason the method works is similar to the discussion in Section 28.2.4.1: essentially the $\mathbf{W}_k$ matrix learns a set of L-dimensional basis functions for the

Figure 28.11: *Random samples from the MixFA model fit to CelebA. Generated by* mix_ppca_celebA.ipynb. *Adapted from Figure 4 of [RW18]. Used with kind permission of Yair Weiss.*

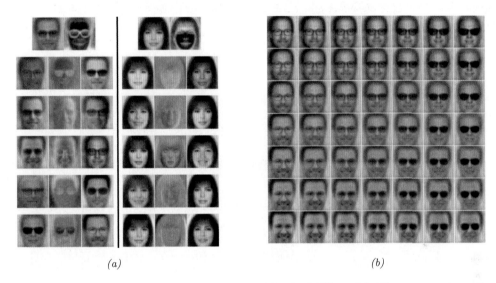

(a)   (b)

Figure 28.12: *(a) Visualization of the parameters learned by the MFA model. The top row shows the mean* $\boldsymbol{\mu}_k$ *and noise variance* $\boldsymbol{\Psi}_k$, *reshaped from 12,288-dimensional vectors to* $64 \times 64 \times 3$ *images, for two mixture components* k. *The next 5 rows show the first 5 (of 10) basis functions (columns of* $\mathbf{W}_k$) *as images. On row* i, *left column, we show* $\boldsymbol{\mu}_k - \mathbf{W}_k[:, i]$; *in the middle, we show* $0.5 + \mathbf{W}_k[:, i]$, *and on the right we show* $\boldsymbol{\mu}_k + \mathbf{W}_k[:, i]$. *(b) Images generated by computing* $\boldsymbol{\mu}_k + z_1 \mathbf{W}_k[:, i] + z_2 \mathbf{W}_k[:, j]$, *for some component* k *and dimensions* i, j, *where* (z_1, z_2) *are drawn from the grid* $[-1 : 1, -1 : 1]$, *so the central image is just* $\boldsymbol{\mu}_k$. *From Figure 6 of [RW18]. Used with kind permission of Yair Weiss.*

subset of face images that get mapped to cluster k. See Figure 28.12 for an illustration.

There are several advantages to this model compared to VAEs and GANs. First, [RW18], showed that this MixFA model captures more of the modes of the data distribution than more sophisticated generative models, such as VAEs (Section 21.2) and GANs (Chapter 26). Second, we can compute the exact likelihood $p(\boldsymbol{x})$, so we can compute outliers or unusual images. This is illustrated in Figure 28.13.

Third, we can perform image imputation from partially observed images given arbitrary missingness patterns. To see this, let us partition $\boldsymbol{x} = (\boldsymbol{x}_1, \boldsymbol{x}_2)$, where $\boldsymbol{x}_1$ (of size D_1) is observed and $\boldsymbol{x}_2$ (of size

Figure 28.13: *Samples from the 100 CelebA images with lowest likelihood under the MFA model. Generated by* mix_ppca_celebA.ipynb. *Adapted from Figure 7a of [RW18]. Used with kind permission of Yair Weiss.*

Figure 28.14: *Illustration of image imputation using an MFA. Left column shows 4 original images. Subsequent pairs of columns show an occluded input, and a predicted output. Generated by* mix_ppca_celebA.ipynb. *Adapted from Figure 7b of [RW18]. Used with kind permission of Yair Weiss.*

$D_2 = D - D_1$) is missing. We can compute the most probable cluster using

$$k^* = \operatorname*{argmax}_{k=1}^{K} p(c = k)p(\boldsymbol{x}_1 | c = k) \tag{28.94}$$

where

$$\log p(\boldsymbol{x}_1 | \boldsymbol{\mu}_k, \mathbf{C}_k) = -\frac{1}{2} \left[D_1 \log(2\pi) + \log \det(\mathbf{C}_{k,11}) + \tilde{\boldsymbol{x}}_1^\mathsf{T} \mathbf{C}_{k,11}^{-1} \tilde{\boldsymbol{x}}_1 \right] \tag{28.95}$$

where $\mathbf{C}_{k,11}$ is the top left $D_1 \times D_1$ block of $\mathbf{W}_k \mathbf{W}_k^\mathsf{T} + \boldsymbol{\Psi}_k$, and $\tilde{\boldsymbol{x}}_1 = \boldsymbol{x}_1 - \boldsymbol{\mu}_k[1 : D_1]$. Once we know which discrete mixture component to use, we can compute the Gaussian posterior $p(\boldsymbol{z} | \boldsymbol{x}_1, k^*)$ using Equation (28.59). Let $\hat{\boldsymbol{z}} = \mathbb{E}\left[\boldsymbol{z} | \boldsymbol{x}_1, k^*\right]$. Given this, we can compute the predicted output for the full

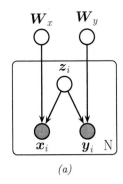
(a)

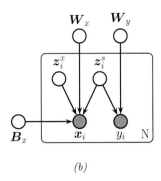
(b)

Figure 28.15: *Gaussian latent factor models for paired data. (a) Supervised PCA. (b) Partial least squares.*

image:

$$\hat{\boldsymbol{x}} = \mathbf{W}_{k^*}\hat{\boldsymbol{z}} + \boldsymbol{\mu}_{k^*} \tag{28.96}$$

We then use the estimate $\boldsymbol{x}' = [\boldsymbol{x}_1, \hat{\boldsymbol{x}}_2]$, so the observed pixels are not changed. This is an example of **image imputation**, and is illustrated in Figure 28.14. Note that we can condition on an arbitrary subset of pixels, and fill in the rest, whereas some other models (e.g., autoregressive models) can only predict the bottom right given the top left (since they assume a generative model which works in raster-scan order).

28.3.4   Factor analysis models for paired data

In this section, we discuss linear-Gaussian factor analysis models when we have two kinds of observed variables, $\boldsymbol{x} \in \mathbb{R}^{D_x}$ and $\boldsymbol{y} \in \mathbb{R}^{D_y}$, which are paired. These often correspond to different sensors or modalities (e.g., images and sound). We follow the presentation of [Vir10].

28.3.4.1   Supervised PCA

If we have two observed signals, we can model the joint $p(\boldsymbol{x}, \boldsymbol{y})$ using a shared low-dimensional representation using the following linear Gaussian model:

$$p(\boldsymbol{z}_n) = \mathcal{N}(\boldsymbol{z}_n|\mathbf{0}, \mathbf{I}_L) \tag{28.97}$$
$$p(\boldsymbol{x}_n|\boldsymbol{z}_n, \boldsymbol{\theta}) = \mathcal{N}(\boldsymbol{x}_n|\mathbf{W}_x\boldsymbol{z}_n, \sigma_x^2\mathbf{I}_{D_x}) \tag{28.98}$$
$$p(\boldsymbol{y}_n|\boldsymbol{z}_n, \boldsymbol{\theta}) = \mathcal{N}(\boldsymbol{y}_n|\mathbf{W}_y\boldsymbol{z}_n, \sigma_y^2\mathbf{I}_{D_y}) \tag{28.99}$$

This is illustrated as a graphical model in Figure 28.15a. The intuition is that $\boldsymbol{z}_n$ is a shared latent subspace, that captures features that $\boldsymbol{x}_n$ and $\boldsymbol{y}_n$ have in common. The variance terms σ_x and σ_y control how much emphasis the model puts on the two different signals.

The above model is called **supervised PCA** [Yu+06]. If we put a prior on the parameters $\boldsymbol{\theta} = (\mathbf{W}_x, \mathbf{W}_y, \sigma_x, \sigma_y)$, it is called **Bayesian factor regression** [Wes03].

We can marginalize out z_n to get $p(y_n | x_n, \boldsymbol{\theta})$. If y_n is a scalar, this becomes

$$p(y_n | \boldsymbol{x}_n, \boldsymbol{\theta}) = \mathcal{N}(y_n | \boldsymbol{x}_n^\mathsf{T} \boldsymbol{v}, \boldsymbol{w}_y^\mathsf{T} \mathbf{C} \boldsymbol{w}_y + \sigma_y^2) \tag{28.100}$$

$$\mathbf{C} = (\mathbf{I} + \sigma_x^{-2} \mathbf{W}_x^\mathsf{T} \mathbf{W}_x)^{-1} \tag{28.101}$$

$$\boldsymbol{v} = \sigma_x^{-2} \mathbf{C} \mathbf{W}_x \boldsymbol{w}_y \tag{28.102}$$

To apply this to the classification setting, we can replace the Gaussian $p(y|z)$ with a logistic regression model:

$$p(y_n | \boldsymbol{z}_n, \boldsymbol{\theta}) = \mathrm{Ber}(y_n | \sigma(\boldsymbol{w}_y^\mathsf{T} \boldsymbol{z}_n)) \tag{28.103}$$

In this case, we can no longer compute the marginal posterior predictive $p(y_n | \boldsymbol{x}_n, \boldsymbol{\theta})$ in closed form, but we can use techniques similar to exponential family PCA (see [Guo09] for details).

The above model is completely symmetric in $\boldsymbol{x}$ and $\boldsymbol{y}$. If our goal is to predict $\boldsymbol{y}$ from $\boldsymbol{x}$ via the latent bottleneck $\boldsymbol{z}$, then we might want to upweight the likelihood term for $\boldsymbol{y}$, as proposed in [Ris+08]. This gives

$$p(\mathbf{X}, \mathbf{Y}, \mathbf{Z} | \boldsymbol{\theta}) = p(\mathbf{Y} | \mathbf{Z}, \mathbf{W}_y) p(\mathbf{X} | \mathbf{Z}, \mathbf{W}_x)^\alpha p(\mathbf{Z}) \tag{28.104}$$

where $\alpha \leq 1$ controls the relative importance of modeling the two sources. The value of α can be chosen by cross-validation.

28.3.4.2   Partial least squares

We now consider an asymmetric or more "discriminative" form of supervised PCA. The key idea is to allow some of the (co)variance in the input features to be explained by its own subspace, $\boldsymbol{z}_i^x$, and to let the rest of the subspace, $\boldsymbol{z}_i^s$, be shared between input and output. The model has the form

$$p(\boldsymbol{z}_i) = \mathcal{N}(\boldsymbol{z}_i^s | \mathbf{0}, \mathbf{I}_{L_s}) \mathcal{N}(\boldsymbol{z}_i^x | \mathbf{0}, \mathbf{I}_{L_x}) \tag{28.105}$$

$$p(\boldsymbol{y}_i | \boldsymbol{z}_i) = \mathcal{N}(\mathbf{W}_y \boldsymbol{z}_i^s + \boldsymbol{\mu}_y, \sigma^2 \mathbf{I}_{D_y}) \tag{28.106}$$

$$p(\boldsymbol{x}_i | \boldsymbol{z}_i) = \mathcal{N}(\mathbf{W}_x \boldsymbol{z}_i^s + \mathbf{B}_x \boldsymbol{z}_i^x + \boldsymbol{\mu}_x, \sigma^2 \mathbf{I}_{D_x}) \tag{28.107}$$

See Figure 28.15b. The corresponding induced distribution on the visible variables has the form

$$p(\boldsymbol{v}_i | \boldsymbol{\theta}) = \int \mathcal{N}(\boldsymbol{v}_i | \mathbf{W} \boldsymbol{z}_i + \boldsymbol{\mu}, \sigma^2 \mathbf{I}) \mathcal{N}(\boldsymbol{z}_i | \mathbf{0}, \mathbf{I}) d\boldsymbol{z}_i = \mathcal{N}(\boldsymbol{v}_i | \boldsymbol{\mu}, \mathbf{W} \mathbf{W}^\mathsf{T} + \sigma^2 \mathbf{I}) \tag{28.108}$$

where $\boldsymbol{v}_i = (\boldsymbol{y}_i; \boldsymbol{x}_i)$, $\boldsymbol{\mu} = (\boldsymbol{\mu}_y; \boldsymbol{\mu}_x)$ and

$$\mathbf{W} = \begin{pmatrix} \mathbf{W}_y & \mathbf{0} \\ \mathbf{W}_x & \mathbf{B}_x \end{pmatrix} \tag{28.109}$$

$$\mathbf{W} \mathbf{W}^\mathsf{T} = \begin{pmatrix} \mathbf{W}_y \mathbf{W}_y^\mathsf{T} & \mathbf{W}_y \mathbf{W}_x^\mathsf{T} \\ \mathbf{W}_x \mathbf{W}_y^\mathsf{T} & \mathbf{W}_x \mathbf{W}_x^\mathsf{T} + \mathbf{B}_x \mathbf{B}_x^\mathsf{T} \end{pmatrix} \tag{28.110}$$

We should choose L large enough so that the shared subspace does not capture covariate-specific variation.

MLE in this model is equivalent to the technique of **partial least squares** (**PLS**) [Gus01; Nou+02; Sun+09]. This model can be also be generalized to discrete data using the exponential family [Vir10].

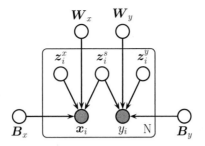

Figure 28.16: Canonical correlation analysis as a PGM.

28.3.4.3 Canonical correlation analysis

We now consider a symmetric unsupervised version of PLS, in which we allow each view to have its own "private" subspace, but there is also a shared subspace. If we have two observed variables, $\boldsymbol{x}_i$ and $\boldsymbol{y}_i$, then we have three latent variables, $\boldsymbol{z}_i^s \in \mathbb{R}^{L_s}$ which is shared, $\boldsymbol{z}_i^x \in \mathbb{R}^{L_x}$ and $\boldsymbol{z}_i^y \in \mathbb{R}^{L_y}$ which are private. We can write the model as follows [BJ05]:

$$p(\boldsymbol{z}_i) = \mathcal{N}(\boldsymbol{z}_i^s|\mathbf{0},\mathbf{I}_{L_s})\mathcal{N}(\boldsymbol{z}_i^x|\mathbf{0},\mathbf{I}_{L_x})\mathcal{N}(\boldsymbol{z}_i^y|\mathbf{0},\mathbf{I}_{L_y}) \tag{28.111}$$

$$p(\boldsymbol{x}_i|\boldsymbol{z}_i) = \mathcal{N}(\boldsymbol{x}_i|\mathbf{B}_x\boldsymbol{z}_i^x + \mathbf{W}_x\boldsymbol{z}_i^s + \boldsymbol{\mu}_x, \sigma^2\mathbf{I}_{D_x}) \tag{28.112}$$

$$p(\boldsymbol{y}_i|\boldsymbol{z}_i) = \mathcal{N}(\boldsymbol{y}_i|\mathbf{B}_y\boldsymbol{z}_i^y + \mathbf{W}_y\boldsymbol{z}_i^s + \boldsymbol{\mu}_y, \sigma^2\mathbf{I}_{D_y}) \tag{28.113}$$

See Figure 28.16 The corresponding observed joint distribution has the form

$$p(\boldsymbol{v}_i|\boldsymbol{\theta}) = \int \mathcal{N}(\boldsymbol{v}_i|\mathbf{W}\boldsymbol{z}_i + \boldsymbol{\mu}, \sigma^2\mathbf{I})\mathcal{N}(\boldsymbol{z}_i|\mathbf{0},\mathbf{I})d\boldsymbol{z}_i = \mathcal{N}(\boldsymbol{v}_i|\boldsymbol{\mu}, \mathbf{W}\mathbf{W}^\mathsf{T} + \sigma^2\mathbf{I}_D) \tag{28.114}$$

where

$$\mathbf{W} = \begin{pmatrix} \mathbf{W}_x & \mathbf{B}_x & \mathbf{0} \\ \mathbf{W}_y & \mathbf{0} & \mathbf{B}_y \end{pmatrix} \tag{28.115}$$

$$\mathbf{W}\mathbf{W}^\mathsf{T} = \begin{pmatrix} \mathbf{W}_x\mathbf{W}_x^\mathsf{T} + \mathbf{B}_x\mathbf{B}_x^\mathsf{T} & \mathbf{W}_x\mathbf{W}_y^\mathsf{T} \\ \mathbf{W}_y\mathbf{W}_x^\mathsf{T} & \mathbf{W}_y\mathbf{W}_y^\mathsf{T} + \mathbf{B}_y\mathbf{B}_y^\mathsf{T} \end{pmatrix} \tag{28.116}$$

[BJ05] showed that MLE for this model is equivalent to a classical statistical method known as **canonical correlation analysis** or **CCA** [Hot36]. However, the PGM perspective allows us to easily generalize to multiple kinds of observations (this is known as **generalized CCA** [Hor61]) or to nonlinear models (this is known as **deep CCA** [WLL16; SNM16]), or exponential family CCA [KVK10]. See [Uur+17] for further discussion of CCA and its extensions, and Section 32.2.2.2 for more details.

28.3.5 Factor analysis with exponential family likelihoods

So far we have assumed the observed data is real-valued, so $\boldsymbol{x}_n \in \mathbb{R}^D$. If we want to model other kinds of data (e.g., binary or categorical), we can simply replace the Gaussian output distribution

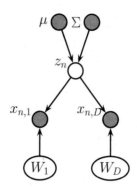

Figure 28.17: Exponential family PCA model as a DPGM.

with a suitable member of the exponential family, where the natural parameters are given by a linear function of $\boldsymbol{z}_n$. That is, we use

$$p(\boldsymbol{x}_n|\boldsymbol{z}_n) = \exp(\mathcal{T}(\boldsymbol{x})^{\mathsf{T}}\boldsymbol{\theta} + h(\boldsymbol{x}) - g(\boldsymbol{\theta})) \tag{28.117}$$

where the $N \times D$ matrix of natural parameters is assumed to be given by the low rank decomposition $\boldsymbol{\Theta} = \mathbf{Z}\mathbf{W}$, where $\mathbf{Z}$ is $N \times L$ and $\mathbf{W}$ is $L \times D$. The resulting model is called **exponential family factor analysis**

Unlike the linear-Gaussian FA, we cannot compute the exact posterior $p(\boldsymbol{z}_n|\boldsymbol{x}_n, \mathbf{W})$ due to the lack of conjugacy between the expfam likelihood and the Gaussian prior. Furthermore, we cannot compute the exact marginal likelihood either, which prevents us from finding the optimal MLE.

[CDS02] proposed a coordinate ascent method for a deterministic variant of this model, known as **exponential family PCA**. This alternates between computing a point estimate of $\boldsymbol{z}_n$ and $\mathbf{W}$. This can be regarded as a degenerate version of variational EM, where the E step uses a delta function posterior for $\boldsymbol{z}_n$. [GS08] present an improved algorithm that finds the global optimum, and [Ude+16] presents an extension called **generalized low rank models**, that covers many different kinds of loss function.

However, it is often preferable to use a probabilistic version of the model, rather than computing point estimates of the latent factors. In this case, we must represent the posterior using a non-degenerate distribution to avoid overfitting, since the number of latent variables is proportional to the number of data cases [WCS08]. Fortunately, we can use a non-degenerate posterior, such as a Gaussian, by optimizing the variational lower bound. We give some examples of this below.

28.3.5.1 Example: binary PCA

Consider a factored Bernoulli likelihood:

$$p(\boldsymbol{x}|\boldsymbol{z}) = \prod_d \text{Ber}(x_d|\sigma(\boldsymbol{w}_d^{\mathsf{T}}\boldsymbol{z})) \tag{28.118}$$

Suppose we observe $N = 150$ bit vectors of length $D = 16$. Each example is generated by choosing one of three binary prototype vectors, and then by flipping bits at random. See Figure 28.18(a)

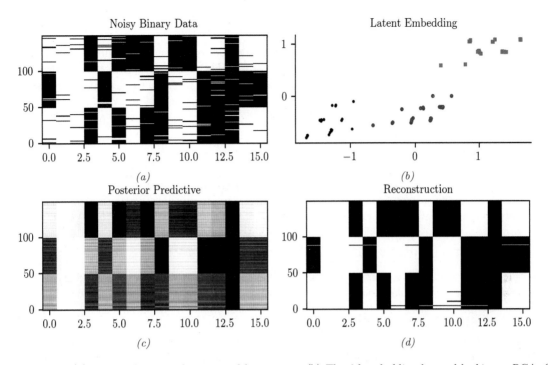

Figure 28.18: (a) 150 synthetic 16 dimensional bit vectors. (b) The 2d embedding learned by binary PCA, fit using variational EM. We have color coded points by the identity of the true "prototype" that generated them. (c) Predicted probability of being on. (d) Thresholded predictions. Generated by binary_fa_demo.ipynb.

for the data. We can fit this using the variational EM algorithm (see [Tip98] for details). We use $L = 2$ latent dimensions to allow us to visualize the latent space. In Figure 28.18(b), we plot $\mathbb{E}\left[\boldsymbol{z}_n | \boldsymbol{x}_n, \hat{\mathbf{W}}\right]$. We see that the projected points group into three distinct clusters, as is to be expected. In Figure 28.18(c), we plot the reconstructed version of the data, which is computed as follows:

$$p(\hat{x}_{nd} = 1 | \boldsymbol{x}_n) = \int d\boldsymbol{z}_n \, p(\boldsymbol{z}_n | \boldsymbol{x}_n) p(\hat{x}_{nd} | \boldsymbol{z}_n) \tag{28.119}$$

If we threshold these probabilities at 0.5 (corresponding to a MAP estimate), we get the "denoised" version of the data in Figure 28.18(d).

28.3.5.2 Example: categorical PCA

We can generalize the model in Section 28.3.5.1 to handle categorical data by using the following likelihood:

$$p(\boldsymbol{x} | \boldsymbol{z}) = \prod_d \text{Cat}(x_d | \text{softmax}(\mathbf{W}_d \boldsymbol{z})) \tag{28.120}$$

We call this **categorical PCA (CatPCA)**. A variational EM algorithm for fitting this is described in [Kha+10].

28.3.6   Factor analysis with DNN likelihoods (VAEs)

The FA model assumes the observed data can be modeled as arising from a linear mapping from a low-dimensional set of Gaussian factors. One way to relax this assumption is to let the mapping from z to x be a nonlinear model, such as a neural network. That is, the likelihood becomes

$$p(x|z) = \mathcal{N}(x|f(w;\theta), \sigma^2 \mathbf{I}) \tag{28.121}$$

We call this "**nonlinear factor analysis**". (We can of course replace the Gaussian likelihood with other distributions, such as categorical, in which case we get nonlinear exponential family factor analysis.) Unfortunately we can no longer compute the posterior or the MLE exactly, so we need to use approximate methods. In Chapter 21, we discuss the variational autoencoder, which fits this nonlinear FA model using amortized variational inference. However, it is also possible to fit the same model using other inference methods, such as MCMC (see e.g., [Hof17]).

28.3.7   Factor analysis with GP likelihoods (GP-LVM)

In this section we discuss a nonlinear version of factor analysis in which we replace the linear decoder $f(z) = \mathbf{W}z$ used in the likelihood $p(y|z) = \mathcal{N}(y|f(z), \sigma^2 \mathbf{I})$ with a nonlinear function, represented by a Gaussian process (Chapter 18), one per output dimension. This is known as a **GP-LVM**, which stands for "Gaussian process latent variable model" [Law05]. (Note that we switch notation a bit from standard FA and define the observed output variable by y, to be consistent with standard supervised GP notation; the inputs to the GP will be latent variables z.)

To explain the method in more detail, we start with PPCA (Section 28.3.2). Recall that the PPCA model is as follows:

$$p(z_i) = \mathcal{N}(z_i|\mathbf{0}, \mathbf{I}) \tag{28.122}$$

$$p(y_i|z_i, \theta) = \mathcal{N}(y_i|\mathbf{W}z_i, \sigma^2 \mathbf{I}) \tag{28.123}$$

We can fit this model by maximum likelihood, by integrating out the z_i and maximizing wrt $\mathbf{W}$ (and σ^2). The objective is given by

$$p(\mathbf{Y}|\mathbf{W}, \sigma^2) = (2\pi)^{-DN/2}|\mathbf{C}|^{-N/2} \exp\left(-\frac{1}{2}\text{tr}(\mathbf{C}^{-1}\mathbf{Y}^\mathsf{T}\mathbf{Y})\right) \tag{28.124}$$

where $\mathbf{C} = \mathbf{W}\mathbf{W}^\mathsf{T} + \sigma^2 \mathbf{I}$. As we showed in Section 28.3.2, the MLE for $\mathbf{W}$ can be computed in terms of the eigenvectors of $\mathbf{Y}^\mathsf{T}\mathbf{Y}$.

Now we consider the dual problem, whereby we maximize wrt $\mathbf{Z}$ and integrate out $\mathbf{W}$. We will use a prior of the form $p(\mathbf{W}) = \prod_j \mathcal{N}(w_j|\mathbf{0}, \mathbf{I})$. The corresponding likelihood becomes

$$p(\mathbf{Y}|\mathbf{Z}, \sigma^2) = \prod_{d=1}^{D} \mathcal{N}(\mathbf{Y}_{:,d}|\mathbf{0}, \mathbf{Z}\mathbf{Z}^\mathsf{T} + \sigma^2 \mathbf{I}) \tag{28.125}$$

$$= (2\pi)^{-DN/2}|\mathbf{K}_z|^{-D/2} \exp\left(-\frac{1}{2}\text{tr}(\mathbf{K}_\sigma^{-1}\mathbf{Y}\mathbf{Y}^\mathsf{T})\right) \tag{28.126}$$

where $\mathbf{K}_\sigma = \mathbf{K} + \sigma^2 \mathbf{I}$, and $\mathbf{K} = \mathbf{Z}\mathbf{Z}^\mathsf{T}$. The MLE for $\mathbf{Z}$ can be computed in terms of the eigenvectors of $\mathbf{K}_\sigma$, and gives the same results as PPCA (see [Law05] for the details).

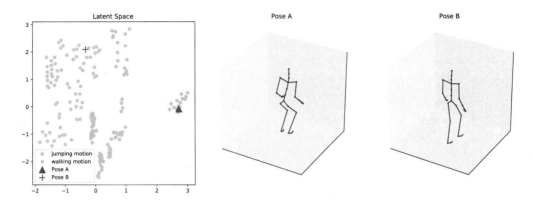

Figure 28.19: Illustration of a 2d embedding of human motion-capture data using a GP-LVM. We show two poses and their corresponding embeddings. Generated by gplvm_mocap.ipynb. Used with kind permission of Aditya Ravuri.

To understand what this process is doing, consider modeling the prior on $f : \mathcal{Z} \to \mathcal{Y}$ with a GP with a linear kernel:

$$\mathcal{K}(\boldsymbol{z}_i, \boldsymbol{z}_j) = \boldsymbol{z}_i^\mathsf{T} \boldsymbol{z}_j + \sigma^2 \delta_{ij} \tag{28.127}$$

The corresponding covariance matrix has the form $\mathbf{K} = \mathbf{ZZ}^\mathsf{T} + \sigma^2 \mathbf{I}$. Thus Equation (28.126) is equivalent to the likelihood of a product of independent GPs. Just as factor analysis is like linear regression with unknown inputs, so GP-LVM is like GP regression with unknown inputs. The goal is then to compute a point estimate of these unknown inputs, i.e., $\hat{\mathbf{Z}}$. (We can also use Bayesian inference.)

The advantage of the dual formulation is that we can use a more general kernel for $\mathbf{K}$ instead of the linear kernel. That is, we can set $K_{ij} = \mathcal{K}(\boldsymbol{z}_i, \boldsymbol{z}_j)$ for any Mercer kernel. The MLE for $\mathbf{Z}$ is no longer be available via eigenvalue methods, but can be computed using gradient-based optimization.

In Figure 28.19, we illustrate the model (with an ARD kernel) applied to some **motion capture** data, from the CMU mocap database at `http://mocap.cs.cmu.edu/`. Each person has 41 markers, whose motion in 3d is tracked using 12 infrared cameras. Each datapoint corresponds to a different body pose. When projected to 2d, we see that similar poses are clustered nearby.

28.4 LFMs with non-Gaussian priors

In this section, we discuss (linear) latent factor models with non-Gaussian priors. See Table 28.1 for a summary of the models we will discuss.

28.4.1 Non-negative matrix factorization (NMF)

Suppose that we use a gamma distribution for the latents: $p(\boldsymbol{z}) = \prod_k \mathrm{Ga}(z_k | \alpha_k, \beta_k)$. This results in a sparse, non-negative hidden representation, which can help interpretability. This is particularly

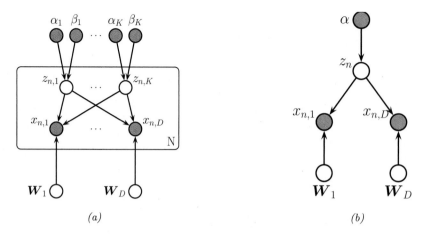

Figure 28.20: (a) Gaussian-Poisson (GAP) model as a DPGM. Here $z_{n,k} \in \mathbb{R}^+$ and $x_{n,d} \in \mathbb{Z}_{\geq 0}$. (b) Simplex FA model as a DPGM. Here $\boldsymbol{z}_n \in \mathbb{S}_K$ and $x_{n,d} \in \{1, \dots, V\}$.

useful when the data is also sparse and non-negative, such as word counts. In this case, it makes sense to use a Poisson likelihood: $p(\boldsymbol{x}|\boldsymbol{z}) = \prod_{d=1}^{D} \mathrm{Poi}(x_d|\boldsymbol{w}_d^\mathsf{T}\boldsymbol{z})$. The overall model has the form

$$p(\boldsymbol{z}, \boldsymbol{x}) = p(\boldsymbol{z})p(\boldsymbol{x}|\boldsymbol{z}) = \left[\prod_k \mathrm{Ga}(z_k|\alpha_k, \beta_k)\right]\left[\prod_{d=1}^{D} \mathrm{Poi}(x_d|\boldsymbol{w}_d^\mathsf{T}\boldsymbol{z})\right] \tag{28.128}$$

The resulting model is called the **GaP** (gamma-Poisson) model [Can04]. See Figure 28.20a for the graphical model.

The parameters α_k and β_k control the sparsity of the latent representation $\boldsymbol{z}_n$. If we set $\alpha_k = \beta_k = 0$, and compute the MLE for $\mathbf{W}$, we recover **non-negative matrix factorization** (**NMF**) [PT94; LS99; LS01], as shown in [BJ06].

Figure 28.21 illustrates the result of applying NMF to a dataset of image patches of faces, where the data correspond to non-negative pixel intensities. We see that the learned basis functions are small localized **parts** of faces. Also, the coefficient vector $\boldsymbol{z}$ is sparse and positive. For PCA, the coefficient vector has negative values, and the resulting basis functions are global, not local. For vector quantization (i.e., GMM model), $\boldsymbol{z}$ is a one-hot vector, with a single mixture component turned on; the resulting weight vectors correspond to entire image prototypes. The reconstruction quality is similar in each case, but the nature of the learned latent representation is quite different.

28.4.2   Multinomial PCA

Suppose we use a Dirichlet prior for the latents, $p(\boldsymbol{z}) = \mathrm{Dir}(\boldsymbol{z}|\boldsymbol{\alpha})$, so $\boldsymbol{z} \in \mathbb{S}_K$, which is the K-dimensional probability simplex. As in Section 28.4.1, the vector $\boldsymbol{z}$ will be sparse and non-negative, but in addition it will satisfy the constraint $\sum_{k=1}^{K} z_k = 1$, so the components are not independent. Now suppose our data is categorical, $x_d \in \{1, \dots, V\}$, so our likelihood has the form $p(\boldsymbol{x}|\boldsymbol{z}) =$

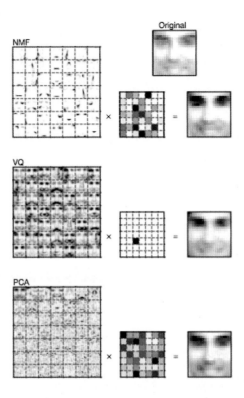

*Figure 28.21: Illustrating the difference between non-negative matrix factorization (NMF), vector quantization (VQ), and principal components analysis (PCA). Left column: filters (columns of **W**) learned from a set of 2429 faces images, each of size 19 × 19. There are 49 basis functions in total, shown in a 7 × 7 montage; each filter is reshaped to a 19 × 19 image for display purposes. (For PCA, negative weights are red, positive weights are black.) Middle column: the 49 latent factors **z** when the model is applied to the original face image shown at the top. Right column: reconstructed face image. From Figure 1 of [LS99].*

$\prod_d \text{Cat}(x_d|\mathbf{W}_d\mathbf{z})$. The overall model is therefore

$$p(\mathbf{z}, \boldsymbol{x}) = \text{Dir}(\mathbf{z}|\boldsymbol{\alpha}) \prod_{d=1}^{D} \text{Cat}(x_d|\mathbf{W}_d\mathbf{z}) \tag{28.129}$$

See Figure 28.20b for the DPGM. This model (or small variants of it) has multiple names: **user rating profile model** [Mar03], **admixture model** [PSD00], **mixed membership model** [EFL04], **multinomial PCA (mPCA)** [BJ06], or **simplex factor analysis (sFA)** [BD11].

28.4.2.1 Example: roll call data

Let us consider the example from [BJ06], who applied this model to analyze some **roll call** data from the US Senate in 2003. Specifically, the data has the form $x_{n,d} \in \{+1, -1, 0\}$ for $n = 1 : 100$

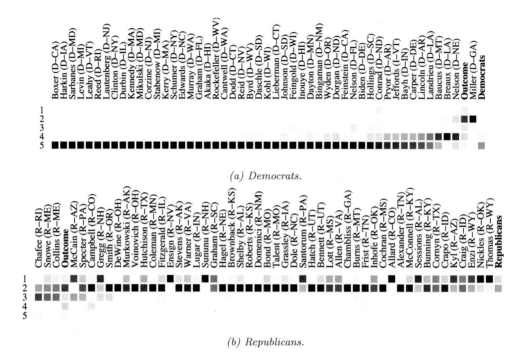

(a) Democrats.

(b) Republicans.

Figure 28.22: *The simplex factor analysis model applied to some roll call data from the US Senate collected in 2003. The senators have been sorted from left to right using the binary PCA method of [Lee06]. See text for details. From Figures 8–9 of [BJ06]. Used with kind permission of Wray Buntine.*

and $d = 1 : 459$, where x_{nd} is the vote of the n'th senator on the d'th bill, where $+1$ means in favor, -1 means against, and 0 means not voting. In addition, we have the overall outcome, which we denote by $x_{101,d} \in \{+1, -1\}$, where $+1$ means the bill was passed, and -1 means it was rejected.

We fit the mPCA model to this data using 5 latent factors using variational EM. Figure 28.22 plots $\mathbb{E}[z_{nk}|\boldsymbol{x}_n] \in [0, 1]$, which is the degree to which senator n belongs to latent component or "bloc" k. We see that component 5 is the Democractic majority, and block 2 is the Republican majority. See [BJ06] for further details.

28.4.2.2 Advantage of Dirichlet prior over Gaussian prior

The main advantage of using a Dirichlet prior compared to a Gaussian prior is that the latent factors are more interpretable. To see this, note that the mean parameters for d'th output distribution have the form $\boldsymbol{\mu}_{nd} = \mathbf{W}^d \boldsymbol{z}_n$, and hence

$$p(x_{nd} = v | \boldsymbol{z}_n) = \sum_k z_{nk} w_{vk}^d \tag{28.130}$$

Thus the latent variables can be additively combined to compute the mean parameters, aiding interpretability. By contrast, the CatPCA model in Section 28.3.5.2 uses a Gaussian prior, so $\mathbf{W}^d \boldsymbol{z}_n$

can be negative; consequently it must pass this vector through a softmax, to convert from natural parameters to mean parameters; this makes $\boldsymbol{z}_n$ harder to interpret.

28.4.2.3 Connection to mixture models

If $\boldsymbol{z}_n$ were a one-hot vector, rather than any point in the probability simplex, then the mPCA model would be equivalent to selecting a single column from $\mathbf{W}_d$ corresponding to the discrete hidden state. This is equivalent to a finite mixture of categorical distributions (see Section 28.2.2), and corresponds to the assumption that $\boldsymbol{x}$ is generated by a single cluster. However, the mPCA model does not require that $\boldsymbol{z}_n$ be one-hot, and instead allows $\boldsymbol{x}_n$ to partially belong to multiple clusters. For this reason, this model is also known as an **admixture mixture** or **mixed membership model** [EFL04].

28.5 Topic models

In this section, we show how to modify the multinomial PCA model of Section 28.4.2 to create latent variable models for sequences of discrete tokens, such as words in text documents, or genes in a DNA sequence. The basic idea is to assume that the words are conditionally independent given a latent **topic vector** $\boldsymbol{z}$. Rather than being a single discrete cluster label, $\boldsymbol{z}$ is a probability distribution over clusters, and each word is sampled from its own "local" cluster. In the NLP community, this kind of model is called a **topic model** (see e.g., [BGHM17]).

28.5.1 Latent Dirichlet allocation (LDA)

In this section, we discuss the most common kind of topic model known as **latent Dirichlet allocation** or **LDA** [BNJ03a; Ble12]. (This usage of the term "LDA" is not to be confused with linear discriminant analysis.) In the genetic community, this model is known as an **admixture model** [PSD00].

28.5.1.1 Model definition

We can define the LDA model as follows. Let $x_{nl} \in \{1, \ldots, V\}$ be the identity of the l'th word in document n, where l can now range from 1 to L_n, the length of the document, and V is the size of the vocabulary. The probability of word v at location l is given by

$$p(x_{nl} = v | \boldsymbol{z}_n) = \sum_k z_{nk} w_{kv} \tag{28.131}$$

where $0 \leq z_{nk} \leq 1$ is the proportion of "topic" k in document n, and $\boldsymbol{z}_n \sim \text{Dir}(\boldsymbol{\alpha})$.

We can rewrite this model by associating a discrete latent variable $m_{nl} \in \{1, \ldots, N_z\}$ with each word in each document, with distribution $p(m_{nl} | \boldsymbol{z}_n) = \text{Cat}(m_{nl} | \boldsymbol{z}_n)$. Thus m_{nl} specifies the topic to use for word l in document n. The full joint model becomes

$$p(\boldsymbol{x}_n, \boldsymbol{z}_n, \boldsymbol{m}_n) = \text{Dir}(\boldsymbol{z}_n | \boldsymbol{\alpha}) \prod_{l=1}^{L_n} \text{Cat}(m_{nl} | \boldsymbol{z}_n) \text{Cat}(x_{nl} | \mathbf{W}[m_{nl}, :]) \tag{28.132}$$

where $\mathbf{W}[k, :] = \boldsymbol{w}_k$ is the distribution over words for the k'th topic. See Figure 28.23 for the corresponding DPGM.

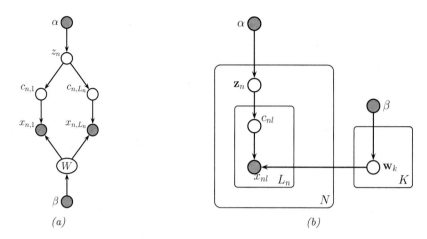

Figure 28.23: *Latent Dirichlet allocation (LDA) as a DPGM. (a) Unrolled form. (b) Plate form.*

We typically use a Dirichlet prior the topic parameters, $p(\boldsymbol{w}_k) = \mathrm{Dir}(\boldsymbol{w}_k|\beta\mathbf{1}_V)$; by setting β small enough, we can encourage these topics to be sparse, so that each topic only predicts a subset of the words. In addition, we use a Dirichlet prior on the latent factors, $p(\boldsymbol{z}_n) = \mathrm{Dir}(\boldsymbol{z}_n|\alpha\mathbf{1}_{N_z})$. If we set α small enough, we can encourage the topic distribution for each document to be sparse, so that each document only contains a subset of the topics. See Figure 28.24 for an illustration.

Note that an earlier version of LDA, known as **probabilistic LSA**, was proposed in [Hof99]. (LSA stands for "**latent semantic analysis**", and refers to the application of PCA to text data; see [Mur22, Sec 20.5.1.2] for details.) The likelihood function, $p(\boldsymbol{x}|\boldsymbol{z})$, is the same as in LDA, but pLSA does not specify a prior for $\boldsymbol{z}$, since it is designed for posterior analysis of a fixed corpus (similar to LSA), rather than being a true generative model.

28.5.1.2   Polysemy

Each topic is a distribution over words that co-occur, and which are therefore semantically related. For example, Figure 28.25 shows 3 topics which were learned from an LDA model fit to the **TASA corpus**[3]. These seem to correspond to 3 different senses of the word "play": playing an instrument, a theatrical play, and playing a sports game.

We can use the inferred document-level topic distribution to overcome **polysemy**, i.e., to disambiguate the meaning of a particular word. This is illustrated in Figure 28.26, where a subset of the words are annotated with the topic to which they were assigned (i.e., we show $\mathrm{argmax}_k\, p(m_{nl} = k|\boldsymbol{x}_n)$). In the first document, the word "music" makes it clear that the musical topic (number 77) is present in the document, which in turn makes it more likely that $m_{nl} = 77$ where l is the index corresponding to the word "play".

---

3. The TASA corpus is an untagged collection of educational materials consisting of 37,651 documents and 12,190,931 word tokens. Words appearing in fewer than 5 documents were replaced with an asterisk, but punctuation was included. The combined vocabulary was of size 37,202 unique words.

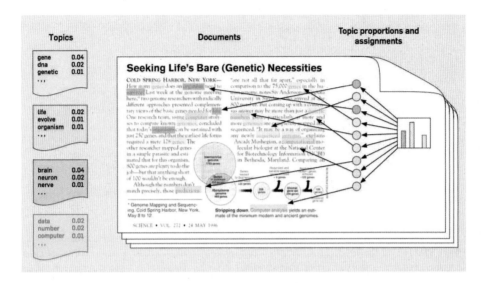

Figure 28.24: *Illustration of latent Dirichlet allocation (LDA). We have color coded certain words by the topic they have been assigned to: yellow represents the genetics cluster, pink represents the evolution cluster, blue represent the data analysis cluster, and green represents the neuroscience cluster. Each topic is in turn defined as a sparse distribution over words. This article is not related to neuroscience, so no words are assigned to the green topic. The overall distribution over topic assignments for this document is shown in the right as a sparse histogram. Adapted from Figure 1 of [Ble12]. Used with kind permission of David Blei.*

Topic 77		Topic 82		Topic 166	
word	prob.	word	prob.	word	prob.
MUSIC	.090	LITERATURE	.031	PLAY	.136
DANCE	.034	POEM	.028	BALL	.129
SONG	.033	POETRY	.027	GAME	.065
PLAY	.030	POET	.020	PLAYING	.042
SING	.026	PLAYS	.019	HIT	.032
SINGING	.026	POEMS	.019	PLAYED	.031
BAND	.026	PLAY	.015	BASEBALL	.027
PLAYED	.023	LITERARY	.013	GAMES	.025
SANG	.022	WRITERS	.013	BAT	.019
SONGS	.021	DRAMA	.012	RUN	.019
DANCING	.020	WROTE	.012	THROW	.016
PIANO	.017	POETS	.011	BALLS	.015
PLAYING	.016	WRITER	.011	TENNIS	.011
RHYTHM	.015	SHAKESPEARE	.010	HOME	.010
ALBERT	.013	WRITTEN	.009	CATCH	.010
MUSICAL	.013	STAGE	.009	FIELD	.010

Figure 28.25: *Three topics related to the word* play. *From Figure 9 of [SG07]. Used with kind permission of Tom Griffiths.*

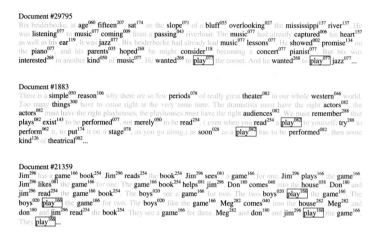

Figure 28.26: *Three documents from the TASA corpus containing different senses of the word* play. *Grayed out words were ignored by the model, because they correspond to uninteresting stop words (such as "and", "the", etc.) or very low frequency words. From Figure 10 of [SG07]. Used with kind permission of Tom Griffiths.*

28.5.1.3 Posterior inference

Many algorithms have been proposed to perform approximate posterior inference in the LDA model. In the original LDA paper, [BNJ03a], they use variational mean field inference (see Section 10.3). In [HBB10], they use stochastic VI (see Supplementary Section 28.1.2). In [GS04], they use collapsed Gibbs sampling, which marginalizes out the discrete latents (see Supplementary Section 28.1.1). In [MB16; SS17b] they discuss how to learned amortized inference networks to perform VI for the collapsed model.

Recently, there has been considerable interest in spectral methods for fitting LDA-like models which are fast and which come with provable guarantees about the quality of the solution they obtain (unlike MCMC and variational methods, where the solution is just an approximation of unknown quality). These methods make certain (reasonable) assumptions beyond the basic model, such as the existence of some anchor words, which uniquely the topic for a document. See [Aro+13] for details.

28.5.1.4 Determining the number of topics

Choosing N_z, the number of topics, is a standard model selection problem. Here are some approaches that have been taken:
- Use annealed importance sampling (Section 11.5.4) to approximate the evidence [Wal+09].
- Cross validation, using the log likelihood on a test set.
- Use the variational lower bound as a proxy for $\log p(\mathcal{D}|N_z)$.
- Use non-parametric Bayesian methods [Teh+06].

28.5.2 Correlated topic model

One weakness of LDA is that it cannot capture correlation between topics. For example, if a document has the "business" topic, it is reasonable to expect the "finance" topic to co-occcur. The source of the problem is the use of a Dirichlet prior for z_n. The problem with the Dirichlet it that it is characterized by just a mean vector $\boldsymbol{\alpha}$, but its covariance is fixed ($\Sigma_{ij} = -\alpha_i \alpha_j$), rather than being a free parameter.

One way around this is to replace the Dirichlet prior with the **logistic normal** distribution, which is defined as follows:

$$p(\boldsymbol{z}) = \int \text{Cat}(\boldsymbol{z}|\text{softmax}(\boldsymbol{\epsilon}))\mathcal{N}(\boldsymbol{\epsilon}|\boldsymbol{\mu}, \boldsymbol{\Sigma})d\boldsymbol{\epsilon} \tag{28.133}$$

This is known as the **correlated topic model** [BL07b];

The difference from categorical PCA discussed in Section 28.3.5.2 is that CTM uses a logistic normal to model the mean parameters, so z_n is sparse and non-negative, whereas CatPCA uses a normal to model the natural parameters, so z_n is dense and can be negative. More precisely, the CTM defines $x_{nl} \sim \text{Cat}(\mathbf{W}\text{softmax}(\boldsymbol{\epsilon}_n))$, but CatPCA defines $\boldsymbol{x}_{nd} \sim \text{Cat}(\text{softmax}(\mathbf{W}_d\boldsymbol{z}_n))$.

Fitting the CTM model is tricky, since the prior for $\boldsymbol{\epsilon}_n$ is no longer conjugate to the multinomial likelihood for m_{nl}. However, we can derive a variational mean field approximation, as described in [BL07b].

Having fit the model, one can then convert $\hat{\boldsymbol{\Sigma}}$ to a sparse precision matrix $\hat{\boldsymbol{\Sigma}}^{-1}$ by pruning low-strength edges, to get a sparse Gaussian graphical model. This allows you to visualize the correlation between topics. Figure 28.27 shows the result of applying this procedure to articles from *Science* magazine, from 1990–1999.

28.5.3 Dynamic topic model

In LDA, the topics (distributions over words) are assumed to be static. In some cases, it makes sense to allow these distributions to evolve smoothly over time. For example, an article might use the topic "neuroscience", but if it was written in the 1900s, it is more likely to use words like "nerve", whereas if it was written in the 2000s, it is more likely to use words like "calcium receptor" (this reflects the general trend of neuroscience towards molecular biology).

One way to model this is to assume the topic distributions evolve according to a Gaussian random walk, as in a state space model (see Section 29.1). We can map these Gaussian vectors to probabilities via the softmax function, resulting in the following model:

$$\boldsymbol{w}_k^t | \boldsymbol{w}_k^{t-1} \sim \mathcal{N}(\boldsymbol{w}_{t-1,k}, \sigma^2 \mathbf{1}_{N_w}) \tag{28.134}$$
$$\boldsymbol{z}_n^t \sim \text{Dir}(\alpha \mathbf{1}_{N_z}) \tag{28.135}$$
$$m_{nl}^t | \boldsymbol{z}_n^t \sim \text{Cat}(\boldsymbol{z}_n^t) \tag{28.136}$$
$$x_{nl}^t | m_{nl}^t = k, \mathbf{W}^t \sim \text{Cat}(\text{softmax}(\boldsymbol{w}_k^t)) \tag{28.137}$$

This is known as a **dynamic topic model** [BL06]. See Figure 28.28 for the DPGM.

One can perform approximate inference in this model using a structured mean field method (Section 10.4.1), that exploits the Kalman smoothing algorithm (Section 8.2.2) to perform exact inference on the linear-Gaussian chain between the $\boldsymbol{w}_k^t$ nodes (see [BL06] for details). Figure 28.29 illustrates a typical output of the system when applied to 100 years of articles from *Science*.

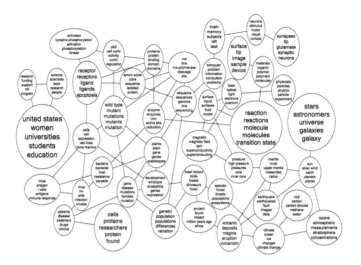

Figure 28.27: Output of the correlated topic model (with $K = 50$ topics) when applied to articles from Science. Nodes represent topics, with the 5 most probable phrases from each topic shown inside. Font size reflects overall prevalence of the topic. See http://www.cs.cmu.edu/~lemur/science/ for an interactive version of this model with 100 topics. Used with kind permission of Figure 2 of [BL07b]. Used with kind permission of David Blei.

It is also possible to use amortized inference, and to learn embeddings for each word, which works much better with rare words. This is called the **dynamic embedded topic model** [DRB19].

28.5.4   LDA-HMM

The Latent dirichlet allocation (LDA) model of Section 28.5.1 assumes words are exchangeable, and thus ignores word order. A simple way to model sequential dependence between words is to use an HMM. The trouble with HMMs is that they can only model short-range dependencies, so they cannot capture the overall gist of a document. Hence they can generate syntactically correct sentences, but not semantically plausible ones.

It is possible to combine LDA with HMM to create a model called **LDA-HMM** [Gri+04]. This model uses the HMM states to model function or syntactic words, such as "and" or "however", and uses the LDA to model content or semantic words, which are harder to predict. There is a distinguished HMM state which specifies when the LDA model should be used to generate the word; the rest of the time, the HMM generates the word.

More formally, for each document n, the model defines an HMM with states $h_{nl} \in \{0, \ldots, H\}$. In addition, each document has an LDA model associated with it. If $h_{nl} = 0$, we generate word x_{nl} from the semantic LDA model, with topic specified by m_{nl}; otherwise we generate word x_{nl} from the

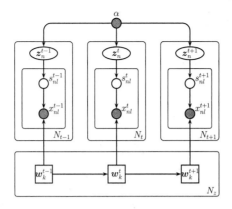

Figure 28.28: The dynamic topic model as a DPGM.

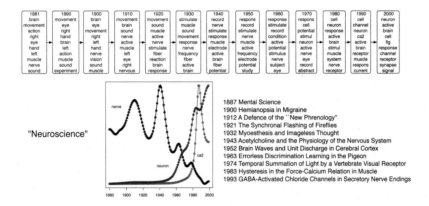

Figure 28.29: Part of the output of the dynamic topic model when applied to articles from Science. At the top, we show the top 10 words for the neuroscience topic over time. On the bottom left, we show the probability of three words within this topic over time. On the bottom right, we list paper titles from different years that contained this topic. From Figure 4 of [BL06]. Used with kind permission of David Blei.

syntactic HMM model. The DPGM is shown in Figure 28.30. The CPDs are as follows:

$$p(\boldsymbol{z}_n) = \mathrm{Dir}(\boldsymbol{z}_n | \alpha \mathbf{1}_{N_z}) \tag{28.138}$$

$$p(m_{nl} = k | \boldsymbol{z}_n) = z_{nk} \tag{28.139}$$

$$p(h_{n,l} = j | h_{n,l-1} = i) = A_{ij} \tag{28.140}$$

$$p(x_{nl} = d | m_{nl} = k, h_{nl} = j) = \begin{cases} W_{kd} & \text{if } j = 0 \\ B_{jd} & \text{if } j > 0 \end{cases} \tag{28.141}$$

where $\mathbf{W}$ is the usual topic-word matrix, $\mathbf{B}$ is the state-word HMM emission matrix, and $\mathbf{A}$ is the state-state HMM transition matrix.

Inference in this model can be done with collapsed Gibbs sampling, analytically integrating out all the continuous quantities. See [Gri+04] for the details.

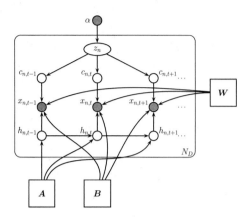

Figure 28.30: *LDA-HMM model as a DPGM.*

the	the	the	the	the	a	the	the	the
blood	,	,	of	a	the	,	,	,
,	and	and	,	of	of	of	a	a
of	of	of	to	,	,	a	of	in
body	a	in	in	in	in	and	and	game
heart	in	land	and	to	water	in	drink	ball
and	trees	to	classes	picture	is	story	alcohol	and
in	tree	farmers	government	film	and	is	to	team
to	with	for	a	image	matter	to	bottle	to
is	on	farm	state	lens	are	as	in	play
blood	forest	farmers	government	light	water	story	drugs	ball
heart	trees	land	state	eye	matter	stories	drug	game
pressure	forests	crops	federal	lens	molecules	poem	alcohol	team
body	land	farm	public	image	liquid	characters	people	*
lungs	soil	food	local	mirror	particles	poetry	drinking	baseball
oxygen	areas	people	act	eyes	gas	character	person	players
vessels	park	farming	states	glass	solid	author	effects	football
arteries	wildlife	wheat	national	object	substance	poems	marijuana	player
*	area	farms	laws	objects	temperature	life	body	field
breathing	rain	corn	department	lenses	changes	poet	use	basketball
the	in	he	*	be	said	can	time	,
a	for	it	new	have	made	would	way	;
his	to	you	other	see	used	will	years	(
this	on	they	first	make	came	could	day	:
their	with	i	same	do	went	may	part	)
these	at	she	great	know	found	had	number	
your	by	we	good	get	called	must	kind	
her	from	there	small	go		do	place	
my	as	this	little	take		have		
some	into	who	old	find		did		

Table 28.2: *Upper row: topics extracted by the LDA model when trained on the combined Brown and TASA corpora. Middle row: topics extracted by LDA part of LDA-HMM model. Bottom row: topics extracted by HMM part of LDA-HMM model. Each column represents a single topic/class, and words appear in order of probability in that topic/class. Since some classes give almost all probability to only a few words, a list is terminated when the words account for 90% of the probability mass. From Figure 2 of [Gri+04]. Used with kind permission of Tom Griffiths.*

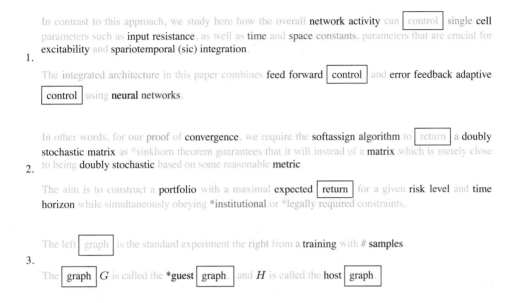

1.

In contrast to this approach, we study here how the overall **network activity** can control single **cell** parameters such as **input resistance**, as well as **time** and **space** constants, parameters that are crucial for excitability and **spariotemporal (sic) integration**.

The integrated architecture in this paper combines **feed forward** control and **error feedback adaptive** control using **neural networks**.

2.

In other words, for our proof of **convergence**, we require the **softassign algorithm** to return a **doubly stochastic matrix** as *sinkhorn theorem guarantees that it will instead of a **matrix** which is merely close to being **doubly stochastic** based on some reasonable **metric**.

The aim is to construct a **portfolio** with a maximal **expected** return for a given **risk** level and **time horizon** while simultaneously obeying *institutional or *legally required constraints.

3.

The left graph is the standard experiment the right from a **training** with # **samples**.

The graph *G* is called the *guest graph, and *H* is called the host graph.

Figure 28.31: Function and content words in the NIPS corpus, as distinguished by the LDA-HMM model. Graylevel indicates posterior probability of assignment to LDA component, with black being highest. The boxed word appears as a function word in one sentence, and as a content word in another sentence. Asterisked words had low frequency, and were treated as a single word type by the model. From Figure 4 of [Gri+04]. Used with kind permission of Tom Griffiths.

The results of applying this model (with $N_z = 200$ LDA topics and $H = 20$ HMM states) to the combined Brown and TASA corpora[4] are shown in Table 28.2. We see that the HMM generally is responsible for syntactic words, and the LDA for semantics words. If we did not have the HMM, the LDA topics would get "polluted" by function words (see top of figure), which is why such words are normally removed during preprocessing.

The model can also help disambiguate when the same word is being used syntactically or semantically. Figure 28.31 shows some examples when the model was applied to the NIPS corpus.[5] We see that the roles of words are distinguished, e.g., "we require the algorithm to *return* a matrix" (verb) vs "the maximal expected *return*" (noun). In principle, a part of speech tagger could disambiguate these two uses, but note that (1) the LDA-HMM method is fully unsupervised (no POS tags were used), and (2) sometimes a word can have the same POS tag, but different senses, e.g., "the left graph" (a synactic role) vs "the graph *G*" (a semantic role).

More recently, [Die+17] proposed topic-RNN, which is similar to LDA-HMM, but replaces the HMM model with an RNN, which is a much more powerful model.

---

4. The Brown corpus consists of 500 documents and 1,137,466 word tokens, with part-of-speech tags for each token. The TASA corpus is an untagged collection of educational materials consisting of 37,651 documents and 12,190,931 word tokens. Words appearing in fewer than 5 documents were replaced with an asterisk, but punctuation was included. The combined vocabulary was of size 37,202 unique words.
5. NIPS stands for "Neural Information Processing Systems". It is one of the top machine learning conferences. The NIPS corpus volumes 1–12 contains 1713 documents.

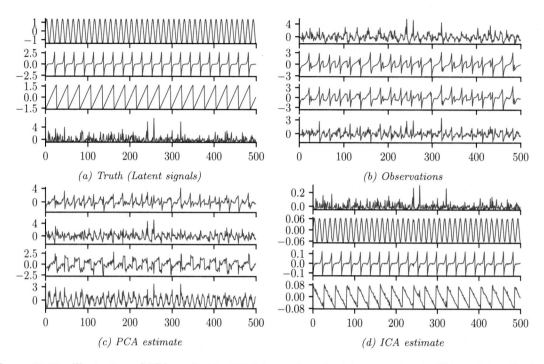

(a) Truth (Latent signals)

(b) Observations

(c) PCA estimate

(d) ICA estimate

Figure 28.32: *Illustration of ICA applied to 500 iid samples of a 4d source signal. This matches the true sources, up to permutation of the dimension indices. Generated by ica_demo.ipynb.*

28.6   Independent components analysis (ICA)

Consider the following situation. You are in a crowded room and many people are speaking. Your ears essentially act as two microphones, which are listening to a linear combination of the different speech signals in the room. Your goal is to deconvolve the mixed signals into their constituent parts. This is known as the **cocktail party problem**, or the **blind source separation (BSS)** problem, where "blind" means we know "nothing" about the source of the signals. Besides the obvious applications to acoustic signal processing, this problem also arises when analyzing EEG and MEG signals, financial data, and any other dataset (not necessarily temporal) where latent sources or factors get mixed together in a linear way. See Figure 28.32 for an example.

28.6.1   Noiseless ICA model

We can formalize the problem as follows. Let $\boldsymbol{x}_n \in \mathbb{R}^D$ be the vector of observed responses, at "time" n, where D is the number of sensors/microphones. Let $\boldsymbol{z}_n \in \mathbb{R}^D$ be the hidden vector of source signals at time n, of the same dimensionality as the observed signal. We assume that

$$\boldsymbol{x}_n = \mathbf{A}\boldsymbol{z}_n \tag{28.142}$$

where $\mathbf{A}$ is an invertible $D \times D$ matrix known as the **mixing matrix** or the **generative weights**. The prior has the form $p(\boldsymbol{z}_n) = \prod_{j=1}^{D} p_j(z_j)$. Typically we assume this is a sparse prior, so only a

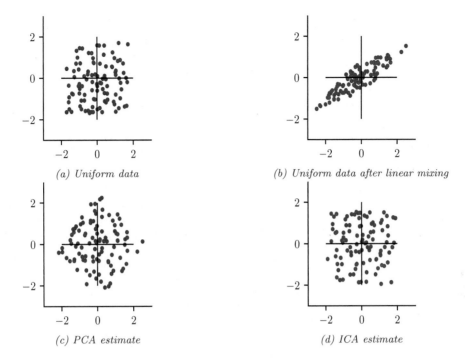

(a) Uniform data

(b) Uniform data after linear mixing

(c) PCA estimate

(d) ICA estimate

Figure 28.33: *Illustration of ICA and PCA applied to 100 iid samples of a 2d source signal with a uniform distribution. Generated by* ica_demo_uniform.ipynb.

subset of the signals are active at any one time (see Section 28.6.2 for further discussion of priors for this model). This model is called **independent components analysis** or **ICA**, since we assume that each observation $\boldsymbol{x}_n$ is a linear combination of independent components represented by sources $\boldsymbol{z}_n$, i.e,

$$x_{nj} = \sum_i A_{ij} z_{nj} \tag{28.143}$$

Our goal is to infer the source signals, $p(\boldsymbol{z}_n|\boldsymbol{x}_n, \mathbf{A})$. Since the model is noiseless, we have

$$p(\boldsymbol{z}_n|\boldsymbol{x}_n, \mathbf{A}) = \delta(\boldsymbol{z}_n - \mathbf{B}\boldsymbol{x}_n) \tag{28.144}$$

where $\mathbf{B} = \mathbf{A}^{-1}$ are the **recognition weights**. (We discuss how to estimate these weights in Section 28.6.3.)

28.6.2 The need for non-Gaussian priors

Since $\boldsymbol{x} = \mathbf{A}\boldsymbol{z}$, we have $\mathbb{E}[\boldsymbol{x}] = \mathbf{A}\mathbb{E}[\boldsymbol{z}]$ and $\text{Cov}[\boldsymbol{x}] = \text{Cov}[\mathbf{A}\boldsymbol{z}] = \mathbf{A}\text{Cov}[\boldsymbol{z}]\mathbf{A}^{\mathsf{T}}$. Without loss of generality, we can assume $\mathbb{E}[\boldsymbol{z}] = \mathbf{0}$, since we can always center the data. Similarly, we can assume $\text{Cov}[\boldsymbol{z}] = \mathbf{I}$, since $\mathbf{A}\mathbf{A}^{\mathsf{T}}$ can capture any correlation in $\boldsymbol{x}$. Thus $\boldsymbol{z}$ is a set of D unit variance, uncorrelated variables, as in factor analysis (Section 28.3.1).

However, this is not sufficient to uniquely identify $\mathbf{A}$ and hence $\mathbf{z}$, as we explained in Section 28.3.1.6. So we need to go beyond an uncorrelated prior and enforce an independent, and non-Gaussian, prior.

To illustrate this, suppose we have two independent sources with uniform distributions, as shown in Figure 28.33(a). Now suppose we have the following mixing matrix

$$\mathbf{A} = 0.3 \begin{pmatrix} 2 & 3 \\ 2 & 1 \end{pmatrix} \tag{28.145}$$

Then we observe the data shown in Figure 28.33(b) (assuming no noise). The full-rank PCA model (where $K = D$) is equivalent to ICA, except it uses a factored Gaussian prior for $\mathbf{z}$. The result of using PCA is shown in Figure 28.33(c). This corresponds to a **whitening** or **sphering** of the data, in which $\mathrm{Cov}\,[\mathbf{z}] = \mathbf{I}$. To uniquely recover the sources, we need to perform an additional rotation. The trouble is, there is no information in the symmetric Gaussian posterior to tell us which angle to rotate by. In a sense, PCA solves "half" of the problem, since it identifies the linear subspace; all that ICA has to do is then to identify the appropriate rotation. To do this, ICA uses an independent, but non-Gaussian, prior. The result is shown in Figure 28.33(d). This shows that ICA can recover the source variables, up to a permutation of the indices and possible sign change.

We typically use a prior which is a super-Gaussian distribution, meaning it has heavy tails; this helps with identifiability. One option is to use a Laplace prior. For mean zero and variance 1, this has a log pdf given by

$$\log p(z) = -\sqrt{2}|z| - \log(\sqrt{2}) \tag{28.146}$$

However, since the Laplace prior is not differentiable at the origin, in ICA it is more common to use the logistic distribution, discussed in Section 15.4.1. If we set the mean to 0 and the variance to 1, we have $\mu = 0$ and $s = \frac{\sqrt{3}}{\pi}$, so the log pdf becomes the following (using the relationship $\mathrm{sech}(x) = 1/\cosh(x)$):

$$\log p(z) = \log \mathrm{sech}^2(z/2s) - \log(4s) = -2\log\cosh(\frac{\pi}{2\sqrt{3}}z) - \log\frac{4\sqrt{3}}{\pi} \tag{28.147}$$

28.6.3 Maximum likelihood estimation

In this section, we discuss how to estimate the mixing matrix $\mathbf{A}$ using maximum likelohood. By the change of variables formula we have

$$p_x(\boldsymbol{x}) = p_z(\boldsymbol{z})|\det(\mathbf{A}^{-1})| = p_z(\mathbf{B}\boldsymbol{x})|\det(\mathbf{B}))| \tag{28.148}$$

where $\mathbf{B} = \mathbf{A}^{-1}$. We can simplify the problem by first whitening the data by computing $\tilde{\boldsymbol{x}} = \mathbf{S}^{-\frac{1}{2}}\mathbf{U}^{\mathsf{T}}(\boldsymbol{x} - \bar{\boldsymbol{x}})$, where $\boldsymbol{\Sigma} = \mathbf{U}\mathbf{S}\mathbf{U}^{\mathsf{T}}$ is the SVD of the covariance matrix. We can now replace the general matrix $\mathbf{B}$ with an orthogonal matrix $\mathbf{V}$. Hence the likelihood becomes

$$p_x(\tilde{\boldsymbol{x}}) = p_z(\mathbf{V}\tilde{\boldsymbol{x}})|\det(\mathbf{V})| \tag{28.149}$$

Since we are constraining $\mathbf{V}$ to be orthogonal, the $|\det(\mathbf{V})|$ term is a constant, so we can drop it. In addition, we drop the tilde symbol, for brevity. Thus the average negative log likelihood can be written as

$$\mathrm{NLL}(\mathbf{V}) = -\frac{1}{N}\log p(\mathbf{X}|\mathbf{V}) = -\frac{1}{N}\sum_{j=1}^{L}\sum_{n=1}^{N}\log p_j(\boldsymbol{v}_j^{\mathsf{T}}\boldsymbol{x}_n) \tag{28.150}$$

where v_j is the j'th row of $\mathbf{V}$, and the prior is factored, so $p(\mathbf{z}) = \prod_j p_j(z_j)$. We can also replace the sum over n with an expectation wrt the empirical distribution to get the following objective

$$\text{NLL}(\mathbf{V}) = \sum_j \mathbb{E}\left[G_j(z_j)\right] \tag{28.151}$$

where $z_j = v_j^\mathsf{T} x$ and $G_j(z_j) \triangleq -\log p_j(z_j)$. We want to minimize this (nonconvex) objective subject to the constraint that $\mathbf{V}$ is an orthogonal matrix.

It is straightforward to derive a (projected) gradient descent algorithm to fit this model. (For some JAX code, see https://github.com/tuananhle7/ica). One can also derive a faster algorithm that follows the natural gradient; see e.g., [Mac03, ch 34] for details. However, the most popular method is to use an approximate Newton method, known as **fast ICA** [HO00]. This was used to produce Figure 28.32.

28.6.4 Alternatives to MLE

In this section, we discuss various alternatives estimators for ICA that have been proposed over the years. We will show that they are equivalent to MLE. However, they bring interesting perspectives to the problem.

28.6.4.1 Maximizing non-Gaussianity

An early approach to ICA was to find a matrix $\mathbf{V}$ such that the distribution $\mathbf{z} = \mathbf{V}x$ is as far from Gaussian as possible. (There is a related approach in statistics called **projection pursuit** [FT74].) One measure of non-Gaussianity is kurtosis, but this can be sensitive to outliers. Another measure is the **negentropy**, defined as

$$\text{negentropy}(z) \triangleq \mathbb{H}\left(\mathcal{N}(\mu, \sigma^2)\right) - \mathbb{H}(z) \tag{28.152}$$

where $\mu = \mathbb{E}[z]$ and $\sigma^2 = \mathbb{V}[z]$. Since the Gaussian is the maximum entropy distribution (for a fixed variance), this measure is always non-negative and becomes large for distributions that are highly non-Gaussian.

We can define our objective as maximizing

$$J(\mathbf{V}) = \sum_j \text{negentropy}(z_j) = \sum_j \mathbb{H}\left(\mathcal{N}(\mu_j, \sigma_j^2)\right) - \mathbb{H}(z_j) \tag{28.153}$$

where $\mathbf{z} = \mathbf{V}x$. Since we assume $\mathbb{E}[\mathbf{z}] = \mathbf{0}$ and $\text{Cov}[\mathbf{z}] = \mathbf{I}$, the first term is a constant. Hence

$$J(\mathbf{V}) = \sum_j -\mathbb{H}(z_j) + \text{const} = \sum_j \mathbb{E}[\log p(z_j)] + \text{const} \tag{28.154}$$

which we see is equal (up to a sign change, and irrelevant constants) to the log-likelihood in Equation (28.151).

28.6.4.2   Minimizing total correlation

In Section 5.3.5.1, we show that the total correlation of z is given by

$$\text{TC}(z) = \sum_j \mathbb{H}(z_j) - \mathbb{H}(z) = D_{\text{KL}}\left(p(z) \,\|\, \prod_j p_k(z_j)\right) \tag{28.155}$$

This is zero iff the components of z are all mutually independent. In Section 21.3.1.1, we show that minimizing this results in a representation that is **disentangled**.

Now since $z = \mathbf{V}x$, we have

$$\text{TC}(z) = \sum_j \mathbb{H}(z_j) - \mathbb{H}(\mathbf{V}x) \tag{28.156}$$

Since we constrain $\mathbf{V}$ to be orthogonal, we can drop the last term, since $\mathbb{H}(\mathbf{V}x) = \mathbb{H}(x) = \text{const}$, since multiplying by $\mathbf{V}$ does not change the shape of the distribution. Hence we have $\text{TC}(z) = \sum_k \mathbb{H}(z_k)$. Minimizing this is equivalent to maximizing the negentropy, which is equivalent to maximum likelihood.

28.6.4.3   Maximizing mutual information (InfoMax)

Let $z_j = \phi(v_j^\mathsf{T} x) + \epsilon$ be the noisy output of an encoder, where ϕ is some nonlinear scalar function, and $\epsilon \sim \mathcal{N}(0, 1)$. It seems reasonable to try to maximize the information flow through this system, a principle known as **infomax** [Lin88b; BS95a]. That is, we want to maximize the mutual information between z (the internal neural representation) and x (the observed input signal). We have $\mathbb{I}(x; z) = \mathbb{H}(z) - \mathbb{H}(z|x)$, where the latter term is constant if we assume the noise has constant variance. One can show that we can approximate the former term as follows

$$\mathbb{H}(z) = \sum_j \mathbb{E}\left[\log \phi'(v_j^\mathsf{T} x)\right] + \log |\det(\mathbf{V})| \tag{28.157}$$

where, as usual, we can drop the last term if $\mathbf{V}$ is orthogonal. If we define $\phi(z)$ to be a cdf, then $\phi'(z)$ is its pdf, and the above expression is equivalent to the log likelihood. In particular, if we use a logistic nonlinearity, $\phi(z) = \sigma(z)$, then the corresponding pdf is the logistic distribution, and $\log \phi'(z) = \log \cosh(z)$, which matches Equation (28.147) (ignoring irrelevant constants). Thus we see that infomax is equivalent to maximum likelihood.

28.6.5   Sparse coding

In this section, we consider an extension of ICA to the case where we allow for observation noise (using a Gaussian likelihood), and we allow for a non-square mixing matrix $\mathbf{W}$. We also use a Laplace prior for z. The resulting model is as follows:

$$p(z, x) = p(z)p(x|z) = \left[\prod_k \text{Laplace}(z_k|0, 1/\lambda)\right] \mathcal{N}(x|\mathbf{W}z, \sigma^2 \mathbf{I}) \tag{28.158}$$

Thus each observation $\boldsymbol{x}$ is approximated by a sparse combination of columns of $\mathbf{W}$, known as **basis functions**; the sparse vector of weights is given by $\boldsymbol{z}$. (This can be thought of as a form of sparse factor analysis, except the sparsity is in the latent code $\boldsymbol{z}$, not the weight matrix $\mathbf{W}$.)

Not all basis functions will be active for any given observation, due to the sparsity penalty. Hence we can allow for more latent factors K than observations D. This is called **overcomplete representation**.

If we have a batch of N examples, stored in the rows of $\mathbf{X}$, the negative log joint becomes

$$-\log p(\mathbf{X}, \mathbf{Z} | \mathbf{W}) = \frac{1}{2\sigma^2} \sum_{n=1}^{N} ||\boldsymbol{x}_n - \mathbf{W} \boldsymbol{z}_n||_2^2 + \lambda ||\boldsymbol{z}_n||_1 + \text{const} \tag{28.159}$$

$$= \frac{1}{2\sigma^2} ||\mathbf{X} - \mathbf{W} \mathbf{Z}||_F^2 + \lambda ||\mathbf{Z}||_{1,1} + \text{const} \tag{28.160}$$

The MAP inference problem consists of estimating $\mathbf{Z}$ for a fixed $\mathbf{W}$; this is known as **sparse coding**, and can be solved using standard algorithms for sparse linear regression (see Section 15.2.6).[6],

The learning problem consists of estimating $\mathbf{W}$, marginalizing out $\mathbf{Z}$. This is called **dictionary learning**. Since this is computationally difficult, it is common to jointly optimize $\mathbf{W}$ and $\mathbf{Z}$ (thus "maxing out" wrt $\mathbf{Z}$ instead of marginalizing it out). We can do this by applying alternating optimization to Equation (28.160): estimating $\mathbf{Z}$ given $\mathbf{W}$ is a sparse linear regression problem, and estimating $\mathbf{W}$ given $\mathbf{Z}$ is a simple least squares problem. (For faster algorithms, see [Mai+10].)

Figure 28.34(a) illustrates the results of dictionary learning when applied to a dataset of natural image patches. (Each patch is first centered and normalized to unit norm.) We see that the method has learned bar and edge detectors that are similar to the simple cells in the primary visual cortex of the mammalian brain [OF96]. By contrast, PCA results in sinusoidal gratings, as shown in Figure 28.34(b).[7]

28.6.6 Nonlinear ICA

There are various ways to extend ICA to the nonlinear case. The resulting methods are similar to variational autoencoders (Chapter 21). For details, see e.g., [KKH20].

---

6. Solving an ℓ_1 optimization problem for each data example can be slow. However, it is possible to train a neural network to approximate the outcome of this process; this is known as **predictive sparse decomposition** [KRL08; GL10].

7. The reason PCA discovers sinusoidal grating patterns is because it is trying to model the covariance of the data, which, in the case of image patches, is translation invariant. This means $\text{Cov}[I(x, y), I(x', y')] = f\left[(x - x')^2 + (y - y')^2\right]$ for some function f, where $I(x, y)$ is the image intensity at location (x, y). One can show (see e.g., [HHH09, p125]) that the eigenvectors of a matrix of this kind are always sinusoids of different phases, i.e., PCA discovers a **Fourier basis**.

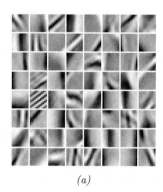

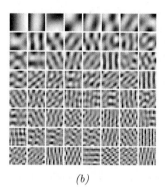

(a)   (b)

Figure 28.34: Illustration of the filters learned by various methods when applied to natural image patches. (a) Sparse coding. (b) PCA. Generated by sparse_dict_demo.ipynb.

29 State-space models

29.1 Introduction

A **state-space model** (**SSM**) is a **partially observed Markov model**, in which the hidden state, z_t, evolves over time according to a Markov process (Section 2.6), and each hidden state generates some observations y_t at each time step. (We focus on discrete time systems.) The main goal is to infer the hidden states given the observations. However, we may also be interested in using the model to predict future observations (e.g., for time-series forecasting).

An SSM can be represented as a stochastic discrete time nonlinear dynamical system of the form

$$z_t = f(z_{t-1}, u_t, q_t) \tag{29.1}$$
$$y_t = h(z_t, u_t, y_{1:t-1}, r_t) \tag{29.2}$$

where $z_t \in \mathbb{R}^{N_z}$ are the hidden states, $u_t \in \mathbb{R}^{N_u}$ are optional observed inputs, $y_t \in \mathbb{R}^{N_y}$ are observed outputs, f is the **transition function**, q_t is the **process noise**, h is the **observation function**, and r_t is the **observation noise**.

Rather than writing this as a deterministic function of random noise, we can represent it as a probabilistic model as follows:

$$p(z_t|z_{t-1}, u_t) = p(z_t|f(z_{t-1}, u_t)) \tag{29.3}$$
$$p(y_t|z_t, u_t, y_{1:t-1}) = p(y_t|h(z_t, u_t, y_{1:t-1})) \tag{29.4}$$

where $p(z_t|z_{t-1}, u_t)$ is the **transition model**, and $p(y_t|z_t, u_t, y_{1:t-1})$ is the **observation model**. Unrolling over time, we get the following joint distribution:

$$p(y_{1:T}, z_{1:T}|u_{1:T}) = \left[p(z_1|u_1) \prod_{t=2}^{T} p(z_t|z_{t-1}, u_t) \right] \left[\prod_{t=1}^{T} p(y_t|z_t, u_t, y_{1:t-1}) \right] \tag{29.5}$$

If we assume the current observation y_t only depends on the current hidden state, z_t, and the previous observation, y_{t-1}, we get the graphical model in Figure 29.1(a). (This is called an autoregressive state-space model.) However, by using a sufficient expressive hidden state z_t, we can implicitly represent all the past observations, $y_{1:t-1}$. Thus it is more common to assume that the observations are conditionally independent of each other (rather than having Markovian dependencies) given the hidden state. In this case the joint simplifies to

$$p(y_{1:T}, z_{1:T}|u_{1:T}) = \left[p(z_1|u_1) \prod_{t=2}^{T} p(z_t|z_{t-1}, u_t) \right] \left[\prod_{t=1}^{T} p(y_t|z_t, u_t) \right] \tag{29.6}$$

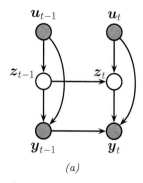
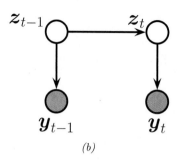

(a)

(b)

Figure 29.1: State-space model represented as a graphical model. (a) Generic form, with inputs $\boldsymbol{u}_t$, hidden state $\boldsymbol{z}_t$, and observations $\boldsymbol{y}_t$. We assume the observation likelihood is first-order auto-regressive. (b) Simplified form, with no inputs, and Markovian observations.

Sometimes there are no external inputs, so the model further simplifies to the following unconditional generative model:

$$p(\boldsymbol{y}_{1:T}, \boldsymbol{z}_{1:T}) = \left[p(\boldsymbol{z}_1) \prod_{t=2}^{T} p(\boldsymbol{z}_t | \boldsymbol{z}_{t-1}) \right] \left[\prod_{t=1}^{T} p(\boldsymbol{y}_t | \boldsymbol{z}_t) \right] \tag{29.7}$$

See Figure 29.1(b) for the simplified graphical model.

29.2 Hidden Markov models (HMMs)

In this section, we discuss the **hidden Markov model** or **HMM**, which is an SSM in which the hidden states are discrete, so $z_t \in \{1, \ldots, K\}$. The observations may be discrete, $y_t \in \{1, \ldots, N_y\}$, or continuous, $\boldsymbol{y}_t \in \mathbb{R}^{N_y}$, or some combination, as we illustrate below. More details on HMMs can be found in Supplementary Chapter 29, as well as other references, such as [Rab89; Fra08; CMR05]. For an interactive introduction, see https://nipunbatra.github.io/hmm/.

29.2.1 Conditional independence properties

The HMM graphical model is shown in Figure 29.1(b). This encodes the assumption that the hidden states are Markovian, and the observations are iid conditioned on the hidden states. All that remains is to specify the form of the conditional probability distributions of each node.

29.2.2 State transition model

The initial state distribution is denoted by

$$p(z_1 = j) = \pi_j \tag{29.8}$$

where $\boldsymbol{\pi}$ is a discrete distribution over the K states.

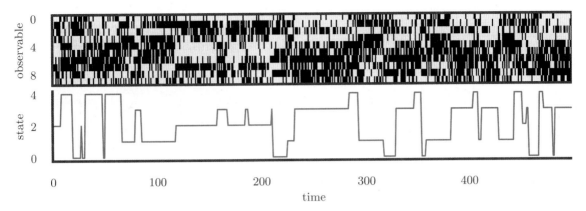

Figure 29.2: *Some samples from an HMM with 10 Bernoulli observables. Generated by bernoulli_hmm_example.ipynb.*

The **transition model** is denoted by

$$p(z_t = j | z_{t-1} = i) = A_{ij} \tag{29.9}$$

Here the i'th row of $\mathbf{A}$ corresponds to the outgoing distribution from state i. This is a **row stochastic matrix**, meaning each row sums to one. We can visualize the non-zero entries in the transition matrix by creating a state transition diagram, as shown in Figure 2.15.

29.2.3 Discrete likelihoods

The **observation model** $p(\boldsymbol{y}_t | z_t = j)$ can take multiple forms, depending on the type of data. For discrete observations we can use

$$p(y_t = k | z_t = j) = y_{jk} \tag{29.10}$$

For example, see the casino HMM example in Section 9.2.1.1.

If we have D discrete observations per time step, we can use a factorial model of the form

$$p(\boldsymbol{y}_t | z_t = j) = \prod_{d=1}^{D} \mathrm{Cat}(y_{td} | \boldsymbol{y}_{d,j,:}) \tag{29.11}$$

In the special case of binary observations, this becomes

$$p(\boldsymbol{y}_t | z_t = j) = \prod_{d=1}^{D} \mathrm{Ber}(y_{td} | y_{d,j}) \tag{29.12}$$

In Figure 29.2, we give an example of an HMM with 5 hidden states and 10 Bernoulli observables.

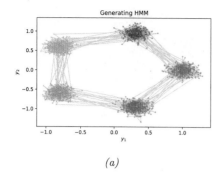

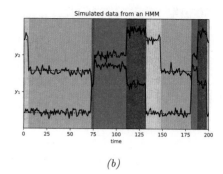

(a)   (b)

Figure 29.3: (a) Some 2d data sampled from a 5 state HMM. Each state emits from a 2d Gaussian. (b) The hidden state sequence is shown by the colors. We superimpose the observed 2d time series (note that we have shifted the vertical scale so the values don't overlap). Generated by gaussian_hmm_2d.ipynb.

29.2.4   Gaussian likelihoods

If $\boldsymbol{y}_t$ is continuous, it is common to use a Gaussian observation model:

$$p(\boldsymbol{y}_t|z_t = j) = \mathcal{N}(\boldsymbol{y}_t|\boldsymbol{\mu}_j, \boldsymbol{\Sigma}_j) \tag{29.13}$$

As a simple example, suppose we have an HMM with 3 hidden states, each of which generates a 2d Gaussian. We can represent these Gaussian distributions as 2d ellipses, as shown in Figure 29.3(a). We call these "**lily pads**", because of their shape. We can imagine a frog hopping from one lily pad to another. (This analogy is due to the late Sam Roweis.) It will stay on a pad for a while (corresponding to remaining in the same discrete state z_t), and then jump to a new pad (corresponding to a transition to a new state). See Figure 29.3(b). The data we see are just the 2d points (e.g., water droplets) coming from near the pad that the frog is currently on. Thus this model is like a Gaussian mixture model (Section 28.2.1), in that it generates clusters of observations, except now there is temporal correlation between the datapoints.

We can also use more flexible observation models. For example, if we use a M-component GMM, then we have

$$p(\boldsymbol{y}_t|z_t = j) = \sum_{k=1}^{M} w_{jk}\mathcal{N}(\boldsymbol{y}_t|\boldsymbol{\mu}_{jk}, \boldsymbol{\Sigma}_{jk}) \tag{29.14}$$

This is called a **GMM-HMM**.

29.2.5   Autoregressive likelihoods

The standard HMM assumes the observations are conditionally independent given the hidden state. In practice this is often not the case. However, it is straightforward to have direct arcs from $\boldsymbol{y}_{t-1}$ to $\boldsymbol{y}_t$ as well as from z_t to $\boldsymbol{y}_t$, as in Figure 29.1(a). This is known as an **auto-regressive HMM**.

For continuous data, we can use an observation model of the form

$$p(\boldsymbol{y}_t|\boldsymbol{y}_{t-1}, z_t = j, \boldsymbol{\theta}) = \mathcal{N}(\boldsymbol{y}_t|\mathbf{E}_j\boldsymbol{y}_{t-1} + \boldsymbol{\mu}_j, \boldsymbol{\Sigma}_j) \tag{29.15}$$

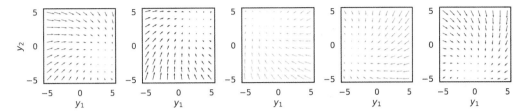

Figure 29.4: Illustration of the observation dynamics for each of the 5 hidden states. The attractor point corresponds to the steady state solution for the corresponding autoregressive process. Generated by hmm_ ar.ipynb.

This is a linear regression model, where the parameters are chosen according to the current hidden state. (We could also use a nonlinear model, such as a neural network.) Such models are widely used in econometrics, where they are called **regime switching Markov model** [Ham90]. Similar models can be defined for discrete observations (see e.g., [SJ99]).

We can also consider higher-order extensions, where we condition on the last L observations:

$$p(\boldsymbol{y}_t|\boldsymbol{y}_{t-L:t-1}, z_t = j, \boldsymbol{\theta}) = \mathcal{N}(\boldsymbol{y}_t|\sum_{\ell=1}^{L} \mathbf{W}_{j,\ell}\boldsymbol{y}_{t-\ell} + \boldsymbol{\mu}_j, \boldsymbol{\Sigma}_j) \qquad (29.16)$$

The AR-HMM essentially combines two Markov chains, one on the hidden variables, to capture long range dependencies, and one on the observed variables, to capture short range dependencies [Ber99]. Since all the visible nodes are observed, adding connections between them just changes the likelihood, but does not complicate the task of posterior inference (see Section 9.2.3).

Let us now consider a 2d example of this, due to Scott Linderman. We use a left-to-right transition matrix with 5 states. In addition, the final state returns to first state, so we just cycle through the states. Let $\boldsymbol{y}_t \in \mathbb{R}^2$, and suppose we set $\mathbf{E}_j$ to a rotation matrix with a small angle of 7 degrees, and we set each $\boldsymbol{\mu}_j$ to 72-degree separated points on a circle about the origin, so each state rotates 1/5 of the way around the circle. If the model stays in the same state j for a long time, the observed dynamics will converge to the steady state $\boldsymbol{y}_{*,j}$, which satisfies $\boldsymbol{y}_{*,j} = \mathbf{E}_j\boldsymbol{y}_{*,j} + \boldsymbol{\mu}_j$; we can solve for the steady state vector using $\boldsymbol{y}_{*,j} = (\mathbf{I} - \mathbf{E}_j)^{-1}\boldsymbol{\mu}_j$. We can visualize the induced 2d flow for each of the 5 states as shown in Figure 29.4.

In Figure 29.5(a), we show a trajectory sampled from this model. We see that the two components of the observation vector undergo different dynamics, depending on the underlying hidden state. In Figure 29.5(b), we show the same data in a 2d scatter plot. The first observation is the yellow dot (from state 2) at $(-0.8, 0.5)$. The dynamics converge to the stationary value of $\boldsymbol{y}_{*,2} = (-2.0, 3.8)$. Then the system jumps to the green state (state 3), so it adds an offset of $\boldsymbol{\mu}_3$ to the last observation, and then converges to the stationary value of $\boldsymbol{y}_{*,3} = (-4.3, -0.8)$. And so on.

29.2.6 Neural network likelihoods

For higher dimensional data, such as images, it can be useful to use a normalizing flow (Chapter 23), one per latent state (see e.g., [HNBK18; Gho+21]), as the class-conditional generative model. However, it is also possible to use discriminative neural network classifiers, which are much easier to train. In

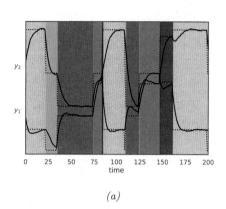
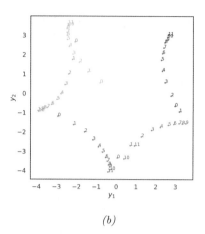

(a)   (b)

Figure 29.5: Samples from the 2d AR-HMM. (a) Time series plot of $y_{t,1}$ and $y_{t,2}$. (The latter are shifted up vertically by 4.7) The background color is the generating state. The dotted lines represent the stationary value for that component of the observation. (b) Scatter plot of observations. Colors denote the generating state. We show the first 12 samples from each state. Generated by hmm_ar.ipynb.

particular, note that the likelihood per state can be rewritten as follows:

$$p(\boldsymbol{y}_t | z_t = j) = \frac{p(z_t = j | \boldsymbol{y}_t) p(\boldsymbol{y}_t)}{p(z_t = j)} \propto \frac{p(z_t = j | \boldsymbol{y}_t)}{p(z_t = j)} \tag{29.17}$$

where we have dropped the $p(\boldsymbol{y}_t)$ term since it is independent of the state z_t. Here $p(z_t = j | \boldsymbol{y}_t)$ is the output of a classifier, and $p(z_t = j)$ is the probability of being in state j, which can be computed from the stationary distribution of the Markov chain (or empirically, if the state sequence is known). We can thus use discriminative classifiers to define the likelihood function when using gradient-based training. This is called the **scaled likelihood trick** [BM93; Ren+94]. [Guo+14] used this to create a **hybrid CNN-HMM** model for estimatng sequences of digits based on street signs.

29.3   HMMs: applications

In this section, we discuss some applications of HMMs.

29.3.1   Time series segmentation

In this section, we give a variant of the casino example from Section 9.2.1.1, where our goal is to segment a time series into different regimes, each of which corresponds to a different statistical distribution. In Figure 29.6a we show the data, corresponding to counts generated from some process (e.g., visits to a web site, or number of infections). We see that the count rate seems to be roughly constant for a while, and then changes at certain points. We would like to segment this data stream into K different regimes or states, each of which is associated with a Poisson observation model with

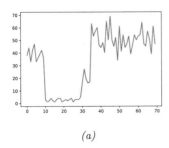 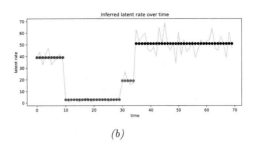

(a) (b)

Figure 29.6: (a) A sample time series dataset of counts. (b) A segmentation of this data using a 4 state HMM. Generated by poisson_hmm_changepoint.ipynb.

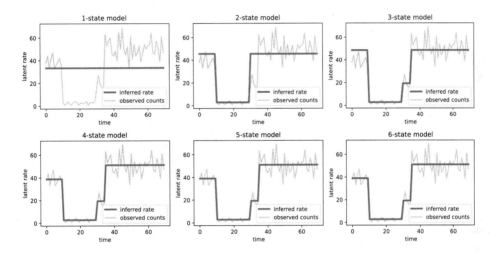

Figure 29.7: Segmentation of the time series using HMMs with 1–6 states. Generated by poisson_hmm_changepoint.ipynb.

rate λ_k:

$$p(y_t|z_t = k) = \text{Poi}(y_t|\lambda_k) \tag{29.18}$$

We use a uniform prior over the initial states. For the transition matrix, we assume the Markov chain stays in the same state with probability $p = 0.95$, and otherwise transitions to one of the other $K - 1$ states uniformly at random:

$$z_1 \sim \text{Categorical}\left(\left\{\frac{1}{4}, \frac{1}{4}, \frac{1}{4}, \frac{1}{4}\right\}\right) \tag{29.19}$$

$$z_t|z_{t-1} \sim \text{Categorical}\left(\left\{\begin{array}{ll} p & \text{if } z_t = z_{t-1} \\ \frac{1-p}{4-1} & \text{otherwise} \end{array}\right\}\right) \tag{29.20}$$

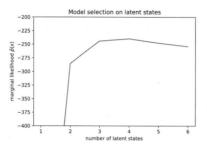

Figure 29.8: Marginal likelihood vs number of states K in the Poisson HMM. Generated by poisson_hmm_changepoint.ipynb.

We compute a MAP estimate for the parameters $\boldsymbol{\lambda}_{1:K}$ using a log-Normal(5,5) prior. We optimize the log of the Poisson rates using gradient descent, initializing the parameters at a random value centered on the log of the overall count means. We show the results in Figure 29.6b. See that the method has successfully partitioned the data into 4 regimes, which is in fact how it was generated. (The generating rates are $\boldsymbol{\lambda} = (40, 3, 20, 50)$, with the changepoints happening at times $(10, 30, 35)$.)

In general we don't know the optimal number of states K. To solve this, we can fit many different models, as shown in Figure 29.7, for $K = 1 : 6$. We see that after $K \geq 3$, the model fits are very similar, since multiple states get associated to the same regime. We can pick the "best" K to be the one with the highest marginal likelihood. Rather than summing over both discrete latent states and integrating over the unknown parameters $\boldsymbol{\lambda}$, we just maximize over the parameters (empirical Bayes approximation):

$$p(\boldsymbol{y}_{1:T}|K) \approx \max_{\boldsymbol{\lambda}} \sum_{\boldsymbol{z}} p(\boldsymbol{y}_{1:T}, \boldsymbol{z}_{1:T}|\boldsymbol{\lambda}, K) \tag{29.21}$$

We show this plot in Figure 29.8. We see the peak is at $K = 3$ or $K = 4$; after that it starts to go down, due to the Bayesian Occam's razor effect.

29.3.2 Protein sequence alignment

An important application of HMMs is to the problem of **protein sequence alignment** [Dur+98]. Here the goal is to determine if a test sequence $\boldsymbol{y}_{1:T}$ belongs to a protein family or not, and if so, how it aligns with the canonical representation of that family. (Similar methods can be used to align DNA and RNA sequences.)

To solve the alignment problem, let us initially assume we have a set of aligned sequences from a protein family, from which we can generate a **consensus sequence**. This defines a probability distribution over symbols at each location t in the string; denote each **position-specific scoring matrix** (PSSM) by $\theta_t(v) = p(y_t = v)$. These parameters can be estimated by counting.

Now we turn the PSSM into an HMM with 3 hidden states, representing the events that the location t matches the consensus sequence, $z_t = M$, or inserts its own unique symbol, $z_t = I$, or deletes (skips) the corresponding consensus symbol, $z_t = D$. We define the observation models for these 3 events as follows. For matches, we use the PSSM $p(y_t = v|z_t = M) = \theta_t(v)$. For insertions

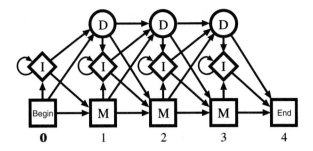

Figure 29.9: *State transition diagram for a profile HMM. From Figure 5.7 of [Dur+98]. Used with kind permission of Richard Durbin.*

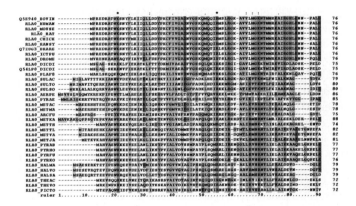

Figure 29.10: *Example of multiple sequence alignment. We show the first 90 positions of the acidic ribosomal protein P0 from several organisms. Colors represent functional properties of the corresponding amino acid. Dashes represent insertions or deletions. From* https://en.wikipedia.org/wiki/Multiple_sequence_alignment. *Used with kind permission of Wikipedia author Miguel Andrade.*

we use the uniform distribution $p(y_t = v|z_t = I) = 1/V$, where V is the size of the vocabulary. For deletions, we use $p(y_t = -|z_t = D)$, where "-" is a special deletion symbol used to pad the generated sequence to the correct length. The corresponding state transition matrix is shown in Figure 29.9: we see that matches and deletions advance one location along the consensus sequence, but insertions stay in the same location (represented by the self-transition from I to I). This model is known as a **profile HMM**.

Given a profile HMM with consensus parameters $\boldsymbol{\theta}$, we can compute $p(\boldsymbol{y}_{1:T}|\boldsymbol{\theta})$ in $O(T)$ time using the forwards algorithm, as described in Section 9.2.2. This can be used to decide if the sequence belongs to this family or not, by thresholding the log-odds score, $L(\boldsymbol{y}) = \log p(\boldsymbol{y}|\boldsymbol{\theta})/p(\boldsymbol{y}|\mathcal{M}_0)$, where $\mathcal{M}_0$ is a baseline model, such as the uniform distribution. If the string matches, we can compute an alignment to the consensus using the Viterbi algorithm, as described in Section 9.2.6. See Figure 29.10 for an illustration of such a **multiple sequence alignment**. If we don't have an initial set of aligned sequences from which to compute the consensus sequence $\boldsymbol{\theta}$, we can use the Baum-Welch algorithm

(Section 29.4.1) to compute the MLE for the parameters $\boldsymbol{\theta}$ from a set of unaligned sequences. For details, see e.g., [Dur+98, Ch.6].

29.3.3   Spelling correction

In this section, we illustrate how to use an HMM for **spelling correction**. The goal is to infer the sequence of words $\boldsymbol{z}_{1:T}$ that the user meant to type, given observations of what they actually did type, $\boldsymbol{y}_{1:T}$.

29.3.3.1   Baseline model

We start by using a simple unigram language model, so $p(\boldsymbol{z}_{1:T}) = \prod_{1:T} p(z_t)$, where $p(z_t = k)$ is the prior probability of word k being used. These probabilities can be estimated by simply normalizing word frequency counts from a large training corpus. We ignore any Markov structure.

Now we turn to the observation model, $p(y_t = v | z_t = k)$, which is the probability the user types word v when they meant to type word k. For this, we use a **noisy channel model**, in which the "message" z_t gets corrupted by one of four kinds of error: substitution error, where we swap one letter for another (e.g., "government" mistyped as "govermment"); transposition errors, where we swap the order of two adjacent letters (e.g., "government" mistyped as "governmnent"); deletion errors, where we omit one letter (e.g., "government" mistyped as "goverment"); and insertion errors, where we add an extra latter (e.g., "government" mistyped as "governmennt"). If y differs from z by d such errors, we say that y and z have an **edit distance** of d. Let $\mathcal{D}(y, d)$ be the set of words that are edit distance d away from y. We can then define the following likelihood function:

$$p(y|z) = \begin{cases} p_1 & y = z \\ p_2 & y \in \mathcal{D}(z, 1) \\ p_3 & y \in \mathcal{D}(z, 2) \\ p_4 & \text{otherwise} \end{cases} \tag{29.22}$$

where $p_1 > p_2 > p_3 > p_4$.

We can combine the likelihood with the prior to get the overall score for each hypothesis (i.e., candidate correction). This simple model, which was proposed by Peter Norvig[1], can work can quite well. However, it also has some flaws. For example, the error model assumes that the smaller the edit distance, the more likely the word, but this is not always valid. For example, "reciet" gets corrected to "recite" instead of "receipt", and "adres" gets corrected to "acres" not "address". We can fix this problem by learning the parameters of the noise model based on a labeled corpus of (z, x) pairs derived from actual spelling errors. One possible way to get such a corpus is to look at web search behavior: if a user types query q_1 and then quickly changes it to q_2 followed by a click on a link, it suggests that q_2 is a manual correction for q_1, so we can set $(z = q_2, y = q_1)$. This heuristic has been used in the Etsy search engine[2]. It is also possible to manually collect such data (see e.g., [Hag+17]), or to algorithmically create $(\boldsymbol{z}, \boldsymbol{y})$ pairs, where $\boldsymbol{y}$ is an automatically generated misspelling of $\boldsymbol{z}$ (see e.g., [ECM18]).

---

1. See his excellent tutorial at `http://norvig.com/spell-correct.html`.
2. See this blogpost by Mohit Nayyar for details: `https://codeascraft.com/2017/05/01/ modeling-spelling-correction-for-search-at-etsy/`.

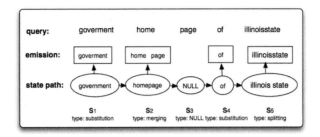

Figure 29.11: Illustration of an HMM applied to spelling correction. The top row, labeled "query", represents the search query $\boldsymbol{y}_{1:T}$ typed by the user, namely "goverment home page of illinoisstate". The bottom row, labeled "state path", represents the most probable assignment to the hidden states, $\boldsymbol{z}_{1:T}$, namely "government homepage of illinois state". (The NULL state is a silent state, that is needed to handle the generation of two tokens from a single hidden state.) The middle row, labeled "emission", represents the words emitted by each state, which match the observed data. From Figure 1 of [LDZ11].

29.3.3.2 HMM model

The baseline model can work well, but has room for improvement. In particular, many errors will be hard to correct without context. For example, suppose the user typed "advice": did they mean "advice" or "advise"? It depends on whether they intended to use a noun or a verb, which is hard to tell without looking at the sequence of words. To do this, we will "upgrade" our model to an HMM. We just have to replace our independence prior $p(\boldsymbol{z}_{1:T}) = \prod_t p(z_t)$ by a standard first-order language model on words, $p(\boldsymbol{z}_{1:T}) = \prod_t p(z_t|z_{t-1})$. The parameters of this model can be estimated by counting bigrams in a large corpus of "clean" text (see Section 2.6.3.1). The observation model $p(y_t|z_t)$ can remain unchanged.

Given this model, we can compute the top N most likely hidden sequences in $O(NTK^2)$ time, where K is the number of hidden states, and T is the length of the sequence, as explained in Section 9.2.6.5. In a naive implementation, the number of hidden states K is the number of words in the vocabulary, which would make the method very slow. However, we can exploit sparsity of the likelihood function (i.e., the fact that $p(y|z)$ is 0 for most values of z) to generate small candidate lists of hidden states for each location in the sequence. This gives us a sparse belief state vector $\boldsymbol{\alpha}_t$.

29.3.3.3 Extended HMM model

We can extend the HMM model to handle higher level errors, in addition to misspellings of individual words. In particular, [LDZ11; LDZ12] proposed modeling the following kinds of errors:

- Two words merged into one, e.g., "home page" → "homepage".

- One word split into two, e.g., "illinoisstate" → "illinois state".

- Within-word errors, such as substitution, transposition, insertion and deletion of letters, as we discussed in Section 29.3.3.2.

We can model this with an HMM, where we augment the state space with a **silent state**, that does not emit any symbols. Figure 29.11 illustrates how this model can "denoise" the observed query "goverment home page of illinoisstate" into the correctly formulated query "government homepage of illinois state".

An alternative to using HMMs is to use supervised learning to fit a sequence-to-sequence translation model, using RNNs or transformers. This can work very well, but often needs much more training data, which can be problematic for **low-resource languages** [ECM18].

29.4   HMMs: parameter learning

In this section, we discuss how to compute a point estimate or the full posterior over the model parameters of an HMM given a set of partially observed sequences.

29.4.1   The Baum-Welch (EM) algorithm

In this section, we discuss how to compute an approximate MLE for the parameters of an HMM using the EM algorithm which is an iterative bound optimization algorithm (see Section 6.5.3 for details). When applied to HMMs, the resulting method is known as the **Baum-Welch** algorithm [Bau+70].

29.4.1.1   Log likelihood

The joint probability of a single sequence is given by

$$p(\boldsymbol{y}_{1:T}, \boldsymbol{z}_{1:T}|\boldsymbol{\theta}) = [p(z_1|\boldsymbol{\pi})] \left[\prod_{t=2}^{T} p(z_t|z_{t-1}, \mathbf{A})\right] \left[\prod_{t=1}^{T} p(\boldsymbol{y}_t|z_t, \mathbf{B})\right] \tag{29.23}$$

$$= \left[\prod_{k=1}^{K} \pi_k^{\mathbb{I}(z_1=k)}\right] \left[\prod_{t=2}^{T}\prod_{j=1}^{K}\prod_{k=1}^{K} A_{jk}^{\mathbb{I}(z_{t-1}=j,z_t=k)}\right] \left[\prod_{t=1}^{T}\prod_{k=1}^{K} p(\boldsymbol{y}_t|\mathbf{B}_k)^{\mathbb{I}(z_t=k)}\right] \tag{29.24}$$

where $\boldsymbol{\theta} = (\boldsymbol{\pi}, \mathbf{A}, \mathbf{B})$. Of course, we cannot compute this objective, since $\boldsymbol{z}_{1:T}$ is hidden. So instead we will optimize the expected complete data log likelihood, where expectations are taken using the parameters from the previous iteration of the algorithm:

$$Q(\boldsymbol{\theta}, \boldsymbol{\theta}^{\text{old}}) = \mathbb{E}_{p(\boldsymbol{z}_{1:T}|\boldsymbol{y}_{1:T}, \boldsymbol{\theta}^{\text{old}})}\left[\log p(\boldsymbol{y}_{1:T}, \boldsymbol{z}_{1:T}|\boldsymbol{\theta})\right] \tag{29.25}$$

This can be easily summed over N sequences. See Figure 29.12 for the graphical model.

The above objective is a lower bound on the observed data log likelihood, $\log p(\boldsymbol{y}_{1:T}|\boldsymbol{\theta})$, so the entire procedure is a bound optimization method that is guaranteed to converge to a local optimum. (In fact, if suitably initialized, the method can be shown to converge to (close to) one of the global optima [YBW15].)

29.4.1.2   E step

Let $A_{jk} = p(z_t = k|z_{t-1} = j)$ be the $K \times K$ transition matrix. For the first time slice, let $\pi_k = p(z_1 = k)$ be the initial state distribution. Let $\boldsymbol{\theta}_k$ represent the parameters of the observation model for state k.

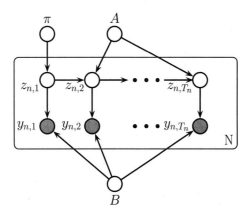

Figure 29.12: HMM with plate notation. A are the parameters for the state transition matrix $p(z_t|z_{t-1})$ and B are the parameters for the discrete observation model $p(x_t|z_t)$. T_n is the length of the n'th sequence.

To compute the expected sufficient statistics, we first run the forwards-backwards algorithm on each sequence (see Section 9.2.3). This returns the following node and edge marginals:

$$\gamma_{n,t}(j) \triangleq p(z_t = j|\boldsymbol{y}_{n,1:T_n}, \boldsymbol{\theta}^{old}) \tag{29.26}$$

$$\xi_{n,t}(j,k) \triangleq p(z_{t-1} = j, z_t = k|\boldsymbol{y}_{n,1:T_n}, \boldsymbol{\theta}^{old}) \tag{29.27}$$

where T_n is the length of sequence n. We can then derive the expected counts as follows (note that we pool the sufficient statistics across time, since the parameters are tied, as well as across sequences):

$$\mathbb{E}\left[N_k^1\right] = \sum_{n=1}^{N} \gamma_{n,1}(k), \ \mathbb{E}\left[N_k\right] = \sum_{n=1}^{N}\sum_{t=2}^{T_n} \gamma_{n,t}(k), \ \mathbb{E}\left[N_{jk}\right] = \sum_{n=1}^{N}\sum_{t=2}^{T_n} \xi_{n,t}(j,k) \tag{29.28}$$

Given the above quantities, we can compute the expected complete data log likelihood as follows:

$$Q(\boldsymbol{\theta}, \boldsymbol{\theta}^{\text{old}}) = \sum_{k=1}^{K} \mathbb{E}\left[N_k^1\right] \log \pi_k + \sum_{j=1}^{K}\sum_{k=1}^{K} \mathbb{E}\left[N_{jk}\right] \log A_{jk}$$
$$+ \sum_{n=1}^{N}\sum_{t=1}^{T_n}\sum_{k=1}^{K} p(z_t = k|\boldsymbol{y}_{n,1:T_n}, \boldsymbol{\theta}^{\text{old}}) \log p(\boldsymbol{y}_{n,t}|\boldsymbol{\theta}_k) \tag{29.29}$$

29.4.1.3 M step

We can estimate the transition matrix and initial state probabilities by maximizing the objective subject to the sum to one constraint. The result is just a normalized version of the expected counts:

$$\hat{A}_{jk} = \frac{\mathbb{E}\left[N_{jk}\right]}{\sum_{k'} \mathbb{E}\left[N_{jk'}\right]}, \ \hat{\pi}_k = \frac{\mathbb{E}\left[N_k^1\right]}{N} \tag{29.30}$$

This result is quite intuitive: we simply add up the expected number of transitions from j to k, and divide by the expected number of times we transition from j to anything else.

For a categorical observation model, the expected sufficient statistics are

$$\mathbb{E}\left[M_{kv}\right] = \sum_{n=1}^{N} \sum_{t=1}^{T_n} \gamma_{n,t}(k) \mathbb{I}\left(y_{n,t} = v\right) = \sum_{n=1}^{N} \sum_{t:y_{n,t}=v} \gamma_{n,t}(k) \tag{29.31}$$

The M step has the form

$$\hat{B}_{kv} = \frac{\mathbb{E}\left[M_{kv}\right]}{\mathbb{E}\left[N_k\right]} \tag{29.32}$$

This result is quite intuitive: we simply add up the expected number of times we are in state k and we see a symbol v, and divide by the expected number of times we are in state k. See Algorithm 11 for the pseudocode.

For a Gaussian observation model, the expected sufficient statistics are given by

$$\overline{\boldsymbol{y}}_k = \sum_{n=1}^{N} \sum_{t=1}^{T_n} \gamma_{n,t}(k) \boldsymbol{y}_{n,t}, \quad \overline{\boldsymbol{y}\boldsymbol{y}^\mathsf{T}}_k = \sum_{n=1}^{N} \sum_{t=1}^{T_n} \gamma_{n,t}(k) \boldsymbol{y}_{n,t} \boldsymbol{y}_{n,t}^\mathsf{T} \tag{29.33}$$

The M step becomes

$$\hat{\boldsymbol{\mu}}_k = \frac{\overline{\boldsymbol{y}}_k}{\mathbb{E}\left[N_k\right]} \tag{29.34}$$

$$\hat{\boldsymbol{\Sigma}}_k = \frac{\overline{\boldsymbol{y}\boldsymbol{y}^\mathsf{T}}_k - \mathbb{E}\left[N_k\right] \hat{\boldsymbol{\mu}}_k \hat{\boldsymbol{\mu}}_k^\mathsf{T}}{\mathbb{E}\left[N_k\right]} \tag{29.35}$$

In practice, we often need to add a log prior to these estimates to ensure the resulting $\hat{\boldsymbol{\Sigma}}_k$ estimate is well-conditioned. See [Mur22, Sec 4.5.2] for details.

Algorithm 29.1: Baum-Welch algorithm for (discrete observation) HMMs

---

1 Initialize parameters $\boldsymbol{\theta}$
2 **for** *each iteration* **do**
3 $\quad$ // E step
4 $\quad$ Initialize expected counts: $\mathbb{E}\left[N_k\right] = 0$, $\mathbb{E}\left[N_{jk}\right] = 0$, $\mathbb{E}\left[M_{kv}\right] = 0$
5 $\quad$ **for** *each datacase n* **do**
6 $\quad\quad$ Use forwards-backwards algorithm on $\boldsymbol{y}_n$ to compute $\gamma_{n,t}$ and $\xi_{n,t}$
$\quad\quad$ (Equations 29.26–29.27)
7 $\quad\quad$ $\mathbb{E}\left[N_k\right] := \mathbb{E}\left[N_k\right] + \sum_{t=2}^{T_n} \gamma_{n,t}(k)$
8 $\quad\quad$ $\mathbb{E}\left[N_{jk}\right] := \mathbb{E}\left[N_{jk}\right] + \sum_{t=2}^{T_n} \xi_{n,t}(j,k)$
9 $\quad\quad$ $\mathbb{E}\left[M_{kv}\right] := \mathbb{E}\left[M_{kv}\right] + \sum_{t:x_{n,t}=v} \gamma_{n,t}(k)$
10 $\quad$ // M step
11 $\quad$ Compute new parameters $\boldsymbol{\theta} = (\mathbf{A}, \mathbf{B}, \boldsymbol{\pi})$ using Equations 29.30

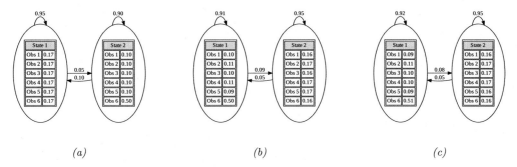

Figure 29.13: *Illustration of the casino HMM. (a) True parameters used to generate the data. (b) Estimated parameters using EM. (c) Estimated parameters using SGD. Generated by casino_hmm_training.ipynb.*

29.4.1.4 Initialization

As usual with EM, we must take care to ensure that we initialize the parameters carefully, to minimize the chance of getting stuck in poor local optima. There are several ways to do this, such as:

- Use some fully labeled data to initialize the parameters.

- Initially ignore the Markov dependencies, and estimate the observation parameters using the standard mixture model estimation methods, such as K-means or EM.

- Randomly initialize the parameters, use multiple restarts, and pick the best solution.

Techniques such as deterministic annealing [UN98; RR01a] can help mitigate the effect of local minima. Also, just as K-means is often used to initialize EM for GMMs, so it is common to initialize EM for HMMs using Viterbi training. The Viterbi algorithm is explained in Section 9.2.6, but basically it is an algorithm to compute the single most probable path. As an approximation to the E step, we can replace the sum over paths with the statistics computed using this single path. Sometimes this can give better results [AG11].

29.4.1.5 Example: casino HMM

In this section, we fit the casino HMM from Section 9.2.1.1. The true generative model is shown in Figure 29.13a. We used this to generate 4 sequences of length 5000, totalling 20,000 observations. We initialized the model with random parameters. We ran EM for 200 iterations and got the results in Figure 29.13b. We see that the learned parameters are close to the true parameters, modulo **label switching** of the states, due to unidentifiability.

29.4.2 Parameter estimation using SGD

Although the EM algorithm is the "traditional" way to fit HMMs, it is inherently a batch algorithm, so it does not scale well to large datasets (with many sequences). Although it is possible to extend bound optimization to the online case (see e.g., [Mai15]), this can take a lot of memory.

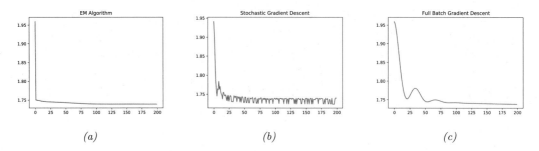

Figure 29.14: Average negative log likelihood per learning step the casino HMM. (a) EM. (b) SGD with minibatch size 1. (b) Full batch gradient descent. Generated by casino_hmm_training.ipynb.

A simple alternative is to optimize $\log p(\boldsymbol{y}_{1:T}|\boldsymbol{\theta})$ using SGD. We can compute this objective using the forwards algorithm, as shown in Equation (8.7):

$$\log p(\boldsymbol{y}_{1:T}|\boldsymbol{\theta}) = \sum_{t=1}^{T} \log p(\boldsymbol{y}_t|\boldsymbol{y}_{1:t-1}, \boldsymbol{\theta}) = \sum_{t=1}^{T} \log Z_t \tag{29.36}$$

where the normalization constant for each time step is given by

$$Z_t \triangleq p(\boldsymbol{y}_t|\boldsymbol{y}_{1:t-1}) = \sum_{j=1}^{K} p(z_t = j|\boldsymbol{y}_{1:t-1})p(\boldsymbol{y}_t|z_t = j) \tag{29.37}$$

Of course, we need to ensure the transition matrix remains a valid row stochastic matrix, i.e., that $0 \le A_{ij} \le 1$ and $\sum_j A_{ij} = 1$. Similarly, if we have categorical observations, we need to ensure B_{jk} is a valid row stochastic matrix, and if we have Gaussian observations, we need to ensure $\boldsymbol{\Sigma}_k$ is a valid psd matrix. These constraints are automatically taken care of in EM. When using SGD, we can reparameterize to an unconstrained form, as proposed in [BC94].

29.4.2.1   Example: casino HMM

In this section, we use SGD to fit the casino HMM using the same data as in Section 29.4.1.5. We show the learning the learning curves in Figure 29.14. We see that SGD converges slightly more slowly than EM, and is not monotonic in how it decreases the NLL loss, even in the full batch case. However, the final parameters are similar, as shown in Figure 29.13.

29.4.3   Parameter estimation using spectral methods

Fitting HMMs using maximum likelihood is difficult, because the log likelihood is not convex. Thus there are many local optima, and EM and SGD can give poor results. An alternative approach is to marginalize out the hidden variables, and work instead with predictive distributions in the visible space. For discrete observation HMMs, with observation matrix $B_{jk} = p(y_t = k|z_t = j)$, such a distribution has the form

$$[\boldsymbol{y}_t]_k \triangleq p(y_t = k|\boldsymbol{y}_{1:t-1}) \tag{29.38}$$

This is called a **predictive state representation** [SJR04].

Suppose there are m possible hidden states, and n possible visible symbols, where $n \geq m$. One can show [HKZ12; Joh12] that the PSR vectors lie in a subspace in $\mathbb{R}^n$ with a dimensionality of $m \leq n$. Intuitively this is because the linear operator $\mathbf{A}$ defining the hidden state update in Equation (9.8), combined with the mapping to observables via $\mathbf{B}$, induces low rank structure in the output space. Furthermore, we can estimate a basis for this low rank subspace using SVD applied to the observable matrix of co-occurrence counts:

$$[\mathbf{P}_2]_{ij} = p(y_t = i, y_{t-1} = j) \tag{29.39}$$

We also need to estimate the third order statistics

$$[\mathbf{P}_3]_{ijk} = p(y_t = i, y_{t-1} = j, y_{t-2} = k) \tag{29.40}$$

Using these quantities, it possible to perform recursive updating of our predictions while working entirely in visible space. This is called **spectral estimation**, or **tensor decomposition** [HKZ12; AHK12; Rod14; Ana+14; RSG17].

We can use spectral methods to get a good initial estimate of the parameters for the latent variable model, which can then be refined using EM (see e.g., [Smi+00]). Alternatively, we can use them "as is", without needing EM at all. See [Mat14] for a comparison of these methods. See also Section 29.8.2 where we discuss spectral methods for fitting linear dynamical systems.

29.4.4 Bayesian HMMs

MLE methods can easily overfit, and can suffer from numerical problems, especially when sample sizes are small. In this section, we briefly discuss some approaches to inferring the posterior over the parameters, $p(\boldsymbol{\theta}|\mathcal{D})$. By adopting a Bayesian approach, we can also allow the number of states to be unbounded by using a hierarchical Dirichlet process (Supplementary Section 31.1) to get a **HDP-HMM** [Fox+08].

There are various algorithms we can use to perform posterior inference, such as variational Bayes EM [Bea03] or blocked Gibbs sampling (see Section 29.4.4.1), that alternates between sampling latent sequences $\boldsymbol{z}_{1:T,1:N}^s$ using the forwards filtering backwards sampling algorithm (Section 9.2.7) and sampling the parameters from their full conditionals, $p(\boldsymbol{\theta}|\boldsymbol{y}_{1:T}, \boldsymbol{z}_{1:T,1:N}^s)$. Unfortuntely, the high correlation between $\boldsymbol{z}$ and $\boldsymbol{\theta}$ makes this coordinate-wise approach rather slow.

A faster approach is to marginalize out the discrete latents (using the forwards algorithm), and then to use MCMC [Fot+14] or SVI [Obe+19] to sample from the following log posterior:

$$\log p(\boldsymbol{\theta}, \mathcal{D}) = \log p(\boldsymbol{\theta}) + \sum_{n=1}^{N} \log p(\boldsymbol{y}_{1:T,n}|\boldsymbol{\theta}) \tag{29.41}$$

This is a form of "collapsed" inference.

29.4.4.1 Blocked Gibbs sampling for HMMs

This section is written by Xinglong Li.

In this section, we discuss Bayesian inference for HMMs using blocked Gibbs sampling [Sco02]. For the observation model, we consider the first-order auto-regressive HMM model in Section 29.2.5, so $p(\boldsymbol{y}_t|\boldsymbol{y}_{t-1}, z_t = j, \boldsymbol{\theta}) = \mathcal{N}(\boldsymbol{y}_t|\mathbf{E}_j\boldsymbol{y}_{t-1} + \boldsymbol{\mu}_j, \boldsymbol{\Sigma}_j)$. For a model with K hidden states, the unknown parameters are $\boldsymbol{\theta} = \{\boldsymbol{\pi}, \mathbf{A}, \mathbf{E}_1, \ldots, \mathbf{E}_K, \boldsymbol{\Sigma}_1, \ldots, \boldsymbol{\Sigma}_K\}$, where we assume (for notational simplicity) that $\boldsymbol{\mu}_j$ of each autoregressive model is known, and that we condition the observations on $\boldsymbol{y}_1$.

We alternate between sampling from $p(\boldsymbol{z}_{1:T}|\boldsymbol{y}_{1:T}, \boldsymbol{\theta})$ using the forwards filtering backwards sampling algorithm (Section 9.2.7), and sampling from $p(\boldsymbol{\theta}|\boldsymbol{z}_{1:T}, \boldsymbol{y}_{1:T})$. Sampling from $p(\boldsymbol{\theta}|\boldsymbol{z}_{1:T}, \boldsymbol{y}_{1:T})$ is easy if we use conjugate priors. Here we use a Dirichlet prior for $\boldsymbol{\pi}$ and each row $\mathbf{A}_{j\cdot}$ of the transition matrix, and choose the matrix normal inverse Wishart distribution as the prior for $\{\mathbf{E}_j, \boldsymbol{\Sigma}_j\}$ of each autoregressive model, similar to Bayesian multivariate linear regression Section 15.2.9. In particular, the prior distributions of $\boldsymbol{\theta}$ are:

$$\boldsymbol{\pi} \sim \text{Dir}(\breve{\boldsymbol{\alpha}}_\pi) \qquad\qquad\qquad \mathbf{A}_{j\cdot} \sim \text{Dir}(\breve{\boldsymbol{\alpha}}_A) \qquad\qquad (29.42)$$

$$\boldsymbol{\Sigma}_j \sim \text{IW}(\breve{\nu}_j, \breve{\boldsymbol{\Psi}}_j) \qquad\qquad\qquad \mathbf{E}_j|\boldsymbol{\Sigma}_j \sim \mathcal{MN}(\breve{\mathbf{M}}_j, \boldsymbol{\Sigma}_j, \breve{\mathbf{V}}_j) \qquad\qquad (29.43)$$

where $\breve{\alpha}_{\pi,k} = \breve{\alpha}_\pi / K$ and $\breve{\alpha}_{A,k} = \breve{\alpha}_A / K$. The log prior probability is

$$\log p(\boldsymbol{\theta}) = c + \sum_{k=1}^{K} \frac{\breve{\alpha}_\pi}{K} \log \pi_k + \sum_{j=1}^{K}\sum_{k=1}^{K} \frac{\breve{\alpha}_A}{K} \log A_{jk} - \sum_{j=1}^{K} \left(\frac{\breve{\nu}_j + N_y + 1}{2} \log|\boldsymbol{\Sigma}_j| + \frac{1}{2}\text{tr}\left(\breve{\boldsymbol{\Psi}}_j \, \boldsymbol{\Sigma}_j^{-1} \right) \right)$$

$$- \sum_{j=1}^{K} \left(\frac{1}{2} \log|\boldsymbol{\Sigma}_j| + \frac{1}{2}\text{tr}((\mathbf{E}_j - \breve{\mathbf{M}}_j)^\mathsf{T} \boldsymbol{\Sigma}_j^{-1} (\mathbf{E}_j - \breve{\mathbf{M}}_j) \, \breve{\mathbf{V}}_j) \right) \qquad (29.44)$$

Given $\boldsymbol{y}_{1:T}$ and $\boldsymbol{z}_{1:T}$ we denote $N_j = \sum_{t=2}^{T} \mathbb{I}(z_t = j)$ and $N_{jk} = \sum_{t=1}^{T-1} \mathbb{I}(z_t = j, z_{t+1} = k)$. The joint likelihood is

$$\log p(\boldsymbol{y}_{1:T}, \boldsymbol{z}_{1:T}|\boldsymbol{\theta}) = c + \sum_{k=1}^{K} \mathbb{I}(z_1 = k) \log \pi_k + \sum_{j=1}^{K}\sum_{k=1}^{K} N_{jk} \log A_{jk}$$

$$- \sum_{j=1}^{K}\sum_{z_t=j} \left(\frac{1}{2}\log|\boldsymbol{\Sigma}_j| + \frac{1}{2}(\boldsymbol{y}_t - \mathbf{E}_j\boldsymbol{y}_{t-1} - \boldsymbol{\mu}_j)^\mathsf{T} \boldsymbol{\Sigma}_j^{-1}(\boldsymbol{y}_t - \mathbf{E}_j\boldsymbol{y}_{t-1} - \boldsymbol{\mu}_j) \right)$$

$$\qquad\qquad\qquad (29.45)$$

$$= c + \sum_{k=1}^{K} \mathbb{I}(z_1 = k) \log \pi_k + \sum_{j=1}^{K}\sum_{k=1}^{K} N_{jk} \log A_{jk}$$

$$- \sum_{j=1}^{K} \left(\frac{N_j}{2}\log|\boldsymbol{\Sigma}_j| + \frac{1}{2}(\hat{\mathbf{Y}}_j - \mathbf{E}_j\tilde{\mathbf{Y}}_j)^\mathsf{T} \boldsymbol{\Sigma}_j^{-1}(\hat{\mathbf{Y}}_j - \mathbf{E}_j\tilde{\mathbf{Y}}_j) \right) \qquad (29.46)$$

where $\hat{\mathbf{Y}}_j = [\boldsymbol{y}_t - \boldsymbol{\mu}_j]_{z_t=j}$ and $\tilde{\mathbf{Y}}_j = [\boldsymbol{y}_{t-1}]_{z_t=j}$, and it can be seen that $\hat{\mathbf{Y}}_j \sim \mathcal{MN}\left(\hat{\mathbf{Y}}_j|\mathbf{E}_j\tilde{\mathbf{Y}}_j, \boldsymbol{\Sigma}_j, \mathbf{I}_{N_j} \right)$.

It is obvious from $\log p(\boldsymbol{\theta}) + \log p(\boldsymbol{y}_{1:T}, \boldsymbol{z}_{1:T}|\boldsymbol{\theta})$ that the posteriors of $\boldsymbol{\pi}$ and $\mathbf{A}_{j\cdot}$ are both still Dirichlet distributions. It can also be shown that the posterior distributions of $\{\mathbf{E}_j, \boldsymbol{\Sigma}_j\}$ are still matrix normal inverse Wishart distributions, whose hyperparameters can be directly obtained by replacing $\mathbf{Y}, \mathbf{A}, \mathbf{X}$ in Equation (15.105) with $\hat{\mathbf{Y}}_j, \mathbf{E}_j$ and $\tilde{\mathbf{Y}}_j$ respectively. To summarize, the posterior

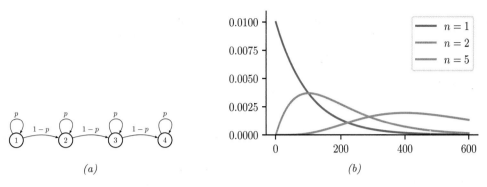

(a)   *(b)*

Figure 29.15: (a) A Markov chain with $n = 4$ repeated states and self loops. (b) The resulting distribution over sequence lengths, for $p = 0.99$ and various n. Generated by hmm_self_loop_dist.ipynb.

distribution $p(\boldsymbol{\theta}|\boldsymbol{z}_{1:T}, \boldsymbol{y}_{1:T})$ is:

$$\boldsymbol{\pi}|\boldsymbol{z}_{1:T} \sim \text{Dir}(\widehat{\boldsymbol{\alpha}}_\pi), \qquad\qquad \widehat{\alpha}_{\pi,k} = \breve{\alpha}_\pi /K + \mathbb{I}(z_1 = k) \qquad (29.47)$$

$$\mathbf{A}_{j\cdot}|\boldsymbol{z}_{1:T} \sim \text{Dir}(\widehat{\boldsymbol{\alpha}}_A), \qquad\qquad \widehat{\alpha}_{A_j,k} = \breve{\alpha}_A /K + N_{jk} \qquad (29.48)$$

$$\boldsymbol{\Sigma}_j|\boldsymbol{z}_{1:T}, \boldsymbol{y}_{1:T} \sim \text{IW}(\widehat{\nu}_j, \widehat{\boldsymbol{\Psi}}_j) \qquad \mathbf{E}_j|\boldsymbol{\Sigma}_j, \boldsymbol{z}_{1:T}, \boldsymbol{y}_{1:T} \sim \mathcal{MN}(\widehat{\mathbf{M}}_j, \boldsymbol{\Sigma}_j, \widehat{\mathbf{V}}_j) \qquad (29.49)$$

29.5 HMMs: generalizations

In this section, we discuss various extensions of the vanilla HMM introduced in Section 29.2.

29.5.1 Hidden semi-Markov model (HSMM)

In a standard HMM (Section 29.2), the probability we remain in state i for exactly d steps is

$$p(d_i = d) = (1 - A_{ii})A_{ii}^d \propto \exp(d \log A_{ii}) \qquad (29.50)$$

where A_{ii} is the self-loop probability. This is called the **geometric distribution**. However, this kind of exponentially decaying function of d is sometimes unrealistic.

A simple way to model non-geometric waiting times is to replace each state with n new states, each with the same emission probabilities as the original state. For example, consider the model in Figure 29.15(a). Obviously the smallest sequence this can generate is of length $n = 4$. Any path of length d through the model has probability $p^{d-n}(1 - p)^n$; multiplying by the number of possible paths we find that the total probability of a path of length d is

$$p(d) = \binom{d - 1}{n - 1} p^{d-n}(1 - p)^n \qquad (29.51)$$

This is equivalent to the negative binomial distribution. By adjusting n and the self-loop probabilities p of each state, we can model a wide range of waiting times: see Figure 29.15(b).

A more general solution is to use a **semi-Markov model**, in which the next state not only depends on the previous state, but also on how how long we've been in that state. When the state-space is

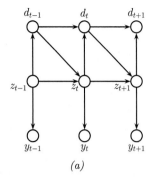
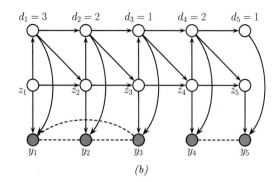

(a)   *(b)*

Figure 29.16: Encoding a hidden semi-Markov model as a DPGM. (a) d_t is a deterministic down counter (duration variable). Each observation is generated independently. (b) Similar to (a), except now we generate the observations within each segment as a block. In this figure, we represent the non-Markovian dependencies between the observations within each segment by using undirected edges. We represent the conditional independence between the observations across different segments by disconnecting $\boldsymbol{y}_{1:3}$ from $\boldsymbol{y}_{4:5}$; this can be enforced by "breaking the link" whenever $d_t = 1$ (representing the end of a segment).

not observed directly, the result is called a **hidden semi-Markov model (HSMM)**, a **variable duration HMM**, or an **explicit duration HMM** [Yu10].

One way to represent a HSMM is to use the graphical model shown in Figure 29.16(a). The $d_t \in \{1, \ldots, D\}$ node is a state duration counter, where D is the maximum duration of any state. When we first enter state j, we sample d_t from the duration distribution for that state, $d_t \sim p_j(\cdot)$. Thereafter, d_t deterministically counts down until $d_t = 1$. More precisely, we define the following CPD:

$$p(d_t = d'|d_{t-1} = d, z_t = j) = \begin{cases} D_j(d') & \text{if } d = 1 \\ 1 & \text{if } d' = d - 1 \text{ and } d > 1 \\ 0 & \text{otherwise} \end{cases} \tag{29.52}$$

Note that $D_j(d)$ could be represented as a table (a non-parametric approach) or as some kind of parametric distribution, such as a gamma distribution. If $D_j(d)$ is a (truncated) geometric distribution, this emulates a standard HMM.

While $d_t > 1$, the state z_t is not allowed to change. When $d_t = 1$, we make a stochastic transition to a new state. (We assume $A_{jj} = 0$.) More precisely, we define the state CPD as follows:

$$p(z_t = k|z_{t-1} = j, d_{t-1} = d) = \begin{cases} 1 & \text{if } d > 0 \text{ and } j = k \\ A_{jk} & \text{if } d = 1 \\ 0 & \text{otherwise} \end{cases} \tag{29.53}$$

This ensures that the model stays in the same state for the entire duration of the segment. At each step within this segment, an observation is generated.

HSMMs are useful not only because they can model the duration of each state explicitly, but also because they can model the distribution of a whole subsequence of observations at once, instead of assuming all observations are generated independently at each time step. That is, they can use likelihood models of the form $p(\boldsymbol{y}_{t:t+l-1}|z_t = k, d_t = l)$, which generate l correlated observations if the duration in state k is for l time steps. This approach, known as a **segmental HMM**, is useful for modeling data that is piecewise linear, or shows other local trends [ODK96]. We can also use an RNN to model each segment, resulting in an **RNN-HSMM** model [Dai+17].

More precisely, we can define a segmental HMM as follows:

$$p(\boldsymbol{y}, \boldsymbol{z}, \boldsymbol{d}) = \left[p(z_1)p(d_1|z_1) \prod_{t=2}^{T} p(z_t|z_{t-1}, d_{t-1})p(d_t|z_t, d_{t-1}) \right] p(\boldsymbol{y}|\boldsymbol{z}, \boldsymbol{d}) \tag{29.54}$$

In a standard HSMM, we assume

$$p(\boldsymbol{y}|\boldsymbol{z}, \boldsymbol{d}) = \prod_{t=1}^{T} p(y_t|z_t) \tag{29.55}$$

so the duration variables only determine the hidden state dynamics. To define $p(\boldsymbol{y}|\boldsymbol{z}, \boldsymbol{d})$ for a segmental HMM, let us use s_i and e_i to denote the start and end times of segment i. This sequence can be computed deterministically from $\boldsymbol{d}$ using $s_1 = 1$, $s_i = s_{i-1} + d_{s_{i-1}}$, and $e_i = s_i + d_{s_i} - 1$. We now define the observation model as follows:

$$p(\boldsymbol{y}|\boldsymbol{z}, \boldsymbol{d}) = \prod_{i=1}^{|\boldsymbol{s}|} p(\boldsymbol{y}_{s_i:e_i}|z_{s_i}, d_{s_i}) \tag{29.56}$$

See Figure 29.16(b) for the DPGM.

If we use an RNN for each segment, we have

$$p(\boldsymbol{y}_{s_i:e_i}|z_{s_i}, d_{s_i}) = \prod_{t=s_i}^{e_i} p(y_t|\boldsymbol{y}_{s_i:t-1}, z_{s_i}) = \prod_{t=s_i}^{e_i} p(y_t|h_t, z_{s_i}) \tag{29.57}$$

where h_t is the hidden state that is deterministically updated given the previous observations in this sequence.

As shown in [Chi14], it is possible to compute $p(z_t, d_t|\boldsymbol{y}_{1:T})$ in $O(TK^2 + TKD)$ time, where T is the sequence length, K is the number of states, and D is the maximum duration of any segment. In [Dai+17], they show how to train an approximate inference algorithm, based on a mean field approximation $q(\boldsymbol{z}, \boldsymbol{d}|\boldsymbol{y}) = \prod_t q(z_t|\boldsymbol{y})q(d_t|\boldsymbol{y})$, to compute the posterior in $O(TK + TD)$ time.

29.5.2 Hierarchical HMMs

A **hierarchical HMM** (HHMM) [FST98] is an extension of the HMM that is designed to model domains with hierarchical structure. Figure 29.17 gives an example of an HHMM used in automatic speech recognition, where words are composed of phones which are composed of subphones. We can always "flatten" an HHMM to a regular HMM, but a factored representation is often easier to interpret, and allows for more efficient inference and model fitting.

HHMMs have been used in many application domains, e.g., speech recognition [Bil01], gene finding [Hu+00], plan recognition [BVW02], monitoring transportation patterns [Lia+07], indoor robot localization [TMK04], etc. HHMMs are less expressive than stochastic context free grammars (SCFGs) since they only allow hierarchies of bounded depth, but they support more efficient inference. In

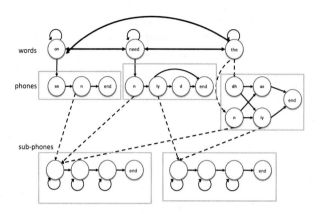

Figure 29.17: *An example of an HHMM for an ASR system which can recognize 3 words. The top level represents bigram word probabilities. The middle level represents the phonetic spelling of each word. The bottom level represents the subphones of each phone. (It is traditional to represent a phone as a 3 state HMM, representing the beginning, middle and end; these are known as subphones.) Adapted from Figure 7.5 of [JM00].*

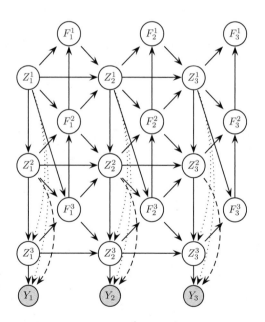

Figure 29.18: *An HHMM represented as a DPGM. Z_t^ℓ is the state at time t, level ℓ; $F_t^\ell = 1$ if the HMM at level ℓ has finished (entered its exit state), otherwise $F_t^\ell = 0$. Shaded nodes are observed; the remaining nodes are hidden. We may optionally clamp $F_T^\ell = 1$, where T is the length of the observation sequence, to ensure all models have finished by the end of the sequence. From Figure 2 of [MP01].*

particular, inference in SCFGs (using the inside outside algorithm, [JM08]) takes $O(T^3)$ whereas inference in an HHMM takes $O(T)$ time [MP01; WM12].

We can represent an HHMM as a directed graphical model as shown in Figure 29.18. Q_t^ℓ represents the state at time t and level ℓ. A state transition at level ℓ is only "allowed" if the chain at the level below has "finished", as determined by the $F_t^{\ell-1}$ node. (The chain below finishes when it chooses to enter its end state.) This mechanism ensures that higher level chains evolve more slowly than lower level chains, i.e., lower levels are nested within higher levels.

A variable duration HMM can be thought of as a special case of an HHMM, where the top level is a deterministic counter, and the bottom level is a regular HMM, which can only change states once the counter has "timed out". See [MP01] for further details.

29.5.3 Factorial HMMs

An HMM represents the hidden state using a single discrete random variable $z_t \in \{1, \dots, K\}$. To represent 10 bits of information would require $K = 2^{10} = 1024$ states. By contrast, consider a **distributed representation** of the hidden state, where each $z_{t,m} \in \{0, 1\}$ represents the m'th bit of the t'th hidden state. Now we can represent 10 bits using just 10 binary variables. This model is called a **factorial HMM** [GJ97].

More precisely, the model is defined as follows:

$$p(\boldsymbol{z}, \boldsymbol{y}) = \prod_t \left[\prod_m p(z_{tm}|z_{t-1,m}) \right] p(\boldsymbol{y}_t|\boldsymbol{z}_t) \tag{29.58}$$

where $p(z_{tm} = k|z_{t-1,m} = j) = A_{mjk}$ is an entry in the transition matrix for chain m, $p(z_{1m} = k|z_{0m}) = p(z_{1m} = k) = \pi_{mk}$, is the initial state distribution for chain m, and

$$p(\boldsymbol{y}_t|\boldsymbol{z}_t) = \mathcal{N}\left(\boldsymbol{y}_t| \sum_{m=1}^{M} \mathbf{W}_m \boldsymbol{z}_{tm}, \boldsymbol{\Sigma}\right) \tag{29.59}$$

is the observation model, where $\boldsymbol{z}_{tm}$ is a 1-of-K encoding of z_{tm} and $\mathbf{W}_m$ is a $D \times K$ matrix (assuming $\boldsymbol{y}_t \in \mathbb{R}^D$). Figure 29.19a illustrates the model for the case where $M = 3$.

An interesting application of FHMMs is to the problem of **energy disaggregation** [KJ12]. In this problem, we observe the total energy usage of a house at each moment in time, i.e., the observation model has the form

$$p(y_t|\boldsymbol{z}_t) = \mathcal{N}(y_t| \sum_{m=1}^{M} w_m z_{tm}, \sigma^2) \tag{29.60}$$

where w_m is the amount of energy used by device m, and $z_{tm} = 1$ if device m is being used at time t and $z_{tm} = 0$ otherwise. The transition model is assumed to be

$$p(z_{t,m} = 1|z_{t-1,m}) = \begin{cases} A_{01} & \text{if } z_{t-1,m} = 0 \\ A_{11} & \text{if } z_{t-1,m} = 1 \end{cases} \tag{29.61}$$

We do not know which devices are turned on at each time step (i.e., the z_{tm} are hidden), but by applying inference in the FHMM over time, we can separate the total energy into its parts, and thereby determine which devices are using the most electricity.

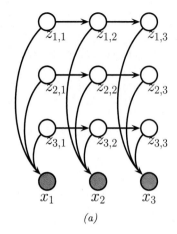
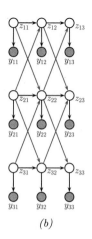

(a)   (b)

Figure 29.19: (a) A factorial HMM with 3 chains. (b) A coupled HMM with 3 chains.

Unfortunately, conditioned on $\boldsymbol{y}_t$, all the hidden variables are correlated (due to explaining away the common observed child $\boldsymbol{y}_t$). This make exact state estimation intractable. However, we can derive efficient approximate inference algorithms, as we discuss in Supplementary Section 10.3.2.

29.5.4   Coupled HMMs

If we have multiple related data streams, we can use a **coupled HMM** [Bra96]. This is a series of HMMs where the state transitions depend on the states of neighboring chains. That is, we represent the conditional distribution for each time slice as

$$p(\boldsymbol{z}_t, \boldsymbol{y}_t | \boldsymbol{z}_{t-1}) = \prod_m p(\boldsymbol{y}_{tm} | z_{tm}) p(z_{tm} | \boldsymbol{z}_{t-1,m-1:m+1}) \tag{29.62}$$

with boundary conditions defined in the obvious way. See Section 29.5.4 for an illustration with $M = 3$ chains.

Coupled HMMs have been used for various tasks, such as **audio-visual speech recognition** [Nef+02], modeling freeway traffic flows [KM00], and modeling conversational interactions between people [Bas+01].

However, there are two drawbacks to this model. First, exact inference takes $O(T(K^M)^2)$, as in a factorial HMM; however, in practice this is not usually a problem, since M is often small. Second, the model requires $O(MK^4)$ parameters to specify, if there are M chains with K states per chain, because each state depends on its own past plus the past of its two neighbors. There is a closely related model, known as the **influence model** [Asa00], which uses fewer parameters, by computing a convex combination of pairwise transition matrices.

29.5.5   Dynamic Bayes nets (DBN)

A **dynamic Bayesian network** (**DBN**) is a way to represent a stochastic process using a directed graphical model [Mur02]. (Note that the network is not dynamic (the structure and parameters are

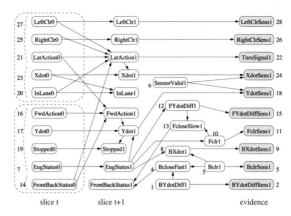

Figure 29.20: The BATnet DBN. The transient nodes are only shown for the second slice, to minimize clutter. The dotted lines are used to group related variables. Used with kind permission of Daphne Koller.

fixed), rather it is a network representation of a dynamical system.) A DBN can be considered as a natural generalization of an HMM.

An example is shown in Figure 29.20, which is a DBN designed to monitor the state of a simulated autonomous car known as the "Bayesian automated taxi", or "BATmobile" [For+95]. To define the model, you just need to specify the structure of the first time-slice, the structure between two time-slices, and the form of the CPDs. For details, see [KF09a].

29.5.6 Changepoint detection

In this section, we discuss **changepoint detection**, which is the task of detecting when there are "abrupt" changes in the distribution of the observed values in a time series. We focus on the online case. (For a review of offline methods to this problem, see e.g., [AC17; TOV18]. (See also [BW20] for a recent empirical evaluation of various methods, focused on the 1d time series case.)

The methods we discuss can (in principle) be used for high-dimensional time series segmentation. Our starting point is the hidden semi-Markov models (HSMM) discussed in Section 29.5.1. This is like an HMM in which we explicitly model the duration spent in each state. This is done by augmenting the latent state z_t with a duration variable d_t which is initialized according to a duration distribution, $d_t \sim D_{z_t}(\cdot)$, and which then *counts down* to 1. An alternative approach is to add a variable $r_t\{0, 1, \ldots, \}$ which encodes the **run length** for the current state; this starts at 0 whenever a new segment is created, and then *counts up* by one at each step. The transition dynamics is specified by

$$p(r_t|r_{t-1}) = \begin{cases} H(r_{t-1}+1) & \text{if } r_t = 0 \\ 1 - H(r_{t-1}+1) & \text{if } r_t = r_{t-1}+1 \\ 0 & \text{otherwise} \end{cases} \qquad (29.63)$$

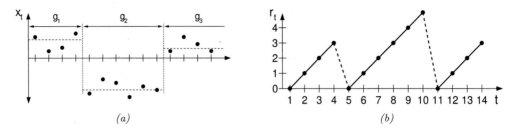

Figure 29.21: *Illustration of Bayesian online changepoint detection (BOCPD). (a) Hypothetical segmentation of a univariate time series divided by changepoints on the mean into three segments of lengths $g_1 = 4$, $g_2 = 6$, and an undetermined length for g_3 (since it the third segment has not yet ended). From Figure 1 of [AM07]. Used with kind permission of Ryan Adams.*

where $H(\tau)$ is a **hazard function**:

$$H(\tau) = \frac{p_g(\tau)}{\sum_{t=\tau}^{\infty} p_g(t)} \tag{29.64}$$

where $p_g(t)$ is the probability of a segment of length t. See Figure 29.21 for an illustration. If we set p_g to be a geometric distribution with parameter λ, then the hazard function is the constant $H(\tau) = 1/\lambda$.

The advantage of the run-length representation is that we can define the observation model for a segment in a causal way (that only depends on past data):

$$p(\boldsymbol{y}_t|\boldsymbol{y}_{1:t-1}, r_t = r, z_t = k) = p(\boldsymbol{y}_t|\boldsymbol{y}_{t-r:t-1}, z_t = k) = \int p(\boldsymbol{y}_t|\boldsymbol{\eta})p(\boldsymbol{\eta}|\boldsymbol{y}_{t-r:t-1}, z_t = k)d\boldsymbol{\eta} \tag{29.65}$$

where $\boldsymbol{\eta}$ are the parameters that are "local" to this segment. This called the **underlying predictive model** or **UPM** for the segment. The posterior over the UPM parameters is given by

$$p(\boldsymbol{\eta}|\boldsymbol{y}_{t-r:t-1}, z_t = k) \propto p(\boldsymbol{\eta}|z_t = k) \prod_{i=t-r}^{t-1} p(\boldsymbol{y}_i|\boldsymbol{\eta}) \tag{29.66}$$

where we initialize the prior for $\boldsymbol{\eta}$ using hyper-parameters chosen by state k. If the model is conjugate exponential, we can compute this marginal likelihood in closed form, and we have

$$\pi_t^{r,k} = p(\boldsymbol{y}_t|\boldsymbol{y}_{t-r:t-1}, z_t = k) = p(\boldsymbol{y}_t|\boldsymbol{\psi}_t^{r,k}) \tag{29.67}$$

where $\boldsymbol{\psi}_t^{r,k}$ are the parameters of the posterior predictive distribution at time t based on the last r observations (and using a prior from state k).

In the special case in which we have $K = 1$ hidden states, then each segment is modeled independently, and we get a **product partition model** [BH92]:

$$p(\boldsymbol{y}|\boldsymbol{r}) = p(\boldsymbol{y}_{s_1:e_1}) \cdots p(\boldsymbol{y}_{s_N:e_N}) \tag{29.68}$$

where s_i and e_i are the start and end of segment i, which can be computed from the run lengths $\boldsymbol{r}$. (We initialize with $r_0 = 0$.) Thus there is no information sharing between segments. This can be

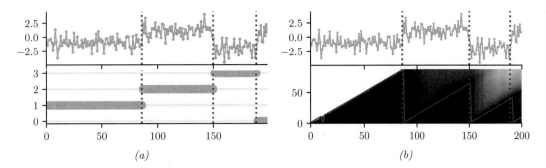

Figure 29.22: Illustration of BOCPD. (a) Synthetic data from a GMM with 4 states. Top row is the data, bottom row is the generating state. (b) Output of algorithm. Top row: Estimated changepoint locations. Bottom row: posterior predicted probability of a changepoint at each step. Generated by changepoint_detection.ipynb.

useful for time series in which there are abrupt changes, and where the new parameters are unrelated to the old ones.

Detecting the locations of these changes is called **changepoint detection**. An exact online algorithm for solving this task was proposed in [FL07] and independently in [AM07]; in the latter paper, they call the method **Bayesian online changepoint detection** or **BOCPD**. We can compute a posterior over the current run length recursively as follows:

$$p(r_t|\boldsymbol{y}_{1:t}) \propto p(\boldsymbol{y}_t|\boldsymbol{y}_{1:t-1}, r_t)p(r_t|\boldsymbol{y}_{1:t-1}) \tag{29.69}$$

where we initialize with $p(r_0 = 0) = 1$. The marginal likelihood $p(\boldsymbol{y}_t|\boldsymbol{y}_{1:t-1}, r_t)$ is given by Equation (29.65) (with $z_t = 1$ dropped, since there is just one state). The prior predictive is given by

$$p(r_t|\boldsymbol{y}_{1:t-1}) = \sum_{r_{t-1}} p(r_t|r_{t-1})p(r_{t-1}|\boldsymbol{y}_{1:t-1}) \tag{29.70}$$

The one step ahead predictive distribution is given by

$$p(\boldsymbol{y}_{t+1}|\boldsymbol{y}_{1:t}) = \sum_{r_t} p(\boldsymbol{y}_{t+1}|\boldsymbol{y}_{1:t}, r_t)p(r_t|\boldsymbol{y}_{1:t}) \tag{29.71}$$

29.5.6.1   Example

We give an example of the method in Figure 29.22 applied to a synthetic 1d dataset generated from a 4 state GMM. The likelihood is a univariate Gaussian, $p(y_t|\mu) = \mathcal{N}(y_t|\mu, \sigma^2)$, where $\sigma^2 = 1$ is fixed, and μ is inferred using a Gaussian prior. The hazard function is set to a geometric distribution with rate N/T, where $N = 4$ is the true number of change points and $T = 200$ is the length of the sequence.

29.5.6.2   Extensions

Although the above method is exact, each update step takes $O(t)$ time, so the total cost of the algorithm is $O(T^2)$. We can reduce this by pruning out states with low probability. In particular, we can use particle filtering (Section 13.2) with N particles, together with a stratified optimal resampling method, to reduce the cost to $O(TN)$. See [FL07] for details.

In addition, the above method relies on a conjugate exponential model in order to compute the marginal likelihood, and update the posterior parameters for each r, in $O(1)$ time. For more complex models, we need to use approximations. In [TBS13], they use variational Bayes (Section 10.3.3), and in [Mav16], they use particle filtering (Section 13.2), which is more general, but much slower.

It is possible to extend the model in various other ways. In [FL11], they allow for Markov dependence between the parameters of neighboring segments. In [STR10], they use a Gaussian process (Chapter 18) to represent the UPM, which captures correlations between observations within the same segment. In [KJD18], they use generalized Bayesian inference (Section 14.1.3) to create a method that is more robust to model misspecification.

In [Gol+17], they extend the model by modeling the probability of a sequence of observations, rather than having to make the decision about whether to insert a changepoint or not based on just the likelihood ratio of a single time step.

In [AE+20], they extend the model by allowing for multiple discrete states, as in an HSMM. In addition, they add both the run length r_t and the duration d_t to the state space. This allows the method to specify not just when the current segment started, but also when it is expected to end. In addition, it allows the UPM to depend on the duration of the segment, and not just on past observations. For example, we can use

$$p(y_t|r_t, d_t, \eta) = \mathcal{N}(y_t|\boldsymbol{\phi}(r_t/d_t)^\mathsf{T}\boldsymbol{\eta}, \sigma^2) \tag{29.72}$$

where $0 \leq r_t/d_t \leq 1$, and $\boldsymbol{\phi}()$ is a set of learned basis functions. This allows observation sequences for the same hidden state to have a common functional shape, even if the time spent in each state is different.

29.6   Linear dynamical systems (LDSs)

In this section, we discuss **linear-Gaussian state-space model** (**LG-SSM**), also called **linear dynamical system** (**LDS**). This is a special case of an SSM in which the transition function and observation function are both linear, and the process noise and observation noise are both Gaussian.

29.6.1   Conditional independence properties

The LDS graphical model is shown in Figure 29.1(a). This encodes the assumption that the hidden states are Markovian, and the observations are iid conditioned on the hidden states. All that remains is to specify the form of the conditional probability distributions of each node.

29.6.2   Parameterization

An LDS model is defined as follows:

$$p(z_t|z_{t-1}, u_t) = \mathcal{N}(z_t|\mathbf{F}_t z_{t-1} + \mathbf{B}_t u_t + b_t, \mathbf{Q}_t) \tag{29.73}$$
$$p(y_t|z_t, u_t) = \mathcal{N}(y_t|\mathbf{H}_t z_t + \mathbf{D}_t u_t + d_t, \mathbf{R}_t) \tag{29.74}$$

We often assume the bias (offset) terms are zero, in which case the model simplifies to

$$p(\boldsymbol{z}_t|\boldsymbol{z}_{t-1}, \boldsymbol{u}_t) = \mathcal{N}(\boldsymbol{z}_t|\mathbf{F}_t\boldsymbol{z}_{t-1} + \mathbf{B}_t\boldsymbol{u}_t, \mathbf{Q}_t) \tag{29.75}$$

$$p(\boldsymbol{y}_t|\boldsymbol{z}_t, \boldsymbol{u}_t) = \mathcal{N}(\boldsymbol{y}_t|\mathbf{H}_t\boldsymbol{z}_t + \mathbf{D}_t\boldsymbol{u}_t, \mathbf{R}_t) \tag{29.76}$$

Furthermore, if there are no inputs, the model further simplifies to

$$p(\boldsymbol{z}_t|\boldsymbol{z}_{t-1}) = \mathcal{N}(\boldsymbol{z}_t|\mathbf{F}_t\boldsymbol{z}_{t-1}, \mathbf{Q}_t) \tag{29.77}$$

$$p(\boldsymbol{y}_t|\boldsymbol{z}_t) = \mathcal{N}(\boldsymbol{y}_t|\mathbf{H}_t\boldsymbol{z}_t, \mathbf{R}_t) \tag{29.78}$$

We can also write this as a structural equation model (Section 4.7.2):

$$\boldsymbol{z}_t = \mathbf{F}_t\boldsymbol{z}_{t-1} + \boldsymbol{q}_t \tag{29.79}$$

$$\boldsymbol{y}_t = \mathbf{H}_t\boldsymbol{z}_t + \boldsymbol{r}_t \tag{29.80}$$

where $\boldsymbol{q}_t \sim \mathcal{N}(\mathbf{0}, \mathbf{Q}_t)$ is the **process noise**, and $\boldsymbol{r}_t \sim \mathcal{N}(\mathbf{0}, \mathbf{R}_t)$ is the **observation noise**.

Typically we assume the parameters $\boldsymbol{\theta}_t = (\mathbf{F}_t, \mathbf{H}_t, \mathbf{B}_t, \mathbf{D}_t, \mathbf{Q}_t, \mathbf{R}_t)$ are independent of time, so the model is stationary. (We discuss how to learn the parameters in Section 29.8.) Given the parameters, we discuss how to perform online posterior inference of the latent states using the Kalman filter in Section 8.2.2, and offline inference using the Kalman smoother in Section 8.2.3.

29.7 LDS: applications

In this section, we discuss some applications of LDS models.

29.7.1 Object tracking and state estimation

Consider an object moving in $\mathbb{R}^2$. Let the state at time t be the position and velocity of the object, $\boldsymbol{z}_t = \begin{pmatrix} u_t & v_t & \dot{u}_t & \dot{v}_t \end{pmatrix}$. (We use u and v for the two coordinates, to avoid confusion with the state and observation variables.) We assume this evolves in continuous time according to a linear **stochastic differential equation** or SDE, in which the dynamics are given by Newton's law of motion, and where the random acceleration corresponds to a **white noise process** (aka **Brownian motion**). However, since the observations occur at discrete time steps t_k, we will only evaluate the system at discrete time points; this is called a **continuous-discrete SSM** [SS19, p199]. (We shall henceforth write t instead of t_k, since in this book we only consider discrete time.) The corresponding discrete time SSM is given by the following [SS19, p82]:

$$\underbrace{\begin{pmatrix} u_t \\ v_t \\ \dot{u}_t \\ \dot{v}_t \end{pmatrix}}_{\boldsymbol{z}_t} = \underbrace{\begin{pmatrix} 1 & 0 & \Delta & 0 \\ 0 & 1 & 0 & \Delta \\ 0 & 0 & 1 & 0 \\ 0 & 0 & 0 & 1 \end{pmatrix}}_{\mathbf{F}} \underbrace{\begin{pmatrix} u_{t-1} \\ v_{t-1} \\ \dot{u}_{t-1} \\ \dot{v}_{t-1} \end{pmatrix}}_{\boldsymbol{z}_{t-1}} + \boldsymbol{q}_t \tag{29.81}$$

where Δ is the step size between consecutive discrete measurement times, $\boldsymbol{q}_t \sim \mathcal{N}(\boldsymbol{0}, \mathbf{Q})$ is the process noise, and the noise covariance matrix $\mathbf{Q}$ is given by

$$
\mathbf{Q} = \begin{pmatrix}
\frac{q_1 \Delta^3}{3} & 0 & \frac{q_1 \Delta^2}{2} & 0 \\
0 & \frac{q_2 \Delta^3}{3} & 0 & \frac{q_2 \Delta^2}{2} \\
\frac{q_1 \Delta^2}{2} & 0 & q_1 \Delta & 0 \\
0 & \frac{q_2 \Delta^2}{2} & 0 & q_2 \Delta
\end{pmatrix}
$$

where q_i are the diffusion coefficients of the white noise process for dimension i (see [SS19, p44] for details).

Now suppose that at each discrete time point we observe the location, corrupted by Gaussian noise. Thus the observation model becomes

$$
\underbrace{\begin{pmatrix} y_{1,t} \\ y_{2,t} \end{pmatrix}}_{\boldsymbol{y}_t} = \underbrace{\begin{pmatrix} 1 & 0 & 0 & 0 \\ 0 & 0 & 1 & 0 \end{pmatrix}}_{\mathbf{H}} \underbrace{\begin{pmatrix} u_t \\ \dot{u}_t \\ v_t \\ \dot{v}_t \end{pmatrix}}_{\boldsymbol{z}_t} + \boldsymbol{r}_t \tag{29.82}
$$

where $\boldsymbol{r}_t \sim \mathcal{N}(\boldsymbol{0}, \mathbf{R})$ is the **observation noise**. We see that the observation matrix $\mathbf{H}$ simply "extracts" the relevant parts of the state vector.

Suppose we sample a trajectory and corresponding set of noisy observations from this model, $(\boldsymbol{z}_{1:T}, \boldsymbol{y}_{1:T}) \sim p(\boldsymbol{z}, \boldsymbol{y} | \boldsymbol{\theta})$. (We use diagonal observation noise, $\mathbf{R} = \mathrm{diag}(\sigma_1^2, \sigma_2^2)$.) The results are shown in Figure 29.23(a). We can use the Kalman filter (Section 8.2.2) to compute $p(\boldsymbol{z}_t | \boldsymbol{y}_{1:t}, \boldsymbol{\theta})$ for each t,. (We initialize the filter with a vague prior, namely $p(\boldsymbol{z}_0) = \mathcal{N}(\boldsymbol{z}_0 | \boldsymbol{0}, 10^5 \mathbf{I})$.) The results are shown in Figure 29.23(b). We see that the posterior mean (red line) is close to the ground truth, but there is considerable uncertainty (shown by the confidence ellipses). To improve results, we can use the Kalman smoother (Section 8.2.3) to compute $p(\boldsymbol{z}_t | \boldsymbol{y}_{1:T}, \boldsymbol{\theta})$, where we condition on all the data, past and future. The results are shown in Figure 29.23(c). Now we see that the resulting estimate is smoother, and the uncertainty is reduced. (The uncertainty is larger at the edges because there is less information in the neighbors to condition on.)

29.7.2 Online Bayesian linear regression (recursive least squares)

In Section 15.2.2, we discuss how to compute $p(\boldsymbol{w} | \sigma^2, \mathcal{D})$ for a linear regression model in batch mode, using a Gaussian prior of the form $p(\boldsymbol{w}) = \mathcal{N}(\boldsymbol{w} | \boldsymbol{\mu}, \boldsymbol{\Sigma})$. In this section, we discuss how to compute this posterior online, by repeatedly performing the following update:

$$
p(\boldsymbol{w} | \mathcal{D}_{1:t}) \propto p(\mathcal{D}_t | \boldsymbol{w}) p(\boldsymbol{w} | \mathcal{D}_{1:t-1}) \tag{29.83}
$$

$$
\propto p(\mathcal{D}_t | \boldsymbol{w}) p(\mathcal{D}_{t-1} | \boldsymbol{w}) \dots p(\mathcal{D}_1 | \boldsymbol{w}) p(\boldsymbol{w}) \tag{29.84}
$$

where $\mathcal{D}_t = (\boldsymbol{u}_t, y_t)$ is the t'th labeled example, and $\mathcal{D}_{1:t-1}$ are the first $t-1$ examples. (For brevity, we drop the conditioning on σ^2.) We see that the previous posterior, $p(\boldsymbol{w} | \mathcal{D}_{1:t-1})$, becomes the current prior, which gets updated by $\mathcal{D}_t$ to become the new posterior, $p(\boldsymbol{w} | \mathcal{D}_{1:t})$. This is an example of sequential Bayesian updating or online Bayesian inference. In the case of linear regression, this process is known as the **recursive least squares** or **RLS** algorithm.

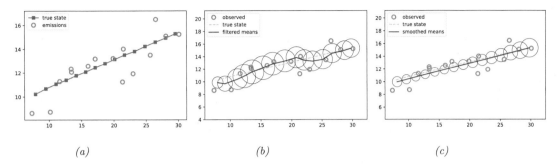

Figure 29.23: Illustration of Kalman filtering and smoothing for a linear dynamical system. (Repeated from Figure 8.2.) (a) Observations (green circles) are generated by an object moving to the right (true location denoted by blue squares). (b) Results of online Kalman filtering. Red cross is the posterior mean, circles are 95% confidence ellipses derived from the posterior covariance. (c) Same as (b), but using offline Kalman smoothing. The MSE in the trajectory for filtering is 3.13, and for smoothing is 1.71. Generated by kf_tracking.ipynb.

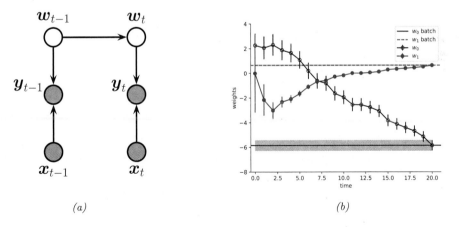

Figure 29.24: (a) A dynamic generalization of linear regression. (b) Illustration of the recursive least squares algorithm applied to the model $p(y|x, \boldsymbol{w}) = \mathcal{N}(y|w_0 + w_1 x, \sigma^2)$. We plot the marginal posterior of w_0 and w_1 vs number of datapoints. (Error bars represent $\mathbb{E}[w_j|\boldsymbol{y}_{1:t}, \boldsymbol{x}_{1:t}] \pm \sqrt{\mathbb{V}[w_j|\boldsymbol{y}_{1:t}, \boldsymbol{x}_{1:t}]}$.) After seeing all the data, we converge to the offline (batch) Bayes solution, represented by the horizontal lines. (Shading represents the marginal posterior variance.) Generated by kf_linreg.ipynb.

We can implement this method by using a linear Gaussian state-space model(Section 29.6). The basic idea is to let the hidden state represent the regression parameters, and to let the (time-varying) observation model $\mathbf{H}_t$ represent the current feature vector $\boldsymbol{x}_t$.[3] That is, the observation model has the form

$$p(y_t|\boldsymbol{w}_t) = \mathcal{N}(y_t|\mathbf{H}_t\boldsymbol{z}_t, \mathbf{R}_t) = \mathcal{N}(y_t|\boldsymbol{x}_t^\mathsf{T}\boldsymbol{w}_t, \sigma^2) \tag{29.85}$$

If we assume the regression parameters do not change, the dynamics model becomes

$$p(\boldsymbol{w}_t|\boldsymbol{w}_{t-1}) = \mathcal{N}(\boldsymbol{w}_t|\boldsymbol{w}_{t-1}, 0) = \delta(\boldsymbol{w}_t - \boldsymbol{w}_{t-1}) \tag{29.86}$$

(If we do let the parameters change over time, we get a so-called **dynamic linear model** [Har90; WH97; PPC09].) See Figure 29.24a for the model, and Supplementary Section 8.1.2 for a simplification of the Kalman filter equations when applied to this special case.

We show a 1d example in Figure 29.24b. We see that online inference converges to the exact batch (offline) posterior in a single pass over the data.

If we approximate the Kalman gain matrix by $\mathbf{K}_t \approx \eta_t \mathbf{1}$, we recover the **least mean squares** or **LMS** algorithm, where η_t is the learning rate. In LMS, we need to adapt the learning rate to ensure convergence to the MLE. Furthermore, the algorithm may require multiple passes through the data to converge to this global optimum. By contrast, the RLS algorithm automatically performs step-size adaptation, and converges to the optimal posterior in a single pass over the data.

In Section 8.6.3, we extend this approach to perform online parameter estimation for logistic regression, and in Section 17.5.2, we extend this approach to perform online parameter estimation for MLPs.

29.7.3   Adaptive filtering

Consider an autoregressive model of order D:

$$y_t = w_1 y_{t-1} + \cdots + w_D y_{t-D} + \epsilon_t \tag{29.87}$$

where $\epsilon_t \sim \mathcal{N}(0, 1)$. The problem of **adaptive filtering** is to estimate the parameters $\boldsymbol{w}_{1:D}$ given the observations $\boldsymbol{y}_{1:t}$.

We can cast this as inference in an LG-SSM by defining the observation matrix to be $\mathbf{H}_t = (y_{t-1} \ldots y_{t-D})$ and defining the state as $\boldsymbol{z}_t = \boldsymbol{w}$. We can also allow the parameters to evolve over time, similar to Section 29.7.2.

29.7.4   Time series forecasting

In Section 29.12 we discuss how to use LDS models to perform time series forecasting.

---

3. It is tempting to think we can just set the input $\boldsymbol{u}_t$ to the covariates $\boldsymbol{x}_t$. Unfortunately this will not work, since the effect of the inputs is to add an offset term to the output in a way which is independent of the hidden state (parameters). That is, since we have $\boldsymbol{y}_t = \mathbf{H}_t\boldsymbol{z}_t + \mathbf{D}_t\boldsymbol{u}_t + \boldsymbol{d} + \boldsymbol{r}_t$, if we set $\boldsymbol{u}_t = \boldsymbol{x}_t$ then the features get multiplied by the constant LDS parameter $\mathbf{D}_t$ instead of the hidden state $\boldsymbol{z}_t$ containing the regression weights.

29.8 LDS: parameter learning

There are many approaches for estimating the parameters of state-space models. (In the control theory community, this is known as **systems identification** [Lju87].) In the case of linear dynamical systems, many of the methods are similar to techniques used to fit HMMs, discussed in Section 29.4. For example, we can use EM, SGD, spectral methods, or Bayesian methods, as we discuss below.

29.8.1 EM for LDS

This section is coauthored with Xinglong Li.

If we only observe the output sequence, we can compute ML or MAP estimates of the parameters using EM. The method is conceptually quite similar to the Baum-Welch algorithm for HMMs (Section 29.4.1), except we use Kalman smoothing (Section 8.2.3) instead of forwards-backwards in the E step, and use different calculations in the M step. The details can be found in [SS82; GH96a]. Here we extend these results to consider the case where the HMM may have an optional input sequence $\boldsymbol{u}_{1:T}$.

Our goal is to maximize the expected complete data log likelihood

$$\mathcal{Q}(\boldsymbol{\theta}, \boldsymbol{\theta}_{k-1}) = \mathbb{E}\left[\log p(\boldsymbol{z}_{1:T}, \boldsymbol{y}_{1:T}|\boldsymbol{\theta})|\boldsymbol{y}_{1:T}, \boldsymbol{u}_{1:T}, \boldsymbol{\theta}_{k-1}\right] \tag{29.88}$$

where the expectations are taken wrt the parameters at the previous iteration $k-1$ of the algorithm. (We initialize with random parameters, or by first fitting a simpler model, such as factor analysis.) For brevity of notations, we assume that the bias terms are included in $\mathbf{D}$ and $\mathbf{B}$ (i.e., the last entry of $\boldsymbol{u}_t$ is 1).

The log joint is given by the following:

$$\log p(\boldsymbol{z}_{1:T}, \boldsymbol{y}_{1:T}|\boldsymbol{\theta}) = -\sum_{t=1}^{T}\left(\frac{1}{2}(\boldsymbol{y}_t - \mathbf{H}\boldsymbol{z}_t - \mathbf{D}\boldsymbol{u}_t)^\mathsf{T}\mathbf{R}^{-1}(\boldsymbol{y}_t - \mathbf{H}\boldsymbol{z}_t - \mathbf{D}\boldsymbol{u}_t)\right) - \frac{T}{2}\log|\mathbf{R}| \tag{29.89}$$

$$-\sum_{t=2}^{T}\left(\frac{1}{2}(\boldsymbol{z}_t - \mathbf{F}\boldsymbol{z}_{t-1} - \mathbf{B}\boldsymbol{u}_t)^\mathsf{T}\mathbf{Q}^{-1}(\boldsymbol{z}_t - \mathbf{F}\boldsymbol{z}_{t-1} - \mathbf{B}\boldsymbol{u}_t)\right) - \frac{T-1}{2}\log|\mathbf{Q}|$$

$$\tag{29.90}$$

$$-\frac{1}{2}(\boldsymbol{z}_1 - \boldsymbol{m}_1)^\mathsf{T}\mathbf{V}_1^{-1}(\boldsymbol{z}_1 - \boldsymbol{m}_1) - \frac{1}{2}\log|\mathbf{V}_1| + \text{const} \tag{29.91}$$

where the prior on the initial state is $p(\boldsymbol{z}_1) = \mathcal{N}(\boldsymbol{z}_1|\boldsymbol{m}_1, \mathbf{V}_1)$.

In the E step, we can run the Kalman smoother to compute $\boldsymbol{\mu}_{t|T} = \mathbb{E}\left[\boldsymbol{z}_t|\boldsymbol{y}_{1:T}\right]$, and $\boldsymbol{\Sigma}_{t|T} = \text{Cov}\left[\boldsymbol{z}_t|\boldsymbol{y}_{1:T}\right]$, from which we can compute $\hat{\boldsymbol{z}}_t = \boldsymbol{\mu}_{t|T}$ and

$$\mathbf{P}_t = \mathbb{E}\left[\boldsymbol{z}_t\boldsymbol{z}_t^\mathsf{T}|\boldsymbol{y}_{1:T}\right] = \boldsymbol{\Sigma}_{t|T} + \boldsymbol{\mu}_{t|T}\boldsymbol{\mu}_{t|T}^\mathsf{T} \tag{29.92}$$

We also need to compute the cross term

$$\mathbf{P}_{t,t-1} = \mathbb{E}\left[\boldsymbol{z}_t\boldsymbol{z}_{t-1}^\mathsf{T}|\boldsymbol{y}_{1:T}\right] = \boldsymbol{\Sigma}_{t,t-1|T} + \boldsymbol{\mu}_{t|T}\boldsymbol{\mu}_{t-1|T}^\mathsf{T} \tag{29.93}$$

where

$$\boldsymbol{\Sigma}_{t-1,t-2|T} = \boldsymbol{\Sigma}_{t-1|t-1}\mathbf{G}_{t-2}^\mathsf{T} + \mathbf{G}_{t-1}(\boldsymbol{\Sigma}_{t,t-1|T} - \mathbf{F}\boldsymbol{\Sigma}_{t-1|t-1})\mathbf{G}_{t-2}^\mathsf{T} \tag{29.94}$$

where $\mathbf{G}_t$ is the backwards Kalman gain matrix defined in Equation (8.67). We initialize this using $\boldsymbol{\Sigma}_{T,T-1|T} = (\mathbf{I} - \mathbf{K}_T \mathbf{H})\mathbf{F}\boldsymbol{\Sigma}_{T-1|T-1}$, where $\mathbf{K}_T$ is the forwards Kalman gain matrix defined in Equation (8.28).

We can derive the M step as follows, using standard matrix calculus. We denote $\mathbf{A}_{\text{out}} = [\mathbf{H}, \mathbf{D}]$, $\hat{\boldsymbol{x}}_{\text{out},t} = [\hat{\boldsymbol{z}}_t^T, \boldsymbol{u}_t^T]^T$, $\mathbf{A}_{\text{dyn}} = [\mathbf{F}, \mathbf{B}]$, $\hat{\boldsymbol{x}}_{\text{dyn},t} = [\hat{\boldsymbol{z}}_{t-1}^T, \boldsymbol{u}_t^T]^T$, and

$$\mathbf{P}_{\text{out},t} = \begin{pmatrix} \mathbf{P}_t & \hat{\boldsymbol{z}}_t \boldsymbol{u}_t^\mathsf{T} \\ \boldsymbol{u}_t \hat{\boldsymbol{z}}_t^\mathsf{T} & \boldsymbol{u}_t \boldsymbol{u}_t^\mathsf{T} \end{pmatrix}, \qquad\qquad \mathbf{P}_{\text{dyn},t} = \begin{pmatrix} \mathbf{P}_{t-1} & \hat{\boldsymbol{z}}_{t-1} \boldsymbol{u}_t^\mathsf{T} \\ \boldsymbol{u}_t \hat{\boldsymbol{z}}_{t-1}^\mathsf{T} & \boldsymbol{u}_t \boldsymbol{u}_t^\mathsf{T} \end{pmatrix}. \tag{29.95}$$

- Output matrices:

$$\frac{\partial \mathcal{Q}}{\partial \mathbf{A}_{\text{out}}} = \sum_{t=1}^{T} \mathbf{R}^{-1} \boldsymbol{y}_t \hat{\boldsymbol{x}}_{\text{out},t}^\mathsf{T} - \sum_{t=1}^{T} \mathbf{R}^{-1} \mathbf{A}_{\text{out}} \mathbf{P}_{\text{out},t} = \mathbf{0} \tag{29.96}$$

$$\mathbf{A}_{\text{out}}^{\text{new}} = \left(\sum_{t=1}^{T} \boldsymbol{y}_t \hat{\boldsymbol{x}}_{\text{out},t}^\mathsf{T} \right) \left(\sum_{t=1}^{T} \mathbf{P}_{\text{out},t} \right)^{-1} \tag{29.97}$$

- Output noise covariance:

$$\frac{\partial \mathcal{Q}(\mathbf{A}_{\text{out}} = \mathbf{A}_{\text{out}}^{\text{new}})}{\partial \mathbf{R}^{-1}} = \frac{T}{2} \mathbf{R} - \frac{1}{2} \sum_{t=1}^{T} \left(\boldsymbol{y}_t \boldsymbol{y}_t^\mathsf{T} - 2 \mathbf{A}_{\text{out}}^{\text{new}} \hat{\boldsymbol{x}}_{\text{out},t} \boldsymbol{y}_t^\mathsf{T} + \mathbf{A}_{\text{out}}^{\text{new}} \mathbf{P}_{\text{out},t} \mathbf{A}_{\text{out}}^{\text{new},\mathsf{T}} \right) = \mathbf{0} \tag{29.98}$$

$$\mathbf{R}^{\text{new}} = \frac{1}{T} \sum_{t=1}^{T} (\boldsymbol{y}_t \boldsymbol{y}_t^\mathsf{T} - \mathbf{A}_{\text{out}}^{\text{new}} \hat{\boldsymbol{x}}_{\text{out},t} \boldsymbol{y}_t^\mathsf{T}) \tag{29.99}$$

- System dynamics matrices:

$$\frac{\partial \mathcal{Q}}{\partial \mathbf{A}_{\text{dyn}}} = - \sum_{t=2}^{T} \mathbf{Q}^{-1} \left[\mathbf{P}_{t,t-1}, \hat{\boldsymbol{z}}_t \boldsymbol{u}_t^\mathsf{T} \right] + \sum_{t=2}^{T} \mathbf{Q}^{-1} \mathbf{A}_{\text{dyn}} \mathbf{P}_{\text{dyn},t} = \mathbf{0} \tag{29.100}$$

$$\mathbf{A}_{\text{dyn}}^{\text{new}} = \left(\sum_{t=2}^{T} [\mathbf{P}_{t,t-1}, \hat{\boldsymbol{z}}_t \boldsymbol{u}_t^\mathsf{T}] \right) \left(\sum_{t=2}^{T} \mathbf{P}_{\text{dyn},t} \right)^{-1} \tag{29.101}$$

- State noise covariance:

$$\frac{\partial \mathcal{Q}(\mathbf{A}_{\text{dyn}} = \mathbf{A}_{\text{dyn}}^{\text{new}})}{\partial \mathbf{Q}^{-1}} = \frac{T-1}{2} \mathbf{Q} - \frac{1}{2} \sum_{t=2}^{T} (\mathbf{P}_t - 2\mathbf{A}_{\text{dyn}}^{\text{new}} \left[\mathbf{P}_{t-1,t}, \boldsymbol{u}_t \hat{\boldsymbol{z}}_t^\mathsf{T} \right] + \mathbf{A}_{\text{dyn}}^{\text{new}} \mathbf{P}_{\text{dyn},t} \mathbf{A}_{\text{dyn}}^{\text{new},\mathsf{T}}) \tag{29.102}$$

$$= \frac{T-1}{2} \mathbf{Q} - \frac{1}{2} \sum_{t=2}^{T} \left(\mathbf{P}_t - \mathbf{A}_{\text{dyn}}^{\text{new}} \left[\mathbf{P}_{t-1,t}, \boldsymbol{u}_t \hat{\boldsymbol{z}}_t^\mathsf{T} \right] \right) = \mathbf{0} \tag{29.103}$$

$$\mathbf{Q}^{\text{new}} = \frac{1}{T-1} \sum_{t=2}^{T} \left(\mathbf{P}_t - \mathbf{A}_{\text{dyn}}^{\text{new}} \left[\mathbf{P}_{t-1,t}, \boldsymbol{u}_t \hat{\boldsymbol{z}}_t^\mathsf{T} \right] \right) \tag{29.104}$$

- Initial state mean:

$$\frac{\partial Q}{\partial \boldsymbol{m}} = (\hat{\boldsymbol{z}}_1 - \boldsymbol{m})\mathbf{V}_1^{-1} = \mathbf{0} \tag{29.105}$$

$$\boldsymbol{m}^{\text{new}} = \hat{\boldsymbol{z}}_1 \tag{29.106}$$

- Initial state covariance:

$$\frac{\partial Q}{\partial \mathbf{V}_1^{-1}} = \frac{\mathbf{V}_1}{2} - \frac{1}{2}(\mathbf{P}_1 - \hat{\boldsymbol{z}}_1 \boldsymbol{m}_1^\mathsf{T} - \boldsymbol{m}_1 \hat{\boldsymbol{z}}_1^\mathsf{T} + \boldsymbol{m}_1 \boldsymbol{m}_1^\mathsf{T}) = \mathbf{0} \tag{29.107}$$

$$\mathbf{V}_1^{\text{new}} = \mathbf{P}_1 - \hat{\boldsymbol{z}}_1 \hat{\boldsymbol{z}}_1^\mathsf{T} \tag{29.108}$$

Note that computing these expected sufficient statistics in the inner loop of EM takes $O(T)$ time, which can be expensive for long sequences. In [Mar10b], a faster method, known as **ASOS** (approximate second order statistics), is proposed. In this approach, various statistics are precomputed in a single pass over the sequence, and from then on, all iterations take constant time (independent of T). Alternatively, if we have multiple processors, we can perform Kalman smoothing in $O(\log T)$ time using parallel scan operations (Section 8.2.3.4).

29.8.2 Subspace identification methods

EM does not always give satisfactory results, because it is sensitive to the initial parameter estimates. One way to avoid this is to use a different approach known as a **subspace identification** (**SSID**) [OM96; Kat05].

To understand this approach, let us initially assume there is no observation noise and no system noise. In this case, we have $\boldsymbol{z}_t = \mathbf{F}\boldsymbol{z}_{t-1}$ and $\boldsymbol{y}_t = \mathbf{H}\boldsymbol{z}_t$, and hence $\boldsymbol{y}_t = \mathbf{H}\mathbf{F}^{t-1}\boldsymbol{z}_1$. Consequently all the observations must be generated from a $\dim(\boldsymbol{z}_t)$-dimensional linear manifold or subspace. We can identify this subspace using PCA. Once we have an estimate of the $\boldsymbol{z}_t$'s, we can fit the model as if it were fully observed. We can either use these estimates in their own right, or use them to initialize EM. Several papers (e.g., [Smi+00; BK15]) have shown that initializing EM this way gives much better results than initializing EM at random, or just using SSID without EM.

Although the theory only works for noise-free data, we can try to estimate the system noise covariance $\mathbf{Q}$ from the residuals in predicting $\boldsymbol{z}_t$ from $\boldsymbol{z}_{t-1}$, and to estimate the observation noise covariance $\mathbf{R}$ from the residuals in predicting $\boldsymbol{y}_t$ from $\boldsymbol{z}_t$. We can either use these estimates in their own right, or use them to initialize EM. Because this method relies on taking an SVD, it is called a **spectral estimation method**. Similar methods can also be used for HMMs (see Section 29.4.3).

29.8.3 Ensuring stability of the dynamical system

When estimating the dynamics matrix $\mathbf{F}$, it is very useful to impose a constraint on its eigenvalues. To see why this is important, consider the case of no system noise. In this case, the hidden state at time t is given by

$$\boldsymbol{z}_t = \mathbf{F}^t \boldsymbol{z}_1 = \mathbf{U}\boldsymbol{\Lambda}^t\mathbf{U}^{-1}\boldsymbol{z}_1 \tag{29.109}$$

where $\mathbf{U}$ is the matrix of eigenvectors for $\mathbf{F}$, and $\boldsymbol{\Lambda} = \text{diag}(\lambda_i)$ contains the eigenvalues. If any $\lambda_i > 1$, then for large t, $\boldsymbol{z}_t$ will blow up in magnitude. Consequently, to ensure stability, it is useful to require that all the eigenvalues are less than 1 [SBG07]. Of course, if all the eigenvalues are less than 1, then $\mathbb{E}[\boldsymbol{z}_t] = \mathbf{0}$ for large t, so the state will return to the origin. Fortunately, when we add noise, the state becomes non-zero, so the model does not degenerate.

29.8.4 Bayesian LDS

SSMs can be quite sensitive to their parameter values, which is a particular concern when they are used for forecasting applications (see Section 29.12.1), or when the latent states or parameters are interpreted for scientific purposes (see e.g., [AM+16]). In such cases, it is wise to represent our uncertainty about the parameters by using Bayesian inference.

There are various algorithms we can use to perform this task. For linear-Gaussian SSMs, it is possible to use variational Bayes EM [Bea03; BC07] (see Section 10.3.5), or blocked Gibbs sampling (see Section 29.8.4.1). Note, however, that $\boldsymbol{\theta}$ and $\boldsymbol{z}$ are highly correlated, so the mean field approximation can be inaccurate, and the blocked Gibbs method can mix slowly. It is also possible to use collapsed MCMC in which we marginalize out $\boldsymbol{z}_{1:T}$ and just work with $p(\boldsymbol{\theta}|\boldsymbol{y}_{1:T})$, which we can sample using HMC.

29.8.4.1 Blocked Gibbs sampling for LDS

This section is written by Xinglong Li.

In this section, we discuss blocked Gibbs sampling for LDS [CK94b; CMR05; FS07]. We alternate between sampling from $p(\boldsymbol{z}_{1:T}|\boldsymbol{y}_{1:T}, \boldsymbol{\theta})$ using the forwards-filter backwards-sampling algorithm (Section 8.2.3.5), and sampling from $p(\boldsymbol{\theta}|\boldsymbol{z}_{1:T}, \boldsymbol{y}_{1:T})$, which is easy to do if we use conjugate priors.

In more detail, we will consider the following linear Gaussian state space model with homogeneous parameters:

$$p(\boldsymbol{z}_t|\boldsymbol{z}_{t-1}, \boldsymbol{u}_t) = \mathcal{N}(\boldsymbol{z}_t|\mathbf{F}\boldsymbol{z}_{t-1} + \mathbf{B}\boldsymbol{u}_t, \mathbf{Q}) \tag{29.110}$$

$$p(\boldsymbol{y}_t|\boldsymbol{z}_t, \boldsymbol{u}_t) = \mathcal{N}(\boldsymbol{y}_t|\mathbf{H}\boldsymbol{z}_t + \mathbf{D}\boldsymbol{u}_t, \mathbf{R}) \tag{29.111}$$

The set of all the parameters is $\boldsymbol{\theta} = \{\mathbf{F}, \mathbf{H}, \mathbf{B}, \mathbf{D}, \mathbf{Q}, \mathbf{R}\}$. For the sake of simplicity, we assume that the regression coefficient matrix $\mathbf{B}$ and $\mathbf{D}$ include the intercept term (i.e., the last entry of $\boldsymbol{u}_t = 1$).

We use conjugate MNIW priors, as in Bayesian multivariate linear regression Section 15.2.9. Specifically,

$$p(\mathbf{Q}, [\mathbf{F}, \mathbf{B}]) = \text{MNIW}(\mathbf{M}_{z0}, \mathbf{V}_{z0}, \nu_{q0}, \boldsymbol{\Psi}_{q0}) \tag{29.112}$$

$$p(\mathbf{R}, [\mathbf{H}, \mathbf{D}]) = \text{MNIW}(\mathbf{M}_{y0}, \mathbf{V}_{y0}, \nu_{r0}, \boldsymbol{\Psi}_{r0}) \tag{29.113}$$

Given $\boldsymbol{z}_{1:T}$, $\boldsymbol{u}_{1:T}$ and $\boldsymbol{y}_{1:T}$, the posteriors are also MNIW. Specifically,

$$\mathbf{Q}|\boldsymbol{z}_{1:T}, \boldsymbol{u}_{1:T} \sim \text{IW}(\nu_{q1}, \boldsymbol{\Psi}_{q1}) \tag{29.114}$$

$$[\mathbf{F}, \mathbf{B}]|\mathbf{Q}, \boldsymbol{z}_{1:T}, \boldsymbol{u}_{1:T} \sim \mathcal{MN}(\mathbf{M}_{z1}, \mathbf{Q}, \mathbf{V}_{z1}) \tag{29.115}$$

where the set of hyperparameters $\{\mathbf{M}_{z1}, \mathbf{V}_{z1}, \nu_{q_1}, \boldsymbol{\Psi}_{q1}\}$ of the posterior MNIW can be obtained by replacing $\mathbf{Y}, \mathbf{A}, \mathbf{X}$ in Equation (15.105) with $\boldsymbol{z}_{2:T}$, $[\mathbf{F}, \mathbf{B}]$, and $[\boldsymbol{z}_{t-1}^{\mathsf{T}}, \boldsymbol{u}_t^{\mathsf{T}}]_{t=2:T}^{\mathsf{T}}$, respectively. Similarly,

$$\mathbf{R}|\boldsymbol{z}_{1:T}, \boldsymbol{u}_{1:T}, \boldsymbol{y}_{1:T} \sim \text{IW}(\nu_{r1}, \boldsymbol{\Psi}_{r1}) \tag{29.116}$$

$$[\mathbf{H}, \mathbf{D}]|\mathbf{R}, \boldsymbol{z}_{1:T}, \boldsymbol{u}_{1:T}, \boldsymbol{y}_{1:T} \sim \mathcal{MN}(\mathbf{M}_{y1}, \mathbf{R}, \mathbf{V}_{y1}), \tag{29.117}$$

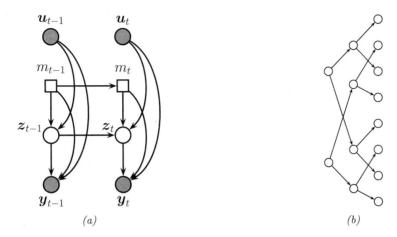

Figure 29.25: (a) A switching SSM. Squares represent discrete random variables, circles represent continuous random variables. (b) Illustration of how the number of modes in the belief state of a switching SSM grows exponentially over time. We assume there are two binary states.

and the hyperparameters $\{\mathbf{M}_{y1}, \mathbf{V}_{y1}, \nu_{r1}, \mathbf{\Psi}_{r1}\}$ of the posterior MNIW can be obtained by replacing $\mathbf{Y}, \mathbf{A}, \mathbf{X}$ in Equation (15.105) with $\boldsymbol{y}_{1:T}, [\mathbf{H}, \mathbf{D}]$, and $[\boldsymbol{y}_t^\mathsf{T}, \boldsymbol{u}_t^\mathsf{T}]_{1;T}^\mathsf{T}$.

29.9   Switching linear dynamical systems (SLDSs)

Consider a state-space modelin which the latent state has both a discrete latent variable, $m_t \in \{1, \ldots, K\}$, and a continuous latent variable, $\boldsymbol{z}_t \in \mathbb{R}^{N_z}$. (A model with discrete and continuous latent variables is known as a **hybrid system** in control theory.) We assume the observed responses are continuous, $\boldsymbol{y}_t \in \mathbb{R}^{N_y}$. We may also have continuous observed inputs $\boldsymbol{u}_t \in \mathbb{R}^{N_u}$. The discrete variable can be used to represent different kinds of system dynamics or operating regimes (e.g., normal or abnormal), or different kinds of observation models (e.g., to handle outliers due to sensor noise or failures). If the system is linear-Gaussian, it is called a **switching linear dynamical system (SLDS)**, a **regime switching Markov model** [Ham90; KN98], or a **jump Markov linear system (JMLS)** [DGK01].

29.9.1   Parameterization

An SLDS model is defined as follows:

$$p(m_t = k | m_{t-1} = j) = A_{jk} \tag{29.118}$$
$$p(\boldsymbol{z}_t | \boldsymbol{z}_{t-1}, m_t = k, \boldsymbol{u}_t) = \mathcal{N}(\boldsymbol{z}_t | \mathbf{F}_k \boldsymbol{z}_{t-1} + \mathbf{B}_k \boldsymbol{u}_t + \boldsymbol{b}_k, \mathbf{Q}_k) \tag{29.119}$$
$$p(\boldsymbol{y}_t | \boldsymbol{z}_t, m_t = k, \boldsymbol{u}_t) = \mathcal{N}(\boldsymbol{y}_t | \mathbf{H}_k \boldsymbol{z}_t + \mathbf{D}_k \boldsymbol{u}_t + \boldsymbol{d}_k, \mathbf{R}_k) \tag{29.120}$$

See Figure 29.25a for the DPGM representation. It is straightforward to make a nonlinear version of this model.

29.9.2   Posterior inference

Unfortunately exact inference in such switching models is intractable, even in the linear Gaussian case. To see why, suppose for simplicity that the latent discrete switching variable m_t is binary, and that only the dynamics matrix $\mathbf{F}$ depend on m_t, not the observation matrix $\mathbf{H}$. Our initial belief state will be a mixture of 2 Gaussians, corresponding to $p(\boldsymbol{z}_1|\boldsymbol{y}_1, m_1 = 1)$ and $p(\boldsymbol{z}_1|\boldsymbol{y}_1, m_1 = 2)$. The one-step-ahead predictive density will be a mixture of 4 Gaussians $p(\boldsymbol{z}_2|\boldsymbol{y}_1, m_1 = 1, m_2 = 1)$, $p(\boldsymbol{z}_2|\boldsymbol{y}_1, m_1 = 1, m_2 = 2)$, $p(\boldsymbol{z}_2|\boldsymbol{y}_1, m_1 = 2, m_2 = 1)$, and $p(\boldsymbol{z}_2|\boldsymbol{y}_1, m_1 = 2, m_2 = 2)$, obtained by passing each of the prior modes through the 2 possible transition models. The belief state at step 2 will also be a mixture of 4 Gaussians, obtained by updating each of the above distributions with $\boldsymbol{y}_2$. At step 3, the belief state will be a mixture of 8 Gaussians. And so on. So we see there is an exponential explosion in the number of modes. Each sequence of discrete values corresponds to a different hypothesis (sometimes called a **track**), which can be represented as a tree, as shown in Figure 29.25b.

Various methods for approximate online inference have been proposed for this model, such as the following:

- Prune off low probability trajectories in the discrete tree. This is widely used in multiple hypothesis tracking methods (see Section 29.9.3).

- Use particle filtering (Section 13.2) where we sample discrete trajectories, and apply the Kalman filter to the continuous variables. See Section 13.4.1 for details.

- Use ADF (Section 8.6), where we approximate the exponentially large mixture of Gaussians with a smaller mixture of Gaussians. See Section 8.6.2 for details.

- Use structured variational inference, where we approximate the posterior as a product of chain-structured distributions, one over the discrete variables and one over the continuous variables, with variational "coupling" terms in between (see e.g., [GH98; PJD21; Wan+22]).

29.9.3   Application: Multitarget tracking

The problem of **multi-target tracking** frequently arises in engineering applications (especially in aerospace and defence). This is a very large topic (see e.g., [BSF88; BSL93; Vo+15] for details), but in this section, we show how switching LDS models (or their nonlinear extensions) can be used to tackle the problem.

29.9.3.1   Warm-up

In the simplest setting, we know there are N objects we want to track, and each one generates its own uniquely identified observation. If we assume the objects are independent, we can apply Kalman filtering and smoothing in parallel, as shown in Figure 29.26. (In this example, each object follows a linear dynamical model with different initial random velocities, as in Section 29.7.1.)

29.9.3.2   Data association

More generally, at each step we may observe M measurements, e.g., "blips" on a radar screen. We can have $M < N$ due to occlusion or missed detections. We can have $M > N$ due to clutter or false

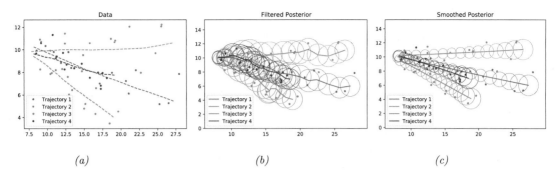

Figure 29.26: Illustration of Kalman filtering and smoothing for tracking multiple moving objects. Generated by kf_parallel.ipynb.

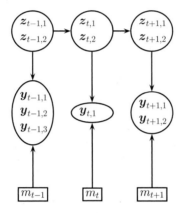

Figure 29.27: A model for tracking two objects in the presence of data-association ambiguity. We observe 3, 1 and 2 detections at time steps $t-1$, t and $t+1$. The m_t hidden variable encodes the association between the observations and the hidden causes.

alarms. Or we can have $M = N$. In any case, we need to figure out the **correspondence** between the M detections $\boldsymbol{x}_t^m$ and the N objects $\boldsymbol{z}_t^i$. This is called the problem of **data association**, and it arises in many application domains.

We can model this problem by augmenting the state space with discrete variables m_t that represent the association matrix between the observations, $\boldsymbol{y}_{t,1:M}$, and the sources, $\boldsymbol{z}_{t,1:N}$. See Figure 29.27 for an illustration, where we have $N = 2$ objects, but a variable number M_t of observations per time step.

As we mentioned in Section 29.9.2, inference in such hybrid (discrete-continouus) models is intractable, due to the exponential number of posterior modes. In the sections below, we briefly mention a few approximate inference methods.

29.9.3.3   Nearest neighbor approximation using Hungarian algorithm

A common way to perform approximate inference in this model is to compute an $N \times M$ weight matrix, where W_{im} measures the "compatibility" between object i and measurement m, typically based on how close m is to where the model thinks i is (the so-called **nearest neighbor data association** heuristic).

We can make this into a square matrix by adding dummy background objects, which can explain all the false alarms, and adding dummy observations, which can explain all the missed detections. We can then compute the maximal weight bipartite matching using the **Hungarian algorithm**, which takes $O(\max(N, M)^3)$ time (see e.g., [BDM09]).

Conditional on knowing the assignments of measurements to tracks, we can perform the usual Bayesian state update procedure (e.g., based on Kalman filtering). Note that objects that are assigned to dummy observations do not perform a measurement update, so their state estimate is just based on forwards prediction from the dynamics model.

29.9.3.4   Other approximate inference schemes

The Hungarian algorithm can be slow (since it is cubic in the number of measurements), and can give poor results since it relies on hard assignment. Better performance can be obtained by using loopy belief propagation (Section 9.4). The basic idea is to approximately marginalize out the unknown assignment variables, rather than perform a MAP estimate. This is known as the **SPADA** method (sum-product algorithm for data association) [WL14b; Mey+18].

The cost of each iteration of the iterative procedure is $O(NM)$. Furthermore, [WL14b] proved this will always converge in a finite number of steps, and [Von13] showed that the corresponding solution will in fact be the global optimum. The SPADA method is more efficient, and more accurate, than earlier heuristic methods, such as **JPDA** (joint probabilistic data association) [BSWT11; Vo+15].

It is also possible to use sequential Monte Carlo methods to solve data association and tracking. See Section 13.2 for a general discussion of SMC, and [RAG04; Wan+17b] for a review of specific techniques for this model family.

29.9.3.5   Handling an unknown number of targets

In general, we do not know the true number of targets N, so we have to deal with variable-sized state space. This is an example of an **open world** model (see Section 4.6.5), which differs from the standard **closed world assumption** where we know how many objects of interest there are.

For example, suppose at each time step we get two "blips" on our radar screen, representing the presence of an object at a given location. These measurements are not tagged with the source of the object that generated them, so the data looks like Figure 29.28(a). In Figure 29.28(b-c) we show two different hypotheses about the underlying object trajectories that could have generated this data. However, how can we know there are two objects? Maybe there are more, but some are just not detected. Maybe there are fewer, and some observations are false alarms due to background clutter. One such more complex hypothesis is shown in Figure 29.28(d). Figuring out what is going on in problems such as this is known as **multiple hypothesis tracking**.

A common approximate solution to this is to create new objects whenever an observation cannot be "explained" (i.e., generated with high likelihood) by any existing objects, and to prune out old objects that have not been detected in a while (in order to keep the computational cost bounded). Sets

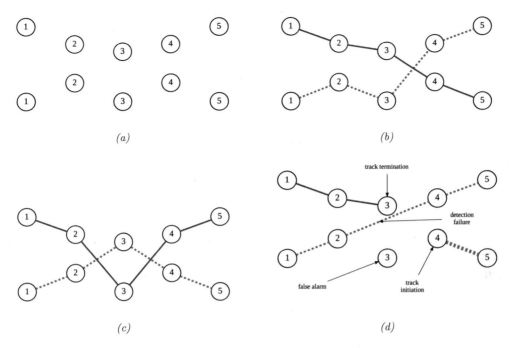

Figure 29.28: Illustration of multi-target tacking in 2d over 5 time steps. (a) We observe 2 measurements per time step. (b-c) Possible hypotheses about the underlying object tracks. (d) A more complex hypothesis in which the red track stops at step 3, the dashed red track starts at step 4, the dotted blue track has a detection failure at step 3, and one of the measurements at step 3 is a false alarm. Adapted from Figure 15.8 of [RN19].

whose size and content are both random are called **random finite sets**. An elegant mathematical framework for dealing with such objects is described in [Mah07; Mah13; Vo+15].

29.10   Nonlinear SSMs

In this section, we consider SSMs with nonlinear transition and/or observation functions, and additive Gaussian noise. That is, we assume the model has the following form

$$\boldsymbol{z}_t = \boldsymbol{f}(\boldsymbol{z}_{t-1}, \boldsymbol{u}_t) + \boldsymbol{q}_t \tag{29.121}$$
$$\boldsymbol{q}_t \sim \mathcal{N}(\boldsymbol{0}, \mathbf{Q}_t) \tag{29.122}$$
$$\boldsymbol{y}_t = \boldsymbol{h}(\boldsymbol{z}_t, \boldsymbol{u}_t) + \boldsymbol{r}_t \tag{29.123}$$
$$\boldsymbol{r}_t \sim \mathcal{N}(\boldsymbol{0}, \mathbf{R}_t) \tag{29.124}$$

This is called a **nonlinear dynamical system (NLDS)**, or **nonlinear Gaussian SSM (NLG-SSM)**.

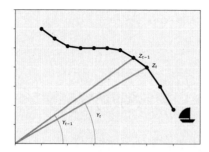

Figure 29.29: Illustration of a bearings-only tracking problem. Adapted from Figure 2.1 of [CP20b].

29.10.1 Example: object tracking and state estimation

In Section 8.3.2.3 we give an example of a 2d tracking problem where the motion model is nonlinear, but the observation model is linear.

Here we consider an example where the motion model is linear, but the observation model is nonlinear. In particular, suppose we use the same 2d linear dynamics as in Section 29.7.1, where the state space contains the position and velocity of the object, $z_t = \begin{pmatrix} u_t & v_t & \dot{u}_t & \dot{v}_t \end{pmatrix}$. (We use u and v for the two coordinates, to avoid confusion with the state and observation variables.) Instead of directly observing the location, suppose we have a **bearings only tracking problem**, in which we just observe the angle to the target:

$$y_t = \tan^{-1}\left(\frac{v_t - s_y}{u_t - s_x} \right) + r_t \tag{29.125}$$

where (s_x, s_y) is the position of the measurement sensor. See Figure 29.29 for an illustration. This nonlinear observation model prevents the use of the Kalman filter, but we can still apply approximate inference methods, as we discuss below.

29.10.2 Posterior inference

Inferring the states of an NLDS model is in general computationally difficult. Fortunately, there are a variety of approximate inference schemes that can be used, such as the extended Kalman filter (Section 8.3.2), the unscented Kalman filter (Section 8.4.2), etc.

29.11 Non-Gaussian SSMs

In this section, we consider SSMs in which the transition and observation noise is non-Gaussian. The transition and observation functions can be linear or nonlinear. We can represent this as a probabilistic model as follows:

$$p(z_t | z_{t-1}, u_t) = p(z_t | f(z_{t-1}, u_t)) \tag{29.126}$$
$$p(y_t | z_t, u_t) = p(y_t | h(z_t, u_t)) \tag{29.127}$$

This is called a **non-Gaussian SSM (NSSM)**.

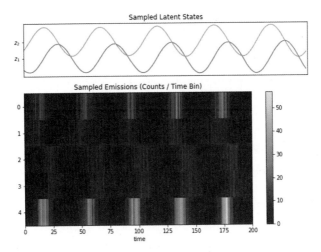

Figure 29.30: *Samples from a 2d LDS with 5 Poisson likelihood terms. Generated by poisson_lds.ipynb.*

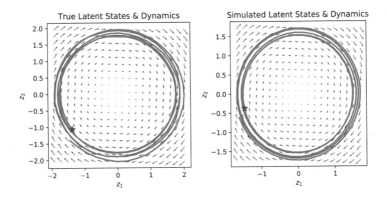

Figure 29.31: *Latent state trajectory (blue lines) and dynamics matrix **A** (arrows) for (left) true model and (right) estimated model. The star marks the start of the trajectory. Generated by poisson_lds.ipynb.*

29.11.1 Example: spike train modeling

In this section we discuss consider an SSM with linear-Gaussian latent dynamics and a Poisson likelihood. Such models are widely used in neuroscience for modeling **neural spike trains**. (see e.g., [Pan+10; Mac+11]). This is an example of an **exponential family state-space model** (see e.g., [Vid99; Hel17]).

We consider a simple example where the model has 2 continuous latent variables, and we set the dynamics matrix **A** to a random rotation matrix. The observation model has the form

$$p(\boldsymbol{y}_t|\boldsymbol{z}_t) = \prod_{d=1}^{D} \text{Poi}(y_{td}|\exp(\boldsymbol{w}_d^\mathsf{T}\boldsymbol{z}_t)) \tag{29.128}$$

where $\boldsymbol{w}_d$ is a random vector, and we use $D = 5$ observations per time step. Some samples from this model are shown in Figure 29.30.

We can fit this model by using EM, where in the E step we approximate $p(\boldsymbol{y}_t|\boldsymbol{z}_t)$ using a Laplace approximation, after which we can use the Kalman smoother to compute $p(\boldsymbol{z}_{1:T}|\boldsymbol{y}_{1:T})$. In the M step, we optimize the expected complete data log likelihood, similar to Section 29.8.1. We show the result in Figure 29.31, where we compare the parameters $\mathbf{A}$ and the posterior trajectory $\mathbb{E}\left[\boldsymbol{z}_t|\boldsymbol{y}_{1:T}\right]$ using the true model and the estimated model. We see good agreement.

29.11.2   Example: stochastic volatility models

In finance, it is common to model the **log-returns**, $y_t = \log(p_t/p_{t-1})$, where p_t is the price of some asset at time t. A common model for this problem, known as a **stochastic volatility model**, (see e.g., [KSC98]), has the following form:

$$y_t = \boldsymbol{u}_t^\mathsf{T}\boldsymbol{\beta} + \exp(z_t/2)r_t \tag{29.129}$$
$$z_t = \mu + \rho(z_{t-1} - \mu) + \sigma q_t \tag{29.130}$$
$$r_t \sim \mathcal{N}(0, 1) \tag{29.131}$$
$$q_t \sim \mathcal{N}(0, 1) \tag{29.132}$$

We see that the dynamical model is a first-order autoregressive process. We typically require that $|\rho| < 1$, to ensure the system is stationary. The observation model is Gaussian, but can be replaced by a heavy-tailed distribution such as a Student.

We can capture longer range temporal correlation by using a higher order auto-regressive process. To do this, we just expand the state-space to contain the past K values. For example, if $K = 2$ we have

$$\begin{pmatrix} z_t - \mu \\ z_{t-1} - \mu \end{pmatrix} = \begin{pmatrix} \rho_1 & \rho_2 \\ 1 & 0 \end{pmatrix} \begin{pmatrix} z_{t-1} - \mu \\ z_{t-2} - \mu \end{pmatrix} + \begin{pmatrix} q_t \\ 0 \end{pmatrix} \tag{29.133}$$

where $q_t \sim \mathcal{N}(0, \sigma_z^2)$. Thus we have

$$z_t = \mu + \rho_1(z_{t-1} - \mu) + \rho_2(z_{t-2} - \mu) + q_t \tag{29.134}$$

29.11.3   Posterior inference

Inferring the states of an NGSSM model is in general computationally difficult. Fortunately, there are a variety of approximate inference schemes that can be used, which we discuss in Chapter 8 and Chapter 13.

29.12   Structural time series models

In this section, we discuss **time series forecasting**, which is the problem of computing the predictive distribution over future observations given the data up until the present, i.e., computing $p(\boldsymbol{y}_{t+h}|\boldsymbol{y}_{1:t})$. (The model may optionally be conditioned on known future inputs, to get $p(\boldsymbol{y}_{t+h}|\boldsymbol{y}_{1:t}, \boldsymbol{u}_{1:t+h})$.) There are many approaches to this problem (see e.g., [HA21]), but in this section, we focus on **structural time series (STS)** models, which are defined in terms of linear-Gaussian SSMs.

Many classical time series methods, such as the **ARMA** (autoregressive moving average) method, can be represented as STS models (see e.g., [Har90; CK07; DK12; PFW21]). However, the STS approach has much more flexibility. For example, we can create nonlinear, non-Gaussian, and even hierarchical extensions, as we discuss below.

29.12.1 Introduction

The basic idea of an STS model is to represent the observed scalar time series as a sum of C individual **components**:

$$f(t) = f_1(t) + f_2(t) + \cdots + f_C(t) + \epsilon_t \tag{29.135}$$

where $\epsilon_t \sim \mathcal{N}(0, \sigma^2)$. For example, we might have a seasonal component that causes the observed values to oscillate up and down, and a growth component, that causes the observed values to get larger over time. Each latent process $f_c(t)$ is modeled by a linear Gaussian state-space model, which (in this context) is also called a **dynamic linear model (DLM)**. Since these are linear, we can combine them altogether into a single LG-SSM. In particular, in the case of scalar observations, the model has the form

$$p(\boldsymbol{z}_t | \boldsymbol{z}_{t-1}, \boldsymbol{\theta}) = \mathcal{N}(\boldsymbol{z}_t | \mathbf{F} \boldsymbol{z}_{t-1}, \mathbf{Q}) \tag{29.136}$$

$$p(y_t | \boldsymbol{z}_t, \boldsymbol{\theta}) = \mathcal{N}(y_t | \mathbf{H} \boldsymbol{z}_t + \boldsymbol{\beta}^\mathsf{T} \boldsymbol{u}_t, \sigma_y^2) \tag{29.137}$$

where $\mathbf{F}$ and $\mathbf{Q}$ are block structured matrices, with one block per component. The vector $\mathbf{H}$ then adds up all the relevant pieces from each component to generate the overall mean. Note that the matrices $\mathbf{F}$ and $\mathbf{H}$ are fixed sparse matrices which can be derived from the form of the corresponding components of the model, as we discuss below. So the only model parameters are the variance terms, $\mathbf{Q}$ and σ_y^2, and the optional regression coefficients $\boldsymbol{\beta}$.[4] We can generalize this to vector-valued observations as follows:

$$p(\boldsymbol{z}_t | \boldsymbol{z}_{t-1}, \boldsymbol{\theta}) = \mathcal{N}(\boldsymbol{z}_t | \mathbf{F} \boldsymbol{z}_{t-1}, \mathbf{Q}) \tag{29.138}$$

$$p(\boldsymbol{y}_t | \boldsymbol{z}_t, \boldsymbol{\theta}) = \mathcal{N}(\boldsymbol{y}_t | \mathbf{H} \boldsymbol{z}_t + \mathbf{D} \boldsymbol{u}_t, \mathbf{R}) \tag{29.139}$$

29.12.2 Structural building blocks

In this section, we discuss the building blocks of common STS models.

29.12.2.1 Local level model

The simplest latent dynamical process is known as the **local level model**. It assumes the observations $y_t \in \mathbb{R}$ are generated by a Gaussian with (latent) mean μ_t, which evolves over time according to a random walk:

$$y_t = \mu_t + \epsilon_{y,t} \quad \epsilon_{y,t} \sim \mathcal{N}(0, \sigma_y^2) \tag{29.140}$$

$$\mu_t = \mu_{t-1} + \epsilon_{\mu,t}, \quad \epsilon_{\mu,t} \sim \mathcal{N}(0, \sigma_\mu^2) \tag{29.141}$$

---

4. In the statistics community, the notation often [DK12], who write the dynamics as $\boldsymbol{\alpha}_t = \mathbf{T}_t \boldsymbol{\alpha}_{t-1} + \boldsymbol{c}_t \mathbf{R}_t \boldsymbol{\eta}_t$ and the observations as $y_t = \mathbf{Z}_t \boldsymbol{\alpha}_t + \boldsymbol{\beta}^\mathsf{T} \boldsymbol{x}_t + H_t \epsilon_t$, where $\boldsymbol{\eta}_t \sim \mathcal{N}(\mathbf{0}, \mathbf{I})$ and $\epsilon_t \sim \mathcal{N}(0, 1)$.

We also assume $\mu_1 \sim \mathcal{N}(0, \sigma_\mu^2)$. Hence the latent mean at any future step has distribution $\mu_t \sim \mathcal{N}(0, t\sigma_\mu^2)$, so the variance grows with time. We can also use an autoregressive (AR) process, $\mu_t = \rho\mu_{t-1} + \epsilon_{\mu,t}$, where $|\rho| < 1$. This has the stationary distribution $\mu_\infty \sim \mathcal{N}(0, \frac{\sigma_\mu^2}{1-\rho^2})$, so the uncertainty grows to a finite asymptote instead of unboundedly.

29.12.2.2   Local linear model

Many time series exhibit linear trends upwards or downwards, at least locally. We can model this by letting the level μ_t change by an amount δ_{t-1} (representing the slope of the line over an interval $\Delta t = 1$) at each step

$$\mu_t = \mu_{t-1} + \delta_{t-1} + \epsilon_{\mu,t} \tag{29.142}$$

The slope itself also follows a random walk,

$$\delta_t = \delta_{t-1} + \epsilon_{\delta,t} \tag{29.143}$$

and $\epsilon_{\delta,t} \sim \mathcal{N}(0, \sigma_\delta^2)$. This is called a **local linear trend** model.

We can combine these two processes by defining the following dynamics model:

$$\underbrace{\begin{pmatrix} \mu_t \\ \delta_t \end{pmatrix}}_{\boldsymbol{z}_t} = \underbrace{\begin{pmatrix} 1 & 1 \\ 0 & 1 \end{pmatrix}}_{\mathbf{F}} \underbrace{\begin{pmatrix} \mu_{t-1} \\ \delta_{t-1} \end{pmatrix}}_{\boldsymbol{z}_{t-1}} + \underbrace{\begin{pmatrix} \epsilon_{\mu,t} \\ \epsilon_{\delta,t} \end{pmatrix}}_{\boldsymbol{\epsilon}_t} \tag{29.144}$$

For the emission model we have

$$y_t = \underbrace{\begin{pmatrix} 1 & 0 \end{pmatrix}}_{\mathbf{H}} \underbrace{\begin{pmatrix} \mu_t \\ \delta_t \end{pmatrix}}_{\boldsymbol{z}_t} + \epsilon_{y,t} \tag{29.145}$$

We can also use an autoregressive model for the slope, i.e.,

$$\delta_t = D + \rho(\delta_{t-1} - D) + \epsilon_{\delta,t} \tag{29.146}$$

where D is the long run slope to which δ will revert. This is called a "**semilocal linear trend**" model, and is useful for longer term forecasts.

29.12.2.3   Adding covariates

We can easily include covariates $\boldsymbol{u}_t$ into the model, to increase prediction accuracy. If we use a linear model, we have

$$y_t = \mu_t + \boldsymbol{\beta}^\mathsf{T} \boldsymbol{u}_t + \epsilon_{y,t} \tag{29.147}$$

See Figure 29.32a for an illustration of the local level model with covariates. Note that, when forecasting into the future, we will need some way to predict the input values of future $\boldsymbol{u}_{t+h}$; a simple approach is just to assume future inputs are the same as the present, $\boldsymbol{u}_{t+h} = \boldsymbol{u}_t$.

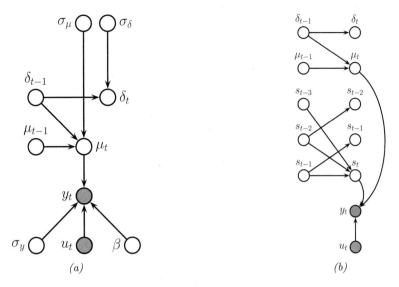

Figure 29.32: (a) A BSTS model with local linear trend and linear regression on inputs. The observed output is y_t. The latent state vector is defined by $\boldsymbol{z}_t = (\mu_t, \delta_t)$. The (static) parameters are $\boldsymbol{\theta} = (\sigma_y, \sigma_\mu, \sigma_\delta, \boldsymbol{\beta})$. The covariates are $\boldsymbol{u}_t$. (b) Adding a latent seasonal process (with $S = 4$ seasons). Parameter nodes are omitted for clarity.

29.12.2.4 Modelling seasonality

Many time series also exhibit **seasonality**, i.e., they fluctuate periodically. This can be modeled by creating a latent process consisting of a series offset terms, s_t. To model cyclicity, we ensure that these sum to zero (on average) over a complete cycle of S steps:

$$s_t = -\sum_{k=1}^{S-1} s_{t-k} + \epsilon_{s,t}, \quad \epsilon_{s,t} \sim \mathcal{N}(0, \sigma_s^2) \tag{29.148}$$

For example, for $S = 4$, we have $s_t = -(s_{t-1} + s_{t-2} + s_{t-3}) + \epsilon_{s,t}$. We can convert this to a first-order model by stacking the last $S - 1$ seasons into the state vector, as shown in Figure 29.32b.

29.12.2.5 Adding it all up

We can combine the various latent processes (local level, linear trend, and seasonal cycles) into a single linear-Gaussian SSM, because the sparse graph structure can be encoded by sparse matrices. More precisely, the transition model becomes

$$\underbrace{\begin{pmatrix} s_t \\ s_{t-1} \\ s_{t-2} \\ \mu_t \\ \delta_t \end{pmatrix}}_{\boldsymbol{z}_t} = \underbrace{\begin{pmatrix} -1 & -1 & -1 & 0 & 0 \\ 1 & 0 & 0 & 0 & 0 \\ 0 & 1 & 0 & 0 & 0 \\ 0 & 0 & 0 & 1 & 1 \\ 0 & 0 & 0 & 0 & 1 \end{pmatrix}}_{\mathbf{F}} \underbrace{\begin{pmatrix} s_{t-1} \\ s_{t-2} \\ s_{t-3} \\ \mu_{t-1} \\ \delta_{t-1} \end{pmatrix}}_{\boldsymbol{z}_{t-1}} + \mathcal{N}\left(\mathbf{0}, \mathrm{diag}([\sigma_s^2, 0, 0, \sigma_\mu^2, \sigma_\delta^2])\right) \tag{29.149}$$

Having defined the model, we can use the Kalman filter to compute $p(z_t|y_{1:t})$, and then make predictions forwards in time by rolling forwards in latent space, and then predicting the outputs:

$$p(y_{t+1}|y_{1:t}) = \int p(y_{t+1}|z_{t+1})p(z_{t+1}|z_t)p(z_t|y_{1:t})dz_t \tag{29.150}$$

This can be computed in closed form, as explained in Section 8.2.2.

29.12.3   Model fitting

Once we have specified the form of the model, we need to learn the model parameters, $\theta = (D, R, Q)$, since F and H fixed to the values specified by the structural blocks, and $B = 0$. Common approaches are based on maximum likelihood estimation (see Section 29.8), and Bayesian inference (see Section 29.8.4). The latter approach is known as **Bayesian structural time series** or **BSTS** modeling [SV14; QRJN18], and often uses the following conjugate prior:

$$p(\theta) = \text{MNIW}(R, D)\text{IW}(Q) \tag{29.151}$$

Alternatively, if there are a large number of covariates, we may use a sparsity-promoting prior (e.g., spike and slab, Section 15.2.5) for the regression coefficients D.

29.12.4   Forecasting

Once the parameters have been estimated on an historical dataset, we can perform inference on a new time series to compute $p(z_t|y_{1:t}, u_{1:t}, \theta)$ using the Kalman filter (Section 8.2.2). Given the current posterior, we can then "roll forwards" in time to forecast future observations h steps ahead by computing $p(y_{t+h}|y_{1:t}, u_{1:t+h}, \theta)$, as in Section 8.2.2.3. If the parameters are uncertain, we can sample from the posterior, $p(\theta|y_{1:t}, u_{1:t})$, and then perform Monte Carlo averaging of the forecasts.

29.12.5   Examples

In this section, we give various examples of STS models.

29.12.5.1   Example: forecasting CO$_2$ levels from Mauna Loa

In this section, we fit an STS model to the monthly atmospheric CO$_2$ readings from the Mauna Loa observatory in Hawaii.[5] The data is from January 1966 to February 2019. We combine a local linear trend model with a seasonal model, where we assume the periodicity is $S = 12$, since the data is monthly (see Figure 29.33a). We fit the model to all the data except for the last 10 years using variational Bayes. The resulting posterior mean and standard deviations for the parameters are $\sigma_y = 0.169 \pm 0.008$, $\sigma_\mu = 0.159 \pm 0.017$, $\sigma_\delta = 0.009 \pm 0.003$, $\sigma_s = 0.038 \pm 0.008$. We can sample 10 parameter vectors from the posterior and then plug them it to create a distribution over forecasts. The results are shown in orange in Figure 29.33a. Finally, in Figure 29.33b, we plot the posterior mean values of the two latent components (linear trend and current seasonal value) over time. We see how the model has successfully decomposed the observed signal into a sum of two simpler signals. (See also Section 18.8.1 where we model this data using a GP.)

---

5. For details, see `https://blog.tensorflow.org/2019/03/structural-time-series-modeling-in.html`.

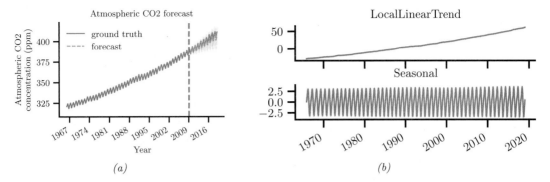

(a)   (b)

Figure 29.33: (a) CO_2 levels from Mauna Loa. In orange plot we show predictions for the most recent 10 years. (b) Underlying components for the STS mode which was fit to Figure 29.33a. Generated by sts.ipynb.

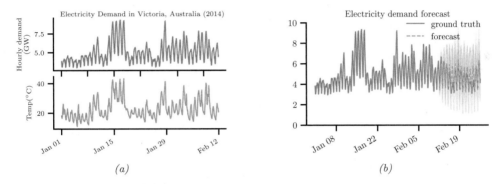

(a)   (b)

Figure 29.34: (a) Hourly temperature and electricity demand in Victoria, Australia in 2014. (b) Electricity forecasts using an STS. Generated by sts.ipynb.

29.12.5.2   Example: forecasting (real-valued) electricity usage

In this section, we consider a more complex example: forecasting electricity demand in Victoria, Australia, as a function of the previous value and the external temperature. (Remember that January is summer in Australia!) The hourly data from the first six weeks of 2014 is shown in Figure 29.34a.[6]

We fit an STS to this using 4 components: a seasonal hourly effect (period 24), a seasonal daily effect (period 7, with 24 steps per season), a linear regression on the temperature, and an autoregressive term on the observations themselves. We fit the model with variational inference. (This takes about a minute on a GPU.) We then draw 10 posterior samples and show the posterior predictive forecasts in Figure 29.34b. We see that the results are reasonable, but there is also considerable uncertainty.

We plot the individual components in Figure 29.35. Note that they have different vertical scales, reflecting their relative importance. We see that the regression on the external temperature is the most important effect. However, the hour of day effect is also quite significant, even after accounting for external temperature. The autoregressive effect is the most uncertain one, since it is responsible

---

6. The data is from https://github.com/robjhyndman/fpp2-package.

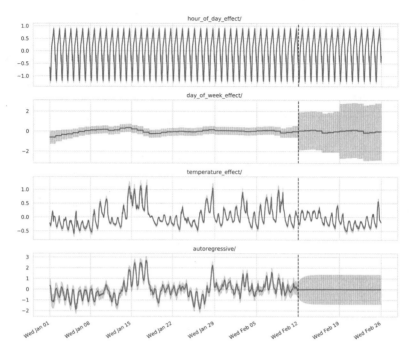

Figure 29.35: Components of the electricity forecasts. Generated by sts.ipynb.

for modeling all of the residual variation in the data beyond what is accounted for by the observation noise.

We can also use the model for **anomaly detection**. To do this, we compute the one-step-ahead predictive distributions, $p(y_t|\boldsymbol{y}_{1:t-1}, \boldsymbol{u}_{1:t})$, for each time step t, and then flag all time steps where the observation is improbable. The results are shown in Figure 29.36.

29.12.5.3   Example: forecasting (integer valued) sales

In Section 29.12.5.2, we used a linear Gaussian STS model to forecast electricity demand. However, for some problems, we have integer valued observations, e.g., for neural spike data (see Section 29.11.1), RNA-Seq data [LJY19], sales data, etc. Here we focus on the case of sales data, where $y_t \in \{0, 1, 2, \ldots\}$ is the number of units of some item that are sold on a given day. Predicting future values of y_t is important for many businesses. (This problem is known as **demand forecasting**.)

We assume the observed counts are due to some latent demand, $z_t \in \mathbb{R}$. Hence we can use a model similar to Section 29.11.1, with a Poisson likelihood, except the linear dynamics are given by an STS model. In [SSF16; See+17], they consider a likelihood of the form $y_t \sim \text{Poi}(y_t|g(d_t^y))$, where $d_t = z_t + \boldsymbol{u}_t^\mathsf{T}\boldsymbol{w}$ is the instantaneous latent demand, $\boldsymbol{u}_t$ are the covariates that encode seasonal indicators (e.g., temporal distance from holidays), and $g(d) = e^d$ or $\log(1+e^d)$ is the transfer function. The dynamics model is a local random walk term, and $z_t = z_{t-1} + \alpha\mathcal{N}(0, 1)$, to capture serial correlation in the data.

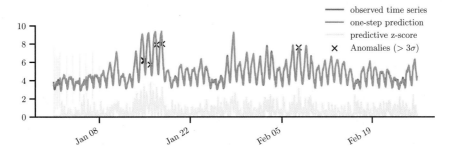

Figure 29.36: *Anomaly detection in a time series. We plot the observed electricity data in blue and the predictions in orange. In gray, we plot the z-score at time t , given by $(y_t - \mu_t)/\sigma_t$, where $p(y_t|\boldsymbol{y}_{1:t-1}, \boldsymbol{u}_{1:t}) = \mathcal{N}(\mu_t, \sigma_t^2)$. Anomalous observations are defined as points where $z_t > 3$ and are marked with red crosses. Generated by sts.ipynb.*

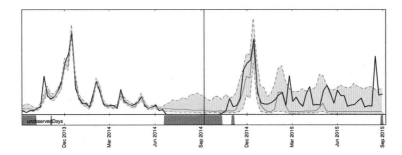

Figure 29.37: *Visualization of a probabilistic demand forecast for a hypothetical product. Note the sudden spike near the Christmas holiday in December 2013. The black line denotes the actual demand. Green lines denote the model samples in the training range, while the red lines show the actual probabilistic forecast on data unseen by the model. The red bars at the bottom indicate out-of-stock events which can explain the observed zeros. From Figure 1 of [Bös+17]. Used with kind permission of Tim Januschowski.*

However, sometimes we observe zero counts, $y_t = 0$, not because there is no demand, but because there is no supply (i.e., we are out of stock). If we do not model this properly, we may incorrectly infer that $z_t = 0$, thus underestimating demand, which may result in not ordering enough inventory for the future, further compounding the error.

One solution is to use a **zero-inflated Poisson (ZIP)** model [Lam92] for the likelihood. This is a mixture model of the form $p(y_t|d_t) = p_0 \mathbb{I}(y_t = 0) + (1 - p_0)\text{Poi}(y_t|e^{d_t})$, where p_0 is the probability of the first mixture component. It is also common to use a (possibly zero-inflated) negative binomial model (Section 2.2.1.4) as the likelihood. This is used in [Cha14; Sal+19b] for the demand forecasting problem. The disadvantage of these likelihoods is that they are not log-concave for $d_t = 0$, which complicates posterior inference. In particular, the Laplace approximation is a poor choice, since it may find a saddle point. In [SSF16], they tackle this using a log-concave **multi-stage likelihood**, in which $y_t = 0$ is emitted with probability $\sigma(d_t^0)$; otherwise $y_t = 1$ is emitted with probability $\sigma(d_t^1)$; otherwise $y_t =$ is emitted with probability $\text{Poi}(d_t^2)$. This generalizes the scheme in [SOB12].

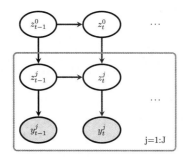

Figure 29.38: Illustration of a hierarchical state-space model.

29.12.5.4 Example: hierarchical SSM for electoral panel data

Suppose we perform a survey for the US presidential elections. Let N_t^j be the number of people who vote at time t in state j, and let y_t^j be the number of those people who vote Democrat. (We assume $N_t^j - y_t^j$ vote Republican.) It is natural to want to model the dependencies in this data both across time (longitudinally) and across space (this is an example of **panel data**).

We can do this using a hierarchical SSM, as illustrated in Figure 29.38. The top level Markov chain, z_t^0, models national-level trends, and the state-specific chains, z_t^j, model local "random effects". In practice we would usually also include covariates at the national level, $\boldsymbol{u}_t^0$ and state level, $\boldsymbol{u}_t^j$. Thus the model becomes

$$y_t^j \sim \text{Bin}(y_t^j | \pi_t^j, N_t^j) \tag{29.152}$$

$$\pi_t^j = \sigma \left[(\boldsymbol{z}_t^0)^\mathsf{T} \boldsymbol{u}_t^0 + (\boldsymbol{z}_t^j)^\mathsf{T} \boldsymbol{u}_t^j \right] \tag{29.153}$$

$$\boldsymbol{z}_t^0 = \boldsymbol{z}_{t-1}^0 + \mathcal{N}(\boldsymbol{0}, \sigma^2 \mathbf{I}) \tag{29.154}$$

$$\boldsymbol{z}_t^j = \boldsymbol{z}_{t-1}^j + \mathcal{N}(\boldsymbol{0}, \tau^2 \mathbf{I}) \tag{29.155}$$

For more details, see [Lin13b].

29.12.6 Causal impact of a time series intervention

In this section, we discuss how to estimate the causal effect on an intervention given some **quasi-experimental** time series data. (The term "quasi-experimental" means the data was collected under an intervention but without using random assignment.) For example, suppose y_t is the click through rate (CTR) of the web page of some company at time t. The company launches an ad campaign at time n, and observes outcomes $\boldsymbol{y}_{1:n}$ before the intervention and $\boldsymbol{y}_{n+1:m}$ after the intervention. (This is an example of an **interrupted time series**, since the "natural" process was perturbed at some point.) A natural question to ask is: what would the CTR have been had the company not run the ad campaign? This is a **counterfactual** question. (We discuss counterfactuals in Section 4.7.4.) If we can predict this counterfactual time series, $\tilde{\boldsymbol{y}}_{n+1:m}$, then we compare the actual y_t to the predicted $\tilde{y}_t$, and use this to estimate the **causal impact** of the intervention.

To predict the counterfactual outcome, we will use a structural time series (STS) model (see Section 29.12), following [Bro+15]. An STS model is a linear-Gaussian state-space model, where

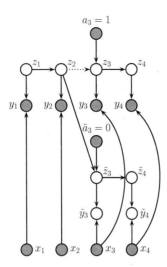

Figure 29.39: Twin network state-space model for estimating causal impact of an intervention that occurs just after time step $n = 2$. We have $m = 4$ actual observations, denoted $\boldsymbol{y}_{1:4}$. We cut the incoming arcs to $\boldsymbol{z}_3$ since we assume $\boldsymbol{z}_{3:T}$ comes from a different distribution, namely the post-intervention distribution. However, in the counterfactual world, shown at the bottom of the figure (with tilde symbols), we assume the distributions are the same as in the past, so information flows along the chain uninterrupted.

arrows have a natural causal interpretation in terms of the **arrow of time**; thus a STS is a kind of structural equation model, and hence a structural causal model (see Section 4.7). The use of an SCM allows us to infer the latent state of the noise variables given the observed data; we can then "roll back time" to the point of intervention, where we explore an alternative "fork in the road" from the one we actually took by "rolling forwards in time" in a new version of the model, using the **twin network** approach to counterfactual inference (see Section 4.7.4).

29.12.6.1 Computing the counterfactual prediction

To explain the method in more detail, consider the twin network in Figure 29.39. The intervention occurs after time $n = 2$, and there are $m = 4$ observations in total. We observe 2 datapoints before the intervention, $\boldsymbol{y}_{1:2}$, and 2 datapoints afterwards, $\boldsymbol{y}_{3:4}$. We assume observations are generated by latent states $\boldsymbol{z}_{1:4}$, which evolve over time. The states are subject to exogenous noise terms, which can represent any set of unmodeled factors, such as the state of the economy. In addition, we have exogenous covariates, $\boldsymbol{x}_{1:m}$.

To predict what would have happened if we had not performed the intervention, (an event denoted by $\tilde{a} = 0$), we replicate the part of the model that occurs after the intervention, and use it to make forecasts. The goal is to compute the counterfactual distribution, $p(\tilde{\boldsymbol{y}}_{n+1:m} | \boldsymbol{y}_{1:n}, \boldsymbol{x}_{1:m})$, where $\tilde{y}_t$ represents counterfactual outcomes if the action had been $\tilde{a} = 0$. We can compute this counterfactual distribution as follows:

$$p(\tilde{\boldsymbol{y}}_{n+1:m}|\boldsymbol{y}_{1:n},\boldsymbol{x}_{1:m}) = \int p(\tilde{\boldsymbol{y}}_{n+1:m}|\tilde{\boldsymbol{z}}_{n+1:m},\boldsymbol{x}_{n+1:m},\boldsymbol{\theta})p(\tilde{\boldsymbol{z}}_{n+1:m}|\boldsymbol{z}_n,\boldsymbol{\theta})\times \qquad (29.156)$$

$$p(\boldsymbol{z}_n,\boldsymbol{\theta}|\boldsymbol{x}_{1:n},\boldsymbol{y}_{1:n})d\boldsymbol{\theta}d\boldsymbol{z}_n d\tilde{\boldsymbol{z}}_{n+1:m} \qquad (29.157)$$

where

$$p(\boldsymbol{z}_n,\boldsymbol{\theta}|\boldsymbol{x}_{1:n},\boldsymbol{y}_{1:n}) = p(\boldsymbol{z}_n|\boldsymbol{x}_{1:n},\boldsymbol{y}_{1:n},\boldsymbol{\theta})p(\boldsymbol{\theta}|\boldsymbol{x}_{1:n},\boldsymbol{y}_{1:n}) \qquad (29.158)$$

For linear Gaussian SSMs, the term $p(\boldsymbol{z}_n|\boldsymbol{x}_{1:n},\boldsymbol{y}_{1:n},\boldsymbol{\theta})$ can be computed using Kalman filtering (Section 8.2.2), and the term $p(\boldsymbol{\theta}|\boldsymbol{y}_{1:n},\boldsymbol{x}_{1:n})$, can be computed using MCMC or variational inference.

We can use samples from the above posterior predictive distribution to compute a Monte Carlo approximation to the distribution of the **treatment effect** per time step, $\tau_t^i = y_t - \tilde{y}_t^i$, where the i index refers to posterior samples. We can also approximate the distribution of the cumulative causal impact using $\sigma_t^i = \sum_{s=n+1}^{t} \tau_t^i$. (There will be uncertainty in these quantities arising both from epistemic uncertainty, about the true parameters controlling the model, and aleatoric uncertainty, due to system and observation noise.)

29.12.6.2   Assumptions needed for the method to work

The validity of the method is based on 3 assumptions: (1) Predictability: we assume that the outcome can be adequately predicted by our model given the data at hand. (We can check this by using **backcasting**, in which we make predictions on part of the historical data.) (2) Unaffectedness: we assume that the intervention does not change future covariates $\boldsymbol{x}_{n+1:m}$. (We can potentially check this by running the method with each of the covariates as an outcome variable.) (3) Stability: we assume that, had the intervention not taken place, the model for the outcome in the pre-treatment period would have continued in the post-treatment period. (We can check this by seeing if we predict an effect if the treatment is shifted earlier in time.)

29.12.6.3   Example

As a concrete example, let us assume we have a local level model and we use linear regression to model the dependence on the covariates, as in Section 29.12.2.3. That is,

$$y_t = \mu_t + \boldsymbol{\beta}^\mathsf{T}\boldsymbol{x}_t + \mathcal{N}(0,\sigma_y^2) \qquad (29.159)$$
$$\mu_t = \mu_{t-1} + \delta_{t-1} + \mathcal{N}(0,\sigma_\mu^2) \qquad (29.160)$$
$$\delta_t = \delta_{t-1} + \mathcal{N}(0,\sigma_\delta^2) \qquad (29.161)$$

See the graphical model in Figure 29.40. The static parameters of the model are $\boldsymbol{\theta} = (\boldsymbol{\beta},\sigma_y^2,\sigma_\mu^2,\sigma_\delta^2)$, the other terms are state or observation variables. (Note that we are free to use any kind of STS model; the local level model is just a simple default.)

For simplicity, let us assume we have a single scalar input x_t, in addition to the scalar output y_t. We create some synthetic data using an autoregressive process on x_t, and then set $y_t = 1.2x_t + \epsilon_t$. We then manually intervene at timestep $t = 70$ by increasing the y_t values by 10. In Figure 29.41, we show the output of the causal impact procedure when applied to this dataset. In the top row, we see

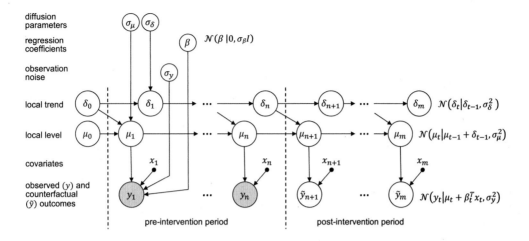

Figure 29.40: A graphical model representation of the local level causal impact model. The dotted line represents the time n at which an intervention occurs. Adapted from Figure 2 of [Bro+15]. Used with kind permission of Kay Brodersen.

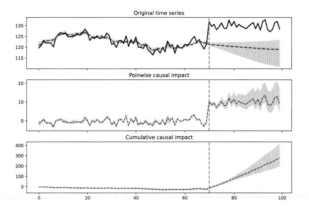

Figure 29.41: Some simulated time series data which we use to estimate the causal impact of some intervention, which occurs at time $n = 70$, Generated by causal_impact_jax.ipynb.

that the forecasted output $\tilde{y}_t$ (blue line) at times $t \geq 70$ follows the general AR trend learned by the model on the pre-interventional period, whereas the actual observations y_t (black line) are quite different. Thus the posterior over the pointwise causal impact, $\tau_t = y_t - \tilde{y}_t$, has a value of about 10 for $t \geq 70$.

29.12.6.4 Comparison to synthetic control

The use of a linear combination of other "**donor**" time series $\boldsymbol{\beta}^\mathsf{T} \boldsymbol{x}_t$ is similar in spirit to the concept of a "**synthetic control**" [Aba; Shi+21]. However we do not restrict ourselves to a convex combination of donors. Indeed, when we have many covariates, we can use a spike-and-slab prior (Section 15.2.5) or horseshoe prior (Section 15.2.7) to select the relevant ones. Furthermore, the STS method can be applied even if we just observe the outcome series y_t, without any other parallel time series.

29.12.7   Prophet

Prophet [TL18a] is a popular time series forecasting library from Facebook. It fits a generalized additive model of the form

$$y(t) = g(t) + s(t) + h(t) + \boldsymbol{w}^\mathsf{T} \boldsymbol{x}(t) + \epsilon_t \tag{29.162}$$

where $g(t)$ is a trend function, $s(t)$ is a seasonal fluctuation (modeled using linear regression applied to a sinusoidal basis set), $h(t)$ is an optional set of sparse "holiday effects", $\boldsymbol{x}(t)$ are an optional set of (possibly lagged) covariates, $\boldsymbol{w}$ are the regression coefficients, and $\epsilon(t)$ is the residual noise term, assumed to be iid Gaussian.

   Prophet is a regression model, not an auto-regressive model, since it predicts the time series $\boldsymbol{y}_{1:T}$ given the time stamp t and the covariates $\boldsymbol{x}_{1:T}$, but without conditioning on past observations of y. To model the dependence on time, the trend function is assumed to be a piecewise linear trend with S changepoints, uniformly spaced in time. (See Main Section 29.5.6 for a discussion of changepoint detection.) That is, the model has the form

$$g(t) = (k + \boldsymbol{a}(t)^T \boldsymbol{\delta})t + (m + \boldsymbol{a}(t)^\mathsf{T} \boldsymbol{\gamma}) \tag{29.163}$$

where k is the growth rate, m is the offset, $a_j(t) = \mathbb{I}(t \geq s_j)$, where s_j is the time of the j'th changepoint, $\delta_t \sim \text{Laplace}(\tau)$ is the magnitude of the change, and $\gamma_j = -s_j \delta_j$ to make the function continuous. The Laplace prior on δ ensures the MAP parameter estimate is sparse, so the difference across change point boundaries is usually 0.

   For an interactive visualization of how Prophet works, see `http://prophet.mbrouns.com/`.

29.12.8   Neural forecasting methods

Classical time series methods work well when there is little data (e.g., short sequences, or few covariates). However, in some cases, we have a lot of data. For example, we might have a single, but very long sequence, such as in anomaly detection from real-time sensors [Ahm+17]. Or we may have multiple, related sequences, such as sales of related products [Sal+19b]. In both cases, larger data means we can afford to fit more complex parametric models. Neural networks are a natural choice, because of their flexibility. Until recently, their performance in forecasting tasks was not competitive with classical methods, but this has recently started to change, as described in [Ben+20; LZ20].

   A common benchmark in the univariate time series forecasting literature is the **M4 forecasting competition** [MSA18], which requires participants to make forecasts on many different kinds of (univariate) time series (without covariates). This was recently won by a neural method [Smy20]. More precisely, the winner of the 2019 M4 competition was a *hybrid* RNN-classical method called **ES-RNN** [Smy20]. The exponential smoothing (ES) part allows data-efficient adaptation to the observed past of the current time series; the recurrent neural network (RNN) part allows for learning of nonlinear components from multiple related time series. (This is known as a **local+global** model, since the ES part is "trained" just on the local time series, whereas the RNN is trained on a global dataset of related time series.)

In [Ran+18] they adopt a different approach for combining RNNs and classical methods, called **DeepSSM**. In particular, they train a single RNN to predict the parameters of a state-space model (see Main Section 29.1). In more detail, let $\boldsymbol{x}_{1:T}^n$ represent the n'th time series, and let $\boldsymbol{\theta}_t^n$ represent the non-stationary parameters of a linear-trend SSM model (see Section 29.12.1). We train an RNN to compute $\boldsymbol{\theta}_t^n = f(\boldsymbol{c}_{1:T}^n; \boldsymbol{\phi})$, where $\boldsymbol{\phi}$ are the RNN parameters shared across all sequences. We can use the predicted parameters to compute the log likelihood of the sequence, $L_n = \log p(\boldsymbol{x}_{1:T}^n | \boldsymbol{c}_{1:T}^n, \boldsymbol{\theta}_{1:T}^n)$, using the Kalman filter. These two modules can be combined to allow for end-to-end training of $\boldsymbol{\phi}$ to maximize $\sum_{n=1}^N L_n$.

In [Wan+19c], they propose a different hybrid model known as **Deep Factors**. The idea is to represent each time series (or its latent function, for non-Gaussian data) as a weighted sum of a global time series, coming from a neural model, and a stochastic local model, such as an SSM or GP. The **DeepGLO** (global-local) approach of [SYD19] proposes a related hybrid method, where the global model uses matrix factorization to learn shared factors. This is then combined with temporal convolutional networks.

It is also possible to train a purely neural model, without resorting to classical methods. For example, the **N-BEATS** model of [Ore+20] trains a residual network to predict the weights of a set of basis functions, corresponding to a polynomial trend and a periodic signal. The weights for the basis functions are predicted for each window of input using the neural network. Another approach is the **DeepAR** model of [Sal+19b], which fits a single RNN to a large number of time series. The original paper used integer (count) time series, modeled with a negative binomial likelihood function. This is a unimodal distribution, which may not be suitable for all tasks. More flexible forms, such as mixtures of Gaussians, have also been proposed [Muk+18]. A popular alternative is to use **quantile regression** [Koe05], in which the model is trained to predict quantiles of the distribution. For example, [Gas+19] proposed **SQF-RNN**, which uses splines to represent the quantile function. They used **CRPS** or **continuous-ranked probability score** as the loss function. This is a proper scoring rule, but is less sensitive to outliers, and is more "distance aware", than log loss.

The above methods all predict a single output (per time step). If there are multiple simultaneous observations, it is best to try to model their interdependencies. In [Sal+19a], they use a (low-rank) **Gaussian copula** for this, and in [Tou+19], they use a **nonparametric copula**.

In [Wen+17], they simultaneously predict quantiles for multiple steps ahead using dilated causal convolution (or an RNN). They call their method **MQ-CNN**. In [WT19], they extend this to predict the full quantile function, taking as input the desired quantile level α, rather than prespecifying a fixed set of levels. They also use a copula to learn the dependencies among multiple univariate marginals.

29.13   Deep SSMs

Traditional state-space model assume linear dynamics and linear observation models, both with additive Gaussian noise. This is obviously very limiting. In this section, we allow the dynamics and/or observation model to be modeled by nonlinear and/or non-Markovian deep neural networks; we call these **deep state-space model**, also known as **dynamical variational autoencoders**. (To be consistent with the literature on VAEs, we denote the observations by $\boldsymbol{x}_t$ instead of $\boldsymbol{y}_t$.) For a detailed review, see [Ged+20; Gir+21].

29.13.1   Deep Markov models

Suppose we create a SSM in which we use a deep neural network for the dynamics model and/or observation model; the result is called a **deep Markov model** [KSS17] or **stochastic RNN** [BO14; Fra+16]. (This is not quite the same as a variational RNN, which we explain in Section 29.13.4.)

We can fit a DMM using SVI (Section 10.1.4). The key is to infer the posterior over the latents. From the first-order Markov properties, the exact posterior is given by

$$p(\boldsymbol{z}_{1:T}|\boldsymbol{x}_{1:T}) = \prod_{t=1}^{T} p(\boldsymbol{z}_t|\boldsymbol{z}_{t-1}, \boldsymbol{x}_{1:T}) = \prod_{t=1}^{T} p(\boldsymbol{z}_t|\boldsymbol{z}_{t-1}, \cancel{\boldsymbol{x}_{1:t-1}}, \boldsymbol{x}_{t:T}) \tag{29.164}$$

where we define $p(\boldsymbol{z}_1|\boldsymbol{z}_0, \boldsymbol{x}_{1:T}) = p(\boldsymbol{z}_1|\boldsymbol{x}_{1:T})$, and the cancelation follows since $\boldsymbol{z}_t \perp \boldsymbol{x}_{1:t-1}|\boldsymbol{z}_{t-1}$, as pointed out in [KSS17].

In general, it is intractable to compute $p(\boldsymbol{z}_{1:T}|\boldsymbol{x}_{1:T})$, so we approximate it with an inference network. There are many choices for q. A simple one is a fully factorized model, $q(\boldsymbol{z}_{1:T}) = \prod_t q(\boldsymbol{z}_t|\boldsymbol{x}_{1:t})$. This is illustrated in Figure 29.42a. Since $\boldsymbol{z}_t$ only depends on past data, $\boldsymbol{x}_{1:t}$ (which is accumulated in the RNN hidden state $\boldsymbol{h}_t$), we can use this inference network at run time for online inference. However, for training the model offline, we can use a more accurate posterior by using

$$q(\boldsymbol{z}_{1:T}|\boldsymbol{x}_{1:T}) = \prod_{t=1}^{T} q(\boldsymbol{z}_t|\boldsymbol{z}_{t-1}, \boldsymbol{x}_{1:T}) = \prod_{t=1}^{T} q(\boldsymbol{z}_t|\boldsymbol{z}_{t-1}, \cancel{\boldsymbol{x}_{1:t-1}}, \boldsymbol{x}_{t:T}) \tag{29.165}$$

Note that the dependence on past observation $\boldsymbol{x}_{1:t-1}$ is already captured by $\boldsymbol{z}_{t-1}$, as in Equation (29.164). The dependencies on future observations, $\boldsymbol{x}_{t:T}$, can be summarized by a backwards RNN, as shown in Figure 29.42b. Thus

$$q(\boldsymbol{z}_{1:T}, \boldsymbol{h}_{1:T}|\boldsymbol{x}_{1:T}) = \prod_{t=T}^{1} \mathbb{I}\left(\boldsymbol{h}_t = f(\boldsymbol{h}_{t+1}, \boldsymbol{x}_t)\right) \prod_{t=1}^{T} q(\boldsymbol{z}_t|\boldsymbol{z}_{t-1}, \boldsymbol{h}_t) \tag{29.166}$$

Given a fully factored $q(\boldsymbol{z}_{1:T})$, we can compute the ELBO as follows.

$$\log p(\boldsymbol{x}_{1:T}) = \log \left[\sum_{\boldsymbol{z}_{1:T}} p(\boldsymbol{x}_{1:T}|\boldsymbol{z}_{1:T}) p(\boldsymbol{z}_{1:T}) \right] \tag{29.167}$$

$$= \log \mathbb{E}_{q(\boldsymbol{z}_{1:T})} \left[p(\boldsymbol{x}_{1:T}|\boldsymbol{z}_{1:T}) \frac{p(\boldsymbol{z}_{1:T})}{q(\boldsymbol{z}_{1:T})} \right] \tag{29.168}$$

$$= \log \mathbb{E}_{q(\boldsymbol{z}_{1:T})} \left[\prod_{t=1}^{T} \frac{p(\boldsymbol{x}_t|\boldsymbol{z}_t) p(\boldsymbol{z}_t|\boldsymbol{z}_{t-1})}{q(\boldsymbol{z}_t)} \right] \tag{29.169}$$

$$\geq \mathbb{E}_{q(\boldsymbol{z}_{1:T})} \left[\sum_{t=1}^{T} \log p(\boldsymbol{x}_t|\boldsymbol{z}_t) + \log p(\boldsymbol{z}_t|\boldsymbol{z}_{t-1}) - \log q(\boldsymbol{z}_t) \right] \tag{29.170}$$

$$= \sum_{t=1}^{T} \mathbb{E}_{q(\boldsymbol{z}_t)} \left[\log p(\boldsymbol{x}_t|\boldsymbol{z}_t) \right] - \mathbb{E}_{q(\boldsymbol{z}_{t-1})} \left[D_{\mathbb{KL}}\left(q(\boldsymbol{z}_t) \,\|\, p(\boldsymbol{z}_t|\boldsymbol{z}_{t-1}) \right) \right] \tag{29.171}$$

If we assume that the variational posteriors are jointly Gaussian, we can use the reparameterization trick to use posterior samples to compute stochastic gradients of the ELBO. Furthermore, since we assumed a Gaussian prior, the KL term can be computed analytically.

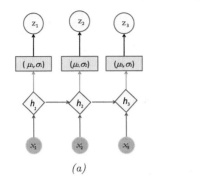
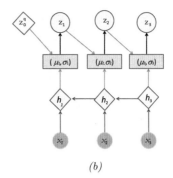

(a)   *(b)*

Figure 29.42: *Inference networks for deep Markov model. (a) Fully factorized causal posterior $q(\boldsymbol{z}_{1:T}|\boldsymbol{x}_{1:T}) = \prod_t q(\boldsymbol{z}_t|\boldsymbol{x}_{1:t})$. The past observations $\boldsymbol{x}_{1:t}$ are stored in the RNN hidden state $\boldsymbol{h}_t$. (b) Markovian posterior $q(\boldsymbol{z}_{1:T}|\boldsymbol{x}_{1:T}) = \prod_t q(\boldsymbol{z}_t|\boldsymbol{z}_{t-1}, \boldsymbol{x}_{t:T})$. The future observations $\boldsymbol{x}_{t:T}$ are stored in the RNN hidden state $\boldsymbol{h}_t$.*

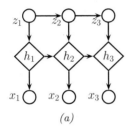
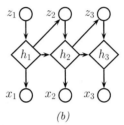

(a)   *(b)*

Figure 29.43: *Recurrent state-space models. (a) Prior is first-order Markov, $p(\boldsymbol{z}_t|\boldsymbol{z}_{t-1})$, but observation model is not Markovian, $p(\boldsymbol{x}_t|\boldsymbol{h}_t) = p(\boldsymbol{x}_t|\boldsymbol{z}_{1:t})$, where $\boldsymbol{h}_t$ summarizes $\boldsymbol{z}_{1:t}$. (b) Prior model is no longer first-order Markov either, $p(\boldsymbol{z}_t|\boldsymbol{h}_{t-1}) = p(\boldsymbol{z}_t|\boldsymbol{z}_{1:t-1})$. Diamonds are deterministic nodes, circles are stochastic.*

29.13.2 Recurrent SSM

In a DMM, the observation model $p(\boldsymbol{x}_t|\boldsymbol{z}_t)$ is first-order Markov, as is the dynamics model $p(\boldsymbol{z}_t|\boldsymbol{z}_{t-1})$. We can modify the model so that it captures long-range dependencies by adding deterministic hidden states as well. We can make the observation model depend on $\boldsymbol{z}_{1:t}$ instead of just $\boldsymbol{z}_t$ by using $p(\boldsymbol{x}_t|\boldsymbol{h}_t)$, where $\boldsymbol{h}_t = f(\boldsymbol{h}_{t-1}, \boldsymbol{z}_t)$, so $\boldsymbol{h}_t$ records all the stochastic choices. This is illustrated in Figure 29.43a. We can also make the dynamical prior depend on $\boldsymbol{z}_{1:t-1}$ by replacing $p(\boldsymbol{z}_t|\boldsymbol{z}_{t-1})$ with $p(\boldsymbol{z}_t|\boldsymbol{h}_{t-1})$. as is illustrated in Figure 29.43b. This is known as a **recurrent SSM**.

We can derive an inference network for an RSSM similar to the one we used for DMMs, except now we use a standard forwards RNN to compute $q(\boldsymbol{z}_t|\boldsymbol{x}_{1:t-1}, \boldsymbol{x}_{1:t})$.

29.13.3 Improving multistep predictions

In Figure 29.44(a), we show the loss terms involved in the ELBO. In particular, the wavy edge $z_{t|t} \rightarrow z_{t|t-1}$ corresponds to $\mathbb{E}_{q(\boldsymbol{z}_{t-1})}\left[D_{\text{KL}}\left(q(\boldsymbol{z}_t) \parallel p(\boldsymbol{z}_t|\boldsymbol{z}_{t-1})\right)\right]$, and the solid edge $z_{t|t} \rightarrow \boldsymbol{x}_t$ corresponds to $\mathbb{E}_{q(\boldsymbol{z}_t)}\left[\log p(\boldsymbol{x}_t|\boldsymbol{z}_t)\right]$. We see that the dynamics model, $p(\boldsymbol{z}_t|\boldsymbol{z}_{t-1})$, is only ever penalized in terms of how it differs from the one-step-ahead posterior $q(\boldsymbol{z}_t)$, which can hurt the ability of the model to make long-term predictions.

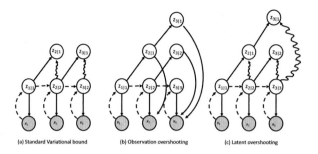

Figure 29.44: *Unrolling schemes for SSMs. The labels $z_{i|j}$ is shorthand for $p(z_i|x_{1:j})$. Solid lines denote the generative process, dashed lines the inference process. Arrows pointing at shaded circles represent log-likelihood loss terms. Wavy arrows indicate KL divergence loss terms. (a) Standard 1 step reconstruction of the observations. (b) Observation overshooting tries to predict future observations by unrolling in latent space. (c) Latent overshooting predicts future latent states and penalizes their KL divergence, but does need to care about future observations. Adapted from Figure 3 of [Haf+19].*

One solution to this is to make multistep forwards predictions using the dynamics model, and use these to reconstruct future observations, and add these errors as extra loss terms. This is called **observation overshooting** [Amo+18], and is illustrated in Figure 29.44(b).

A faster approach, proposed in [Haf+19], is to apply a similar idea but in latent space. More precisely, let us compute the multi-step prediction model, by repeatedly applying the transition model and integrating out the intermediate states to get $p(z_t|z_{t-d})$. We can then compute the ELBO for this as follows:

$$\log p_d(\boldsymbol{x}_{1:T}) \triangleq \log \int \prod_{t=1}^{T} p(\boldsymbol{z}_t|\boldsymbol{z}_{t-d})p(\boldsymbol{x}_t|\boldsymbol{z}_t)d\boldsymbol{z}_{1:T} \tag{29.172}$$

$$\geq \sum_{t=1}^{T} \mathbb{E}_{q(\boldsymbol{z}_t)}\left[\log p(\boldsymbol{x}_t|\boldsymbol{z}_t)\right] - \mathbb{E}_{p(\boldsymbol{z}_{t-1}|\boldsymbol{z}_{t-d})q(\boldsymbol{z}_{t-d})}\left[D_{\mathrm{KL}}\left(q(\boldsymbol{z}_t) \parallel p(\boldsymbol{z}_t|\boldsymbol{z}_{t-1})\right)\right] \tag{29.173}$$

To train the model so it is good at predicting at different future horizon depths d, we can average the above over all $1 \leq d \leq D$. However, for computational reasons, we can instead just average the KL terms, using weights β_d. This is called **latent overshooting** [Haf+19], and is illustrated in Figure 29.44(c). The new objective becomes

$$\frac{1}{D}\sum_{d=1}^{D} \log p_d(\boldsymbol{x}_{1:T}) \geq \sum_{t=1}^{T} \mathbb{E}_{q(\boldsymbol{z}_t)}\left[\log p(\boldsymbol{x}_t|\boldsymbol{z}_t)\right] \tag{29.174}$$

$$- \frac{1}{D}\sum_{d=1}^{D} \beta_d \mathbb{E}_{p(\boldsymbol{z}_{t-1}|\boldsymbol{z}_{t-d})q(\boldsymbol{z}_{t-d})}\left[D_{\mathrm{KL}}\left(q(\boldsymbol{z}_t) \parallel p(\boldsymbol{z}_t|\boldsymbol{z}_{t-1})\right)\right] \tag{29.175}$$

29.13.4   Variational RNNs

A **variational RNN** (**VRNN**) [Chu+15] is similar to a recurrent SSM except the hidden states are generated conditional on all past hidden states *and* all past observations, rather than just the past

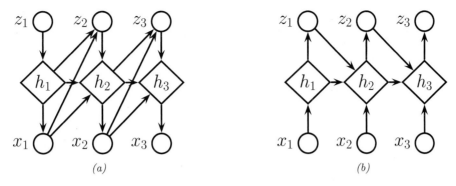

Figure 29.45: Variational RNN. (a) Generative model. (b) Inference model. The diamond-shaped nodes are deterministic.

hidden states. This is a more expressive model, but is slower to use for forecasting, since unrolling into the future requires generating observations $\boldsymbol{x}_{t+1}, \boldsymbol{x}_{t+2}, \ldots$ to "feed into" the hidden states, which controls the dynamics. This makes the model less useful for forecasting and model-based RL (see Section 35.4.5.2).

More precisely, the generative model is as follows:

$$p(\boldsymbol{x}_{1:T}, \boldsymbol{z}_{1:T}, \boldsymbol{h}_{1:T}) = \prod_{t=1}^{T} p(\boldsymbol{z}_t | \boldsymbol{h}_{t-1}, \boldsymbol{x}_{t-1}) \mathbb{I}\left(\boldsymbol{h}_t = f(\boldsymbol{h}_{t-1}, \boldsymbol{x}_{t-1}, \boldsymbol{z}_t)\right) p(\boldsymbol{x}_t | \boldsymbol{h}_t) \tag{29.176}$$

where $p(\boldsymbol{z}_1 | \boldsymbol{h}_0, \boldsymbol{x}_0) = p(\boldsymbol{z}_0)$ and $\boldsymbol{h}_1 = f(\boldsymbol{h}_0, \boldsymbol{x}_0, \boldsymbol{z}_1) = f(\boldsymbol{z}_1)$. Thus $\boldsymbol{h}_t = (\boldsymbol{z}_{1:t}, \boldsymbol{x}_{1:t-1})$ is a summary of the past observations and past and current stochastic latent samples. If we marginalize out these deterministic hidden nodes, we see that the dynamical prior on the stochastic latents is $p(\boldsymbol{z}_t | \boldsymbol{h}_{t-1}, \boldsymbol{x}_{t-1}) = p(\boldsymbol{z}_t | \boldsymbol{z}_{1:t-1}, \boldsymbol{x}_{1:t-1})$, whereas in a DMM, it is $p(\boldsymbol{z}_t | \boldsymbol{z}_{t-1})$, and in an RSSM, it is $p(\boldsymbol{z}_t | \boldsymbol{z}_{1:t-1})$. See Figure 29.45a for an illustration.

We can train VRNNs using SVI. In [Chu+15], they use the following inference network:

$$q(\boldsymbol{z}_{1:T}, \boldsymbol{h}_{1:T} | \boldsymbol{x}_{1:T}) = \prod_{t=1}^{T} \mathbb{I}\left(\boldsymbol{h}_t = f(\boldsymbol{h}_{t-1}, \boldsymbol{z}_{t-1}, \boldsymbol{x}_t)\right) q(\boldsymbol{z}_t | \boldsymbol{h}_t) \tag{29.177}$$

Thus $\boldsymbol{h}_t = (\boldsymbol{z}_{1:t-1}, \boldsymbol{x}_{1:t})$. Marginalizing out these deterministic nodes, we see that the filtered posterior has the form $q(\boldsymbol{z}_{1:T} | \boldsymbol{x}_{1:T}) = \prod_t q(\boldsymbol{z}_t | \boldsymbol{z}_{1:t-1}, \boldsymbol{x}_{1:t})$. See Figure 29.45b for an illustration. (We can also optionally replace $\boldsymbol{x}_t$ with the output of a bidirectional RNN to get the smoothed posterior, $q(\boldsymbol{z}_{1:T} | \boldsymbol{x}_{1:T}) = \prod_t q(\boldsymbol{z}_t | \boldsymbol{z}_{1:t-1}, \boldsymbol{x}_{1:T})$.)

This approach was used in [DF18] to generate simple videos of moving objects (e.g., a robot pushing a block); they call their method **stochastic video generation** or **SVG**. This was scaled up in [Vil+19], using simpler but larger architectures.

30 Graph learning

30.1 Introduction

Graphs are a very common way to represent data. In this chapter we discuss probability models for graphs. In Section 30.2, we assume the graph structure G is known, but we want to "explain" it in terms of a set of meaningful latent features; for this we use various kinds of latent variable models. In Section 30.3, we assume the graph structure G is unknown and needs to be inferred from correlated data, $\boldsymbol{x}_n \in \mathbb{R}^D$; for this, we will use probabilistic graphical models with unknown topology. (See also Section 16.3.6, where we discuss graph neural networks, for performing supervised learning using graph-structured data.)

30.2 Latent variable models for graphs

Graphs arise in many application areas, such as modeling social networks, protein-protein interaction networks, or patterns of disease transmission between people or animals. To try to find "interesting structure" in such graphs, such as clusters or communities, it is common to fit latent variable generative models of various forms, such as the **stochastic blocks model**. See Supplementary Section 30.1 for details.

30.3 Graphical model structure learning

In this section, we discuss how to learn the structure of a probabilistic graphical model given sample observations of some or all of its nodes. That is, the input is an $N \times D$ data matrix, and the output is a graph G (directed or undirected) with N_G nodes. (Usually $N_G = D$, but we also consider the case where we learn extra latent nodes that are not present in the input.)

There are many different methods for learning PGM graph structures. See Supplementary Chapter 30 for details.

In terms of applications, there are three main reasons to perform structure learning for PGMs: understanding, prediction, and causal inference (which involves both understanding and prediction), as we summarize below.

Learning sparse PGMs can be useful for gaining an understanding of multiple interacting variables. For example, consider a problem that arises in systems biology: we measure the phosphorylation status of some proteins in a cell [Sac+05] and want to infer how they interact. Figure 30.1 gives an example of a graph structure that was learned from this data, using a method called graphical lasso

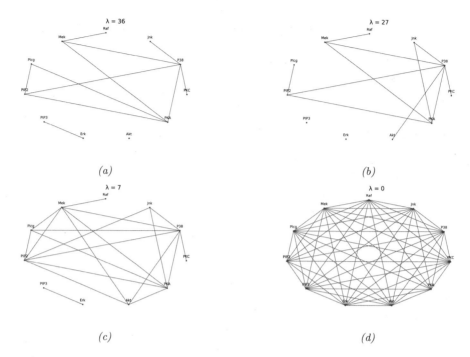

Figure 30.1: *A sparse undirected Gaussian graphical model learned using graphical lasso applied to some flow cytometry data (from [Sac+05]), which measures the phosphorylation status of 11 proteins. The sparsity level is controlled by λ. (a) λ = 36. (b) λ = 27. (c) λ = 7. (d) λ = 0. Adapted from Figure 17.5 of [HTF09]. Generated by* ggm_lasso_demo.ipynb.

[FHT08; MH12], which is explained in Supplementary Section 30.4.2. As another example, [Smi+06] showed that one can recover the neural "wiring diagram" of a certain kind of bird from multivariate time-series EEG data. The recovered structure closely matched the known functional connectivity of this part of the bird brain.

In some cases, we are not interested in interpreting the graph structure, we just want to use it to make predictions. One example of this is in financial portfolio management, where accurate models of the covariance between large numbers of different stocks is important. [CW07] show that by learning a sparse graph, and then using this as the basis of a trading strategy, it is possible to outperform (i.e., make more money than) methods that do not exploit sparse graphs. Another example is predicting traffic jams on the freeway. [Hor+05] describe a deployed system called JamBayes for predicting traffic flow in the Seattle area, using a directed graphical model whose structure was learned from data.

Structure learning is also an important pre-requisite for causal inference. In particular, to predict the effects of interventions on a system, or to perform counterfactual reasoning, we need to know the structural causal model (SCM), as we discuss in Section 4.7. An SCM is a kind of directed graphical model where the relationships between nodes are deterministic (functional), except for stochastic root (exogenous) variables. Consequently one can use techniques for learning DAG structures as a way to learn SCMs, if we make some assumptions about (lack of) confounders. This is called **causal discovery**. See Supplementary Section 30.5 for details.

31 Nonparametric Bayesian models

This chapter is written by Vinayak Rao.

31.1 Introduction

The defining characteristic of a **parametric model** is that the objects being modeled, whether regression or classification functions, probability densities, or something more modern like graphs or shapes, are indexed by a finite-dimensional parameter vector. For instance, neural networks have a fixed number of parameters, independent of the dataset. In a **parametric Bayesian model**, a prior probability distribution on these parameters is used to define a prior distribution on the objects of interest. By contrast, in a **Bayesian nonparametric (BNP)** model (also called a **non-parametric Bayesian** model) we directly place prior distributions on the objects of interest, such as functions, graphs, probability distributions, etc. This is usually done via some kind of **stochastic process**, which is a probability distribution over a potentially infinite set of random variables.

One example is a **Gaussian process**. As explained in Chapter 18, this defines a probability distribution over an unknown function $f : \mathcal{X} \to \mathbb{R}$, such that the joint distribution of $f(\mathbf{X}) = (f(\boldsymbol{x}_1), \ldots, f(\boldsymbol{x}_N))$ is jointly Gaussian for any finite set of values $\mathbf{X} = \{\boldsymbol{x}_n \in \mathcal{X}\}_{n=1}^N$ i.e., $p(f(\mathbf{X})) = \mathcal{N}(f(\mathbf{X})|\boldsymbol{\mu}(\mathbf{X}), \mathbf{K}(\mathbf{X}))$ where $\boldsymbol{\mu}(\mathbf{X}) = [\mu(\boldsymbol{x}_1), \ldots, \mu(\boldsymbol{x}_N)]$ is the mean, $\mathbf{K}(\mathbf{X}) = [\mathcal{K}(\boldsymbol{x}_i), \mathcal{K}(\boldsymbol{x}_j)]$ is the $N \times N$ Gram matrix, and $\mathcal{K}$ is a positive definite kernel function. The complexity of the posterior over functions can grow with the amount of data, avoiding underfitting, since we maintain a full posterior distribution over the infinite set of unknown "parameters" (i.e., function evaluations at all points $\boldsymbol{x} \in \mathcal{X}$). But by taking a Bayesian approach, we avoid overfitting this infinitely flexible model. Despite involving infinite-parameter objects, practitioners are often only interested in inferences on a finite training dataset and predictions on a finite test dataset. This often allows these models to be surprisingly tractable. We can also define probability distributions over probability distributions, as well as other kinds of objects.

We discuss these topics in more detail in Supplementary Chapter 31. For even more information, see e.g., [Hjo+10; GV17].

32 Representation learning

This chapter is written by Ben Poole and Simon Kornblith.

32.1 Introduction

Representation learning is a paradigm for training machine learning models to transform raw inputs into a form that makes it easier to solve new tasks. Unlike supervised learning, where the task is known at training time, representation learning often assumes that we do not know what task we wish to solve ahead of time. Without this knowledge, are there transformations of the input we can learn that are useful for a variety of tasks we might care about?

One point of evidence that representation learning is possible comes from us. Humans can rapidly form rich representations of new classes [LST15] that can support diverse behaviors: finding more instances of that class, decomposing that instance into parts, and generating new instances from that class. However, it is hard to directly specify what representations we would like our machine learning systems to learn. We may want it make it easy to solve new tasks with small amounts of data, we may want to construct novel inputs or answer questions about similarities between inputs, and we may want the representation to encode certain information while discarding other information.

In building methods for representation learning, the goal is to design a task whose solution requires learning an improved representation of the input instead of directly specifying what the representation should do. These tasks can vary greatly, from building generative models of the dataset to learning to cluster datapoints. Different methods often involve different assumptions on the dataset, different kinds of data, and induce different biases on the learned representation. In this chapter we first discuss methods for evaluating learned representations, then approaches for learning representations based on supervised learning, generative modeling, and self-supervised learning, and finally the theory behind when representation learning is possible.

32.2 Evaluating and comparing learned representations

How can we make sense of representations learned by different neural networks, or of the differences between representations learned in different layers of the same network? Although it is tempting to imagine representations of neural networks as points in a space, this space is high-dimensional. In order to determine the quality of representations and how different representations differ, we need ways to summarize these high-dimensional representations or their relationships with a few

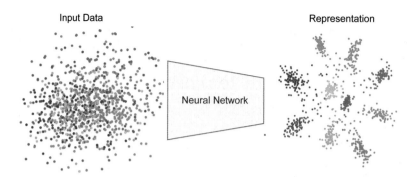

Figure 32.1: Representation learning transforms input data (left) where data from different classes (color) are mixed together to a representation (right) where attributes like class are more easily distinguished. Generated by vib_demo.ipynb.

relevant scalars. Doing so requires making assumptions about what structure in the representations is important.

32.2.1   Downstream performance

The most common way to evaluate the quality of a representation is to adapt it to one or more downstream tasks thought to be representative of real-world scenarios. In principle, one could choose any strategy to adapt the representation, but a small number of adaptation strategies dominate the literature. We discuss these strategies below.

Clearly, downstream performance can only differ from pretraining performance if the downstream task is different from the pretraining task. Downstream tasks can differ from the pretraining task in their input distributions, target distributions, or both. The downstream tasks used to evaluate unsupervised or self-supervised representation learning often involve the same distribution of inputs as the pretraining task, but require predicting targets that were not provided during pretraining. For example, in self-supervised visual representation learning, representations learned on the ImageNet dataset without using the accompanying labels are evaluated on ImageNet using labels, either by performing linear evaluation with all the data or by fine-tuning using subsets of the data. By contrast, in **transfer learning** (Section 19.5.1), the input distribution of the downstream task differs from the distribution of the pretraining task. For example, we might pretrain the representation on a large variety of natural images and then ask how the representation performs at distinguishing different species of birds not seen during pretraining.

32.2.1.1   Linear classifiers and linear evaluation

Linear evaluation treats the trained neural network as a fixed feature extractor and trains a linear classifier on top of fixed features extracted from a chosen network layer. In earlier work, this linear classifier was often a support vector machine [Don+14; SR+14; Cha+14], but in more recent work, it is typically an L^2-regularized multinomial logistic regression classifier [ZIE17; KSL19; KZB19]. The process of training this classifier is equivalent to attaching a new layer to the chosen representation layer and training only this new layer, with the rest of the network's weights frozen and any normalization/regularization layers set to "inference mode" (see Figure 32.2).

Although linear classifiers are conceptually simple compared to deep neural networks, they are not necessarily simple to train. Unlike deep neural network training, objectives associated with commonly-used linear classifiers are convex and thus it is possible to find global minima, but it can be challenging to do so with stochastic gradient methods. When using SGD, it is important to tune both the learning rate schedule and weight decay. Even with careful tuning, SGD may still require substantially more epochs to converge when training the classifier than when training the original neural network [KZB19]. Nonetheless, linear evaluation with SGD remains a commonly used approach in the representation learning literature.

When it is possible to maintain all features in memory simultaneously, it is possible to use full-batch optimization method with line search such as L-BFGS in place of SGD [KSL19; Rad+21]. These optimization methods ensure that the loss decreases at every iteration of training, and thus do not require manual tuning of learning rates. To obtain maximal accuracy, it is still important to tune the amount of regularization, but this can be done efficiently by sweeping this hyperparameter and using the optimal weights for the previous value of the hyperparameter as a warm start. Using a full-batch optimizer typically implies precomputing the features before performing the optimization, rather than recomputing features on each minibatch. Precomputing features can save a substantial amount of computation, since the forwards passes through the frozen model are typically much more expensive than computing the gradient of the linear classifier. However, precomputing features also limits the number of augmentations of each example that can be considered.

It is important to keep in mind that the accuracy obtainable by training a linear classifier on a finite dataset is only a lower bound on the accuracy of the Bayes-optimal linear classifier. The datasets used for linear evaluation are often small relative to the number of parameters to be trained, and the classifier typically needs to be regularized to obtain maximal accuracy. Thus, linear evaluation accuracy depends not only on whether it is possible to linearly separate different classes in the representation, but also on how much data is required to find a good decision boundary with a given training objective and regularizer. In practice, even an invertible linear transformation of a representation can affect linear evaluation accuracy.

32.2.1.2 Fine-tuning

It is also possible to adapt all layers from the pretraining task to the downstream task. This process is typically referred to as **fine-tuning** [HS06b; Gir+14]. In its simplest form, fine-tuning, like linear evaluation, involves attaching a new layer to a chosen representation layer, but unlike linear evaluation, all network parameters, and not simply those of the new layer, are updated according to gradients computed on the downstream task. The new layer may be initialized with zeros or using the solution obtained by training it with all other parameters frozen. Typically, the best results are obtained when the network is fine-tuned at a lower learning rate than was used for pretraining.

Fine-tuning is substantially more expensive than training a linear classifier on top of fixed feature representations, since each training step requires backpropagating through multiple layers. However, fine-tuned networks typically outperform linear classifiers, especially when the pretraining and downstream tasks are very different [KSL19; AGM14; Cha+14; Azi+15]. Linear classifiers perform better only when the number of training examples is very small (~5 per class) [KSL19].

Fine-tuning can also involve adding several new network layers. For detection and segmentation tasks, which require fine-grained knowledge of spatial position, it is common to add a *feature pyramid network* (FPN) [Lin+17b] that incorporates information from different feature maps in the pretrained network. Alternatively, new layers can be interspersed between old layers and initialized to preserve the network's output. *Net2Net* [CGS15] follows this approach to construct a higher-capacity network that makes use of representations contained in the pretrained weights of a smaller network, whereas *adapter modules* [Hou+19] incorporate new, parameter-efficient modules into a pretrained network and freeze the old ones to reduce the number of parameters that need to be stored when adapting models to different tasks.

32.2.1.3 Disentanglement

Given knowledge about how a dataset was generated, for example that there are certain factors of variation such as position, shape, and color that generated the data, we often wish to estimate how well we can recover those factors in our learned representation. This requires using disentangled representation learning methods (see Section 21.3.1.1). While there are a variety of metrics for disentanglement, most measure to what extent there is a one-to-one correspondence between latent factors and dimensions of the learned representation.

32.2.2 Representational similarity

Rather than measure compatibility between a representation and a downstream task, we might seek to directly examine relationships between two fixed representations without reference to a task. In this section, we assume that we have two sets of fixed representations corresponding to the same n examples. These representations could be extracted from different layers of the same network or layers of different neural networks, and need not have the same dimensionality. For notational convenience, we assume that each set of representations has been stacked row-wise to form matrices $\boldsymbol{X} \in \mathbb{R}^{n \times p_1}$ and $\boldsymbol{Y} \in \mathbb{R}^{n \times p_2}$ such that $\boldsymbol{X}_{i,:}$ and $\boldsymbol{Y}_{i,:}$ are two different representations of the same example.

32.2.2.1 Representational similarity analysis and centered kernel alignment

Representational similarity analysis (RSA) is the dominant technique for measuring similarity of representations in neuroscience [KMB08], but has also been applied in machine learning. RSA reduces the problem of measuring similarity between representation matrices to measuring the similarities between representations of individual examples. RSA begins by forming representational similarity matrices (RSMs) from each representation. Given functions $k : \mathcal{X} \times \mathcal{X} \mapsto \mathbb{R}$ and $k' : \mathcal{Y} \times \mathcal{Y} \mapsto \mathbb{R}$ that measure the similarity between pairs of representations of individual examples $\boldsymbol{x}, \boldsymbol{x}' \in \mathcal{X}$, and $\boldsymbol{y}, \boldsymbol{y}' \in \mathcal{Y}$, the corresponding representational similarity matrices $\boldsymbol{K}, \boldsymbol{K}' \in \mathbb{R}^{n \times n}$ contain the similarities between the representations of all pairs of examples $\boldsymbol{K}_{ij} = k(\boldsymbol{X}_{i,:}, \boldsymbol{X}_{j,:})$ and $\boldsymbol{K}'_{ij} = k'(\boldsymbol{Y}_{i,:}, \boldsymbol{Y}_{j,:})$. These representational similarity matrices are transformed into a scalar similarity value by applying a matrix similarity function $s(\boldsymbol{K}, \boldsymbol{K}')$.

The RSA framework can encompass many different forms of similarity through the selection of the similarity functions $k(\cdot, \cdot)$, $k'(\cdot, \cdot)$, and $s(\cdot, \cdot)$. How these functions should be selected is a contentious topic [BS+20; Kri19]. In practice, it is common to choose $k(\boldsymbol{x}, \boldsymbol{x}') = k'(\boldsymbol{x}, \boldsymbol{x}') = \text{corr}[\boldsymbol{x}, \boldsymbol{x}']$, the Pearson correlation coefficient between examples. $s(\cdot, \cdot)$ is often chosen to be the Spearman rank correlation between the representational similarity matrices, which is computed by reshaping $\boldsymbol{K}$ and

K' to vectors, computing the rankings of their elements, and measuring the Pearson correlation between these rankings.

Centered kernel alignment (CKA) is a technique that was first proposed in machine learning literature [Cri+02; CMR12] but that can be interpreted as a form of RSA. In centered kernel alignment, the per-example similarity functions k and k' are chosen to be positive semi-definite kernels so that K and K' are kernel matrices. The matrix similarity function s is the cosine similarity between centered kernel matrices

$$s(K, K') = \frac{\langle HKH, HK'H \rangle_{\mathrm{F}}}{\|HKH\|_{\mathrm{F}} \|HK'H\|_{\mathrm{F}}}, \tag{32.1}$$

where $\langle A, B \rangle_{\mathrm{F}} = \mathrm{vec}(A)^\top \mathrm{vec}(B) = \mathrm{tr}(A^\top B)$ is the Frobenius product, and $H = I - \frac{1}{n}\mathbf{1}\mathbf{1}^\top$ is the centering matrix. As it is applied above, the centering matrix subtracts the means from the rows and columns of the similarity index.

A special case of centered kernel alignment arises when k and k' are chosen to be the linear kernel $k(x, x') = k'(x, x') = x^\top x'$. In this case, $K = XX^\top$ and $K' = YY^\top$, allowing for an alternative expression for CKA in terms of the similarities between pairs of *features* rather than pairs of examples. The representations themselves must first be centered by subtracting the means from their columns, yielding $\tilde{X} = HX$ and $\tilde{Y} = HY$. Then, so-called linear centered kernel alignment is given by

$$s(K, K') = \frac{\langle \tilde{X}\tilde{X}^\top, \tilde{Y}\tilde{Y}^\top \rangle_{\mathrm{F}}}{\|\tilde{X}\tilde{X}^\top\|_{\mathrm{F}} \|\tilde{Y}\tilde{Y}^\top\|_{\mathrm{F}}} = \frac{\|\tilde{X}^\top \tilde{Y}\|_{\mathrm{F}}^2}{\|\tilde{X}^\top \tilde{X}\|_{\mathrm{F}} \|\tilde{Y}^\top \tilde{Y}\|_{\mathrm{F}}}. \tag{32.2}$$

Linear centered kernel alignment is equivalent to the RV coefficient [RE76] between centered features, as shown in [Kor+19].

32.2.2.2 Canonical correlation analysis and related methods

Given two datasets (in this case, the representation matrices X and Y), canonical correlation analysis or CCA (Section 28.3.4.3) seeks to map both datasets to a shared latent space such that they are maximally correlated in this space. The ith pair of canonical weights (w_i, w_i') maximize the correlation between the corresponding canonical vectors $\rho_i = \mathrm{corr}[Xw_i, Yw_i']$ subject to the constraint that the new canonical vectors are orthogonal to previous canonical vectors,

$$\begin{aligned} \text{maximize } &\mathrm{corr}[Xw_i, Yw_i'] \\ \text{subject to } &\forall_{j<i} \;\; Xw_i \perp Xw_j \\ &\forall_{j<i} \;\; Yw_i' \perp Yw_j' \\ &\|Xw_i\| = \|Yw_i'\| = 1. \end{aligned} \tag{32.3}$$

The maximum number of non-zero canonical correlations is the minimum of the ranks, $p = \min(\mathrm{rk}(X), \mathrm{rk}(Y))$.

The standard algorithm for computing the canonical weights and correlations [BG73] first decomposes the individual representations as the product of an orthogonal matrix and a second matrix, $\tilde{X} = QR : Q^\top Q = I$ and $\tilde{Y} = Q'R' : Q'^\top Q' = I$. These decompositions can be obtained either by QR factorization or singular value decomposition. A second singular value decomposition of $Q^\top Q' = U\Sigma V^\top$ provides the quantities needed to determine the canonical weights and correlations.

Specifically, the canonical correlations are the singular values $\boldsymbol{\rho} = \text{diag}(\boldsymbol{\Sigma})$; the canonical vectors are the columns of $\boldsymbol{XW} = \boldsymbol{QU}$ and $\boldsymbol{YW'} = \boldsymbol{Q'V}$; and the canonical weights are $\boldsymbol{W} = \boldsymbol{R}^{-1}\boldsymbol{U}$ and $\boldsymbol{W'} = \boldsymbol{R}'^{-1}\boldsymbol{V}$.

Two common strategies to turn the resulting vector of canonical correlations into a scalar are to take the **mean squared canonical correlation**,

$$R_{\text{CCA}}^2(\boldsymbol{X}, \boldsymbol{Y}) = \|\boldsymbol{\rho}\|_2^2/p = \|\boldsymbol{Q}^\top \boldsymbol{Q}'\|_F^2/p, \tag{32.4}$$

or the **mean canonical correlation**,

$$\bar{\rho} = \sum_{i=1}^p \rho_i/p = \|\boldsymbol{Q}^\top \boldsymbol{Q}'\|_*/p, \tag{32.5}$$

where $\|\cdot\|_*$ denotes the nuclear norm. The mean squared canonical correlation has several alternative names, including Yanai's GCD [Yan74; RBS84], Pillai's trace, or the eigenspace overlap score [May+19].

Although CCA is a powerful tool, it suffers from the curse of dimensionality. If at least one representation has more neurons than examples and each neuron is linearly independent of the others, then all canonical correlations are 1. In practice, because neural network representations are high-dimensional, we can find ourselves in the regime where there are not enough data to accurately estimate the canonical correlations. Moreover, even when we can accurately estimate the canonical correlations, it may be desirable for a similarity measure to place less emphasis on the similarity of low-variance directions.

Singular vector CCA (SVCCA) mitigates these problems by retaining only the largest principal components of $\tilde{\boldsymbol{X}}$ and $\tilde{\boldsymbol{Y}}$ when performing CCA. Given the singular value decomposition of the representations $\tilde{\boldsymbol{X}} = \boldsymbol{U\Sigma V}^\top$ and $\tilde{\boldsymbol{Y}} = \boldsymbol{U'\Sigma'V'}^\top$, SVCCA retains only the first k columns of $\boldsymbol{U}$ corresponding to the largest k singular values of $\boldsymbol{\sigma} = \text{diag}(\boldsymbol{\Sigma})$ (i.e., the k largest principal components) and the first k' columns of $\boldsymbol{U'}$ corresponding to the largest k' singular values $\boldsymbol{\sigma}' = \text{diag}(\boldsymbol{\Sigma}')$. With these singular value decompositions, the canonical correlations, vectors, and weights can then be computed using the algorithm of Björck and Golub [BG73] described above, by setting

$$\boldsymbol{Q} = \boldsymbol{U}_{:,1:k}, \qquad \boldsymbol{R} = \boldsymbol{\Sigma}_{1:k,1:k}\boldsymbol{V}_{:,1:k}^\top, \qquad \boldsymbol{Q}' = \boldsymbol{U}'_{:,1:k}, \qquad \boldsymbol{R}' = \boldsymbol{\Sigma}'_{1:k,1:k}\boldsymbol{V}'^\top_{:,1:k}. \tag{32.6}$$

Raghu et al. [Rag+17] suggest retaining enough components to explain 99% of the variance, i.e., setting k to the minimum value such that $\|\boldsymbol{\sigma}_{1:k}\|^2/\|\boldsymbol{\sigma}\|^2 = 0.99$ and k' to the minimum value such that $\|\boldsymbol{\sigma}'_{1:k'}\|^2/\|\boldsymbol{\sigma}'\|^2 = 0.99$. However, for a fixed value of $\min(k, k')$, CCA-based similarity measures increase with the value of $\max(k, k')$. Representations that require more components to explain 99% of the variance of representations may thus appear "more similar" to all other representations than representations with more rapidly decaying singular value spectra. In practice, it is often better to set k and k' to the same fixed value.

Projection-weighted CCA (PWCCA) [MRB18] instead weights the correlations by a measure of the variability in the original representation that they explain. The resulting similarity measure is

$$\text{PWCCA}(\boldsymbol{X}, \boldsymbol{Y}) = \frac{\sum_{i=1}^p \alpha_i \rho_i}{\sum_{i=1}^p \alpha_i}, \qquad \alpha_i = \|(\boldsymbol{Y}\boldsymbol{w}'_i)^\top \boldsymbol{Y}\|_1. \tag{32.7}$$

PWCCA enjoys somewhat widespread use in representational similarity literature, but it has potentially undesirable properties. First, it is asymmetric; its value depends on which of the two representations is used for the weighting. Second, it is unclear why weightings should be determined using the L^1 norm, which is not invariant to rotations of the representation. It is arguably more intuitive to weight the correlations directly by the amount of variance in the representation that the canonical component explains, which corresponds to replacing the L^1 norm with the squared L^2 norm. The resulting similarity measure is

$$R_{\text{LR}}^2(\boldsymbol{X}, \boldsymbol{Y}) = \frac{\sum_{i=1}^{p} \alpha_i' \rho_i^2}{\sum_{i=1}^{p} \alpha_i'}, \qquad\qquad \alpha_i' = \sum_{j=1}^{p_2} \|(\boldsymbol{Y}\boldsymbol{w}_i')^{\top}\boldsymbol{Y}\|_2^2. \tag{32.8}$$

As shown by Kornblith et al. [Kor+19], when $p_2 \geq p_1$, this alternative similarity measure is equivalent to the overall variance explained by using linear regression to fit every neuron in $\tilde{\boldsymbol{Y}}$ using the representation $\tilde{\boldsymbol{X}}$,

$$R_{\text{LR}}^2(\boldsymbol{X}, \boldsymbol{Y}) = 1 - \sum_{i=1}^{p_2} \min_{\boldsymbol{\beta}} \|\tilde{\boldsymbol{Y}}_{:,i} - \tilde{\boldsymbol{X}}\boldsymbol{\beta}\|^2 / \|\tilde{\boldsymbol{Y}}\|_{\text{F}}^2. \tag{32.9}$$

Finally, there is also a close relationship between CCA and linear CKA. This relationship can be clarified by writing similarity indexes directly in terms of the singular value decompositions $\tilde{\boldsymbol{X}} = \boldsymbol{U}\boldsymbol{\Sigma}\boldsymbol{V}^{\top}$ and $\tilde{\boldsymbol{Y}} = \boldsymbol{U}'\boldsymbol{\Sigma}'\boldsymbol{V}'^{\top}$. The left-singular vectors $\boldsymbol{u}_i = \boldsymbol{U}_{:,i}$ correspond to the principal components of $\boldsymbol{X}$ normalized to unit length, and the squared singular values $\lambda_i = \Sigma_{ii}^2$ are the amount of variance that those principal components explain (up to a factor of $1/n$). Given these singular value decompositions, R_{CCA}^2, R_{LR}^2, and linear CKA become:

$$R_{\text{CCA}}^2(\boldsymbol{X}, \boldsymbol{Y}) = \sum_{i=1}^{p_1}\sum_{j=1}^{p_2} \left(\boldsymbol{u}_i^{\top}\boldsymbol{u}_j'\right)^2 / p_1 \tag{32.10}$$

$$R_{\text{LR}}^2(\boldsymbol{X}, \boldsymbol{Y}) = \sum_{i=1}^{p_2}\sum_{j=1}^{p_2} \lambda_j' \left(\boldsymbol{u}_i^{\top}\boldsymbol{u}_j'\right)^2 / \sum_{j=1}^{p_2} \lambda_j' \tag{32.11}$$

$$\text{CKA}_{\text{linear}}(\boldsymbol{X}, \boldsymbol{Y}) = \frac{\sum_{i=1}^{p_1}\sum_{j=1}^{p_2} \lambda_i \lambda_j' \left(\boldsymbol{u}_i^{\top}\boldsymbol{u}_j'\right)^2}{\sqrt{\sum_{i=1}^{p_1} \lambda_i^2}\sqrt{\sum_{j=1}^{p_2} \lambda_j'^2}}. \tag{32.12}$$

Thus, these similarity indexes all involve the similarities between all pairs of principal components from $\boldsymbol{X}$ and $\boldsymbol{Y}$, but place different weightings on these similarities according to the fraction of variance that these principal components explain.

32.2.2.3 Comparing representational similarity measures

What properties are desirable in a representational similarity measure is an open question, and this question may not have a unique answer. Whereas evaluations of downstream accuracy approximate real-world use cases for neural network representations, the goal of representational similarity is instead to develop understanding of how representations evolve across neural networks, or how they differ between neural networks with different architectures or training settings.

One way to taxonomize different similarity measures is through the transformations of a representation that they are invariant to. The minimum form of invariance is invariance to permutation of a representation's constituent neurons, which is needed because neurons in neural networks generally have no canonical ordering: for commonly-used initialization strategies, any permutation of a given initialization is equiprobable, and nearly all architectures and optimizers produce training trajectories that are equivariant under permutation. On the other hand, invariance to arbitrary invertible transformations, as provided by mutual information, is clearly undesirable, since many realistic neural networks are injective functions of the input [Gol+19] and thus there always exists an invertible transformation between any pair of representations. In practice, most similarity measures in common use are invariant to rotations (orthogonal transformations) of representations, which implies invariance to permutation. Similarity measures based solely on CCA correlations, such as R_{CCA}^2 and $\bar{\rho}$, are invariant to all invertible linear transformations of representations. However, SVCCA and PWCCA are not.

A different way to distinguish similarity measures is to investigate situations where we know the relationships among representations and to empirically evaluate their ability to recover these relationships. Kornblith et al. [Kor+19] propose a simple "sanity check": Given two architecturally identical networks A and B trained from different random initializations, any layer in network A should be more similar to the architecturally corresponding layer in network B than to any other layer. They show that, when considering flattened representations of CNNs, similarity measures based on centered kernel alignment satisfy this sanity check whereas other similarity measures do not. By contrast, when considering representations of individual tokens in Transformers, all similarity measures perform reasonably well. However, Maheswaranathan et al. [Mah+19] show that both CCA and linear CKA are highly sensitive to seemingly innocuous RNN design choices such as the activation function, even though analysis of the fixed points of the dynamics of different networks suggests they all operate similarly.

32.3   Approaches for learning representations

The goal of representation learning is to learn a transformation of the inputs that makes it easier to solve future tasks. Typically the tasks we want the representation to be useful for are not known when learning the representation, so we cannot directly train to improve performance on the task. Learning such generic representations requires collecting large-scale unlabeled or weakly-labeled datasets, and identifying tasks or priors for the representations that one can solve without direct access to the downstream tasks. Most methods focus on learning a parametric mapping $z = f_\theta(x)$ that takes an input x and transforms it into a representation z using a neural network with parameters θ.

The main challenge in representation learning is coming up with a task that requires learning a good representation to solve. If the task is too easy, then it can be solved without learning an interesting transformation of the inputs, or by learning a *shortcut*. If a task is too different from the downstream task that the representation will be evaluated on, then the representation may also not be useful. For example, if the downstream task is object detection, then the representation needs to encode both the identity and location of objects in the image. However, if we only care about classification, then the representation can discard information about position. This leads to approaches for learning representations that are often not generic: different training tasks may perform better for different downstream tasks.

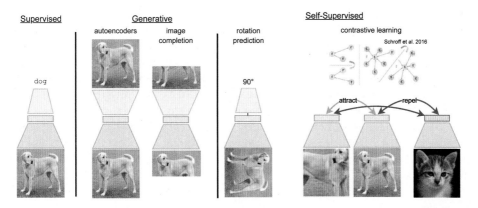

Figure 32.2: Approaches for representation learning from images. An input image is encoded through a deep neural network (green) to produce a representation (blue). An additional shallow or deep neural network (yellow) is often used to train the representation, but is thrown out after the representation is learned when solving downstream tasks. In the supervised case, the mapping from the representation to logits is typically linear, while for autoencoders the mapping from representation to images can be highly complex and stochastic. Unlike supervised or generative approaches, contrastive methods rely on other datapoints in the form of positive pairs (often created through data augmentation) and negative pairs (typically other datapoints) to learn a representation.

In Figue 32.2, we outline three approaches we will discuss for representation learning. **Supervised** approaches train on large-scale supervised or weakly-supervised data using standard supervised losses. **Generative** approaches aim to learn generative models of the dataset or parts of a dataset. **Self-supervised** approaches are based on transformation prediction or multi-view learning, where we design a task that where labels can be easily synthesized without needing human input.

32.3.1   Supervised representation learning and transfer

The first major successes in visual representation learning with deep learning came from networks trained on large labeled datasets. Following the discovery that supervised deep neural networks could outperform classical computer vision models for natural image classification [KSH12b; CMS12], it became clear that the representations learned by these networks could outperform handcrafted features used across a wide variety of tasks [Don+14; SR+14; Oqu+14; Gir+14]. Although unsupervised visual representation learning has recently achieved competitive results on many domains, supervised representation learning remains the dominant approach.

Larger networks trained on larger datasets generally achieve better performance on both pretraining and downstream tasks. When other design choices are held fixed, architectures that achieve higher accuracy during pretraining on natural image datasets such as ImageNet also learn better representations for downstream natural image tasks, as measured by both linear evaluation and fine-tuned accuracy [KSL19; TL19; Zha+19a; Zha+21; Abn+21]. However, when the domain shift from the pretraining task to the downstream task becomes larger (e.g., from ImageNet to medical imaging), the correlation between pretraining and downstream accuracy can be much lower [Rag+19;

Ke+21; Abn+21]. Studies that vary pretraining dataset size generally find that larger pretraining datasets yield better representations for downstream tasks [HAE16; Mah+18; Kol+20; Zha+21; Abn+21], although there is an interaction between model size and dataset. When training small models with the intention of transferring to a specific downstream task, it is sometimes preferable to pretrain on a smaller dataset that is more closely related to that task rather than a larger dataset that is less closely related [Cui+18; Mah+18; Ngi+18; Kol+20], but larger models seem to derive greater benefit from larger, more diverse datasets [Mah+18; Kol+20].

Whereas scaling the architecture and dataset size generally improves both pretraining and downstream accuracy, other design choices can improve pretraining accuracy at the expense of transfer, or vice versa. Regularizers such as penultimate layer dropout and label smoothing improve accuracy on pretraining tasks but produce worse representations for downstream tasks [KSL19; Kor+21]. Although most convolutional neural networks are trained with batch normalization, Kolesnikov et al. [Kol+20] find that the combination of group normalization and weight standardization leads to networks that perform similarly on pretraining tasks but substantially better on transfer tasks. Adversarial training produces networks that perform worse on pretraining tasks as compared to standard training, but these representations transfer better to other tasks [Sal+20]. For certain combinations of pretraining and downstream datasets, increasing the amount of weight decay on the network's final layer can improve transferability at the cost of pretraining accuracy [Zha+21; Abn+21].

The challenge of collecting ever-larger pretraining datasets has led to the emergence of **weakly-supervised representation learning**, which eschews the expensive human annotations of datasets such as ImageNet and instead relies on data that can be readily collected from the Internet, but which may have greater label noise. Supervision sources include hashtags accompanying images on websites such as Instagram and Flickr [CG15; Iza+15; Jou+16; Mah+18], image labels obtained automatically using proprietary algorithms involving user feedback signals [Sun+17; Kol+20], or image captions/alt text [Li+17a; SPL20; DJ21; Rad+21; Jia+21]. Hashtags and automatic labeling give rise to image classification problems that closely resemble their more strongly supervised counterparts. The primary difference versus standard supervised representation learning is that the data are noisier, but in practice, the benefits of more data often outweigh the detrimental effects of the noise.

Image-text supervision has provided more fertile ground for innovation, as there are many different ways of jointly processing text and images. The simplest approach is again to convert the data into an image classification problem, where the network is trained to predict which words or n-grams appear in the text accompanying a given image [Li+17a]. More sophisticated approaches train image-conditional language models [DJ21] or masked language models [SPL20], which can make better use of the structure of the text. Recently, there has been a surge in interest in *contrastive* image/text pretraining models such as CLIP [Rad+21] and ALIGN [Jia+21], details of which we discuss in Section 32.3.4. These models process images and text independently using two separate "towers", and learn an embedding space where embeddings of images lie close to the embeddings of the corresponding text. As shown by Radford et al. [Rad+21], contrastive image/text pretraining learns high-quality representations faster than alternative approaches.

Beyond simply learning good visual representations, pretrained models that embed image and text in a common space enable **zero-shot transfer** of learned representations. In zero-shot transfer, an image classifier is constructed using only textual descriptions of the classes of interest, without any images from the downstream task. Early co-embedding models relied on pretrained image models and word embeddings that were then adapted to a common space [Fro+13], but contrastive image/text pretraining provides a means to learn co-embedding models end-to-end. Compared to linear classifiers trained using image embeddings, zero-shot classifiers typically perform worse, but zero-shot classifiers are far more robust to distribution shift [Rad+21].

32.3.2 Generative representation learning

Supervised representation learning often fails to learn representations for tasks that differ significantly from the task the representation was trained on. How can we learn representations when the task we wish to solve differs a lot from tasks where we have large labeled datasets?

Generative representation learning aims to model the entire distribution of a dataset $q(x)$ with a parametric model $p_\theta(x)$. The hope of generative representation learning is that. if we can build models that can create all the data that we have seen, then we implicitly may learn a representation that can be used to answer any question about the data, not just the questions that are related to a supervised task for which we have labels. For example, in the case of digit classification, it is hard to collect labels for the style of a handwritten digit, but if the model has to product all possible handwritten digits in our dataset it needs to learn to produce digits with different styles. On the other hand, supervised learning to classify digits aims to learn a representation that is invariant to style.

There are two main approaches for learning representations with generative models: (1) latent-variable models that aim to capture the underlying factors of variation in data with latent variables z that act as the representation (see the chapter on VAEs, Chapter 21), and (2) fully-observed models where a neural architecture is trained with a tractable generative objective (see the chapters on AR models, Chapter 22, and flow models, Chapter 23), and then a representation is extracted from the learned architecture.

32.3.2.1 Latent-variable models

One criterion for learning a good representation of the world is that it is useful for synthesizing observed data. If we can build a model that can create new observations, and has a simple set of latent variables, then hopefully this model will learn variables that are related to the underlying physical process that created the observations. For example, if we are trying to model a dataset of 2d images of shapes, knowing the position, size, and type of the shape would enable easy synthesis of the image. This approach to learning is known as **analysis-by-synthesis**, and is a theory of perception that aims at identifying a set of underlying latent factors (analysis) that could be used to synthesize observations [Rob63; Bau74; LM03]. Our goal is to learn a generative model $p_\theta(x, z)$ over the observations x and latents z, with parameters θ. Given an observation x, performing the analysis step to extract a representation requires running inference to sample or compute the posterior mean of $p_\theta(z|x)$. Different choices for the model $p_\theta(x, z)$ and inference procedure for $p_\theta(z|x)$ represent different ways of learning representations from a dataset.

Early work on deep latent-variable generative models aimed to learn stacks of features often based on training simple energy-based models or directed sparse coding models, each of which could explain the previous set of latent factors, and which learned increasingly abstract representation [HOT06b; Lee+09; Ran+06]. Bengio, Courville, and Vincent [BCV13] provide an overview of several methods based on stacking latent-variable generative modeling approaches to learn increasingly abstract representation. However greedy approaches to generative representation learning have failed to scale to larger natural datasets.

If the generative process that created the data is simple and can be described, then encoding that structure into a generative model is a tremendously powerful way of learning useful and robust representations. Lake, Salakhutdinov, and Tenenbaum [LST15] and George et al. [Geo+17] use knowledge of how characters are composed of strokes to build hierarchical generative models with representations that excel at several downstream tasks. However, for many real-world datasets the generative structure is not known, and the generative model must also be learned. There is often a tradeoff between imposing structure in the generative process (such as sparsity) vs. learning that structure from data.

Directed latent-variable generative models have proven easier to train and scale to natural datasets. Variational autoencoders (Chapter 21) train a directed latent-variable generative model with variational inference, and learn a prior $p_\theta(z)$, decoder $p_\theta(x|z)$, and an amortized inference network $q_\phi(z|x)$ that can be used to extract a representation on new datapoints. Higgins et al. [Hig+17b] show β-VAEs (Section 21.3.1) are capable of learning latent variables that correspond to factors of variation on simple synthetic datasets. Kingma et al. [Kin+14b] and Rasmus et al. [Ras+15] demonstrate improved performing on semi-supervised learning with VAEs. While there have been several recent advances to scale up VAEs to natural datasets [VK20b; Chi21b], none of these methods have yet led to representations that are competitive for downstream tasks such as classification or segmentation.

Adversarial methods for training directed latent-variable models have also proven useful for representation learning. In particular, GANs (Chapter 26) trained with encoders such as BiGAN [DKD17], ALI [Dum+17], and [Che+16] were able to learn representations on small scale datasets that performed well at object classification. The discriminators from GANs have also proven useful for learning representations [RMC16b]. More recently, these methods were scaled up to ImageNet in BigBiGAN [DS19], with learned representations that performed strongly on classification and segmentation tasks.

32.3.2.2　Fully observed models

The neural network architectures used in fully observed generative models can also learn useful representations without the presence of latent-variables. ImageGPT [Che+20a] demonstrate that an autoregressive model trained on pixels can learn internal representations that excel at image classification. Unlike with latent-variable models where the representation is often thought of as the latent variables, ImageGPT extracted representations from the deterministic layers of the transformer architecture used to compute future tokens. Similar approaches have shown progress for learning features in language modeling [Raf+20b], however alternative objectives, based on masked training (as in BERT, [Dev+19]), often leads to better performance.

32.3.2.3　Autoencoders

A related set of methods for representation learning are based on learning a representation from which the original data can be reconstructed. These methods are often called **autoencoders** (see Section 16.3.3), as the data is encoded in a way such that the input data itself can be recreated. However, unlike generative models, they cannot typically be used to synthesize observations from scratch or assign likelihoods to observations. Autoencoders learn an encoder that outputs a representation $z = f_\theta(x)$, and a decoder $g_\phi(z)$ that takes the representation z and tries to recreate the input data, x. The quality of the approximate reconstruction , $\hat{x} = g_\phi(z)$ is often measured using a domain-specific loss, for example mean-squared error for images:

$$\mathcal{L}(\theta, \phi) = \frac{1}{|\mathcal{D}|} \sum_{x \in \mathcal{D}} \|x - g_\phi(f_\theta(x))\|_2^2. \tag{32.13}$$

If there are no constraints on the encoder or decoder, and the dimensionality of the representation z matches the dimensionality of the input x, then there exists a trivial solution to minimize the autoencoding objective: set both f_θ and g_ϕ to identity functions. In this case the representation has not learned anything interesting, and thus in practice an additional regularizer is often placed on the learned representation.

Reducing the dimensionality of the representation z is one effective mechanism to avoid trivial solutions to the autoencoding objective. If both the encoder and decoder networks are linear, and the loss is mean-squared-error, then the resulting linear autoencoder model can learn the principal components of a dataset [Pla18].

Other methods maintain higher-dimensional representations by adding sparsity (for example, penalties on $\|z\|_1$ in Ng et al. [Ng+11]) or smoothness regularizers [Rif+11], or adding noise to the input [Vin+08] or intermediate layers of the network [Sri+14b; PSDG14]. These added regularizers aim to bias the encoder and decoder to learn representations that are not just the identity function, but instead are nonlinear transformations of the input that may be useful for downstream tasks. See Bengio, Courville, and Vincent [BCV13] for a more detailed discussion of regularized autoencoders and their applications. A recent re-evaluation of several algorithms based on iteratively learning features by stacked regularized autoencoders have been shown to degrade performance versus training end-to-end from scratch [Pai+14]. However, we will see in Section 32.3.3.1 that denoising autoencoders have shown promise for representation learning in discrete domains and when applied with more complex noise and masking patterns.

32.3.2.4 Challenges in generative representation learning

Despite several success in generative representation learning, they have empirically fallen behind. Generative methods for representation learning have to learn to match complex high-dimensional and diverse training datasets, which requires modeling all axis of variation of the inputs, regardless of whether they are semantically relevant for downstream tasks. For example, the exact pattern of blades of grass in an image matter for generation quality, but are unlikely to be useful for many of the semantic evaluations that are typically used. Ways to bias generative models to focus on the semantic features and ignore "noise" in the input is an open area of research.

32.3.3 Self-supervised representation learning

When given large amounts of labeled data, standard supervised learning is a powerful mechanism for training deep neural networks. When only presented with unlabeled data, building generative models requires modeling all variations in a dataset, and is often not explicit about what is the signal and noise that we aim to capture in a representation. The methods and architectures for building these generative models also differs substantially from those of supervised learning, where largely feedforward architectures are used to predict low-dimensional representations. Instead of trying to model all aspects of variation, self-supervised learning aims to design tasks where labels can be generated cheaply, and help to encode the structure of what we may care about for other downstream tasks. Self-supervised learning methods allow us to apply the tools and techniques of supervised learning to unlabeled data by designing a task for which we can cheaply produce labels.

In the image domain, several self-supervised tasks, also known as **pretext tasks**, have been proven effective for learning representations. Models are trained to perform these tasks in a supervised fashion using data generated by the pretext task, and then the learned representation is transferred to a target task of interest (such as object recognition), by training a linear classifier or fine-tuning the model in a supervised fashion.

32.3.3.1   Denoising and masked prediction

Generative representation learning is challenging because generative models must learn to produce the entire data distribution. A simpler option is *denoising*, in which some variety of noise is added to the input and the model is trained to reconstruct the noiseless input. A particularly successful variant of denoising is *masked prediction*, in which input patches or tokens are replaced with uninformative masks and the network is trained to predict only these missing patches or tokens.

The **denoising autoencoder** [Vin+08; Vin+10a] was the first deep model to exploit denoising for representation learning. A denoising autoencoder resembles a standard autoencoder architecturally, but it is trained to perform a different task. Whereas a standard autoencoder attempts to reconstruct its input exactly, a denoising autoencoder attempts to produce a noiseless output from a noisy input. Vincent et al. [Vin+08] argue that the network must learn the structure of the data manifold in order to solve the denoising task.

Newer approaches retain the conceptual approach of the denoising autoencoder, but adjust the masking strategy and objective. **BERT** [Dev+18] introduced the **masked language modeling** task, where 15% of the input tokens are selected for masking and the network is trained to predict them. 80% of the time, these tokens are replaced with an uninformative [MASK] token. However, the [MASK] token does not appear at fine-tuning time, producing some domain shift between pretraining and fine-tuning. Thus, 10% of the time, tokens are replaced with random tokens, and 10% of the time, they are left intact. BERT and the masked language modeling task have been extremely influential for representation learning in natural language processing, inspiring substantial follow-up work [Liu+19c; Jos+20].

Although denoising-based approaches to representation learning were first employed for computer vision, they received little attention for the decade that followed. Vincent et al. [Vin+08] greedily trained stacks of up to three denoising autoencoders that were then fine-tuned end-to-end to perform digit classification, but greedy unsupervised pretraining was abandoned as it was shown that it was possible to attain good performance using CNNs and other architectures trained end-to-end. Context encoders [Pat+16] mask contiguous image regions and train models to perform inpainting, achieving transfer learning performance competitive with other contemporary unsupervised visual representation learning methods. The use of image colorization as a pretext task [ZIE16; ZIE17] is also related to denoising in that colorization involves reconstructing the original image from a corrupted input, although generally color is dropped in a deterministic fashion rather than stochastically.

Recently, the success of BERT in NLP has inspired new approaches to visual representation learning based on masked prediction. Image GPT [Che+20a] trained a transformer directly upon pixels to perform a BERT-style masked image modeling task. While the resulting model achieves very high accuracy when fine-tuned CIFAR-10, the cost of self-attention is quadratic in the number of pixels,

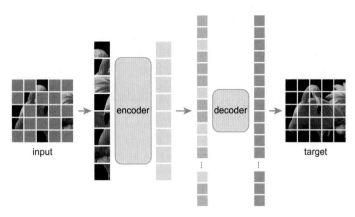

Figure 32.3: Masked autoencoders learn a representation of images by randomly masking out input patches and trying to predict them (from He et al. [He+21]).

limiting applicability to larger image sizes. **BEiT** [Bao+22b] addresses this challenge by combining the idea of masked image modeling with the patch-based architecture of vision transformers [Dos+21]. BEiT splits images into 16×16 pixel image patches and then discretizes these patches using a discrete VAE [Ram+21b]. At training time, 40% of tokens are masked. The network receives continuous patches as input and is trained to predict the discretized missing tokens using a softmax over all possible tokens.

The **masked autoencoder** or **MAE** [He+22] further simplifies the masked image modeling task (see Figure 32.3). The MAE eliminates the need to discretize patches and instead predicts the constituent pixels of each patch directly using a shallow decoder trained with L_2 loss. Because the MAE encoder operates only on the unmasked tokens, it can be trained efficiently even while masking most (75%) of the tokens. Models pretrained using masked prediction and then fine-tuned with labels currently hold the top positions on the ImageNet leaderboard among models trained without additional data [He+22; Don+21].

32.3.3.2 Transformation prediction

An even simpler approach to representation learning involves applying a transformation to the input image and then predicting the transformation that was applied (see Figure 32.4). This prediction task is usually formulated as a classification problem. For visual representation learning, transformation prediction is appealing because it allows reusing exactly the same training pipelines as standard supervised image classification. However, it is not clear that networks trained to perform transformation prediction tasks learn rich visual representations. Transformation prediction tasks are potentially susceptible to "shortcut" solutions, where networks learn trivial features that are nonetheless sufficient to solve the task with high accuracy. For many years, self-supervised learning methods based on transformation prediction were among the top-performing methods, but they have since been displaced by newer methods based on contrastive learning and masked prediction.

Some pretext tasks operate by cutting images into patches and training networks to recover the spatial arrangement of the patches. In context prediction [DGE15], a network receives two adjacent

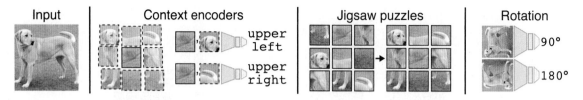

Figure 32.4: Transformation prediction involves training neural networks to predict a transformation applied to the input. Context encoders predict the position of a second crop relative to the first. The jigsaw puzzle task involves predicting the way in which patches have been permuted. Rotation prediction involves predicting the rotation that was applied to the input.

image patches as input and is trained to recover their spatial relationship by performing an eight-class classification problem. To prevent the network from directly matching the pixels at the patch borders, the two patches must be separated by a small variable gap. In addition, to prevent networks from using chromatic aberration to localize the patches relative to the lens, color channels must be distorted or stochastically dropped. Other work has trained networks to solve jigsaw puzzles by splitting images into a 3×3 grid of patches [NF16]. The network receives shuffled patches as input and learns to predict how they were permuted. By limiting the permutations to a subset of all possibilities, the jigsaw puzzle task can be formulated as a standard classification task [NF16].

Another widely used pretext task is rotation prediction [GSK18], where input images are rotated 0, 90, 180, or 270 degrees and networks are trained to classify which rotation was applied. Although this task is extremely simple, the learned representations often perform better than those learned using patch-based methods [GSK18; KZB19]. However, all approaches based on transformation prediction currently underperform masked prediction and multiview approaches on standard benchmark datasets such as CIFAR-10 and ImageNet.

32.3.4 Multiview representation learning

The field of **multiview representation learning** aims to learn a representation where "similar" inputs or *views* of an input are mapped nearby in the representation space, and "dissimilar" inputs are mapped further apart. This representation space is often high-dimensional, and relies on collecting data or designing a task where one can generative "positive" pairs of examples that are similar, and "negative" pairs of examples that are dissimilar. There are many motivations and objectives for multiview representation learning, but all rely on coming up with sets of positive pairs, and a mechanism to prevent all representations from collapsing to the same point. Here we use the term multiview representation learning to encompass **contrastive learning** which combines positive and negative pairs, metric learning, and "non-contrastive" learning which eliminates the need for negative pairs.

Unlike generative methods for representation learning, multiview representation learning makes it easy to incorporate prior knowledge about what inputs should be closer in the embedding space. Furthermore, these inputs need not be from the same modality, and thus multiview representation learning can be applied with rich multimodal datasets. The simplicity of the way in which prior knowledge can be incorporated into a model through data has made multiview representation learning one of the most powerful and performant methods for learning representations.

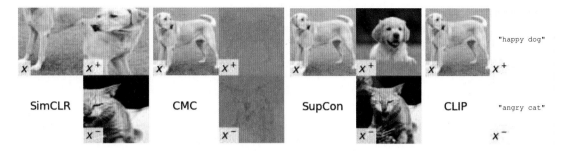

Figure 32.5: Positive and negative pairs used by different multiview representation learning methods.

While there are a variety of methods for multiview representation learning, they all involve a repulsion component that pulls positive pairs closer together in embedding space, and a mechanism to prevent collapse of the representation to a single point in embedding space. We begin by describing loss functions for multiview representation learning and how they combine attractive and repulsive terms to shape the representation, then discuss the role of view generation, and finally practical considerations in deploying multiview representation learning.

32.3.4.1 View selection

Multiview representation learning depends on a datapoint or "anchor" x, a positive example x^+ that x will be attracted to, and zero or more negative examples x^- that x is repelled from. We assume access to a data-generating process for the positive pair: $p^+(x, x^+)$, and a process that generates the negative examples given the datapoint x: $p^-(x^-|x)$. Typically $p^+(x, x^+)$ generate (x, x^+) that are different augmentations of an underlying image from the dataset, and x^- represents an augmented view of a different random image from the dataset. The generative process for x^- is then independent of x, i.e., $p^-(x^-|x) = p^-(x^-)$.

The choice of views used to generate positive and negative pairs is critical to the success of representation learning. Figure 32.5 shows the positive pair (x, x^+) and negative x^- for several methods which we discuss below: SimCLR, CMC, SupCon, and CLIP.

SimCLR [Che+20c] creates positive pairs by applying two different data augmentations defined by transformations t and t' to an initial image x_0 twice: $x = t(x_0), x^+ = t(x_0)$. The data augmentations used are random crops (with horizontal flips and resize), color distortion, and Gaussian blur. The strengths of these augmentations (e.g., the amount of blur) impact performance and are typically treated as a hyperparameter.

If we access to additional information, such as a categorical label, we can use this to select positive pairs with the same label, and negative pairs with different labels. The resulting objective, when used with a contrastive loss, is called **SupCon** [Kho+20], and resembles neighborhood component analysis [Gol+04]. It was shown to improve robustness when compared to standard supervised learning.

Contrastive multiview coding (CMC) [TKI20] generates views by splitting an initial image into orthogonal dimensions, such as the luma and chroma dimensions. These views are now no longer in the same space (or same dimensionality), and thus we must learn different encoders for the different inputs. However, the output of these encoders all live in the same-dimensional embedding space, and can be used in contrastive losses. At test-time, we can then combine embeddings from these different views through averaging or concatenation.

Views do not need to be from the same modality. **CLIP** [Rad+21] uses contrastive learning on image-text pairs, where x is an image, and x^+ and x^- are text descriptions. When applied to massive datasets of image-text pairs scraped from the Internet, CLIP is able to learn robust representations without any of the additional data augmentation needed by SimCLR or other image-only contrastive methods.

In most contrastive methods, negative examples are selected by randomly choosing x^+ from other elements in a minibatch. However, if the batch size is small it may be the case that none of the negative examples are close in embedding space to the positive example, and so learning may be slow. Instead of randomly choosing negatives, they may be chosen more intelligently through **hard negative mining** that selects negative examples that are close to the positive example in embedding space [Fag+18]. This typically requires maintaining and updating a database of negative examples over the course of training; this incurs enough computational overhead that the technique is infrequently used. However, reweighting examples within a minibatch can also lead to improved performance [Rob+21].

The choice of positive and negative views directly impacts what features are learned and what invariances are encouraged. Tian et al. [Tia+20] discusses the role of view selection on the learned representations, showing how choosing positives based on shared attributes (as in SupCon) can lead to learning those attributes or ignoring them. They also present a method for learning views (whereas all prior approaches fix views) based on targeting a "sweet spot" in the level of mutual information between the views that is neither too high or too low. However, understanding what views will work well for what downstream tasks remains an open area of study.

32.3.4.2 Contrastive losses

Given p^+ and p^-, we seek loss functions that learn an embedding $f_\theta(x)$ where x and x^+ are close in the embedding space, while x and x^- are far apart. This is called **metric learning**.

Chopra, Hadsell, LeCun, et al. [CHL+05] present a family of objectives that implements this intuition by enforcing the distance between negative pairs to always be at least ϵ bigger than the distance between positive pairs. The contrastive loss as instantiated in [HCL06] is:

$$\mathcal{L}_{\text{contrastive}} = \mathbb{E}_{x,x^+,x^-} \left[\|f_\theta(x) - f_\theta(x^+)\|^2 + \max(0, \epsilon - \|f_\theta(x) - f_\theta(x^-)\|^2) \right]. \tag{32.14}$$

This loss pulls together the positive pairs by making the squared ℓ_2 distance between them small, and tries to ensure that negative pairs are at least a distance of ϵ apart. One challenge with using the contrastive loss in practice is tuning the hyperparameter ϵ.

Similarly, the **triplet loss** [SKP15] tries to ensure that the positive pair (x, x^+) is always at least some distance ϵ closer to each other than the negative pair (x, x^-):

$$\mathcal{L}_{\text{triplet}} = \mathbb{E}_{x,x^+,x^-} \left[\max(0, \|f_\theta(x) - f_\theta(x^+)\|^2 - \|f_\theta(x) - f_\theta(x^-)\|^2 + \epsilon) \right]. \tag{32.15}$$

A downside to the triplet loss approach is that one has to be careful about choosing hard negatives: if the negative pair is already sufficiently far away then the objective function is zero and no learning occurs.

An alternative contrastive loss which has gained popularity due to its lack of hyperparameters and empirical effectiveness is known as the **InfoNCE loss** [OLV18b] or the **multiclass N-pair loss**

[Soh16]:

$$\mathcal{L}_{\text{InfoNCE}} = -\mathbb{E}_{x,x^+,x_{1:M}^-} \left[\log \frac{\exp f_\theta(x)^T g_\phi(x^+)}{\exp f_\theta(x)^T g_\phi(x^+) + \sum_{i=1}^M \exp f_\theta(x)^T g_\phi(x_i^-)} \right], \tag{32.16}$$

where M are the number of negative examples. Typically the embeddings $f(x)$ and $g(x')$ are ℓ_2-normalized, and an additional hyperparameter τ can be introduced to rescale the inner products [Che+20c]. Unlike the triplet loss, which uses a hard threshold of ϵ, $\mathcal{L}_{\text{InfoNCE}}$ can always be improved by pushing negative examples further away. Intuitively, the InfoNCE loss ensures that the positive pair is closer together than any of the M negative pairs in the minibatch. The InfoNCE loss can be related to a lower bound on the mutual information between the input x and the learned representation z [OLV18b; Poo+19a]:

$$I(X; Z) \geq \log M - \mathcal{L}_{\text{InfoNCE}}, \tag{32.17}$$

and has also been motivated as a way of learning representations through the InfoMax principle [OLV18b; Hje+18; BHB19]. When applying the InfoNCE loss to parallel views that are the same modality and dimension, the encoder f_θ for the anchor x and the positive and negative examples g_ϕ can be shared.

32.3.4.3 Negative-free losses

Negative-free representation learning (sometimes called **non-contrastive representation learning**) learns representations using only positive pairs, without explicitly constructing negative pairs. Whereas contrastive methods prevent collapse by enforcing that positive pairs are closer together than negative pairs, negative-free methods make use of other mechanisms. One class of negative-free objectives includes both attractive terms and terms that prevent collapse. Another class of methods uses objectives that include only attractive terms, and instead relies on the learning dynamics to prevent collapse.

The **Barlow Twins** loss [Zbo+21] is

$$\mathcal{L}_{\text{BT}} = \sum_{i=1}^p (1 - C_{ii})^2 + \lambda \sum_{i=1}^p \sum_{j \neq i} C_{ij}^2 \tag{32.18}$$

where C is the cross-correlation matrix between two batches of features that arise from the two views. The first term is an attractive term that encourages high similarity between the representations of the two views, whereas the second term prevents collapse to a low-rank representation. The loss is minimized when C is the identity matrix. Similar losses based on ensuring the variance of features being non-zero have also been useful for preventing collapse [BPL21b]. The Barlow Twins loss can be related to kernel-based independence criterion such as HSIC which have also been useful as losses for representation learning [Li+21; Tsa+21].

BYOL (bootstrap your own latents) [Gri+20] and SimSiam [Che+20c] simply minimize the mean squared error between two representations:

$$\mathcal{L}_{\text{BYOL}} = \mathbb{E}_{\boldsymbol{x},\boldsymbol{x}^+} \left[\|g_\phi(f_\theta(\boldsymbol{x})) - f_{\theta'}(\boldsymbol{x}^+)\|^2 \right]. \tag{32.19}$$

Following Grill et al. [Gri+20], g_ϕ is known as the *predictor*, f_θ is the *online network*, and $f_{\theta'}$ is the *target network*. When optimizing this loss function, weights are backpropagated to update ϕ and θ, but optimizing θ' directly leads the representation to collapse [Che+20c]. Instead, BYOL sets θ' as an exponential moving average of θ, and SimSiam sets $\theta' \leftarrow \theta$ at each iteration of training. The reasons why BYOL and SimSiam avoid collapse are not entirely clear, but Tian, Chen, and Ganguli [TCG21] analyze the gradient flow dynamics of a simplified linear BYOL model and show that collapse can indeed be avoided given properly set hyperparameters.

DINO (self-distillation with no labels) [Car+21] is another non-contrastive loss that relies on the dynamics of learning to avoid collapse. Like BYOL, DINO uses a loss that consists only of an attractive term between an online network and a target network formed by an exponential moving average of the online network weights. Unlike BYOL, DINO uses a cross-entropy loss where the target network produces the targets for the online network, and avoids the need for a predictor network. The DINO loss is:

$$\mathcal{L}_{\text{DINO}} = \mathbb{E}_{\boldsymbol{x},\boldsymbol{x}^+} \left[H(f_{\theta'}(\boldsymbol{x})/\tau, \text{center}(f_\theta(\boldsymbol{x}^+))/\tau') \right]. \tag{32.20}$$

where, with some abuse of notation, center is a mean-centering operation applied across the minibatch that contains x^+. Centering the output of the target network is necessary to prevent collapse to a single "class", whereas using a lower temperature $\tau' < \tau$ for the target network is necessary to prevent collapse to a uniform distribution. The DINO loss provides marginal gains over the BYOL loss when performing self-supervised representation learning with vision transformers on ImageNet [Car+21].

32.3.4.4 Tricks of the trade

Beyond view selection and losses, there are a number of useful architectures and modifications that enable more effective multiview representation learning.

Normalizing the output of the encoders and computing cosine similarity instead of predicting unconstrained representations has shown to improve performance [Che+20c]. This normalization bounds the similarity between points between -1 and 1, so an additional temperature parameter τ is typically introduced and fixed or annealed over the course of learning.

While the learned representation with multiview learning are often useful for downstream tasks, the losses when combined with data augmentation typically lead to too much invariance for some tasks. Instead, one can extract an earlier layer in the encoder as the representation, or alternatively, add an additional layer known as a projection head to the encoder before computing the loss [Che+20c]. When training we compute the loss on the output of the projection head, but when evaluating the quality of the representation we discard this additional layer.

Given the summation over negative examples in the denominator of the InfoNCE loss, it is often sensitive to the batch size used for training. In practice, large batch sizes of 4096 or more are needed to achieve good performance with this loss, which can be computationally burdensome. **MoCo** (momentum contrast) [He+20] introduced a memory queue to store negative examples from previous minibatches to expand the size of negatives at each iteration. Additionally, they use a momentum encoder, where the encoder for the positive and negative examples uses an exponential moving average of the anchor encoder parameters. This momentum encoder approach was also found useful in BYOL to prevent collapse. As in BYOL, adding an extra predictor network that maps from the online network to the target network has shown to improve the performance of MoCo, and removes the requirement of a memory queue [CXH21].

The backbone architectures of the encoder networks play a large role in the quality of representations. For representation learning in vision, recent work has switched from ConvNet-based backbones to vision transformers, resulting in larger-scale models with improved performance on several downstream tasks [CXH21].

32.4 Theory of representation learning

While deep representation learning has replaced hand-designed features for most applications, the theory behind what features are learned and what guarantees these methods provide are limited. Here we review several theoretical directions in understanding representation learning: identifiability, information maximization, and transfer bounds.

32.4.1 Identifiability

In this section, we assume a latent-variable generative model that generated the data, where $z \sim p(z)$ are the latent variables, and $x = g(z)$ is a deterministic generator that maps from the latent variables to observations. Our goal is to learn a representation $h = f_\theta(x)$ that inverts the generative model and recovers $h = z$. If we can do this, we say the model is **identifiable**. Oftentimes we are not able to recover the true latent variables exactly, for example the dimensions of the latent variables may be permuted, or individual dimensions may be transformed version of an underlying latent variable: $h_i = f_i(z_i)$. Thus most theoretical work on identifiability focuses on the case of learning a representation that can be permuted and elementwise transformed to match the true latent variables. Such representations are referred to as **disentangled** as the dimensions of the learned representation do not mix together multiple dimensions of the true latent variables.

Methods for recovering are typically based around latent-variable models such as VAEs combined with various regularizers (see Section 21.3.1.1). While several publications showed promising empirical progress, a large-scale study by Locatello et al. [Loc+20a] on disentangled representation learning methods showed that several existing approaches cannot work without additional assumptions on the data or model. Their argument relies on the observation that we can form a bijection f that takes samples from a factorial prior $p(z) = \prod_i p_i(z_i)$ and maps to $z' = f(z)$ that (1) preservers the marginal distribution, and (2) has entirely entangled latents (each dimension of z influences every dimension of z'). Transforming the marginal in this way changes the representation, but preserves the marginal likelihood of the data, and thus one cannot use marginal likelihood alone to identify or distinguish between the entangled and disentangled model. Empirically, they show that past methods largely succeeded due to careful hyperparameter selection on the target disentanglement metrics that require supervised labels. While further work has developed unsupervised methods for hyperparameter that address several of these issues [Dua+20], at this point there are no known robust methods for learning disentangled representations without further assumptions.

To address the empirical and theoretical gap in learning disentangled representations, several papers have proposed using additional sources of information in the form of weakly-labeled data to provide guarantees. In theoretical work on nonlinear ICA [RMK21; Khe+20; Häl+21], this information comes in the form of additional observations for each datapoint that are related to the underlying latent variable through an exponential family. Work on **causal representation learning** has expanded the applicability of these methods and highlighted the settings where such strong assumptions on weakly-labeled data may be attainable [Sch+21c; WJ21; Rei+22]

Alternatively, one can assume access to pairs of observations where the relationship between latent variables is known. In Shu et al. [Shu+19b], they show that one can provably learn a disentangled representation of data when given access to pairs of data where only one of the latent variables is changed at a time. In real world datasets, having access to pairs of data like this is challenging, as not all the latent-variables of the model may be under the control of the data collector, and covering the full space of settings of the latent variable may be prohibitively expensive. Locatello et al. [Loc+20b] develops this method further but leverages a heuristic to detect which latent variable has changed, and shows this performs empirically well, and under some restricted settings may lead to learning disentangled representations.

More recently, [Kiv+21; Kiv+22] showed that it is possible to identify deep latent variable models, such as VAEs, without any side information, provided the latent space prior has the form of a mixture.

32.4.2   Information maximization

When learning representations of an input x, one desideratum is to preserve as much information about x as possible. Any information we discard cannot be recovered, and if that information is useful for a downstream task then performance will decrease. Early work on understanding biological learning by Linsker [Lin88c] and Bell and Sejnowski [BS95b] argued that information maximization or **InfoMax** is a good learning principle for biological systems as it enables the downstream processing systems access to as much sensory input as possible. However, these biological systems aim to communicate information subject to strong constraints, and these constraints can likely be tuned over time by evolution to sculpt the kinds of representations that are learned.

When applying information maximization to neural networks, we are often able to realize trivial solutions which biological systems may not face: being able to losslessly copy the input. Information theory does not "color" the bits, it does not tell us which bits of an input are more important than others. Simply sending the image losslessly maximizes information, but does not provide a transformation of the input that can improve performance according to the metrics in Section 32.2. Architectural and optimization constraints can guide the bits we learn and the bits we dispose of, but we can also leverage additional sources of information, for example labels, to identify which bits to extract.

The **information bottleneck** method (Section 5.6) aims to learn representations Z of an input X that are predictive of another observed variable Y, while being as compressed as possible. The observed variable Y guides the bits learned in the representation Z towards those that are predictive, and penalizes content that does not predict Y. We can formalize the information bottleneck as an optimization problem [TPB00]:

$$\text{maximize}_\theta I(Z; Y) - \beta I(X; Z). \tag{32.21}$$

Estimating mutual information in high dimensions is challenging, but we can form variational bounds on mutual information that are amenable to optimization with modern neural networks, such as variational information bottleneck (VIB, see Section 5.6.2). Approaches built on VIB have shown improved robustness to adversarial examples and natural variations [FA20].

Unlike information bottleneck methods, many recent approaches motivated by InfoMax have no explicit compression objective [Hje+18; BHB19; OLV18b]. They aim to maximize information subject to constraints, but without any explicit penalty on the information contained in the representation.

In spite of the appeal of explaining representation learning with information theory, there are a number of challenges. One of the greatest challenges in applying information theory to understand the content in learned representations is that most learned representations have determinstic encoders, $z = f_\theta(x)$ that map from a continuous input x to a continuous representation z. These mappings can typically preserve infinite information about the input. As mutual information estimators scale poorly with the true mutual information, estimating MI in this setting is difficult and typically results in weak lower bounds.

In the absence of constraints, maximizing information between an input and a learned representation has trivial solutions that do not result in any interesting transformation of the input. For example, the identity mapping $z = x$ maximizes information but does not alter the input. Tschannen et al. [Tsc+19] show that for invertible networks where the true mutual information between the input and representation is infinite, maximizing estimators of mutual information can result in meaningful learned represenations. This highlights that the geometric dependence and bias of these estimators may have more to do with their success for representation learning than the information itself (as it is infinite throughout training).

There have been several proposed methods for learning stochastic representations that constrain the amount of information in learned representations [Ale+17]. However, these approaches have not yet resulted in improved performance on most downstream tasks. Fischer and Alemi [FA20] shows that constraining information can improve robustness on some benchmarks, but scaling up models and datasets with determinstic representations currently presents the best results [Rad+21]. More work is needed to identify whether constraining information can improve learned representations.

33 Interpretability

This chapter is written by Been Kim and Finale Doshi-Velez.

33.1 Introduction

As machine learning models become increasingly commonplace, there exists increasing pressure to ensure that these models' behaviors align with our values and expectations. It is essential that models that automate even mundane tasks (e.g., processing paperwork, flagging potential fraud) do not harm their users or society at large. Models with large impacts on health and welfare (e.g., recommending treatment, driving autonomously) must not only be safe but often also function collaboratively with their users.

However, determining whether a model is harmful is not easy. Specific performance metrics may be too narrowly focused—e.g., just because an autonomous car stays in lane does not mean it is safe. Indeed, the narrow objectives used in common decision formalisms such as Bayesian decision theory (Section 34.1), multi-step decision problems (Chapter 34), and reinforcement learning (Chapter 35) can often be easily exploited (e.g.,, reward hacking). Incomplete sets of metrics also result in models that learn shortcuts that do not generalize to new situations (e.g., [Gei+20b]). Even when one knows the desired metrics, those metrics can be hard to estimate with limited data or a distribution shift (Chapter 19). Finally, normative concepts, such as fairness, may be impossible to fully formalize. As a result, not only may unexpected and irreversible harms occur (e.g., an adverse drug reaction) but more subtle harms may go unnoticed until sufficient reporting data accrues [Amo+16].

Interpretability allows human experts to inspect a model. Alongside traditional statistical measures of performance, this human inspection can help expose issues and thus mitigate potential harms. Exposing the workings of a model can also help people identify ways to incorporate information they have into a final decision. More broadly, even when we are satisfied with a model's performance, we may be interested in understanding *why* they work to gain scientific and operational insights. For example, one might gain insights in language structure by asking why a language model performs so well; understanding why patient data cluster along particular axes may result in a better understanding of disease and the common treatment pathways. Ultimately, interpretation helps humans to communicate better with machines to accomplish our tasks better.

In this chapter, we lay out the role and terminologies in interpretable ML before introducing methods, properties, and evaluation of interpretability methods.

33.1.1   The role of interpretability: unknowns and under-specifications

As noted above, ensuring that models behave as desired is challenging. In some cases, the desired behavior can be guaranteed by design, such as certain notions of privacy via differentially-private learning algorithms or some chosen mathematical metric of fairness. In other cases, tracking various metrics, such as adverse events or subgroup error rates, may be the appropriate and sufficient way to identify concerns. Much of this textbook deals with uncertainty quantification: basic models in Chapter 3, Bayesian neural networks in Chapter 17, Gaussian processes in Chapter 18). When well-calibrated uncertainties can be computed, they may provide sufficient warning that a model's output may be suspect.

However, in many cases, the ultimate goal may be fundamentally impossible to fully specify and thus formalize. For example, Section 20.4.8 discusses the challenge of evaluating the quality of samples from a generative model. In such cases, human inspection of the machine learning model may be necessary. Below we describe several examples.

Blindspot discovery. Inspection may reveal **blindspots** in our modeling, objective, or data [Bad+18; Zec+18b; Gur+18]. For example, suppose a company has trained a machine learning system for credit scoring. The model was trained on a relatively affluent, middle-aged population, and now the company is considering using it on a different, college-aged population. Suppose that inspection of the model reveals that it relies heavily on the applicant's mortgage payments. Not only might this suggest that the model might not transfer well to the college population, but it might encourage us to check for bias in the existing application because we know historical biases have prevented certain populations from achieving home ownership (something that a purely quantitative definition of fairness may not be able to recognize). Indeed, the most common application of interpretability in industry settings is for engineers to debug models and make deployment decisions [Pai].

Novel insights. Inspection may catalyze the discovery of **novel insights.** For example, suppose an algorithm determines that surgical procedures fall into three clusters. The surgeries in one of the clusters of patients seem to consistently take longer than expected. A human inspecting these clusters may determine that a common factor in the cluster with the delays is that those surgeries occur in a different part of the hospital, a feature not in the original dataset. This insight may result in ideas to improve on-time surgery performance.

Human+ML teaming. Inspection may empower effective **human+ML interaction and teaming**. For example, suppose an anxiety treatment recommendation algorithm reveals the patient's comorbid insomnia constrained its recommendations. If the patient reports that they no longer have trouble sleeping, the algorithm could be re-run with that constraint removed to get additional treatment options. More broadly, inspection can reveal places where people may wish to adjust the model, such as correcting an incorrect input or assumption. It can also help people use only part of a model in their own decision-making, such as using a model's computation of which treatments unsafe vs. which treatments are best. In these ways, the human+ML team may be able to produce better combined performance than either alone (e.g., [Ame+19; Kam16]).

Individual-level recourse. Inspection can help determine whether a specific harm or error happened in a specific context. For example, if a loan applicant knows what features were used to deny them a loan, they have a starting point to argue that an error might have been made, or that the algorithm denied them unjustly. For this reason, inspectability is sometimes a legal requirement [Zer+19; GF17; Cou16].

As we look at the examples above, we see that one common element is that *interpretability is needed when we need to combine human insights with the ML algorithm to achieve the ultimate goal.*[1] However, looking at the list above also emphasizes that beyond this very basic commonality, *each application and task represents very different needs.* A scientist seeking to glean insights from a clustering on molecules may be interested in global patterns — such as all molecules with certain loop structures are more stable — and be willing to spend hours puzzling over a model's outputs. In contrast, a clinician seeking to make a specific treatment decision may only care about aspects of the model relevant to the specific patient; they must also reach their decision within the time-pressure of an office visit. This brings us to our most important point: the best form of explanation depends on the *context*; interpretability is a means to an end.

33.1.2 Terminology and framework

In broad strokes, "to interpret means to explain or present in understandable terms" [Mer]. Understanding, in turn, involves an alignment of mental models. In interpretable machine learning, that alignment is between what (perhaps part of) the machine learning model is doing and what the user thinks the model is doing.

As a result, interpretable machine learning ecosystem includes not only standard machine learning (e.g., a prediction task) but also what information is provided to the human user, in what context, and the user's ultimate goal. The broader *socio-technical system* — the collection of interactions between human, social, organizational, and technical (hardware and software) factors — cannot be ignored [Sel+19]. The goal of interpretable machine learning is to help a user do *their* task, with *their* cognitive strengths and weaknesses, with *their* focus and distractions [Mil19]. Below we define the key terms of this expanded ecosystem and describe how they relate to each other. Before continuing, however, we note that the field of interpretable machine learning is relatively new, and a consensus around terminology is still evolving. Thus, it is always important to define terms.

Two core **social** or **human factors** elements in interpretable machine learning are the *context* and the *end-task*.

Context. We use the term *context* to describe the setting in which an interpretable machine learning system will be used. Who is the user? What information do they have? What constraints are present on their time, cognition, or attention? We will use the terms context and application interchangeably [Sta].

End-task. We use the term *end-task* to refer to the user's ultimate goal. What are they ultimately trying to achieve? We will use the terms end-task and downstream tasks interchangeably.

Three core **technical** elements in interpretable machine learning are the *method*, the *metrics*, and the *properties* of the methods.

---

1. We emphasize that interpretability is different from manipulation or persuasion, where the goal is to intentionally deceive or convince users of a predetermined choice.

Method. How do we does the interpretability happen? We use the term *explanation* to mean the output provided by the method to the user: interpretable machine learning *methods* provide *explanations* to the users. If the explanation is the model itself, we call the method *inherently interpretable* or *interpretable by design*. In other cases, the model may be too complex for a human to inspect it in its entirety: perhaps it is a large neural network that no human could expect to comprehend; perhaps it is a medium-sized decision tree that could be inspected if one had twenty minutes but not if one needs to make a decision in two minutes. In such cases, the explanation may be a *partial view* of the model, one that is ideally suited for performing the end-task in the given context. Finally, we note that even inherently interpretable models do not reveal everything: one might be able to fully inspect the function (e.g., a two-node decision tree) but not know what data it was trained on or which datapoints were most influential.

Metrics. How is the interpretability method evaluated? Evaluation is one of the most essential and challenging aspects of interpretable machine learning, because we are interested in the **end-task** performance of the *human*, when explanation is provided. We call this the *downstream performance*. Just as different goals in ML require different metrics (e.g., positive predictive value, log likelihood, AUC), different **contexts** and **end-tasks** will have different metrics. For example, the model with the best predictive performance (e.g., log likelihood loss) may not be the model that results in the best downstream performance.

Properties. What characteristics does the explanation have in relation to the model, the context and the end-tasks? Different **contexts** and different **end-tasks** might require different properties. For example, suppose that an explanation is being used to identify ways in which a denied loan applicant could improve their application. Then, it may be important that the explanation only include factors that, if changed, would change the outcome. In contrast, suppose the explanation is being used to determine if the denial was fair. Then, it may be important that the explanation does not leave out any relevant factors. In this way, properties serve as a glue between interpretability methods, contexts and end-tasks: properties allow us to specify and quantify aspects of the explanation relevant to our ultimate end-task goals. Then we can make sure that our interpretability method has those properties.

How they all relate. Formulating an interpretable machine learning problem generally starts by specifying the context and the end-task. Together the context and the end-task imply what metrics are appropriate to evaluate the downstream performance on the end-task and suggest what properties will be important in the explanation. Meanwhile, the context also determines the data and training metric for the ML model. The appropriate choice of explanation methods will depend on the model and properties desired, and it will be evaluated with respect to the end-task metric to determine the downstream performance. Figure 33.1 shows these relationships.

Interpretable machine learning involves many challenges, from computing explanations and optimizing interpretable models and creating explanations with certain properties to understanding the associated human factors. That said, the grand challenge is to (1) understand what properties are needed for different contexts and end-tasks and (2) identify and create interpretable machxine learning methods that have those properties.

A simple example In the following sections, we will expand upon methods for interpretability,

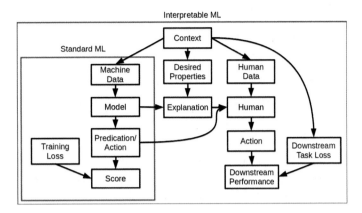

Figure 33.1: The interpretable machine learning ecosystem. While standard machine learning can often abstract away elements of the context and consider only the process of learning models given a data distribution and a loss, interpretable machine is inextricably tied to a socio-technical context.

metrics for evaluation, and types of properties. First, however, we provide a simple example connecting all of the concepts we discussed above.

Suppose our *context* is that we have a lemonade stand, and our *end-task* is to understand when the stand is most successful in order to prioritize which days it is worth setting it up. (We have heard that sometimes machine learning models latch on to incorrect mechanisms and want to check the model before using it to inform our business strategy.) Our *metric* for the downstream performance is whether we correctly determine if the model can be trusted; this could be quantified as the amount of profit that we make by opening on busy days and being closed on quiet days.

To train our model, we collect data on two input features — the average temperature for the day (measured in degrees Fahrenheit) and the cleanliness of the sidewalk near our stand (measured as a proportion of the sidewalk that is free of litter, between 0 and 1) — and the output feature of whether the day was profitable. Two models seem to fit the data approximately equally well:

Model 1:

$$p(\texttt{profit}) = .9 * (\texttt{temperature} > 75) + .1(\texttt{howCleanSidewalk}) \tag{33.1}$$

Model 2:

$$p(\texttt{profit}) = \sigma(.9(\texttt{temperature} - 75)/\texttt{maxTemperature} + .1(\texttt{howCleanSidewalk} - .5)) \tag{33.2}$$

These models are illustrated in Figure 33.2. Both of these models are inherently interpretable in the sense that they are easy to inspect and understand. While we were not explicitly seeking causal models (for that, see Chapter 36), both rely mostly on the temperature, which seems reasonable.

For the sake of this example, suppose that the models above were black boxes, and we could only request partial views of it. We decide to ask the model for the most important features. Let us see what happens when we consider two different ways of computing important features.[2]

---

2. In the remainder of the chapter we will describe many other ways of creating and computing explanations.

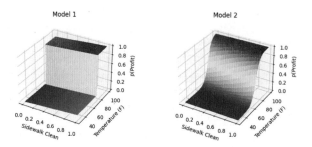

Figure 33.2: Models described in the simple example. Both of these models have the same qualitative characteristics, but different explanation methods will describe these models quite differently, potentially causing confusion.

Our first (feature-based) explanation method computes, for each training point, whether individually changing each feature to its max or min value changes the prediction. Important features are those that change the prediction for many training points. One can think of this explanation method as a variant of computing feature importance based on how important a feature is to the coalition that produces the prediction. In this case, both models will report temperature to be the dominating feature. If we used this explanation to vet our models, we would correctly conclude that both models use the features in a sensible way (and thus may be worth considering for deciding when to open our lemonade stand).

Our second (feature-based) explanation method computes the magnitude of the derivatives of the output with respect to the inputs for each training point. Important features are those that have a large sum of absolute derivatives across the training set. One can think of this explanation method as a variant of computing feature importances based on local geometry. In this case, Model 2 will still report that temperature has higher derivatives. However, Model 1, which has very similar behavior to Model 2, will report that sidewalk cleanliness is the dominating feature because the derivative with respect to temperature is zero nearly everywhere. If we used this explanation to vet our models, we would incorrectly conclude that Model 1 relies on an unimportant feature (and that Model 1 and 2 rely on different features).

What happened? The different explanations had different properties. The first explanation had the property of fidelity with respect to identifying features that, if changed, will affect the prediction, whereas the second explanation had the property of correctly identifying features that have the most local curvature. In this example, the first property is more important for the task of determining whether our model can be used to determine our business strategy. [3]

33.2   Methods for interpretable machine learning

There exist many methods for interpretable machine learning. Each method has different properties and the right choice will depend on context and end-tasks. As we noted in Section 33.1.2, the grand challenge in interpretable machine learning is determining what kinds of properties are needed for

---

3. Other properties may be important for this end-task. This example is just the simplest one.

what contexts, and what explanation methods satisfy those properties. Thus, one should consider this section a high-level snapshot of the rapidly changing options of methods that one may want to choose for interpretable machine learning.

33.2.1 Inherently interpretable models: the model is its explanation

We consider certain classes of models inherently interpretable: a person can inspect the full model and, with reasonable effort, understand how inputs become outputs.[4] Specifically, we define inherently interpretable models as those that require no additional process or proxies in order for them to be used as explanation for the end-task. For example, suppose a model consists of a relatively small set of rules. Then, those rules might suffice as the explanation for end-tasks that do not involve extreme time pressure. (Note: in this way, a model might be inherently interpretable for one end-task and not another.)

Inherently interpretable models fall into two main categories: sparse (or otherwise compact) models and logic-based models.

Compact or **sparse** feature-based models include various kinds of sparse regressions. Earlier in this textbook, we discussed simple models such as HMMs (Section 29.2), generalized linear models (Chapter 15), and various latent variable models (Chapter 28). When small enough, these are generally inherently interpretable. More advanced models in this category include super-sparse linear integer models and other checklist models [DMV15; UTR14].

While simple functionally, sparsity has its drawbacks when it comes to inspection and interpretation. For example, if a model picks only one of several correlated features, it may be harder to identify what signal is actually driving the prediction. A model might also assign correlated features different signs that ultimately cancel, rendering an interpretion of weights meaningless.

To handle these issues, as well as to express more complex functions, some models in this category impose hierarchical or modular structures in which each component is still relatively compact and can be inspected. Examples include topic models (e.g., [BNJ03b], (small) discrete time series models (e.g., [FHDV20]), generalized additive models (e.g., [HT17]) and monotonicity-enforced models (e.g., [Gup+16]).

Logic-based models use logical statements as basis. Models in this category include decision-trees [Bre+17], decision lists [Riv87; WR15; Let+15a; Ang+18; DMV15] , decision tables, decision sets [Hau+10; Wan+17a; LBL16; Mal+17; Bén+21], and logic programming [MDR94]. A broader discussion, as well as a survey of user studies on these methods, can be found in [Fre14]. Logic-based models easily model non-linear relationships but can have trouble modeling continuous relationships between the input and output (e.g., expressing a linear function vs. a step-wise constant function). Like the compact models, hierarchies and other forms of modularity can be used to extend the expressivity of the model while keeping it human-inspectable. For example, one can define a new concept as a formula based on some literals, and then use the new concept to build more complex rules.

When using inherently interpretable models, three key decisions need to be made: the choice of the model class, how to manage uninterpretable input features, and the choice of optimization method.

---

4. There may be other questions, such as how training data influenced the model, which may still require additional computation or information.

Decision: model class. Since the model is its own explanation, the decision on the model class becomes the decision on the form of explanation. Thus, we need to consider both whether the model class is a good choice for modeling the data as well as providing the necessary information to the user. For example, if one chooses to use a linear model to describe one's data, then it is important that the intended users can understand or manipulate the linear model. Moreover, if the fitting process produces a model that is too large to be human-inspectable, then it is no longer inherently interpretable, even if it belongs to one of the model classes described above.

Decision: optimization methods for training. The kinds of model classes that are typically inherently interpretable often require more advanced methods for optimization: compact, sparse, and logic-based models all involve learning discrete parameters. Fortunately, there is a long and continuing history of research for optimizing such models, including directly via optimization programs, relaxation and rounding techniques, and search-based approaches. Another popular optimization approach is via distillation or mimics: one first trains a complex model (e.g., a neural network) and then uses the complex model's output to train a simpler model to mimic the more complex model. The more complex model is then discarded. These optimization techniques are beyond the scope of this chapter but covered in optimization textbooks.

Decision: how to manage uninterpretable input features. Sometimes the input features themselves are not directly interpretable (e.g., pixels of an image or individual amplitudes spectrogram); only collections of inputs have semantic meaning for human users. This situation challenges our ability not only to create inherently interpretable models but also explanations in general.

To address this issue, more advanced methods attempt to add a "concept" layer that first converts the uninterpretable raw input to a set of human-interpretable concept features. Next, these concepts are mapped to the model's output [Kim+18a; Bau+17]. This second stage can still be inherently interpretable. For example, one could first map a pattern of spectrogram to a semantically meaningful sound (e.g., people chatting, cups clinking) and then from those sounds to a scene classification (e.g., in a cafe). While promising, one must ensure that the initial data-to-concept mapping truly maps the raw data to concepts as the user understands them, no more and no less. Creating and validating that machine-derived concepts correspond to a semantically meaningful human concepts remains an open research challenge.

When might we want to consider inherently interpretable models? When not? Inherently interpretable models have several advantages over other approaches. When the model is its explanation, one need not worry about whether the explanation is faithful to the model or whether it provides the right partial view of the model for the intended task. Relatedly, if a person vets the model and finds nothing amiss, they might feel more confident about avoiding surprises. For all these reasons, inherently interpretable models have been advocated for in high-stakes scenarios, as well as generally being the first go-to to try [Rud19].

That said, these models do have their drawbacks. They typically require more specialized optimization approaches. With appropriate optimization, inherently interpretable models can often match the performance of more complex models, but there are domains — in particular, images, waveforms, and language — in which deep models or other more complex models typically give significantly higher performance. Trying to fit complex behavior with a simple function may result not only in high bias in the trained model but also invite people to (incorrectly) rationalize why that highly biased model is sensible [Lun+20]. In an industry setting, seeking a migration away from a legacy, uninterpretable, business-critical model that has been tuned over decades would run into resistance.

Lastly, we note that just because a model is inherently interpretable, it does not guard against all kinds of surprises: as noted in Section 33.1, interpretability is just one form of validation mechanism. For example, if the data distribution shifts, then one may observe unexpected model behavior.

33.2.2 Semi-inherently interpretable models: example-based methods

Example-based models use examples as their basis for their predictions. For example, an example-based classifier might predict the class of a new input by first identifying the outputs for similar instances in the training set and next taking a vote. K-nearest neighbors is one of the best known models in this class. Extensions include methods to identify exemplars for predicted classes and clusters (e.g., [KRS14; KL17b; JL15a; FD07b; RT16; Arn+10]), to generate exemplars (e.g., [Li+17d]), to define similarities between instances via sophisticated embeddings (e.g.,[PM18a]), and to first decompose an instance into parts and then find neighbors or exemplars between the parts (e.g., [Che+18b]). Like logic-based models, example-based models can describe highly non-linear boundaries.

On one hand, individual decisions made by example-based methods seem fully inspectable: one can provide the user with exactly the training instances (including their output labels) that were used to classify a particular input in a particular way. However, it may be difficult to convey a potentially complex distance metric used to define "similarity". As a result, the user may incorrectly infer what features or patterns made examples similar. It is also often difficult to convey the intuition behind the global decision boundary using examples.

33.2.3 Post-hoc or joint training: the explanation gives a partial view of the model

Inherently interpretable models are a subset of all machine learning models, and circumstances may require working with a model that is not inherently interpretable. As noted above, large neural models (Chapter 16) have demonstrated large performance benefits for certain kinds of data (e.g., images, waveform, and text); one might have to work with a legacy, business critical model that has been tuned for decades; one might be trying to understand a system of interconnected models.

In these cases, the view that the explanation gives into the model will necessarily be *partial*: the explanation may only be an approximation of the model or be otherwise incomplete. Thus, more decisions have to be made. Below, we split these decisions into two broad categories — what the explanation should consist of to best serve the context and how the explanation should be computed from the trained model. More detail on the abilities and limitations of these partial explanation methods can be found in [Sla+20; Yeh+19a; Kin+19; Ade+20a].

33.2.3.1 What does the explanation consist of?

One set of decisions center around the content of the explanation and what properties it should have. One choice is the form: Should the explanation be a list of important features? The top interactions? One must also choose the scope of the explanation: Is it trying to explain the whole model (global)?

The model's behavior near a specific input (local)? Something else? Determining what properties the explanation must have will help answer these and other questions. We expand on each of these points below; the right choice, as always, will depend on the user — whom the explanation is for —and their end-task.

Decision: form of the explanation. In the case of inherently interpretable models, the model class used to fit the data was also the explanation. Now, the model class and the explanation are two different entities. For example, the model could be a deep network and the explanation a decision tree.

Works in interpretable machine learning have used a large variety of forms of explanations. The form could be a list of "important" input features [RSG16b; Lun+20; STY17; Smi+17; FV17] or "important" concepts [Kim+18a; Bau+20; Bau+18]. Or it could be a simpler model that approximates the complex model (e.g., a local linear approximation, an approximating rule set)[FH17; BKB17; Aga+21b; Yin+19c]. Another choice could be a set of similar or prototypical examples [KRS14; AA18; Li+17d; JL15a; JL15b; Arn+10]. Finally, one can choose whether the explanation should include a contrast against an alternative (also sometimes described as a counterfactual explanation) [Goy+19; WMR18; Kar+20a] or include or influential examples [KL17b].

Different forms of explanations will facilitate different tasks in different contexts. For example, a contrastive explanation of why treatment A is better than treatment B may help a clinician decide between treatments A and B. However, a contrast between treatments A and B may not be useful when comparing treatments A and C. Given the large number of choices, literature on how people communicate in the desired context can often provide some guidance. For example, if the domain involves making quick, high-stakes decisions, one might turn to how trauma nurses and firefighters explain their decisions (known as recognition-primed decision making, [Kle17]).

Decision: scope of the explanation: global or local. Another major decision regarding the parameters of the explanation is its scope.

Local explanation: In some cases, we may only need to interrogate an existing model about a specific decision. For example, why was this image predicted as a bird? Why was this patient predicted to have diabetes? Local explanations can help see if a consequential decision was made incorrectly or determine what could have been done differently to produce a different outcome (i.e., provide a recourse).

Local explanations can take many forms. A family of methods called saliency maps or attribution maps [STY17; Smi+17; ZF14; Sel+17; Erh+09; Spr+14; Shr+16] estimate the importances of each input dimension (e.g., via first-order derivatives with respect to the input). More generally, one might locally-fit simpler model in the neighborhood of the input of interest (e.g., LIME [RSG16b]). A local explanation may also consist of representative examples, including identifying which training points were most influential for a particular decision [KL17b] or identifying nearby datapoints with different predictions [MRW19; LHR20; Kar+20a].

All local explanation methods are partial views because they only attempt to explain the model around an input of interest. A key risk is that the user may overgeneralize the explanation to a wider region than it applies. They may also interpolate an incorrect mental model of the model based on a few local explanations.

Global explanation: In other cases, we may desire insight into the model as a whole or for a collection of datapoints (e.g., all inputs predicted to one class). For example, suppose that our end-task is to decide whether to deploy a model. Then, we care about understanding the *entire* model.

Global explanations can take many forms. One choice is to fit a simpler model (e.g., an inherently interpretable model) that approximates the original model (e.g., [HVD14]). One can also identify concepts or features that affect decisions across many inputs (e.g., [Kim+18b]). Another approach is to provide a carefully chosen set of representative examples [Yeh+18]. These examples might be chosen to be somehow characteristic of, or providing coverage of, a class (e.g., [AA18]), to draw attention to decision boundaries (e.g., [Zhu+18]), or to identify inputs particularly influential in training the model.

Unless a model is inherently interpretable, it is still important to remember that a global explanation is still a partial view. To make a complex model accessible to the user, the global explanation will need to leave some things out.

Decision: determining what properties the context needs. Different forms of explanations have different levels of expressivity. For example, an explanation listing important features, or fitting a local linear model around a particular input, does not expose interactions—but fitting a local decision tree would. For each form, there will also be many ways to compute an explanation of that form (more on this in Section 33.2.3.2). How do we choose amongst all of these different ways to compute the explanation? We suggest that the first step in determining the form and computation of an explanation should be to determine what properties are needed from it.

Specifying properties is especially important because not only may different forms of explanations have different intrinsic properties—e.g., can it model interactions?—but the properties may depend on the model being explained. For example, if the model is relatively smooth, then a feature-based explanation relying on local gradients may be fairly faithful to the original model. However if the model has spiky contours, the same explanation may not adequately capture the model's behavior. Once the desired properties are determined, one can determine what kind of computation is necessary to achieve them. We will list commonly desirable properties in Section 33.3.

33.2.3.2 How the explanation is computed

Another set of decisions has to do with how the explanation is computed.

Decision: computation of explanation. Once we make the decisions above, we must decide how the explanation will actually be computed. This choice will have a large impact on the explanation's properties. Thus, it is crucial to carefully choose a computational approach that provides the properties needed for the context and end-task.

For example, suppose one is seeking to identify the most "important" input features that change a prediction. Different computations correspond to different definitions of importance. One definition of importance might be the smallest region in an image that, when changed, changes the prediction—a perturbation-based analysis. Even within this definition, we would need to specify how that perturbation will be computed: Do we keep the pixel values within the training distribution? Do we preserve correlations between pixels? Different works take different approaches [SVZ13; DG17; FV17; DSZ16; Adl+18; Bac+15a].

A related approach is to define importance in terms of sensitivity (e.g., largest gradients of the output with respect to the input feature). Even then, there are many computational decisions to be made [STY17; Smi+17; Sel+17; Erh+09; Shr+16]. Yet another common definition of importance is how often the input feature is part of a "winning coalition" that drives the prediction, e.g., a Shapley or Banzaf score [LL17]. Each of these definitions have different properties, as well as require different amounts of computation.

Similar issues come up with other forms of explanations. For example, for an example-based explanation, one has to define what it means to be similar or otherwise representative: Is it the cosine similarity between activations? A uniform L2 ball of a certain size between inputs? Likewise, there are many different ways to obtain counterfactuals. One can rely on distance functions to identify nearby inputs that with different outputs [WMR17; LHR20], causal frameworks [Kus+18], or SAT formulations [Kar+20a], among other choices.

Decision: joint training vs. post-hoc application. So far, we have described our partial explanation techniques as extracting some information from an already-trained model. This approach is called deriving a post-hoc explanation. As noted above, post-hoc, partial explanations may have some limitations: for example, an explanation based on a local linear approximation may be great if the model is generally smooth, but provide little insight if the model has high curvature. Note that this limitation is not because the partial explanation is wrong, but because the view that local gradients provide isn't sufficient if the true decision boundary is curvy.

One approach to getting explanations to have desired properties we is to train the model and the explanation jointly. For example, a regularizer that penalizes violations of desired properties can help steer the overall optimization process towards learning models that both perform well and are amenable to the desired explanation [Plu+20]. It is often possible to find such a model because most complex model classes have multiple high-performing optima [Bre01].

The choice of regularization will depend on the desired properties, the form of the explanation, and its computation. For example, in some settings, we may desire the explanation use the same features that people do for the task (e.g., lower frequency vs. higher frequency features in image classifiers [Wan+20b]) — and still be faithful to the model. In other settings, we may want to control the input dimensions used or not used in the explanation, or for the explanation to be somehow compact (e.g., a small decision tree) while still being faithful to the underlying model, [RHDV17; Shu+19a; Vel+17; Nei+18; Wu+19b; Plu+20]. (Certain attention models fall into this category [JW19; WP19].) We may also have constraints on the properties of concepts or other intermediate features [AMJ18b; Koh+20a; Hen+16; BH20; CBR20; Don+17b]. In all of these cases, these desired properties could be included as a regularizer when training the model.

When choosing between a post-hoc explanation or joint training, one key consideration is that joint training assumes that one can re-train the model or the system of interest. In many cases in practice, this may not be possible. Replacing a complex and well-validated system in deployment for a decade may not be possible or take a prohibitively long time. In that case, one can still extract approximated explanations using post-hoc methods. Finally, a joint optimization, even when it can be performed, is not a panacea: optimization for some properties may result in unexpected violations of other (unspecified but desired) properties. For this reason, explanations from jointly trained models are still partial.

When might we want to consider post-hoc methods, and when not?. The advantage of post-hoc interpretability methods is that they can be applied to any model. This family of methods is especially useful in real-world scenarios where one needs to work with a system that contains many models as its parts, where one cannot expect to replace the whole system with one model. These approaches can also provide at least some broader knowledge about the model to identify unexpected concerns.

That said, post-hoc explanations, as approximations of the true model, may not be fully faithful to the model nor cover the model completely. As such, an explanation method tailored for one context may not be transferable in another; even in the intended context, there may be blindspots about the model that the explanation misses completely. For these reasons, in high stakes situations, one should attempt to use an inherently interpretable model first if possible [Rud19]. In all situations when post-hoc explanations are used, one must keep in mind that they are only one tool in a broader accountability toolkit and warn users appropriately.

33.2.4   Transparency and visualization

The scope of interpretable machine learning is around methods that expose the process by which a trained model makes a decision. However, the behavior of a model also depends on the objective function, the training data, how the training data were collected and processed, and how the model was trained and tested. Conveying to a human these other aspects of what goes into the creation of a model can be as important as explaining the trained model itself. While a full discussion of transparency and visualization is outside the scope of this chapter, we provide a brief discussion here to describe these important adjacent concepts.

Transparency is an umbrella term for the many things that one could expose about the modeling process and its context. Interpreting models is one aspect. However, one could also be transparent about other aspects, such as the data collection process or the training process (e.g., [Geb+21; Mit+19; Dnp]). There are also situations in which a trained model is released (whether or not it is inherently interpretable), and thus the software can be inspected and run directly.

Visualization is one way to create transparency. One can visualize the data directly or various aspects of the model's process (e.g., [Str+17]). Interactive visualizations can convey more than text or code descriptions [ZF14; OMS17; MOT15; Ngu+16; Hoh+20]. Finally, in the specific context of interpretable machine learning, how the explanation is presented — the visualization — can make a large difference in how easily users can consume it. Even something as simple as a rule list has many choices of layout, highlighting, and other organization.

When might we want to consider transparency and visualization? When not? In many cases, the trouble with a model comes not from the model itself, but parts of its training pipeline. The problem might be the training data. For example, since policing data contain historical bias, predictions of crime hot spots based on that data will be biased. Similarly, if clinicians only order tests when they are concerned about a patient's condition, then a model trained to predict risk based on tests ordered will only recapitulate what the clinicians already know. Transparency about the properties of the data, and how training and testing were performed, can help identify these issues.

Of course, inspecting the data and the model generation process is something that takes time and attention. Thus, visualizations of this kind and other descriptions to increase transparency are best-suited to situations in which a human inspector is not under time pressure to sift through potentially complex patterns for sources of trouble. These methods are not well-suited for situations in which a specific decision must be made in a relatively short amount of time, e.g., providing decision-support to a clinician at the bedside.

Finally, transparency in the form of making code available can potentially assist in understanding how a model works, identifying bugs, and allowing independent testing by a third party (e.g., testing with a new set of inputs, evaluating counterfactuals in different testing distributions). However, if a model is sufficiently complex, as many modern models are, then simply having access to the code is likely not be enough for a human to gain sufficient understanding for their task.

33.3   Properties: the abstraction between context and method

Recall from the terminology and framework in Section 33.1.2 that the context and end-task determine what properties are needed for the explanation. For example, in a high-stakes setting — such as advising on interventions for an unstable patient — it may be important that the explanation completely and accurately reflects the model (fidelity). In contrast, in a discovery-oriented setting, it might be more important for any explanation to allow for efficient iterative refinement, revealing different aspects of the model in turn (interactivity). Not all contexts and end-tasks need all properties, and the lack of a key property may result in poor downstream performance.

While the research is still evolving, there exists a growing informal understanding about how properties may work as an abstraction between methods and contexts. Many interpretability methods from Section 33.2 share the same properties, and methods with the same properties may have similar downstream performance in a specific end-task and context. If two contexts and end-tasks require the same properties, then a method that works well for one may work well for the other. A method with properties well-matched for one context could miserably fail in another context.

How to find desired properties? Of course, identifying what properties are important for a particular context and end-task is not trivial. Indeed, identifying what properties are important for what contexts, end-tasks, and downstream performance metrics is one facet of the grand challenge of interpretable machine learning. For the present, the process of identifying the correct properties will likely require iteration via user studies. However, iterating over properties is still a much smaller space than iterating over methods. For example, if one wants to test whether the sparsity of the explanation is key to good downstream performance, one could intentionally create explanations of varying levels of sparsity to test that hypothesis. This is a much more precise knob to test than exhaustively trying out different explanation methods with different hyperparameters.

Below, we first describe examples of properties that have been discussed in the interpretable machine learning literature. Many of these properties are purely computational — that is, they can be determined purely from the model and the explanation. A few have some user-centric elements. Next we list examples of properties of explanation from cognitive science (on human to human explanations) and human-computer interaction (on machine to human explanations). Some of these properties have analogs in the machine learning list, while others may serve as inspiration for areas to formalize.

33.3.1   Properties of explanations from interpretable machine learning

Many lists of potentially-important properties of interpretable machine learning models have been compiled, sometimes using different terms for similar concepts and sometimes using the similar terms for different concepts. Below we list some commonly-described properties of explanations, knowing that this list will evolve over time as the field advances.

Faithfulness, fidelity (e.g., as described in [JG20; JG21]). When the explanation is only a partial view of the model, how well does it match the model? There are many ways to make this notion precise. For example, suppose a mimic (simple model) is used to provide a global explanation of a more complex model. One possible measure of faithfulness could be how often the mimic gives the same outputs as the original. Another could be how often the mimic has the same first derivatives (local slope) as the original. In the context of a local explanation consisting of the 'key' features for a prediction, one could measure faithfulness by whether the prediction changes if the supposedly important features are flipped. Another measure could check to make sure the prediction does not change if a supposedly unimportant feature is flipped. The appropriate formalization will depend on the context.

Compactness, sparsity (e.g., as described in [Lip18; Mur+19]). In general, an explanation must be small enough such that the user can process it within the constraints of the task (e.g., how quickly a decision must be made). Sparsity generally corresponds to some notion of smallness (a few features, a few parameters, $L1$ norm etc.). Compactness generally carries an additional notion of not including anything irrelevant (that is, even if the explanation is small enough, it could be made smaller). Each must be formalized for the context

Completeness (e.g., as described in [Yeh+19b]). If the explanation is not the model, does it still include all of the relevant elements? For example, if an explanation consists of important features for a prediction, does it include all of them, or leave some out? Moreover, if the explanation uses derived quantities that are not the raw input features — for example, some notion of higher-level concepts — are they expressive enough to explain all possible directions of variation that could change the prediction? Note that one can have a faithful explanation in certain ways but not complete in others: Fore example, an explanation may be faithful in the sense that flipping features considered important flips the prediction and flipping features considered unimportant does not. However, the explanation may fail to include that flipping a set of unimportant features does change the prediction.

Stability (e.g., as described in [AMJ18a]) To what extent are the explanations similar for similar inputs? Note that the underlying model will naturally affect whether the explanation can be stable. For example, if the underlying model has high curvature and the explanation has limited expressiveness, then it may not be possible to have a stable explanation.

Actionability (e.g., as described in [Kar+20b; Poy+20]). Actionability implies filtering the content of the explanation to focus on only aspects of the model that the user might be able to intervene on. For example, if a patient is predicted to be at high risk of heart disease, an actionable explanation might only include mutable factors such as exercise and not immutable factors such as age or genetics. The notion of recourse corresponds to actionability in a justice context.

Modularity (e.g., as described in [Lip18; Mur+19]). Modularity implies that the explanation can be broken down into understandable parts. While modularity does not guarantee that the user can explain the system as a whole, for more complex models, modular explanations — where the user can inspect each part — can be an effective way to provide a reasonable level of insight into the model's workings.

Interactivity (e.g., [Ten+20]) Does the explanation allow the user to ask questions, such as how the explanation changes for a related input, or how an output changes given a change in input? In some contexts, providing everything that a user might want or need to know from the start might be overwhelming, but it might be possible to provide a way for the user to navigate the information about the model in their own way.

Translucence (e.g., as described in [SF20; Lia+19]). Is the explanation clear about its limitations? For example, if a linear model is locally fit to a deep model at a particular input, is there a mechanism that reports that this explanation may be limited if there are strong feature interactions around that input? We emphasize that translucence is about exposing limitations in the explanation, rather than the model. As with all accountability methods, the goal of the explanation is to expose the limitations of the model.

Simulability (e.g., as described in [Lip18; Mur+19]). A model is simulable if a user can take the model and an input and compute the output (within any constraints of time and cognition). A simulable explanation is an explanation that is a simulable model. For example, a list of features is not simulable, because a list of features alone does not tell us how to compute the output. In contrast, an explanation in the form of a decision tree does include a computation process: the user can follow the logic of the tree, as long as it is not too deep. This example also points out an important difference between compactness and simulability: if an explanation is too large, it may not be simulable. However, just because an explanation is compact — such as a short list of features — does not mean that a person can compute the model's output with it.

It may seem that simulability is different from the other properties because its definition involves human input. However, in practice, we often know what kinds of explanations are easy for people to simulate (e.g., decision trees with short path lengths, rule lists with small formulas, etc.). This knowledge can be turned into a purely computational training constraint where we seek simulatable explanations.

Alignment to the user's vocabulary and mental model. (e.g., as described in [Kim+18a]). Is the content of the explanation designed for the user's vocabulary? For example, the explanation could be given in the semantics a user knows, such as medical conditions vs. raw sensor readings. Doing so can help the user more easily connect the explanation to their knowledge and existing decision-making guidelines [Clo+19]. Of course, the right vocabulary will depend on the user: an explanation in terms of parameter variances and influential points may be comprehensible to an engineer debugging a lending model but not to a loan applicant.

Like simulability, mental-model alignment is more human-centric. However, just as before, we can imagine an abstraction between eliciting vocabulary and mental models from users (i.e., determining how they define their terms and how to think), and ensuring that an explanation is provided in alignment with whatever that elicited user vocabulary and mental model is.

Once desired properties are identified, we need to operationalize them. For example, if sparsity is a desired property, would using the L1 norm be enough? Or does a more sophisticated loss term need to be designed? This decision will necessarily be human-centric: how small an explanation needs to be, or in what ways it needs to be small, is a decision that needs to consider how people will be using the explanation. Once operationalized, most properties can be optimized computationally. That said, the properties should be evaluated with the context, end-task, model, and chosen explanation methods. Once evaluated, one may revisit the choice of the explanation and model.

Finally, we emphasize that the ability to achieve a particular property will depend on the *intrinsic* characteristics of the model. For example, the behavior of a highly nonlinear model with interactions between the inputs will, in general, be harder to understand than a linear model. No matter how we try to explain it, if we are trying to explain something complicated, then users will have a harder time understanding it.

33.3.2 Properties of explanations from cognitive science

Above we focused on computational properties between models and explanations. The fields of cognitive science and human-computer interaction have long examined what people consider good properties of an explanation. These more human-centered properties may be ones that researchers in machine learning may be less aware of, yet essential for communicating information to people.

Unsurprisingly, the literature on human explanation concurs that the explanation must fit the context [VF+80]; different contexts require different properties and different explanations. That said, human explanations are also social constructs, often including post-hoc rationalizations and other biases. We should focus on properties that help users achieve their goals, not ones simply "because people sometimes do it".

Below we list several of these properties.

Soundness (e.g., as described in [Kul+13]). Explanations should contain nothing but the truth with respect to whatever they are describing. Soundness corresponds to notions of *compactness* and *faithfulness* above.

Completeness (e.g., as described in [Kul+13]). Explanations should contain the whole truth with respect to whatever they are describing. Completeness corresponds to notions of *completeness* and *faithfulness* above.

Generality (e.g., as described in [Mil19]). Overall, people understand that an explanation for one context may not apply in another. That said, there is an expectation that an explanation should reflect some underlying mechanism or principle and will thus apply to similar cases — for whatever notion of similarity is in the person's mental model. Explanations that do not generalize to similar cases may be misinterpreted. Generality corresponds to notions of *stability* above.

Simplicity (e.g., as described in [Mil19]). All of the above being equal, simpler explanations are generally preferred. Simplicity relates to notions of *sparsity* and *complexity* above.

Contrastiveness (e.g., as described in [Mil19]). Contrastive explanations provide information of how something differs from an alternate decision or prediction. For example, instead of providing a list of features for why a particular drug is recommended, it might provide a list of features that explain why one drug is recommended over another. Contrastiveness relates to notions of *actionability* above, and more generally explanation types that include *counterfactuals*.

Finally, the cognitive science literature also notes that explanations are often goal directed. This matches the notion of explanation in ML as information that helps a person improve performance on their end-task. Different information may help with different goals, and thus human explanations take many forms. Examples include deductive-nomological forms (i.e. a logical proofs) [HO48], forms that provide a sense of an underlying mechanism [BA05; Gle02; CO06], and forms that conveying understanding [Kei06]. Knowing these forms can help us consider what options might be best among different sets of interpretable machine learning methods.

33.4   Evaluation of interpretable machine learning models

One cannot formalize the notion of interpretability without specifying the context, the end-task, and the downstream performance metric [VF+80]. If one explanation empowers the human to get better performance on their end-task over another explanation, then it is more useful. While the grand challenge of interpretable machine learning is to develop a general understanding of what properties are needed for good downstream performance on different end-tasks in different contexts, in this section, we will focus on rigorous evaluation within one context [DVK17].

Specifically, we describe two major categories for evaluating interpretable machine learning methods:

Computational evaluations of properties (without people). Computational evaluations of whether explanations have desired properties do not user studies. For example, one can computationally measure whether a particular explanation satisfies a definition of faithfulness under different training and test data distributions or whether the outputs of one explanation are more sparse than another. Such measures are valuable when one already knows that certain properties may be important for certain contexts. Computational evaluations also serve as intermediate evaluations and sanity checks to identify undesirable explanation behavior prior to a more expensive user study-based evaluation.

User studies (with people). Ultimately, user studies are needed to measure how well an interpretable machine learning method enables the user to complete their end-task in a given context. Performing a rigorous, well-designed user study in a real context is significant work — much more so than computing a test likelihood on benchmark datasets. It requires significant asks of not only the researchers but also the target users. Methods for different contexts will also have different evaluation challenges: while a system designed to assist with optimizing music recommendations might be testable on a wide population, a system designed to help a particle physicist identify new kinds of interactions might only be tested with one or two physicists because people with that expertise are hard to find. In all cases, the evaluation can be done rigorously given careful attention to experimental design.

33.4.1   Computational evaluation: does the method have desired properties?

While the ultimate measure of interpretability is whether the method successfully empowers the user to perform their task, properties can serve as a valuable abstraction. Checking whether an explanation has the right computational and desired properties can ensure that the method works as expected (e.g., no implementation errors, no obviously odd behaviors). One can iterate on novel, computationally-efficient methods to optimize the quantitative formalization of a property before conducting expensive human experiments. Computational checks can also ensure whether properties that held for one model continue to hold when applied to another model. Finally, checking for specific properties can also help pinpoint in what way an explanation is falling short, which may be less clear from a user study due to confounding.

In some cases, one might be able to prove mathematically that an explanation has certain properties, while in others the test must be empirical. For empirical testing, one umbrella strategy is to use a hypothesis-based sanity check; if we think a phenomenon X should never occur (hypothesis), we can test whether we can create situations where X may occur. If it does, then the method fails this sanity check. Another umbrella strategy is to create datasets with known characteristics or ground truth explanations. These could be purely synthetic constructions (e.g., generated tables with intentionally correlated features), semi-synthetic approaches (e.g., intentionally changing the labels on an image dataset), or taking slices of a real dataset (e.g., introduce intentional bias by only selecting real image, label pairs that are of outdoor environments). Note that these tests

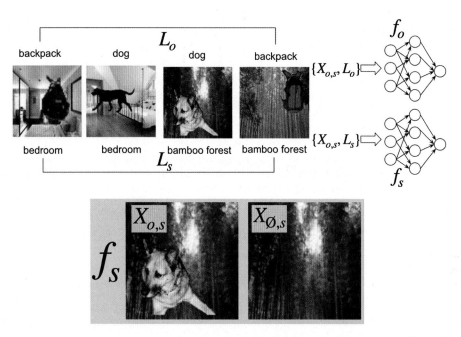

Figure 33.3: An example of computational evaluation using (semi-)synthetic datasets from [YK19]: foreground images (e.g., dogs, backpacks) are placed on different backgrounds (e.g., indoors, outdoors) to test what an explanation is looking for.

can only tell us if something is wrong; if a method passes a check, there may still be missing blindspots.

Examples of sanity checks. One strategy is to come up statements of the form "if this explanation is working, then phenomenon X should not be occurring" and then try to create a situation in which phenomenon X occurs. If we succeed, then the sanity check fails. By asking about out-of-the-box phenomena, this strategy can reveal some surprising failure modes of explanation methods.

For example, [Ade+20a] operates under the assumption that a faithful explanation should be a function of a model's prediction. The hypothesis is that the explanation should significantly change when comparing a trained model to an untrained model (where prediction is random). They show that many existing methods fail to pass this sanity check (Figure 33.4).

In another example, [Kin+19] hypothesize that a faithful explanation should be invariant to input transformations that do not affect model predictions or weights, such as constant shift of inputs (e.g., all inputs are added by 10). This hypothesis can be seen as testing both faithfulness and stability properties. Their work shows that some methods fail this sanity check.

Adversarial attacks on explanations also fall into this category. For example, [GAZ19] shows that two perceptively indistinguishable inputs with the same predicted label can be assigned very different explanations.

Examples using (semi)synthetic datasets. Constructed datasets can also help score properties

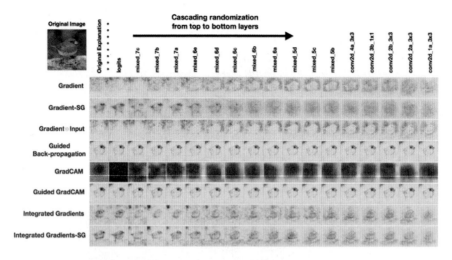

Figure 33.4: *Interpretability methods (each row) and their explanations as we randomize layers starting from the logits, and cumulatively to the bottom layer (each column), in the context of image classification task. The rightmost column is showing a completely randomized network. Most methods output similar explanations for the first two columns; one predicts the bird, and the other predicts randomly. This sanity check tests the hypothesis that the explanation should significantly change (quantitatively and qualitatively) when comparing a trained model and an untrained model [Ade+20a].*

of various methods. We use the work of [YK19] as an example. Here, the authors were interested in explanations with the properties of compactness and faithfulness: it should not identify features as important if they are not. To test for these properties, the authors generate images with known correlations. Specifically, they generate multiple datasets, each with a different rate of how often each particular foreground object co-occurs with each particular background (see Figure 33.3). Each dataset comes with two labels per image: for the object and the background.

Now, the authors compare two models: one trained to classify objects and one trained to classify backgrounds (left, Figure 33.3). If a model is trained to classify objects and they all happen to have the same background, the background should be less important than in a model trained to classify backgrounds ([YK19] call this 'model contrast score'). They also checked that the model trained to predict backgrounds was not providing attributions to the foreground objects (see right Figure 33.3). Other works using similar strategies include [Wil+20b; Gha+21; PMT18; KPT21; Yeh+19b; Kim+18b].

Examples with real datasets. While more difficult, it is possible to at least partially check for certain kinds of properties on real datasets that have no ground-truth.

For example, suppose an explanation ranks features from most to least important. We want to determine if this ranking is faithful. Further, suppose we can assume that the features do not interact. Then, one can attempt to make the prediction just with the top-1 most important feature, just the top-2 ranked features, etc. and observe if the change in prediction accuracy exhibits diminishing returns as more features are added. (If the features do interact, this test will not work. For example,

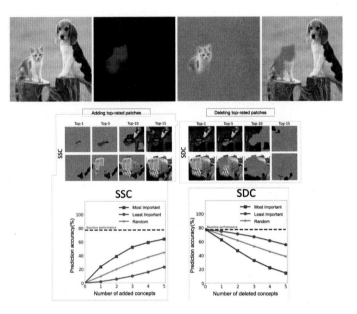

Figure 33.5: Examples of computational evaluation with real datasets. Top row is from Figure 1 of [DG17], used with kind permission of Yarin Gal. Bottom row is from Figure 4 of [Gho+19]. One would expect that adding or deleting patches rated as most 'relevant' for an image classification would have a large effect on the classification compared to patches not rated as important.

if features A, B, C are the top-3 features, but C is only important if feature B is present, the test above would over-estimate the importance of the feature C.)

Figure 33.5 shows an example of this kind of test [Gho+19]. Their method outputs a set of image patches (e.g., a set of connected pixels) that correlates with the prediction. They add top-n image patches provided by the explanation one by one and observe the desired trend in accuracy. A similar experiment in reverse direction (i.e., deleting top-n most important image patches one by one) provides additional evidence. Similar experiments are also conducted in [FV17; RSG16a].

For example, in [DG17], authors define properties in plain English first: smallest sufficient region (smallest region of the image that alone allows a confident classification) and smallest destroying region (smallest region of the image that when removed, prevents a confident classification), followed by careful operationalization of these properties such that they become the objective for optimization. Then, separately, an evaluation metric of saliency is defined to be "the tightest rectangular crop that contains the entire salient region and to feed that rectangular region to the classifier to directly verify whether it is able to recognise the requested class". While the "rectangular" constraint may introduce artifacts, it is a neat trick to make evaluation possible. By checking expected behavior as described above, authors confirm that methods' behavior on the real data is aligned with the defined property compared to baselines.

Evaluating the evaluations. As we have seen so far, there are many ways to formalize a given property and many empirical tests to determine whether a property is present. Each empirical test will have different qualities. As an illustration, in [Tom+20], the authors ask whether popular saliency metrics give consistent results across literature. They tested whether different metrics for assessing the quality of saliency-based explanations (explanations that identify important pixels or regions in images) is evaluating similar properties. In other words, this work tests consistency and stability properties of *metrics*. They show many metrics are statistically unreliable and inconsistent. While each metric may still have a particular use [Say+19], knowing this inconsistency exists helps us better understand the landscape and limitations of evaluation approaches. Developing good evaluations for computational properties is an ongoing area of research.

33.4.2 User study-based evaluation: does the method help a user perform a target task?

User study-based evaluations measure whether an interpretable machine learning method helps a human perform some task. This task could be the ultimate end-task of interest (e.g., does a method help a doctor make better treatment decisions) or a synthetic task that mirrors contexts of interest (e.g., a simplified situation with artificial diseases and symptoms). In both cases, rigorous experimental design is critical to ensuring that the experiment measures what we want it to measure. Understanding experimental design for user studies is essential for research in interpretable machine learning.

33.4.2.1 User studies in real contexts.

The gold standard for testing whether an explanation is useful is to test it in the intended context: Do clinicians make better decisions with a certain kind of decision support? Do programmers debug code faster with a certain kind of explanation about model errors? Do product teams create more fair models for their businesses? A complete guide on how to design and conduct user studies is out of scope for this chapter; below we point out some basic considerations.

33.4.2.2 Basic elements of user studies

Performing a high-quality user study is a nuanced and non-trivial endeavor. There are many sources of bias, some obvious (e.g., learning and fatigue effects during a study) and some less obvious (e.g., participants willing to work with us are more optimistic about AI technology than those we could not recruit, or different participants may have different needs for cognition).

Interface design. The explanation must be presented to the user. Unlike the *intrinsic* difficulty of explaining a model (i.e., complex models are harder to explain than simple ones), the design of the interface is an *extrinsic* source of difficulty that can confound the experimental results. For example, it may be easier, in general, to scan a list of features ordered by importance rather than alphabetically.

When we perform an evaluation with respect to an end-task, intrinsic and extrinsic difficulties can get conflated. Does one explanation type work better because it does a better job of explaining the complex system? Or does it work better simply because it was presented in a way that was easier for people to use? Especially if the goal is to test the difference between one explanation and another in the experiment, it is important that the interface for each is designed to tease out the effect from the explanations and their presentations. (Note that good presentations and visualization are an important but different object of study.) Moreover, if using the interface requires training, it is important to deliver the training to users in a way that is neutral in each testing condition. For example, how the end-task and goals of the study are described during training (e.g., with practice questions) will have a large impact on how users approach the task.

Baselines. Simply the presence of an explanation may change the way in which people interact with an ML system. Thus, it is often important to consider how a human performs with no ML system, with an ML system and no explanation, with an ML system and a placebo explanation (an explanation that provides no information), and with an ML system and hand-crafted explanations (manually generated by humans who are presumably good communicators).

Experimental design and hypothesis testing. Independent and dependent variables, hypotheses, and inclusion and exclusion criteria must be clearly defined prior to the start of the study. For example, suppose that one hypothesizes that a particular explanation will help a developer debug an image classifier. In this case, the independent variable would be a form of assistance: the particular explanation, competing explanation methods, and the baselines above. The dependent variable would be whether the developer can identify bugs. Inclusion and exclusion criteria might include a requirement that the developer has sufficient experience training image classifiers (as determined by an initial survey, or a pre-test), demonstrates engagement (as measured by a base level of performance on practice rounds), and does not have prior experience with the particular explanation types (as determined by an initial survey). Other exclusion criteria could be removing outliers. For example, one could decide, in advance, to exclude data from any participant that takes an unusually long or short time to perform task as a proxy for engagement.

As noted in Section 33.2, there are many decisions that go into any interpretable machine learning method, and each context is nuanced. Studies of the form "Does explanation X (computed via some pipeline Y) help users in context Z compared to explanation X'?" may not provide much insight as to *why* that particular explanation is better or worse — making it harder not only to iterate on a particular explanation but also to generalize to other explanations or contexts. There are many factors of potential variation in the results, ranging from the properties of the explanation and its presentation to the difficulty of the task.

To reduce this variance, and to get more useful and generalizable insights, we can manipulate some factors of variation directly. For example, suppose the research question is whether complete explanations are better than incomplete explanations in a particular context. One might write out hand-crafted explanations that are complete in what features they implicate, explanations in which one important feature is missing, and explanations in which several important features are missing. Doing so ensures even coverage of the different experimental regimes of interest, which may not occur if the explanations were simply output from a pipeline. As another example, one might intentionally create an image classifier with known bugs, or simply pretend to have an image classifier that makes certain predictions (as done in [Ade+20b]). These kinds of studies are called *wizard-of-Oz* studies, and they can help us more precisely uncover the science of why an explanation is useful (e.g., as done in [Jac+21]).

Once the independent and dependent variables, hypotheses, and participant criteria (including how the independent and dependent variables may be manipulated) are determined, the next step is setting up the study design itself. Broadly speaking, *randomization* marginalizes over potential confounds. For example, randomization in assigning subjects to tasks marginalizes the subject's prior knowledge; randomization in the order of tasks marginalizes out learning effects. *Matching* and *repeated measures* reduce variance. An example of matching would be asking the same subject to perform the same end-task with two different explanations. An example of repeated measures would be asking the subject to perform the end-task for several different inputs.

Other techniques for designing user studies include block randomized designs/Latin square designs that randomize the order of explanation types while keeping tasks associated with each explanation type grouped together. This can be used to marginalize the effects of learning and fatigue without too much context switching. Careful consideration should be given to what will be compared within subjects and across subjects. Comparisons of task performance within subjects will have lower variance but a potential bias from learning effects from the first task to the second. Comparisons across subjects will have higher variance and also potential bias from population shift during experimental recruitment. Finally, each of these study designs, as well as the choice of independent and dependent variables, will imply an appropriate significance test. It is essential to choose the right test and multiple hypothesis correction to avoid inflated significance values while retaining power.

Qualitative studies. So far, we have described the standard approach for the design of a quantitative user study–one in which the dependent variable is numerically measured (e.g., time taken to correctly identify a bug, % bugs detected). While quantitative studies provide value by demonstrating that there is a consistent, quantifiable effect across many users, they usually do not tell us *why* a certain explanation worked. In contrast, qualitative studies, often performed with a "think-aloud" or other discussion-based protocol in which users expose their thought process as they perform the experiment, can help identify why a particular form of explanation seems to be useful or not. The experimenter can gain insights by hearing how the user was using the information, and depending on the protocol, can ask for clarifications.

For example, suppose one is interested in how people use an example-based explanation to understand a video-game agent's policy. The idea is to show a few video clips of an automated agent in the video game, and then ask the user what the agent might do in novel situations. In a think-aloud study, the user would perform this task while talking through how they are connecting the videos they have seen to the new situation. By hearing these thoughts, a researcher might not only gain deeper insight into how users make these connections — e.g., users might see the agent collect coins in one video and presume that the agent will always go after coins — but they might also identify surprising bugs: for example, a user might see the agent fall into a pit and attribute it to a one-off sloppy fingers, not internalizing that an automated agent might make that mistake every time.

While a participant in a think-aloud study is typically more engaged in the study than they might be otherwise (because they are describing their thinking), knowing their thoughts can provide insight into the causal process between what information is being provided by the explanation and the action that the human user takes, ultimately helping advance the science of how people interact with machine-provided information.

Pilot studies: The above descriptions are just a very high-level overview of the many factors that must be designed properly for a high-quality evaluation. In practice, one does not typically get all of these right the first time. Small scale pilot studies are essential to checking factors such as whether participants attend to the provided information in unexpected ways or whether instructions are clear and well-designed. Modifying the experiments after iterative small scale pilot studies can save a lot of time and energy down the road. In these pilots, one should collect not only the usual information about users and the dependent variables, but also discuss with the participants how they approached the study tasks and whether any aspects of the study were confusing. These discussions will lead to insights and confidence that the study is testing what it is intended to test. The results from pilot studies should not be included in the final results.

Finally, as the number of factors to test increases (e.g., baselines, independent variables), the study design becomes more complex and may require more participants and longer participation times to determine if the results are significant — which can in turn increase costs and effects of fatigue. Pilots, think-aloud studies, and careful thinking about what aspects of the evaluation require user studies and what can be completed computationally can all help distill down a user-based evaluation to the most important factors.

33.4.2.3 User studies in synthetic contexts

It is not always appropriate or possible to test an interpretable machine learning method in the real context: for example, it would be unethical to test a prototype explanation system on patients each time one has a new way to convey information about a treatment recommendation. In such cases, we might want to run an experiment in which clinicians perform a task on made-up patients, or in some analogous non-medical context where the participant pool is bigger and more affordable. Similarly, one might create a relatively accessible image classification debugging context where one can control the incorrect labels, distribution shifts, etc. (e.g., [Ade+20b]) and see what explanations help users detect problems in this simpler setting. The convenience and scalability of using a simpler setting could shed light on what properties of explanations are important generally (e.g., for debugging image classification). For example, we can test how different forms of explanation have different cognitive loads or how a particular property affects performance with a relatively large pool of subjects (e.g., [Lag+19]). The same principles we outlined above for user studies in real contexts continue to apply, but there are some important cautions.

Cautions regarding synthetic contexts: While user studies with synthetic contexts can be valuable for identifying scientific principles, one must be cautious. For example, experimental subjects in a synthetic high-stakes context may not treat the stakes of the problem as seriously, may be relatively unburdened with respect to distractions or other demands on their time and attention (e.g., a quiet study environment vs. a chaotic hospital floor), and ignore important factors of the task (e.g., clicking through to complete the task as quickly as possible). Moreover, small differences in task definition can have big effects: even the difference between asking users to simply perform a task with an explanation available vs. asking users to answer some questions about the explanation first, may create very different results as the latter forces the user to pay attention to the explanation and the former does not. Priming users by giving them a specific scenario where they can put themselves into a mindset could help. For example: "Imagine now you are an engineer at a company selling a risk calculator. A deadline is approaching and your boss wants to make sure the product will work for a new client. Describe how you would use the following explanation".

33.5   Discussion: how to think about interpretable machine learning

Interpretable machine learning is a young, interdisciplinary field of study. As a result, consensus on definitions, evaluation methods, and appropriate abstractions is still forming. The goal of this section is to lay out a core set of principles about interpretable machine learning. While specifics in the previous sections may change, the principles below will be durable.

There is no universal, mathematical definition of interpretability, and there never will be. Defining a downstream performance metric (and justifying it) for each context is a must. The information that best communicates to the human what is needed to perform a task will necessarily vary: for example, what a clinical expert needs to determine whether to try a new treatment policy is very different than what a person to determine how to get a denied loan approved. Similarly, methods to communicate characteristics of models built on pixel data may not be appropriate for communicating characteristics of models built on language data. We may hope to identify desired properties in explanations to maximize downstream task performance for different classes of end tasks — that is the grand challenge of interpretable machine learning — but there will never be one metric for all contexts.

While this lack of a universal metric may feel disappointing, other areas of machine learning also lack universal metrics. For example, not only is it impossible to satisfy the many metrics on fairness at the same time [KMR16], but also in a particular situation, none may exactly match the desires of the stakeholders. Even in a standard classification setting, there are many metrics that correspond to making the predicted and true labels as close as possible. Does one care about overall accuracy? Precision? Recall? It is unlikely that one objective captures everything that is needed in one situation, much less across different contexts. Evaluation can still be rigorous as long as assumptions and requirements are made precise.

What sets interpretable machine learning apart from other areas of machine learning, however, is that a large class of evaluations require human input. As a necessarily interdisciplinary area, rigorous work in interpretable machine learning requires not only knowledge of computation and statistics but also experimental design and user studies.

Interpretability is only a part of the solution for fairness, calibrated trust, accountability, causality, and other important problems. Learning models that are fair, safe, causal, or engender calibrated trust are all goals, whereas interpretability is one *means* towards that goal.

In some cases, we don't need interpretability. For example, if the goal can be fully formalized in mathematical terms (e.g., a regulatory requirement may mandate a model satisfy certain fairness metrics), we do not need any human input. If a model behaves as expected across an exhaustive set of pre-defined inputs, then it may be less important to understand how it produced its outputs. Similarly, if a model performs well across a variety of regimes, that might (appropriately) increase one's trust in it; if it makes errors, that might (appropriately) decrease trust without an inspection of any of the system's internals.

In other cases, human input is needed to achieve the end-task. For example, while there is much work in the identification of causal models (see Chapter 36), under many circumstances, it is not possible to learn a model that is *guaranteed* to be causal from a dataset alone. Here, interpretability could assist the end-task of "Is the model causal?" by allowing a human to inspect the model's prediction process.

As another example, one could measure the safety of a clinical decision support system by tracking how often its recommendations causes harm to patients — and stop using the system if it causes too much harm. However, if we use this approach to safety, we will only discover that the system is unsafe *after* a significant number of patients have been harmed. Here, interpretability could support the end-task of safety by allowing clinical experts to inspect the model's decision process for red flags *prior* to deployment.

In general, complex contexts and end-tasks will require a constellation of methods (and people) to achieve them. For example, formalizing a complex notion such as accountability will require a broad collection of people — from policy makers and ethicists to corporations, engineers, and users — unifying vocabularies, exchanging domain knowledge, and identifying goals. Evaluating or monitoring it will involve various empirical measures of quality and insights from interpretability.

Interpretability is not about understanding everything about the model; it is about understanding enough to do the end-task. The ultimate measure of an interpretable machine learning method is whether it helps the user perform their end-task. Suppose the end-task is to fix an overheating laptop. An explanation that lists the likely sources of heat is probably sufficient to address the issue, even if one does not know the chemical properties of its components. On the other hand, if the laptop keeps freezing up, knowing about the sources of heat may not be the right information. Importantly, both end-tasks have clear downstream performance metrics: we can observe whether the information helped the user perform actions that make the laptop overheat or freeze up less.

As another example, consider AlphaGo, Google DeepMind's AI go player that beat the human world champion, Lee SeDol. The model is so complex that one cannot fully understand its decision process, including surprising moves like its famous move 37[Met16]. That said, partial probes (e.g., does AlphaGo believe the same move would have made a different impact if it was made earlier but similar position in the game) might still help a go expert gain insights on the rationale for the move in the context of what they already know about the game.

Relatedly, interpretability is distinct from full transparency into the model or knowing the model's code. Staring at the weights of every neuron in a large network is likely to be as effective as taking one's laptop apart to understand a bug in your code. There are many good reasons for open source projects and models, but open source code itself may or may not be sufficient for a user to accomplish their end-task. For example, a typical user will not be able to reason through $100K$ lines of parameters despite having all the pieces available.

That said, any partial view of a model is, necessarily, only a partial view; it does not tell the full story. While we just argued that many end-tasks do not require knowing everything about a model, we also must acknowledge that a partial view does not convey the full model. For example, the set of features needed to change a loan decision may be the right partial view for a denied applicant, but convey nothing about whether the model is discriminatory. Any probe will only return what it is designed to compute (e.g., an approximation of a complex function with a simpler one). Different probes may be able to reveal different properties at different levels of quality. Incorrectly believing the partial view is the full story could result in incorrect insights.

Partial views can lack stability and enable attacks. Relatedly, any explanation that reveals only certain parts of a model can lack stability (e.g., [AMJ18a]) and can be more easily attacked (e.g., see [Yeh+19a; GAZ19; Dom+19; Sla+20]). Especially when models are overparameterized such as neural networks, it is possible to learn models whose explanations say one thing (e.g., a feature is not important, according to some formalization of feature importance) while the model does another (e.g., uses the prohibited feature). Joint training can also exacerbate the issue, as it allows the model to learn boundaries that pass some partial-view test while in reality violating the underlying constraint. Other adversarial approaches can work on the input, minimally perturbing it to change the explanation's partial view while keeping the prediction constant or to change the prediction while keeping the explanation constant.

These concerns highlight an important open area: We need to improve ways to endow explanations with the property of translucence, that is, explanations that communicate what they can and cannot say about the model. Translucence is important because misinterpreted explanations that happen to favor a user's views create false basis for trust.

Trade-offs between inherently interpretable models and performance often do not exist; partial views can help when they do. While some have claimed that there exists an inherent trade-off between using an inherently-interpretable model and performance (defined as a model's performance on some test data), this trade-off does not always exist in practice for several reasons [Rud19].

First, in many cases, the data can be surprisingly well-fit by a fairly simple model (due to high noise, for example) or a model that can be decomposed into interpretable parts. One can often find a combination of architecture, regularizer, and optimizer that produces inherently interpretable models with performance comparable to, or sometimes even better than, blackbox approaches [Wan+17a; LCG12; Car+15; Let+15b; UR16; FHDV20; KRS14]. In fact, interpretability and performance can be synergistic: methods for encoding a preference for simpler models (e.g., L1 regularizer for sparsity property) were initially developed to increase performance and avoid overfitting, and interpretable models are often more robust [RDV18].

Second, a narrow focus on the trade-off between using inherently interpretable models and a predefined metric of performance, as usually measured on a validation set, overlooks a broader issue: that predefined metric of performance may not tell the full story about the quality of the model. For example, using an inherently interpretable model may enable a person to realize that a prediction is based on confounding, not causation—or other ways it might fail in deployment. In this way, one might get better performance with an inherently interpretable model in practice even if a blackbox appears to have better performance numbers in validation. An inherently interpretable model may also enable better human+model teaming by allowing the human user to step in and override the system appropriately.

Human factors are essential. All machine learning systems ultimately connect to broader socio-technical contexts. However, in many cases, many aspects of model construction and optimization can be performed in a purely computational setting: there are techniques to check for appropriate model capacity, techniques for tuning a gradient descent or convex optimization. In contrast, interpretable machine learning must consider human factors *from the beginning*: there is no point optimizing an explanation to have various properties if it still fails to improve the user's performance on the end-task.

Over-reliance. Just because an explanation is present, does not mean that the user will analytically and reasonably incorporate the information provided into their ultimate decision-making task. The presence of *any* explanation can increase a user's trust in the model, exacerbating the general issue

Original Image

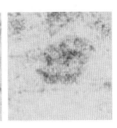

Figure 33.6: *(Potential) perception issues: an explanation from a trained network (left) is visually indistinguishable to humans from one from an untrained network (right)—even if they are not exactly identical.*

of over-trust in human+ML teams. Recent studies have found that even data scientists over-trust explanations in unintended ways [Kau+20]; their excitement about the tool led them to take it at face-value rather than dig deeper. [LM20] reports a similar finding, noting that inaccurate but evocative presentations can create a feeling of comprehension.

Over-reliance can be combated with explicit measures to force the user to engage analytically and skeptically with the information in the explanation. For example, one could ask the user to submit their decision first and only then show the recommendation and accompanying explanation to pique their interest in why their choice and the recommendation might disagree (and prompting whether they want to change their choice). Another option is to ask the user some basic questions about the explanation prior to submitting their decision to force them to look at the explanation carefully. Yet another option is to provide only the relevant information (the explanation) without the recommendation, forcing the user to synthesize the additional information on their own. However, in all these cases, there is a delicate balance: users will often be amenable to expending additional cognitive effort if they can see it achieves better results, but if they feel the effort is too much, they may start ignoring the information entirely.

Potential for misuse. A malicious version of over-reliance is when explanations are used to manipulate a user rather than facilitating the user's end-task. Further, users may report that they *like* explanations that are simple, require little cognitive effort, etc. even when those explanations do not help them perform their end-task. As creators of interpretable machine learning methods, one must be on alert to ensure that the explanations help the user achieve what they want to (ideally in a way that they also like).

Misunderstandings from a lack of understanding of machine learning. Even when correctly engaged, users in different contexts will have different levels of knowledge about machine learning. For example, not everyone may understand concepts such as additive factors or Shapley values [Sha16]. Users may also attribute more understanding to a model than it actually has. For example, if they see a set of pixels highlighted around a beak, or a set of topic model terms about a disease, they may mistakenly believe that the machine learning model has some notion of concepts that matches theirs, when the truth might be quite different.

Related: perception issues in image explanations. The nature of our visual processing system adds another layer of nuance when it comes to interpreting and misinterpreting explanations. In Figure 33.6, two explanations (in terms of important pixels in a bird image) seem to communicate a similar message; for most people, both explanations seem to suggest that the belly and cheek of the bird are the important parts for this prediction. However, one of them is generated from a trained network (left), but the other one is from a network that returns random predictions (right). While the two saliency maps aren't identical to machines, they look similar because humans don't parse an image as pixel values, but as whole, they see a bird in both pictures.

Another common issue with pixel-based explanations is that explanation creators often multiply the original image with an importance "mask" (black and clear saliency mask, where black pixel represents no importance and a clear pixel represents maximum importance), introducing the arbitrary artifact that black objects never appear important [Smi+17]. In addition, this binary mask is produced by clipping important pixels in a certain percentile (e.g., only taking 99−th percentile), which can also introduce another artifact [Sun+19c]. The balancing act between artifacts introduced by visualization for the ease of understanding and faithfully representing the explanation remains a challenge.

Together, all of these points on human factors emphasize what we said from the start: we cannot divorce the study and practice of interpretable machine learning from its intended socio-technical context.

PART VI

Action

34 Decision making under uncertainty

34.1 Statistical decision theory

Bayesian inference provides the optimal way to update our beliefs about hidden quantities H given observed data $\mathbf{X} = \boldsymbol{x}$ by computing the posterior $p(H|\boldsymbol{x})$. However, at the end of the day, we need to turn our beliefs into **actions** that we can perform in the world. How can we decide which action is best? This is where **decision theory** comes in. In this section, we give a brief introduction. For more details, see e.g., [DeG70; Ber85b; KWW22].

34.1.1 Basics

In **statistical decision theory**, we have an **agent** or decision maker, who wants to choose an **action** from has a set of possible actions, $a \in \mathcal{A}$, given some observations or data $\boldsymbol{x}$. We assume the data comes from some environment that is external to the agent; we characterize the state of this environment by a hidden or unknown variable $h \in \mathcal{H}$, known as the **state of nature**. Finally, we assume we know a **loss function** $\ell(h, a)$, that specifies the loss we incur if we take action a when the state of nature is h. The goal is to define a **policy**, also called an **estimator** or **decision procedure**, which specifies which action to take in response to each possible observation, $a = \delta(\boldsymbol{x})$, so as to minimize the expected loss, also called the **risk**:

$$\delta^*(\cdot) = \underset{\delta}{\operatorname{argmin}}\, R(\delta) \tag{34.1}$$

where the risk is given by

$$R(\delta) = \mathbb{E}\left[\ell(h, \delta(\mathbf{X}))\right] \tag{34.2}$$

The key question is how to define the above expectation. We can use a frequentist or Bayesian approach, as we discuss below.

34.1.2 Frequentist decision theory

In **frequentist decision theory**, we treat the state of nature h as a fixed but unknown quantity, and treat the data $\mathbf{X}$ as random. Hence we take expectations wrt the data, which gives us the **frequentist risk**:

$$r(\delta|h) = \mathbb{E}_{p(\boldsymbol{x}|h)}\left[\ell(h, \delta(\boldsymbol{x}))\right] = \int p(\boldsymbol{x}|h)\ell(h, \delta(\boldsymbol{x}))d\boldsymbol{x} \tag{34.3}$$

The idea is that a good estimator will have low risk across many different datasets.

Unfortunately, the state of nature is not known, so the above quantity cannot be computed. There are several possible solutions to this. One idea is to put a prior distribution on h, and then to compute the **Bayes risk**, also called the **integrated risk**:

$$R_B(\delta) \triangleq \mathbb{E}_{p(h)}\left[r(\delta|h)\right] = \int p(h)p(\boldsymbol{x}|h)\ell(h, \delta(\boldsymbol{x}))\, dh\, d\boldsymbol{x} \tag{34.4}$$

A decision rule that minimizes the Bayes risk is known as a **Bayes estimator**.

Of course the use of a prior might seem undesirable in the context of frequentist statistics. We can therefore use the **maximum risk** instead. This is defined as follows:

$$R_{\max}(\delta) = \max_h r(\delta|h) \tag{34.5}$$

Minimizing the maximum risk gives rise to a **minimax estimator**:

$$\delta^* = \min_\delta \max_h r_h(\delta) \tag{34.6}$$

Minimax estimators have a certain appeal. However, computing them can be hard. And furthermore, they are very pessimistic. In fact, one can show that all minimax estimators are equivalent to Bayes estimators under a **least favorable prior**. In most statistical situations (excluding game theoretic ones), assuming nature is an adversary is not a reasonable assumption. See [BS94, p449] for further discussion of this point.

34.1.3   Bayesian decision theory

In **Bayesian decision theory**, we treat the data as an observed constant, $\boldsymbol{x}$, and the state of nature as an unknown random variable. The **posterior expected loss** for picking action a is defined as follows:

$$\rho(a|\boldsymbol{x}) \triangleq \mathbb{E}_{p(h|\boldsymbol{x})}\left[\ell(h, a)\right] = \int \ell(h, a)p(h|\boldsymbol{x})dh \tag{34.7}$$

We can define the posterior expected loss, or **Bayesian risk**, for an estimator using

$$\rho(\delta|\boldsymbol{x}) = \rho(\delta(\boldsymbol{x})|\boldsymbol{x}) \tag{34.8}$$

The **optimal policy** specifies what action to take so as to minimize the expected loss. This is given by

$$\delta^*(\boldsymbol{x}) = \operatorname*{argmin}_{a \in \mathcal{A}} \mathbb{E}_{p(h|\boldsymbol{x})}\left[\ell(h, a)\right] \tag{34.9}$$

An alternative, but equivalent, way of stating this result is as follows. Let us define a **utility function** $U(h, a)$ to be the desirability of each possible action in each possible state. If we set $U(h, a) = -\ell(h, a)$, then the optimal policy is as follows:

$$\delta^*(\boldsymbol{x}) = \operatorname*{argmax}_{a \in \mathcal{A}} \mathbb{E}_h\left[U(h, a)\right] \tag{34.10}$$

This is called the **maximum expected utility principle**.

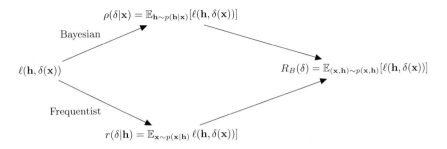

Figure 34.1: *Illustration of how the Bayesian and frequentist approaches to decision making incur the same Bayes risk.*

34.1.4 Frequentist optimality of the Bayesian approach

We see that the Bayesian approach, given by Equation (34.9), which picks the best action for each individual observation $\boldsymbol{x}$, will also optimize the Bayes risk in Equation (34.4), which picks the best policy for all possible observations. This follows from **Fubini's theorem**, which lets us exchange the order of integration in a double integral:

$$R_B(\delta) = \mathbb{E}_{p(\boldsymbol{x})}\left[\rho(\delta|\boldsymbol{x})\right] = \mathbb{E}_{p(h|\boldsymbol{x})p(\boldsymbol{x})}\left[\ell(h, \delta(\boldsymbol{x}))\right] \tag{34.11}$$

$$= \mathbb{E}_{p(h)}\left[r(\delta|h)\right] = \mathbb{E}_{p(h)p(\boldsymbol{x}|h)}\left[\ell(h, \delta(\boldsymbol{x}))\right] \tag{34.12}$$

See Figure 34.1 for an illustration. The above result tells us that the Bayesian approach has optimal frequentist properties.

More generally, one can show that any **admissable policy**[1] is a Bayes policy with respect to some, possibly improper, prior distribution, a result known as **Wald's theorem** [Wal47]. (See [DR21] for a more general version of this result.) Thus we arguably lose nothing by "restricting" ourselves to the Bayesian approach (although we need to check that our modeling assumptions are adequate, a topic we discuss in Section 3.9). See [BS94, p448] for further discussion of this point.

Another advantage of the Bayesian approach is that is constructive, that is, it specifies how to create the optimal policy (estimator) given a particular dataset. By contrast, the frequentist approach allows you to use any estimator you like; it just derives the properties of this estimator across multiple datasets, but does not tell you how to create the estimator.

34.1.5 Examples of one-shot decision making problems

In the sections below, we give some common examples of **one-shot** decision making problems (i.e., making a single decision, not a sequence of decisions) that arise in ML applications.

---

1. An estimator is said to be **admissible** if it is not strictly dominated by any other estimator. We say that δ^1 **dominates** δ^2 if $R(\boldsymbol{\theta}, \delta^1) \leq R(\boldsymbol{\theta}, \delta^2)$ for all $\boldsymbol{\theta}$. The domination is said to be strict if the inequality is strict for some $\boldsymbol{\theta}^*$.

34.1.5.1   Classification

Suppose the states of nature correspond to class labels, so $\mathcal{H} = \mathcal{Y} = \{1, \ldots, C\}$. Furthermore, suppose the actions also correspond to class labels, so $\mathcal{A} = \mathcal{Y}$. In this setting, a very commonly used loss function is the **zero-one loss** $\ell_{01}(y^*, \hat{y})$, defined as follows:

$$
\begin{array}{c|cc}
 & \hat{y} = 0 & \hat{y} = 1 \\
\hline
y^* = 0 & 0 & 1 \\
y^* = 1 & 1 & 0
\end{array}
\tag{34.13}
$$

We can write this more concisely as follows:

$$
\ell_{01}(y^*, \hat{y}) = \mathbb{I}(y^* \neq \hat{y})
\tag{34.14}
$$

In this case, the posterior expected loss is

$$
\rho(\hat{y}|\boldsymbol{x}) = p(\hat{y} \neq y^*|\boldsymbol{x}) = 1 - p(y^* = \hat{y}|\boldsymbol{x})
\tag{34.15}
$$

Hence the action that minimizes the expected loss is to choose the most probable label:

$$
\delta(\boldsymbol{x}) = \operatorname*{argmax}_{y \in \mathcal{Y}} p(y|\boldsymbol{x})
\tag{34.16}
$$

This corresponds to the **mode** of the posterior distribution, also known as the **maximum a posteriori** or **MAP estimate**.

We can generalize the loss function to associate different costs for false positives and false negatives. We can also allow for a "**reject action**", in which the decision maker abstains from classifying when it is not sufficiently confident. This is called **selective prediction**; see Section 19.3.3 for details.

34.1.5.2   Regression

Now suppose the hidden state of nature is a scalar $h \in \mathbb{R}$, and the corresponding action is also a scalar, $y \in \mathbb{R}$. The most common loss for continuous states and actions is the ℓ_2 **loss**, also called **squared error** or **quadratic loss**, which is defined as follows:

$$
\ell_2(h, y) = (h - y)^2
\tag{34.17}
$$

In this case, the risk is given by

$$
\rho(y|\boldsymbol{x}) = \mathbb{E}\left[(h - y)^2|\boldsymbol{x}\right] = \mathbb{E}\left[h^2|\boldsymbol{x}\right] - 2y\mathbb{E}\left[h|\boldsymbol{x}\right] + y^2
\tag{34.18}
$$

The optimal action must satisfy the condition that the derivative of the risk (at that point) is zero (as explained in Chapter 6). Hence the optimal action is to pick the posterior mean:

$$
\frac{\partial}{\partial y}\rho(y|\boldsymbol{x}) = -2\mathbb{E}\left[h|\boldsymbol{x}\right] + 2y = 0 \;\Rightarrow\; \delta(\boldsymbol{x}) = \mathbb{E}\left[h|\boldsymbol{x}\right] = \int h \, p(h|\boldsymbol{x}) dh
\tag{34.19}
$$

This is often called the **minimum mean squared error** estimate or **MMSE** estimate.

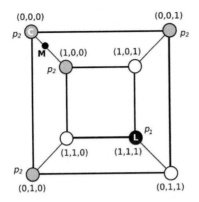

Figure 34.2: A distribution on a discrete space in which the mode (black point L, with probability p_1) is untypical of most of the probability mass (gray circles, with probability $p_2 < p_1$). The small black circle labeled M (near the top left) is the posterior mean, which is not well defined in a discrete state space. C (the top left vertex) is the centroid estimator, made up of the maximizer of the posterior marginals. See text for details. From Figure 1 of [CL07]. Used with kind permission of Luis Carvalho.

34.1.5.3 Parameter estimation

Suppose the states of nature correspond to unknown parameters, so $\mathcal{H} = \Theta = \mathbb{R}^D$. Furthermore, suppose the actions also correspond to parameters, so $\mathcal{A} = \Theta$. Finally, we assume the observed data (that is input to the policy/estimator) is a dataset, such as $\mathcal{D} = \{(\boldsymbol{x}_n, \boldsymbol{y}_n) : n = 1 : N\}$. If we use quadratic loss, then the optimal action is to pick the posterior mean. If we use 0-1 loss, then the optimal action is to pick the posterior mode, i.e., the MAP estimate:

$$\delta(\mathcal{D}) = \hat{\boldsymbol{\theta}} = \underset{\boldsymbol{\theta} \in \Theta}{\operatorname{argmax}}\, p(\boldsymbol{\theta}|\mathcal{D}) \tag{34.20}$$

34.1.5.4 Estimating discrete parameters

The MAP estimate is the optimal estimate when the loss function is 0-1 loss, $\ell(\boldsymbol{\theta}, \hat{\boldsymbol{\theta}}) = \mathbb{I}\left(\boldsymbol{\theta} \neq \hat{\boldsymbol{\theta}}\right)$, as we show in Section 34.1.5.1. However, this does not give any "partial credit" for estimating some of the components of $\boldsymbol{\theta}$ correctly. An alternative is to use the **Hamming loss**:

$$\ell(\boldsymbol{\theta}, \hat{\boldsymbol{\theta}}) = \sum_{d=1}^{D} \mathbb{I}\left(\theta_d \neq \hat{\theta}_d\right) \tag{34.21}$$

In this case, one can show that the optimal estimator is the vector of **max marginals**

$$\hat{\boldsymbol{\theta}} = \left[\underset{\theta_d}{\operatorname{argmax}} \int_{\boldsymbol{\theta}_{-d}} p(\boldsymbol{\theta}|\mathcal{D}) d\boldsymbol{\theta}_{-d}\right]_{d=1}^{D} \tag{34.22}$$

This is also called the **maximizer of posterior marginals** or **MPM** estimate. Note that computing the max marginals involves marginalization and maximization, and thus depends on the whole distribution; this tends to be more robust than the MAP estimate [MMP87].

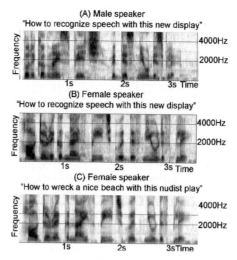

Figure 34.3: Spectograms for three different spoken sentences. The x-axis shows progression of time and the y-axis shows different frequency bands. The energy of the signal in different bands is shown as intensity in grayscale values with progression of time. (A) and (B) show spectrograms of the same sentence "How to recognize speech with this new display" spoken by two different speakers, male and female. Although the frequency characterization is similar, the formant frequencies are much more clearly defined in the speech of the female speaker. (C) shows the spectrogram of the utterance "How to wreck a nice beach with this nudist play" spoken by the same female speaker as in (B). (A) and (B) are not identical even though they are composed of the same words. (B) and (C) are similar to each other even though they are not the same sentences. From Figure 1.2 of [Gan07]. Used with kind permission of Madhavi Ganapathiraju.

For example, consider a problem in which we must estimate a vector of binary variables. Figure 34.2 shows a distribution on $\{0, 1\}^3$, where points are arranged such that they are connected to their nearest neighbors, as measured by Hamming distance. The black state (circle) labeled L (configuration (1,1,1)) has probability p_1, and corresponds to the MAP estimate. The 4 gray states have probability $p_2 < p_1$; and the 3 white states have probability 0. Although the black state is the most probable, it is untypical of the posterior: all its nearest neighbors have probability zero, meaning it is very isolated. By contrast, the gray states, although slightly less probable, are all connected to other gray states, and together they constitute much more of the total probability mass.

In the example in Figure 34.2, we have $p(\theta_j = 0) = 3p_2$ and $p(\theta_j = 1) = p_2 + p_1$ for $j = 1 : 3$. If $2p_2 > p_1$, the vector of max marginals is $(0, 0, 0)$. This MPM estimate can be shown to be a **centroid estimator**, in the sense that it minimizes the squared distance to the posterior mean (the center of mass), yet it (usually) represents a valid configuration, unlike the actual mean (fractional estimates do not make sense for discrete problems). See [CL07] for further discussion of this point.

34.1.5.5 Structured prediction

In some problems, such as natural language processing or computer vision, the desired action is to return an output object $y \in \mathcal{Y}$, such as a set of labels or body poses, that not only is probable given the input x, but is also internally consistent. For example, suppose x is a sequence of phonemes and

$\boldsymbol{y}$ is a sequence of words. Although $\boldsymbol{x}$ might sound more like $\boldsymbol{y}$ = "How to wreck a nice beach" on a word-by-word basis, if we take the sequence of words into account then we may find (under a language model prior) that $\boldsymbol{y}$ = "How to recognize speech" is more likely overall. (See Figure 34.3.) We can capture this kind of dependency amongst outputs, given inputs, using a **structured prediction model**, such as a conditional random field (see Section 4.4).

In addition to modeling dependencies in $p(\boldsymbol{y}|\boldsymbol{x})$, we may prefer certain action choices $\hat{\boldsymbol{y}}$, which we capture in the loss function $\ell(\boldsymbol{y}, \hat{\boldsymbol{y}})$. For example, referring to Figure 34.3, we may be reluctant to assume the user said $\hat{y}_t$="nudist" at step t unless we are very confident of this prediction, since the cost of mis-categorizing this word may be higher than for other words.

Given a loss function, we can pick the optimal action using **minimum Bayes risk** decoding:

$$\hat{\boldsymbol{y}} = \min_{\hat{\boldsymbol{y}} \in \mathcal{Y}} \sum_{\boldsymbol{y} \in \mathcal{Y}} p(\boldsymbol{y}|\boldsymbol{x}) \ell(\boldsymbol{y}, \hat{\boldsymbol{y}}) \tag{34.23}$$

We can approximate the expectation empirically by sampling M solutions $\boldsymbol{y}^m \sim p(\boldsymbol{y}|\boldsymbol{x})$ from the posterior predictive distribution. (Ideally these are diverse from each other.) We use the same set of M samples to approximate the minimization to get

$$\hat{\boldsymbol{y}} \approx \min_{\boldsymbol{y}^i, i \in \{1,\dots,M\}} \sum_{j \in \{1,\dots,M\}} p(\boldsymbol{y}^j|\boldsymbol{x}) \ell(\boldsymbol{y}^j, \boldsymbol{y}^i) \tag{34.24}$$

This is called **empirical MBR** [Pre+17a], who applied it to computer vision problems. A similar approach was adopted in [Fre+22], who applied it to neural machine translation.

34.1.5.6 Fairness

Models trained with ML are increasingly being used to high-stakes applications, such as deciding whether someone should be released from prison or not, etc. In such applications, it is important that we focus not only on accuracy, but also on **fairness**. A variety of definitions for what is meant by fairness have been proposed (see e.g., [VR18]), many of which entail conflicting goals [Kle18]. Below we mention a few common definitions, which can all be interpreted decision theoretically.

We consider a binary classification problem with true label Y, predicted label $\hat{Y}$ and **sensitive attribute** S (such as gender or race). The concept of **equal opportunity** requires equal true positive rates across subgroups, i.e., $p(\hat{Y} = 1|Y = 1, S = 0) = p(\hat{Y} = 1|Y = 1, S = 1)$. The concept of **equal odds** requires equal true positive rates across subgroups, and also equal false positive rates across subgroups, i.e., $p(\hat{Y} = 1|Y = 0, S = 0) = p(\hat{Y} = 1|Y = 0, S = 1)$. The concept of **statistical parity** requires positive predictions to be unaffected by the value of the protected attribute, regardless of the true label, i.e., $p(\hat{Y} = 1|S = 0) = p(\hat{Y} = 1|S = 1)$.

For more details on this topic, see e.g., [KR19].

34.2 Decision (influence) diagrams

When dealing with structured multi-stage decision problems, it is useful to use a graphical notation called an **influence diagram** [HM81; KM08], also called a **decision diagram**. This extends directed probabilistic graphical models (Chapter 4) by adding **decision nodes** (also called **action nodes**), represented by rectangles, and **utility nodes** (also called **value nodes**), represented by diamonds. The original random variables are called **chance nodes**, and are represented by ovals, as usual.

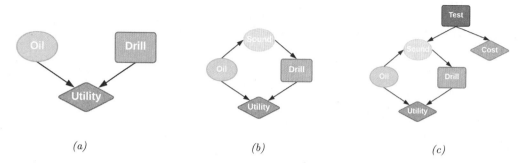

(a) (b) (c)

Figure 34.4: Influence diagrams for the oil wildcatter problem. Ovals are random variables (chance nodes), squares are decision (action) nodes, diamonds are utility (value) nodes. (a) Basic model. (b) An extension in which we have an information arc from the Sound chance node to the Drill decision node. (c) An extension in which we get to decide whether to perform a test or not, as well as whether to drill or not.

34.2.1   Example: oil wildcatter

As an example (from [Rai68]), consider creating a model for the decision problem faced by an oil **"wildcatter"**, which is a person who drills wildcat wells, which are exploration wells drilled in areas not known to be oil fields.

Suppose you have to decide whether to drill an oil well or not at a given location. You have two possible actions: $d = 1$ means drill, $d = 0$ means don't drill. You assume there are 3 states of nature: $o = 0$ means the well is dry, $o = 1$ means it is wet (has some oil), and $o = 2$ means it is soaking (has a lot of oil). We can represent this as a decision diagram as shown in Figure 34.4(a).

Suppose your prior beliefs are $p(o) = [0.5, 0.3, 0.2]$, and your utility function $U(d, o)$ is specified by the following table:

	$o = 0$	$o = 1$	$o = 2$
$d = 0$	0	0	0
$d = 1$	-70	50	200

We see that if you don't drill, you incur no costs, but also make no money. If you drill a dry well, you lose \$70; if you drill a wet well, you gain \$50; and if you drill a soaking well, you gain \$200.

What action should you take if you have no information beyond your prior knowledge? Your prior expected utility for taking action d is

$$\text{EU}(d) = \sum_{o=0}^{2} p(o) U(d, o) \tag{34.25}$$

We find $\text{EU}(d = 0) = 0$ and $\text{EU}(d = 1) = 20$ and hence the maximum expected utility is

$$\text{MEU} = \max\{\text{EU}(d = 0), \text{EU}(d = 1)\} = \max\{0, 20\} = 20 \tag{34.26}$$

Thus the optimal action is to drill, $d^* = 1$.

34.2.2 Information arcs

Now let us consider a slight extension to the model, in which you have access to a measurement (called a "sounding"), which is a noisy indicator about the state of the oil well. Hence we add an $O \rightarrow S$ arc to the model. In addition, we assume that the outcome of the sounding test will be available before we decide whether to drill or not; hence we add an **information arc** from S to D. This is illustrated in Figure 34.4(b). Note that the utility depends on the action and the true state of the world, but not the measurement.

We assume the sounding variable can be in one of 3 states: $s = 0$ is a diffuse reflection pattern, suggesting no oil; $s = 1$ is an open reflection pattern, suggesting some oil; and $s = 2$ is a closed reflection pattern, indicating lots of oil. Since S is caused by O, we add an $O \rightarrow S$ arc to our model. Let us model the reliability of our sensor using the following conditional distribution for $p(S|O)$:

	$s = 0$	$s = 1$	$s = 2$
$o = 0$	0.6	0.3	0.1
$o = 1$	0.3	0.4	0.3
$o = 2$	0.1	0.4	0.5

Suppose the sounding observation is s. The posterior expected utility of performing action d is

$$\mathrm{EU}(d|s) = \sum_{o=0}^{2} p(o|s)U(o, d) \tag{34.27}$$

We need to compute this for each possible observation, $s \in \{0, 1, 2\}$, and each possible action, $d \in \{0, 1\}$. If $s = 0$, we find the posterior over the oil state is $p(o|s = 0) = [0.732, 0.219, 0.049]$, and hence $\mathrm{EU}(d = 0|s = 0) = 0$ and $\mathrm{EU}(d = 1|s = 0) = -30.5$. If $s = 1$, we similarly find $\mathrm{EU}(d = 0|s = 1) = 0$ and $\mathrm{EU}(d = 1|s = 1) = 32.9$. If $s = 2$, we find $\mathrm{EU}(d = 0|s = 2) = 0$ and $\mathrm{EU}(d = 1|s = 2) = 87.5$. Hence the optimal policy $d^*(s)$ is as follows: if $s = 0$, choose $d = 0$ and get $0; if $s = 1$, choose $d = 1$ and get $32.9; and if $s = 2$, choose $d = 1$ and get $87.5.

The maximum expected utility of the wildcatter, before seeing the experimental sounding, can be computed using

$$\mathrm{MEU} = \sum_{s} p(s)\mathrm{EU}(d^*(s)|s) \tag{34.28}$$

where prior marginal on the outcome of the test is $p(s) = \sum_{o} p(o)p(s|o) = [0.41, 0.35, 0.24]$. Hence the MEU is

$$\mathrm{MEU} = 0.41 \times 0 + 0.35 \times 32.9 + 0.24 \times 87.5 = 32.2 \tag{34.29}$$

These numbers can be summarized in the **decision tree** shown in Figure 34.5.

34.2.3 Value of information

Now suppose you can choose whether to do the test or not. This can be modelled as shown in Figure 34.4(c), where we add a new test node T. If $T = 1$, we do the test, and S can enter states $\{0, 1, 2\}$, determined by O, exactly as above. If $T = 0$, we don't do the test, and S enters a special unknown state. There is also some cost associated with performing the test.

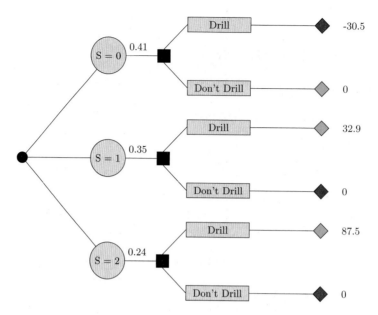

Figure 34.5: Decision tree for the oil wildcatter problem. Black circles are chance variables, black squares are decision nodes, diamonds are the resulting utilities. Green leaf nodes have higher utility than red leaf nodes.

Is it worth doing the test? This depends on how much our MEU changes if we know the outcome of the test (namely the state of S). If you don't do the test, we have MEU = 20 from Equation (34.26). If you do the test, you have MEU = 32.2 from Equation (34.29). So the improvement in utility if you do the test (and act optimally on its outcome) is \$12.2. This is called the **value of perfect information** (VPI). So we should do the test as long as it costs less than \$12.2.

In terms of graphical models, the VPI of a variable S can be determined by computing the MEU for the base influence diagram, $\mathcal{G}$, in Figure 34.4(b), and then computing the MEU for the same influence diagram where we add information arcs from S to the action node, and then computing the difference. In other words,

$$\text{VPI} = \text{MEU}(\mathcal{G} + S \rightarrow D) - \text{MEU}(\mathcal{G}) \tag{34.30}$$

where D is the decision node and S is the variable we are measuring. This will tell us whether it is worth adding obtaining measurement S.

34.2.4 Computing the optimal policy

In general, given an influence diagram, we can compute the optimal policy automatically by modifying the variable elimination algorithm (Section 9.5), as explained in [LN01; KM08]. The basic idea is to work backwards from the final action, computing the optimal decision at each step, assuming all following actions are chosen optimally. When the influence diagram has a simple chain structure, as in a Markov decision process (Section 34.5), the result is equivalent to Bellman's equation (Section 34.5.5).

34.3   A/B testing

Suppose you are trying to decide which version of a product is likely to sell more, or which version of a drug is likely to work better. Let us call the versions you are choosing between A and B; sometimes version A is called the **control**, and version B is called the **treatment**. (Sometimes the different actions are called **"arms"**.)

A very common approach to such problems is to use an **A/B test**, in which you try both actions out for a while, by randomly assigning a different action to different subsets of the population, and then you measure the resulting accumulated **reward** from each action, and you pick the winner. (This is sometimes called a "**test and roll**" approach, since you test which method is best, and then roll it out for the rest of the population.)

A key problem in A/B testing is to come up with a decision rule, or policy, for deciding which action is best, after obtaining potentially noisy results during the test phase. Another problem is to choose how many people to assign to the treatment, n_1, and how many to the control, n_0. The fundamental tradeoff is that using larger values of n_1 and n_0 will help you collect more data and hence be more confident in picking the best action, but this incurs an **opportunity cost**, because the testing phase involves performing actions that may not result in the highest reward. (This is an example of the exploration-exploitation tradeoff, which we discuss more in Section 34.4.3.) In this section, we give a simple Bayesian decision theoretic analysis of this problem, following the presentation of [FB19].[2] More details on A/B testing can be found in [KTX20].

34.3.1   A Bayesian approach

We assume the i'th reward for action j is given by $Y_{ij} \sim \mathcal{N}(\mu_j, \sigma_j^2)$ for $i = 1 : n_j$ and $j = 0 : 1$, where $j = 0$ corresponds to the control (action A), $j = 1$ corresponds to the treatment (action B), and n_j is the number of samples you collect from group j. The parameters μ_j are the expected reward for action j; our goal is to estimate these parameters. (For simplicity, we assume the σ_j^2 are known.)

We will adopt a Bayesian approach, which is well suited to sequential decision problems. For simplicity, we will use Gaussian priors for the unknowns, $\mu_j \sim \mathcal{N}(m_j, \tau_j^2)$, where m_j is the prior mean reward for action j, and τ_j is our confidence in this prior. We assume the prior parameters are known. (In practice we can use an empirical Bayes approach, as we discuss in Section 34.3.2.)

34.3.1.1   Optimal policy

Initially we assume the sample size of the experiment (i.e., the values n_1 for the treatment and n_0 for the control) are known. Our goal is to compute the optimal policy or decision rule $\pi(\boldsymbol{y}_1, \boldsymbol{y}_0)$, which specifies which action to deploy, where $\boldsymbol{y}_j = (y_{1j}, \dots, y_{n_j,j})$ is the data from action j.

The optimal policy is simple: choose the action with the greater expected posterior expected reward:

$$\pi^*(\boldsymbol{y}_1, \boldsymbol{y}_0) = \begin{cases} 1 & \text{if } \mathbb{E}\left[\mu_1 | \boldsymbol{y}_1\right] \geq \mathbb{E}\left[\mu_0 | \boldsymbol{y}_0\right] \\ 0 & \text{if } \mathbb{E}\left[\mu_1 | \boldsymbol{y}_1\right] < \mathbb{E}\left[\mu_0 | \boldsymbol{y}_0\right] \end{cases} \tag{34.31}$$

---

2. For a similar set of results in the time-discounted setting, see `https://chris-said.io/2020/01/10/optimizing-sample-sizes-in-ab-testing-part-I`.

All that remains is to compute the posterior. over the unknown parameters, μ_j. Applying Bayes' rule for Gaussians (Equation (2.121)), we find that the corresponding posterior is given by

$$p(\mu_j | \boldsymbol{y}_j, n_j) = \mathcal{N}(\mu_j | \, \widehat{m}_j, \widehat{\tau}_j^2) \tag{34.32}$$

$$1/\, \widehat{\tau}_j = n_j/\sigma_j^2 + 1/\tau_j^2 \tag{34.33}$$

$$\widehat{m}_j \, / \, \widehat{\tau}_j = n_j \bar{y}_j/\sigma_j^2 + m_j/\tau_j^2 \tag{34.34}$$

We see that the posterior precision (inverse variance) is a weighted sum of the prior precision plus n_j units of measurement precision. We also see that the posterior precision weighted mean is a sum of the prior precision weighted mean and the measurement precision weighted mean.

Given the posterior, we can plug $\widehat{m}_j$ into Equation (34.31). In the fully symmetric case, where $n_1 = n_0$, $m_1 = m_0 = m$, $\tau_1 = \tau_0 = \tau$, and $\sigma_1 = \sigma_0 = \sigma$, we find that the optimal policy is to simply "pick the winner", which is the arm with higher empirical performance:

$$\pi^*(\boldsymbol{y}_1, \boldsymbol{y}_0) = \mathbb{I}\left(\frac{m}{\tau^2} + \frac{\bar{y}_1}{\sigma^2} > \frac{m}{\tau^2} + \frac{\bar{y}_0}{\sigma^2} \right) = \mathbb{I}\left(\bar{y}_1 > \bar{y}_0 \right) \tag{34.35}$$

However, when the problem is asymmetric, we need to take into account the different sample sizes and/or different prior beliefs.

34.3.1.2 Optimal sample size

We now discuss how to compute the optimal sample size for each arm of the experiment, i.e, the values n_0 and n_1. We assume the total population size is N, and we cannot reuse people from the testing phase,

The prior expected reward in the testing phase is given by

$$\mathbb{E}[R_{\text{test}}] = n_0 m_0 + n_1 m_1 \tag{34.36}$$

The expected reward in the roll phase depends on the decision rule $\pi(\boldsymbol{y}_1, \boldsymbol{y}_0)$ that we use:

$$\mathbb{E}_\pi[R_{\text{roll}}] = \int_{\mu_1} \int_{\mu_0} \int_{\boldsymbol{y}_1} \int_{\boldsymbol{y}_0} (N - n_1 - n_0)\left(\pi(\boldsymbol{y}_1, \boldsymbol{y}_0)\mu_1 + (1 - \pi(\boldsymbol{y}_1, \boldsymbol{y}_0))\mu_0 \right) \tag{34.37}$$

$$\times \, p(\boldsymbol{y}_0 | \mu_0) p(\boldsymbol{y}_1 | \mu_1) p(\mu_0) p(\mu_1) d\boldsymbol{y}_0 d\boldsymbol{y}_1 d\mu_0 d\mu_1 \tag{34.38}$$

For $\pi = \pi^*$ one can show that this equals

$$\mathbb{E}[R_{\text{roll}}] \triangleq \mathbb{E}_{\pi*}[R_{\text{roll}}] = (N - n_1 - n_0)\left(m_1 + e\Phi(\frac{e}{v}) + v\phi(\frac{e}{v}) \right) \tag{34.39}$$

where ϕ is the Gaussian pdf, Φ is the Gaussian cdf, $e = m_0 - m_1$ and

$$v = \sqrt{\frac{\tau_1^4}{\tau_1^2 + \sigma_1^2/n_1} + \frac{\tau_0^4}{\tau_0^2 + \sigma_0^2/n_0}} \tag{34.40}$$

In the fully symmetric case, Equation (34.39) simplifies to

$$\mathbb{E}[R_{\text{roll}}] = \underbrace{(N - 2n)m}_{R_a} + \underbrace{(N - 2n)\frac{\sqrt{2}\tau^2}{\sqrt{\pi}\sqrt{2\tau^2 + \frac{2}{n}\sigma^2}}}_{R_b} \tag{34.41}$$

This has an intuitive interpretation. The first term, R_a, is the prior reward we expect to get before we learn anything about the arms. The second term, R_b, is the reward we expect to see by virtue of picking the optimal action to deploy.

Let us we write $R_b = (N - 2n)R_i$, where R_i is the incremental gain. We see that the incremental gain increases with n, because we are more likely to pick the correct action with a larger sample size; however, this gain can only be accrued for a smaller number of people, as shown by the $N - 2n$ prefactor. (This is a consequence of the explore-exploit tradeoff.)

The total expected reward is given by adding Equation (34.36) and Equation (34.41):

$$\mathbb{E}[R] = \mathbb{E}[R_{\text{test}}] + \mathbb{E}[R_{\text{roll}}] = Nm + (N - 2n)\left(\frac{\sqrt{2}\tau^2}{\sqrt{\pi}\sqrt{2\tau^2 + \frac{2}{n}\sigma^2}} \right) \tag{34.42}$$

(The equation for the nonsymmetric case is given in [FB19].)

We can maximize the expected reward in Equation (34.42) to find the optimal sample size for the testing phase, which (from symmetry) satisfies $n_1^* = n_2^* = n^*$, and from $\frac{d}{dn^*}\mathbb{E}[R] = 0$ satisfies

$$n^* = \sqrt{\frac{N}{4}u^2 + \left(\frac{3}{4}u^2\right)^2} - \frac{3}{4}u^2 \leq \sqrt{N}\frac{\sigma}{2\tau} \tag{34.43}$$

where $u^2 = \frac{\sigma^2}{\tau^2}$. Thus we see that the optimal sample size n^* increases as the observation noise σ increases, since we need to collect more data to be confident of the right decision. However, the optimal sample size decreases with τ, since a prior belief that the effect size $\delta = \mu_1 - \mu_0$ will be large implies we expect to need less data to reach a confident conclusion.

34.3.1.3 Regret

Given a policy, it is natural to wonder how good it is. We define the **regret** of a policy to be the difference between the expected reward given **perfect information** (PI) about the true best action and the expected reward due to our policy. Minimizing regret is equivalent to making the expected reward of our policy equal to the best possible reward (which may be high or low, depending on the problem).

An oracle with perfect information about which μ_j is bigger would pick the highest scoring action, and hence get an expected reward of $N\mathbb{E}[\max(\mu_1, \mu_2)]$. Since we assume $\mu_j \sim \mathcal{N}(m, \tau^2)$, we have

$$\mathbb{E}[R|PI] = N\left(m + \frac{\tau}{\sqrt{\pi}}\right) \tag{34.44}$$

Therefore the regret from the optimal policy is given by

$$\mathbb{E}[R|PI] - (\mathbb{E}[R_{\text{test}}|\pi^*] + \mathbb{E}[R_{\text{roll}}|\pi^*]) = N\frac{\tau}{\sqrt{\pi}}\left(1 - \frac{\tau}{\sqrt{\tau^2 + \frac{\sigma^2}{n^*}}}\right) + \frac{2n^*\tau^2}{\sqrt{\pi}\sqrt{\tau^2 + \frac{\sigma^2}{n^*}}} \tag{34.45}$$

One can show that the regret is $O(\sqrt{N})$, which is optimal for this problem when using a time horizon (population size) of N [AG13].

34.3.1.4 Expected error rate

Sometimes the goal is posed as **best arm identification**, which means identifying whether $\mu_1 > \mu_0$ or not. That is, if we define $\delta = \mu_1 - \mu_0$, we want to know if $\delta > 0$ or $\delta < 0$. This is naturally phrased as a **hypothesis test**. However, this is arguably the wrong objective, since it is usually not worth spending money on collecting a large sample size to be confibeny that $\delta > 0$ (say) if the magnitude of δ is small. Instead, it makes more sense to optimize total expected reward, using the method in Section 34.3.1.1.

Nevertheless, we may want to know the probability that we have picked the wrong arm if we use the policy from Section 34.3.1.1. In the symmetric case, this is given by the following:

$$\Pr(\pi(\boldsymbol{y}_1, \boldsymbol{y}_0) = 1 | \mu_1 < \mu_0) = \Pr(Y_1 - Y_0 > 0 | \mu_1 < \mu_0) = 1 - \Phi\left(\frac{\mu_1 - \mu_0}{\sigma\sqrt{\frac{1}{n_1} + \frac{1}{n_0}}}\right) \tag{34.46}$$

The above expression assumed that μ_j are known. Since they are not known, we can compute the expected error rate using $\mathbb{E}\left[\Pr(\pi(\boldsymbol{y}_1, \boldsymbol{y}_0) = 1 | \mu_1 < \mu_0)\right]$. By symmetry, the quantity $\mathbb{E}\left[\Pr(\pi(\boldsymbol{y}_1, \boldsymbol{y}_0) = 0 | \mu_1 > \mu_0)\right]$ is the same. One can show that both quantities are given by

$$\text{Prob. error} = \frac{1}{4} - \frac{1}{2\pi} \arctan\left(\frac{\sqrt{2}\tau}{\sigma}\sqrt{\frac{n_1 n_0}{n_1 + n_0}}\right) \tag{34.47}$$

As expected, the error rate decreases with the sample size n_1 and n_0, increases with observation noise σ, and decreases with variance of the effect size τ. Thus a policy that minimizes the classification error will also maximize expected reward, but it may pick an overly large sample size, since it does not take into account the magnitude of δ.

34.3.2 Example

In this section, we give a simple example of the above framework. Suppose our goal is to do **website testing**, where have two different versions of a webpage that we want to compare in terms of their **click through rate**. The observed data is now binary, $y_{ij} \sim \text{Ber}(\mu_j)$, so it is natural to use a beta prior, $\mu_j \sim \text{Beta}(\alpha, \beta)$ (see Section 3.4.1). However, in this case the optimal sample size and decision rule is harder to compute (see [FB19; Sta+17] for details). As a simple approximation, we can assume $\overline{y}_{ij} \sim \mathcal{N}(\mu_j, \sigma^2)$, where $\mu_j \sim \mathcal{N}(m, \tau^2)$, $m = \frac{\alpha}{\alpha+\beta}$, $\tau^2 = \frac{\alpha\beta}{(\alpha+\beta)^2(\alpha+\beta+1)}$, and $\sigma^2 = m(1 - m)$.

To set the Gaussian prior, [FB19] used empirical data from about 2000 prior A/B tests. For each test, they observed the number of times the page was served with each of the two variations, as well as the total number of times a user clicked on each version. Given this data, they used a hierarchical Bayesian model to infer $\mu_j \sim \mathcal{N}(m = 0.68, \tau = 0.03)$. This prior implies that the expected effect size is quite small, $\mathbb{E}\left[|\mu_1 - \mu_0|\right] = 0.023$. (This is consistent with the results in [Aze+20], who found that most changes made to the Microsoft Bing EXP platform had negligible effect, although there were occasionally some "big hits".)

With this prior, and assuming a population of $N = 100,000$, Equation (34.43) says that the optimal number of trials to run is $n_1^* = n_0^* = 2284$. The expected reward (number of clicks or **conversions**) in the testing phase is $\mathbb{E}\left[R_{\text{test}}\right] = 3106$, and in the deployment phase $\mathbb{E}\left[R_{\text{roll}}\right] = 66,430$, for a total reward of $69,536$. The expected error rate is 10%.

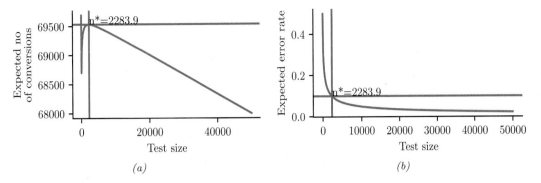

Figure 34.6: Total expected profit (a) and error rate (b) as a function of the sample size used for website testing. Generated by ab_test_demo.ipynb.

In Figure 34.6a, we plot the expected reward vs the size of the test phase n. We see that the reward increases sharply with n to the global maximum at $n^* = 2284$, and then drops off more slowly. This indicates that it is better to have a slightly larger test than one that is too small by the same amount. (However, when using a heavy tailed model, [Aze+20] finds that it is better to do lots of smaller tests.)

In Figure 34.6b, we plot the probability of picking the wrong action vs n. We see that tests that are larger than optimal only reduce this error rate marginally. Consequently, if you want to make the misclassification rate low, you may need a large sample size, particularly if $\mu_1 - \mu_0$ is small, since then it will be hard to detect the true best action. However, it is also less important to identify the best action in this case, since both actions have very similar expected reward. This explains why classical methods for A/B testing based on frequentist statistics, which use hypothesis testing methods to determine if A is better than B, may often recommend sample sizes that are much larger than necessary. (See [FB19] and references therein for further discussion.)

34.4 Contextual bandits

This section is co-authored with Lihong Li.

In Section 34.3, we discussed A/B testing, in which the decision maker tries two different actions, a_0 and a_1, a fixed number of times, n_1 and n_0, measures the resulting sequence of rewards, $\boldsymbol{y}_1$ and $\boldsymbol{y}_0$, and then picks the best action to use for the rest of time (or the rest of the population) so as to maximize expected reward.

We can obviously generalize this beyond two actions. More importantly, we can generalize this beyond a one-stage decision problem. In particular, suppose we allow the decision maker to try an action a_t, observe the reward r_t, and then decide what to do at time step $t + 1$, rather than waiting until $n_1 + n_0$ experiments are finished. This immediate feedback allows for **adaptive policies** that can result in much higher expected reward (lower regret). We have converted a one-stage decision problem into a **sequential decision problem**. There are many kinds of sequential decision problems, but in this section, we consider the simplest kind, known as a **bandit problem** (see e.g., [LS19; Sli19]).

34.4.1 Types of bandit

In a **multi-armed bandit** problem (MAB) there is an agent (decision maker) that can choose an **action** from some **policy** $a_t \sim \pi_t$ at each step, after which it receives a **reward** sampled from the **environment**, $r_t \sim p_R(a_t)$, with expected value $R(s, a) = \mathbb{E}[R|a]$.[3]

We can think of this in terms of an agent at a casino who is faced with multiple slot machines, each of which pays out rewards at a different rate. A slot machine is sometimes called a **one-armed bandit**, so a set of K such machines is called a **multi-armed bandit**; each different action corresponds to pulling the arm of a different slot machine, $a_t \in \{1, \ldots, K\}$. The goal is to quickly figure out which machine pays out the most money, and then to keep playing that one until you become as rich as possible.

We can extend this model by defining a **contextual bandit**, in which the input to the policy at each step is a randomly chosen state or context $s_t \in \mathcal{S}$. The states evolve over time according to some arbitrary process, $s_t \sim p(s_t | \mathbf{s}_{1:t-1})$, independent of the actions of the agent. The policy now has the form $a_t \sim \pi_t(a_t | s_t)$, and the reward function now has the form $r_t \sim p_R(r_t | s_t, a_t)$, with expected value $R(s, a) = \mathbb{E}[R|s, a]$. At each step, the agent can use the observed data, $\mathcal{D}_{1:t}$ where $\mathcal{D}_t = (s_t, a_t, r_t)$, to update its policy, to maximize expected reward.

In the **finite horizon** formulation of (contextual) bandits, the goal is to maximize the expected **cumulative reward**:

$$J \triangleq \sum_{t=1}^{T} \mathbb{E}_{p_R(r_t|s_t,a_t)\pi_t(a_t|s_t)p(s_t|\mathbf{s}_{1:t-1})}[r_t] = \sum_{t=1}^{T} \mathbb{E}[r_t] \tag{34.48}$$

(Note that the reward is accrued at each step, even while the agent updates its policy; this is sometimes called "**earning while learning**".) In the **infinite horizon** formulation, where $T = \infty$, the cumulative reward may be infinite. To prevent J from being unbounded, we introduce a **discount factor** $0 < \gamma < 1$, so that

$$J \triangleq \sum_{t=1}^{\infty} \gamma^{t-1} \mathbb{E}[r_t] \tag{34.49}$$

The quantity γ can be interpreted as the probability that the agent is terminated at any moment in time (in which case it will cease to accumulate reward).

Another way to write this is as follows:

$$J = \sum_{t=1}^{\infty} \gamma^{t-1} \mathbb{E}[r_t] = \sum_{t=1}^{\infty} \gamma^{t-1} \mathbb{E}\left[\sum_{a=1}^{K} R_a(s_t, a_t)\right] \tag{34.50}$$

where we define

$$R_a(s_t, a_t) = \begin{cases} R(s_t, a) & \text{if } a_t = a \\ 0 & \text{otherwise} \end{cases} \tag{34.51}$$

---

3. This is known as a **stochastic bandit**. It is also possible to allow the reward, and possibly the state, to be chosen in an adversarial manner, where nature tries to minimize the reward of the agent. This is known as an **adversarial bandit**.

Thus we conceptually evaluate the reward for all arms, but only the one that was actually chosen (namely a_t) gives a non-zero value to the agent, namely r_t.

There are many extensions of the basic bandit problem. A natural one is to allow the agent to perform **multiple plays**, choosing $M \leq K$ distinct arms at once. Let $\boldsymbol{a}_t$ be the corresponding action vector which specifies the identity of the chosen arms. Then we define the reward to be

$$r_t = \sum_{a=1}^{K} R_a(s_t, \boldsymbol{a}_t) \tag{34.52}$$

where

$$R_a(s_t, \boldsymbol{a}_t) = \begin{cases} R(s_t, a) & \text{if } a \in \boldsymbol{a}_t \\ 0 & \text{otherwise} \end{cases} \tag{34.53}$$

This is useful for modeling **resource allocation** problems.

Another variant is known as a **restless bandit** [Whi88]. This is the same as the multiple play formulation, except we additionally assume that each arm has its own state vector s_t^a associated with it, which evolves according to some stochastic process, regardless of whether arm a was chosen or not. We then define

$$r_t = \sum_{a=1}^{K} R_a(s_t^a, \boldsymbol{a}_t) \tag{34.54}$$

where $s_t^a \sim p(s_t^a | \boldsymbol{s}_{1:t-1}^a)$ is some arbitrary distribution, often assumed to be Markovian. (The fact that the states associated with each arm evolve even if the arm is not picked is what gives rise to the term "restless".) This can be used to model serial dependence between the rewards given by each arm.

34.4.2 Applications

Contextual bandits have many applications. For example, consider an **online advertising system**. In this case, the state s_t represents features of the web page that the user is currently looking at, and the action a_t represents the identity of the ad which the system chooses to show. Since the relevance of the ad depends on the page, the reward function has the form $R(s_t, a_t)$, and hence the problem is contextual. The goal is to maximize the expected reward, which is equivalent to the expected number of times people click on ads; this is known as the **click through rate** or **CTR**. (See e.g., [Gra+10; Li+10; McM+13; Aga+14; Du+21; YZ22] for more information about this application.)

Another application of contextual bandits arises in **clinical trials** [VBW15]. In this case, the state s_t are features of the current patient we are treating, and the action a_t is the treatment the doctor chooses to give them (e.g., a new drug or a **placebo**). Our goal is to maximize expected reward, i.e., the expected number of people who get cured. (An alternative goal is to determine which treatment is best as quickly as possible, rather than maximizing expected reward; this variant is known as **best-arm identification** [ABM10].)

34.4.3 Exploration-exploitation tradeoff

The fundamental difficulty in solving bandit problems is known as the **exploration-exploitation tradeoff**. This refers to the fact that the agent needs to try multiple state/action combinations (this

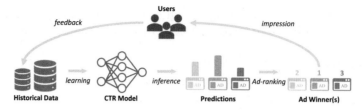

Figure 34.7: *Illustration of the feedback problem in online advertising and recommendation systems. The click through rate (CTR) model is used to decide what ads to show, which affects what data is collected, which affects how the model learns. From Figure 1–2 of [Du+21]. Used with kind permission of Chao Du.*

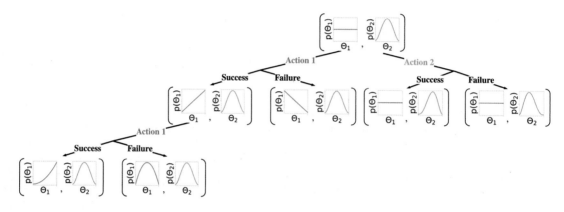

Figure 34.8: *Illustration of sequential belief updating for a two-armed beta-Bernoulli bandit. The prior for the reward for action 1 is the (blue) uniform distribution* Beta(1,1)*; the prior for the reward for action 2 is the (orange) unimodal distribution* Beta(2,2)*. We update the parameters of the belief state based on the chosen action, and based on whether the observed reward is success (1) or failure (0).*

is known as exploration) in order to collect enough data so it can reliably learn the reward function $R(s,a)$; it can then exploit its knowledge by picking the predicted best action for each state. If the agent starts exploiting an incorrect model too early, it will collect suboptimal data, and will get stuck in a negative **feedback loop**, as illustrated in Figure 34.7. This is different from supervised learning, where the data is drawn iid from a fixed distribution (see e.g., [Jeu+19] for details).

We discuss some solutions to the exploration-exploitation problem below.

34.4.4   The optimal solution

In this section, we discuss the optimal solution to the exploration-exploitation tradeoff. Let us denote the posterior over the parameters of the reward function by $b_t = p(\theta|h_t)$, where $h_t = \{s_{1:t-1}, a_{1:t-1}, r_{1:t-1}\}$ is the history of observations; this is known as the **belief state** or **information state**. It is a finite sufficient statistic for the history h_t. The belief state can be updated deterministically using Bayes' rule:

$$b_t = \text{BayesRule}(b_{t-1}, a_t, r_t) \tag{34.55}$$

For example, consider a context-free **Bernoulli bandit**, where $p_R(r|a) = \text{Ber}(r|\mu_a)$, and $\mu_a = p_R(r = 1|a) = R(a)$ is the expected reward for taking action a. Suppose we use a factored beta prior

$$p_0(\boldsymbol{\theta}) = \prod_a \text{Beta}(\mu_a|\alpha_0^a, \beta_0^a) \tag{34.56}$$

where $\boldsymbol{\theta} = (\mu_1, \ldots, \mu_K)$. We can compute the posterior in closed form, as we discuss in Section 3.4.1. In particular, we find

$$p(\boldsymbol{\theta}|\mathcal{D}_t) = \prod_a \text{Beta}(\mu_a| \underbrace{\alpha_0^a + N_t^0(a)}_{\alpha_t^a}, \underbrace{\beta_0^a + N_t^1(a)}_{\beta_t^a}) \tag{34.57}$$

where

$$N_t^r(a) = \sum_{s=1}^{t-1} \mathbb{I}(a_t = a, r_t = r) \tag{34.58}$$

This is illustrated in Figure 34.8 for a two-armed Bernoulli bandit.

We can use a similar method for a **Gaussian bandit**, where $p_R(r|a) = \mathcal{N}(r|\mu_a, \sigma_a^2)$, using results from Section 3.4.3. In the case of contextual bandits, the problem becomes more complicated. If we assume a **linear regression bandit**, $p_R(r|s, a; \boldsymbol{\theta}) = \mathcal{N}(r|\phi(s,a)^\mathsf{T}\boldsymbol{\theta}, \sigma^2)$, we can use Bayesian linear regression to compute $p(\boldsymbol{\theta}|\mathcal{D}_t)$ in closed form, as we discuss in Section 15.2. If we assume a **logistic regression bandit**, $p_R(r|s, a; \boldsymbol{\theta}) = \text{Ber}(r|\sigma(\phi(s,a)^\mathsf{T}\boldsymbol{\theta}))$, we can use Bayesian logistic regression to compute $p(\boldsymbol{\theta}|\mathcal{D}_t)$, as we discuss in Section 15.3.5. If we have a **neural bandit** of the form $p_R(r|s, a; \boldsymbol{\theta}) = \text{GLM}(r|f(s,a;\boldsymbol{\theta}))$ for some nonlinear function f, then posterior inference becomes more challenging, as we discuss in Chapter 17. However, standard techniques, such as the extended Kalman filter (Section 17.5.2) can be applied. (For a way to scale this approach to large DNNs, see the "**subspace neural bandit**" approach of [DMKM22].)

Regardless of the algorithmic details, we can represent the belief state update as follows:

$$p(\boldsymbol{b}_t|\boldsymbol{b}_{t-1}, a_t, r_t) = \mathbb{I}(\boldsymbol{b}_t = \text{BayesRule}(\boldsymbol{b}_{t-1}, a_t, r_t)) \tag{34.59}$$

The observed reward at each step is then predicted to be

$$p(r_t|\boldsymbol{b}_t) = \int p_R(r_t|s_t, a_t; \boldsymbol{\theta}) p(\boldsymbol{\theta}|\boldsymbol{b}_t) d\boldsymbol{\theta} \tag{34.60}$$

We see that this is a special form of a (controlled) Markov decision process (Section 34.5) known as a **belief-state MDP**.

In the special case of context-free bandits with a finite number of arms, the optimal policy of this belief state MDP can be computed using dynamic programming (see Section 34.6); the result can be represented as a table of action probabilities, $\pi_t(a_1, \ldots, a_K)$, for each step; this is known as the **Gittins index** [Git89]. However, computing the optimal policy for general contextual bandits is intractable [PT87], so we have to resort to approximations, as we discuss below.

34.4.5 Upper confidence bounds (UCBs)

The optimal solution to explore-exploit is intractable. However, an intuitively sensible approach is based on the principle known as "**optimism in the face of uncertainty**". The principle selects actions greedily, but based on optimistic estimates of their rewards. The most important class of strategies with this principle are collectively called **upper confidence bound** or **UCB** methods.

To use a UCB strategy, the agent maintains an optimistic reward function estimate $\tilde{R}_t$, so that $\tilde{R}_t(s_t, a) \geq R(s_t, a)$ for all a with high probability, and then chooses the greedy action accordingly:

$$a_t = \operatorname*{argmax}_a \tilde{R}_t(s_t, a) \tag{34.61}$$

UCB can be viewed a form of **exploration bonus**, where the optimistic estimate encourages exploration. Typically, the amount of optimism, $\tilde{R}_t - R$, decreases over time so that the agent gradually reduces exploration. With properly constructed optimistic reward estimates, the UCB strategy has been shown to achieve near-optimal regret in many variants of bandits [LS19]. (We discuss regret in Section 34.4.7.)

The optimistic function $\tilde{R}$ can be obtained in different ways, sometimes in closed forms, as we discuss below.

34.4.5.1   Frequentist approach

One approach is to use a **concentration inequality** [BLM16] to derive a high-probability upper bound of the estimation error: $|\hat{R}_t(s, a) - R_t(s, a)| \leq \delta_t(s, a)$, where $\hat{R}_t$ is a usual estimate of R (often the MLE), and δ_t is a properly selected function. An optimistic reward is then obtained by setting $\tilde{R}_t(s, a) = \hat{R}_t(s, a) + \delta_t(s, a)$.

As an example, consider again the context-free Bernoulli bandit, $R(a) \sim \text{Ber}(\mu(a))$. The MLE $\hat{R}_t(a) = \hat{\mu}_t(a)$ is given by the empirical average of observed rewards whenever action a was taken:

$$\hat{\mu}_t(a) = \frac{N_t^1(a)}{N_t(a)} = \frac{N_t^1(a)}{N_t^0(a) + N_t^1(a)} \tag{34.62}$$

where $N_t^r(a)$ is the number of times (up to step $t-1$) that action a has been tried and the observed reward was r, and $N_t(a)$ is the total number of times action a has been tried:

$$N_t(a) = \sum_{s=1}^{t-1} \mathbb{I}(a_t = a) \tag{34.63}$$

Then the **Chernoff-Hoeffding inequality** [BLM16] leads to $\delta_t(a) = c/\sqrt{N_t(a)}$ for some proper constant c, so

$$\tilde{R}_t(a) = \hat{\mu}_t(a) + \frac{c}{\sqrt{N_t(a)}} \tag{34.64}$$

34.4.5.2   Bayesian approach

We may also derive $\tilde{R}$ from Bayesian inference. If we use a beta prior, we can compute the posterior in closed form, as shown in Equation (34.57). The posterior mean is $\hat{\mu}_t(a) = \mathbb{E}[\mu(a)|\boldsymbol{h}_t] = \frac{\alpha_t^a}{\alpha_t^a + \beta_t^a}$. From Equation (3.17), the posterior standard deviation is approximately

$$\hat{\sigma}_t(a) = \sqrt{\mathbb{V}[\mu(a)|\boldsymbol{h}_t]} \approx \sqrt{\frac{\hat{\mu}_t(a)(1 - \hat{\mu}_t(a))}{N_t(a)}} \tag{34.65}$$

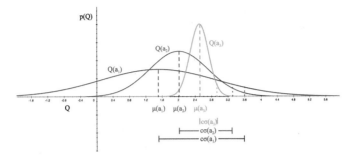

Figure 34.9: Illustration of the reward distribution $Q(a)$ for 3 different actions, and the corresponding lower and upper confidence bounds. From [Sil18]. Used with kind permission of David Silver.

We can use similar techniques for a Gaussian bandit, where $p_R(R|a, \boldsymbol{\theta}) = \mathcal{N}(R|\mu_a, \sigma_a^2)$, μ_a is the expected reward, and σ_a^2 the variance. If we use a conjugate prior, we can compute $p(\mu_a, \sigma_a|\mathcal{D}_t)$ in closed form (see Section 3.4.3). Using an uninformative version of the conjugate prior, we find $\mathbb{E}[\mu_a|\boldsymbol{h}_t] = \hat{\mu}_t(a)$, which is just the empirical mean of rewards for action a. The uncertainty in this estimate is the standard error of the mean, given by Equation (3.133), i.e., $\sqrt{\mathbb{V}[\mu_a|\boldsymbol{h}_t]} = \hat{\sigma}_t(a)/\sqrt{N_t(a)}$, where $\hat{\sigma}_t(a)$ is the empirical standard deviation of the rewards for action a.

This approach can also be extended to contextual bandits, modulo the difficulty of computing the belief state.

Once we have computed the mean and posterior standard deviation, we define the optimistic reward estimate as

$$\tilde{R}_t(a) = \hat{\mu}_t(a) + c\hat{\sigma}_t(a) \tag{34.66}$$

for some constant c that controls how greedy the policy is. We see that this is similar to the frequentist method based on concentration inequalities, but is more general.

34.4.5.3 Example

Figure 34.9 illustrates the UCB principle for a Gaussian bandit. We assume there are 3 actions, and we represent $p(R(a)|\mathcal{D}_t)$ using a Gaussian. We show the posterior means $Q(a) = \mu(a)$ with a vertical dotted line, and the scaled posterior standard deviations $c\sigma(a)$ as a horizontal solid line.

34.4.6 Thompson sampling

A common alternative to UCB is to use **Thompson sampling** [Tho33], also called **probability matching** [Sco10]. In this approach, we define the policy at step t to be $\pi_t(a|s_t, \boldsymbol{h}_t) = p_a$, where p_a is the probability that a is the optimal action. This can be computed using

$$p_a = \Pr(a = a_*|s_t, \boldsymbol{h}_t) = \int \mathbb{I}\left(a = \operatorname*{argmax}_{a'} R(s_t, a'; \boldsymbol{\theta})\right) p(\boldsymbol{\theta}|\boldsymbol{h}_t) d\boldsymbol{\theta} \tag{34.67}$$

If the posterior is uncertain, the agent will sample many different actions, automatically resulting in exploration. As the uncertainty decreases, it will start to exploit its knowledge.

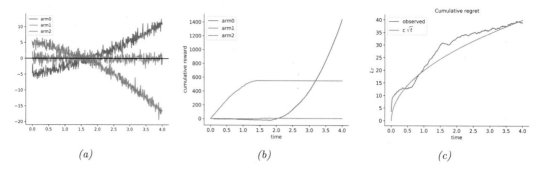

Figure 34.10: Illustration of Thompson sampling applied to a linear-Gaussian contextual bandit. The context has the form $s_t = (1, t, t^2)$. (a) True reward for each arm vs time. (b) Cumulative reward per arm vs time. (c) Cumulative regret vs time. Generated by thompson_sampling_linear_gaussian.ipynb.

To see how we can implement this method, note that we can compute the expression in Equation (34.67) by using a single Monte Carlo sample $\tilde{\boldsymbol{\theta}}_t \sim p(\boldsymbol{\theta}|\boldsymbol{h}_t)$. We then plug in this parameter into our reward model, and greedily pick the best action:

$$a_t = \underset{a'}{\operatorname{argmax}} R(s_t, a'; \tilde{\boldsymbol{\theta}}_t) \tag{34.68}$$

This sample-then-exploit approach will choose actions with exactly the desired probability, since

$$p_a = \int \mathbb{I}\left(a = \underset{a'}{\operatorname{argmax}} R(s_t, a'; \tilde{\boldsymbol{\theta}}_t)\right) p(\tilde{\boldsymbol{\theta}}_t|\boldsymbol{h}_t) = \underset{\tilde{\boldsymbol{\theta}}_t \sim p(\boldsymbol{\theta}|\boldsymbol{h}_t)}{\operatorname{Pr}}\left(a = \underset{a'}{\operatorname{argmax}} R(s_t, a'; \tilde{\boldsymbol{\theta}}_t)\right) \tag{34.69}$$

Despite its simplicity, this approach can be shown to achieve optimal (logarithmic) regret (see e.g., [Rus+18] for a survey). In addition, it is very easy to implement, and hence is widely used in practice [Gra+10; Sco10; CL11].

In Figure 34.10, we give a simple example of Thompson sampling applied to a linear regression bandit. The context has the form $s_t = (1, t, t^2)$. The true reward function has the form $R(s_t, a) = \boldsymbol{w}_a^\mathsf{T} s_t$. The weights per arm are chosen as follows: $\boldsymbol{w}_0 = (-5, 2, 0.5)$, $\boldsymbol{w}_1 = (0, 0, 0)$, $\boldsymbol{w}_2 = (5, -1.5, -1)$. Thus we see that arm 0 is initially worse (large negative bias) but gets better over time (positive slope), arm 1 is useless, and arm 2 is initially better (large positive bias) but gets worse over time. The observation noise is the same for all arms, $\sigma^2 = 1$. See Figure 34.10(a) for a plot of the reward function.

We use a conjugate Gaussian-gamma prior and perform exact Bayesian updating. Thompson sampling quickly discovers that arm 1 is useless. Initially it pulls arm 2 more, but it adapts to the non-stationary nature of the problem and switches over to arm 0, as shown in Figure 34.10(b).

34.4.7   Regret

We have discussed several methods for solving the exploration-exploitation tradeoff. It is useful to quantify the degree of suboptimality of these methods. A common approach is to compute the **regret**, which is defined as the difference between the expected reward under the agent's policy and the oracle policy π_*, which knows the true reward function. (Note that the oracle policy will in general be better than the Bayes optimal policy, which we disucssed in Section 34.4.4.)

Specifically, let π_t be the agent's policy at time t. Then the **per-step regret** at t is defined as

$$l_t \triangleq \mathbb{E}_{p(s_t)}\left[R(s_t, \pi_*(s_t))\right] - \mathbb{E}_{\pi_t(a_t|s_t)p(s_t)}\left[R(s_t, a_t)\right] \tag{34.70}$$

If we only care about the final performance of the best discovered arm, as in most optimization problems, it is enough to look at the **simple regret** at the last step, namely l_T. Optimizing simple regret results in a problem known as **pure exploration** [BMS11], since there is no need to exploit the information during the learning process. However, it is more common to focus on the **cumulative regret**, also called the **total regret** or just the **regret**, which is defined as

$$L_T \triangleq \mathbb{E}\left[\sum_{t=1}^{T} l_t\right] \tag{34.71}$$

Here the expectation is with respect to randomness in determining π_t, which depends on earlier states, actions and rewards, as well as other potential sources of randomness.

Under the typical assumption that rewards are bounded, L_T is at most linear in T. If the agent's policy converges to the optimal policy as T increases, then the regret is sublinear: $L_T = o(T)$. In general, the slower L_T grows, the more efficient the agent is in trading off exploration and exploitation.

To understand its growth rate, it is helpful to consider again a simple context-free bandit, where $R_* = \text{argmax}_a R(a)$ is the optimal reward. The total regret in the first T steps can be written as

$$L_T = \mathbb{E}\left[\sum_{t=1}^{T} R_* - R(a_t)\right] = \sum_{a \in \mathcal{A}} \mathbb{E}\left[N_{T+1}(a)\right](R_* - R(a)) = \sum_{a \in \mathcal{A}} \mathbb{E}\left[N_{T+1}(a)\right]\Delta_a \tag{34.72}$$

where $N_{T+1}(a)$ is the total number of times the agent picks action a up to step T, and $\Delta_a = R_* - R(a)$ is the reward **gap**. If the agent under-explores and converges to choosing a suboptimal action (say, $\hat{a}$), then a linear regret is suffered with a per-step regret of $\Delta_{\hat{a}}$. On the other hand, if the agent over-explores, then $N_t(a)$ will be too large for suboptimal actions, and the agent also suffers a linear regret.

Fortunately, it is possible to achieve sublinear regrets, using some of the methods discussed above, such as UCB and Thompson sampling. For example, one can show that Thompson sampling has $O(\sqrt{KT \log T})$ regret [RR14]. This is shown empirically in Figure 34.10(c).

In fact, both UCB and Thompson sampling are optimal, in the sense that their regrets are essentially not improvable; that is, they match regret lower bounds. To establish such a lower bound, note that the agent needs to collect enough data to distinguish different reward distributions, before identifying the optimal action. Typically, the deviation of the reward estimate from the true reward decays at the rate of $1/\sqrt{N}$, where N is the sample size (see e.g., Equation (3.133)). Therefore, if two reward distributions are similar, distinguishing them becomes harder and requires more samples. (For example, consider the case of a bandit with Gaussian rewards with slightly different means and large variance, as shown in Figure 34.9.)

The following fundamental result is proved by [LR85] for the asymptotic regret (under certain mild assumptions not given here):

$$\liminf_{T \to \infty} L_T \geq \log T \sum_{a:\Delta_a > 0} \frac{\Delta_a}{D_{\mathrm{KL}}\left(p_R(a) \,\|\, p_R(a_*)\right)} \tag{34.73}$$

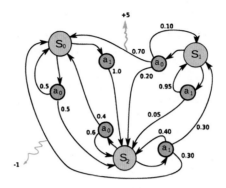

Figure 34.11: Illustration of an MDP as a finite state machine (FSM). The MDP has three discrete states (green cirlces), two discrete actions (orange circles), and two non-zero rewards (orange arrows). The numbers on the black edges represent state transition probabilities, e.g., $p(s' = s_0 | a = a_0, s' = s_0) = 0.7$; most state transitions are impossible (probability 0), so the graph is sparse. The numbers on the yellow wiggly edges represent expected rewards, e.g., $R(s = s_1, a = a_0, s' = s_0) = +5$; state transitions with zero reward are not annotated. From https://en.wikipedia.org/wiki/Markov_decision_process. *Used with kind permission of Wikipedia author waldoalvarez.*

Thus, we see that the best we can achieve is logarithmic growth in the total regret. Similar lower bounds have also been obtained for various bandits variants.

34.5   Markov decision problems

In this section, we generalize the discussion of contextual bandits by allowing the state of nature to change depending on the actions chosen by the agent. The resulting model is called a **Markov decision process** or **MDP**, as we explain in detail below. This model forms the foundation of reinforcement learning, which we discuss in Chapter 35.

34.5.1   Basics

A **Markov decision process** [Put94] can be used to model the interaction of an **agent** and an **environment**. It is often described by a tuple $\langle \mathcal{S}, \mathcal{A}, p_T, p_R, p_0 \rangle$, where $\mathcal{S}$ is a set of environment states, $\mathcal{A}$ a set of actions the agent can take, p_T a **transition model**, p_R a **reward model**, and p_0 the initial state distribution. The interaction starts at time $t = 0$, where the initial state $s_0 \sim p_0$. Then, at time $t \geq 0$, the agent observes the environment state $s_t \in \mathcal{S}$, and follows a **policy** π to take an action $a_t \in \mathcal{A}$. In response, the environment emits a real-valued reward signal $r_t \in \mathcal{R}$ and enters a new state $s_{t+1} \in \mathcal{S}$. The policy is in general stochastic, with $\pi(a|s)$ being the probability of choosing action a in state s. We use $\pi(s)$ to denote the conditional probability over $\mathcal{A}$ if the policy is stochastic, or the action it chooses if it is deterministic. The process at every step is called a **transition**; at time t, it consists of the tuple (s_t, a_t, r_t, s_{t+1}), where $a_t \sim \pi(s_t)$, $s_{t+1} \sim p_T(s_t, a_t)$, and $r_t \sim p_R(s_t, a_t, s_{t+1})$. Hence, under policy π, the probability of generating a trajectory $\boldsymbol{\tau}$ of length T can be written explicitly as

$$p(\boldsymbol{\tau}) = p_0(s_0) \prod_{t=0}^{T-1} \pi(a_t|s_t) p_T(s_{t+1}|s_t, a_t) p_R(r_t|s_t, a_t, s_{t+1}) \tag{34.74}$$

It is useful to define the **reward function** from the reward model p_R, as the average immediate reward of taking action a in state s, with the next state marginalized:

$$R(s, a) \triangleq \mathbb{E}_{p_T(s'|s,a)} \left[\mathbb{E}_{p(r|s,a,s')} [r] \right] \tag{34.75}$$

Eliminating the dependence on next states does not lead to loss of generality in the following discussions, as our subject of interest is the total (additive) expected reward along the trajectory. For this reason, we often use the tuple $\langle \mathcal{S}, \mathcal{A}, p_T, R, p_0 \rangle$ to describe an MDP.

In general, the state and action sets of an MDP can be discrete or continuous. When both sets are finite, we can represent these functions as lookup tables; this is known as a **tabular representation**. In this case, we can represent the MDP as a **finite state machine**, which is a graph where nodes correspond to states, and edges correspond to actions and the resulting rewards and next states. Figure 34.11 gives a simple example of an MDP with 3 states and 2 actions.

The field of **control theory**, which is very closely related to RL, uses slightly different terminology. In particular, the environment is called the **plant**, and the agent is called the **controller**. States are denoted by $\boldsymbol{x}_t \in \mathcal{X} \subseteq \mathbb{R}^D$, actions are denoted by $\boldsymbol{u}_t \in \mathcal{U} \subseteq \mathbb{R}^K$, and rewards are denoted by costs $c_t \in \mathbb{R}$. Apart from this notational difference, the fields of RL and control theory are very similar (see e.g., [Son98; Rec19]), although control theory tends to focus on provably optimal methods (by making strong modeling assumptions), whereas RL tends to tackle harder problems with heuristic methods, for which optimality guarantees are often hard to obtain.

34.5.2 Partially observed MDPs

An important generalization of the MDP framework relaxes the assumption that the agent sees the hidden world state s_t directly; instead we assume it only sees a potentially noisy observation generated from the hidden state, $x_t \sim p(\cdot|s_t, a_t)$. The resulting model is called a **partially observable Markov decision process** or **POMDP** (pronounced "pom-dee-pee"). Now the agent's policy is a mapping from all the available data to actions, $a_t \sim \pi(\mathcal{D}_{1:t-1}, x_t)$, $\mathcal{D}_t = (x_t, a_t, r_t)$. See Figure 34.12 for an illustration. MDPs are a special case where $x_t = s_t$.

In general, POMDPs are much harder to solve than MDPs. A common approximation is to use the last several observed inputs, say $\boldsymbol{x}_{t-h:t}$ for history of size h, as a proxy for the hidden state, and then to treat this as a fully observed MDP.

34.5.3 Episodes and returns

The Markov decision process describes how a trajectory $\boldsymbol{\tau} = (s_0, a_0, r_0, s_1, a_1, r_1, \ldots)$ is stochastically generated. If the agent can potentially interact with the environment forever, we call it a **continuing task**. Alternatively, the agent is in an **episodic task**, if its interaction terminates once the system enters a **terminal state** or **absorbing state**; s is absorbing if the next state from s is always s with 0 reward. After entering a terminal state, we may start a new **epsiode** from a new initial state $s_0 \sim p_0$. The episode length is in general random. For example, the amount of time a robot takes to

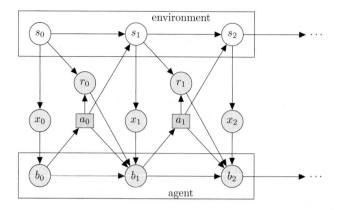

Figure 34.12: Illustration of a partially observable Markov decision process (POMDP) with hidden environment state s_t which generates the observation x_t, controlled by an agent with internal belief state b_t which generates the action a_t. The reward r_t depends on s_t and a_t. Nodes in this graph represent random variables (circles) and decision variables (squares).

reach its goal may be quite variable, depending on the decisions it makes, and the randomness in the environment. Note that we can convert an episodic MDP to a continuing MDP by redefining the transition model in absorbing states to be the initial-state distribution p_0. Finally, if the trajectory length T in an episodic task is fixed and known, it is called a **finite horizon problem**.

Let $\boldsymbol{\tau}$ be a trajectory of length T, where T may be ∞ if the task is continuing. We define the **return** for the state at time t to be the sum of expected rewards obtained going forwards, where each reward is multiplied by a **discount factor** $\gamma \in [0, 1]$:

$$G_t \triangleq r_t + \gamma r_{t+1} + \gamma^2 r_{t+2} + \cdots + \gamma^{T-t-1} r_{T-1} \tag{34.76}$$

$$= \sum_{k=0}^{T-t-1} \gamma^k r_{t+k} = \sum_{j=t}^{T-1} \gamma^{j-t} r_j \tag{34.77}$$

G_t is sometimes called the **reward-to-go**. For episodic tasks that terminate at time T, we define $G_t = 0$ for $t \geq T$. Clearly, the return satisfies the following recursive relationship:

$$G_t = r_t + \gamma(r_{t+1} + \gamma r_{t+2} + \cdots) = r_t + \gamma G_{t+1} \tag{34.78}$$

The discount factor γ plays two roles. First, it ensures the return is finite even if $T = \infty$ (i.e., infinite horizon), provided we use $\gamma < 1$ and the rewards r_t are bounded. Second, it puts more weight on short-term rewards, which generally has the effect of encouraging the agent to achieve its goals more quickly (see Section 34.5.5.1 for an example). However, if γ is too small, the agent will become too greedy. In the extreme case where $\gamma = 0$, the agent is completely **myopic**, and only tries to maximize its immediate reward. In general, the discount factor reflects the assumption that there is a probability of $1 - \gamma$ that the interaction will end at the next step. For finite horizon problems, where T is known, we can set $\gamma = 1$, since we know the life time of the agent a priori.[4]

---

4. We may also use $\gamma = 1$ for continuing tasks, targeting the (undiscounted) average reward criterion [Put94].

34.5.4 Value functions

Let π be a given policy. We define the **state-value function**, or **value function** for short, as follows (with $\mathbb{E}_\pi [\cdot]$ indicating that actions are selected by π):

$$V_\pi(s) \triangleq \mathbb{E}_\pi [G_0|s_0 = s] = \mathbb{E}_\pi \left[\sum_{t=0}^{\infty} \gamma^t r_t | s_0 = s \right] \tag{34.79}$$

This is the expected return obtained if we start in state s and follow π to choose actions in a continuing task (i.e., $T = \infty$).

Similarly, we define the **action-value function**, also known as the Q-**function**, as follows:

$$Q_\pi(s,a) \triangleq \mathbb{E}_\pi [G_0|s_0 = s, a_0 = a] = \mathbb{E}_\pi \left[\sum_{t=0}^{\infty} \gamma^t r_t | s_0 = s, a_0 = a \right] \tag{34.80}$$

This quantity represents the expected return obtained if we start by taking action a in state s, and then follow π to choose actions thereafter.

Finally, we define the **advantage function** as follows:

$$A_\pi(s,a) \triangleq Q_\pi(s,a) - V_\pi(s) \tag{34.81}$$

This tells us the benefit of picking action a in state s then switching to policy π, relative to the baseline return of always following π. Note that $A_\pi(s,a)$ can be both positive and negative, and $\mathbb{E}_{\pi(a|s)} [A_\pi(s,a)] = 0$ due to a useful equality: $V_\pi(s) = \mathbb{E}_{\pi(a|s)} [Q_\pi(s,a)]$.

34.5.5 Optimal value functions and policies

Suppose π_* is a policy such that $V_{\pi_*} \geq V_\pi$ for all $s \in \mathcal{S}$ and all policy π, then it is an **optimal policy**. There can be multiple optimal policies for the same MDP, but by definition their value functions must be the same, and are denoted by V_* and Q_*, respectively. We call V_* the **optimal state-value function**, and Q_* the **optimal action-value function**. Furthermore, any finite MDP must have at least one deterministic optimal policy [Put94].

A fundamental result about the optimal value function is **Bellman's optimality equations**:

$$V_*(s) = \max_a R(s,a) + \gamma \mathbb{E}_{p_T(s'|s,a)} [V_*(s')] \tag{34.82}$$

$$Q_*(s,a) = R(s,a) + \gamma \mathbb{E}_{p_T(s'|s,a)} \left[\max_{a'} Q_*(s',a') \right] \tag{34.83}$$

Conversely, the optimal value functions are the only solutions that satisfy the equations. In other words, although the value function is defined as the expectation of a sum of infinitely many rewards, it can be characterized by a recursive equation that involves only one-step transition and reward models of the MDP. Such a recursion play a central role in many RL algorithms we will see later in this chapter. Given a value function (V or Q), the discrepancy between the right- and left-hand sides of Equations (34.82) and (34.83) are called **Bellman error** or **Bellman residual**.

Furthermore, given the optimal value function, we can derive an optimal policy using

$$\pi_*(s) = \underset{a}{\operatorname{argmax}} \, Q_*(s,a) \tag{34.84}$$

$$= \underset{a}{\operatorname{argmax}} \left[R(s,a) + \gamma \mathbb{E}_{p_T(s'|s,a)} [V_*(s')] \right] \tag{34.85}$$

Following such an optimal policy ensures the agent achieves maximum expected return starting from any state. The problem of solving for V_*, Q_* or π_* is called **policy optimization**. In contrast, solving for V_π or Q_π for a given policy π is called **policy evaluation**, which constitutes an important subclass of RL problems as will be discussed in later sections. For policy evaluation, we have similar Bellman equations, which simply replace $\max_a\{\cdot\}$ in Equations (34.82) and (34.83) with $\mathbb{E}_{\pi(a|s)}[\cdot]$.

In Equations (34.84) and (34.85), as in the Bellman optimality equations, we must take a maximum over all actions in $\mathcal{A}$, and the maximizing action is called the **greedy action** with respect to the value functions, Q_* or V_*. Finding greedy actions is computationally easy if $\mathcal{A}$ is a small finite set. For high dimensional continuous spaces, we can treat a as a sequence of actions, and optimize one dimension at a time [Met+17], or use gradient-free optimizers such as cross-entropy method (Section 6.7.5), as used in the **QT-Opt** method [Kal+18a]. Recently, **CAQL** (continuous action Q-learning, [Ryu+20]) proposed to use mixed integer programming to solve the argmax problem, leveraging the ReLU structure of the Q-network. We can also amortize the cost of this optimization by training a policy $a_* = \pi_*(s)$ after learning the optimal Q-function.

34.5.5.1   Example

In this section, we show a simple example, to make concepts like value functions more concrete. Consider the 1d **grid world** shown in Figure 34.13(a). There are 5 possible states, among them S_{T1} and S_{T2} are absorbing states, since the interaction ends once the agent enters them. There are 2 actions, $\uparrow$ and $\downarrow$. The reward function is zero everywhere except at the goal state, S_{T2}, which gives a reward of 1 upon entering. Thus the optimal action in every state is to move down.

Figure 34.13(b) shows the Q_* function for $\gamma = 0$. Note that we only show the function for non-absorbing states, as the optimal Q-values are 0 in absorbing states by definition. We see that $Q_*(s_3, \downarrow) = 1.0$, since the agent will get a reward of 1.0 on the next step if it moves down from s_3; however, $Q_*(s, a) = 0$ for all other state-action pairs, since they do not provide nonzero immediate reward. This optimal Q-function reflects the fact that using $\gamma = 0$ is completely myopic, and ignores the future.

Figure 34.13(c) shows Q_* when $\gamma = 1$. In this case, we care about all future rewards equally. Thus $Q_*(s, a) = 1$ for all state-action pairs, since the agent can always reach the goal eventually. This is infinitely far-sighted. However, it does not give the agent any short-term guidance on how to behave. For example, in s_2, it is not clear if it is should go up or down, since both actions will eventually reach the goal with identical Q_*-values.

Figure 34.13(d) shows Q_* when $\gamma = 0.9$. This reflects a preference for near-term rewards, while also taking future reward into account. This encourages the agent to seek the shortest path to the goal, which is usually what we desire. A proper choice of γ is up to the agent designer, just like the design of the reward function, and has to reflect the desired behavior of the agent.

34.6   Planning in an MDP

In this section, we discuss how to compute an optimal policy when the MDP model is known. This problem is called **planning**, in contrast to the learning problem where the models are unknown, which is tackled using reinforcement learning Chapter 35. The planning algorithms we discuss are based on **dynamic programming** (DP) and **linear programming** (LP).

For simplicity, in this section, we assume discrete state and action sets with $\gamma < 1$. However, exact

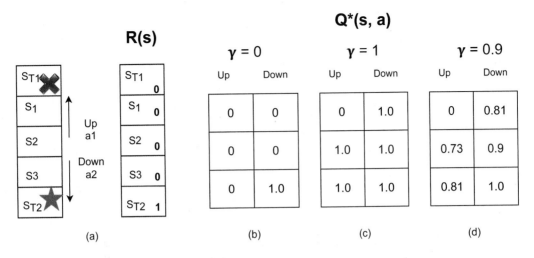

Figure 34.13: *Left: illustration of a simple MDP corresponding to a 1d grid world of 3 non-absorbing states and 2 actions. Right: optimal Q-functions for different values of γ. Adapted from Figures 3.1, 3.2, 3.4 of [GK19].*

calculation of optimal policies often depends polynomially on the sizes of $\mathcal{S}$ and $\mathcal{A}$, and is intractable, for example, when the state space is a Cartesian product of several finite sets. This challenge is known as the **curse of dimensionality**. Therefore, approximations are typically needed, such as using parametric or nonparametric representations of the value function or policy, both for computational tractability and for extending the methods to handle MDPs with general state and action sets. In this case, we have **approximate dynamic programming** (ADP) and **approximate linear programming** (ALP) algorithms (see e.g., [Ber19]).

34.6.1 Value iteration

A popular and effective DP method for solving an MDP is **value iteration** (VI). Starting from an initial value function estimate V_0, the algorithm iteratively updates the estimate by

$$V_{k+1}(s) = \max_a \left[R(s, a) + \gamma \sum_{s'} p(s'|s, a) V_k(s') \right] \tag{34.86}$$

Note that the update rule, sometimes called a **Bellman backup**, is exactly the right-hand side of the Bellman optimality equation Equation (34.82), with the unknown V_* replaced by the current estimate V_k. A fundamental property of Equation (34.86) is that the update is a **contraction**: it can be verified that

$$\max_s |V_{k+1}(s) - V_*(s)| \leq \gamma \max_s |V_k(s) - V_*(s)| \tag{34.87}$$

In other words, every iteration will reduce the maximum value function error by a constant factor. It follows immediately that V_k will converge to V_*, after which an optimal policy can be extracted using Equation (34.85). In practice, we can often terminate VI when V_k is close enough to V_*, since the resulting greedy policy wrt V_k will be near optimal. Value iteration can be adapted to learn the optimal action-value function Q_*.

In value iteration, we compute $V_*(s)$ and $\pi_*(s)$ for all possible states s, averaging over all possible next states s' at each iteration, as illustrated in Figure 34.14(right). However, for some problems, we may only be interested in the value (and policy) for certain special starting states. This is the case, for example, in **shortest path problems** on graphs, where we are trying to find the shortest route from the current state to a goal state. This can be modeled as an episodic MDP by defining a transition matrix $p_T(s'|s, a)$ where taking edge a from node s leads to the neighboring node s' with probability 1. The reward function is defined as $R(s, a) = -1$ for all states s except the goal states, which are modeled as absorbing states.

In problems such as this, we can use a method known as **real-time dynamic programming** (RTDP) [BBS95], to efficiently compute an **optimal partial policy**, which only specifies what to do for the reachable states. RTDP maintains a value function estimate V. At each step, it performs a Bellman backup for the current state s by $V(s) \leftarrow \max_a \mathbb{E}_{p_T(s'|s,a)} [R(s, a) + \gamma V(s')]$. It can picks an action a (often with some exploration), reaches a next state s', and repeats the process. This can be seen as a form of the more general **asynchronous value iteration**, that focuses its computational effort on parts of the state space that are more likely to be reachable from the current state, rather than synchronously updating all states at each iteration.

34.6.2   Policy iteration

Another effective DP method for computing π_* is **policy iteration**. It is an iterative algorithm that searches in the space of deterministic policies until converging to an optimal policy. Each iteration consists of two steps, **policy evaluation** and **policy improvement**.

The policy evaluation step, as mentioned earlier, computes the value function for the current policy. Let π represent the current policy, $\boldsymbol{v}(s) = V_\pi(s)$ represent the value function encoded as a vector indexed by states, $\boldsymbol{r}(s) = \sum_a \pi(a|s)R(s, a)$ represent the reward vector, and $\mathbf{T}(s'|s) = \sum_a \pi(a|s)p(s'|s, a)$ represent the state transition matrix. Bellman's equation for policy evaluation can be written in the matrix-vector form as

$$\boldsymbol{v} = \boldsymbol{r} + \gamma \mathbf{T} \boldsymbol{v} \qquad (34.88)$$

This is a linear system of equations in $|\mathcal{S}|$ unknowns, We can solve it using matrix inversion: $\boldsymbol{v} = (\mathbf{I} - \gamma \mathbf{T})^{-1} \boldsymbol{r}$. Alternatively, we can use value iteration by computing $\boldsymbol{v}_{t+1} = \boldsymbol{r} + \gamma \mathbf{T} \boldsymbol{v}_t$ until near convergence, or some form of asynchronous variant that is computationally more efficient.

Once we have evaluated V_π for the current policy π, we can use it to derive a better policy π', thus the name policy improvement. To do this, we simply compute a deterministic policy π' that acts greedily with respect to V_π in every state; that is, $\pi'(s) = \text{argmax}_a\{R(s, a) + \gamma \mathbb{E}[V_\pi(s')]\}$. We can guarantee that $V_{\pi'} \geq V_\pi$. To see this, define $\boldsymbol{r}'$, $\mathbf{T}'$ and $\boldsymbol{v}'$ as before, but for the new policy π'. The definition of π' implies $\boldsymbol{r}' + \gamma \mathbf{T}' \boldsymbol{v} \geq \boldsymbol{r} + \gamma \mathbf{T} \boldsymbol{v} = \boldsymbol{v}$, where the equality is due to Bellman's equation. Repeating the same equality, we have

$$\boldsymbol{v} \leq \boldsymbol{r}' + \gamma \mathbf{T}' \boldsymbol{v} \leq \boldsymbol{r}' + \gamma \mathbf{T}'(\boldsymbol{r}' + \gamma \mathbf{T}' \boldsymbol{v}) \leq \boldsymbol{r}' + \gamma \mathbf{T}'(\boldsymbol{r}' + \gamma \mathbf{T}'(\boldsymbol{r}' + \gamma \mathbf{T}' \boldsymbol{v})) \leq \cdots \qquad (34.89)$$

$$= (\mathbf{I} + \gamma \mathbf{T}' + \gamma^2 \mathbf{T}'^2 + \cdots)\boldsymbol{r} = (\mathbf{I} - \gamma \mathbf{T}')^{-1} \boldsymbol{r} = \boldsymbol{v}' \qquad (34.90)$$

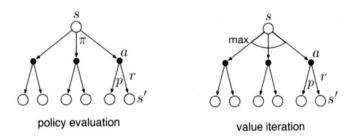

Figure 34.14: *Policy iteration vs value iteration represented as backup diagrams. Empty circles represent states, solid (filled) circles represent states and actions. Adapted from Figure 8.6 of [SB18].*

Starting from an initial policy π_0, policy iteration alternates between policy evaluation (E) and improvement (I) steps, as illustrated below:

$$\pi_0 \xrightarrow{E} V_{\pi_0} \xrightarrow{I} \pi_1 \xrightarrow{E} V_{\pi_1} \cdots \xrightarrow{I} \pi_* \xrightarrow{E} V_* \tag{34.91}$$

The algorithm stops at iteration k, if the policy π_k is greedy with respect to its own value function V_{π_k}. In this case, the policy is optimal. Since there are at most $|\mathcal{A}|^{|\mathcal{S}|}$ deterministic policies, and every iteration strictly improves the policy, the algorithm must converge after finite iterations.

In PI, we alternate between policy evaluation (which involves multiple iterations, until convergence of V_π), and policy improvement. In VI, we alternate between one iteration of policy evaluation followed by one iteration of policy improvement (the "max" operator in the update rule). In **generalized policy improvement**, we are free to intermix any number of these steps in any order. The process will converge once the policy is greedy wrt its own value function.

Note that policy evaluation computes V_π whereas value iteration computes V_*. This difference is illustrated in Figure 34.14, using a **backup diagram**. Here the root node represents any state s, nodes at the next level represent state-action combinations (solid circles), and nodes at the leaves representing the set of possible resulting next state s' for each possible action. In the former case, we average over all actions according to the policy, whereas in the latter, we take the maximum over all actions.

34.6.3 Linear programming

While dynamic programming is effective and popular, linear programming (LP) provides an alternative that finds important uses, such as in off-policy RL (Section 35.5). The primal form of LP is given by

$$\min_V \sum_s p_0(s)V(s) \quad \text{s.t.} \quad V(s) \geq R(s,a) + \gamma \sum_{s'} p_T(s'|s,a)V(s), \quad \forall (s,a) \in \mathcal{S} \times \mathcal{A} \tag{34.92}$$

where $p_0(s) > 0$ for all $s \in \mathcal{S}$, and can be interpreted as the initial state distribution. It can be verified that any V satisfying the constraint in Equation (34.92) is optimistic [Put94], that is, $V \geq V_*$. When the objective is minimized, the solution V will be "pushed" to the smallest possible, which is V_*. Once V_* is found, any action a that makes the constraint tight in state s is optimal in that state.

The dual LP form is sometimes more intuitive:

$$\max_{d \geq 0} \sum_{s,a} d(s,a)R(s,a) \quad \text{s.t.} \quad \sum_{a} d(s,a) = (1-\gamma)p_0(s) + \gamma \sum_{\bar{s},\bar{a}} p_T(s|\bar{s},\bar{a})d(\bar{s},\bar{a}) \quad \forall s \in \mathcal{S} \quad (34.93)$$

Any nonnegative d satisfying the constraint above is the **normalized occupancy distribution** of some corresponding policy $\pi_d(a|s) \triangleq d(s,a)/\sum_{a'} d(s,a')$: [5]

$$d(s,a) = (1-\gamma)\sum_{t=0}^{\infty} \gamma^t p\big(s_t = s, a_t = a | s_0 \sim p_0, a_t \sim \pi_d(s_t)\big) \quad (34.94)$$

The constant $(1-\gamma)$ normalizes d to be a valid distribution, so that it sums to unity. With this interpretation of d, the objective in Equation (34.93) is just the average per-step reward under the normalized occupancy distribution. Once an optimal solution d_* is found, an optimal policy can be immediately obtained by $\pi_*(a|s) = d_*(s,a)/\sum_{a'} d_*(s,a')$.

A challenge in solving the primal or dual LPs for MDPs is the large number of constraints and variables. Approximations are needed, where the variables are parameterized (either linearly or nonlinearly), and the constraints are sampled or approximated (see e.g., [dV04; LBS17; CLW18]).

34.7   Active learning

This section is coauthored with Zeel B Patel.

In this section, we discuss **active learning** (AL), in which the agent gets to choose which data it wants to use so as to learn the underlying predictive function as quickly as possible, i.e., using the smallest amount of labeled data. This can be much more efficient than using randomly collected data, as illustrated in Figure 34.15. This is useful when labels are expensive to collect, e.g., for medical image classification [GIG17; Wal+20].

There are many approaches to AL, as reviewed in [Set12]. In this section, we just consider a few methods.

34.7.1   Active learning scenarios

One of the earliest AL methods is known as **membership query synthesis** [Ang88]. In this scenario the agent can generate an arbitrary query $x \sim p(x)$ and then ask the oracle for its label, $y = f(x)$. (An "oracle" is the term given to a system that knows the true answer to every possible question.) This scenario is mostly of theoretical interest, since it is hard to learn good generative models, and it is rarely possible to have access to an oracle on demand (although human-power **crowd computing** platforms can be considered as oracles with high latency).

Another scenario is **stream-based selective sampling** [ACL89], where the agent receives a stream of inputs, $x_1, x_2, \ldots$, and at each step must decide whether to request the label or not. Again, this scenario is mostly of theoretical interest.

The last and widely used setting for machine learning is **pool-based-sampling** [LG94], where the pool of unlabeled samples $\mathcal{X}$ is available from the beginning. At each step we apply an **acquisition**

---

5. If $\sum_{a'} d(s,a') = 0$ for some state s, then $\pi_d(s)$ may be defined arbitrarily, since s is not visited under the policy.

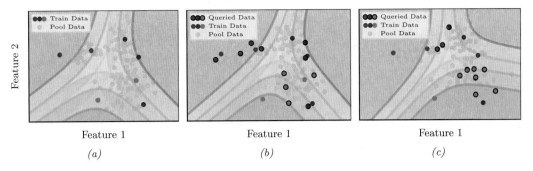

Figure 34.15: *Decision boundaries for a logistic regression model applied to a 2-dimensional, 3-class dataset. (a) Results after fitting the model on the initial training data; the test accuracy is 0.818. (b) results after further training on 11 randomly sampled points; accuracy is 0.848. (c) Results after further training on 11 points chosen with margin sampling (see Section 34.7.3); accuracy is 0.969. Generated by* active_learning_visualization_class.ipynb.

Problem	Goal	Action space
Active learning	$\operatorname{argmin}_f \mathbb{E}_{p(\boldsymbol{x})} \left[\ell(f^*(\boldsymbol{x}), f(\boldsymbol{x})) \right]$	choose $\boldsymbol{x}$ at which to get $\boldsymbol{y} = f^*(\boldsymbol{x})$
Bayesian optimization	$\operatorname{argmax}_{\boldsymbol{x} \in \mathcal{X}} f^*(\boldsymbol{x})$	choose $\boldsymbol{x}$ at which to evaluate $f^*(\boldsymbol{x})$
Contextual bandits	$\operatorname{argmax}_\pi \mathbb{E}_{p(\boldsymbol{x})\pi(a|\boldsymbol{x})} \left[R^*(\boldsymbol{x}, a) \right]$	choose a at which to evaluate $R^*(\boldsymbol{x}, a)$

Table 34.1: *Comparison among active learning, Bayesian optimization, and contextual bandits in terms of goal and action space.*

function to each candidate in the batch, to decide which one to collect the label for. We then collect the label, update the model with the new data, and repeat the process until we exhaust the pool, run out of time, or reach some desired performance. In the subsequent sections, we will focus only on pool-based sampling.

34.7.2   Relationship to other forms of sequential decision making

(Pool-based) active learning is closely related to Bayesian optimization (BO, Section 6.6) and contexual bandit problems (Section 34.4). The connections are discussed at length [Tou14], but in brief, the methods differ because they solve slightly different objective functions, as summarized in Table 34.1. In particular, in active learning, our goal is to identify a function $f : \mathcal{X} \to \mathcal{Y}$ that will incur minimum expected loss when applied to random inputs $\boldsymbol{x}$; in BO, our goal is to identify an input point $\boldsymbol{x}$ where the function output $f(\boldsymbol{x})$ is maximal; and in bandits, our goal is to identify a policy $\pi : \mathcal{X} \to \mathcal{A}$ that will give maximum expected reward when applied to random inputs (contexts) $\boldsymbol{x}$. (We see that the goal in AL and bandits is similar, but in bandits the agent only gets to choose the action, not the state, so only has partial control over where the (reward) function is evaluated.)

In all three problems, we want to find the optimum with as few actions as possible, so we have to solve the exploration-exploitation problem (Section 34.4.3). One approach is to represent our uncertainty about the function using a method such as a Gaussian process (Chapter 18), which lets

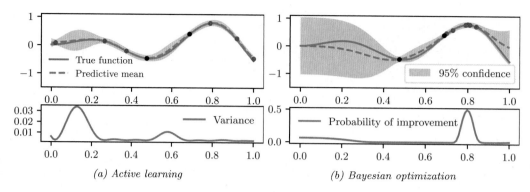

Figure 34.16: Active learning vs Bayesian optimization. Active learning tries to approximate the true function well. Bayesian optimization tries to find maximum value of the true function. Initial and queried points are denoted as black and red dots respectively. Generated by bayes_opt_vs_active_learning.ipynb.

us compute $p(f|\mathcal{D}_{1:t})$. We then define some acquisition function $\alpha(\boldsymbol{x})$ that evaluates how useful it would be to query the function at input location $\boldsymbol{x}$, given the belief state $p(f|\mathcal{D}_{1:t})$ and we pick as our next query $\boldsymbol{x}_{t+1} = \operatorname{argmax}_{\boldsymbol{x}} \alpha(\boldsymbol{x})$. (In the bandit setting, the agent does not get to choose the state $\boldsymbol{x}$, but does get to choose action a.) For example, in BO, it is common to use probability of improvement (Section 6.6.3.1), and for AL of a regression task, we can use the posterior predictive variance. The objective for AL will cause the agent to query "all over the place", whereas for BO, the agent will "zoom in" on the most promising regions, as shown in Figure 34.16. We discuss other acquisition functions for AL in Section 34.7.3.

34.7.3   Acquisition strategies

In this section, we discuss some common AL heuristics for choosing which points to query.

34.7.3.1   Uncertainty sampling

An intuitive heuristic for choosing which example to label next is to pick the one for which the model is currently most uncertain. This is called **uncertainty sampling**. We already illustrated this in the case of regression in Figure 34.16, where we represented uncertainty in terms of the posterior variance.

For classification problems, we can measure uncertainty in various ways. Let $\boldsymbol{p}_n = [p(y = c|\boldsymbol{x}_n)]_{c=1}^{C}$ be the vector of class probabilities for each unlabeled input $\boldsymbol{x}_n$. Let $U_n = \alpha(\boldsymbol{p}_n)$ be the uncertainty for example n, where α is an acquisition function. Some common choices for α are: **entropy sampling** [SW87a], which uses $\alpha(\boldsymbol{p}) = -\sum_{c=1}^{C} p_c \log p_c$; **margin sampling**, which uses $\alpha(\boldsymbol{p}) = p_2 - p_1$, where p_1 is the probability of the most probable class, and p_2 is the probability of the second most probable class; and **least confident sampling**, which uses $\alpha(\boldsymbol{p}) = 1 - p_{c^*}$, where $c^* = \operatorname{argmax}_c p_c$. The difference between these strategies is shown in Figure 34.17. In practice it is often found that margin sampling works the best [Chu+19].

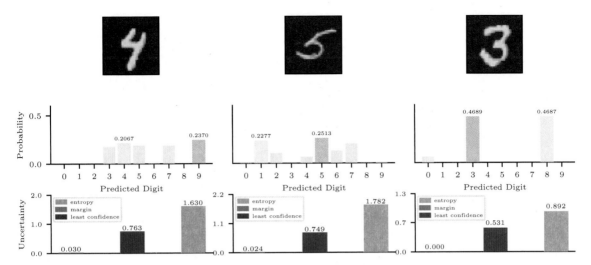

Figure 34.17: *Outputs of a logistic regression model fit on some training points, and then applied to 3 candidate query inputs. We show the predicted probabilites for each class label. The highlighted dark gray is the max probability, the light gray bar is the 2nd highest probability. The least confident scores for the 3 inputs are: $1 - 0.23 = 0.76$, $1 - 0.25 = 0.75$, and $1 - 0.47 = 0.53$, so we pick the first query. The entropy scores are: 1.63, 1.78 and 0.89, so we pick the second query. The margin scores are: $0.237 - 0.2067 = 0.0303$, $0.2513 - 0.2277 = 0.0236$, and $0.4689 - 0.4687 = 0.0002$, so we pick the third query. Generated by active_learning_comparison_mnist.ipynb.*

34.7.3.2   Query by committee

In this section, we discuss how to apply uncertainty sampling to models, such as support vector machines (SVMs), that only return a point prediction rather than a probability distribution. The basic approach is to create an ensemble of diverse models, and to use disagreement between the model predictions as a form of uncertainty. (This can be useful even for probabilistic models, such as DNNs, since model uncertainty can often be larger than parametric uncertainty, as we discuss in the section on deep ensembles, Section 17.3.9.)

In more detail, suppose we have K ensemble members, and let c_n^k be the predicted class from member k on input $\boldsymbol{x}_n$. Let $v_{nc} = \sum_{k=1}^K \mathbb{I}\left(c_n^k = c\right)$ be the number of votes cast for class c, and $q_{nc} = v_{nc}/C$ be the induced distribution. (A similar method can be used for regression models, where we use the standard deviation of the prediction across the members.) We can then use margin sampling or entropy sampling with distribution $\boldsymbol{q}_n$. This approach is called **query by committee (QBC)** [SOS92], and can often out-perform vanilla uncertainty sampling with a single model, as we show in Figure 34.18.

34.7.3.3   Information theoretic methods

A natural acquisition strategy is to pick points whose labels will maximimally reduce our uncertainty about the model parameters $\boldsymbol{w}$. This is known as the **information gain** criterion, and was first

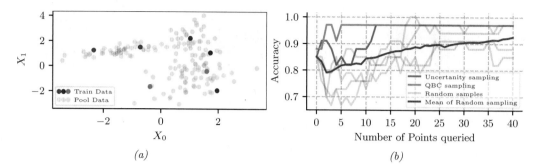

Figure 34.18: (a) Random forest (RF) classifier applied to a 2-dimensional, 3-class dataset. (b) Accuracy vs number of query points for margin sampling vs random sampling. We represent uncertainty using either a single RF (based on the predicted distribution over labels induced by the trees in the forest), or a committee containing an RF and a logistic regression model. Generated by active_learning_compare_class.ipynb.

proposed in [Lin56]. It is defined as follows:

$$\alpha(\boldsymbol{x}) \triangleq \mathbb{H}\left(p(\boldsymbol{w}|\mathcal{D})\right) - \mathbb{E}_{p(y|\boldsymbol{x},\mathcal{D})}\left[\mathbb{H}\left(p(\boldsymbol{w}|\mathcal{D},\boldsymbol{x},y)\right)\right] \tag{34.95}$$

(Note that the first term is a constant wrt $\boldsymbol{x}$, but we include it for later convenience.) This is equivalent to the expected change in the posterior over the parameters which is given by

$$\alpha'(\boldsymbol{x}) \triangleq \mathbb{E}_{p(y|\boldsymbol{x},\mathcal{D})}\left[D_{\mathrm{KL}}\left(p(\boldsymbol{w}|\mathcal{D},\boldsymbol{x},y) \parallel p(\boldsymbol{w}|\mathcal{D})\right)\right] \tag{34.96}$$

Using symmetry of the mutual information, we can rewrite Equation (34.95) as follows:

$$\alpha(\boldsymbol{x}) = \mathbb{H}\left(\boldsymbol{w}|\mathcal{D}\right) - \mathbb{E}_{p(y|\boldsymbol{x},\mathcal{D})}\left[\mathbb{H}\left(\boldsymbol{w}|\mathcal{D},\boldsymbol{x},y\right)\right] \tag{34.97}$$

$$= \mathbb{I}(\boldsymbol{w},y|\mathcal{D},\boldsymbol{x}) \tag{34.98}$$

$$= \mathbb{H}\left(y|\boldsymbol{x},\mathcal{D}\right) - \mathbb{E}_{p(\boldsymbol{w}|\mathcal{D})}\left[\mathbb{H}\left(y|\boldsymbol{x},\boldsymbol{w},\mathcal{D}\right)\right] \tag{34.99}$$

The advantage of this approach is that we now only have to reason about the uncertainty of the predictive distribution over outputs y, not over the parameters $\boldsymbol{w}$. This approach is called **Bayesian active learning by disagreement** or **BALD** [Hou+12].

Equation (34.99) has an interesting interpretation. The first term prefers examples $\boldsymbol{x}$ for which there is uncertainty in the predicted label. Just using this as a selection criterion is equivalent to uncertainty sampling, which we discussed above. However, this can have problems with examples which are inherently ambiguous or mislabeled. By adding the second term, we penalize such behavior, since we add a large negative weight to points whose predictive distribution is entropic even when we know the parameters. Thus we ignore aleatoric (intrinsic) uncertainty and focus on epistemic uncertainty.

34.7.4   Batch active learning

In many applications, we need to select a batch of unlabeled examples at once, since training a model on single examples is too slow. This is called **batch active learning**. The key challenge is that we need to ensure the different queries that we request are diverse, so we maximize the information gain. Various methods for this problem have been devised; here we focus on the **BatchBALD** method of [KAG19], which extends the BALD method of Section 34.7.3.3.

34.7.4.1 BatchBALD

The naive way to extend the BALD score to a batch of b candidate query points is to define

$$\alpha_{\text{BALD}}(\{\boldsymbol{x}_1, \ldots, \boldsymbol{x}_B\}, p(\boldsymbol{w}|\mathcal{D})) = \alpha_{\text{BALD}}(\boldsymbol{x}_{1:B}, p(\boldsymbol{w}|\mathcal{D})) = \sum_{i=1}^{B} \mathbb{I}(y_i; \boldsymbol{w}|\boldsymbol{x}_i, \mathcal{D}) \tag{34.100}$$

However this may pick points that are quite similar in terms of their information content. In BatchBALD, we use joint conditional mutual information between the set of labels and the parameters:

$$\alpha_{\text{BBALD}}(\boldsymbol{x}_{1:B}, p(\boldsymbol{w}|\mathcal{D})) = \mathbb{I}(\boldsymbol{y}_{1:B}; \boldsymbol{w}|\boldsymbol{x}_{1:B}, \mathcal{D}) = \mathbb{H}(\boldsymbol{y}_{1:b}|\boldsymbol{x}_{1:B}, \mathcal{D}) - \mathbb{E}_{p(\boldsymbol{w}|\mathcal{D})}\left[\mathbb{H}(\boldsymbol{y}_{1:B}|\boldsymbol{x}_{1:B}, \boldsymbol{w}, \mathcal{D})\right] \tag{34.101}$$

To understand how this differs from BALD, we will use information diagrams for representing MI in terms of Venn diagrams, as explained in Section 5.3.2. In particular, [Yeu91a] showed that we can define a signed measure, μ^*, for discrete random variables x and y such that $\mathbb{I}(x; y) = \mu^*(x \cap y)$, $\mathbb{H}(x, y) = \mu^*(x \cup y)$, $\mathbb{E}_{p(y)}[\mathbb{H}(x|y)] = \mu^*(x \setminus y)$, etc. Using this, we can interpret standard BALD as the sum of the individual intersections, $\sum_i \mu^*(y_i \cap \boldsymbol{w})$, which double counts overlaps between the y_i, as shown in Figure 34.19(a). By contrast, BatchBALD takes overlap into account by computing

$$\mathbb{I}(\boldsymbol{y}_{1:B}; \boldsymbol{w}|\boldsymbol{x}_{1:B}, \mathcal{D}) = \mu^*(\cup_i y_i \cap \boldsymbol{w}) = \mu^*(\cup_i y_i) - \mu^*(\cup_i y_i \setminus \boldsymbol{w}) \tag{34.102}$$

This is illustrated in Figure 34.19(b). From this, we can see that $\alpha_{\text{BBALD}} \leq \alpha_{\text{BALD}}$. Indeed, one can show[6]

$$\mathbb{I}(\boldsymbol{y}_{1:B}, \boldsymbol{w}|\boldsymbol{x}_{1:B}, \mathcal{D}) = \sum_{i=1}^{B} \mathbb{I}(y_i, \boldsymbol{w}|\boldsymbol{x}_{1:B}, \mathcal{D}) - \mathbb{TC}(\boldsymbol{y}_{1:B}|\boldsymbol{x}_{1:B}, \mathcal{D}) \tag{34.103}$$

where TC is the total correlation (see Section 5.3.5.1).

34.7.4.2 Optimizing BatchBALD

To avoid the combinatorial explosion that arises from jointly scoring subsets of points, we can use a a greedy approximation for computing BatchBALD one point at a time. In particular, suppose at step $n-1$ we already have a partial batch $\mathcal{A}_{n-1}$. The next point is chosen using

$$\boldsymbol{x}_n = \operatorname*{argmax}_{\boldsymbol{x} \in \mathcal{D}_{\text{pool}} \setminus \mathcal{A}_{n-1}} \alpha_{\text{BBALD}}(\mathcal{A}_{n-1} \cup \{\boldsymbol{x}\}, p(\boldsymbol{w}|\mathcal{D})) \tag{34.104}$$

We then add $\boldsymbol{x}_n$ to $\mathcal{A}_{n-1}$ to get $\mathcal{A}_n$. Fortunately the BatchBALD acquisition function is submodular, as shown in [KAG19]. Hence this greedy algorithm is within $1 - 1/e \approx 0.63$ of optimal (see Section 6.9.4.1).

---

6. See http://blog.blackhc.net/2022/07/kbald/

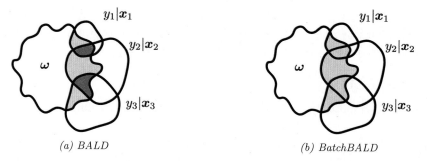

Figure 34.19: Intuition behind BALD and BatchBALD. D_{pool} is an unlabelled dataset (from which $x_{1:b}$ are taken), D_{train} is the current training set, w is set of model parameters, $p(y|x,w,D_{train})$ are output predictions for datapoint x. BALD overestimates the joint mutual information whereas BatchBALD takes the overlap between variables into account. Areas contributing to the respective score are shown in grey, and areas that are double-counted in dark grey. From Figure 3 of [KAG19]. Used with kind permission of Andreas Kirsch.

34.7.4.3   Computing BatchBALD

Computing the joint (conditional) mutual information is intractable, so in this section, we discuss how to approximate it. For brevity we drop the conditioning on x and $\mathcal{D}$. With this new notation, the objective becomes

$$\alpha_{\text{BBALD}}(x_{1:B}, p(w|\mathcal{D})) = \mathbb{H}(y_1, \ldots, y_B) - \mathbb{E}_{p(w)}\left[\mathbb{H}(y_1, \ldots, y_B|w)\right] \tag{34.105}$$

Note that the y_i are conditionally independent given w, so $\mathbb{H}(y_1, \ldots, y_B|w) = \sum_{i=1}^B \mathbb{H}(y_i|w)$. Hence we can approximate the second term with Monte Carlo:

$$\mathbb{E}_{p(w)}\left[\mathbb{H}(y_1, \ldots, y_B|w)\right] \approx \frac{1}{S}\sum_{i=1}^n \sum_s \mathbb{H}(y_i|\hat{w}_s) \tag{34.106}$$

where $\hat{w}_s \sim p(w|\mathcal{D})$.

The first term, $\mathbb{H}(y_1, \ldots, y_B)$, is a joint entropy, so is harder to compute. [KAG19] propose the following approximation, summing over all possible label sequences in the batch, and leveraging the fact that $p(y) = \mathbb{E}_{p(w)}[p(y|w)]$:

$$\mathbb{H}(y_{1:B}) = \mathbb{E}_{p(w)p(y_{1:B}|vw)}\left[-\log p(y_{1:B}|w)\right] \tag{34.107}$$

$$\approx \sum_{\hat{y}_{1:B}} \left(\frac{1}{S}\sum_{s=1}^S p(\hat{y}_{1:B}|\hat{w}_s)\right) \log\left(\frac{1}{S}\sum_{s=1}^S p(\hat{y}_{1:B}|\hat{w}_s)\right) \tag{34.108}$$

The sum over all possible labels sequences can be made more efficient by noting that $p(y_{1:n}|w) = p(y_n|w)p(y_{1:n-1}|w)$, so when we implement the greedy algorithm, we can incrementally update the probabilities, reusing previous computations. See [KAG19] for the details.

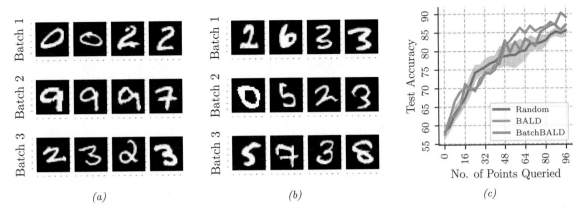

Figure 34.20: *Three batches (each of size 4) queried from the MNIST pool by (a) BALD and (b) BatchBALD. (c) Plot of accuracy vs number of points queried. BALD may select replicas of single informative datapoint while BatchBALD selects diverse points, thus increasing data efficiency. Generated by* batch_bald_mnist.ipynb.

34.7.4.4   Experimental comparison of BALD vs BatchBALD on MNIST

In this section, we show some experimental results applying BALD and BatchBALD to train a CNN on the standard MNIST dataset. We use a batch size of 4, and approximate the posterior over parameters $p(\boldsymbol{w}|\mathcal{D})$ using MC dropout (Section 17.3.1). In Figure 34.20(a), we see that BALD selects examples that are very similar to each other, whereas in Figure 34.20(b), we see that BatchBALD selects a greater diversity of points. In Figure 34.20(c), we see that BatchBALD results in more efficient learning than BALD, which in turn is more efficient than randomly sampling data.

35 Reinforcement learning

This chapter is co-authored with Lihong Li.

35.1 Introduction

Reinforcement learning or **RL** is a paradigm of learning where an agent sequentially interacts with an initially unknown environment. The interaction typically results in a **trajectory**, or multiple trajectories. Let $\boldsymbol{\tau} = (s_0, a_0, r_0, s_1, a_1, r_1, s_2, \ldots, s_T)$ be a trajectory of length T, consisting of a sequence of states s_t, actions a_t, and rewards r_t.[1] The goal of the agent is to optimize her action-selection policy, so that the discounted cumulative reward, $G_0 \triangleq \sum_{t=0}^{T-1} \gamma^t r_t$, is maximized for some given **discount factor** $\gamma \in [0, 1]$.

In general, G_0 is a random variable. We will focus on maximizing its expectation, inspired by the maximum expected utility principle (Section 34.1.3), but note other possibilities such as **conditional value at risk**[2] that can be more appropriate in risk-sensitive applications.

We will focus on the Markov decision process, where the generative model for the trajectory $\boldsymbol{\tau}$ can be factored into single-step models. When these model parameters are known, solving for an optimal policy is called **planning** (see Section 34.6); otherwise, RL algorithms may be used to obtain an optimal policy from trajectories, a process called **learning**.

In **model-free RL**, we try to learn the policy without explicitly representing and learning the models, but directly from the trajectories. In **model-based RL**, we first learn a model from the trajectories, and then use a planning algorithm on the learned model to solve for the policy. See Figure 35.1 for an overview. This chapter will introduce some of the key concepts and techniques, and will mostly follow the notation from [SB18]. More details can be found in textbooks such as [Sze10; SB18; Ber19; Aga+21a; Mey22; Aga+22], and reviews such as [WO12; Aru+17; FL+18; Li18].

35.1.1 Overview of methods

In this section, we give a brief overview of how to compute optimal policies when the MDP model is not known. Instead, the agent interacts with the environment and learns from the observed

---

1. Note that the time starts at 0 here, while it starts at 1 when we discuss bandits (Section 34.4). Our choices of notation are to be consistent with conventions in respective literature.
2. The conditional value at risk, or CVaR, is the expected reward conditioned on being in the worst 5% (say) of samples. See [Cho+15] for an example application in RL.

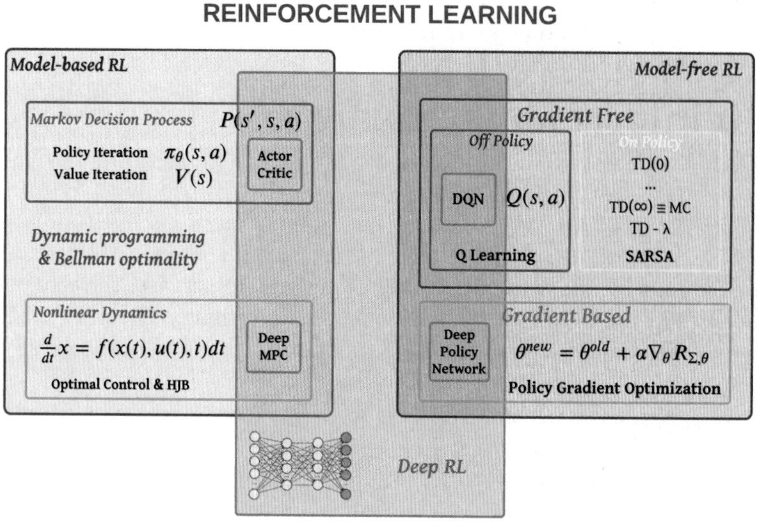

REINFORCEMENT LEARNING

Figure 35.1: Overview of RL methods. Abbreviations: DQN = Deep Q network (Section 35.2.6); MPC = Model Predictive Control (Section 35.4); HJB = Hamilton-Jacobi-Bellman equation; TD = temporal difference learning (Section 35.2.2). Adapted from a slide by Steve Brunton.

Method	Functions learned	On/Off	Section
SARSA	$Q(s, a)$	On	Section 35.2.4
Q-learning	$Q(s, a)$	Off	Section 35.2.5
REINFORCE	$\pi(a|s)$	On	Section 35.3.2
A2C	$\pi(a|s), V(s)$	On	Section 35.3.3.1
TRPO/PPO	$\pi(a|s), A(s, a)$	On	Section 35.3.4
DDPG	$a = \pi(s), Q(s, a)$	Off	Section 35.3.5
Soft actor-critic	$\pi(a|s), Q(s, a)$	Off	Section 35.6.1
Model-based RL	$p(s'|s, a)$	Off	Section 35.4

Table 35.1: Summary of some popular methods for RL. On/off refers to on-policy vs off-policy methods.

trajectories. This is the core focus of RL. We will go into more details into later sections, but first provide this roadmap.

We may categorize RL methods by the quantity the agent represents and learns: value function, policy, and model; or by how actions are selected: on-policy (actions must be selected by the agent's current policy), and off-policy. Table 35.1 lists a few representative examples. More details are given in the subsequent sections. We will also discuss at greater depth two important topics of off-policy learning and inference-based control in Sections 35.5 and 35.6.

35.1.2   Value-based methods

In a value-based method, we often try to learn the optimal Q-function from experience, and then derive a policy from it using Equation (34.84). Typically, a function approximator (e.g., a neural network), $Q_{\boldsymbol{w}}$, is used to represent the Q-function, which is trained iteratively. Given a transition (s, a, r, s'), we define the **temporal difference** (also called the **TD error**) as

$$r + \gamma \max_{a'} Q_{\boldsymbol{w}}(s', a') - Q_{\boldsymbol{w}}(s, a)$$

Clearly, the expected TD error is the Bellman error evaluated at (s, a). Therefore, if $Q_{\boldsymbol{w}} = Q_*$, the TD error is 0 on average by Bellman's optimality equation. Otherwise, the error provides a signal for the agent to change $\boldsymbol{w}$ to make $Q_{\boldsymbol{w}}(s, a)$ closer to $R(s, a) + \gamma \max_{a'} Q_{\boldsymbol{w}}(s', a')$. The update on $Q_{\boldsymbol{w}}$ is based on a target that is computed using $Q_{\boldsymbol{w}}$. This kind of update is known as **bootstrapping** in RL, and should not be confused with the statistical bootstrap (Section 3.3.2). Value based methods such as **Q-learning** and **SARSA** are discussed in Section 35.2.

35.1.3   Policy search methods

In **policy search**, we try to directly maximize $J(\pi_{\boldsymbol{\theta}})$ wrt the policy parameter $\boldsymbol{\theta}$. If $J(\pi_{\boldsymbol{\theta}})$ is differentiable wrt $\boldsymbol{\theta}$, we can use stochastic gradient ascent to optimize $\boldsymbol{\theta}$, which is known as **policy gradient**, as described in Section 35.3.1. The basic idea is to perform **Monte Carlo rollouts**, in which we sample trajectories by interacting with the environment, and then use the score function estimator (Section 6.3.4) to estimate $\nabla_{\boldsymbol{\theta}} J(\pi_{\boldsymbol{\theta}})$. Here, $J(\pi_{\boldsymbol{\theta}})$ is defined as an expectation whose distribution depends on $\boldsymbol{\theta}$, so it is invalid to swap ∇ and $\mathbb{E}$ in computing the gradient, and the score function estimator can be used instead. An example of policy gradient is **REINFORCE**.

Policy gradient methods have the advantage that they provably converge to a local optimum for many common policy classes, whereas Q-learning may diverge when approximation is used (Section 35.5.3). In addition, policy gradient methods can easily be applied to continuous action spaces, since they do not need to compute $\mathrm{argmax}_a Q(s, a)$. Unfortunately, the score function estimator for $\nabla_{\boldsymbol{\theta}} J(\pi_{\boldsymbol{\theta}})$ can have a very high variance, so the resulting method can converge slowly.

One way to reduce the variance is to learn an approximate value function, $V_{\boldsymbol{w}}(s)$. and to use it as a baseline in the score function estimator. We can learn $V_{\boldsymbol{w}}(s)$ using one of the value function methods similar to Q-learning. Alternatively, we can learn an advantage function, $A_{\boldsymbol{w}}(s, a)$, and use it to estimate the gradient. These policy gradient variants are called **actor critic** methods, where the actor refers to the policy $\pi_{\boldsymbol{\theta}}$ and the critic refers to $V_{\boldsymbol{w}}$ or $A_{\boldsymbol{w}}$. See Section 35.3.3 for details.

35.1.4   Model-based RL

Value-based methods, such as Q-learning, and policy search methods, such as policy gradient, can be very **sample inefficient**, which means they may need to interact with the environment many times before finding a good policy. If an agent has prior knowledge of the MDP model, it can be more sample efficient to first learn the model, and then compute an optimal (or near-optimal) policy of the model without having to interact with the environment any more.

This approach is called **model-based RL**. The first step is to learn the MDP model including the $p_T(s'|s, a)$ and $R(s, a)$ functions, e.g., using DNNs. Given a collection of (s, a, r, s') tuples, such a model can be learned using standard supervised learning methods. The second step can be done by running an RL algorithm on synthetic experiences generated from the model, or by running a planning algorithm on the model directly (Section 34.6). In practice, we often interleave the model learning and planning phases, so we can use the partially learned policy to decide what data to collect. We discuss model-based RL in more detail in Section 35.4.

35.1.5   Exploration-exploitation tradeoff

A fundamental problem in RL with unknown transition and reward models is to decide between choosing actions that the agent knows will yield high reward, or choosing actions whose reward is uncertain, but which may yield information that helps the agent get to parts of state-action space with even higher reward. This is called the **exploration-exploitation tradeoff**, which has been discussed in the simpler contextual bandit setting in Section 34.4. The literature on efficient exploration is huge. In this section, we briefly describe several representative techniques.

35.1.5.1 ϵ-greedy

A common heuristic is to use an ϵ-**greedy** policy π_ϵ, parameterized by $\epsilon \in [0, 1]$. In this case, we pick the greedy action wrt the current model, $a_t = \text{argmax}_a \hat{R}_t(s_t, a)$ with probability $1 - \epsilon$, and a random action with probability ϵ. This rule ensures the agent's continual exploration of all state-action combinations. Unfortunately, this heuristic can be shown to be suboptimal, since it explores every action with at least a constant probability $\epsilon/|\mathcal{A}|$.

35.1.5.2   Boltzmann exploration

A source of inefficiency in the ϵ-greedy rule is that exploration occurs uniformly over all actions. The **Boltzmann policy** can be more efficient, by assigning higher probabilities to explore more promising actions:

$$\pi_\tau(a|s) = \frac{\exp(\hat{R}_t(s_t, a)/\tau)}{\sum_{a'} \exp(\hat{R}_t(s_t, a')/\tau)} \tag{35.1}$$

where $\tau > 0$ is a temperature parameter that controls how entropic the distribution is. As τ gets close to 0, π_τ becomes close to a greedy policy. On the other hand, higher values of τ will make $\pi(a|s)$ more uniform, and encourage more exploration. Its action selection probabilities can be much "smoother" with respect to changes in the reward estimates than ϵ-greedy, as illustrated in Table 35.2.

35.1.5.3   Upper confidence bounds and Thompson sampling

The upper confidence bound (UCB) (Section 34.4.5) and Thompson sampling (Section 34.4.6) approaches may also be extended to MDPs. In contrast to the contextual bandit case, where the only uncertainty is in the reward function, here we must also take into account uncertainty in the transition probabilities.

   As in the bandit case, the UCB approach requires to estimate an upper confidence bound for all actions' Q-values in the current state, and then take the action with the highest UCB score. One way to obtain UCBs of the Q-values is to use **count-based exploration**, where we learn the optimal

$\hat{R}(s,a_1)$	$\hat{R}(s,a_2)$	$\pi_\epsilon(a\|s_1)$	$\pi_\epsilon(a\|s_2)$	$\pi_\tau(a\|s_1)$	$\pi_\tau(a\|s_2)$
1.00	9.00	0.05	0.95	0.00	1.00
4.00	6.00	0.05	0.95	0.12	0.88
4.90	5.10	0.05	0.95	0.45	0.55
5.05	4.95	0.95	0.05	0.53	0.48
7.00	3.00	0.95	0.05	0.98	0.02
8.00	2.00	0.95	0.05	1.00	0.00

Table 35.2: *Comparison of ϵ-greedy policy (with $\epsilon = 0.1$) and Boltzmann policy (with $\tau = 1$) for a simple MDP with 6 states and 2 actions. Adapted from Table 4.1 of [GK19].*

Q-function with an **exploration bonus** added to the reward in a transition (s, a, r, s'):

$$\tilde{r} = r + \alpha / \sqrt{N_{s,a}} \tag{35.2}$$

where $N_{s,a}$ is the number of times action a has been taken in state s, and $\alpha \geq 0$ is a weighting term that controls the degree of exploration. This is the approach taken by the **MBIE-EB** method [SL08] for finite-state MDPs, and in the generalization to continuous-state MDPs through the use of hashing [Bel+16]. Other approaches also explicitly maintain uncertainty in state transition probabilities, and use that information to obtain UCBs. Examples are **MBIE** [SL08], **UCRL2** [JOA10], and **UCBVI** [AOM17], among many others.

Thompson sampling can be similarly adapted, by maintaining the posterior distribution of the reward and transition model parameters. In finite-state MDPs, for example, the transition model is a categorical distribution conditioned on the state. We may use the conjugate prior of Dirichlet distributions (Section 3.4) for the transition model, so that the posterior distribution can be conveniently computed and sampled from. More details on this approach are found in [Rus+18].

Both UCB and Thompson sampling methods have been shown to yield efficient exploration with provably strong regret bounds (Section 34.4.7) [JOA10], or related PAC bounds [SLL09; DLB17], often under necessary assumptions such as finiteness of the MDPs. In practice, these methods may be combined with function approximation like neural networks and implemented approximately.

35.1.5.4 Optimal solution using Bayes-adaptive MDPs

The Bayes optimal solution to the exploration-exploitation tradeoff can be computed by formulating the problem as a special kind of POMDP known as a **Bayes-adaptive MDP** or **BAMDP** [Duf02]. This extends the Gittins index approach in Section 34.4.4 to the MDP setting.

In particular, a BAMDP has a **belief state** space, $\mathcal{B}$, representing uncertainty about the reward model $p_R(r|s, a, s')$ and transition model $p_T(s'|s, a)$. The transition model on this augmented MDP can be written as follows:

$$T^+(s_{t+1}, b_{t+1}|s_t, b_t, a_t, r_t) = T^+(s_{t+1}|s_t, a_t, b_t)T^+(b_{t+1}|s_t, a_t, r_t, s_{t+1}) \tag{35.3}$$

$$= \mathbb{E}_{b_t}[T(s_{t+1}|s_t, a_t)] \times \mathbb{I}(b_{t+1} = p(R, T|\boldsymbol{h}_{t+1})) \tag{35.4}$$

where $\mathbb{E}_{b_t}[T(s_{t+1}|s_t, a_t)]$ is the posterior predictive distribution over next states, and $p(R, T|\boldsymbol{h}_{t+1})$ is the new belief state given $\boldsymbol{h}_{t+1} = (s_{1:t+1}, a_{1:t+1}, r_{1:t+1})$, which can be computed using Bayes' rule.

Similarly, the reward function for the augmented MDP is given by

$$R^+(r|s_t, b_t, a_t, s_{t+1}, b_{t+1}) = \mathbb{E}_{b_{t+1}} \left[R(s_t, a_t, s_{t+1}) \right] \tag{35.5}$$

For small problems, we can solve the resulting augmented MDP optimally. However, in general this is computationally intractable. [Gha+15] surveys many methods to solve it more efficiently. For example, [KN09] develop an algorithm that behaves similarly to Bayes optimal policies, except in a provably small number of steps; [GSD13] propose an approximate method based on Monte Carlo rollouts. More recently, [Zin+20] propose an approximate method based on meta-learning (Section 19.6.4), in which they train a (model-free) policy for multiple related tasks. Each task is represented by a task embedding vector m, which is inferred from $\boldsymbol{h}_t$ using a VAE (Section 21.2). The posterior $p(m|\boldsymbol{h}_t)$ is used as a proxy for the belief state b_t, and the policy is trained to perform well given s_t and b_t. At test time, the policy is applied to the incrementally computed belief state; this allows the method to infer what kind of task this is, and then to use a pre-trained policy to quickly solve it.

35.2 Value-based RL

In this section, we assume the agent has access to samples from p_T and p_R by interacting with the environment. We will show how to use these samples to learn optimal Q-functions from which we can derive optimal policies.

35.2.1 Monte Carlo RL

Recall that $Q_\pi(s, a) = \mathbb{E}\left[G_t | s_t = s, a_t = a\right]$ for any t. A simple way to estimate this is to take action a, and then sample the rest of the trajectory according to π, and then compute the average sum of discounted rewards. The trajectory ends when we reach a terminal state, if the task is episodic, or when the discount factor γ^t becomes negligibly small, whichever occurs first. This is the **Monte Carlo estimation** of the value function.

We can use this technique together with policy iteration (Section 34.6.2) to learn an optimal policy. Specifically, at iteration k, we compute a new, improved policy using $\pi_{k+1}(s) = \text{argmax}_a Q_k(s, a)$, where Q_k is approximated using MC estimation. This update can be applied to all the states visited on the sampled trajectory. This overall technique is called **Monte Carlo control**.

To ensure this method converges to the optimal policy, we need to collect data for every (state, action) pair, at least in the tabular case, since there is no generalization across different values of $Q(s, a)$. One way to achieve this is to use an ϵ-greedy policy. Since this is an on-policy algorithm, the resulting method will converge to the optimal ϵ-soft policy, as opposed to the optimal policy. It is possible to use importance sampling to estimate the value function for the optimal policy, even if actions are chosen according to the ϵ-greedy policy. However, it is simpler to just gradually reduce ϵ.

35.2.2 Temporal difference (TD) learning

The Monte Carlo (MC) method in Section 35.2.1 results in an estimator for $Q_\pi(s, a)$ with very high variance, since it has to unroll many trajectories, whose returns are a sum of many random rewards generated by stochastic state transitions. In addition, it is limited to episodic tasks (or finite horizon

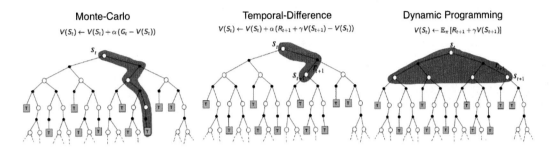

Figure 35.2: Backup diagrams of $V(s_t)$ for Monte Carlo, temporal difference, and dynamic programming updates of the state-value function. Used with kind permission of Andy Barto.

truncation of continuing tasks), since it must unroll to the end of the episode before each update step, to ensure it reliably estimates the long term return.

In this section, we discuss a more efficient technique called **temporal difference** or **TD** learning [Sut88]. The basic idea is to incrementally reduce the Bellman error for sampled states or state-actions, based on transitions instead of a long trajectory. More precisely, suppose we are to learn the value function V_π for a fixed policy π. Given a state transition (s, a, r, s') where $a \sim \pi(s)$, we change the estimate $V(s)$ so that it moves towards the bootstrapping target (Section 35.1.2)

$$V(s_t) \leftarrow V(s_t) + \eta\,[r_t + \gamma V(s_{t+1}) - V(s_t)] \tag{35.6}$$

where η is the learning rate. The term multiplied by η above is known as the **TD error**. A more general form of TD update for parametric value function representations is

$$\boldsymbol{w} \leftarrow \boldsymbol{w} + \eta\,[r_t + \gamma V_{\boldsymbol{w}}(s_{t+1}) - V_{\boldsymbol{w}}(s_t)]\,\nabla_{\boldsymbol{w}} V_{\boldsymbol{w}}(s_t) \tag{35.7}$$

of which Equation (35.6) is a special case. The TD update rule for learning Q_π is similar.

It can be shown that TD learning in the tabular case, Equation (35.6), converges to the correct value function, under proper conditions [Ber19]. However, it may diverge when approximation is used (Equation (35.7)), an issue we will discuss further in Section 35.5.3.

The potential divergence of TD is also consistent with the fact that Equation (35.7) is not SGD (Section 6.3.1) on any objective function, despite a very similar form. Instead, it is an example of **bootstrapping**, in which the estimate, $V_{\boldsymbol{w}}(s_t)$, is updated to approach a target, $r_t + \gamma V_{\boldsymbol{w}}(s_{t+1})$, which is defined by the value function estimate itself. This idea is shared by DP methods like value iteration, although they rely on the complete MDP model to compute an exact Bellman backup. In contrast, TD learning can be viewed as using sampled transitions to approximate such backups. An example of non-bootstrapping approach is the Monte Carlo estimation in the previous section. It samples a complete trajectory, rather than individual transitions, to perform an update, and is often much less efficient. Figure 35.2 illustrates the difference between MC, TD, and DP.

35.2.3 TD learning with eligibility traces

A key difference between TD and MC is the way they estimate returns. Given a trajectory $\boldsymbol{\tau} = (s_0, a_0, r_0, s_1, \ldots, s_T)$, TD estimates the return from state s_t by one-step lookahead, $G_{t:t+1} = r_t +$

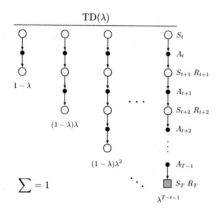

Figure 35.3: The backup diagram for TD(λ). Standard TD learning corresponds to $\lambda = 0$, and standard MC learning corresponds to $\lambda = 1$. From Figure 12.1 of [SB18]. Used with kind permission of Richard Sutton.

$\gamma V(s_{t+1})$, where the return from time $t + 1$ is replaced by its value function estimate. In contrast, MC waits until the end of the episode or until T is large enough, then uses the estimate $G_{t:T} = r_t + \gamma r_{t+1} + \cdots + \gamma^{T-t-1} r_{T-1}$. It is possible to interpolate between these by performing an n-step rollout, and then using the value function to approximate the return for the rest of the trajectory, similar to heuristic search (Section 35.4.1.1). That is, we can use the n-step estimate

$$G_{t:t+n} = r_t + \gamma r_{t+1} + \cdots + \gamma^{n-1} r_{t+n-1} + \gamma^n V(s_{t+n}) \tag{35.8}$$

The corresponding n-step version of the TD update becomes

$$V(s_t) \leftarrow V(s_t) + \eta \left[G_{t:t+n} - V(s_t) \right] \tag{35.9}$$

Rather than picking a specific lookahead value, n, we can take a weighted average of all possible values, with a single parameter $\lambda \in [0, 1]$, by using

$$G_t^\lambda \triangleq (1 - \lambda) \sum_{n=1}^{\infty} \lambda^{n-1} G_{t:t+n} \tag{35.10}$$

This is called the **λ-return**. The coefficient of $1 - \lambda = (1 + \lambda + \lambda^2 + \cdots)^{-1}$ in the front ensures this is a convex combination of n-step returns. See Figure 35.3 for an illustration.

An important benefit of using the geometric weighting in Equation (35.10) is that the corresponding TD learning update can be efficiently implemented, through the use of **eligibility traces**, even though G_t^λ is a sum of infinitely many terms. The method is called **TD(λ)**, and can be combined with many algorithms to be studied in the rest of the chapter. See [SB18] for a detailed discussion.

35.2.4 SARSA: on-policy TD control

TD learning is for policy evaluation, as it estimates the value function for a fixed policy. In order to find an optimal policy, we may use the algorithm as a building block inside generalized policy iteration (Section 34.6.2). In this case, it is more convenient to work with the action-value function, Q, and a policy π that is greedy with respect to Q. The agent follows π in every step to choose actions, and upon a transition (s, a, r, s') the TD update rule is

$$Q(s,a) \leftarrow Q(s,a) + \eta \left[r + \gamma Q(s',a') - Q(s,a) \right] \tag{35.11}$$

where $a' \sim \pi(s')$ is the action the agent will take in state s'. After Q is updated (for policy evaluation), π also changes accordingly as it is greedy with respect to Q (for policy improvement). This algorithm, first proposed by [RN94], was further studied and renamed to **SARSA** by [Sut96]; the name comes from its update rule that involves an augmented transition (s, a, r, s', a').

In order for SARSA to converge to Q_*, every state-action pair must be visited infinitely often, at least in the tabular case, since the algorithm only updates $Q(s,a)$ for (s,a) that it visits. One way to ensure this condition is to use a "greedy in the limit with infinite exploration" (**GLIE**) policy. An example is the ϵ-greedy policy, with ϵ vanishing to 0 gradually. It can be shown that SARSA with a GLIE policy will converge to Q_* and π_* [Sin+00].

35.2.5 Q-learning: off-policy TD control

SARSA is an **on-policy** algorithm, which means it learns the Q-function for the policy it is currently using, which is typically not the optimal policy (except in the limit for a GLIE policy). However, with a simple modification, we can convert this to an **off-policy** algorithm that learns Q_*, even if a suboptimal policy is used to choose actions.

The idea is to replace the sampled next action $a' \sim \pi(s')$ in Equation (35.11) with a greedy action in s': $a' = \operatorname{argmax}_b Q(s',b)$. This results in the following update when a transition (s, a, r, s') happens

$$Q(s,a) \leftarrow Q(s,a) + \eta \left[r + \gamma \max_b Q(s',b) - Q(s,a) \right] \tag{35.12}$$

This is the update rule of **Q-learning** for the tabular case [WD92]. The extension to work with function approximation can be done in a way similar to Equation (35.7). Since it is off-policy, the method can use (s, a, r, s') triples coming from any data source, such as older versions of the policy, or log data from an existing (non-RL) system. If every state-action pair is visited infinitely often, the algorithm provably converges to Q_* in the tabular case, with properly decayed learning rates [Ber19]. Algorithm 35.1 gives a vanilla implementation of Q-learning with ϵ-greedy exploration.

35.2.5.1 Example

Figure 35.4 gives an example of Q-learning applied to the simple 1d grid world from Figure 34.13, using $\gamma = 0.9$. We show the Q-functon at the start and end of each episode, after performing actions chosen by an ϵ-greedy policy. We initialize $Q(s,a) = 0$ for all entries, and use a step size of $\eta = 1$, so the update becomes $Q_*(s,a) = r + \gamma Q_*(s',a_*)$, where $a_* = \downarrow$ for all states.

35.2.5.2 Double Q-learning

Standard Q-learning suffers from a problem known as the **optimizer's curse** [SW06], or the **maximization bias**. The problem refers to the simple statistical inequality, $\mathbb{E}\left[\max_a X_a\right] \geq \max_a \mathbb{E}\left[X_a\right]$,

---

Algorithm 35.1: Q-learning with ϵ-greedy exploration

---

1 Initialize value function parameters $\boldsymbol{w}$

2 repeat

3   Sample starting state s of new episode

4   **repeat**

5   Sample action $a = \begin{cases} \mathrm{argmax}_b\, Q_{\boldsymbol{w}}(s,b), & \text{with probability } 1 - \epsilon \\ \text{random action}, & \text{with probability } \epsilon \end{cases}$

6   Observe state s', reward r

7   Compute the TD error: $\delta = r + \gamma \max_{a'} Q_{\boldsymbol{w}}(s',a') - Q_{\boldsymbol{w}}(s,a)$

8 $\boldsymbol{w} \leftarrow \boldsymbol{w} + \eta \delta \nabla_{\boldsymbol{w}} Q_{\boldsymbol{w}}(s,a)$

9 $s \leftarrow s'$

10   **until** *state s is terminal*

11 until *converged*

---

for a set of random variables $\{X_a\}$. Thus, if we pick actions greedily according to their random scores $\{X_a\}$, we might pick a wrong action just because random noise makes it appealing.

Figure 35.5 gives a simple example of how this can happen in an MDP. The start state is A. The right action gives a reward 0 and terminates the episode. The left action also gives a reward of 0, but then enters state B, from which there are many possible actions, with rewards drawn from $\mathcal{N}(-0.1, 1.0)$. Thus the expected return for any trajectory starting with the left action is -0.1, making it suboptimal. Nevertheless, the RL algorithm may pick the left action due to the maximization bias making B appear to have a positive value.

One solution to avoid the maximization bias is to use two separate Q-functions, Q_1 and Q_2, one for selecting the greedy action, and the other for estimating the corresponding Q-value. In particular, upon seeing a transition (s, a, r, s'), we perform the following update

$$Q_1(s,a) \leftarrow Q_1(s,a) + \eta \left[r + \gamma Q_2\big(s', \operatorname*{argmax}_{a'} Q_1(s',a')\big) - Q_1(s,a) \right] \tag{35.13}$$

and may repeat the same update but with the roles of Q_1 and Q_2 swapped. This technique is called **double Q-learning** [Has10]. Figure 35.5 shows the benefits of the algorithm over standard Q-learning in a toy problem.

35.2.6   Deep Q-network (DQN)

When function approximation is used, Q-learning may be hard to use in practice due to instability problems. Here, we will describe two important heuristics, popularized by the **deep Q-network** or **DQN** work [Mni+15], which was able to train agents to outperform humans at playing Atari games, using CNN-structured Q-networks.

The first technique, originally proposed in [Lin92], is to leverage an **experience replace** buffer, which stores the most recent (s, a, r, s') transition tuples. In contrast to standard Q-learning which updates the Q-function when a new transition occurs, the DQN agent also performs additional updates using transitions sampled from the buffer. This modification has two advantages. First, it

Q-function episode start

	UP	DOWN
Q_1 S_1	0	0
S_2	0	0
S_3	0	0

	UP	DOWN
Q_2 S_1	0	0
S_2	0	0
S_3	0	1

	UP	DOWN
Q_3 S_1	0	0
S_2	0	0.9
S_3	0	1

	UP	DOWN
Q_4 S_1	0	0.81
S_2	0	0.9
S_3	0.81	1

	UP	DOWN
Q_5 S_1	0	0.81
S_2	0.73	0.9
S_3	0.81	1

Transitions

Episode	Time Step	Action	(s, a, r, s')	$r + \gamma Q^*(s', a)$
1	1	↓	$(S_1, D, 0, S_2)$	$0 + 0.9 \times 0 = 0$
1	2	↑	$(S_2, U, 0, S_1)$	$0 + 0.9 \times 0 = 0$
1	3	↓	$(S_1, D, 0, S_2)$	$0 + 0.9 \times 0 = 0$
1	4	↓	$(S_2, U, 0, S_1)$	$0 + 0.9 \times 0 = 0$
1	5	↓	$(S_3, D, 1, S_{T2})$	1
2	1	↓	$(S_1, D, 0, S_2)$	$0 + 0.9 \times 0 = 0$
2	2	↓	$(S_2, D, 0, S_3)$	$0 + 0.9 \times 1 = 0.9$
2	3	↓	$(S_3, D, 0, S_{T2})$	1
3	1	↓	$(S_1, D, 0, S_2)$	$0 + 0.9 \times 0.9 = 0.81$
3	2	↓	$(S_2, D, 0, S_3)$	$0 + 0.9 \times 1 = 0.9$
3	3	↑	$(S_3, D, 0, S_2)$	$0 + 0.9 \times 0.9 = 0.81$
3	4	↓	$(S_2, D, 0, S_3)$	$0 + 0.9 \times 1 = 0.9$
3	5	↓	$(S_3, D, 0, S_{T2})$	1
4	1	↓	$(S_1, D, 0, S_2)$	$0 + 0.9 \times 0.9 = 0.81$
4	2	↑	$(S_2, U, 0, S_1)$	$0 + 0.9 \times 0.81 = 0.73$
4	3	↓	$(S_1, D, 0, S_2)$	$0 + 0.9 \times 0.9 = 0.81$
4	4	↑	$(S_2, U, 0, S_3)$	$0 + 0.9 \times 0.81 = 0.73$
4	5	↓	$(S_1, D, 0, S_3)$	$0 + 0.9 \times 0.9 = 0.81$
4	6	↓	$(S_2, D, 0, S_3)$	$0 + 0.9 \times 1 = 0.9$
4	7	↓	$(S_2, D, 0, S_3)$	1
5	1	↑	$(S1, U, 0, S_{T1})$	0

Q-function episode end

	UP	DOWN
S_1	0	0
S_2	0	0
S_3	0	1

	UP	DOWN
S_1	0	0
S_2	0	0.9
S_3	0	1

	UP	DOWN
S_1	0	0.81
S_2	0	0.9
S_3	0.81	1

	UP	DOWN
S_1	0	0.81
S_2	0.73	0.9
S_3	0.81	1

	UP	DOWN
S_1	0	0.81
S_2	0.73	0.9
S_3	0.81	1

Figure 35.4: *Illustration of Q learning for the 1d grid world in Figure 34.13 using ϵ-greedy exploration. At the end of episode 1, we make a transition from S_3 to S_{T2} and get a reward of $r = 1$, so we estimate $Q(S_3, \downarrow) = 1$. In episode 2, we make a transition from S_2 to S_3, so S_2 gets incremented by $\gamma Q(S_3, \downarrow) = 0.9$. Adapted from Figure 3.3 of [GK19].*

improves data efficiency as every transition can be used multiple times. Second, it improves stability in training, by reducing the correlation of the data samples that the network is trained on.

The second idea to improve stability is to regress the Q-network to a "frozen" **target network** computed at an earlier iteration, rather than trying to chase a constantly moving target. Specifically, we maintain an extra, frozen copy of the Q-network, $Q_{\boldsymbol{w}^-}$, of the same structure as $Q_{\boldsymbol{w}}$. This new Q-network is to compute bootstrapping targets for training $Q_{\boldsymbol{w}}$, in which the loss function is

$$\mathcal{L}^{\text{DQN}}(\boldsymbol{w}) = \mathbb{E}_{(s,a,r,s') \sim U(\mathcal{D})} \left[\left(r + \gamma \max_{a'} Q_{\boldsymbol{w}^-}(s', a') - Q_{\boldsymbol{w}}(s, a) \right)^2 \right] \tag{35.14}$$

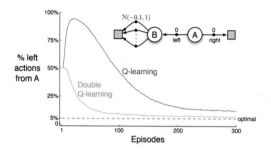

Figure 35.5: *Comparison of Q-learning and double Q-learning on a simple episodic MDP using ϵ-greedy action selection with $\epsilon = 0.1$. The initial state is A, and squares denote absorbing states. The data are averaged over 10,000 runs. From Figure 6.5 of [SB18]. Used with kind permission of Richard Sutton.*

where $U(\mathcal{D})$ is a uniform distribution over the replay buffer $\mathcal{D}$. We then periodically set $\boldsymbol{w}^- \leftarrow \boldsymbol{w}$, usually after a few episodes. This approach is an instance of **fitted value iteration** [SB18].

Various improvements to DQN have been proposed. One is **double DQN** [HGS16], which uses the double learning technique (Section 35.2.5.2) to remove the maximization bias. The second is to replace the uniform distribution in Equation (35.14) with one that favors more important transition tuples, resulting in the use of **prioritized experience replay** [Sch+16a]. For example, we can sample transitions from $\mathcal{D}$ with probability $p(s, a, r, s') \propto (|\delta| + \varepsilon)^{\eta}$, where δ is the corresponding TD error (under the current Q-function), $\varepsilon > 0$ a hyperparameter to ensure every experience is chosen with nonzero probability, and $\eta \geq 0$ controls the "inverse temperature" of the distribution (so $\eta = 0$ corresponds to uniform sampling). The third is to learn a value function $V_{\boldsymbol{w}}$ and an advantage function $A_{\boldsymbol{w}}$, with shared parameter $\boldsymbol{w}$, instead of learning $Q_{\boldsymbol{w}}$. The resulting **dueling DQN** [Wan+16] is shown to be more sample efficient, especially when there are many actions with similar Q-values.

The **rainbow** method [Hes+18] combines all three improvements, as well as others, including multi-step returns (Section 35.2.3), distributional RL [BDM17] (which predicts the distribution of returns, not just the expected return), and noisy nets [For+18b] (which adds random noise to the network weights to encourage exploration). It produces state-of-the-art results on the Atari benchmark.

35.3   Policy-based RL

In the previous section, we considered methods that estimate the action-value function, $Q(s, a)$, from which we derive a policy, which may be greedy or softmax. However, these methods have three main disadvantages: (1) they can be difficult to apply to continuous action spaces; (2) they may diverge if function approximation is used; and (3) the training of Q, often based on TD-style updates, is not directly related to the expected return garnered by the learned policy.

In this section, we discuss **policy search** methods, which directly optimize the parameters of the policy so as to maximize its expected return. However, we will see that these methods often benefit from estimating a value or advantage function to reduce the variance in the policy search process.

35.3.1 The policy gradient theorem

We start by defining the objective function for policy learning, and then derive its gradient. We consider the episodic case. A similar result can be derived for the continuing case with the average reward criterion [SB18, Sec 13.6].

We define the objective to be the expected return of a policy, which we aim to maximize:

$$J(\pi) \triangleq \mathbb{E}_{p_0,\pi}[G_0] = \mathbb{E}_{p_0(s_0)}[V_\pi(s_0)] = \mathbb{E}_{p_0(s_0)\pi(a_0|s_0)}[Q_\pi(s_0, a_0)] \tag{35.15}$$

We consider policies $\pi_{\boldsymbol{\theta}}$ parameterized by $\boldsymbol{\theta}$, and compute the gradient of Equation (35.15) wrt $\boldsymbol{\theta}$:

$$\nabla_{\boldsymbol{\theta}} J(\pi_{\boldsymbol{\theta}}) = \mathbb{E}_{p_0(s_0)}\left[\nabla_{\boldsymbol{\theta}}\left(\sum_{a_0} \pi_{\boldsymbol{\theta}}(a_0|s_0)Q_{\pi_{\boldsymbol{\theta}}}(s_0, a_0)\right)\right] \tag{35.16}$$

$$= \mathbb{E}_{p_0(s_0)}\left[\sum_{a_0} \nabla_{\boldsymbol{\theta}}\pi_{\boldsymbol{\theta}}(a_0|s_0)Q_{\pi_{\boldsymbol{\theta}}}(s_0, a_0)\right] + \mathbb{E}_{p_0(s_0)\pi_{\boldsymbol{\theta}}(a_0|s_0)}[\nabla_{\boldsymbol{\theta}}Q_{\pi_{\boldsymbol{\theta}}}(s_0, a_0)] \tag{35.17}$$

Now we calculate the term $\nabla_{\boldsymbol{\theta}}Q_{\pi_{\boldsymbol{\theta}}}(s_0, a_0)$:

$$\nabla_{\boldsymbol{\theta}}Q_{\pi_{\boldsymbol{\theta}}}(s_0, a_0) = \nabla_{\boldsymbol{\theta}}\left[R(s_0, a_0) + \gamma\mathbb{E}_{p_T(s_1|s_0,a_0)}[V_{\pi_{\boldsymbol{\theta}}}(s_1)]\right] = \gamma\nabla_{\boldsymbol{\theta}}\mathbb{E}_{p_T(s_1|s_0,a_0)}[V_{\pi_{\boldsymbol{\theta}}}(s_1)] \tag{35.18}$$

The right-hand side above is in a form similar to $\nabla_{\boldsymbol{\theta}} J(\pi_{\boldsymbol{\theta}})$. Repeating the same steps as before gives

$$\nabla_{\boldsymbol{\theta}} J(\pi_{\boldsymbol{\theta}}) = \sum_{t=0}^{\infty} \gamma^t \mathbb{E}_{p_t(s)}\left[\sum_a \nabla_{\boldsymbol{\theta}}\pi_{\boldsymbol{\theta}}(a|s)Q_{\pi_{\boldsymbol{\theta}}}(s, a)\right] \tag{35.19}$$

$$= \frac{1}{1-\gamma}\mathbb{E}_{p_{\pi_{\boldsymbol{\theta}}}^{\infty}(s)}\left[\sum_a \nabla_{\boldsymbol{\theta}}\pi_{\boldsymbol{\theta}}(a|s)Q_{\pi_{\boldsymbol{\theta}}}(s, a)\right] \tag{35.20}$$

$$= \frac{1}{1-\gamma}\mathbb{E}_{p_{\pi_{\boldsymbol{\theta}}}^{\infty}(s)\pi_{\boldsymbol{\theta}}(a|s)}[\nabla_{\boldsymbol{\theta}}\log \pi_{\boldsymbol{\theta}}(a|s)\, Q_{\pi_{\boldsymbol{\theta}}}(s, a)] \tag{35.21}$$

where $p_t(s)$ is the probability of visiting s in time t if we start with $s_0 \sim p_0$ and follow $\pi_{\boldsymbol{\theta}}$, and $p_{\pi_{\boldsymbol{\theta}}}^{\infty}(s) = (1-\gamma)\sum_{t=0}^{\infty}\gamma^t p_t(s)$ is the normalized discounted state visitation distribution. Equation (35.21) is known as the **policy gradient theorem** [Sut+99].

In practice, estimating the policy gradient using Equation (35.21) can have a high variance. A baseline $b(s)$ can be used for variance reduction (Section 6.3.4.1):

$$\nabla_{\boldsymbol{\theta}} J(\pi_{\boldsymbol{\theta}}) = \frac{1}{1-\gamma}\mathbb{E}_{p_{\pi_{\boldsymbol{\theta}}}^{\infty}(s)\pi_{\boldsymbol{\theta}}(a|s)}[\nabla_{\boldsymbol{\theta}}\log \pi_{\boldsymbol{\theta}}(a|s)(Q_{\pi_{\boldsymbol{\theta}}}(s, a) - b(s))] \tag{35.22}$$

A common choice for the baseline is $b(s) = V_{\pi_{\boldsymbol{\theta}}}(s)$. We will discuss how to estimate it below.

35.3.2 REINFORCE

One way to apply the policy gradient theorem to optimize a policy is to use stochastic gradient ascent. Suppose $\boldsymbol{\tau} = (s_0, a_0, r_0, s_1, \ldots, s_T)$ is a trajectory with $s_0 \sim p_0$ and $\pi_{\boldsymbol{\theta}}$. Then,

$$\nabla_{\boldsymbol{\theta}} J(\pi_{\boldsymbol{\theta}}) = \frac{1}{1-\gamma} \mathbb{E}_{p_{\pi_{\boldsymbol{\theta}}}^{\infty}(s)\pi_{\boldsymbol{\theta}}(a|s)} \left[\nabla_{\boldsymbol{\theta}} \log \pi_{\boldsymbol{\theta}}(a|s) Q_{\pi_{\boldsymbol{\theta}}}(s, a) \right] \tag{35.23}$$

$$\approx \sum_{t=0}^{T-1} \gamma^t G_t \nabla_{\boldsymbol{\theta}} \log \pi_{\boldsymbol{\theta}}(a_t|s_t) \tag{35.24}$$

where the return G_t is defined in Equation (34.76), and the factor γ^t is due to the definition of $p_{\pi_{\boldsymbol{\theta}}}^{\infty}$ where the state at time t is discounted.

We can use a baseline in the gradient estimate to get the following update rule:

$$\boldsymbol{\theta} \leftarrow \boldsymbol{\theta} + \eta \sum_{t=0}^{T-1} \gamma^t (G_t - b(s_t)) \nabla_{\boldsymbol{\theta}} \log \pi_{\boldsymbol{\theta}}(a_t|s_t) \tag{35.25}$$

This is called the **REINFORCE** algorithm [Wil92].[3] The udpate equation can be interepreted as follows: we compute the sum of discounted future rewards induced by a trajectory, compared to a baseline, and if this is positive, we increase $\boldsymbol{\theta}$ so as to make this trajectory more likely, otherwise we decrease $\boldsymbol{\theta}$. Thus, we reinforce good behaviors, and reduce the chances of generating bad ones.

We can use a constant (state-independent) baseline, or we can use a state-dependent baseline, $b(s_t)$ to further lower the variance. A natural choice is to use an estimated value function, $V_{\boldsymbol{w}}(s)$, which can be learned, e.g., with MC. Algorithm 35.2 gives the pseudocode where stochastic gradient updates are used with separate learning rates.

Algorithm 35.2: REINFORCE with value function baseline

---

1   Initialize policy parameters $\boldsymbol{\theta}$, baseline parameters $\boldsymbol{w}$
2   **repeat**
3   Sample an episode $\boldsymbol{\tau} = (s_0, a_0, r_0, s_1, \ldots, s_T)$ using $\pi_{\boldsymbol{\theta}}$
4   Compute G_t for all $t \in \{0, 1, \ldots, T-1\}$ using Equation (34.76)
5   **for** $t = 0, 1, \ldots, T-1$ **do**
6          $\delta = G_t - V_{\boldsymbol{w}}(s_t)$ // scalar error
7          $\boldsymbol{w} \leftarrow \boldsymbol{w} + \eta_{\boldsymbol{w}} \delta \nabla_{\boldsymbol{w}} V_{\boldsymbol{w}}(s_t)$
8          $\boldsymbol{\theta} \leftarrow \boldsymbol{\theta} + \eta_{\boldsymbol{\theta}} \gamma^t \delta \nabla_{\boldsymbol{\theta}} \log \pi_{\boldsymbol{\theta}}(a_t|s_t)$
9   **until** *converged*

35.3.3 Actor-critic methods

An **actor-critic** method [BSA83] uses the policy gradient method, but where the expected return is estimated using temporal difference learning of a value function instead of MC rollouts. The term

---

3. The term "REINFORCE" is an acronym for "REward Increment = nonnegative Factor x Offset Reinforcement x Characteristic Eligibility". The phrase "characteristic eligibility" refers to the $\nabla \log \pi_{\boldsymbol{\theta}}(a_t|s_t)$ term; the phrase "offset reinforcement" refers to the $G_t - b(s_t)$ term; and the phrase "nonnegative factor" refers to the learning rate η of SGD.

"actor" refers to the policy, and the term "critic" refers to the value function. The use of bootstrapping in TD updates allows more efficient learning of the value function compared to MC. In addition, it allows us to develop a fully online, incremental algorithm, that does not need to wait until the end of the trajectory before updating the parameters (as in Algorithm 35.2).

Concretely, consider the use of the one-step TD(0) method to estimate the return in the episodic csae, i.e., we replace G_t with $G_{t:t+1} = r_t + \gamma V_{\boldsymbol{w}}(s_{t+1})$. If we use $V_{\boldsymbol{w}}(s_t)$ as a baseline, the REINFORCE update in Equation (35.25) becomes

$$\boldsymbol{\theta} \leftarrow \boldsymbol{\theta} + \eta \sum_{t=0}^{T-1} \gamma^t \left(G_{t:t+1} - V_{\boldsymbol{w}}(s_t)\right) \nabla_{\boldsymbol{\theta}} \log \pi_{\boldsymbol{\theta}}(a_t|s_t) \tag{35.26}$$

$$= \boldsymbol{\theta} + \eta \sum_{t=0}^{T-1} \gamma^t \left(r_t + \gamma V_{\boldsymbol{w}}(s_{t+1}) - V_{\boldsymbol{w}}(s_t)\right) \nabla_{\boldsymbol{\theta}} \log \pi_{\boldsymbol{\theta}}(a_t|s_t) \tag{35.27}$$

35.3.3.1   A2C and A3C

Note that $r_{t+1} + \gamma V_{\boldsymbol{w}}(s_{t+1}) - V_{\boldsymbol{w}}(s_t)$ is a single sample approximation to the advantage function $A(s_t, a_t) = Q(s_t, a_t) - V(s_t)$. This method is therefore called **advantage actor critic** or **A2C** (Algorithm 35.3). If we run the actors in parallel and asynchronously update their shared parameters, the method is called **asynchrononous advantage actor critic** or **A3C** [Mni+16].

Algorithm 35.3: Advantage actor critic (A2C) algorithm

---

1 Initialize actor parameters $\boldsymbol{\theta}$, critic parameters $\boldsymbol{w}$
2 **repeat**
3   Sample starting state s_0 of a new episode
4   **for** $t = 0, 1, 2, \ldots$ **do**
5   Sample action $a_t \sim \pi_{\boldsymbol{\theta}}(\cdot|s_t)$
6   Observe next state s_{t+1} and reward r_t
7          $\delta = r_t + \gamma V_{\boldsymbol{w}}(s_{t+1}) - V_{\boldsymbol{w}}(s_t)$
8          $\boldsymbol{w} \leftarrow \boldsymbol{w} + \eta_{\boldsymbol{w}} \delta \nabla_{\boldsymbol{w}} V_{\boldsymbol{w}}(s_t)$
9          $\boldsymbol{\theta} \leftarrow \boldsymbol{\theta} + \eta_{\boldsymbol{\theta}} \gamma^t \delta \nabla_{\boldsymbol{\theta}} \log \pi_{\boldsymbol{\theta}}(a_t|s_t)$
10 **until** *converged*

35.3.3.2   Eligibility traces

In A2C, we use a single step rollout, and then use the value function in order to approximate the expected return for the trajectory. More generally, we can use the n-step estimate

$$G_{t:t+n} = r_t + \gamma r_{t+1} + \gamma^2 r_{t+2} + \cdots + \gamma^{n-1} r_{t+n-1} + \gamma^n V_{\boldsymbol{w}}(s_{t+n}) \tag{35.28}$$

and obtain an n-step advantage estimate as follows:

$$A_{\pi_{\boldsymbol{\theta}}}^{(n)}(s_t, a_t) = G_{t:t+n} - V_{\boldsymbol{w}}(s_t) \tag{35.29}$$

The n steps of actual rewards are an unbiased sample, but have high variance. By contrast, $V_{\boldsymbol{w}}(s_{t+n+1})$ has lower variance, but is biased. By changing n, we can control the bias-variance tradeoff. Instead of using a single value of n, we can take an weighted average, with weight proportional to λ^n for $A_{\pi_{\boldsymbol{\theta}}}^{(n)}(s_t, a_t)$, as in TD($\lambda$). The average can be shown to be equivalent to

$$A_{\pi_{\boldsymbol{\theta}}}^{(\lambda)}(s_t, a_t) \triangleq \sum_{\ell=0}^{\infty} (\gamma\lambda)^{\ell} \delta_{t+l} \tag{35.30}$$

where $\delta_t = r_t + \gamma V_{\boldsymbol{w}}(s_{t+1}) - V_{\boldsymbol{w}}(s_t)$ is the TD error at time t. Here, $\lambda \in [0, 1]$ is a parameter that controls the bias-variance tradeoff: larger values decrease the bias but increase the variance, as in TD(λ). We can implement Equation (35.30) efficiently using eligibility traces, as shown in Algorithm 35.4, as an example of **generalized advantage estimation** (**GAE**) [Sch+16b]. See [SB18, Ch.12] for further details.

Algorithm 35.4: Actor critic with eligibility traces

---

1 Initialize actor parameters $\boldsymbol{\theta}$, critic parameters $\boldsymbol{w}$
2 repeat
3 $\quad$ Initialize eligibility trace vectors: $\boldsymbol{z_{\theta}} \leftarrow \boldsymbol{0}$, $\boldsymbol{z_w} \leftarrow \boldsymbol{0}$
4 $\quad$ Sample starting state s_0 of a new episode
5 $\quad$ **for** $t = 0, 1, 2, \dots$ **do**
6 $\quad\quad$ Sample action $a_t \sim \pi_{\boldsymbol{\theta}}(\cdot|s_t)$
7 $\quad\quad$ Observe state s_{t+1} and reward r_t
8 $\quad\quad$ Compute the TD error: $\delta = r_t + \gamma V_{\boldsymbol{w}}(s_{t+1}) - V_{\boldsymbol{w}}(s_t)$
9 $\quad\quad$ $\boldsymbol{z_w} \leftarrow \gamma\lambda_{\boldsymbol{w}} \boldsymbol{z_w} + \nabla_{\boldsymbol{w}} V_{\boldsymbol{w}}(s)$
10 $\quad\quad$ $\boldsymbol{z_{\theta}} \leftarrow \gamma\lambda_{\boldsymbol{\theta}} \boldsymbol{z_{\theta}} + \gamma^t \nabla_{\boldsymbol{\theta}} \log \pi_{\boldsymbol{\theta}}(a_t|s_t)$
11 $\quad\quad$ $\boldsymbol{w} \leftarrow \boldsymbol{w} + \eta_{\boldsymbol{w}} \delta \boldsymbol{z_w}$
12 $\quad\quad$ $\boldsymbol{\theta} \leftarrow \boldsymbol{\theta} + \eta_{\boldsymbol{\theta}} \delta \boldsymbol{z_{\theta}}$
13 until *converged*

35.3.4 Bound optimization methods

In policy gradient methods, the objective $J(\boldsymbol{\theta})$ does not necessarily increase monotonically, but rather can collapse especially if the learning rate is not small enough. We now describe methods that guarantee monotonic improvement, similar to bound optimization algorithms (Section 6.5). We start with a useful fact that relate the policy values of two arbitrary policies [KL02]:

$$J(\pi') - J(\pi) = \frac{1}{1-\gamma} \mathbb{E}_{p_{\pi'}^{\infty}(s)} \left[\mathbb{E}_{\pi'(a|s)} \left[A_{\pi}(s, a) \right] \right] \tag{35.31}$$

where π can be interpreted as the current policy during policy optimization, and π' a candidate new policy (such as the greedy policy wrt Q_{π}). As in the policy improvement theorem (Section 34.6.2), if $\mathbb{E}_{\pi'(a|s)}[A_{\pi}(s, a)] \geq 0$ for all s, then $J(\pi') \geq J(\pi)$. However, we cannot ensure this condition to hold when function approximation is used, as such a uniformly improving policy π' may not be representable by our parametric family, $\{\pi_\theta\}_{\theta \in \Theta}$. Therefore, nonnegativity of Equation (35.31) is not easy to ensure, when we do not have a direct way to sample states from p_π^∞.

One way to ensure monotonic improvement of J is to improve the policy conservatively. Define $\pi_\theta = \theta\pi' + (1-\theta)\pi$ for $\theta \in [0,1]$. It follows from the policy gradient theorem (Equation (35.21), with $\boldsymbol{\theta} = [\theta]$) that $J(\pi_\theta) - J(\pi) = \theta L(\pi') + O(\theta^2)$, where

$$L(\pi') \triangleq \frac{1}{1-\gamma}\mathbb{E}_{p_\pi^\infty(s)}\left[\mathbb{E}_{\pi'(a|s)}\left[A_\pi(s,a)\right]\right] = \frac{1}{1-\gamma}\mathbb{E}_{p_\pi^\infty(s)\pi(a|s)}\left[\frac{\pi'(a|s)}{\pi(a|s)}A_\pi(s,a)\right] \tag{35.32}$$

In the above, we have switched the state distribution from $p_{\pi'}^\infty$ in Equation (35.31) to p_π^∞, while at the same time introducing a higher order residual term of $O(\theta^2)$. The linear term, $\theta L(\pi')$, can be estimated and optimized based on episodes sampled by π. The higher order term can be bounded in various ways, resulting in different lower bounds of $J(\pi_\theta) - J(\pi)$. We can then optimize θ to make sure this lower bound is positive, which would imply $J(\pi_\theta) - J(\pi) > 0$. In **conservative policy iteration** [KL02], the following (slightly simplified) lower bound is used

$$J^{\mathrm{CPI}}(\pi_\theta) \triangleq J(\pi) + \theta L(\pi') - \frac{2\varepsilon\gamma}{(1-\gamma)^2}\theta^2 \tag{35.33}$$

where $\varepsilon = \max_s |\mathbb{E}_{\pi'(a|s)}[A_\pi(s,a)]|$.

This idea can be generalized to policies beyond those in the form of π_θ, where the condition of a small enough θ is replaced by a small enough divergence between π' and π. In **safe policy iteration** [Pir+13], the divergence is the maximum total variation, while in **trust region policy optimization (TRPO)** [Sch+15b], the divergence is the maximum KL-divergence. In the latter case, π' may be found by optimizing the following lower bound

$$J^{\mathrm{TRPO}}(\pi') \triangleq J(\pi) + L(\pi') - \frac{\varepsilon\gamma}{(1-\gamma)^2}\max_s D_{\mathbb{KL}}\left(\pi(s) \,\|\, \pi'(s)\right) \tag{35.34}$$

where $\varepsilon = \max_{s,a} |A_\pi(s,a)|$.

In practice, the above update rule can be overly conservative, and approximations are used. [Sch+15b] propose a version that implements two ideas: one is to replace the point-wise maximum KL-divergence by some average KL-divergence (usually averaged over $p_{\pi_\theta}^\infty$); the second is to maximize the first two terms in Equation (35.34), with π' lying in a KL-ball centered at π. That is, we solve

$$\underset{\pi'}{\mathrm{argmax}}\, L(\pi') \ \ \text{s.t.} \ \ \mathbb{E}_{p_\pi^\infty(s)}\left[D_{\mathbb{KL}}\left(\pi(s) \,\|\, \pi'(s)\right)\right] \le \delta \tag{35.35}$$

for some threshold $\delta > 0$.

In Section 6.4.2.1, we show that the trust region method, using a KL penalty at each step, is equivalent to natural gradient descent (see e.g., [Kak02; PS08b]). This is important, because a step of size η in parameter space does not always correspond to a step of size η in the policy space:

$$d_{\boldsymbol{\theta}}(\boldsymbol{\theta}_1, \boldsymbol{\theta}_2) = d_{\boldsymbol{\theta}}(\boldsymbol{\theta}_2, \boldsymbol{\theta}_3) \not\Rightarrow d_\pi(\pi_{\boldsymbol{\theta}_1}, \pi_{\boldsymbol{\theta}_2}) = d_\pi(\pi_{\boldsymbol{\theta}_2}, \pi_{\boldsymbol{\theta}_3}) \tag{35.36}$$

where $d_{\boldsymbol{\theta}}(\boldsymbol{\theta}_1, \boldsymbol{\theta}_2) = \|\boldsymbol{\theta}_1 - \boldsymbol{\theta}_2\|$ is the Euclidean distance, and $d_\pi(\pi_1, \pi_2) = D_{\mathbb{KL}}(\pi_1 \,\|\, \pi_2)$ the KL distance. In other words, the effect on the policy of any given change to the parameters depends on where we are in parameter space. This is taken into account by the natural gradient method, resulting in faster and more robust optimization. The natural policy gradient can be approximated using the KFAC method (Section 6.4.4), as done in [Wu+17].

Other than TRPO, another approach inspired by Equation (35.34) is to use the KL-divergence as a penalty term, replacing the factor $2\varepsilon\gamma/(1-\gamma)^2$ by a tuning parameter. However, it often works better, and is simpler, by using the following clipped objective, which results in the **proximal policy optimization** or **PPO** method [Sch+17]:

$$J^{\text{PPO}}(\pi') \triangleq \frac{1}{1-\gamma} \mathbb{E}_{p_\pi^\infty(s)\pi(a|s)} \left[\kappa_\epsilon \left(\frac{\pi'(a|s)}{\pi(a|s)} \right) A_\pi(s,a) \right] \tag{35.37}$$

where $\kappa_\epsilon(x) \triangleq \text{clip}(x, 1-\epsilon, 1+\epsilon)$ ensures $|\kappa(x) - 1| \leq \epsilon$. This method can be modified to ensure monotonic improvement as discussed in [WHT19], making it a true bound optimization method.

35.3.5   Deterministic policy gradient methods

In this section, we consider the case of a deterministic policy, that predicts a unique action for each state, so $a_t = \mu_\theta(s_t)$, rather than $a_t \sim \pi_\theta(s_t)$. We assume the states and actions are continuous, and define the objective as

$$J(\mu_\theta) \triangleq \frac{1}{1-\gamma} \mathbb{E}_{p_{\mu_\theta}^\infty(s)} [R(s, \mu_\theta(s))] \tag{35.38}$$

The **deterministic policy gradient theorem** [Sil+14] provides a way to compute the gradient:

$$\nabla_\theta J(\mu_\theta) = \frac{1}{1-\gamma} \mathbb{E}_{p_{\mu_\theta}^\infty(s)} [\nabla_\theta Q_{\mu_\theta}(s, \mu_\theta(s))] \tag{35.39}$$

$$= \frac{1}{1-\gamma} \mathbb{E}_{p_{\mu_\theta}^\infty(s)} \left[\nabla_\theta \mu_\theta(s) \nabla_a Q_{\mu_\theta}(s, a)|_{a=\mu_\theta(s)} \right] \tag{35.40}$$

where $\nabla_\theta \mu_\theta(s)$ is the $M \times N$ Jacobian matrix, and M and N are the dimensions of $\mathcal{A}$ and θ, respectively. For stochastic policies of the form $\pi_\theta(a|s) = \mu_\theta(s) + \text{noise}$, the standard policy gradient theorem reduces to the above form as the noise level goes to zero.

Note that the gradient estimate in Equation (35.40) integrates over the states but not over the actions, which helps reduce the variance in gradient estimation from sampled trajectories. However, since the deterministic policy does not do any exploration, we need to use an off-policy method, that collects data from a stochastic behavior policy β, whose stationary state distribution is p_β^∞. The original objective, $J(\mu_\theta)$, is approximated by the following:

$$J_b(\mu_\theta) \triangleq \mathbb{E}_{p_\beta^\infty(s)} [V_{\mu_\theta}(s)] = \mathbb{E}_{p_\beta^\infty(s)} [Q_{\mu_\theta}(s, \mu_\theta(s))] \tag{35.41}$$

with the off-policy deterministic policy gradient approximated by (see also Section 35.5.1.2)

$$\nabla_\theta J_b(\mu_\theta) \approx \mathbb{E}_{p_\beta^\infty(s)} [\nabla_\theta [Q_{\mu_\theta}(s, \mu_\theta(s))]] = \mathbb{E}_{p_\beta^\infty(s)} \left[\nabla_\theta \mu_\theta(s) \nabla_a Q_{\mu_\theta}(s, a)|_{a=\mu_\theta(s)} ds \right] \tag{35.42}$$

where we have a dropped a term that depends on $\nabla_\theta Q_{\mu_\theta}(s, a)$ and is hard to estimate [Sil+14].

To apply Equation (35.42), we may learn $Q_w \approx Q_{\mu_\theta}$ with TD, giving rise to the following updates:

$$\delta = r_t + \gamma Q_w(s_{t+1}, \mu_\theta(s_{t+1})) - Q_w(s_t, a_t) \tag{35.43}$$

$$w_{t+1} \leftarrow w_t + \eta_w \delta \nabla_w Q_w(s_t, a_t) \tag{35.44}$$

$$\theta_{t+1} \leftarrow \theta_t + \eta_\theta \nabla_\theta \mu_\theta(s_t) \nabla_a Q_w(s_t, a)|_{a=\mu_\theta(s_t)} \tag{35.45}$$

This avoids importance sampling in the actor update because of the deterministic policy gradient, and avoids importance sampling in the critic update because of the use of Q-learning.

If Q_w is linear in w, and uses features of the form $\phi(s, a) = a^\mathsf{T} \nabla_\theta \mu_\theta(s)$, where a is the vector representation of a, then we say the function approximator for the critic is **compatible** with the actor; in this case, one can show that the above approximation does not bias the overall gradient. The method has been extended in various ways. The **DDPG** algorithm of [Lil+16], which stands for "deep deterministic policy gradient", uses the DQN method (Section 35.2.6) to update Q that is represented by deep neural networks. The **TD3** algorithm [FHM18], which stands for "twin delayed DDPG", extends DDPG by using double DQN (Section 35.2.5.2) and other heuristics to further improve performance. Finally, the **D4PG** algorithm [BM+18], which stands for "distributed distributional DDPG", extends DDPG to handle distributed training, and to handle **distributional RL** (i.e., working with distributions of rewards instead of expected rewards [BDM17]).

35.3.6 Gradient-free methods

The policy gradient estimator computes a "zeroth order" gradient, which essentially evaluates the function with randomly sampled trajectories. Sometimes it can be more efficient to use a derivative-free optimizer (Section 6.7), that does not even attempt to estimate the gradient. For example, [MGR18] obtain good results by training linear policies with random search, and [Sal+17b] show how to use evolutionary strategies to optimize the policy of a robotic controller.

35.4 Model-based RL

Model-free approaches to RL typically need a lot of interactions with the environment to achieve good performance. For example, state of the art methods for the Atari benchmark, such as rainbow (Section 35.2.6), use millions of frames, equivalent to many days of playing at the standard frame rate. By contrast, humans can achieve the same performance in minutes [Tsi+17]. Similarly, OpenAI's robot hand controller [And+20] learns to manipulate a cube using 100 years of simulated data.

One promising approach to greater sample efficiency is **model-based RL** (**MBRL**). In this approach, we first learn the transition model and reward function, $p_T(s'|s, a)$ and $R(s, a)$, then use them to compute a near-optimal policy. This approach can significantly reduce the amount of real-world data that the agent needs to collect, since it can "try things out" in its imagination (i.e., the models), rather than having to try them out empirically.

There are several ways we can use a model, and many different kinds of model we can create. Some of the algorithms mentioned earlier, such as MBIE and UCLR2 for provably efficient exploration (Section 35.1.5.3), are examples of model-based methods. MBRL also provides a natural connection between RL and planning (Section 34.6) [Sut90]. We discuss some examples in the sections below, and refer to [MBJ20; PKP21; MH20] for more detailed reviews.

35.4.1 Model predictive control (MPC)

So far in this chapter, we have focused on trying to learn an optimal policy $\pi_*(s)$, which can then be used at run time to quickly pick the best action for any given state s. However, we can also avoid performing all this work in advance, and wait until we know what state we are in, call it s_t, and then use a model to predict future states and rewards that might follow for each possible sequence of

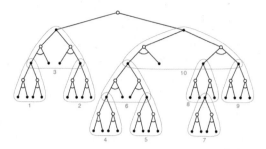

Figure 35.6: Illustration of heuristic search. In this figure, the subtrees are ordered according to a depth-first search procedure. From Figure 8.9 of [SB18]. Used with kind permission of Richard Sutton.

future actions we might pursue. We then take the action that looks most promising, and repeat the process at the next step. More precisely, we compute

$$a^*_{t:t+H-1} = \underset{a_{t:t+H-1}}{\operatorname{argmax}} \mathbb{E} \left[\sum_{h=0}^{H-1} R(s_{t+h}, a_{t+h}) + \hat{V}(s_{t+H}) \right] \tag{35.46}$$

where the expectation is over state sequences that might result from executing $a_{t:t+H-1}$ from state s_t. Here, H is called the **planning horizon**, and $\hat{V}(s_{t+H})$ is an estimate of the reward-to-go at the end of this H-step look-ahead process. This is known as **receeding horizon control** or **model predictive control (MPC)** [MM90; CA13]. We discuss some special cases of this below.

35.4.1.1 Heuristic search

If the state and action spaces are finite, we can solve Equation (35.46) exactly, although the time complexity will typically be exponential in H. However, in many situations, we can prune off unpromising trajectories, thus making the approach feasible in large scale problems.

In particular, consider a discrete, deterministic MDP where reward maximization corresponds to finding a shortest path to a goal state. We can expand the successors of the current state according to all possible actions, trying to find the goal state. Since the search tree grows exponentially with depth, we can use a **heuristic function** to prioritize which nodes to expand; this is called **best-first search**, as illustrated in Figure 35.6.

If the heuristic function is an optimistic lower bound on the true distance to the goal, it is called **admissible**; If we aim to maximize total rewards, admissibility means the heuristic function is an upper bound of the true value function. Admissibility ensures we will never incorrectly prune off parts of the search space. In this case, the resulting algorithm is known as A^* **search**, and is optimal. For more details on classical AI **heuristic search** methods, see [Pea84; RN19].

35.4.1.2 Monte Carlo tree search (MCTS)

Monte Carlo tree search or **MCTS** is similar to heuristic search, but learns a value function for each encountered state, rather than relying on a manually designed heuristic (see e.g., [Mun14] for details). MCTS is inspired by UCB for bandits (Section 34.4.5), but applies to general sequential decision making problems including MDPs [KS06].

The MCTS method forms the basis of the famous **AlphaGo** and **AlphaZero** programs [Sil+16; Sil+18], which can play expert-level Go, chess, and shogi (Japanese chess), using a known model of the environment. The **MuZero** method of [Sch+20] and the **Stochastic MuZero** method of [Ant+22] extend this to the case where the world model is also learned. The action-value functions for the intermediate nodes in the search tree are represented by deep neural networks, and updated using temporal difference methods that we discuss in Section 35.2. MCTS can also be applied to many other kinds of seqential decision problems, such as experiment design for sequentially creating molecules [SPW18].

35.4.1.3   Trajectory optimization for continuous actions

For continuous actions, we cannot enumerate all possible branches in the search tree. Instead, Equation (35.46) can be viewed as a nonlinear program, where $a_{t:t+H-1}$ are the real-valued variables to be optimized. If the system dynamics are linear and the reward function corresponds to negative quadratic cost, the optimal action sequence can be solved mathematically, as in the **linear-quadratic-Gaussian (LQG)** controller (see e.g., [AM89; HR17]). However, this problem is hard in general and often solved by numerical methods such as **shooting** and **collocation** [Die+07; Rao10; Kal+11]. Many of them work in an iterative fashion, starting with an initial action sequence followed by a step to improve it. This process repeats until convergence of the cost.

An example is **differential dynamic programming (DDP)** [JM70; TL05]. In each iteration, DDP starts with a reference trajectory, and linearizes the system dynamics around states on the trajectory to form a locally quadratic approximation of the reward function. This system can be solved using LQG, whose optimal solution results in a new trajectory. The algorithm then moves to the next iteration, with the new trajectory as the reference trajectory.

Other alternatives are possible, including black-box (gradient-free) optimization methods like the cross-entropy method. (see Section 6.7.5).

35.4.2   Combining model-based and model-free

In Section 35.4.1, we discussed MPC, which uses the model to decide which action to take at each step. However, this can be slow, and can suffer from problems when the model is inaccurate. An alternative is to use the learned model to help reduce the sample complexity of policy learning.

There are many ways to do this. One approach is to generate rollouts from the model, and then train a policy or Q-function on the "hallucinated" data. This is the basis of the famous **dyna** method [Sut90]. In [Jan+19], they propose a similar method, but generate short rollouts from previously visited real states; this ensures the model only has to extrapolate locally.

In [Web+17], they train a model to predict future states and rewards, but then use the hidden states of this model as additional context for a policy-based learning method. This can help overcome partial observability. They call their method **imagination-augmented agents**. A related method appears in [Jad+17], who propose to train a model to jointly predict future rewards and other auxiliary signals, such as future states. This can help in situations when rewards are sparse or absent.

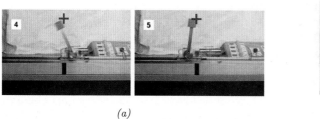

(a)   (b)

Figure 35.7: (a) A cart-pole system being controlled by a policy learned by PILCO using just 17.5 seconds of real-world interaction. The goal state is marked by the red cross. The initial state is where the cart is stationary on the right edge of the workspace, and the pendulum is horizontal. For a video of the system learning, see `https://bit.ly/35fpLmR`. *(b) A low-quality robot arm being controlled by a block-stacking policy learned by PILCO using just 230 seconds of real-world interaction. From Figures 11, 12 from [DFR15]. Used with kind permission of Marc Deisenroth.*

35.4.3 MBRL using Gaussian processes

This section gives some examples of dynamics models that have been learned for low-dimensional continuous control problems. Such problems frequently arise in robotics. Since the dynamics are often nonlinear, it is useful to use a flexible and sample-efficient model family, such as Gaussian processes (Section 18.1). We will use notation like s and a for states and actions to emphasize they are vectors.

35.4.3.1 PILCO

We first describe the **PILCO** method [DR11; DFR15], which stands for "probabilistic inference for learning control". It is extremely data efficient for continuous control problems, enabling learning from scratch on real physical robots in a matter of minutes.

PILCO assumes the world model has the form $s_{t+1} = f(s_t, a_t) + \epsilon_t$, where $\epsilon_t \sim \mathcal{N}(0, \Sigma)$, and f is an unknown, continuous function.[4] The basic idea is to learn a Gaussian process (Section 18.1)) approximation of f based on some initial random trajectories, and then to use this model to generate "fantasy" rollout trajectories of length T, that can be used to evaluate the expected cost of the current policy, $J(\pi_\theta) = \sum_{t=1}^{T} \mathbb{E}_{a_t \sim \pi_\theta} [c(s_t)]$, where $s_0 \sim p_0$. This function and its gradients wrt θ can be computed deterministically, if a Gaussian assumption about the state distribution at each step is made, because the Gaussian belief state can be propagated deterministically through the GP model. Therefore, we can use deterministic batch optimization methods, such as Levenberg-Marquardt, to optimize the policy parameters θ, instead of applying SGD to sampled trajectories. (See `https://github.com/mathDR/jax-pilco` for some JAX code.)

Due to its data efficiency, it is possible to apply PILCO to real robots. Figure 35.7a shows the results of applying it to solve a **cart-pole swing-up** task, where the goal is to make the inverted pendulum swing up by applying a horizontal force to move the cart back and forth. The state of the system $s \in \mathbb{R}^4$ consists of the position x of the cart (with $x = 0$ being the center of the track), the

---

4. An alternative, which often works better, is to use f to model the residual, so that $s_{t+1} = s_t + f(s_t, a_t) + \epsilon_t$.

velocity $\dot{x}$, the angle θ of the pendulum (measured from hanging downward), and the angular velocity $\dot{\theta}$. The control signal $a \in \mathbb{R}$ is the force applied to the cart. The target state is $\boldsymbol{s}_* = (0, \star, \pi, \star)$, corresponding to the cart being in the middle and the pendulum being vertical, with velocities unspecified. The authors used an RBF controller with 50 basis functions, amounting to a total of 305 policy parameters. The controller was successfully trained using just 7 real world trials.[5]

Figure 35.7b shows the results of applying PILCO to solve a **block stacking** task using a low-quality robot arm with 6 degrees of freedom. A separate controller was trained for each block. The state space $\boldsymbol{s} \in \mathbb{R}^3$ is the 3d location of the center of the block in the arm's gripper (derived from an RGBD sensor), and the control $\boldsymbol{a} \in \mathbb{R}^4$ corresponds to the pulse widths of four servo motors. A linear policy was successfully trained using as few as 10 real world trials.

35.4.3.2 GP-MPC

[KD18a] have proposed an extension to PILCO that they call **GP-MPC**, since it combines a GP dynamics model with model predictive control (Section 35.4.1). In particular, they use an open-loop control policy to propose a sequence of actions, $\boldsymbol{a}_{t:t+H-1}$, as opposed to sampling them from a policy. They compute a Gaussian approximation to the future state trajectory, $p(\boldsymbol{s}_{t+1:t+H}|\boldsymbol{a}_{t:t+H-1}, \boldsymbol{s}_t)$, by moment matching, and use this to deterministically compute the expected reward and its gradient wrt $\boldsymbol{a}_{t:t+H-1}$ (as opposed to the policy parameters $\boldsymbol{\theta}$). Using this, they can solve Equation (35.46) to find $\boldsymbol{a}_{t:t+H-1}^*$; finally, they execute the first step of this plan, a_t^*, and repeat the whole process.

The advantage of GP-MPC over policy-based PILCO is that it can handle constraints more easily, and it can be more data efficient, since it continually updates the GP model after every step (instead of at the end of an trajectory).

35.4.4 MBRL using DNNs

Gaussian processes do not scale well to large sample sizes and high dimensional data. Deep neural networks (DNNs) work much better in this regime. However, they do not naturally model uncertainty, which can cause MPC methods to fail. We discuss various methods for representing uncertainty with DNNs in Section 17.1. Here, we mention a few approaches that have been used for MBRL.

The **deep PILCO** method uses DNNs together with Monte Carlo dropout (Section 17.3.1) to represent uncertainty [GMAR16]. [Chu+18] proposed **probabilistic ensembles with trajectory sampling** or **PETS**, which represents uncertainty using an ensemble of DNNs (Section 17.3.9). Many other approaches are possible, depending on the details of the problem being tackled.

Since these are all stochastic methods (as opposed to the GP methods above), they can suffer from a high variance in the predicted returns, which can make it difficult for the MPC controller to pick the best action. We can reduce variance with the **common random number** trick [KSN99], where all rollouts share the same random seed, so differences in $J(\pi_\theta)$ can be attributed to changes in $\boldsymbol{\theta}$ but not other factors. This technique was used in **PEGASUS** [NJ00][6] and in [HMD18].

---

5. 2 random initial trials, each 5 seconds, and then 5 policy-generated trials, each 2.5 seconds, totalling 17.5 seeconds.
6. PEGASUS stands for "Policy Evaluation-of-Goodness And Search Using Scenarios", where the term "scenario" refers to one of the shared random samples.

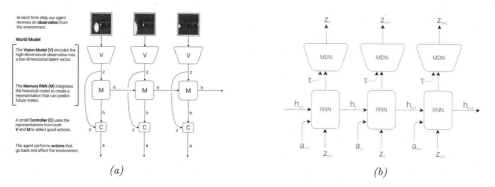

Figure 35.8: (a) Illustration of an agent interacting with the VizDoom environment. (The yellow blobs represent fireballs being thrown towards the agent by various enemies.) The agent has a world model, composed of a vision system V and a memory RNN M, and has a controller C. (b) Detailed representation of the memory model. Here h_t is the deterministic hidden state of the RNN at time t, which is used to predict the next latent of the VAE, z_{t+1}, using a mixture density network (MDN). Here τ is a temperature parameter used to increase the variance of the predictions, to prevent the controller from exploiting model inaccuracies. From Figures 4, 6 of [HS18]. Used with kind permission of David Ha.

35.4.5 MBRL using latent-variable models

In this section, we describe some methods that learn latent variable models, rather than trying to predict dynamics directly in the observed space, which is hard to do when the states are images.

35.4.5.1 World models

The "world models" paper [HS18] showed how to learn a generative model of two simple video games (CarRacing and a VizDoom-like environment), such that the model can be used to train a policy entirely in simulation. The basic idea is shown in Figure 35.8. First, we collect some random experience, and use this to fit a VAE model (Section 21.2) to reduce the dimensionality of the images, $x_t \in \mathbb{R}^{64 \times 64 \times 3}$, to a latent $z_t \in \mathbb{R}^{64}$. Next, we train an RNN to predict $p(z_{t+1}|z_t, a_t, h_t)$, where h_t is the deterministic RNN state, and a_t is the continuous action vector (3-dimensional in both cases). The emission model for the RNN is a mixture density network, in order to model multi-modal futures. Finally, we train the controller using z_t and h_t as inputs; here z_t is a compact representation of the current frame, and h_t is a compact representation of the predicted distribution over z_{t+1}.

The authors of [HS18] trained the controller using a derivative free optimizer called **CMA-ES** (covariance matrix adaptation evolutionary strategy, see Section 6.7.6.2). It can work better than policy gradient methods, as discussed in Section 35.3.6. However, it does not scale to high dimensions. To tackle this, the authors use a linear controller, which has only 867 parameters.[7] By contrast, VAE has 4.3M parameters and MDN-RNN 422k. Fortunately, these two models can be trained in an unsupervised way from random rollouts, so sample efficiency is less critical than when training the policy.

---

7. The input is a 32-dimensional z_t plus a 256-dimensional h_t, and there are 3 outputs. So the number of parameters is $(32 + 256) \times 3 + 3 = 867$, to account for the weights and biases.

So far, we have described how to use the representation learned by the generative model as informative features for the controller, but the controller is still learned by interacting with the real world. Surprisingly, we can also train the controller entirely in "dream mode", in which the generated images from the VAE decoder at time t are fed as input to the VAE encoder at time $t+1$, and the MDN-RNN is trained to predict the next reward r_{t+1} as well as z_{t+1}. Unfortunately, this method does not always work, since the model (which is trained in an unsupervised way) may fail to capture task-relevant features (due to underfitting) and may memorize task-irrelevant features (due to overfitting). The controller can learn to exploit weaknesses in the model (similar to an adversarial attack) and achieve high simulated reward, but such a controller may not work well when transferred to the real world.

One approach to combat this is to artificially increase the variance of the MDN model (by using a temperature parameter τ), in order to make the generated samples more stochastic. This forces the controller to be robust to large variations; the controller will then treat the real world as just another kind of noise. This is similar to the technique of domain randomization, which is sometimes used for sim-to-real applications; see e.g., [MAZA18].

35.4.5.2   PlaNet and Dreamer

In [HS18], they first learn the world model on random rollouts, and then train a controller. On harder problems, it is necessary to iterate these two steps, so the model can be trained on data collected by the controller, in an iterative fashion.

In this section, we describe one method of this kind, known as **PlaNet** [Haf+19]. PlaNet uses a POMDP model, where z_t are the latent states, s_t are the observations, a_t are the actions, and r_t are the rewards. It fits a recurrent state space model (Section 29.13.2) of the form $p(z_t|z_{t-1}, a_{t-1})p(s_t|z_t)p(r_t|z_t)$ using variational inference, where the posterior is approximated by $q(z_t|s_{1:t}, a_{1:t-1})$. After fitting the model to some random trajectories, the system uses the inference model to compute the current belief state, and then uses the cross entropy method to find an action sequence for the next H steps to maximize expected reward, by optimizing in latent space. The system then executes a_t^*, updates the model, and repeats the whole process. To encourage the dynamics model to capture long term trajectories, they use the "latent overshooting" training method described in Section 29.13.3. The PlaNet method outperforms model-free methods, such as A3C (Section 35.3.3.1) and D4PG (Section 35.3.5), on various image-based continuous control tasks, illustrated in Figure 35.9.

Although PlaNet is sample efficient, it is not computationally efficient. For example, they use CEM with 1000 samples and 10 iterations to optimize trajectories with a horizon of length 12, which requires $120,000$ evaluations of the transition dynamics to choose a single action. [AY19] improve this by replacing CEM with differentiable CEM, and then optimize in a latent space of action sequences. This is much faster, but the results are not quite as good. However, since the whole policy is now differentiable, it can be fine-tuned using PPO (Section 35.3.4), which closes the performance gap at negligible cost.

A recent extension of the PlaNet paper, known as **Dreamer**, was proposed in [Haf+20]. In this paper, the online MPC planner is replaced by a policy network, $\pi(a_t|z_t)$, which is learned using gradient-based actor-critic in latent space. The inference and generative models are trained by maximizing the ELBO, as in PlaNet. The policy is trained by SGD to maximize expected total reward as predicted by the value function, and the value function is trained by SGD to minimize

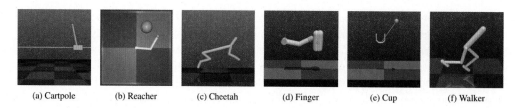

| (a) Cartpole | (b) Reacher | (c) Cheetah | (d) Finger | (e) Cup | (f) Walker |

Figure 35.9: Illustration of some image-based control problems used in the PlaNet paper. Inputs are $64 \times 64 \times 3$. (a) The cartpole swingup task has a fixed camera so the cart can move out of sight, making this a partially observable problem. (b) The reacher task has a sparse reward. (c) The cheetah running task includes both contacts and a larger number of joints. (d) The finger spinning task includes contacts between the finger and the object. (e) The cup task has a sparse reward that is only given once the ball is caught. (f) The walker task requires balance and predicting difficult interactions with the ground when the robot is lying down. From Figure 1 of [Haf+19]. Used with kind permission of Danijar Hafner.

MSE between predicted future reward and the TD-λ estimate (Section 35.2.2). They show that Dreamer gives better results than PlaNet, presumably because they learn a policy to optimize the long term reward (as estimated by the value function), rather than relying on MPC based on short-term rollouts.

35.4.6   Robustness to model errors

The main challenge with MBRL is that errors in the model can result in poor performance of the resulting policy, due to the distribution shift problem (Section 19.2). That is, the model is trained to predict states and rewards that it has seen using some behavior policy (e.g., the current policy), and then is used to compute an optimal policy under the learned model. When the latter policy is followed, the agent will experience a different distribution of states, under which the learned model may not be a good approximation of the real environment.

We require the model to generalize in a robust way to new states and actions. (This is related to the off-policy learning problem that we discuss in Section 35.5.) Failing that, the model should at least be able to quantify its uncertainty (Section 19.3). These topics are the focus of much recent research (see e.g., [Luo+19; Kur+19; Jan+19; Isl+19; Man+19; WB20; Eys+21]).

35.5   Off-policy learning

We have seen examples of off-policy methods such as Q-learning. They do not require that training data be generated by the policy it tries to evaluate or improve. Therefore, they tend to have greater data efficiency than their on-policy counterparts, by taking advantage of data generated by other policies. They are also easier to be applied in practice, especially in domains where costs and risks of following a new policy must be considered. This section covers this important topic.

A key challenge in off-policy learning is that the data distribution is typically different from the desired one, and this mismatch must be dealt with. For example, the probability of visiting a state s at time t in a trajectory depends not only on the MDP's transition model, but also on the policy that is being followed. If we are to estimate $J(\pi)$, as defined in Equation (35.15), but the trajectories are generated by a different policy π', simply averaging rewards in the data gives us $J(\pi')$, not $J(\pi)$. We have to somehow correct for the gap, or "bias". Another challenge is that off-policy data can also make an algorithm unstable and divergent, which we will discuss in Section 35.5.3.

Removing distribution mismatches is not unique in off-policy learning, and is also needed in supervised learning to handle covariate shift (Section 19.2.3.1), and in causal effect estimation (Chapter 36), among others. Off-policy learning is also closely related to **offline reinforcement learning** (also called **batch reinforcement learning**): the former emphasizes the distributional mismatch between data and the agent's policy, and the latter emphasizes that the data is static and no further online interaction with the environment is allowed [LP03; EGW05; Lev+20]. Clearly, in the offline scenario with fixed data, off-policy learning is typically a critical technical component. Recently, several datasets have been prepared to facilitate empirical comparisons of offline RL methods (see e.g., [Gul+20; Fu+20]).

Finally, while this section focuses on MDPs, most methods can be simplified and adapted to the special case of contextual bandits (Section 34.4). In fact, off-policy methods have been successfully used in numerous industrial bandit applications (see e.g., [Li+10; Bot+13; SJ15; HLR16]).

35.5.1 Basic techniques

We start with four basic techniques, and will consider more sophisticated ones in subsequent sections. The off-policy data is assumed to be a collection of trajectories: $\mathcal{D} = \{\tau^{(i)}\}_{1 \leq i \leq n}$, where each trajectory is a sequence as before: $\tau^{(i)} = (s_0^{(i)}, a_0^{(i)}, r_0^{(i)}, s_1^{(i)} \ldots)$. Here, the reward and next states are sampled according to the reward and transition models; the actions are chosen by a **behavior policy**, denoted π_b, which is different from the **target policy**, π_e, that the agent is evaluating or improving. When π_b is unknown, we are in a **behavior-agnostic off-policy** setting.

35.5.1.1 Direct method

A natural approach to off-policy learning starts with estimating the unknown reward and transition models of the MDP from off-policy data. This can be done using regression and density estimation methods on the reward and transition models, respectively, to obtain $\hat{R}$ and $\hat{P}$; see Section 35.4 for further discussions. These estimated models then give us an inexpensive way to (approximately) simulate the original MDP, and we can apply on-policy methods on the simulated data. This method directly models the outcome of taking an action in a state, thus the name **direct method**, and is sometimes known as **regression estimator** and **plug-in estimator**.

While the direct method is natural and sometimes effective, it has a few limitations. First, a small estimation error in the simulator has a compounding effect in long-horizon problems (or equivalently, when the discount factor γ is close to 1). Therefore, an agent that is optimized against an MDP simulator may overfit the estimation errors. Unfortunately, learning the MDP model, especially the transition model, is generally difficult, making the method limited in domains where $\hat{R}$ and $\hat{P}$ can be learned to high fidelity. See Section 35.4.6 for a related discussion.

35.5.1.2 Importance sampling

The second approach relies on importance sampling (IS) (Section 11.5) to correct for distributional mismatches in the off-policy data. To demonstrate the idea, consider the problem of estimating the target policy value $J(\pi_e)$ with a fixed horizon T. Correspondingly, the trajectories in $\mathcal{D}$ are also of length T. Then, the IS off-policy estimator, first adopted by [PSS00], is given by

$$\hat{J}_{\text{IS}}(\pi_e) \triangleq \frac{1}{n} \sum_{i=1}^{n} \frac{p(\boldsymbol{\tau}^{(i)}|\pi_e)}{p(\boldsymbol{\tau}^{(i)}|\pi_b)} \sum_{t=0}^{T-1} \gamma^t r_t^{(i)} \tag{35.47}$$

It can be verified that $\mathbb{E}_{\pi_b}\left[\hat{J}_{\text{IS}}(\pi_e)\right] = J(\pi_e)$, that is, $\hat{J}_{\text{IS}}(\pi_e)$ is **unbiased**, provided that $p(\boldsymbol{\tau}|\pi_b) > 0$ whenever $p(\boldsymbol{\tau}|\pi_e) > 0$. The **importance ratio**, $\frac{p(\boldsymbol{\tau}^{(i)}|\pi_e)}{p(\boldsymbol{\tau}^{(i)}|\pi_b)}$, is used to compensate for the fact that the data is sampled from π_b and not π_e. Furthermore, this ratio does *not* depend on the MDP models, because for any trajectory $\boldsymbol{\tau} = (s_0, a_0, r_0, s_1, \ldots, s_T)$, we have from Equation (34.74) that

$$\frac{p(\boldsymbol{\tau}|\pi_e)}{p(\boldsymbol{\tau}|\pi_b)} = \frac{p(s_0) \prod_{t=0}^{T-1} \pi_e(a_t|s_t) p_T(s_{t+1}|s_t, a_t) p_R(r_t|s_t, a_t, s_{t+1})}{p(s_0) \prod_{t=0}^{T-1} \pi_b(a_t|s_t) p_T(s_{t+1}|s_t, a_t) p_R(r_t|s_t, a_t, s_{t+1})} = \prod_{t=0}^{T-1} \frac{\pi_e(a_t|s_t)}{\pi_b(a_t|s_t)} \tag{35.48}$$

This simplification makes it easy to apply IS, as long as the target and behavior policies are known. If the behavior policy is unknown, we can estimate it from $\mathcal{D}$ (using, e.g., logistic regression or DNNs), and replace π_b by its estimate $\hat{\pi}_b$ in Equation (35.48). For convenience, define the **per-step importance ratio** at time t by $\rho_t(\boldsymbol{\tau}) \triangleq \pi_e(a_t|s_t)/\pi_b(a_t|s_t)$, and similarly, $\hat{\rho}_t(\boldsymbol{\tau}) \triangleq \pi_e(a_t|s_t)/\hat{\pi}_b(a_t|s_t)$.

Although IS can in principle eliminate distributional mismatches, in practice its usability is often limited by its potentially high variance. Indeed, the importance ratio in Equation (35.47) can be arbitrarily large if $p(\boldsymbol{\tau}^{(i)}|\pi_e) \gg p(\boldsymbol{\tau}^{(i)}|\pi_b)$. There are many improvements to the basic IS estimator. One improvement is based on the observation that the reward r_t is independent of the trajectory beyond time t. This leads to a **per-decision importance sampling** variant that often yields lower variance (see Section 11.6.2 for a statistical motivation, and [LBB20] for a further discussion):

$$\hat{J}_{\text{PDIS}}(\pi_e) \triangleq \frac{1}{n} \sum_{i=1}^{n} \sum_{t=0}^{T-1} \prod_{t' \leq t} \rho_{t'}(\boldsymbol{\tau}^{(i)}) \gamma^t r_t^{(i)} \tag{35.49}$$

There are many other variants such as self-normalized IS and truncated IS, both of which aim to reduce variance possibly at the cost of a small bias; precise expressions of these alternatives are found, e.g., in [Liu+18b]. In the next subsection, we will discuss another systematic way to improve IS.

IS may also be applied to improve a policy against the policy value given in Equation (35.15). However, directly applying the calculation of Equation (35.48) runs into a fundamental issue with IS, which we will discuss in Section 35.5.2. For now, we may consider the following approximation of policy value, averaging over the state distribution of the behavior policy:

$$J_b(\pi_{\boldsymbol{\theta}}) \triangleq \mathbb{E}_{p_\beta^\infty(s)}\left[V_\pi(s)\right] = \mathbb{E}_{p_\beta^\infty(s)}\left[\sum_a \pi_{\boldsymbol{\theta}}(a|s) Q_\pi(s, a)\right] \tag{35.50}$$

Differentiating this and ignoring the term $\nabla_{\boldsymbol{\theta}} Q_\pi(s, a)$, as suggested by [DWS12], gives a way to (approximately) estimate the **off-policy policy-gradient** using a one-step IS correction ratio:

$$\nabla_{\boldsymbol{\theta}} J_b(\pi_{\boldsymbol{\theta}}) \approx \mathbb{E}_{p_\beta^\infty(s)} \left[\sum_a \nabla_{\boldsymbol{\theta}} \pi_{\boldsymbol{\theta}}(a|s) Q_\pi(s,a) \right]$$

$$= \mathbb{E}_{p_\beta^\infty(s)\beta(a|s)} \left[\frac{\pi_{\boldsymbol{\theta}}(a|s)}{\beta(a|s)} \nabla_{\boldsymbol{\theta}} \log \pi_{\boldsymbol{\theta}}(a|s) Q_\pi(s,a) \right]$$

Finally, we note that in the tabular MDP case, there exists a policy π_* that is optimal in all states (Section 34.5.5). This policy maximizes J and J_b simultaneously, so Equation (35.50) can be a good proxy for Equation (35.15) as long as all states are "covered" by the behavior policy π_b. The situation is similar when the set of value functions or policies under consideration is sufficiently expressive: an example is a Q-learning like algorithm called Retrace [Mun+16; ASN20]. Unfortunately, in general when we work with parametric families of value functions or policies, such a uniform optimality is lost, and the distribution of states has a direct impact on the solution found by the algorithm. We will revisit this problem in Section 35.5.2.

35.5.1.3 Doubly robust

It is possible to combine the direct and importance sampling methods discussed previously. To develop intuition, consider the problem of estimating $J(\pi_e)$ in a contextual bandit (Section 34.4), that is, when $T = 1$ in $\mathcal{D}$. The **doubly robust** (DR) estimator is given by

$$\hat{J}_{\mathrm{DR}}(\pi_e) \triangleq \frac{1}{n} \sum_{i=1}^n \left(\frac{\pi_e(a_0^{(i)}|s_0^{(i)})}{\hat{\pi}_b(a_0^{(i)}|s_0^{(i)})} \left(r_0^{(i)} - \hat{Q}(s_0^{(i)}, a_0^{(i)}) \right) + \hat{V}(s_0^{(i)}) \right) \qquad (35.51)$$

where $\hat{Q}$ is an estimate of Q_{π_e}, which can be obtained using methods discussed in Section 35.2, and $\hat{V}(s) = \mathbb{E}_{\pi_e(a|s)} \left[\hat{Q}(s,a) \right]$. If $\hat{\pi}_b = \pi_b$, the term $\hat{Q}$ is canceled by $\hat{V}$ on average, and we get the IS estimate that is unbiased; if $\hat{Q} = Q_{\pi_e}$, the term $\hat{Q}$ is canceled by the reward on average, and we get the estimator as in the direct method that is also unbiased. In other words, the estimator Equation (35.51) is unbiased, as long as one of the estimates, $\hat{\pi}_b$ and $\hat{Q}$, is right. This observation justifies the name doubly robust, which has its origin in causal inference (see e.g., [BR05]).

The above DR estimator may be extended to MDPs recursively, starting from the last step. Given a length-T trajectory $\boldsymbol{\tau}$, define $\hat{J}_{\mathrm{DR}}[T] \triangleq 0$, and for $t < T$,

$$\hat{J}_{\mathrm{DR}}[t] \triangleq \hat{V}(s_t) + \hat{\rho}_t(\boldsymbol{\tau}) \left(r_t + \gamma \hat{J}_{\mathrm{DR}}[t+1] - \hat{Q}(s_t, a_t) \right) \qquad (35.52)$$

where $\hat{Q}(s_t, a_t)$ is the estimated cumulative reward for the remaining $T - t$ steps. The DR estimator of $J(\pi_e)$, denoted $\hat{J}_{\mathrm{DR}}(\pi_e)$, is the average of $\hat{J}_{\mathrm{DR}}[0]$ over all n trajectories in $\mathcal{D}$ [JL16]. It can be verified (as an exercise) that the recursive definition is equivalent to

$$\hat{J}_{\mathrm{DR}}[0] = \hat{V}(s_0) + \sum_{t=0}^{T-1} \left(\prod_{t'=0}^t \hat{\rho}_{t'}(\boldsymbol{\tau}) \right) \gamma^t \left(r_t + \gamma \hat{V}(s_{t+1}) - \hat{Q}(s_t, a_t) \right) \qquad (35.53)$$

This form can be easily generalized to the infinite-horizon setting by letting $T \to \infty$ [TB16]. Other than double robustness, the estimator is also shown to result in minimum variance under certain conditions [JL16]. Finally, the DR estimator can be incorporated into policy gradient for policy optimization, to reduce gradient estimation variance [HJ20].

35.5.1.4   Behavior regularized method

The three methods discussed previously do not impose any constraint on the target policy π_e. Typically, the more different π_e is from π_b, the less accurate our off-policy estimation can be. Therefore, when we optimize a policy in offline RL, a natural strategy is to favor target policies that are "close" to the behavior policy. Similar ideas are discussed in the context of conservative policy gradient (Section 35.3.4).

One approach is to impose a hard constraint on the proximity between the two policies. For example, we may modify the loss function of DQN (Equation (35.14)) as follows

$$\mathcal{L}_1^{\text{DQN}}(\boldsymbol{w}) \triangleq \mathbb{E}_{(s,a,r,s')\sim\mathcal{D}}\left[\left(r + \gamma \max_{\pi:D(\pi,\pi_b)\leq\varepsilon}\mathbb{E}_{\pi(a'|s')}\left[Q_{\boldsymbol{w}^-}(s',a')\right] - Q_{\boldsymbol{w}}(s,a)\right)^2\right] \qquad (35.54)$$

In the above, we replace the $\max_{a'}$ operation by an expectation over a policy that stays close enough to the behavior policy, measured by some distance function D. For various instantiations and further details, see e.g., [FMP19; Kum+19a].

We may also impose a soft constraint on the proximity, by penalizing target policies that are too different. The DQN loss function can be adapted accordingly:

$$\mathcal{L}_2^{\text{DQN}}(\boldsymbol{w}) \triangleq \mathbb{E}_{(s,a,r,s')\sim\mathcal{D}}\left[\left(r + \gamma \max_{\pi}\mathbb{E}_{\pi(a'|s')}\left[Q_{\boldsymbol{w}^-}(s',a')\right] - \alpha\gamma D(\pi(s'),\pi_b(s')) - Q_{\boldsymbol{w}}(s,a)\right)^2\right] \qquad (35.55)$$

This idea has been used in contextual bandits [SJ15] and empirically studied in MDPs by [WTN19].

There are many choices for the function D, such as the KL-divergence, for both hard and soft constraints. More detailed discussions and examples can be found in [Lev+20].

Finally, behavior regularization and previous methods like IS can be combined, where the former ensures lower variance and greater generalization of the latter (e.g., [SJ15]). Furthermore, most proposed behavior regularized methods consider one-step difference in D, comparing $\pi(s)$ and $\pi_b(s)$ conditioned on s. In many cases, it is desired to consider the difference between the long-term distributions, p_β^∞ and p^∞, which we will discuss next.

35.5.2   The curse of horizon

The IS and DR approaches presented in the previous section all rely on an importance ratio to correct distributional mismatches. The ratio depends on the entire trajectory, and its variance grows exponentially in the trajectory length T. Correspondingly, the off-policy estimate of either the policy value or policy gradient can suffer an exponentially large variance (and thus very low accuracy), a challenge called the **curse of horizon** [Liu+18b]. Policies found by approximate algorithms like Q-learning and off-policy actor-critic often have hard-to-control error due to distribution mismatches.

This section discusses an approach to tackling this challenge, by considering corrections in the state-action distribution, rather than in the trajectory distribution. This change is critical: [Liu+18b] describes an example, where the state-action distributions under the behavior and target policies are identical, but the importance ratio of a trajectory grows exponentially large. It is now more convenient to assume the off-policy data consists of a set of transitions: $\mathcal{D} = \{(s_i, a_i, r_i, s_i')\}_{1 \leq i \leq m}$, where $(s_i, a_i) \sim p_{\mathcal{D}}$ (some fixed but unknown sampling distribution, such as p_β^∞), and r_i and s_i' are sampled from the MDP's reward and transition models. Given a policy π, we aim to estimate the correction ratio $\zeta_*(s, a) = p_\pi^\infty(s, a)/p_{\mathcal{D}}(s, a)$, as it allows us to rewrite the policy value (Equation (35.15)) as

$$J(\pi) = \frac{1}{1 - \gamma} \mathbb{E}_{p_\pi^\infty(s,a)} [R(s, a)] = \frac{1}{1 - \gamma} \mathbb{E}_{p_\beta^\infty(s,a)} [\zeta_*(s, a) R(s, a)] \tag{35.56}$$

For simplicity, we assume the initial state distribution p_0 is known, or can be easily sampled from. This assumption is often easy to satisfy in practice.

The starting point is the following linear program formulation for any given π:

$$\max_{d \geq 0} - \mathrm{D_f} (d \| p_{\mathcal{D}})) \quad \text{s.t.} \quad d(s, a) = (1 - \gamma)\mu_0(s)\pi(a|s) + \gamma \sum_{\bar{s}, \bar{a}} p(s|\bar{s}, \bar{a})d(\bar{s}, \bar{a})\pi(a|s) \quad \forall(s, a)$$
$$\tag{35.57}$$

where $\mathrm{D_f}$ is the *f*-divergence (Section 2.7.1). The constraint is a variant of Equation (34.93), giving similar flow conditions in the space of $\mathcal{S} \times \mathcal{A}$ under policy π. Under mild conditions, p_π^∞ is only solution that satisfies the flow constraints, so the objective does not affect the solution, but will facilitate the derivation below. We can now obtain the Lagrangian, with multipliers $\{\nu(s, a)\}$, and use the change-of-variables $\zeta(s, a) = d(s, a)/p_{\mathcal{D}}(s, a)$ to obtain the following optimization problem:

$$\max_{\zeta \geq 0} \min_{\nu} \mathcal{L}(\zeta, \nu) = \mathbb{E}_{p_{\mathcal{D}}(s,a)} [-f(\zeta(s, a)] + (1 - \gamma)\mathbb{E}_{p_0(s)\pi(a|s)} [\nu(s, a)] \tag{35.58}$$
$$+ \mathbb{E}_{\pi(a'|s')p(s'|s,a)p_{\mathcal{D}}(s,a)} [\zeta(s, a) (\gamma\nu(s', a') - \nu(s, a))]$$

It can be shown that the saddle point to Equation (35.58) must coincide with the desired correction ratio ζ_*. In practice, we may parameterize ζ and ν, and apply two-timescales stochastic gradient descent/ascent on the off-policy data $\mathcal{D}$ to solve for an approximate saddle-point. This is the **DualDICE** method [Nac+19a], which is extended to **GenDICE** [Zha+20c].

Compared to the IS or DR approaches, Equation (35.58) does not compute the importance ratio of a trajectory, thus generally has a lower variance. Furthermore, it is behavior-agnostic, without having to estimate the behavior policy, or even to assume data consists of a collection of trajectories. Finally, this approach can be extended to be doubly robust (e.g., [UHJ20]), and to optimize a policy [Nac+19b] against the true policy value $J(\pi)$ (as opposed to approximations like Equation (35.50)). For more examples along this line of approach, see [ND20] and the references therein.

35.5.3 The deadly triad

Other than introducing bias, off-policy data may also make a value-based RL method unstable and even divergent. Consider the simple MDP depicted in Figure 35.10a, due to [Bai95]. It has 7 states and 2 actions. Taking the dashed action takes the environment to the 6 upper states uniformly at random, while the solid action takes it to the bottom state. The reward is 0 in all transitions, and $\gamma = 0.99$. The value function $V_{\boldsymbol{w}}$ uses a linear parameterization indicated by the expressions shown inside the states, with $\boldsymbol{w} \in \mathbb{R}^8$. The target policies π always chooses the solid action in every state. Clearly, the true value function, $V_\pi(s) = 0$, can be exactly represented by setting $\boldsymbol{w} = \boldsymbol{0}$.

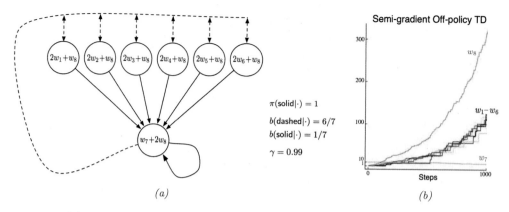

Figure 35.10: (a) A simple MDP. (b) Parameters of the policy diverge over time. From Figures 11.1 and 11.2 of [SB18]. Used with kind permission of Richard Sutton.

Suppose we use a behavior policy b to generate a trajectory, which chooses the dashed and solid actions with probabilities 6/7 and 1/7, respectively, in every state. If we apply TD(0) on this trajectory, the parameters diverge to ∞ (Figure 35.10b), even though the problem appears simple! In contrast, with on-policy data (that is, when b is the same as π), TD(0) with linear approximation can be guaranteed to converge to a good value function approximate [TR97].

The divergence behavior is demonstrated in many value-based bootstrapping methods, including TD, Q-learning, and related approximate dynamic programming algorithms, where the value function is represented either linearly (like the example above) or nonlinearly [Gor95; Ber19]. The root cause of these divergence phenomena is that the contraction property in the tabular case (Equation (34.87)) may no longer hold when V is approximated by $V_{\boldsymbol{w}}$. An RL algorithm can become unstable when it has these three components: off-policy learning, bootstrapping (for faster learning, compared to MC), function approximation (for generalization in large scale MDPs). This combination is known as **the deadly triad** [SB18]. It highlights another important challenge introduced by off-policy learning, and is a subject of ongoing research (e.g., [van+18; Kum+19a]).

A general way to ensure convergence in off-policy learning is to construct an objective function function, the minimization of which leads to a good value function approximation; see [SB18, Ch. 11] for more background. A natural candidate is the discrepancy between the left and right hand sides of the Bellman optimality Equation (34.82), whose unique solution is V_*. However, the "max" operator is not friendly to optimization. Instead, we may introduce an entropy term to smooth the greedy policy, resulting in a differential square loss in **path consistency learning** (**PCL**) [Nac+17]:

$$\min_{V,\pi} \mathcal{L}^{\text{PCL}}(V, \pi) \triangleq \mathbb{E}\left[\frac{1}{2}\big(r + \gamma V(s') - \lambda \log \pi(a|s) - V(s)\big)^2\right] \tag{35.59}$$

where the expectation is over (s, a, r, s') tuples drawn from some off-policy distribution (e.g., uniform over $\mathcal{D}$). Minimizing this loss, however, does not result in the optimal value function and policy in general, due to an issue known as "double sampling" [SB18, Sec. 11.5].

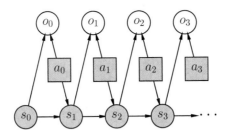

Figure 35.11: A graphical model for optimal control. States and actions are observed, while optimality variables are not. Adapted from Figure 1b of [Lev18].

This problem can be mitigated by introducing a dual function in the optimization [Dai+18]

$$\min_{V,\pi} \max_{\nu} \mathcal{L}^{\text{SBEED}}(V, \pi; \nu) \triangleq \mathbb{E}\left[\nu(s,a)\big(r + \gamma V(s') - \lambda \log \pi(a|s) - V(s)\big)^2 - \nu(s,a)^2/2\right] \quad (35.60)$$

where ν belongs to some function class (e.g., a DNN [Dai+18] or RKHS [FLL19]). It can be shown that optimizing Equation (35.60) forces ν to model the Bellman error. So this approach is called **smoothed Bellman error embedding**, or **SBEED**. In both PCL and SBEED, the objective can be optimized by gradient-based methods on parameterized value functions and policies.

35.6 Control as inference

In this section, we will discuss another approach to policy optimization, by reducing it to probabilistic inference. This is called **control as inference**, see e.g., [Att03; TS06; Tou09; BT12; KGO12; HR17; Lev18]. This approach allows one to incorporate domain knowledge in modeling, and apply powerful tools from approximate inference (see e.g., Chapter 7), in a consistent and flexible framework.

35.6.1 Maximum entropy reinforcement learning

We now describe a graphical model that exemplifies such a reduction, which results in RL algorithms that are closely related to some discussed previously. The model allows a trade-off between reward and entropy maximization, and recovers the standard RL setting when the entropy part vanishes in the trade-off. Our discussion mostly follows the approach of [Lev18].

Figure 35.11 gives a probabilistic model, which not only captures state transitions as before, but also introduces a new variable, o_t. This variable is binary, indicating whether the action at time t is optimal or not, and has the following probability distribution:

$$p(o_t = 1|s_t, a_t) = \exp(\lambda^{-1} R(s_t, a_t)) \quad (35.61)$$

for some temperature parameter $\lambda > 0$ whose role will be clear soon. In the above, we have assumed without much loss of generality that $R(s,a) < 0$, so that Equation (35.61) gives a valid probability. Furthermore, we can assume a non-informative, uniform action prior, $p(a_t|s_t)$, to simplify the exposition, for we can always push $p(a_t|s_t)$ into Equation (35.61). Under these assumptions, the likelihood of observing a length-T trajectory $\boldsymbol{\tau}$, when optimality achieved in every step, is:

$$p(\boldsymbol{\tau}|\mathbf{o}_{0:T-1}=\mathbf{1}) \propto p(\boldsymbol{\tau},\mathbf{o}_{0:T-1}=\mathbf{1}) \propto p(s_0)\prod_{t=0}^{T-1}p(o_t=1|s_t,a_t)p_T(s_{t+1}|s_t,a_t)$$

$$= p(s_0)\prod_{t=0}^{T-1}p_T(s_{t+1}|s_t,a_t)\exp\left(\frac{1}{\lambda}\sum_{t=0}^{T-1}R(s_t,a_t)\right) \quad (35.62)$$

The intuition of Equation (35.62) is clearest when the state transitions are deterministic. In this case, $p_T(s_{t+1}|s_t,a_t)$ is either 1 or 0, depending on whether the transition is dynamically feasible or not. Hence, $p(\boldsymbol{\tau}|\mathbf{o}_{0:T-1}=\mathbf{1})$ is either proportional to $\exp(\lambda^{-1}\sum_{t=0}^{T-1}R(s_t,a_t))$ if $\boldsymbol{\tau}$ is feasible, or 0 otherwise. Maximizing reward is equivalent to inferring a trajectory with maximum $p(\boldsymbol{\tau}|\mathbf{o}_{0:T-1}=\mathbf{1})$.

The optimal policy in this probabilistic model is given by

$$p(a_t|s_t,\mathbf{o}_{t:T-1}=\mathbf{1}) = \frac{p(s_t,a_t|\mathbf{o}_{t:T-1}=\mathbf{1})}{p(s_t|\mathbf{o}_{t:T-1}=\mathbf{1})} = \frac{p(\mathbf{o}_{t:T-1}=\mathbf{1}|s_t,a_t)p(a_t|s_t)p(s_t)}{p(\mathbf{o}_{t:T-1}=\mathbf{1}|s_t)p(s_t)}$$

$$\propto \frac{p(\mathbf{o}_{t:T-1}=\mathbf{1}|s_t,a_t)}{p(\mathbf{o}_{t:T-1}=\mathbf{1}|s_t)} \quad (35.63)$$

The two probabilities in Equation (35.63) can be computed as follows, starting with $p(o_{T-1}=1|s_{T-1},a_{T-1})=\exp(\lambda^{-1}R(s_{T-1},a_{T-1}))$,

$$p(\mathbf{o}_{t:T-1}=\mathbf{1}|s_t,a_t) = \int_{\mathcal{S}}p(\mathbf{o}_{t+1:T-1}=\mathbf{1}|s_{t+1})p_T(s_{t+1}|s_t,a_t)\exp(\lambda^{-1}R(s_t,a_t))ds_{t+1} \quad (35.64)$$

$$p(\mathbf{o}_{t:T-1}=\mathbf{1}|s_t) = \int_{\mathcal{A}}p(\mathbf{o}_{t:T-1}=\mathbf{1}|s_t,a_t)p(a_t|s_t)da_t \quad (35.65)$$

The calculation above is expensive. In practice, we can approximate the optimal policy using a parametric form, $\pi_\theta(a_t|s_t)$. The resulted probability of trajectory $\boldsymbol{\tau}$ now becomes

$$p_\theta(\boldsymbol{\tau}) = p(s_1)\prod_{t=0}^{T-1}p_T(s_{t+1}|s_t,a_t)\pi_\theta(a_t|s_t) \quad (35.66)$$

If we optimize θ so that $D_{\mathrm{KL}}\left(p_\theta(\boldsymbol{\tau}) \parallel p(\boldsymbol{\tau}|\mathbf{o}_{0:T-1}=\mathbf{1})\right)$ is minimized, which can be simplified to

$$D_{\mathrm{KL}}\left(p_\theta(\boldsymbol{\tau}) \parallel p(\boldsymbol{\tau}|\mathbf{o}_{0:T-1}=\mathbf{1})\right) = -\mathbb{E}_{p_\theta}\left[\sum_{t=0}^{T-1}\lambda^{-1}R(s_t,a_t)+\mathbb{H}(\pi_\theta(s_t))\right]+\mathrm{const} \quad (35.67)$$

where the constant term only depends on the uniform action prior $p(a_t|s_t)$, but not $\boldsymbol{\theta}$. In other words, the objective is to maximize total reward, with an entropy regularization favoring more uniform policies. Thus this approach is called **maximum entropy RL**, or **MERL**. If π_θ can represent all stochastic policies, a softmax version of the Bellman equation can be obtained for Equation (35.67):

$$Q_*(s_t,a_t) = \lambda^{-1}R(s_t,a_t)+\mathbb{E}_{p_T(s_{t+1}|s_t,a_t)}\left[\log\int_{\mathcal{A}}\exp(Q_*(s_{t+1},a_{t+1}))da\right] \quad (35.68)$$

with the convention that $Q_*(s_T, a) = 0$ for all a, and the optimal policy has a softmax form: $\pi_*(a_t|s_t) \propto \exp(Q_*(s_t, a_t))$. Note that the Q_* above is different from the usual optimal Q-function (Equation (34.83)), due to the introduction of the entropy term. However, as $\lambda \to 0$, their difference vanishes, and the softmax policy becomes greedy, recovering the standard RL setting.

The **soft actor-critic (SAC)** algorithm [Haa+18b; Haa+18c] is an off-policy actor-critic method whose objective function is equivalent to Equation (35.67) (by taking T to ∞):

$$J^{\text{SAC}}(\boldsymbol{\theta}) \triangleq \mathbb{E}_{p_{\pi_{\boldsymbol{\theta}}}^{\infty}(s)\pi_{\boldsymbol{\theta}}(a|s)} [R(s, a) + \lambda \, \mathbb{H}(\pi_{\boldsymbol{\theta}}(s))] \tag{35.69}$$

Note that the entropy term has also the added benefit of encouraging exploration.

To compute the optimal policy, similar to other actor-critic algorithms, we will work with the "soft" state- and action-function approximations, parameterized by $\boldsymbol{w}$ and $\boldsymbol{u}$, respectively:

$$Q_{\boldsymbol{w}}(s, a) = R(s, a) + \gamma \mathbb{E}_{p_T(s'|s,a)} [V_{\boldsymbol{u}}(s', a') - \lambda \log \pi_{\boldsymbol{\theta}}(a'|s')] \tag{35.70}$$

$$V_{\boldsymbol{u}}(s, a) = \lambda \log \sum_a \exp(\lambda^{-1} Q_{\boldsymbol{w}}(s, a)) \tag{35.71}$$

This induces an improved policy (with entropy regularization): $\pi_{\boldsymbol{w}}(a|s) = \exp(\lambda^{-1} Q_{\boldsymbol{w}}(s, a))/Z_{\boldsymbol{w}}(s)$, where $Z_{\boldsymbol{w}}(s) = \sum_a \exp(\lambda^{-1} Q_{\boldsymbol{w}}(s, a))$ is the normalization constant. We then perform a soft policy improvement step to update $\boldsymbol{\theta}$ by minimizing $\mathbb{E}[D_{\text{KL}}(\pi_{\boldsymbol{\theta}}(s) \, \| \, \pi_{\boldsymbol{w}}(s))]$ where the expectation may be approximated by sampling s from a replay buffer D.

In [Haa+18c; Haa+18b], they show that the SAC method outperforms the off-policy DDPG algorithm (Section 35.3.5) and the on-policy PPO algorithm (Section 35.3.4) by a wide margin on various continuous control tasks. For more details, see [Haa+18c].

There is a variant of soft actor-critic, which only requires to model the action-value function. It is based on the observation that both the policy and soft value function can be induced by the soft action-value function as follows:

$$V_{\boldsymbol{w}}(s) = \lambda \log \sum_a \exp\left(\lambda^{-1} Q_{\boldsymbol{w}}(s, a)\right) \tag{35.72}$$

$$\pi_{\boldsymbol{w}}(a|s) = \exp\left(\lambda^{-1}(Q_{\boldsymbol{w}}(s, a) - V_{\boldsymbol{w}}(s))\right) \tag{35.73}$$

We then only need to learn $\boldsymbol{w}$, using approaches similar to DQN (Section 35.2.6). The resulting algorithm, **soft Q-learning** [SAC17], is convenient if the number of actions is small (when $\mathcal{A}$ is discrete), or if the integral in obtaining $V_{\boldsymbol{w}}$ from $Q_{\boldsymbol{w}}$ is easy to compute (when $\mathcal{A}$ is continuous).

It is interesting to see that algorithms derived in the maximum entropy RL framework bears a resemblance to PCL and SBEED in Section 35.5.3, both of which were to minimize an objective function resulting from the entropy-smoothed Bellman equation.

35.6.2 Other approaches

VIREL is an alternative model to maximum entropy RL [Fel+19]. Similar to soft actor-critic, it uses an approximate action-value function, $Q_{\boldsymbol{w}}$, a stochastic policy, $\pi_{\boldsymbol{\theta}}$, and a binary optimality random variable o_t at time t. A different probability model for o_t is used

$$p(o_t = 1|s_t, a_t) = \exp\left(\frac{Q_{\boldsymbol{w}}(s_t, a_t) - \max_a Q_{\boldsymbol{w}}(s_t, a)}{\lambda_{\boldsymbol{w}}}\right) \tag{35.74}$$

The temperature parameter $\lambda_{\boldsymbol{w}}$ is also part of the parameterization, and can be updated from data. An EM method can be used to maximize the objective

$$\mathcal{L}(\boldsymbol{w}, \boldsymbol{\theta}) = \mathbb{E}_{p(s)} \left[\mathbb{E}_{\pi_{\boldsymbol{\theta}}(a|s)} \left[\frac{Q_{\boldsymbol{w}}(s, a)}{\lambda_{\boldsymbol{w}}} \right] + \mathbb{H}(\pi_{\boldsymbol{\theta}}(s)) \right] \tag{35.75}$$

for some distribution p that can be conveniently sampled from (e.g., in a replay buffer). The algorithm may be interpreted as an instance of actor-critic. In the E-step, the critic parameter $\boldsymbol{w}$ is fixed, and the actor parameter $\boldsymbol{\theta}$ is updated using gradient accent with stepsize $\eta_{\boldsymbol{\theta}}$ (for policy improvement):

$$\boldsymbol{\theta} \leftarrow \boldsymbol{\theta} + \eta_{\boldsymbol{\theta}} \nabla_{\boldsymbol{\theta}} \mathcal{L}(\boldsymbol{w}, \boldsymbol{\theta}) \tag{35.76}$$

In the M-step, the actor parameter is fixed, and the critic parameter is updated (for policy evaluation):

$$\boldsymbol{w} \leftarrow \boldsymbol{w} + \eta_{\boldsymbol{w}} \nabla_{\boldsymbol{w}} \mathcal{L}(\boldsymbol{w}, \boldsymbol{\theta}) \tag{35.77}$$

Finally, there are other possibilities of reducing optimal control to probabilistic inference, in addition to MERL and VIREL. For example, we may aim to maximize the expectation of the trajectory return G, by optimizing the policy parameter $\boldsymbol{\theta}$:

$$J(\pi_{\boldsymbol{\theta}}) = \int G(\boldsymbol{\tau}) p(\boldsymbol{\tau}|\boldsymbol{\theta}) d\boldsymbol{\tau} \tag{35.78}$$

It can be interpreted as a pseudo-likelihood function, when the $G(\boldsymbol{\tau})$ is treated as probability density, and solved (approximately) by a range of algorithms (see e.g., [PS07; Neu11; Abd+18]). Interestingly, some of these methods have a similar objective as MERL (Equation (35.67)), although the distribution involving $\boldsymbol{\theta}$ appears in the second argument of D_{KL}. As discussed in Section 2.7.1, this forwards KL-divergence is mode-covering, which in the context of RL is argued to be less preferred than the mode-seeking, reverse KL-divergence used by MERL. For more details and references, see [Lev18].

Control as inference is also closely related to **active inference**; this is based on the **free energy principle** which is popular in neuroscience (see e.g., [Fri09; Buc+17; SKM18; Ger19; Maz+22]). The FEP is equivalent to using variational inference (see Section 10.1) to perform state estimation (perception) and parameter estimation (learning). In particular, consider a latent variable model with hidden states $\boldsymbol{s}$, observations $\boldsymbol{y}$, and parameters $\boldsymbol{\theta}$. Following Section 10.1.1.1, we define the variational free energy to be $\mathcal{F}(\boldsymbol{o}) = D_{\text{KL}}(q(\boldsymbol{s}, \boldsymbol{\theta}|\boldsymbol{y}) \parallel p(\boldsymbol{s}, \boldsymbol{y}, \boldsymbol{\theta}))$. State estimation corresponds to solving $\min_{q(\boldsymbol{s}|\boldsymbol{y})} \mathcal{F}(\boldsymbol{y})$, and parameter estimation corresponds to solving $\min_{q(\boldsymbol{\theta}|\boldsymbol{y})} \mathcal{F}(\boldsymbol{y})$, just as in variational Bayes EM (Section 10.3.5). (Minimizing the VFE for certain hierarchical Gaussian models also forms the foundation of predictive coding, which we discuss in Supplementary Section 8.1.4.)

To extend this to decision making problems we can define the **expected free energy** as $\overline{\mathcal{F}}(\boldsymbol{a}) = \mathbb{E}_{q(\boldsymbol{y}|\boldsymbol{a})}[\mathcal{F}(\boldsymbol{y})]$, where $q(\boldsymbol{y}|\boldsymbol{a})$ is the posterior predictive distribution over observations given actions sequence $\boldsymbol{a}$. The connection to control as inference is explained in [Mil+20; WIP20; LÖW21].

35.6.3   Imitation learning

In previous sections, an RL agent is to learn an optimal sequential decision making policy so that the total reward is maximized. **Imitation learning** (IL), also known as **apprenticeship learning** and **learning from demonstration** (LfD), is a different setting, in which the agent does not observe rewards, but has access to a collection $\mathcal{D}_{\exp}$ of trajectories generated by an expert policy $\pi_{\exp}$; that is, $\boldsymbol{\tau} = (s_0, a_0, s_1, a_1, \ldots, s_T)$ and $a_t \sim \pi_{\exp}(s_t)$ for $\boldsymbol{\tau} \in \mathcal{D}_{\exp}$. The goal is to learn a good policy by imitating the expert, in the absence of reward signals. IL finds many applications in scenarios where we have demonstrations of experts (often humans) but designing a good reward function is not easy, such as car driving and conversational systems. See [Osa+18] for a survey up to 2018.

35.6.3.1 Imitation learning by behavior cloning

A natural method is **behavior cloning**, which reduces IL to supervised learning; see [Pom89] for an early application to autonomous driving. It interprets a policy as a classifier that maps states (inputs) to actions (labels), and finds a policy by minimizing the imitation error, such as

$$\min_{\pi} \mathbb{E}_{p^\infty_{\pi_{\exp}}(s)} \left[D_{\mathrm{KL}} \left(\pi_{\exp}(s) \parallel \pi(s) \right) \right] \tag{35.79}$$

where the expectation wrt $p^\infty_{\pi_{\exp}}$ may be approximated by averaging over states in $\mathcal{D}_{\exp}$. A challenge with this method is that the loss does not consider the sequential nature of IL: future state distribution is not fixed but instead depends on earlier actions. Therefore, if we learn a policy $\hat{\pi}$ that has a low imitation error under distribution $p^\infty_{\pi_{\exp}}$, as defined in Equation (35.79), it may still incur a large error under distribution $p^\infty_{\hat{\pi}}$ (when the policy $\hat{\pi}$ is actually run). Further expert demonstrations or algorithmic augmentations are often needed to handle the distribution mismatch (see e.g., [DLM09; RGB11]).

35.6.3.2 Imitation learning by inverse reinforcement learning

An effective approach to IL is **inverse reinforcement learning** (IRL) or **inverse optimal control** (IOC). Here, we first infer a reward function that "explains" the observed expert trajectories, and then compute a (near-)optimal policy against this learned reward using any standard RL algorithms studied in earlier sections. The key step of reward learning (from expert trajectories) is the opposite of standard RL, thus called inverse RL [NR00a].

It is clear that there are infinitely many reward functions for which the expert policy is optimal, for example by several optimality-preserving transformations [NHR99]. To address this challenge, we can follow the maximum entropy principle (Section 2.4.7), and use an energy-based probability model to capture how expert trajectories are generated [Zie+08]:

$$p(\boldsymbol{\tau}) \propto \exp\left(\sum_{t=0}^{T-1} R_{\boldsymbol{\theta}}(s_t, a_t) \right) \tag{35.80}$$

where $R_{\boldsymbol{\theta}}$ is an unknown reward function with parameter $\boldsymbol{\theta}$. Abusing notation slightly, we denote by $R_{\boldsymbol{\theta}}(\boldsymbol{\tau}) = \sum_{t=0}^{T-1} R_{\boldsymbol{\theta}}(s_t, a_t))$ the cumulative reward along the trajectory $\boldsymbol{\tau}$. This model assigns exponentially small probabilities to trajectories with lower cumulative rewards. The partition function, $Z_{\boldsymbol{\theta}} \triangleq \int_{\boldsymbol{\tau}} \exp(R_{\boldsymbol{\theta}}(\boldsymbol{\tau}))$, is in general intractable to compute, and must be approximated. Here, we can take a sample-based approach. Let $\mathcal{D}_{\exp}$ and $\mathcal{D}$ be the sets of trajectories generated by an expert, and by some known distribution q, respectively. We may infer $\boldsymbol{\theta}$ by maximizing the likelihood, $p(\mathcal{D}_{\exp}|\boldsymbol{\theta})$, or equivalently, minimizing the negative log-likelihood loss

$$\mathcal{L}(\boldsymbol{\theta}) = -\frac{1}{|\mathcal{D}_{\exp}|} \sum_{\boldsymbol{\tau} \in \mathcal{D}_{\exp}} R_{\boldsymbol{\theta}}(\boldsymbol{\tau}) + \log \frac{1}{|\mathcal{D}|} \sum_{\boldsymbol{\tau} \in \mathcal{D}} \frac{\exp(R_{\boldsymbol{\theta}}(\boldsymbol{\tau}))}{q(\boldsymbol{\tau})} \tag{35.81}$$

The term inside the log of the loss is an importance sampling estimate of Z that is unbiased as long as $q(\boldsymbol{\tau}) > 0$ for all $\boldsymbol{\tau}$. However, in order to reduce the variance, we can choose q adaptively as $\boldsymbol{\theta}$ is being updated. The optimal sampling distribution (Section 11.5), $q_*(\boldsymbol{\tau}) \propto \exp(R_{\boldsymbol{\theta}}(\boldsymbol{\tau}))$, is hard to obtain. Instead, we may find a policy $\hat{\pi}$ which induces a distribution that is close to q_*, for instance, using methods of maximum entropy RL discussed in Section 35.6.1. Interestingly, the process above produces the inferred reward $R_{\boldsymbol{\theta}}$ as well as an approximate optimal policy $\hat{\pi}$. This approach is used by **guided cost learning** [FLA16], and found effective in robotics applications.

35.6.3.3   Imitation learning by divergence minimization

We now discuss a different, but related, approach to IL. Recall that the reward function depends only on the state and action in an MDP. It implies that if we can find a policy π, so that $p_{\pi}^{\infty}(s, a)$ and $p_{\pi_{\exp}}^{\infty}(s, a)$ are close, then π receives similar long-term reward as $\pi_{\exp}$, and is a good imitation of $\pi_{\exp}$ in this regard. A number of IL algorithms find π by minimizing the divergence between p_{π}^{∞} and $p_{\pi_{\exp}}^{\infty}$. We will largely follow the exposition of [GZG19]; see [Ke+19b] for a similar derivation.

Let f be a convex function, and D_f the f-divergence (Section 2.7.1). From the above intuition, we want to minimize $D_f \left(p_{\pi_{\exp}}^{\infty} \middle\| p_{\pi}^{\infty} \right)$. Then, using a variational approximation of D_f [NWJ10a], we can solve the following optimization problem for π:

$$\min_{\pi} \max_{\boldsymbol{w}} \mathbb{E}_{p_{\pi_{\exp}}^{\infty}(s,a)} [T_{\boldsymbol{w}}(s, a)] - \mathbb{E}_{p_{\pi}^{\infty}(s,a)} [f^*(T_{\boldsymbol{w}}(s, a))] \tag{35.82}$$

where $T_{\boldsymbol{w}} : \mathcal{S} \times \mathcal{A} \to \mathbb{R}$ is a function parameterizd by $\boldsymbol{w}$. The first expectation can be estimated using $\mathcal{D}_{\exp}$, as in behavior cloning, and the second can be estimated using trajectories generated by policy π. Furthermore, to implement this algorithm, we often use a parametric policy representation $\pi_{\boldsymbol{\theta}}$, and then perform stochastic gradient updates to find a saddle-point to Equation (35.82).

With different choices of the convex function f, we can obtain many existing IL algorithms, such as **generative adversarial imitation learning** (**GAIL**) [HE16b] and **adversarial inverse RL** (**AIRL**) [FLL18], as well as new algorithms like **f-divergence max-ent IRL** (*f*-**MAX**) and **forward adversarial inverse RL** (**FAIRL**) [GZG19; Ke+19b].

Finally, the algorithms above typically require running the learned policy π to approximate the second expectation in Equation (35.82). In risk- or cost-sensitive scenarios, collecting more data is not always possible, Instead, we are in the off-policy IL setting, working with trajectories collected by some policy other than π. Hence, we need to correct the mismatch between p_{π}^{∞} and the off-policy trajectory distribution, for which techniques from Section 35.5 can be used. An example is **ValueDICE** [KNT20], which uses a similar distribution correction method of DualDICE (Section 35.5.2).

36 Causality

This chapter is written by Victor Veitch and Alex D'Amour.

36.1 Introduction

The bulk of machine learning considers relationships between observed variables with the goal of summarizing these relationships in a manner that allows predictions on similar data. However, for many problems, our main interest is to predict how system would change if it were observed under different conditions. For instance, in healthcare, we are interested in whether a patient will recover if given a certain treatment (as opposed to whether treatment and recovery are associated in the observed data). **Causal inference** addresses how to formalize such problems, determine whether they can be solved, and, if so, how to solve them. This chapter covers the fundamentals of this subject. Code examples for the discussed methods are available at `https://github.com/vveitch/causality-tutorials`. For more information on the connections between ML and causal inference, see e.g., [Kad+22; Xia+21a].

To make the gap between observed data modeling and causal inference concrete, consider the relationships depicted in Figure 36.1a and Figure 36.1b. Figure 36.1a shows the relationship between deaths by drowning and ice cream production in the United States in 1931 (the pattern holds across most years). Figure 36.1b shows the relationship between smoking and lung cancer across various countries. In each case, there is a strong positive association. Faced with this association, we might ask: could we reduce drowning deaths by banning ice cream? Could we reduce lung cancer by banning cigarettes? We intuitively understand that these interventional questions have different answers, despite the fact that the observed associations are similar. Determining the causal effect of some intervention in the world requires some such causal hypothesis about the world.

For concreteness, consider three possible explanations for the association between ice cream and drowning. Perhaps eating ice cream does cause people to drown — due to stomach cramps or similar. Or, perhaps, drownings increase demand for ice cream — the survivors eat huge quantities of ice cream to handle their grief. Or, the association may be due (at least in part) to a common cause: warm weather makes people more likely to eat ice cream and more likely to go swimming (and, hence, to drown). Under all three scenarios, we can observe exactly the same data, but the implications for an ice cream ban are very different. Hence, answering questions about what will happen under an intervention requires us to incorporate some causal knowledge of the world — e.g., which of these scenarios is plausible?

Our goal in this chapter to introduce the essentials of estimating causal effects. The high-level

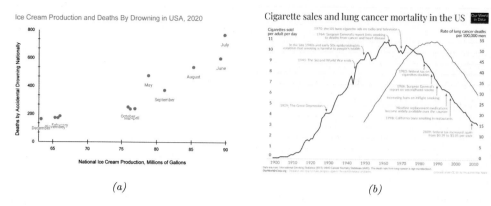

Figure 36.1: Correlation is not causation. (a) Ice cream production is strongly associated with deaths by drowning. Ice cream production data from the US Department of Agriculture National Agricultural Statistics Service. Drowning data from the National Center for Health Statistics at the United States Centers for Disease Control. (b) Smoking is strongly associated with lung cancer. From `ourworldindata.org/smoking-big-problem-in-brief`*. Used with kind permission of Max Roser.*

approach has three steps.

- **Causal estimands**: The first step is to formally define the quantities we want to estimate. These are summaries of how the world would change under intervention, rather than summaries of the world as it has already been observed. E.g., we want to formalize "The expected number of drownings in the United States if we ban ice cream".

- **Identification**: The next step is to identify the causal estimands with quantities that can, in principle, be estimated from observational data. This step involves codifying our causal knowledge of the world and translating this into a statement such as, "The causal effect is equal to the expected number of drownings after adjusting for month". This step tells us what causal questions we could answer with perfect knowledge of the observed data distribution.

- **Estimation**: Finally, we must estimate the observable quantity using a finite data sample. The form of causal estimands favors certain efficient estimation procedures that allow us to exploit non-parametric (e.g., machine learning) predictive models.

In this chapter, we'll mainly focus on the estimation of the causal effect of an intervention averaged over all members of a population, known as the **average treatment effect** or **ATE**. This is the most common problem in applied causal inference work. It is in some sense the simplest problem, and will allow us to concretely explain the use and importance of the fundamental causal concepts. These causal concepts include structural causal models, causal graphical models, the do-calculus, and efficient estimation using influence function techniques. This problem is also useful for understanding the role that standard predictive modeling and machine learning play in estimating causal quantities.

36.2 Causal formalism

In causal inference, the goal is to use data to learn about how the outcome in the world would change under intervention. In order to make such inferences, we must also make use of our causal knowledge of the world. This requires a formalism that lets us make the notion of intervention precise and lets us encode our causal knowledge as assumptions.

36.2.1 Structural causal models

Consider a setting in which we observe four variables from a population of people: A_i, an indicator of whether or not person i smoked at a particular age, Y_i, an indicator of whether or not person i developed lung cancer at a later age, H_i, a "health consciousness" index that measures a person's health-consciousness (perhaps constructed from a set of survey responses about attitudes towards health), and G_i, an indicator for whether the person has a genetic predisposition towards cancer. Suppose we observe a dataset of these variables drawn independently and identically from a population, $(A_i, Y_i, H_i) \overset{\text{iid}}{\sim} P^{\text{obs}}$, where "obs" stands for "observed".

In standard practice, we model data like these using probabilistic models. Notably, there are many different ways to specify a probabilistic model for the same observed distribution. For example, we could write a probabilistic model for P^{obs} as

$$A \sim P^{\text{obs}}(A) \tag{36.1}$$

$$H|A \sim P^{\text{obs}}(H|A) \tag{36.2}$$

$$Y|A, H \sim P^{\text{obs}}(Y|H, A) \tag{36.3}$$

$$G|A, H, Y \sim P^{\text{obs}}(G|A, H, Y) \tag{36.4}$$

This is a valid factorization, and sampling variables in this order would yield valid samples from the joint distribution P^{obs}. However, this factorization does not map well to a mechanistic understanding of how these variables are causally related in the world. In particular, it is perhaps more plausible that health-consciousness H causally precedes smoking status A, since a person's health-consciousness would influence their decision to smoke.

These intuitions about causal ordering are intimately tied to the notion of intervention. Here, we will focus on a notion of intervention that can be represented in terms of "structural" models that describe mechanistic relationships between variables. The fundamental objects that we will reason about are **structural causal models**, or SCM's. SCM's resemble probabilistic models, but they encode additional assumptions (see also Section 4.7). Specifically, SCM's serve two purposes: they describe a probabilistic model *and* they provide semantics for transforming the data-generating process through intervention.

Formally, SCM's describe a mechanistic data generating process with an ordered sequence of equations that resemble assignment operations in a program. Each variable in a system is determined by combining other modeled variables (the causes) with exogenous "noise" according to some (unknown) deterministic function. For instance, a plausible SCM for P^{obs} might be

$$G \leftarrow f_G(\xi_0) \tag{36.5}$$

$$H \leftarrow f_H(\xi_1) \tag{36.6}$$

$$A \leftarrow f_A(H, \xi_2) \tag{36.7}$$

$$Y \leftarrow f_Y(G, H, A, \xi_3) \tag{36.8}$$

where the (unknown) functions f are fixed, and the variables ξ are unmeasured causes, modeled as independent random "noise" variables. Conceptually, the functions f_G, f_H, f_A, f_Y describe deterministic physical relationships in the real world, while the variables ξ are hidden causes that are sufficient to distinguish each unit i in the population. Because we assume that each observed unit i is drawn at random from the population, we model ξ as random noise.

SCM's imply probabilistic models, but not the other way around. For example, our example SCM implies probabilistic model for the observed data based on the factorization $P^{\text{obs}}(G, H, A, Y) = P^{\text{obs}}(G)P^{\text{obs}}(H)P^{\text{obs}}(A \mid H)P^{\text{obs}}(Y \mid A, H)$. Thus, we could sample from the SCM in the same way we would from a probabilistic model: draw a set of noise variables ξ and evaluate each assignment operation in the SCM in order.

Beyond the probabilistic model, an SCM encodes additional assumptions about the effects of **interventions**. This can be formalized using the **do-calculus** (as in the verb "to do"), which we describe in Section 36.8; But in brief, interventions are represented by replacing assignment statements. For example, if we were interested in the distribution of Y in the hypothetical scenario that smoking were eliminated, we could set the second line of the SCM to be $A \leftarrow 0$. We would denote this by $P(Y|\text{do}(A = 0), H)$. Because the f functions in the SCM are assumed to be invariant mechanistic relationships, the SCM encodes the assumption that this edited SCM generates data that we would see if we really applied this intervention in the world. Thus, the ordering of statements in an SCM are load-bearing: they imply substantive assumptions about how the world changes in response to interventions. This is in contrast to more standard probabilistic models where variables can be rearranged by applications of Bayes' Rule without changing the substantive implications of the model. (See also Section 4.7.3.)

We note that structural causal model may not incorporate all possible notions of causality. For example, laws based on conserved quantities or equilibria — e.g., the ideal gas law — do not trivially map to SCMs, though these are fundamental in disciplines such as physics and economics. Nonetheless, we will confine our discussion to SCMs.

36.2.2 Causal DAGs

SCM's encode many details about the assumed generative process of a system, but often it is useful to reason about causal problems at a higher level of abstraction. In particular, it is often useful to separate the causal structure of a problem from the particular functional form of those causal relationships. **Causal graphs** provide this level of abstraction. A causal graph specifies which variables causally affect other variables, but leaves the parametric form of the structural equations f unspecified. Given an SCM, the corresponding causal graph can be drawn as follows: for each line of the SCM, draw arrows from the variables on the right hand side to variables on the left hand side. The causal DAG for our smoking-cancer example is shown in Figure 36.2. In this way, causal DAGs are related to SCMs in the same way that probabilistic graphical models (PGMs) are related

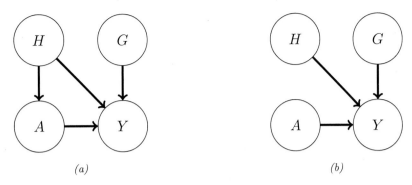

Figure 36.2: (a) Causal graph illustrating relationships between smoking A, cancer Y, health conciousness H, and genetic cancer pre-disposition G. (b) "Mutilated" causal graph illustrating relationships under an intervention on smoking A.

to probabilistic models.

In fact, in the same way that SCMs imply a probabilistic model, causal DAGs imply a PGM. Functionally, causal graphs behave as probabilistic graphical models (Chapter 4). They imply conditional independence relationships between the variables in the observed data in same way. They obey the Markov property: If $X \leftarrow Y \rightarrow Z$ then $X \perp Z|Y$; recall d-separation (Section 4.2.4.1). Additionally, if $X \rightarrow Y \leftarrow Z$ then, usually, $X \not\perp Z|Y$ (even if X and Z are marginally independent). In this case, Y is called a **collider** for X and Z.

Conceptually, the difference between causal DAGs and PGMs is that probabilistic graphical models encode our assumptions about statistical relationships, whereas causal graphs encode our (stronger) assumptions about causal relationships. Such causal relationships can be used to derive how statistical relationships would change under intervention.

Causal graphs also allow us to reason about the causal and non-causal origins of statistical dependencies in observed data without specifying a full SCM. In a causal graph, two variables — say, A and D — can be statistically associated in different ways. First, there can be a directed path from (ancestor) A to (descendant) D. In this case, A is a causal ancestor of D and interventions on A will propagate through to change D; $P(D|\text{do}(A = a)) \neq P(D|\text{do}(A = a'))$. For example, smoking is a causal ancestor of cancer in our example. Alternatively, A and D could share a common cause — there is some variable C such that there is a directed path from C to A and from C to D. If A and D are associated only through such a path then interventions on A will not change the distribution of D. However, it is still the case that $P(D|A = a) \neq P(D|A = a')$ — observing different values of A changes our guess for the value of D. The reason is that A carries information about C, which carries information about D. For example, suppose we lived in a world where there was no effect of smoking on developing cancer (e.g., everybody vapes), there would nevertheless be an association between smoking and cancer because of the path $A \leftarrow H \rightarrow Y$. The existence of such "backdoor paths" is one core reason that statistical and causal association are not the same. Of course, more complicated variants of these associations are possible — e.g., C is itself only associated with A through a backdoor path — but this already captures the key distinction between causal and non-causal paths.

Recall that our aim in introducing SCMs and causal graphs is to enable us to formalize our causal knowledge of the world and to make precise what interventional quantities we'd like to estimate. Writing down a causal graph gives a simple formal way to encode our knowledge of the causal structure of a problem. Usefully, this causal structure is sufficient to directly reason about the implications of interventions without fully specifying the underlying SCM. The key observation is that if a variable A is intervened on then, after intervention, none of the other variables are causes of A. That is, when we replace a line of an SCM with a statement directly assigning a variable a particular value, we cut off all dependencies that variable had on its causal parents. Accordingly, in the causal graph, the intervened on variable has no parents. This leads us to the **graph surgery** notion of intervention: an intervention that sets A to a is the operation that deletes all incoming edges to A in the graph, and then conditions on $A = a$ in the resulting probability distribution (which is defined by the conditional independence structure of the post-surgery graph). We'll use Pearl's do notation to denote this operation. $P(\mathbf{X}|\text{do}(A = a))$ is the distribution of $\mathbf{X}$ given $A = a$ under the mutilated graph that results from deleting all edges going into A. Similarly, $\mathbb{E}[\mathbf{X}|\text{do}(A = a)] \triangleq \mathbb{E}_{P(\mathbf{X}|\text{do}(A=a))}[\mathbf{X}]$. Thus, we can formalize statements such as "the average effect of receiving drug A" as

$$\text{ATE} = E[Y|\text{do}(A = 1)] - \mathbb{E}[Y|\text{do}(A = 0)], \tag{36.9}$$

where ATE stands for average treatment effect.

For concreteness, consider our running example. We contrast the distribution that results by conditioning on A with the distribution that results from intervening on A:

$$P(Y, H, G|A = a) = P(Y|H, G, A = a)P(G)P(H|A = a) \tag{36.10}$$
$$P(Y, H, G|\text{do}(A = a)) = P(Y|H, G, A = a)P(G)P(H) \tag{36.11}$$

The key difference between these two distributions is that the standard conditional distribution describes a population where health consciousness H has the distribution that we observe among individuals with smoking status $A = a$, while the interventional distribution described a population where health consciousness H follows the marginal distribution among all individuals. For example, we would expect $P(H \mid A = \texttt{smoker})$ to put more mass on lower values of H than the marginal health consciousness distribution than the marginal distribution $P(H)$, which would also include non-smokers. The intervention distribution thus incorporates a hypothesis of how smoking would affect the subpopulation individuals who tend to be too health conscious to smoke in the observed data.

36.2.3   Identification

A central challenge in causal inference is that many different SCM's can produce identical distributions of observed data. This means that, on the basis of observed data alone, we cannot uniquely identify the SCM that generated it. This is true no matter how large of a data sample is available to us.

For example, consider the setting where there is a treatment A that may or may not have an effect on outcome Y, and where both the treatment and outcome are known to be affected by some *unobserved* common binary cause U. Now, we might be interested in the causal estimand $E[Y|\text{do}(A = 1)]$. In general, we can't learn this quantity from the observed data. The problem is that, we can't tell apart the case where the treatment has a strong effect from the case where the treatment has no effect, but $U = 1$ both causes people to tend to be treated and increases the probability of a positive outcome. The same observation shows we can't learn the (more complicated) interventional distribution $P(Y|do(A = 1))$ (if we could learn this, then we'd get the average effect automatically).

Thus, an important part of causal inference is to augment the observed data with knowledge about the underlying causal structure of the process under consideration. Often, these assumptions can narrow the space of SCM's sufficiently so that there is only one value of the causal estimand that is compatible with the observed data. We say that the causal estimand is **identified** or **identifiable** under a given set of assumptions if those assumptions are sufficient to provide a unique answer. There are many different sets of sufficient conditions that yield identifiable causal effects; we call each set of sufficient conditions an **identification strategy**.

Given a set of assumptions about the underlying SCM, the most common way to show that a causal estimand is identified is by construction. Specifically, if the causal estimand can be written entirely in terms of observable probability distributions, then it is identifed. We call such a function of observed distributions a **statistical estimand**. Once such a statistical estimand has been recovered, we can then construct and analyze an estimator for that quantity using standard statistical tools. As an example of a statistical estimand, in the SCM above, it can be shown the ATE as defined in Equation (36.9), is equal to the following statistical estimand

$$\text{ATE} \overset{(*)}{=} \tau^{\text{ATE}} \triangleq \mathbb{E}[\mathbb{E}[Y|H, A = 1] - \mathbb{E}[Y|H, A = 0]], \tag{36.12}$$

where the equality $(*)$ only holds because of some specific properties of the SCM. Note that the RHS above only involves conditional expectations between observed variables (there are no do operators), so τ^{ATE} is only a function of observable probability distributions.

There are many kinds of assumptions we might make about the SCM governing the process under consideration. For example, the following are assertions we might make about the system in our running example:

1. The probability of developing cancer is additive on the logit scale in A, G, and H (i.e., logistic regression is a well-specified model).

2. For each individual, smoking can never decrease the probability of developing cancer.

3. Whether someone smokes is influenced by their health consciousness H, but not by their genetic predisposition to cancer G.

These assumptions range from strong parametric assumptions fully specifying the form of the SCM equations, to non-parametric assumptions that only specify what the inputs to each equation are, leaving the form fully unspecified. Typically, assumptions that fully specify the parametric form are very strong, and would require far more detailed knowledge of the system under consideration than we actually have. The goal in identification arguments is to find a set of assumptions that are weak enough that they might be plausibly true for the system under consideration, but which are also strong enough to allow for identification of the causal effect.

If we are not willing to make any assumptions about the functional form of the SCM, then our assumptions are just about which variables affect (and do not affect) the other variables. In this sense, such which-affects-which assumptions are minimal. These assumptions are exactly the assumptions captured by writing down a (possibly incomplete) causal DAG, showing which variables are parents of each other variable. The graph may be incomplete because we may not know whether each possible edge is present in the physical system. For example, we might be unsure whether the gene G actually has a causal effect on health consciousness H. It is natural to ask to what extent we can identify causal effects only on the basis of partially specified causal DAGs. It turns out much progress can be made based on such non-parametric assumptions; we discuss this in detail in Section 36.8.

We will also discuss certain assumptions that cannot be encoded in a causal graph, but that are still weaker than assuming that full functional forms are known. For example, we might assume that the outcome is affected additively by the treatment and any confounders, with no interaction terms between them. These weaker assumptions can enable causal identification even when assuming the causal graph alone does not.

It is worth emphasizing that every causal identification strategy relies on assumptions that have some content that cannot be validated in the observed data. This follows directly from the ill-posedness of causal problems: if the assumptions used to identify causal quantities could be validated, that would imply that the causal estimand was identifiable from the observed data alone. However, since we know that there are many values of the causal estimand that are compatible with observed data, it follows that the assumptions in our identification strategy must have unobservable implications.

36.2.4   Counterfactuals and the causal hierarchy

Structural causal models let us formalize and study a hierarchy of different kinds of query about the system under consideration. The most familiar is observational queries: questions that are purely about statistical associations (e.g., "Are smoking and lung cancer associated in the population this sample was drawn from?"). Next is interventional queries: questions about causal relationships at the population level (e.g., "How much does smoking increase the probability of cancer in a given population?"). The rest of this chapter is focused on the defintion, identification, and estimation of interventional queries. Finally, there are counterfactual queries: questions about causal relationships at the level of specific individuals, had something been different (e.g., "Would Alice have developed cancer had she not smoked?"). This causal hierarchy was popularized by [Pea09a, Ch. 1].

Interventional queries concern the prospective effect of an intervention on an outcome; for example, if we intervene and prevent a randomly sampled individual from smoking, what is the probability they develop lung cancer? Ultimately, the probability statement here is about our uncertainty about the "noise" variables ξ in the SCM. These are the unmeasured factors specific to the randomly selected individual. The distribution is determined by the population from which that individual is sampled. Thus, interventional queries are statements about populations. Interventional queries can be written in terms of conditional distributions using do-notation, e.g., $P(Y|\text{do}(A = 0))$. In our example, this represents the distribution of lung cancer outcomes for an individual selected at random and prevented from smoking.

Counterfactual queries concern how an observed outcome might have been different had an intervention been applied in the past. Counterfactual queries are often framed in terms of attributing a given outcome to a particular cause. For example, would Alice have developed cancer had she not smoked? Did most smokers with lung cancer develop cancer because they smoked? Counterfactual queries are so called because they require a comparison of counterfactual outcomes within individuals. In the formalism of SCM's, counterfactual outcomes for an individual i are generated by running the same values of ξ_i through differently intervened SCMs. Counterfactual outcomes are often written in terms of **potential outcomes** notation. In our running smoking example, this would look like:

$$Y_i(a) \triangleq f_Y(G_i, H_i, a, \xi_{3,i}). \tag{36.13}$$

That is, $Y_i(a)$ is the outcome we would have seen had A been set to a while all of $G_i, H_i, \xi_{3,i}$ were kept fixed.

It is important to understand what distinguishes interventional and fundamentally counterfactual queries. Just because a query can be written in terms of potential outcomes does not make it a counterfactual query. For example, the average treatment effect, which is the canonical interventional query, is easy to write in potential outcomes notation:

$$\text{ATE} = \mathbb{E}[Y_i(1) - Y_i(0)]. \tag{36.14}$$

Instead, the key dividing line between counterfactual and interventional queries is whether the query requires knowing the joint distribution of potential outcomes within individuals, or whether marginal distributions of potential outcomes across individuals will suffice. An important signature of a counterfactual query is conditioning on the value of one potential outcome. For example, "the lung cancer rate among smokers who developed cancer, had they not smoked" is a counterfactual query, and can be written as:

$$\mathbb{E}[Y_i(0) \mid Y_i(1) = 1, A_i = 1] \tag{36.15}$$

Answering this query requires knowing how individual-level cancer outcomes are related (through $\xi_{3,i}$) across the worlds where the each individual i did and did not smoke. Notably, this query cannot be rewritten using do-notation, because it requires a distinction between $Y(0)$ and $Y(1)$ while the ATE can: $\mathbb{E}[Y \mid \text{do}(A = 1)] - \mathbb{E}[Y \mid \text{do}(A = 0)]$.

Counterfactual queries require categorically more assumptions for identification than interventional ones. For identifying interventional queries, knowing the DAG structure of an SCM is often sufficient, while for counterfactual queries, some assumptions about the functional forms in the SCM are necessary. This is because only one potential outcome is ever observed for each individual, so the dependence between potential outcomes within individuals is not observable. For example, the data in our running example provide no information on how individual-level smoking and non-smoking cancer risk are related. Thus, answering a question like "Did smokers who developed cancer have lower non-smoking cancer risk than smokers who did not develop cancer?", requires additional assumptions about how characteristics encoded in ξ_i are translated to cancer outcomes. To answer this question without such assumptions, we would need to observe smokers who developed cancer in the alternate world where they did not smoke. Because they compare how individuals would have turned out under different generating processes, counterfactual queries are often referred to as "cross-world" quantities. On the other hand, interventional queries only require understanding the marginal distributions of potential outcomes $Y_i(0)$ and $Y_i(1)$ across individuals; thus, no cross-world information is necessary at the individual level.

We conclude this section by noting that counterfactual outcomes and potential outcomes notation are often conceptually useful, even if they are not used to explicitly answer counterfactual queries. Many causal queries are more intuitive to formalize in terms of potential outcomes. E.g., "Would I have smoked if I was more health conscious?" may be more intuitive than "Would a randomly sampled individual from the same population have smoked had they been subject to an intervention that made them more health concious?". In fact, some schools of causal inference use potential outcomes, rather than DAGs, as their primary conceptual building block [See IR15]. Causal graphs and potential outcomes both provide ways to formulate interventional queries and causal assumptions. Ultimately, these are mathematically equivalent. Nevertheless, practically, they have different strengths. The main advantage of potential outcomes is that counterfactual statements often map more directly to our mechanistic understanding of the world. This can make it easier to articulate causal desiderata and causal assumptions we may wish to use. On the other hand, the potential outcomes notation does not automatically distinguish between interventional and counterfactual queries. Additionally, causal graphs often give an intuitive and easy way of articulating assumptions about structural causal models involving many variables—potential outcomes get quickly unwieldy. In short: both formalizations have distinct advantages, and those advantages are simply about how easy it is to translate our causal understanding of the world into crisp mathematical assumptions.

36.3   Randomized control trials

We now turn to the business of estimating causal effects from data. We begin with **randomized control trials**, which are experiments designed to make the causal concerns as simple as possible.

The simplest situation for causal estimation is when there are no common causes of A and Y. The world is rarely so obliging as to make this the case. However, sometimes we can design an experiment to enforce the no-common-causes structure. In randomized control trials we assign each participant to either the treatment or control group at random. Because random assignment does not depend on any property of the units in the study, there are no causes of treatment assignment, and hence also no common causes of Y and A.

In this case, it's straightforward to see that $P(Y|\text{do}(A = a)) = P(Y|a)$. This is essentially by definition of the graph surgery: since A has no parents, the mutilated graph is the same as the original graph. Indeed, the graph surgery definition is chosen to make this true: any sensible formalization of causality should have this identification result.

It is common to use RCTs to study the average treatment effect,

$$\text{ATE} = E[Y|\text{do}(A = 1)] - \mathbb{E}[Y|\text{do}(A = 0)]. \tag{36.16}$$

This is the expected difference between being assigned treatment and assigned no treatment for a randomly chosen member of the population. It's easy to see that in an RCT this causal quantity is identified as a parameter τ^{RCT} of the observational distribution:

$$\tau^{\text{RCT}} = \mathbb{E}[Y|A = 1] - \mathbb{E}[Y|A = 0].$$

Then, a natural estimator is:

$$\hat{\tau}^{\text{RCT}} \triangleq \frac{1}{n_A} \sum_{i:A_i=1} Y_i - \frac{1}{n - n_A} \sum_{i:A_i=0} Y_i, \tag{36.17}$$

where n_A is the number of units who received treatment. That is, we estimate the average treatment effect as the difference between the average outcome of the treated group and the average outcome of the untreated (control) group.[1]

Randomized control trials are the gold standard for estimating causal effects. This is because we know *by design* that there are no confounders that can produce alternative causal explanations of the

---

1. There is a literature on efficient estimation of causal effects in RCT's going back to Fisher [Fis25] that employ more sophisticated estimators. See also Lin [Lin13a] and Bloniarz et al. [Blo+16] for more modern treatments.

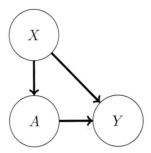

Figure 36.3: A causal DAG illustrating a situation where treatment A and outcome Y are both influenced by observed confounders X.

data. In particular, the assumption of the triangle DAG—there are no unobserved confounders—is enforced by design. However, there are limitations. Most obviously, randomized control trials are sometimes infeasible to conduct. This could be due to expense, regulatory restrictions, or more fundamental difficulties (e.g., in developmental economics, the response of interest is sometimes collected decades after treatment). Additionally, it may be difficult to ensure that the participants in an RCT are representative of the population where the treatment will be deployed. For instance, participants in drug trials may skew younger and poorer than the population of patients who will ultimately take the drug.

36.4 Confounder adjustment

We now turn to the problem of estimating causal effects using observational (i.e., not experimental) data. The most common application of causal inference is estimating the average treatment effect (ATE) of an intervention. The ATE is also commonly called the **average causal effect**, or ACE. Here, we focus on the important special case where the treatment A is binary, and we observe the outcome Y as well as a set of common causes X that influence both A and Y.

36.4.1 Causal estimand, statistical estimand, and identification

Consider a problem where we observe treatment A, outcome Y, and covariates X, which are drawn iid from some unknown distribution P. We wish to learn the average treatment effect: the expected difference between being assigned treatment and assigned no treatment for a randomly chosen member of the population. Following the discussion in the introduction, there are three steps to learning this quantity: mathematically formalize the causal estimand, give conditions for the causal estimand to be identified as a statistical estimand, and, finally, estimate this statistical estimand from data. We now turn to the first two steps.

The average treatment effect is defined to be the difference between the average outcome if we *intervened* and set A to be 0, versus the average outcome if we intervened and set A to be 1. Using the do notation, we can write this formally as

$$\text{ATE} = \mathbb{E}[Y|\text{do}(A = 1)] - \mathbb{E}[Y|\text{do}(A = 0)]. \tag{36.18}$$

The next step is to articulate sufficient conditions for the ATE to be identified as a statistical estimand (a parameter of distribution P). The key issue is the possible presence of **confounders**. Confounders are "common cause" variables that affect both the treatment and outcome. When there are confounding variables in observed data, the sub-population of people who are observed to have received one level of the treatment A will differ from the rest of the population in ways that are relevant to their observed Y. For example, there is a strong positive association between horseback riding in childhood (treatment) and healthiness as an adult (outcome) [RB16]. However, both of these quantities are influenced by wealth X. The population of people who rode horses as children ($A = 1$) is wealthier than the population of people who did not. Accordingly, the horseback-riding population will have better health outcomes even if there is no actual causal benefit of horseback riding for adult health.

We'll express the assumptions required for causal identification in the form of a causal DAG. Namely, we consider the simple triangle DAG in Figure 36.3, where the treatment and outcome are influenced by *observed* confounders X. It turns out that the assumption encoded by this DAG suffices for identification. To understand why this is so, recall that the target causal effect is defined according to the distribution we would see if the edge from X to A was removed (that's the meaning of do). The key insight is that because the intervention only modifies the relationship between X and A, the structural equation that generates outcomes Y given X and A, illustrated in Figure 36.3 as the $A \rightarrow Y \leftarrow X$, is the same even after the $X \rightarrow Y$ edge is removed. For example, we might believe that the physiological processes by which smoking status A and confounders X produce lung cancer Y remain the same, regardless of how the decision to smoke or not smoke was made. Second, because the intervention does not change the composition of the population, we would also expect the distribution of background characteristics X to be the same between the observational and intervened processes.

With these insights about invariances between observed and interventional data, we can derive a statistical estimand for the ATE as follows.

Theorem 2 (Adjustment with no unobserved confounders). *We observe $A, Y, X \sim P$. Suppose that*

1. *(Confounders observed) The data obeys the causal structure in Figure 36.3. In particular, X contains all common causes of A and Y and no variable in X is caused by A or Y.*

2. *(Overlap) $0 < \mathrm{P}(A = 1 | X = x) < 1$ for all values of x. That is, there are no individuals for whom treatment is always or never assigned.*

Then, the average treatment effect is identified as $\mathrm{ATE} = \tau$, *where*

$$\tau = \mathbb{E}[\mathbb{E}[Y | A = 1, X]] - \mathbb{E}[\mathbb{E}[Y | A = 0, X]]. \tag{36.19}$$

Proof. First, we expand the ATE using the tower property of expectation, conditioning on X. Then, we apply the invariances discussed above:

$$ATE = \mathbb{E}[Y | \mathrm{do}(A = 1)] - \mathbb{E}[Y | \mathrm{do}(A = 0)] \tag{36.20}$$

$$= \mathbb{E}[\mathbb{E}[Y | \mathrm{do}(A = 1), X]] - \mathbb{E}[\mathbb{E}[Y | \mathrm{do}(A = 0), X]] \tag{36.21}$$

$$= \mathbb{E}[\mathbb{E}[Y | A = 1, X]] - \mathbb{E}[\mathbb{E}[Y | A = 0, X]] \tag{36.22}$$

The final equality is the key to passing from a causal to observational quantity. This follows because, from the causal graph, the conditional distribution of Y given A, X is the same in both the original graph and in the mutilated graph created by removing the edge from X to A. This mutilated graph defines $P(Y|\text{do}(A = 1), X)$, so the equality holds.

The condition that $0 < P(A = 1|X = x) < 1$ is required for the first equality (the tower property) to be well defined. $\square$

Note that Equation (36.19) is a function of only conditional expectations and distributions that appear in the observed data distribution (in particular, it contains no "do" operators). Thus, if we can fully characterize the observed data distribution P, we can map that distribution to a unique ATE.

It is useful to note how τ differs from the naive estimand $\mathbb{E}[Y|A = 1] - \mathbb{E}[Y|A = 0]$ that just reports the treatment-outcome association without adjusting for confounding. The comparison is especially clear when we write out the outer expectation in τ explicitly as an integral over X:

$$\tau = \int \mathbb{E}[Y \mid A = 1, X]P(X)dX - \int \mathbb{E}[Y \mid A = 0, X]P(X)dX \tag{36.23}$$

We can write the naive estimand in a similar form by applying the tower property of expectation:

$$\mathbb{E}[Y \mid A = 1] - \mathbb{E}[Y \mid A = 0] = \int \mathbb{E}[Y \mid A = 1, X]P(X \mid A = 1)dX - \int \mathbb{E}[Y \mid A = 0, X]P(X \mid A = 0)dX \tag{36.24}$$

The key difference is the probability distribuiton over X that is being integrated over. The observational difference in means integrates over the distinct conditional distributions of confounders X, depending on the value of A. On the other hand, in the ATE estimand τ, we integrate over the same distribution $P(X)$ for both levels of the treatment.

Overlap In addition to the assumption on the causal structure, identification requires that there is sufficient random variation in how treatments are assigned.

Definition 1. *A distribution P on A, X satisfies* **overlap** *if $0 < P(A = 1|x) < 1$ for all x. It satisfies* **strict overlap** *if $\epsilon < P(A = 1|x) < 1 - \epsilon$ for all x and some $\epsilon > 0$.*

Overlap is the requirement that any unit could have either recieved the treatment or not.

To see the necessity of overlap, consider estimating the effectiveness of a drug in a study where patient sex is a confounder, but the drug was only ever prescribed to male patients. Then, conditional on a patient being female, we would know that patient was assigned to control. Without further assumptions, it's impossible to know the effect of the drug on a population with female patients, because there would be no data to inform the expected outcome for treated female patients, that is, $\mathbb{E}[Y \mid A = 1, X = \texttt{female}]$. In this case, the statistical estimand equation 36.19 would not be identifiable. In the same vein, strict overlap ensures that the conditional distributions at each stratum of X can be estimated in finite samples.

Overlap can be particularly limiting in settings where we are adjusting for a large number of covariates (in an effort to satisfy no unobserved confounding). Then, certain combinations of traits may be very highly predictive of treatment assignment, even if individual traits are not. E.g., male patients over age 70 with BMI greater than 25 are very rarely assigned the drug. If such groups represent a significant fraction of the target population, or have significantly different treatment effects, then this issue can be problematic. In this case, the strict overlap assumption puts very strong restrictions on observational studies: for an observational study to satisfy overlap, most dimensions of the confounders X would need to closely mimic the balance we would expect in an RCT [D'A+21].

36.4.2   ATE estimation with observed confounders

We now return to estimating the ATE using observed — i.e., not experimental — data. We've shown that in the case where we observe all common causes of the treatment and outcome, the ATE is causally identified with a statistical estimand τ. We now consider several strategies for estimating this quantity using a finite data sample. Broadly, these techniques are known as backdoor adjustment.[2]

Recall that the defining characteristic of a confounding variable is that it affects both treatment and outcome. Thus, an adjustment strategy may aim to account for the influence of confounders on the observed outcome, the influence of confounders on treatment, or both. We discuss each of these strategies in turn.

36.4.2.1   Outcome model adjustment

We begin with an approach to covariate adjustment that relies on modeling the conditional expectation of the outcome Y given treatment A and confounders X. This strategy is often referred to as g-computation or outcome adjustment.[3] To begin, we define

Definition 2. *The **conditional expected outcome** is the function Q given by*

$$Q(a, x) = \mathbb{E}[Y | A = a, X = x]. \tag{36.25}$$

Substituting this definition into the definition of our estimand τ, Equation (36.19), we have $\tau = \mathbb{E}[Q(1, x) - Q(0, x)]$. This suggests a procedure for estimating τ: fit a model $\hat{Q}$ for Q and then report

$$\hat{\tau}^Q \triangleq \frac{1}{n} \sum_i \hat{Q}(1, x_i) - \hat{Q}(0, x_i). \tag{36.26}$$

To fit $\hat{Q}$, recall that $E[Y|a, x] = \operatorname{argmin}_Q \mathbb{E}[(Y - Q(A, X)^2]$. That is, the minimizer (among all functions) of the squared loss risk is the conditional expected outcome.[4] So, to approximate Q, we simply use mean squared error to fit a predictor that predicts Y from A and X.

The estimation procedure takes several steps. We first fit a model $\hat{Q}$ to predict Y. Then, for each unit i, we predict that unit's outcome had they received treatment $\hat{Q}(1, x_i)$ and we predict their outcome had they not received treatment $\hat{Q}(0, x_i)$.[5] If the unit actually did receive treatment ($a_i = 1$)

---

2. As we discuss in Section 36.8, this backdoor adjustment references the estimand returned by the do-calculus to eliminate confounding from a backdoor path. This also generalizes the approaches discussed here to some cases where we do not observe all common causes.

3. The "g" stands for generalized, for now-inscrutable historical reasons [Rob86].

4. To be precise, this definition applies when X and Y are square-integrable, and the minimzation taken over measurable functions.

5. This interpretation is justified by the same conditions as Theorem 2.

then $\hat{Q}(0, x_i)$ is our guess about what would have happened in the counterfactual case that they did not. The estimated expected gain from treatment for this individual is $\hat{Q}(1, x_i) - \hat{Q}(0, x_i)$—the difference in expected outcome between being treated and not treated. Finally, we estimate the outer expectation with respect to $P(X)$ — the true population distribution of the confounders — using the empirical distribution $\hat{P}(X) = 1/n \sum_i \delta_{x_i}$. In effect, this means we substitute the expectation (over an unknown distribution) by an average over the observed data.

Linear regression It's worth saying something more about the special case where Q is modeled as a linear function of both the treatment and all the covariates. That is, the case where we assume the identification conditions of Theorem 2 and we additionally assume that the true, causal law (the SCM) governing Y yields: $Q(A, X) = \mathbb{E}[Y|A, X] = \mathbb{E}[f_Y(A, X, \xi)|A, X] = \beta_0 + \beta_A A + \beta_X X$. Plugging in, we see that $Q(1, X) - Q(0, X) = \beta_A$ (and so also $\tau = \beta_A$). Then, the estimator for the average treatment effect reduces to the estimator for the regression coefficient β_A. This "fit linear regression and report the regression coefficient" remains a common way of estimating the association between two variables in practice. The expected-outcome-adjustment procedure here may be viewed as a generalization of this procedure that removes the linear parametric assumption.

36.4.2.2 Propensity Score Adjustment

Outcome model adjustment relies on modeling the relationship between the confounders and the outcome. A popular alternative is to model the relationship between the confounders and the treatment. This strategy adjusts for confounding by directly addressing sampling bias in the treated and control groups. This bias arises from the relationship between the confounders and the treatment. Intuitively, the effect of confounding may be viewed as due to the difference between $P(X|A = 1)$ and $P(X|A = 0)$ — e.g., the population of people who rode horses as children is wealthier than the population of people who did not. When we observe all confounding variables X, this degree of over- or under-representation can be adjusted away by reweighting samples such that the confounders X have the same distribution in the treated and control groups. When the confounders are balanced between the two groups, then any differences between them must be attributable to the treatment.

A key quantity for balancing treatment and control groups is the **propensity score**, which summarises the relationship between confounders and treatment.

Definition 3. *The* **propensity score** *is the function g given by $g(x) = P(A = 1|X = x)$.*

To make use of the propensity score in adjustment, we first rewrite the estimand τ in a suggestive form, leveraging the fact that $A \in \{0, 1\}$:

$$\tau = \mathbb{E}\left[\frac{YA}{g(X)} - \frac{Y(1 - A)}{1 - g(X)}\right]. \tag{36.27}$$

This identity can be verified by noting that $\mathbb{E}[YA|X] = \mathbb{E}[Y|A = 1, X]P(A = 1|X) + 0$, rearranging for $\mathbb{E}[Y|A = 1, X]$, doing the same for $\mathbb{E}[Y|A = 0, X]$, and substituting in to Equation (36.19). Note that the identity is just a mathematical fact about the statistical estimand — it does not rely on any causal assumptions, and holds whether or not τ can be interpreted as a causal effect.

This expression suggests the **inverse probability of treatment weighted estimator**, or IPTW estimator:

$$\hat{\tau}^{\text{IPTW}} \triangleq \frac{1}{n} \sum_i \frac{Y_i A_i}{\hat{g}(X_i)} - \frac{Y_i(1 - A_i)}{1 - \hat{g}(X_i)}. \tag{36.28}$$

Here, $\hat{g}$ is an estimate of the propensity score function. Recall from Section 14.2.1 that if a model is well-specified and the loss function is a proper scoring rule then risk minimizer $g^* = \text{argmin}_g \mathbb{E}[L(A, g(X))]$ will be $g^*(X) = P(A = 1|X)$. That is, we can estimate the propensity score by fitting a model that predicts A from X. Cross-entropy and squared loss are both proper scoring rules, so we may use standard supervised learning methods.

In summary, the procedure is to estimate the propensity score function (with machine learning), and then to plug the estimated propensity scores $\hat{g}(x_i)$ into Equation (36.28). The IPTW estimator computes a difference of weighted averages between the treated and untreated group. The effect is to upweight the outcomes of units who were unlikely to be treated but who nevertheless actually, by chance, recieved treatment (and similarly for untreated). Intuitively, such units are typical for the untreated population. So, their outcomes under treatment are informative about what would have happened had a typical untreated unit received treatment.

A word of warning is in order. Although the IPTW is asymtotically valid and popular in practice, it can be very unstable in finite samples. If estimated propensity scores are extreme for some values of x (that is, very close to 0 or 1), then the corresponding IPTW weights can be very large, resulting in a high-variance estimator. In some cases, this instability can be mitigated by instead using the Hajek version of the estimator.

$$\hat{\tau}^{\text{h-IPTW}} \triangleq \sum_i Y_i A_i \frac{1/\hat{g}(X_i)}{\sum_i A_i/\hat{g}(X_i)} - \sum_i Y_i(1 - A_i) \frac{1/(1-\hat{g}(X_i))}{\sum_i (1-A_i)/(1-\hat{g}(X_i))}. \tag{36.29}$$

However, extreme weights can persist even after self-normalization, either because there are truly strata of X where treatment assignment is highly imbalanced, or because the propensity score estimation method has overfit. In such cases, it is common to apply heuristics such as weight clipping.

See Khan and Ugander [KU21] for a longer discussion of inverse-propensity type estimators, including some practical improvements.

36.4.2.3 Double machine learning

We have seen how to estimate the average treatment effect using either the relationship between confounders and outcome, or the relationship between confounders and treatment. In each case, we follow a two step estimation procedure. First, we fit models for the expected outcome or the propensity score. Second, we plug these fitted models into a downstream estimator of the effect.

Unsurprisingly, the quality of the estimate of τ depends on the quality of the estimates $\hat{Q}$ or $\hat{g}$. This is problematic because Q and g may be complex functions that require large numbers of samples to estimate. Even though we're only interested in the 1-dimensional parameter τ, the naive estimators described thus far can have very slow rates of convergence. This leads to unreliable inference or very large confidence intervals.

Remarkably, there are strategies for combining Q and g in estimators that, in principle, do better than using either Q or g alone. The **augmented inverse probability of treatment weighted**

estimator (AIPTW) is one such estimator. It is defined as

$$\hat{\tau}^{\text{AIPTW}} \triangleq \frac{1}{n} \sum_i \hat{Q}(1, X_i) - \hat{Q}(0, X_i) + A_i \frac{Y_i - \hat{Q}(1, X_i)}{\hat{g}(x_i)} - (1 - A_i) \frac{Y_i - \hat{Q}(0, X_i)}{1 - \hat{g}(X_i)}. \tag{36.30}$$

That is, $\hat{\tau}^{\text{AIPTW}}$ is the outcome adjustment estimator plus a stabilization term that depends on the propensity score. This estimator is a particular case of a broader class of estimators that are refered to as **semi-parametrically efficient** or **double machine-learning** estimators [Che+17e; Che+17d]. We'll use the later terminology here.

We now turn to understanding the sense in which double machine learning estimators are robust to misestimation of the **nuisance functions** Q and g. To this end, we define the **influence curve** of τ to be the function ϕ defined by[6]

$$\phi(X_i, A_i, Y_i; Q, g, \tau) \triangleq Q(1, X_i) - Q(0, X_i) + A_i \frac{Y_i - Q(1, X_i)}{g(x_i)} - (1 - A_i) \frac{Y_i - Q(0, X_i)}{1 - g(X_i)} - \tau. \tag{36.31}$$

By design, $\hat{\tau}^{\text{AIPTW}} - \tau = \frac{1}{n} \sum_i \phi(\mathbf{X}_i; \hat{Q}, \hat{g}, \tau)$. We begin by considering what would happen if we simply knew Q and g, and didn't have to estimate them. In this case, the estimator would be $\hat{\tau}^{\text{ideal}} = \frac{1}{n} \sum_i \phi(\mathbf{X}_i; Q, g, \tau)$ and, by the central limit theorem, we would have:

$$\sqrt{n}(\hat{\tau}^{\text{ideal}} - \tau) \xrightarrow{d} \text{Normal}(0, \mathbb{E}[\phi(\mathbf{X}_i; Q, g, \tau)^2]). \tag{36.32}$$

This result characterizes the estimation uncertainty in the best possible case. If we knew Q and g, we could rely on this result for, e.g., finding confidence intervals for our estimate.

The question is: what happens when Q and g need to be estimated? For general estimators and nuisance function models, we don't expect the $\sqrt{n}$-rate of Equation (36.32) to hold. For instance, $\sqrt{n}(\hat{\tau}^Q - \tau)$ only converges if $\sqrt{n}\mathbb{E}[(\hat{Q} - Q)^2]^{\frac{1}{2}} \to 0$. That is, for the naive estimator we only get the $\sqrt{n}$ rate for estimating τ if we can also estimate Q at the $\sqrt{n}$ rate — a much harder task! This is the issue that the double machine learning estimator helps with.

To understand how, we decompose the error in estimating τ as follows:

$$\sqrt{n}(\hat{\tau}^{\text{AIPTW}} - \tau) \tag{36.33}$$

$$= \frac{1}{\sqrt{n}} \sum_i \phi(\mathbf{X}_i; Q, g, \tau) \tag{36.34}$$

$$+ \frac{1}{\sqrt{n}} \sum_i \phi(\mathbf{X}_i; \hat{Q}, \hat{g}, \tau) - \phi(\mathbf{X}_i; Q, g, \tau) - \mathbb{E}[\phi(\mathbf{X}; \hat{Q}, \hat{g}, \tau) - \phi(\mathbf{X}; Q, g, \tau)] \tag{36.35}$$

$$+ \sqrt{n}\mathbb{E}[\phi(\mathbf{X}; \hat{Q}, \hat{g}, \tau) - \phi(\mathbf{X}; Q, g, \tau)] \tag{36.36}$$

We recognize the first term, Equation (36.34), as $\sqrt{n}(\hat{\tau}^{\text{ideal}} - \tau)$, the estimation error in the optimal case where we know Q and g. Ideally, we'd like the error of $\hat{\tau}^{\text{AIPTW}}$ to be asymptotically equal to this ideal case—which will happen if the other two terms go to 0.

---

6. Influence curves are the foundation of what follows, and the key to generalizing the analysis beyond the ATE. Unfortunately, going into the general mathematics would require a major digression, so we omit it. However, see references at the end of the chapter for some pointers to the relevant literature.

The second term, Equation (36.35), is a penalty we pay for using the same data to estimate Q, g and to compute τ. For many model classes, it can be shown that such "empirical process" terms go to 0. This can also be guaranteed in general by using different data for fitting the nuisance functions and for computing the estimator (see the next section).

The third term, Equation (36.36), captures the penalty we pay for misestimating the nuisance functions. This is where the particular form of the AIPTW is key. With a little algebra, we can show that

$$\mathbb{E}[\phi(\mathbf{X}; \hat{Q}, \hat{g}) - \phi(\mathbf{X}; Q, g)] = \mathbb{E}[\frac{1}{g(X)}(\hat{g}(X) - g(X))(\hat{Q}(1, X) - Q(1, X)) \tag{36.37}$$

$$+ \frac{1}{1 - g(X)}(\hat{g}(X) - g(X))(\hat{Q}(0, X) - Q(0, X))]. \tag{36.38}$$

The important point is that estimation errors of Q and g are multiplied together. Using the Cauchy-Schwarz inequality, we find that $\sqrt{n}\mathbb{E}[\phi(\mathbf{X}; \hat{Q}, \hat{g}) - \phi(\mathbf{X}; Q, g)] \to 0$ as long as $\sqrt{n} \max_a \mathbb{E}[(\hat{Q}(a, X) - Q(a, X))^2]^{\frac{1}{2}}\mathbb{E}[(\hat{g}(X) - g(X))^2]^{\frac{1}{2}} \to 0$. That is, the misestimation penalty will vanish so long as the *product* of the misestimation errors is $o(\sqrt{n})$. For example, this means that τ can be estimated at the (optimal) $\sqrt{n}$ rate even when the estimation error of each of Q and g only decreases as $o(n^{-1/4})$.

The upshot here is that the double machine learning estimator has the special property that the weak condition $\sqrt{n}\mathbb{E}(\hat{Q}(T, X) - Q(T, X))^2\mathbb{E}(\hat{g}(X) - g(X))^2 \to 0$ suffices to imply that

$$\sqrt{n}(\hat{\tau}^{\text{AIPTW}} - \tau) \xrightarrow{d} \text{Normal}(0, \mathbb{E}[\phi(\mathbf{X}_i; Q, g, \tau)^2]) \tag{36.39}$$

(though strictly speaking this requires some additional technical conditions we haven't discussed). This is *not* true for the earlier estimators we discussed, which require a much faster rate of convergence for the nuisance function estimation.

The AIPTW estimator has two further nice properties that are worth mentioning. First, it is **non-parametrically efficient**. This means that this estimator has the smallest possible variance of any estimator that does not make parametric assumptions; namely, $\mathbb{E}[\phi(\mathbf{X}_i; Q, g, \tau)^2]$. This means, for example, that this estimator yields the smallest confidence intervals of any approach that does not rely on parametric assumptions. Second, it is **doubly robust**: the estimator is consistent (converges to the true τ as $n \to \infty$) as long as at least one of either $\hat{Q}$ or $\hat{g}$ is consistent.

36.4.2.4   Cross fitting

The term Equation (36.35) in the error decomposition above is the penalty we pay for reusing the same data to both fit Q, g and to compute the estimator. For many choices of model for Q, g, this term goes to 0 quickly as n gets large and we achieve the (best case) $\sqrt{n}$ error rate. However, this property doesn't always hold.

As an alternative, we can always randomly split the available data and use one part for model fitting, and the other to compute the estimator. Effectively, this means the nuisance function estimation and estimator computation are done using independent samples. It can then be shown that the reuse penalty will vanish. However, this comes at the price of reducing the amount of data available for each of nuisance function estimation and estimator computation.

This strategy can be improved upon by a **cross fitting** approach. We divide the data into K folds. For each fold j we use the other $K - 1$ folds to fit the nuisance function models $\hat{Q}^{-j}, \hat{g}^{-j}$.

Then, for each datapoint i in fold j, we take $\hat{Q}(a_i, x_i) = \hat{Q}^{-j}(a_i, x_i)$ and $\hat{g}(x_i) = \hat{g}^{-j}(x_i)$. That is, the estimated conditional outcomes and propensity score for each datapoint are predictions from a model that was not trained on that datapoint. Then, we estimate τ by plugging $\{\hat{Q}(a_i, x_i), \hat{g}(x_i)\}_i$ into Equation (36.30). It can be shown that this cross fitting procedure has the same asymptotic guarantee — the central limit theorem at the $\sqrt{n}$ rate — as described above.

36.4.3 Uncertainty quantification

In addition to the point estimate $\hat{\tau}$ of the average treatment effect, we'd also like to report a measure of the uncertainty in our estimate. For example, in the form of a confidence interval. The asymptotic normality of $\sqrt{n}\hat{\tau}$ (Equation (36.39)) provides a means for this quantification. Namely, we could base confidence intervals and similar on the limiting variance $\mathbb{E}[\phi(\mathbf{X}_i; Q, g, \tau)^2]$. Of course, we don't actually know any of Q, g, or τ. However, it turns out that it suffices to estimate the asymptotic variance with $\frac{1}{n}\sum_i \phi(\mathbf{X}_i; \hat{Q}, \hat{g}, \hat{\tau})^2$ [Che+17e]. That is, we can estimate the uncertainty by simply plugging in our fitted nuisance models and our point estimate of τ into

$$\hat{\mathbb{V}}[\hat{\tau}] = 1/n \sum_i \phi(\mathbf{X}_i; \hat{Q}, \hat{g}, \hat{\tau})^2. \tag{36.40}$$

This estimated variance can then be used to compute confidence intervals in the usual manner. E.g., we'd report a 95% confidence interval for τ as $\hat{\tau} \pm 1.96\sqrt{\hat{\mathbb{V}}[\hat{\tau}]/n}$.

Alternatively, we could quantify the uncertainty by bootstrapping. Note, however, that this would require refitting the nuisance functions with each bootstrap model. Depending on the model and data, this can be prohibitively computationally expensive.

36.4.4 Matching

One particularly popular approach to adjustment-based causal estimation is **matching**. Intuitively, the idea is to match each treated to unit to an untreated unit that has the same (or at least similar) values of the confounding variables and then compare the observed outcomes of the treated unit and its matched control. If we match on the full set of common causes, then the difference in outcomes is, intuitively, a noisy estimate of the effect the treatment had on that treated unit. We'll now build this up a bit more carefully. In the process we'll see that matching can be understood as, essentially, a particular kind of outcome model adjustment.

For simplicity, consider the case where X is a discrete random variable. Define $\mathcal{A}_x$ to be the set of treated units with covariate value x, and $\mathcal{C}_x$ to be the set of untreated units with covariate value x. In this case, the matching estimator is:

$$\hat{\tau}^{\text{matching}} = \sum_x \hat{P}(x)\Big(\frac{1}{|\mathcal{A}_x|}\sum_{i \in \mathcal{A}_x} Y_i - \frac{1}{|\mathcal{C}_x|}\sum_{j \in \mathcal{C}_x} Y_j\Big), \tag{36.41}$$

where $\hat{P}(x)$ is an estimator of $P(X = x)$ — e.g., the fraction of units with $X = x$. Now, we can rewrite $Y_i = Q(A_i, X_i) + \xi_i$ where ξ_i is a unit-specific noise term defined by the equation. In particular, we have that $\mathbb{E}[\xi_i | A_i, X_i] = 0$. Substituting this in, we have:

$$\hat{\tau}^{\text{matching}} = \sum_x \hat{P}(x)\big(Q(1, x) - Q(0, x)\big) + \sum_x \frac{1}{|\mathcal{A}_x|}\sum_{i \in \mathcal{A}_x} \xi_i - \frac{1}{|\mathcal{C}_x|}\sum_{j \in \mathcal{C}_x} \xi_j. \tag{36.42}$$

We can recognize the first term as an estimator of usual target parameter τ (it will be equal to τ if $\hat{P}(x) = P(x)$). The second term is a difference of averages of random variables with expectation 0, and so each term will converge to 0 as long as $|\mathcal{A}_x|$ and $|\mathcal{C}_x|$ each go to infinity as we see more and more data. Thus, we see that the matching estimator is a particular way of estimating the parameter τ. The procedure can be extended to continuous covariates by introducing some notion of values of X being close, and then matching close treatment and control variables.

There are two points we should emphasize here. First, notice that the argument here has nothing to do with causal identification. Matching is a particular technique for estimating the observational parameter τ. Whether or not τ can be interpreted as an average treatment effect is determined by the conditions of Theorem 2 — the particular estimation strategy doesn't say anything about this. Second, notice that in essence matching amounts to a particular choice of model for $\hat{Q}$. Namely, $\hat{Q}(1, x) = \frac{1}{|\mathcal{A}_x|} \sum_{i \in \mathcal{A}_x} Y_i$ and similarly for $\hat{Q}(0, x)$. That is, we estimate the conditional expected outcome as a sample mean over units with the same covariate value. Whether this is a good idea depends on the quality of our model for Q. In situations where better models are possible (e.g., a machine-learning model fits the data well), we might expect to get a more accurate estimate by using the conditional expected outcome predictor directly.

There is another important case we mention in passing. In general, when using adjustment based identification, it suffices to adjust for any function $\phi(X)$ of X such that $A \perp\!\!\!\perp X | \phi(X)$. To see that adjusting for only $\phi(X)$ suffices, first notice that $g(X) = P(A = 1|X) = P(A = 1|\phi(X))$ only depends on $\phi(X)$, and then recall that can write the target parameter as $\tau = \mathbb{E}[\frac{YA}{g(X)} - \frac{Y(1-A)}{1-g(X)}]$, whence τ only depends on X through $g(X)$. That is: replacing X by a reduced version $\phi(X)$ such that $g(X) = P(A = 1|\phi(X))$ can't make any difference to τ. Indeed, the most popular choice of $\phi(X)$ is the propensity score itself, $\phi(X) = g(X)$. This leads to **propensity score matching**, a two step procedure where we first fit a model for the propensity score, and then run matching based on the estimated propensity score values for each unit. Again, this is just a particular estimation procedure for the observational parameter τ, and says nothing about whether it's valid to interpret τ as a causal effect.

36.4.5   Practical considerations and procedures

when performing causal analysis, many issues can arise in practice, some of which we discuss below.

36.4.5.1   What to adjust for

Choosing which variables to adjust for is a key detail in estimating causal effects using covariate adjustment. The criterion is clear when one has a full causal graph relating A, Y, and all covariates X to each other. Namely, adjust for all variables that are actually causal parents of A and Y. In fact, with access to the full graph, this criterion can be generalized somewhat — see Section 36.8.

In practice, we often don't actually know the full causal graph relating all of our variables. As a result, it is common to apply simple heuristics to determine which variables to adjust for. Unfortunately, these heuristics have serious limitations. However, exploring these is instructive.

A key condition in Theorem 2 is that the covariates X that we adjust for must include all the common causes. In the absence of a full causal graph, it is tempting to condition on as many observed variables as possible to try to ensure this condition holds. However, this can be problematic. For instance, suppose that M is a mediator of the effect of A on Y — i.e., M lies on one of the directed

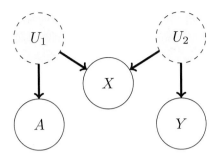

Figure 36.4: The M-bias causal graph. Here, A and Y are not confounded. However, conditioning on the covariate X opens a backdoor path, passing through U_1 and U_2 (because X is a colider). Thus, adjusting for X creates bias. This is true even though X need not be a pre-treatment variable.

paths between A and Y. Then, conditioning on M will block this path, removing some of the causal effect. Note that this does not always result in an attenuated, or smaller-magnitude, effect estimate. The effect through a given mediator may run in the opposite direction of other causal pathways from the treatment; thus conditioning on a mediator can inflate or even flip the sign of a treatment effect. Alternatively, if C is a collider between A and Y — a variable that is caused by both — then conditioning on C will induce an extra statistical dependency between A and Y.

Both pitfalls of the "condition on everything" heuristic discussed above both involve conditioning on variables that are downstream of the treatment A. A natural response is to this is to limit conditioning to all pre-treatment variables, or those that are causally upstream of the treatment. Importantly, if there is a valid adjustment set in the observed covariates X, then there will also be a valid adjustment set among the pre-treatment covariates. This is because any open backdoor path between A and Y must include a parent of A, and the set of pre-treatment covariates includes these parents. However, it is still possible that conditioning on the full set of pre-treatment variables can induce new backdoor paths between A and Y through colliders. In particular, if there is a covariate D that is separately confounded with the treatment A and the outcome Y then D is a collider, and conditioning on D opens a new backdoor path. This phenomenon is known as m-bias because of the shape of the graph [Pea09c], see Figure 36.4.

A practical refinement of the pre-treatment variable heuristic is given in VanderWeele and Shpitser [VS11]. Their heuristic suggests conditioning on all pre-treatment variables that are causes of the treatment, outcome, or both. The essential qualifier in this heuristic is that the variable is causally upstream of treatment and/or outcome. This eliminates the possibility of conditioning on covariates that are only confounded with treatment and outcome, avoiding m-bias. Notably, this heuristic requires more causal knowledge than the above heuristics, but does not require detailed knowledge of how different covariates are causally related to each other.

The VanderWeele and Shpitser [VS11] criterion is a useful rule of thumb, but other practical considerations often arise. For example, if one has more knowledge about the causal structure among covariates, it is possible to optimize adjustment sets to minimize the variance of the resulting estimator [RS20]. One important example of reducing variance by pruning adjustment sets is the exclusion of variables that are known to only be a parent of the treatment, and not of the outcome (so called instruments, as discussed in Section 36.5).

Finally, adjustment set selection criteria operate under the assumption that there actually exists a valid adjustment set among observed covariates. When there is no set of observed covariates in X that block all backdoor paths, then any adjusted estimate will be biased. Importantly, in this case, the bias does not necessarily decrease as one conditions on more variables. For example, conditioning on an instrumental variable often results in an estimate that has higher bias, in addition to the higher variance discussed above. This phenomenon is known as bias amplification or z-bias; see Section 36.7.2. A general rule of thumb is that variables that explain away much more variation in the treatment than in the outcome can potentially amplify bias, and should be treated with caution.

36.4.5.2   Overlap

Recall that in addition to no-unobserved-confounders, identification of the average treatment effect requires overlap: the condition that $0 < P(A = 1|x) < 1$ for the population distribution P. With infinite data, any amount of overlap will suffice for estimating the causal effect. In realistic settings, even near failures can be problematic. Equation (36.39) gives an expression for the (asymptotic) variance of our estimate: $\mathbb{E}[\phi(\mathbf{X}_i; \hat{Q}, \hat{g}, \hat{\tau})^2]/n$. Notice that $\phi(\mathbf{X}_i; \hat{Q}, \hat{g}, \hat{\tau})^2$ involves terms that are proportional to $1/g(X)$ and $1/(1 - g(X))$. Accordingly, the variance of our estimator will balloon if there are units where $g(x) \approx 0$ or $g(x) \approx 1$ (unless such units are rare enough that they don't contribute much to the expectation).

In practice, a simple way to deal with potential overlap violation is to fit a model $\hat{g}$ for the treatment assignment probability — which we need to do anyways — and check that the values $\hat{g}(x)$ are not too extreme. In the case that some values are too extreme, the simplest resolution is to cheat. We can simply exclude all the data with extreme values of $\hat{g}(x)$. This is equivalent to considering the average treatment effect over only the subpopulation where overlap is satisfied. This changes the interpretation of the estimand. The restricted subpopulation ATE may or may not provide a satisfactory answer to the real-world problem at hand, and this needs to be justified based on knowledge of the real-world problem.

36.4.5.3   Choice of estimand and average treatment effect on the treated

Usually, our goal in estimating a causal effect is qualitative. We want to know what the sign of the effect is, and whether it's large or small. The utility of the ATE is that it provides a concrete query we can use to get a handle on the qualitative question. However, it is not sacrosanct; sometimes we're better off choosing an alternative causal estimand that still answers the qualitative question but which is easier to estimate statistically. The **average treatment effect on the treated** or **ATT**,

$$\text{ATT} \triangleq \mathbb{E}_{X|A=1}[\mathbb{E}[Y|X, \text{do}(A = 1)] - E[Y|X, \text{do}(A = 0)]], \tag{36.43}$$

is one such an estimand that is frequently useful.

The ATT is useful when many members of the population are very unlikely to receive treatment, but the treated units had a reasonably high probability of receiving the control. This can happen if, e.g., we sample control units from the general population, but the treatment units all self-selected into treatment from a smaller subpopulation. In this case, it's not possible to (non-parametrically) determine the treatment effect for the control units where no similar unit took treatment. The ATT solves this obstacle by simply omitting such units from the average.

If we have the causal structure Figure 36.3, and the overlap condition $P(A = 1|X = x) < 1$ for all $X = x$ then the ATT is causally identified as

$$\tau^{\text{ATT}} = \mathbb{E}_{X|A=1}[\mathbb{E}[Y|A = 1, X] - E[Y|A = 0, X]]. \tag{36.44}$$

Note that the required overlap condition here is weaker than for identifying the ATE. (The proof is the same as Theorem 2.)

The estimation strategies for the ATE translate readily to estimation strategies for the ATT. Namely, estimate the nuisance functions the same way and then simply replace averages over all datapoints by averages over the treated datapoints only. In principle, it's possible to do a little better than this by making use of the untreated datapoints as well. A corresponding double machine learning estimator is

$$\hat{\tau}^{\text{ATT}-\text{AIPTW}} \triangleq \frac{1}{n} \sum_i \frac{A_i}{P(A = 1)} (Y - \hat{Q}(0, X_i)) - \frac{(1 - A_i)g(X)}{P(A = 1)(1 - g(X))} (Y - \hat{Q}(0, X_i)). \tag{36.45}$$

. The variance of this estimator can be estimated by

$$\phi^{\text{ATT}}(\mathbf{X}_i; Q, g, \tau) \triangleq \frac{1}{n} \sum_i \left[\frac{A_i}{P(A = 1)} (Y - \hat{Q}(0, X_i)) \right.$$

$$\left. - \frac{(1 - A_i)g(X)}{P(A = 1)(1 - g(X))} (Y - \hat{Q}(0, X_i) - \frac{A\tau}{P(A = 1)} \right] \tag{36.46}$$

$$\hat{\mathbb{V}}[\hat{\tau}^{\text{ATT}-\text{AIPTW}}] \triangleq \frac{1}{n} \sum_i \phi^{\text{ATT}}(\mathbf{X}_i; \hat{Q}, \hat{g}, \hat{\tau}^{\text{ATT}-\text{AIPTW}}). \tag{36.47}$$

Notice that the estimator for the ATT doesn't require estimating $Q(1, X)$. This can be a considerable advantage when the treated units are rare. See Chernozhukov et al. [Che+17e] for details.

36.4.6 Summary and practical advice

We have seen a number of estimators that follow the general procedure:

1. Fit statistical or machine-learning models $\hat{Q}(a, x)$ as a predictor for Y, and/or $\hat{g}(x)$ as a predictor for A

2. Compute the predictions $\hat{Q}(0, x_i), \hat{Q}(1, x_i), \hat{g}(x_i)$ for each datapoint, and

3. Combine these predictions into an estimate of the average treatment effect.

Importantly, no single estimation approach is a silver bullet. For example, the double machine-learning estimator has appealing theoretical properties, such as asymptotic efficiency guarantees and a recipe for estimating uncertainty without needing to bootstrap the model fitting. However, in terms of the quality of point estimates, the double ML estimators can sometimes underperform their more naive counterparts [KS07]. In fact, there are cases where each of outcome regression, propensity weighting, or doubly robust methods will outperform the others.

One difficulty in choosing an estimator in practice is that there are fewer guardrails in causal inference than there are in standard predictive modeling. In predictive modeling, we construct a train-test split and validate our prediction models using the true labels or outcomes in the held-out dataset. However, for causal problems, the causal estimands are functionals of a different data-generating process from the one that we actually observed. As a result, it is impossible to empirically validate many aspects of causal estimation using standard techniques.

The effectiveness of a given approach is often determined by how much we trust the specification of our propensity score or outcome regression models $\hat{g}(x)$ and $\hat{Q}(a, x)$, and how well the treatment and control groups overlap in the dataset. Using flexible models for the nuisance functions g and Q can alleviate some of the concerns about model misspecification, but our freedom to use such models is often constrained by dataset size. When we have the luxury of large data, we can use flexible models; on the other hand, when the dataset is relatively small, we may need to use a smaller parametric family or stringent regularization to obtain stable estimates of Q and g. Similarly, if overlap is poor in some regions of the covariate space, then flexible models for Q may be highly variable, and inverse propensity score weights may be large. In these cases, IPTW or AIPTW estimates may fluctuate wildly as a function of large weights. Meanwhile, outcome regression estimates will be sensitive to the specification of the Q model and its regularization, and can incur bias that is difficult to measure if the specification or regularization does not match the true outcome process.

There are a number of practical steps that we can take to sanity-check causal estimates. The simplest check is to compute many different ATE estimators (e.g., outcome regression, IPTW, doubly robust) using several comparably complex estimators of Q and g. We can then check whether they agree, at least qualitatively. If they do agree then this can provide some peace of mind (although it is not a guarantee of accuracy). If they disagree, caution is warranted, particularly in choosing the specification of the Q and g models.

It is also important to check for failures of overlap. Often, issues such as disagreement between alternative estimators can be traced back to poor overlap. A common way to do this, particularly with high-dimensional data, is to examine the estimated (ideally cross-fitted) propensity scores $\hat{g}(x_i)$. This is a useful diagnostic, even if the intention is to use an outcome regression approach that only incorporates and estimated outcome regression function $\hat{Q}(a, x_i)$. If overlap issues are relevant, it may be better to instead estimate either the average treatment effect on the treated, or the "trimmed" estimand given by discarding units with extreme propensities.

Uncertainty quantification is also an essential part of most causal analyses. This frequently takes the form of an estimate of the estimator's variance, or a confidence interval. This may be important for downstream decision-making, and can also be a useful diagnostic. We can calculate variance either by bootstrapping the entire procedure (including refitting the models in each bootstrap replicate), or computing analytical variance estimates from the AIPTW estimator. Generally, large variance estimates may indicate issues with the analysis. For example, poor overlap will often (although not always) manifest as extremely large variances under either of these methods. Small variance estimates should be treated with caution, unless other checks, such as overlap checks, or stability across different Q and g models, also pass.

The previous advice only addresses the statistical problem of estimating τ from a data sample. It does not speak to whether or not τ can reasonably be interpreted as an average treatment effect. Considerable care should be devoted to whether or not the assumption that there are no unobserved confounders is reasonable. There are several methods for assessing the sensitivity of the ATE estimate to violations of this assumption. See Section 36.7. Bias due to unobserved confounding can be substantial in practice—often overwhelming bias due to estimation error—so it is wise to conduct such an analysis.

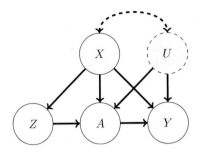

Figure 36.5: Causal graph illustrating the instrumental variable setup. The treatment A and outcome Y are both influenced by unobserved confounder U. Nevertheless, identification is sometimes possible due to the presence of the instrument Z. We also allow for observed covariates X that we may need to adjust for. The dashed arrow between U and X indicates a statistical dependency where we remain agnostic to the particular causal relationship.

36.5 Instrumental variable strategies

Adjustment-based methods rely on observing all confounders affecting the treatment and outcome. In some situations, it is possible to identify interesting causal effects even when there are unobserved confounders. We now consider strategies based on **instrumental variables**. The instrumental variable graph is shown in Figure 36.5. The key ingredient is the instrumental variable Z, a variable that has a causal effect on Y only through its causal effect on A. Informally, the identification strategy is to determine to the causal effect of Z on Y, the causal effect of Z on A, and then combine these into an estimate of the causal effect of A on Y.

For this identification to strategy to work the instrument must satisfy three conditions. There are observed variables (confounders) X such that:

1. **Instrument relevance** $Z \not\perp A|X$: the instrument must actually affect the treatment assignment.

2. **Instrument unconfoundedness** Any backdoor path between Z and Y is blocked by X, even conditional on A.

3. **Exclusion restriction** All directed paths from Z to Y pass through A. That is, the instrument affects the outcome *only* through its effect on A.

(It may help conceptually to first think through the case where X is the empty set — i.e., where the only confounder is the unobserved U). These assumptions are necessary for using instrumental variables for causal identification, but they are not quite sufficient. In practice, they must be supplemented by an additional assumption that depends more closely on the details of the problem at hand. Historically, this additional assumption was usually that both the instrument-treatment and treatment-outcome relationships are linear. We'll examine some less restrictive alternatives below.

Before moving on to how to use instrumental variables for identification, let's consider how we might encounter instruments in practice. The key is that its often possible to find, and measure, variables that affect treatment and that are assigned (as if) at random. For example, suppose we are interested in measuring the effect of taking a drug A on some health outcome Y. The challenge is that whether a study participant actually takes the drug can be confounded with Y—e.g., sicker people may be more likely to take their medication, but have worse outcomes. However, the assignment of treatments to patients can be randomized and this random assignment can be viewed as an instrument. This **random assignment with non-compliance** scenario is common in practice. The random assignment — the instrument — satisfies relevance (so long as assigning the drug affects the probability of the patient taking the drug). It also satisfies unconfoundedness (because the instrument is randomized). And, it plausibly satisfies exclusion restriction: telling (or not telling) a patient to take a drug has no effect on their health outcome except through influencing whether or not they actually take the drug. As a second example, the **judge fixed effects** research design uses the identity of the judge assigned to each criminal case to infer the effect of incarceration on some life outcome of interest (e.g., total lifetime earnings). Relevance will be satisfied so long as different judges have different propensities to hand out severe sentences. The assignment of trial judges to cases is randomized, so unconfoundedness will also be satisfied. And, exclusion restriction is also plausible: the particular identity of the judge assigned to your case has no bearing on your years-later life outcomes, except through the particular sentence that you're subjected to.

It's important to note that these assumptions require some care, particularly exclusion restriction. Relevance can be checked directly from the data, by fitting a model to predict the treatment from the instrument (or vice versa). Unconfoundedness is often satisfied by design: the instrument is randomly assigned. Even when literal random assignment doesn't hold, we often restrict to instruments where unconfoundedness is "obviously" satisfied — e.g., using number of rainy days in a month as an instrument for sun exposure. Exclusion restriction is trickier. For example, it might fail in the drug assignment case if patients who are not told to take a drug respond by seeking out alternative treatment. Or, it might fail in the judge fixed effects case if judges hand out additional, unrecorded, punishments in addition to incarceration. Assessing the plausibility of exclusion restriction requires careful consideration based on domain expertise.

We now return to the question of how to make use of an instrument once we have it in hand. As previously mentioned, getting causal identification using instrumental variables requires supplementing the IV assumptions with some additional assumption about the causal process.

36.5.1 Additive unobserved confounding

We first consider **additive unobserved confounding**. That is, we assume that the structural caual model for the outcome has the form:[7]

$$Y \leftarrow f(A, X) + f_U(U). \tag{36.48}$$

In words, we assume that there are no interaction effects between the treatment and the unobserved confounder — everyone responds to treatment in the same way. With this additional assumption, we see that $\mathbb{E}[Y|X, \mathrm{do}(A = a)] - \mathbb{E}[Y|X, \mathrm{do}(A = a')] = f(a, X) - f(a', X)$. In this setting, our goal is to learn this contrast.

Theorem 3 (Additive confounding identification). *If the instrumental variables assumptions hold and also additive unobserved confounding holds, then there is a function $\tilde{f}(a, x)$ where*

$$\mathbb{E}[Y|x, \mathrm{do}(A = a)] - \mathbb{E}[Y|x, \mathrm{do}(A = a')] = \tilde{f}(a, x) - \tilde{f}(a', x), \tag{36.49}$$

---

7. We roll the unit-specific variables ξ into U to avoid notational overload.

for all x, a, a' and such that $\tilde{f}$ satisfies

$$\mathbb{E}[Y|z, x] = \int \tilde{f}(a, x) p(a|z, x) \mathrm{d}a. \tag{36.50}$$

Here, $p(a|z, x)$ is the conditional probability density of treatment.

In particular, if there is a unique function g that satisfies

$$\mathbb{E}[Y|z, x] = \int g(a, x) p(a|z, x) \mathrm{d}a, \tag{36.51}$$

then $g = \tilde{f}$ and this relation identifies the target causal effect.

Before giving the proof, lets understand the point of this identification result. The key insight is that both the left hand side of Equation (36.51) and $p(a|z, x)$ (appearing in the integrand) are identified by the data, since they involve only observational relationships between observed variables. So, $\tilde{f}$ is identified implicitly as one of the functions that makes Equation (36.51) true. If there is a unique such function, then this fully identifies the causal effect.

Proof. With the additive unobserved confounding assumption, the instrument unconfoundedness implies that $U \perp\!\!\!\perp Z|X$. Then, we have that:

$$\mathbb{E}[Y|Z, X] = \mathbb{E}[f(A, X)|Z, X] + \mathbb{E}[f_U(U)|Z, X] \tag{36.52}$$
$$= \mathbb{E}[f(A, X)|Z, X] + \mathbb{E}[f_U(U)|X] \tag{36.53}$$
$$= \mathbb{E}[\tilde{f}(A, X)|Z, X], \tag{36.54}$$

where $\tilde{f} = f(A, X) + \mathbb{E}[f_U(U)|X]$. Now, identifying just $\tilde{f}$ would suffice for us, because we could then identify contrasts between treatements: $f(a, x) - f(a', x) = \tilde{f}(a, x) - \tilde{f}(a', x)$. (The term $\mathbb{E}[f_U(U)|x]$ cancels out). Accordingly, we rewrite Equation (36.54) as:

$$\mathbb{E}[Y|z, x] = \int \tilde{f}(a, x) p(a|z, x) \mathrm{d}a. \tag{36.55}$$

$\square$

It's worth dwelling briefly on how the IV assumptions come into play here. The exclusion restriction is implied by the additive unobserved confounding assumption, which we use explicilty. We also use the unconfoundedness assumption to conclude $U \perp\!\!\!\perp Z|X$. However, we do not use relevance. The role of relevance here is in ensuring that few functions solve the relation Equation (36.51). Informally, the solution g is constrained by the requirement that it hold for all values of Z. However, different values of Z only add non-trivial constraints if $p(a|z, x)$ differ depending on the value of z — this is exactly the relevance condition.

Estimation The basic estimation strategy is to fit models for $\mathbb{E}[Y|z, x]$ and $p(a|z, x)$ from the data, and then solve the implicit equation Equation (36.51) to find g consistent with the fitted models. The procedures for doing this can vary considerably depending on the particulars of the data (e.g., if Z is discrete or continuous) and the choice of modeling strategy. We omit a detailed discussion, but see e.g., [NP03; Dar+11; Har+17; SSG19; BKS19; Mua+20; Dik+20] for various concrete approaches.

It's also worth mentioning an additional nuance to the general procedure. Even if relevance holds, there will often be more than one function that satisfies Equation (36.51). So, we have only identified $\tilde{f}$ as a member of this set of functions. In practice, this ambiguity is defeated by making some additional structural assumption about $\tilde{f}$. For example, we model $\tilde{f}$ with a neural network, and then choose the network satisfying Equation (36.51) that has minimum $l2$-norm on the parameters (i.e., we pick the $l2$-regularized solution).

36.5.2   Instrument monotonicity and local average treatment effect

We now consider an alternative assumption to additive unobserved confounding that is applicable when both the instrument and treatment are binary. It will be convenient to conceptualize the instrument as assignment-to-treatment. Then, the population divides into four subpopulations:

1. Compliers, who take the treatment if assigned to it, and who don't take the treatment otherwise.

2. Always takers, who take the treatment no matter their assignment.

3. Never takers, who refuse the treatment no matter their assignment.

4. Defiers, who refuse the treatment if assigned to it, and who take the treatment if not assigned.

Our goal in this setting will be to identify the average treatment effect among the compliers. The **local average treatment effect** (or **complier average treatment effect**) is defined to be[8]

$$\text{LATE} = \mathbb{E}[Y|\text{do}(A=1), \text{complier}] - \mathbb{E}[Y|\text{do}(A=0), \text{complier}]. \tag{36.56}$$

The LATE requires an additional assumption for identification. Namely, **instrument monotonicity**: being assigned (not assigned) the treatment only increases (decreases) the probability that each unit will take the treatment. Equivalently, $P(\text{defier}) = 0$.

We can then write down the identification result.

Theorem 4. *Given the instrumental variable assumptions and instrument monotonicty, the local average treatment is identified as a parameter τ^{LATE} of the observational distributional; that is,* LATE $= \tau^{\text{LATE}}$. *Namely,*

$$\tau^{\text{LATE}} = \frac{\mathbb{E}[\mathbb{E}[Y|X, Z=1] - \mathbb{E}[Y|X, Z=0]]}{\mathbb{E}[P(A=1|X, Z=1) - P(A=1|X, Z=0)]}. \tag{36.57}$$

Proof. We now show that, given the IV assumptions and monotonicity, LATE $= \tau^{\text{LATE}}$. First, notice that

$$\tau^{\text{LATE}} = \frac{\mathbb{E}[Y|\text{do}(Z=1)] - \mathbb{E}[Y|\text{do}(Z=0)]}{P(A=1|\text{do}(Z=1)) - P(A=1|\text{do}(Z=0))}. \tag{36.58}$$

This follows from backdoor adjustment, Theorem 2, applied to the numerator and denominator separately. Our strategy will be to decompose $\mathbb{E}[Y|\text{do}(Z=z)]$ into the contributions from the

---

8. We follow the econometrics literature in using "LATE" because "CATE" is already commonly used for conditional average treatment effect.

compliers, the units that ignore the instrument (the always/never takers), and the defiers. To that end, note that $P(\text{complier}|\text{do}(Z = z)) = P(\text{complier})$ and similarly for always/never takers and defiers — interventions on the instrument don't change the composition of the population. Then,

$$\mathbb{E}[Y|\text{do}(Z = 1)] - \mathbb{E}[Y|\text{do}(Z = 1)] \tag{36.59}$$

$$= \big(\mathbb{E}[Y|\text{complier}, \text{do}(Z = 1)] - \mathbb{E}[Y|\text{complier}, \text{do}(Z = 0)]\big)\,P(\text{complier}) \tag{36.60}$$

$$+ \big(\mathbb{E}[Y|\text{always/never}, \text{do}(Z = 1)] - \mathbb{E}[Y|\text{always/never}, \text{do}(Z = 0)]\big)\,P(\text{always/never}) \tag{36.61}$$

$$+ \big(\mathbb{E}[Y|\text{defier}, \text{do}(Z = 1)] - \mathbb{E}[Y|\text{defier}, \text{do}(Z = 0)]\big)\,P(\text{defier}). \tag{36.62}$$

The key is the effect on the complier subpopulation, Equation (36.60). First, by definition of the complier population, we have that:

$$\mathbb{E}[Y|\text{complier}, \text{do}(Z = z)] = \mathbb{E}[Y|\text{complier}, \text{do}(A = z)]. \tag{36.63}$$

That is, the causal effect of the treatment is the same as the causal effect of the instrument in this subpopulation — this is the core reason why access to an instrument allows identification of the local average treatment effect. This means that

$$\text{LATE} = \mathbb{E}[Y|\text{complier}, \text{do}(Z = 1)] - \mathbb{E}[Y|\text{complier}, \text{do}(Z = 0)]. \tag{36.64}$$

Further, we have that $P(\text{complier}) = P(A = 1|\text{do}(Z = 1)) - P(A = 1|\text{do}(Z = 0))$. The reason is simply that, by definition of the subpopulations,

$$P(A = 1|\text{do}(Z = 1)) = P(\text{complier}) + P(\text{always taker}) \tag{36.65}$$

$$P(A = 1|\text{do}(Z = 0)) = P(\text{always taker}). \tag{36.66}$$

Now, plugging the expression for $P(\text{complier})$ and Equation (36.64) into Equation (36.60) we have that:

$$\big(\mathbb{E}[Y|\text{complier}, \text{do}(Z = 1)] - \mathbb{E}[Y|\text{complier}, \text{do}(Z = 0)]\big)\,P(\text{complier}) \tag{36.67}$$

$$= \text{LATE} \times \big(P(A = 1|\text{do}(Z = 1)) - P(A = 1|\text{do}(Z = 0))\big) \tag{36.68}$$

This gives us an expression for the local average treatment effect in terms of the effect of the instrument on the compliers and the probability that a unit takes the treatment when assigned/not-assigned.

The next step is to show that the remaining instrument effect decomposition terms, Equations (36.61) and (36.62), are both 0. Equation (36.61) is the causal effect of the instrument on the always/never takers. It's equal to 0 because, by definition of this subpopulation, the instrument has no causal effect in the subpopulation — they ignore the instrument! Mathematically, this is just $\mathbb{E}[Y|\text{always/never}, \text{do}(Z = 1)] = \mathbb{E}[Y|\text{always/never}, \text{do}(Z = 0)]$. Finally, Equation (36.62) is 0 by the instrument monotonicity assumption: we assumed that $P(\text{defier}) = 0$.

In totality, we now have that Equations (36.60) to (36.62) reduces to:

$$\mathbb{E}[Y|\text{do}(Z = 1)] - \mathbb{E}[Y|\text{do}(Z = 1)] \tag{36.69}$$

$$= \text{LATE} \times \big(P(A = 1|\text{do}(Z = 1)) - P(A = 1|\text{do}(Z = 0))\big) + 0 + 0 \tag{36.70}$$

Rearranging for LATE and plugging in to Equation (36.58) gives the claimed identification result. $\qquad\square$

36.5.2.1 Estimation

For estimating the local average treatment effect under the monotone instrument assumption, there is a double-machine learning approach that works with generic supervised learning approaches. Here, we want an estimator $\hat{\tau}^{\text{LATE}}$ for the parameter

$$\tau^{\text{LATE}} = \frac{\mathbb{E}[\mathbb{E}[Y|X, Z = 1] - \mathbb{E}[Y|X, Z = 0]]}{\mathbb{E}[\text{P}(A = 1|X, Z = 1) - \text{P}(A = 1|X, Z = 0)]}. \tag{36.71}$$

To define the estimator, it's convenient to introduce some additional notation. First, we define the nuisance functions:

$$\mu(z, x) = \mathbb{E}[Y|z, x] \tag{36.72}$$

$$m(z, x) = \text{P}(A = 1|x, z) \tag{36.73}$$

$$p(x) = \text{P}(Z = 1|x). \tag{36.74}$$

We also define the score ϕ by:

$$\phi_{Z \to Y}(\mathbf{X}; \mu, p) \triangleq \mu(1, X) - \mu(0, X) + \frac{Z(Y - \mu(1, X))}{p(X)} - \frac{(1 - Z)(Y - \mu(0, X))}{1 - p(X)} \tag{36.75}$$

$$\phi_{Z \to A}(\mathbf{X}; m, p) \triangleq m(1, X) - m(0, X) + \frac{Z(A - m(1, X))}{p(X)} - \frac{(1 - Z)(A - m(0, X))}{1 - p(X)} \tag{36.76}$$

$$\phi(\mathbf{X}; \mu, m, p, \tau) \triangleq \phi_{Z \to Y}(\mathbf{X}; \mu, p) - \phi_{Z \to A}(\mathbf{X}; m, p) \times \tau \tag{36.77}$$

Then, the estimator is defined by a two stage procedure:

1. Fit models $\hat{\mu}, \hat{m}, \hat{p}$ for each of μ, m, p (using supervised machine learning).

2. Define $\hat{\tau}^{\text{LATE}}$ as the solution to $\frac{1}{n} \sum_i \phi(\mathbf{X}_i; \hat{\mu}, \hat{m}, \hat{p}, \hat{\tau}^{\text{LATE}}) = 0$. That is,

$$\hat{\tau}^{\text{LATE}} = \frac{\frac{1}{n} \sum_i \phi_{Z \to Y}(\mathbf{X}_i; \hat{\mu}, \hat{p})}{\frac{1}{n} \sum_i \phi_{Z \to A}(\mathbf{X}_i; \hat{m}, \hat{p})} \tag{36.78}$$

It may help intuitions to notice that the double machine learning estimator of the LATE is effectively the double machine learning estimator of of the average treatment effect of Z on Y divided by the double machine learning estimator of the average treatment effect of Z on A.

Similarly to Section 36.4, the nuisance functions can be estimated by:

1. Fit a model $\hat{\mu}$ that predicts Y from Z, X by minimizing mean square error.

2. Fit a model $\hat{m}$ that predicts A from Z, X by minimizing mean cross-entropy.

3. Fit a model $\hat{p}$ that predicts Z from X by minimizing mean cross-entropy.

As in Section 36.4, reusing the same data for model fitting and computing the estimator can potentially cause problems. This can be avoided with use a cross-fitting procedure as described in Section 36.4.2.4. In this case, we split the data into K folds and, for each fold k, use all the but the k'th fold to compute estimates $\hat{\mu}_{-k}, \hat{m}_{-k}, \hat{p}_{-k}$ of the nuisance parameters. Then we compute the nuisance estimates for each datapoint i in fold k by predicting the required quantity using the nuisance model fit on the other folds. That is, if unit i is in fold k, we compute $\hat{\mu}(z_i, x_i) \triangleq \hat{\mu}^{-k}(z_i, x_i)$ and so forth.

The key result is that if we use the cross-fit version of the estimator and the estimators for the nuisance functions converge to their true values in the sense that

1. $\mathbb{E}(\hat{\mu}(Z, X) - \mu(Z, X))^2 \to 0$, $\mathbb{E}(\hat{m}(Z, X) - m(Z, X))^2 \to 0$, and $\mathbb{E}(\hat{p}(X) - p(X))^2 \to 0$

2. $\sqrt{\mathbb{E}[(\hat{p}(X) - p(X))^2]} \times \left(\sqrt{\mathbb{E}[(\hat{\mu}(Z, X) - \mu(Z, X))^2]} + \sqrt{\mathbb{E}[(\hat{m}(Z, X) - m(Z, X))^2]} \right) = o(\sqrt{n})$

then (with some omitted technical conditions) we have asymptotic normality at the $\sqrt{n}$-rate:

$$\sqrt{n}(\hat{\tau}^{\mathrm{LATE-cf}} - \tau^{\mathrm{LATE}}) \xrightarrow{d} \mathrm{Normal}(0, \frac{\mathbb{E}[\phi(\mathbf{X}; \mu, m, p, \tau^{\mathrm{LATE}})^2]}{\mathbb{E}[m(1, X) - m(0, X)]^2}). \tag{36.79}$$

As with double machine learning for the confounder adjustment strategy, the key point here is that we can achieve the (optimal) $\sqrt{n}$ rate for estimating the LATE under a relatively weak condition on how well we estimate the nuisance functions — what matters is the *product* of the error in p and the errors in μ, m. So, for example, a very good model for how the instrument is assigned (p) can make up for errors in the estimation of the treatment-assignment (m) and outcome (μ) models.

The double machine learning estimator also gives a recipe for quantifying uncertainty. To that end, define

$$\hat{\tau}_{Z \to A} \triangleq \frac{1}{n} \sum_i \phi_{Z \to A}(\mathbf{X}_i; \hat{m}, \hat{p}) \tag{36.80}$$

$$\hat{\mathbb{V}}[\hat{\tau}^{\mathrm{LATE}}] \triangleq \frac{1}{\hat{\tau}_{Z \to A}^2} \frac{1}{n} \sum_i \phi(\mathbf{X}_i; \hat{\mu}, \hat{m}, \hat{p}, \hat{\tau}^{\mathrm{LATE}})^2. \tag{36.81}$$

Then, subject to suitable technical conditions, $\hat{\mathbb{V}}[\hat{\tau}^{\mathrm{LATE-cf}}]$ can be used as an estimate of the variance of the estimator. More precisely,

$$\sqrt{n}(\hat{\tau}^{\mathrm{LATE}} - \tau^{\mathrm{LATE}}) \xrightarrow{d} \mathrm{Normal}(0, \hat{\mathbb{V}}[\hat{\tau}^{\mathrm{LATE}}]). \tag{36.82}$$

Then, confidence intervals or p-values can be computed using this variance in the usual way. The main extra condition required for the variance estimator to be valid is that the nuisance parameters must all converge at rate $O(n^{-1/4})$ (so an excellent estimator for one can't fully compensate for terrible estimators of the others). In fact, even this condition is unnecessary in certain special cases — e.g., when p is known exactly, which occurs when the instrument is randomly assigned. See Chernozhukov et al. [Che+17e] for technical details.

36.5.3 Two stage least squares

Commonly, the IV assumptions are supplemented with the following linear model assumptions:

$$A_i \leftarrow \alpha_0 + \alpha Z_i + \delta_A X_i + \gamma_A X_i + \xi_i^A \tag{36.83}$$

$$Y_i \leftarrow \beta_0 + \beta A_i + \delta_Y X_i + \gamma_Y X_i + \xi_i^Y \tag{36.84}$$

That is, we assume that the real-world process for treatment assignment and the outcome are both linear. In this case, plugging Equation (36.83) into Equation (36.84) yields

$$Y_i \leftarrow \tilde{\beta}_0 + \beta\alpha Z_i + \tilde{\delta}X_i + \tilde{\gamma}X_i + \tilde{\xi}_i. \tag{36.85}$$

The point is that β, the average treatment effect of A on Y, is equal to the coefficient $\beta\alpha$ of the instrument in the outcome-instrument model divided by the coefficient α of the instrument in the treatment-instrument model. So, to estimate the treatment effect, we simply fit both linear models and divide the estimated coefficients. This procedure is called **two stage least squares**.

The simplicity of this procedure is seductive. However, the required linearity assumptions are hard to satisfy in practice and frequently lead to severe issues. A particularly pernicious version of this is that linear-model misspecfication together with weak relevance can yield standard errors for the estimate that are far too small. In practice, this can lead us to find large, significant estimates from two stage least squares when the truth is actually a weak or null effect. See [Rei16; You19; ASS19; Lal+21] for critical evaluations of two stage least squares in practice.

36.6 Difference in differences

Unsurprisingly, time plays an important role in causality. Causes precede effects, and we should be able to incorporate this knowledge into causal identification. We now turn to a particular strategy for causal identification that relies on observing each unit at multiple time points. Data of this kind is sometimes called **panel data**. We'll consider the simplest case. There are two time periods. In the first period, none of the units are treated, and we observe an outcome Y_{0i} for each unit. Then, a subset of the units are treated, denoted by $A_i = 1$. In the second time period, we again observe the outcomes Y_{1i} for each unit, where now the outcomes of the treated units are affected by the treatment. Our goal is to determine the average effect receiving the treatment had on the treated units. That is, we want to know the average difference between the outcomes we actually observed for the treated units, and the outcomes we would have observed on those same units if they had not been treated. The general strategy we look at is called **difference in differences**.[9]

As a concrete motivating example, consider trying to determine the effect raising minimum wage on employment. The concern here is that, in an efficient labor market, increasing the price of workers will reduce the demand for them, thereby driving down employment. As such, it seems increasing minimum wage may hurt the people the policy is nominally intended to help. The question is: how strong is this effect in practice? Card and Krueger [CK94a] studied this effect using difference in differences. The Philadelphia metropolitan area includes regions in both Pennsylvania and New Jersey (different US states). On April 1st 1992, New Jersey raised its minimum wage from \$4.25 to \$5.05. In Pennsylvania, the wage remained constant at \$4.25. The strategy is to collect employment data from fast food restaurants (which pay many employees minimum wage) in each state before and after the change in minimum wage. In this case, for restaurant i, we have Y_{0i}, the number of full time employees in February 1992, and Y_{1i}, the number of full time employees in November 1992. The treatment is simply $A_i = 1$ if the restaurant was located in New Jersey, and $A_i = 0$ if located in Pennsylvania. Our goal is to estimate the average effect of the minimum wage hike on employment in the restaurants affected by it (i.e., the ones in New Jersey).

---

9. See github.com/vveitch/causality-tutorials/blob/main/difference_in_differences.ipynb.

The assumption in classical difference-in-differences is the following structural equation:

$$Y_{ti} \leftarrow W_i + S_t + \tau A_i \mathbb{I}(t = 1) + \xi_{ti}, \tag{36.86}$$

with $\mathbb{E}[\xi_{ti}|W_i, S_t, A_i] = 0$. Here, W_i is a unit specific effect that is constant across time (e.g., the location of the restuarant or competence of the management) and S_t is a time-specific effect that applies to all units (e.g., the state of the US economy at each time). Both of these quantities are treated as unobserved, and not explicitly accounted for. The parameter τ captures the target causal effect. The (strong) assumption here is that unit, time, and treatment effects are all additive. This assumption is called **parallel trends**, because it is equivalent to assuming that, in the absence of treatment, the trend over time would be the same in both groups. It's easy to see that under this assumption, we have:

$$\tau = \mathbb{E}[Y_{1i} - Y_{0i}|A = 1] - \mathbb{E}[Y_{1i} - Y_{0i}|A = 0]. \tag{36.87}$$

That is, the estimand first computes the difference across time for both the treated and untreated group, and then computes the difference between these differences across the groups. The obvious estimator is then

$$\hat{\tau} = \frac{1}{n_A} \sum_{i:A_i=1} Y_{1i} - Y_{0i} - \frac{1}{n - n_A} \sum_{i:A_i=0} Y_{1i} - Y_{0i}, \tag{36.88}$$

where n_A is the number of treated units.

The root identification problem addressed by difference-in-differences is that $\mathbb{E}[W_i|A_i = 1] \neq \mathbb{E}[W_i|A_i = 0]$. That is, restaurants in New Jersey may be systematically different from restuarants in Pennsylvania in unobserved ways that affect employment.[10] This is why we can't simply compare average outcomes for the treated and untreated. The identification assumption is that this unit-specific effect is the only source of statistical association with treatment; in particular we assume the time-specific effect has no such issue: $\mathbb{E}[S_{1i} - S_{0i}|A_i = 1] = \mathbb{E}[S_{1i} - S_{0i}|A_i = 0]$. Unfortunately, this assumption can be too strong. For instance, administrative data shows employment in Pennsylvania falling relative to employment in New Jersey between 1993 and 1996 [AP08, §5.2]. Although this doesn't directly contradict the parallel trends assumption used for indentification, which needs to hold only in 1992, it does make it seem less credible.

To weaken the assumption, we'll look at a version that requires parallel trends to hold only after adjusting for covariates. To motivate this, we note that there were several different types of fast food restaurant included in the employment data. These vary, e.g., in the type of food they serve, and in cost per meal. Now, it seems reasonable the trend in employment may depend on the type of restuarant. For example, more expensive chains (such as KFC) might be more affected by recessions than cheaper chains (such as McDonald's). If expensive chains are more common in New Jersey than in Pennsylvania, this effect can create a violation of parallel trends — if there's recession affecting both states, we'd expect employment to go down more in New Jersey than in Pennsylvania. However, we may find it credible that McDonald's restaurants in New Jersey have the same trend as McDonald's in Pennsylvania, and similarly for KFC.

---

10. This is similar to the issue that arises from unobserved confounding, except W_i need not be a cause of the treatment assignment.

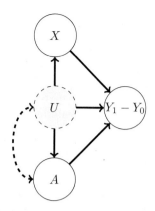

Figure 36.6: Causal graph assumed for the difference-in-differences setting. Here, the outcome of interest is the difference between the pre- and post-treatment period, $Y_1 - Y_0$. This difference is influenced by the treatment, unobserved factors U, and observed covariates X. The dashed arrow between U and A indicates a statistical dependency between the variables, but where we remain agnostic to the precise causal mechanism. For example, in the minimum wage example, U might be the average income in restaurant's neighbourhood, which is dependent on the state, and hence also the treatment.

The next step is to give a definition of the target causal effect that doesn't depend on a parametric model, and a non-parametric statement of the identification assumption to go with it. In words, the causal estimand will be the average treatment effect on the units that received the treatment. To make sense of this mathematically, we'll introduce a new piece of notation:

$$\mathrm{P}^{A=1}(Y|\mathrm{do}(A=a)) \triangleq \int \mathrm{P}(Y|A=a, \text{parents of } Y)\mathrm{dP}(\text{parents of } Y|A=1) \tag{36.89}$$

$$\mathbb{E}^{A=1}[Y|\mathrm{do}(A=a)] \triangleq \mathbb{E}_{\mathrm{P}^{A=1}(Y|\mathrm{do}(A=a))}[Y]. \tag{36.90}$$

In words: recall that the ordinary do operator works by replacing $\mathrm{P}(\text{parents}|A=a)$ by the marginal distribution $\mathrm{P}(\text{parents})$, thereby breaking the backdoor associations. Now, we're replacing the distribution $\mathrm{P}(\text{parents}|A=a)$ by $\mathrm{P}(\text{parents}|A=1)$, irrespective of the actual treatment value. This still breaks all backdoor associations, but is a better match for our target of estimating the treatment effect only among the treated units.

To formalize a causal estimand using the do-calculus, we need to assume some partial causal structure. We'll use the graph in Figure 36.6. With this in hand, our causal estimand is the average treatment effect on the units that received the treatment, namely:

$$\mathrm{ATT}^{\mathrm{DiD}} = \mathbb{E}^{A=1}[Y_1 - Y_0|\mathrm{do}(A=1)] - \mathbb{E}^{A=1}[Y_1 - Y_0|\mathrm{do}(A=0)]] \tag{36.91}$$

In the minimum wage example, this is the average effect of the minimum wage hike on employment in the restaurants affected by it (i.e., the ones in New Jersey).

Finally, we formalize the identification assumption that, conditional on X, the trends in the treated and untreated groups are the same. The **conditional parallel trends** assumption is:

$$\mathbb{E}^{A=1}[Y_1 - Y_0|X, \mathrm{do}(A=0)] = \mathbb{E}[Y_1 - Y_0|X, A=0]. \tag{36.92}$$

In words, this says that for treated units with covariates X, the trend we would have seen had we not assigned treatment is the same as the trend we actually saw for the untreated units with covariates X. That is, if New Jersey had not raised its minimum wage, then McDonald's in New Jersey would have the same expected change in employment as McDonald's in Pennsylvania.

With this in hand, we can give the main identification result:

Theorem 5 (Difference in differences identification)**.** *We observe* $A, Y_0, Y_1, X \sim P$. *Suppose that*

1. *(Causal structure) The data follows the causal graph in Figure 36.6.*

2. *(Conditional parallel trends)* $\mathbb{E}^{A=1}[Y_1 - Y_0|X, \mathrm{do}(A = 0)] = \mathbb{E}[Y_1 - Y_0|X, A = 0]$.

3. *(Overlap)* $\mathrm{P}(A = 1) > 0$ *and* $\mathrm{P}(A = 1|X = x) < 1$ *for all values of x in the sample space. That is, there are no covariate values that only exist in the treated group.*

Then, the average treatment effect on the treated is identified as $\mathrm{ATT}^{\mathrm{DiD}} = \tau^{\mathrm{DiD}}$, *where*

$$\tau^{\mathrm{DiD}} = \mathbb{E}[\mathbb{E}[Y_1 - Y_0|A = 1, X] - \mathbb{E}[Y_1 - Y_0|A = 0, X]|A = 1]. \tag{36.93}$$

Proof. First, by unrolling definitions, we have that

$$\mathbb{E}^{A=1}[Y_1 - Y_0|\mathrm{do}(A = 1), X] = \mathbb{E}[Y_1 - Y_0|A = 1, X]. \tag{36.94}$$

The interpretation is the near-tautology that the average effect among the treated under treatment is equal to the actually observed average effect among the treated. Next,

$$\mathbb{E}^{A=1}[Y_1 - Y_0|\mathrm{do}(A = 0), X] = \mathbb{E}[Y_1 - Y_0|A = 0, X]. \tag{36.95}$$

is just the conditional parallel trends assumption. The result follows immediately.

(The overlap assumption is required to make sure all the conditional expectations are well defined). $\square$

36.6.1 Estimation

With the identification result in hand, the next task is to estimate the observational estimand Equation (36.93). To that end, we define $\tilde{Y} \triangleq Y_1 - Y_0$. Then, we've assumed that $\tilde{Y}, X, A \overset{\text{iid}}{\sim} P$ for some unknown distribution P, and our target estimand is $\mathbb{E}[\mathbb{E}[\tilde{Y}|A = 1, X] - \mathbb{E}[\tilde{Y}|A = 0, X]|A = 1]$. We can immediately recognize this as the observational estimand that occurs in estimating the average treatment effect through adjustment, described in Section 36.4.5.3. That is, even though the causal situation and the identification argument are different between the adjustment setting and the difference in differences setting, the statistical estimation task we end up with is the same. Accordingly, we can use all of the estimation tools we developed for adjustment. That is, all of the techniques there — expected outcome modeling, propensity score methods, double machine learning, and so forth — were purely about the *statistical* task, which is the same between the two scenarios.

So, we're left with the same general recipe for estimation we saw in Section 36.4.6. Namely,

1. Fit statistical or machine-learning models $\hat{Q}(a, x)$ as a predictor for $\tilde{Y} = Y_1 - Y_0$, and/or $\hat{g}(x)$ as a predictor for A.

2. Compute the predictions $\hat{Q}(0, x_i), \hat{Q}(1, x_i), \hat{g}(x_i)$ for each datapoint.

3. Combine these predictions into an estimate of the average treatment effect on the treated.

The estimator in the third step can be the expected outcome model estimator, the propensity weighted estimator, the double machine learning estimator, or any other strategy that's valid in the adjustment setting.

36.7   Credibility checks

Once we've chosen an identification strategy, fit our models, and produced an estimate, we're faced with a basic question: should we believe it? Whether the reported estimate succeeds in capturing the true causal effect depends on whether the assumptions required for causal identification hold, the quality of the machine learning models, and the variability in the estimate due to only having access to a finite data sample. The latter two problems are already familiar from machine learning and statistical practice. We should, e.g., assess our models by checking performance on held out data, examining feature importance, and so forth. Similarly, we should report measures of the uncertainty due to finite sample (e.g., in the form of confidence intervals). Because these procedures are already familiar practice, we will not dwell on them further. However, model evaluation and uncertainty quantification are key parts of any credible causal analysis.

Assessing the validity of identification assumptions is trickier. First, there are assumptions that can in fact be checked from data. For example, overlap should be checked in analysis using backdoor adjustment or difference in differences, and relevance should be checked in the instrumental variable setting. Again, checking these conditions is absolutely necessary for a credible causal analysis. But, again, this involves only familiar data analysis, so we will not discuss it further. Next, there are the causal assumptions that cannot be verified from data; e.g., no unobserved confounding in backdoor adjustment, the exclusion restriction in IV, and conditional parallel trends in DiD. Ultimately, the validity of these assumptions must be assessed using substantive causal knowledge of the particular problem under consideration. However, it is possible to conduct some supplementary analyses that make the required judgement easier. We now discuss two such two such techniques.

36.7.1   Placebo checks

In many situations we may be able to find a variable that can be interepreted as a "treatment" that is known to have no effect on the outcome, but which we expect to be confounded with the outcome in a very similar fashion to the true treatment of interest. For example, if we're trying to estimate the efficacy of a COVID vaccine in preventing symptomatic COVID, we might take our placebo treatment to be vaccination against HPV. We do not expect that there's any causal effect here. However, it seems plausible that latent factors that cause an individual to seek (or avoid) HPV vaccination and COVID vaccination are similar; e.g., health concientiousness, fear of needles, and so forth. Then, if our identification strategy is valid for the COVID vaccine, we'd also expect it to be to be valid for HPV vaccination. Accordingly, our estimation procedure we use for estimating the COVID effect should, when applied to HPV, yield $\hat{\tau} \approx 0$. Or, more precisely, the confidence interval should contain 0. If this does not happen, then we may suspect that there are still some confounding factors lurking that are not adequately handled by the identification procedure.

A similar procedure works when there is a variable that can be interpreted as an outcome which is known to not be affected by the treatment, but that shares confounders with the outcome we're actually interested in. For example, in the COVID vaccination case, we might take the null outcome to be symptomatic COVID within 7 days of vaccination [Dag+21]. Our knowledge of both the biological mechanism of vaccination and the amount of time it takes to develop symptoms after COVID infection (at least 2 days) lead us to conclude that it's unlikely that the treatment has a causal effect on the outcome. However, the properties of the treated people that affect how likely they are to develop symptomatic COVID are largely the same in the 7 day and, e.g., 6 month window. That includes factors such as risk aversion, baseline health, and so forth. Again, we can apply our identification strategy to estimate the causal effect of the treatment on the null outcome. If the confidence interval does not include 0, then we should doubt the credibility of the analysis.

36.7.2 Sensitivity analysis to unobserved confounding

We now specialize to the case of estimating the average causal effect of a binary treatment by adjusting for confounding variables, as described in Section 36.4. In this case, causal identification is based on the assumption of 'no unobserved confounding'; i.e., the assumption that the observed covariates include all common causes of the treatment assignment and outcome. This assumption is fundamentally untestable from observed data, but its violation can induce bias in the estimation of the treatment effect — the unobserved confounding may completely or in part explain the observed association. Our aim in this part is to develop a sensitivity analysis tool to aid in reasoning about potential bias induced by unobserved confounding.

Intuitively, if we estimate a large positive effect then we might expect the real effect is also positive, even in the presence of mild unobserved confounding. For example, consider the association between smoking and lung cancer. One could argue that this association arises from a hormone that both predisposes carriers to both an increased desire to smoke and to a greater risk of lung cancer. However, the association between smoking and lung cancer is large — is it plausible that some unknown hormonal association could have a strong enough influence to explain the association? Cornfield et al. [Cor+59] showed that, for a particular observational dataset, such an umeasured hormone would need to increase the probability of smoking by at least a factor of nine. This is an unreasonable effect size for a hormone, so they conclude it's unlikely the causal effect can be explained away.

We would like a general procedure to allow domain experts to make judgments about whether plausible confounding is "mild" relative to the "large" effect. In particular, the domain expert must translate judgments about the strength of the unobserved confounding into judgments about the bias induced in the estimate of the effect. Accordingly, we must formalize what is meant by strength of unobserved confounding, and to show how to translate judgments about confounding strength into judgments about bias.

A prototypical example, due to Imbens [Imb03] (building on [RR83]), illustrates the broad approach. As above, the observed data consists of a treatment A, an outcome Y, and covariates X that may causally affect the treatment and outcome. Imbens [Imb03] then posits an additional unobserved binary confounder U for each patient, and supposes that the observed data and unobserved confounder were generated according to the following assumption, known as **Imbens' Sensitivity Model**:

$$U_i \overset{\text{iid}}{\sim} \text{Bern}(1/2) \tag{36.96}$$

$$A_i | X_i, U_i \overset{\text{ind}}{\sim} \text{Bern}(\text{sig}(\gamma X_i + \alpha U_i)) \tag{36.97}$$

$$Y_i | X_i, A_i, U_i \overset{\text{ind}}{\sim} \mathcal{N}(\tau A_i + \beta X_i + \delta U_i, \sigma^2). \tag{36.98}$$

where sig is the sigmoid function.

If we had observed U_i, we could estimate $(\hat{\tau}, \hat{\gamma}, \hat{\beta}, \hat{\alpha}, \hat{\delta}, \hat{\sigma}^2)$ from the data and report $\hat{\tau}$ as the estimate of the average treatment effect. Since U_i is not observed, it is not possible to identify the parameters from the data. Instead, we make (subjective) judgments about plausible values of α — how strongly U_i affects the treatment assignment — and δ — how strongly U_i affects the outcome. Contingent on plausible $\alpha = \alpha^*$ and $\delta = \delta^*$, the other parameters can be estimated. This yields an estimate of the treatment effect $\hat{\tau}(\alpha^*, \delta^*)$ under the presumed values of the sensitivity parameters.

The approach just outlined has a major drawback: it relies on a parametric model for the full data generating process. The assumed model is equivalent to assuming that, had U been observed, it would have been appropriate to use logistic regression to model treatment assignment, and linear regression to model the outcome. This assumption also implies a simple, parametric model for the relationships governing the observed data. This restriction is out of step with modern practice, where we use flexible machine-learning methods to model these relationships. For example, the assumption forbids the use of neural networks or random forests, though such methods are often state-of-the-art for causal effect estimation.

Austen plots   We now turn to developing an alternative an adaptation of Imbens' approach that fully decouples sensitivity analysis and modeling of the observed data. Namely, the **Austen plots** of [VZ20]. An example Austen plot is shown in Figure 36.7. The high-level idea is to posit a generative model that uses a simple, interpretable parametric form for the influence of the unobserved confounder, but that *puts no constraints on the model for the observed data*. We then use the parametric part of the model to formalize "confounding strength" and to compute the induced bias as a function of the confounding.

Austen plots further adapt two strategies pioneered by Imbens [Imb03]. First, we find a parameterization of the model so that the sensitivity parameters, measuring strength of confounding, are on a standardized, unitless scale. This allows us to compare the strength of hypothetical unobserved confounding to the strength of observed covariates, measured from data. Second, we plot the curve of all values of the sensitivity parameter that would yield given level of bias. This moves the analyst judgment from "what are plausible values of the sensitivity parameters?" to "are sensitivity parameters this extreme plausible?"

Figure 36.7, an Austen plot for an observational study of the effect of combination medications on diastolic blood pressure, illustrates the idea. A bias of 2 would suffice to undermine the qualitative conclusion that the blood-pressure treatment is effective. Examining the plot, an unobserved confounder as strong as age could induce this amount of confounding, but no other (group of) observed confounders has so much influence. Accordingly, if a domain expert thinks an unobserved confounder as strong as age is unlikely then they may conclude that the treatment is likely effective. Or, if such a confounder is plausible, they may conclude that the study fails to establish efficacy.

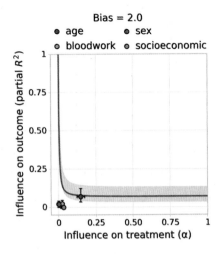

Figure 36.7: Austen plot showing how strong an unobserved confounder would need to be to induce a bias of 2 in an observational study of the effect of combination blood pressure medications on diastolic blood pressure [Dor+16]. We chose this bias to equal the nominal average treatment effect estimated from the data. We model the outcome with Bayesian Additive Regression Trees and the treatment assignment with logistic regression. The curve shows all values treatment and outcome influence that would induce a bias of 2. The colored dots show the influence strength of (groups of) observed covariates, given all other covariates. For example, an unobserved confounder with as much influence as the patient's age might induce a bias of about 2.

Setup The data are generated independently and identically $(Y_i, A_i, X_i, U_i) \overset{\text{iid}}{\sim} P$, where U_i is not observed and P is some unknown probability distribution. The approach in Section 36.4 assumes that the observed covariates X contain all common causes of Y and A. If this 'no unobserved confounding' assumption holds, then the ATE is equal to parameter, τ, of the observed data distribution, where

$$\tau = \mathbb{E}[\mathbb{E}[Y|X, A = 1] - \mathbb{E}[Y|X, A = 0]]. \tag{36.99}$$

This observational parameter is then estimated from a finite data sample. Recall from Section 36.4 that this involves estimating the conditional expected outcome $Q(A, X) = \mathbb{E}[Y|A, X]$ and the propensity score $g(X) = P(A = 1|X)$, then plugging these into an estimator $\hat{\tau}$.

We are now concerned with the case of possible unobserved confounding. That is, where U causally affects Y and A. If there is unobserved confounding then the parameter τ is not equal to the ATE, so $\hat{\tau}$ is a biased estimate. Inference about the ATE then divides into two tasks. First, the statistical task: estimating τ as accurately as possible from the observed data. And, second, the causal (domain-specific) problem of assessing bias = ATE $- \tau$. We emphasize that our focus here is bias due to causal misidentification, not the statistical bias of the estimator. Our aim is to reason about the bias induced by unobserved confounding — the second task — in a way that imposes no constraints on the modeling choices for $\hat{Q}$, $\hat{g}$, and $\hat{\tau}$ used in the statistical analysis.

Sensitivity model   Our sensitivity analysis should impose no constraints on how the *observed* data is modeled. However, sensitivity analysis demands some assumption on the relationship between the observed data and the *unobserved* confounder. It is convenient to formalize such assumptions by specifying a probabilistic model for how the data is generated. The strength of confounding is then formalized in terms of the parameters of the model (the sensitivity parameters). Then, the bias induced by the confounding can be derived from the assumed model. Our task is to posit a generative model that both yields a useful and easily interpretable sensitivity analysis, and that avoids imposing any assumptions about the observed data.

To begin, consider the functional form of the sensitivity model used by Imbens [Imb03].

$$\text{logit}(\text{P}(A = 1|x, u)) = h(x) + \alpha u \tag{36.100}$$
$$\mathbb{E}[Y|a, x, u] = l(a, x) + \delta u, \tag{36.101}$$

for some functions h and l. That is, the propensity score is logit-linear in the unobserved confounder, and the conditional expected outcome is linear.

By rearranging Equation (36.100) to solve for u and plugging in to Equation (36.101), we see that it's equivalent to assume $\mathbb{E}[Y|t, x, u] = \tilde{l}(t, x) + \tilde{\delta}\text{logit}\text{P}(A = 1|x, u)$. That is, the unobserved confounder u only influences the outcome through the propensity score. Accordingly, by positing a distribution on $\text{P}(A = 1|x, u)$ directly, we can circumvent the need to explicitly articulate U (and h).

Definition 36.7.1. *Let* $\tilde{g}(x, u) = \text{P}(A = 1|x, u)$ *denote the propensity score given observed covariates* x *and the unobserved confounder* u.

The insight is that we can posit a sensitivity model by defining a distribution on $\tilde{g}$ directly. We choose:

$$\tilde{g}(X, U)|X \ \sim \ \text{Beta}(g(X)(1/\alpha - 1), (1 - g(X))(1/\alpha - 1)).$$

That is, the full propensity score $\tilde{g}(X, U)$ for each unit is assumed to be sampled from a Beta distribution centered at the observed propensity score $g(X)$. The sensitivity parameter α plays the same role as in Imbens' model: it controls the influence of the unobserved confounder U on treatment assignment. When α is close to 0 then $\tilde{g}(X, U)|X$ is tightly concentrated around $g(X)$, and the unobserved confounder has little influence. That is, U minimally affects our belief about who is likely to receive treatment. Conversely, when α is close to 1 then $\tilde{g}$ concentrates near 0 and 1; i.e., knowing U would let us accurately predict treatment assignment. Indeed, it can be shown that α is the change in our belief about how likely a unit was to have gotten the treatment, given that they were actually observed to be treated (or not):

$$\alpha = \mathbb{E}[\tilde{g}(X, U)|A = 1] - \mathbb{E}[\tilde{g}(X, U)|A = 0]. \tag{36.102}$$

With the $\tilde{g}$ model in hand, we define the **Austen sensitivity model** as follows:

$$\tilde{g}(X, U)|X \ \sim \ \text{Beta}(g(X)(1/\alpha - 1), (1 - g(X))(1/\alpha - 1)) \tag{36.103}$$
$$A|X, U \ \sim \ \text{Bern}(\tilde{g}(X, U)) \tag{36.104}$$
$$\mathbb{E}[Y|A, X, U] = Q(A, X) + \delta\big(\text{logit}\tilde{g}(X, U) - \mathbb{E}[\text{logit}\tilde{g}(X, U)|A, X]\big). \tag{36.105}$$

This model has been constructed to satisfy the requirement that the propensity score and conditional expected outcome are the g and Q actually present in the observed data:

$$P(A = 1|X) = \mathbb{E}[\mathbb{E}[T|X, U]|X] = \mathbb{E}[\tilde{g}(X, U)|X] = g(X)$$
$$\mathbb{E}[Y|A, X] = \mathbb{E}[\mathbb{E}[Y|A, X, U]|A, X] = Q(A, X).$$

The sensitivity parameters are α, controlling the dependence between the unobserved confounder the treatment assignment, and δ, controlling the relationship with the outcome.

Bias We now turn to calculating the bias induced by unobserved confounding. By assumption, X and U together suffice to render the average treatment effect identifiable as:

$$\texttt{ATE} = \mathbb{E}[\mathbb{E}[Y|A = 1, X, U] - \mathbb{E}[Y|A = 0, X, U]].$$

Plugging in our sensitivity model yields,

$$\texttt{ATE} = \mathbb{E}[Q(1, X) - Q(0, X)] + \delta(\mathbb{E}[\text{logit}\tilde{g}(X, U)|X, A = 1] - \mathbb{E}[\text{logit}\tilde{g}(X, U)|X, A = 0]).$$

The first term is the observed-data estimate τ, so

$$\texttt{bias} = \delta(\mathbb{E}[\text{logit}\tilde{g}(X, U)|X, A = 1] - \mathbb{E}[\text{logit}\tilde{g}(X, U)|X, A = 0]).$$

Then, by invoking beta-Bernoulli conjugacy and standard beta identities,[11] we arrive at,

Theorem 6. *Under the Austen sensitivity model, Equation* (36.105), *an unobserved confounder with influence α and δ induces bias in the estimated treatment effect equal to*

$$\texttt{bias} = \frac{\delta}{1/\alpha - 1}\mathbb{E}\Big[\frac{1}{g(X)} + \frac{1}{1 - g(X)}\Big].$$

That is, the amount of bias is determined by the sensitivity parameters and by the *realized* propensity score. Notice that more extreme propensity scores lead to more extreme bias in response to unobserved confounding. This means, in particular, that conditioning on a covariate that affects the treatment but that does not directly affect the outcome (an instrument) will increase any bias due to unobserved confounding. This general phenomena is known as **z-bias**.

Sensitivity parameters The Austen model provides a formalization of confounding strength in terms of the parameters α and δ and tells us how much bias is induced by a given strength of confounding. This lets us translate judgments about confounding strength to judgments about bias. However, it is not immediately obvious how to translate qualitative judgements such as "I think any unobserved confounder would be much less important than age" to judgements about the possible values of the sensitivity parameters.

First, because the scale of δ is not fixed, it may be difficult to compare the influence of potential unobserved confounders to the influence of reference variables. To resolve this, we reexpress the outcome-confounder strength in terms of the (non-parametric) partial coefficient of determination:

$$R^2_{Y,\text{par}}(\alpha, \delta) = 1 - \frac{\mathbb{E}(Y - \mathbb{E}[Y|A, X, U])^2}{\mathbb{E}(Y - Q(A, X))^2}.$$

The key to computing the reparameterization is the following result

---

11. We also use the recurrence relation $\psi(x + 1) - \psi(x) = 1/x$, where ψ is the digamma function.

Theorem 7. *Under the Austen sensitivity model, Equation (36.105), the outcome influence is*

$$R^2_{Y,\mathrm{par}}(\alpha, \delta) = \delta^2 \sum_{a=0}^{1} \frac{\mathbb{E}\big[\psi_1\big(g(X)^a(1-g(X))^{1-a}(1/\alpha - 1) + 1[A = a]\big)\big]}{\mathbb{E}[(Y - Q(A, X))^2]},$$

where ψ_1 is the trigamma function.

See Veitch and Zaveri [VZ20] for the proof.

By design, α — the strength of confounding influence on on treatment assignment — is already on a fixed, unitless scale. However, because the measure is tied to the model it may be difficult to interpret, and it is not obvious how to compute reference confounding strength values from the observed data. The next result clarifies these issues.

Theorem 8. *Under the Austen sensitivity model, Equation (36.105),*

$$\alpha = 1 - \frac{\mathbb{E}[\tilde{g}(X, U)(1 - \tilde{g}(X, U))]}{\mathbb{E}[g(X)(1 - g(X))]}.$$

See Veitch and Zaveri [VZ20] for the proof. That is, the sensitivity parameter α is measures how much more extreme the propensity scores become when we condition on U. That is, α is a measure of the extra predictive power U adds for A, above and beyond the predictive power in X. It may also be insightful to notice that

$$\alpha = R^2_{A,\mathrm{par}} = 1 - \frac{\mathbb{E}[(A - \tilde{g}(X, U))^2]}{\mathbb{E}[(A - g(X))^2]}. \tag{36.106}$$

That is, α is just the (non-parametric) partial coefficient of determination of U on A—the same measure used for the outcome influence. (To see this, just expand the expectations conditional on $A = 1$ and $A = 0$).

Estimating bias   In combination, Theorems 6 and 7 yield an expression for the bias in terms of α and $R^2_{Y,\mathrm{par}}$. In practice, we can estimate the bias induced by confounding by fitting models for $\hat{Q}$ and $\hat{g}$ and replacing the expectations by means over the data.

36.7.2.1   Calibration using observed data

The analyst must make judgments about the influence a hypothetical unobserved confounder might have on treatment assignment and outcome. To calibrate such judgments, we'd like to have a reference point for how much the observed covariates influence the treatment assignment and outcome. In the sensitivity model, the degree of influence is measured by partial R^2_Y and α. We want to measure the degree of influence of an observed covariate Z given the other observed covariates $X \setminus Z$.

For the outcome, this can be measured as:

$$R^2_{Y \cdot Z | T, X \setminus Z} \triangleq 1 - \frac{\mathbb{E}(Y - Q(A, X))^2}{\mathbb{E}(Y - \mathbb{E}[Y | A, X \setminus Z])^2}.$$

In practice, we can estimate the quantity by fitting a new regression model $\hat{Q}_Z$ that predicts Y from A and $X \backslash Z$. Then we compute

$$R^2_{Y \cdot Z | T, X \backslash Z} = 1 - \frac{\frac{1}{n} \sum_i (y_i - \hat{Q}(t_i, x_i))^2}{\frac{1}{n} \sum_i (y_i - \hat{Q}_Z(t_i, x_i \backslash z_i))^2}.$$

Using Theorem 8, we can measure influence of observed covariate Z on treatment assignment given $X \backslash Z$ in an analogous fashion to the outcome. We define $g_{X \backslash Z}(X \backslash Z) = P(A = 1 | X \backslash Z)$, then fit a model for $g_{X \backslash Z}$ by predicting A from $X \backslash Z$, and estimate

$$\hat{\alpha}_{Z | X \backslash Z} = 1 - \frac{\frac{1}{n} \sum_i \hat{g}(x_i)(1 - \hat{g}(x_i))}{\frac{1}{n} \sum_i \hat{g}_{X \backslash Z}(x_i \backslash z_i)(1 - \hat{g}_{X \backslash Z}(x_i \backslash z_i))}.$$

Grouping covariates The estimated values $\hat{\alpha}_{X \backslash Z}$ and $\hat{R}^2_{Y, X \backslash Z}$ measure the influence of Z conditioned on all the other confounders. In some cases, this can be misleading. For example, if some piece of information is important but there are multiple covariates providing redundant measurements, then the estimated influence of each covariate will be small. To avoid this, group together related or strongly dependent covariates and compute the influence of the entire group in aggregate. For example, grouping income, location, and race as 'socioeconomic variables'.

36.7.2.2 Practical use

We now have sufficient results to produce Austen plots such as Figure 36.7. At a high level, the procedure is:

1. Produce an estimate $\hat{\tau}$ using any modeling tools. As a component of this, estimate the propensity score $\hat{g}$ and conditional outcome model $\hat{Q}$.

2. Pick a level of bias that would suffice to change the qualitative interpretation of the estimate (e.g., the lower bound of a 95% confidence interval).

3. Plot the values of α and $R^2_{Y, \text{par}}$ that would suffice to induce that much bias. This is the black curve on the plot. To calculate these values, use Theorems 6 and 7 together with the estimated $\hat{g}$ and $\hat{Q}$.

4. Finally, compute reference influence level for (groups of) observed covariates. In particular, this requires fitting reduced models for the conditional expected outcome and propensity that do not use the reference covariate as a feature.

In practice, an analyst only needs to do the model fitting parts themselves. The bias calculations, reference value calculations, and plotting can be done automatically with standard libraries.[12].

Austen plots are predicated on Equation (36.105). This assumption replaces the purely parametric Equation (36.98) with a version that eliminates any parametric requirements on the observed data. However, we emphasize that Equation (36.105) does, implicitly, impose some parametric assumption on the structural causal relationship between U and A, Y. Ultimately, any conclusion drawn from

---

12. See github.com/vveitch/causality-tutorials/blob/main/Sensitivity_Analysis.ipynb.

the sensitivity analysis depends on this assumption, which is not justified on any substantive grounds. Accordingly, such sensitivity analyses can only be used to informally guide domain experts. They do not circumvent the need to thoroughly adjust for confounding. This reliance on a structural assumption is a generic property of sensitivity analysis.[13] Indeed, there are now many sensitivity analysis models that allow the use of any machine learning model in the data analysis [e.g., RRS00; FDF19; She+11; HS13; BK19; Ros10; Yad+18; ZSB19; Sch+21a]. However, none of these are yet in routine use in practice. We have presented Austen plots here not because they make an especially virtuous modeling assumption, but because they are (relatively) easy to understand and interpret.

Austen plots are most useful in situations where the conclusion from the plot would be 'obvious' to a domain expert. For instance, in Figure 36.7, we can be confident that an unobserved confounder similar to socioeconomic status would not induce enough bias to change the qualitative conclusion. By contrast, Austen plots should not be used to draw conclusions such as, "I think a latent confounder could only be 90% as strong as 'age', so there is evidence of a small non-zero effect". Such nuanced conclusions might depend on issues such as the particular sensitivity model we use, or finite-sample variation of our bias and influence estimates, or on incautious interpretation of the calibration dots. These issues are subtle, and it would be difficult resolve them to a sufficient degree that a sensitivity analysis would make an analysis credible.

Calibration using observed data The interpretation of the observed-data calibration requires some care. The sensitivity analysis requires the analyst to make judgements about the strength of influence of the unobserved confounder U, *conditional on the observed covariates X*. However, we report the strength of influence of observed covariate(s) Z, *conditional on the other observed covariates $X \backslash Z$*. The difference in conditioning sets can have subtle effects.

Cinelli and Hazlett [CH20] give an example where Z and U are identical variables in the true model, but where influence of U given A, X is larger than the influence of Z given $A, X \backslash Z$. (The influence of Z given $X \backslash Z, U$ would be the same as the influence of U given X). Accordingly, an analyst is *not* justified in a judgment such as, "I know that U and Z are very similar. I see Z has substantial influence, but the dot is below the line. Thus, U will not undo the study conclusions". In essence, if the domain expert suspects a strong interaction between U and Z then naively eyeballing the dot-vs-line position may be misleading. A particular subtle case is when U and Z are independent variables that both strongly influence A and Y. The joint influence on A creates an interaction effect between them when A is conditioned on (the treatment is a collider). This affects the interpretation of $R^2_{Y \cdot U | X, A}$. Indeed, we should generally be skeptical of sensitivity analysis interpretation when it is expected that a strong confounder has been omitted. In such cases, our conclusions may depend substantively on the particular form of our sensitivity model, or other unjustifiable assumptions.

Although the interaction problem is conceptually important, its practical significance is unclear. We often expect the opposite effect: if U and Z are dependent (e.g., race and wealth) then omitting U should increase the apparent importance of Z — leading to a conservative judgement (a dot artifically towards the top right part of the plot).

---

13. In extreme cases, there can be so little unexplained variation in A or Y that only a very weak confounder could be compatible with the data. In this case, essentially assumption free sensitivity analysis is possible [Man90].

36.8 The do-calculus

We have seen several strategies for identifying causal effects as parameters of observational distributions. Confounder adjustment (Section 36.4) relied only on the assumed causal graph (and overlap), which specified that we observe all common causes of A and Y. On the other hand, instrumental variable methods and difference-in-differences each relied on both an assumed causal graph and partial functional form assumptions about the underlying structural causal model. Because functional form assumptions can be quite difficult to justify on substantive grounds, it's natural to ask when causal identification is possible from the causal graph alone. That is, when can we be agnostic to the particular functional form of the structural causal models?

There is a general "**calculus of intervention**", known as the **do-calculus**, that gives a general recipe for determining when the causal assumptions expressed in a causal graph can be used to identify causal effects [Pea09c]. The do-calculus is a set of three rewrite rules that allows us to replace statements where we condition on variables being set by intervention, e.g. $P(Y|\text{do}(A = a))$, with statements involving only observational quantities, e.g. $\mathbb{E}_X[P(Y|A = a, X)]$. When causal identification is possible, we can repeatedly apply the three rules to boil down our target causal parameter into an expression involving only the observational distribution.

36.8.1 The three rules

To express the rules, let X, Y, Z, and W be arbitrary disjoint sets of variables in a causal DAG G.

Rule 1 The first rule allows us to insert or delete observations z:

$$p(y|\text{do}(x), z, w) = p(y|\text{do}(x), w) \text{ if } (Y \perp Z | X, W)_{G_{\overline{X}}} \tag{36.107}$$

where $G_{\overline{X}}$ denotes cuting edges going into X, and $(Y \perp Z | X, W)_{G_{\overline{X}}}$ denotes conditional independence in the mutilated graph. The rule follows from d-separation in the mutilated graph. This rule just says that conditioniong on irrelevant variables leaves the distribution invariant (as we would expect).

Rule 2 The second rule allows us to replace $\text{do}(z)$ with conditioning on (seeing) z. The simplest case where can do this is: if Z is a root of the causal graph (i.e., it has no causal parents) then $p(y|\text{do}(z)) = p(y|z)$. The reason is that the do operator is equivalent to conditioning in the mutilated causal graph where all the edges into Z are removed, but, because Z is a root, the mutilated graph is just the original causal graph. The general form of this rule is:

$$p(y|\text{do}(x), \text{do}(z), w) = p(y|\text{do}(x), z, w) \text{ if } (Y \perp Z | X, W)_{G_{\overline{X}\underline{Z}}} \tag{36.108}$$

where $G_{\overline{X}\underline{Z}}$ cuts edges going into X and out of Z. Intuitively, we can replace $\text{do}(z)$ by z as long as there are no backdoor (non-directed) paths between z and y. If there are in fact no such paths, then cutting all the edges going out of Z will mean there are no paths connecting Z and Y, so that $Y \perp Z$. The rule just generalizes this line of reasoning to allow for extra observed and intervened variables.

Rule 3 The third rule allows us to insert or delete actions $\text{do}(z)$:

$$p(y|\text{do}(x), \text{do}(z), w) = p(y|\text{do}(x), w) \text{ if } (Y \perp Z | X, W)_{G_{\overline{X}\overline{Z^*}}} \tag{36.109}$$

where $G_{\overline{X}\underline{Z}^*}$ cuts edges going into X and Z^*, and where Z^* is the set of Z-nodes that are not ancestors of any W-node in $G_{\overline{X}}$. Intuitively, this condition corresponds to intervening on X, and checking whether the distribution of Y is invariant to *any* intervention that we could apply on Z.

36.8.2   Revisiting backdoor adjustment

We begin with a more general form of the adjustment formula we used in Section 36.4.

First, suppose we observe all of A's parents, call them X. For notational simplicity, we'll assume for the moment that X is discrete. Then,

$$p(Y = y | \mathrm{do}(A = a)) = \sum_{x} p(Y = y | x, \mathrm{do}(A = a)) p(x | \mathrm{do}(A = a)) \tag{36.110}$$

$$= \sum_{x} p(Y = y | x, A = a) p(x). \tag{36.111}$$

The first line is just a standard probability relation (marginalizing over z). We are using causal assumptions in two ways in the second line. First, $p(x | \mathrm{do}(A = a)) = p(x)$: the treatment has no causal effect on Z, so interventions on A don't change the distribution of Z. This is rule 3, Equation (36.109). Second, $p(Y = y | z, \mathrm{do}(A = a)) = p(Y = y | z, A = a)$. This equality holds because conditioning on the parents blocks all non-directed paths from A to Y, reducing the causal effect to be the same as the observational effect. The equality is an application of rule 2, Equation (36.108).

Now, what if we don't observe all the parents of A? The key issue is **backdoor paths**: paths between A and Y that contain an arrow into A. These paths are the general form of the problem that occurs when A and Y share a common cause. Suppose that we can find a set of variables S such that (1) no node in S is a descendant of A; and (2) S blocks every backdoor path between A and Y. Such a set is said to satisfy the **backdoor criterion**. In this case, we can use S instead of the parents of X in the adjustment formula, Equation (36.111). That is,

$$p(Y = y | \mathrm{do}(A = a)) = \mathbb{E}_S[p(Y = y | S, A = a)]. \tag{36.112}$$

The proof follows the invocation of rules 3 and 2, in the same way as for the case where S is just the parents of A. Notice that requiring S to not contain any descendants of A means that we don't risk conditioning on any variables that mediate the effect, nor any variables that might be colliders — either would undermine the estimate.

The backdoor adjustment formula generalizes the adjust-for-parents approach and adjust-for-all-common-causes approach of Section 36.4. That's because both the parents of A and the common causes satisfy the backdoor criterion.

In practice, the full distribution $p(Y = y | \mathrm{do}(A = a))$ is rarely used as the causal target. Instead, we try to estimate a low-dimensional parameter of this distribution, such as the average treatment effect. The adjustment formula immediately translates in the obvious way. If we define

$$\tau = \mathbb{E}_S[\mathbb{E}[Y | A = 1, S] - \mathbb{E}[Y | A = 0, S]],$$

then we have that $\mathrm{ATE} = \tau$ whenever S satisfies the backdoor criteria. The parameter τ can then be estimated from finite data using the methods described in Section 36.4, using S in place of the common causes X.

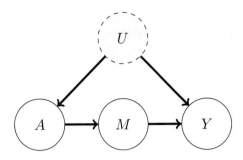

Figure 36.8: Causal graph illustrating the frontdoor criterion setup. The effect of the treatment A on outcome Y is entirely mediated by mediator M. This allows us infer the causal effect even if the treatment and outcome are confounded by U.

36.8.3 Frontdoor adjustment

Backdoor adjustment is applicable if there's at least one observed variable on every backdoor path between A and Y. As we have seen, identification is sometimes still possible even when this condition doesn't hold. Frontdoor adjustment is another strategy of this kind. Figure 36.8 shows the causal structure that allows this kind of adjustment strategy. Suppose we're interested in the effect of smoking A on developing cancer Y, but we're concerned about some latent genetic confounder U.

Suppose that all of the directed paths from A to Y pass through some set of variables M. Such variables are called **mediators**. For example, the effect of smoking on lung cancer might be entirely mediated by the amount of tar in the lungs and measured tissue damage. It turns out that if all such mediators are observed, and the mediators do not have an unobserved common cause with A or Y, then causal identification is possible. To understand why this is true, first notice that we can identify the causal effect of A on M and the causal effect of M on A, both by backdoor adjustment. Further, the mechanism of action of A on Y is: A changes M which in turn changes Y. Then, we can combine these as:

$$p(Y|\text{do}(A = a)) = \sum_m p(Y|\text{do}(M = m))p(M = m|\text{do}(A = a)) \tag{36.113}$$

$$= \sum_m \sum_{a'} p(Y|a', m)p(a')p(m|a) \tag{36.114}$$

The second line is just backdoor adjustment applied to identify each of the do expressions (note that A blocks the M-Y backdoor path through U).

Equation (36.114) is called the **front-door formula** [Pea09b, §3.3.2]. To state the result in more general terms, let us introduce a definition. We say a set of variables M satisfies the **front-door criterion** relative to an ordered pair of variables (A, Y) if (1) M intercepts all directed paths from A to Y; (2) there is no unblocked backdoor path from A to M; and (3) all backdoor paths from M to Y are blocked by A. If M satisfies this criterion, and if $p(A, M) > 0$ for all values of A and M, then the causal effect of A on Y is identifiable and is given by Equation (36.114).

Let us interpret this theorem in terms of our smoking example. Condition 1 means that smoking A should have no effect on cancer Y except via tar and tissue damage M. Conditions 2 and 3 mean that the genotype U cannot have any effect on M except via smoking A. Finally, the requirement that $p(A, M) > 0$ for all values implies that high levels of tar in the lungs must arise not only due to smoking, but also other factors (e.g., pollutants). In other words, we require $p(A = 0, M = 1) > 0$ so we can assess the impact of the mediator in the untreated setting.

We can now use the do-calculus to derive the frontdoor criterion; following [PM18b, p236]. Assuming the causal graph G shown in Figure 36.8:

$$p(y|\text{do}(a)) = \sum_m p(y|\text{do}(a), m)p(m|\text{do}(a)) \qquad \text{(probability axioms)}$$

$$= \sum_m p(y|\text{do}(a), \text{do}(m))p(m|\text{do}(a)) \qquad \text{(rule 2 using } G_{\overline{S}\underline{T}})$$

$$= \sum_m p(y|\text{do}(a), \text{do}(m))p(m|a) \qquad \text{(rule 2 using } G_{\underline{S}})$$

$$= \sum_m p(y|\text{do}(m))p(m|a) \qquad \text{(rule 3 using } G_{\overline{ST^*}})$$

$$= \sum_{a'}\sum_m p(y|\text{do}(m), a')p(a'|\text{do}(m))p(m|a) \qquad \text{(probability axioms)}$$

$$= \sum_{a'}\sum_m p(y|m, a')p(a'|\text{do}(m))p(m|a) \qquad \text{(rule 2 using } G_{\underline{T}})$$

$$= \sum_{a'}\sum_m p(y|m, a')p(a')p(m|a) \qquad \text{(rule 3 using } G_{\overline{T^*}})$$

Estimation   To estimate the causal distribution from data using the frontdoor criterion we need to estimate each of $p(y|m, a)$, $p(a)$, and $p(m|a)$. In practice, we can fit models $\hat{p}(y|m, a)$ by predicting Y from M and A, and $\hat{p}(m|a)$ by predicting M from A. Then, using the empirical distribution to estimate $p(a)$, the final estimate is:

$$\frac{1}{|A|}\sum_{a'}\sum_m \hat{p}(y|m, a')\hat{p}(m|a), \qquad (36.115)$$

where $|A|$ is the number of treatments.

We usually have more modest targets than the full distribution $p(y|\text{do}(a))$. For instance, we may be content with just estimating the average treatment effect. It's straightforward to derive a formula for this using the frontdoor adjustment. Similarly to backdoor adjustment, more advanced estimators of the ATE through frontdoor effect are possible in principle. For example, we might combine fitted models for $\mathbb{E}[Y|m, a]$ and $P(M|a)$. See Fulcher et al. [Ful+20] for an approach to robust estimation via front door adjustment, as well as a generalization of the front door approach to more general settings.

36.9   Further reading

There is an enormous and growing literature on the intersection of causality and machine learning.

First, there are many textbooks on theoretical and practical elements of causal inference. These include Pearl [Pea09c], focused on causal graphs, Angrist and Pischke [AP08], focused on econometrics,

Hernán and Robins [HR20b], with roots in epidemiology, Imbens and Rubin [IR15], with origin in statistics, and Morgan and Winship [MW15], for a social sciences perspective. The introduction to causality in Shalizi [Sha22, §7] is also recommended, particularly the treatment of matching.

Double machine-learning has featured prominently in this chapter. This is a particular instantiation of non-parametric estimation. This topic has substantial theoretical and practical importance in modern causal inference. The double machine learning work includes estimators for many commonly encountered scenarios [Che+17e; Che+17d]. Good references for a lucid explanation of how and why non-parametric estimation works include [Ken16; Ken17; FK21]. Usually, the key guarantees of non-parametric estimator are asymptotic. Generally, there are many estimators that share optimal asymptotic guarantees (e.g., the AIPTW estimator given in Equation (36.30)). Although these are asymptotically equivalent, in finite samples their behavior can be very different. There are estimators that preserve asymptotic guarantees but aim to improve performance in practical finite sample regimes [e.g., vR11].

There is also considerable interest in the estimation of heterogeneous treatment effects. The question here is: what effect would this treatment have when applied to a unit with such-and-such specific characteristics? E.g., what is the effect of this drug on women over the age of 50? The causal identification arguments used here are more-or-less the same as for the estimation of average case effects. However, the estimation problems can be substantially more involved. Some reading includes [Kün+19; NW20; Ken20; Yad+21].

There are several commonly applicable causal identification and estimation strategies beyond the ones we've covered in this chapter. **Regression discontinuity designs** rely on the presence of some sharp, arbitrary non-linearity in treatment assignment. For example, eligibility for some aid programs is determined by whether an individual has income below or above a fixed amount. The effect of the treatment can be studied by comparing units just below and just above this threshhold. **Synthetic controls** are a class of methods that try to study the effect of a treatment on a given unit by constructing a synthetic version of that unit that acts as a control. For example, to study the effect of legislation banning smoking indoors in California, we can construct a synthetic California as a weighted average of other states, with weights chosen to balance demographic characteristics. Then, we can compare the observed outcome of California with the outcome of the synthetic control, constructed as the weighted average of the outcomes of the donor states. See Angrist and Pischke [AP08] for a textbook treatment of both strategies. Closely related are methods that use time series modeling to create synthetic outcomes. For example, to study the effect of an advertising campaign beginning at time T on product sales Y_t, we might build a time series model for Y_t using data in the $t < T$ period, and then use this model to predict the values of $(\hat{Y}_t)_{t>T}$ we would have seen had the campaign not been run. We can estimate the causal effect by comparing the factual, realized Y_t to the predicted, counterfactual, $\hat{Y}_t$. See Brodersen et al. [Bro+15] for an instantiation of this idea.

In this chapter, our focus has been on using machine learning tools to estimate causal effects. There is also a growing interest in using the ideas of causality to improve machine learning tools. This is mainly aimed at building predictors that are robust when deployed in new domains [SS18b; SCS19; Arj+20; Mei18b; PBM16a; RC+18; Zha+13a; Sch+12b; Vei+21] or that do not rely on particular 'spurious' correlations in the training data [RPH21; Wu+21; Gar+19; Mit+20; WZ19; KCC20; KHL20; TAH20; Vei+21].

Index

Bibliography

pling". In: *Advances in neural information processing systems* 2 (1989).

[ACP87]   S. Arnborg, D. G. Corneil, and A. Proskurowski. "Complexity of finding embeddings in a k-tree". In: *SIAM J. on Algebraic and Discrete Methods* 8 (1987), pp. 277–284.

[Ada00]   L. Adamic. *Zipf, Power-laws, and Pareto - a ranking tutorial*. Tech. rep. 2000.

[Ada+20]   V. Adam, S. Eleftheriadis, N. Durrande, A. Artemev, and J. Hensman. "Doubly Sparse Variational Gaussian Processes". In: *AISTATS*. 2020.

[Ade+20a]   J. Adebayo, J. Gilmer, M. Muelly, I. Goodfellow, M. Hardt, and B. Kim. *Sanity Checks for Saliency Maps*. 2020. arXiv: 1810.03292 [cs.CV].

[Ade+20b]   J. Adebayo, M. Muelly, I. Liccardi, and B. Kim. "Debugging tests for model explanations". In: *arXiv preprint arXiv:2011.05429* (2020).

[Adl+18]   P. Adler, C. Falk, S. A. Friedler, T. Nix, G. Rybeck, C. Scheidegger, B. Smith, and S. Venkatasubramanian. "Auditing black-box models for indirect influence". In: *Knowledge and Information Systems* 54.1 (2018), pp. 95–122.

[Ado]   *Taking It to the MAX: Adobe Photoshop Gets New NVIDIA AI-Powered Neural Filters*. https://blogs.nvidia.com/blog/2020/10/20/adobe-max-ai/. Accessed: 2021-08-12.

[AE+20]   D. Agudelo-España, S. Gomez-Gonzalez, S. Bauer, B. Schölkopf, and J. Peters. "Bayesian Online Prediction of Change Points". In: *UAI*. Vol. 124. Proceedings of Machine Learning Research. PMLR, 2020, pp. 320–329.

[AFD01]   C. Andrieu, N. de Freitas, and A. Doucet. "Robust Full Bayesian Learning for Radial Basis Networks". In: *Neural Computation* 13.10 (2001), pp. 2359–2407.

[AFG19]   M. Akten, R. Fiebrink, and M. Grierson. "Learning to See: You Are What You See". In: *ACM SIGGRAPH 2019 Art Gallery*. SIGGRAPH '19. Association for Computing Machinery, 2019.

[AG11]   A. Allahverdyan and A. Galstyan. "Comparative Analysis of Viterbi Training and Maximum Likelihood Estimation for HMMs". In: *NIPS*. 2011, pp. 1674–1682.

[AG13]   S. Agrawal and N. Goyal. "Further Optimal Regret Bounds for Thompson Sampling". In: *AISTATS*. 2013.

[Aga+14]   D. Agarwal, B. Long, J. Traupman, D. Xin, and L. Zhang. "LASER: a scalable response prediction platform for online advertising". In: *WSDM*. 2014.

[Aga+21a]   A. Agarwal, N. Jiang, S. M. Kakade, and W. Sun. *Reinforcement Learning: Theory and Algorithms*. 2021.

[Aga+21b]   R. Agarwal, L. Melnick, N. Frosst, X. Zhang, B. Lengerich, R. Caruana, and G. Hinton. *Neural Additive Models: Interpretable Machine Learning with Neural Nets*. 2021. arXiv: 2004.13912 [cs.LG].

[Aga+22]   A. Agarwal, N. Jiang, S. Kakade, and W. Sun. *Reinforcement Learning:Theory and Algorithms*. 2022.

[AGM14]   P. Agrawal, R. Girshick, and J. Malik. "Analyzing the performance of multilayer neural networks for object recognition". In: *European conference on computer vision*. Springer. 2014, pp. 329–344.

[AA18]   D. Amir and O. Amir. "Highlights: Summarizing agent behavior to people". In: *Proceedings of the 17th International Conference on Autonomous Agents and MultiAgent Systems*. 2018, pp. 1168–1176.

[AB08]   C. Archambeau and F. Bach. "Sparse probabilistic projections". In: *NIPS*. 2008.

[AB17]   M. Arjovsky and L. Bottou. "Towards principled methods for training generative adversarial networks". In: (2017).

[AB21]   A. N. Angelopoulos and S. Bates. "A Gentle Introduction to Conformal Prediction and Distribution-Free Uncertainty Quantification". In: (2021). arXiv: 2107.07511 [cs.LG].

[Aba]   A. Abadie. "Using Synthetic Controls: Feasibility, Data Requirements, and Methodological Aspects". In: *J. of Economic Literature* ().

[Abd+18]   A. Abdolmaleki, J. T. Springenberg, Y. Tassa, R. Munos, N. Heess, and M. A. Riedmiller. "Maximum a Posteriori Policy Optimisation". In: *ICLR*. 2018.

[ABM10]   J.-Y. Audibert, S. Bubeck, and R. Munos. "Best Arm Identification in Multi-Armed Bandits". In: *COLT*. 2010, pp. 41–53.

[Abn+21]   S. Abnar, M. Dehghani, B. Neyshabur, and H. Sedghi. "Exploring the limits of large scale pre-training". In: *ICLR*. 2021.

[ABV21]   S. Akbayrak, I. Bocharov, and B. de Vries. "Extended Variational Message Passing for Automated Approximate Bayesian Inference". In: *Entropy* 23.7 (2021).

[AC17]   S. Aminikhanghahi and D. J. Cook. "A Survey of Methods for Time Series Change Point Detection". en. In: *Knowl. Inf. Syst.* 51.2 (2017), pp. 339–367.

[AC93]   J. Albert and S. Chib. "Bayesian analysis of binary and polychotomous response data". In: *JASA* 88.422 (1993), pp. 669–679.

[ACB17]   M. Arjovsky, S. Chintala, and L. Bottou. "Wasserstein generative adversarial networks". In: *ICML*. 2017, pp. 214–223.

[ACL16]   L. Aitchison, N. Corradi, and P. E. Latham. "Zipf's Law Arises Naturally When There Are Underlying, Unobserved Variables". en. In: *PLoS Comput. Biol.* 12.12 (2016), e1005110.

[ACL89]   L. Atlas, D. Cohn, and R. Ladner. "Training connectionist networks with queries and selective sam-

[AGM19] V. Amrhein, S. Greenland, and B. McShane. "Scientists rise up against statistical significance". In: *Nature* 567.7748 (2019), p. 305.

[AH09] I. Arasaratnam and S. Haykin. "Cubature Kalman Filters". In: *IEEE Trans. Automat. Contr.* 54.6 (2009), pp. 1254–1269.

[AHE07] I. Arasaratnam, S. Haykin, and R. J. Elliott. "Discrete-Time Nonlinear Filtering Algorithms Using Gauss–Hermite Quadrature". In: *Proc. IEEE* 95.5 (2007), pp. 953–977.

[AHG20] L. Ambrogioni, M. Hinne, and M. van Gerven. "Automatic structured variational inference". In: (2020). arXiv: 2002.00643 [stat.ML].

[AHK01] C. C. Aggarwal, A. Hinneburg, and D. A. Keim. "On the Surprising Behavior of Distance Metrics in High Dimensional Space". In: *Database Theory — ICDT 2001*. Springer Berlin Heidelberg, 2001, pp. 420–434.

[AHK12] A. Anandkumar, D. Hsu, and S. M. Kakade. "A Method of Moments for Mixture Models and Hidden Markov Models". In: *COLT*. Vol. 23. Proceedings of Machine Learning Research. PMLR, 2012, pp. 33.1–33.34.

[AHK65] K. Abend, T. J. Harley, and L. N. Kanal. "Classification of Binary Random Patterns". In: *IEEE Transactions on Information Theory* 11(4) (1965), pp. 538–544.

[Ahm+17] S. Ahmad, A. Lavin, S. Purdy, and Z. Agha. "Unsupervised real-time anomaly detection for streaming data". In: *Neurocomputing* 262 (2017), pp. 134–147.

[AHP+05] P. K. Agarwal, S. Har-Peled, et al. "Geometric approximation via coresets". In: *Combinatorial and computational geometry* 52.1-30 (2005), p. 3.

[AHS85] D. Ackley, G. Hinton, and T. Sejnowski. "A Learning Algorithm for Boltzmann Machines". In: *Cognitive Science* 9 (1985), pp. 147–169.

[AHT07] Y. Altun, T. Hofmann, and I. Tsochantaridis. "Support Vector Machine Learning for Interdependent and Structured Output Spaces". In: *Predicting Structured Data*. Ed. by G. Bakir, T. Hofmann, B. Scholkopf, A. Smola, B. Taskar, and S. Vishwanathan. MIT Press, 2007.

[Ahu+21] K. Ahuja, J. Wang, A. Dhurandhar, K. Shanmugam, and K. R. Varshney. "Empirical or Invariant Risk Minimization? A Sample Complexity Perspective". In: *ICLR*. 2021.

[AI 19] AI Artists. *Creative Tools to Generate AI Art*. 2019.

[Ait21] L. Aitchison. "A statistical theory of cold posteriors in deep neural networks". In: *ICLR*. 2021.

[Aka74] H. Akaike. "A new look at the statistical model identification". In: *IEEE Trans. on Automatic Control* 19.6 (1974).

[AKO18] S.-I. Amari, R. Karakida, and M. Oizumi. "Fisher Information and Natural Gradient Learning of Random Deep Networks". In: (2018). arXiv: 1808.07172 [cs.LG].

[AKZK19] B. Amos, V. Koltun, and J Zico Kolter. "The Limited Multi-Label Projection Layer". In: (2019). arXiv: 1906.08707 [cs.LG].

[AL+16] J. Ala-Luhtala, N. Whiteley, K. Heine, and R. Piche. "An Introduction to Twisted Particle Filters and Parameter Estimation in Non-linear State-space Models". In: *IEEE Trans. Signal Process.* 64.18 (2016), pp. 4875–4890.

[al21] M. A. et al. *Understanding Dataset Shift and Potential Remedies*. Tech. rep. Vector Institute, 2021.

[Ale+16] A. A. Alemi, I. Fischer, J. V. Dillon, and K. Murphy. "Deep Variational Information Bottleneck". In: *ICLR*. 2016.

[Ale+17] A. A. Alemi, I. S. Fischer, J. V. Dillon, and K. P. Murphy. "Deep Variational Information Bottleneck". In: *ArXiv* abs/1612.00410 (2017).

[Ale+18] A. A. Alemi, B. Poole, I. Fischer, J. V. Dillon, R. A. Saurous, and K. Murphy. "Fixing a broken ELBO". In: *ICML*. 2018.

[Alq21] P. Alquier. "User-friendly introduction to PAC-Bayes bounds". In: (2021). arXiv: 2110.11216 [stat.ML].

[Alq22] P. Alquier. "Approximate Bayesian Inference". In: *Entropy* 22.11 (2022).

[Als+19] J. Alsing, T. Charnock, S. Feeney, and B. Wandelt. "Fast likelihood-free cosmology with neural density estimators and active learning". In: *Monthly Notices of the Royal Astronomical Society* 488.3 (2019), pp. 4440–4458.

[ALS20] B. Axelrod, Y. P. Liu, and A. Sidford. "Near-optimal approximate discrete and continuous submodular function minimization". In: *Proceedings of the Fourteenth Annual ACM-SIAM Symposium on Discrete Algorithms*. SIAM. 2020, pp. 837–853.

[AM07] R. P. Adams and D. J. C. MacKay. "Bayesian Online Changepoint Detection". In: (2007). arXiv: 0710.3742 [stat.ML].

[AM+16] M. Auger-Méthé, C. Field, C. M. Albertsen, A. E. Derocher, M. A. Lewis, I. D. Jonsen, and J. Mills Flemming. "State-space models' dirty little secrets: even simple linear Gaussian models can have estimation problems". en. In: *Sci. Rep.* 6 (2016), p. 26677.

[AM74] D. Andrews and C. Mallows. "Scale mixtures of Normal distributions". In: *J. of Royal Stat. Soc. Series B* 36 (1974), pp. 99–102.

[AM89] B. D. Anderson and J. B. Moore. *Optimal Control: Linear Quadratic Methods*. Prentice-Hall International, Inc., 1989.

[Ama09] S.-I. Amari. "α-Divergence Is Unique, Belonging to Both *f*-Divergence and Bregman Divergence Classes". In: *IEEE Trans. Inf. Theory* 55.11 (2009), pp. 4925–4931.

[Ama98] S Amari. "Natural Gradient Works Efficiently in Learning". In: *Neural Comput.* 10.2 (1998), pp. 251–276.

[Ame+19] S. Amershi, D. Weld, M. Vorvoreanu, A. Fourney, B. Nushi, P. Collisson, J. Suh, S. Iqbal, P. N. Bennett, K. Inkpen, et al. "Guidelines for human-AI interaction". In: *Proceedings of the 2019 chi conference on human factors in computing systems*. 2019, pp. 1–13.

[Ami01] E. Amir. "Efficient Approximation for Triangulation of Minimum Treewidth". In: *UAI*. 2001.

[AMJ18a] D. Alvarez-Melis and T. S. Jaakkola. "On the robustness of interpretability methods". In: *arXiv preprint arXiv:1806.08049* (2018).

[AMJ18b] D. Alvarez-Melis and T. S. Jaakkola. "Towards robust interpretability with self-explaining neural networks". In: *arXiv preprint arXiv:1806.07538* (2018).

[Amo+16]   D. Amodei, C. Olah, J. Steinhardt, P. F. Christiano, J. Schulman, and D. Mané. "Concrete Problems in AI Safety". In: *CoRR* abs/1606.06565 (2016). arXiv: 1606.06565.

[Amo+18]   B. Amos, L. Dinh, S. Cabi, T. Rothörl, S. G. Colmenarejo, A. Muldal, T. Erez, Y. Tassa, N. de Freitas, and M. Denil. "Learning Awareness Models". In: *ICLR*. 2018.

[Amo22]   B. Amos. "Tutorial on amortized optimization for learning to optimize over continuous domains". In: (2022). arXiv: 2202.00665 [cs.LG].

[AMO88]   R. K. Ahuja, T. L. Magnanti, and J. B. Orlin. "Network flows". In: (1988).

[Ana+14]   A. Anandkumar, R. Ge, D. Hsu, S. M. Kakade, and M. Telgarsky. "Tensor Decompositions for Learning Latent Variable Models". In: *JMLR* 15 (2014), pp. 2773–2832.

[And+03]   C. Andrieu, N. de Freitas, A. Doucet, and M. Jordan. "An introduction to MCMC for machine learning". In: *Machine Learning* 50 (2003), pp. 5–43.

[And+20]   O. M. Andrychowicz et al. "Learning dexterous in-hand manipulation". In: *Int. J. Rob. Res.* 39.1 (2020), pp. 3–20.

[And82]   B. D. O. Anderson. "Reverse-time diffusion equation models". In: *Stochastic Processes and thei Applications* 12.3 (May 1982), pp. 313–326.

[Ang+18]   E. Angelino, N. Larus-Stone, D. Alabi, M. Seltzer, and C. Rudin. *Learning Certifiably Optimal Rule Lists for Categorical Data*. 2018. arXiv: 1704.01701 [stat.ML].

[Ang+20]   C. Angermueller, D. Dohan, D. Belanger, R. Deshpande, K. Murphy, and L. Colwell. "Model-based reinforcement learning for biological sequence design". In: *ICLR*. 2020.

[Ang+21]   A. N. Angelopoulos, S. Bates, E. J. Candès, M. I. Jordan, and L. Lei. "Learn then Test: Calibrating Predictive Algorithms to Achieve Risk Control". In: (2021). arXiv: 2110.01052 [cs.LG].

[Ang88]   D. Angluin. "Queries and concept learning". In: *Machine learning* 2.4 (1988), pp. 319–342.

[Ani+18]   R. Anirudh, J. J. Thiagarajan, B. Kailkhura, and T. Bremer. "An Unsupervised Approach to Solving Inverse Problems using Generative Adversarial Networks". In: (2018). arXiv: 1805.07281 [cs.CV].

[Ano19]   Anonymous. "Neural Tangents: Fast and Easy Infinite Neural Networks in Python". In: (2019).

[Ant+22]   I. Antonoglou, J. Schrittwieser, S. Ozair, T. K. Hubert, and D. Silver. "Planning in Stochastic Environments with a Learned Model". In: *ICLR*. 2022.

[AO03]   J.-H. Ahn and J.-H. Oh. "A Constrained EM Algorithm for Principal Component Analysis". In: *Neural Computation* 15 (2003), pp. 57–65.

[AOM17]   M. G. Azar, I. Osband, and R. Munos. "Minimax Regret Bounds for Reinforcement Learning". In: *ICML*. 2017, pp. 263–272.

[AP08]   J. D. Angrist and J.-S. Pischke. *Mostly harmless econometrics: An empiricist's companion*. Princeton university press, 2008.

[AP09]   J. Angrist and J.-S. Pischke. *Mostly Harmless Econometrics*. 2009.

[AP19]   M. Abadi and G. D. Plotkin. "A simple differentiable programming language". In: *Proceedings of the ACM on Programming Languages* 4.POPL (2019), pp. 1–28.

[Ara+09]   A. Aravkin, B. Bell, J. Burke, and G. Pillonetto. *An L1-Laplace Robust Kalman Smoother*. Tech. rep. U. Washington, 2009.

[Ara10]   A. Aravkin. *Student's t Kalman Smoother*. Tech. rep. U. Washington, 2010.

[Ara+17]   A. Aravkin, J. V. Burke, L. Ljung, A. Lozano, and G. Pillonetto. "Generalized Kalman smoothing: Modeling and algorithms". In: *Automatica* 86 (2017), pp. 63–86.

[Arb+18]   M. Arbel, D. Sutherland, M. Bińkowski, and A. Gretton. "On gradient regularizers for MMD GANs". In: *Advances in neural information processing systems*. 2018, pp. 6700–6710.

[Arj+19]   M. Arjovsky, L. Bottou, I. Gulrajani, and D. Lopez-Paz. "Invariant Risk Minimization". In: (2019). arXiv: 1907.02893 [stat.ML].

[Arj+20]   M. Arjovsky, L. Bottou, I. Gulrajani, and D. Lopez-Paz. *Invariant Risk Minimization*. 2020. arXiv: 1907.02893 [stat.ML].

[Arn+10]   C. W. Arnold, S. M. El-Saden, A. A. Bui, and R. Taira. "Clinical case-based retrieval using latent topic analysis". In: *AMIA annual symposium proceedings*. Vol. 2010. American Medical Informatics Association. 2010, p. 26.

[Aro+13]   S. Arora, R. Ge, Y. Halpern, D. Mimno, A. Moitra, D. Sontag, Y. Wu, and M. Zhu. "A Practical Algorithm for Topic Modeling with Provable Guarantees". In: *ICML*. 2013.

[Aro+19]   S. Arora, S. S. Du, W. Hu, Z. Li, R. Salakhutdinov, and R. Wang. "On Exact Computation with an Infinitely Wide Neural Net". In: (2019). arXiv: 1904.11955 [cs.LG].

[Aro+21]   R. Arora et al. *Theory of deep learning*. 2021.

[ARS13]   N. S. Arora, S. Russell, and E. Sudderth. "NET-VISA: Network Processing Vertically Integrated Seismic AnalysisNET-VISA: Network Processing Vertically Integrated Seismic Analysis". In: *Bull. Seismol. Soc. Am.* 103.2A (2013), pp. 709–729.

[Aru+02]   M. Arulampalam, S. Maskell, N. Gordon, and T. Clapp. "A Tutorial on Particle Filters for Online Nonlinear/Non-Gaussian Bayesian Tracking". In: *IEEE Trans. on Signal Processing* 50.2 (2002), pp. 174–189.

[Aru+17]   K. Arulkumaran, M. P. Deisenroth, M. Brundage, and A. A. Bharath. "A Brief Survey of Deep Reinforcement Learning". In: *IEEE Signal Processing Magazine, Special Issue on Deep Learning for Image Understanding* (2017).

[AS17]   A. Achille and S. Soatto. "On the Emergence of Invariance and Disentangling in Deep Representations". In: (2017). arXiv: 1706.01350 [cs.LG].

[AS18]   A. Achille and S. Soatto. "On the Emergence of Invariance and Disentangling in Deep Representations". In: *JMLR* 18 (2018), pp. 1–34.

[AS66]   S. M. Ali and S. D. Silvey. "A General Class of Coefficients of Divergence of One Distribution from Another". In: *J. R. Stat. Soc. Series B Stat. Methodol.* 28.1 (1966), pp. 131–142.

[Asa00]   C. Asavathiratham. "The Influence Model: A Tractable Representation for the Dynamics of Networked Markov Chains". PhD thesis. MIT, Dept. EECS, 2000.

[ASD20]   A. Agrawal, D. Sheldon, and J. Domke. "Advances in Black-Box VI: Normalizing Flows, Importance Weighting, and Optimization". In: *NIPS*. 2020.

[ASM17]   A. Azuma, M. Shimbo, and Y. Matsumoto. "An Algebraic Formalization of Forward and Forward-backward Algorithms". In: (2017). arXiv: 1702.06941 [cs.LG].

[ASN20]   R. Agarwal, D. Schuurmans, and M. Norouzi. "An Optimistic Perspective on Offline Reinforcement Learning". In: *ICML*. 2020.

[ASS19]   I. Andrews, J. H. Stock, and L. Sun. "Weak Instruments in Instrumental Variables Regression: Theory and Practice". In: *Annual Review of Economics* 11.1 (2019).

[AT08]   C. Andrieu and J. Thoms. "A tutorial on adaptive MCMC". In: *Statistical Computing* 18 (2008), pp. 343–373.

[AT20]   E. Agustsson and L. Theis. "Universally Quantized Neural Compression". 2020.

[Att00]   H. Attias. "A Variational Bayesian Framework for Graphical Models". In: *NIPS-12*. 2000.

[Att03]   H. Attias. "Planning by Probabilistic Inference". In: *AI-Stats*. 2003.

[Aue12]   J. E. Auerbach. "Automated evolution of interesting images". In: *Artificial Life 13*. 2012.

[Aus+21]   J. Austin, D. D. Johnson, J. Ho, D. Tarlow, and R. van den Berg. "Structured Denoising Diffusion Models in Discrete State-Spaces". In: *NIPS*. July 2021.

[AWR17]   J. Altschuler, J. Weed, and P. Rigollet. "Near-linear time approximation algorithms for optimal transport via Sinkhorn iteration". In: *arXiv preprint arXiv:1705.09634* (2017).

[AXK17]   B. Amos, L. Xu, and J. Z. Kolter. "Input convex neural networks". In: *International Conference on Machine Learning*. PMLR. 2017, pp. 146–155.

[AY19]   B. Amos and D. Yarats. "The Differentiable Cross-Entropy Method". In: (2019). arXiv: 1909.12830 [cs.LG].

[AZ17]   S. Arora and Y. Zhang. "Do gans actually learn the distribution? an empirical study". In: *arXiv preprint arXiv:1706.08224* (2017).

[Aze+20]   E. M. Azevedo, A. Deng, J. L. Montiel Olea, J. Rao, and E. G. Weyl. "A/B Testing with Fat Tails". In: *J. Polit. Econ.* (2020), pp. 000–000.

[Azi+15]   H. Azizpour, A. Sharif Razavian, J. Sullivan, A. Maki, and S. Carlsson. "From generic to specific deep representations for visual recognition". In: *Proceedings of the IEEE conference on computer vision and pattern recognition workshops*. 2015, pp. 36–45.

[BA03]   D. Barber and F. Agakov. "The IM Algorithm: A Variational Approach to Information Maximization". In: *NIPS*. NIPS'03. MIT Press, 2003, pp. 201–208.

[BA05]   W. Bechtel and A. Abrahamsen. "Explanation: A mechanist alternative". In: *Studies in History and Philosophy of Science Part C: Studies in History and Philosophy of Biological and Biomedical Sciences* 36.2 (2005), pp. 421–441.

[Bac09]   F. Bach. "High-Dimensional Non-Linear Variable Selection through Hierarchical Kernel Learning". In: (2009). arXiv: 0909.0844 [cs.LG].

[Bac+13]   F. Bach et al. "Learning with Submodular Functions: A Convex Optimization Perspective". In:

Foundations and Trends® in Machine Learning 6.2-3 (2013), pp. 145–373.

[Bac+15a]   S. Bach, A. Binder, G. Montavon, F. Klauschen, K.-R. Müller, and W. Samek. "On pixel-wise explanations for non-linear classifier decisions by layer-wise relevance propagation". In: *PloS one* 10.7 (2015), e0130140.

[Bac+15b]   S. H. Bach, M. Broecheler, B. Huang, and L. Getoor. "Hinge-Loss Markov Random Fields and Probabilistic Soft Logic". In: (2015). arXiv: 1505.04406 [cs.LG].

[Bac+18]   E. Bach, J. Dusart, L. Hellerstein, and D. Kletenik. "Submodular goal value of Boolean functions". In: *Discrete Applied Mathematics* 238 (2018), pp. 1–13.

[Bad+18]   M. A. Badgeley, J. R. Zech, L. Oakden-Rayner, B. S. Glicksberg, M. Liu, W. Gale, M. V. McConnell, B. Percha, T. M. Snyder, and J. T. Dudley. "Deep Learning Predicts Hip Fracture using Confounding Patient and Healthcare Variables". In: *CoRR* abs/1811.03695 (2018). arXiv: 1811.03695.

[Bah+20]   Y. Bahri, J. Kadmon, J. Pennington, S. Schoenholz, J. Sohl-Dickstein, and S. Ganguli. "Statistical Mechanics of Deep Learning". In: *Annu. Rev. Condens. Matter Phys.* (2020).

[Bai+15]   R. Bairi, R. Iyer, G. Ramakrishnan, and J. Bilmes. "Summarization of multi-document topic hierarchies using submodular mixtures". In: *Proceedings of the 53rd Annual Meeting of the Association for Computational Linguistics and the 7th International Joint Conference on Natural Language Processing (Volume 1: Long Papers)*. 2015, pp. 553–563.

[Bai95]   L. C. Baird. "Residual Algorithms: Reinforcement Learning with Function Approximation". In: *ICML*. 1995, pp. 30–37.

[Bak+17]   J. Baker, P. Fearnhead, E. B. Fox, and C. Nemeth. "Control Variates for Stochastic Gradient MCMC". In: (2017). arXiv: 1706.05439 [stat.CO].

[Bal17]   S. Baluja. "Learning deep models of optimization landscapes". In: *IEEE Symposium Series on Computational Intelligence (SSCI)* (2017).

[Bal+18]   D. Balduzzi, S. Racaniere, J. Martens, J. Foerster, K. Tuyls, and T. Graepel. "The mechanics of n-player differentiable games". In: *International Conference on Machine Learning*. PMLR. 2018, pp. 354–363.

[Ban+05]   A. Banerjee, I. S. Dhillon, J. Ghosh, and S. Sra. "Clustering on the unit hypersphere using von Mises-Fisher distributions". In: *JMLR*. 2005, pp. 1345–1382.

[Ban06]   A. Banerjee. "On bayesian bounds". In: *ICML*. 2006, pp. 81–88.

[Ban+18]   A. Bansal, S. Ma, D. Ramanan, and Y. Sheikh. "Recycle-gan: Unsupervised video retargeting". In: *Proceedings of the European conference on computer vision (ECCV)*. 2018, pp. 119–135.

[Bao+22a]   F. Bao, S. Nie, K. Xue, Y. Cao, C. Li, H. Su, and J. Zhu. "All are Worth Words: A ViT Backbone for Diffusion Models". In: (Sept. 2022). arXiv: 2209.12152 [cs.CV].

[Bao+22b]   H. Bao, L. Dong, S. Piao, and F. Wei. "BEiT: BERT Pre-Training of Image Transformers". In: *International Conference on Learning Representations*. 2022.

[Bas+01]   S. Basu, T. Choudhury, B. Clarkson, and A. Pentland. *Learning Human Interactions with the Influence Model*. Tech. rep. 539. MIT Media Lab, 2001.

[Bat+12]   D. Batra, P. Yadollahpour, A. Guzman-Rivera, and G. Shakhnarovich. "Diverse M-Best Solutions in Markov Random Fields". In: *ECCV*. Springer Berlin Heidelberg, 2012, pp. 1–16.

[Bau+17]   D. Bau, B. Zhou, A. Khosla, A. Oliva, and A. Torralba. "Network Dissection: Quantifying Interpretability of Deep Visual Representations". In: *Computer Vision and Pattern Recognition*. 2017.

[Bau+18]   D. Bau, J.-Y. Zhu, H. Strobelt, B. Zhou, J. B. Tenenbaum, W. T. Freeman, and A. Torralba. "Gan dissection: Visualizing and understanding generative adversarial networks". In: *arXiv preprint arXiv:1811.10597* (2018).

[Bau+20]   D. Bau, J.-Y. Zhu, H. Strobelt, A. Lapedriza, B. Zhou, and A. Torralba. "Understanding the role of individual units in a deep neural network". In: *Proceedings of the National Academy of Sciences* (2020).

[Bau+70]   L. E. Baum, T. Petrie, G. Soules, and N. Weiss. "A maximization technique occuring in the statistical analysis of probabalistic functions in Markov chains". In: *The Annals of Mathematical Statistics* 41 (1970), pp. 164–171.

[Bau74]   B. G. Baumgart. "Geometric modeling for computer vision." In: 1974.

[Bax00]   J Baxter. "A Model of Inductive Bias Learning". In: *JAIR* (2000).

[Bay+15]   A. G. Baydin, B. A. Pearlmutter, A. A. Radul, and J. M. Siskind. "Automatic differentiation in machine learning: a survey". In: (2015). arXiv: 1502.05767 [cs.SC].

[BB08]   O. Bousquet and L. Bottou. "The Tradeoffs of Large Scale Learning". In: *NIPS*. 2008, pp. 161–168.

[BB11]   L. Bottou and O. Bousquet. "The Tradeoffs of Large Scale Learning". In: *Optimization for Machine Learning*. Ed. by S. Sra, S. Nowozin, and S. J. Wright. MIT Press, 2011, pp. 351–368.

[BB12]   J. Bergstra and Y. Bengio. "Random Search for Hyper-Parameter Optimization". In: *JMLR* 13 (2012), pp. 281–305.

[BB15a]   A. Bendale and T. Boult. "Towards Open World Recognition". In: *CVPR*. 2015.

[BB15b]   J. Bornschein and Y. Bengio. "Reweighted Wake-Sleep". In: *ICLR*. 2015.

[BB17]   J. Bilmes and W. Bai. "Deep Submodular Functions". In: *Arxiv* abs/1701.08939 (2017).

[BB18]   W. Bai and J. Bilmes. "Greed is Still Good: Maximizing Monotone Submodular+Supermodular (BP) Functions". In: *International Conference on Machine Learning (ICML)*. http://proceedings.mlr.press/v80/bai18a.html. Stockholm, Sweden, 2018.

[BBM10]   N. Bhatnagar, C. Bogdanov, and E. Mossel. *The Computational Complexity of Estimating Convergence Time*. Tech. rep. arxiv, 2010.

[BBS09]   J. O. Berger, J. M. Bernardo, and D. Sun. "The Formal Definition of Reference Priors". In: *Ann. Stat.* 37.2 (2009), pp. 905–938.

[BBS95]   A. G. Barto, S. J. Bradtke, and S. P. Singh. "Learning to act using real-time dynamic programming". In: *AIJ* 72.1 (1995), pp. 81–138.

[BBV11a]   R. Benassi, J. Bect, and E. Vazquez. "Bayesian optimization using sequential Monte Carlo". In: (2011). arXiv: 1111.4802 [math.OC].

[BBV11b]   R. Benassi, J. Bect, and E. Vazquez. "Robust Gaussian Process-Based Global Optimization Using a Fully Bayesian Expected Improvement Criterion". en. In: *Intl. Conf. on Learning and Intelligent Optimization (LION)*. 2011, pp. 176–190.

[BC07]   D. Barber and S. Chiappa. "Unified inference for variational Bayesian linear Gaussian state space models". In: *NIPS*. 2007.

[BC08]   M. Bădoiu and K. L. Clarkson. "Optimal coresets for balls". In: *Computational Geometry* 40.1 (2008), pp. 14–22.

[BC14]   J. Ba and R. Caruana. "Do Deep Nets Really Need to be Deep?" In: *Advances in Neural Information Processing Systems* 27 (2014).

[BC17]   D. Beck and T. Cohn. "Learning Kernels over Strings using Gaussian Processes". In: *Proceedings of the Eighth International Joint Conference on Natural Language Processing (Volume 2: Short Papers)*. Vol. 2. 2017, pp. 67–73.

[BC89]   D. P. Bertsekas and D. A. Castanon. "The auction algorithm for the transportation problem". In: *Annals of Operations Research* 20.1 (1989), pp. 67–96.

[BC93]   B. M. Bell and F. W. Cathey. "The iterated Kalman filter update as a Gauss-Newton method". In: *IEEE Trans. Automat. Contr.* 38.2 (Feb. 1993), pp. 294–297.

[BC94]   P. Baldi and Y. Chauvin. "Smooth online learning algorithms for Hidden Markov Models". In: *Neural Computation* 6 (1994), pp. 305–316.

[BC95]   S. Baluja and R. Caruana. "Removing the Genetics from the Standard Genetic Algorithm". In: *ICML*. 1995, pp. 38–46.

[BCF10]   E. Brochu, V. M. Cora, and N. de Freitas. "A Tutorial on Bayesian Optimization of Expensive Cost Functions, with Application to Active User Modeling and Hierarchical Reinforcement Learning". In: (2010). arXiv: 1012.2599 [cs.LG].

[BCH20]   M. Briers, M. Charalambides, and C. Holmes. "Risk scoring calculation for the current NHSx contact tracing app". In: (2020). arXiv: 2005.11057 [cs.CY].

[BCJ20]   A. Buchholz, N. Chopin, and P. E. Jacob. "Adaptive Tuning Of Hamiltonian Monte Carlo Within Sequential Monte Carlo". In: *Bayesian Anal.* (2020).

[BCN18]   L. Bottou, F. E. Curtis, and J. Nocedal. "Optimization Methods for Large-Scale Machine Learning". In: *SIAM Rev.* 60.2 (2018), pp. 223–311.

[BCNM06]   C. Bucilă, R. Caruana, and A. Niculescu-Mizil. "Model compression". In: *Proceedings of the 12th ACM SIGKDD international conference on Knowledge discovery and data mining*. 2006, pp. 535–541.

[BCV13]   Y. Bengio, A. Courville, and P. Vincent. "Representation learning: A review and new perspectives". In: *IEEE transactions on pattern analysis and machine intelligence* 35.8 (2013), pp. 1798–1828.

[BD+10]   S. Ben-David, J. Blitzer, K. Crammer, A. Kulesza, F. Pereira, and J. W. Vaughan. "A theory of learning from different domains". In: *Mach. Learn.* 79.1 (May 2010), pp. 151–175.

[BD11]   A. Bhattacharya and D. B. Dunson. "Simplex factor models for multivariate unordered categorical data". In: *JASA* (2011).

[BD87]   G. Box and N. Draper. *Empirical Model-Building and Response Surfaces.* Wiley, 1987.

[BD92]   D. Bayer and P. Diaconis. "Trailing the dovetail shuffle to its lair". In: *The Annals of Applied Probability* 2.2 (1992), pp. 294–313.

[BD97]   S. Baluja and S. Davies. "Using Optimal Dependency-Trees for Combinatorial Optimization: Learning the Structure of the Search Space". In: *ICML.* 1997.

[BDM09]   R. Burkard, M. Dell'Amico, and S. Martello. *Assignment Problems.* SIAM, 2009.

[BDM10]   M. Briers, A. Doucet, and S. Maskel. "Smoothing algorithms for state-space models". In: *Annals of the Institute of Statistical Mathematics* 62.1 (2010), pp. 61–89.

[BDM17]   M. G. Bellemare, W. Dabney, and R. Munos. "A Distributional Perspective on Reinforcement Learning". In: *ICML.* 2017.

[BDM18]   N. Brosse, A. Durmus, and E. Moulines. "The promises and pitfalls of Stochastic Gradient Langevin Dynamics". In: *NIPS.* 2018.

[BDS18]   A. Brock, J. Donahue, and K. Simonyan. "Large Scale GAN Training for High Fidelity Natural Image Synthesis". In: (2018). arXiv: 1809.11096 [cs.LG].

[Bea03]   M. Beal. "Variational Algorithms for Approximate Bayesian Inference". PhD thesis. Gatsby Unit, 2003.

[Bea19]   M. A. Beaumont. "Approximate Bayesian Computation". In: *Annual Review of Statistics and Its Application* 6.1 (2019), pp. 379–403.

[Béd08]   M. Bédard. "Optimal acceptance rates for Metropolis algorithms: Moving beyond 0.234". In: *Stochastic Process. Appl.* 118.12 (2008), pp. 2198–2222.

[Beh+19]   J. Behrmann, W. Grathwohl, R. T. Q. Chen, D. Duvenaud, and J.-H. Jacobsen. "Invertible Residual Networks". In: *ICML.* 2019.

[Bel03]   A. J. Bell. "The co-information lattice". In: *ICA conference.* 2003.

[Bel+16]   M. G. Bellemare, S. Srinivasan, G. Ostrovski, T. Schaul, D. Saxton, and R. Munos. "Unifying Count-Based Exploration and Intrinsic Motivation". In: *NIPS.* 2016.

[Bel+18]   M. I. Belghazi, A. Baratin, S. Rajeshwar, S. Ozair, Y. Bengio, A. Courville, and D. Hjelm. "Mutual Information Neural Estimation". In: *ICML.* Ed. by J. Dy and A. Krause. Vol. 80. Proceedings of Machine Learning Research. PMLR, 2018, pp. 531–540.

[Bel+19]   D. Belanger, S. Vora, Z. Mariet, R. Deshpande, D. Dohan, C. Angermueller, K. Murphy, O. Chapelle, and L. Colwell. "Biological Sequence Design using Batched Bayesian Optimization". In: *NIPS workshop on ML for the sciences.* 2019.

[Bel94]   B. M. Bell. "The Iterated Kalman Smoother as a Gauss–Newton Method". In: *SIAM J. Optim.* 4.3 (Aug. 1994), pp. 626–636.

[Ben13]   Y. Bengio. "Estimating or Propagating Gradients Through Stochastic Neurons". In: (2013). arXiv: 1305.2982 [cs.LG].

[Ben+20]   K. Benidis et al. "Neural forecasting: Introduction and literature overview". In: (2020). arXiv: 2004.10240 [cs.LG].

[Bén+21]   C. Bénard, G. Biau, S. Veiga, and E. Scornet. "Interpretable random forests via rule extraction". In: *International Conference on Artificial Intelligence and Statistics.* PMLR. 2021, pp. 937–945.

[Ben+21a]   Y. Bengio, T. Deleu, E. J. Hu, S. Lahlou, M. Tiwari, and E. Bengio. "GFlowNet Foundations". In: (Nov. 2021). arXiv: 2111.09266 [cs.LG].

[Ben+21b]   G. W. Benton, W. J. Maddox, S. Lotfi, and A. G. Wilson. "Loss Surface Simplexes for Mode Connecting Volumes and Fast Ensembling". In: *ICML.* 2021.

[Ber05]   J. M. Bernardo. "Reference Analysis". In: *Handbook of Statistics.* Ed. by D. K. Dey and C. R. Rao. Vol. 25. Elsevier, 2005, pp. 17–90.

[Ber15]   D. Bertsekas. *Convex Optimization Algorithms.* Athena Scientific, 2015.

[Ber16]   D. Bertsekas. *Nonlinear Programming.* Third. Athena Scientific, 2016.

[Ber+18]   R. van den Berg, L. Hasenclever, J. M. Tomczak, and M. Welling. "Sylvester normalizing flows for variational inference". In: *AISTATS.* 2018.

[Ber+19]   H. Berard, G. Gidel, A. Almahairi, P. Vincent, and S. Lacoste-Julien. "A Closer Look at the Optimization Landscapes of Generative Adversarial Networks". In: *International Conference on Learning Representations.* 2019.

[Ber19]   D. Bertsekas. *Reinforcement learning and optimal control.* Athena Scientific, 2019.

[Ber+21]   J. Berner, P. Grohs, G. Kutyniok, and P. Petersen. "The Modern Mathematics of Deep Learning". In: (2021). arXiv: 2105.04026 [cs.LG].

[Ber85a]   J. Berger. "Bayesian Salesmanship". In: *Bayesian Inference and Decision Techniques with Applications: Essays in Honor of Bruno deFinetti.* Ed. by P. K. Goel and A. Zellner. North-Holland, 1985.

[Ber85b]   J. Berger. *Statistical Decision Theory and Bayesian Analysis (2nd edition).* Springer-Verlag, 1985.

[Ber97a]   D. A. Berry. "Teaching Elementary Bayesian Statistics with Real Applications in Science". In: *Am. Stat.* 51.3 (1997), pp. 241–246.

[Ber97b]   D. Bertsekas. *Parallel and Distribution Computation: Numerical Methods.* Athena Scientific, 1997.

[Ber99]   A. Berchtold. "The double chain Markov model". In: *Comm. Stat. Theor. Methods* 28 (1999), pp. 2569–2589.

[Bes75]   J. Besag. "Statistical analysis of non-lattice data". In: *The Statistician* 24 (1975), pp. 179–196.

[Bet13]   M. Betancourt. "A General Metric for Riemannian Manifold Hamiltonian Monte Carlo". In: *Geometric Science of Information.* Springer Berlin Heidelberg, 2013, pp. 327–334.

[Bet17]   M. Betancourt. "A Conceptual Introduction to Hamiltonian Monte Carlo". In: (2017). arXiv: 1701.02434 [stat.ME].

[Bet18]   M. Betancourt. *Probability Theory (For Scientists and Engineers).* 2018.

[Bey+20]   L. Beyer, O. J. Hénaff, A. Kolesnikov, X. Zhai, and A. van den Oord. "Are we done with ImageNet?" In: (2020). arXiv: 2006.07159 [cs.CV].

[BFH75]   Y. Bishop, S. Fienberg, and P. Holland. *Discrete Multivariate Analysis: Theory and Practice.* MIT Press, 1975.

[BFY20]   T. D. Barfoot, J. R. Forbes, and D. Yoon. "Exactly Sparse Gaussian Variational Inference with Application to Derivative-Free Batch Nonlinear State Estimation". In: *Intl. J. of Robotics Research* (2020).

[BG06]   M. Beal and Z. Ghahramani. "Variational Bayesian Learning of Directed Graphical Models with Hidden Variables". In: *Bayesian Analysis* 1.4 (2006).

[BG13]   M. J. Betancourt and M. Girolami. "Hamiltonian Monte Carlo for Hierarchical Models". In: (2013). arXiv: 1312.0906 [stat.ME].

[BG73]   A. Björck and G. H. Golub. "Numerical methods for computing angles between linear subspaces". In: *Mathematics of computation* 27.123 (1973), pp. 579–594.

[BG96]   A. Becker and D. Geiger. "A sufficiently fast algorithm for finding close to optimal junction trees". In: *UAI.* 1996.

[BGHM17]   J. Boyd-Graber, Y. Hu, and D. Mimno. "Applications of Topic Models". In: *Foundations and Trends® in Information Retrieval* 11.2-3 (2017), pp. 143–296.

[BGM17]   J Ba, R Grosse, and J Martens. "Distributed Second-Order Optimization using Kronecker-Factored Approximations". In: *ICLR.* openreview.net, 2017.

[BGS16]   Y. Burda, R. Grosse, and R. Salakhutdinov. "Importance Weighted Autoencoders". In: *ICLR.* 2016.

[BGT93]   C. Berrou, A. Glavieux, and P. Thitimajashima. "Near Shannon limit error-correcting coding and decoding: Turbo codes". In: *Proc. IEEE Intl. Comm. Conf.* (1993).

[BH11]   M.-F. Balcan and N. J. Harvey. "Learning submodular functions". In: *Proceedings of the forty-third annual ACM symposium on Theory of computing.* 2011, pp. 793–802.

[BH20]   M. T. Bahadori and D. Heckerman. "Debiasing Concept-based Explanations with Causal Analysis". In: *International Conference on Learning Representations.* 2020.

[BH92]   D. Barry and J. A. Hartigan. "Product partition models for change point problems". In: *Annals of statistics* 20 (1992), pp. 260–279.

[Bha+19]   A. Bhadra, J. Datta, N. G. Polson, and B. T. Willard. "Lasso Meets Horseshoe: a survey". In: *Bayesian Anal.* 34.3 (2019), pp. 405–427.

[Bha+21]   K. Bhatia, N. Kuang, Y. Ma, and Y. Wang. *Statistical and computational tradeoffs in variational Bayes: a case study of inferential model selection.* Tech. rep. 2021.

[BHB19]   P. Bachman, R. D. Hjelm, and W. Buchwalter. *Learning Representations by Maximizing Mutual Information Across Views.* 2019. arXiv: 1906.00910 [cs.LG].

[BHB22]   F. Berns, J. Hüwel, and C. Beecks. "Automated Model Inference for Gaussian Processes: An Overview of State-of-the-Art Methods and Algorithms". en. In: *SN Comput Sci* 3.4 (May 2022), p. 300.

[BHC19]   M. Binkowski, D. Hjelm, and A. Courville. "Batch weight for domain adaptation with mass shift". In: *Proceedings of the IEEE/CVF International Conference on Computer Vision.* 2019, pp. 1844–1853.

[BHO75]   P. J. Bickel, E. A. Hammel, and J. W. O'connell. "Sex bias in graduate admissions: data from berkeley". en. In: *Science* 187.4175 (1975), pp. 398–404.

[BHPI02]   M. Bădoiu, S. Har-Peled, and P. Indyk. "Approximate clustering via core-sets". In: *Proceedings of the thiry-fourth annual ACM symposium on Theory of computing.* 2002, pp. 250–257.

[BHW16]   P. G. Bissiri, C. Holmes, and S. Walker. "A General Framework for Updating Belief Distributions". In: *JRSSB* 78.5 (2016), 1103–1130.

[Bic09]   D. Bickson. "Gaussian Belief Propagation: Theory and Application". PhD thesis. Hebrew University of Jerusalem, 2009.

[Bie06]   G. J. Bierman. *Factorization Methods for Discrete Sequential Estimation (Dover Books on Mathematics).* en. Illustrated edition. Dover Publications, 2006.

[Big+11]   B. Biggio, G. Fumera, I. Pillai, and F. Roli. "A survey and experimental evaluation of image spam filtering techniques". In: *Pattern recognition letters* 32.10 (2011), pp. 1436–1446.

[Bil01]   J. A. Bilmes. *Graphical Models and Automatic Speech Recognition.* Tech. rep. UWEETR-2001-0005. Univ. Washington, Dept. of Elec. Eng., 2001.

[Bil22]   J. Bilmes. "Submodularity In Machine Learning and Artificial Intelligence". In: (2022). arXiv: 2202.00132 [cs.LG].

[Biń+18]   M. Bińkowski, D. J. Sutherland, M. Arbel, and A. Gretton. "Demystifying MMD GANs". In: *ICLR.* 2018.

[Bin+18]   M. Binkowski, D. J. Sutherland, M. Arbel, and A. Gretton. "Demystifying MMD GANs". In: *International Conference on Learning Representations.* 2018.

[Bin+19]   E. Bingham, J. P. Chen, M. Jankowiak, F. Obermeyer, N. Pradhan, T. Karaletsos, R. Singh, P. Szerlip, P. Horsfall, and N. D. Goodman. "Pyro: Deep Universal Probabilistic Programming". In: *JMLR* 20.28 (2019), pp. 1–6.

[Biń+19]   M. Bińkowski, J. Donahue, S. Dieleman, A. Clark, E. Elsen, N. Casagrande, L. C. Cobo, and K. Simonyan. "High Fidelity Speech Synthesis with Adversarial Networks". In: *International Conference on Learning Representations.* 2019.

[Bin+97]   J. Binder, D. Koller, S. J. Russell, and K. Kanazawa. "Adaptive Probabilistic Networks with Hidden Variables". In: *Machine Learning* 29 (1997), pp. 213–244.

[Bis06]   C. Bishop. *Pattern recognition and machine learning.* Springer, 2006.

[Bis99]   C. Bishop. "Bayesian PCA". In: *NIPS.* 1999.

[Bit16]   S. Bitzer. *The UKF exposed: How it works, when it works and when it's better to sample.* 2016.

[Bit+21]   J. Bitterwolf, A. Meinke, M. Augustin, and M. Hein. "Revisiting out-of-distribution detection: A simple baseline is surprisingly effective". In: *ICML Workshop on Uncertainty in Deep Learning (UDL).* 2021.

[BJ05] F. Bach and M. Jordan. *A probabilistic interpretation of canonical correlation analysis*. Tech. rep. 688. U. C. Berkeley, 2005.

[BJ06] W. Buntine and A. Jakulin. "Discrete Component Analysis". In: *Subspace, Latent Structure and Feature Selection: Statistical and Optimization Perspectives Workshop*. 2006.

[BJV97] J. S. D. Bonet, C. L. I. Jr., and P. A. Viola. "MIMIC: Finding Optima by Estimating Probability Densities". In: *NIPS*. MIT Press, 1997, pp. 424–430.

[BK10] R. Bardenet and B. Kegl. "Surrogating the surrogate: accelerating Gaussian-process-based global optimization with a mixture cross-entropy algorithm". In: *ICML*. 2010.

[BK15] D. Belanger and S. Kakade. "A Linear Dynamical System Model for Text". en. In: *ICML*. 2015, pp. 833–842.

[BK19] M. Bonvini and E. H. Kennedy. "Sensitivity Analysis via the Proportion of Unmeasured Confounding". In: *arXiv e-prints*, arXiv:1912.02793 (Dec. 2019), arXiv:1912.02793. arXiv: 1912.02793 [stat.ME].

[BKB17] O. Bastani, C. Kim, and H. Bastani. "Interpreting blackbox models via model extraction". In: *arXiv preprint arXiv:1705.08504* (2017).

[BKH16] J. L. Ba, J. R. Kiros, and G. E. Hinton. "Layer Normalization". In: (2016). arXiv: 1607.06450 [stat.ML].

[BKM16] D. M. Blei, A. Kucukelbir, and J. D. McAuliffe. "Variational Inference: A Review for Statisticians". In: *JASA* (2016).

[BKS19] A. Bennett, N. Kallus, and T. Schnabel. "Deep Generalized Method of Moments for Instrumental Variable Analysis". In: *Advances in Neural Information Processing Systems*. 2019, pp. 3564–3574.

[BL06] D. Blei and J. Lafferty. "Dynamic topic models". In: *ICML*. 2006, pp. 113–120.

[BL07a] C. M. Bishop and J. Lasserre. "Generative or discriminative? Getting the best of both worlds". In: *Bayesian Statistics 8*. 2007.

[BL07b] D. Blei and J. Lafferty. "A Correlated Topic Model of "Science"". In: *Annals of Applied Stat.* 1.1 (2007), pp. 17–35.

[BLC18] A. J. Bose, H. Ling, and Y. Cao. "Adversarial Contrastive Estimation". In: *Proceedings of the 56th Annual Meeting of the Association for Computational Linguistics (Volume 1: Long Papers)*. 2018, pp. 1021–1032.

[Ble12] D. M. Blei. "Probabilistic topic models". In: *Commun. ACM* 55.4 (2012), pp. 77–84.

[BLH21] Y. Bengio, Y. Lecun, and G. Hinton. "Deep learning for AI". In: *Comm. of the ACM* 64.7 (June 2021), pp. 58–65.

[BLH22] J. Bornschein, Y. Li, and M. Hutter. "Sequential Learning Of Neural Networks for Prequential MDL". In: (Oct. 2022). arXiv: 2210.07931 [stat.ML].

[BLM16] S. Boucheron, G. Lugosi, and P. Massart. *Concentration Inequalities: A Nonasymptotic Theory of Independence*. Oxford University Press, 2016.

[Blo+16] A. Bloniarz, H. Liu, C.-H. Zhang, J. S. Sekhon, and B. Yu. "Lasso adjustments of treatment effect estimates in randomized experiments". In: *Proceedings of the National Academy of Sciences* 113.27 (2016), pp. 7383–7390.

[BLS11] G. Blanchard, G. Lee, and C. Scott. "Generalizing from several related classification tasks to a new unlabeled sample". In: *NIPS*. 2011.

[BLS17] J. Ballé, V. Laparra, and E. P. Simoncelli. "End-to-end Optimized Image Compression". In: *ICLR*. 2017.

[Blu+15] C. Blundell, J. Cornebise, K. Kavukcuoglu, and D. Wierstra. "Weight Uncertainty in Neural Networks". In: *ICML*. 2015.

[BM+18] G. Barth-Maron, M. W. Hoffman, D. Budden, W. Dabney, D. Horgan, T. B. Dhruva, A. Muldal, N. Heess, and T. Lillicrap. "Distributed Distributional Deterministic Policy Gradients". In: *ICLR*. 2018.

[BM19] Y. Blau and T. Michaeli. "Rethinking Lossy Compression: The Rate-Distortion-Perception Tradeoff". In: *ICML*. 2019.

[BM93] H. A. Bourlard and N. Morgan. *Connectionist Speech Recognition: A Hybrid Approach*. USA: Kluwer Academic Publishers, 1993.

[BMK20] Z. Borsos, M. Mutny, and A. Krause. "Coresets via Bilevel Optimization for Continual Learning and Streaming". In: *Advances in Neural Information Processing Systems* 33 (2020).

[BMM00] J. Barnard, R. Mcculloch, and X.-L. Meng. "Modeling covariance matrices in terms of standard deviations and correlations, with application to shrinkage". In: *Stat. Sin.* 10 (2000).

[BMP19] A. Brunel, D. Mazza, and M. Pagani. "Backpropagation in the Simply Typed Lambda-Calculus with Linear Negation". In: *Proc. ACM Program. Lang.* 4.POPL (2019).

[BMR97] J. Binder, K. Murphy, and S. Russell. "Space-efficient inference in dynamic probabilistic networks". In: *IJCAI*. 1997.

[BMS11] S. Bubeck, R. Munos, and G. Stoltz. "Pure Exploration in Finitely-armed and Continuous-armed Bandits". In: *Theoretical Computer Science* 412.19 (2011), pp. 1832–1852.

[BNJ03a] D. Blei, A. Ng, and M. Jordan. "Latent Dirichlet allocation". In: *JMLR* 3 (2003), pp. 993–1022.

[BNJ03b] D. M. Blei, A. Y. Ng, and M. I. Jordan. "Latent dirichlet allocation". In: *JMLR* 3 (2003), pp. 993–1022.

[BO14] J. Bayer and C. Osendorfer. "Learning Stochastic Recurrent Networks". In: *Workshop on Advances in Variational Inference*. 2014.

[Boe+05] P.-T. de Boer, D. P. Kroese, S. Mannor, and R. Y. Rubinstein. "A Tutorial on the Cross-Entropy Method". en. In: *Ann. Oper. Res.* 134.1 (2005), pp. 19–67.

[Boh92] D. Bohning. "Multinomial logistic regression algorithm". In: *Annals of the Inst. of Statistical Math.* 44 (1992), pp. 197–200.

[Bol02] W. Bolstad. "Teaching Bayesian Statistics to Undergraduates: Who, What, Where, When, Why and How". In: *ICOTS6 Intl. Conf. on Teaching Statistics*. 2002.

[Bol89] K. Bollen. *Structural Equation Models with Latent Variables*. John Wiley & Sons, 1989.

[Bon64] G. Bonnet. "Transformations des signaux aléatoires a travers les systemes non lineáires sans memóire". In: *Annales des Telecommuncations* 19 (1964).

[Bös+17] J.-H. Böse, V. Flunkert, J. Gasthaus, T. Januschowski, D. Lange, D. Salinas, D. Schelter, M. Seeger, and Y. Wang. "Probabilistic Demand Forecasting at Scale". In: *Proceedings VLDB Endowment* 10.12 (2017), pp. 1694–1705.

[Bot+13] L. Bottou, J. Peters, J. Quiñonero-Candela, D. X. Charles, D. M. Chickering, E. Portugaly, D. Ray, P. Simard, and E. Snelson. "Counterfactual Reasoning and Learning Systems: The Example of Computational Advertising". In: *JMLR* 14 (2013), pp. 3207–3260.

[Bow+16a] S. R. Bowman, L. Vilnis, O. Vinyals, A. M. Dai, R. Jozefowicz, and S. Bengio. "Generating Sentences from a Continuous Space". In: *CONLL*. 2016.

[Bow+16b] S. R. Bowman, L. Vilnis, O. Vinyals, A. M. Dai, R. Jozefowicz, and S. Bengio. "Generating Sentences from a Continuous Space". In: *CONLL*. 2016.

[Box80] G. E. P. Box. "Sampling and Bayes' Inference in Scientific Modelling and Robustness". In: *J. of Royal Stat. Soc. Series A* 143.4 (1980), pp. 383–430.

[BP13] K. A. Bollen and J. Pearl. "Eight Myths About Causality and Structural Equation Models". In: *Handbook of Causal Analysis for Social Research*. Ed. by S. L. Morgan. Springer Netherlands, 2013, pp. 301–328.

[BP16] E. Bareinboim and J. Pearl. "Causal inference and the data-fusion problem". en. In: *Proc. Natl. Acad. Sci. U. S. A.* 113.27 (2016), pp. 7345–7352.

[BP21] T. Bricken and C. Pehlevan. "Attention Approximates Sparse Distributed Memory". In: *NIPS*. 2021.

[BPK16] S. Bulo, L. Porzi, and P. Kontschieder. "Distillation dropout". In: *ICML*. 2016.

[BPL21a] R. Balestriero, J. Pesenti, and Y. LeCun. "Learning in High Dimension Always Amounts to Extrapolation". In: (Oct. 2021). arXiv: 2110 . 09485 [cs.LG].

[BPL21b] A. Bardes, J. Ponce, and Y. LeCun. "Vicreg: Variance-invariance-covariance regularization for self-supervised learning". In: *arXiv preprint arXiv:2105.04906* (2021).

[BPS16] A. G. Baydin, B. A. Pearlmutter, and J. M. Siskind. "DiffSharp: An AD library for .NET languages". In: *arXiv preprint arXiv:1611.03423* (2016).

[BR05] H. Bang and J. M. Robins. "Doubly Robust Estimation in Missing Data and Causal Inference Models". In: *Biometrics* 61.4 (2005), pp. 962–973.

[BR18] B. Biggio and F. Roli. "Wild patterns: Ten years after the rise of adversarial machine learning". In: *Pattern Recognition* 84 (2018), pp. 317–331.

[BR98] S. Brooks and G. Roberts. "Assessing convergence of Markov Chain Monte Carlo algorithms". In: *Statistics and Computing* 8 (1998), pp. 319–335.

[Bra+18] J. Bradbury, R. Frostig, P. Hawkins, M. J. Johnson, C. Leary, D. Maclaurin, and S. Wanderman-Milne. *JAX: composable transformations of Python+NumPy programs*. Version 0.1.55. 2018.

[Bra96] M. Brand. *Coupled hidden Markov models for modeling interacting processes*. Tech. rep. 405. MIT Lab for Perceptual Computing, 1996.

[Bre01] L. Breiman. "Statistical modeling: The two cultures (with comments and a rejoinder by the author)". In: *Statistical science* 16.3 (2001), pp. 199–231.

[Bre+17] L. Breiman, J. H. Friedman, R. A. Olshen, and C. J. Stone. *Classification and regression trees*. Routledge, 2017.

[Bre+20a] J. Brehmer, G. Louppe, J. Pavez, and K. Cranmer. "Mining gold from implicit models to improve likelihood-free inference". en. In: *Proc. Natl. Acad. Sci. U. S. A.* 117.10 (2020), pp. 5242–5249.

[Bre+20b] R. Brekelmans, V. Masrani, F. Wood, G. Ver Steeg, and A. Galstyan. "All in the Exponential Family: Bregman Duality in Thermodynamic Variational Inference". In: *ICML*. 2020.

[Bre67] L. M. Bregman. "The relaxation method of finding the common point of convex sets and its application to the solution of problems in convex programming". In: *USSR Computational Mathematics and Mathematical Physics* 7.3 (1967), pp. 200–217.

[Bre91] Y. Brenier. "Polar factorization and monotone rearrangement of vector-valued functions". In: *Communications on pure and applied mathematics* 44.4 (1991), pp. 375–417.

[Bre92] J. Breese. "Construction of belief and decision networks". In: *Computational Intelligence* 8 (1992), 624–647.

[Bre96] L. Breiman. "Stacked regressions". In: *Mach. Learn.* 24.1 (1996), pp. 49–64.

[BRG20] R. Bai, V. Rockova, and E. I. George. "Spike-and-slab meets LASSO: A review of the spike-and-slab LASSO". In: (2020). arXiv: 2010.06451 [stat.ME].

[Bri12] W. M. Briggs. "It is Time to Stop Teaching Frequentism to Non-statisticians". In: *arXiv* (2012). arXiv: 1201.2590 [stat.OT].

[Bri50] G. W. Brier. "Verification of forecasts expressed in terms of probability". In: *Monthly Weather Review* 78.1 (1950), pp. 1–3.

[Bro09] G. Brown. "A new perspective on information theoretic feature selection". In: *AISTATS*. 2009.

[Bro+13] T. Broderick, N. Boyd, A. Wibisono, A. C. Wilson, and M. I. Jordan. "Streaming Variational Bayes". In: *NIPS*. 2013.

[Bro+15] K. H. Brodersen, F. Gallusser, J. Koehler, N. Remy, and S. L. Scott. "Inferring causal impact using Bayesian structural time-series models". In: *Ann. Appl. Stat.* 9.1 (2015), pp. 247–274.

[Bro18] T. Broderick. *Tutorial: Variational Bayes and Beyond*. 2018.

[Bro19] J. Brownlee. *Generative Adversarial Networks with Python*. Accessed: 2019-8-27. Machine Learning Mastery, 2019.

[Bro+20a] D. Brookes, A. Busia, C. Fannjiang, K. Murphy, and J. Listgarten. "A view of estimation of distribution algorithms through the lens of expectation-maximization". In: *GECCO*. GECCO '20. Association for Computing Machinery, 2020, pp. 189–190.

[Bro+20b] P. Brouillard, S. Lachapelle, A. Lacoste, S. Lacoste-Julien, and A. Drouin. "Differentiable Causal Discovery from Interventional Data". In: *NIPS*. July 2020.

[Bro+20c] D. Brown, R. Coleman, R. Srinivasan, and S. Niekum. "Safe imitation learning via fast bayesian reward inference from preferences". In: *International Conference on Machine Learning*. PMLR. 2020, pp. 1165–1177.

[Bro+20d] T. B. Brown et al. "Language Models are Few-Shot Learners". In: (2020). arXiv: 2005.14165 [cs.CL].

[BRS17] E. Balkanski, A. Rubinstein, and Y. Singer. "The Limitations of Optimization from Samples". In: *Proceedings of the 49th Annual ACM SIGACT Symposium on Theory of Computing*. STOC 2017. Montreal, Canada: Association for Computing Machinery, 2017, 1016–1027.

[BRSS18] N. Bou-Rabee and J. M. Sanz-Serna. "Geometric integrators and the Hamiltonian Monte Carlo method". In: *Acta Numer.* (2018).

[Bru+18] M. Brundage et al. "The Malicious Use of Artificial Intelligence: Forecasting, Prevention, and Mitigation". In: (2018). arXiv: 1802.07228 [cs.AI].

[BS17] E. Balkanski and Y. Singer. "Minimizing a Submodular Function from Samples." In: *NIPS*. 2017, pp. 814–822.

[BS18] S. Barratt and R. Sharma. "A note on the inception score". In: *arXiv preprint arXiv:1801.01973* (2018).

[BS20] E. Balkanski and Y. Singer. "A lower bound for parallel submodular minimization". In: *Proceedings of the 52nd Annual ACM SIGACT Symposium on Theory of Computing*. 2020, pp. 130–139.

[BS+20] S. Bobadilla-Suarez, C. Ahlheim, A. Mehrotra, A. Panos, and B. C. Love. "Measures of neural similarity". In: *Computational Brain & Behavior* 3.4 (2020), pp. 369–383.

[BS94] J. Bernardo and A. Smith. *Bayesian Theory*. John Wiley, 1994.

[BS95a] A. J. Bell and T. J. Sejnowski. "An information maximisation approach to blind separation and blind deconvolution". In: *Neural Computation* 7.6 (1995), pp. 1129–1159.

[BS95b] A. J. Bell and T. J. Sejnowski. "An information-maximization approach to blind separation and blind deconvolution". In: *Neural computation* 7.6 (1995), pp. 1129–1159.

[BSA83] A. G. Barto, R. S. Sutton, and C. W. Anderson. "Neuronlike adaptive elements that can solve difficult learning control problems". In: *SMC* 13.5 (1983), pp. 834–846.

[BSF88] Y. Bar-Shalom and T. Fortmann. *Tracking and data association*. Academic Press, 1988.

[BSL93] Y. Bar-Shalom and X. Li. *Estimation and Tracking: Principles, Techniques and Software*. Artech House, 1993.

[BSWT11] Y. Bar-Shalom, P. K. Willett, and X. Tian. *Tracking and Data Fusion: A Handbook of Algorithms*. en. Yaakov Bar-Shalom, 2011.

[BT00] C. Bishop and M. Tipping. "Variational relevance vector machines". In: *UAI*. 2000.

[BT04] G. Bouchard and B. Triggs. "The tradeoff between generative and discriminative classifiers". In: *IASC International Symposium on Computational Statistics (COMPSTAT '04)*. 2004.

[BT08] D. Bertsekas and J. Tsitsiklis. *Introduction to Probability*. 2nd Edition. Athena Scientific, 2008.

[BT12] M. Botvinick and M. Toussaint. "Planning as inference". en. In: *Trends Cogn. Sci.* 16.10 (2012), pp. 485–488.

[BT73] G. Box and G. Tiao. *Bayesian inference in statistical analysis*. Addison-Wesley, 1973.

[BTEGN09] A. Ben-Tal, L. El Ghaoui, and A. Nemirovski. *Robust optimization*. Vol. 28. Princeton University Press, 2009.

[Buc+12] N. Buchbinder, M. Feldman, J. Naor, and R. Schwartz. "A tight (1/2) linear-time approximation to unconstrained submodular maximization". In: *In FOCS* (2012).

[Buc+17] C. L. Buckley, C. S. Kim, S. McGregor, and A. K. Seth. "The free energy principle for action and perception: A mathematical review". In: *J. Math. Psychol.* 81 (2017), pp. 55–79.

[Buc21] J. Buchner. "Nested Sampling Methods". In: (Jan. 2021). arXiv: 2101.09675 [stat.CO].

[Bud+21] K. Budhathoki, D. Janzing, P. Bloebaum, and H. Ng. "Why did the distribution change?" In: *AISTATS*. Ed. by A. Banerjee and K. Fukumizu. Vol. 130. Proceedings of Machine Learning Research. PMLR, 2021, pp. 1666–1674.

[Bul11] A. D. Bull. "Convergence rates of efficient global optimization algorithms". In: *JMLR* 12 (2011), 2879–2904.

[Bul+20] S. Bulusu, B. Kailkhura, B. Li, P. K. Varshney, and D. Song. "Anomalous Example Detection in Deep Learning: A Survey". In: *IEEE Access* 8 (2020), pp. 132330–132347.

[BV04] S. Boyd and L. Vandenberghe. *Convex optimization*. Cambridge, 2004.

[BVHP18] S. Beery, G. Van Horn, and P. Perona. "Recognition in terra incognita". In: *Proceedings of the European Conference on Computer Vision (ECCV)*. 2018, pp. 456–473.

[BVW02] H. Bui, S. Venkatesh, and G. West. "Policy Recognition in the Abstract Hidden Markov Model". In: *JAIR* 17 (2002), pp. 451–499.

[BW20] G. J. J. van den Burg and C. K. I. Williams. "An Evaluation of Change Point Detection Algorithms". In: (2020). arXiv: 2003.06222 [stat.ML].

[BW21] G. J. van den Burg and C. K. Williams. "On Memorization in Probabilistic Deep Generative Models". In: *NIPS*. 2021.

[BWM18] A. Buchholz, F. Wenzel, and S. Mandt. "Quasi-Monte Carlo Variational Inference". In: *ICML*. 2018.

[BWR16] M. Bauer, M. van der Wilk, and C. E. Rasmussen. "Understanding Probabilistic Sparse Gaussian Process Approximations". In: *NIPS*. 2016, pp. 1533–1541.

[BYH20] O. Bohdal, Y. Yang, and T. Hospedales. "Flexible Dataset Distillation: Learn Labels Instead of Images". In: *arXiv preprint arXiv:2006.08572* (2020).

[BYM17] D. Belanger, B. Yang, and A. McCallum. "End-to-End Learning for Structured Prediction Energy Networks". In: *ICML*. Ed. by D. Precup and Y. W. Teh. Vol. 70. Proceedings of Machine Learning Research. PMLR, 2017, pp. 429–439.

[Byr+16] R Byrd, S Hansen, J Nocedal, and Y Singer. "A Stochastic Quasi-Newton Method for Large-Scale Optimization". In: *SIAM J. Optim.* 26.2 (2016), pp. 1008–1031.

[BZ20] A. Barbu and S.-C. Zhu. *Monte Carlo Methods*. en. Springer, 2020.

[CA13]   E. F. Camacho and C. B. Alba. *Model predictive control*. Springer, 2013.

[Cac+18]   M. Caccia, L. Caccia, W. Fedus, H. Larochelle, J. Pineau, and L. Charlin. "Language GANs Falling Short". In: *CoRR* abs/1811.02549 (2018). arXiv: 1811.02549.

[CAII20]   V. Coscrato, M. H. de Almeida Inácio, and R. Izbicki. "The NN-Stacking: Feature weighted linear stacking through neural networks". In: *Neurocomputing* (2020).

[Cal+07]   G. Calinescu, C. Chekuri, M. Pál, and J. Vondrák. "Maximizing a submodular set function subject to a matroid constraint". In: *Proceedings of the 12th International Conference on Integer Programming and Combinatorial Optimization (IPCO)*. 2007, pp. 182–196.

[Cal20]   O. Calin. *Deep Learning Architectures: A Mathematical Approach*. en. 1st ed. Springer, 2020.

[Cam+21]   A. Campbell, Y. Shi, T. Rainforth, and A. Doucet. "Online Variational Filtering and Parameter Learning". In: *NIPS*. 2021.

[Can04]   J. Canny. "GaP: a factor model for discrete data". In: *SIGIR*. 2004, pp. 122–129.

[Cao+15]   Y. Cao, M. A Brubaker, D. J Fleet, and A. Hertzmann. "Efficient Optimization for Sparse Gaussian Process Regression". en. In: *IEEE PAMI* 37.12 (2015), pp. 2415–2427.

[Cao+22]   H. Cao, C. Tan, Z. Gao, G. Chen, P.-A. Heng, and S. Z. Li. "A Survey on Generative Diffusion Model". In: (Sept. 2022). arXiv: 2209.02646 [cs.AI].

[Cap+22]   T. Capretto, C. Piho, R. Kumar, J. Westfall, T. Yarkoni, and O. A. Martin. "Bambi: A Simple Interface for Fitting Bayesian Linear Models in Python". In: *Journal of Statistical Software* 103.15 (2022), 1–29.

[Car03]   P. Carbonetto. "Unsupervised Statistical Models for General Object Recognition". MA thesis. University of British Columbia, 2003.

[Car+15]   R. Caruana, Y. Lou, J. Gehrke, P. Koch, M. Sturm, and N. Elhadad. "Intelligible models for healthcare: Predicting pneumonia risk and hospital 30-day readmission". In: *Proceedings of the 21th ACM SIGKDD international conference on knowledge discovery and data mining*. 2015, pp. 1721–1730.

[Car+19]   N. Carlini, A. Athalye, N. Papernot, W. Brendel, J. Rauber, D. Tsipras, I. Goodfellow, A. Madry, and A. Kurakin. "On evaluating adversarial robustness". In: *arXiv preprint arXiv:1902.06705* (2019).

[Car+21]   M. Caron, H. Touvron, I. Misra, H. Jégou, J. Mairal, P. Bojanowski, and A. Joulin. *Emerging Properties in Self-Supervised Vision Transformers*. 2021. arXiv: 2104.14294 [cs.CV].

[Car97]   R. Caruana. "Multitask Learning". In: *Machine Learning* 28.1 (1997), pp. 41–75.

[Cat08]   A. Caticha. *Lectures on Probability, Entropy, and Statistical Physics*. 2008. arXiv: 0808.0012 [physics.data-an].

[Cat+11]   A. Caticha, A. Mohammad-Djafari, J.-F. Bercher, and P. Bessiére. "Entropic Inference". In: *AIP Conference Proceedings* 1305.1 (2011), pp. 20–29. eprint: https://aip.scitation.org/doi/pdf/10.1063/1.3573619.

[CB20]   Y. Chen and P. Bühlmann. "Domain adaptation under structural causal models". In: *JMLR* (2020).

[CBL20]   K. Cranmer, J. Brehmer, and G. Louppe. "The frontier of simulation-based inference". In: *Proceedings of the National Academy of Sciences* 117.48 (2020), pp. 30055–30062.

[CBR20]   Z. Chen, Y. Bei, and C. Rudin. "Concept whitening for interpretable image recognition". In: *Nature Machine Intelligence* 2.12 (2020), pp. 772–782.

[CC84]   M. Conforti and G. Cornuejols. "Submodular set functions, matroids and the greedy algorithm: tight worst-case bounds and some generalizations of the Rado-Edmonds theorem". In: *Discrete Applied Mathematics* 7.3 (1984), pp. 251–274.

[CC96]   M. Cowles and B. Carlin. "Markov Chain Monte Carlo Convergence Diagnostics: A Comparative Review". In: *JASA* 91 (1996), pp. 883–904.

[CCS22]   A. Corenflos, N. Chopin, and S. Särkkä. "DeSequentialized Monte Carlo: a parallel-in-time particle smoother". In: (2022). arXiv: 2202.02264 [stat.CO].

[CDC15]   C. Chen, N. Ding, and L. Carin. "On the Convergence of Stochastic Gradient MCMC Algorithms with High-Order Integrators". In: *NIPS*. 2015.

[CDS02]   M. Collins, S. Dasgupta, and R. E. Schapire. "A Generalization of Principal Components Analysis to the Exponential Family". In: *NIPS-14*. 2002.

[CDS19]   A. Clark, J. Donahue, and K. Simonyan. "Adversarial video generation on complex datasets". In: *arXiv preprint arXiv:1907.06571* (2019).

[Cér+12]   F Cérou, P Del Moral, T Furon, and A Guyader. "Sequential Monte Carlo for rare event estimation". In: *Stat. Comput.* 22.3 (2012), pp. 795–808.

[CFG14]   T. Chen, E. B. Fox, and C. Guestrin. "Stochastic Gradient Hamiltonian Monte Carlo". In: *ICML*. 2014.

[CG00]   S. S. Chen and R. A. Gopinath. "Gaussianization". In: *NIPS*. 2000, pp. 423–429.

[CG15]   X. Chen and A. Gupta. "Webly supervised learning of convolutional networks". In: *Proceedings of the IEEE International Conference on Computer Vision*. 2015, pp. 1431–1439.

[CG18]   C. Ceylan and M. U. Gutmann. "Conditional Noise-Contrastive Estimation of Unnormalised Models". In: *International Conference on Machine Learning*. 2018, pp. 726–734.

[CG96]   S. Chen and J. Goodman. "An empirical study of smoothing techniques for language modeling". In: *Proc. 34th ACL*. 1996, pp. 310–318.

[CG98]   S. Chen and J. Goodman. *An empirical study of smoothing techniques for language modeling*. Tech. rep. TR-10-98. Dept. Comp. Sci., Harvard, 1998.

[CGR06]   S. R. Cook, A. Gelman, and D. B. Rubin. "Validation of Software for Bayesian Models Using Posterior Quantiles". In: *J. Comput. Graph. Stat.* 15.3 (2006), pp. 675–692.

[CGS15]   T. Chen, I. Goodfellow, and J. Shlens. "Net2net: Accelerating learning via knowledge transfer". In: *International Conference on Learning Representations*. 2015.

[CH20]   C. Cinelli and C. Hazlett. "Making sense of sensitivity: extending omitted variable bias". In: *Journal of the Royal Statistical Society: Series B (Statistical*

Methodology) 82.1 (2020), pp. 39–67. eprint: https://rss.onlinelibrary.wiley.com/doi/pdf/10.1111/rssb.12348.

[Cha12] K. M. A. Chai. "Variational Multinomial Logit Gaussian Process". In: *JMLR* 13.Jun (2012), pp. 1745–1808.

[Cha14] N. Chapados. "Effective Bayesian Modeling of Groups of Related Count Time Series". In: *ICML*. 2014.

[Cha+14] K. Chatfield, K. Simonyan, A. Vedaldi, and A. Zisserman. "Return of the devil in the details: Delving deep into convolutional nets". In: *British Machine Vision Conference*. 2014.

[Cha+17] D. Chakrabarty, Y. T. Lee, A. Sidford, and S. C.-w. Wong. "Subquadratic submodular function minimization". In: *Proceedings of the 49th Annual ACM SIGACT Symposium on Theory of Computing*. 2017, pp. 1220–1231.

[Cha+18] N. S. Chatterji, N. Flammarion, Y.-A. Ma, P. L. Bartlett, and M. I. Jordan. "On the theory of variance reduction for stochastic gradient Monte Carlo". In: *ICML*. 2018.

[Cha+19a] C. Chan, S. Ginosar, T. Zhou, and A. A. Efros. "Everybody dance now". In: *Proceedings of the IEEE/CVF International Conference on Computer Vision*. 2019, pp. 5933–5942.

[Cha+19b] J. J. Chandler, I. Martinez, M. M. Finucane, J. G. Terziev, and A. M. Resch. "Speaking on Data's Behalf: What Researchers Say and How Audiences Choose". en. In: *Eval. Rev.* (2019), p. 193841X19834968.

[Cha+19c] T. Chavdarova, G. Gidel, F. Fleuret, and S. Lacoste-Julien. "Reducing noise in GAN training with variance reduced extragradient". In: *Advances in Neural Information Processing Systems*. 2019, pp. 393–403.

[Cha21] S. H. Chan. *Introduction to Probability for Data Science*. Michigan Publishing, 2021.

[Cha+22] H. Chang, H. Zhang, L. Jiang, C. Liu, and W. T. Freeman. "MaskGIT: Masked Generative Image Transformer". In: *CVPR*. Feb. 2022.

[Che+05] G. Chechik, A. Globerson, N. Tishby, and Y. Weiss. "Information Bottleneck for Gaussian Variables". In: *JMLR* 6.Jan (2005), pp. 165–188.

[Che+15] L.-C. Chen, G. Papandreou, I. Kokkinos, K. Murphy, and A. L. Yuille. "Semantic Image Segmentation with Deep Convolutional Nets and Fully Connected CRFs". In: *ICLR*. 2015.

[Che+16] X. Chen, Y. Duan, R. Houthooft, J. Schulman, I. Sutskever, and P. Abbeel. "InfoGAN: Interpretable Representation Learning by Information Maximizing Generative Adversarial Nets". In: *NIPS*. 2016.

[Che+17] T. Che, Y. Li, R. Zhang, R. D. Hjelm, W. Li, Y. Song, and Y. Bengio. "Maximum-likelihood augmented discrete generative adversarial networks". In: *arXiv preprint arXiv:1702.07983* (2017).

[Che17] C. Chelba. *Language Modeling in the Era of Abundant Data*. AI with the best. 2017.

[Che+17a] L.-C. Chen, G. Papandreou, I. Kokkinos, K. Murphy, and A. L. Yuille. "DeepLab: Semantic Image Segmentation with Deep Convolutional Nets, Atrous Convolution, and Fully Connected CRFs". In: *IEEE PAMI* (2017).

[Che+17b] X. Chen, D. P. Kingma, T. Salimans, Y. Duan, P. Dhariwal, J. Schulman, I. Sutskever, and P.

Abbeel. "Variational Lossy Autoencoder". In: *ICLR*. 2017.

[Che+17c] X. Chen, N. Mishra, M. Rohaninejad, and P. Abbeel. "PixelSNAIL: An Improved Autoregressive Generative Model". In: (2017). arXiv: 1712.09763 [cs.LG].

[Che+17d] V. Chernozhukov, D. Chetverikov, M. Demirer, E. Duflo, C. Hansen, and W. Newey. "Double/Debiased/Neyman Machine Learning of Treatment Effects". In: *American Economic Review* 107.5 (2017), pp. 261–65.

[Che+17e] V. Chernozhukov, D. Chetverikov, M. Demirer, E. Duflo, C. Hansen, W. Newey, and J. Robins. "Double/Debiased Machine Learning for Treatment and Structural parameters". In: *The Econometrics Journal* (2017).

[Che+18a] C. Chen, W. Wang, Y. Zhang, Q. Su, and L. Carin. "A convergence analysis for a class of practical variance-reduction stochastic gradient MCMC". In: *Sci. China Inf. Sci.* 62.1 (2018), p. 12101.

[Che+18b] C. Chen, O. Li, C. Tao, A. J. Barnett, J. Su, and C. Rudin. "This looks like that: deep learning for interpretable image recognition". In: *arXiv preprint arXiv:1806.10574* (2018).

[Che+18c] R. T. Q. Chen, Y. Rubanova, J. Bettencourt, and D. Duvenaud. "Neural Ordinary Differential Equations". In: *NIPS*. 2018.

[Che+18d] X. Cheng, N. S. Chatterji, P. L. Bartlett, and M. I. Jordan. "Underdamped Langevin MCMC: A non-asymptotic analysis". In: *COLT*. 2018.

[Che+19] R. T. Q. Chen, J. Behrmann, D. Duvenaud, and J.-H. Jacobsen. "Residual Flows for Invertible Generative Modeling". In: *NIPS*. 2019.

[Che+20a] M. Chen, A. Radford, R. Child, J. Wu, H. Jun, D. Luan, and I. Sutskever. "Generative pretraining from pixels". In: *International Conference on Machine Learning*. PMLR. 2020, pp. 1691–1703.

[Che+20b] M. Chen, Y. Wang, T. Liu, Z. Yang, X. Li, Z. Wang, and T. Zhao. "On computation and generalization of generative adversarial imitation learning". In: *arXiv preprint arXiv:2001.02792* (2020).

[Che+20c] T. Chen, S. Kornblith, M. Norouzi, and G. Hinton. "A simple framework for contrastive learning of visual representations". In: *ICML*. 2020.

[Che+22] D. Chen, D. Wang, T. Darrell, and S. Ebrahimi. "Contrastive Test-Time Adaptation". In: *CVPR*. Apr. 2022.

[Che95] Y. Cheng. "Mean shift, mode seeking, and clustering". In: *IEEE PAMI* 17.8 (1995).

[Chi14] S. Chiappa. "Explicit-Duration Markov Switching Models". In: *Foundations and Trends in Machine Learning* 7.6 (2014), pp. 803–886.

[Chi21a] R. Child. "Very Deep VAEs Generalize Autoregressive Models and Can Outperform Them on Images". In: *ICLR*. 2021.

[Chi21b] R. Child. "Very Deep VAEs Generalize Autoregressive Models and Can Outperform Them on Images". In: *ArXiv* abs/2011.10650 (2021).

[CHL+05] S. Chopra, R. Hadsell, Y. LeCun, et al. "Learning a similarity metric discriminatively, with application to face verification". In: *CVPR*. 2005, pp. 539–546.

[CHM97] D. M. Chickering, D. Heckerman, and C. Meek. "A Bayesian Approach to Learning Bayesian Networks with Local Structure". In: *UAI*. UAI'97. 1997, pp. 80–89.

[Cho02] N. Chopin. "A Sequential Particle Filter Method for Static Models". In: *Biometrika* 89.3 (2002), pp. 539–551.

[Cho11] M. J. Choi. "Trees and Beyond: Exploiting and Improving Tree-Structured Graphical Models". PhD thesis. MIT, 2011.

[Cho+15] Y. Chow, A. Tamar, S. Mannor, and M. Pavone. "Risk-Sensitive and Robust Decision-Making: A CVaR Optimization Approach". In: *NIPS*. 2015, pp. 1522–1530.

[Cho21] F. Chollet. *Deep learning with Python (second edition)*. Manning, 2021.

[Cho+22] J. Choi, J. Lee, C. Shin, S. Kim, H. Kim, and S. Yoon. "Perception Prioritized Training of Diffusion Models". In: *CVPR*. Apr. 2022.

[Cho57] N. Chomsky. *Syntactic Structures*. Mouton, 1957.

[Chr+21] R. Christiansen, N. Pfister, M. E. Jakobsen, N. Gnecco, and J. Peters. "A causal framework for distribution generalization". In: *IEEE PAMI* (2021).

[Chu+15] J. Chung, K. Kastner, L. Dinh, K. Goel, A. Courville, and Y. Bengio. "A Recurrent Latent Variable Model for Sequential Data". In: *NIPS*. 2015.

[Chu+18] K. Chua, R. Calandra, R. McAllister, and S. Levine. "Deep Reinforcement Learning in a Handful of Trials using Probabilistic Dynamics Models". In: *NIPS*. 2018.

[Chu+19] G. Chuang, G. DeSalvo, L. Karydas, J.-F. Kagy, A. Rostamizadeh, and A Theeraphol. "Active Learning Empirical Study". In: *NeurIPS LIRE Workshop*. 2019.

[Chw+15] K. Chwialkowski, A. Ramdas, D. Sejdinovic, and A. Gretton. "Fast Two-Sample Testing with Analytic Representations of Probability Measures". In: *NIPS*. 2015.

[CI13] M. Clydec and E. S. Iversen. "Bayesian model averaging in the M-open framework". In: *Bayesian Theory and Applications*. Ed. by P. Damien. Jan. 2013.

[CI81] W. J. Conover and R. L. Iman. "Rank Transformations as a Bridge Between Parametric and Nonparametric Statistics". In: *Am. Stat.* 35.3 (1981), pp. 124–129.

[CJ21] A. D. Cobb and B. Jalaian. "Scaling Hamiltonian Monte Carlo inference for Bayesian neural networks with symmetric splitting". In: *UAI*. Vol. 161. Proceedings of Machine Learning Research. PMLR, 2021, pp. 675–685.

[CK05] M. Collins and T. Koo. "Discriminative Reranking for Natural Language Parsing". In: *Proc. ACL*. 2005.

[CK07] J. J. F. Commandeur and S. J. Koopman. *An Introduction to State Space Time Series Analysis (Practical Econometrics)*. en. 1st ed. Oxford University Press, 2007.

[CK21] D. Chakrabarty and S. Khanna. "Better and simpler error analysis of the Sinkhorn–Knopp algorithm for matrix scaling". In: *Mathematical Programming* 188.1 (2021), pp. 395–407.

[CK94a] D. Card and A. B. Krueger. "Minimum Wages and Employment: A Case Study of the Fast-Food Industry in New Jersey and Pennsylvania". In: *American Economic Review* 84.4 (1994), pp. 772–793.

[CK94b] C. Carter and R. Kohn. "On Gibbs sampling for state space models". In: *Biometrika* 81.3 (1994), pp. 541–553.

[CK96] C. Carter and R. Kohn. "Markov Chain Monte Carlo in Conditionally Gaussian State Space Models". In: *Biometrika* 83 (1996), pp. 589–601.

[CKK17] L. Chen, A. Krause, and A. Karbasi. "Interactive Submodular Bandit." In: *NIPS*. 2017, pp. 141–152.

[CL00] R. Chen and S. Liu. "Mixture Kalman Filters". In: *J. Royal Stat. Soc. B* (2000).

[CL07] L. Carvahlo and C. Lawrence. "Centroid estimation in discrete high-dimensional spaces with applications in biology". In: *PNAS* 105.4 (2007).

[CL11] O. Chapelle and L. Li. "An empirical evaluation of Thompson sampling". In: *NIPS*. 2011.

[CL18] Z. Chen and B. Liu. *Lifelong Machine Learning*. Synthesis Lectures on Artificial Intelligence and Machine Learning. Morgan Claypool, 2018.

[CL96] B. P. Carlin and T. A. Louis. *Bayes and Empirical Bayes Methods for Data Analysis*. Chapman and Hall, 1996.

[Cla20] P. Clavier. "Sum-Product Network in the context of missing data". en. MA thesis. KTH, 2020.

[Cla21] A. Clayton. *Bernoulli's Fallacy: Statistical Illogic and the Crisis of Modern Science*. en. Columbia University Press, 2021.

[CLD18] C. Cremer, X. Li, and D. Duvenaud. "Inference Suboptimality in Variational Autoencoders". In: *ICML*. 2018.

[Clo+19] J. R. Clough, I. Oksuz, E. Puyol-Antón, B. Ruijsink, A. P. King, and J. A. Schnabel. "Global and local interpretability for cardiac MRI classification". In: *International Conference on Medical Image Computing and Computer-Assisted Intervention*. Springer. 2019, pp. 656–664.

[Clo20] Cloudera. *Causality for ML*. 2020.

[CLV19] M. Cox, T. van de Laar, and B. de Vries. "A factor graph approach to automated design of Bayesian signal processing algorithms". In: *Int. J. Approx. Reason.* 104 (2019), pp. 185–204.

[CLW18] Y. Chen, L. Li, and M. Wang. "Scalable Bilinear π-Learning Using State and Action Features". In: *ICML*. 2018, pp. 833–842.

[CM09] O. Cappé and E. Moulines. "Online EM Algorithm for Latent Data Models". In: *J. of Royal Stat. Soc. Series B* 71.3 (2009), pp. 593–613.

[CMD17] C. Cremer, Q. Morris, and D. Duvenaud. "Reinterpreting Importance-Weighted Autoencoders". In: *ICLR Workshop*. 2017.

[CMJ22] P. G. Chang, K. P. Murphy, and M. Jones. "On diagonal approximations to the extended Kalman filter for online training of Bayesian neural networks". In: *Continual Lifelong Learning Workshop at ACML 2022*. Dec. 2022.

[CMR05] O. Cappe, E. Moulines, and T. Ryden. *Inference in Hidden Markov Models*. Springer, 2005.

[CMR12] C. Cortes, M. Mohri, and A. Rostamizadeh. "Algorithms for learning kernels based on centered alignment". In: *The Journal of Machine Learning Research* 13.1 (2012), pp. 795–828.

[CMS12] D. Ciregan, U. Meier, and J. Schmidhuber. "Multi-column deep neural networks for image classification". In: *2012 IEEE conference on computer vision and pattern recognition*. IEEE. 2012, pp. 3642–3649.

[CN01] H. Choset and K. Nagatani. "Topological simultaneous localization and mapping (SLAM): toward exact localization without explicit localization". In: *IEEE Trans. Robotics and Automation* 17.2 (2001).

[CNW20] M. Collier, A. Nazabal, and C. K. I. Williams. "VAEs in the Presence of Missing Data". In: *ICML Workshop on the Art of Learning with Missing Values*. 2020.

[CO06] N. Chater and M. Oaksford. "Mental mechanisms". In: *Information sampling and adaptive cognition* (2006), pp. 210–236.

[COB18] L. Chizat, E. Oyallon, and F. Bach. "On Lazy Training in Differentiable Programming". In: (2018). arXiv: 1812.07956 [math.OC].

[Coh94] J. Cohen. "The earth is round (p < .05)". In: *American Psychologist* 49.12 (1994), pp. 997–1003.

[Col21] E. Collins. *LaMDA: our breakthrough conversation technology*. https://blog.google/technology/ai/lamda/. Accessed: NA-NA-NA. May 2021.

[Coo05] J. Cook. *Exact Calculation of Beta Inequalities*. Tech. rep. M. D. Anderson Cancer Center, Dept. Biostatistics, 2005.

[Cor+12] G. Cormode, M. Garofalakis, P. J. Haas, and C. Jermaine. "Synopses for massive data: Samples, histograms, wavelets, sketches". In: *Foundations and Trends in Databases* 4.1–3 (2012), pp. 1–294.

[Cor17] G. Cormode. "Data sketching". In: *Communications of the ACM* 60.9 (2017), pp. 48–55.

[Cor+59] J. Cornfield, W. Haenszel, E. C. Hammond, A. M. Lilienfeld, M. B. Shimkin, and E. L. Wynder. "Smoking and Lung Cancer: Recent Evidence and a Discussion of Some Questions". In: *JNCI: Journal of the National Cancer Institute* 22.1 (Jan. 1959), pp. 173–203. eprint: https://academic.oup.com/jnci/article-pdf/22/1/173/2704718/22-1-173.pdf.

[Cor+87] A Corana, M Marchesi, C Martini, and S Ridella. "Minimizing Multimodal Functions of Continuous Variables with the "Simulated Annealing" Algorithm". In: *ACM Trans. Math. Softw.* 13.3 (1987), pp. 262–280.

[Cou16] Council of European Union. *General Data Protection Regulation*. 2016.

[Cou+20] J. Courts, A. Wills, T. Schön, and B. Ninness. "Variational System Identification for Nonlinear State-Space Models". In: (2020). arXiv: 2012.05072 [stat.ML].

[Cou+21] J. Courts, J. Hendriks, A. Wills, T. Schön, and B. Ninness. "Variational State and Parameter Estimation". In: *19th IFAC Symposium on System Identification SYSID 2021*. 2021.

[Cov99] T. M. Cover. *Elements of information theory*. John Wiley & Sons, 1999.

[Cox06] D. R. Cox. *Principles of Statistical Inference*. en. Illustrated edition. Cambridge University Press, Aug. 2006.

[Cox46] R. T. Cox. "Probability, Frequency and Reasonable Expectation". In: *Am. J. Phys.* 14.1 (Jan. 1946), pp. 1–13.

[Cox61] R. Cox. *Algebra of Probable Inference*. en. Johns Hopkins University Press, 1961.

[CP20a] R. Chen and I. C. Paschalidis. *Distributionally Robust Learning*. NOW Foundations and Trends in Optimization, 2020.

[CP20b] N. Chopin and O. Papaspiliopoulos. *An Introduction to Sequential Monte Carlo*. en. 1st ed. Springer, 2020.

[CPD17] P. Constantinou and A Philip Dawid. "Extended conditional independence and applications in causal inference". en. In: *Ann. Stat.* 45.6 (2017), pp. 2618–2653.

[CPS10] C. Carvalho, N. Polson, and J. Scott. "The horseshoe estimator for sparse signals". In: *Biometrika* 97.2 (2010), p. 465.

[Cri+02] N. Cristianini, J. Shawe-Taylor, A. Elisseeff, and J. S. Kandola. "On Kernel-Target Alignment". In: *Advances in Neural Information Processing Systems*. 2002, pp. 367–373.

[CRK19] J. M. Cohen, E. Rosenfeld, and J. Z. Kolter. "Certified adversarial robustness via randomized smoothing". In: *arXiv preprint arXiv:1902.02918* (2019).

[Cro+11] D. F. Crouse, P. Willett, K. Pattipati, and L. Svensson. "A look at Gaussian mixture reduction algorithms". In: *14th International Conference on Information Fusion*. 2011, pp. 1–8.

[CS04] I. Csiszár and P. C. Shields. "Information theory and statistics: A tutorial". In: (2004).

[CS09] Y. Cho and L. K. Saul. "Kernel Methods for Deep Learning". In: *NIPS*. 2009, pp. 342–350.

[CS18] P. Chaudhari and S. Soatto. "Stochastic gradient descent performs variational inference, converges to limit cycles for deep networks". In: *ICLR*. 2018.

[CSF16] A. W. Churchill, S. Sigtia, and C. Fernando. "Learning to Generate Genotypes with Neural Networks". In: (2016). arXiv: 1604.04153 [cs.NE].

[Csi67] I. Csiszar. "Information-Type Measures of Difference of Probability Distributions and Indirect Observations". In: *Studia Scientiarum Mathematicarum Hungarica* 2 (1967), pp. 299–318.

[CSN21] J. Coullon, L. South, and C. Nemeth. "Stochastic Gradient MCMC with Multi-Armed Bandit Tuning". In: (2021). arXiv: 2105.13059 [stat.CO].

[CSZ06] O. Chapelle, B. Scholkopf, and A. Zien, eds. *Semi-Supervised Learning*. MIT Press, 2006.

[CT06] T. M. Cover and J. A. Thomas. *Elements of Information Theory*. 2nd edition. John Wiley, 2006.

[CT+19] M. F. Cusumano-Towner, F. A. Saad, A. K. Lew, and V. K. Mansinghka. "Gen: a general-purpose probabilistic programming system with programmable inference". In: *Proceedings of the 40th ACM SIGPLAN Conference on Programming Language Design and Implementation*. PLDI 2019. Association for Computing Machinery, 2019, pp. 221–236.

[CT91] T. M. Cover and J. A. Thomas. *Elements of Information Theory*. John Wiley, 1991.

[CTM17] M. F. Cusumano-Towner and V. K. Mansinghka. "AIDE: An algorithm for measuring the accuracy of probabilistic inference algorithms". In: *NIPS*. 2017.

[CTN17]   Y. Chali, M. Tanvee, and M. T. Nayeem. "Towards abstractive multi-document summarization using submodular function-based framework, sentence compression and merging". In: *Proceedings of the Eighth International Joint Conference on Natural Language Processing (Volume 2: Short Papers)*. 2017, pp. 418–424.

[CTS78]   C. Cannings, E. A. Thompson, and M. H. Skolnick. "Probability functions in complex pedigrees". In: *Advances in Applied Probability* 10 (1978), pp. 26–61.

[CUH16]   D.-A. Clevert, T. Unterthiner, and S. Hochreiter. "Fast and Accurate Deep Network Learning by Exponential Linear Units (ELUs)". In: *ICLR*. 2016.

[Cui+18]   Y. Cui, Y. Song, C. Sun, A. Howard, and S. Belongie. "Large scale fine-grained categorization and domain-specific transfer learning". In: *Proceedings of the IEEE conference on computer vision and pattern recognition*. 2018, pp. 4109–4118.

[Cun22]   Y. L. Cun. *A path towards autonomous AI*. 2022.

[Cun83]   W. H. Cunningham. "Decomposition of submodular functions". In: *Combinatorica* 3.1 (1983), pp. 53–68.

[Cut13]   M. Cuturi. "Sinkhorn Distances: Lightspeed Computation of Optimal Transportation Distances". In: *NIPS*. 2013.

[CW07]   C. M. Carvahlo and M. West. "Dynamic Matrix-Variate Graphical Models". In: *Bayesian Analysis* 2.1 (2007), pp. 69–98.

[CW16]   T. Cohen and M. Welling. "Group Equivariant Convolutional Networks". en. In: *ICML*. 2016, pp. 2990–2999.

[CWG20]   D. C. Castro, I. Walker, and B. Glocker. "Causality matters in medical imaging". en. In: *Nat. Commun.* 11.1 (2020), p. 3673.

[CWS21]   J. Courts, A. G. Wills, and T. B. Schön. "Gaussian Variational State Estimation for Nonlinear State-Space Models". In: *IEEE Trans. Signal Process.* 69 (2021), pp. 5979–5993.

[CXH21]   X. Chen, S. Xie, and K. He. "An empirical study of training self-supervised vision transformers". In: *arXiv preprint arXiv:2104.02057* (2021).

[CY20]   G. Cormode and K. Yi. *Small Summaries for Big Data*. Cambridge University Press, 2020.

[Cza+20]   J. Czarnowski, T. Laidlow, R. Clark, and A. J. Davison. "DeepFactors: Real-Time Probabilistic Dense Monocular SLAM". In: *ICRA*. 2020.

[CZG20]   B. Charpentier, D. Zügner, and S. Günnemann. "Posterior network: Uncertainty estimation without ood samples via density-based pseudo-counts". In: *arXiv preprint arXiv:2006.09239* (2020).

[CZS22]   A. Corenflos, Z. Zhao, and S. Särkkä. "Temporal Gaussian Process Regression in Logarithmic Time". In: *2022 25th International Conference on Information Fusion (FUSION)*. July 2022, pp. 1–5.

[D'A+20]   A. D'Amour et al. "Underspecification Presents Challenges for Credibility in Modern Machine Learning". In: (2020). arXiv: 2011.03395 [cs.LG].

[D'A+21]   A. D'Amour, P. Ding, A. Feller, L. Lei, and J. Sekhon. "Overlap in observational studies with high-dimensional covariates". In: *Journal of Econometrics* 221.2 (2021), pp. 644–654.

[Dag+21]   N. Dagan, N. Barda, E. Kepten, O. Miron, S. Perchik, M. A. Katz, M. A. Hernán, M. Lipsitch, B. Reis, and R. D. Balicer. "BNT162b2 mRNA Covid-19 Vaccine in a Nationwide Mass Vaccination Setting". In: *New England Journal of Medicine* 384.15 (2021), pp. 1412–1423. eprint: https://doi.org/10.1056/NEJMoa2101765.

[Dai+17]   H. Dai, B. Dai, Y.-M. Zhang, S. Li, and L. Song. "Recurrent Hidden Semi-Markov Model". In: *ICLR*. 2017.

[Dai+18]   B. Dai, A. Shaw, L. Li, L. Xiao, N. He, Z. Liu, J. Chen, and L. Song. "SBEED: Convergent Reinforcement Learning with Nonlinear Function Approximation". In: *ICML*. 2018, pp. 1133–1142.

[Dai+19a]   B. Dai, H. Dai, A. Gretton, L. Song, D. Schuurmans, and N. He. "Kernel exponential family estimation via doubly dual embedding". In: *AISTATS*. PMLR. 2019, pp. 2321–2330.

[Dai+19b]   B. Dai, Z. Liu, H. Dai, N. He, A. Gretton, L. Song, and D. Schuurmans. "Exponential family estimation via adversarial dynamics embedding". In: *Advances in Neural Information Processing Systems*. 2019, pp. 10979–10990.

[Dai+20a]   C. Dai, J. Heng, P. E. Jacob, and N. Whiteley. "An invitation to sequential Monte Carlo samplers". In: (2020). arXiv: 2007.11936 [stat.CO].

[Dai+20b]   Z. Dai, G. Lai, Y. Yang, and Q. V. Le. "Funnel-Transformer: Filtering out Sequential Redundancy for Efficient Language Processing". In: *NIPS*. 2020.

[Dal+04]   N. Dalvi, P. Domingos, S. Sanghai, and D. Verma. "Adversarial classification". In: *Proceedings of the tenth ACM SIGKDD international conference on Knowledge discovery and data mining*. 2004, pp. 99–108.

[Dar03]   A. Darwiche. "A Differential Approach to Inference in Bayesian Networks". In: *J. ACM* 50.3 (2003), pp. 280–305.

[Dar09]   A. Darwiche. *Modeling and Reasoning with Bayesian Networks*. Cambridge, 2009.

[Dar+11]   S. Darolles, Y. Fan, J.-P. Florens, and E. Renault. "Nonparametric instrumental regression". In: *Econometrica* 79.5 (2011), pp. 1541–1565.

[Dar80]   R. A. Darton. "Rotation in Factor Analysis". In: *Journal of the Royal Statistical Society. Series D (The Statistician)* 29.3 (1980), pp. 167–194.

[Dau05]   F Daum. "Nonlinear filters: beyond the Kalman filter". In: *IEEE Aerospace and Electronic Systems Magazine* 20.8 (Aug. 2005), pp. 57–69.

[Dav+04]   T. A. Davis, J. R. Gilbert, S. I. Larimore, and E. G. Ng. "A Column Approximate Minimum Degree Ordering Algorithm". In: *ACM Trans. Math. Softw.* 30.3 (2004), pp. 353–376.

[Dav+18]   T. R. Davidson, L. Falorsi, N. De Cao, T. Kipf, and J. M. Tomczak. "Hyperspherical Variational Auto-Encoders". In: *UAI*. 2018.

[Daw00]   A. P. Dawid. "Causal Inference Without Counterfactuals". In: *JASA* 95.450 (2000), pp. 407–424.

[Daw02]   A. P. Dawid. "Influence diagrams for causal modelling and inference". In: *Intl. Stat. Review* 70 (2002). Corrections p437, pp. 161–189.

[Daw15]   A. P. Dawid. "Statistical Causality from a Decision-Theoretic Perspective". In: *Annu. Rev. Stat. Appl.* 2.1 (2015), pp. 273–303.

[Daw82]   A. P. Dawid. "The Well-Calibrated Bayesian". In: *JASA* 77.379 (1982), pp. 605–610.

[Dax+21]   E. Daxberger, A. Kristiadi, A. Immer, R. Eschenhagen, M. Bauer, and P. Hennig. "Laplace Redux–Effortless Bayesian Deep Learning". In: *NIPS*. 2021.

[Day+95]   P. Dayan, G. Hinton, R. Neal, and R. Zemel. "The Helmholtz machine". In: *Neural Networks* 9.8 (1995).

[DBB20]   S. Daulton, M. Balandat, and E. Bakshy. "Differentiable Expected Hypervolume Improvement for Parallel Multi-Objective Bayesian Optimization". In: *NIPS*. 2020.

[DBP19]   C. Durkan, A. Bekasov, and I. M. G. Papamakarios. "Neural Spline Flows". In: *NIPS*. 2019.

[DBW20]   I. A. Delbridge, D. S. Bindel, and A. G. Wilson. "Randomly Projected Additive Gaussian Processes for Regression". In: *International Conference on Machine Learning*. 2020.

[DCF+15]   E. Denton, S. Chintala, R. Fergus, et al. "Deep generative image models using a Laplacian pyramid of adversarial networks". In: *NIPS*. 2015.

[DD22]   S. Doyen and N. B. Dadario. "12 Plagues of AI in Healthcare: A Practical Guide to Current Issues With Using Machine Learning in a Medical Context". en. In: *Front Digit Health* 4 (May 2022), p. 765406.

[DDL97]   S. DellaPietra, V. DellaPietra, and J. Lafferty. "Inducing features of random fields". In: *IEEE PAMI* 19.4 (1997).

[DE00]   R. Dahlhaus and M. Eichler. "Causality and graphical models for time series". In: *Highly structured stochastic systems*. Ed. by P. Green, N. Hjort, and S. Richardson. Oxford University Press, 2000.

[DE04]   J. Dow and J. Endersby. "Multinomial probit and multinomial logit: a comparison of choice models for voting research". In: *Electoral Studies* 23.1 (2004), pp. 107–122.

[Dec96]   R. Dechter. "Bucket elimination: a unifying framework for probabilistic inference". In: *UAI*. 1996.

[DeG70]   M. DeGroot. *Optimal Statistical Decisions.* McGraw-Hill, 1970.

[DEL20]   H. M. Dolatabadi, S. Erfani, and C. Leckie. "Invertible Generative Modeling using Linear Rational Splines". In: *AISTATS*. 2020, pp. 4236–4246.

[Del+21]   M. Delange, R. Aljundi, M. Masana, S. Parisot, X. Jia, A. Leonardis, G. Slabaugh, and T. Tuytelaars. "A continual learning survey: Defying forgetting in classification tasks". en. In: *IEEE PAMI* (2021).

[Den+02]   D. Denison, C. Holmes, B. Mallick, and A. Smith. *Bayesian methods for nonlinear classification and regression.* Wiley, 2002.

[Den+20]   Y. Deng, A. Bakhtin, M. Ott, A. Szlam, and M. Ranzato. "Residual Energy-Based Models for Text Generation". In: *International Conference on Learning Representations*. 2020.

[Dev+18]   J. Devlin, M.-W. Chang, K. Lee, and K. Toutanova. "Bert: Pre-training of deep bidirectional transformers for language understanding". In: *arXiv preprint arXiv:1810.04805* (2018).

[Dev+19]   J. Devlin, M.-W. Chang, K. Lee, and K. Toutanova. "BERT: Pre-training of Deep Bidirectional Transformers for Language Understanding". In: *NAACL*. 2019.

[Dev+21]   L. Devlin, P. Horridge, P. L. Green, and S. Maskell. "The No-U-Turn Sampler as a Proposal Distribution in a Sequential Monte Carlo Sampler with a Near-Optimal L-Kernel". In: (2021). arXiv: 2108.02498 [stat.CO].

[Dev85]   P. A. Devijver. "Baum's forward-backward algorithm revisited". In: *Pattern Recognition Letters* 3.6 (1985), pp. 369–373.

[Dex]   *Dex: Research language for array processing in the Haskell/ML family.* https://github.com/google-research/dex-lang. 2019.

[DF18]   E. Denton and R. Fergus. "Stochastic Video Generation with a Learned Prior". In: *ICML*. 2018.

[DF19]   X. Ding and D. J. Freedman. "Learning Deep Generative Models with Annealed Importance Sampling". In: (2019). arXiv: 1906.04904 [stat.ML].

[DF21]   F. D'Angelo and V. Fortuin. "Repulsive Deep Ensembles are Bayesian". In: *NIPS*. May 2021.

[DFF21]   S. Dozinski, U. Feige, and M. Feldman. "Are Gross Substitutes a Substitute for Submodular Valuations?" In: *arXiv preprint arXiv:2102.13343* (2021).

[DFO20]   M. Deisenroth, A. Faisal, and C. S. Ong. *Mathematics for machine learning.* Cambridge, 2020.

[DFR15]   M. P. Deisenroth, D. Fox, and C. E. Rasmussen. "Gaussian Processes for Data-Efficient Learning in Robotics and Control". en. In: *IEEE PAMI* 37.2 (2015), pp. 408–423.

[DFS16]   A. Daniely, R. Frostig, and Y. Singer. "Toward Deeper Understanding of Neural Networks: The Power of Initialization and a Dual View on Expressivity". In: *NIPS*. 2016, pp. 2253–2261.

[DG17]   P. Dabkowski and Y. Gal. "Real time image saliency for black box classifiers". In: *NeurIPS* (2017).

[DG84]   P. J. Diggle and R. J. Gratton. "Monte Carlo methods of inference for implicit statistical models". In: *Journal of the Royal Statistical Society. Series B (Methodological)* (1984), pp. 193–227.

[DGA00]   A. Doucet, S. Godsill, and C. Andrieu. "On sequential Monte Carlo Sampling Methods for Bayesian Filtering". In: *Statistics and Computing* 10.3 (2000), pp. 197–208.

[DGE15]   C. Doersch, A. Gupta, and A. A. Efros. "Unsupervised visual representation learning by context prediction". In: *Proceedings of the IEEE international conference on computer vision*. 2015, pp. 1422–1430.

[DGK01]   A. Doucet, N. Gordon, and V. Krishnamurthy. "Particle Filters for State Estimation of Jump Markov Linear Systems". In: *IEEE Trans. on Signal Processing* 49.3 (2001), pp. 613–624.

[DH22]   F. Dellaert and S. Hutchinson. *Introducion to Robotics and Perception.* 2022.

[DHK14]   A. Deshpande, L. Hellerstein, and D. Kletenik. "Approximation algorithms for stochastic boolean function evaluation and stochastic submodular set cover". In: *Proceedings of the twenty-fifth annual ACM-SIAM Symposium on Discrete Algorithms*. SIAM. 2014, pp. 1453–1466.

[Dia88a]   P Diaconis. "Recent progress on de Finetti's notions of exchangeability". In: *Bayesian Statistics* 3 (1988).

[Dia88b] P. Diaconis. "Sufficiency as statistical symmetry". In: *Proceedings of the AMS Centennial Symposium*. 1988, pp. 15–26.

[Die00] T. G. Dietterich. "Ensemble Methods in Machine Learning". In: *Multiple Classifier Systems*. Springer Berlin Heidelberg, 2000, pp. 1–15.

[Die+07] M. Diehl, H. G. Bock, H. Diedam, and P.-B. Wieber. "Fast Direct Multiple Shooting Algorithms for Optimal Robot Control". In: *Lecture Notes in Control and Inform. Sci.* 340 (2007).

[Die10] L. Dietz. *Directed Factor Graph Notation for Generative Models*. Tech. rep. MPI, 2010.

[Die+17] A. B. Dieng, C. Wang, J. Gao, and J. Paisley. "TopicRNN: A Recurrent Neural Network with Long-Range Semantic Dependency". In: *ICLR*. 2017.

[Die+19a] A. B. Dieng, Y. Kim, A. M. Rush, and D. M. Blei. "Avoiding Latent Variable Collapse With Generative Skip Models". In: *AISTATS*. 2019.

[Die+19b] A. B. Dieng, F. J. Ruiz, D. M. Blei, and M. K. Titsias. "Prescribed generative adversarial networks". In: *arXiv preprint arXiv:1910.04302* (2019).

[Dik+20] N. Dikkala, G. Lewis, L. Mackey, and V. Syrgkanis. "Minimax Estimation of Conditional Moment Models". In: *Advances in Neural Information Processing Systems*. 2020.

[Din+17] L. Dinh, R. Pascanu, S. Bengio, and Y. Bengio. "Sharp Minima Can Generalize For Deep Nets". In: (2017). arXiv: 1703.04933 [cs.LG].

[DJ11] A. Doucet and A. M. Johansen. "A Tutorial on Particle Filtering and Smoothing: Fifteen years later". In: *Handbook of Nonlinear Filtering*. Ed. by D Crisan and B Rozovsk. 2011.

[DJ21] K. Desai and J. Johnson. *VirTex: Learning Visual Representations from Textual Annotations*. 2021. arXiv: 2006.06666 [cs.CV].

[DJK18] J. Djolonga, S. Jegelka, and A. Krause. "Provable Variational Inference for Constrained Log-Submodular Models". In: *NeurIPS*. 2018.

[DK12] J. Durbin and S. J. Koopman. *Time Series Analysis by State Space Methods (Second Edition)*. en. Revised ed. edition. Oxford University Press, 2012.

[DK14] J. Djolonga and A. Krause. "From map to marginals: Variational inference in bayesian submodular models". In: *Advances in Neural Information Processing Systems*. 2014, pp. 244–252.

[DK15a] J. Djolonga and A. Krause. "Scalable variational inference in log-supermodular models". In: *International Conference on Machine Learning*. PMLR. 2015, pp. 1804–1813.

[DK15b] G. Durrett and D. Klein. "Neural CRF Parsing". In: *Proc. ACL*. 2015.

[DKB15] L. Dinh, D. Krueger, and Y. Bengio. "NICE: Non-linear Independent Components Estimation". In: *ICLR*. 2015.

[DKD16] J. Donahue, P. Krahenbuhl, and T. Darrell. "Adversarial feature learning". In: *arXiv preprint arXiv:1605.09782* (2016).

[DKD17] J. Donahue, P. Krähenbühl, and T. Darrell. *Adversarial Feature Learning*. 2017. arXiv: 1605.09782 [cs.LG].

[DKS13] J. Dick, F. Y. Kuo, and I. H. Sloan. "High-dimensional integration: the quasi-Monte Carlo way". In: *Acta Numerica* 22 (2013), 133–288.

[DL09] P. Domingos and D. Lowd. *Markov Logic: An Interface Layer for AI*. Morgan & Claypool, 2009.

[DL10] J. V. Dillon and G. Lebanon. "Stochastic Composite Likelihood". In: *J. Mach. Learn. Res.* 11 (2010), pp. 2597–2633.

[DL13] A. Damianou and N. Lawrence. "Deep Gaussian Processes". en. In: *AISTATS*. 2013, pp. 207–215.

[DL93] P. Dagum and M. Luby. "Approximating probabilistic inference in Bayesian belief networks is NP-hard". In: *Artificial Intelligence* 60 (1993), pp. 141–153.

[DLB17] C. Dann, T. Lattimore, and E. Brunskill. "Unifying PAC and Regret: Uniform PAC Bounds for Episodic Reinforcement Learning". In: *NIPS*. 2017, pp. 5717–5727.

[DLM09] H. Daumé III, J. Langford, and D. Marcu. "Search-based Structured Prediction". In: *MLJ* 75.3 (2009), pp. 297–325.

[DLM99] B. Delyon, M. Lavielle, and E. Moulines. "Convergence of a stochastic approximation version of the EM algorithm". In: *Annals of Statistics* 27.1 (1999), pp. 94–128.

[DLR77] A. P. Dempster, N. M. Laird, and D. B. Rubin. "Maximum likelihood from incomplete data via the EM algorithm". In: *J. of the Royal Statistical Society, Series B* 34 (1977), pp. 1–38.

[DLT21] M. De Lange and T. Tuytelaars. "Continual Prototype Evolution: Learning Online from Non-Stationary Data Streams". In: *ICCV*. 2021.

[DM01] D. van Dyk and X.-L. Meng. "The Art of Data Augmentation". In: *J. Computational and Graphical Statistics* 10.1 (2001), pp. 1–50.

[DM19a] Y. Du and I. Mordatch. "Implicit Generation and Generalization in Energy-Based Models". In: (2019). arXiv: 1903.08689 [cs.LG].

[DM19b] Y. Du and I. Mordatch. "Implicit Generation and Modeling with Energy Based Models". In: *NIPS*. 2019, pp. 3608–3618.

[DM22] A. P. Dawid and M. Musio. "Effects of Causes and Causes of Effects". In: *Annu. Rev. Stat. Appl.* 9.1 (Mar. 2022), pp. 261–287.

[DMDJ12] P. Del Moral, A. Doucet, and A. Jasra. "An adaptive sequential Monte Carlo method for approximate Bayesian computation". In: *Stat. Comput.* 22.5 (2012), pp. 1009–1020.

[DMKM22] G. Duran-Martin, A. Kara, and K. Murphy. "Efficient Online Bayesian Inference for Neural Bandits". In: *AISTATS*. 2022.

[DMM17] A. P. Dawid, M. Musio, and R. Murtas. "The probability of causation". In: *Law, Probability and Risk* 16.4 (2017), pp. 163–179.

[DMP18] C. Donahue, J. McAuley, and M. Puckette. "Adversarial Audio Synthesis". In: *International Conference on Learning Representations*. 2018.

[DMV15] S. Dash, D. M. Malioutov, and K. R. Varshney. "Learning interpretable classification rules using sequential rowsampling". In: *2015 IEEE International Conference on Acoustics, Speech and Signal Processing (ICASSP)*. IEEE. 2015, pp. 3337–3341.

[DN21a] P. Dhariwal and A. Nichol. "Diffusion Models Beat GANs on Image Synthesis". In: *NIPS*. May 2021.

[DN21b] P. Dhariwal and A. Q. Nichol. "Diffusion Models Beat GANs on Image Synthesis". In: *NIPS*. May 2021.

[Dnp] .

[DNR11] D. Duvenaud, H. Nickisch, and C. E. Rasmussen. "Additive Gaussian Processes". In: *NIPS*. 2011.

[Dom+06] P. Domingos, S. Kok, H. Poon, M. Richardson, and P. Singla. "Unifying Logical and Statistical AI". In: *IJCAI*. 2006.

[Dom+19] A.-K. Dombrowski, M. Alber, C. J. Anders, M. Ackermann, K.-R. Müller, and P. Kessel. "Explanations can be manipulated and geometry is to blame". In: *arXiv preprint arXiv:1906.07983* (2019).

[Don+14] J. Donahue, Y. Jia, O. Vinyals, J. Hoffman, N. Zhang, E. Tzeng, and T. Darrell. "Decaf: A deep convolutional activation feature for generic visual recognition". In: *International conference on machine learning*. 2014, pp. 647–655.

[Don+17a] K. Dong, D. Eriksson, H. Nickisch, D. Bindel, and A. G. Wilson. "Scalable Log Determinants for Gaussian Process Kernel Learning". In: *NIPS*. 2017, pp. 6327–6337.

[Don+17b] Y. Dong, H. Su, J. Zhu, and F. Bao. "Towards interpretable deep neural networks by leveraging adversarial examples". In: *arXiv preprint arXiv:1708.05493* (2017).

[Don+21] X. Dong, J. Bao, T. Zhang, D. Chen, W. Zhang, L. Yuan, D. Chen, F. Wen, and N. Yu. "Peco: Perceptual codebook for bert pre-training of vision transformers". In: *arXiv preprint arXiv:2111.12710* (2021).

[Doo+17] J. van Doorn, A. Ly, M. Marsman, and E.-J. Wagenmakers. "Bayesian Rank-Based Hypothesis Testing for the Rank Sum Test, the Signed Rank Test, and Spearman's ρ". In: (Dec. 2017). arXiv: 1712.06941 [stat.ME].

[Dor+16] V. Dorie, M. Harada, N. B. Carnegie, and J. Hill. "A flexible, interpretable framework for assessing sensitivity to unmeasured confounding". In: *Statistics in Medicine* 35.20 (2016), pp. 3453–3470. eprint: https://onlinelibrary.wiley.com/doi/pdf/10.1002/sim.6973.

[Dos+21] A. Dosovitskiy et al. "An Image is Worth 16x16 Words: Transformers for Image Recognition at Scale". In: *International Conference on Learning Representations*. 2021.

[Doy+07] K. Doya, S. Ishii, A. Pouget, and R. P. N. Rao, eds. *Bayesian Brain: Probabilistic Approaches to Neural Coding*. MIT Press, 2007.

[DR11] M. P. Deisenroth and C. E. Rasmussen. "PILCO: A Model-Based and Data-Efficient Approach to Policy Search". In: *ICML*. 2011.

[DR17] G. K. Dziugaite and D. M. Roy. "Computing nonvacuous generalization bounds for deep (stochastic) neural networks with many more parameters than training data". In: *UAI*. 2017.

[DR21] H. Duanmu and D. M. Roy. "On extended admissibale procedures and their nonstandard Bayes risk". In: *Annals of Statistics* (2021).

[DRB19] A. B. Dieng, F. J. R. Ruiz, and D. M. Blei. "The Dynamic Embedded Topic Model". In: (2019). arXiv: 1907.05545 [cs.CL].

[DRG15] G. K. Dziugaite, D. M. Roy, and Z. Ghahramani. "Training generative neural networks via Max-

imum Mean Discrepancy optimization". In: *ICML*. 2015.

[Dru08] J. Drugowitsch. *Bayesian linear regression*. Tech. rep. U. Rochester, 2008.

[DS18] J. Domke and D. R. Sheldon. "Importance Weighting and Variational Inference". In: *NIPS*. 2018, pp. 4474–4483.

[DS19] J. Donahue and K. Simonyan. "Large scale adversarial representation learning". In: *arXiv preprint arXiv:1907.02544* (2019).

[DSDB17] L. Dinh, J. Sohl-Dickstein, and S. Bengio. "Density estimation using Real NVP". In: *ICLR*. 2017.

[DSK16] V. Dumoulin, J. Shlens, and M. Kudlur. "A Learned Representation For Artistic Style". In: (2016).

[DSP21] M. Dowling, P. Sokół, and I. M. Park. "Hida-Matérn Kernel". In: (July 2021). arXiv: 2107.07098 [stat.ML].

[DSZ16] A. Datta, S. Sen, and Y. Zick. "Algorithmic transparency via quantitative input influence: Theory and experiments with learning systems". In: *2016 IEEE symposium on security and privacy (SP)*. IEEE. 2016, pp. 598–617.

[DTK16] J. Djolonga, S. Tschiatschek, and A. Krause. "Variational inference in mixed probabilistic submodular models". In: *Advances in Neural Information Processing Systems*. 2016, pp. 1759–1767.

[Du+18] J. Du, S. Ma, Y.-C. Wu, S. Kar, and J. M. F. Moura. "Convergence Analysis of Distributed Inference with Vector-Valued Gaussian Belief Propagation". In: *JMLR* 18.172 (2018), pp. 1–38.

[Du+19] S. S. Du, K. Hou, B. Póczos, R. Salakhutdinov, R. Wang, and K. Xu. "Graph Neural Tangent Kernel: Fusing Graph Neural Networks with Graph Kernels". In: (2019). arXiv: 1905.13192 [cs.LG].

[Du+20] Y. Du, S. Li, J. Tenenbaum, and I. Mordatch. "Improved Contrastive Divergence Training of Energy Based Models". In: *arXiv preprint arXiv:2012.01316* (2020).

[Du+21] C. Du, Z. Gao, S. Yuan, L. Gao, Z. Li, Y. Zeng, X. Zhu, J. Xu, K. Gai, and K.-C. Lee. "Exploration in Online Advertising Systems with Deep Uncertainty-Aware Learning". In: *KDD*. KDD '21. Association for Computing Machinery, 2021, pp. 2792–2801.

[Dua+20] S. Duan, N. Watters, L. Matthey, C. P. Burgess, A. Lerchner, and I. Higgins. "A Heuristic for Unsupervised Model Selection for Variational Disentangled Representation Learning". In: *ArXiv* abs/1905.12614 (2020).

[Dua+87] S. Duane, A. Kennedy, B. Pendleton, and D. Roweth. "Hybrid Monte Carlo". In: *Physics Letters B* 195.2 (1987), pp. 216–222.

[Dub+16] A. Dubey, S. J. Reddi, B. Póczos, A. J. Smola, E. P. Xing, and S. A. Williamson. "Variance Reduction in Stochastic Gradient Langevin Dynamics". en. In: *NIPS*. Vol. 29. 2016, pp. 1154–1162.

[Dub20] Y. Dubois. *Neural Process Family*. http://yanndubs.github.io/Neural-Process-Family/. 2020.

[Dud13] J. Duda. "Asymmetric numeral systems: entropy coding combining speed of Huffman coding with compression rate of arithmetic coding". In: (2013). arXiv: 1311.2540 [cs.IT].

[Duf02] M. Duff. "Optimal Learning: Computational procedures for Bayes-adaptive Markov decision processes". PhD thesis. U. Mass. Dept. Comp. Sci., 2002.

[Dum+16] V. Dumoulin, I. Belghazi, B. Poole, O. Mastropietro, A. Lamb, M. Arjovsky, and A. Courville. "Adversarially learned inference". In: *arXiv preprint arXiv:1606.00704* (2016).

[Dum+17] V. Dumoulin, I. Belghazi, B. Poole, O. Mastropietro, A. Lamb, M. Arjovsky, and A. Courville. *Adversarially Learned Inference*. 2017. arXiv: 1606.00704 [stat.ML].

[Dum+18] A. Dumitrache, O. Inel, B. Timmermans, C. Ortiz, R.-J. Sips, L. Aroyo, and C. Welty. "Empirical Methodology for Crowdsourcing Ground Truth". In: *Semantic Web Journal* (2018).

[Dur+19] C. Durkan, A. Bekasov, I. Murray, and G. Papamakarios. "Cubic-Spline Flows". In: *ICML Workshop on Invertible Neural Networks and Normalizing Flows*. 2019.

[Dur+98] R. Durbin, S. Eddy, A. Krogh, and G. Mitchison. *Biological Sequence Analysis: Probabilistic Models of Proteins and Nucleic Acids*. Cambridge University Press, 1998.

[Duv+13] D. Duvenaud, J. Lloyd, R. Grosse, J. Tenenbaum, and G. Zoubin. "Structure Discovery in Nonparametric Regression through Compositional Kernel Search". en. In: *ICML*. 2013, pp. 1166–1174.

[Duv14] D. Duvenaud. "Automatic Model Construction with Gaussian Processes". PhD thesis. Computational and Biological Learning Laboratory, University of Cambridge, 2014.

[dV04] D. P. de Farias and B. Van Roy. "On Constraint Sampling in the Linear Programming Approach to Approximate Dynamic Programming". In: *Mathematics of Operations Research* 29.3 (2004), pp. 462–478.

[DV+17] H. De Vries, F. Strub, J. Mary, H. Larochelle, O. Pietquin, and A. C. Courville. "Modulating early visual processing by language". In: *Advances in Neural Information Processing Systems*. 2017, pp. 6594–6604.

[DV75] M. D. Donsker and S. S. Varadhan. "Asymptotic evaluation of certain Markov process expectations for large time, I". In: *Communications on Pure and Applied Mathematics* 28.1 (1975), pp. 1–47.

[DV99] A. P. Dawid and V. Vovk. "Prequential probability: Principles and properties". In: *Bernoulli* 5 (1999), pp. 125–162.

[DVK17] F. Doshi-Velez and B. Kim. *Towards A Rigorous Science of Interpretable Machine Learning*. 2017. eprint: 1702.08608 (stat.ML).

[DW19] B. Dai and D. Wipf. "Diagnosing and Enhancing VAE Models". In: *ICLR*. 2019.

[DWS12] T. Degris, M. White, and R. S. Sutton. "Off-Policy Actor-Critic". In: *ICML*. 2012.

[DWW19] B. Dai, Z. Wang, and D. Wipf. "The Usual Suspects? Reassessing Blame for VAE Posterior Collapse". In: (2019). arXiv: 1912.10702 [cs.LG].

[DWW20] B. Dai, Z. Wang, and D. Wipf. "The Usual Suspects? Reassessing Blame for VAE Posterior Collapse". In: *ICML*. Ed. by H. D. Iii and A. Singh. Vol. 119. Proceedings of Machine Learning Research. PMLR, 2020, pp. 2313–2322.

[DY79] P. Diaconis and D. Ylvisaker. "Conjugate priors for exponential families". In: vol. 7. 1979, pp. 269–281.

[ECM18] P. Etoori, M. Chinnakotla, and R. Mamidi. "Automatic Spelling Correction for Resource-Scarce Languages using Deep Learning". In: *Proceedings of ACL 2018, Student Research Workshop*. Association for Computational Linguistics, 2018, pp. 146–152.

[ED05] D. Earl and M. Deem. "Parallel tempering: Theory, applications, and new perspectives". In: *Phys. Chem. Chem. Phys.* 7 (2005), p. 3910.

[Edm69] H. P. Edmundson. "New methods in automatic extracting". In: *Journal of the ACM (JACM)* 16.2 (1969), pp. 264–285.

[Edm70] J. Edmonds. "Matroids, submodular functions, and certain polyhedra". In: *Combinatorial Structures and Their Applications* (1970), pp. 69–87.

[EFL04] E. Erosheva, S. Fienberg, and J. Lafferty. "Mixed-membership models of scientific publications". In: *PNAS* 101 (2004), pp. 5220–2227.

[Efr86] B. Efron. "Why Isn't Everyone a Bayesian?" In: *The American Statistician* 40.1 (1986).

[EGW05] D. Ernst, P. Geurts, and L. Wehenkel. "Tree-Based Batch Mode Reinforcement Learning". In: *JMLR* 6 (2005), pp. 503–556.

[EH16] B. Efron and T. Hastie. *Computer Age Statistical Inference, Student Edition: Algorithms, Evidence, and Data Science*. en. Cambridge University Press, June 2016.

[Eis16] J. Eisner. "Inside-Outside and Forward-Backward Algorithms Are Just Backprop (Tutorial Paper)". In: *EMNLP Workshop on Structured Prediction for NLP*. 2016.

[Eke+13] M. Ekeberg, C. Lövkvist, Y. Lan, M. Weigt, and E. Aurell. "Improved contact prediction in proteins: using pseudolikelihoods to infer Potts models". en. In: *Phys. Rev. E Stat. Nonlin. Soft Matter Phys.* 87.1 (2013), p. 012707.

[EM07] D. Eaton and K. Murphy. "Exact Bayesian structure learning from uncertain interventions". In: *AI/Statistics*. 2007.

[EMH19] T. Elsken, J. H. Metzen, and F. Hutter. "Neural Architecture Search: A Survey". In: *JMLR* 20 (2019), pp. 1–21.

[EMK06] G. Elidan, I. McGraw, and D. Koller. "Residual belief propagation: Informed scheduling for asynchronous message passing". In: *UAI*. 2006.

[Eng+18] J. Engel, K. K. Agrawal, S. Chen, I. Gulrajani, C. Donahue, and A. Roberts. "GANSynth: Adversarial Neural Audio Synthesis". In: *International Conference on Learning Representations*. 2018.

[Erh+09] D. Erhan, Y. Bengio, A. Courville, and P. Vincent. "Visualizing higher-layer features of a deep network". In: *University of Montreal* 1341.3 (2009), p. 1.

[Erm+13] S. Ermon, C. P. Gomes, A. Sabharwal, and B. Selman. "Taming the Curse of Dimensionality: Discrete Integration by Hashing and Optimization". In: *ICML*. Feb. 2013.

[ERO21] P. Esser, R. Rombach, and B. Ommer. "Taming Transformers for High-Resolution Image Synthesis". In: *CVPR*. 2021.

[ET93] B. Efron and R. J. Tibshirani. *An Introduction to the Bootstrap*. en. 1st ed. Chapman and Hall/CRC, Jan. 1993.

[Etz+18]   A. Etz, J. M. Haaf, J. N. Rouder, and J. Vandekerckhove. "Bayesian Inference and Testing Any Hypothesis You Can Specify". In: *Advances in Methods and Practices in Psychological Science* 1.2 (June 2018), pp. 281–295.

[Eva+18]   R. Evans et al. "De novo structure prediction with deep-learning based scoring". In: (2018).

[Eve09]   G. Evensen. *Data Assimilation: The Ensemble Kalman Filter*. en. 2nd ed. 2009 edition. Springer, 2009.

[EW10]   El-Yaniv and Wiener. "On the Foundations of Noise-free Selective Classification". In: *JMLR* (2010).

[EY09]   M. Elad and I. Yavnch. "A plurality of sparse representations is better than the sparsest one alone". In: *IEEE Trans. on Info. Theory* 55.10 (2009), pp. 4701–4714.

[Eyk+18]   K. Eykholt, I. Evtimov, E. Fernandes, B. Li, A. Rahmati, C. Xiao, A. Prakash, T. Kohno, and D. Song. "Robust Physical-World Attacks on Deep Learning Models". In: *CVPR*. 2018.

[Eys+21]   B. Eysenbach, A. Khazatsky, S. Levine, and R. Salakhutdinov. "Mismatched No More: Joint Model-Policy Optimization for Model-Based RL". In: (2021). arXiv: 2110.02758 [cs.LG].

[FA20]   I. Fischer and A. A. Alemi. "CEB Improves Model Robustness". In: *Entropy* 22.10 (2020), p. 1081.

[Fad+20]   S. G. Fadel, S. Mair, R. da S. Torres, and U. Brefeld. "Principled Interpolation in Normalizing Flows". In: (2020). arXiv: 2010.12059 [stat.ML].

[Fag+18]   F. Faghri, D. J. Fleet, J. R. Kiros, and S. Fidler. "VSE++: Improving Visual-Semantic Embeddings with Hard Negatives". In: *BMVC*. 2018.

[FAL17]   C. Finn, P. Abbeel, and S. Levine. "Model-Agnostic Meta-Learning for Fast Adaptation of Deep Networks". In: *ICML*. 2017.

[Far22]   S. Farquhar. "Understanding Approximation for Bayesian Inference in Neural Networks". PhD thesis. Oxford, Nov. 2022.

[Fau+18]   L. Faury, F. Vasile, C. Calauzènes, and O. Fercoq. "Neural Generative Models for Global Optimization with Gradients". In: (2018). arXiv: 1805.08594 [cs.NE].

[FB19]   E. M. Feit and R. Berman. "Test & Roll: Profit-Maximizing A/B Tests". In: *Marketing Science* 38.6 (2019), pp. 1038–1058.

[FBW21]   M. Finzi, G. Benton, and A. G. Wilson. "Residual Pathway Priors for Soft Equivariance Constraints". In: *NIPS*. 2021.

[FC03]   P. Fearnhead and P. Clifford. "On-line inference for hidden Markov models via particle filters". en. In: *J. of Royal Stat. Soc. Series B* 65.4 (2003), pp. 887–899.

[FD07a]   B. Frey and D. Dueck. "Clustering by Passing Messages Between Data Points". In: *Science* 315 (2007), 972–976.

[FD07b]   B. J. Frey and D. Dueck. "Clustering by passing messages between data points". In: *science* 315.5814 (2007), pp. 972–976.

[FDF19]   A. M. Franks, A. D'Amour, and A. Feller. "Flexible Sensitivity Analysis for Observational Studies Without Observable Implications". In: *Journal of the American Statistical Association* 0.0 (2019),

pp. 1–33. eprint: https://doi.org/10.1080/01621459.2019.1604369.

[FDZ19]   A. Fasano, D. Durante, and G. Zanella. "Scalable and Accurate Variational Bayes for High-Dimensional Binary Regression Models". In: (2019). arXiv: 1911.06743 [stat.ME].

[FE73]   M. Fischler and R. Elschlager. "The representation and matching of pictorial structures". In: *IEEE Trans. on Computer* 22.1 (1973).

[Fed+18]   W. Fedus, M. Rosca, B. Lakshminarayanan, A. M. Dai, S. Mohamed, and I. Goodfellow. "Many Paths to Equilibrium: GANs Do Not Need to Decrease a Divergence At Every Step". In: *International Conference on Learning Representations*. 2018.

[Fei98]   U. Feige. "A threshold of ln n for approximating set cover". In: *Journal of the ACM (JACM)* (1998).

[Fel+10]   P. Felzenszwalb, R. Girshick, D. McAllester, and D. Ramanan. "Object Detection with Discriminatively Trained Part Based Models". In: *IEEE PAMI* 32.9 (2010).

[Fel+19]   M. Fellows, A. Mahajan, T. G. J. Rudner, and S. Whiteson. "VIREL: A Variational Inference Framework for Reinforcement Learning". In: *NeurIPS*. 2019, pp. 7120–7134.

[Fen+21]   S. Y. Feng, V. Gangal, J. Wei, S. Chandar, S. Vosoughi, T. Mitamura, and E. Hovy. "A Survey of Data Augmentation Approaches for NLP". In: (2021). arXiv: 2105.03075 [cs.CL].

[Feu+15]   M. Feurer, A. Klein, K. Eggensperger, J. Springenberg, M. Blum, and F. Hutter. "Efficient and Robust Automated Machine Learning". In: *NIPS*. 2015, pp. 2962–2970.

[FG15]   N. Fournier and A. Guillin. "On the rate of convergence in Wasserstein distance of the empirical measure". In: *Probability Theory and Related Fields* 162.3 (2015), pp. 707–738.

[FG18]   S. Farquhar and Y. Gal. "Towards Robust Evaluations of Continual Learning". In: (2018). arXiv: 1805.09733 [stat.ML].

[FGG97]   N. Friedman, D. Geiger, and M. Goldszmidt. "Bayesian network classifiers". In: *MLJ* 29 (1997), pp. 131–163.

[FH12]   P. F. Felzenszwalb and D. P. Huttenlocher. "Distance Transforms of Sampled Functions". In: *Theory of Computing* 8.19 (2012), pp. 415–428.

[FH17]   N. Frosst and G. Hinton. *Distilling a Neural Network Into a Soft Decision Tree*. 2017. arXiv: 1711.09784 [cs.LG].

[FH20]   E. Fong and C. Holmes. "On the marginal likelihood and cross-validation". In: *Biometrika* 107.2 (2020).

[FH75]   K Fukunaga and L Hostetler. "The estimation of the gradient of a density function, with applications in pattern recognition". In: *IEEE Trans. Inf. Theory* 21.1 (1975), pp. 32–40.

[FH97]   B. J. Frey and G. Hinton. "Efficient stochastic source coding and an application to a Bayesian network source model". In: *Computer Journal* (1997).

[FHDV20]   J. Futoma, M. C. Hughes, and F. Doshi-Velez. "Popcorn: Partially observed prediction constrained reinforcement learning". In: *AISTATS* (2020).

[FHHL20] G. Flamich, M. Havasi, and J. M. Hernández-Lobato. "Compressing images by encoding their latent representations with relative entropy coding". In: vol. 33. 2020, pp. 16131–16141.

[FHK03] P. Felzenszwalb, D. Huttenlocher, and J. Kleinberg. "Fast Algorithms for Large State Space HMMs with Applications to Web Usage Analysis". In: *NIPS*. 2003.

[FHL19] S. Fort, H. Hu, and B. Lakshminarayanan. "Deep Ensembles: A Loss Landscape Perspective". In: (2019). arXiv: 1912.02757 [stat.ML].

[FHM18] S. Fujimoto, H. van Hoof, and D. Meger. "Addressing Function Approximation Error in Actor-Critic Methods". In: *ICLR*. 2018.

[FHT08] J. Friedman, T. Hastie, and R. Tibshirani. "Sparse inverse covariance estimation the graphical lasso". In: *Biostatistics* 9.3 (2008), pp. 432–441.

[FI10] A. Fischer and C. Igel. "Empirical analysis of the divergence of Gibbs sampling based learning algorithms for restricted Boltzmann machines". In: *International conference on artificial neural networks*. Springer. 2010, pp. 208–217.

[Fie70] S. Fienberg. "An Iterative Procedure for Estimation in Contingency Tables". In: *Annals of Mathematical Statistics* 41.3 (1970), pp. 907–917.

[Fin+16] C. Finn, P. Christiano, P. Abbeel, and S. Levine. "A connection between generative adversarial networks, inverse reinforcement learning, and energy-based models". In: *arXiv preprint arXiv:1611.03852* (2016).

[Fis20] I. Fischer. "The Conditional Entropy Bottleneck". In: *Entropy* 22.9 (2020).

[Fis25] R. Fisher. *Statistical Methods for Research Workers*. Biological monographs and manuals. Oliver and Boyd, 1925.

[FJ02] M. A. T. Figueiredo and A. K. Jain. "Unsupervised Learning of Finite Mixture Models". In: *IEEE PAMI* 24.3 (2002), pp. 381–396.

[FJL18] R. Frostig, M. J. Johnson, and C. Leary. "Compiling machine learning programs via high-level tracing". In: *Machine Learning and Systems (MLSys)* (2018).

[FK13a] V. Feldman and P. Kothari. "Learning Coverage Functions". In: *CoRR* abs/1304.2079 (2013). arXiv: 1304.2079.

[FK13b] M Frei and H. R. Künsch. "Bridging the ensemble Kalman and particle filters". In: *Biometrika* 100.4 (2013), pp. 781–800.

[FK14] V. Feldman and P. Kothari. "Learning Coverage Functions and Private Release of Marginals". In: *Proceedings of The 27th Conference on Learning Theory*. Ed. by M. F. Balcan, V. Feldman, and C. Szepesvári. Vol. 35. Proceedings of Machine Learning Research. Barcelona, Spain: PMLR, 2014, pp. 679–702.

[FK21] A. Fisher and E. H. Kennedy. "Visually Communicating and Teaching Intuition for Influence Functions". In: *The American Statistician* 75.2 (2021), pp. 162–172. eprint: https://doi.org/10.1080/00031305.2020.1717620.

[FKH17] S. Falkner, A. Klein, and F. Hutter. "Combining Hyperband and Bayesian Optimization". In: *NIPS 2017 Bayesian Optimization Workshop*. 2017.

[FKV13] V. Feldman, P. Kothari, and J. Vondrák. "Representation, Approximation and Learning of Submodular Functions Using Low-rank Decision Trees". In: *Proceedings of the 26th Annual Conference on Learning Theory*. Ed. by S. Shalev-Shwartz and I. Steinwart. Vol. 30. Proceedings of Machine Learning Research. Princeton, NJ, USA: PMLR, 2013, pp. 711–740.

[FKV14] V. Feldman, P. Kothari, and J. Vondrák. "Nearly tight bounds on l1 approximation of self-bounding functions". In: *CoRR, abs/1404.4702* 1 (2014).

[FKV17] V. Feldman, P. Kothari, and J. Vondrák. "Tight Bounds on ℓ_1 Approximation and Learning of Self-Bounding Functions". In: *International Conference on Algorithmic Learning Theory*. PMLR. 2017, pp. 540–559.

[FKV20] V. Feldman, P. Kothari, and J. Vondrák. "Tight bounds on ℓ_1 approximation and learning of self-bounding functions". In: *Theoretical Computer Science* 808 (2020), pp. 86–98.

[FL07] P. Fearnhead and Z. Liu. "Online Inference for Multiple Changepoint Problems". In: *J. of Royal Stat. Soc. Series B* 69 (2007), pp. 589–605.

[FL11] P. Fearnhead and Z. Liu. "Efficient Bayesian analysis of multiple changepoint models with dependence across segments". In: *Statistics and Computing* 21.2 (2011), pp. 217–229.

[FL+18] V. François-Lavet, P. Henderson, R. Islam, M. G. Bellemare, and J. Pineau. "An Introduction to Deep Reinforcement Learning". In: *Foundations and Trends in Machine Learning* 11.3 (2018).

[FLA16] C. Finn, S. Levine, and P. Abbeel. "Guided Cost Learning: Deep Inverse Optimal Control via Policy Optimization". In: *ICML*. 2016, pp. 49–58.

[Fla+16] S. Flaxman, D. Sejdinovic, J. P. Cunningham, and S. Filippi. "Bayesian Learning of Kernel Embeddings". In: *UAI*. 2016.

[FLL18] J. Fu, K. Luo, and S. Levine. "Learning Robust Rewards with Adverserial Inverse Reinforcement Learning". In: *ICLR*. 2018.

[FLL19] Y. Feng, L. Li, and Q. Liu. "A Kernel Loss for Solving the Bellman Equation". In: *NeurIPS*. 2019, pp. 15430–15441.

[FLMM21] D. T. Frazier, R. Loaiza-Maya, and G. M. Martin. "Variational Bayes in State Space Models: Inferential and Predictive Accuracy". In: (June 2021). arXiv: 2106.12262 [stat.ME].

[FMM18] M. Figurnov, S. Mohamed, and A. Mnih. "Implicit Reparameterization Gradients". In: *NIPS*. 2018.

[FMP19] S. Fujimoto, D. Meger, and D. Precup. "Off-Policy Deep Reinforcement Learning without Exploration". In: *ICML*. 2019, pp. 2052–2062.

[FNG00] N. de Freitas, M. Niranjan, and A. Gee. "Hierarchical Bayesian models for regularisation in sequential learning". In: *Neural Computation* 12.4 (2000), pp. 955–993.

[FNW78] M. Fisher, G. Nemhauser, and L. Wolsey. "An analysis of approximations for maximizing submodular set functions—II". In: *Polyhedral combinatorics* (1978), pp. 73–87.

[FO20] F. Farnia and A. Ozdaglar. "Do GANs always have Nash equilibria?" In: *Proceedings of the 37th International Conference on Machine Learning*. Ed. by

H. D. III and A. Singh. Vol. 119. Proceedings of Machine Learning Research. PMLR, 2020, pp. 3029–3039.

[Fon+21]   D. Fontanel, F. Cermelli, M. Mancini, and B. Caputo. "On the Challenges of Open World Recognition under Shifting Visual Domains". In: *ICRA*. 2021.

[For01]   G. D. Forney. "Codes on graphs: normal realizations". In: *IEEE Trans. Inf. Theory* 47.2 (2001), pp. 520–548.

[For+18a]   V. Fortuin, G. Dresdner, H. Strathmann, and G. Rätsch. "Scalable Gaussian Processes on Discrete Domains". In: (2018). arXiv: 1810.10368 [stat.ML].

[For+18b]   M. Fortunato et al. "Noisy Networks for Exploration". In: *ICLR*. 2018.

[For+19]   N. Ford, J. Gilmer, N. Carlini, and D. Cubuk. "Adversarial Examples Are a Natural Consequence of Test Error in Noise". In: (2019). arXiv: 1901.10513 [cs.LG].

[For22]   V. Fortuin. "Priors in Bayesian Deep Learning: A Review". In: *Intl. Statisical Review* (2022). arXiv: 2105.06868 [stat.ML].

[For+95]   J. Forbes, T. Huang, K. Kanazawa, and S. Russell. "The BATmobile: Towards a Bayesian Automated Taxi". In: *IJCAI*. 1995.

[Fot+14]   N. Foti, J. Xu, D. Laird, and E. Fox. "Stochastic variational inference for hidden Markov models". In: *NIPS*. 2014, pp. 3599–3607.

[Fox+08]   E. Fox, E. Sudderth, M. Jordan, and A. Willsky. "An HDP-HMM for Systems with State Persistence". In: *ICML*. 2008.

[Fox09]   E. B. Fox. "Bayesian nonparametric learning of complex dynamical phenomena". PhD thesis. Massachusetts Institute of Technology, 2009.

[FP08]   N Friel and A. N. Pettitt. "Marginal Likelihood Estimation via Power Posteriors". In: *J. of Royal Stat. Soc. Series B* 70.3 (2008), pp. 589–607.

[FP69]   D. C. Fraser and J. E. Potter. "The optimum linear smoother as a combination of two optimum linear filters". In: *IEEE Trans. on Automatical Control* (1969), pp. 387–390.

[FPD09]   P. Frazier, W. Powell, and S. Dayanik. "The knowledge-gradient policy for correlated normal beliefs". In: *INFORMS J. on Computing* 21.4 (2009), pp. 599–613.

[Fra08]   A. Fraser. *Hidden Markov Models and Dynamical Systems*. SIAM Press, 2008.

[Fra+16]   M. Fraccaro, S. K. Sønderby, U. Paquet, and O. Winther. "Sequential Neural Models with Stochastic Layers". In: *NIPS*. 2016.

[Fra18]   P. I. Frazier. "Bayesian Optimization". In: *Recent Advances in Optimization and Modeling of Contemporary Problems*. INFORMS TutORials in Operations Research. INFORMS, 2018, pp. 255–278.

[Fre14]   A. A. Freitas. "Comprehensible classification models: a position paper". In: *ACM SIGKDD explorations newsletter* 15.1 (2014), pp. 1–10.

[Fre+22]   M. Freitag, D. Grangier, Q. Tan, and B. Liang. "High Quality Rather than High Model Probability: Minimum Bayes Risk Decoding with Neural Metrics". In: *TACL*. 2022.

[Fre98]   B. Frey. *Graphical Models for Machine Learning and Digital Communication*. MIT Press, 1998.

[Fre99]   R. M. French. "Catastrophic forgetting in connectionist networks". In: *Trends in Cognitive Science* (1999).

[Fri09]   K. Friston. "The free-energy principle: a rough guide to the brain?" en. In: *Trends Cogn. Sci.* 13.7 (2009), pp. 293–301.

[Fro+13]   A. Frome, G. Corrado, J. Shlens, S. Bengio, J. Dean, M. Ranzato, and T. Mikolov. "Devise: A deep visual-semantic embedding model". In: (2013).

[Fro+21]   R. Frostig, M. Johnson, D. Maclaurin, A. Paszke, and A. Radul. "Decomposing reverse-mode automatic differentiation". In: *LAFI workshop at POPL 2021*. 2021.

[FS07]   S. Fruhwirth-Schnatter. *Finite Mixture and Markov Switching Models*. Springer, 2007.

[FSF10]   S. Fruhwirth-Schnatter and R. Fruhwirth. "Data Augmentation and MCMC for Binary and Multinomial Logit Models". In: *Statistical Modelling and Regression Structures*. Ed. by T. Kneib and G. Tutz. Springer, 2010, pp. 111–132.

[FST98]   S. Fine, Y. Singer, and N. Tishby. "The Hierarchical Hidden Markov Model: Analysis and Applications". In: *Machine Learning* 32 (1998), p. 41.

[FT05]   M. Fashing and C. Tomasi. "Mean shift is a bound optimization". en. In: *IEEE Trans. Pattern Anal. Mach. Intell.* 27.3 (2005), pp. 471–474.

[FT19]   A. Finke and A. H. Thiery. "On the relationship between variational inference and adaptive importance sampling". In: (July 2019). arXiv: 1907.10477 [stat.ML].

[FT74]   J. H. Friedman and J. W. Tukey. "A Projection Pursuit Algorithm for Exploratory Data Analysis". In: *IEEE Trans. Comput.* C-23.9 (1974), pp. 881–890.

[Fu15]   M. Fu, ed. *Handbook of Simulation Optimization*. 1st ed. Springer-Verlag New York, 2015.

[Fu+17]   Z. Fu, X. Tan, N. Peng, D. Zhao, and R. Yan. "Style transfer in text: Exploration and evaluation". In: *arXiv preprint arXiv:1711.06861* (2017).

[Fu+19]   H. Fu, C. Li, X. Liu, J. Gao, A. Celikyilmaz, and L. Carin. "Cyclical Annealing Schedule: A Simple Approach to Mitigating KL Vanishing". In: *NAACL*. 2019.

[Fu+20]   J. Fu, A. Kumar, O. Nachum, G. Tucker, and S. Levine. *D4RL: Datasets for Deep Data-Driven Reinforcement Learning*. arXiv:2004.07219. 2020.

[Fuj05]   S. Fujishige. *Submodular functions and optimization*. Vol. 58. Elsevier Science, 2005.

[Ful+20]   I. R. Fulcher, I. Shpitser, S. Marealle, and E. J. Tchetgen Tchetgen. "Robust inference on population indirect causal effects: the generalized front door criterion". In: *Journal of the Royal Statistical Society: Series B (Statistical Methodology)* 82.1 (2020), pp. 199–214. eprint: https://rss.onlinelibrary.wiley.com/doi/pdf/10.1111/rssb.12345.

[FV15]   V. Feldman and J. Vondrák. "Tight Bounds on Low-Degree Spectral Concentration of Submodular and XOS Functions". In: *2015 IEEE 56th Annual Symposium on Foundations of Computer Science*. 2015, pp. 923–942.

[FV16]   V. Feldman and J. Vondrák. "Optimal bounds on approximation of submodular and XOS functions by juntas". In: *SIAM Journal on Computing* 45.3 (2016), pp. 1129–1170.

[FV17]   R. C. Fong and A. Vedaldi. "Interpretable explanations of black boxes by meaningful perturbation". In: *Proceedings of the IEEE international conference on computer vision*. 2017, pp. 3429–3437.

[FW12]   N. Friel and J. Wyse. "Estimating the evidence – a review". In: *Stat. Neerl.* 66.3 (2012), pp. 288–308.

[FW21]   R. Friedman and Y. Weiss. "Posterior Sampling for Image Restoration using Explicit Patch Priors". In: (2021). arXiv: 2104.09895 [cs.CV].

[FWW21]   M. Finzi, M. Welling, and A. G. Wilson. "A Practical Method for Constructing Equivariant Multilayer Perceptrons for Arbitrary Matrix Groups". In: *ICML*. 2021.

[Gaj+19]   A. Gajewski, J. Clune, K. O. Stanley, and J. Lehman. "Evolvability ES: Scalable and Direct Optimization of Evolvability". In: *Proc. of the Conf. on Genetic and Evolutionary Computation*. 2019.

[Gan07]   M Ganapathiraju. "Application of language technologies in biology: Feature extraction and modeling for transmembrane helix prediction". en. PhD thesis. 2007.

[Gan+16a]   Y Ganin, E Ustinova, H Ajakan, P Germain, and others. "Domain-adversarial training of neural networks". In: *JMLR* (2016).

[Gan+16b]   Y. Ganin, E. Ustinova, H. Ajakan, P. Germain, H. Larochelle, F. Laviolette, M. Marchand, and V. Lempitsky. "Domain-adversarial training of neural networks". In: *The journal of machine learning research* 17.1 (2016), pp. 2096–2030.

[Gan+23]   A. Gane et al. "ProtNLM: Model-based Natural Language Protein Annotation". In: (2023).

[Gao+18]   R. Gao, J. Xie, S.-C. Zhu, and Y. N. Wu. "Learning Grid-like Units with Vector Representation of Self-Position and Matrix Representation of Self-Motion". In: *arXiv preprint arXiv:1810.05597* (2018).

[Gao+20]   R. Gao, E. Nijkamp, D. P. Kingma, Z. Xu, A. M. Dai, and Y. N. Wu. "Flow contrastive estimation of energy-based models". In: *Proceedings of the IEEE/CVF Conference on Computer Vision and Pattern Recognition*. 2020, pp. 7518–7528.

[Gao+21]   R. Gao, Y. Song, B. Poole, Y. N. Wu, and D. P. Kingma. "Learning Energy-Based Models by Diffusion Recovery Likelihood". In: *ICLR*. 2021.

[Gär03]   T. Gärtner. "A Survey of Kernels for Structured Data". In: *SIGKDD Explor. Newsl.* 5.1 (2003), pp. 49–58.

[GAR16]   R. B. Grosse, S. Ancha, and D. M. Roy. "Measuring the reliability of MCMC inference with bidirectional Monte Carlo". In: *NIPS*. 2016.

[Gar+18a]   J. Gardner, G. Pleiss, K. Q. Weinberger, D. Bindel, and A. G. Wilson. "GPyTorch: Blackbox Matrix-Matrix Gaussian Process Inference with GPU Acceleration". In: *NIPS*. Ed. by S Bengio, H Wallach, H Larochelle, K Grauman, N Cesa-Bianchi, and R Garnett. Curran Associates, Inc., 2018, pp. 7576–7586.

[Gar+18b]   J. R. Gardner, G. Pleiss, R. Wu, K. Q. Weinberger, and A. G. Wilson. "Product Kernel Interpolation for Scalable Gaussian Processes". In: *AISTATS*. 2018.

[Gar+18c]   T. Garipov, P. Izmailov, D. Podoprikhin, D. Vetrov, and A. G. Wilson. "Loss Surfaces, Mode Connectivity, and Fast Ensembling of DNNs". In: *NIPS*. 2018.

[Gar+18d]   M. Garnelo, D. Rosenbaum, C. Maddison, T. Ramalho, D. Saxton, M. Shanahan, Y. W. Teh, D. Rezende, and S. M. A. Eslami. "Conditional Neural Processes". In: *ICML*. Ed. by J. Dy and A. Krause. Vol. 80. Proceedings of Machine Learning Research. PMLR, 2018, pp. 1704–1713.

[Gar+18e]   M. Garnelo, J. Schwarz, D. Rosenbaum, F. Viola, D. J. Rezende, S. M. Ali Eslami, and Y. W. Teh. "Neural Processes". In: *ICML workshop on Theoretical Foundations and Applications of Deep Generative Models*. 2018.

[Gar+19]   S. Garg, V. Perot, N. Limtiaco, A. Taly, E. H. Chi, and A. Beutel. "Counterfactual Fairness in Text Classification through Robustness". In: *Proceedings of the 2019 AAAI/ACM Conference on AI, Ethics, and Society*. AIES '19. Association for Computing Machinery, 2019, 219–226.

[Gar+20]   S. Garg, Y. Wu, S. Balakrishnan, and Z. C. Lipton. "A unified view of label shift estimation". In: *NIPS*. Mar. 2020.

[Gar23]   R. Garnett. *Bayesian Optimization*. Cambridge University Press, 2023.

[GARD18]   G. Gur-Ari, D. A. Roberts, and E. Dyer. "Gradient Descent Happens in a Tiny Subspace". In: (2018). arXiv: 1812.04754 [cs.LG].

[Gas+19]   J. Gasthaus, K. Benidis, Y. Wang, S. S. Rangapuram, D. Salinas, V. Flunkert, and T. Januschowski. "Probabilistic Forecasting with Spline Quantile Function RNNs". In: *ICML*. Vol. 89. Proceedings of Machine Learning Research. PMLR, 2019, pp. 1901–1910.

[GAZ19]   A. Ghorbani, A. Abid, and J. Zou. "Interpretation of neural networks is fragile". In: *Proceedings of the AAAI Conference on Artificial Intelligence*. Vol. 33. 01. 2019, pp. 3681–3688.

[GB00]   Z. Ghahramani and M. Beal. "Variational inference for Bayesian mixtures of factor analysers". In: *NIPS-12*. 2000.

[GB09]   A. Guillory and J. Bilmes. "Label Selection on Graphs". In: *NIPS*. Vancouver, Canada, 2009.

[GB10]   X. Glorot and Y. Bengio. "Understanding the difficulty of training deep feedforward neural networks". In: *AISTATS*. 2010, pp. 249–256.

[GB11]   A. Guillory and J. Bilmes. "Active Semi-Supervised Learning using Submodular Functions". In: *UAI*. Barcelona, Spain: AUAI, 2011.

[GB+18]   R. Gómez-Bombarelli, J. N. Wei, D. Duvenaud, J. M. Hernández-Lobato, B. Sánchez-Lengeling, D. Sheberla, J. Aguilera-Iparraguirre, T. D. Hirzel, R. P. Adams, and A. Aspuru-Guzik. "Automatic Chemical Design Using a Data-Driven Continuous Representation of Molecules". en. In: *American Chemical Society Central Science* 4.2 (2018), pp. 268–276.

[GBB11]   X. Glorot, A. Bordes, and Y. Bengio. "Deep Sparse Rectifier Neural Networks". In: *AISTATS*. 2011.

[GBC16]   I. Goodfellow, Y. Bengio, and A. Courville. *Deep Learning*. http://www.deeplearningbook.org. MIT Press, 2016.

[GBGM23]   R. Gozalo-Brizuela and E. C. Garrido-Merchan. "ChatGPT is not all you need. A State of the Art Review of large Generative AI models". In: (Jan. 2023). arXiv: 2301.04655 [cs.LG].

[GBJ18]   R. Giordano, T. Broderick, and M. I. Jordan. "Covariances, Robustness, and Variational Bayes". In: *JMLR* 19.51 (2018), pp. 1–49.

[GBP18]   C. Gurau, A. Bewley, and I. Posner. "Dropout Distillation for Efficiently Estimating Model Confidence". 2018.

[GC11]   M. Girolami and B. Calderhead. "Riemann manifold Langevin and Hamiltonian Monte Carlo methods". In: *J. of Royal Stat. Soc. Series B* 73.2 (2011), pp. 123–214.

[GC90]   R. P. Goldman and E. Charniak. "Dynamic Construction of Belief Networks". In: *UAI*. 1990.

[GCW19]   M. Gerber, N. Chopin, and N. Whiteley. "Negative association, ordering and convergence of resampling methods". In: *Ann. Stat.* 47.4 (2019), pp. 2236–2260.

[GD20]   T. Geffner and J. Domke. "A Rule for Gradient Estimator Selection, with an Application to Variational Inference". In: *AISTATS*. Ed. by S. Chiappa and R. Calandra. Vol. 108. Proceedings of Machine Learning Research. PMLR, 2020, pp. 1803–1812.

[GDFY16]   S. Ghosh, F. M. Delle Fave, and J. Yedidia. "Assumed Density Filtering Methods for Learning Bayesian Neural Networks". In: *AAAI*. 2016.

[Geb+21]   T. Gebru, J. Morgenstern, B. Vecchione, J. W. Vaughan, H. Wallach, H. D. Iii, and K. Crawford. "Datasheets for datasets". In: *Communications of the ACM* 64.12 (2021), pp. 86–92.

[Ged+20]   D. Gedon, N. Wahlström, T. B. Schön, and L. Ljung. "Deep State Space Models for Nonlinear System Identification". In: (Mar. 2020). arXiv: 2003.14162 [eess.SY].

[Gei+20a]   R. Geirhos, J.-H. Jacobsen, C. Michaelis, R. Zemel, W. Brendel, M. Bethge, and F. A. Wichmann. "Shortcut Learning in Deep Neural Networks". In: *Nature Machine Intelligence* (2020).

[Gei+20b]   R. Geirhos, J. Jacobsen, C. Michaelis, R. S. Zemel, W. Brendel, M. Bethge, and F. A. Wichmann. "Shortcut Learning in Deep Neural Networks". In: *CoRR* abs/2004.07780 (2020). arXiv: 2004.07780.

[Gel+04]   A. Gelman, J. Carlin, H. Stern, and D. Rubin. *Bayesian data analysis*. 2nd edition. Chapman and Hall, 2004.

[Gel06]   A. Gelman. "Prior distributions for variance parameters in hierarchical models (comment on article by Browne and Draper)". en. In: *Bayesian Anal.* 1.3 (2006), pp. 515–534.

[Gel+08]   A. Gelman, A. Jakulin, M. G. Pittau, and Y.-S. Su. "A weakly informative default prior distribution for logistic and other regression models". en. In: *The Annals of Applied Statistics* 2.4 (2008), pp. 1360–1383.

[Gel+14a]   A. Gelman, J. B. Carlin, H. S. Stern, D. B. Dunson, A. Vehtari, and D. B. Rubin. *Bayesian Data Analysis, Third Edition*. Third edition. Chapman and Hall/CRC, 2014.

[Gel+14b]   A. Gelman, A. Vehtari, P. Jylänki, C. Robert, N. Chopin, and J. P. Cunningham. "Expectation propagation as a way of life". In: (2014). arXiv: 1412.4869 [stat.CO].

[Gel16]   A. Gelman. "The problems with p-values are not just with p-values". In: *American Statistician* (2016).

[Gel+20]   A. Gelman, A. Vehtari, D. Simpson, C. C. Margossian, B. Carpenter, Y. Yao, L. Kennedy, J. Gabry, P.-C. Bürkner, and M. Modrák. "Bayesian Workflow". In: (2020). arXiv: 2011.01808 [stat.ME].

[Gel+22]   A. Gelman, J. Hill, B. Goodrich, J. Gabry, D. Simpson, and A. Vehtari. *Applied Regression and Multilevel Models*. To appear. 2022.

[Gel90]   M. Gelbrich. "On a formula for the L2 Wasserstein metric between measures on Euclidean and Hilbert spaces". In: *Mathematische Nachrichten* 147.1 (1990), pp. 185–203.

[Gen+19]   A. Genevay, L. Chizat, F. Bach, M. Cuturi, and G. Peyré. "Sample complexity of sinkhorn divergences". In: *The 22nd International Conference on Artificial Intelligence and Statistics*. PMLR. 2019, pp. 1574–1583.

[Geo+17]   D. George et al. "A generative vision model that trains with high data efficiency and breaks text-based CAPTCHAs". In: *Science* 358.6368 (2017), eaag2612. eprint: https://www.science.org/doi/pdf/10.1126/science.aag2612.

[Geo+18]   T. George, C. Laurent, X. Bouthillier, N. Ballas, and P. Vincent. "Fast Approximate Natural Gradient Descent in a Kronecker Factored Eigenbasis". In: *NIPS*. Curran Associates, Inc., 2018, pp. 9550–9560.

[Geo88]   H.-O. Georgii. *Gibbs Measures and Phase Transitions*. en. Walter De Gruyter Inc, 1988.

[Ger+15]   M. Germain, K. Gregor, I. Murray, and H. Larochelle. "MADE: Masked Autoencoder for Distribution Estimation". In: *ICML*. Ed. by F. Bach and D. Blei. Vol. 37. Proceedings of Machine Learning Research. PMLR, 2015, pp. 881–889.

[Gér19]   A. Géron. *Hands-On Machine Learning with Scikit-Learn and TensorFlow: Concepts, Tools, and Techniques for Building Intelligent Systems (2nd edition)*. en. O'Reilly Media, Incorporated, 2019.

[Ger19]   S. J. Gershman. "What does the free energy principle tell us about the brain?" In: *Neurons, Behavior, Data Analysis, and Theory* (2019).

[GEY19]   Y. Geifman and R. El-Yaniv. "SelectiveNet: A Deep Neural Network with an Integrated Reject Option". In: *ICML*. 2019.

[Gey92]   C. Geyer. "Practical Markov chain Monte Carlo". In: *Statistical Science* 7 (1992), pp. 473–483.

[GF00]   E. George and D. Foster. "Calibration and empirical Bayes variable selection". In: *Biometrika* 87.4 (2000), pp. 731–747.

[GF09]   I. E. Givoni and B. J. Frey. "A Binary Variable Model for Affinity Propagation". In: *Neural Computation* 21.6 (2009), pp. 1589–1600.

[GF+15]   Á. F. García-Fernández, L. Svensson, M. R. Morelande, and S. Särkkä. "Posterior Linearization Filter: Principles and Implementation Using Sigma Points". In: *IEEE Trans. Signal Process.* 63.20 (Oct. 2015), pp. 5561–5573.

[GF17]   B. Goodman and S. Flaxman. "European Union regulations on algorithmic decision-making and a "right to explanation"". In: *AI magazine* 38.3 (2017), pp. 50–57.

[GF21]   A. Grim and P. Felzenszwalb. "Convex Combination Belief Propagation Algorithms". In: (May 2021). arXiv: 2105.12815 [cs.AI].

[GFSS17]   Á. F. García-Fernández, L. Svensson, and S. Särkkä. "Iterated Posterior Linearization Smoother". In: *IEEE Trans. Automat. Contr.* 62.4 (2017), pp. 2056–2063.

[GFTS19] Á. F. García-Fernández, F. Tronarp, and S. Särkkä. "Gaussian Process Classification Using Posterior Linearization". In: *IEEE Signal Process. Lett.* 26.5 (2019), pp. 735–739.

[GFWO20] T. Galy-Fajou, F. Wenzel, and M. Opper. "Automated Augmented Conjugate Inference for Nonconjugate Gaussian Process Models". In: *AISTATS*. 2020.

[GG14] S. J. Gershman and N. D. Goodman. "Amortized Inference in Probabilistic Reasoning". In: *36th Annual Conference of the Cognitive Science Society*. 2014.

[GG16] Y. Gal and Z. Ghahramani. "Dropout as a Bayesian Approximation: Representing Model Uncertainty in Deep Learning". In: *ICML*. 2016.

[GG84] S. Geman and D. Geman. "Stochastic Relaxation, Gibbs Distributions, and the Bayesian Restoration of Images". In: *IEEE PAMI* 6.6 (1984).

[GGG15] M. Gygli, H. Grabner, and L. Gool. "Video summarization by learning submodular mixtures of objectives". In: *2015 IEEE Conference on Computer Vision and Pattern Recognition (CVPR)* (2015), pp. 3090–3098.

[GGS21] M. Grcic, I. Grubisic, and S. Segvic. "DenseFlow: Official implementation of Densely connected normalizing flows". en. In: *NIPS*. 2021.

[GH07] A. Gelman and J. Hill. *Data analysis using regression and multilevel/ hierarchical models*. Cambridge, 2007.

[GH10] M. Gutmann and A. Hyvärinen. "Noise-contrastive estimation: A new estimation principle for unnormalized statistical models". In: *Proceedings of the Thirteenth International Conference on Artificial Intelligence and Statistics*. 2010, pp. 297–304.

[GH12] M. Gutmann and J.-i. Hirayama. "Bregman divergence as general framework to estimate unnormalized statistical models". In: *arXiv:1202.3727* (2012).

[GH96a] Z. Ghahramani and G. Hinton. *Parameter estimation for linear dynamical systems*. Tech. rep. CRG-TR-96-2. Dept. Comp. Sci., Univ. Toronto, 1996.

[GH96b] Z. Ghahramani and G. Hinton. *The EM Algorithm for Mixtures of Factor Analyzers*. Tech. rep. Dept. of Comp. Sci., Uni. Toronto, 1996.

[GH98] Z. Ghahramani and G. Hinton. "Variational learning for switching state-space models". In: *Neural Computation* 12.4 (1998), pp. 963–996.

[Gha+15] M. Ghavamzadeh, S. Mannor, J. Pineau, and A. Tamar. "Bayesian Reinforcement Learning: A Survey". In: *Foundations and Trends in ML* (2015).

[Gha+19] M. Ghazvininejad, O. Levy, Y. Liu, and L. Zettlemoyer. "Mask-Predict: Parallel Decoding of Conditional Masked Language Models". In: *EMNLP*. Hong Kong, China: Association for Computational Linguistics, Nov. 2019, pp. 6112–6121.

[Gha+21] A. Ghandeharioun, B. Kim, C.-L. Li, B. Jou, B. Eoff, and R. W. Picard. *DISSECT: Disentangled Simultaneous Explanations via Concept Traversals*. 2021. arXiv: 2105.15164 [cs.LG].

[GHC20] C. Geng, S.-J. Huang, and S. Chen. "Recent Advances in Open Set Recognition: A Survey". In: *IEEE PAMI* (2020).

[GHC21] S. Gould, R. Hartley, and D. J. Campbell. "Deep Declarative Networks". en. In: *IEEE PAMI* PP (2021).

[GHK17] Y. Gal, J. Hron, and A. Kendall. "Concrete Dropout". In: (2017). arXiv: 1705.07832 [stat.ML].

[Gho+19] A. Ghorbani, J. Wexler, J. Zou, and B. Kim. *Towards Automatic Concept-based Explanations*. 2019. arXiv: 1902.03129 [stat.ML].

[Gho+21] A. Ghosh, A. Honoré, D. Liu, G. E. Henter, and S. Chatterjee. "Normalizing Flow based Hidden Markov Models for Classification of Speech Phones with Explainability". In: (July 2021). arXiv: 2107.00730 [cs.LG].

[GHV14] A. Gelman, J. Hwang, and A. Vehtari. "Understanding predictive information criteria for Bayesian models". In: *Statistics and Computing* 24.6 (2014), pp. 997–1016.

[GHV20a] A. Gelman, J. Hill, and A. Vehtari. *Regression and Other Stories*. en. 1st ed. Cambridge University Press, 2020.

[GHV20b] A. Gelman, J. Hill, and A. Vehtari. *Regression and Other Stories*. Cambridge, 2020.

[Gib97] M. Gibbs. "Bayesian Gaussian Processes for Regression and Classification". PhD thesis. U. Cambridge, 1997.

[GIG17] Y. Gal, R. Islam, and Z. Ghahramani. "Deep bayesian active learning with image data". In: *International Conference on Machine Learning*. PMLR. 2017, pp. 1183–1192.

[Gil+18a] J. Gilmer, R. P. Adams, I. Goodfellow, D. Andersen, and G. E. Dahl. "Motivating the rules of the game for adversarial example research". In: *arXiv preprint arXiv:1807.06732* (2018).

[Gil+18b] J. Gilmer, L. Metz, F. Faghri, S. S. Schoenholz, M. Raghu, M. Wattenberg, and I. Goodfellow. "Adversarial spheres". In: *arXiv preprint arXiv:1801.02774* (2018).

[Gil88] J. R. Gilbert. "Some nested dissection order is nearly optimal". In: *Inf. Process. Lett.* 26.6 (1988), pp. 325–328.

[Gir+14] R. Girshick, J. Donahue, T. Darrell, and J. Malik. "Rich feature hierarchies for accurate object detection and semantic segmentation". In: *Proceedings of the IEEE conference on computer vision and pattern recognition*. 2014, pp. 580–587.

[Gir+15] R. Girshick, F. Iandola, T. Darrell, and J. Malik. "Deformable Part Models are Convolutional Neural Networks". In: *CVPR*. 2015.

[Gir+21] L. Girin, S. Leglaive, X. Bie, J. Diard, T. Hueber, and X. Alameda-Pineda. "Dynamical Variational Autoencoders: A Comprehensive Review". In: *Foundations and Trends® in Machine Learning* 15.1-2 (2021), pp. 1–175.

[Git89] J. Gittins. *Multi-armed Bandit Allocation Indices*. Wiley, 1989.

[GJ97] Z. Ghahramani and M. Jordan. "Factorial Hidden Markov Models". In: *Machine Learning* 29 (1997), pp. 245–273.

[GK19] L. Graesser and W. L. Keng. *Foundations of Deep Reinforcement Learning: Theory and Practice in Python*. en. 1 edition. Addison-Wesley Professional, 2019.

[GKS05] C. Guestrin, A. Krause, and A. P. Singh. "Near-optimal sensor placements in gaussian processes". In: *Proceedings of the 22nd international conference on Machine learning*. 2005, pp. 265–272.

[GL10]   K. Gregor and Y. LeCun. "Learning fast approximations of sparse coding". In: *ICML*. 2010, pp. 399–406.

[GL97]   F. Glover and M. Laguna. *Tabu Search*. Kluwer Academic Publishers, 1997.

[Gla03]   P. Glasserman. *Monte Carlo Methods in Financial Engineering*. 1st ed. Stochastic Modelling and Applied Probability. Springer-Verlag New York, 2003.

[Gle02]   S. Glennan. "Rethinking mechanistic explanation". In: *Philosophy of science* 69.S3 (2002), S342–S353.

[GLM15]   J. Ghosh, Y. Li, and R. Mitra. "On the Use of Cauchy Prior Distributions for Bayesian Logistic Regression". In: (2015). arXiv: 1507.07170 [stat.ME].

[GLP21]   I. Gulrajani and D. Lopez-Paz. "In Search of Lost Domain Generalization". In: *ICLR*. 2021.

[GLS81]   M. Grötschel, L. Lovász, and A. Schrijver. "The ellipsoid method and its consequences in combinatorial optimization". In: *Combinatorica* 1.2 (1981), pp. 169–197.

[GM12]   G. Gordon and J. McNulty. *Matroids: a geometric introduction*. Cambridge University Press, 2012.

[GM15]   J. Gorham and L. Mackey. "Measuring sample quality with Stein's method". In: *Advances in Neural Information Processing Systems*. 2015, pp. 226–234.

[GM16]   R. Grosse and J. Martens. "A Kronecker-factored approximate Fisher matrix for convolution layers". In: *ICML*. 2016.

[GM17]   P. L. Green and S Maskell. "Estimating the parameters of dynamical systems from Big Data using Sequential Monte Carlo samplers". In: *Mech. Syst. Signal Process.* 93 (2017), pp. 379–396.

[GM98]   A. Gelman and X.-L. Meng. "Simulating normalizing constants: from importance sampling to bridge sampling to path sampling". In: *Statisical Science* 13 (1998), pp. 163–185.

[GMAR16] Y. Gal, R. T. Mc Allister, and C. E. Rasmussen. "Improving PILCO with Bayesian Neural Network Dynamics Models". In: *ICML workshop on Data-efficient machine learning*. 2016.

[GMH20]   M. Gorinova, D. Moore, and M. Hoffman. "Automatic Reparameterisation of Probabilistic Programs". In: *ICML*. Vol. 119. Proceedings of Machine Learning Research. PMLR, 2020, pp. 3648–3657.

[GNM19]   D. Greenberg, M. Nonnenmacher, and J. Macke. "Automatic Posterior Transformation for Likelihood-Free Inference". In: *ICML*. 2019.

[Goe+09] M. X. Goemans, N. J. Harvey, S. Iwata, and V. Mirrokni. "Approximating submodular functions everywhere". In: *Proceedings of the twentieth annual ACM-SIAM symposium on Discrete algorithms*. SIAM. 2009, pp. 535–544.

[Gol+04] J. Goldberger, S. T. Roweis, G. E. Hinton, and R. Salakhutdinov. "Neighbourhood Components Analysis". In: *NIPS*. 2004.

[Gol+17] N. Gold, M. G. Frasch, C. Herry, B. S. Richardson, and X. Wang. "A Doubly Stochastic Change Point Detection Algorithm for Noisy Biological Signals". en. In: *Front. Physiol.* (2017), p. 106088.

[Gol17]   Y. Goldberg. *Neural Network Methods for Natural Language Processing*. Morgan & Claypool Publishers, 2017.

[Gol+19] Z. Goldfeld, E. van den Berg, K. H. Greenewald, I. Melnyk, N. Nguyen, B. Kingsbury, and Y. Polyanskiy. "Estimating Information Flow in Deep Neural Networks". In: *ICML*. 2019.

[Gol89]   D. E. Goldberg. *Genetic Algorithms in Search, Optimization and Machine Learning*. 1st. Addison-Wesley Longman Publishing Co., Inc., 1989.

[Gom+17] A. N. Gomez, M. Ren, R. Urtasun, and R. B. Grosse. "The Reversible Residual Network: Backpropagation Without Storing Activations". In: *NIPS*. 2017.

[Gon+11] J. Gonzalez, Y. Low, A. Gretton, and C. Guestrin. "Parallel gibbs sampling: From colored fields to thin junction trees". In: *AISTATS*. 2011, pp. 324–332.

[Gon+14] B. Gong, W.-L. Chao, K. Grauman, and F. Sha. "Diverse sequential subset selection for supervised video summarization". In: *Advances in neural information processing systems* 27 (2014), pp. 2069–2077.

[Gon+20] P. J. Goncalves et al. "Training deep neural density estimators to identify mechanistic models of neural dynamics". In: *Elife* 9 (2020).

[Goo+14] I. J. Goodfellow, J. Pouget-Abadie, M. Mirza, B. Xu, D. Warde-Farley, S. Ozair, A. Courville, and Y. Bengio. "Generative Adversarial Networks". In: *NIPS*. 2014.

[Goo16]   I. Goodfellow. "NIPS 2016 Tutorial: Generative Adversarial Networks". In: *NIPS Tutorial*. 2016.

[Goo85]   I. Good. "Weight of evidence: A brief survey". In: *Bayesian statistics* 2 (1985), pp. 249–270.

[Gor+14] A. D. Gordon, T. A. Henzinger, A. V. Nori, and S. K. Rajamani. "Probabilistic programming". In: *Intl. Conf. on Software Engineering*. 2014.

[Gor+19] J. Gordon, J. Bronskill, M. Bauer, S. Nowozin, and R. E. Turner. "Meta-Learning Probabilistic Inference For Prediction". In: *ICLR*. 2019.

[Gor93]   N. Gordon. "Novel Approach to Nonlinear/Non-Gaussian Bayesian State Estimation". In: *IEE Proceedings (F)* 140.2 (1993), pp. 107–113.

[Gor95]   G. J. Gordon. "Stable Function Approximation in Dynamic Programming". In: *ICML*. 1995, pp. 261–268.

[Gou+96] C. Gourieroux, M. Gourieroux, A. Monfort, and D. A. Monfort. *Simulation-based econometric methods*. Oxford university press, 1996.

[Goy+19] Y. Goyal, Z. Wu, J. Ernst, D. Batra, D. Parikh, and S. Lee. *Counterfactual Visual Explanations*. 2019. arXiv: 1904.07451 [cs.LG].

[Goy+22] S. Goyal, M. Sun, A. Raghunathan, and Z. Kolter. "Test-Time Adaptation via Conjugate Pseudo-labels". In: (July 2022). arXiv: 2207.09640 [cs.LG].

[GPS89]   D. Greig, B. Porteous, and A. Seheult. "Exact maximum a posteriori estimation for binary images". In: *J. of Royal Stat. Soc. Series B* 51.2 (1989), pp. 271–279.

[GR06a]   M Girolami and S Rogers. "Variational Bayesian Multinomial Probit Regression with Gaussian Process Priors". In: *Neural Comput.* 18.8 (2006), pp. 1790–1817.

[GR06b]   M. Girolami and S. Rogers. "Variational Bayesian multinomial probit regression with Gaussian process priors". In: *Neural Comptuation* 18.8 (2006), pp. 1790 –1817.

[GR07a] T. Gneiting and A. E. Raftery. "Strictly Proper Scoring Rules, Prediction, and Estimation". In: *JASA* 102.477 (2007), pp. 359–378.

[GR07b] T. Gneiting and A. E. Raftery. "Strictly proper scoring rules, prediction, and estimation". In: *Journal of the American statistical Association* 102.477 (2007), pp. 359–378.

[Gra+10] T. Graepel, J. Quinonero-Candela, T. Borchert, and R. Herbrich. "Web-Scale Bayesian Click-Through Rate Prediction for Sponsored Search Advertising in Microsoft's Bing Search Engine". In: *ICML*. 2010.

[Gra11] A. Graves. "Practical Variational Inference for Neural Networks". In: *NIPS*. 2011.

[Gra+19] W. Grathwohl, R. T. Q. Chen, J. Bettencourt, I. Sutskever, and D. Duvenaud. "FFJORD: Free-form Continuous Dynamics for Scalable Reversible Generative Models". In: (2019).

[Gra+20a] W. Grathwohl, J. Kelly, M. Hashemi, M. Norouzi, K. Swersky, and D. Duvenaud. "No MCMC for me: Amortized sampling for fast and stable training of energy-based models". In: *arXiv preprint arXiv:2010.04230* (2020).

[Gra+20b] W. Grathwohl, K.-C. Wang, J.-H. Jacobsen, D. Duvenaud, M. Norouzi, and K. Swersky. "Your classifier is secretly an energy based model and you should treat it like one". In: *ICLR*. 2020.

[Gra+20c] W. Grathwohl, K.-C. Wang, J.-H. Jacobsen, D. Duvenaud, and R. Zemel. "Cutting out the Middle-Man: Training and Evaluating Energy-Based Models without Sampling". In: *arXiv preprint arXiv:2002.05616* (2020).

[Gre03] P. Green. "Tutorial on trans-dimensional MCMC". In: *Highly Structured Stochastic Systems*. Ed. by P. Green, N. Hjort, and S. Richardson. OUP, 2003.

[Gre+12] A. Gretton, K. M. Borgwardt, M. J. Rasch, B. Schölkopf, and A. Smola. "A Kernel Two-Sample Test". In: *JMLR* 13.Mar (2012), pp. 723–773.

[Gre+14] K. Gregor, I. Danihelka, A. Mnih, C. Blundell, and D. Wierstra. "Deep AutoRegressive Networks". In: *ICML*. 2014.

[Gre20] F. Greenlee. *Transformer VAE*. 2020.

[Gre+22] P. L. Green, R. E. Moore, R. J. Jackson, J. Li, and S. Maskell. "Increasing the efficiency of Sequential Monte Carlo samplers through the use of approximately optimal L-kernels". In: *Mech. Syst. Signal Process.* 162 (2022).

[Gre98] P. Green. "Reversible Jump Markov Chain Monte Carlo computation and Bayesian model determination". In: *Biometrika* 82 (1998), pp. 711–732.

[Gri+04] T. Griffiths, M. Steyvers, D. Blei, and J. Tenenbaum. "Integrating Topics and Syntax". In: *NIPS*. 2004.

[Gri+20] J.-B. Grill, F. Strub, F. Altché, C. Tallec, P. H. Richemond, E. Buchatskaya, C. Doersch, B. A. Pires, Z. D. Guo, M. G. Azar, et al. "Bootstrap your own latent: A new approach to self-supervised learning". In: *arXiv preprint arXiv:2006.07733* (2020).

[GRS96] W. Gilks, S. Richardson, and D. Spiegelhalter. *Markov Chain Monte Carlo in Practice*. Chapman and Hall, 1996.

[GS04] T. Griffiths and M. Steyvers. "Finding scientific topics". In: *PNAS* 101 (2004), pp. 5228–5235.

[GS08] Y Guo and D Schuurmans. "Efficient global optimization for exponential family PCA and low-rank matrix factorization". In: *2008 46th Annual Allerton Conference on Communication, Control, and Computing*. 2008, pp. 1100–1107.

[GS13] A. Gelman and C. R. Shalizi. "Philosophy and the practice of Bayesian statistics". en. In: *Br. J. Math. Stat. Psychol.* 66.1 (Feb. 2013), pp. 8–38.

[GS15] R. B. Grosse and R. Salakhutdinov. "Scaling Up Natural Gradient by Sparsely Factorizing the Inverse Fisher Matrix". In: *ICML*. 2015.

[GS90] A. Gelfand and A. Smith. "Sampling-based approaches to calculating marginal densities". In: *JASA* 85 (1990), pp. 385–409.

[GS92] G. Grimmett and D. Stirzaker. *Probability and Random Processes*. Oxford, 1992.

[GS97] C. M. Grinstead and J. L. Snell. *Introduction to probability (2nd edition)*. American Mathematical Society, 1997.

[GSA14] M. A. Gelbart, J. Snoek, and R. P. Adams. "Bayesian Optimization with Unknown Constraints". In: *UAI*. 2014.

[GSD13] A. Guez, D. Silver, and P. Dayan. "Scalable and Efficient Bayes-Adaptive Reinforcement Learning Based on Monte-Carlo Tree Search". In: *JAIR* 48 (2013), pp. 841–883.

[GSJ19] A. Gretton, D. Sutherland, and W. Jitkrittum. *NIPS tutorial on interpretable comparison of distributions and models*. 2019.

[GSK18] S. Gidaris, P. Singh, and N. Komodakis. "Unsupervised Representation Learning by Predicting Image Rotations". In: *International Conference on Learning Representations*. 2018.

[GSM18] U. Garciarena, R. Santana, and A. Mendiburu. "Expanding Variational Autoencoders for Learning and Exploiting Latent Representations in Search Distributions". In: *Proc. of the Conf. on Genetic and Evolutionary Computation*. 2018, pp. 849–856.

[GSR12] S. Garg, A. Singh, and F. Ramos. "Learning non-stationary Space-Time models for environmental monitoring". In: *AAAI* 26.1 (2012), pp. 288–294.

[GSR13] J. Gama, R. Sebastião, and P. P. Rodrigues. "On evaluating stream learning algorithms". In: *MLJ* 90.3 (Mar. 2013), pp. 317–346.

[GSS15] I. J. Goodfellow, J. Shlens, and C. Szegedy. "Explaining and Harnessing Adversarial Examples". In: *ICLR*. 2015.

[GSZ21] P. Grünwald, T. Steinke, and L. Zakynthinou. "PAC-Bayes, MAC-Bayes and Conditional Mutual Information: Fast rate bounds that handle general VC classes". In: *COLT*. 2021.

[GT86] J. R. Gilbert and R. E. Tarjan. "The analysis of a nested dissection algorithm". In: *Numer. Math.* 50.4 (1986), pp. 377–404.

[GU16] C. A. Gomez-Uribe. "Online Algorithms For Parameter Mean And Variance Estimation In Dynamic Regression Models". In: (May 2016). arXiv: 1605.05697 [stat.ML].

[Gue19] B. Guedj. "A primer on PAC-Bayesian learning". In: *arXiv preprint arXiv:1901.05353* (2019).

[GUK21] C. A. Gomez-Uribe and B. Karrer. "The Decoupled Extended Kalman Filter for Dynamic

Exponential-Family Factorization Models". In: *JMLR* 22.5 (2021), pp. 1–25.

[Gul+17]   I. Gulrajani, F. Ahmed, M. Arjovsky, V. Dumoulin, and A. C. Courville. "Improved training of wasserstein gans". In: *NIPS*. 2017, pp. 5767–5777.

[Gul+20]   C. Gulcehre et al. *RL Unplugged: Benchmarks for Offline Reinforcement Learning*. arXiv:2006.13888. 2020.

[Gum54]   E. J. Gumbel. *Statistical theory of extreme values and some practical applications;: A series of lectures (United States. National Bureau of Standards. Applied mathematics series)*. en. 1st edition. U.S. Govt. Print. Office, 1954.

[Guo09]   Y. Guo. "Supervised exponential family principal component analysis via convex optimization". In: *NIPS*. 2009.

[Guo+14]   Q. Guo, D. Tu, J. Lei, and G. Li. "Hybrid CNN-HMM model for street view house number recognition". In: *ACCV Workshops*. Lecture notes in computer science. Cham: Springer International Publishing, 2014, pp. 303–315.

[Guo+17]   C. Guo, G. Pleiss, Y. Sun, and K. Q. Weinberger. "On Calibration of Modern Neural Networks". In: *ICML*. 2017.

[Gup+16]   M. Gupta, A. Cotter, J. Pfeifer, K. Voevodski, K. Canini, A. Mangylov, W. Moczydlowski, and A. van Esbroeck. "Monotonic Calibrated Interpolated Look-Up Tables". In: *Journal of Machine Learning Research* 17.109 (2016), pp. 1–47.

[Gur+18]   S. Gururangan, S. Swayamdipta, O. Levy, R. Schwartz, S. R. Bowman, and N. A. Smith. "Annotation Artifacts in Natural Language Inference Data". In: *CoRR* abs/1803.02324 (2018). arXiv: 1803.02324.

[Gus01]   M. Gustafsson. "A probabilistic derivation of the partial least-squares algorithm". In: *Journal of Chemical Information and Modeling* 41 (2001), pp. 288–294.

[Gut+14]   M. U. Gutmann, R. Dutta, S. Kaski, and J. Corander. "Statistical inference of intractable generative models via classification". In: *arXiv preprint arXiv:1407.4981* (2014).

[Gut22]   M. U. Gutmann. "Pen and Paper Exercises in Machine Learning". In: (June 2022). arXiv: 2206.13446 [cs.LG].

[GV17]   S. Ghosal and A. van der Vaart. *Fundamentals of Nonparametric Bayesian Inference*. en. 1st ed. Cambridge University Press, 2017.

[GW08]   A. Griewank and A. Walther. *Evaluating Derivatives: Principles and Techniques of Algorithmic Differentiation*. Second. Society for Industrial and Applied Mathematics, 2008.

[GW92]   W. Gilks and P. Wild. "Adaptive rejection sampling for Gibbs sampling". In: *Applied Statistics* 41 (1992), pp. 337–348.

[GXG18]   H. Ge, K. Xu, and Z. Ghahramani. "Turing: a language for flexible probabilistic inference". In: *AISTATS*. 2018, pp. 1682–1690.

[GZG19]   S. K. S. Ghasemipour, R. S. Zemel, and S. Gu. "A Divergence Minimization Perspective on Imitation Learning Methods". In: *CORL*. 2019, pp. 1259–1277.

[HA21]   R. J. Hyndman and G. Athanasopoulos. *Forecasting: Principles and Practice*. en. 3rd ed. Otexts, 2021.

[Haa+17]   T. Haarnoja, H. Tang, P. Abbeel, and S. Levine. "Reinforcement learning with deep energy-based policies". In: *Proceedings of the 34th International Conference on Machine Learning-Volume 70*. 2017, pp. 1352–1361.

[Haa+18a]   T. Haarnoja, A. Zhou, P. Abbeel, and S. Levine. "Soft Actor-Critic: Off-Policy Maximum Entropy Deep Reinforcement Learning with a Stochastic Actor". In: *International Conference on Machine Learning*. 2018, pp. 1861–1870.

[Haa+18b]   T. Haarnoja, A. Zhou, P. Abbeel, and S. Levine. "Soft Actor-Critic: Off-Policy Maximum Entropy Deep Reinforcement Learning with a Stochastic Actor". In: *ICML*. 2018.

[Haa+18c]   T. Haarnoja et al. "Soft Actor-Critic Algorithms and Applications". In: (2018). arXiv: 1812.05905 [cs.LG].

[HAB17]   J. H. Huggins, R. P. Adams, and T. Broderick. "PASS-GLM: polynomial approximate sufficient statistics for scalable Bayesian GLM inference". In: *NIPS*. 2017.

[Had+20]   R. Hadsell, D. Rao, A. A. Rusu, and R. Pascanu. "Embracing Change: Continual Learning in Deep Neural Networks". en. In: *Trends Cogn. Sci.* 24.12 (2020), pp. 1028–1040.

[HAE16]   M. Huh, P. Agrawal, and A. A. Efros. "What makes ImageNet good for transfer learning?" In: *arXiv preprint arXiv:1608.08614* (2016).

[Haf18]   D. Hafner. *Building Variational Auto-Encoders in TensorFlow*. Blog post. 2018.

[Haf+19]   D. Hafner, T. Lillicrap, I. Fischer, R. Villegas, D. Ha, H. Lee, and J. Davidson. "Learning Latent Dynamics for Planning from Pixels". In: *ICML*. 2019.

[Haf+20]   D. Hafner, T. Lillicrap, J. Ba, and M. Norouzi. "Dream to Control: Learning Behaviors by Latent Imagination". In: *ICLR*. 2020.

[Hag+17]   M. Hagen, M. Potthast, M. Gohsen, A. Rathgeber, and B. Stein. "A Large-Scale Query Spelling Correction Corpus". In: *Proceedings of the 40th International ACM SIGIR Conference on Research and Development in Information Retrieval*. SIGIR '17. ACM, 2017, pp. 1261–1264.

[Haj88]   B. Hajek. "Cooling Schedules for Optimal Annealing". In: *Math. Oper. Res.* 13.2 (1988), pp. 311–329.

[Häl+21]   H. Hälvä, S. L. Corff, L. Leh'ericy, J. So, Y. Zhu, E. Gassiat, and A. Hyvärinen. "Disentangling Identifiable Features from Noisy Data with Structured Nonlinear ICA". In: *NIPS*. 2021.

[Ham90]   J. Hamilton. "Analysis of time series subject to changes in regime". In: *J. Econometrics* 45 (1990), pp. 39–70.

[Han16]   N. Hansen. "The CMA Evolution Strategy: A Tutorial". In: (2016). arXiv: 1604.00772 [cs.LG].

[Han+20]   K. Han et al. "A Survey on Vision Transformer". In: (2020). arXiv: 2012.12556 [cs.CV].

[Han80]   T. S. Han. "Multiple mutual informations and multiple interactions in frequency data". In: *Information and Control* 46.1 (1980), pp. 26–45.

[Har+17]   J. Hartford, G. Lewis, K. Leyton-Brown, and M. Taddy. "Deep IV: A flexible approach for counterfactual prediction". In: *Proceedings of the 34th International Conference on Machine Learning-Volume 70*. JMLR. org, 2017, pp. 1414–1423.

[Har18]   K. Hartnett. "To Build Truly Intelligent Machines, Teach Them Cause and Effect". In: *Quanta Magazine* (2018).

[Har90]   A. C. Harvey. *Forecasting, Structural Time Series Models, and the Kalman Filter.* Cambridge Univerity Press, 1990.

[Has10]   H. van Hasselt. "Double Q-learning". In: *NIPS*. Ed. by J. D. Lafferty, C. K. I. Williams, J Shawe-Taylor, R. S. Zemel, and A Culotta. Curran Associates, Inc., 2010, pp. 2613–2621.

[Has70]   W. Hastings. "Monte Carlo Sampling Methods Using Markov Chains and Their Applications". In: *Biometrika* 57.1 (1970), pp. 97–109.

[Hau+10]   J. R. Hauser, O. Toubia, T. Evgeniou, R. Befurt, and D. Dzyabura. "Disjunctions of conjunctions, cognitive simplicity, and consideration sets". In: *Journal of Marketing Research* 47.3 (2010), pp. 485–496.

[Hau+11]   M. Hauschild, M. Pelikan, M. Hauschild, and M. Pelikan. "An introduction and survey of estimation of distribution algorithms". In: *Swarm and Evolutionary Computation.* 2011.

[HBB10]   M. Hoffman, D. Blei, and F. Bach. "Online learning for latent Dirichlet allocation". In: *NIPS*. 2010.

[HBW19]   E. Hoogeboom, R. van den Berg, and M. Welling. "Emerging Convolutions for Generative Normalizing Flows". In: *ICML*. 2019.

[HC93]   G. Hinton and D. V. Camp. "Keeping Neural Networks Simple by Minimizing the Description Length of the Weights". In: *in Proc. of the 6th Ann. ACM Conf. on Computational Learning Theory.* ACM Press, 1993, pp. 5–13.

[HCG20]   S. Huang, Y. Cao, and R. Grosse. "Evaluating Lossy Compression Rates of Deep Generative Models". In: *ICML*. 2020.

[HCL06]   R. Hadsell, S. Chopra, and Y. LeCun. "Dimensionality Reduction by Learning an Invariant Mapping". In: *2006 IEEE Computer Society Conference on Computer Vision and Pattern Recognition (CVPR'06)* 2 (2006), pp. 1735–1742.

[HD19]   D. Hendrycks and T. Dietterich. "Benchmarking Neural Network Robustness to Common Corruptions and Perturbations". In: *ICLR*. 2019.

[HDL17]   D. Ha, A. M. Dai, and Q. V. Le. "HyperNetworks". In: *ICLR*. 2017.

[He+16a]   K. He, X. Zhang, S. Ren, and J. Sun. "Deep Residual Learning for Image Recognition". In: *CVPR*. 2016.

[HE16a]   J. Ho and S. Ermon. "Generative adversarial imitation learning". In: *Proceedings of the 30th International Conference on Neural Information Processing Systems.* 2016, pp. 4572–4580.

[He+16b]   K. He, X. Zhang, S. Ren, and J. Sun. "Identity Mappings in Deep Residual Networks". In: *ECCV*. 2016.

[HE16b]   J. Ho and S. Ermon. "Generative Adversarial Imitation Learning". In: *NIPS*. 2016, pp. 4565–4573.

[HE18]   D. Ha and D. Eck. "A Neural Representation of Sketch Drawings". In: *ICLR*. 2018.

[He+19]   J. He, D. Spokoyny, G. Neubig, and T. Berg-Kirkpatrick. "Lagging Inference Networks and Posterior Collapse in Variational Autoencoders". In: *ICLR*. 2019.

[He+20]   K. He, H. Fan, Y. Wu, S. Xie, and R. Girshick. "Momentum contrast for unsupervised visual representation learning". In: *CVPR*. 2020, pp. 9729–9738.

[He+21]   K. He, X. Chen, S. Xie, Y. Li, P. Dollár, and R. Girshick. *Masked Autoencoders Are Scalable Vision Learners.* 2021. arXiv: 2111.06377 [cs.CV].

[He+22]   K. He, X. Chen, S. Xie, Y. Li, P. Dollár, and R. Girshick. "Masked autoencoders are scalable vision learners". In: *Proceedings of the IEEE/CVF Conference on Computer Vision and Pattern Recognition.* 2022, pp. 16000–16009.

[Heg06]   P. Heggernes. "Minimal triangulations of graphs: A survey". In: *Discrete Math.* 306.3 (2006), pp. 297–317.

[Hei+16]   M. Heinonen, H. Mannerström, J. Rousu, S. Kaski, and H. Lähdesmäki. "Non-Stationary Gaussian Process Regression with Hamiltonian Monte Carlo". In: *AISTATS*. Ed. by A. Gretton and C. C. Robert. Vol. 51. Proceedings of Machine Learning Research. Cadiz, Spain: PMLR, 2016, pp. 732–740.

[Hel17]   J. Helske. "KFAS: Exponential Family State Space Models in R". In: *J. Stat. Softw.* (2017).

[Hen+15]   J. Hensman, A. Matthews, M. Filippone, and Z. Ghahramani. "MCMC for Variationally Sparse Gaussian Processes". In: *NIPS*. 2015, pp. 1648–1656.

[Hen+16]   L. A. Hendricks, Z. Akata, M. Rohrbach, J. Donahue, B. Schiele, and T. Darrell. "Generating visual explanations". In: *European conference on computer vision.* Springer. 2016, pp. 3–19.

[Hen+18]   G. E. Henter, J. Lorenzo-Trueba, X. Wang, and J. Yamagishi. "Deep Encoder-Decoder Models for Unsupervised Learning of Controllable Speech Synthesis". In: (2018). arXiv: 1807.11470 [eess.AS].

[Hen+19a]   O. J. Henaff, A. Razavi, C. Doersch, S. M. Ali Eslami, and A. van den Oord. "Data-Efficient Image Recognition with Contrastive Predictive Coding". In: *arXiv [cs.CV]* (2019).

[Hen+19b]   D. Hendrycks, S. Basart, M. Mazeika, A. Zou, J. Kwon, M. Mostajabi, J. Steinhardt, and D. Song. "Scaling Out-of-Distribution Detection for Real-World Settings". In: (2019). arXiv: 1911.11132 [cs.CV].

[Hen+20]   D. Hendrycks*, N. Mu*, E. D. Cubuk, B. Zoph, J. Gilmer, and B. Lakshminarayanan. "AugMix: A Simple Data Processing Method to Improve Robustness and Uncertainty". In: *ICLR*. 2020.

[Hen+21]   C. Henning, M. R. Cervera, F. D'Angelo, J. von Oswald, R. Traber, B. Ehret, S. Kobayashi, B. F. Grewe, and J. Sacramento. "Posterior Meta-Replay for Continual Learning". In: *NIPS*. 2021.

[Hes00]   T. Heskes. "On "Natural" Learning and Pruning in Multilayered Perceptrons". In: *Neural Comput.* 12.4 (2000), pp. 881–901.

[Hes+18]   M. Hessel, J. Modayil, H. van Hasselt, T. Schaul, G. Ostrovski, W. Dabney, D. Horgan, B. Piot, M. Azar, and D. Silver. "Rainbow: Combining Improvements in Deep Reinforcement Learning". In: *AAAI*. 2018.

[Heu+17a]   M. Heusel, H. Ramsauer, T. Unterthiner, B. Nessler, and S. Hochreiter. "GANs Trained by a Two Time-Scale Update Rule Converge to a Local Nash Equilibrium". In: *NIPS*. 2017.

[Heu+17b]   M. Heusel, H. Ramsauer, T. Unterthiner, B. Nessler, and S. Hochreiter. "Gans trained by a two time-scale update rule converge to a local nash equilibrium". In: *Advances in neural information processing systems.* 2017, pp. 6626–6637.

[HFL13]   J. Hensman, N. Fusi, and N. D. Lawrence. "Gaussian Processes for Big Data". In: *UAI*. 2013.

[HFM17]   D. W. Hogg and D. Foreman-Mackey. "Data analysis recipes: Using Markov Chain Monte Carlo". In: (2017). arXiv: 1710.06068 [astro-ph.IM].

[HG12]   D. I. Hastie and P. J. Green. "Model Choice using Reversible Jump Markov Chain Monte Carlo". In: *Statistica Neerlandica* 66 (2012), pp. 309–338.

[HG14]   M. D. Hoffman and A. Gelman. "The No-U-Turn Sampler: Adaptively Setting Path Lengths in Hamiltonian Monte Carlo". In: *JMLR* 15 (2014), pp. 1593–1623.

[HG16]   D. Hendrycks and K. Gimpel. "Gaussian Error Linear Units (GELUs)". In: *arXiv [cs.LG]* (2016).

[HGMG18]   J. Hron, A. G. de G. Matthews, and Z. Ghahramani. "Variational Bayesian dropout: pitfalls and fixes". In: *ICML*. 2018.

[HGS16]   H. van Hasselt, A. Guez, and D. Silver. "Deep Reinforcement Learning with Double Q-Learning". In: *AAAI*. AAAI'16. AAAI Press, 2016, pp. 2094–2100.

[HH06]   C. Holmes and L. Held. "Bayesian auxiliary variable models for binary and multinomial regression". In: *Bayesian Analysis* 1.1 (2006), pp. 145–168.

[HHH09]   A. Hyvarinen, J. Hurri, and P. Hoyer. *Natural Image Statistics: a probabilistic approach to early computational vision*. Springer, 2009.

[HHK19]   M. Haußmann, F. A. Hamprecht, and M. Kandemir. "Sampling-Free Variational Inference of Bayesian Neural Networks by Variance Backpropagation". In: *UAI*. 2019.

[HHLB11]   F. Hutter, H. H. Hoos, and K. Leyton-Brown. "Sequential Model-Based Optimization for General Algorithm Configuration". In: *Intl. Conf. on Learning and Intelligent Optimization (LION)*. 2011, pp. 507–523.

[Hig+17a]   I. Higgins, L. Matthey, A. Pal, C. Burgess, X. Glorot, M. Botvinick, S. Mohamed, and A. Lerchner. "beta-VAE: Learning Basic Visual Concepts with a Constrained Variational Framework". In: *ICLR*. 2017.

[Hig+17b]   I. Higgins, L. Matthey, A. Pal, C. P. Burgess, X. Glorot, M. M. Botvinick, S. Mohamed, and A. Lerchner. "beta-VAE: Learning Basic Visual Concepts with a Constrained Variational Framework". In: *ICLR*. 2017.

[Hin02]   G. E. Hinton. "Training products of experts by minimizing contrastive divergence". en. In: *Neural Computation* 14.8 (2002), pp. 1771–1800.

[Hin10]   G. Hinton. *A Practical Guide to Training Restricted Boltzmann Machines*. Tech. rep. U. Toronto, 2010.

[Hin+95]   G. E. Hinton, P Dayan, B. J. Frey, and R. M. Neal. "The "wake-sleep" algorithm for unsupervised neural networks". en. In: *Science* 268.5214 (1995), pp. 1158–1161.

[HIY19]   K. Hayashi, M. Imaizumi, and Y. Yoshida. "On Random Subsampling of Gaussian Process Regression: A Graphon-Based Analysis". In: (2019). arXiv: 1901.09541 [stat.ML].

[HJ12]   T. Hazan and T. Jaakkola. "On the Partition Function and Random Maximum A-Posteriori Perturbations". In: *ICML*. June 2012.

[HJ20]   J. Huang and N. Jiang. "From Importance Sampling to Doubly Robust Policy Gradient". In: *ICML*. 2020.

[HJA20]   J. Ho, A. Jain, and P. Abbeel. "Denoising Diffusion Probabilistic Models". In: *NIPS*. 2020.

[Hje+18]   R. D. Hjelm, A. Fedorov, S. Lavoie-Marchildon, K. Grewal, P. Bachman, A. Trischler, and Y. Bengio. "Learning deep representations by mutual information estimation and maximization". In: *International Conference on Learning Representations*. 2018.

[Hjo+10]   N. Hjort, C. Holmes, P. Muller, and S. Walker, eds. *Bayesian Nonparametrics*. Cambridge, 2010.

[HJT18]   M. D. Hoffman, M. J. Johnson, and D. Tran. "Autoconj: Recognizing and Exploiting Conjugacy Without a Domain-Specific Language". In: *NIPS*. 2018.

[HKH22]   M. Hobbhahn, A. Kristiadi, and P. Hennig. "Fast Predictive Uncertainty for Classification with Bayesian Deep Networks". In: *UAI*. 2022.

[HKO22]   P. Hennig, H. Kersting, and M. Osborne. *Probabilistic Numerics: Computation as Machine Learning*. 2022.

[HKP91]   J. Hertz, A. Krogh, and R. G. Palmer. *An Introduction to the Theory of Neural Comptuation*. Addison-Wesley, 1991.

[HKZ12]   D. Hsu, S. Kakade, and T. Zhang. "A spectral algorithm for learning hidden Markov models". In: *J. of Computer and System Sciences* 78.5 (2012), pp. 1460–1480.

[HL04]   D. R. Hunter and K. Lange. "A Tutorial on MM Algorithms". In: *The American Statistician* 58 (2004), pp. 30–37.

[HL+16a]   J. Hernandez-Lobato, Y. Li, M. Rowland, T. Bui, D. Hernandez-Lobato, and R. Turner. "Black-Box Alpha Divergence Minimization". en. In: *ICML*. 2016, pp. 1511–1520.

[HL+16b]   M. Hernandez-Lobato, M. A. Gelbart, R. P. Adams, M. W. Hoffman, and Z. Ghahramani. "A General Framework for Constrained Bayesian Optimization using Information-based Search". In: *JMLR* (2016).

[HL20]   X. Hu and J. Lei. "A Distribution-Free Test of Covariate Shift Using Conformal Prediction". In: (2020). arXiv: 2010.07147 [stat.ME].

[HLA15a]   J. M. Hernández-Lobato and R. P. Adams. "Probabilistic Backpropagation for Scalable Learning of Bayesian Neural Networks". In: *ICML*. 2015.

[HLA15b]   J. M. Hernández-Lobato and R. P. Adams. "Probabilistic Backpropagation for Scalable Learning of Bayesian Neural Networks". In: *ICML*. 2015.

[HLA19]   J. Ho, E. Lohn, and P. Abbeel. "Compression with Flows via Local Bits-Back Coding". In: *NeurIPS*. 2019.

[HLC19]   Y.-P. Hsieh, C. Liu, and V. Cevher. "Finding mixed nash equilibria of generative adversarial networks". In: *International Conference on Machine Learning*. 2019, pp. 2810–2819.

[HLHG14]   J. Hernandez-Lobato, M. W. Hoffman, and Z. Ghahramani. "Predictive entropy search for efficient global optimization of black-box functions". In: *NIPS*. 2014.

[HLR16]   K. Hofmann, L. Li, and F. Radlinski. "Online Evaluation for Information Retrieval". In: *Foun-*

dations and Trends in Information Retrieval 10.1 (2016), pp. 1–117.

[HLRW14] J. R. Hershey, J. Le Roux, and F. Weninger. "Deep Unfolding: Model-Based Inspiration of Novel Deep Architectures". In: (2014). arXiv: 1409.2574 [cs.LG].

[HLS03] R. Herbrich, N. D. Lawrence, and M. Seeger. "Fast Sparse Gaussian Process Methods: The Informative Vector Machine". In: NIPS. MIT Press, 2003, pp. 625–632.

[HM81] R. Howard and J. Matheson. "Influence diagrams". In: Readings on the Principles and Applications of Decision Analysis, volume II. Ed. by R. Howard and J. Matheson. Strategic Decisions Group, 1981.

[HMD18] J. C. Higuera, D Meger, and G Dudek. "Synthesizing Neural Network Controllers with Probabilistic Model-Based Reinforcement Learning". In: IROS. 2018, pp. 2538–2544.

[HMD19] D. Hendrycks, M. Mazeika, and T. Dietterich. "Deep Anomaly Detection with Outlier Exposure". In: ICLR. 2019.

[HMK04] D. Heckerman, C. Meek, and D. Koller. Probabilistic Models for Relational Data. Tech. rep. MSR-TR-2004-30. Microsoft Research, 2004.

[HNBK18] J. He, G. Neubig, and T. Berg-Kirkpatrick. "Unsupervised Learning of Syntactic Structure with Invertible Neural Projections". In: EMNLP. 2018.

[HNP09] A. Halevy, P. Norvig, and F. Pereira. "The unreasonable effectiveness of data". In: IEEE Intelligent Systems 24.2 (2009), pp. 8–12.

[HO00] A. Hyvarinen and E. Oja. "Independent component analysis: algorithms and applications". In: Neural Networks 13 (2000), pp. 411–430.

[Ho+21] J. Ho, C. Saharia, W. Chan, D. J. Fleet, M. Norouzi, and T. Salimans. "Cascaded Diffusion Models for High Fidelity Image Generation". In: (May 2021). arXiv: 2106.15282 [cs.CV].

[HO48] C. G. Hempel and P. Oppenheim. "Studies in the Logic of Explanation". In: Philosophy of science 15.2 (1948), pp. 135–175.

[Hob69] A. Hobson. "A new theorem of information theory". In: Journal of Statistical Physics 1.3 (1969), pp. 383–391.

[Hoe+14] R. Hoekstra, R. D. Morey, J. N. Rouder, and E.-J. Wagenmakers. "Robust misinterpretation of confidence intervals". en. In: Psychon. Bull. Rev. 21.5 (2014), pp. 1157–1164.

[Hoe+21] T. Hoefler, D. Alistarh, T. Ben-Nun, N. Dryden, and A. Peste. "Sparsity in Deep Learning: Pruning and growth for efficient inference and training in neural networks". In: (2021). arXiv: 2102.00554 [cs.LG].

[Hoe+99] J. Hoeting, D. Madigan, A. Raftery, and C. Volinsky. "Bayesian Model Averaging: A Tutorial". In: Statistical Science 4.4 (1999).

[Hof09] P. D. Hoff. A First Course in Bayesian Statistical Methods. Springer, 2009.

[Hof13] M. D. Hoffman, D. M. Blei, C. Wang, and J. Paisley. "Stochastic Variational Inference". In: JMLR 14 (2013), pp. 1303–1347.

[Hof17] M. D. Hoffman. "Learning Deep Latent Gaussian Models with Markov Chain Monte Carlo". In: ICML. 2017, pp. 1510–1519.

[Hof+18] J. Hoffman, E. Tzeng, T. Park, J.-Y. Zhu, P. Isola, K. Saenko, A. Efros, and T. Darrell. "Cycada: Cycle-consistent adversarial domain adaptation". In: International conference on machine learning. PMLR. 2018, pp. 1989–1998.

[Hof+19] M. Hoffman, P. Sountsov, J. V. Dillon, I. Langmore, D. Tran, and S. Vasudevan. "NeuTra-lizing Bad Geometry in Hamiltonian Monte Carlo Using Neural Transport". In: (2019). arXiv: 1903.03704 [stat.CO].

[Hof99] T. Hofmann. "Probabilistic latent semantic indexing". In: Research and Development in Information Retrieval (1999), pp. 50–57.

[Hoh+20] F. Hohman, M. Conlen, J. Heer, and D. H. P. Chau. "Communicating with interactive articles". In: Distill 5.9 (2020), e28.

[Hol86] P. W. Holland. "Statistics and Causal Inference". In: JASA 81.396 (1986), pp. 945–960.

[Hol92] J. H. Holland. Adaptation in Natural and Artificial Systems. https://mitpress.mit.edu/books/adaptation-natural-and-artificial-systems. Accessed: 2017-11-26. 1992.

[Hon+10] A. Honkela, T. Raiko, M. Kuusela, M. Tornio, and J. Karhunen. "Approximate Riemannian Conjugate Gradient Learning for Fixed-Form Variational Bayes". In: JMLR 11.Nov (2010), pp. 3235–3268.

[Hoo+21] E. Hoogeboom, D. Nielsen, P. Jaini, P. Forré, and M. Welling. "Argmax Flows and Multinomial Diffusion: Learning Categorical Distributions". In: NIPS. Feb. 2021.

[Hop82] J. J. Hopfield. "Neural networks and physical systems with emergent collective computational abilities". In: PNAS 79.8 (1982), 2554–2558.

[Hor+05] E. Horvitz, J. Apacible, R. Sarin, and L. Liao. "Prediction, Expectation, and Surprise: Methods, Designs, and Study of a Deployed Traffic Forecasting Service". In: UAI. 2005.

[Hor61] P Horst. "Generalized canonical correlations and their applications to experimental data". en. In: J. Clin. Psychol. 17 (1961), pp. 331–347.

[Hos+20a] T. Hospedales, A. Antoniou, P. Micaelli, and A. Storkey. "Meta-Learning in Neural Networks: A Survey". In: (2020). arXiv: 2004.05439 [cs.LG].

[Hos+20b] R. Hostettler, F. Tronarp, Á. F. García-Fernández, and S. Särkkä. "Importance Densities for Particle Filtering Using Iterated Conditional Expectations". In: IEEE Signal Process. Lett. 27 (2020), pp. 211–215.

[HOT06a] G. Hinton, S. Osindero, and Y. Teh. "A fast learning algorithm for deep belief nets". In: Neural Computation 18 (2006), pp. 1527–1554.

[HOT06b] G. E. Hinton, S. Osindero, and Y. W. Teh. "A Fast Learning Algorithm for Deep Belief Nets". In: Neural Computation 18 (2006), pp. 1527–1554.

[Hot36] H. Hotelling. "Relations Between Two Sets of Variates". In: Biometrika 28.3/4 (1936), pp. 321–377.

[Hou+12] N. Houlsby, F. Huszar, Z. Ghahramani, and J. M. Hernández-lobato. "Collaborative Gaussian Processes for Preference Learning". In: NIPS. 2012, pp. 2096–2104.

[Hou+19]   N. Houlsby, A. Giurgiu, S. Jastrzebski, B. Morrone, Q. De Laroussilhe, A. Gesmundo, M. Attariyan, and S. Gelly. "Parameter-efficient transfer learning for NLP". In: *International Conference on Machine Learning*. PMLR. 2019, pp. 2790–2799.

[HOW11]   P. Hall, J. T. Ormerod, and M. P. Wand. "Theory of Gaussian Variational Approximation for a Generalised Linear Mixed Model". In: *Statistica Sinica* 21 (2011), pp. 269–389.

[HP10]   J. Hacker and P. Pierson. *Winner-Take-All Politics: How Washington Made the Rich Richer — and Turned Its Back on the Middle Class*. Simon & Schuster, 2010.

[HPHL19]   M. Havasi, R. Peharz, and J. M. Hernández-Lobato. "Minimal Random Code Learning: Getting Bits Back from Compressed Model Parameters". In: 2019.

[HPR19]   C. Herzog né Hoffmann, E. Petersen, and P. Rostalski. "Iterative Approximate Nonlinear Inference via Gaussian Message Passing on Factor Graphs". In: *IEEE Control Systems Letters* 3.4 (2019), pp. 978–983.

[HR17]   C. Hoffmann and P. Rostalski. "Linear Optimal Control on Factor Graphs — A Message Passing Perspective". In: *Intl. Federation of Automatic Control* 50.1 (2017), pp. 6314–6319.

[HR20a]   M. Hernan and J. Robins. *Causal Inference: What If*. CRC Press, 2020.

[HR20b]   M. Hernán and J. Robins. *Causal Inference: What If*. Boca Raton: Chapman & Hall/CRC., 2020.

[HS05]   H. Hoos and T. Stutzle. *Stochastic local search: Foundations and applications*. Morgan Kauffman, 2005.

[HS06a]   G. Hinton and R. Salakhutdinov. "Reducing the dimensionality of data with neural networks". In: *Science* 313.5786 (2006), pp. 504–507.

[HS06b]   G. E. Hinton and R. R. Salakhutdinov. "Reducing the dimensionality of data with neural networks". In: *science* 313.5786 (2006), pp. 504–507.

[HS09]   M. Heaton and J. Scott. *Bayesian computation and the linear model*. Tech. rep. Duke, 2009.

[HS10]   J. Hartikainen and S. Särkkä. "Kalman filtering and smoothing solutions to temporal Gaussian process regression models". In: *2010 IEEE International Workshop on Machine Learning for Signal Processing*. Aug. 2010, pp. 379–384.

[HS12]   P. Hennig and C. Schuler. "Entropy search for information-efficient global optimization". In: *JMLR* 13 (2012), pp. 1809–1837.

[HS13]   J. Y. Hsu and D. S. Small. "Calibrating Sensitivity Analyses to Observed Covariates in Observational Studies". In: *Biometrics* 69.4 (2013), pp. 803–811. eprint: https://onlinelibrary.wiley.com/doi/pdf/10.1111/biom.12101.

[HS18]   D. Ha and J. Schmidhuber. "World Models". In: *NIPS*. 2018.

[HS21]   J. Ho and T. Salimans. "Classifier-Free Diffusion Guidance". In: *NIPS Workshop on Deep Generative Models and Downstream Applications*. 2021.

[HS88]   D. S. Hochbaum and D. B. Shmoys. "A polynomial approximation scheme for scheduling on uniform processors: Using the dual approximation approach". In: *SICOMP*. 1988.

[HS97]   S Hochreiter and J Schmidhuber. "Flat minima". en. In: *Neural Comput.* 9.1 (1997), pp. 1–42.

[HSDK12]   C. Hillar, J. Sohl-Dickstein, and K. Koepsell. *Efficient and Optimal Binary Hopfield Associative Memory Storage Using Minimum Probability Flow*. Tech. rep. 2012. arXiv: 1204.2916.

[HSG06]   J. D. Hol, T. B. Schon, and F. Gustafsson. "On Resampling Algorithms for Particle Filters". In: *IEEE Nonlinear Statistical Signal Processing Workshop*. 2006, pp. 79–82.

[HSGF21]   S. Hassan, S. Sarkka, and A. F. Garcia-Fernandez. "Temporal Parallelization of Inference in Hidden Markov Models". In: *IEEE Trans. Signal Processing* 69 (2021), pp. 4875–4887.

[Hsu+18]   Y.-C. Hsu, Y.-C. Liu, A. Ramasamy, and Z. Kira. "Re-evaluating Continual Learning Scenarios: A Categorization and Case for Strong Baselines". In: *NIPS Continual Learning Workshop*. 2018.

[HT01]   G. E. Hinton and Y. Teh. "Discovering multiple constraints that are frequently approximately satisfied". In: *UAI*. 2001.

[HT09]   H. Hoefling and R. Tibshirani. "Estimation of Sparse Binary Pairwise Markov Networks using Pseudo-likelihoods". In: *JMLR* 10 (2009).

[HT15]   J. H. Huggins and J. B. Tenenbaum. "Risk and regret of hierarchical Bayesian learners". In: *ICML*. 2015.

[HT17]   T. J. Hastie and R. J. Tibshirani. *Generalized additive models*. Routledge, 2017.

[HTF01]   T. Hastie, R. Tibshirani, and J. Friedman. *The Elements of Statistical Learning*. Springer, 2001.

[HTF09]   T. Hastie, R. Tibshirani, and J. Friedman. *The Elements of Statistical Learning*. 2nd edition. Springer, 2009.

[HTW15]   T. Hastie, R. Tibshirani, and M. Wainwright. *Statistical Learning with Sparsity: The Lasso and Generalizations*. CRC Press, 2015.

[Hu+00]   M. Hu, C. Ingram, M.Sirski, C. Pal, S. Swamy, and C. Patten. *A Hierarchical HMM Implementation for Vertebrate Gene Splice Site Prediction*. Tech. rep. Dept. Computer Science, Univ. Waterloo, 2000.

[Hu+12]   J. Hu, Y. Wang, E. Zhou, M. C. Fu, and S. I. Marcus. "A Survey of Some Model-Based Methods for Global Optimization". en. In: *Optimization, Control, and Applications of Stochastic Systems*. Systems & Control: Foundations & Applications. Birkhäuser, Boston, 2012, pp. 157–179.

[Hu+17]   W. Hu, C. J. Li, L. Li, and J.-G. Liu. "On the diffusion approximation of nonconvex stochastic gradient descent". In: (2017). arXiv: 1705.07562 [stat.ML].

[Hu+18]   W. Hu, G. Niu, I. Sato, and M. Sugiyama. "Does Distributionally Robust Supervised Learning Give Robust Classifiers?" In: *ICML*. 2018.

[Hua+17a]   G. Huang, Y. Li, G. Pleiss, Z. Liu, J. Hopcroft, and K. Weinberger. "Snapshot ensembles: train 1, get M for free". In: *ICLR*. 2017.

[Hua+17b]   Y Huang, Y Zhang, N Li, Z Wu, and J. A. Chambers. "A Novel Robust Student's t-Based Kalman Filter". In: *IEEE Trans. Aerosp. Electron. Syst.* 53.3 (2017), pp. 1545–1554.

[Hua+18a]   C.-Z. A. Huang, A. Vaswani, I. Uszkoreit, N. Shazeer, I. Simon, C. Hawthorne, A. M. Dai, M. D. Hoffman, M. Dinculescu, and D. Eck. "Music Transformer". In: (2018). arXiv: 1809.04281 [cs.LG].

[Hua+18b] C.-W. Huang, D. Krueger, A. Lacoste, and A. Courville. "Neural Autoregressive Flows". In: *ICML*. 2018.

[Hua+19] Y. Huang, Y. Zhang, Y. Zhao, and J. A. Chambers. "A Novel Robust Gaussian–Student's t Mixture Distribution Based Kalman Filter". In: *IEEE Trans. Signal Process.* 67.13 (2019), pp. 3606–3620.

[Hug+19] J. H. Huggins, T. Campbell, M. Kasprzak, and T. Broderick. "Scalable Gaussian Process Inference with Finite-data Mean and Variance Guarantees". In: *AISTATS*. 2019.

[Hug+20] J. Huggins, M. Kasprzak, T. Campbell, and T. Broderick. "Validated Variational Inference via Practical Posterior Error Bounds". In: *AISTATS*. Ed. by S. Chiappa and R. Calandra. Vol. 108. Proceedings of Machine Learning Research. PMLR, 2020, pp. 1792–1802.

[Hus17a] F. Huszár. *Is Maximum Likelihood Useful for Representation Learning?* 2017.

[Hus17b] F. Huszár. "Variational inference using implicit distributions". In: *arXiv preprint arXiv:1702.08235* (2017).

[Hut89] M. F. Hutchinson. "A stochastic estimator of the trace of the influence matrix for Laplacian smoothing splines". In: *Communications in Statistics-Simulation and Computation* 18.3 (1989), pp. 1059–1076.

[HVD14] G. Hinton, O. Vinyals, and J. Dean. "Distilling the Knowledge in a Neural Network". In: *NIPS DL workshop*. 2014.

[HW13] A. Huang and M. P. Wand. "Simple Marginally Noninformative Prior Distributions for Covariance Matrices". en. In: *Bayesian Analysis* 8.2 (2013), pp. 439–452.

[HXW17] H. He, B. Xin, and D. Wipf. "From Bayesian Sparsity to Gated Recurrent Nets". In: *NIPS*. 2017.

[HY01] M. Hansen and B. Yu. "Model selection and the principle of minimum description length". In: *JASA* (2001).

[Hyv05] A. Hyvärinen. "Estimation of non-normalized statistical models by score matching". In: *JMLR* 6.Apr (2005), pp. 695–709.

[Hyv07a] A. Hyvarinen. "Connections between score matching, contrastive divergence, and pseudolikelihood for continuous-valued variables". In: *IEEE Transactions on neural networks* 18.5 (2007), pp. 1529–1531.

[Hyv07b] A. Hyvärinen. "Some extensions of score matching". In: *Computational statistics & data analysis* 51.5 (2007), pp. 2499–2512.

[IB12] R. Iyer and J. Bilmes. "Algorithms for Approximate Minimization of the Difference Between Submodular Functions, with Applications". In: *Uncertainty in Artificial Intelligence (UAI)*. Catalina Island, USA: AUAI, 2012.

[IB13] R. Iyer and J. Bilmes. "Submodular Optimization with Submodular Cover and Submodular Knapsack Constraints". In: *Neural Information Processing Society (NeurIPS, formerly NIPS)*. Lake Tahoe, CA, 2013.

[IB15] R. K. Iyer and J. A. Bilmes. "Polyhedral aspects of Submodularity, Convexity and Concavity". In: *Arxiv, CoRR* abs/1506.07329 (2015).

[IB98] M. Isard and A. Blake. "CONDENSATION - conditional density propagation for visual tracking". In: *Intl. J. of Computer Vision* 29.1 (1998), pp. 5–18.

[IBK06] E. L. Ionides, C Bretó, and A. A. King. "Inference for nonlinear dynamical systems". en. In: *PNAS* 103.49 (2006), pp. 18438–18443.

[IFF00] S. Iwata, L. Fleischer, and S. Fujishige. "A combinatorial strongly polynomial algorithm for minimizing submodular functions". In: *Journal of the ACM* (2000).

[IFW05] A. T. Ihler, J. W. Fischer III, and A. S. Willsky. "Loopy Belief Propagation: Convergence and Effects of Message Errors". In: *JMLR* 6 (2005), pp. 905–936.

[IJB13] R. Iyer, S. Jegelka, and J. Bilmes. "Curvature and Optimal Algorithms for Learning and Minimizing Submodular Functions". In: *NIPS*. Lake Tahoe, CA, 2013.

[IKB21] A. Immer, M. Korzepa, and M. Bauer. "Improving predictions of Bayesian neural nets via local linearization". In: *AISTATS*. Ed. by A. Banerjee and K. Fukumizu. Vol. 130. Proceedings of Machine Learning Research. PMLR, 2021, pp. 703–711.

[IM17] J. Ingraham and D. Marks. "Bayesian Sparsity for Intractable Undirected Models". In: *ICML*. 2017.

[Imb03] G. Imbens. "Sensitivity to Exogeneity Assumptions in Program Evaluation". In: *The American Economic Review* (2003).

[Imb19] G. W. Imbens. "Potential Outcome and Directed Acyclic Graph Approaches to Causality: Relevance for Empirical Practice in Economics". In: (2019). arXiv: 1907.07271 [stat.ME].

[Imm+21] A. Immer, M. Bauer, V. Fortuin, G. Rätsch, and M. E. Khan. "Scalable Marginal Likelihood Estimation for Model Selection in Deep Learning". In: *ICML*. 2021.

[IN09] S. Iwata and K. Nagano. "Submodular function minimization under covering constraints". In: *Proceedings of the 50th Annual IEEE Symposium on Foundations of Computer Science (FOCS)*. 2009, pp. 671–680.

[Ing20] M. Ingram. *Deterministic ADVI in JAX (blog post)*. https://martiningram.github.io/deterministic-advi/. 2020.

[INK18] P. Izmailov, A. Novikov, and D. Kropotov. "Scalable Gaussian Processes with Billions of Inducing Inputs via Tensor Train Decomposition". In: *ICML*. 2018.

[Inn20] M. Innes. "Sense & Sensitivities: The Path to General-Purpose Algorithmic Differentiation". In: *Proceedings of Machine Learning and Systems*. Ed. by I. Dhillon, D. Papailiopoulos, and V. Sze. Vol. 2. 2020, pp. 58–69.

[IO09] S. Iwata and J. B. Orlin. "A simple combinatorial algorithm for submodular function minimization". In: *Proceedings of the twentieth annual ACM-SIAM symposium on Discrete algorithms*. SIAM. 2009, pp. 1230–1237.

[IR00] D. R. Insua and F. Ruggeri. *Robust Bayesian Analysis*. Springer, 2000.

[IR15] G. Imbens and D. Rubin. *Causal Inference in Statistics, Social and Biomedical Sciences: An Introduction*. Cambridge University Press, 2015.

[IS15] S. Ioffe and C. Szegedy. "Batch Normalization: Accelerating Deep Network Training by Reducing Internal Covariate Shift". In: *ICML*. 2015, pp. 448–456.

[Isa03]   M. Isard. "PAMPAS: Real-Valued Graphical Models for Computer Vision". In: *CVPR*. Vol. 1. 2003, p. 613.

[Isl+19]   R. Islam, R. Seraj, S. Y. Arnob, and D. Precup. "Doubly Robust Off-Policy Actor-Critic Algorithms for Reinforcement Learning". In: *NeurIPS Workshop on Safety and Robustness in Decision Making*. 2019.

[Iso+17]   P. Isola, J.-Y. Zhu, T. Zhou, and A. A. Efros. "Image-to-Image Translation with Conditional Adversarial Networks". In: *CVPR*. 2017.

[IX00]   K Ito and K Xiong. "Gaussian filters for nonlinear filtering problems". In: *IEEE Trans. Automat. Contr.* 45.5 (2000), pp. 910–927.

[Iye+21]   R. Iyer, N. Khargonkar, J. Bilmes, and H. Asnani. "Generalized Submodular Information Measures: Theoretical Properties, Examples, Optimization Algorithms, and Applications". In: *IEEE Transactions on Information Theory* (2021).

[Iza+15]   H. Izadinia, B. C. Russell, A. Farhadi, M. D. Hoffman, and A. Hertzmann. "Deep classifiers from image tags in the wild". In: *Proceedings of the 2015 Workshop on Community-Organized Multimodal Mining: Opportunities for Novel Solutions*. 2015, pp. 13–18.

[Izm+18]   P. Izmailov, D. Podoprikhin, T. Garipov, D. Vetrov, and A. G. Wilson. "Averaging Weights Leads to Wider Optima and Better Generalization". In: *UAI*. 2018.

[Izm+19]   P. Izmailov, W. J. Maddox, P. Kirichenko, T. Garipov, D. Vetrov, and A. G. Wilson. "Subspace Inference for Bayesian Deep Learning". In: *UAI*. 2019.

[Izm+21a] P. Izmailov, P. Nicholson, S. Lotfi, and A. G. Wilson. "Dangers of Bayesian Model Averaging under Covariate Shift". In: *NIPS*. 2021.

[Izm+21b] P. Izmailov, S. Vikram, M. D. Hoffman, and A. G. Wilson. "What Are Bayesian Neural Network Posteriors Really Like?" In: *ICML*. 2021.

[Jaa01]   T. Jaakkola. "Tutorial on variational approximation methods". In: *Advanced mean field methods*. Ed. by M. Opper and D. Saad. MIT Press, 2001.

[Jac+21]   M. Jacobs, M. F. Pradier, T. H. McCoy, R. H. Perlis, F. Doshi-Velez, and K. Z. Gajos. "How machine-learning recommendations influence clinician treatment selections: the example of antidepressant selection". In: *Translational psychiatry* 11.1 (2021), pp. 1–9.

[Jad+17]   M. Jaderberg, V. Mnih, W. M. Czarnecki, T. Schaul, J. Z. Leibo, D. Silver, and K. Kavukcuoglu. "Reinforcement Learning with Unsupervised Auxiliary Tasks". In: *ICLR*. 2017.

[Jak21]   K. Jakkala. "Deep Gaussian Processes: A Survey". In: (2021). arXiv: 2106.12135 [cs.LG].

[Jan+17]   P. A. Jang, A. Loeb, M. Davidow, and A. G. Wilson. "Scalable Levy Process Priors for Spectral Kernel Learning". In: *Advances in Neural Information Processing Systems*. 2017.

[Jan18]   E. Jang. *Normalizing Flows Tutorial*. 2018.

[Jan+19]   M. Janner, J. Fu, M. Zhang, and S. Levine. "When to Trust Your Model: Model-Based Policy Optimization". In: *NIPS*. 2019.

[Jas]   Jason Antic and Jeremy Howard and Uri Manor. *Decrappification, DeOldification, and Super Resolution (Blog post)*.

[Jay03]   E. T. Jaynes. *Probability theory: the logic of science*. Cambridge university press, 2003.

[Jay+20]   S. M. Jayakumar, W. M. Czarnecki, J. Menick, J. Schwarz, J. Rae, S. Osindero, Y. W. Teh, T. Harley, and R. Pascanu. "Multiplicative Interactions and Where to Find Them". In: *ICLR*. 2020.

[Jay76]   E. T. Jaynes. "Confidence intervals vs Bayesian intervals". In: *Foundations of Probability Theory, Statistical Inference, and Statistical Theories of Science, vol II*. Ed. by W. L. Harper and C. A. Hooker. Reidel Publishing Co., 1976.

[JB03]   A. Jakulin and I. Bratko. "Analyzing Attribute Dependencies". In: *Proc. 7th European Conf. on Principles and Practice of Knowledge Discovery in Databases*. 2003.

[JB16]   S. Jegelka and J. Bilmes. "Graph cuts with interacting edge weights: examples, approximations, and algorithms". In: *Mathematical Programming* (2016), pp. 1–42.

[JB65]   C. Jacobi and C. W. Borchardt. "De investigando ordine systematis aequationum differentialium vulgarium cujuscunque." In: *Journal für die reine und angewandte Mathematik* 1865.64 (1865), pp. 297–320.

[JBB09]   D. Jian, A. Barthels, and M. Beetz. "Adaptive Markov logic networks: Learning statistical relational models with dynamic parameters". In: *9th European Conf. on AI*. 2009, 937–942.

[Jef04]   R. Jeffrey. *Subjective Probability: The Real Thing*. Cambridge, 2004.

[Jen+17]   R. Jenatton, C. Archambeau, J. González, and M. Seeger. "Bayesian Optimization with Tree-structured Dependencies". en. In: *ICML*. 2017, pp. 1655–1664.

[Jeu+19]   O. Jeunen, D. Mykhaylov, D. Rohde, F. Vasile, A. Gilotte, and M. Bompaire. "Learning from Bandit Feedback: An Overview of the State-of-the-art". In: (2019). arXiv: 1909.08471 [cs.IR].

[JG20]   A. Jacovi and Y. Goldberg. "Towards faithfully interpretable NLP systems: How should we define and evaluate faithfulness?" In: *arXiv preprint arXiv:2004.03685* (2020).

[JG21]   A. Jacovi and Y. Goldberg. "Aligning faithful interpretations with their social attribution". In: *Transactions of the Association for Computational Linguistics* 9 (2021), pp. 294–310.

[JGH18]   A. Jacot, F. Gabriel, and C. Hongler. "Neural Tangent Kernel: Convergence and Generalization in Neural Networks". In: *NIPS*. 2018.

[JGP17]   E. Jang, S. Gu, and B. Poole. "Categorical Reparameterization with Gumbel-Softmax". In: *ICLR*. 2017.

[Jha+22]   S. Jha, D. Gong, X. Wang, R. E. Turner, and L. Yao. "The Neural Process Family: Survey, Applications and Perspectives". In: (Sept. 2022). arXiv: 2209.00517 [cs.LG].

[Ji+22]   Z. Ji et al. "Survey of Hallucination in Natural Language Generation". In: *ACM Computing Surveys* (Feb. 2022).

[Jia+19]   R. Jia, A. Raghunathan, K. Göksel, and P. Liang. "Certified Robustness to Adversarial Word Substitutions". In: *EMNLP*. 2019.

[Jia+21]   C. Jia, Y. Yang, Y. Xia, Y.-T. Chen, Z. Parekh, H. Pham, Q. V. Le, Y. Sung, Z. Li, and T. Duerig. *Scaling Up Visual and Vision-Language Representation Learning With Noisy Text Supervision*. 2021. arXiv: 2102.05918 [cs.CV].

[Jia21] H. Jiang. "Minimizing convex functions with integral minimizers". In: *Proceedings of the 2021 ACM-SIAM Symposium on Discrete Algorithms (SODA)*. SIAM. 2021, pp. 976–985.

[Jih+12] Jihong Min, J Kim, Seunghak Shin, and I. S. Kweon. "Efficient Data-Driven MCMC sampling for vision-based 6D SLAM". In: *ICRA*. 2012, pp. 3025–3032.

[Jin11] Y. Jin. "Surrogate-assisted evolutionary computation: Recent advances and future challenges". In: *Swarm and Evolutionary Computation* 1.2 (2011), pp. 61–70.

[Jit+16] W. Jitkrittum, Z. Szabó, K. P. Chwialkowski, and A. Gretton. "Interpretable Distribution Features with Maximum Testing Power". In: *NIPS*. Curran Associates, Inc., 2016, pp. 181–189.

[JJ00] T. S. Jaakkola and M. I. Jordan. "Bayesian parameter estimation via variational methods". In: *Statistics and Computing* 10 (2000), pp. 25–37.

[JKG18] H. Jiang, B. Kim, and M. Y. Guan. "To Trust Or Not To Trust A Classifier". In: *NIPS*. 2018.

[JKK95] C. S. Jensen, A. Kong, and U. Kjaerulff. "Blocking-Gibbs Sampling in Very Large Probabilistic Expert Systems". In: *Intl. J. Human-Computer Studies* (1995), pp. 647–666.

[JL15a] V. Jalali and D. Leake. "CBR meets big data: A case study of large-scale adaptation rule generation". In: *International Conference on Case-Based Reasoning*. Springer. 2015, pp. 181–196.

[JL15b] V. Jalali and D. B. Leake. "Enhancing case-based regression with automatically-generated ensembles of adaptations". In: *Journal of Intelligent Information Systems* 46 (2015), pp. 237–258.

[JL16] N. Jiang and L. Li. "Doubly Robust Off-policy Evaluation for Reinforcement Learning". In: *ICML*. 2016, pp. 652–661.

[JM00] D. Jurafsky and J. H. Martin. *Speech and language processing: An Introduction to Natural Language Processing, Computational Linguistics, and Speech Recognition*. Prentice-Hall, 2000.

[JM08] D. Jurafsky and J. H. Martin. *Speech and language processing: An Introduction to Natural Language Processing, Computational Linguistics, and Speech Recognition*. 2nd edition. Prentice-Hall, 2008.

[JM18] A. Jolicoeur-Martineau. "The relativistic discriminator: a key element missing from standard GAN". In: *arXiv preprint arXiv:1807.00734* (2018).

[JM70] D. H. Jacobson and D. Q. Mayne. *Differential Dynamic Programming*. Elsevier Press, 1970.

[JMW06] J. K. Johnson, D. M. Malioutov, and A. S. Willsky. "Walk-sum interpretation and analysis of Gaussian belief propagation". In: *NIPS*. 2006, pp. 579–586.

[JNJ20] C. Jin, P. Netrapalli, and M. I. Jordan. "What is local optimality in nonconvex-nonconcave minimax optimization?" In: *Proceedings of the 34th International Conference on Machine Learning-Volume 73*. 2020.

[JO18] M. Jankowiak and F. Obermeyer. "Pathwise Derivatives Beyond the Reparameterization Trick". In: *ICML*. 2018.

[JOA10] T. Jaksch, R. Ortner, and P. Auer. "Near-optimal Regret Bounds for Reinforcement Learning". In: *JMLR* 11 (2010), pp. 1563–1600.

[JOA17] P. E. Jacob, J. O'Leary, and Y. F. Atchadé. "Unbiased Markov Chain Monte Carlo with couplings". In: *arXiv preprint arXiv:1708.03625* (2017).

[Joh12] M. J. Johnson. "A Simple Explanation of A Spectral Algorithm for Learning Hidden Markov Models". In: (2012). arXiv: 1204.2477 [stat.ME].

[Jon01] D. R. Jones. "A Taxonomy of Global Optimization Methods Based on Response Surfaces". In: *J. Global Optimiz.* 21.4 (2001), pp. 345–383.

[Jor07] M. I. Jordan. *An Introduction to Probabilistic Graphical Models*. In preparation. 2007.

[Jor+22] J. Jordon, L. Szpruch, F. Houssiau, M. Bottarelli, G. Cherubin, C. Maple, S. N. Cohen, and A. Weller. "Synthetic Data – what, why and how?" In: (May 2022). arXiv: 2205.03257 [cs.LG].

[Jor+98] M. I. Jordan, Z. Ghahramani, T. S. Jaakkola, and L. K. Saul. "An introduction to variational methods for graphical models". In: *Learning in Graphical Models*. Ed. by M. Jordan. MIT Press, 1998.

[Jos+17] A. Joshi, S. Ghosh, M. Betke, S. Sclaroff, and H. Pfister. "Personalizing gesture recognition using hierarchical Bayesian neural networks". In: *CVPR*. Honolulu, HI: IEEE, July 2017.

[Jos20] C. Joshi. *Transformers are Graph Neural Networks*. Tech. rep. 2020.

[Jos+20] M. Joshi, D. Chen, Y. Liu, D. S. Weld, L. Zettlemoyer, and O. Levy. "Spanbert: Improving pre-training by representing and predicting spans". In: *Transactions of the Association for Computational Linguistics* 8 (2020), pp. 64–77.

[Jos+22] L. V. Jospin, W. Buntine, F. Boussaid, H. Laga, and M. Bennamoun. "Hands-on Bayesian Neural Networks — a Tutorial for Deep Learning Users". In: (2022).

[Jou+16] A. Joulin, L. Van Der Maaten, A. Jabri, and N. Vasilache. "Learning visual features from large weakly supervised data". In: *European Conference on Computer Vision*. Springer. 2016, pp. 67–84.

[JP95] R. Jirousek and S. Preucil. "On the effective implementation of the iterative proportional fitting procedure". In: *Computational Statistics & Data Analysis* 19 (1995), pp. 177–189.

[JS93] M. Jerrum and A. Sinclair. "Polynomial-time approximation algorithms for the Ising model". In: *SIAM J. on Computing* 22 (1993), pp. 1087–1116.

[JS96] M. Jerrum and A. Sinclair. "The Markov chain Monte Carlo method: an approach to approximate counting and integration". In: *Approximation Algorithms for NP-hard problems*. Ed. by D. S. Hochbaum. PWS Publishing, 1996.

[JSY19] P. Jaini, K. A. Selby, and Y. Yu. "Sum-of-Squares Polynomial Flow". In: *ICML*. 2019, pp. 3009–3018.

[JU97] S. Julier and J. Uhlmann. "A New Extension of the Kalman Filter to Nonlinear Systems". In: *Proc. of AeroSense: The 11th Intl. Symp. on Aerospace/Defence Sensing, Simulation and Controls*. 1997.

[JUDW00] S Julier, J Uhlmann, and H. F. Durrant-Whyte. "A new method for the nonlinear transformation of means and covariances in filters and estimators". In: *IEEE Trans. Automat. Contr.* 45.3 (Mar. 2000), pp. 477–482.

[JW14]   M. Johnson and A. Willsky. "Stochastic Variational Inference for Bayesian Time Series Models". en. In: *ICML*. 2014, pp. 1854–1862.

[JW19]   S. Jain and B. C. Wallace. "Attention is not explanation". In: *arXiv preprint arXiv:1902.10186* (2019).

[Kaa12]   Kaare Brandt Petersen and Michael Syskind Pedersen. *The Matrix Cookbook*. 2012.

[Kad+22]   J. Kaddour, A. Lynch, Q. Liu, M. J. Kusner, and R. Silva. "Causal Machine Learning: A Survey and Open Problems". In: (June 2022). arXiv: 2206.15475 [cs.LG].

[KAG19]   A. Kirsch, J. van Amersfoort, and Y. Gal. "BatchBALD: Efficient and Diverse Batch Acquisition for Deep Bayesian Active Learning". In: *NIPS*. 2019.

[KAH19]   F. H. Kingma, P. Abbeel, and J. Ho. "Bit-Swap: Recursive Bits-Back Coding for Lossless Compression with Hierarchical Latent Variables". In: *ICML*. 2019.

[Kai58]   H. Kaiser. "The varimax criterion for analytic rotation in factor analysis". In: *Psychometrika* 23.3 (1958).

[Kak02]   S. M. Kakade. "A Natural Policy Gradient". In: *NIPS*. 2002, pp. 1531–1538.

[Kal+11]   M. Kalakrishnan, S. Chitta, E. A. Theodorou, P. Pastor, and S. Schaal. "STOMP: Stochastic Trajectory Optimization for Motion Planning". In: *ICRA*. 2011, pp. 4569–4574.

[Kal+18a]   D. Kalashnikov et al. "QT-Opt: Scalable Deep Reinforcement Learning for Vision-Based Robotic Manipulation". In: *CORL*. 2018.

[Kal+18b]   N. Kalchbrenner, E. Elsen, K. Simonyan, S. Noury, N. Casagrande, E. Lockhart, F. Stimberg, A. Oord, S. Dieleman, and K. Kavukcuoglu. "Efficient neural audio synthesis". In: *International Conference on Machine Learning*. PMLR. 2018, pp. 2410–2419.

[Kam16]   E. Kamar. "Directions in Hybrid Intelligence: Complementing AI Systems with Human Intelligence." In: *IJCAI*. 2016, pp. 4070–4073.

[Kam+22]   S. Kamthe, S. Takao, S. Mohamed, and M. P. Deisenroth. "Iterative state estimation in non-linear dynamical systems using approximate expectation propagation". In: *Trans. on Machine Learning Research* (2022).

[Kan+20]   T. Kaneko, H. Kameoka, K. Tanaka, and N. Hojo. "CycleGAN-VC3: Examining and Improving CycleGAN-VCs for Mel-spectrogram Conversion". In: *Interspeech conference proceedings* (2020).

[Kan42]   L. Kantorovich. "On the transfer of masses (in Russian)". In: *Doklady Akademii Nauk* 37.2 (1942), pp. 227–229.

[Kap+22]   S. Kapoor, W. J. Maddox, P. Izmailov, and A. G. Wilson. "On Uncertainty, Tempering, and Data Augmentation in Bayesian Classification". In: *arXiv preprint arXiv:2203.16481* (2022).

[Kar+18]   T. Karras, T. Aila, S. Laine, and J. Lehtinen. "Progressive Growing of GANs for Improved Quality, Stability, and Variation". In: *ICLR*. 2018.

[Kar+20a]   A.-H. Karimi, G. Barthe, B. Balle, and I. Valera. *Model-Agnostic Counterfactual Explanations for Consequential Decisions*. 2020. arXiv: 1905.11190 [cs.LG].

[Kar+20b]   A.-H. Karimi, G. Barthe, B. Schölkopf, and I. Valera. "A survey of algorithmic recourse: defi-

nitions, formulations, solutions, and prospects". In: *arXiv preprint arXiv:2010.04050* (2020).

[Kar+20c]   T. Karras, S. Laine, M. Aittala, J. Hellsten, J. Lehtinen, and T. Aila. "Analyzing and improving the image quality of stylegan". In: *Proceedings of the IEEE/CVF Conference on Computer Vision and Pattern Recognition*. 2020, pp. 8110–8119.

[Kar+21]   T. Karras, M. Aittala, S. Laine, E. Härkönen, J. Hellsten, J. Lehtinen, and T. Aila. "Alias-Free Generative Adversarial Networks". In: *arXiv preprint arXiv:2106.12423* (2021).

[Kar+22]   T. Karras, M. Aittala, T. Aila, and S. Laine. "Elucidating the Design Space of Diffusion-Based Generative Models". In: *NIPS*. June 2022.

[Kat05]   T. Katayama. *Subspace Methods for Systems Identification*. Springer Verlag, 2005.

[Kat+06]   H. G. Katzgraber, S. Trebst, D. A. Huse, and M. Troyer. "Feedback-optimized parallel tempering Monte Carlo". In: *Journal of Statistical Mechanics: Theory and Experiment* 2006.03 (2006), P03018.

[Kat+17]   G. Katz, C. Barrett, D. L. Dill, K. Julian, and M. J. Kochenderfer. "Reluplex: An efficient SMT solver for verifying deep neural networks". In: *International Conference on Computer Aided Verification*. Springer. 2017, pp. 97–117.

[Kat+19]   N. Kato, H. Osone, K. Oomori, C. W. Ooi, and Y. Ochiai. "GANs-Based Clothes Design: Pattern Maker Is All You Need to Design Clothing". In: *Proceedings of the 10th Augmented Human International Conference 2019*. Association for Computing Machinery, 2019.

[Kau+19]   V. Kaushal, R. Iyer, S. Kothawade, R. Mahadev, K. Doctor, and G. Ramakrishnan. "Learning from less data: A unified data subset selection and active learning framework for computer vision". In: *2019 IEEE Winter Conference on Applications of Computer Vision (WACV)*. IEEE. 2019, pp. 1289–1299.

[Kau+20]   H. Kaur, H. Nori, S. Jenkins, R. Caruana, H. Wallach, and J. Wortman Vaughan. "Interpreting interpretability: understanding data scientists' use of interpretability tools for machine learning". In: *Proceedings of the 2020 CHI conference on human factors in computing systems*. 2020, pp. 1–14.

[Kau+21]   D. Kaushik, A. Setlur, E. Hovy, and Z. C. Lipton. "Explaining The Efficacy of Counterfactually Augmented Data". In: *ICLR*. 2021.

[KB00]   H. J. Kushner and A. S. Budhiraja. "A nonlinear filtering algorithm based on an approximation of the conditional distribution". In: *IEEE Trans. Automat. Contr.* 45.3 (2000), pp. 580–585.

[KB14a]   D. P. Kingma and J. Ba. "Adam: A method for stochastic optimization". In: *arXiv preprint arXiv:1412.6980* (2014).

[KB14b]   K. Kirchhoff and J. Bilmes. "Submodularity for Data Selection in Machine Translation". In: *Empirical Methods in Natural Language Processing (EMNLP)*. 2014.

[KB16]   T. Kim and Y. Bengio. "Deep directed generative models with energy-based probability estimation". In: *arXiv preprint arXiv:1606.03439* (2016).

[KBH19]   F. Kunstner, L. Balles, and P. Hennig. "Limitations of the Empirical Fisher Approximation". In: (2019). arXiv: 1905.12558 [cs.LG].

[KCC20]   V. Kumar, A. Choudhary, and E. Cho. "Data Augmentation using Pre-trained Transformer Models". In: *Proceedings of the 2nd Workshop on Lifelong Learning for Spoken Language Systems*. Suzhou, China: Association for Computational Linguistics, Dec. 2020, pp. 18–26.

[KD18a] S. Kamthe and M. P. Deisenroth. "Data-Efficient Reinforcement Learning with Probabilistic Model Predictive Control". In: *AISTATS*. 2018.

[KD18b] D. P. Kingma and P. Dhariwal. "Glow: Generative Flow with Invertible 1×1 Convolutions". In: *NIPS*. 2018.

[Ke+19a] L. Ke, M. Barnes, W. Sun, G. Lee, S. Choudhury, and S. Srinivasa. "Imitation Learning as *f*-Divergence Minimization". In: *arXiv preprint arXiv:1905.12888* (2019).

[Ke+19b] L. Ke, S. Choudhury, M. Barnes, W. Sun, G. Lee, and S. Srinivasa. *Imitation Learning as f-Divergence Minimization*. arXiv:1905.12888. 2019.

[Ke+21] A. Ke, W. Ellsworth, O. Banerjee, A. Y. Ng, and P. Rajpurkar. "CheXtransfer: performance and parameter efficiency of ImageNet models for chest X-Ray interpretation". In: *Proceedings of the Conference on Health, Inference, and Learning*. 2021, pp. 116–124.

[Kei06] F. C. Keil. "Explanation and understanding". In: *Annu. Rev. Psychol.* 57 (2006), pp. 227–254.

[Kel+20] J. Kelly, J. Bettencourt, M. J. Johnson, and D. Duvenaud. "Learning Differential Equations that are Easy to Solve". In: *Neural Information Processing Systems*. 2020.

[Kel21] R. Kelter. "Bayesian model selection in the M-open setting — Approximate posterior inference and subsampling for efficient large-scale leave-one-out cross-validation via the difference estimator". In: *J. Math. Psychol.* 100 (Feb. 2021), p. 102474.

[Ken16] E. H. Kennedy. "Semiparametric theory and empirical processes in causal inference". In: *Statistical causal inferences and their applications in public health research*. ICSA Book Ser. Stat. Springer, [Cham], 2016, pp. 141–167.

[Ken17] E. H. Kennedy. *Semiparametric theory*. 2017. arXiv: 1709.06418 [stat.ME].

[Ken20] E. H. Kennedy. *Optimal doubly robust estimation of heterogeneous causal effects*. 2020. arXiv: 2004.14497 [math.ST].

[Ken93] G. Kenji. *100 Statistical Tests*. Sage Publications, 1993.

[Kes+17] N. S. Keskar, D. Mudigere, J. Nocedal, M. Smelyanskiy, and P. T. P. Tang. "On Large-Batch Training for Deep Learning: Generalization Gap and Sharp Minima". In: *ICLR*. 2017.

[KF09a] D. Koller and N. Friedman. *Probabilistic Graphical Models: Principles and Techniques*. MIT Press, 2009.

[KF09b] D. Krishnan and R. Fergus. "Fast Image Deconvolution using Hyper-Laplacian Priors". In: *NIPS*. 2009, pp. 1033–1041.

[KFL01] F. Kschischang, B. Frey, and H.-A. Loeliger. "Factor Graphs and the Sum-Product Algorithm". In: *IEEE Trans Info. Theory* (2001).

[KG05] A. Krause and C. Guestrin. "Near-optimal Nonmyopic Value of Information in Graphical Models". In: *Proc. of the 21st Annual Conf. on Uncertainty in Artificial Intelligence (UAI 2005)*. AUAI Press, 2005, pp. 324–331.

[KG17] A. Kendall and Y. Gal. "What Uncertainties Do We Need in Bayesian Deep Learning for Computer Vision?" In: *NIPS*. Curran Associates, Inc., 2017, pp. 5574–5584.

[KGO12] H. J. Kappen, V. Gómez, and M. Opper. "Optimal control as a graphical model inference problem". In: *Mach. Learn.* 87.2 (2012), pp. 159–182.

[KGV22] K. Kreis, R. Gao, and A. Vahdat. *Denoising diffusion-based generative modeling: foundations and applications*. CVPR Tutorial. 2022.

[KH22] L. Kurscheidt and M. Hein. "Lost in Translation: Modern Image Classifiers still degrade even under simple Translations". In: *ICML 2022 Shift Happens Workshop*. July 2022.

[Kha+10] M. E. Khan, B. Marlin, G. Bouchard, and K. P. Murphy. "Variational bounds for mixed-data factor analysis". In: *NIPS*. 2010.

[Kha+18] M. E. Khan, D. Nielsen, V. Tangkaratt, W. Lin, Y. Gal, and A. Srivastava. "Fast and Scalable Bayesian Deep Learning by Weight-Perturbation in Adam". In: *ICML*. 2018.

[Kha20] M. E. Khan. *Deep learning with Bayesian principles*. NeurIPS tutorial. 2020.

[Kha+21] S. Khan, M. Naseer, M. Hayat, S. W. Zamir, F. S. Khan, and M. Shah. "Transformers in Vision: A Survey". In: *ACM Computing Surveys December* (2021).

[Khe+20] I. Khemakhem, R. Monti, D. Kingma, and A. Hyvarinen. "ICE-BeeM: Identifiable Conditional Energy-Based Deep Models Based on Nonlinear ICA". In: *NIPS*. Vol. 33. 2020, pp. 12768–12778.

[KHH20] A. Kristiadi, M. Hein, and P. Hennig. "Being Bayesian, Even Just a Bit, Fixes Overconfidence in ReLU Networks". In: *ICML*. 2020.

[KHL20] D. Kaushik, E. Hovy, and Z. C. Lipton. *Learning the Difference that Makes a Difference with Counterfactually-Augmented Data*. 2020. arXiv: 1909.12434 [cs.CL].

[Kho+20] P. Khosla, P. Teterwak, C. Wang, A. Sarna, Y. Tian, P. Isola, A. Maschinot, C. Liu, and D. Krishnan. "Supervised Contrastive Learning". In: *ArXiv* abs/2004.11362 (2020).

[Kil+20] K. Killamsetty, D. Sivasubramanian, G. Ramakrishnan, and R. Iyer. "GLISTER: Generalization based Data Subset Selection for Efficient and Robust Learning". In: *arXiv preprint arXiv:2012.10630* (2020).

[Kim+18a] B. Kim, M. Wattenberg, J. Gilmer, C. Cai, J. Wexler, F. Viegas, and R. Sayres. "Interpretability Beyond Feature Attribution: Quantitative Testing with Concept Activation Vectors (TCAV)". In: *ICML*. 2018.

[Kim+18b] B. Kim, M. Wattenberg, J. Gilmer, C. Cai, J. Wexler, F. Viegas, et al. "Interpretability beyond feature attribution: Quantitative testing with concept activation vectors (tcav)". In: *International conference on machine learning*. PMLR. 2018, pp. 2668–2677.

[Kim+18c] Y. Kim, S. Wiseman, A. C. Miller, D. Sontag, and A. M. Rush. "Semi-Amortized Variational Autoencoders". In: *ICML*. 2018.

[Kim+19] S. Kim, S.-G. Lee, J. Song, J. Kim, and S. Yoon. "FloWaveNet : A Generative Flow for Raw Audio". In: *Proceedings of the 36th International Conference on Machine Learning*. 2019, pp. 3370–3378.

[Kim+22] S. Kim, P. Y. Lu, C. Loh, J. Smith, J. Snoek, and M. Soljačić. "Deep Learning for

Bayesian Optimization of Scientific Problems with High-Dimensional Structure". In: *TMLR* (2022).

[Kin+14a] D. P. Kingma, D. J. Rezende, S. Mohamed, and M. Welling. "Semi-Supervised Learning with Deep Generative Models". In: *NIPS*. 2014.

[Kin+14b] D. P. Kingma, D. J. Rezende, S. Mohamed, and M. Welling. *Semi-Supervised Learning with Deep Generative Models*. 2014. arXiv: 1406.5298 [cs.LG].

[Kin+16] D. P. Kingma, T. Salimans, R. Jozefowicz, X. Chen, I. Sutskever, and M. Welling. "Improved Variational Inference with Inverse Autoregressive Flow". In: *NIPS*. 2016.

[Kin+19] P.-J. Kindermans, S. Hooker, J. Adebayo, M. Alber, K. T. Schütt, S. Dähne, D. Erhan, and B. Kim. "The (un) reliability of saliency methods". In: *Explainable AI: Interpreting, Explaining and Visualizing Deep Learning*. Springer, 2019, pp. 267–280.

[Kin+21] D. P. Kingma, T. Salimans, B. Poole, and J. Ho. "Variational Diffusion Models". In: *NIPS*. July 2021.

[Kir+17] J. Kirkpatrick et al. "Overcoming catastrophic forgetting in neural networks". en. In: *PNAS* 114.13 (2017), pp. 3521–3526.

[Kir+21] A. Kirsch, J. M. J. van Amersfoort, P. H. S. Torr, and Y. Gal. "On pitfalls in OoD detection: Predictive entropy considered harmful". In: *ICML Workshop on Uncertainty in Deep Learning*. 2021.

[Kit04] G. Kitagawa. "The two-filter formula for smoothing and an implementation of the Gaussian-sum smoother". In: *Annals of the Institute of Statistical Mathematics* 46.4 (2004), pp. 605–623.

[Kiv+21] B. Kivva, G. Rajendran, P. Ravikumar, and B. Aragam. "Learning latent causal graphs via mixture oracles". In: *NIPS*. June 2021.

[Kiv+22] B. Kivva, G. Rajendran, P. Ravikumar, and B. Aragam. "Identifiability of deep generative models under mixture priors without auxiliary information". In: (June 2022). arXiv: 2206.10044 [cs.LG].

[KIW20] P. Kirichenko, P. Izmailov, and A. G. Wilson. "Why Normalizing Flows Fail to Detect Out-of-Distribution Data". In: (2020). arXiv: 2006.08545 [stat.ML].

[KJ12] J. Z. Kolter and T. S. Jaakkola. "Approximate Inference in Additive Factorial HMMs with Application to Energy Disaggregation". In: *AISTATS*. 2012.

[Kja90] U. Kjaerulff. *Triangulation of graphs – algorithms giving small total state space*. Tech. rep. R-90-09. Dept. of Math. and Comp. Sci., Aalborg Univ., Denmark, 1990.

[Kja92] U. Kjaerulff. "Optimal decomposition of probabilistic networks by simulated annealing". In: *Statistics and Computing*. Vol. 2. 1992, pp. 7–17.

[KJD18] J. Knoblauch, J. Jewson, and T. Damoulas. "Doubly Robust Bayesian Inference for Non-Stationary Streaming Data with β-Divergences". In: *NIPS*. 2018.

[KJD19] J. Knoblauch, J. Jewson, and T. Damoulas. "Generalized Variational Inference: Three arguments for deriving new Posteriors". In: (2019). arXiv: 1904.02063 [stat.ML].

[KJD21] J. Knoblauch, J. Jewson, and T. Damoulas. "An Optimization-centric View on Bayes' Rule: Reviewing and Generalizing Variational Inference". In: *JMLR* (2021).

[KJM19] N. M. Kriege, F. D. Johansson, and C. Morris. "A Survey on Graph Kernels". In: (2019). arXiv: 1903.11835 [cs.LG].

[KJV83] S. Kirkpatrick, C. G. Jr., and M. Vecchi. "Optimization by simulated annealing". In: *Science* 220 (1983), pp. 671–680.

[KK11] P. Krähenbühl and V. Koltun. "Efficient Inference in Fully Connected CRFs with Gaussian Edge Potentials". In: *NIPS*. 2011.

[KKG22] A. Kirsch, J. Kossen, and Y. Gal. "Marginal and Joint Cross-Entropies & Predictives for Online Bayesian Inference, Active Learning, and Active Sampling". In: (May 2022). arXiv: 2205.08766 [cs.LG].

[KKH20] I. Khemakhem, D. P. Kingma, and A. Hyvärinen. "Variational Autoencoders and Nonlinear ICA: A Unifying Framework". In: *AISTATS*. 2020.

[KKL20] N. Kitaev, L. Kaiser, and A. Levskaya. "Reformer: The Efficient Transformer". In: *8th International Conference on Learning Representations, ICLR 2020, Addis Ababa, Ethiopia, April 26-30, 2020*. OpenReview.net, 2020.

[KKR95] K. Kanazawa, D. Koller, and S. Russell. "Stochastic Simulation Algorithms for Dynamic Probabilistic Networks". In: *UAI*. 1995.

[KKS20] F. Kunstner, R. Kumar, and M. Schmidt. "Homeomorphic-Invariance of EM: Non-Asymptotic Convergence in KL Divergence for Exponential Families via Mirror Descent". In: (2020). arXiv: 2011.01170 [cs.LG].

[KKT03] D. Kempe, J. Kleinberg, and É. Tardos. "Maximizing the spread of influence through a social network". In: *Proceedings of the ninth ACM SIGKDD international conference on Knowledge discovery and data mining*. 2003, pp. 137–146.

[KL02] S. Kakade and J. Langford. "Approximately Optimal Approximate Reinforcement Learning". In: *ICML*. ICML '02. Morgan Kaufmann Publishers Inc., 2002, pp. 267–274.

[KL09] H. Kawakatsu and A. Largey. "EM algorithms for ordered probit models with endogenous regressors". In: *The Econometrics Journal* 12.1 (2009), pp. 164–186.

[KL10] D. P. Kingma and Y. LeCun. "Regularized estimation of image statistics by score matching". In: *Advances in neural information processing systems*. 2010, pp. 1126–1134.

[KL17a] M. E. Khan and W. Lin. "Conjugate-Computation Variational Inference : Converting Variational Inference in Non-Conjugate Models to Inferences in Conjugate Models". In: *AISTATS*. 2017.

[KL17b] P. W. Koh and P. Liang. "Understanding black-box predictions via influence functions". In: *International Conference on Machine Learning*. PMLR. 2017, pp. 1885–1894.

[KL17c] J. K. Kruschke and T. M. Liddell. "The Bayesian New Statistics: Hypothesis testing, estimation, meta-analysis, and power analysis from a Bayesian perspective". In: *Psychon. Bull. Rev.* (2017).

[KL21] W. M. Kouw and M. Loog. "A review of domain adaptation without target labels". en. In: *IEEE Trans. Pattern Anal. Mach. Intell.* (2021).

[Kla+06] M. Klaas, M. Briers, N. de Freitas, A. Doucet, S. Maskell, and D. Lang. "Fast Particle Smoothing: If I Had a Million Particles". In: *ICML*. 2006.

[KLA19]   T. Karras, S. Laine, and T. Aila. "A Style-Based Generator Architecture for Generative Adversarial Networks". In: *CVPR*. 2019.

[Kle+11]   A. Kleiner, A. Talwalkar, P. Sarkar, and M. I. Jordan. *A scalable bootstrap for massive data*. Tech. rep. UC Berkeley, 2011.

[Kle17]   G. A. Klein. *Sources of power: How people make decisions*. MIT press, 2017.

[Kle18]   J. Kleinberg. "Inherent Trade-Offs in Algorithmic Fairness". In: *ACM International Conference on Measurement and Modeling of Computer Systems*. SIGMETRICS '18. Irvine, CA, USA: Association for Computing Machinery, June 2018, p. 40.

[KLM19]   A. Kumar, P. Liang, and T. Ma. "Verified Uncertainty Calibration". In: *NIPS*. 2019.

[KM00]   J. Kwon and K. Murphy. *Modeling Freeway Traffic with Coupled HMMs*. Tech. rep. Univ. California, Berkeley, 2000.

[KM08]   U. Kjaerulff and A. Madsen. *Bayesian Networks and Influence Diagrams: A Guide to Construction and Analysis*. Springer, 2008.

[KM22]   J. Kuan and J. Mueller. "Back to the Basics: Revisiting Out-of-Distribution Detection Baselines". In: *ICML PODS Workshop*. July 2022.

[KMB08]   N. Kriegeskorte, M. Mur, and P. Bandettini. "Representational similarity analysis - connecting the branches of systems neuroscience". en. In: *Front. Syst. Neurosci.* 2 (Nov. 2008), p. 4.

[KML20]   A. Kumar, T. Ma, and P. Liang. "Understanding Self-Training for Gradual Domain Adaptation". In: *ICML*. Ed. by H. D. Iii and A. Singh. Vol. 119. Proceedings of Machine Learning Research. PMLR, 2020, pp. 5468–5479.

[KMR16]   J. Kleinberg, S. Mullainathan, and M. Raghavan. "Inherent trade-offs in the fair determination of risk scores". In: *arXiv preprint arXiv:1609.05807* (2016).

[KMY04]   D. Kersten, P. Mamassian, and A. Yuille. "Object perception as Bayesian inference". en. In: *Annu. Rev. Psychol.* 55 (2004), pp. 271–304.

[KN09]   J. Z. Kolter and A. Y. Ng. "Near-Bayesian Exploration in Polynomial Time". In: *ICML*. 2009.

[KN95]   R. Kneser and H. Ney. "Improved backing-off for n-gram language modeling". In: *ICASSP*. Vol. 1. 1995, pp. 181–184.

[KN98]   C.-J. Kim and C. Nelson. *State-Space Models with Regime-Switching: Classical and Gibbs-Sampling Approaches with Applications*. MIT Press, 1998.

[KNP11]   K. Kersting, S. Natarajan, and D. Poole. *Statistical Relational AI: Logic, Probability and Computation*. Tech. rep. UBC, 2011.

[KNT20]   I. Kostrikov, O. Nachum, and J. Tompson. "Imitation Learning via Off-Policy Distribution Matching". In: *ICLR*. 2020.

[Koe05]   R. Koenker. *Quantile Regression*. en. Cambridge University Press, 2005.

[Koh+20a]   P. W. Koh, T. Nguyen, Y. S. Tang, S. Mussmann, E. Pierson, B. Kim, and P. Liang. "Concept bottleneck models". In: *International Conference on Machine Learning*. PMLR. 2020, pp. 5338–5348.

[Koh+20b]   P. W. Koh et al. "WILDS: A Benchmark of in-the-Wild Distribution Shifts". In: (Dec. 2020). arXiv: 2012.07421 [cs.LG].

[Kol+20]   A. Kolesnikov, L. Beyer, X. Zhai, J. Puigcerver, J. Yung, S. Gelly, and N. Houlsby. "Big transfer (BiT): General visual representation learning". In: *ECCV*. Springer. 2020, pp. 491–507.

[Koo03]   G. Koop. *Bayesian econometrics*. Wiley, 2003.

[Kor+15]   A. Korattikara, V. Rathod, K. Murphy, and M. Welling. "Bayesian Dark Knowledge". In: *NIPS*. 2015.

[Kor+19]   S. Kornblith, M. Norouzi, H. Lee, and G. Hinton. "Similarity of neural network representations revisited". In: *arXiv preprint arXiv:1905.00414* (2019).

[Kor+20]   A. Korotin, V. Egiazarian, A. Asadulaev, A. Safin, and E. Burnaev. "Wasserstein-2 Generative Networks". In: *International Conference on Learning Representations*. 2020.

[Kor+21]   S. Kornblith, T. Chen, H. Lee, and M. Norouzi. "Why do better loss functions lead to less transferable features?" In: *Advances in Neural Information Processing Systems*. Vol. 34. 2021.

[Kot+17]   L. Kotthoff, C. Thornton, H. H. Hoos, F. Hutter, and K. Leyton-Brown. "Auto-WEKA 2.0: Automatic model selection and hyperparameter optimization in WEKA". In: *JMLR* 18.25 (2017), pp. 1–5.

[Kot+22]   S. Kothawade, V. Kaushal, G. Ramakrishnan, J. Bilmes, and R. Iyer. "PRISM: A Rich Class of Parameterized Submodular Information Measures for Guided Subset Selection". In: *Proceedings of the AAAI Conference on Artificial Intelligence*. 2022.

[Koy+10]   S. Koyama, L. C. Pérez-Bolde, C. R. Shalizi, and R. E. Kass. "Approximate Methods for State-Space Models". en. In: *JASA* 105.489 (2010), pp. 170–180.

[Koz92]   J. R. Koza. *Genetic Programming*. https://mitpress.mit.edu/books/genetic-programming. Accessed: 2017-11-26. 1992.

[KP20]   A. Kumar and B. Poole. "On Implicit Regularization in β-VAEs". In: *ICML*. 2020.

[KPB19]   I. Kobyzev, S. Prince, and M. A. Brubaker. "Normalizing Flows: An Introduction and Review of Current Methods". In: (2019). arXiv: 1908.09257 [stat.ML].

[KPHL17]   M. J. Kusner, B. Paige, and J. M. Hernández-Lobato. "Grammar Variational Autoencoder". In: *ICML*. 2017.

[KPS98]   J. T. Key, L. R. Pericchi, and A. F. Smith. "Choosing among models when none of them are true". In: *Proc. of the Workshop on Model Selection* (1998).

[KPS99]   J. T. Key, L. R. Pericchi, and A. F. Smith. "Bayesian model choice: what and why". In: *Bayesian statistics 6* 6 (1999), pp. 343–370.

[KPT21]   J. S. Kim, G. Plumb, and A. Talwalkar. "Sanity Simulations for Saliency Methods". In: *arXiv preprint arXiv:2105.06506* (2021).

[KR19]   M. Kearns and A. Roth. *The Ethical Algorithm: The Science of Socially Aware Algorithm Design*. en. Oxford University Press, 2019.

[KR21a]   M. Khan and H. Rue. "The Bayesian Learning Rule". In: (2021). arXiv: 2107.04562 [stat.ME].

[KR21b]   S. Kong and D. Ramanan. "OpenGAN: Open-Set Recognition via Open Data Generation". In: *ICCV*. 2021.

[Kra+08] A. Krause, H Brendan McMahan, C. Guestrin, and A. Gupta. "Robust Submodular Observation Selection". In: *JMLR* 9 (2008), pp. 2761–2801.

[Kri+05] B. Krishnapuram, L. Carin, M. Figueiredo, and A. Hartemink. "Learning sparse Bayesian classifiers: multi-class formulation, fast algorithms, and generalization bounds". In: *IEEE Transaction on Pattern Analysis and Machine Intelligence* (2005).

[Kri19] N. Kriegeskorte. *What's the best measure of representational dissimilarity?* 2019.

[KRL08] K. Kavukcuoglu, M. Ranzato, and Y. LeCun. "Fast Inference in Sparse Coding Algorithms with Applications to Object Recognition". In: *NIPS workshop on optimization in machine learning*. 2008.

[KRS14] B. Kim, C. Rudin, and J. A. Shah. "The bayesian case model: A generative approach for case-based reasoning and prototype classification". In: *Advances in neural information processing systems*. 2014, pp. 1952–1960.

[Kru10] J. Kruschke. *An open letter on Bayesian Data Analysis*. Tech. rep. U. Indiana, 2010.

[Kru13] J. K. Kruschke. "Bayesian estimation supersedes the t test". In: *J. Experimental Psychology: General* 142.2 (2013), pp. 573–603.

[Kru15] J. Kruschke. *Doing Bayesian Data Analysis: A Tutorial with R, JAGS and STAN*. Second edition. Academic Press, 2015.

[KS06] L. Kocsis and C. Szepesvári. "Bandit Based Monte-Carlo Planning". In: *ECML*. 2006, pp. 282–293.

[KS07] J. D. Y. Kang and J. L. Schafer. "Demystifying double robustness: a comparison of alternative strategies for estimating a population mean from incomplete data". In: *Statist. Sci.* 22.4 (2007), pp. 523–539.

[KS15] H. Kaya and A. A. Salah. "Adaptive Mixtures of Factor Analyzers". In: (2015). arXiv: 1507.02801 [stat.ML].

[KSB21] B. Kompa, J. Snoek, and A. Beam. "Empirical Frequentist Coverage of Deep Learning Uncertainty Quantification Procedures". In: *Entropy* 23.12 (2021).

[KSC98] S. Kim, N. Shephard, and S. Chib. "Stochastic Volatility: Likelihood Inference and Comparison with ARCH Models". In: *Review of Economic Studies* 65.3 (1998), pp. 361–393.

[KSH12a] A. Krizhevsky, I. Sutskever, and G. Hinton. "Imagenet classification with deep convolutional neural networks". In: *NIPS*. 2012.

[KSH12b] A. Krizhevsky, I. Sutskever, and G. E. Hinton. "Imagenet classification with deep convolutional neural networks". In: *Advances in neural information processing systems*. 2012, pp. 1097–1105.

[KSL19] S. Kornblith, J. Shlens, and Q. V. Le. "Do better ImageNet models transfer better?" In: *Proceedings of the IEEE/CVF Conference on Computer Vision and Pattern Recognition*. 2019, pp. 2661–2671.

[KSL21] S. Kim, Q. Song, and F. Liang. "Stochastic gradient Langevin dynamics with adaptive drifts". In: *J. Stat. Comput. Simul.* (2021), pp. 1–19.

[KSN99] N. L. Kleinman, J. C. Spall, and D. Q. Naiman. "Simulation-Based Optimization with Stochastic Approximation Using Common Random Numbers". In: *Manage. Sci.* 45.11 (1999), pp. 1570–1578.

[KSS17] R. G. Krishnan, U. Shalit, and D. Sontag. "Structured Inference Networks for Nonlinear State Space Models". In: *AAAI*. 2017.

[KSW15] D. P. Kingma, T. Salimans, and M. Welling. "Variational Dropout and the Local Reparameterization Trick". In: *NIPS*. 2015.

[KT11] A. Kulesza and B. Taskar. "k-DPPs: Fixed-size determinantal point processes". In: *ICML*. 2011.

[KTB11] D. P. Kroese, T. Taimre, and Z. I. Botev. *Handbook of Monte Carlo Methods*. en. 1 edition. Wiley, 2011.

[KTX20] R. Kohavi, D. Tang, and Y. Xu. *Trustworthy Online Controlled Experiments: A Practical Guide to A/B Testing*. en. 1st ed. Cambridge University Press, 2020.

[KU21] S. Khan and J. Ugander. *Adaptive normalization for IPW estimation*. 2021. arXiv: 2106.07695 [stat.ME].

[Kua+09] P. Kuan, G. Pan, J. A. Thomson, R. Stewart, and S. Keles. *A hierarchical semi-Markov model for detecting enrichment with application to ChIP-Seq experiments*. Tech. rep. U. Wisconsin, 2009.

[Kub04] M. Kubale. *Graph colorings*. Vol. 352. American Mathematical Society, 2004.

[Kuc+16] A. Kucukelbir, D. Tran, R. Ranganath, A. Gelman, and D. M. Blei. "Automatic Differentiation Variational Inference". In: *JMLR* (2016).

[Kuh55] H. W. Kuhn. "The Hungarian method for the assignment problem". In: *Naval Research Logistics Quarterly* 2 (1955), pp. 83–97.

[Kul+13] T. Kulesza, S. Stumpf, M. Burnett, S. Yang, I. Kwan, and W.-K. Wong. "Too much, too little, or just right? Ways explanations impact end users' mental models". In: *2013 IEEE Symposium on visual languages and human centric computing*. IEEE. 2013, pp. 3–10.

[Kul+19] M. Kull, M. Perello-Nieto, M. Kängsepp, T. S. Filho, H. Song, and P. Flach. "Beyond temperature scaling: Obtaining well-calibrated multiclass probabilities with Dirichlet calibration". In: *NIPS*. 2019.

[Kum+19a] A. Kumar, J. Fu, M. Soh, G. Tucker, and S. Levine. "Stabilizing Off-Policy Q-Learning via Bootstrapping Error Reduction". In: *NeurIPS*. 2019, pp. 11761–11771.

[Kum+19b] M. Kumar, M. Babaeizadeh, D. Erhan, C. Finn, S. Levine, L. Dinh, and D. P. Kingma. "VideoFlow: A flow-based generative model for video". In: *ICML Workshop on Invertible Neural Networks and Normalizing Flows* (2019).

[Kum+19c] R. Kumar, S. Ozair, A. Goyal, A. Courville, and Y. Bengio. "Maximum entropy generators for energy-based models". In: *arXiv preprint arXiv:1901.08508* (2019).

[Kün+19] S. R. Künzel, J. S. Sekhon, P. J. Bickel, and B. Yu. "Metalearners for estimating heterogeneous treatment effects using machine learning". In: *Proceedings of the National Academy of Sciences* 116.10 (2019), pp. 4156–4165. eprint: https://www.pnas.org/content/116/10/4156.full.pdf.

[Kun20] J. Kuntz. "Markov chains revisited". In: (Jan. 2020). arXiv: 2001.02183 [math.PR].

[Kur+19] T. Kurutach, I. Clavera, Y. Duan, A. Tamar, and P. Abbeel. "Model-Ensemble Trust-Region Policy Optimization". In: *ICLR*. 2019.

[Kur+20]   R. Kurle, B. Cseke, A. Klushyn, P. van der Smagt, and S. Günnemann. "Continual Learning with Bayesian Neural Networks for Non-Stationary Data". In: *ICLR*. 2020.

[Kus+18]   M. J. Kusner, J. R. Loftus, C. Russell, and R. Silva. *Counterfactual Fairness*. 2018. arXiv: 1703.06856 [stat.ML].

[Kus64]   H. J. Kushner. "A New Method of Locating the Maximum Point of an Arbitrary Multipeak Curve in the Presence of Noise". In: *J. Basic Eng* 86.1 (1964), pp. 97–106.

[KVK10]   A. Klami, S. Virtanen, and S. Kaski. "Bayesian exponential family projections for coupled data sources". In: *UAI*. 2010.

[KW14]   D. P. Kingma and M. Welling. "Auto-encoding variational Bayes". In: *ICLR*. 2014.

[KW18]   A. S. I. Kim and M. P. Wand. "On expectation propagation for generalised, linear and mixed models". In: *Aust. N. Z. J. Stat.* 60.1 (2018), pp. 75–102.

[KW19a]   D. P. Kingma and M. Welling. "An Introduction to Variational Autoencoders". In: *Foundations and Trends in Machine Learning* 12.4 (2019), pp. 307–392.

[KW19b]   M. J. Kochenderfer and T. A. Wheeler. *Algorithms for Optimization*. en. The MIT Press, 2019.

[KW70]   G. S. Kimeldorf and G. Wahba. "A Correspondence Between Bayesian Estimation on Stochastic Processes and Smoothing by Splines". en. In: *Ann. Math. Stat.* 41.2 (1970), pp. 495–502.

[KW96]   R. E. Kass and L. Wasserman. "The Selection of Prior Distributions by Formal Rules". In: *JASA* 91.435 (1996), pp. 1343–1370.

[KWW22]   M. J. Kochenderfer, T. A. Wheeler, and K. Wray. *Algorithms for Decision Making*. The MIT Press, 2022.

[KY94]   J. J. Kosowsky and A. L. Yuille. "The invisible hand algorithm: Solving the assignment problem with statistical physics". In: *Neural networks* 7.3 (1994), pp. 477–490.

[Kyn+19]   T. Kynkäänniemi, T. Karras, S. Laine, J. Lehtinen, and T. Aila. "Improved Precision and Recall Metric for Assessing Generative Models". In: *NeurIPS*. 2019.

[KZ02]   V. Kolmogorov and R. Zabih. "What energy functions can be minimized via graph cuts?" In: *Computer Vision—ECCV 2002* (2002), pp. 185–208.

[KZB19]   A. Kolesnikov, X. Zhai, and L. Beyer. "Revisiting self-supervised visual representation learning". In: *Proceedings of the IEEE/CVF conference on computer vision and pattern recognition*. 2019, pp. 1920–1929.

[LA87]   P. J. M. Laarhoven and E. H. L. Aarts, eds. *Simulated Annealing: Theory and Applications*. Kluwer Academic Publishers, 1987.

[Lag+19]   I. Lage, E. Chen, J. He, M. Narayanan, B. Kim, S. J. Gershman, and F. Doshi-Velez. "Human evaluation of models built for interpretability". In: *Proceedings of the AAAI Conference on Human Computation and Crowdsourcing*. Vol. 7. 1. 2019, pp. 59–67.

[Lak+17]   B. M. Lake, T. D. Ullman, J. B. Tenenbaum, and S. J. Gershman. "Building Machines That Learn and Think Like People". en. In: *Behav. Brain Sci.* (2017), pp. 1–101.

[Lal+21]   A. Lal, M. W. Lockhart, Y. Xu, and Z. Zu. "How Much Should We Trust Instrumental Variable Estimates in Political Science? Practical Advice based on Over 60 Replicated Studies". In: (2021).

[Lam18]   B. Lambert. *A Student's Guide to Bayesian Statistics*. en. 1st ed. SAGE Publications Ltd, 2018.

[Lam92]   D. Lambert. "Zero-Inflated Poisson Regression, with an Application to Defects in Manufacturing". In: *Technometrics* 34.1 (1992), pp. 1–14.

[Lan95a]   K. Lange. "A gradient algorithm locally equivalent to the em algorithm". en. In: *J. of Royal Stat. Soc. Series B* 57.2 (July 1995), pp. 425–437.

[Lan95b]   K. Lange. "A QUASI-NEWTON ACCELERATION OF THE EM ALGORITHM". In: *Statistica Sinica* 5.1 (1995), pp. 1–18.

[Lao+20]   J. Lao, C. Suter, I. Langmore, C. Chimisov, A. Saxena, P. Sountsov, D. Moore, R. A. Saurous, M. D. Hoffman, and J. V. Dillon. "tfp.mcmc: Modern Markov Chain Monte Carlo Tools Built for Modern Hardware". In: *PROBPROG*. 2020.

[Lar+16]   A. B. L. Larsen, S. K. Sonderby, H. Larochelle, and O. Winther. "Autoencoding beyond pixels using a learned similarity metric". In: *International conference on machine learning*. PMLR. 2016, pp. 1558–1566.

[Lar+22]   B. W. Larsen, S. Fort, N. Becker, and S. Ganguli. "How many degrees of freedom do we need to train deep networks: a loss landscape perspective". In: *ICLR*. 2022.

[Las08]   K. B. Laskey. "MEBN: A language for first-order Bayesian knowledge bases". In: *Artif. Intell.* 172.2 (2008), pp. 140–178.

[Lau92]   S. L. Lauritzen. "Propagation of probabilities, means and variances in mixed graphical association models". In: *JASA* 87.420 (1992), pp. 1098–1108.

[Lau95]   S. L. Lauritzen. "The EM algorithm for graphical association models with missing data". In: *Computational Statistics and Data Analysis* 19 (1995), pp. 191–201.

[Lav00]   M. Lavine. *What is Bayesian statistics and why everything else is wrong*. Tech. rep. Duke, 2000.

[Law05]   N. D. Lawrence. "Probabilistic non-linear principal component analysis with Gaussian process latent variable models". In: *JMLR* 6 (2005), pp. 1783–1816.

[Law+22]   D. Lawson, A. Raventós, A. Warrington, and S. Linderman. "SIXO: Smoothing Inference with Twisted Objectives". In: (June 2022). arXiv: 2206.05952 [cs.LG].

[LB09]   H. Lin and J. A. Bilmes. "How to Select a Good Training-data Subset for Transcription: Submodular Active Selection for Sequences". In: *Proc. Annual Conference of the International Speech Communication Association (INTERSPEECH)*. Brighton, UK, 2009.

[LB10a]   H. Lin and J. Bilmes. "Multi-document Summarization via Budgeted Maximization of Submodular Functions". In: *North American chapter of the Association for Computational Linguistics/Human Language Technology Conference (NAACL/HLT-2010)*. Los Angeles, CA, 2010.

[LB10b]   H. Lin and J. A. Bilmes. "An Application of the Submodular Principal Partition to Training Data Subset Selection". In: *Neural Information Processing Society (NeurIPS, formerly NIPS) Workshop*. NeurIPS (formerly NIPS) Workshop on Discrete Optimization in Machine Learning: Submodularity, Sparsity & Polyhedra (DISCML). Vancouver, Canada, 2010.

[LB11]   H. Lin and J. Bilmes. "A Class of Submodular Functions for Document Summarization". In: *The 49th Annual Meeting of the Association for Computational Linguistics: Human Language Technologies (ACL/HLT-2011)*. (long paper). Portland, OR, 2011.

[LB12]   H. Lin and J. Bilmes. "Learning Mixtures of Submodular Shells with Application to Document Summarization". In: *Uncertainty in Artificial Intelligence (UAI)*. Catalina Island, USA: AUAI, 2012.

[LB19]   A. Levray and V. Belle. "Learning Tractable Probabilistic Models in Open Worlds". In: (2019). arXiv: 1901.05847 [cs.LG].

[LBB20]   Y. Liu, P.-L. Bacon, and E. Brunskill. "Understanding the Curse of Horizon in Off-Policy Evaluation via Conditional Importance Sampling". In: *ICML*. 2020.

[LBH15]   Y. LeCun, Y. Bengio, and G. Hinton. "Deep learning". en. In: *Nature* 521.7553 (May 2015), pp. 436–444.

[LBH22]   X. Lu, A. Boukouvalas, and J. Hensman. "Additive Gaussian Processes Revisited". In: *ICML*. June 2022.

[LBL16]   H. Lakkaraju, S. H. Bach, and J. Leskovec. "Interpretable decision sets: A joint framework for description and prediction". In: *Proceedings of the 22nd ACM SIGKDD international conference on knowledge discovery and data mining*. 2016, pp. 1675–1684.

[LBM06]   J. A. Lasserre, C. M. Bishop, and T. P. Minka. "Principled Hybrids of Generative and Discriminative Models". In: *CVPR*. Vol. 1. June 2006, pp. 87–94.

[LBS01]   T. Lefebvre, H. Bruyninckx, and J. D. Schutter. "Comment on "A New Method for the Nonlinear Transformation of Means and Covariances in Filters and Estimators"". In: *IEEE Trans. on Automatic Control* 47.8 (2001), pp. 1406–1409.

[LBS17]   C. Lakshminarayanan, S. Bhatnagar, and C. Szepesvári. "A Linearly Relaxed Approximate Linear Program for Markov Decision Processes". In: *IEEE Transactions on Automatic Control* 63.4 (2017), pp. 1185–1191.

[LBW17]   T. A. Le, A. G. Baydin, and F. Wood. "Inference Compilation and Universal Probabilistic Programming". In: *AISTATS*. 2017.

[LC02]   J. Langford and R. Caruana. "(Not) bounding the true error". In: *NIPS*. 2002.

[LCG12]   Y. Lou, R. Caruana, and J. Gehrke. "Intelligible models for classification and regression". In: *Proceedings of the 18th ACM SIGKDD international conference on Knowledge discovery and data mining*. 2012, pp. 150–158.

[LCR21]   T. Lesort, M. Caccia, and I. Rish. "Understanding Continual Learning Settings with Data Distribution Drift Analysis". In: (2021). arXiv: 2104.01678 [cs.LG].

[LDZ11]   Y Li, H Duan, and C. X. Zhai. "Cloudspeller: Spelling correction for search queries by using a unified hidden markov model with web-scale resources". In: *SIGIR*. 2011.

[LDZ12]   Y. Li, H. Duan, and C. Zhai. "A Generalized Hidden Markov Model with Discriminative Training for Query Spelling Correction". In: *SIGIR*. 2012, pp. 611–620.

[Le+18]   T. A. Le, M. Igl, T. Rainforth, T. Jin, and F. Wood. "Auto-Encoding Sequential Monte Carlo". In: *ICLR*. 2018.

[L'E18]   P. L'Ecuyer. "Randomized Quasi-Monte Carlo: An Introduction for Practitioners". In: *Monte Carlo and Quasi-Monte Carlo Methods*. Springer International Publishing, 2018, pp. 29–52.

[Le+19]   T. A. Le, A. R. Kosiorek, N Siddharth, Y. W. Teh, and F. Wood. "Revisiting Reweighted Wake-Sleep for Models with Stochastic Control Flow". In: *UAI*. 2019.

[LeC+89]   Y. LeCun, B. Boser, J. S. Denker, D. Henderson, R. E. Howard, W. Hubbard, and L. D. Jackel. "Backpropagation Applied to Handwritten Zip Code Recognition". In: *Neural Computation* 1.4 (1989), pp. 541–551.

[LeC+98]   Y. LeCun, L. Bottou, G. B. Orr, and K.-R. Müller. "Efficient BackProp". en. In: *Neural Networks: Tricks of the Trade*. Lecture Notes in Computer Science. Springer, Berlin, Heidelberg, 1998, pp. 9–50.

[Lee04]   M. D. Lee. "Models, parameters and priors in Bayesian inference". 2004.

[Lee06]   J. de Leeuw. "Principal Component Analysis of Binary Data by Iterated Singular Value Decomposition". In: *Comput. Stat. Data Anal.* 50.1 (2006), pp. 21–39.

[Lee+09]   H. Lee, R. B. Grosse, R. Ranganath, and A. Ng. "Convolutional deep belief networks for scalable unsupervised learning of hierarchical representations". In: *ICML '09*. 2009.

[Lee+10]   J. Lee, V. Mirrokni, V. Nagarajan, and M. Sviridenko. "Maximizing Nonmonotone Submodular Functions under Matroid or Knapsack Constraints". In: *SIAM Journal on Discrete Mathematics* 23.4 (2010), pp. 2053–2078.

[Lee+18]   J. Lee, Y. Bahri, R. Novak, S. S. Schoenholz, J. Pennington, and J. Sohl-Dickstein. "Deep Neural Networks as Gaussian Processes". In: *ICLR*. 2018.

[Lei+18]   J. Lei, M. G'Sell, A. Rinaldo, R. J. Tibshirani, and L. Wasserman. "Distribution-Free Predictive Inference For Regression". In: *JASA* (2018).

[Lei+20]   F. Leibfried, V. Dutordoir, S. T. John, and N. Durrande. "A Tutorial on Sparse Gaussian Processes and Variational Inference". In: (2020). arXiv: 2012.13962 [cs.LG].

[Lem09]   C. Lemieux. *Monte Carlo and Quasi-Monte Carlo Sampling*. Springer, New York, NY, 2009.

[Léo14]   C. Léonard. "A survey of the Schrödinger problem and some of its connections with optimal transport". In: *Discrete & Continuous Dynamical Systems* 34.4 (2014), p. 1533.

[Let+15a]   B. Letham, C. Rudin, T. H. McCormick, and D. Madigan. "Interpretable classifiers using rules and Bayesian analysis: Building a better stroke prediction model". In: *The Annals of Applied Statistics* 9.3 (2015).

[Let+15b]   B. Letham, C. Rudin, T. H. McCormick, and D. Madigan. "Interpretable classifiers using rules and bayesian analysis: Building a better stroke prediction model". In: *The Annals of Applied Statistics* 9.3 (2015), pp. 1350–1371.

[Lev18]   S. Levine. "Reinforcement Learning and Control as Probabilistic Inference: Tutorial and Review". In: (2018). arXiv: 1805.00909 [cs.LG].

[Lev+20] S. Levine, A. Kumar, G. Tucker, and J. Fu. *Offline Reinforcement Learning: Tutorial, Review, and Perspectives on Open Problems.* arXiv:2005.01643. 2020.

[LF+21] L. Le Folgoc, V. Baltatzis, S. Desai, A. Devaraj, S. Ellis, O. E. Martinez Manzanera, A. Nair, H. Qiu, J. Schnabel, and B. Glocker. "Is MC Dropout Bayesian?" In: (2021). arXiv: 2110.04286 [cs.LG].

[LFG21] F. Lin, X. Fang, and Z. Gao. "Distributionally Robust Optimization: A review on theory and applications". In: *Numer. Algebra Control Optim.* 12.1 (2021), pp. 159–212.

[LG94] D. D. Lewis and W. A. Gale. "A sequential algorithm for training text classifiers". In: *SIGIR94.* Springer. 1994, pp. 3–12.

[LGMT11] F. Le Gland, V. Monbet, and V.-D. Tran. "Large Sample Asymptotics for the Ensemble Kalman Filter". In: *Oxford Handbook of Nonlinear Filtering.* Ed. by D Crisan And. 2011.

[LHF17] R. M. Levy, A. Haldane, and W. F. Flynn. "Potts Hamiltonian models of protein co-variation, free energy landscapes, and evolutionary fitness". en. In: *Curr. Opin. Struct. Biol.* 43 (2017), pp. 55–62.

[LHF20] J. Liang, D. Hu, and J. Feng. "Do We Really Need to Access the Source Data? Source Hypothesis Transfer for Unsupervised Domain Adaptation". In: *ICML.* Ed. by H. D. Iii and A. Singh. Vol. 119. Proceedings of Machine Learning Research. PMLR, 2020, pp. 6028–6039.

[LHLT15] Y. Li, J. M. Hernandez-Lobato, and R. E. Turner. "Stochastic Expectation Propagation". In: *NIPS.* 2015.

[LHR20] A. Lucic, H. Haned, and M. de Rijke. "Why does my model fail? contrastive local explanations for retail forecasting". In: *Proceedings of the 2020 Conference on Fairness, Accountability, and Transparency.* 2020, pp. 90–98.

[Li+10] L. Li, W. Chu, J. Langford, and R. E. Schapire. "A contextual-bandit approach to personalized news article recommendation". In: *WWW.* 2010.

[Li+16] C. Li, C. Chen, D. Carlson, and L. Carin. "Preconditioned Stochastic Gradient Langevin Dynamics for Deep Neural Networks". In: *AAAI.* 2016.

[Li+17a] A. Li, A. Jabri, A. Joulin, and L. van der Maaten. "Learning visual n-grams from web data". In: *Proceedings of the IEEE International Conference on Computer Vision.* 2017, pp. 4183–4192.

[Li+17b] C.-L. Li, W.-C. Chang, Y. Cheng, Y. Yang, and B. Poczos. "Mmd gan: Towards deeper understanding of moment matching network". In: *Advances in Neural Information Processing Systems.* 2017, pp. 2203–2213.

[Li+17c] L. Li, K. Jamieson, G. De Salvo, A. Rostamizadeh, and A. Talwalkar. "Hyperband: bandit-based configuration evaluation for hyperparameter optimization". In: *ICLR.* 2017.

[Li+17d] O. Li, H. Liu, C. Chen, and C. Rudin. *Deep Learning for Case-Based Reasoning through Prototypes: A Neural Network that Explains Its Predictions.* 2017. arXiv: 1710.04806 [cs.AI].

[Li+17e] T.-C. Li, J.-Y. Su, W. Liu, and J. M. Corchado. "Approximate Gaussian conjugacy: parametric recursive filtering under nonlinearity, multimodality, uncertainty, and constraint, and beyond". In: *Frontiers of Information Technology & Electronic Engineering* 18.12 (2017), pp. 1913–1939.

[Li18] Y. Li. "Deep Reinforcement Learning". In: (2018). arXiv: 1810.06339 [cs.LG].

[Li+18a] C. Li, H. Farkhoor, R. Liu, and J. Yosinski. "Measuring the Intrinsic Dimension of Objective Landscapes". In: *ICLR.* 2018.

[Li+18b] C. Li, H. Farkhoor, R. Liu, and J. Yosinski. "Measuring the Intrinsic Dimension of Objective Landscapes". In: *ICLR.* 2018.

[Li+18c] X. Li, C. Li, J. Chi, J. Ouyang, and W. Wang. "Black-box Expectation Propagation for Bayesian Models". In: *ICDM.* Proceedings. Society for Industrial and Applied Mathematics, 2018, pp. 603–611.

[Li+19] J. Li, S. Qu, X. Li, J. Szurley, J. Z. Kolter, and F. Metze. "Adversarial Music: Real world Audio Adversary against Wake-word Detection System". In: *NIPS.* Curran Associates, Inc., 2019, pp. 11908–11918.

[Li+20] C. Li, X. Gao, Y. Li, B. Peng, X. Li, Y. Zhang, and J. Gao. "Optimus: Organizing Sentences via Pre-trained Modeling of a Latent Space". In: *EMNLP.* 2020.

[Li+21] Y. Li, R. Pogodin, D. J. Sutherland, and A. Gretton. "Self-Supervised Learning with Kernel Dependence Maximization". In: *NeurIPS.* 2021.

[Li+22] R. Li, W. Li, Y. Yang, H. Wei, J. Jiang, and Q. Bai. "Swinv2-Imagen: Hierarchical Vision Transformer Diffusion Models for Text-to-Image Generation". In: (Oct. 2022). arXiv: 2210.09549 [cs.CV].

[Lia+] P. Liang, R. Bommasani, T. Lee, D. Tsipras, D. Soylu, M. Yasunaga, Y. Zhang, D. Narayanan, and Y. Wu. "Helm: Holistic Evaluation of Language Models (HELM), a framework to increase the transparency of language models (https://arxiv.org/abs/2211.09110)". en.

[Lia+07] L. Liao, D. J. Patterson, D. Fox, and H. Kautz. "Learning and Inferring Transportation Routines". In: *Artificial Intelligence* 171.5 (2007), pp. 311–331.

[Lia+08] F. Liang, R. Paulo, G. Molina, M. Clyde, and J. Berger. "Mixtures of g-priors for Bayesian Variable Selection". In: *JASA* 103.481 (2008), pp. 410–423.

[Lia+19] V. Liao, R. Ballamy, M. Muller, and H. Candello. "Human-AI Collaboration: Towards Socially-Guided Machine Learning". In: *CHI Workshop on Human-Centered Machine Learning Perspectives.* 2019.

[Lil+16] T. P. Lillicrap, J. J. Hunt, A. Pritzel, N. Heess, T. Erez, Y. Tassa, D. Silver, and D. Wierstra. "Continuous control with deep reinforcement learning". In: *ICLR.* 2016.

[Lin13a] W. Lin. "Agnostic notes on regression adjustments to experimental data: Reexamining Freedman's critique". In: *The Annals of Applied Statistics* 7.1 (2013), pp. 295–318.

[Lin13b] D. A. Linzer. "Dynamic Bayesian Forecasting of Presidential Elections in the States". In: *JASA* 108.501 (2013), pp. 124–134.

[Lin+17a] K. Lin, D. Li, X. He, Z. Zhang, and M.-T. Sun. "Adversarial ranking for language generation". In: *Advances in Neural Information Processing Systems.* 2017, pp. 3155–3165.

[Lin+17b] T.-Y. Lin, P. Dollár, R. Girshick, K. He, B. Hariharan, and S. Belongie. "Feature pyramid networks for object detection". In: *Proceedings of the IEEE conference on computer vision and pattern recognition.* 2017, pp. 2117–2125.

[Lin19]   J. K. Lindelov. *Common statistical tests are linear models (or: how to teach stats)*. Blog post. 2019.

[Lin+20]   H. Lin, H. Chen, T. Zhang, C. Laroche, and K. Choromanski. "Demystifying Orthogonal Monte Carlo and Beyond". In: (2020). arXiv: 2005.13590 [cs.LG].

[Lin+21a]   T. Lin, Y. Wang, X. Liu, and X. Qiu. "A Survey of Transformers". In: (2021). arXiv: 2106.04554 [cs.LG].

[Lin+21b]   A. Lindholm, N. Wahlström, F. Lindsten, and T. B. Schön. *Machine Learning - A First Course for Engineers and Scientists*. 2021.

[Lin+21c]   J. Lindqvist, S. Särkkä, Á. F. García-Fernández, M. Raitoharju, and L. Svensson. "Posterior linearisation smoothing with robust iterations". In: (Dec. 2021). arXiv: 2112.03969 [math.OC].

[Lin+22]   Z. Lin, J. Shi, D. Pathak, and D. Ramanan. "The CLEAR Benchmark: Continual LEArning on Real-World Imagery". In: *NIPS Datasets and Benchmarks Track*. Jan. 2022.

[Lin56]   D. Lindley. "On a measure of the information provided by an experiment". In: *The Annals of Math. Stat.* (1956), 986–1005.

[Lin88a]   B. Lindsay. "Composite Likelihood Methods". In: *Contemporary Mathematics* 80.1 (1988), pp. 221–239.

[Lin88b]   R Linsker. "Self-organization in a perceptual network". In: *Computer* 21.3 (1988), pp. 105–117.

[Lin88c]   R. Linsker. "Self-organization in a perceptual network". In: *Computer* 21.3 (1988), pp. 105–117.

[Lin92]   L.-J. Lin. "Self-Improving Reactive Agents Based on Reinforcement Learning, Planning and Teaching". In: *Mach. Learn.* 8.3-4 (1992), pp. 293–321.

[Lip18]   Z. C. Lipton. "The Mythos of Model Interpretability: In machine learning, the concept of interpretability is both important and slippery." In: *Queue* 16.3 (2018), pp. 31–57.

[LIS20]   Z. Lu, E. Ie, and F. Sha. "Mean-Field Approximation to Gaussian-Softmax Integral with Application to Uncertainty Estimation". In: (June 2020). arXiv: 2006.07584 [cs.LG].

[Liu01]   J. Liu. *Monte Carlo Strategies in Scientific Computation*. Springer, 2001.

[Liu+15]   Z. Liu, P. Luo, X. Wang, and X. Tang. "Deep Learning Face Attributes in the Wild". In: *ICCV*. 2015.

[Liu+18a]   L. Liu, X. Liu, C.-J. Hsieh, and D. Tao. "Stochastic Second-order Methods for Non-convex Optimization with Inexact Hessian and Gradient". In: (2018). arXiv: 1809.09853 [math.OC].

[Liu+18b]   Q. Liu, L. Li, Z. Tang, and D. Zhou. "Breaking the Curse of Horizon: Infinite-horizon Off-policy Estimation". In: *NeurIPS*. Curran Associates Inc., 2018, pp. 5361–5371.

[Liu+19a]   H. Liu, Y.-S. Ong, Z. Yu, J. Cai, and X. Shen. "Scalable Gaussian Process Classification with Additive Noise for Various Likelihoods". In: (2019). arXiv: 1909.06541 [stat.ML].

[Liu+19b]   R. Liu, J. Regier, N. Tripuraneni, M. I. Jordan, and J. McAuliffe. "Rao-Blackwellized Stochastic Gradients for Discrete Distributions". In: *ICML*. 2019.

[Liu+19c]   Y. Liu, M. Ott, N. Goyal, J. Du, M. Joshi, D. Chen, O. Levy, M. Lewis, L. Zettlemoyer, and V. Stoy-

anov. "Roberta: A robustly optimized bert pretraining approach". In: *arXiv preprint arXiv:1907.11692* (2019).

[Liu+20a]   F. Liu, W. Xu, J. Lu, G. Zhang, A. Gretton, and D. J. Sutherland. "Learning Deep Kernels for Non-Parametric Two-Sample Tests". In: *ICML*. 2020.

[Liu+20b]   F. Liu, W. Xu, J. Lu, G. Zhang, A. Gretton, and D. J. Sutherland. "Learning deep kernels for non-parametric two-sample tests". In: *International Conference on Machine Learning*. PMLR. 2020, pp. 6316–6326.

[Liu+20c]   H. Liu, Y.-S. Ong, X. Shen, and J. Cai. "When Gaussian Process Meets Big Data: A Review of Scalable GPs". In: *IEEE Transactions on Neural Networks and Learning Systems* 31.1 (2020).

[Liu+20d]   J. Z. Liu, Z. Lin, S. Padhy, D. Tran, T. Bedrax-Weiss, and B. Lakshminarayanan. "Simple and Principled Uncertainty Estimation with Deterministic Deep Learning via Distance Awareness". In: *NIPS*. 2020.

[Liu+21a]   P. Liu, W. Yuan, J. Fu, Z. Jiang, H. Hayashi, and G. Neubig. "Pre-train, Prompt, and Predict: A Systematic Survey of Prompting Methods in Natural Language Processing". In: (2021). arXiv: 2107.13586 [cs.CL].

[Liu+21b]   W. Liu, X. Wang, J. D. Owens, and Y. Li. "Energy-based Out-of-distribution Detection". In: *NIPS*. 2021.

[Liu+22a]   J. Z. Liu, S. Padhy, J. Ren, Z. Lin, Y. Wen, G. Jerfel, Z. Nado, J. Snoek, D. Tran, and B. Lakshminarayanan. "A Simple Approach to Improve Single-Model Deep Uncertainty via Distance-Awareness". In: *JMLR* 23 (May 2022), pp. 1–62.

[Liu+22b]   Z. Liu, H. Mao, C.-Y. Wu, C. Feichtenhofer, T. Darrell, and S. Xie. "A ConvNet for the 2020s". In: (2022). arXiv: 2201.03545 [cs.CV].

[LJ08]   P. Liang and M. I. Jordan. "An Asymptotic Analysis of Generative, Discriminative, and Pseudo-likelihood Estimators". In: *International Conference on Machine Learning (ICML)*. 2008.

[Lju87]   L. Ljung. *System Identificiation: Theory for the User*. Prentice Hall, 1987.

[LJY19]   S. Liu, Y. Jiang, and T. Yu. "Modelling RNA-Seq data with a zero-inflated mixture Poisson linear model". en. In: *Genet. Epidemiol.* 43.7 (2019), pp. 786–799.

[LK07]   P. Liang and D. Klein. *Structured Bayesian Nonparametric Models with Variational Inference*. ACL Tutorial. 2007.

[LK09]   P. Liang and D. Klein. "Online EM for Unsupervised Models". In: *NAACL*. 2009.

[LKJ09]   D. Lewandowski, D. Kurowicka, and H. Joe. "Generating random correlation matrices based on vines and extended onion method". In: *J. Multivar. Anal.* 100.9 (2009), pp. 1989–2001.

[LL02]   P. Larranaga and J. A. Lozano. *Estimation of Distribution Algorithms: A New Tool for Evolutionary Computation*. Kluwer Academic Publishers, 2002.

[LL17]   S. M. Lundberg and S.-I. Lee. "A unified approach to interpreting model predictions". In: *NIPS*. 2017, pp. 4765–4774.

[LLC20]   M. Locher, K. B. Laskey, and P. C. G. Costa. "Design patterns for modeling first-order expressive Bayesian networks". In: *Knowl. Eng. Rev.* 35 (2020).

[LLJ16]   Q. Liu, J. Lee, and M. Jordan. "A kernelized Stein discrepancy for goodness-of-fit tests". In: *International conference on machine learning*. 2016, pp. 276–284.

[LLN06]   B. Lehmann, D. Lehmann, and N. Nisan. "Combinatorial auctions with decreasing marginal utilities". In: *Games and Economic Behavior* 55.2 (2006), pp. 270–296.

[Llo+14]   J. R. Lloyd, D. Duvenaud, R. Grosse, J. B. Tenenbaum, and Z. Ghahramani. "Automatic Construction and Natural-Language Description of Nonparametric Regression Models". In: *AAAI*. 2014.

[LM03]   T. S. Lee and D. Mumford. "Hierarchical Bayesian inference in the visual cortex." In: *Journal of the Optical Society of America. A, Optics, image science, and vision* 20 7 (2003), pp. 1434–48.

[LM11]   H. Larochelle and I. Murray. "The neural autoregressive distribution estimator". In: *AISTATS*. Vol. 15. 2011, pp. 29–37.

[LM20]   M. L. Leavitt and A. Morcos. "Towards falsifiable interpretability research". In: *arXiv preprint arXiv:2010.12016* (2020).

[LMP01]   J. Lafferty, A. McCallum, and F. Pereira. "Conditional Random Fields: Probabilistic Models for Segmenting and Labeling Sequence Data". In: *ICML*. 2001.

[LMS16]   B. Leimkuhler, C. Matthews, and G. Stoltz. "The computation of averages from equilibrium and nonequilibrium Langevin molecular dynamics". In: *IMA J. Numer. Anal.* 36.1 (2016), pp. 13–79.

[LN01]   S. Lauritzen and D. Nilsson. "Representing and solving decision problems with limited information". In: *Management Science* 47 (2001), pp. 1238–1251.

[LN19]   H. Lin and V. Ng. "Abstractive summarization: A survey of the state of the art". In: *Proceedings of the AAAI Conference on Artificial Intelligence*. Vol. 33. 01. 2019, pp. 9815–9822.

[LN96]   o. Lee and J. A. Nelder. "Hierarchical Generalized Linear Models". In: *J. of Royal Stat. Soc. Series B* 58.4 (1996), pp. 619–678.

[Loc+18]   F. Locatello, S. Bauer, M. Lucic, G. Rätsch, S. Gelly, B. Schölkopf, and O. Bachem. "Challenging Common Assumptions in the Unsupervised Learning of Disentangled Representations". In: (2018). arXiv: 1811.12359 [cs.LG].

[Loc+20a]   F. Locatello, S. Bauer, M. Lucic, G. Raetsch, S. Gelly, B. Schölkopf, and O. Bachem. "A Sober Look at the Unsupervised Learning of Disentangled Representations and their Evaluation". In: *Journal of Machine Learning Research* 21.209 (2020), pp. 1–62.

[Loc+20b]   F. Locatello, B. Poole, G. Rätsch, B. Schölkopf, O. Bachem, and M. Tschannen. "Weakly-supervised disentanglement without compromises". In: *International Conference on Machine Learning*. PMLR. 2020, pp. 6348–6359.

[Lod+02]   H. Lodhi, C. Saunders, J. Shawe-Taylor, N. Cristianini, and C. Watkins. "Text classification using string kernels". en. In: *J. Mach. Learn. Res.* (2002).

[Loe04]   H Loeliger. "An introduction to factor graphs". In: *IEEE Signal Process. Magazine* 21.1 (2004), pp. 28–41.

[Loe+07]   H Loeliger, J Dauwels, J Hu, S Korl, L Ping, and F. R. Kschischang. "The Factor Graph Approach to Model-Based Signal Processing". In: *Proc. IEEE* 95.6 (2007), pp. 1295–1322.

[Loe+16]   H.-A. Loeliger, L. Bruderer, H. Malmberg, F. Wadehn, and N. Zalmai. "On Sparsity by NUV-EM, Gaussian Message Passing, and Kalman Smoothing". In: *ITA Workshop*. 2016.

[Loi+21]   N. Loizou, S. Vaswani, I. Laradji, and S. Lacoste-Julien. "Stochastic Polyak step-size for SGD: An adaptive learning rate for fast convergence". In: *AISTATS*. 2021.

[Lon+18]   M. Long, Z. Cao, J. Wang, and M. I. Jordan. "Conditional adversarial domain adaptation". In: *Neural Information Processing Systems* (2018).

[Lot+22]   S. Lotfi, P. Izmailov, G. Benton, M. Goldblum, and A. G. Wilson. "Bayesian Model Selection, the Marginal Likelihood, and Generalization". In: *ICML*. 2022.

[Lov+20]   T. Lovett, M. Briers, M. Charalambides, R. Jersakova, J. Lomax, and C. Holmes. "Inferring proximity from Bluetooth Low Energy RSSI with Unscented Kalman Smoothers". In: (2020). arXiv: 2007.05057 [eess.SP].

[Lov83]   L. Lovász. "Submodular functions and convexity". In: *Mathematical programming the state of the art*. Springer, 1983, pp. 235–257.

[LÖW21]   T. van de Laar, A. Özçelikkale, and H. Wymeersch. "Application of the Free Energy Principle to Estimation and Control". In: *IEEE Trans. Signal Process.* 69 (2021), pp. 4234–4244.

[LP01]   U. Lerner and R. Parr. "Inference in Hybrid Networks: Theoretical Limits and Practical Algorithms". In: *UAI*. 2001.

[LP03]   M. G. Lagoudakis and R. Parr. "Least-Squares Policy Iteration". In: *JMLR* 4 (2003), pp. 1107–1149.

[LP06]   N. Lartillot and H. Philippe. "Computing Bayes factors using thermodynamic integration". en. In: *Systematic Biology* 55.2 (2006), pp. 195–207.

[LP20]   P. Lemberger and I. Panico. "A Primer on Domain Adaptation". In: (Jan. 2020). arXiv: 2001.09994 [cs.LG].

[LPB17]   B. Lakshminarayanan, A. Pritzel, and C. Blundell. "Simple and Scalable Predictive Uncertainty Estimation using Deep Ensembles". In: *NIPS*. 2017.

[LPO17]   D. Lopez-Paz and M. Oquab. "Revisiting classifier two-sample tests". In: *International Conference on Learning Representations*. 2017.

[LPR17]   D. Lopez-Paz and M. Ranzato. "Gradient Episodic Memory for Continual Learning". In: *NIPS*. 2017.

[LR19]   F. Lattimore and D. Rohde. "Replacing the do-calculus with Bayes rule". In: (2019). arXiv: 1906.07125 [stat.ML].

[LR85]   T. L. Lai and H. Robbins. "Asymptotically efficient adaptive allocation rules". en. In: *Adv. Appl. Math.* (1985).

[LR87]   R. J. Little and D. B. Rubin. *Statistical Analysis with Missing Data*. Wiley and Son, 1987.

[LR95]   C. Liu and D. Rubin. "ML Estimation of the T distribution using EM and its extensions, ECM and ECME". In: *Statistica Sinica* 5 (1995), pp. 19–39.

[LRC19]   Y. Li, B. I. P. Rubinstein, and T. Cohn. "Truth Inference at Scale: A Bayesian Model for Adjudicating Highly Redundant Crowd Annotations". In: *WWW*. 2019.

[LS01]   D. Lee and S. Seung. "Algorithms for non-negative matrix factorization". In: *NIPS*. 2001.

[LS19]   T. Lattimore and C. Szepesvari. *Bandit Algorithms*. Cambridge, 2019.

[LS99]   D. D. Lee and H. S. Seung. "Learning the parts of objects by non-negative matrix factorization". In: *Nature* 401.6755 (1999), pp. 788–791.

[LST15]   B. M. Lake, R. Salakhutdinov, and J. B. Tenenbaum. "Human-level concept learning through probabilistic program induction". In: *Science* 350 (2015), pp. 1332 –1338.

[LST21]   N. Loo, S. Swaroop, and R. E. Turner. "Generalized Variational Continual Learning". In: *ICLR*. 2021.

[LST90]   J. K. Lenstra, D. B. Shmoys, and É. Tardos. "Approximation algorithms for scheduling unrelated parallel machines". In: *Mathematical programming*. 1990.

[LSV09]   J. Lee, M. Sviridenko, and J. Vondrák. "Submodular maximization over multiple matroids via generalized exchange properties". In: *Approximation, Randomization, and Combinatorial Optimization. Algorithms and Techniques* (2009), pp. 244–257.

[LSW15]   Y. T. Lee, A. Sidford, and S. C.-w. Wong. "A faster cutting plane method and its implications for combinatorial and convex optimization". In: *2015 IEEE 56th Annual Symposium on Foundations of Computer Science*. IEEE. 2015, pp. 1049–1065.

[LSZ15]   Y. Li, K. Swersky, and R. Zemel. "Generative Moment Matching Networks". In: *ICML*. 2015.

[LT16]   M.-Y. Liu and O. Tuzel. "Coupled Generative Adversarial Networks". In: *NIPS*. 2016, pp. 469–477.

[LTW15]   Q. Li, C. Tai, and E Weinan. "Stochastic modified equations and adaptive stochastic gradient algorithms". In: *ICML*. 2015.

[Lu+21a] X. Lu, I. Osband, B. Van Roy, and Z. Wen. "Evaluating Probabilistic Inference in Deep Learning: Beyond Marginal Predictions". In: (2021). arXiv: 2107.09224 [cs.LG].

[Lu+21b] X. Lu, B. Van Roy, V. Dwaracherla, M. Ibrahimi, I. Osband, and Z. Wen. "Reinforcement Learning, Bit by Bit". In: (Mar. 2021). arXiv: 2103.04047 [cs.LG].

[Lu+22]   X. Lu, I. Osband, B. Van Roy, and Z. Wen. "From Predictions to Decisions: The Importance of Joint Predictive Distributions". In: (2022). arXiv: 2107.09224 [cs.LG].

[Luc+18] A Lucas, M Iliadis, R Molina, and A. K. Katsaggelos. "Using Deep Neural Networks for Inverse Problems in Imaging: Beyond Analytical Methods". In: *IEEE Signal Process. Mag.* 35.1 (2018), pp. 20–36.

[Luc+19] J. Lucas, G. Tucker, R. Grosse, and M. Norouzi. "Don't blame the ELBO! A linear VAE perspective on posterior collapse". In: *NIPS*. 2019.

[Luh58]   H. P. Luhn. "The automatic creation of literature abstracts". In: *IBM Journal of research and development* 2.2 (1958), pp. 159–165.

[Lun+20] S. M. Lundberg, G. Erion, H. Chen, A. DeGrave, J. M. Prutkin, B. Nair, R. Katz, J. Himmelfarb, N. Bansal, and S.-I. Lee. "From local explanations to global understanding with explainable AI for trees". In: *Nature machine intelligence* 2.1 (2020), pp. 56–67.

[Luo+19] Y. Luo, H. Xu, Y. Li, Y. Tian, T. Darrell, and T. Ma. "Algorithmic Framework for Model-based Deep Reinforcement Learning with Theoretical Guarantees". In: *ICLR*. 2019.

[Lut16]   J Luttinen. "BayesPy: variational Bayesian inference in Python". In: *JMLR* (2016).

[LV06]   F. Liese and I. Vajda. "On divergences and informations in statistics and information theory". In: *IEEE Transactions on Information Theory* 52.10 (2006), pp. 4394–4412.

[LW04]   H. Lopes and M. West. "Bayesian model assessment in factor analysis". In: *Statisica Sinica* 14 (2004), pp. 41–67.

[LW16]   C. Louizos and M. Welling. "Structured and Efficient Variational Deep Learning with Matrix Gaussian Posteriors". In: *ICML*. 2016.

[LW17]   C. Louizos and M. Welling. "Multiplicative Normalizing Flows for Variational Bayesian Neural Networks". In: *Proceedings of the 34th International Conference on Machine Learning*. 2017, pp. 2218–2227.

[LWS18]   Z. C. Lipton, Y.-X. Wang, and A. Smola. "Detecting and Correcting for Label Shift with Black Box Predictors". In: *ICML*. 2018.

[LY17]   J. H. Lim and J. C. Ye. "Geometric gan". In: *arXiv preprint arXiv:1705.02894* (2017).

[Ly+20]   A. Ly et al. "The Bayesian Methodology of Sir Harold Jeffreys as a Practical Alternative to the P Value Hypothesis Test". In: *Computational Brain & Behavior* 3.2 (June 2020), pp. 153–161.

[Lyu11]   S. Lyu. "Unifying non-maximum likelihood learning objectives with minimum KL contraction". In: *Advances in Neural Information Processing Systems*. 2011, pp. 64–72.

[Lyu12]   S. Lyu. "Interpretation and generalization of score matching". In: *arXiv preprint arXiv:1205.2629* (2012).

[Lyu+20] X.-K. Lyu, Y. Xu, X.-F. Zhao, X.-N. Zuo, and C.-P. Hu. "Beyond psychology: prevalence of p value and confidence interval misinterpretation across different fields". In: *Journal of Pacific Rim Psychology* 14 (2020).

[LZ20]   B. Lim and S. Zohren. "Time Series Forecasting With Deep Learning: A Survey". In: (2020). arXiv: 2004.13408 [stat.ML].

[MA10]   I. Murray and R. P. Adams. "Slice sampling covariance hyperparameters of latent Gaussian models". In: *NIPS*. 2010, pp. 1732–1740.

[Maa+16] L. Maaløe, C. K. Sønderby, S. K. Sønderby, and O. Winther. "Auxiliary Deep Generative Models". In: *ICML*. 2016.

[Maa+19] L. Maaløe, M. Fraccaro, V. Liévin, and O. Winther. "BIVA: A Very Deep Hierarchy of Latent Variables for Generative Modeling". In: *NIPS*. 2019.

[Mac03]   D. MacKay. *Information Theory, Inference, and Learning Algorithms*. Cambridge University Press, 2003.

[Mac+11] J. H. Macke, L. Büsing, J. P. Cunningham, B. M. Y. Ece, K. V. Shenoy, and M. Sahani. "Empirical models of spiking in neural populations". In: *NIPS*. 2011.

[Mac+15] D. Maclaurin, D. Duvenaud, M. Johnson, and R. P. Adams. *Autograd: Reverse-mode differentiation of native Python*. 2015.

[Mac+19]   D. Maclaurin, A. Radul, M. J. Johnson, and D. Vytiniotis. "Dex: array programming with typed indices". In: *NeurIPS workshop: Program Transformations for Machine Learning* (2019).

[Mac92a]   D. MacKay. "The evidence framework applied to classification networks". In: *Neural Computation* 4.5 (1992), pp. 720–736.

[Mac92b]   D. J. C. MacKay. "A Practical Bayesian Framework for Backpropagation Networks". In: *Neural Comput.* 4.3 (1992), pp. 448–472.

[Mac95]   D. MacKay. "Probable networks and plausible predictions — a review of practical Bayesian methods for supervised neural networks". In: *Network: Computation in Neural Systems* 6.3 (1995), pp. 469–505.

[Mac98]   D. MacKay. "Introduction to Gaussian Processes". In: *Neural Networks and Machine Learning.* Ed. by C. Bishop. 1998.

[Mac99]   D. MacKay. "Comparision of approximate methods for handling hyperparameters". In: *Neural Computation* 11.5 (1999), pp. 1035–1068.

[Mad+17]   C. J. Maddison, D. Lawson, G. Tucker, N. Heess, M. Norouzi, A. Mnih, A. Doucet, and Y. W. Teh. "Filtering Variational Objectives". In: *NIPS.* 2017.

[Mad+18]   A. Madry, A. Makelov, L. Schmidt, D. Tsipras, and A. Vladu. "Towards Deep Learning Models Resistant to Adversarial Attacks". In: *ICLR.* 2018.

[Mad+19]   W. J. Maddox, P. Izmailov, T. Garipov, D. P. Vetrov, and A. G. Wilson. "A Simple Baseline for Bayesian Uncertainty in Deep Learning". In: *NIPS.* Curran Associates, Inc., 2019, pp. 13153–13164.

[MAD20]   W. R. Morningstar, A. A. Alemi, and J. V. Dillon. "PAC^m-Bayes: Narrowing the Empirical Risk Gap in the Misspecified Bayesian Regime". In: (2020). arXiv: 2010.09629 [cs.LG].

[Mah07]   R. P. S. Mahler. *Statistical Multisource-Multitarget Information Fusion.* Artech House, Inc., 2007.

[Mah13]   R Mahler. "Statistics 102 for Multisource-Multitarget Detection and Tracking". In: *IEEE J. Sel. Top. Signal Process.* 7.3 (2013), pp. 376–389.

[Mah+18]   D. Mahajan, R. Girshick, V. Ramanathan, K. He, M. Paluri, Y. Li, A. Bharambe, and L. van der Maaten. "Exploring the limits of weakly supervised pretraining". In: *Proceedings of the European Conference on Computer Vision (ECCV).* 2018, pp. 181–196.

[Mah+19]   N. Maheswaranathan, A. H. Williams, M. D. Golub, S. Ganguli, and D. Sussillo. "Universality and individuality in neural dynamics across large populations of recurrent networks". In: *Advances in Neural Information Processing Systems* 2019 (2019), p. 15629.

[Mah+23]   K. Mahowald, A. A. Ivanova, I. A. Blank, N. Kanwisher, J. B. Tenenbaum, and E. Fedorenko. "Dissociating language and thought in large language models: a cognitive perspective". In: (Jan. 2023). arXiv: 2301.06627 [cs.CL].

[Mai+10]   J. Mairal, F. Bach, J. Ponce, and G. Sapiro. "Online learning for matrix factorization and sparse coding". In: *JMLR* 11 (2010), pp. 19–60.

[Mai13]   J. Mairal. "Stochastic Majorization-minimization Algorithms for Large-scale Optimization". In: *NIPS.* 2013, pp. 2283–2291.

[Mai15]   J Mairal. "Incremental Majorization-Minimization Optimization with Application to Large-Scale Machine Learning". In: *SIAM J. Optim.* 25.2 (2015), pp. 829–855.

[Mai+22]   Z. Mai, R. Li, J. Jeong, D. Quispe, H. Kim, and S. Sanner. "Online continual learning in image classification: An empirical survey". In: *Neurocomputing* 469 (2022), pp. 28–51.

[Mak+15a]   A. Makhzani, J. Shlens, N. Jaitly, I. Goodfellow, and B. Frey. "Adversarial Autoencoders". In: (2015). arXiv: 1511.05644 [cs.LG].

[Mak+15b]   A. Makhzani, J. Shlens, N. Jaitly, I. Goodfellow, and B. Frey. "Adversarial autoencoders". In: *arXiv preprint arXiv:1511.05644* (2015).

[Mak+20]   A. Makkuva, A. Taghvaei, S. Oh, and J. Lee. "Optimal transport mapping via input convex neural networks". In: *International Conference on Machine Learning.* PMLR. 2020, pp. 6672–6681.

[Mal+17]   D. M. Malioutov, K. R. Varshney, A. Emad, and S. Dash. "Learning interpretable classification rules with boolean compressed sensing". In: *Transparent Data Mining for Big and Small Data.* Springer, 2017, pp. 95–121.

[Man]   B. Mann. *How many times should you shuffle a deck of cards?* Tech. rep. Dartmouth.

[Man+19]   D. J. Mankowitz, N. Levine, R. Jeong, Y. Shi, J. Kay, A. Abdolmaleki, J. T. Springenberg, T. Mann, T. Hester, and M. Riedmiller. "Robust Reinforcement Learning for Continuous Control with Model Misspecification". In: (2019). arXiv: 1906.07516 [cs.LG].

[Man22a]   V. Manokhin. *Awesome Conformal Prediction.* Version v1.0.0. "If you use Awesome Conformal Prediction, please cite it as below.". Apr. 2022.

[Man22b]   V. Manokhin. "Machine Learning for Probabilistic Prediction". PhD thesis. Royal Holloway, University of London, June 2022.

[Man90]   C. F. Manski. "Nonparametric Bounds on Treatment Effects". In: *The American Economic Review* 80.2 (1990), pp. 319–323.

[Mao+17]   X. Mao, Q. Li, H. Xie, R. Y. K. Lau, Z. Wang, and S. P. Smolley. "Least Squares Generative Adversarial Networks". In: *ICCV.* 2017.

[MAP17]   H. Martínez Alonso and B. Plank. "When is multitask learning effective? Semantic sequence prediction under varying data conditions". In: *Proc. European ACL.* Valencia, Spain: Association for Computational Linguistics, Apr. 2017, pp. 44–53.

[Mar03]   B. Marlin. "Modeling User Rating Profiles for Collaborative Filtering". In: *NIPS.* 2003.

[Mar+06]   A. Margolin, I. Nemenman, K. Basso, C. Wiggins, G. Stolovitzky, and R. F. abd A. Califano. "ARACNE: An Algorithm for the Reconstruction of Gene Regulatory Networks in a Mammalian Cellular Context". In: *BMC Bioinformatics* 7 (2006).

[Mar+10]   B. M. Marlin, K. Swersky, B. Chen, and N. de Freitas. "Inductive Principles for Restricted Boltzmann Machine Learning". In: *AISTATS.* 2010.

[Mar10a]   J Martens. "Deep learning via Hessian-free optimization". In: *ICML.* 2010.

[Mar10b]   J. Martens. "Learning the Linear Dynamical System with ASOS". In: *ICML.* ICML'10. Omnipress, 2010, pp. 743–750.

[Mar16]   J. Martens. "Second-order optimization for neural networks". PhD thesis. Toronto, 2016.

[Mar18]   O. Martin. *Bayesian analysis with Python*. Packt, 2018.

[Mar20]   J. Martens. "New insights and perspectives on the natural gradient method". In: *JMLR* (2020).

[Mas+20]   M. Masana, X. Liu, B. Twardowski, M. Menta, A. D. Bagdanov, and J. van de Weijer. "Class-incremental learning: survey and performance evaluation on image classification". In: (2020). arXiv: 2010.15277 [cs.LG].

[Mat14]   C. Mattfeld. "Implementing spectral methods for hidden Markov models with real-valued emissions". MA thesis. ETH Zurich, 2014.

[Mat+16]   A. Matthews, J. Hensman, R. Turner, and Z. Ghahramani. "On Sparse Variational Methods and the Kullback-Leibler Divergence between Stochastic Processes". en. In: *AISTATS*. 2016, pp. 231–239.

[Mav16]   Mavrogonatou, L And Vyshemirsky, "Sequential Importance Sampling for Online Bayesian Change-point Detection". In: *22nd International Conference on Computational Statistics*. 2016.

[May+19]   A. May, J. Zhang, T. Dao, and C. Ré. "On the downstream performance of compressed word embeddings". In: *Advances in neural information processing systems* 32 (2019), p. 11782.

[May79]   P. Maybeck. *Stochastic models, estimation, and control*. Academic Press, 1979.

[Maz+22]   P. Mazzaglia, T. Verbelen, O. Çatal, and B. Dhoedt. "The Free Energy Principle for Perception and Action: A Deep Learning Perspective". en. In: *Entropy* 24.2 (2022).

[MAZA18]   X. B. P. amd Marcin Andrychowicz, W. Zaremba, and P. Abbeel. "Sim-to-Real Transfer of Robotic Control with Dynamics Randomization". In: *ICRA*. 2018, pp. 1–8.

[MB16]   Y. Miao and P. Blunsom. "Language as a Latent Variable: Discrete Generative Models for Sentence Compression". In: *EMNLP*. 2016.

[MB18]   A. Mensch and M. Blondel. "Differentiable Dynamic Programming for Structured Prediction and Attention". In: *ICML*. 2018.

[MB21]   M. Y. Michelis and Q. Becker. "On Linear Interpolation in the Latent Space of Deep Generative Models". In: *ICLR Workshop on Geometrical and Topological Representation Learning*. 2021.

[MB88]   T. Mitchell and J. Beauchamp. "Bayesian Variable Selection in Linear Regression". In: *JASA* 83 (1988), pp. 1023–1036.

[MBJ20]   T. M. Moerland, J. Broekens, and C. M. Jonker. "Model-based Reinforcement Learning: A Survey". In: (2020). arXiv: 2006.16712 [cs.LG].

[MBL20]   B. Mirzasoleiman, J. Bilmes, and J. Leskovec. "Coresets for data-efficient training of machine learning models". In: *International Conference on Machine Learning*. PMLR. 2020, pp. 6950–6960.

[MBW20]   W. J. Maddox, G. Benton, and A. G. Wilson. "Rethinking Parameter Counting in Deep Models: Effective Dimensionality Revisited". In: *arXiv preprint arXiv:2003.02139* (2020).

[MC03]   P. Moscato and C. Cotta. "A Gentle Introduction to Memetic Algorithms". en. In: *Handbook of Metaheuristics*. International Series in Operations Research & Management Science. Springer, Boston, MA, 2003, pp. 105–144.

[MC19]   P. Moreno Comellas. "Vision as inverse graphics for detailed scene understanding". en. PhD thesis. 2019.

[McA99]   D. A. McAllester. "PAC-Bayesian model averaging". In: *Proceedings of the twelfth annual conference on computational learning theory*. 1999.

[McE20]   R. McElreath. *Statistical Rethinking: A Bayesian Course with Examples in R and Stan (2nd edition)*. en. Chapman and Hall/CRC, 2020.

[McG54]   W. McGill. "Multivariate information transmission". In: *Psychometrika* 19 (1954), pp. 97–116.

[McM+13]   H. B. McMahan, G. Holt, D Sculley, M. Young, D. Ebner, J. Grady, L. Nie, T. Phillips, E. Davydov, D. Golovin, et al. "Ad click prediction: a view from the trenches". In: *KDD*. 2013, pp. 1222–1230.

[Md+19]   C. de Masson d'Autume, M. Rosca, J. Rae, and S. Mohamed. "Training language GANs from Scratch". In: (2019). arXiv: 1905.09922 [cs.CL].

[MD97]   X. L. Meng and D. van Dyk. "The EM algorithm — an old folk song sung to a fast new tune (with Discussion)". In: *J. Royal Stat. Soc. B* 59 (1997), pp. 511–567.

[MDA15]   D. Maclaurin, D. Duvenaud, and R. P. Adams. "Gradient-based Hyperparameter Optimization through Reversible Learning". In: *ICML*. 2015.

[MDM19]   S. Mahloujifar, D. I. Diochnos, and M. Mahmoody. "The curse of concentration in robust learning: Evasion and poisoning attacks from concentration of measure". In: *Proceedings of the AAAI Conference on Artificial Intelligence*. Vol. 33. 2019, pp. 4536–4543.

[MDR94]   S. Muggleton and L. De Raedt. "Inductive logic programming: Theory and methods". In: *The Journal of Logic Programming* 19 (1994), pp. 629–679.

[Med+21]   M. A. Medina, J. L. M. Olea, C. Rush, and A. Velez. "On the Robustness to Misspecification of α-Posteriors and Their Variational Approximations". In: (2021). arXiv: 2104.08324 [stat.ML].

[Mee+18]   J.-W. van de Meent, B. Paige, H. Yang, and F. Wood. *An introduction to probabilistic programming*. Foundations and Trends in Machine Learning, 2018.

[Mei18a]   N. Meinshausen. "Causality from a distributional robustness point of view". In: *IEEE Data Science Workshop (DSW)*. 2018, pp. 6–10.

[Mei18b]   N. Meinshausen. "CAUSALITY FROM A DISTRIBUTIONAL ROBUSTNESS POINT OF VIEW". In: *2018 IEEE Data Science Workshop (DSW)*. 2018, pp. 6–10.

[Men+21]   A. K. Menon, S. Jayasumana, A. S. Rawat, H. Jain, A. Veit, and S. Kumar. "Long-tail learning via logit adjustment". In: *ICLR*. 2021.

[Mer]   *Definition of interpret*. 2022. URL: https://www.merriam-webster.com/dictionary/interpret.

[Mer+00]   R. van der Merwe, A. Doucet, N. de Freitas, and E. Wan. "The Unscented Particle Filter". In: *NIPS-13*. 2000.

[Met16]   C. Metz. *In Two Moves, AlphaGo and Lee Sedol Redefined the Future*. 2016. URL: https://www.wired.com/2016/03/two-moves-alphago-lee-sedol-redefined-future/ (visited on 01/07/2022).

[Met+16] L. Metz, B. Poole, D. Pfau, and J. Sohl-Dickstein. "Unrolled Generative Adversarial Networks". In: (2016).

[Met+17] L. Metz, J. Ibarz, N. Jaitly, and J. Davidson. "Discrete Sequential Prediction of Continuous Actions for Deep RL". In: (2017). arXiv: 1705.05035 [cs.LG].

[Met+53] N. Metropolis, A. Rosenbluth, M. Rosenbluth, A. Teller, and E. Teller. "Equation of state calculations by fast computing machines". In: *J. of Chemical Physics* 21 (1953), pp. 1087–1092.

[Mey+18] F. Meyer, T. Kropfreiter, J. Williams, R. Lau, F. Hlawatsch, P. Braca, and M. Win. "Message passing algorithms for scalable multitarget tracking". In: *Proc. IEEE* 106.2 (2018).

[Mey+21] R. A. Meyer, C. Musco, C. Musco, and D. P. Woodruff. "Hutch++: Optimal Stochastic Trace Estimation". In: *SIAM Symposium on Simplicity in Algorithms (SOSA21)*. 2021.

[Mey22] S. Meyn. *Control Systems and Reinforcement Learning*. Cambridge, 2022.

[MFP00] A. McCallum, D. Freitag, and F. Pereira. "Maximum Entropy Markov Models for Information Extraction and Segmentation". In: *ICML*. 2000.

[MFR20] G. M. Martin, D. T. Frazier, and C. P. Robert. "Computing Bayes: Bayesian Computation from 1763 to the 21st Century". In: (2020). arXiv: 2004.06425 [stat.CO].

[MG05] I. Murray and Z. Ghahramani. *A note on the evidence and Bayesian Occam's razor*. Tech. rep. Gatsby, 2005.

[MG15] J. Martens and R. Grosse. "Optimizing Neural Networks with Kronecker-factored Approximate Curvature". In: *ICML*. 2015.

[MG18] A. Malinin and M. Gales. "Predictive Uncertainty Estimation via Prior Networks". In: (2018). arXiv: 1802.10501 [stat.ML].

[MGM06] I. Murray, Z. Ghahramani, and D. J. C. MacKay. "MCMC for doubly-intractable distributions". In: *Proceedings of the 22nd Annual Conference on Uncertainty in Artificial Intelligence (UAI-06)*. AUAI Press, 2006, pp. 359–366.

[MGN18a] L. Mescheder, A. Geiger, and S. Nowozin. "Which Training Methods for GANs do actually Converge?" In: *ICML*. 2018.

[MGN18b] L. Mescheder, A. Geiger, and S. Nowozin. "Which training methods for GANs do actually converge?" In: *International conference on machine learning*. PMLR. 2018, pp. 3481–3490.

[MGR18] H. Mania, A. Guy, and B. Recht. "Simple random search of static linear policies is competitive for reinforcement learning". In: *NIPS*. Ed. by S Bengio, H Wallach, H Larochelle, K Grauman, N Cesa-Bianchi, and R Garnett. Curran Associates, Inc., 2018, pp. 1800–1809.

[MH12] R. Mazumder and T. Hastie. *The Graphical Lasso: New Insights and Alternatives*. Tech. rep. Stanford Dept. Statistics, 2012.

[MH20] I. Mordatch and J. Hamrick. *ICML tutorial on model-based methods in reinforcement learning*. https://sites.google.com/corp/view/mbrl-tutorial. 2020.

[MHB17] S. Mandt, M. D. Hoffman, and D. M. Blei. "Stochastic Gradient Descent As Approximate Bayesian Inference". In: *JMLR* 18.1 (2017), pp. 4873–4907.

[MHH14] F. Meyer, O. Hlinka, and F. Hlawatsch. "Sigma point belief propagation". In: *IEEE Signal Processing Letters* 21.2 (2014), pp. 145–149.

[MHN13] A. L. Maas, A. Y. Hannun, and A. Y. Ng. "Rectifier Nonlinearities Improve Neural Network Acoustic Models". In: *ICML*. Vol. 28. 2013.

[Mik+13] T. Mikolov, I. Sutskever, K. Chen, G. S. Corrado, and J. Dean. "Distributed representations of words and phrases and their compositionality". In: *NIPS*. 2013, pp. 3111–3119.

[Mil+05] B. Milch, B. Marthi, S. Russell, D. Sontag, D. Ong, and A. Kolobov. "BLOG: Probabilistic Models with Unknown Objects". In: *IJCAI*. 2005.

[Mil19] T. Miller. "Explanation in artificial intelligence: Insights from the social sciences". In: *Artificial intelligence* 267 (2019), pp. 1–38.

[Mil+20] B. Millidge, A. Tschantz, A. K. Seth, and C. L. Buckley. "On the Relationship Between Active Inference and Control as Inference". In: *International Workshop on Active Inference*. 2020.

[Mil+21] J. P. Miller, R. Taori, A. Raghunathan, S. Sagawa, P. W. Koh, V. Shankar, P. Liang, Y. Carmon, and L. Schmidt. "Accuracy on the Line: on the Strong Correlation Between Out-of-Distribution and In-Distribution Generalization". In: *ICML*. Ed. by M. Meila and T. Zhang. Vol. 139. Proceedings of Machine Learning Research. PMLR, 2021, pp. 7721–7735.

[Min00a] T. Minka. *Bayesian linear regression*. Tech. rep. MIT, 2000.

[Min00b] T. Minka. *Bayesian model averaging is not model combination*. Tech. rep. MIT Media Lab, 2000.

[Min00c] T. Minka. *Estimating a Dirichlet distribution*. Tech. rep. MIT, 2000.

[Min01a] T. Minka. "A family of algorithms for approximate Bayesian inference". PhD thesis. MIT, 2001.

[Min01b] T. Minka. "Expectation Propagation for approximate Bayesian inference". In: *UAI*. 2001.

[Min04] T. Minka. *Power EP*. Tech. rep. MSR-TR-2004-149. 2004.

[Min05] T. Minka. *Divergence measures and message passing*. Tech. rep. MSR Cambridge, 2005.

[Min+18] T. Minka, J. Winn, J. Guiver, Y. Zaykov, D. Fabian, and J. Bronskill. *Infer.NET 0.3*. Microsoft Research Cambridge. 2018.

[Min78] M. Minoux. "Accelerated greedy algorithms for maximizing submodular set functions". In: *Optimization Techniques*. Ed. by J. Stoer. Vol. 7. Lecture Notes in Control and Information Sciences. 10.1007/BFb0006528. Springer Berlin / Heidelberg, 1978, pp. 234–243.

[Min99] T. Minka. *Pathologies of Orthodox Statisics*. Tech. rep. MIT Media Lab, 1999.

[Mis+16] I. Misra, A. Shrivastava, A. Gupta, and M. Hebert. "Cross-stitch Networks for Multi-task Learning". In: *CVPR*. 2016.

[Mis+18] A. Mishkin, F. Kunstner, D. Nielsen, M. Schmidt, and M. E. Khan. "SLANG: Fast Structured Covariance Approximations for Bayesian Deep Learning with Natural Gradient". In: *NIPS*. Curran Associates, Inc., 2018, pp. 6245–6255.

[Mit+19] M. Mitchell, S. Wu, A. Zaldivar, P. Barnes, L. Vasserman, B. Hutchinson, E. Spitzer, I. D. Raji, and T. Gebru. "Model cards for model reporting". In: *Proceedings of the conference on fairness, accountability, and transparency*. 2019, pp. 220–229.

[Mit+20] J. Mitrovic, B. McWilliams, J. Walker, L. Buesing, and C. Blundell. *Representation Learning via Invariant Causal Mechanisms*. 2020. arXiv: 2010.07922 [cs.LG].

[Mit97] T. Mitchell. *Machine Learning*. McGraw Hill, 1997.

[Miy+18a] T. Miyato, T. Kataoka, M. Koyama, and Y. Yoshida. "Spectral Normalization for Generative Adversarial Networks". In: *ICLR*. 2018.

[Miy+18b] T. Miyato, T. Kataoka, M. Koyama, and Y. Yoshida. "Spectral Normalization for Generative Adversarial Networks". In: *ICLR*. 2018.

[Miy+18c] T. Miyato, T. Kataoka, M. Koyama, and Y. Yoshida. "Spectral Normalization for Generative Adversarial Networks". In: *International Conference on Learning Representations*. 2018.

[MJ97] M. Meila and M. Jordan. *Triangulation by continuous embedding*. Tech. rep. 1605. MIT AI Lab, 1997.

[MK05] J. Mooij and H. Kappen. "Sufficient conditions for convergence of loopy belief propagation". In: *UAI*. 2005.

[MK07] G. J. McLachlan and T. Krishnan. *The EM Algorithm and Extensions (Second Edition)*. Wiley, 2007.

[MK18] T. Miyato and M. Koyama. "cGANs with Projection Discriminator". In: *International Conference on Learning Representations*. 2018.

[MK19] J. Menick and N. Kalchbrenner. "Generating high fidelity images with subscale pixel networks and multidimensional upscaling". In: *ICLR*. 2019.

[MK97] G. J. McLachlan and T. Krishnan. *The EM Algorithm and Extensions*. Wiley, 1997.

[MKH19] R. Müller, S. Kornblith, and G. E. Hinton. "When does label smoothing help?" In: *NIPS*. 2019, pp. 4694–4703.

[MKL11] O. Martin, R. Kumar, and J. Lao. *Bayesian Modeling and Computation in Python*. CRC Press, 2011.

[MKL21] O. A. Martin, R. Kumar, and J. Lao. *Bayesian Modeling and Computation in Python*. CRC Press, 2021.

[MKS21] K. Murphy, A. Kumar, and S. Serghiou. "Risk score learning for COVID-19 contact tracing apps". In: *Machine Learning for Healthcare*. 2021.

[ML02] T. Minka and J. Lafferty. "Expectation-propagation for the Generative Aspect Model". In: *UAI*. Morgan Kaufmann Publishers Inc., 2002, pp. 352–359.

[ML16] S. Mohamed and B. Lakshminarayanan. "Learning in Implicit Generative Models". In: (2016). arXiv: 1610.03483 [stat.ML].

[MLN19] P. Michel, O. Levy, and G. Neubig. "Are Sixteen Heads Really Better than One?" In: *NIPS*. 2019.

[MLW19] V. Masrani, T. A. Le, and F. Wood. "The Thermodynamic Variational Objective". In: *NIPS*. Curran Associates, Inc., 2019, pp. 11521–11530.

[MM01] T. K. Marks and J. R. Movellan. *Diffusion networks, products of experts, and factor analysis*. Tech. rep. University of California San Diego, 2001.

[MM90] D. Q. Mayne and H Michalska. "Receding horizon control of nonlinear systems". In: *IEEE Trans. Automat. Contr.* 35.7 (1990), pp. 814–824.

[MMC98] R. J. McEliece, D. J. C. MacKay, and J. F. Cheng. "Turbo decoding as an instance of Pearl's 'belief propagation' algorithm". In: *IEEE J. on Selected Areas in Comm.* 16.2 (1998), pp. 140–152.

[MMP87] J. Marroquin, S. Mitter, and T. Poggio. "Probabilistic solution of ill-posed problems in computational vision". In: *JASA* 82.297 (1987), pp. 76–89.

[MMT17] C. J. Maddison, A. Mnih, and Y. W. Teh. "The Concrete Distribution: A Continuous Relaxation of Discrete Random Variables". In: *ICLR*. 2017.

[MN89] P. McCullagh and J. Nelder. *Generalized linear models*. 2nd edition. Chapman and Hall, 1989.

[MNG17a] L. Mescheder, S. Nowozin, and A. Geiger. "Adversarial variational bayes: Unifying variational autoencoders and generative adversarial networks". In: *International Conference on Machine Learning*. PMLR. 2017, pp. 2391–2400.

[MNG17b] L. Mescheder, S. Nowozin, and A. Geiger. "The numerics of gans". In: *Advances in Neural Information Processing Systems*. 2017, pp. 1825–1835.

[Mni+15] V. Mnih et al. "Human-level control through deep reinforcement learning". In: *Nature* 518.7540 (2015), pp. 529–533.

[Mni+16] V. Mnih, A. P. Badia, M. Mirza, A. Graves, T. P. Lillicrap, T. Harley, D. Silver, and K. Kavukcuoglu. "Asynchronous Methods for Deep Reinforcement Learning". In: *ICML*. 2016.

[MO14] M. Mirza and S. Osindero. "Conditional generative adversarial nets". In: *arXiv preprint arXiv:1411.1784* (2014).

[Moc+96] J. Mockus, W. Eddy, A. Mockus, L. Mockus, and G. Reklaitis. *Bayesian Heuristic Approach to Discrete and Global Optimization: Algorithms, Visualization, Software, and Applications*. Kluwer, 1996.

[Moh+20] S. Mohamed, M. Rosca, M. Figurnov, and A. Mnih. "Monte Carlo Gradient Estimation in Machine Learning". In: *JMLR* 21.132 (2020), pp. 1–62.

[Mon81] G. Monge. "Mémoire sur la théorie des déblais et des remblais". In: *Histoire de l'Académie Royale des Sciences* (1781), pp. 666–704.

[Mor+11] F. Morcos, A. Pagnani, B. Lunt, A. Bertolino, D. S. Marks, C. Sander, R. Zecchina, J. N. Onuchic, T. Hwa, and M. Weigt. "Direct-coupling analysis of residue coevolution captures native contacts across many protein families". en. In: *Proc. Natl. Acad. Sci. U. S. A.* 108.49 (2011), E1293–301.

[Mor+16] R. D. Morey, R. Hoekstra, J. N. Rouder, M. D. Lee, and E.-J. Wagenmakers. "The fallacy of placing confidence in confidence intervals". en. In: *Psychon. Bull. Rev.* 23.1 (2016), pp. 103–123.

[Mor+21a] W. Morningstar, C. Ham, A. Gallagher, B. Lakshminarayanan, A. Alemi, and J. Dillon. "Density of States Estimation for Out of Distribution Detection". In: *AISTATS*. Ed. by A. Banerjee and K. Fukumizu. Vol. 130. Proceedings of Machine Learning Research. PMLR, 2021, pp. 3232–3240.

[Mor+21b] W. Morningstar, S. Vikram, C. Ham, A. Gallagher, and J. Dillon. "Automatic Differentiation Variational Inference with Mixtures". In: *AISTATS*. Ed. by A. Banerjee and K. Fukumizu. Vol. 130. Proceedings of Machine Learning Research. PMLR, 2021, pp. 3250–3258.

[Mor63]   T. Morimoto. "Markov Processes and the H-Theorem". In: *J. Phys. Soc. Jpn.* 18.3 (1963), pp. 328–331.

[MOT15]   A. Mordvintsev, C. Olah, and M. Tyka. *Inceptionism: Going Deeper into Neural Networks.* https://ai.googleblog.com/2015/06/inceptionism-going-deeper-into-neural.html. Accessed: NA-NA-NA. 2015.

[Mov08]   J. R. Movellan. "A minimum velocity approach to learning". In: *unpublished draft, Jan* (2008).

[MP01]   K. Murphy and M. Paskin. "Linear time inference in hierarchical HMMs". In: *NIPS.* 2001.

[MP21]   D. Mazza and M. Pagani. "Automatic Differentiation in PCF". In: *Proc. ACM Program. Lang.* 5.POPL (2021).

[MP95]   D. MacKay and L. Peto. "A hierarchical dirichlet language model". In: *Natural Language Engineering* 1.3 (1995), pp. 289–307.

[MPS18]   O. Mangoubi, N. S. Pillai, and A. Smith. "Does Hamiltonian Monte Carlo mix faster than a random walk on multimodal densities?" In: (2018). arXiv: 1808.03230 [math.PR].

[MPT13]   K. Mohan, J. Pearl, and J. Tian. "Graphical models for inference with missing data". In: *NIPS.* 2013.

[MR09]   A. Melkumyan and F. Ramos. "A Sparse Covariance Function for Exact Gaussian Process Inference in Large Datasets". In: *IJCAI.* 2009, pp. 1936–1942.

[MR10]   B. Milch and S. Russell. "Extending Bayesian Networks to the Open-Universe Case". In: *Heuristics, Probability and Causality. A Tribute to Judea Pearl.* Ed. by R. Dechter, H. Geffner, and J. Y. Halper. College Publications, 2010.

[MRB18]   A. S. Morcos, M. Raghu, and S. Bengio. "Insights on representational similarity in neural networks with canonical correlation". In: *Advances in neural information processing systems* (2018).

[MRW19]   B. Mittelstadt, C. Russell, and S. Wachter. "Explaining explanations in AI". In: *Proceedings of the conference on fairness, accountability, and transparency.* 2019, pp. 279–288.

[MS67]   J McNamee and F Stenger. "Construction of fully symmetric numerical integration formulas of fully symmetric numerical integration formulas". In: *Numer. Math.* 10.4 (Nov. 1967), pp. 327–344.

[MS96]   V Matveev V and R Shrock. "Complex-temperature singularities in Potts models on the square lattice". en. In: *Phys. Rev. E Stat. Phys. Plasmas Fluids Relat. Interdiscip. Topics* 54.6 (1996), pp. 6174–6185.

[MS99]   C. Manning and H. Schuetze. *Foundations of statistical natural language processing.* MIT Press, 1999.

[MSA18]   S. Makridakis, E. Spiliotis, and V. Assimakopoulos. "The M4 Competition: Results, findings, conclusion and way forward". In: *Int. J. Forecast.* 34.4 (2018), pp. 802–808.

[MT12]   A. Mnih and Y. W. Teh. "A fast and simple algorithm for training neural probabilistic language models". In: *ICML.* 2012, pp. 419–426.

[MTM14]   C. J. Maddison, D. Tarlow, and T. Minka. "A* Sampling". In: *NIPS.* 2014.

[MTS22]   Y. Ma, D. Tsao, and H.-Y. Shum. "On the Principles of Parsimony and Self-Consistency for the Emergence of Intelligence". In: (July 2022). arXiv: 2207.04630 [cs.AI].

[Mua+17]   K. Muandet, K. Fukumizu, B. Sriperumbudur, and B. Schölkopf. "Kernel Mean Embedding of Distributions: A Review and Beyond". In: *Foundations and Trends* 10.1-2 (2017), pp. 1–141.

[Mua+20]   K. Muandet, A. Mehrjou, S. K. Lee, and A. Raj. *Dual Instrumental Variable Regression.* 2020.

[Muk+18]   S. Mukherjee, D. Shankar, A. Ghosh, N. Tathawadekar, P. Kompalli, S. Sarawagi, and K. Chaudhury. "ARMDN: Associative and Recurrent Mixture Density Networks for eRetail Demand Forecasting". In: (2018). arXiv: 1803.03800 [cs.LG].

[Mül+19a]   T. Müller, B. McWilliams, F. Rousselle, M. Gross, and J. Novák. "Neural Importance Sampling". In: *SIGGRAPH.* 2019.

[Mül+19b]   T. Müller, B. McWilliams, F. Rousselle, M. Gross, and J. Novák. "Neural importance sampling". In: *ACM Transactions on Graphics* 38.5 (2019), p. 145.

[Mun14]   R. Munos. "From Bandits to Monte-Carlo Tree Search: The Optimistic Principle Applied to Optimization and Planning". In: *Foundations and Trends in Machine Learning* 7.1 (2014), pp. 1–129.

[Mun+16]   R. Munos, T. Stepleton, A. Harutyunyan, and M. G. Bellemare. "Safe and Efficient Off-Policy Reinforcement Learning". In: *NIPS.* 2016, pp. 1046–1054.

[Mun57]   J. Munkres. "Algorithms for the assignment and transportation problems". In: *Journal of the society for industrial and applied mathematics* 5.1 (1957), pp. 32–38.

[Mur00]   K. Murphy. "Bayesian Map Learning in Dynamic Environments". In: *NIPS.* Vol. 12. 2000.

[Mur02]   K. Murphy. "Dynamic Bayesian Networks: Representation, Inference and Learning". PhD thesis. Dept. Computer Science, UC Berkeley, 2002.

[Mur+19]   W. J. Murdoch, C. Singh, K. Kumbier, R. Abbasi-Asl, and B. Yu. "Definitions, methods, and applications in interpretable machine learning". In: *Proceedings of the National Academy of Sciences* 116.44 (2019), pp. 22071–22080.

[Mur22]   K. P. Murphy. *Probabilistic Machine Learning: An introduction.* MIT Press, 2022.

[MW15]   S. Morgan and C. Winship. *Counterfactuals and Causal Inference.* 2nd. Cambridge University Press, 2015.

[MWJ99]   K. Murphy, Y. Weiss, and M. Jordan. "Loopy Belief Propagation for Approximate Inference: an Empirical Study". In: *UAI.* 1999.

[MYM18]   J. Marino, Y. Yue, and S. Mandt. "Iterative Amortized Inference". In: *ICML.* 2018.

[Nac+17]   O. Nachum, M. Norouzi, K. Xu, and D. Schuurmans. "Bridging the Gap Between Value and Policy Based Reinforcement Learning". In: *NIPS.* 2017, pp. 2772–2782.

[Nac+19a]   O. Nachum, Y. Chow, B. Dai, and L. Li. "DualDICE: Behavior-agnostic Estimation of Discounted Stationary Distribution Corrections". In: *NeurIPS.* 2019, pp. 2315–2325.

[Nac+19b]   O. Nachum, B. Dai, I. Kostrikov, Y. Chow, L. Li, and D. Schuurmans. *Algae: Policy Gradient from Arbitrary Experience.* CoRR abs/1912.02074. 2019.

[Nad+19] S. Naderi, K. He, R. Aghajani, S. Sclaroff, and P. Felzenszwalb. "Generalized Majorization-Minimization". In: *ICML*. 2019.

[Nae+18] C. A. Naesseth, S. W. Linderman, R. Ranganath, and D. M. Blei. "Variational Sequential Monte Carlo". In: *AISTATS*. 2018.

[Nal18] E. T. Nalisnick. "On Priors for Bayesian Neural Networks". PhD thesis. UC Irvine, 2018.

[Nal+19a] E. Nalisnick, A. Matsukawa, Y. W. Teh, D. Gorur, and B. Lakshminarayanan. "Do Deep Generative Models Know What They Don't Know?" In: *ICLR*. 2019.

[Nal+19b] E. Nalisnick, A. Matsukawa, Y. W. Teh, D. Gorur, and B. Lakshminarayanan. "Hybrid Models with Deep and Invertible Features". In: *ICML*. 2019, pp. 4723–4732.

[Nau04] J. Naudts. "Estimators, escort probabilities and ϕ-exponential families in statistical physics". In: *J. of Inequalities in Pure and Applied Mathematics* 5.4 (2004).

[NB05] M. Narasimhan and J. Bilmes. "A Submodular-Supermodular Procedure with Applications to Discriminative Structure Learning". In: *Uncertainty in Artificial Intelligence: Proceedings of the Twentieth Conference (UAI-2004)*. Edinburgh, Scotland: Morgan Kaufmann Publishers, 2005.

[NB06] M. Narasimhan and J. Bilmes. *Learning Graphical Models over partial k-trees*. Tech. rep. UWEETR-2006-0001. https://vannevar.ece.uw.edu/techsite/papers/refer/UWEETR-2006-0001.html. University of Washington, Department of Electrical Engineering, 2006.

[NBS18] B. Neyshabur, S. Bhojanapalli, and N. Srebro. "A PAC-Bayesian Approach to Spectrally-Normalized Margin Bounds for Neural Networks". In: *ICLR*. 2018.

[NCH15] M. Naeini, G. Cooper, and M. Hauskrecht. "Obtaining well calibrated probabilities using Bayesian binning". In: *AAAI*. 2015.

[NCL20] T. Nguyen, Z. Chen, and J. Lee. "Dataset Meta-Learning from Kernel Ridge-Regression". In: *International Conference on Learning Representations*. 2020.

[NCT16a] S. Nowozin, B. Cseke, and R. Tomioka. "f-GAN: Training Generative Neural Samplers using Variational Divergence Minimization". In: *NIPS*. Ed. by D. D. Lee, M Sugiyama, U. V. Luxburg, I Guyon, and R Garnett. Curran Associates, Inc., 2016, pp. 271–279.

[NCT16b] S. Nowozin, B. Cseke, and R. Tomioka. "f-gan: Training generative neural samplers using variational divergence minimization". In: *NIPS*. 2016, pp. 271–279.

[NCT16c] S. Nowozin, B. Cseke, and R. Tomioka. "f-gan: Training generative neural samplers using variational divergence minimization". In: *Advances in neural information processing systems*. 2016, pp. 271–279.

[ND20] O. Nachum and B. Dai. "Reinforcement Learning via Fenchel-Rockafellar Duality". In: (2020). arXiv: 2001.01866 [cs.LG].

[ND21] A. Nichol and P. Dhariwal. "Improved denoising diffusion probabilistic models". In: *ICML*. 2021.

[NDL20] A. Nishimura, D. Dunson, and J. Lu. "Discontinuous Hamiltonian Monte Carlo for discrete parameters and discontinuous likelihoods". In: *Biometrika* (2020).

[Nea01] R. M. Neal. "Annealed Importance Sampling". In: *Statistics and Computing* 11 (2001), pp. 125–139.

[Nea03] R. Neal. "Slice sampling". In: *Annals of Statistics* 31.3 (2003), pp. 7–5–767.

[Nea+08] R. Neal et al. "Computing likelihood functions for high-energy physics experiments when distributions are defined by simulators with nuisance parameters". In: (2008).

[Nea10] R. Neal. "MCMC using Hamiltonian Dynamics". In: *Handbook of Markov Chain Monte Carlo*. Ed. by S. Brooks, A. Gelman, G. Jones, and X.-L. Meng. Chapman & Hall, 2010.

[Nea12] R. C. Neath. "On Convergence Properties of the Monte Carlo EM Algorithm". In: *arXiv [math.ST]* (2012).

[Nea20] B. Neal. *Introduction to Causal Inference from a Machine Learning Perspective*. 2020.

[Nea92] R. Neal. "Connectionist learning of belief networks". In: *Artificial Intelligence* 56 (1992), pp. 71–113.

[Nea93] R. M. Neal. *Probabilistic Inference using Markov Chain Monte Carlo Methods*. Tech. rep. CRG-TR-93-1. 144pp. Dept. of Computer Science, University of Toronto, 1993.

[Nea96] R. Neal. *Bayesian learning for neural networks*. Springer, 1996.

[Nef+02] A. Nefian, L. Liang, X. Pi, X. Liu, and K. Murphy. "Dynamic Bayesian Networks for Audio-Visual Speech Recognition". In: *J. Applied Signal Processing* (2002).

[Neg+21] J. Negrea, J. Yang, H. Feng, D. M. Roy, and J. H. Huggins. "Statistical inference with stochastic gradient algorithms". 2021.

[Nei+18] D. Neil, J. Briody, A. Lacoste, A. Sim, P. Creed, and A. Saffari. "Interpretable graph convolutional neural networks for inference on noisy knowledge graphs". In: *arXiv preprint arXiv:1812.00279* (2018).

[Nel21] Nelson Elhage and Neel Nanda and Catherine Olsson and Tom Henighan and Nicholas Joseph and Ben Mann and Amanda Askell and Yuntao Bai and Anna Chen and Tom Conerly and Nova DasSarma and Dawn Drain and Deep Ganguli and Zac Hatfield-Dodds and Danny Hernandez and Andy Jones and Jackson Kernion and Liane Lovitt and Kamal Ndousse and Dario Amodei and Tom Brown and Jack Clark and Jared Kaplan and Sam McCandlish and Chris Olah. *A Mathematical Framework for Transformer Circuits*. Tech. rep. Anthropic, 2021.

[Neu11] G. Neumann. "Variational Inference for Policy Search in Changing Situations". In: *ICML*. 2011, pp. 817–824.

[Ney+17] B. Neyshabur, S. Bhojanapalli, D. McAllester, and N. Srebro. "Exploring generalization in deep learning". In: *NIPS*. 2017.

[NF16] M. Noroozi and P. Favaro. "Unsupervised learning of visual representations by solving jigsaw puzzles". In: *European conference on computer vision*. Springer. 2016, pp. 69–84.

[NG01] D. Nilsson and J. Goldberger. "Sequentially finding the N-Best List in Hidden Markov Models". In: *IJCAI*. 2001, pp. 1280–1285.

[Ng+11] A. Ng et al. "Sparse autoencoder". In: *CS294A Lecture notes* 72.2011 (2011), pp. 1–19.

[Ngi+11] J. Ngiam, Z. Chen, P. W. Koh, and A. Y. Ng. "Learning deep energy models". In: *Proceedings of the 28th international conference on machine learning (ICML-11)*. 2011, pp. 1105–1112.

[Ngi+18] J. Ngiam, D. Peng, V. Vasudevan, S. Kornblith, Q. V. Le, and R. Pang. "Domain adaptive transfer learning with specialist models". In: *arXiv preprint arXiv:1811.07056* (2018).

[Ngu+16] A. Nguyen, A. Dosovitskiy, J. Yosinski, T. Brox, and J. Clune. *Synthesizing the preferred inputs for neurons in neural networks via deep generator networks.* 2016. arXiv: 1605.09304 [cs.NE].

[Ngu+18] C. V. Nguyen, Y. Li, T. D. Bui, and R. E. Turner. "Variational Continual Learning". In: *ICLR*. 2018.

[Ngu+19] T. T. Nguyen, Q. V. H. Nguyen, D. T. Nguyen, D. T. Nguyen, Thien Huynh-The, S. Nahavandi, T. T. Nguyen, Q.-V. Pham, and C. M. Nguyen. "Deep Learning for Deepfakes Creation and Detection: A Survey". In: (2019). arXiv: 1909.11573 [cs.CV].

[Ngu+21] T. Nguyen, R. Novak, L. Xiao, and J. Lee. "Dataset Distillation with Infinitely Wide Convolutional Networks". In: *Advances in Neural Information Processing Systems*. Ed. by A. Beygelzimer, Y. Dauphin, P. Liang, and J. W. Vaughan. 2021.

[NH98a] R. M. Neal and G. E. Hinton. "A new view of the EM algorithm that justifies incremental and other variants". In: *Learning in Graphical Models*. Ed. by M. Jordan. MIT Press, 1998.

[NH98b] R. M. Neal and G. E. Hinton. "A View of the EM Algorithm that Justifies Incremental, Sparse, and other Variants". In: *Learning in Graphical Models*. Ed. by M. I. Jordan. Springer Netherlands, 1998, pp. 355–368.

[NHLS19] E. Nalisnick, J. M. Hernández-Lobato, and P. Smyth. "Dropout as a Structured Shrinkage Prior". In: *ICML*. 2019.

[NHR99] A. Ng, D. Harada, and S. Russell. "Policy invariance under reward transformations: Theory and application to reward shaping". In: *ICML*. 1999.

[NI92] H. Nagamochi and T. Ibaraki. "Computing edge-connectivity of multigraphs and capacitated graphs". In: *SIAM J. Discrete Math.* 5 (1992), pp. 54–66.

[Nig+00] K. Nigam, A. K. Mccallum, S. Thrun, and T. Mitchell. "Text Classification from Labeled and Unlabeled Documents using EM". In: *MLJ* 39.2 (May 2000), pp. 103–134.

[Nij+19] E. Nijkamp, M. Hill, S.-C. Zhu, and Y. N. Wu. "Learning non-convergent non-persistent short-run MCMC toward energy-based model". In: *NIPS*. 2019, pp. 5232–5242.

[Nix+19] J. Nixon, M. Dusenberry, L. Zhang, G. Jerfel, and D. Tran. "Measuring Calibration in Deep Learning". In: (2019). arXiv: 1904.01685 [cs.LG].

[NJ00] A. Y. Ng and M. Jordan. "PEGASUS: A policy search method for large MDPs and POMDPs". In: *UAI*. 2000.

[NJB05] M. Narasimhan, N. Jojic, and J. A. Bilmes. "Q-clustering". In: *Advances in Neural Information Processing Systems* 18 (2005), pp. 979–986.

[NK17] V. Nagarajan and J. Z. Kolter. "Gradient descent GAN optimization is locally stable". In: *Advances in neural information processing systems*. 2017, pp. 5585–5595.

[NKI10] K. Nagano, Y. Kawahara, and S. Iwata. "Minimum average cost clustering". In: *Advances in Neural Information Processing Systems* 23 (2010), pp. 1759–1767.

[NLS15] C. A. Naesseth, F. Lindsten, and T. B. Schön. "Nested Sequential Monte Carlo Methods". In: *ICML*. 2015.

[NLS19] C. A. Naesseth, F. Lindsten, and T. B. Schön. "Elements of Sequential Monte Carlo". In: *Foundations and Trends in Machine Learning* (2019).

[NM12] A. Nenkova and K. McKeown. "A survey of text summarization techniques". In: *Mining text data*. Springer, 2012, pp. 43–76.

[NMC05] A. Niculescu-Mizil and R. Caruana. "Predicting Good Probabilities with Supervised Learning". In: *ICML*. 2005.

[NNP19] W. Nie, N. Narodytska, and A. Patel. "RelGAN: Relational Generative Adversarial Networks for Text Generation". In: *International Conference on Learning Representations*. 2019.

[Noc+21] L. Noci, K. Roth, G. Bachmann, S. Nowozin, and T. Hofmann. "Disentangling the Roles of Curation, Data-Augmentation and the Prior in the Cold Posterior Effect". In: *NIPS*. 2021.

[Noé+19] F. Noé, S. Olsson, J. Köhler, and H. Wu. "Boltzmann generators: Sampling equilibrium states of many-body systems with deep learning". In: *Science* 365 (2019).

[Nou+02] M. N. Nounou, B. R. Bakshi, P. K. Goel, and X. Shen. "Process modeling by Bayesian latent variable regression". In: *Am. Inst. Chemical Engineers Journal* 48.8 (2002), pp. 1775–1793.

[Nov+19] R. Novak, L. Xiao, J. Lee, Y. Bahri, G. Yang, J. Hron, D. A. Abolafia, J. Pennington, and J. Sohl-Dickstein. "Bayesian Deep Convolutional Networks with Many Channels are Gaussian Processes". In: *ICLR*. 2019.

[NP03] W. K. Newey and J. L. Powell. "Instrumental variable estimation of nonparametric models". In: *Econometrica* 71.5 (2003), pp. 1565–1578.

[NR00a] A. Ng and S. Russell. "Algorithms for inverse reinforcement learning". In: *ICML*. 2000.

[NR00b] A. Y. Ng and S. Russell. "Algorithms for Inverse Reinforcement Learning". In: *in Proc. 17th International Conf. on Machine Learning*. Citeseer. 2000.

[NR94] M. Newton and A. Raftery. "Approximate Bayesian Inference with the Weighted Likelihood Bootstrap". In: *J. of Royal Stat. Soc. Series B* 56.1 (1994), pp. 3–48.

[NS17] E. Nalisnick and P. Smyth. "Variational Reference Priors". In: *ICLR Workshop*. 2017.

[NS18] E. Nalisnick and P. Smyth. "Learning Priors for Invariance". In: *AISTATS*. 2018.

[NW06] J. Nocedal and S. Wright. *Numerical Optimization*. Springer, 2006.

[NW20] X Nie and S Wager. "Quasi-oracle estimation of heterogeneous treatment effects". In: *Biometrika* 108.2 (Sept. 2020), pp. 299–319. eprint: https://academic.oup.com/biomet/article-pdf/108/2/299/37938939/asaa076.pdf.

[NWF78] G. Nemhauser, L. Wolsey, and M. Fisher. "An analysis of approximations for maximizing submodular set functions—I". In: *Mathematical Programming* 14.1 (1978), pp. 265–294.

[NWJ09]   X. Nguyen, M. J. Wainwright, and M. I. Jordan. "On Surrogate Loss Functions and f-Divergences". In: *Ann. Stat.* 37.2 (2009), pp. 876–904.

[NWJ+09]   X. Nguyen, M. J. Wainwright, M. I. Jordan, et al. "On surrogate loss functions and f-divergences". In: *The Annals of Statistics* 37.2 (2009), pp. 876–904.

[NWJ10a]   X Nguyen, M. J. Wainwright, and M. I. Jordan. "Estimating Divergence Functionals and the Likelihood Ratio by Convex Risk Minimization". In: *IEEE Trans. Inf. Theory* 56.11 (2010), pp. 5847–5861.

[NWJ10b]   X. Nguyen, M. J. Wainwright, and M. I. Jordan. "Estimating divergence functionals and the likelihood ratio by convex risk minimization". In: *IEEE Transactions on Information Theory* 56.11 (2010), pp. 5847–5861.

[NYC15]   A. Nguyen, J. Yosinski, and J. Clune. "Deep Neural Networks are Easily Fooled: High Confidence Predictions for Unrecognizable Images". In: *CVPR.* 2015.

[OA09]   M. Opper and C. Archambeau. "The variational Gaussian approximation revisited". en. In: *Neural Comput.* 21.3 (2009), pp. 786–792.

[OAC18]   I. Osband, J. Aslanides, and A. Cassirer. "Randomized prior functions for deep reinforcement learning". In: *NIPS.* 2018.

[Obe+19]   F. Obermeyer, E. Bingham, M. Jankowiak, J. Chiu, N. Pradhan, A. Rush, and N. Goodman. "Tensor Variable Elimination for Plated Factor Graphs". In: *ICML.* 2019.

[OCM21]   L. A. Ortega, R. Cabañas, and A. R. Masegosa. "Diversity and Generalization in Neural Network Ensembles". In: (2021). arXiv: 2110 . 13786 [cs.LG].

[ODK96]   M. Ostendorf, V. Digalakis, and O. Kimball. "From HMMs to segment models: a unified view of stochastic modeling for speech recognition". In: *IEEE Trans. on Speech and Audio Processing* 4.5 (1996), pp. 360–378.

[OED21]   J. Ortiz, T. Evans, and A. J. Davison. "A visual introduction to Gaussian Belief Propagation". In: *arXiv preprint arXiv:2107.02308* (2021).

[OF96]   B. A. Olshausen and D. J. Field. "Emergence of simple cell receptive field properties by learning a sparse code for natural images". In: *Nature* 381 (1996), pp. 607–609.

[O'H78]   A. O'Hagan. "Curve Fitting and Optimal Design for Prediction". In: *J. of Royal Stat. Soc. Series B* 40 (1978), pp. 1–42.

[OKK16]   A. Van den Oord, N. Kalchbrenner, and K. Kavukcuoglu. "Pixel Recurrent Neural Networks". In: *ICML.* 2016.

[Oll+17]   Y. Ollivier, L. Arnold, A. Auger, and N. Hansen. "Information-Geometric Optimization Algorithms: A Unifying Picture via Invariance Principles". In: *JMLR* 18 (2017), pp. 1–65.

[Oll18]   Y. Ollivier. "Online natural gradient as a Kalman filter". en. In: *Electron. J. Stat.* 12.2 (2018), pp. 2930–2961.

[OLV18a]   A. van den Oord, Y. Li, and O. Vinyals. "Representation Learning with Contrastive Predictive Coding". In: (2018). arXiv: 1807.03748 [cs.LG].

[OLV18b]   A. v. d. Oord, Y. Li, and O. Vinyals. "Representation learning with contrastive predictive coding". In: *arXiv preprint arXiv:1807.03748* (2018).

[OM96]   P. V. Overschee and B. D. Moor. *Subspace Identification for Linear Systems: Theory, Implementation, Applications.* Kluwer Academic Publishers, 1996.

[OMS17]   C. Olah, A. Mordvintsev, and L. Schubert. "Feature Visualization". In: *Distill* 2.11 (2017).

[O'N09]   B. O'Neill. "Exchangeability, Correlation, and Bayes' Effect". In: *Int. Stat. Rev.* 77.2 (2009), pp. 241–250.

[ONS18]   V. M.-H. Ong, D. J. Nott, and M. S. Smith. "Gaussian Variational Approximation With a Factor Covariance Structure". In: *J. Comput. Graph. Stat.* 27.3 (2018), pp. 465–478.

[oor+16]   A. Van den oord, S. Dieleman, H. Zen, K. Simonyan, O. Vinyals, A. Graves, N. Kalchbrenner, A. Senior, and K. Kavukcuoglu. "WaveNet: A Generative Model for Raw Audio". In: (2016). arXiv: 1609.03499 [cs.SD].

[Oor+16]   A. van den Oord, N. Kalchbrenner, O. Vinyals, L. Espeholt, A. Graves, and K. Kavukcuoglu. "Conditional Image Generation with PixelCNN Decoders". In: (2016). arXiv: 1606.05328 [cs.CV].

[Oor+18]   A. van den Oord et al. "Parallel WaveNet: Fast High-Fidelity Speech Synthesis". In: *ICML.* Ed. by J. Dy and A. Krause. Vol. 80. Proceedings of Machine Learning Research. PMLR, 2018, pp. 3918–3926.

[Oor+19]   A. van den Oord, B. Poole, O. Vinyals, and A. Razavi. "Fixing Posterior Collapse with delta-VAEs". In: *ICLR.* 2019.

[OOS17]   A. Odena, C. Olah, and J. Shlens. "Conditional image synthesis with auxiliary classifier gans". In: *International conference on machine learning.* 2017, pp. 2642–2651.

[Ope]   OpenAI. *ChatGPT: Optimizing Language Models for Dialogue.* Blog.

[Oqu+14]   M. Oquab, L. Bottou, I. Laptev, and J. Sivic. "Learning and transferring mid-level image representations using convolutional neural networks". In: *Proceedings of the IEEE conference on computer vision and pattern recognition.* 2014, pp. 1717–1724.

[OR20]   A. Owen and D. Rudolf. "A strong law of large numbers for scrambled net integration". In: (2020). arXiv: 2002.07859 [math.NA].

[Ore+20]   B. N. Oreshkin, D. Carpov, N. Chapados, and Y. Bengio. "N-BEATS: Neural basis expansion analysis for interpretable time series forecasting". In: *ICLR.* 2020.

[ORW21]   S. W. Ober, C. E. Rasmussen, and M. van der Wilk. "The Promises and Pitfalls of Deep Kernel Learning". In: *ICML.* Feb. 2021.

[Osa+18]   T. Osa, J. Pajarinen, G. Neumann, J. A. Bagnell, P. Abbeel, and J. Peters. "An Algorithmic Perspective on Imitation Learning". In: *Foundations and Trends in Robotics* 7.1–2 (2018), pp. 1–179.

[Osa+19a]   K. Osawa, S. Swaroop, A. Jain, R. Eschenhagen, R. E. Turner, R. Yokota, and M. E. Khan. "Practical Deep Learning with Bayesian Principles". In: *NIPS.* 2019.

[Osa+19b]   K. Osawa, Y. Tsuji, Y. Ueno, A. Naruse, R. Yokota, and S. Matsuoka. "Large-Scale Distributed Second-Order Optimization Using Kronecker-

Factored Approximate Curvature for Deep Convolutional Neural Networks". In: *CVPR*. 2019.

[Osb16] I. Osband. "Risk versus Uncertainty in Deep Learning: Bayes, Bootstrap and the Dangers of Dropout". In: *NIPS workshop on Bayesian deep learning*. 2016.

[Osb+21] I. Osband, Z. Wen, S. M. Asghari, V. Dwaracherla, B. Hao, M. Ibrahimi, D. Lawson, X. Lu, B. O'Donoghue, and B. Van Roy. "The Neural Testbed: Evaluating Predictive Distributions". In: (2021). arXiv: 2110.04629 [cs.LG].

[Ose11] I. V. Oseledets. "Tensor-Train Decomposition". In: *SIAM J. Sci. Comput.* 33.5 (2011), pp. 2295–2317.

[OT05] A. B. Owen and S. D. Tribble. "A quasi-Monte Carlo Metropolis algorithm". en. In: *PNAS* 102.25 (2005), pp. 8844–8849.

[Ouy+22] L. Ouyang et al. "Training language models to follow instructions with human feedback". In: (Mar. 2022). arXiv: 2203.02155 [cs.CL].

[Ova+19] Y. Ovadia, E. Fertig, J. Ren, Z. Nado, D Sculley, S. Nowozin, J. V. Dillon, B. Lakshminarayanan, and J. Snoek. "Can You Trust Your Model's Uncertainty? Evaluating Predictive Uncertainty Under Dataset Shift". In: *NIPS*. 2019.

[OVK17] A. van den Oord, O. Vinyals, and K. Kavukcuoglu. "Neural Discrete Representation Learning". In: *NIPS*. 2017.

[Owe13] A. B. Owen. *Monte Carlo theory, methods and examples*. 2013.

[Owe17] A. B. Owen. "A randomized Halton algorithm in R". In: *arXiv [stat.CO]* (2017).

[Oxl11] J. Oxley. *Matroid Theory: Second Edition*. Oxford University Press, 2011.

[Pac+14] J. Pacheco, S. Zuffi, M. Black, and E. Sudderth. "Preserving Modes and Messages via Diverse Particle Selection". en. In: *ICML*. 2014, pp. 1152–1160.

[Pai] *Explainable AI in Practice Falls Short of Transparency Goals*. https://partnershiponai.org/xai-in-practice/. Accessed: 2021-11-23.

[Pai+14] T. L. Paine, P. Khorrami, W. Han, and T. S. Huang. "An analysis of unsupervised pre-training in light of recent advances". In: *arXiv preprint arXiv:1412.6597* (2014).

[Pan+10] L. Paninski, Y. Ahmadian, D. G. Ferreira, S. Koyama, K. Rahnama Rad, M. Vidne, J. Vogelstein, and W. Wu. "A new look at state-space models for neural data". en. In: *J. Comput. Neurosci.* 29.1-2 (2010), pp. 107–126.

[Pan+21] G. Pang, C. Shen, L. Cao, and A. Van Den Hengel. "Deep Learning for Anomaly Detection: A Review". In: *ACM Comput. Surv.* 54.2 (2021), pp. 1–38.

[Pan+22] K. Pandey, A. Mukherjee, P. Rai, and A. Kumar. "DiffuseVAE: Efficient, Controllable and High-Fidelity Generation from Low-Dimensional Latents". In: *Transactions on Machine Learning Research* (Jan. 2022).

[Pap+17] N. Papernot, P. McDaniel, I. Goodfellow, S. Jha, Z Berkay Celik, and A. Swami. "Practical Black-Box Attacks against Deep Learning Systems using Adversarial Examples". In: *ACM Asia Conference on Computer and Communications Security*. 2017.

[Pap+19] G. Papamakarios, E. Nalisnick, D. J. Rezende, S. Mohamed, and B. Lakshminarayanan.

"Normalizing Flows for Probabilistic Modeling and Inference". In: (2019). arXiv: 1912.02762 [stat.ML].

[Par+19] S Parameswaran, C Deledalle, L Denis, and T. Q. Nguyen. "Accelerating GMM-Based Patch Priors for Image Restoration: Three Ingredients for a 100× Speed-Up". In: *IEEE Trans. Image Process.* 28.2 (2019), pp. 687–698.

[Par81] G. Parisi. "Correlation functions and computer simulations". In: *Nuclear Physics B* 180.3 (1981), pp. 378–384.

[Pas+02] H. Pasula, B. Marthi, B. Milch, S. Russell, and I. Shpitser. "Identity Uncertainty and Citation Matching". In: *NIPS*. 2002.

[Pas+21a] A. Paszke, D. Johnson, D. Duvenaud, D. Vytiniotis, A. Radul, M. Johnson, J. Ragan-Kelley, and D. Maclaurin. "Getting to the Point: Index Sets and Parallelism-Preserving Autodiff for Pointful Array Programming". In: *Proc. ACM Program. Lang.* 5.ICFP (2021).

[Pas+21b] A. Paszke, M. J. Johnson, R. Frostig, and D. Maclaurin. "Parallelism-Preserving Automatic Differentiation for Second-Order Array Languages". In: *Proceedings of the 9th ACM SIGPLAN International Workshop on Functional High-Performance and Numerical Computing*. FHPNC 2021. Association for Computing Machinery, 2021, 13–23.

[Pat+16] D. Pathak, P. Krahenbuhl, J. Donahue, T. Darrell, and A. A. Efros. "Context encoders: Feature learning by inpainting". In: *Proceedings of the IEEE conference on computer vision and pattern recognition*. 2016, pp. 2536–2544.

[Pat+22] Z. B. Patel, P. Purohit, H. M. Patel, S. Sahni, and N. Batra. "Accurate and Scalable Gaussian Processes for Fine-Grained Air Quality Inference". en. In: *AAAI* 36.11 (June 2022), pp. 12080–12088.

[PB14] R. Pascanu and Y. Bengio. "Revisiting Natural Gradient for Deep Networks". In: *ICLR*. 2014.

[PBM16a] J. Peters, P. Bühlmann, and N. Meinshausen. "Causal inference by using invariant prediction: identification and confidence intervals". In: *Journal of the Royal Statistical Society. Series B (Statistical Methodology)* 78.5 (2016), pp. 947–1012.

[PBM16b] J. Peters, P. Bühlmann, and N. Meinshausen. "Causal inference using invariant prediction: identification and confidence intervals". In: *J. of Royal Stat. Soc. Series B* 78.5 (2016), pp. 947–1012.

[PC08] T. Park and G. Casella. "The Bayesian Lasso". In: *JASA* 103.482 (2008), pp. 681–686.

[PC09] J. Paisley and L. Carin. "Nonparametric Factor Analysis with Beta Process Priors". In: *ICML*. 2009.

[PC12] N. Pinto and D. D. Cox. "High-throughput-derived biologically-inspired features for unconstrained face recognition". In: *Image Vis. Comput.* 30.3 (2012), pp. 159–168.

[PD03] J. D. Park and A. Darwiche. "A Differential Semantics for Jointree Algorithms". In: *NIPS*. MIT Press, 2003, pp. 801–808.

[PD11] H. Poon and P. Domingos. "Sum-Product Networks: A New Deep Architecture". In: *UAI*. Java code at http://alchemy.cs.washington.edu/spn/. Short intro at http://lessoned.blogspot.com/2011/10/intro-to-sum-product-networks.html. 2011.

[PdC20] F.-P. Paty, A. d'Aspremont, and M. Cuturi. "Regularity as Regularization: Smooth and Strongly Convex Brenier Potentials in Optimal Transport". In:

Proceedings of the Twenty Third International Conference on Artificial Intelligence and Statistics. Ed. by S. Chiappa and R. Calandra. Vol. 108. Proceedings of Machine Learning Research. PMLR, 2020, pp. 1222–1232.

[PDL+12] M. Parry, A. P. Dawid, S. Lauritzen, et al. "Proper local scoring rules". In: *The Annals of Statistics* 40.1 (2012), pp. 561–592.

[PE16] V. Papyan and M. Elad. "Multi-Scale Patch-Based Image Restoration". en. In: *IEEE Trans. Image Process.* 25.1 (2016), pp. 249–261.

[Pea09a] J. Pearl. *Causality*. 2nd. Cambridge University Press, 2009.

[Pea09b] J. Pearl. *Causality: Models, Reasoning and Inference (Second Edition)*. Cambridge Univ. Press, 2009.

[Pea09c] J. Pearl. "Causal inference in statistics: An overview". In: *Stat. Surv.* 3.0 (2009), pp. 96–146.

[Pea12] J. Pearl. "The Causal Foundations of Structural Equation Modeling". In: *Handbook of structural equation modeling*. Ed. by R. H. Hoyle. Vol. 68. 2012.

[Pea19] J. Pearl. "The Seven Tools of Causal Inference, with Reflections on Machine Learning". In: *Comm. of the ACM* 62.3 (2019), pp. 54–60.

[Pea36] K. Pearson. "Method of moments and method of maximum likelihood". In: *Biometrika* 28.1/2 (1936), pp. 34–59.

[Pea84] J. Pearl. *Heuristics: Intelligent Search Strategies for Computer Problem Solving*. Addison-Wesley Longman Publishing Co., Inc., 1984.

[Pea88] J. Pearl. *Probabilistic Reasoning in Intelligent Systems: Networks of Plausible Inference*. Morgan Kaufmann, 1988.

[Pea94] B. A. Pearlmutter. "Fast Exact Multiplication by the Hessian". In: *Neural Comput.* 6.1 (1994), pp. 147–160.

[Peh+20] R. Peharz, S. Lang, A. Vergari, K. Stelzner, A. Molina, M. Trapp, G. Van den Broeck, K. Kersting, and Z. Ghahramani. "Einsum Networks: Fast and Scalable Learning of Tractable Probabilistic Circuits". In: (2020). arXiv: 2004.06231 [cs.LG].

[Pel05] M. Pelikan. *Hierarchical Bayesian Optimization Algorithm: Toward a New Generation of Evolutionary Algorithms*. en. Softcover reprint of hardcover 1st ed. 2005 edition. Springer, 2005.

[Pen13] J. Pena. "Reading dependencies from covariance graphs". In: *Intl. J. of Approximate Reasoning* 54.1 (2013).

[Per+18] E. Perez, F. Strub, H. de Vries, V. Dumoulin, and A. Courville. "FiLM: Visual Reasoning with a General Conditioning Layer". In: *AAAI*. 2018.

[Pes+21] H. Pesonen et al. "ABC of the Future". In: (2021). arXiv: 2112.12841 [stat.AP].

[Pey20] G. Peyre. "Course notes on Optimization for Machine Learning". 2020.

[Pez+21] M. Pezeshki, S.-O. Kaba, Y. Bengio, A. Courville, D. Precup, and G. Lajoie. "Gradient Starvation: A Learning Proclivity in Neural Networks". In: *NIPS*. 2021.

[PF03] G. V. Puskorius and L. A. Feldkamp. "Parameter-based Kalman filter training: Theory and implementation". In: *Kalman Filtering and Neural Networks*. Ed. by S. Haykin. John Wiley & Sons, Inc., 2003, pp. 23–67.

[PF91] G. V. Puskorius and L. A. Feldkamp. "Decoupled extended Kalman filter training of feedforward layered networks". In: *International Joint Conference on Neural Networks*. Vol. i. 1991, 771–777 vol.1.

[PFW21] R. Prado, M. Ferreira, and M. West. *Time Series: Modelling, Computation and Inference (2nd ed)*. CRC Press, 2021.

[PG98] M. Popescu and P. D. Gader. "Image content retrieval from image databases using feature integration by Choquet integral". In: *Storage and Retrieval for Image and Video Databases VII*. Ed. by M. M. Yeung, B.-L. Yeo, and C. A. Bouman. Vol. 3656. International Society for Optics and Photonics. SPIE, 1998, pp. 552 –560.

[PGCP00] M Pelikan, D. E. Goldberg, and E Cantú-Paz. "Linkage problem, distribution estimation, and Bayesian networks". en. In: *Evol. Comput.* 8.3 (2000), pp. 311–340.

[PGJ16] J. Pearl, M. Glymour, and N. Jewell. *Causal inference in statistics: a primer*. Wiley, 2016.

[PH22] M. Phuong and M. Hutter. "Formal Algorithms for Transformers". In: (July 2022). arXiv: 2207.09238 [cs.LG].

[PHL12] M. Pelikan, M. Hausschild, and F. Lobo. *Introduction to estimation of distribution algorithms*. Tech. rep. U. Missouri, 2012.

[PHR18] E. Petersen, C. Hoffmann, and P. Rostalski. "On Approximate Nonlinear Gaussian Message Passing On Factor Graphs". In: *IEEE Statistical Signal Processing Workshop (SSP)*. 2018.

[Phu+18] M. Phuong, M. Welling, N. Kushman, R. Tomioka, and S. Nowozin. "The Mutual Autoencoder: Controlling Information in Latent Code Representations". In: *Arxiv* (2018).

[Pir+13] M. Pirotta, M. Restelli, A. Pecorino, and D. Calandriello. "Safe Policy Iteration". In: *ICML*. 3. 2013, pp. 307–317.

[PJD21] Y. Petetin, Y. Janati, and F. Desbouvries. "Structured Variational Bayesian Inference for Gaussian State-Space Models With Regime Switching". In: *IEEE Signal Process. Lett.* 28 (2021), pp. 1953–1957.

[PJS17] J. Peters, D. Janzing, and B. Schölkopf. *Elements of Causal Inference: Foundations and Learning Algorithms (Adaptive Computation and Machine Learning series)*. The MIT Press, 2017.

[PKP21] A. Plaat, W. Kosters, and M. Preuss. "High-Accuracy Model-Based Reinforcement Learning, a Survey". In: (2021). arXiv: 2107.08241 [cs.LG].

[PL03] M. A. Paskin and G. D. Lawrence. *Junction Tree Algorithms for Solving Sparse Linear Systems*. Tech. rep. UCB/CSD-03-1271. UC Berkeley, 2003.

[Pla00] J. Platt. "Probabilities for SV machines". In: *Advances in Large Margin Classifiers*. Ed. by A. Smola, P. Bartlett, B. Schoelkopf, and D. Schuurmans. MIT Press, 2000.

[Pla18] E. Plaut. "From Principal Subspaces to Principal Components with Linear Autoencoders". In: *ArXiv* abs/1804.10253 (2018).

[Ple+18] G. Pleiss, J. R. Gardner, K. Q. Weinberger, and A. G. Wilson. "Constant-Time Predictive Distributions for Gaussian Processes". In: *International Conference on Machine Learning*. 2018.

[Plu+20] G. Plumb, M. Al-Shedivat, Á. A. Cabrera, A. Perer, E. Xing, and A. Talwalkar. "Regularizing black-box models for improved interpretability". In: *Advances in Neural Information Processing Systems* 33 (2020).

[PM18a] N. Papernot and P. McDaniel. *Deep k-Nearest Neighbors: Towards Confident, Interpretable and Robust Deep Learning*. 2018. arXiv: 1803.04765 [cs.LG].

[PM18b] J. Pearl and D. Mackenzie. *The book of why: the new science of cause and effect*. 2018.

[PMT18] G. Plumb, D. Molitor, and A. Talwalkar. "Supervised Local Modeling for Interpretability". In: *CoRR* abs/1807.02910 (2018). arXiv: 1807.02910.

[Pol+19] A. A. Pol, V. Berger, G. Cerminara, C. Germain, and M. Pierini. "Anomaly Detection With Conditional Variational Autoencoders". In: *IEEE International Conference on Machine Learning and Applications*. 2019.

[Pom89] D. Pomerleau. "ALVINN: An Autonomous Land Vehicle in a Neural Network". In: *NIPS*. 1989, pp. 305–313.

[Poo+12] D. Poole, D. Buchman, S. Natarajan, and K. Kersting. "Aggregation and Population Growth: The Relational Logistic Regression and Markov Logic Cases". In: *Statistical Relational AI workshop*. 2012.

[Poo+19a] B. Poole, S. Ozair, A. van den Oord, A. A. Alemi, and G. Tucker. "On Variational Bounds of Mutual Information". In: *ICML*. 2019.

[Poo+19b] B. Poole, S. Ozair, A. van den Oord, A. A. Alemi, and G. Tucker. "On variational lower bounds of mutual information". In: *ICML*. 2019.

[Pou04] M. Pourahmadi. *Simultaneous Modelling of Covariance Matrices: GLM, Bayesian and Nonparametric Perspectives*. Tech. rep. Northern Illinois University, 2004.

[Poy+20] R. Poyiadzi, K. Sokol, R. Santos-Rodriguez, T. De Bie, and P. Flach. "FACE: Feasible and actionable counterfactual explanations". In: *Proceedings of the AAAI/ACM Conference on AI, Ethics, and Society*. 2020, pp. 344–350.

[PPC09] G. Petris, S. Petrone, and P. Campagnoli. *Dynamic linear models with R*. Springer, 2009.

[PPG91] C. S. Pomerleau, O. F. Pomerleau, and A. W. Garcia. "Biobehavioral research on nicotine use in women". In: *British Journal of Addiction* 86.5 (1991), pp. 527–531.

[PPM17] G. Papamakarios, T. Pavlakou, and I. Murray. "Masked Autoregressive Flow for Density Estimation". In: *NIPS*. 2017.

[PPR22] B. Paria, B. Pòczos, and P. Ravikumar. "Be greedy – a simple algorithm for blackbox optimization using neural networks". In: *ICML Workshop on Adaptive Experimental Design and Active Learning in the Real World*. 2022.

[PPS18] T. Pierrot, N. Perrin, and O. Sigaud. "First-order and second-order variants of the gradient descent in a unified framework". In: (2018). arXiv: 1810.08102 [cs.LG].

[PR03] O. Papaspiliopoulos and G. O. Roberts. "Non-Centered Parameterisations for Hierarchical Models and Data Augmentation". In: *Bayesian Statistics* 7 (2003), pp. 307–326.

[Pra+18] S. Prabhumoye, Y. Tsvetkov, R. Salakhutdinov, and A. W. Black. "Style Transfer Through Back-Translation". In: *Proceedings of the 56th Annual Meeting of the Association for Computational Linguistics (Volume 1: Long Papers)*. 2018, pp. 866–876.

[Pre05] S. J. Press. *Applied multivariate analysis, using Bayesian and frequentist methods of inference*. Second edition. Dover, 2005.

[Pre+17a] V. Premachandran, D. Tarlow, A. L. Yuille, and D. Batra. "Empirical Minimum Bayes Risk Prediction". en. In: *IEEE PAMI* 39.1 (Jan. 2017), pp. 75–86.

[Pre+17b] O. Press, A. Bar, B. Bogin, J. Berant, and L. Wolf. "Language generation with recurrent generative adversarial networks without pre-training". In: *arXiv preprint arXiv:1706.01399* (2017).

[Pre+88] W. Press, W. Vetterling, S. Teukolosky, and B. Flannery. *Numerical Recipes in C: The Art of Scientific Computing*. Second. Cambridge University Press, 1988.

[PRG17] M. Probst, F. Rothlauf, and J. Grahl. "Scalability of using Restricted Boltzmann Machines for combinatorial optimization". In: *Eur. J. Oper. Res.* 256.2 (2017), pp. 368–383.

[Pri58] R. Price. "A useful theorem for nonlinear devices having Gaussian inputs". In: *IRE Trans. Info. Theory* 4.2 (1958), pp. 69–72.

[PS07] J. Peters and S. Schaal. "Reinforcement Learning by Reward-Weighted Regression for Operational Space Control". In: *ICML*. 2007, pp. 745–750.

[PS08a] B. A. Pearlmutter and J. M. Siskind. "Reverse-Mode AD in a Functional Framework: Lambda the Ultimate Backpropagator". In: *ACM Trans. Program. Lang. Syst.* 30.2 (2008).

[PS08b] J. Peters and S. Schaal. "Reinforcement Learning of Motor Skills with Policy Gradients". In: *Neural Networks* 21.4 (2008), pp. 682–697.

[PS12] N. G. Polson and J. G. Scott. "On the Half-Cauchy Prior for a Global Scale Parameter". en. In: *Bayesian Anal.* 7.4 (2012), pp. 887–902.

[PS17] N. G. Polson and V. Sokolov. "Deep Learning: A Bayesian Perspective". en. In: *Bayesian Anal.* 12.4 (2017), pp. 1275–1304.

[PSCP06] M. Pelikan, K. Sastry, and E. Cantú-Paz. *Scalable Optimization via Probabilistic Modeling: From Algorithms to Applications (Studies in Computational Intelligence)*. Springer-Verlag New York, Inc., 2006.

[PSD00] J. K. Pritchard, M Stephens, and P Donnelly. "Inference of population structure using multilocus genotype data". In: *Genetics* 155.2 (2000), pp. 945–959.

[PSDG14] B. Poole, J. Sohl-Dickstein, and S. Ganguli. "Analyzing noise in autoencoders and deep networks". In: *arXiv preprint arXiv:1406.1831* (2014).

[PSM19] G. Papamakarios, D. Sterratt, and I. Murray. "Sequential Neural Likelihood: Fast Likelihood-free Inference with Autoregressive Flows". In: *AISTATS*. 2019.

[PSS00] D. Precup, R. S. Sutton, and S. P. Singh. "Eligibility Traces for Off-Policy Policy Evaluation". In: *ICML*. ICML '00. Morgan Kaufmann Publishers Inc., 2000, pp. 759–766.

[PT13] S. Patterson and Y. W. Teh. "Stochastic Gradient Riemannian Langevin Dynamics on the Probability Simplex". In: *NIPS*. 2013.

[PT87]   C. Papadimitriou and J. Tsitsiklis. "The complexity of Markov decision processes". In: *Mathematics of Operations Research* 12.3 (1987), pp. 441–450.

[PT94]   P. Paatero and U. Tapper. "Positive Matrix Factorization: A Non-negative Factor Model with Optimal Utilization of Error Estimates of Data Values". In: *Environmetrics* 5 (1994), pp. 111–126.

[PTD20]   A. Prabhu, P. H. S. Torr, and P. K. Dokania. "GDumb: A simple approach that questions our progress in continual learning". In: *ECCV.* Lecture notes in computer science. Springer International Publishing, 2020, pp. 524–540.

[Put94]   M. L. Puterman. *Markov Decision Processes: Discrete Stochastic Dynamic Programming.* Wiley, 1994.

[PVC19]   R. Prenger, R. Valle, and B. Catanzaro. "WaveGLOW: A flow-based generative network for speech synthesis". In: *Proceedings of the 2019 IEEE International Conference on Acoustics, Speech and Signal Processing.* IEEE. 2019, pp. 3617–3621.

[PW05]   S. Parise and M. Welling. "Learning in Markov Random Fields: An Empirical Study". In: *Joint Statistical Meeting.* 2005.

[PX22]   W. Peebles and S. Xie. "Scalable Diffusion Models with Transformers". In: (Dec. 2022). arXiv: 2212.09748 [cs.CV].

[PY10]   G. Papandreou and A. L. Yuille. "Gaussian sampling by local perturbations". In: *NIPS.* 2010.

[PY11]   G Papandreou and A. L. Yuille. "Perturb-and-MAP random fields: Using discrete optimization to learn and sample from energy models". In: *ICCV.* Nov. 2011, pp. 193–200.

[PY14]   G. Papandreou and A. Yuille. "Perturb-and-MAP Random Fields: Reducing Random Sampling to Optimization, with Applications in Computer Vision". In: *Advanced Structured Prediction.* Ed. by S. Nowozin, P. Gehler, J. Jancsary, C. Lampert. MIT Press, 2014.

[QC+06]   J. Quiñonero-Candela, C. E. Rasmussen, F. Sinz, O. Bousquet, and B. Schölkopf. "Evaluating Predictive Uncertainty Challenge". In: *Machine Learning Challenges. Evaluating Predictive Uncertainty, Visual Object Classification, and Recognising Tectual Entailment.* Lecture Notes in Computer Science. Springer Berlin Heidelberg, 2006, pp. 1–27.

[QC+08]   J. Quinonero-Candela, M. Sugiyama, A. Schwaighofer, and N. D. Lawrence, eds. *Dataset Shift in Machine Learning.* en. The MIT Press, 2008.

[QCR05]   J. Quinonero-Candela and C. Rasmussen. "A unifying view of sparse approximate Gaussian process regression". In: *JMLR* 6.3 (2005), pp. 1939–1959.

[Qin+20] C. Qin, Y. Wu, J. T. Springenberg, A. Brock, J. Donahue, T. P. Lillicrap, and P. Kohli. "Training Generative Adversarial Networks by Solving Ordinary Differential Equations". In: *arXiv preprint arXiv:2010.15040* (2020).

[QRJN18] J. Qiu, S Rao Jammalamadaka, and N. Ning. "Multivariate Bayesian Structural Time Series Model". In: *JMLR* 19.68 (2018), pp. 1–33.

[Qu+21]   H. Qu, H. Rahmani, L. Xu, B. Williams, and J. Liu. "Recent Advances of Continual Learning in Computer Vision: An Overview". In: (2021). arXiv: 2109.11369 [cs.CV].

[Qua+07] A. Quattoni, S. Wang, L.-P. Morency, M. Collins, and T. Darrell. "Hidden conditional random fields". In: *IEEE PAMI* 29.10 (2007), pp. 1848–1852.

[Que98]   M. Queyranne. "Minimizing symmetric submodular functions". In: *Math. Programming* 82 (1998), pp. 3–12.

[QZW19]   Y. Qiu, L. Zhang, and X. Wang. "Unbiased Contrastive Divergence Algorithm for Training Energy-Based Latent Variable Models". In: *ICLR.* 2019.

[RA13]   O. Rippel and R. P. Adams. "High-dimensional probability estimation with deep density models". In: *ArXiv Preprint arXiv:1302.5125* (2013).

[Rab89]   L. R. Rabiner. "A Tutorial on Hidden Markov Models and Selected Applications in Speech Recognition". In: *Proc. of the IEEE* 77.2 (1989), pp. 257–286.

[Rad+18] A. Radford, K. Narasimhan, T. Salimans, and I. Sutskever. *Improving Language Understanding by Generative Pre-Training.* Tech. rep. OpenAI, 2018.

[Rad+19] A. Radford, J. Wu, R. Child, D. Luan, D. Amodei, and I. Sutskever. *Language Models are Unsupervised Multitask Learners.* Tech. rep. OpenAI, 2019.

[Rad+21] A. Radford, J. W. Kim, C. Hallacy, A. Ramesh, G. Goh, S. Agarwal, G. Sastry, A. Askell, P. Mishkin, J. Clark, et al. "Learning transferable visual models from natural language supervision". In: *arXiv preprint arXiv:2103.00020* (2021).

[Raf+20a] C. Raffel, N. Shazeer, A. Roberts, K. Lee, S. Narang, M. Matena, Y. Zhou, W. Li, and P. J. Liu. "Exploring the Limits of Transfer Learning with a Unified Text-to-Text Transformer". In: *JMLR* (2020).

[Raf+20b] C. Raffel, N. M. Shazeer, A. Roberts, K. Lee, S. Narang, M. Matena, Y. Zhou, W. Li, and P. J. Liu. "Exploring the Limits of Transfer Learning with a Unified Text-to-Text Transformer". In: *ArXiv* abs/1910.10683 (2020).

[Raf22]   E. Raff. *Inside Deep Learning: Math, Algorithms, Models.* en. Annotated edition. Manning, May 2022.

[RAG04]   B. Ristic, S. Arulampalam, and N. Gordon. *Beyond the Kalman Filter: Particle Filters for Tracking Applications.* Artech House Radar Library, 2004.

[Rag+17] M. Raghu, J. Gilmer, J. Yosinski, and J. Sohl-Dickstein. "Svcca: Singular vector canonical correlation analysis for deep learning dynamics and interpretability". In: *Advances in Neural Information Processing Systems.* 2017, pp. 6076–6085.

[Rag+19] M. Raghu, C. Zhang, J. Kleinberg, and S. Bengio. "Transfusion: Understanding transfer learning for medical imaging". In: *NIPS.* 2019, pp. 3347–3357.

[Rag+21] M. Raghu, T. Unterthiner, S. Kornblith, C. Zhang, and A. Dosovitskiy. "Do Vision Transformers See Like Convolutional Neural Networks?" In: *NIPS.* 2021.

[Rai+18a] T. Rainforth, A. R. Kosiorek, T. A. Le, C. J. Maddison, M. Igl, F. Wood, and Y. W. Teh. "Tighter Variational Bounds are Not Necessarily Better". In: *ICML.* 2018.

[Rai+18b] M. Raitoharju, L. Svensson, Á. F. García-Fernández, and R. Piché. "Damped Posterior Linearization Filter". In: *IEEE Signal Process. Lett.* 25.4 (2018).

[Rai+20] T. Rainforth, A. Golinski, F. Wood, and S. Zaidi. "Target–Aware Bayesian Inference: How to Beat Optimal Conventional Estimators". In: *JMLR* 21.88 (2020), pp. 1–54.

[Rai68] H. Raiffa. *Decision Analysis*. Addison Wesley, 1968.

[Rak+08] A. Rakotomamonjy, F. Bach, S. Canu, and Y. Grandvalet. "SimpleMKL". In: *JMLR* 9 (2008), pp. 2491–2521.

[Ram+21a] A. Ramesh, M. Pavlov, G. Goh, S. Gray, C. Voss, A. Radford, M. Chen, and I. Sutskever. "Zero-Shot Text-to-Image Generation". In: (2021). arXiv: 2102.12092 [cs.CV].

[Ram+21b] A. Ramesh, M. Pavlov, G. Goh, S. Gray, C. Voss, A. Radford, M. Chen, and I. Sutskever. "Zero-shot text-to-image generation". In: *International Conference on Machine Learning*. PMLR. 2021, pp. 8821–8831.

[Ram+22] A. Ramesh, P. Dhariwal, A. Nichol, C. Chu, and M. Chen. "Hierarchical Text-Conditional Image Generation with CLIP Latents". In: (Apr. 2022). arXiv: 2204.06125 [cs.CV].

[Ran+06] M. Ranzato, C. S. Poultney, S. Chopra, and Y. LeCun. "Efficient Learning of Sparse Representations with an Energy-Based Model". In: *NIPS*. 2006.

[Ran16] R. Ranganath. "Hierarchical Variational Models". In: *ICML*. 2016.

[Ran+18] S. S. Rangapuram, M. W. Seeger, J. Gasthaus, L. Stella, Y. Wang, and T. Januschowski. "Deep State Space Models for Time Series Forecasting". In: *NIPS*. Curran Associates, Inc., 2018, pp. 7796–7805.

[Rao10] A. V. Rao. "A Survey of Numerical Methods for Optimal Control". In: *Adv. Astronaut. Sci.* 135.1 (2010).

[Rao99] R. P. Rao. "An optimal estimation approach to visual perception and learning". en. In: *Vision Res.* 39.11 (1999), pp. 1963–1989.

[Ras+15] A. Rasmus, H. Valpola, M. Honkala, M. Berglund, and T. Raiko. *Semi-Supervised Learning with Ladder Networks*. 2015. arXiv: 1507 . 02672 [cs.NE].

[Rat+09] M. Rattray, O. Stegle, K. Sharp, and J. Winn. "Inference algorithms and learning theory for Bayesian sparse factor analysis". In: *Proc. Intl. Workshop on Statistical-Mechanical Informatics*. 2009.

[Rav+18] S. Ravuri, S. Mohamed, M. Rosca, and O. Vinyals. "Learning Implicit Generative Models with the Method of Learned Moments". In: *International Conference on Machine Learning*. 2018, pp. 4314–4323.

[RB16] G. P. Rigby BR. "The Efficacy of Equine-Assisted Activities and Therapies on Improving Physical Function." In: *J Altern Complement Med.* (2016).

[RBB18a] H. Ritter, A. Botev, and D. Barber. "A Scalable Laplace Approximation for Neural Networks". In: *ICLR*. 2018.

[RBB18b] H. Ritter, A. Botev, and D. Barber. "Online Structured Laplace Approximations for Overcoming Catastrophic Forgetting". In: *NIPS*. Curran Associates, Inc., 2018, pp. 3738–3748.

[RBS16] L. J. Ratliff, S. A. Burden, and S. S. Sastry. "On the characterization of local Nash equilibria in continuous games". In: *IEEE transactions on automatic control* 61.8 (2016), pp. 2301–2307.

[RBS84] J. Ramsay, J. ten Berge, and G. Styan. "Matrix correlation". In: *Psychometrika* 49.3 (1984), pp. 403–423.

[RC04] C. Robert and G. Casella. *Monte Carlo Statistical Methods*. 2nd edition. Springer, 2004.

[RC+18] M. Rojas-Carulla, B. Schölkopf, R. Turner, and J. Peters. "Invariant Models for Causal Transfer Learning". In: *Journal of Machine Learning Research* 19.36 (2018), pp. 1–34.

[RD06] M. Richardson and P. Domingos. "Markov logic networks". In: *Machine Learning* 62 (2006), pp. 107–136.

[RDV18] A. S. Ross and F. Doshi-Velez. "Improving the adversarial robustness and interpretability of deep neural networks by regularizing their input gradients". In: *Thirty-second AAAI conference on artificial intelligence*. 2018.

[RE76] P Robert and Y Escoufier. "A unifying tool for linear multivariate statistical methods: The RV- coefficient". In: *J. R. Stat. Soc. Ser. C Appl. Stat.* 25.3 (1976), p. 257.

[Rea+19] E. Real, A. Aggarwal, Y. Huang, and Q. V. Le. "Regularized Evolution for Image Classifier Architecture Search". In: *AAAI*. 2019.

[Rec19] B. Recht. "A Tour of Reinforcement Learning: The View from Continuous Control". In: *Annual Review of Control, Robotics, and Autonomous Systems* 2 (2019), pp. 253–279.

[Ree+17] S. Reed, A. van den Oord, N. Kalchbrenner, S. G. Colmenarejo, Z. Wang, D. Belov, and N. de Freitas. "Parallel Multiscale Autoregressive Density Estimation". In: (2017). arXiv: 1703.03664 [cs.CV].

[Rei+10] J. Reisinger, A. Waters, B. Silverthorn, and R. Mooney. "Spherical topic models". In: *ICML*. 2010.

[Rei13] S. Reich. "A Nonparametric Ensemble Transform Method for Bayesian Inference". In: *SIAM J. Sci. Comput.* 35.4 (2013), A2013–A2024.

[Rei16] P. C. Reiss. "Just How Sensitive are Instrumental Variable Estimates?" In: *Foundations and Trends in Accounting* 10.2-4 (2016).

[Rei+22] P. Reizinger, L. Gresele, J. Brady, J. von Kügelgen, D. Zietlow, B. Scholkopf, G. Martius, W. Brendel, and M. Besserve. "Embrace the Gap: VAEs Perform Independent Mechanism Analysis". In: 2022.

[Ren+19] J. Ren, P. J. Liu, E. Fertig, J. Snoek, R. Poplin, M. A. DePristo, J. V. Dillon, and B. Lakshminarayanan. "Likelihood Ratios for Out-of-Distribution Detection". In: *NIPS*. 2019.

[Rén61] A. Rényi. "On Measures of Entropy and Information". en. In: *Proceedings of the Fourth Berkeley Symposium on Mathematical Statistics and Probability, Volume 1: Contributions to the Theory of Statistics*. The Regents of the University of California, 1961.

[Ren+94] S Renals, N Morgan, H Bourlard, M Cohen, and H Franco. "Connectionist probability estimators in HMM speech recognition". In: *IEEE Trans. Audio Speech Lang. Processing* 2.1 (Jan. 1994), pp. 161–174.

[RFB15] O. Ronneberger, P. Fischer, and T. Brox. "U-Net: Convolutional Networks for Biomedical Image Segmentation". In: *MICCAI (Intl. Conf. on Medical Image Computing and Computer Assisted Interventions)*. 2015.

[RG17] M Roth and F Gustafsson. "Computation and visualization of posterior densities in scalar nonlinear and non-Gaussian Bayesian filtering and smoothing problems". In: *ICASSP*. 2017, pp. 4686–4690.

[RGB11] S. Ross, G. J. Gordon, and D. Bagnell. "A Reduction of Imitation Learning and Structured Prediction to No-Regret Online Learning". In: *AISTATS*. 2011, pp. 627–635.

[RGB14]   R. Ranganath, S. Gerrish, and D. M. Blei. "Black Box Variational Inference". In: *AISTATS*. 2014.

[RGL19]   S. Rabanser, S. Günnemann, and Z. C. Lipton. "Failing Loudly: An Empirical Study of Methods for Detecting Dataset Shift". In: *NIPS*. 2019.

[RH05]   H. Rue and L. Held. *Gaussian Markov Random Fields: Theory and Applications*. Vol. 104. Monographs on Statistics and Applied Probability. London: Chapman & Hall, 2005.

[RHDV17]   A. S. Ross, M. C. Hughes, and F. Doshi-Velez. "Right for the right reasons: Training differentiable models by constraining their explanations". In: *IJCAI* (2017).

[RHG16]   D. Ritchie, P. Horsfall, and N. D. Goodman. "Deep Amortized Inference for Probabilistic Programs". In: (2016). arXiv: 1610.05735 [cs.AI].

[RHK17]   S. Remes, M. Heinonen, and S. Kaski. "Non-Stationary Spectral Kernels". In: *NIPS*. May 2017.

[RHW86a]   D. Rumelhart, G. Hinton, and R. Williams. "Learning internal representations by error propagation". In: *Parallel Distributed Processing: Explorations in the Microstructure of Cognition*. Ed. by D. Rumelhart, J. McClelland, and the PDD Research Group. MIT Press, 1986.

[RHW86b]   D. Rumelhart, G. E. Hinton, and R. J. Williams. "Learning representations by back-propagating errors". In: *Nature* 323 (1986), pp. 533–536.

[Ric03]   T. Richardson. "Markov properties for acyclic directed mixed graphs". In: *Scandinavian J. of Statistics* 30 (2003), pp. 145–157.

[Ric95]   J. Rice. *Mathematical statistics and data analysis*. 2nd edition. Duxbury, 1995.

[Rif+11]   S. Rifai, P. Vincent, X. Muller, X. Glorot, and Y. Bengio. "Contractive auto-encoders: Explicit invariance during feature extraction". In: *Icml*. 2011.

[Ris+08]   I. Rish, G. Grabarnik, G. Cecchi, F. Pereira, and G. Gordon. "Closed-form supervised dimensionality reduction with generalized linear models". In: *ICML*. 2008.

[Riv87]   R. L. Rivest. "Learning decision lists". In: *Machine learning* 2.3 (1987), pp. 229–246.

[RK04]   R. Rubinstein and D. Kroese. *The Cross-Entropy Method: A Unified Approach to Combinatorial Optimization, Monte-Carlo Simulation, and Machine Learning*. Springer-Verlag, 2004.

[RL17]   S. Ravi and H. Larochelle. "Optimization as a Model for Few-Shot Learning". In: *ICLR*. 2017.

[RM15]   D. J. Rezende and S. Mohamed. "Variational Inference with Normalizing Flows". In: *ICML*. 2015.

[RMB08]   N. L. Roux, P.-A. Manzagol, and Y. Bengio. "Topmoumoute Online Natural Gradient Algorithm". In: *NIPS*. 2008, pp. 849–856.

[RMC09]   H. Rue, S. Martino, and N. Chopin. "Approximate Bayesian Inference for Latent Gaussian Models Using Integrated Nested Laplace Approximations". In: *J. of Royal Stat. Soc. Series B* 71 (2009), pp. 319–392.

[RMC15]   A. Radford, L. Metz, and S. Chintala. "Unsupervised Representation Learning with Deep Convo-

lutional Generative Adversarial Networks". In: *arXiv* (2015).

[RMC16a]   A. Radford, L. Metz, and S. Chintala. "Unsupervised Representation Learning with Deep Convolutional Generative Adversarial Networks". In: *ICLR*. 2016.

[RMC16b]   A. Radford, L. Metz, and S. Chintala. "Unsupervised Representation Learning with Deep Convolutional Generative Adversarial Networks". In: *CoRR* abs/1511.06434 (2016).

[RMK21]   G. Roeder, L. Metz, and D. P. Kingma. "On Linear Identifiability of Learned Representations". In: *ICML*. 2021.

[RMW14a]   D. Rezende, S. Mohamed, and D. Wierstra. "Stochastic backpropagation and approximate inference in deep generative models". In: *ICML*. 2014.

[RMW14b]   D. J. Rezende, S. Mohamed, and D. Wierstra. "Stochastic Backpropagation and Approximate Inference in Deep Generative Models". In: *ICML*. Ed. by E. P. Xing and T. Jebara. Vol. 32. Proceedings of Machine Learning Research. PMLR, 2014, pp. 1278–1286.

[RN02]   S. Russell and P. Norvig. *Artificial Intelligence: A Modern Approach*. 2nd edition. Prentice Hall, 2002.

[RN10]   S. Russell and P. Norvig. *Artificial Intelligence: A Modern Approach*. 3rd edition. Prentice Hall, 2010.

[RN19]   S. Russell and P. Norvig. *Artificial Intelligence: A Modern Approach*. 4th edition. Prentice Hall, 2019.

[RN94]   G. A. Rummery and M Niranjan. *On-Line Q-Learning Using Connectionist Systems*. Tech. rep. Cambridge Univ. Engineering Dept., 1994.

[RN95]   S. Russell and P. Norvig. *Artificial Intelligence: A Modern Approach*. Prentice Hall, 1995.

[RNA22]   L. Regenwetter, A. H. Nobari, and F. Ahmed. "Deep Generative Models in Engineering Design: A Review". In: *J. Mech. Des.* (2022).

[Rob07]   C. P. Robert. *The Bayesian Choice: From Decision-Theoretic Foundations to Computational Implementation*. en. 2nd edition. Springer Verlag, New York, 2007.

[Rob+13]   S Roberts, M Osborne, M Ebden, S Reece, N Gibson, and S Aigrain. "Gaussian processes for time-series modelling". en. In: *Philos. Trans. A Math. Phys. Eng. Sci.* 371.1984 (2013), p. 20110550.

[Rob+18]   C. P. Robert, V. Elvira, N. Tawn, and C. Wu. "Accelerating MCMC Algorithms". In: (2018). arXiv: 1804.02719 [stat.CO].

[Rob+21]   J. Robinson, C.-Y. Chuang, S. Sra, and S. Jegelka. "Contrastive Learning with Hard Negative Samples". In: *ArXiv* abs/2010.04592 (2021).

[Rob63]   L. G. Roberts. "Machine Perception of Three-Dimensional Solids". In: *Outstanding Dissertations in the Computer Sciences*. 1963.

[Rob86]   J. Robins. "A new approach to causal inference in mortality studies with a sustained exposure period—application to control of the healthy worker survivor effect". In: *Mathematical Modelling* 7.9 (1986), pp. 1393–1512.

[Rob95a]   C. Robert. "Simulation of truncated normal distributions". In: *Statistics and computing* 5 (1995), pp. 121–125.

[Rob95b] A. Robins. "Catastrophic Forgetting, Rehearsal and Pseudorehearsal". In: *Conn. Sci.* 7.2 (1995), pp. 123–146.

[Rod14] J. Rodu. "Spectral estimation of hidden Markov models". PhD thesis. U. Penn, 2014.

[RÖG13] M. Roth, E. Özkan, and F. Gustafsson. "A Student's t filter for heavy tailed process and measurement noise". In: *ICASSP*. 2013, pp. 5770–5774.

[Roh21] D. Rohde. "Causal Inference, is just Inference: A beautifully simple idea that not everyone accepts". In: *I (Still) Can't Believe It's Not Better! NeurIPS 2021 Workshop*. 2021.

[Rom+22] R. Rombach, A. Blattmann, D. Lorenz, P. Esser, and B. Ommer. "High-Resolution Image Synthesis with Latent Diffusion Models". In: *CVPR*. 2022.

[Ros10] P. Rosenbaum. *Design of Observational Studies*. 2010.

[Ros+21] M. Rosca, Y. Wu, B. Dherin, and D. G. Barrett. "Discretization Drift in Two-Player Games". In: (2021).

[Ros+22] C. Rosato, L. Devlin, V. Beraud, P. Horridge, T. B. Schön, and S. Maskell. "Efficient Learning of the Parameters of Non-Linear Models Using Differentiable Resampling in Particle Filters". In: *IEEE Trans. Signal Process.* 70 (2022), pp. 3676–3692.

[Ros22] C. Ross. *AI gone astray: How subtle shifts in patient data send popular algorithms reeling, undermining patient safety*. en. https://www.statnews.com/2022/02/28/sepsis-hospital-algorithms-data-shift/. Accessed: 2022-3-2. 2022.

[Rot+17] M. Roth, G. Hendeby, C. Fritsche, and F. Gustafsson. "The Ensemble Kalman filter: a signal processing perspective". In: *EURASIP J. Adv. Signal Processing* 2017.1 (2017), p. 56.

[Rot+18] W. Roth, R. Peharz, S. Tschiatschek, and F. Pernkopf. "Hybrid generative-discriminative training of Gaussian mixture models". In: *Pattern Recognit. Lett.* 112 (Sept. 2018), pp. 131–137.

[Rot96] D. Roth. "On the hardness of approximate reasoning". In: *Artificial Intelligence* 82.1-2 (1996), pp. 273–302.

[ROV19] A. Razavi, A. van den Oord, and O. Vinyals. "Generating diverse high resolution images with VA-VAE-2". In: *NIPS*. 2019.

[Row97] S. Roweis. "EM algorithms for PCA and SPCA". In: *NIPS*. 1997.

[Roy+21] N. Roy et al. "From Machine Learning to Robotics: Challenges and Opportunities for Embodied Intelligence". In: (Oct. 2021). arXiv: 2110.15245 [cs.RO].

[RPC19] Y. Romano, E. Patterson, and E. J. Candès. "Conformalized Quantile Regression". In: *NIPS*. 2019.

[RPH21] A. Robey, G. J. Pappas, and H. Hassani. *Model-Based Domain Generalization*. 2021. arXiv: 2102.11436 [stat.ML].

[RR01a] A. Rao and K. Rose. "Deterministically Annealed Design of Hidden Markov Model Speech Recognizers". In: *IEEE Trans. on Speech and Audio Proc.* 9.2 (2001), pp. 111–126.

[RR01b] G. Roberts and J. Rosenthal. "Optimal scaling for various Metropolis-Hastings algorithms". In: *Statistical Science* 16 (2001), pp. 351–367.

[RR08] A. Rahimi and B. Recht. "Random Features for Large-Scale Kernel Machines". In: *NIPS*. Curran Associates, Inc., 2008, pp. 1177–1184.

[RR09] A. Rahimi and B. Recht. "Weighted Sums of Random Kitchen Sinks: Replacing minimization with randomization in learning". In: *NIPS*. Curran Associates, Inc., 2009, pp. 1313–1320.

[RR11] T. S. Richardson and J. M. Robins. "Single World Intervention Graphs: A Primer". In: *Second UAI workshop on causal structure learning*. 2011.

[RR13] T. S. Richardson and J. M. Robins. "Single World Intervention Graphs (SWIGs): A Unification of the Counterfactual and Graphical Approaches to Causality". 2013.

[RR14] D. Russo and B. V. Roy. "Learning to Optimize via Posterior Sampling". In: *Math. Oper. Res.* 39.4 (2014), pp. 1221–1243.

[RR83] P. R. Rosenbaum and D. B. Rubin. "Assessing Sensitivity to an Unobserved Binary Covariate in an Observational Study with Binary Outcome". In: *Journal of the Royal Statistical Society. Series B (Methodological)* 45.2 (1983), pp. 212–218.

[RRR21] E. Rosenfeld, P. Ravikumar, and A. Risteski. "The Risks of Invariant Risk Minimization". In: *ICML*. 2021.

[RRS00] J. M. Robins, A. Rotnitzky, and D. O. Scharfstein. "Sensitivity analysis for selection bias and unmeasured confounding in missing data and causal inference models". In: *Statistical models in epidemiology, the environment, and clinical trials*. Springer, 2000, pp. 1–94.

[RS07] M. Raphan and E. P. Simoncelli. "Learning to be Bayesian without supervision". In: *Advances in neural information processing systems*. 2007, pp. 1145–1152.

[RS11] M. Raphan and E. P. Simoncelli. "Least squares estimation without priors or supervision". In: *Neural computation* 23.2 (2011), pp. 374–420.

[RS20] A. Rotnitzky and E. Smucler. "Efficient Adjustment Sets for Population Average Causal Treatment Effect Estimation in Graphical Models." In: *J. Mach. Learn. Res.* 21 (2020), pp. 188–1.

[RS97a] G. O. Roberts and S. K. Sahu. "Updating Schemes, Correlation Structure, Blocking and Parameterization for the Gibbs Sampler". In: *J. of Royal Stat. Soc. Series B* 59.2 (1997), pp. 291–317.

[RS97b] G. O. Roberts and S. K. Sahu. "Updating schemes, correlation structure, blocking and parameterization for the Gibbs sampler". In: *J. of Royal Stat. Soc. Series B* 59.2 (1997), pp. 291–317.

[RSC20] Y. Romano, M. Sesia, and E. J. Candès. "Classification with Valid and Adaptive Coverage". In: *NIPS*. 2020.

[RSG16a] M. T. Ribeiro, S. Singh, and C. Guestrin. "" Why should i trust you?" Explaining the predictions of any classifier". In: *Proceedings of the 22nd ACM SIGKDD international conference on knowledge discovery and data mining*. 2016, pp. 1135–1144.

[RSG16b] M. T. Ribeiro, S. Singh, and C. Guestrin. "Model-agnostic interpretability of machine learning". In: *arXiv preprint arXiv:1606.05386* (2016).

[RSG17] S. Rabanser, O. Shchur, and S. Günnemann. "Introduction to Tensor Decompositions and their Applications in Machine Learning". In: (2017). arXiv: 1711.10781 [stat.ML].

[RT16]   S. Reid and R. Tibshirani. "Sparse regression and marginal testing using cluster prototypes". In: *Biostatistics* 17.2 (2016), pp. 364–376.

[RT82]   D. B. Rubin and D. T. Thayer. "EM algorithms for ML factor analysis". In: *Psychometrika* 47.1 (1982), pp. 69–76.

[RT96]   G. O. Roberts and R. L. Tweedie. "Exponential convergence of Langevin distributions and their discrete approximations". en. In: *Bernoulli* 2.4 (1996), pp. 341–363.

[RTS18]   C. Riquelme, G. Tucker, and J. Snoek. "Deep Bayesian Bandits Showdown: An Empirical Comparison of Bayesian Deep Networks for Thompson Sampling". In: *ICLR*. 2018.

[RTS65]   H. E. Rauch, F. Tung, and C. T. Striebel. "Maximum likelihood estimates of linear dynamic systems". In: *AIAA Journal* 3.8 (1965), pp. 1445–1450.

[Rub+20]   Y. Rubanova, D. Dohan, K. Swersky, and K. Murphy. "Amortized Bayesian Optimization over Discrete Spaces". In: *UAI*. 2020.

[Rub74]   D. B. Rubin. "Estimating causal effects of treatments in randomized and nonrandomized studies". In: *J. Educ. Psychol.* 66.5 (1974), pp. 688–701.

[Rub76]   D. B. Rubin. "Inference and Missing Data". In: *Biometrika* 63.3 (1976), pp. 581–592.

[Rub84]   D. B. Rubin. "Bayesianly Justifiable and Relevant Frequency Calculations for the Applied Statistician". In: *Ann. Stat.* 12.4 (1984), pp. 1151–1172.

[Rub97]   R. Y. Rubinstein. "Optimization of computer simulation models with rare events". In: *Eur. J. Oper. Res.* 99.1 (1997), pp. 89–112.

[Rud19]   C. Rudin. *Stop Explaining Black Box Machine Learning Models for High Stakes Decisions and Use Interpretable Models Instead.* 2019. arXiv: 1811.10154 [stat.ML].

[Ruf+21]   L. Ruff, J. R. Kauffmann, R. A. Vandermeulen, G. Montavon, W. Samek, M. Kloft, T. G. Dietterich, and K.-R. Müller. "A Unifying Review of Deep and Shallow Anomaly Detection". In: *Proc. IEEE* 109.5 (2021), pp. 756–795.

[Rus15]   S. Russell. "Unifying Logic and Probability". In: *Commun. ACM* 58.7 (2015), pp. 88–97.

[Rus+16]   A. A. Rusu, N. C. Rabinowitz, G. Desjardins, H. Soyer, J. Kirkpatrick, K. Kavukcuoglu, R. Pascanu, and R. Hadsell. "Progressive Neural Networks". In: (2016). arXiv: 1606.04671 [cs.LG].

[Rus+18]   D. J. Russo, B. Van Roy, A. Kazerouni, I. Osband, and Z. Wen. "A Tutorial on Thompson Sampling". In: *Foundations and Trends in Machine Learning* 11.1 (2018), pp. 1–96.

[Rus+95]   S. Russell, J. Binder, D. Koller, and K. Kanazawa. "Local learning in probabilistic networks with hidden variables". In: *IJCAI*. 1995.

[RV19]   S. Ravuri and O. Vinyals. "Classification accuracy score for conditional generative models". In: *Advances in Neural Information Processing Systems*. 2019, pp. 12268–12279.

[RW06]   C. E. Rasmussen and C. K. I. Williams. *Gaussian Processes for Machine Learning.* MIT Press, 2006.

[RW11]   M. D. Reid and R. C. Williamson. "Information, Divergence and Risk for Binary Experiments". In: *Journal of Machine Learning Research* 12.3 (2011).

[RW15]   D. Rosenbaum and Y. Weiss. "The Return of the Gating Network: Combining Generative Models and Discriminative Training in Natural Image Priors". In: *NIPS*. 2015, pp. 2665–2673.

[RW18]   E. Richardson and Y. Weiss. "On GANs and GMMs". In: *NIPS*. 2018.

[RWD17]   G. Roeder, Y. Wu, and D. Duvenaud. "Sticking the Landing: An Asymptotically Zero-Variance Gradient Estimator for Variational Inference". In: *NIPS*. 2017.

[RY21]   D. Roberts and S. Yaida. *The Principles of Deep Learning Theory: An Effective Theory Approach to Understanding Neural Network.* 2021.

[Ryc+19]   B. Rychalska, D. Basaj, A. Gosiewska, and P. Biecek. "Models in the Wild: On Corruption Robustness of Neural NLP Systems". In: *International Conference on Neural Information Processing (ICONIP)*. Springer International Publishing, 2019, pp. 235–247.

[Ryu+20]   M. Ryu, Y. Chow, R. Anderson, C. Tjandraatmadja, and C. Boutilier. "CAQL: Continuous Action Q-Learning". In: *ICLR*. 2020.

[RZL17]   P. Ramachandran, B. Zoph, and Q. V. Le. "Searching for Activation Functions". In: (2017). arXiv: 1710.05941 [cs.NE].

[SA19]   F. Schafer and A. Anandkumar. "Competitive gradient descent". In: *NIPS*. 2019, pp. 7625–7635.

[Sac+05]   K. Sachs, O. Perez, D. Pe'er, D. Lauffenburger, and G. Nolan. "Causal Protein-Signaling Networks Derived from Multiparameter Single-Cell Data". In: *Science* 308 (2005).

[SAC17]   J. Schulman, P. Abbeel, and X. Chen. *Equivalence Between Policy Gradients and Soft Q-Learning.* arXiv:1704.06440. 2017.

[Sag+20]   S. Sagawa, P. W. Koh, T. B. Hashimoto, and P. Liang. "Distributionally Robust Neural Networks for Group Shifts: On the Importance of Regularization for Worst-Case Generalization". In: *ICLR*. 2020.

[Sah+21]   C. Saharia, W. Chan, H. Chang, C. A. Lee, J. Ho, T. Salimans, D. J. Fleet, and M. Norouzi. "Palette: Image-to-Image Diffusion Models". In: (Nov. 2021). arXiv: 2111.05826 [cs.CV].

[Sah+22]   C. Saharia et al. "Photorealistic Text-to-Image Diffusion Models with Deep Language Understanding". In: (May 2022). arXiv: 2205.11487 [cs.CV].

[Sai+20]   M. Saito, S. Saito, M. Koyama, and S. Kobayashi. "Train Sparsely, Generate Densely: Memory-Efficient Unsupervised Training of High-Resolution Temporal GAN". In: *International Journal of Computer Vision* 128 (2020), pp. 2586–2606.

[Saj+18]   M. S. Sajjadi, O. Bachem, M. Lucic, O. Bousquet, and S. Gelly. "Assessing generative models via precision and recall". In: *Proceedings of the 32nd International Conference on Neural Information Processing Systems*. 2018, pp. 5234–5243.

[Sal16]   T. Salimans. "A Structured Variational Autoencoder for Learning Deep Hierarchies of Sparse Features". In: (2016). arXiv: 1602.08734 [stat.ML].

[Sal+16]   T. Salimans, I. Goodfellow, W. Zaremba, V. Cheung, A. Radford, and X. Chen. "Improved Techniques for Training GANs". In: (2016). arXiv: 1606.03498 [cs.LG].

[Sal+17a]   M. Salehi, A. Karbasi, D. Scheinost, and R. T. Constable. "A Submodular Approach to Create Individualized Parcellations of the Human Brain". In:

Medical Image Computing and Computer Assisted Intervention - MICCAI 2017. Ed. by M. Descoteaux, L. Maier-Hein, A. Franz, P. Jannin, D. L. Collins, and S. Duchesne. Cham: Springer International Publishing, 2017, pp. 478–485.

[Sal+17b] T. Salimans, J. Ho, X. Chen, and I. Sutskever. "Evolution Strategies as a Scalable Alternative to Reinforcement Learning". In: (2017). arXiv: 1703.03864 [stat.ML].

[Sal+17c] T. Salimans, A. Karpathy, X. Chen, and D. P. Kingma. "PixelCNN++: Improving the Pixel-CNN with Discretized Logistic Mixture Likelihood and Other Modifications". In: *ICLR*. 2017.

[Sal+19a] D. Salinas, M. Bohlke-Schneider, L. Callot, R. Medico, and J. Gasthaus. "High-Dimensional Multivariate Forecasting with Low-Rank Gaussian Copula Processes". In: *NIPS*. 2019.

[Sal+19b] D. Salinas, V. Flunkert, J. Gasthaus, and T. Januschowski. "DeepAR: Probabilistic forecasting with autoregressive recurrent networks". In: *International Journal of Forecasting* (2019).

[Sal+20] H. Salman, A. Ilyas, L. Engstrom, A. Kapoor, and A. Madry. "Do Adversarially Robust ImageNet Models Transfer Better?" In: *arXiv preprint arXiv:2007.08489* (2020).

[Sal+21] M. Salehi, H. Mirzaei, D. Hendrycks, Y. Li, M. H. Rohban, and M. Sabokrou. "A Unified Survey on Anomaly, Novelty, Open-Set, and Out-of-Distribution Detection: Solutions and Future Challenges". In: (2021). arXiv: 2110.14051 [cs.CV].

[Sam74] P. A. Samuelson. "Complementarity: An essay on the 40th anniversary of the Hicks-Allen revolution in demand theory". In: *Journal of Economic literature* 12.4 (1974), pp. 1255–1289.

[San17] R. Santana. "Gray-box optimization and factorized distribution algorithms: where two worlds collide". In: (2017). arXiv: 1707.03093 [cs.NE].

[San+17] A. Santoro, D. Raposo, D. G. Barrett, M. Malinowski, R. Pascanu, P. Battaglia, and T. Lillicrap. "A simple neural network module for relational reasoning". In: *Advances in neural information processing systems*. 2017, pp. 4967–4976.

[Sar08] S. Sarkka. "Unscented Rauch–Tung–Striebel Smoother". In: *IEEE Trans. Automat. Contr.* 53.3 (Apr. 2008), pp. 845–849.

[Sar13] S. Sarkka. *Bayesian Filtering and Smoothing.* Cambridge University Press, 2013.

[Sar18] H. Sarin. "Playing a game of GANstruction". In: *The Gradient* (2018).

[Say+19] R. Sayres, S. Xu, T Saensuksopa, M. Le, and D. R. Webster. "Assistance from a deep learning system improves diabetic retinopathy assessment in optometrists". In: *Investigative Ophthalmology & Visual Science* 60.9 (2019), pp. 1433–1433.

[SB01] A. J. Smola and P. L. Bartlett. "Sparse Greedy Gaussian Process Regression". In: *NIPS*. Ed. by T. K. Leen, T. G. Dietterich, and V Tresp. MIT Press, 2001, pp. 619–625.

[SB18] R. Sutton and A. Barto. *Reinforcement learning: an introduction (2nd edn).* MIT Press, 2018.

[SBG07] S. Siddiqi, B. Boots, and G. Gordon. "A constraint generation approach to learning stable linear dynamical systems". In: *NIPS*. 2007.

[SBP17] Y Sun, P Babu, and D. P. Palomar. "Majorization-Minimization Algorithms in Signal Processing, Communications, and Machine Learning". In: *IEEE Trans. Signal Process.* 65.3 (2017), pp. 794–816.

[SC13] C. Schäfer and N. Chopin. "Sequential Monte Carlo on large binary sampling spaces". In: *Stat. Comput.* 23.2 (2013), pp. 163–184.

[SC86] R. Smith and P. Cheeseman. "On the Representation and Estimation of Spatial Uncertainty". In: *Intl. J. Robotics Research* 5.4 (1986), pp. 56–68.

[SC90] R. Schwarz and Y. Chow. "The n-best algorithm: an efficient and exact procedure for finding the n most likely hypotheses". In: *ICASSP*. 1990.

[Sca21] S. Scardapane. *Lecture 8: Beyond single-task supervised learning.* 2021.

[Sch00] A. Schrijver. "A combinatorial algorithm minimizing submodular functions in strongly polynomial time". In: *Journal of Combinatorial Theory, Series B* 80.2 (2000), pp. 346–355.

[Sch02] N. N. Schraudolph. "Fast Curvature Matrix-Vector Products for Second-Order Gradient Descent". In: *Neural Computation* 14 (2002).

[Sch04] A. Schrijver. *Combinatorial Optimization.* Springer, 2004.

[Sch+12a] B. Schoelkopf, D. Janzing, J. Peters, E. Sgouritsa, K. Zhang, and J. Mooij. "On Causal and Anticausal Learning". In: *ICML*. 2012.

[Sch+12b] B. Schölkopf, D. Janzing, J. Peters, E. Sgouritsa, K. Zhang, and J. Mooij. "On causal and anticausal learning". In: *Proceedings of the 29th International Coference on International Conference on Machine Learning*. 2012, pp. 459–466.

[Sch14] J. Schmidhuber. *Deep Learning in Neural Networks: An Overview.* Tech. rep. 2014.

[Sch+15a] J. Schulman, N. Heess, T. Weber, and P. Abbeel. "Gradient Estimation Using Stochastic Computation Graphs". In: *NIPS*. 2015.

[Sch+15b] J. Schulman, S. Levine, P. Moritz, M. I. Jordan, and P. Abbeel. "Trust Region Policy Optimization". In: *ICML*. 2015.

[Sch+16a] T. Schaul, J. Quan, I. Antonoglou, and D. Silver. "Prioritized Experience Replay". In: *ICLR*. 2016.

[Sch+16b] J. Schulman, P. Moritz, S. Levine, M. Jordan, and P. Abbeel. "High-Dimensional Continuous Control Using Generalized Advantage Estimation". In: *ICLR*. 2016.

[Sch+17] J. Schulman, F. Wolski, P. Dhariwal, A. Radford, and O. Klimov. "Proximal Policy Optimization Algorithms". In: (2017). arXiv: 1707.06347 [cs.LG].

[Sch+18] J. Schwarz, J. Luketina, W. M. Czarnecki, A. Grabska-Barwinska, Y. W. Teh, R. Pascanu, and R. Hadsell. "Progress & Compress: A scalable framework for continual learning". In: *ICML*. 2018.

[Sch19] B. Schölkopf. "Causality for Machine Learning". In: (2019). arXiv: 1911.10500 [cs.LG].

[Sch20] J. Schmidhuber. *Planning & Reinforcement Learning with Recurrent World Models and Artificial Curiosity.* 2020.

[Sch+20] J. Schrittwieser et al. "Mastering Atari, Go, Chess and Shogi by Planning with a Learned Model". In: *Nature* (2020).

[Sch+21a] D. O. Scharfstein, R. Nabi, E. H. Kennedy, M.-Y. Huang, M. Bonvini, and M. Smid. *Semipara-*

ography

[...] *metric Sensitivity Analysis: Unmeasured Confounding In Observational Studies.* 2021. arXiv: 2104.08300 [stat.ME].

[Sch+21b] B. Schölkopf, F. Locatello, S. Bauer, N. R. Ke, N. Kalchbrenner, A. Goyal, and Y. Bengio. "Toward Causal Representation Learning". In: *Proc. IEEE* 109.5 (2021), pp. 612–634.

[Sch+21c] B. Schölkopf, F. Locatello, S. Bauer, N. R. Ke, N. Kalchbrenner, A. Goyal, and Y. Bengio. "Towards Causal Representation Learning". In: *CoRR* abs/2102.11107 (2021). arXiv: 2102.11107.

[Sch78] G. Schwarz. "Estimating the dimension of a model". In: *Annals of Statistics* 6.2 (1978), pp. 461–464.

[Sco02] S Scott. "Bayesian methods for hidden Markov models: Recursive computing in the 21st century." In: *JASA* (2002).

[Sco09] S. Scott. "Data augmentation, frequentist estimation, and the Bayesian analysis of multinomial logit models". In: *Statistical Papers* (2009).

[Sco10] S. Scott. "A modern Bayesian look at the multi-armed bandit". In: *Applied Stochastic Models in Business and Industry* 26 (2010), pp. 639–658.

[SCPD22] R. Sanchez-Cauce, I. Paris, and F. J. Diez. "Sum-Product Networks: A Survey". en. In: *IEEE PAMI* 44.7 (July 2022), pp. 3821–3839.

[SCS19] A. Subbaswamy, B. Chen, and S. Saria. *A Universal Hierarchy of Shift-Stable Distributions and the Tradeoff Between Stability and Performance.* 2019. arXiv: 1905.11374 [stat.ML].

[SCS22] A. Subbaswamy, B. Chen, and S. Saria. "A unifying causal framework for analyzing dataset shift-stable learning algorithms". en. In: *Journal of Causal Inference* 10.1 (Jan. 2022), pp. 64–89.

[SD12] J. Sohl-Dickstein. "The Natural Gradient by Analogy to Signal Whitening, and Recipes and Tricks for its Use". In: (2012). arXiv: 1205.1828 [cs.LG].

[SD+15a] J. Sohl-Dickstein, E. Weiss, N. Maheswaranathan, and S. Ganguli. "Deep Unsupervised Learning using Nonequilibrium Thermodynamics". In: *ICML.* 2015, pp. 2256–2265.

[SD+15b] J. Sohl-Dickstein, E. A. Weiss, N. Maheswaranathan, and S. Ganguli. "Deep Unsupervised Learning using Nonequilibrium Thermodynamics". In: *ICML.* 2015.

[SDBD11] J. Sohl-Dickstein, P. Battaglino, and M. R. DeWeese. "Minimum probability flow learning". In: *Proceedings of the 28th International Conference on International Conference on Machine Learning.* 2011, pp. 905–912.

[SE19] Y. Song and S. Ermon. "Generative Modeling by Estimating Gradients of the Data Distribution". In: *NIPS.* 2019, pp. 11895–11907.

[SE20a] J. Song and S. Ermon. "Multi-label Contrastive Predictive Coding". In: *NIPS.* 2020.

[SE20b] Y. Song and S. Ermon. "Improved Techniques for Training Score-Based Generative Models". In: *NIPS.* 2020.

[See+17] M. Seeger, S. Rangapuram, Y. Wang, D. Salinas, J. Gasthaus, T. Januschowski, and V. Flunkert. "Approximate Bayesian Inference in Linear State Space Models for Intermittent Demand Forecasting at Scale". In: (2017). arXiv: 1709.07638 [stat.ML].

[Sej20] T. J. Sejnowski. "The unreasonable effectiveness of deep learning in artificial intelligence". en. In: *PNAS* 117.48 (Dec. 2020), pp. 30033–30038.

[Sel+17] R. R. Selvaraju, M. Cogswell, A. Das, R. Vedantam, D. Parikh, and D. Batra. "Grad-cam: Visual explanations from deep networks via gradient-based localization". In: *Proceedings of the IEEE international conference on computer vision.* 2017, pp. 618–626.

[Sel+19] A. D. Selbst, D. Boyd, S. A. Friedler, S. Venkatasubramanian, and J. Vertesi. "Fairness and Abstraction in Sociotechnical Systems". In: *Proceedings of the Conference on Fairness, Accountability, and Transparency.* FAT* '19. Atlanta, GA, USA: Association for Computing Machinery, 2019, 59–68.

[Sen+08] P. Sen, G. Namata, M. Bilgic, L. Getoor, B. Galligher, and T. Eliassi-Rad. "Collective Classification in Network Data". en. In: *AI Magazine* 29.3 (2008), pp. 93–93.

[Ser+20] J. Serrà, D. Álvarez, V. Gómez, O. Slizovskaia, J. F. Núñez, and J. Luque. "Input complexity and out-of-distribution detection with likelihood-based generative models". In: *ICLR.* 2020.

[Set12] B. Settles. "Active learning". In: *Synthesis Lectures on Artificial Intelligence and Machine Learning* 6 (2012), 1–114.

[SF08] Z. Svitkina and L. Fleischer. "Submodular approximation: Sampling-based algorithms and lower bounds". In: *FOCS.* 2008.

[SF20] K. Sokol and P. Flach. "Explainability fact sheets: a framework for systematic assessment of explainable approaches". In: *Proceedings of the 2020 Conference on Fairness, Accountability, and Transparency.* 2020, pp. 56–67.

[SFB18] S. A. Sisson, Y. Fan, and M. A. Beaumont. "Overview of ABC". In: *Handbook of approximate Bayesian computation.* Chapman and Hall/CRC, 2018, pp. 3–54.

[SG02] J. L. Schafer and J. W. Graham. "Missing data: our view of the state of the art". en. In: *Psychol. Methods* 7.2 (June 2002), pp. 147–177.

[SG05] E. Snelson and Z. Ghahramani. "Compact Approximations to Bayesian Predictive Distributions". In: *ICML.* 2005.

[SG06a] E. Snelson and Z. Ghahramani. "Sparse Gaussian processes using pseudo-inputs". In: *NIPS.* 2006.

[SG06b] E. Snelson and Z. Ghahramani. "Sparse Gaussian Processes using Pseudo-inputs". In: *Advances in Neural Information Processing Systems.* Ed. by Y. Weiss, B. Schölkopf, and J. Platt. Vol. 18. MIT Press, 2006.

[SG07] M. Steyvers and T. Griffiths. "Probabilistic topic models". In: *Latent Semantic Analysis: A Road to Meaning.* Ed. by T. Landauer, D McNamara, S. Dennis, and W. Kintsch. Laurence Erlbaum, 2007.

[SG09] R. Silva and Z. Ghahramani. "The Hidden Life of Latent Variables: Bayesian Learning with Mixed Graph Models". In: *JMLR* 10 (2009), pp. 1187–1238.

[SGF21] S. Särkkä and Á. F. García-Fernández. "Temporal Parallelization of Bayesian Filters and Smoothers". In: *IEEE Trans. Automat. Contr.* 66.1 (2021).

[SGS16] A. Sharghi, B. Gong, and M. Shah. "Query-focused extractive video summarization". In: *European Conference on Computer Vision.* Springer. 2016, pp. 3–19.

[SH07] R. Salakhutdinov and G. Hinton. "Using Deep Belief Nets to Learn Covariance Kernels for Gaussian Processes". In: *NIPS*. 2007.

[SH09] R. Salakhutdinov and G. Hinton. "Deep Boltzmann Machines". In: *AISTATS*. Vol. 5. 2009, pp. 448–455.

[SH10] R. Salakhutdinov and G. Hinton. "Replicated Softmax: an Undirected Topic Model". In: *NIPS*. 2010.

[SH21] T. Salimans and J. Ho. "Should EBMs model the energy or the score?" In: *ICLR Energy Based Models Workshop*. Apr. 2021.

[SH22] T. Salimans and J. Ho. "Progressive Distillation for Fast Sampling of Diffusion Models". In: *ICLR*. Feb. 2022.

[SHA15] M. A. Skoglund, G. Hendeby, and D. Axehill. "Extended Kalman filter modifications based on an optimization view point". In: *2015 18th International Conference on Information Fusion (Fusion)*. July 2015, pp. 1856–1861.

[Sha+16] B Shahriari, K Swersky, Z. Wang, R. P. Adams, and N de Freitas. "Taking the Human Out of the Loop: A Review of Bayesian Optimization". In: *Proc. IEEE* 104.1 (2016), pp. 148–175.

[Sha16] L. S. Shapley. *17. A value for n-person games.* Princeton University Press, 2016.

[Sha+16] M. Sharif, S. Bhagavatula, L. Bauer, and M. K. Reiter. "Accessorize to a Crime: Real and Stealthy Attacks on State-of-the-Art Face Recognition". In: *Proceedings of the 2016 ACM SIGSAC Conference on Computer and Communications Security*. ACM, 2016, pp. 1528–1540.

[Sha+19] A. Shaikhha, A. Fitzgibbon, D. Vytiniotis, and S. Peyton Jones. "Efficient differentiable programming in a functional array-processing language". In: *Proceedings of the ACM on Programming Languages* 3.ICFP (2019), pp. 1–30.

[Sha+20] H. Shah, K. Tamuly, A. Raghunathan, P. Jain, and P. Netrapalli. "The Pitfalls of Simplicity Bias in Neural Networks". In: *NIPS*. 2020.

[Sha22] C. Shalizi. *Advanced Data Analysis from an Elementary Point of View*. Cambridge University Press, 2022.

[Sha48] C. Shannon. "A mathematical theory of communication". In: *Bell Systems Tech. Journal* 27 (1948), pp. 379–423.

[Sha98] R. Shachter. "Bayes-Ball: The Rational Pastime (for determining Irrelevance and Requisite Information in Belief Networks and Influence Diagrams)". In: *UAI*. 1998.

[She+11] C. Shen, X. Li, L. Li, and M. C. Were. "Sensitivity analysis for causal inference using inverse probability weighting". In: *Biometrical Journal* 53.5 (2011), pp. 822–837. eprint: https://onlinelibrary.wiley.com/doi/pdf/10.1002/bimj.201100042.

[She+17] T. Shen, T. Lei, R. Barzilay, and T. Jaakkola. "Style transfer from non-parallel text by cross-alignment". In: *Advances in neural information processing systems* 30 (2017), pp. 6830–6841.

[She+20] T. Shen, J. Mueller, R. Barzilay, and T. Jaakkola. "Educating Text Autoencoders: Latent Representation Guidance via Denoising". In: *ICML*. 2020.

[She+21] Z. Shen, J. Liu, Y. He, X. Zhang, R. Xu, H. Yu, and P. Cui. "Towards Out-Of-Distribution Generalization: A Survey". In: (2021). arXiv: 2108.13624 [cs.LG].

[SHF15] R. Steorts, R. Hall, and S. Fienberg. "A Bayesian Approach to Graphical Record Linkage and De-duplication". In: *JASA* (2015).

[Shi00a] H. Shimodaira. "Improving predictive inference under covariate shift by weighting the log-likelihood function". In: *J. Stat. Plan. Inference* 90.2 (2000), pp. 227–244.

[Shi00b] B. Shipley. *Cause and Correlation in Biology: A User's Guide to Path Analysis, Structural Equations and Causal Inference*. Cambridge, 2000.

[Shi+21] C. Shi, D. Sridhar, V. Misra, and D. M. Blei. "On the Assumptions of Synthetic Control Methods". In: (2021). arXiv: 2112.05671 [stat.ME].

[SHM14] D. Soudry, I. Hubara, and R. Meir. "Expectation backpropagation: Parameter-free training of multilayer neural networks with continuous or discrete weights". In: *NIPS*. 2014.

[Shr+16] A. Shrikumar, P. Greenside, A. Shcherbina, and A. Kundaje. "Not just a black box: Learning important features through propagating activation differences". In: *arXiv preprint arXiv:1605.01713* (2016).

[SHS] D. Stutz, M. Hein, and B. Schiele. "Confidence-calibrated adversarial training: Generalizing to unseen attacks". In: ().

[SHS01] B. Schölkopf, R. Herbrich, and A. J. Smola. "A Generalized Representer Theorem". In: *COLT*. COLT '01/EuroCOLT '01. Springer-Verlag, 2001, pp. 416–426.

[Shu+19a] K. Shu, L. Cui, S. Wang, D. Lee, and H. Liu. "defend: Explainable fake news detection". In: *Proceedings of the 25th ACM SIGKDD international conference on knowledge discovery & data mining*. 2019, pp. 395–405.

[Shu+19b] R. Shu, Y. Chen, A. Kumar, S. Ermon, and B. Poole. "Weakly supervised disentanglement with guarantees". In: *arXiv preprint arXiv:1910.09772* (2019).

[SI00] M. Sato and S. Ishii. "On-line EM algorithm for the normalized Gaussian network". In: *Neural Computation* 12 (2000), pp. 407–432.

[Sil+14] D. Silver, G. Lever, N. Heess, T. Degris, D. Wierstra, and M. Riedmiller. "Deterministic Policy Gradient Algorithms". In: *ICML*. ICML'14. JMLR.org, 2014, pp. I–387–I–395.

[Sil+16] D. Silver et al. "Mastering the game of Go with deep neural networks and tree search". en. In: *Nature* 529.7587 (2016), pp. 484–489.

[Sil18] D. Silver. *Lecture 9L Exploration and Exploitation*. 2018.

[Sil+18] D. Silver et al. "A general reinforcement learning algorithm that masters chess, shogi, and Go through self-play". en. In: *Science* 362.6419 (2018), pp. 1140–1144.

[Sil85] B. W. Silverman. "Some Aspects of the Spline Smoothing Approach to Non-Parametric Regression Curve Fitting". In: *J. R. Stat. Soc. Series B Stat. Methodol.* 47.1 (1985), pp. 1–52.

[Sim02] D. Simon. "Training radial basis neural networks with the extended Kalman Filter". In: *Neurocomputing* (2002).

[Sim06] D. Simon. *Optimal State Estimation: Kalman, H Infinity, and Nonlinear Approaches.* Wiley, 2006.

[Sin+00] S. Singh, T. Jaakkola, M. L. Littman, and C. Szepesvári. "Convergence Results for Single-Step On-PolicyReinforcement-Learning Algorithms". In: *MLJ* 38.3 (2000), pp. 287–308.

[Sin67] R. Sinkhorn. "Diagonal Equivalence to Matrices with Prescribed Row and Column Sums". In: *The American Mathematical Monthly* 74.4 (1967), pp. 402–405.

[Siv+20] T. Sivula, M. Magnusson, A. A. Matamoros, and A. Vehtari. "Uncertainty in Bayesian Leave-One-Out Cross-Validation Based Model Comparison". In: (Aug. 2020). arXiv: 2008.10296 [stat.ME].

[SJ08] S. Shirdhonkar and D. W. Jacobs. "Approximate earth mover's distance in linear time". In: *2008 IEEE Conference on Computer Vision and Pattern Recognition.* IEEE. 2008, pp. 1–8.

[SJ15] A. Swaminathan and T. Joachims. "Batch Learning from Logged Bandit Feedback through Counterfactual Risk Minimization". In: *JMLR* 16.1 (2015), pp. 1731–1755.

[SJ95] L. Saul and M. Jordan. "Exploiting tractable substructures in intractable networks". In: *NIPS.* Vol. 8. 1995.

[SJ99] L. Saul and M. Jordan. "Mixed memory Markov models: Decomposing complex stochastic processes as mixture of simpler ones". In: *Machine Learning* 37.1 (1999), pp. 75–87.

[SJJ96] L. Saul, T. Jaakkola, and M. Jordan. "Mean Field Theory for Sigmoid Belief Networks". In: *JAIR* 4 (1996), pp. 61–76.

[SJR04] S. Singh, M. James, and M. Rudary. "Predictive state representations: A new theory for modeling dynamical systems". In: *UAI.* 2004.

[SK19] C. Shorten and T. M. Khoshgoftaar. "A survey on Image Data Augmentation for Deep Learning". en. In: *Journal of Big Data* 6.1 (2019), pp. 1–48.

[SK20] S. Singh and S. Krishnan. "Filter Response Normalization Layer: Eliminating Batch Dependence in the Training of Deep Neural Networks". In: *CVPR.* 2020.

[SK89] R. Shachter and C. R. Kenley. "Gaussian Influence Diagrams". In: *Managment Science* 35.5 (1989), pp. 527–550.

[Ski06] J. Skilling. "Nested sampling for general Bayesian computation". In: *Bayesian Analysis* 1.4 (2006), pp. 833–860.

[Ski89] J. Skilling. "The eigenvalues of megadimensional matrices". In: *Maximum Entropy and Bayesian Methods.* Springer, 1989, pp. 455–466.

[SKM07] M. Sugiyama, M. Krauledat, and K.-R. Müller. "Covariate Shift Adaptation by Importance Weighted Cross Validation". In: *J. Mach. Learn. Res.* 8.35 (2007), pp. 985–1005.

[SKM18] S. Schwöbel, S. Kiebel, and D. Marković. "Active Inference, Belief Propagation, and the Bethe Approximation". en. In: *Neural Comput.* 30.9 (2018), pp. 2530–2567.

[SKM21] M. Shanahan, C. Kaplanis, and J. Mitrović. "Encoders and Ensembles for Task-Free Continual Learning". In: (2021). arXiv: 2105.13327 [cs.LG].

[SKP15] F. Schroff, D. Kalenichenko, and J. Philbin. "Facenet: A unified embedding for face recognition and clustering". In: *Proceedings of the IEEE conference on computer vision and pattern recognition.* 2015, pp. 815–823.

[SKTF18] H. Shao, A. Kumar, and P Thomas Fletcher. "The Riemannian Geometry of Deep Generative Models". In: *CVPR.* 2018, pp. 315–323.

[SKW15] T. Salimans, D. Kingma, and M. Welling. "Markov Chain Monte Carlo and Variational Inference: Bridging the Gap". In: *ICML.* 2015, pp. 1218–1226.

[SL08] A. L. Strehl and M. L. Littman. "An Analysis of Model-based Interval Estimation for Markov Decision Processes". In: *J. of Comp. and Sys. Sci.* 74.8 (2008), pp. 1309–1331.

[SL18] S. L. Smith and Q. V. Le. "A Bayesian Perspective on Generalization and Stochastic Gradient Descent". In: *ICLR.* 2018.

[SL90] D. J. Spiegelhalter and S. L. Lauritzen. "Sequential updating of conditional probabilities on directed graphical structures". In: *Networks* 20 (1990).

[Sla+20] D. Slack, S. Hilgard, E. Jia, S. Singh, and H. Lakkaraju. "Fooling lime and shap: Adversarial attacks on post hoc explanation methods". In: *Proceedings of the AAAI/ACM Conference on AI, Ethics, and Society.* 2020, pp. 180–186.

[SLG17] A. Sharghi, J. S. Laurel, and B. Gong. "Query-focused video summarization: Dataset, evaluation, and a memory network based approach". In: *Proceedings of the IEEE Conference on Computer Vision and Pattern Recognition.* 2017, pp. 4788–4797.

[Sli19] A. Slivkins. "Introduction to Multi-Armed Bandits". In: *Foundations and Trends in Machine Learning* (2019).

[SLL09] A. L. Strehl, L. Li, and M. L. Littman. "Reinforcement Learning in Finite MDPs: PAC Analysis". In: *JMLR* 10 (2009), pp. 2413–2444.

[SLM92] B. Selman, H. Levesque, and D. Mitchell. "A New Method for Solving Hard Satisfiability Problems". In: *Proceedings of the Tenth National Conference on Artificial Intelligence.* AAAI'92. AAAI Press, 1992, pp. 440–446.

[SLW19] M. Sadinle, J. Lei, and L. Wasserman. "Least Ambiguous Set-Valued Classifiers With Bounded Error Levels". In: *JASA* 114.525 (2019), pp. 223–234.

[SM07] C. Sutton and A. McCallum. "Improved Dynamic Schedules for Belief Propagation". In: *UAI.* 2007.

[SM12] Y Saika and K Morimoto. "Generalized MAP estimation via parameter scheduling and maximizer of the posterior marginal estimate for image reconstruction using multiple halftone images". In: *12th International Conference on Control, Automation and Systems.* 2012, pp. 1285–1289.

[SMB10] H. Schulz, A. Müller, and S. Behnke. "Investigating convergence of restricted Boltzmann machine learning". In: *NIPS 2010 Workshop on Deep Learning and Unsupervised Feature Learning.* Vol. 1. 2. 2010, pp. 6–1.

[SME21] J. Song, C. Meng, and S. Ermon. "Denoising Diffusion Implicit Models". In: *ICLR.* 2021.

[SMH07] R. R. Salakhutdinov, A. Mnih, and G. E. Hinton. "Restricted Boltzmann machines for collaborative filtering". In: *ICML.* Vol. 24. 2007, pp. 791–798.

[Smi+00] G. Smith, J. F. G. de Freitas, T. Robinson, and M. Niranjan. "Speech Modelling Using Subspace and EM Techniques". In: *NIPS*. MIT Press, 2000, pp. 796–802.

[Smi+06] V. Smith, J. Yu, T. Smulders, A. Hartemink, and E. Jarvis. "Computational Inference of Neural Information Flow Networks". In: *PLOS Computational Biology* 2 (2006), pp. 1436–1439.

[Smi11] N. Smith. *Linguistic structure prediction.* Morgan Claypool, 2011.

[Smi+17] D. Smilkov, N. Thorat, B. Kim, F. Viégas, and M. Wattenberg. *SmoothGrad: removing noise by adding noise.* 2017. arXiv: 1706.03825 [cs.LG].

[Smo86] P. Smolensky. "Information processing in dynamical systems: foundations of harmony theory". In: *Parallel Distributed Processing: Explorations in the Microstructure of Cognition. Volume 1.* Ed. by D. Rumehart and J. McClelland. McGraw-Hill, 1986.

[SMS17] M. Saito, E. Matsumoto, and S. Saito. "Temporal Generative Adversarial Nets with Singular Value Clipping". In: *ICCV*. 2017.

[SMT18] M. R. U. Saputra, A. Markham, and N. Trigoni. "Visual SLAM and Structure from Motion in Dynamic Environments: A Survey". In: *ACM Computing Surveys* 51.2 (2018), pp. 1–36.

[Smy20] S. Smyl. "A hybrid method of exponential smoothing and recurrent neural networks for time series forecasting". In: *Int. J. Forecast.* 36.1 (2020), pp. 75–85.

[Sn+16] C. K. Sø nderby, T. Raiko, L. Maalø e, S. R. K. Sø nderby, and O. Winther. "Ladder Variational Autoencoders". In: *NIPS*. Curran Associates, Inc., 2016, pp. 3738–3746.

[SNM16] M. Suzuki, K. Nakayama, and Y. Matsuo. "Joint Multimodal Learning with Deep Generative Models". In: (2016). arXiv: 1611.01891 [stat.ML].

[SOB12] R. Snyder, J. K. Ord, and A. Beaumont. "Forecasting the intermittent demand for slow-moving inventories: A modelling approach". In: *Int. J. Forecast.* 28.2 (2012), pp. 485–496.

[Soh16] K. Sohn. "Improved deep metric learning with multi-class n-pair loss objective". In: *Advances in Neural Information Processing Systems*. 2016, pp. 1857–1865.

[Søn+16] C. Sønderby, T. Raiko, L. Maaløe, S. Sønderby, and O. Winther. "How to Train Deep Variational Autoencoders and Probabilistic Ladder Networks". In: *ICML*. 2016.

[Son+19] Y. Song, S. Garg, J. Shi, and S. Ermon. "Sliced Score Matching: A Scalable Approach to Density and Score Estimation". In: *Proceedings of the Thirty-Fifth Conference on Uncertainty in Artificial Intelligence, UAI 2019, Tel Aviv, Israel, July 22-25, 2019.* 2019, p. 204.

[Son+21a] Y. Song, C. Durkan, I. Murray, and S. Ermon. "Maximum Likelihood Training of Score-Based Diffusion Models". In: *NIPS*. 2021.

[Son+21b] Y. Song, J. Sohl-Dickstein, D. P. Kingma, A. Kumar, S. Ermon, and B. Poole. "Score-Based Generative Modeling through Stochastic Differential Equations". In: *ICLR*. 2021.

[Son98] E. D. Sontag. *Mathematical Control Theory: Deterministic Finite Dimensional Systems.* 2nd. Vol. 6. Texts in Applied Mathematics. Springer, 1998.

[SOS92] H. Seung, M. Opper, and H. Sompolinsky. "Query by committee". In: *5th Annual Workshop on Computational Learning Theory*. 1992, 287–294.

[SPD92] S. Shah, F. Palmieri, and M. Datum. "Optimal filtering algorithms for fast learning in feedforward neural networks". In: *Neural Netw.* 5.5 (1992), pp. 779–787.

[Spi71] M. Spivak. *Calculus On Manifolds: A Modern Approach To Classical Theorems Of Advanced Calculus.* Westview Press; 5th edition, 1971.

[SPL20] M. B. Sariyildiz, J. Perez, and D. Larlus. "Learning visual representations with caption annotations". In: *Computer Vision–ECCV 2020: 16th European Conference, Glasgow, UK, August 23–28, 2020, Proceedings, Part VIII 16.* Springer. 2020, pp. 153–170.

[Spr+14] J. T. Springenberg, A. Dosovitskiy, T. Brox, and M. Riedmiller. "Striving for simplicity: The all convolutional net". In: *arXiv preprint arXiv:1412.6806* (2014).

[Spr+16] J. T. Springenberg, A. Klein, S. Falkner, and F. Hutter. "Bayesian Optimization with Robust Bayesian Neural Networks". In: *NIPS*. 2016, pp. 4141–4149.

[SPW18] M. H. S. Segler, M. Preuss, and M. P. Waller. "Planning chemical syntheses with deep neural networks and symbolic AI". en. In: *Nature* 555.7698 (2018), pp. 604–610.

[SPZ09] P. Schniter, L. C. Potter, and J. Ziniel. "Fast Bayesian Matching Pursuit: Model Uncertainty and Parameter Estimation for Sparse Linear Models". In: *IEEE Trans. on Signal Processing* (2009).

[SQ05] V. Smidl and A. Quinn. *The Variational Bayes Method in Signal Processing.* Springer, 2005.

[SR+14] A. Sharif Razavian, H. Azizpour, J. Sullivan, and S. Carlsson. "CNN features off-the-shelf: an astounding baseline for recognition". In: *Proceedings of the IEEE conference on computer vision and pattern recognition workshops*. 2014, pp. 806–813.

[SRG03] R. Salakhutdinov, S. T. Roweis, and Z. Ghahramani. "Optimization with EM and Expectation-Conjugate-Gradient". In: *ICML*. 2003.

[Sri+09] B. K. Sriperumbudur, K. Fukumizu, A. Gretton, B. Schölkopf, and G. R. G. Lanckriet. "On integral probability metrics, φ-divergences and binary classification". In: (2009). arXiv: 0901.2698 [cs.IT].

[Sri+10] N. Srinivas, A. Krause, S. Kakade, and M. Seeger. "Gaussian Process Optimization in the Bandit Setting: No Regret and Experimental Design". In: *ICML*. 2010, pp. 1015–1022.

[Sri+14a] N. Srivastava, G. Hinton, A. Krizhevsky, I. Sutskever, and R. Salakhutdinov. "Dropout: A Simple Way to Prevent Neural Networks from Over tting". In: *JMLR* (2014).

[Sri+14b] N. Srivastava, G. E. Hinton, A. Krizhevsky, I. Sutskever, and R. Salakhutdinov. "Dropout: a simple way to prevent neural networks from overfitting". In: *J. Mach. Learn. Res.* 15 (2014), pp. 1929–1958.

[Sri+17] A. Srivastava, L. Valkov, C. Russell, M. U. Gutmann, and C. Sutton. "Veegan: Reducing mode collapse in gans using implicit variational learning". In: *Proceedings of the 31st International Conference on Neural Information Processing Systems*. 2017, pp. 3310–3320.

[SRS10]   P. Schnitzspan, S. Roth, and B. Schiele. "Automatic discovery of meaningful object parts with latent CRFs". In: *CVPR*. 2010.

[SS15]   D. J. Sutherland and J. Schneider. "On the Error of Random Fourier Features". In: *UAI*. June 2015.

[SS17a]   A. Srivastava and C. Sutton. "Autoencoding Variational Inference For Topic Models". In: *ICLR*. 2017.

[SS17b]   A. Srivastava and C. Sutton. "Autoencoding Variational Inference For Topic Models". In: *ICLR*. 2017.

[SS18a]   O. Sener and S. Savarese. "Active Learning for Convolutional Neural Networks: A Core-Set Approach". In: *International Conference on Learning Representations*. 2018.

[SS18b]   A. Subbaswamy and S. Saria. "Counterfactual Normalization: Proactively Addressing Dataset Shift and Improving Reliability Using Causal Mechanisms". In: *Proceedings of the 34th Conference on Uncertainty in Artificial Intelligence (UAI), 2018*. 2018.

[SS19]   S. Sarkka and A. Solin. *Applied stochastic differential equations*. en. Cambridge University Press, 2019.

[SS20a]   S. Sarkka and L. Svensson. "Levenberg-Marquardt and Line-Search Extended Kalman Smoothers". In: *ICASSP*. Barcelona, Spain: IEEE, May 2020.

[SS20b]   K. E. Smith and A. O. Smith. "Conditional GAN for timeseries generation". In: *arXiv preprint arXiv:2006.16477* (2020).

[SS21]   I. Sucholutsky and M. Schonlau. "Soft-Label Dataset Distillation and Text Dataset Distillation". In: *2021 International Joint Conference on Neural Networks (IJCNN)*. 2021, pp. 1–8.

[SS23]   S. Sarkka and L. Svensson. *Bayesian Filtering and Smoothing (2nd edition)*. Cambridge University Press, 2023.

[SS82]   R. H. Shumway and D. S. Stoffer. "An approach to time series smoothing and forecasting using the em algorithm". en. In: *J. Time Ser. Anal.* 3.4 (July 1982), pp. 253–264.

[SSA14]   K. Swersky, J. Snoek, and R. P. Adams. "Freeze-Thaw Bayesian Optimization". In: (2014). arXiv: 1406.3896 [stat.ML].

[SSA18]   K. Shmelkov, C. Schmid, and K. Alahari. "How good is my GAN?" In: *Proceedings of the European Conference on Computer Vision (ECCV)*. 2018, pp. 213–229.

[SSB17]   S. Semeniuta, A. Severyn, and E. Barth. "A Hybrid Convolutional Variational Autoencoder for Text Generation". In: (2017). arXiv: 1702.02390 [cs.CL].

[SSE18]   Y. Song, J. Song, and S. Ermon. "Accelerating Natural Gradient with Higher-Order Invariance". In: *ICML*. 2018.

[SSF16]   M. W. Seeger, D. Salinas, and V. Flunkert. "Bayesian Intermittent Demand Forecasting for Large Inventories". In: *NIPS*. 2016, pp. 4646–4654.

[SSG18a]   S. Semeniuta, A. Severyn, and S. Gelly. "On Accurate Evaluation of GANs for Language Generation". In: *arXiv preprint arXiv:1806.04936* (2018).

[SSG18b]   S. Semeniuta, A. Severyn, and S. Gelly. "On Accurate Evaluation of GANs for Language Generation". In: (2018). arXiv: 1806.04936 [cs.CL].

[SSG19]   R. Singh, M. Sahani, and A. Gretton. "Kernel Instrumental Variable Regression". In: *Advances in Neural Information Processing Systems*. 2019, pp. 4593–4605.

[SSH13]   S. Sarkka, A. Solin, and J. Hartikainen. "Spatio-Temporal Learning via Infinite-Dimensional Bayesian Filtering and Smoothing: A look at Gaussian process regression through Kalman filtering". In: *IEEE Signal Processing Magazine* (2013).

[SSJ12]   R. Sipos, P. Shivaswamy, and T. Joachims. "Large-margin learning of submodular summarization models". In: *Proceedings of the 13th Conference of the European Chapter of the Association for Computational Linguistics*. 2012, pp. 224–233.

[SSK12]   M. Sugiyama, T. Suzuki, and T. Kanamori. *Density Ratio Estimation in Machine Learning*. en. Cambridge University Press, 2012.

[SSM18]   S. Santurkar, L. Schmidt, and A. Madry. "A classification-based study of covariate shift in gan distributions". In: *International Conference on Machine Learning*. PMLR. 2018, pp. 4480–4489.

[SSZ17]   J. Snell, K. Swersky, and R. Zemel. "Prototypical networks for few-shot learning". In: *NIPS*. 2017, pp. 4077–4087.

[Sta]   *Scientific Explanation*. https://plato.stanford.edu/entries/scientific-explanation/#ConcOpenIssuFutuDire. Accessed: 2021-11-23.

[Sta07]   K. O. Stanley. "Compositional pattern producing networks: A novel abstraction of development". In: *Genet. Program. Evolvable Mach.* 8.2 (2007), pp. 131–162.

[Sta+17]   N. Stallard, F. Miller, S. Day, S. W. Hee, J. Madan, S. Zohar, and M. Posch. "Determination of the optimal sample size for a clinical trial accounting for the population size". en. In: *Biom. J.* 59.4 (2017), pp. 609–625.

[Sta+19]   K. O. Stanley, J. Clune, J. Lehman, and R. Miikkulainen. "Designing neural networks through neuroevolution". In: *Nature Machine Intelligence* 1.1 (2019).

[Sta+20]   T. Standley, A. R. Zamir, D. Chen, L. Guibas, J. Malik, and S. Savarese. "Which Tasks Should Be Learned Together in Multi-task Learning?" In: *ICML*. 2020.

[Ste81]   C. M. Stein. "Estimation of the mean of a multivariate normal distribution". In: *The annals of Statistics* (1981), pp. 1135–1151.

[Sto09]   A. J. Storkey. "When Training and Test Sets are Different: Characterising Learning Transfer". In: *Dataset Shift in Machine Learning*. 2009.

[Sto17]   J. Stoehr. "A review on statistical inference methods for discrete Markov random fields". In: (2017). arXiv: 1704.03331 [stat.ME].

[STR10]   Y. Saatchi, R. Turner, and C. E. Rasmussen. "Gaussian Process Change Point Models". In: *ICML*. unknown, 2010, pp. 927–934.

[Str+17]   H. Strobelt, S. Gehrmann, H. Pfister, and A. M. Rush. "Lstmvis: A tool for visual analysis of hidden state dynamics in recurrent neural networks". In: *IEEE transactions on visualization and computer graphics* 24.1 (2017), pp. 667–676.

[Str19]   M. Streeter. "Bayes Optimal Early Stopping Policies for Black-Box Optimization". In: (2019). arXiv: 1902.08285 [cs.LG].

[Stu+22]   D. Stutz, Krishnamurthy, Dvijotham, A. T. Cemgil, and A. Doucet. "Learning Optimal Conformal Classifiers". In: *ICLR*. 2022.

[STY17]   M. Sundararajan, A. Taly, and Q. Yan. *Axiomatic Attribution for Deep Networks*. 2017. arXiv: 1703.01365 [cs.LG].

[Suc+20]   F. P. Such, A. Rawal, J. Lehman, K. Stanley, and J. Clune. "Generative teaching networks: Accelerating neural architecture search by learning to generate synthetic training data". In: *International Conference on Machine Learning*. PMLR. 2020, pp. 9206–9216.

[Sud+03]   E. Sudderth, A. Ihler, W. Freeman, and A. Willsky. "Nonparametric Belief Propagation". In: *CVPR*. 2003.

[Sud06]   E. Sudderth. "Graphical Models for Visual Object Recognition and Tracking". PhD thesis. MIT, 2006.

[Sud+10]   E. Sudderth, A. Ihler, M. Isard, W. Freeman, and A. Willsky. "Nonparametric Belief Propagation". In: *Comm. of the ACM* 53.10 (2010).

[Sug+13]   M. Sugiyama, T. Kanamori, T. Suzuki, M. C. du Plessis, S. Liu, and I. Takeuchi. "Density-difference estimation". en. In: *Neural Comput.* 25.10 (2013), pp. 2734–2775.

[Sun+09]   L. Sun, S. Ji, S. Yu, and J. Ye. "On the Equivalence Between Canonical Correlation Analysis and Orthonormalized Partial Least Squares". In: *IJCAI*. 2009.

[Sun+17]   C. Sun, A. Shrivastava, S. Singh, and A. Gupta. "Revisiting unreasonable effectiveness of data in deep learning era". In: *Proceedings of the IEEE international conference on computer vision*. 2017, pp. 843–852.

[Sun+18]   S. Sun, G. Zhang, C. Wang, W. Zeng, J. Li, and R. Grosse. "Differentiable Compositional Kernel Learning for Gaussian Processes". In: *ICML*. 2018.

[Sun+19a]   S. Sun, G. Zhang, J. Shi, and R. Grosse. "Functional variational bayesian neural networks". In: *arXiv preprint arXiv:1903.05779* (2019).

[Sun+19b]   S. Sun, Z. Cao, H. Zhu, and J. Zhao. "A Survey of Optimization Methods from a Machine Learning Perspective". In: (2019). arXiv: 1906.06821 [cs.LG].

[Sun+19c]   M. Sundararajan, J. Xu, A. Taly, R. Sayres, and A. Najmi. "Exploring Principled Visualizations for Deep Network Attributions." In: *IUI Workshops*. Vol. 4. 2019.

[Sun+20]   Y. Sun, X. Wang, Z. Liu, J. Miller, A. Efros, and M. Hardt. "Test-Time Training with Self-Supervision for Generalization under Distribution Shifts". In: *ICML*. Vol. 119. Proceedings of Machine Learning Research. PMLR, 2020, pp. 9229–9248.

[Sun+22]   T. Sun, M. Segu, J. Postels, Y. Wang, L. Van Gool, B. Schiele, F. Tombari, and F. Yu. "SHIFT: A Synthetic Driving Dataset for Continuous Multi-Task Domain Adaptation". In: *CVPR*. June 2022.

[Sut+17]   D. J. Sutherland, H.-Y. Tung, H. Strathmann, S. De, A. Ramdas, A. Smola, and A. Gretton. "Generative Models and Model Criticism via Optimized Maximum Mean Discrepancy". In: *ICLR*. 2017.

[Sut19]   R. Sutton. *The Bitter Lesson*. 2019.

[Sut88]   R. Sutton. "Learning to predict by the methods of temporal differences". In: *Machine Learning* 3.1 (1988), pp. 9–44.

[Sut90]   R. S. Sutton. "Integrated Architectures for Learning, Planning, and Reacting Based on Approximating Dynamic Programming". In: *ICML*. Ed. by B. Porter and R. Mooney. Morgan Kaufmann, 1990, pp. 216–224.

[Sut96]   R. S. Sutton. "Generalization in Reinforcement Learning: Successful Examples Using Sparse Coarse Coding". In: *NIPS*. Ed. by D. S. Touretzky, M. C. Mozer, and M. E. Hasselmo. MIT Press, 1996, pp. 1038–1044.

[Sut+99]   R. Sutton, D. McAllester, S. Singh, and Y. Mansour. "Policy Gradient Methods for Reinforcement Learning with Function Approximation". In: *NIPS*. 1999.

[SV08]   G. Shafer and V. Vovk. "A Tutorial on Conformal Prediction". In: *JMLR* 9.Mar (2008), pp. 371–421.

[SV14]   S. L. Scott and H. R. Varian. "Predicting the present with Bayesian structural time series". In: *International Journal of Mathematical Modelling and Numerical Optimisation* 5.1-2 (2014), pp. 4–23.

[SV98]   M. Studenty and J. Vejnarova. "The multi-information function as a tool for measuring stochastic dependence". In: *Learning in graphical models*. Ed. by M. Jordan. MIT Press, 1998, pp. 261–297.

[SVE04]   A. Smola, S. V. N. Vishwanathan, and E. Eskin. "Laplace Propagation". In: *NIPS*. MIT Press, 2004, pp. 441–448.

[Svi04]   M. Sviridenko. "A note on maximizing a submodular set function subject to a knapsack constraint". In: *Operations Research Letters* 32.1 (2004), pp. 41–43.

[SVK19]   J. Su, D. V. Vargas, and S. Kouichi. "One pixel attack for fooling deep neural networks". In: *IEEE Trans. Evol. Comput.* 23.5 (2019).

[SVZ13]   K. Simonyan, A. Vedaldi, and A. Zisserman. "Deep inside convolutional networks: Visualising image classification models and saliency maps". In: *arXiv preprint arXiv:1312.6034* (2013).

[SW06]   J. E. Smith and R. L. Winkler. "The Optimizer's Curse: Skepticism and Postdecision Surprise in Decision Analysis". In: *Manage. Sci.* 52.3 (2006), pp. 311–322.

[SW13]   G. J. Sussman and J. Wisdom. *Functional Differential Geometry*. Functional Differential Geometry. MIT Press, 2013.

[SW20]   V. G. Satorras and M. Welling. "Neural Enhanced Belief Propagation on Factor Graphs". In: (2020). arXiv: 2003.01998 [cs.LG].

[SW87a]   M. Shewry and H. Wynn. "Maximum entropy sampling". In: *J. Applied Statistics* 14 (1987), 165–170.

[SW87b]   R. Swendsen and J.-S. Wang. "Nonuniversal critical dynamics in Monte Carlo simulations". In: *Physical Review Letters* 58 (1987), pp. 86–88.

[SW89]   S. Singhal and L. Wu. "Training Multilayer Perceptrons with the Extended Kalman Algorithm". In: *NIPS*. Vol. 1. 1989.

[Swe+10]   K. Swersky, B. Chen, B. Marlin, and N. de Freitas. "A Tutorial on Stochastic Approximation Algorithms for Training Restricted Boltzmann Machines and Deep Belief Nets". In: *Information Theory and Applications (ITA) Workshop*. 2010.

[Swe+13]   K. Swersky, D. Duvenaud, J. Snoek, F. Hutter, and M. A. Osborne. "Raiders of the Lost Architecture: Kernels for Bayesian Optimization in Conditional Parameter Spaces". In: *NIPS BayesOpt workshop*. 2013.

[SWL03] M. Seeger, C. K. I. Williams, and N. D. Lawrence. "Fast Forward Selection to Speed Up Sparse Gaussian Process Regression". In: *AISTATS*. 2003.

[SYD19] R. Sen, H.-F. Yu, and I. Dhillon. "Think Globally, Act Locally: A Deep Neural Network Approach to High-Dimensional Time Series Forecasting". In: *NIPS*. 2019.

[SZ22] R. Shwartz-Ziv. "Information Flow in Deep Neural Networks". PhD thesis. 2022.

[SZ+22] R. Shwartz-Ziv, M. Goldblum, H. Souri, S. Kapoor, C. Zhu, Y. LeCun, and A. G. Wilson. "Pre-Train Your Loss: Easy Bayesian Transfer Learning with Informative Priors". In: (May 2022). arXiv: 2205.10279 [cs.LG].

[Sze10] C. Szepesvari. *Algorithms for Reinforcement Learning*. Morgan Claypool, 2010.

[Sze+14] C. Szegedy, W. Zaremba, I. Sutskever, J. Bruna, D. Erhan, I. Goodfellow, and R. Fergus. "Intriguing properties of neural networks". In: *ICLR*. 2014.

[Sze+15a] C. Szegedy, W. Liu, Y. Jia, P. Sermanet, S. Reed, D. Anguelov, D. Erhan, V. Vanhoucke, and A. Rabinovich. "Going Deeper with Convolutions". In: *CVPR*. 2015.

[Sze+15b] C. Szegedy, V. Vanhoucke, S. Ioffe, J. Shlens, and Z. Wojna. "Rethinking the Inception Architecture for Computer Vision". In: (2015). arXiv: 1512.00567 [cs.CV].

[TAH20] D. Teney, E. Abbasnejad, and A. van den Hengel. "Learning What Makes a Difference from Counterfactual Examples and Gradient Supervision". In: *CoRR* abs/2004.09034 (2020). arXiv: 2004.09034.

[TB16] P. S. Thomas and E. Brunskill. "Data-Efficient Off-Policy Policy Evaluation for Reinforcement Learning". In: *ICML*. 2016, pp. 2139–2148.

[TB22] A. Tiulpin and M. B. Blaschko. "Greedy Bayesian Posterior Approximation with Deep Ensembles". In: *Trans. on Machine Learning Research* (2022).

[TB99] M. Tipping and C. Bishop. "Probabilistic principal component analysis". In: *J. of Royal Stat. Soc. Series B* 21.3 (1999), pp. 611–622.

[TBA19] N. Tremblay, S. Barthelmé, and P.-O. Amblard. "Determinantal Point Processes for Coresets." In: *J. Mach. Learn. Res.* 20 (2019), pp. 168–1.

[TBB19] J. Townsend, T. Bird, and D. Barber. "Practical Lossless Compression with Latent Variables using Bits Back Coding". In: *ICLR*. 2019.

[TBF06] S. Thrun, W. Burgard, and D. Fox. *Probabilistic Robotics*. MIT Press, 2006.

[TBS13] R. Turner, S. Bottone, and C. Stanek. "Online variational approximations to non-exponential family change point models: With application to radar tracking". In: *NIPS*. 2013.

[TCG21] Y. Tian, X. Chen, and S. Ganguli. "Understanding self-supervised learning dynamics without contrastive pairs". In: *International Conference on Machine Learning*. PMLR. 2021, pp. 10268–10278.

[Teh06] Y. W. Teh. "A hierarchical Bayesian language model based on Pitman-Yor processes". In: *Proc. of the Assoc. for Computational Linguistics*. 2006, 985=992.

[Teh+06] Y.-W. Teh, M. Jordan, M. Beal, and D. Blei. "Hierarchical Dirichlet processes". In: *JASA* 101.476 (2006), pp. 1566–1581.

[Teh+20] N. Tehrani, N. S. Arora, Y. L. Li, K. D. Shah, D. Noursi, M. Tingley, N. Torabi, S. Masouleh, E. Lippert, and E. Meijer. "Bean Machine: A Declarative Probabilistic Programming Language For Efficient Programmable Inference". In: *Proceedings of the 10th International Conference on Probabilistic Graphical Models*. Ed. by M. Jaeger and T. D. Nielsen. Vol. 138. Proceedings of Machine Learning Research. PMLR, 2020, pp. 485–496.

[Ten+20] I. Tenney, J. Wexler, J. Bastings, T. Bolukbasi, A. Coenen, S. Gehrmann, E. Jiang, M. Pushkarna, C. Radebaugh, E. Reif, et al. "The language interpretability tool: Extensible, interactive visualizations and analysis for NLP models". In: *arXiv preprint arXiv:2008.05122* (2020).

[TF03] M. Tipping and A. Faul. "Fast marginal likelihood maximisation for sparse Bayesian models". In: *AI/Stats*. 2003.

[TG18] L. Tu and K. Gimpel. "Learning Approximate Inference Networks for Structured Prediction". In: *ICLR*. 2018.

[TGFS18] F. Tronarp, Á. F. García-Fernández, and S. Särkkä. "Iterative Filtering and Smoothing in Nonlinear and Non-Gaussian Systems Using Conditional Moments". In: *IEEE Signal Process. Lett.* 25.3 (2018), pp. 408–412.

[TGK03] B. Taskar, C. Guestrin, and D. Koller. "Max-Margin Markov Networks". In: *NIPS*. 2003.

[TH09] T. Tieleman and G. Hinton. "Using Fast Weights to Improve Persistent Contrastive Divergence". In: *ICML*. 2009, pp. 1033–1040.

[Tho+19] V. Thomas, F. Pedregosa, B. van Merriënboer, P.-A. Mangazol, Y. Bengio, and N. Le Roux. "Information matrices and generalization". In: (2019). arXiv: 1906.07774 [cs.LG].

[Tho33] W. R. Thompson. "On the Likelihood that One Unknown Probability Exceeds Another in View of the Evidence of Two Samples". In: *Biometrika* 25.3/4 (1933), pp. 285–294.

[Thr+04] S. Thrun, M. Montemerlo, D. Koller, B. Wegbreit, J. Nieto, and E. Nebot. "FastSLAM: An efficient solution to the simultaneous localization and mapping problem with unknown data association". In: *JMLR* 2004 (2004).

[Thr98] S. Thrun. "Lifelong learning algorithms". In: *Learning to learn*. Ed. by S. Thrun and L. Pratt. Kluwer, 1998, pp. 181–209.

[Thu+21] S. Thulasidasan, S. Thapa, S. Dhaubhadel, G. Chennupati, T. Bhattacharya, and J. Bilmes. "An Effective Baseline for Robustness to Distributional Shift". In: (2021). arXiv: 2105.07107 [cs.LG].

[Tia+20] Y. Tian, C. Sun, B. Poole, D. Krishnan, C. Schmid, and P. Isola. "What makes for good views for contrastive learning". In: *ArXiv* abs/2005.10243 (2020).

[Tib96] R. Tibshirani. "Regression shrinkage and selection via the lasso". In: *J. Royal. Statist. Soc B* 58.1 (1996), pp. 267–288.

[Tie08] T. Tieleman. "Training restricted Boltzmann machines using approximations to the likelihood gradient". In: *ICML*. ACM New York, NY, USA. 2008, pp. 1064–1071.

[Tip01]   M. Tipping. "Sparse Bayesian learning and the relevance vector machine". In: *JMLR* 1 (2001), pp. 211–244.

[Tip98]   M. Tipping. "Probabilistic visualization of high-dimensional binary data". In: *NIPS*. 1998.

[Tit09]   M. K. Titsias. "Variational Learning of Inducing Variables in Sparse Gaussian Processes". In: *AISTATS*. 2009.

[TK86]   L. Tierney and J. Kadane. "Accurate approximations for posterior moments and marginal densities". In: *JASA* 81.393 (1986).

[TKI20]   Y. Tian, D. Krishnan, and P. Isola. "Contrastive Multiview Coding". In: *ECCV*. 2020.

[TL05]   E. Todorov and W. Li. "A Generalized Iterative LQG Method for Locally-optimal Feedback Control of Constrained Nonlinear Stochastic Systems". In: *ACC*. 2005, pp. 300–306.

[TL18a]   S. J. Taylor and B. Letham. "Forecasting at scale". en. In: *The American Statistician* 72.1 (2018), pp. 37–45.

[TL18b]   G. Tucker and D. Lawson. "Doubly Reparameterized Gradient Estimators for Monte Carlo Objectives". In: *1st Symposium on Advances in Approximate Bayesian Inference*. 2018.

[TL19]   M. Tan and Q. Le. "Efficientnet: Rethinking model scaling for convolutional neural networks". In: *International Conference on Machine Learning*. PMLR. 2019, pp. 6105–6114.

[TLG08]   D. G. Tzikas, A. C. Likas, and N. P. Galatsanos. "The variational approximation for Bayesian inference". In: *IEEE Signal Process. Mag.* 25.6 (Nov. 2008), pp. 131–146.

[TLG14]   M. Titsias and M. Lázaro-Gredilla. "Doubly Stochastic Variational Bayes for non-Conjugate Inference". In: *ICML*. 2014, pp. 1971–1979.

[TM15]   D. Trafimow and M. Marks. "Editorial". In: *Basic Appl. Soc. Psych.* 37.1 (2015), pp. 1–2.

[TMD12]   A. Talhouk, K. Murphy, and A. Doucet. "Efficient Bayesian Inference for Multivariate Probit Models with Sparse Inverse Correlation Matrices". In: *J. Comp. Graph. Statist.* 21.3 (2012), pp. 739–757.

[TMK04]   G. Theocharous, K. Murphy, and L. Kaelbling. "Representing hierarchical POMDPs as DBNs for multi-scale robot localization". In: *ICRA*. 2004.

[TN13]   L. S. L. Tan and D. J. Nott. "Variational Inference for Generalized Linear Mixed Models Using Partially Noncentered Parametrizations". In: *Stat. Sci.* (2013).

[TND21]   M.-N. Tran, T.-N. Nguyen, and V.-H. Dao. "A practical tutorial on Variational Bayes". In: (2021). arXiv: 2103.01327 [stat.CO].

[TOB16]   L. Theis, A. van den Oord, and M. Bethge. "A note on the evaluation of generative models". In: *ICLR*. 2016.

[Tol22]   S. Toledo. "UltimateKalman: Flexible Kalman Filtering and Smoothing Using Orthogonal Transformations". In: (July 2022). arXiv: 2207 . 13526 [math.NA].

[Tom+20]   R. Tomsett, D. Harborne, S. Chakraborty, P. Gurram, and A. Preece. "Sanity checks for saliency metrics". In: *Proceedings of the AAAI conference on artificial intelligence*. Vol. 34. 04. 2020, pp. 6021–6029.

[Tom22]   J. M. Tomczak. *Deep Generative Modeling*. en. 1st ed. Springer, 2022.

[Tou09]   M. Toussaint. "Robot Rrajectory Optimization using Approximate Inference". In: *ICML*. 2009, pp. 1049–1056.

[Tou14]   M. Toussaint. *Bandits, Global Optimization, Active Learning, and Bayesian RL – understanding the common ground*. Autonomous Learning Summer School. 2014.

[Tou+19]   J Toubeau, J Bottieau, F Vallée, and Z De Grève. "Deep Learning-Based Multivariate Probabilistic Forecasting for Short-Term Scheduling in Power Markets". In: *IEEE Trans. Power Syst.* 34.2 (2019), pp. 1203–1215.

[TOV18]   C. Truong, L. Oudre, and N. Vayatis. "Selective review of offline change point detection methods". In: (2018). arXiv: 1801.00718 [cs.CE].

[TP97]   S. Thrun and L. Pratt, eds. *Learning to learn*. Kluwer, 1997.

[TPB00]   N. Tishby, F. C. Pereira, and W. Bialek. "The information bottleneck method". In: *ArXiv physics/0004057* (2000).

[TPB99]   N. Tishby, F. Pereira, and W. Biale. "The Information Bottleneck method". In: *The 37th annual Allerton Conf. on Communication, Control, and Computing*. 1999, pp. 368–377.

[TR19]   M. K. Titsias and F. Ruiz. "Unbiased Implicit Variational Inference". In: *AISTATS*. Ed. by K. Chaudhuri and M. Sugiyama. Vol. 89. Proceedings of Machine Learning Research. PMLR, 2019, pp. 167–176.

[TR97]   J. Tsitsiklis and B. V. Roy. "An analysis of temporal-difference learning with function approximation". In: *IEEE Trans. on Automatic Control* 42.5 (1997), pp. 674–690.

[Tra+19]   D. Tran, K. Vafa, K. K. Agrawal, L. Dinh, and B. Poole. "Discrete Flows: Invertible Generative Models of Discrete Data". In: *Advances in Neural Information Processing Systems*. 2019.

[Tra+20a]   L. Tran, B. S. Veeling, K. Roth, J. Swiatkowski, J. V. Dillon, J. Snoek, S. Mandt, T. Salimans, S. Nowozin, and R. Jenatton. "Hydra: Preserving Ensemble Diversity for Model Distillation". In: (2020). arXiv: 2001.04694 [cs.LG].

[Tra+20b]   M.-N. Tran, N Nguyen, D Nott, and R Kohn. "Bayesian Deep Net GLM and GLMM". In: *J. Comput. Graph. Stat.* 29.1 (2020), pp. 97–113.

[TRB16]   D. Tran, R. Ranganath, and D. M. Blei. "The Variational Gaussian Process". In: *ICLR*. 2016.

[Tri21]   K. Triantafyllopoulos. *Bayesian Inference of State Space Models: Kalman Filtering and Beyond*. en. 1st ed. Springer, 2021.

[TS06]   M. Toussaint and A. Storkey. "Probabilistic inference for solving discrete and continuous state Markov Decision Processes". In: *ICML*. 2006, pp. 945–952.

[Tsa+18]   Y.-H. Tsai, W.-C. Hung, S. Schulter, K. Sohn, M.-H. Yang, and M. Chandraker. "Learning to adapt structured output space for semantic segmentation". In: *Proceedings of the IEEE conference on computer vision and pattern recognition*. 2018, pp. 7472–7481.

[Tsa+19]   Y.-H. H. Tsai, S. Bai, M. Yamada, L.-P. Morency, and R. Salakhutdinov. "Transformer Dissection: An Unified Understanding for Transformer's Attention via the Lens of Kernel". In: *EMNLP*. Association for Computational Linguistics, 2019, pp. 4344–4353.

[Tsa+21] Y.-H. H. Tsai, S. Bai, L.-P. Morency, and R. Salakhutdinov. "A Note on Connecting Barlow Twins with Negative-Sample-Free Contrastive Learning". In: *ArXiv* abs/2104.13712 (2021).

[Tsa88] C. Tsallis. "Possible generalization of Boltzmann-Gibbs statistics". In: *J. of Statistical Physics* 52 (1988), pp. 479–487.

[Tsc+14] S. Tschiatschek, R. Iyer, H. Wei, and J. Bilmes. "Learning Mixtures of Submodular Functions for Image Collection Summarization". In: *NIPS*. Montreal, Canada, 2014.

[Tsc+19] M. Tschannen, J. Djolonga, P. K. Rubenstein, S. Gelly, and M. Lucic. "On Mutual Information Maximization for Representation Learning". In: *arXiv preprint arXiv:1907.13625* (2019).

[Tsi+17] P. A. Tsividis, T. Pouncy, J. L. Xu, J. B. Tenenbaum, and S. J. Gershman. "Human Learning in Atari". en. In: *AAAI Spring Symposium Series*. 2017.

[Tso+05] I. Tsochantaridis, T. Joachims, T. Hofmann, and Y. Altun. "Large Margin Methods for Structured and Interdependent Output Variables". In: *JMLR* 6 (2005), pp. 1453–1484.

[TT13] E. G. Tabak and C. V. Turner. "A family of nonparametric density estimation algorithms". In: *Communications on Pure and Applied Mathematics* 66.2 (2013), pp. 145–164.

[TT17] B. Trippe and R. Turner. "Overpruning in Variational Bayesian Neural Networks". In: *NIPS Workshop on Advances in Approximate Bayesian Inference*. 2017.

[Tuc+19] G. Tucker, D. Lawson, B. Dai, and R. Ranganath. "Revisiting auxiliary latent variables in generative models". In: (2019).

[TUI17] T. Taketomi, H. Uchiyama, and S. Ikeda. "Visual SLAM algorithms: a survey from 2010 to 2016". en. In: *IPSJ Transactions on Computer Vision and Applications* 9.1 (2017), p. 16.

[Tul+18] S. Tulyakov, M.-Y. Liu, X. Yang, and J. Kautz. "Mocogan: Decomposing motion and content for video generation". In: *Proceedings of the IEEE conference on computer vision and pattern recognition*. 2018, pp. 1526–1535.

[Tur+08] R. Turner, P. Berkes, M. Sahani, and D. Mackay. *Counterexamples to variational free energy compactness folk theorems*. Tech. rep. U. Cambridge, 2008.

[TVE10] E. G. Tabak and E. Vanden-Eijnden. "Density estimation by dual ascent of the log-likelihood". In: *Communications in Mathematical Sciences* 8.1 (2010), pp. 217–233.

[TW16] J. M. Tomczak and M. Welling. "Improving variational auto-encoders using Householder flow". In: *NeurIPS Workshop on Bayesian Deep Learning* (2016).

[TX00] J. B. Tenenbaum and F. Xu. "Word learning as Bayesian inference". In: *Proc. 22nd Annual Conf. of the Cognitive Science Society*. 2000.

[TZ02] Z. Tu and S. Zhu. "Image Segmentation by Data-Driven Markov Chain Monte Carlo". In: *IEEE PAMI* 24.5 (2002), pp. 657–673.

[Tze+17] E. Tzeng, J. Hoffman, K. Saenko, and T. Darrell. "Adversarial discriminative domain adaptation".
In: *Proceedings of the IEEE conference on computer vision and pattern recognition*. 2017, pp. 7167–7176.

[UAP22] A. Ulhaq, N. Akhtar, and G. Pogrebna. "Efficient Diffusion Models for Vision: A Survey". In: (Oct. 2022). arXiv: 2210.09292 [cs.CV].

[UCS17] S. Ubaru, J. Chen, and Y. Saad. "Fast Estimation of $tr(f(A))$ via Stochastic Lanczos Quadrature". In: *SIAM J. Matrix Anal. Appl.* 38.4 (2017), pp. 1075–1099.

[Ude+16] M. Udell, C. Horn, R. Zadeh, and S. Boyd. "Generalized Low Rank Models". In: *Foundations and Trends in Machine Learning* 9.1 (2016), pp. 1–118.

[UHJ20] M. Uehara, J. Huang, and N. Jiang. "Minimax Weight and Q-Function Learning for Off-Policy Evaluation". In: *ICML*. 2020.

[UML13] B. Uria, I. Murray, and H. Larochelle. "RNADE: The real-valued neural autoregressive density-estimator". In: *NIPS*. 2013.

[UML14] B. Uria, I. Murray, and H. Larochelle. "A Deep and Tractable Density Estimator". In: *ICML*. 2014.

[UN98] N. Ueda and R. Nakano. "Deterministic annealing EM algorithm". In: *Neural Networks* 11 (1998), pp. 271–282.

[UR16] B. Ustun and C. Rudin. "Supersparse linear integer models for optimized medical scoring systems". In: *Machine Learning* 102.3 (2016), pp. 349–391.

[Uri+16] B. Uria, M.-A. Côté, K. Gregor, I. Murray, and H. Larochelle. "Neural Autoregressive Distribution Estimation". In: *JMLR* (2016).

[UTR14] B. Ustun, S. Tracà, and C. Rudin. *Supersparse Linear Integer Models for Interpretable Classification*. 2014. arXiv: 1306.6677 [stat.ML].

[Uur+17] V. Uurtio, J. M. Monteiro, J. Kandola, J. Shawe-Taylor, D. Fernandez-Reyes, and J. Rousu. "A Tutorial on Canonical Correlation Methods". In: *ACM Computing Surveys* (2017).

[UVL16] D. Ulyanov, A. Vedaldi, and V. Lempitsky. "Instance Normalization: The Missing Ingredient for Fast Stylization". In: (2016). arXiv: 1607.08022 [cs.CV].

[UVL18] D. Ulyanov, A. Vedaldi, and V. Lempitsky. "Deep Image Prior". In: *CVPR*. 2018.

[Vaa00] A. W. Van der Vaart. *Asymptotic statistics*. Vol. 3. Cambridge university press, 2000.

[Val00] H. Valpola. "Bayesian Ensemble Learning for Nonlinear Factor Analysis". PhD thesis. Helsinki University of Technology, 2000.

[Van10] J. Vanhatalo. "Speeding up the inference in Gaussian process models". PhD thesis. Helsinki Univ. Technology, 2010.

[Van14] J. VanderPlas. *Frequentism and Bayesianism III: Confidence, Credibility, and why Frequentism and Science do not Mix*. Blog post. 2014.

[van+18] H. van Hasselt, Y. Doron, F. Strub, M. Hessel, N. Sonnerat, and J. Modayil. *Deep Reinforcement Learning and the Deadly Triad*. arXiv:1812.02648. 2018.

[Vas+17a] A. B. Vasudevan, M. Gygli, A. Volokitin, and L. Van Gool. "Query-adaptive video summarization via quality-aware relevance estimation". In: *Proceedings of the 25th ACM international conference on Multimedia*. 2017, pp. 582–590.

[Vas+17b] A. Vaswani, N. Shazeer, N. Parmar, J. Uszkoreit, L. Jones, A. N. Gomez, Ł. Kaiser, and I. Polosukhin. "Attention is all you need". In: *NIPS*. 2017, pp. 5998–6008.

[Vas+17c] A. Vaswani, N. Shazeer, N. Parmar, J. Uszkoreit, L. Jones, A. N. Gomez, L. Kaiser, and I. Polosukhin. "Attention Is All You Need". In: *NIPS*. 2017.

[Vaz+22] S. Vaze, K. Han, A. Vedaldi, and A. Zisserman. "Open-Set Recognition: A Good Closed-Set Classifier is All You Need". In: *ICLR*. 2022.

[VBW15] S. S. Villar, J. Bowden, and J. Wason. "Multi-armed Bandit Models for the Optimal Design of Clinical Trials: Benefits and Challenges". en. In: *Stat. Sci.* 30.2 (2015), pp. 199–215.

[VDMW03] R. Van Der Merwe and E. Wan. "Sigma-Point Kalman Filters for probabilistic inference in dynamic state-space models". In: *Workshop on Advances in ML*. 2003.

[Ved+18] R. Vedantam, I. Fischer, J. Huang, and K. Murphy. "Generative Models of Visually Grounded Imagination". In: *ICLR*. 2018.

[Veh+15] A. Vehtari, D. Simpson, A. Gelman, Y. Yao, and J. Gabry. "Pareto Smoothed Importance Sampling". In: (July 2015). arXiv: 1507.02646 [stat.CO].

[Veh+19] A. Vehtari, A. Gelman, D. Simpson, B. Carpenter, and P.-C. Bürkner. "Rank-normalization, folding, and localization: An improved $\hat{R}$ for assessing convergence of MCMC". In: (2019). arXiv: 1903.08008 [stat.CO].

[Vei+21] V. Veitch, A. D'Amour, S. Yadlowsky, and J. Eisenstein. "Counterfactual Invariance to Spurious Correlations: Why and How to Pass Stress Tests". In: *Advances in Neural Information Processing Systems*. 2021.

[Vel+17] P. Veličković, G. Cucurull, A. Casanova, A. Romero, P. Lio, and Y. Bengio. "Graph attention networks". In: *arXiv preprint arXiv:1710.10903* (2017).

[Ver18] R. Vershynin. *High-Dimensional Probability: An Introduction with Applications in Data Science.* en. 1 edition. Cambridge University Press, 2018.

[Ver+19] A. Vergari, A. Molina, R. Peharz, Z. Ghahramani, K. Kersting, and I. Valera. "Automatic Bayesian Density Analysis". In: *AAAI*. 2019.

[VF+80] B. C. Van Fraassen et al. *The scientific image.* Oxford University Press, 1980.

[VGG17] A. Vehtari, A. Gelman, and J. Gabry. "Practical Bayesian model evaluation using leave-one-out cross-validation and WAIC". In: *Stat. Comput.* 27.5 (2017), pp. 1413–1432.

[VGS05] V. Vovk, A. Gammerman, and G. Shafer. *Algorithmic Learning in a Random World.* en. 2005th ed. Springer, 2005.

[Vid99] P. Vidoni. "Exponential Family State Space Models Based on a Conjugate Latent Process". In: *J. R. Stat. Soc. Series B Stat. Methodol.* 61.1 (1999), pp. 213–221.

[Vil08] C. Villani. *Optimal Transport: Old and New.* Grundlehren der mathematischen Wissenschaften. Springer Berlin Heidelberg, 2008.

[Vil+19] R. Villegas, A. Pathak, H. Kannan, D. Erhan, Q. V. Le, and H. Lee. "High Fidelity Video Prediction with Large Stochastic Recurrent Neural Networks". In: *NIPS*. 2019.

[Vin+08] P. Vincent, H. Larochelle, Y. Bengio, and P.-A. Manzagol. "Extracting and composing robust features with denoising autoencoders". In: *Proceedings of the 25th international conference on Machine learning*. 2008, pp. 1096–1103.

[Vin+10a] P. Vincent, H. Larochelle, I. Lajoie, Y. Bengio, and P.-A. Manzagol. "Stacked denoising autoencoders: Learning useful representations in a deep network with a local denoising criterion". In: *Journal of machine learning research* 11.Dec (2010), pp. 3371–3408.

[Vin+10b] M. Vinyals, J. Cerquides, J. Rodriguez-Aguilar, and A. Farinelli. "Worst-case bounds on the quality of max-product fixed-points". In: *NIPS*. 2010.

[Vin11] P. Vincent. "A connection between score matching and denoising autoencoders". In: *Neural computation* 23.7 (2011), pp. 1661–1674.

[Vir10] S. Virtanen. "Bayesian exponential family projections". MA thesis. Aalto University, 2010.

[Vis+06] S. V. N. Vishwanathan, N. N. Schraudolph, M. W. Schmidt, and K. P. Murphy. "Accelerated training of conditional random fields with stochastic gradient methods". In: *ICML*. ACM Press, 2006.

[Vis+10] S. V. N. Vishwanathan, N. N. Schraudolph, R. Kondor, and K. M. Borgward. "Graph Kernels". In: *JMLR* 11 (2010), pp. 1201–1242.

[Vit67] A. Viterbi. "Error bounds for convolutional codes and an asymptotically optimal decoding algorithm". In: *IEEE Trans. on Information Theory* 13.2 (1967), pp. 260–269.

[VJV09] J. Vanhatalo, P. Jylänki, and A. Vehtari. "Gaussian process regression with Student-t likelihood". In: *NIPS*. Vol. 22. 2009.

[VK20a] A. Vahdat and J. Kautz. "NVAE: A Deep Hierarchical Variational Autoencoder". In: *NIPS*. 2020.

[VK20b] A. Vahdat and J. Kautz. "Nvae: A deep hierarchical variational autoencoder". In: *arXiv preprint arXiv:2007.03898* (2020).

[VKK21] A. Vahdat, K. Kreis, and J. Kautz. "Score-based Generative Modeling in Latent Space". In: *NIPS*. June 2021.

[VLT21] G. M. van de Ven, Z. Li, and A. S. Tolias. "Class-Incremental Learning with Generative Classifiers". In: *CVPR workshop on Continual Learning in Computer Vision (CLVision)*. 2021.

[Vo+15] B.-N. Vo, M. Mallick, Y. Bar-Shalom, S. Coraluppi, R. Osborne, R. Mahler, B. t Vo, and J. Webster. *Multitarget tracking.* John Wiley and Sons, 2015.

[Von13] P. Vontobel. "The Bethe permanent of a nonnegative matrix". In: *IEEE Trans. Info. Theory* 59.3 (2013).

[Vov13] V. Vovk. "Kernel Ridge Regression". In: *Empirical Inference: Festschrift in Honor of Vladimir N. Vapnik.* Ed. by B. Schölkopf, Z. Luo, and V. Vovk. Springer Berlin Heidelberg, 2013, pp. 105–116.

[VPV10] J. Vanhatalo, V. Pietilainen, and A. Vehtari. "Approximate inference for disease mapping with sparse Gaussian processes". In: *Statistics in Medicine* 29.15 (2010), pp. 1580–1607.

[vR11] M. van der Laan and S. Rose. *Targeted Learning: Causal Inference for Observational and Experimental Data.* Jan. 2011.

[VR18]   S. Verma and J. Rubin. "Fairness Definitions Explained". In: *2018 IEEE/ACM International Workshop on Software Fairness (FairWare)*. May 2018, pp. 1–7.

[VRF11]   C. Varin, N. Reid, and D. Firth. "An overview of composite likelihood methods". In: *Stat. Sin.* 21.1 (2011), pp. 5–42.

[VS11]   T. J. VanderWeele and I. Shpitser. "A new criterion for confounder selection". In: *Biometrics* (2011).

[VT18]   G. M. van de Ven and A. S. Tolias. "Three scenarios for continual learning". In: *NeurIPS Continual Learning workshop.* 2018.

[Vyt+19] D. Vytiniotis, D. Belov, R. Wei, G. Plotkin, and M. Abadi. "The differentiable curry". In: *NeurIPS 2019 Workshop Program Transformations.* 2019.

[VZ20]   V. Veitch and A. Zaveri. "Sense and Sensitivity Analysis: Simple Post-Hoc Analysis of Bias Due to Unobserved Confounding". In: *Advances in Neural Information Processing Systems.* Ed. by H. Larochelle, M. Ranzato, R. Hadsell, M. F. Balcan, and H. Lin. Vol. 33. Curran Associates, Inc., 2020, pp. 10999–11009.

[WA13]   A. Wilson and R. Adams. "Gaussian process kernels for pattern discovery and extrapolation". In: *International conference on machine learning.* 2013, pp. 1067–1075.

[Wal+09] H. Wallach, I. Murray, R. Salakhutdinov, and D. Mimno. "Evaluation Methods for Topic Models". In: *ICML.* 2009.

[Wal+20] M. Walmsley et al. "Galaxy Zoo: probabilistic morphology through Bayesian CNNs and active learning". In: *Monthly Notices Royal Astronomial Society* 491.2 (2020), pp. 1554–1574.

[Wal47]   A. Wald. "An Essentially Complete Class of Admissible Decision Functions". en. In: *Ann. Math. Stat.* 18.4 (1947), pp. 549–555.

[Wan+16] Z. Wang, T. Schaul, M. Hessel, H. van Hasselt, M. Lanctot, and N. de Freitas. "Dueling Network Architectures for Deep Reinforcement Learning". In: *ICML.* 2016.

[Wan17]   M. P. Wand. "Fast Approximate Inference for Arbitrarily Large Semiparametric Regression Models via Message Passing". In: *JASA* 112.517 (2017), pp. 137–168.

[Wan+17a] T. Wang, C. Rudin, F. Doshi-Velez, Y. Liu, E. Klampfl, and P. MacNeille. "A bayesian framework for learning rule sets for interpretable classification". In: *The Journal of Machine Learning Research* 18.1 (2017), pp. 2357–2393.

[Wan+17b] X. Wang, T. Li, S. Sun, and J. M. Corchado. "A Survey of Recent Advances in Particle Filters and Remaining Challenges for Multitarget Tracking". en. In: *Sensors* 17.12 (2017).

[Wan+17c] Y. Wang et al. "Tacotron: Towards End-to-End Speech Synthesis". In: *Interspeech.* 2017.

[Wan+18] T.-C. Wang, M.-Y. Liu, J.-Y. Zhu, G. Liu, A. Tao, J. Kautz, and B. Catanzaro. "Video-to-video synthesis". In: *Proceedings of the 32nd International Conference on Neural Information Processing Systems.* 2018, pp. 1152–1164.

[Wan+19a] K. Wang, G. Pleiss, J. Gardner, S. Tyree, K. Q. Weinberger, and A. G. Wilson. "Exact Gaussian Processes on a Million Data Points". In: *NIPS.* 2019, pp. 14622–14632.

[Wan+19b] S. Wang, W. Bai, C. Lavania, and J. Bilmes. "Fixing Mini-batch Sequences with Hierarchical Robust Partitioning". In: *Proceedings of the Twenty-Second International Conference on Artificial Intelligence and Statistics.* Ed. by K. Chaudhuri and M. Sugiyama. Vol. 89. Proceedings of Machine Learning Research. PMLR, 2019, pp. 3352–3361.

[Wan+19c] Y. Wang, A. Smola, D. C. Maddix, J. Gasthaus, D. Foster, and T. Januschowski. "Deep Factors for Forecasting". In: *ICML.* 2019.

[Wan+20a] D. Wang, E. Shelhamer, S. Liu, B. Olshausen, and T. Darrell. "Tent: Fully Test-Time Adaptation by Entropy Minimization". In: *ICLR.* 2020.

[Wan+20b] H. Wang, X. Wu, Z. Huang, and E. P. Xing. "High-frequency component helps explain the generalization of convolutional neural networks". In: *Proceedings of the IEEE/CVF Conference on Computer Vision and Pattern Recognition.* 2020, pp. 8684–8694.

[Wan+20c] T. Wang, J.-Y. Zhu, A. Torralba, and A. A. Efros. *Dataset Distillation.* 2020. arXiv: 1811.10959 [cs.LG].

[Wan+20d] Z. Wang, S. Cheng, L. Yueru, J. Zhu, and B. Zhang. "A Wasserstein Minimum Velocity Approach to Learning Unnormalized Models". In: *Proceedings of the Twenty Third International Conference on Artificial Intelligence and Statistics.* Ed. by S. Chiappa and R. Calandra. Vol. 108. Proceedings of Machine Learning Research. PMLR, 2020, pp. 3728–3738.

[Wan+21] J. Wang, C. Lan, C. Liu, Y. Ouyang, W. Zeng, and T. Qin. "Generalizing to Unseen Domains: A Survey on Domain Generalization". In: *IJCAI.* 2021.

[Wan+22] H. Wang, Y. Yang, D. Pati, and A. Bhattacharya. "Structured Variational Inference in Bayesian State-Space Models". In: (2022).

[Was04]   L. Wasserman. *All of statistics. A concise course in statistical inference.* Springer, 2004.

[Was06]   L. Wasserman. *All of Nonparametric Statistics.* Springer, 2006.

[Wat10]   S. Watanabe. "Asymptotic Equivalence of Bayes Cross Validation and Widely Applicable Information Criterion in Singular Learning Theory". In: *JMLR* 11 (2010), pp. 3571–3594.

[Wat13]   S. Watanabe. "A Widely Applicable Bayesian Information Criterion". In: *JMLR* 14 (2013), pp. 867–897.

[Wat60]   S. Watanabe. "Information theoretical analysis of multivariate correlation". In: *IBM J. of Research and Development* 4 (1960), pp. 66–82.

[WB05]   J. Winn and C. Bishop. "Variational Message Passing". In: *JMLR* 6 (2005), pp. 661–694.

[WB20]   T. Wang and J. Ba. "Exploring Model-based Planning with Policy Networks". In: *ICLR.* 2020.

[WBC21]   Y. Wang, D. M. Blei, and J. P. Cunningham. "Posterior Collapse and Latent Variable Non-identifiability". In: *NIPS.* 2021.

[WC19]   A. Wang and K. Cho. "BERT has a Mouth, and It Must Speak: BERT as a Markov Random Field Language Model". In: *Proc. Workshop on Methods for Optimizing and Evaluating Neural Language Generation.* Minneapolis, Minnesota: Association for Computational Linguistics, June 2019, pp. 30–36.

[WCS08]   M. Welling, C. Chemudugunta, and N. Sutter. "Deterministic Latent Variable Models and their Pitfalls". In: *ICDM.* 2008.

[WD92]   C. Watkins and P. Dayan. "Q-learning". In: *Machine Learning* 8.3 (1992), pp. 279–292.

[WDN15]   A. G. Wilson, C. Dann, and H. Nickisch. "Thoughts on Massively Scalable Gaussian Processes". In: *arXiv preprint arXiv:1511.01870* (2015). https://arxiv.org/abs/1511.01870.

[Web+17]   T. Weber et al. "Imagination-Augmented Agents for Deep Reinforcement Learning". In: *NIPS*. 2017.

[Wei00]   Y. Weiss. "Correctness of local probability propagation in graphical models with loops". In: *Neural Computation* 12 (2000), pp. 1–41.

[Wei+13]   K. Wei, Y. Liu, K. Kirchhoff, and J. Bilmes. "Using Document Summarization Techniques for Speech Data Subset Selection." In: *HLT-NAACL*. 2013, pp. 721–726.

[Wei+14]   K. Wei, Y. Liu, K. Kirchhoff, and J. Bilmes. "Unsupervised Submodular Subset Selection for Speech Data". In: *Proc. IEEE Intl. Conf. on Acoustics, Speech, and Signal Processing*. Florence, Italy, 2014.

[Wei+15a]   K. Wei, R. Iyer, S. Wang, W. Bai, and J. Bilmes. "How to Intelligently Distribute Training Data to Multiple Compute Nodes: Distributed Machine Learning via Submodular Partitioning". In: *Neural Information Processing Society (NeurIPS, formerly NIPS) Workshop*. LearningSys Workshop, http://learningsys.org. Montreal, Canada, 2015.

[Wei+15b]   K. Wei, R. Iyer, S. Wang, W. Bai, and J. Bilmes. "Mixed Robust/Average Submodular Partitioning: Fast Algorithms, Guarantees, and Applications". In: *Neural Information Processing Society (NeurIPS, formerly NIPS)*. Montreal, Canada, 2015.

[Wei+22]   J. Wei et al. "Emergent Abilities of Large Language Models". In: *TMLR* (June 2022).

[Wel11]   M. Welling. "Bayesian Learning via Stochastic Gradient Langevin Dynamics". In: *ICML*. 2011.

[Wen+17]   R. Wen, K. Torkkola, B. Narayanaswamy, and D. Madeka. "A Multi-Horizon Quantile Recurrent Forecaster". In: *NIPS Time Series Workshop*. 2017.

[Wen+19a]   L. Wenliang, D. Sutherland, H. Strathmann, and A. Gretton. "Learning deep kernels for exponential family densities". In: *International Conference on Machine Learning*. 2019, pp. 6737–6746.

[Wen+19b]   F. Wenzel, T. Galy-Fajou, C. Donner, M. Kloft, and M. Opper. "Efficient Gaussian Process Classification Using Polya-Gamma Data Augmentation". In: *AAAI*. 2019.

[Wen+20a]   C. Wendler, A. Amrollahi, B. Seifert, A. Krause, and M. Püschel. "Learning set functions that are sparse in non-orthogonal Fourier bases". In: *arXiv preprint arXiv:2010.00439* (2020).

[Wen+20b]   F. Wenzel, K. Roth, B. S. Veeling, J. Świątkowski, L. Tran, S. Mandt, J. Snoek, T. Salimans, R. Jenatton, and S. Nowozin. "How Good is the Bayes Posterior in Deep Neural Networks Really?" In: *ICML*. 2020.

[Wen+20c]   F. Wenzel, J. Snoek, D. Tran, and R. Jenatton. "Hyperparameter Ensembles for Robustness and Uncertainty Quantification". In: *NIPS*. 2020.

[Wen21]   L. Weng. "What are diffusion models?" In: *lilianweng.github.io/lil-log* (2021).

[Wes03]   M. West. "Bayesian Factor Regression Models in the "Large p, Small n" Paradigm". In: *Bayesian Statistics* 7 (2003).

[Wes87]   M. West. "On scale mixtures of normal distributions". In: *Biometrika* 74 (1987), pp. 646–648.

[WF01a]   Y. Weiss and W. T. Freeman. "Correctness of belief propagation in Gaussian graphical models of arbitrary topology". In: *Neural Computation* 13.10 (2001), pp. 2173–2200.

[WF01b]   Y. Weiss and W. T. Freeman. "On the optimality of solutions of the max-product belief propagation algorithm in arbitrary graphs". In: *IEEE Trans. Information Theory, Special Issue on Codes on Graphs and Iterative Algorithms* 47.2 (2001), pp. 723–735.

[WF14]   Z. Wang and N. de Freitas. "Theoretical Analysis of Bayesian Optimisation with Unknown Gaussian Process Hyper-Parameters". In: (2014). arXiv: 1406.7758 [stat.ML].

[WF16]   Z. Wang and N. de Freitas. "Theoretical Analysis of Bayesian Optimisation with Unknown Gaussian Process Hyper-Parameters". In: *BayesOpt Workshop*. 2016.

[WG17]   P. White and S. Gorard. "Against Inferential Statistics: How and Why Current Statistics Teaching Gets It Wrong". en. In: *J. Educ. Behav. Stat.* 16.1 (2017), pp. 55–65.

[WG18]   M. Wu and N. Goodman. "Multimodal Generative Models for Scalable Weakly-Supervised Learning". In: *NIPS*. 2018.

[WGY21]   G. Weiss, Y. Goldberg, and E. Yahav. "Thinking Like Transformers". In: *ICML*. 2021.

[WH02]   M. Welling and G. E. Hinton. "A new learning algorithm for mean field Boltzmann machines". In: *International Conference on Artificial Neural Networks*. Springer. 2002, pp. 351–357.

[WH18]   Y. Wu and K. He. "Group Normalization". In: *ECCV*. 2018.

[WH97]   M. West and J. Harrison. *Bayesian forecasting and dynamic models*. Springer, 1997.

[WHD18]   J. T. Wilson, F. Hutter, and M. P. Deisenroth. "Maximizing acquisition functions for Bayesian optimization". In: *NIPS*. 2018.

[Whi16]   T. White. "Sampling Generative Networks". In: *arXiv* (2016).

[Whi88]   P Whittle. "Restless bandits: activity allocation in a changing world". In: *J. Appl. Probab.* 25.A (1988), pp. 287–298.

[WHT19]   Y. Wang, H. He, and X. Tan. "Truly Proximal Policy Optimization". In: *UAI*. 2019.

[WI20]   A. G. Wilson and P. Izmailov. "Bayesian Deep Learning and a Probabilistic Perspective of Generalization". In: *NIPS*. 2020.

[WIB15]   K. Wei, R. Iyer, and J. Bilmes. "Submodularity in Data Subset Selection and Active Learning". In: *Proceedings of the 32nd international conference on Machine learning*. Lille, France, 2015.

[Wie+14]   D Wierstra, T Schaul, J Peters, and J Schmidhuber. "Natural Evolution Strategies". In: *JMLR* 15.1 (2014), pp. 949–980.

[Wik21]   Wikipedia contributors. *CliffsNotes — Wikipedia, The Free Encyclopedia*. [Online; accessed 29-December-2021]. 2021.

[Wil+14]   A. G. Wilson, E. Gilboa, A. Nehorai, and J. P. Cunningham. "Fast kernel learning for multidimensional pattern extrapolation". In: *Advances in Neu-*

ral Information Processing Systems. 2014, pp. 3626–3634.

[Wil14] A. G. Wilson. "Covariance kernels for fast automatic pattern discovery and extrapolation with Gaussian processes". PhD thesis. University of Cambridge, 2014.

[Wil+16] A. G. Wilson, Z. Hu, R. Salakhutdinov, and E. P. Xing. "Deep Kernel Learning". en. In: *AISTATS.* 2016, pp. 370–378.

[Wil+17] A. G. Wills, J. Hendriks, C. Renton, and B. Ninness. "A Bayesian Filtering Algorithm for Gaussian Mixture Models". In: (2017). arXiv: 1705.05495 [stat.ML].

[Wil+20] H. Wilde, J. Jewson, S. Vollmer, and C. Holmes. "Foundations of Bayesian Learning from Synthetic Data". In: (Nov. 2020). arXiv: 2011.08299 [cs.LG].

[Wil20] A. G. Wilson. "The Case for Bayesian Deep Learning". In: (2020). arXiv: 2001.10995 [cs.LG].

[Wil+20a] J. T. Wilson, V. Borovitskiy, A. Terenin, P. Mostowsky, and M. P. Deisenroth. "Efficiently Sampling Functions from Gaussian Process Posteriors". In: *ICML.* 2020.

[Wil+20b] A. B. Wiltschko, B. Sanchez-Lengeling, B. Lee, E. Reif, J. Wei, K. J. McCloskey, L. Colwell, W. Qian, and Y. Wang. "Evaluating Attribution for Graph Neural Networks". In: (2020).

[Wil69] A. G. Wilson. "The use of entropy maximising models, in the theory of trip distribution, mode split and route split". In: *Journal of transport economics and policy* (1969), pp. 108–126.

[Wil92] R. J. Williams. "Simple statistical gradient-following algorithms for connectionist reinforcement learning". In: *MLJ* 8.3-4 (1992), pp. 229–256.

[Wil98] C. Williams. "Computation with infinite networks". In: *Neural Computation* 10.5 (1998), pp. 1203–1216.

[Win] J. Winn. *VIBES.*

[Win+19] J. Winn, C. Bishop, T. Diethe, J. Guiver, and Y. Zaykov. *Model-based Machine Learning.* 2019.

[WIP20] J. Watson, A. Imohiosen, and J. Peters. "Active Inference or Control as Inference? A Unifying View". In: *International Workshop on Active Inference.* 2020.

[Wit] *DEEPFAKES: PREPARE NOW (PERSPECTIVES FROM BRAZIL).* https://lab.witness.org/brazil-deepfakes-prepare-now/. Accessed: 2021-08-18.

[Wiy+19] R. R. Wiyatno, A. Xu, O. Dia, and A. de Berker. "Adversarial Examples in Modern Machine Learning: A Review". In: (2019). arXiv: 1911.05268 [cs.LG].

[WJ08] M. J. Wainwright and M. I. Jordan. "Graphical models, exponential families, and variational inference". In: *Foundations and Trends in Machine Learning* 1–2 (2008), pp. 1–305.

[WJ21] Y. Wang and M. I. Jordan. *Desiderata for Representation Learning: A Causal Perspective.* 2021. arXiv: 2109.03795 [stat.ML].

[WJW03] M. J. Wainwright, T. S. Jaakkola, and A. S. Willsky. "Tree-based reparameterization framework for analysis of sum-product and related algorithms". In: *IEEE Trans. on Information Theory* 49.5 (2003), pp. 1120–1146.

[WK18] E. Wong and Z. Kolter. "Provable defenses against adversarial examples via the convex outer adversarial polytope". In: *International Conference on Machine Learning.* PMLR. 2018, pp. 5286–5295.

[WK96] G. Widmer and M. Kubat. "Learning in the presence of concept drift and hidden contexts". In: *Mach. Learn.* 23.1 (1996), pp. 69–101.

[WKS21] V. Wild, M. Kanagawa, and D. Sejdinovic. "Connections and Equivalences between the Nyström Method and Sparse Variational Gaussian Processes". In: (2021). arXiv: 2106.01121 [stat.ML].

[WL14a] N. Whiteley and A. Lee. "Twisted particle filters". en. In: *Annals of Statistics* 42.1 (Feb. 2014), pp. 115–141.

[WL14b] J. L. Williams and R. A. Lau. "Approximate evaluation of marginal association probabilities with belief propagation". In: *IEEE Trans. Aerosp. Electron. Syst.* 50.4 (2014).

[WL19] A. Wehenkel and G. Louppe. "Unconstrained Monotonic Neural Networks". In: *NIPS.* 2019.

[WLL16] W. Wang, H. Lee, and K. Livescu. "Deep Variational Canonical Correlation Analysis". In: *arXiv* (2016).

[WLZ19] D. Widmann, F. Lindsten, and D. Zachariah. "Calibration tests in multi-class classification: A unifying framework". In: *NIPS.* Curran Associates, Inc., 2019, pp. 12236–12246.

[WM12] K. Wakabayashi and T. Miura. "Forward-Backward Activation Algorithm for Hierarchical Hidden Markov Models". In: *NIPS.* 2012.

[WMR17] S. Wachter, B. Mittelstadt, and C. Russell. "Counterfactual explanations without opening the black box: Automated decisions and the GDPR". In: *Harv. JL & Tech.* 31 (2017), p. 841.

[WMR18] S. Wachter, B. Mittelstadt, and C. Russell. *Counterfactual Explanations without Opening the Black Box: Automated Decisions and the GDPR.* 2018. arXiv: 1711.00399 [cs.AI].

[WN01] E. A. Wan and A. T. Nelson. "Dual EKF Methods". In: *Kalman Filtering and Neural Networks.* Ed. by S. Haykin. Wiley, 2001.

[WN07] D. Wipf and S. Nagarajan. "A new view of automatic relevancy determination". In: *NIPS.* 2007.

[WN10] D. Wipf and S. Nagarajan. "Iterative Reweighted ℓ_1 and ℓ_2 Methods for Finding Sparse Solutions". In: *J. of Selected Topics in Signal Processing (Special Issue on Compressive Sensing)* 4.2 (2010).

[WN15] A. G. Wilson and H. Nickisch. "Kernel Interpolation for Scalable Structured Gaussian Processes (KISS-GP)". In: *ICML.* ICML'15. JMLR.org, 2015, pp. 1775–1784.

[WN18] C. K. I. Williams and C. Nash. "Autoencoders and Probabilistic Inference with Missing Data: An Exact Solution for The Factor Analysis Case". In: (2018). arXiv: 1801.03851 [cs.LG].

[WO12] M. Wiering and M. van Otterlo, eds. *Reinforcement learning: State-of-the-art.* Springer, 2012.

[Woł+21] M. Wołczyk, M. Zając, R. Pascanu, Ł. Kuciński, and P. Miłoś. "Continual World: A Robotic Benchmark For Continual Reinforcement Learning". In: *NIPS.* 2021.

[Wol76]   P. Wolfe. "Finding the nearest point in a polytope". In: *Mathematical Programming* 11 (1976), pp. 128–149.

[Wol92]   D. Wolpert. "Stacked Generalization". In: *Neural Networks* 5.2 (1992), pp. 241–259.

[Woo+09]   F. Wood, C. Archambeau, J. Gasthaus, L. James, and Y. W. Teh. "A Stochastic Memoizer for Sequence Data". In: *ICML*. 2009.

[Woo+19]   B. Woodworth, S. Gunasekar, P. Savarese, E. Moroshko, I. Golan, J. Lee, D. Soudry, and N. Srebro. "Kernel and Rich Regimes in Overparametrized Models". In: (2019). arXiv: 1906.05827 [cs.LG].

[WP18]   H. Wang and H. Poon. "Deep Probabilistic Logic: A Unifying Framework for Indirect Supervision". In: *EMNLP*. 2018.

[WP19]   S. Wiegreffe and Y. Pinter. "Attention is not not explanation". In: *arXiv preprint arXiv:1908.04626* (2019).

[WR15]   F. Wang and C. Rudin. "Falling Rule Lists". In: *Proceedings of the Eighteenth International Conference on Artificial Intelligence and Statistics*. Ed. by G. Lebanon and S. V. N. Vishwanathan. Vol. 38. Proceedings of Machine Learning Research. San Diego, California, USA: PMLR, 2015, pp. 1013–1022.

[WRN10]   D. Wipf, B. Rao, and S. Nagarajan. "Latent Variable Bayesian Models for Promoting Sparsity". In: *IEEE Transactions on Information Theory* (2010).

[WRZH04]   M. Welling, M. Rosen-Zvi, and G. Hinton. "Exponential family harmoniums with an application to information retrieval". In: *NIPS-14*. 2004.

[WS01]   C. K. I. Williams and M. Seeger. "Using the Nyström Method to Speed Up Kernel Machines". In: *NIPS*. Ed. by T. K. Leen, T. G. Dietterich, and V Tresp. MIT Press, 2001, pp. 682–688.

[WS05]   M. Welling and C. Sutton. "Learning in Markov Random Fields with Contrastive Free Energies". In: *Tenth International Workshop on Artificial Intelligence and Statistics (AISTATS)*. 2005.

[WS93]   D. Wolpert and C. Strauss. "What Bayes has to say about the evidence procedure". In: *Proc. Workshop on Maximum Entropy and Bayesian methods*. 1993.

[WSG21]   C. Wang, S. Sun, and R. Grosse. "Beyond Marginal Uncertainty: How Accurately can Bayesian Regression Models Estimate Posterior Predictive Correlations?" In: *AISTATS*. Ed. by A. Banerjee and K. Fukumizu. Vol. 130. Proceedings of Machine Learning Research. PMLR, 2021, pp. 2476–2484.

[WSL19]   R. L. Wasserstein, A. L. Schirm, and N. A. Lazar. "Moving to a World Beyond "p < 0.05"". In: *The American Statistician* 73.sup1 (2019), pp. 1–19.

[WSN00]   B. Williams, T. Santner, and W. Notz. "Sequential design of computer experiments to minimize integrated response functions". In: *Statistica Sinica* 10 (2000), pp. 1133–1152.

[WSS21]   W. J. Wilkinson, S. Särkkä, and A. Solin. "Bayes-Newton Methods for Approximate Bayesian Inference with PSD Guarantees". In: (2021). arXiv: 2111.01721 [stat.ML].

[WT01]   M. Welling and Y.-W. Teh. "Belief Optimization for Binary Networks: a Stable Alternative to Loopy Belief Propagation". In: *UAI*. 2001.

[WT19]   R. Wen and K. Torkkola. "Deep Generative Quantile-Copula Models for Probabilistic Forecasting". In: *ICML*. 2019.

[WT90]   G. Wei and M. Tanner. "A Monte Carlo implementation of the EM algorithm and the poor man's data augmentation algorithms". In: *JASA* 85.411 (1990), pp. 699–704.

[WTB20]   Y. Wen, D. Tran, and J. Ba. "BatchEnsemble: an Alternative Approach to Efficient Ensemble and Lifelong Learning". In: *ICLR*. 2020.

[WTN19]   Y. Wu, G. Tucker, and O. Nachum. *Behavior Regularized Offline Reinforcement Learning*. arXiv:1911.11361. 2019.

[Wu+06]   Y Wu, D Hu, M Wu, and X Hu. "A Numerical-Integration Perspective on Gaussian Filters". In: *IEEE Trans. Signal Process.* 54.8 (2006), pp. 2910–2921.

[Wu+17]   Y. Wu, E. Mansimov, S. Liao, R. Grosse, and J. Ba. "Scalable trust-region method for deep reinforcement learning using Kronecker-factored approximation". In: *NIPS*. 2017.

[Wu+19a]   A. Wu, S. Nowozin, E. Meeds, R. E. Turner, J. M. Hernández-Lobato, and A. L. Gaunt. "Fixing Variational Bayes: Deterministic Variational Inference for Bayesian Neural Networks". In: *ICLR*. 2019.

[Wu+19b]   M. Wu, S. Parbhoo, M. Hughes, R. Kindle, L. Celi, M. Zazzi, V. Roth, and F. Doshi-Velez. "Regional tree regularization for interpretability in black box models". In: *AAAI* (2019).

[Wu+21]   T. Wu, M. T. Ribeiro, J. Heer, and D. S. Weld. "Polyjuice: Generating Counterfactuals for Explaining, Evaluating, and Improving Models". In: *Proceedings of the 59th Annual Meeting of the Association for Computational Linguistics*. Association for Computational Linguistics, 2021.

[Wüt+16]   M. Wüthrich, S. Trimpe, C. Garcia Cifuentes, D. Kappler, and S. Schaal. "A new perspective and extension of the Gaussian Filter". en. In: *The International Journal of Robotics Research* 35.14 (2016), pp. 1731–1749.

[WW12]   Y. Wu and D. P. Wipf. "Dual-Space Analysis of the Sparse Linear Model". In: *NIPS*. 2012.

[WY02]   D. Wilkinson and S. Yeung. "Conditional simulation from highly structured Gaussian systems with application to blocking-MCMC for the Bayesian analysis of very large linear models". In: *Statistics and Computing* 12 (2002), pp. 287–300.

[WYG14]   J. Wen, C.-N. Yu, and R. Greiner. "Robust Learning under Uncertain Test Distributions: Relating Covariate Shift to Model Misspecification". In: *ICML*. Vol. 32. Proceedings of Machine Learning Research. PMLR, 2014, pp. 631–639.

[WZ19]   J. Wei and K. Zou. "EDA: Easy Data Augmentation Techniques for Boosting Performance on Text Classification Tasks". In: *Proceedings of the 2019 Conference on Empirical Methods in Natural Language Processing and the 9th International Joint Conference on Natural Language Processing (EMNLP-IJCNLP)*. Hong Kong, China: Association for Computational Linguistics, Nov. 2019, pp. 6382–6388.

[WZR20]   S. Wu, H. R. Zhang, and C. Ré. "Understanding and Improving Information Transfer in Multi-Task Learning". In: *International Conference on Learning Representations*. 2020.

[XC19]   Z. Xia and A. Chakrabarti. "Training Image Estimators without Image Ground-Truth". In: *NIPS*. 2019.

[XD18]   J. Xu and G. Durrett. "Spherical Latent Spaces for Stable Variational Autoencoders". In: *EMNLP*. 2018.

[Xia+21a]   K. Xia, K.-Z. Lee, Y. Bengio, and E. Barein-boim. "The Causal-Neural Connection: Expressiveness, Learnability, and Inference". In: *NIPS*. July 2021.

[Xia+21b]   K. Xiao, L. Engstrom, A. Ilyas, and A. Madry. "Noise or Signal: The Role of Image Backgrounds in Object Recognition". In: *ICLR*. 2021.

[Xie+16]   J. Xie, Y. Lu, S.-C. Zhu, and Y. N. Wu. "A Theory of Generative ConvNet". In: *ICML*. 2016.

[Xie+18]   J. Xie, Y. Lu, R. Gao, and Y. N. Wu. "Cooperative Learning of Energy-Based Model and Latent Variable Model via MCMC Teaching." In: *AAAI*. Vol. 1. 6. 2018, p. 7.

[Xie+22]   S. M. Xie, A. Raghunathan, P. Liang, and T. Ma. "An Explanation of In-context Learning as Implicit Bayesian Inference". In: *ICLR*. 2022.

[XJ96]   L. Xu and M. I. Jordan. "On Convergence Properties of the EM Algorithm for Gaussian Mixtures". In: *Neural Computation* 8 (1996), pp. 129–151.

[XKV22]   Z. Xiao, K. Kreis, and A. Vahdat. "Tackling the Generative Learning Trilemma with Denoising Diffusion GANs". In: *ICLR*. 2022.

[Xu+15]   J. Xu, L. Mukherjee, Y. Li, J. Warner, J. M. Rehg, and V. Singh. "Gaze-enabled egocentric video summarization via constrained submodular maximization". In: *Proceedings of the IEEE conference on computer vision and pattern recognition*. 2015, pp. 2235–2244.

[Xu18]   J. Xu. "Distance-based Protein Folding Powered by Deep Learning". In: (2018). arXiv: 1811.03481 [q-bio.BM].

[Yad+18]   S. Yadlowsky, H. Namkoong, S. Basu, J. Duchi, and L. Tian. "Bounds on the conditional and average treatment effect with unobserved confounding factors". In: *arXiv e-prints*, arXiv:1808.09521 (Aug. 2018), arXiv:1808.09521. arXiv: 1808.09521 [stat.ME].

[Yad+21]   S. Yadlowsky, S. Fleming, N. Shah, E. Brunskill, and S. Wager. *Evaluating Treatment Prioritization Rules via Rank-Weighted Average Treatment Effects*. 2021. arXiv: 2111.07966 [stat.ME].

[Yan+17]   S Yang, L Xie, X Chen, X Lou, X Zhu, D Huang, and H Li. "Statistical parametric speech synthesis using generative adversarial networks under a multi-task learning framework". In: *IEEE Automatic Speech Recognition and Understanding Workshop (ASRU)*. 2017, pp. 685–691.

[Yan19]   G. Yang. "Scaling Limits of Wide Neural Networks with Weight Sharing: Gaussian Process Behavior, Gradient Independence, and Neural Tangent Kernel Derivation". In: (2019). arXiv: 1902.04760 [cs.NE].

[Yan+21]   J. Yang, K. Zhou, Y. Li, and Z. Liu. "Generalized OOD Detection: A Survey". In: (2021).

[Yan+22]   L. Yang, Z. Zhang, Y. Song, S. Hong, R. Xu, Y. Zhao, Y. Shao, W. Zhang, B. Cui, and M.-H. Yang. "Diffusion Models: A Comprehensive Survey of Methods and Applications". In: (Sept. 2022). arXiv: 2209.00796 [cs.LG].

[Yan74]   H Yanai. "Unification of various techniques of multivariate analysis by means of generalized coefficient of determination (GCD)". In: *J. Behaviormetrics* 1.1 (1974), pp. 45–54.

[Yan81]   M. Yannakakis. "Computing the minimum fill-in is NP-complete". In: *SIAM J. Alg. Discrete Methods* 2 (1981), pp. 77–79.

[Yao+18a]   Y. Yao, A. Vehtari, D. Simpson, and A. Gelman. "Using Stacking to Average Bayesian Predictive Distributions (with Discussion)". en. In: *Bayesian Analysis* 13.3 (2018), pp. 917–1007.

[Yao+18b]   Y. Yao, A. Vehtari, D. Simpson, and A. Gelman. "Yes, but Did It Work?: Evaluating Variational Inference". In: *ICML*. Vol. 80. Proceedings of Machine Learning Research. PMLR, 2018, pp. 5581–5590.

[YBM20]   Y. Yang, R. Bamler, and S. Mandt. *Improving Inference for Neural Image Compression*. 2020. arXiv: 2006.04240 [eess.IV].

[YBW15]   F. Yang, S. Balakrishnan, and M. J. Wainwright. "Statistical and Computational Guarantees for the Baum-Welch Algorithm". In: (2015). arXiv: 1512.08269 [stat.ML].

[Yed11]   J. S. Yedidia. "Message-Passing Algorithms for Inference and Optimization". In: *J. Stat. Phys.* 145.4 (2011), pp. 860–890.

[Yeh+18]   C.-K. Yeh, J. S. Kim, I. E. H. Yen, and P. Ravikumar. *Representer Point Selection for Explaining Deep Neural Networks*. 2018. arXiv: 1811.09720 [cs.LG].

[Yeh+19a]   C.-K. Yeh, C.-Y. Hsieh, A. Suggala, D. I. Inouye, and P. K. Ravikumar. "On the (in) fidelity and sensitivity of explanations". In: *Advances in Neural Information Processing Systems* 32 (2019), pp. 10967–10978.

[Yeh+19b]   C.-K. Yeh, B. Kim, S. O. Arik, C.-L. Li, T. Pfister, and P. Ravikumar. "On completeness-aware concept-based explanations in deep neural networks". In: *arXiv preprint arXiv:1910.07969* (2019).

[Yeu+17]   S. Yeung, A. Kannan, Y. Dauphin, and L. Fei-Fei. "Tackling Over-pruning in Variational Autoencoders". In: *ICML Workshop on "Principled Approaches to Deep Learning"*. 2017.

[Yeu91a]   R. W. Yeung. "A new outlook on Shannon's information measures". In: *IEEE Trans. Inf. Theory* 37.3 (1991), pp. 466–474.

[Yeu91b]   R. W. Yeung. "A new outlook on Shannon's information measures". In: *IEEE Trans. on Information Theory* 37 (1991), pp. 466–474.

[YFW00]   J. Yedidia, W. T. Freeman, and Y. Weiss. "Generalized Belief Propagation". In: *NIPS*. 2000.

[YH21]   G. Yang and E. J. Hu. "Feature Learning in Infinite-Width Neural Networks". In: *ICML*. 2021.

[Yin+19a]   D. Yin, R. G. Lopes, J. Shlens, E. D. Cubuk, and J. Gilmer. "A Fourier Perspective on Model Robustness in Computer Vision". In: *NIPS*. 2019.

[Yin+19b]   P. Yin, J. Lyu, S. Zhang, S. Osher, Y. Qi, and J. Xin. "Understanding Straight-Through Estimator in Training Activation Quantized Neural Nets". In: *ICLR*. 2019.

[Yin+19c]   R. Ying, D. Bourgeois, J. You, M. Zitnik, and J. Leskovec. "Gnnexplainer: Generating explanations for graph neural networks". In: *Advances in neural information processing systems* 32 (2019), p. 9240.

[Yin+20]   D. Yin, M. Farajtabar, A. Li, N. Levine, and A. Mott. "Optimization and Generalization of Regularization-Based Continual Learning: a Loss Approximation Viewpoint". In: (2020). arXiv: 2006.10974 [cs.LG].

[YK06]   A. Yuille and D. Kersten. "Vision as Bayesian inference: analysis by synthesis?" en. In: *Trends Cogn. Sci.* 10.7 (2006), pp. 301–308.

[YK19]   M. Yang and B. Kim. *Benchmarking Attribution Methods with Relative Feature Importance.* 2019. arXiv: 1907.09701 [cs.LG].

[YMT22]   Y. Yang, S. Mandt, and L. Theis. "An Introduction to Neural Data Compression". In: (2022). arXiv: 2202.06533 [cs.LG].

[Yoo+18]   K. Yoon, R. Liao, Y. Xiong, L. Zhang, E. Fetaya, R. Urtasun, R. Zemel, and X. Pitkow. "Inference in Probabilistic Graphical Models by Graph Neural Networks". In: *ICLR Workshop.* 2018.

[You19]   A. Young. "Consistency without inference: Instrumental variables in practical application". In: (2019).

[You89]   L. Younes. "Parameter estimation for imperfectly observed Gibbsian fields". In: *Probab. Theory and Related Fields* 82 (1989), pp. 625–645.

[You99]   L. Younes. "On the convergence of Markovian stochastic algorithms with rapidly decreasing ergodicity rates". In: *Stochastics: An International Journal of Probability and Stochastic Processes* 65.3-4 (1999), pp. 177–228.

[YS10]   G. A. Young and R. L. Smith. *Essentials of Statistical Inference.* en. Illustrated edition. Cambridge University Press, Mar. 2010.

[Yu+06]   S. Yu, K. Yu, V. Tresp, K. H.-P., and M. Wu. "Supervised probabilistic principal component analysis". In: *KDD.* 2006.

[Yu10]   S.-Z. Yu. "Hidden Semi-Markov Models". In: *Artificial Intelligence J.* 174.2 (2010).

[Yu+16]   F. X. X. Yu, A. T. Suresh, K. M. Choromanski, D. N. Holtmann-Rice, and S. Kumar. "Orthogonal Random Features". In: *NIPS.* Curran Associates, Inc., 2016, pp. 1975–1983.

[Yu+17]   L. Yu, W. Zhang, J. Wang, and Y. Yu. "Seqgan: Sequence generative adversarial nets with policy gradient". In: *Thirty-first AAAI conference on artificial intelligence.* 2017.

[Yu+18]   Y. Yu et al. "Dynamic Control Flow in Large-Scale Machine Learning". In: *Proceedings of the Thirteenth EuroSys Conference.* EuroSys '18. Association for Computing Machinery, 2018.

[Yu+20]   L. Yu, Y. Song, J. Song, and S. Ermon. "Training Deep Energy-Based Models with f-Divergence Minimization". In: *arXiv preprint arXiv:2003.03463* (2020).

[Yu+21]   J. Yu, X. Li, J. Y. Koh, H. Zhang, R. Pang, J. Qin, A. Ku, Y. Xu, J. Baldridge, and Y. Wu. "Vector-quantized Image Modeling with Improved VQGAN". In: (2021). arXiv: 2110.04627 [cs.CV].

[Yu+22]   J. Yu et al. "Scaling Autoregressive Models for Content-Rich Text-to-Image Generation". 2022.

[Yua+19]   X. Yuan, P. He, Q. Zhu, and X. Li. "Adversarial Examples: Attacks and Defenses for Deep Learning". en. In: *IEEE Trans. Neural Networks and Learning Systems* 30.9 (2019), pp. 2805–2824.

[Yui01]   A. Yuille. "CCCP algorithms to minimze the Bethe and Kikuchi free energies: convergent alternatives to belief propagation". In: *Neural Computation* 14 (2001), pp. 1691–1722.

[YW04]   C. Yanover and Y. Weiss. "Finding the M Most Probable Configurations in Arbitrary Graphical Models". In: *NIPS.* 2004.

[YWX17]   J.-g. Yao, X. Wan, and J. Xiao. "Recent advances in document summarization". In: *Knowledge and Information Systems* 53.2 (2017), pp. 297–336.

[YZ19]   G. Yaroslavtsev and S. Zhou. "Approximate F_2-Sketching of Valuation Functions". In: *Approximation, Randomization, and Combinatorial Optimization. Algorithms and Techniques (APPROX /RANDOM 2019).* Ed. by D. Achlioptas and L. A. Végh. Vol. 145. Leibniz International Proceedings in Informatics (LIPIcs). Dagstuhl, Germany: Schloss Dagstuhl–Leibniz-Zentrum fuer Informatik, 2019, 69:1–69:21.

[YZ22]   Y. Yang and P. Zhai. "Click-through rate prediction in online advertising: A literature review". In: *Inf. Process. Manag.* 59.2 (2022), p. 102853.

[ZA12]   J. Zou and R. Adams. "Priors for Diversity in Generative Latent Variable Models". In: *NIPS.* 2012.

[Zaf+22]   M. Zaffran, A. Dieuleveut, O. Féron, Y. Goude, and J. Josse. "Adaptive Conformal Predictions for Time Series". In: (2022). arXiv: 2202.07282 [stat.ML].

[Zai+20]   S. Zaidi, A. Zela, T. Elsken, C. Holmes, F. Hutter, and Y. W. Teh. "Neural Ensemble Search for Performant and Calibrated Predictions". In: (2020). arXiv: 2006.08573 [cs.LG].

[Zan21]   N. Zanichelli. *IAML Distill Blog: Transformers in Vision.* 2021.

[ZB18]   T. Zhou and J. Bilmes. "Minimax curriculum learning: Machine teaching with desirable difficulties and scheduled diversity". In: *International Conference on Learning Representations.* 2018.

[ZB21]   B. Zhao and H. Bilen. "Dataset Condensation with Differentiable Siamese Augmentation". In: *Proceedings of the 38th International Conference on Machine Learning, ICML 2021, 18-24 July 2021, Virtual Event.* Ed. by M. Meila and T. Z. 0001. Vol. 139. Proceedings of Machine Learning Research. PMLR, 2021, pp. 12674–12685.

[Zbo+21]   J. Zbontar, L. Jing, I. Misra, Y. LeCun, and S. Deny. "Barlow twins: Self-supervised learning via redundancy reduction". In: *arXiv preprint arXiv:2103.03230* (2021).

[ZDK15]   J. Zhang, J. Djolonga, and A. Krause. "Higher-order inference for multi-class log-supermodular models". In: *Proceedings of the IEEE International Conference on Computer Vision.* 2015, pp. 1859–1867.

[ZE01a]   B. Zadrozny and C. Elkan. "Obtaining calibrated probability estimaets from decision trees and naive Bayesian classifiers". In: *ICML.* 2001.

[ZE01b]   B. Zadrozny and C. Elkan. "Transforming classifier scores into accurate multiclass probability estimates". In: *KDD.* 2001.

[Zec+18a]   J. R. Zech, M. A. Badgeley, M. Liu, A. B. Costa, J. J. Titano, and E. K. Oermann. "Variable generalization performance of a deep learning model to detect pneumonia in chest radiographs: A cross-sectional study". en. In: *PLoS Med.* 15.11 (Nov. 2018), e1002683.

[Zec+18b]   J. R. Zech, M. A. Badgeley, M. Liu, A. B. Costa, J. J. Titano, and E. K. Oermann. "Variable generalization performance of a deep learning model to detect pneumonia in chest radiographs: a cross-sectional study". In: *PLoS medicine* 15.11 (2018), e1002683.

[Zel76]   A. Zellner. "Bayesian and non-Bayesian analysis of the regression model with multivariate Student-t error terms". In: *JASA* 71.354 (1976), pp. 400–405.

[Zel86]   A. Zellner. "On assessing prior distributions and Bayesian regression analysis with g-prior distributions". In: *Bayesian inference and decision techniques, Studies of Bayesian and Econometrics and Statistics volume 6*. North Holland, 1986.

[Zen+18]   C. Zeno, I. Golan, E. Hoffer, and D. Soudry. "Task Agnostic Continual Learning Using Online Variational Bayes". In: (2018). arXiv: 1803 . 10123 [stat.ML].

[Zen+21]   C. Zeno, I. Golan, E. Hoffer, and D. Soudry. "Task-Agnostic Continual Learning Using Online Variational Bayes With Fixed-Point Updates". en. In: *Neural Comput.* 33.11 (2021), pp. 3139–3177.

[Zer+19]   J. Zerilli, A. Knott, J. Maclaurin, and C. Gavaghan. "Transparency in algorithmic and human decision-making: is there a double standard?" In: *Philosophy & Technology* 32.4 (2019), pp. 661–683.

[ZF14]   M. D. Zeiler and R. Fergus. "Visualizing and understanding convolutional networks". In: *European conference on computer vision*. Springer. 2014, pp. 818–833.

[ZFV20]   G. Zeni, M. Fontana, and S. Vantini. "Conformal Prediction: a Unified Review of Theory and New Challenges". In: (2020). arXiv: 2005.07972 [cs.LG].

[ZG21]   D. Zou and Q. Gu. "On the Convergence of Hamiltonian Monte Carlo with Stochastic Gradients". In: *ICML*. Ed. by M. Meila and T. Zhang. Vol. 139. Proceedings of Machine Learning Research. PMLR, 2021, pp. 13012–13022.

[ZGR21]   L. Zhang, M. Goldstein, and R. Ranganath. "Understanding Failures in Out-of-Distribution Detection with Deep Generative Models". In: *ICML*. Ed. by M. Meila and T. Zhang. Vol. 139. Proceedings of Machine Learning Research. PMLR, 2021, pp. 12427–12436.

[Zha+13a] K. Zhang, B. Schölkopf, K. Muandet, and Z. Wang. "Domain Adaptation under Target and Conditional Shift". In: *Proceedings of the 30th International Conference on Machine Learning*. 2013, pp. 819–827.

[Zha+13b] K. Zhang, B. Scholkopf, K. Muandet, and Z. Wang. "Domain Adaptation under Target and Conditional Shift". In: *ICML*. Vol. 28. 2013.

[Zha+16]   S. Zhai, Y. Cheng, R. Feris, and Z. Zhang. "Generative adversarial networks as variational training of energy based models". In: *arXiv preprint arXiv:1611.01799* (2016).

[Zha+17]   C. Zhang, S. Bengio, M. Hardt, B. Recht, and O. Vinyals. "Understanding deep learning requires rethinking generalization". In: *ICLR*. 2017.

[Zha+18]   G. Zhang, S. Sun, D. Duvenaud, and R. Grosse. "Noisy Natural Gradient as Variational Inference". In: *ICML*. 2018.

[Zha+19a] X. Zhai, J. Puigcerver, A. Kolesnikov, P. Ruyssen, C. Riquelme, M. Lucic, J. Djolonga, A. S. Pinto, M. Neumann, A. Dosovitskiy, et al. "A large-scale study of representation learning with the visual task adaptation benchmark". In: *arXiv preprint arXiv:1910.04867* (2019).

[Zha+19b] C. Zhang, J. Butepage, H. Kjellstrom, and S. Mandt. "Advances in Variational Inference". In: *IEEE PAMI* (2019), pp. 2008–2026.

[Zha+19c] H. Zhang, I. Goodfellow, D. Metaxas, and A. Odena. "Self-attention generative adversarial networks". In: *International conference on machine learning*. PMLR. 2019, pp. 7354–7363.

[Zha+19d] L. Zhao, K. Korovina, W. Si, and. M. Cheung. "Approximate inference with Graph Neural Networks". 2019.

[Zha+20a] A. Zhang, Z. Lipton, M. Li, and A. Smola. *Dive into deep learning*. 2020.

[Zha+20b] H. Zhang, A. Li, J. Guo, and Y. Guo. "Hybrid models for open set recognition". In: *European Conference on Computer Vision*. Springer. 2020, pp. 102–117.

[Zha+20c] R. Zhang, B. Dai, L. Li, and D. Schuurmans. "GenDICE: Generalized Offline Estimation of Stationary Values". In: *ICLR*. 2020.

[Zha+20d] R. Zhang, C. Li, J. Zhang, C. Chen, and A. G. Wilson. "Cyclical stochastic gradient MCMC for Bayesian deep learning". In: *ICLR*. 2020.

[Zha+20e] X. Zhang, Y. Li, Z. Zhang, and Z.-L. Zhang. "f-GAIL: Learning f-Divergence for Generative Adversarial Imitation Learning". In: *Neural Information Processing Systems* (2020).

[Zha+20f] Y. Zhang, X. Chen, Y. Yang, A. Ramamurthy, B. Li, Y. Qi, and L. Song. "Efficient Probabilistic Logic Reasoning with Graph Neural Networks". In: *ICLR*. 2020.

[Zha+21]   X. Zhai, A. Kolesnikov, N. Houlsby, and L. Beyer. "Scaling vision transformers". In: *arXiv preprint arXiv:2106.04560* (2021).

[Zhe+15]   S. Zheng, S. Jayasumana, B. Romera-Paredes, V. Vineet, Z. Su, D. Du, C. Huang, and P. Torr. "Conditional Random Fields as Recurrent Neural Networks". In: *ICCV*. 2015.

[Zho+19a] S. Zhou, M. Gordon, R. Krishna, A. Narcomey, L. F. Fei-Fei, and M. Bernstein. "HYPE: A Benchmark for Human eYe Perceptual Evaluation of Generative Models". In: *NIPS*. Curran Associates, Inc., 2019, pp. 3444–3456.

[Zho+19b] S. Zhou, M. L. Gordon, R. Krishna, A. Narcomey, L. Fei-Fei, and M. S. Bernstein. "HYPE: a benchmark for human eye perceptual evaluation of generative models". In: *Proceedings of the 33rd International Conference on Neural Information Processing Systems*. 2019, pp. 3449–3461.

[Zho20]   G. Zhou. "Mixed Hamiltonian Monte Carlo for Mixed Discrete and Continuous Variable". In: (2020). arXiv: 1909.04852 [stat.CO].

[ZHT06]   H. Zou, T. Hastie, and R. Tibshirani. "Sparse principal component analysis". In: *JCGS* 15.2 (2006), pp. 262–286.

[Zhu+17]   J.-Y. Zhu, T. Park, P. Isola, and A. A. Efros. "Unpaired Image-to-Image Translation using Cycle-Consistent Adversarial Networks". In: *ICCV*. 2017.

[Zhu+18]   X. Zhu, A. Singla, S. Zilles, and A. N. Rafferty. "An overview of machine teaching". In: *arXiv preprint arXiv:1801.05927* (2018).

[Zhu+21]   F. Zhuang, Z. Qi, K. Duan, D. Xi, Y. Zhu, H. Zhu, H. Xiong, and Q. He. "A Comprehensive Survey on Transfer Learning". In: *Proc. IEEE* 109.1 (2021).

[Zie+08]   B. D. Ziebart, A. L. Maas, J. A. Bagnell, and A. K. Dey. "Maximum Entropy Inverse Reinforcement Learning". In: *AAAI*. 2008, pp. 1433–1438.

[ZIE16]   R. Zhang, P. Isola, and A. A. Efros. "Colorful image colorization". In: *European conference on computer vision*. Springer. 2016, pp. 649–666.

[ZIE17]   R. Zhang, P. Isola, and A. A. Efros. "Split-brain autoencoders: Unsupervised learning by cross-channel prediction". In: *Proceedings of the IEEE Conference on Computer Vision and Pattern Recognition*. 2017, pp. 1058–1067.

[Zin+20]   L. Zintgraf, K. Shiarlis, M. Igl, S. Schulze, Y. Gal, K. Hofmann, and S. Whiteson. "VariBAD: A Very Good Method for Bayes-Adaptive Deep RL via Meta-Learning". In: *ICLR*. 2020.

[Ziy+19]   L. Ziyin, Z. Wang, P. P. Liang, R. Salakhutdinov, L.-P. Morency, and M. Ueda. "Deep gamblers: Learning to abstain with portfolio theory". In: *NIPS*. June 2019.

[ZL21]   A. Zhou and S. Levine. "Training on Test Data with Bayesian Adaptation for Covariate Shift". In: *NIPS*. 2021.

[ZLF21]   M. Zhang, S. Levine, and C. Finn. "MEMO: Test Time Robustness via Adaptation and Augmentation". In: (2021). arXiv: 2110.09506 [cs.LG].

[ZLG20]   R. Zivan, O. Lev, and R. Galiki. "Beyond Trees: Analysis and Convergence of Belief Propagation in Graphs with Multiple Cycles". In: *AAAI*. 2020.

[ZMB21]   B. Zhao, K. R. Mopuri, and H. Bilen. "Dataset Condensation with Gradient Matching". In: *International Conference on Learning Representations*. 2021.

[ZMG19]   G. Zhang, J. Martens, and R. B. Grosse. "Fast Convergence of Natural Gradient Descent for Over-Parameterized Neural Networks". In: *NIPS*. 2019, pp. 8082–8093.

[ZML16]   J. J. Zhao, M. Mathieu, and Y. LeCun. "Energy-based Generative Adversarial Network". In: (2016).

[Zoe07]   O. Zoeter. "Bayesian generalized linear models in a terabyte world". In: *Proc. 5th International Symposium on image and Signal Processing and Analysis*. 2007.

[Zon+18]   B. Zong, Q. Song, M. R. Min, W. Cheng, C. Lumezanu, D. Cho, and H. Chen. "Deep Autoencoding Gaussian Mixture Model for Unsupervised Anomaly Detection". In: *ICLR*. 2018.

[ZP00]   G. Zweig and M. Padmanabhan. "Exact alpha-beta computation in logarithmic space with application to map word graph construction". In: *ICSLP*. 2000.

[ZP96]   N. Zhang and D. Poole. "Exploiting causal independence in Bayesian network inference". In: *JAIR* (1996), pp. 301–328.

[ZR19a]   Z. Ziegler and A. Rush. "Latent Normalizing Flows for Discrete Sequences". In: *Proceedings of the 36th International Conference on Machine Learning*. 2019, pp. 7673–7682.

[ZR19b]   Z. M. Ziegler and A. M. Rush. "Latent Normalizing Flows for Discrete Sequences". In: *ICML*. 2019.

[ZSB19]   Q. Zhao, D. S. Small, and B. B. Bhattacharya. "Sensitivity analysis for inverse probability weighting estimators via the percentile bootstrap". In: *Journal of the Royal Statistical Society: Series B (Statistical Methodology)* 81.4 (2019), pp. 735–761. eprint: https://rss.onlinelibrary.wiley.com/doi/pdf/10.1111/rssb.12327.

[ZSE19]   S. Zhao, J. Song, and S. Ermon. "InfoVAE: Information Maximizing Variational Autoencoders". In: *AAAI*. 2019.

[ZW11]   D Zoran and Y Weiss. "From learning models of natural image patches to whole image restoration". In: *ICCV*. 2011.

[ZW12]   D. Zoran and Y. Weiss. "Natural Images, Gaussian Mixtures and Dead Leaves". In: *NIPS*. 2012, pp. 1736–1744.

[ZWM97]   C. S. Zhu, N. Y. Wu, and D. Mumford. "Minimax Entropy Principle and Its Application to Texture Modeling". In: *Neural Computation* 9.8 (1997).

[ZY08]   J.-H. Zhao and P. L. H. Yu. "Fast ML Estimation for the Mixture of Factor Analyzers via an ECM Algorithm". In: *IEEE. Trans. on Neural Networks* 19.11 (2008).

[ZY21]   Y. Zhang and Q. Yang. "A Survey on Multi-Task Learning". In: *IEEE Trans. Knowl. Data Eng.* (2021).

[ZY97]   Z. Zhang and R. W. Yeung. "A non-Shannon-type conditional inequality of information quantities". In: *IEEE Transactions on Information Theory* 43.6 (1997), pp. 1982–1986.

[ZY98]   Z. Zhang and R. W. Yeung. "On characterization of entropy function via information inequalities". In: *IEEE Transactions on Information Theory* 44.4 (1998), pp. 1440–1452.